THE PRAYER BIBLE

PRESENTED

to

____

by

____

on

____

THE PRAYER BIBLE

THOMAS NELSON

NEW INTERNATIONAL VERSION

THE PRAYER BIBLE

THOMAS NELSON
Since 1798

www.ThomasNelson.com

The Prayer Bible, NIV

Published in Nashville, Tennessee, by Thomas Nelson.

Thomas Nelson is a registered trademark of HarperCollins Christian Publishing, Inc.
The Holy Bible, New International Version®, NIV®

Library of Congress Control Number: 2024946600

Printed in India

---

25 26 27 28 29 30 31 32 33 34 35 36 /BPI/ 13 12 11 10 9 8 7 6 5 4 3 2 1

CONTENTS

THE OLD TESTAMENT

THE NEW TESTAMENT

INTRODUCTION TO *THE PRAYER BIBLE*

COME EXPERIENCE THE LORD

Prayer is a wonderful gift given to us by God. Throughout the centuries, it has been described in a multitude of ways. Some defined it as crying out to God in a time of need and others as praising God for his goodness. Prayer encompasses many facets: speaking to God, being silent before God, listening for the Holy Spirit's guidance to understand Scripture, pleading for help, asking for forgiveness, interceding for others in their time of need and worshiping God. Prayer is a deeply personal conversation with God in which—the Bible assures us—he listens and responds (Psalm 91:15; Jeremiah 33:3).

Because prayer is key to our walk with God, we want to do it regularly, effectively and passionately. However, we are not always confident about our prayer lives. It's why we are glad to offer this edition. *The Prayer Bible* is designed to help you engage more deeply and confidently in prayer. Inside, you'll find prayer prompts located alongside every chapter of the Bible. By combining your daily Bible reading with your prayer life, your prayer life will find its direction from the Scripture. But what does it mean to pray Scripture? It can either mean saying the prayers of the Bible word for word as our own prayers, personalizing portions of the Scriptures in prayer or praying through the different topics of the Bible.

How to Use this Edition:

Read the Bible passage first. We are happy to provide the Scripture engagement prompts, but they are always secondary to God's Word.

Read the Praying Scripture prompt slowly. It will give a brief insight into the passage that can enlighten your understanding and guide you to deeper study of the passage.

Use the Praying Scripture prompt to guide your prayer time. The prompt gives you one way to pray according to the content of the passage. These prompts offer different types of guidance that will encourage deeper introspection, inspire you to worship, offer hope or motivate you to pray about an action to take.

Pray with the words of Scripture. Whether at a loss for words or not, allow the words of the Bible to fill your prayers before God.

Be confident and filled with hope. God gave us the practice of prayer because he desires a close relationship with us.

It's our hope that as you engage God's Word through prayer that you will increasingly know its author, become rooted in his unshakable truth and bear much fruit for his glory. As part of the Abide Initiative, this Bible edition falls in line with the other Abide resources of Bibles, Scripture journals and studies. Through Abide, there is a grand opportunity that awaits: to meet the God of the Word. These resources allow you to move into Bible reading and study with the assurance that you will encounter the Lord. To that end, the Scripture engagement practices offered in the Abide line will aid you to grow ever deeper in your walk with Christ.

ABBREVIATIONS

Book abbreviations used in the notes and articles:
OT = Old Testament
NT = New Testament

1Ch	1 Chronicles	OT	Hos	Hosea	OT
1Co	1 Corinthians	NT	Isa	Isaiah	OT
1Jn	1 John	NT	Jas	James	NT
1Ki	1 Kings	OT	Jer	Jeremiah	OT
1Pe	1 Peter	NT	Job	Job	OT
1Sa	1 Samuel	OT	Joel	Joel	OT
1Th	1 Thessalonians	NT	Jn	John	NT
1Ti	1 Timothy	NT	Jnh	Jonah	OT
2Ch	2 Chronicles	OT	Jos	Joshua	OT
2Co	2 Corinthians	NT	Jude	Jude	NT
2Jn	2 John	NT	Jdg	Judges	OT
2Ki	2 Kings	OT	La	Lamentations	OT
2Pe	2 Peter	NT	Lev	Leviticus	OT
2Sa	2 Samuel	OT	Lk	Luke	NT
2Th	2 Thessalonians	NT	Mal	Malachi	OT
2Ti	2 Timothy	NT	Mk	Mark	NT
3Jn	3 John	NT	Mt	Matthew	NT
Ac	Acts	NT	Mic	Micah	OT
Am	Amos	OT	Na	Nahum	OT
Col	Colossians	NT	Ne	Nehemiah	OT
Da	Daniel	OT	Nu	Numbers	OT
Dt	Deuteronomy	OT	Ob	Obadiah	OT
Ecc	Ecclesiastes	OT	Php	Philippians	NT
Eph	Ephesians	NT	Phm	Philemon	NT
Est	Esther	OT	Pr	Proverbs	OT
Ex	Exodus	OT	Ps	Psalms	OT
Eze	Ezekiel	OT	Rev	Revelation	NT
Ezr	Ezra	OT	Ro	Romans	NT
Gal	Galatians	NT	Ru	Ruth	OT
Ge	Genesis	OT	SS	Song of Songs	OT
Hab	Habakkuk	OT	Titus	Titus	NT
Hag	Haggai	OT	Zec	Zechariah	OT
Heb	Hebrews	NT	Zep	Zephaniah	OT

365-DAY BIBLE-READING PLAN

DAY	READING
☐ 1	Ge 1–3
☐ 2	Ge 4–5
☐ 3	Ge 6:1—9:19
☐ 4	Ge 9:20—12:9
☐ 5	Ge 12:10—16:16
☐ 6	Ge 17:1—19:29
☐ 7	Ge 19:30—22:24
☐ 8	Ge 23–24
☐ 9	Ge 25–26
☐ 10	Ge 27:1—29:14
☐ 11	Ge 29:15—31:21
☐ 12	Ge 31:22—33:20
☐ 13	Ge 34:1—36:30
☐ 14	Ge 36:31—38:30
☐ 15	Ge 39:1—41:36
☐ 16	Ge 41:37—43:34
☐ 17	Ge 44–45
☐ 18	Ge 46–48
☐ 19	Ge 49–Ex 1
☐ 20	Ex 2–4
☐ 21	Ex 5–7
☐ 22	Ex 8:1—10:20
☐ 23	Ex 10:21—13:16
☐ 24	Ex 13:17—16:36
☐ 25	Ex 17–20
☐ 26	Ex 21:1—23:13
☐ 27	Ex 23:14—25:40
☐ 28	Ex 26–28
☐ 29	Ex 29–30
☐ 30	Ex 31:1—33:10
☐ 31	Ex 33:11—36:7
☐ 32	Ex 36:8—38:20
☐ 33	Ex 38:21—40:38
☐ 34	Lev 1:1—5:13
☐ 35	Lev 5:14—7:38
☐ 36	Lev 8–10
☐ 37	Lev 11:1—13:46
☐ 38	Lev 13:47—14:57
☐ 39	Lev 15–17
☐ 40	Lev 18–20
☐ 41	Lev 21:1—23:25
☐ 42	Lev 23:26—25:55
☐ 43	Lev 26–27
☐ 44	Nu 1–2
☐ 45	Nu 3:1—4:33
☐ 46	Nu 4:34—6:27
☐ 47	Nu 7
☐ 48	Nu 8–10
☐ 49	Nu 11–13
☐ 50	Nu 14–15
☐ 51	Nu 16–18
☐ 52	Nu 19–21
☐ 53	Nu 22–24
☐ 54	Nu 25–26
☐ 55	Nu 27–29
☐ 56	Nu 30–31
☐ 57	Nu 32–33
☐ 58	Nu 34–36
☐ 59	Dt 1:1—3:7
☐ 60	Dt 3:8—5:33
☐ 61	Dt 6:1—9:6
☐ 62	Dt 9:7—11:32
☐ 63	Dt 12–14
☐ 64	Dt 15–18
☐ 65	Dt 19–21
☐ 66	Dt 22–25
☐ 67	Dt 26:1—28:14
☐ 68	Dt 28:15—29:29
☐ 69	Dt 30:1—32:47
☐ 70	Dt 32:48—Jos 2:24
☐ 71	Jos 3–6
☐ 72	Jos 7–9
☐ 73	Jos 10–12
☐ 74	Jos 13–15
☐ 75	Jos 16:1—19:31
☐ 76	Jos 19:32—21:45
☐ 77	Jos 22–24
☐ 78	Jdg 1–3
☐ 79	Jdg 4–6
☐ 80	Jdg 7–8
☐ 81	Jdg 9–10
☐ 82	Jdg 11–13
☐ 83	Jdg 14–17
☐ 84	Jdg 18–19
☐ 85	Jdg 20–Ru 1
☐ 86	Ru 2–4
☐ 87	1Sa 1–4
☐ 88	1Sa 5–8
☐ 89	1Sa 9–12
☐ 90	1Sa 13–14
☐ 91	1Sa 15–16
☐ 92	1Sa 17–18
☐ 93	1Sa 19–21
☐ 94	1Sa 22–24
☐ 95	1Sa 25–27
☐ 96	1Sa 28–31
☐ 97	2Sa 1:1—3:21
☐ 98	2Sa 3:22—6:23
☐ 99	2Sa 7–10
☐ 100	2Sa 11:1—13:22
☐ 101	2Sa 13:23—15:37
☐ 102	2Sa 16:1—19:8
☐ 103	2Sa 19:9—21:22
☐ 104	2Sa 22–23
☐ 105	2Sa 24:1—1Ki 2:11
☐ 106	1Ki 2:12—4:21
☐ 107	1Ki 4:22—7:14
☐ 108	1Ki 7:15—8:66
☐ 109	1Ki 9–11
☐ 110	1Ki 12–13
☐ 111	1Ki 14:1—16:20
☐ 112	1Ki 16:21—18:46
☐ 113	1Ki 19–21
☐ 114	1Ki 22–2Ki 2
☐ 115	2Ki 3–4
☐ 116	2Ki 5–7
☐ 117	2Ki 8:1—10:17
☐ 118	2Ki 10:18—13:25
☐ 119	2Ki 14–16
☐ 120	2Ki 17–19

DAY	READING
☐ **121**	2Ki 20–22
☐ **122**	2Ki 23–25
☐ **123**	1Ch 1:1—2:2
☐ **124**	1Ch 2:3—4:23
☐ **125**	1Ch 4:24—5:26
☐ **126**	1Ch 6:1—7:5
☐ **127**	1Ch 7:6—8:40
☐ **128**	1Ch 9:1—11:14
☐ **129**	1Ch 11:15—13:14
☐ **130**	1Ch 14–16
☐ **131**	1Ch 17–20
☐ **132**	1Ch 21–23
☐ **133**	1Ch 24–26
☐ **134**	1Ch 27–29
☐ **135**	2Ch 1–4
☐ **136**	2Ch 5–7
☐ **137**	2Ch 8–11
☐ **138**	2Ch 12–16
☐ **139**	2Ch 17–20
☐ **140**	2Ch 21–24
☐ **141**	2Ch 25–28
☐ **142**	2Ch 29–31
☐ **143**	2Ch 32–34
☐ **144**	2Ch 35–36
☐ **145**	Ezr 1–3
☐ **146**	Ezr 4–7
☐ **147**	Ezr 8–10
☐ **148**	Ne 1–4
☐ **149**	Ne 5–7
☐ **150**	Ne 8–10
☐ **151**	Ne 11–13
☐ **152**	Est 1–4
☐ **153**	Est 5–10
☐ **154**	Job 1–3
☐ **155**	Job 4–7
☐ **156**	Job 8–10
☐ **157**	Job 11–14
☐ **158**	Job 15–18
☐ **159**	Job 19–21
☐ **160**	Job 22–25
☐ **161**	Job 26–31
☐ **162**	Job 32–37
☐ **163**	Job 38–42
☐ **164**	Ps 1–7
☐ **165**	Ps 8–15
☐ **166**	Ps 16–19
☐ **167**	Ps 20–25
☐ **168**	Ps 26–31
☐ **169**	Ps 32–35
☐ **170**	Ps 36–39
☐ **171**	Ps 40–45
☐ **172**	Ps 46–50
☐ **173**	Ps 51–57
☐ **174**	Ps 58–64
☐ **175**	Ps 65–68
☐ **176**	Ps 69–72
☐ **177**	Ps 73–77
☐ **178**	Ps 78–79
☐ **179**	Ps 80–85
☐ **180**	Ps 86–89
☐ **181**	Ps 90–95
☐ **182**	Ps 96–102
☐ **183**	Ps 103–105
☐ **184**	Ps 106–107
☐ **185**	Ps 108–114
☐ **186**	Ps 115–118
☐ **187**	Ps 119:1–88
☐ **188**	Ps 119:89–176
☐ **189**	Ps 120–131
☐ **190**	Ps 132–138
☐ **191**	Ps 139–144
☐ **192**	Ps 145–150
☐ **193**	Pr 1–3
☐ **194**	Pr 4–6
☐ **195**	Pr 7–9
☐ **196**	Pr 10–12
☐ **197**	Pr 13–15
☐ **198**	Pr 16–18
☐ **199**	Pr 19–21
☐ **200**	Pr 22–24
☐ **201**	Pr 25–27
☐ **202**	Pr 28–31
☐ **203**	Ecc 1–3
☐ **204**	Ecc 4–7
☐ **205**	Ecc 8–12
☐ **206**	SS 1–8
☐ **207**	Is 1–4
☐ **208**	Is 5–8
☐ **209**	Is 9–12
☐ **210**	Is 13–17
☐ **211**	Is 18–22
☐ **212**	Is 23–27
☐ **213**	Is 28–30
☐ **214**	Is 31–35
☐ **215**	Is 36–38
☐ **216**	Is 39–42
☐ **217**	Is 43–45
☐ **218**	Is 46–50
☐ **219**	Is 51–56
☐ **220**	Is 57–61
☐ **221**	Is 62–66
☐ **222**	Jer 1–3
☐ **223**	Jer 4–5
☐ **224**	Jer 6–8
☐ **225**	Jer 9–11
☐ **226**	Jer 12–15
☐ **227**	Jer 16–19
☐ **228**	Jer 20–23
☐ **229**	Jer 24–26
☐ **230**	Jer 27–29
☐ **231**	Jer 30–31
☐ **232**	Jer 32:1—34:7
☐ **233**	Jer 34:8—37:21
☐ **234**	Jer 38–41
☐ **235**	Jer 42–45
☐ **236**	Jer 46–48
☐ **237**	Jer 49
☐ **238**	Jer 50–51
☐ **239**	Jer 52
☐ **240**	La 1–5
☐ **241**	Eze 1–5
☐ **242**	Eze 6–10
☐ **243**	Eze 11–13
☐ **244**	Eze 14–16
☐ **245**	Eze 17–19
☐ **246**	Eze 20–21
☐ **247**	Eze 22–23
☐ **248**	Eze 24–27
☐ **249**	Eze 28–31

DAY	READING
☐ 250	Eze 32–34
☐ 251	Eze 35–37
☐ 252	Eze 38–40
☐ 253	Eze 41–43
☐ 254	Eze 44–46
☐ 255	Eze 47–48
☐ 256	Da 1–3
☐ 257	Da 4–6
☐ 258	Da 7–9
☐ 259	Da 10–12
☐ 260	Hos 1–5
☐ 261	Hos 6–10
☐ 262	Hos 11–14
☐ 263	Joel 1–3
☐ 264	Am 1–4
☐ 265	Am 5–Ob 1
☐ 266	Jnh 1–Mic 4
☐ 267	Mic 5–Na 3
☐ 268	Hab 1–Zep 3
☐ 269	Hag 1–Zec 3
☐ 270	Zec 4–10
☐ 271	Zec 11–Mal 4
☐ 272	Mt 1–2
☐ 273	Mt 3–4
☐ 274	Mt 5–7
☐ 275	Mt 8–9
☐ 276	Mt 10–11
☐ 277	Mt 12–13
☐ 278	Mt 14–15
☐ 279	Mt 16–18
☐ 280	Mt 19–20
☐ 281	Mt 21–22
☐ 282	Mt 23–24
☐ 283	Mt 25–26
☐ 284	Mt 27–28
☐ 285	Mk 1–2
☐ 286	Mk 3–4
☐ 287	Mk 5–6
☐ 288	Mk 7–8
☐ 289	Mk 9–10
☐ 290	Mk 11–12
☐ 291	Mk 13–14
☐ 292	Mk 15–16
☐ 293	Lk 1
☐ 294	Lk 2
☐ 295	Lk 3–4
☐ 296	Lk 5–6
☐ 297	Lk 7–8
☐ 298	Lk 9
☐ 299	Lk 10–11
☐ 300	Lk 12–13
☐ 301	Lk 14–15
☐ 302	Lk 16–17
☐ 303	Lk 18–19
☐ 304	Lk 20–21
☐ 305	Lk 22:1—23:25
☐ 306	Lk 23:26—24:53
☐ 307	Jn 1–2
☐ 308	Jn 3–4
☐ 309	Jn 5–6
☐ 310	Jn 7
☐ 311	Jn 8–9
☐ 312	Jn 10:1—11:44
☐ 313	Jn 11:45—12:50
☐ 314	Jn 13–14
☐ 315	Jn 15–17
☐ 316	Jn 18–19
☐ 317	Jn 20–21
☐ 318	Ac 1–3
☐ 319	Ac 4–6
☐ 320	Ac 7–8
☐ 321	Ac 9–10
☐ 322	Ac 11:1—13:12
☐ 323	Ac 13:13—14:28
☐ 324	Ac 15–16
☐ 325	Ac 17–19
☐ 326	Ac 20–21
☐ 327	Ac 22–24
☐ 328	Ac 25–26
☐ 329	Ac 27–28
☐ 330	Ro 1–4
☐ 331	Ro 5–8
☐ 332	Ro 9–11
☐ 333	Ro 12–14
☐ 334	Ro 15–16
☐ 335	1Co 1–4
☐ 336	1Co 5–9
☐ 337	1Co 10–12
☐ 338	1Co 13–16
☐ 339	2Co 1–3
☐ 340	2Co 4–6
☐ 341	2Co 7–9
☐ 342	2Co 10–13
☐ 343	Gal 1–3
☐ 344	Gal 4–6
☐ 345	Eph 1–3
☐ 346	Eph 4–6
☐ 347	Php 1–4
☐ 348	Col 1–4
☐ 349	1Th 1–5
☐ 350	2Th 1–3
☐ 351	1Ti 1–6
☐ 352	2Ti 1–4
☐ 353	Titus 1–Phm 1
☐ 354	Heb 1–6
☐ 355	Heb 7–13
☐ 356	Jas 1–3
☐ 357	Jas 4–5
☐ 358	1Pe 1–5
☐ 359	2Pe 1–3
☐ 360	1Jn 1–Jude 1
☐ 361	Rev 1–3
☐ 362	Rev 4–9
☐ 363	Rev 10–13
☐ 364	Rev 14–18
☐ 365	Rev 19–22

PREFACE TO THE NEW INTERNATIONAL VERSION

The goal of the New International Version (NIV) is to enable English-speaking people from around the world to read and hear God's eternal Word in their own language. Our work as translators is motivated by our conviction that the Bible is God's Word in written form. We believe that the Bible contains the divine answer to the deepest needs of humanity, sheds unique light on our path in a dark world and sets forth the way to our eternal well-being. Out of these deep convictions, we have sought to recreate as far as possible the experience of the original audience—blending transparency to the original text with accessibility for the millions of English speakers around the world. We have prioritized accuracy, clarity and literary quality with the goal of creating a translation suitable for public and private reading, evangelism, teaching, preaching, memorizing and liturgical use. We have also sought to preserve a measure of continuity with the long tradition of translating the Scriptures into English.

The complete NIV Bible was first published in 1978. It was a completely new translation made by over a hundred scholars working directly from the best available Hebrew, Aramaic and Greek texts. The translators came from the United States, Great Britain, Canada, Australia and New Zealand, giving the translation an international scope. They were from many denominations and churches—including Anglican, Assemblies of God, Baptist, Brethren, Christian Reformed, Church of Christ, Evangelical Covenant, Evangelical Free, Lutheran, Mennonite, Methodist, Nazarene, Presbyterian, Wesleyan and others. This breadth of denominational and theological perspective helped to safeguard the translation from sectarian bias. For these reasons, and by the grace of God, the NIV has gained a wide readership in all parts of the English-speaking world.

The work of translating the Bible is never finished. As good as they are, English translations must be regularly updated so that they will continue to communicate accurately the meaning of God's Word. Updates are needed in order to reflect the latest developments in our understanding of the biblical world and its languages and to keep pace with changes in English usage. Recognizing, then, that the NIV would retain its ability to communicate God's Word accurately only if it were regularly updated, the original translators established the Committee on Bible Translation (CBT). The Committee is a self-perpetuating group of biblical scholars charged with keeping abreast of advances in biblical scholarship and changes in English and issuing periodic updates to the NIV. The CBT is an independent, self-governing body and has sole responsibility for the NIV text. The Committee mirrors the original group of translators in its diverse international and denominational makeup and in its unifying commitment to the Bible as God's inspired Word.

In obedience to its mandate, the Committee has issued periodic updates to the NIV. An initial revision was released in 1984. A more thorough revision process was completed in 2005, resulting in the separately published TNIV. The updated NIV you now have in your hands builds on both the original NIV and the TNIV and represents the latest effort of the Committee to articulate God's unchanging Word in the way the original authors might have said it had they been speaking in English to the global English-speaking audience today.

TRANSLATION PHILOSOPHY

The Committee's translating work has been governed by three widely accepted principles about the way people use words and about the way we understand them.

First, the meaning of words is determined by the way that users of the language actually use them at any given time. For the biblical languages, therefore, the Committee utilizes the best and most recent scholarship on the way Hebrew, Aramaic and Greek words were being used in biblical times. At the same time, the Committee carefully studies the state of modern English. Good translation is like good communication: one must know the target audience so that the appropriate choices can be made about which English words to use to represent the original words of Scripture. From its inception, the NIV has had as its target the general English-speaking population all over the world, the "International" in its title reflecting this concern. The aim of the Committee is to put the Scriptures into natural English that will communicate effectively with the broadest possible audience of English speakers.

Modern technology has enhanced the Committee's ability to choose the right English words to convey the meaning of the original text. The field of computational linguistics harnesses the power of computers to provide broadly applicable and current data about the state of the language. Translators can now access huge databases of modern English to better understand the current meaning and usage of key words. The Committee utilized this resource in preparing the 2011 edition of the NIV. An area of especially rapid and significant change in English is the way certain nouns and pronouns are used to refer to human beings. The Committee therefore requested experts in computational linguistics at Collins Dictionaries to pose some key questions about this usage to its database of English—the largest in the world, with over 4.4 billion words, gathered from several English-speaking countries and including both spoken and written English. (The Collins Study, called "The Development and Use of Gender Language in Contemporary English," can be accessed at *http://www.thenivbible.com/about-the-niv/about-the-2011-edition/*.) The study revealed that the most popular words to describe the human race in modern U.S. English were "humanity," "man" and "mankind." The Committee then used this data in the updated NIV, choosing from among these three words (and occasionally others also) depending on the context.

A related issue creates a larger problem for modern translations: the move away from using the third-person masculine singular pronouns—"he/him/his"—to refer to men and women equally. This usage does persist in some forms of English, and this revision therefore occasionally uses these pronouns in a generic sense. But the tendency, recognized in day-to-day usage and confirmed by the Collins study, is away from the generic use of "he," "him" and "his." In recognition of this shift in language and in an effort to translate into the natural English that people are actually using, this revision of the NIV generally uses other constructions when the biblical text is plainly addressed to men and women equally. The reader will encounter especially frequently a "they," "their" or "them" to express a generic singular idea. Thus, for instance, Mark 8:36 reads: "What good is it for someone to gain the whole world, yet forfeit their soul?" This generic use of the "distributive" or "singular" "they/them/their" has been used for many centuries by respected writers of English and has now become established as standard English, spoken and written, all over the world.

A second linguistic principle that feeds into the Committee's translation work is that meaning is found not in individual words, as vital as they are, but in larger clusters: phrases, clauses, sentences, discourses. Translation is not, as many people think, a matter of word substitution: English word *x* in place of Hebrew word *y*. Translators must first determine the meaning of the words of the biblical languages in the context of the passage and then select English words that accurately communicate that meaning to modern listeners and readers. This means that accurate translation will not always reflect the exact structure of the original language. To be sure, there is debate over the degree to which translators should try to preserve the "form" of the original text in English. From the beginning, the NIV has taken a mediating position on this issue. The manual produced when the translation that became the NIV was first being planned states: "If the Greek or Hebrew syntax has a good parallel in modern English, it should be used. But if there is no good parallel, the English syntax appropriate to the meaning of the original is to be chosen." It is fine, in other words, to carry over the form of the biblical languages into English—but not at the expense of natural expression. The principle that meaning resides in larger clusters of words means that the Committee has not insisted on a "word-for-word" approach to translation. We certainly believe that every word of Scripture is inspired by God and therefore to be carefully studied to determine what God is saying to us. It is for this reason that the Committee labors over every single word of the original texts, working hard to determine how each of those words contributes to what the text is saying. Ultimately, however, it is how these individual words function in combination with other words that determines meaning.

A third linguistic principle guiding the Committee in its translation work is the recognition that words have a spectrum of meaning. It is popular to define a word by using another word, or "gloss," to substitute for it. This substitute word is then sometimes called the "literal" meaning of a word. In fact, however, words have a range of possible meanings. Those meanings will vary depending on the context, and words in one language will usually not occupy the same semantic range as words in another language. The Committee therefore studies each original word of Scripture in its context to identify its meaning in a particular verse and then chooses an appropriate English word (or phrase) to represent it. It is impossible, then, to translate any given Hebrew, Aramaic or Greek word with the same English word all the time. The Committee does try to translate related occurrences of a word in the original languages with the same English word in order to preserve the connection for the English reader. But the Committee generally privileges clear natural meaning over a concern with consistency in rendering particular words.

TEXTUAL BASIS

For the Old Testament the standard Hebrew text, the Masoretic Text as published in the latest edition of *Biblia Hebraica*, has been used throughout. The Masoretic Text tradition contains marginal notations that offer variant readings. These have sometimes been followed instead of the text itself. Because such instances involve variants within the Masoretic tradition, they have not been indicated in the textual notes. In a few cases, words in the basic consonantal text have been divided differently than in the Masoretic Text. Such cases are usually indicated in the textual footnotes. The Dead Sea Scrolls contain biblical texts that represent an earlier stage of the transmission of the Hebrew text. They have been consulted, as have been the Samaritan Pentateuch and the ancient scribal traditions concerning deliberate textual changes. The translators also consulted the more important early versions. Readings from these versions, the Dead Sea Scrolls and the scribal traditions were occasionally followed where the Masoretic Text seemed doubtful and where accepted principles of textual criticism showed that one or more of these textual witnesses appeared to provide the correct reading. In rare cases, the translators have emended the Hebrew text where it appears to have become corrupted at an even earlier stage of its transmission. These departures from the Masoretic Text are also indicated in the textual footnotes. Sometimes the vowel indicators (which are later additions to the basic consonantal text) found in the Masoretic Text did not, in the judgment of the translators, represent the correct vowels for the original text. Accordingly, some words have been read with a different set of vowels. These instances are usually not indicated in the footnotes.

The Greek text used in translating the New Testament has been an eclectic one, based on the latest editions of the Nestle-Aland/United Bible Societies' Greek New Testament. The translators have made their choices among the variant readings in accordance with widely accepted principles of New Testament textual criticism. Footnotes call attention to places where uncertainty remains.

The New Testament authors, writing in Greek, often quote the Old Testament from its ancient Greek version, the Septuagint. This is one reason why some of the Old Testament quotations in the NIV New Testament are not identical to the corresponding passages in the NIV Old Testament. Such quotations in the New Testament are indicated with the footnote "(see Septuagint)."

FOOTNOTES AND FORMATTING

Footnotes in this version are of several kinds, most of which need no explanation. Those giving alternative translations begin with "Or" and generally introduce the alternative with the last word preceding it in the text, except when it is a single-word alternative. When poetry is quoted in a footnote a slash mark indicates a line division.

It should be noted that references to diseases, minerals, flora and fauna, architectural details, clothing, jewelry, musical instruments and other articles cannot always be identified with precision. Also, linear measurements and measures of capacity can only be approximated (see the Table of Weights and Measures). Although *Selah*, used mainly in the Psalms, is probably a musical term, its meaning is uncertain. Since it may interrupt reading and distract the reader, this word has not been kept in the English text, but every occurrence has been signaled by a footnote.

As an aid to the reader, sectional headings have been inserted. They are not to be regarded as part of the biblical text and are not intended for oral reading. It is the Committee's hope that these headings may prove more helpful to the reader than the traditional chapter divisions, which were introduced long after the Bible was written.

Sometimes the chapter and/or verse numbering in English translations of the Old Testament differs from that found in published Hebrew texts. This is particularly the case in the Psalms, where the traditional titles are included in the Hebrew verse numbering. Such differences are indicated in the footnotes at the bottom of the page. In the New Testament, verse numbers that marked off portions of the traditional English text not supported by the best Greek manuscripts now appear in brackets, with a footnote indicating the text that has been omitted (see, for example, Matthew 17:[21]).

Mark 16:9–20 and John 7:53—8:11, although long accorded virtually equal status with the rest of the Gospels in which they stand, have a questionable standing in the textual history of the New Testament, as noted in the bracketed annotations with which they are set off. A different typeface has been chosen for these passages to indicate their uncertain status.

Basic formatting of the text, such as lining the poetry, paragraphing (both prose and poetry), setting up of (administrative-like) lists, indenting letters and lengthy prayers within narratives and the insertion of sectional headings, has been the work of the Committee. However, the choice between single-column and double-column formats has been left to the publishers. Also the issuing of "red-letter" editions is a publisher's choice—one that the Committee does not endorse.

The Committee has again been reminded that every human effort is flawed—including this revision of the NIV. We trust, however, that many will find in it an improved representation of the Word of God, through which they hear his call to faith in our Lord Jesus Christ and to service in his kingdom. We offer this version of the Bible to him in whose name and for whose glory it has been made.

The Committee on Bible Translation

OLD TESTAMENT

GENESIS

Genesis introduces readers to the Bible's main character: the triune God. It reveals the Bible's storyline and its major themes. While we find many of the narratives of the Bible's heroes inspiring and instructive, the main character introduces himself in the first verse: "In the beginning God." Through his words and actions in Genesis, we learn that God is all-powerful, all-knowing, ever-present, holy, just, righteous, loving, kind, gracious and faithful to his promises. The Bible's first book also portrays God as the One who knows and loves his people.

Chapters 1 and 2 explain how God created the world and everything in it. The beauty and majesty of creation should drive us toward prayer of awe and wonder. The vastness of the universe and the intricacy of the world at the cellular level, the harmony of the planets and the balance of earth's systems, all speak to the glory of the Creator who deserves our praise. The crowning jewels of creation were two human beings—one male and one female—both made in God's image. However, these image bearers fell into sin. They did not take God at his word, believing instead the words of the tempter, Satan. Their sin brought degradation into the perfect world that God had created, eventually forcing them from the perfect Eden made just for them.

Early in the Genesis narrative, after the fall, we are introduced to prayer: "At that time people began to call on the name of the LORD" (4:26). Perhaps the effects of sin were becoming evident. Or perhaps humans realized how deeply their separation from God cut. Whatever their reason, people began to pray. Enoch walked with the Lord, and the Lord took him up to heaven. The Lord made personal promises to Noah and fulfilled those promises as "Noah found favor in the eyes of the LORD" (6:8).

Genesis reveals how God will bring redemption to all the nations of the world through one family, fulfilling his promise to Eve. God's interactions with Abraham, then Isaac and Jacob, form the center of the Genesis narrative arc. Abraham prayed to God in person, interceding for the lives of the righteous in Sodom and Gomorrah. Isaac pleaded with God to give children to Rebekah, the wife he loved. Jacob wrestled with an angel, praying that God would bless him.

The final chapters of Genesis tell us of Joseph and his sojourn in Egypt, which ultimately led to the salvation of Joseph's family from a famine and their relocation to Egypt in fulfillment of God's promise. We don't read of Joseph's specific prayers, but there is no doubt that he prayed from the bottom of a cistern, while in prison, while in Pharaoh's house and when he discovered his father was still alive. No matter how difficult life became for Joseph in Egypt, Genesis tells us, "The LORD was with Joseph" (39:2,23).

The revelation of God's plan so long ago to redeem a people for himself should drive us to worship, and our introduction to a God who listens should encourage us to pray.

PRAYING SCRIPTURE

Genesis 1

The Bible opens with the reason we should praise God for all things: He is the Creator. He is the only one with enough power and wisdom to create the universe and everything in it from nothing, including the human race created in his image.

Stop for a moment and ponder God's unlimited power that brought galaxies into being. Marvel that he made you. Praise him for making you and loving you.

THE BEGINNING

1 In the beginning God created the heavens and the earth. 2Now
the earth was formless and empty, darkness was over the surface
of the deep, and the Spirit of God was hovering over the waters.
3And God said, "Let there be light," and there was light. 4God saw
that the light was good, and he separated the light from the
darkness. 5God called the light "day," and the darkness he called
"night." And there was evening, and there was morning — the
first day.
6And God said, "Let there be a vault between the waters to separate
water from water." 7So God made the vault and separated the wa-
ter under the vault from the water above it. And it was so. 8God
called the vault "sky." And there was evening, and there was morn-
ing — the second day.
9And God said, "Let the water under the sky be gathered to one place,
and let dry ground appear." And it was so. 10God called the dry
ground "land," and the gathered waters he called "seas." And God
saw that it was good.
11Then God said, "Let the land produce vegetation: seed-bearing
plants and trees on the land that bear fruit with seed in it, ac-
cording to their various kinds." And it was so. 12The land produced
vegetation: plants bearing seed according to their kinds and trees
bearing fruit with seed in it according to their kinds. And God saw
that it was good. 13And there was evening, and there was morn-
ing — the third day.
14And God said, "Let there be lights in the vault of the sky to separate
the day from the night, and let them serve as signs to mark sacred
times, and days and years, 15and let them be lights in the vault of
the sky to give light on the earth." And it was so. 16God made two
great lights — the greater light to govern the day and the lesser
light to govern the night. He also made the stars. 17God set them in
the vault of the sky to give light on the earth, 18to govern the day
and the night, and to separate light from darkness. And God saw
that it was good. 19And there was evening, and there was morn-
ing — the fourth day.
20And God said, "Let the water teem with living creatures, and let birds
fly above the earth across the vault of the sky." 21So God created
the great creatures of the sea and every living thing with which
the water teems and that moves about in it, according to their
kinds, and every winged bird according to its kind. And God saw
that it was good. 22God blessed them and said, "Be fruitful and in-
crease in number and fill the water in the seas, and let the birds
increase on the earth." 23And there was evening, and there was
morning — the fifth day.
24And God said, "Let the land produce living creatures according
to their kinds: the livestock, the creatures that move along the
ground, and the wild animals, each according to its kind." And it
was so. 25God made the wild animals according to their kinds, the
livestock according to their kinds, and all the creatures that move
along the ground according to their kinds. And God saw that it was
good.
26Then God said, "Let us make mankind in our image, in our
likeness, so that they may rule over the fish in the sea and the

birds in the sky, over the livestock and all the wild animals,[a] and
over all the creatures that move along the ground."

27 So God created mankind in his own image,
in the image of God he created them;
male and female he created them.

28 God blessed them and said to them, "Be fruitful and increase
in number; fill the earth and subdue it. Rule over the fish in the
sea and the birds in the sky and over every living creature that
moves on the ground."
29 Then God said, "I give you every seed-bearing plant on the
face of the whole earth and every tree that has fruit with seed in
it. They will be yours for food. 30 And to all the beasts of the earth
and all the birds in the sky and all the creatures that move along
the ground—everything that has the breath of life in it—I give
every green plant for food." And it was so.
31 God saw all that he had made, and it was very good. And there
was evening, and there was morning—the sixth day.

2 Thus the heavens and the earth were completed in all their vast
array.
2 By the seventh day God had finished the work he had been doing; so
on the seventh day he rested from all his work. 3 Then God blessed
the seventh day and made it holy, because on it he rested from all
the work of creating that he had done.

ADAM AND EVE

4 This is the account of the heavens and the earth when they were
created, when the LORD God made the earth and the heavens.

5 Now no shrub had yet appeared on the earth[b] and no plant had
yet sprung up, for the LORD God had not sent rain on the earth and
there was no one to work the ground, 6 but streams[c] came up from the
earth and watered the whole surface of the ground. 7 Then the LORD
God formed a man[d] from the dust of the ground and breathed into his
nostrils the breath of life, and the man became a living being.
8 Now the LORD God had planted a garden in the east, in Eden; and
there he put the man he had formed. 9 The LORD God made all kinds of
trees grow out of the ground—trees that were pleasing to the eye and
good for food. In the middle of the garden were the tree of life and the
tree of the knowledge of good and evil.
10 A river watering the garden flowed from Eden; from there it was
separated into four headwaters. 11 The name of the first is the Pishon;
it winds through the entire land of Havilah, where there is gold. 12 (The
gold of that land is good; aromatic resin[e] and onyx are also there.)
13 The name of the second river is the Gihon; it winds through the en-
tire land of Cush.[f] 14 The name of the third river is the Tigris; it runs
along the east side of Ashur. And the fourth river is the Euphrates.
15 The LORD God took the man and put him in the Garden of Eden to

PRAYING SCRIPTURE

Genesis 2

Genesis 2 begins with God resting from his work on the seventh day. This serves as a pattern for us to make time to rest each week. In our go, go, go, "what's next" world, such a pattern can be a nearly insurmountable challenge.

Every part of our being—physical, mental, emotional and spiritual needs rest. Ask God to help you remember to rest; then be intentional in taking time to do it.

---

[a] *26* Probable reading of the original Hebrew text (see Syriac); Masoretic Text *the earth* [b] *5* Or *land*; also in verse 6 [c] *6* Or *mist* [d] *7* The Hebrew for *man (adam)* sounds like and may be related to the Hebrew for *ground (adamah)*; it is also the name *Adam* (see verse 20). [e] *12* Or *good; pearls* [f] *13* Possibly southeast Mesopotamia

work it and take care of it. 16And the LORD God commanded the man,
"You are free to eat from any tree in the garden; 17but you must not
eat from the tree of the knowledge of good and evil, for when you eat
from it you will certainly die."
18The LORD God said, "It is not good for the man to be alone. I will
make a helper suitable for him."
19Now the LORD God had formed out of the ground all the wild an-
imals and all the birds in the sky. He brought them to the man to see
what he would name them; and whatever the man called each living
creature, that was its name. 20So the man gave names to all the live-
stock, the birds in the sky and all the wild animals.
But for Adam[a] no suitable helper was found. 21So the LORD God
caused the man to fall into a deep sleep; and while he was sleeping,
he took one of the man's ribs[b] and then closed up the place with flesh.
22Then the LORD God made a woman from the rib[c] he had taken out of
the man, and he brought her to the man.
23The man said,

"This is now bone of my bones
  and flesh of my flesh;
she shall be called 'woman,'
  for she was taken out of man."

24That is why a man leaves his father and mother and is united to his
wife, and they become one flesh.
25Adam and his wife were both naked, and they felt no shame.

THE FALL

3 Now the serpent was more crafty than any of the wild animals the
LORD God had made. He said to the woman, "Did God really say,
'You must not eat from any tree in the garden'?"
2The woman said to the serpent, "We may eat fruit from the trees
in the garden, 3but God did say, 'You must not eat fruit from the tree
that is in the middle of the garden, and you must not touch it, or you
will die.'"
4"You will not certainly die," the serpent said to the woman. 5"For
God knows that when you eat from it your eyes will be opened, and
you will be like God, knowing good and evil."
6When the woman saw that the fruit of the tree was good for food
and pleasing to the eye, and also desirable for gaining wisdom, she
took some and ate it. She also gave some to her husband, who was with
her, and he ate it. 7Then the eyes of both of them were opened, and
they realized they were naked; so they sewed fig leaves together and
made coverings for themselves.
8Then the man and his wife heard the sound of the LORD God as he
was walking in the garden in the cool of the day, and they hid from the
LORD God among the trees of the garden. 9But the LORD God called to
the man, "Where are you?"
10He answered, "I heard you in the garden, and I was afraid because
I was naked; so I hid."
11And he said, "Who told you that you were naked? Have you eaten
from the tree that I commanded you not to eat from?"
12The man said, "The woman you put here with me — she gave me
some fruit from the tree, and I ate it."

PRAYING SCRIPTURE

Genesis 3

Humanity was cast into a tailspin when Adam and Eve rebelled against God. Placed in a garden with all they could ever need, they chose to violate the single restriction God placed on them, becoming separated from him. But God showed them mercy.

We often feel as if God's only response to our disobedience is anger, but it isn't. If you've sinned, confess it to God and receive his covering mercy.

[a] 20 *Or the man* [b] 21 *Or took part of the man's side* [c] 22 *Or part*

13Then the LORD God said to the woman, "What is this you have
done?"
The woman said, "The serpent deceived me, and I ate."
14So the LORD God said to the serpent, "Because you have done this,

"Cursed are you above all livestock
and all wild animals!
You will crawl on your belly
and you will eat dust
all the days of your life.
15 And I will put enmity
between you and the woman,
and between your offspring[a] and hers;
he will crush[b] your head,
and you will strike his heel."

16To the woman he said,

"I will make your pains in childbearing very severe;
with painful labor you will give birth to children.
Your desire will be for your husband,
and he will rule over you."

17To Adam he said, "Because you listened to your wife and ate fruit
from the tree about which I commanded you, 'You must not eat from it,'

"Cursed is the ground because of you;
through painful toil you will eat food from it
all the days of your life.
18 It will produce thorns and thistles for you,
and you will eat the plants of the field.
19 By the sweat of your brow
you will eat your food
until you return to the ground,
since from it you were taken;
for dust you are
and to dust you will return."

20Adam[c] named his wife Eve,[d] because she would become the
mother of all the living.
21The LORD God made garments of skin for Adam and his wife and
clothed them. 22And the LORD God said, "The man has now become like
one of us, knowing good and evil. He must not be allowed to reach out
his hand and take also from the tree of life and eat, and live forever."
23So the LORD God banished him from the Garden of Eden to work the
ground from which he had been taken. 24After he drove the man out,
he placed on the east side[e] of the Garden of Eden cherubim and a flaming sword flashing back and forth to guard the way to the tree of life.

CAIN AND ABEL

4 Adam[c] made love to his wife Eve, and she became pregnant and
gave birth to Cain.[f] She said, "With the help of the LORD I have
brought forth[g] a man." 2Later she gave birth to his brother Abel.

PRAYING SCRIPTURE

Genesis 4

When God addressed Cain, he focused on the attitude of Cain's heart. Cain's angry response to God's rejection of his offering was the outward expression of the inward reality God had seen.

When you come to God, are you trying to hide an attitude you know displeases God? He already knows what's in us, so be honest and open with him. Confess it so that your prayers are not hindered.

[a] 15 Or *seed* [b] 15 Or *strike* [c] 20,1 Or *The man* [d] 20 *Eve* probably means *living.* [e] 24 Or *placed in front* [f] 1 *Cain* sounds like the Hebrew for *brought forth* or *acquired.* [g] 1 Or *have acquired*

Now Abel kept flocks, and Cain worked the soil. 3In the course of
time Cain brought some of the fruits of the soil as an offering to the
LORD. 4And Abel also brought an offering — fat portions from some of
the firstborn of his flock. The LORD looked with favor on Abel and his
offering, 5but on Cain and his offering he did not look with favor. So
Cain was very angry, and his face was downcast.

6Then the LORD said to Cain, "Why are you angry? Why is your face
downcast? 7If you do what is right, will you not be accepted? But if you
do not do what is right, sin is crouching at your door; it desires to have
you, but you must rule over it."

8Now Cain said to his brother Abel, "Let's go out to the field."[a] While
they were in the field, Cain attacked his brother Abel and killed him.

9Then the LORD said to Cain, "Where is your brother Abel?"

"I don't know," he replied. "Am I my brother's keeper?"

10The LORD said, "What have you done? Listen! Your brother's
blood cries out to me from the ground. 11Now you are under a curse
and driven from the ground, which opened its mouth to receive your
brother's blood from your hand. 12When you work the ground, it will
no longer yield its crops for you. You will be a restless wanderer on
the earth."

13Cain said to the LORD, "My punishment is more than I can bear.
14Today you are driving me from the land, and I will be hidden from
your presence; I will be a restless wanderer on the earth, and whoever
finds me will kill me."

15But the LORD said to him, "Not so[b]; anyone who kills Cain will suf-
fer vengeance seven times over." Then the LORD put a mark on Cain so
that no one who found him would kill him. 16So Cain went out from
the LORD's presence and lived in the land of Nod,[c] east of Eden.

17Cain made love to his wife, and she became pregnant and gave
birth to Enoch. Cain was then building a city, and he named it after his
son Enoch. 18To Enoch was born Irad, and Irad was the father of Mehu-
jael, and Mehujael was the father of Methushael, and Methushael was
the father of Lamech.

19Lamech married two women, one named Adah and the other Zil-
lah. 20Adah gave birth to Jabal; he was the father of those who live in
tents and raise livestock. 21His brother's name was Jubal; he was the
father of all who play stringed instruments and pipes. 22Zillah also had
a son, Tubal-Cain, who forged all kinds of tools out of[d] bronze and iron.
Tubal-Cain's sister was Naamah.

23Lamech said to his wives,

"Adah and Zillah, listen to me;
 wives of Lamech, hear my words.
I have killed a man for wounding me,
 a young man for injuring me.
24If Cain is avenged seven times,
 then Lamech seventy-seven times."

25Adam made love to his wife again, and she gave birth to a son and
named him Seth,[e] saying, "God has granted me another child in place

[a] 8 Samaritan Pentateuch, Septuagint, Vulgate and Syriac; Masoretic Text does not have *"Let's go out to the field."* [b] 15 Septuagint, Vulgate and Syriac; Hebrew *Very well* [c] 16 *Nod* means *wandering* (see verses 12 and 14). [d] 22 Or *who instructed all who work in* [e] 25 *Seth* probably means *granted.*

of Abel, since Cain killed him." 26Seth also had a son, and he named
him Enosh.

At that time people began to call on[a] the name of the LORD.

FROM ADAM TO NOAH

5 This is the written account of Adam's family line.

When God created mankind, he made them in the likeness of God.
2He created them male and female and blessed them. And he named
them "Mankind"[b] when they were created.

3When Adam had lived 130 years, he had a son in his own likeness,
in his own image; and he named him Seth. 4After Seth was born, Adam
lived 800 years and had other sons and daughters. 5Altogether, Adam
lived a total of 930 years, and then he died.

6When Seth had lived 105 years, he became the father[c] of Enosh. 7Af-
ter he became the father of Enosh, Seth lived 807 years and had other
sons and daughters. 8Altogether, Seth lived a total of 912 years, and
then he died.

9When Enosh had lived 90 years, he became the father of Kenan.
10After he became the father of Kenan, Enosh lived 815 years and had
other sons and daughters. 11Altogether, Enosh lived a total of 905 years,
and then he died.

12When Kenan had lived 70 years, he became the father of Mahalalel.
13After he became the father of Mahalalel, Kenan lived 840 years and
had other sons and daughters. 14Altogether, Kenan lived a total of 910
years, and then he died.

15When Mahalalel had lived 65 years, he became the father of Jared.
16After he became the father of Jared, Mahalalel lived 830 years and
had other sons and daughters. 17Altogether, Mahalalel lived a total of
895 years, and then he died.

18When Jared had lived 162 years, he became the father of Enoch.
19After he became the father of Enoch, Jared lived 800 years and had
other sons and daughters. 20Altogether, Jared lived a total of 962 years,
and then he died.

21When Enoch had lived 65 years, he became the father of Methu-
selah. 22After he became the father of Methuselah, Enoch walked
faithfully with God 300 years and had other sons and daughters. 23Al-
together, Enoch lived a total of 365 years. 24Enoch walked faithfully
with God; then he was no more, because God took him away.

25When Methuselah had lived 187 years, he became the father of La-
mech. 26After he became the father of Lamech, Methuselah lived 782
years and had other sons and daughters. 27Altogether, Methuselah
lived a total of 969 years, and then he died.

28When Lamech had lived 182 years, he had a son. 29He named him
Noah[d] and said, "He will comfort us in the labor and painful toil of our
hands caused by the ground the LORD has cursed." 30After Noah was
born, Lamech lived 595 years and had other sons and daughters. 31Al-
together, Lamech lived a total of 777 years, and then he died.

32After Noah was 500 years old, he became the father of Shem, Ham
and Japheth.

PRAYING SCRIPTURE

Genesis 5

Through this genealogy, the writer of Genesis reminds us that unless God takes us straight to heaven, as he did Enoch (see verse 24), we are going to die. It is the overarching reality of life on earth. It comes to an end for all of us.

Ask God to help you see your time on this earth through his eyes and with his purposes in mind so that you leave nothing behind and nothing unfinished.

---

[a] 26 Or *to proclaim* [b] 2 Hebrew *adam* [c] 6 *Father* may mean *ancestor;* also in verses 7-26. [d] 29 *Noah* sounds like the Hebrew for *comfort.*

PRAYING SCRIPTURE

Genesis 6

The narrative of Noah often focuses on the wickedness of the earth, the dimensions of the ark or the total number and kind of the animals. But the hinge of the story is this: "But Noah found favor in the eyes of the LORD" (verse 8). What a heart-helping reality! God shows grace even in dark times.

No one deserves grace; we all find it extended to us from God's hand, from the heart of a good Father. Ask him for his grace in confidence.

WICKEDNESS IN THE WORLD

6 When human beings began to increase in number on the earth and daughters were born to them, 2the sons of God saw that the daughters of humans were beautiful, and they married any of them they chose. 3Then the LORD said, "My Spirit will not contend with[a] humans forever, for they are mortal[b]; their days will be a hundred and twenty years."

4The Nephilim were on the earth in those days — and also afterward — when the sons of God went to the daughters of humans and had children by them. They were the heroes of old, men of renown.

5The LORD saw how great the wickedness of the human race had become on the earth, and that every inclination of the thoughts of the human heart was only evil all the time. 6The LORD regretted that he had made human beings on the earth, and his heart was deeply troubled. 7So the LORD said, "I will wipe from the face of the earth the human race I have created — and with them the animals, the birds and the creatures that move along the ground — for I regret that I have made them." 8But Noah found favor in the eyes of the LORD.

NOAH AND THE FLOOD

9This is the account of Noah and his family.

Noah was a righteous man, blameless among the people of his time, and he walked faithfully with God. 10Noah had three sons: Shem, Ham and Japheth.

11Now the earth was corrupt in God's sight and was full of violence. 12God saw how corrupt the earth had become, for all the people on earth had corrupted their ways. 13So God said to Noah, "I am going to put an end to all people, for the earth is filled with violence because of them. I am surely going to destroy both them and the earth. 14So make yourself an ark of cypress[c] wood; make rooms in it and coat it with pitch inside and out. 15This is how you are to build it: The ark is to be three hundred cubits long, fifty cubits wide and thirty cubits high.[d] 16Make a roof for it, leaving below the roof an opening one cubit[e] high all around.[f] Put a door in the side of the ark and make lower, middle and upper decks. 17I am going to bring floodwaters on the earth to destroy all life under the heavens, every creature that has the breath of life in it. Everything on earth will perish. 18But I will establish my covenant with you, and you will enter the ark — you and your sons and your wife and your sons' wives with you. 19You are to bring into the ark two of all living creatures, male and female, to keep them alive with you. 20Two of every kind of bird, of every kind of animal and of every kind of creature that moves along the ground will come to you to be kept alive. 21You are to take every kind of food that is to be eaten and store it away as food for you and for them."

22Noah did everything just as God commanded him.

7 The LORD then said to Noah, "Go into the ark, you and your whole family, because I have found you righteous in this generation. 2Take with you seven pairs of every kind of clean animal, a male and

PRAYING SCRIPTURE

Genesis 7

Sometimes God's keeping his promises means he fulfills his threats about sin. As Noah and his family, along with many animals, were saved from the floodwaters, the rest of humanity perished in judgment.

Remember that God saved Noah *in* judgment *from* judgment; the ark was in the storm. Ask God to give you faith to endure in his grace when those around you are enduring the tragic effects of their sin.

---

[a] *3* Or *My spirit will not remain in* [b] *3* Or *corrupt* [c] *14* The meaning of the Hebrew for this word is uncertain. [d] *15* That is, about 450 feet long, 75 feet wide and 45 feet high or about 135 meters long, 23 meters wide and 14 meters high [e] *16* That is, about 18 inches or about 45 centimeters
[f] *16* The meaning of the Hebrew for this clause is uncertain.

its mate, and one pair of every kind of unclean animal, a male and its
mate, 3and also seven pairs of every kind of bird, male and female, to
keep their various kinds alive throughout the earth. 4Seven days from
now I will send rain on the earth for forty days and forty nights, and I
will wipe from the face of the earth every living creature I have made."
5And Noah did all that the LORD commanded him.
6Noah was six hundred years old when the floodwaters came on the
earth. 7And Noah and his sons and his wife and his sons' wives entered
the ark to escape the waters of the flood. 8Pairs of clean and unclean
animals, of birds and of all creatures that move along the ground,
9male and female, came to Noah and entered the ark, as God had com-
manded Noah. 10And after the seven days the floodwaters came on
the earth.
11In the six hundredth year of Noah's life, on the seventeenth day of
the second month — on that day all the springs of the great deep burst
forth, and the floodgates of the heavens were opened. 12And rain fell
on the earth forty days and forty nights.
13On that very day Noah and his sons, Shem, Ham and Japheth, to-
gether with his wife and the wives of his three sons, entered the ark.
14They had with them every wild animal according to its kind, all live-
stock according to their kinds, every creature that moves along the
ground according to its kind and every bird according to its kind, ev-
erything with wings. 15Pairs of all creatures that have the breath of life
in them came to Noah and entered the ark. 16The animals going in
were male and female of every living thing, as God had commanded
Noah. Then the LORD shut him in.
17For forty days the flood kept coming on the earth, and as the waters
increased they lifted the ark high above the earth. 18The waters rose
and increased greatly on the earth, and the ark floated on the surface
of the water. 19They rose greatly on the earth, and all the high moun-
tains under the entire heavens were covered. 20The waters rose and
covered the mountains to a depth of more than fifteen cubits.[a,b] 21Ev-
ery living thing that moved on land perished — birds, livestock, wild
animals, all the creatures that swarm over the earth, and all mankind.
22Everything on dry land that had the breath of life in its nostrils died.
23Every living thing on the face of the earth was wiped out; people and
animals and the creatures that move along the ground and the birds
were wiped from the earth. Only Noah was left, and those with him
in the ark.
24The waters flooded the earth for a hundred and fifty days.

8 But God remembered Noah and all the wild animals and the live-
stock that were with him in the ark, and he sent a wind over the
earth, and the waters receded. 2Now the springs of the deep and the
floodgates of the heavens had been closed, and the rain had stopped
falling from the sky. 3The water receded steadily from the earth. At the
end of the hundred and fifty days the water had gone down, 4and on
the seventeenth day of the seventh month the ark came to rest on the
mountains of Ararat. 5The waters continued to recede until the tenth
month, and on the first day of the tenth month the tops of the moun-
tains became visible.

[a] *20* That is, about 23 feet or about 6.8 meters [b] *20* Or *rose more than fifteen cubits, and the mountains were covered*

PRAYING SCRIPTURE

Genesis 8

The center of the flood narrative is Moses' assertion that "God remembered Noah" (verse 1) and caused the waters to subside. God does not forget his children even in the aftermath of judgment. Noah and his family were confined to the ark for months as the water subsided.

When you feel as though things around you have fallen apart and will never come back together, thank God that he does not forget you.

6After forty days Noah opened a window he had made in the ark
7and sent out a raven, and it kept flying back and forth until the wa-
ter had dried up from the earth. 8Then he sent out a dove to see if
the water had receded from the surface of the ground. 9But the dove
could find nowhere to perch because there was water over all the sur-
face of the earth; so it returned to Noah in the ark. He reached out his
hand and took the dove and brought it back to himself in the ark. 10He
waited seven more days and again sent out the dove from the ark.
11When the dove returned to him in the evening, there in its beak was
a freshly plucked olive leaf! Then Noah knew that the water had re-
ceded from the earth. 12He waited seven more days and sent the dove
out again, but this time it did not return to him.

13By the first day of the first month of Noah's six hundred and first
year, the water had dried up from the earth. Noah then removed the
covering from the ark and saw that the surface of the ground was dry.
14By the twenty-seventh day of the second month the earth was com-
pletely dry.

15Then God said to Noah, 16"Come out of the ark, you and your wife
and your sons and their wives. 17Bring out every kind of living creature
that is with you — the birds, the animals, and all the creatures that
move along the ground — so they can multiply on the earth and be
fruitful and increase in number on it."

18So Noah came out, together with his sons and his wife and his
sons' wives. 19All the animals and all the creatures that move along
the ground and all the birds — everything that moves on land — came
out of the ark, one kind after another.

20Then Noah built an altar to the LORD and, taking some of all the
clean animals and clean birds, he sacrificed burnt offerings on it. 21The
LORD smelled the pleasing aroma and said in his heart: "Never again
will I curse the ground because of humans, even though[a] every incli-
nation of the human heart is evil from childhood. And never again will
I destroy all living creatures, as I have done.

22"As long as the earth endures,
seedtime and harvest,
cold and heat,
summer and winter,
day and night
will never cease."

PRAYING SCRIPTURE

Genesis 9

This chapter contains one of the best-known promises in the entire Bible: God will never flood the world again, as indicated by the rainbow. Of particular interest is that God's promise extends to humans and animals (see verses 10–11). The animal kingdom was not spared from the judgment humans invoked.

Ask God to help you be aware of the extended effects of your own sin and to live in obedience to him.

GOD'S COVENANT WITH NOAH

9 Then God blessed Noah and his sons, saying to them, "Be fruitful
and increase in number and fill the earth. 2The fear and dread of
you will fall on all the beasts of the earth, and on all the birds in the
sky, on every creature that moves along the ground, and on all the fish
in the sea; they are given into your hands. 3Everything that lives and
moves about will be food for you. Just as I gave you the green plants, I
now give you everything.

4"But you must not eat meat that has its lifeblood still in it. 5And for
your lifeblood I will surely demand an accounting. I will demand an
accounting from every animal. And from each human being, too, I will
demand an accounting for the life of another human being.

[a] 21 Or *humans, for*

6“Whoever sheds human blood,
by humans shall their blood be shed;
for in the image of God
has God made mankind.
7As for you, be fruitful and increase in number; multiply on the earth
and increase upon it.”
8Then God said to Noah and to his sons with him: 9“I now establish
my covenant with you and with your descendants after you 10and with
every living creature that was with you — the birds, the livestock and
all the wild animals, all those that came out of the ark with you — ev-
ery living creature on earth. 11I establish my covenant with you: Never
again will all life be destroyed by the waters of a flood; never again will
there be a flood to destroy the earth.”
12And God said, “This is the sign of the covenant I am making be-
tween me and you and every living creature with you, a covenant for
all generations to come: 13I have set my rainbow in the clouds, and it
will be the sign of the covenant between me and the earth. 14Whenever
I bring clouds over the earth and the rainbow appears in the clouds, 15I
will remember my covenant between me and you and all living crea-
tures of every kind. Never again will the waters become a flood to de-
stroy all life. 16Whenever the rainbow appears in the clouds, I will see
it and remember the everlasting covenant between God and all living
creatures of every kind on the earth.”
17So God said to Noah, “This is the sign of the covenant I have estab-
lished between me and all life on the earth.”

THE SONS OF NOAH

18The sons of Noah who came out of the ark were Shem, Ham and
Japheth. (Ham was the father of Canaan.) 19These were the three sons
of Noah, and from them came the people who were scattered over the
whole earth.
20Noah, a man of the soil, proceeded[a] to plant a vineyard. 21When he
drank some of its wine, he became drunk and lay uncovered inside his
tent. 22Ham, the father of Canaan, saw his father naked and told his
two brothers outside. 23But Shem and Japheth took a garment and laid
it across their shoulders; then they walked in backward and covered
their father's naked body. Their faces were turned the other way so that
they would not see their father naked.
24When Noah awoke from his wine and found out what his youngest
son had done to him, 25he said,

“Cursed be Canaan!
The lowest of slaves
will he be to his brothers.”

26He also said,

“Praise be to the LORD, the God of Shem!
May Canaan be the slave of Shem.
27May God extend Japheth's[b] territory;
may Japheth live in the tents of Shem,
and may Canaan be the slave of Japheth.”

---

[a] *20* Or *soil, was the first* [b] *27* *Japheth* sounds like the Hebrew for *extend.*

28 After the flood Noah lived 350 years. 29 Noah lived a total of 950
years, and then he died.

THE TABLE OF NATIONS

10 This is the account of Shem, Ham and Japheth, Noah's sons,
who themselves had sons after the flood.

THE JAPHETHITES

2 The sons[a] of Japheth:
Gomer, Magog, Madai, Javan, Tubal, Meshek and Tiras.
3 The sons of Gomer:
Ashkenaz, Riphath and Togarmah.
4 The sons of Javan:
Elishah, Tarshish, the Kittites and the Rodanites.[b] 5 (From these
the maritime peoples spread out into their territories by their
clans within their nations, each with its own language.)

THE HAMITES

6 The sons of Ham:
Cush, Egypt, Put and Canaan.
7 The sons of Cush:
Seba, Havilah, Sabtah, Raamah and Sabteka.
The sons of Raamah:
Sheba and Dedan.

8 Cush was the father[c] of Nimrod, who became a mighty warrior on
the earth. 9 He was a mighty hunter before the LORD; that is why it
is said, "Like Nimrod, a mighty hunter before the LORD." 10 The first
centers of his kingdom were Babylon, Uruk, Akkad and Kalneh, in[d]
Shinar.[e] 11 From that land he went to Assyria, where he built Nineveh,
Rehoboth Ir,[f] Calah 12 and Resen, which is between Nineveh and Ca-
lah—which is the great city.

13 Egypt was the father of
the Ludites, Anamites, Lehabites, Naphtuhites, 14 Pathrusites,
Kasluhites (from whom the Philistines came) and Caphtorites.
15 Canaan was the father of
Sidon his firstborn,[g] and of the Hittites, 16 Jebusites, Amorites,
Girgashites, 17 Hivites, Arkites, Sinites, 18 Arvadites, Zemarites
and Hamathites.

Later the Canaanite clans scattered 19 and the borders of Canaan
reached from Sidon toward Gerar as far as Gaza, and then toward
Sodom, Gomorrah, Admah and Zeboyim, as far as Lasha.

20 These are the sons of Ham by their clans and languages, in their
territories and nations.

THE SEMITES

21 Sons were also born to Shem, whose older brother was[h] Japheth;
Shem was the ancestor of all the sons of Eber.

PRAYING SCRIPTURE

Genesis 10

The oft-called "Table of Nations" catalogs the descendants of Noah who were about to be scattered among the nations after humankind began building the tower of Babel. This record should fill us with hope that God remembers not only us but all of our family members.

Pray today for the members of your immediate and extended family. If you don't have family, pray that the families you know will come to know God.

---

[a] 2 *Sons* may mean *descendants* or *successors* or *nations*; also in verses 3, 4, 6, 7, 20-23, 29 and 31. [b] 4 Some manuscripts of the Masoretic Text and Samaritan Pentateuch (see also Septuagint and 1 Chron. 1:7); most manuscripts of the Masoretic Text *Dodanites* [c] 8 *Father* may mean *ancestor* or *predecessor* or *founder*; also in verses 13, 15, 24 and 26. [d] 10 Or *Uruk and Akkad—all of them in* [e] 10 That is, Babylonia [f] 11 Or *Nineveh with its city squares* [g] 15 Or *of the Sidonians, the foremost* [h] 21 Or *Shem, the older brother of*

22 The sons of Shem:
Elam, Ashur, Arphaxad, Lud and Aram.
23 The sons of Aram:
Uz, Hul, Gether and Meshek.[a]
24 Arphaxad was the father of[b] Shelah,
and Shelah the father of Eber.
25 Two sons were born to Eber:
One was named Peleg,[c] because in his time the earth was divided; his brother was named Joktan.
26 Joktan was the father of
Almodad, Sheleph, Hazarmaveth, Jerah, 27 Hadoram, Uzal, Diklah, 28 Obal, Abimael, Sheba, 29 Ophir, Havilah and Jobab. All these were sons of Joktan.
30 The region where they lived stretched from Mesha toward Sephar, in the eastern hill country.
31 These are the sons of Shem by their clans and languages, in their territories and nations.

32 These are the clans of Noah's sons, according to their lines of descent, within their nations. From these the nations spread out over the earth after the flood.

THE TOWER OF BABEL

11 Now the whole world had one language and a common speech.
2 As people moved eastward,[d] they found a plain in Shinar[e] and
settled there.
3 They said to each other, "Come, let's make bricks and bake them
thoroughly." They used brick instead of stone, and tar for mortar.
4 Then they said, "Come, let us build ourselves a city, with a tower that
reaches to the heavens, so that we may make a name for ourselves;
otherwise we will be scattered over the face of the whole earth."
5 But the LORD came down to see the city and the tower the people
were building. 6 The LORD said, "If as one people speaking the same
language they have begun to do this, then nothing they plan to do will
be impossible for them. 7 Come, let us go down and confuse their language so they will not understand each other."
8 So the LORD scattered them from there over all the earth, and they
stopped building the city. 9 That is why it was called Babel[f] — because
there the LORD confused the language of the whole world. From there
the LORD scattered them over the face of the whole earth.

FROM SHEM TO ABRAM

10 This is the account of Shem's family line.

Two years after the flood, when Shem was 100 years old, he became
the father[g] of Arphaxad. 11 And after he became the father of Arphaxad,
Shem lived 500 years and had other sons and daughters.

PRAYING SCRIPTURE

Genesis 11

From our earliest days, humanity has organized to defy God. When everyone decided to make a name for themselves, to exalt themselves above God, he scattered them to the four corners of the earth, confusing the language over all the earth and stopping their efforts. They did not realize God was saving them from themselves.

Pride is never a way to God. Search your own heart for any sin that seeks to elevate self above God.

---

[a] 23 See Septuagint and 1 Chron. 1:17; Hebrew *Mash.* [b] 24 Hebrew; Septuagint *father of Cainan, and Cainan was the father of* [c] 25 *Peleg* means *division.* [d] 2 Or *from the east*; or *in the east* [e] 2 That is, Babylonia [f] 9 That is, Babylon; *Babel* sounds like the Hebrew for *confused.* [g] 10 *Father* may mean *ancestor*; also in verses 11-25.

12When Arphaxad had lived 35 years, he became the father of Shelah.
13And after he became the father of Shelah, Arphaxad lived 403 years
and had other sons and daughters.[a]
14When Shelah had lived 30 years, he became the father of Eber.
15And after he became the father of Eber, Shelah lived 403 years and
had other sons and daughters.
16When Eber had lived 34 years, he became the father of Peleg. 17And
after he became the father of Peleg, Eber lived 430 years and had other
sons and daughters.
18When Peleg had lived 30 years, he became the father of Reu. 19And
after he became the father of Reu, Peleg lived 209 years and had other
sons and daughters.
20When Reu had lived 32 years, he became the father of Serug. 21And
after he became the father of Serug, Reu lived 207 years and had other
sons and daughters.
22When Serug had lived 30 years, he became the father of Nahor.
23And after he became the father of Nahor, Serug lived 200 years and
had other sons and daughters.
24When Nahor had lived 29 years, he became the father of Terah.
25And after he became the father of Terah, Nahor lived 119 years and
had other sons and daughters.
26After Terah had lived 70 years, he became the father of Abram, Na-
hor and Haran.

ABRAM'S FAMILY

27This is the account of Terah's family line.

Terah became the father of Abram, Nahor and Haran. And Haran be-
came the father of Lot. 28While his father Terah was still alive, Haran
died in Ur of the Chaldeans, in the land of his birth. 29Abram and Nahor
both married. The name of Abram's wife was Sarai, and the name of
Nahor's wife was Milkah; she was the daughter of Haran, the father of
both Milkah and Iskah. 30Now Sarai was childless because she was not
able to conceive.
31Terah took his son Abram, his grandson Lot son of Haran, and his
daughter-in-law Sarai, the wife of his son Abram, and together they set
out from Ur of the Chaldeans to go to Canaan. But when they came to
Harran, they settled there.
32Terah lived 205 years, and he died in Harran.

PRAYING SCRIPTURE

Genesis 12

The first three verses of Genesis 12 set the stage for the rest of the Bible as God promises to bless all nations through Abraham's family. Abraham was a pagan in Ur before God called him, likely a worshiper of a moon god.

Thank God today that he called Abraham to be the father of faith and that he called you from your unbelief to a life of blessing in Jesus.

THE CALL OF ABRAM

12 The LORD had said to Abram, "Go from your country, your people
and your father's household to the land I will show you.

2"I will make you into a great nation,
and I will bless you;
I will make your name great,
and you will be a blessing.[b]

[a] 12,13 Hebrew; Septuagint (see also Luke 3:35,36 and note at Gen. 10:24) *35 years, he became the father of Cainan. 13And after he became the father of Cainan, Arphaxad lived 430 years and had other sons and daughters, and then he died. When Cainan had lived 130 years, he became the father of Shelah. And after he became the father of Shelah, Cainan lived 330 years and had other sons and daughters* [b] 2 *Or be seen as blessed*

3 I will bless those who bless you,
and whoever curses you I will curse;
and all peoples on earth
will be blessed through you."[a]

4 So Abram went, as the LORD had told him; and Lot went with him.
Abram was seventy-five years old when he set out from Harran. 5 He
took his wife Sarai, his nephew Lot, all the possessions they had accu-
mulated and the people they had acquired in Harran, and they set out
for the land of Canaan, and they arrived there.
6 Abram traveled through the land as far as the site of the great tree
of Moreh at Shechem. At that time the Canaanites were in the land.
7 The LORD appeared to Abram and said, "To your offspring[b] I will give
this land." So he built an altar there to the LORD, who had appeared
to him.
8 From there he went on toward the hills east of Bethel and pitched
his tent, with Bethel on the west and Ai on the east. There he built an
altar to the LORD and called on the name of the LORD.
9 Then Abram set out and continued toward the Negev.

ABRAM IN EGYPT

10 Now there was a famine in the land, and Abram went down to
Egypt to live there for a while because the famine was severe. 11 As he
was about to enter Egypt, he said to his wife Sarai, "I know what a
beautiful woman you are. 12 When the Egyptians see you, they will say,
'This is his wife.' Then they will kill me but will let you live. 13 Say you
are my sister, so that I will be treated well for your sake and my life will
be spared because of you."
14 When Abram came to Egypt, the Egyptians saw that Sarai was a
very beautiful woman. 15 And when Pharaoh's officials saw her, they
praised her to Pharaoh, and she was taken into his palace. 16 He treated
Abram well for her sake, and Abram acquired sheep and cattle, male
and female donkeys, male and female servants, and camels.
17 But the LORD inflicted serious diseases on Pharaoh and his house-
hold because of Abram's wife Sarai. 18 So Pharaoh summoned Abram.
"What have you done to me?" he said. "Why didn't you tell me she was
your wife? 19 Why did you say, 'She is my sister,' so that I took her to be
my wife? Now then, here is your wife. Take her and go!" 20 Then Phar-
aoh gave orders about Abram to his men, and they sent him on his way,
with his wife and everything he had.

ABRAM AND LOT SEPARATE

13 So Abram went up from Egypt to the Negev, with his wife and
everything he had, and Lot went with him. 2 Abram had become
very wealthy in livestock and in silver and gold.
3 From the Negev he went from place to place until he came to Bethel,
to the place between Bethel and Ai where his tent had been earlier
4 and where he had first built an altar. There Abram called on the name
of the LORD.
5 Now Lot, who was moving about with Abram, also had flocks and
herds and tents. 6 But the land could not support them while they
stayed together, for their possessions were so great that they were not

PRAYING SCRIPTURE

Genesis 13

To avoid the constant bickering of their herdsmen, Abraham and Lot separated their families and flocks. Abraham was willing to give up the best land, giving his nephew first choice. Lot chose an area that was "well watered," seemingly superior to the land remaining for Abraham (verse 10).

How much are you willing to give up to create peace with those around you? Ask God to give you the heart of a peacemaker.

[a] 3 Or *earth / will use your name in blessings* (see 48:20) [b] 7 Or *seed*

able to stay together. 7And quarreling arose between Abram's herders
and Lot's. The Canaanites and Perizzites were also living in the land
at that time.
8So Abram said to Lot, "Let's not have any quarreling between you
and me, or between your herders and mine, for we are close relatives.
9Is not the whole land before you? Let's part company. If you go to the
left, I'll go to the right; if you go to the right, I'll go to the left."
10Lot looked around and saw that the whole plain of the Jordan to-
ward Zoar was well watered, like the garden of the LORD, like the land
of Egypt. (This was before the LORD destroyed Sodom and Gomorrah.)
11So Lot chose for himself the whole plain of the Jordan and set out to-
ward the east. The two men parted company: 12Abram lived in the land
of Canaan, while Lot lived among the cities of the plain and pitched his
tents near Sodom. 13Now the people of Sodom were wicked and were
sinning greatly against the LORD.
14The LORD said to Abram after Lot had parted from him, "Look
around from where you are, to the north and south, to the east and
west. 15All the land that you see I will give to you and your offspring[a]
forever. 16I will make your offspring like the dust of the earth, so that
if anyone could count the dust, then your offspring could be counted.
17Go, walk through the length and breadth of the land, for I am giving
it to you."
18So Abram went to live near the great trees of Mamre at Hebron,
where he pitched his tents. There he built an altar to the LORD.

ABRAM RESCUES LOT

14 At the time when Amraphel was king of Shinar,[b] Arioch king
of Ellasar, Kedorlaomer king of Elam and Tidal king of Goyim,
2these kings went to war against Bera king of Sodom, Birsha king of
Gomorrah, Shinab king of Admah, Shemeber king of Zeboyim, and the
king of Bela (that is, Zoar). 3All these latter kings joined forces in the
Valley of Siddim (that is, the Dead Sea Valley). 4For twelve years they
had been subject to Kedorlaomer, but in the thirteenth year they
rebelled.
5In the fourteenth year, Kedorlaomer and the kings allied with him
went out and defeated the Rephaites in Ashteroth Karnaim, the Zu-
zites in Ham, the Emites in Shaveh Kiriathaim 6and the Horites in
the hill country of Seir, as far as El Paran near the desert. 7Then they
turned back and went to En Mishpat (that is, Kadesh), and they con-
quered the whole territory of the Amalekites, as well as the Amorites
who were living in Hazezon Tamar.
8Then the king of Sodom, the king of Gomorrah, the king of Admah,
the king of Zeboyim and the king of Bela (that is, Zoar) marched out
and drew up their battle lines in the Valley of Siddim 9against Kedor-
laomer king of Elam, Tidal king of Goyim, Amraphel king of Shinar
and Arioch king of Ellasar — four kings against five. 10Now the Valley
of Siddim was full of tar pits, and when the kings of Sodom and Go-
morrah fled, some of the men fell into them and the rest fled to the
hills. 11The four kings seized all the goods of Sodom and Gomorrah
and all their food; then they went away. 12They also carried off Abram's
nephew Lot and his possessions, since he was living in Sodom.
13A man who had escaped came and reported this to Abram the

PRAYING SCRIPTURE

Genesis 14

In this unusual narrative, we are introduced to a man named Melchizedek, whom Abraham met following a battle with an Elamite king. He was said to be both a king and a priest and will later be referenced in explaining Jesus' ministry as both.

In prayer today, recognize Jesus as the King who has all authority, and trust him as the High Priest to hear and answer your requests as you offer them in faith.

[a] *15* Or *seed*; also in verse 16 [b] *1* That is, Babylonia; also in verse 9

Hebrew. Now Abram was living near the great trees of Mamre the
Amorite, a brother[a] of Eshkol and Aner, all of whom were allied with
Abram. 14When Abram heard that his relative had been taken captive,
he called out the 318 trained men born in his household and went
in pursuit as far as Dan. 15During the night Abram divided his men
to attack them and he routed them, pursuing them as far as Hobah,
north of Damascus. 16He recovered all the goods and brought back his
relative Lot and his possessions, together with the women and the
other people.

17After Abram returned from defeating Kedorlaomer and the kings
allied with him, the king of Sodom came out to meet him in the Valley
of Shaveh (that is, the King's Valley).

18Then Melchizedek king of Salem brought out bread and wine. He
was priest of God Most High, 19and he blessed Abram, saying,

"Blessed be Abram by God Most High,
  Creator of heaven and earth.
20 And praise be to God Most High,
  who delivered your enemies into your hand."

Then Abram gave him a tenth of everything.

21The king of Sodom said to Abram, "Give me the people and keep
the goods for yourself."

22But Abram said to the king of Sodom, "With raised hand I have
sworn an oath to the LORD, God Most High, Creator of heaven and
earth, 23that I will accept nothing belonging to you, not even a thread
or the strap of a sandal, so that you will never be able to say, 'I made
Abram rich.' 24I will accept nothing but what my men have eaten and
the share that belongs to the men who went with me — to Aner, Eshkol
and Mamre. Let them have their share."

THE LORD'S COVENANT WITH ABRAM

15 After this, the word of the LORD came to Abram in a vision:

"Do not be afraid, Abram.
  I am your shield,[b]
  your very great reward.[c]"

2But Abram said, "Sovereign LORD, what can you give me since I re-
main childless and the one who will inherit[d] my estate is Eliezer of
Damascus?" 3And Abram said, "You have given me no children; so a
servant in my household will be my heir."

4Then the word of the LORD came to him: "This man will not be your
heir, but a son who is your own flesh and blood will be your heir." 5He
took him outside and said, "Look up at the sky and count the stars — if
indeed you can count them." Then he said to him, "So shall your off-
spring[e] be."

6Abram believed the LORD, and he credited it to him as righteousness.

7He also said to him, "I am the LORD, who brought you out of Ur of
the Chaldeans to give you this land to take possession of it."

8But Abram said, "Sovereign LORD, how can I know that I will gain
possession of it?"

PRAYING SCRIPTURE

Genesis 15

When many people read the Old Testament, they mistakenly think that keeping the law is the way to God. But Moses shows that even before he inscribed God's law, faith accessed the righteousness of God (see verse 6). It was Abraham's belief in God's promise that was recorded, not his works as a result of God's promise.

Are you trusting God's promise or your works for salvation? Believe God's promise; he has done the work.

---

[a] 13 Or *a relative;* or *an ally* [b] 1 Or *sovereign* [c] 1 Or *shield; / your reward will be very great* [d] 2 The meaning of the Hebrew for this phrase is uncertain. [e] 5 Or *seed*

9 So the LORD said to him, "Bring me a heifer, a goat and a ram, each
three years old, along with a dove and a young pigeon."
10 Abram brought all these to him, cut them in two and arranged the
halves opposite each other; the birds, however, he did not cut in half.
11 Then birds of prey came down on the carcasses, but Abram drove
them away.
12 As the sun was setting, Abram fell into a deep sleep, and a thick and
dreadful darkness came over him. 13 Then the LORD said to him, "Know
for certain that for four hundred years your descendants will be strang-
ers in a country not their own and that they will be enslaved and mis-
treated there. 14 But I will punish the nation they serve as slaves, and
afterward they will come out with great possessions. 15 You, however,
will go to your ancestors in peace and be buried at a good old age. 16 In
the fourth generation your descendants will come back here, for the
sin of the Amorites has not yet reached its full measure."
17 When the sun had set and darkness had fallen, a smoking firepot
with a blazing torch appeared and passed between the pieces. 18 On that
day the LORD made a covenant with Abram and said, "To your descen-
dants I give this land, from the Wadi[a] of Egypt to the great river, the Eu-
phrates— 19 the land of the Kenites, Kenizzites, Kadmonites, 20 Hittites,
Perizzites, Rephaites, 21 Amorites, Canaanites, Girgashites and Jebusites."

HAGAR AND ISHMAEL

16 Now Sarai, Abram's wife, had borne him no children. But she
had an Egyptian slave named Hagar; 2 so she said to Abram,
"The LORD has kept me from having children. Go, sleep with my slave;
perhaps I can build a family through her."
Abram agreed to what Sarai said. 3 So after Abram had been living
in Canaan ten years, Sarai his wife took her Egyptian slave Hagar and
gave her to her husband to be his wife. 4 He slept with Hagar, and she
conceived.
When she knew she was pregnant, she began to despise her mistress.
5 Then Sarai said to Abram, "You are responsible for the wrong I am
suffering. I put my slave in your arms, and now that she knows she is
pregnant, she despises me. May the LORD judge between you and me."
6 "Your slave is in your hands," Abram said. "Do with her whatever
you think best." Then Sarai mistreated Hagar; so she fled from her.
7 The angel of the LORD found Hagar near a spring in the desert; it
was the spring that is beside the road to Shur. 8 And he said, "Hagar,
slave of Sarai, where have you come from, and where are you going?"
"I'm running away from my mistress Sarai," she answered.
9 Then the angel of the LORD told her, "Go back to your mistress and
submit to her." 10 The angel added, "I will increase your descendants so
much that they will be too numerous to count."
11 The angel of the LORD also said to her:

"You are now pregnant
  and you will give birth to a son.
You shall name him Ishmael,[b]
  for the LORD has heard of your misery.
12 He will be a wild donkey of a man;
  his hand will be against everyone
  and everyone's hand against him,

PRAYING SCRIPTURE

Genesis 16

We tend to doubt God's promises when we cannot see how they will be fulfilled. The longer we have to wait for promises to be fulfilled, the more likely our faith is to waver. Surely, we think, we need to help God out.

Ask God today for faith that endures and doesn't fade with time or circumstances. This is the kind of faith that truly pleases God.

[a] 18 Or *river* [b] 11 *Ishmael* means *God hears.*

and he will live in hostility
toward[a] all his brothers."

13She gave this name to the LORD who spoke to her: "You are the
God who sees me," for she said, "I have now seen[b] the One who sees
me." 14That is why the well was called Beer Lahai Roi[c]; it is still there,
between Kadesh and Bered.
15So Hagar bore Abram a son, and Abram gave the name Ishmael to
the son she had borne. 16Abram was eighty-six years old when Hagar
bore him Ishmael.

THE COVENANT OF CIRCUMCISION

17 When Abram was ninety-nine years old, the LORD appeared to
him and said, "I am God Almighty[d]; walk before me faithfully
and be blameless. 2Then I will make my covenant between me and you
and will greatly increase your numbers."
3Abram fell facedown, and God said to him, 4"As for me, this is my
covenant with you: You will be the father of many nations. 5No lon-
ger will you be called Abram[e]; your name will be Abraham,[f] for I have
made you a father of many nations. 6I will make you very fruitful; I
will make nations of you, and kings will come from you. 7I will estab-
lish my covenant as an everlasting covenant between me and you and
your descendants after you for the generations to come, to be your God
and the God of your descendants after you. 8The whole land of Canaan,
where you now reside as a foreigner, I will give as an everlasting pos-
session to you and your descendants after you; and I will be their God."
9Then God said to Abraham, "As for you, you must keep my covenant,
you and your descendants after you for the generations to come. 10This
is my covenant with you and your descendants after you, the covenant
you are to keep: Every male among you shall be circumcised. 11You are
to undergo circumcision, and it will be the sign of the covenant be-
tween me and you. 12For the generations to come every male among
you who is eight days old must be circumcised, including those born in
your household or bought with money from a foreigner — those who
are not your offspring. 13Whether born in your household or bought
with your money, they must be circumcised. My covenant in your flesh
is to be an everlasting covenant. 14Any uncircumcised male, who has
not been circumcised in the flesh, will be cut off from his people; he
has broken my covenant."
15God also said to Abraham, "As for Sarai your wife, you are no lon-
ger to call her Sarai; her name will be Sarah. 16I will bless her and will
surely give you a son by her. I will bless her so that she will be the
mother of nations; kings of peoples will come from her."
17Abraham fell facedown; he laughed and said to himself, "Will a son
be born to a man a hundred years old? Will Sarah bear a child at the
age of ninety?" 18And Abraham said to God, "If only Ishmael might live
under your blessing!"
19Then God said, "Yes, but your wife Sarah will bear you a son, and
you will call him Isaac.[g] I will establish my covenant with him as
an everlasting covenant for his descendants after him. 20And as for

PRAYING SCRIPTURE

Genesis 17

When God appeared to 99-year-old Abram and reiterated his promise that he would have a son, it seemed even more unlikely from a human perspective than the first time Abram heard the promise. Understandably, Abraham himself raised age—his and Sarah's—as an objection.

God is the God of the impossible. There is no circumstance he cannot overcome, so don't hesitate to ask him to overcome those around you.

---

[a] 12 Or *live to the east / of* [b] 13 Or *seen the back of* [c] 14 *Beer Lahai Roi* means *well of the Living One who sees me.* [d] 1 Hebrew *El-Shaddai*
[e] 5 *Abram* means *exalted father.* [f] 5 *Abraham* probably means *father of many.* [g] 19 *Isaac* means *he laughs.*

Ishmael, I have heard you: I will surely bless him; I will make him
fruitful and will greatly increase his numbers. He will be the father of
twelve rulers, and I will make him into a great nation. 21But my cov-
enant I will establish with Isaac, whom Sarah will bear to you by this
time next year." 22When he had finished speaking with Abraham, God
went up from him.

23On that very day Abraham took his son Ishmael and all those
born in his household or bought with his money, every male in his
household, and circumcised them, as God told him. 24Abraham was
ninety-nine years old when he was circumcised, 25and his son Ishmael
was thirteen; 26Abraham and his son Ishmael were both circumcised
on that very day. 27And every male in Abraham's household, including
those born in his household or bought from a foreigner, was circum-
cised with him.

PRAYING SCRIPTURE

Genesis 18

How would you pray if God gave you the opportunity to save a city? Would you be overwhelmed? Speechless? Abraham modeled intercessory prayer for us as he begged God to spare Sodom and Gomorrah. He did not hesitate to plead with God to save lives from judgment.

Ask God today to have mercy on people who might be facing judgment so that his mercy is revealed to them.

THE THREE VISITORS

18 The LORD appeared to Abraham near the great trees of Mamre
while he was sitting at the entrance to his tent in the heat of the
day. 2Abraham looked up and saw three men standing nearby. When
he saw them, he hurried from the entrance of his tent to meet them
and bowed low to the ground.

3He said, "If I have found favor in your eyes, my lord,[a] do not pass
your servant by. 4Let a little water be brought, and then you may all
wash your feet and rest under this tree. 5Let me get you something to
eat, so you can be refreshed and then go on your way — now that you
have come to your servant."

"Very well," they answered, "do as you say."

6So Abraham hurried into the tent to Sarah. "Quick," he said, "get
three seahs[b] of the finest flour and knead it and bake some bread."

7Then he ran to the herd and selected a choice, tender calf and gave
it to a servant, who hurried to prepare it. 8He then brought some curds
and milk and the calf that had been prepared, and set these before
them. While they ate, he stood near them under a tree.

9"Where is your wife Sarah?" they asked him.

"There, in the tent," he said.

10Then one of them said, "I will surely return to you about this time
next year, and Sarah your wife will have a son."

Now Sarah was listening at the entrance to the tent, which was
behind him. 11Abraham and Sarah were already very old, and Sarah
was past the age of childbearing. 12So Sarah laughed to herself as she
thought, "After I am worn out and my lord is old, will I now have this
pleasure?"

13Then the LORD said to Abraham, "Why did Sarah laugh and say,
'Will I really have a child, now that I am old?' 14Is anything too hard
for the LORD? I will return to you at the appointed time next year, and
Sarah will have a son."

15Sarah was afraid, so she lied and said, "I did not laugh."

But he said, "Yes, you did laugh."

ABRAHAM PLEADS FOR SODOM

16When the men got up to leave, they looked down toward Sodom,
and Abraham walked along with them to see them on their way. 17Then

[a] 3 Or *eyes, Lord* [b] 6 That is, probably about 36 pounds or about 16 kilograms

the LORD said, "Shall I hide from Abraham what I am about to do?
18Abraham will surely become a great and powerful nation, and all na-
tions on earth will be blessed through him.[a] 19For I have chosen him,
so that he will direct his children and his household after him to keep
the way of the LORD by doing what is right and just, so that the LORD
will bring about for Abraham what he has promised him."

20Then the LORD said, "The outcry against Sodom and Gomorrah is
so great and their sin so grievous 21that I will go down and see if what
they have done is as bad as the outcry that has reached me. If not, I
will know."

22The men turned away and went toward Sodom, but Abraham re-
mained standing before the LORD.[b] 23Then Abraham approached him
and said: "Will you sweep away the righteous with the wicked? 24What
if there are fifty righteous people in the city? Will you really sweep it
away and not spare[c] the place for the sake of the fifty righteous people
in it? 25Far be it from you to do such a thing — to kill the righteous with
the wicked, treating the righteous and the wicked alike. Far be it from
you! Will not the Judge of all the earth do right?"

26The LORD said, "If I find fifty righteous people in the city of Sodom,
I will spare the whole place for their sake."

27Then Abraham spoke up again: "Now that I have been so bold as to
speak to the Lord, though I am nothing but dust and ashes, 28what if
the number of the righteous is five less than fifty? Will you destroy the
whole city for lack of five people?"

"If I find forty-five there," he said, "I will not destroy it."

29Once again he spoke to him, "What if only forty are found there?"

He said, "For the sake of forty, I will not do it."

30Then he said, "May the Lord not be angry, but let me speak. What
if only thirty can be found there?"

He answered, "I will not do it if I find thirty there."

31Abraham said, "Now that I have been so bold as to speak to the
Lord, what if only twenty can be found there?"

He said, "For the sake of twenty, I will not destroy it."

32Then he said, "May the Lord not be angry, but let me speak just
once more. What if only ten can be found there?"

He answered, "For the sake of ten, I will not destroy it."

33When the LORD had finished speaking with Abraham, he left, and
Abraham returned home.

SODOM AND GOMORRAH DESTROYED

19 The two angels arrived at Sodom in the evening, and Lot was
sitting in the gateway of the city. When he saw them, he got
up to meet them and bowed down with his face to the ground. 2"My
lords," he said, "please turn aside to your servant's house. You can wash
your feet and spend the night and then go on your way early in the
morning."

"No," they answered, "we will spend the night in the square."

3But he insisted so strongly that they did go with him and entered
his house. He prepared a meal for them, baking bread without yeast,
and they ate. 4Before they had gone to bed, all the men from every part

[a] 18 Or *will use his name in blessings* (see 48:20) [b] 22 Masoretic Text; an ancient Hebrew scribal tradition *but the LORD remained standing before Abraham* [c] 24 Or *forgive*; also in verse 26

PRAYING SCRIPTURE

Genesis 19

The wrath of God falling upon Sodom and Gomorrah demonstrates the unflinching justice of God. What a tragedy of death and destruction for cities so wicked that their names still invoke the sinfulness of humans and God's anger at sin.

Reflect for a moment on the depth of sin that brings the wrath of God. Thank God that ultimate justice is found through his judgment poured out on our sin in his Son, Jesus.

of the city of Sodom — both young and old — surrounded the house.
5They called to Lot, "Where are the men who came to you tonight?
Bring them out to us so that we can have sex with them."

6Lot went outside to meet them and shut the door behind him 7and
said, "No, my friends. Don't do this wicked thing. 8Look, I have two
daughters who have never slept with a man. Let me bring them out to
you, and you can do what you like with them. But don't do anything
to these men, for they have come under the protection of my roof."

9"Get out of our way," they replied. "This fellow came here as a for-
eigner, and now he wants to play the judge! We'll treat you worse than
them." They kept bringing pressure on Lot and moved forward to
break down the door.

10But the men inside reached out and pulled Lot back into the house
and shut the door. 11Then they struck the men who were at the door of
the house, young and old, with blindness so that they could not find
the door.

12The two men said to Lot, "Do you have anyone else here — sons-in-
law, sons or daughters, or anyone else in the city who belongs to you?
Get them out of here, 13because we are going to destroy this place. The
outcry to the LORD against its people is so great that he has sent us to
destroy it."

14So Lot went out and spoke to his sons-in-law, who were pledged to
marry[a] his daughters. He said, "Hurry and get out of this place, because
the LORD is about to destroy the city!" But his sons-in-law thought he
was joking.

15With the coming of dawn, the angels urged Lot, saying, "Hurry!
Take your wife and your two daughters who are here, or you will be
swept away when the city is punished."

16When he hesitated, the men grasped his hand and the hands of his
wife and of his two daughters and led them safely out of the city, for
the LORD was merciful to them. 17As soon as they had brought them
out, one of them said, "Flee for your lives! Don't look back, and don't
stop anywhere in the plain! Flee to the mountains or you will be swept
away!"

18But Lot said to them, "No, my lords,[b] please! 19Your[c] servant has
found favor in your[c] eyes, and you[c] have shown great kindness to me
in sparing my life. But I can't flee to the mountains; this disaster will
overtake me, and I'll die. 20Look, here is a town near enough to run to,
and it is small. Let me flee to it — it is very small, isn't it? Then my life
will be spared."

21He said to him, "Very well, I will grant this request too; I will not
overthrow the town you speak of. 22But flee there quickly, because
I cannot do anything until you reach it." (That is why the town was
called Zoar.[d])

23By the time Lot reached Zoar, the sun had risen over the land.
24Then the LORD rained down burning sulfur on Sodom and Gomor-
rah — from the LORD out of the heavens. 25Thus he overthrew those cit-
ies and the entire plain, destroying all those living in the cities — and
also the vegetation in the land. 26But Lot's wife looked back, and she
became a pillar of salt.

27Early the next morning Abraham got up and returned to the place

---

[a] 14 Or *were married to* [b] 18 Or *No, Lord;* or *No, my lord* [c] 19 The Hebrew is singular. [d] 22 *Zoar* means *small.*

where he had stood before the LORD. 28He looked down toward Sodom
and Gomorrah, toward all the land of the plain, and he saw dense
smoke rising from the land, like smoke from a furnace.
29So when God destroyed the cities of the plain, he remembered
Abraham, and he brought Lot out of the catastrophe that overthrew
the cities where Lot had lived.

LOT AND HIS DAUGHTERS

30Lot and his two daughters left Zoar and settled in the mountains,
for he was afraid to stay in Zoar. He and his two daughters lived in a
cave. 31One day the older daughter said to the younger, "Our father is
old, and there is no man around here to give us children — as is the
custom all over the earth. 32Let's get our father to drink wine and then
sleep with him and preserve our family line through our father."
33That night they got their father to drink wine, and the older daugh-
ter went in and slept with him. He was not aware of it when she lay
down or when she got up.
34The next day the older daughter said to the younger, "Last night I
slept with my father. Let's get him to drink wine again tonight, and you
go in and sleep with him so we can preserve our family line through
our father." 35So they got their father to drink wine that night also, and
the younger daughter went in and slept with him. Again he was not
aware of it when she lay down or when she got up.
36So both of Lot's daughters became pregnant by their father. 37The
older daughter had a son, and she named him Moab[a]; he is the fa-
ther of the Moabites of today. 38The younger daughter also had a son,
and she named him Ben-Ammi[b]; he is the father of the Ammonites[c]
of today.

ABRAHAM AND ABIMELEK

20 Now Abraham moved on from there into the region of the
Negev and lived between Kadesh and Shur. For a while he
stayed in Gerar, 2and there Abraham said of his wife Sarah, "She is my
sister." Then Abimelek king of Gerar sent for Sarah and took her.
3But God came to Abimelek in a dream one night and said to him,
"You are as good as dead because of the woman you have taken; she is
a married woman."
4Now Abimelek had not gone near her, so he said, "Lord, will you
destroy an innocent nation? 5Did he not say to me, 'She is my sister,'
and didn't she also say, 'He is my brother'? I have done this with a clear
conscience and clean hands."
6Then God said to him in the dream, "Yes, I know you did this with
a clear conscience, and so I have kept you from sinning against me.
That is why I did not let you touch her. 7Now return the man's wife,
for he is a prophet, and he will pray for you and you will live. But if
you do not return her, you may be sure that you and all who belong
to you will die."
8Early the next morning Abimelek summoned all his officials, and
when he told them all that had happened, they were very much afraid.
9Then Abimelek called Abraham in and said, "What have you done to
us? How have I wronged you that you have brought such great guilt

PRAYING SCRIPTURE

Genesis 20

It seems Abraham was a slow learner. He didn't learn the lesson he should have in an earlier instance when he lied to protect himself and said Sarah was his sister. Not only that, but God threatened to kill the person whom Abraham deceived!

Sometimes it takes more than one experience to learn a lesson, but our disobedience could mean problems for others. Pray that God will make you quickly obedient to his commands.

---

[a] 37 *Moab* sounds like the Hebrew for *from father.* [b] 38 *Ben-Ammi* means *son of my father's people.* [c] 38 Hebrew *Bene-Ammon*

upon me and my kingdom? You have done things to me that should
never be done." 10And Abimelek asked Abraham, "What was your rea-
son for doing this?"
11Abraham replied, "I said to myself, 'There is surely no fear of God
in this place, and they will kill me because of my wife.' 12Besides, she
really is my sister, the daughter of my father though not of my mother;
and she became my wife. 13And when God had me wander from my fa-
ther's household, I said to her, 'This is how you can show your love to
me: Everywhere we go, say of me, "He is my brother."'"
14Then Abimelek brought sheep and cattle and male and female
slaves and gave them to Abraham, and he returned Sarah his wife to
him. 15And Abimelek said, "My land is before you; live wherever you
like."
16To Sarah he said, "I am giving your brother a thousand shekels[a] of
silver. This is to cover the offense against you before all who are with
you; you are completely vindicated."
17Then Abraham prayed to God, and God healed Abimelek, his wife
and his female slaves so they could have children again, 18for the LORD
had kept all the women in Abimelek's household from conceiving be-
cause of Abraham's wife Sarah.

THE BIRTH OF ISAAC

21 Now the LORD was gracious to Sarah as he had said, and the LORD
did for Sarah what he had promised. 2Sarah became pregnant
and bore a son to Abraham in his old age, at the very time God had
promised him. 3Abraham gave the name Isaac[b] to the son Sarah bore
him. 4When his son Isaac was eight days old, Abraham circumcised
him, as God commanded him. 5Abraham was a hundred years old
when his son Isaac was born to him.
6Sarah said, "God has brought me laughter, and everyone who hears
about this will laugh with me." 7And she added, "Who would have said
to Abraham that Sarah would nurse children? Yet I have borne him a
son in his old age."

HAGAR AND ISHMAEL SENT AWAY

8The child grew and was weaned, and on the day Isaac was weaned
Abraham held a great feast. 9But Sarah saw that the son whom Hagar
the Egyptian had borne to Abraham was mocking, 10and she said to
Abraham, "Get rid of that slave woman and her son, for that woman's
son will never share in the inheritance with my son Isaac."
11The matter distressed Abraham greatly because it concerned his
son. 12But God said to him, "Do not be so distressed about the boy and
your slave woman. Listen to whatever Sarah tells you, because it is
through Isaac that your offspring[c] will be reckoned. 13I will make the
son of the slave into a nation also, because he is your offspring."
14Early the next morning Abraham took some food and a skin of
water and gave them to Hagar. He set them on her shoulders and then
sent her off with the boy. She went on her way and wandered in the
Desert of Beersheba.
15When the water in the skin was gone, she put the boy under one of
the bushes. 16Then she went off and sat down about a bowshot away,

PRAYING SCRIPTURE

Genesis 21

After many years of life and long after God first gave the promise to Abraham and Sarah, their son Isaac was born. Abraham was 100 years old; Sarah was 90. Isaac was the son through whom God's promise of a blessing for the world would come.

Is there a promise from God for which you are still waiting? Pray with hope and wait in faith for him to fulfill it.

[a] 16 That is, about 25 pounds or about 12 kilograms [b] 3 *Isaac* means *he laughs.* [c] 12 Or *seed*

for she thought, "I cannot watch the boy die." And as she sat there,
she[a] began to sob.
17God heard the boy crying, and the angel of God called to Hagar
from heaven and said to her, "What is the matter, Hagar? Do not be
afraid; God has heard the boy crying as he lies there. 18Lift the boy up
and take him by the hand, for I will make him into a great nation."
19Then God opened her eyes and she saw a well of water. So she went
and filled the skin with water and gave the boy a drink.
20God was with the boy as he grew up. He lived in the desert and
became an archer. 21While he was living in the Desert of Paran, his
mother got a wife for him from Egypt.

THE TREATY AT BEERSHEBA

22At that time Abimelek and Phicol the commander of his forces said
to Abraham, "God is with you in everything you do. 23Now swear to me
here before God that you will not deal falsely with me or my children
or my descendants. Show to me and the country where you now reside
as a foreigner the same kindness I have shown to you."
24Abraham said, "I swear it."
25Then Abraham complained to Abimelek about a well of water that
Abimelek's servants had seized. 26But Abimelek said, "I don't know
who has done this. You did not tell me, and I heard about it only today."
27So Abraham brought sheep and cattle and gave them to Abimelek,
and the two men made a treaty. 28Abraham set apart seven ewe lambs
from the flock, 29and Abimelek asked Abraham, "What is the meaning
of these seven ewe lambs you have set apart by themselves?"
30He replied, "Accept these seven lambs from my hand as a witness
that I dug this well."
31So that place was called Beersheba,[b] because the two men swore
an oath there.
32After the treaty had been made at Beersheba, Abimelek and Phicol
the commander of his forces returned to the land of the Philistines.
33Abraham planted a tamarisk tree in Beersheba, and there he called
on the name of the LORD, the Eternal God. 34And Abraham stayed in
the land of the Philistines for a long time.

ABRAHAM TESTED

22 Some time later God tested Abraham. He said to him,
"Abraham!"
"Here I am," he replied.
2Then God said, "Take your son, your only son, whom you love—
Isaac—and go to the region of Moriah. Sacrifice him there as a burnt
offering on a mountain I will show you."
3Early the next morning Abraham got up and loaded his donkey.
He took with him two of his servants and his son Isaac. When he had
cut enough wood for the burnt offering, he set out for the place God
had told him about. 4On the third day Abraham looked up and saw
the place in the distance. 5He said to his servants, "Stay here with the
donkey while I and the boy go over there. We will worship and then we
will come back to you."
6Abraham took the wood for the burnt offering and placed it on his

[a] 16 Hebrew; Septuagint *the child* [b] 31 *Beersheba* can mean *well of seven* and *well of the oath.*

PRAYING SCRIPTURE

Genesis 22

Would God truly demand a child sacrifice? Why would Abraham go through with killing the one through whom all the world would be blessed? Because he believed God would raise Isaac.

God's command wasn't for a human sacrifice, but for a substitute, a ram that would die in Isaac's place. God's test of Abraham previews the death of Jesus for all humanity. Thank God both for his wisdom and his provision.

son Isaac, and he himself carried the fire and the knife. As the two of
them went on together, 7Isaac spoke up and said to his father Abra-
ham, "Father?"
"Yes, my son?" Abraham replied.
"The fire and wood are here," Isaac said, "but where is the lamb for
the burnt offering?"
8Abraham answered, "God himself will provide the lamb for the
burnt offering, my son." And the two of them went on together.
9When they reached the place God had told him about, Abraham
built an altar there and arranged the wood on it. He bound his son
Isaac and laid him on the altar, on top of the wood. 10Then he reached
out his hand and took the knife to slay his son. 11But the angel of the
LORD called out to him from heaven, "Abraham! Abraham!"
"Here I am," he replied.
12"Do not lay a hand on the boy," he said. "Do not do anything to him.
Now I know that you fear God, because you have not withheld from me
your son, your only son."
13Abraham looked up and there in a thicket he saw a ram[a] caught by
its horns. He went over and took the ram and sacrificed it as a burnt
offering instead of his son. 14So Abraham called that place The LORD
Will Provide. And to this day it is said, "On the mountain of the LORD
it will be provided."
15The angel of the LORD called to Abraham from heaven a second
time 16and said, "I swear by myself, declares the LORD, that because you
have done this and have not withheld your son, your only son, 17I will
surely bless you and make your descendants as numerous as the stars
in the sky and as the sand on the seashore. Your descendants will take
possession of the cities of their enemies, 18and through your offspring[b]
all nations on earth will be blessed,[c] because you have obeyed me."
19Then Abraham returned to his servants, and they set off together
for Beersheba. And Abraham stayed in Beersheba.

NAHOR'S SONS

20Some time later Abraham was told, "Milkah is also a mother;
she has borne sons to your brother Nahor: 21Uz the firstborn, Buz his
brother, Kemuel (the father of Aram), 22Kesed, Hazo, Pildash, Jidlaph
and Bethuel." 23Bethuel became the father of Rebekah. Milkah bore
these eight sons to Abraham's brother Nahor. 24His concubine, whose
name was Reumah, also had sons: Tebah, Gaham, Tahash and Maakah.

THE DEATH OF SARAH

23 Sarah lived to be a hundred and twenty-seven years old. 2She
died at Kiriath Arba (that is, Hebron) in the land of Canaan, and
Abraham went to mourn for Sarah and to weep over her.
3Then Abraham rose from beside his dead wife and spoke to the Hit-
tites.[d] He said, 4"I am a foreigner and stranger among you. Sell me
some property for a burial site here so I can bury my dead."
5The Hittites replied to Abraham, 6"Sir, listen to us. You are a mighty

PRAYING SCRIPTURE

Genesis 23

We rarely like to think of how God works in death, but he does. After the death of Sarah, Abraham purchased the land for her burial. God, in the natural flow of earthly existence, worked to expand Abraham's property in accordance with promises he'd already made.

How might God be working in your life right now? Consider it, and then thank God for his wisdom and power that always sees, knows and provides.

[a] *13* Many manuscripts of the Masoretic Text, Samaritan Pentateuch, Septuagint and Syriac; most manuscripts of the Masoretic Text *a ram behind him* [b] *18* Or *seed* [c] *18* Or *and all nations on earth will use the name of your offspring in blessings* (see 48:20) [d] *3* Or *the descendants of Heth*; also in verses 5, 7, 10, 16, 18 and 20

prince among us. Bury your dead in the choicest of our tombs. None of
us will refuse you his tomb for burying your dead."
7 Then Abraham rose and bowed down before the people of the land,
the Hittites. 8 He said to them, "If you are willing to let me bury my
dead, then listen to me and intercede with Ephron son of Zohar on my
behalf 9 so he will sell me the cave of Machpelah, which belongs to him
and is at the end of his field. Ask him to sell it to me for the full price
as a burial site among you."
10 Ephron the Hittite was sitting among his people and he replied to
Abraham in the hearing of all the Hittites who had come to the gate
of his city. 11 "No, my lord," he said. "Listen to me; I give[a] you the field,
and I give[a] you the cave that is in it. I give[a] it to you in the presence of
my people. Bury your dead."
12 Again Abraham bowed down before the people of the land 13 and
he said to Ephron in their hearing, "Listen to me, if you will. I will pay
the price of the field. Accept it from me so I can bury my dead there."
14 Ephron answered Abraham, 15 "Listen to me, my lord; the land is
worth four hundred shekels[b] of silver, but what is that between you
and me? Bury your dead."
16 Abraham agreed to Ephron's terms and weighed out for him the
price he had named in the hearing of the Hittites: four hundred shek-
els of silver, according to the weight current among the merchants.
17 So Ephron's field in Machpelah near Mamre — both the field and
the cave in it, and all the trees within the borders of the field — was
deeded 18 to Abraham as his property in the presence of all the Hittites
who had come to the gate of the city. 19 Afterward Abraham buried his
wife Sarah in the cave in the field of Machpelah near Mamre (which is
at Hebron) in the land of Canaan. 20 So the field and the cave in it were
deeded to Abraham by the Hittites as a burial site.

ISAAC AND REBEKAH

24 Abraham was now very old, and the LORD had blessed him in
every way. 2 He said to the senior servant in his household, the
one in charge of all that he had, "Put your hand under my thigh. 3 I
want you to swear by the LORD, the God of heaven and the God of earth,
that you will not get a wife for my son from the daughters of the Ca-
naanites, among whom I am living, 4 but will go to my country and my
own relatives and get a wife for my son Isaac."
5 The servant asked him, "What if the woman is unwilling to come
back with me to this land? Shall I then take your son back to the coun-
try you came from?"
6 "Make sure that you do not take my son back there," Abraham said.
7 "The LORD, the God of heaven, who brought me out of my father's
household and my native land and who spoke to me and promised me
on oath, saying, 'To your offspring[c] I will give this land' — he will send
his angel before you so that you can get a wife for my son from there.
8 If the woman is unwilling to come back with you, then you will be
released from this oath of mine. Only do not take my son back there."
9 So the servant put his hand under the thigh of his master Abraham
and swore an oath to him concerning this matter.
10 Then the servant left, taking with him ten of his master's camels

PRAYING SCRIPTURE

Genesis 24

God's promise to Abraham — that he would make of him many nations — was only partially fulfilled with the birth of Isaac. Isaac, too, needed descendants. In a beautiful metaphor of salvation, a father (God) sent his servant (the Holy Spirit) to seek a bride (the church) for his son (Jesus).

This reminder of God's love and faithfulness to fulfill his promises through multiple generations should awaken us to praise his name.

[a] *11* Or *sell* [b] *15* That is, about 10 pounds or about 4.6 kilograms
[c] *7* Or *seed*

loaded with all kinds of good things from his master. He set out for
Aram Naharaim[a] and made his way to the town of Nahor. 11He had the
camels kneel down near the well outside the town; it was toward eve-
ning, the time the women go out to draw water.

12Then he prayed, "LORD, God of my master Abraham, make me suc-
cessful today, and show kindness to my master Abraham. 13See, I am
standing beside this spring, and the daughters of the townspeople are
coming out to draw water. 14May it be that when I say to a young wom-
an, 'Please let down your jar that I may have a drink,' and she says,
'Drink, and I'll water your camels too' — let her be the one you have
chosen for your servant Isaac. By this I will know that you have shown
kindness to my master."

15Before he had finished praying, Rebekah came out with her jar on
her shoulder. She was the daughter of Bethuel son of Milkah, who was
the wife of Abraham's brother Nahor. 16The woman was very beautiful,
a virgin; no man had ever slept with her. She went down to the spring,
filled her jar and came up again.

17The servant hurried to meet her and said, "Please give me a little
water from your jar."

18"Drink, my lord," she said, and quickly lowered the jar to her hands
and gave him a drink.

19After she had given him a drink, she said, "I'll draw water for your
camels too, until they have had enough to drink." 20So she quickly
emptied her jar into the trough, ran back to the well to draw more wa-
ter, and drew enough for all his camels. 21Without saying a word, the
man watched her closely to learn whether or not the LORD had made
his journey successful.

22When the camels had finished drinking, the man took out a gold
nose ring weighing a beka[b] and two gold bracelets weighing ten shek-
els.[c] 23Then he asked, "Whose daughter are you? Please tell me, is there
room in your father's house for us to spend the night?"

24She answered him, "I am the daughter of Bethuel, the son that
Milkah bore to Nahor." 25And she added, "We have plenty of straw and
fodder, as well as room for you to spend the night."

26Then the man bowed down and worshiped the LORD, 27saying,
"Praise be to the LORD, the God of my master Abraham, who has not
abandoned his kindness and faithfulness to my master. As for me, the
LORD has led me on the journey to the house of my master's relatives."

28The young woman ran and told her mother's household about
these things. 29Now Rebekah had a brother named Laban, and he hur-
ried out to the man at the spring. 30As soon as he had seen the nose
ring, and the bracelets on his sister's arms, and had heard Rebekah
tell what the man said to her, he went out to the man and found him
standing by the camels near the spring. 31"Come, you who are blessed
by the LORD," he said. "Why are you standing out here? I have prepared
the house and a place for the camels."

32So the man went to the house, and the camels were unloaded.
Straw and fodder were brought for the camels, and water for him and
his men to wash their feet. 33Then food was set before him, but he said,
"I will not eat until I have told you what I have to say."

"Then tell us," Laban said.

---

[a] *10* That is, Northwest Mesopotamia [b] *22* That is, about 1/5 ounce or about 5.7 grams [c] *22* That is, about 4 ounces or about 115 grams

34So he said, "I am Abraham's servant. 35The LORD has blessed my
master abundantly, and he has become wealthy. He has given him
sheep and cattle, silver and gold, male and female servants, and cam-
els and donkeys. 36My master's wife Sarah has borne him a son in her
old age, and he has given him everything he owns. 37And my master
made me swear an oath, and said, 'You must not get a wife for my son
from the daughters of the Canaanites, in whose land I live, 38but go
to my father's family and to my own clan, and get a wife for my son.'

39"Then I asked my master, 'What if the woman will not come back
with me?'

40"He replied, 'The LORD, before whom I have walked faithfully, will
send his angel with you and make your journey a success, so that you
can get a wife for my son from my own clan and from my father's fam-
ily. 41You will be released from my oath if, when you go to my clan, they
refuse to give her to you — then you will be released from my oath.'

42"When I came to the spring today, I said, 'LORD, God of my master
Abraham, if you will, please grant success to the journey on which I have
come. 43See, I am standing beside this spring. If a young woman comes
out to draw water and I say to her, "Please let me drink a little water from
your jar," 44and if she says to me, "Drink, and I'll draw water for your
camels too," let her be the one the LORD has chosen for my master's son.'

45"Before I finished praying in my heart, Rebekah came out, with her
jar on her shoulder. She went down to the spring and drew water, and
I said to her, 'Please give me a drink.'

46"She quickly lowered her jar from her shoulder and said, 'Drink,
and I'll water your camels too.' So I drank, and she watered the camels
also.

47"I asked her, 'Whose daughter are you?'

"She said, 'The daughter of Bethuel son of Nahor, whom Milkah bore
to him.'

"Then I put the ring in her nose and the bracelets on her arms, 48and
I bowed down and worshiped the LORD. I praised the LORD, the God
of my master Abraham, who had led me on the right road to get the
granddaughter of my master's brother for his son. 49Now if you will
show kindness and faithfulness to my master, tell me; and if not, tell
me, so I may know which way to turn."

50Laban and Bethuel answered, "This is from the LORD; we can say
nothing to you one way or the other. 51Here is Rebekah; take her and
go, and let her become the wife of your master's son, as the LORD has
directed."

52When Abraham's servant heard what they said, he bowed down to
the ground before the LORD. 53Then the servant brought out gold and
silver jewelry and articles of clothing and gave them to Rebekah; he
also gave costly gifts to her brother and to her mother. 54Then he and
the men who were with him ate and drank and spent the night there.

When they got up the next morning, he said, "Send me on my way
to my master."

55But her brother and her mother replied, "Let the young woman
remain with us ten days or so; then you[a] may go."

56But he said to them, "Do not detain me, now that the LORD has
granted success to my journey. Send me on my way so I may go to my
master."

---

[a] 55 Or *she*

57 Then they said, "Let's call the young woman and ask her about it."
58 So they called Rebekah and asked her, "Will you go with this man?"
"I will go," she said.
59 So they sent their sister Rebekah on her way, along with her nurse
and Abraham's servant and his men. 60 And they blessed Rebekah and
said to her,

"Our sister, may you increase
  to thousands upon thousands;
may your offspring possess
  the cities of their enemies."

61 Then Rebekah and her attendants got ready and mounted the cam-
els and went back with the man. So the servant took Rebekah and left.
62 Now Isaac had come from Beer Lahai Roi, for he was living in the
Negev. 63 He went out to the field one evening to meditate,[a] and as he
looked up, he saw camels approaching. 64 Rebekah also looked up and
saw Isaac. She got down from her camel 65 and asked the servant, "Who
is that man in the field coming to meet us?"
"He is my master," the servant answered. So she took her veil and
covered herself.
66 Then the servant told Isaac all he had done. 67 Isaac brought her
into the tent of his mother Sarah, and he married Rebekah. So she
became his wife, and he loved her; and Isaac was comforted after his
mother's death.

THE DEATH OF ABRAHAM

25 Abraham had taken another wife, whose name was Keturah.
2 She bore him Zimran, Jokshan, Medan, Midian, Ishbak and
Shuah. 3 Jokshan was the father of Sheba and Dedan; the descendants
of Dedan were the Ashurites, the Letushites and the Leummites. 4 The
sons of Midian were Ephah, Epher, Hanok, Abida and Eldaah. All these
were descendants of Keturah.
5 Abraham left everything he owned to Isaac. 6 But while he was still
living, he gave gifts to the sons of his concubines and sent them away
from his son Isaac to the land of the east.
7 Abraham lived a hundred and seventy-five years. 8 Then Abraham
breathed his last and died at a good old age, an old man and full of
years; and he was gathered to his people. 9 His sons Isaac and Ish-
mael buried him in the cave of Machpelah near Mamre, in the field of
Ephron son of Zohar the Hittite, 10 the field Abraham had bought from
the Hittites.[b] There Abraham was buried with his wife Sarah. 11 After
Abraham's death, God blessed his son Isaac, who then lived near Beer
Lahai Roi.

PRAYING SCRIPTURE

Genesis 25

God often uses bizarre circumstances and foolish men to accomplish his purposes. Such was the case with Jacob and Esau, the former a schemer and the latter a man controlled by appetite. The younger would be stronger than the older, perhaps the source of sibling jealousy.

God has only flawed people to use. Thank God you don't have to be perfect for him to fulfill his purposes through you. Live expecting him to use you.

ISHMAEL'S SONS

12 This is the account of the family line of Abraham's son Ishmael,
whom Sarah's slave, Hagar the Egyptian, bore to Abraham.

13 These are the names of the sons of Ishmael, listed in the order
of their birth: Nebaioth the firstborn of Ishmael, Kedar, Adbeel, Mib-
sam, 14 Mishma, Dumah, Massa, 15 Hadad, Tema, Jetur, Naphish and

[a] *63* The meaning of the Hebrew for this word is uncertain. [b] *10* Or *the descendants of Heth*

Kedemah. [16]These were the sons of Ishmael, and these are the names
of the twelve tribal rulers according to their settlements and camps.
[17]Ishmael lived a hundred and thirty-seven years. He breathed his last
and died, and he was gathered to his people. [18]His descendants settled
in the area from Havilah to Shur, near the eastern border of Egypt, as
you go toward Ashur. And they lived in hostility toward[a] all the tribes
related to them.

JACOB AND ESAU

[19]This is the account of the family line of Abraham's son Isaac.

Abraham became the father of Isaac, [20]and Isaac was forty years old
when he married Rebekah daughter of Bethuel the Aramean from Pad-
dan Aram[b] and sister of Laban the Aramean.
[21]Isaac prayed to the LORD on behalf of his wife, because she was
childless. The LORD answered his prayer, and his wife Rebekah became
pregnant. [22]The babies jostled each other within her, and she said,
"Why is this happening to me?" So she went to inquire of the LORD.
[23]The LORD said to her,

"Two nations are in your womb,
  and two peoples from within you will be separated;
one people will be stronger than the other,
  and the older will serve the younger."

[24]When the time came for her to give birth, there were twin boys
in her womb. [25]The first to come out was red, and his whole body was
like a hairy garment; so they named him Esau.[c] [26]After this, his brother
came out, with his hand grasping Esau's heel; so he was named Jacob.[d]
Isaac was sixty years old when Rebekah gave birth to them.
[27]The boys grew up, and Esau became a skillful hunter, a man of
the open country, while Jacob was content to stay at home among the
tents. [28]Isaac, who had a taste for wild game, loved Esau, but Rebekah
loved Jacob.
[29]Once when Jacob was cooking some stew, Esau came in from the
open country, famished. [30]He said to Jacob, "Quick, let me have some
of that red stew! I'm famished!" (That is why he was also called Edom.[e])
[31]Jacob replied, "First sell me your birthright."
[32]"Look, I am about to die," Esau said. "What good is the birthright
to me?"
[33]But Jacob said, "Swear to me first." So he swore an oath to him,
selling his birthright to Jacob.
[34]Then Jacob gave Esau some bread and some lentil stew. He ate and
drank, and then got up and left.
So Esau despised his birthright.

ISAAC AND ABIMELEK

26 Now there was a famine in the land — besides the previous
famine in Abraham's time — and Isaac went to Abimelek king
of the Philistines in Gerar. [2]The LORD appeared to Isaac and said, "Do
not go down to Egypt; live in the land where I tell you to live. [3]Stay in
this land for a while, and I will be with you and will bless you. For to

PRAYING SCRIPTURE

Genesis 26

Human beings often repeat the sinful actions and patterns they learned from their families, and it happened here with Isaac. Under pressure from a famine, he lied to a regional king, calling Rebekah his sister.

Breaking cycles of sin or patterns of destructive behavior can seem nearly impossible, but God can deliver you. Commit to him in prayer anything that has you bound, and trust him for deliverance.

---

[a] 18 Or *lived to the east of* [b] 20 That is, Northwest Mesopotamia
[c] 25 *Esau* may mean *hairy.* [d] 26 *Jacob* means *he grasps the heel,* a Hebrew idiom for *he deceives.* [e] 30 *Edom* means *red.*

you and your descendants I will give all these lands and will confirm the oath I swore to your father Abraham. 4I will make your descendants as numerous as the stars in the sky and will give them all these lands, and through your offspring[a] all nations on earth will be blessed,[b] 5because Abraham obeyed me and did everything I required of him, keeping my commands, my decrees and my instructions." 6So Isaac stayed in Gerar.

7When the men of that place asked him about his wife, he said, "She is my sister," because he was afraid to say, "She is my wife." He thought, "The men of this place might kill me on account of Rebekah, because she is beautiful."

8When Isaac had been there a long time, Abimelek king of the Philistines looked down from a window and saw Isaac caressing his wife Rebekah. 9So Abimelek summoned Isaac and said, "She is really your wife! Why did you say, 'She is my sister'?"

Isaac answered him, "Because I thought I might lose my life on account of her."

10Then Abimelek said, "What is this you have done to us? One of the men might well have slept with your wife, and you would have brought guilt upon us."

11So Abimelek gave orders to all the people: "Anyone who harms this man or his wife shall surely be put to death."

12Isaac planted crops in that land and the same year reaped a hundredfold, because the LORD blessed him. 13The man became rich, and his wealth continued to grow until he became very wealthy. 14He had so many flocks and herds and servants that the Philistines envied him. 15So all the wells that his father's servants had dug in the time of his father Abraham, the Philistines stopped up, filling them with earth.

16Then Abimelek said to Isaac, "Move away from us; you have become too powerful for us."

17So Isaac moved away from there and encamped in the Valley of Gerar, where he settled. 18Isaac reopened the wells that had been dug in the time of his father Abraham, which the Philistines had stopped up after Abraham died, and he gave them the same names his father had given them.

19Isaac's servants dug in the valley and discovered a well of fresh water there. 20But the herders of Gerar quarreled with those of Isaac and said, "The water is ours!" So he named the well Esek,[c] because they disputed with him. 21Then they dug another well, but they quarreled over that one also; so he named it Sitnah.[d] 22He moved on from there and dug another well, and no one quarreled over it. He named it Rehoboth,[e] saying, "Now the LORD has given us room and we will flourish in the land."

23From there he went up to Beersheba. 24That night the LORD appeared to him and said, "I am the God of your father Abraham. Do not be afraid, for I am with you; I will bless you and will increase the number of your descendants for the sake of my servant Abraham."

25Isaac built an altar there and called on the name of the LORD. There he pitched his tent, and there his servants dug a well.

26Meanwhile, Abimelek had come to him from Gerar, with Ahuzzath

---

[a] 4 Or *seed* [b] 4 Or *and all nations on earth will use the name of your offspring in blessings* (see 48:20) [c] 20 *Esek* means *dispute.* [d] 21 *Sitnah* means *opposition.* [e] 22 *Rehoboth* means *room.*

his personal adviser and Phicol the commander of his forces. 27Isaac
asked them, "Why have you come to me, since you were hostile to me
and sent me away?"
28They answered, "We saw clearly that the LORD was with you; so we
said, 'There ought to be a sworn agreement between us' — between us
and you. Let us make a treaty with you 29that you will do us no harm,
just as we did not harm you but always treated you well and sent you
away peacefully. And now you are blessed by the LORD."
30Isaac then made a feast for them, and they ate and drank. 31Early
the next morning the men swore an oath to each other. Then Isaac sent
them on their way, and they went away peacefully.
32That day Isaac's servants came and told him about the well they
had dug. They said, "We've found water!" 33He called it Shibah,[a] and to
this day the name of the town has been Beersheba.[b]

JACOB TAKES ESAU'S BLESSING

34When Esau was forty years old, he married Judith daughter of Be-
eri the Hittite, and also Basemath daughter of Elon the Hittite. 35They
were a source of grief to Isaac and Rebekah.

27 When Isaac was old and his eyes were so weak that he could
no longer see, he called for Esau his older son and said to him,
"My son."
"Here I am," he answered.
2Isaac said, "I am now an old man and don't know the day of my
death. 3Now then, get your equipment — your quiver and bow — and
go out to the open country to hunt some wild game for me. 4Prepare
me the kind of tasty food I like and bring it to me to eat, so that I may
give you my blessing before I die."
5Now Rebekah was listening as Isaac spoke to his son Esau. When
Esau left for the open country to hunt game and bring it back, 6Rebekah
said to her son Jacob, "Look, I overheard your father say to your brother
Esau, 7'Bring me some game and prepare me some tasty food to eat, so
that I may give you my blessing in the presence of the LORD before I
die.' 8Now, my son, listen carefully and do what I tell you: 9Go out to the
flock and bring me two choice young goats, so I can prepare some tasty
food for your father, just the way he likes it. 10Then take it to your father
to eat, so that he may give you his blessing before he dies."
11Jacob said to Rebekah his mother, "But my brother Esau is a hairy
man while I have smooth skin. 12What if my father touches me? I
would appear to be tricking him and would bring down a curse on
myself rather than a blessing."
13His mother said to him, "My son, let the curse fall on me. Just do
what I say; go and get them for me."
14So he went and got them and brought them to his mother, and she
prepared some tasty food, just the way his father liked it. 15Then Re-
bekah took the best clothes of Esau her older son, which she had in the
house, and put them on her younger son Jacob. 16She also covered his
hands and the smooth part of his neck with the goatskins. 17Then she
handed to her son Jacob the tasty food and the bread she had made.
18He went to his father and said, "My father."
"Yes, my son," he answered. "Who is it?"

PRAYING SCRIPTURE

Genesis 27

Dysfunctional families didn't suddenly appear in our era. Rebekah and Jacob conspired together to steal Esau's blessing from his father. Even so, God would ultimately use the descendants of duplicitous Jacob—the heir of the promise—to bring redemption through Christ.

Don't think that God cannot use you in spite of a bad family situation; he can. Commit yourself and your ways to him to be used by him.

[a] 33 *Shibah* can mean *oath* or *seven.* [b] 33 *Beersheba* can mean *well of the oath* and *well of seven.*

19 Jacob said to his father, "I am Esau your firstborn. I have done as
you told me. Please sit up and eat some of my game, so that you may
give me your blessing."

20 Isaac asked his son, "How did you find it so quickly, my son?"

"The LORD your God gave me success," he replied.

21 Then Isaac said to Jacob, "Come near so I can touch you, my son, to
know whether you really are my son Esau or not."

22 Jacob went close to his father Isaac, who touched him and said,
"The voice is the voice of Jacob, but the hands are the hands of Esau."
23 He did not recognize him, for his hands were hairy like those of his
brother Esau; so he proceeded to bless him. 24 "Are you really my son
Esau?" he asked.

"I am," he replied.

25 Then he said, "My son, bring me some of your game to eat, so that
I may give you my blessing."

Jacob brought it to him and he ate; and he brought some wine and
he drank. 26 Then his father Isaac said to him, "Come here, my son, and
kiss me."

27 So he went to him and kissed him. When Isaac caught the smell of
his clothes, he blessed him and said,

"Ah, the smell of my son
  is like the smell of a field
  that the LORD has blessed.
28 May God give you heaven's dew
  and earth's richness —
  an abundance of grain and new wine.
29 May nations serve you
  and peoples bow down to you.
Be lord over your brothers,
  and may the sons of your mother bow down to you.
May those who curse you be cursed
  and those who bless you be blessed."

30 After Isaac finished blessing him, and Jacob had scarcely left his
father's presence, his brother Esau came in from hunting. 31 He too pre-
pared some tasty food and brought it to his father. Then he said to him,
"My father, please sit up and eat some of my game, so that you may
give me your blessing."

32 His father Isaac asked him, "Who are you?"

"I am your son," he answered, "your firstborn, Esau."

33 Isaac trembled violently and said, "Who was it, then, that hunted
game and brought it to me? I ate it just before you came and I blessed
him — and indeed he will be blessed!"

34 When Esau heard his father's words, he burst out with a loud and
bitter cry and said to his father, "Bless me — me too, my father!"

35 But he said, "Your brother came deceitfully and took your blessing."

36 Esau said, "Isn't he rightly named Jacob[a]? This is the second time
he has taken advantage of me: He took my birthright, and now he's
taken my blessing!" Then he asked, "Haven't you reserved any bless-
ing for me?"

37 Isaac answered Esau, "I have made him lord over you and have

---

[a] *36* *Jacob* means *he grasps the heel,* a Hebrew idiom for *he takes advantage of* or *he deceives.*

made all his relatives his servants, and I have sustained him with grain
and new wine. So what can I possibly do for you, my son?"
38 Esau said to his father, "Do you have only one blessing, my father?
Bless me too, my father!" Then Esau wept aloud.
39 His father Isaac answered him,

"Your dwelling will be
  away from the earth's richness,
  away from the dew of heaven above.
40 You will live by the sword
  and you will serve your brother.
But when you grow restless,
  you will throw his yoke
  from off your neck."

41 Esau held a grudge against Jacob because of the blessing his father
had given him. He said to himself, "The days of mourning for my fa-
ther are near; then I will kill my brother Jacob."
42 When Rebekah was told what her older son Esau had said, she sent
for her younger son Jacob and said to him, "Your brother Esau is plan-
ning to avenge himself by killing you. 43 Now then, my son, do what I
say: Flee at once to my brother Laban in Harran. 44 Stay with him for a
while until your brother's fury subsides. 45 When your brother is no lon-
ger angry with you and forgets what you did to him, I'll send word for
you to come back from there. Why should I lose both of you in one day?"
46 Then Rebekah said to Isaac, "I'm disgusted with living because of
these Hittite women. If Jacob takes a wife from among the women
of this land, from Hittite women like these, my life will not be worth
living."

28 So Isaac called for Jacob and blessed him. Then he commanded
him: "Do not marry a Canaanite woman. 2 Go at once to Pad-
dan Aram,[a] to the house of your mother's father Bethuel. Take a wife
for yourself there, from among the daughters of Laban, your mother's
brother. 3 May God Almighty[b] bless you and make you fruitful and in-
crease your numbers until you become a community of peoples. 4 May
he give you and your descendants the blessing given to Abraham, so
that you may take possession of the land where you now reside as a
foreigner, the land God gave to Abraham." 5 Then Isaac sent Jacob on
his way, and he went to Paddan Aram, to Laban son of Bethuel the Ara-
mean, the brother of Rebekah, who was the mother of Jacob and Esau.
6 Now Esau learned that Isaac had blessed Jacob and had sent him to
Paddan Aram to take a wife from there, and that when he blessed him
he commanded him, "Do not marry a Canaanite woman," 7 and that Ja-
cob had obeyed his father and mother and had gone to Paddan Aram.
8 Esau then realized how displeasing the Canaanite women were to his
father Isaac; 9 so he went to Ishmael and married Mahalath, the sister
of Nebaioth and daughter of Ishmael son of Abraham, in addition to
the wives he already had.

JACOB'S DREAM AT BETHEL

10 Jacob left Beersheba and set out for Harran. 11 When he reached a
certain place, he stopped for the night because the sun had set. Taking

PRAYING SCRIPTURE

Genesis 28

Do you ever wish you could have a personal encounter with God? Jacob had one in a dream. In it, God confirmed the promise to his grandfather and father: He would give Jacob descendants like the sands of the seashore.

Whether you have had a personal encounter with God or not, have confidence that he knows where you are and what you need. Thank him for watching over you.

---

[a] *2* That is, Northwest Mesopotamia; also in verses 5, 6 and 7 [b] *3* Hebrew *El-Shaddai*

one of the stones there, he put it under his head and lay down to sleep.
12He had a dream in which he saw a stairway resting on the earth, with
its top reaching to heaven, and the angels of God were ascending and
descending on it. 13There above it[a] stood the LORD, and he said: "I am
the LORD, the God of your father Abraham and the God of Isaac. I will
give you and your descendants the land on which you are lying. 14Your
descendants will be like the dust of the earth, and you will spread out
to the west and to the east, to the north and to the south. All peoples
on earth will be blessed through you and your offspring.[b] 15I am with
you and will watch over you wherever you go, and I will bring you back
to this land. I will not leave you until I have done what I have prom-
ised you."

16When Jacob awoke from his sleep, he thought, "Surely the LORD is
in this place, and I was not aware of it." 17He was afraid and said, "How
awesome is this place! This is none other than the house of God; this
is the gate of heaven."

18Early the next morning Jacob took the stone he had placed under
his head and set it up as a pillar and poured oil on top of it. 19He called
that place Bethel,[c] though the city used to be called Luz.

20Then Jacob made a vow, saying, "If God will be with me and will
watch over me on this journey I am taking and will give me food to eat
and clothes to wear 21so that I return safely to my father's household,
then the LORD[d] will be my God 22and[e] this stone that I have set up as
a pillar will be God's house, and of all that you give me I will give you
a tenth."

JACOB ARRIVES IN PADDAN ARAM

29 Then Jacob continued on his journey and came to the land of
the eastern peoples. 2There he saw a well in the open country,
with three flocks of sheep lying near it because the flocks were watered
from that well. The stone over the mouth of the well was large. 3When
all the flocks were gathered there, the shepherds would roll the stone
away from the well's mouth and water the sheep. Then they would re-
turn the stone to its place over the mouth of the well.

4Jacob asked the shepherds, "My brothers, where are you from?"

"We're from Harran," they replied.

5He said to them, "Do you know Laban, Nahor's grandson?"

"Yes, we know him," they answered.

6Then Jacob asked them, "Is he well?"

"Yes, he is," they said, "and here comes his daughter Rachel with
the sheep."

7"Look," he said, "the sun is still high; it is not time for the flocks to
be gathered. Water the sheep and take them back to pasture."

8"We can't," they replied, "until all the flocks are gathered and the
stone has been rolled away from the mouth of the well. Then we will
water the sheep."

9While he was still talking with them, Rachel came with her father's
sheep, for she was a shepherd. 10When Jacob saw Rachel daughter of
his uncle Laban, and Laban's sheep, he went over and rolled the stone

PRAYING SCRIPTURE

Genesis 29

If Scripture teaches us anything, it's that the Lord works even in the most broken human situations. Jacob, deceived by his uncle as he had deceived his brother and father, unknowingly married a woman he did not love.

When you've been used or feel disdained, know that God is sovereign in your situation. Cry out to him in your anguish and pain, and then trust him to heal you.

---

[a] 13 Or *There beside him* [b] 14 Or *will use your name and the name of your offspring in blessings* (see 48:20) [c] 19 *Bethel* means *house of God.*
[d] 20,21 Or *Since God . . . father's household, the LORD* [e] 21,22 Or *household, and the LORD will be my God, 22then*

away from the mouth of the well and watered his uncle's sheep. 11Then
Jacob kissed Rachel and began to weep aloud. 12He had told Rachel that
he was a relative of her father and a son of Rebekah. So she ran and
told her father.

13As soon as Laban heard the news about Jacob, his sister's son, he
hurried to meet him. He embraced him and kissed him and brought
him to his home, and there Jacob told him all these things. 14Then La-
ban said to him, "You are my own flesh and blood."

JACOB MARRIES LEAH AND RACHEL

After Jacob had stayed with him for a whole month, 15Laban said to
him, "Just because you are a relative of mine, should you work for me
for nothing? Tell me what your wages should be."

16Now Laban had two daughters; the name of the older was Leah,
and the name of the younger was Rachel. 17Leah had weak[a] eyes, but
Rachel had a lovely figure and was beautiful. 18Jacob was in love with
Rachel and said, "I'll work for you seven years in return for your youn-
ger daughter Rachel."

19Laban said, "It's better that I give her to you than to some other
man. Stay here with me." 20So Jacob served seven years to get Rachel,
but they seemed like only a few days to him because of his love for her.

21Then Jacob said to Laban, "Give me my wife. My time is completed,
and I want to make love to her."

22So Laban brought together all the people of the place and gave
a feast. 23But when evening came, he took his daughter Leah and
brought her to Jacob, and Jacob made love to her. 24And Laban gave
his servant Zilpah to his daughter as her attendant.

25When morning came, there was Leah! So Jacob said to Laban,
"What is this you have done to me? I served you for Rachel, didn't I?
Why have you deceived me?"

26Laban replied, "It is not our custom here to give the younger
daughter in marriage before the older one. 27Finish this daughter's
bridal week; then we will give you the younger one also, in return for
another seven years of work."

28And Jacob did so. He finished the week with Leah, and then Laban
gave him his daughter Rachel to be his wife. 29Laban gave his servant
Bilhah to his daughter Rachel as her attendant. 30Jacob made love to
Rachel also, and his love for Rachel was greater than his love for Leah.
And he worked for Laban another seven years.

JACOB'S CHILDREN

31When the Lord saw that Leah was not loved, he enabled her to
conceive, but Rachel remained childless. 32Leah became pregnant and
gave birth to a son. She named him Reuben,[b] for she said, "It is be-
cause the Lord has seen my misery. Surely my husband will love me
now."

33She conceived again, and when she gave birth to a son she said,
"Because the Lord heard that I am not loved, he gave me this one too."
So she named him Simeon.[c]

34Again she conceived, and when she gave birth to a son she said,

---

[a] 17 Or *delicate* [b] 32 *Reuben* sounds like the Hebrew for *he has seen my misery*; the name means *see, a son.* [c] 33 *Simeon* probably means *one who hears.*

PRAYING
SCRIPTURE

Genesis 30

God's promise to Abraham seemed absurd when he made it, but eventually Abraham's family grew. His grandson Jacob had a rapidly multiplying family while his trickster nature had made him a man rich in livestock. In spite of his wealth, trouble was brewing in his marriages and extended family.

When you pray, thank God that he will bless you even if you are mistreated and taken advantage of by friends or family.

"Now at last my husband will become attached to me, because I have
borne him three sons." So he was named Levi.[a]
35 She conceived again, and when she gave birth to a son she said,
"This time I will praise the LORD." So she named him Judah.[b] Then she
stopped having children.

30 When Rachel saw that she was not bearing Jacob any children,
she became jealous of her sister. So she said to Jacob, "Give me
children, or I'll die!"
2 Jacob became angry with her and said, "Am I in the place of God,
who has kept you from having children?"
3 Then she said, "Here is Bilhah, my servant. Sleep with her so that
she can bear children for me and I too can build a family through her."
4 So she gave him her servant Bilhah as a wife. Jacob slept with her,
5 and she became pregnant and bore him a son. 6 Then Rachel said, "God
has vindicated me; he has listened to my plea and given me a son." Be-
cause of this she named him Dan.[c]
7 Rachel's servant Bilhah conceived again and bore Jacob a second
son. 8 Then Rachel said, "I have had a great struggle with my sister, and
I have won." So she named him Naphtali.[d]
9 When Leah saw that she had stopped having children, she took her
servant Zilpah and gave her to Jacob as a wife. 10 Leah's servant Zil-
pah bore Jacob a son. 11 Then Leah said, "What good fortune!"[e] So she
named him Gad.[f]
12 Leah's servant Zilpah bore Jacob a second son. 13 Then Leah said,
"How happy I am! The women will call me happy." So she named him
Asher.[g]
14 During wheat harvest, Reuben went out into the fields and found
some mandrake plants, which he brought to his mother Leah. Rachel
said to Leah, "Please give me some of your son's mandrakes."
15 But she said to her, "Wasn't it enough that you took away my hus-
band? Will you take my son's mandrakes too?"
"Very well," Rachel said, "he can sleep with you tonight in return for
your son's mandrakes."
16 So when Jacob came in from the fields that evening, Leah went
out to meet him. "You must sleep with me," she said. "I have hired you
with my son's mandrakes." So he slept with her that night.
17 God listened to Leah, and she became pregnant and bore Jacob a
fifth son. 18 Then Leah said, "God has rewarded me for giving my ser-
vant to my husband." So she named him Issachar.[h]
19 Leah conceived again and bore Jacob a sixth son. 20 Then Leah said,
"God has presented me with a precious gift. This time my husband will
treat me with honor, because I have borne him six sons." So she named
him Zebulun.[i]
21 Some time later she gave birth to a daughter and named her Dinah.
22 Then God remembered Rachel; he listened to her and enabled her
to conceive. 23 She became pregnant and gave birth to a son and said,
"God has taken away my disgrace." 24 She named him Joseph,[j] and said,
"May the LORD add to me another son."

---

[a] 34 *Levi* sounds like and may be derived from the Hebrew for *attached.*
[b] 35 *Judah* sounds like and may be derived from the Hebrew for *praise.*
[c] 6 *Dan* here means *he has vindicated.* [d] 8 *Naphtali* means *my struggle.*
[e] 11 Or *"A troop is coming!"* [f] 11 *Gad* can mean *good fortune* or *a troop.*
[g] 13 *Asher* means *happy.* [h] 18 *Issachar* sounds like the Hebrew for *reward.*
[i] 20 *Zebulun* probably means *honor.* [j] 24 *Joseph* means *may he add.*

JACOB'S FLOCKS INCREASE

25After Rachel gave birth to Joseph, Jacob said to Laban, "Send me
on my way so I can go back to my own homeland. 26Give me my wives
and children, for whom I have served you, and I will be on my way. You
know how much work I've done for you."
27But Laban said to him, "If I have found favor in your eyes, please
stay. I have learned by divination that the LORD has blessed me be-
cause of you." 28He added, "Name your wages, and I will pay them."
29Jacob said to him, "You know how I have worked for you and how
your livestock has fared under my care. 30The little you had before I
came has increased greatly, and the LORD has blessed you wherever I
have been. But now, when may I do something for my own household?"
31"What shall I give you?" he asked.
"Don't give me anything," Jacob replied. "But if you will do this one
thing for me, I will go on tending your flocks and watching over them:
32Let me go through all your flocks today and remove from them every
speckled or spotted sheep, every dark-colored lamb and every spotted
or speckled goat. They will be my wages. 33And my honesty will testify
for me in the future, whenever you check on the wages you have paid
me. Any goat in my possession that is not speckled or spotted, or any
lamb that is not dark-colored, will be considered stolen."
34"Agreed," said Laban. "Let it be as you have said." 35That same day
he removed all the male goats that were streaked or spotted, and all
the speckled or spotted female goats (all that had white on them) and
all the dark colored lambs, and he placed them in the care of his sons.
36Then he put a three-day journey between himself and Jacob, while
Jacob continued to tend the rest of Laban's flocks.
37Jacob, however, took fresh-cut branches from poplar, almond and
plane trees and made white stripes on them by peeling the bark and
exposing the white inner wood of the branches. 38Then he placed the
peeled branches in all the watering troughs, so that they would be di-
rectly in front of the flocks when they came to drink. When the flocks
were in heat and came to drink, 39they mated in front of the branches.
And they bore young that were streaked or speckled or spotted. 40Ja-
cob set apart the young of the flock by themselves, but made the rest
face the streaked and dark-colored animals that belonged to Laban.
Thus he made separate flocks for himself and did not put them with
Laban's animals. 41Whenever the stronger females were in heat, Jacob
would place the branches in the troughs in front of the animals so
they would mate near the branches, 42but if the animals were weak, he
would not place them there. So the weak animals went to Laban and
the strong ones to Jacob. 43In this way the man grew exceedingly pros-
perous and came to own large flocks, and female and male servants,
and camels and donkeys.

JACOB FLEES FROM LABAN

31 Jacob heard that Laban's sons were saying, "Jacob has taken ev-
erything our father owned and has gained all this wealth from
what belonged to our father." 2And Jacob noticed that Laban's attitude
toward him was not what it had been.
3Then the LORD said to Jacob, "Go back to the land of your fathers
and to your relatives, and I will be with you."
4So Jacob sent word to Rachel and Leah to come out to the fields
where his flocks were. 5He said to them, "I see that your father's

PRAYING SCRIPTURE

Genesis 31

Despite Laban's scheming to take advantage of Jacob and Jacob's deception to escape Laban's ongoing mistreatment by making a covenant between them, Jacob and Laban acknowledged that God sees and knows everything. God was, they agreed, the Judge between them.

Do you have a strained or broken relationship with anyone? Ask God to bring reconciliation so that he is honored and his name exalted.

attitude toward me is not what it was before, but the God of my father
has been with me. 6You know that I've worked for your father with all
my strength, 7yet your father has cheated me by changing my wages
ten times. However, God has not allowed him to harm me. 8If he said,
'The speckled ones will be your wages,' then all the flocks gave birth to
speckled young; and if he said, 'The streaked ones will be your wages,'
then all the flocks bore streaked young. 9So God has taken away your
father's livestock and has given them to me.
10"In breeding season I once had a dream in which I looked up and
saw that the male goats mating with the flock were streaked, speckled
or spotted. 11The angel of God said to me in the dream, 'Jacob.' I an-
swered, 'Here I am.' 12And he said, 'Look up and see that all the male
goats mating with the flock are streaked, speckled or spotted, for I have
seen all that Laban has been doing to you. 13I am the God of Bethel,
where you anointed a pillar and where you made a vow to me. Now
leave this land at once and go back to your native land.'"
14Then Rachel and Leah replied, "Do we still have any share in the
inheritance of our father's estate? 15Does he not regard us as foreign-
ers? Not only has he sold us, but he has used up what was paid for us.
16Surely all the wealth that God took away from our father belongs to
us and our children. So do whatever God has told you."
17Then Jacob put his children and his wives on camels, 18and he drove
all his livestock ahead of him, along with all the goods he had accumu-
lated in Paddan Aram,[a] to go to his father Isaac in the land of Canaan.
19When Laban had gone to shear his sheep, Rachel stole her father's
household gods. 20Moreover, Jacob deceived Laban the Aramean by
not telling him he was running away. 21So he fled with all he had,
crossed the Euphrates River, and headed for the hill country of Gilead.

LABAN PURSUES JACOB

22On the third day Laban was told that Jacob had fled. 23Taking his
relatives with him, he pursued Jacob for seven days and caught up
with him in the hill country of Gilead. 24Then God came to Laban the
Aramean in a dream at night and said to him, "Be careful not to say
anything to Jacob, either good or bad."
25Jacob had pitched his tent in the hill country of Gilead when Laban
overtook him, and Laban and his relatives camped there too. 26Then
Laban said to Jacob, "What have you done? You've deceived me, and
you've carried off my daughters like captives in war. 27Why did you run
off secretly and deceive me? Why didn't you tell me, so I could send you
away with joy and singing to the music of timbrels and harps? 28You
didn't even let me kiss my grandchildren and my daughters goodbye.
You have done a foolish thing. 29I have the power to harm you; but last
night the God of your father said to me, 'Be careful not to say anything to
Jacob, either good or bad.' 30Now you have gone off because you longed
to return to your father's household. But why did you steal my gods?"
31Jacob answered Laban, "I was afraid, because I thought you would
take your daughters away from me by force. 32But if you find anyone who
has your gods, that person shall not live. In the presence of our relatives,
see for yourself whether there is anything of yours here with me; and
if so, take it." Now Jacob did not know that Rachel had stolen the gods.
33So Laban went into Jacob's tent and into Leah's tent and into the tent

---

[a] *18* That is, Northwest Mesopotamia

of the two female servants, but he found nothing. After he came out of
Leah's tent, he entered Rachel's tent. 34Now Rachel had taken the house-
hold gods and put them inside her camel's saddle and was sitting on
them. Laban searched through everything in the tent but found nothing.
35Rachel said to her father, "Don't be angry, my lord, that I cannot
stand up in your presence; I'm having my period." So he searched but
could not find the household gods.
36Jacob was angry and took Laban to task. "What is my crime?" he
asked Laban. "How have I wronged you that you hunt me down? 37Now
that you have searched through all my goods, what have you found
that belongs to your household? Put it here in front of your relatives
and mine, and let them judge between the two of us.
38"I have been with you for twenty years now. Your sheep and goats
have not miscarried, nor have I eaten rams from your flocks. 39I did not
bring you animals torn by wild beasts; I bore the loss myself. And you
demanded payment from me for whatever was stolen by day or night.
40This was my situation: The heat consumed me in the daytime and
the cold at night, and sleep fled from my eyes. 41It was like this for the
twenty years I was in your household. I worked for you fourteen years
for your two daughters and six years for your flocks, and you changed
my wages ten times. 42If the God of my father, the God of Abraham and
the Fear of Isaac, had not been with me, you would surely have sent me
away empty-handed. But God has seen my hardship and the toil of my
hands, and last night he rebuked you."
43Laban answered Jacob, "The women are my daughters, the chil-
dren are my children, and the flocks are my flocks. All you see is mine.
Yet what can I do today about these daughters of mine, or about the
children they have borne? 44Come now, let's make a covenant, you and
I, and let it serve as a witness between us."
45So Jacob took a stone and set it up as a pillar. 46He said to his rel-
atives, "Gather some stones." So they took stones and piled them in a
heap, and they ate there by the heap. 47Laban called it Jegar Sahadutha,
and Jacob called it Galeed.[a]
48Laban said, "This heap is a witness between you and me today."
That is why it was called Galeed. 49It was also called Mizpah,[b] because
he said, "May the LORD keep watch between you and me when we are
away from each other. 50If you mistreat my daughters or if you take
any wives besides my daughters, even though no one is with us, re-
member that God is a witness between you and me."
51Laban also said to Jacob, "Here is this heap, and here is this pillar
I have set up between you and me. 52This heap is a witness, and this
pillar is a witness, that I will not go past this heap to your side to harm
you and that you will not go past this heap and pillar to my side to
harm me. 53May the God of Abraham and the God of Nahor, the God of
their father, judge between us."
So Jacob took an oath in the name of the Fear of his father Isaac. 54He
offered a sacrifice there in the hill country and invited his relatives to
a meal. After they had eaten, they spent the night there.
55Early the next morning Laban kissed his grandchildren and his
daughters and blessed them. Then he left and returned home.[c]

---

[a] *47* The Aramaic *Jegar Sahadutha* and the Hebrew *Galeed* both mean *witness heap.* [b] *49* *Mizpah* means *watchtower.* [c] *55* In Hebrew texts this verse (31:55) is numbered 32:1.

PRAYING SCRIPTURE

Genesis 32

Many people get so hung up on who Jacob wrestled that they miss *why* Jacob wrestled. Two things stand out: The man came to Jacob to wrestle, and his purpose was to push Jacob into securing a blessing on his life. Jacob overcame (see verse 28) and was spared (see verse 30).

This passage may have birthed the phrase "prevailing prayer," prayer that does not stop until answered. Today, take your great burden to God again. Keep praying with the anticipation that God will answer.

JACOB PREPARES TO MEET ESAU

32[a] Jacob also went on his way, and the angels of God met him.
2When Jacob saw them, he said, "This is the camp of God!" So
he named that place Mahanaim.[b]
3Jacob sent messengers ahead of him to his brother Esau in the land
of Seir, the country of Edom. 4He instructed them: "This is what you
are to say to my lord Esau: 'Your servant Jacob says, I have been staying
with Laban and have remained there till now. 5I have cattle and don-
keys, sheep and goats, male and female servants. Now I am sending
this message to my lord, that I may find favor in your eyes.' "
6When the messengers returned to Jacob, they said, "We went to
your brother Esau, and now he is coming to meet you, and four hun-
dred men are with him."
7In great fear and distress Jacob divided the people who were with
him into two groups,[c] and the flocks and herds and camels as well. 8He
thought, "If Esau comes and attacks one group,[d] the group[d] that is left
may escape."
9Then Jacob prayed, "O God of my father Abraham, God of my father
Isaac, LORD, you who said to me, 'Go back to your country and your
relatives, and I will make you prosper,' 10I am unworthy of all the kind-
ness and faithfulness you have shown your servant. I had only my staff
when I crossed this Jordan, but now I have become two camps. 11Save
me, I pray, from the hand of my brother Esau, for I am afraid he will
come and attack me, and also the mothers with their children. 12But
you have said, 'I will surely make you prosper and will make your de-
scendants like the sand of the sea, which cannot be counted.' "
13He spent the night there, and from what he had with him he se-
lected a gift for his brother Esau: 14two hundred female goats and
twenty male goats, two hundred ewes and twenty rams, 15thirty fe-
male camels with their young, forty cows and ten bulls, and twenty
female donkeys and ten male donkeys. 16He put them in the care of
his servants, each herd by itself, and said to his servants, "Go ahead of
me, and keep some space between the herds."
17He instructed the one in the lead: "When my brother Esau meets
you and asks, 'Who do you belong to, and where are you going, and
who owns all these animals in front of you?' 18then you are to say, 'They
belong to your servant Jacob. They are a gift sent to my lord Esau, and
he is coming behind us.' "
19He also instructed the second, the third and all the others who fol-
lowed the herds: "You are to say the same thing to Esau when you
meet him. 20And be sure to say, 'Your servant Jacob is coming behind
us.' " For he thought, "I will pacify him with these gifts I am sending on
ahead; later, when I see him, perhaps he will receive me." 21So Jacob's
gifts went on ahead of him, but he himself spent the night in the camp.

JACOB WRESTLES WITH GOD

22That night Jacob got up and took his two wives, his two female ser-
vants and his eleven sons and crossed the ford of the Jabbok. 23After
he had sent them across the stream, he sent over all his possessions.
24So Jacob was left alone, and a man wrestled with him till daybreak.
25When the man saw that he could not overpower him, he touched the

[a] In Hebrew texts 32:1-32 is numbered 32:2-33. [b] 2 *Mahanaim* means *two camps.* [c] 7 Or *camps* [d] 8 Or *camp*

socket of Jacob's hip so that his hip was wrenched as he wrestled with the man. 26Then the man said, "Let me go, for it is daybreak."

But Jacob replied, "I will not let you go unless you bless me."

27The man asked him, "What is your name?"

"Jacob," he answered.

28Then the man said, "Your name will no longer be Jacob, but Israel,[a] because you have struggled with God and with humans and have overcome."

29Jacob said, "Please tell me your name."

But he replied, "Why do you ask my name?" Then he blessed him there.

30So Jacob called the place Peniel,[b] saying, "It is because I saw God face to face, and yet my life was spared."

31The sun rose above him as he passed Peniel,[c] and he was limping because of his hip. 32Therefore to this day the Israelites do not eat the tendon attached to the socket of the hip, because the socket of Jacob's hip was touched near the tendon.

JACOB MEETS ESAU

33 Jacob looked up and there was Esau, coming with his four hundred men; so he divided the children among Leah, Rachel and the two female servants. 2He put the female servants and their children in front, Leah and her children next, and Rachel and Joseph in the rear. 3He himself went on ahead and bowed down to the ground seven times as he approached his brother.

4But Esau ran to meet Jacob and embraced him; he threw his arms around his neck and kissed him. And they wept. 5Then Esau looked up and saw the women and children. "Who are these with you?" he asked.

Jacob answered, "They are the children God has graciously given your servant."

6Then the female servants and their children approached and bowed down. 7Next, Leah and her children came and bowed down. Last of all came Joseph and Rachel, and they too bowed down.

8Esau asked, "What's the meaning of all these flocks and herds I met?"

"To find favor in your eyes, my lord," he said.

9But Esau said, "I already have plenty, my brother. Keep what you have for yourself."

10"No, please!" said Jacob. "If I have found favor in your eyes, accept this gift from me. For to see your face is like seeing the face of God, now that you have received me favorably. 11Please accept the present that was brought to you, for God has been gracious to me and I have all I need." And because Jacob insisted, Esau accepted it.

12Then Esau said, "Let us be on our way; I'll accompany you."

13But Jacob said to him, "My lord knows that the children are tender and that I must care for the ewes and cows that are nursing their young. If they are driven hard just one day, all the animals will die. 14So let my lord go on ahead of his servant, while I move along slowly at the pace of the flocks and herds before me and the pace of the children, until I come to my lord in Seir."

15Esau said, "Then let me leave some of my men with you."

[a] 28 *Israel* probably means *he struggles with God.* [b] 30 *Peniel* means *face of God.* [c] 31 Hebrew *Penuel,* a variant of *Peniel*

PRAYING SCRIPTURE

Genesis 33

In a remarkable narrative of Jacob's returning home to meet his brother, God protected him and gave him favor with Esau, whom he had deceived then double-crossed. Esau forgave Jacob, greeting him with hugs and kisses.

Given their history, we might have expected Esau to have become consumed with bitterness or bent on revenge, yet he chose to forgive. Ask God to protect you from the bitterness of unforgiveness.

"But why do that?" Jacob asked. "Just let me find favor in the eyes of my lord."

16So that day Esau started on his way back to Seir. 17Jacob, however, went to Sukkoth, where he built a place for himself and made shelters for his livestock. That is why the place is called Sukkoth.[a]

18After Jacob came from Paddan Aram,[b] he arrived safely at the city of Shechem in Canaan and camped within sight of the city. 19For a hundred pieces of silver,[c] he bought from the sons of Hamor, the father of Shechem, the plot of ground where he pitched his tent. 20There he set up an altar and called it El Elohe Israel.[d]

DINAH AND THE SHECHEMITES

34 Now Dinah, the daughter Leah had borne to Jacob, went out to visit the women of the land. 2When Shechem son of Hamor the Hivite, the ruler of that area, saw her, he took her and raped her. 3His heart was drawn to Dinah daughter of Jacob; he loved the young woman and spoke tenderly to her. 4And Shechem said to his father Hamor, "Get me this girl as my wife."

5When Jacob heard that his daughter Dinah had been defiled, his sons were in the fields with his livestock; so he did nothing about it until they came home.

6Then Shechem's father Hamor went out to talk with Jacob. 7Meanwhile, Jacob's sons had come in from the fields as soon as they heard what had happened. They were shocked and furious, because Shechem had done an outrageous thing in[e] Israel by sleeping with Jacob's daughter — a thing that should not be done.

8But Hamor said to them, "My son Shechem has his heart set on your daughter. Please give her to him as his wife. 9Intermarry with us; give us your daughters and take our daughters for yourselves. 10You can settle among us; the land is open to you. Live in it, trade[f] in it, and acquire property in it."

11Then Shechem said to Dinah's father and brothers, "Let me find favor in your eyes, and I will give you whatever you ask. 12Make the price for the bride and the gift I am to bring as great as you like, and I'll pay whatever you ask me. Only give me the young woman as my wife."

13Because their sister Dinah had been defiled, Jacob's sons replied deceitfully as they spoke to Shechem and his father Hamor. 14They said to them, "We can't do such a thing; we can't give our sister to a man who is not circumcised. That would be a disgrace to us. 15We will enter into an agreement with you on one condition only: that you become like us by circumcising all your males. 16Then we will give you our daughters and take your daughters for ourselves. We'll settle among you and become one people with you. 17But if you will not agree to be circumcised, we'll take our sister and go."

18Their proposal seemed good to Hamor and his son Shechem. 19The young man, who was the most honored of all his father's family, lost no time in doing what they said, because he was delighted with Jacob's daughter. 20So Hamor and his son Shechem went to the gate of

PRAYING SCRIPTURE

Genesis 34

Taking things into our own hands often feels right yet ends badly. Jacob's sons took vengeance for themselves rather than waiting for God's justice, bringing about negative consequences for the family.

Having the patience to wait for God's justice is not always easy. When tempted to "help God out," confess your impatience and commit to wait on his perfect justice and timing.

[a] *17 Sukkoth* means *shelters.* [b] *18* That is, Northwest Mesopotamia
[c] *19* Hebrew *hundred kesitahs*; a kesitah was a unit of money of unknown weight and value. [d] *20 El Elohe Israel* can mean *El is the God of Israel* or *mighty is the God of Israel.* [e] *7* Or *against* [f] *10* Or *move about freely*; also in verse 21

their city to speak to the men of their city. 21“These men are friendly toward us,” they said. “Let them live in our land and trade in it; the land has plenty of room for them. We can marry their daughters and they can marry ours. 22But the men will agree to live with us as one people only on the condition that our males be circumcised, as they themselves are. 23Won’t their livestock, their property and all their other animals become ours? So let us agree to their terms, and they will settle among us.”

24All the men who went out of the city gate agreed with Hamor and his son Shechem, and every male in the city was circumcised.

25Three days later, while all of them were still in pain, two of Jacob’s sons, Simeon and Levi, Dinah’s brothers, took their swords and attacked the unsuspecting city, killing every male. 26They put Hamor and his son Shechem to the sword and took Dinah from Shechem’s house and left. 27The sons of Jacob came upon the dead bodies and looted the city where[a] their sister had been defiled. 28They seized their flocks and herds and donkeys and everything else of theirs in the city and out in the fields. 29They carried off all their wealth and all their women and children, taking as plunder everything in the houses.

30Then Jacob said to Simeon and Levi, “You have brought trouble on me by making me obnoxious to the Canaanites and Perizzites, the people living in this land. We are few in number, and if they join forces against me and attack me, I and my household will be destroyed.”

31But they replied, “Should he have treated our sister like a prostitute?”

JACOB RETURNS TO BETHEL

35 Then God said to Jacob, “Go up to Bethel and settle there, and build an altar there to God, who appeared to you when you were fleeing from your brother Esau.”

2So Jacob said to his household and to all who were with him, “Get rid of the foreign gods you have with you, and purify yourselves and change your clothes. 3Then come, let us go up to Bethel, where I will build an altar to God, who answered me in the day of my distress and who has been with me wherever I have gone.” 4So they gave Jacob all the foreign gods they had and the rings in their ears, and Jacob buried them under the oak at Shechem. 5Then they set out, and the terror of God fell on the towns all around them so that no one pursued them.

6Jacob and all the people with him came to Luz (that is, Bethel) in the land of Canaan. 7There he built an altar, and he called the place El Bethel,[b] because it was there that God revealed himself to him when he was fleeing from his brother.

8Now Deborah, Rebekah’s nurse, died and was buried under the oak outside Bethel. So it was named Allon Bakuth.[c]

9After Jacob returned from Paddan Aram,[d] God appeared to him again and blessed him. 10God said to him, “Your name is Jacob,[e] but you will no longer be called Jacob; your name will be Israel.[f]” So he named him Israel.

11And God said to him, “I am God Almighty[g]; be fruitful and increase

[a] 27 Or *because* [b] 7 *El Bethel* means *God of Bethel.* [c] 8 *Allon Bakuth* means *oak of weeping.* [d] 9 That is, Northwest Mesopotamia; also in verse 26 [e] 10 *Jacob* means *he grasps the heel,* a Hebrew idiom for *he deceives.* [f] 10 *Israel* probably means *he struggles with God.* [g] 11 Hebrew *El-Shaddai*

PRAYING SCRIPTURE

Genesis 35

At Bethel God reiterated to Jacob the same promise he’d made to Abraham, then to Isaac. God made his promise personal and changed Jacob’s name to Israel. He expanded the promise to include kings in the line of Abraham, Isaac and Jacob.

Eventually one of those kings would be Jesus himself. Praise God for his wisdom in providing for this family in pursuit of bringing salvation to the world.

in number. A nation and a community of nations will come from you,
and kings will be among your descendants. 12 The land I gave to Abra-
ham and Isaac I also give to you, and I will give this land to your de-
scendants after you." 13 Then God went up from him at the place where
he had talked with him.
14 Jacob set up a stone pillar at the place where God had talked with
him, and he poured out a drink offering on it; he also poured oil on it.
15 Jacob called the place where God had talked with him Bethel.[a]

THE DEATHS OF RACHEL AND ISAAC

16 Then they moved on from Bethel. While they were still some dis-
tance from Ephrath, Rachel began to give birth and had great difficulty.
17 And as she was having great difficulty in childbirth, the midwife said
to her, "Don't despair, for you have another son." 18 As she breathed her
last — for she was dying — she named her son Ben-Oni.[b] But his father
named him Benjamin.[c]
19 So Rachel died and was buried on the way to Ephrath (that is, Beth-
lehem). 20 Over her tomb Jacob set up a pillar, and to this day that pillar
marks Rachel's tomb.
21 Israel moved on again and pitched his tent beyond Migdal Eder.
22 While Israel was living in that region, Reuben went in and slept with
his father's concubine Bilhah, and Israel heard of it.

Jacob had twelve sons:
23 The sons of Leah:
Reuben the firstborn of Jacob,
Simeon, Levi, Judah, Issachar and Zebulun.
24 The sons of Rachel:
Joseph and Benjamin.
25 The sons of Rachel's servant Bilhah:
Dan and Naphtali.
26 The sons of Leah's servant Zilpah:
Gad and Asher.
These were the sons of Jacob, who were born to him in Paddan Aram.
27 Jacob came home to his father Isaac in Mamre, near Kiriath Arba
(that is, Hebron), where Abraham and Isaac had stayed. 28 Isaac lived a
hundred and eighty years. 29 Then he breathed his last and died and
was gathered to his people, old and full of years. And his sons Esau
and Jacob buried him.

ESAU'S DESCENDANTS

36 This is the account of the family line of Esau (that is, Edom).

2 Esau took his wives from the women of Canaan: Adah daughter
of Elon the Hittite, and Oholibamah daughter of Anah and grand-
daughter of Zibeon the Hivite — 3 also Basemath daughter of Ish-
mael and sister of Nebaioth.
4 Adah bore Eliphaz to Esau, Basemath bore Reuel, 5 and Oholi-
bamah bore Jeush, Jalam and Korah. These were the sons of Esau,
who were born to him in Canaan.
6 Esau took his wives and sons and daughters and all the

PRAYING SCRIPTURE

Genesis 36

Despite Jacob's trickery and theft, God honored Esau, blessing him immensely with possessions and a multitude of descendants. Esau's descendants were so numerous they made up the Edomite people. God more than restored what Jacob had stolen from him.

When we are wronged, we can still trust God completely because he has done no wrong. Ask God to help you have faith even when people cheat or take advantage.

[a] 15 *Bethel* means *house of God.* [b] 18 *Ben-Oni* means *son of my trouble.*
[c] 18 *Benjamin* means *son of my right hand.*

members of his household, as well as his livestock and all his other
animals and all the goods he had acquired in Canaan, and moved
to a land some distance from his brother Jacob.
7 Their possessions
were too great for them to remain together; the land where they
were staying could not support them both because of their livestock.
8 So Esau (that is, Edom) settled in the hill country of Seir.

9 This is the account of the family line of Esau the father of the Edomites in the hill country of Seir.

10 These are the names of Esau's sons:

Eliphaz, the son of Esau's wife Adah, and Reuel, the son of Esau's wife Basemath.

11 The sons of Eliphaz:

Teman, Omar, Zepho, Gatam and Kenaz.

12 Esau's son Eliphaz also had a concubine named Timna, who bore him Amalek. These were grandsons of Esau's wife Adah.

13 The sons of Reuel:

Nahath, Zerah, Shammah and Mizzah. These were grandsons of Esau's wife Basemath.

14 The sons of Esau's wife Oholibamah daughter of Anah and granddaughter of Zibeon, whom she bore to Esau:

Jeush, Jalam and Korah.

15 These were the chiefs among Esau's descendants:

The sons of Eliphaz the firstborn of Esau:

Chiefs Teman, Omar, Zepho, Kenaz,
16 Korah,[a] Gatam and Amalek. These were the chiefs descended from Eliphaz in Edom; they were grandsons of Adah.

17 The sons of Esau's son Reuel:

Chiefs Nahath, Zerah, Shammah and Mizzah. These were the chiefs descended from Reuel in Edom; they were grandsons of Esau's wife Basemath.

18 The sons of Esau's wife Oholibamah:

Chiefs Jeush, Jalam and Korah. These were the chiefs descended from Esau's wife Oholibamah daughter of Anah.

19 These were the sons of Esau (that is, Edom), and these were their chiefs.

20 These were the sons of Seir the Horite, who were living in the region:

Lotan, Shobal, Zibeon, Anah,
21 Dishon, Ezer and Dishan. These sons of Seir in Edom were Horite chiefs.

22 The sons of Lotan:

Hori and Homam.[b] Timna was Lotan's sister.

23 The sons of Shobal:

Alvan, Manahath, Ebal, Shepho and Onam.

24 The sons of Zibeon:

Aiah and Anah. This is the Anah who discovered the hot springs[c] in the desert while he was grazing the donkeys of his father Zibeon.

---

[a] *16* Masoretic Text; Samaritan Pentateuch (also verse 11 and 1 Chron. 1:36) does not have *Korah.* [b] *22* Hebrew *Hemam,* a variant of *Homam* (see 1 Chron. 1:39) [c] *24* Vulgate; Syriac *discovered water;* the meaning of the Hebrew for this word is uncertain.

25 The children of Anah:
Dishon and Oholibamah daughter of Anah.
26 The sons of Dishon[a]:
Hemdan, Eshban, Ithran and Keran.
27 The sons of Ezer:
Bilhan, Zaavan and Akan.
28 The sons of Dishan:
Uz and Aran.
29 These were the Horite chiefs:
Lotan, Shobal, Zibeon, Anah, 30 Dishon, Ezer and Dishan. These
were the Horite chiefs, according to their divisions, in the land
of Seir.

THE RULERS OF EDOM

31 These were the kings who reigned in Edom before any Israelite
king reigned:
32 Bela son of Beor became king of Edom. His city was named
Dinhabah.
33 When Bela died, Jobab son of Zerah from Bozrah succeeded him
as king.
34 When Jobab died, Husham from the land of the Temanites succeeded him as king.
35 When Husham died, Hadad son of Bedad, who defeated Midian in
the country of Moab, succeeded him as king. His city was named
Avith.
36 When Hadad died, Samlah from Masrekah succeeded him as king.
37 When Samlah died, Shaul from Rehoboth on the river succeeded
him as king.
38 When Shaul died, Baal-Hanan son of Akbor succeeded him as king.
39 When Baal-Hanan son of Akbor died, Hadad[b] succeeded him as
king. His city was named Pau, and his wife's name was Meheta-
bel daughter of Matred, the daughter of Me-Zahab.

40 These were the chiefs descended from Esau, by name, according to
their clans and regions:
Timna, Alvah, Jetheth, 41 Oholibamah, Elah, Pinon, 42 Kenaz,
Teman, Mibzar, 43 Magdiel and Iram. These were the chiefs of
Edom, according to their settlements in the land they occupied.

This is the family line of Esau, the father of the Edomites.

JOSEPH'S DREAMS

37 Jacob lived in the land where his father had stayed, the land
of Canaan.

2 This is the account of Jacob's family line.

Joseph, a young man of seventeen, was tending the flocks with his brothers, the sons of Bilhah and the sons of Zilpah, his father's wives, and he brought their father a bad report about them.

3 Now Israel loved Joseph more than any of his other sons, because
he had been born to him in his old age; and he made an ornate[c] robe

PRAYING SCRIPTURE

Genesis 37

It didn't look as though Joseph's dreams were going to come to pass. Rather than ruling over his brothers, he was sold into slavery in Egypt by those same brothers. Like Joseph, many of us have experienced betrayal and injustice.

Do you have hopes, dreams or goals that seem dead? Tell God you trust that he has not abandoned you, and recommit your future to him.

---

[a] 26 Hebrew *Dishan,* a variant of *Dishon* [b] 39 Many manuscripts of the Masoretic Text, Samaritan Pentateuch and Syriac (see also 1 Chron. 1:50); most manuscripts of the Masoretic Text *Hadar* [c] 3 The meaning of the Hebrew for this word is uncertain; also in verses 23 and 32.

for him. 4When his brothers saw that their father loved him more than
any of them, they hated him and could not speak a kind word to him.
5Joseph had a dream, and when he told it to his brothers, they hated
him all the more. 6He said to them, "Listen to this dream I had: 7We
were binding sheaves of grain out in the field when suddenly my sheaf
rose and stood upright, while your sheaves gathered around mine and
bowed down to it."
8His brothers said to him, "Do you intend to reign over us? Will
you actually rule us?" And they hated him all the more because of his
dream and what he had said.
9Then he had another dream, and he told it to his brothers. "Listen,"
he said, "I had another dream, and this time the sun and moon and
eleven stars were bowing down to me."
10When he told his father as well as his brothers, his father rebuked
him and said, "What is this dream you had? Will your mother and I
and your brothers actually come and bow down to the ground before
you?" 11His brothers were jealous of him, but his father kept the mat-
ter in mind.

JOSEPH SOLD BY HIS BROTHERS

12Now his brothers had gone to graze their father's flocks near She-
chem, 13and Israel said to Joseph, "As you know, your brothers are graz-
ing the flocks near Shechem. Come, I am going to send you to them."
"Very well," he replied.
14So he said to him, "Go and see if all is well with your brothers and
with the flocks, and bring word back to me." Then he sent him off from
the Valley of Hebron.
When Joseph arrived at Shechem, 15a man found him wandering
around in the fields and asked him, "What are you looking for?"
16He replied, "I'm looking for my brothers. Can you tell me where
they are grazing their flocks?"
17"They have moved on from here," the man answered. "I heard
them say, 'Let's go to Dothan.'"
So Joseph went after his brothers and found them near Dothan.
18But they saw him in the distance, and before he reached them, they
plotted to kill him.
19"Here comes that dreamer!" they said to each other. 20"Come now,
let's kill him and throw him into one of these cisterns and say that
a ferocious animal devoured him. Then we'll see what comes of his
dreams."
21When Reuben heard this, he tried to rescue him from their hands.
"Let's not take his life," he said. 22"Don't shed any blood. Throw him
into this cistern here in the wilderness, but don't lay a hand on him."
Reuben said this to rescue him from them and take him back to his
father.
23So when Joseph came to his brothers, they stripped him of his
robe — the ornate robe he was wearing — 24and they took him and
threw him into the cistern. The cistern was empty; there was no water
in it.
25As they sat down to eat their meal, they looked up and saw a cara-
van of Ishmaelites coming from Gilead. Their camels were loaded with
spices, balm and myrrh, and they were on their way to take them down
to Egypt.
26Judah said to his brothers, "What will we gain if we kill our brother

and cover up his blood? 27Come, let's sell him to the Ishmaelites and not lay our hands on him; after all, he is our brother, our own flesh and blood." His brothers agreed.

28So when the Midianite merchants came by, his brothers pulled Joseph up out of the cistern and sold him for twenty shekels[a] of silver to the Ishmaelites, who took him to Egypt.

29When Reuben returned to the cistern and saw that Joseph was not there, he tore his clothes. 30He went back to his brothers and said, "The boy isn't there! Where can I turn now?"

31Then they got Joseph's robe, slaughtered a goat and dipped the robe in the blood. 32They took the ornate robe back to their father and said, "We found this. Examine it to see whether it is your son's robe."

33He recognized it and said, "It is my son's robe! Some ferocious animal has devoured him. Joseph has surely been torn to pieces."

34Then Jacob tore his clothes, put on sackcloth and mourned for his son many days. 35All his sons and daughters came to comfort him, but he refused to be comforted. "No," he said, "I will continue to mourn until I join my son in the grave." So his father wept for him.

36Meanwhile, the Midianites[b] sold Joseph in Egypt to Potiphar, one of Pharaoh's officials, the captain of the guard.

JUDAH AND TAMAR

38 At that time, Judah left his brothers and went down to stay with a man of Adullam named Hirah. 2There Judah met the daughter of a Canaanite man named Shua. He married her and made love to her; 3she became pregnant and gave birth to a son, who was named Er. 4She conceived again and gave birth to a son and named him Onan. 5She gave birth to still another son and named him Shelah. It was at Kezib that she gave birth to him.

6Judah got a wife for Er, his firstborn, and her name was Tamar. 7But Er, Judah's firstborn, was wicked in the LORD's sight; so the LORD put him to death.

8Then Judah said to Onan, "Sleep with your brother's wife and fulfill your duty to her as a brother-in-law to raise up offspring for your brother." 9But Onan knew that the child would not be his; so whenever he slept with his brother's wife, he spilled his semen on the ground to keep from providing offspring for his brother. 10What he did was wicked in the LORD's sight; so the LORD put him to death also.

11Judah then said to his daughter-in-law Tamar, "Live as a widow in your father's household until my son Shelah grows up." For he thought, "He may die too, just like his brothers." So Tamar went to live in her father's household.

12After a long time Judah's wife, the daughter of Shua, died. When Judah had recovered from his grief, he went up to Timnah, to the men who were shearing his sheep, and his friend Hirah the Adullamite went with him.

13When Tamar was told, "Your father-in-law is on his way to Timnah to shear his sheep," 14she took off her widow's clothes, covered herself with a veil to disguise herself, and then sat down at the entrance to Enaim, which is on the road to Timnah. For she saw that, though Shelah had now grown up, she had not been given to him as his wife.

PRAYING SCRIPTURE

Genesis 38

Tamar's actions in this passage seem underhanded, but when confronted with evidence, Judah admitted she was in the right. In spite of this sordid tale, Tamar is included in Jesus' genealogy in Matthew 1.

Have you ever thought God could not use you because of some sin or ugly event in your family? Ask God to use you as one in your family who can bring glory to his name.

[a] *28* That is, about 8 ounces or about 230 grams [b] *36* Samaritan Pentateuch, Septuagint, Vulgate and Syriac (see also verse 28); Masoretic Text *Medanites*

15 When Judah saw her, he thought she was a prostitute, for she had covered her face. 16 Not realizing that she was his daughter-in-law, he went over to her by the roadside and said, "Come now, let me sleep with you."

"And what will you give me to sleep with you?" she asked.

17 "I'll send you a young goat from my flock," he said.

"Will you give me something as a pledge until you send it?" she asked.

18 He said, "What pledge should I give you?"

"Your seal and its cord, and the staff in your hand," she answered. So he gave them to her and slept with her, and she became pregnant by him. 19 After she left, she took off her veil and put on her widow's clothes again.

20 Meanwhile Judah sent the young goat by his friend the Adullamite in order to get his pledge back from the woman, but he did not find her. 21 He asked the men who lived there, "Where is the shrine prostitute who was beside the road at Enaim?"

"There hasn't been any shrine prostitute here," they said.

22 So he went back to Judah and said, "I didn't find her. Besides, the men who lived there said, 'There hasn't been any shrine prostitute here.'"

23 Then Judah said, "Let her keep what she has, or we will become a laughingstock. After all, I did send her this young goat, but you didn't find her."

24 About three months later Judah was told, "Your daughter-in-law Tamar is guilty of prostitution, and as a result she is now pregnant."

Judah said, "Bring her out and have her burned to death!"

25 As she was being brought out, she sent a message to her father-in-law. "I am pregnant by the man who owns these," she said. And she added, "See if you recognize whose seal and cord and staff these are."

26 Judah recognized them and said, "She is more righteous than I, since I wouldn't give her to my son Shelah." And he did not sleep with her again.

27 When the time came for her to give birth, there were twin boys in her womb. 28 As she was giving birth, one of them put out his hand; so the midwife took a scarlet thread and tied it on his wrist and said, "This one came out first." 29 But when he drew back his hand, his brother came out, and she said, "So this is how you have broken out!" And he was named Perez.[a] 30 Then his brother, who had the scarlet thread on his wrist, came out. And he was named Zerah.[b]

JOSEPH AND POTIPHAR'S WIFE

39 Now Joseph had been taken down to Egypt. Potiphar, an Egyptian who was one of Pharaoh's officials, the captain of the guard, bought him from the Ishmaelites who had taken him there.

2 The LORD was with Joseph so that he prospered, and he lived in the house of his Egyptian master. 3 When his master saw that the LORD was with him and that the LORD gave him success in everything he did, 4 Joseph found favor in his eyes and became his attendant. Potiphar put him in charge of his household, and he entrusted to his care everything he owned. 5 From the time he put him in charge of his household and of all that he owned, the LORD blessed the household of the

[a] 29 *Perez* means *breaking out.* [b] 30 *Zerah* can mean *scarlet* or *brightness.*

PRAYING SCRIPTURE

Genesis 39

As the record of Joseph's life continues, we find a most practical application: When the temptation to sin presents itself, run away from it. When this mistress of the house where he worked attempted to seduce Joseph, he ran from her, literally leaving his robe in her hand. The temptation to sin can be accompanied by immense pressure. Ask God to give you the willingness to physically remove yourself from temptation.

Egyptian because of Joseph. The blessing of the LORD was on every-
thing Potiphar had, both in the house and in the field. 6So Potiphar left
everything he had in Joseph's care; with Joseph in charge, he did not
concern himself with anything except the food he ate.

Now Joseph was well-built and handsome, 7and after a while his
master's wife took notice of Joseph and said, "Come to bed with me!"

8But he refused. "With me in charge," he told her, "my master does
not concern himself with anything in the house; everything he owns
he has entrusted to my care. 9No one is greater in this house than I am.
My master has withheld nothing from me except you, because you are
his wife. How then could I do such a wicked thing and sin against God?"
10And though she spoke to Joseph day after day, he refused to go to bed
with her or even be with her.

11One day he went into the house to attend to his duties, and none of
the household servants was inside. 12She caught him by his cloak and
said, "Come to bed with me!" But he left his cloak in her hand and ran
out of the house.

13When she saw that he had left his cloak in her hand and had run
out of the house, 14she called her household servants. "Look," she said
to them, "this Hebrew has been brought to us to make sport of us! He
came in here to sleep with me, but I screamed. 15When he heard me
scream for help, he left his cloak beside me and ran out of the house."

16She kept his cloak beside her until his master came home. 17Then
she told him this story: "That Hebrew slave you brought us came to me
to make sport of me. 18But as soon as I screamed for help, he left his
cloak beside me and ran out of the house."

19When his master heard the story his wife told him, saying, "This is
how your slave treated me," he burned with anger. 20Joseph's master
took him and put him in prison, the place where the king's prisoners
were confined.

But while Joseph was there in the prison, 21the LORD was with him;
he showed him kindness and granted him favor in the eyes of the
prison warden. 22So the warden put Joseph in charge of all those held
in the prison, and he was made responsible for all that was done there.
23The warden paid no attention to anything under Joseph's care, be-
cause the LORD was with Joseph and gave him success in whatever he
did.

PRAYING SCRIPTURE

Genesis 39

Sold into slavery, then falsely accused by his master's wife, Joseph found himself in prison. But no matter how dire Joseph's situation became, Scripture tells us the Lord was with him. Joseph's life reminds us that God never loses track of his children.

Have you ever been falsely accused? Ask God to remind you of his presence, and call on him, believing that he is attentive to your prayer.

THE CUPBEARER AND THE BAKER

40 Some time later, the cupbearer and the baker of the king of
Egypt offended their master, the king of Egypt. 2Pharaoh was
angry with his two officials, the chief cupbearer and the chief baker,
3and put them in custody in the house of the captain of the guard, in
the same prison where Joseph was confined. 4The captain of the guard
assigned them to Joseph, and he attended them.

After they had been in custody for some time, 5each of the two
men — the cupbearer and the baker of the king of Egypt, who were
being held in prison — had a dream the same night, and each dream
had a meaning of its own.

6When Joseph came to them the next morning, he saw that they
were dejected. 7So he asked Pharaoh's officials who were in custody
with him in his master's house, "Why do you look so sad today?"

8"We both had dreams," they answered, "but there is no one to in-
terpret them."

PRAYING SCRIPTURE

Genesis 40

As a young adult, Joseph moved from one trial to another. Every time he had reason to hope, a new calamity crashed on him. His hope to leave prison was dashed when his prison mates, two men close to Pharaoh, forgot to tell him about Joseph.

Sometimes we help people in need only to have them forget us. Whatever your current situation, praise God that he will deliver you in due season.

Then Joseph said to them, "Do not interpretations belong to God?
Tell me your dreams."
9So the chief cupbearer told Joseph his dream. He said to him, "In
my dream I saw a vine in front of me, 10and on the vine were three
branches. As soon as it budded, it blossomed, and its clusters ripened
into grapes. 11Pharaoh's cup was in my hand, and I took the grapes,
squeezed them into Pharaoh's cup and put the cup in his hand."
12"This is what it means," Joseph said to him. "The three branches
are three days. 13Within three days Pharaoh will lift up your head and
restore you to your position, and you will put Pharaoh's cup in his
hand, just as you used to do when you were his cupbearer. 14But when
all goes well with you, remember me and show me kindness; mention
me to Pharaoh and get me out of this prison. 15I was forcibly carried
off from the land of the Hebrews, and even here I have done nothing
to deserve being put in a dungeon."
16When the chief baker saw that Joseph had given a favorable in-
terpretation, he said to Joseph, "I too had a dream: On my head were
three baskets of bread.[a] 17In the top basket were all kinds of baked
goods for Pharaoh, but the birds were eating them out of the basket
on my head."
18"This is what it means," Joseph said. "The three baskets are three
days. 19Within three days Pharaoh will lift off your head and impale
your body on a pole. And the birds will eat away your flesh."
20Now the third day was Pharaoh's birthday, and he gave a feast for
all his officials. He lifted up the heads of the chief cupbearer and the
chief baker in the presence of his officials: 21He restored the chief cup-
bearer to his position, so that he once again put the cup into Pharaoh's
hand — 22but he impaled the chief baker, just as Joseph had said to
them in his interpretation.
23The chief cupbearer, however, did not remember Joseph; he for-
got him.

PHARAOH'S DREAMS

41 When two full years had passed, Pharaoh had a dream: He was
standing by the Nile, 2when out of the river there came up
seven cows, sleek and fat, and they grazed among the reeds. 3After
them, seven other cows, ugly and gaunt, came up out of the Nile and
stood beside those on the riverbank. 4And the cows that were ugly and
gaunt ate up the seven sleek, fat cows. Then Pharaoh woke up.
5He fell asleep again and had a second dream: Seven heads of grain,
healthy and good, were growing on a single stalk. 6After them, seven
other heads of grain sprouted — thin and scorched by the east wind.
7The thin heads of grain swallowed up the seven healthy, full heads.
Then Pharaoh woke up; it had been a dream.
8In the morning his mind was troubled, so he sent for all the magi-
cians and wise men of Egypt. Pharaoh told them his dreams, but no
one could interpret them for him.
9Then the chief cupbearer said to Pharaoh, "Today I am reminded
of my shortcomings. 10Pharaoh was once angry with his servants, and
he imprisoned me and the chief baker in the house of the captain of
the guard. 11Each of us had a dream the same night, and each dream
had a meaning of its own. 12Now a young Hebrew was there with us,

PRAYING SCRIPTURE

Genesis 41

Two years later, when Pharaoh himself was troubled by dreams, the king's cupbearer remembered Joseph, who then interpreted Pharaoh's dreams. The Lord raised Joseph to a position he never could have reached had he not gone to prison in Egypt.

Sometimes our darkest hour is the time just before God does his greatest work. Ask God to strengthen your heart, and expect him to raise you up.

[a] 16 Or *three wicker baskets*

a servant of the captain of the guard. We told him our dreams, and
he interpreted them for us, giving each man the interpretation of his
dream. 13 And things turned out exactly as he interpreted them to us: I
was restored to my position, and the other man was impaled."

14 So Pharaoh sent for Joseph, and he was quickly brought from the
dungeon. When he had shaved and changed his clothes, he came be-
fore Pharaoh.

15 Pharaoh said to Joseph, "I had a dream, and no one can interpret
it. But I have heard it said of you that when you hear a dream you can
interpret it."

16 "I cannot do it," Joseph replied to Pharaoh, "but God will give Phar-
aoh the answer he desires."

17 Then Pharaoh said to Joseph, "In my dream I was standing on the
bank of the Nile, 18 when out of the river there came up seven cows, fat
and sleek, and they grazed among the reeds. 19 After them, seven other
cows came up — scrawny and very ugly and lean. I had never seen such
ugly cows in all the land of Egypt. 20 The lean, ugly cows ate up the
seven fat cows that came up first. 21 But even after they ate them, no
one could tell that they had done so; they looked just as ugly as before.
Then I woke up.

22 "In my dream I saw seven heads of grain, full and good, growing
on a single stalk. 23 After them, seven other heads sprouted — withered
and thin and scorched by the east wind. 24 The thin heads of grain swal-
lowed up the seven good heads. I told this to the magicians, but none
of them could explain it to me."

25 Then Joseph said to Pharaoh, "The dreams of Pharaoh are one and
the same. God has revealed to Pharaoh what he is about to do. 26 The
seven good cows are seven years, and the seven good heads of grain
are seven years; it is one and the same dream. 27 The seven lean, ugly
cows that came up afterward are seven years, and so are the seven
worthless heads of grain scorched by the east wind: They are seven
years of famine.

28 "It is just as I said to Pharaoh: God has shown Pharaoh what he is
about to do. 29 Seven years of great abundance are coming throughout
the land of Egypt, 30 but seven years of famine will follow them. Then
all the abundance in Egypt will be forgotten, and the famine will rav-
age the land. 31 The abundance in the land will not be remembered,
because the famine that follows it will be so severe. 32 The reason the
dream was given to Pharaoh in two forms is that the matter has been
firmly decided by God, and God will do it soon.

33 "And now let Pharaoh look for a discerning and wise man and put
him in charge of the land of Egypt. 34 Let Pharaoh appoint commis-
sioners over the land to take a fifth of the harvest of Egypt during the
seven years of abundance. 35 They should collect all the food of these
good years that are coming and store up the grain under the authority
of Pharaoh, to be kept in the cities for food. 36 This food should be held
in reserve for the country, to be used during the seven years of famine
that will come upon Egypt, so that the country may not be ruined by
the famine."

37 The plan seemed good to Pharaoh and to all his officials. 38 So Phar-
aoh asked them, "Can we find anyone like this man, one in whom is
the spirit of God[a]?"

---

[a] 38 Or *of the gods*

39Then Pharaoh said to Joseph, "Since God has made all this known to you, there is no one so discerning and wise as you. 40You shall be in charge of my palace, and all my people are to submit to your orders. Only with respect to the throne will I be greater than you."

JOSEPH IN CHARGE OF EGYPT

41So Pharaoh said to Joseph, "I hereby put you in charge of the whole land of Egypt." 42Then Pharaoh took his signet ring from his finger and put it on Joseph's finger. He dressed him in robes of fine linen and put a gold chain around his neck. 43He had him ride in a chariot as his second-in-command,[a] and people shouted before him, "Make way[b]!" Thus he put him in charge of the whole land of Egypt.

44Then Pharaoh said to Joseph, "I am Pharaoh, but without your word no one will lift hand or foot in all Egypt." 45Pharaoh gave Joseph the name Zaphenath-Paneah and gave him Asenath daughter of Potiphera, priest of On,[c] to be his wife. And Joseph went throughout the land of Egypt.

46Joseph was thirty years old when he entered the service of Pharaoh king of Egypt. And Joseph went out from Pharaoh's presence and traveled throughout Egypt. 47During the seven years of abundance the land produced plentifully. 48Joseph collected all the food produced in those seven years of abundance in Egypt and stored it in the cities. In each city he put the food grown in the fields surrounding it. 49Joseph stored up huge quantities of grain, like the sand of the sea; it was so much that he stopped keeping records because it was beyond measure.

50Before the years of famine came, two sons were born to Joseph by Asenath daughter of Potiphera, priest of On. 51Joseph named his firstborn Manasseh[d] and said, "It is because God has made me forget all my trouble and all my father's household." 52The second son he named Ephraim[e] and said, "It is because God has made me fruitful in the land of my suffering."

53The seven years of abundance in Egypt came to an end, 54and the seven years of famine began, just as Joseph had said. There was famine in all the other lands, but in the whole land of Egypt there was food. 55When all Egypt began to feel the famine, the people cried to Pharaoh for food. Then Pharaoh told all the Egyptians, "Go to Joseph and do what he tells you."

56When the famine had spread over the whole country, Joseph opened all the storehouses and sold grain to the Egyptians, for the famine was severe throughout Egypt. 57And all the world came to Egypt to buy grain from Joseph, because the famine was severe everywhere.

JOSEPH'S BROTHERS GO TO EGYPT

42 When Jacob learned that there was grain in Egypt, he said to his sons, "Why do you just keep looking at each other?" 2He continued, "I have heard that there is grain in Egypt. Go down there and buy some for us, so that we may live and not die."

3Then ten of Joseph's brothers went down to buy grain from Egypt. 4But Jacob did not send Benjamin, Joseph's brother, with the others,

[a] 43 Or *in the chariot of his second-in-command*; or *in his second chariot*
[b] 43 Or *Bow down* [c] 45 That is, Heliopolis; also in verse 50 [d] 51 *Manasseh* sounds like and may be derived from the Hebrew for *forget.* [e] 52 *Ephraim* sounds like the Hebrew for *twice fruitful.*

PRAYING SCRIPTURE

Genesis 42

Years into a severe famine, Joseph's brothers, who had betrayed him, arrived in Egypt to buy grain. Joseph showed uncommon kindness to his brothers who had treated him so cruelly. Though they did not recognize him, he purposed to bless them.

Think about what you would do if given the opportunity to thoroughly bless someone who had deeply wronged you. Ask God to give you his love toward even them.

because he was afraid that harm might come to him. [5]So Israel's sons were among those who went to buy grain, for there was famine in the land of Canaan also.

[6]Now Joseph was the governor of the land, the person who sold grain to all its people. So when Joseph's brothers arrived, they bowed down to him with their faces to the ground. [7]As soon as Joseph saw his brothers, he recognized them, but he pretended to be a stranger and spoke harshly to them. "Where do you come from?" he asked.

"From the land of Canaan," they replied, "to buy food."

[8]Although Joseph recognized his brothers, they did not recognize him. [9]Then he remembered his dreams about them and said to them, "You are spies! You have come to see where our land is unprotected."

[10]"No, my lord," they answered. "Your servants have come to buy food. [11]We are all the sons of one man. Your servants are honest men, not spies."

[12]"No!" he said to them. "You have come to see where our land is unprotected."

[13]But they replied, "Your servants were twelve brothers, the sons of one man, who lives in the land of Canaan. The youngest is now with our father, and one is no more."

[14]Joseph said to them, "It is just as I told you: You are spies! [15]And this is how you will be tested: As surely as Pharaoh lives, you will not leave this place unless your youngest brother comes here. [16]Send one of your number to get your brother; the rest of you will be kept in prison, so that your words may be tested to see if you are telling the truth. If you are not, then as surely as Pharaoh lives, you are spies!" [17]And he put them all in custody for three days.

[18]On the third day, Joseph said to them, "Do this and you will live, for I fear God: [19]If you are honest men, let one of your brothers stay here in prison, while the rest of you go and take grain back for your starving households. [20]But you must bring your youngest brother to me, so that your words may be verified and that you may not die." This they proceeded to do.

[21]They said to one another, "Surely we are being punished because of our brother. We saw how distressed he was when he pleaded with us for his life, but we would not listen; that's why this distress has come on us."

[22]Reuben replied, "Didn't I tell you not to sin against the boy? But you wouldn't listen! Now we must give an accounting for his blood." [23]They did not realize that Joseph could understand them, since he was using an interpreter.

[24]He turned away from them and began to weep, but then came back and spoke to them again. He had Simeon taken from them and bound before their eyes.

[25]Joseph gave orders to fill their bags with grain, to put each man's silver back in his sack, and to give them provisions for their journey. After this was done for them, [26]they loaded their grain on their donkeys and left.

[27]At the place where they stopped for the night one of them opened his sack to get feed for his donkey, and he saw his silver in the mouth of his sack. [28]"My silver has been returned," he said to his brothers. "Here it is in my sack."

Their hearts sank and they turned to each other trembling and said, "What is this that God has done to us?"

[29]When they came to their father Jacob in the land of Canaan, they

told him all that had happened to them. They said, 30"The man who
is lord over the land spoke harshly to us and treated us as though we
were spying on the land. 31But we said to him, 'We are honest men; we
are not spies. 32We were twelve brothers, sons of one father. One is no
more, and the youngest is now with our father in Canaan.'
33"Then the man who is lord over the land said to us, 'This is how I
will know whether you are honest men: Leave one of your brothers
here with me, and take food for your starving households and go. 34But
bring your youngest brother to me so I will know that you are not spies
but honest men. Then I will give your brother back to you, and you can
trade[a] in the land.'"
35As they were emptying their sacks, there in each man's sack was his
pouch of silver! When they and their father saw the money pouches,
they were frightened. 36Their father Jacob said to them, "You have de-
prived me of my children. Joseph is no more and Simeon is no more,
and now you want to take Benjamin. Everything is against me!"
37Then Reuben said to his father, "You may put both of my sons to
death if I do not bring him back to you. Entrust him to my care, and I
will bring him back."
38But Jacob said, "My son will not go down there with you; his
brother is dead and he is the only one left. If harm comes to him on
the journey you are taking, you will bring my gray head down to the
grave in sorrow."

THE SECOND JOURNEY TO EGYPT

43 Now the famine was still severe in the land. 2So when they had
eaten all the grain they had brought from Egypt, their father
said to them, "Go back and buy us a little more food."
3But Judah said to him, "The man warned us solemnly, 'You will not
see my face again unless your brother is with you.' 4If you will send
our brother along with us, we will go down and buy food for you. 5But
if you will not send him, we will not go down, because the man said to
us, 'You will not see my face again unless your brother is with you.'"
6Israel asked, "Why did you bring this trouble on me by telling the
man you had another brother?"
7They replied, "The man questioned us closely about ourselves and
our family. 'Is your father still living?' he asked us. 'Do you have an-
other brother?' We simply answered his questions. How were we to
know he would say, 'Bring your brother down here'?"
8Then Judah said to Israel his father, "Send the boy along with me
and we will go at once, so that we and you and our children may live
and not die. 9I myself will guarantee his safety; you can hold me per-
sonally responsible for him. If I do not bring him back to you and set
him here before you, I will bear the blame before you all my life. 10As
it is, if we had not delayed, we could have gone and returned twice."
11Then their father Israel said to them, "If it must be, then do this: Put
some of the best products of the land in your bags and take them down
to the man as a gift — a little balm and a little honey, some spices and
myrrh, some pistachio nuts and almonds. 12Take double the amount of
silver with you, for you must return the silver that was put back into the
mouths of your sacks. Perhaps it was a mistake. 13Take your brother also
and go back to the man at once. 14And may God Almighty[b] grant you

PRAYING SCRIPTURE

Genesis 43

Joseph decided to test his brothers, putting them in a position of fear and uncertainty. They had no idea this Egyptian ruler, who demanded things from them and framed them for stealing, was their long-departed brother.

Do you ever wish you could get the upper hand on someone who wronged you? Trust God with payback. It's easy to lose control of a desire for vengeance.

[a] 34 Or *move about freely* [b] 14 Hebrew *El-Shaddai*

mercy before the man so that he will let your other brother and Benja-
min come back with you. As for me, if I am bereaved, I am bereaved."
15So the men took the gifts and double the amount of silver, and
Benjamin also. They hurried down to Egypt and presented them-
selves to Joseph. 16When Joseph saw Benjamin with them, he said to
the steward of his house, "Take these men to my house, slaughter an
animal and prepare a meal; they are to eat with me at noon."
17The man did as Joseph told him and took the men to Joseph's
house. 18Now the men were frightened when they were taken to his
house. They thought, "We were brought here because of the silver that
was put back into our sacks the first time. He wants to attack us and
overpower us and seize us as slaves and take our donkeys."
19So they went up to Joseph's steward and spoke to him at the en-
trance to the house. 20"We beg your pardon, our lord," they said, "we
came down here the first time to buy food. 21But at the place where we
stopped for the night we opened our sacks and each of us found his sil-
ver — the exact weight — in the mouth of his sack. So we have brought
it back with us. 22We have also brought additional silver with us to buy
food. We don't know who put our silver in our sacks."
23"It's all right," he said. "Don't be afraid. Your God, the God of your
father, has given you treasure in your sacks; I received your silver."
Then he brought Simeon out to them.
24The steward took the men into Joseph's house, gave them water
to wash their feet and provided fodder for their donkeys. 25They pre-
pared their gifts for Joseph's arrival at noon, because they had heard
that they were to eat there.
26When Joseph came home, they presented to him the gifts they
had brought into the house, and they bowed down before him to the
ground. 27He asked them how they were, and then he said, "How is
your aged father you told me about? Is he still living?"
28They replied, "Your servant our father is still alive and well." And
they bowed down, prostrating themselves before him.
29As he looked about and saw his brother Benjamin, his own moth-
er's son, he asked, "Is this your youngest brother, the one you told me
about?" And he said, "God be gracious to you, my son." 30Deeply moved
at the sight of his brother, Joseph hurried out and looked for a place to
weep. He went into his private room and wept there.
31After he had washed his face, he came out and, controlling himself,
said, "Serve the food."
32They served him by himself, the brothers by themselves, and the
Egyptians who ate with him by themselves, because Egyptians could
not eat with Hebrews, for that is detestable to Egyptians. 33The men
had been seated before him in the order of their ages, from the first-
born to the youngest; and they looked at each other in astonishment.
34When portions were served to them from Joseph's table, Benjamin's
portion was five times as much as anyone else's. So they feasted and
drank freely with him.

A SILVER CUP IN A SACK

44 Now Joseph gave these instructions to the steward of his
house: "Fill the men's sacks with as much food as they can
carry, and put each man's silver in the mouth of his sack. 2Then put my
cup, the silver one, in the mouth of the youngest one's sack, along with
the silver for his grain." And he did as Joseph said.

PRAYING SCRIPTURE

Genesis 44

The trial Joseph put his brothers through took a perhaps unexpected turn: They refused to allow their youngest brother to be harmed, citing their father's love for him. Their decision was a total reversal of what they had done to Joseph so many years before.

Sometimes heart change takes a long time. Ask God for his own patience as you pray and wait for him to work in people around you.

3As morning dawned, the men were sent on their way with their
donkeys. 4They had not gone far from the city when Joseph said to
his steward, "Go after those men at once, and when you catch up with
them, say to them, 'Why have you repaid good with evil? 5Isn't this
the cup my master drinks from and also uses for divination? This is a
wicked thing you have done.'"

6When he caught up with them, he repeated these words to them.
7But they said to him, "Why does my lord say such things? Far be it
from your servants to do anything like that! 8We even brought back
to you from the land of Canaan the silver we found inside the mouths
of our sacks. So why would we steal silver or gold from your master's
house? 9If any of your servants is found to have it, he will die; and the
rest of us will become my lord's slaves."

10"Very well, then," he said, "let it be as you say. Whoever is found to
have it will become my slave; the rest of you will be free from blame."

11Each of them quickly lowered his sack to the ground and opened it.
12Then the steward proceeded to search, beginning with the oldest and
ending with the youngest. And the cup was found in Benjamin's sack.
13At this, they tore their clothes. Then they all loaded their donkeys
and returned to the city.

14Joseph was still in the house when Judah and his brothers came
in, and they threw themselves to the ground before him. 15Joseph said
to them, "What is this you have done? Don't you know that a man like
me can find things out by divination?"

16"What can we say to my lord?" Judah replied. "What can we say?
How can we prove our innocence? God has uncovered your servants'
guilt. We are now my lord's slaves—we ourselves and the one who was
found to have the cup."

17But Joseph said, "Far be it from me to do such a thing! Only the
man who was found to have the cup will become my slave. The rest of
you, go back to your father in peace."

18Then Judah went up to him and said: "Pardon your servant, my
lord, let me speak a word to my lord. Do not be angry with your ser-
vant, though you are equal to Pharaoh himself. 19My lord asked his
servants, 'Do you have a father or a brother?' 20And we answered, 'We
have an aged father, and there is a young son born to him in his old
age. His brother is dead, and he is the only one of his mother's sons left,
and his father loves him.'

21"Then you said to your servants, 'Bring him down to me so I can
see him for myself.' 22And we said to my lord, 'The boy cannot leave
his father; if he leaves him, his father will die.' 23But you told your ser-
vants, 'Unless your youngest brother comes down with you, you will
not see my face again.' 24When we went back to your servant my father,
we told him what my lord had said.

25"Then our father said, 'Go back and buy a little more food.' 26But we
said, 'We cannot go down. Only if our youngest brother is with us will we
go. We cannot see the man's face unless our youngest brother is with us.'

27"Your servant my father said to us, 'You know that my wife bore
me two sons. 28One of them went away from me, and I said, "He has
surely been torn to pieces." And I have not seen him since. 29If you take
this one from me too and harm comes to him, you will bring my gray
head down to the grave in misery.'

30"So now, if the boy is not with us when I go back to your servant my
father, and if my father, whose life is closely bound up with the boy's

life, 31sees that the boy isn't there, he will die. Your servants will bring
the gray head of our father down to the grave in sorrow. 32Your servant
guaranteed the boy's safety to my father. I said, 'If I do not bring him
back to you, I will bear the blame before you, my father, all my life!'
33"Now then, please let your servant remain here as my lord's slave
in place of the boy, and let the boy return with his brothers. 34How can
I go back to my father if the boy is not with me? No! Do not let me see
the misery that would come on my father."

JOSEPH MAKES HIMSELF KNOWN

45 Then Joseph could no longer control himself before all his
attendants, and he cried out, "Have everyone leave my pres-
ence!" So there was no one with Joseph when he made himself known
to his brothers. 2And he wept so loudly that the Egyptians heard him,
and Pharaoh's household heard about it.
3Joseph said to his brothers, "I am Joseph! Is my father still living?"
But his brothers were not able to answer him, because they were ter-
rified at his presence.
4Then Joseph said to his brothers, "Come close to me." When they
had done so, he said, "I am your brother Joseph, the one you sold into
Egypt! 5And now, do not be distressed and do not be angry with your-
selves for selling me here, because it was to save lives that God sent me
ahead of you. 6For two years now there has been famine in the land,
and for the next five years there will be no plowing and reaping. 7But
God sent me ahead of you to preserve for you a remnant on earth and
to save your lives by a great deliverance.[a]
8"So then, it was not you who sent me here, but God. He made me
father to Pharaoh, lord of his entire household and ruler of all Egypt.
9Now hurry back to my father and say to him, 'This is what your son Jo-
seph says: God has made me lord of all Egypt. Come down to me; don't
delay. 10You shall live in the region of Goshen and be near me — you,
your children and grandchildren, your flocks and herds, and all you
have. 11I will provide for you there, because five years of famine are
still to come. Otherwise you and your household and all who belong
to you will become destitute.'
12"You can see for yourselves, and so can my brother Benjamin, that
it is really I who am speaking to you. 13Tell my father about all the
honor accorded me in Egypt and about everything you have seen. And
bring my father down here quickly."
14Then he threw his arms around his brother Benjamin and wept,
and Benjamin embraced him, weeping. 15And he kissed all his brothers
and wept over them. Afterward his brothers talked with him.
16When the news reached Pharaoh's palace that Joseph's brothers
had come, Pharaoh and all his officials were pleased. 17Pharaoh said to
Joseph, "Tell your brothers, 'Do this: Load your animals and return
to the land of Canaan, 18and bring your father and your families back
to me. I will give you the best of the land of Egypt and you can enjoy
the fat of the land.'
19"You are also directed to tell them, 'Do this: Take some carts from
Egypt for your children and your wives, and get your father and come.
20Never mind about your belongings, because the best of all Egypt will
be yours.'"
21So the sons of Israel did this. Joseph gave them carts, as Pharaoh

[a] 7 Or *save you as a great band of survivors*

PRAYING SCRIPTURE

Genesis 45

Have you ever wondered whether God could bring good out of your bad situation? Despite severe mistreatment at the hands of his brothers, Joseph determined that the hand of God had brought him to Egypt to save the lives of his family. He was able to see a bigger picture of God's providence.

Ask God to help you see below the surface. Perhaps he intends to use you to save others.

had commanded, and he also gave them provisions for their journey.
22 To each of them he gave new clothing, but to Benjamin he gave three
hundred shekels[a] of silver and five sets of clothes. 23 And this is what
he sent to his father: ten donkeys loaded with the best things of Egypt,
and ten female donkeys loaded with grain and bread and other pro-
visions for his journey. 24 Then he sent his brothers away, and as they
were leaving he said to them, "Don't quarrel on the way!"
25 So they went up out of Egypt and came to their father Jacob in the
land of Canaan. 26 They told him, "Joseph is still alive! In fact, he is ruler
of all Egypt." Jacob was stunned; he did not believe them. 27 But when
they told him everything Joseph had said to them, and when he saw
the carts Joseph had sent to carry him back, the spirit of their father
Jacob revived. 28 And Israel said, "I'm convinced! My son Joseph is still
alive. I will go and see him before I die."

JACOB GOES TO EGYPT

46 So Israel set out with all that was his, and when he reached
Beersheba, he offered sacrifices to the God of his father Isaac.
2 And God spoke to Israel in a vision at night and said, "Jacob! Jacob!"
"Here I am," he replied.
3 "I am God, the God of your father," he said. "Do not be afraid to go
down to Egypt, for I will make you into a great nation there. 4 I will go
down to Egypt with you, and I will surely bring you back again. And
Joseph's own hand will close your eyes."
5 Then Jacob left Beersheba, and Israel's sons took their father Jacob
and their children and their wives in the carts that Pharaoh had sent
to transport him. 6 So Jacob and all his offspring went to Egypt, taking
with them their livestock and the possessions they had acquired in
Canaan. 7 Jacob brought with him to Egypt his sons and grandsons and
his daughters and granddaughters — all his offspring.
8 These are the names of the sons of Israel (Jacob and his descen-
dants) who went to Egypt:

Reuben the firstborn of Jacob.
9 The sons of Reuben:
Hanok, Pallu, Hezron and Karmi.
10 The sons of Simeon:
Jemuel, Jamin, Ohad, Jakin, Zohar and Shaul the son of a Canaanite woman.
11 The sons of Levi:
Gershon, Kohath and Merari.
12 The sons of Judah:
Er, Onan, Shelah, Perez and Zerah (but Er and Onan had died in the land of Canaan).
The sons of Perez:
Hezron and Hamul.
13 The sons of Issachar:
Tola, Puah,[b] Jashub[c] and Shimron.
14 The sons of Zebulun:
Sered, Elon and Jahleel.

PRAYING SCRIPTURE

Genesis 46

You can imagine the joy Israel felt when God revealed he would see Joseph before he died. Long had Israel believed his favored son was dead. Not only was Joseph alive, but he had taken personal responsibility for rescuing his family.

Has God ever blessed you so unexpectedly that you were overwhelmed? Take a moment to praise God for unexpected blessings that cause you to break forth in praise.

---

[a] *22* That is, about 7 1/2 pounds or about 3.5 kilograms [b] *13* Samaritan Pentateuch and Syriac (see also 1 Chron. 7:1); Masoretic Text *Puvah*
[c] *13* Samaritan Pentateuch and some Septuagint manuscripts (see also Num. 26:24 and 1 Chron. 7:1); Masoretic Text *Iob*

15These were the sons Leah bore to Jacob in Paddan Aram,[a] besides
his daughter Dinah. These sons and daughters of his were thirty-three
in all.

16The sons of Gad:
Zephon,[b] Haggi, Shuni, Ezbon, Eri, Arodi and Areli.
17The sons of Asher:
Imnah, Ishvah, Ishvi and Beriah.
Their sister was Serah.
The sons of Beriah:
Heber and Malkiel.
18These were the children born to Jacob by Zilpah, whom Laban had
given to his daughter Leah — sixteen in all.
19The sons of Jacob's wife Rachel:
Joseph and Benjamin. 20In Egypt, Manasseh and Ephraim were
born to Joseph by Asenath daughter of Potiphera, priest of On.[c]
21The sons of Benjamin:
Bela, Beker, Ashbel, Gera, Naaman, Ehi, Rosh, Muppim, Huppim
and Ard.
22These were the sons of Rachel who were born to Jacob — fourteen
in all.

23The son of Dan:
Hushim.
24The sons of Naphtali:
Jahziel, Guni, Jezer and Shillem.
25These were the sons born to Jacob by Bilhah, whom Laban had
given to his daughter Rachel — seven in all.

26All those who went to Egypt with Jacob — those who were his di-
rect descendants, not counting his sons' wives — numbered sixty-six
persons. 27With the two sons[d] who had been born to Joseph in Egypt,
the members of Jacob's family, which went to Egypt, were seventy[e]
in all.

28Now Jacob sent Judah ahead of him to Joseph to get directions to
Goshen. When they arrived in the region of Goshen, 29Joseph had his
chariot made ready and went to Goshen to meet his father Israel. As
soon as Joseph appeared before him, he threw his arms around his fa-
ther[f] and wept for a long time.
30Israel said to Joseph, "Now I am ready to die, since I have seen for
myself that you are still alive."
31Then Joseph said to his brothers and to his father's household, "I
will go up and speak to Pharaoh and will say to him, 'My brothers and
my father's household, who were living in the land of Canaan, have
come to me. 32The men are shepherds; they tend livestock, and they
have brought along their flocks and herds and everything they own.'
33When Pharaoh calls you in and asks, 'What is your occupation?' 34you
should answer, 'Your servants have tended livestock from our boyhood
on, just as our fathers did.' Then you will be allowed to settle in the
region of Goshen, for all shepherds are detestable to the Egyptians."

---

[a] *15* That is, Northwest Mesopotamia [b] *16* Samaritan Pentateuch and Septuagint (see also Num. 26:15); Masoretic Text *Ziphion* [c] *20* That is, Heliopolis [d] *27* Hebrew; Septuagint *the nine children* [e] *27* Hebrew (see also Exodus 1:5 and note); Septuagint (see also Acts 7:14) *seventy-five* [f] *29* Hebrew *around him*

47 Joseph went and told Pharaoh, "My father and brothers, with
their flocks and herds and everything they own, have come
from the land of Canaan and are now in Goshen." 2He chose five of his
brothers and presented them before Pharaoh.
3Pharaoh asked the brothers, "What is your occupation?"
"Your servants are shepherds," they replied to Pharaoh, "just as our
fathers were." 4They also said to him, "We have come to live here for a
while, because the famine is severe in Canaan and your servants' flocks
have no pasture. So now, please let your servants settle in Goshen."
5Pharaoh said to Joseph, "Your father and your brothers have come
to you, 6and the land of Egypt is before you; settle your father and your
brothers in the best part of the land. Let them live in Goshen. And if
you know of any among them with special ability, put them in charge
of my own livestock."
7Then Joseph brought his father Jacob in and presented him before
Pharaoh. After Jacob blessed[a] Pharaoh, 8Pharaoh asked him, "How old
are you?"
9And Jacob said to Pharaoh, "The years of my pilgrimage are a hun-
dred and thirty. My years have been few and difficult, and they do not
equal the years of the pilgrimage of my fathers." 10Then Jacob blessed[b]
Pharaoh and went out from his presence.
11So Joseph settled his father and his brothers in Egypt and gave them
property in the best part of the land, the district of Rameses, as Pharaoh
directed. 12Joseph also provided his father and his brothers and all his
father's household with food, according to the number of their children.

JOSEPH AND THE FAMINE

13There was no food, however, in the whole region because the
famine was severe; both Egypt and Canaan wasted away because of
the famine. 14Joseph collected all the money that was to be found in
Egypt and Canaan in payment for the grain they were buying, and
he brought it to Pharaoh's palace. 15When the money of the people of
Egypt and Canaan was gone, all Egypt came to Joseph and said, "Give
us food. Why should we die before your eyes? Our money is all gone."
16"Then bring your livestock," said Joseph. "I will sell you food in ex-
change for your livestock, since your money is gone." 17So they brought
their livestock to Joseph, and he gave them food in exchange for their
horses, their sheep and goats, their cattle and donkeys. And he brought
them through that year with food in exchange for all their livestock.
18When that year was over, they came to him the following year and
said, "We cannot hide from our lord the fact that since our money is gone
and our livestock belongs to you, there is nothing left for our lord except
our bodies and our land. 19Why should we perish before your eyes—we
and our land as well? Buy us and our land in exchange for food, and we
with our land will be in bondage to Pharaoh. Give us seed so that we may
live and not die, and that the land may not become desolate."
20So Joseph bought all the land in Egypt for Pharaoh. The Egyptians,
one and all, sold their fields, because the famine was too severe for
them. The land became Pharaoh's, 21and Joseph reduced the people to
servitude,[c] from one end of Egypt to the other. 22However, he did not
buy the land of the priests, because they received a regular allotment

PRAYING SCRIPTURE

Genesis 47

God is always preparing for us well before we know what we need. When Joseph went to Pharaoh on behalf of his family, the Egyptian leader gave Joseph and his family free choice of the best part of the land.

Israel's family was not only reunited, but God used Joseph to keep the line of the Messiah intact. Praise God for working in the details of your life to accomplish his purposes.

---

[a] 7 Or *greeted* [b] 10 Or *said farewell to* [c] 21 Samaritan Pentateuch and Septuagint (see also Vulgate); Masoretic Text *and he moved the people into the cities*

from Pharaoh and had food enough from the allotment Pharaoh gave
them. That is why they did not sell their land.
23 Joseph said to the people, “Now that I have bought you and your
land today for Pharaoh, here is seed for you so you can plant the
ground. 24 But when the crop comes in, give a fifth of it to Pharaoh. The
other four-fifths you may keep as seed for the fields and as food for
yourselves and your households and your children.”
25 “You have saved our lives,” they said. “May we find favor in the
eyes of our lord; we will be in bondage to Pharaoh.”
26 So Joseph established it as a law concerning land in Egypt — still
in force today — that a fifth of the produce belongs to Pharaoh. It was
only the land of the priests that did not become Pharaoh’s.
27 Now the Israelites settled in Egypt in the region of Goshen. They
acquired property there and were fruitful and increased greatly in
number.
28 Jacob lived in Egypt seventeen years, and the years of his life were
a hundred and forty-seven. 29 When the time drew near for Israel to
die, he called for his son Joseph and said to him, “If I have found favor
in your eyes, put your hand under my thigh and promise that you will
show me kindness and faithfulness. Do not bury me in Egypt, 30 but
when I rest with my fathers, carry me out of Egypt and bury me where
they are buried.”
“I will do as you say,” he said.
31 “Swear to me,” he said. Then Joseph swore to him, and Israel wor-
shiped as he leaned on the top of his staff.[a]

MANASSEH AND EPHRAIM

48 Some time later Joseph was told, “Your father is ill.” So he took
his two sons Manasseh and Ephraim along with him. 2 When
Jacob was told, “Your son Joseph has come to you,” Israel rallied his
strength and sat up on the bed.
3 Jacob said to Joseph, “God Almighty[b] appeared to me at Luz in the
land of Canaan, and there he blessed me 4 and said to me, ‘I am going
to make you fruitful and increase your numbers. I will make you a
community of peoples, and I will give this land as an everlasting pos-
session to your descendants after you.’
5 “Now then, your two sons born to you in Egypt before I came to you
here will be reckoned as mine; Ephraim and Manasseh will be mine,
just as Reuben and Simeon are mine. 6 Any children born to you after
them will be yours; in the territory they inherit they will be reckoned
under the names of their brothers. 7 As I was returning from Paddan,[c]
to my sorrow Rachel died in the land of Canaan while we were still on
the way, a little distance from Ephrath. So I buried her there beside the
road to Ephrath” (that is, Bethlehem).
8 When Israel saw the sons of Joseph, he asked, “Who are these?”
9 “They are the sons God has given me here,” Joseph said to his father.
Then Israel said, “Bring them to me so I may bless them.”
10 Now Israel’s eyes were failing because of old age, and he could
hardly see. So Joseph brought his sons close to him, and his father
kissed them and embraced them.
11 Israel said to Joseph, “I never expected to see your face again, and
now God has allowed me to see your children too.”

PRAYING SCRIPTURE

Genesis 48

In the same way God chose Jacob—the younger brother—for the line of blessing, Jacob (Israel) chose to bless Ephraim—Joseph’s youngest son—over the oldest, Manasseh. Ephraim was to head a greater tribe than his brother.

God sometimes reveals his ways through those around us. Joseph would not have chosen Israel’s way. Ask God to help you be sensitive when he directs your ways through others.

[a] 31 Or *Israel bowed down at the head of his bed* [b] 3 Hebrew *El-Shaddai*
[c] 7 That is, Northwest Mesopotamia

12 Then Joseph removed them from Israel's knees and bowed down
with his face to the ground. 13 And Joseph took both of them, Ephraim
on his right toward Israel's left hand and Manasseh on his left toward
Israel's right hand, and brought them close to him. 14 But Israel reached
out his right hand and put it on Ephraim's head, though he was the
younger, and crossing his arms, he put his left hand on Manasseh's
head, even though Manasseh was the firstborn.
15 Then he blessed Joseph and said,

"May the God before whom my fathers
  Abraham and Isaac walked faithfully,
the God who has been my shepherd
  all my life to this day,
16 the Angel who has delivered me from all harm
  — may he bless these boys.
May they be called by my name
  and the names of my fathers Abraham and Isaac,
and may they increase greatly
  on the earth."

17 When Joseph saw his father placing his right hand on Ephraim's
head he was displeased; so he took hold of his father's hand to move
it from Ephraim's head to Manasseh's head. 18 Joseph said to him, "No,
my father, this one is the firstborn; put your right hand on his head."
19 But his father refused and said, "I know, my son, I know. He too will
become a people, and he too will become great. Nevertheless, his youn-
ger brother will be greater than he, and his descendants will become a
group of nations." 20 He blessed them that day and said,

"In your[a] name will Israel pronounce this blessing:
  'May God make you like Ephraim and Manasseh.'"

So he put Ephraim ahead of Manasseh.
21 Then Israel said to Joseph, "I am about to die, but God will be with
you[b] and take you[b] back to the land of your[b] fathers. 22 And to you I give
one more ridge of land[c] than to your brothers, the ridge I took from the
Amorites with my sword and my bow."

JACOB BLESSES HIS SONS

49 Then Jacob called for his sons and said: "Gather around so I
can tell you what will happen to you in days to come.

2 "Assemble and listen, sons of Jacob;
  listen to your father Israel.

3 "Reuben, you are my firstborn,
  my might, the first sign of my strength,
  excelling in honor, excelling in power.
4 Turbulent as the waters, you will no longer excel,
  for you went up onto your father's bed,
  onto my couch and defiled it.

5 "Simeon and Levi are brothers —
  their swords[d] are weapons of violence.

[a] *20* The Hebrew is singular. [b] *21* The Hebrew is plural. [c] *22* The Hebrew for *ridge of land* is identical with the place name Shechem. [d] *5* The meaning of the Hebrew for this word is uncertain.

PRAYING SCRIPTURE

Genesis 49

Have you ever thought about what your last words would be if you could choose them? Would you try to be pithy? Profound? Reflective? Israel uttered prophetic words about the futures of his sons, some positive and some negative.

Why wait until your deathbed to bless those around you? Ask God to help you be intentional in blessing and encouraging others now, while you have the opportunity.

6 Let me not enter their council,
let me not join their assembly,
for they have killed men in their anger
and hamstrung oxen as they pleased.
7 Cursed be their anger, so fierce,
and their fury, so cruel!
I will scatter them in Jacob
and disperse them in Israel.

8 "Judah,[a] your brothers will praise you;
your hand will be on the neck of your enemies;
your father's sons will bow down to you.
9 You are a lion's cub, Judah;
you return from the prey, my son.
Like a lion he crouches and lies down,
like a lioness — who dares to rouse him?
10 The scepter will not depart from Judah,
nor the ruler's staff from between his feet,[b]
until he to whom it belongs[c] shall come
and the obedience of the nations shall be his.
11 He will tether his donkey to a vine,
his colt to the choicest branch;
he will wash his garments in wine,
his robes in the blood of grapes.
12 His eyes will be darker than wine,
his teeth whiter than milk.[d]

13 "Zebulun will live by the seashore
and become a haven for ships;
his border will extend toward Sidon.

14 "Issachar is a rawboned[e] donkey
lying down among the sheep pens.[f]
15 When he sees how good is his resting place
and how pleasant is his land,
he will bend his shoulder to the burden
and submit to forced labor.

16 "Dan[g] will provide justice for his people
as one of the tribes of Israel.
17 Dan will be a snake by the roadside,
a viper along the path,
that bites the horse's heels
so that its rider tumbles backward.

18 "I look for your deliverance, LORD.

19 "Gad[h] will be attacked by a band of raiders,
but he will attack them at their heels.

20 "Asher's food will be rich;
he will provide delicacies fit for a king.

---

[a] 8 *Judah* sounds like and may be derived from the Hebrew for *praise.*
[b] 10 Or *from his descendants* [c] 10 Or *to whom tribute belongs*; the meaning of the Hebrew for this phrase is uncertain. [d] 12 Or *will be dull from wine, / his teeth white from milk* [e] 14 Or *strong* [f] 14 Or *the campfires*; or *the saddlebags* [g] 16 *Dan* here means *he provides justice.* [h] 19 *Gad* sounds like the Hebrew for *attack* and also for *band of raiders.*

21 "Naphtali is a doe set free
that bears beautiful fawns.[a]

22 "Joseph is a fruitful vine,
a fruitful vine near a spring,
whose branches climb over a wall.[b]
23 With bitterness archers attacked him;
they shot at him with hostility.
24 But his bow remained steady,
his strong arms stayed[c] limber,
because of the hand of the Mighty One of Jacob,
because of the Shepherd, the Rock of Israel,
25 because of your father's God, who helps you,
because of the Almighty,[d] who blesses you
with blessings of the skies above,
blessings of the deep springs below,
blessings of the breast and womb.
26 Your father's blessings are greater
than the blessings of the ancient mountains,
than[e] the bounty of the age-old hills.
Let all these rest on the head of Joseph,
on the brow of the prince among[f] his brothers.

27 "Benjamin is a ravenous wolf;
in the morning he devours the prey,
in the evening he divides the plunder."

28 All these are the twelve tribes of Israel, and this is what their father
said to them when he blessed them, giving each the blessing appro-
priate to him.

THE DEATH OF JACOB

29 Then he gave them these instructions: "I am about to be gath-
ered to my people. Bury me with my fathers in the cave in the field of
Ephron the Hittite, 30 the cave in the field of Machpelah, near Mamre in
Canaan, which Abraham bought along with the field as a burial place
from Ephron the Hittite. 31 There Abraham and his wife Sarah were bur-
ied, there Isaac and his wife Rebekah were buried, and there I buried
Leah. 32 The field and the cave in it were bought from the Hittites.[g]"

33 When Jacob had finished giving instructions to his sons, he drew his
feet up into the bed, breathed his last and was gathered to his people.

50 Joseph threw himself on his father and wept over him and
kissed him. 2 Then Joseph directed the physicians in his ser-
vice to embalm his father Israel. So the physicians embalmed him,
3 taking a full forty days, for that was the time required for embalming.
And the Egyptians mourned for him seventy days.

4 When the days of mourning had passed, Joseph said to Pharaoh's
court, "If I have found favor in your eyes, speak to Pharaoh for me. Tell
him, 5 'My father made me swear an oath and said, "I am about to die;
bury me in the tomb I dug for myself in the land of Canaan." Now let
me go up and bury my father; then I will return.'"

PRAYING SCRIPTURE

Genesis 50

Most people have experienced situations in which forgiveness was not easy. Many sins deeply wound. Crimes can cause lasting trauma to the mind and body. We should remember that forgiveness does not mean nothing bad ever happened. It means we've decided to let God handle our offenders as he sees fit.

Joseph experienced a most horrific betrayal, yet through God's grace he forgave his brothers. Ask God for the grace to leave all retribution to him.

---

[a] 21 Or *free; / he utters beautiful words* [b] 22 Or *Joseph is a wild colt, / a wild colt near a spring, / a wild donkey on a terraced hill* [c] 23,24 Or *archers will attack . . . will shoot . . . will remain . . . will stay* [d] 25 Hebrew *Shaddai*
[e] 26 Or *of my progenitors, / as great as* [f] 26 Or *of the one separated from*
[g] 32 Or *the descendants of Heth*

6 Pharaoh said, "Go up and bury your father, as he made you swear to do."

7 So Joseph went up to bury his father. All Pharaoh's officials accompanied him — the dignitaries of his court and all the dignitaries of Egypt — 8 besides all the members of Joseph's household and his brothers and those belonging to his father's household. Only their children and their flocks and herds were left in Goshen. 9 Chariots and horsemen[a] also went up with him. It was a very large company.

10 When they reached the threshing floor of Atad, near the Jordan, they lamented loudly and bitterly; and there Joseph observed a seven-day period of mourning for his father. 11 When the Canaanites who lived there saw the mourning at the threshing floor of Atad, they said, "The Egyptians are holding a solemn ceremony of mourning." That is why that place near the Jordan is called Abel Mizraim.[b]

12 So Jacob's sons did as he had commanded them: 13 They carried him to the land of Canaan and buried him in the cave in the field of Machpelah, near Mamre, which Abraham had bought along with the field as a burial place from Ephron the Hittite. 14 After burying his father, Joseph returned to Egypt, together with his brothers and all the others who had gone with him to bury his father.

JOSEPH REASSURES HIS BROTHERS

15 When Joseph's brothers saw that their father was dead, they said, "What if Joseph holds a grudge against us and pays us back for all the wrongs we did to him?" 16 So they sent word to Joseph, saying, "Your father left these instructions before he died: 17 'This is what you are to say to Joseph: I ask you to forgive your brothers the sins and the wrongs they committed in treating you so badly.' Now please forgive the sins of the servants of the God of your father." When their message came to him, Joseph wept.

18 His brothers then came and threw themselves down before him. "We are your slaves," they said.

19 But Joseph said to them, "Don't be afraid. Am I in the place of God? 20 You intended to harm me, but God intended it for good to accomplish what is now being done, the saving of many lives. 21 So then, don't be afraid. I will provide for you and your children." And he reassured them and spoke kindly to them.

THE DEATH OF JOSEPH

22 Joseph stayed in Egypt, along with all his father's family. He lived a hundred and ten years 23 and saw the third generation of Ephraim's children. Also the children of Makir son of Manasseh were placed at birth on Joseph's knees.[c]

24 Then Joseph said to his brothers, "I am about to die. But God will surely come to your aid and take you up out of this land to the land he promised on oath to Abraham, Isaac and Jacob." 25 And Joseph made the Israelites swear an oath and said, "God will surely come to your aid, and then you must carry my bones up from this place."

26 So Joseph died at the age of a hundred and ten. And after they embalmed him, he was placed in a coffin in Egypt.

---

[a] *9* Or *charioteers* [b] *11* *Abel Mizraim* means *mourning of the Egyptians.*
[c] *23* That is, were counted as his

EXODUS

The story of the exodus picks up almost four hundred years after the close of Genesis. God's promise that Abraham's descendants would be as numerous as the stars in the sky was coming to fruition, as the Egyptians grew fearful of the expanding Israelite nation in their midst. They chose to enslave and oppress Israel, and their cruelty became the backdrop for what would become God's greatest act of salvation in the Old Testament.

Exodus reveals that God is approachable and shows how his people can know him. In chapter 3, he made himself known to Moses in the burning bush and revealed his name to the reluctant leader. He spoke to Moses throughout the plagues and the exodus from Egypt. He personally led his people out of slavery and across the Red Sea into the salvation he had prepared for them.

Exodus established Moses as the mediator for God's people. When God spoke to the people at Sinai, they were afraid and asked for Moses to stand in the middle, receiving the words of the Lord and then communicating them to the people. When Israel sinned in the wilderness, Moses approached God and interceded for the people. He appealed to God's character and asked him to save his people.

Moses' role as mediator prepared God's people for the work of Christ. He came to earth and spoke God's words directly. His death split the veil of fear that God's people often face so that we can approach the Lord "in the name of Jesus." Jesus now serves as our new Moses, the great intercessor who prays for his people in the presence of his Father.

In Exodus 34, Moses experienced the Old Testament's most intimate recorded encounter with God. He asked the Lord if he could see his glory, the resplendent light that accompanies God's holiness. The Lord responded that no one could see his glory and live. As a concession, God hid Moses in the cleft of a rock and allowed Moses to see his back. As he passed by Moses, God proclaimed the heart of his character, and those words became a statement of faith for Israel, repeated often throughout the rest of the Old Testament. Old Testament believers would frequently refer to the descriptive words God used of himself in their prayers to remind themselves of the Lord's gracious character.

Moses' consistent intercession for the children of Israel is a pattern for all God's people. Standing in the gap before God on behalf of others is one of the most meaningful things a child of God can do. Few things have greater eternal impact than intercession. Whether praying for a friend to know God, for a family member to get a job, for a parent to be healed or for a member of our church family to know the will of God, praying for others is both a great responsibility and a great honor.

THE ISRAELITES OPPRESSED

1 These are the names of the sons of Israel who went to Egypt with
Jacob, each with his family: 2Reuben, Simeon, Levi and Judah; 3Is-
sachar, Zebulun and Benjamin; 4Dan and Naphtali; Gad and Asher. 5The
descendants of Jacob numbered seventy[a] in all; Joseph was already in
Egypt.
6Now Joseph and all his brothers and all that generation died, 7but the
Israelites were exceedingly fruitful; they multiplied greatly, increased in
numbers and became so numerous that the land was filled with them.
8Then a new king, to whom Joseph meant nothing, came to power
in Egypt. 9"Look," he said to his people, "the Israelites have become
far too numerous for us. 10Come, we must deal shrewdly with them or
they will become even more numerous and, if war breaks out, will join
our enemies, fight against us and leave the country."
11So they put slave masters over them to oppress them with forced
labor, and they built Pithom and Rameses as store cities for Pharaoh.
12But the more they were oppressed, the more they multiplied and
spread; so the Egyptians came to dread the Israelites 13and worked
them ruthlessly. 14They made their lives bitter with harsh labor in brick
and mortar and with all kinds of work in the fields; in all their harsh
labor the Egyptians worked them ruthlessly.
15The king of Egypt said to the Hebrew midwives, whose names
were Shiphrah and Puah, 16"When you are helping the Hebrew women
during childbirth on the delivery stool, if you see that the baby is a boy,
kill him; but if it is a girl, let her live." 17The midwives, however, feared
God and did not do what the king of Egypt had told them to do; they let
the boys live. 18Then the king of Egypt summoned the midwives and
asked them, "Why have you done this? Why have you let the boys live?"
19The midwives answered Pharaoh, "Hebrew women are not like
Egyptian women; they are vigorous and give birth before the mid-
wives arrive."
20So God was kind to the midwives and the people increased and be-
came even more numerous. 21And because the midwives feared God,
he gave them families of their own.
22Then Pharaoh gave this order to all his people: "Every Hebrew boy
that is born you must throw into the Nile, but let every girl live."

PRAYING SCRIPTURE

Exodus 1

History has repeatedly shown that the evil one attacks children whenever he can in the same way that Pharaoh attempted to stamp out the Israelites by killing their children. God rewarded the heroism of the midwives, blessing them with families of their own.

Are there children around you at home, work or church? Ask God for opportunities to show his love to them.

THE BIRTH OF MOSES

2 Now a man of the tribe of Levi married a Levite woman, 2and she
became pregnant and gave birth to a son. When she saw that he
was a fine child, she hid him for three months. 3But when she could
hide him no longer, she got a papyrus basket[b] for him and coated it
with tar and pitch. Then she placed the child in it and put it among the
reeds along the bank of the Nile. 4His sister stood at a distance to see
what would happen to him.
5Then Pharaoh's daughter went down to the Nile to bathe, and her
attendants were walking along the riverbank. She saw the basket
among the reeds and sent her female slave to get it. 6She opened it
and saw the baby. He was crying, and she felt sorry for him. "This is
one of the Hebrew babies," she said.

PRAYING SCRIPTURE

Exodus 2

Have you ever had a moment of anger that ended in a very bad situation? That is what happened to Moses. Although he was defending his own countryman, his violent response put him directly in Pharaoh's crosshairs. And so Moses fled.

If you are given to outbursts of anger, ask God to deliver you in his power before you find yourself far away, living in fear.

[a] 5 Masoretic Text (see also Gen. 46:27); Dead Sea Scrolls and Septuagint (see also Acts 7:14 and note at Gen. 46:27) *seventy-five* [b] 3 The Hebrew can also mean *ark*, as in Gen. 6:14.

7Then his sister asked Pharaoh's daughter, "Shall I go and get one of
the Hebrew women to nurse the baby for you?"
8"Yes, go," she answered. So the girl went and got the baby's mother.
9Pharaoh's daughter said to her, "Take this baby and nurse him for
me, and I will pay you." So the woman took the baby and nursed him.
10When the child grew older, she took him to Pharaoh's daughter and
he became her son. She named him Moses,[a] saying, "I drew him out
of the water."

MOSES FLEES TO MIDIAN

11One day, after Moses had grown up, he went out to where his own
people were and watched them at their hard labor. He saw an Egyptian
beating a Hebrew, one of his own people. 12Looking this way and that
and seeing no one, he killed the Egyptian and hid him in the sand.
13The next day he went out and saw two Hebrews fighting. He asked
the one in the wrong, "Why are you hitting your fellow Hebrew?"
14The man said, "Who made you ruler and judge over us? Are you
thinking of killing me as you killed the Egyptian?" Then Moses was
afraid and thought, "What I did must have become known."
15When Pharaoh heard of this, he tried to kill Moses, but Moses fled
from Pharaoh and went to live in Midian, where he sat down by a well.
16Now a priest of Midian had seven daughters, and they came to draw
water and fill the troughs to water their father's flock. 17Some shep-
herds came along and drove them away, but Moses got up and came to
their rescue and watered their flock.
18When the girls returned to Reuel their father, he asked them, "Why
have you returned so early today?"
19They answered, "An Egyptian rescued us from the shepherds. He
even drew water for us and watered the flock."
20"And where is he?" Reuel asked his daughters. "Why did you leave
him? Invite him to have something to eat."
21Moses agreed to stay with the man, who gave his daughter Zipporah
to Moses in marriage. 22Zipporah gave birth to a son, and Moses named
him Gershom,[b] saying, "I have become a foreigner in a foreign land."
23During that long period, the king of Egypt died. The Israelites
groaned in their slavery and cried out, and their cry for help because
of their slavery went up to God. 24God heard their groaning and he re-
membered his covenant with Abraham, with Isaac and with Jacob. 25So
God looked on the Israelites and was concerned about them.

MOSES AND THE BURNING BUSH

3 Now Moses was tending the flock of Jethro his father-in-law, the
priest of Midian, and he led the flock to the far side of the wil-
derness and came to Horeb, the mountain of God. 2There the angel of
the LORD appeared to him in flames of fire from within a bush. Moses
saw that though the bush was on fire it did not burn up. 3So Moses
thought, "I will go over and see this strange sight — why the bush does
not burn up."
4When the LORD saw that he had gone over to look, God called to him
from within the bush, "Moses! Moses!"
And Moses said, "Here I am."

PRAYING SCRIPTURE

Exodus 3

Wouldn't it be easy if God always spoke to us through miraculous means? The term "a burning bush experience" refers to those rare experiences.

The presence of the Holy Spirit and the Word of God removes the need for burning bushes. Ask the Spirit to speak to you through the Word on a daily basis.

---

[a] *10* *Moses* sounds like the Hebrew for *draw out.* [b] *22* *Gershom* sounds like the Hebrew for *a foreigner there.*

5“Do not come any closer,” God said. “Take off your sandals, for the
place where you are standing is holy ground.” 6Then he said, “I am the
God of your father,[a] the God of Abraham, the God of Isaac and the God of
Jacob.” At this, Moses hid his face, because he was afraid to look at God.
7The LORD said, “I have indeed seen the misery of my people in
Egypt. I have heard them crying out because of their slave drivers,
and I am concerned about their suffering. 8So I have come down to res-
cue them from the hand of the Egyptians and to bring them up out of
that land into a good and spacious land, a land flowing with milk and
honey — the home of the Canaanites, Hittites, Amorites, Perizzites, Hi-
vites and Jebusites. 9And now the cry of the Israelites has reached me,
and I have seen the way the Egyptians are oppressing them. 10So now,
go. I am sending you to Pharaoh to bring my people the Israelites out
of Egypt.”

11But Moses said to God, “Who am I that I should go to Pharaoh and
bring the Israelites out of Egypt?”

12And God said, “I will be with you. And this will be the sign to you
that it is I who have sent you: When you have brought the people out
of Egypt, you[b] will worship God on this mountain.”

13Moses said to God, “Suppose I go to the Israelites and say to them,
‘The God of your fathers has sent me to you,’ and they ask me, ‘What is
his name?’ Then what shall I tell them?”

14God said to Moses, “I AM WHO I AM.[c] This is what you are to say to
the Israelites: ‘I AM has sent me to you.’ ”

15God also said to Moses, “Say to the Israelites, ‘The LORD,[d] the God
of your fathers — the God of Abraham, the God of Isaac and the God of
Jacob — has sent me to you.’

“This is my name forever,
  the name you shall call me
  from generation to generation.

16“Go, assemble the elders of Israel and say to them, ‘The LORD, the
God of your fathers — the God of Abraham, Isaac and Jacob — appeared
to me and said: I have watched over you and have seen what has been
done to you in Egypt. 17And I have promised to bring you up out of
your misery in Egypt into the land of the Canaanites, Hittites, Amo-
rites, Perizzites, Hivites and Jebusites — a land flowing with milk and
honey.’

18“The elders of Israel will listen to you. Then you and the elders are
to go to the king of Egypt and say to him, ‘The LORD, the God of the
Hebrews, has met with us. Let us take a three-day journey into the wil-
derness to offer sacrifices to the LORD our God.’ 19But I know that the
king of Egypt will not let you go unless a mighty hand compels him.
20So I will stretch out my hand and strike the Egyptians with all the
wonders that I will perform among them. After that, he will let you go.
21“And I will make the Egyptians favorably disposed toward this
people, so that when you leave you will not go empty-handed. 22Every
woman is to ask her neighbor and any woman living in her house for
articles of silver and gold and for clothing, which you will put on your
sons and daughters. And so you will plunder the Egyptians.”

---

[a] *6* Masoretic Text; Samaritan Pentateuch (see Acts 7:32) *fathers* [b] *12* The Hebrew is plural. [c] *14* Or *I WILL BE WHAT I WILL BE* [d] *15* The Hebrew for *LORD* sounds like and may be related to the Hebrew for *I AM* in verse 14.

SIGNS FOR MOSES

4 Moses answered, "What if they do not believe me or listen to me
and say, 'The LORD did not appear to you'?"
2Then the LORD said to him, "What is that in your hand?"
"A staff," he replied.
3The LORD said, "Throw it on the ground."
Moses threw it on the ground and it became a snake, and he ran
from it. 4Then the LORD said to him, "Reach out your hand and take
it by the tail." So Moses reached out and took hold of the snake and it
turned back into a staff in his hand. 5"This," said the LORD, "is so that
they may believe that the LORD, the God of their fathers — the God of
Abraham, the God of Isaac and the God of Jacob — has appeared to
you."
6Then the LORD said, "Put your hand inside your cloak." So Moses
put his hand into his cloak, and when he took it out, the skin was lep-
rous[a] — it had become as white as snow.
7"Now put it back into your cloak," he said. So Moses put his hand
back into his cloak, and when he took it out, it was restored, like the
rest of his flesh.
8Then the LORD said, "If they do not believe you or pay attention to
the first sign, they may believe the second. 9But if they do not believe
these two signs or listen to you, take some water from the Nile and
pour it on the dry ground. The water you take from the river will be-
come blood on the ground."
10Moses said to the LORD, "Pardon your servant, Lord. I have never
been eloquent, neither in the past nor since you have spoken to your
servant. I am slow of speech and tongue."
11The LORD said to him, "Who gave human beings their mouths? Who
makes them deaf or mute? Who gives them sight or makes them blind?
Is it not I, the LORD? 12Now go; I will help you speak and will teach you
what to say."
13But Moses said, "Pardon your servant, Lord. Please send someone
else."
14Then the LORD's anger burned against Moses and he said, "What
about your brother, Aaron the Levite? I know he can speak well. He is
already on his way to meet you, and he will be glad to see you. 15You
shall speak to him and put words in his mouth; I will help both of you
speak and will teach you what to do. 16He will speak to the people for
you, and it will be as if he were your mouth and as if you were God to
him. 17But take this staff in your hand so you can perform the signs
with it."

MOSES RETURNS TO EGYPT

18Then Moses went back to Jethro his father-in-law and said to him,
"Let me return to my own people in Egypt to see if any of them are
still alive."
Jethro said, "Go, and I wish you well."
19Now the LORD had said to Moses in Midian, "Go back to Egypt, for
all those who wanted to kill you are dead." 20So Moses took his wife and
sons, put them on a donkey and started back to Egypt. And he took the
staff of God in his hand.

PRAYING SCRIPTURE

Exodus 4

Often Christians face doubt or fear when they ponder God's plan for their lives. God rarely confirms his plan via miracles as he did with Moses. We usually have to walk by faith, not by sight, praying and hoping to avoid mistakes.

But this doesn't bother God. Thank him for bearing with you when you are uncertain and for increasing your faith so you can follow his plan with confidence.

[a] 6 The Hebrew word for *leprous* was used for various diseases affecting the skin.

21The LORD said to Moses, "When you return to Egypt, see that you
perform before Pharaoh all the wonders I have given you the power
to do. But I will harden his heart so that he will not let the people go.
22Then say to Pharaoh, 'This is what the LORD says: Israel is my first-
born son, 23and I told you, "Let my son go, so he may worship me." But
you refused to let him go; so I will kill your firstborn son.'"
24At a lodging place on the way, the LORD met Moses[a] and was about
to kill him. 25But Zipporah took a flint knife, cut off her son's foreskin
and touched Moses' feet with it.[b] "Surely you are a bridegroom of blood
to me," she said. 26So the LORD let him alone. (At that time she said
"bridegroom of blood," referring to circumcision.)
27The LORD said to Aaron, "Go into the wilderness to meet Moses." So
he met Moses at the mountain of God and kissed him. 28Then Moses
told Aaron everything the LORD had sent him to say, and also about all
the signs he had commanded him to perform.
29Moses and Aaron brought together all the elders of the Israelites,
30and Aaron told them everything the LORD had said to Moses. He also
performed the signs before the people, 31and they believed. And when
they heard that the LORD was concerned about them and had seen
their misery, they bowed down and worshiped.

BRICKS WITHOUT STRAW

5 Afterward Moses and Aaron went to Pharaoh and said, "This is
what the LORD, the God of Israel, says: 'Let my people go, so that
they may hold a festival to me in the wilderness.'"
2Pharaoh said, "Who is the LORD, that I should obey him and let Is-
rael go? I do not know the LORD and I will not let Israel go."
3Then they said, "The God of the Hebrews has met with us. Now let
us take a three-day journey into the wilderness to offer sacrifices to
the LORD our God, or he may strike us with plagues or with the sword."
4But the king of Egypt said, "Moses and Aaron, why are you taking
the people away from their labor? Get back to your work!" 5Then Phar-
aoh said, "Look, the people of the land are now numerous, and you are
stopping them from working."
6That same day Pharaoh gave this order to the slave drivers and
overseers in charge of the people: 7"You are no longer to supply the
people with straw for making bricks; let them go and gather their own
straw. 8But require them to make the same number of bricks as before;
don't reduce the quota. They are lazy; that is why they are crying out,
'Let us go and sacrifice to our God.' 9Make the work harder for the peo-
ple so that they keep working and pay no attention to lies."
10Then the slave drivers and the overseers went out and said to the
people, "This is what Pharaoh says: 'I will not give you any more straw.
11Go and get your own straw wherever you can find it, but your work
will not be reduced at all.'" 12So the people scattered all over Egypt
to gather stubble to use for straw. 13The slave drivers kept pressing
them, saying, "Complete the work required of you for each day, just as
when you had straw." 14And Pharaoh's slave drivers beat the Israelite
overseers they had appointed, demanding, "Why haven't you met your
quota of bricks yesterday or today, as before?"
15Then the Israelite overseers went and appealed to Pharaoh: "Why

PRAYING SCRIPTURE

Exodus 5

Approaching powerful people is not easy because they can be unpredictable. Moses asked Pharaoh to free the Israelites so they could go worship. But Pharaoh was loath to release all that free labor and made things worse as punishment. The Israelites' frustration was turned back on Moses and Aaron.

Have you ever been wrongly blamed for following God? Do what Moses did: Go back and speak to God about it.

---

[a] *24* Hebrew *him* [b] *25* The meaning of the Hebrew for this clause is uncertain.

have you treated your servants this way? 16Your servants are given no
straw, yet we are told, 'Make bricks!' Your servants are being beaten,
but the fault is with your own people."

17Pharaoh said, "Lazy, that's what you are — lazy! That is why you keep
saying, 'Let us go and sacrifice to the LORD.' 18Now get to work. You will
not be given any straw, yet you must produce your full quota of bricks."

19The Israelite overseers realized they were in trouble when they
were told, "You are not to reduce the number of bricks required of you
for each day." 20When they left Pharaoh, they found Moses and Aaron
waiting to meet them, 21and they said, "May the LORD look on you and
judge you! You have made us obnoxious to Pharaoh and his officials
and have put a sword in their hand to kill us."

GOD PROMISES DELIVERANCE

22Moses returned to the LORD and said, "Why, Lord, why have you
brought trouble on this people? Is this why you sent me? 23Ever since I
went to Pharaoh to speak in your name, he has brought trouble on this
people, and you have not rescued your people at all."

6 Then the LORD said to Moses, "Now you will see what I will do to
Pharaoh: Because of my mighty hand he will let them go; because
of my mighty hand he will drive them out of his country."

2God also said to Moses, "I am the LORD. 3I appeared to Abraham, to
Isaac and to Jacob as God Almighty,[a] but by my name the LORD[b] I did
not make myself fully known to them. 4I also established my covenant
with them to give them the land of Canaan, where they resided as for-
eigners. 5Moreover, I have heard the groaning of the Israelites, whom
the Egyptians are enslaving, and I have remembered my covenant.

6"Therefore, say to the Israelites: 'I am the LORD, and I will bring you
out from under the yoke of the Egyptians. I will free you from being
slaves to them, and I will redeem you with an outstretched arm and
with mighty acts of judgment. 7I will take you as my own people, and
I will be your God. Then you will know that I am the LORD your God,
who brought you out from under the yoke of the Egyptians. 8And I will
bring you to the land I swore with uplifted hand to give to Abraham, to
Isaac and to Jacob. I will give it to you as a possession. I am the LORD.'"

9Moses reported this to the Israelites, but they did not listen to him
because of their discouragement and harsh labor.

10Then the LORD said to Moses, 11"Go, tell Pharaoh king of Egypt to
let the Israelites go out of his country."

12But Moses said to the LORD, "If the Israelites will not listen to me,
why would Pharaoh listen to me, since I speak with faltering lips[c]?"

FAMILY RECORD OF MOSES AND AARON

13Now the LORD spoke to Moses and Aaron about the Israelites and
Pharaoh king of Egypt, and he commanded them to bring the Israel-
ites out of Egypt.

14These were the heads of their families[d]:

The sons of Reuben the firstborn son of Israel were Hanok and
Pallu, Hezron and Karmi. These were the clans of Reuben.

[a] 3 Hebrew *El-Shaddai* [b] 3 See note at 3:15. [c] 12 Hebrew *I am uncircumcised of lips*; also in verse 30 [d] 14 The Hebrew for *families* here and in verse 25 refers to units larger than clans.

PRAYING SCRIPTURE

Exodus 6

Generations after the deaths of Abraham, Isaac and Jacob, God reiterated his long-standing promise, this time to Moses. His covenant was the basis of delivering his children. God promised to rescue them from bondage and lead them to the land associated with the covenant.

God never forgets his promises. Never hesitate to claim the promises of God when you pray. You will find them all throughout his Word.

15 The sons of Simeon were Jemuel, Jamin, Ohad, Jakin, Zohar and Shaul the son of a Canaanite woman. These were the clans of Simeon.

16 These were the names of the sons of Levi according to their records: Gershon, Kohath and Merari. Levi lived 137 years.

17 The sons of Gershon, by clans, were Libni and Shimei.

18 The sons of Kohath were Amram, Izhar, Hebron and Uzziel. Kohath lived 133 years.

19 The sons of Merari were Mahli and Mushi.

These were the clans of Levi according to their records.

20 Amram married his father's sister Jochebed, who bore him Aaron and Moses. Amram lived 137 years.

21 The sons of Izhar were Korah, Nepheg and Zikri.

22 The sons of Uzziel were Mishael, Elzaphan and Sithri.

23 Aaron married Elisheba, daughter of Amminadab and sister of Nahshon, and she bore him Nadab and Abihu, Eleazar and Ithamar.

24 The sons of Korah were Assir, Elkanah and Abiasaph. These were the Korahite clans.

25 Eleazar son of Aaron married one of the daughters of Putiel, and she bore him Phinehas.

These were the heads of the Levite families, clan by clan.

26 It was this Aaron and Moses to whom the LORD said, "Bring the Israelites out of Egypt by their divisions." 27 They were the ones who spoke to Pharaoh king of Egypt about bringing the Israelites out of Egypt — this same Moses and Aaron.

AARON TO SPEAK FOR MOSES

28 Now when the LORD spoke to Moses in Egypt, 29 he said to him, "I am the LORD. Tell Pharaoh king of Egypt everything I tell you."

30 But Moses said to the LORD, "Since I speak with faltering lips, why would Pharaoh listen to me?"

7 Then the LORD said to Moses, "See, I have made you like God to Pharaoh, and your brother Aaron will be your prophet. 2 You are to say everything I command you, and your brother Aaron is to tell Pharaoh to let the Israelites go out of his country. 3 But I will harden Pharaoh's heart, and though I multiply my signs and wonders in Egypt, 4 he will not listen to you. Then I will lay my hand on Egypt and with mighty acts of judgment I will bring out my divisions, my people the Israelites. 5 And the Egyptians will know that I am the LORD when I stretch out my hand against Egypt and bring the Israelites out of it."

6 Moses and Aaron did just as the LORD commanded them. 7 Moses was eighty years old and Aaron eighty-three when they spoke to Pharaoh.

AARON'S STAFF BECOMES A SNAKE

8 The LORD said to Moses and Aaron, 9 "When Pharaoh says to you, 'Perform a miracle,' then say to Aaron, 'Take your staff and throw it down before Pharaoh,' and it will become a snake."

10 So Moses and Aaron went to Pharaoh and did just as the LORD commanded. Aaron threw his staff down in front of Pharaoh and his officials, and it became a snake. 11 Pharaoh then summoned wise men and sorcerers, and the Egyptian magicians also did the same things by their

PRAYING SCRIPTURE

Exodus 7

Convincing the most powerful man in the world to free his slaves seemed like an overwhelming task for Moses and Aaron, both in their eighties. And without God's presence and assurance, it would have been. God gave an indication of what he would do, but he did not go into detail.

God doesn't always reveal his entire plan. Tell him that you trust him as he reveals it in his good time.

secret arts: 12Each one threw down his staff and it became a snake. But
Aaron's staff swallowed up their staffs. 13Yet Pharaoh's heart became
hard and he would not listen to them, just as the LORD had said.

THE PLAGUE OF BLOOD

14Then the LORD said to Moses, "Pharaoh's heart is unyielding; he
refuses to let the people go. 15Go to Pharaoh in the morning as he goes
out to the river. Confront him on the bank of the Nile, and take in your
hand the staff that was changed into a snake. 16Then say to him, 'The
LORD, the God of the Hebrews, has sent me to say to you: Let my people
go, so that they may worship me in the wilderness. But until now you
have not listened. 17This is what the LORD says: By this you will know
that I am the LORD: With the staff that is in my hand I will strike the
water of the Nile, and it will be changed into blood. 18The fish in the
Nile will die, and the river will stink; the Egyptians will not be able to
drink its water.'"

19The LORD said to Moses, "Tell Aaron, 'Take your staff and stretch
out your hand over the waters of Egypt — over the streams and canals,
over the ponds and all the reservoirs — and they will turn to blood.'
Blood will be everywhere in Egypt, even in vessels[a] of wood and stone."

20Moses and Aaron did just as the LORD had commanded. He raised
his staff in the presence of Pharaoh and his officials and struck the
water of the Nile, and all the water was changed into blood. 21The fish
in the Nile died, and the river smelled so bad that the Egyptians could
not drink its water. Blood was everywhere in Egypt.

22But the Egyptian magicians did the same things by their secret
arts, and Pharaoh's heart became hard; he would not listen to Moses
and Aaron, just as the LORD had said. 23Instead, he turned and went
into his palace, and did not take even this to heart. 24And all the Egyp-
tians dug along the Nile to get drinking water, because they could not
drink the water of the river.

THE PLAGUE OF FROGS

8[b] 25Seven days passed after the LORD struck the Nile. 1Then the
LORD said to Moses, "Go to Pharaoh and say to him, 'This is what
the LORD says: Let my people go, so that they may worship me. 2If you
refuse to let them go, I will send a plague of frogs on your whole coun-
try. 3The Nile will teem with frogs. They will come up into your palace
and your bedroom and onto your bed, into the houses of your officials
and on your people, and into your ovens and kneading troughs. 4The
frogs will come up on you and your people and all your officials.'"

5Then the LORD said to Moses, "Tell Aaron, 'Stretch out your hand
with your staff over the streams and canals and ponds, and make frogs
come up on the land of Egypt.'"

6So Aaron stretched out his hand over the waters of Egypt, and the
frogs came up and covered the land. 7But the magicians did the same
things by their secret arts; they also made frogs come up on the land
of Egypt.

8Pharaoh summoned Moses and Aaron and said, "Pray to the LORD to
take the frogs away from me and my people, and I will let your people
go to offer sacrifices to the LORD."

PRAYING SCRIPTURE

Exodus 8

In the face of plague after plague, Pharaoh continually hardened his heart toward God. Moses made clear that God's purpose was for Pharaoh to know and recognize God's power. Even Pharaoh's own magicians recognized the "finger of God" (verse 19).

Some people simply will not repent and come to faith in God. Ask God to make you a consistent witness in the face of persistent unbelief.

---

[a] 19 Or *even on their idols* [b] In Hebrew texts 8:1-4 is numbered 7:26-29, and 8:5-32 is numbered 8:1-28.

9 Moses said to Pharaoh, "I leave to you the honor of setting the time for me to pray for you and your officials and your people that you and your houses may be rid of the frogs, except for those that remain in the Nile."

10 "Tomorrow," Pharaoh said.

Moses replied, "It will be as you say, so that you may know there is no one like the LORD our God. 11 The frogs will leave you and your houses, your officials and your people; they will remain only in the Nile."

12 After Moses and Aaron left Pharaoh, Moses cried out to the LORD about the frogs he had brought on Pharaoh. 13 And the LORD did what Moses asked. The frogs died in the houses, in the courtyards and in the fields. 14 They were piled into heaps, and the land reeked of them. 15 But when Pharaoh saw that there was relief, he hardened his heart and would not listen to Moses and Aaron, just as the LORD had said.

THE PLAGUE OF GNATS

16 Then the LORD said to Moses, "Tell Aaron, 'Stretch out your staff and strike the dust of the ground,' and throughout the land of Egypt the dust will become gnats." 17 They did this, and when Aaron stretched out his hand with the staff and struck the dust of the ground, gnats came on people and animals. All the dust throughout the land of Egypt became gnats. 18 But when the magicians tried to produce gnats by their secret arts, they could not.

Since the gnats were on people and animals everywhere, 19 the magicians said to Pharaoh, "This is the finger of God." But Pharaoh's heart was hard and he would not listen, just as the LORD had said.

THE PLAGUE OF FLIES

20 Then the LORD said to Moses, "Get up early in the morning and confront Pharaoh as he goes to the river and say to him, 'This is what the LORD says: Let my people go, so that they may worship me. 21 If you do not let my people go, I will send swarms of flies on you and your officials, on your people and into your houses. The houses of the Egyptians will be full of flies; even the ground will be covered with them.

22 " 'But on that day I will deal differently with the land of Goshen, where my people live; no swarms of flies will be there, so that you will know that I, the LORD, am in this land. 23 I will make a distinction[a] between my people and your people. This sign will occur tomorrow.' "

24 And the LORD did this. Dense swarms of flies poured into Pharaoh's palace and into the houses of his officials; throughout Egypt the land was ruined by the flies.

25 Then Pharaoh summoned Moses and Aaron and said, "Go, sacrifice to your God here in the land."

26 But Moses said, "That would not be right. The sacrifices we offer the LORD our God would be detestable to the Egyptians. And if we offer sacrifices that are detestable in their eyes, will they not stone us? 27 We must take a three-day journey into the wilderness to offer sacrifices to the LORD our God, as he commands us."

28 Pharaoh said, "I will let you go to offer sacrifices to the LORD your God in the wilderness, but you must not go very far. Now pray for me."

29 Moses answered, "As soon as I leave you, I will pray to the LORD, and tomorrow the flies will leave Pharaoh and his officials and his

[a] 23 Septuagint and Vulgate; Hebrew *will put a deliverance*

people. Only let Pharaoh be sure that he does not act deceitfully again
by not letting the people go to offer sacrifices to the LORD."
[30]Then Moses left Pharaoh and prayed to the LORD, [31]and the LORD
did what Moses asked. The flies left Pharaoh and his officials and his
people; not a fly remained. [32]But this time also Pharaoh hardened his
heart and would not let the people go.

THE PLAGUE ON LIVESTOCK

9 Then the LORD said to Moses, "Go to Pharaoh and say to him, 'This
is what the LORD, the God of the Hebrews, says: "Let my people
go, so that they may worship me." [2]If you refuse to let them go and
continue to hold them back, [3]the hand of the LORD will bring a terrible
plague on your livestock in the field — on your horses, donkeys and
camels and on your cattle, sheep and goats. [4]But the LORD will make
a distinction between the livestock of Israel and that of Egypt, so that
no animal belonging to the Israelites will die.'"
[5]The LORD set a time and said, "Tomorrow the LORD will do this in
the land." [6]And the next day the LORD did it: All the livestock of the
Egyptians died, but not one animal belonging to the Israelites died.
[7]Pharaoh investigated and found that not even one of the animals of
the Israelites had died. Yet his heart was unyielding and he would not
let the people go.

THE PLAGUE OF BOILS

[8]Then the LORD said to Moses and Aaron, "Take handfuls of soot
from a furnace and have Moses toss it into the air in the presence of
Pharaoh. [9]It will become fine dust over the whole land of Egypt, and
festering boils will break out on people and animals throughout the
land."
[10]So they took soot from a furnace and stood before Pharaoh. Mo-
ses tossed it into the air, and festering boils broke out on people and
animals. [11]The magicians could not stand before Moses because of the
boils that were on them and on all the Egyptians. [12]But the LORD hard-
ened Pharaoh's heart and he would not listen to Moses and Aaron, just
as the LORD had said to Moses.

THE PLAGUE OF HAIL

[13]Then the LORD said to Moses, "Get up early in the morning, con
front Pharaoh and say to him, 'This is what the LORD, the God of the
Hebrews, says: Let my people go, so that they may worship me, [14]or this
time I will send the full force of my plagues against you and against
your officials and your people, so you may know that there is no one
like me in all the earth. [15]For by now I could have stretched out my
hand and struck you and your people with a plague that would have
wiped you off the earth. [16]But I have raised you up[a] for this very pur-
pose, that I might show you my power and that my name might be
proclaimed in all the earth. [17]You still set yourself against my people
and will not let them go. [18]Therefore, at this time tomorrow I will send
the worst hailstorm that has ever fallen on Egypt, from the day it was
founded till now. [19]Give an order now to bring your livestock and ev-
erything you have in the field to a place of shelter, because the hail will

PRAYING SCRIPTURE

Exodus 9

In the season of plagues, Pharaoh sometimes expressed sorrow over his sin until the consequences disappeared. But after the plague was over or God showed mercy, Pharaoh returned to his hard heart and disobedience. Moses, however, was not fooled by Pharaoh's act.

When you see people hardening their hearts toward God, pray that they will be turned to repentance so they can experience his mercy, forgiveness and grace.

[a] 16 Or *have spared you*

fall on every person and animal that has not been brought in and is
still out in the field, and they will die.'"
20 Those officials of Pharaoh who feared the word of the LORD hur-
ried to bring their slaves and their livestock inside. 21 But those who
ignored the word of the LORD left their slaves and livestock in the field.
22 Then the LORD said to Moses, "Stretch out your hand toward the
sky so that hail will fall all over Egypt — on people and animals and on
everything growing in the fields of Egypt." 23 When Moses stretched out
his staff toward the sky, the LORD sent thunder and hail, and lightning
flashed down to the ground. So the LORD rained hail on the land of
Egypt; 24 hail fell and lightning flashed back and forth. It was the worst
storm in all the land of Egypt since it had become a nation. 25 Through-
out Egypt hail struck everything in the fields — both people and ani-
mals; it beat down everything growing in the fields and stripped every
tree. 26 The only place it did not hail was the land of Goshen, where the
Israelites were.
27 Then Pharaoh summoned Moses and Aaron. "This time I have
sinned," he said to them. "The LORD is in the right, and I and my people
are in the wrong. 28 Pray to the LORD, for we have had enough thunder
and hail. I will let you go; you don't have to stay any longer."
29 Moses replied, "When I have gone out of the city, I will spread out
my hands in prayer to the LORD. The thunder will stop and there will
be no more hail, so you may know that the earth is the LORD's. 30 But I
know that you and your officials still do not fear the LORD God."
31 (The flax and barley were destroyed, since the barley had headed
and the flax was in bloom. 32 The wheat and spelt, however, were not
destroyed, because they ripen later.)
33 Then Moses left Pharaoh and went out of the city. He spread out
his hands toward the LORD; the thunder and hail stopped, and the rain
no longer poured down on the land. 34 When Pharaoh saw that the rain
and hail and thunder had stopped, he sinned again: He and his officials
hardened their hearts. 35 So Pharaoh's heart was hard and he would not
let the Israelites go, just as the LORD had said through Moses.

THE PLAGUE OF LOCUSTS

10 Then the LORD said to Moses, "Go to Pharaoh, for I have hard-
ened his heart and the hearts of his officials so that I may per-
form these signs of mine among them 2 that you may tell your children
and grandchildren how I dealt harshly with the Egyptians and how I
performed my signs among them, and that you may know that I am
the LORD."
3 So Moses and Aaron went to Pharaoh and said to him, "This is what
the LORD, the God of the Hebrews, says: 'How long will you refuse to
humble yourself before me? Let my people go, so that they may wor-
ship me. 4 If you refuse to let them go, I will bring locusts into your
country tomorrow. 5 They will cover the face of the ground so that it
cannot be seen. They will devour what little you have left after the hail,
including every tree that is growing in your fields. 6 They will fill your
houses and those of all your officials and all the Egyptians — something
neither your parents nor your ancestors have ever seen from the day
they settled in this land till now.'" Then Moses turned and left Pharaoh.
7 Pharaoh's officials said to him, "How long will this man be a snare
to us? Let the people go, so that they may worship the LORD their God.
Do you not yet realize that Egypt is ruined?"

PRAYING SCRIPTURE

Exodus 10

Time after time, God protected his people from the judgment happening around them in Egypt. Plagues that fell on Egypt were kept from Goshen; punishments that bombarded the Egyptians avoided God's people. God was willing and able to separate judgment from mercy.

If you belong to God, you never need fear when his judgment falls on others. He will sustain you; commit yourself to him and trust him completely.

8Then Moses and Aaron were brought back to Pharaoh. "Go, worship
the LORD your God," he said. "But tell me who will be going."
9Moses answered, "We will go with our young and our old, with our
sons and our daughters, and with our flocks and herds, because we are
to celebrate a festival to the LORD."
10Pharaoh said, "The LORD be with you — if I let you go, along with
your women and children! Clearly you are bent on evil.[a] 11No! Have
only the men go and worship the LORD, since that's what you have
been asking for." Then Moses and Aaron were driven out of Pharaoh's
presence.
12And the LORD said to Moses, "Stretch out your hand over Egypt so
that locusts swarm over the land and devour everything growing in
the fields, everything left by the hail."
13So Moses stretched out his staff over Egypt, and the LORD made
an east wind blow across the land all that day and all that night. By
morning the wind had brought the locusts; 14they invaded all Egypt
and settled down in every area of the country in great numbers. Never
before had there been such a plague of locusts, nor will there ever be
again. 15They covered all the ground until it was black. They devoured
all that was left after the hail — everything growing in the fields and
the fruit on the trees. Nothing green remained on tree or plant in all
the land of Egypt.
16Pharaoh quickly summoned Moses and Aaron and said, "I have
sinned against the LORD your God and against you. 17Now forgive my
sin once more and pray to the LORD your God to take this deadly plague
away from me."
18Moses then left Pharaoh and prayed to the LORD. 19And the LORD
changed the wind to a very strong west wind, which caught up the
locusts and carried them into the Red Sea.[b] Not a locust was left any-
where in Egypt. 20But the LORD hardened Pharaoh's heart, and he
would not let the Israelites go.

THE PLAGUE OF DARKNESS

21Then the LORD said to Moses, "Stretch out your hand toward the
sky so that darkness spreads over Egypt — darkness that can be felt."
22So Moses stretched out his hand toward the sky, and total darkness
covered all Egypt for three days. 23No one could see anyone else or
move about for three days. Yet all the Israelites had light in the places
where they lived.
24Then Pharaoh summoned Moses and said, "Go, worship the LORD.
Even your women and children may go with you; only leave your flocks
and herds behind."
25But Moses said, "You must allow us to have sacrifices and burnt
offerings to present to the LORD our God. 26Our livestock too must go
with us; not a hoof is to be left behind. We have to use some of them in
worshiping the LORD our God, and until we get there we will not know
what we are to use to worship the LORD."
27But the LORD hardened Pharaoh's heart, and he was not willing to let
them go. 28Pharaoh said to Moses, "Get out of my sight! Make sure you
do not appear before me again! The day you see my face you will die."
29"Just as you say," Moses replied. "I will never appear before you
again."

---

[a] 10 Or *Be careful, trouble is in store for you!* [b] 19 Or *the Sea of Reeds*

PRAYING SCRIPTURE

Exodus 11

Sin rarely affects just one person. The entirety of Egypt felt God's judgment on Pharaoh's sinful lack of repentance. Then God warned of a final, horrific plague that would take the life of every firstborn in Egypt.

Have you been tempted to believe that your sin would not affect other people? Like acid, sin is corrosive! Ask God now to deliver you from any temptation you will face today.

THE PLAGUE ON THE FIRSTBORN

11 Now the LORD had said to Moses, "I will bring one more plague
on Pharaoh and on Egypt. After that, he will let you go from here,
and when he does, he will drive you out completely. 2Tell the people
that men and women alike are to ask their neighbors for articles of
silver and gold." 3(The LORD made the Egyptians favorably disposed
toward the people, and Moses himself was highly regarded in Egypt
by Pharaoh's officials and by the people.)
4So Moses said, "This is what the LORD says: 'About midnight I will
go throughout Egypt. 5Every firstborn son in Egypt will die, from the
firstborn son of Pharaoh, who sits on the throne, to the firstborn son
of the female slave, who is at her hand mill, and all the firstborn of the
cattle as well. 6There will be loud wailing throughout Egypt—worse
than there has ever been or ever will be again. 7But among the Israel-
ites not a dog will bark at any person or animal.' Then you will know
that the LORD makes a distinction between Egypt and Israel. 8All these
officials of yours will come to me, bowing down before me and saying,
'Go, you and all the people who follow you!' After that I will leave."
Then Moses, hot with anger, left Pharaoh.
9The LORD had said to Moses, "Pharaoh will refuse to listen to you—
so that my wonders may be multiplied in Egypt." 10Moses and Aaron
performed all these wonders before Pharaoh, but the LORD hard-
ened Pharaoh's heart, and he would not let the Israelites go out of his
country.

PRAYING SCRIPTURE

Exodus 12

Few narratives in all the Bible hold more historic, symbolic and theological significance than the institution of the Passover. God rescued his people; God protected his people; God taught his people. The blood symbolized that of Jesus, the spotless Lamb who was to come, by which God would rescue all those who believe in him.

The Passover is a story of the hope of the Messiah's salvation to come. Ask God to strengthen your faith in his ability to take care of you.

THE PASSOVER AND THE FESTIVAL OF UNLEAVENED BREAD

12 The LORD said to Moses and Aaron in Egypt, 2"This month is to
be for you the first month, the first month of your year. 3Tell
the whole community of Israel that on the tenth day of this month
each man is to take a lamb[a] for his family, one for each household.
4If any household is too small for a whole lamb, they must share one
with their nearest neighbor, having taken into account the number of
people there are. You are to determine the amount of lamb needed in
accordance with what each person will eat. 5The animals you choose
must be year-old males without defect, and you may take them from
the sheep or the goats. 6Take care of them until the fourteenth day of
the month, when all the members of the community of Israel must
slaughter them at twilight. 7Then they are to take some of the blood
and put it on the sides and tops of the doorframes of the houses where
they eat the lambs. 8That same night they are to eat the meat roasted
over the fire, along with bitter herbs, and bread made without yeast.
9Do not eat the meat raw or boiled in water, but roast it over a fire—
with the head, legs and internal organs. 10Do not leave any of it till
morning; if some is left till morning, you must burn it. 11This is how
you are to eat it: with your cloak tucked into your belt, your sandals on
your feet and your staff in your hand. Eat it in haste; it is the LORD's
Passover.
12"On that same night I will pass through Egypt and strike down ev-
ery firstborn of both people and animals, and I will bring judgment on
all the gods of Egypt. I am the LORD. 13The blood will be a sign for you

[a] 3 The Hebrew word can mean *lamb* or *kid*; also in verse 4.

on the houses where you are, and when I see the blood, I will pass over you. No destructive plague will touch you when I strike Egypt.

14“This is a day you are to commemorate; for the generations to come you shall celebrate it as a festival to the LORD—a lasting ordinance. 15For seven days you are to eat bread made without yeast. On the first day remove the yeast from your houses, for whoever eats anything with yeast in it from the first day through the seventh must be cut off from Israel. 16On the first day hold a sacred assembly, and another one on the seventh day. Do no work at all on these days, except to prepare food for everyone to eat; that is all you may do.

17“Celebrate the Festival of Unleavened Bread, because it was on this very day that I brought your divisions out of Egypt. Celebrate this day as a lasting ordinance for the generations to come. 18In the first month you are to eat bread made without yeast, from the evening of the fourteenth day until the evening of the twenty-first day. 19For seven days no yeast is to be found in your houses. And anyone, whether foreigner or native-born, who eats anything with yeast in it must be cut off from the community of Israel. 20Eat nothing made with yeast. Wherever you live, you must eat unleavened bread.”

21Then Moses summoned all the elders of Israel and said to them, “Go at once and select the animals for your families and slaughter the Passover lamb. 22Take a bunch of hyssop, dip it into the blood in the basin and put some of the blood on the top and on both sides of the doorframe. None of you shall go out of the door of your house until morning. 23When the LORD goes through the land to strike down the Egyptians, he will see the blood on the top and sides of the doorframe and will pass over that doorway, and he will not permit the destroyer to enter your houses and strike you down.

24“Obey these instructions as a lasting ordinance for you and your descendants. 25When you enter the land that the LORD will give you as he promised, observe this ceremony. 26And when your children ask you, ‘What does this ceremony mean to you?’ 27then tell them, ‘It is the Passover sacrifice to the LORD, who passed over the houses of the Israelites in Egypt and spared our homes when he struck down the Egyptians.’” Then the people bowed down and worshiped. 28The Israelites did just what the LORD commanded Moses and Aaron.

29At midnight the LORD struck down all the firstborn in Egypt, from the firstborn of Pharaoh, who sat on the throne, to the firstborn of the prisoner, who was in the dungeon, and the firstborn of all the livestock as well. 30Pharaoh and all his officials and all the Egyptians got up during the night, and there was loud wailing in Egypt, for there was not a house without someone dead.

THE EXODUS

31During the night Pharaoh summoned Moses and Aaron and said, “Up! Leave my people, you and the Israelites! Go, worship the LORD as you have requested. 32Take your flocks and herds, as you have said, and go. And also bless me.”

33The Egyptians urged the people to hurry and leave the country. “For otherwise,” they said, “we will all die!” 34So the people took their dough before the yeast was added, and carried it on their shoulders in kneading troughs wrapped in clothing. 35The Israelites did as Moses instructed and asked the Egyptians for articles of silver and gold and for clothing. 36The LORD had made the Egyptians favorably disposed toward the people, and they gave them what they asked for; so they plundered the Egyptians.

37 The Israelites journeyed from Rameses to Sukkoth. There were about six hundred thousand men on foot, besides women and children. 38 Many other people went up with them, and also large droves of livestock, both flocks and herds. 39 With the dough the Israelites had brought from Egypt, they baked loaves of unleavened bread. The dough was without yeast because they had been driven out of Egypt and did not have time to prepare food for themselves.

40 Now the length of time the Israelite people lived in Egypt[a] was 430 years. 41 At the end of the 430 years, to the very day, all the LORD's divisions left Egypt. 42 Because the LORD kept vigil that night to bring them out of Egypt, on this night all the Israelites are to keep vigil to honor the LORD for the generations to come.

PASSOVER RESTRICTIONS

43 The LORD said to Moses and Aaron, "These are the regulations for the Passover meal:

"No foreigner may eat it. 44 Any slave you have bought may eat it after you have circumcised him, 45 but a temporary resident or a hired worker may not eat it.

46 "It must be eaten inside the house; take none of the meat outside the house. Do not break any of the bones. 47 The whole community of Israel must celebrate it.

48 "A foreigner residing among you who wants to celebrate the LORD's Passover must have all the males in his household circumcised; then he may take part like one born in the land. No uncircumcised male may eat it. 49 The same law applies both to the native-born and to the foreigner residing among you."

50 All the Israelites did just what the LORD had commanded Moses and Aaron. 51 And on that very day the LORD brought the Israelites out of Egypt by their divisions.

CONSECRATION OF THE FIRSTBORN

13 The LORD said to Moses, 2 "Consecrate to me every firstborn male. The first offspring of every womb among the Israelites belongs to me, whether human or animal."

3 Then Moses said to the people, "Commemorate this day, the day you came out of Egypt, out of the land of slavery, because the LORD brought you out of it with a mighty hand. Eat nothing containing yeast. 4 Today, in the month of Aviv, you are leaving. 5 When the LORD brings you into the land of the Canaanites, Hittites, Amorites, Hivites and Jebusites — the land he swore to your ancestors to give you, a land flowing with milk and honey — you are to observe this ceremony in this month: 6 For seven days eat bread made without yeast and on the seventh day hold a festival to the LORD. 7 Eat unleavened bread during those seven days; nothing with yeast in it is to be seen among you, nor shall any yeast be seen anywhere within your borders. 8 On that day tell your son, 'I do this because of what the LORD did for me when I came out of Egypt.' 9 This observance will be for you like a sign on your hand and a reminder on your forehead that this law of the LORD is to be on

PRAYING SCRIPTURE

Exodus 13

Memory is a powerful thing. When memories are connected to meaning, we have the experience of going beyond the memory itself to a transcendent truth. God intended for the Israelites to celebrate the Festival of Unleavened Bread regularly so they would remember how he delivered them from Egypt.

Do you have any memories that are connected to God's working in your life? Thank God for the memories that encourage you to keep serving him.

[a] *40* Masoretic Text; Samaritan Pentateuch and Septuagint *Egypt and Canaan*

your lips. For the LORD brought you out of Egypt with his mighty hand.
10You must keep this ordinance at the appointed time year after year.
11"After the LORD brings you into the land of the Canaanites and
gives it to you, as he promised on oath to you and your ancestors, 12you
are to give over to the LORD the first offspring of every womb. All the
firstborn males of your livestock belong to the LORD. 13Redeem with
a lamb every firstborn donkey, but if you do not redeem it, break its
neck. Redeem every firstborn among your sons.
14"In days to come, when your son asks you, 'What does this mean?'
say to him, 'With a mighty hand the LORD brought us out of Egypt, out
of the land of slavery. 15When Pharaoh stubbornly refused to let us go,
the LORD killed the firstborn of both people and animals in Egypt. This
is why I sacrifice to the LORD the first male offspring of every womb
and redeem each of my firstborn sons.' 16And it will be like a sign on
your hand and a symbol on your forehead that the LORD brought us
out of Egypt with his mighty hand."

CROSSING THE SEA

17When Pharaoh let the people go, God did not lead them on the road
through the Philistine country, though that was shorter. For God said,
"If they face war, they might change their minds and return to Egypt."
18So God led the people around by the desert road toward the Red Sea.[a]
The Israelites went up out of Egypt ready for battle.
19Moses took the bones of Joseph with him because Joseph had
made the Israelites swear an oath. He had said, "God will surely come
to your aid, and then you must carry my bones up with you from this
place."[b]
20After leaving Sukkoth they camped at Etham on the edge of the
desert. 21By day the LORD went ahead of them in a pillar of cloud to
guide them on their way and by night in a pillar of fire to give them
light, so that they could travel by day or night. 22Neither the pillar of
cloud by day nor the pillar of fire by night left its place in front of the
people.

14 Then the LORD said to Moses, 2"Tell the Israelites to turn back
and encamp near Pi Hahiroth, between Migdol and the sea.
They are to encamp by the sea, directly opposite Baal Zephon. 3Phar-
aoh will think, 'The Israelites are wandering around the land in confu-
sion, hemmed in by the desert.' 4And I will harden Pharaoh's heart, and
he will pursue them. But I will gain glory for myself through Pharaoh
and all his army, and the Egyptians will know that I am the LORD." So
the Israelites did this.
5When the king of Egypt was told that the people had fled, Pharaoh
and his officials changed their minds about them and said, "What have
we done? We have let the Israelites go and have lost their services!" 6So
he had his chariot made ready and took his army with him. 7He took
six hundred of the best chariots, along with all the other chariots of
Egypt, with officers over all of them. 8The LORD hardened the heart
of Pharaoh king of Egypt, so that he pursued the Israelites, who were
marching out boldly. 9The Egyptians — all Pharaoh's horses and chari-
ots, horsemen[c] and troops — pursued the Israelites and overtook them
as they camped by the sea near Pi Hahiroth, opposite Baal Zephon.

PRAYING SCRIPTURE

Exodus 14

Finally freed from enslavement to Pharaoh, the children of Israel were stuck between his army and the sea. To go forward was to die; to go back was unthinkable. But God was not caught off guard. Moses challenged the people, "Do not be afraid. Stand firm and you will see the deliverance the LORD will bring you today" (verse 13).

Often the way forward is to wait. Pray for patience as you watch for God's deliverance. Trust his timing and his purposes.

---

[a] 18 Or *the Sea of Reeds* [b] 19 See Gen. 50:25. [c] 9 Or *charioteers*; also in verses 17, 18, 23, 26 and 28

10 As Pharaoh approached, the Israelites looked up, and there were
the Egyptians, marching after them. They were terrified and cried out
to the LORD. 11 They said to Moses, "Was it because there were no graves
in Egypt that you brought us to the desert to die? What have you done
to us by bringing us out of Egypt? 12 Didn't we say to you in Egypt,
'Leave us alone; let us serve the Egyptians'? It would have been better
for us to serve the Egyptians than to die in the desert!"

13 Moses answered the people, "Do not be afraid. Stand firm and you
will see the deliverance the LORD will bring you today. The Egyptians
you see today you will never see again. 14 The LORD will fight for you;
you need only to be still."

15 Then the LORD said to Moses, "Why are you crying out to me? Tell
the Israelites to move on. 16 Raise your staff and stretch out your hand
over the sea to divide the water so that the Israelites can go through
the sea on dry ground. 17 I will harden the hearts of the Egyptians so
that they will go in after them. And I will gain glory through Pharaoh
and all his army, through his chariots and his horsemen. 18 The Egyp-
tians will know that I am the LORD when I gain glory through Pharaoh,
his chariots and his horsemen."

19 Then the angel of God, who had been traveling in front of Israel's
army, withdrew and went behind them. The pillar of cloud also moved
from in front and stood behind them, 20 coming between the armies
of Egypt and Israel. Throughout the night the cloud brought darkness
to the one side and light to the other side; so neither went near the
other all night long.

21 Then Moses stretched out his hand over the sea, and all that night
the LORD drove the sea back with a strong east wind and turned it into
dry land. The waters were divided, 22 and the Israelites went through
the sea on dry ground, with a wall of water on their right and on their
left.

23 The Egyptians pursued them, and all Pharaoh's horses and chariots
and horsemen followed them into the sea. 24 During the last watch of
the night the LORD looked down from the pillar of fire and cloud at the
Egyptian army and threw it into confusion. 25 He jammed[a] the wheels
of their chariots so that they had difficulty driving. And the Egyptians
said, "Let's get away from the Israelites! The LORD is fighting for them
against Egypt."

26 Then the LORD said to Moses, "Stretch out your hand over the sea
so that the waters may flow back over the Egyptians and their chari-
ots and horsemen." 27 Moses stretched out his hand over the sea, and
at daybreak the sea went back to its place. The Egyptians were fleeing
toward[b] it, and the LORD swept them into the sea. 28 The water flowed
back and covered the chariots and horsemen—the entire army of
Pharaoh that had followed the Israelites into the sea. Not one of them
survived.

29 But the Israelites went through the sea on dry ground, with a wall
of water on their right and on their left. 30 That day the LORD saved Is-
rael from the hands of the Egyptians, and Israel saw the Egyptians ly-
ing dead on the shore. 31 And when the Israelites saw the mighty hand
of the LORD displayed against the Egyptians, the people feared the
LORD and put their trust in him and in Moses his servant.

---

[a] *25* See Samaritan Pentateuch, Septuagint and Syriac; Masoretic Text *removed* [b] *27* Or *from*

THE SONG OF MOSES AND MIRIAM

15 Then Moses and the Israelites sang this song to the LORD:

"I will sing to the LORD,
for he is highly exalted.
Both horse and driver
he has hurled into the sea.

2 "The LORD is my strength and my defense[a];
he has become my salvation.
He is my God, and I will praise him,
my father's God, and I will exalt him.
3 The LORD is a warrior;
the LORD is his name.
4 Pharaoh's chariots and his army
he has hurled into the sea.
The best of Pharaoh's officers
are drowned in the Red Sea.[b]
5 The deep waters have covered them;
they sank to the depths like a stone.
6 Your right hand, LORD,
was majestic in power.
Your right hand, LORD,
shattered the enemy.

7 "In the greatness of your majesty
you threw down those who opposed you.
You unleashed your burning anger;
it consumed them like stubble.
8 By the blast of your nostrils
the waters piled up.
The surging waters stood up like a wall;
the deep waters congealed in the heart of the sea.
9 The enemy boasted,
'I will pursue, I will overtake them.
I will divide the spoils;
I will gorge myself on them.
I will draw my sword
and my hand will destroy them.'
10 But you blew with your breath,
and the sea covered them.
They sank like lead
in the mighty waters.
11 Who among the gods
is like you, LORD?
Who is like you—
majestic in holiness,
awesome in glory,
working wonders?

12 "You stretch out your right hand,
and the earth swallows your enemies.
13 In your unfailing love you will lead
the people you have redeemed.

[a] 2 Or *song* [b] 4 Or *the Sea of Reeds*; also in verse 22

PRAYING SCRIPTURE

Exodus 15

God's deliverance from Pharaoh was so profound that Moses and the people burst into a song of praise. The song vividly describes their experience of watching the Egyptian army be swept away by the waters of the Red Sea. They knew when the story of God's salvation swept through the nations, the peoples would fear the God of Israel (see verses 14–16).

The song ends with a declaration: "The LORD reigns for ever and ever" (verse 18). Join Moses in praising the Lord.

In your strength you will guide them
to your holy dwelling.
14 The nations will hear and tremble;
anguish will grip the people of Philistia.
15 The chiefs of Edom will be terrified,
the leaders of Moab will be seized with trembling,
the people[a] of Canaan will melt away;
16 terror and dread will fall on them.
By the power of your arm
they will be as still as a stone —
until your people pass by, LORD,
until the people you bought[b] pass by.
17 You will bring them in and plant them
on the mountain of your inheritance —
the place, LORD, you made for your dwelling,
the sanctuary, Lord, your hands established.

18 "The LORD reigns
for ever and ever."

19 When Pharaoh's horses, chariots and horsemen[c] went into the sea,
the LORD brought the waters of the sea back over them, but the Israel-
ites walked through the sea on dry ground. 20 Then Miriam the prophet,
Aaron's sister, took a timbrel in her hand, and all the women followed
her, with timbrels and dancing. 21 Miriam sang to them:

"Sing to the LORD,
for he is highly exalted.
Both horse and driver
he has hurled into the sea."

THE WATERS OF MARAH AND ELIM

22 Then Moses led Israel from the Red Sea and they went into the
Desert of Shur. For three days they traveled in the desert without find-
ing water. 23 When they came to Marah, they could not drink its water
because it was bitter. (That is why the place is called Marah.[d]) 24 So the
people grumbled against Moses, saying, "What are we to drink?"
25 Then Moses cried out to the LORD, and the LORD showed him a
piece of wood. He threw it into the water, and the water became fit to
drink.

There the LORD issued a ruling and instruction for them and put
them to the test. 26 He said, "If you listen carefully to the LORD your God
and do what is right in his eyes, if you pay attention to his commands
and keep all his decrees, I will not bring on you any of the diseases I
brought on the Egyptians, for I am the LORD, who heals you."
27 Then they came to Elim, where there were twelve springs and sev-
enty palm trees, and they camped there near the water.

MANNA AND QUAIL

16 The whole Israelite community set out from Elim and came to
the Desert of Sin, which is between Elim and Sinai, on the fif-
teenth day of the second month after they had come out of Egypt. 2 In

PRAYING SCRIPTURE

Exodus 16

Have you ever doubted the Lord's ability to provide for you? When we focus on our circumstances, things can look hopeless. God provided Israel with food daily. For 40 years he provided them the bread of heaven: manna. All they had to do was gather it.

Have you praised God lately for your food, shelter and clothing? Make a list of blessings, and then set aside some time to honor God for it.

---

[a] 15 Or *rulers* [b] 16 Or *created* [c] 19 Or *charioteers* [d] 23 *Marah* means *bitter.*

the desert the whole community grumbled against Moses and Aaron.
3The Israelites said to them, "If only we had died by the LORD's hand
in Egypt! There we sat around pots of meat and ate all the food we
wanted, but you have brought us out into this desert to starve this en-
tire assembly to death."
4Then the LORD said to Moses, "I will rain down bread from heaven
for you. The people are to go out each day and gather enough for that
day. In this way I will test them and see whether they will follow my
instructions. 5On the sixth day they are to prepare what they bring in,
and that is to be twice as much as they gather on the other days."
6So Moses and Aaron said to all the Israelites, "In the evening you
will know that it was the LORD who brought you out of Egypt, 7and in
the morning you will see the glory of the LORD, because he has heard
your grumbling against him. Who are we, that you should grumble
against us?" 8Moses also said, "You will know that it was the LORD
when he gives you meat to eat in the evening and all the bread you
want in the morning, because he has heard your grumbling against
him. Who are we? You are not grumbling against us, but against the
LORD."
9Then Moses told Aaron, "Say to the entire Israelite community,
'Come before the LORD, for he has heard your grumbling.'"
10While Aaron was speaking to the whole Israelite community, they
looked toward the desert, and there was the glory of the LORD appear-
ing in the cloud.
11The LORD said to Moses, 12"I have heard the grumbling of the Is-
raelites. Tell them, 'At twilight you will eat meat, and in the morning
you will be filled with bread. Then you will know that I am the LORD
your God.'"
13That evening quail came and covered the camp, and in the morn-
ing there was a layer of dew around the camp. 14When the dew was
gone, thin flakes like frost on the ground appeared on the desert floor.
15When the Israelites saw it, they said to each other, "What is it?" For
they did not know what it was.
Moses said to them, "It is the bread the LORD has given you to eat.
16This is what the LORD has commanded: 'Everyone is to gather as
much as they need. Take an omer[a] for each person you have in your
tent.'"
17The Israelites did as they were told; some gathered much, some
little. 18And when they measured it by the omer, the one who gathered
much did not have too much, and the one who gathered little did not
have too little. Everyone had gathered just as much as they needed.
19Then Moses said to them, "No one is to keep any of it until
morning."
20However, some of them paid no attention to Moses; they kept part
of it until morning, but it was full of maggots and began to smell. So
Moses was angry with them.
21Each morning everyone gathered as much as they needed, and
when the sun grew hot, it melted away. 22On the sixth day, they gath-
ered twice as much — two omers[b] for each person — and the lead-
ers of the community came and reported this to Moses. 23He said to
them, "This is what the LORD commanded: 'Tomorrow is to be a day

[a] *16* That is, possibly about 3 pounds or about 1.4 kilograms; also in verses 18, 32, 33 and 36 [b] *22* That is, possibly about 6 pounds or about 2.8 kilograms

of sabbath rest, a holy sabbath to the LORD. So bake what you want to
bake and boil what you want to boil. Save whatever is left and keep it
until morning.' "
24 So they saved it until morning, as Moses commanded, and it did
not stink or get maggots in it. 25 "Eat it today," Moses said, "because to-
day is a sabbath to the LORD. You will not find any of it on the ground
today. 26 Six days you are to gather it, but on the seventh day, the Sab-
bath, there will not be any."
27 Nevertheless, some of the people went out on the seventh day to
gather it, but they found none. 28 Then the LORD said to Moses, "How
long will you[a] refuse to keep my commands and my instructions?
29 Bear in mind that the LORD has given you the Sabbath; that is why
on the sixth day he gives you bread for two days. Everyone is to stay
where they are on the seventh day; no one is to go out." 30 So the people
rested on the seventh day.
31 The people of Israel called the bread manna.[b] It was white like cori-
ander seed and tasted like wafers made with honey. 32 Moses said, "This
is what the LORD has commanded: 'Take an omer of manna and keep
it for the generations to come, so they can see the bread I gave you to
eat in the wilderness when I brought you out of Egypt.' "
33 So Moses said to Aaron, "Take a jar and put an omer of manna in it.
Then place it before the LORD to be kept for the generations to come."
34 As the LORD commanded Moses, Aaron put the manna with the
tablets of the covenant law, so that it might be preserved. 35 The Israel-
ites ate manna forty years, until they came to a land that was settled;
they ate manna until they reached the border of Canaan.
36 (An omer is one-tenth of an ephah.)

WATER FROM THE ROCK

17 The whole Israelite community set out from the Desert of Sin,
traveling from place to place as the LORD commanded. They
camped at Rephidim, but there was no water for the people to drink.
2 So they quarreled with Moses and said, "Give us water to drink."
Moses replied, "Why do you quarrel with me? Why do you put the
LORD to the test?"
3 But the people were thirsty for water there, and they grumbled
against Moses. They said, "Why did you bring us up out of Egypt to
make us and our children and livestock die of thirst?"
4 Then Moses cried out to the LORD, "What am I to do with these peo-
ple? They are almost ready to stone me."
5 The LORD answered Moses, "Go out in front of the people. Take with
you some of the elders of Israel and take in your hand the staff with
which you struck the Nile, and go. 6 I will stand there before you by the
rock at Horeb. Strike the rock, and water will come out of it for the people
to drink." So Moses did this in the sight of the elders of Israel. 7 And he
called the place Massah[c] and Meribah[d] because the Israelites quarreled
and because they tested the LORD saying, "Is the LORD among us or not?"

THE AMALEKITES DEFEATED

8 The Amalekites came and attacked the Israelites at Rephidim. 9 Mo-
ses said to Joshua, "Choose some of our men and go out to fight the

PRAYING SCRIPTURE

Exodus 17

The Israelites continually forgot all that God had done to redeem them from Egypt and sustain them in the wilderness. They elevated complaining to an art form. Did they really think God had provided food every day to allow them to die of thirst?

Have you ever had people around you who so lacked faith that they frustrated you? Ask God to handle complainers so you can focus on his grace to you.

[a] 28 The Hebrew is plural. [b] 31 *Manna* sounds like the Hebrew for *What is it?* (see verse 15). [c] 7 *Massah* means *testing.* [d] 7 *Meribah* means *quarreling.*

Amalekites. Tomorrow I will stand on top of the hill with the staff of
God in my hands."
10So Joshua fought the Amalekites as Moses had ordered, and Moses,
Aaron and Hur went to the top of the hill. 11As long as Moses held up
his hands, the Israelites were winning, but whenever he lowered his
hands, the Amalekites were winning. 12When Moses' hands grew tired,
they took a stone and put it under him and he sat on it. Aaron and Hur
held his hands up — one on one side, one on the other — so that his
hands remained steady till sunset. 13So Joshua overcame the Amalek-
ite army with the sword.
14Then the LORD said to Moses, "Write this on a scroll as something
to be remembered and make sure that Joshua hears it, because I will
completely blot out the name of Amalek from under heaven."
15Moses built an altar and called it The LORD is my Banner. 16He
said, "Because hands were lifted up against[a] the throne of the LORD,[b]
the LORD will be at war against the Amalekites from generation to
generation."

JETHRO VISITS MOSES

18 Now Jethro, the priest of Midian and father-in-law of Moses,
heard of everything God had done for Moses and for his people
Israel, and how the LORD had brought Israel out of Egypt.
2After Moses had sent away his wife Zipporah, his father-in-law Jeth-
ro received her 3and her two sons. One son was named Gershom,[c] for
Moses said, "I have become a foreigner in a foreign land"; 4and the
other was named Eliezer,[d] for he said, "My father's God was my helper;
he saved me from the sword of Pharaoh."
5Jethro, Moses' father-in-law, together with Moses' sons and wife,
came to him in the wilderness, where he was camped near the moun-
tain of God. 6Jethro had sent word to him, "I, your father-in-law Jethro,
am coming to you with your wife and her two sons."
7So Moses went out to meet his father-in-law and bowed down and
kissed him. They greeted each other and then went into the tent. 8Mo-
ses told his father-in-law about everything the LORD had done to Phar-
aoh and the Egyptians for Israel's sake and about all the hardships they
had met along the way and how the LORD had saved them.
9Jethro was delighted to hear about all the good things the LORD
had done for Israel in rescuing them from the hand of the Egyptians.
10He said, "Praise be to the LORD, who rescued you from the hand of
the Egyptians and of Pharaoh, and who rescued the people from the
hand of the Egyptians. 11Now I know that the LORD is greater than all
other gods, for he did this to those who had treated Israel arrogantly."
12Then Jethro, Moses' father-in-law, brought a burnt offering and other
sacrifices to God, and Aaron came with all the elders of Israel to eat a
meal with Moses' father-in-law in the presence of God.
13The next day Moses took his seat to serve as judge for the people,
and they stood around him from morning till evening. 14When his
father-in-law saw all that Moses was doing for the people, he said, "What
is this you are doing for the people? Why do you alone sit as judge, while
all these people stand around you from morning till evening?"

PRAYING SCRIPTURE

Exodus 18

Moses was working himself to death dispensing advice to the people. His father-in-law noticed his heavy load and encouraged Moses to share the burden. The advice Jethro gave was accompanied by an assurance of God's presence.

When someone offers you unsolicited advice, what is your response? Ask God to help you be sensitive and ready when he chooses to guide you through the words of others.

[a] *16* Or *to* [b] *16* The meaning of the Hebrew for this clause is uncertain.
[c] *3* *Gershom* sounds like the Hebrew for *a foreigner there.* [d] *4* *Eliezer* means *my God is helper.*

15Moses answered him, "Because the people come to me to seek
God's will. 16Whenever they have a dispute, it is brought to me, and
I decide between the parties and inform them of God's decrees and
instructions."
17Moses' father-in-law replied, "What you are doing is not good. 18You
and these people who come to you will only wear yourselves out. The
work is too heavy for you; you cannot handle it alone. 19Listen now
to me and I will give you some advice, and may God be with you. You
must be the people's representative before God and bring their dis-
putes to him. 20Teach them his decrees and instructions, and show
them the way they are to live and how they are to behave. 21But se-
lect capable men from all the people — men who fear God, trustwor-
thy men who hate dishonest gain — and appoint them as officials over
thousands, hundreds, fifties and tens. 22Have them serve as judges for
the people at all times, but have them bring every difficult case to you;
the simple cases they can decide themselves. That will make your load
lighter, because they will share it with you. 23If you do this and God so
commands, you will be able to stand the strain, and all these people
will go home satisfied."
24Moses listened to his father-in-law and did everything he said. 25He
chose capable men from all Israel and made them leaders of the peo-
ple, officials over thousands, hundreds, fifties and tens. 26They served
as judges for the people at all times. The difficult cases they brought to
Moses, but the simple ones they decided themselves.
27Then Moses sent his father-in-law on his way, and Jethro returned
to his own country.

AT MOUNT SINAI

19 On the first day of the third month after the Israelites left
Egypt — on that very day — they came to the Desert of Sinai.
2After they set out from Rephidim, they entered the Desert of Sinai,
and Israel camped there in the desert in front of the mountain.
3Then Moses went up to God, and the LORD called to him from the
mountain and said, "This is what you are to say to the descendants of
Jacob and what you are to tell the people of Israel: 4'You yourselves
have seen what I did to Egypt, and how I carried you on eagles' wings
and brought you to myself. 5Now if you obey me fully and keep my
covenant, then out of all nations you will be my treasured possession.
Although the whole earth is mine, 6you[a] will be for me a kingdom of
priests and a holy nation.' These are the words you are to speak to the
Israelites."
7So Moses went back and summoned the elders of the people and
set before them all the words the LORD had commanded him to speak.
8The people all responded together, "We will do everything the LORD
has said." So Moses brought their answer back to the LORD.
9The LORD said to Moses, "I am going to come to you in a dense
cloud, so that the people will hear me speaking with you and will al-
ways put their trust in you." Then Moses told the LORD what the people
had said.
10And the LORD said to Moses, "Go to the people and consecrate them
today and tomorrow. Have them wash their clothes 11and be ready by
the third day, because on that day the LORD will come down on Mount

[a] 5,6 Or *possession, for the whole earth is mine.* 6*You*

PRAYING SCRIPTURE

Exodus 19

Few moments in the Bible are more powerful than when the children of Israel arrived at Mount Sinai. God's intention was to set them apart as a people unique among all peoples on earth. They were to be a holy nation, dedicated to him alone.

Think about what it means to be committed to God. Is there anything in your life that has divided your attention? If so, reconsecrate yourself to him now.

Sinai in the sight of all the people. 12Put limits for the people around
the mountain and tell them, 'Be careful that you do not approach the
mountain or touch the foot of it. Whoever touches the mountain is
to be put to death. 13They are to be stoned or shot with arrows; not a
hand is to be laid on them. No person or animal shall be permitted to
live.' Only when the ram's horn sounds a long blast may they approach
the mountain."
14After Moses had gone down the mountain to the people, he con-
secrated them, and they washed their clothes. 15Then he said to the
people, "Prepare yourselves for the third day. Abstain from sexual
relations."
16On the morning of the third day there was thunder and lightning,
with a thick cloud over the mountain, and a very loud trumpet blast.
Everyone in the camp trembled. 17Then Moses led the people out of the
camp to meet with God, and they stood at the foot of the mountain.
18Mount Sinai was covered with smoke, because the LORD descended
on it in fire. The smoke billowed up from it like smoke from a furnace,
and the whole mountain[a] trembled violently. 19As the sound of the
trumpet grew louder and louder, Moses spoke and the voice of God
answered him.[b]
20The LORD descended to the top of Mount Sinai and called Moses to
the top of the mountain. So Moses went up 21and the LORD said to him,
"Go down and warn the people so they do not force their way through
to see the LORD and many of them perish. 22Even the priests, who ap-
proach the LORD, must consecrate themselves, or the LORD will break
out against them."
23Moses said to the LORD, "The people cannot come up Mount Sinai,
because you yourself warned us, 'Put limits around the mountain and
set it apart as holy.'"
24The LORD replied, "Go down and bring Aaron up with you. But the
priests and the people must not force their way through to come up to
the LORD, or he will break out against them."
25So Moses went down to the people and told them.

THE TEN COMMANDMENTS

20 And God spoke all these words:

2"I am the LORD your God, who brought you out of Egypt, out
of the land of slavery.
3"You shall have no other gods before[c] me.
4"You shall not make for yourself an image in the form of anything
in heaven above or on the earth beneath or in the waters be-
low. 5You shall not bow down to them or worship them; for I,
the LORD your God, am a jealous God, punishing the children
for the sin of the parents to the third and fourth generation
of those who hate me, 6but showing love to a thousand gen-
erations of those who love me and keep my commandments.
7"You shall not misuse the name of the LORD your God, for the LORD
will not hold anyone guiltless who misuses his name.
8"Remember the Sabbath day by keeping it holy. 9Six days you shall

[a] 18 Most Hebrew manuscripts; a few Hebrew manuscripts and Septuagint *and all the people* [b] 19 Or *and God answered him with thunder* [c] 3 Or *besides*

PRAYING SCRIPTURE

Exodus 20

As the Lord continued leading Israel through Moses, he provided them with the guidelines they needed to follow as his people. The law would distinguish them from the nations around them, uniquely qualifying them as his own. The most prominent of these were the Ten Commandments, which endure as the foundation of legal systems today.

Pray through verses 1–17. Confess any recent violations of God's commandments whether outwardly or inwardly.

labor and do all your work, 10but the seventh day is a sabbath
to the LORD your God. On it you shall not do any work, nei-
ther you, nor your son or daughter, nor your male or female
servant, nor your animals, nor any foreigner residing in your
towns. 11For in six days the LORD made the heavens and the
earth, the sea, and all that is in them, but he rested on the
seventh day. Therefore the LORD blessed the Sabbath day and
made it holy.
12"Honor your father and your mother, so that you may live long in
the land the LORD your God is giving you.
13"You shall not murder.
14"You shall not commit adultery.
15"You shall not steal.
16"You shall not give false testimony against your neighbor.
17"You shall not covet your neighbor's house. You shall not covet
your neighbor's wife, or his male or female servant, his ox or
donkey, or anything that belongs to your neighbor."

18When the people saw the thunder and lightning and heard the
trumpet and saw the mountain in smoke, they trembled with fear.
They stayed at a distance 19and said to Moses, "Speak to us yourself
and we will listen. But do not have God speak to us or we will die."
20Moses said to the people, "Do not be afraid. God has come to test
you, so that the fear of God will be with you to keep you from sinning."
21The people remained at a distance, while Moses approached the
thick darkness where God was.

IDOLS AND ALTARS

22Then the LORD said to Moses, "Tell the Israelites this: 'You have
seen for yourselves that I have spoken to you from heaven: 23Do not
make any gods to be alongside me; do not make for yourselves gods
of silver or gods of gold.
24" 'Make an altar of earth for me and sacrifice on it your burnt of-
ferings and fellowship offerings, your sheep and goats and your cat-
tle. Wherever I cause my name to be honored, I will come to you and
bless you. 25If you make an altar of stones for me, do not build it with
dressed stones, for you will defile it if you use a tool on it. 26And do
not go up to my altar on steps, or your private parts may be exposed.'

21

"These are the laws you are to set before them:

HEBREW SERVANTS

2"If you buy a Hebrew servant, he is to serve you for six years. But
in the seventh year, he shall go free, without paying anything. 3If he
comes alone, he is to go free alone; but if he has a wife when he comes,
she is to go with him. 4If his master gives him a wife and she bears him
sons or daughters, the woman and her children shall belong to her
master, and only the man shall go free.
5"But if the servant declares, 'I love my master and my wife and
children and do not want to go free,' 6then his master must take him
before the judges.[a] He shall take him to the door or the doorpost and
pierce his ear with an awl. Then he will be his servant for life.

PRAYING SCRIPTURE

Exodus 21

The laws God instituted for Israel had many provisions about human life. It's easy to see that God expected the Israelites to respect the dignity of human life because humans are made in God's image.

Do you value every person as created in God's image, having dignity and worth? Ask him to help you see all people as he sees them.

[a] 6 Or *before God*

7“If a man sells his daughter as a servant, she is not to go free as male servants do. 8If she does not please the master who has selected her for himself,[a] he must let her be redeemed. He has no right to sell her to foreigners, because he has broken faith with her. 9If he selects her for his son, he must grant her the rights of a daughter. 10If he marries another woman, he must not deprive the first one of her food, clothing and marital rights. 11If he does not provide her with these three things, she is to go free, without any payment of money.

PERSONAL INJURIES

12“Anyone who strikes a person with a fatal blow is to be put to death. 13However, if it is not done intentionally, but God lets it happen, they are to flee to a place I will designate. 14But if anyone schemes and kills someone deliberately, that person is to be taken from my altar and put to death.

15“Anyone who attacks[b] their father or mother is to be put to death.

16“Anyone who kidnaps someone is to be put to death, whether the victim has been sold or is still in the kidnapper’s possession.

17“Anyone who curses their father or mother is to be put to death.

18“If people quarrel and one person hits another with a stone or with their fist[c] and the victim does not die but is confined to bed, 19the one who struck the blow will not be held liable if the other can get up and walk around outside with a staff; however, the guilty party must pay the injured person for any loss of time and see that the victim is completely healed.

20“Anyone who beats their male or female slave with a rod must be punished if the slave dies as a direct result, 21but they are not to be punished if the slave recovers after a day or two, since the slave is their property.

22“If people are fighting and hit a pregnant woman and she gives birth prematurely[d] but there is no serious injury, the offender must be fined whatever the woman’s husband demands and the court allows. 23But if there is serious injury, you are to take life for life, 24eye for eye, tooth for tooth, hand for hand, foot for foot, 25burn for burn, wound for wound, bruise for bruise.

26“An owner who hits a male or female slave in the eye and destroys it must let the slave go free to compensate for the eye. 27And an owner who knocks out the tooth of a male or female slave must let the slave go free to compensate for the tooth.

28“If a bull gores a man or woman to death, the bull is to be stoned to death, and its meat must not be eaten. But the owner of the bull will not be held responsible. 29If, however, the bull has had the habit of goring and the owner has been warned but has not kept it penned up and it kills a man or woman, the bull is to be stoned and its owner also is to be put to death. 30However, if payment is demanded, the owner may redeem his life by the payment of whatever is demanded. 31This law also applies if the bull gores a son or daughter. 32If the bull gores a male or female slave, the owner must pay thirty shekels[e] of silver to the master of the slave, and the bull is to be stoned to death.

33“If anyone uncovers a pit or digs one and fails to cover it and an

---

[a] 8 Or *master so that he does not choose her* [b] 15 Or *kills* [c] 18 Or *with a tool* [d] 22 Or *she has a miscarriage* [e] 32 That is, about 12 ounces or about 345 grams

ox or a donkey falls into it, 34the one who opened the pit must pay the
owner for the loss and take the dead animal in exchange.
35"If anyone's bull injures someone else's bull and it dies, the two
parties are to sell the live one and divide both the money and the dead
animal equally. 36However, if it was known that the bull had the habit
of goring, yet the owner did not keep it penned up, the owner must
pay, animal for animal, and take the dead animal in exchange.

PROTECTION OF PROPERTY

22[a] "Whoever steals an ox or a sheep and slaughters it or sells it
must pay back five head of cattle for the ox and four sheep
for the sheep.
2"If a thief is caught breaking in at night and is struck a fatal blow,
the defender is not guilty of bloodshed; 3but if it happens after sunrise,
the defender is guilty of bloodshed.
"Anyone who steals must certainly make restitution, but if they have
nothing, they must be sold to pay for their theft. 4If the stolen animal
is found alive in their possession—whether ox or donkey or sheep—
they must pay back double.
5"If anyone grazes their livestock in a field or vineyard and lets them
stray and they graze in someone else's field, the offender must make
restitution from the best of their own field or vineyard.
6"If a fire breaks out and spreads into thornbushes so that it burns
shocks of grain or standing grain or the whole field, the one who
started the fire must make restitution.
7"If anyone gives a neighbor silver or goods for safekeeping and they
are stolen from the neighbor's house, the thief, if caught, must pay
back double. 8But if the thief is not found, the owner of the house
must appear before the judges, and they must[b] determine whether the
owner of the house has laid hands on the other person's property. 9In
all cases of illegal possession of an ox, a donkey, a sheep, a garment,
or any other lost property about which somebody says, 'This is mine,'
both parties are to bring their cases before the judges.[c] The one whom
the judges declare[d] guilty must pay back double to the other.
10"If anyone gives a donkey, an ox, a sheep or any other animal to
their neighbor for safekeeping and it dies or is injured or is taken away
while no one is looking, 11the issue between them will be settled by the
taking of an oath before the LORD that the neighbor did not lay hands
on the other person's property. The owner is to accept this, and no res-
titution is required. 12But if the animal was stolen from the neighbor,
restitution must be made to the owner. 13If it was torn to pieces by a
wild animal, the neighbor shall bring in the remains as evidence and
shall not be required to pay for the torn animal.
14"If anyone borrows an animal from their neighbor and it is injured
or dies while the owner is not present, they must make restitution.
15But if the owner is with the animal, the borrower will not have to pay.
If the animal was hired, the money paid for the hire covers the loss.

SOCIAL RESPONSIBILITY

16"If a man seduces a virgin who is not pledged to be married and
sleeps with her, he must pay the bride-price, and she shall be his wife.

PRAYING SCRIPTURE

Exodus 22

The Law of Moses was intended to guide God's people in the many ways they interacted in society. There were laws about morality, personal property of all kinds and protections for vulnerable people. God ensured that his people knew how to relate to others.

These laws teach us that God is concerned with our personal relationships. If you struggle with anyone relationally, ask God to help you love that person.

[a] In Hebrew texts 22:1 is numbered 21:37, and 22:2-31 is numbered 22:1-30.
[b] 8 Or *before God, and he will* [c] 9 Or *before God* [d] 9 Or *whom God declares*

17 If her father absolutely refuses to give her to him, he must still pay
the bride-price for virgins.
18 "Do not allow a sorceress to live.
19 "Anyone who has sexual relations with an animal is to be put to
death.
20 "Whoever sacrifices to any god other than the LORD must be
destroyed.[a]
21 "Do not mistreat or oppress a foreigner, for you were foreigners
in Egypt.
22 "Do not take advantage of the widow or the fatherless. 23 If you do
and they cry out to me, I will certainly hear their cry. 24 My anger will
be aroused, and I will kill you with the sword; your wives will become
widows and your children fatherless.
25 "If you lend money to one of my people among you who is needy,
do not treat it like a business deal; charge no interest. 26 If you take
your neighbor's cloak as a pledge, return it by sunset, 27 because that
cloak is the only covering your neighbor has. What else can they sleep
in? When they cry out to me, I will hear, for I am compassionate.
28 "Do not blaspheme God[b] or curse the ruler of your people.
29 "Do not hold back offerings from your granaries or your vats.[c]
"You must give me the firstborn of your sons. 30 Do the same with
your cattle and your sheep. Let them stay with their mothers for seven
days, but give them to me on the eighth day.
31 "You are to be my holy people. So do not eat the meat of an animal
torn by wild beasts; throw it to the dogs.

LAWS OF JUSTICE AND MERCY

23 "Do not spread false reports. Do not help a guilty person by
being a malicious witness.
2 "Do not follow the crowd in doing wrong. When you give testimony
in a lawsuit, do not pervert justice by siding with the crowd, 3 and do
not show favoritism to a poor person in a lawsuit.
4 "If you come across your enemy's ox or donkey wandering off, be
sure to return it. 5 If you see the donkey of someone who hates you
fallen down under its load, do not leave it there; be sure you help them
with it.
6 "Do not deny justice to your poor people in their lawsuits. 7 Have
nothing to do with a false charge and do not put an innocent or honest
person to death, for I will not acquit the guilty.
8 "Do not accept a bribe, for a bribe blinds those who see and twists
the words of the innocent.
9 "Do not oppress a foreigner; you yourselves know how it feels to be
foreigners, because you were foreigners in Egypt.

SABBATH LAWS

10 "For six years you are to sow your fields and harvest the crops,
11 but during the seventh year let the land lie unplowed and unused.
Then the poor among your people may get food from it, and the wild
animals may eat what is left. Do the same with your vineyard and your
olive grove.

PRAYING SCRIPTURE

Exodus 23

Many of the commands in this chapter can be summarized in the words, "Love your neighbor as yourself." Indeed, that's how Jesus himself summarized the Law of Moses (see Mark 12:31). We tend to get caught up in the dos and don'ts of the law, missing the relationship aspect between God and humanity.

Ask God to give you opportunities to love him and your neighbors, fulfilling both major aspects of the law.

---

[a] *20* The Hebrew term refers to the irrevocable giving over of things or persons to the LORD, often by totally destroying them. [b] *28* Or *Do not revile the judges* [c] *29* The meaning of the Hebrew for this phrase is uncertain.

12"Six days do your work, but on the seventh day do not work, so
that your ox and your donkey may rest, and so that the slave born in
your household and the foreigner living among you may be refreshed.
13"Be careful to do everything I have said to you. Do not invoke the
names of other gods; do not let them be heard on your lips.

THE THREE ANNUAL FESTIVALS

14"Three times a year you are to celebrate a festival to me.
15"Celebrate the Festival of Unleavened Bread; for seven days eat
bread made without yeast, as I commanded you. Do this at the ap-
pointed time in the month of Aviv, for in that month you came out
of Egypt.

"No one is to appear before me empty-handed.

16"Celebrate the Festival of Harvest with the firstfruits of the crops
you sow in your field.

"Celebrate the Festival of Ingathering at the end of the year, when
you gather in your crops from the field.

17"Three times a year all the men are to appear before the Sovereign
LORD.

18"Do not offer the blood of a sacrifice to me along with anything
containing yeast.

"The fat of my festival offerings must not be kept until morning.

19"Bring the best of the firstfruits of your soil to the house of the
LORD your God.

"Do not cook a young goat in its mother's milk.

GOD'S ANGEL TO PREPARE THE WAY

20"See, I am sending an angel ahead of you to guard you along the
way and to bring you to the place I have prepared. 21Pay attention to
him and listen to what he says. Do not rebel against him; he will not
forgive your rebellion, since my Name is in him. 22If you listen care-
fully to what he says and do all that I say, I will be an enemy to your
enemies and will oppose those who oppose you. 23My angel will go
ahead of you and bring you into the land of the Amorites, Hittites,
Perizzites, Canaanites, Hivites and Jebusites, and I will wipe them out.
24Do not bow down before their gods or worship them or follow their
practices. You must demolish them and break their sacred stones to
pieces. 25Worship the LORD your God, and his blessing will be on your
food and water. I will take away sickness from among you, 26and none
will miscarry or be barren in your land. I will give you a full life span.

27"I will send my terror ahead of you and throw into confusion every
nation you encounter. I will make all your enemies turn their backs
and run. 28I will send the hornet ahead of you to drive the Hivites,
Canaanites and Hittites out of your way. 29But I will not drive them
out in a single year, because the land would become desolate and the
wild animals too numerous for you. 30Little by little I will drive them
out before you, until you have increased enough to take possession of
the land.

31"I will establish your borders from the Red Sea[a] to the Mediterra-
nean Sea,[b] and from the desert to the Euphrates River. I will give into
your hands the people who live in the land, and you will drive them
out before you. 32Do not make a covenant with them or with their gods.

---

[a] 31 Or *the Sea of Reeds* [b] 31 Hebrew *to the Sea of the Philistines*

33 Do not let them live in your land or they will cause you to sin against
me, because the worship of their gods will certainly be a snare to you."

THE COVENANT CONFIRMED

24 Then the LORD said to Moses, "Come up to the LORD, you and
Aaron, Nadab and Abihu, and seventy of the elders of Israel.
You are to worship at a distance, 2 but Moses alone is to approach the
LORD; the others must not come near. And the people may not come
up with him."
3 When Moses went and told the people all the LORD's words and laws,
they responded with one voice, "Everything the LORD has said we will
do." 4 Moses then wrote down everything the LORD had said.
He got up early the next morning and built an altar at the foot of
the mountain and set up twelve stone pillars representing the twelve
tribes of Israel. 5 Then he sent young Israelite men, and they offered
burnt offerings and sacrificed young bulls as fellowship offerings to
the LORD. 6 Moses took half of the blood and put it in bowls, and the
other half he splashed against the altar. 7 Then he took the Book of the
Covenant and read it to the people. They responded, "We will do every-
thing the LORD has said; we will obey."
8 Moses then took the blood, sprinkled it on the people and said,
"This is the blood of the covenant that the LORD has made with you in
accordance with all these words."
9 Moses and Aaron, Nadab and Abihu, and the seventy elders of Israel
went up 10 and saw the God of Israel. Under his feet was something like
a pavement made of lapis lazuli, as bright blue as the sky. 11 But God did
not raise his hand against these leaders of the Israelites; they saw God,
and they ate and drank.
12 The LORD said to Moses, "Come up to me on the mountain and stay
here, and I will give you the tablets of stone with the law and com-
mandments I have written for their instruction."
13 Then Moses set out with Joshua his aide, and Moses went up on
the mountain of God. 14 He said to the elders, "Wait here for us until we
come back to you. Aaron and Hur are with you, and anyone involved
in a dispute can go to them."
15 When Moses went up on the mountain, the cloud covered it, 16 and
the glory of the LORD settled on Mount Sinai. For six days the cloud
covered the mountain, and on the seventh day the LORD called to Mo-
ses from within the cloud. 17 To the Israelites the glory of the LORD
looked like a consuming fire on top of the mountain. 18 Then Moses
entered the cloud as he went on up the mountain. And he stayed on
the mountain forty days and forty nights.

OFFERINGS FOR THE TABERNACLE

25 The LORD said to Moses, 2 "Tell the Israelites to bring me an
offering. You are to receive the offering for me from everyone
whose heart prompts them to give. 3 These are the offerings you are to
receive from them: gold, silver and bronze; 4 blue, purple and scarlet
yarn and fine linen; goat hair; 5 ram skins dyed red and another type
of durable leather[a]; acacia wood; 6 olive oil for the light; spices for the
anointing oil and for the fragrant incense; 7 and onyx stones and other
gems to be mounted on the ephod and breastpiece.

[a] *5* Possibly the hides of large aquatic mammals

PRAYING SCRIPTURE

Exodus 24

Sometimes the talk of blood in the Old Testament rattles our modern sensibilities. But Moses led the Israelites to ratify the covenant with God by sprinkling sacrificial blood on the altar and then on the people themselves.

It's easy to see that this dedication ceremony was a prefiguring of Jesus dying for the sins of the world. Thank God now for the gift of Jesus, who reconciles us to God through his blood.

PRAYING SCRIPTURE

Exodus 25

The Lord instructed the Israelites to build a tabernacle for worship along with furnishings for it. Among them was the ark of the covenant law, which had two gold cherubim bowing toward each other on the mercy seat. Only the priests could move it. Worshiping God was serious and meaningful.

Pause for a moment to contemplate the majesty and power of God. Worship him for his wisdom, beauty, light and love.

8"Then have them make a sanctuary for me, and I will dwell among them. 9Make this tabernacle and all its furnishings exactly like the pattern I will show you.

THE ARK

10"Have them make an ark[a] of acacia wood — two and a half cubits long, a cubit and a half wide, and a cubit and a half high.[b] 11Overlay it with pure gold, both inside and out, and make a gold molding around it. 12Cast four gold rings for it and fasten them to its four feet, with two rings on one side and two rings on the other. 13Then make poles of acacia wood and overlay them with gold. 14Insert the poles into the rings on the sides of the ark to carry it. 15The poles are to remain in the rings of this ark; they are not to be removed. 16Then put in the ark the tablets of the covenant law, which I will give you.

17"Make an atonement cover of pure gold — two and a half cubits long and a cubit and a half wide. 18And make two cherubim out of hammered gold at the ends of the cover. 19Make one cherub on one end and the second cherub on the other; make the cherubim of one piece with the cover, at the two ends. 20The cherubim are to have their wings spread upward, overshadowing the cover with them. The cherubim are to face each other, looking toward the cover. 21Place the cover on top of the ark and put in the ark the tablets of the covenant law that I will give you. 22There, above the cover between the two cherubim that are over the ark of the covenant law, I will meet with you and give you all my commands for the Israelites.

THE TABLE

23"Make a table of acacia wood — two cubits long, a cubit wide and a cubit and a half high.[c] 24Overlay it with pure gold and make a gold molding around it. 25Also make around it a rim a handbreadth[d] wide and put a gold molding on the rim. 26Make four gold rings for the table and fasten them to the four corners, where the four legs are. 27The rings are to be close to the rim to hold the poles used in carrying the table. 28Make the poles of acacia wood, overlay them with gold and carry the table with them. 29And make its plates and dishes of pure gold, as well as its pitchers and bowls for the pouring out of offerings. 30Put the bread of the Presence on this table to be before me at all times.

THE LAMPSTAND

31"Make a lampstand of pure gold. Hammer out its base and shaft, and make its flowerlike cups, buds and blossoms of one piece with them. 32Six branches are to extend from the sides of the lampstand — three on one side and three on the other. 33Three cups shaped like almond flowers with buds and blossoms are to be on one branch, three on the next branch, and the same for all six branches extending from the lampstand. 34And on the lampstand there are to be four cups shaped like almond flowers with buds and blossoms. 35One bud shall be under the first pair of branches extending from the lampstand, a

[a] *10* That is, a chest [b] *10* That is, about 3 3/4 feet long and 2 1/4 feet wide and high or about 1.1 meters long and 68 centimeters wide and high; similarly in verse 17 [c] *23* That is, about 3 feet long, 1 1/2 feet wide and 2 1/4 feet high or about 90 centimeters long, 45 centimeters wide and 68 centimeters high [d] *25* That is, about 3 inches or about 7.5 centimeters

second bud under the second pair, and a third bud under the third pair—six branches in all. 36The buds and branches shall all be of one piece with the lampstand, hammered out of pure gold.

37"Then make its seven lamps and set them up on it so that they light the space in front of it. 38Its wick trimmers and trays are to be of pure gold. 39A talent[a] of pure gold is to be used for the lampstand and all these accessories. 40See that you make them according to the pattern shown you on the mountain.

THE TABERNACLE

26 "Make the tabernacle with ten curtains of finely twisted linen and blue, purple and scarlet yarn, with cherubim woven into them by a skilled worker. 2All the curtains are to be the same size—twenty-eight cubits long and four cubits wide.[b] 3Join five of the curtains together, and do the same with the other five. 4Make loops of blue material along the edge of the end curtain in one set, and do the same with the end curtain in the other set. 5Make fifty loops on one curtain and fifty loops on the end curtain of the other set, with the loops opposite each other. 6Then make fifty gold clasps and use them to fasten the curtains together so that the tabernacle is a unit.

7"Make curtains of goat hair for the tent over the tabernacle—eleven altogether. 8All eleven curtains are to be the same size—thirty cubits long and four cubits wide.[c] 9Join five of the curtains together into one set and the other six into another set. Fold the sixth curtain double at the front of the tent. 10Make fifty loops along the edge of the end curtain in one set and also along the edge of the end curtain in the other set. 11Then make fifty bronze clasps and put them in the loops to fasten the tent together as a unit. 12As for the additional length of the tent curtains, the half curtain that is left over is to hang down at the rear of the tabernacle. 13The tent curtains will be a cubit[d] longer on both sides; what is left will hang over the sides of the tabernacle so as to cover it. 14Make for the tent a covering of ram skins dyed red, and over that a covering of the other durable leather.[e]

15"Make upright frames of acacia wood for the tabernacle. 16Each frame is to be ten cubits long and a cubit and a half wide,[f] 17with two projections set parallel to each other. Make all the frames of the tabernacle in this way. 18Make twenty frames for the south side of the tabernacle 19and make forty silver bases to go under them—two bases for each frame, one under each projection. 20For the other side, the north side of the tabernacle, make twenty frames 21and forty silver bases—two under each frame. 22Make six frames for the far end, that is, the west end of the tabernacle, 23and make two frames for the corners at the far end. 24At these two corners they must be double from the bottom all the way to the top and fitted into a single ring; both shall be like that. 25So there will be eight frames and sixteen silver bases—two under each frame.

26"Also make crossbars of acacia wood: five for the frames on one side of the tabernacle, 27five for those on the other side, and five for the

[a] *39* That is, about 75 pounds or about 34 kilograms [b] *2* That is, about 42 feet long and 6 feet wide or about 13 meters long and 1.8 meters wide [c] *8* That is, about 45 feet long and 6 feet wide or about 13.5 meters long and 1.8 meters wide [d] *13* That is, about 18 inches or about 45 centimeters [e] *14* Possibly the hides of large aquatic mammals (see 25:5) [f] *16* That is, about 15 feet long and 2 1/4 feet wide or about 4.5 meters long and 68 centimeters wide

PRAYING SCRIPTURE

Exodus 26

The Lord carefully laid out instructions that showed how to build the tent where his people would approach him. Lengths and sections had to be precise. Various materials—skins, wood, gold, yarn, linen—and various colors would adorn it.

The Israelites were learning the God-ordered way in which worship was to take place. Ask God to help you worship him the way he deserves to be worshiped.

frames on the west, at the far end of the tabernacle. 28The center cross-
bar is to extend from end to end at the middle of the frames. 29Overlay
the frames with gold and make gold rings to hold the crossbars. Also
overlay the crossbars with gold.
30"Set up the tabernacle according to the plan shown you on the
mountain.
31"Make a curtain of blue, purple and scarlet yarn and finely twisted
linen, with cherubim woven into it by a skilled worker. 32Hang it with
gold hooks on four posts of acacia wood overlaid with gold and stand-
ing on four silver bases. 33Hang the curtain from the clasps and place
the ark of the covenant law behind the curtain. The curtain will sep-
arate the Holy Place from the Most Holy Place. 34Put the atonement
cover on the ark of the covenant law in the Most Holy Place. 35Place the
table outside the curtain on the north side of the tabernacle and put
the lampstand opposite it on the south side.
36"For the entrance to the tent make a curtain of blue, purple and
scarlet yarn and finely twisted linen — the work of an embroiderer.
37Make gold hooks for this curtain and five posts of acacia wood over-
laid with gold. And cast five bronze bases for them.

THE ALTAR OF BURNT OFFERING

27 "Build an altar of acacia wood, three cubits[a] high; it is to be
square, five cubits long and five cubits wide.[b] 2Make a horn at
each of the four corners, so that the horns and the altar are of one piece,
and overlay the altar with bronze. 3Make all its utensils of bronze — its
pots to remove the ashes, and its shovels, sprinkling bowls, meat forks
and firepans. 4Make a grating for it, a bronze network, and make a
bronze ring at each of the four corners of the network. 5Put it under
the ledge of the altar so that it is halfway up the altar. 6Make poles of
acacia wood for the altar and overlay them with bronze. 7The poles
are to be inserted into the rings so they will be on two sides of the al-
tar when it is carried. 8Make the altar hollow, out of boards. It is to be
made just as you were shown on the mountain.

PRAYING SCRIPTURE

Exodus 27

The Lord gave Israel careful instructions for building the altar where sacrifices would be made to him. He also ordered that the lamp be fueled by pure olive oil and burned constantly. Animal sacrifices were to be offered, and light would regularly shine.

The tabernacle foretold of a sacrifice who would be the light of the world. Thank God that through the tabernacle, he was showing us Jesus.

THE COURTYARD

9"Make a courtyard for the tabernacle. The south side shall be a hun-
dred cubits[c] long and is to have curtains of finely twisted linen, 10with
twenty posts and twenty bronze bases and with silver hooks and bands
on the posts. 11The north side shall also be a hundred cubits long and is
to have curtains, with twenty posts and twenty bronze bases and with
silver hooks and bands on the posts.
12"The west end of the courtyard shall be fifty cubits[d] wide and have
curtains, with ten posts and ten bases. 13On the east end, toward the
sunrise, the courtyard shall also be fifty cubits wide. 14Curtains fifteen
cubits[e] long are to be on one side of the entrance, with three posts and
three bases, 15and curtains fifteen cubits long are to be on the other
side, with three posts and three bases.
16"For the entrance to the courtyard, provide a curtain twenty cubits[f]
long, of blue, purple and scarlet yarn and finely twisted linen — the

[a] *1* That is, about 4 1/2 feet or about 1.4 meters [b] *1* That is, about 7 1/2 feet or about 2.3 meters long and wide [c] *9* That is, about 150 feet or about 45 meters; also in verse 11 [d] *12* That is, about 75 feet or about 23 meters; also in verse 13 [e] *14* That is, about 23 feet or about 6.8 meters; also in verse 15 [f] *16* That is, about 30 feet or about 9 meters

work of an embroiderer—with four posts and four bases. 17All the posts around the courtyard are to have silver bands and hooks, and bronze bases. 18The courtyard shall be a hundred cubits long and fifty cubits wide,[a] with curtains of finely twisted linen five cubits[b] high, and with bronze bases. 19All the other articles used in the service of the tabernacle, whatever their function, including all the tent pegs for it and those for the courtyard, are to be of bronze.

OIL FOR THE LAMPSTAND

20"Command the Israelites to bring you clear oil of pressed olives for the light so that the lamps may be kept burning. 21In the tent of meeting, outside the curtain that shields the ark of the covenant law, Aaron and his sons are to keep the lamps burning before the LORD from evening till morning. This is to be a lasting ordinance among the Israelites for the generations to come.

THE PRIESTLY GARMENTS

28 "Have Aaron your brother brought to you from among the Israelites, along with his sons Nadab and Abihu, Eleazar and Ithamar, so they may serve me as priests. 2Make sacred garments for your brother Aaron to give him dignity and honor. 3Tell all the skilled workers to whom I have given wisdom in such matters that they are to make garments for Aaron, for his consecration, so he may serve me as priest. 4These are the garments they are to make: a breastpiece, an ephod, a robe, a woven tunic, a turban and a sash. They are to make these sacred garments for your brother Aaron and his sons, so they may serve me as priests. 5Have them use gold, and blue, purple and scarlet yarn, and fine linen.

THE EPHOD

6"Make the ephod of gold, and of blue, purple and scarlet yarn, and of finely twisted linen—the work of skilled hands. 7It is to have two shoulder pieces attached to two of its corners, so it can be fastened. 8Its skillfully woven waistband is to be like it—of one piece with the ephod and made with gold, and with blue, purple and scarlet yarn, and with finely twisted linen.

9"Take two onyx stones and engrave on them the names of the sons of Israel 10in the order of their birth—six names on one stone and the remaining six on the other. 11Engrave the names of the sons of Israel on the two stones the way a gem cutter engraves a seal. Then mount the stones in gold filigree settings 12and fasten them on the shoulder pieces of the ephod as memorial stones for the sons of Israel. Aaron is to bear the names on his shoulders as a memorial before the LORD. 13Make gold filigree settings 14and two braided chains of pure gold, like a rope, and attach the chains to the settings.

THE BREASTPIECE

15"Fashion a breastpiece for making decisions—the work of skilled hands. Make it like the ephod: of gold, and of blue, purple and scarlet yarn, and of finely twisted linen. 16It is to be square—a span[c] long and

[a] *18* That is, about 150 feet long and 75 feet wide or about 45 meters long and 23 meters wide [b] *18* That is, about 7 1/2 feet or about 2.3 meters
[c] *16* That is, about 9 inches or about 23 centimeters

PRAYING SCRIPTURE

Exodus 28

The Lord instituted a line of priests to mediate between the people and him. They were responsible for offering sacrifices that atoned for sins. God gave clear instructions about their garments including a plate that read "HOLY TO THE LORD" (verse 36).

Not just anyone could approach God, and even the priests had specific requirements to follow. Thank God that he is near you in prayer, and take your requests to him.

a span wide — and folded double. 17 Then mount four rows of precious
stones on it. The first row shall be carnelian, chrysolite and beryl; 18 the
second row shall be turquoise, lapis lazuli and emerald; 19 the third row
shall be jacinth, agate and amethyst; 20 the fourth row shall be topaz,
onyx and jasper.[a] Mount them in gold filigree settings. 21 There are to
be twelve stones, one for each of the names of the sons of Israel, each
engraved like a seal with the name of one of the twelve tribes.

22 "For the breastpiece make braided chains of pure gold, like a rope.
23 Make two gold rings for it and fasten them to two corners of the
breastpiece. 24 Fasten the two gold chains to the rings at the corners of
the breastpiece, 25 and the other ends of the chains to the two settings,
attaching them to the shoulder pieces of the ephod at the front. 26 Make
two gold rings and attach them to the other two corners of the breast-
piece on the inside edge next to the ephod. 27 Make two more gold rings
and attach them to the bottom of the shoulder pieces on the front of
the ephod, close to the seam just above the waistband of the ephod.
28 The rings of the breastpiece are to be tied to the rings of the ephod
with blue cord, connecting it to the waistband, so that the breastpiece
will not swing out from the ephod.

29 "Whenever Aaron enters the Holy Place, he will bear the names of
the sons of Israel over his heart on the breastpiece of decision as a con-
tinuing memorial before the LORD. 30 Also put the Urim and the Thum-
mim in the breastpiece, so they may be over Aaron's heart whenever he
enters the presence of the LORD. Thus Aaron will always bear the means
of making decisions for the Israelites over his heart before the LORD.

OTHER PRIESTLY GARMENTS

31 "Make the robe of the ephod entirely of blue cloth, 32 with an open-
ing for the head in its center. There shall be a woven edge like a collar[b]
around this opening, so that it will not tear. 33 Make pomegranates of
blue, purple and scarlet yarn around the hem of the robe, with gold
bells between them. 34 The gold bells and the pomegranates are to al-
ternate around the hem of the robe. 35 Aaron must wear it when he
ministers. The sound of the bells will be heard when he enters the Holy
Place before the LORD and when he comes out, so that he will not die.

36 "Make a plate of pure gold and engrave on it as on a seal: HOLY TO
THE LORD. 37 Fasten a blue cord to it to attach it to the turban; it is to
be on the front of the turban. 38 It will be on Aaron's forehead, and he
will bear the guilt involved in the sacred gifts the Israelites consecrate,
whatever their gifts may be. It will be on Aaron's forehead continually
so that they will be acceptable to the LORD.

39 "Weave the tunic of fine linen and make the turban of fine linen.
The sash is to be the work of an embroiderer. 40 Make tunics, sashes and
caps for Aaron's sons to give them dignity and honor. 41 After you put
these clothes on your brother Aaron and his sons, anoint and ordain
them. Consecrate them so they may serve me as priests.

42 "Make linen undergarments as a covering for the body, reaching
from the waist to the thigh. 43 Aaron and his sons must wear them
whenever they enter the tent of meeting or approach the altar to min-
ister in the Holy Place, so that they will not incur guilt and die.

"This is to be a lasting ordinance for Aaron and his descendants.

---

[a] *20* The precise identification of some of these precious stones is uncertain.
[b] *32* The meaning of the Hebrew for this word is uncertain.

CONSECRATION OF THE PRIESTS

29 "This is what you are to do to consecrate them, so they may serve me as priests: Take a young bull and two rams without defect. 2And from the finest wheat flour make round loaves without yeast, thick loaves without yeast and with olive oil mixed in, and thin loaves without yeast and brushed with olive oil. 3Put them in a basket and present them along with the bull and the two rams. 4Then bring Aaron and his sons to the entrance to the tent of meeting and wash them with water. 5Take the garments and dress Aaron with the tunic, the robe of the ephod, the ephod itself and the breastpiece. Fasten the ephod on him by its skillfully woven waistband. 6Put the turban on his head and attach the sacred emblem to the turban. 7Take the anointing oil and anoint him by pouring it on his head. 8Bring his sons and dress them in tunics 9and fasten caps on them. Then tie sashes on Aaron and his sons.[a] The priesthood is theirs by a lasting ordinance.

"Then you shall ordain Aaron and his sons.

10"Bring the bull to the front of the tent of meeting, and Aaron and his sons shall lay their hands on its head. 11Slaughter it in the LORD's presence at the entrance to the tent of meeting. 12Take some of the bull's blood and put it on the horns of the altar with your finger, and pour out the rest of it at the base of the altar. 13Then take all the fat on the internal organs, the long lobe of the liver, and both kidneys with the fat on them, and burn them on the altar. 14But burn the bull's flesh and its hide and its intestines outside the camp. It is a sin offering.[b]

15"Take one of the rams, and Aaron and his sons shall lay their hands on its head. 16Slaughter it and take the blood and splash it against the sides of the altar. 17Cut the ram into pieces and wash the internal organs and the legs, putting them with the head and the other pieces. 18Then burn the entire ram on the altar. It is a burnt offering to the LORD, a pleasing aroma, a food offering presented to the LORD.

19"Take the other ram, and Aaron and his sons shall lay their hands on its head. 20Slaughter it, take some of its blood and put it on the lobes of the right ears of Aaron and his sons, on the thumbs of their right hands, and on the big toes of their right feet. Then splash blood against the sides of the altar. 21And take some blood from the altar and some of the anointing oil and sprinkle it on Aaron and his garments and on his sons and their garments. Then he and his sons and their garments will be consecrated.

22"Take from this ram the fat, the fat tail, the fat on the internal organs, the long lobe of the liver, both kidneys with the fat on them, and the right thigh. (This is the ram for the ordination.) 23From the basket of bread made without yeast, which is before the LORD, take one round loaf, one thick loaf with olive oil mixed in, and one thin loaf. 24Put all these in the hands of Aaron and his sons and have them wave them before the LORD as a wave offering. 25Then take them from their hands and burn them on the altar along with the burnt offering for a pleasing aroma to the LORD, a food offering presented to the LORD. 26After you take the breast of the ram for Aaron's ordination, wave it before the LORD as a wave offering, and it will be your share.

27"Consecrate those parts of the ordination ram that belong to Aaron and his sons: the breast that was waved and the thigh that was presented. 28This is always to be the perpetual share from the Israelites

[a] 9 Hebrew; Septuagint *on them* [b] 14 Or *purification offering*; also in verse 36

PRAYING SCRIPTURE

Exodus 29

In an extraordinary consecration ceremony, Aaron and his sons were set aside to serve the Lord. After they were consecrated, God promised to dwell with the children of Israel, committing to them in a unique relationship between God and people.

Stop for a moment and praise the One who created the universe, keeps it by his power and has consecrated you as his own.

for Aaron and his sons. It is the contribution the Israelites are to make
to the LORD from their fellowship offerings.
29“Aaron’s sacred garments will belong to his descendants so that
they can be anointed and ordained in them. 30The son who succeeds
him as priest and comes to the tent of meeting to minister in the Holy
Place is to wear them seven days.
31“Take the ram for the ordination and cook the meat in a sacred
place. 32At the entrance to the tent of meeting, Aaron and his sons are to
eat the meat of the ram and the bread that is in the basket. 33They are to
eat these offerings by which atonement was made for their ordination
and consecration. But no one else may eat them, because they are sa-
cred. 34And if any of the meat of the ordination ram or any bread is left
over till morning, burn it up. It must not be eaten, because it is sacred.
35“Do for Aaron and his sons everything I have commanded you, tak-
ing seven days to ordain them. 36Sacrifice a bull each day as a sin offer-
ing to make atonement. Purify the altar by making atonement for it,
and anoint it to consecrate it. 37For seven days make atonement for the
altar and consecrate it. Then the altar will be most holy, and whatever
touches it will be holy.
38“This is what you are to offer on the altar regularly each day: two
lambs a year old. 39Offer one in the morning and the other at twilight.
40With the first lamb offer a tenth of an ephah[a] of the finest flour
mixed with a quarter of a hin[b] of oil from pressed olives, and a quar-
ter of a hin of wine as a drink offering. 41Sacrifice the other lamb at
twilight with the same grain offering and its drink offering as in the
morning — a pleasing aroma, a food offering presented to the LORD.
42“For the generations to come this burnt offering is to be made reg-
ularly at the entrance to the tent of meeting, before the LORD. There I
will meet you and speak to you; 43there also I will meet with the Isra-
elites, and the place will be consecrated by my glory.
44“So I will consecrate the tent of meeting and the altar and will con-
secrate Aaron and his sons to serve me as priests. 45Then I will dwell
among the Israelites and be their God. 46They will know that I am the
LORD their God, who brought them out of Egypt so that I might dwell
among them. I am the LORD their God.

PRAYING SCRIPTURE

Exodus 30

God continued to instruct his people that certain things and certain people were to be holy. That is, they were to be set apart for his use. These items and people were not for common use; they had a special role in service to God.

Think about what it means to be holy, set apart for God’s use. See yourself as designated for God’s use, and make yourself available to him today.

THE ALTAR OF INCENSE

30 “Make an altar of acacia wood for burning incense. 2It is to be
square, a cubit long and a cubit wide, and two cubits high[c] —
its horns of one piece with it. 3Overlay the top and all the sides and
the horns with pure gold, and make a gold molding around it. 4Make
two gold rings for the altar below the molding — two on each of the
opposite sides — to hold the poles used to carry it. 5Make the poles of
acacia wood and overlay them with gold. 6Put the altar in front of the
curtain that shields the ark of the covenant law — before the atone-
ment cover that is over the tablets of the covenant law — where I will
meet with you.
7“Aaron must burn fragrant incense on the altar every morning
when he tends the lamps. 8He must burn incense again when he lights

[a] *40* That is, probably about 3 1/2 pounds or about 1.6 kilograms [b] *40* That is, probably about 1 quart or about 1 liter [c] *2* That is, about 1 1/2 feet long and wide and 3 feet high or about 45 centimeters long and wide and 90 centimeters high

the lamps at twilight so incense will burn regularly before the LORD
for the generations to come. 9Do not offer on this altar any other in-
cense or any burnt offering or grain offering, and do not pour a drink
offering on it. 10Once a year Aaron shall make atonement on its horns.
This annual atonement must be made with the blood of the atoning
sin offering[a] for the generations to come. It is most holy to the LORD."

ATONEMENT MONEY

11Then the LORD said to Moses, 12"When you take a census of the Isra-
elites to count them, each one must pay the LORD a ransom for his life
at the time he is counted. Then no plague will come on them when you
number them. 13Each one who crosses over to those already counted is
to give a half shekel,[b] according to the sanctuary shekel, which weighs
twenty gerahs. This half shekel is an offering to the LORD. 14All who
cross over, those twenty years old or more, are to give an offering to the
LORD. 15The rich are not to give more than a half shekel and the poor
are not to give less when you make the offering to the LORD to atone
for your lives. 16Receive the atonement money from the Israelites and
use it for the service of the tent of meeting. It will be a memorial for the
Israelites before the LORD, making atonement for your lives."

BASIN FOR WASHING

17Then the LORD said to Moses, 18"Make a bronze basin, with its
bronze stand, for washing. Place it between the tent of meeting and
the altar, and put water in it. 19Aaron and his sons are to wash their
hands and feet with water from it. 20Whenever they enter the tent of
meeting, they shall wash with water so that they will not die. Also,
when they approach the altar to minister by presenting a food offering
to the LORD, 21they shall wash their hands and feet so that they will not
die. This is to be a lasting ordinance for Aaron and his descendants for
the generations to come."

ANOINTING OIL

22Then the LORD said to Moses, 23"Take the following fine spices:
500 shekels[c] of liquid myrrh, half as much (that is, 250 shekels) of fra-
grant cinnamon, 250 shekels[d] of fragrant calamus, 24500 shekels of
cassia — all according to the sanctuary shekel — and a hin[e] of olive oil.
25Make these into a sacred anointing oil, a fragrant blend, the work of
a perfumer. It will be the sacred anointing oil. 26Then use it to anoint
the tent of meeting, the ark of the covenant law, 27the table and all its
articles, the lampstand and its accessories, the altar of incense, 28the
altar of burnt offering and all its utensils, and the basin with its stand.
29You shall consecrate them so they will be most holy, and whatever
touches them will be holy.

30"Anoint Aaron and his sons and consecrate them so they may serve
me as priests. 31Say to the Israelites, 'This is to be my sacred anointing
oil for the generations to come. 32Do not pour it on anyone else's body
and do not make any other oil using the same formula. It is sacred, and
you are to consider it sacred. 33Whoever makes perfume like it and puts
it on anyone other than a priest must be cut off from their people.'"

---

[a] *10* Or *purification offering*; also in verse 15 [b] *13* That is, about 1/5 ounce or about 5.8 grams [c] *23* That is, about 12 1/2 pounds or about 5.8 kilograms; also in verse 24 [d] *23* That is, about 6 1/4 pounds or about 2.9 kilograms [e] *24* That is, probably about 1 gallon or about 3.8 liters

INCENSE

[34]Then the LORD said to Moses, "Take fragrant spices—gum resin, onycha and galbanum—and pure frankincense, all in equal amounts, [35]and make a fragrant blend of incense, the work of a perfumer. It is to be salted and pure and sacred. [36]Grind some of it to powder and place it in front of the ark of the covenant law in the tent of meeting, where I will meet with you. It shall be most holy to you. [37]Do not make any incense with this formula for yourselves; consider it holy to the LORD. [38]Whoever makes incense like it to enjoy its fragrance must be cut off from their people."

BEZALEL AND OHOLIAB

31 Then the LORD said to Moses, [2]"See, I have chosen Bezalel son of Uri, the son of Hur, of the tribe of Judah, [3]and I have filled him with the Spirit of God, with wisdom, with understanding, with knowledge and with all kinds of skills—[4]to make artistic designs for work in gold, silver and bronze, [5]to cut and set stones, to work in wood, and to engage in all kinds of crafts. [6]Moreover, I have appointed Oholiab son of Ahisamak, of the tribe of Dan, to help him. Also I have given ability to all the skilled workers to make everything I have commanded you: [7]the tent of meeting, the ark of the covenant law with the atonement cover on it, and all the other furnishings of the tent—[8]the table and its articles, the pure gold lampstand and all its accessories, the altar of incense, [9]the altar of burnt offering and all its utensils, the basin with its stand—[10]and also the woven garments, both the sacred garments for Aaron the priest and the garments for his sons when they serve as priests, [11]and the anointing oil and fragrant incense for the Holy Place. They are to make them just as I commanded you."

PRAYING SCRIPTURE

Exodus 31

God was deadly serious about his people observing the Sabbath day because it was holy. Violating the Sabbath was a capital offense. This commanded rest was not only for the people's benefit physically but also to remind them of God's rest after his creation week.

It's hard to equate rest with holiness. Think of ways you can plan rest, and ask God to lead you into practicing a regular Sabbath.

THE SABBATH

[12]Then the LORD said to Moses, [13]"Say to the Israelites, 'You must observe my Sabbaths. This will be a sign between me and you for the generations to come, so you may know that I am the LORD, who makes you holy.

[14]" 'Observe the Sabbath, because it is holy to you. Anyone who desecrates it is to be put to death; those who do any work on that day must be cut off from their people. [15]For six days work is to be done, but the seventh day is a day of sabbath rest, holy to the LORD. Whoever does any work on the Sabbath day is to be put to death. [16]The Israelites are to observe the Sabbath, celebrating it for the generations to come as a lasting covenant. [17]It will be a sign between me and the Israelites forever, for in six days the LORD made the heavens and the earth, and on the seventh day he rested and was refreshed.' "

[18]When the LORD finished speaking to Moses on Mount Sinai, he gave him the two tablets of the covenant law, the tablets of stone inscribed by the finger of God.

PRAYING SCRIPTURE

Exodus 32

While Moses was on the mountain with God, the people turned to idolatry. It's easy to blame them for sinning, but often we turn to idols also. When they sinned against the Lord, Moses served as a mediator, interceding with God on their behalf.

God's children today have a mediator too. When you are tempted to turn from God to idols, turn to our mediator, Jesus Christ, for strength to stand.

THE GOLDEN CALF

32 When the people saw that Moses was so long in coming down from the mountain, they gathered around Aaron and said, "Come, make us gods[a] who will go before us. As for this fellow Moses who brought us up out of Egypt, we don't know what has happened to him."

[a] *1* Or *a god;* also in verses 23 and 31

2Aaron answered them, "Take off the gold earrings that your wives,
your sons and your daughters are wearing, and bring them to me."
3So all the people took off their earrings and brought them to Aaron.
4He took what they handed him and made it into an idol cast in the
shape of a calf, fashioning it with a tool. Then they said, "These are
your gods,[a] Israel, who brought you up out of Egypt."

5When Aaron saw this, he built an altar in front of the calf and an-
nounced, "Tomorrow there will be a festival to the LORD." 6So the next
day the people rose early and sacrificed burnt offerings and presented
fellowship offerings. Afterward they sat down to eat and drink and got
up to indulge in revelry.

7Then the LORD said to Moses, "Go down, because your people, whom
you brought up out of Egypt, have become corrupt. 8They have been
quick to turn away from what I commanded them and have made
themselves an idol cast in the shape of a calf. They have bowed down
to it and sacrificed to it and have said, 'These are your gods, Israel, who
brought you up out of Egypt.'

9"I have seen these people," the LORD said to Moses, "and they are a
stiff-necked people. 10Now leave me alone so that my anger may burn
against them and that I may destroy them. Then I will make you into
a great nation."

11But Moses sought the favor of the LORD his God. "LORD," he said,
"why should your anger burn against your people, whom you brought
out of Egypt with great power and a mighty hand? 12Why should the
Egyptians say, 'It was with evil intent that he brought them out, to kill
them in the mountains and to wipe them off the face of the earth'?
Turn from your fierce anger; relent and do not bring disaster on your
people. 13Remember your servants Abraham, Isaac and Israel, to whom
you swore by your own self: 'I will make your descendants as numer-
ous as the stars in the sky and I will give your descendants all this
land I promised them, and it will be their inheritance forever.'" 14Then
the LORD relented and did not bring on his people the disaster he had
threatened.

15Moses turned and went down the mountain with the two tablets
of the covenant law in his hands. They were inscribed on both sides,
front and back. 16The tablets were the work of God; the writing was the
writing of God, engraved on the tablets.

17When Joshua heard the noise of the people shouting, he said to
Moses, "There is the sound of war in the camp."

18Moses replied:

"It is not the sound of victory,
  it is not the sound of defeat;
  it is the sound of singing that I hear."

19When Moses approached the camp and saw the calf and the danc-
ing, his anger burned and he threw the tablets out of his hands, break-
ing them to pieces at the foot of the mountain. 20And he took the calf
the people had made and burned it in the fire; then he ground it to
powder, scattered it on the water and made the Israelites drink it.

21He said to Aaron, "What did these people do to you, that you led
them into such great sin?"

22"Do not be angry, my lord," Aaron answered. "You know how prone

[a] 4 Or *This is your god*; also in verse 8

these people are to evil. 23They said to me, 'Make us gods who will go before us. As for this fellow Moses who brought us up out of Egypt, we don't know what has happened to him.' 24So I told them, 'Whoever has any gold jewelry, take it off.' Then they gave me the gold, and I threw it into the fire, and out came this calf!"

25Moses saw that the people were running wild and that Aaron had let them get out of control and so become a laughingstock to their enemies. 26So he stood at the entrance to the camp and said, "Whoever is for the LORD, come to me." And all the Levites rallied to him.

27Then he said to them, "This is what the LORD, the God of Israel, says: 'Each man strap a sword to his side. Go back and forth through the camp from one end to the other, each killing his brother and friend and neighbor.'" 28The Levites did as Moses commanded, and that day about three thousand of the people died. 29Then Moses said, "You have been set apart to the LORD today, for you were against your own sons and brothers, and he has blessed you this day."

30The next day Moses said to the people, "You have committed a great sin. But now I will go up to the LORD; perhaps I can make atonement for your sin."

31So Moses went back to the LORD and said, "Oh, what a great sin these people have committed! They have made themselves gods of gold. 32But now, please forgive their sin—but if not, then blot me out of the book you have written."

33The LORD replied to Moses, "Whoever has sinned against me I will blot out of my book. 34Now go, lead the people to the place I spoke of, and my angel will go before you. However, when the time comes for me to punish, I will punish them for their sin."

35And the LORD struck the people with a plague because of what they did with the calf Aaron had made.

PRAYING SCRIPTURE

Exodus 33

Because of God's welcoming presence as our Father, we sometimes forget his utter holiness and power. Moses could see only the back of God's glory; to see him fully would have killed a mere human. God blocked Moses' view for his own good.

Spend some time thinking about the absolute holiness and power of God. Thank him that you can, through Jesus, go to him with any request or concern.

33 Then the LORD said to Moses, "Leave this place, you and the people you brought up out of Egypt, and go up to the land I promised on oath to Abraham, Isaac and Jacob, saying, 'I will give it to your descendants.' 2I will send an angel before you and drive out the Canaanites, Amorites, Hittites, Perizzites, Hivites and Jebusites. 3Go up to the land flowing with milk and honey. But I will not go with you, because you are a stiff-necked people and I might destroy you on the way."

4When the people heard these distressing words, they began to mourn and no one put on any ornaments. 5For the LORD had said to Moses, "Tell the Israelites, 'You are a stiff-necked people. If I were to go with you even for a moment, I might destroy you. Now take off your ornaments and I will decide what to do with you.'" 6So the Israelites stripped off their ornaments at Mount Horeb.

THE TENT OF MEETING

7Now Moses used to take a tent and pitch it outside the camp some distance away, calling it the "tent of meeting." Anyone inquiring of the LORD would go to the tent of meeting outside the camp. 8And whenever Moses went out to the tent, all the people rose and stood at the entrances to their tents, watching Moses until he entered the tent. 9As Moses went into the tent, the pillar of cloud would come down and stay at the entrance, while the LORD spoke with Moses. 10Whenever the people saw the pillar of cloud standing at the entrance to the tent, they all stood and worshiped, each at the entrance to their tent. 11The

LORD would speak to Moses face to face, as one speaks to a friend. Then
Moses would return to the camp, but his young aide Joshua son of Nun
did not leave the tent.

MOSES AND THE GLORY OF THE LORD

12 Moses said to the LORD, "You have been telling me, 'Lead these
people,' but you have not let me know whom you will send with me.
You have said, 'I know you by name and you have found favor with
me.' 13 If you are pleased with me, teach me your ways so I may know
you and continue to find favor with you. Remember that this nation
is your people."

14 The LORD replied, "My Presence will go with you, and I will give
you rest."

15 Then Moses said to him, "If your Presence does not go with us, do
not send us up from here. 16 How will anyone know that you are pleased
with me and with your people unless you go with us? What else will
distinguish me and your people from all the other people on the face
of the earth?"

17 And the LORD said to Moses, "I will do the very thing you have
asked, because I am pleased with you and I know you by name."

18 Then Moses said, "Now show me your glory."

19 And the LORD said, "I will cause all my goodness to pass in front
of you, and I will proclaim my name, the LORD, in your presence. I will
have mercy on whom I will have mercy, and I will have compassion on
whom I will have compassion. 20 But," he said, "you cannot see my face,
for no one may see me and live."

21 Then the LORD said, "There is a place near me where you may stand
on a rock. 22 When my glory passes by, I will put you in a cleft in the
rock and cover you with my hand until I have passed by. 23 Then I will
remove my hand and you will see my back; but my face must not be
seen."

THE NEW STONE TABLETS

34 The LORD said to Moses, "Chisel out two stone tablets like
the first ones, and I will write on them the words that were
on the first tablets, which you broke. 2 Be ready in the morning, and
then come up on Mount Sinai. Present yourself to me there on top of
the mountain. 3 No one is to come with you or be seen anywhere on
the mountain; not even the flocks and herds may graze in front of the
mountain."

4 So Moses chiseled out two stone tablets like the first ones and went
up Mount Sinai early in the morning, as the LORD had commanded
him; and he carried the two stone tablets in his hands. 5 Then the LORD
came down in the cloud and stood there with him and proclaimed his
name, the LORD. 6 And he passed in front of Moses, proclaiming, "The
LORD, the LORD, the compassionate and gracious God, slow to anger,
abounding in love and faithfulness, 7 maintaining love to thousands,
and forgiving wickedness, rebellion and sin. Yet he does not leave the
guilty unpunished; he punishes the children and their children for the
sin of the parents to the third and fourth generation."

8 Moses bowed to the ground at once and worshiped. 9 "Lord," he said,
"if I have found favor in your eyes, then let the Lord go with us. Al-
though this is a stiff-necked people, forgive our wickedness and our
sin, and take us as your inheritance."

PRAYING SCRIPTURE

Exodus 34

After Moses broke the tablets of the commandments in anger, God, rather than banishing him, invited Moses back to Sinai to replace them. Moses again spent 40 days and 40 nights on the mountain, fasting in God's presence as God rewrote the Ten Commandments for his people.

God is a God of second chances. He remembers that we are frail and meets us in our weaknesses. Thank him for his infinite compassion.

PRAYING SCRIPTURE

Exodus 34

The Lord had declared his glory as he passed Moses in the cleft of the rock. The time spent in God's presence on the mountain caused Moses' face to shine.

Have you ever been around someone you could tell had spent time with God? Perhaps it was the way he or she talked or shone with joy. Ask God to make it obvious that you've been in his presence.

10Then the LORD said: "I am making a covenant with you. Before
all your people I will do wonders never before done in any nation in
all the world. The people you live among will see how awesome is the
work that I, the LORD, will do for you. 11Obey what I command you
today. I will drive out before you the Amorites, Canaanites, Hittites,
Perizzites, Hivites and Jebusites. 12Be careful not to make a treaty with
those who live in the land where you are going, or they will be a snare
among you. 13Break down their altars, smash their sacred stones and
cut down their Asherah poles.[a] 14Do not worship any other god, for the
LORD, whose name is Jealous, is a jealous God.

15"Be careful not to make a treaty with those who live in the land;
for when they prostitute themselves to their gods and sacrifice to
them, they will invite you and you will eat their sacrifices. 16And when
you choose some of their daughters as wives for your sons and those
daughters prostitute themselves to their gods, they will lead your sons
to do the same.

17"Do not make any idols.

18"Celebrate the Festival of Unleavened Bread. For seven days eat
bread made without yeast, as I commanded you. Do this at the ap-
pointed time in the month of Aviv, for in that month you came out
of Egypt.

19"The first offspring of every womb belongs to me, including all the
firstborn males of your livestock, whether from herd or flock. 20Re-
deem the firstborn donkey with a lamb, but if you do not redeem it,
break its neck. Redeem all your firstborn sons.

"No one is to appear before me empty-handed.

21"Six days you shall labor, but on the seventh day you shall rest;
even during the plowing season and harvest you must rest.

22"Celebrate the Festival of Weeks with the firstfruits of the wheat
harvest, and the Festival of Ingathering at the turn of the year.[b] 23Three
times a year all your men are to appear before the Sovereign LORD, the
God of Israel. 24I will drive out nations before you and enlarge your
territory, and no one will covet your land when you go up three times
each year to appear before the LORD your God.

25"Do not offer the blood of a sacrifice to me along with anything
containing yeast, and do not let any of the sacrifice from the Passover
Festival remain until morning.

26"Bring the best of the firstfruits of your soil to the house of the
LORD your God.

"Do not cook a young goat in its mother's milk."

27Then the LORD said to Moses, "Write down these words, for in ac-
cordance with these words I have made a covenant with you and with
Israel." 28Moses was there with the LORD forty days and forty nights
without eating bread or drinking water. And he wrote on the tablets
the words of the covenant — the Ten Commandments.

THE RADIANT FACE OF MOSES

29When Moses came down from Mount Sinai with the two tablets of
the covenant law in his hands, he was not aware that his face was ra-
diant because he had spoken with the LORD. 30When Aaron and all the
Israelites saw Moses, his face was radiant, and they were afraid to come

[a] *13* That is, wooden symbols of the goddess Asherah [b] *22* That is, in the autumn

near him. 31But Moses called to them; so Aaron and all the leaders of the community came back to him, and he spoke to them. 32Afterward all the Israelites came near him, and he gave them all the commands the LORD had given him on Mount Sinai.

33When Moses finished speaking to them, he put a veil over his face. 34But whenever he entered the LORD's presence to speak with him, he removed the veil until he came out. And when he came out and told the Israelites what he had been commanded, 35they saw that his face was radiant. Then Moses would put the veil back over his face until he went in to speak with the LORD.

SABBATH REGULATIONS

35 Moses assembled the whole Israelite community and said to them, "These are the things the LORD has commanded you to do: 2For six days, work is to be done, but the seventh day shall be your holy day, a day of sabbath rest to the LORD. Whoever does any work on it is to be put to death. 3Do not light a fire in any of your dwellings on the Sabbath day."

MATERIALS FOR THE TABERNACLE

4Moses said to the whole Israelite community, "This is what the LORD has commanded: 5From what you have, take an offering for the LORD. Everyone who is willing is to bring to the LORD an offering of gold, silver and bronze; 6blue, purple and scarlet yarn and fine linen; goat hair; 7ram skins dyed red and another type of durable leather[a]; acacia wood; 8olive oil for the light; spices for the anointing oil and for the fragrant incense; 9and onyx stones and other gems to be mounted on the ephod and breastpiece.

10"All who are skilled among you are to come and make everything the LORD has commanded: 11the tabernacle with its tent and its covering, clasps, frames, crossbars, posts and bases; 12the ark with its poles and the atonement cover and the curtain that shields it; 13the table with its poles and all its articles and the bread of the Presence; 14the lampstand that is for light with its accessories, lamps and oil for the light; 15the altar of incense with its poles, the anointing oil and the fragrant incense; the curtain for the doorway at the entrance to the tabernacle; 16the altar of burnt offering with its bronze grating, its poles and all its utensils; the bronze basin with its stand; 17the curtains of the courtyard with its posts and bases, and the curtain for the entrance to the courtyard; 18the tent pegs for the tabernacle and for the courtyard, and their ropes; 19the woven garments worn for ministering in the sanctuary — both the sacred garments for Aaron the priest and the garments for his sons when they serve as priests."

20Then the whole Israelite community withdrew from Moses' presence, 21and everyone who was willing and whose heart moved them came and brought an offering to the LORD for the work on the tent of meeting, for all its service, and for the sacred garments. 22All who were willing, men and women alike, came and brought gold jewelry of all kinds: brooches, earrings, rings and ornaments. They all presented their gold as a wave offering to the LORD. 23Everyone who had blue, purple or scarlet yarn or fine linen, or goat hair, ram skins dyed red or the other durable leather brought them. 24Those presenting an

[a] 7 Possibly the hides of large aquatic mammals; also in verse 23

PRAYING SCRIPTURE

Exodus 35

Part of the construction of the tabernacle and its furnishings required the children of Israel to bring offerings. Their gifts varied: jewelry, yarn, furs, silver, gold, bronze and wood. Each Israelite was moved in his or her heart to give.

Has there been a recent opportunity where you were moved to be generous to someone or some cause? Thank God for the privilege of giving to him.

offering of silver or bronze brought it as an offering to the LORD, and
everyone who had acacia wood for any part of the work brought it.
25 Every skilled woman spun with her hands and brought what she had
spun — blue, purple or scarlet yarn or fine linen. 26 And all the women
who were willing and had the skill spun the goat hair. 27 The leaders
brought onyx stones and other gems to be mounted on the ephod and
breastpiece. 28 They also brought spices and olive oil for the light and
for the anointing oil and for the fragrant incense. 29 All the Israelite
men and women who were willing brought to the LORD freewill offer-
ings for all the work the LORD through Moses had commanded them
to do.

BEZALEL AND OHOLIAB

30 Then Moses said to the Israelites, "See, the LORD has chosen Bezalel
son of Uri, the son of Hur, of the tribe of Judah, 31 and he has filled him
with the Spirit of God, with wisdom, with understanding, with knowl-
edge and with all kinds of skills — 32 to make artistic designs for work
in gold, silver and bronze, 33 to cut and set stones, to work in wood and
to engage in all kinds of artistic crafts. 34 And he has given both him and
Oholiab son of Ahisamak, of the tribe of Dan, the ability to teach others.
35 He has filled them with skill to do all kinds of work as engravers, de-
signers, embroiderers in blue, purple and scarlet yarn and fine linen, and
36 weavers — all of them skilled workers and designers. 1 So Bezalel,
Oholiab and every skilled person to whom the LORD has given
skill and ability to know how to carry out all the work of constructing
the sanctuary are to do the work just as the LORD has commanded."
2 Then Moses summoned Bezalel and Oholiab and every skilled per-
son to whom the LORD had given ability and who was willing to come
and do the work. 3 They received from Moses all the offerings the Is-
raelites had brought to carry out the work of constructing the sanc-
tuary. And the people continued to bring freewill offerings morning
after morning. 4 So all the skilled workers who were doing all the work
on the sanctuary left what they were doing 5 and said to Moses, "The
people are bringing more than enough for doing the work the LORD
commanded to be done."
6 Then Moses gave an order and they sent this word throughout the
camp: "No man or woman is to make anything else as an offering for
the sanctuary." And so the people were restrained from bringing more,
7 because what they already had was more than enough to do all the
work.

PRAYING SCRIPTURE

Exodus 36

Construction on the tabernacle did not begin until after the people brought offerings, but the actual construction was carried out by skilled craftsmen. The people who did the work knew what they were doing.

What kinds of skills do you have? Have you been intentional about using them for kingdom purposes? Ask God to give you opportunities to use your talent for his glory.

THE TABERNACLE

8 All those who were skilled among the workers made the tabernacle
with ten curtains of finely twisted linen and blue, purple and scarlet
yarn, with cherubim woven into them by expert hands. 9 All the cur-
tains were the same size — twenty-eight cubits long and four cubits
wide.[a] 10 They joined five of the curtains together and did the same
with the other five. 11 Then they made loops of blue material along the
edge of the end curtain in one set, and the same was done with the end
curtain in the other set. 12 They also made fifty loops on one curtain and
fifty loops on the end curtain of the other set, with the loops opposite

[a] 9 That is, about 42 feet long and 6 feet wide or about 13 meters long and 1.8 meters wide

each other. 13 Then they made fifty gold clasps and used them to fasten the two sets of curtains together so that the tabernacle was a unit.

14 They made curtains of goat hair for the tent over the tabernacle — eleven altogether. 15 All eleven curtains were the same size — thirty cubits long and four cubits wide.[a] 16 They joined five of the curtains into one set and the other six into another set. 17 Then they made fifty loops along the edge of the end curtain in one set and also along the edge of the end curtain in the other set. 18 They made fifty bronze clasps to fasten the tent together as a unit. 19 Then they made for the tent a covering of ram skins dyed red, and over that a covering of the other durable leather.[b]

20 They made upright frames of acacia wood for the tabernacle. 21 Each frame was ten cubits long and a cubit and a half wide,[c] 22 with two projections set parallel to each other. They made all the frames of the tabernacle in this way. 23 They made twenty frames for the south side of the tabernacle 24 and made forty silver bases to go under them — two bases for each frame, one under each projection. 25 For the other side, the north side of the tabernacle, they made twenty frames 26 and forty silver bases — two under each frame. 27 They made six frames for the far end, that is, the west end of the tabernacle, 28 and two frames were made for the corners of the tabernacle at the far end. 29 At these two corners the frames were double from the bottom all the way to the top and fitted into a single ring; both were made alike. 30 So there were eight frames and sixteen silver bases — two under each frame.

31 They also made crossbars of acacia wood: five for the frames on one side of the tabernacle, 32 five for those on the other side, and five for the frames on the west, at the far end of the tabernacle. 33 They made the center crossbar so that it extended from end to end at the middle of the frames. 34 They overlaid the frames with gold and made gold rings to hold the crossbars. They also overlaid the crossbars with gold.

35 They made the curtain of blue, purple and scarlet yarn and finely twisted linen, with cherubim woven into it by a skilled worker. 36 They made four posts of acacia wood for it and overlaid them with gold. They made gold hooks for them and cast their four silver bases. 37 For the entrance to the tent they made a curtain of blue, purple and scarlet yarn and finely twisted linen — the work of an embroiderer; 38 and they made five posts with hooks for them. They overlaid the tops of the posts and their bands with gold and made their five bases of bronze.

THE ARK

37 Bezalel made the ark of acacia wood — two and a half cubits long, a cubit and a half wide, and a cubit and a half high.[d] 2 He overlaid it with pure gold, both inside and out, and made a gold molding around it. 3 He cast four gold rings for it and fastened them to its four feet, with two rings on one side and two rings on the other. 4 Then he made poles of acacia wood and overlaid them with gold. 5 And he inserted the poles into the rings on the sides of the ark to carry it.

PRAYING SCRIPTURE

Exodus 37

The ark of the covenant law would be the visible symbol of God's presence among his people. God's glory would descend over the top of it, called "the atonement cover," where God showed mercy to his people.

The presence of God under the old covenant was limited and periodic, unlike the new covenant, in which each believer knows God's presence. Thank God that he is now and always with his children.

---

[a] *15* That is, about 45 feet long and 6 feet wide or about 14 meters long and 1.8 meters wide [b] *19* Possibly the hides of large aquatic mammals (see 35:7)
[c] *21* That is, about 15 feet long and 2 1/4 feet wide or about 4.5 meters long and 68 centimeters wide [d] *1* That is, about 3 3/4 feet long and 2 1/4 feet wide and high or about 1.1 meters long and 68 centimeters wide and high; similarly in verse 6

6He made the atonement cover of pure gold — two and a half cu-
bits long and a cubit and a half wide. 7Then he made two cherubim
out of hammered gold at the ends of the cover. 8He made one cherub
on one end and the second cherub on the other; at the two ends he
made them of one piece with the cover. 9The cherubim had their wings
spread upward, overshadowing the cover with them. The cherubim
faced each other, looking toward the cover.

THE TABLE

10They[a] made the table of acacia wood — two cubits long, a cubit
wide and a cubit and a half high.[b] 11Then they overlaid it with pure
gold and made a gold molding around it. 12They also made around it
a rim a handbreadth[c] wide and put a gold molding on the rim. 13They
cast four gold rings for the table and fastened them to the four corners,
where the four legs were. 14The rings were put close to the rim to hold
the poles used in carrying the table. 15The poles for carrying the table
were made of acacia wood and were overlaid with gold. 16And they
made from pure gold the articles for the table — its plates and dishes
and bowls and its pitchers for the pouring out of drink offerings.

THE LAMPSTAND

17They made the lampstand of pure gold. They hammered out its
base and shaft, and made its flowerlike cups, buds and blossoms of one
piece with them. 18Six branches extended from the sides of the lamp-
stand — three on one side and three on the other. 19Three cups shaped
like almond flowers with buds and blossoms were on one branch, three
on the next branch and the same for all six branches extending from
the lampstand. 20And on the lampstand were four cups shaped like al-
mond flowers with buds and blossoms. 21One bud was under the first
pair of branches extending from the lampstand, a second bud under
the second pair, and a third bud under the third pair — six branches in
all. 22The buds and the branches were all of one piece with the lamp-
stand, hammered out of pure gold.
23They made its seven lamps, as well as its wick trimmers and trays,
of pure gold. 24They made the lampstand and all its accessories from
one talent[d] of pure gold.

THE ALTAR OF INCENSE

25They made the altar of incense out of acacia wood. It was square,
a cubit long and a cubit wide and two cubits high[e] — its horns of one
piece with it. 26They overlaid the top and all the sides and the horns
with pure gold, and made a gold molding around it. 27They made two
gold rings below the molding — two on each of the opposite sides — to
hold the poles used to carry it. 28They made the poles of acacia wood
and overlaid them with gold.
29They also made the sacred anointing oil and the pure, fragrant in-
cense — the work of a perfumer.

---

[a] *10* Or *He*; also in verses 11-29 [b] *10* That is, about 3 feet long, 1 1/2 feet wide and 2 1/4 feet high or about 90 centimeters long, 45 centimeters wide and 68 centimeters high [c] *12* That is, about 3 inches or about 7.5 centimeters [d] *24* That is, about 75 pounds or about 34 kilograms [e] *25* That is, about 1 1/2 feet long and wide and 3 feet high or about 45 centimeters long and wide and 90 centimeters high

THE ALTAR OF BURNT OFFERING

38 They[a] built the altar of burnt offering of acacia wood, three cu-
bits[b] high; it was square, five cubits long and five cubits wide.[c]
2They made a horn at each of the four corners, so that the horns and
the altar were of one piece, and they overlaid the altar with bronze.
3They made all its utensils of bronze — its pots, shovels, sprinkling
bowls, meat forks and firepans. 4They made a grating for the altar,
a bronze network, to be under its ledge, halfway up the altar. 5They
cast bronze rings to hold the poles for the four corners of the bronze
grating. 6They made the poles of acacia wood and overlaid them with
bronze. 7They inserted the poles into the rings so they would be on the
sides of the altar for carrying it. They made it hollow, out of boards.

THE BASIN FOR WASHING

8They made the bronze basin and its bronze stand from the mirrors
of the women who served at the entrance to the tent of meeting.

THE COURTYARD

9Next they made the courtyard. The south side was a hundred cu-
bits[d] long and had curtains of finely twisted linen, 10with twenty posts
and twenty bronze bases, and with silver hooks and bands on the
posts. 11The north side was also a hundred cubits long and had twenty
posts and twenty bronze bases, with silver hooks and bands on the posts.
12The west end was fifty cubits[e] wide and had curtains, with ten posts
and ten bases, with silver hooks and bands on the posts. 13The east
end, toward the sunrise, was also fifty cubits wide. 14Curtains fifteen
cubits[f] long were on one side of the entrance, with three posts and
three bases, 15and curtains fifteen cubits long were on the other side of
the entrance to the courtyard, with three posts and three bases. 16All
the curtains around the courtyard were of finely twisted linen. 17The
bases for the posts were bronze. The hooks and bands on the posts
were silver, and their tops were overlaid with silver; so all the posts of
the courtyard had silver bands.
18The curtain for the entrance to the courtyard was made of blue,
purple and scarlet yarn and finely twisted linen — the work of an em-
broiderer. It was twenty cubits[g] long and, like the curtains of the court-
yard, five cubits[h] high, 19with four posts and four bronze bases. Their
hooks and bands were silver, and their tops were overlaid with silver.
20All the tent pegs of the tabernacle and of the surrounding courtyard
were bronze.

THE MATERIALS USED

21These are the amounts of the materials used for the tabernacle, the
tabernacle of the covenant law, which were recorded at Moses' com-
mand by the Levites under the direction of Ithamar son of Aaron, the
priest. 22(Bezalel son of Uri, the son of Hur, of the tribe of Judah, made
everything the LORD commanded Moses; 23with him was Oholiab son
of Ahisamak, of the tribe of Dan — an engraver and designer, and an

PRAYING SCRIPTURE

Exodus 38

The tabernacle was made with great care, reflecting the same concern we should show as we approach the Lord. Each component had specific dimensions and directions for its fabrication. Worshiping God would not happen according to what each person wanted to do.

There is a difference between going to God as we are and recognizing God for who he is. Ask God to help you avoid a lackadaisical approach to worship.

---

[a] *1* Or *He*; also in verses 2-9 [b] *1* That is, about 4 1/2 feet or about 1.4 meters [c] *1* That is, about 7 1/2 feet or about 2.3 meters long and wide [d] *9* That is, about 150 feet or about 45 meters [e] *12* That is, about 75 feet or about 23 meters [f] *14* That is, about 22 feet or about 6.8 meters [g] *18* That is, about 30 feet or about 9 meters [h] *18* That is, about 7 1/2 feet or about 2.3 meters

embroiderer in blue, purple and scarlet yarn and fine linen.) 24The to-
tal amount of the gold from the wave offering used for all the work on
the sanctuary was 29 talents and 730 shekels,[a] according to the sanc-
tuary shekel.
25The silver obtained from those of the community who were
counted in the census was 100 talents[b] and 1,775 shekels,[c] according to
the sanctuary shekel — 26one beka per person, that is, half a shekel,[d]
according to the sanctuary shekel, from everyone who had crossed
over to those counted, twenty years old or more, a total of 603,550 men.
27The 100 talents of silver were used to cast the bases for the sanctu-
ary and for the curtain — 100 bases from the 100 talents, one talent
for each base. 28They used the 1,775 shekels to make the hooks for the
posts, to overlay the tops of the posts, and to make their bands.
29The bronze from the wave offering was 70 talents and 2,400 shek-
els.[e] 30They used it to make the bases for the entrance to the tent of
meeting, the bronze altar with its bronze grating and all its utensils,
31the bases for the surrounding courtyard and those for its entrance
and all the tent pegs for the tabernacle and those for the surrounding
courtyard.

THE PRIESTLY GARMENTS

39 From the blue, purple and scarlet yarn they made woven gar-
ments for ministering in the sanctuary. They also made sacred
garments for Aaron, as the LORD commanded Moses.

THE EPHOD

2They[f] made the ephod of gold, and of blue, purple and scarlet yarn,
and of finely twisted linen. 3They hammered out thin sheets of gold
and cut strands to be worked into the blue, purple and scarlet yarn and
fine linen — the work of skilled hands. 4They made shoulder pieces
for the ephod, which were attached to two of its corners, so it could
be fastened. 5Its skillfully woven waistband was like it — of one piece
with the ephod and made with gold, and with blue, purple and scarlet
yarn, and with finely twisted linen, as the LORD commanded Moses.
6They mounted the onyx stones in gold filigree settings and en-
graved them like a seal with the names of the sons of Israel. 7Then
they fastened them on the shoulder pieces of the ephod as memorial
stones for the sons of Israel, as the LORD commanded Moses.

THE BREASTPIECE

8They fashioned the breastpiece — the work of a skilled craftsman.
They made it like the ephod: of gold, and of blue, purple and scarlet
yarn, and of finely twisted linen. 9It was square — a span[g] long and
a span wide — and folded double. 10Then they mounted four rows of
precious stones on it. The first row was carnelian, chrysolite and beryl;
11the second row was turquoise, lapis lazuli and emerald; 12the third
row was jacinth, agate and amethyst; 13the fourth row was topaz, onyx

PRAYING SCRIPTURE

Exodus 39

The Israelites built the tabernacle according to God's design. But it wasn't only the structure involved. The priestly ephod, breastpiece, robe and other pieces had to be made following specific and detailed instructions. Nothing was left to personal preference.

The God of Abraham, Isaac and Jacob is not like the false gods of the nations. Thank God today that he invites you to spend time with him in prayer.

---

[a] *24* The weight of the gold was a little over a ton or about 1 metric ton.
[b] *25* That is, about 3 3/4 tons or about 3.4 metric tons; also in verse 27
[c] *25* That is, about 44 pounds or about 20 kilograms; also in verse 28
[d] *26* That is, about 1/5 ounce or about 5.7 grams [e] *29* The weight of the bronze was about 2 1/2 tons or about 2.4 metric tons. [f] *2* Or *He*; also in verses 7, 8 and 22 [g] *9* That is, about 9 inches or about 23 centimeters

and jasper.[a] They were mounted in gold filigree settings. 14There were twelve stones, one for each of the names of the sons of Israel, each engraved like a seal with the name of one of the twelve tribes.

15For the breastpiece they made braided chains of pure gold, like a rope. 16They made two gold filigree settings and two gold rings, and fastened the rings to two of the corners of the breastpiece. 17They fastened the two gold chains to the rings at the corners of the breastpiece, 18and the other ends of the chains to the two settings, attaching them to the shoulder pieces of the ephod at the front. 19They made two gold rings and attached them to the other two corners of the breastpiece on the inside edge next to the ephod. 20Then they made two more gold rings and attached them to the bottom of the shoulder pieces on the front of the ephod, close to the seam just above the waistband of the ephod. 21They tied the rings of the breastpiece to the rings of the ephod with blue cord, connecting it to the waistband so that the breastpiece would not swing out from the ephod—as the LORD commanded Moses.

OTHER PRIESTLY GARMENTS

22They made the robe of the ephod entirely of blue cloth—the work of a weaver— 23with an opening in the center of the robe like the opening of a collar,[b] and a band around this opening, so that it would not tear. 24They made pomegranates of blue, purple and scarlet yarn and finely twisted linen around the hem of the robe. 25And they made bells of pure gold and attached them around the hem between the pomegranates. 26The bells and pomegranates alternated around the hem of the robe to be worn for ministering, as the LORD commanded Moses.

27For Aaron and his sons, they made tunics of fine linen—the work of a weaver— 28and the turban of fine linen, the linen caps and the undergarments of finely twisted linen. 29The sash was made of finely twisted linen and blue, purple and scarlet yarn—the work of an embroiderer—as the LORD commanded Moses.

30They made the plate, the sacred emblem, out of pure gold and engraved on it, like an inscription on a seal: HOLY TO THE LORD. 31Then they fastened a blue cord to it to attach it to the turban, as the LORD commanded Moses.

MOSES INSPECTS THE TABERNACLE

32So all the work on the tabernacle, the tent of meeting, was completed. The Israelites did everything just as the LORD commanded Moses. 33Then they brought the tabernacle to Moses: the tent and all its furnishings, its clasps, frames, crossbars, posts and bases; 34the covering of ram skins dyed red and the covering of another durable leather[c] and the shielding curtain; 35the ark of the covenant law with its poles and the atonement cover; 36the table with all its articles and the bread of the Presence; 37the pure gold lampstand with its row of lamps and all its accessories, and the olive oil for the light; 38the gold altar, the anointing oil, the fragrant incense, and the curtain for the entrance to the tent; 39the bronze altar with its bronze grating, its poles and all its

[a] *13* The precise identification of some of these precious stones is uncertain.
[b] *23* The meaning of the Hebrew for this word is uncertain. [c] *34* Possibly the hides of large aquatic mammals

utensils; the basin with its stand; [40]the curtains of the courtyard with
its posts and bases, and the curtain for the entrance to the courtyard;
the ropes and tent pegs for the courtyard; all the furnishings for the
tabernacle, the tent of meeting; [41]and the woven garments worn for
ministering in the sanctuary, both the sacred garments for Aaron the
priest and the garments for his sons when serving as priests.
[42]The Israelites had done all the work just as the LORD had com-
manded Moses. [43]Moses inspected the work and saw that they had
done it just as the LORD had commanded. So Moses blessed them.

SETTING UP THE TABERNACLE

40 Then the LORD said to Moses: [2]"Set up the tabernacle, the tent
of meeting, on the first day of the first month. [3]Place the ark
of the covenant law in it and shield the ark with the curtain. [4]Bring
in the table and set out what belongs on it. Then bring in the lamp-
stand and set up its lamps. [5]Place the gold altar of incense in front of
the ark of the covenant law and put the curtain at the entrance to the
tabernacle.
[6]"Place the altar of burnt offering in front of the entrance to the
tabernacle, the tent of meeting; [7]place the basin between the tent of
meeting and the altar and put water in it. [8]Set up the courtyard around
it and put the curtain at the entrance to the courtyard.
[9]"Take the anointing oil and anoint the tabernacle and everything
in it; consecrate it and all its furnishings, and it will be holy. [10]Then
anoint the altar of burnt offering and all its utensils; consecrate the
altar, and it will be most holy. [11]Anoint the basin and its stand and
consecrate them.
[12]"Bring Aaron and his sons to the entrance to the tent of meeting
and wash them with water. [13]Then dress Aaron in the sacred garments,
anoint him and consecrate him so he may serve me as priest. [14]Bring
his sons and dress them in tunics. [15]Anoint them just as you anointed
their father, so they may serve me as priests. Their anointing will be to
a priesthood that will continue throughout their generations." [16]Moses
did everything just as the LORD commanded him.
[17]So the tabernacle was set up on the first day of the first month
in the second year. [18]When Moses set up the tabernacle, he put the
bases in place, erected the frames, inserted the crossbars and set up
the posts. [19]Then he spread the tent over the tabernacle and put the
covering over the tent, as the LORD commanded him.
[20]He took the tablets of the covenant law and placed them in the
ark, attached the poles to the ark and put the atonement cover over it.
[21]Then he brought the ark into the tabernacle and hung the shielding
curtain and shielded the ark of the covenant law, as the LORD com-
manded him.
[22]Moses placed the table in the tent of meeting on the north side of
the tabernacle outside the curtain [23]and set out the bread on it before
the LORD, as the LORD commanded him.
[24]He placed the lampstand in the tent of meeting opposite the table
on the south side of the tabernacle [25]and set up the lamps before the
LORD, as the LORD commanded him.
[26]Moses placed the gold altar in the tent of meeting in front of the
curtain [27]and burned fragrant incense on it, as the LORD commanded
him.
[28]Then he put up the curtain at the entrance to the tabernacle. [29]He

PRAYING SCRIPTURE

Exodus 40

Israel's portable place of worship was the structure where God visited his people. The tabernacle was the center of Israel's camp, reminding them that worship should be central. After the furniture and utensils were consecrated, the glory of God filled the tabernacle so that Moses could not even enter.

The tabernacle and everything in it were holy to God, as we are to be. Ask God to set you apart for his glory.

set the altar of burnt offering near the entrance to the tabernacle, the
tent of meeting, and offered on it burnt offerings and grain offerings,
as the LORD commanded him.
30He placed the basin between the tent of meeting and the altar and
put water in it for washing, 31and Moses and Aaron and his sons used
it to wash their hands and feet. 32They washed whenever they entered
the tent of meeting or approached the altar, as the LORD commanded
Moses.
33Then Moses set up the courtyard around the tabernacle and altar
and put up the curtain at the entrance to the courtyard. And so Moses
finished the work.

THE GLORY OF THE LORD

34Then the cloud covered the tent of meeting, and the glory of the
LORD filled the tabernacle. 35Moses could not enter the tent of meeting
because the cloud had settled on it, and the glory of the LORD filled the
tabernacle.
36In all the travels of the Israelites, whenever the cloud lifted from
above the tabernacle, they would set out; 37but if the cloud did not lift,
they did not set out — until the day it lifted. 38So the cloud of the LORD
was over the tabernacle by day, and fire was in the cloud by night, in
the sight of all the Israelites during all their travels.

LEVITICUS

Many view Leviticus as a boring list of rules that has nothing to do with God's people today. Yet Leviticus reveals that God has made a way for his people to experience forgiveness and redemption, to know him personally and to live in ways that honor him. Far from being irrelevant, this book lays a foundation for eternal redemption to come.

The first seven chapters of Leviticus detail the requirements for sacrificial offerings the Israelites must offer. Chapters 8–10 narrate the setting aside of Aaron's sons as priests, the assumption of their duties and the danger of performing those duties outside of God's instruction. The next seven chapters explain how the Israelites must deal with ceremonial uncleanness, including the instructions for the Day of Atonement, the most important day on the Hebrew calendar. The final chapters contain moral laws that govern both personal conduct and how God's people should treat each other.

Leviticus reveals an important truth for our prayer lives—God is approachable. Each law governing sacrifice and uncleanness shows how a person can be made ready to come before God. Our sins stand between us and him. In the old covenant, these laws gave the people a method for approaching God—through the Aaronic priesthood. Under the Law of Moses, only priests could come to God, and only then through sacrifices that provided limited-term efficacy. The blood of these offerings was insufficient for eternity, but they did point the way. They prepared us for the work of Christ in the New Testament, as he is the final sacrifice offered to bring people back to God forever.

The work that the high priest did on the Day of Atonement has been forever replaced by Christ's offer of his own blood in the Most Holy Place in heaven. We can come before God, but we must do so through the sacrifice of the great mediator, the Lord Jesus. Our privilege to come before the throne of God is because of Jesus Christ. No one comes to God in any way except through him.

Leviticus also reveals the logic behind God's moral law. For example, in chapter 19 God offered an assortment of moral laws governing life in Israel and repeatedly followed them with the refrain, "I am the LORD your God." He rooted these commands in the name he revealed to Moses at the burning bush: "I AM" (Exodus 3:14). This was the personal name he made known to the Israelites as he prepared to lead them out of Egypt. By reminding them of this, he was pointing them back to the salvation he worked for them in the exodus.

Leviticus leads us to pray to the Lord, the one true God who has the power to answer, deliver and redeem. Prayers offered to God through Jesus are never in vain. As the final sacrifice, the One to whom the lambs, bulls and goats pointed, Jesus' blood has opened an eternal living way to the Father.

THE BURNT OFFERING

1 The LORD called to Moses and spoke to him from the tent of meet-
ing. He said, 2"Speak to the Israelites and say to them: 'When any-
one among you brings an offering to the LORD, bring as your offering
an animal from either the herd or the flock.
3" 'If the offering is a burnt offering from the herd, you are to offer a
male without defect. You must present it at the entrance to the tent of
meeting so that it will be acceptable to the LORD. 4You are to lay your
hand on the head of the burnt offering, and it will be accepted on your
behalf to make atonement for you. 5You are to slaughter the young
bull before the LORD, and then Aaron's sons the priests shall bring the
blood and splash it against the sides of the altar at the entrance to the
tent of meeting. 6You are to skin the burnt offering and cut it into
pieces. 7The sons of Aaron the priest are to put fire on the altar and
arrange wood on the fire. 8Then Aaron's sons the priests shall arrange
the pieces, including the head and the fat, on the wood that is burning
on the altar. 9You are to wash the internal organs and the legs with wa-
ter, and the priest is to burn all of it on the altar. It is a burnt offering,
a food offering, an aroma pleasing to the LORD.
10" 'If the offering is a burnt offering from the flock, from either the
sheep or the goats, you are to offer a male without defect. 11You are to
slaughter it at the north side of the altar before the LORD, and Aaron's
sons the priests shall splash its blood against the sides of the altar.
12You are to cut it into pieces, and the priest shall arrange them, in-
cluding the head and the fat, on the wood that is burning on the altar.
13You are to wash the internal organs and the legs with water, and the
priest is to bring all of them and burn them on the altar. It is a burnt
offering, a food offering, an aroma pleasing to the LORD.
14" 'If the offering to the LORD is a burnt offering of birds, you are to
offer a dove or a young pigeon. 15The priest shall bring it to the altar,
wring off the head and burn it on the altar; its blood shall be drained
out on the side of the altar. 16He is to remove the crop and the feath-
ers[a] and throw them down east of the altar where the ashes are. 17He
shall tear it open by the wings, not dividing it completely, and then
the priest shall burn it on the wood that is burning on the altar. It is a
burnt offering, a food offering, an aroma pleasing to the LORD.

THE GRAIN OFFERING

2 " 'When anyone brings a grain offering to the LORD, their offer-
ing is to be of the finest flour. They are to pour olive oil on it, put
incense on it 2and take it to Aaron's sons the priests. The priest shall
take a handful of the flour and oil, together with all the incense, and
burn this as a memorial[b] portion on the altar, a food offering, an aroma
pleasing to the LORD. 3The rest of the grain offering belongs to Aaron
and his sons; it is a most holy part of the food offerings presented to
the LORD.
4" 'If you bring a grain offering baked in an oven, it is to consist of
the finest flour: either thick loaves made without yeast and with olive
oil mixed in or thin loaves made without yeast and brushed with ol-
ive oil. 5If your grain offering is prepared on a griddle, it is to be made
of the finest flour mixed with oil, and without yeast. 6Crumble it and

[a] *16* Or *crop with its contents*; the meaning of the Hebrew for this word is uncertain. [b] *2* Or *representative*; also in verses 9 and 16

PRAYING SCRIPTURE

Leviticus 1

Every sacrifice brought before the Lord had to be without blemish. This requirement prevented people from offering sickly or malformed animals to God in order to keep the healthiest animals for themselves. Their offerings were completely consumed by fire.

Are you ever tempted to offer God less than your best, like the money left over after an unnecessary shopping spree? Ask God to help you give him the best of everything, always.

PRAYING SCRIPTURE

Leviticus 2

When the people brought their grain offerings, they gave to the Lord out of their firstfruits. This offering was a test of faith in that second- or third-fruits were not guaranteed. Giving God the first was trusting that he would supply the rest.

Do you struggle to believe God can or will supply your needs? If so, ask him to increase your faith to believe he is able.

pour oil on it; it is a grain offering. 7If your grain offering is cooked
in a pan, it is to be made of the finest flour and some olive oil. 8Bring
the grain offering made of these things to the LORD; present it to the
priest, who shall take it to the altar. 9He shall take out the memorial
portion from the grain offering and burn it on the altar as a food of-
fering, an aroma pleasing to the LORD. 10The rest of the grain offering
belongs to Aaron and his sons; it is a most holy part of the food offer-
ings presented to the LORD.

11"'Every grain offering you bring to the LORD must be made without
yeast, for you are not to burn any yeast or honey in a food offering pre-
sented to the LORD. 12You may bring them to the LORD as an offering of
the firstfruits, but they are not to be offered on the altar as a pleasing
aroma. 13Season all your grain offerings with salt. Do not leave the salt
of the covenant of your God out of your grain offerings; add salt to all
your offerings.

14"'If you bring a grain offering of firstfruits to the LORD, offer
crushed heads of new grain roasted in the fire. 15Put oil and incense on
it; it is a grain offering. 16The priest shall burn the memorial portion
of the crushed grain and the oil, together with all the incense, as a food
offering presented to the LORD.

THE FELLOWSHIP OFFERING

3 "'If your offering is a fellowship offering, and you offer an animal
from the herd, whether male or female, you are to present before
the LORD an animal without defect. 2You are to lay your hand on the
head of your offering and slaughter it at the entrance to the tent of
meeting. Then Aaron's sons the priests shall splash the blood against
the sides of the altar. 3From the fellowship offering you are to bring
a food offering to the LORD: the internal organs and all the fat that is
connected to them, 4both kidneys with the fat on them near the loins,
and the long lobe of the liver, which you will remove with the kidneys.
5Then Aaron's sons are to burn it on the altar on top of the burnt offer-
ing that is lying on the burning wood; it is a food offering, an aroma
pleasing to the LORD.

6"'If you offer an animal from the flock as a fellowship offering to
the LORD, you are to offer a male or female without defect. 7If you of-
fer a lamb, you are to present it before the LORD, 8lay your hand on its
head and slaughter it in front of the tent of meeting. Then Aaron's sons
shall splash its blood against the sides of the altar. 9From the fellow-
ship offering you are to bring a food offering to the LORD: its fat, the
entire fat tail cut off close to the backbone, the internal organs and all
the fat that is connected to them, 10both kidneys with the fat on them
near the loins, and the long lobe of the liver, which you will remove
with the kidneys. 11The priest shall burn them on the altar as a food
offering presented to the LORD.

12"'If your offering is a goat, you are to present it before the LORD,
13lay your hand on its head and slaughter it in front of the tent of meet-
ing. Then Aaron's sons shall splash its blood against the sides of the
altar. 14From what you offer you are to present this food offering to
the LORD: the internal organs and all the fat that is connected to them,
15both kidneys with the fat on them near the loins, and the long lobe
of the liver, which you will remove with the kidneys. 16The priest shall
burn them on the altar as a food offering, a pleasing aroma. All the fat
is the LORD's.

PRAYING SCRIPTURE

Leviticus 3

The children of Israel went to the tabernacle repeatedly to offer blood sacrifices for their sins. As with other aspects of their worship, God gave explicit details on how to treat nearly every part of the animal: blood, fat and organs.

The blood sacrifices were a type of the ultimate sacrifice, Jesus. Thank God that we no longer need to offer up temporary sacrifices for our sins.

17"'This is a lasting ordinance for the generations to come, wherever
you live: You must not eat any fat or any blood.'"

THE SIN OFFERING

4 The LORD said to Moses, 2"Say to the Israelites: 'When anyone sins
unintentionally and does what is forbidden in any of the LORD's
commands—

3"'If the anointed priest sins, bringing guilt on the people, he must
bring to the LORD a young bull without defect as a sin offering[a] for the
sin he has committed. 4He is to present the bull at the entrance to the
tent of meeting before the LORD. He is to lay his hand on its head and
slaughter it there before the LORD. 5Then the anointed priest shall take
some of the bull's blood and carry it into the tent of meeting. 6He is to
dip his finger into the blood and sprinkle some of it seven times before
the LORD, in front of the curtain of the sanctuary. 7The priest shall then
put some of the blood on the horns of the altar of fragrant incense that
is before the LORD in the tent of meeting. The rest of the bull's blood he
shall pour out at the base of the altar of burnt offering at the entrance
to the tent of meeting. 8He shall remove all the fat from the bull of the
sin offering—all the fat that is connected to the internal organs, 9both
kidneys with the fat on them near the loins, and the long lobe of the
liver, which he will remove with the kidneys— 10just as the fat is re-
moved from the ox[b] sacrificed as a fellowship offering. Then the priest
shall burn them on the altar of burnt offering. 11But the hide of the bull
and all its flesh, as well as the head and legs, the internal organs and
the intestines 12that is, all the rest of the bull he must take outside
the camp to a place ceremonially clean, where the ashes are thrown,
and burn it there in a wood fire on the ash heap.

13"'If the whole Israelite community sins unintentionally and does
what is forbidden in any of the LORD's commands, even though the
community is unaware of the matter, when they realize their guilt
14and the sin they committed becomes known, the assembly must
bring a young bull as a sin offering and present it before the tent of
meeting. 15The elders of the community are to lay their hands on the
bull's head before the LORD, and the bull shall be slaughtered before
the LORD. 16Then the anointed priest is to take some of the bull's blood
into the tent of meeting. 17He shall dip his finger into the blood and
sprinkle it before the LORD seven times in front of the curtain. 18He is
to put some of the blood on the horns of the altar that is before the
LORD in the tent of meeting. The rest of the blood he shall pour out
at the base of the altar of burnt offering at the entrance to the tent of
meeting. 19He shall remove all the fat from it and burn it on the altar,
20and do with this bull just as he did with the bull for the sin offering.
In this way the priest will make atonement for the community, and
they will be forgiven. 21Then he shall take the bull outside the camp
and burn it as he burned the first bull. This is the sin offering for the
community.

22"'When a leader sins unintentionally and does what is forbidden
in any of the commands of the LORD his God, when he realizes his guilt
23and the sin he has committed becomes known, he must bring as his

PRAYING SCRIPTURE

Leviticus 4

We often sin without intending to, but this does not lessen the seriousness of it. A special sacrifice offered for such sins indicates that God does not wink at accidental sin but demands it be covered as surely as intentional transgressions are. All sin is offensive to God.

Spend some time reflecting on the last few days. Ask God to show you any sins committed without your realizing it, and thank him for forgiving them.

---

[a] 3 Or *purification offering*; here and throughout this chapter [b] *10* The Hebrew word can refer to either male or female.

offering a male goat without defect. [24]He is to lay his hand on the goat's
head and slaughter it at the place where the burnt offering is slaugh-
tered before the LORD. It is a sin offering. [25]Then the priest shall take
some of the blood of the sin offering with his finger and put it on the
horns of the altar of burnt offering and pour out the rest of the blood
at the base of the altar. [26]He shall burn all the fat on the altar as he
burned the fat of the fellowship offering. In this way the priest will
make atonement for the leader's sin, and he will be forgiven.

[27]" 'If any member of the community sins unintentionally and does
what is forbidden in any of the LORD's commands, when they realize
their guilt [28]and the sin they have committed becomes known, they
must bring as their offering for the sin they committed a female goat
without defect. [29]They are to lay their hand on the head of the sin of-
fering and slaughter it at the place of the burnt offering. [30]Then the
priest is to take some of the blood with his finger and put it on the
horns of the altar of burnt offering and pour out the rest of the blood
at the base of the altar. [31]They shall remove all the fat, just as the fat is
removed from the fellowship offering, and the priest shall burn it on
the altar as an aroma pleasing to the LORD. In this way the priest will
make atonement for them, and they will be forgiven.

[32]" 'If someone brings a lamb as their sin offering, they are to bring
a female without defect. [33]They are to lay their hand on its head and
slaughter it for a sin offering at the place where the burnt offering is
slaughtered. [34]Then the priest shall take some of the blood of the sin
offering with his finger and put it on the horns of the altar of burnt of-
fering and pour out the rest of the blood at the base of the altar. [35]They
shall remove all the fat, just as the fat is removed from the lamb of the
fellowship offering, and the priest shall burn it on the altar on top of
the food offerings presented to the LORD. In this way the priest will
make atonement for them for the sin they have committed, and they
will be forgiven.

5 " 'If anyone sins because they do not speak up when they hear a
public charge to testify regarding something they have seen or
learned about, they will be held responsible.

[2]" 'If anyone becomes aware that they are guilty — if they unwit-
tingly touch anything ceremonially unclean (whether the carcass of
an unclean animal, wild or domestic, or of any unclean creature that
moves along the ground) and they are unaware that they have become
unclean, but then they come to realize their guilt; [3]or if they touch
human uncleanness (anything that would make them unclean) even
though they are unaware of it, but then they learn of it and realize
their guilt; [4]or if anyone thoughtlessly takes an oath to do anything,
whether good or evil (in any matter one might carelessly swear about)
even though they are unaware of it, but then they learn of it and real-
ize their guilt — [5]when anyone becomes aware that they are guilty in
any of these matters, they must confess in what way they have sinned.
[6]As a penalty for the sin they have committed, they must bring to the
LORD a female lamb or goat from the flock as a sin offering[a]; and the
priest shall make atonement for them for their sin.

[7]" 'Anyone who cannot afford a lamb is to bring two doves or two
young pigeons to the LORD as a penalty for their sin — one for a sin

[a] 6 Or *purification offering*; here and throughout this chapter

PRAYING SCRIPTURE

Leviticus 5

When we sin, we should seek forgiveness immediately. Part of this process is simply to admit that we've sinned. That can be a hard thing to do. Our pride often leads us to rationalize sins rather than admit them.

Confessing sin is the same in the Old and New Testaments. Confess to God when you have sinned so you can walk in the light.

offering and the other for a burnt offering. 8 They are to bring them
to the priest, who shall first offer the one for the sin offering. He is
to wring its head from its neck, not dividing it completely, 9 and is to
splash some of the blood of the sin offering against the side of the al-
tar; the rest of the blood must be drained out at the base of the altar.
It is a sin offering. 10 The priest shall then offer the other as a burnt
offering in the prescribed way and make atonement for them for the
sin they have committed, and they will be forgiven.
11 " 'If, however, they cannot afford two doves or two young pigeons,
they are to bring as an offering for their sin a tenth of an ephah[a] of the
finest flour for a sin offering. They must not put olive oil or incense
on it, because it is a sin offering. 12 They are to bring it to the priest,
who shall take a handful of it as a memorial[b] portion and burn it on
the altar on top of the food offerings presented to the LORD. It is a sin
offering. 13 In this way the priest will make atonement for them for
any of these sins they have committed, and they will be forgiven. The
rest of the offering will belong to the priest, as in the case of the grain
offering.' "

THE GUILT OFFERING

14 The LORD said to Moses: 15 "When anyone is unfaithful to the LORD
by sinning unintentionally in regard to any of the LORD's holy things,
they are to bring to the LORD as a penalty a ram from the flock, one
without defect and of the proper value in silver, according to the sanc-
tuary shekel.[c] It is a guilt offering. 16 They must make restitution for
what they have failed to do in regard to the holy things, pay an ad-
ditional penalty of a fifth of its value and give it all to the priest. The
priest will make atonement for them with the ram as a guilt offering,
and they will be forgiven.
17 "If anyone sins and does what is forbidden in any of the LORD's
commands, even though they do not know it, they are guilty and will
be held responsible. 18 They are to bring to the priest as a guilt offering
a ram from the flock, one without defect and of the proper value. In
this way the priest will make atonement for them for the wrong they
have committed unintentionally, and they will be forgiven. 19 It is a
guilt offering; they have been guilty of[d] wrongdoing against the LORD."
6 [e] The LORD said to Moses: 2 "If anyone sins and is unfaithful to the
LORD by deceiving a neighbor about something entrusted to
them or left in their care or about something stolen, or if they cheat
their neighbor, 3 or if they find lost property and lie about it, or if they
swear falsely about any such sin that people may commit— 4 when
they sin in any of these ways and realize their guilt, they must return
what they have stolen or taken by extortion, or what was entrusted to
them, or the lost property they found, 5 or whatever it was they swore
falsely about. They must make restitution in full, add a fifth of the
value to it and give it all to the owner on the day they present their
guilt offering. 6 And as a penalty they must bring to the priest, that
is, to the LORD, their guilt offering, a ram from the flock, one with-
out defect and of the proper value. 7 In this way the priest will make

PRAYING SCRIPTURE

Leviticus 6

God does not only see sin in offenses toward him. He wants his people to walk in righteousness in their dealings with each other too. Offerings to God were acceptable until any required restitution was made in an interpersonal offense.

This requirement is echoed by Jesus. Before you pray, consider whether there is an offense between you and another. Take any necessary steps toward reconciliation.

[a] *11* That is, probably about 3 1/2 pounds or about 1.6 kilograms [b] *12* Or *representative* [c] *15* That is, about 2/5 ounce or about 12 grams [d] *19* Or *offering; atonement has been made for their* [e] In Hebrew texts 6:1-7 is numbered 5:20-26, and 6:8-30 is numbered 6:1-23.

atonement for them before the LORD, and they will be forgiven for any
of the things they did that made them guilty."

THE BURNT OFFERING

8The LORD said to Moses: 9"Give Aaron and his sons this command:
'These are the regulations for the burnt offering: The burnt offering
is to remain on the altar hearth throughout the night, till morning,
and the fire must be kept burning on the altar. 10The priest shall then
put on his linen clothes, with linen undergarments next to his body,
and shall remove the ashes of the burnt offering that the fire has con-
sumed on the altar and place them beside the altar. 11Then he is to take
off these clothes and put on others, and carry the ashes outside the
camp to a place that is ceremonially clean. 12The fire on the altar must
be kept burning; it must not go out. Every morning the priest is to add
firewood and arrange the burnt offering on the fire and burn the fat of
the fellowship offerings on it. 13The fire must be kept burning on the
altar continuously; it must not go out.

THE GRAIN OFFERING

14" 'These are the regulations for the grain offering: Aaron's sons are
to bring it before the LORD, in front of the altar. 15The priest is to take
a handful of the finest flour and some olive oil, together with all the
incense on the grain offering, and burn the memorial[a] portion on the
altar as an aroma pleasing to the LORD. 16Aaron and his sons shall eat
the rest of it, but it is to be eaten without yeast in the sanctuary area;
they are to eat it in the courtyard of the tent of meeting. 17It must not
be baked with yeast; I have given it as their share of the food offerings
presented to me. Like the sin offering[b] and the guilt offering, it is most
holy. 18Any male descendant of Aaron may eat it. For all generations
to come it is his perpetual share of the food offerings presented to the
LORD. Whatever touches them will become holy.[c]' "
19The LORD also said to Moses, 20"This is the offering Aaron and his
sons are to bring to the LORD on the day he[d] is anointed: a tenth of an
ephah[e] of the finest flour as a regular grain offering, half of it in the
morning and half in the evening. 21It must be prepared with oil on a
griddle; bring it well-mixed and present the grain offering broken[f] in
pieces as an aroma pleasing to the LORD. 22The son who is to succeed
him as anointed priest shall prepare it. It is the LORD's perpetual share
and is to be burned completely. 23Every grain offering of a priest shall
be burned completely; it must not be eaten."

THE SIN OFFERING

24The LORD said to Moses, 25"Say to Aaron and his sons: 'These are
the regulations for the sin offering: The sin offering is to be slaugh-
tered before the LORD in the place the burnt offering is slaughtered; it
is most holy. 26The priest who offers it shall eat it; it is to be eaten in
the sanctuary area, in the courtyard of the tent of meeting. 27Whatever
touches any of the flesh will become holy, and if any of the blood is
spattered on a garment, you must wash it in the sanctuary area. 28The

---

[a] *15* Or *representative* [b] *17* Or *purification offering*; also in verses 25 and 30
[c] *18* Or *Whoever touches them must be holy*; similarly in verse 27 [d] *20* Or
each [e] *20* That is, probably about 3 1/2 pounds or about 1.6 kilograms
[f] *21* The meaning of the Hebrew for this word is uncertain.

clay pot the meat is cooked in must be broken; but if it is cooked in a
bronze pot, the pot is to be scoured and rinsed with water. 29 Any male
in a priest's family may eat it; it is most holy. 30 But any sin offering
whose blood is brought into the tent of meeting to make atonement
in the Holy Place must not be eaten; it must be burned up.

THE GUILT OFFERING

7 " 'These are the regulations for the guilt offering, which is most
holy: 2 The guilt offering is to be slaughtered in the place where the
burnt offering is slaughtered, and its blood is to be splashed against
the sides of the altar. 3 All its fat shall be offered: the fat tail and the fat
that covers the internal organs, 4 both kidneys with the fat on them
near the loins, and the long lobe of the liver, which is to be removed
with the kidneys. 5 The priest shall burn them on the altar as a food
offering presented to the LORD. It is a guilt offering. 6 Any male in a
priest's family may eat it, but it must be eaten in the sanctuary area;
it is most holy.

7 " 'The same law applies to both the sin offering[a] and the guilt of-
fering: They belong to the priest who makes atonement with them.
8 The priest who offers a burnt offering for anyone may keep its hide
for himself. 9 Every grain offering baked in an oven or cooked in a pan
or on a griddle belongs to the priest who offers it, 10 and every grain
offering, whether mixed with olive oil or dry, belongs equally to all
the sons of Aaron.

THE FELLOWSHIP OFFERING

11 " 'These are the regulations for the fellowship offering anyone may
present to the LORD:

12 " 'If they offer it as an expression of thankfulness, then along
with this thank offering they are to offer thick loaves made without
yeast and with olive oil mixed in, thin loaves made without yeast and
brushed with oil, and thick loaves of the finest flour well-kneaded and
with oil mixed in. 13 Along with their fellowship offering of thanksgiv-
ing they are to present an offering with thick loaves of bread made
with yeast. 14 They are to bring one of each kind as an offering, a con-
tribution to the LORD; it belongs to the priest who splashes the blood of
the fellowship offering against the altar. 15 The meat of their fellowship
offering of thanksgiving must be eaten on the day it is offered; they
must leave none of it till morning.

16 " 'If, however, their offering is the result of a vow or is a freewill of-
fering, the sacrifice shall be eaten on the day they offer it, but anything
left over may be eaten on the next day. 17 Any meat of the sacrifice left
over till the third day must be burned up. 18 If any meat of the fellow-
ship offering is eaten on the third day, the one who offered it will not
be accepted. It will not be reckoned to their credit, for it has become
impure; the person who eats any of it will be held responsible.

19 " 'Meat that touches anything ceremonially unclean must not be
eaten; it must be burned up. As for other meat, anyone ceremonially
clean may eat it. 20 But if anyone who is unclean eats any meat of the
fellowship offering belonging to the LORD, they must be cut off from
their people. 21 Anyone who touches something unclean — whether
human uncleanness or an unclean animal or any unclean creature

PRAYING SCRIPTURE

Leviticus 7

The peace offering could be made either for thanksgiving or making a vow. We should be thankful for God's bountiful blessings and be careful to follow through on any promises we make to him.

Consider your many blessings from God, and thank him for them now. Ask him to bring to mind any commitments you need to keep and for the strength to complete them.

[a] 7 Or *purification offering*; also in verse 37

that moves along the ground[a] — and then eats any of the meat of the
fellowship offering belonging to the LORD must be cut off from their
people.'"

EATING FAT AND BLOOD FORBIDDEN

22The LORD said to Moses, 23"Say to the Israelites: 'Do not eat any of
the fat of cattle, sheep or goats. 24The fat of an animal found dead or
torn by wild animals may be used for any other purpose, but you must
not eat it. 25Anyone who eats the fat of an animal from which a food
offering may be[b] presented to the LORD must be cut off from their peo-
ple. 26And wherever you live, you must not eat the blood of any bird or
animal. 27Anyone who eats blood must be cut off from their people.'"

THE PRIESTS' SHARE

28The LORD said to Moses, 29"Say to the Israelites: 'Anyone who
brings a fellowship offering to the LORD is to bring part of it as their
sacrifice to the LORD. 30With their own hands they are to present the
food offering to the LORD; they are to bring the fat, together with the
breast, and wave the breast before the LORD as a wave offering. 31The
priest shall burn the fat on the altar, but the breast belongs to Aaron
and his sons. 32You are to give the right thigh of your fellowship offer-
ings to the priest as a contribution. 33The son of Aaron who offers the
blood and the fat of the fellowship offering shall have the right thigh
as his share. 34From the fellowship offerings of the Israelites, I have
taken the breast that is waved and the thigh that is presented and have
given them to Aaron the priest and his sons as their perpetual share
from the Israelites.'"

35This is the portion of the food offerings presented to the LORD that
were allotted to Aaron and his sons on the day they were presented to
serve the LORD as priests. 36On the day they were anointed, the LORD
commanded that the Israelites give this to them as their perpetual
share for the generations to come.

37These, then, are the regulations for the burnt offering, the grain of-
fering, the sin offering, the guilt offering, the ordination offering and
the fellowship offering, 38which the LORD gave Moses at Mount Sinai
in the Desert of Sinai on the day he commanded the Israelites to bring
their offerings to the LORD.

PRAYING SCRIPTURE

Leviticus 8

The Lord dealt with his people through intermediaries. In Israel's case, it was the priests. Aaron and his sons bridged the gap between the people and God, offering sacrifices on their behalf so their sins might be temporarily covered.

The priesthood exemplified the ultimate great high priest, Jesus Christ, who intercedes for us with the Father. Ask God how you can become an intercessor for others like Christ is for you.

THE ORDINATION OF AARON AND HIS SONS

8 The LORD said to Moses, 2"Bring Aaron and his sons, their gar-
ments, the anointing oil, the bull for the sin offering,[c] the two
rams and the basket containing bread made without yeast, 3and gather
the entire assembly at the entrance to the tent of meeting." 4Moses
did as the LORD commanded him, and the assembly gathered at the
entrance to the tent of meeting.

5Moses said to the assembly, "This is what the LORD has commanded
to be done." 6Then Moses brought Aaron and his sons forward and
washed them with water. 7He put the tunic on Aaron, tied the sash
around him, clothed him with the robe and put the ephod on him. He
also fastened the ephod with a decorative waistband, which he tied

---

[a] *21* A few Hebrew manuscripts, Samaritan Pentateuch, Syriac and Targum (see 5:2); most Hebrew manuscripts *any unclean, detestable thing* [b] *25* Or *offering is* [c] *2* Or *purification offering*; also in verse 14

around him. [8]He placed the breastpiece on him and put the Urim and
Thummim in the breastpiece. [9]Then he placed the turban on Aaron's
head and set the gold plate, the sacred emblem, on the front of it, as
the LORD commanded Moses.

[10]Then Moses took the anointing oil and anointed the tabernacle
and everything in it, and so consecrated them. [11]He sprinkled some of
the oil on the altar seven times, anointing the altar and all its utensils
and the basin with its stand, to consecrate them. [12]He poured some
of the anointing oil on Aaron's head and anointed him to consecrate
him. [13]Then he brought Aaron's sons forward, put tunics on them, tied
sashes around them and fastened caps on them, as the LORD com-
manded Moses.

[14]He then presented the bull for the sin offering, and Aaron and his
sons laid their hands on its head. [15]Moses slaughtered the bull and took
some of the blood, and with his finger he put it on all the horns of the
altar to purify the altar. He poured out the rest of the blood at the base
of the altar. So he consecrated it to make atonement for it. [16]Moses also
took all the fat around the internal organs, the long lobe of the liver,
and both kidneys and their fat, and burned it on the altar. [17]But the
bull with its hide and its flesh and its intestines he burned up outside
the camp, as the LORD commanded Moses.

[18]He then presented the ram for the burnt offering, and Aaron and
his sons laid their hands on its head. [19]Then Moses slaughtered the ram
and splashed the blood against the sides of the altar. [20]He cut the ram
into pieces and burned the head, the pieces and the fat. [21]He washed
the internal organs and the legs with water and burned the whole ram
on the altar. It was a burnt offering, a pleasing aroma, a food offering
presented to the LORD, as the LORD commanded Moses.

[22]He then presented the other ram, the ram for the ordination, and
Aaron and his sons laid their hands on its head. [23]Moses slaughtered
the ram and took some of its blood and put it on the lobe of Aaron's
right ear, on the thumb of his right hand and on the big toe of his
right foot. [24]Moses also brought Aaron's sons forward and put some
of the blood on the lobes of their right ears, on the thumbs of their
right hands and on the big toes of their right feet. Then he splashed
blood against the sides of the altar. [25]After that, he took the fat, the fat
tail, all the fat around the internal organs, the long lobe of the liver,
both kidneys and their fat and the right thigh. [26]And from the basket
of bread made without yeast, which was before the LORD, he took one
thick loaf, one thick loaf with olive oil mixed in, and one thin loaf,
and he put these on the fat portions and on the right thigh. [27]He put
all these in the hands of Aaron and his sons, and they waved them be-
fore the LORD as a wave offering. [28]Then Moses took them from their
hands and burned them on the altar on top of the burnt offering as an
ordination offering, a pleasing aroma, a food offering presented to the
LORD. [29]Moses also took the breast, which was his share of the ordina-
tion ram, and waved it before the LORD as a wave offering, as the LORD
commanded Moses.

[30]Then Moses took some of the anointing oil and some of the blood
from the altar and sprinkled them on Aaron and his garments and
on his sons and their garments. So he consecrated Aaron and his gar-
ments and his sons and their garments.

[31]Moses then said to Aaron and his sons, "Cook the meat at the en-
trance to the tent of meeting and eat it there with the bread from the

basket of ordination offerings, as I was commanded: 'Aaron and his sons are to eat it.' [32]Then burn up the rest of the meat and the bread. [33]Do not leave the entrance to the tent of meeting for seven days, until the days of your ordination are completed, for your ordination will last seven days. [34]What has been done today was commanded by the LORD to make atonement for you. [35]You must stay at the entrance to the tent of meeting day and night for seven days and do what the LORD requires, so you will not die; for that is what I have been commanded."

[36]So Aaron and his sons did everything the LORD commanded through Moses.

THE PRIESTS BEGIN THEIR MINISTRY

9 On the eighth day Moses summoned Aaron and his sons and the elders of Israel. [2]He said to Aaron, "Take a bull calf for your sin offering[a] and a ram for your burnt offering, both without defect, and present them before the LORD. [3]Then say to the Israelites: 'Take a male goat for a sin offering, a calf and a lamb — both a year old and without defect — for a burnt offering, [4]and an ox[b] and a ram for a fellowship offering to sacrifice before the LORD, together with a grain offering mixed with olive oil. For today the LORD will appear to you.'"

[5]They took the things Moses commanded to the front of the tent of meeting, and the entire assembly came near and stood before the LORD. [6]Then Moses said, "This is what the LORD has commanded you to do, so that the glory of the LORD may appear to you."

[7]Moses said to Aaron, "Come to the altar and sacrifice your sin offering and your burnt offering and make atonement for yourself and the people; sacrifice the offering that is for the people and make atonement for them, as the LORD has commanded."

[8]So Aaron came to the altar and slaughtered the calf as a sin offering for himself. [9]His sons brought the blood to him, and he dipped his finger into the blood and put it on the horns of the altar; the rest of the blood he poured out at the base of the altar. [10]On the altar he burned the fat, the kidneys and the long lobe of the liver from the sin offering, as the LORD commanded Moses; [11]the flesh and the hide he burned up outside the camp.

[12]Then he slaughtered the burnt offering. His sons handed him the blood, and he splashed it against the sides of the altar. [13]They handed him the burnt offering piece by piece, including the head, and he burned them on the altar. [14]He washed the internal organs and the legs and burned them on top of the burnt offering on the altar.

[15]Aaron then brought the offering that was for the people. He took the goat for the people's sin offering and slaughtered it and offered it for a sin offering as he did with the first one.

[16]He brought the burnt offering and offered it in the prescribed way. [17]He also brought the grain offering, took a handful of it and burned it on the altar in addition to the morning's burnt offering.

[18]He slaughtered the ox and the ram as the fellowship offering for the people. His sons handed him the blood, and he splashed it against the sides of the altar. [19]But the fat portions of the ox and the ram — the fat tail, the layer of fat, the kidneys and the long lobe of the liver — [20]these they laid on the breasts, and then Aaron burned the fat on the

PRAYING SCRIPTURE

Leviticus 9

The law provided for the priests, who had to offer sacrifices for themselves before they offered sacrifices for the people. God would not allow them in his presence on behalf of others if they themselves were not cleansed.

The inauguration of this priesthood was confirmed when God's glory fell from heaven, consuming the entire offering (see verses 23–24). Thank God that the sacrifices started under Aaron are no longer necessary because of Jesus.

---

[a] 2 Or *purification offering*; here and throughout this chapter [b] 4 The Hebrew word can refer to either male or female; also in verses 18 and 19.

altar. 21Aaron waved the breasts and the right thigh before the LORD as
a wave offering, as Moses commanded.
22Then Aaron lifted his hands toward the people and blessed them.
And having sacrificed the sin offering, the burnt offering and the fel-
lowship offering, he stepped down.
23Moses and Aaron then went into the tent of meeting. When they
came out, they blessed the people; and the glory of the LORD appeared
to all the people. 24Fire came out from the presence of the LORD and
consumed the burnt offering and the fat portions on the altar. And
when all the people saw it, they shouted for joy and fell facedown.

THE DEATH OF NADAB AND ABIHU

10 Aaron's sons Nadab and Abihu took their censers, put fire in
them and added incense; and they offered unauthorized fire
before the LORD, contrary to his command. 2So fire came out from the
presence of the LORD and consumed them, and they died before the
LORD. 3Moses then said to Aaron, "This is what the LORD spoke of when
he said:

"'Among those who approach me
 I will be proved holy;
in the sight of all the people
 I will be honored.'"

Aaron remained silent.
4Moses summoned Mishael and Elzaphan, sons of Aaron's uncle
Uzziel, and said to them, "Come here; carry your cousins outside the
camp, away from the front of the sanctuary." 5So they came and carried
them, still in their tunics, outside the camp, as Moses ordered.
6Then Moses said to Aaron and his sons Eleazar and Ithamar, "Do
not let your hair become unkempt[a] and do not tear your clothes, or
you will die and the LORD will be angry with the whole community.
But your relatives, all the Israelites, may mourn for those the LORD has
destroyed by fire. 7Do not leave the entrance to the tent of meeting or
you will die, because the LORD's anointing oil is on you." So they did
as Moses said.
8Then the LORD said to Aaron, 9"You and your sons are not to drink
wine or other fermented drink whenever you go into the tent of meet-
ing, or you will die. This is a lasting ordinance for the generations to
come, 10so that you can distinguish between the holy and the common,
between the unclean and the clean, 11and so you can teach the Israel-
ites all the decrees the LORD has given them through Moses."
12Moses said to Aaron and his remaining sons, Eleazar and Ithamar,
"Take the grain offering left over from the food offerings prepared
without yeast and presented to the LORD and eat it beside the altar, for
it is most holy. 13Eat it in the sanctuary area, because it is your share
and your sons' share of the food offerings presented to the LORD; for so
I have been commanded. 14But you and your sons and your daughters
may eat the breast that was waved and the thigh that was presented.
Eat them in a ceremonially clean place; they have been given to you
and your children as your share of the Israelites' fellowship offerings.
15The thigh that was presented and the breast that was waved must be
brought with the fat portions of the food offerings, to be waved before

PRAYING SCRIPTURE

Leviticus 10

God has always taken seriously how people render worship. Because God is holy, the way we worship him is a matter of grave importance. Different cultures might worship in various appropriate ways, but God does not accept an "anything goes" approach. Aaron's sons found out in judgment.

When going to God in prayer or worship, begin with self-examination. Ask God to cleanse you completely so you can offer acceptable worship.

[a] 6 Or *Do not uncover your heads*

the LORD as a wave offering. This will be the perpetual share for you
and your children, as the LORD has commanded."
16When Moses inquired about the goat of the sin offering[a] and found
that it had been burned up, he was angry with Eleazar and Ithamar,
Aaron's remaining sons, and asked, 17"Why didn't you eat the sin of-
fering in the sanctuary area? It is most holy; it was given to you to take
away the guilt of the community by making atonement for them be-
fore the LORD. 18Since its blood was not taken into the Holy Place, you
should have eaten the goat in the sanctuary area, as I commanded."
19Aaron replied to Moses, "Today they sacrificed their sin offering
and their burnt offering before the LORD, but such things as this have
happened to me. Would the LORD have been pleased if I had eaten the
sin offering today?" 20When Moses heard this, he was satisfied.

CLEAN AND UNCLEAN FOOD

11 The LORD said to Moses and Aaron, 2"Say to the Israelites: 'Of all
the animals that live on land, these are the ones you may eat: 3You
may eat any animal that has a divided hoof and that chews the cud.
4" 'There are some that only chew the cud or only have a divided
hoof, but you must not eat them. The camel, though it chews the cud,
does not have a divided hoof; it is ceremonially unclean for you. 5The
hyrax, though it chews the cud, does not have a divided hoof; it is un-
clean for you. 6The rabbit, though it chews the cud, does not have a di-
vided hoof; it is unclean for you. 7And the pig, though it has a divided
hoof, does not chew the cud; it is unclean for you. 8You must not eat
their meat or touch their carcasses; they are unclean for you.
9" 'Of all the creatures living in the water of the seas and the streams
you may eat any that have fins and scales. 10But all creatures in the
seas or streams that do not have fins and scales — whether among all
the swarming things or among all the other living creatures in the
water — you are to regard as unclean. 11And since you are to regard
them as unclean, you must not eat their meat; you must regard their
carcasses as unclean. 12Anything living in the water that does not have
fins and scales is to be regarded as unclean by you.
13" 'These are the birds you are to regard as unclean and not eat be-
cause they are unclean: the eagle,[b] the vulture, the black vulture, 14the
red kite, any kind of black kite, 15any kind of raven, 16the horned owl,
the screech owl, the gull, any kind of hawk, 17the little owl, the cormo-
rant, the great owl, 18the white owl, the desert owl, the osprey, 19the
stork, any kind of heron, the hoopoe and the bat.
20" 'All flying insects that walk on all fours are to be regarded as un-
clean by you. 21There are, however, some flying insects that walk on all
fours that you may eat: those that have jointed legs for hopping on the
ground. 22Of these you may eat any kind of locust, katydid, cricket or
grasshopper. 23But all other flying insects that have four legs you are
to regard as unclean.
24" 'You will make yourselves unclean by these; whoever touches
their carcasses will be unclean till evening. 25Whoever picks up one
of their carcasses must wash their clothes, and they will be unclean
till evening.

PRAYING SCRIPTURE

Leviticus 11

The law includes many instructions about food. The Lord forbids us to do what would be detrimental to our bodies and souls. Some animals might have been deemed unclean as tests of obedience while other laws brought attention to cleanliness.

None of this was pointless; God wanted his people to be holy because he is holy. Ask God to help you live a holy life that points others to him.

[a] *16* Or *purification offering*; also in verses 17 and 19 [b] *13* The precise identification of some of the birds, insects and animals in this chapter is uncertain.

26“‘Every animal that does not have a divided hoof or that does not
chew the cud is unclean for you; whoever touches the carcass of any of
them will be unclean. 27Of all the animals that walk on all fours, those
that walk on their paws are unclean for you; whoever touches their
carcasses will be unclean till evening. 28Anyone who picks up their car-
casses must wash their clothes, and they will be unclean till evening.
These animals are unclean for you.

29“‘Of the animals that move along the ground, these are unclean
for you: the weasel, the rat, any kind of great lizard, 30the gecko, the
monitor lizard, the wall lizard, the skink and the chameleon. 31Of all
those that move along the ground, these are unclean for you. Whoever
touches them when they are dead will be unclean till evening. 32When
one of them dies and falls on something, that article, whatever its use,
will be unclean, whether it is made of wood, cloth, hide or sackcloth.
Put it in water; it will be unclean till evening, and then it will be clean.
33If one of them falls into a clay pot, everything in it will be unclean,
and you must break the pot. 34Any food you are allowed to eat that has
come into contact with water from any such pot is unclean, and any
liquid that is drunk from such a pot is unclean. 35Anything that one
of their carcasses falls on becomes unclean; an oven or cooking pot
must be broken up. They are unclean, and you are to regard them as
unclean. 36A spring, however, or a cistern for collecting water remains
clean, but anyone who touches one of these carcasses is unclean. 37If
a carcass falls on any seeds that are to be planted, they remain clean.
38But if water has been put on the seed and a carcass falls on it, it is
unclean for you.

39“‘If an animal that you are allowed to eat dies, anyone who touches
its carcass will be unclean till evening. 40Anyone who eats some of its
carcass must wash their clothes, and they will be unclean till evening.
Anyone who picks up the carcass must wash their clothes, and they will
be unclean till evening.

41“‘Every creature that moves along the ground is to be regarded
as unclean; it is not to be eaten. 42You are not to eat any creature that
moves along the ground, whether it moves on its belly or walks on all
fours or on many feet; it is unclean. 43Do not defile yourselves by any
of these creatures. Do not make yourselves unclean by means of them
or be made unclean by them. 44I am the LORD your God; consecrate
yourselves and be holy, because I am holy. Do not make yourselves
unclean by any creature that moves along the ground. 45I am the LORD,
who brought you up out of Egypt to be your God; therefore be holy,
because I am holy.

46“‘These are the regulations concerning animals, birds, every living
thing that moves about in the water and every creature that moves
along the ground. 47You must distinguish between the unclean and
the clean, between living creatures that may be eaten and those that
may not be eaten.’”

PURIFICATION AFTER CHILDBIRTH

12 The LORD said to Moses, 2“Say to the Israelites: ‘A woman who
becomes pregnant and gives birth to a son will be ceremonially
unclean for seven days, just as she is unclean during her monthly pe-
riod. 3On the eighth day the boy is to be circumcised. 4Then the woman
must wait thirty-three days to be purified from her bleeding. She must
not touch anything sacred or go to the sanctuary until the days of her

PRAYING SCRIPTURE

Leviticus 12

Childbearing in ancient Israel was treated with a great deal of attention. Each birth required sacrifices. This reminded the people that they needed to confess general sinfulness to God. Giving birth was not a sin, but God used it as a reminder that we sin.

It is good to be mindful of our struggle against sin. Ask God to reveal any sin in your life, and then confess it to him.

purification are over. [5]If she gives birth to a daughter, for two weeks the woman will be unclean, as during her period. Then she must wait sixty-six days to be purified from her bleeding.

[6]"'When the days of her purification for a son or daughter are over, she is to bring to the priest at the entrance to the tent of meeting a year-old lamb for a burnt offering and a young pigeon or a dove for a sin offering.[a] [7]He shall offer them before the LORD to make atonement for her, and then she will be ceremonially clean from her flow of blood.

"'These are the regulations for the woman who gives birth to a boy or a girl. [8]But if she cannot afford a lamb, she is to bring two doves or two young pigeons, one for a burnt offering and the other for a sin offering. In this way the priest will make atonement for her, and she will be clean.'"

REGULATIONS ABOUT DEFILING SKIN DISEASES

13 The LORD said to Moses and Aaron, [2]"When anyone has a swelling or a rash or a shiny spot on their skin that may be a defiling skin disease,[b] they must be brought to Aaron the priest or to one of his sons[c] who is a priest. [3]The priest is to examine the sore on the skin, and if the hair in the sore has turned white and the sore appears to be more than skin deep, it is a defiling skin disease. When the priest examines that person, he shall pronounce them ceremonially unclean. [4]If the shiny spot on the skin is white but does not appear to be more than skin deep and the hair in it has not turned white, the priest is to isolate the affected person for seven days. [5]On the seventh day the priest is to examine them, and if he sees that the sore is unchanged and has not spread in the skin, he is to isolate them for another seven days. [6]On the seventh day the priest is to examine them again, and if the sore has faded and has not spread in the skin, the priest shall pronounce them clean; it is only a rash. They must wash their clothes, and they will be clean. [7]But if the rash does spread in their skin after they have shown themselves to the priest to be pronounced clean, they must appear before the priest again. [8]The priest is to examine that person, and if the rash has spread in the skin, he shall pronounce them unclean; it is a defiling skin disease.

[9]"When anyone has a defiling skin disease, they must be brought to the priest. [10]The priest is to examine them, and if there is a white swelling in the skin that has turned the hair white and if there is raw flesh in the swelling, [11]it is a chronic skin disease and the priest shall pronounce them unclean. He is not to isolate them, because they are already unclean.

[12]"If the disease breaks out all over their skin and, so far as the priest can see, it covers all the skin of the affected person from head to foot, [13]the priest is to examine them, and if the disease has covered their whole body, he shall pronounce them clean. Since it has all turned white, they are clean. [14]But whenever raw flesh appears on them, they will be unclean. [15]When the priest sees the raw flesh, he shall pronounce them unclean. The raw flesh is unclean; they have a defiling disease. [16]If the raw flesh changes and turns white, they must go to the priest. [17]The priest is to examine them, and if the sores have turned

PRAYING SCRIPTURE

Leviticus 13

Although there was no knowledge of germs and viruses in ancient Israel, God went to great lengths to ensure that his people were protected. Leprosy was an infectious disease with close examinations required. Garments that were contaminated had to be destroyed.

How should God's concerns about health inform us? Thank God for times he has healed you. Ask him to help you to glorify him in any illness you suffer.

[a] *6* Or *purification offering*; also in verse 8 [b] *2* The Hebrew word for *defiling skin disease*, traditionally translated "leprosy," was used for various diseases affecting the skin; here and throughout verses 3-46. [c] *2* Or *descendants*

white, the priest shall pronounce the affected person clean; then they
will be clean.

18“When someone has a boil on their skin and it heals, 19and in the
place where the boil was, a white swelling or reddish-white spot ap-
pears, they must present themselves to the priest. 20The priest is to
examine it, and if it appears to be more than skin deep and the hair
in it has turned white, the priest shall pronounce that person unclean.
It is a defiling skin disease that has broken out where the boil was.
21But if, when the priest examines it, there is no white hair in it and it
is not more than skin deep and has faded, then the priest is to isolate
them for seven days. 22If it is spreading in the skin, the priest shall
pronounce them unclean; it is a defiling disease. 23But if the spot is
unchanged and has not spread, it is only a scar from the boil, and the
priest shall pronounce them clean.

24“When someone has a burn on their skin and a reddish-white or
white spot appears in the raw flesh of the burn, 25the priest is to ex-
amine the spot, and if the hair in it has turned white, and it appears to
be more than skin deep, it is a defiling disease that has broken out in
the burn. The priest shall pronounce them unclean; it is a defiling skin
disease. 26But if the priest examines it and there is no white hair in the
spot and if it is not more than skin deep and has faded, then the priest
is to isolate them for seven days. 27On the seventh day the priest is to
examine that person, and if it is spreading in the skin, the priest shall
pronounce them unclean; it is a defiling skin disease. 28If, however, the
spot is unchanged and has not spread in the skin but has faded, it is a
swelling from the burn, and the priest shall pronounce them clean; it
is only a scar from the burn.

29“If a man or woman has a sore on their head or chin, 30the priest
is to examine the sore, and if it appears to be more than skin deep and
the hair in it is yellow and thin, the priest shall pronounce them un-
clean; it is a defiling skin disease on the head or chin. 31But if, when the
priest examines the sore, it does not seem to be more than skin deep
and there is no black hair in it, then the priest is to isolate the affected
person for seven days. 32On the seventh day the priest is to examine
the sore, and if it has not spread and there is no yellow hair in it and it
does not appear to be more than skin deep, 33then the man or woman
must shave themselves, except for the affected area, and the priest is to
keep them isolated another seven days. 34On the seventh day the priest
is to examine the sore, and if it has not spread in the skin and appears
to be no more than skin deep, the priest shall pronounce them clean.
They must wash their clothes, and they will be clean. 35But if the sore
does spread in the skin after they are pronounced clean, 36the priest is
to examine them, and if he finds that the sore has spread in the skin,
he does not need to look for yellow hair; they are unclean. 37If, how-
ever, the sore is unchanged so far as the priest can see, and if black hair
has grown in it, the affected person is healed. They are clean, and the
priest shall pronounce them clean.

38“When a man or woman has white spots on the skin, 39the priest is
to examine them, and if the spots are dull white, it is a harmless rash
that has broken out on the skin; they are clean.

40“A man who has lost his hair and is bald is clean. 41If he has lost
his hair from the front of his scalp and has a bald forehead, he is clean.
42But if he has a reddish-white sore on his bald head or forehead, it is
a defiling disease breaking out on his head or forehead. 43The priest

is to examine him, and if the swollen sore on his head or forehead is reddish-white like a defiling skin disease, 44the man is diseased and is unclean. The priest shall pronounce him unclean because of the sore on his head.

45"Anyone with such a defiling disease must wear torn clothes, let their hair be unkempt,[a] cover the lower part of their face and cry out, 'Unclean! Unclean!' 46As long as they have the disease they remain unclean. They must live alone; they must live outside the camp.

REGULATIONS ABOUT DEFILING MOLDS

47"As for any fabric that is spoiled with a defiling mold — any woolen or linen clothing, 48any woven or knitted material of linen or wool, any leather or anything made of leather — 49if the affected area in the fabric, the leather, the woven or knitted material, or any leather article, is greenish or reddish, it is a defiling mold and must be shown to the priest. 50The priest is to examine the affected area and isolate the article for seven days. 51On the seventh day he is to examine it, and if the mold has spread in the fabric, the woven or knitted material, or the leather, whatever its use, it is a persistent defiling mold; the article is unclean. 52He must burn the fabric, the woven or knitted material of wool or linen, or any leather article that has been spoiled; because the defiling mold is persistent, the article must be burned.

53"But if, when the priest examines it, the mold has not spread in the fabric, the woven or knitted material, or the leather article, 54he shall order that the spoiled article be washed. Then he is to isolate it for another seven days. 55After the article has been washed, the priest is to examine it again, and if the mold has not changed its appearance, even though it has not spread, it is unclean. Burn it, no matter which side of the fabric has been spoiled. 56If, when the priest examines it, the mold has faded after the article has been washed, he is to tear the spoiled part out of the fabric, the leather, or the woven or knitted material. 57But if it reappears in the fabric, in the woven or knitted material, or in the leather article, it is a spreading mold; whatever has the mold must be burned. 58Any fabric, woven or knitted material, or any leather article that has been washed and is rid of the mold, must be washed again. Then it will be clean."

59These are the regulations concerning defiling molds in woolen or linen clothing, woven or knitted material, or any leather article, for pronouncing them clean or unclean.

CLEANSING FROM DEFILING SKIN DISEASES

14 The LORD said to Moses, 2"These are the regulations for any diseased person at the time of their ceremonial cleansing, when they are brought to the priest: 3The priest is to go outside the camp and examine them. If they have been healed of their defiling skin disease,[b] 4the priest shall order that two live clean birds and some cedar wood, scarlet yarn and hyssop be brought for the person to be cleansed. 5Then the priest shall order that one of the birds be killed over fresh water in a clay pot. 6He is then to take the live bird and dip it, together with the cedar wood, the scarlet yarn and the hyssop, into the blood of the bird

PRAYING SCRIPTURE

Leviticus 14

Offerings for cleansing were deeply embedded in the old covenant. These were constant reminders that human beings are unclean before God and in need of sacrifices to cover them—or a final sacrifice to accomplish a once-and-for-all cleansing.

The sacrifice of the Lord Jesus on the cross completely cleanses us from uncleanness. Thank God that the blood of Jesus is sufficient for all sins forever.

[a] 45 Or *clothes, uncover their head* [b] 3 The Hebrew word for *defiling skin disease*, traditionally translated "leprosy," was used for various diseases affecting the skin; also in verses 7, 32, 54 and 57.

that was killed over the fresh water. 7Seven times he shall sprinkle the one to be cleansed of the defiling disease, and then pronounce them clean. After that, he is to release the live bird in the open fields.

8"The person to be cleansed must wash their clothes, shave off all their hair and bathe with water; then they will be ceremonially clean. After this they may come into the camp, but they must stay outside their tent for seven days. 9On the seventh day they must shave off all their hair; they must shave their head, their beard, their eyebrows and the rest of their hair. They must wash their clothes and bathe themselves with water, and they will be clean.

10"On the eighth day they must bring two male lambs and one ewe lamb a year old, each without defect, along with three-tenths of an ephah[a] of the finest flour mixed with olive oil for a grain offering, and one log[b] of oil. 11The priest who pronounces them clean shall present both the one to be cleansed and their offerings before the LORD at the entrance to the tent of meeting.

12"Then the priest is to take one of the male lambs and offer it as a guilt offering, along with the log of oil; he shall wave them before the LORD as a wave offering. 13He is to slaughter the lamb in the sanctuary area where the sin offering[c] and the burnt offering are slaughtered. Like the sin offering, the guilt offering belongs to the priest; it is most holy. 14The priest is to take some of the blood of the guilt offering and put it on the lobe of the right ear of the one to be cleansed, on the thumb of their right hand and on the big toe of their right foot. 15The priest shall then take some of the log of oil, pour it in the palm of his own left hand, 16dip his right forefinger into the oil in his palm, and with his finger sprinkle some of it before the LORD seven times. 17The priest is to put some of the oil remaining in his palm on the lobe of the right ear of the one to be cleansed, on the thumb of their right hand and on the big toe of their right foot, on top of the blood of the guilt offering. 18The rest of the oil in his palm the priest shall put on the head of the one to be cleansed and make atonement for them before the LORD.

19"Then the priest is to sacrifice the sin offering and make atonement for the one to be cleansed from their uncleanness. After that, the priest shall slaughter the burnt offering 20and offer it on the altar, together with the grain offering, and make atonement for them, and they will be clean.

21"If, however, they are poor and cannot afford these, they must take one male lamb as a guilt offering to be waved to make atonement for them, together with a tenth of an ephah[d] of the finest flour mixed with olive oil for a grain offering, a log of oil, 22and two doves or two young pigeons, such as they can afford, one for a sin offering and the other for a burnt offering.

23"On the eighth day they must bring them for their cleansing to the priest at the entrance to the tent of meeting, before the LORD. 24The priest is to take the lamb for the guilt offering, together with the log of oil, and wave them before the LORD as a wave offering. 25He shall slaughter the lamb for the guilt offering and take some of its blood

---

[a] *10* That is, probably about 11 pounds or about 5 kilograms [b] *10* That is, about 1/3 quart or about 0.3 liter; also in verses 12, 15, 21 and 24 [c] *13* Or *purification offering*; also in verses 19, 22 and 31 [d] *21* That is, probably about 3 1/2 pounds or about 1.6 kilograms

and put it on the lobe of the right ear of the one to be cleansed, on the
thumb of their right hand and on the big toe of their right foot. [26]The
priest is to pour some of the oil into the palm of his own left hand,
[27]and with his right forefinger sprinkle some of the oil from his palm
seven times before the LORD. [28]Some of the oil in his palm he is to
put on the same places he put the blood of the guilt offering — on the
lobe of the right ear of the one to be cleansed, on the thumb of their
right hand and on the big toe of their right foot. [29]The rest of the oil in
his palm the priest shall put on the head of the one to be cleansed, to
make atonement for them before the LORD. [30]Then he shall sacrifice
the doves or the young pigeons, such as the person can afford, [31]one as
a sin offering and the other as a burnt offering, together with the grain
offering. In this way the priest will make atonement before the LORD
on behalf of the one to be cleansed."

[32]These are the regulations for anyone who has a defiling skin dis-
ease and who cannot afford the regular offerings for their cleansing.

CLEANSING FROM DEFILING MOLDS

[33]The LORD said to Moses and Aaron, [34]"When you enter the land of
Canaan, which I am giving you as your possession, and I put a spread-
ing mold in a house in that land, [35]the owner of the house must go and
tell the priest, 'I have seen something that looks like a defiling mold
in my house.' [36]The priest is to order the house to be emptied before
he goes in to examine the mold, so that nothing in the house will be
pronounced unclean. After this the priest is to go in and inspect the
house. [37]He is to examine the mold on the walls, and if it has greenish
or reddish depressions that appear to be deeper than the surface of
the wall, [38]the priest shall go out the doorway of the house and close
it up for seven days. [39]On the seventh day the priest shall return to
inspect the house. If the mold has spread on the walls, [40]he is to order
that the contaminated stones be torn out and thrown into an unclean
place outside the town. [41]He must have all the inside walls of the house
scraped and the material that is scraped off dumped into an unclean
place outside the town. [42]Then they are to take other stones to replace
these and take new clay and plaster the house.

[43]"If the defiling mold reappears in the house after the stones have
been torn out and the house scraped and plastered, [44]the priest is to go
and examine it and, if the mold has spread in the house, it is a persis-
tent defiling mold; the house is unclean. [45]It must be torn down — its
stones, timbers and all the plaster — and taken out of the town to an
unclean place.

[46]"Anyone who goes into the house while it is closed up will be un-
clean till evening. [47]Anyone who sleeps or eats in the house must wash
their clothes.

[48]"But if the priest comes to examine it and the mold has not spread
after the house has been plastered, he shall pronounce the house clean,
because the defiling mold is gone. [49]To purify the house he is to take
two birds and some cedar wood, scarlet yarn and hyssop. [50]He shall kill
one of the birds over fresh water in a clay pot. [51]Then he is to take the
cedar wood, the hyssop, the scarlet yarn and the live bird, dip them
into the blood of the dead bird and the fresh water, and sprinkle the
house seven times. [52]He shall purify the house with the bird's blood,
the fresh water, the live bird, the cedar wood, the hyssop and the scar-
let yarn. [53]Then he is to release the live bird in the open fields outside

the town. In this way he will make atonement for the house, and it will be clean."

54These are the regulations for any defiling skin disease, for a sore, 55for defiling molds in fabric or in a house, 56and for a swelling, a rash or a shiny spot, 57to determine when something is clean or unclean.

These are the regulations for defiling skin diseases and defiling molds.

DISCHARGES CAUSING UNCLEANNESS

15 The LORD said to Moses and Aaron, 2"Speak to the Israelites and say to them: 'When any man has an unusual bodily discharge, such a discharge is unclean. 3Whether it continues flowing from his body or is blocked, it will make him unclean. This is how his discharge will bring about uncleanness:

4" 'Any bed the man with a discharge lies on will be unclean, and anything he sits on will be unclean. 5Anyone who touches his bed must wash their clothes and bathe with water, and they will be unclean till evening. 6Whoever sits on anything that the man with a discharge sat on must wash their clothes and bathe with water, and they will be unclean till evening.

7" 'Whoever touches the man who has a discharge must wash their clothes and bathe with water, and they will be unclean till evening.

8" 'If the man with the discharge spits on anyone who is clean, they must wash their clothes and bathe with water, and they will be unclean till evening.

9" 'Everything the man sits on when riding will be unclean, 10and whoever touches any of the things that were under him will be unclean till evening; whoever picks up those things must wash their clothes and bathe with water, and they will be unclean till evening.

11" 'Anyone the man with a discharge touches without rinsing his hands with water must wash their clothes and bathe with water, and they will be unclean till evening.

12" 'A clay pot that the man touches must be broken, and any wooden article is to be rinsed with water.

13" 'When a man is cleansed from his discharge, he is to count off seven days for his ceremonial cleansing; he must wash his clothes and bathe himself with fresh water, and he will be clean. 14On the eighth day he must take two doves or two young pigeons and come before the LORD to the entrance to the tent of meeting and give them to the priest. 15The priest is to sacrifice them, the one for a sin offering[a] and the other for a burnt offering. In this way he will make atonement before the LORD for the man because of his discharge.

16" 'When a man has an emission of semen, he must bathe his whole body with water, and he will be unclean till evening. 17Any clothing or leather that has semen on it must be washed with water, and it will be unclean till evening. 18When a man has sexual relations with a woman and there is an emission of semen, both of them must bathe with water, and they will be unclean till evening.

19" 'When a woman has her regular flow of blood, the impurity of her monthly period will last seven days, and anyone who touches her will be unclean till evening.

20" 'Anything she lies on during her period will be unclean, and

[a] *15* Or *purification offering*; also in verse 30

PRAYING SCRIPTURE

Leviticus 15

We can enter the presence of the Lord only if we go to him clean and free from the stain of impurity or for the purpose of being cleansed. Under the Law of Moses, bodily discharges marked both men and women as unclean and in need of washing. Even things touched by an unclean person had to be cleansed.

Are there impurities in your life that are affecting others? Ask God to cleanse you.

anything she sits on will be unclean. [21]Anyone who touches her bed will be unclean; they must wash their clothes and bathe with water, and they will be unclean till evening. [22]Anyone who touches anything she sits on will be unclean; they must wash their clothes and bathe with water, and they will be unclean till evening. [23]Whether it is the bed or anything she was sitting on, when anyone touches it, they will be unclean till evening.

[24]“ ‘If a man has sexual relations with her and her monthly flow touches him, he will be unclean for seven days; any bed he lies on will be unclean.

[25]“ ‘When a woman has a discharge of blood for many days at a time other than her monthly period or has a discharge that continues beyond her period, she will be unclean as long as she has the discharge, just as in the days of her period. [26]Any bed she lies on while her discharge continues will be unclean, as is her bed during her monthly period, and anything she sits on will be unclean, as during her period. [27]Anyone who touches them will be unclean; they must wash their clothes and bathe with water, and they will be unclean till evening.

[28]“ ‘When she is cleansed from her discharge, she must count off seven days, and after that she will be ceremonially clean. [29]On the eighth day she must take two doves or two young pigeons and bring them to the priest at the entrance to the tent of meeting. [30]The priest is to sacrifice one for a sin offering and the other for a burnt offering. In this way he will make atonement for her before the LORD for the uncleanness of her discharge.

[31]“ ‘You must keep the Israelites separate from things that make them unclean, so they will not die in their uncleanness for defiling my dwelling place,[a] which is among them.’ ”

[32]These are the regulations for a man with a discharge, for anyone made unclean by an emission of semen, [33]for a woman in her monthly period, for a man or a woman with a discharge, and for a man who has sexual relations with a woman who is ceremonially unclean.

THE DAY OF ATONEMENT

16 The LORD spoke to Moses after the death of the two sons of Aaron who died when they approached the LORD. [2]The LORD said to Moses: “Tell your brother Aaron that he is not to come whenever he chooses into the Most Holy Place behind the curtain in front of the atonement cover on the ark, or else he will die. For I will appear in the cloud over the atonement cover.

[3]“This is how Aaron is to enter the Most Holy Place: He must first bring a young bull for a sin offering[b] and a ram for a burnt offering. [4]He is to put on the sacred linen tunic, with linen undergarments next to his body; he is to tie the linen sash around him and put on the linen turban. These are sacred garments; so he must bathe himself with water before he puts them on. [5]From the Israelite community he is to take two male goats for a sin offering and a ram for a burnt offering.

[6]“Aaron is to offer the bull for his own sin offering to make atonement for himself and his household. [7]Then he is to take the two goats and present them before the LORD at the entrance to the tent of meeting. [8]He is to cast lots for the two goats — one lot for the LORD and the

[a] *31* Or *my tabernacle* [b] *3* Or *purification offering*; here and throughout this chapter

PRAYING SCRIPTURE

Leviticus 16

No single day on Israel’s calendar was imbued with as much significance as the Day of Atonement. It featured three specific things: the high priest, a goat for sacrifice and a scapegoat, which symbolically carried the people’s cumulative annual sins far from the camp into the wilderness.

Eventually Jesus would come and serve as the perfect, final sacrifice. Thank God that Jesus is the complete sacrifice for all your sins.

other for the scapegoat.[a] 9Aaron shall bring the goat whose lot falls to
the LORD and sacrifice it for a sin offering. 10But the goat chosen by lot
as the scapegoat shall be presented alive before the LORD to be used for
making atonement by sending it into the wilderness as a scapegoat.
11"Aaron shall bring the bull for his own sin offering to make atone-
ment for himself and his household, and he is to slaughter the bull for
his own sin offering. 12He is to take a censer full of burning coals from
the altar before the LORD and two handfuls of finely ground fragrant
incense and take them behind the curtain. 13He is to put the incense
on the fire before the LORD, and the smoke of the incense will conceal
the atonement cover above the tablets of the covenant law, so that he
will not die. 14He is to take some of the bull's blood and with his finger
sprinkle it on the front of the atonement cover; then he shall sprinkle
some of it with his finger seven times before the atonement cover.
15"He shall then slaughter the goat for the sin offering for the people
and take its blood behind the curtain and do with it as he did with the
bull's blood: He shall sprinkle it on the atonement cover and in front
of it. 16In this way he will make atonement for the Most Holy Place be-
cause of the uncleanness and rebellion of the Israelites, whatever their
sins have been. He is to do the same for the tent of meeting, which is
among them in the midst of their uncleanness. 17No one is to be in the
tent of meeting from the time Aaron goes in to make atonement in
the Most Holy Place until he comes out, having made atonement for
himself, his household and the whole community of Israel.
18"Then he shall come out to the altar that is before the LORD and
make atonement for it. He shall take some of the bull's blood and some
of the goat's blood and put it on all the horns of the altar. 19He shall
sprinkle some of the blood on it with his finger seven times to cleanse
it and to consecrate it from the uncleanness of the Israelites.
20"When Aaron has finished making atonement for the Most Holy
Place, the tent of meeting and the altar, he shall bring forward the
live goat. 21He is to lay both hands on the head of the live goat and
confess over it all the wickedness and rebellion of the Israelites — all
their sins — and put them on the goat's head. He shall send the goat
away into the wilderness in the care of someone appointed for the
task. 22The goat will carry on itself all their sins to a remote place; and
the man shall release it in the wilderness.
23"Then Aaron is to go into the tent of meeting and take off the linen
garments he put on before he entered the Most Holy Place, and he is
to leave them there. 24He shall bathe himself with water in the sanctu-
ary area and put on his regular garments. Then he shall come out and
sacrifice the burnt offering for himself and the burnt offering for the
people, to make atonement for himself and for the people. 25He shall
also burn the fat of the sin offering on the altar.
26"The man who releases the goat as a scapegoat must wash his
clothes and bathe himself with water; afterward he may come into the
camp. 27The bull and the goat for the sin offerings, whose blood was
brought into the Most Holy Place to make atonement, must be taken
outside the camp; their hides, flesh and intestines are to be burned up.
28The man who burns them must wash his clothes and bathe himself
with water; afterward he may come into the camp.

[a] *8* The meaning of the Hebrew for this word is uncertain; also in verses 10 and 26.

29“This is to be a lasting ordinance for you: On the tenth day of the seventh month you must deny yourselves[a] and not do any work—whether native-born or a foreigner residing among you— 30because on this day atonement will be made for you, to cleanse you. Then, before the LORD, you will be clean from all your sins. 31It is a day of sabbath rest, and you must deny yourselves; it is a lasting ordinance. 32The priest who is anointed and ordained to succeed his father as high priest is to make atonement. He is to put on the sacred linen garments 33and make atonement for the Most Holy Place, for the tent of meeting and the altar, and for the priests and all the members of the community.

34“This is to be a lasting ordinance for you: Atonement is to be made once a year for all the sins of the Israelites.”

And it was done, as the LORD commanded Moses.

EATING BLOOD FORBIDDEN

17 The LORD said to Moses, 2“Speak to Aaron and his sons and to all the Israelites and say to them: ‘This is what the LORD has commanded: 3Any Israelite who sacrifices an ox,[b] a lamb or a goat in the camp or outside of it 4instead of bringing it to the entrance to the tent of meeting to present it as an offering to the LORD in front of the tabernacle of the LORD—that person shall be considered guilty of bloodshed; they have shed blood and must be cut off from their people. 5This is so the Israelites will bring to the LORD the sacrifices they are now making in the open fields. They must bring them to the priest, that is, to the LORD, at the entrance to the tent of meeting and sacrifice them as fellowship offerings. 6The priest is to splash the blood against the altar of the LORD at the entrance to the tent of meeting and burn the fat as an aroma pleasing to the LORD. 7They must no longer offer any of their sacrifices to the goat idols[c] to whom they prostitute themselves. This is to be a lasting ordinance for them and for the generations to come.’

8“Say to them: ‘Any Israelite or any foreigner residing among them who offers a burnt offering or sacrifice 9and does not bring it to the entrance to the tent of meeting to sacrifice it to the LORD must be cut off from the people of Israel.

10“ ‘I will set my face against any Israelite or any foreigner residing among them who eats blood, and I will cut them off from the people. 11For the life of a creature is in the blood, and I have given it to you to make atonement for yourselves on the altar; it is the blood that makes atonement for one’s life.[d] 12Therefore I say to the Israelites, “None of you may eat blood, nor may any foreigner residing among you eat blood.”

13“ ‘Any Israelite or any foreigner residing among you who hunts any animal or bird that may be eaten must drain out the blood and cover it with earth, 14because the life of every creature is its blood. That is why I have said to the Israelites, “You must not eat the blood of any creature, because the life of every creature is its blood; anyone who eats it must be cut off.”

15“ ‘Anyone, whether native-born or foreigner, who eats anything found dead or torn by wild animals must wash their clothes and bathe

PRAYING SCRIPTURE

Leviticus 17

The law contained specific admonitions for Israel, and sacrifices were at the center. What kind of offering would God accept or reject? God very clearly forbade sacrifices to demons, but even acceptable sacrifices had to be properly offered for God to be pleased.

As you pray today, thank God for the blood of his perfect Lamb, Jesus Christ, sacrificed acceptably for you and sufficient to save all who believe.

[a] *29* Or *must fast;* also in verse 31 [b] *3* The Hebrew word can refer to either male or female. [c] *7* Or *the demons* [d] *11* Or *atonement by the life in the blood*

with water, and they will be ceremonially unclean till evening; then
they will be clean. 16But if they do not wash their clothes and bathe
themselves, they will be held responsible.'"

UNLAWFUL SEXUAL RELATIONS

18 The LORD said to Moses, 2"Speak to the Israelites and say to
them: 'I am the LORD your God. 3You must not do as they do in
Egypt, where you used to live, and you must not do as they do in the
land of Canaan, where I am bringing you. Do not follow their practices.
4You must obey my laws and be careful to follow my decrees. I am the
LORD your God. 5Keep my decrees and laws, for the person who obeys
them will live by them. I am the LORD.
6" 'No one is to approach any close relative to have sexual relations.
I am the LORD.
7" 'Do not dishonor your father by having sexual relations with your
mother. She is your mother; do not have relations with her.
8" 'Do not have sexual relations with your father's wife; that would
dishonor your father.
9" 'Do not have sexual relations with your sister, either your father's
daughter or your mother's daughter, whether she was born in the same
home or elsewhere.
10" 'Do not have sexual relations with your son's daughter or your
daughter's daughter; that would dishonor you.
11" 'Do not have sexual relations with the daughter of your father's
wife, born to your father; she is your sister.
12" 'Do not have sexual relations with your father's sister; she is your
father's close relative.
13" 'Do not have sexual relations with your mother's sister, because
she is your mother's close relative.
14" 'Do not dishonor your father's brother by approaching his wife to
have sexual relations; she is your aunt.
15" 'Do not have sexual relations with your daughter-in-law. She is
your son's wife; do not have relations with her.
16" 'Do not have sexual relations with your brother's wife; that would
dishonor your brother.
17" 'Do not have sexual relations with both a woman and her daugh-
ter. Do not have sexual relations with either her son's daughter or her
daughter's daughter; they are her close relatives. That is wickedness.
18" 'Do not take your wife's sister as a rival wife and have sexual rela-
tions with her while your wife is living.
19" 'Do not approach a woman to have sexual relations during the
uncleanness of her monthly period.
20" 'Do not have sexual relations with your neighbor's wife and defile
yourself with her.
21" 'Do not give any of your children to be sacrificed to Molek, for you
must not profane the name of your God. I am the LORD.
22" 'Do not have sexual relations with a man as one does with a
woman; that is detestable.
23" 'Do not have sexual relations with an animal and defile yourself
with it. A woman must not present herself to an animal to have sexual
relations with it; that is a perversion.
24" 'Do not defile yourselves in any of these ways, because this is how
the nations that I am going to drive out before you became defiled.
25Even the land was defiled; so I punished it for its sin, and the land

PRAYING SCRIPTURE

Leviticus 18

It is easy for Christians to absorb cultural preferences about sex. But our obedience to the Lord in matters of sex reflects the reality that our bodies belong to him. God's children cannot simply make up their own rules about sexuality.

Think about the various ways sex is presented in the culture around you. Ask God to help you adhere to the sexual ethics he presents in his Word.

PRAYING SCRIPTURE

Leviticus 19

In a lengthy summary, the Lord instructed Moses to revisit the law for his people. He began by reminding them of his holiness and ended by reminding them of his covenant name: *Yahweh* (translated "LORD," verse 37). Everything about the law—sacrifices, offerings and relationships—was to teach them about God's name and character.

Do you know God? If so, thank him for saving you. If not, ask him to bring you into a loving relationship with him.

vomited out its inhabitants. [26]But you must keep my decrees and my
laws. The native-born and the foreigners residing among you must
not do any of these detestable things, [27]for all these things were done
by the people who lived in the land before you, and the land became
defiled. [28]And if you defile the land, it will vomit you out as it vomited
out the nations that were before you.
[29]"'Everyone who does any of these detestable things—such persons
must be cut off from their people. [30]Keep my requirements and do not
follow any of the detestable customs that were practiced before you
came and do not defile yourselves with them. I am the LORD your God.'"

VARIOUS LAWS

19 The LORD said to Moses, [2]"Speak to the entire assembly of Israel
and say to them: 'Be holy because I, the LORD your God, am holy.
[3]"'Each of you must respect your mother and father, and you must
observe my Sabbaths. I am the LORD your God.
[4]"'Do not turn to idols or make metal gods for yourselves. I am the
LORD your God.
[5]"'When you sacrifice a fellowship offering to the LORD, sacrifice it
in such a way that it will be accepted on your behalf. [6]It shall be eaten
on the day you sacrifice it or on the next day; anything left over until
the third day must be burned up. [7]If any of it is eaten on the third day,
it is impure and will not be accepted. [8]Whoever eats it will be held re-
sponsible because they have desecrated what is holy to the LORD; they
must be cut off from their people.
[9]"'When you reap the harvest of your land, do not reap to the very
edges of your field or gather the gleanings of your harvest. [10]Do not
go over your vineyard a second time or pick up the grapes that have
fallen. Leave them for the poor and the foreigner. I am the LORD your
God.
[11]"'Do not steal.
"'Do not lie.
"'Do not deceive one another.
[12]"'Do not swear falsely by my name and so profane the name of
your God. I am the LORD.
[13]"'Do not defraud or rob your neighbor.
"'Do not hold back the wages of a hired worker overnight.
[14]"'Do not curse the deaf or put a stumbling block in front of the
blind, but fear your God. I am the LORD.
[15]"'Do not pervert justice; do not show partiality to the poor or favor-
itism to the great, but judge your neighbor fairly.
[16]"'Do not go about spreading slander among your people.
"'Do not do anything that endangers your neighbor's life. I am the
LORD.
[17]"'Do not hate a fellow Israelite in your heart. Rebuke your neighbor
frankly so you will not share in their guilt.
[18]"'Do not seek revenge or bear a grudge against anyone among your
people, but love your neighbor as yourself. I am the LORD.
[19]"'Keep my decrees.
"'Do not mate different kinds of animals.
"'Do not plant your field with two kinds of seed.
"'Do not wear clothing woven of two kinds of material.
[20]"'If a man sleeps with a female slave who is promised to another
man but who has not been ransomed or given her freedom, there must

be due punishment.[a] Yet they are not to be put to death, because she
had not been freed. 21 The man, however, must bring a ram to the en-
trance to the tent of meeting for a guilt offering to the LORD. 22 With the
ram of the guilt offering the priest is to make atonement for him be-
fore the LORD for the sin he has committed, and his sin will be forgiven.
23 " 'When you enter the land and plant any kind of fruit tree, regard
its fruit as forbidden.[b] For three years you are to consider it forbidden[b];
it must not be eaten. 24 In the fourth year all its fruit will be holy, an of-
fering of praise to the LORD. 25 But in the fifth year you may eat its fruit.
In this way your harvest will be increased. I am the LORD your God.
26 " 'Do not eat any meat with the blood still in it.
" 'Do not practice divination or seek omens.
27 " 'Do not cut the hair at the sides of your head or clip off the edges
of your beard.
28 " 'Do not cut your bodies for the dead or put tattoo marks on your-
selves. I am the LORD.
29 " 'Do not degrade your daughter by making her a prostitute, or the
land will turn to prostitution and be filled with wickedness.
30 " 'Observe my Sabbaths and have reverence for my sanctuary. I am
the LORD.
31 " 'Do not turn to mediums or seek out spiritists, for you will be de-
filed by them. I am the LORD your God.
32 " 'Stand up in the presence of the aged, show respect for the elderly
and revere your God. I am the LORD.
33 " 'When a foreigner resides among you in your land, do not mis-
treat them. 34 The foreigner residing among you must be treated as
your native-born. Love them as yourself, for you were foreigners in
Egypt. I am the LORD your God.
35 " 'Do not use dishonest standards when measuring length, weight or
quantity. 36 Use honest scales and honest weights, an honest ephah[c] and
an honest hin.[d] I am the LORD your God, who brought you out of Egypt.
37 " 'Keep all my decrees and all my laws and follow them. I am the
LORD.' "

PUNISHMENTS FOR SIN

20 The LORD said to Moses, 2 "Say to the Israelites: 'Any Israelite or
any foreigner residing in Israel who sacrifices any of his chil-
dren to Molek is to be put to death. The members of the community are
to stone him. 3 I myself will set my face against him and will cut him off
from his people; for by sacrificing his children to Molek, he has defiled
my sanctuary and profaned my holy name. 4 If the members of the com-
munity close their eyes when that man sacrifices one of his children
to Molek and if they fail to put him to death, 5 I myself will set my face
against him and his family and will cut them off from their people to-
gether with all who follow him in prostituting themselves to Molek.
6 " 'I will set my face against anyone who turns to mediums and spir-
itists to prostitute themselves by following them, and I will cut them
off from their people.
7 " 'Consecrate yourselves and be holy, because I am the LORD your God.
8 Keep my decrees and follow them. I am the LORD, who makes you holy.

[a] *20* Or *be an inquiry* [b] *23* Hebrew *uncircumcised* [c] *36* An ephah was a dry measure having the capacity of about 3/5 of a bushel or about 22 liters. [d] *36* A hin was a liquid measure having the capacity of about 1 gallon or about 3.8 liters.

PRAYING SCRIPTURE

Leviticus 20

The Lord commands us to be holy because his people's lives should reflect his character to the world. Sin of any kind is a stain on God's character, whether worshiping a false god, committing immoral acts with another person or practicing forbidden spiritism. God's judgment is as real as his love.

In prayer we admit we've sinned, one time or many times. Avail yourself of God's mercy as you pray.

9“ ‘Anyone who curses their father or mother is to be put to death.
Because they have cursed their father or mother, their blood will be
on their own head.

10“ ‘If a man commits adultery with another man’s wife — with the
wife of his neighbor — both the adulterer and the adulteress are to be
put to death.

11“ ‘If a man has sexual relations with his father’s wife, he has dishon-
ored his father. Both the man and the woman are to be put to death;
their blood will be on their own heads.

12“ ‘If a man has sexual relations with his daughter-in-law, both of
them are to be put to death. What they have done is a perversion; their
blood will be on their own heads.

13“ ‘If a man has sexual relations with a man as one does with a
woman, both of them have done what is detestable. They are to be put
to death; their blood will be on their own heads.

14“ ‘If a man marries both a woman and her mother, it is wicked.
Both he and they must be burned in the fire, so that no wickedness
will be among you.

15“ ‘If a man has sexual relations with an animal, he is to be put to
death, and you must kill the animal.

16“ ‘If a woman approaches an animal to have sexual relations with
it, kill both the woman and the animal. They are to be put to death;
their blood will be on their own heads.

17“ ‘If a man marries his sister, the daughter of either his father or his
mother, and they have sexual relations, it is a disgrace. They are to be
publicly removed from their people. He has dishonored his sister and
will be held responsible.

18“ ‘If a man has sexual relations with a woman during her monthly
period, he has exposed the source of her flow, and she has also uncov-
ered it. Both of them are to be cut off from their people.

19“ ‘Do not have sexual relations with the sister of either your mother
or your father, for that would dishonor a close relative; both of you
would be held responsible.

20“ ‘If a man has sexual relations with his aunt, he has dishonored
his uncle. They will be held responsible; they will die childless.

21“ ‘If a man marries his brother’s wife, it is an act of impurity; he has
dishonored his brother. They will be childless.

22“ ‘Keep all my decrees and laws and follow them, so that the land
where I am bringing you to live may not vomit you out. 23You must
not live according to the customs of the nations I am going to drive out
before you. Because they did all these things, I abhorred them. 24But I
said to you, “You will possess their land; I will give it to you as an inher-
itance, a land flowing with milk and honey.” I am the LORD your God,
who has set you apart from the nations.

25“ ‘You must therefore make a distinction between clean and un-
clean animals and between unclean and clean birds. Do not defile
yourselves by any animal or bird or anything that moves along the
ground — those that I have set apart as unclean for you. 26You are to be
holy to me because I, the LORD, am holy, and I have set you apart from
the nations to be my own.

27“ ‘A man or woman who is a medium or spiritist among you must
be put to death. You are to stone them; their blood will be on their
own heads.’ ”

RULES FOR PRIESTS

21 The LORD said to Moses, "Speak to the priests, the sons of Aaron,
and say to them: 'A priest must not make himself ceremonially
unclean for any of his people who die, [2]except for a close relative, such
as his mother or father, his son or daughter, his brother, [3]or an unmar-
ried sister who is dependent on him since she has no husband — for
her he may make himself unclean. [4]He must not make himself unclean
for people related to him by marriage,[a] and so defile himself.
[5]" 'Priests must not shave their heads or shave off the edges of their
beards or cut their bodies. [6]They must be holy to their God and must
not profane the name of their God. Because they present the food of-
ferings to the LORD, the food of their God, they are to be holy.
[7]" 'They must not marry women defiled by prostitution or divorced
from their husbands, because priests are holy to their God. [8]Regard
them as holy, because they offer up the food of your God. Consider
them holy, because I the LORD am holy — I who make you holy.
[9]" 'If a priest's daughter defiles herself by becoming a prostitute, she
disgraces her father; she must be burned in the fire.
[10]" 'The high priest, the one among his brothers who has had the
anointing oil poured on his head and who has been ordained to wear
the priestly garments, must not let his hair become unkempt[b] or tear
his clothes. [11]He must not enter a place where there is a dead body. He
must not make himself unclean, even for his father or mother, [12]nor
leave the sanctuary of his God or desecrate it, because he has been ded-
icated by the anointing oil of his God. I am the LORD.
[13]" 'The woman he marries must be a virgin. [14]He must not marry
a widow, a divorced woman, or a woman defiled by prostitution, but
only a virgin from his own people, [15]so that he will not defile his off-
spring among his people. I am the LORD, who makes him holy.' "
[16]The LORD said to Moses, [17]"Say to Aaron: 'For the generations to
come none of your descendants who has a defect may come near to
offer the food of his God. [18]No man who has any defect may come near:
no man who is blind or lame, disfigured or deformed; [19]no man with a
crippled foot or hand, [20]or who is a hunchback or a dwarf, or who has
any eye defect, or who has festering or running sores or damaged testi-
cles. [21]No descendant of Aaron the priest who has any defect is to come
near to present the food offerings to the LORD. He has a defect; he must
not come near to offer the food of his God. [22]He may eat the most holy
food of his God, as well as the holy food; [23]yet because of his defect, he
must not go near the curtain or approach the altar, and so desecrate
my sanctuary. I am the LORD, who makes them holy.' "
[24]So Moses told this to Aaron and his sons and to all the Israelites.

22 The LORD said to Moses, [2]"Tell Aaron and his sons to treat with
respect the sacred offerings the Israelites consecrate to me, so
they will not profane my holy name. I am the LORD.
[3]"Say to them: 'For the generations to come, if any of your descen-
dants is ceremonially unclean and yet comes near the sacred offerings
that the Israelites consecrate to the LORD, that person must be cut off
from my presence. I am the LORD.
[4]" 'If a descendant of Aaron has a defiling skin disease[c] or a bodily

[a] 4 Or *unclean as a leader among his people* [b] 10 Or *not uncover his head*
[c] 4 The Hebrew word for *defiling skin disease,* traditionally translated "leprosy," was used for various diseases affecting the skin.

PRAYING SCRIPTURE

Leviticus 21

Under the old covenant, the priests were a specially set-apart class. Under the new covenant, however, every Christian is a priest who may appear before the Lord. The sacrifice of Jesus fulfilled the temporary sacrifices of the old covenant. God's people no longer need sacrifices to approach him; the way is eternally opened.

Use your position as a priest to intercede for someone today. Take that person's burdens before God on his or her behalf.

PRAYING SCRIPTURE

Leviticus 22

Intertwined with God's law was the memory of the exodus. God ended this section of laws by reminding the people that it was he who had delivered them from Egypt. His power to deliver them showed his authority to demand their obedience to the laws he instituted.

The exodus is a physical example of a spiritual truth: God delivers his people from their bondage to oppressive rulers who do not serve him. Thank God for your freedom to serve Christ, King of all.

discharge, he may not eat the sacred offerings until he is cleansed. He
will also be unclean if he touches something defiled by a corpse or by
anyone who has an emission of semen, 5or if he touches any crawling
thing that makes him unclean, or any person who makes him unclean,
whatever the uncleanness may be. 6The one who touches any such
thing will be unclean till evening. He must not eat any of the sacred
offerings unless he has bathed himself with water. 7When the sun goes
down, he will be clean, and after that he may eat the sacred offerings,
for they are his food. 8He must not eat anything found dead or torn by
wild animals, and so become unclean through it. I am the LORD.

9" 'The priests are to perform my service in such a way that they do
not become guilty and die for treating it with contempt. I am the LORD,
who makes them holy.

10" 'No one outside a priest's family may eat the sacred offering, nor
may the guest of a priest or his hired worker eat it. 11But if a priest buys
a slave with money, or if slaves are born in his household, they may eat
his food. 12If a priest's daughter marries anyone other than a priest, she
may not eat any of the sacred contributions. 13But if a priest's daughter
becomes a widow or is divorced, yet has no children, and she returns to
live in her father's household as in her youth, she may eat her father's
food. No unauthorized person, however, may eat it.

14" 'Anyone who eats a sacred offering by mistake must make resti-
tution to the priest for the offering and add a fifth of the value to it.
15The priests must not desecrate the sacred offerings the Israelites pre-
sent to the LORD 16by allowing them to eat the sacred offerings and so
bring upon them guilt requiring payment. I am the LORD, who makes
them holy.' "

UNACCEPTABLE SACRIFICES

17The LORD said to Moses, 18"Speak to Aaron and his sons and to all
the Israelites and say to them: 'If any of you — whether an Israelite or a
foreigner residing in Israel — presents a gift for a burnt offering to the
LORD, either to fulfill a vow or as a freewill offering, 19you must present
a male without defect from the cattle, sheep or goats in order that it
may be accepted on your behalf. 20Do not bring anything with a defect,
because it will not be accepted on your behalf. 21When anyone brings
from the herd or flock a fellowship offering to the LORD to fulfill a spe-
cial vow or as a freewill offering, it must be without defect or blemish
to be acceptable. 22Do not offer to the LORD the blind, the injured or the
maimed, or anything with warts or festering or running sores. Do not
place any of these on the altar as a food offering presented to the LORD.
23You may, however, present as a freewill offering an ox[a] or a sheep
that is deformed or stunted, but it will not be accepted in fulfillment of
a vow. 24You must not offer to the LORD an animal whose testicles are
bruised, crushed, torn or cut. You must not do this in your own land,
25and you must not accept such animals from the hand of a foreigner
and offer them as the food of your God. They will not be accepted on
your behalf, because they are deformed and have defects.' "

26The LORD said to Moses, 27"When a calf, a lamb or a goat is born, it
is to remain with its mother for seven days. From the eighth day on,
it will be acceptable as a food offering presented to the LORD. 28Do not
slaughter a cow or a sheep and its young on the same day.

[a] *23* The Hebrew word can refer to either male or female.

29"When you sacrifice a thank offering to the LORD, sacrifice it in
such a way that it will be accepted on your behalf. 30It must be eaten
that same day; leave none of it till morning. I am the LORD.
31"Keep my commands and follow them. I am the LORD. 32Do not
profane my holy name, for I must be acknowledged as holy by the Is-
raelites. I am the LORD, who made you holy 33and who brought you out
of Egypt to be your God. I am the LORD."

THE APPOINTED FESTIVALS

23 The LORD said to Moses, 2"Speak to the Israelites and say to
them: 'These are my appointed festivals, the appointed festi-
vals of the LORD, which you are to proclaim as sacred assemblies.

THE SABBATH

3"'There are six days when you may work, but the seventh day is a
day of sabbath rest, a day of sacred assembly. You are not to do any
work; wherever you live, it is a sabbath to the LORD.

THE PASSOVER AND THE FESTIVAL OF UNLEAVENED BREAD

4"'These are the LORD's appointed festivals, the sacred assemblies
you are to proclaim at their appointed times: 5The LORD's Passover
begins at twilight on the fourteenth day of the first month. 6On the
fifteenth day of that month the LORD's Festival of Unleavened Bread
begins; for seven days you must eat bread made without yeast. 7On the
first day hold a sacred assembly and do no regular work. 8For seven
days present a food offering to the LORD. And on the seventh day hold
a sacred assembly and do no regular work.'"

OFFERING THE FIRSTFRUITS

9The LORD said to Moses, 10"Speak to the Israelites and say to them:
'When you enter the land I am going to give you and you reap its har-
vest, bring to the priest a sheaf of the first grain you harvest. 11He is to
wave the sheaf before the LORD so it will be accepted on your behalf;
the priest is to wave it on the day after the Sabbath. 12On the day you
wave the sheaf, you must sacrifice as a burnt offering to the LORD a
lamb a year old without defect, 13together with its grain offering of
two-tenths of an ephah[a] of the finest flour mixed with olive oil—a
food offering presented to the LORD, a pleasing aroma—and its drink
offering of a quarter of a hin[b] of wine. 14You must not eat any bread,
or roasted or new grain, until the very day you bring this offering to
your God. This is to be a lasting ordinance for the generations to come,
wherever you live.

THE FESTIVAL OF WEEKS

15"'From the day after the Sabbath, the day you brought the sheaf
of the wave offering, count off seven full weeks. 16Count off fifty days
up to the day after the seventh Sabbath, and then present an offering
of new grain to the LORD. 17From wherever you live, bring two loaves
made of two-tenths of an ephah of the finest flour, baked with yeast,
as a wave offering of firstfruits to the LORD. 18Present with this bread
seven male lambs, each a year old and without defect, one young bull
and two rams. They will be a burnt offering to the LORD, together with
their grain offerings and drink offerings—a food offering, an aroma

[a] 13 That is, probably about 7 pounds or about 3.2 kilograms; also in verse 17
[b] 13 That is, about 1 quart or about 1 liter

PRAYING SCRIPTURE

Leviticus 23

The festivals, or feasts, that God commanded Israel to celebrate were not merely about food. They were to be holy convocations; they were the Lord's festivals. The Lord instituted them as reminders: Keep the Sabbath day, keep the Passover, celebrate the harvest.

Pray that God's people will recapture the spirit of celebrating with the Lord as expressed in the festivals.

pleasing to the LORD. 19Then sacrifice one male goat for a sin offering[a]
and two lambs, each a year old, for a fellowship offering. 20The priest
is to wave the two lambs before the LORD as a wave offering, together
with the bread of the firstfruits. They are a sacred offering to the LORD
for the priest. 21On that same day you are to proclaim a sacred assem-
bly and do no regular work. This is to be a lasting ordinance for the
generations to come, wherever you live.

22" 'When you reap the harvest of your land, do not reap to the very
edges of your field or gather the gleanings of your harvest. Leave them
for the poor and for the foreigner residing among you. I am the LORD
your God.' "

THE FESTIVAL OF TRUMPETS

23The LORD said to Moses, 24"Say to the Israelites: 'On the first day
of the seventh month you are to have a day of sabbath rest, a sacred
assembly commemorated with trumpet blasts. 25Do no regular work,
but present a food offering to the LORD.' "

THE DAY OF ATONEMENT

26The LORD said to Moses, 27"The tenth day of this seventh month is
the Day of Atonement. Hold a sacred assembly and deny yourselves,[b]
and present a food offering to the LORD. 28Do not do any work on that
day, because it is the Day of Atonement, when atonement is made for
you before the LORD your God. 29Those who do not deny themselves
on that day must be cut off from their people. 30I will destroy from
among their people anyone who does any work on that day. 31You shall
do no work at all. This is to be a lasting ordinance for the generations
to come, wherever you live. 32It is a day of sabbath rest for you, and you
must deny yourselves. From the evening of the ninth day of the month
until the following evening you are to observe your sabbath."

THE FESTIVAL OF TABERNACLES

33The LORD said to Moses, 34"Say to the Israelites: 'On the fifteenth
day of the seventh month the LORD's Festival of Tabernacles begins,
and it lasts for seven days. 35The first day is a sacred assembly; do no
regular work. 36For seven days present food offerings to the LORD, and
on the eighth day hold a sacred assembly and present a food offering
to the LORD. It is the closing special assembly; do no regular work.

37(" 'These are the LORD's appointed festivals, which you are to pro-
claim as sacred assemblies for bringing food offerings to the LORD —
the burnt offerings and grain offerings, sacrifices and drink offerings
required for each day. 38These offerings are in addition to those for the
LORD's Sabbaths and[c] in addition to your gifts and whatever you have
vowed and all the freewill offerings you give to the LORD.)

39" 'So beginning with the fifteenth day of the seventh month, af-
ter you have gathered the crops of the land, celebrate the festival to
the LORD for seven days; the first day is a day of sabbath rest, and the
eighth day also is a day of sabbath rest. 40On the first day you are to
take branches from luxuriant trees — from palms, willows and other
leafy trees — and rejoice before the LORD your God for seven days.
41Celebrate this as a festival to the LORD for seven days each year. This
is to be a lasting ordinance for the generations to come; celebrate it

---

[a] 19 Or *purification offering* [b] 27 Or *and fast*; similarly in verses 29 and 32
[c] 38 Or *These festivals are in addition to the LORD's Sabbaths, and these offerings are*

in the seventh month. 42Live in temporary shelters for seven days: All
native-born Israelites are to live in such shelters 43so your descendants
will know that I had the Israelites live in temporary shelters when I
brought them out of Egypt. I am the LORD your God.'"
44So Moses announced to the Israelites the appointed festivals of
the LORD.

OLIVE OIL AND BREAD SET BEFORE THE LORD

24 The LORD said to Moses, 2"Command the Israelites to bring you
clear oil of pressed olives for the light so that the lamps may
be kept burning continually. 3Outside the curtain that shields the ark
of the covenant law in the tent of meeting, Aaron is to tend the lamps
before the LORD from evening till morning, continually. This is to be a
lasting ordinance for the generations to come. 4The lamps on the pure
gold lampstand before the LORD must be tended continually.
5"Take the finest flour and bake twelve loaves of bread, using two-
tenths of an ephah[a] for each loaf. 6Arrange them in two stacks, six in
each stack, on the table of pure gold before the LORD. 7By each stack
put some pure incense as a memorial[b] portion to represent the bread
and to be a food offering presented to the LORD. 8This bread is to be
set out before the LORD regularly, Sabbath after Sabbath, on behalf of
the Israelites, as a lasting covenant. 9It belongs to Aaron and his sons,
who are to eat it in the sanctuary area, because it is a most holy part
of their perpetual share of the food offerings presented to the LORD."

A BLASPHEMER PUT TO DEATH

10Now the son of an Israelite mother and an Egyptian father went
out among the Israelites, and a fight broke out in the camp between
him and an Israelite. 11The son of the Israelite woman blasphemed
the Name with a curse; so they brought him to Moses. (His mother's
name was Shelomith, the daughter of Dibri the Danite.) 12They put
him in custody until the will of the LORD should be made clear to
them.
13Then the LORD said to Moses: 14"Take the blasphemer outside the
camp. All those who heard him are to lay their hands on his head, and
the entire assembly is to stone him. 15Say to the Israelites: 'Anyone who
curses their God will be held responsible; 16anyone who blasphemes
the name of the LORD is to be put to death. The entire assembly must
stone them. Whether foreigner or native-born, when they blaspheme
the Name they are to be put to death.
17"'Anyone who takes the life of a human being is to be put to death.
18Anyone who takes the life of someone's animal must make restitu-
tion — life for life. 19Anyone who injures their neighbor is to be in-
jured in the same manner: 20fracture for fracture, eye for eye, tooth
for tooth. The one who has inflicted the injury must suffer the same
injury. 21Whoever kills an animal must make restitution, but whoever
kills a human being is to be put to death. 22You are to have the same
law for the foreigner and the native-born. I am the LORD your God.'"
23Then Moses spoke to the Israelites, and they took the blasphemer
outside the camp and stoned him. The Israelites did as the LORD com-
manded Moses.

PRAYING SCRIPTURE

Leviticus 24

The Lord is holy. We should treat his name in accordance with his holy nature. To blaspheme the name of the Lord was a death-penalty offense under Israel's law, because to curse God's name was to curse him.

Think about how you use God's name. Do you use it casually or with the esteem that it—and God—is due? Ask him to help you honor his name as you honor God himself.

---

[a] 5 That is, probably about 7 pounds or about 3.2 kilograms [b] 7 Or *representative*

PRAYING SCRIPTURE

Leviticus 25

The principle of Sabbath concerned more than one day a week and more than personal rest. Even the land was to have rest. The law reminded Israel's children that everything, including the earth, belonged to God.

Because we belong to the Lord, we should value the dignity of every person made in his image as well as the land he gave us to cultivate. Ask God to help you reflect his love to every part of his creation.

THE SABBATH YEAR

25 The LORD said to Moses at Mount Sinai, 2"Speak to the Isra-
elites and say to them: 'When you enter the land I am going
to give you, the land itself must observe a sabbath to the LORD. 3For
six years sow your fields, and for six years prune your vineyards and
gather their crops. 4But in the seventh year the land is to have a year
of sabbath rest, a sabbath to the LORD. Do not sow your fields or prune
your vineyards. 5Do not reap what grows of itself or harvest the grapes
of your untended vines. The land is to have a year of rest. 6Whatever
the land yields during the sabbath year will be food for you — for your-
self, your male and female servants, and the hired worker and tem-
porary resident who live among you, 7as well as for your livestock and
the wild animals in your land. Whatever the land produces may be
eaten.

THE YEAR OF JUBILEE

8" 'Count off seven sabbath years — seven times seven years — so
that the seven sabbath years amount to a period of forty-nine years.
9Then have the trumpet sounded everywhere on the tenth day of
the seventh month; on the Day of Atonement sound the trumpet
throughout your land. 10Consecrate the fiftieth year and proclaim lib-
erty throughout the land to all its inhabitants. It shall be a jubilee for
you; each of you is to return to your family property and to your own
clan. 11The fiftieth year shall be a jubilee for you; do not sow and do
not reap what grows of itself or harvest the untended vines. 12For it
is a jubilee and is to be holy for you; eat only what is taken directly
from the fields.

13" 'In this Year of Jubilee everyone is to return to their own property.

14" 'If you sell land to any of your own people or buy land from them,
do not take advantage of each other. 15You are to buy from your own
people on the basis of the number of years since the Jubilee. And they
are to sell to you on the basis of the number of years left for harvesting
crops. 16When the years are many, you are to increase the price, and
when the years are few, you are to decrease the price, because what is
really being sold to you is the number of crops. 17Do not take advan-
tage of each other, but fear your God. I am the LORD your God.

18" 'Follow my decrees and be careful to obey my laws, and you will
live safely in the land. 19Then the land will yield its fruit, and you will
eat your fill and live there in safety. 20You may ask, "What will we
eat in the seventh year if we do not plant or harvest our crops?" 21I
will send you such a blessing in the sixth year that the land will yield
enough for three years. 22While you plant during the eighth year, you
will eat from the old crop and will continue to eat from it until the
harvest of the ninth year comes in.

23" 'The land must not be sold permanently, because the land is mine
and you reside in my land as foreigners and strangers. 24Throughout
the land that you hold as a possession, you must provide for the re-
demption of the land.

25" 'If one of your fellow Israelites becomes poor and sells some of
their property, their nearest relative is to come and redeem what they
have sold. 26If, however, there is no one to redeem it for them but later
on they prosper and acquire sufficient means to redeem it themselves,
27they are to determine the value for the years since they sold it and
refund the balance to the one to whom they sold it; they can then go

back to their own property. 28But if they do not acquire the means to repay, what was sold will remain in the possession of the buyer until the Year of Jubilee. It will be returned in the Jubilee, and they can then go back to their property.

29" 'Anyone who sells a house in a walled city retains the right of redemption a full year after its sale. During that time the seller may redeem it. 30If it is not redeemed before a full year has passed, the house in the walled city shall belong permanently to the buyer and the buyer's descendants. It is not to be returned in the Jubilee. 31But houses in villages without walls around them are to be considered as belonging to the open country. They can be redeemed, and they are to be returned in the Jubilee.

32" 'The Levites always have the right to redeem their houses in the Levitical towns, which they possess. 33So the property of the Levites is redeemable — that is, a house sold in any town they hold — and is to be returned in the Jubilee, because the houses in the towns of the Levites are their property among the Israelites. 34But the pastureland belonging to their towns must not be sold; it is their permanent possession.

35" 'If any of your fellow Israelites become poor and are unable to support themselves among you, help them as you would a foreigner and stranger, so they can continue to live among you. 36Do not take interest or any profit from them, but fear your God, so that they may continue to live among you. 37You must not lend them money at interest or sell them food at a profit. 38I am the Lord your God, who brought you out of Egypt to give you the land of Canaan and to be your God.

39" 'If any of your fellow Israelites become poor and sell themselves to you, do not make them work as slaves. 40They are to be treated as hired workers or temporary residents among you; they are to work for you until the Year of Jubilee. 41Then they and their children are to be released, and they will go back to their own clans and to the property of their ancestors. 42Because the Israelites are my servants, whom I brought out of Egypt, they must not be sold as slaves. 43Do not rule over them ruthlessly, but fear your God.

44" 'Your male and female slaves are to come from the nations around you; from them you may buy slaves. 45You may also buy some of the temporary residents living among you and members of their clans born in your country, and they will become your property. 46You can bequeath them to your children as inherited property and can make them slaves for life, but you must not rule over your fellow Israelites ruthlessly.

47" 'If a foreigner residing among you becomes rich and any of your fellow Israelites become poor and sell themselves to the foreigner or to a member of the foreigner's clan, 48they retain the right of redemption after they have sold themselves. One of their relatives may redeem them: 49An uncle or a cousin or any blood relative in their clan may redeem them. Or if they prosper, they may redeem themselves. 50They and their buyer are to count the time from the year they sold themselves up to the Year of Jubilee. The price for their release is to be based on the rate paid to a hired worker for that number of years. 51If many years remain, they must pay for their redemption a larger share of the price paid for them. 52If only a few years remain until the Year of Jubilee, they are to compute that and pay for their redemption accordingly. 53They are to be treated as workers hired from year

to year; you must see to it that those to whom they owe service do not
rule over them ruthlessly.
54“ ‘Even if someone is not redeemed in any of these ways, they and
their children are to be released in the Year of Jubilee, 55for the Israel-
ites belong to me as servants. They are my servants, whom I brought
out of Egypt. I am the LORD your God.

REWARD FOR OBEDIENCE

26 “ ‘Do not make idols or set up an image or a sacred stone for
yourselves, and do not place a carved stone in your land to bow
down before it. I am the LORD your God.
2“ ‘Observe my Sabbaths and have reverence for my sanctuary. I am
the LORD.
3“ ‘If you follow my decrees and are careful to obey my commands, 4I
will send you rain in its season, and the ground will yield its crops and
the trees their fruit. 5Your threshing will continue until grape harvest
and the grape harvest will continue until planting, and you will eat all
the food you want and live in safety in your land.
6“ ‘I will grant peace in the land, and you will lie down and no one
will make you afraid. I will remove wild beasts from the land, and the
sword will not pass through your country. 7You will pursue your ene-
mies, and they will fall by the sword before you. 8Five of you will chase
a hundred, and a hundred of you will chase ten thousand, and your
enemies will fall by the sword before you.
9“ ‘I will look on you with favor and make you fruitful and increase
your numbers, and I will keep my covenant with you. 10You will still
be eating last year’s harvest when you will have to move it out to make
room for the new. 11I will put my dwelling place[a] among you, and I will
not abhor you. 12I will walk among you and be your God, and you will
be my people. 13I am the LORD your God, who brought you out of Egypt
so that you would no longer be slaves to the Egyptians; I broke the bars
of your yoke and enabled you to walk with heads held high.

PUNISHMENT FOR DISOBEDIENCE

14“ ‘But if you will not listen to me and carry out all these commands,
15and if you reject my decrees and abhor my laws and fail to carry out
all my commands and so violate my covenant, 16then I will do this to
you: I will bring on you sudden terror, wasting diseases and fever that
will destroy your sight and sap your strength. You will plant seed in
vain, because your enemies will eat it. 17I will set my face against you
so that you will be defeated by your enemies; those who hate you will
rule over you, and you will flee even when no one is pursuing you.
18“ ‘If after all this you will not listen to me, I will punish you for
your sins seven times over. 19I will break down your stubborn pride
and make the sky above you like iron and the ground beneath you like
bronze. 20Your strength will be spent in vain, because your soil will not
yield its crops, nor will the trees of your land yield their fruit.
21“ ‘If you remain hostile toward me and refuse to listen to me, I will
multiply your afflictions seven times over, as your sins deserve. 22I will
send wild animals against you, and they will rob you of your children,
destroy your cattle and make you so few in number that your roads
will be deserted.

PRAYING SCRIPTURE

Leviticus 26

God’s promises to Israel included blessings for obedience and punishment for disobedience. He never intended to bless his people if they lived any way they pleased. Yet he keeps every covenant promise that he ever made.

God never forgets any of his promises. If you need to claim one of them today—for yourself or someone else—take it to him as you pray.

---

[a] *11* Or *my tabernacle*

23“ ‘If in spite of these things you do not accept my correction but
continue to be hostile toward me, 24I myself will be hostile toward you
and will afflict you for your sins seven times over. 25And I will bring
the sword on you to avenge the breaking of the covenant. When you
withdraw into your cities, I will send a plague among you, and you will
be given into enemy hands. 26When I cut off your supply of bread, ten
women will be able to bake your bread in one oven, and they will dole
out the bread by weight. You will eat, but you will not be satisfied.

27“ ‘If in spite of this you still do not listen to me but continue to be
hostile toward me, 28then in my anger I will be hostile toward you,
and I myself will punish you for your sins seven times over. 29You
will eat the flesh of your sons and the flesh of your daughters. 30I will
destroy your high places, cut down your incense altars and pile your
dead bodies[a] on the lifeless forms of your idols, and I will abhor you.
31I will turn your cities into ruins and lay waste your sanctuaries, and I
will take no delight in the pleasing aroma of your offerings. 32I myself
will lay waste the land, so that your enemies who live there will be
appalled. 33I will scatter you among the nations and will draw out my
sword and pursue you. Your land will be laid waste, and your cities will
lie in ruins. 34Then the land will enjoy its sabbath years all the time
that it lies desolate and you are in the country of your enemies; then
the land will rest and enjoy its sabbaths. 35All the time that it lies des-
olate, the land will have the rest it did not have during the sabbaths
you lived in it.

36“ ‘As for those of you who are left, I will make their hearts so fearful
in the lands of their enemies that the sound of a windblown leaf will
put them to flight. They will run as though fleeing from the sword,
and they will fall, even though no one is pursuing them. 37They will
stumble over one another as though fleeing from the sword, even
though no one is pursuing them. So you will not be able to stand be-
fore your enemies. 38You will perish among the nations; the land of
your enemies will devour you. 39Those of you who are left will waste
away in the lands of their enemies because of their sins; also because
of their ancestors’ sins they will waste away.

40“ ‘But if they will confess their sins and the sins of their ances-
tors — their unfaithfulness and their hostility toward me, 41which
made me hostile toward them so that I sent them into the land of
their enemies — then when their uncircumcised hearts are humbled
and they pay for their sin, 42I will remember my covenant with Jacob
and my covenant with Isaac and my covenant with Abraham, and I
will remember the land. 43For the land will be deserted by them and
will enjoy its sabbaths while it lies desolate without them. They will
pay for their sins because they rejected my laws and abhorred my de-
crees. 44Yet in spite of this, when they are in the land of their enemies,
I will not reject them or abhor them so as to destroy them completely,
breaking my covenant with them. I am the LORD their God. 45But for
their sake I will remember the covenant with their ancestors whom I
brought out of Egypt in the sight of the nations to be their God. I am
the LORD.’ ”

46These are the decrees, the laws and the regulations that the LORD
established at Mount Sinai between himself and the Israelites through
Moses.

---

[a] *30* Or *your funeral offerings*

PRAYING SCRIPTURE

Leviticus 27

The theme of redemption permeates the law for good reason. It's the story of how God saves people through history: He redeems us. He buys us back from death. The law emphasizes what God emphasizes. These redemptive commands point to Jesus.

Have you reflected recently on what it means to be redeemed from sin? Thank God for the redemption he provides from sin through Jesus.

REDEEMING WHAT IS THE LORD'S

27 The LORD said to Moses, 2"Speak to the Israelites and say to them: 'If anyone makes a special vow to dedicate a person to the LORD by giving the equivalent value, 3set the value of a male between the ages of twenty and sixty at fifty shekels[a] of silver, according to the sanctuary shekel[b]; 4for a female, set her value at thirty shekels[c]; 5for a person between the ages of five and twenty, set the value of a male at twenty shekels[d] and of a female at ten shekels[e]; 6for a person between one month and five years, set the value of a male at five shekels[f] of silver and that of a female at three shekels[g] of silver; 7for a person sixty years old or more, set the value of a male at fifteen shekels[h] and of a female at ten shekels. 8If anyone making the vow is too poor to pay the specified amount, the person being dedicated is to be presented to the priest, who will set the value according to what the one making the vow can afford.

9" 'If what they vowed is an animal that is acceptable as an offering to the LORD, such an animal given to the LORD becomes holy. 10They must not exchange it or substitute a good one for a bad one, or a bad one for a good one; if they should substitute one animal for another, both it and the substitute become holy. 11If what they vowed is a ceremonially unclean animal — one that is not acceptable as an offering to the LORD — the animal must be presented to the priest, 12who will judge its quality as good or bad. Whatever value the priest then sets, that is what it will be. 13If the owner wishes to redeem the animal, a fifth must be added to its value.

14" 'If anyone dedicates their house as something holy to the LORD, the priest will judge its quality as good or bad. Whatever value the priest then sets, so it will remain. 15If the one who dedicates their house wishes to redeem it, they must add a fifth to its value, and the house will again become theirs.

16" 'If anyone dedicates to the LORD part of their family land, its value is to be set according to the amount of seed required for it — fifty shekels of silver to a homer[i] of barley seed. 17If they dedicate a field during the Year of Jubilee, the value that has been set remains. 18But if they dedicate a field after the Jubilee, the priest will determine the value according to the number of years that remain until the next Year of Jubilee, and its set value will be reduced. 19If the one who dedicates the field wishes to redeem it, they must add a fifth to its value, and the field will again become theirs. 20If, however, they do not redeem the field, or if they have sold it to someone else, it can never be redeemed. 21When the field is released in the Jubilee, it will become holy, like a field devoted to the LORD; it will become priestly property.

22" 'If anyone dedicates to the LORD a field they have bought, which is not part of their family land, 23the priest will determine its value up to the Year of Jubilee, and the owner must pay its value on that day as something holy to the LORD. 24In the Year of Jubilee the field

---

[a] *3* That is, about 1 1/4 pounds or about 575 grams; also in verse 16 [b] *3* That is, about 2/5 ounce or about 12 grams; also in verse 25 [c] *4* That is, about 12 ounces or about 345 grams [d] *5* That is, about 8 ounces or about 230 grams [e] *5* That is, about 4 ounces or about 115 grams; also in verse 7 [f] *6* That is, about 2 ounces or about 58 grams [g] *6* That is, about 1 1/4 ounces or about 35 grams [h] *7* That is, about 6 ounces or about 175 grams [i] *16* That is, probably about 300 pounds or about 135 kilograms

will revert to the person from whom it was bought, the one whose
land it was. 25Every value is to be set according to the sanctuary shekel,
twenty gerahs to the shekel.

26"'No one, however, may dedicate the firstborn of an animal, since
the firstborn already belongs to the LORD; whether an ox[a] or a sheep,
it is the LORD's. 27If it is one of the unclean animals, it may be bought
back at its set value, adding a fifth of the value to it. If it is not redeemed, it is to be sold at its set value.

28"'But nothing that a person owns and devotes[b] to the LORD—whether a human being or an animal or family land—may be sold or redeemed; everything so devoted is most holy to the LORD.

29"'No person devoted to destruction[c] may be ransomed; they are to be put to death.

30"'A tithe of everything from the land, whether grain from the soil
or fruit from the trees, belongs to the LORD; it is holy to the LORD.
31Whoever would redeem any of their tithe must add a fifth of the
value to it. 32Every tithe of the herd and flock—every tenth animal
that passes under the shepherd's rod—will be holy to the LORD. 33No
one may pick out the good from the bad or make any substitution. If anyone does make a substitution, both the animal and its substitute become holy and cannot be redeemed.'"

34These are the commands the LORD gave Moses at Mount Sinai for the Israelites.

---

[a] *26* The Hebrew word can refer to either male or female. [b] *28* The Hebrew term refers to the irrevocable giving over of things or persons to the LORD.
[c] *29* The Hebrew term refers to the irrevocable giving over of things or persons to the LORD, often by totally destroying them.

NUMBERS

The Hebrew name for the book of Numbers is "In the Wilderness" and is a fitting summary for the events it describes. It begins with a census of the children of Israel and closes with their wandering in the wilderness for 40 years until the generation that refused to enter the promised land—the generation of unbelief—died off.

While some people wonder about the significance of such a list of names and the numbers of them, the census of the children of Israel makes an important theological point—God kept his promise to Abraham. The promise, repeated in Genesis 15 and 17, guaranteed that Abraham would have descendants as numerous as the stars in the sky. The same Lord who made that promise to Abraham promised Israel's children that he would lead them out of Egypt and into the land of promise. God emphasized that he would keep *that* promise just as he kept the first promise to Abraham.

The first ten chapters of Numbers chronicle the preparations the Israelites made to leave for the promised land, a land flowing with milk and honey. After the numbering of the children of Israel, they sanctified the tabernacle, put the priesthood in place and celebrated the Passover. Chapters 11–25 narrate the Israelites' wilderness wanderings, with particular attention focused on their breaking faith with the Lord. The people had previously doubted God's ability to keep his promise. Their doubt reached a crescendo when they refused to believe the spies' reports about the land. The final chapters take place on the plains of Moab as the first generation died out and their children prepared to enter the land in their place. Significant to this section is a prayer of Moses that challenged God to remember his word because of his reputation (see 14:13–19). God was so angry with the Israelites that he threatened to destroy the entire nation and raise a new people from Moses' descendants. Moses reminded God that the nations around Israel would see that as God's inability to bring them into the land, indicating his hand had fallen short of his famed might. God heard Moses' prayer and relented.

The Israelites' struggle in the book of Numbers mirrors many of the struggles we face in a fallen world. We put our focus on our circumstances instead of the God who has mightily delivered us. We doubt his ability to come through for us in spite of the fact that we are better off now than in the place we once were. The goodness and kindness of God is all around us. Still, we wonder whether God will keep his promises even though we know his record of doing everything he has said he will do. This struggle often leads us to prayerlessness. We say to ourselves, *Things have remained unchanged for so long, why even pray? What's the point?*

But the thing to remember is that the people *would enter* the land. The prayers of Abraham, Isaac, Jacob, Moses, Joshua, Caleb and a new generation would be answered. God would honor his promises and do what he said he would do, just as he honors the totality of his promises in Scripture even today and hears every prayer of his people offered in faith and according to his will.

THE CENSUS

1 The LORD spoke to Moses in the tent of meeting in the Desert of
Sinai on the first day of the second month of the second year after
the Israelites came out of Egypt. He said: 2"Take a census of the whole
Israelite community by their clans and families, listing every man by
name, one by one. 3You and Aaron are to count according to their divi-
sions all the men in Israel who are twenty years old or more and able
to serve in the army. 4One man from each tribe, each of them the head
of his family, is to help you. 5These are the names of the men who are
to assist you:

from Reuben, Elizur son of Shedeur;
6 from Simeon, Shelumiel son of Zurishaddai;
7 from Judah, Nahshon son of Amminadab;
8 from Issachar, Nethanel son of Zuar;
9 from Zebulun, Eliab son of Helon;
10 from the sons of Joseph:
from Ephraim, Elishama son of Ammihud;
from Manasseh, Gamaliel son of Pedahzur;
11 from Benjamin, Abidan son of Gideoni;
12 from Dan, Ahiezer son of Ammishaddai;
13 from Asher, Pagiel son of Okran;
14 from Gad, Eliasaph son of Deuel;
15 from Naphtali, Ahira son of Enan."

16These were the men appointed from the community, the leaders of
their ancestral tribes. They were the heads of the clans of Israel.
17Moses and Aaron took these men whose names had been specified,
18and they called the whole community together on the first day of the
second month. The people registered their ancestry by their clans and
families, and the men twenty years old or more were listed by name,
one by one, 19as the LORD commanded Moses. And so he counted them
in the Desert of Sinai:

20 From the descendants of Reuben the firstborn son of Israel:
All the men twenty years old or more who were able to serve in
the army were listed by name, one by one, according to the rec-
ords of their clans and families. 21The number from the tribe of
Reuben was 46,500.

22 From the descendants of Simeon:
All the men twenty years old or more who were able to serve
in the army were counted and listed by name, one by one, ac-
cording to the records of their clans and families. 23The number
from the tribe of Simeon was 59,300.

24 From the descendants of Gad:
All the men twenty years old or more who were able to serve
in the army were listed by name, according to the records of
their clans and families. 25The number from the tribe of Gad was
45,650.

26 From the descendants of Judah:
All the men twenty years old or more who were able to serve in
the army were listed by name, according to the records of their
clans and families. 27The number from the tribe of Judah was
74,600.

PRAYING SCRIPTURE

Numbers 1

The remarkable census of Israel in the wilderness affirms God's faithfulness to his promises. He had sustained them through the exodus and escape through the Red Sea. He had given them the laws they needed to live according to his will. Recording their population was a practical means of showing that God had kept them alive as a nation.

Thank God for your family, for friends who are your family and for his family.

28 From the descendants of Issachar:
All the men twenty years old or more who were able to serve in the army were listed by name, according to the records of their clans and families. 29 The number from the tribe of Issachar was 54,400.

30 From the descendants of Zebulun:
All the men twenty years old or more who were able to serve in the army were listed by name, according to the records of their clans and families. 31 The number from the tribe of Zebulun was 57,400.

32 From the sons of Joseph:
From the descendants of Ephraim:
All the men twenty years old or more who were able to serve in the army were listed by name, according to the records of their clans and families. 33 The number from the tribe of Ephraim was 40,500.
34 From the descendants of Manasseh:
All the men twenty years old or more who were able to serve in the army were listed by name, according to the records of their clans and families. 35 The number from the tribe of Manasseh was 32,200.

36 From the descendants of Benjamin:
All the men twenty years old or more who were able to serve in the army were listed by name, according to the records of their clans and families. 37 The number from the tribe of Benjamin was 35,400.

38 From the descendants of Dan:
All the men twenty years old or more who were able to serve in the army were listed by name, according to the records of their clans and families. 39 The number from the tribe of Dan was 62,700.

40 From the descendants of Asher:
All the men twenty years old or more who were able to serve in the army were listed by name, according to the records of their clans and families. 41 The number from the tribe of Asher was 41,500.

42 From the descendants of Naphtali:
All the men twenty years old or more who were able to serve in the army were listed by name, according to the records of their clans and families. 43 The number from the tribe of Naphtali was 53,400.

44 These were the men counted by Moses and Aaron and the twelve
leaders of Israel, each one representing his family. 45 All the Israelites
twenty years old or more who were able to serve in Israel's army were
counted according to their families. 46 The total number was 603,550.
47 The ancestral tribe of the Levites, however, was not counted along
with the others. 48 The LORD had said to Moses: 49 "You must not count
the tribe of Levi or include them in the census of the other Israelites.
50 Instead, appoint the Levites to be in charge of the tabernacle of the
covenant law — over all its furnishings and everything belonging to it.

They are to carry the tabernacle and all its furnishings; they are to take
care of it and encamp around it. 51 Whenever the tabernacle is to move,
the Levites are to take it down, and whenever the tabernacle is to be set
up, the Levites shall do it. Anyone else who approaches it is to be put
to death. 52 The Israelites are to set up their tents by divisions, each of
them in their own camp under their standard. 53 The Levites, however,
are to set up their tents around the tabernacle of the covenant law so
that my wrath will not fall on the Israelite community. The Levites are
to be responsible for the care of the tabernacle of the covenant law."
54 The Israelites did all this just as the LORD commanded Moses.

THE ARRANGEMENT OF THE TRIBAL CAMPS

2 The LORD said to Moses and Aaron: 2 "The Israelites are to camp
around the tent of meeting some distance from it, each of them
under their standard and holding the banners of their family."

3 On the east, toward the sunrise, the divisions of the camp of Ju-
dah are to encamp under their standard. The leader of the people
of Judah is Nahshon son of Amminadab. 4 His division numbers
74,600.
5 The tribe of Issachar will camp next to them. The leader of the
people of Issachar is Nethanel son of Zuar. 6 His division numbers
54,400.
7 The tribe of Zebulun will be next. The leader of the people of
Zebulun is Eliab son of Helon. 8 His division numbers 57,400.
9 All the men assigned to the camp of Judah, according to their
divisions, number 186,400. They will set out first.

10 On the south will be the divisions of the camp of Reuben un-
der their standard. The leader of the people of Reuben is Elizur son
of Shedeur. 11 His division numbers 46,500.
12 The tribe of Simeon will camp next to them. The leader of the
people of Simeon is Shelumiel son of Zurishaddai. 13 His division
numbers 59,300.
14 The tribe of Gad will be next. The leader of the people of Gad is
Eliasaph son of Deuel.[a] 15 His division numbers 45,650.
16 All the men assigned to the camp of Reuben, according to
their divisions, number 151,450. They will set out second.
17 Then the tent of meeting and the camp of the Levites will set
out in the middle of the camps. They will set out in the same or-
der as they encamp, each in their own place under their standard.

18 On the west will be the divisions of the camp of Ephraim un-
der their standard. The leader of the people of Ephraim is Elish-
ama son of Ammihud. 19 His division numbers 40,500.
20 The tribe of Manasseh will be next to them. The leader of the
people of Manasseh is Gamaliel son of Pedahzur. 21 His division
numbers 32,200.
22 The tribe of Benjamin will be next. The leader of the people of
Benjamin is Abidan son of Gideoni. 23 His division numbers 35,400.
24 All the men assigned to the camp of Ephraim, according to
their divisions, number 108,100. They will set out third.

PRAYING SCRIPTURE

Numbers 2

When Israel camped, the tabernacle was in the center, signifying God's presence. Whenever Israel left a campsite, the tabernacle went with them, signifying that the Lord was among his people.

How often do you need to be reminded that God is with you? Thank him for being close to you wherever you are.

[a] *14* Many manuscripts of the Masoretic Text, Samaritan Pentateuch and Vulgate (see also 1:14); most manuscripts of the Masoretic Text *Reuel*

25On the north will be the divisions of the camp of Dan under
their standard. The leader of the people of Dan is Ahiezer son of
Ammishaddai. 26His division numbers 62,700.
27The tribe of Asher will camp next to them. The leader of the
people of Asher is Pagiel son of Okran. 28His division numbers
41,500.
29The tribe of Naphtali will be next. The leader of the people
of Naphtali is Ahira son of Enan. 30His division numbers 53,400.
31All the men assigned to the camp of Dan number 157,600. They
will set out last, under their standards.

32These are the Israelites, counted according to their families.
All the men in the camps, by their divisions, number 603,550.
33The Levites, however, were not counted along with the other Is-
raelites, as the LORD commanded Moses.

34So the Israelites did everything the LORD commanded Moses; that
is the way they encamped under their standards, and that is the way
they set out, each of them with their clan and family.

THE LEVITES

3 This is the account of the family of Aaron and Moses at the time
the LORD spoke to Moses at Mount Sinai.
2The names of the sons of Aaron were Nadab the firstborn and
Abihu, Eleazar and Ithamar. 3Those were the names of Aaron's sons,
the anointed priests, who were ordained to serve as priests. 4Nadab
and Abihu, however, died before the LORD when they made an offering
with unauthorized fire before him in the Desert of Sinai. They had no
sons, so Eleazar and Ithamar served as priests during the lifetime of
their father Aaron.
5The LORD said to Moses, 6"Bring the tribe of Levi and present them
to Aaron the priest to assist him. 7They are to perform duties for him
and for the whole community at the tent of meeting by doing the work
of the tabernacle. 8They are to take care of all the furnishings of the
tent of meeting, fulfilling the obligations of the Israelites by doing the
work of the tabernacle. 9Give the Levites to Aaron and his sons; they
are the Israelites who are to be given wholly to him.[a] 10Appoint Aaron
and his sons to serve as priests; anyone else who approaches the sanc-
tuary is to be put to death."
11The LORD also said to Moses, 12"I have taken the Levites from
among the Israelites in place of the first male offspring of every Is-
raelite woman. The Levites are mine, 13for all the firstborn are mine.
When I struck down all the firstborn in Egypt, I set apart for myself
every firstborn in Israel, whether human or animal. They are to be
mine. I am the LORD."
14The LORD said to Moses in the Desert of Sinai, 15"Count the Levites
by their families and clans. Count every male a month old or more."
16So Moses counted them, as he was commanded by the word of the
LORD.
17These were the names of the sons of Levi:
Gershon, Kohath and Merari.

PRAYING SCRIPTURE

Numbers 3

The Lord commanded a census to be taken of the Levites. Then he said, "The Levites are to be mine. I am the LORD" (verse 45). God claimed them for himself. This statement foreshadowed Paul's declaration that God "predestined us for adoption to sonship through Jesus Christ" (Ephesians 1:5).

We are more than servants—we are his sons! How does it feel to be a child of God?

[a] 9 Most manuscripts of the Masoretic Text; some manuscripts of the Masoretic Text, Samaritan Pentateuch and Septuagint (see also 8:16) *to me*

18 These were the names of the Gershonite clans:
Libni and Shimei.
19 The Kohathite clans:
Amram, Izhar, Hebron and Uzziel.
20 The Merarite clans:
Mahli and Mushi.
These were the Levite clans, according to their families.

21 To Gershon belonged the clans of the Libnites and Shimeites; these
were the Gershonite clans. 22 The number of all the males a month old
or more who were counted was 7,500. 23 The Gershonite clans were to
camp on the west, behind the tabernacle. 24 The leader of the families
of the Gershonites was Eliasaph son of Lael. 25 At the tent of meeting
the Gershonites were responsible for the care of the tabernacle and
tent, its coverings, the curtain at the entrance to the tent of meet-
ing, 26 the curtains of the courtyard, the curtain at the entrance to the
courtyard surrounding the tabernacle and altar, and the ropes—and
everything related to their use.

27 To Kohath belonged the clans of the Amramites, Izharites, Hebron-
ites and Uzzielites; these were the Kohathite clans. 28 The number of
all the males a month old or more was 8,600.[a] The Kohathites were
responsible for the care of the sanctuary. 29 The Kohathite clans were to
camp on the south side of the tabernacle. 30 The leader of the families
of the Kohathite clans was Elizaphan son of Uzziel. 31 They were respon-
sible for the care of the ark, the table, the lampstand, the altars, the ar-
ticles of the sanctuary used in ministering, the curtain, and everything
related to their use. 32 The chief leader of the Levites was Eleazar son of
Aaron, the priest. He was appointed over those who were responsible
for the care of the sanctuary.

33 To Merari belonged the clans of the Mahlites and the Mushites;
these were the Merarite clans. 34 The number of all the males a month
old or more who were counted was 6,200. 35 The leader of the families
of the Merarite clans was Zuriel son of Abihail; they were to camp on
the north side of the tabernacle. 36 The Merarites were appointed to take
care of the frames of the tabernacle, its crossbars, posts, bases, all its
equipment, and everything related to their use, 37 as well as the posts of
the surrounding courtyard with their bases, tent pegs and ropes.

38 Moses and Aaron and his sons were to camp to the east of the tab-
ernacle, toward the sunrise, in front of the tent of meeting. They were
responsible for the care of the sanctuary on behalf of the Israelites.
Anyone else who approached the sanctuary was to be put to death.

39 The total number of Levites counted at the LORD's command by
Moses and Aaron according to their clans, including every male a
month old or more, was 22,000.

40 The LORD said to Moses, "Count all the firstborn Israelite males
who are a month old or more and make a list of their names. 41 Take
the Levites for me in place of all the firstborn of the Israelites, and the

[a] *28* Hebrew; some Septuagint manuscripts *8,300*

livestock of the Levites in place of all the firstborn of the livestock of the Israelites. I am the LORD."

42 So Moses counted all the firstborn of the Israelites, as the LORD commanded him. 43 The total number of firstborn males a month old or more, listed by name, was 22,273.

44 The LORD also said to Moses, 45 "Take the Levites in place of all the firstborn of Israel, and the livestock of the Levites in place of their livestock. The Levites are to be mine. I am the LORD. 46 To redeem the 273 firstborn Israelites who exceed the number of the Levites, 47 collect five shekels[a] for each one, according to the sanctuary shekel, which weighs twenty gerahs. 48 Give the money for the redemption of the additional Israelites to Aaron and his sons."

49 So Moses collected the redemption money from those who exceeded the number redeemed by the Levites. 50 From the firstborn of the Israelites he collected silver weighing 1,365 shekels,[b] according to the sanctuary shekel. 51 Moses gave the redemption money to Aaron and his sons, as he was commanded by the word of the LORD.

THE KOHATHITES

4 The LORD said to Moses and Aaron: 2 "Take a census of the Kohathite branch of the Levites by their clans and families. 3 Count all the men from thirty to fifty years of age who come to serve in the work at the tent of meeting.

4 "This is the work of the Kohathites at the tent of meeting: the care of the most holy things. 5 When the camp is to move, Aaron and his sons are to go in and take down the shielding curtain and put it over the ark of the covenant law. 6 Then they are to cover the curtain with a durable leather,[c] spread a cloth of solid blue over that and put the poles in place.

7 "Over the table of the Presence they are to spread a blue cloth and put on it the plates, dishes and bowls, and the jars for drink offerings; the bread that is continually there is to remain on it. 8 They are to spread a scarlet cloth over them, cover that with the durable leather and put the poles in place.

9 "They are to take a blue cloth and cover the lampstand that is for light, together with its lamps, its wick trimmers and trays, and all its jars for the olive oil used to supply it. 10 Then they are to wrap it and all its accessories in a covering of the durable leather and put it on a carrying frame.

11 "Over the gold altar they are to spread a blue cloth and cover that with the durable leather and put the poles in place.

12 "They are to take all the articles used for ministering in the sanctuary, wrap them in a blue cloth, cover that with the durable leather and put them on a carrying frame.

13 "They are to remove the ashes from the bronze altar and spread a purple cloth over it. 14 Then they are to place on it all the utensils used for ministering at the altar, including the firepans, meat forks, shovels and sprinkling bowls. Over it they are to spread a covering of the durable leather and put the poles in place.

15 "After Aaron and his sons have finished covering the holy

PRAYING SCRIPTURE

Numbers 4

As with the construction of the tabernacle, the ongoing system of worship involved many people. The Lord designated families to safeguard the tabernacle's sections in transit, spreading the ministry among the Israelites.

How are you involved in the ministry of your local church? Is there a role for which you are responsible? Ask God to help you fulfill your ministry as an act of worship to him.

[a] *47* That is, about 2 ounces or about 58 grams [b] *50* That is, about 35 pounds or about 16 kilograms [c] *6* Possibly the hides of large aquatic mammals; also in verses 8, 10, 11, 12, 14 and 25

furnishings and all the holy articles, and when the camp is ready to move, only then are the Kohathites to come and do the carrying. But they must not touch the holy things or they will die. The Kohathites are to carry those things that are in the tent of meeting.

16“Eleazar son of Aaron, the priest, is to have charge of the oil for the light, the fragrant incense, the regular grain offering and the anointing oil. He is to be in charge of the entire tabernacle and everything in it, including its holy furnishings and articles.”

17The LORD said to Moses and Aaron, 18“See that the Kohathite tribal clans are not destroyed from among the Levites. 19So that they may live and not die when they come near the most holy things, do this for them: Aaron and his sons are to go into the sanctuary and assign to each man his work and what he is to carry. 20But the Kohathites must not go in to look at the holy things, even for a moment, or they will die.”

THE GERSHONITES

21The LORD said to Moses, 22“Take a census also of the Gershonites by their families and clans. 23Count all the men from thirty to fifty years of age who come to serve in the work at the tent of meeting.

24“This is the service of the Gershonite clans in their carrying and their other work: 25They are to carry the curtains of the tabernacle, that is, the tent of meeting, its covering and its outer covering of durable leather, the curtains for the entrance to the tent of meeting, 26the curtains of the courtyard surrounding the tabernacle and altar, the curtain for the entrance to the courtyard, the ropes and all the equipment used in the service of the tent. The Gershonites are to do all that needs to be done with these things. 27All their service, whether carrying or doing other work, is to be done under the direction of Aaron and his sons. You shall assign to them as their responsibility all they are to carry. 28This is the service of the Gershonite clans at the tent of meeting. Their duties are to be under the direction of Ithamar son of Aaron, the priest.

THE MERARITES

29“Count the Merarites by their clans and families. 30Count all the men from thirty to fifty years of age who come to serve in the work at the tent of meeting. 31As part of all their service at the tent, they are to carry the frames of the tabernacle, its crossbars, posts and bases, 32as well as the posts of the surrounding courtyard with their bases, tent pegs, ropes, all their equipment and everything related to their use. Assign to each man the specific things he is to carry. 33This is the service of the Merarite clans as they work at the tent of meeting under the direction of Ithamar son of Aaron, the priest.”

THE NUMBERING OF THE LEVITE CLANS

34Moses, Aaron and the leaders of the community counted the Kohathites by their clans and families. 35All the men from thirty to fifty years of age who came to serve in the work at the tent of meeting, 36counted by clans, were 2,750. 37This was the total of all those in the Kohathite clans who served at the tent of meeting. Moses and Aaron counted them according to the LORD’s command through Moses.

38The Gershonites were counted by their clans and families. 39All the men from thirty to fifty years of age who came to serve in the work at

the tent of meeting, 40counted by their clans and families, were 2,630.
41This was the total of those in the Gershonite clans who served at
the tent of meeting. Moses and Aaron counted them according to the
LORD's command.
42The Merarites were counted by their clans and families. 43All the
men from thirty to fifty years of age who came to serve in the work at
the tent of meeting, 44counted by their clans, were 3,200. 45This was
the total of those in the Merarite clans. Moses and Aaron counted them
according to the LORD's command through Moses.
46So Moses, Aaron and the leaders of Israel counted all the Levites by
their clans and families. 47All the men from thirty to fifty years of age
who came to do the work of serving and carrying the tent of meeting
48numbered 8,580. 49At the LORD's command through Moses, each was
assigned his work and told what to carry.
Thus they were counted, as the LORD commanded Moses.

THE PURITY OF THE CAMP

5 The LORD said to Moses, 2"Command the Israelites to send away
from the camp anyone who has a defiling skin disease[a] or a dis-
charge of any kind, or who is ceremonially unclean because of a dead
body. 3Send away male and female alike; send them outside the camp
so they will not defile their camp, where I dwell among them." 4The
Israelites did so; they sent them outside the camp. They did just as the
LORD had instructed Moses.

> **PRAYING SCRIPTURE**
>
> **Numbers 5**
>
> God desires his people to walk in fellowship with him. When sin breaks that fellowship, God commands us to confess our sins, to agree with him that we sinned. God desires that we avoid sin because our sin doesn't just affect us, it also impacts the people around us.
>
> Is there any sin in your life? If so, take time to confess, and then seek forgiveness from anyone you've sinned against.

RESTITUTION FOR WRONGS

5The LORD said to Moses, 6"Say to the Israelites: 'Any man or woman
who wrongs another in any way[b] and so is unfaithful to the LORD is
guilty 7and must confess the sin they have committed. They must
make full restitution for the wrong they have done, add a fifth of the
value to it and give it all to the person they have wronged. 8But if
that person has no close relative to whom restitution can be made for
the wrong, the restitution belongs to the LORD and must be given to
the priest, along with the ram with which atonement is made for the
wrongdoer. 9All the sacred contributions the Israelites bring to a priest
will belong to him. 10Sacred things belong to their owners, but what
they give to the priest will belong to the priest.' "

THE TEST FOR AN UNFAITHFUL WIFE

11Then the LORD said to Moses, 12"Speak to the Israelites and say to
them: 'If a man's wife goes astray and is unfaithful to him 13so that
another man has sexual relations with her, and this is hidden from
her husband and her impurity is undetected (since there is no witness
against her and she has not been caught in the act), 14and if feelings of
jealousy come over her husband and he suspects his wife and she is im-
pure — or if he is jealous and suspects her even though she is not im-
pure — 15then he is to take his wife to the priest. He must also take an
offering of a tenth of an ephah[c] of barley flour on her behalf. He must
not pour olive oil on it or put incense on it, because it is a grain offer-
ing for jealousy, a reminder-offering to draw attention to wrongdoing.

---

[a] *2* The Hebrew word for *defiling skin disease,* traditionally translated "leprosy," was used for various diseases affecting the skin. [b] *6* Or *woman who commits any wrong common to mankind* [c] *15* That is, probably about 3 1/2 pounds or about 1.6 kilograms

16"'The priest shall bring her and have her stand before the LORD.
17Then he shall take some holy water in a clay jar and put some dust
from the tabernacle floor into the water. 18After the priest has had the
woman stand before the LORD, he shall loosen her hair and place in her
hands the reminder-offering, the grain offering for jealousy, while he
himself holds the bitter water that brings a curse. 19Then the priest shall
put the woman under oath and say to her, "If no other man has had
sexual relations with you and you have not gone astray and become im-
pure while married to your husband, may this bitter water that brings
a curse not harm you. 20But if you have gone astray while married to
your husband and you have made yourself impure by having sexual
relations with a man other than your husband"— 21here the priest is to
put the woman under this curse—"may the LORD cause you to become
a curse[a] among your people when he makes your womb miscarry and
your abdomen swell. 22May this water that brings a curse enter your
body so that your abdomen swells or your womb miscarries."

"'Then the woman is to say, "Amen. So be it."

23"'The priest is to write these curses on a scroll and then wash them
off into the bitter water. 24He shall make the woman drink the bitter
water that brings a curse, and this water that brings a curse and causes
bitter suffering will enter her. 25The priest is to take from her hands
the grain offering for jealousy, wave it before the LORD and bring it to
the altar. 26The priest is then to take a handful of the grain offering as
a memorial[b] offering and burn it on the altar; after that, he is to have
the woman drink the water. 27If she has made herself impure and been
unfaithful to her husband, this will be the result: When she is made to
drink the water that brings a curse and causes bitter suffering, it will
enter her, her abdomen will swell and her womb will miscarry, and
she will become a curse. 28If, however, the woman has not made her-
self impure, but is clean, she will be cleared of guilt and will be able
to have children.

29"'This, then, is the law of jealousy when a woman goes astray and
makes herself impure while married to her husband, 30or when feel-
ings of jealousy come over a man because he suspects his wife. The
priest is to have her stand before the LORD and is to apply this entire
law to her. 31The husband will be innocent of any wrongdoing, but the
woman will bear the consequences of her sin.'"

THE NAZIRITE

6 The LORD said to Moses, 2"Speak to the Israelites and say to them:
'If a man or woman wants to make a special vow, a vow of ded-
ication to the LORD as a Nazirite, 3they must abstain from wine and
other fermented drink and must not drink vinegar made from wine or
other fermented drink. They must not drink grape juice or eat grapes
or raisins. 4As long as they remain under their Nazirite vow, they must
not eat anything that comes from the grapevine, not even the seeds
or skins.

5"'During the entire period of their Nazirite vow, no razor may be
used on their head. They must be holy until the period of their dedica-
tion to the LORD is over; they must let their hair grow long.

PRAYING SCRIPTURE

Numbers 6

It's worth considering the innumerable times the Aaronic blessing (see verses 24–26) has been prayed by God's saints through the centuries. Many worship gatherings end with these verses being spoken over the congregation. They are words of hope, encouragement and promise.

Think about how you can incorporate the Aaronic blessing into your personal prayer life and when you gather with other believers in the community of faith.

---

[a] *21* That is, may he cause your name to be used in cursing (see Jer. 29:22); or, may others see that you are cursed; similarly in verse 27. [b] *26* Or *representative*

6“ ‘Throughout the period of their dedication to the LORD, the Naz-
irite must not go near a dead body. 7Even if their own father or mother
or brother or sister dies, they must not make themselves ceremonially
unclean on account of them, because the symbol of their dedication to
God is on their head. 8Throughout the period of their dedication, they
are consecrated to the LORD.

9“ ‘If someone dies suddenly in the Nazirite’s presence, thus defiling
the hair that symbolizes their dedication, they must shave their head
on the seventh day — the day of their cleansing. 10Then on the eighth
day they must bring two doves or two young pigeons to the priest at
the entrance to the tent of meeting. 11The priest is to offer one as a
sin offering[a] and the other as a burnt offering to make atonement for
the Nazirite because they sinned by being in the presence of the dead
body. That same day they are to consecrate their head again. 12They
must rededicate themselves to the LORD for the same period of ded-
ication and must bring a year-old male lamb as a guilt offering. The
previous days do not count, because they became defiled during their
period of dedication.

13“ ‘Now this is the law of the Nazirite when the period of their ded-
ication is over. They are to be brought to the entrance to the tent of
meeting. 14There they are to present their offerings to the LORD: a year-
old male lamb without defect for a burnt offering, a year-old ewe lamb
without defect for a sin offering, a ram without defect for a fellowship
offering, 15together with their grain offerings and drink offerings, and
a basket of bread made with the finest flour and without yeast — thick
loaves with olive oil mixed in, and thin loaves brushed with olive oil.

16“ ‘The priest is to present all these before the LORD and make the
sin offering and the burnt offering. 17He is to present the basket of un-
leavened bread and is to sacrifice the ram as a fellowship offering to
the LORD, together with its grain offering and drink offering.

18“ ‘Then at the entrance to the tent of meeting, the Nazirite must
shave off the hair that symbolizes their dedication. They are to take
the hair and put it in the fire that is under the sacrifice of the fellow-
ship offering.

19“ ‘After the Nazirite has shaved off the hair that symbolizes their
dedication, the priest is to place in their hands a boiled shoulder of the
ram, and one thick loaf and one thin loaf from the basket, both made
without yeast. 20The priest shall then wave these before the LORD as a
wave offering; they are holy and belong to the priest, together with the
breast that was waved and the thigh that was presented. After that, the
Nazirite may drink wine.

21“ ‘This is the law of the Nazirite who vows offerings to the LORD in
accordance with their dedication, in addition to whatever else they can
afford. They must fulfill the vows they have made, according to the law
of the Nazirite.’ ”

THE PRIESTLY BLESSING

22The LORD said to Moses, 23“Tell Aaron and his sons, ‘This is how you
are to bless the Israelites. Say to them:

24“ ‘ “The LORD bless you
and keep you;

[a] 11 Or *purification offering*; also in verses 14 and 16

25 the LORD make his face shine on you
and be gracious to you;
26 the LORD turn his face toward you
and give you peace."'
27 "So they will put my name on the Israelites, and I will bless them."

OFFERINGS AT THE DEDICATION OF THE TABERNACLE

7 When Moses finished setting up the tabernacle, he anointed and
consecrated it and all its furnishings. He also anointed and con-
secrated the altar and all its utensils. 2 Then the leaders of Israel, the
heads of families who were the tribal leaders in charge of those who
were counted, made offerings. 3 They brought as their gifts before the
LORD six covered carts and twelve oxen — an ox from each leader and a
cart from every two. These they presented before the tabernacle.
4 The LORD said to Moses, 5 "Accept these from them, that they may
be used in the work at the tent of meeting. Give them to the Levites as
each man's work requires."
6 So Moses took the carts and oxen and gave them to the Levites.
7 He gave two carts and four oxen to the Gershonites, as their work re-
quired, 8 and he gave four carts and eight oxen to the Merarites, as
their work required. They were all under the direction of Ithamar son
of Aaron, the priest. 9 But Moses did not give any to the Kohathites, be-
cause they were to carry on their shoulders the holy things, for which
they were responsible.
10 When the altar was anointed, the leaders brought their offerings
for its dedication and presented them before the altar. 11 For the LORD
had said to Moses, "Each day one leader is to bring his offering for the
dedication of the altar."

12 The one who brought his offering on the first day was Nahshon son
of Amminadab of the tribe of Judah.
13 His offering was one silver plate weighing a hundred and thirty
shekels[a] and one silver sprinkling bowl weighing seventy shek-
els,[b] both according to the sanctuary shekel, each filled with the
finest flour mixed with olive oil as a grain offering; 14 one gold dish
weighing ten shekels,[c] filled with incense; 15 one young bull, one
ram and one male lamb a year old for a burnt offering; 16 one male
goat for a sin offering[d]; 17 and two oxen, five rams, five male goats
and five male lambs a year old to be sacrificed as a fellowship of-
fering. This was the offering of Nahshon son of Amminadab.

18 On the second day Nethanel son of Zuar, the leader of Issachar,
brought his offering.
19 The offering he brought was one silver plate weighing a hundred
and thirty shekels and one silver sprinkling bowl weighing sev-
enty shekels, both according to the sanctuary shekel, each filled
with the finest flour mixed with olive oil as a grain offering; 20 one
gold dish weighing ten shekels, filled with incense; 21 one young
bull, one ram and one male lamb a year old for a burnt offering;

PRAYING SCRIPTURE

Numbers 7

After all the tribes had given offerings, the Lord spoke to Moses in the tabernacle. His voice came to Moses from the mercy seat on the ark of the covenant, from between the wings of the cherubim. Moses was the only person to experience God this way.

Think about the difference between Moses' conversation with God and your own. Thank God that the door to approach him is eternally open through Jesus.

---

[a] *13* That is, about 3 1/4 pounds or about 1.5 kilograms; also elsewhere in this chapter [b] *13* That is, about 1 3/4 pounds or about 800 grams; also elsewhere in this chapter [c] *14* That is, about 4 ounces or about 115 grams; also elsewhere in this chapter [d] *16* Or *purification offering*; also elsewhere in this chapter

22one male goat for a sin offering; 23and two oxen, five rams, five
male goats and five male lambs a year old to be sacrificed as a
fellowship offering. This was the offering of Nethanel son of Zuar.

24On the third day, Eliab son of Helon, the leader of the people of Zeb-
ulun, brought his offering.

25His offering was one silver plate weighing a hundred and thirty
shekels and one silver sprinkling bowl weighing seventy shekels,
both according to the sanctuary shekel, each filled with the fin-
est flour mixed with olive oil as a grain offering; 26one gold dish
weighing ten shekels, filled with incense; 27one young bull, one
ram and one male lamb a year old for a burnt offering; 28one male
goat for a sin offering; 29and two oxen, five rams, five male goats
and five male lambs a year old to be sacrificed as a fellowship of-
fering. This was the offering of Eliab son of Helon.

30On the fourth day Elizur son of Shedeur, the leader of the people of
Reuben, brought his offering.

31His offering was one silver plate weighing a hundred and thirty
shekels and one silver sprinkling bowl weighing seventy shekels,
both according to the sanctuary shekel, each filled with the fin-
est flour mixed with olive oil as a grain offering; 32one gold dish
weighing ten shekels, filled with incense; 33one young bull, one
ram and one male lamb a year old for a burnt offering; 34one male
goat for a sin offering; 35and two oxen, five rams, five male goats
and five male lambs a year old to be sacrificed as a fellowship of-
fering. This was the offering of Elizur son of Shedeur.

36On the fifth day Shelumiel son of Zurishaddai, the leader of the peo-
ple of Simeon, brought his offering.

37His offering was one silver plate weighing a hundred and thirty
shekels and one silver sprinkling bowl weighing seventy shekels,
both according to the sanctuary shekel, each filled with the fin-
est flour mixed with olive oil as a grain offering; 38one gold dish
weighing ten shekels, filled with incense; 39one young bull, one
ram and one male lamb a year old for a burnt offering; 40one male
goat for a sin offering; 41and two oxen, five rams, five male goats
and five male lambs a year old to be sacrificed as a fellowship of-
fering. This was the offering of Shelumiel son of Zurishaddai.

42On the sixth day Eliasaph son of Deuel, the leader of the people of
Gad, brought his offering.

43His offering was one silver plate weighing a hundred and thirty
shekels and one silver sprinkling bowl weighing seventy shekels,
both according to the sanctuary shekel, each filled with the fin-
est flour mixed with olive oil as a grain offering; 44one gold dish
weighing ten shekels, filled with incense; 45one young bull, one
ram and one male lamb a year old for a burnt offering; 46one male
goat for a sin offering; 47and two oxen, five rams, five male goats
and five male lambs a year old to be sacrificed as a fellowship of-
fering. This was the offering of Eliasaph son of Deuel.

48On the seventh day Elishama son of Ammihud, the leader of the peo-
ple of Ephraim, brought his offering.

49His offering was one silver plate weighing a hundred and thirty
shekels and one silver sprinkling bowl weighing seventy shekels,

both according to the sanctuary shekel, each filled with the fin-
est flour mixed with olive oil as a grain offering; 50one gold dish
weighing ten shekels, filled with incense; 51one young bull, one
ram and one male lamb a year old for a burnt offering; 52one male
goat for a sin offering; 53and two oxen, five rams, five male goats
and five male lambs a year old to be sacrificed as a fellowship of-
fering. This was the offering of Elishama son of Ammihud.

54On the eighth day Gamaliel son of Pedahzur, the leader of the people
of Manasseh, brought his offering.
55His offering was one silver plate weighing a hundred and thirty
shekels and one silver sprinkling bowl weighing seventy shekels,
both according to the sanctuary shekel, each filled with the fin-
est flour mixed with olive oil as a grain offering; 56one gold dish
weighing ten shekels, filled with incense; 57one young bull, one
ram and one male lamb a year old for a burnt offering; 58one male
goat for a sin offering; 59and two oxen, five rams, five male goats
and five male lambs a year old to be sacrificed as a fellowship of-
fering. This was the offering of Gamaliel son of Pedahzur.

60On the ninth day Abidan son of Gideoni, the leader of the people of
Benjamin, brought his offering.
61His offering was one silver plate weighing a hundred and thirty
shekels and one silver sprinkling bowl weighing seventy shekels,
both according to the sanctuary shekel, each filled with the fin-
est flour mixed with olive oil as a grain offering; 62one gold dish
weighing ten shekels, filled with incense; 63one young bull, one
ram and one male lamb a year old for a burnt offering; 64one male
goat for a sin offering; 65and two oxen, five rams, five male goats
and five male lambs a year old to be sacrificed as a fellowship of-
fering. This was the offering of Abidan son of Gideoni.

66On the tenth day Ahiezer son of Ammishaddai, the leader of the peo-
ple of Dan, brought his offering.
67His offering was one silver plate weighing a hundred and thirty
shekels and one silver sprinkling bowl weighing seventy shekels,
both according to the sanctuary shekel, each filled with the fin-
est flour mixed with olive oil as a grain offering; 68one gold dish
weighing ten shekels, filled with incense; 69one young bull, one
ram and one male lamb a year old for a burnt offering; 70one male
goat for a sin offering; 71and two oxen, five rams, five male goats
and five male lambs a year old to be sacrificed as a fellowship of-
fering. This was the offering of Ahiezer son of Ammishaddai.

72On the eleventh day Pagiel son of Okran, the leader of the people of
Asher, brought his offering.
73His offering was one silver plate weighing a hundred and thirty
shekels and one silver sprinkling bowl weighing seventy shekels,
both according to the sanctuary shekel, each filled with the fin-
est flour mixed with olive oil as a grain offering; 74one gold dish
weighing ten shekels, filled with incense; 75one young bull, one
ram and one male lamb a year old for a burnt offering; 76one male
goat for a sin offering; 77and two oxen, five rams, five male goats
and five male lambs a year old to be sacrificed as a fellowship of-
fering. This was the offering of Pagiel son of Okran.

78On the twelfth day Ahira son of Enan, the leader of the people of
Naphtali, brought his offering.
79His offering was one silver plate weighing a hundred and thirty
shekels and one silver sprinkling bowl weighing seventy shekels,
both according to the sanctuary shekel, each filled with the fin-
est flour mixed with olive oil as a grain offering; 80one gold dish
weighing ten shekels, filled with incense; 81one young bull, one
ram and one male lamb a year old for a burnt offering; 82one male
goat for a sin offering; 83and two oxen, five rams, five male goats
and five male lambs a year old to be sacrificed as a fellowship of-
fering. This was the offering of Ahira son of Enan.

84These were the offerings of the Israelite leaders for the dedication
of the altar when it was anointed: twelve silver plates, twelve silver
sprinkling bowls and twelve gold dishes. 85Each silver plate weighed
a hundred and thirty shekels, and each sprinkling bowl seventy shek-
els. Altogether, the silver dishes weighed two thousand four hundred
shekels,[a] according to the sanctuary shekel. 86The twelve gold dishes
filled with incense weighed ten shekels each, according to the sanctu-
ary shekel. Altogether, the gold dishes weighed a hundred and twenty
shekels.[b] 87The total number of animals for the burnt offering came
to twelve young bulls, twelve rams and twelve male lambs a year old,
together with their grain offering. Twelve male goats were used for
the sin offering. 88The total number of animals for the sacrifice of the
fellowship offering came to twenty-four oxen, sixty rams, sixty male
goats and sixty male lambs a year old. These were the offerings for the
dedication of the altar after it was anointed.
89When Moses entered the tent of meeting to speak with the LORD,
he heard the voice speaking to him from between the two cherubim
above the atonement cover on the ark of the covenant law. In this way
the LORD spoke to him.

SETTING UP THE LAMPS

8 The LORD said to Moses, 2"Speak to Aaron and say to him, 'When
you set up the lamps, see that all seven light up the area in front
of the lampstand.'"
3Aaron did so; he set up the lamps so that they faced forward on
the lampstand, just as the LORD commanded Moses. 4This is how the
lampstand was made: It was made of hammered gold—from its base
to its blossoms. The lampstand was made exactly like the pattern the
LORD had shown Moses.

THE SETTING APART OF THE LEVITES

5The LORD said to Moses: 6"Take the Levites from among all the Is-
raelites and make them ceremonially clean. 7To purify them, do this:
Sprinkle the water of cleansing on them; then have them shave their
whole bodies and wash their clothes. And so they will purify them-
selves. 8Have them take a young bull with its grain offering of the fin-
est flour mixed with olive oil; then you are to take a second young bull
for a sin offering.[c] 9Bring the Levites to the front of the tent of meet-
ing and assemble the whole Israelite community. 10You are to bring
the Levites before the LORD, and the Israelites are to lay their hands

PRAYING SCRIPTURE

Numbers 8

One theme of the tabernacle was light. Seven lamps were arranged close to the lampstand so the light could be easily seen. It reminded the priests that God was the light of the world, and it was in his illumination that they ministered.

Without light we walk in darkness. Ask God to provide light as you seek to follow him and commit to walk in the light he provides.

[a] *85* That is, about 60 pounds or about 28 kilograms [b] *86* That is, about 3 pounds or about 1.4 kilograms [c] *8* Or *purification offering*; also in verse 12

on them. 11Aaron is to present the Levites before the LORD as a wave
offering from the Israelites, so that they may be ready to do the work
of the LORD.
12"Then the Levites are to lay their hands on the heads of the bulls,
using one for a sin offering to the LORD and the other for a burnt of-
fering, to make atonement for the Levites. 13Have the Levites stand in
front of Aaron and his sons and then present them as a wave offering
to the LORD. 14In this way you are to set the Levites apart from the other
Israelites, and the Levites will be mine.
15"After you have purified the Levites and presented them as a wave
offering, they are to come to do their work at the tent of meeting.
16They are the Israelites who are to be given wholly to me. I have taken
them as my own in place of the firstborn, the first male offspring from
every Israelite woman. 17Every firstborn male in Israel, whether hu-
man or animal, is mine. When I struck down all the firstborn in Egypt,
I set them apart for myself. 18And I have taken the Levites in place of
all the firstborn sons in Israel. 19From among all the Israelites, I have
given the Levites as gifts to Aaron and his sons to do the work at the
tent of meeting on behalf of the Israelites and to make atonement for
them so that no plague will strike the Israelites when they go near the
sanctuary."
20Moses, Aaron and the whole Israelite community did with the
Levites just as the LORD commanded Moses. 21The Levites purified
themselves and washed their clothes. Then Aaron presented them as
a wave offering before the LORD and made atonement for them to pu-
rify them. 22After that, the Levites came to do their work at the tent of
meeting under the supervision of Aaron and his sons. They did with
the Levites just as the LORD commanded Moses.
23The LORD said to Moses, 24"This applies to the Levites: Men
twenty-five years old or more shall come to take part in the work at
the tent of meeting, 25but at the age of fifty, they must retire from their
regular service and work no longer. 26They may assist their brothers
in performing their duties at the tent of meeting, but they themselves
must not do the work. This, then, is how you are to assign the respon-
sibilities of the Levites."

THE PASSOVER

9 The LORD spoke to Moses in the Desert of Sinai in the first month
of the second year after they came out of Egypt. He said, 2"Have
the Israelites celebrate the Passover at the appointed time. 3Celebrate
it at the appointed time, at twilight on the fourteenth day of this
month, in accordance with all its rules and regulations."
4So Moses told the Israelites to celebrate the Passover, 5and they did
so in the Desert of Sinai at twilight on the fourteenth day of the first
month. The Israelites did everything just as the LORD commanded
Moses.
6But some of them could not celebrate the Passover on that day be-
cause they were ceremonially unclean on account of a dead body. So
they came to Moses and Aaron that same day 7and said to Moses, "We
have become unclean because of a dead body, but why should we be
kept from presenting the LORD's offering with the other Israelites at
the appointed time?"
8Moses answered them, "Wait until I find out what the LORD com-
mands concerning you."

PRAYING SCRIPTURE

Numbers 9

Have you ever wondered if you can be sure about God's leading in your life? Whether you can know which step comes next? The children of Israel were led alternately by a pillar of cloud and pillar of fire. God's leading was unmistakable, and their obedience was expected.

If you are uncertain about your next step, ask God to make it clear so you can be sure of your obedience.

[9]Then the LORD said to Moses, [10]"Tell the Israelites: 'When any of you or your descendants are unclean because of a dead body or are away on a journey, they are still to celebrate the LORD's Passover, [11]but they are to do it on the fourteenth day of the second month at twilight. They are to eat the lamb, together with unleavened bread and bitter herbs. [12]They must not leave any of it till morning or break any of its bones. When they celebrate the Passover, they must follow all the regulations. [13]But if anyone who is ceremonially clean and not on a journey fails to celebrate the Passover, they must be cut off from their people for not presenting the LORD's offering at the appointed time. They will bear the consequences of their sin.

[14]" 'A foreigner residing among you is also to celebrate the LORD's Passover in accordance with its rules and regulations. You must have the same regulations for both the foreigner and the native-born.' "

THE CLOUD ABOVE THE TABERNACLE

[15]On the day the tabernacle, the tent of the covenant law, was set up, the cloud covered it. From evening till morning the cloud above the tabernacle looked like fire. [16]That is how it continued to be; the cloud covered it, and at night it looked like fire. [17]Whenever the cloud lifted from above the tent, the Israelites set out; wherever the cloud settled, the Israelites encamped. [18]At the LORD's command the Israelites set out, and at his command they encamped. As long as the cloud stayed over the tabernacle, they remained in camp. [19]When the cloud remained over the tabernacle a long time, the Israelites obeyed the LORD's order and did not set out. [20]Sometimes the cloud was over the tabernacle only a few days; at the LORD's command they would encamp, and then at his command they would set out. [21]Sometimes the cloud stayed only from evening till morning, and when it lifted in the morning, they set out. Whether by day or by night, whenever the cloud lifted, they set out. [22]Whether the cloud stayed over the tabernacle for two days or a month or a year, the Israelites would remain in camp and not set out; but when it lifted, they would set out. [23]At the LORD's command they encamped, and at the LORD's command they set out. They obeyed the LORD's order, in accordance with his command through Moses.

THE SILVER TRUMPETS

10 The LORD said to Moses: [2]"Make two trumpets of hammered silver, and use them for calling the community together and for having the camps set out. [3]When both are sounded, the whole community is to assemble before you at the entrance to the tent of meeting. [4]If only one is sounded, the leaders—the heads of the clans of Israel—are to assemble before you. [5]When a trumpet blast is sounded, the tribes camping on the east are to set out. [6]At the sounding of a second blast, the camps on the south are to set out. The blast will be the signal for setting out. [7]To gather the assembly, blow the trumpets, but not with the signal for setting out.

[8]"The sons of Aaron, the priests, are to blow the trumpets. This is to be a lasting ordinance for you and the generations to come. [9]When you go into battle in your own land against an enemy who is oppressing you, sound a blast on the trumpets. Then you will be remembered by the LORD your God and rescued from your enemies. [10]Also at your times of rejoicing—your appointed festivals and New Moon

PRAYING SCRIPTURE

Numbers 10

One of the ways God chose to remind his people of his goodness was by means of memorials. Festivals and sacrifices were more than food and offerings; they had deeper meanings, pointing to God's faithfulness to them.

Many Christians find encouragement in memorials, whether pages in a journal, notes in their Bible or testimonies. Ask God to give you memorials that will serve as reminders of his presence.

feasts—you are to sound the trumpets over your burnt offerings and
fellowship offerings, and they will be a memorial for you before your
God. I am the LORD your God."

THE ISRAELITES LEAVE SINAI

11 On the twentieth day of the second month of the second year, the
cloud lifted from above the tabernacle of the covenant law. 12 Then the
Israelites set out from the Desert of Sinai and traveled from place to
place until the cloud came to rest in the Desert of Paran. 13 They set out,
this first time, at the LORD's command through Moses.

14 The divisions of the camp of Judah went first, under their stan-
dard. Nahshon son of Amminadab was in command. 15 Nethanel son of
Zuar was over the division of the tribe of Issachar, 16 and Eliab son of
Helon was over the division of the tribe of Zebulun. 17 Then the taber-
nacle was taken down, and the Gershonites and Merarites, who carried
it, set out.

18 The divisions of the camp of Reuben went next, under their stan-
dard. Elizur son of Shedeur was in command. 19 Shelumiel son of Zu-
rishaddai was over the division of the tribe of Simeon, 20 and Eliasaph
son of Deuel was over the division of the tribe of Gad. 21 Then the Ko-
hathites set out, carrying the holy things. The tabernacle was to be set
up before they arrived.

22 The divisions of the camp of Ephraim went next, under their stan-
dard. Elishama son of Ammihud was in command. 23 Gamaliel son of
Pedahzur was over the division of the tribe of Manasseh, 24 and Abidan
son of Gideoni was over the division of the tribe of Benjamin.

25 Finally, as the rear guard for all the units, the divisions of the camp
of Dan set out under their standard. Ahiezer son of Ammishaddai was
in command. 26 Pagiel son of Okran was over the division of the tribe
of Asher, 27 and Ahira son of Enan was over the division of the tribe of
Naphtali. 28 This was the order of march for the Israelite divisions as
they set out.

29 Now Moses said to Hobab son of Reuel the Midianite, Moses' fa-
ther-in-law, "We are setting out for the place about which the LORD
said, 'I will give it to you.' Come with us and we will treat you well, for
the LORD has promised good things to Israel."

30 He answered, "No, I will not go; I am going back to my own land
and my own people."

31 But Moses said, "Please do not leave us. You know where we should
camp in the wilderness, and you can be our eyes. 32 If you come with
us, we will share with you whatever good things the LORD gives us."

33 So they set out from the mountain of the LORD and traveled for
three days. The ark of the covenant of the LORD went before them dur-
ing those three days to find them a place to rest. 34 The cloud of the
LORD was over them by day when they set out from the camp.

35 Whenever the ark set out, Moses said,

"Rise up, LORD!
  May your enemies be scattered;
  may your foes flee before you."

36 Whenever it came to rest, he said,

"Return, LORD,
  to the countless thousands of Israel."

PRAYING SCRIPTURE

Numbers 11

Eventually the people forgot the ways the Lord had delivered and provided for them. Rather than expressing amazement and gratitude for the provision of daily manna, they coveted the food they ate while in bondage in Egypt. This led to complaining against God and Moses.

Are you ever tempted to desire things that enslave you? Ask God to help you reject them and seek true freedom instead.

FIRE FROM THE LORD

11 Now the people complained about their hardships in the hear-
ing of the LORD, and when he heard them his anger was aroused.
Then fire from the LORD burned among them and consumed some
of the outskirts of the camp. 2When the people cried out to Moses, he
prayed to the LORD and the fire died down. 3So that place was called
Taberah,[a] because fire from the LORD had burned among them.

QUAIL FROM THE LORD

4The rabble with them began to crave other food, and again the
Israelites started wailing and said, "If only we had meat to eat! 5We
remember the fish we ate in Egypt at no cost—also the cucumbers,
melons, leeks, onions and garlic. 6But now we have lost our appetite;
we never see anything but this manna!"

7The manna was like coriander seed and looked like resin. 8The peo-
ple went around gathering it, and then ground it in a hand mill or
crushed it in a mortar. They cooked it in a pot or made it into loaves.
And it tasted like something made with olive oil. 9When the dew set-
tled on the camp at night, the manna also came down.

10Moses heard the people of every family wailing at the entrance to
their tents. The LORD became exceedingly angry, and Moses was trou-
bled. 11He asked the LORD, "Why have you brought this trouble on your
servant? What have I done to displease you that you put the burden
of all these people on me? 12Did I conceive all these people? Did I give
them birth? Why do you tell me to carry them in my arms, as a nurse
carries an infant, to the land you promised on oath to their ancestors?
13Where can I get meat for all these people? They keep wailing to me,
'Give us meat to eat!' 14I cannot carry all these people by myself; the
burden is too heavy for me. 15If this is how you are going to treat me,
please go ahead and kill me—if I have found favor in your eyes—and
do not let me face my own ruin."

16The LORD said to Moses: "Bring me seventy of Israel's elders who
are known to you as leaders and officials among the people. Have them
come to the tent of meeting, that they may stand there with you. 17I will
come down and speak with you there, and I will take some of the power
of the Spirit that is on you and put it on them. They will share the bur-
den of the people with you so that you will not have to carry it alone.

18"Tell the people: 'Consecrate yourselves in preparation for tomor-
row, when you will eat meat. The LORD heard you when you wailed,
"If only we had meat to eat! We were better off in Egypt!" Now the
LORD will give you meat, and you will eat it. 19You will not eat it for
just one day, or two days, or five, ten or twenty days, 20but for a whole
month—until it comes out of your nostrils and you loathe it—be-
cause you have rejected the LORD, who is among you, and have wailed
before him, saying, "Why did we ever leave Egypt?"'"

21But Moses said, "Here I am among six hundred thousand men on
foot, and you say, 'I will give them meat to eat for a whole month!'
22Would they have enough if flocks and herds were slaughtered for
them? Would they have enough if all the fish in the sea were caught
for them?"

23The LORD answered Moses, "Is the LORD's arm too short? Now you
will see whether or not what I say will come true for you."

---

[a] 3 *Taberah* means *burning.*

24So Moses went out and told the people what the LORD had said. He
brought together seventy of their elders and had them stand around
the tent. 25Then the LORD came down in the cloud and spoke with him,
and he took some of the power of the Spirit that was on him and put
it on the seventy elders. When the Spirit rested on them, they prophe-
sied — but did not do so again.
26However, two men, whose names were Eldad and Medad, had re-
mained in the camp. They were listed among the elders, but did not go
out to the tent. Yet the Spirit also rested on them, and they prophesied
in the camp. 27A young man ran and told Moses, "Eldad and Medad are
prophesying in the camp."
28Joshua son of Nun, who had been Moses' aide since youth, spoke
up and said, "Moses, my lord, stop them!"
29But Moses replied, "Are you jealous for my sake? I wish that all the
LORD's people were prophets and that the LORD would put his Spirit
on them!" 30Then Moses and the elders of Israel returned to the camp.
31Now a wind went out from the LORD and drove quail in from the sea.
It scattered them up to two cubits[a] deep all around the camp, as far as a
day's walk in any direction. 32All that day and night and all the next day
the people went out and gathered quail. No one gathered less than ten
homers.[b] Then they spread them out all around the camp. 33But while
the meat was still between their teeth and before it could be consumed,
the anger of the LORD burned against the people, and he struck them
with a severe plague. 34Therefore the place was named Kibroth Hattaa-
vah,[c] because there they buried the people who had craved other food.
35From Kibroth Hattaavah the people traveled to Hazeroth and
stayed there.

MIRIAM AND AARON OPPOSE MOSES

12 Miriam and Aaron began to talk against Moses because of his
Cushite wife, for he had married a Cushite. 2"Has the LORD spo-
ken only through Moses?" they asked. "Hasn't he also spoken through
us?" And the LORD heard this.
3(Now Moses was a very humble man, more humble than anyone
else on the face of the earth.)
4At once the LORD said to Moses, Aaron and Miriam, "Come out to the
tent of meeting, all three of you." So the three of them went out. 5Then
the LORD came down in a pillar of cloud; he stood at the entrance to the
tent and summoned Aaron and Miriam. When the two of them stepped
forward, 6he said, "Listen to my words:

"When there is a prophet among you,
  I, the LORD, reveal myself to them in visions,
  I speak to them in dreams.
7But this is not true of my servant Moses;
  he is faithful in all my house.
8With him I speak face to face,
  clearly and not in riddles;
  he sees the form of the LORD.
Why then were you not afraid
  to speak against my servant Moses?"

[a] *31* That is, about 3 feet or about 90 centimeters [b] *32* That is, possibly about 1 3/4 tons or about 1.6 metric tons [c] *34* *Kibroth Hattaavah* means *graves of craving*.

PRAYING SCRIPTURE

Numbers 12

Have you ever asked God to deliver someone in spite of his or her sin? We often take a posture of judgment and hope people will experience what they deserve rather than the mercy and grace of God. The Lord commended Moses for his meekness in the face of criticism about his marriage, then heard his prayer for those who had sinned.

Ask God for the meekness to pray for anyone who speaks against you.

9The anger of the LORD burned against them, and he left them.

10When the cloud lifted from above the tent, Miriam's skin was leprous[a] — it became as white as snow. Aaron turned toward her and saw that she had a defiling skin disease, 11and he said to Moses, "Please, my lord, I ask you not to hold against us the sin we have so foolishly committed. 12Do not let her be like a stillborn infant coming from its mother's womb with its flesh half eaten away."

13So Moses cried out to the LORD, "Please, God, heal her!"

14The LORD replied to Moses, "If her father had spit in her face, would she not have been in disgrace for seven days? Confine her outside the camp for seven days; after that she can be brought back." 15So Miriam was confined outside the camp for seven days, and the people did not move on till she was brought back.

16After that, the people left Hazeroth and encamped in the Desert of Paran.

EXPLORING CANAAN

13 The LORD said to Moses, 2"Send some men to explore the land of Canaan, which I am giving to the Israelites. From each ancestral tribe send one of its leaders."

3So at the LORD's command Moses sent them out from the Desert of Paran. All of them were leaders of the Israelites. 4These are their names:

from the tribe of Reuben, Shammua son of Zakkur;
5from the tribe of Simeon, Shaphat son of Hori;
6from the tribe of Judah, Caleb son of Jephunneh;
7from the tribe of Issachar, Igal son of Joseph;
8from the tribe of Ephraim, Hoshea son of Nun;
9from the tribe of Benjamin, Palti son of Raphu;
10from the tribe of Zebulun, Gaddiel son of Sodi;
11from the tribe of Manasseh (a tribe of Joseph), Gaddi son of Susi;
12from the tribe of Dan, Ammiel son of Gemalli;
13from the tribe of Asher, Sethur son of Michael;
14from the tribe of Naphtali, Nahbi son of Vophsi;
15from the tribe of Gad, Geuel son of Maki.

16These are the names of the men Moses sent to explore the land. (Moses gave Hoshea son of Nun the name Joshua.)

17When Moses sent them to explore Canaan, he said, "Go up through the Negev and on into the hill country. 18See what the land is like and whether the people who live there are strong or weak, few or many. 19What kind of land do they live in? Is it good or bad? What kind of towns do they live in? Are they unwalled or fortified? 20How is the soil? Is it fertile or poor? Are there trees in it or not? Do your best to bring back some of the fruit of the land." (It was the season for the first ripe grapes.)

21So they went up and explored the land from the Desert of Zin as far as Rehob, toward Lebo Hamath. 22They went up through the Negev and came to Hebron, where Ahiman, Sheshai and Talmai, the descendants of Anak, lived. (Hebron had been built seven years before Zoan in Egypt.) 23When they reached the Valley of Eshkol,[b] they cut off a

[a] *10* The Hebrew for *leprous* was used for various diseases affecting the skin.
[b] *23* *Eshkol* means *cluster*; also in verse 24.

PRAYING SCRIPTURE

Numbers 13

Faith distinguishes between those who see God on life's path and those who see only obstacles in the way. Two spies saw that the land was as lush as God had promised. But the majority could not see past the obstacles.

Faith is not about denying reality but about seeing reality as God sees it. Faith enables us to do that. Ask God for the faith to see beyond obstacles in your life.

branch bearing a single cluster of grapes. Two of them carried it on a
pole between them, along with some pomegranates and figs. 24That
place was called the Valley of Eshkol because of the cluster of grapes
the Israelites cut off there. 25At the end of forty days they returned
from exploring the land.

REPORT ON THE EXPLORATION

26They came back to Moses and Aaron and the whole Israelite com-
munity at Kadesh in the Desert of Paran. There they reported to them
and to the whole assembly and showed them the fruit of the land.
27They gave Moses this account: "We went into the land to which you
sent us, and it does flow with milk and honey! Here is its fruit. 28But
the people who live there are powerful, and the cities are fortified and
very large. We even saw descendants of Anak there. 29The Amalekites
live in the Negev; the Hittites, Jebusites and Amorites live in the hill
country; and the Canaanites live near the sea and along the Jordan."
30Then Caleb silenced the people before Moses and said, "We should
go up and take possession of the land, for we can certainly do it."
31But the men who had gone up with him said, "We can't attack those
people; they are stronger than we are." 32And they spread among the
Israelites a bad report about the land they had explored. They said,
"The land we explored devours those living in it. All the people we saw
there are of great size. 33We saw the Nephilim there (the descendants
of Anak come from the Nephilim). We seemed like grasshoppers in our
own eyes, and we looked the same to them."

THE PEOPLE REBEL

14 That night all the members of the community raised their voices
and wept aloud. 2All the Israelites grumbled against Moses and
Aaron, and the whole assembly said to them, "If only we had died in
Egypt! Or in this wilderness! 3Why is the LORD bringing us to this land
only to let us fall by the sword? Our wives and children will be taken
as plunder. Wouldn't it be better for us to go back to Egypt?" 4And they
said to each other, "We should choose a leader and go back to Egypt."
5Then Moses and Aaron fell facedown in front of the whole Israelite
assembly gathered there. 6Joshua son of Nun and Caleb son of Jephun-
neh, who were among those who had explored the land, tore their
clothes 7and said to the entire Israelite assembly, "The land we passed
through and explored is exceedingly good. 8If the LORD is pleased with
us, he will lead us into that land, a land flowing with milk and honey,
and will give it to us. 9Only do not rebel against the LORD. And do not
be afraid of the people of the land, because we will devour them. Their
protection is gone, but the LORD is with us. Do not be afraid of them."
10But the whole assembly talked about stoning them. Then the glory
of the LORD appeared at the tent of meeting to all the Israelites. 11The
LORD said to Moses, "How long will these people treat me with con-
tempt? How long will they refuse to believe in me, in spite of all the
signs I have performed among them? 12I will strike them down with
a plague and destroy them, but I will make you into a nation greater
and stronger than they."
13Moses said to the LORD, "Then the Egyptians will hear about it! By
your power you brought these people up from among them. 14And
they will tell the inhabitants of this land about it. They have already
heard that you, LORD, are with these people and that you, LORD, have

PRAYING SCRIPTURE

Numbers 14

Fear has uprooted countless blessings since the Israelites' refusal to enter the promised land. The people were so afraid of the giant inhabitants and the fortified cities of Canaan that though God would subdue them on their behalf, they preferred to return to bondage in Egypt. They had no faith that God was able to do what he said.

Do you struggle with fear? It will kill your walk of faith, so ask God for courage to believe him when you need it.

been seen face to face, that your cloud stays over them, and that you
go before them in a pillar of cloud by day and a pillar of fire by night.
15 If you put all these people to death, leaving none alive, the nations
who have heard this report about you will say, 16 'The LORD was not able
to bring these people into the land he promised them on oath, so he
slaughtered them in the wilderness.'

17 "Now may the Lord's strength be displayed, just as you have de-
clared: 18 'The LORD is slow to anger, abounding in love and forgiving
sin and rebellion. Yet he does not leave the guilty unpunished; he pun-
ishes the children for the sin of the parents to the third and fourth
generation.' 19 In accordance with your great love, forgive the sin of
these people, just as you have pardoned them from the time they left
Egypt until now."

20 The LORD replied, "I have forgiven them, as you asked. 21 Never-
theless, as surely as I live and as surely as the glory of the LORD fills
the whole earth, 22 not one of those who saw my glory and the signs
I performed in Egypt and in the wilderness but who disobeyed me
and tested me ten times— 23 not one of them will ever see the land I
promised on oath to their ancestors. No one who has treated me with
contempt will ever see it. 24 But because my servant Caleb has a differ-
ent spirit and follows me wholeheartedly, I will bring him into the land
he went to, and his descendants will inherit it. 25 Since the Amalekites
and the Canaanites are living in the valleys, turn back tomorrow and
set out toward the desert along the route to the Red Sea.[a]"

26 The LORD said to Moses and Aaron: 27 "How long will this wicked
community grumble against me? I have heard the complaints of these
grumbling Israelites. 28 So tell them, 'As surely as I live, declares the
LORD, I will do to you the very thing I heard you say: 29 In this wil-
derness your bodies will fall—every one of you twenty years old or
more who was counted in the census and who has grumbled against
me. 30 Not one of you will enter the land I swore with uplifted hand
to make your home, except Caleb son of Jephunneh and Joshua son
of Nun. 31 As for your children that you said would be taken as plun-
der, I will bring them in to enjoy the land you have rejected. 32 But as
for you, your bodies will fall in this wilderness. 33 Your children will be
shepherds here for forty years, suffering for your unfaithfulness, until
the last of your bodies lies in the wilderness. 34 For forty years—one
year for each of the forty days you explored the land—you will suf-
fer for your sins and know what it is like to have me against you.' 35 I,
the LORD, have spoken, and I will surely do these things to this whole
wicked community, which has banded together against me. They will
meet their end in this wilderness; here they will die."

36 So the men Moses had sent to explore the land, who returned and
made the whole community grumble against him by spreading a bad
report about it— 37 these men who were responsible for spreading the
bad report about the land were struck down and died of a plague be-
fore the LORD. 38 Of the men who went to explore the land, only Joshua
son of Nun and Caleb son of Jephunneh survived.

39 When Moses reported this to all the Israelites, they mourned bit-
terly. 40 Early the next morning they set out for the highest point in the
hill country, saying, "Now we are ready to go up to the land the LORD
promised. Surely we have sinned!"

---

[a] 25 Or *the Sea of Reeds*

41But Moses said, "Why are you disobeying the LORD's command?
This will not succeed! 42Do not go up, because the LORD is not with you.
You will be defeated by your enemies, 43for the Amalekites and the Ca-
naanites will face you there. Because you have turned away from the
LORD, he will not be with you and you will fall by the sword."

44Nevertheless, in their presumption they went up toward the high-
est point in the hill country, though neither Moses nor the ark of the
LORD's covenant moved from the camp. 45Then the Amalekites and
the Canaanites who lived in that hill country came down and attacked
them and beat them down all the way to Hormah.

SUPPLEMENTARY OFFERINGS

15 The LORD said to Moses, 2"Speak to the Israelites and say to
them: 'After you enter the land I am giving you as a home 3and
you present to the LORD food offerings from the herd or the flock, as
an aroma pleasing to the LORD—whether burnt offerings or sacrifices,
for special vows or freewill offerings or festival offerings—4then the
person who brings an offering shall present to the LORD a grain offer-
ing of a tenth of an ephah[a] of the finest flour mixed with a quarter of a
hin[b] of olive oil. 5With each lamb for the burnt offering or the sacrifice,
prepare a quarter of a hin of wine as a drink offering.

6" 'With a ram prepare a grain offering of two-tenths of an ephah[c]
of the finest flour mixed with a third of a hin[d] of olive oil, 7and a third
of a hin of wine as a drink offering. Offer it as an aroma pleasing to
the LORD.

8" 'When you prepare a young bull as a burnt offering or sacrifice, for
a special vow or a fellowship offering to the LORD, 9bring with the bull
a grain offering of three-tenths of an ephah[e] of the finest flour mixed
with half a hin[f] of olive oil, 10and also bring half a hin of wine as a drink
offering. This will be a food offering, an aroma pleasing to the LORD.
11Each bull or ram, each lamb or young goat, is to be prepared in this
manner. 12Do this for each one, for as many as you prepare.

13" 'Everyone who is native-born must do these things in this way
when they present a food offering as an aroma pleasing to the LORD.
14For the generations to come, whenever a foreigner or anyone else
living among you presents a food offering as an aroma pleasing to the
LORD, they must do exactly as you do. 15The community is to have the
same rules for you and for the foreigner residing among you; this is a
lasting ordinance for the generations to come. You and the foreigner
shall be the same before the LORD: 16The same laws and regulations
will apply both to you and to the foreigner residing among you.' "

17The LORD said to Moses, 18"Speak to the Israelites and say to them:
'When you enter the land to which I am taking you 19and you eat the
food of the land, present a portion as an offering to the LORD. 20Present
a loaf from the first of your ground meal and present it as an offering
from the threshing floor. 21Throughout the generations to come you
are to give this offering to the LORD from the first of your ground meal.

PRAYING SCRIPTURE

Numbers 15

The Lord often commanded Israel to enact visible reminders of his redemption. Offerings, altars and the design of garments served as God's means of turning the people's minds toward him. Such visuals were not idols; they directed the people to God rather than replacing him.

What reminders can you use to turn your attention to God? Notes with Scripture? Godward art? Photo reminders of God's working in your faith journey?

---

[a] 4 That is, probably about 3 1/2 pounds or about 1.6 kilograms [b] 4 That is, about 1 quart or about 1 liter; also in verse 5 [c] 6 That is, probably about 7 pounds or about 3.2 kilograms [d] 6 That is, about 1 1/3 quarts or about 1.3 liters; also in verse 7 [e] 9 That is, probably about 11 pounds or about 5 kilograms [f] 9 That is, about 2 quarts or about 1.9 liters; also in verse 10

OFFERINGS FOR UNINTENTIONAL SINS

22“ ‘Now if you as a community unintentionally fail to keep any of
these commands the LORD gave Moses — 23any of the LORD’s commands
to you through him, from the day the LORD gave them and continuing
through the generations to come — 24and if this is done unintention-
ally without the community being aware of it, then the whole commu-
nity is to offer a young bull for a burnt offering as an aroma pleasing to
the LORD, along with its prescribed grain offering and drink offering,
and a male goat for a sin offering.[a] 25The priest is to make atonement
for the whole Israelite community, and they will be forgiven, for it was
not intentional and they have presented to the LORD for their wrong a
food offering and a sin offering. 26The whole Israelite community and
the foreigners residing among them will be forgiven, because all the
people were involved in the unintentional wrong.

27“ ‘But if just one person sins unintentionally, that person must
bring a year-old female goat for a sin offering. 28The priest is to make
atonement before the LORD for the one who erred by sinning unin-
tentionally, and when atonement has been made, that person will be
forgiven. 29One and the same law applies to everyone who sins un-
intentionally, whether a native-born Israelite or a foreigner residing
among you.

30“ ‘But anyone who sins defiantly, whether native-born or foreigner,
blasphemes the LORD and must be cut off from the people of Israel.
31Because they have despised the LORD’s word and broken his com-
mands, they must surely be cut off; their guilt remains on them.’ ”

THE SABBATH-BREAKER PUT TO DEATH

32While the Israelites were in the wilderness, a man was found
gathering wood on the Sabbath day. 33Those who found him gather-
ing wood brought him to Moses and Aaron and the whole assembly,
34and they kept him in custody, because it was not clear what should
be done to him. 35Then the LORD said to Moses, “The man must die. The
whole assembly must stone him outside the camp.” 36So the assembly
took him outside the camp and stoned him to death, as the LORD com-
manded Moses.

TASSELS ON GARMENTS

37The LORD said to Moses, 38“Speak to the Israelites and say to them:
‘Throughout the generations to come you are to make tassels on the
corners of your garments, with a blue cord on each tassel. 39You will
have these tassels to look at and so you will remember all the com-
mands of the LORD, that you may obey them and not prostitute your-
selves by chasing after the lusts of your own hearts and eyes. 40Then
you will remember to obey all my commands and will be consecrated
to your God. 41I am the LORD your God, who brought you out of Egypt
to be your God. I am the LORD your God.’ ”

KORAH, DATHAN AND ABIRAM

16 Korah son of Izhar, the son of Kohath, the son of Levi, and cer-
tain Reubenites — Dathan and Abiram, sons of Eliab, and On son
of Peleth — became insolent[b] 2and rose up against Moses. With them
were 250 Israelite men, well-known community leaders who had been

PRAYING SCRIPTURE

Numbers 16

Leadership often involves a significant amount of undeserved criticism. Although God had affirmed Moses’ leadership over Israel, a group of 250 tribal leaders were displeased, questioning Moses and asserting their own authority. God responded by destroying all of them.

Ask God to reveal to you any jealousy or pride that is lurking in your heart. Ask him to give you wisdom to follow godly leaders without sinning against them.

[a] 24 Or *purification offering*; also in verses 25 and 27 [b] 1 Or *Peleth — took men*

appointed members of the council. 3They came as a group to oppose
Moses and Aaron and said to them, "You have gone too far! The whole
community is holy, every one of them, and the LORD is with them. Why
then do you set yourselves above the LORD's assembly?"
4When Moses heard this, he fell facedown. 5Then he said to Korah
and all his followers: "In the morning the LORD will show who belongs
to him and who is holy, and he will have that person come near him.
The man he chooses he will cause to come near him. 6You, Korah,
and all your followers are to do this: Take censers 7and tomorrow put
burning coals and incense in them before the LORD. The man the LORD
chooses will be the one who is holy. You Levites have gone too far!"
8Moses also said to Korah, "Now listen, you Levites! 9Isn't it enough
for you that the God of Israel has separated you from the rest of the
Israelite community and brought you near himself to do the work at
the LORD's tabernacle and to stand before the community and minister
to them? 10He has brought you and all your fellow Levites near him-
self, but now you are trying to get the priesthood too. 11It is against
the LORD that you and all your followers have banded together. Who is
Aaron that you should grumble against him?"
12Then Moses summoned Dathan and Abiram, the sons of Eliab. But
they said, "We will not come! 13Isn't it enough that you have brought
us up out of a land flowing with milk and honey to kill us in the wil-
derness? And now you also want to lord it over us! 14Moreover, you
haven't brought us into a land flowing with milk and honey or given
us an inheritance of fields and vineyards. Do you want to treat these
men like slaves[a]? No, we will not come!"
15Then Moses became very angry and said to the LORD, "Do not ac-
cept their offering. I have not taken so much as a donkey from them,
nor have I wronged any of them."
16Moses said to Korah, "You and all your followers are to appear be-
fore the LORD tomorrow—you and they and Aaron. 17Each man is to
take his censer and put incense in it—250 censers in all—and present
it before the LORD. You and Aaron are to present your censers also."
18So each of them took his censer, put burning coals and incense in it,
and stood with Moses and Aaron at the entrance to the tent of meeting.
19When Korah had gathered all his followers in opposition to them at
the entrance to the tent of meeting, the glory of the LORD appeared to
the entire assembly. 20The LORD said to Moses and Aaron, 21"Separate
yourselves from this assembly so I can put an end to them at once."
22But Moses and Aaron fell facedown and cried out, "O God, the God
who gives breath to all living things, will you be angry with the entire
assembly when only one man sins?"
23Then the LORD said to Moses, 24"Say to the assembly, 'Move away
from the tents of Korah, Dathan and Abiram.'"
25Moses got up and went to Dathan and Abiram, and the elders of
Israel followed him. 26He warned the assembly, "Move back from the
tents of these wicked men! Do not touch anything belonging to them,
or you will be swept away because of all their sins." 27So they moved
away from the tents of Korah, Dathan and Abiram. Dathan and Abiram
had come out and were standing with their wives, children and little
ones at the entrances to their tents.
28Then Moses said, "This is how you will know that the LORD has sent

[a] 14 Or *to deceive these men*; Hebrew *Will you gouge out the eyes of these men*

me to do all these things and that it was not my idea: 29If these men
die a natural death and suffer the fate of all mankind, then the LORD
has not sent me. 30But if the LORD brings about something totally new,
and the earth opens its mouth and swallows them, with everything
that belongs to them, and they go down alive into the realm of the
dead, then you will know that these men have treated the LORD with
contempt."

31As soon as he finished saying all this, the ground under them split
apart 32and the earth opened its mouth and swallowed them and their
households, and all those associated with Korah, together with their
possessions. 33They went down alive into the realm of the dead, with
everything they owned; the earth closed over them, and they perished
and were gone from the community. 34At their cries, all the Israelites
around them fled, shouting, "The earth is going to swallow us too!"

35And fire came out from the LORD and consumed the 250 men who
were offering the incense.

36The LORD said to Moses, 37"Tell Eleazar son of Aaron, the priest,
to remove the censers from the charred remains and scatter the coals
some distance away, for the censers are holy— 38the censers of the
men who sinned at the cost of their lives. Hammer the censers into
sheets to overlay the altar, for they were presented before the LORD and
have become holy. Let them be a sign to the Israelites."

39So Eleazar the priest collected the bronze censers brought by those
who had been burned to death, and he had them hammered out to
overlay the altar, 40as the LORD directed him through Moses. This was
to remind the Israelites that no one except a descendant of Aaron
should come to burn incense before the LORD, or he would become
like Korah and his followers.

41The next day the whole Israelite community grumbled against Mo-
ses and Aaron. "You have killed the LORD's people," they said.

42But when the assembly gathered in opposition to Moses and Aaron
and turned toward the tent of meeting, suddenly the cloud covered it
and the glory of the LORD appeared. 43Then Moses and Aaron went to
the front of the tent of meeting, 44and the LORD said to Moses, 45"Get
away from this assembly so I can put an end to them at once." And
they fell facedown.

46Then Moses said to Aaron, "Take your censer and put incense in
it, along with burning coals from the altar, and hurry to the assem-
bly to make atonement for them. Wrath has come out from the LORD;
the plague has started." 47So Aaron did as Moses said, and ran into the
midst of the assembly. The plague had already started among the peo-
ple, but Aaron offered the incense and made atonement for them. 48He
stood between the living and the dead, and the plague stopped. 49But
14,700 people died from the plague, in addition to those who had died
because of Korah. 50Then Aaron returned to Moses at the entrance to
the tent of meeting, for the plague had stopped.[a]

THE BUDDING OF AARON'S STAFF

17[b] The LORD said to Moses, 2"Speak to the Israelites and get twelve
staffs from them, one from the leader of each of their ancestral
tribes. Write the name of each man on his staff. 3On the staff of Levi

[a] 50 In Hebrew texts 16:36-50 is numbered 17:1-15. [b] In Hebrew texts 17:1-13 is numbered 17:16-28.

PRAYING SCRIPTURE

Numbers 17

It would be nice to have miraculous guidance every step of the way—as when the Israelites received direction through a wooden staff that produced blossoms and mature almonds in a single night. We often feel as though such solid, tangible signs would keep us from making mistakes.

The good news is that the same God who gave life to dead wood lives in us. If you need direction, ask and trust his guidance.

write Aaron's name, for there must be one staff for the head of each
ancestral tribe. 4Place them in the tent of meeting in front of the ark
of the covenant law, where I meet with you. 5The staff belonging to the
man I choose will sprout, and I will rid myself of this constant grum-
bling against you by the Israelites."

6So Moses spoke to the Israelites, and their leaders gave him twelve
staffs, one for the leader of each of their ancestral tribes, and Aaron's
staff was among them. 7Moses placed the staffs before the LORD in the
tent of the covenant law.

8The next day Moses entered the tent and saw that Aaron's staff,
which represented the tribe of Levi, had not only sprouted but had
budded, blossomed and produced almonds. 9Then Moses brought out
all the staffs from the LORD's presence to all the Israelites. They looked
at them, and each of the leaders took his own staff.

10The LORD said to Moses, "Put back Aaron's staff in front of the ark
of the covenant law, to be kept as a sign to the rebellious. This will put
an end to their grumbling against me, so that they will not die." 11Mo-
ses did just as the LORD commanded him.

12The Israelites said to Moses, "We will die! We are lost, we are all lost!
13Anyone who even comes near the tabernacle of the LORD will die. Are
we all going to die?"

DUTIES OF PRIESTS AND LEVITES

18 The LORD said to Aaron, "You, your sons and your family are to
bear the responsibility for offenses connected with the sanctu-
ary, and you and your sons alone are to bear the responsibility for of-
fenses connected with the priesthood. 2Bring your fellow Levites from
your ancestral tribe to join you and assist you when you and your sons
minister before the tent of the covenant law. 3They are to be responsi-
ble to you and are to perform all the duties of the tent, but they must
not go near the furnishings of the sanctuary or the altar. Otherwise
both they and you will die. 4They are to join you and be responsible
for the care of the tent of meeting — all the work at the tent — and no
one else may come near where you are.

5"You are to be responsible for the care of the sanctuary and the al-
tar, so that my wrath will not fall on the Israelites again. 6I myself have
selected your fellow Levites from among the Israelites as a gift to you,
dedicated to the LORD to do the work at the tent of meeting. 7But only
you and your sons may serve as priests in connection with everything
at the altar and inside the curtain. I am giving you the service of the
priesthood as a gift. Anyone else who comes near the sanctuary is to
be put to death."

OFFERINGS FOR PRIESTS AND LEVITES

8Then the LORD said to Aaron, "I myself have put you in charge of the
offerings presented to me; all the holy offerings the Israelites give me
I give to you and your sons as your portion, your perpetual share. 9You
are to have the part of the most holy offerings that is kept from the
fire. From all the gifts they bring me as most holy offerings, whether
grain or sin[a] or guilt offerings, that part belongs to you and your sons.
10Eat it as something most holy; every male shall eat it. You must re-
gard it as holy.

[a] 9 Or *purification*

PRAYING SCRIPTURE

Numbers 18

The priests and the Levites had their physical needs met through the offerings given by the people, and they were responsible for tithing from those offerings. All Israelites had to demonstrate obedience in how they managed the income God provided for them.

Do you find it difficult to trust that God will provide for your needs? Ask God to increase your faith so that you can give without fear.

11“This also is yours: whatever is set aside from the gifts of all the wave offerings of the Israelites. I give this to you and your sons and daughters as your perpetual share. Everyone in your household who is ceremonially clean may eat it.

12“I give you all the finest olive oil and all the finest new wine and grain they give the LORD as the firstfruits of their harvest. 13All the land’s firstfruits that they bring to the LORD will be yours. Everyone in your household who is ceremonially clean may eat it.

14“Everything in Israel that is devoted[a] to the LORD is yours. 15The first offspring of every womb, both human and animal, that is offered to the LORD is yours. But you must redeem every firstborn son and every firstborn male of unclean animals. 16When they are a month old, you must redeem them at the redemption price set at five shekels[b] of silver, according to the sanctuary shekel, which weighs twenty gerahs.

17“But you must not redeem the firstborn of a cow, a sheep or a goat; they are holy. Splash their blood against the altar and burn their fat as a food offering, an aroma pleasing to the LORD. 18Their meat is to be yours, just as the breast of the wave offering and the right thigh are yours. 19Whatever is set aside from the holy offerings the Israelites present to the LORD I give to you and your sons and daughters as your perpetual share. It is an everlasting covenant of salt before the LORD for both you and your offspring.”

20The LORD said to Aaron, “You will have no inheritance in their land, nor will you have any share among them; I am your share and your inheritance among the Israelites.

21“I give to the Levites all the tithes in Israel as their inheritance in return for the work they do while serving at the tent of meeting. 22From now on the Israelites must not go near the tent of meeting, or they will bear the consequences of their sin and will die. 23It is the Levites who are to do the work at the tent of meeting and bear the responsibility for any offenses they commit against it. This is a lasting ordinance for the generations to come. They will receive no inheritance among the Israelites. 24Instead, I give to the Levites as their inheritance the tithes that the Israelites present as an offering to the LORD. That is why I said concerning them: ‘They will have no inheritance among the Israelites.’ ”

25The LORD said to Moses, 26“Speak to the Levites and say to them: ‘When you receive from the Israelites the tithe I give you as your inheritance, you must present a tenth of that tithe as the LORD’s offering. 27Your offering will be reckoned to you as grain from the threshing floor or juice from the winepress. 28In this way you also will present an offering to the LORD from all the tithes you receive from the Israelites. From these tithes you must give the LORD’s portion to Aaron the priest. 29You must present as the LORD’s portion the best and holiest part of everything given to you.’

30“Say to the Levites: ‘When you present the best part, it will be reckoned to you as the product of the threshing floor or the winepress. 31You and your households may eat the rest of it anywhere, for it is your wages for your work at the tent of meeting. 32By presenting the best part of it you will not be guilty in this matter; then you will not defile the holy offerings of the Israelites, and you will not die.’ ”

---

[a] *14* The Hebrew term refers to the irrevocable giving over of things or persons to the LORD. [b] *16* That is, about 2 ounces or about 58 grams

THE WATER OF CLEANSING

19 The LORD said to Moses and Aaron: 2"This is a requirement of the
law that the LORD has commanded: Tell the Israelites to bring
you a red heifer without defect or blemish and that has never been un-
der a yoke. 3Give it to Eleazar the priest; it is to be taken outside the
camp and slaughtered in his presence. 4Then Eleazar the priest is to
take some of its blood on his finger and sprinkle it seven times toward
the front of the tent of meeting. 5While he watches, the heifer is to be
burned — its hide, flesh, blood and intestines. 6The priest is to take
some cedar wood, hyssop and scarlet wool and throw them onto the
burning heifer. 7After that, the priest must wash his clothes and bathe
himself with water. He may then come into the camp, but he will be cer-
emonially unclean till evening. 8The man who burns it must also wash
his clothes and bathe with water, and he too will be unclean till evening.
9"A man who is clean shall gather up the ashes of the heifer and put
them in a ceremonially clean place outside the camp. They are to be
kept by the Israelite community for use in the water of cleansing; it is
for purification from sin. 10The man who gathers up the ashes of the
heifer must also wash his clothes, and he too will be unclean till eve-
ning. This will be a lasting ordinance both for the Israelites and for the
foreigners residing among them.
11"Whoever touches a human corpse will be unclean for seven days.
12They must purify themselves with the water on the third day and
on the seventh day; then they will be clean. But if they do not purify
themselves on the third and seventh days, they will not be clean. 13If
they fail to purify themselves after touching a human corpse, they de-
file the LORD's tabernacle. They must be cut off from Israel. Because
the water of cleansing has not been sprinkled on them, they are un-
clean; their uncleanness remains on them.
14"This is the law that applies when a person dies in a tent: Anyone
who enters the tent and anyone who is in it will be unclean for seven
days, 15and every open container without a lid fastened on it will be
unclean.
16"Anyone out in the open who touches someone who has been killed
with a sword or someone who has died a natural death, or anyone who
touches a human bone or a grave, will be unclean for seven days.
17"For the unclean person, put some ashes from the burned purifica-
tion offering into a jar and pour fresh water over them. 18Then a man
who is ceremonially clean is to take some hyssop, dip it in the water
and sprinkle the tent and all the furnishings and the people who were
there. He must also sprinkle anyone who has touched a human bone or
a grave or anyone who has been killed or anyone who has died a natu-
ral death. 19The man who is clean is to sprinkle those who are unclean
on the third and seventh days, and on the seventh day he is to purify
them. Those who are being cleansed must wash their clothes and bathe
with water, and that evening they will be clean. 20But if those who are
unclean do not purify themselves, they must be cut off from the com-
munity, because they have defiled the sanctuary of the LORD. The wa-
ter of cleansing has not been sprinkled on them, and they are unclean.
21This is a lasting ordinance for them.
"The man who sprinkles the water of cleansing must also wash his
clothes, and anyone who touches the water of cleansing will be un-
clean till evening. 22Anything that an unclean person touches becomes
unclean, and anyone who touches it becomes unclean till evening."

PRAYING SCRIPTURE

Numbers 19

Laws about ritual uncleanness pointed the Israelites to all of the impurity that existed in their lives because of sin. Such laws pointed to a deeper reality than burning clothes, sprinkling water or bathing. If our external person needs to be cleansed, how much more do our hearts need to be cleansed before an almighty God?

Ask God to examine you for any uncleanness, and then thank him for cleansing you in Jesus.

PRAYING SCRIPTURE

Numbers 20

Sometimes our solution to a problem is not God's solution. We can find ourselves going against God while thinking we are going with him. Moses' sin in striking the rock showed he did not believe speaking to it was enough. His disobedience denigrated God in the eyes of the people.

Are you tempted to take matters out of God's hands and into yours? Ask him for patience to wait for his ways.

WATER FROM THE ROCK

20 In the first month the whole Israelite community arrived at
the Desert of Zin, and they stayed at Kadesh. There Miriam
died and was buried.
2Now there was no water for the community, and the people gath-
ered in opposition to Moses and Aaron. 3They quarreled with Moses
and said, "If only we had died when our brothers fell dead before the
LORD! 4Why did you bring the LORD's community into this wilderness,
that we and our livestock should die here? 5Why did you bring us up
out of Egypt to this terrible place? It has no grain or figs, grapevines or
pomegranates. And there is no water to drink!"
6Moses and Aaron went from the assembly to the entrance to the
tent of meeting and fell facedown, and the glory of the LORD ap-
peared to them. 7The LORD said to Moses, 8"Take the staff, and you
and your brother Aaron gather the assembly together. Speak to that
rock before their eyes and it will pour out its water. You will bring
water out of the rock for the community so they and their livestock
can drink."
9So Moses took the staff from the LORD's presence, just as he com-
manded him. 10He and Aaron gathered the assembly together in front
of the rock and Moses said to them, "Listen, you rebels, must we bring
you water out of this rock?" 11Then Moses raised his arm and struck the
rock twice with his staff. Water gushed out, and the community and
their livestock drank.
12But the LORD said to Moses and Aaron, "Because you did not trust
in me enough to honor me as holy in the sight of the Israelites, you will
not bring this community into the land I give them."
13These were the waters of Meribah,[a] where the Israelites quarreled
with the LORD and where he was proved holy among them.

EDOM DENIES ISRAEL PASSAGE

14Moses sent messengers from Kadesh to the king of Edom, saying:

"This is what your brother Israel says: You know about all the
hardships that have come on us. 15Our ancestors went down into
Egypt, and we lived there many years. The Egyptians mistreated
us and our ancestors, 16but when we cried out to the LORD, he
heard our cry and sent an angel and brought us out of Egypt.
"Now we are here at Kadesh, a town on the edge of your ter-
ritory. 17Please let us pass through your country. We will not go
through any field or vineyard, or drink water from any well. We
will travel along the King's Highway and not turn to the right or
to the left until we have passed through your territory."

18But Edom answered:

"You may not pass through here; if you try, we will march out
and attack you with the sword."

19The Israelites replied:

"We will go along the main road, and if we or our livestock drink
any of your water, we will pay for it. We only want to pass through
on foot — nothing else."

---

[a] 13 *Meribah* means *quarreling.*

20Again they answered:

"You may not pass through."

Then Edom came out against them with a large and powerful army.
21Since Edom refused to let them go through their territory, Israel
turned away from them.

THE DEATH OF AARON

22The whole Israelite community set out from Kadesh and came to
Mount Hor. 23At Mount Hor, near the border of Edom, the LORD said
to Moses and Aaron, 24"Aaron will be gathered to his people. He will
not enter the land I give the Israelites, because both of you rebelled
against my command at the waters of Meribah. 25Get Aaron and his son
Eleazar and take them up Mount Hor. 26Remove Aaron's garments and
put them on his son Eleazar, for Aaron will be gathered to his people;
he will die there."

27Moses did as the LORD commanded: They went up Mount Hor in
the sight of the whole community. 28Moses removed Aaron's garments
and put them on his son Eleazar. And Aaron died there on top of the
mountain. Then Moses and Eleazar came down from the mountain,
29and when the whole community learned that Aaron had died, all the
Israelites mourned for him thirty days.

ARAD DESTROYED

21 When the Canaanite king of Arad, who lived in the Negev, heard
that Israel was coming along the road to Atharim, he attacked
the Israelites and captured some of them. 2Then Israel made this vow
to the LORD: "If you will deliver these people into our hands, we will
totally destroy[a] their cities." 3The LORD listened to Israel's plea and
gave the Canaanites over to them. They completely destroyed them
and their towns; so the place was named Hormah.[b]

THE BRONZE SNAKE

4They traveled from Mount Hor along the route to the Red Sea,[c] to go
around Edom. But the people grew impatient on the way; 5they spoke
against God and against Moses, and said, "Why have you brought us
up out of Egypt to die in the wilderness? There is no bread! There is no
water! And we detest this miserable food!"

6Then the LORD sent venomous snakes among them; they bit the peo
ple and many Israelites died. 7The people came to Moses and said, "We
sinned when we spoke against the LORD and against you. Pray that the
LORD will take the snakes away from us." So Moses prayed for the people.

8The LORD said to Moses, "Make a snake and put it up on a pole;
anyone who is bitten can look at it and live." 9So Moses made a bronze
snake and put it up on a pole. Then when anyone was bitten by a snake
and looked at the bronze snake, they lived.

THE JOURNEY TO MOAB

10The Israelites moved on and camped at Oboth. 11Then they set out
from Oboth and camped in Iye Abarim, in the wilderness that faces

PRAYING SCRIPTURE

Numbers 21

One of Scripture's more unusual stories is filled with meaning. The Lord judged the people's complaining by sending "venomous snakes" whose bites would bring death. Moses made a bronze replica of a snake and put it on a pole. Anyone bitten needed only to look at it and they would live.

The rich symbolism of Jesus is plain: Look to the Lord and live. Pray to the Lord about the deliverance you need today.

---

[a] 2 The Hebrew term refers to the irrevocable giving over of things or persons to the LORD, often by totally destroying them; also in verse 3. [b] 3 *Hormah* means *destruction*. [c] 4 Or *the Sea of Reeds*

Moab toward the sunrise. 12From there they moved on and camped in
the Zered Valley. 13They set out from there and camped alongside the
Arnon, which is in the wilderness extending into Amorite territory.
The Arnon is the border of Moab, between Moab and the Amorites.
14That is why the Book of the Wars of the LORD says:

"... Zahab[a] in Suphah and the ravines,
  the Arnon 15and[b] the slopes of the ravines
that lead to the settlement of Ar
  and lie along the border of Moab."

16From there they continued on to Beer, the well where the LORD said
to Moses, "Gather the people together and I will give them water."
17Then Israel sang this song:

"Spring up, O well!
  Sing about it,
18 about the well that the princes dug,
  that the nobles of the people sank—
  the nobles with scepters and staffs."

Then they went from the wilderness to Mattanah, 19from Mattanah to
Nahaliel, from Nahaliel to Bamoth, 20and from Bamoth to the valley in
Moab where the top of Pisgah overlooks the wasteland.

DEFEAT OF SIHON AND OG

21Israel sent messengers to say to Sihon king of the Amorites:

22"Let us pass through your country. We will not turn aside into any field or vineyard, or drink water from any well. We will travel along the King's Highway until we have passed through your territory."

23But Sihon would not let Israel pass through his territory. He mus-
tered his entire army and marched out into the wilderness against Is-
rael. When he reached Jahaz, he fought with Israel. 24Israel, however,
put him to the sword and took over his land from the Arnon to the
Jabbok, but only as far as the Ammonites, because their border was
fortified. 25Israel captured all the cities of the Amorites and occupied
them, including Heshbon and all its surrounding settlements. 26Hesh-
bon was the city of Sihon king of the Amorites, who had fought against
the former king of Moab and had taken from him all his land as far as
the Arnon.
27That is why the poets say:

"Come to Heshbon and let it be rebuilt;
  let Sihon's city be restored.
28 "Fire went out from Heshbon,
  a blaze from the city of Sihon.
It consumed Ar of Moab,
  the citizens of Arnon's heights.
29 Woe to you, Moab!
  You are destroyed, people of Chemosh!
He has given up his sons as fugitives

---

[a] 14 Septuagint; Hebrew *Waheb* [b] 14,15 Or *"I have been given from Suphah and the ravines / of the Arnon* 15*to*

and his daughters as captives
to Sihon king of the Amorites.

30 "But we have overthrown them;
Heshbon's dominion has been destroyed all the way to Dibon.
We have demolished them as far as Nophah,
which extends to Medeba."

31 So Israel settled in the land of the Amorites.
32 After Moses had sent spies to Jazer, the Israelites captured its sur-
rounding settlements and drove out the Amorites who were there.
33 Then they turned and went up along the road toward Bashan, and
Og king of Bashan and his whole army marched out to meet them in
battle at Edrei.
34 The LORD said to Moses, "Do not be afraid of him, for I have de-
livered him into your hands, along with his whole army and his land.
Do to him what you did to Sihon king of the Amorites, who reigned in
Heshbon."
35 So they struck him down, together with his sons and his whole
army, leaving them no survivors. And they took possession of his land.

BALAK SUMMONS BALAAM

22 Then the Israelites traveled to the plains of Moab and camped
along the Jordan across from Jericho.
2 Now Balak son of Zippor saw all that Israel had done to the Am-
orites, 3 and Moab was terrified because there were so many people.
Indeed, Moab was filled with dread because of the Israelites.
4 The Moabites said to the elders of Midian, "This horde is going to
lick up everything around us, as an ox licks up the grass of the field."
So Balak son of Zippor, who was king of Moab at that time, 5 sent
messengers to summon Balaam son of Beor, who was at Pethor, near
the Euphrates River, in his native land. Balak said:

"A people has come out of Egypt; they cover the face of the
land and have settled next to me. 6 Now come and put a curse on
these people, because they are too powerful for me. Perhaps then
I will be able to defeat them and drive them out of the land. For
I know that whoever you bless is blessed, and whoever you curse
is cursed."

7 The elders of Moab and Midian left, taking with them the fee for
divination. When they came to Balaam, they told him what Balak had
said.
8 "Spend the night here," Balaam said to them, "and I will report back
to you with the answer the LORD gives me." So the Moabite officials
stayed with him.
9 God came to Balaam and asked, "Who are these men with you?"
10 Balaam said to God, "Balak son of Zippor, king of Moab, sent me
this message: 11 'A people that has come out of Egypt covers the face of
the land. Now come and put a curse on them for me. Perhaps then I
will be able to fight them and drive them away.'"
12 But God said to Balaam, "Do not go with them. You must not put a
curse on those people, because they are blessed."
13 The next morning Balaam got up and said to Balak's officials, "Go
back to your own country, for the LORD has refused to let me go with
you."

PRAYING SCRIPTURE

Numbers 22

It is all too easy to seek out teachers who will tell us what we want to hear. Our desire to be right or comfortable can lead us to reject sound teaching that might challenge our attitudes or actions, leading us to repentance. Seeking the approval of other people is not the way to truth.

Examine your heart for harmful preferences. Ask God to correct you by the Spirit and the Word.

14So the Moabite officials returned to Balak and said, "Balaam refused to come with us."

15Then Balak sent other officials, more numerous and more distinguished than the first. 16They came to Balaam and said:

> "This is what Balak son of Zippor says: Do not let anything keep you from coming to me, 17because I will reward you handsomely and do whatever you say. Come and put a curse on these people for me."

18But Balaam answered them, "Even if Balak gave me all the silver and gold in his palace, I could not do anything great or small to go beyond the command of the LORD my God. 19Now spend the night here so that I can find out what else the LORD will tell me."

20That night God came to Balaam and said, "Since these men have come to summon you, go with them, but do only what I tell you."

BALAAM'S DONKEY

21Balaam got up in the morning, saddled his donkey and went with the Moabite officials. 22But God was very angry when he went, and the angel of the LORD stood in the road to oppose him. Balaam was riding on his donkey, and his two servants were with him. 23When the donkey saw the angel of the LORD standing in the road with a drawn sword in his hand, it turned off the road into a field. Balaam beat it to get it back on the road.

24Then the angel of the LORD stood in a narrow path through the vineyards, with walls on both sides. 25When the donkey saw the angel of the LORD, it pressed close to the wall, crushing Balaam's foot against it. So he beat the donkey again.

26Then the angel of the LORD moved on ahead and stood in a narrow place where there was no room to turn, either to the right or to the left. 27When the donkey saw the angel of the LORD, it lay down under Balaam, and he was angry and beat it with his staff. 28Then the LORD opened the donkey's mouth, and it said to Balaam, "What have I done to you to make you beat me these three times?"

29Balaam answered the donkey, "You have made a fool of me! If only I had a sword in my hand, I would kill you right now."

30The donkey said to Balaam, "Am I not your own donkey, which you have always ridden, to this day? Have I been in the habit of doing this to you?"

"No," he said.

31Then the LORD opened Balaam's eyes, and he saw the angel of the LORD standing in the road with his sword drawn. So he bowed low and fell facedown.

32The angel of the LORD asked him, "Why have you beaten your donkey these three times? I have come here to oppose you because your path is a reckless one before me.[a] 33The donkey saw me and turned away from me these three times. If it had not turned away, I would certainly have killed you by now, but I would have spared it."

34Balaam said to the angel of the LORD, "I have sinned. I did not realize you were standing in the road to oppose me. Now if you are displeased, I will go back."

35The angel of the LORD said to Balaam, "Go with the men, but speak only what I tell you." So Balaam went with Balak's officials.

---

[a] *32* The meaning of the Hebrew for this clause is uncertain.

36When Balak heard that Balaam was coming, he went out to meet
him at the Moabite town on the Arnon border, at the edge of his terri-
tory. 37Balak said to Balaam, "Did I not send you an urgent summons?
Why didn't you come to me? Am I really not able to reward you?"
38"Well, I have come to you now," Balaam replied. "But I can't say
whatever I please. I must speak only what God puts in my mouth."
39Then Balaam went with Balak to Kiriath Huzoth. 40Balak sacrificed
cattle and sheep, and gave some to Balaam and the officials who were
with him. 41The next morning Balak took Balaam up to Bamoth Baal,
and from there he could see the outskirts of the Israelite camp.

BALAAM'S FIRST MESSAGE

23 Balaam said, "Build me seven altars here, and prepare seven
bulls and seven rams for me." 2Balak did as Balaam said, and
the two of them offered a bull and a ram on each altar.
3Then Balaam said to Balak, "Stay here beside your offering while I
go aside. Perhaps the LORD will come to meet with me. Whatever he
reveals to me I will tell you." Then he went off to a barren height.
4God met with him, and Balaam said, "I have prepared seven altars,
and on each altar I have offered a bull and a ram."
5The LORD put a word in Balaam's mouth and said, "Go back to Balak
and give him this word."
6So he went back to him and found him standing beside his offering,
with all the Moabite officials. 7Then Balaam spoke his message:

"Balak brought me from Aram,
the king of Moab from the eastern mountains.
'Come,' he said, 'curse Jacob for me;
come, denounce Israel.'
8 How can I curse
those whom God has not cursed?
How can I denounce
those whom the LORD has not denounced?
9 From the rocky peaks I see them,
from the heights I view them.
I see a people who live apart
and do not consider themselves one of the nations.
10 Who can count the dust of Jacob
or number even a fourth of Israel?
Let me die the death of the righteous,
and may my final end be like theirs!"

11Balak said to Balaam, "What have you done to me? I brought you to
curse my enemies, but you have done nothing but bless them!"
12He answered, "Must I not speak what the LORD puts in my mouth?"

BALAAM'S SECOND MESSAGE

13Then Balak said to him, "Come with me to another place where you
can see them; you will not see them all but only the outskirts of their
camp. And from there, curse them for me." 14So he took him to the field
of Zophim on the top of Pisgah, and there he built seven altars and of-
fered a bull and a ram on each altar.
15Balaam said to Balak, "Stay here beside your offering while I meet
with him over there."

PRAYING SCRIPTURE

Numbers 23

We often conclude that God cannot be trusted to keep his promises; that somehow he will fail to follow through or leave us in a jam. This passage reminds us that God doesn't lie and doesn't fail. He protected and blessed his chosen people as he said he would.

If you are struggling to trust God, let this reminder encourage you to approach him in absolute confidence.

16The LORD met with Balaam and put a word in his mouth and said,
"Go back to Balak and give him this word."
17So he went to him and found him standing beside his offering,
with the Moabite officials. Balak asked him, "What did the LORD say?"
18Then he spoke his message:

"Arise, Balak, and listen;
  hear me, son of Zippor.
19 God is not human, that he should lie,
  not a human being, that he should change his mind.
Does he speak and then not act?
  Does he promise and not fulfill?
20 I have received a command to bless;
  he has blessed, and I cannot change it.
21 "No misfortune is seen in Jacob,
  no misery observed[a] in Israel.
The LORD their God is with them;
  the shout of the King is among them.
22 God brought them out of Egypt;
  they have the strength of a wild ox.
23 There is no divination against[b] Jacob,
  no evil omens against[b] Israel.
It will now be said of Jacob
  and of Israel, 'See what God has done!'
24 The people rise like a lioness;
  they rouse themselves like a lion
that does not rest till it devours its prey
  and drinks the blood of its victims."

25Then Balak said to Balaam, "Neither curse them at all nor bless
them at all!"
26Balaam answered, "Did I not tell you I must do whatever the LORD
says?"

BALAAM'S THIRD MESSAGE

27Then Balak said to Balaam, "Come, let me take you to another place.
Perhaps it will please God to let you curse them for me from there."
28And Balak took Balaam to the top of Peor, overlooking the wasteland.
29Balaam said, "Build me seven altars here, and prepare seven bulls
and seven rams for me." 30Balak did as Balaam had said, and offered a
bull and a ram on each altar.

24 Now when Balaam saw that it pleased the LORD to bless Israel,
he did not resort to divination as at other times, but turned his
face toward the wilderness. 2When Balaam looked out and saw Israel
encamped tribe by tribe, the Spirit of God came on him 3and he spoke
his message:

"The prophecy of Balaam son of Beor,
  the prophecy of one whose eye sees clearly,
4 the prophecy of one who hears the words of God,
  who sees a vision from the Almighty,[c]
  who falls prostrate, and whose eyes are opened:

PRAYING SCRIPTURE

Numbers 24

Sometimes we can find ourselves in a position where someone asks us to do something wrong. Giving in to such a temptation is never pleasing to God, even if the person asking is in a position of authority over us. Obeying God is always right.

Scripture says "the Spirit of God came on" the prophet Balaam (verse 2). Ask the Holy Spirit to lead you in his ways at all times.

[a] *21* Or *He has not looked on Jacob's offenses / or on the wrongs found*
[b] *23* Or *in* [c] *4* Hebrew *Shaddai*; also in verse 16

5 "How beautiful are your tents, Jacob,
your dwelling places, Israel!

6 "Like valleys they spread out,
like gardens beside a river,
like aloes planted by the LORD,
like cedars beside the waters.
7 Water will flow from their buckets;
their seed will have abundant water.

"Their king will be greater than Agag;
their kingdom will be exalted.

8 "God brought them out of Egypt;
they have the strength of a wild ox.
They devour hostile nations
and break their bones in pieces;
with their arrows they pierce them.
9 Like a lion they crouch and lie down,
like a lioness — who dares to rouse them?

"May those who bless you be blessed
and those who curse you be cursed!"

10 Then Balak's anger burned against Balaam. He struck his hands
together and said to him, "I summoned you to curse my enemies, but
you have blessed them these three times. 11 Now leave at once and go
home! I said I would reward you handsomely, but the LORD has kept
you from being rewarded."
12 Balaam answered Balak, "Did I not tell the messengers you sent
me, 13 'Even if Balak gave me all the silver and gold in his palace, I could
not do anything of my own accord, good or bad, to go beyond the command of the LORD — and I must say only what the LORD says'? 14 Now I
am going back to my people, but come, let me warn you of what this
people will do to your people in days to come."

BALAAM'S FOURTH MESSAGE

15 Then he spoke his message:

"The prophecy of Balaam son of Beor,
the prophecy of one whose eye sees clearly,
16 the prophecy of one who hears the words of God,
who has knowledge from the Most High,
who sees a vision from the Almighty,
who falls prostrate, and whose eyes are opened:

17 "I see him, but not now;
I behold him, but not near.
A star will come out of Jacob;
a scepter will rise out of Israel.
He will crush the foreheads of Moab,
the skulls[a] of[b] all the people of Sheth.[c]
18 Edom will be conquered;
Seir, his enemy, will be conquered,

[a] 17 Samaritan Pentateuch (see also Jer. 48:45); the meaning of the word in the Masoretic Text is uncertain. [b] 17 Or possibly *Moab, / batter* [c] 17 Or *all the noisy boasters*

but Israel will grow strong.
19 A ruler will come out of Jacob
and destroy the survivors of the city."

BALAAM'S FIFTH MESSAGE

20 Then Balaam saw Amalek and spoke his message:

"Amalek was first among the nations,
but their end will be utter destruction."

BALAAM'S SIXTH MESSAGE

21 Then he saw the Kenites and spoke his message:

"Your dwelling place is secure,
your nest is set in a rock;
22 yet you Kenites will be destroyed
when Ashur takes you captive."

BALAAM'S SEVENTH MESSAGE

23 Then he spoke his message:

"Alas! Who can live when God does this?[a]
24 Ships will come from the shores of Cyprus;
they will subdue Ashur and Eber,
but they too will come to ruin."

25 Then Balaam got up and returned home, and Balak went his own
way.

MOAB SEDUCES ISRAEL

25 While Israel was staying in Shittim, the men began to indulge
in sexual immorality with Moabite women, 2 who invited them
to the sacrifices to their gods. The people ate the sacrificial meal and
bowed down before these gods. 3 So Israel yoked themselves to the Baal
of Peor. And the LORD's anger burned against them.
4 The LORD said to Moses, "Take all the leaders of these people, kill
them and expose them in broad daylight before the LORD, so that the
LORD's fierce anger may turn away from Israel."
5 So Moses said to Israel's judges, "Each of you must put to death
those of your people who have yoked themselves to the Baal of Peor."
6 Then an Israelite man brought into the camp a Midianite woman
right before the eyes of Moses and the whole assembly of Israel while
they were weeping at the entrance to the tent of meeting. 7 When Phin-
ehas son of Eleazar, the son of Aaron, the priest, saw this, he left the
assembly, took a spear in his hand 8 and followed the Israelite into the
tent. He drove the spear into both of them, right through the Israelite
man and into the woman's stomach. Then the plague against the Israel-
ites was stopped; 9 but those who died in the plague numbered 24,000.
10 The LORD said to Moses, 11 "Phinehas son of Eleazar, the son of
Aaron, the priest, has turned my anger away from the Israelites. Since
he was as zealous for my honor among them as I am, I did not put an
end to them in my zeal. 12 Therefore tell him I am making my covenant
of peace with him. 13 He and his descendants will have a covenant of a

PRAYING SCRIPTURE

Numbers 25

Worshiping idols is always an abomination to God. The Israelites provoked God by committing idolatry and brought judgment on themselves. Idolatry is substituting anything in God's place—whether one of God's gifts or a preference.

Is there anything that has become an idol in your life? If so, repent of substituting it for God, and allow him the utmost position in your heart.

[a] *23* Masoretic Text; with a different word division of the Hebrew *The people from the islands will gather from the north.*

lasting priesthood, because he was zealous for the honor of his God and
made atonement for the Israelites."
14 The name of the Israelite who was killed with the Midianite woman
was Zimri son of Salu, the leader of a Simeonite family. 15 And the name
of the Midianite woman who was put to death was Kozbi daughter of
Zur, a tribal chief of a Midianite family.
16 The LORD said to Moses, 17 "Treat the Midianites as enemies and kill
them. 18 They treated you as enemies when they deceived you in the
Peor incident involving their sister Kozbi, the daughter of a Midianite
leader, the woman who was killed when the plague came as a result of
that incident."

THE SECOND CENSUS

26 After the plague the LORD said to Moses and Eleazar son of
Aaron, the priest, 2 "Take a census of the whole Israelite com-
munity by families — all those twenty years old or more who are able
to serve in the army of Israel." 3 So on the plains of Moab by the Jordan
across from Jericho, Moses and Eleazar the priest spoke with them and
said, 4 "Take a census of the men twenty years old or more, as the LORD
commanded Moses."

These were the Israelites who came out of Egypt:

5 The descendants of Reuben, the firstborn son of Israel, were:
through Hanok, the Hanokite clan;
through Pallu, the Palluite clan;
6 through Hezron, the Hezronite clan;
through Karmi, the Karmite clan.
7 These were the clans of Reuben; those numbered were 43,730.

8 The son of Pallu was Eliab, 9 and the sons of Eliab were Nemuel,
Dathan and Abiram. The same Dathan and Abiram were the commu-
nity officials who rebelled against Moses and Aaron and were among
Korah's followers when they rebelled against the LORD. 10 The earth
opened its mouth and swallowed them along with Korah, whose fol-
lowers died when the fire devoured the 250 men. And they served as a
warning sign. 11 The line of Korah, however, did not die out.

12 The descendants of Simeon by their clans were:
through Nemuel, the Nemuelite clan;
through Jamin, the Jaminite clan;
through Jakin, the Jakinite clan;
13 through Zerah, the Zerahite clan;
through Shaul, the Shaulite clan.
14 These were the clans of Simeon; those numbered were 22,200.

15 The descendants of Gad by their clans were:
through Zephon, the Zephonite clan;
through Haggi, the Haggite clan;
through Shuni, the Shunite clan;
16 through Ozni, the Oznite clan;
through Eri, the Erite clan;
17 through Arodi,[a] the Arodite clan;
through Areli, the Arelite clan.
18 These were the clans of Gad; those numbered were 40,500.

PRAYING SCRIPTURE

Numbers 26

As we read the census of the families of Israel, remember the promise of judgment God invoked after the last census. The unbelief exhibited after the spies went into Canaan limited the number of people who would subsequently enter the land of promise. God was not mocked.

Sometimes it's easy to think that God overlooks sin, but he doesn't. Ask God to help you walk in faith today and every day.

[a] 17 Samaritan Pentateuch and Syriac (see also Gen. 46:16); Masoretic Text *Arod*

19 Er and Onan were sons of Judah, but they died in Canaan.
20 The descendants of Judah by their clans were:
through Shelah, the Shelanite clan;
through Perez, the Perezite clan;
through Zerah, the Zerahite clan.
21 The descendants of Perez were:
through Hezron, the Hezronite clan;
through Hamul, the Hamulite clan.
22 These were the clans of Judah; those numbered were 76,500.

23 The descendants of Issachar by their clans were:
through Tola, the Tolaite clan;
through Puah, the Puite[a] clan;
24 through Jashub, the Jashubite clan;
through Shimron, the Shimronite clan.
25 These were the clans of Issachar; those numbered were 64,300.

26 The descendants of Zebulun by their clans were:
through Sered, the Seredite clan;
through Elon, the Elonite clan;
through Jahleel, the Jahleelite clan.
27 These were the clans of Zebulun; those numbered were 60,500.

28 The descendants of Joseph by their clans through Manasseh and Ephraim were:

29 The descendants of Manasseh:
through Makir, the Makirite clan (Makir was the father of Gilead);
through Gilead, the Gileadite clan.
30 These were the descendants of Gilead:
through Iezer, the Iezerite clan;
through Helek, the Helekite clan;
31 through Asriel, the Asrielite clan;
through Shechem, the Shechemite clan;
32 through Shemida, the Shemidaite clan;
through Hepher, the Hepherite clan.
33 (Zelophehad son of Hepher had no sons; he had only daughters, whose names were Mahlah, Noah, Hoglah, Milkah and Tirzah.)
34 These were the clans of Manasseh; those numbered were 52,700.

35 These were the descendants of Ephraim by their clans:
through Shuthelah, the Shuthelahite clan;
through Beker, the Bekerite clan;
through Tahan, the Tahanite clan.
36 These were the descendants of Shuthelah:
through Eran, the Eranite clan.
37 These were the clans of Ephraim; those numbered were 32,500.

These were the descendants of Joseph by their clans.

38 The descendants of Benjamin by their clans were:
through Bela, the Belaite clan;
through Ashbel, the Ashbelite clan;
through Ahiram, the Ahiramite clan;

---

[a] *23* Samaritan Pentateuch, Septuagint, Vulgate and Syriac (see also 1 Chron. 7:1); Masoretic Text *through Puvah, the Punite*

39 through Shupham,[a] the Shuphamite clan;
through Hupham, the Huphamite clan.
40 The descendants of Bela through Ard and Naaman were:
through Ard,[b] the Ardite clan;
through Naaman, the Naamite clan.
41 These were the clans of Benjamin; those numbered were 45,600.

42 These were the descendants of Dan by their clans:
through Shuham, the Shuhamite clan.
These were the clans of Dan: 43 All of them were Shuhamite clans; and
those numbered were 64,400.

44 The descendants of Asher by their clans were:
through Imnah, the Imnite clan;
through Ishvi, the Ishvite clan;
through Beriah, the Beriite clan;
45 and through the descendants of Beriah:
through Heber, the Heberite clan;
through Malkiel, the Malkielite clan.
46 (Asher had a daughter named Serah.)
47 These were the clans of Asher; those numbered were 53,400.

48 The descendants of Naphtali by their clans were:
through Jahzeel, the Jahzeelite clan;
through Guni, the Gunite clan;
49 through Jezer, the Jezerite clan;
through Shillem, the Shillemite clan.
50 These were the clans of Naphtali; those numbered were 45,400.

51 The total number of the men of Israel was 601,730.

52 The LORD said to Moses, 53 "The land is to be allotted to them as an
inheritance based on the number of names. 54 To a larger group give a
larger inheritance, and to a smaller group a smaller one; each is to re-
ceive its inheritance according to the number of those listed. 55 Be sure
that the land is distributed by lot. What each group inherits will be ac-
cording to the names for its ancestral tribe. 56 Each inheritance is to be
distributed by lot among the larger and smaller groups."

57 These were the Levites who were counted by their clans:
through Gershon, the Gershonite clan;
through Kohath, the Kohathite clan;
through Merari, the Merarite clan.
58 These also were Levite clans:
the Libnite clan,
the Hebronite clan,
the Mahlite clan,
the Mushite clan,
the Korahite clan.
(Kohath was the forefather of Amram; 59 the name of Amram's wife
was Jochebed, a descendant of Levi, who was born to the Levites[c]

---

[a] *39* A few manuscripts of the Masoretic Text, Samaritan Pentateuch, Vulgate and Syriac (see also Septuagint); most manuscripts of the Masoretic Text *Shephupham* [b] *40* Samaritan Pentateuch and Vulgate (see also Septuagint); Masoretic Text does not have *through Ard.* [c] *59* Or *Jochebed, a daughter of Levi, who was born to Levi*

in Egypt. To Amram she bore Aaron, Moses and their sister Mir-
iam. [60]Aaron was the father of Nadab and Abihu, Eleazar and Ith-
amar. [61]But Nadab and Abihu died when they made an offering
before the LORD with unauthorized fire.)

[62]All the male Levites a month old or more numbered 23,000. They
were not counted along with the other Israelites because they received
no inheritance among them.

[63]These are the ones counted by Moses and Eleazar the priest when
they counted the Israelites on the plains of Moab by the Jordan across
from Jericho. [64]Not one of them was among those counted by Moses
and Aaron the priest when they counted the Israelites in the Desert of
Sinai. [65]For the LORD had told those Israelites they would surely die in
the wilderness, and not one of them was left except Caleb son of Je-
phunneh and Joshua son of Nun.

ZELOPHEHAD'S DAUGHTERS

27 The daughters of Zelophehad son of Hepher, the son of Gilead,
the son of Makir, the son of Manasseh, belonged to the clans
of Manasseh son of Joseph. The names of the daughters were Mahlah,
Noah, Hoglah, Milkah and Tirzah. They came forward [2]and stood be-
fore Moses, Eleazar the priest, the leaders and the whole assembly at
the entrance to the tent of meeting and said, [3]"Our father died in the
wilderness. He was not among Korah's followers, who banded together
against the LORD, but he died for his own sin and left no sons. [4]Why
should our father's name disappear from his clan because he had no
son? Give us property among our father's relatives."
[5]So Moses brought their case before the LORD, [6]and the LORD said
to him, [7]"What Zelophehad's daughters are saying is right. You must
certainly give them property as an inheritance among their father's
relatives and give their father's inheritance to them.
[8]"Say to the Israelites, 'If a man dies and leaves no son, give his in-
heritance to his daughter. [9]If he has no daughter, give his inheritance
to his brothers. [10]If he has no brothers, give his inheritance to his fa-
ther's brothers. [11]If his father had no brothers, give his inheritance to
the nearest relative in his clan, that he may possess it. This is to have
the force of law for the Israelites, as the LORD commanded Moses.'"

JOSHUA TO SUCCEED MOSES

[12]Then the LORD said to Moses, "Go up this mountain in the Abarim
Range and see the land I have given the Israelites. [13]After you have
seen it, you too will be gathered to your people, as your brother Aaron
was, [14]for when the community rebelled at the waters in the Desert of
Zin, both of you disobeyed my command to honor me as holy before
their eyes." (These were the waters of Meribah Kadesh, in the Desert
of Zin.)
[15]Moses said to the LORD, [16]"May the LORD, the God who gives breath
to all living things, appoint someone over this community [17]to go out
and come in before them, one who will lead them out and bring them
in, so the LORD's people will not be like sheep without a shepherd."
[18]So the LORD said to Moses, "Take Joshua son of Nun, a man in
whom is the spirit of leadership,[a] and lay your hand on him. [19]Have

PRAYING SCRIPTURE

Numbers 27

Many times people don't think about inheritance until a loved one has passed away. Then, rather than mourning, the survivors get caught up in "who gets what." This often leads to hurt feelings and damaged or even ruptured relationships in families.

What is your attitude or expectation about a potential inheritance? Thank God that no matter how much or little earthly inheritance you receive, an eternal one is reserved for you.

[a] 18 Or *the Spirit*

him stand before Eleazar the priest and the entire assembly and com-
mission him in their presence. 20 Give him some of your authority so
the whole Israelite community will obey him. 21 He is to stand before
Eleazar the priest, who will obtain decisions for him by inquiring of the
Urim before the LORD. At his command he and the entire community
of the Israelites will go out, and at his command they will come in."
22 Moses did as the LORD commanded him. He took Joshua and had
him stand before Eleazar the priest and the whole assembly. 23 Then he
laid his hands on him and commissioned him, as the LORD instructed
through Moses.

DAILY OFFERINGS

28 The LORD said to Moses, 2 "Give this command to the Israelites
and say to them: 'Make sure that you present to me at the ap-
pointed time my food offerings, as an aroma pleasing to me.' 3 Say to
them: 'This is the food offering you are to present to the LORD: two
lambs a year old without defect, as a regular burnt offering each day.
4 Offer one lamb in the morning and the other at twilight, 5 together
with a grain offering of a tenth of an ephah[a] of the finest flour mixed
with a quarter of a hin[b] of oil from pressed olives. 6 This is the regular
burnt offering instituted at Mount Sinai as a pleasing aroma, a food
offering presented to the LORD. 7 The accompanying drink offering is
to be a quarter of a hin of fermented drink with each lamb. Pour out
the drink offering to the LORD at the sanctuary. 8 Offer the second lamb
at twilight, along with the same kind of grain offering and drink of-
fering that you offer in the morning. This is a food offering, an aroma
pleasing to the LORD.

SABBATH OFFERINGS

9 " 'On the Sabbath day, make an offering of two lambs a year old
without defect, together with its drink offering and a grain offering of
two-tenths of an ephah[c] of the finest flour mixed with olive oil. 10 This
is the burnt offering for every Sabbath, in addition to the regular burnt
offering and its drink offering.

MONTHLY OFFERINGS

11 " 'On the first of every month, present to the LORD a burnt offer-
ing of two young bulls, one ram and seven male lambs a year old,
all without defect. 12 With each bull there is to be a grain offering of
three-tenths of an ephah[d] of the finest flour mixed with oil; with the
ram, a grain offering of two-tenths of an ephah of the finest flour
mixed with oil; 13 and with each lamb, a grain offering of a tenth of an
ephah of the finest flour mixed with oil. This is for a burnt offering,
a pleasing aroma, a food offering presented to the LORD. 14 With each
bull there is to be a drink offering of half a hin[e] of wine; with the ram,
a third of a hin[f]; and with each lamb, a quarter of a hin. This is the
monthly burnt offering to be made at each new moon during the year.

[a] *5* That is, probably about 3 1/2 pounds or about 1.6 kilograms; also in verses 13, 21 and 29 [b] *5* That is, about 1 quart or about 1 liter; also in verses 7 and 14 [c] *9* That is, probably about 7 pounds or about 3.2 kilograms; also in verses 12, 20 and 28 [d] *12* That is, probably about 11 pounds or about 5 kilograms; also in verses 20 and 28 [e] *14* That is, about 2 quarts or about 1.9 liters [f] *14* That is, about 1 1/3 quarts or about 1.3 liters

PRAYING SCRIPTURE

Numbers 28

Offerings were a regular part of the Israelites' worship, reminding them of their sinfulness and God's provision. The primary expression of their worship was giving offerings of different kinds. One particular offering had to be made each morning and evening.

Contrast that with the once-for-all offering of Jesus Christ. Because of him, no further animal sacrifices are needed. Thank God for his eternal provision for sin.

15Besides the regular burnt offering with its drink offering, one male
goat is to be presented to the LORD as a sin offering.[a]

THE PASSOVER

16"'On the fourteenth day of the first month the LORD's Passover is
to be held. 17On the fifteenth day of this month there is to be a festival;
for seven days eat bread made without yeast. 18On the first day hold a
sacred assembly and do no regular work. 19Present to the LORD a food
offering consisting of a burnt offering of two young bulls, one ram and
seven male lambs a year old, all without defect. 20With each bull offer
a grain offering of three-tenths of an ephah of the finest flour mixed
with oil; with the ram, two-tenths; 21and with each of the seven lambs,
one-tenth. 22Include one male goat as a sin offering to make atone-
ment for you. 23Offer these in addition to the regular morning burnt
offering. 24In this way present the food offering every day for seven
days as an aroma pleasing to the LORD; it is to be offered in addition to
the regular burnt offering and its drink offering. 25On the seventh day
hold a sacred assembly and do no regular work.

THE FESTIVAL OF WEEKS

26"'On the day of firstfruits, when you present to the LORD an offer-
ing of new grain during the Festival of Weeks, hold a sacred assembly
and do no regular work. 27Present a burnt offering of two young bulls,
one ram and seven male lambs a year old as an aroma pleasing to the
LORD. 28With each bull there is to be a grain offering of three-tenths of
an ephah of the finest flour mixed with oil; with the ram, two-tenths;
29and with each of the seven lambs, one-tenth. 30Include one male
goat to make atonement for you. 31Offer these together with their
drink offerings, in addition to the regular burnt offering and its grain
offering. Be sure the animals are without defect.

THE FESTIVAL OF TRUMPETS

29 "'On the first day of the seventh month hold a sacred assembly
and do no regular work. It is a day for you to sound the trum-
pets. 2As an aroma pleasing to the LORD, offer a burnt offering of one
young bull, one ram and seven male lambs a year old, all without de-
fect. 3With the bull offer a grain offering of three-tenths of an ephah[b]
of the finest flour mixed with olive oil; with the ram, two-tenths[c]; 4and
with each of the seven lambs, one-tenth.[d] 5Include one male goat as a
sin offering[e] to make atonement for you. 6These are in addition to the
monthly and daily burnt offerings with their grain offerings and drink
offerings as specified. They are food offerings presented to the LORD,
a pleasing aroma.

THE DAY OF ATONEMENT

7"'On the tenth day of this seventh month hold a sacred assembly.
You must deny yourselves[f] and do no work. 8Present as an aroma
pleasing to the LORD a burnt offering of one young bull, one ram and

PRAYING SCRIPTURE

Numbers 29

One scenario that repeats itself through the law is this: When the Lord issued commands to the Israelites, Moses would tell them everything. Moses acted as a faithful spokesman for God so God's people would know exactly what he expected of them.

A real danger within God's people is changing God's words to suit our own desires. Ask God to help you faithfully teach his Word to others.

[a] *15* Or *purification offering*; also in verse 22 [b] *3* That is, probably about 11 pounds or about 5 kilograms; also in verses 9 and 14 [c] *3* That is, probably about 7 pounds or about 3.2 kilograms; also in verses 9 and 14 [d] *4* That is, probably about 3 1/2 pounds or about 1.6 kilograms; also in verses 10 and 15 [e] *5* Or *purification offering*; also elsewhere in this chapter [f] *7* Or *must fast*

seven male lambs a year old, all without defect. 9With the bull offer
a grain offering of three-tenths of an ephah of the finest flour mixed
with oil; with the ram, two-tenths; 10and with each of the seven lambs,
one-tenth. 11Include one male goat as a sin offering, in addition to
the sin offering for atonement and the regular burnt offering with its
grain offering, and their drink offerings.

THE FESTIVAL OF TABERNACLES

12" 'On the fifteenth day of the seventh month, hold a sacred as-
sembly and do no regular work. Celebrate a festival to the LORD for
seven days. 13Present as an aroma pleasing to the LORD a food offer-
ing consisting of a burnt offering of thirteen young bulls, two rams
and fourteen male lambs a year old, all without defect. 14With each of
the thirteen bulls offer a grain offering of three-tenths of an ephah of
the finest flour mixed with oil; with each of the two rams, two-tenths;
15and with each of the fourteen lambs, one-tenth. 16Include one male
goat as a sin offering, in addition to the regular burnt offering with its
grain offering and drink offering.

17" 'On the second day offer twelve young bulls, two rams and four-
teen male lambs a year old, all without defect. 18With the bulls, rams
and lambs, offer their grain offerings and drink offerings according
to the number specified. 19Include one male goat as a sin offering, in
addition to the regular burnt offering with its grain offering, and their
drink offerings.

20" 'On the third day offer eleven bulls, two rams and fourteen male
lambs a year old, all without defect. 21With the bulls, rams and lambs,
offer their grain offerings and drink offerings according to the num-
ber specified. 22Include one male goat as a sin offering, in addition to
the regular burnt offering with its grain offering and drink offering.

23" 'On the fourth day offer ten bulls, two rams and fourteen male
lambs a year old, all without defect. 24With the bulls, rams and lambs,
offer their grain offerings and drink offerings according to the num-
ber specified. 25Include one male goat as a sin offering, in addition to
the regular burnt offering with its grain offering and drink offering.

26" 'On the fifth day offer nine bulls, two rams and fourteen male
lambs a year old, all without defect. 27With the bulls, rams and lambs,
offer their grain offerings and drink offerings according to the num-
ber specified. 28Include one male goat as a sin offering, in addition to
the regular burnt offering with its grain offering and drink offering.

29" 'On the sixth day offer eight bulls, two rams and fourteen male
lambs a year old, all without defect. 30With the bulls, rams and lambs,
offer their grain offerings and drink offerings according to the num-
ber specified. 31Include one male goat as a sin offering, in addition to
the regular burnt offering with its grain offering and drink offering.

32" 'On the seventh day offer seven bulls, two rams and fourteen
male lambs a year old, all without defect. 33With the bulls, rams and
lambs, offer their grain offerings and drink offerings according to the
number specified. 34Include one male goat as a sin offering, in addition
to the regular burnt offering with its grain offering and drink offering.

35" 'On the eighth day hold a closing special assembly and do no reg-
ular work. 36Present as an aroma pleasing to the LORD a food offering
consisting of a burnt offering of one bull, one ram and seven male
lambs a year old, all without defect. 37With the bull, the ram and the
lambs, offer their grain offerings and drink offerings according to the

number specified. [38]Include one male goat as a sin offering, in addition
to the regular burnt offering with its grain offering and drink offering.
[39]" 'In addition to what you vow and your freewill offerings, offer
these to the LORD at your appointed festivals: your burnt offerings,
grain offerings, drink offerings and fellowship offerings.' "
[40]Moses told the Israelites all that the LORD commanded him.[a]

VOWS

30 [b] Moses said to the heads of the tribes of Israel: "This is what
the LORD commands: [2]When a man makes a vow to the LORD
or takes an oath to obligate himself by a pledge, he must not break his
word but must do everything he said.
[3]"When a young woman still living in her father's household makes
a vow to the LORD or obligates herself by a pledge [4]and her father hears
about her vow or pledge but says nothing to her, then all her vows
and every pledge by which she obligated herself will stand. [5]But if her
father forbids her when he hears about it, none of her vows or the
pledges by which she obligated herself will stand; the LORD will release
her because her father has forbidden her.
[6]"If she marries after she makes a vow or after her lips utter a rash
promise by which she obligates herself [7]and her husband hears about
it but says nothing to her, then her vows or the pledges by which she
obligated herself will stand. [8]But if her husband forbids her when he
hears about it, he nullifies the vow that obligates her or the rash prom-
ise by which she obligates herself, and the LORD will release her.
[9]"Any vow or obligation taken by a widow or divorced woman will
be binding on her.
[10]"If a woman living with her husband makes a vow or obligates her-
self by a pledge under oath [11]and her husband hears about it but says
nothing to her and does not forbid her, then all her vows or the pledges
by which she obligated herself will stand. [12]But if her husband nullifies
them when he hears about them, then none of the vows or pledges
that came from her lips will stand. Her husband has nullified them,
and the LORD will release her. [13]Her husband may confirm or nullify
any vow she makes or any sworn pledge to deny herself.[c] [14]But if her
husband says nothing to her about it from day to day, then he confirms
all her vows or the pledges binding on her. He confirms them by saying
nothing to her when he hears about them. [15]If, however, he nullifies
them some time after he hears about them, then he must bear the con-
sequences of her wrongdoing."
[16]These are the regulations the LORD gave Moses concerning rela-
tionships between a man and his wife, and between a father and his
young daughter still living at home.

VENGEANCE ON THE MIDIANITES

31 The LORD said to Moses, [2]"Take vengeance on the Midianites for
the Israelites. After that, you will be gathered to your people."
[3]So Moses said to the people, "Arm some of your men to go to war
against the Midianites so that they may carry out the LORD's vengeance
on them. [4]Send into battle a thousand men from each of the tribes of
Israel." [5]So twelve thousand men armed for battle, a thousand from

[a] *40* In Hebrew texts this verse (29:40) is numbered 30:1. [b] In Hebrew texts 30:1-16 is numbered 30:2-17. [c] *13* Or *to fast*

PRAYING SCRIPTURE

Numbers 30

The Mosaic Law required that people who made vows keep their word. A person's word was to be his or her bond, and this was especially true in families. Husbands, wives and children were guided by a number of interrelated laws to ensure the keeping of oaths.

Think about the last time you failed to keep your word. Ask God's forgiveness and ask forgiveness from anyone—especially family—who was affected by it.

PRAYING SCRIPTURE

Numbers 31

War is a complex issue, one addressed in the Scriptures. The Israelites received instructions on handling the spoils. They were to keep some of the confiscated gold in the tabernacle, a reminder of the Lord's deliverance.

War affects not only warriors, but also those left behind. In some places even today, as in ancient times, spoils include people. Pray that the Prince of Peace soon comes to end all wars.

each tribe, were supplied from the clans of Israel. 6Moses sent them into battle, a thousand from each tribe, along with Phinehas son of Eleazar, the priest, who took with him articles from the sanctuary and the trumpets for signaling.

7They fought against Midian, as the LORD commanded Moses, and killed every man. 8Among their victims were Evi, Rekem, Zur, Hur and Reba — the five kings of Midian. They also killed Balaam son of Beor with the sword. 9The Israelites captured the Midianite women and children and took all the Midianite herds, flocks and goods as plunder. 10They burned all the towns where the Midianites had settled, as well as all their camps. 11They took all the plunder and spoils, including the people and animals, 12and brought the captives, spoils and plunder to Moses and Eleazar the priest and the Israelite assembly at their camp on the plains of Moab, by the Jordan across from Jericho.

13Moses, Eleazar the priest and all the leaders of the community went to meet them outside the camp. 14Moses was angry with the officers of the army — the commanders of thousands and commanders of hundreds — who returned from the battle.

15"Have you allowed all the women to live?" he asked them. 16"They were the ones who followed Balaam's advice and enticed the Israelites to be unfaithful to the LORD in the Peor incident, so that a plague struck the LORD's people. 17Now kill all the boys. And kill every woman who has slept with a man, 18but save for yourselves every girl who has never slept with a man.

19"Anyone who has killed someone or touched someone who was killed must stay outside the camp seven days. On the third and seventh days you must purify yourselves and your captives. 20Purify every garment as well as everything made of leather, goat hair or wood."

21Then Eleazar the priest said to the soldiers who had gone into battle, "This is what is required by the law that the LORD gave Moses: 22Gold, silver, bronze, iron, tin, lead 23and anything else that can withstand fire must be put through the fire, and then it will be clean. But it must also be purified with the water of cleansing. And whatever cannot withstand fire must be put through that water. 24On the seventh day wash your clothes and you will be clean. Then you may come into the camp."

DIVIDING THE SPOILS

25The LORD said to Moses, 26"You and Eleazar the priest and the family heads of the community are to count all the people and animals that were captured. 27Divide the spoils equally between the soldiers who took part in the battle and the rest of the community. 28From the soldiers who fought in the battle, set apart as tribute for the LORD one out of every five hundred, whether people, cattle, donkeys or sheep. 29Take this tribute from their half share and give it to Eleazar the priest as the LORD's part. 30From the Israelites' half, select one out of every fifty, whether people, cattle, donkeys, sheep or other animals. Give them to the Levites, who are responsible for the care of the LORD's tabernacle." 31So Moses and Eleazar the priest did as the LORD commanded Moses.

32The plunder remaining from the spoils that the soldiers took was 675,000 sheep, 3372,000 cattle, 3461,000 donkeys 35and 32,000 women who had never slept with a man.

36The half share of those who fought in the battle was:

337,500 sheep, 37of which the tribute for the LORD was 675;
38 36,000 cattle, of which the tribute for the LORD was 72;
39 30,500 donkeys, of which the tribute for the LORD was 61;
40 16,000 people, of whom the tribute for the LORD was 32.

41Moses gave the tribute to Eleazar the priest as the LORD's part, as
the LORD commanded Moses.
42The half belonging to the Israelites, which Moses set apart from
that of the fighting men— 43the community's half—was 337,500
sheep, 4436,000 cattle, 4530,500 donkeys 46and 16,000 people. 47From
the Israelites' half, Moses selected one out of every fifty people and
animals, as the LORD commanded him, and gave them to the Levites,
who were responsible for the care of the LORD's tabernacle.
48Then the officers who were over the units of the army—the com-
manders of thousands and commanders of hundreds—went to Moses
49and said to him, "Your servants have counted the soldiers under our
command, and not one is missing. 50So we have brought as an offering
to the LORD the gold articles each of us acquired—armlets, bracelets,
signet rings, earrings and necklaces—to make atonement for our-
selves before the LORD."
51Moses and Eleazar the priest accepted from them the gold—all the
crafted articles. 52All the gold from the commanders of thousands and
commanders of hundreds that Moses and Eleazar presented as a gift
to the LORD weighed 16,750 shekels.[a] 53Each soldier had taken plunder
for himself. 54Moses and Eleazar the priest accepted the gold from the
commanders of thousands and commanders of hundreds and brought
it into the tent of meeting as a memorial for the Israelites before the
LORD.

THE TRANSJORDAN TRIBES

32 The Reubenites and Gadites, who had very large herds and
flocks, saw that the lands of Jazer and Gilead were suitable for
livestock. 2So they came to Moses and Eleazar the priest and to the
leaders of the community, and said, 3"Ataroth, Dibon, Jazer, Nimrah,
Heshbon, Elealeh, Sebam, Nebo and Beon— 4the land the LORD sub-
dued before the people of Israel—are suitable for livestock, and your
servants have livestock. 5If we have found favor in your eyes," they
said, "let this land be given to your servants as our possession. Do not
make us cross the Jordan."
6Moses said to the Gadites and Reubenites, "Should your fellow Is-
raelites go to war while you sit here? 7Why do you discourage the Isra-
elites from crossing over into the land the LORD has given them? 8This
is what your fathers did when I sent them from Kadesh Barnea to look
over the land. 9After they went up to the Valley of Eshkol and viewed
the land, they discouraged the Israelites from entering the land the
LORD had given them. 10The LORD's anger was aroused that day and he
swore this oath: 11'Because they have not followed me wholeheartedly,
not one of those who were twenty years old or more when they came
up out of Egypt will see the land I promised on oath to Abraham, Isaac
and Jacob— 12not one except Caleb son of Jephunneh the Kenizzite
and Joshua son of Nun, for they followed the LORD wholeheartedly.'
13The LORD's anger burned against Israel and he made them wander

PRAYING SCRIPTURE

Numbers 32

As the tribes prepared to settle on the eastern side of the Jordan, Moses reminded them of the long journey that brought them to this point, including the disobedience that caused 40 years of wandering aimlessly in the wilderness.

It helps to reflect on the victories and losses along our faith journey. Take some time for such a reflection, and thank God for bringing you this far and for being with you.

[a] *52* That is, about 420 pounds or about 190 kilograms

in the wilderness forty years, until the whole generation of those who
had done evil in his sight was gone.

14"And here you are, a brood of sinners, standing in the place of your
fathers and making the LORD even more angry with Israel. 15If you turn
away from following him, he will again leave all this people in the wil-
derness, and you will be the cause of their destruction."

16Then they came up to him and said, "We would like to build pens
here for our livestock and cities for our women and children. 17But we
will arm ourselves for battle[a] and go ahead of the Israelites until we
have brought them to their place. Meanwhile our women and children
will live in fortified cities, for protection from the inhabitants of the
land. 18We will not return to our homes until each of the Israelites has
received their inheritance. 19We will not receive any inheritance with
them on the other side of the Jordan, because our inheritance has
come to us on the east side of the Jordan."

20Then Moses said to them, "If you will do this — if you will arm
yourselves before the LORD for battle 21and if all of you who are armed
cross over the Jordan before the LORD until he has driven his enemies
out before him — 22then when the land is subdued before the LORD,
you may return and be free from your obligation to the LORD and to
Israel. And this land will be your possession before the LORD.

23"But if you fail to do this, you will be sinning against the LORD;
and you may be sure that your sin will find you out. 24Build cities for
your women and children, and pens for your flocks, but do what you
have promised."

25The Gadites and Reubenites said to Moses, "We your servants will
do as our lord commands. 26Our children and wives, our flocks and
herds will remain here in the cities of Gilead. 27But your servants, every
man who is armed for battle, will cross over to fight before the LORD,
just as our lord says."

28Then Moses gave orders about them to Eleazar the priest and
Joshua son of Nun and to the family heads of the Israelite tribes. 29He
said to them, "If the Gadites and Reubenites, every man armed for
battle, cross over the Jordan with you before the LORD, then when the
land is subdued before you, you must give them the land of Gilead as
their possession. 30But if they do not cross over with you armed, they
must accept their possession with you in Canaan."

31The Gadites and Reubenites answered, "Your servants will do what
the LORD has said. 32We will cross over before the LORD into Canaan
armed, but the property we inherit will be on this side of the Jordan."

33Then Moses gave to the Gadites, the Reubenites and the half-tribe
of Manasseh son of Joseph the kingdom of Sihon king of the Amorites
and the kingdom of Og king of Bashan — the whole land with its cities
and the territory around them.

34The Gadites built up Dibon, Ataroth, Aroer, 35Atroth Shophan, Jazer,
Jogbehah, 36Beth Nimrah and Beth Haran as fortified cities, and built
pens for their flocks. 37And the Reubenites rebuilt Heshbon, Elealeh
and Kiriathaim, 38as well as Nebo and Baal Meon (these names were
changed) and Sibmah. They gave names to the cities they rebuilt.

39The descendants of Makir son of Manasseh went to Gilead, cap-
tured it and drove out the Amorites who were there. 40So Moses gave
Gilead to the Makirites, the descendants of Manasseh, and they settled

[a] 17 Septuagint; Hebrew *will be quick to arm ourselves*

there. 41Jair, a descendant of Manasseh, captured their settlements and
called them Havvoth Jair.[a] 42And Nobah captured Kenath and its sur-
rounding settlements and called it Nobah after himself.

STAGES IN ISRAEL'S JOURNEY

33 Here are the stages in the journey of the Israelites when they
came out of Egypt by divisions under the leadership of Moses
and Aaron. 2At the LORD's command Moses recorded the stages in their
journey. This is their journey by stages:

3The Israelites set out from Rameses on the fifteenth day of the
first month, the day after the Passover. They marched out defi-
antly in full view of all the Egyptians, 4who were burying all their
firstborn, whom the LORD had struck down among them; for the
LORD had brought judgment on their gods.
5The Israelites left Rameses and camped at Sukkoth.
6They left Sukkoth and camped at Etham, on the edge of the
desert.
7They left Etham, turned back to Pi Hahiroth, to the east of Baal
Zephon, and camped near Migdol.
8They left Pi Hahiroth[b] and passed through the sea into the des-
ert, and when they had traveled for three days in the Desert of
Etham, they camped at Marah.
9They left Marah and went to Elim, where there were twelve
springs and seventy palm trees, and they camped there.
10They left Elim and camped by the Red Sea.[c]
11They left the Red Sea and camped in the Desert of Sin.
12They left the Desert of Sin and camped at Dophkah.
13They left Dophkah and camped at Alush.
14They left Alush and camped at Rephidim, where there was no
water for the people to drink.
15They left Rephidim and camped in the Desert of Sinai.
16They left the Desert of Sinai and camped at Kibroth Hattaavah.
17They left Kibroth Hattaavah and camped at Hazeroth.
18They left Hazeroth and camped at Rithmah.
19They left Rithmah and camped at Rimmon Perez.
20They left Rimmon Perez and camped at Libnah.
21They left Libnah and camped at Rissah.
22They left Rissah and camped at Kehelathah.
23They left Kehelathah and camped at Mount Shepher.
24They left Mount Shepher and camped at Haradah.
25They left Haradah and camped at Makheloth.
26They left Makheloth and camped at Tahath.
27They left Tahath and camped at Terah.
28They left Terah and camped at Mithkah.
29They left Mithkah and camped at Hashmonah.
30They left Hashmonah and camped at Moseroth.
31They left Moseroth and camped at Bene Jaakan.
32They left Bene Jaakan and camped at Hor Haggidgad.
33They left Hor Haggidgad and camped at Jotbathah.
34They left Jotbathah and camped at Abronah.

PRAYING SCRIPTURE

Numbers 33

Remembering the ways God has worked in our lives encourages us to trust him continually. With the Jordan before him, Moses rehearsed the Israelites' exodus from Egypt as they prepared to cross it. God's work in our past prepares us for God's work in our future.

Spend some time reviewing the highs and lows of your walk, noting how God worked along the way. Ask him to strengthen your faith for whatever is ahead.

---

[a] 41 Or *them the settlements of Jair* [b] 8 Many manuscripts of the Masoretic Text, Samaritan Pentateuch and Vulgate; most manuscripts of the Masoretic Text *left from before Hahiroth* [c] 10 Or *the Sea of Reeds*; also in verse 11

35They left Abronah and camped at Ezion Geber.
36They left Ezion Geber and camped at Kadesh, in the Desert
of Zin.
37They left Kadesh and camped at Mount Hor, on the border of
Edom. 38At the LORD's command Aaron the priest went up Mount
Hor, where he died on the first day of the fifth month of the for-
tieth year after the Israelites came out of Egypt. 39Aaron was a
hundred and twenty-three years old when he died on Mount Hor.
40The Canaanite king of Arad, who lived in the Negev of Canaan,
heard that the Israelites were coming.
41They left Mount Hor and camped at Zalmonah.
42They left Zalmonah and camped at Punon.
43They left Punon and camped at Oboth.
44They left Oboth and camped at Iye Abarim, on the border of
Moab.
45They left Iye Abarim and camped at Dibon Gad.
46They left Dibon Gad and camped at Almon Diblathaim.
47They left Almon Diblathaim and camped in the mountains of
Abarim, near Nebo.
48They left the mountains of Abarim and camped on the plains
of Moab by the Jordan across from Jericho. 49There on the plains
of Moab they camped along the Jordan from Beth Jeshimoth to
Abel Shittim.

50On the plains of Moab by the Jordan across from Jericho the LORD
said to Moses, 51"Speak to the Israelites and say to them: 'When you
cross the Jordan into Canaan, 52drive out all the inhabitants of the land
before you. Destroy all their carved images and their cast idols, and
demolish all their high places. 53Take possession of the land and settle
in it, for I have given you the land to possess. 54Distribute the land by
lot, according to your clans. To a larger group give a larger inheritance,
and to a smaller group a smaller one. Whatever falls to them by lot will
be theirs. Distribute it according to your ancestral tribes.
55" 'But if you do not drive out the inhabitants of the land, those you
allow to remain will become barbs in your eyes and thorns in your
sides. They will give you trouble in the land where you will live. 56And
then I will do to you what I plan to do to them.' "

BOUNDARIES OF CANAAN

34 The LORD said to Moses, 2"Command the Israelites and say to
them: 'When you enter Canaan, the land that will be allotted
to you as an inheritance is to have these boundaries:

3" 'Your southern side will include some of the Desert of Zin along
the border of Edom. Your southern boundary will start in the east from
the southern end of the Dead Sea, 4cross south of Scorpion Pass, con-
tinue on to Zin and go south of Kadesh Barnea. Then it will go to Hazar
Addar and over to Azmon, 5where it will turn, join the Wadi of Egypt
and end at the Mediterranean Sea.
6" 'Your western boundary will be the coast of the Mediterranean
Sea. This will be your boundary on the west.
7" 'For your northern boundary, run a line from the Mediterranean
Sea to Mount Hor 8and from Mount Hor to Lebo Hamath. Then the
boundary will go to Zedad, 9continue to Ziphron and end at Hazar
Enan. This will be your boundary on the north.

PRAYING SCRIPTURE

Numbers 34

It is God's prerogative to establish the boundaries of every place. He appointed the tribal boundaries of Canaan with respect to his promise to Abraham, Isaac and Jacob. There was a defined and divine order to how the people of Israel should divide the promised land.

The fulfillment of God's promises sometimes takes decades or longer. Ask God for the patience and faith to endure well as you wait on him.

10" 'For your eastern boundary, run a line from Hazar Enan to She-
pham. 11The boundary will go down from Shepham to Riblah on the
east side of Ain and continue along the slopes east of the Sea of Gal-
ilee.[a] 12Then the boundary will go down along the Jordan and end at
the Dead Sea.

" 'This will be your land, with its boundaries on every side.' "

13Moses commanded the Israelites: "Assign this land by lot as an in-
heritance. The LORD has ordered that it be given to the nine and a half
tribes, 14because the families of the tribe of Reuben, the tribe of Gad
and the half-tribe of Manasseh have received their inheritance. 15These
two and a half tribes have received their inheritance east of the Jordan
across from Jericho, toward the sunrise."

16The LORD said to Moses, 17"These are the names of the men who
are to assign the land for you as an inheritance: Eleazar the priest and
Joshua son of Nun. 18And appoint one leader from each tribe to help
assign the land. 19These are their names:

Caleb son of Jephunneh,
  from the tribe of Judah;
20 Shemuel son of Ammihud,
  from the tribe of Simeon;
21 Elidad son of Kislon,
  from the tribe of Benjamin;
22 Bukki son of Jogli,
  the leader from the tribe of Dan;
23 Hanniel son of Ephod,
  the leader from the tribe of Manasseh son of Joseph;
24 Kemuel son of Shiphtan,
  the leader from the tribe of Ephraim son of Joseph;
25 Elizaphan son of Parnak,
  the leader from the tribe of Zebulun;
26 Paltiel son of Azzan,
  the leader from the tribe of Issachar;
27 Ahihud son of Shelomi,
  the leader from the tribe of Asher;
28 Pedahel son of Ammihud,
  the leader from the tribe of Naphtali."

29These are the men the LORD commanded to assign the inheritance
to the Israelites in the land of Canaan.

TOWNS FOR THE LEVITES

35 On the plains of Moab by the Jordan across from Jericho, the
LORD said to Moses, 2"Command the Israelites to give the Le-
vites towns to live in from the inheritance the Israelites will possess.
And give them pasturelands around the towns. 3Then they will have
towns to live in and pasturelands for the cattle they own and all their
other animals.

4"The pasturelands around the towns that you give the Levites will
extend a thousand cubits[b] from the town wall. 5Outside the town, mea-
sure two thousand cubits[c] on the east side, two thousand on the south
side, two thousand on the west and two thousand on the north, with the
town in the center. They will have this area as pastureland for the towns.

PRAYING SCRIPTURE

Numbers 35

God's grace to the Israelites in Canaan was demonstrated in part by the construction of cities of refuge, where a person who killed someone accidentally could go and be protected from retribution. The strident requirements of the law met the fullness of God's mercy. What are some ways that God has demonstrated his mercy toward you? Thank him for all the times mercy has overcome judgment.

[a] *11* Hebrew *Kinnereth* [b] *4* That is, about 1,500 feet or about 450 meters
[c] *5* That is, about 3,000 feet or about 900 meters

CITIES OF REFUGE

6“Six of the towns you give the Levites will be cities of refuge, to
which a person who has killed someone may flee. In addition, give
them forty-two other towns. 7In all you must give the Levites forty-
eight towns, together with their pasturelands. 8The towns you give the
Levites from the land the Israelites possess are to be given in propor-
tion to the inheritance of each tribe: Take many towns from a tribe
that has many, but few from one that has few.”

9Then the LORD said to Moses: 10“Speak to the Israelites and say to
them: ‘When you cross the Jordan into Canaan, 11select some towns
to be your cities of refuge, to which a person who has killed someone
accidentally may flee. 12They will be places of refuge from the avenger,
so that anyone accused of murder may not die before they stand trial
before the assembly. 13These six towns you give will be your cities of
refuge. 14Give three on this side of the Jordan and three in Canaan as
cities of refuge. 15These six towns will be a place of refuge for Israelites
and for foreigners residing among them, so that anyone who has killed
another accidentally can flee there.

16“ ‘If anyone strikes someone a fatal blow with an iron object, that
person is a murderer; the murderer is to be put to death. 17Or if anyone
is holding a stone and strikes someone a fatal blow with it, that per-
son is a murderer; the murderer is to be put to death. 18Or if anyone is
holding a wooden object and strikes someone a fatal blow with it, that
person is a murderer; the murderer is to be put to death. 19The avenger
of blood shall put the murderer to death; when the avenger comes
upon the murderer, the avenger shall put the murderer to death. 20If
anyone with malice aforethought shoves another or throws something
at them intentionally so that they die 21or if out of enmity one person
hits another with their fist so that the other dies, that person is to be
put to death; that person is a murderer. The avenger of blood shall put
the murderer to death when they meet.

22“ ‘But if without enmity someone suddenly pushes another or
throws something at them unintentionally 23or, without seeing them,
drops on them a stone heavy enough to kill them, and they die, then
since that other person was not an enemy and no harm was intended,
24the assembly must judge between the accused and the avenger of
blood according to these regulations. 25The assembly must protect the
one accused of murder from the avenger of blood and send the ac-
cused back to the city of refuge to which they fled. The accused must
stay there until the death of the high priest, who was anointed with
the holy oil.

26“ ‘But if the accused ever goes outside the limits of the city of ref-
uge to which they fled 27and the avenger of blood finds them outside
the city, the avenger of blood may kill the accused without being guilty
of murder. 28The accused must stay in the city of refuge until the death
of the high priest; only after the death of the high priest may they re-
turn to their own property.

29“ ‘This is to have the force of law for you throughout the genera-
tions to come, wherever you live.

30“ ‘Anyone who kills a person is to be put to death as a murderer
only on the testimony of witnesses. But no one is to be put to death on
the testimony of only one witness.

31“ ‘Do not accept a ransom for the life of a murderer, who deserves
to die. They are to be put to death.

32“ ‘Do not accept a ransom for anyone who has fled to a city of ref-
uge and so allow them to go back and live on their own land before the
death of the high priest.
33“ ‘Do not pollute the land where you are. Bloodshed pollutes the
land, and atonement cannot be made for the land on which blood has
been shed, except by the blood of the one who shed it. 34Do not defile
the land where you live and where I dwell, for I, the LORD, dwell among
the Israelites.’ ”

INHERITANCE OF ZELOPHEHAD’S DAUGHTERS

36 The family heads of the clan of Gilead son of Makir, the son of
Manasseh, who were from the clans of the descendants of Jo-
seph, came and spoke before Moses and the leaders, the heads of the
Israelite families. 2They said, “When the LORD commanded my lord to
give the land as an inheritance to the Israelites by lot, he ordered you
to give the inheritance of our brother Zelophehad to his daughters.
3Now suppose they marry men from other Israelite tribes; then their
inheritance will be taken from our ancestral inheritance and added to
that of the tribe they marry into. And so part of the inheritance allot-
ted to us will be taken away. 4When the Year of Jubilee for the Israelites
comes, their inheritance will be added to that of the tribe into which
they marry, and their property will be taken from the tribal inheri-
tance of our ancestors.”
5Then at the LORD’s command Moses gave this order to the Israel-
ites: “What the tribe of the descendants of Joseph is saying is right.
6This is what the LORD commands for Zelophehad’s daughters: They
may marry anyone they please as long as they marry within their fa-
ther’s tribal clan. 7No inheritance in Israel is to pass from one tribe to
another, for every Israelite shall keep the tribal inheritance of their an-
cestors. 8Every daughter who inherits land in any Israelite tribe must
marry someone in her father’s tribal clan, so that every Israelite will
possess the inheritance of their ancestors. 9No inheritance may pass
from one tribe to another, for each Israelite tribe is to keep the land
it inherits.”
10So Zelophehad’s daughters did as the LORD commanded Mo-
ses. 11Zelophehad’s daughters — Mahlah, Tirzah, Hoglah, Milkah and
Noah — married their cousins on their father’s side. 12They married
within the clans of the descendants of Manasseh son of Joseph, and
their inheritance remained in their father’s tribe and clan.

13These are the commands and regulations the LORD gave through
Moses to the Israelites on the plains of Moab by the Jordan across from
Jericho.

PRAYING SCRIPTURE

Numbers 36

Whom and when to marry are important questions. God restricted marriage in some cases, threatening a loss of inheritance to discourage intertribal unions. While this might seem strange in some ways, it was important that the tribal line of Christ remain distinct.

As the saying goes, “God works in mysterious ways.” Commit to be obedient to God even if he leads you in a way that doesn’t immediately make sense.

DEUTERONOMY

Deuteronomy opens with Israel on the plains of Moab, awaiting entry to the promised land. Because he had sinned against God, Moses could not cross the Jordan with them, but he prepared them for their conquest with three discourses. His speeches reminded the Israelites that theirs was a unique nation because they were delivered by God from Egypt through the exodus, they were sustained by him in the wilderness and they belonged totally to him. Because he was their God and they were his people, they should have stood apart from the other people in the land they were about to conquer. The book is, in essence, an adaptation and expansion of the law Israel had already received from the Lord.

The book's outline is divided into Moses' three speeches and his concluding words before his death on Mount Nebo. First, Moses rehearsed the exodus and the wanderings in the wilderness, reminding them of lessons they should have learned from that experience. The second address begins in chapter 4 and carries through to the end of chapter 28. Within it, Moses told the people of their obligations to love and obey God. It includes a restatement of the Ten Commandments.

Chapters 12–26 contain specific laws related to life as God's covenant people in Israel. Moses laid out the blessings and curses related to keeping or disobeying the covenant. The third speech in chapters 29–30 renewed the covenant between God and Israel. The final chapters cover the song of Moses, Moses' final words and his death.

As Moses prepared the new generation for life in the land, he wanted them to know that they were to love God and obey him. Moses told them to love God "with all your heart and with all your soul and with all your strength" (6:5). They could not proclaim that they loved God while flouting his commandments. They had to demonstrate their love for God by obeying him; otherwise they would invoke judgment on themselves and possibly their children too.

Little is said directly about prayer in Deuteronomy, but there are manifold implications. How are we to obey God without seeking him? How can we follow God without seeking his paths? How do we love him without telling him? How do we love our neighbors well without asking for God's help?

When we pray, we remember our call to love and obey God. This command is rooted in his relationship with us. Just as he led Israel out of Egypt, he redeemed us through the miraculous work of Christ and brought us out of bondage to sin. He leads us through the difficulties and trials of life in the same way he led Israel in the wilderness and provided for them. God is not distant; he is near to his people whom he loves. Prayer is not a duty; it is a heavenward privilege, an opportunity to be in conversation with the author of the law, the One who fulfills all his promises.

So we pray, expressing thankfulness for the salvation he offers and his presence in our lives.

PRAYING SCRIPTURE

Deuteronomy 1

As the Israelites stood poised to enter the promised land, God reminded them of their sin in the wilderness so they would not be inclined to disobey again. God spoke clearly, yet they did not listen. This led to the second giving of the law.

Can you remember a time when God spoke clearly to you yet you did not obey? Ask him for the humility to listen and obey when he speaks.

THE COMMAND TO LEAVE HOREB

1 These are the words Moses spoke to all Israel in the wilderness east
of the Jordan — that is, in the Arabah — opposite Suph, between Pa-
ran and Tophel, Laban, Hazeroth and Dizahab. 2 (It takes eleven days to
go from Horeb to Kadesh Barnea by the Mount Seir road.)
3 In the fortieth year, on the first day of the eleventh month, Moses
proclaimed to the Israelites all that the LORD had commanded him
concerning them. 4 This was after he had defeated Sihon king of the
Amorites, who reigned in Heshbon, and at Edrei had defeated Og king
of Bashan, who reigned in Ashtaroth.
5 East of the Jordan in the territory of Moab, Moses began to expound
this law, saying:

6 The LORD our God said to us at Horeb, "You have stayed long
enough at this mountain. 7 Break camp and advance into the hill coun-
try of the Amorites; go to all the neighboring peoples in the Arabah,
in the mountains, in the western foothills, in the Negev and along the
coast, to the land of the Canaanites and to Lebanon, as far as the great
river, the Euphrates. 8 See, I have given you this land. Go in and take
possession of the land the LORD swore he would give to your fathers —
to Abraham, Isaac and Jacob — and to their descendants after them."

THE APPOINTMENT OF LEADERS

9 At that time I said to you, "You are too heavy a burden for me to
carry alone. 10 The LORD your God has increased your numbers so that to-
day you are as numerous as the stars in the sky. 11 May the LORD, the God
of your ancestors, increase you a thousand times and bless you as he has
promised! 12 But how can I bear your problems and your burdens and
your disputes all by myself? 13 Choose some wise, understanding and
respected men from each of your tribes, and I will set them over you."
14 You answered me, "What you propose to do is good."
15 So I took the leading men of your tribes, wise and respected men,
and appointed them to have authority over you — as commanders of
thousands, of hundreds, of fifties and of tens and as tribal officials.
16 And I charged your judges at that time, "Hear the disputes between
your people and judge fairly, whether the case is between two Israel-
ites or between an Israelite and a foreigner residing among you. 17 Do
not show partiality in judging; hear both small and great alike. Do not
be afraid of anyone, for judgment belongs to God. Bring me any case
too hard for you, and I will hear it." 18 And at that time I told you every-
thing you were to do.

SPIES SENT OUT

19 Then, as the LORD our God commanded us, we set out from Horeb
and went toward the hill country of the Amorites through all that vast
and dreadful wilderness that you have seen, and so we reached Ka-
desh Barnea. 20 Then I said to you, "You have reached the hill country
of the Amorites, which the LORD our God is giving us. 21 See, the LORD
your God has given you the land. Go up and take possession of it as the
LORD, the God of your ancestors, told you. Do not be afraid; do not be
discouraged."
22 Then all of you came to me and said, "Let us send men ahead to
spy out the land for us and bring back a report about the route we are
to take and the towns we will come to."

23The idea seemed good to me; so I selected twelve of you, one man
from each tribe. 24They left and went up into the hill country, and came
to the Valley of Eshkol and explored it. 25Taking with them some of the
fruit of the land, they brought it down to us and reported, "It is a good
land that the LORD our God is giving us."

REBELLION AGAINST THE LORD

26But you were unwilling to go up; you rebelled against the com-
mand of the LORD your God. 27You grumbled in your tents and said,
"The LORD hates us; so he brought us out of Egypt to deliver us into the
hands of the Amorites to destroy us. 28Where can we go? Our brothers
have made our hearts melt in fear. They say, 'The people are stronger
and taller than we are; the cities are large, with walls up to the sky. We
even saw the Anakites there.' "

29Then I said to you, "Do not be terrified; do not be afraid of them.
30The LORD your God, who is going before you, will fight for you, as he
did for you in Egypt, before your very eyes, 31and in the wilderness.
There you saw how the LORD your God carried you, as a father carries
his son, all the way you went until you reached this place."

32In spite of this, you did not trust in the LORD your God, 33who went
ahead of you on your journey, in fire by night and in a cloud by day,
to search out places for you to camp and to show you the way you
should go.

34When the LORD heard what you said, he was angry and solemnly
swore: 35"No one from this evil generation shall see the good land I
swore to give your ancestors, 36except Caleb son of Jephunneh. He will
see it, and I will give him and his descendants the land he set his feet
on, because he followed the LORD wholeheartedly."

37Because of you the LORD became angry with me also and said, "You
shall not enter it, either. 38But your assistant, Joshua son of Nun, will
enter it. Encourage him, because he will lead Israel to inherit it. 39And
the little ones that you said would be taken captive, your children who
do not yet know good from bad — they will enter the land. I will give
it to them and they will take possession of it. 40But as for you, turn
around and set out toward the desert along the route to the Red Sea.[a]"

41Then you replied, "We have sinned against the LORD. We will go
up and fight, as the LORD our God commanded us." So every one of
you put on his weapons, thinking it easy to go up into the hill country.

42But the LORD said to me, "Tell them, 'Do not go up and fight, be-
cause I will not be with you. You will be defeated by your enemies.' "

43So I told you, but you would not listen. You rebelled against the
LORD's command and in your arrogance you marched up into the hill
country. 44The Amorites who lived in those hills came out against you;
they chased you like a swarm of bees and beat you down from Seir all
the way to Hormah. 45You came back and wept before the LORD, but he
paid no attention to your weeping and turned a deaf ear to you. 46And
so you stayed in Kadesh many days — all the time you spent there.

WANDERINGS IN THE WILDERNESS

2 Then we turned back and set out toward the wilderness along the
route to the Red Sea,[a] as the LORD had directed me. For a long time
we made our way around the hill country of Seir.

[a] 40,1 Or *the Sea of Reeds*

PRAYING SCRIPTURE

Deuteronomy 2

Moses rehearsed Israel's history not only to remind them of their sin but also to remind them of how God worked in their past for their good by keeping his word. God loved Israel. He did not leave them helpless but provided the guidance they needed in Canaan.

God is always at work doing good for his people. Spend a few minutes thanking him for the good things he has done for you.

2Then the LORD said to me, 3"You have made your way around this
hill country long enough; now turn north. 4Give the people these or-
ders: 'You are about to pass through the territory of your relatives the
descendants of Esau, who live in Seir. They will be afraid of you, but be
very careful. 5Do not provoke them to war, for I will not give you any
of their land, not even enough to put your foot on. I have given Esau
the hill country of Seir as his own. 6You are to pay them in silver for
the food you eat and the water you drink.' "

7The LORD your God has blessed you in all the work of your hands.
He has watched over your journey through this vast wilderness. These
forty years the LORD your God has been with you, and you have not
lacked anything.

8So we went on past our relatives the descendants of Esau, who live
in Seir. We turned from the Arabah road, which comes up from Elath
and Ezion Geber, and traveled along the desert road of Moab.

9Then the LORD said to me, "Do not harass the Moabites or provoke
them to war, for I will not give you any part of their land. I have given
Ar to the descendants of Lot as a possession."

10(The Emites used to live there—a people strong and numerous,
and as tall as the Anakites. 11Like the Anakites, they too were consid-
ered Rephaites, but the Moabites called them Emites. 12Horites used
to live in Seir, but the descendants of Esau drove them out. They de-
stroyed the Horites from before them and settled in their place, just as
Israel did in the land the LORD gave them as their possession.)

13And the LORD said, "Now get up and cross the Zered Valley." So we
crossed the valley.

14Thirty-eight years passed from the time we left Kadesh Barnea
until we crossed the Zered Valley. By then, that entire generation of
fighting men had perished from the camp, as the LORD had sworn to
them. 15The LORD's hand was against them until he had completely
eliminated them from the camp.

16Now when the last of these fighting men among the people had
died, 17the LORD said to me, 18"Today you are to pass by the region of
Moab at Ar. 19When you come to the Ammonites, do not harass them
or provoke them to war, for I will not give you possession of any land
belonging to the Ammonites. I have given it as a possession to the de-
scendants of Lot."

20(That too was considered a land of the Rephaites, who used to live
there; but the Ammonites called them Zamzummites. 21They were a
people strong and numerous, and as tall as the Anakites. The LORD
destroyed them from before the Ammonites, who drove them out and
settled in their place. 22The LORD had done the same for the descen-
dants of Esau, who lived in Seir, when he destroyed the Horites from
before them. They drove them out and have lived in their place to this
day. 23And as for the Avvites who lived in villages as far as Gaza, the
Caphtorites coming out from Caphtor[a] destroyed them and settled in
their place.)

DEFEAT OF SIHON KING OF HESHBON

24"Set out now and cross the Arnon Gorge. See, I have given into
your hand Sihon the Amorite, king of Heshbon, and his country. Be-
gin to take possession of it and engage him in battle. 25This very day

[a] *23* That is, Crete

I will begin to put the terror and fear of you on all the nations under
heaven. They will hear reports of you and will tremble and be in an-
guish because of you."
26From the Desert of Kedemoth I sent messengers to Sihon king of
Heshbon offering peace and saying, 27"Let us pass through your coun-
try. We will stay on the main road; we will not turn aside to the right
or to the left. 28Sell us food to eat and water to drink for their price in
silver. Only let us pass through on foot — 29as the descendants of Esau,
who live in Seir, and the Moabites, who live in Ar, did for us — until we
cross the Jordan into the land the LORD our God is giving us." 30But Si-
hon king of Heshbon refused to let us pass through. For the LORD your
God had made his spirit stubborn and his heart obstinate in order to
give him into your hands, as he has now done.
31The LORD said to me, "See, I have begun to deliver Sihon and his
country over to you. Now begin to conquer and possess his land."
32When Sihon and all his army came out to meet us in battle at Ja-
haz, 33the LORD our God delivered him over to us and we struck him
down, together with his sons and his whole army. 34At that time we
took all his towns and completely destroyed[a] them — men, women
and children. We left no survivors. 35But the livestock and the plunder
from the towns we had captured we carried off for ourselves. 36From
Aroer on the rim of the Arnon Gorge, and from the town in the gorge,
even as far as Gilead, not one town was too strong for us. The LORD our
God gave us all of them. 37But in accordance with the command of the
LORD our God, you did not encroach on any of the land of the Ammon-
ites, neither the land along the course of the Jabbok nor that around
the towns in the hills.

DEFEAT OF OG KING OF BASHAN

3 Next we turned and went up along the road toward Bashan, and
Og king of Bashan with his whole army marched out to meet us
in battle at Edrei. 2The LORD said to me, "Do not be afraid of him, for
I have delivered him into your hands, along with his whole army and
his land. Do to him what you did to Sihon king of the Amorites, who
reigned in Heshbon."
3So the LORD our God also gave into our hands Og king of Bashan
and all his army. We struck them down, leaving no survivors. 4At that
time we took all his cities. There was not one of the sixty cities that we
did not take from them — the whole region of Argob, Og's kingdom
in Bashan. 5All these cities were fortified with high walls and with
gates and bars, and there were also a great many unwalled villages.
6We completely destroyed[a] them, as we had done with Sihon king
of Heshbon, destroying[a] every city — men, women and children. 7But
all the livestock and the plunder from their cities we carried off for
ourselves.
8So at that time we took from these two kings of the Amorites the
territory east of the Jordan, from the Arnon Gorge as far as Mount
Hermon. 9(Hermon is called Sirion by the Sidonians; the Amorites call
it Senir.) 10We took all the towns on the plateau, and all Gilead, and
all Bashan as far as Salekah and Edrei, towns of Og's kingdom in Ba-
shan. 11(Og king of Bashan was the last of the Rephaites. His bed was

PRAYING SCRIPTURE

Deuteronomy 3

In one of Scripture's saddest accounts, God told Moses that because of disobedience, he would not enter the promised land. As much as Moses wanted to enter, God said no. But God did not leave Israel without a leader; he appointed Joshua in Moses' stead.

God's kingdom is never dependent on one person alone, no matter how influential. We should prayerfully commit to God's leadership over any one person's.

[a] *34,6* The Hebrew term refers to the irrevocable giving over of things or persons to the LORD, often by totally destroying them.

decorated with iron and was more than nine cubits long and four cu-
bits wide.[a] It is still in Rabbah of the Ammonites.)

DIVISION OF THE LAND

12Of the land that we took over at that time, I gave the Reubenites
and the Gadites the territory north of Aroer by the Arnon Gorge, in-
cluding half the hill country of Gilead, together with its towns. 13The
rest of Gilead and also all of Bashan, the kingdom of Og, I gave to the
half-tribe of Manasseh. (The whole region of Argob in Bashan used to
be known as a land of the Rephaites. 14Jair, a descendant of Manasseh,
took the whole region of Argob as far as the border of the Geshurites
and the Maakathites; it was named after him, so that to this day Ba-
shan is called Havvoth Jair.[b]) 15And I gave Gilead to Makir. 16But to the
Reubenites and the Gadites I gave the territory extending from Gilead
down to the Arnon Gorge (the middle of the gorge being the border)
and out to the Jabbok River, which is the border of the Ammonites.
17Its western border was the Jordan in the Arabah, from Kinnereth to
the Sea of the Arabah (that is, the Dead Sea), below the slopes of Pisgah.
18I commanded you at that time: "The LORD your God has given you
this land to take possession of it. But all your able-bodied men, armed
for battle, must cross over ahead of the other Israelites. 19However,
your wives, your children and your livestock (I know you have much
livestock) may stay in the towns I have given you, 20until the LORD
gives rest to your fellow Israelites as he has to you, and they too have
taken over the land that the LORD your God is giving them across the
Jordan. After that, each of you may go back to the possession I have
given you."

MOSES FORBIDDEN TO CROSS THE JORDAN

21At that time I commanded Joshua: "You have seen with your own
eyes all that the LORD your God has done to these two kings. The LORD
will do the same to all the kingdoms over there where you are going.
22Do not be afraid of them; the LORD your God himself will fight for you."
23At that time I pleaded with the LORD: 24"Sovereign LORD, you have
begun to show to your servant your greatness and your strong hand.
For what god is there in heaven or on earth who can do the deeds and
mighty works you do? 25Let me go over and see the good land beyond
the Jordan — that fine hill country and Lebanon."
26But because of you the LORD was angry with me and would not
listen to me. "That is enough," the LORD said. "Do not speak to me any-
more about this matter. 27Go up to the top of Pisgah and look west and
north and south and east. Look at the land with your own eyes, since
you are not going to cross this Jordan. 28But commission Joshua, and
encourage and strengthen him, for he will lead this people across and
will cause them to inherit the land that you will see." 29So we stayed in
the valley near Beth Peor.

OBEDIENCE COMMANDED

4 Now, Israel, hear the decrees and laws I am about to teach you. Fol-
low them so that you may live and may go in and take possession
of the land the LORD, the God of your ancestors, is giving you. 2Do not

PRAYING SCRIPTURE

Deuteronomy 4

The Lord wanted his people to remember what great things he had done for them so they would tell them to future generations. Moses framed his reminder around God's special relationship to Israel, that God was "near" them (verse 7). Israel's God lives! He was not carved from wood or chiseled from stone.

That God is close to his people is a tremendous comfort. Thank God he is always near to us.

---

[a] *11* That is, about 14 feet long and 6 feet wide or about 4 meters long and 1.8 meters wide [b] *14* Or *called the settlements of Jair*

add to what I command you and do not subtract from it, but keep the
commands of the LORD your God that I give you.
3You saw with your own eyes what the LORD did at Baal Peor. The
LORD your God destroyed from among you everyone who followed the
Baal of Peor, 4but all of you who held fast to the LORD your God are still
alive today.
5See, I have taught you decrees and laws as the LORD my God com-
manded me, so that you may follow them in the land you are enter-
ing to take possession of it. 6Observe them carefully, for this will show
your wisdom and understanding to the nations, who will hear about
all these decrees and say, "Surely this great nation is a wise and un-
derstanding people." 7What other nation is so great as to have their
gods near them the way the LORD our God is near us whenever we pray
to him? 8And what other nation is so great as to have such righteous
decrees and laws as this body of laws I am setting before you today?
9Only be careful, and watch yourselves closely so that you do not
forget the things your eyes have seen or let them fade from your heart
as long as you live. Teach them to your children and to their children
after them. 10Remember the day you stood before the LORD your God
at Horeb, when he said to me, "Assemble the people before me to hear
my words so that they may learn to revere me as long as they live in
the land and may teach them to their children." 11You came near and
stood at the foot of the mountain while it blazed with fire to the very
heavens, with black clouds and deep darkness. 12Then the LORD spoke
to you out of the fire. You heard the sound of words but saw no form;
there was only a voice. 13He declared to you his covenant, the Ten Com-
mandments, which he commanded you to follow and then wrote them
on two stone tablets. 14And the LORD directed me at that time to teach
you the decrees and laws you are to follow in the land that you are
crossing the Jordan to possess.

IDOLATRY FORBIDDEN

15You saw no form of any kind the day the LORD spoke to you at Ho-
reb out of the fire. Therefore watch yourselves very carefully, 16so that
you do not become corrupt and make for yourselves an idol, an image
of any shape, whether formed like a man or a woman, 17or like any an-
imal on earth or any bird that flies in the air, 18or like any creature that
moves along the ground or any fish in the waters below. 19And when
you look up to the sky and see the sun, the moon and the stars — all
the heavenly array — do not be enticed into bowing down to them and
worshiping things the LORD your God has apportioned to all the na-
tions under heaven. 20But as for you, the LORD took you and brought
you out of the iron-smelting furnace, out of Egypt, to be the people of
his inheritance, as you now are.
21The LORD was angry with me because of you, and he solemnly
swore that I would not cross the Jordan and enter the good land the
LORD your God is giving you as your inheritance. 22I will die in this
land; I will not cross the Jordan; but you are about to cross over and
take possession of that good land. 23Be careful not to forget the cov-
enant of the LORD your God that he made with you; do not make for
yourselves an idol in the form of anything the LORD your God has for-
bidden. 24For the LORD your God is a consuming fire, a jealous God.
25After you have had children and grandchildren and have lived in
the land a long time — if you then become corrupt and make any kind

of idol, doing evil in the eyes of the LORD your God and arousing his anger, [26]I call the heavens and the earth as witnesses against you this day that you will quickly perish from the land that you are crossing the Jordan to possess. You will not live there long but will certainly be destroyed. [27]The LORD will scatter you among the peoples, and only a few of you will survive among the nations to which the LORD will drive you. [28]There you will worship man-made gods of wood and stone, which cannot see or hear or eat or smell. [29]But if from there you seek the LORD your God, you will find him if you seek him with all your heart and with all your soul. [30]When you are in distress and all these things have happened to you, then in later days you will return to the LORD your God and obey him. [31]For the LORD your God is a merciful God; he will not abandon or destroy you or forget the covenant with your ancestors, which he confirmed to them by oath.

THE LORD IS GOD

[32]Ask now about the former days, long before your time, from the day God created human beings on the earth; ask from one end of the heavens to the other. Has anything so great as this ever happened, or has anything like it ever been heard of? [33]Has any other people heard the voice of God[a] speaking out of fire, as you have, and lived? [34]Has any god ever tried to take for himself one nation out of another nation, by testings, by signs and wonders, by war, by a mighty hand and an outstretched arm, or by great and awesome deeds, like all the things the LORD your God did for you in Egypt before your very eyes?

[35]You were shown these things so that you might know that the LORD is God; besides him there is no other. [36]From heaven he made you hear his voice to discipline you. On earth he showed you his great fire, and you heard his words from out of the fire. [37]Because he loved your ancestors and chose their descendants after them, he brought you out of Egypt by his Presence and his great strength, [38]to drive out before you nations greater and stronger than you and to bring you into their land to give it to you for your inheritance, as it is today.

[39]Acknowledge and take to heart this day that the LORD is God in heaven above and on the earth below. There is no other. [40]Keep his decrees and commands, which I am giving you today, so that it may go well with you and your children after you and that you may live long in the land the LORD your God gives you for all time.

CITIES OF REFUGE

[41]Then Moses set aside three cities east of the Jordan, [42]to which anyone who had killed a person could flee if they had unintentionally killed a neighbor without malice aforethought. They could flee into one of these cities and save their life. [43]The cities were these: Bezer in the wilderness plateau, for the Reubenites; Ramoth in Gilead, for the Gadites; and Golan in Bashan, for the Manassites.

INTRODUCTION TO THE LAW

[44]This is the law Moses set before the Israelites. [45]These are the stipulations, decrees and laws Moses gave them when they came out of Egypt [46]and were in the valley near Beth Peor east of the Jordan, in the land of Sihon king of the Amorites, who reigned in Heshbon and was

---

[a] 33 Or *of a god*

defeated by Moses and the Israelites as they came out of Egypt. 47They
took possession of his land and the land of Og king of Bashan, the two
Amorite kings east of the Jordan. 48This land extended from Aroer on
the rim of the Arnon Gorge to Mount Sirion[a] (that is, Hermon), 49and
included all the Arabah east of the Jordan, as far as the Dead Sea,[b] be-
low the slopes of Pisgah.

THE TEN COMMANDMENTS

5 Moses summoned all Israel and said:
Hear, Israel, the decrees and laws I declare in your hearing today.
Learn them and be sure to follow them. 2The LORD our God made a cov-
enant with us at Horeb. 3It was not with our ancestors[c] that the LORD
made this covenant, but with us, with all of us who are alive here today.
4The LORD spoke to you face to face out of the fire on the mountain.
5(At that time I stood between the LORD and you to declare to you the
word of the LORD, because you were afraid of the fire and did not go up
the mountain.) And he said:

6"I am the LORD your God, who brought you out of Egypt, out
of the land of slavery.
7"You shall have no other gods before[d] me.
8"You shall not make for yourself an image in the form of anything
in heaven above or on the earth beneath or in the waters be-
low. 9You shall not bow down to them or worship them; for I,
the LORD your God, am a jealous God, punishing the children
for the sin of the parents to the third and fourth generation
of those who hate me, 10but showing love to a thousand gen-
erations of those who love me and keep my commandments.
11"You shall not misuse the name of the LORD your God, for the LORD
will not hold anyone guiltless who misuses his name.
12"Observe the Sabbath day by keeping it holy, as the LORD your God
has commanded you. 13Six days you shall labor and do all your
work, 14but the seventh day is a sabbath to the LORD your God.
On it you shall not do any work, neither you, nor your son or
daughter, nor your male or female servant, nor your ox, your
donkey or any of your animals, nor any foreigner residing in
your towns, so that your male and female servants may rest,
as you do. 15Remember that you were slaves in Egypt and that
the LORD your God brought you out of there with a mighty
hand and an outstretched arm. Therefore the LORD your God
has commanded you to observe the Sabbath day.
16"Honor your father and your mother, as the LORD your God has
commanded you, so that you may live long and that it may
go well with you in the land the LORD your God is giving you.
17"You shall not murder.
18"You shall not commit adultery.
19"You shall not steal.
20"You shall not give false testimony against your neighbor.
21"You shall not covet your neighbor's wife. You shall not set your
desire on your neighbor's house or land, his male or female
servant, his ox or donkey, or anything that belongs to your
neighbor."

---

[a] 48 Syriac (see also 3:9); Hebrew *Siyon* [b] 49 Hebrew *the Sea of the Arabah*
[c] 3 Or *not only with our parents* [d] 7 Or *besides*

PRAYING SCRIPTURE

Deuteronomy 5

Moses' review of the Ten Commandments had a purpose: that the people would "be sure to follow them" (verse 1). Obedience does not happen unless we are observing God's statutes; people don't stumble into following God's commands.

What would happen if God's people were careful to observe God's will? If we were more careful than when purchasing a car or deciding on a college? Ask God for that kind of intention to do his will.

22These are the commandments the LORD proclaimed in a loud voice to your whole assembly there on the mountain from out of the fire, the cloud and the deep darkness; and he added nothing more. Then he wrote them on two stone tablets and gave them to me.

23When you heard the voice out of the darkness, while the mountain was ablaze with fire, all the leaders of your tribes and your elders came to me. 24And you said, "The LORD our God has shown us his glory and his majesty, and we have heard his voice from the fire. Today we have seen that a person can live even if God speaks with them. 25But now, why should we die? This great fire will consume us, and we will die if we hear the voice of the LORD our God any longer. 26For what mortal has ever heard the voice of the living God speaking out of fire, as we have, and survived? 27Go near and listen to all that the LORD our God says. Then tell us whatever the LORD our God tells you. We will listen and obey."

28The LORD heard you when you spoke to me, and the LORD said to me, "I have heard what this people said to you. Everything they said was good. 29Oh, that their hearts would be inclined to fear me and keep all my commands always, so that it might go well with them and their children forever!

30"Go, tell them to return to their tents. 31But you stay here with me so that I may give you all the commands, decrees and laws you are to teach them to follow in the land I am giving them to possess."

32So be careful to do what the LORD your God has commanded you; do not turn aside to the right or to the left. 33Walk in obedience to all that the LORD your God has commanded you, so that you may live and prosper and prolong your days in the land that you will possess.

LOVE THE LORD YOUR GOD

6 These are the commands, decrees and laws the LORD your God directed me to teach you to observe in the land that you are crossing the Jordan to possess, 2so that you, your children and their children after them may fear the LORD your God as long as you live by keeping all his decrees and commands that I give you, and so that you may enjoy long life. 3Hear, Israel, and be careful to obey so that it may go well with you and that you may increase greatly in a land flowing with milk and honey, just as the LORD, the God of your ancestors, promised you.

4Hear, O Israel: The LORD our God, the LORD is one.[a] 5Love the LORD your God with all your heart and with all your soul and with all your strength. 6These commandments that I give you today are to be on your hearts. 7Impress them on your children. Talk about them when you sit at home and when you walk along the road, when you lie down and when you get up. 8Tie them as symbols on your hands and bind them on your foreheads. 9Write them on the doorframes of your houses and on your gates.

10When the LORD your God brings you into the land he swore to your fathers, to Abraham, Isaac and Jacob, to give you — a land with large, flourishing cities you did not build, 11houses filled with all kinds of good things you did not provide, wells you did not dig, and vineyards and olive groves you did not plant — then when you eat and are satisfied, 12be careful that you do not forget the LORD, who brought you out of Egypt, out of the land of slavery.

PRAYING SCRIPTURE

Deuteronomy 6

In this passage is the well-known *shema*, the section Jesus drew on when he was asked about the greatest commandment in the law: to love the Lord with all our heart, soul and strength, and to love our neighbor as we love ourselves.

How can you love God more? Ask him.

---

[a] 4 Or *The LORD our God is one LORD*; or *The LORD is our God, the LORD is one*; or *The LORD is our God, the LORD alone*

[13]Fear the LORD your God, serve him only and take your oaths in his
name. [14]Do not follow other gods, the gods of the peoples around you;
[15]for the LORD your God, who is among you, is a jealous God and his an-
ger will burn against you, and he will destroy you from the face of the
land. [16]Do not put the LORD your God to the test as you did at Massah.
[17]Be sure to keep the commands of the LORD your God and the stipula-
tions and decrees he has given you. [18]Do what is right and good in the
LORD's sight, so that it may go well with you and you may go in and
take over the good land the LORD promised on oath to your ancestors,
[19]thrusting out all your enemies before you, as the LORD said.

[20]In the future, when your son asks you, "What is the meaning of the
stipulations, decrees and laws the LORD our God has commanded you?"
[21]tell him: "We were slaves of Pharaoh in Egypt, but the LORD brought
us out of Egypt with a mighty hand. [22]Before our eyes the LORD sent
signs and wonders — great and terrible — on Egypt and Pharaoh and
his whole household. [23]But he brought us out from there to bring us in
and give us the land he promised on oath to our ancestors. [24]The LORD
commanded us to obey all these decrees and to fear the LORD our God,
so that we might always prosper and be kept alive, as is the case today.
[25]And if we are careful to obey all this law before the LORD our God, as
he has commanded us, that will be our righteousness."

DRIVING OUT THE NATIONS

7 When the LORD your God brings you into the land you are en-
tering to possess and drives out before you many nations — the
Hittites, Girgashites, Amorites, Canaanites, Perizzites, Hivites and Jeb-
usites, seven nations larger and stronger than you — [2]and when the
LORD your God has delivered them over to you and you have defeated
them, then you must destroy them totally.[a] Make no treaty with them,
and show them no mercy. [3]Do not intermarry with them. Do not give
your daughters to their sons or take their daughters for your sons, [4]for
they will turn your children away from following me to serve other
gods, and the LORD's anger will burn against you and will quickly de-
stroy you. [5]This is what you are to do to them: Break down their altars,
smash their sacred stones, cut down their Asherah poles[b] and burn
their idols in the fire. [6]For you are a people holy to the LORD your God.
The LORD your God has chosen you out of all the peoples on the face of
the earth to be his people, his treasured possession.

[7]The LORD did not set his affection on you and choose you because
you were more numerous than other peoples, for you were the fewest
of all peoples. [8]But it was because the LORD loved you and kept the
oath he swore to your ancestors that he brought you out with a mighty
hand and redeemed you from the land of slavery, from the power of
Pharaoh king of Egypt. [9]Know therefore that the LORD your God is God;
he is the faithful God, keeping his covenant of love to a thousand gen-
erations of those who love him and keep his commandments. [10]But

> those who hate him he will repay to their face by destruction;
>
> he will not be slow to repay to their face those who hate him.

[11]Therefore, take care to follow the commands, decrees and laws I give
you today.

---

[a] *2* The Hebrew term refers to the irrevocable giving over of things or persons to the LORD, often by totally destroying them; also in verse 26. [b] *5* That is, wooden symbols of the goddess Asherah; here and elsewhere in Deuteronomy

PRAYING SCRIPTURE

Deuteronomy 7

Israel was not a special nation because of anything she had done but because the Lord had chosen to set his love upon her. This is the definition of grace: getting something we do not deserve. Grace cannot be earned; it is always freely given.

Thank God for his grace, demonstrated in sending Jesus to die for the sins of the world. Rejoice that his grace is all you need.

12If you pay attention to these laws and are careful to follow them,
then the LORD your God will keep his covenant of love with you, as he
swore to your ancestors. 13He will love you and bless you and increase
your numbers. He will bless the fruit of your womb, the crops of your
land — your grain, new wine and olive oil — the calves of your herds
and the lambs of your flocks in the land he swore to your ancestors to
give you. 14You will be blessed more than any other people; none of
your men or women will be childless, nor will any of your livestock be
without young. 15The LORD will keep you free from every disease. He
will not inflict on you the horrible diseases you knew in Egypt, but he
will inflict them on all who hate you. 16You must destroy all the peo-
ples the LORD your God gives over to you. Do not look on them with
pity and do not serve their gods, for that will be a snare to you.

17You may say to yourselves, "These nations are stronger than we
are. How can we drive them out?" 18But do not be afraid of them; re-
member well what the LORD your God did to Pharaoh and to all Egypt.
19You saw with your own eyes the great trials, the signs and wonders,
the mighty hand and outstretched arm, with which the LORD your God
brought you out. The LORD your God will do the same to all the peo-
ples you now fear. 20Moreover, the LORD your God will send the hornet
among them until even the survivors who hide from you have per-
ished. 21Do not be terrified by them, for the LORD your God, who is
among you, is a great and awesome God. 22The LORD your God will
drive out those nations before you, little by little. You will not be al-
lowed to eliminate them all at once, or the wild animals will multiply
around you. 23But the LORD your God will deliver them over to you,
throwing them into great confusion until they are destroyed. 24He will
give their kings into your hand, and you will wipe out their names
from under heaven. No one will be able to stand up against you; you
will destroy them. 25The images of their gods you are to burn in the
fire. Do not covet the silver and gold on them, and do not take it for
yourselves, or you will be ensnared by it, for it is detestable to the LORD
your God. 26Do not bring a detestable thing into your house or you, like
it, will be set apart for destruction. Regard it as vile and utterly detest
it, for it is set apart for destruction.

DO NOT FORGET THE LORD

8 Be careful to follow every command I am giving you today, so that
you may live and increase and may enter and possess the land the
LORD promised on oath to your ancestors. 2Remember how the LORD
your God led you all the way in the wilderness these forty years, to
humble and test you in order to know what was in your heart, whether
or not you would keep his commands. 3He humbled you, causing you
to hunger and then feeding you with manna, which neither you nor
your ancestors had known, to teach you that man does not live on
bread alone but on every word that comes from the mouth of the LORD.
4Your clothes did not wear out and your feet did not swell during these
forty years. 5Know then in your heart that as a man disciplines his son,
so the LORD your God disciplines you.

6Observe the commands of the LORD your God, walking in obedience
to him and revering him. 7For the LORD your God is bringing you into
a good land — a land with brooks, streams, and deep springs gushing
out into the valleys and hills; 8a land with wheat and barley, vines and
fig trees, pomegranates, olive oil and honey; 9a land where bread will

PRAYING SCRIPTURE

Deuteronomy 8

Moses implored the Israelites to remember God when they entered the land of promise lest they be chastened by him. He reminded them that God was bringing them into a good land filled with good things, and that they should bless the Lord because of it.

When tempted to forget God in spite of all the good he's done, remember that he chastens those he loves. Spend some time thanking God for his goodness.

not be scarce and you will lack nothing; a land where the rocks are iron
and you can dig copper out of the hills.
10 When you have eaten and are satisfied, praise the LORD your God
for the good land he has given you. 11 Be careful that you do not forget
the LORD your God, failing to observe his commands, his laws and his
decrees that I am giving you this day. 12 Otherwise, when you eat and
are satisfied, when you build fine houses and settle down, 13 and when
your herds and flocks grow large and your silver and gold increase and
all you have is multiplied, 14 then your heart will become proud and you
will forget the LORD your God, who brought you out of Egypt, out of the
land of slavery. 15 He led you through the vast and dreadful wilderness,
that thirsty and waterless land, with its venomous snakes and scorpi-
ons. He brought you water out of hard rock. 16 He gave you manna to
eat in the wilderness, something your ancestors had never known, to
humble and test you so that in the end it might go well with you. 17 You
may say to yourself, "My power and the strength of my hands have
produced this wealth for me." 18 But remember the LORD your God, for
it is he who gives you the ability to produce wealth, and so confirms his
covenant, which he swore to your ancestors, as it is today.
19 If you ever forget the LORD your God and follow other gods and
worship and bow down to them, I testify against you today that you
will surely be destroyed. 20 Like the nations the LORD destroyed before
you, so you will be destroyed for not obeying the LORD your God.

NOT BECAUSE OF ISRAEL'S RIGHTEOUSNESS

9 Hear, Israel: You are now about to cross the Jordan to go in and
dispossess nations greater and stronger than you, with large cities
that have walls up to the sky. 2 The people are strong and tall — Ana-
kites! You know about them and have heard it said: "Who can stand
up against the Anakites?" 3 But be assured today that the LORD your
God is the one who goes across ahead of you like a devouring fire. He
will destroy them; he will subdue them before you. And you will drive
them out and annihilate them quickly, as the LORD has promised you.
4 After the LORD your God has driven them out before you, do not say
to yourself, "The LORD has brought me here to take possession of this
land because of my righteousness." No, it is on account of the wicked-
ness of these nations that the LORD is going to drive them out before
you. 5 It is not because of your righteousness or your integrity that you
are going in to take possession of their land; but on account of the
wickedness of these nations, the LORD your God will drive them out
before you, to accomplish what he swore to your fathers, to Abraham,
Isaac and Jacob. 6 Understand, then, that it is not because of your righ-
teousness that the LORD your God is giving you this good land to pos-
sess, for you are a stiff-necked people.

THE GOLDEN CALF

7 Remember this and never forget how you aroused the anger of the
LORD your God in the wilderness. From the day you left Egypt until you
arrived here, you have been rebellious against the LORD. 8 At Horeb
you aroused the LORD's wrath so that he was angry enough to destroy
you. 9 When I went up on the mountain to receive the tablets of stone,
the tablets of the covenant that the LORD had made with you, I stayed
on the mountain forty days and forty nights; I ate no bread and drank
no water. 10 The LORD gave me two stone tablets inscribed by the finger

PRAYING SCRIPTURE

Deuteronomy 9

Many times on the journey to the promised land the Israelites provoked God's wrath. God warned the people strongly against thinking their victories in Canaan were due to their inherent righteousness. God was judging the wickedness of the inhabitants; Israel was his instrument.

Sometimes when God uses us, we are tempted to feel pride. Express thanks to God that he chooses to use you in spite of your shortcomings.

of God. On them were all the commandments the LORD proclaimed to
you on the mountain out of the fire, on the day of the assembly.
11 At the end of the forty days and forty nights, the LORD gave me the
two stone tablets, the tablets of the covenant. 12 Then the LORD told me,
"Go down from here at once, because your people whom you brought
out of Egypt have become corrupt. They have turned away quickly
from what I commanded them and have made an idol for themselves."
13 And the LORD said to me, "I have seen this people, and they are a
stiff-necked people indeed! 14 Let me alone, so that I may destroy them
and blot out their name from under heaven. And I will make you into
a nation stronger and more numerous than they."
15 So I turned and went down from the mountain while it was ablaze
with fire. And the two tablets of the covenant were in my hands.
16 When I looked, I saw that you had sinned against the LORD your God;
you had made for yourselves an idol cast in the shape of a calf. You had
turned aside quickly from the way that the LORD had commanded you.
17 So I took the two tablets and threw them out of my hands, breaking
them to pieces before your eyes.
18 Then once again I fell prostrate before the LORD for forty days and
forty nights; I ate no bread and drank no water, because of all the sin
you had committed, doing what was evil in the LORD's sight and so
arousing his anger. 19 I feared the anger and wrath of the LORD, for he
was angry enough with you to destroy you. But again the LORD listened
to me. 20 And the LORD was angry enough with Aaron to destroy him,
but at that time I prayed for Aaron too. 21 Also I took that sinful thing of
yours, the calf you had made, and burned it in the fire. Then I crushed
it and ground it to powder as fine as dust and threw the dust into a
stream that flowed down the mountain.
22 You also made the LORD angry at Taberah, at Massah and at Kib-
roth Hattaavah.
23 And when the LORD sent you out from Kadesh Barnea, he said, "Go
up and take possession of the land I have given you." But you rebelled
against the command of the LORD your God. You did not trust him or
obey him. 24 You have been rebellious against the LORD ever since I
have known you.
25 I lay prostrate before the LORD those forty days and forty nights be-
cause the LORD had said he would destroy you. 26 I prayed to the LORD
and said, "Sovereign LORD, do not destroy your people, your own inheri-
tance that you redeemed by your great power and brought out of Egypt
with a mighty hand. 27 Remember your servants Abraham, Isaac and
Jacob. Overlook the stubbornness of this people, their wickedness and
their sin. 28 Otherwise, the country from which you brought us will say,
'Because the LORD was not able to take them into the land he had prom-
ised them, and because he hated them, he brought them out to put them
to death in the wilderness.' 29 But they are your people, your inheritance
that you brought out by your great power and your outstretched arm."

TABLETS LIKE THE FIRST ONES

10 At that time the LORD said to me, "Chisel out two stone tablets
like the first ones and come up to me on the mountain. Also
make a wooden ark.[a] 2 I will write on the tablets the words that were on
the first tablets, which you broke. Then you are to put them in the ark."

[a] 1 That is, a chest

PRAYING SCRIPTURE

Deuteronomy 10

The second part of this chapter gives the heartbeat of the law: Fear the Lord, keep his commands, recognize God's mercy, power and justice. This heartbeat should be in Israel's breast. God was to be her praise. Not simply "praise him," but he was her praise in totality.

What are some of the things that compete for your praise? Pray that you will see God as your utmost praise.

3So I made the ark out of acacia wood and chiseled out two stone
tablets like the first ones, and I went up on the mountain with the two
tablets in my hands. 4The LORD wrote on these tablets what he had
written before, the Ten Commandments he had proclaimed to you on
the mountain, out of the fire, on the day of the assembly. And the LORD
gave them to me. 5Then I came back down the mountain and put the
tablets in the ark I had made, as the LORD commanded me, and they
are there now.

6(The Israelites traveled from the wells of Bene Jaakan to Moserah.
There Aaron died and was buried, and Eleazar his son succeeded him
as priest. 7From there they traveled to Gudgodah and on to Jotbathah,
a land with streams of water. 8At that time the LORD set apart the tribe
of Levi to carry the ark of the covenant of the LORD, to stand before the
LORD to minister and to pronounce blessings in his name, as they still
do today. 9That is why the Levites have no share or inheritance among
their fellow Israelites; the LORD is their inheritance, as the LORD your
God told them.)

10Now I had stayed on the mountain forty days and forty nights, as
I did the first time, and the LORD listened to me at this time also. It
was not his will to destroy you. 11“Go,” the LORD said to me, “and lead
the people on their way, so that they may enter and possess the land I
swore to their ancestors to give them.”

FEAR THE LORD

12And now, Israel, what does the LORD your God ask of you but to fear
the LORD your God, to walk in obedience to him, to love him, to serve
the LORD your God with all your heart and with all your soul, 13and to
observe the LORD’s commands and decrees that I am giving you today
for your own good?

14To the LORD your God belong the heavens, even the highest heav-
ens, the earth and everything in it. 15Yet the LORD set his affection
on your ancestors and loved them, and he chose you, their descen-
dants, above all the nations—as it is today. 16Circumcise your hearts,
therefore, and do not be stiff-necked any longer. 17For the LORD your
God is God of gods and Lord of lords, the great God, mighty and awe-
some, who shows no partiality and accepts no bribes. 18He defends the
cause of the fatherless and the widow, and loves the foreigner resid-
ing among you, giving them food and clothing. 19And you are to love
those who are foreigners, for you yourselves were foreigners in Egypt.
20Fear the LORD your God and serve him. Hold fast to him and take
your oaths in his name. 21He is the one you praise; he is your God, who
performed for you those great and awesome wonders you saw with
your own eyes. 22Your ancestors who went down into Egypt were sev-
enty in all, and now the LORD your God has made you as numerous as
the stars in the sky.

LOVE AND OBEY THE LORD

11 Love the LORD your God and keep his requirements, his decrees,
his laws and his commands always. 2Remember today that your
children were not the ones who saw and experienced the discipline of
the LORD your God: his majesty, his mighty hand, his outstretched arm;
3the signs he performed and the things he did in the heart of Egypt,
both to Pharaoh king of Egypt and to his whole country; 4what he did
to the Egyptian army, to its horses and chariots, how he overwhelmed

PRAYING SCRIPTURE

Deuteronomy 11

After 40 years of wandering in the wilderness, the children of Israel were finally ready to enter Canaan. The many warnings and promises God gave them as they stood at the gate to the promised land are summarized in verse 1: Love the Lord and keep all his words.

Love the Lord and obey him: Israel would struggle with that for generations. Pray that you will love and obey the Lord every day of your life.

them with the waters of the Red Sea[a] as they were pursuing you, and
how the LORD brought lasting ruin on them. 5It was not your children
who saw what he did for you in the wilderness until you arrived at
this place, 6and what he did to Dathan and Abiram, sons of Eliab the
Reubenite, when the earth opened its mouth right in the middle of all
Israel and swallowed them up with their households, their tents and
every living thing that belonged to them. 7But it was your own eyes
that saw all these great things the LORD has done.

8Observe therefore all the commands I am giving you today, so that
you may have the strength to go in and take over the land that you
are crossing the Jordan to possess, 9and so that you may live long in
the land the LORD swore to your ancestors to give to them and their
descendants, a land flowing with milk and honey. 10The land you are
entering to take over is not like the land of Egypt, from which you
have come, where you planted your seed and irrigated it by foot as
in a vegetable garden. 11But the land you are crossing the Jordan to
take possession of is a land of mountains and valleys that drinks rain
from heaven. 12It is a land the LORD your God cares for; the eyes of the
LORD your God are continually on it from the beginning of the year to
its end.

13So if you faithfully obey the commands I am giving you today — to
love the LORD your God and to serve him with all your heart and with
all your soul — 14then I will send rain on your land in its season, both
autumn and spring rains, so that you may gather in your grain, new
wine and olive oil. 15I will provide grass in the fields for your cattle, and
you will eat and be satisfied.

16Be careful, or you will be enticed to turn away and worship other
gods and bow down to them. 17Then the LORD's anger will burn against
you, and he will shut up the heavens so that it will not rain and the
ground will yield no produce, and you will soon perish from the good
land the LORD is giving you. 18Fix these words of mine in your hearts
and minds; tie them as symbols on your hands and bind them on your
foreheads. 19Teach them to your children, talking about them when
you sit at home and when you walk along the road, when you lie down
and when you get up. 20Write them on the doorframes of your houses
and on your gates, 21so that your days and the days of your children
may be many in the land the LORD swore to give your ancestors, as
many as the days that the heavens are above the earth.

22If you carefully observe all these commands I am giving you to
follow — to love the LORD your God, to walk in obedience to him and
to hold fast to him — 23then the LORD will drive out all these nations
before you, and you will dispossess nations larger and stronger than
you. 24Every place where you set your foot will be yours: Your territory
will extend from the desert to Lebanon, and from the Euphrates River
to the Mediterranean Sea. 25No one will be able to stand against you.
The LORD your God, as he promised you, will put the terror and fear of
you on the whole land, wherever you go.

26See, I am setting before you today a blessing and a curse — 27the
blessing if you obey the commands of the LORD your God that I am
giving you today; 28the curse if you disobey the commands of the LORD
your God and turn from the way that I command you today by fol-
lowing other gods, which you have not known. 29When the LORD your

[a] 4 Or *the Sea of Reeds*

God has brought you into the land you are entering to possess, you are
to proclaim on Mount Gerizim the blessings, and on Mount Ebal the
curses. 30As you know, these mountains are across the Jordan, west-
ward, toward the setting sun, near the great trees of Moreh, in the ter-
ritory of those Canaanites living in the Arabah in the vicinity of Gilgal.
31You are about to cross the Jordan to enter and take possession of the
land the LORD your God is giving you. When you have taken it over and
are living there, 32be sure that you obey all the decrees and laws I am
setting before you today.

THE ONE PLACE OF WORSHIP

12 These are the decrees and laws you must be careful to follow
in the land that the LORD, the God of your ancestors, has given
you to possess—as long as you live in the land. 2Destroy completely
all the places on the high mountains, on the hills and under every
spreading tree, where the nations you are dispossessing worship their
gods. 3Break down their altars, smash their sacred stones and burn
their Asherah poles in the fire; cut down the idols of their gods and
wipe out their names from those places.
4You must not worship the LORD your God in their way. 5But you are
to seek the place the LORD your God will choose from among all your
tribes to put his Name there for his dwelling. To that place you must
go; 6there bring your burnt offerings and sacrifices, your tithes and
special gifts, what you have vowed to give and your freewill offerings,
and the firstborn of your herds and flocks. 7There, in the presence of
the LORD your God, you and your families shall eat and shall rejoice in
everything you have put your hand to, because the LORD your God has
blessed you.
8You are not to do as we do here today, everyone doing as they see
fit, 9since you have not yet reached the resting place and the inheri-
tance the LORD your God is giving you. 10But you will cross the Jordan
and settle in the land the LORD your God is giving you as an inher-
itance, and he will give you rest from all your enemies around you
so that you will live in safety. 11Then to the place the LORD your God
will choose as a dwelling for his Name—there you are to bring every-
thing I command you: your burnt offerings and sacrifices, your tithes
and special gifts, and all the choice possessions you have vowed to the
LORD. 12And there rejoice before the LORD your God—you, your sons
and daughters, your male and female servants, and the Levites from
your towns who have no allotment or inheritance of their own. 13Be
careful not to sacrifice your burnt offerings anywhere you please. 14Of-
fer them only at the place the LORD will choose in one of your tribes,
and there observe everything I command you.
15Nevertheless, you may slaughter your animals in any of your towns
and eat as much of the meat as you want, as if it were gazelle or deer,
according to the blessing the LORD your God gives you. Both the cere-
monially unclean and the clean may eat it. 16But you must not eat the
blood; pour it out on the ground like water. 17You must not eat in your
own towns the tithe of your grain and new wine and olive oil, or the
firstborn of your herds and flocks, or whatever you have vowed to give,
or your freewill offerings or special gifts. 18Instead, you are to eat them
in the presence of the LORD your God at the place the LORD your God
will choose—you, your sons and daughters, your male and female ser-
vants, and the Levites from your towns—and you are to rejoice before

PRAYING SCRIPTURE

Deuteronomy 12

The Lord made it clear that life would go well in the land as long as the people obeyed him and walked in his ways. God warned them not to import pagan worship into true worship. He wanted them to worship exactly as he instructed them.

Do you ever find yourself uninterested in worship? Seek God as he desires to be sought, and praise him as he desires to be praised.

the LORD your God in everything you put your hand to. [19]Be careful not
to neglect the Levites as long as you live in your land.
[20]When the LORD your God has enlarged your territory as he prom-
ised you, and you crave meat and say, "I would like some meat," then
you may eat as much of it as you want. [21]If the place where the LORD
your God chooses to put his Name is too far away from you, you may
slaughter animals from the herds and flocks the LORD has given you, as
I have commanded you, and in your own towns you may eat as much
of them as you want. [22]Eat them as you would gazelle or deer. Both the
ceremonially unclean and the clean may eat. [23]But be sure you do not
eat the blood, because the blood is the life, and you must not eat the
life with the meat. [24]You must not eat the blood; pour it out on the
ground like water. [25]Do not eat it, so that it may go well with you and
your children after you, because you will be doing what is right in the
eyes of the LORD.
[26]But take your consecrated things and whatever you have vowed
to give, and go to the place the LORD will choose. [27]Present your burnt
offerings on the altar of the LORD your God, both the meat and the
blood. The blood of your sacrifices must be poured beside the altar
of the LORD your God, but you may eat the meat. [28]Be careful to obey
all these regulations I am giving you, so that it may always go well
with you and your children after you, because you will be doing what
is good and right in the eyes of the LORD your God.
[29]The LORD your God will cut off before you the nations you are
about to invade and dispossess. But when you have driven them out
and settled in their land, [30]and after they have been destroyed before
you, be careful not to be ensnared by inquiring about their gods, say-
ing, "How do these nations serve their gods? We will do the same."
[31]You must not worship the LORD your God in their way, because in
worshiping their gods, they do all kinds of detestable things the LORD
hates. They even burn their sons and daughters in the fire as sacrifices
to their gods.
[32]See that you do all I command you; do not add to it or take away
from it.[a]

WORSHIPING OTHER GODS

13 [b] If a prophet, or one who foretells by dreams, appears among
you and announces to you a sign or wonder, [2]and if the sign
or wonder spoken of takes place, and the prophet says, "Let us follow
other gods" (gods you have not known) "and let us worship them,"
[3]you must not listen to the words of that prophet or dreamer. The LORD
your God is testing you to find out whether you love him with all your
heart and with all your soul. [4]It is the LORD your God you must follow,
and him you must revere. Keep his commands and obey him; serve
him and hold fast to him. [5]That prophet or dreamer must be put to
death for inciting rebellion against the LORD your God, who brought
you out of Egypt and redeemed you from the land of slavery. That
prophet or dreamer tried to turn you from the way the LORD your God
commanded you to follow. You must purge the evil from among you.
[6]If your very own brother, or your son or daughter, or the wife you
love, or your closest friend secretly entices you, saying, "Let us go and

PRAYING SCRIPTURE

Deuteronomy 13

God takes idol worship seriously. Under the law, the punishment for idol worship was death. False prophets, false dreamers and those who tried to deceive the people into worshiping false gods were all subject to death by stoning. But God desired to show compassion instead.

Thank God for the mercy he shows when our hearts are captured by idols. Then pray that you can live in complete devotion to him.

[a] *32* In Hebrew texts this verse (12:32) is numbered 13:1. [b] In Hebrew texts 13:1-18 is numbered 13:2-19.

worship other gods" (gods that neither you nor your ancestors have known, 7gods of the peoples around you, whether near or far, from one end of the land to the other), 8do not yield to them or listen to them. Show them no pity. Do not spare them or shield them. 9You must certainly put them to death. Your hand must be the first in putting them to death, and then the hands of all the people. 10Stone them to death, because they tried to turn you away from the LORD your God, who brought you out of Egypt, out of the land of slavery. 11Then all Israel will hear and be afraid, and no one among you will do such an evil thing again.

12If you hear it said about one of the towns the LORD your God is giving you to live in 13that troublemakers have arisen among you and have led the people of their town astray, saying, "Let us go and worship other gods" (gods you have not known), 14then you must inquire, probe and investigate it thoroughly. And if it is true and it has been proved that this detestable thing has been done among you, 15you must certainly put to the sword all who live in that town. You must destroy it completely,[a] both its people and its livestock. 16You are to gather all the plunder of the town into the middle of the public square and completely burn the town and all its plunder as a whole burnt offering to the LORD your God. That town is to remain a ruin forever, never to be rebuilt, 17and none of the condemned things[a] are to be found in your hands. Then the LORD will turn from his fierce anger, will show you mercy, and will have compassion on you. He will increase your numbers, as he promised on oath to your ancestors— 18because you obey the LORD your God by keeping all his commands that I am giving you today and doing what is right in his eyes.

CLEAN AND UNCLEAN FOOD

14 You are the children of the LORD your God. Do not cut yourselves or shave the front of your heads for the dead, 2for you are a people holy to the LORD your God. Out of all the peoples on the face of the earth, the LORD has chosen you to be his treasured possession.

3Do not eat any detestable thing. 4These are the animals you may eat: the ox, the sheep, the goat, 5the deer, the gazelle, the roe deer, the wild goat, the ibex, the antelope and the mountain sheep.[b] 6You may eat any animal that has a divided hoof and that chews the cud. 7However, of those that chew the cud or that have a divided hoof you may not eat the camel, the rabbit or the hyrax. Although they chew the cud, they do not have a divided hoof; they are ceremonially unclean for you. 8The pig is also unclean; although it has a divided hoof, it does not chew the cud. You are not to eat their meat or touch their carcasses.

9Of all the creatures living in the water, you may eat any that has fins and scales. 10But anything that does not have fins and scales you may not eat; for you it is unclean.

11You may eat any clean bird. 12But these you may not eat: the eagle, the vulture, the black vulture, 13the red kite, the black kite, any kind of falcon, 14any kind of raven, 15the horned owl, the screech owl, the gull, any kind of hawk, 16the little owl, the great owl, the white owl, 17the desert owl, the osprey, the cormorant, 18the stork, any kind of heron, the hoopoe and the bat.

PRAYING SCRIPTURE

Deuteronomy 14

God instructed the Israelites not to mourn like the unbelieving people in the nations around them. Mutilating themselves for the dead did not reveal God as holy. Connected to this instruction was the unique relationship between them and God. How they viewed death reflected how they viewed God.

How do you mourn? When believers die, we honor God as holy by believing that we will see them again in the resurrection.

[a] *15,17* The Hebrew term refers to the irrevocable giving over of things or persons to the LORD, often by totally destroying them. [b] *5* The precise identification of some of the birds and animals in this chapter is uncertain.

19All flying insects are unclean to you; do not eat them. 20But any
winged creature that is clean you may eat.
21Do not eat anything you find already dead. You may give it to the
foreigner residing in any of your towns, and they may eat it, or you
may sell it to any other foreigner. But you are a people holy to the
LORD your God.

Do not cook a young goat in its mother's milk.

TITHES

22Be sure to set aside a tenth of all that your fields produce each year.
23Eat the tithe of your grain, new wine and olive oil, and the firstborn
of your herds and flocks in the presence of the LORD your God at the
place he will choose as a dwelling for his Name, so that you may learn
to revere the LORD your God always. 24But if that place is too distant
and you have been blessed by the LORD your God and cannot carry your
tithe (because the place where the LORD will choose to put his Name is
so far away), 25then exchange your tithe for silver, and take the silver
with you and go to the place the LORD your God will choose. 26Use the
silver to buy whatever you like: cattle, sheep, wine or other fermented
drink, or anything you wish. Then you and your household shall eat
there in the presence of the LORD your God and rejoice. 27And do not
neglect the Levites living in your towns, for they have no allotment or
inheritance of their own.
28At the end of every three years, bring all the tithes of that year's
produce and store it in your towns, 29so that the Levites (who have no
allotment or inheritance of their own) and the foreigners, the father-
less and the widows who live in your towns may come and eat and be
satisfied, and so that the LORD your God may bless you in all the work
of your hands.

THE YEAR FOR CANCELING DEBTS

15 At the end of every seven years you must cancel debts. 2This is
how it is to be done: Every creditor shall cancel any loan they
have made to a fellow Israelite. They shall not require payment from
anyone among their own people, because the LORD's time for cancel-
ing debts has been proclaimed. 3You may require payment from a for-
eigner, but you must cancel any debt your fellow Israelite owes you.
4However, there need be no poor people among you, for in the land
the LORD your God is giving you to possess as your inheritance, he will
richly bless you, 5if only you fully obey the LORD your God and are care-
ful to follow all these commands I am giving you today. 6For the LORD
your God will bless you as he has promised, and you will lend to many
nations but will borrow from none. You will rule over many nations
but none will rule over you.
7If anyone is poor among your fellow Israelites in any of the towns
of the land the LORD your God is giving you, do not be hardhearted or
tightfisted toward them. 8Rather, be openhanded and freely lend them
whatever they need. 9Be careful not to harbor this wicked thought:
"The seventh year, the year for canceling debts, is near," so that you do
not show ill will toward the needy among your fellow Israelites and
give them nothing. They may then appeal to the LORD against you,
and you will be found guilty of sin. 10Give generously to them and do
so without a grudging heart; then because of this the LORD your God
will bless you in all your work and in everything you put your hand to.

PRAYING SCRIPTURE

Deuteronomy 15

To alleviate burdensome debt and ensure no long-lasting cycles of poverty, God commanded that all debts for fellow Israelites be canceled every seven years. Even further, to prevent generational poverty, God commanded that every 50 years all ancestral property be returned to the family who owned it, debts be canceled and indentured servants freed.

God wants his people to know freedom. Celebrate when you hear of God's people getting free from poverty and debt.

11There will always be poor people in the land. Therefore I command
you to be openhanded toward your fellow Israelites who are poor and
needy in your land.

FREEING SERVANTS

12If any of your people — Hebrew men or women — sell them-
selves to you and serve you six years, in the seventh year you must let
them go free. 13And when you release them, do not send them away
empty-handed. 14Supply them liberally from your flock, your thresh-
ing floor and your winepress. Give to them as the LORD your God has
blessed you. 15Remember that you were slaves in Egypt and the LORD
your God redeemed you. That is why I give you this command today.
16But if your servant says to you, "I do not want to leave you," be-
cause he loves you and your family and is well off with you, 17then
take an awl and push it through his earlobe into the door, and he will
become your servant for life. Do the same for your female servant.
18Do not consider it a hardship to set your servant free, because their
service to you these six years has been worth twice as much as that
of a hired hand. And the LORD your God will bless you in everything
you do.

THE FIRSTBORN ANIMALS

19Set apart for the LORD your God every firstborn male of your herds
and flocks. Do not put the firstborn of your cows to work, and do not
shear the firstborn of your sheep. 20Each year you and your family are
to eat them in the presence of the LORD your God at the place he will
choose. 21If an animal has a defect, is lame or blind, or has any serious
flaw, you must not sacrifice it to the LORD your God. 22You are to eat it
in your own towns. Both the ceremonially unclean and the clean may
eat it, as if it were gazelle or deer. 23But you must not eat the blood;
pour it out on the ground like water.

THE PASSOVER

16 Observe the month of Aviv and celebrate the Passover of the
LORD your God, because in the month of Aviv he brought you
out of Egypt by night. 2Sacrifice as the Passover to the LORD your God
an animal from your flock or herd at the place the LORD will choose
as a dwelling for his Name. 3Do not eat it with bread made with yeast,
but for seven days eat unleavened bread, the bread of affliction, be-
cause you left Egypt in haste — so that all the days of your life you
may remember the time of your departure from Egypt. 4Let no yeast
be found in your possession in all your land for seven days. Do not let
any of the meat you sacrifice on the evening of the first day remain
until morning.
5You must not sacrifice the Passover in any town the LORD your
God gives you 6except in the place he will choose as a dwelling for
his Name. There you must sacrifice the Passover in the evening, when
the sun goes down, on the anniversary[a] of your departure from Egypt.
7Roast it and eat it at the place the LORD your God will choose. Then in
the morning return to your tents. 8For six days eat unleavened bread
and on the seventh day hold an assembly to the LORD your God and
do no work.

PRAYING SCRIPTURE

Deuteronomy 16

In the land, the people would regularly feast to remember God's grace to them. These feasts, or festivals, were connected to God's desire for justice. In the Scripture, justice and righteousness are the same. To pervert justice was to defame God's righteousness and defile the land.

What are some ways you can pursue justice in your context? Seek God's righteousness that you might find what is altogether just.

[a] 6 Or *down, at the time of day*

THE FESTIVAL OF WEEKS

[9]Count off seven weeks from the time you begin to put the sickle
to the standing grain. [10]Then celebrate the Festival of Weeks to the
LORD your God by giving a freewill offering in proportion to the bless-
ings the LORD your God has given you. [11]And rejoice before the LORD
your God at the place he will choose as a dwelling for his Name — you,
your sons and daughters, your male and female servants, the Levites
in your towns, and the foreigners, the fatherless and the widows liv-
ing among you. [12]Remember that you were slaves in Egypt, and follow
carefully these decrees.

THE FESTIVAL OF TABERNACLES

[13]Celebrate the Festival of Tabernacles for seven days after you have
gathered the produce of your threshing floor and your winepress. [14]Be
joyful at your festival — you, your sons and daughters, your male and
female servants, and the Levites, the foreigners, the fatherless and the
widows who live in your towns. [15]For seven days celebrate the festival
to the LORD your God at the place the LORD will choose. For the LORD
your God will bless you in all your harvest and in all the work of your
hands, and your joy will be complete.

[16]Three times a year all your men must appear before the LORD your
God at the place he will choose: at the Festival of Unleavened Bread,
the Festival of Weeks and the Festival of Tabernacles. No one should
appear before the LORD empty-handed: [17]Each of you must bring a gift
in proportion to the way the LORD your God has blessed you.

JUDGES

[18]Appoint judges and officials for each of your tribes in every town
the LORD your God is giving you, and they shall judge the people fairly.
[19]Do not pervert justice or show partiality. Do not accept a bribe, for a
bribe blinds the eyes of the wise and twists the words of the innocent.
[20]Follow justice and justice alone, so that you may live and possess the
land the LORD your God is giving you.

WORSHIPING OTHER GODS

[21]Do not set up any wooden Asherah pole beside the altar you build
to the LORD your God, [22]and do not erect a sacred stone, for these the
LORD your God hates.

17 Do not sacrifice to the LORD your God an ox or a sheep that has
any defect or flaw in it, for that would be detestable to him.

[2]If a man or woman living among you in one of the towns the LORD
gives you is found doing evil in the eyes of the LORD your God in vio-
lation of his covenant, [3]and contrary to my command has worshiped
other gods, bowing down to them or to the sun or the moon or the
stars in the sky, [4]and this has been brought to your attention, then you
must investigate it thoroughly. If it is true and it has been proved that
this detestable thing has been done in Israel, [5]take the man or woman
who has done this evil deed to your city gate and stone that person to
death. [6]On the testimony of two or three witnesses a person is to be put
to death, but no one is to be put to death on the testimony of only one
witness. [7]The hands of the witnesses must be the first in putting that
person to death, and then the hands of all the people. You must purge
the evil from among you.

PRAYING SCRIPTURE

Deuteronomy 17

God acknowledged that Israel would eventually seek a king. Kings were to be men who loved God and obeyed his commandments. They were not to enrich themselves or to follow the ways of the nations by marrying multiple wives. They were to read God's law every day of their lives and seek to live by it.

God prioritizes his Word over all. Ask God that his priorities will always be yours.

LAW COURTS

8If cases come before your courts that are too difficult for you to
judge — whether bloodshed, lawsuits or assaults — take them to the
place the LORD your God will choose. 9Go to the Levitical priests and
to the judge who is in office at that time. Inquire of them and they
will give you the verdict. 10You must act according to the decisions
they give you at the place the LORD will choose. Be careful to do ev-
erything they instruct you to do. 11Act according to whatever they
teach you and the decisions they give you. Do not turn aside from
what they tell you, to the right or to the left. 12Anyone who shows
contempt for the judge or for the priest who stands ministering there
to the LORD your God is to be put to death. You must purge the evil
from Israel. 13All the people will hear and be afraid, and will not be
contemptuous again.

THE KING

14When you enter the land the LORD your God is giving you and have
taken possession of it and settled in it, and you say, "Let us set a king
over us like all the nations around us," 15be sure to appoint over you a
king the LORD your God chooses. He must be from among your fellow
Israelites. Do not place a foreigner over you, one who is not an Israel-
ite. 16The king, moreover, must not acquire great numbers of horses
for himself or make the people return to Egypt to get more of them,
for the LORD has told you, "You are not to go back that way again." 17He
must not take many wives, or his heart will be led astray. He must not
accumulate large amounts of silver and gold.

18When he takes the throne of his kingdom, he is to write for himself
on a scroll a copy of this law, taken from that of the Levitical priests.
19It is to be with him, and he is to read it all the days of his life so that
he may learn to revere the LORD his God and follow carefully all the
words of this law and these decrees 20and not consider himself better
than his fellow Israelites and turn from the law to the right or to the
left. Then he and his descendants will reign a long time over his king-
dom in Israel.

OFFERINGS FOR PRIESTS AND LEVITES

18 The Levitical priests — indeed, the whole tribe of Levi — are to
have no allotment or inheritance with Israel. They shall live on
the food offerings presented to the LORD, for that is their inheritance.
2They shall have no inheritance among their fellow Israelites; the LORD
is their inheritance, as he promised them.

3This is the share due the priests from the people who sacrifice a bull
or a sheep: the shoulder, the internal organs and the meat from the
head. 4You are to give them the firstfruits of your grain, new wine and
olive oil, and the first wool from the shearing of your sheep, 5for the
LORD your God has chosen them and their descendants out of all your
tribes to stand and minister in the LORD's name always.

6If a Levite moves from one of your towns anywhere in Israel where
he is living, and comes in all earnestness to the place the LORD will
choose, 7he may minister in the name of the LORD his God like all his
fellow Levites who serve there in the presence of the LORD. 8He is to
share equally in their benefits, even though he has received money
from the sale of family possessions.

PRAYING SCRIPTURE

Deuteronomy 18

In one of the most significant prophecies in the Old Testament, Moses looked forward to a prophet like himself. This prophet, whom the Lord would raise up, would speak his own words. This prophet is revealed in the Gospels as none other than Jesus Christ.

Think about how this prophecy was fulfilled more than a thousand years later. Praise God that he fulfills every prophecy he inspires.

OCCULT PRACTICES

9When you enter the land the LORD your God is giving you, do not learn to imitate the detestable ways of the nations there. 10Let no one be found among you who sacrifices their son or daughter in the fire, who practices divination or sorcery, interprets omens, engages in witchcraft, 11or casts spells, or who is a medium or spiritist or who consults the dead. 12Anyone who does these things is detestable to the LORD; because of these same detestable practices the LORD your God will drive out those nations before you. 13You must be blameless before the LORD your God.

THE PROPHET

14The nations you will dispossess listen to those who practice sorcery or divination. But as for you, the LORD your God has not permitted you to do so. 15The LORD your God will raise up for you a prophet like me from among you, from your fellow Israelites. You must listen to him. 16For this is what you asked of the LORD your God at Horeb on the day of the assembly when you said, "Let us not hear the voice of the LORD our God nor see this great fire anymore, or we will die."

17The LORD said to me: "What they say is good. 18I will raise up for them a prophet like you from among their fellow Israelites, and I will put my words in his mouth. He will tell them everything I command him. 19I myself will call to account anyone who does not listen to my words that the prophet speaks in my name. 20But a prophet who presumes to speak in my name anything I have not commanded, or a prophet who speaks in the name of other gods, is to be put to death."

21You may say to yourselves, "How can we know when a message has not been spoken by the LORD?" 22If what a prophet proclaims in the name of the LORD does not take place or come true, that is a message the LORD has not spoken. That prophet has spoken presumptuously, so do not be alarmed.

CITIES OF REFUGE

19 When the LORD your God has destroyed the nations whose land he is giving you, and when you have driven them out and settled in their towns and houses, 2then set aside for yourselves three cities in the land the LORD your God is giving you to possess. 3Determine the distances involved and divide into three parts the land the LORD your God is giving you as an inheritance, so that a person who kills someone may flee for refuge to one of these cities.

4This is the rule concerning anyone who kills a person and flees there for safety — anyone who kills a neighbor unintentionally, without malice aforethought. 5For instance, a man may go into the forest with his neighbor to cut wood, and as he swings his ax to fell a tree, the head may fly off and hit his neighbor and kill him. That man may flee to one of these cities and save his life. 6Otherwise, the avenger of blood might pursue him in a rage, overtake him if the distance is too great, and kill him even though he is not deserving of death, since he did it to his neighbor without malice aforethought. 7This is why I command you to set aside for yourselves three cities.

8If the LORD your God enlarges your territory, as he promised on oath to your ancestors, and gives you the whole land he promised them, 9because you carefully follow all these laws I command you today — to love the LORD your God and to walk always in obedience to

PRAYING SCRIPTURE

Deuteronomy 19

Legal procedures under the Law of Moses were intended to ensure fairness and justice. Witnesses in legal proceedings were to tell the truth, and judges were to make "thorough" inquiries to expose false witnesses (see verses 18–19). Why? So that evil would be removed from Israel.

Although we are often tempted to lie, lying is at odds with the character of God. Ask God to help you be truthful at all times.

him — then you are to set aside three more cities. 10Do this so that innocent blood will not be shed in your land, which the LORD your God is giving you as your inheritance, and so that you will not be guilty of bloodshed.

11But if out of hate someone lies in wait, assaults and kills a neighbor, and then flees to one of these cities, 12the killer shall be sent for by the town elders, be brought back from the city, and be handed over to the avenger of blood to die. 13Show no pity. You must purge from Israel the guilt of shedding innocent blood, so that it may go well with you.

14Do not move your neighbor's boundary stone set up by your predecessors in the inheritance you receive in the land the LORD your God is giving you to possess.

WITNESSES

15One witness is not enough to convict anyone accused of any crime or offense they may have committed. A matter must be established by the testimony of two or three witnesses.

16If a malicious witness takes the stand to accuse someone of a crime, 17the two people involved in the dispute must stand in the presence of the LORD before the priests and the judges who are in office at the time. 18The judges must make a thorough investigation, and if the witness proves to be a liar, giving false testimony against a fellow Israelite, 19then do to the false witness as that witness intended to do to the other party. You must purge the evil from among you. 20The rest of the people will hear of this and be afraid, and never again will such an evil thing be done among you. 21Show no pity: life for life, eye for eye, tooth for tooth, hand for hand, foot for foot.

GOING TO WAR

20 When you go to war against your enemies and see horses and chariots and an army greater than yours, do not be afraid of them, because the LORD your God, who brought you up out of Egypt, will be with you. 2When you are about to go into battle, the priest shall come forward and address the army. 3He shall say: "Hear, Israel: Today you are going into battle against your enemies. Do not be fainthearted or afraid; do not panic or be terrified by them. 4For the LORD your God is the one who goes with you to fight for you against your enemies to give you victory."

5The officers shall say to the army: "Has anyone built a new house and not yet begun to live in it? Let him go home, or he may die in battle and someone else may begin to live in it. 6Has anyone planted a vineyard and not begun to enjoy it? Let him go home, or he may die in battle and someone else enjoy it. 7Has anyone become pledged to a woman and not married her? Let him go home, or he may die in battle and someone else marry her." 8Then the officers shall add, "Is anyone afraid or fainthearted? Let him go home so that his fellow soldiers will not become disheartened too." 9When the officers have finished speaking to the army, they shall appoint commanders over it.

10When you march up to attack a city, make its people an offer of peace. 11If they accept and open their gates, all the people in it shall be subject to forced labor and shall work for you. 12If they refuse to make peace and they engage you in battle, lay siege to that city. 13When the LORD your God delivers it into your hand, put to the sword all the men in it. 14As for the women, the children, the livestock and everything

PRAYING SCRIPTURE

Deuteronomy 20

As the Israelites went into battle, they needed to remember that the Lord was with them. But they also had to remember they were not warring for war's sake. God did not want them to adopt the abominations of the pagan nations, which would prove an ongoing challenge for them.

We need not go to literal war to gain victory over sin, but spiritual warfare is inevitable. Ask God to give you victory.

else in the city, you may take these as plunder for yourselves. And you may use the plunder the LORD your God gives you from your enemies. 15This is how you are to treat all the cities that are at a distance from you and do not belong to the nations nearby.

16However, in the cities of the nations the LORD your God is giving you as an inheritance, do not leave alive anything that breathes. 17Completely destroy[a] them — the Hittites, Amorites, Canaanites, Perizzites, Hivites and Jebusites — as the LORD your God has commanded you. 18Otherwise, they will teach you to follow all the detestable things they do in worshiping their gods, and you will sin against the LORD your God.

19When you lay siege to a city for a long time, fighting against it to capture it, do not destroy its trees by putting an ax to them, because you can eat their fruit. Do not cut them down. Are the trees people, that you should besiege them?[b] 20However, you may cut down trees that you know are not fruit trees and use them to build siege works until the city at war with you falls.

ATONEMENT FOR AN UNSOLVED MURDER

21 If someone is found slain, lying in a field in the land the LORD your God is giving you to possess, and it is not known who the killer was, 2your elders and judges shall go out and measure the distance from the body to the neighboring towns. 3Then the elders of the town nearest the body shall take a heifer that has never been worked and has never worn a yoke 4and lead it down to a valley that has not been plowed or planted and where there is a flowing stream. There in the valley they are to break the heifer's neck. 5The Levitical priests shall step forward, for the LORD your God has chosen them to minister and to pronounce blessings in the name of the LORD and to decide all cases of dispute and assault. 6Then all the elders of the town nearest the body shall wash their hands over the heifer whose neck was broken in the valley, 7and they shall declare: "Our hands did not shed this blood, nor did our eyes see it done. 8Accept this atonement for your people Israel, whom you have redeemed, LORD, and do not hold your people guilty of the blood of an innocent person." Then the bloodshed will be atoned for, 9and you will have purged from yourselves the guilt of shedding innocent blood, since you have done what is right in the eyes of the LORD.

PRAYING SCRIPTURE

Deuteronomy 21

At the end of this section of the law, Moses included instructions about corpses from capital punishment. They should not leave the body on a pole overnight. Paul quoted this part of the chapter in Galatians 3:13 to show that Jesus died bearing our curse, being hanged on a pole.

Think about how Jesus' death was directly connected to the law. Thank God that Jesus fulfilled the law since we are totally unable to do so.

MARRYING A CAPTIVE WOMAN

10When you go to war against your enemies and the LORD your God delivers them into your hands and you take captives, 11if you notice among the captives a beautiful woman and are attracted to her, you may take her as your wife. 12Bring her into your home and have her shave her head, trim her nails 13and put aside the clothes she was wearing when captured. After she has lived in your house and mourned her father and mother for a full month, then you may go to her and be her husband and she shall be your wife. 14If you are not pleased with her, let her go wherever she wishes. You must not sell her or treat her as a slave, since you have dishonored her.

---

[a] 17 The Hebrew term refers to the irrevocable giving over of things or persons to the LORD, often by totally destroying them. [b] 19 Or *down to use in the siege, for the fruit trees are for the benefit of people.*

THE RIGHT OF THE FIRSTBORN

15If a man has two wives, and he loves one but not the other, and
both bear him sons but the firstborn is the son of the wife he does not
love, 16when he wills his property to his sons, he must not give the
rights of the firstborn to the son of the wife he loves in preference to
his actual firstborn, the son of the wife he does not love. 17He must ac-
knowledge the son of his unloved wife as the firstborn by giving him
a double share of all he has. That son is the first sign of his father's
strength. The right of the firstborn belongs to him.

A REBELLIOUS SON

18If someone has a stubborn and rebellious son who does not obey
his father and mother and will not listen to them when they discipline
him, 19his father and mother shall take hold of him and bring him to
the elders at the gate of his town. 20They shall say to the elders, "This
son of ours is stubborn and rebellious. He will not obey us. He is a glut-
ton and a drunkard." 21Then all the men of his town are to stone him
to death. You must purge the evil from among you. All Israel will hear
of it and be afraid.

VARIOUS LAWS

22If someone guilty of a capital offense is put to death and their body
is exposed on a pole, 23you must not leave the body hanging on the
pole overnight. Be sure to bury it that same day, because anyone who
is hung on a pole is under God's curse. You must not desecrate the land
the LORD your God is giving you as an inheritance.

22 If you see your fellow Israelite's ox or sheep straying, do not
ignore it but be sure to take it back to its owner. 2If they do not
live near you or if you do not know who owns it, take it home with you
and keep it until they come looking for it. Then give it back. 3Do the
same if you find their donkey or cloak or anything else they have lost.
Do not ignore it.

4If you see your fellow Israelite's donkey or ox fallen on the road, do
not ignore it. Help the owner get it to its feet.

5A woman must not wear men's clothing, nor a man wear women's
clothing, for the LORD your God detests anyone who does this.

6If you come across a bird's nest beside the road, either in a tree or
on the ground, and the mother is sitting on the young or on the eggs,
do not take the mother with the young. 7You may take the young, but
be sure to let the mother go, so that it may go well with you and you
may have a long life.

8When you build a new house, make a parapet around your roof so
that you may not bring the guilt of bloodshed on your house if some-
one falls from the roof.

9Do not plant two kinds of seed in your vineyard; if you do, not only
the crops you plant but also the fruit of the vineyard will be defiled.[a]

10Do not plow with an ox and a donkey yoked together.

11Do not wear clothes of wool and linen woven together.

12Make tassels on the four corners of the cloak you wear.

MARRIAGE VIOLATIONS

13If a man takes a wife and, after sleeping with her, dislikes her 14and
slanders her and gives her a bad name, saying, "I married this woman,

[a] 9 Or *be forfeited to the sanctuary*

PRAYING SCRIPTURE

Deuteronomy 22

It is impossible to miss, when reading the law, that sexual mores were important to God. God did not allow his people to take a do-whatever-you-feel-is-right approach to sexual relationships. Rapists were punished, as were adulterers. Purity was the goal.

Think about how far most modern cultures are from the Biblical standards of morality. Ask God to help you pursue holiness in spirit, soul and body.

but when I approached her, I did not find proof of her virginity," 15then
the young woman's father and mother shall bring to the town elders at
the gate proof that she was a virgin. 16Her father will say to the elders,
"I gave my daughter in marriage to this man, but he dislikes her. 17Now
he has slandered her and said, 'I did not find your daughter to be a vir-
gin.' But here is the proof of my daughter's virginity." Then her parents
shall display the cloth before the elders of the town, 18and the elders
shall take the man and punish him. 19They shall fine him a hundred
shekels[a] of silver and give them to the young woman's father, because
this man has given an Israelite virgin a bad name. She shall continue
to be his wife; he must not divorce her as long as he lives.

20If, however, the charge is true and no proof of the young woman's
virginity can be found, 21she shall be brought to the door of her father's
house and there the men of her town shall stone her to death. She has
done an outrageous thing in Israel by being promiscuous while still in
her father's house. You must purge the evil from among you.

22If a man is found sleeping with another man's wife, both the man
who slept with her and the woman must die. You must purge the evil
from Israel.

23If a man happens to meet in a town a virgin pledged to be married
and he sleeps with her, 24you shall take both of them to the gate of that
town and stone them to death — the young woman because she was in
a town and did not scream for help, and the man because he violated
another man's wife. You must purge the evil from among you.

25But if out in the country a man happens to meet a young woman
pledged to be married and rapes her, only the man who has done this
shall die. 26Do nothing to the woman; she has committed no sin de-
serving death. This case is like that of someone who attacks and mur-
ders a neighbor, 27for the man found the young woman out in the
country, and though the betrothed woman screamed, there was no
one to rescue her.

28If a man happens to meet a virgin who is not pledged to be mar-
ried and rapes her and they are discovered, 29he shall pay her father
fifty shekels[b] of silver. He must marry the young woman, for he has
violated her. He can never divorce her as long as he lives.

30A man is not to marry his father's wife; he must not dishonor his
father's bed.[c]

PRAYING SCRIPTURE

Deuteronomy 23

God is intimately concerned with his people's relationships. These laws reminded the children of Israel that their interpersonal dealings reflected their unique relationship with God. Food should be shared rather than hoarded, money loaned at no interest.

What are some ways your relationships with other believers differ from those with unbelievers? Do your relationships with believers exemplify sacrificial love? Ask God for relationships that reflect being in his family.

EXCLUSION FROM THE ASSEMBLY

23[d] No one who has been emasculated by crushing or cutting may
enter the assembly of the LORD.

2No one born of a forbidden marriage[e] nor any of their descendants
may enter the assembly of the LORD, not even in the tenth generation.
3No Ammonite or Moabite or any of their descendants may enter
the assembly of the LORD, not even in the tenth generation. 4For they
did not come to meet you with bread and water on your way when you
came out of Egypt, and they hired Balaam son of Beor from Pethor in
Aram Naharaim[f] to pronounce a curse on you. 5However, the LORD your
God would not listen to Balaam but turned the curse into a blessing

[a] *19* That is, about 2 1/2 pounds or about 1.2 kilograms [b] *29* That is, about 1 1/4 pounds or about 575 grams [c] *30* In Hebrew texts this verse (22:30) is numbered 23:1. [d] In Hebrew texts 23:1-25 is numbered 23:2-26. [e] *2* Or *one of illegitimate birth* [f] *4* That is, Northwest Mesopotamia

for you, because the LORD your God loves you. 6Do not seek a treaty of
friendship with them as long as you live.
7Do not despise an Edomite, for the Edomites are related to you. Do
not despise an Egyptian, because you resided as foreigners in their
country. 8The third generation of children born to them may enter the
assembly of the LORD.

UNCLEANNESS IN THE CAMP

9When you are encamped against your enemies, keep away from
everything impure. 10If one of your men is unclean because of a noc-
turnal emission, he is to go outside the camp and stay there. 11But as
evening approaches he is to wash himself, and at sunset he may return
to the camp.
12Designate a place outside the camp where you can go to relieve
yourself. 13As part of your equipment have something to dig with, and
when you relieve yourself, dig a hole and cover up your excrement.
14For the LORD your God moves about in your camp to protect you and
to deliver your enemies to you. Your camp must be holy, so that he will
not see among you anything indecent and turn away from you.

MISCELLANEOUS LAWS

15If a slave has taken refuge with you, do not hand them over to their
master. 16Let them live among you wherever they like and in whatever
town they choose. Do not oppress them.
17No Israelite man or woman is to become a shrine prostitute. 18You
must not bring the earnings of a female prostitute or of a male prosti-
tute[a] into the house of the LORD your God to pay any vow, because the
LORD your God detests them both.
19Do not charge a fellow Israelite interest, whether on money or food
or anything else that may earn interest. 20You may charge a foreigner
interest, but not a fellow Israelite, so that the LORD your God may bless
you in everything you put your hand to in the land you are entering
to possess.
21If you make a vow to the LORD your God, do not be slow to pay it,
for the LORD your God will certainly demand it of you and you will be
guilty of sin. 22But if you refrain from making a vow, you will not be
guilty. 23Whatever your lips utter you must be sure to do, because you
made your vow freely to the LORD your God with your own mouth.
24If you enter your neighbor's vineyard, you may eat all the grapes
you want, but do not put any in your basket. 25If you enter your neigh-
bor's grainfield, you may pick kernels with your hands, but you must
not put a sickle to their standing grain.

24 If a man marries a woman who becomes displeasing to him
because he finds something indecent about her, and he writes
her a certificate of divorce, gives it to her and sends her from his house,
2and if after she leaves his house she becomes the wife of another man,
3and her second husband dislikes her and writes her a certificate of di-
vorce, gives it to her and sends her from his house, or if he dies, 4then
her first husband, who divorced her, is not allowed to marry her again
after she has been defiled. That would be detestable in the eyes of the
LORD. Do not bring sin upon the land the LORD your God is giving you
as an inheritance.

[a] 18 Hebrew *of a dog*

PRAYING SCRIPTURE

Deuteronomy 24

The law in Israel called upon every one to look out for the widows, orphans and foreigners among them. To mistreat these people—those most likely to be taken advantage of—was unjust. God saw it as a perversion of his law. Having been slaves in Egypt should have led the Israelites to demonstrate justice in their society.

Do you show mercy to others because mercy has been shown to you? This is God's way.

5If a man has recently married, he must not be sent to war or have
any other duty laid on him. For one year he is to be free to stay at home
and bring happiness to the wife he has married.
6Do not take a pair of millstones — not even the upper one — as se-
curity for a debt, because that would be taking a person's livelihood
as security.
7If someone is caught kidnapping a fellow Israelite and treating or
selling them as a slave, the kidnapper must die. You must purge the
evil from among you.
8In cases of defiling skin diseases,[a] be very careful to do exactly as
the Levitical priests instruct you. You must follow carefully what I have
commanded them. 9Remember what the LORD your God did to Miriam
along the way after you came out of Egypt.
10When you make a loan of any kind to your neighbor, do not go
into their house to get what is offered to you as a pledge. 11Stay out-
side and let the neighbor to whom you are making the loan bring the
pledge out to you. 12If the neighbor is poor, do not go to sleep with
their pledge in your possession. 13Return their cloak by sunset so that
your neighbor may sleep in it. Then they will thank you, and it will be
regarded as a righteous act in the sight of the LORD your God.
14Do not take advantage of a hired worker who is poor and needy,
whether that worker is a fellow Israelite or a foreigner residing in one
of your towns. 15Pay them their wages each day before sunset, because
they are poor and are counting on it. Otherwise they may cry to the
LORD against you, and you will be guilty of sin.
16Parents are not to be put to death for their children, nor children
put to death for their parents; each will die for their own sin.
17Do not deprive the foreigner or the fatherless of justice, or take the
cloak of the widow as a pledge. 18Remember that you were slaves in
Egypt and the LORD your God redeemed you from there. That is why I
command you to do this.
19When you are harvesting in your field and you overlook a sheaf,
do not go back to get it. Leave it for the foreigner, the fatherless and
the widow, so that the LORD your God may bless you in all the work
of your hands. 20When you beat the olives from your trees, do not go
over the branches a second time. Leave what remains for the foreigner,
the fatherless and the widow. 21When you harvest the grapes in your
vineyard, do not go over the vines again. Leave what remains for the
foreigner, the fatherless and the widow. 22Remember that you were
slaves in Egypt. That is why I command you to do this.

25 When people have a dispute, they are to take it to court and
the judges will decide the case, acquitting the innocent and
condemning the guilty. 2If the guilty person deserves to be beaten, the
judge shall make them lie down and have them flogged in his presence
with the number of lashes the crime deserves, 3but the judge must not
impose more than forty lashes. If the guilty party is flogged more than
that, your fellow Israelite will be degraded in your eyes.
4Do not muzzle an ox while it is treading out the grain.
5If brothers are living together and one of them dies without a son,
his widow must not marry outside the family. Her husband's brother
shall take her and marry her and fulfill the duty of a brother-in-law

PRAYING SCRIPTURE

Deuteronomy 25

Israel's law ensured that the guilty were punished. In non-death penalty cases requiring physical punishment, no more than 40 lashes could be given. The guilty were to be punished for their crimes, but they were not to be humiliated as a result. Punishment was not to be a source of pride for the judges.

Pray God will give you a heart of compassion for people who have paid or are paying for their crimes.

---

[a] 8 The Hebrew word for *defiling skin diseases*, traditionally translated "leprosy," was used for various diseases affecting the skin.

to her. 6The first son she bears shall carry on the name of the dead brother so that his name will not be blotted out from Israel.

7However, if a man does not want to marry his brother's wife, she shall go to the elders at the town gate and say, "My husband's brother refuses to carry on his brother's name in Israel. He will not fulfill the duty of a brother-in-law to me." 8Then the elders of his town shall summon him and talk to him. If he persists in saying, "I do not want to marry her," 9his brother's widow shall go up to him in the presence of the elders, take off one of his sandals, spit in his face and say, "This is what is done to the man who will not build up his brother's family line." 10That man's line shall be known in Israel as The Family of the Unsandaled.

11If two men are fighting and the wife of one of them comes to rescue her husband from his assailant, and she reaches out and seizes him by his private parts, 12you shall cut off her hand. Show her no pity.

13Do not have two differing weights in your bag — one heavy, one light. 14Do not have two differing measures in your house — one large, one small. 15You must have accurate and honest weights and measures, so that you may live long in the land the LORD your God is giving you. 16For the LORD your God detests anyone who does these things, anyone who deals dishonestly.

17Remember what the Amalekites did to you along the way when you came out of Egypt. 18When you were weary and worn out, they met you on your journey and attacked all who were lagging behind; they had no fear of God. 19When the LORD your God gives you rest from all the enemies around you in the land he is giving you to possess as an inheritance, you shall blot out the name of Amalek from under heaven. Do not forget!

FIRSTFRUITS AND TITHES

26 When you have entered the land the LORD your God is giving you as an inheritance and have taken possession of it and settled in it, 2take some of the firstfruits of all that you produce from the soil of the land the LORD your God is giving you and put them in a basket. Then go to the place the LORD your God will choose as a dwelling for his Name 3and say to the priest in office at the time, "I declare today to the LORD your God that I have come to the land the LORD swore to our ancestors to give us." 4The priest shall take the basket from your hands and set it down in front of the altar of the LORD your God. 5Then you shall declare before the LORD your God: "My father was a wandering Aramean, and he went down into Egypt with a few people and lived there and became a great nation, powerful and numerous. 6But the Egyptians mistreated us and made us suffer, subjecting us to harsh labor. 7Then we cried out to the LORD, the God of our ancestors, and the LORD heard our voice and saw our misery, toil and oppression. 8So the LORD brought us out of Egypt with a mighty hand and an outstretched arm, with great terror and with signs and wonders. 9He brought us to this place and gave us this land, a land flowing with milk and honey; 10and now I bring the firstfruits of the soil that you, LORD, have given me." Place the basket before the LORD your God and bow down before him. 11Then you and the Levites and the foreigners residing among you shall rejoice in all the good things the LORD your God has given to you and your household.

12When you have finished setting aside a tenth of all your produce

PRAYING SCRIPTURE

Deuteronomy 26

Keeping God's commands demonstrates that we belong to him, that we are his people. How we live demonstrates whom we serve. In the New Testament it's called bearing fruit (see Galatians 5:22–23). The Israelites were expected to "listen to him," and then he would exalt them among the surrounding nations (see verses 17–19).

What kind of fruit are you bearing? Does it show a life connected to Jesus? Ask God to produce in you fruit that honors him.

in the third year, the year of the tithe, you shall give it to the Levite,
the foreigner, the fatherless and the widow, so that they may eat in
your towns and be satisfied. 13Then say to the LORD your God: "I have
removed from my house the sacred portion and have given it to the
Levite, the foreigner, the fatherless and the widow, according to all you
commanded. I have not turned aside from your commands nor have
I forgotten any of them. 14I have not eaten any of the sacred portion
while I was in mourning, nor have I removed any of it while I was un-
clean, nor have I offered any of it to the dead. I have obeyed the LORD
my God; I have done everything you commanded me. 15Look down
from heaven, your holy dwelling place, and bless your people Israel
and the land you have given us as you promised on oath to our ances-
tors, a land flowing with milk and honey."

FOLLOW THE LORD'S COMMANDS

16The LORD your God commands you this day to follow these de-
crees and laws; carefully observe them with all your heart and with all
your soul. 17You have declared this day that the LORD is your God and
that you will walk in obedience to him, that you will keep his decrees,
commands and laws — that you will listen to him. 18And the LORD has
declared this day that you are his people, his treasured possession as
he promised, and that you are to keep all his commands. 19He has de-
clared that he will set you in praise, fame and honor high above all the
nations he has made and that you will be a people holy to the LORD
your God, as he promised.

THE ALTAR ON MOUNT EBAL

27 Moses and the elders of Israel commanded the people: "Keep
all these commands that I give you today. 2When you have
crossed the Jordan into the land the LORD your God is giving you, set
up some large stones and coat them with plaster. 3Write on them all
the words of this law when you have crossed over to enter the land
the LORD your God is giving you, a land flowing with milk and honey,
just as the LORD, the God of your ancestors, promised you. 4And when
you have crossed the Jordan, set up these stones on Mount Ebal, as I
command you today, and coat them with plaster. 5Build there an altar
to the LORD your God, an altar of stones. Do not use any iron tool on
them. 6Build the altar of the LORD your God with fieldstones and offer
burnt offerings on it to the LORD your God. 7Sacrifice fellowship offer-
ings there, eating them and rejoicing in the presence of the LORD your
God. 8And you shall write very clearly all the words of this law on these
stones you have set up."

PRAYING SCRIPTURE

Deuteronomy 27

When the Israelites arrived in the land, they built an altar of stones as a reminder of God's promise to them. Writing the law on large, uncut stones provided a visual record of what God required of his people.

Do you use any visual cues to remind you of God's Word or to pray? Ask God for creative reminders that continually turn your mind and heart to him.

CURSES FROM MOUNT EBAL

9Then Moses and the Levitical priests said to all Israel, "Be silent,
Israel, and listen! You have now become the people of the LORD your
God. 10Obey the LORD your God and follow his commands and decrees
that I give you today."

11On the same day Moses commanded the people:

12When you have crossed the Jordan, these tribes shall stand on
Mount Gerizim to bless the people: Simeon, Levi, Judah, Issachar, Jo-
seph and Benjamin. 13And these tribes shall stand on Mount Ebal to
pronounce curses: Reuben, Gad, Asher, Zebulun, Dan and Naphtali.

14The Levites shall recite to all the people of Israel in a loud voice:

15"Cursed is anyone who makes an idol—a thing detestable to the LORD, the work of skilled hands—and sets it up in secret."

Then all the people shall say, "Amen!"

16"Cursed is anyone who dishonors their father or mother."

Then all the people shall say, "Amen!"

17"Cursed is anyone who moves their neighbor's boundary stone."

Then all the people shall say, "Amen!"

18"Cursed is anyone who leads the blind astray on the road."

Then all the people shall say, "Amen!"

19"Cursed is anyone who withholds justice from the foreigner, the fatherless or the widow."

Then all the people shall say, "Amen!"

20"Cursed is anyone who sleeps with his father's wife, for he dishonors his father's bed."

Then all the people shall say, "Amen!"

21"Cursed is anyone who has sexual relations with any animal."

Then all the people shall say, "Amen!"

22"Cursed is anyone who sleeps with his sister, the daughter of his father or the daughter of his mother."

Then all the people shall say, "Amen!"

23"Cursed is anyone who sleeps with his mother-in-law."

Then all the people shall say, "Amen!"

24"Cursed is anyone who kills their neighbor secretly."

Then all the people shall say, "Amen!"

25"Cursed is anyone who accepts a bribe to kill an innocent person."

Then all the people shall say, "Amen!"

26"Cursed is anyone who does not uphold the words of this law by carrying them out."

Then all the people shall say, "Amen!"

BLESSINGS FOR OBEDIENCE

28 If you fully obey the LORD your God and carefully follow all his
commands I give you today, the LORD your God will set you
high above all the nations on earth. 2All these blessings will come on
you and accompany you if you obey the LORD your God:

3You will be blessed in the city and blessed in the country.

4The fruit of your womb will be blessed, and the crops of your land and the young of your livestock—the calves of your herds and the lambs of your flocks.

5Your basket and your kneading trough will be blessed.

6You will be blessed when you come in and blessed when you go out.

7The LORD will grant that the enemies who rise up against you will be defeated before you. They will come at you from one direction but flee from you in seven.

8The LORD will send a blessing on your barns and on everything you put your hand to. The LORD your God will bless you in the land he is giving you.

9The LORD will establish you as his holy people, as he promised you
on oath, if you keep the commands of the LORD your God and walk in
obedience to him. 10Then all the peoples on earth will see that you are

PRAYING SCRIPTURE

Deuteronomy 28

The law was a system that instituted rewards and punishments. From Moses through the prophets, the Israelites were promised blessings when they obeyed and curses when they disobeyed. Many times when God pronounced judgment for disobedience, repentance was framed in the blessings God would bring if the people would simply obey him.

In Jesus, however, God's children have no curses. Praise God because of his Son and the unending blessings we have in Christ.

called by the name of the LORD, and they will fear you. 11The LORD will grant you abundant prosperity — in the fruit of your womb, the young of your livestock and the crops of your ground — in the land he swore to your ancestors to give you.

12The LORD will open the heavens, the storehouse of his bounty, to send rain on your land in season and to bless all the work of your hands. You will lend to many nations but will borrow from none. 13The LORD will make you the head, not the tail. If you pay attention to the commands of the LORD your God that I give you this day and carefully follow them, you will always be at the top, never at the bottom. 14Do not turn aside from any of the commands I give you today, to the right or to the left, following other gods and serving them.

CURSES FOR DISOBEDIENCE

15However, if you do not obey the LORD your God and do not carefully follow all his commands and decrees I am giving you today, all these curses will come on you and overtake you:

16You will be cursed in the city and cursed in the country.
17Your basket and your kneading trough will be cursed.
18The fruit of your womb will be cursed, and the crops of your land, and the calves of your herds and the lambs of your flocks.
19You will be cursed when you come in and cursed when you go out.

20The LORD will send on you curses, confusion and rebuke in everything you put your hand to, until you are destroyed and come to sudden ruin because of the evil you have done in forsaking him.[a] 21The LORD will plague you with diseases until he has destroyed you from the land you are entering to possess. 22The LORD will strike you with wasting disease, with fever and inflammation, with scorching heat and drought, with blight and mildew, which will plague you until you perish. 23The sky over your head will be bronze, the ground beneath you iron. 24The LORD will turn the rain of your country into dust and powder; it will come down from the skies until you are destroyed.

25The LORD will cause you to be defeated before your enemies. You will come at them from one direction but flee from them in seven, and you will become a thing of horror to all the kingdoms on earth. 26Your carcasses will be food for all the birds and the wild animals, and there will be no one to frighten them away. 27The LORD will afflict you with the boils of Egypt and with tumors, festering sores and the itch, from which you cannot be cured. 28The LORD will afflict you with madness, blindness and confusion of mind. 29At midday you will grope about like a blind person in the dark. You will be unsuccessful in everything you do; day after day you will be oppressed and robbed, with no one to rescue you.

30You will be pledged to be married to a woman, but another will take her and rape her. You will build a house, but you will not live in it. You will plant a vineyard, but you will not even begin to enjoy its fruit. 31Your ox will be slaughtered before your eyes, but you will eat none of it. Your donkey will be forcibly taken from you and will not be returned. Your sheep will be given to your enemies, and no one will rescue them. 32Your sons and daughters will be given to another

[a] *20* Hebrew *me*

nation, and you will wear out your eyes watching for them day after
day, powerless to lift a hand. 33 A people that you do not know will eat
what your land and labor produce, and you will have nothing but cruel
oppression all your days. 34 The sights you see will drive you mad. 35 The
LORD will afflict your knees and legs with painful boils that cannot be
cured, spreading from the soles of your feet to the top of your head.

36 The LORD will drive you and the king you set over you to a nation
unknown to you or your ancestors. There you will worship other gods,
gods of wood and stone. 37 You will become a thing of horror, a byword
and an object of ridicule among all the peoples where the LORD will
drive you.

38 You will sow much seed in the field but you will harvest little, be-
cause locusts will devour it. 39 You will plant vineyards and cultivate
them but you will not drink the wine or gather the grapes, because
worms will eat them. 40 You will have olive trees throughout your
country but you will not use the oil, because the olives will drop off.
41 You will have sons and daughters but you will not keep them, be-
cause they will go into captivity. 42 Swarms of locusts will take over all
your trees and the crops of your land.

43 The foreigners who reside among you will rise above you higher and
higher, but you will sink lower and lower. 44 They will lend to you, but
you will not lend to them. They will be the head, but you will be the tail.

45 All these curses will come on you. They will pursue you and over-
take you until you are destroyed, because you did not obey the LORD
your God and observe the commands and decrees he gave you. 46 They
will be a sign and a wonder to you and your descendants forever. 47 Be-
cause you did not serve the LORD your God joyfully and gladly in the
time of prosperity, 48 therefore in hunger and thirst, in nakedness and
dire poverty, you will serve the enemies the LORD sends against you.
He will put an iron yoke on your neck until he has destroyed you.

49 The LORD will bring a nation against you from far away, from the
ends of the earth, like an eagle swooping down, a nation whose lan-
guage you will not understand, 50 a fierce-looking nation without re-
spect for the old or pity for the young. 51 They will devour the young of
your livestock and the crops of your land until you are destroyed. They
will leave you no grain, new wine or olive oil, nor any calves of your
herds or lambs of your flocks until you are ruined. 52 They will lay siege
to all the cities throughout your land until the high fortified walls in
which you trust fall down. They will besiege all the cities throughout
the land the LORD your God is giving you.

53 Because of the suffering your enemy will inflict on you during
the siege, you will eat the fruit of the womb, the flesh of the sons and
daughters the LORD your God has given you. 54 Even the most gentle
and sensitive man among you will have no compassion on his own
brother or the wife he loves or his surviving children, 55 and he will not
give to one of them any of the flesh of his children that he is eating. It
will be all he has left because of the suffering your enemy will inflict on
you during the siege of all your cities. 56 The most gentle and sensitive
woman among you — so sensitive and gentle that she would not ven-
ture to touch the ground with the sole of her foot — will begrudge the
husband she loves and her own son or daughter 57 the afterbirth from
her womb and the children she bears. For in her dire need she intends
to eat them secretly because of the suffering your enemy will inflict on
you during the siege of your cities.

58If you do not carefully follow all the words of this law, which are written in this book, and do not revere this glorious and awesome name — the LORD your God — 59the LORD will send fearful plagues on you and your descendants, harsh and prolonged disasters, and severe and lingering illnesses. 60He will bring on you all the diseases of Egypt that you dreaded, and they will cling to you. 61The LORD will also bring on you every kind of sickness and disaster not recorded in this Book of the Law, until you are destroyed. 62You who were as numerous as the stars in the sky will be left but few in number, because you did not obey the LORD your God. 63Just as it pleased the LORD to make you prosper and increase in number, so it will please him to ruin and destroy you. You will be uprooted from the land you are entering to possess.

64Then the LORD will scatter you among all nations, from one end of the earth to the other. There you will worship other gods — gods of wood and stone, which neither you nor your ancestors have known. 65Among those nations you will find no repose, no resting place for the sole of your foot. There the LORD will give you an anxious mind, eyes weary with longing, and a despairing heart. 66You will live in constant suspense, filled with dread both night and day, never sure of your life. 67In the morning you will say, "If only it were evening!" and in the evening, "If only it were morning!" — because of the terror that will fill your hearts and the sights that your eyes will see. 68The LORD will send you back in ships to Egypt on a journey I said you should never make again. There you will offer yourselves for sale to your enemies as male and female slaves, but no one will buy you.

RENEWAL OF THE COVENANT

29 [a] These are the terms of the covenant the LORD commanded Moses to make with the Israelites in Moab, in addition to the covenant he had made with them at Horeb.

2Moses summoned all the Israelites and said to them:

Your eyes have seen all that the LORD did in Egypt to Pharaoh, to all his officials and to all his land. 3With your own eyes you saw those great trials, those signs and great wonders. 4But to this day the LORD has not given you a mind that understands or eyes that see or ears that hear. 5Yet the LORD says, "During the forty years that I led you through the wilderness, your clothes did not wear out, nor did the sandals on your feet. 6You ate no bread and drank no wine or other fermented drink. I did this so that you might know that I am the LORD your God."

7When you reached this place, Sihon king of Heshbon and Og king of Bashan came out to fight against us, but we defeated them. 8We took their land and gave it as an inheritance to the Reubenites, the Gadites and the half-tribe of Manasseh.

9Carefully follow the terms of this covenant, so that you may prosper in everything you do. 10All of you are standing today in the presence of the LORD your God — your leaders and chief men, your elders and officials, and all the other men of Israel, 11together with your children and your wives, and the foreigners living in your camps who chop your wood and carry your water. 12You are standing here in order to enter into a covenant with the LORD your God, a covenant the LORD is

PRAYING SCRIPTURE

Deuteronomy 29

Over and over Moses reviewed the things God had done for the people of Israel to sustain them and give life. While in Moab, Moses reminded them of the terms of God's covenant with them, that those things had been revealed for the purpose of obedience.

God will often bring things to mind that bear witness to his previous working in our lives. Ask for those things to spur you on to obedience.

[a] In Hebrew texts 29:1 is numbered 28:69, and 29:2-29 is numbered 29:1-28.

making with you this day and sealing with an oath, 13 to confirm you
this day as his people, that he may be your God as he promised you and
as he swore to your fathers, Abraham, Isaac and Jacob. 14 I am making
this covenant, with its oath, not only with you 15 who are standing here
with us today in the presence of the LORD our God but also with those
who are not here today.

16 You yourselves know how we lived in Egypt and how we passed
through the countries on the way here. 17 You saw among them their
detestable images and idols of wood and stone, of silver and gold.
18 Make sure there is no man or woman, clan or tribe among you today
whose heart turns away from the LORD our God to go and worship the
gods of those nations; make sure there is no root among you that pro-
duces such bitter poison.

19 When such a person hears the words of this oath and they invoke a
blessing on themselves, thinking, "I will be safe, even though I persist
in going my own way," they will bring disaster on the watered land as
well as the dry. 20 The LORD will never be willing to forgive them; his
wrath and zeal will burn against them. All the curses written in this
book will fall on them, and the LORD will blot out their names from
under heaven. 21 The LORD will single them out from all the tribes of
Israel for disaster, according to all the curses of the covenant written
in this Book of the Law.

22 Your children who follow you in later generations and foreigners
who come from distant lands will see the calamities that have fallen
on the land and the diseases with which the LORD has afflicted it.
23 The whole land will be a burning waste of salt and sulfur—nothing
planted, nothing sprouting, no vegetation growing on it. It will be like
the destruction of Sodom and Gomorrah, Admah and Zeboyim, which
the LORD overthrew in fierce anger. 24 All the nations will ask: "Why
has the LORD done this to this land? Why this fierce, burning anger?"

25 And the answer will be: "It is because this people abandoned the
covenant of the LORD, the God of their ancestors, the covenant he
made with them when he brought them out of Egypt. 26 They went
off and worshiped other gods and bowed down to them, gods they did
not know, gods he had not given them. 27 Therefore the LORD's anger
burned against this land, so that he brought on it all the curses written
in this book. 28 In furious anger and in great wrath the LORD uprooted
them from their land and thrust them into another land, as it is now."

29 The secret things belong to the LORD our God, but the things re-
vealed belong to us and to our children forever, that we may follow all
the words of this law.

PROSPERITY AFTER TURNING TO THE LORD

30 When all these blessings and curses I have set before you come
on you and you take them to heart wherever the LORD your
God disperses you among the nations, 2 and when you and your chil-
dren return to the LORD your God and obey him with all your heart and
with all your soul according to everything I command you today, 3 then
the LORD your God will restore your fortunes[a] and have compassion on
you and gather you again from all the nations where he scattered you.
4 Even if you have been banished to the most distant land under the
heavens, from there the LORD your God will gather you and bring you

[a] 3 Or *will bring you back from captivity*

PRAYING SCRIPTURE

Deuteronomy 30

In a most picturesque section, God reminded the people that his commands were not mysterious or hard to find. No one need scale mountains or swim the ocean to understand how God wanted him or her to live. God set life and death before them and his Word very near them.

The Word of God is near us. How glorious a truth! Thank God that you have access to his Word.

back. [5]He will bring you to the land that belonged to your ancestors,
and you will take possession of it. He will make you more prosperous
and numerous than your ancestors. [6]The LORD your God will circum-
cise your hearts and the hearts of your descendants, so that you may
love him with all your heart and with all your soul, and live. [7]The LORD
your God will put all these curses on your enemies who hate and per-
secute you. [8]You will again obey the LORD and follow all his commands
I am giving you today. [9]Then the LORD your God will make you most
prosperous in all the work of your hands and in the fruit of your womb,
the young of your livestock and the crops of your land. The LORD will
again delight in you and make you prosperous, just as he delighted
in your ancestors, [10]if you obey the LORD your God and keep his com-
mands and decrees that are written in this Book of the Law and turn to
the LORD your God with all your heart and with all your soul.

THE OFFER OF LIFE OR DEATH

[11]Now what I am commanding you today is not too difficult for you
or beyond your reach. [12]It is not up in heaven, so that you have to ask,
"Who will ascend into heaven to get it and proclaim it to us so we may
obey it?" [13]Nor is it beyond the sea, so that you have to ask, "Who will
cross the sea to get it and proclaim it to us so we may obey it?" [14]No,
the word is very near you; it is in your mouth and in your heart so you
may obey it.

[15]See, I set before you today life and prosperity, death and destruc-
tion. [16]For I command you today to love the LORD your God, to walk in
obedience to him, and to keep his commands, decrees and laws; then
you will live and increase, and the LORD your God will bless you in the
land you are entering to possess.

[17]But if your heart turns away and you are not obedient, and if you
are drawn away to bow down to other gods and worship them, [18]I de-
clare to you this day that you will certainly be destroyed. You will not
live long in the land you are crossing the Jordan to enter and possess.

[19]This day I call the heavens and the earth as witnesses against you
that I have set before you life and death, blessings and curses. Now
choose life, so that you and your children may live [20]and that you may
love the LORD your God, listen to his voice, and hold fast to him. For the
LORD is your life, and he will give you many years in the land he swore
to give to your fathers, Abraham, Isaac and Jacob.

JOSHUA TO SUCCEED MOSES

31 Then Moses went out and spoke these words to all Israel: [2]"I am
now a hundred and twenty years old and I am no longer able
to lead you. The LORD has said to me, 'You shall not cross the Jordan.'
[3]The LORD your God himself will cross over ahead of you. He will de-
stroy these nations before you, and you will take possession of their
land. Joshua also will cross over ahead of you, as the LORD said. [4]And
the LORD will do to them what he did to Sihon and Og, the kings of the
Amorites, whom he destroyed along with their land. [5]The LORD will de-
liver them to you, and you must do to them all that I have commanded
you. [6]Be strong and courageous. Do not be afraid or terrified because
of them, for the LORD your God goes with you; he will never leave you
nor forsake you."

[7]Then Moses summoned Joshua and said to him in the presence of
all Israel, "Be strong and courageous, for you must go with this people

PRAYING SCRIPTURE

Deuteronomy 31

Because the Lord is always with us, we can live with humble confidence and courage. Those who lead in God's power can have courage, and those who follow can do so with faith in God's wisdom. Moses encouraged Joshua to be strong and courageous because he had to lead the people.

Ask God to fill you with strength and courage that you can boldly follow wherever he leads you.

into the land that the LORD swore to their ancestors to give them, and you must divide it among them as their inheritance. 8The LORD himself goes before you and will be with you; he will never leave you nor forsake you. Do not be afraid; do not be discouraged."

PUBLIC READING OF THE LAW

9So Moses wrote down this law and gave it to the Levitical priests, who carried the ark of the covenant of the LORD, and to all the elders of Israel. 10Then Moses commanded them: "At the end of every seven years, in the year for canceling debts, during the Festival of Tabernacles, 11when all Israel comes to appear before the LORD your God at the place he will choose, you shall read this law before them in their hearing. 12Assemble the people — men, women and children, and the foreigners residing in your towns — so they can listen and learn to fear the LORD your God and follow carefully all the words of this law. 13Their children, who do not know this law, must hear it and learn to fear the LORD your God as long as you live in the land you are crossing the Jordan to possess."

ISRAEL'S REBELLION PREDICTED

14The LORD said to Moses, "Now the day of your death is near. Call Joshua and present yourselves at the tent of meeting, where I will commission him." So Moses and Joshua came and presented themselves at the tent of meeting.

15Then the LORD appeared at the tent in a pillar of cloud, and the cloud stood over the entrance to the tent. 16And the LORD said to Moses: "You are going to rest with your ancestors, and these people will soon prostitute themselves to the foreign gods of the land they are entering. They will forsake me and break the covenant I made with them. 17And in that day I will become angry with them and forsake them; I will hide my face from them, and they will be destroyed. Many disasters and calamities will come on them, and in that day they will ask, 'Have not these disasters come on us because our God is not with us?' 18And I will certainly hide my face in that day because of all their wickedness in turning to other gods.

19"Now write down this song and teach it to the Israelites and have them sing it, so that it may be a witness for me against them. 20When I have brought them into the land flowing with milk and honey, the land I promised on oath to their ancestors, and when they eat their fill and thrive, they will turn to other gods and worship them, rejecting me and breaking my covenant. 21And when many disasters and calamities come on them, this song will testify against them, because it will not be forgotten by their descendants. I know what they are disposed to do, even before I bring them into the land I promised them on oath." 22So Moses wrote down this song that day and taught it to the Israelites.

23The LORD gave this command to Joshua son of Nun: "Be strong and courageous, for you will bring the Israelites into the land I promised them on oath, and I myself will be with you."

24After Moses finished writing in a book the words of this law from beginning to end, 25he gave this command to the Levites who carried the ark of the covenant of the LORD: 26"Take this Book of the Law and place it beside the ark of the covenant of the LORD your God. There it will remain as a witness against you. 27For I know how rebellious and

stiff-necked you are. If you have been rebellious against the LORD while
I am still alive and with you, how much more will you rebel after I die!
28 Assemble before me all the elders of your tribes and all your officials,
so that I can speak these words in their hearing and call the heavens
and the earth to testify against them. 29 For I know that after my death
you are sure to become utterly corrupt and to turn from the way I have
commanded you. In days to come, disaster will fall on you because you
will do evil in the sight of the LORD and arouse his anger by what your
hands have made."

THE SONG OF MOSES

30 And Moses recited the words of this song from beginning to end in
the hearing of the whole assembly of Israel:

32 Listen, you heavens, and I will speak;
hear, you earth, the words of my mouth.
2 Let my teaching fall like rain
and my words descend like dew,
like showers on new grass,
like abundant rain on tender plants.

3 I will proclaim the name of the LORD.
Oh, praise the greatness of our God!
4 He is the Rock, his works are perfect,
and all his ways are just.
A faithful God who does no wrong,
upright and just is he.

5 They are corrupt and not his children;
to their shame they are a warped and crooked generation.
6 Is this the way you repay the LORD,
you foolish and unwise people?
Is he not your Father, your Creator,[a]
who made you and formed you?
7 Remember the days of old;
consider the generations long past.
Ask your father and he will tell you,
your elders, and they will explain to you.
8 When the Most High gave the nations their inheritance,
when he divided all mankind,
he set up boundaries for the peoples
according to the number of the sons of Israel.[b]
9 For the LORD's portion is his people,
Jacob his allotted inheritance.

10 In a desert land he found him,
in a barren and howling waste.
He shielded him and cared for him;
he guarded him as the apple of his eye,
11 like an eagle that stirs up its nest
and hovers over its young,
that spreads its wings to catch them
and carries them aloft.

PRAYING SCRIPTURE

Deuteronomy 32

God intended for his people to teach his Word to their children. Moses encouraged the people to "take to heart" God's words because they were the very life of God imparted to them (see verse 46). This, God said, was not futile; it would prolong their days. His Word is power!

Knowing God's Word is never without benefit. Ask God to help you see the eternal blessing of knowing and keeping his Word.

---

[a] 6 Or *Father, who bought you* [b] 8 Masoretic Text; Dead Sea Scrolls (see also Septuagint) *sons of God*

12 The LORD alone led him;
no foreign god was with him.

13 He made him ride on the heights of the land
and fed him with the fruit of the fields.
He nourished him with honey from the rock,
and with oil from the flinty crag,
14 with curds and milk from herd and flock
and with fattened lambs and goats,
with choice rams of Bashan
and the finest kernels of wheat.
You drank the foaming blood of the grape.

15 Jeshurun[a] grew fat and kicked;
filled with food, they became heavy and sleek.
They abandoned the God who made them
and rejected the Rock their Savior.
16 They made him jealous with their foreign gods
and angered him with their detestable idols.
17 They sacrificed to false gods, which are not God—
gods they had not known,
gods that recently appeared,
gods your ancestors did not fear.
18 You deserted the Rock, who fathered you;
you forgot the God who gave you birth.

19 The LORD saw this and rejected them
because he was angered by his sons and daughters.
20 "I will hide my face from them," he said,
"and see what their end will be;
for they are a perverse generation,
children who are unfaithful.
21 They made me jealous by what is no god
and angered me with their worthless idols.
I will make them envious by those who are not a people;
I will make them angry by a nation that has no understanding.
22 For a fire will be kindled by my wrath,
one that burns down to the realm of the dead below.
It will devour the earth and its harvests
and set afire the foundations of the mountains.

23 "I will heap calamities on them
and spend my arrows against them.
24 I will send wasting famine against them,
consuming pestilence and deadly plague;
I will send against them the fangs of wild beasts,
the venom of vipers that glide in the dust.
25 In the street the sword will make them childless;
in their homes terror will reign.
The young men and young women will perish,
the infants and those with gray hair.
26 I said I would scatter them
and erase their name from human memory,
27 but I dreaded the taunt of the enemy,
lest the adversary misunderstand

[a] 15 *Jeshurun* means *the upright one*, that is, Israel.

and say, 'Our hand has triumphed;
the LORD has not done all this.' "

28 They are a nation without sense,
there is no discernment in them.
29 If only they were wise and would understand this
and discern what their end will be!
30 How could one man chase a thousand,
or two put ten thousand to flight,
unless their Rock had sold them,
unless the LORD had given them up?
31 For their rock is not like our Rock,
as even our enemies concede.
32 Their vine comes from the vine of Sodom
and from the fields of Gomorrah.
Their grapes are filled with poison,
and their clusters with bitterness.
33 Their wine is the venom of serpents,
the deadly poison of cobras.

34 "Have I not kept this in reserve
and sealed it in my vaults?
35 It is mine to avenge; I will repay.
In due time their foot will slip;
their day of disaster is near
and their doom rushes upon them."

36 The LORD will vindicate his people
and relent concerning his servants
when he sees their strength is gone
and no one is left, slave or free.[a]
37 He will say: "Now where are their gods,
the rock they took refuge in,
38 the gods who ate the fat of their sacrifices
and drank the wine of their drink offerings?
Let them rise up to help you!
Let them give you shelter!

39 "See now that I myself am he!
There is no god besides me.
I put to death and I bring to life,
I have wounded and I will heal,
and no one can deliver out of my hand.
40 I lift my hand to heaven and solemnly swear:
As surely as I live forever,
41 when I sharpen my flashing sword
and my hand grasps it in judgment,
I will take vengeance on my adversaries
and repay those who hate me.
42 I will make my arrows drunk with blood,
while my sword devours flesh:
the blood of the slain and the captives,
the heads of the enemy leaders."

---

[a] 36 Or *and they are without a ruler or leader*

43 Rejoice, you nations, with his people,[a,b]
for he will avenge the blood of his servants;
he will take vengeance on his enemies
and make atonement for his land and people.

44 Moses came with Joshua[c] son of Nun and spoke all the words of
this song in the hearing of the people. 45 When Moses finished reciting
all these words to all Israel, 46 he said to them, "Take to heart all the
words I have solemnly declared to you this day, so that you may command your children to obey carefully all the words of this law. 47 They
are not just idle words for you — they are your life. By them you will
live long in the land you are crossing the Jordan to possess."

MOSES TO DIE ON MOUNT NEBO

48 On that same day the LORD told Moses, 49 "Go up into the Abarim
Range to Mount Nebo in Moab, across from Jericho, and view Canaan,
the land I am giving the Israelites as their own possession. 50 There on
the mountain that you have climbed you will die and be gathered to
your people, just as your brother Aaron died on Mount Hor and was
gathered to his people. 51 This is because both of you broke faith with
me in the presence of the Israelites at the waters of Meribah Kadesh in
the Desert of Zin and because you did not uphold my holiness among
the Israelites. 52 Therefore, you will see the land only from a distance;
you will not enter the land I am giving to the people of Israel."

MOSES BLESSES THE TRIBES

33 This is the blessing that Moses the man of God pronounced on
the Israelites before his death. 2 He said:

"The LORD came from Sinai
and dawned over them from Seir;
he shone forth from Mount Paran.
He came with[d] myriads of holy ones
from the south, from his mountain slopes.[e]
3 Surely it is you who love the people;
all the holy ones are in your hand.
At your feet they all bow down,
and from you receive instruction,
4 the law that Moses gave us,
the possession of the assembly of Jacob.
5 He was king over Jeshurun[f]
when the leaders of the people assembled,
along with the tribes of Israel.

6 "Let Reuben live and not die,
nor[g] his people be few."

7 And this he said about Judah:

"Hear, LORD, the cry of Judah;
bring him to his people.

PRAYING SCRIPTURE

Deuteronomy 33

Moses' final words to the people celebrated God's love for them. Their great leader, who had led them from Egypt to the Jordan River, imparted a blessing to them, tribe by tribe. What a moment of impact this must have been!

What people in your faith journey have spoken to you the most life-giving words of blessing? Thank God for them, and if they are still living, thank them personally.

[a] 43 Or *Make his people rejoice, you nations* [b] 43 Masoretic Text; Dead Sea Scrolls (see also Septuagint) *people, / and let all the angels worship him, /* [c] 44 Hebrew *Hoshea*, a variant of *Joshua* [d] 2 Or *from* [e] 2 The meaning of the Hebrew for this phrase is uncertain. [f] 5 *Jeshurun* means *the upright one*, that is, Israel; also in verse 26. [g] 6 Or *but let*

With his own hands he defends his cause.
  Oh, be his help against his foes!"

8 About Levi he said:

"Your Thummim and Urim belong
  to your faithful servant.
You tested him at Massah;
  you contended with him at the waters of Meribah.
9 He said of his father and mother,
  'I have no regard for them.'
He did not recognize his brothers
  or acknowledge his own children,
but he watched over your word
  and guarded your covenant.
10 He teaches your precepts to Jacob
  and your law to Israel.
He offers incense before you
  and whole burnt offerings on your altar.
11 Bless all his skills, LORD,
  and be pleased with the work of his hands.
Strike down those who rise against him,
  his foes till they rise no more."

12 About Benjamin he said:

"Let the beloved of the LORD rest secure in him,
  for he shields him all day long,
  and the one the LORD loves rests between his shoulders."

13 About Joseph he said:

"May the LORD bless his land
  with the precious dew from heaven above
  and with the deep waters that lie below;
14 with the best the sun brings forth
  and the finest the moon can yield;
15 with the choicest gifts of the ancient mountains
  and the fruitfulness of the everlasting hills;
16 with the best gifts of the earth and its fullness
  and the favor of him who dwelt in the burning bush.
Let all these rest on the head of Joseph,
  on the brow of the prince among[a] his brothers.
17 In majesty he is like a firstborn bull;
  his horns are the horns of a wild ox.
With them he will gore the nations,
  even those at the ends of the earth.
Such are the ten thousands of Ephraim;
  such are the thousands of Manasseh."

18 About Zebulun he said:

"Rejoice, Zebulun, in your going out,
  and you, Issachar, in your tents.
19 They will summon peoples to the mountain
  and there offer the sacrifices of the righteous;

---

[a] 16 Or *of the one separated from*

they will feast on the abundance of the seas,
on the treasures hidden in the sand."

20 About Gad he said:

"Blessed is he who enlarges Gad's domain!
Gad lives there like a lion,
tearing at arm or head.
21 He chose the best land for himself;
the leader's portion was kept for him.
When the heads of the people assembled,
he carried out the LORD's righteous will,
and his judgments concerning Israel."

22 About Dan he said:

"Dan is a lion's cub,
springing out of Bashan."

23 About Naphtali he said:

"Naphtali is abounding with the favor of the LORD
and is full of his blessing;
he will inherit southward to the lake."

24 About Asher he said:

"Most blessed of sons is Asher;
let him be favored by his brothers,
and let him bathe his feet in oil.
25 The bolts of your gates will be iron and bronze,
and your strength will equal your days.

26 "There is no one like the God of Jeshurun,
who rides across the heavens to help you
and on the clouds in his majesty.
27 The eternal God is your refuge,
and underneath are the everlasting arms.
He will drive out your enemies before you,
saying, 'Destroy them!'
28 So Israel will live in safety;
Jacob will dwell[a] secure
in a land of grain and new wine,
where the heavens drop dew.
29 Blessed are you, Israel!
Who is like you,
a people saved by the LORD?
He is your shield and helper
and your glorious sword.
Your enemies will cower before you,
and you will tread on their heights."

THE DEATH OF MOSES

34 Then Moses climbed Mount Nebo from the plains of Moab to
the top of Pisgah, across from Jericho. There the LORD showed
him the whole land — from Gilead to Dan, 2 all of Naphtali, the territory

[a] 28 Septuagint; Hebrew *Jacob's spring is*

PRAYING SCRIPTURE

Deuteronomy 34

The miraculous life of Moses came to an end at the age of 120. This chapter records that his eyesight had not grown weak, nor had his physical strength diminished. So great was his impact, the Israelites mourned for 30 days after his death.

What spiritual leader has had the biggest impact for good on your life? Thank God for placing that person in your life to help you become like Jesus.

of Ephraim and Manasseh, all the land of Judah as far as the Mediterra-
nean Sea, 3the Negev and the whole region from the Valley of Jericho,
the City of Palms, as far as Zoar. 4Then the LORD said to him, "This is
the land I promised on oath to Abraham, Isaac and Jacob when I said,
'I will give it to your descendants.' I have let you see it with your eyes,
but you will not cross over into it."

5And Moses the servant of the LORD died there in Moab, as the LORD
had said. 6He buried him[a] in Moab, in the valley opposite Beth Peor,
but to this day no one knows where his grave is. 7Moses was a hundred
and twenty years old when he died, yet his eyes were not weak nor his
strength gone. 8The Israelites grieved for Moses in the plains of Moab
thirty days, until the time of weeping and mourning was over.

9Now Joshua son of Nun was filled with the spirit[b] of wisdom be-
cause Moses had laid his hands on him. So the Israelites listened to
him and did what the LORD had commanded Moses.

10Since then, no prophet has risen in Israel like Moses, whom the
LORD knew face to face, 11who did all those signs and wonders the LORD
sent him to do in Egypt — to Pharaoh and to all his officials and to his
whole land. 12For no one has ever shown the mighty power or per-
formed the awesome deeds that Moses did in the sight of all Israel.

[a] 6 Or *He was buried* [b] 9 Or *Spirit*

JOSHUA

The book that bears his name tells the story of Joshua leading the Israelites across the Jordan River and into the land of promise. Little by little, they conquered the land and, in accordance with God's promise, drove out almost all the people who lived there. Then they apportioned the land to each of the tribes. Joshua and Israel displayed great courage in their conquest of the land but also made crucial missteps that would plague Israel for years to come. The lack of complete obedience became a hallmark of the people.

Joshua begins with a commission from the Lord to Joshua. The task to which he was called was a difficult one, but the Lord assured Joshua he would be with him wherever he went. In the early chapters, the Israelites made the long-awaited trek across the Jordan and into the land. As he had at the Red Sea, God miraculously parted the Jordan River so the people could follow the priests across. After entering the land, Israel defeated the inhabitants and took control of it, fulfilling the promise God made to Abraham years before. In chapters 13–21, Joshua divided the land between the tribes of Israel. The book closes with Joshua's final instructions, the renewal of the covenant and Joshua's death.

The presence of the Lord among his people is one of Joshua's major themes. God's repeated commands to Joshua not to fear but to be strong were based on that promise: "for the LORD your God will be with you wherever you go" (1:9). It calls to mind Moses' plea not to let the Israelites go up from the wilderness unless God was with them. In every battle, the key issue for Israel's success was whether or not the Lord was with them.

As Christians reflect on Joshua, we remember that God dwells in us through his Spirit. Just as Joshua needed courage to conquer the promised land, we need strength to walk in obedience to God's commands each day. We pray for courage because we need it, and then we live courageously knowing that God is always with us. Joshua should encourage us to pray every time we face an enemy or a challenge for which we are unprepared.

Joshua's closing speech has inspired God's people throughout the generations. He charged Israel to fear the Lord by loving him and obeying him. He also called upon them to put away their foreign gods and idols. Then he issued a challenge for them to choose whom they would serve, declaring, "But as for me and my household, we will serve the LORD" (24:15).

Families serve the Lord as a result of prayer. God hears the prayers of parents, grandparents, siblings, aunts, uncles and cousins who call on him. In a world of innumerable temptations and distractions, of false gods at every turn, we need to ask God in faith to help our families serve him.

PRAYING SCRIPTURE

Joshua 1

As the Israelites prepared to enter the promised land, God told Joshua, their leader, three times, “Be strong and courageous” (verses 6,7,9). The basis of this charge was that God had promises waiting on the other side.

Rather than manufacturing courage, God’s faithfulness should be the source of it. Look to God’s Word, and then ask him to make you strong and courageous in your faith in him as you read.

JOSHUA INSTALLED AS LEADER

1 After the death of Moses the servant of the LORD, the LORD said to Joshua son of Nun, Moses’ aide: 2“Moses my servant is dead. Now then, you and all these people, get ready to cross the Jordan River into the land I am about to give to them — to the Israelites. 3I will give you every place where you set your foot, as I promised Moses. 4Your territory will extend from the desert to Lebanon, and from the great river, the Euphrates — all the Hittite country — to the Mediterranean Sea in the west. 5No one will be able to stand against you all the days of your life. As I was with Moses, so I will be with you; I will never leave you nor forsake you. 6Be strong and courageous, because you will lead these people to inherit the land I swore to their ancestors to give them.

7“Be strong and very courageous. Be careful to obey all the law my servant Moses gave you; do not turn from it to the right or to the left, that you may be successful wherever you go. 8Keep this Book of the Law always on your lips; meditate on it day and night, so that you may be careful to do everything written in it. Then you will be prosperous and successful. 9Have I not commanded you? Be strong and courageous. Do not be afraid; do not be discouraged, for the LORD your God will be with you wherever you go.”

10So Joshua ordered the officers of the people: 11“Go through the camp and tell the people, ‘Get your provisions ready. Three days from now you will cross the Jordan here to go in and take possession of the land the LORD your God is giving you for your own.’ ”

12But to the Reubenites, the Gadites and the half-tribe of Manasseh, Joshua said, 13“Remember the command that Moses the servant of the LORD gave you after he said, ‘The LORD your God will give you rest by giving you this land.’ 14Your wives, your children and your livestock may stay in the land that Moses gave you east of the Jordan, but all your fighting men, ready for battle, must cross over ahead of your fellow Israelites. You are to help them 15until the LORD gives them rest, as he has done for you, and until they too have taken possession of the land the LORD your God is giving them. After that, you may go back and occupy your own land, which Moses the servant of the LORD gave you east of the Jordan toward the sunrise.”

16Then they answered Joshua, “Whatever you have commanded us we will do, and wherever you send us we will go. 17Just as we fully obeyed Moses, so we will obey you. Only may the LORD your God be with you as he was with Moses. 18Whoever rebels against your word and does not obey it, whatever you may command them, will be put to death. Only be strong and courageous!”

PRAYING SCRIPTURE

Joshua 2

Rahab hid the spies because she had heard of the miracles God performed during the exodus. She believed God gave the Israelites victory over their enemies before crossing the Jordan and that he would do so in Canaan. In Hebrews 11 we are told that it was Rahab’s faith that motivated her.

Ask God to give you faith for your future challenges based on what he has already done in your journey.

RAHAB AND THE SPIES

2 Then Joshua son of Nun secretly sent two spies from Shittim. “Go, look over the land,” he said, “especially Jericho.” So they went and entered the house of a prostitute named Rahab and stayed there.

2The king of Jericho was told, “Look, some of the Israelites have come here tonight to spy out the land.” 3So the king of Jericho sent this message to Rahab: “Bring out the men who came to you and entered your house, because they have come to spy out the whole land.”

4But the woman had taken the two men and hidden them. She said, “Yes, the men came to me, but I did not know where they had come from. 5At dusk, when it was time to close the city gate, they left. I don’t know which way they went. Go after them quickly. You may catch up

with them." 6(But she had taken them up to the roof and hidden them
under the stalks of flax she had laid out on the roof.) 7So the men set
out in pursuit of the spies on the road that leads to the fords of the
Jordan, and as soon as the pursuers had gone out, the gate was shut.

8Before the spies lay down for the night, she went up on the roof
9and said to them, "I know that the LORD has given you this land and
that a great fear of you has fallen on us, so that all who live in this
country are melting in fear because of you. 10We have heard how the
LORD dried up the water of the Red Sea[a] for you when you came out of
Egypt, and what you did to Sihon and Og, the two kings of the Amo-
rites east of the Jordan, whom you completely destroyed.[b] 11When we
heard of it, our hearts melted in fear and everyone's courage failed
because of you, for the LORD your God is God in heaven above and on
the earth below.

12"Now then, please swear to me by the LORD that you will show
kindness to my family, because I have shown kindness to you. Give
me a sure sign 13that you will spare the lives of my father and mother,
my brothers and sisters, and all who belong to them — and that you
will save us from death."

14"Our lives for your lives!" the men assured her. "If you don't tell
what we are doing, we will treat you kindly and faithfully when the
LORD gives us the land."

15So she let them down by a rope through the window, for the house
she lived in was part of the city wall. 16She said to them, "Go to the hills
so the pursuers will not find you. Hide yourselves there three days un-
til they return, and then go on your way."

17Now the men had said to her, "This oath you made us swear will not
be binding on us 18unless, when we enter the land, you have tied this
scarlet cord in the window through which you let us down, and unless
you have brought your father and mother, your brothers and all your
family into your house. 19If any of them go outside your house into the
street, their blood will be on their own heads; we will not be responsi-
ble. As for those who are in the house with you, their blood will be on
our head if a hand is laid on them. 20But if you tell what we are doing,
we will be released from the oath you made us swear."

21"Agreed," she replied. "Let it be as you say."

So she sent them away, and they departed. And she tied the scarlet
cord in the window.

22When they left, they went into the hills and stayed there three
days, until the pursuers had searched all along the road and returned
without finding them. 23Then the two men started back. They went
down out of the hills, forded the river and came to Joshua son of Nun
and told him everything that had happened to them. 24They said to
Joshua, "The LORD has surely given the whole land into our hands; all
the people are melting in fear because of us."

CROSSING THE JORDAN

3 Early in the morning Joshua and all the Israelites set out from
Shittim and went to the Jordan, where they camped before cross-
ing over. 2After three days the officers went throughout the camp, 3giv-
ing orders to the people: "When you see the ark of the covenant of the

[a] 10 Or *the Sea of Reeds* [b] 10 The Hebrew term refers to the irrevocable giving over of things or persons to the LORD, often by totally destroying them.

PRAYING SCRIPTURE

Joshua 3

In many ways, the Israelites' crossing of the Jordan repeated the Red Sea crossing; it was a similar miracle for a new generation. This crossing had a twist, though. Before, Moses stretched out his rod and God parted the Red Sea. At the Jordan, the priests' feet had to touch the water before God stopped the river.

God wants our faith to increase so we will increasingly trust him. Ask him for this.

LORD your God, and the Levitical priests carrying it, you are to move
out from your positions and follow it. 4Then you will know which way
to go, since you have never been this way before. But keep a distance
of about two thousand cubits[a] between you and the ark; do not go
near it."
5Joshua told the people, "Consecrate yourselves, for tomorrow the
LORD will do amazing things among you."
6Joshua said to the priests, "Take up the ark of the covenant and pass
on ahead of the people." So they took it up and went ahead of them.
7And the LORD said to Joshua, "Today I will begin to exalt you in the
eyes of all Israel, so they may know that I am with you as I was with
Moses. 8Tell the priests who carry the ark of the covenant: 'When you
reach the edge of the Jordan's waters, go and stand in the river.' "
9Joshua said to the Israelites, "Come here and listen to the words of
the LORD your God. 10This is how you will know that the living God is
among you and that he will certainly drive out before you the Canaan-
ites, Hittites, Hivites, Perizzites, Girgashites, Amorites and Jebusites.
11See, the ark of the covenant of the Lord of all the earth will go into the
Jordan ahead of you. 12Now then, choose twelve men from the tribes
of Israel, one from each tribe. 13And as soon as the priests who carry
the ark of the LORD — the Lord of all the earth — set foot in the Jordan,
its waters flowing downstream will be cut off and stand up in a heap."
14So when the people broke camp to cross the Jordan, the priests car-
rying the ark of the covenant went ahead of them. 15Now the Jordan is
at flood stage all during harvest. Yet as soon as the priests who carried
the ark reached the Jordan and their feet touched the water's edge,
16the water from upstream stopped flowing. It piled up in a heap a
great distance away, at a town called Adam in the vicinity of Zarethan,
while the water flowing down to the Sea of the Arabah (that is, the
Dead Sea) was completely cut off. So the people crossed over opposite
Jericho. 17The priests who carried the ark of the covenant of the LORD
stopped in the middle of the Jordan and stood on dry ground, while
all Israel passed by until the whole nation had completed the crossing
on dry ground.

4 When the whole nation had finished crossing the Jordan, the
LORD said to Joshua, 2"Choose twelve men from among the peo-
ple, one from each tribe, 3and tell them to take up twelve stones from
the middle of the Jordan, from right where the priests are standing,
and carry them over with you and put them down at the place where
you stay tonight."
4So Joshua called together the twelve men he had appointed from
the Israelites, one from each tribe, 5and said to them, "Go over before
the ark of the LORD your God into the middle of the Jordan. Each of
you is to take up a stone on his shoulder, according to the number of
the tribes of the Israelites, 6to serve as a sign among you. In the future,
when your children ask you, 'What do these stones mean?' 7tell them
that the flow of the Jordan was cut off before the ark of the covenant of
the LORD. When it crossed the Jordan, the waters of the Jordan were cut
off. These stones are to be a memorial to the people of Israel forever."
8So the Israelites did as Joshua commanded them. They took twelve
stones from the middle of the Jordan, according to the number of the
tribes of the Israelites, as the LORD had told Joshua; and they carried

PRAYING SCRIPTURE

Joshua 4

After decades of wandering around in the wilderness, when Israel entered the promised land, Joshua wanted to ensure that future generations would know the miracle of crossing the Jordan. With the flow of the river still halted, Joshua instructed that 12 large stones be placed as an altar where the Israelites crossed.

Memorials to God's work in our spiritual journey are important. Ask God how you can mark the stages in your growth.

[a] 4 That is, about 3,000 feet or about 900 meters

them over with them to their camp, where they put them down.
9Joshua set up the twelve stones that had been[a] in the middle of the
Jordan at the spot where the priests who carried the ark of the cov-
enant had stood. And they are there to this day.

10Now the priests who carried the ark remained standing in the mid-
dle of the Jordan until everything the LORD had commanded Joshua
was done by the people, just as Moses had directed Joshua. The people
hurried over, 11and as soon as all of them had crossed, the ark of the
LORD and the priests came to the other side while the people watched.
12The men of Reuben, Gad and the half-tribe of Manasseh crossed over,
ready for battle, in front of the Israelites, as Moses had directed them.
13About forty thousand armed for battle crossed over before the LORD
to the plains of Jericho for war.

14That day the LORD exalted Joshua in the sight of all Israel; and
they stood in awe of him all the days of his life, just as they had stood
in awe of Moses.

15Then the LORD said to Joshua, 16"Command the priests carrying the
ark of the covenant law to come up out of the Jordan."

17So Joshua commanded the priests, "Come up out of the Jordan."

18And the priests came up out of the river carrying the ark of the
covenant of the LORD. No sooner had they set their feet on the dry
ground than the waters of the Jordan returned to their place and ran
at flood stage as before.

19On the tenth day of the first month the people went up from the
Jordan and camped at Gilgal on the eastern border of Jericho. 20And
Joshua set up at Gilgal the twelve stones they had taken out of the Jor-
dan. 21He said to the Israelites, "In the future when your descendants
ask their parents, 'What do these stones mean?' 22tell them, 'Israel
crossed the Jordan on dry ground.' 23For the LORD your God dried up
the Jordan before you until you had crossed over. The LORD your God
did to the Jordan what he had done to the Red Sea[b] when he dried it up
before us until we had crossed over. 24He did this so that all the peoples
of the earth might know that the hand of the LORD is powerful and so
that you might always fear the LORD your God."

5 Now when all the Amorite kings west of the Jordan and all the Ca-
naanite kings along the coast heard how the LORD had dried up the
Jordan before the Israelites until they[c] had crossed over, their hearts
melted in fear and they no longer had the courage to face the Israelites.

CIRCUMCISION AND PASSOVER AT GILGAL

2At that time the LORD said to Joshua, "Make flint knives and cir-
cumcise the Israelites again." 3So Joshua made flint knives and circum-
cised the Israelites at Gibeath Haaraloth.[d]

4Now this is why he did so: All those who came out of Egypt—all the
men of military age—died in the wilderness on the way after leaving
Egypt. 5All the people that came out had been circumcised, but all the
people born in the wilderness during the journey from Egypt had not.
6The Israelites had moved about in the wilderness forty years until all
the men who were of military age when they left Egypt had died, since
they had not obeyed the LORD. For the LORD had sworn to them that
they would not see the land he had solemnly promised their ancestors

PRAYING SCRIPTURE

Joshua 5

As with Moses, Joshua had an encounter with the "commander of the LORD's army" who reminded him of God's holiness (see verse 15). This surely encouraged Joshua that God was with him exactly as he had been with Moses all the way down to requesting he remove his shoes because of holy ground.

Think about any "holy ground" encounter you've had with God, and remember that he's the God of Moses and Joshua too. Thank him for that.

[a] 9 Or *Joshua also set up twelve stones* [b] 23 Or *the Sea of Reeds* [c] 1 Another textual tradition *we* [d] 3 *Gibeath Haaraloth* means *the hill of foreskins.*

to give us, a land flowing with milk and honey. 7So he raised up their sons in their place, and these were the ones Joshua circumcised. They were still uncircumcised because they had not been circumcised on the way. 8And after the whole nation had been circumcised, they remained where they were in camp until they were healed.

9Then the LORD said to Joshua, "Today I have rolled away the reproach of Egypt from you." So the place has been called Gilgal[a] to this day.

10On the evening of the fourteenth day of the month, while camped at Gilgal on the plains of Jericho, the Israelites celebrated the Passover. 11The day after the Passover, that very day, they ate some of the produce of the land: unleavened bread and roasted grain. 12The manna stopped the day after[b] they ate this food from the land; there was no longer any manna for the Israelites, but that year they ate the produce of Canaan.

THE FALL OF JERICHO

13Now when Joshua was near Jericho, he looked up and saw a man standing in front of him with a drawn sword in his hand. Joshua went up to him and asked, "Are you for us or for our enemies?"

14"Neither," he replied, "but as commander of the army of the LORD I have now come." Then Joshua fell facedown to the ground in reverence, and asked him, "What message does my Lord[c] have for his servant?"

15The commander of the LORD's army replied, "Take off your sandals, for the place where you are standing is holy." And Joshua did so.

6 Now the gates of Jericho were securely barred because of the Israelites. No one went out and no one came in.

2Then the LORD said to Joshua, "See, I have delivered Jericho into your hands, along with its king and its fighting men. 3March around the city once with all the armed men. Do this for six days. 4Have seven priests carry trumpets of rams' horns in front of the ark. On the seventh day, march around the city seven times, with the priests blowing the trumpets. 5When you hear them sound a long blast on the trumpets, have the whole army give a loud shout; then the wall of the city will collapse and the army will go up, everyone straight in."

6So Joshua son of Nun called the priests and said to them, "Take up the ark of the covenant of the LORD and have seven priests carry trumpets in front of it." 7And he ordered the army, "Advance! March around the city, with an armed guard going ahead of the ark of the LORD."

8When Joshua had spoken to the people, the seven priests carrying the seven trumpets before the LORD went forward, blowing their trumpets, and the ark of the LORD's covenant followed them. 9The armed guard marched ahead of the priests who blew the trumpets, and the rear guard followed the ark. All this time the trumpets were sounding. 10But Joshua had commanded the army, "Do not give a war cry, do not raise your voices, do not say a word until the day I tell you to shout. Then shout!" 11So he had the ark of the LORD carried around the city, circling it once. Then the army returned to camp and spent the night there.

12Joshua got up early the next morning and the priests took up the ark of the LORD. 13The seven priests carrying the seven trumpets went

PRAYING SCRIPTURE

Joshua 6

Few stories are as memorable as the battle of Jericho. With marching, trumpets, shouting and the miraculous wall collapse, the victory at Jericho is an amazing example of God's power. The first battle of the promised land bolstered the people's faith.

Think about how your faith increases when God comes through for you. Ask him to build faith on faith, and then trust him during increasing challenges in your walk with him.

[a] 9 *Gilgal* sounds like the Hebrew for *roll.* [b] 12 Or *the day* [c] 14 Or *lord*

forward, marching before the ark of the LORD and blowing the trum-
pets. The armed men went ahead of them and the rear guard followed
the ark of the LORD, while the trumpets kept sounding. 14So on the sec-
ond day they marched around the city once and returned to the camp.
They did this for six days.
15On the seventh day, they got up at daybreak and marched around
the city seven times in the same manner, except that on that day
they circled the city seven times. 16The seventh time around, when
the priests sounded the trumpet blast, Joshua commanded the army,
"Shout! For the LORD has given you the city! 17The city and all that is in
it are to be devoted[a] to the LORD. Only Rahab the prostitute and all who
are with her in her house shall be spared, because she hid the spies we
sent. 18But keep away from the devoted things, so that you will not
bring about your own destruction by taking any of them. Otherwise
you will make the camp of Israel liable to destruction and bring trou-
ble on it. 19All the silver and gold and the articles of bronze and iron
are sacred to the LORD and must go into his treasury."
20When the trumpets sounded, the army shouted, and at the sound
of the trumpet, when the men gave a loud shout, the wall collapsed;
so everyone charged straight in, and they took the city. 21They devoted
the city to the LORD and destroyed with the sword every living thing
in it — men and women, young and old, cattle, sheep and donkeys.
22Joshua said to the two men who had spied out the land, "Go into
the prostitute's house and bring her out and all who belong to her, in
accordance with your oath to her." 23So the young men who had done
the spying went in and brought out Rahab, her father and mother, her
brothers and sisters and all who belonged to her. They brought out
her entire family and put them in a place outside the camp of Israel.
24Then they burned the whole city and everything in it, but they put
the silver and gold and the articles of bronze and iron into the trea-
sury of the LORD's house. 25But Joshua spared Rahab the prostitute,
with her family and all who belonged to her, because she hid the men
Joshua had sent as spies to Jericho — and she lives among the Israel-
ites to this day.
26At that time Joshua pronounced this solemn oath: "Cursed before
the LORD is the one who undertakes to rebuild this city, Jericho:

"At the cost of his firstborn son
he will lay its foundations;
at the cost of his youngest
he will set up its gates."

27So the LORD was with Joshua, and his fame spread throughout the
land.

ACHAN'S SIN

7 But the Israelites were unfaithful in regard to the devoted things[b];
Achan son of Karmi, the son of Zimri,[c] the son of Zerah, of the tribe
of Judah, took some of them. So the LORD's anger burned against Israel.
2Now Joshua sent men from Jericho to Ai, which is near Beth Aven

[a] 17 The Hebrew term refers to the irrevocable giving over of things or persons to the LORD, often by totally destroying them; also in verses 18 and 21.
[b] 1 The Hebrew term refers to the irrevocable giving over of things or persons to the LORD, often by totally destroying them; also in verses 11, 12, 13 and 15.
[c] 1 See Septuagint and 1 Chron. 2:6; Hebrew *Zabdi*; also in verses 17 and 18.

PRAYING SCRIPTURE

Joshua 7

With the battle of Jericho under their belts, defeating tiny Ai should have been no trouble for the Israelites. But there was a problem. Unlike some future battles, they were forbidden from plundering things from the city. One soldier, Achan, took some money and clothes, bringing judgment on himself and his family.

Sin always affects those around us. Ask God to reveal any sin in your heart. Abandon it for the protection of your family.

to the east of Bethel, and told them, "Go up and spy out the region." So
the men went up and spied out Ai.
3When they returned to Joshua, they said, "Not all the army will have
to go up against Ai. Send two or three thousand men to take it and do
not weary the whole army, for only a few people live there." 4So about
three thousand went up; but they were routed by the men of Ai, 5who
killed about thirty-six of them. They chased the Israelites from the city
gate as far as the stone quarries and struck them down on the slopes.
At this the hearts of the people melted in fear and became like water.
6Then Joshua tore his clothes and fell facedown to the ground before
the ark of the LORD, remaining there till evening. The elders of Israel
did the same, and sprinkled dust on their heads. 7And Joshua said,
"Alas, Sovereign LORD, why did you ever bring this people across the
Jordan to deliver us into the hands of the Amorites to destroy us? If
only we had been content to stay on the other side of the Jordan! 8Par-
don your servant, Lord. What can I say, now that Israel has been routed
by its enemies? 9The Canaanites and the other people of the country
will hear about this and they will surround us and wipe out our name
from the earth. What then will you do for your own great name?"
10The LORD said to Joshua, "Stand up! What are you doing down on
your face? 11Israel has sinned; they have violated my covenant, which
I commanded them to keep. They have taken some of the devoted
things; they have stolen, they have lied, they have put them with their
own possessions. 12That is why the Israelites cannot stand against their
enemies; they turn their backs and run because they have been made
liable to destruction. I will not be with you anymore unless you destroy
whatever among you is devoted to destruction.
13"Go, consecrate the people. Tell them, 'Consecrate yourselves in
preparation for tomorrow; for this is what the LORD, the God of Israel,
says: There are devoted things among you, Israel. You cannot stand
against your enemies until you remove them.
14" 'In the morning, present yourselves tribe by tribe. The tribe
the LORD chooses shall come forward clan by clan; the clan the LORD
chooses shall come forward family by family; and the family the LORD
chooses shall come forward man by man. 15Whoever is caught with the
devoted things shall be destroyed by fire, along with all that belongs
to him. He has violated the covenant of the LORD and has done an out-
rageous thing in Israel!' "
16Early the next morning Joshua had Israel come forward by tribes,
and Judah was chosen. 17The clans of Judah came forward, and the Ze-
rahites were chosen. He had the clan of the Zerahites come forward by
families, and Zimri was chosen. 18Joshua had his family come forward
man by man, and Achan son of Karmi, the son of Zimri, the son of Ze-
rah, of the tribe of Judah, was chosen.
19Then Joshua said to Achan, "My son, give glory to the LORD, the
God of Israel, and honor him. Tell me what you have done; do not hide
it from me."
20Achan replied, "It is true! I have sinned against the LORD, the God
of Israel. This is what I have done: 21When I saw in the plunder a beau-
tiful robe from Babylonia,[a] two hundred shekels[b] of silver and a bar
of gold weighing fifty shekels,[c] I coveted them and took them. They
are hidden in the ground inside my tent, with the silver underneath."

---

[a] *21* Hebrew *Shinar* [b] *21* That is, about 5 pounds or about 2.3 kilograms
[c] *21* That is, about 1 1/4 pounds or about 575 grams

22So Joshua sent messengers, and they ran to the tent, and there it
was, hidden in his tent, with the silver underneath. 23They took the
things from the tent, brought them to Joshua and all the Israelites and
spread them out before the LORD.
24Then Joshua, together with all Israel, took Achan son of Zerah, the
silver, the robe, the gold bar, his sons and daughters, his cattle, don-
keys and sheep, his tent and all that he had, to the Valley of Achor.
25Joshua said, "Why have you brought this trouble on us? The LORD will
bring trouble on you today."
Then all Israel stoned him, and after they had stoned the rest, they
burned them. 26Over Achan they heaped up a large pile of rocks, which
remains to this day. Then the LORD turned from his fierce anger. There-
fore that place has been called the Valley of Achor[a] ever since.

AI DESTROYED

8 Then the LORD said to Joshua, "Do not be afraid; do not be dis-
couraged. Take the whole army with you, and go up and attack Ai.
For I have delivered into your hands the king of Ai, his people, his city
and his land. 2You shall do to Ai and its king as you did to Jericho and
its king, except that you may carry off their plunder and livestock for
yourselves. Set an ambush behind the city."
3So Joshua and the whole army moved out to attack Ai. He chose
thirty thousand of his best fighting men and sent them out at night
4with these orders: "Listen carefully. You are to set an ambush behind
the city. Don't go very far from it. All of you be on the alert. 5I and all
those with me will advance on the city, and when the men come out
against us, as they did before, we will flee from them. 6They will pursue
us until we have lured them away from the city, for they will say, 'They
are running away from us as they did before.' So when we flee from
them, 7you are to rise up from ambush and take the city. The LORD your
God will give it into your hand. 8When you have taken the city, set it on
fire. Do what the LORD has commanded. See to it; you have my orders."
9Then Joshua sent them off, and they went to the place of ambush
and lay in wait between Bethel and Ai, to the west of Ai — but Joshua
spent that night with the people.
10Early the next morning Joshua mustered his army, and he and the
leaders of Israel marched before them to Ai. 11The entire force that was
with him marched up and approached the city and arrived in front of
it. They set up camp north of Ai, with the valley between them and
the city. 12Joshua had taken about five thousand men and set them in
ambush between Bethel and Ai, to the west of the city. 13So the soldiers
took up their positions — with the main camp to the north of the city
and the ambush to the west of it. That night Joshua went into the valley.
14When the king of Ai saw this, he and all the men of the city hurried
out early in the morning to meet Israel in battle at a certain place over-
looking the Arabah. But he did not know that an ambush had been set
against him behind the city. 15Joshua and all Israel let themselves be
driven back before them, and they fled toward the wilderness. 16All the
men of Ai were called to pursue them, and they pursued Joshua and
were lured away from the city. 17Not a man remained in Ai or Bethel
who did not go after Israel. They left the city open and went in pursuit
of Israel.

PRAYING SCRIPTURE

Joshua 8

After Israel won the second battle against Ai, Joshua built an altar on which were written the words of the law. He then read the law to the people as a reminder of the blessings and curses God had promised. In doing this, Joshua connected his leadership to that of Moses.

How often do you read God's Word for the purpose of being reminded? It's a powerful way to bring yourself to thankfulness and praise.

---

[a] 26 *Achor* means *trouble.*

18 Then the LORD said to Joshua, "Hold out toward Ai the javelin that is in your hand, for into your hand I will deliver the city." So Joshua held out toward the city the javelin that was in his hand. 19 As soon as he did this, the men in the ambush rose quickly from their position and rushed forward. They entered the city and captured it and quickly set it on fire.

20 The men of Ai looked back and saw the smoke of the city rising up into the sky, but they had no chance to escape in any direction; the Israelites who had been fleeing toward the wilderness had turned back against their pursuers. 21 For when Joshua and all Israel saw that the ambush had taken the city and that smoke was going up from it, they turned around and attacked the men of Ai. 22 Those in the ambush also came out of the city against them, so that they were caught in the middle, with Israelites on both sides. Israel cut them down, leaving them neither survivors nor fugitives. 23 But they took the king of Ai alive and brought him to Joshua.

24 When Israel had finished killing all the men of Ai in the fields and in the wilderness where they had chased them, and when every one of them had been put to the sword, all the Israelites returned to Ai and killed those who were in it. 25 Twelve thousand men and women fell that day — all the people of Ai. 26 For Joshua did not draw back the hand that held out his javelin until he had destroyed[a] all who lived in Ai. 27 But Israel did carry off for themselves the livestock and plunder of this city, as the LORD had instructed Joshua.

28 So Joshua burned Ai[b] and made it a permanent heap of ruins, a desolate place to this day. 29 He impaled the body of the king of Ai on a pole and left it there until evening. At sunset, Joshua ordered them to take the body from the pole and throw it down at the entrance of the city gate. And they raised a large pile of rocks over it, which remains to this day.

THE COVENANT RENEWED AT MOUNT EBAL

30 Then Joshua built on Mount Ebal an altar to the LORD, the God of Israel, 31 as Moses the servant of the LORD had commanded the Israelites. He built it according to what is written in the Book of the Law of Moses — an altar of uncut stones, on which no iron tool had been used. On it they offered to the LORD burnt offerings and sacrificed fellowship offerings. 32 There, in the presence of the Israelites, Joshua wrote on stones a copy of the law of Moses. 33 All the Israelites, with their elders, officials and judges, were standing on both sides of the ark of the covenant of the LORD, facing the Levitical priests who carried it. Both the foreigners living among them and the native-born were there. Half of the people stood in front of Mount Gerizim and half of them in front of Mount Ebal, as Moses the servant of the LORD had formerly commanded when he gave instructions to bless the people of Israel.

34 Afterward, Joshua read all the words of the law — the blessings and the curses — just as it is written in the Book of the Law. 35 There was not a word of all that Moses had commanded that Joshua did not read to the whole assembly of Israel, including the women and children, and the foreigners who lived among them.

---

[a] *26* The Hebrew term refers to the irrevocable giving over of things or persons to the LORD, often by totally destroying them. [b] *28* *Ai* means *the ruin.*

THE GIBEONITE DECEPTION

9 Now when all the kings west of the Jordan heard about these
things — the kings in the hill country, in the western foothills, and
along the entire coast of the Mediterranean Sea as far as Lebanon (the
kings of the Hittites, Amorites, Canaanites, Perizzites, Hivites and Jeb-
usites) — 2they came together to wage war against Joshua and Israel.
3However, when the people of Gibeon heard what Joshua had done
to Jericho and Ai, 4they resorted to a ruse: They went as a delegation
whose donkeys were loaded[a] with worn-out sacks and old wineskins,
cracked and mended. 5They put worn and patched sandals on their
feet and wore old clothes. All the bread of their food supply was dry
and moldy. 6Then they went to Joshua in the camp at Gilgal and said
to him and the Israelites, "We have come from a distant country; make
a treaty with us."
7The Israelites said to the Hivites, "But perhaps you live near us, so
how can we make a treaty with you?"
8"We are your servants," they said to Joshua.
But Joshua asked, "Who are you and where do you come from?"
9They answered: "Your servants have come from a very distant
country because of the fame of the LORD your God. For we have heard
reports of him: all that he did in Egypt, 10and all that he did to the two
kings of the Amorites east of the Jordan — Sihon king of Heshbon, and
Og king of Bashan, who reigned in Ashtaroth. 11And our elders and all
those living in our country said to us, 'Take provisions for your jour-
ney; go and meet them and say to them, "We are your servants; make
a treaty with us."' 12This bread of ours was warm when we packed it
at home on the day we left to come to you. But now see how dry and
moldy it is. 13And these wineskins that we filled were new, but see how
cracked they are. And our clothes and sandals are worn out by the very
long journey."
14The Israelites sampled their provisions but did not inquire of the
LORD. 15Then Joshua made a treaty of peace with them to let them live,
and the leaders of the assembly ratified it by oath.
16Three days after they made the treaty with the Gibeonites, the Isra-
elites heard that they were neighbors, living near them. 17So the Israel-
ites set out and on the third day came to their cities: Gibeon, Kephirah,
Beeroth and Kiriath Jearim. 18But the Israelites did not attack them,
because the leaders of the assembly had sworn an oath to them by the
LORD, the God of Israel.
The whole assembly grumbled against the leaders, 19but all the lead-
ers answered, "We have given them our oath by the LORD, the God of
Israel, and we cannot touch them now. 20This is what we will do to
them: We will let them live, so that God's wrath will not fall on us for
breaking the oath we swore to them." 21They continued, "Let them live,
but let them be woodcutters and water carriers in the service of the
whole assembly." So the leaders' promise to them was kept.
22Then Joshua summoned the Gibeonites and said, "Why did you de-
ceive us by saying, 'We live a long way from you,' while actually you live
near us? 23You are now under a curse: You will never be released from
service as woodcutters and water carriers for the house of my God."
24They answered Joshua, "Your servants were clearly told how the

[a] 4 Most Hebrew manuscripts; some Hebrew manuscripts, Vulgate and Syriac (see also Septuagint) *They prepared provisions and loaded their donkeys*

PRAYING SCRIPTURE

Joshua 9

Israel made the foolish decision to enter into a covenant with Gibeon after being deceived by its representatives. Pretending to be from a far country and fearing the same fate as Ai—and knowing God's commands—the Gibeonites secured a treaty to provide for their own security.

Few things are more frustrating than being tricked. Ask God for wisdom in all your dealings and for a heart to heed all his commands.

LORD your God had commanded his servant Moses to give you the
whole land and to wipe out all its inhabitants from before you. So we
feared for our lives because of you, and that is why we did this. 25We are
now in your hands. Do to us whatever seems good and right to you."
26So Joshua saved them from the Israelites, and they did not kill
them. 27That day he made the Gibeonites woodcutters and water carri-
ers for the assembly, to provide for the needs of the altar of the LORD at
the place the LORD would choose. And that is what they are to this day.

THE SUN STANDS STILL

10 Now Adoni-Zedek king of Jerusalem heard that Joshua had
taken Ai and totally destroyed[a] it, doing to Ai and its king as
he had done to Jericho and its king, and that the people of Gibeon had
made a treaty of peace with Israel and had become their allies. 2He and
his people were very much alarmed at this, because Gibeon was an im-
portant city, like one of the royal cities; it was larger than Ai, and all its
men were good fighters. 3So Adoni-Zedek king of Jerusalem appealed
to Hoham king of Hebron, Piram king of Jarmuth, Japhia king of La-
chish and Debir king of Eglon. 4"Come up and help me attack Gibeon,"
he said, "because it has made peace with Joshua and the Israelites."
5Then the five kings of the Amorites — the kings of Jerusalem, He-
bron, Jarmuth, Lachish and Eglon — joined forces. They moved up with
all their troops and took up positions against Gibeon and attacked it.
6The Gibeonites then sent word to Joshua in the camp at Gilgal: "Do
not abandon your servants. Come up to us quickly and save us! Help
us, because all the Amorite kings from the hill country have joined
forces against us."
7So Joshua marched up from Gilgal with his entire army, including
all the best fighting men. 8The LORD said to Joshua, "Do not be afraid
of them; I have given them into your hand. Not one of them will be
able to withstand you."
9After an all-night march from Gilgal, Joshua took them by surprise.
10The LORD threw them into confusion before Israel, so Joshua and the
Israelites defeated them completely at Gibeon. Israel pursued them
along the road going up to Beth Horon and cut them down all the way
to Azekah and Makkedah. 11As they fled before Israel on the road down
from Beth Horon to Azekah, the LORD hurled large hailstones down
on them, and more of them died from the hail than were killed by the
swords of the Israelites.
12On the day the LORD gave the Amorites over to Israel, Joshua said
to the LORD in the presence of Israel:

"Sun, stand still over Gibeon,
and you, moon, over the Valley of Aijalon."
13So the sun stood still,
and the moon stopped,
till the nation avenged itself on[b] its enemies,

as it is written in the Book of Jashar.
The sun stopped in the middle of the sky and delayed going down
about a full day. 14There has never been a day like it before or since, a

PRAYING SCRIPTURE
Joshua 10

The Lord often used miraculous means to fight for his people, and this passage recounts one of the most startling: The sun stood still so Israel could win a battle. Where God's promises are concerned, there is no power he will not exercise to keep them so that he will be glorified.

Do you need God to keep a specific promise today? Pray that Scripture to him, and expect him to be faithful to his Word.

---

[a] *1* The Hebrew term refers to the irrevocable giving over of things or persons to the LORD, often by totally destroying them; also in verses 28, 35, 37, 39 and 40.
[b] *13* Or *nation triumphed over*

day when the LORD listened to a human being. Surely the LORD was
fighting for Israel!
15Then Joshua returned with all Israel to the camp at Gilgal.

FIVE AMORITE KINGS KILLED

16Now the five kings had fled and hidden in the cave at Makkedah.
17When Joshua was told that the five kings had been found hiding in
the cave at Makkedah, 18he said, "Roll large rocks up to the mouth of
the cave, and post some men there to guard it. 19But don't stop; pursue
your enemies! Attack them from the rear and don't let them reach their
cities, for the LORD your God has given them into your hand."
20So Joshua and the Israelites defeated them completely, but a few
survivors managed to reach their fortified cities. 21The whole army
then returned safely to Joshua in the camp at Makkedah, and no one
uttered a word against the Israelites.
22Joshua said, "Open the mouth of the cave and bring those five
kings out to me." 23So they brought the five kings out of the cave — the
kings of Jerusalem, Hebron, Jarmuth, Lachish and Eglon. 24When they
had brought these kings to Joshua, he summoned all the men of Israel
and said to the army commanders who had come with him, "Come
here and put your feet on the necks of these kings." So they came for-
ward and placed their feet on their necks.
25Joshua said to them, "Do not be afraid; do not be discouraged. Be
strong and courageous. This is what the LORD will do to all the ene-
mies you are going to fight." 26Then Joshua put the kings to death and
exposed their bodies on five poles, and they were left hanging on the
poles until evening.
27At sunset Joshua gave the order and they took them down from the
poles and threw them into the cave where they had been hiding. At the
mouth of the cave they placed large rocks, which are there to this day.

SOUTHERN CITIES CONQUERED

28That day Joshua took Makkedah. He put the city and its king to the
sword and totally destroyed everyone in it. He left no survivors. And
he did to the king of Makkedah as he had done to the king of Jericho.
29Then Joshua and all Israel with him moved on from Makkedah to
Libnah and attacked it. 30The LORD also gave that city and its king into
Israel's hand. The city and everyone in it Joshua put to the sword. He
left no survivors there. And he did to its king as he had done to the
king of Jericho.
31Then Joshua and all Israel with him moved on from Libnah to La-
chish; he took up positions against it and attacked it. 32The LORD gave
Lachish into Israel's hands, and Joshua took it on the second day. The
city and everyone in it he put to the sword, just as he had done to Lib-
nah. 33Meanwhile, Horam king of Gezer had come up to help Lachish,
but Joshua defeated him and his army — until no survivors were left.
34Then Joshua and all Israel with him moved on from Lachish to Eg-
lon; they took up positions against it and attacked it. 35They captured
it that same day and put it to the sword and totally destroyed everyone
in it, just as they had done to Lachish.
36Then Joshua and all Israel with him went up from Eglon to Hebron
and attacked it. 37They took the city and put it to the sword, together
with its king, its villages and everyone in it. They left no survivors. Just
as at Eglon, they totally destroyed it and everyone in it.

[38]Then Joshua and all Israel with him turned around and attacked
Debir. [39]They took the city, its king and its villages, and put them to
the sword. Everyone in it they totally destroyed. They left no survivors.
They did to Debir and its king as they had done to Libnah and its king
and to Hebron.
[40]So Joshua subdued the whole region, including the hill country,
the Negev, the western foothills and the mountain slopes, together
with all their kings. He left no survivors. He totally destroyed all who
breathed, just as the LORD, the God of Israel, had commanded. [41]Joshua
subdued them from Kadesh Barnea to Gaza and from the whole re-
gion of Goshen to Gibeon. [42]All these kings and their lands Joshua con-
quered in one campaign, because the LORD, the God of Israel, fought
for Israel.
[43]Then Joshua returned with all Israel to the camp at Gilgal.

NORTHERN KINGS DEFEATED

11 When Jabin king of Hazor heard of this, he sent word to Jobab
king of Madon, to the kings of Shimron and Akshaph, [2]and to
the northern kings who were in the mountains, in the Arabah south of
Kinnereth, in the western foothills and in Naphoth Dor on the west; [3]to
the Canaanites in the east and west; to the Amorites, Hittites, Perizzites
and Jebusites in the hill country; and to the Hivites below Hermon in
the region of Mizpah. [4]They came out with all their troops and a large
number of horses and chariots — a huge army, as numerous as the
sand on the seashore. [5]All these kings joined forces and made camp
together at the Waters of Merom to fight against Israel.
[6]The LORD said to Joshua, "Do not be afraid of them, because by this
time tomorrow I will hand all of them, slain, over to Israel. You are to
hamstring their horses and burn their chariots."
[7]So Joshua and his whole army came against them suddenly at the
Waters of Merom and attacked them, [8]and the LORD gave them into
the hand of Israel. They defeated them and pursued them all the way
to Greater Sidon, to Misrephoth Maim, and to the Valley of Mizpah on
the east, until no survivors were left. [9]Joshua did to them as the LORD
had directed: He hamstrung their horses and burned their chariots.
[10]At that time Joshua turned back and captured Hazor and put its
king to the sword. (Hazor had been the head of all these kingdoms.)
[11]Everyone in it they put to the sword. They totally destroyed[a] them,
not sparing anyone that breathed, and he burned Hazor itself.
[12]Joshua took all these royal cities and their kings and put them
to the sword. He totally destroyed them, as Moses the servant of the
LORD had commanded. [13]Yet Israel did not burn any of the cities built
on their mounds — except Hazor, which Joshua burned. [14]The Israel-
ites carried off for themselves all the plunder and livestock of these
cities, but all the people they put to the sword until they completely
destroyed them, not sparing anyone that breathed. [15]As the LORD com-
manded his servant Moses, so Moses commanded Joshua, and Joshua
did it; he left nothing undone of all that the LORD commanded Moses.
[16]So Joshua took this entire land: the hill country, all the Negev, the
whole region of Goshen, the western foothills, the Arabah and the

PRAYING SCRIPTURE

Joshua 11

As he had numerous times before, God again told Joshua, "Do not be afraid" (verse 6). This is a theme throughout the Scriptures. Think about the countless times fear creeps into your life. Have you been fearful recently? What about? Did you take that fear to God immediately?

God does not want us to fear. Ask him to increase your faith so that your fear is replaced by his presence.

---

[a] *11* The Hebrew term refers to the irrevocable giving over of things or persons to the LORD, often by totally destroying them; also in verses 12, 20 and 21.

mountains of Israel with their foothills, 17 from Mount Halak, which
rises toward Seir, to Baal Gad in the Valley of Lebanon below Mount
Hermon. He captured all their kings and put them to death. 18 Joshua
waged war against all these kings for a long time. 19 Except for the Hi-
vites living in Gibeon, not one city made a treaty of peace with the
Israelites, who took them all in battle. 20 For it was the LORD himself
who hardened their hearts to wage war against Israel, so that he might
destroy them totally, exterminating them without mercy, as the LORD
had commanded Moses.

21 At that time Joshua went and destroyed the Anakites from the hill
country: from Hebron, Debir and Anab, from all the hill country of
Judah, and from all the hill country of Israel. Joshua totally destroyed
them and their towns. 22 No Anakites were left in Israelite territory;
only in Gaza, Gath and Ashdod did any survive.

23 So Joshua took the entire land, just as the LORD had directed Mo-
ses, and he gave it as an inheritance to Israel according to their tribal
divisions. Then the land had rest from war.

LIST OF DEFEATED KINGS

12 These are the kings of the land whom the Israelites had defeated
and whose territory they took over east of the Jordan, from the
Arnon Gorge to Mount Hermon, including all the eastern side of the
Arabah:

2 Sihon king of the Amorites, who reigned in Heshbon.
He ruled from Aroer on the rim of the Arnon Gorge — from the
middle of the gorge to the Jabbok River, which is the border
of the Ammonites. This included half of Gilead. 3 He also ruled
over the eastern Arabah from the Sea of Galilee[a] to the Sea of
the Arabah (that is, the Dead Sea), to Beth Jeshimoth, and then
southward below the slopes of Pisgah.

4 And the territory of Og king of Bashan, one of the last of the
Rephaites, who reigned in Ashtaroth and Edrei.

5 He ruled over Mount Hermon, Salekah, all of Bashan to the bor-
der of the people of Geshur and Maakah, and half of Gilead to
the border of Sihon king of Heshbon.

6 Moses, the servant of the LORD, and the Israelites conquered them.
And Moses the servant of the LORD gave their land to the Reubenites,
the Gadites and the half-tribe of Manasseh to be their possession.

7 Here is a list of the kings of the land that Joshua and the Israelites
conquered on the west side of the Jordan, from Baal Gad in the Valley
of Lebanon to Mount Halak, which rises toward Seir. Joshua gave their
lands as an inheritance to the tribes of Israel according to their tribal
divisions. 8 The lands included the hill country, the western foothills,
the Arabah, the mountain slopes, the wilderness and the Negev. These
were the lands of the Hittites, Amorites, Canaanites, Perizzites, Hivites
and Jebusites. These were the kings:

9 the king of Jericho	one
the king of Ai (near Bethel)	one
10 the king of Jerusalem	one
the king of Hebron	one

[a] 3 Hebrew *Kinnereth*

PRAYING SCRIPTURE

Joshua 12

As Joshua listed the kings conquered by Israel, each name was a promise of God fulfilled. Moses led the people to conquer kings before crossing the Jordan while Joshua led them to conquer dozens of kings after entering the land.

Israel's victories recorded here were in battle. But God's power to deliver in life and spirit is available to all his children, so don't hesitate to call on his name.

11 the king of Jarmuth one
the king of Lachish one
12 the king of Eglon one
the king of Gezer one
13 the king of Debir one
the king of Geder one
14 the king of Hormah one
the king of Arad one
15 the king of Libnah one
the king of Adullam one
16 the king of Makkedah one
the king of Bethel one
17 the king of Tappuah one
the king of Hepher one
18 the king of Aphek one
the king of Lasharon one
19 the king of Madon one
the king of Hazor one
20 the king of Shimron Meron one
the king of Akshaph one
21 the king of Taanach one
the king of Megiddo one
22 the king of Kedesh one
the king of Jokneam in Carmel one
23 the king of Dor (in Naphoth Dor) one
the king of Goyim in Gilgal one
24 the king of Tirzah one
thirty-one kings in all.

LAND STILL TO BE TAKEN

13 When Joshua had grown old, the LORD said to him, "You are
now very old, and there are still very large areas of land to be
taken over.

2"This is the land that remains: all the regions of the Philistines and
Geshurites, 3from the Shihor River on the east of Egypt to the ter-
ritory of Ekron on the north, all of it counted as Canaanite though
held by the five Philistine rulers in Gaza, Ashdod, Ashkelon, Gath
and Ekron; the territory of the Avvites 4on the south; all the land
of the Canaanites, from Arah of the Sidonians as far as Aphek and
the border of the Amorites; 5the area of Byblos; and all Lebanon
to the east, from Baal Gad below Mount Hermon to Lebo Hamath.

6"As for all the inhabitants of the mountain regions from Lebanon
to Misrephoth Maim, that is, all the Sidonians, I myself will drive them
out before the Israelites. Be sure to allocate this land to Israel for an
inheritance, as I have instructed you, 7and divide it as an inheritance
among the nine tribes and half of the tribe of Manasseh."

DIVISION OF THE LAND EAST OF THE JORDAN

8The other half of Manasseh,[a] the Reubenites and the Gadites had re-
ceived the inheritance that Moses had given them east of the Jordan,
as he, the servant of the LORD, had assigned it to them.

[a] 8 Hebrew *With it* (that is, with the other half of Manasseh)

PRAYING SCRIPTURE

Joshua 13

As God continued to apportion the promised land to the tribes, he reminded Israel's leader that although he was advancing in age, still there were "very large areas of land" left to take over according to God's promises (verse 1).

God is not finished with us when we get old. Ask God to help you serve him with all the strength and ability you have until your dying day.

[9]It extended from Aroer on the rim of the Arnon Gorge, and from
the town in the middle of the gorge, and included the whole pla-
teau of Medeba as far as Dibon, [10]and all the towns of Sihon king
of the Amorites, who ruled in Heshbon, out to the border of the
Ammonites. [11]It also included Gilead, the territory of the people of
Geshur and Maakah, all of Mount Hermon and all Bashan as far as
Salekah — [12]that is, the whole kingdom of Og in Bashan, who had
reigned in Ashtaroth and Edrei. (He was the last of the Rephaites.)
Moses had defeated them and taken over their land. [13]But the Isra-
elites did not drive out the people of Geshur and Maakah, so they
continue to live among the Israelites to this day.

[14]But to the tribe of Levi he gave no inheritance, since the food of-
ferings presented to the LORD, the God of Israel, are their inheritance,
as he promised them.

[15]This is what Moses had given to the tribe of Reuben, according to its
clans:

[16]The territory from Aroer on the rim of the Arnon Gorge, and
from the town in the middle of the gorge, and the whole plateau
past Medeba [17]to Heshbon and all its towns on the plateau, in-
cluding Dibon, Bamoth Baal, Beth Baal Meon, [18]Jahaz, Kedemoth,
Mephaath, [19]Kiriathaim, Sibmah, Zereth Shahar on the hill in the
valley, [20]Beth Peor, the slopes of Pisgah, and Beth Jeshimoth —
[21]all the towns on the plateau and the entire realm of Sihon king
of the Amorites, who ruled at Heshbon. Moses had defeated him
and the Midianite chiefs, Evi, Rekem, Zur, Hur and Reba — princes
allied with Sihon — who lived in that country. [22]In addition to
those slain in battle, the Israelites had put to the sword Balaam
son of Beor, who practiced divination. [23]The boundary of the Reu-
benites was the bank of the Jordan. These towns and their villages
were the inheritance of the Reubenites, according to their clans.

[24]This is what Moses had given to the tribe of Gad, according to its
clans:

[25]The territory of Jazer, all the towns of Gilead and half the Am-
monite country as far as Aroer, near Rabbah; [26]and from Hesh-
bon to Ramath Mizpah and Betonim, and from Mahanaim to the
territory of Debir; [27]and in the valley, Beth Haram, Beth Nimrah,
Sukkoth and Zaphon with the rest of the realm of Sihon king of
Heshbon (the east side of the Jordan, the territory up to the end
of the Sea of Galilee[a]). [28]These towns and their villages were the
inheritance of the Gadites, according to their clans.

[29]This is what Moses had given to the half-tribe of Manasseh, that is, to
half the family of the descendants of Manasseh, according to its clans:

[30]The territory extending from Mahanaim and including all of Ba-
shan, the entire realm of Og king of Bashan — all the settlements
of Jair in Bashan, sixty towns, [31]half of Gilead, and Ashtaroth and
Edrei (the royal cities of Og in Bashan). This was for the descen-
dants of Makir son of Manasseh — for half of the sons of Makir,
according to their clans.

---

[a] *27* Hebrew *Kinnereth*

32This is the inheritance Moses had given when he was in the plains of Moab across the Jordan east of Jericho. 33But to the tribe of Levi, Moses had given no inheritance; the LORD, the God of Israel, is their inheritance, as he promised them.

DIVISION OF THE LAND WEST OF THE JORDAN

14 Now these are the areas the Israelites received as an inheritance in the land of Canaan, which Eleazar the priest, Joshua son of Nun and the heads of the tribal clans of Israel allotted to them. 2Their inheritances were assigned by lot to the nine and a half tribes, as the LORD had commanded through Moses. 3Moses had granted the two and a half tribes their inheritance east of the Jordan but had not granted the Levites an inheritance among the rest, 4for Joseph's descendants had become two tribes — Manasseh and Ephraim. The Levites received no share of the land but only towns to live in, with pasturelands for their flocks and herds. 5So the Israelites divided the land, just as the LORD had commanded Moses.

PRAYING SCRIPTURE

Joshua 14

Along with Joshua, only one spy had demonstrated faith that God would give Israel the promised land decades before they entered: Caleb. Now, 40 years later, neither his strength nor his faith failed as he asked Joshua for the portion God promised.

Is there something for which you've asked God for a long time, so long you're wondering if he will answer? Ask again today with as much faith as in the beginning!

ALLOTMENT FOR CALEB

6Now the people of Judah approached Joshua at Gilgal, and Caleb son of Jephunneh the Kenizzite said to him, "You know what the LORD said to Moses the man of God at Kadesh Barnea about you and me. 7I was forty years old when Moses the servant of the LORD sent me from Kadesh Barnea to explore the land. And I brought him back a report according to my convictions, 8but my fellow Israelites who went up with me made the hearts of the people melt in fear. I, however, followed the LORD my God wholeheartedly. 9So on that day Moses swore to me, 'The land on which your feet have walked will be your inheritance and that of your children forever, because you have followed the LORD my God wholeheartedly.'[a]

10"Now then, just as the LORD promised, he has kept me alive for forty-five years since the time he said this to Moses, while Israel moved about in the wilderness. So here I am today, eighty-five years old! 11I am still as strong today as the day Moses sent me out; I'm just as vigorous to go out to battle now as I was then. 12Now give me this hill country that the LORD promised me that day. You yourself heard then that the Anakites were there and their cities were large and fortified, but, the LORD helping me, I will drive them out just as he said."

13Then Joshua blessed Caleb son of Jephunneh and gave him Hebron as his inheritance. 14So Hebron has belonged to Caleb son of Jephunneh the Kenizzite ever since, because he followed the LORD, the God of Israel, wholeheartedly. 15(Hebron used to be called Kiriath Arba after Arba, who was the greatest man among the Anakites.)

Then the land had rest from war.

PRAYING SCRIPTURE

Joshua 15

The list of cities in Judah is remarkable in light of Israel's founding by a man who was childless until he was almost a hundred years old. God's promise that Abraham's descendants would be as the sand of the seashore was well on the way to fulfillment.

God's promise opened the door for anyone to become a spiritual descendant of Abraham. Praise God for sustaining his people until the Messiah came.

ALLOTMENT FOR JUDAH

15 The allotment for the tribe of Judah, according to its clans, extended down to the territory of Edom, to the Desert of Zin in the extreme south.

2Their southern boundary started from the bay at the southern end of the Dead Sea, 3crossed south of Scorpion Pass, continued on to Zin and went over to the south of Kadesh Barnea. Then it

[a] 9 Deut. 1:36

ran past Hezron up to Addar and curved around to Karka. 4It then
passed along to Azmon and joined the Wadi of Egypt, ending at
the Mediterranean Sea. This is their[a] southern boundary.

5The eastern boundary is the Dead Sea as far as the mouth of
the Jordan.

The northern boundary started from the bay of the sea at the
mouth of the Jordan, 6went up to Beth Hoglah and continued
north of Beth Arabah to the Stone of Bohan son of Reuben. 7The
boundary then went up to Debir from the Valley of Achor and
turned north to Gilgal, which faces the Pass of Adummim south
of the gorge. It continued along to the waters of En Shemesh and
came out at En Rogel. 8Then it ran up the Valley of Ben Hinnom
along the southern slope of the Jebusite city (that is, Jerusalem).
From there it climbed to the top of the hill west of the Hinnom
Valley at the northern end of the Valley of Rephaim. 9From the
hilltop the boundary headed toward the spring of the waters of
Nephtoah, came out at the towns of Mount Ephron and went down
toward Baalah (that is, Kiriath Jearim). 10Then it curved westward
from Baalah to Mount Seir, ran along the northern slope of Mount
Jearim (that is, Kesalon), continued down to Beth Shemesh and
crossed to Timnah. 11It went to the northern slope of Ekron, turned
toward Shikkeron, passed along to Mount Baalah and reached Jab-
neel. The boundary ended at the sea.

12The western boundary is the coastline of the Mediterranean
Sea.

These are the boundaries around the people of Judah by their clans.

13In accordance with the LORD's command to him, Joshua gave to
Caleb son of Jephunneh a portion in Judah — Kiriath Arba, that is, He-
bron. (Arba was the forefather of Anak.) 14From Hebron Caleb drove
out the three Anakites — Sheshai, Ahiman and Talmai, the sons of
Anak. 15From there he marched against the people living in Debir (for-
merly called Kiriath Sepher). 16And Caleb said, "I will give my daughter
Aksah in marriage to the man who attacks and captures Kiriath Se-
pher." 17Othniel son of Kenaz, Caleb's brother, took it; so Caleb gave his
daughter Aksah to him in marriage.

18One day when she came to Othniel, she urged him[b] to ask her fa-
ther for a field. When she got off her donkey, Caleb asked her, "What
can I do for you?"

19She replied, "Do me a special favor. Since you have given me land
in the Negev, give me also springs of water." So Caleb gave her the up-
per and lower springs.

20This is the inheritance of the tribe of Judah, according to its clans:

21The southernmost towns of the tribe of Judah in the Negev toward
the boundary of Edom were:

Kabzeel, Eder, Jagur, 22Kinah, Dimonah, Adadah, 23Kedesh, Ha-
zor, Ithnan, 24Ziph, Telem, Bealoth, 25Hazor Hadattah, Kerioth
Hezron (that is, Hazor), 26Amam, Shema, Moladah, 27Hazar Gad-
dah, Heshmon, Beth Pelet, 28Hazar Shual, Beersheba, Biziothiah,

---

[a] 4 Septuagint; Hebrew *your* [b] 18 Hebrew and some Septuagint manuscripts; other Septuagint manuscripts (see also note at Judges 1:14) *Othniel, he urged her*

29 Baalah, Iyim, Ezem, 30 Eltolad, Kesil, Hormah, 31 Ziklag, Madman-
nah, Sansannah, 32 Lebaoth, Shilhim, Ain and Rimmon — a total of
twenty-nine towns and their villages.

33 In the western foothills:
Eshtaol, Zorah, Ashnah, 34 Zanoah, En Gannim, Tappuah, Enam,
35 Jarmuth, Adullam, Sokoh, Azekah, 36 Shaaraim, Adithaim and
Gederah (or Gederothaim)[a] — fourteen towns and their villages.
37 Zenan, Hadashah, Migdal Gad, 38 Dilean, Mizpah, Joktheel,
39 Lachish, Bozkath, Eglon, 40 Kabbon, Lahmas, Kitlish, 41 Gederoth,
Beth Dagon, Naamah and Makkedah — sixteen towns and their
villages.
42 Libnah, Ether, Ashan, 43 Iphtah, Ashnah, Nezib, 44 Keilah, Akzib
and Mareshah — nine towns and their villages.
45 Ekron, with its surrounding settlements and villages; 46 west
of Ekron, all that were in the vicinity of Ashdod, together with
their villages; 47 Ashdod, its surrounding settlements and villages;
and Gaza, its settlements and villages, as far as the Wadi of Egypt
and the coastline of the Mediterranean Sea.

48 In the hill country:
Shamir, Jattir, Sokoh, 49 Dannah, Kiriath Sannah (that is, Debir),
50 Anab, Eshtemoh, Anim, 51 Goshen, Holon and Giloh — eleven
towns and their villages.
52 Arab, Dumah, Eshan, 53 Janim, Beth Tappuah, Aphekah, 54 Hum-
tah, Kiriath Arba (that is, Hebron) and Zior — nine towns and their
villages.
55 Maon, Carmel, Ziph, Juttah, 56 Jezreel, Jokdeam, Zanoah,
57 Kain, Gibeah and Timnah — ten towns and their villages.
58 Halhul, Beth Zur, Gedor, 59 Maarath, Beth Anoth and Eltekon —
six towns and their villages.[b]
60 Kiriath Baal (that is, Kiriath Jearim) and Rabbah — two towns
and their villages.

61 In the wilderness:
Beth Arabah, Middin, Sekakah, 62 Nibshan, the City of Salt and
En Gedi — six towns and their villages.
63 Judah could not dislodge the Jebusites, who were living in Jeru-
salem; to this day the Jebusites live there with the people of Judah.

ALLOTMENT FOR EPHRAIM AND MANASSEH

16 The allotment for Joseph began at the Jordan, east of the
springs of Jericho, and went up from there through the des-
ert into the hill country of Bethel. 2 It went on from Bethel (that
is, Luz),[c] crossed over to the territory of the Arkites in Ataroth,
3 descended westward to the territory of the Japhletites as far as
the region of Lower Beth Horon and on to Gezer, ending at the
Mediterranean Sea.
4 So Manasseh and Ephraim, the descendants of Joseph, received their
inheritance.
5 This was the territory of Ephraim, according to its clans:

PRAYING SCRIPTURE

Joshua 16

Bad things often happen when God's people don't do things God's way. In this case, some of the people in the cities refused to drive out the existing inhabitants of Canaan as God had instructed them. Ephraim chose to enslave the Canaanites in their region instead.

It never works to circumvent God's desires with our own. Ask God to search your heart for any temptation to substitute your will for his.

---

[a] 36 Or *Gederah and Gederothaim* [b] 59 The Septuagint adds another district of eleven towns, including Tekoa and Ephrathah (Bethlehem).
[c] 2 Septuagint; Hebrew *Bethel to Luz*

The boundary of their inheritance went from Ataroth Addar in
the east to Upper Beth Horon 6and continued to the Mediterranean
Sea. From Mikmethath on the north it curved eastward to Taanath
Shiloh, passing by it to Janoah on the east. 7Then it went down
from Janoah to Ataroth and Naarah, touched Jericho and came out
at the Jordan. 8From Tappuah the border went west to the Kanah
Ravine and ended at the Mediterranean Sea. This was the inheri-
tance of the tribe of the Ephraimites, according to its clans. 9It also
included all the towns and their villages that were set aside for the
Ephraimites within the inheritance of the Manassites.
10They did not dislodge the Canaanites living in Gezer; to this day the
Canaanites live among the people of Ephraim but are required to do
forced labor.

17 This was the allotment for the tribe of Manasseh as Joseph's
firstborn, that is, for Makir, Manasseh's firstborn. Makir was the
ancestor of the Gileadites, who had received Gilead and Bashan be-
cause the Makirites were great soldiers. 2So this allotment was for the
rest of the people of Manasseh — the clans of Abiezer, Helek, Asriel,
Shechem, Hepher and Shemida. These are the other male descendants
of Manasseh son of Joseph by their clans.

3Now Zelophehad son of Hepher, the son of Gilead, the son of Makir,
the son of Manasseh, had no sons but only daughters, whose names
were Mahlah, Noah, Hoglah, Milkah and Tirzah. 4They went to Eleazar
the priest, Joshua son of Nun, and the leaders and said, "The LORD
commanded Moses to give us an inheritance among our relatives." So
Joshua gave them an inheritance along with the brothers of their fa-
ther, according to the LORD's command. 5Manasseh's share consisted
of ten tracts of land besides Gilead and Bashan east of the Jordan, 6be-
cause the daughters of the tribe of Manasseh received an inheritance
among the sons. The land of Gilead belonged to the rest of the descen-
dants of Manasseh.

7The territory of Manasseh extended from Asher to Mikmethath
east of Shechem. The boundary ran southward from there to in-
clude the people living at En Tappuah. 8(Manasseh had the land
of Tappuah, but Tappuah itself, on the boundary of Manasseh, be-
longed to the Ephraimites.) 9Then the boundary continued south
to the Kanah Ravine. There were towns belonging to Ephraim lying
among the towns of Manasseh, but the boundary of Manasseh was
the northern side of the ravine and ended at the Mediterranean
Sea. 10On the south the land belonged to Ephraim, on the north to
Manasseh. The territory of Manasseh reached the Mediterranean
Sea and bordered Asher on the north and Issachar on the east.

11Within Issachar and Asher, Manasseh also had Beth Shan, Ibleam
and the people of Dor, Endor, Taanach and Megiddo, together with
their surrounding settlements (the third in the list is Naphoth[a]).
12Yet the Manassites were not able to occupy these towns, for the Ca-
naanites were determined to live in that region. 13However, when the
Israelites grew stronger, they subjected the Canaanites to forced labor
but did not drive them out completely.

14The people of Joseph said to Joshua, "Why have you given us only
one allotment and one portion for an inheritance? We are a numerous
people, and the LORD has blessed us abundantly."

[a] *11* That is, Naphoth Dor

PRAYING SCRIPTURE

Joshua 17

This passage gives a hint as to why certain of the tribes hesitated to drive out the Canaanites: They were strong. They had chariots of iron. Driving out the inhabitants would not be easy. The Israelites had to work for the victory God promised.

It would be nice if following Jesus was easy, wouldn't it? But God will help us walk in the victory he has already won.

15“If you are so numerous,” Joshua answered, “and if the hill country
of Ephraim is too small for you, go up into the forest and clear land for
yourselves there in the land of the Perizzites and Rephaites.”
16The people of Joseph replied, “The hill country is not enough for
us, and all the Canaanites who live in the plain have chariots fitted
with iron, both those in Beth Shan and its settlements and those in
the Valley of Jezreel.”
17But Joshua said to the tribes of Joseph — to Ephraim and Manas-
seh — “You are numerous and very powerful. You will have not only
one allotment 18but the forested hill country as well. Clear it, and its
farthest limits will be yours; though the Canaanites have chariots fit-
ted with iron and though they are strong, you can drive them out.”

DIVISION OF THE REST OF THE LAND

18 The whole assembly of the Israelites gathered at Shiloh and set
up the tent of meeting there. The country was brought under
their control, 2but there were still seven Israelite tribes who had not
yet received their inheritance.
3So Joshua said to the Israelites: “How long will you wait before you
begin to take possession of the land that the LORD, the God of your
ancestors, has given you? 4Appoint three men from each tribe. I will
send them out to make a survey of the land and to write a description
of it, according to the inheritance of each. Then they will return to me.
5You are to divide the land into seven parts. Judah is to remain in its
territory on the south and the tribes of Joseph in their territory on the
north. 6After you have written descriptions of the seven parts of the
land, bring them here to me and I will cast lots for you in the presence
of the LORD our God. 7The Levites, however, do not get a portion among
you, because the priestly service of the LORD is their inheritance. And
Gad, Reuben and the half-tribe of Manasseh have already received
their inheritance on the east side of the Jordan. Moses the servant of
the LORD gave it to them.”
8As the men started on their way to map out the land, Joshua in-
structed them, “Go and make a survey of the land and write a descrip-
tion of it. Then return to me, and I will cast lots for you here at Shiloh
in the presence of the LORD.” 9So the men left and went through the
land. They wrote its description on a scroll, town by town, in seven
parts, and returned to Joshua in the camp at Shiloh. 10Joshua then
cast lots for them in Shiloh in the presence of the LORD, and there he
distributed the land to the Israelites according to their tribal divisions.

PRAYING SCRIPTURE

Joshua 18

Neglecting to do God’s will is as much a sin as violating his commands. When tribes simply refused to possess their sections of the land, Joshua pressed them to obey. The comfort they experienced in inactivity was apparently good enough for them.

Sometimes God uses people in our lives to push us and challenge us to obey. Thank God for every person like that whom he has placed in your path.

ALLOTMENT FOR BENJAMIN

11The first lot came up for the tribe of Benjamin according to its clans.
Their allotted territory lay between the tribes of Judah and Joseph:
12On the north side their boundary began at the Jordan, passed
the northern slope of Jericho and headed west into the hill coun-
try, coming out at the wilderness of Beth Aven. 13From there it
crossed to the south slope of Luz (that is, Bethel) and went down
to Ataroth Addar on the hill south of Lower Beth Horon.
14From the hill facing Beth Horon on the south the boundary
turned south along the western side and came out at Kiriath Baal
(that is, Kiriath Jearim), a town of the people of Judah. This was
the western side.
15The southern side began at the outskirts of Kiriath Jearim on

the west, and the boundary came out at the spring of the waters
of Nephtoah. 16The boundary went down to the foot of the hill
facing the Valley of Ben Hinnom, north of the Valley of Rephaim.
It continued down the Hinnom Valley along the southern slope of
the Jebusite city and so to En Rogel. 17It then curved north, went to
En Shemesh, continued to Geliloth, which faces the Pass of Adum-
mim, and ran down to the Stone of Bohan son of Reuben. 18It con-
tinued to the northern slope of Beth Arabah[a] and on down into
the Arabah. 19It then went to the northern slope of Beth Hoglah
and came out at the northern bay of the Dead Sea, at the mouth of
the Jordan in the south. This was the southern boundary.
20The Jordan formed the boundary on the eastern side.
These were the boundaries that marked out the inheritance of the
clans of Benjamin on all sides.

21The tribe of Benjamin, according to its clans, had the following towns:
Jericho, Beth Hoglah, Emek Keziz, 22Beth Arabah, Zemaraim,
Bethel, 23Avvim, Parah, Ophrah, 24Kephar Ammoni, Ophni and
Geba — twelve towns and their villages.
25Gibeon, Ramah, Beeroth, 26Mizpah, Kephirah, Mozah, 27Re-
kem, Irpeel, Taralah, 28Zelah, Haeleph, the Jebusite city (that is, Je-
rusalem), Gibeah and Kiriath — fourteen towns and their villages.
This was the inheritance of Benjamin for its clans.

ALLOTMENT FOR SIMEON

19 The second lot came out for the tribe of Simeon according to
its clans. Their inheritance lay within the territory of Judah. 2It
included:
Beersheba (or Sheba),[b] Moladah, 3Hazar Shual, Balah, Ezem,
4Eltolad, Bethul, Hormah, 5Ziklag, Beth Markaboth, Hazar Susah,
6Beth Lebaoth and Sharuhen — thirteen towns and their villages;
7Ain, Rimmon, Ether and Ashan — four towns and their vil-
lages — 8and all the villages around these towns as far as Baalath
Beer (Ramah in the Negev).
This was the inheritance of the tribe of the Simeonites, according to
its clans. 9The inheritance of the Simeonites was taken from the share
of Judah, because Judah's portion was more than they needed. So the
Simeonites received their inheritance within the territory of Judah.

ALLOTMENT FOR ZEBULUN

10The third lot came up for Zebulun according to its clans:
The boundary of their inheritance went as far as Sarid. 11Going
west it ran to Maralah, touched Dabbesheth, and extended to the
ravine near Jokneam. 12It turned east from Sarid toward the sun-
rise to the territory of Kisloth Tabor and went on to Daberath and
up to Japhia. 13Then it continued eastward to Gath Hepher and Eth
Kazin; it came out at Rimmon and turned toward Neah. 14There
the boundary went around on the north to Hannathon and ended
at the Valley of Iphtah El. 15Included were Kattath, Nahalal, Shim-
ron, Idalah and Bethlehem. There were twelve towns and their
villages.

PRAYING SCRIPTURE

Joshua 19

By God's command, the Israelites gave an inheritance to Joshua for his leadership in conquering the land. He received his allotment in Shiloh near the door of the tabernacle, a constant reminder of the priority of worship in Israel. The dividing of the land then ended.

Like Joshua, Christians live in the presence of the One who deserves our worship. Pause now and several times today to worship God.

[a] 18 Septuagint; Hebrew *slope facing the Arabah* [b] 2 Or *Beersheba, Sheba*; 1 Chron. 4:28 does not have *Sheba.*

16These towns and their villages were the inheritance of Zebulun, ac-
cording to its clans.

ALLOTMENT FOR ISSACHAR

17The fourth lot came out for Issachar according to its clans. 18Their
territory included:

Jezreel, Kesulloth, Shunem, 19Hapharaim, Shion, Anaharath,
20Rabbith, Kishion, Ebez, 21Remeth, En Gannim, En Haddah and
Beth Pazzez. 22The boundary touched Tabor, Shahazumah and
Beth Shemesh, and ended at the Jordan. There were sixteen towns
and their villages.

23These towns and their villages were the inheritance of the tribe of
Issachar, according to its clans.

ALLOTMENT FOR ASHER

24The fifth lot came out for the tribe of Asher according to its clans.
25Their territory included:

Helkath, Hali, Beten, Akshaph, 26Allammelek, Amad and Mishal.
On the west the boundary touched Carmel and Shihor Libnath. 27It
then turned east toward Beth Dagon, touched Zebulun and the
Valley of Iphtah El, and went north to Beth Emek and Neiel, pass-
ing Kabul on the left. 28It went to Abdon,[a] Rehob, Hammon and
Kanah, as far as Greater Sidon. 29The boundary then turned back
toward Ramah and went to the fortified city of Tyre, turned to-
ward Hosah and came out at the Mediterranean Sea in the region
of Akzib, 30Ummah, Aphek and Rehob. There were twenty-two
towns and their villages.

31These towns and their villages were the inheritance of the tribe of
Asher, according to its clans.

ALLOTMENT FOR NAPHTALI

32The sixth lot came out for Naphtali according to its clans:

33Their boundary went from Heleph and the large tree in Zaa-
nannim, passing Adami Nekeb and Jabneel to Lakkum and ending
at the Jordan. 34The boundary ran west through Aznoth Tabor and
came out at Hukkok. It touched Zebulun on the south, Asher on
the west and the Jordan[b] on the east. 35The fortified towns were
Ziddim, Zer, Hammath, Rakkath, Kinnereth, 36Adamah, Ramah,
Hazor, 37Kedesh, Edrei, En Hazor, 38Iron, Migdal El, Horem, Beth
Anath and Beth Shemesh. There were nineteen towns and their
villages.

39These towns and their villages were the inheritance of the tribe of
Naphtali, according to its clans.

ALLOTMENT FOR DAN

40The seventh lot came out for the tribe of Dan according to its clans.
41The territory of their inheritance included:

Zorah, Eshtaol, Ir Shemesh, 42Shaalabbin, Aijalon, Ithlah, 43Elon,
Timnah, Ekron, 44Eltekeh, Gibbethon, Baalath, 45Jehud, Bene Be-
rak, Gath Rimmon, 46Me Jarkon and Rakkon, with the area facing
Joppa.

---

[a] *28* Some Hebrew manuscripts (see also 21:30); most Hebrew manuscripts *Ebron* [b] *34* Septuagint; Hebrew *west, and Judah, the Jordan,*

47(When the territory of the Danites was lost to them, they went up
and attacked Leshem, took it, put it to the sword and occupied it. They
settled in Leshem and named it Dan after their ancestor.)
48These towns and their villages were the inheritance of the tribe of
Dan, according to its clans.

ALLOTMENT FOR JOSHUA

49When they had finished dividing the land into its allotted portions,
the Israelites gave Joshua son of Nun an inheritance among them, 50as
the LORD had commanded. They gave him the town he asked for—
Timnath Serah[a] in the hill country of Ephraim. And he built up the
town and settled there.

51These are the territories that Eleazar the priest, Joshua son of Nun
and the heads of the tribal clans of Israel assigned by lot at Shiloh in
the presence of the LORD at the entrance to the tent of meeting. And
so they finished dividing the land.

CITIES OF REFUGE

20 Then the LORD said to Joshua: 2"Tell the Israelites to designate
the cities of refuge, as I instructed you through Moses, 3so that
anyone who kills a person accidentally and unintentionally may flee
there and find protection from the avenger of blood. 4When they flee
to one of these cities, they are to stand in the entrance of the city gate
and state their case before the elders of that city. Then the elders are
to admit the fugitive into their city and provide a place to live among
them. 5If the avenger of blood comes in pursuit, the elders must not
surrender the fugitive, because the fugitive killed their neighbor unin-
tentionally and without malice aforethought. 6They are to stay in that
city until they have stood trial before the assembly and until the death
of the high priest who is serving at that time. Then they may go back
to their own home in the town from which they fled."

7So they set apart Kedesh in Galilee in the hill country of Naphtali,
Shechem in the hill country of Ephraim, and Kiriath Arba (that is, He-
bron) in the hill country of Judah. 8East of the Jordan (on the other
side from Jericho) they designated Bezer in the wilderness on the pla-
teau in the tribe of Reuben, Ramoth in Gilead in the tribe of Gad, and
Golan in Bashan in the tribe of Manasseh. 9Any of the Israelites or any
foreigner residing among them who killed someone accidentally could
flee to these designated cities and not be killed by the avenger of blood
prior to standing trial before the assembly.

TOWNS FOR THE LEVITES

21 Now the family heads of the Levites approached Eleazar the
priest, Joshua son of Nun, and the heads of the other tribal
families of Israel 2at Shiloh in Canaan and said to them, "The LORD
commanded through Moses that you give us towns to live in, with pas-
turelands for our livestock." 3So, as the LORD had commanded, the Is-
raelites gave the Levites the following towns and pasturelands out of
their own inheritance:

4The first lot came out for the Kohathites, according to their clans.
The Levites who were descendants of Aaron the priest were allotted
thirteen towns from the tribes of Judah, Simeon and Benjamin. 5The

[a] *50* Also known as *Timnath Heres* (see Judges 2:9)

PRAYING SCRIPTURE

Joshua 20

Israel was finally in position to establish cities of refuge to prevent people from taking undue vengeance upon others. God made it clear that vengeance belongs to him, so any expression of earthly recompense should reflect God's righteous judgment.

Most people are, at some time or another, tempted to deliver vengeance. Ask God to help you show mercy while you leave revenge to him.

PRAYING SCRIPTURE

Joshua 21

With the land finally and completely settled, a declaration was made that every one of God's promises to Israel had come to pass. Not only had God given them victory, but Joshua said that God "gave them rest on every side" (verse 44). What a blessed thought!

Israel's rest is a picture of the rest God promises in Hebrews 4. It's a rest we enter. Ask God to help you live in the rest he has given in Jesus.

rest of Kohath's descendants were allotted ten towns from the clans of
the tribes of Ephraim, Dan and half of Manasseh.

6The descendants of Gershon were allotted thirteen towns from the
clans of the tribes of Issachar, Asher, Naphtali and the half-tribe of Ma-
nasseh in Bashan.

7The descendants of Merari, according to their clans, received twelve
towns from the tribes of Reuben, Gad and Zebulun.

8So the Israelites allotted to the Levites these towns and their pas-
turelands, as the LORD had commanded through Moses.

9From the tribes of Judah and Simeon they allotted the following
towns by name 10(these towns were assigned to the descendants of
Aaron who were from the Kohathite clans of the Levites, because the
first lot fell to them):

11They gave them Kiriath Arba (that is, Hebron), with its sur-
rounding pastureland, in the hill country of Judah. (Arba was the
forefather of Anak.) 12But the fields and villages around the city
they had given to Caleb son of Jephunneh as his possession.

13So to the descendants of Aaron the priest they gave Hebron
(a city of refuge for one accused of murder), Libnah, 14Jattir, Esh-
temoa, 15Holon, Debir, 16Ain, Juttah and Beth Shemesh, together
with their pasturelands — nine towns from these two tribes.

17And from the tribe of Benjamin they gave them Gibeon, Geba,
18Anathoth and Almon, together with their pasturelands — four
towns.

19The total number of towns for the priests, the descendants of Aaron,
came to thirteen, together with their pasturelands.

20The rest of the Kohathite clans of the Levites were allotted towns
from the tribe of Ephraim:

21In the hill country of Ephraim they were given Shechem (a
city of refuge for one accused of murder) and Gezer, 22Kibzaim
and Beth Horon, together with their pasturelands — four towns.

23Also from the tribe of Dan they received Eltekeh, Gibbethon,
24Aijalon and Gath Rimmon, together with their pasturelands —
four towns.

25From half the tribe of Manasseh they received Taanach and
Gath Rimmon, together with their pasturelands — two towns.

26All these ten towns and their pasturelands were given to the rest of
the Kohathite clans.

27The Levite clans of the Gershonites were given:
from the half-tribe of Manasseh,
Golan in Bashan (a city of refuge for one accused of murder) and
Be Eshterah, together with their pasturelands — two towns;
28from the tribe of Issachar,
Kishion, Daberath, 29Jarmuth and En Gannim, together with their
pasturelands — four towns;
30from the tribe of Asher,
Mishal, Abdon, 31Helkath and Rehob, together with their pasture-
lands — four towns;
32from the tribe of Naphtali,
Kedesh in Galilee (a city of refuge for one accused of murder),
Hammoth Dor and Kartan, together with their pasturelands —
three towns.

33 The total number of towns of the Gershonite clans came to thirteen,
together with their pasturelands.

34 The Merarite clans (the rest of the Levites) were given:
from the tribe of Zebulun,
Jokneam, Kartah, 35 Dimnah and Nahalal, together with their pas-
turelands — four towns;
36 from the tribe of Reuben,
Bezer, Jahaz, 37 Kedemoth and Mephaath, together with their pas-
turelands — four towns;
38 from the tribe of Gad,
Ramoth in Gilead (a city of refuge for one accused of murder), Ma-
hanaim, 39 Heshbon and Jazer, together with their pasturelands —
four towns in all.
40 The total number of towns allotted to the Merarite clans, who were
the rest of the Levites, came to twelve.
41 The towns of the Levites in the territory held by the Israelites were
forty-eight in all, together with their pasturelands. 42 Each of these
towns had pasturelands surrounding it; this was true for all these
towns.
43 So the LORD gave Israel all the land he had sworn to give their an-
cestors, and they took possession of it and settled there. 44 The LORD
gave them rest on every side, just as he had sworn to their ancestors.
Not one of their enemies withstood them; the LORD gave all their en-
emies into their hands. 45 Not one of all the LORD's good promises to
Israel failed; every one was fulfilled.

EASTERN TRIBES RETURN HOME

22 Then Joshua summoned the Reubenites, the Gadites and the
half-tribe of Manasseh 2 and said to them, "You have done all
that Moses the servant of the LORD commanded, and you have obeyed
me in everything I commanded. 3 For a long time now — to this very
day — you have not deserted your fellow Israelites but have carried
out the mission the LORD your God gave you. 4 Now that the LORD your
God has given them rest as he promised, return to your homes in the
land that Moses the servant of the LORD gave you on the other side of
the Jordan. 5 But be very careful to keep the commandment and the
law that Moses the servant of the LORD gave you: to love the LORD your
God, to walk in obedience to him, to keep his commands, to hold fast
to him and to serve him with all your heart and with all your soul."
6 Then Joshua blessed them and sent them away, and they went to
their homes. 7 (To the half-tribe of Manasseh Moses had given land in
Bashan, and to the other half of the tribe Joshua gave land on the west
side of the Jordan along with their fellow Israelites.) When Joshua sent
them home, he blessed them, 8 saying, "Return to your homes with
your great wealth — with large herds of livestock, with silver, gold,
bronze and iron, and a great quantity of clothing — and divide the
plunder from your enemies with your fellow Israelites."
9 So the Reubenites, the Gadites and the half-tribe of Manasseh left
the Israelites at Shiloh in Canaan to return to Gilead, their own land,
which they had acquired in accordance with the command of the LORD
through Moses.
10 When they came to Geliloth near the Jordan in the land of Canaan,
the Reubenites, the Gadites and the half-tribe of Manasseh built an

PRAYING SCRIPTURE

Joshua 22

Not content to rest, some of Israel's tribes nearly went to war. Discovering that no wrong had been committed, they decided against fighting, choosing peace instead. The tribes of Rueben and Gad with Manasseh's half tribe had built an altar on the frontier, which they now named "A Witness Between Us" (verse 34).

How often we forget that God is a witness to everything we say and do. Pray that you remember that God witnesses the fruit of your lips, loves and life.

imposing altar there by the Jordan. 11And when the Israelites heard
that they had built the altar on the border of Canaan at Geliloth near
the Jordan on the Israelite side, 12the whole assembly of Israel gath-
ered at Shiloh to go to war against them.

13So the Israelites sent Phinehas son of Eleazar, the priest, to the land
of Gilead — to Reuben, Gad and the half-tribe of Manasseh. 14With him
they sent ten of the chief men, one from each of the tribes of Israel,
each the head of a family division among the Israelite clans.

15When they went to Gilead — to Reuben, Gad and the half-tribe of
Manasseh — they said to them: 16"The whole assembly of the LORD
says: 'How could you break faith with the God of Israel like this? How
could you turn away from the LORD and build yourselves an altar in
rebellion against him now? 17Was not the sin of Peor enough for us?
Up to this very day we have not cleansed ourselves from that sin, even
though a plague fell on the community of the LORD! 18And are you now
turning away from the LORD?

"'If you rebel against the LORD today, tomorrow he will be angry
with the whole community of Israel. 19If the land you possess is de-
filed, come over to the LORD's land, where the LORD's tabernacle stands,
and share the land with us. But do not rebel against the LORD or against
us by building an altar for yourselves, other than the altar of the LORD
our God. 20When Achan son of Zerah was unfaithful in regard to the de-
voted things,[a] did not wrath come on the whole community of Israel?
He was not the only one who died for his sin.'"

21Then Reuben, Gad and the half-tribe of Manasseh replied to the
heads of the clans of Israel: 22"The Mighty One, God, the LORD! The
Mighty One, God, the LORD! He knows! And let Israel know! If this has
been in rebellion or disobedience to the LORD, do not spare us this day.
23If we have built our own altar to turn away from the LORD and to offer
burnt offerings and grain offerings, or to sacrifice fellowship offerings
on it, may the LORD himself call us to account.

24"No! We did it for fear that some day your descendants might say
to ours, 'What do you have to do with the LORD, the God of Israel? 25The
LORD has made the Jordan a boundary between us and you — you Reu-
benites and Gadites! You have no share in the LORD.' So your descen-
dants might cause ours to stop fearing the LORD.

26"That is why we said, 'Let us get ready and build an altar — but not
for burnt offerings or sacrifices.' 27On the contrary, it is to be a witness
between us and you and the generations that follow, that we will wor-
ship the LORD at his sanctuary with our burnt offerings, sacrifices and
fellowship offerings. Then in the future your descendants will not be
able to say to ours, 'You have no share in the LORD.'

28"And we said, 'If they ever say this to us, or to our descendants, we
will answer: Look at the replica of the LORD's altar, which our ancestors
built, not for burnt offerings and sacrifices, but as a witness between
us and you.'

29"Far be it from us to rebel against the LORD and turn away from
him today by building an altar for burnt offerings, grain offerings and
sacrifices, other than the altar of the LORD our God that stands before
his tabernacle."

30When Phinehas the priest and the leaders of the community — the

---

[a] *20* The Hebrew term refers to the irrevocable giving over of things or
persons to the LORD, often by totally destroying them.

heads of the clans of the Israelites — heard what Reuben, Gad and Ma-
nasseh had to say, they were pleased. 31And Phinehas son of Eleazar,
the priest, said to Reuben, Gad and Manasseh, "Today we know that
the LORD is with us, because you have not been unfaithful to the LORD
in this matter. Now you have rescued the Israelites from the LORD's
hand."
32Then Phinehas son of Eleazar, the priest, and the leaders returned
to Canaan from their meeting with the Reubenites and Gadites in Gil-
ead and reported to the Israelites. 33They were glad to hear the report
and praised God. And they talked no more about going to war against
them to devastate the country where the Reubenites and the Gadites
lived.
34And the Reubenites and the Gadites gave the altar this name: A
Witness Between Us — that the LORD is God.

JOSHUA'S FAREWELL TO THE LEADERS

23 After a long time had passed and the LORD had given Israel rest
from all their enemies around them, Joshua, by then a very
old man, 2summoned all Israel — their elders, leaders, judges and offi-
cials — and said to them: "I am very old. 3You yourselves have seen ev-
erything the LORD your God has done to all these nations for your sake;
it was the LORD your God who fought for you. 4Remember how I have
allotted as an inheritance for your tribes all the land of the nations
that remain — the nations I conquered — between the Jordan and the
Mediterranean Sea in the west. 5The LORD your God himself will push
them out for your sake. He will drive them out before you, and you
will take possession of their land, as the LORD your God promised you.
6"Be very strong; be careful to obey all that is written in the Book of
the Law of Moses, without turning aside to the right or to the left. 7Do
not associate with these nations that remain among you; do not invoke
the names of their gods or swear by them. You must not serve them or
bow down to them. 8But you are to hold fast to the LORD your God, as
you have until now.
9"The LORD has driven out before you great and powerful nations;
to this day no one has been able to withstand you. 10One of you routs a
thousand, because the LORD your God fights for you, just as he prom-
ised. 11So be very careful to love the LORD your God.
12"But if you turn away and ally yourselves with the survivors of
these nations that remain among you and if you intermarry with them
and associate with them, 13then you may be sure that the LORD your
God will no longer drive out these nations before you. Instead, they
will become snares and traps for you, whips on your backs and thorns
in your eyes, until you perish from this good land, which the LORD your
God has given you.
14"Now I am about to go the way of all the earth. You know with all
your heart and soul that not one of all the good promises the LORD
your God gave you has failed. Every promise has been fulfilled; not
one has failed. 15But just as all the good things the LORD your God has
promised you have come to you, so he will bring on you all the evil
things he has threatened, until the LORD your God has destroyed you
from this good land he has given you. 16If you violate the covenant of
the LORD your God, which he commanded you, and go and serve other
gods and bow down to them, the LORD's anger will burn against you,
and you will quickly perish from the good land he has given you."

PRAYING SCRIPTURE

Joshua 23

At the end of Joshua's life, the great leader gave an exhortation for the people to follow God. Using a poetic phrase—"I am about to go the way of all the earth"—Joshua reminds us that our days on earth will end (verse 14).

If God gives you 70 to 80 years, how will you steward the ones you have left? Ask God to help you use your time encouraging people to follow him.

PRAYING SCRIPTURE

Joshua 24

When Joshua finished recounting the history of God's involvement with the people of Israel, beginning with the call of Abraham on through Isaac, Jacob and Moses, he charged those in his hearing to choose which god to serve. Joshua stated firmly, "But as for me and my household, we will serve the LORD" (verse 15).

Joshua's declaration serves as a reminder to us. Make the same declaration today in your prayer that you and your family will seek and serve the Lord.

THE COVENANT RENEWED AT SHECHEM

24 Then Joshua assembled all the tribes of Israel at Shechem. He
summoned the elders, leaders, judges and officials of Israel,
and they presented themselves before God.
[2]Joshua said to all the people, "This is what the LORD, the God of
Israel, says: 'Long ago your ancestors, including Terah the father of
Abraham and Nahor, lived beyond the Euphrates River and worshiped
other gods. [3]But I took your father Abraham from the land beyond
the Euphrates and led him throughout Canaan and gave him many
descendants. I gave him Isaac, [4]and to Isaac I gave Jacob and Esau. I
assigned the hill country of Seir to Esau, but Jacob and his family went
down to Egypt.
[5]" 'Then I sent Moses and Aaron, and I afflicted the Egyptians by
what I did there, and I brought you out. [6]When I brought your people
out of Egypt, you came to the sea, and the Egyptians pursued them
with chariots and horsemen[a] as far as the Red Sea.[b] [7]But they cried
to the LORD for help, and he put darkness between you and the Egyp-
tians; he brought the sea over them and covered them. You saw with
your own eyes what I did to the Egyptians. Then you lived in the wil-
derness for a long time.
[8]" 'I brought you to the land of the Amorites who lived east of the
Jordan. They fought against you, but I gave them into your hands. I de-
stroyed them from before you, and you took possession of their land.
[9]When Balak son of Zippor, the king of Moab, prepared to fight against
Israel, he sent for Balaam son of Beor to put a curse on you. [10]But I
would not listen to Balaam, so he blessed you again and again, and I
delivered you out of his hand.
[11]" 'Then you crossed the Jordan and came to Jericho. The citizens
of Jericho fought against you, as did also the Amorites, Perizzites, Ca-
naanites, Hittites, Girgashites, Hivites and Jebusites, but I gave them
into your hands. [12]I sent the hornet ahead of you, which drove them
out before you — also the two Amorite kings. You did not do it with
your own sword and bow. [13]So I gave you a land on which you did not
toil and cities you did not build; and you live in them and eat from
vineyards and olive groves that you did not plant.'
[14]"Now fear the LORD and serve him with all faithfulness. Throw
away the gods your ancestors worshiped beyond the Euphrates River
and in Egypt, and serve the LORD. [15]But if serving the LORD seems un-
desirable to you, then choose for yourselves this day whom you will
serve, whether the gods your ancestors served beyond the Euphrates,
or the gods of the Amorites, in whose land you are living. But as for me
and my household, we will serve the LORD."
[16]Then the people answered, "Far be it from us to forsake the LORD
to serve other gods! [17]It was the LORD our God himself who brought us
and our parents up out of Egypt, from that land of slavery, and per-
formed those great signs before our eyes. He protected us on our entire
journey and among all the nations through which we traveled. [18]And
the LORD drove out before us all the nations, including the Amorites,
who lived in the land. We too will serve the LORD, because he is our
God."
[19]Joshua said to the people, "You are not able to serve the LORD. He
is a holy God; he is a jealous God. He will not forgive your rebellion

[a] 6 Or *charioteers* [b] 6 Or *the Sea of Reeds*

and your sins. 20 If you forsake the LORD and serve foreign gods, he
will turn and bring disaster on you and make an end of you, after he
has been good to you."
21 But the people said to Joshua, "No! We will serve the LORD."
22 Then Joshua said, "You are witnesses against yourselves that you
have chosen to serve the LORD."
"Yes, we are witnesses," they replied.
23 "Now then," said Joshua, "throw away the foreign gods that are
among you and yield your hearts to the LORD, the God of Israel."
24 And the people said to Joshua, "We will serve the LORD our God
and obey him."
25 On that day Joshua made a covenant for the people, and there at
Shechem he reaffirmed for them decrees and laws. 26 And Joshua re-
corded these things in the Book of the Law of God. Then he took a large
stone and set it up there under the oak near the holy place of the LORD.
27 "See!" he said to all the people. "This stone will be a witness against
us. It has heard all the words the LORD has said to us. It will be a witness
against you if you are untrue to your God."
28 Then Joshua dismissed the people, each to their own inheritance.

BURIED IN THE PROMISED LAND

29 After these things, Joshua son of Nun, the servant of the LORD, died
at the age of a hundred and ten. 30 And they buried him in the land
of his inheritance, at Timnath Serah[a] in the hill country of Ephraim,
north of Mount Gaash.
31 Israel served the LORD throughout the lifetime of Joshua and of
the elders who outlived him and who had experienced everything the
LORD had done for Israel.
32 And Joseph's bones, which the Israelites had brought up from
Egypt, were buried at Shechem in the tract of land that Jacob bought
for a hundred pieces of silver[b] from the sons of Hamor, the father of
Shechem. This became the inheritance of Joseph's descendants.
33 And Eleazar son of Aaron died and was buried at Gibeah, which
had been allotted to his son Phinehas in the hill country of Ephraim.

---

[a] *30* Also known as *Timnath Heres* (see Judges 2:9) [b] *32* Hebrew *hundred kesitahs*; a kesitah was a unit of money of unknown weight and value.

JUDGES

Following Joshua's death, Israel entered one of the worst periods of its entire history. Judges demonstrates what happens when God's people turn from him at the first opportunity, then make that the pattern of their existence. The narrative of Judges repeats in cycles: The people would abandon the Lord, and then God would allow their enemies to overrun them as judgment. Israel would respond to the judgment by calling out to the Lord in repentance, and then God would raise up a judge who delivered Israel from their trouble. The cycle repeated itself numerous times over the course of more than two hundred years.

After the death of Joshua, whom the people recognized as God's anointed leader, the people ran after their own sinful desires. In the absence of a clear leader, chaos reigned. The people lived as if God had never given them his law. The refrain running through the book amplifies the theological point the writer wanted to make: "In those days Israel had no king; everyone did as they saw fit" (17:6; 21:25). Prayer gave way to preference and sacrifice to self-sufficiency. In one case, an Israelite hired his own priest and effectively started his own religion. In another a Levite dismembered his own concubine, sending body parts to each of the 12 tribes as a ghoulish message.

After an introduction to Israel's spiritual malignancy in the first two chapters, the book follows the careers of the judges. They rise, they fall, they live, they die, and then another judge is chosen to deliver the nation. Many of their names are familiar: Deborah, Gideon, Samson. Many are not: Shamgar, Tola, Jair. Even the judges were not immune to disobedience. The tragic end of Samson, whose life started under a promise, was due to living his life how he wanted rather than how God commanded. The final refrain reminds us of the degradation throughout the land.

When we consider the setting of Judges, it is remarkable to see Gideon, Barak, Samson, and Jephthah counted with Abraham, Moses and David in the Hebrews 11 Hall of Faith. While it is unexpected, it is also encouraging. Even in the darkest days we could imagine, God is at work in unlikely places. He still raises up those who love and trust him to perform mighty works in his name. His light can shine in the deepest darkness. We are also reminded of God's forgiveness and deliverance when his people repent of their rebellion.

Many Christians bemoan the societal decay that we see around us. It is tempting to throw our hands up in disgust, but Judges offers us a way forward. We pray for God to be at work among us in little ways and in the lives of the individuals around us. Others may do what is right in their own eyes, but we have the Word of God that instructs us in serving him. While we mourn the sin that surrounds us, we should also give thanks for the evidence of God's grace that we see.

ISRAEL FIGHTS THE REMAINING CANAANITES

1 After the death of Joshua, the Israelites asked the LORD, "Who of us is to go up first to fight against the Canaanites?"

2The LORD answered, "Judah shall go up; I have given the land into their hands."

3The men of Judah then said to the Simeonites their fellow Israelites, "Come up with us into the territory allotted to us, to fight against the Canaanites. We in turn will go with you into yours." So the Simeonites went with them.

4When Judah attacked, the LORD gave the Canaanites and Perizzites into their hands, and they struck down ten thousand men at Bezek. 5It was there that they found Adoni-Bezek and fought against him, putting to rout the Canaanites and Perizzites. 6Adoni-Bezek fled, but they chased him and caught him, and cut off his thumbs and big toes.

7Then Adoni-Bezek said, "Seventy kings with their thumbs and big toes cut off have picked up scraps under my table. Now God has paid me back for what I did to them." They brought him to Jerusalem, and he died there.

8The men of Judah attacked Jerusalem also and took it. They put the city to the sword and set it on fire.

9After that, Judah went down to fight against the Canaanites living in the hill country, the Negev and the western foothills. 10They advanced against the Canaanites living in Hebron (formerly called Kiriath Arba) and defeated Sheshai, Ahiman and Talmai. 11From there they advanced against the people living in Debir (formerly called Kiriath Sepher).

12And Caleb said, "I will give my daughter Aksah in marriage to the man who attacks and captures Kiriath Sepher." 13Othniel son of Kenaz, Caleb's younger brother, took it; so Caleb gave his daughter Aksah to him in marriage.

14One day when she came to Othniel, she urged him[a] to ask her father for a field. When she got off her donkey, Caleb asked her, "What can I do for you?"

15She replied, "Do me a special favor. Since you have given me land in the Negev, give me also springs of water." So Caleb gave her the upper and lower springs.

16The descendants of Moses' father-in-law, the Kenite, went up from the City of Palms[b] with the people of Judah to live among the inhabitants of the Desert of Judah in the Negev near Arad.

17Then the men of Judah went with the Simeonites their fellow Israelites and attacked the Canaanites living in Zephath, and they totally destroyed[c] the city. Therefore it was called Hormah.[d] 18Judah also took[e] Gaza, Ashkelon and Ekron—each city with its territory.

19The LORD was with the men of Judah. They took possession of the hill country, but they were unable to drive the people from the plains, because they had chariots fitted with iron. 20As Moses had promised, Hebron was given to Caleb, who drove from it the three sons of Anak. 21The Benjamites, however, did not drive out the Jebusites, who were living in Jerusalem; to this day the Jebusites live there with the Benjamites.

[a] 14 Hebrew; Septuagint and Vulgate *Othniel, he urged her* [b] 16 That is, Jericho [c] 17 The Hebrew term refers to the irrevocable giving over of things or persons to the LORD, often by totally destroying them. [d] 17 *Hormah* means *destruction.* [e] 18 Hebrew; Septuagint *Judah did not take*

PRAYING SCRIPTURE

Judges 1

Some of the tribes successfully defeated the people of the land, but others could not. Strongholds were scattered around, including those of the Jebusites who occupied Jerusalem. These losses occurred despite God's assurances of victory for them.

All Christians have experienced setbacks in their walk despite God's power over sin, death and hell. Ask God for the faith to trust him completely in your ongoing struggle against sin.

[22]Now the tribes of Joseph attacked Bethel, and the LORD was with them. [23]When they sent men to spy out Bethel (formerly called Luz), [24]the spies saw a man coming out of the city and they said to him, "Show us how to get into the city and we will see that you are treated well." [25]So he showed them, and they put the city to the sword but spared the man and his whole family. [26]He then went to the land of the Hittites, where he built a city and called it Luz, which is its name to this day.

[27]But Manasseh did not drive out the people of Beth Shan or Taanach or Dor or Ibleam or Megiddo and their surrounding settlements, for the Canaanites were determined to live in that land. [28]When Israel became strong, they pressed the Canaanites into forced labor but never drove them out completely. [29]Nor did Ephraim drive out the Canaanites living in Gezer, but the Canaanites continued to live there among them. [30]Neither did Zebulun drive out the Canaanites living in Kitron or Nahalol, so these Canaanites lived among them, but Zebulun did subject them to forced labor. [31]Nor did Asher drive out those living in Akko or Sidon or Ahlab or Akzib or Helbah or Aphek or Rehob. [32]The Asherites lived among the Canaanite inhabitants of the land because they did not drive them out. [33]Neither did Naphtali drive out those living in Beth Shemesh or Beth Anath; but the Naphtalites too lived among the Canaanite inhabitants of the land, and those living in Beth Shemesh and Beth Anath became forced laborers for them. [34]The Amorites confined the Danites to the hill country, not allowing them to come down into the plain. [35]And the Amorites were determined also to hold out in Mount Heres, Aijalon and Shaalbim, but when the power of the tribes of Joseph increased, they too were pressed into forced labor. [36]The boundary of the Amorites was from Scorpion Pass to Sela and beyond.

THE ANGEL OF THE LORD AT BOKIM

2 The angel of the LORD went up from Gilgal to Bokim and said, "I brought you up out of Egypt and led you into the land I swore to give to your ancestors. I said, 'I will never break my covenant with you, [2]and you shall not make a covenant with the people of this land, but you shall break down their altars.' Yet you have disobeyed me. Why have you done this? [3]And I have also said, 'I will not drive them out before you; they will become traps for you, and their gods will become snares to you.' "

[4]When the angel of the LORD had spoken these things to all the Israelites, the people wept aloud, [5]and they called that place Bokim.[a] There they offered sacrifices to the LORD.

DISOBEDIENCE AND DEFEAT

[6]After Joshua had dismissed the Israelites, they went to take possession of the land, each to their own inheritance. [7]The people served the LORD throughout the lifetime of Joshua and of the elders who outlived him and who had seen all the great things the LORD had done for Israel.

[8]Joshua son of Nun, the servant of the LORD, died at the age of a hundred and ten. [9]And they buried him in the land of his inheritance, at Timnath Heres[b] in the hill country of Ephraim, north of Mount Gaash.

PRAYING SCRIPTURE

Judges 2

Soon after the death of Joshua, the nation of Israel entered cycles of rebellion. This was partly because the generation who had witnessed God's miraculous works had utterly failed to pass along the remembrance of what he had done. As a result, the second generation after the exodus did not know God at all (see verse 10).

Teaching the next generation to seek and know God is critical. Ask God to make you successful in this area whether your descendants are physical or spiritual ones.

[a] 5 *Bokim* means *weepers.* [b] 9 Also known as *Timnath Serah* (see Joshua 19:50 and 24:30)

10After that whole generation had been gathered to their ancestors, another generation grew up who knew neither the LORD nor what he had done for Israel. 11Then the Israelites did evil in the eyes of the LORD and served the Baals. 12They forsook the LORD, the God of their ancestors, who had brought them out of Egypt. They followed and worshiped various gods of the peoples around them. They aroused the LORD's anger 13because they forsook him and served Baal and the Ashtoreths. 14In his anger against Israel the LORD gave them into the hands of raiders who plundered them. He sold them into the hands of their enemies all around, whom they were no longer able to resist. 15Whenever Israel went out to fight, the hand of the LORD was against them to defeat them, just as he had sworn to them. They were in great distress.

16Then the LORD raised up judges,[a] who saved them out of the hands of these raiders. 17Yet they would not listen to their judges but prostituted themselves to other gods and worshiped them. They quickly turned from the ways of their ancestors, who had been obedient to the LORD's commands. 18Whenever the LORD raised up a judge for them, he was with the judge and saved them out of the hands of their enemies as long as the judge lived; for the LORD relented because of their groaning under those who oppressed and afflicted them. 19But when the judge died, the people returned to ways even more corrupt than those of their ancestors, following other gods and serving and worshiping them. They refused to give up their evil practices and stubborn ways.

20Therefore the LORD was very angry with Israel and said, "Because this nation has violated the covenant I ordained for their ancestors and has not listened to me, 21I will no longer drive out before them any of the nations Joshua left when he died. 22I will use them to test Israel and see whether they will keep the way of the LORD and walk in it as their ancestors did." 23The LORD had allowed those nations to remain; he did not drive them out at once by giving them into the hands of Joshua.

3 These are the nations the LORD left to test all those Israelites who had not experienced any of the wars in Canaan 2(he did this only to teach warfare to the descendants of the Israelites who had not had previous battle experience): 3the five rulers of the Philistines, all the Canaanites, the Sidonians, and the Hivites living in the Lebanon mountains from Mount Baal Hermon to Lebo Hamath. 4They were left to test the Israelites to see whether they would obey the LORD's commands, which he had given their ancestors through Moses.

5The Israelites lived among the Canaanites, Hittites, Amorites, Perizzites, Hivites and Jebusites. 6They took their daughters in marriage and gave their own daughters to their sons, and served their gods.

OTHNIEL

7The Israelites did evil in the eyes of the LORD; they forgot the LORD their God and served the Baals and the Asherahs. 8The anger of the LORD burned against Israel so that he sold them into the hands of Cushan-Rishathaim king of Aram Naharaim,[b] to whom the Israelites were subject for eight years. 9But when they cried out to the LORD, he raised up for them a deliverer, Othniel son of Kenaz, Caleb's younger brother, who saved them. 10The Spirit of the LORD came on him, so that he became Israel's judge[c] and went to war. The LORD gave Cushan-Rishathaim king

PRAYING SCRIPTURE

Judges 3

Israel's greatest sin against the Lord was abandoning him and turning to idols. Idolatry was a sin they committed repeatedly, bringing God's judgment each time. To deliver Israel, God sent his Spirit to empower a deliverer to save them.

Today the Spirit of God empowers every believer to overcome this world and live a life that fully reflects that of Jesus. Prayerfully yield yourself to the Holy Spirit's power every day.

[a] *16* Or *leaders*; similarly in verses 17-19 [b] *8* That is, Northwest Mesopotamia [c] *10* Or *leader*

of Aram into the hands of Othniel, who overpowered him. 11So the land
had peace for forty years, until Othniel son of Kenaz died.

EHUD

12Again the Israelites did evil in the eyes of the LORD, and because
they did this evil the LORD gave Eglon king of Moab power over Israel.
13Getting the Ammonites and Amalekites to join him, Eglon came and
attacked Israel, and they took possession of the City of Palms.[a] 14The
Israelites were subject to Eglon king of Moab for eighteen years.

15Again the Israelites cried out to the LORD, and he gave them a de-
liverer — Ehud, a left-handed man, the son of Gera the Benjamite. The
Israelites sent him with tribute to Eglon king of Moab. 16Now Ehud had
made a double-edged sword about a cubit[b] long, which he strapped to
his right thigh under his clothing. 17He presented the tribute to Eglon
king of Moab, who was a very fat man. 18After Ehud had presented the
tribute, he sent on their way those who had carried it. 19But on reach-
ing the stone images near Gilgal he himself went back to Eglon and
said, "Your Majesty, I have a secret message for you."

The king said to his attendants, "Leave us!" And they all left.

20Ehud then approached him while he was sitting alone in the upper
room of his palace[c] and said, "I have a message from God for you." As
the king rose from his seat, 21Ehud reached with his left hand, drew the
sword from his right thigh and plunged it into the king's belly. 22Even
the handle sank in after the blade, and his bowels discharged. Ehud
did not pull the sword out, and the fat closed in over it. 23Then Ehud
went out to the porch[d]; he shut the doors of the upper room behind
him and locked them.

24After he had gone, the servants came and found the doors of the
upper room locked. They said, "He must be relieving himself in the in-
ner room of the palace." 25They waited to the point of embarrassment,
but when he did not open the doors of the room, they took a key and
unlocked them. There they saw their lord fallen to the floor, dead.

26While they waited, Ehud got away. He passed by the stone images
and escaped to Seirah. 27When he arrived there, he blew a trumpet in
the hill country of Ephraim, and the Israelites went down with him
from the hills, with him leading them.

28"Follow me," he ordered, "for the LORD has given Moab, your en-
emy, into your hands." So they followed him down and took possession
of the fords of the Jordan that led to Moab; they allowed no one to
cross over. 29At that time they struck down about ten thousand Mo-
abites, all vigorous and strong; not one escaped. 30That day Moab was
made subject to Israel, and the land had peace for eighty years.

SHAMGAR

31After Ehud came Shamgar son of Anath, who struck down six hun-
dred Philistines with an oxgoad. He too saved Israel.

DEBORAH

4 Again the Israelites did evil in the eyes of the LORD, now that Ehud
was dead. 2So the LORD sold them into the hands of Jabin king of
Canaan, who reigned in Hazor. Sisera, the commander of his army, was

PRAYING SCRIPTURE

Judges 4

The prophet and judge Deborah responded to God's command by deploying troops against Sisera. Hebrews 11 says Barak, charged with carrying out the assault, did so "through faith" (11:33). God used both a judge and a warrior to deliver Israel from oppression.

God often uses partnerships to advance his kingdom purposes; no one need go it alone. Ask God for wisdom to know when to join forces with others for his glory.

[a] *13* That is, Jericho [b] *16* That is, about 18 inches or about 45 centimeters
[c] *20* The meaning of the Hebrew for this word is uncertain; also in verse 24.
[d] *23* The meaning of the Hebrew for this word is uncertain.

based in Harosheth Haggoyim. 3Because he had nine hundred chari-
ots fitted with iron and had cruelly oppressed the Israelites for twenty
years, they cried to the LORD for help.
4Now Deborah, a prophet, the wife of Lappidoth, was leading[a] Is-
rael at that time. 5She held court under the Palm of Deborah between
Ramah and Bethel in the hill country of Ephraim, and the Israelites
went up to her to have their disputes decided. 6She sent for Barak son
of Abinoam from Kedesh in Naphtali and said to him, "The LORD, the
God of Israel, commands you: 'Go, take with you ten thousand men of
Naphtali and Zebulun and lead them up to Mount Tabor. 7I will lead
Sisera, the commander of Jabin's army, with his chariots and his troops
to the Kishon River and give him into your hands.'"
8Barak said to her, "If you go with me, I will go; but if you don't go
with me, I won't go."
9"Certainly I will go with you," said Deborah. "But because of the
course you are taking, the honor will not be yours, for the LORD will de-
liver Sisera into the hands of a woman." So Deborah went with Barak to
Kedesh. 10There Barak summoned Zebulun and Naphtali, and ten thou-
sand men went up under his command. Deborah also went up with him.
11Now Heber the Kenite had left the other Kenites, the descendants
of Hobab, Moses' brother-in-law,[b] and pitched his tent by the great tree
in Zaanannim near Kedesh.
12When they told Sisera that Barak son of Abinoam had gone up to
Mount Tabor, 13Sisera summoned from Harosheth Haggoyim to the Ki-
shon River all his men and his nine hundred chariots fitted with iron.
14Then Deborah said to Barak, "Go! This is the day the LORD has given
Sisera into your hands. Has not the LORD gone ahead of you?" So Barak
went down Mount Tabor, with ten thousand men following him. 15At
Barak's advance, the LORD routed Sisera and all his chariots and army
by the sword, and Sisera got down from his chariot and fled on foot.
16Barak pursued the chariots and army as far as Harosheth Hag-
goyim, and all Sisera's troops fell by the sword; not a man was left.
17Sisera, meanwhile, fled on foot to the tent of Jael, the wife of Heber
the Kenite, because there was an alliance between Jabin king of Hazor
and the family of Heber the Kenite.
18Jael went out to meet Sisera and said to him, "Come, my lord, come
right in. Don't be afraid." So he entered her tent, and she covered him
with a blanket.
19"I'm thirsty," he said. "Please give me some water." She opened a
skin of milk, gave him a drink, and covered him up.
20"Stand in the doorway of the tent," he told her. "If someone comes
by and asks you, 'Is anyone in there?' say 'No.'"
21But Jael, Heber's wife, picked up a tent peg and a hammer and went
quietly to him while he lay fast asleep, exhausted. She drove the peg
through his temple into the ground, and he died.
22Just then Barak came by in pursuit of Sisera, and Jael went out to
meet him. "Come," she said, "I will show you the man you're looking
for." So he went in with her, and there lay Sisera with the tent peg
through his temple — dead.
23On that day God subdued Jabin king of Canaan before the Israel-
ites. 24And the hand of the Israelites pressed harder and harder against
Jabin king of Canaan until they destroyed him.

---

[a] 4 Traditionally *judging* [b] 11 Or *father-in-law*

PRAYING SCRIPTURE

Judges 5

The song of Deborah and Barak recounted the victories God had given the judges in liberating Israel. After their victory, God gave Israel rest for 40 years.

Do you ever think of singing about the victories over sin or attacks God wins for you? This song of praise is based on literal life events. Ask God for a melody in your heart that celebrates his work in your life.

THE SONG OF DEBORAH

5 On that day Deborah and Barak son of Abinoam sang this song:

2 "When the princes in Israel take the lead,
when the people willingly offer themselves—
praise the LORD!

3 "Hear this, you kings! Listen, you rulers!
I, even I, will sing to[a] the LORD;
I will praise the LORD, the God of Israel, in song.

4 "When you, LORD, went out from Seir,
when you marched from the land of Edom,
the earth shook, the heavens poured,
the clouds poured down water.
5 The mountains quaked before the LORD, the One of Sinai,
before the LORD, the God of Israel.

6 "In the days of Shamgar son of Anath,
in the days of Jael, the highways were abandoned;
travelers took to winding paths.
7 Villagers in Israel would not fight;
they held back until I, Deborah, arose,
until I arose, a mother in Israel.
8 God chose new leaders
when war came to the city gates,
but not a shield or spear was seen
among forty thousand in Israel.
9 My heart is with Israel's princes,
with the willing volunteers among the people.
Praise the LORD!

10 "You who ride on white donkeys,
sitting on your saddle blankets,
and you who walk along the road,
consider 11 the voice of the singers[b] at the watering places.
They recite the victories of the LORD,
the victories of his villagers in Israel.

"Then the people of the LORD
went down to the city gates.
12 'Wake up, wake up, Deborah!
Wake up, wake up, break out in song!
Arise, Barak!
Take captive your captives, son of Abinoam.'

13 "The remnant of the nobles came down;
the people of the LORD came down to me against the mighty.
14 Some came from Ephraim, whose roots were in Amalek;
Benjamin was with the people who followed you.
From Makir captains came down,
from Zebulun those who bear a commander's[b] staff.
15 The princes of Issachar were with Deborah;
yes, Issachar was with Barak,
sent under his command into the valley.

---

[a] *3* Or *of* [b] *11,14* The meaning of the Hebrew for this word is uncertain.

In the districts of Reuben
there was much searching of heart.
16 Why did you stay among the sheep pens[a]
to hear the whistling for the flocks?
In the districts of Reuben
there was much searching of heart.
17 Gilead stayed beyond the Jordan.
And Dan, why did he linger by the ships?
Asher remained on the coast
and stayed in his coves.
18 The people of Zebulun risked their very lives;
so did Naphtali on the terraced fields.

19 "Kings came, they fought,
the kings of Canaan fought.
At Taanach, by the waters of Megiddo,
they took no plunder of silver.
20 From the heavens the stars fought,
from their courses they fought against Sisera.
21 The river Kishon swept them away,
the age-old river, the river Kishon.
March on, my soul; be strong!
22 Then thundered the horses' hooves —
galloping, galloping go his mighty steeds.
23 'Curse Meroz,' said the angel of the LORD.
'Curse its people bitterly,
because they did not come to help the LORD,
to help the LORD against the mighty.'

24 "Most blessed of women be Jael,
the wife of Heber the Kenite,
most blessed of tent-dwelling women.
25 He asked for water, and she gave him milk;
in a bowl fit for nobles she brought him curdled milk.
26 Her hand reached for the tent peg,
her right hand for the workman's hammer.
She struck Sisera, she crushed his head,
she shattered and pierced his temple.
27 At her feet he sank,
he fell; there he lay.
At her feet he sank, he fell;
where he sank, there he fell — dead.
28 "Through the window peered Sisera's mother;
behind the lattice she cried out,
'Why is his chariot so long in coming?
Why is the clatter of his chariots delayed?'
29 The wisest of her ladies answer her;
indeed, she keeps saying to herself,
30 'Are they not finding and dividing the spoils:
a woman or two for each man,
colorful garments as plunder for Sisera,
colorful garments embroidered,

[a] 16 Or *the campfires*; or *the saddlebags*

highly embroidered garments for my neck —
all this as plunder?'

[31]"So may all your enemies perish, LORD!
But may all who love you be like the sun
when it rises in its strength."

Then the land had peace forty years.

PRAYING SCRIPTURE

Judges 6

We often marvel at the miraculous victory God gave Gideon. But we don't always remember that Gideon was the weakest in his family, which was in the weakest tribe. So, when the Lord called Gideon, he sensed that the task was too big to handle.

God often presents us with challenges that appear too big. When that happens, ask God for the faith to trust in his ability to deliver you.

GIDEON

6 The Israelites did evil in the eyes of the LORD, and for seven years
he gave them into the hands of the Midianites. [2]Because the power
of Midian was so oppressive, the Israelites prepared shelters for them-
selves in mountain clefts, caves and strongholds. [3]Whenever the Isra-
elites planted their crops, the Midianites, Amalekites and other eastern
peoples invaded the country. [4]They camped on the land and ruined the
crops all the way to Gaza and did not spare a living thing for Israel, nei-
ther sheep nor cattle nor donkeys. [5]They came up with their livestock
and their tents like swarms of locusts. It was impossible to count them
or their camels; they invaded the land to ravage it. [6]Midian so impov-
erished the Israelites that they cried out to the LORD for help.
[7]When the Israelites cried out to the LORD because of Midian, [8]he
sent them a prophet, who said, "This is what the LORD, the God of Is-
rael, says: I brought you up out of Egypt, out of the land of slavery. [9]I
rescued you from the hand of the Egyptians. And I delivered you from
the hand of all your oppressors; I drove them out before you and gave
you their land. [10]I said to you, 'I am the LORD your God; do not worship
the gods of the Amorites, in whose land you live.' But you have not
listened to me."
[11]The angel of the LORD came and sat down under the oak in Oph-
rah that belonged to Joash the Abiezrite, where his son Gideon was
threshing wheat in a winepress to keep it from the Midianites. [12]When
the angel of the LORD appeared to Gideon, he said, "The LORD is with
you, mighty warrior."
[13]"Pardon me, my lord," Gideon replied, "but if the LORD is with us,
why has all this happened to us? Where are all his wonders that our
ancestors told us about when they said, 'Did not the LORD bring us up
out of Egypt?' But now the LORD has abandoned us and given us into
the hand of Midian."
[14]The LORD turned to him and said, "Go in the strength you have and
save Israel out of Midian's hand. Am I not sending you?"
[15]"Pardon me, my lord," Gideon replied, "but how can I save Israel?
My clan is the weakest in Manasseh, and I am the least in my family."
[16]The LORD answered, "I will be with you, and you will strike down
all the Midianites, leaving none alive."
[17]Gideon replied, "If now I have found favor in your eyes, give me a
sign that it is really you talking to me. [18]Please do not go away until I
come back and bring my offering and set it before you."
And the LORD said, "I will wait until you return."
[19]Gideon went inside, prepared a young goat, and from an ephah[a]
of flour he made bread without yeast. Putting the meat in a basket
and its broth in a pot, he brought them out and offered them to him
under the oak.

---

[a] *19* That is, probably about 36 pounds or about 16 kilograms

20The angel of God said to him, "Take the meat and the unleavened
bread, place them on this rock, and pour out the broth." And Gideon
did so. 21Then the angel of the LORD touched the meat and the unleav-
ened bread with the tip of the staff that was in his hand. Fire flared
from the rock, consuming the meat and the bread. And the angel of
the LORD disappeared. 22When Gideon realized that it was the angel of
the LORD, he exclaimed, "Alas, Sovereign LORD! I have seen the angel
of the LORD face to face!"

23But the LORD said to him, "Peace! Do not be afraid. You are not
going to die."

24So Gideon built an altar to the LORD there and called it The LORD Is
Peace. To this day it stands in Ophrah of the Abiezrites.

25That same night the LORD said to him, "Take the second bull from
your father's herd, the one seven years old.[a] Tear down your father's
altar to Baal and cut down the Asherah pole[b] beside it. 26Then build a
proper kind of[c] altar to the LORD your God on the top of this height. Us-
ing the wood of the Asherah pole that you cut down, offer the second[d]
bull as a burnt offering."

27So Gideon took ten of his servants and did as the LORD told him.
But because he was afraid of his family and the townspeople, he did it
at night rather than in the daytime.

28In the morning when the people of the town got up, there was
Baal's altar, demolished, with the Asherah pole beside it cut down and
the second bull sacrificed on the newly built altar!

29They asked each other, "Who did this?"

When they carefully investigated, they were told, "Gideon son of Jo-
ash did it."

30The people of the town demanded of Joash, "Bring out your son.
He must die, because he has broken down Baal's altar and cut down the
Asherah pole beside it."

31But Joash replied to the hostile crowd around him, "Are you going
to plead Baal's cause? Are you trying to save him? Whoever fights for
him shall be put to death by morning! If Baal really is a god, he can
defend himself when someone breaks down his altar." 32So because
Gideon broke down Baal's altar, they gave him the name Jerub-Baal[e]
that day, saying, "Let Baal contend with him."

33Now all the Midianites, Amalekites and other eastern peoples
joined forces and crossed over the Jordan and camped in the Valley of
Jezreel. 34Then the Spirit of the LORD came on Gideon, and he blew a
trumpet, summoning the Abiezrites to follow him. 35He sent messen-
gers throughout Manasseh, calling them to arms, and also into Asher,
Zebulun and Naphtali, so that they too went up to meet them.

36Gideon said to God, "If you will save Israel by my hand as you have
promised — 37look, I will place a wool fleece on the threshing floor.
If there is dew only on the fleece and all the ground is dry, then I will
know that you will save Israel by my hand, as you said." 38And that is
what happened. Gideon rose early the next day; he squeezed the fleece
and wrung out the dew — a bowlful of water.

39Then Gideon said to God, "Do not be angry with me. Let me make

---

[a] *25* Or *Take a full-grown, mature bull from your father's herd* [b] *25* That is, a wooden symbol of the goddess Asherah; also in verses 26, 28 and 30
[c] *26* Or *build with layers of stone an* [d] *26* Or *full-grown*; also in verse 28
[e] *32* *Jerub-Baal* probably means *let Baal contend.*

just one more request. Allow me one more test with the fleece, but
this time make the fleece dry and let the ground be covered with dew."
40That night God did so. Only the fleece was dry; all the ground was
covered with dew.

GIDEON DEFEATS THE MIDIANITES

7 Early in the morning, Jerub-Baal (that is, Gideon) and all his men
camped at the spring of Harod. The camp of Midian was north of
them in the valley near the hill of Moreh. 2The LORD said to Gideon,
"You have too many men. I cannot deliver Midian into their hands, or
Israel would boast against me, 'My own strength has saved me.' 3Now
announce to the army, 'Anyone who trembles with fear may turn back
and leave Mount Gilead.'" So twenty-two thousand men left, while ten
thousand remained.
4But the LORD said to Gideon, "There are still too many men. Take
them down to the water, and I will thin them out for you there. If I say,
'This one shall go with you,' he shall go; but if I say, 'This one shall not
go with you,' he shall not go."
5So Gideon took the men down to the water. There the LORD told
him, "Separate those who lap the water with their tongues as a dog
laps from those who kneel down to drink." 6Three hundred of them
drank from cupped hands, lapping like dogs. All the rest got down on
their knees to drink.
7The LORD said to Gideon, "With the three hundred men that lapped
I will save you and give the Midianites into your hands. Let all the
others go home." 8So Gideon sent the rest of the Israelites home but
kept the three hundred, who took over the provisions and trumpets
of the others.
Now the camp of Midian lay below him in the valley. 9During that
night the LORD said to Gideon, "Get up, go down against the camp,
because I am going to give it into your hands. 10If you are afraid to at-
tack, go down to the camp with your servant Purah 11and listen to what
they are saying. Afterward, you will be encouraged to attack the camp."
So he and Purah his servant went down to the outposts of the camp.
12The Midianites, the Amalekites and all the other eastern peoples had
settled in the valley, thick as locusts. Their camels could no more be
counted than the sand on the seashore.
13Gideon arrived just as a man was telling a friend his dream. "I had
a dream," he was saying. "A round loaf of barley bread came tumbling
into the Midianite camp. It struck the tent with such force that the tent
overturned and collapsed."
14His friend responded, "This can be nothing other than the sword
of Gideon son of Joash, the Israelite. God has given the Midianites and
the whole camp into his hands."
15When Gideon heard the dream and its interpretation, he bowed
down and worshiped. He returned to the camp of Israel and called out,
"Get up! The LORD has given the Midianite camp into your hands." 16Di-
viding the three hundred men into three companies, he placed trum-
pets and empty jars in the hands of all of them, with torches inside.
17"Watch me," he told them. "Follow my lead. When I get to the edge
of the camp, do exactly as I do. 18When I and all who are with me blow
our trumpets, then from all around the camp blow yours and shout,
'For the LORD and for Gideon.'"
19Gideon and the hundred men with him reached the edge of the

PRAYING SCRIPTURE

Judges 7

The story of Gideon and his 300 men is a story of trust. Called to face an army of Midianite oppressors with only torches and trumpets, Gideon's attack was an act of complete trust in God's wisdom and power. In no human's reckoning should Gideon's men have been successful, yet they were.

You may be called to trust God in circumstances where victory looks impossible. Trust his word and trust his power.

camp at the beginning of the middle watch, just after they had changed the guard. They blew their trumpets and broke the jars that were in their hands. 20 The three companies blew the trumpets and smashed the jars. Grasping the torches in their left hands and holding in their right hands the trumpets they were to blow, they shouted, "A sword for the LORD and for Gideon!" 21 While each man held his position around the camp, all the Midianites ran, crying out as they fled.

22 When the three hundred trumpets sounded, the LORD caused the men throughout the camp to turn on each other with their swords. The army fled to Beth Shittah toward Zererah as far as the border of Abel Meholah near Tabbath. 23 Israelites from Naphtali, Asher and all Manasseh were called out, and they pursued the Midianites. 24 Gideon sent messengers throughout the hill country of Ephraim, saying, "Come down against the Midianites and seize the waters of the Jordan ahead of them as far as Beth Barah."

So all the men of Ephraim were called out and they seized the waters of the Jordan as far as Beth Barah. 25 They also captured two of the Midianite leaders, Oreb and Zeeb. They killed Oreb at the rock of Oreb, and Zeeb at the winepress of Zeeb. They pursued the Midianites and brought the heads of Oreb and Zeeb to Gideon, who was by the Jordan.

ZEBAH AND ZALMUNNA

8 Now the Ephraimites asked Gideon, "Why have you treated us like this? Why didn't you call us when you went to fight Midian?" And they challenged him vigorously.

2 But he answered them, "What have I accomplished compared to you? Aren't the gleanings of Ephraim's grapes better than the full grape harvest of Abiezer? 3 God gave Oreb and Zeeb, the Midianite leaders, into your hands. What was I able to do compared to you?" At this, their resentment against him subsided.

4 Gideon and his three hundred men, exhausted yet keeping up the pursuit, came to the Jordan and crossed it. 5 He said to the men of Sukkoth, "Give my troops some bread; they are worn out, and I am still pursuing Zebah and Zalmunna, the kings of Midian."

6 But the officials of Sukkoth said, "Do you already have the hands of Zebah and Zalmunna in your possession? Why should we give bread to your troops?"

7 Then Gideon replied, "Just for that, when the LORD has given Zebah and Zalmunna into my hand, I will tear your flesh with desert thorns and briers."

8 From there he went up to Peniel[a] and made the same request of them, but they answered as the men of Sukkoth had. 9 So he said to the men of Peniel, "When I return in triumph, I will tear down this tower."

10 Now Zebah and Zalmunna were in Karkor with a force of about fifteen thousand men, all that were left of the armies of the eastern peoples; a hundred and twenty thousand swordsmen had fallen. 11 Gideon went up by the route of the nomads east of Nobah and Jogbehah and attacked the unsuspecting army. 12 Zebah and Zalmunna, the two kings of Midian, fled, but he pursued them and captured them, routing their entire army.

13 Gideon son of Joash then returned from the battle by the Pass of Heres. 14 He caught a young man of Sukkoth and questioned him, and

PRAYING SCRIPTURE

Judges 8

Despite his impressive victories in battle, Gideon refused to be elevated into a king or ruler, reminding the people the Lord was their ruler. Nevertheless, he led them into idolatry when he fashioned a gold ephod from the plunder of war and set it up in his city.

God's people should be aware that they could lead people astray, even unintentionally, and should ask God to keep them from it.

[a] 8 Hebrew *Penuel*, a variant of *Peniel*; also in verses 9 and 17

the young man wrote down for him the names of the seventy-seven
officials of Sukkoth, the elders of the town. 15 Then Gideon came and
said to the men of Sukkoth, "Here are Zebah and Zalmunna, about
whom you taunted me by saying, 'Do you already have the hands of
Zebah and Zalmunna in your possession? Why should we give bread
to your exhausted men?'" 16 He took the elders of the town and taught
the men of Sukkoth a lesson by punishing them with desert thorns
and briers. 17 He also pulled down the tower of Peniel and killed the
men of the town.

18 Then he asked Zebah and Zalmunna, "What kind of men did you
kill at Tabor?"

"Men like you," they answered, "each one with the bearing of a
prince."

19 Gideon replied, "Those were my brothers, the sons of my own
mother. As surely as the LORD lives, if you had spared their lives, I
would not kill you." 20 Turning to Jether, his oldest son, he said, "Kill
them!" But Jether did not draw his sword, because he was only a boy
and was afraid.

21 Zebah and Zalmunna said, "Come, do it yourself. 'As is the man, so
is his strength.'" So Gideon stepped forward and killed them, and took
the ornaments off their camels' necks.

GIDEON'S EPHOD

22 The Israelites said to Gideon, "Rule over us — you, your son and
your grandson — because you have saved us from the hand of Midian."

23 But Gideon told them, "I will not rule over you, nor will my son
rule over you. The LORD will rule over you." 24 And he said, "I do have
one request, that each of you give me an earring from your share of the
plunder." (It was the custom of the Ishmaelites to wear gold earrings.)

25 They answered, "We'll be glad to give them." So they spread out
a garment, and each of them threw a ring from his plunder onto it.
26 The weight of the gold rings he asked for came to seventeen hundred
shekels,[a] not counting the ornaments, the pendants and the purple
garments worn by the kings of Midian or the chains that were on their
camels' necks. 27 Gideon made the gold into an ephod, which he placed
in Ophrah, his town. All Israel prostituted themselves by worshiping it
there, and it became a snare to Gideon and his family.

GIDEON'S DEATH

28 Thus Midian was subdued before the Israelites and did not raise its
head again. During Gideon's lifetime, the land had peace forty years.

29 Jerub-Baal son of Joash went back home to live. 30 He had seventy
sons of his own, for he had many wives. 31 His concubine, who lived in
Shechem, also bore him a son, whom he named Abimelek. 32 Gideon
son of Joash died at a good old age and was buried in the tomb of his
father Joash in Ophrah of the Abiezrites.

33 No sooner had Gideon died than the Israelites again prostituted
themselves to the Baals. They set up Baal-Berith as their god 34 and did
not remember the LORD their God, who had rescued them from the
hands of all their enemies on every side. 35 They also failed to show any
loyalty to the family of Jerub-Baal (that is, Gideon) in spite of all the
good things he had done for them.

---

[a] *26* That is, about 43 pounds or about 20 kilograms

ABIMELEK

9 Abimelek son of Jerub-Baal went to his mother's brothers in She-
chem and said to them and to all his mother's clan, 2"Ask all the
citizens of Shechem, 'Which is better for you: to have all seventy of
Jerub-Baal's sons rule over you, or just one man?' Remember, I am
your flesh and blood."
3When the brothers repeated all this to the citizens of Shechem, they
were inclined to follow Abimelek, for they said, "He is related to us."
4They gave him seventy shekels[a] of silver from the temple of Baal-
Berith, and Abimelek used it to hire reckless scoundrels, who became
his followers. 5He went to his father's home in Ophrah and on one
stone murdered his seventy brothers, the sons of Jerub-Baal. But Jo-
tham, the youngest son of Jerub-Baal, escaped by hiding. 6Then all the
citizens of Shechem and Beth Millo gathered beside the great tree at
the pillar in Shechem to crown Abimelek king.
7When Jotham was told about this, he climbed up on the top of
Mount Gerizim and shouted to them, "Listen to me, citizens of She-
chem, so that God may listen to you. 8One day the trees went out to
anoint a king for themselves. They said to the olive tree, 'Be our king.'
9"But the olive tree answered, 'Should I give up my oil, by which
both gods and humans are honored, to hold sway over the trees?'
10"Next, the trees said to the fig tree, 'Come and be our king.'
11"But the fig tree replied, 'Should I give up my fruit, so good and
sweet, to hold sway over the trees?'
12"Then the trees said to the vine, 'Come and be our king.'
13"But the vine answered, 'Should I give up my wine, which cheers
both gods and humans, to hold sway over the trees?'
14"Finally all the trees said to the thornbush, 'Come and be our king.'
15"The thornbush said to the trees, 'If you really want to anoint me
king over you, come and take refuge in my shade; but if not, then let
fire come out of the thornbush and consume the cedars of Lebanon!'
16"Have you acted honorably and in good faith by making Abime-
lek king? Have you been fair to Jerub-Baal and his family? Have you
treated him as he deserves? 17Remember that my father fought for you
and risked his life to rescue you from the hand of Midian. 18But today
you have revolted against my father's family. You have murdered his
seventy sons on a single stone and have made Abimelek, the son of
his female slave, king over the citizens of Shechem because he is re-
lated to you. 19So have you acted honorably and in good faith toward
Jerub-Baal and his family today? If you have, may Abimelek be your
joy, and may you be his, too! 20But if you have not, let fire come out
from Abimelek and consume you, the citizens of Shechem and Beth
Millo, and let fire come out from you, the citizens of Shechem and Beth
Millo, and consume Abimelek!"
21Then Jotham fled, escaping to Beer, and he lived there because he
was afraid of his brother Abimelek.
22After Abimelek had governed Israel three years, 23God stirred up
animosity between Abimelek and the citizens of Shechem so that they
acted treacherously against Abimelek. 24God did this in order that the
crime against Jerub-Baal's seventy sons, the shedding of their blood,
might be avenged on their brother Abimelek and on the citizens of
Shechem, who had helped him murder his brothers. 25In opposition

[a] 4 That is, about 1 3/4 pounds or about 800 grams

PRAYING SCRIPTURE

Judges 9

Double-dealing and conspiratorial behavior are not God's way for his people. A conflict that started when Abimelek, a son of Jerubbaal, murdered his brothers, continued until God intervened, bringing judgment on him, ending in his death.

Israel's story continues to show what happens when God is continually disregarded. Sin always begets tragic ends. Ask God to keep your heart and mind pure and focused on him.

to him these citizens of Shechem set men on the hilltops to ambush
and rob everyone who passed by, and this was reported to Abimelek.
26 Now Gaal son of Ebed moved with his clan into Shechem, and its
citizens put their confidence in him. 27 After they had gone out into the
fields and gathered the grapes and trodden them, they held a festival
in the temple of their god. While they were eating and drinking, they
cursed Abimelek. 28 Then Gaal son of Ebed said, "Who is Abimelek, and
why should we Shechemites be subject to him? Isn't he Jerub-Baal's
son, and isn't Zebul his deputy? Serve the family of Hamor, Shechem's
father! Why should we serve Abimelek? 29 If only this people were un-
der my command! Then I would get rid of him. I would say to Abime-
lek, 'Call out your whole army!' "[a]

30 When Zebul the governor of the city heard what Gaal son of Ebed
said, he was very angry. 31 Under cover he sent messengers to Abimelek,
saying, "Gaal son of Ebed and his clan have come to Shechem and are
stirring up the city against you. 32 Now then, during the night you and
your men should come and lie in wait in the fields. 33 In the morning
at sunrise, advance against the city. When Gaal and his men come out
against you, seize the opportunity to attack them."

34 So Abimelek and all his troops set out by night and took up con-
cealed positions near Shechem in four companies. 35 Now Gaal son of
Ebed had gone out and was standing at the entrance of the city gate
just as Abimelek and his troops came out from their hiding place.

36 When Gaal saw them, he said to Zebul, "Look, people are coming
down from the tops of the mountains!"

Zebul replied, "You mistake the shadows of the mountains for men."

37 But Gaal spoke up again: "Look, people are coming down from the
central hill,[b] and a company is coming from the direction of the di-
viners' tree."

38 Then Zebul said to him, "Where is your big talk now, you who said,
'Who is Abimelek that we should be subject to him?' Aren't these the
men you ridiculed? Go out and fight them!"

39 So Gaal led out[c] the citizens of Shechem and fought Abimelek.
40 Abimelek chased him all the way to the entrance of the gate, and
many were killed as they fled. 41 Then Abimelek stayed in Arumah, and
Zebul drove Gaal and his clan out of Shechem.

42 The next day the people of Shechem went out to the fields, and
this was reported to Abimelek. 43 So he took his men, divided them
into three companies and set an ambush in the fields. When he saw
the people coming out of the city, he rose to attack them. 44 Abime-
lek and the companies with him rushed forward to a position at the
entrance of the city gate. Then two companies attacked those in the
fields and struck them down. 45 All that day Abimelek pressed his at-
tack against the city until he had captured it and killed its people. Then
he destroyed the city and scattered salt over it.

46 On hearing this, the citizens in the tower of Shechem went into
the stronghold of the temple of El-Berith. 47 When Abimelek heard that
they had assembled there, 48 he and all his men went up Mount Zal-
mon. He took an ax and cut off some branches, which he lifted to his
shoulders. He ordered the men with him, "Quick! Do what you have

[a] 29 Septuagint; Hebrew *him." Then he said to Abimelek, "Call out your whole army!"* [b] 37 The Hebrew for this phrase means *the navel of the earth.*
[c] 39 Or *Gaal went out in the sight of*

seen me do!" 49So all the men cut branches and followed Abimelek.
They piled them against the stronghold and set it on fire with the peo-
ple still inside. So all the people in the tower of Shechem, about a thou-
sand men and women, also died.

50Next Abimelek went to Thebez and besieged it and captured it.
51Inside the city, however, was a strong tower, to which all the men
and women — all the people of the city — had fled. They had locked
themselves in and climbed up on the tower roof. 52Abimelek went to
the tower and attacked it. But as he approached the entrance to the
tower to set it on fire, 53a woman dropped an upper millstone on his
head and cracked his skull.

54Hurriedly he called to his armor-bearer, "Draw your sword and kill
me, so that they can't say, 'A woman killed him.'" So his servant ran
him through, and he died. 55When the Israelites saw that Abimelek was
dead, they went home.

56Thus God repaid the wickedness that Abimelek had done to his
father by murdering his seventy brothers. 57God also made the people
of Shechem pay for all their wickedness. The curse of Jotham son of
Jerub-Baal came on them.

TOLA

10 After the time of Abimelek, a man of Issachar named Tola son
of Puah, the son of Dodo, rose to save Israel. He lived in Shamir,
in the hill country of Ephraim. 2He led[a] Israel twenty-three years; then
he died, and was buried in Shamir.

JAIR

3He was followed by Jair of Gilead, who led Israel twenty-two years.
4He had thirty sons, who rode thirty donkeys. They controlled thirty
towns in Gilead, which to this day are called Havvoth Jair.[b] 5When Jair
died, he was buried in Kamon.

JEPHTHAH

6Again the Israelites did evil in the eyes of the LORD. They served
the Baals and the Ashtoreths, and the gods of Aram, the gods of Si-
don, the gods of Moab, the gods of the Ammonites and the gods of the
Philistines. And because the Israelites forsook the LORD and no longer
served him, 7he became angry with them. He sold them into the hands
of the Philistines and the Ammonites, 8who that year shattered and
crushed them. For eighteen years they oppressed all the Israelites on
the east side of the Jordan in Gilead, the land of the Amorites. 9The
Ammonites also crossed the Jordan to fight against Judah, Benjamin
and Ephraim; Israel was in great distress. 10Then the Israelites cried
out to the LORD, "We have sinned against you, forsaking our God and
serving the Baals."

11The LORD replied, "When the Egyptians, the Amorites, the Ammon-
ites, the Philistines, 12the Sidonians, the Amalekites and the Maonites[c]
oppressed you and you cried to me for help, did I not save you from
their hands? 13But you have forsaken me and served other gods, so I
will no longer save you. 14Go and cry out to the gods you have chosen.
Let them save you when you are in trouble!"

[a] 2 Traditionally *judged*; also in verse 3 [b] 4 Or *called the settlements of Jair*
[c] 12 Hebrew; some Septuagint manuscripts *Midianites*

PRAYING SCRIPTURE

Judges 10

When we trust in human solutions rather than the Lord, we find they cannot deliver us the way he can. Turning to our own way is like serving "the Baals" as Israel did (see verse 10). God calls it forsaking him.

Christians are tempted by the false gods of money, position and power. Following them is to forsake God. Pray that your love for the true God will keep you from false gods.

15But the Israelites said to the LORD, "We have sinned. Do with us whatever you think best, but please rescue us now." 16Then they got rid of the foreign gods among them and served the LORD. And he could bear Israel's misery no longer.

17When the Ammonites were called to arms and camped in Gilead, the Israelites assembled and camped at Mizpah. 18The leaders of the people of Gilead said to each other, "Whoever will take the lead in attacking the Ammonites will be head over all who live in Gilead."

11 Jephthah the Gileadite was a mighty warrior. His father was Gilead; his mother was a prostitute. 2Gilead's wife also bore him sons, and when they were grown up, they drove Jephthah away. "You are not going to get any inheritance in our family," they said, "because you are the son of another woman." 3So Jephthah fled from his brothers and settled in the land of Tob, where a gang of scoundrels gathered around him and followed him.

4Some time later, when the Ammonites were fighting against Israel, 5the elders of Gilead went to get Jephthah from the land of Tob. 6"Come," they said, "be our commander, so we can fight the Ammonites."

7Jephthah said to them, "Didn't you hate me and drive me from my father's house? Why do you come to me now, when you're in trouble?"

8The elders of Gilead said to him, "Nevertheless, we are turning to you now; come with us to fight the Ammonites, and you will be head over all of us who live in Gilead."

9Jephthah answered, "Suppose you take me back to fight the Ammonites and the LORD gives them to me — will I really be your head?"

10The elders of Gilead replied, "The LORD is our witness; we will certainly do as you say." 11So Jephthah went with the elders of Gilead, and the people made him head and commander over them. And he repeated all his words before the LORD in Mizpah.

12Then Jephthah sent messengers to the Ammonite king with the question: "What do you have against me that you have attacked my country?"

13The king of the Ammonites answered Jephthah's messengers, "When Israel came up out of Egypt, they took away my land from the Arnon to the Jabbok, all the way to the Jordan. Now give it back peaceably."

14Jephthah sent back messengers to the Ammonite king, 15saying:

"This is what Jephthah says: Israel did not take the land of Moab or the land of the Ammonites. 16But when they came up out of Egypt, Israel went through the wilderness to the Red Sea[a] and on to Kadesh. 17Then Israel sent messengers to the king of Edom, saying, 'Give us permission to go through your country,' but the king of Edom would not listen. They sent also to the king of Moab, and he refused. So Israel stayed at Kadesh.

18"Next they traveled through the wilderness, skirted the lands of Edom and Moab, passed along the eastern side of the country of Moab, and camped on the other side of the Arnon. They did not enter the territory of Moab, for the Arnon was its border.

19"Then Israel sent messengers to Sihon king of the Amorites, who ruled in Heshbon, and said to him, 'Let us pass through your

[a] 16 Or *the Sea of Reeds*

PRAYING SCRIPTURE

Judges 11

After making a bizarre and foolish vow, Jephthah blamed his daughter for becoming a sacrifice. He tried to justify his decision by giving her time with her friends to mourn her coming death. So painful was her death, Israel's women lamented for her four days each year.

Jephthah's vow reminds us of the danger of rash or arrogant promises. Ask God to help you think carefully and biblically when giving your word.

country to our own place.' 20Sihon, however, did not trust Israel[a]
to pass through his territory. He mustered all his troops and en-
camped at Jahaz and fought with Israel.

21"Then the LORD, the God of Israel, gave Sihon and his whole
army into Israel's hands, and they defeated them. Israel took over
all the land of the Amorites who lived in that country, 22capturing
all of it from the Arnon to the Jabbok and from the desert to the
Jordan.

23"Now since the LORD, the God of Israel, has driven the Am-
orites out before his people Israel, what right have you to take
it over? 24Will you not take what your god Chemosh gives you?
Likewise, whatever the LORD our God has given us, we will pos-
sess. 25Are you any better than Balak son of Zippor, king of Moab?
Did he ever quarrel with Israel or fight with them? 26For three
hundred years Israel occupied Heshbon, Aroer, the surrounding
settlements and all the towns along the Arnon. Why didn't you
retake them during that time? 27I have not wronged you, but you
are doing me wrong by waging war against me. Let the LORD, the
Judge, decide the dispute this day between the Israelites and the
Ammonites."

28The king of Ammon, however, paid no attention to the message
Jephthah sent him.

29Then the Spirit of the LORD came on Jephthah. He crossed Gilead
and Manasseh, passed through Mizpah of Gilead, and from there he
advanced against the Ammonites. 30And Jephthah made a vow to the
LORD: "If you give the Ammonites into my hands, 31whatever comes
out of the door of my house to meet me when I return in triumph
from the Ammonites will be the LORD's, and I will sacrifice it as a burnt
offering."

32Then Jephthah went over to fight the Ammonites, and the LORD
gave them into his hands. 33He devastated twenty towns from Aroer
to the vicinity of Minnith, as far as Abel Keramim. Thus Israel subdued
Ammon.

34When Jephthah returned to his home in Mizpah, who should come
out to meet him but his daughter, dancing to the sound of timbrels!
She was an only child. Except for her he had neither son nor daughter.
35When he saw her, he tore his clothes and cried, "Oh no, my daughter!
You have brought me down and I am devastated. I have made a vow
to the LORD that I cannot break."

36"My father," she replied, "you have given your word to the LORD.
Do to me just as you promised, now that the LORD has avenged you of
your enemies, the Ammonites. 37But grant me this one request," she
said. "Give me two months to roam the hills and weep with my friends,
because I will never marry."

38"You may go," he said. And he let her go for two months. She and
her friends went into the hills and wept because she would never
marry. 39After the two months, she returned to her father, and he did
to her as he had vowed. And she was a virgin.

From this comes the Israelite tradition 40that each year the young
women of Israel go out for four days to commemorate the daughter of
Jephthah the Gileadite.

---

[a] 20 Or *however, would not make an agreement for Israel*

PRAYING SCRIPTURE

Judges 12

The internal division in Israel was a sign of the nation's fall from God. An ongoing list of judges, their families and their lengths of rule, along with conflict fills the storyline. Jealousy wreaked havoc in the nation.

It is impossible to know the total damage caused by any single act of disobedience because more disobedience usually follows. Pray that God keeps you mindful of the ongoing, rotten fruit of sin.

JEPHTHAH AND EPHRAIM

12 The Ephraimite forces were called out, and they crossed over
to Zaphon. They said to Jephthah, "Why did you go to fight the
Ammonites without calling us to go with you? We're going to burn
down your house over your head."
2 Jephthah answered, "I and my people were engaged in a great
struggle with the Ammonites, and although I called, you didn't save
me out of their hands. 3 When I saw that you wouldn't help, I took my
life in my hands and crossed over to fight the Ammonites, and the
LORD gave me the victory over them. Now why have you come up today to fight me?"
4 Jephthah then called together the men of Gilead and fought against
Ephraim. The Gileadites struck them down because the Ephraimites
had said, "You Gileadites are renegades from Ephraim and Manasseh."
5 The Gileadites captured the fords of the Jordan leading to Ephraim,
and whenever a survivor of Ephraim said, "Let me cross over," the men
of Gilead asked him, "Are you an Ephraimite?" If he replied, "No," 6 they
said, "All right, say 'Shibboleth.'" If he said, "Sibboleth," because he
could not pronounce the word correctly, they seized him and killed
him at the fords of the Jordan. Forty-two thousand Ephraimites were
killed at that time.
7 Jephthah led[a] Israel six years. Then Jephthah the Gileadite died and
was buried in a town in Gilead.

IBZAN, ELON AND ABDON

8 After him, Ibzan of Bethlehem led Israel. 9 He had thirty sons and
thirty daughters. He gave his daughters away in marriage to those outside his clan, and for his sons he brought in thirty young women as
wives from outside his clan. Ibzan led Israel seven years. 10 Then Ibzan
died and was buried in Bethlehem.
11 After him, Elon the Zebulunite led Israel ten years. 12 Then Elon
died and was buried in Aijalon in the land of Zebulun.
13 After him, Abdon son of Hillel, from Pirathon, led Israel. 14 He had
forty sons and thirty grandsons, who rode on seventy donkeys. He led
Israel eight years. 15 Then Abdon son of Hillel died and was buried at
Pirathon in Ephraim, in the hill country of the Amalekites.

PRAYING SCRIPTURE

Judges 13

An "angel of the LORD" foretold the coming of Israel's strongest judge, Samson, a man of supernatural strength, who would honor the Nazirite vows (see verse 3). His parents saw the prophecy confirmed when the angel ascended toward heaven in the sacrificial fire from the altar!

Most Christians have known dark, difficult places when we need God to act on our behalf. Pause and ask God to reassure you that he will fulfill his plans for you.

THE BIRTH OF SAMSON

13 Again the Israelites did evil in the eyes of the LORD, so the LORD
delivered them into the hands of the Philistines for forty years.
2 A certain man of Zorah, named Manoah, from the clan of the Danites, had a wife who was childless, unable to give birth. 3 The angel of
the LORD appeared to her and said, "You are barren and childless, but
you are going to become pregnant and give birth to a son. 4 Now see
to it that you drink no wine or other fermented drink and that you do
not eat anything unclean. 5 You will become pregnant and have a son
whose head is never to be touched by a razor because the boy is to be
a Nazirite, dedicated to God from the womb. He will take the lead in
delivering Israel from the hands of the Philistines."
6 Then the woman went to her husband and told him, "A man of God
came to me. He looked like an angel of God, very awesome. I didn't ask
him where he came from, and he didn't tell me his name. 7 But he said

---

[a] 7 Traditionally *judged*; also in verses 8-14

to me, 'You will become pregnant and have a son. Now then, drink
no wine or other fermented drink and do not eat anything unclean,
because the boy will be a Nazirite of God from the womb until the day
of his death.'"
8Then Manoah prayed to the LORD: "Pardon your servant, Lord. I beg
you to let the man of God you sent to us come again to teach us how to
bring up the boy who is to be born."
9God heard Manoah, and the angel of God came again to the woman
while she was out in the field; but her husband Manoah was not with
her. 10The woman hurried to tell her husband, "He's here! The man
who appeared to me the other day!"
11Manoah got up and followed his wife. When he came to the man,
he said, "Are you the man who talked to my wife?"
"I am," he said.
12So Manoah asked him, "When your words are fulfilled, what is to
be the rule that governs the boy's life and work?"
13The angel of the LORD answered, "Your wife must do all that I have
told her. 14She must not eat anything that comes from the grapevine,
nor drink any wine or other fermented drink nor eat anything un-
clean. She must do everything I have commanded her."
15Manoah said to the angel of the LORD, "We would like you to stay
until we prepare a young goat for you."
16The angel of the LORD replied, "Even though you detain me, I will
not eat any of your food. But if you prepare a burnt offering, offer it to
the LORD." (Manoah did not realize that it was the angel of the LORD.)
17Then Manoah inquired of the angel of the LORD, "What is your
name, so that we may honor you when your word comes true?"
18He replied, "Why do you ask my name? It is beyond understand-
ing.[a]" 19Then Manoah took a young goat, together with the grain of-
fering, and sacrificed it on a rock to the LORD. And the LORD did an
amazing thing while Manoah and his wife watched: 20As the flame
blazed up from the altar toward heaven, the angel of the LORD as-
cended in the flame. Seeing this, Manoah and his wife fell with their
faces to the ground. 21When the angel of the LORD did not show himself
again to Manoah and his wife, Manoah realized that it was the angel
of the LORD.
22"We are doomed to die!" he said to his wife. "We have seen God!"
23But his wife answered, "If the LORD had meant to kill us, he would
not have accepted a burnt offering and grain offering from our hands,
nor shown us all these things or now told us this."
24The woman gave birth to a boy and named him Samson. He grew
and the LORD blessed him, 25and the Spirit of the LORD began to stir
him while he was in Mahaneh Dan, between Zorah and Eshtaol.

SAMSON'S MARRIAGE

14 Samson went down to Timnah and saw there a young Philistine
woman. 2When he returned, he said to his father and mother,
"I have seen a Philistine woman in Timnah; now get her for me as my
wife."
3His father and mother replied, "Isn't there an acceptable woman
among your relatives or among all our people? Must you go to the un-
circumcised Philistines to get a wife?"

PRAYING SCRIPTURE

Judges 14

Samson carried out many of his supernatural acts by the power of the Holy Spirit. The Spirit of the Lord came on Samson and enabled him to easily kill a lion in one instance and 30 Philistine oppressors in another.

Too often we fail to appreciate what God in his power can do. We can share the gospel with anyone! Ask God's Spirit to empower you for every task.

[a] 18 Or *is wonderful*

But Samson said to his father, "Get her for me. She's the right one for
me." 4(His parents did not know that this was from the LORD, who was
seeking an occasion to confront the Philistines; for at that time they
were ruling over Israel.)
5Samson went down to Timnah together with his father and mother.
As they approached the vineyards of Timnah, suddenly a young lion
came roaring toward him. 6The Spirit of the LORD came powerfully
upon him so that he tore the lion apart with his bare hands as he might
have torn a young goat. But he told neither his father nor his mother
what he had done. 7Then he went down and talked with the woman,
and he liked her.
8Some time later, when he went back to marry her, he turned aside
to look at the lion's carcass, and in it he saw a swarm of bees and some
honey. 9He scooped out the honey with his hands and ate as he went
along. When he rejoined his parents, he gave them some, and they too
ate it. But he did not tell them that he had taken the honey from the
lion's carcass.
10Now his father went down to see the woman. And there Samson
held a feast, as was customary for young men. 11When the people saw
him, they chose thirty men to be his companions.
12"Let me tell you a riddle," Samson said to them. "If you can give
me the answer within the seven days of the feast, I will give you thirty
linen garments and thirty sets of clothes. 13If you can't tell me the
answer, you must give me thirty linen garments and thirty sets of
clothes."
"Tell us your riddle," they said. "Let's hear it."
14He replied,

"Out of the eater, something to eat;
out of the strong, something sweet."

For three days they could not give the answer.
15On the fourth[a] day, they said to Samson's wife, "Coax your husband
into explaining the riddle for us, or we will burn you and your father's
household to death. Did you invite us here to steal our property?"
16Then Samson's wife threw herself on him, sobbing, "You hate me!
You don't really love me. You've given my people a riddle, but you
haven't told me the answer."
"I haven't even explained it to my father or mother," he replied, "so
why should I explain it to you?" 17She cried the whole seven days of the
feast. So on the seventh day he finally told her, because she continued
to press him. She in turn explained the riddle to her people.
18Before sunset on the seventh day the men of the town said to him,

"What is sweeter than honey?
What is stronger than a lion?"

Samson said to them,

"If you had not plowed with my heifer,
you would not have solved my riddle."

19Then the Spirit of the LORD came powerfully upon him. He went
down to Ashkelon, struck down thirty of their men, stripped them
of everything and gave their clothes to those who had explained the

[a] *15* Some Septuagint manuscripts and Syriac; Hebrew *seventh*

riddle. Burning with anger, he returned to his father's home. 20And
Samson's wife was given to one of his companions who had attended
him at the feast.

SAMSON'S VENGEANCE ON THE PHILISTINES

15 Later on, at the time of wheat harvest, Samson took a young
goat and went to visit his wife. He said, "I'm going to my wife's
room." But her father would not let him go in.
2"I was so sure you hated her," he said, "that I gave her to your com-
panion. Isn't her younger sister more attractive? Take her instead."
3Samson said to them, "This time I have a right to get even with the
Philistines; I will really harm them." 4So he went out and caught three
hundred foxes and tied them tail to tail in pairs. He then fastened a
torch to every pair of tails, 5lit the torches and let the foxes loose in the
standing grain of the Philistines. He burned up the shocks and stand-
ing grain, together with the vineyards and olive groves.
6When the Philistines asked, "Who did this?" they were told,
"Samson, the Timnite's son-in-law, because his wife was given to his
companion."
So the Philistines went up and burned her and her father to death.
7Samson said to them, "Since you've acted like this, I swear that I won't
stop until I get my revenge on you." 8He attacked them viciously and
slaughtered many of them. Then he went down and stayed in a cave
in the rock of Etam.
9The Philistines went up and camped in Judah, spreading out near
Lehi. 10The people of Judah asked, "Why have you come to fight us?"
"We have come to take Samson prisoner," they answered, "to do to
him as he did to us."
11Then three thousand men from Judah went down to the cave in the
rock of Etam and said to Samson, "Don't you realize that the Philistines
are rulers over us? What have you done to us?"
He answered, "I merely did to them what they did to me."
12They said to him, "We've come to tie you up and hand you over to
the Philistines."
Samson said, "Swear to me that you won't kill me yourselves."
13"Agreed," they answered. "We will only tie you up and hand you
over to them. We will not kill you." So they bound him with two new
ropes and led him up from the rock. 14As he approached Lehi, the Phi-
listines came toward him shouting. The Spirit of the LORD came pow-
erfully upon him. The ropes on his arms became like charred flax, and
the bindings dropped from his hands. 15Finding a fresh jawbone of a
donkey, he grabbed it and struck down a thousand men.
16Then Samson said,

"With a donkey's jawbone
I have made donkeys of them.[a]
With a donkey's jawbone
I have killed a thousand men."

17When he finished speaking, he threw away the jawbone; and the
place was called Ramath Lehi.[b]
18Because he was very thirsty, he cried out to the LORD, "You have

[a] 16 Or *made a heap or two;* the Hebrew for *donkey* sounds like the Hebrew for *heap.* [b] 17 *Ramath Lehi* means *jawbone hill.*

PRAYING SCRIPTURE

Judges 15

Although Samson was a mighty warrior—he killed a thousand men with a donkey's jawbone in this case—he had to rely on the Lord for other necessities. Samson's supernatural abilities did not mean he could live apart from God's sustaining power.

Isn't it easy to forget how desperately we need the Lord? We are so quickly tempted to self-sufficiency that we should constantly ask God for humility to depend on him always.

PRAYING SCRIPTURE

Judges 16

Samson's 20-year rule over Israel came to a tragic end when he fell for the temptations of a Philistine prostitute. Samson was not above reproach, and his eventual death amid thousands of Philistine royals occurred in spite of God's blessing on his life.

It is sometimes said, "God uses crooked sticks," but we should not rejoice in our crookedness. Thank God when he uses you despite your flaws and weaknesses.

given your servant this great victory. Must I now die of thirst and fall
into the hands of the uncircumcised?" 19Then God opened up the hol-
low place in Lehi, and water came out of it. When Samson drank, his
strength returned and he revived. So the spring was called En Hak-
kore,[a] and it is still there in Lehi.
20Samson led[b] Israel for twenty years in the days of the Philistines.

SAMSON AND DELILAH

16 One day Samson went to Gaza, where he saw a prostitute. He
went in to spend the night with her. 2The people of Gaza were
told, "Samson is here!" So they surrounded the place and lay in wait
for him all night at the city gate. They made no move during the night,
saying, "At dawn we'll kill him."
3But Samson lay there only until the middle of the night. Then he
got up and took hold of the doors of the city gate, together with the
two posts, and tore them loose, bar and all. He lifted them to his shoul-
ders and carried them to the top of the hill that faces Hebron.
4Some time later, he fell in love with a woman in the Valley of Sorek
whose name was Delilah. 5The rulers of the Philistines went to her and
said, "See if you can lure him into showing you the secret of his great
strength and how we can overpower him so we may tie him up and sub-
due him. Each one of us will give you eleven hundred shekels[c] of silver."
6So Delilah said to Samson, "Tell me the secret of your great strength
and how you can be tied up and subdued."
7Samson answered her, "If anyone ties me with seven fresh bow-
strings that have not been dried, I'll become as weak as any other man."
8Then the rulers of the Philistines brought her seven fresh bow-
strings that had not been dried, and she tied him with them. 9With
men hidden in the room, she called to him, "Samson, the Philistines
are upon you!" But he snapped the bowstrings as easily as a piece
of string snaps when it comes close to a flame. So the secret of his
strength was not discovered.
10Then Delilah said to Samson, "You have made a fool of me; you lied
to me. Come now, tell me how you can be tied."
11He said, "If anyone ties me securely with new ropes that have never
been used, I'll become as weak as any other man."
12So Delilah took new ropes and tied him with them. Then, with
men hidden in the room, she called to him, "Samson, the Philistines
are upon you!" But he snapped the ropes off his arms as if they were
threads.
13Delilah then said to Samson, "All this time you have been making a
fool of me and lying to me. Tell me how you can be tied."
He replied, "If you weave the seven braids of my head into the fab-
ric on the loom and tighten it with the pin, I'll become as weak as any
other man." So while he was sleeping, Delilah took the seven braids of
his head, wove them into the fabric 14and[d] tightened it with the pin.
Again she called to him, "Samson, the Philistines are upon you!" He
awoke from his sleep and pulled up the pin and the loom, with the
fabric.
15Then she said to him, "How can you say, 'I love you,' when you

[a] 19 *En Hakkore* means *caller's spring.* [b] 20 Traditionally *judged* [c] 5 That is, about 28 pounds or about 13 kilograms [d] 13,14 Some Septuagint manuscripts; Hebrew *replied, "I can if you weave the seven braids of my head into the fabric on the loom."* [14]*So she*

won't confide in me? This is the third time you have made a fool of me and haven't told me the secret of your great strength." [16]With such nagging she prodded him day after day until he was sick to death of it.

[17]So he told her everything. "No razor has ever been used on my head," he said, "because I have been a Nazirite dedicated to God from my mother's womb. If my head were shaved, my strength would leave me, and I would become as weak as any other man."

[18]When Delilah saw that he had told her everything, she sent word to the rulers of the Philistines, "Come back once more; he has told me everything." So the rulers of the Philistines returned with the silver in their hands. [19]After putting him to sleep on her lap, she called for someone to shave off the seven braids of his hair, and so began to subdue him.[a] And his strength left him.

[20]Then she called, "Samson, the Philistines are upon you!"

He awoke from his sleep and thought, "I'll go out as before and shake myself free." But he did not know that the LORD had left him.

[21]Then the Philistines seized him, gouged out his eyes and took him down to Gaza. Binding him with bronze shackles, they set him to grinding grain in the prison. [22]But the hair on his head began to grow again after it had been shaved.

THE DEATH OF SAMSON

[23]Now the rulers of the Philistines assembled to offer a great sacrifice to Dagon their god and to celebrate, saying, "Our god has delivered Samson, our enemy, into our hands."

[24]When the people saw him, they praised their god, saying,

"Our god has delivered our enemy
  into our hands,
the one who laid waste our land
  and multiplied our slain."

[25]While they were in high spirits, they shouted, "Bring out Samson to entertain us." So they called Samson out of the prison, and he performed for them.

When they stood him among the pillars, [26]Samson said to the servant who held his hand, "Put me where I can feel the pillars that support the temple, so that I may lean against them." [27]Now the temple was crowded with men and women; all the rulers of the Philistines were there, and on the roof were about three thousand men and women watching Samson perform. [28]Then Samson prayed to the LORD, "Sovereign LORD, remember me. Please, God, strengthen me just once more, and let me with one blow get revenge on the Philistines for my two eyes." [29]Then Samson reached toward the two central pillars on which the temple stood. Bracing himself against them, his right hand on the one and his left hand on the other, [30]Samson said, "Let me die with the Philistines!" Then he pushed with all his might, and down came the temple on the rulers and all the people in it. Thus he killed many more when he died than while he lived.

[31]Then his brothers and his father's whole family went down to get him. They brought him back and buried him between Zorah and Eshtaol in the tomb of Manoah his father. He had led[b] Israel twenty years.

---

[a] *19* Hebrew; some Septuagint manuscripts *and he began to weaken*
[b] *31* Traditionally *judged*

MICAH'S IDOLS

17 Now a man named Micah from the hill country of Ephraim 2said to his mother, "The eleven hundred shekels[a] of silver that were taken from you and about which I heard you utter a curse — I have that silver with me; I took it."

Then his mother said, "The LORD bless you, my son!"

3When he returned the eleven hundred shekels of silver to his mother, she said, "I solemnly consecrate my silver to the LORD for my son to make an image overlaid with silver. I will give it back to you."

4So after he returned the silver to his mother, she took two hundred shekels[b] of silver and gave them to a silversmith, who used them to make the idol. And it was put in Micah's house.

5Now this man Micah had a shrine, and he made an ephod and some household gods and installed one of his sons as his priest. 6In those days Israel had no king; everyone did as they saw fit.

7A young Levite from Bethlehem in Judah, who had been living within the clan of Judah, 8left that town in search of some other place to stay. On his way[c] he came to Micah's house in the hill country of Ephraim.

9Micah asked him, "Where are you from?"

"I'm a Levite from Bethlehem in Judah," he said, "and I'm looking for a place to stay."

10Then Micah said to him, "Live with me and be my father and priest, and I'll give you ten shekels[d] of silver a year, your clothes and your food." 11So the Levite agreed to live with him, and the young man became like one of his sons to him. 12Then Micah installed the Levite, and the young man became his priest and lived in his house. 13And Micah said, "Now I know that the LORD will be good to me, since this Levite has become my priest."

PRAYING SCRIPTURE

Judges 17

Without stable spiritual leadership, the Israelite people were free to create their own religions. Micah and his mother held to a form of spirituality but made an idol of silver, then recruited his own paid priest. In this invented religion, he hoped to gain God's favor.

People who deny God's Word always end up creating an alternate, false belief system. Ask God to keep you close to him and far from idolatry.

THE DANITES SETTLE IN LAISH

18 In those days Israel had no king.

And in those days the tribe of the Danites was seeking a place of their own where they might settle, because they had not yet come into an inheritance among the tribes of Israel. 2So the Danites sent five of their leading men from Zorah and Eshtaol to spy out the land and explore it. These men represented all the Danites. They told them, "Go, explore the land."

So they entered the hill country of Ephraim and came to the house of Micah, where they spent the night. 3When they were near Micah's house, they recognized the voice of the young Levite; so they turned in there and asked him, "Who brought you here? What are you doing in this place? Why are you here?"

4He told them what Micah had done for him, and said, "He has hired me and I am his priest."

5Then they said to him, "Please inquire of God to learn whether our journey will be successful."

6The priest answered them, "Go in peace. Your journey has the LORD's approval."

7So the five men left and came to Laish, where they saw that the

PRAYING SCRIPTURE

Judges 18

As Israel continued to spiral, the Danites took by force the carved image Micah had made and paid his priest to come serve them. They adopted Micah's false religion as their own, then took it over, rejecting the God of Israel until the next cycle of captivity.

We are reminded repeatedly that the people did what was right in their own eyes. Ask God to provide godly leaders who adhere to God's Word.

---

[a] *2* That is, about 28 pounds or about 13 kilograms [b] *4* That is, about 5 pounds or about 2.3 kilograms [c] *8* Or *To carry on his profession*
[d] *10* That is, about 4 ounces or about 115 grams

people were living in safety, like the Sidonians, at peace and secure.
And since their land lacked nothing, they were prosperous.[a] Also, they
lived a long way from the Sidonians and had no relationship with any-
one else.[b]
8 When they returned to Zorah and Eshtaol, their fellow Danites
asked them, "How did you find things?"
9 They answered, "Come on, let's attack them! We have seen the land,
and it is very good. Aren't you going to do something? Don't hesitate to
go there and take it over. 10 When you get there, you will find an unsus-
pecting people and a spacious land that God has put into your hands,
a land that lacks nothing whatever."
11 Then six hundred men of the Danites, armed for battle, set out
from Zorah and Eshtaol. 12 On their way they set up camp near Kiriath
Jearim in Judah. This is why the place west of Kiriath Jearim is called
Mahaneh Dan[c] to this day. 13 From there they went on to the hill country
of Ephraim and came to Micah's house.
14 Then the five men who had spied out the land of Laish said to their
fellow Danites, "Do you know that one of these houses has an ephod,
some household gods and an image overlaid with silver? Now you
know what to do." 15 So they turned in there and went to the house of
the young Levite at Micah's place and greeted him. 16 The six hundred
Danites, armed for battle, stood at the entrance of the gate. 17 The five
men who had spied out the land went inside and took the idol, the
ephod and the household gods while the priest and the six hundred
armed men stood at the entrance of the gate.
18 When the five men went into Micah's house and took the idol, the
ephod and the household gods, the priest said to them, "What are you
doing?"
19 They answered him, "Be quiet! Don't say a word. Come with us, and
be our father and priest. Isn't it better that you serve a tribe and clan in
Israel as priest rather than just one man's household?" 20 The priest was
very pleased. He took the ephod, the household gods and the idol and
went along with the people. 21 Putting their little children, their live-
stock and their possessions in front of them, they turned away and left.
22 When they had gone some distance from Micah's house, the men
who lived near Micah were called together and overtook the Danites.
23 As they shouted after them, the Danites turned and said to Micah,
"What's the matter with you that you called out your men to fight?"
24 He replied, "You took the gods I made, and my priest, and went
away. What else do I have? How can you ask, 'What's the matter with
you?' "
25 The Danites answered, "Don't argue with us, or some of the men
may get angry and attack you, and you and your family will lose your
lives." 26 So the Danites went their way, and Micah, seeing that they
were too strong for him, turned around and went back home.
27 Then they took what Micah had made, and his priest, and went on
to Laish, against a people at peace and secure. They attacked them with
the sword and burned down their city. 28 There was no one to rescue
them because they lived a long way from Sidon and had no relation-
ship with anyone else. The city was in a valley near Beth Rehob.

---

[a] 7 The meaning of the Hebrew for this clause is uncertain. [b] 7 Hebrew; some Septuagint manuscripts *with the Arameans* [c] 12 *Mahaneh Dan* means *Dan's camp.*

The Danites rebuilt the city and settled there. 29They named it Dan
after their ancestor Dan, who was born to Israel — though the city used
to be called Laish. 30There the Danites set up for themselves the idol,
and Jonathan son of Gershom, the son of Moses,[a] and his sons were
priests for the tribe of Dan until the time of the captivity of the land.
31They continued to use the idol Micah had made, all the time the
house of God was in Shiloh.

A LEVITE AND HIS CONCUBINE

19 In those days Israel had no king.
Now a Levite who lived in a remote area in the hill country of
Ephraim took a concubine from Bethlehem in Judah. 2But she was un-
faithful to him. She left him and went back to her parents' home in
Bethlehem, Judah. After she had been there four months, 3her hus-
band went to her to persuade her to return. He had with him his ser-
vant and two donkeys. She took him into her parents' home, and when
her father saw him, he gladly welcomed him. 4His father-in-law, the
woman's father, prevailed on him to stay; so he remained with him
three days, eating and drinking, and sleeping there.
5On the fourth day they got up early and he prepared to leave, but
the woman's father said to his son-in-law, "Refresh yourself with some-
thing to eat; then you can go." 6So the two of them sat down to eat and
drink together. Afterward the woman's father said, "Please stay tonight
and enjoy yourself." 7And when the man got up to go, his father-in-law
persuaded him, so he stayed there that night. 8On the morning of the
fifth day, when he rose to go, the woman's father said, "Refresh your-
self. Wait till afternoon!" So the two of them ate together.
9Then when the man, with his concubine and his servant, got up to
leave, his father-in-law, the woman's father, said, "Now look, it's almost
evening. Spend the night here; the day is nearly over. Stay and enjoy
yourself. Early tomorrow morning you can get up and be on your way
home." 10But, unwilling to stay another night, the man left and went
toward Jebus (that is, Jerusalem), with his two saddled donkeys and
his concubine.
11When they were near Jebus and the day was almost gone, the ser-
vant said to his master, "Come, let's stop at this city of the Jebusites
and spend the night."
12His master replied, "No. We won't go into any city whose people
are not Israelites. We will go on to Gibeah." 13He added, "Come, let's try
to reach Gibeah or Ramah and spend the night in one of those places."
14So they went on, and the sun set as they neared Gibeah in Benjamin.
15There they stopped to spend the night. They went and sat in the city
square, but no one took them in for the night.
16That evening an old man from the hill country of Ephraim, who
was living in Gibeah (the inhabitants of the place were Benjamites),
came in from his work in the fields. 17When he looked and saw the
traveler in the city square, the old man asked, "Where are you going?
Where did you come from?"
18He answered, "We are on our way from Bethlehem in Judah to a
remote area in the hill country of Ephraim where I live. I have been to

PRAYING SCRIPTURE

Judges 19

It's difficult to determine which is most heinous in this story: the brutality of the demonic mob or the callousness of the Levite toward his brutalized concubine. Sin is sin, and God hates it—whether it is committed by the unrighteous or the allegedly righteous.

This Scripture reminds us how inhumanely people can act apart from God. Ask him to keep you from actual violence and from attitudes leading to it.

---

[a] *30* Many Hebrew manuscripts, some Septuagint manuscripts and Vulgate; many other Hebrew manuscripts and some other Septuagint manuscripts *Manasseh*

Bethlehem in Judah and now I am going to the house of the LORD.[a] No one has taken me in for the night. 19We have both straw and fodder for our donkeys and bread and wine for ourselves your servants — me, the woman and the young man with us. We don't need anything."

20"You are welcome at my house," the old man said. "Let me supply whatever you need. Only don't spend the night in the square." 21So he took him into his house and fed his donkeys. After they had washed their feet, they had something to eat and drink.

22While they were enjoying themselves, some of the wicked men of the city surrounded the house. Pounding on the door, they shouted to the old man who owned the house, "Bring out the man who came to your house so we can have sex with him."

23The owner of the house went outside and said to them, "No, my friends, don't be so vile. Since this man is my guest, don't do this outrageous thing. 24Look, here is my virgin daughter, and his concubine. I will bring them out to you now, and you can use them and do to them whatever you wish. But as for this man, don't do such an outrageous thing."

25But the men would not listen to him. So the man took his concubine and sent her outside to them, and they raped her and abused her throughout the night, and at dawn they let her go. 26At daybreak the woman went back to the house where her master was staying, fell down at the door and lay there until daylight.

27When her master got up in the morning and opened the door of the house and stepped out to continue on his way, there lay his concubine, fallen in the doorway of the house, with her hands on the threshold. 28He said to her, "Get up; let's go." But there was no answer. Then the man put her on his donkey and set out for home.

29When he reached home, he took a knife and cut up his concubine, limb by limb, into twelve parts and sent them into all the areas of Israel. 30Everyone who saw it was saying to one another, "Such a thing has never been seen or done, not since the day the Israelites came up out of Egypt. Just imagine! We must do something! So speak up!"

THE ISRAELITES PUNISH THE BENJAMITES

20 Then all Israel from Dan to Beersheba and from the land of Gilead came together as one and assembled before the LORD in Mizpah. 2The leaders of all the people of the tribes of Israel took their places in the assembly of God's people, four hundred thousand men armed with swords. 3(The Benjamites heard that the Israelites had gone up to Mizpah.) Then the Israelites said, "Tell us how this awful thing happened."

4So the Levite, the husband of the murdered woman, said, "I and my concubine came to Gibeah in Benjamin to spend the night. 5During the night the men of Gibeah came after me and surrounded the house, intending to kill me. They raped my concubine, and she died. 6I took my concubine, cut her into pieces and sent one piece to each region of Israel's inheritance, because they committed this lewd and outrageous act in Israel. 7Now, all you Israelites, speak up and tell me what you have decided to do."

8All the men rose up together as one, saying, "None of us will go home. No, not one of us will return to his house. 9But now this is what

PRAYING SCRIPTURE

Judges 20

Don't all people have a tendency to try to make themselves look innocent? It's part of our fallen nature. When the Levite spoke about the incident involving his concubine, he told the story in a way that minimized his own guilt, placing most of the blame on others.

Taking the blame when appropriate is a mark of spiritual maturity; passing blame is not. Ask God to help you take responsibility for your own decisions.

[a] *18* Hebrew, Vulgate, Syriac and Targum; Septuagint *going home*

we'll do to Gibeah: We'll go up against it in the order decided by cast-
ing lots. 10We'll take ten men out of every hundred from all the tribes
of Israel, and a hundred from a thousand, and a thousand from ten
thousand, to get provisions for the army. Then, when the army arrives
at Gibeah[a] in Benjamin, it can give them what they deserve for this
outrageous act done in Israel." 11So all the Israelites got together and
united as one against the city.

12The tribes of Israel sent messengers throughout the tribe of Benja-
min, saying, "What about this awful crime that was committed among
you? 13Now turn those wicked men of Gibeah over to us so that we may
put them to death and purge the evil from Israel."

But the Benjamites would not listen to their fellow Israelites. 14From
their towns they came together at Gibeah to fight against the Israelites.
15At once the Benjamites mobilized twenty-six thousand swordsmen
from their towns, in addition to seven hundred able young men from
those living in Gibeah. 16Among all these soldiers there were seven
hundred select troops who were left-handed, each of whom could sling
a stone at a hair and not miss.

17Israel, apart from Benjamin, mustered four hundred thousand
swordsmen, all of them fit for battle.

18The Israelites went up to Bethel[b] and inquired of God. They said,
"Who of us is to go up first to fight against the Benjamites?"

The LORD replied, "Judah shall go first."

19The next morning the Israelites got up and pitched camp near
Gibeah. 20The Israelites went out to fight the Benjamites and took up
battle positions against them at Gibeah. 21The Benjamites came out of
Gibeah and cut down twenty-two thousand Israelites on the battlefield
that day. 22But the Israelites encouraged one another and again took
up their positions where they had stationed themselves the first day.
23The Israelites went up and wept before the LORD until evening, and
they inquired of the LORD. They said, "Shall we go up again to fight
against the Benjamites, our fellow Israelites?"

The LORD answered, "Go up against them."

24Then the Israelites drew near to Benjamin the second day. 25This
time, when the Benjamites came out from Gibeah to oppose them,
they cut down another eighteen thousand Israelites, all of them armed
with swords.

26Then all the Israelites, the whole army, went up to Bethel, and
there they sat weeping before the LORD. They fasted that day until
evening and presented burnt offerings and fellowship offerings to the
LORD. 27And the Israelites inquired of the LORD. (In those days the ark
of the covenant of God was there, 28with Phinehas son of Eleazar, the
son of Aaron, ministering before it.) They asked, "Shall we go up again
to fight against the Benjamites, our fellow Israelites, or not?"

The LORD responded, "Go, for tomorrow I will give them into your
hands."

29Then Israel set an ambush around Gibeah. 30They went up against
the Benjamites on the third day and took up positions against Gib-
eah as they had done before. 31The Benjamites came out to meet them
and were drawn away from the city. They began to inflict casualties on
the Israelites as before, so that about thirty men fell in the open field

---

[a] *10* One Hebrew manuscript; most Hebrew manuscripts *Geba,* a variant of *Gibeah* [b] *18* Or *to the house of God;* also in verse 26

and on the roads — the one leading to Bethel and the other to Gibeah.
32While the Benjamites were saying, "We are defeating them as be-
fore," the Israelites were saying, "Let's retreat and draw them away
from the city to the roads."
33All the men of Israel moved from their places and took up posi-
tions at Baal Tamar, and the Israelite ambush charged out of its place
on the west[a] of Gibeah.[b] 34Then ten thousand of Israel's able young
men made a frontal attack on Gibeah. The fighting was so heavy that
the Benjamites did not realize how near disaster was. 35The LORD de-
feated Benjamin before Israel, and on that day the Israelites struck
down 25,100 Benjamites, all armed with swords. 36Then the Benjamites
saw that they were beaten.

Now the men of Israel had given way before Benjamin, because they
relied on the ambush they had set near Gibeah. 37Those who had been
in ambush made a sudden dash into Gibeah, spread out and put the
whole city to the sword. 38The Israelites had arranged with the ambush
that they should send up a great cloud of smoke from the city, 39and
then the Israelites would counterattack.

The Benjamites had begun to inflict casualties on the Israelites
(about thirty), and they said, "We are defeating them as in the first bat-
tle." 40But when the column of smoke began to rise from the city, the
Benjamites turned and saw the whole city going up in smoke. 41Then
the Israelites counterattacked, and the Benjamites were terrified, be-
cause they realized that disaster had come on them. 42So they fled be-
fore the Israelites in the direction of the wilderness, but they could
not escape the battle. And the Israelites who came out of the towns cut
them down there. 43They surrounded the Benjamites, chased them and
easily[c] overran them in the vicinity of Gibeah on the east. 44Eighteen
thousand Benjamites fell, all of them valiant fighters. 45As they turned
and fled toward the wilderness to the rock of Rimmon, the Israelites
cut down five thousand men along the roads. They kept pressing after
the Benjamites as far as Gidom and struck down two thousand more.
46On that day twenty-five thousand Benjamite swordsmen fell, all of
them valiant fighters. 47But six hundred of them turned and fled into
the wilderness to the rock of Rimmon, where they stayed four months.
48The men of Israel went back to Benjamin and put all the towns to the
sword, including the animals and everything else they found. All the
towns they came across they set on fire.

WIVES FOR THE BENJAMITES

21 The men of Israel had taken an oath at Mizpah: "Not one of us
will give his daughter in marriage to a Benjamite."
2The people went to Bethel,[d] where they sat before God until eve-
ning, raising their voices and weeping bitterly. 3"LORD, God of Israel,"
they cried, "why has this happened to Israel? Why should one tribe be
missing from Israel today?"
4Early the next day the people built an altar and presented burnt
offerings and fellowship offerings.
5Then the Israelites asked, "Who from all the tribes of Israel has

PRAYING SCRIPTURE

Judges 21

In the final scene of Judges, after decades of sad, sordid, sinful history, we are reminded of the ongoing problem. Without a king, "everyone did as they saw fit" (verse 25). They forgot the law, neglected worship of their covenant God and lived like unbelievers. The whole book tells the tale.

Pray that God will help you die to self so that you can live for him.

---

[a] *33* Some Septuagint manuscripts and Vulgate; the meaning of the Hebrew for this word is uncertain. [b] *33* Hebrew *Geba,* a variant of *Gibeah*
[c] *43* The meaning of the Hebrew for this word is uncertain. [d] *2* Or *to the house of God*

failed to assemble before the LORD?" For they had taken a solemn oath
that anyone who failed to assemble before the LORD at Mizpah was to
be put to death.

6 Now the Israelites grieved for the tribe of Benjamin, their fellow
Israelites. "Today one tribe is cut off from Israel," they said. 7 "How can
we provide wives for those who are left, since we have taken an oath by
the LORD not to give them any of our daughters in marriage?" 8 Then
they asked, "Which one of the tribes of Israel failed to assemble before
the LORD at Mizpah?" They discovered that no one from Jabesh Gilead
had come to the camp for the assembly. 9 For when they counted the
people, they found that none of the people of Jabesh Gilead were there.

10 So the assembly sent twelve thousand fighting men with instruc-
tions to go to Jabesh Gilead and put to the sword those living there,
including the women and children. 11 "This is what you are to do," they
said. "Kill every male and every woman who is not a virgin." 12 They
found among the people living in Jabesh Gilead four hundred young
women who had never slept with a man, and they took them to the
camp at Shiloh in Canaan.

13 Then the whole assembly sent an offer of peace to the Benjamites
at the rock of Rimmon. 14 So the Benjamites returned at that time and
were given the women of Jabesh Gilead who had been spared. But
there were not enough for all of them.

15 The people grieved for Benjamin, because the LORD had made a
gap in the tribes of Israel. 16 And the elders of the assembly said, "With
the women of Benjamin destroyed, how shall we provide wives for
the men who are left? 17 The Benjamite survivors must have heirs,"
they said, "so that a tribe of Israel will not be wiped out. 18 We can't
give them our daughters as wives, since we Israelites have taken this
oath: 'Cursed be anyone who gives a wife to a Benjamite.' 19 But look,
there is the annual festival of the LORD in Shiloh, which lies north of
Bethel, east of the road that goes from Bethel to Shechem, and south
of Lebonah."

20 So they instructed the Benjamites, saying, "Go and hide in the
vineyards 21 and watch. When the young women of Shiloh come out to
join in the dancing, rush from the vineyards and each of you seize one
of them to be your wife. Then return to the land of Benjamin. 22 When
their fathers or brothers complain to us, we will say to them, 'Do us the
favor of helping them, because we did not get wives for them during
the war. You will not be guilty of breaking your oath because you did
not give your daughters to them.'"

23 So that is what the Benjamites did. While the young women were
dancing, each man caught one and carried her off to be his wife. Then
they returned to their inheritance and rebuilt the towns and settled
in them.

24 At that time the Israelites left that place and went home to their
tribes and clans, each to his own inheritance.

25 In those days Israel had no king; everyone did as they saw fit.

RUTH

The book of Ruth moves from ashes to beauty. It tells the story of a family on the brink of disaster and the glory of redeeming love. It contains some of the most well-known words of commitment and faithfulness while also setting the stage for the coming Redeemer. Chapter 1 contains a passage used often at weddings today; however, in Ruth it is a commitment from the title character to her mother-in-law. It is one of the most beautiful declarations of love in any literature (see verses 16–17).

Elimelek and his family lived in Bethlehem during the period of the judges. As if this time were not dark enough, a famine struck the land and they had to leave Bethlehem, which ironically suggests "house of bread," for their own survival. The family fled to the land of Moab and lived among Israel's enemies. While there, Elimelek's sons took Moabite wives—Ruth and Orpah. Elimelek then died, followed by both of his sons, leaving behind his wife, Naomi and her two daughters-in-law. Naomi found herself in the most vulnerable position a woman could experience.

Chapter 1 concludes with Naomi leaving Moab and imploring her daughters-in-law to stay in their own land and find husbands. Orpah relented and went back, but Ruth pledged her faithfulness to Naomi, her people and her God. The first chapter includes a word of hope, as they arrived during the beginning of barley harvest.

The middle chapters introduce the readers to Boaz, a relative of Elimelek. Ruth, in order to provide for Naomi and herself, went to glean in Boaz's fields. Boaz showed uncommon kindness to Ruth by having his men look after her in the field and intentionally leave extra grain for her to take home. Naomi encouraged Ruth to meet Boaz as he was threshing the harvest. She spoke with Boaz about redeeming Naomi's land, which would include marriage to her. Boaz proclaimed her kindness in this arrangement but revealed a complication in Ruth's plan: Another relative legally had the first opportunity to redeem Ruth.

The writer of Ruth thought so little of the nearer redeemer that readers are never told his name. This relative refused to redeem the land and marry Ruth because doing so would dilute his inheritance, so Boaz redeemed Naomi's land and married Ruth. They would later have a son named Obed, and the people would celebrate Naomi's reversal of fortune. Ruth closes with a genealogy, showing that Obed would be grandfather to David. Later in the genealogy in Matthew's Gospel, Ruth is one of only four women mentioned in the line of the Messiah.

Ruth reminds us that there is no situation we face in which we should not seek the Lord. Ruth's life was marked by deaths in the family, including that of her husband, relocation, new customs, support of her mother-in-law and dependence on others for enough to live on. Every part of our lives can be taken to God in prayer. There is nothing too big for him to handle nor too small to bring to his attention.

NAOMI LOSES HER HUSBAND AND SONS

1 In the days when the judges ruled,[a] there was a famine in the land.
So a man from Bethlehem in Judah, together with his wife and two
sons, went to live for a while in the country of Moab. 2The man's name
was Elimelek, his wife's name was Naomi, and the names of his two
sons were Mahlon and Kilion. They were Ephrathites from Bethlehem,
Judah. And they went to Moab and lived there.
3Now Elimelek, Naomi's husband, died, and she was left with her two
sons. 4They married Moabite women, one named Orpah and the other
Ruth. After they had lived there about ten years, 5both Mahlon and Kil-
ion also died, and Naomi was left without her two sons and her husband.

NAOMI AND RUTH RETURN TO BETHLEHEM

6When Naomi heard in Moab that the LORD had come to the aid of
his people by providing food for them, she and her daughters-in-law
prepared to return home from there. 7With her two daughters-in-law
she left the place where she had been living and set out on the road
that would take them back to the land of Judah.
8Then Naomi said to her two daughters-in-law, "Go back, each of
you, to your mother's home. May the LORD show you kindness, as you
have shown kindness to your dead husbands and to me. 9May the LORD
grant that each of you will find rest in the home of another husband."
Then she kissed them goodbye and they wept aloud 10and said to
her, "We will go back with you to your people."
11But Naomi said, "Return home, my daughters. Why would you
come with me? Am I going to have any more sons, who could become
your husbands? 12Return home, my daughters; I am too old to have
another husband. Even if I thought there was still hope for me — even
if I had a husband tonight and then gave birth to sons — 13would you
wait until they grew up? Would you remain unmarried for them? No,
my daughters. It is more bitter for me than for you, because the LORD's
hand has turned against me!"
14At this they wept aloud again. Then Orpah kissed her mother-in-
law goodbye, but Ruth clung to her.
15"Look," said Naomi, "your sister-in-law is going back to her people
and her gods. Go back with her."
16But Ruth replied, "Don't urge me to leave you or to turn back from
you. Where you go I will go, and where you stay I will stay. Your people
will be my people and your God my God. 17Where you die I will die, and
there I will be buried. May the LORD deal with me, be it ever so severely,
if even death separates you and me." 18When Naomi realized that Ruth
was determined to go with her, she stopped urging her.
19So the two women went on until they came to Bethlehem. When
they arrived in Bethlehem, the whole town was stirred because of
them, and the women exclaimed, "Can this be Naomi?"
20"Don't call me Naomi,[b]" she told them. "Call me Mara,[c] because
the Almighty[d] has made my life very bitter. 21I went away full, but the
LORD has brought me back empty. Why call me Naomi? The LORD has
afflicted[e] me; the Almighty has brought misfortune upon me."
22So Naomi returned from Moab accompanied by Ruth the Moabite,
her daughter-in-law, arriving in Bethlehem as the barley harvest was
beginning.

PRAYING SCRIPTURE

Ruth 1

Recited at more weddings than perhaps any other passage, Ruth's declaration of commitment wasn't even to a spouse; it was to her mother-in-law. Left widowed, Ruth and Naomi returned to Israel, Naomi's homeland. It was here the mercy of God interacted with their needs.

Faithfulness is a marker of the Christian life. If you lack it, ask God to develop it in you so those around you can trust you.

---

[a] 1 Traditionally *judged* [b] 20 *Naomi* means *pleasant.* [c] 20 *Mara* means *bitter.* [d] 20 Hebrew *Shaddai;* also in verse 21 [e] 21 Or *has testified against*

RUTH MEETS BOAZ IN THE GRAIN FIELD

2 Now Naomi had a relative on her husband's side, a man of stand-
ing from the clan of Elimelek, whose name was Boaz.
2And Ruth the Moabite said to Naomi, "Let me go to the fields and
pick up the leftover grain behind anyone in whose eyes I find favor."
Naomi said to her, "Go ahead, my daughter." 3So she went out, en-
tered a field and began to glean behind the harvesters. As it turned
out, she was working in a field belonging to Boaz, who was from the
clan of Elimelek.
4Just then Boaz arrived from Bethlehem and greeted the harvesters,
"The LORD be with you!"
"The LORD bless you!" they answered.
5Boaz asked the overseer of his harvesters, "Who does that young
woman belong to?"
6The overseer replied, "She is the Moabite who came back from
Moab with Naomi. 7She said, 'Please let me glean and gather among
the sheaves behind the harvesters.' She came into the field and has
remained here from morning till now, except for a short rest in the
shelter."
8So Boaz said to Ruth, "My daughter, listen to me. Don't go and
glean in another field and don't go away from here. Stay here with the
women who work for me. 9Watch the field where the men are harvest-
ing, and follow along after the women. I have told the men not to lay
a hand on you. And whenever you are thirsty, go and get a drink from
the water jars the men have filled."
10At this, she bowed down with her face to the ground. She asked
him, "Why have I found such favor in your eyes that you notice me — a
foreigner?"
11Boaz replied, "I've been told all about what you have done for your
mother-in-law since the death of your husband — how you left your
father and mother and your homeland and came to live with a people
you did not know before. 12May the LORD repay you for what you have
done. May you be richly rewarded by the LORD, the God of Israel, under
whose wings you have come to take refuge."
13"May I continue to find favor in your eyes, my lord," she said. "You
have put me at ease by speaking kindly to your servant — though I do
not have the standing of one of your servants."
14At mealtime Boaz said to her, "Come over here. Have some bread
and dip it in the wine vinegar."
When she sat down with the harvesters, he offered her some roasted
grain. She ate all she wanted and had some left over. 15As she got up to
glean, Boaz gave orders to his men, "Let her gather among the sheaves
and don't reprimand her. 16Even pull out some stalks for her from the
bundles and leave them for her to pick up, and don't rebuke her."
17So Ruth gleaned in the field until evening. Then she threshed the
barley she had gathered, and it amounted to about an ephah.[a] 18She
carried it back to town, and her mother-in-law saw how much she had
gathered. Ruth also brought out and gave her what she had left over
after she had eaten enough.
19Her mother-in-law asked her, "Where did you glean today? Where
did you work? Blessed be the man who took notice of you!"
Then Ruth told her mother-in-law about the one at whose place she

[a] 17 That is, probably about 30 pounds or about 13 kilograms

PRAYING SCRIPTURE

Ruth 2

Boaz showed Ruth and Naomi uncommon kindness—a requirement of the law and then some. The law commanded that the edges of the fields be left unharvested for strangers and the poor. Boaz allowed that for Ruth but also instructed his field hands to drop some grain for her to harvest.

Have God's people ever shown you unexpected kindnesses? Pray for ways you might show such kindness to someone today.

had been working. "The name of the man I worked with today is Boaz,"
she said.
20"The LORD bless him!" Naomi said to her daughter-in-law. "He
has not stopped showing his kindness to the living and the dead."
She added, "That man is our close relative; he is one of our guardian-
redeemers.[a]"
21Then Ruth the Moabite said, "He even said to me, 'Stay with my
workers until they finish harvesting all my grain.'"
22Naomi said to Ruth her daughter-in-law, "It will be good for you,
my daughter, to go with the women who work for him, because in
someone else's field you might be harmed."
23So Ruth stayed close to the women of Boaz to glean until the
barley and wheat harvests were finished. And she lived with her
mother-in-law.

RUTH AND BOAZ AT THE THRESHING FLOOR

3 One day Ruth's mother-in-law Naomi said to her, "My daughter,
I must find a home[b] for you, where you will be well provided for.
2Now Boaz, with whose women you have worked, is a relative of ours.
Tonight he will be winnowing barley on the threshing floor. 3Wash,
put on perfume, and get dressed in your best clothes. Then go down
to the threshing floor, but don't let him know you are there until he
has finished eating and drinking. 4When he lies down, note the place
where he is lying. Then go and uncover his feet and lie down. He will
tell you what to do."
5"I will do whatever you say," Ruth answered. 6So she went down
to the threshing floor and did everything her mother-in-law told her
to do.
7When Boaz had finished eating and drinking and was in good spir-
its, he went over to lie down at the far end of the grain pile. Ruth ap-
proached quietly, uncovered his feet and lay down. 8In the middle of
the night something startled the man; he turned — and there was a
woman lying at his feet!
9"Who are you?" he asked.
"I am your servant Ruth," she said. "Spread the corner of your gar-
ment over me, since you are a guardian-redeemer[c] of our family."
10"The LORD bless you, my daughter," he replied. "This kindness is
greater than that which you showed earlier: You have not run after the
younger men, whether rich or poor. 11And now, my daughter, don't be
afraid. I will do for you all you ask. All the people of my town know that
you are a woman of noble character. 12Although it is true that I am a
guardian-redeemer of our family, there is another who is more closely
related than I. 13Stay here for the night, and in the morning if he wants
to do his duty as your guardian-redeemer, good; let him redeem you.
But if he is not willing, as surely as the LORD lives I will do it. Lie here
until morning."
14So she lay at his feet until morning, but got up before anyone could
be recognized; and he said, "No one must know that a woman came to
the threshing floor."

[a] 20 The Hebrew word for *guardian-redeemer* is a legal term for one who has the obligation to redeem a relative in serious difficulty (see Lev. 25:25-55).
[b] 1 Hebrew *find rest* (see 1:9)
[c] 9 The Hebrew word for *guardian-redeemer* is a legal term for one who has the obligation to redeem a relative in serious difficulty (see Lev. 25:25-55); also in verses 12 and 13.

PRAYING SCRIPTURE

Ruth 3

Naomi and Ruth conceived a plan to ensure Boaz would accept his familial responsibility to Ruth. Through a unique ritual, Ruth secured his commitment to redeem her, bringing her into his family. Yet Ruth was forced to wait to see how the matter turned out.

It's difficult to wait on God after we've done all we can do, so ask God for patience and faith to let him do his work.

15He also said, "Bring me the shawl you are wearing and hold it out."
When she did so, he poured into it six measures of barley and placed
the bundle on her. Then he[a] went back to town.
16When Ruth came to her mother-in-law, Naomi asked, "How did it
go, my daughter?"
Then she told her everything Boaz had done for her 17and added, "He
gave me these six measures of barley, saying, 'Don't go back to your
mother-in-law empty-handed.'"
18Then Naomi said, "Wait, my daughter, until you find out what hap-
pens. For the man will not rest until the matter is settled today."

BOAZ MARRIES RUTH

4 Meanwhile Boaz went up to the town gate and sat down there just
as the guardian-redeemer[b] he had mentioned came along. Boaz
said, "Come over here, my friend, and sit down." So he went over and
sat down.
2Boaz took ten of the elders of the town and said, "Sit here," and they
did so. 3Then he said to the guardian-redeemer, "Naomi, who has come
back from Moab, is selling the piece of land that belonged to our rel-
ative Elimelek. 4I thought I should bring the matter to your attention
and suggest that you buy it in the presence of these seated here and
in the presence of the elders of my people. If you will redeem it, do so.
But if you[c] will not, tell me, so I will know. For no one has the right to
do it except you, and I am next in line."
"I will redeem it," he said.
5Then Boaz said, "On the day you buy the land from Naomi, you also
acquire Ruth the Moabite, the[d] dead man's widow, in order to maintain
the name of the dead with his property."
6At this, the guardian-redeemer said, "Then I cannot redeem it be-
cause I might endanger my own estate. You redeem it yourself. I can-
not do it."
7(Now in earlier times in Israel, for the redemption and transfer of
property to become final, one party took off his sandal and gave it to
the other. This was the method of legalizing transactions in Israel.)
8So the guardian-redeemer said to Boaz, "Buy it yourself." And he
removed his sandal.
9Then Boaz announced to the elders and all the people, "Today you
are witnesses that I have bought from Naomi all the property of Elim-
elek, Kilion and Mahlon. 10I have also acquired Ruth the Moabite, Mah-
lon's widow, as my wife, in order to maintain the name of the dead
with his property, so that his name will not disappear from among his
family or from his hometown. Today you are witnesses!"
11Then the elders and all the people at the gate said, "We are wit-
nesses. May the LORD make the woman who is coming into your
home like Rachel and Leah, who together built up the family of Israel.
May you have standing in Ephrathah and be famous in Bethlehem.

PRAYING SCRIPTURE

Ruth 4

Boaz took advantage of a legal loophole to complete the circle of God's provision. He informed the nearest relative that if he bought the property from Naomi, he would also acquire Ruth the Moabite to maintain the name of the dead man with his property. The relative declined, not wanting to endanger his own estate. Boaz then stepped in. In this way, God provided for the two women.

And in doing so, God also provided for us, for Boaz and Ruth became ancestors to David and to Jesus, our Savior. Praise God for his perfect provision.

---

[a] *15* Most Hebrew manuscripts; many Hebrew manuscripts, Vulgate and Syriac *she* [b] *1* The Hebrew word for *guardian-redeemer* is a legal term for one who has the obligation to redeem a relative in serious difficulty (see Lev. 25:25-55); also in verses 3, 6, 8 and 14. [c] *4* Many Hebrew manuscripts, Septuagint, Vulgate and Syriac; most Hebrew manuscripts *he* [d] *5* Vulgate and Syriac; Hebrew (see also Septuagint) *Naomi and from Ruth the Moabite, you acquire the*

12Through the offspring the LORD gives you by this young woman, may
your family be like that of Perez, whom Tamar bore to Judah."

NAOMI GAINS A SON

13So Boaz took Ruth and she became his wife. When he made love
to her, the LORD enabled her to conceive, and she gave birth to a son.
14The women said to Naomi: "Praise be to the LORD, who this day has
not left you without a guardian-redeemer. May he become famous
throughout Israel! 15He will renew your life and sustain you in your
old age. For your daughter-in-law, who loves you and who is better to
you than seven sons, has given him birth."

16Then Naomi took the child in her arms and cared for him. 17The
women living there said, "Naomi has a son!" And they named him
Obed. He was the father of Jesse, the father of David.

THE GENEALOGY OF DAVID

18This, then, is the family line of Perez:

Perez was the father of Hezron,
19 Hezron the father of Ram,
Ram the father of Amminadab,
20 Amminadab the father of Nahshon,
Nahshon the father of Salmon,[a]
21 Salmon the father of Boaz,
Boaz the father of Obed,
22 Obed the father of Jesse,
and Jesse the father of David.

---

[a] *20* A few Hebrew manuscripts, some Septuagint manuscripts and Vulgate (see also verse 21 and Septuagint of 1 Chron. 2:11); most Hebrew manuscripts *Salma*

1 SAMUEL

First Samuel provides the antidote to the chaos of the judges: a king chosen by God. It introduces Samuel, a prophet of the Lord who would take the place of the corrupt priests who exploited God's people, and the final judge. As the people cried out for a king, Samuel anointed Saul, even as he warned the people that they would be exploited by an earthly king. The people were no longer without a king, as in the years covered by the book of Judges, but Saul often did that which was right in his own eyes. After the Lord rejected Saul—due to his repeated disobedience—Samuel anointed David as the next king. This set off a long struggle to determine who would be king over Israel.

Saul viewed David as a threat to his throne and repeatedly tried to kill him. In Saul's violence and rage, he employed his son Jonathan, David's best friend, in his schemes, but his plans were always thwarted. David continually showed his personal integrity by refusing to kill Saul, while Jonathan showed his trust in God by refusing to betray David, even though it would cost him the throne. Saul and Jonathan died in battle in the book's final chapter, clearing the way for David to be recognized as the rightful ruler of God's people.

First Samuel contains two beautiful stories of God working in unlikely places to bring redemption to his people. The author introduced us to "a certain man . . . whose name was Elkanah" (1:1). Elkanah had two wives. The wife he loved more, Hannah, was barren and suffered many indignities at the hands of his other wife.

When the family went to the house of the Lord, Hannah prayed with such intensity that the priest Eli believed she was drunk. This prayer is one of the most well-known in all the Scriptures. She promised to dedicate her first child to the Lord if he would bless her with children. The next year, she conceived and gave birth to a son named Samuel.

After the Lord rejected King Saul for his wickedness, he sent Samuel to the house of Jesse to anoint one of his sons as the new king. The Lord told Samuel not to evaluate the new king by his physical appearance for the Lord was more concerned with the inner person, the heart. David, merely a shepherd boy who had never faced combat, became Israel's hero by killing Goliath—a giant Philistine warrior—with a sling and a single stone.

As a man after God's own heart, David was a man of ongoing prayer. The dozens of psalms attributed to him reveal a man always pursuing God in prayer and in his commandments. The contrast between Saul, who used the faith to his own ends, and David, who pursued God with his whole heart, could not be more stark. We would do well to learn to pray like Hannah and pursue God like David.

PRAYING SCRIPTURE

1 Samuel 1

Many a woman can identify with Hannah. Desiring children, a woman may plead with God to intervene and open her womb. God may act, or she may never give birth and choose to adopt. In doing so, God makes the woman a parent to a beautiful child who desires parents as much as the woman desires a child.

Pray today for women in Hannah's position, especially if it is you yourself. God heard Hannah, and he will hear you.

THE BIRTH OF SAMUEL

1 There was a certain man from Ramathaim, a Zuphite[a] from the hill country of Ephraim, whose name was Elkanah son of Jeroham, the son of Elihu, the son of Tohu, the son of Zuph, an Ephraimite. 2He had two wives; one was called Hannah and the other Peninnah. Peninnah had children, but Hannah had none.

3Year after year this man went up from his town to worship and sacrifice to the LORD Almighty at Shiloh, where Hophni and Phinehas, the two sons of Eli, were priests of the LORD. 4Whenever the day came for Elkanah to sacrifice, he would give portions of the meat to his wife Peninnah and to all her sons and daughters. 5But to Hannah he gave a double portion because he loved her, and the LORD had closed her womb. 6Because the LORD had closed Hannah's womb, her rival kept provoking her in order to irritate her. 7This went on year after year. Whenever Hannah went up to the house of the LORD, her rival provoked her till she wept and would not eat. 8Her husband Elkanah would say to her, "Hannah, why are you weeping? Why don't you eat? Why are you downhearted? Don't I mean more to you than ten sons?"

9Once when they had finished eating and drinking in Shiloh, Hannah stood up. Now Eli the priest was sitting on his chair by the doorpost of the LORD's house. 10In her deep anguish Hannah prayed to the LORD, weeping bitterly. 11And she made a vow, saying, "LORD Almighty, if you will only look on your servant's misery and remember me, and not forget your servant but give her a son, then I will give him to the LORD for all the days of his life, and no razor will ever be used on his head."

12As she kept on praying to the LORD, Eli observed her mouth. 13Hannah was praying in her heart, and her lips were moving but her voice was not heard. Eli thought she was drunk 14and said to her, "How long are you going to stay drunk? Put away your wine."

15"Not so, my lord," Hannah replied, "I am a woman who is deeply troubled. I have not been drinking wine or beer; I was pouring out my soul to the LORD. 16Do not take your servant for a wicked woman; I have been praying here out of my great anguish and grief."

17Eli answered, "Go in peace, and may the God of Israel grant you what you have asked of him."

18She said, "May your servant find favor in your eyes." Then she went her way and ate something, and her face was no longer downcast.

19Early the next morning they arose and worshiped before the LORD and then went back to their home at Ramah. Elkanah made love to his wife Hannah, and the LORD remembered her. 20So in the course of time Hannah became pregnant and gave birth to a son. She named him Samuel,[b] saying, "Because I asked the LORD for him."

HANNAH DEDICATES SAMUEL

21When her husband Elkanah went up with all his family to offer the annual sacrifice to the LORD and to fulfill his vow, 22Hannah did not go. She said to her husband, "After the boy is weaned, I will take him and present him before the LORD, and he will live there always."[c]

---

[a] *1* See Septuagint and 1 Chron. 6:26-27,33-35; or *from Ramathaim Zuphim.*
[b] *20* *Samuel* sounds like the Hebrew for *heard by God.*
[c] *22* Masoretic Text; Dead Sea Scrolls *always. I have dedicated him as a Nazirite — all the days of his life."*

23“Do what seems best to you,” her husband Elkanah told her. “Stay
here until you have weaned him; only may the LORD make good his[a]
word.” So the woman stayed at home and nursed her son until she had
weaned him.

24After he was weaned, she took the boy with her, young as he was,
along with a three-year-old bull,[b] an ephah[c] of flour and a skin of wine,
and brought him to the house of the LORD at Shiloh. 25When the bull
had been sacrificed, they brought the boy to Eli, 26and she said to him,
“Pardon me, my lord. As surely as you live, I am the woman who stood
here beside you praying to the LORD. 27I prayed for this child, and the
LORD has granted me what I asked of him. 28So now I give him to the
LORD. For his whole life he will be given over to the LORD.” And he wor-
shiped the LORD there.

HANNAH'S PRAYER

2 Then Hannah prayed and said:

“My heart rejoices in the LORD;
  in the LORD my horn[d] is lifted high.
My mouth boasts over my enemies,
  for I delight in your deliverance.

2“There is no one holy like the LORD;
  there is no one besides you;
  there is no Rock like our God.

3“Do not keep talking so proudly
  or let your mouth speak such arrogance,
for the LORD is a God who knows,
  and by him deeds are weighed.

4“The bows of the warriors are broken,
  but those who stumbled are armed with strength.
5Those who were full hire themselves out for food,
  but those who were hungry are hungry no more.
She who was barren has borne seven children,
  but she who has had many sons pines away.

6“The LORD brings death and makes alive;
  he brings down to the grave and raises up.
7The LORD sends poverty and wealth;
  he humbles and he exalts.
8He raises the poor from the dust
  and lifts the needy from the ash heap;
he seats them with princes
  and has them inherit a throne of honor.

“For the foundations of the earth are the LORD's;
  on them he has set the world.
9He will guard the feet of his faithful servants,
  but the wicked will be silenced in the place of darkness.

PRAYING SCRIPTURE

1 Samuel 2

Hannah's prayer celebrated God's exalting the humble and humbling the proud. Moreover, she acknowledged God's absolute sovereignty over his entire creation and ultimate victory over all his enemies.

Hannah's prayer of praise patterns our own praise. Recognition of God's greatness, majesty and utterly unequaled being is the foundation for our praying. Without his supremacy, we have no basis for faith. Remember to recognize God's attributes when you pray.

[a] *23* Masoretic Text; Dead Sea Scrolls, Septuagint and Syriac *your*
[b] *24* Dead Sea Scrolls, Septuagint and Syriac; Masoretic Text *with three bulls*
[c] *24* That is, probably about 36 pounds or about 16 kilograms [d] *1* *Horn* here symbolizes strength; also in verse 10.

"It is not by strength that one prevails;
10 those who oppose the LORD will be broken.
The Most High will thunder from heaven;
the LORD will judge the ends of the earth.

"He will give strength to his king
and exalt the horn of his anointed."

11Then Elkanah went home to Ramah, but the boy ministered before
the LORD under Eli the priest.

ELI'S WICKED SONS

12Eli's sons were scoundrels; they had no regard for the LORD. 13Now
it was the practice of the priests that, whenever any of the people of-
fered a sacrifice, the priest's servant would come with a three-pronged
fork in his hand while the meat was being boiled 14and would plunge
the fork into the pan or kettle or caldron or pot. Whatever the fork
brought up the priest would take for himself. This is how they treated
all the Israelites who came to Shiloh. 15But even before the fat was
burned, the priest's servant would come and say to the person who
was sacrificing, "Give the priest some meat to roast; he won't accept
boiled meat from you, but only raw."

16If the person said to him, "Let the fat be burned first, and then take
whatever you want," the servant would answer, "No, hand it over now;
if you don't, I'll take it by force."

17This sin of the young men was very great in the LORD's sight, for
they[a] were treating the LORD's offering with contempt.

18But Samuel was ministering before the LORD — a boy wearing a
linen ephod. 19Each year his mother made him a little robe and took it
to him when she went up with her husband to offer the annual sacri-
fice. 20Eli would bless Elkanah and his wife, saying, "May the LORD give
you children by this woman to take the place of the one she prayed for
and gave to[b] the LORD." Then they would go home. 21And the LORD was
gracious to Hannah; she gave birth to three sons and two daughters.
Meanwhile, the boy Samuel grew up in the presence of the LORD.

22Now Eli, who was very old, heard about everything his sons were
doing to all Israel and how they slept with the women who served at
the entrance to the tent of meeting. 23So he said to them, "Why do you
do such things? I hear from all the people about these wicked deeds
of yours. 24No, my sons; the report I hear spreading among the LORD's
people is not good. 25If one person sins against another, God[c] may me-
diate for the offender; but if anyone sins against the LORD, who will
intercede for them?" His sons, however, did not listen to their father's
rebuke, for it was the LORD's will to put them to death.

26And the boy Samuel continued to grow in stature and in favor with
the LORD and with people.

PROPHECY AGAINST THE HOUSE OF ELI

27Now a man of God came to Eli and said to him, "This is what the
LORD says: 'Did I not clearly reveal myself to your ancestor's family
when they were in Egypt under Pharaoh? 28I chose your ancestor out
of all the tribes of Israel to be my priest, to go up to my altar, to burn

---

[a] 17 Dead Sea Scrolls and Septuagint; Masoretic Text *people* [b] 20 Dead Sea Scrolls; Masoretic Text *and asked from* [c] 25 Or *the judges*

incense, and to wear an ephod in my presence. I also gave your ancestor's family all the food offerings presented by the Israelites. 29 Why do you[a] scorn my sacrifice and offering that I prescribed for my dwelling? Why do you honor your sons more than me by fattening yourselves on the choice parts of every offering made by my people Israel?'

30 "Therefore the LORD, the God of Israel, declares: 'I promised that members of your family would minister before me forever.' But now the LORD declares: 'Far be it from me! Those who honor me I will honor, but those who despise me will be disdained. 31 The time is coming when I will cut short your strength and the strength of your priestly house, so that no one in it will reach old age, 32 and you will see distress in my dwelling. Although good will be done to Israel, no one in your family line will ever reach old age. 33 Every one of you that I do not cut off from serving at my altar I will spare only to destroy your sight and sap your strength, and all your descendants will die in the prime of life.

34 " 'And what happens to your two sons, Hophni and Phinehas, will be a sign to you — they will both die on the same day. 35 I will raise up for myself a faithful priest, who will do according to what is in my heart and mind. I will firmly establish his priestly house, and they will minister before my anointed one always. 36 Then everyone left in your family line will come and bow down before him for a piece of silver and a loaf of bread and plead, "Appoint me to some priestly office so I can have food to eat." ' "

THE LORD CALLS SAMUEL

3 The boy Samuel ministered before the LORD under Eli. In those days the word of the LORD was rare; there were not many visions.

2 One night Eli, whose eyes were becoming so weak that he could barely see, was lying down in his usual place. 3 The lamp of God had not yet gone out, and Samuel was lying down in the house of the LORD, where the ark of God was. 4 Then the LORD called Samuel.

Samuel answered, "Here I am." 5 And he ran to Eli and said, "Here I am; you called me."

But Eli said, "I did not call; go back and lie down." So he went and lay down.

6 Again the LORD called, "Samuel!" And Samuel got up and went to Eli and said, "Here I am; you called me."

"My son," Eli said, "I did not call; go back and lie down."

7 Now Samuel did not yet know the LORD: The word of the LORD had not yet been revealed to him.

8 A third time the LORD called, "Samuel!" And Samuel got up and went to Eli and said, "Here I am; you called me."

Then Eli realized that the LORD was calling the boy. 9 So Eli told Samuel, "Go and lie down, and if he calls you, say, 'Speak, LORD, for your servant is listening.' " So Samuel went and lay down in his place.

10 The LORD came and stood there, calling as at the other times, "Samuel! Samuel!"

Then Samuel said, "Speak, for your servant is listening."

11 And the LORD said to Samuel: "See, I am about to do something in Israel that will make the ears of everyone who hears about it tingle. 12 At that time I will carry out against Eli everything I spoke against his family — from beginning to end. 13 For I told him that I would judge his

PRAYING SCRIPTURE

1 Samuel 3

Most people do not experience the call to ministry as uniquely as did Samuel. Roused from sleep four times by the word of the Lord, the boy child was chosen to deliver a message against the priest Eli. The Lord would use Samuel to lead Israel spiritually for many years.

Has God called you to a ministry? Have you said yes? If God is calling you, pray a prayer of surrender to obedience.

[a] 29 The Hebrew is plural.

family forever because of the sin he knew about; his sons blasphemed
God,[a] and he failed to restrain them. 14Therefore I swore to the house
of Eli, 'The guilt of Eli's house will never be atoned for by sacrifice or
offering.'"
15Samuel lay down until morning and then opened the doors of the
house of the LORD. He was afraid to tell Eli the vision, 16but Eli called
him and said, "Samuel, my son."
Samuel answered, "Here I am."
17"What was it he said to you?" Eli asked. "Do not hide it from me. May
God deal with you, be it ever so severely, if you hide from me anything
he told you." 18So Samuel told him everything, hiding nothing from
him. Then Eli said, "He is the LORD; let him do what is good in his eyes."
19The LORD was with Samuel as he grew up, and he let none of Sam-
uel's words fall to the ground. 20And all Israel from Dan to Beersheba
recognized that Samuel was attested as a prophet of the LORD. 21The
LORD continued to appear at Shiloh, and there he revealed himself to
Samuel through his word.

PRAYING SCRIPTURE

1 Samuel 4

At some point, the Israelites forgot that the ark of the covenant was part of their worship and began treating it like a good luck charm. They took it into battle believing it would give them victory. Instead, they were routed by their enemies and the ark was taken.

Whenever we lose our first love, we can start treating God as if he owes us something. Ask God to help you love him wholeheartedly.

4 And Samuel's word came to all Israel.

THE PHILISTINES CAPTURE THE ARK

Now the Israelites went out to fight against the Philistines. The Is-
raelites camped at Ebenezer, and the Philistines at Aphek. 2The Phi-
listines deployed their forces to meet Israel, and as the battle spread,
Israel was defeated by the Philistines, who killed about four thousand
of them on the battlefield. 3When the soldiers returned to camp, the el-
ders of Israel asked, "Why did the LORD bring defeat on us today before
the Philistines? Let us bring the ark of the LORD's covenant from Shiloh,
so that he may go with us and save us from the hand of our enemies."
4So the people sent men to Shiloh, and they brought back the ark
of the covenant of the LORD Almighty, who is enthroned between the
cherubim. And Eli's two sons, Hophni and Phinehas, were there with
the ark of the covenant of God.
5When the ark of the LORD's covenant came into the camp, all Israel
raised such a great shout that the ground shook. 6Hearing the uproar,
the Philistines asked, "What's all this shouting in the Hebrew camp?"
When they learned that the ark of the LORD had come into the camp,
7the Philistines were afraid. "A god has[b] come into the camp," they said.
"Oh no! Nothing like this has happened before. 8We're doomed! Who
will deliver us from the hand of these mighty gods? They are the gods
who struck the Egyptians with all kinds of plagues in the wilderness.
9Be strong, Philistines! Be men, or you will be subject to the Hebrews,
as they have been to you. Be men, and fight!"
10So the Philistines fought, and the Israelites were defeated and ev-
ery man fled to his tent. The slaughter was very great; Israel lost thirty
thousand foot soldiers. 11The ark of God was captured, and Eli's two
sons, Hophni and Phinehas, died.

DEATH OF ELI

12That same day a Benjamite ran from the battle line and went to
Shiloh with his clothes torn and dust on his head. 13When he arrived,
there was Eli sitting on his chair by the side of the road, watching,

[a] *13* An ancient Hebrew scribal tradition (see also Septuagint); Masoretic Text *sons made themselves contemptible* [b] *7* Or "*Gods have* (see Septuagint)

because his heart feared for the ark of God. When the man entered
the town and told what had happened, the whole town sent up a cry.
14 Eli heard the outcry and asked, "What is the meaning of this
uproar?"
The man hurried over to Eli, 15 who was ninety-eight years old and
whose eyes had failed so that he could not see. 16 He told Eli, "I have just
come from the battle line; I fled from it this very day."
Eli asked, "What happened, my son?"
17 The man who brought the news replied, "Israel fled before the Phi-
listines, and the army has suffered heavy losses. Also your two sons,
Hophni and Phinehas, are dead, and the ark of God has been captured."
18 When he mentioned the ark of God, Eli fell backward off his chair
by the side of the gate. His neck was broken and he died, for he was an
old man, and he was heavy. He had led[a] Israel forty years.
19 His daughter-in-law, the wife of Phinehas, was pregnant and near
the time of delivery. When she heard the news that the ark of God had
been captured and that her father-in-law and her husband were dead,
she went into labor and gave birth, but was overcome by her labor
pains. 20 As she was dying, the women attending her said, "Don't de-
spair; you have given birth to a son." But she did not respond or pay
any attention.
21 She named the boy Ichabod,[b] saying, "The Glory has departed from
Israel"—because of the capture of the ark of God and the deaths of
her father-in-law and her husband. 22 She said, "The Glory has departed
from Israel, for the ark of God has been captured."

THE ARK IN ASHDOD AND EKRON

5 After the Philistines had captured the ark of God, they took it from
Ebenezer to Ashdod. 2 Then they carried the ark into Dagon's tem-
ple and set it beside Dagon. 3 When the people of Ashdod rose early the
next day, there was Dagon, fallen on his face on the ground before the
ark of the LORD! They took Dagon and put him back in his place. 4 But
the following morning when they rose, there was Dagon, fallen on his
face on the ground before the ark of the LORD! His head and hands
had been broken off and were lying on the threshold; only his body
remained. 5 That is why to this day neither the priests of Dagon nor
any others who enter Dagon's temple at Ashdod step on the threshold.
6 The LORD's hand was heavy on the people of Ashdod and its vicin-
ity; he brought devastation on them and afflicted them with tumors.[c]
7 When the people of Ashdod saw what was happening, they said, "The
ark of the god of Israel must not stay here with us, because his hand
is heavy on us and on Dagon our god." 8 So they called together all the
rulers of the Philistines and asked them, "What shall we do with the
ark of the god of Israel?"
They answered, "Have the ark of the god of Israel moved to Gath." So
they moved the ark of the God of Israel.
9 But after they had moved it, the LORD's hand was against that city,
throwing it into a great panic. He afflicted the people of the city, both
young and old, with an outbreak of tumors.[d] 10 So they sent the ark of
God to Ekron.

[a] 18 Traditionally *judged* [b] 21 *Ichabod* means *no glory.* [c] 6 Hebrew; Septuagint and Vulgate *tumors. And rats appeared in their land, and there was death and destruction throughout the city* [d] 9 Or *with tumors in the groin* (see Septuagint)

PRAYING SCRIPTURE

1 Samuel 5

After being taken to Ashdod, the ark was placed in the pagan temple of Dagon. Dagon was shown to be utterly powerless in the presence of the ark, being thrown to the ground and broken in pieces. God smote the Philistines with tumors for keeping the ark.

We do well to remember that our own false gods are destroyed in the presence of Jesus. Commit to worshiping him alone.

As the ark of God was entering Ekron, the people of Ekron cried out, "They have brought the ark of the god of Israel around to us to kill us and our people." 11So they called together all the rulers of the Philistines and said, "Send the ark of the god of Israel away; let it go back to its own place, or it[a] will kill us and our people." For death had filled the city with panic; God's hand was very heavy on it. 12Those who did not die were afflicted with tumors, and the outcry of the city went up to heaven.

THE ARK RETURNED TO ISRAEL

6 When the ark of the LORD had been in Philistine territory seven months, 2the Philistines called for the priests and the diviners and said, "What shall we do with the ark of the LORD? Tell us how we should send it back to its place."

3They answered, "If you return the ark of the god of Israel, do not send it back to him without a gift; by all means send a guilt offering to him. Then you will be healed, and you will know why his hand has not been lifted from you."

4The Philistines asked, "What guilt offering should we send to him?"

They replied, "Five gold tumors and five gold rats, according to the number of the Philistine rulers, because the same plague has struck both you and your rulers. 5Make models of the tumors and of the rats that are destroying the country, and give glory to Israel's god. Perhaps he will lift his hand from you and your gods and your land. 6Why do you harden your hearts as the Egyptians and Pharaoh did? When Israel's god dealt harshly with them, did they not send the Israelites out so they could go on their way?

7"Now then, get a new cart ready, with two cows that have calved and have never been yoked. Hitch the cows to the cart, but take their calves away and pen them up. 8Take the ark of the LORD and put it on the cart, and in a chest beside it put the gold objects you are sending back to him as a guilt offering. Send it on its way, 9but keep watching it. If it goes up to its own territory, toward Beth Shemesh, then the LORD has brought this great disaster on us. But if it does not, then we will know that it was not his hand that struck us but that it happened to us by chance."

10So they did this. They took two such cows and hitched them to the cart and penned up their calves. 11They placed the ark of the LORD on the cart and along with it the chest containing the gold rats and the models of the tumors. 12Then the cows went straight up toward Beth Shemesh, keeping on the road and lowing all the way; they did not turn to the right or to the left. The rulers of the Philistines followed them as far as the border of Beth Shemesh.

13Now the people of Beth Shemesh were harvesting their wheat in the valley, and when they looked up and saw the ark, they rejoiced at the sight. 14The cart came to the field of Joshua of Beth Shemesh, and there it stopped beside a large rock. The people chopped up the wood of the cart and sacrificed the cows as a burnt offering to the LORD. 15The Levites took down the ark of the LORD, together with the chest containing the gold objects, and placed them on the large rock. On that day the people of Beth Shemesh offered burnt offerings and made sacrifices to the LORD. 16The five rulers of the Philistines saw all this and then returned that same day to Ekron.

17These are the gold tumors the Philistines sent as a guilt offering

PRAYING SCRIPTURE

1 Samuel 6

The Philistines, like the Egyptians, learned that they should not harden their hearts against God or treat him lightly. Judgment always followed when God's people were persecuted or when nations exerted themselves against God.

Ask God to give you the wisdom to be a witness to those people around you who are nearest to God's judgment. Ask him to make you a testimony to the goodness and grace he gives to his people.

[a] 11 Or *he*

to the LORD — one each for Ashdod, Gaza, Ashkelon, Gath and Ekron.
18And the number of the gold rats was according to the number of Phi-
listine towns belonging to the five rulers — the fortified towns with
their country villages. The large rock on which the Levites set the ark of
the LORD is a witness to this day in the field of Joshua of Beth Shemesh.
19But God struck down some of the inhabitants of Beth Shemesh,
putting seventy[a] of them to death because they looked into the ark
of the LORD. The people mourned because of the heavy blow the LORD
had dealt them. 20And the people of Beth Shemesh asked, "Who can
stand in the presence of the LORD, this holy God? To whom will the ark
go up from here?"
21Then they sent messengers to the people of Kiriath Jearim, saying,
"The Philistines have returned the ark of the LORD. Come down and
7 take it up to your town." 1So the men of Kiriath Jearim came and
took up the ark of the LORD. They brought it to Abinadab's house
on the hill and consecrated Eleazar his son to guard the ark of the LORD.
2The ark remained at Kiriath Jearim a long time — twenty years in all.

SAMUEL SUBDUES THE PHILISTINES AT MIZPAH

Then all the people of Israel turned back to the LORD. 3So Samuel
said to all the Israelites, "If you are returning to the LORD with all your
hearts, then rid yourselves of the foreign gods and the Ashtoreths and
commit yourselves to the LORD and serve him only, and he will deliver
you out of the hand of the Philistines." 4So the Israelites put away their
Baals and Ashtoreths, and served the LORD only.
5Then Samuel said, "Assemble all Israel at Mizpah, and I will inter-
cede with the LORD for you." 6When they had assembled at Mizpah,
they drew water and poured it out before the LORD. On that day they
fasted and there they confessed, "We have sinned against the LORD."
Now Samuel was serving as leader[b] of Israel at Mizpah.
7When the Philistines heard that Israel had assembled at Mizpah, the
rulers of the Philistines came up to attack them. When the Israelites
heard of it, they were afraid because of the Philistines. 8They said to
Samuel, "Do not stop crying out to the LORD our God for us, that he
may rescue us from the hand of the Philistines." 9Then Samuel took a
suckling lamb and sacrificed it as a whole burnt offering to the LORD.
He cried out to the LORD on Israel's behalf, and the LORD answered him.
10While Samuel was sacrificing the burnt offering, the Philistines
drew near to engage Israel in battle. But that day the LORD thundered
with loud thunder against the Philistines and threw them into such a
panic that they were routed before the Israelites. 11The men of Israel
rushed out of Mizpah and pursued the Philistines, slaughtering them
along the way to a point below Beth Kar.
12Then Samuel took a stone and set it up between Mizpah and Shen.
He named it Ebenezer,[c] saying, "Thus far the LORD has helped us."
13So the Philistines were subdued and they stopped invading Isra-
el's territory. Throughout Samuel's lifetime, the hand of the LORD was
against the Philistines. 14The towns from Ekron to Gath that the Phi-
listines had captured from Israel were restored to Israel, and Israel
delivered the neighboring territory from the hands of the Philistines.
And there was peace between Israel and the Amorites.

[a] 19 A few Hebrew manuscripts; most Hebrew manuscripts and Septuagint *50,070* [b] 6 Traditionally *judge*; also in verse 15 [c] 12 *Ebenezer* means *stone of help.*

PRAYING SCRIPTURE

1 Samuel 7

The Lord demands our whole-hearted allegiance to him and him alone. To demonstrate such commitment, Samuel called for the people to repent and to prepare their hearts to serve the Lord only. What would it mean for us to prepare our hearts to serve God only? At the least, we would need to examine our attitudes and actions, then repent from sin and return to our first-priority love.

15Samuel continued as Israel's leader all the days of his life. 16From
year to year he went on a circuit from Bethel to Gilgal to Mizpah, judg-
ing Israel in all those places. 17But he always went back to Ramah,
where his home was, and there he also held court for Israel. And he
built an altar there to the LORD.

ISRAEL ASKS FOR A KING

8 When Samuel grew old, he appointed his sons as Israel's leaders.[a]
2The name of his firstborn was Joel and the name of his second
was Abijah, and they served at Beersheba. 3But his sons did not follow
his ways. They turned aside after dishonest gain and accepted bribes
and perverted justice.

4So all the elders of Israel gathered together and came to Samuel at
Ramah. 5They said to him, "You are old, and your sons do not follow
your ways; now appoint a king to lead[b] us, such as all the other nations
have."

6But when they said, "Give us a king to lead us," this displeased Sam-
uel; so he prayed to the LORD. 7And the LORD told him: "Listen to all
that the people are saying to you; it is not you they have rejected, but
they have rejected me as their king. 8As they have done from the day I
brought them up out of Egypt until this day, forsaking me and serving
other gods, so they are doing to you. 9Now listen to them; but warn
them solemnly and let them know what the king who will reign over
them will claim as his rights."

10Samuel told all the words of the LORD to the people who were ask-
ing him for a king. 11He said, "This is what the king who will reign over
you will claim as his rights: He will take your sons and make them
serve with his chariots and horses, and they will run in front of his
chariots. 12Some he will assign to be commanders of thousands and
commanders of fifties, and others to plow his ground and reap his har-
vest, and still others to make weapons of war and equipment for his
chariots. 13He will take your daughters to be perfumers and cooks and
bakers. 14He will take the best of your fields and vineyards and olive
groves and give them to his attendants. 15He will take a tenth of your
grain and of your vintage and give it to his officials and attendants.
16Your male and female servants and the best of your cattle[c] and don-
keys he will take for his own use. 17He will take a tenth of your flocks,
and you yourselves will become his slaves. 18When that day comes, you
will cry out for relief from the king you have chosen, but the LORD will
not answer you in that day."

19But the people refused to listen to Samuel. "No!" they said. "We
want a king over us. 20Then we will be like all the other nations, with a
king to lead us and to go out before us and fight our battles."

21When Samuel heard all that the people said, he repeated it before
the LORD. 22The LORD answered, "Listen to them and give them a king."

Then Samuel said to the Israelites, "Everyone go back to your own
town."

SAMUEL ANOINTS SAUL

9 There was a Benjamite, a man of standing, whose name was
Kish son of Abiel, the son of Zeror, the son of Bekorath, the son
of Aphiah of Benjamin. 2Kish had a son named Saul, as handsome a

PRAYING SCRIPTURE

1 Samuel 8

Few things bring the people of God low like lusting after the world. God had been the only king in Israel's history. Yet, seeing the surrounding nations, the people wanted a human king; someone of flesh and blood like themselves. God saw through it, knowing they were rejecting *him* from leading them.

That which is convenient and popular is not always the best thing. Pray for wisdom always to recognize and accept God's best.

PRAYING SCRIPTURE

1 Samuel 9

Although Saul was the tallest and handsomest man in Israel, as well as from a family of some renown, he seemed surprised at Samuel's interest. But God had spoken, identifying Saul as the man to anoint as king.

Are you still surprised when God chooses you to join his work? Ask him to help you retain the faith of a child and wonder at his ways.

[a] *1* Traditionally *judges* [b] *5* Traditionally *judge*; also in verses 6 and 20
[c] *16* Septuagint; Hebrew *young men*

young man as could be found anywhere in Israel, and he was a head taller than anyone else.

[3]Now the donkeys belonging to Saul's father Kish were lost, and Kish said to his son Saul, "Take one of the servants with you and go and look for the donkeys." [4]So he passed through the hill country of Ephraim and through the area around Shalisha, but they did not find them. They went on into the district of Shaalim, but the donkeys were not there. Then he passed through the territory of Benjamin, but they did not find them.

[5]When they reached the district of Zuph, Saul said to the servant who was with him, "Come, let's go back, or my father will stop thinking about the donkeys and start worrying about us."

[6]But the servant replied, "Look, in this town there is a man of God; he is highly respected, and everything he says comes true. Let's go there now. Perhaps he will tell us what way to take."

[7]Saul said to his servant, "If we go, what can we give the man? The food in our sacks is gone. We have no gift to take to the man of God. What do we have?"

[8]The servant answered him again. "Look," he said, "I have a quarter of a shekel[a] of silver. I will give it to the man of God so that he will tell us what way to take." [9](Formerly in Israel, if someone went to inquire of God, they would say, "Come, let us go to the seer," because the prophet of today used to be called a seer.)

[10]"Good," Saul said to his servant. "Come, let's go." So they set out for the town where the man of God was.

[11]As they were going up the hill to the town, they met some young women coming out to draw water, and they asked them, "Is the seer here?"

[12]"He is," they answered. "He's ahead of you. Hurry now; he has just come to our town today, for the people have a sacrifice at the high place. [13]As soon as you enter the town, you will find him before he goes up to the high place to eat. The people will not begin eating until he comes, because he must bless the sacrifice; afterward, those who are invited will eat. Go up now; you should find him about this time."

[14]They went up to the town, and as they were entering it, there was Samuel, coming toward them on his way up to the high place.

[15]Now the day before Saul came, the LORD had revealed this to Samuel: [16]"About this time tomorrow I will send you a man from the land of Benjamin. Anoint him ruler over my people Israel; he will deliver them from the hand of the Philistines. I have looked on my people, for their cry has reached me."

[17]When Samuel caught sight of Saul, the LORD said to him, "This is the man I spoke to you about; he will govern my people."

[18]Saul approached Samuel in the gateway and asked, "Would you please tell me where the seer's house is?"

[19]"I am the seer," Samuel replied. "Go up ahead of me to the high place, for today you are to eat with me, and in the morning I will send you on your way and will tell you all that is in your heart. [20]As for the donkeys you lost three days ago, do not worry about them; they have been found. And to whom is all the desire of Israel turned, if not to you and your whole family line?"

[21]Saul answered, "But am I not a Benjamite, from the smallest tribe

---

[a] *8* That is, about 1/10 ounce or about 3 grams

of Israel, and is not my clan the least of all the clans of the tribe of Ben-
jamin? Why do you say such a thing to me?"
22Then Samuel brought Saul and his servant into the hall and seated
them at the head of those who were invited — about thirty in number.
23Samuel said to the cook, "Bring the piece of meat I gave you, the one
I told you to lay aside."
24So the cook took up the thigh with what was on it and set it in front
of Saul. Samuel said, "Here is what has been kept for you. Eat, because
it was set aside for you for this occasion from the time I said, 'I have
invited guests.'" And Saul dined with Samuel that day.
25After they came down from the high place to the town, Samuel
talked with Saul on the roof of his house. 26They rose about daybreak,
and Samuel called to Saul on the roof, "Get ready, and I will send you on
your way." When Saul got ready, he and Samuel went outside together.
27As they were going down to the edge of the town, Samuel said to Saul,
"Tell the servant to go on ahead of us" — and the servant did so — "but
you stay here for a while, so that I may give you a message from God."

10 Then Samuel took a flask of olive oil and poured it on Saul's
head and kissed him, saying, "Has not the LORD anointed you
ruler over his inheritance?[a] 2When you leave me today, you will meet
two men near Rachel's tomb, at Zelzah on the border of Benjamin.
They will say to you, 'The donkeys you set out to look for have been
found. And now your father has stopped thinking about them and is
worried about you. He is asking, "What shall I do about my son?"'
3"Then you will go on from there until you reach the great tree of
Tabor. Three men going up to worship God at Bethel will meet you
there. One will be carrying three young goats, another three loaves of
bread, and another a skin of wine. 4They will greet you and offer you
two loaves of bread, which you will accept from them.
5"After that you will go to Gibeah of God, where there is a Philis-
tine outpost. As you approach the town, you will meet a procession of
prophets coming down from the high place with lyres, timbrels, pipes
and harps being played before them, and they will be prophesying.
6The Spirit of the LORD will come powerfully upon you, and you will
prophesy with them; and you will be changed into a different person.
7Once these signs are fulfilled, do whatever your hand finds to do, for
God is with you.
8"Go down ahead of me to Gilgal. I will surely come down to you to
sacrifice burnt offerings and fellowship offerings, but you must wait
seven days until I come to you and tell you what you are to do."

SAUL MADE KING

9As Saul turned to leave Samuel, God changed Saul's heart, and all
these signs were fulfilled that day. 10When he and his servant arrived
at Gibeah, a procession of prophets met him; the Spirit of God came
powerfully upon him, and he joined in their prophesying. 11When all
those who had formerly known him saw him prophesying with the
prophets, they asked each other, "What is this that has happened to
the son of Kish? Is Saul also among the prophets?"

PRAYING SCRIPTURE

1 Samuel 10

The anointing of Saul was the clear sign that Israel had rejected the God of the covenant as their king. Jealousy over other nations drove them to demand a human monarch. Israel was never as strong under human kings as when God was their king.

Fame, acceptance and fear are some of the reasons we follow people rather than God. Ask God for the wisdom and faith to serve him foremost.

---

[a] 1 Hebrew; Septuagint and Vulgate *over his people Israel? You will reign over the LORD's people and save them from the power of their enemies round about. And this will be a sign to you that the LORD has anointed you ruler over his inheritance:*

12A man who lived there answered, "And who is their father?" So
it became a saying: "Is Saul also among the prophets?" 13After Saul
stopped prophesying, he went to the high place.
14Now Saul's uncle asked him and his servant, "Where have you
been?"
"Looking for the donkeys," he said. "But when we saw they were not
to be found, we went to Samuel."
15Saul's uncle said, "Tell me what Samuel said to you."
16Saul replied, "He assured us that the donkeys had been found."
But he did not tell his uncle what Samuel had said about the kingship.
17Samuel summoned the people of Israel to the LORD at Mizpah
18and said to them, "This is what the LORD, the God of Israel, says: 'I
brought Israel up out of Egypt, and I delivered you from the power of
Egypt and all the kingdoms that oppressed you.' 19But you have now
rejected your God, who saves you out of all your disasters and calam-
ities. And you have said, 'No, appoint a king over us.' So now present
yourselves before the LORD by your tribes and clans."
20When Samuel had all Israel come forward by tribes, the tribe of
Benjamin was taken by lot. 21Then he brought forward the tribe of Ben-
jamin, clan by clan, and Matri's clan was taken. Finally Saul son of Kish
was taken. But when they looked for him, he was not to be found. 22So
they inquired further of the LORD, "Has the man come here yet?"
And the LORD said, "Yes, he has hidden himself among the supplies."
23They ran and brought him out, and as he stood among the people
he was a head taller than any of the others. 24Samuel said to all the
people, "Do you see the man the LORD has chosen? There is no one like
him among all the people."
Then the people shouted, "Long live the king!"
25Samuel explained to the people the rights and duties of kingship.
He wrote them down on a scroll and deposited it before the LORD. Then
Samuel dismissed the people to go to their own homes.
26Saul also went to his home in Gibeah, accompanied by valiant men
whose hearts God had touched. 27But some scoundrels said, "How can
this fellow save us?" They despised him and brought him no gifts. But
Saul kept silent.

SAUL RESCUES THE CITY OF JABESH

11 Nahash[a] the Ammonite went up and besieged Jabesh Gilead. And
all the men of Jabesh said to him, "Make a treaty with us, and we
will be subject to you."
2But Nahash the Ammonite replied, "I will make a treaty with you
only on the condition that I gouge out the right eye of every one of you
and so bring disgrace on all Israel."
3The elders of Jabesh said to him, "Give us seven days so we can send
messengers throughout Israel; if no one comes to rescue us, we will
surrender to you."
4When the messengers came to Gibeah of Saul and reported these
terms to the people, they all wept aloud. 5Just then Saul was returning

PRAYING SCRIPTURE

1 Samuel 11

Israel "held a great celebration" after Saul led them to victory in battle, proving we can be happy when we choose our own way instead of God's way (see verse 15). The people offered sacrifices because of a military victory yet expressed no remorse over choosing a king.

Have you ever been happy about something, then realized later it wasn't a good thing? Ask God to give you a heart that rejoices in what is right.

[a] *1* Masoretic Text; Dead Sea Scrolls *gifts. Now Nahash king of the Ammonites oppressed the Gadites and Reubenites severely. He gouged out all their right eyes and struck terror and dread in Israel. Not a man remained among the Israelites beyond the Jordan whose right eye was not gouged out by Nahash king of the Ammonites, except that seven thousand men fled from the Ammonites and entered Jabesh Gilead. About a month later,* [1]Nahash

from the fields, behind his oxen, and he asked, "What is wrong with everyone? Why are they weeping?" Then they repeated to him what the men of Jabesh had said.

6 When Saul heard their words, the Spirit of God came powerfully upon him, and he burned with anger. 7 He took a pair of oxen, cut them into pieces, and sent the pieces by messengers throughout Israel, proclaiming, "This is what will be done to the oxen of anyone who does not follow Saul and Samuel." Then the terror of the LORD fell on the people, and they came out together as one. 8 When Saul mustered them at Bezek, the men of Israel numbered three hundred thousand and those of Judah thirty thousand.

9 They told the messengers who had come, "Say to the men of Jabesh Gilead, 'By the time the sun is hot tomorrow, you will be rescued.'" When the messengers went and reported this to the men of Jabesh, they were elated. 10 They said to the Ammonites, "Tomorrow we will surrender to you, and you can do to us whatever you like."

11 The next day Saul separated his men into three divisions; during the last watch of the night they broke into the camp of the Ammonites and slaughtered them until the heat of the day. Those who survived were scattered, so that no two of them were left together.

SAUL CONFIRMED AS KING

12 The people then said to Samuel, "Who was it that asked, 'Shall Saul reign over us?' Turn these men over to us so that we may put them to death."

13 But Saul said, "No one will be put to death today, for this day the LORD has rescued Israel."

14 Then Samuel said to the people, "Come, let us go to Gilgal and there renew the kingship." 15 So all the people went to Gilgal and made Saul king in the presence of the LORD. There they sacrificed fellowship offerings before the LORD, and Saul and all the Israelites held a great celebration.

SAMUEL'S FAREWELL SPEECH

12 Samuel said to all Israel, "I have listened to everything you said to me and have set a king over you. 2 Now you have a king as your leader. As for me, I am old and gray, and my sons are here with you. I have been your leader from my youth until this day. 3 Here I stand. Testify against me in the presence of the LORD and his anointed. Whose ox have I taken? Whose donkey have I taken? Whom have I cheated? Whom have I oppressed? From whose hand have I accepted a bribe to make me shut my eyes? If I have done any of these things, I will make it right."

4 "You have not cheated or oppressed us," they replied. "You have not taken anything from anyone's hand."

5 Samuel said to them, "The LORD is witness against you, and also his anointed is witness this day, that you have not found anything in my hand."

"He is witness," they said.

6 Then Samuel said to the people, "It is the LORD who appointed Moses and Aaron and brought your ancestors up out of Egypt. 7 Now then, stand here, because I am going to confront you with evidence before the LORD as to all the righteous acts performed by the LORD for you and your ancestors.

PRAYING SCRIPTURE

1 Samuel 12

In Samuel's address to the people of Israel, he directly and prophetically challenged their disobedience, reminding them of the sins their forefathers committed in spite of God's goodness to them. Finally, the Israelites acknowledged that they had sinned in asking for a king.

God is so gracious to forgive. He would always rather bless than discipline. If there is any sin in your life, repent and ask for God's blessing.

8"After Jacob entered Egypt, they cried to the LORD for help, and the
LORD sent Moses and Aaron, who brought your ancestors out of Egypt
and settled them in this place.
9"But they forgot the LORD their God; so he sold them into the hand
of Sisera, the commander of the army of Hazor, and into the hands of
the Philistines and the king of Moab, who fought against them. 10They
cried out to the LORD and said, 'We have sinned; we have forsaken the
LORD and served the Baals and the Ashtoreths. But now deliver us from
the hands of our enemies, and we will serve you.' 11Then the LORD sent
Jerub-Baal,[a] Barak,[b] Jephthah and Samuel,[c] and he delivered you from
the hands of your enemies all around you, so that you lived in safety.
12"But when you saw that Nahash king of the Ammonites was mov-
ing against you, you said to me, 'No, we want a king to rule over us'—
even though the LORD your God was your king. 13Now here is the king
you have chosen, the one you asked for; see, the LORD has set a king
over you. 14If you fear the LORD and serve and obey him and do not
rebel against his commands, and if both you and the king who reigns
over you follow the LORD your God — good! 15But if you do not obey the
LORD, and if you rebel against his commands, his hand will be against
you, as it was against your ancestors.
16"Now then, stand still and see this great thing the LORD is about
to do before your eyes! 17Is it not wheat harvest now? I will call on the
LORD to send thunder and rain. And you will realize what an evil thing
you did in the eyes of the LORD when you asked for a king."
18Then Samuel called on the LORD, and that same day the LORD sent
thunder and rain. So all the people stood in awe of the LORD and of
Samuel.
19The people all said to Samuel, "Pray to the LORD your God for your
servants so that we will not die, for we have added to all our other sins
the evil of asking for a king."
20"Do not be afraid," Samuel replied. "You have done all this evil;
yet do not turn away from the LORD, but serve the LORD with all your
heart. 21Do not turn away after useless idols. They can do you no good,
nor can they rescue you, because they are useless. 22For the sake of
his great name the LORD will not reject his people, because the LORD
was pleased to make you his own. 23As for me, far be it from me that I
should sin against the LORD by failing to pray for you. And I will teach
you the way that is good and right. 24But be sure to fear the LORD and
serve him faithfully with all your heart; consider what great things he
has done for you. 25Yet if you persist in doing evil, both you and your
king will perish."

SAMUEL REBUKES SAUL

13 Saul was thirty[d] years old when he became king, and he reigned
over Israel forty-[e]two years.
2Saul chose three thousand men from Israel; two thousand were
with him at Mikmash and in the hill country of Bethel, and a thou-
sand were with Jonathan at Gibeah in Benjamin. The rest of the men
he sent back to their homes.

PRAYING SCRIPTURE

1 Samuel 13

It did not take long before Saul's pride led him to the sin that doomed his kingdom. Rather than waiting for Samuel, Saul offered sacrifices himself instead of going to battle. His lack of patience and willingness to twist worship to his own ends secured God's judgment.

God will not be mocked or manipulated. Search your life and repent of any attempt to use God for your own ends.

---

[a] 11 Also called *Gideon* [b] 11 Some Septuagint manuscripts and Syriac; Hebrew *Bedan* [c] 11 Hebrew; some Septuagint manuscripts and Syriac *Samson* [d] 1 A few late manuscripts of the Septuagint; Hebrew does not have *thirty*. [e] 1 Probable reading of the original Hebrew text (see Acts 13:21); Masoretic Text does not have *forty-*.

3Jonathan attacked the Philistine outpost at Geba, and the Philistines heard about it. Then Saul had the trumpet blown throughout the land and said, "Let the Hebrews hear!" 4So all Israel heard the news: "Saul has attacked the Philistine outpost, and now Israel has become obnoxious to the Philistines." And the people were summoned to join Saul at Gilgal.

5The Philistines assembled to fight Israel, with three thousand[a] chariots, six thousand charioteers, and soldiers as numerous as the sand on the seashore. They went up and camped at Mikmash, east of Beth Aven. 6When the Israelites saw that their situation was critical and that their army was hard pressed, they hid in caves and thickets, among the rocks, and in pits and cisterns. 7Some Hebrews even crossed the Jordan to the land of Gad and Gilead.

Saul remained at Gilgal, and all the troops with him were quaking with fear. 8He waited seven days, the time set by Samuel; but Samuel did not come to Gilgal, and Saul's men began to scatter. 9So he said, "Bring me the burnt offering and the fellowship offerings." And Saul offered up the burnt offering. 10Just as he finished making the offering, Samuel arrived, and Saul went out to greet him.

11"What have you done?" asked Samuel.

Saul replied, "When I saw that the men were scattering, and that you did not come at the set time, and that the Philistines were assembling at Mikmash, 12I thought, 'Now the Philistines will come down against me at Gilgal, and I have not sought the LORD's favor.' So I felt compelled to offer the burnt offering."

13"You have done a foolish thing," Samuel said. "You have not kept the command the LORD your God gave you; if you had, he would have established your kingdom over Israel for all time. 14But now your kingdom will not endure; the LORD has sought out a man after his own heart and appointed him ruler of his people, because you have not kept the LORD's command."

15Then Samuel left Gilgal[b] and went up to Gibeah in Benjamin, and Saul counted the men who were with him. They numbered about six hundred.

ISRAEL WITHOUT WEAPONS

16Saul and his son Jonathan and the men with them were staying in Gibeah[c] in Benjamin, while the Philistines camped at Mikmash. 17Raiding parties went out from the Philistine camp in three detachments. One turned toward Ophrah in the vicinity of Shual, 18another toward Beth Horon, and the third toward the borderland overlooking the Valley of Zeboyim facing the wilderness.

19Not a blacksmith could be found in the whole land of Israel, because the Philistines had said, "Otherwise the Hebrews will make swords or spears!" 20So all Israel went down to the Philistines to have their plow points, mattocks, axes and sickles[d] sharpened. 21The price was two-thirds of a shekel[e] for sharpening plow points and mattocks, and a third of a shekel[f] for sharpening forks and axes and for repointing goads.

[a] *5* Some Septuagint manuscripts and Syriac; Hebrew *thirty thousand*
[b] *15* Hebrew; Septuagint *Gilgal and went his way; the rest of the people went after Saul to meet the army, and they went out of Gilgal* [c] *16* Two Hebrew manuscripts; most Hebrew manuscripts *Geba*, a variant of *Gibeah*
[d] *20* Septuagint; Hebrew *plow points* [e] *21* That is, about 1/4 ounce or about 8 grams [f] *21* That is, about 1/8 ounce or about 4 grams

22So on the day of the battle not a soldier with Saul and Jonathan had
a sword or spear in his hand; only Saul and his son Jonathan had them.

JONATHAN ATTACKS THE PHILISTINES

23Now a detachment of Philistines had gone out to the pass at
14 Mikmash. 1One day Jonathan son of Saul said to his young ar-
mor-bearer, "Come, let's go over to the Philistine outpost on the
other side." But he did not tell his father.

2Saul was staying on the outskirts of Gibeah under a pomegranate
tree in Migron. With him were about six hundred men, 3among whom
was Ahijah, who was wearing an ephod. He was a son of Ichabod's
brother Ahitub son of Phinehas, the son of Eli, the LORD's priest in Shi-
loh. No one was aware that Jonathan had left.

4On each side of the pass that Jonathan intended to cross to reach
the Philistine outpost was a cliff; one was called Bozez and the other
Seneh. 5One cliff stood to the north toward Mikmash, the other to the
south toward Geba.

6Jonathan said to his young armor-bearer, "Come, let's go over to
the outpost of those uncircumcised men. Perhaps the LORD will act
in our behalf. Nothing can hinder the LORD from saving, whether by
many or by few."

7"Do all that you have in mind," his armor-bearer said. "Go ahead; I
am with you heart and soul."

8Jonathan said, "Come on, then; we will cross over toward them and
let them see us. 9If they say to us, 'Wait there until we come to you,' we
will stay where we are and not go up to them. 10But if they say, 'Come
up to us,' we will climb up, because that will be our sign that the LORD
has given them into our hands."

11So both of them showed themselves to the Philistine outpost.
"Look!" said the Philistines. "The Hebrews are crawling out of the holes
they were hiding in." 12The men of the outpost shouted to Jonathan
and his armor-bearer, "Come up to us and we'll teach you a lesson."

So Jonathan said to his armor-bearer, "Climb up after me; the LORD
has given them into the hand of Israel."

13Jonathan climbed up, using his hands and feet, with his armor-
bearer right behind him. The Philistines fell before Jonathan, and his
armor-bearer followed and killed behind him. 14In that first attack
Jonathan and his armor-bearer killed some twenty men in an area of
about half an acre.

ISRAEL ROUTS THE PHILISTINES

15Then panic struck the whole army — those in the camp and field,
and those in the outposts and raiding parties — and the ground shook.
It was a panic sent by God.[a]

16Saul's lookouts at Gibeah in Benjamin saw the army melting away
in all directions. 17Then Saul said to the men who were with him, "Mus-
ter the forces and see who has left us." When they did, it was Jonathan
and his armor-bearer who were not there.

18Saul said to Ahijah, "Bring the ark of God." (At that time it was with
the Israelites.)[b] 19While Saul was talking to the priest, the tumult in the
Philistine camp increased more and more. So Saul said to the priest,
"Withdraw your hand."

PRAYING SCRIPTURE

1 Samuel 14

Some people think of faith as an abundance of confidence or absolute certainty; a faith-filled person never doubts a victorious outcome. Such was not the case with Jonathan as he prepared to attack the Philistines. Although he knew God was able, he was not certain in this case that God was willing.

But Jonathan was willing to trust God with the results. Ask God for that kind of faith.

---

[a] 15 Or *a terrible panic* [b] 18 Hebrew; Septuagint *"Bring the ephod." (At that time he wore the ephod before the Israelites.)*

20Then Saul and all his men assembled and went to the battle. They
found the Philistines in total confusion, striking each other with their
swords. 21Those Hebrews who had previously been with the Philistines
and had gone up with them to their camp went over to the Israelites
who were with Saul and Jonathan. 22When all the Israelites who had
hidden in the hill country of Ephraim heard that the Philistines were
on the run, they joined the battle in hot pursuit. 23So on that day the
LORD saved Israel, and the battle moved on beyond Beth Aven.

JONATHAN EATS HONEY

24Now the Israelites were in distress that day, because Saul had
bound the people under an oath, saying, "Cursed be anyone who eats
food before evening comes, before I have avenged myself on my ene-
mies!" So none of the troops tasted food.
25The entire army entered the woods, and there was honey on the
ground. 26When they went into the woods, they saw the honey ooz-
ing out; yet no one put his hand to his mouth, because they feared
the oath. 27But Jonathan had not heard that his father had bound the
people with the oath, so he reached out the end of the staff that was in
his hand and dipped it into the honeycomb. He raised his hand to his
mouth, and his eyes brightened.[a] 28Then one of the soldiers told him,
"Your father bound the army under a strict oath, saying, 'Cursed be
anyone who eats food today!' That is why the men are faint."
29Jonathan said, "My father has made trouble for the country. See
how my eyes brightened when I tasted a little of this honey. 30How
much better it would have been if the men had eaten today some of
the plunder they took from their enemies. Would not the slaughter of
the Philistines have been even greater?"
31That day, after the Israelites had struck down the Philistines from
Mikmash to Aijalon, they were exhausted. 32They pounced on the
plunder and, taking sheep, cattle and calves, they butchered them on
the ground and ate them, together with the blood. 33Then someone
said to Saul, "Look, the men are sinning against the LORD by eating
meat that has blood in it."
"You have broken faith," he said. "Roll a large stone over here at
once." 34Then he said, "Go out among the men and tell them, 'Each of
you bring me your cattle and sheep, and slaughter them here and eat
them. Do not sin against the LORD by eating meat with blood still in it.'"
So everyone brought his ox that night and slaughtered it there.
35Then Saul built an altar to the LORD; it was the first time he had done
this.
36Saul said, "Let us go down and pursue the Philistines by night and
plunder them till dawn, and let us not leave one of them alive."
"Do whatever seems best to you," they replied.
But the priest said, "Let us inquire of God here."
37So Saul asked God, "Shall I go down and pursue the Philistines?
Will you give them into Israel's hand?" But God did not answer him
that day.
38Saul therefore said, "Come here, all you who are leaders of the
army, and let us find out what sin has been committed today. 39As
surely as the LORD who rescues Israel lives, even if the guilt lies with
my son Jonathan, he must die." But not one of them said a word.

[a] 27 Or *his strength was renewed*; similarly in verse 29

40Saul then said to all the Israelites, "You stand over there; I and
Jonathan my son will stand over here."
"Do what seems best to you," they replied.
41Then Saul prayed to the LORD, the God of Israel, "Why have you not
answered your servant today? If the fault is in me or my son Jonathan,
respond with Urim, but if the men of Israel are at fault,[a] respond with
Thummim." Jonathan and Saul were taken by lot, and the men were
cleared. 42Saul said, "Cast the lot between me and Jonathan my son."
And Jonathan was taken.
43Then Saul said to Jonathan, "Tell me what you have done."
So Jonathan told him, "I tasted a little honey with the end of my
staff. And now I must die!"
44Saul said, "May God deal with me, be it ever so severely, if you do
not die, Jonathan."
45But the men said to Saul, "Should Jonathan die — he who has
brought about this great deliverance in Israel? Never! As surely as the
LORD lives, not a hair of his head will fall to the ground, for he did this
today with God's help." So the men rescued Jonathan, and he was not
put to death.
46Then Saul stopped pursuing the Philistines, and they withdrew to
their own land.
47After Saul had assumed rule over Israel, he fought against their en-
emies on every side: Moab, the Ammonites, Edom, the kings[b] of Zobah,
and the Philistines. Wherever he turned, he inflicted punishment on
them.[c] 48He fought valiantly and defeated the Amalekites, delivering
Israel from the hands of those who had plundered them.

SAUL'S FAMILY

49Saul's sons were Jonathan, Ishvi and Malki-Shua. The name of his
older daughter was Merab, and that of the younger was Michal. 50His
wife's name was Ahinoam daughter of Ahimaaz. The name of the com-
mander of Saul's army was Abner son of Ner, and Ner was Saul's uncle.
51Saul's father Kish and Abner's father Ner were sons of Abiel.
52All the days of Saul there was bitter war with the Philistines, and
whenever Saul saw a mighty or brave man, he took him into his service.

THE LORD REJECTS SAUL AS KING

15 Samuel said to Saul, "I am the one the LORD sent to anoint
you king over his people Israel; so listen now to the message
from the LORD. 2This is what the LORD Almighty says: 'I will punish
the Amalekites for what they did to Israel when they waylaid them as
they came up from Egypt. 3Now go, attack the Amalekites and totally
destroy[d] all that belongs to them. Do not spare them; put to death
men and women, children and infants, cattle and sheep, camels and
donkeys.'"
4So Saul summoned the men and mustered them at Telaim — two
hundred thousand foot soldiers and ten thousand from Judah. 5Saul
went to the city of Amalek and set an ambush in the ravine. 6Then
he said to the Kenites, "Go away, leave the Amalekites so that I do not

PRAYING SCRIPTURE

1 Samuel 15

Saul's spiral of disobedience continued with blatant disregard for God's direct command given through Samuel. In an overt display of hardness of heart, Saul lied to Samuel's face about his disobedience: "I have carried out the LORD's instructions" (verse 13).

Invoking the name of God in justifying disobedience is dangerous ground indeed. Ask God to help you hallow his name at every step of your faith journey.

[a] *41* Septuagint; Hebrew does not have *"Why . . . at fault.* [b] *47* Masoretic Text; Dead Sea Scrolls and Septuagint *king* [c] *47* Hebrew; Septuagint *he was victorious* [d] *3* The Hebrew term refers to the irrevocable giving over of things or persons to the LORD, often by totally destroying them; also in verses 8, 9, 15, 18, 20 and 21.

destroy you along with them; for you showed kindness to all the Isra-
elites when they came up out of Egypt." So the Kenites moved away
from the Amalekites.
[7]Then Saul attacked the Amalekites all the way from Havilah to Shur,
near the eastern border of Egypt. [8]He took Agag king of the Amalekites
alive, and all his people he totally destroyed with the sword. [9]But Saul
and the army spared Agag and the best of the sheep and cattle, the fat
calves[a] and lambs — everything that was good. These they were unwill-
ing to destroy completely, but everything that was despised and weak
they totally destroyed.
[10]Then the word of the LORD came to Samuel: [11]"I regret that I have
made Saul king, because he has turned away from me and has not car-
ried out my instructions." Samuel was angry, and he cried out to the
LORD all that night.
[12]Early in the morning Samuel got up and went to meet Saul, but he
was told, "Saul has gone to Carmel. There he has set up a monument in
his own honor and has turned and gone on down to Gilgal."
[13]When Samuel reached him, Saul said, "The LORD bless you! I have
carried out the LORD's instructions."
[14]But Samuel said, "What then is this bleating of sheep in my ears?
What is this lowing of cattle that I hear?"
[15]Saul answered, "The soldiers brought them from the Amalekites;
they spared the best of the sheep and cattle to sacrifice to the LORD
your God, but we totally destroyed the rest."
[16]"Enough!" Samuel said to Saul. "Let me tell you what the LORD said
to me last night."
"Tell me," Saul replied.
[17]Samuel said, "Although you were once small in your own eyes, did
you not become the head of the tribes of Israel? The LORD anointed
you king over Israel. [18]And he sent you on a mission, saying, 'Go and
completely destroy those wicked people, the Amalekites; wage war
against them until you have wiped them out.' [19]Why did you not obey
the LORD? Why did you pounce on the plunder and do evil in the eyes
of the LORD?"
[20]"But I did obey the LORD," Saul said. "I went on the mission the
LORD assigned me. I completely destroyed the Amalekites and brought
back Agag their king. [21]The soldiers took sheep and cattle from the
plunder, the best of what was devoted to God, in order to sacrifice them
to the LORD your God at Gilgal."
[22]But Samuel replied:

"Does the LORD delight in burnt offerings and sacrifices
  as much as in obeying the LORD?
To obey is better than sacrifice,
  and to heed is better than the fat of rams.
[23]For rebellion is like the sin of divination,
  and arrogance like the evil of idolatry.
Because you have rejected the word of the LORD,
  he has rejected you as king."

[24]Then Saul said to Samuel, "I have sinned. I violated the LORD's
command and your instructions. I was afraid of the men and so I gave

---

[a] 9 Or *the grown bulls*; the meaning of the Hebrew for this phrase is uncertain.

in to them. 25 Now I beg you, forgive my sin and come back with me, so
that I may worship the LORD."
26 But Samuel said to him, "I will not go back with you. You have
rejected the word of the LORD, and the LORD has rejected you as king
over Israel!"
27 As Samuel turned to leave, Saul caught hold of the hem of his robe,
and it tore. 28 Samuel said to him, "The LORD has torn the kingdom of
Israel from you today and has given it to one of your neighbors — to
one better than you. 29 He who is the Glory of Israel does not lie or
change his mind; for he is not a human being, that he should change
his mind."
30 Saul replied, "I have sinned. But please honor me before the elders
of my people and before Israel; come back with me, so that I may wor-
ship the LORD your God." 31 So Samuel went back with Saul, and Saul
worshiped the LORD.
32 Then Samuel said, "Bring me Agag king of the Amalekites."
Agag came to him in chains.[a] And he thought, "Surely the bitterness
of death is past."
33 But Samuel said,

"As your sword has made women childless,
so will your mother be childless among women."

And Samuel put Agag to death before the LORD at Gilgal.
34 Then Samuel left for Ramah, but Saul went up to his home in
Gibeah of Saul. 35 Until the day Samuel died, he did not go to see Saul
again, though Samuel mourned for him. And the LORD regretted that
he had made Saul king over Israel.

SAMUEL ANOINTS DAVID

16 The LORD said to Samuel, "How long will you mourn for Saul,
since I have rejected him as king over Israel? Fill your horn with
oil and be on your way; I am sending you to Jesse of Bethlehem. I have
chosen one of his sons to be king."
2 But Samuel said, "How can I go? If Saul hears about it, he will
kill me."
The LORD said, "Take a heifer with you and say, 'I have come to sacri-
fice to the LORD.' 3 Invite Jesse to the sacrifice, and I will show you what
to do. You are to anoint for me the one I indicate."
4 Samuel did what the LORD said. When he arrived at Bethlehem, the
elders of the town trembled when they met him. They asked, "Do you
come in peace?"
5 Samuel replied, "Yes, in peace; I have come to sacrifice to the LORD.
Consecrate yourselves and come to the sacrifice with me." Then he con-
secrated Jesse and his sons and invited them to the sacrifice.
6 When they arrived, Samuel saw Eliab and thought, "Surely the
LORD's anointed stands here before the LORD."
7 But the LORD said to Samuel, "Do not consider his appearance or his
height, for I have rejected him. The LORD does not look at the things
people look at. People look at the outward appearance, but the LORD
looks at the heart."
8 Then Jesse called Abinadab and had him pass in front of Samuel.
But Samuel said, "The LORD has not chosen this one either." 9 Jesse

PRAYING SCRIPTURE

1 Samuel 16

As Saul's reign declined, marked by disobedience, God prepared a young shepherd to become Israel's next king. Samuel went to Jesse's house expecting to find one like Saul: strong and handsome. But God had other plans, instructing Samuel, "Do not consider his appearance" (verse 7). God was looking at the hearts of Jesse's sons.

Could it be said that you are a person after God's heart? Pray to be like him in your deepest being.

[a] 32 The meaning of the Hebrew for this phrase is uncertain.

then had Shammah pass by, but Samuel said, "Nor has the LORD chosen
this one." 10 Jesse had seven of his sons pass before Samuel, but Samuel
said to him, "The LORD has not chosen these." 11 So he asked Jesse, "Are
these all the sons you have?"

"There is still the youngest," Jesse answered. "He is tending the
sheep."

Samuel said, "Send for him; we will not sit down until he arrives."

12 So he sent for him and had him brought in. He was glowing with
health and had a fine appearance and handsome features.

Then the LORD said, "Rise and anoint him; this is the one."

13 So Samuel took the horn of oil and anointed him in the presence
of his brothers, and from that day on the Spirit of the LORD came pow-
erfully upon David. Samuel then went to Ramah.

DAVID IN SAUL'S SERVICE

14 Now the Spirit of the LORD had departed from Saul, and an evil[a]
spirit from the LORD tormented him.

15 Saul's attendants said to him, "See, an evil spirit from God is tor-
menting you. 16 Let our lord command his servants here to search for
someone who can play the lyre. He will play when the evil spirit from
God comes on you, and you will feel better."

17 So Saul said to his attendants, "Find someone who plays well and
bring him to me."

18 One of the servants answered, "I have seen a son of Jesse of Bethle-
hem who knows how to play the lyre. He is a brave man and a warrior.
He speaks well and is a fine-looking man. And the LORD is with him."

19 Then Saul sent messengers to Jesse and said, "Send me your son
David, who is with the sheep." 20 So Jesse took a donkey loaded with
bread, a skin of wine and a young goat and sent them with his son
David to Saul.

21 David came to Saul and entered his service. Saul liked him very
much, and David became one of his armor-bearers. 22 Then Saul sent
word to Jesse, saying, "Allow David to remain in my service, for I am
pleased with him."

23 Whenever the spirit from God came on Saul, David would take up
his lyre and play. Then relief would come to Saul; he would feel better,
and the evil spirit would leave him.

DAVID AND GOLIATH

17 Now the Philistines gathered their forces for war and assem-
bled at Sokoh in Judah. They pitched camp at Ephes Dammim,
between Sokoh and Azekah. 2 Saul and the Israelites assembled and
camped in the Valley of Elah and drew up their battle line to meet
the Philistines. 3 The Philistines occupied one hill and the Israelites an-
other, with the valley between them.

4 A champion named Goliath, who was from Gath, came out of the
Philistine camp. His height was six cubits and a span.[b] 5 He had a
bronze helmet on his head and wore a coat of scale armor of bronze
weighing five thousand shekels[c]; 6 on his legs he wore bronze greaves,
and a bronze javelin was slung on his back. 7 His spear shaft was like

PRAYING SCRIPTURE

1 Samuel 17

In this narrative, David faces a warrior so imposing that the entire army of Israel, including Saul, was paralyzed with fear. But David remembered what they forgot: The Lord is bigger than Goliath. Israel's army faced an obstacle, but the Lord did not, so David went in his strength.

We often lose battles because we trust our strength rather than God's. Ask for the strength he gives as you face the world each day.

[a] 14 Or *and a harmful*; similarly in verses 15, 16 and 23 [b] 4 That is, about 9 feet 9 inches or about 3 meters [c] 5 That is, about 125 pounds or about 58 kilograms

a weaver's rod, and its iron point weighed six hundred shekels.[a] His
shield bearer went ahead of him.

8Goliath stood and shouted to the ranks of Israel, "Why do you come
out and line up for battle? Am I not a Philistine, and are you not the
servants of Saul? Choose a man and have him come down to me. 9If he
is able to fight and kill me, we will become your subjects; but if I over-
come him and kill him, you will become our subjects and serve us."
10Then the Philistine said, "This day I defy the armies of Israel! Give me
a man and let us fight each other." 11On hearing the Philistine's words,
Saul and all the Israelites were dismayed and terrified.

12Now David was the son of an Ephrathite named Jesse, who was
from Bethlehem in Judah. Jesse had eight sons, and in Saul's time he
was very old. 13Jesse's three oldest sons had followed Saul to the war:
The firstborn was Eliab; the second, Abinadab; and the third, Sham-
mah. 14David was the youngest. The three oldest followed Saul, 15but
David went back and forth from Saul to tend his father's sheep at
Bethlehem.

16For forty days the Philistine came forward every morning and eve-
ning and took his stand.

17Now Jesse said to his son David, "Take this ephah[b] of roasted grain
and these ten loaves of bread for your brothers and hurry to their
camp. 18Take along these ten cheeses to the commander of their unit.
See how your brothers are and bring back some assurance[c] from them.
19They are with Saul and all the men of Israel in the Valley of Elah,
fighting against the Philistines."

20Early in the morning David left the flock in the care of a shepherd,
loaded up and set out, as Jesse had directed. He reached the camp as
the army was going out to its battle positions, shouting the war cry.
21Israel and the Philistines were drawing up their lines facing each
other. 22David left his things with the keeper of supplies, ran to the bat-
tle lines and asked his brothers how they were. 23As he was talking with
them, Goliath, the Philistine champion from Gath, stepped out from
his lines and shouted his usual defiance, and David heard it. 24When-
ever the Israelites saw the man, they all fled from him in great fear.

25Now the Israelites had been saying, "Do you see how this man
keeps coming out? He comes out to defy Israel. The king will give great
wealth to the man who kills him. He will also give him his daughter in
marriage and will exempt his family from taxes in Israel."

26David asked the men standing near him, "What will be done for
the man who kills this Philistine and removes this disgrace from Is-
rael? Who is this uncircumcised Philistine that he should defy the ar-
mies of the living God?"

27They repeated to him what they had been saying and told him,
"This is what will be done for the man who kills him."

28When Eliab, David's oldest brother, heard him speaking with the
men, he burned with anger at him and asked, "Why have you come
down here? And with whom did you leave those few sheep in the wil-
derness? I know how conceited you are and how wicked your heart is;
you came down only to watch the battle."

29"Now what have I done?" said David. "Can't I even speak?" 30He

---

[a] *7* That is, about 15 pounds or about 6.9 kilograms [b] *17* That is, probably about 36 pounds or about 16 kilograms [c] *18* Or *some token*; or *some pledge of spoils*

then turned away to someone else and brought up the same matter,
and the men answered him as before. 31 What David said was overheard
and reported to Saul, and Saul sent for him.

32 David said to Saul, "Let no one lose heart on account of this Philis-
tine; your servant will go and fight him."

33 Saul replied, "You are not able to go out against this Philistine and
fight him; you are only a young man, and he has been a warrior from
his youth."

34 But David said to Saul, "Your servant has been keeping his father's
sheep. When a lion or a bear came and carried off a sheep from the
flock, 35 I went after it, struck it and rescued the sheep from its mouth.
When it turned on me, I seized it by its hair, struck it and killed it.
36 Your servant has killed both the lion and the bear; this uncircum-
cised Philistine will be like one of them, because he has defied the
armies of the living God. 37 The LORD who rescued me from the paw of
the lion and the paw of the bear will rescue me from the hand of this
Philistine."

Saul said to David, "Go, and the LORD be with you."

38 Then Saul dressed David in his own tunic. He put a coat of armor
on him and a bronze helmet on his head. 39 David fastened on his
sword over the tunic and tried walking around, because he was not
used to them.

"I cannot go in these," he said to Saul, "because I am not used to
them." So he took them off. 40 Then he took his staff in his hand,
chose five smooth stones from the stream, put them in the pouch
of his shepherd's bag and, with his sling in his hand, approached the
Philistine.

41 Meanwhile, the Philistine, with his shield bearer in front of him,
kept coming closer to David. 42 He looked David over and saw that he
was little more than a boy, glowing with health and handsome, and he
despised him. 43 He said to David, "Am I a dog, that you come at me with
sticks?" And the Philistine cursed David by his gods. 44 "Come here," he
said, "and I'll give your flesh to the birds and the wild animals!"

45 David said to the Philistine, "You come against me with sword and
spear and javelin, but I come against you in the name of the LORD Al-
mighty, the God of the armies of Israel, whom you have defied. 46 This
day the LORD will deliver you into my hands, and I'll strike you down
and cut off your head. This very day I will give the carcasses of the Phi-
listine army to the birds and the wild animals, and the whole world
will know that there is a God in Israel. 47 All those gathered here will
know that it is not by sword or spear that the LORD saves; for the battle
is the LORD's, and he will give all of you into our hands."

48 As the Philistine moved closer to attack him, David ran quickly
toward the battle line to meet him. 49 Reaching into his bag and tak-
ing out a stone, he slung it and struck the Philistine on the forehead.
The stone sank into his forehead, and he fell facedown on the ground.

50 So David triumphed over the Philistine with a sling and a stone;
without a sword in his hand he struck down the Philistine and killed
him.

51 David ran and stood over him. He took hold of the Philistine's
sword and drew it from the sheath. After he killed him, he cut off his
head with the sword.

When the Philistines saw that their hero was dead, they turned and
ran. 52 Then the men of Israel and Judah surged forward with a shout

and pursued the Philistines to the entrance of Gath[a] and to the gates
of Ekron. Their dead were strewn along the Shaaraim road to Gath and
Ekron. 53When the Israelites returned from chasing the Philistines,
they plundered their camp.
54David took the Philistine's head and brought it to Jerusalem; he
put the Philistine's weapons in his own tent.
55As Saul watched David going out to meet the Philistine, he said
to Abner, commander of the army, "Abner, whose son is that young
man?"
Abner replied, "As surely as you live, Your Majesty, I don't know."
56The king said, "Find out whose son this young man is."
57As soon as David returned from killing the Philistine, Abner took
him and brought him before Saul, with David still holding the Philis-
tine's head.
58"Whose son are you, young man?" Saul asked him.
David said, "I am the son of your servant Jesse of Bethlehem."

SAUL'S GROWING FEAR OF DAVID

18 After David had finished talking with Saul, Jonathan became
one in spirit with David, and he loved him as himself. 2From
that day Saul kept David with him and did not let him return home
to his family. 3And Jonathan made a covenant with David because he
loved him as himself. 4Jonathan took off the robe he was wearing and
gave it to David, along with his tunic, and even his sword, his bow and
his belt.
5Whatever mission Saul sent him on, David was so successful that
Saul gave him a high rank in the army. This pleased all the troops, and
Saul's officers as well.
6When the men were returning home after David had killed the Phi-
listine, the women came out from all the towns of Israel to meet King
Saul with singing and dancing, with joyful songs and with timbrels
and lyres. 7As they danced, they sang:

"Saul has slain his thousands,
  and David his tens of thousands."

8Saul was very angry; this refrain displeased him greatly. "They have
credited David with tens of thousands," he thought, "but me with only
thousands. What more can he get but the kingdom?" 9And from that
time on Saul kept a close eye on David.
10The next day an evil[b] spirit from God came forcefully on Saul. He
was prophesying in his house, while David was playing the lyre, as he
usually did. Saul had a spear in his hand 11and he hurled it, saying to
himself, "I'll pin David to the wall." But David eluded him twice.
12Saul was afraid of David, because the LORD was with David but had
departed from Saul. 13So he sent David away from him and gave him
command over a thousand men, and David led the troops in their cam-
paigns. 14In everything he did he had great success, because the LORD
was with him. 15When Saul saw how successful he was, he was afraid
of him. 16But all Israel and Judah loved David, because he led them in
their campaigns.
17Saul said to David, "Here is my older daughter Merab. I will give her
to you in marriage; only serve me bravely and fight the battles of the

PRAYING SCRIPTURE

1 Samuel 18

Saul's unwillingness to repent and follow God with his whole heart poisoned his attitude toward David. After the people deservedly celebrated David's victory over Goliath more than Saul's own exploits, the king became murderously enraged, even more so because the Lord was with David.

Disobedience carries the seeds of all kinds of poisoned fruit. Ask God to root out any jealousy or bitterness that would destroy your relationships.

---

[a] 52 Some Septuagint manuscripts; Hebrew *of a valley* [b] 10 Or *a harmful*

LORD." For Saul said to himself, "I will not raise a hand against him. Let
the Philistines do that!"
18But David said to Saul, "Who am I, and what is my family or my
clan in Israel, that I should become the king's son-in-law?" 19So[a] when
the time came for Merab, Saul's daughter, to be given to David, she was
given in marriage to Adriel of Meholah.
20Now Saul's daughter Michal was in love with David, and when they
told Saul about it, he was pleased. 21"I will give her to him," he thought,
"so that she may be a snare to him and so that the hand of the Phi-
listines may be against him." So Saul said to David, "Now you have a
second opportunity to become my son-in-law."
22Then Saul ordered his attendants: "Speak to David privately and
say, 'Look, the king likes you, and his attendants all love you; now be-
come his son-in-law.'"
23They repeated these words to David. But David said, "Do you think
it is a small matter to become the king's son-in-law? I'm only a poor
man and little known."
24When Saul's servants told him what David had said, 25Saul replied,
"Say to David, 'The king wants no other price for the bride than a hun-
dred Philistine foreskins, to take revenge on his enemies.'" Saul's plan
was to have David fall by the hands of the Philistines.
26When the attendants told David these things, he was pleased to
become the king's son-in-law. So before the allotted time elapsed, 27Da-
vid took his men with him and went out and killed two hundred Phi-
listines and brought back their foreskins. They counted out the full
number to the king so that David might become the king's son-in-law.
Then Saul gave him his daughter Michal in marriage.
28When Saul realized that the LORD was with David and that his
daughter Michal loved David, 29Saul became still more afraid of him,
and he remained his enemy the rest of his days.
30The Philistine commanders continued to go out to battle, and as
often as they did, David met with more success than the rest of Saul's
officers, and his name became well known.

SAUL TRIES TO KILL DAVID

19 Saul told his son Jonathan and all the attendants to kill David.
But Jonathan had taken a great liking to David 2and warned
him, "My father Saul is looking for a chance to kill you. Be on your
guard tomorrow morning; go into hiding and stay there. 3I will go out
and stand with my father in the field where you are. I'll speak to him
about you and will tell you what I find out."
4Jonathan spoke well of David to Saul his father and said to him, "Let
not the king do wrong to his servant David; he has not wronged you,
and what he has done has benefited you greatly. 5He took his life in his
hands when he killed the Philistine. The LORD won a great victory for
all Israel, and you saw it and were glad. Why then would you do wrong
to an innocent man like David by killing him for no reason?"
6Saul listened to Jonathan and took this oath: "As surely as the LORD
lives, David will not be put to death."
7So Jonathan called David and told him the whole conversation. He
brought him to Saul, and David was with Saul as before.
8Once more war broke out, and David went out and fought the Phi-
listines. He struck them with such force that they fled before him.

PRAYING SCRIPTURE

1 Samuel 19

Although Saul, continuously vexed by an "evil spirit," sought to kill David (see verse 9), Saul's son Jonathan was committed to protecting God's anointed. He attempted to reason with Saul, reminding the king that God had given Israel the victory.

Do you ever feel as though someone seriously seeks your harm, whether physical, emotional or even career harm? Pray for that person. Ask God to change that person's heart toward you.

[a] 19 Or *However,*

9But an evil[a] spirit from the LORD came on Saul as he was sitting in
his house with his spear in his hand. While David was playing the lyre,
10Saul tried to pin him to the wall with his spear, but David eluded him
as Saul drove the spear into the wall. That night David made good his
escape.
11Saul sent men to David's house to watch it and to kill him in the
morning. But Michal, David's wife, warned him, "If you don't run for
your life tonight, tomorrow you'll be killed." 12So Michal let David
down through a window, and he fled and escaped. 13Then Michal took
an idol and laid it on the bed, covering it with a garment and putting
some goats' hair at the head.
14When Saul sent the men to capture David, Michal said, "He is ill."
15Then Saul sent the men back to see David and told them, "Bring
him up to me in his bed so that I may kill him." 16But when the men
entered, there was the idol in the bed, and at the head was some goats'
hair.
17Saul said to Michal, "Why did you deceive me like this and send my
enemy away so that he escaped?"
Michal told him, "He said to me, 'Let me get away. Why should I kill
you?'"
18When David had fled and made his escape, he went to Samuel at
Ramah and told him all that Saul had done to him. Then he and Sam-
uel went to Naioth and stayed there. 19Word came to Saul: "David is in
Naioth at Ramah"; 20so he sent men to capture him. But when they saw
a group of prophets prophesying, with Samuel standing there as their
leader, the Spirit of God came on Saul's men, and they also prophesied.
21Saul was told about it, and he sent more men, and they prophesied
too. Saul sent men a third time, and they also prophesied. 22Finally, he
himself left for Ramah and went to the great cistern at Seku. And he
asked, "Where are Samuel and David?"
"Over in Naioth at Ramah," they said.
23So Saul went to Naioth at Ramah. But the Spirit of God came even
on him, and he walked along prophesying until he came to Naioth.
24He stripped off his garments, and he too prophesied in Samuel's
presence. He lay naked all that day and all that night. This is why peo-
ple say, "Is Saul also among the prophets?"

DAVID AND JONATHAN

20 Then David fled from Naioth at Ramah and went to Jonathan
and asked, "What have I done? What is my crime? How have I
wronged your father, that he is trying to kill me?"
2"Never!" Jonathan replied. "You are not going to die! Look, my fa-
ther doesn't do anything, great or small, without letting me know. Why
would he hide this from me? It isn't so!"
3But David took an oath and said, "Your father knows very well that
I have found favor in your eyes, and he has said to himself, 'Jonathan
must not know this or he will be grieved.' Yet as surely as the LORD lives
and as you live, there is only a step between me and death."
4Jonathan said to David, "Whatever you want me to do, I'll do for
you."
5So David said, "Look, tomorrow is the New Moon feast, and I am
supposed to dine with the king; but let me go and hide in the field

PRAYING SCRIPTURE

1 Samuel 20

Jonathan's affection and sense of responsibility for David grew to the point that he had to protect David from his father. Facing Saul's wrath, Jonathan refused to turn on his friend even though he knew it meant he himself would not inherit the throne.

Jonathan was a man of faith, valor and integrity. Despite condemnation from his own father, he obeyed God. Ask God to give you that same heart for him.

[a] 9 Or *But a harmful*

until the evening of the day after tomorrow. 6If your father misses me at all, tell him, 'David earnestly asked my permission to hurry to Bethlehem, his hometown, because an annual sacrifice is being made there for his whole clan.' 7If he says, 'Very well,' then your servant is safe. But if he loses his temper, you can be sure that he is determined to harm me. 8As for you, show kindness to your servant, for you have brought him into a covenant with you before the LORD. If I am guilty, then kill me yourself! Why hand me over to your father?"

9"Never!" Jonathan said. "If I had the least inkling that my father was determined to harm you, wouldn't I tell you?"

10David asked, "Who will tell me if your father answers you harshly?"

11"Come," Jonathan said, "let's go out into the field." So they went there together.

12Then Jonathan said to David, "I swear by the LORD, the God of Israel, that I will surely sound out my father by this time the day after tomorrow! If he is favorably disposed toward you, will I not send you word and let you know? 13But if my father intends to harm you, may the LORD deal with Jonathan, be it ever so severely, if I do not let you know and send you away in peace. May the LORD be with you as he has been with my father. 14But show me unfailing kindness like the LORD's kindness as long as I live, so that I may not be killed, 15and do not ever cut off your kindness from my family — not even when the LORD has cut off every one of David's enemies from the face of the earth."

16So Jonathan made a covenant with the house of David, saying, "May the LORD call David's enemies to account." 17And Jonathan had David reaffirm his oath out of love for him, because he loved him as he loved himself.

18Then Jonathan said to David, "Tomorrow is the New Moon feast. You will be missed, because your seat will be empty. 19The day after tomorrow, toward evening, go to the place where you hid when this trouble began, and wait by the stone Ezel. 20I will shoot three arrows to the side of it, as though I were shooting at a target. 21Then I will send a boy and say, 'Go, find the arrows.' If I say to him, 'Look, the arrows are on this side of you; bring them here,' then come, because, as surely as the LORD lives, you are safe; there is no danger. 22But if I say to the boy, 'Look, the arrows are beyond you,' then you must go, because the LORD has sent you away. 23And about the matter you and I discussed — remember, the LORD is witness between you and me forever."

24So David hid in the field, and when the New Moon feast came, the king sat down to eat. 25He sat in his customary place by the wall, opposite Jonathan,[a] and Abner sat next to Saul, but David's place was empty. 26Saul said nothing that day, for he thought, "Something must have happened to David to make him ceremonially unclean — surely he is unclean." 27But the next day, the second day of the month, David's place was empty again. Then Saul said to his son Jonathan, "Why hasn't the son of Jesse come to the meal, either yesterday or today?"

28Jonathan answered, "David earnestly asked me for permission to go to Bethlehem. 29He said, 'Let me go, because our family is observing a sacrifice in the town and my brother has ordered me to be there. If I have found favor in your eyes, let me get away to see my brothers.' That is why he has not come to the king's table."

30Saul's anger flared up at Jonathan and he said to him, "You son of a

---

[a] *25* Septuagint; Hebrew *wall. Jonathan arose*

perverse and rebellious woman! Don't I know that you have sided with
the son of Jesse to your own shame and to the shame of the mother
who bore you? 31As long as the son of Jesse lives on this earth, neither
you nor your kingdom will be established. Now send someone to bring
him to me, for he must die!"
32"Why should he be put to death? What has he done?" Jonathan
asked his father. 33But Saul hurled his spear at him to kill him. Then
Jonathan knew that his father intended to kill David.
34Jonathan got up from the table in fierce anger; on that second
day of the feast he did not eat, because he was grieved at his father's
shameful treatment of David.
35In the morning Jonathan went out to the field for his meeting with
David. He had a small boy with him, 36and he said to the boy, "Run and
find the arrows I shoot." As the boy ran, he shot an arrow beyond him.
37When the boy came to the place where Jonathan's arrow had fallen,
Jonathan called out after him, "Isn't the arrow beyond you?" 38Then he
shouted, "Hurry! Go quickly! Don't stop!" The boy picked up the arrow
and returned to his master. 39(The boy knew nothing about all this;
only Jonathan and David knew.) 40Then Jonathan gave his weapons to
the boy and said, "Go, carry them back to town."
41After the boy had gone, David got up from the south side of the
stone and bowed down before Jonathan three times, with his face to
the ground. Then they kissed each other and wept together — but Da-
vid wept the most.
42Jonathan said to David, "Go in peace, for we have sworn friendship
with each other in the name of the LORD, saying, 'The LORD is witness
between you and me, and between your descendants and my descen-
dants forever.'" Then David left, and Jonathan went back to the town.[a]

DAVID AT NOB

21 [b] David went to Nob, to Ahimelek the priest. Ahimelek trembled
when he met him, and asked, "Why are you alone? Why is no
one with you?"
2David answered Ahimelek the priest, "The king sent me on a mis-
sion and said to me, 'No one is to know anything about the mission I
am sending you on.' As for my men, I have told them to meet me at
a certain place. 3Now then, what do you have on hand? Give me five
loaves of bread, or whatever you can find."
4But the priest answered David, "I don't have any ordinary bread on
hand; however, there is some consecrated bread here — provided the
men have kept themselves from women."
5David replied, "Indeed women have been kept from us, as usual
whenever[c] I set out. The men's bodies are holy even on missions that
are not holy. How much more so today!" 6So the priest gave him the
consecrated bread, since there was no bread there except the bread
of the Presence that had been removed from before the LORD and re-
placed by hot bread on the day it was taken away.
7Now one of Saul's servants was there that day, detained before the
LORD; he was Doeg the Edomite, Saul's chief shepherd.
8David asked Ahimelek, "Don't you have a spear or a sword here?
I haven't brought my sword or any other weapon, because the king's
mission was urgent."

PRAYING SCRIPTURE

1 Samuel 21

Sometimes God's ways are unknowable. In a moment of hunger, David asked a priest for food for himself and his men. Lacking any ordinary food, the priest gave them holy bread to eat—bread that had been consecrated to God.

God's ways are so much higher than ours and his goodness better than we can imagine. God's wisdom should be a source of ongoing praise when we pray.

---

[a] *42* In Hebrew texts this sentence (20:42b) is numbered 21:1. [b] In Hebrew texts 21:1-15 is numbered 21:2-16. [c] *5* Or *from us in the past few days since*

9 The priest replied, "The sword of Goliath the Philistine, whom you
killed in the Valley of Elah, is here; it is wrapped in a cloth behind the
ephod. If you want it, take it; there is no sword here but that one."
David said, "There is none like it; give it to me."

DAVID AT GATH

10 That day David fled from Saul and went to Achish king of Gath.
11 But the servants of Achish said to him, "Isn't this David, the king of
the land? Isn't he the one they sing about in their dances:

"'Saul has slain his thousands,
and David his tens of thousands'?"

12 David took these words to heart and was very much afraid of Achish
king of Gath. 13 So he pretended to be insane in their presence; and
while he was in their hands he acted like a madman, making marks on
the doors of the gate and letting saliva run down his beard.
14 Achish said to his servants, "Look at the man! He is insane! Why
bring him to me? 15 Am I so short of madmen that you have to bring
this fellow here to carry on like this in front of me? Must this man
come into my house?"

DAVID AT ADULLAM AND MIZPAH

22 David left Gath and escaped to the cave of Adullam. When his
brothers and his father's household heard about it, they went
down to him there. 2 All those who were in distress or in debt or discon-
tented gathered around him, and he became their commander. About
four hundred men were with him.
3 From there David went to Mizpah in Moab and said to the king of
Moab, "Would you let my father and mother come and stay with you
until I learn what God will do for me?" 4 So he left them with the king of
Moab, and they stayed with him as long as David was in the stronghold.
5 But the prophet Gad said to David, "Do not stay in the stronghold.
Go into the land of Judah." So David left and went to the forest of
Hereth.

SAUL KILLS THE PRIESTS OF NOB

6 Now Saul heard that David and his men had been discovered. And
Saul was seated, spear in hand, under the tamarisk tree on the hill
at Gibeah, with all his officials standing at his side. 7 He said to them,
"Listen, men of Benjamin! Will the son of Jesse give all of you fields
and vineyards? Will he make all of you commanders of thousands and
commanders of hundreds? 8 Is that why you have all conspired against
me? No one tells me when my son makes a covenant with the son of
Jesse. None of you is concerned about me or tells me that my son has
incited my servant to lie in wait for me, as he does today."
9 But Doeg the Edomite, who was standing with Saul's officials, said,
"I saw the son of Jesse come to Ahimelek son of Ahitub at Nob. 10 Ahim-
elek inquired of the LORD for him; he also gave him provisions and the
sword of Goliath the Philistine."
11 Then the king sent for the priest Ahimelek son of Ahitub and all
the men of his family, who were the priests at Nob, and they all came
to the king. 12 Saul said, "Listen now, son of Ahitub."
"Yes, my lord," he answered.
13 Saul said to him, "Why have you conspired against me, you and

PRAYING SCRIPTURE

1 Samuel 22

As David's popularity grew in Israel, Saul descended further into ungodliness, ordering the slaughter of 85 priests because one of them had helped David. At any time during his sinful falling, Saul could have repented and turned back to God. Instead, he continued in disobedience.

Do you know anyone whose life is spiraling like Saul's? Intercede for that person. Ask God to open his or her eyes.

the son of Jesse, giving him bread and a sword and inquiring of God
for him, so that he has rebelled against me and lies in wait for me, as
he does today?"

14Ahimelek answered the king, "Who of all your servants is as loyal
as David, the king's son-in-law, captain of your bodyguard and highly
respected in your household? 15Was that day the first time I inquired
of God for him? Of course not! Let not the king accuse your servant or
any of his father's family, for your servant knows nothing at all about
this whole affair."

16But the king said, "You will surely die, Ahimelek, you and your
whole family."

17Then the king ordered the guards at his side: "Turn and kill the
priests of the LORD, because they too have sided with David. They knew
he was fleeing, yet they did not tell me."

But the king's officials were unwilling to raise a hand to strike the
priests of the LORD.

18The king then ordered Doeg, "You turn and strike down the
priests." So Doeg the Edomite turned and struck them down. That day
he killed eighty-five men who wore the linen ephod. 19He also put to
the sword Nob, the town of the priests, with its men and women, its
children and infants, and its cattle, donkeys and sheep.

20But one son of Ahimelek son of Ahitub, named Abiathar, escaped
and fled to join David. 21He told David that Saul had killed the priests
of the LORD. 22Then David said to Abiathar, "That day, when Doeg the
Edomite was there, I knew he would be sure to tell Saul. I am responsi-
ble for the death of your whole family. 23Stay with me; don't be afraid.
The man who wants to kill you is trying to kill me too. You will be safe
with me."

DAVID SAVES KEILAH

23 When David was told, "Look, the Philistines are fighting against
Keilah and are looting the threshing floors," 2he inquired of the
LORD, saying, "Shall I go and attack these Philistines?"

The LORD answered him, "Go, attack the Philistines and save Keilah."

3But David's men said to him, "Here in Judah we are afraid. How
much more, then, if we go to Keilah against the Philistine forces!"

4Once again David inquired of the LORD, and the LORD answered him,
"Go down to Keilah, for I am going to give the Philistines into your
hand." 5So David and his men went to Keilah, fought the Philistines and
carried off their livestock. He inflicted heavy losses on the Philistines
and saved the people of Keilah. 6(Now Abiathar son of Ahimelek had
brought the ephod down with him when he fled to David at Keilah.)

SAUL PURSUES DAVID

7Saul was told that David had gone to Keilah, and he said, "God has
delivered him into my hands, for David has imprisoned himself by en-
tering a town with gates and bars." 8And Saul called up all his forces for
battle, to go down to Keilah to besiege David and his men.

9When David learned that Saul was plotting against him, he said to
Abiathar the priest, "Bring the ephod." 10David said, "LORD, God of Is-
rael, your servant has heard definitely that Saul plans to come to Kei-
lah and destroy the town on account of me. 11Will the citizens of Keilah
surrender me to him? Will Saul come down, as your servant has heard?
LORD, God of Israel, tell your servant."

PRAYING SCRIPTURE

1 Samuel 23

Are there times in life when you feel as David must have felt when being pursued by Saul? At every turn it seems someone is intent on injuring you. The Lord, however, will be on your side as he was with David.

Trials and persecution are to be expected in life. Yet God's people can believe he will carry them through trials. Ask him for confidence in him and peace.

PRAYING
SCRIPTURE

1 Samuel 24

We are never more like Jesus than when we bless our enemies. Scripture teaches us to bless those who persecute us. Nonbelievers can practice hate, but we are to show love. They can practice vengeance, but we must show mercy.

This is one of the hardest aspects of following Jesus. Ask God to help you love the world the way he does.

And the LORD said, "He will."
12Again David asked, "Will the citizens of Keilah surrender me and
my men to Saul?"
And the LORD said, "They will."
13So David and his men, about six hundred in number, left Keilah
and kept moving from place to place. When Saul was told that David
had escaped from Keilah, he did not go there.
14David stayed in the wilderness strongholds and in the hills of the
Desert of Ziph. Day after day Saul searched for him, but God did not
give David into his hands.
15While David was at Horesh in the Desert of Ziph, he learned that[a]
Saul had come out to take his life. 16And Saul's son Jonathan went
to David at Horesh and helped him find strength in God. 17"Don't be
afraid," he said. "My father Saul will not lay a hand on you. You will
be king over Israel, and I will be second to you. Even my father Saul
knows this." 18The two of them made a covenant before the LORD. Then
Jonathan went home, but David remained at Horesh.
19The Ziphites went up to Saul at Gibeah and said, "Is not David
hiding among us in the strongholds at Horesh, on the hill of Haki-
lah, south of Jeshimon? 20Now, Your Majesty, come down whenever
it pleases you to do so, and we will be responsible for giving him into
your hands."
21Saul replied, "The LORD bless you for your concern for me. 22Go
and get more information. Find out where David usually goes and who
has seen him there. They tell me he is very crafty. 23Find out about all
the hiding places he uses and come back to me with definite informa-
tion. Then I will go with you; if he is in the area, I will track him down
among all the clans of Judah."
24So they set out and went to Ziph ahead of Saul. Now David and his
men were in the Desert of Maon, in the Arabah south of Jeshimon.
25Saul and his men began the search, and when David was told about
it, he went down to the rock and stayed in the Desert of Maon. When
Saul heard this, he went into the Desert of Maon in pursuit of David.
26Saul was going along one side of the mountain, and David and his
men were on the other side, hurrying to get away from Saul. As Saul
and his forces were closing in on David and his men to capture them,
27a messenger came to Saul, saying, "Come quickly! The Philistines are
raiding the land." 28Then Saul broke off his pursuit of David and went
to meet the Philistines. That is why they call this place Sela Hammah-
lekoth.[b] 29And David went up from there and lived in the strongholds
of En Gedi.[c]

DAVID SPARES SAUL'S LIFE

24 [d] After Saul returned from pursuing the Philistines, he was told,
"David is in the Desert of En Gedi." 2So Saul took three thou-
sand able young men from all Israel and set out to look for David and
his men near the Crags of the Wild Goats.
3He came to the sheep pens along the way; a cave was there, and
Saul went in to relieve himself. David and his men were far back in the
cave. 4The men said, "This is the day the LORD spoke of when he said[e]

[a] 15 Or *he was afraid because* [b] 28 *Sela Hammahlekoth* means *rock of parting.* [c] 29 In Hebrew texts this verse (23:29) is numbered 24:1. [d] In Hebrew texts 24:1-22 is numbered 24:2-23. [e] 4 Or *"Today the LORD is saying*

to you, 'I will give your enemy into your hands for you to deal with
as you wish.'" Then David crept up unnoticed and cut off a corner of
Saul's robe.
5Afterward, David was conscience-stricken for having cut off a cor-
ner of his robe. 6He said to his men, "The LORD forbid that I should do
such a thing to my master, the LORD's anointed, or lay my hand on him;
for he is the anointed of the LORD." 7With these words David sharply
rebuked his men and did not allow them to attack Saul. And Saul left
the cave and went his way.
8Then David went out of the cave and called out to Saul, "My lord the
king!" When Saul looked behind him, David bowed down and prostrated
himself with his face to the ground. 9He said to Saul, "Why do you lis-
ten when men say, 'David is bent on harming you'? 10This day you have
seen with your own eyes how the LORD delivered you into my hands in
the cave. Some urged me to kill you, but I spared you; I said, 'I will not
lay my hand on my lord, because he is the LORD's anointed.' 11See, my
father, look at this piece of your robe in my hand! I cut off the corner of
your robe but did not kill you. See that there is nothing in my hand to
indicate that I am guilty of wrongdoing or rebellion. I have not wronged
you, but you are hunting me down to take my life. 12May the LORD judge
between you and me. And may the LORD avenge the wrongs you have
done to me, but my hand will not touch you. 13As the old saying goes,
'From evildoers come evil deeds,' so my hand will not touch you.
14"Against whom has the king of Israel come out? Who are you pur-
suing? A dead dog? A flea? 15May the LORD be our judge and decide be-
tween us. May he consider my cause and uphold it; may he vindicate
me by delivering me from your hand."
16When David finished saying this, Saul asked, "Is that your voice,
David my son?" And he wept aloud. 17"You are more righteous than
I," he said. "You have treated me well, but I have treated you badly.
18You have just now told me about the good you did to me; the LORD
delivered me into your hands, but you did not kill me. 19When a man
finds his enemy, does he let him get away unharmed? May the LORD
reward you well for the way you treated me today. 20I know that you
will surely be king and that the kingdom of Israel will be established
in your hands. 21Now swear to me by the LORD that you will not kill off
my descendants or wipe out my name from my father's family."
22So David gave his oath to Saul. Then Saul returned home, but David
and his men went up to the stronghold.

DAVID, NABAL AND ABIGAIL

25 Now Samuel died, and all Israel assembled and mourned for
him; and they buried him at his home in Ramah. Then David
moved down into the Desert of Paran.[a]
2A certain man in Maon, who had property there at Carmel, was very
wealthy. He had a thousand goats and three thousand sheep, which he
was shearing in Carmel. 3His name was Nabal and his wife's name was
Abigail. She was an intelligent and beautiful woman, but her husband
was surly and mean in his dealings — he was a Calebite.
4While David was in the wilderness, he heard that Nabal was shear-
ing sheep. 5So he sent ten young men and said to them, "Go up to Nabal

[a] 1 Hebrew and some Septuagint manuscripts; other Septuagint manuscripts *Maon*

PRAYING SCRIPTURE

1 Samuel 25

Abigail, the wife of a rich man, understood the role David played in God's plan. She confirmed the promise of "a lasting dynasty" for David, understanding that David was on God's side (see verse 28). After Nabal's sudden death, David took Abigail as his wife.

David's throne was established in God's promise and would be eternally secured in the resurrection of Christ. Praise God for his ability to keep his redemptive promises!

at Carmel and greet him in my name. 6Say to him: 'Long life to you!
Good health to you and your household! And good health to all that
is yours!
7" 'Now I hear that it is sheep-shearing time. When your shepherds
were with us, we did not mistreat them, and the whole time they were
at Carmel nothing of theirs was missing. 8Ask your own servants and
they will tell you. Therefore be favorable toward my men, since we
come at a festive time. Please give your servants and your son David
whatever you can find for them.' "
9When David's men arrived, they gave Nabal this message in David's
name. Then they waited.
10Nabal answered David's servants, "Who is this David? Who is this
son of Jesse? Many servants are breaking away from their masters
these days. 11Why should I take my bread and water, and the meat I
have slaughtered for my shearers, and give it to men coming from
who knows where?"
12David's men turned around and went back. When they arrived,
they reported every word. 13David said to his men, "Each of you strap
on your sword!" So they did, and David strapped his on as well. About
four hundred men went up with David, while two hundred stayed with
the supplies.
14One of the servants told Abigail, Nabal's wife, "David sent mes-
sengers from the wilderness to give our master his greetings, but he
hurled insults at them. 15Yet these men were very good to us. They
did not mistreat us, and the whole time we were out in the fields near
them nothing was missing. 16Night and day they were a wall around
us the whole time we were herding our sheep near them. 17Now think
it over and see what you can do, because disaster is hanging over our
master and his whole household. He is such a wicked man that no one
can talk to him."
18Abigail acted quickly. She took two hundred loaves of bread, two
skins of wine, five dressed sheep, five seahs[a] of roasted grain, a hun-
dred cakes of raisins and two hundred cakes of pressed figs, and loaded
them on donkeys. 19Then she told her servants, "Go on ahead; I'll fol-
low you." But she did not tell her husband Nabal.
20As she came riding her donkey into a mountain ravine, there
were David and his men descending toward her, and she met them.
21David had just said, "It's been useless — all my watching over this
fellow's property in the wilderness so that nothing of his was miss-
ing. He has paid me back evil for good. 22May God deal with David,[b]
be it ever so severely, if by morning I leave alive one male of all who
belong to him!"
23When Abigail saw David, she quickly got off her donkey and
bowed down before David with her face to the ground. 24She fell at
his feet and said: "Pardon your servant, my lord, and let me speak to
you; hear what your servant has to say. 25Please pay no attention, my
lord, to that wicked man Nabal. He is just like his name — his name
means Fool, and folly goes with him. And as for me, your servant, I
did not see the men my lord sent. 26And now, my lord, as surely as
the LORD your God lives and as you live, since the LORD has kept you
from bloodshed and from avenging yourself with your own hands,

---

[a] *18* That is, probably about 60 pounds or about 27 kilograms [b] *22* Some Septuagint manuscripts; Hebrew *with David's enemies*

may your enemies and all who are intent on harming my lord be like Nabal. 27And let this gift, which your servant has brought to my lord, be given to the men who follow you.

28"Please forgive your servant's presumption. The LORD your God will certainly make a lasting dynasty for my lord, because you fight the LORD's battles, and no wrongdoing will be found in you as long as you live. 29Even though someone is pursuing you to take your life, the life of my lord will be bound securely in the bundle of the living by the LORD your God, but the lives of your enemies he will hurl away as from the pocket of a sling. 30When the LORD has fulfilled for my lord every good thing he promised concerning him and has appointed him ruler over Israel, 31my lord will not have on his conscience the staggering burden of needless bloodshed or of having avenged himself. And when the LORD your God has brought my lord success, remember your servant."

32David said to Abigail, "Praise be to the LORD, the God of Israel, who has sent you today to meet me. 33May you be blessed for your good judgment and for keeping me from bloodshed this day and from avenging myself with my own hands. 34Otherwise, as surely as the LORD, the God of Israel, lives, who has kept me from harming you, if you had not come quickly to meet me, not one male belonging to Nabal would have been left alive by daybreak."

35Then David accepted from her hand what she had brought him and said, "Go home in peace. I have heard your words and granted your request."

36When Abigail went to Nabal, he was in the house holding a banquet like that of a king. He was in high spirits and very drunk. So she told him nothing at all until daybreak. 37Then in the morning, when Nabal was sober, his wife told him all these things, and his heart failed him and he became like a stone. 38About ten days later, the LORD struck Nabal and he died.

39When David heard that Nabal was dead, he said, "Praise be to the LORD, who has upheld my cause against Nabal for treating me with contempt. He has kept his servant from doing wrong and has brought Nabal's wrongdoing down on his own head."

Then David sent word to Abigail, asking her to become his wife. 40His servants went to Carmel and said to Abigail, "David has sent us to you to take you to become his wife."

41She bowed down with her face to the ground and said, "I am your servant and am ready to serve you and wash the feet of my lord's servants." 42Abigail quickly got on a donkey and, attended by her five female servants, went with David's messengers and became his wife. 43David had also married Ahinoam of Jezreel, and they both were his wives. 44But Saul had given his daughter Michal, David's wife, to Paltiel[a] son of Laish, who was from Gallim.

DAVID AGAIN SPARES SAUL'S LIFE

26 The Ziphites went to Saul at Gibeah and said, "Is not David hiding on the hill of Hakilah, which faces Jeshimon?"

2So Saul went down to the Desert of Ziph, with his three thousand select Israelite troops, to search there for David. 3Saul made his camp beside the road on the hill of Hakilah facing Jeshimon, but David stayed

[a] 44 Hebrew *Palti*, a variant of *Paltiel*

PRAYING SCRIPTURE

1 Samuel 26

Few things bear witness to the character of God more than showing mercy rather than deserved judgment. For a second time, David was within killing distance of Saul yet spared his life. Jesus blesses the merciful as those who will receive mercy themselves.

Mercy is something all people hope to receive, yet many people struggle to express it. Ask God to help you show mercy that you might also experience it.

in the wilderness. When he saw that Saul had followed him there, 4he
sent out scouts and learned that Saul had definitely arrived.
5Then David set out and went to the place where Saul had camped.
He saw where Saul and Abner son of Ner, the commander of the army,
had lain down. Saul was lying inside the camp, with the army en-
camped around him.
6David then asked Ahimelek the Hittite and Abishai son of Zeruiah,
Joab's brother, "Who will go down into the camp with me to Saul?"
"I'll go with you," said Abishai.
7So David and Abishai went to the army by night, and there was Saul,
lying asleep inside the camp with his spear stuck in the ground near
his head. Abner and the soldiers were lying around him.
8Abishai said to David, "Today God has delivered your enemy into
your hands. Now let me pin him to the ground with one thrust of the
spear; I won't strike him twice."
9But David said to Abishai, "Don't destroy him! Who can lay a hand
on the LORD's anointed and be guiltless? 10As surely as the LORD lives,"
he said, "the LORD himself will strike him, or his time will come and he
will die, or he will go into battle and perish. 11But the LORD forbid that I
should lay a hand on the LORD's anointed. Now get the spear and water
jug that are near his head, and let's go."
12So David took the spear and water jug near Saul's head, and they
left. No one saw or knew about it, nor did anyone wake up. They were
all sleeping, because the LORD had put them into a deep sleep.
13Then David crossed over to the other side and stood on top of the
hill some distance away; there was a wide space between them. 14He
called out to the army and to Abner son of Ner, "Aren't you going to
answer me, Abner?"
Abner replied, "Who are you who calls to the king?"
15David said, "You're a man, aren't you? And who is like you in Israel?
Why didn't you guard your lord the king? Someone came to destroy
your lord the king. 16What you have done is not good. As surely as the
LORD lives, you and your men must die, because you did not guard
your master, the LORD's anointed. Look around you. Where are the
king's spear and water jug that were near his head?"
17Saul recognized David's voice and said, "Is that your voice, David
my son?"
David replied, "Yes it is, my lord the king." 18And he added, "Why is
my lord pursuing his servant? What have I done, and what wrong am
I guilty of? 19Now let my lord the king listen to his servant's words.
If the LORD has incited you against me, then may he accept an offer-
ing. If, however, people have done it, may they be cursed before the
LORD! They have driven me today from my share in the LORD's inheri-
tance and have said, 'Go, serve other gods.' 20Now do not let my blood
fall to the ground far from the presence of the LORD. The king of Is-
rael has come out to look for a flea — as one hunts a partridge in the
mountains."
21Then Saul said, "I have sinned. Come back, David my son. Because
you considered my life precious today, I will not try to harm you again.
Surely I have acted like a fool and have been terribly wrong."
22"Here is the king's spear," David answered. "Let one of your young
men come over and get it. 23The LORD rewards everyone for their righ-
teousness and faithfulness. The LORD delivered you into my hands to-
day, but I would not lay a hand on the LORD's anointed. 24As surely as

I valued your life today, so may the LORD value my life and deliver me from all trouble."

25 Then Saul said to David, "May you be blessed, David my son; you will do great things and surely triumph."

So David went on his way, and Saul returned home.

DAVID AMONG THE PHILISTINES

27 But David thought to himself, "One of these days I will be destroyed by the hand of Saul. The best thing I can do is to escape to the land of the Philistines. Then Saul will give up searching for me anywhere in Israel, and I will slip out of his hand."

2 So David and the six hundred men with him left and went over to Achish son of Maok king of Gath. 3 David and his men settled in Gath with Achish. Each man had his family with him, and David had his two wives: Ahinoam of Jezreel and Abigail of Carmel, the widow of Nabal. 4 When Saul was told that David had fled to Gath, he no longer searched for him.

5 Then David said to Achish, "If I have found favor in your eyes, let a place be assigned to me in one of the country towns, that I may live there. Why should your servant live in the royal city with you?"

6 So on that day Achish gave him Ziklag, and it has belonged to the kings of Judah ever since. 7 David lived in Philistine territory a year and four months.

8 Now David and his men went up and raided the Geshurites, the Girzites and the Amalekites. (From ancient times these peoples had lived in the land extending to Shur and Egypt.) 9 Whenever David attacked an area, he did not leave a man or woman alive, but took sheep and cattle, donkeys and camels, and clothes. Then he returned to Achish.

10 When Achish asked, "Where did you go raiding today?" David would say, "Against the Negev of Judah" or "Against the Negev of Jerahmeel" or "Against the Negev of the Kenites." 11 He did not leave a man or woman alive to be brought to Gath, for he thought, "They might inform on us and say, 'This is what David did.'" And such was his practice as long as he lived in Philistine territory. 12 Achish trusted David and said to himself, "He has become so obnoxious to his people, the Israelites, that he will be my servant for life."

PRAYING SCRIPTURE

1 Samuel 27

In an attempt to escape Saul's grasp, David and his men moved their base of operations to the land of their perpetual enemies, the Philistines. From there they executed multiple raids back in Judah, victorious at every turn.

Have you ever been forced into a position you did not desire? God does not abandon us when life throws curves. Pray that he will make you victorious in unexpected circumstances.

28 In those days the Philistines gathered their forces to fight against Israel. Achish said to David, "You must understand that you and your men will accompany me in the army."

2 David said, "Then you will see for yourself what your servant can do."

Achish replied, "Very well, I will make you my bodyguard for life."

SAUL AND THE MEDIUM AT ENDOR

3 Now Samuel was dead, and all Israel had mourned for him and buried him in his own town of Ramah. Saul had expelled the mediums and spiritists from the land.

4 The Philistines assembled and came and set up camp at Shunem, while Saul gathered all Israel and set up camp at Gilboa. 5 When Saul saw the Philistine army, he was afraid; terror filled his heart. 6 He inquired of the LORD, but the LORD did not answer him by dreams or Urim or prophets. 7 Saul then said to his attendants, "Find me a woman who is a medium, so I may go and inquire of her."

"There is one in Endor," they said.

PRAYING SCRIPTURE

1 Samuel 28

After the prophet Samuel's death, King Saul had no one to ask about God's will. He had previously dispelled mediums from the land, but he unwisely sought a medium for insight in the face of the gathered Philistine army.

Scripture prohibits seeking advice from spirits. To do so is to expose ourselves to demons. God, instead, gives us direction from his Word and in prayer.

8 So Saul disguised himself, putting on other clothes, and at night
he and two men went to the woman. "Consult a spirit for me," he said,
"and bring up for me the one I name."
9 But the woman said to him, "Surely you know what Saul has done.
He has cut off the mediums and spiritists from the land. Why have you
set a trap for my life to bring about my death?"
10 Saul swore to her by the LORD, "As surely as the LORD lives, you will
not be punished for this."
11 Then the woman asked, "Whom shall I bring up for you?"
"Bring up Samuel," he said.
12 When the woman saw Samuel, she cried out at the top of her voice
and said to Saul, "Why have you deceived me? You are Saul!"
13 The king said to her, "Don't be afraid. What do you see?"
The woman said, "I see a ghostly figure[a] coming up out of the earth."
14 "What does he look like?" he asked.
"An old man wearing a robe is coming up," she said.
Then Saul knew it was Samuel, and he bowed down and prostrated
himself with his face to the ground.
15 Samuel said to Saul, "Why have you disturbed me by bringing
me up?"
"I am in great distress," Saul said. "The Philistines are fighting against
me, and God has departed from me. He no longer answers me, either by
prophets or by dreams. So I have called on you to tell me what to do."
16 Samuel said, "Why do you consult me, now that the LORD has de-
parted from you and become your enemy? 17 The LORD has done what
he predicted through me. The LORD has torn the kingdom out of your
hands and given it to one of your neighbors — to David. 18 Because you
did not obey the LORD or carry out his fierce wrath against the Amalek-
ites, the LORD has done this to you today. 19 The LORD will deliver both
Israel and you into the hands of the Philistines, and tomorrow you and
your sons will be with me. The LORD will also give the army of Israel
into the hands of the Philistines."
20 Immediately Saul fell full length on the ground, filled with fear
because of Samuel's words. His strength was gone, for he had eaten
nothing all that day and all that night.
21 When the woman came to Saul and saw that he was greatly shaken,
she said, "Look, your servant has obeyed you. I took my life in my
hands and did what you told me to do. 22 Now please listen to your
servant and let me give you some food so you may eat and have the
strength to go on your way."
23 He refused and said, "I will not eat."
But his men joined the woman in urging him, and he listened to
them. He got up from the ground and sat on the couch.
24 The woman had a fattened calf at the house, which she butchered
at once. She took some flour, kneaded it and baked bread without
yeast. 25 Then she set it before Saul and his men, and they ate. That
same night they got up and left.

ACHISH SENDS DAVID BACK TO ZIKLAG

29 The Philistines gathered all their forces at Aphek, and Israel
camped by the spring in Jezreel. 2 As the Philistine rulers
marched with their units of hundreds and thousands, David and his

[a] 13 Or *see spirits*; or *see gods*

PRAYING SCRIPTURE

1 Samuel 29

Have you ever felt like an outsider where you were once welcomed? Maybe in a group at school or a church where people turned against you? Being shunned or ostracized for no reason is a powerfully negative experience.

The emotion of being rejected by a community can be overwhelming. Thankfully, God has promised never to leave or forsake his children. Thank him for that promise and rest in it.

men were marching at the rear with Achish. 3 The commanders of the
Philistines asked, "What about these Hebrews?"
Achish replied, "Is this not David, who was an officer of Saul king of
Israel? He has already been with me for over a year, and from the day
he left Saul until now, I have found no fault in him."
4 But the Philistine commanders were angry with Achish and said,
"Send the man back, that he may return to the place you assigned him.
He must not go with us into battle, or he will turn against us during the
fighting. How better could he regain his master's favor than by taking
the heads of our own men? 5 Isn't this the David they sang about in
their dances:

"'Saul has slain his thousands,
and David his tens of thousands'?"

6 So Achish called David and said to him, "As surely as the LORD lives,
you have been reliable, and I would be pleased to have you serve with
me in the army. From the day you came to me until today, I have found
no fault in you, but the rulers don't approve of you. 7 Now turn back and
go in peace; do nothing to displease the Philistine rulers."
8 "But what have I done?" asked David. "What have you found against
your servant from the day I came to you until now? Why can't I go and
fight against the enemies of my lord the king?"
9 Achish answered, "I know that you have been as pleasing in my
eyes as an angel of God; nevertheless, the Philistine commanders have
said, 'He must not go up with us into battle.' 10 Now get up early, along
with your master's servants who have come with you, and leave in the
morning as soon as it is light."
11 So David and his men got up early in the morning to go back to the
land of the Philistines, and the Philistines went up to Jezreel.

DAVID DESTROYS THE AMALEKITES

30 David and his men reached Ziklag on the third day. Now the
Amalekites had raided the Negev and Ziklag. They had at-
tacked Ziklag and burned it, 2 and had taken captive the women and
everyone else in it, both young and old. They killed none of them, but
carried them off as they went on their way.
3 When David and his men reached Ziklag, they found it destroyed by
fire and their wives and sons and daughters taken captive. 4 So David
and his men wept aloud until they had no strength left to weep. 5 Da-
vid's two wives had been captured — Ahinoam of Jezreel and Abigail,
the widow of Nabal of Carmel. 6 David was greatly distressed because
the men were talking of stoning him; each one was bitter in spirit be-
cause of his sons and daughters. But David found strength in the LORD
his God.
7 Then David said to Abiathar the priest, the son of Ahimelek, "Bring
me the ephod." Abiathar brought it to him, 8 and David inquired of the
LORD, "Shall I pursue this raiding party? Will I overtake them?"
"Pursue them," he answered. "You will certainly overtake them and
succeed in the rescue."
9 David and the six hundred men with him came to the Besor Val-
ley, where some stayed behind. 10 Two hundred of them were too
exhausted to cross the valley, but David and the other four hundred
continued the pursuit.
11 They found an Egyptian in a field and brought him to David. They

PRAYING SCRIPTURE

1 Samuel 30

In the midst of overwhelming calamity—their city was burned, and the families of David and his men taken captive—David found strength in the Lord his God. David refused to let his circumstances dictate his spirit and emotions.

When life is overwhelming, when family relations are strained, when calamity strikes, God will provide the strength you need to overcome. Strengthen yourself in him! Call on his name, and he will help you.

gave him water to drink and food to eat— 12part of a cake of pressed
figs and two cakes of raisins. He ate and was revived, for he had not
eaten any food or drunk any water for three days and three nights.
13David asked him, "Who do you belong to? Where do you come
from?"
He said, "I am an Egyptian, the slave of an Amalekite. My master
abandoned me when I became ill three days ago. 14We raided the
Negev of the Kerethites, some territory belonging to Judah and the
Negev of Caleb. And we burned Ziklag."
15David asked him, "Can you lead me down to this raiding party?"
He answered, "Swear to me before God that you will not kill me or
hand me over to my master, and I will take you down to them."
16He led David down, and there they were, scattered over the coun-
tryside, eating, drinking and reveling because of the great amount of
plunder they had taken from the land of the Philistines and from Ju-
dah. 17David fought them from dusk until the evening of the next day,
and none of them got away, except four hundred young men who rode
off on camels and fled. 18David recovered everything the Amalekites
had taken, including his two wives. 19Nothing was missing: young or
old, boy or girl, plunder or anything else they had taken. David brought
everything back. 20He took all the flocks and herds, and his men drove
them ahead of the other livestock, saying, "This is David's plunder."
21Then David came to the two hundred men who had been too ex-
hausted to follow him and who were left behind at the Besor Valley.
They came out to meet David and the men with him. As David and
his men approached, he asked them how they were. 22But all the evil
men and troublemakers among David's followers said, "Because they
did not go out with us, we will not share with them the plunder we re-
covered. However, each man may take his wife and children and go."
23David replied, "No, my brothers, you must not do that with what
the LORD has given us. He has protected us and delivered into our
hands the raiding party that came against us. 24Who will listen to what
you say? The share of the man who stayed with the supplies is to be
the same as that of him who went down to the battle. All will share
alike." 25David made this a statute and ordinance for Israel from that
day to this.
26When David reached Ziklag, he sent some of the plunder to the el-
ders of Judah, who were his friends, saying, "Here is a gift for you from
the plunder of the LORD's enemies."
27David sent it to those who were in Bethel, Ramoth Negev and Jattir;
28to those in Aroer, Siphmoth, Eshtemoa 29and Rakal; to those in the
towns of the Jerahmeelites and the Kenites; 30to those in Hormah, Bor
Ashan, Athak 31and Hebron; and to those in all the other places where
he and his men had roamed.

SAUL TAKES HIS LIFE

31 Now the Philistines fought against Israel; the Israelites fled be-
fore them, and many fell dead on Mount Gilboa. 2The Philis-
tines were in hot pursuit of Saul and his sons, and they killed his sons
Jonathan, Abinadab and Malki-Shua. 3The fighting grew fierce around
Saul, and when the archers overtook him, they wounded him critically.
4Saul said to his armor-bearer, "Draw your sword and run me
through, or these uncircumcised fellows will come and run me through
and abuse me."

PRAYING SCRIPTURE

1 Samuel 31

Saul's ignominious decline came to a tragic end as he was running from the Philistines. Three of Saul's sons were killed, while Saul was severely wounded. In a desperate ploy to avoid capture, Saul committed suicide.

God uses the courses of this world to accomplish his ends. God sovereignly rules over all; this cannot be denied. Thank God that he is working all things to his glory.

But his armor-bearer was terrified and would not do it; so Saul took
his own sword and fell on it. 5When the armor-bearer saw that Saul was
dead, he too fell on his sword and died with him. 6So Saul and his three
sons and his armor-bearer and all his men died together that same day.

7When the Israelites along the valley and those across the Jordan
saw that the Israelite army had fled and that Saul and his sons had
died, they abandoned their towns and fled. And the Philistines came
and occupied them.

8The next day, when the Philistines came to strip the dead, they
found Saul and his three sons fallen on Mount Gilboa. 9They cut off his
head and stripped off his armor, and they sent messengers throughout
the land of the Philistines to proclaim the news in the temple of their
idols and among their people. 10They put his armor in the temple of
the Ashtoreths and fastened his body to the wall of Beth Shan.

11When the people of Jabesh Gilead heard what the Philistines had
done to Saul, 12all their valiant men marched through the night to Beth
Shan. They took down the bodies of Saul and his sons from the wall of
Beth Shan and went to Jabesh, where they burned them. 13Then they
took their bones and buried them under a tamarisk tree at Jabesh, and
they fasted seven days.

2 SAMUEL

The second book of Samuel picks up where the first left off, with the deaths of Saul and Jonathan. The rebellious life of Saul comes to an ignominious end with him committing suicide on the battlefield after being wounded severely. David, who steadfastly refused to attack God's anointed king, mourned the deaths of the king and his best friend, Saul's son, Jonathan. We might have reason to expect David to become king upon Saul's death, given that Samuel had anointed him while at Jesse's house. Instead, Saul's son Ish-Bosheth was anointed king by most of the tribes. Judah accepted David as king, setting off a brutal civil war.

The Lord gave David victory in the civil war, fulfilling Samuel's promise that David would become king over Israel. In chapters 6 and 7, the ark came to rest in Jerusalem, resulting in a celebration of God's goodness to Israel. When David sought to build a physical house for the Lord, he was rebuffed. The Lord promised to build a symbolic house for David instead. In a moment that carries immense implications for Biblical narrative, God made a covenant with David and promised that someone from his family would rule on the throne forever. David could not have known exactly that this descendant would be Jesus Christ the Messiah, born hundreds of years after David's death.

If one were to read 2 Samuel from beginning to end in one sitting, they would notice a distinct turn in the book's direction, starting with chapter 11. David sinned in his sexual encounter with Bathsheba, then covered it up by having her husband, Uriah, murdered. The prophet Nathan confronted David with a parable about a rich man stealing a lamb from his neighbor. As David grew angry and plotted for the man to make restitution and suffer his fate, Nathan informed him, "You are the man!" (12:7). David, despite being king and having many wives and concubines, could not resist taking another man's wife.

After David's sin, the circumstances of his life and within his family fell apart. His son Amnon raped David's daughter, Amnon's half sister Tamar. Tamar was avenged by her brother Absalom, who killed Amnon. Absalom then turned on David, leading a revolt to try to kill his father and take his throne. Even when David's armies finally won a victory over Absalom, David could not rejoice in his deliverance because it meant the death of his son. David's reign ended with a pestilence upon the people because David sinned against the Lord by numbering the military men in Israel rather than taking a full census.

Second Samuel should remind us of our need not only to pray in all of life's circumstances but to combine obedience with our prayers. Offering perfunctory, ritualistic prayers is useless. If we pray and sin anyway, what good has been accomplished? Prayer brings us into the presence of God to leave with his power. Obedience is the evidence that our prayers were sincere.

DAVID HEARS OF SAUL'S DEATH

1 After the death of Saul, David returned from striking down the
Amalekites and stayed in Ziklag two days. 2On the third day a man
arrived from Saul's camp with his clothes torn and dust on his head.
When he came to David, he fell to the ground to pay him honor.
3"Where have you come from?" David asked him.
He answered, "I have escaped from the Israelite camp."
4"What happened?" David asked. "Tell me."
"The men fled from the battle," he replied. "Many of them fell and
died. And Saul and his son Jonathan are dead."
5Then David said to the young man who brought him the report,
"How do you know that Saul and his son Jonathan are dead?"
6"I happened to be on Mount Gilboa," the young man said, "and
there was Saul, leaning on his spear, with the chariots and their driv-
ers in hot pursuit. 7When he turned around and saw me, he called out
to me, and I said, 'What can I do?'
8"He asked me, 'Who are you?'
"'An Amalekite,' I answered.
9"Then he said to me, 'Stand here by me and kill me! I'm in the
throes of death, but I'm still alive.'
10"So I stood beside him and killed him, because I knew that after he
had fallen he could not survive. And I took the crown that was on his
head and the band on his arm and have brought them here to my lord."
11Then David and all the men with him took hold of their clothes and
tore them. 12They mourned and wept and fasted till evening for Saul
and his son Jonathan, and for the army of the LORD and for the nation
of Israel, because they had fallen by the sword.
13David said to the young man who brought him the report, "Where
are you from?"
"I am the son of a foreigner, an Amalekite," he answered.
14David asked him, "Why weren't you afraid to lift your hand to de-
stroy the LORD's anointed?"
15Then David called one of his men and said, "Go, strike him down!"
So he struck him down, and he died. 16For David had said to him, "Your
blood be on your own head. Your own mouth testified against you
when you said, 'I killed the LORD's anointed.'"

DAVID'S LAMENT FOR SAUL AND JONATHAN

17David took up this lament concerning Saul and his son Jonathan,
18and he ordered that the people of Judah be taught this lament of the
bow (it is written in the Book of Jashar):

19 "A gazelle[a] lies slain on your heights, Israel.
    How the mighty have fallen!

20 "Tell it not in Gath,
    proclaim it not in the streets of Ashkelon,
lest the daughters of the Philistines be glad,
    lest the daughters of the uncircumcised rejoice.

21 "Mountains of Gilboa,
    may you have neither dew nor rain,
    may no showers fall on your terraced fields.[b]

PRAYING SCRIPTURE

2 Samuel 1

Do you ever lament over the death of someone who has opposed you? Most of us do not have enemies who try to kill us, but some do have people who make life difficult. When Saul and Jonathan were killed in battle, David lamented not only his dear friend but also Saul, who'd tried numerous times to kill him.

Ask God to help you genuinely love those who oppose you.

[a] 19 *Gazelle* here symbolizes a human dignitary. [b] 21 Or / *nor fields that yield grain for offerings*

For there the shield of the mighty was despised,
the shield of Saul—no longer rubbed with oil.

22 "From the blood of the slain,
from the flesh of the mighty,
the bow of Jonathan did not turn back,
the sword of Saul did not return unsatisfied.
23 Saul and Jonathan—
in life they were loved and admired,
and in death they were not parted.
They were swifter than eagles,
they were stronger than lions.

24 "Daughters of Israel,
weep for Saul,
who clothed you in scarlet and finery,
who adorned your garments with ornaments of gold.

25 "How the mighty have fallen in battle!
Jonathan lies slain on your heights.
26 I grieve for you, Jonathan my brother;
you were very dear to me.
Your love for me was wonderful,
more wonderful than that of women.
27 "How the mighty have fallen!
The weapons of war have perished!"

DAVID ANOINTED KING OVER JUDAH

2 In the course of time, David inquired of the LORD. "Shall I go up to
one of the towns of Judah?" he asked.
The LORD said, "Go up."
David asked, "Where shall I go?"
"To Hebron," the LORD answered.
2 So David went up there with his two wives, Ahinoam of Jezreel and
Abigail, the widow of Nabal of Carmel. 3 David also took the men who
were with him, each with his family, and they settled in Hebron and
its towns. 4 Then the men of Judah came to Hebron, and there they
anointed David king over the tribe of Judah.
When David was told that it was the men from Jabesh Gilead who
had buried Saul, 5 he sent messengers to them to say to them, "The
LORD bless you for showing this kindness to Saul your master by bury-
ing him. 6 May the LORD now show you kindness and faithfulness, and
I too will show you the same favor because you have done this. 7 Now
then, be strong and brave, for Saul your master is dead, and the people
of Judah have anointed me king over them."

WAR BETWEEN THE HOUSES OF DAVID AND SAUL

8 Meanwhile, Abner son of Ner, the commander of Saul's army, had
taken Ish-Bosheth son of Saul and brought him over to Mahanaim. 9 He
made him king over Gilead, Ashuri and Jezreel, and also over Ephraim,
Benjamin and all Israel.
10 Ish-Bosheth son of Saul was forty years old when he became king
over Israel, and he reigned two years. The tribe of Judah, however, re-
mained loyal to David. 11 The length of time David was king in Hebron
over Judah was seven years and six months.

PRAYING SCRIPTURE

2 Samuel 2

The death of Saul and anointing of David as king did not result in a smooth succession. Instead, a civil war broke out between David's house and those who supported the line of Saul. God sovereignly kept his promise of a Messianic line while allowing the negative impacts an earthly king had on the people.

God can work good from our mistakes, but we should pray that he works through our obedience instead.

12Abner son of Ner, together with the men of Ish-Bosheth son of Saul,
left Mahanaim and went to Gibeon. 13Joab son of Zeruiah and David's
men went out and met them at the pool of Gibeon. One group sat down
on one side of the pool and one group on the other side.
14Then Abner said to Joab, "Let's have some of the young men get up
and fight hand to hand in front of us."
"All right, let them do it," Joab said.
15So they stood up and were counted off — twelve men for Benjamin
and Ish-Bosheth son of Saul, and twelve for David. 16Then each man
grabbed his opponent by the head and thrust his dagger into his op-
ponent's side, and they fell down together. So that place in Gibeon was
called Helkath Hazzurim.[a]
17The battle that day was very fierce, and Abner and the Israelites
were defeated by David's men.
18The three sons of Zeruiah were there: Joab, Abishai and Asahel.
Now Asahel was as fleet-footed as a wild gazelle. 19He chased Abner,
turning neither to the right nor to the left as he pursued him. 20Abner
looked behind him and asked, "Is that you, Asahel?"
"It is," he answered.
21Then Abner said to him, "Turn aside to the right or to the left; take
on one of the young men and strip him of his weapons." But Asahel
would not stop chasing him.
22Again Abner warned Asahel, "Stop chasing me! Why should I strike
you down? How could I look your brother Joab in the face?"
23But Asahel refused to give up the pursuit; so Abner thrust the butt
of his spear into Asahel's stomach, and the spear came out through his
back. He fell there and died on the spot. And every man stopped when
he came to the place where Asahel had fallen and died.
24But Joab and Abishai pursued Abner, and as the sun was setting,
they came to the hill of Ammah, near Giah on the way to the wasteland
of Gibeon. 25Then the men of Benjamin rallied behind Abner. They
formed themselves into a group and took their stand on top of a hill.
26Abner called out to Joab, "Must the sword devour forever? Don't
you realize that this will end in bitterness? How long before you order
your men to stop pursuing their fellow Israelites?"
27Joab answered, "As surely as God lives, if you had not spoken, the
men would have continued pursuing them until morning."
28So Joab blew the trumpet, and all the troops came to a halt; they
no longer pursued Israel, nor did they fight anymore.
29All that night Abner and his men marched through the Arabah.
They crossed the Jordan, continued through the morning hours[b] and
came to Mahanaim.
30Then Joab stopped pursuing Abner and assembled the whole
army. Besides Asahel, nineteen of David's men were found missing.
31But David's men had killed three hundred and sixty Benjamites who
were with Abner. 32They took Asahel and buried him in his father's
tomb at Bethlehem. Then Joab and his men marched all night and ar-
rived at Hebron by daybreak.

3 The war between the house of Saul and the house of David lasted
a long time. David grew stronger and stronger, while the house of
Saul grew weaker and weaker.

[a] 16 *Helkath Hazzurim* means *field of daggers* or *field of hostilities.* [b] 29 See Septuagint; the meaning of the Hebrew for this phrase is uncertain.

PRAYING SCRIPTURE

2 Samuel 3

Murder and mayhem marked the struggle for the throne. When life is ravaged by the pursuit of earthly power, the results can be tragic, as seen in Joab's treachery. David, for his part, considered his kingdom guiltless.

There are more ways to execute treachery than by physical harm. Gossip, slander and double-dealing all grow from the same heart. Ask God to keep you free from the sins that destroy others.

2 Sons were born to David in Hebron:
His firstborn was Amnon the son of Ahinoam of Jezreel;
3 his second, Kileab the son of Abigail the widow of Nabal of Carmel;
the third, Absalom the son of Maakah daughter of Talmai king of Geshur;
4 the fourth, Adonijah the son of Haggith;
the fifth, Shephatiah the son of Abital;
5 and the sixth, Ithream the son of David's wife Eglah.
These were born to David in Hebron.

ABNER GOES OVER TO DAVID

6 During the war between the house of Saul and the house of David,
Abner had been strengthening his own position in the house of Saul.
7 Now Saul had had a concubine named Rizpah daughter of Aiah. And Ish-
Bosheth said to Abner, "Why did you sleep with my father's concubine?"
8 Abner was very angry because of what Ish-Bosheth said. So he answered, "Am I a dog's head — on Judah's side? This very day I am loyal to the house of your father Saul and to his family and friends. I haven't handed you over to David. Yet now you accuse me of an offense involv-
ing this woman! 9 May God deal with Abner, be it ever so severely, if I do
not do for David what the LORD promised him on oath 10 and transfer
the kingdom from the house of Saul and establish David's throne over
Israel and Judah from Dan to Beersheba." 11 Ish-Bosheth did not dare to
say another word to Abner, because he was afraid of him.
12 Then Abner sent messengers on his behalf to say to David, "Whose land is it? Make an agreement with me, and I will help you bring all Israel over to you."
13 "Good," said David. "I will make an agreement with you. But I demand one thing of you: Do not come into my presence unless you
bring Michal daughter of Saul when you come to see me." 14 Then Da-
vid sent messengers to Ish-Bosheth son of Saul, demanding, "Give me my wife Michal, whom I betrothed to myself for the price of a hundred Philistine foreskins."
15 So Ish-Bosheth gave orders and had her taken away from her hus-
band Paltiel son of Laish. 16 Her husband, however, went with her, weeping behind her all the way to Bahurim. Then Abner said to him, "Go back home!" So he went back.
17 Abner conferred with the elders of Israel and said, "For some time
you have wanted to make David your king. 18 Now do it! For the LORD
promised David, 'By my servant David I will rescue my people Israel from the hand of the Philistines and from the hand of all their enemies.'"
19 Abner also spoke to the Benjamites in person. Then he went to Hebron to tell David everything that Israel and the whole tribe of Ben-
jamin wanted to do. 20 When Abner, who had twenty men with him,
came to David at Hebron, David prepared a feast for him and his men.
21 Then Abner said to David, "Let me go at once and assemble all Israel for my lord the king, so that they may make a covenant with you, and that you may rule over all that your heart desires." So David sent Abner away, and he went in peace.

JOAB MURDERS ABNER

22 Just then David's men and Joab returned from a raid and brought with them a great deal of plunder. But Abner was no longer with David

in Hebron, because David had sent him away, and he had gone in
peace. 23When Joab and all the soldiers with him arrived, he was told
that Abner son of Ner had come to the king and that the king had sent
him away and that he had gone in peace.

24So Joab went to the king and said, "What have you done? Look, Ab-
ner came to you. Why did you let him go? Now he is gone! 25You know
Abner son of Ner; he came to deceive you and observe your move-
ments and find out everything you are doing."

26Joab then left David and sent messengers after Abner, and they
brought him back from the cistern at Sirah. But David did not know
it. 27Now when Abner returned to Hebron, Joab took him aside into an
inner chamber, as if to speak with him privately. And there, to avenge
the blood of his brother Asahel, Joab stabbed him in the stomach, and
he died.

28Later, when David heard about this, he said, "I and my kingdom
are forever innocent before the LORD concerning the blood of Abner
son of Ner. 29May his blood fall on the head of Joab and on his whole
family! May Joab's family never be without someone who has a run-
ning sore or leprosy[a] or who leans on a crutch or who falls by the sword
or who lacks food."

30(Joab and his brother Abishai murdered Abner because he had
killed their brother Asahel in the battle at Gibeon.)

31Then David said to Joab and all the people with him, "Tear your
clothes and put on sackcloth and walk in mourning in front of Abner."
King David himself walked behind the bier. 32They buried Abner in He-
bron, and the king wept aloud at Abner's tomb. All the people wept also.

33The king sang this lament for Abner:

"Should Abner have died as the lawless die?
34 Your hands were not bound,
your feet were not fettered.
You fell as one falls before the wicked."

And all the people wept over him again.

35Then they all came and urged David to eat something while it was
still day; but David took an oath, saying, "May God deal with me, be it
ever so severely, if I taste bread or anything else before the sun sets!"

36All the people took note and were pleased; indeed, everything the
king did pleased them. 37So on that day all the people there and all Is-
rael knew that the king had no part in the murder of Abner son of Ner.

38Then the king said to his men, "Do you not realize that a commander
and a great man has fallen in Israel this day? 39And today, though I am
the anointed king, I am weak, and these sons of Zeruiah are too strong
for me. May the LORD repay the evildoer according to his evil deeds!"

ISH-BOSHETH MURDERED

4 When Ish-Bosheth son of Saul heard that Abner had died in He-
bron, he lost courage, and all Israel became alarmed. 2Now Saul's
son had two men who were leaders of raiding bands. One was named
Baanah and the other Rekab; they were sons of Rimmon the Beerothite
from the tribe of Benjamin — Beeroth is considered part of Benjamin,
3because the people of Beeroth fled to Gittaim and have resided there
as foreigners to this day.

[a] 29 The Hebrew for *leprosy* was used for various diseases affecting the skin.

PRAYING SCRIPTURE

2 Samuel 4

As the bloodletting continued with killing and reprisal killings, prayer became conspicuous for its absence. God is referenced on occasion, but we don't read of anyone calling on the name of the Lord or asking for wisdom.

It is easy for life to snowball into a series of events to which we react. Asking God for wisdom and seeking his face in trying times is the better way.

4(Jonathan son of Saul had a son who was lame in both feet. He was
five years old when the news about Saul and Jonathan came from Jez-
reel. His nurse picked him up and fled, but as she hurried to leave, he
fell and became disabled. His name was Mephibosheth.)
5Now Rekab and Baanah, the sons of Rimmon the Beerothite, set out
for the house of Ish-Bosheth, and they arrived there in the heat of the
day while he was taking his noonday rest. 6They went into the inner
part of the house as if to get some wheat, and they stabbed him in the
stomach. Then Rekab and his brother Baanah slipped away.
7They had gone into the house while he was lying on the bed in his
bedroom. After they stabbed and killed him, they cut off his head. Tak-
ing it with them, they traveled all night by way of the Arabah. 8They
brought the head of Ish-Bosheth to David at Hebron and said to the
king, "Here is the head of Ish-Bosheth son of Saul, your enemy, who
tried to kill you. This day the LORD has avenged my lord the king
against Saul and his offspring."
9David answered Rekab and his brother Baanah, the sons of Rim-
mon the Beerothite, "As surely as the LORD lives, who has delivered
me out of every trouble, 10when someone told me, 'Saul is dead,' and
thought he was bringing good news, I seized him and put him to death
in Ziklag. That was the reward I gave him for his news! 11How much
more — when wicked men have killed an innocent man in his own
house and on his own bed — should I not now demand his blood from
your hand and rid the earth of you!"
12So David gave an order to his men, and they killed them. They cut
off their hands and feet and hung the bodies by the pool in Hebron.
But they took the head of Ish-Bosheth and buried it in Abner's tomb
at Hebron.

DAVID BECOMES KING OVER ISRAEL

5 All the tribes of Israel came to David at Hebron and said, "We are
your own flesh and blood. 2In the past, while Saul was king over
us, you were the one who led Israel on their military campaigns. And
the LORD said to you, 'You will shepherd my people Israel, and you will
become their ruler.'"
3When all the elders of Israel had come to King David at Hebron, the
king made a covenant with them at Hebron before the LORD, and they
anointed David king over Israel.
4David was thirty years old when he became king, and he reigned forty
years. 5In Hebron he reigned over Judah seven years and six months,
and in Jerusalem he reigned over all Israel and Judah thirty-three years.

PRAYING SCRIPTURE

2 Samuel 5

Finally, all the elders surrendered to God's will and anointed David as king over all of Israel, initiating a 40-year reign. And we see again David inquiring of God and God answering him.

Sometimes we can feel too busy to pray. Before long, prayer is crowded out altogether. Ask God to help you prioritize prayer so that it happens all through your day.

DAVID CONQUERS JERUSALEM

6The king and his men marched to Jerusalem to attack the Jebu-
sites, who lived there. The Jebusites said to David, "You will not get
in here; even the blind and the lame can ward you off." They thought,
"David cannot get in here." 7Nevertheless, David captured the fortress
of Zion — which is the City of David.
8On that day David had said, "Anyone who conquers the Jebusites
will have to use the water shaft to reach those 'lame and blind' who
are David's enemies.[a]" That is why they say, "The 'blind and lame' will
not enter the palace."

---

[a] 8 Or *are hated by David*

9David then took up residence in the fortress and called it the City of
David. He built up the area around it, from the terraces[a] inward. 10And
he became more and more powerful, because the LORD God Almighty
was with him.
11Now Hiram king of Tyre sent envoys to David, along with cedar logs
and carpenters and stonemasons, and they built a palace for David.
12Then David knew that the LORD had established him as king over
Israel and had exalted his kingdom for the sake of his people Israel.
13After he left Hebron, David took more concubines and wives in
Jerusalem, and more sons and daughters were born to him. 14These
are the names of the children born to him there: Shammua, Shobab,
Nathan, Solomon, 15Ibhar, Elishua, Nepheg, Japhia, 16Elishama, Eliada
and Eliphelet.

DAVID DEFEATS THE PHILISTINES

17When the Philistines heard that David had been anointed king over
Israel, they went up in full force to search for him, but David heard
about it and went down to the stronghold. 18Now the Philistines had
come and spread out in the Valley of Rephaim; 19so David inquired of
the LORD, "Shall I go and attack the Philistines? Will you deliver them
into my hands?"
The LORD answered him, "Go, for I will surely deliver the Philistines
into your hands."
20So David went to Baal Perazim, and there he defeated them. He
said, "As waters break out, the LORD has broken out against my enemies
before me." So that place was called Baal Perazim.[b] 21The Philistines
abandoned their idols there, and David and his men carried them off.
22Once more the Philistines came up and spread out in the Valley of
Rephaim; 23so David inquired of the LORD, and he answered, "Do not
go straight up, but circle around behind them and attack them in front
of the poplar trees. 24As soon as you hear the sound of marching in the
tops of the poplar trees, move quickly, because that will mean the LORD
has gone out in front of you to strike the Philistine army." 25So David
did as the LORD commanded him, and he struck down the Philistines
all the way from Gibeon[c] to Gezer.

THE ARK BROUGHT TO JERUSALEM

6 David again brought together all the able young men of Israel—
thirty thousand. 2He and all his men went to Baalah[d] in Judah to
bring up from there the ark of God, which is called by the Name,[e] the
name of the LORD Almighty, who is enthroned between the cherubim
on the ark. 3They set the ark of God on a new cart and brought it from
the house of Abinadab, which was on the hill. Uzzah and Ahio, sons of
Abinadab, were guiding the new cart 4with the ark of God on it,[f] and
Ahio was walking in front of it. 5David and all Israel were celebrating
with all their might before the LORD, with castanets,[g] harps, lyres, tim-
brels, sistrums and cymbals.

[a] 9 Or *the Millo* [b] 20 *Baal Perazim* means *the lord who breaks out.*
[c] 25 Septuagint (see also 1 Chron. 14:16); Hebrew *Geba* [d] 2 That is, Kiriath Jearim (see 1 Chron. 13:6) [e] 2 Hebrew; Septuagint and Vulgate do not have *the Name.* [f] 3,4 Dead Sea Scrolls and some Septuagint manuscripts; Masoretic Text *cart* 4*and they brought it with the ark of God from the house of Abinadab, which was on the hill* [g] 5 Masoretic Text; Dead Sea Scrolls and Septuagint (see also 1 Chron. 13:8) *songs*

PRAYING SCRIPTURE

2 Samuel 6

It was time for the ark of the covenant to return to Jerusalem. But after many years in the house of Abinadab, familiarity bred disaster. Rather than being carried on the priests' shoulders, it was loaded on a cart. When the ox stumbled, Uzzah touched the ark and was struck dead.

Treating the things of God as ordinary is dangerous. Pray that God will help you keep everything holy that is holy.

6When they came to the threshing floor of Nakon, Uzzah reached
out and took hold of the ark of God, because the oxen stumbled. 7The
LORD's anger burned against Uzzah because of his irreverent act; there-
fore God struck him down, and he died there beside the ark of God.
8Then David was angry because the LORD's wrath had broken out
against Uzzah, and to this day that place is called Perez Uzzah.[a]
9David was afraid of the LORD that day and said, "How can the ark
of the LORD ever come to me?" 10He was not willing to take the ark of
the LORD to be with him in the City of David. Instead, he took it to the
house of Obed-Edom the Gittite. 11The ark of the LORD remained in
the house of Obed-Edom the Gittite for three months, and the LORD
blessed him and his entire household.
12Now King David was told, "The LORD has blessed the household of
Obed-Edom and everything he has, because of the ark of God." So Da-
vid went to bring up the ark of God from the house of Obed-Edom to
the City of David with rejoicing. 13When those who were carrying the
ark of the LORD had taken six steps, he sacrificed a bull and a fattened
calf. 14Wearing a linen ephod, David was dancing before the LORD with
all his might, 15while he and all Israel were bringing up the ark of the
LORD with shouts and the sound of trumpets.
16As the ark of the LORD was entering the City of David, Michal
daughter of Saul watched from a window. And when she saw King
David leaping and dancing before the LORD, she despised him in her
heart.
17They brought the ark of the LORD and set it in its place inside the
tent that David had pitched for it, and David sacrificed burnt offerings
and fellowship offerings before the LORD. 18After he had finished sac-
rificing the burnt offerings and fellowship offerings, he blessed the
people in the name of the LORD Almighty. 19Then he gave a loaf of
bread, a cake of dates and a cake of raisins to each person in the whole
crowd of Israelites, both men and women. And all the people went to
their homes.
20When David returned home to bless his household, Michal daugh-
ter of Saul came out to meet him and said, "How the king of Israel has
distinguished himself today, going around half-naked in full view of
the slave girls of his servants as any vulgar fellow would!"
21David said to Michal, "It was before the LORD, who chose me rather
than your father or anyone from his house when he appointed me
ruler over the LORD's people Israel — I will celebrate before the LORD.
22I will become even more undignified than this, and I will be humil-
iated in my own eyes. But by these slave girls you spoke of, I will be
held in honor."
23And Michal daughter of Saul had no children to the day of her
death.

GOD'S PROMISE TO DAVID

7 After the king was settled in his palace and the LORD had given
him rest from all his enemies around him, 2he said to Nathan the
prophet, "Here I am, living in a house of cedar, while the ark of God
remains in a tent."
3Nathan replied to the king, "Whatever you have in mind, go ahead
and do it, for the LORD is with you."

[a] 8 *Perez Uzzah* means *outbreak against Uzzah.*

PRAYING SCRIPTURE

2 Samuel 7

Although Israel had a number of leaders since their deliverance from Egypt—Moses, Joshua, many judges—the Messiah's line, the promised seed of Abraham, had not yet been announced. When God made a covenant with David, he established David's house (see verse 11). He promised that his offspring would build a house for the Lord's name and that his kingdom would endure forever (see verse 13).

Establishing David's throne foretold the coming of the Messiah. Thank God that his wisdom and power flawlessly established the way for Jesus.

4But that night the word of the LORD came to Nathan, saying:

5"Go and tell my servant David, 'This is what the LORD says: Are
you the one to build me a house to dwell in? 6I have not dwelt in
a house from the day I brought the Israelites up out of Egypt to
this day. I have been moving from place to place with a tent as
my dwelling. 7Wherever I have moved with all the Israelites, did
I ever say to any of their rulers whom I commanded to shepherd
my people Israel, "Why have you not built me a house of cedar?"'

8"Now then, tell my servant David, 'This is what the LORD Al-
mighty says: I took you from the pasture, from tending the flock,
and appointed you ruler over my people Israel. 9I have been with
you wherever you have gone, and I have cut off all your enemies
from before you. Now I will make your name great, like the names
of the greatest men on earth. 10And I will provide a place for my
people Israel and will plant them so that they can have a home of
their own and no longer be disturbed. Wicked people will not op-
press them anymore, as they did at the beginning 11and have done
ever since the time I appointed leaders[a] over my people Israel. I
will also give you rest from all your enemies.

"'The LORD declares to you that the LORD himself will estab-
lish a house for you: 12When your days are over and you rest with
your ancestors, I will raise up your offspring to succeed you, your
own flesh and blood, and I will establish his kingdom. 13He is the
one who will build a house for my Name, and I will establish the
throne of his kingdom forever. 14I will be his father, and he will be
my son. When he does wrong, I will punish him with a rod wielded
by men, with floggings inflicted by human hands. 15But my love
will never be taken away from him, as I took it away from Saul,
whom I removed from before you. 16Your house and your king-
dom will endure forever before me[b]; your throne will be estab-
lished forever.'"

17Nathan reported to David all the words of this entire revelation.

DAVID'S PRAYER

18Then King David went in and sat before the LORD, and he said:

"Who am I, Sovereign LORD, and what is my family, that you
have brought me this far? 19And as if this were not enough in your
sight, Sovereign LORD, you have also spoken about the future of
the house of your servant — and this decree, Sovereign LORD, is
for a mere human![c]

20"What more can David say to you? For you know your servant,
Sovereign LORD. 21For the sake of your word and according to your
will, you have done this great thing and made it known to your
servant.

22"How great you are, Sovereign LORD! There is no one like you,
and there is no God but you, as we have heard with our own ears.
23And who is like your people Israel — the one nation on earth
that God went out to redeem as a people for himself, and to make
a name for himself, and to perform great and awesome wonders

---

[a] *11* Traditionally *judges* [b] *16* Some Hebrew manuscripts and Septuagint; most Hebrew manuscripts *you* [c] *19* Or *for the human race*

by driving out nations and their gods from before your people,
whom you redeemed from Egypt?[a] 24You have established your
people Israel as your very own forever, and you, LORD, have be-
come their God.
25"And now, LORD God, keep forever the promise you have made
concerning your servant and his house. Do as you promised, 26so
that your name will be great forever. Then people will say, 'The
LORD Almighty is God over Israel!' And the house of your servant
David will be established in your sight.
27"LORD Almighty, God of Israel, you have revealed this to your
servant, saying, 'I will build a house for you.' So your servant has
found courage to pray this prayer to you. 28Sovereign LORD, you
are God! Your covenant is trustworthy, and you have promised
these good things to your servant. 29Now be pleased to bless the
house of your servant, that it may continue forever in your sight;
for you, Sovereign LORD, have spoken, and with your blessing the
house of your servant will be blessed forever."

DAVID'S VICTORIES

PRAYING SCRIPTURE

2 Samuel 8

As David's military exploits continued and his star was on the rise, he dedicated the captured gold and silver to the Lord. These offerings started a pattern of dedication and generosity that would mark David's life.

When God blesses us with financial increase, what should be our response? Ask God to help you generously steward his gifts.

8 In the course of time, David defeated the Philistines and sub-
dued them, and he took Metheg Ammah from the control of the
Philistines.
2David also defeated the Moabites. He made them lie down on
the ground and measured them off with a length of cord. Every two
lengths of them were put to death, and the third length was allowed to
live. So the Moabites became subject to David and brought him tribute.
3Moreover, David defeated Hadadezer son of Rehob, king of Zobah,
when he went to restore his monument at[b] the Euphrates River. 4David
captured a thousand of his chariots, seven thousand charioteers[c] and
twenty thousand foot soldiers. He hamstrung all but a hundred of the
chariot horses.
5When the Arameans of Damascus came to help Hadadezer king of
Zobah, David struck down twenty-two thousand of them. 6He put gar-
risons in the Aramean kingdom of Damascus, and the Arameans be-
came subject to him and brought tribute. The LORD gave David victory
wherever he went.
7David took the gold shields that belonged to the officers of Hadade-
zer and brought them to Jerusalem. 8From Tebah[d] and Berothai, towns
that belonged to Hadadezer, King David took a great quantity of bronze.
9When Tou[e] king of Hamath heard that David had defeated the en-
tire army of Hadadezer, 10he sent his son Joram[f] to King David to greet
him and congratulate him on his victory in battle over Hadadezer, who
had been at war with Tou. Joram brought with him articles of silver, of
gold and of bronze.
11King David dedicated these articles to the LORD, as he had done with
the silver and gold from all the nations he had subdued: 12Edom[g] and

[a] *23* See Septuagint and 1 Chron. 17:21; Hebrew *wonders for your land and before your people, whom you redeemed from Egypt, from the nations and their gods.* [b] *3* Or *his control along* [c] *4* Septuagint (see also Dead Sea Scrolls and 1 Chron. 18:4); Masoretic Text *captured seventeen hundred of his charioteers* [d] *8* See some Septuagint manuscripts (see also 1 Chron. 18:8); Hebrew *Betah.* [e] *9* Hebrew *Toi,* a variant of *Tou;* also in verse 10
[f] *10* A variant of *Hadoram* [g] *12* Some Hebrew manuscripts, Septuagint and Syriac (see also 1 Chron. 18:11); most Hebrew manuscripts *Aram*

Moab, the Ammonites and the Philistines, and Amalek. He also dedi-
cated the plunder taken from Hadadezer son of Rehob, king of Zobah.
13 And David became famous after he returned from striking down
eighteen thousand Edomites[a] in the Valley of Salt.
14 He put garrisons throughout Edom, and all the Edomites became
subject to David. The LORD gave David victory wherever he went.

DAVID'S OFFICIALS

15 David reigned over all Israel, doing what was just and right for all
his people. 16 Joab son of Zeruiah was over the army; Jehoshaphat son
of Ahilud was recorder; 17 Zadok son of Ahitub and Ahimelek son of
Abiathar were priests; Seraiah was secretary; 18 Benaiah son of Jehoiada
was over the Kerethites and Pelethites; and David's sons were priests.[b]

DAVID AND MEPHIBOSHETH

9 David asked, "Is there anyone still left of the house of Saul to
whom I can show kindness for Jonathan's sake?"
2 Now there was a servant of Saul's household named Ziba. They
summoned him to appear before David, and the king said to him, "Are
you Ziba?"
"At your service," he replied.
3 The king asked, "Is there no one still alive from the house of Saul to
whom I can show God's kindness?"
Ziba answered the king, "There is still a son of Jonathan; he is lame
in both feet."
4 "Where is he?" the king asked.
Ziba answered, "He is at the house of Makir son of Ammiel in Lo
Debar."
5 So King David had him brought from Lo Debar, from the house of
Makir son of Ammiel.
6 When Mephibosheth son of Jonathan, the son of Saul, came to Da-
vid, he bowed down to pay him honor.
David said, "Mephibosheth!"
"At your service," he replied.
7 "Don't be afraid," David said to him, "for I will surely show you kind-
ness for the sake of your father Jonathan. I will restore to you all the
land that belonged to your grandfather Saul, and you will always eat
at my table."
8 Mephibosheth bowed down and said, "What is your servant, that
you should notice a dead dog like me?"
9 Then the king summoned Ziba, Saul's steward, and said to him, "I
have given your master's grandson everything that belonged to Saul
and his family. 10 You and your sons and your servants are to farm the
land for him and bring in the crops, so that your master's grandson may
be provided for. And Mephibosheth, grandson of your master, will al-
ways eat at my table." (Now Ziba had fifteen sons and twenty servants.)
11 Then Ziba said to the king, "Your servant will do whatever my lord
the king commands his servant to do." So Mephibosheth ate at David's[c]
table like one of the king's sons.

PRAYING SCRIPTURE

2 Samuel 9

The story of David and Mephibosheth is a beautiful story of God's love for his enemies. David sought to show mercy on behalf of his dear friend Jonathan. God shows mercy to us and has reconciled us to himself through his beloved Son, Jesus Christ. Mephibosheth did not deserve the king's table; we do not deserve the King's blessings.

Pause and praise God for his mercy on undeserving sinners everywhere through Jesus.

---

[a] *13* A few Hebrew manuscripts, Septuagint and Syriac (see also 1 Chron. 18:12); most Hebrew manuscripts *Aram* (that is, Arameans) [b] *18* Or *were chief officials* (see Septuagint and Targum; see also 1 Chron. 18:17)
[c] *11* Septuagint; Hebrew *my*

12Mephibosheth had a young son named Mika, and all the members
of Ziba's household were servants of Mephibosheth. 13And Mephibo-
sheth lived in Jerusalem, because he always ate at the king's table; he
was lame in both feet.

DAVID DEFEATS THE AMMONITES

10 In the course of time, the king of the Ammonites died, and his
son Hanun succeeded him as king. 2David thought, "I will show
kindness to Hanun son of Nahash, just as his father showed kindness
to me." So David sent a delegation to express his sympathy to Hanun
concerning his father.
When David's men came to the land of the Ammonites, 3the Am-
monite commanders said to Hanun their lord, "Do you think David is
honoring your father by sending envoys to you to express sympathy?
Hasn't David sent them to you only to explore the city and spy it out
and overthrow it?" 4So Hanun seized David's envoys, shaved off half
of each man's beard, cut off their garments at the buttocks, and sent
them away.
5When David was told about this, he sent messengers to meet the
men, for they were greatly humiliated. The king said, "Stay at Jericho
till your beards have grown, and then come back."
6When the Ammonites realized that they had become obnoxious to
David, they hired twenty thousand Aramean foot soldiers from Beth
Rehob and Zobah, as well as the king of Maakah with a thousand men,
and also twelve thousand men from Tob.
7On hearing this, David sent Joab out with the entire army of fight-
ing men. 8The Ammonites came out and drew up in battle formation
at the entrance of their city gate, while the Arameans of Zobah and Re-
hob and the men of Tob and Maakah were by themselves in the open
country.
9Joab saw that there were battle lines in front of him and behind
him; so he selected some of the best troops in Israel and deployed them
against the Arameans. 10He put the rest of the men under the com-
mand of Abishai his brother and deployed them against the Ammon-
ites. 11Joab said, "If the Arameans are too strong for me, then you are to
come to my rescue; but if the Ammonites are too strong for you, then I
will come to rescue you. 12Be strong, and let us fight bravely for our peo-
ple and the cities of our God. The LORD will do what is good in his sight."
13Then Joab and the troops with him advanced to fight the Arame-
ans, and they fled before him. 14When the Ammonites realized that
the Arameans were fleeing, they fled before Abishai and went inside
the city. So Joab returned from fighting the Ammonites and came to
Jerusalem.
15After the Arameans saw that they had been routed by Israel, they
regrouped. 16Hadadezer had Arameans brought from beyond the Eu-
phrates River; they went to Helam, with Shobak the commander of
Hadadezer's army leading them.
17When David was told of this, he gathered all Israel, crossed the Jor-
dan and went to Helam. The Arameans formed their battle lines to
meet David and fought against him. 18But they fled before Israel, and
David killed seven hundred of their charioteers and forty thousand
of their foot soldiers.[a] He also struck down Shobak the commander of

PRAYING SCRIPTURE

2 Samuel 10

Sometimes a goodwill gesture is met with someone taking advantage. The best intentions can be misread or used to harm us. How we respond to mistreatment is a reflection of whether we are yielded to the Spirit of God.

Scripture teaches we should treat people the way we desire to be treated, not to repay evil for evil. Ask God to help you repay evil with good and hate with love.

---

[a] *18* Some Septuagint manuscripts (see also 1 Chron. 19:18); Hebrew *horsemen*

their army, and he died there. 19When all the kings who were vassals of Hadadezer saw that they had been routed by Israel, they made peace with the Israelites and became subject to them.

So the Arameans were afraid to help the Ammonites anymore.

DAVID AND BATHSHEBA

11 In the spring, at the time when kings go off to war, David sent Joab out with the king's men and the whole Israelite army. They destroyed the Ammonites and besieged Rabbah. But David remained in Jerusalem.

2One evening David got up from his bed and walked around on the roof of the palace. From the roof he saw a woman bathing. The woman was very beautiful, 3and David sent someone to find out about her. The man said, "She is Bathsheba, the daughter of Eliam and the wife of Uriah the Hittite." 4Then David sent messengers to get her. She came to him, and he slept with her. (Now she was purifying herself from her monthly uncleanness.) Then she went back home. 5The woman conceived and sent word to David, saying, "I am pregnant."

6So David sent this word to Joab: "Send me Uriah the Hittite." And Joab sent him to David. 7When Uriah came to him, David asked him how Joab was, how the soldiers were and how the war was going. 8Then David said to Uriah, "Go down to your house and wash your feet." So Uriah left the palace, and a gift from the king was sent after him. 9But Uriah slept at the entrance to the palace with all his master's servants and did not go down to his house.

10David was told, "Uriah did not go home." So he asked Uriah, "Haven't you just come from a military campaign? Why didn't you go home?"

11Uriah said to David, "The ark and Israel and Judah are staying in tents,[a] and my commander Joab and my lord's men are camped in the open country. How could I go to my house to eat and drink and make love to my wife? As surely as you live, I will not do such a thing!"

12Then David said to him, "Stay here one more day, and tomorrow I will send you back." So Uriah remained in Jerusalem that day and the next. 13At David's invitation, he ate and drank with him, and David made him drunk. But in the evening Uriah went out to sleep on his mat among his master's servants; he did not go home.

14In the morning David wrote a letter to Joab and sent it with Uriah. 15In it he wrote, "Put Uriah out in front where the fighting is fiercest. Then withdraw from him so he will be struck down and die."

16So while Joab had the city under siege, he put Uriah at a place where he knew the strongest defenders were. 17When the men of the city came out and fought against Joab, some of the men in David's army fell; moreover, Uriah the Hittite died.

18Joab sent David a full account of the battle. 19He instructed the messenger: "When you have finished giving the king this account of the battle, 20the king's anger may flare up, and he may ask you, 'Why did you get so close to the city to fight? Didn't you know they would shoot arrows from the wall? 21Who killed Abimelek son of Jerub-Besheth[b]? Didn't a woman drop an upper millstone on him from the wall, so that he died in Thebez? Why did you get so close to the wall?' If he asks you this, then say to him, 'Moreover, your servant Uriah the Hittite is dead.'"

PRAYING SCRIPTURE

2 Samuel 11

David's sin against God and Bathsheba and the murder of her husband, Uriah, show how quickly and how far a person can stray from God, even a person known as "a man after God's heart." Without constant vigilance, any temptation can lead to a spiral of disobedience and negative consequences.

Are you guarding your heart in all areas of your life? Ask God to help you recognize and avoid sin's pitfalls.

---

[a] *11* Or *staying at Sukkoth* [b] *21* Also known as *Jerub-Baal* (that is, Gideon)

22The messenger set out, and when he arrived he told David every-
thing Joab had sent him to say. 23The messenger said to David, "The
men overpowered us and came out against us in the open, but we
drove them back to the entrance of the city gate. 24Then the archers
shot arrows at your servants from the wall, and some of the king's men
died. Moreover, your servant Uriah the Hittite is dead."
25David told the messenger, "Say this to Joab: 'Don't let this upset
you; the sword devours one as well as another. Press the attack against
the city and destroy it.' Say this to encourage Joab."
26When Uriah's wife heard that her husband was dead, she mourned
for him. 27After the time of mourning was over, David had her brought
to his house, and she became his wife and bore him a son. But the
thing David had done displeased the LORD.

NATHAN REBUKES DAVID

12 The LORD sent Nathan to David. When he came to him, he said,
"There were two men in a certain town, one rich and the other
poor. 2The rich man had a very large number of sheep and cattle, 3but
the poor man had nothing except one little ewe lamb he had bought.
He raised it, and it grew up with him and his children. It shared his
food, drank from his cup and even slept in his arms. It was like a
daughter to him.
4"Now a traveler came to the rich man, but the rich man refrained
from taking one of his own sheep or cattle to prepare a meal for the
traveler who had come to him. Instead, he took the ewe lamb that be-
longed to the poor man and prepared it for the one who had come to
him."
5David burned with anger against the man and said to Nathan, "As
surely as the LORD lives, the man who did this must die! 6He must pay
for that lamb four times over, because he did such a thing and had no
pity."
7Then Nathan said to David, "You are the man! This is what the LORD,
the God of Israel, says: 'I anointed you king over Israel, and I delivered
you from the hand of Saul. 8I gave your master's house to you, and
your master's wives into your arms. I gave you all Israel and Judah.
And if all this had been too little, I would have given you even more.
9Why did you despise the word of the LORD by doing what is evil in his
eyes? You struck down Uriah the Hittite with the sword and took his
wife to be your own. You killed him with the sword of the Ammonites.
10Now, therefore, the sword will never depart from your house, because
you despised me and took the wife of Uriah the Hittite to be your own.'
11"This is what the LORD says: 'Out of your own household I am going
to bring calamity on you. Before your very eyes I will take your wives
and give them to one who is close to you, and he will sleep with your
wives in broad daylight. 12You did it in secret, but I will do this thing
in broad daylight before all Israel.'"
13Then David said to Nathan, "I have sinned against the LORD."
Nathan replied, "The LORD has taken away your sin. You are not go-
ing to die. 14But because by doing this you have shown utter contempt
for[a] the LORD, the son born to you will die."
15After Nathan had gone home, the LORD struck the child that Uriah's
wife had borne to David, and he became ill. 16David pleaded with God

PRAYING SCRIPTURE

2 Samuel 12

God loves his children too much to allow us to continue sinning without reprimand—even if that child is a king. David likely thought he had gotten away with his ungodliness. But God sent his prophet to confront David, revealing the selfishness and lust in the king's heart. David was without excuse.

Repentance must be our first response to sin. If you are hiding anything, repent and seek God's restoration.

---

[a] 14 An ancient Hebrew scribal tradition; Masoretic Text *for the enemies of*

for the child. He fasted and spent the nights lying in sackcloth[a] on the
ground. 17The elders of his household stood beside him to get him up
from the ground, but he refused, and he would not eat any food with
them.
18On the seventh day the child died. David's attendants were afraid
to tell him that the child was dead, for they thought, "While the child
was still living, he wouldn't listen to us when we spoke to him. How can
we now tell him the child is dead? He may do something desperate."
19David noticed that his attendants were whispering among them-
selves, and he realized the child was dead. "Is the child dead?" he
asked.
"Yes," they replied, "he is dead."
20Then David got up from the ground. After he had washed, put on
lotions and changed his clothes, he went into the house of the LORD
and worshiped. Then he went to his own house, and at his request they
served him food, and he ate.
21His attendants asked him, "Why are you acting this way? While the
child was alive, you fasted and wept, but now that the child is dead,
you get up and eat!"
22He answered, "While the child was still alive, I fasted and wept.
I thought, 'Who knows? The LORD may be gracious to me and let the
child live.' 23But now that he is dead, why should I go on fasting? Can
I bring him back again? I will go to him, but he will not return to me."
24Then David comforted his wife Bathsheba, and he went to her and
made love to her. She gave birth to a son, and they named him Solo-
mon. The LORD loved him; 25and because the LORD loved him, he sent
word through Nathan the prophet to name him Jedidiah.[b]
26Meanwhile Joab fought against Rabbah of the Ammonites and
captured the royal citadel. 27Joab then sent messengers to David, say-
ing, "I have fought against Rabbah and taken its water supply. 28Now
muster the rest of the troops and besiege the city and capture it. Oth-
erwise I will take the city, and it will be named after me."
29So David mustered the entire army and went to Rabbah, and at-
tacked and captured it. 30David took the crown from their king's[c] head,
and it was placed on his own head. It weighed a talent[d] of gold, and it
was set with precious stones. David took a great quantity of plunder
from the city 31and brought out the people who were there, consigning
them to labor with saws and with iron picks and axes, and he made
them work at brickmaking.[e] David did this to all the Ammonite towns.
Then he and his entire army returned to Jerusalem.

AMNON AND TAMAR

13 In the course of time, Amnon son of David fell in love with Ta-
mar, the beautiful sister of Absalom son of David.
2Amnon became so obsessed with his sister Tamar that he made
himself ill. She was a virgin, and it seemed impossible for him to do
anything to her.
3Now Amnon had an adviser named Jonadab son of Shimeah, Da-
vid's brother. Jonadab was a very shrewd man. 4He asked Amnon,

PRAYING SCRIPTURE

2 Samuel 13

David's inconsistent life would trouble him more than once. The violence of his abuse of Bathsheba and murder of Uriah spread when David's daughter Tamar was raped by her half brother, Amnon. Then, in a version of an honor killing, Tamar's brother Absalom murdered Amnon.

Have you ever had your heart broken by brokenness in your family? God understands, so take that brokenness to him for healing.

---

[a] *16* Dead Sea Scrolls and Septuagint; Masoretic Text does not have *in sackcloth.* [b] *25* *Jedidiah* means *loved by the LORD.* [c] *30* Or *from Milkom's* (that is, Molek's) [d] *30* That is, about 75 pounds or about 34 kilograms
[e] *31* The meaning of the Hebrew for this clause is uncertain.

"Why do you, the king's son, look so haggard morning after morning?
Won't you tell me?"
Amnon said to him, "I'm in love with Tamar, my brother Absalom's
sister."
5"Go to bed and pretend to be ill," Jonadab said. "When your father
comes to see you, say to him, 'I would like my sister Tamar to come and
give me something to eat. Let her prepare the food in my sight so I may
watch her and then eat it from her hand.'"
6So Amnon lay down and pretended to be ill. When the king came
to see him, Amnon said to him, "I would like my sister Tamar to come
and make some special bread in my sight, so I may eat from her hand."
7David sent word to Tamar at the palace: "Go to the house of your
brother Amnon and prepare some food for him." 8So Tamar went to
the house of her brother Amnon, who was lying down. She took some
dough, kneaded it, made the bread in his sight and baked it. 9Then she
took the pan and served him the bread, but he refused to eat.
"Send everyone out of here," Amnon said. So everyone left him.
10Then Amnon said to Tamar, "Bring the food here into my bedroom
so I may eat from your hand." And Tamar took the bread she had pre-
pared and brought it to her brother Amnon in his bedroom. 11But when
she took it to him to eat, he grabbed her and said, "Come to bed with
me, my sister."
12"No, my brother!" she said to him. "Don't force me! Such a thing
should not be done in Israel! Don't do this wicked thing. 13What about
me? Where could I get rid of my disgrace? And what about you? You
would be like one of the wicked fools in Israel. Please speak to the king;
he will not keep me from being married to you." 14But he refused to
listen to her, and since he was stronger than she, he raped her.
15Then Amnon hated her with intense hatred. In fact, he hated her
more than he had loved her. Amnon said to her, "Get up and get out!"
16"No!" she said to him. "Sending me away would be a greater wrong
than what you have already done to me."
But he refused to listen to her. 17He called his personal servant and
said, "Get this woman out of my sight and bolt the door after her." 18So
his servant put her out and bolted the door after her. She was wearing
an ornate[a] robe, for this was the kind of garment the virgin daughters
of the king wore. 19Tamar put ashes on her head and tore the ornate
robe she was wearing. She put her hands on her head and went away,
weeping aloud as she went.
20Her brother Absalom said to her, "Has that Amnon, your brother,
been with you? Be quiet for now, my sister; he is your brother. Don't
take this thing to heart." And Tamar lived in her brother Absalom's
house, a desolate woman.
21When King David heard all this, he was furious. 22And Absalom
never said a word to Amnon, either good or bad; he hated Amnon be-
cause he had disgraced his sister Tamar.

ABSALOM KILLS AMNON

23Two years later, when Absalom's sheepshearers were at Baal Ha-
zor near the border of Ephraim, he invited all the king's sons to come
there. 24Absalom went to the king and said, "Your servant has had
shearers come. Will the king and his attendants please join me?"

[a] *18* The meaning of the Hebrew for this word is uncertain; also in verse 19.

25“No, my son,” the king replied. “All of us should not go; we would
only be a burden to you.” Although Absalom urged him, he still refused
to go but gave him his blessing.
26Then Absalom said, “If not, please let my brother Amnon come
with us.”
The king asked him, “Why should he go with you?” 27But Absalom
urged him, so he sent with him Amnon and the rest of the king’s sons.
28Absalom ordered his men, “Listen! When Amnon is in high spirits
from drinking wine and I say to you, ‘Strike Amnon down,’ then kill
him. Don’t be afraid. Haven’t I given you this order? Be strong and
brave.” 29So Absalom’s men did to Amnon what Absalom had ordered.
Then all the king’s sons got up, mounted their mules and fled.
30While they were on their way, the report came to David: “Absalom
has struck down all the king’s sons; not one of them is left.” 31The king
stood up, tore his clothes and lay down on the ground; and all his at-
tendants stood by with their clothes torn.
32But Jonadab son of Shimeah, David’s brother, said, “My lord should
not think that they killed all the princes; only Amnon is dead. This has
been Absalom’s express intention ever since the day Amnon raped his
sister Tamar. 33My lord the king should not be concerned about the re-
port that all the king’s sons are dead. Only Amnon is dead.”
34Meanwhile, Absalom had fled.
Now the man standing watch looked up and saw many people on
the road west of him, coming down the side of the hill. The watchman
went and told the king, “I see men in the direction of Horonaim, on
the side of the hill.”[a]
35Jonadab said to the king, “See, the king’s sons have come; it has
happened just as your servant said.”
36As he finished speaking, the king’s sons came in, wailing loudly.
The king, too, and all his attendants wept very bitterly.
37Absalom fled and went to Talmai son of Ammihud, the king of Ge-
shur. But King David mourned many days for his son.
38After Absalom fled and went to Geshur, he stayed there three years.
39And King David longed to go to Absalom, for he was consoled con-
cerning Amnon’s death.

ABSALOM RETURNS TO JERUSALEM

14 Joab son of Zeruiah knew that the king’s heart longed for Ab-
salom. 2So Joab sent someone to Tekoa and had a wise woman
brought from there. He said to her, “Pretend you are in mourning.
Dress in mourning clothes, and don’t use any cosmetic lotions. Act
like a woman who has spent many days grieving for the dead. 3Then
go to the king and speak these words to him.” And Joab put the words
in her mouth.
4When the woman from Tekoa went[b] to the king, she fell with her
face to the ground to pay him honor, and she said, “Help me, Your
Majesty!”
5The king asked her, “What is troubling you?”
She said, “I am a widow; my husband is dead. 6I your servant had
two sons. They got into a fight with each other in the field, and no

PRAYING SCRIPTURE

2 Samuel 14

Absalom, like Saul, was recognized in Israel for his good looks. And, like Saul, he had a heart of disobedience. God’s perspective on David—looking at the heart rather than the outer appearance—would again prove important, this time with David’s rebellious son.

In today’s culture that overemphasizes physical beauty, it can be easy to forget to develop our hearts. Ask God to help you keep the proper balance.

[a] *34* Septuagint; Hebrew does not have this sentence. [b] *4* Many Hebrew manuscripts, Septuagint, Vulgate and Syriac; most Hebrew manuscripts *spoke*

one was there to separate them. One struck the other and killed him.
7Now the whole clan has risen up against your servant; they say, 'Hand
over the one who struck his brother down, so that we may put him to
death for the life of his brother whom he killed; then we will get rid
of the heir as well.' They would put out the only burning coal I have
left, leaving my husband neither name nor descendant on the face of
the earth."

8The king said to the woman, "Go home, and I will issue an order in
your behalf."

9But the woman from Tekoa said to him, "Let my lord the king par-
don me and my family, and let the king and his throne be without
guilt."

10The king replied, "If anyone says anything to you, bring them to
me, and they will not bother you again."

11She said, "Then let the king invoke the LORD his God to prevent the
avenger of blood from adding to the destruction, so that my son will
not be destroyed."

"As surely as the LORD lives," he said, "not one hair of your son's head
will fall to the ground."

12Then the woman said, "Let your servant speak a word to my lord
the king."

"Speak," he replied.

13The woman said, "Why then have you devised a thing like this
against the people of God? When the king says this, does he not con-
vict himself, for the king has not brought back his banished son? 14Like
water spilled on the ground, which cannot be recovered, so we must
die. But that is not what God desires; rather, he devises ways so that a
banished person does not remain banished from him.

15"And now I have come to say this to my lord the king because the
people have made me afraid. Your servant thought, 'I will speak to the
king; perhaps he will grant his servant's request. 16Perhaps the king
will agree to deliver his servant from the hand of the man who is try-
ing to cut off both me and my son from God's inheritance.'

17"And now your servant says, 'May the word of my lord the king
secure my inheritance, for my lord the king is like an angel of God in
discerning good and evil. May the LORD your God be with you.'"

18Then the king said to the woman, "Don't keep from me the answer
to what I am going to ask you."

"Let my lord the king speak," the woman said.

19The king asked, "Isn't the hand of Joab with you in all this?"

The woman answered, "As surely as you live, my lord the king, no
one can turn to the right or to the left from anything my lord the king
says. Yes, it was your servant Joab who instructed me to do this and
who put all these words into the mouth of your servant. 20Your servant
Joab did this to change the present situation. My lord has wisdom like
that of an angel of God—he knows everything that happens in the
land."

21The king said to Joab, "Very well, I will do it. Go, bring back the
young man Absalom."

22Joab fell with his face to the ground to pay him honor, and he
blessed the king. Joab said, "Today your servant knows that he has
found favor in your eyes, my lord the king, because the king has
granted his servant's request."

23Then Joab went to Geshur and brought Absalom back to Jerusalem.

24But the king said, "He must go to his own house; he must not see
my face." So Absalom went to his own house and did not see the face
of the king.
25In all Israel there was not a man so highly praised for his hand-
some appearance as Absalom. From the top of his head to the sole of
his foot there was no blemish in him. 26Whenever he cut the hair of his
head — he used to cut his hair once a year because it became too heavy
for him — he would weigh it, and its weight was two hundred shekels[a]
by the royal standard.
27Three sons and a daughter were born to Absalom. His daughter's
name was Tamar, and she became a beautiful woman.
28Absalom lived two years in Jerusalem without seeing the king's
face. 29Then Absalom sent for Joab in order to send him to the king,
but Joab refused to come to him. So he sent a second time, but he re-
fused to come. 30Then he said to his servants, "Look, Joab's field is next
to mine, and he has barley there. Go and set it on fire." So Absalom's
servants set the field on fire.
31Then Joab did go to Absalom's house, and he said to him, "Why
have your servants set my field on fire?"
32Absalom said to Joab, "Look, I sent word to you and said, 'Come
here so I can send you to the king to ask, "Why have I come from Ge-
shur? It would be better for me if I were still there!"' Now then, I want
to see the king's face, and if I am guilty of anything, let him put me
to death."
33So Joab went to the king and told him this. Then the king sum-
moned Absalom, and he came in and bowed down with his face to the
ground before the king. And the king kissed Absalom.

ABSALOM'S CONSPIRACY

15 In the course of time, Absalom provided himself with a chariot
and horses and with fifty men to run ahead of him. 2He would
get up early and stand by the side of the road leading to the city gate.
Whenever anyone came with a complaint to be placed before the king
for a decision, Absalom would call out to him, "What town are you
from?" He would answer, "Your servant is from one of the tribes of
Israel." 3Then Absalom would say to him, "Look, your claims are valid
and proper, but there is no representative of the king to hear you."
4And Absalom would add, "If only I were appointed judge in the land!
Then everyone who has a complaint or case could come to me and I
would see that they receive justice."
5Also, whenever anyone approached him to bow down before him,
Absalom would reach out his hand, take hold of him and kiss him.
6Absalom behaved in this way toward all the Israelites who came to
the king asking for justice, and so he stole the hearts of the people of
Israel.
7At the end of four[b] years, Absalom said to the king, "Let me go to
Hebron and fulfill a vow I made to the LORD. 8While your servant was
living at Geshur in Aram, I made this vow: 'If the LORD takes me back
to Jerusalem, I will worship the LORD in Hebron.[c]'"
9The king said to him, "Go in peace." So he went to Hebron.

PRAYING SCRIPTURE

2 Samuel 15

In the midst of an enormous personal tragedy, David prayed. Betrayed by Absalom and again on the run for his life, David asked God to intervene and bring foolish counsel to Absalom. Then David stopped to worship.

The man after God's own heart was not perfect, but we find an instructive pattern here: Even in the darkest of days, he found time to pray and to worship God Almighty.

[a] *26* That is, about 5 pounds or about 2.3 kilograms [b] *7* Some Septuagint manuscripts, Syriac and Josephus; Hebrew *forty* [c] *8* Some Septuagint manuscripts; Hebrew does not have *in Hebron.*

10Then Absalom sent secret messengers throughout the tribes of Israel to say, "As soon as you hear the sound of the trumpets, then say, 'Absalom is king in Hebron.'" 11Two hundred men from Jerusalem had accompanied Absalom. They had been invited as guests and went quite innocently, knowing nothing about the matter. 12While Absalom was offering sacrifices, he also sent for Ahithophel the Gilonite, David's counselor, to come from Giloh, his hometown. And so the conspiracy gained strength, and Absalom's following kept on increasing.

DAVID FLEES

13A messenger came and told David, "The hearts of the people of Israel are with Absalom."

14Then David said to all his officials who were with him in Jerusalem, "Come! We must flee, or none of us will escape from Absalom. We must leave immediately, or he will move quickly to overtake us and bring ruin on us and put the city to the sword."

15The king's officials answered him, "Your servants are ready to do whatever our lord the king chooses."

16The king set out, with his entire household following him; but he left ten concubines to take care of the palace. 17So the king set out, with all the people following him, and they halted at the edge of the city. 18All his men marched past him, along with all the Kerethites and Pelethites; and all the six hundred Gittites who had accompanied him from Gath marched before the king.

19The king said to Ittai the Gittite, "Why should you come along with us? Go back and stay with King Absalom. You are a foreigner, an exile from your homeland. 20You came only yesterday. And today shall I make you wander about with us, when I do not know where I am going? Go back, and take your people with you. May the LORD show you kindness and faithfulness."[a]

21But Ittai replied to the king, "As surely as the LORD lives, and as my lord the king lives, wherever my lord the king may be, whether it means life or death, there will your servant be."

22David said to Ittai, "Go ahead, march on." So Ittai the Gittite marched on with all his men and the families that were with him.

23The whole countryside wept aloud as all the people passed by. The king also crossed the Kidron Valley, and all the people moved on toward the wilderness.

24Zadok was there, too, and all the Levites who were with him were carrying the ark of the covenant of God. They set down the ark of God, and Abiathar offered sacrifices until all the people had finished leaving the city.

25Then the king said to Zadok, "Take the ark of God back into the city. If I find favor in the LORD's eyes, he will bring me back and let me see it and his dwelling place again. 26But if he says, 'I am not pleased with you,' then I am ready; let him do to me whatever seems good to him."

27The king also said to Zadok the priest, "Do you understand? Go back to the city with my blessing. Take your son Ahimaaz with you, and also Abiathar's son Jonathan. You and Abiathar return with your two sons. 28I will wait at the fords in the wilderness until word comes from you to inform me." 29So Zadok and Abiathar took the ark of God back to Jerusalem and stayed there.

[a] *20* Septuagint; Hebrew *May kindness and faithfulness be with you*

30 But David continued up the Mount of Olives, weeping as he went; his head was covered and he was barefoot. All the people with him covered their heads too and were weeping as they went up. 31 Now David had been told, "Ahithophel is among the conspirators with Absalom." So David prayed, "LORD, turn Ahithophel's counsel into foolishness."

32 When David arrived at the summit, where people used to worship God, Hushai the Arkite was there to meet him, his robe torn and dust on his head. 33 David said to him, "If you go with me, you will be a burden to me. 34 But if you return to the city and say to Absalom, 'Your Majesty, I will be your servant; I was your father's servant in the past, but now I will be your servant,' then you can help me by frustrating Ahithophel's advice. 35 Won't the priests Zadok and Abiathar be there with you? Tell them anything you hear in the king's palace. 36 Their two sons, Ahimaaz son of Zadok and Jonathan son of Abiathar, are there with them. Send them to me with anything you hear."

37 So Hushai, David's confidant, arrived at Jerusalem as Absalom was entering the city.

DAVID AND ZIBA

16 When David had gone a short distance beyond the summit, there was Ziba, the steward of Mephibosheth, waiting to meet him. He had a string of donkeys saddled and loaded with two hundred loaves of bread, a hundred cakes of raisins, a hundred cakes of figs and a skin of wine.

2 The king asked Ziba, "Why have you brought these?"

Ziba answered, "The donkeys are for the king's household to ride on, the bread and fruit are for the men to eat, and the wine is to refresh those who become exhausted in the wilderness."

3 The king then asked, "Where is your master's grandson?"

Ziba said to him, "He is staying in Jerusalem, because he thinks, 'Today the Israelites will restore to me my grandfather's kingdom.'"

4 Then the king said to Ziba, "All that belonged to Mephibosheth is now yours."

"I humbly bow," Ziba said. "May I find favor in your eyes, my lord the king."

SHIMEI CURSES DAVID

5 As King David approached Bahurim, a man from the same clan as Saul's family came out from there. His name was Shimei son of Gera, and he cursed as he came out. 6 He pelted David and all the king's officials with stones, though all the troops and the special guard were on David's right and left. 7 As he cursed, Shimei said, "Get out, get out, you murderer, you scoundrel! 8 The LORD has repaid you for all the blood you shed in the household of Saul, in whose place you have reigned. The LORD has given the kingdom into the hands of your son Absalom. You have come to ruin because you are a murderer!"

9 Then Abishai son of Zeruiah said to the king, "Why should this dead dog curse my lord the king? Let me go over and cut off his head."

10 But the king said, "What does this have to do with you, you sons of Zeruiah? If he is cursing because the LORD said to him, 'Curse David,' who can ask, 'Why do you do this?'"

11 David then said to Abishai and all his officials, "My son, my own flesh and blood, is trying to kill me. How much more, then, this Benjamite! Leave him alone; let him curse, for the LORD has told him to. 12 It

PRAYING SCRIPTURE

2 Samuel 16

When David and some of his men came across one of Saul's family, Shimei, this man assaulted David with rocks and words, cursing David to his face. David, identifying with the man's hurt, would not let his men kill him.

Do you find it hard to empathize with people who are attacking you? This is why Scripture commands us to pray for our enemies. We need it as much as they do.

may be that the LORD will look upon my misery and restore to me his
covenant blessing instead of his curse today."
13 So David and his men continued along the road while Shimei was
going along the hillside opposite him, cursing as he went and throw-
ing stones at him and showering him with dirt. 14 The king and all the
people with him arrived at their destination exhausted. And there he
refreshed himself.

THE ADVICE OF AHITHOPHEL AND HUSHAI

15 Meanwhile, Absalom and all the men of Israel came to Jerusalem,
and Ahithophel was with him. 16 Then Hushai the Arkite, David's confi-
dant, went to Absalom and said to him, "Long live the king! Long live
the king!"
17 Absalom said to Hushai, "So this is the love you show your friend?
If he's your friend, why didn't you go with him?"
18 Hushai said to Absalom, "No, the one chosen by the LORD, by these
people, and by all the men of Israel — his I will be, and I will remain
with him. 19 Furthermore, whom should I serve? Should I not serve the
son? Just as I served your father, so I will serve you."
20 Absalom said to Ahithophel, "Give us your advice. What should
we do?"
21 Ahithophel answered, "Sleep with your father's concubines whom
he left to take care of the palace. Then all Israel will hear that you have
made yourself obnoxious to your father, and the hands of everyone with
you will be more resolute." 22 So they pitched a tent for Absalom on the
roof, and he slept with his father's concubines in the sight of all Israel.
23 Now in those days the advice Ahithophel gave was like that of one
who inquires of God. That was how both David and Absalom regarded
all of Ahithophel's advice.
17 Ahithophel said to Absalom, "I would[a] choose twelve thousand
men and set out tonight in pursuit of David. 2 I would attack him
while he is weary and weak. I would strike him with terror, and then all
the people with him will flee. I would strike down only the king 3 and
bring all the people back to you. The death of the man you seek will
mean the return of all; all the people will be unharmed." 4 This plan
seemed good to Absalom and to all the elders of Israel.
5 But Absalom said, "Summon also Hushai the Arkite, so we can hear
what he has to say as well." 6 When Hushai came to him, Absalom said,
"Ahithophel has given this advice. Should we do what he says? If not,
give us your opinion."
7 Hushai replied to Absalom, "The advice Ahithophel has given is not
good this time. 8 You know your father and his men; they are fighters,
and as fierce as a wild bear robbed of her cubs. Besides, your father is
an experienced fighter; he will not spend the night with the troops.
9 Even now, he is hidden in a cave or some other place. If he should at-
tack your troops first,[b] whoever hears about it will say, 'There has been
a slaughter among the troops who follow Absalom.' 10 Then even the
bravest soldier, whose heart is like the heart of a lion, will melt with
fear, for all Israel knows that your father is a fighter and that those
with him are brave.
11 "So I advise you: Let all Israel, from Dan to Beersheba — as numer-
ous as the sand on the seashore — be gathered to you, with you yourself

PRAYING SCRIPTURE

2 Samuel 17

Absalom could not have known that the conflicting advice he received from his counselors was part of God's plan to defeat him and restore David to the throne. Ahithophel, whose advice was spurned, hanged himself in despair.

It is impossible to see everything God is doing behind the scenes, but we can be sure he is always working. Ask God to give you the faith to trust his invisible hand.

[a] 1 Or *Let me* [b] 9 Or *When some of the men fall at the first attack*

leading them into battle. 12Then we will attack him wherever he may be
found, and we will fall on him as dew settles on the ground. Neither he
nor any of his men will be left alive. 13If he withdraws into a city, then all
Israel will bring ropes to that city, and we will drag it down to the valley
until not so much as a pebble is left."

14Absalom and all the men of Israel said, "The advice of Hushai the
Arkite is better than that of Ahithophel." For the LORD had determined
to frustrate the good advice of Ahithophel in order to bring disaster
on Absalom.

15Hushai told Zadok and Abiathar, the priests, "Ahithophel has ad-
vised Absalom and the elders of Israel to do such and such, but I have
advised them to do so and so. 16Now send a message at once and tell
David, 'Do not spend the night at the fords in the wilderness; cross
over without fail, or the king and all the people with him will be swal-
lowed up.' "

17Jonathan and Ahimaaz were staying at En Rogel. A female servant
was to go and inform them, and they were to go and tell King David,
for they could not risk being seen entering the city. 18But a young man
saw them and told Absalom. So the two of them left at once and went
to the house of a man in Bahurim. He had a well in his courtyard, and
they climbed down into it. 19His wife took a covering and spread it out
over the opening of the well and scattered grain over it. No one knew
anything about it.

20When Absalom's men came to the woman at the house, they asked,
"Where are Ahimaaz and Jonathan?"

The woman answered them, "They crossed over the brook."[a] The
men searched but found no one, so they returned to Jerusalem.

21After they had gone, the two climbed out of the well and went to
inform King David. They said to him, "Set out and cross the river at
once; Ahithophel has advised such and such against you." 22So David
and all the people with him set out and crossed the Jordan. By day-
break, no one was left who had not crossed the Jordan.

23When Ahithophel saw that his advice had not been followed, he
saddled his donkey and set out for his house in his hometown. He put
his house in order and then hanged himself. So he died and was buried
in his father's tomb.

ABSALOM'S DEATH

24David went to Mahanaim, and Absalom crossed the Jordan with all
the men of Israel. 25Absalom had appointed Amasa over the army in
place of Joab. Amasa was the son of Jether,[b] an Ishmaelite[c] who had mar-
ried Abigail,[d] the daughter of Nahash and sister of Zeruiah the mother of
Joab. 26The Israelites and Absalom camped in the land of Gilead.

27When David came to Mahanaim, Shobi son of Nahash from Rabbah
of the Ammonites, and Makir son of Ammiel from Lo Debar, and Bar-
zillai the Gileadite from Rogelim 28brought bedding and bowls and ar-
ticles of pottery. They also brought wheat and barley, flour and roasted
grain, beans and lentils,[e] 29honey and curds, sheep, and cheese from

---

[a] 20 Or *"They passed by the sheep pen toward the water."* [b] 25 Hebrew *Ithra,* a variant of *Jether* [c] 25 Some Septuagint manuscripts (see also 1 Chron. 2:17); Hebrew and other Septuagint manuscripts *Israelite* [d] 25 Hebrew *Abigal,* a variant of *Abigail* [e] 28 Most Septuagint manuscripts and Syriac; Hebrew *lentils, and roasted grain*

PRAYING SCRIPTURE

2 Samuel 18

As David's hand in battle strengthened and made Absalom's defeat likely, David instructed that his son be taken alive. But after Absalom was caught in the boughs of a tree, Joab found and promptly killed him. When David heard this news, he was utterly distraught.

God is mighty to save us in dire situations even when we are brokenhearted over outcomes. Pray for the Lord to give you his peace in every trial.

cows' milk for David and his people to eat. For they said, "The people
have become exhausted and hungry and thirsty in the wilderness."

18 David mustered the men who were with him and appointed
over them commanders of thousands and commanders of hun-
dreds. 2David sent out his troops, a third under the command of Joab,
a third under Joab's brother Abishai son of Zeruiah, and a third under
Ittai the Gittite. The king told the troops, "I myself will surely march
out with you."

3But the men said, "You must not go out; if we are forced to flee, they
won't care about us. Even if half of us die, they won't care; but you are
worth ten thousand of us.[a] It would be better now for you to give us
support from the city."

4The king answered, "I will do whatever seems best to you."

So the king stood beside the gate while all his men marched out
in units of hundreds and of thousands. 5The king commanded Joab,
Abishai and Ittai, "Be gentle with the young man Absalom for my
sake." And all the troops heard the king giving orders concerning Ab-
salom to each of the commanders.

6David's army marched out of the city to fight Israel, and the battle
took place in the forest of Ephraim. 7There Israel's troops were routed
by David's men, and the casualties that day were great — twenty thou-
sand men. 8The battle spread out over the whole countryside, and the
forest swallowed up more men that day than the sword.

9Now Absalom happened to meet David's men. He was riding his
mule, and as the mule went under the thick branches of a large oak,
Absalom's hair got caught in the tree. He was left hanging in midair,
while the mule he was riding kept on going.

10When one of the men saw what had happened, he told Joab, "I just
saw Absalom hanging in an oak tree."

11Joab said to the man who had told him this, "What! You saw him?
Why didn't you strike him to the ground right there? Then I would
have had to give you ten shekels[b] of silver and a warrior's belt."

12But the man replied, "Even if a thousand shekels[c] were weighed
out into my hands, I would not lay a hand on the king's son. In our
hearing the king commanded you and Abishai and Ittai, 'Protect the
young man Absalom for my sake.[d]' 13And if I had put my life in jeop-
ardy[e] — and nothing is hidden from the king — you would have kept
your distance from me."

14Joab said, "I'm not going to wait like this for you." So he took three
javelins in his hand and plunged them into Absalom's heart while Ab-
salom was still alive in the oak tree. 15And ten of Joab's armor-bearers
surrounded Absalom, struck him and killed him.

16Then Joab sounded the trumpet, and the troops stopped pursuing
Israel, for Joab halted them. 17They took Absalom, threw him into a
big pit in the forest and piled up a large heap of rocks over him. Mean-
while, all the Israelites fled to their homes.

18During his lifetime Absalom had taken a pillar and erected it in the

[a] *3* Two Hebrew manuscripts, some Septuagint manuscripts and Vulgate; most Hebrew manuscripts *care; for now there are ten thousand like us*
[b] *11* That is, about 4 ounces or about 115 grams [c] *12* That is, about 25 pounds or about 12 kilograms [d] *12* A few Hebrew manuscripts, Septuagint, Vulgate and Syriac; most Hebrew manuscripts may be translated *Absalom, whoever you may be.* [e] *13* Or *Otherwise, if I had acted treacherously toward him*

King's Valley as a monument to himself, for he thought, "I have no son
to carry on the memory of my name." He named the pillar after him-
self, and it is called Absalom's Monument to this day.

DAVID MOURNS

19 Now Ahimaaz son of Zadok said, "Let me run and take the news to
the king that the LORD has vindicated him by delivering him from the
hand of his enemies."
20 "You are not the one to take the news today," Joab told him. "You
may take the news another time, but you must not do so today, be-
cause the king's son is dead."
21 Then Joab said to a Cushite, "Go, tell the king what you have seen."
The Cushite bowed down before Joab and ran off.
22 Ahimaaz son of Zadok again said to Joab, "Come what may, please
let me run behind the Cushite."
But Joab replied, "My son, why do you want to go? You don't have
any news that will bring you a reward."
23 He said, "Come what may, I want to run."
So Joab said, "Run!" Then Ahimaaz ran by way of the plain[a] and out-
ran the Cushite.
24 While David was sitting between the inner and outer gates, the
watchman went up to the roof of the gateway by the wall. As he looked
out, he saw a man running alone. 25 The watchman called out to the
king and reported it.
The king said, "If he is alone, he must have good news." And the run-
ner came closer and closer.
26 Then the watchman saw another runner, and he called down to the
gatekeeper, "Look, another man running alone!"
The king said, "He must be bringing good news, too."
27 The watchman said, "It seems to me that the first one runs like
Ahimaaz son of Zadok."
"He's a good man," the king said. "He comes with good news."
28 Then Ahimaaz called out to the king, "All is well!" He bowed down
before the king with his face to the ground and said, "Praise be to
the LORD your God! He has delivered up those who lifted their hands
against my lord the king."
29 The king asked, "Is the young man Absalom safe?"
Ahimaaz answered, "I saw great confusion just as Joab was about to
send the king's servant and me, your servant, but I don't know what
it was."
30 The king said, "Stand aside and wait here." So he stepped aside
and stood there.
31 Then the Cushite arrived and said, "My lord the king, hear the good
news! The LORD has vindicated you today by delivering you from the
hand of all who rose up against you."
32 The king asked the Cushite, "Is the young man Absalom safe?"
The Cushite replied, "May the enemies of my lord the king and all
who rise up to harm you be like that young man."
33 The king was shaken. He went up to the room over the gateway and
wept. As he went, he said: "O my son Absalom! My son, my son Absa-
lom! If only I had died instead of you — O Absalom, my son, my son!"[b]

---

[a] *23* That is, the plain of the Jordan [b] *33* In Hebrew texts this verse (18:33) is numbered 19:1.

PRAYING SCRIPTURE

2 Samuel 19

When David returned to Jerusalem, sons of Saul met him to assure him of their favor and support. David's willingness to show grace to Saul's descendants for Jonathan's sake and his ability to navigate political decisions helped reestablish his kingship.

This world will never lack for situations that require wisdom and integrity, so call on God daily to fill you with both so you may be known for them.

19[a] Joab was told, "The king is weeping and mourning for Absalom." 2And for the whole army the victory that day was turned into mourning, because on that day the troops heard it said, "The king is grieving for his son." 3The men stole into the city that day as men steal in who are ashamed when they flee from battle. 4The king covered his face and cried aloud, "O my son Absalom! O Absalom, my son, my son!"

5Then Joab went into the house to the king and said, "Today you have humiliated all your men, who have just saved your life and the lives of your sons and daughters and the lives of your wives and concubines. 6You love those who hate you and hate those who love you. You have made it clear today that the commanders and their men mean nothing to you. I see that you would be pleased if Absalom were alive today and all of us were dead. 7Now go out and encourage your men. I swear by the LORD that if you don't go out, not a man will be left with you by nightfall. This will be worse for you than all the calamities that have come on you from your youth till now."

8So the king got up and took his seat in the gateway. When the men were told, "The king is sitting in the gateway," they all came before him.

Meanwhile, the Israelites had fled to their homes.

DAVID RETURNS TO JERUSALEM

9Throughout the tribes of Israel, all the people were arguing among themselves, saying, "The king delivered us from the hand of our enemies; he is the one who rescued us from the hand of the Philistines. But now he has fled the country to escape from Absalom; 10and Absalom, whom we anointed to rule over us, has died in battle. So why do you say nothing about bringing the king back?"

11King David sent this message to Zadok and Abiathar, the priests: "Ask the elders of Judah, 'Why should you be the last to bring the king back to his palace, since what is being said throughout Israel has reached the king at his quarters? 12You are my relatives, my own flesh and blood. So why should you be the last to bring back the king?' 13And say to Amasa, 'Are you not my own flesh and blood? May God deal with me, be it ever so severely, if you are not the commander of my army for life in place of Joab.'"

14He won over the hearts of the men of Judah so that they were all of one mind. They sent word to the king, "Return, you and all your men." 15Then the king returned and went as far as the Jordan.

Now the men of Judah had come to Gilgal to go out and meet the king and bring him across the Jordan. 16Shimei son of Gera, the Benjamite from Bahurim, hurried down with the men of Judah to meet King David. 17With him were a thousand Benjamites, along with Ziba, the steward of Saul's household, and his fifteen sons and twenty servants. They rushed to the Jordan, where the king was. 18They crossed at the ford to take the king's household over and to do whatever he wished.

When Shimei son of Gera crossed the Jordan, he fell prostrate before the king 19and said to him, "May my lord not hold me guilty. Do not remember how your servant did wrong on the day my lord the king left Jerusalem. May the king put it out of his mind. 20For I your servant know that I have sinned, but today I have come here as the first from the tribes of Joseph to come down and meet my lord the king."

[a] In Hebrew texts 19:1-43 is numbered 19:2-44.

21Then Abishai son of Zeruiah said, "Shouldn't Shimei be put to
death for this? He cursed the LORD's anointed."
22David replied, "What does this have to do with you, you sons of
Zeruiah? What right do you have to interfere? Should anyone be put to
death in Israel today? Don't I know that today I am king over Israel?"
23So the king said to Shimei, "You shall not die." And the king prom-
ised him on oath.
24Mephibosheth, Saul's grandson, also went down to meet the king.
He had not taken care of his feet or trimmed his mustache or washed
his clothes from the day the king left until the day he returned safely.
25When he came from Jerusalem to meet the king, the king asked him,
"Why didn't you go with me, Mephibosheth?"
26He said, "My lord the king, since I your servant am lame, I said, 'I
will have my donkey saddled and will ride on it, so I can go with the
king.' But Ziba my servant betrayed me. 27And he has slandered your
servant to my lord the king. My lord the king is like an angel of God;
so do whatever you wish. 28All my grandfather's descendants deserved
nothing but death from my lord the king, but you gave your servant
a place among those who eat at your table. So what right do I have to
make any more appeals to the king?"
29The king said to him, "Why say more? I order you and Ziba to di-
vide the land."
30Mephibosheth said to the king, "Let him take everything, now that
my lord the king has returned home safely."
31Barzillai the Gileadite also came down from Rogelim to cross the
Jordan with the king and to send him on his way from there. 32Now
Barzillai was very old, eighty years of age. He had provided for the king
during his stay in Mahanaim, for he was a very wealthy man. 33The
king said to Barzillai, "Cross over with me and stay with me in Jerusa-
lem, and I will provide for you."
34But Barzillai answered the king, "How many more years will I live,
that I should go up to Jerusalem with the king? 35I am now eighty
years old. Can I tell the difference between what is enjoyable and what
is not? Can your servant taste what he eats and drinks? Can I still hear
the voices of male and female singers? Why should your servant be an
added burden to my lord the king? 36Your servant will cross over the
Jordan with the king for a short distance, but why should the king re-
ward me in this way? 37Let your servant return, that I may die in my
own town near the tomb of my father and mother. But here is your
servant Kimham. Let him cross over with my lord the king. Do for him
whatever you wish."
38The king said, "Kimham shall cross over with me, and I will do
for him whatever you wish. And anything you desire from me I will
do for you."
39So all the people crossed the Jordan, and then the king crossed
over. The king kissed Barzillai and bid him farewell, and Barzillai re-
turned to his home.
40When the king crossed over to Gilgal, Kimham crossed with him.
All the troops of Judah and half the troops of Israel had taken the king
over.
41Soon all the men of Israel were coming to the king and saying to
him, "Why did our brothers, the men of Judah, steal the king away
and bring him and his household across the Jordan, together with all
his men?"

42 All the men of Judah answered the men of Israel, "We did this be-
cause the king is closely related to us. Why are you angry about it?
Have we eaten any of the king's provisions? Have we taken anything
for ourselves?"
43 Then the men of Israel answered the men of Judah, "We have ten
shares in the king; so we have a greater claim on David than you have.
Why then do you treat us with contempt? Weren't we the first to speak
of bringing back our king?"
But the men of Judah pressed their claims even more forcefully than
the men of Israel.

PRAYING SCRIPTURE

2 Samuel 20

David survived every rebellion for the singular purpose of having his throne established in the line of the Messiah. David's throne was for one from David's line: Jesus Christ. God's servant sat on a throne reserved for God's Servant.

Reflect on what it means for Jesus to be enthroned forever. Rebels and rebellions will be no more. Thank God for his perfect rule that is to come.

SHEBA REBELS AGAINST DAVID

20 Now a troublemaker named Sheba son of Bikri, a Benjamite,
happened to be there. He sounded the trumpet and shouted,

"We have no share in David,
no part in Jesse's son!
Every man to his tent, Israel!"

2 So all the men of Israel deserted David to follow Sheba son of Bikri.
But the men of Judah stayed by their king all the way from the Jordan
to Jerusalem.
3 When David returned to his palace in Jerusalem, he took the ten
concubines he had left to take care of the palace and put them in a
house under guard. He provided for them but had no sexual relations
with them. They were kept in confinement till the day of their death,
living as widows.
4 Then the king said to Amasa, "Summon the men of Judah to come to
me within three days, and be here yourself." 5 But when Amasa went to
summon Judah, he took longer than the time the king had set for him.
6 David said to Abishai, "Now Sheba son of Bikri will do us more harm
than Absalom did. Take your master's men and pursue him, or he will
find fortified cities and escape from us."[a] 7 So Joab's men and the Ker-
ethites and Pelethites and all the mighty warriors went out under the
command of Abishai. They marched out from Jerusalem to pursue
Sheba son of Bikri.
8 While they were at the great rock in Gibeon, Amasa came to meet
them. Joab was wearing his military tunic, and strapped over it at his
waist was a belt with a dagger in its sheath. As he stepped forward, it
dropped out of its sheath.
9 Joab said to Amasa, "How are you, my brother?" Then Joab took
Amasa by the beard with his right hand to kiss him. 10 Amasa was not
on his guard against the dagger in Joab's hand, and Joab plunged it
into his belly, and his intestines spilled out on the ground. Without
being stabbed again, Amasa died. Then Joab and his brother Abishai
pursued Sheba son of Bikri.
11 One of Joab's men stood beside Amasa and said, "Whoever favors
Joab, and whoever is for David, let him follow Joab!" 12 Amasa lay wal-
lowing in his blood in the middle of the road, and the man saw that all
the troops came to a halt there. When he realized that everyone who
came up to Amasa stopped, he dragged him from the road into a field
and threw a garment over him. 13 After Amasa had been removed from
the road, everyone went on with Joab to pursue Sheba son of Bikri.

[a] 6 Or *and do us serious injury*

14Sheba passed through all the tribes of Israel to Abel Beth Maakah
and through the entire region of the Bikrites,[a] who gathered together
and followed him. 15All the troops with Joab came and besieged Sheba
in Abel Beth Maakah. They built a siege ramp up to the city, and it
stood against the outer fortifications. While they were battering the
wall to bring it down, 16a wise woman called from the city, "Listen!
Listen! Tell Joab to come here so I can speak to him." 17He went toward
her, and she asked, "Are you Joab?"

"I am," he answered.

She said, "Listen to what your servant has to say."

"I'm listening," he said.

18She continued, "Long ago they used to say, 'Get your answer at
Abel,' and that settled it. 19We are the peaceful and faithful in Israel.
You are trying to destroy a city that is a mother in Israel. Why do you
want to swallow up the LORD's inheritance?"

20"Far be it from me!" Joab replied, "Far be it from me to swallow
up or destroy! 21That is not the case. A man named Sheba son of Bikri,
from the hill country of Ephraim, has lifted up his hand against the
king, against David. Hand over this one man, and I'll withdraw from
the city."

The woman said to Joab, "His head will be thrown to you from the wall."

22Then the woman went to all the people with her wise advice, and
they cut off the head of Sheba son of Bikri and threw it to Joab. So
he sounded the trumpet, and his men dispersed from the city, each
returning to his home. And Joab went back to the king in Jerusalem.

DAVID'S OFFICIALS

23Joab was over Israel's entire army; Benaiah son of Jehoiada was
over the Kerethites and Pelethites; 24Adoniram[b] was in charge of forced
labor; Jehoshaphat son of Ahilud was recorder; 25Sheva was secretary;
Zadok and Abiathar were priests; 26and Ira the Jairite[c] was David's
priest.

THE GIBEONITES AVENGED

21 During the reign of David, there was a famine for three succes-
sive years; so David sought the face of the LORD. The LORD said,
"It is on account of Saul and his blood-stained house; it is because he
put the Gibeonites to death."

2The king summoned the Gibeonites and spoke to them. (Now the
Gibeonites were not a part of Israel but were survivors of the Amorites;
the Israelites had sworn to spare them, but Saul in his zeal for Israel
and Judah had tried to annihilate them.) 3David asked the Gibeonites,
"What shall I do for you? How shall I make atonement so that you will
bless the LORD's inheritance?"

4The Gibeonites answered him, "We have no right to demand silver
or gold from Saul or his family, nor do we have the right to put anyone
in Israel to death."

"What do you want me to do for you?" David asked.

5They answered the king, "As for the man who destroyed us and

[a] 14 See Septuagint and Vulgate; Hebrew *Berites.* [b] 24 Some Septuagint manuscripts (see also 1 Kings 4:6 and 5:14); Hebrew *Adoram* [c] 26 Hebrew; some Septuagint manuscripts and Syriac (see also 23:38) *Ithrite*

PRAYING SCRIPTURE

2 Samuel 21

David's habit of praying is recorded again as he endured a famine. He asked God for its cause, and God revealed that it was because of a sin committed by Saul, which was avenged. Do sin's effects linger? Absolutely. Saul had been dead for a while, yet judgment was still being levied for his disobedience.

Confession is prayer in which we agree with God about our sin so that fellowship is restored. Ask the Holy Spirit to reveal any place in your life or in the lives of your family members where confession might take place.

plotted against us so that we have been decimated and have no place anywhere in Israel, 6let seven of his male descendants be given to us to be killed and their bodies exposed before the LORD at Gibeah of Saul — the LORD's chosen one."

So the king said, "I will give them to you."

7The king spared Mephibosheth son of Jonathan, the son of Saul, because of the oath before the LORD between David and Jonathan son of Saul. 8But the king took Armoni and Mephibosheth, the two sons of Aiah's daughter Rizpah, whom she had borne to Saul, together with the five sons of Saul's daughter Merab,[a] whom she had borne to Adriel son of Barzillai the Meholathite. 9He handed them over to the Gibeonites, who killed them and exposed their bodies on a hill before the LORD. All seven of them fell together; they were put to death during the first days of the harvest, just as the barley harvest was beginning.

10Rizpah daughter of Aiah took sackcloth and spread it out for herself on a rock. From the beginning of the harvest till the rain poured down from the heavens on the bodies, she did not let the birds touch them by day or the wild animals by night. 11When David was told what Aiah's daughter Rizpah, Saul's concubine, had done, 12he went and took the bones of Saul and his son Jonathan from the citizens of Jabesh Gilead. (They had stolen their bodies from the public square at Beth Shan, where the Philistines had hung them after they struck Saul down on Gilboa.) 13David brought the bones of Saul and his son Jonathan from there, and the bones of those who had been killed and exposed were gathered up.

14They buried the bones of Saul and his son Jonathan in the tomb of Saul's father Kish, at Zela in Benjamin, and did everything the king commanded. After that, God answered prayer in behalf of the land.

WARS AGAINST THE PHILISTINES

15Once again there was a battle between the Philistines and Israel. David went down with his men to fight against the Philistines, and he became exhausted. 16And Ishbi-Benob, one of the descendants of Rapha, whose bronze spearhead weighed three hundred shekels[b] and who was armed with a new sword, said he would kill David. 17But Abishai son of Zeruiah came to David's rescue; he struck the Philistine down and killed him. Then David's men swore to him, saying, "Never again will you go out with us to battle, so that the lamp of Israel will not be extinguished."

18In the course of time, there was another battle with the Philistines, at Gob. At that time Sibbekai the Hushathite killed Saph, one of the descendants of Rapha.

19In another battle with the Philistines at Gob, Elhanan son of Jair[c] the Bethlehemite killed the brother of[d] Goliath the Gittite, who had a spear with a shaft like a weaver's rod.

20In still another battle, which took place at Gath, there was a huge man with six fingers on each hand and six toes on each foot — twenty-four in all. He also was descended from Rapha. 21When he taunted Israel, Jonathan son of Shimeah, David's brother, killed him.

---

[a] *8* Two Hebrew manuscripts, some Septuagint manuscripts and Syriac (see also 1 Samuel 18:19); most Hebrew and Septuagint manuscripts *Michal*
[b] *16* That is, about 7 1/2 pounds or about 3.5 kilograms [c] *19* See 1 Chron. 20:5; Hebrew *Jaare-Oregim.* [d] *19* See 1 Chron. 20:5; Hebrew does not have *the brother of.*

22 These four were descendants of Rapha in Gath, and they fell at the
hands of David and his men.

DAVID'S SONG OF PRAISE

22 David sang to the LORD the words of this song when the LORD
delivered him from the hand of all his enemies and from the
hand of Saul. 2 He said:

"The LORD is my rock, my fortress and my deliverer;
3 my God is my rock, in whom I take refuge,
my shield[a] and the horn[b] of my salvation.
He is my stronghold, my refuge and my savior—
from violent people you save me.

4 "I called to the LORD, who is worthy of praise,
and have been saved from my enemies.
5 The waves of death swirled about me;
the torrents of destruction overwhelmed me.
6 The cords of the grave coiled around me;
the snares of death confronted me.

7 "In my distress I called to the LORD;
I called out to my God.
From his temple he heard my voice;
my cry came to his ears.
8 The earth trembled and quaked,
the foundations of the heavens[c] shook;
they trembled because he was angry.
9 Smoke rose from his nostrils;
consuming fire came from his mouth,
burning coals blazed out of it.
10 He parted the heavens and came down;
dark clouds were under his feet.
11 He mounted the cherubim and flew;
he soared[d] on the wings of the wind.
12 He made darkness his canopy around him—
the dark[e] rain clouds of the sky.
13 Out of the brightness of his presence
bolts of lightning blazed forth.
14 The LORD thundered from heaven;
the voice of the Most High resounded.
15 He shot his arrows and scattered the enemy,
with great bolts of lightning he routed them.
16 The valleys of the sea were exposed
and the foundations of the earth laid bare
at the rebuke of the LORD,
at the blast of breath from his nostrils.

17 "He reached down from on high and took hold of me;
he drew me out of deep waters.
18 He rescued me from my powerful enemy,
from my foes, who were too strong for me.

PRAYING SCRIPTURE

2 Samuel 22

This chapter consists almost totally of David's song of praise to God. Notice it is personal, practical and poetic. David spoke plainly of how God had blessed him, protected him and delivered him. He used poetry to describe God's greatness and might.

Following David's pattern, write out a poem, prayer, song or letter to God. Fill it with descriptive praise as he brings to your mind the ways he has blessed you.

---

[a] 3 Or *sovereign* [b] 3 *Horn* here symbolizes strength. [c] 8 Hebrew; Vulgate and Syriac (see also Psalm 18:7) *mountains* [d] 11 Many Hebrew manuscripts (see also Psalm 18:10); most Hebrew manuscripts *appeared* [e] 12 Septuagint (see also Psalm 18:11); Hebrew *massed*

19 They confronted me in the day of my disaster,
but the LORD was my support.
20 He brought me out into a spacious place;
he rescued me because he delighted in me.

21 "The LORD has dealt with me according to my righteousness;
according to the cleanness of my hands he has
rewarded me.
22 For I have kept the ways of the LORD;
I am not guilty of turning from my God.
23 All his laws are before me;
I have not turned away from his decrees.
24 I have been blameless before him
and have kept myself from sin.
25 The LORD has rewarded me according to my righteousness,
according to my cleanness[a] in his sight.

26 "To the faithful you show yourself faithful,
to the blameless you show yourself blameless,
27 to the pure you show yourself pure,
but to the devious you show yourself shrewd.
28 You save the humble,
but your eyes are on the haughty to bring them low.
29 You, LORD, are my lamp;
the LORD turns my darkness into light.
30 With your help I can advance against a troop[b];
with my God I can scale a wall.

31 "As for God, his way is perfect:
The LORD's word is flawless;
he shields all who take refuge in him.
32 For who is God besides the LORD?
And who is the Rock except our God?
33 It is God who arms me with strength[c]
and keeps my way secure.
34 He makes my feet like the feet of a deer;
he causes me to stand on the heights.
35 He trains my hands for battle;
my arms can bend a bow of bronze.
36 You make your saving help my shield;
your help has made[d] me great.
37 You provide a broad path for my feet,
so that my ankles do not give way.

38 "I pursued my enemies and crushed them;
I did not turn back till they were destroyed.
39 I crushed them completely, and they could not rise;
they fell beneath my feet.
40 You armed me with strength for battle;
you humbled my adversaries before me.

---

[a] *25* Hebrew; Septuagint and Vulgate (see also Psalm 18:24) *to the cleanness of my hands* [b] *30* Or *can run through a barricade* [c] *33* Dead Sea Scrolls, some Septuagint manuscripts, Vulgate and Syriac (see also Psalm 18:32); Masoretic Text *who is my strong refuge* [d] *36* Dead Sea Scrolls; Masoretic Text *shield; / you stoop down to make*

41 You made my enemies turn their backs in flight,
and I destroyed my foes.
42 They cried for help, but there was no one to save them —
to the LORD, but he did not answer.
43 I beat them as fine as the dust of the earth;
I pounded and trampled them like mud in the streets.

44 "You have delivered me from the attacks of the peoples;
you have preserved me as the head of nations.
People I did not know now serve me,
45 foreigners cower before me;
as soon as they hear of me, they obey me.
46 They all lose heart;
they come trembling[a] from their strongholds.

47 "The LORD lives! Praise be to my Rock!
Exalted be my God, the Rock, my Savior!
48 He is the God who avenges me,
who puts the nations under me,
49 who sets me free from my enemies.
You exalted me above my foes;
from a violent man you rescued me.
50 Therefore I will praise you, LORD, among the nations;
I will sing the praises of your name.

51 "He gives his king great victories;
he shows unfailing kindness to his anointed,
to David and his descendants forever."

DAVID'S LAST WORDS

23 These are the last words of David:

"The inspired utterance of David son of Jesse,
the utterance of the man exalted by the Most High,
the man anointed by the God of Jacob,
the hero of Israel's songs:

2 "The Spirit of the LORD spoke through me;
his word was on my tongue.
3 The God of Israel spoke,
the Rock of Israel said to me:
'When one rules over people in righteousness,
when he rules in the fear of God,
4 he is like the light of morning at sunrise
on a cloudless morning,
like the brightness after rain
that brings grass from the earth.'

5 "If my house were not right with God,
surely he would not have made with me an everlasting covenant,
arranged and secured in every part;
surely he would not bring to fruition my salvation
and grant me my every desire.

PRAYING SCRIPTURE

2 Samuel 23

Of David's mighty men, many are named only once in Scripture. But David knew them. They'd been with him through thick and thin, supported him on the run and established him as king.

Think about the people in your life who'd be on such a list. Whose list might you be on? Praise God that even if your name never makes it on a list, he still knows your name.

---

[a] 46 Some Septuagint manuscripts and Vulgate (see also Psalm 18:45); Masoretic Text *they arm themselves*

6 But evil men are all to be cast aside like thorns,
which are not gathered with the hand.
7 Whoever touches thorns
uses a tool of iron or the shaft of a spear;
they are burned up where they lie."

DAVID'S MIGHTY WARRIORS

8 These are the names of David's mighty warriors:

Josheb-Basshebeth,[a] a Tahkemonite,[b] was chief of the Three; he raised his spear against eight hundred men, whom he killed[c] in one encounter.

9 Next to him was Eleazar son of Dodai the Ahohite. As one of the
three mighty warriors, he was with David when they taunted the Phi-
listines gathered at Pas Dammim[d] for battle. Then the Israelites re-
treated, 10 but Eleazar stood his ground and struck down the Philistines
till his hand grew tired and froze to the sword. The LORD brought about
a great victory that day. The troops returned to Eleazar, but only to
strip the dead.

11 Next to him was Shammah son of Agee the Hararite. When the Phi-
listines banded together at a place where there was a field full of len-
tils, Israel's troops fled from them. 12 But Shammah took his stand in
the middle of the field. He defended it and struck the Philistines down,
and the LORD brought about a great victory.

13 During harvest time, three of the thirty chief warriors came down
to David at the cave of Adullam, while a band of Philistines was en-
camped in the Valley of Rephaim. 14 At that time David was in the
stronghold, and the Philistine garrison was at Bethlehem. 15 David
longed for water and said, "Oh, that someone would get me a drink of
water from the well near the gate of Bethlehem!" 16 So the three mighty
warriors broke through the Philistine lines, drew water from the well
near the gate of Bethlehem and carried it back to David. But he refused
to drink it; instead, he poured it out before the LORD. 17 "Far be it from
me, LORD, to do this!" he said. "Is it not the blood of men who went at
the risk of their lives?" And David would not drink it.

Such were the exploits of the three mighty warriors.

18 Abishai the brother of Joab son of Zeruiah was chief of the Three.[e]
He raised his spear against three hundred men, whom he killed, and so
he became as famous as the Three. 19 Was he not held in greater honor
than the Three? He became their commander, even though he was not
included among them.

20 Benaiah son of Jehoiada, a valiant fighter from Kabzeel, per-
formed great exploits. He struck down Moab's two mightiest warriors.
He also went down into a pit on a snowy day and killed a lion. 21 And
he struck down a huge Egyptian. Although the Egyptian had a spear in
his hand, Benaiah went against him with a club. He snatched the spear
from the Egyptian's hand and killed him with his own spear. 22 Such
were the exploits of Benaiah son of Jehoiada; he too was as famous as

[a] 8 Hebrew; some Septuagint manuscripts suggest *Ish-Bosheth,* that is, *Esh-Baal* (see also 1 Chron. 11:11 *Jashobeam*). [b] 8 Probably a variant of *Hakmonite* (see 1 Chron. 11:11) [c] 8 Some Septuagint manuscripts (see also 1 Chron. 11:11); Hebrew and other Septuagint manuscripts *Three; it was Adino the Eznite who killed eight hundred men* [d] 9 See 1 Chron. 11:13; Hebrew *gathered there.* [e] 18 Most Hebrew manuscripts (see also 1 Chron. 11:20); two Hebrew manuscripts and Syriac *Thirty*

the three mighty warriors. 23 He was held in greater honor than any of
the Thirty, but he was not included among the Three. And David put
him in charge of his bodyguard.

24 Among the Thirty were:
Asahel the brother of Joab,
Elhanan son of Dodo from Bethlehem,
25 Shammah the Harodite,
Elika the Harodite,
26 Helez the Paltite,
Ira son of Ikkesh from Tekoa,
27 Abiezer from Anathoth,
Sibbekai[a] the Hushathite,
28 Zalmon the Ahohite,
Maharai the Netophathite,
29 Heled[b] son of Baanah the Netophathite,
Ithai son of Ribai from Gibeah in Benjamin,
30 Benaiah the Pirathonite,
Hiddai[c] from the ravines of Gaash,
31 Abi-Albon the Arbathite,
Azmaveth the Barhumite,
32 Eliahba the Shaalbonite,
the sons of Jashen,
Jonathan 33 son of[d] Shammah the Hararite,
Ahiam son of Sharar[e] the Hararite,
34 Eliphelet son of Ahasbai the Maakathite,
Eliam son of Ahithophel the Gilonite,
35 Hezro the Carmelite,
Paarai the Arbite,
36 Igal son of Nathan from Zobah,
the son of Hagri,[f]
37 Zelek the Ammonite,
Naharai the Beerothite, the armor-bearer of Joab son of Zeruiah,
38 Ira the Ithrite,
Gareb the Ithrite
39 and Uriah the Hittite.
There were thirty-seven in all.

DAVID ENROLLS THE FIGHTING MEN

24 Again the anger of the LORD burned against Israel, and he in-
cited David against them, saying, "Go and take a census of Is-
rael and Judah."
2 So the king said to Joab and the army commanders[g] with him, "Go
throughout the tribes of Israel from Dan to Beersheba and enroll the
fighting men, so that I may know how many there are."

PRAYING SCRIPTURE

2 Samuel 24

Faced with the need to offer a sacrifice to God while away from home, David asked Araunah if he could purchase his threshing floor for an altar. The king refused to accept the threshing floor and oxen as a gift, reasoning that his offering needed to cost him something.

How often are we tempted to give less than our best effort, offering or ministry to God? Ask him to help you always give what honors him.

[a] *27* Some Septuagint manuscripts (see also 21:18; 1 Chron. 11:29); Hebrew *Mebunnai* [b] *29* Some Hebrew manuscripts and Vulgate (see also 1 Chron. 11:30); most Hebrew manuscripts *Heleb* [c] *30* Hebrew; some Septuagint manuscripts (see also 1 Chron. 11:32) *Hurai* [d] *33* Some Septuagint manuscripts (see also 1 Chron. 11:34); Hebrew does not have *son of.*
[e] *33* Hebrew; some Septuagint manuscripts (see also 1 Chron. 11:35) *Sakar*
[f] *36* Some Septuagint manuscripts (see also 1 Chron. 11:38); Hebrew *Haggadi*
[g] *2* Septuagint (see also verse 4 and 1 Chron. 21:2); Hebrew *Joab the army commander*

3But Joab replied to the king, "May the LORD your God multiply the
troops a hundred times over, and may the eyes of my lord the king see
it. But why does my lord the king want to do such a thing?"

4The king's word, however, overruled Joab and the army command-
ers; so they left the presence of the king to enroll the fighting men of
Israel.

5After crossing the Jordan, they camped near Aroer, south of the
town in the gorge, and then went through Gad and on to Jazer. 6They
went to Gilead and the region of Tahtim Hodshi, and on to Dan Jaan
and around toward Sidon. 7Then they went toward the fortress of Tyre
and all the towns of the Hivites and Canaanites. Finally, they went on
to Beersheba in the Negev of Judah.

8After they had gone through the entire land, they came back to Je-
rusalem at the end of nine months and twenty days.

9Joab reported the number of the fighting men to the king: In Israel
there were eight hundred thousand able-bodied men who could han-
dle a sword, and in Judah five hundred thousand.

10David was conscience-stricken after he had counted the fighting
men, and he said to the LORD, "I have sinned greatly in what I have
done. Now, LORD, I beg you, take away the guilt of your servant. I have
done a very foolish thing."

11Before David got up the next morning, the word of the LORD had
come to Gad the prophet, David's seer: 12"Go and tell David, 'This is
what the LORD says: I am giving you three options. Choose one of them
for me to carry out against you.' "

13So Gad went to David and said to him, "Shall there come on you
three[a] years of famine in your land? Or three months of fleeing from
your enemies while they pursue you? Or three days of plague in your
land? Now then, think it over and decide how I should answer the one
who sent me."

14David said to Gad, "I am in deep distress. Let us fall into the hands
of the LORD, for his mercy is great; but do not let me fall into human
hands."

15So the LORD sent a plague on Israel from that morning until the
end of the time designated, and seventy thousand of the people from
Dan to Beersheba died. 16When the angel stretched out his hand to
destroy Jerusalem, the LORD relented concerning the disaster and said
to the angel who was afflicting the people, "Enough! Withdraw your
hand." The angel of the LORD was then at the threshing floor of Arau-
nah the Jebusite.

17When David saw the angel who was striking down the people, he
said to the LORD, "I have sinned; I, the shepherd,[b] have done wrong.
These are but sheep. What have they done? Let your hand fall on me
and my family."

DAVID BUILDS AN ALTAR

18On that day Gad went to David and said to him, "Go up and build an
altar to the LORD on the threshing floor of Araunah the Jebusite." 19So
David went up, as the LORD had commanded through Gad. 20When Arau-
nah looked and saw the king and his officials coming toward him, he
went out and bowed down before the king with his face to the ground.

---

[a] *13* Septuagint (see also 1 Chron. 21:12); Hebrew *seven* [b] *17* Dead Sea Scrolls and Septuagint; Masoretic Text does not have *the shepherd*.

[21]Araunah said, "Why has my lord the king come to his servant?"
"To buy your threshing floor," David answered, "so I can build an altar to the LORD, that the plague on the people may be stopped."
[22]Araunah said to David, "Let my lord the king take whatever he wishes and offer it up. Here are oxen for the burnt offering, and here
are threshing sledges and ox yokes for the wood. [23]Your Majesty, Arau-
nah[a] gives all this to the king." Araunah also said to him, "May the LORD your God accept you."
[24]But the king replied to Araunah, "No, I insist on paying you for it. I will not sacrifice to the LORD my God burnt offerings that cost me nothing."

So David bought the threshing floor and the oxen and paid fifty
shekels[b] of silver for them. [25]David built an altar to the LORD there and
sacrificed burnt offerings and fellowship offerings. Then the LORD answered his prayer in behalf of the land, and the plague on Israel was stopped.

[a] *23* Some Hebrew manuscripts and Septuagint; most Hebrew manuscripts *King Araunah* [b] *24* That is, about 1 1/4 pounds or about 575 grams

1 KINGS

The two books of Kings conclude the narrative arc that started with God's promise to Abraham. The first begins with the death of David and the struggle for his throne. It ends with Israel divided, conquered and sent into exile.

First Kings is not all bad news. It shows Israel at the height of its glory during the reign of Solomon. After he became king following the death of David, Solomon appeared to be the one through whom God would fulfill the promise he made to Abraham to bless all the families of the earth. In chapter 3, the Lord appeared to Solomon in a dream and told him to ask for whatever he wanted. Solomon replied by asking for an understanding mind so he could discern good from evil and lead God's people in righteousness.

Solomon's response to the Lord in chapter 3 is instructive for every Christian. The Lord offered to give Solomon whatever he asked. Rather than asking for long life or wealth or the death of his enemies, he asked for wisdom. Instead of seeking to have an easy life, he sought to have a godly life. He asked that his character would match the enormous task he had been given. While it is right and good to pray for our physical needs, these should not be the sum of our prayers. We should also focus on asking the Lord to mold our character so that we bring glory to him. Solomon's prayer has thus been used as an example of a leader humbly seeking God ever since he offered the prayer.

With God's blessing, Solomon was able to accomplish David's forbidden vision. He built an ornate temple and dedicated it to the Lord. When the queen of Sheba came to visit Solomon, she marveled at the wisdom he offered. Israel had reached its greatest moment, its zenith. Leaders from the known world came to Solomon for counsel, bringing all manner of tribute for him. However, Solomon, like his father, took up multiple wives, against God's design for marriage. In total he would eventually have 700 wives and 300 concubines. Many of these did not serve Israel's God, so they turned his heart away from the Lord.

Israel was unable to regain its heights after Solomon died, resulting in a divided kingdom. The tribes of Judah and Benjamin formed the southern kingdom (Judah), while the other ten tribes formed the northern kingdom (Israel). The remainder of the books of the Kings shift back and forth between these two kingdoms, each of which spiraled lower and lower.

First Kings 17 introduces the prophet Elijah, who would play a key role in Israel's history. He and the prophets who followed him spoke God's word to the kings, both interpreting current events in light of the nation's unfaithfulness and predicting what would happen to them in the future. Elijah's prayer on Mount Carmel when facing the prophets of Baal is a pattern of calling on the Lord for big things so his power can be demonstrated.

ADONIJAH SETS HIMSELF UP AS KING

1 When King David was very old, he could not keep warm even when
they put covers over him. 2So his attendants said to him, "Let us
look for a young virgin to serve the king and take care of him. She can
lie beside him so that our lord the king may keep warm."
3Then they searched throughout Israel for a beautiful young woman
and found Abishag, a Shunammite, and brought her to the king. 4The
woman was very beautiful; she took care of the king and waited on
him, but the king had no sexual relations with her.
5Now Adonijah, whose mother was Haggith, put himself forward and
said, "I will be king." So he got chariots and horses[a] ready, with fifty
men to run ahead of him. 6(His father had never rebuked him by ask-
ing, "Why do you behave as you do?" He was also very handsome and
was born next after Absalom.)
7Adonijah conferred with Joab son of Zeruiah and with Abiathar the
priest, and they gave him their support. 8But Zadok the priest, Bena-
iah son of Jehoiada, Nathan the prophet, Shimei and Rei and David's
special guard did not join Adonijah.
9Adonijah then sacrificed sheep, cattle and fattened calves at the
Stone of Zoheleth near En Rogel. He invited all his brothers, the king's
sons, and all the royal officials of Judah, 10but he did not invite Nathan
the prophet or Benaiah or the special guard or his brother Solomon.
11Then Nathan asked Bathsheba, Solomon's mother, "Have you not
heard that Adonijah, the son of Haggith, has become king, and our
lord David knows nothing about it? 12Now then, let me advise you how
you can save your own life and the life of your son Solomon. 13Go in to
King David and say to him, 'My lord the king, did you not swear to me
your servant: "Surely Solomon your son shall be king after me, and he
will sit on my throne"? Why then has Adonijah become king?' 14While
you are still there talking to the king, I will come in and add my word
to what you have said."
15So Bathsheba went to see the aged king in his room, where Abishag
the Shunammite was attending him. 16Bathsheba bowed down, pros-
trating herself before the king.
"What is it you want?" the king asked.
17She said to him, "My lord, you yourself swore to me your servant by
the LORD your God: 'Solomon your son shall be king after me, and he
will sit on my throne.' 18But now Adonijah has become king, and you,
my lord the king, do not know about it. 19He has sacrificed great num-
bers of cattle, fattened calves, and sheep, and has invited all the king's
sons, Abiathar the priest and Joab the commander of the army, but he
has not invited Solomon your servant. 20My lord the king, the eyes of
all Israel are on you, to learn from you who will sit on the throne of
my lord the king after him. 21Otherwise, as soon as my lord the king
is laid to rest with his ancestors, I and my son Solomon will be treated
as criminals."
22While she was still speaking with the king, Nathan the prophet
arrived. 23And the king was told, "Nathan the prophet is here." So he
went before the king and bowed with his face to the ground.
24Nathan said, "Have you, my lord the king, declared that Adonijah
shall be king after you, and that he will sit on your throne? 25Today he
has gone down and sacrificed great numbers of cattle, fattened calves,

[a] 5 Or *charioteers*

PRAYING SCRIPTURE

1 Kings 1

With David near death and his wishes not clear, his son Adonijah attempted to take the throne. A power play commenced with rivals supporting Adonijah or Solomon. Nathan and Bathsheba feared Solomon would be killed if Adonijah kept the throne.

Sometimes political intrigue or upheaval causes us to worry about unknown outcomes. When things are out of your control, take your concerns to the throne of grace. You'll find peace there.

and sheep. He has invited all the king's sons, the commanders of the army and Abiathar the priest. Right now they are eating and drinking with him and saying, 'Long live King Adonijah!' 26But me your servant, and Zadok the priest, and Benaiah son of Jehoiada, and your servant Solomon he did not invite. 27Is this something my lord the king has done without letting his servants know who should sit on the throne of my lord the king after him?"

DAVID MAKES SOLOMON KING

28Then King David said, "Call in Bathsheba." So she came into the king's presence and stood before him.

29The king then took an oath: "As surely as the LORD lives, who has delivered me out of every trouble, 30I will surely carry out this very day what I swore to you by the LORD, the God of Israel: Solomon your son shall be king after me, and he will sit on my throne in my place."

31Then Bathsheba bowed down with her face to the ground, prostrating herself before the king, and said, "May my lord King David live forever!"

32King David said, "Call in Zadok the priest, Nathan the prophet and Benaiah son of Jehoiada." When they came before the king, 33he said to them: "Take your lord's servants with you and have Solomon my son mount my own mule and take him down to Gihon. 34There have Zadok the priest and Nathan the prophet anoint him king over Israel. Blow the trumpet and shout, 'Long live King Solomon!' 35Then you are to go up with him, and he is to come and sit on my throne and reign in my place. I have appointed him ruler over Israel and Judah."

36Benaiah son of Jehoiada answered the king, "Amen! May the LORD, the God of my lord the king, so declare it. 37As the LORD was with my lord the king, so may he be with Solomon to make his throne even greater than the throne of my lord King David!"

38So Zadok the priest, Nathan the prophet, Benaiah son of Jehoiada, the Kerethites and the Pelethites went down and had Solomon mount King David's mule, and they escorted him to Gihon. 39Zadok the priest took the horn of oil from the sacred tent and anointed Solomon. Then they sounded the trumpet and all the people shouted, "Long live King Solomon!" 40And all the people went up after him, playing pipes and rejoicing greatly, so that the ground shook with the sound.

41Adonijah and all the guests who were with him heard it as they were finishing their feast. On hearing the sound of the trumpet, Joab asked, "What's the meaning of all the noise in the city?"

42Even as he was speaking, Jonathan son of Abiathar the priest arrived. Adonijah said, "Come in. A worthy man like you must be bringing good news."

43"Not at all!" Jonathan answered. "Our lord King David has made Solomon king. 44The king has sent with him Zadok the priest, Nathan the prophet, Benaiah son of Jehoiada, the Kerethites and the Pelethites, and they have put him on the king's mule, 45and Zadok the priest and Nathan the prophet have anointed him king at Gihon. From there they have gone up cheering, and the city resounds with it. That's the noise you hear. 46Moreover, Solomon has taken his seat on the royal throne. 47Also, the royal officials have come to congratulate our lord King David, saying, 'May your God make Solomon's name more famous than yours and his throne greater than yours!' And the king bowed in worship on his bed 48and said, 'Praise be to the LORD,

the God of Israel, who has allowed my eyes to see a successor on my
throne today.'"
49At this, all Adonijah's guests rose in alarm and dispersed. 50But Ad-
onijah, in fear of Solomon, went and took hold of the horns of the altar.
51Then Solomon was told, "Adonijah is afraid of King Solomon and is
clinging to the horns of the altar. He says, 'Let King Solomon swear to
me today that he will not put his servant to death with the sword.'"
52Solomon replied, "If he shows himself to be worthy, not a hair of
his head will fall to the ground; but if evil is found in him, he will die."
53Then King Solomon sent men, and they brought him down from the
altar. And Adonijah came and bowed down to King Solomon, and Sol-
omon said, "Go to your home."

DAVID'S CHARGE TO SOLOMON

2 When the time drew near for David to die, he gave a charge to Sol-
omon his son.
2"I am about to go the way of all the earth," he said. "So be strong,
act like a man, 3and observe what the LORD your God requires: Walk in
obedience to him, and keep his decrees and commands, his laws and
regulations, as written in the Law of Moses. Do this so that you may
prosper in all you do and wherever you go 4and that the LORD may
keep his promise to me: 'If your descendants watch how they live, and
if they walk faithfully before me with all their heart and soul, you will
never fail to have a successor on the throne of Israel.'
5"Now you yourself know what Joab son of Zeruiah did to me—what
he did to the two commanders of Israel's armies, Abner son of Ner and
Amasa son of Jether. He killed them, shedding their blood in peace-
time as if in battle, and with that blood he stained the belt around his
waist and the sandals on his feet. 6Deal with him according to your
wisdom, but do not let his gray head go down to the grave in peace.
7"But show kindness to the sons of Barzillai of Gilead and let them
be among those who eat at your table. They stood by me when I fled
from your brother Absalom.
8"And remember, you have with you Shimei son of Gera, the Benja-
mite from Bahurim, who called down bitter curses on me the day I went
to Mahanaim. When he came down to meet me at the Jordan, I swore
to him by the LORD: 'I will not put you to death by the sword.' 9But now,
do not consider him innocent. You are a man of wisdom; you will know
what to do to him. Bring his gray head down to the grave in blood."
10Then David rested with his ancestors and was buried in the City of
David. 11He had reigned forty years over Israel—seven years in Hebron
and thirty-three in Jerusalem. 12So Solomon sat on the throne of his
father David, and his rule was firmly established.

SOLOMON'S THRONE ESTABLISHED

13Now Adonijah, the son of Haggith, went to Bathsheba, Solomon's
mother. Bathsheba asked him, "Do you come peacefully?"
He answered, "Yes, peacefully." 14Then he added, "I have something
to say to you."
"You may say it," she replied.
15"As you know," he said, "the kingdom was mine. All Israel looked
to me as their king. But things changed, and the kingdom has gone to
my brother; for it has come to him from the LORD. 16Now I have one
request to make of you. Do not refuse me."

PRAYING SCRIPTURE

1 Kings 2

Every father should impart meaningful wisdom to his offspring. As David was preparing to die, he called Solomon, the heir to the throne, charging him to "observe what the LORD your God requires" (verse 3). Solomon would walk in God's ways, keeping his statutes, commandments, judgments and testimonies—his word.

Pray that parents will impart godly wisdom to their children as David did. There is no more important legacy.

"You may make it," she said.
17So he continued, "Please ask King Solomon — he will not refuse
you — to give me Abishag the Shunammite as my wife."
18"Very well," Bathsheba replied, "I will speak to the king for you."
19When Bathsheba went to King Solomon to speak to him for Ado-
nijah, the king stood up to meet her, bowed down to her and sat down
on his throne. He had a throne brought for the king's mother, and she
sat down at his right hand.
20"I have one small request to make of you," she said. "Do not re-
fuse me."
The king replied, "Make it, my mother; I will not refuse you."
21So she said, "Let Abishag the Shunammite be given in marriage to
your brother Adonijah."
22King Solomon answered his mother, "Why do you request Abishag
the Shunammite for Adonijah? You might as well request the kingdom
for him — after all, he is my older brother — yes, for him and for Abia-
thar the priest and Joab son of Zeruiah!"
23Then King Solomon swore by the LORD: "May God deal with me,
be it ever so severely, if Adonijah does not pay with his life for this
request! 24And now, as surely as the LORD lives — he who has estab-
lished me securely on the throne of my father David and has founded
a dynasty for me as he promised — Adonijah shall be put to death to-
day!" 25So King Solomon gave orders to Benaiah son of Jehoiada, and
he struck down Adonijah and he died.
26To Abiathar the priest the king said, "Go back to your fields in Ana-
thoth. You deserve to die, but I will not put you to death now, because
you carried the ark of the Sovereign LORD before my father David and
shared all my father's hardships." 27So Solomon removed Abiathar
from the priesthood of the LORD, fulfilling the word the LORD had spo-
ken at Shiloh about the house of Eli.
28When the news reached Joab, who had conspired with Adonijah
though not with Absalom, he fled to the tent of the LORD and took hold
of the horns of the altar. 29King Solomon was told that Joab had fled to
the tent of the LORD and was beside the altar. Then Solomon ordered
Benaiah son of Jehoiada, "Go, strike him down!"
30So Benaiah entered the tent of the LORD and said to Joab, "The
king says, 'Come out!'"
But he answered, "No, I will die here."
Benaiah reported to the king, "This is how Joab answered me."
31Then the king commanded Benaiah, "Do as he says. Strike him
down and bury him, and so clear me and my whole family of the guilt
of the innocent blood that Joab shed. 32The LORD will repay him for
the blood he shed, because without my father David knowing it he at-
tacked two men and killed them with the sword. Both of them — Abner
son of Ner, commander of Israel's army, and Amasa son of Jether, com-
mander of Judah's army — were better men and more upright than he.
33May the guilt of their blood rest on the head of Joab and his descen-
dants forever. But on David and his descendants, his house and his
throne, may there be the LORD's peace forever."
34So Benaiah son of Jehoiada went up and struck down Joab and
killed him, and he was buried at his home out in the country. 35The
king put Benaiah son of Jehoiada over the army in Joab's position and
replaced Abiathar with Zadok the priest.
36Then the king sent for Shimei and said to him, "Build yourself a

house in Jerusalem and live there, but do not go anywhere else. 37 The
day you leave and cross the Kidron Valley, you can be sure you will die;
your blood will be on your own head."
38 Shimei answered the king, "What you say is good. Your servant
will do as my lord the king has said." And Shimei stayed in Jerusalem
for a long time.
39 But three years later, two of Shimei's slaves ran off to Achish son of
Maakah, king of Gath, and Shimei was told, "Your slaves are in Gath."
40 At this, he saddled his donkey and went to Achish at Gath in search
of his slaves. So Shimei went away and brought the slaves back from
Gath.
41 When Solomon was told that Shimei had gone from Jerusalem to
Gath and had returned, 42 the king summoned Shimei and said to him,
"Did I not make you swear by the LORD and warn you, 'On the day you
leave to go anywhere else, you can be sure you will die'? At that time
you said to me, 'What you say is good. I will obey.' 43 Why then did you
not keep your oath to the LORD and obey the command I gave you?"
44 The king also said to Shimei, "You know in your heart all the wrong
you did to my father David. Now the LORD will repay you for your
wrongdoing. 45 But King Solomon will be blessed, and David's throne
will remain secure before the LORD forever."
46 Then the king gave the order to Benaiah son of Jehoiada, and he
went out and struck Shimei down and he died.
The kingdom was now established in Solomon's hands.

SOLOMON ASKS FOR WISDOM

3 Solomon made an alliance with Pharaoh king of Egypt and mar-
ried his daughter. He brought her to the City of David until he
finished building his palace and the temple of the LORD, and the wall
around Jerusalem. 2 The people, however, were still sacrificing at the
high places, because a temple had not yet been built for the Name of
the LORD. 3 Solomon showed his love for the LORD by walking accord-
ing to the instructions given him by his father David, except that he
offered sacrifices and burned incense on the high places.
4 The king went to Gibeon to offer sacrifices, for that was the most im
portant high place, and Solomon offered a thousand burnt offerings on
that altar. 5 At Gibeon the LORD appeared to Solomon during the night
in a dream, and God said, "Ask for whatever you want me to give you."
6 Solomon answered, "You have shown great kindness to your ser-
vant, my father David, because he was faithful to you and righteous
and upright in heart. You have continued this great kindness to him
and have given him a son to sit on his throne this very day.
7 "Now, LORD my God, you have made your servant king in place of
my father David. But I am only a little child and do not know how to
carry out my duties. 8 Your servant is here among the people you have
chosen, a great people, too numerous to count or number. 9 So give
your servant a discerning heart to govern your people and to distin-
guish between right and wrong. For who is able to govern this great
people of yours?"
10 The Lord was pleased that Solomon had asked for this. 11 So God
said to him, "Since you have asked for this and not for long life or
wealth for yourself, nor have asked for the death of your enemies but
for discernment in administering justice, 12 I will do what you have
asked. I will give you a wise and discerning heart, so that there will

PRAYING SCRIPTURE

1 Kings 3

If you could ask for anything in the world, what would it be? A house of your own? A certain car? A promotion or better job? Survival skills? Many of our requests might not reflect a spiritual end.

When Solomon took the throne, he knew he wasn't completely ready, so he asked God for "a discerning heart to govern your people" (verse 9). Ask God in faith for the wisdom you need.

never have been anyone like you, nor will there ever be. [13]Moreover, I
will give you what you have not asked for — both wealth and honor —
so that in your lifetime you will have no equal among kings. [14]And
if you walk in obedience to me and keep my decrees and commands
as David your father did, I will give you a long life." [15]Then Solomon
awoke — and he realized it had been a dream.

He returned to Jerusalem, stood before the ark of the Lord's covenant and sacrificed burnt offerings and fellowship offerings. Then he gave a feast for all his court.

A WISE RULING

[16]Now two prostitutes came to the king and stood before him. [17]One
of them said, "Pardon me, my lord. This woman and I live in the same
house, and I had a baby while she was there with me. [18]The third day
after my child was born, this woman also had a baby. We were alone;
there was no one in the house but the two of us.

[19]"During the night this woman's son died because she lay on him.
[20]So she got up in the middle of the night and took my son from my
side while I your servant was asleep. She put him by her breast and put
her dead son by my breast. [21]The next morning, I got up to nurse my
son — and he was dead! But when I looked at him closely in the morning light, I saw that it wasn't the son I had borne."

[22]The other woman said, "No! The living one is my son; the dead
one is yours."

But the first one insisted, "No! The dead one is yours; the living one is mine." And so they argued before the king.

[23]The king said, "This one says, 'My son is alive and your son is dead,'
while that one says, 'No! Your son is dead and mine is alive.'"

[24]Then the king said, "Bring me a sword." So they brought a sword
for the king. [25]He then gave an order: "Cut the living child in two and
give half to one and half to the other."

[26]The woman whose son was alive was deeply moved out of love for
her son and said to the king, "Please, my lord, give her the living baby!
Don't kill him!"

But the other said, "Neither I nor you shall have him. Cut him in two!"

[27]Then the king gave his ruling: "Give the living baby to the first
woman. Do not kill him; she is his mother."

[28]When all Israel heard the verdict the king had given, they held
the king in awe, because they saw that he had wisdom from God to
administer justice.

SOLOMON'S OFFICIALS AND GOVERNORS

4 So King Solomon ruled over all Israel. [2]And these were his chief
officials:

Azariah son of Zadok — the priest;
[3]Elihoreph and Ahijah, sons of Shisha — secretaries;
Jehoshaphat son of Ahilud — recorder;
[4]Benaiah son of Jehoiada — commander in chief;
Zadok and Abiathar — priests;
[5]Azariah son of Nathan — in charge of the district governors;
Zabud son of Nathan — a priest and adviser to the king;
[6]Ahishar — palace administrator;
Adoniram son of Abda — in charge of forced labor.

PRAYING SCRIPTURE

1 Kings 4

Under Solomon's reign and partly because of his great wisdom, Israel experienced its greatest era. God's promise to Abraham, Isaac and Jacob was fulfilled as the population exploded. Peace was known throughout the land. Everyone was safe "under their own vine and under their own fig tree," an expression of blessing (verse 25).

It is right to praise God when he blesses us. Every good gift comes from him, so take some time to thank him.

7Solomon had twelve district governors over all Israel, who supplied
provisions for the king and the royal household. Each one had to pro-
vide supplies for one month in the year. 8These are their names:

Ben-Hur — in the hill country of Ephraim;
9 Ben-Deker — in Makaz, Shaalbim, Beth Shemesh and Elon
Bethhanan;
10 Ben-Hesed — in Arubboth (Sokoh and all the land of Hepher were
his);
11 Ben-Abinadab — in Naphoth Dor (he was married to Taphath
daughter of Solomon);
12 Baana son of Ahilud — in Taanach and Megiddo, and in all of Beth
Shan next to Zarethan below Jezreel, from Beth Shan to Abel
Meholah across to Jokmeam;
13 Ben-Geber — in Ramoth Gilead (the settlements of Jair son of Ma-
nasseh in Gilead were his, as well as the region of Argob in Ba-
shan and its sixty large walled cities with bronze gate bars);
14 Ahinadab son of Iddo — in Mahanaim;
15 Ahimaaz — in Naphtali (he had married Basemath daughter of
Solomon);
16 Baana son of Hushai — in Asher and in Aloth;
17 Jehoshaphat son of Paruah — in Issachar;
18 Shimei son of Ela — in Benjamin;
19 Geber son of Uri — in Gilead (the country of Sihon king of the Am-
orites and the country of Og king of Bashan). He was the only
governor over the district.

SOLOMON'S DAILY PROVISIONS

20The people of Judah and Israel were as numerous as the sand on
the seashore; they ate, they drank and they were happy. 21And Sol-
omon ruled over all the kingdoms from the Euphrates River to the
land of the Philistines, as far as the border of Egypt. These countries
brought tribute and were Solomon's subjects all his life.

22Solomon's daily provisions were thirty cors[a] of the finest flour and
sixty cors[b] of meal, 23ten head of stall-fed cattle, twenty of pasture-fed
cattle and a hundred sheep and goats, as well as deer, gazelles, roe-
bucks and choice fowl. 24For he ruled over all the kingdoms west of
the Euphrates River, from Tiphsah to Gaza, and had peace on all sides.
25During Solomon's lifetime Judah and Israel, from Dan to Beersheba,
lived in safety, everyone under their own vine and under their own
fig tree.

26Solomon had four[c] thousand stalls for chariot horses, and twelve
thousand horses.[d]

27The district governors, each in his month, supplied provisions for
King Solomon and all who came to the king's table. They saw to it that
nothing was lacking. 28They also brought to the proper place their quo-
tas of barley and straw for the chariot horses and the other horses.

SOLOMON'S WISDOM

29God gave Solomon wisdom and very great insight, and a breadth
of understanding as measureless as the sand on the seashore.

---

[a] *22* That is, probably about 5 1/2 tons or about 5 metric tons [b] *22* That is, probably about 11 tons or about 10 metric tons [c] *26* Some Septuagint manuscripts (see also 2 Chron. 9:25); Hebrew *forty* [d] *26* Or *charioteers*

30Solomon's wisdom was greater than the wisdom of all the people of the East, and greater than all the wisdom of Egypt. 31He was wiser than anyone else, including Ethan the Ezrahite—wiser than Heman, Kalkol and Darda, the sons of Mahol. And his fame spread to all the surrounding nations. 32He spoke three thousand proverbs and his songs numbered a thousand and five. 33He spoke about plant life, from the cedar of Lebanon to the hyssop that grows out of walls. He also spoke about animals and birds, reptiles and fish. 34From all nations people came to listen to Solomon's wisdom, sent by all the kings of the world, who had heard of his wisdom.[a]

PREPARATIONS FOR BUILDING THE TEMPLE

5 [b] When Hiram king of Tyre heard that Solomon had been anointed king to succeed his father David, he sent his envoys to Solomon, because he had always been on friendly terms with David. 2Solomon sent back this message to Hiram:

> 3"You know that because of the wars waged against my father David from all sides, he could not build a temple for the Name of the LORD his God until the LORD put his enemies under his feet. 4But now the LORD my God has given me rest on every side, and there is no adversary or disaster. 5I intend, therefore, to build a temple for the Name of the LORD my God, as the LORD told my father David, when he said, 'Your son whom I will put on the throne in your place will build the temple for my Name.'
>
> 6"So give orders that cedars of Lebanon be cut for me. My men will work with yours, and I will pay you for your men whatever wages you set. You know that we have no one so skilled in felling timber as the Sidonians."

7When Hiram heard Solomon's message, he was greatly pleased and said, "Praise be to the LORD today, for he has given David a wise son to rule over this great nation."

8So Hiram sent word to Solomon:

> "I have received the message you sent me and will do all you want in providing the cedar and juniper logs. 9My men will haul them down from Lebanon to the Mediterranean Sea, and I will float them as rafts by sea to the place you specify. There I will separate them and you can take them away. And you are to grant my wish by providing food for my royal household."

10In this way Hiram kept Solomon supplied with all the cedar and juniper logs he wanted, 11and Solomon gave Hiram twenty thousand cors[c] of wheat as food for his household, in addition to twenty thousand baths[d,e] of pressed olive oil. Solomon continued to do this for Hiram year after year. 12The LORD gave Solomon wisdom, just as he had promised him. There were peaceful relations between Hiram and Solomon, and the two of them made a treaty.

13King Solomon conscripted laborers from all Israel—thirty thousand men. 14He sent them off to Lebanon in shifts of ten thousand a month, so that they spent one month in Lebanon and two months at

PRAYING SCRIPTURE

1 Kings 5

Solomon's wisdom in creating alliances was of great benefit when it came time to build the temple. Not only could he secure needed supplies, but he knew how to organize its construction. Besides construction supplies, Solomon organized a massive rotating labor force.

We don't always think of praying for mundane things like grocery shopping or car buying. Don't forget to ask God for wisdom concerning all of your daily tasks.

---

[a] *34* In Hebrew texts 4:21-34 is numbered 5:1-14. [b] In Hebrew texts 5:1-18 is numbered 5:15-32. [c] *11* That is, probably about 3,600 tons or about 3,250 metric tons [d] *11* Septuagint (see also 2 Chron. 2:10); Hebrew *twenty cors* [e] *11* That is, about 120,000 gallons or about 440,000 liters

home. Adoniram was in charge of the forced labor. 15 Solomon had sev-
enty thousand carriers and eighty thousand stonecutters in the hills,
16 as well as thirty-three hundred[a] foremen who supervised the project
and directed the workers. 17 At the king's command they removed from
the quarry large blocks of high-grade stone to provide a foundation of
dressed stone for the temple. 18 The craftsmen of Solomon and Hiram
and workers from Byblos cut and prepared the timber and stone for
the building of the temple.

SOLOMON BUILDS THE TEMPLE

6 In the four hundred and eightieth[b] year after the Israelites came
out of Egypt, in the fourth year of Solomon's reign over Israel, in
the month of Ziv, the second month, he began to build the temple of
the LORD.
2 The temple that King Solomon built for the LORD was sixty cu-
bits long, twenty wide and thirty high.[c] 3 The portico at the front of
the main hall of the temple extended the width of the temple, that is
twenty cubits,[d] and projected ten cubits[e] from the front of the temple.
4 He made narrow windows high up in the temple walls. 5 Against the
walls of the main hall and inner sanctuary he built a structure around
the building, in which there were side rooms. 6 The lowest floor was
five cubits[f] wide, the middle floor six cubits[g] and the third floor seven.[h]
He made offset ledges around the outside of the temple so that noth-
ing would be inserted into the temple walls.
7 In building the temple, only blocks dressed at the quarry were used,
and no hammer, chisel or any other iron tool was heard at the temple
site while it was being built.
8 The entrance to the lowest[i] floor was on the south side of the tem-
ple; a stairway led up to the middle level and from there to the third.
9 So he built the temple and completed it, roofing it with beams and
cedar planks. 10 And he built the side rooms all along the temple. The
height of each was five cubits, and they were attached to the temple
by beams of cedar.
11 The word of the LORD came to Solomon: 12 "As for this temple you
are building, if you follow my decrees, observe my laws and keep all
my commands and obey them, I will fulfill through you the promise
I gave to David your father. 13 And I will live among the Israelites and
will not abandon my people Israel."
14 So Solomon built the temple and completed it. 15 He lined its interior
walls with cedar boards, paneling them from the floor of the temple to
the ceiling, and covered the floor of the temple with planks of juniper.
16 He partitioned off twenty cubits at the rear of the temple with cedar
boards from floor to ceiling to form within the temple an inner sanctu-
ary, the Most Holy Place. 17 The main hall in front of this room was forty
cubits[j] long. 18 The inside of the temple was cedar, carved with gourds
and open flowers. Everything was cedar; no stone was to be seen.

PRAYING SCRIPTURE

1 Kings 6

During the temple construction, the Lord appeared to Solomon and made it clear that a building was not enough. God reminded Solomon that his promise never to abandon his people was connected to their obedience. It was a command Israel had forsaken many times.

Scripture teaches us that clothes, buildings, and rank don't impress God. In what worldly way are you tempted to impress him? Lay that on the altar and commit to obedience.

[a] *16* Hebrew; some Septuagint manuscripts (see also 2 Chron. 2:2,18) *thirty-six hundred* [b] *1* Hebrew; Septuagint *four hundred and fortieth* [c] *2* That is, about 90 feet long, 30 feet wide and 45 feet high or about 27 meters long, 9 meters wide and 14 meters high [d] *3* That is, about 30 feet or about 9 meters; also in verses 16 and 20 [e] *3* That is, about 15 feet or about 4.5 meters; also in verses 23-26 [f] *6* That is, about 7 1/2 feet or about 2.3 meters; also in verses 10 and 24 [g] *6* That is, about 9 feet or about 2.7 meters [h] *6* That is, about 11 feet or about 3.2 meters [i] *8* Septuagint; Hebrew *middle* [j] *17* That is, about 60 feet or about 18 meters

[19]He prepared the inner sanctuary within the temple to set the ark
of the covenant of the LORD there. [20]The inner sanctuary was twenty
cubits long, twenty wide and twenty high. He overlaid the inside with
pure gold, and he also overlaid the altar of cedar. [21]Solomon covered
the inside of the temple with pure gold, and he extended gold chains
across the front of the inner sanctuary, which was overlaid with gold.
[22]So he overlaid the whole interior with gold. He also overlaid with
gold the altar that belonged to the inner sanctuary.

[23]For the inner sanctuary he made a pair of cherubim out of olive
wood, each ten cubits high. [24]One wing of the first cherub was five
cubits long, and the other wing five cubits — ten cubits from wing tip
to wing tip. [25]The second cherub also measured ten cubits, for the two
cherubim were identical in size and shape. [26]The height of each cherub
was ten cubits. [27]He placed the cherubim inside the innermost room
of the temple, with their wings spread out. The wing of one cherub
touched one wall, while the wing of the other touched the other wall,
and their wings touched each other in the middle of the room. [28]He
overlaid the cherubim with gold.

[29]On the walls all around the temple, in both the inner and outer
rooms, he carved cherubim, palm trees and open flowers. [30]He also
covered the floors of both the inner and outer rooms of the temple
with gold.

[31]For the entrance to the inner sanctuary he made doors out of olive
wood that were one fifth of the width of the sanctuary. [32]And on the two
olive-wood doors he carved cherubim, palm trees and open flowers, and
overlaid the cherubim and palm trees with hammered gold. [33]In the
same way, for the entrance to the main hall he made doorframes out of
olive wood that were one fourth of the width of the hall. [34]He also made
two doors out of juniper wood, each having two leaves that turned in
sockets. [35]He carved cherubim, palm trees and open flowers on them
and overlaid them with gold hammered evenly over the carvings.

[36]And he built the inner courtyard of three courses of dressed stone
and one course of trimmed cedar beams.

[37]The foundation of the temple of the LORD was laid in the fourth
year, in the month of Ziv. [38]In the eleventh year in the month of Bul,
the eighth month, the temple was finished in all its details according
to its specifications. He had spent seven years building it.

SOLOMON BUILDS HIS PALACE

7 It took Solomon thirteen years, however, to complete the construc-
tion of his palace. [2]He built the Palace of the Forest of Lebanon
a hundred cubits long, fifty wide and thirty high,[a] with four rows of
cedar columns supporting trimmed cedar beams. [3]It was roofed with
cedar above the beams that rested on the columns — forty-five beams,
fifteen to a row. [4]Its windows were placed high in sets of three, facing
each other. [5]All the doorways had rectangular frames; they were in the
front part in sets of three, facing each other.[b]

[6]He made a colonnade fifty cubits long and thirty wide.[c] In front of
it was a portico, and in front of that were pillars and an overhanging
roof.

[a] 2 That is, about 150 feet long, 75 feet wide and 45 feet high or about 45 meters long, 23 meters wide and 14 meters high [b] 5 The meaning of the Hebrew for this verse is uncertain. [c] 6 That is, about 75 feet long and 45 feet wide or about 23 meters long and 14 meters wide

PRAYING SCRIPTURE

1 Kings 7

The skill shown in the building of the temple demonstrates that work has dignity and worth in God's view. The craftsmen were just as important as David who envisioned the temple or Solomon who brought it to construction.

If you are not a pastor, ministry leader or missionary, do you wonder whether your work matters to God? It does! Ask him to glorify himself as you honor him in your work.

7He built the throne hall, the Hall of Justice, where he was to judge, and he covered it with cedar from floor to ceiling.[a] 8And the palace in which he was to live, set farther back, was similar in design. Solomon also made a palace like this hall for Pharaoh's daughter, whom he had married.

9All these structures, from the outside to the great courtyard and from foundation to eaves, were made of blocks of high-grade stone cut to size and smoothed on their inner and outer faces. 10The foundations were laid with large stones of good quality, some measuring ten cubits[b] and some eight.[c] 11Above were high-grade stones, cut to size, and cedar beams. 12The great courtyard was surrounded by a wall of three courses of dressed stone and one course of trimmed cedar beams, as was the inner courtyard of the temple of the LORD with its portico.

THE TEMPLE'S FURNISHINGS

13King Solomon sent to Tyre and brought Huram,[d] 14whose mother was a widow from the tribe of Naphtali and whose father was from Tyre and a skilled craftsman in bronze. Huram was filled with wisdom, with understanding and with knowledge to do all kinds of bronze work. He came to King Solomon and did all the work assigned to him.

15He cast two bronze pillars, each eighteen cubits high and twelve cubits in circumference.[e] 16He also made two capitals of cast bronze to set on the tops of the pillars; each capital was five cubits[f] high. 17A network of interwoven chains adorned the capitals on top of the pillars, seven for each capital. 18He made pomegranates in two rows[g] encircling each network to decorate the capitals on top of the pillars.[h] He did the same for each capital. 19The capitals on top of the pillars in the portico were in the shape of lilies, four cubits[i] high. 20On the capitals of both pillars, above the bowl-shaped part next to the network, were the two hundred pomegranates in rows all around. 21He erected the pillars at the portico of the temple. The pillar to the south he named Jakin[j] and the one to the north Boaz.[k] 22The capitals on top were in the shape of lilies. And so the work on the pillars was completed.

23He made the Sea of cast metal, circular in shape, measuring ten cubits from rim to rim and five cubits high. It took a line of thirty cubits[l] to measure around it. 24Below the rim, gourds encircled it—ten to a cubit. The gourds were cast in two rows in one piece with the Sea.

25The Sea stood on twelve bulls, three facing north, three facing west, three facing south and three facing east. The Sea rested on top of them, and their hindquarters were toward the center. 26It was a handbreadth[m] in thickness, and its rim was like the rim of a cup, like a lily blossom. It held two thousand baths.[n]

---

[a] *7* Vulgate and Syriac; Hebrew *floor* [b] *10* That is, about 15 feet or about 4.5 meters; also in verse 23 [c] *10* That is, about 12 feet or about 3.6 meters [d] *13* Hebrew *Hiram,* a variant of *Huram;* also in verses 40 and 45 [e] *15* That is, about 27 feet high and 18 feet in circumference or about 8.1 meters high and 5.4 meters in circumference [f] *16* That is, about 7 1/2 feet or about 2.3 meters; also in verse 23 [g] *18* Two Hebrew manuscripts and Septuagint; most Hebrew manuscripts *made the pillars, and there were two rows* [h] *18* Many Hebrew manuscripts and Syriac; most Hebrew manuscripts *pomegranates* [i] *19* That is, about 6 feet or about 1.8 meters; also in verse 38 [j] *21* *Jakin* probably means *he establishes.* [k] *21* *Boaz* probably means *in him is strength.* [l] *23* That is, about 45 feet or about 14 meters [m] *26* That is, about 3 inches or about 7.5 centimeters [n] *26* That is, about 12,000 gallons or about 44,000 liters; the Septuagint does not have this sentence.

27 He also made ten movable stands of bronze; each was four cubits
long, four wide and three high.[a] 28 This is how the stands were made:
They had side panels attached to uprights. 29 On the panels between the
uprights were lions, bulls and cherubim — and on the uprights as well.
Above and below the lions and bulls were wreaths of hammered work.
30 Each stand had four bronze wheels with bronze axles, and each had a
basin resting on four supports, cast with wreaths on each side. 31 On the
inside of the stand there was an opening that had a circular frame one
cubit[b] deep. This opening was round, and with its basework it measured
a cubit and a half.[c] Around its opening there was engraving. The panels
of the stands were square, not round. 32 The four wheels were under the
panels, and the axles of the wheels were attached to the stand. The di-
ameter of each wheel was a cubit and a half. 33 The wheels were made like
chariot wheels; the axles, rims, spokes and hubs were all of cast metal.

34 Each stand had four handles, one on each corner, projecting from
the stand. 35 At the top of the stand there was a circular band half a
cubit[d] deep. The supports and panels were attached to the top of the
stand. 36 He engraved cherubim, lions and palm trees on the surfaces of
the supports and on the panels, in every available space, with wreaths
all around. 37 This is the way he made the ten stands. They were all cast
in the same molds and were identical in size and shape.

38 He then made ten bronze basins, each holding forty baths[e] and
measuring four cubits across, one basin to go on each of the ten stands.
39 He placed five of the stands on the south side of the temple and five
on the north. He placed the Sea on the south side, at the southeast
corner of the temple. 40 He also made the pots[f] and shovels and sprin-
kling bowls.

So Huram finished all the work he had undertaken for King Solomon
in the temple of the LORD:

41 the two pillars;
the two bowl-shaped capitals on top of the pillars;
the two sets of network decorating the two bowl-shaped capitals
on top of the pillars;
42 the four hundred pomegranates for the two sets of network (two
rows of pomegranates for each network decorating the bowl-
shaped capitals on top of the pillars);
43 the ten stands with their ten basins;
44 the Sea and the twelve bulls under it;
45 the pots, shovels and sprinkling bowls.

All these objects that Huram made for King Solomon for the temple
of the LORD were of burnished bronze. 46 The king had them cast in clay
molds in the plain of the Jordan between Sukkoth and Zarethan. 47 Sol-
omon left all these things unweighed, because there were so many; the
weight of the bronze was not determined.

48 Solomon also made all the furnishings that were in the LORD's
temple:

---

[a] *27* That is, about 6 feet long and wide and about 4 1/2 feet high or about 1.8 meters long and wide and 1.4 meters high [b] *31* That is, about 18 inches or about 45 centimeters [c] *31* That is, about 2 1/4 feet or about 68 centimeters; also in verse 32 [d] *35* That is, about 9 inches or about 23 centimeters [e] *38* That is, about 240 gallons or about 880 liters [f] *40* Many Hebrew manuscripts, Septuagint, Syriac and Vulgate (see also verse 45 and 2 Chron. 4:11); many other Hebrew manuscripts *basins*

the golden altar;
the golden table on which was the bread of the Presence;
49 the lampstands of pure gold (five on the right and five on the left,
in front of the inner sanctuary);
the gold floral work and lamps and tongs;
50 the pure gold basins, wick trimmers, sprinkling bowls, dishes and
censers;
and the gold sockets for the doors of the innermost room, the
Most Holy Place, and also for the doors of the main hall of the
temple.

51When all the work King Solomon had done for the temple of the
LORD was finished, he brought in the things his father David had dedi-
cated — the silver and gold and the furnishings — and he placed them
in the treasuries of the LORD's temple.

THE ARK BROUGHT TO THE TEMPLE

8 Then King Solomon summoned into his presence at Jerusalem the
elders of Israel, all the heads of the tribes and the chiefs of the Is-
raelite families, to bring up the ark of the LORD's covenant from Zion,
the City of David. 2All the Israelites came together to King Solomon at
the time of the festival in the month of Ethanim, the seventh month.
3When all the elders of Israel had arrived, the priests took up the ark,
4and they brought up the ark of the LORD and the tent of meeting and
all the sacred furnishings in it. The priests and Levites carried them up,
5and King Solomon and the entire assembly of Israel that had gathered
about him were before the ark, sacrificing so many sheep and cattle
that they could not be recorded or counted.
6The priests then brought the ark of the LORD's covenant to its place
in the inner sanctuary of the temple, the Most Holy Place, and put it
beneath the wings of the cherubim. 7The cherubim spread their wings
over the place of the ark and overshadowed the ark and its carrying
poles. 8These poles were so long that their ends could be seen from
the Holy Place in front of the inner sanctuary, but not from outside
the Holy Place; and they are still there today. 9There was nothing in the
ark except the two stone tablets that Moses had placed in it at Horeb,
where the LORD made a covenant with the Israelites after they came
out of Egypt.
10When the priests withdrew from the Holy Place, the cloud filled the
temple of the LORD. 11And the priests could not perform their service
because of the cloud, for the glory of the LORD filled his temple.
12Then Solomon said, "The LORD has said that he would dwell in a
dark cloud; 13I have indeed built a magnificent temple for you, a place
for you to dwell forever."
14While the whole assembly of Israel was standing there, the king
turned around and blessed them. 15Then he said:

"Praise be to the LORD, the God of Israel, who with his own hand
has fulfilled what he promised with his own mouth to my father
David. For he said, 16'Since the day I brought my people Israel out
of Egypt, I have not chosen a city in any tribe of Israel to have a
temple built so that my Name might be there, but I have chosen
David to rule my people Israel.'
17"My father David had it in his heart to build a temple for the
Name of the LORD, the God of Israel. 18But the LORD said to my

PRAYING SCRIPTURE

1 Kings 8

When the priests brought the ark into the Most Holy Place amid the sacrificial offerings, God's glory—the light that emanates from his absolute holiness—appeared in a cloud and filled the entire temple. Solomon's dedicatory prayer asked that God's eyes would always be on the people who came to it.

Today the temple is the bodies of Jesus' followers; we are God's temple. How does that inform your praying?

father David, 'You did well to have it in your heart to build a tem-
ple for my Name. 19Nevertheless, you are not the one to build the
temple, but your son, your own flesh and blood — he is the one
who will build the temple for my Name.'
20"The LORD has kept the promise he made: I have succeeded
David my father and now I sit on the throne of Israel, just as the
LORD promised, and I have built the temple for the Name of the
LORD, the God of Israel. 21I have provided a place there for the ark,
in which is the covenant of the LORD that he made with our ances-
tors when he brought them out of Egypt."

SOLOMON'S PRAYER OF DEDICATION

22Then Solomon stood before the altar of the LORD in front of the
whole assembly of Israel, spread out his hands toward heaven 23and
said:

"LORD, the God of Israel, there is no God like you in heaven
above or on earth below — you who keep your covenant of love
with your servants who continue wholeheartedly in your way.
24You have kept your promise to your servant David my father;
with your mouth you have promised and with your hand you have
fulfilled it — as it is today.
25"Now LORD, the God of Israel, keep for your servant David my
father the promises you made to him when you said, 'You shall
never fail to have a successor to sit before me on the throne of
Israel, if only your descendants are careful in all they do to walk
before me faithfully as you have done.' 26And now, God of Israel,
let your word that you promised your servant David my father
come true.
27"But will God really dwell on earth? The heavens, even the
highest heaven, cannot contain you. How much less this temple I
have built! 28Yet give attention to your servant's prayer and his plea
for mercy, LORD my God. Hear the cry and the prayer that your ser-
vant is praying in your presence this day. 29May your eyes be open
toward this temple night and day, this place of which you said, 'My
Name shall be there,' so that you will hear the prayer your servant
prays toward this place. 30Hear the supplication of your servant
and of your people Israel when they pray toward this place. Hear
from heaven, your dwelling place, and when you hear, forgive.
31"When anyone wrongs their neighbor and is required to take
an oath and they come and swear the oath before your altar in
this temple, 32then hear from heaven and act. Judge between your
servants, condemning the guilty by bringing down on their heads
what they have done, and vindicating the innocent by treating
them in accordance with their innocence.
33"When your people Israel have been defeated by an enemy
because they have sinned against you, and when they turn back
to you and give praise to your name, praying and making suppli-
cation to you in this temple, 34then hear from heaven and forgive
the sin of your people Israel and bring them back to the land you
gave to their ancestors.
35"When the heavens are shut up and there is no rain because
your people have sinned against you, and when they pray toward
this place and give praise to your name and turn from their sin

because you have afflicted them, [36]then hear from heaven and for-
give the sin of your servants, your people Israel. Teach them the
right way to live, and send rain on the land you gave your people
for an inheritance.

[37]"When famine or plague comes to the land, or blight or mil-
dew, locusts or grasshoppers, or when an enemy besieges them in
any of their cities, whatever disaster or disease may come, [38]and
when a prayer or plea is made by anyone among your people Is-
rael — being aware of the afflictions of their own hearts, and
spreading out their hands toward this temple — [39]then hear from
heaven, your dwelling place. Forgive and act; deal with everyone
according to all they do, since you know their hearts (for you alone
know every human heart), [40]so that they will fear you all the time
they live in the land you gave our ancestors.

[41]"As for the foreigner who does not belong to your people Israel
but has come from a distant land because of your name — [42]for
they will hear of your great name and your mighty hand and your
outstretched arm — when they come and pray toward this tem-
ple, [43]then hear from heaven, your dwelling place. Do whatever
the foreigner asks of you, so that all the peoples of the earth may
know your name and fear you, as do your own people Israel, and
may know that this house I have built bears your Name.

[44]"When your people go to war against their enemies, wherever
you send them, and when they pray to the LORD toward the city
you have chosen and the temple I have built for your Name, [45]then
hear from heaven their prayer and their plea, and uphold their
cause.

[46]"When they sin against you — for there is no one who does
not sin — and you become angry with them and give them over to
their enemies, who take them captive to their own lands, far away
or near; [47]and if they have a change of heart in the land where
they are held captive, and repent and plead with you in the land
of their captors and say, 'We have sinned, we have done wrong, we
have acted wickedly'; [48]and if they turn back to you with all their
heart and soul in the land of their enemies who took them cap-
tive, and pray to you toward the land you gave their ancestors, to-
ward the city you have chosen and the temple I have built for your
Name; [49]then from heaven, your dwelling place, hear their prayer
and their plea, and uphold their cause. [50]And forgive your people,
who have sinned against you; forgive all the offenses they have
committed against you, and cause their captors to show them
mercy; [51]for they are your people and your inheritance, whom you
brought out of Egypt, out of that iron-smelting furnace.

[52]"May your eyes be open to your servant's plea and to the plea
of your people Israel, and may you listen to them whenever they
cry out to you. [53]For you singled them out from all the nations of
the world to be your own inheritance, just as you declared through
your servant Moses when you, Sovereign LORD, brought our an-
cestors out of Egypt."

[54]When Solomon had finished all these prayers and supplications
to the LORD, he rose from before the altar of the LORD, where he had
been kneeling with his hands spread out toward heaven. [55]He stood
and blessed the whole assembly of Israel in a loud voice, saying:

56“Praise be to the LORD, who has given rest to his people Israel
just as he promised. Not one word has failed of all the good prom-
ises he gave through his servant Moses. 57May the LORD our God
be with us as he was with our ancestors; may he never leave us nor
forsake us. 58May he turn our hearts to him, to walk in obedience
to him and keep the commands, decrees and laws he gave our
ancestors. 59And may these words of mine, which I have prayed
before the LORD, be near to the LORD our God day and night, that
he may uphold the cause of his servant and the cause of his people
Israel according to each day’s need, 60so that all the peoples of the
earth may know that the LORD is God and that there is no other.
61And may your hearts be fully committed to the LORD our God, to
live by his decrees and obey his commands, as at this time.”

THE DEDICATION OF THE TEMPLE

62Then the king and all Israel with him offered sacrifices before the
LORD. 63Solomon offered a sacrifice of fellowship offerings to the LORD:
twenty-two thousand cattle and a hundred and twenty thousand sheep
and goats. So the king and all the Israelites dedicated the temple of
the LORD.

64On that same day the king consecrated the middle part of the
courtyard in front of the temple of the LORD, and there he offered
burnt offerings, grain offerings and the fat of the fellowship offerings,
because the bronze altar that stood before the LORD was too small to
hold the burnt offerings, the grain offerings and the fat of the fellow-
ship offerings.

65So Solomon observed the festival at that time, and all Israel with
him — a vast assembly, people from Lebo Hamath to the Wadi of Egypt.
They celebrated it before the LORD our God for seven days and seven
days more, fourteen days in all. 66On the following day he sent the
people away. They blessed the king and then went home, joyful and
glad in heart for all the good things the LORD had done for his servant
David and his people Israel.

THE LORD APPEARS TO SOLOMON

9 When Solomon had finished building the temple of the LORD and
the royal palace, and had achieved all he had desired to do, 2the
LORD appeared to him a second time, as he had appeared to him at
Gibeon. 3The LORD said to him:

“I have heard the prayer and plea you have made before me; I
have consecrated this temple, which you have built, by putting my
Name there forever. My eyes and my heart will always be there.

4“As for you, if you walk before me faithfully with integrity of
heart and uprightness, as David your father did, and do all I com-
mand and observe my decrees and laws, 5I will establish your
royal throne over Israel forever, as I promised David your father
when I said, ‘You shall never fail to have a successor on the throne
of Israel.’

6“But if you[a] or your descendants turn away from me and do
not observe the commands and decrees I have given you[a] and go
off to serve other gods and worship them, 7then I will cut off Israel

PRAYING SCRIPTURE

1 Kings 9

The Lord appeared to Solomon again and implored him to walk with integrity and an upright heart. God reiterated the promise he’d made to David, extending it to Solomon and his sons as long as they kept his laws.

Solomon’s inconsistency proved his downfall. He sponsored lavish offerings on one hand but intermarried pagan wives on the other. Ask God to help you keep solely to his ways.

[a] 6 The Hebrew is plural.

from the land I have given them and will reject this temple I have
consecrated for my Name. Israel will then become a byword and
an object of ridicule among all peoples. 8This temple will become
a heap of rubble. All[a] who pass by will be appalled and will scoff
and say, 'Why has the LORD done such a thing to this land and to
this temple?' 9People will answer, 'Because they have forsaken the
LORD their God, who brought their ancestors out of Egypt, and
have embraced other gods, worshiping and serving them — that
is why the LORD brought all this disaster on them.'"

SOLOMON'S OTHER ACTIVITIES

10At the end of twenty years, during which Solomon built these two
buildings — the temple of the LORD and the royal palace — 11King Sol-
omon gave twenty towns in Galilee to Hiram king of Tyre, because
Hiram had supplied him with all the cedar and juniper and gold he
wanted. 12But when Hiram went from Tyre to see the towns that Sol-
omon had given him, he was not pleased with them. 13"What kind of
towns are these you have given me, my brother?" he asked. And he
called them the Land of Kabul,[b] a name they have to this day. 14Now
Hiram had sent to the king 120 talents[c] of gold.

15Here is the account of the forced labor King Solomon conscripted
to build the LORD's temple, his own palace, the terraces,[d] the wall of
Jerusalem, and Hazor, Megiddo and Gezer. 16(Pharaoh king of Egypt
had attacked and captured Gezer. He had set it on fire. He killed its
Canaanite inhabitants and then gave it as a wedding gift to his daugh-
ter, Solomon's wife. 17And Solomon rebuilt Gezer.) He built up Lower
Beth Horon, 18Baalath, and Tadmor[e] in the desert, within his land, 19as
well as all his store cities and the towns for his chariots and for his
horses[f] — whatever he desired to build in Jerusalem, in Lebanon and
throughout all the territory he ruled.

20There were still people left from the Amorites, Hittites, Perizzites,
Hivites and Jebusites (these peoples were not Israelites). 21Solomon
conscripted the descendants of all these peoples remaining in the
land — whom the Israelites could not exterminate[g] — to serve as slave
labor, as it is to this day. 22But Solomon did not make slaves of any of
the Israelites; they were his fighting men, his government officials, his
officers, his captains, and the commanders of his chariots and chari-
oteers. 23They were also the chief officials in charge of Solomon's proj-
ects — 550 officials supervising those who did the work.

24After Pharaoh's daughter had come up from the City of David to
the palace Solomon had built for her, he constructed the terraces.

25Three times a year Solomon sacrificed burnt offerings and fel-
lowship offerings on the altar he had built for the LORD, burning in-
cense before the LORD along with them, and so fulfilled the temple
obligations.

26King Solomon also built ships at Ezion Geber, which is near Elath in
Edom, on the shore of the Red Sea.[h] 27And Hiram sent his men — sailors

[a] *8* See some Septuagint manuscripts, Old Latin, Syriac, Arabic and Targum; Hebrew *And though this temple is now imposing, all* [b] *13* *Kabul* sounds like the Hebrew for *good-for-nothing.* [c] *14* That is, about 4 1/2 tons or about 4 metric tons [d] *15* Or *the Millo*; also in verse 24 [e] *18* The Hebrew may also be read *Tamar.* [f] *19* Or *charioteers* [g] *21* The Hebrew term refers to the irrevocable giving over of things or persons to the LORD, often by totally destroying them. [h] *26* Or *the Sea of Reeds*

who knew the sea — to serve in the fleet with Solomon's men. 28They
sailed to Ophir and brought back 420 talents[a] of gold, which they de-
livered to King Solomon.

THE QUEEN OF SHEBA VISITS SOLOMON

10 When the queen of Sheba heard about the fame of Solomon
and his relationship to the LORD, she came to test Solomon with
hard questions. 2Arriving at Jerusalem with a very great caravan —
with camels carrying spices, large quantities of gold, and precious
stones — she came to Solomon and talked with him about all that she
had on her mind. 3Solomon answered all her questions; nothing was
too hard for the king to explain to her. 4When the queen of Sheba saw
all the wisdom of Solomon and the palace he had built, 5the food on his
table, the seating of his officials, the attending servants in their robes,
his cupbearers, and the burnt offerings he made at[b] the temple of the
LORD, she was overwhelmed.
6She said to the king, "The report I heard in my own country about
your achievements and your wisdom is true. 7But I did not believe
these things until I came and saw with my own eyes. Indeed, not even
half was told me; in wisdom and wealth you have far exceeded the
report I heard. 8How happy your people must be! How happy your offi-
cials, who continually stand before you and hear your wisdom! 9Praise
be to the LORD your God, who has delighted in you and placed you on
the throne of Israel. Because of the LORD's eternal love for Israel, he has
made you king to maintain justice and righteousness."
10And she gave the king 120 talents[c] of gold, large quantities of
spices, and precious stones. Never again were so many spices brought
in as those the queen of Sheba gave to King Solomon.
11(Hiram's ships brought gold from Ophir; and from there they
brought great cargoes of almugwood[d] and precious stones. 12The king
used the almugwood to make supports[e] for the temple of the LORD and
for the royal palace, and to make harps and lyres for the musicians. So
much almugwood has never been imported or seen since that day.)
13King Solomon gave the queen of Sheba all she desired and asked
for, besides what he had given her out of his royal bounty. Then she left
and returned with her retinue to her own country.

PRAYING SCRIPTURE

1 Kings 10

The queen of Sheba's visit marked a moment where God's people were bringing blessings to the other families of the earth. Solomon's wisdom was now preceding him, becoming known to political leaders in neighboring countries.

Solomon showed willingness to work with other leaders for mutual benefit. Ask God to help you be a bridge builder when you can. Partnerships can move kingdom work forward in ways that exceed our individual efforts.

SOLOMON'S SPLENDOR

14The weight of the gold that Solomon received yearly was 666 tal-
ents,[f] 15not including the revenues from merchants and traders and
from all the Arabian kings and the governors of the territories.
16King Solomon made two hundred large shields of hammered gold;
six hundred shekels[g] of gold went into each shield. 17He also made
three hundred small shields of hammered gold, with three minas[h] of
gold in each shield. The king put them in the Palace of the Forest of
Lebanon.

---

[a] *28* That is, about 16 tons or about 14 metric tons [b] *5* Or *the ascent by which he went up to* [c] *10* That is, about 4 1/2 tons or about 4 metric tons [d] *11* Probably a variant of *algumwood;* also in verse 12 [e] *12* The meaning of the Hebrew for this word is uncertain. [f] *14* That is, about 25 tons or about 23 metric tons [g] *16* That is, about 15 pounds or about 6.9 kilograms; also in verse 29 [h] *17* That is, about 3 3/4 pounds or about 1.7 kilograms; or perhaps reference is to double minas, that is, about 7 1/2 pounds or about 3.5 kilograms.

18Then the king made a great throne covered with ivory and overlaid with fine gold. 19The throne had six steps, and its back had a rounded top. On both sides of the seat were armrests, with a lion standing beside each of them. 20Twelve lions stood on the six steps, one at either end of each step. Nothing like it had ever been made for any other kingdom. 21All King Solomon's goblets were gold, and all the household articles in the Palace of the Forest of Lebanon were pure gold. Nothing was made of silver, because silver was considered of little value in Solomon's days. 22The king had a fleet of trading ships[a] at sea along with the ships of Hiram. Once every three years it returned, carrying gold, silver and ivory, and apes and baboons.

23King Solomon was greater in riches and wisdom than all the other kings of the earth. 24The whole world sought audience with Solomon to hear the wisdom God had put in his heart. 25Year after year, everyone who came brought a gift—articles of silver and gold, robes, weapons and spices, and horses and mules.

26Solomon accumulated chariots and horses; he had fourteen hundred chariots and twelve thousand horses,[b] which he kept in the chariot cities and also with him in Jerusalem. 27The king made silver as common in Jerusalem as stones, and cedar as plentiful as sycamore-fig trees in the foothills. 28Solomon's horses were imported from Egypt and from Kue[c]—the royal merchants purchased them from Kue at the current price. 29They imported a chariot from Egypt for six hundred shekels of silver, and a horse for a hundred and fifty.[d] They also exported them to all the kings of the Hittites and of the Arameans.

SOLOMON'S WIVES

11 King Solomon, however, loved many foreign women besides Pharaoh's daughter—Moabites, Ammonites, Edomites, Sidonians and Hittites. 2They were from nations about which the LORD had told the Israelites, "You must not intermarry with them, because they will surely turn your hearts after their gods." Nevertheless, Solomon held fast to them in love. 3He had seven hundred wives of royal birth and three hundred concubines, and his wives led him astray. 4As Solomon grew old, his wives turned his heart after other gods, and his heart was not fully devoted to the LORD his God, as the heart of David his father had been. 5He followed Ashtoreth the goddess of the Sidonians, and Molek the detestable god of the Ammonites. 6So Solomon did evil in the eyes of the LORD; he did not follow the LORD completely, as David his father had done.

7On a hill east of Jerusalem, Solomon built a high place for Chemosh the detestable god of Moab, and for Molek the detestable god of the Ammonites. 8He did the same for all his foreign wives, who burned incense and offered sacrifices to their gods.

9The LORD became angry with Solomon because his heart had turned away from the LORD, the God of Israel, who had appeared to him twice. 10Although he had forbidden Solomon to follow other gods, Solomon did not keep the LORD's command. 11So the LORD said to Solomon, "Since this is your attitude and you have not kept my covenant and my decrees, which I commanded you, I will most certainly tear the kingdom away from you and give it to one of your subordinates.

PRAYING SCRIPTURE

1 Kings 11

Immorality has turned many of God's people away from him. As king, Solomon could have any woman his heart desired, and he desired many. Marriage of political convenience led him to violate God's warning against intermarriage with women who did not know or serve God.

Temptation often comes in the form of what we desire too strongly. Ask God to keep your desires holy and reflective of his purposes for you.

[a] 22 Hebrew *of ships of Tarshish* [b] 26 Or *charioteers* [c] 28 Probably *Cilicia*
[d] 29 That is, about 3 3/4 pounds or about 1.7 kilograms

[12]Nevertheless, for the sake of David your father, I will not do it during
your lifetime. I will tear it out of the hand of your son. [13]Yet I will not
tear the whole kingdom from him, but will give him one tribe for the
sake of David my servant and for the sake of Jerusalem, which I have
chosen."

SOLOMON'S ADVERSARIES

[14]Then the LORD raised up against Solomon an adversary, Hadad the
Edomite, from the royal line of Edom. [15]Earlier when David was fight-
ing with Edom, Joab the commander of the army, who had gone up to
bury the dead, had struck down all the men in Edom. [16]Joab and all
the Israelites stayed there for six months, until they had destroyed
all the men in Edom. [17]But Hadad, still only a boy, fled to Egypt with
some Edomite officials who had served his father. [18]They set out from
Midian and went to Paran. Then taking people from Paran with them,
they went to Egypt, to Pharaoh king of Egypt, who gave Hadad a house
and land and provided him with food.

[19]Pharaoh was so pleased with Hadad that he gave him a sister of his
own wife, Queen Tahpenes, in marriage. [20]The sister of Tahpenes bore
him a son named Genubath, whom Tahpenes brought up in the royal
palace. There Genubath lived with Pharaoh's own children.

[21]While he was in Egypt, Hadad heard that David rested with his
ancestors and that Joab the commander of the army was also dead.
Then Hadad said to Pharaoh, "Let me go, that I may return to my own
country."

[22]"What have you lacked here that you want to go back to your own
country?" Pharaoh asked.

"Nothing," Hadad replied, "but do let me go!"

[23]And God raised up against Solomon another adversary, Rezon son
of Eliada, who had fled from his master, Hadadezer king of Zobah.
[24]When David destroyed Zobah's army, Rezon gathered a band of men
around him and became their leader; they went to Damascus, where
they settled and took control. [25]Rezon was Israel's adversary as long as
Solomon lived, adding to the trouble caused by Hadad. So Rezon ruled
in Aram and was hostile toward Israel.

JEROBOAM REBELS AGAINST SOLOMON

[26]Also, Jeroboam son of Nebat rebelled against the king. He was one
of Solomon's officials, an Ephraimite from Zeredah, and his mother
was a widow named Zeruah.

[27]Here is the account of how he rebelled against the king: Solomon
had built the terraces[a] and had filled in the gap in the wall of the city
of David his father. [28]Now Jeroboam was a man of standing, and when
Solomon saw how well the young man did his work, he put him in
charge of the whole labor force of the tribes of Joseph.

[29]About that time Jeroboam was going out of Jerusalem, and Ahijah
the prophet of Shiloh met him on the way, wearing a new cloak. The
two of them were alone out in the country, [30]and Ahijah took hold of
the new cloak he was wearing and tore it into twelve pieces. [31]Then
he said to Jeroboam, "Take ten pieces for yourself, for this is what the
LORD, the God of Israel, says: 'See, I am going to tear the kingdom out
of Solomon's hand and give you ten tribes. [32]But for the sake of my

[a] *27* Or *the Millo*

servant David and the city of Jerusalem, which I have chosen out of
all the tribes of Israel, he will have one tribe. 33 I will do this because
they have[a] forsaken me and worshiped Ashtoreth the goddess of the
Sidonians, Chemosh the god of the Moabites, and Molek the god of the
Ammonites, and have not walked in obedience to me, nor done what
is right in my eyes, nor kept my decrees and laws as David, Solomon's
father, did.
34 "'But I will not take the whole kingdom out of Solomon's hand; I
have made him ruler all the days of his life for the sake of David my
servant, whom I chose and who obeyed my commands and decrees.
35 I will take the kingdom from his son's hands and give you ten tribes.
36 I will give one tribe to his son so that David my servant may always
have a lamp before me in Jerusalem, the city where I chose to put my
Name. 37 However, as for you, I will take you, and you will rule over all
that your heart desires; you will be king over Israel. 38 If you do what-
ever I command you and walk in obedience to me and do what is right
in my eyes by obeying my decrees and commands, as David my servant
did, I will be with you. I will build you a dynasty as enduring as the
one I built for David and will give Israel to you. 39 I will humble David's
descendants because of this, but not forever.'"
40 Solomon tried to kill Jeroboam, but Jeroboam fled to Egypt, to
Shishak the king, and stayed there until Solomon's death.

SOLOMON'S DEATH

41 As for the other events of Solomon's reign — all he did and the wis-
dom he displayed — are they not written in the book of the annals of
Solomon? 42 Solomon reigned in Jerusalem over all Israel forty years.
43 Then he rested with his ancestors and was buried in the city of David
his father. And Rehoboam his son succeeded him as king.

ISRAEL REBELS AGAINST REHOBOAM

12 Rehoboam went to Shechem, for all Israel had gone there to
make him king. 2 When Jeroboam son of Nebat heard this (he
was still in Egypt, where he had fled from King Solomon), he returned
from[b] Egypt. 3 So they sent for Jeroboam, and he and the whole assem-
bly of Israel went to Rehoboam and said to him: 4 "Your father put a
heavy yoke on us, but now lighten the harsh labor and the heavy yoke
he put on us, and we will serve you."
5 Rehoboam answered, "Go away for three days and then come back
to me." So the people went away.
6 Then King Rehoboam consulted the elders who had served his fa-
ther Solomon during his lifetime. "How would you advise me to an-
swer these people?" he asked.
7 They replied, "If today you will be a servant to these people and
serve them and give them a favorable answer, they will always be your
servants."
8 But Rehoboam rejected the advice the elders gave him and con-
sulted the young men who had grown up with him and were serving
him. 9 He asked them, "What is your advice? How should we answer
these people who say to me, 'Lighten the yoke your father put on us'?"
10 The young men who had grown up with him replied, "These

PRAYING SCRIPTURE

1 Kings 12

After Solomon's death, the kingdom quickly fell apart. When King Rehoboam listened to foolish counsel, a portion of the tribes installed Jeroboam as king. The kingdom was divided, and the people quickly turned away from God to idol worship. Again.

God calls his people to unity, but it is a hard thing to bring about. Ask God to help you have a spirit of unity.

---

[a] 33 Hebrew; Septuagint, Vulgate and Syriac *because he has* [b] 2 Or *he remained in*

people have said to you, 'Your father put a heavy yoke on us, but make our yoke lighter.' Now tell them, 'My little finger is thicker than my father's waist. 11My father laid on you a heavy yoke; I will make it even heavier. My father scourged you with whips; I will scourge you with scorpions.' "

12Three days later Jeroboam and all the people returned to Rehoboam, as the king had said, "Come back to me in three days." 13The king answered the people harshly. Rejecting the advice given him by the elders, 14he followed the advice of the young men and said, "My father made your yoke heavy; I will make it even heavier. My father scourged you with whips; I will scourge you with scorpions." 15So the king did not listen to the people, for this turn of events was from the LORD, to fulfill the word the LORD had spoken to Jeroboam son of Nebat through Ahijah the Shilonite.

16When all Israel saw that the king refused to listen to them, they answered the king:

"What share do we have in David,
  what part in Jesse's son?
To your tents, Israel!
  Look after your own house, David!"

So the Israelites went home. 17But as for the Israelites who were living in the towns of Judah, Rehoboam still ruled over them.

18King Rehoboam sent out Adoniram,[a] who was in charge of forced labor, but all Israel stoned him to death. King Rehoboam, however, managed to get into his chariot and escape to Jerusalem. 19So Israel has been in rebellion against the house of David to this day.

20When all the Israelites heard that Jeroboam had returned, they sent and called him to the assembly and made him king over all Israel. Only the tribe of Judah remained loyal to the house of David.

21When Rehoboam arrived in Jerusalem, he mustered all Judah and the tribe of Benjamin—a hundred and eighty thousand able young men—to go to war against Israel and to regain the kingdom for Rehoboam son of Solomon.

22But this word of God came to Shemaiah the man of God: 23"Say to Rehoboam son of Solomon king of Judah, to all Judah and Benjamin, and to the rest of the people, 24'This is what the LORD says: Do not go up to fight against your brothers, the Israelites. Go home, every one of you, for this is my doing.' " So they obeyed the word of the LORD and went home again, as the LORD had ordered.

GOLDEN CALVES AT BETHEL AND DAN

25Then Jeroboam fortified Shechem in the hill country of Ephraim and lived there. From there he went out and built up Peniel.[b]

26Jeroboam thought to himself, "The kingdom will now likely revert to the house of David. 27If these people go up to offer sacrifices at the temple of the LORD in Jerusalem, they will again give their allegiance to their lord, Rehoboam king of Judah. They will kill me and return to King Rehoboam."

28After seeking advice, the king made two golden calves. He said to the people, "It is too much for you to go up to Jerusalem. Here are

[a] *18* Some Septuagint manuscripts and Syriac (see also 4:6 and 5:14); Hebrew *Adoram* [b] *25* Hebrew *Penuel*, a variant of *Peniel*

your gods, Israel, who brought you up out of Egypt." 29One he set up
in Bethel, and the other in Dan. 30And this thing became a sin; the
people came to worship the one at Bethel and went as far as Dan to
worship the other.[a]
31Jeroboam built shrines on high places and appointed priests from
all sorts of people, even though they were not Levites. 32He instituted
a festival on the fifteenth day of the eighth month, like the festival
held in Judah, and offered sacrifices on the altar. This he did in Bethel,
sacrificing to the calves he had made. And at Bethel he also installed
priests at the high places he had made. 33On the fifteenth day of the
eighth month, a month of his own choosing, he offered sacrifices on
the altar he had built at Bethel. So he instituted the festival for the Israelites and went up to the altar to make offerings.

THE MAN OF GOD FROM JUDAH

13 By the word of the LORD a man of God came from Judah to Bethel,
as Jeroboam was standing by the altar to make an offering. 2By
the word of the LORD he cried out against the altar: "Altar, altar! This is
what the LORD says: 'A son named Josiah will be born to the house of
David. On you he will sacrifice the priests of the high places who make
offerings here, and human bones will be burned on you.'" 3That same
day the man of God gave a sign: "This is the sign the LORD has declared:
The altar will be split apart and the ashes on it will be poured out."
4When King Jeroboam heard what the man of God cried out against
the altar at Bethel, he stretched out his hand from the altar and said,
"Seize him!" But the hand he stretched out toward the man shriveled
up, so that he could not pull it back. 5Also, the altar was split apart and
its ashes poured out according to the sign given by the man of God by
the word of the LORD.
6Then the king said to the man of God, "Intercede with the LORD
your God and pray for me that my hand may be restored." So the man
of God interceded with the LORD, and the king's hand was restored and
became as it was before.
7The king said to the man of God, "Come home with me for a meal,
and I will give you a gift."
8But the man of God answered the king, "Even if you were to give
me half your possessions, I would not go with you, nor would I eat
bread or drink water here. 9For I was commanded by the word of the
LORD: 'You must not eat bread or drink water or return by the way you
came.'" 10So he took another road and did not return by the way he
had come to Bethel.
11Now there was a certain old prophet living in Bethel, whose sons
came and told him all that the man of God had done there that day.
They also told their father what he had said to the king. 12Their father
asked them, "Which way did he go?" And his sons showed him which
road the man of God from Judah had taken. 13So he said to his sons,
"Saddle the donkey for me." And when they had saddled the donkey
for him, he mounted it 14and rode after the man of God. He found him
sitting under an oak tree and asked, "Are you the man of God who came
from Judah?"
"I am," he replied.

[a] 30 Probable reading of the original Hebrew text; Masoretic Text *people went to the one as far as Dan*

PRAYING SCRIPTURE

1 Kings 13

Have you ever gotten bad advice from a person you thought you could trust—but after taking that advice, you realized you had taken the wrong counsel? The results can be devastating.

We all depend on others for counsel and often turn to people we trust. But when an adviser contradicts God's Word, we must obey God. Ask God to help you discern the difference.

15So the prophet said to him, "Come home with me and eat."
16The man of God said, "I cannot turn back and go with you, nor can
I eat bread or drink water with you in this place. 17I have been told by
the word of the LORD: 'You must not eat bread or drink water there or
return by the way you came.'"
18The old prophet answered, "I too am a prophet, as you are. And an
angel said to me by the word of the LORD: 'Bring him back with you to
your house so that he may eat bread and drink water.'" (But he was ly-
ing to him.) 19So the man of God returned with him and ate and drank
in his house.
20While they were sitting at the table, the word of the LORD came to
the old prophet who had brought him back. 21He cried out to the man
of God who had come from Judah, "This is what the LORD says: 'You
have defied the word of the LORD and have not kept the command the
LORD your God gave you. 22You came back and ate bread and drank wa-
ter in the place where he told you not to eat or drink. Therefore your
body will not be buried in the tomb of your ancestors.'"
23When the man of God had finished eating and drinking, the
prophet who had brought him back saddled his donkey for him. 24As
he went on his way, a lion met him on the road and killed him, and
his body was left lying on the road, with both the donkey and the lion
standing beside it. 25Some people who passed by saw the body lying
there, with the lion standing beside the body, and they went and re-
ported it in the city where the old prophet lived.
26When the prophet who had brought him back from his journey
heard of it, he said, "It is the man of God who defied the word of the
LORD. The LORD has given him over to the lion, which has mauled him
and killed him, as the word of the LORD had warned him."
27The prophet said to his sons, "Saddle the donkey for me," and they
did so. 28Then he went out and found the body lying on the road, with
the donkey and the lion standing beside it. The lion had neither eaten
the body nor mauled the donkey. 29So the prophet picked up the body
of the man of God, laid it on the donkey, and brought it back to his own
city to mourn for him and bury him. 30Then he laid the body in his
own tomb, and they mourned over him and said, "Alas, my brother!"
31After burying him, he said to his sons, "When I die, bury me in the
grave where the man of God is buried; lay my bones beside his bones.
32For the message he declared by the word of the LORD against the altar
in Bethel and against all the shrines on the high places in the towns of
Samaria will certainly come true."
33Even after this, Jeroboam did not change his evil ways, but once
more appointed priests for the high places from all sorts of people.
Anyone who wanted to become a priest he consecrated for the high
places. 34This was the sin of the house of Jeroboam that led to its down-
fall and to its destruction from the face of the earth.

AHIJAH'S PROPHECY AGAINST JEROBOAM

14 At that time Abijah son of Jeroboam became ill, 2and Jeroboam
said to his wife, "Go, disguise yourself, so you won't be recog-
nized as the wife of Jeroboam. Then go to Shiloh. Ahijah the prophet
is there — the one who told me I would be king over this people. 3Take
ten loaves of bread with you, some cakes and a jar of honey, and go to
him. He will tell you what will happen to the boy." 4So Jeroboam's wife
did what he said and went to Ahijah's house in Shiloh.

PRAYING SCRIPTURE

1 Kings 14

Jeroboam's sin brought about terrible consequences for his home and those around him. Rehoboam's sin brought Judah ever lower into sin and degradation. The people provoked God repeatedly as they failed to hearken back to God's initial warning that he is a jealous God.

Have you ever experienced jealousy in a relationship? God's jealousy is different in that it's never unrighteous. Pray for God to keep your heart pursuing him alone.

Now Ahijah could not see; his sight was gone because of his age. 5But the LORD had told Ahijah, "Jeroboam's wife is coming to ask you about her son, for he is ill, and you are to give her such and such an answer. When she arrives, she will pretend to be someone else."

6So when Ahijah heard the sound of her footsteps at the door, he said, "Come in, wife of Jeroboam. Why this pretense? I have been sent to you with bad news. 7Go, tell Jeroboam that this is what the LORD, the God of Israel, says: 'I raised you up from among the people and appointed you ruler over my people Israel. 8I tore the kingdom away from the house of David and gave it to you, but you have not been like my servant David, who kept my commands and followed me with all his heart, doing only what was right in my eyes. 9You have done more evil than all who lived before you. You have made for yourself other gods, idols made of metal; you have aroused my anger and turned your back on me.

10" 'Because of this, I am going to bring disaster on the house of Jeroboam. I will cut off from Jeroboam every last male in Israel — slave or free.[a] I will burn up the house of Jeroboam as one burns dung, until it is all gone. 11Dogs will eat those belonging to Jeroboam who die in the city, and the birds will feed on those who die in the country. The LORD has spoken!'

12"As for you, go back home. When you set foot in your city, the boy will die. 13All Israel will mourn for him and bury him. He is the only one belonging to Jeroboam who will be buried, because he is the only one in the house of Jeroboam in whom the LORD, the God of Israel, has found anything good.

14"The LORD will raise up for himself a king over Israel who will cut off the family of Jeroboam. Even now this is beginning to happen.[b] 15And the LORD will strike Israel, so that it will be like a reed swaying in the water. He will uproot Israel from this good land that he gave to their ancestors and scatter them beyond the Euphrates River, because they aroused the LORD's anger by making Asherah poles.[c] 16And he will give Israel up because of the sins Jeroboam has committed and has caused Israel to commit."

17Then Jeroboam's wife got up and left and went to Tirzah. As soon as she stepped over the threshold of the house, the boy died. 18They buried him, and all Israel mourned for him, as the LORD had said through his servant the prophet Ahijah.

19The other events of Jeroboam's reign, his wars and how he ruled, are written in the book of the annals of the kings of Israel. 20He reigned for twenty-two years and then rested with his ancestors. And Nadab his son succeeded him as king

REHOBOAM KING OF JUDAH

21Rehoboam son of Solomon was king in Judah. He was forty-one years old when he became king, and he reigned seventeen years in Jerusalem, the city the LORD had chosen out of all the tribes of Israel in which to put his Name. His mother's name was Naamah; she was an Ammonite.

22Judah did evil in the eyes of the LORD. By the sins they committed

---

[a] *10* Or *Israel — every ruler or leader* [b] *14* The meaning of the Hebrew for this sentence is uncertain. [c] *15* That is, wooden symbols of the goddess Asherah; here and elsewhere in 1 Kings

they stirred up his jealous anger more than those who were before them had done. 23They also set up for themselves high places, sacred stones and Asherah poles on every high hill and under every spreading tree. 24There were even male shrine prostitutes in the land; the people engaged in all the detestable practices of the nations the LORD had driven out before the Israelites.

25In the fifth year of King Rehoboam, Shishak king of Egypt attacked Jerusalem. 26He carried off the treasures of the temple of the LORD and the treasures of the royal palace. He took everything, including all the gold shields Solomon had made. 27So King Rehoboam made bronze shields to replace them and assigned these to the commanders of the guard on duty at the entrance to the royal palace. 28Whenever the king went to the LORD's temple, the guards bore the shields, and afterward they returned them to the guardroom.

29As for the other events of Rehoboam's reign, and all he did, are they not written in the book of the annals of the kings of Judah? 30There was continual warfare between Rehoboam and Jeroboam. 31And Rehoboam rested with his ancestors and was buried with them in the City of David. His mother's name was Naamah; she was an Ammonite. And Abijah[a] his son succeeded him as king.

ABIJAH KING OF JUDAH

PRAYING SCRIPTURE

1 Kings 15

God often assessed the kings based on whether they walked in the ways of David. David's life of pursuing God was a standard of obedience that God held out for the kings to remember. Few did.

Is anyone in your life a kind of David to you? If not, ask God to give you a person of impact who shows a pattern of following him.

15 In the eighteenth year of the reign of Jeroboam son of Nebat, Abijah[b] became king of Judah, 2and he reigned in Jerusalem three years. His mother's name was Maakah daughter of Abishalom.[c]

3He committed all the sins his father had done before him; his heart was not fully devoted to the LORD his God, as the heart of David his forefather had been. 4Nevertheless, for David's sake the LORD his God gave him a lamp in Jerusalem by raising up a son to succeed him and by making Jerusalem strong. 5For David had done what was right in the eyes of the LORD and had not failed to keep any of the LORD's commands all the days of his life — except in the case of Uriah the Hittite.

6There was war between Abijah[d] and Jeroboam throughout Abijah's lifetime. 7As for the other events of Abijah's reign, and all he did, are they not written in the book of the annals of the kings of Judah? There was war between Abijah and Jeroboam. 8And Abijah rested with his ancestors and was buried in the City of David. And Asa his son succeeded him as king.

ASA KING OF JUDAH

9In the twentieth year of Jeroboam king of Israel, Asa became king of Judah, 10and he reigned in Jerusalem forty-one years. His grandmother's name was Maakah daughter of Abishalom.

11Asa did what was right in the eyes of the LORD, as his father David had done. 12He expelled the male shrine prostitutes from the land and got rid of all the idols his ancestors had made. 13He even deposed his grandmother Maakah from her position as queen mother, because she had made a repulsive image for the worship of Asherah. Asa cut it

[a] *31* Some Hebrew manuscripts and Septuagint (see also 2 Chron. 12:16); most Hebrew manuscripts *Abijam* [b] *1* Some Hebrew manuscripts and Septuagint (see also 2 Chron. 12:16); most Hebrew manuscripts *Abijam*; also in verses 7 and 8 [c] *2* A variant of *Absalom*; also in verse 10 [d] *6* Some Hebrew manuscripts and Syriac *Abijam* (that is, Abijah); most Hebrew manuscripts *Rehoboam*

down and burned it in the Kidron Valley. 14Although he did not remove
the high places, Asa's heart was fully committed to the LORD all his life.
15He brought into the temple of the LORD the silver and gold and the
articles that he and his father had dedicated.

16There was war between Asa and Baasha king of Israel throughout
their reigns. 17Baasha king of Israel went up against Judah and forti-
fied Ramah to prevent anyone from leaving or entering the territory
of Asa king of Judah.

18Asa then took all the silver and gold that was left in the treasuries of
the LORD's temple and of his own palace. He entrusted it to his officials
and sent them to Ben-Hadad son of Tabrimmon, the son of Hezion, the
king of Aram, who was ruling in Damascus. 19"Let there be a treaty be-
tween me and you," he said, "as there was between my father and your
father. See, I am sending you a gift of silver and gold. Now break your
treaty with Baasha king of Israel so he will withdraw from me."

20Ben-Hadad agreed with King Asa and sent the commanders of
his forces against the towns of Israel. He conquered Ijon, Dan, Abel
Beth Maakah and all Kinnereth in addition to Naphtali. 21When Ba-
asha heard this, he stopped building Ramah and withdrew to Tirzah.
22Then King Asa issued an order to all Judah — no one was exempt —
and they carried away from Ramah the stones and timber Baasha had
been using there. With them King Asa built up Geba in Benjamin, and
also Mizpah.

23As for all the other events of Asa's reign, all his achievements, all
he did and the cities he built, are they not written in the book of the
annals of the kings of Judah? In his old age, however, his feet became
diseased. 24Then Asa rested with his ancestors and was buried with
them in the city of his father David. And Jehoshaphat his son suc-
ceeded him as king.

NADAB KING OF ISRAEL

25Nadab son of Jeroboam became king of Israel in the second year of
Asa king of Judah, and he reigned over Israel two years. 26He did evil in
the eyes of the LORD, following the ways of his father and committing
the same sin his father had caused Israel to commit.

27Baasha son of Ahijah from the tribe of Issachar plotted against
him, and he struck him down at Gibbethon, a Philistine town, while
Nadab and all Israel were besieging it. 28Baasha killed Nadab in the
third year of Asa king of Judah and succeeded him as king.

29As soon as he began to reign, he killed Jeroboam's whole family.
He did not leave Jeroboam anyone that breathed, but destroyed them
all, according to the word of the LORD given through his servant Ahi-
jah the Shilonite. 30This happened because of the sins Jeroboam had
committed and had caused Israel to commit, and because he aroused
the anger of the LORD, the God of Israel.

31As for the other events of Nadab's reign, and all he did, are they not
written in the book of the annals of the kings of Israel? 32There was war
between Asa and Baasha king of Israel throughout their reigns.

BAASHA KING OF ISRAEL

33In the third year of Asa king of Judah, Baasha son of Ahijah became
king of all Israel in Tirzah, and he reigned twenty-four years. 34He did
evil in the eyes of the LORD, following the ways of Jeroboam and com-
mitting the same sin Jeroboam had caused Israel to commit.

PRAYING SCRIPTURE

1 Kings 16

The high places were the areas erected for idol worship. Most kings built them or left them; a few tore them down. Among the most egregious idolaters was Ahab, a king in Israel. Ahab looked on sinning as "trivial" (verse 31).

God's people even today are tempted to overlook sin. We are forgiven, but that doesn't allow a lazy attitude. Ask God to help you hate sin the way he does.

16 Then the word of the LORD came to Jehu son of Hanani concern-
ing Baasha: 2"I lifted you up from the dust and appointed you
ruler over my people Israel, but you followed the ways of Jeroboam
and caused my people Israel to sin and to arouse my anger by their
sins. 3So I am about to wipe out Baasha and his house, and I will make
your house like that of Jeroboam son of Nebat. 4Dogs will eat those
belonging to Baasha who die in the city, and birds will feed on those
who die in the country."
5As for the other events of Baasha's reign, what he did and his
achievements, are they not written in the book of the annals of the
kings of Israel? 6Baasha rested with his ancestors and was buried in
Tirzah. And Elah his son succeeded him as king.
7Moreover, the word of the LORD came through the prophet Jehu son
of Hanani to Baasha and his house, because of all the evil he had done
in the eyes of the LORD, arousing his anger by the things he did, be-
coming like the house of Jeroboam — and also because he destroyed it.

ELAH KING OF ISRAEL

8In the twenty-sixth year of Asa king of Judah, Elah son of Baasha
became king of Israel, and he reigned in Tirzah two years.
9Zimri, one of his officials, who had command of half his chariots,
plotted against him. Elah was in Tirzah at the time, getting drunk in
the home of Arza, the palace administrator at Tirzah. 10Zimri came in,
struck him down and killed him in the twenty-seventh year of Asa
king of Judah. Then he succeeded him as king.
11As soon as he began to reign and was seated on the throne, he killed
off Baasha's whole family. He did not spare a single male, whether rel-
ative or friend. 12So Zimri destroyed the whole family of Baasha, in
accordance with the word of the LORD spoken against Baasha through
the prophet Jehu — 13because of all the sins Baasha and his son Elah
had committed and had caused Israel to commit, so that they aroused
the anger of the LORD, the God of Israel, by their worthless idols.
14As for the other events of Elah's reign, and all he did, are they not
written in the book of the annals of the kings of Israel?

ZIMRI KING OF ISRAEL

15In the twenty-seventh year of Asa king of Judah, Zimri reigned in
Tirzah seven days. The army was encamped near Gibbethon, a Phi-
listine town. 16When the Israelites in the camp heard that Zimri had
plotted against the king and murdered him, they proclaimed Omri,
the commander of the army, king over Israel that very day there in
the camp. 17Then Omri and all the Israelites with him withdrew from
Gibbethon and laid siege to Tirzah. 18When Zimri saw that the city was
taken, he went into the citadel of the royal palace and set the palace on
fire around him. So he died, 19because of the sins he had committed,
doing evil in the eyes of the LORD and following the ways of Jeroboam
and committing the same sin Jeroboam had caused Israel to commit.
20As for the other events of Zimri's reign, and the rebellion he car-
ried out, are they not written in the book of the annals of the kings of
Israel?

OMRI KING OF ISRAEL

21Then the people of Israel were split into two factions; half sup-
ported Tibni son of Ginath for king, and the other half supported Omri.

22But Omri's followers proved stronger than those of Tibni son of Gi-
nath. So Tibni died and Omri became king.
23In the thirty-first year of Asa king of Judah, Omri became king of
Israel, and he reigned twelve years, six of them in Tirzah. 24He bought
the hill of Samaria from Shemer for two talents[a] of silver and built a
city on the hill, calling it Samaria, after Shemer, the name of the for-
mer owner of the hill.
25But Omri did evil in the eyes of the LORD and sinned more than
all those before him. 26He followed completely the ways of Jeroboam
son of Nebat, committing the same sin Jeroboam had caused Israel to
commit, so that they aroused the anger of the LORD, the God of Israel,
by their worthless idols.
27As for the other events of Omri's reign, what he did and the things
he achieved, are they not written in the book of the annals of the kings
of Israel? 28Omri rested with his ancestors and was buried in Samaria.
And Ahab his son succeeded him as king.

AHAB BECOMES KING OF ISRAEL

29In the thirty-eighth year of Asa king of Judah, Ahab son of Omri be-
came king of Israel, and he reigned in Samaria over Israel twenty-two
years. 30Ahab son of Omri did more evil in the eyes of the LORD than
any of those before him. 31He not only considered it trivial to com-
mit the sins of Jeroboam son of Nebat, but he also married Jezebel
daughter of Ethbaal king of the Sidonians, and began to serve Baal and
worship him. 32He set up an altar for Baal in the temple of Baal that he
built in Samaria. 33Ahab also made an Asherah pole and did more to
arouse the anger of the LORD, the God of Israel, than did all the kings
of Israel before him.
34In Ahab's time, Hiel of Bethel rebuilt Jericho. He laid its founda-
tions at the cost of his firstborn son Abiram, and he set up its gates at
the cost of his youngest son Segub, in accordance with the word of the
LORD spoken by Joshua son of Nun.

ELIJAH ANNOUNCES A GREAT DROUGHT

17 Now Elijah the Tishbite, from Tishbe[b] in Gilead, said to Ahab,
"As the LORD, the God of Israel, lives, whom I serve, there will be
neither dew nor rain in the next few years except at my word."

ELIJAH FED BY RAVENS

2Then the word of the LORD came to Elijah: 3"Leave here, turn east-
ward and hide in the Kerith Ravine, east of the Jordan. 4You will drink
from the brook, and I have directed the ravens to supply you with food
there."
5So he did what the LORD had told him. He went to the Kerith Ravine,
east of the Jordan, and stayed there. 6The ravens brought him bread
and meat in the morning and bread and meat in the evening, and he
drank from the brook.

ELIJAH AND THE WIDOW AT ZAREPHATH

7Some time later the brook dried up because there had been no rain
in the land. 8Then the word of the LORD came to him: 9"Go at once

[a] 24 That is, about 150 pounds or about 68 kilograms [b] 1 Or *Tishbite, of the settlers*

PRAYING SCRIPTURE

1 Kings 17

God often performs his miracles in absurd situations. Elijah instructed a widow on the verge of starvation to prepare her last meal—for him. It seems like a selfish request, but God was testing her faith to the extreme. Rather than letting her starve, God miraculously provided for her every day until the drought ended.

God will come through in our most difficult times. Ask in faith and trust him daily to provide your needs.

to Zarephath in the region of Sidon and stay there. I have directed
a widow there to supply you with food." 10So he went to Zarephath.
When he came to the town gate, a widow was there gathering sticks. He
called to her and asked, "Would you bring me a little water in a jar so
I may have a drink?" 11As she was going to get it, he called, "And bring
me, please, a piece of bread."
12"As surely as the LORD your God lives," she replied, "I don't have any
bread — only a handful of flour in a jar and a little olive oil in a jug. I
am gathering a few sticks to take home and make a meal for myself
and my son, that we may eat it — and die."
13Elijah said to her, "Don't be afraid. Go home and do as you have
said. But first make a small loaf of bread for me from what you have
and bring it to me, and then make something for yourself and your
son. 14For this is what the LORD, the God of Israel, says: 'The jar of flour
will not be used up and the jug of oil will not run dry until the day the
LORD sends rain on the land.'"
15She went away and did as Elijah had told her. So there was food
every day for Elijah and for the woman and her family. 16For the jar of
flour was not used up and the jug of oil did not run dry, in keeping with
the word of the LORD spoken by Elijah.
17Some time later the son of the woman who owned the house be-
came ill. He grew worse and worse, and finally stopped breathing.
18She said to Elijah, "What do you have against me, man of God? Did
you come to remind me of my sin and kill my son?"
19"Give me your son," Elijah replied. He took him from her arms,
carried him to the upper room where he was staying, and laid him
on his bed. 20Then he cried out to the LORD, "LORD my God, have you
brought tragedy even on this widow I am staying with, by causing
her son to die?" 21Then he stretched himself out on the boy three
times and cried out to the LORD, "LORD my God, let this boy's life re-
turn to him!"
22The LORD heard Elijah's cry, and the boy's life returned to him, and
he lived. 23Elijah picked up the child and carried him down from the
room into the house. He gave him to his mother and said, "Look, your
son is alive!"
24Then the woman said to Elijah, "Now I know that you are a man
of God and that the word of the LORD from your mouth is the truth."

ELIJAH AND OBADIAH

18 After a long time, in the third year, the word of the LORD came
to Elijah: "Go and present yourself to Ahab, and I will send rain
on the land." 2So Elijah went to present himself to Ahab.
Now the famine was severe in Samaria, 3and Ahab had summoned
Obadiah, his palace administrator. (Obadiah was a devout believer in
the LORD. 4While Jezebel was killing off the LORD's prophets, Obadiah
had taken a hundred prophets and hidden them in two caves, fifty in
each, and had supplied them with food and water.) 5Ahab had said to
Obadiah, "Go through the land to all the springs and valleys. Maybe we
can find some grass to keep the horses and mules alive so we will not
have to kill any of our animals." 6So they divided the land they were to
cover, Ahab going in one direction and Obadiah in another.
7As Obadiah was walking along, Elijah met him. Obadiah recognized
him, bowed down to the ground, and said, "Is it really you, my lord
Elijah?"

PRAYING SCRIPTURE

1 Kings 18

God's prophet Elijah was outnumbered four hundred to one. Alone, against a raving multitude of Baal-worshiping false prophets, Elijah issued a challenge to demonstrate the true God of Israel. God answered literally by fire, reminding his people that he indeed was the true God.

Have you ever had to stand for truth against a group of doubters? Pray for courage to rise to every opportunity to show that the Lord alone is God.

8“Yes,” he replied. “Go tell your master, ‘Elijah is here.’ ”
9“What have I done wrong,” asked Obadiah, “that you are handing
your servant over to Ahab to be put to death? 10As surely as the LORD
your God lives, there is not a nation or kingdom where my master has
not sent someone to look for you. And whenever a nation or kingdom
claimed you were not there, he made them swear they could not find
you. 11But now you tell me to go to my master and say, ‘Elijah is here.’
12I don’t know where the Spirit of the LORD may carry you when I leave
you. If I go and tell Ahab and he doesn’t find you, he will kill me. Yet I
your servant have worshiped the LORD since my youth. 13Haven’t you
heard, my lord, what I did while Jezebel was killing the prophets of the
LORD? I hid a hundred of the LORD’s prophets in two caves, fifty in each,
and supplied them with food and water. 14And now you tell me to go to
my master and say, ‘Elijah is here.’ He will kill me!”
15Elijah said, “As the LORD Almighty lives, whom I serve, I will surely
present myself to Ahab today.”

ELIJAH ON MOUNT CARMEL

16So Obadiah went to meet Ahab and told him, and Ahab went to
meet Elijah. 17When he saw Elijah, he said to him, “Is that you, you
troubler of Israel?”
18“I have not made trouble for Israel,” Elijah replied. “But you and
your father’s family have. You have abandoned the LORD’s commands
and have followed the Baals. 19Now summon the people from all over
Israel to meet me on Mount Carmel. And bring the four hundred and
fifty prophets of Baal and the four hundred prophets of Asherah, who
eat at Jezebel’s table.”
20So Ahab sent word throughout all Israel and assembled the proph-
ets on Mount Carmel. 21Elijah went before the people and said, “How
long will you waver between two opinions? If the LORD is God, follow
him; but if Baal is God, follow him.”
But the people said nothing.
22Then Elijah said to them, “I am the only one of the LORD’s prophets
left, but Baal has four hundred and fifty prophets. 23Get two bulls for
us. Let Baal’s prophets choose one for themselves, and let them cut it
into pieces and put it on the wood but not set fire to it. I will prepare
the other bull and put it on the wood but not set fire to it. 24Then you
call on the name of your god, and I will call on the name of the LORD.
The god who answers by fire — he is God.”
Then all the people said, “What you say is good.”
25Elijah said to the prophets of Baal, “Choose one of the bulls and
prepare it first, since there are so many of you. Call on the name of
your god, but do not light the fire.” 26So they took the bull given them
and prepared it.
Then they called on the name of Baal from morning till noon. “Baal,
answer us!” they shouted. But there was no response; no one answered.
And they danced around the altar they had made.
27At noon Elijah began to taunt them. “Shout louder!” he said.
“Surely he is a god! Perhaps he is deep in thought, or busy, or traveling.
Maybe he is sleeping and must be awakened.” 28So they shouted louder
and slashed themselves with swords and spears, as was their custom,
until their blood flowed. 29Midday passed, and they continued their
frantic prophesying until the time for the evening sacrifice. But there
was no response, no one answered, no one paid attention.

30Then Elijah said to all the people, "Come here to me." They came to him, and he repaired the altar of the LORD, which had been torn down. 31Elijah took twelve stones, one for each of the tribes descended from Jacob, to whom the word of the LORD had come, saying, "Your name shall be Israel." 32With the stones he built an altar in the name of the LORD, and he dug a trench around it large enough to hold two seahs[a] of seed. 33He arranged the wood, cut the bull into pieces and laid it on the wood. Then he said to them, "Fill four large jars with water and pour it on the offering and on the wood."

34"Do it again," he said, and they did it again.

"Do it a third time," he ordered, and they did it the third time. 35The water ran down around the altar and even filled the trench.

36At the time of sacrifice, the prophet Elijah stepped forward and prayed: "LORD, the God of Abraham, Isaac and Israel, let it be known today that you are God in Israel and that I am your servant and have done all these things at your command. 37Answer me, LORD, answer me, so these people will know that you, LORD, are God, and that you are turning their hearts back again."

38Then the fire of the LORD fell and burned up the sacrifice, the wood, the stones and the soil, and also licked up the water in the trench.

39When all the people saw this, they fell prostrate and cried, "The LORD—he is God! The LORD—he is God!"

40Then Elijah commanded them, "Seize the prophets of Baal. Don't let anyone get away!" They seized them, and Elijah had them brought down to the Kishon Valley and slaughtered there.

41And Elijah said to Ahab, "Go, eat and drink, for there is the sound of a heavy rain." 42So Ahab went off to eat and drink, but Elijah climbed to the top of Carmel, bent down to the ground and put his face between his knees.

43"Go and look toward the sea," he told his servant. And he went up and looked.

"There is nothing there," he said.

Seven times Elijah said, "Go back."

44The seventh time the servant reported, "A cloud as small as a man's hand is rising from the sea."

So Elijah said, "Go and tell Ahab, 'Hitch up your chariot and go down before the rain stops you.'"

45Meanwhile, the sky grew black with clouds, the wind rose, a heavy rain started falling and Ahab rode off to Jezreel. 46The power of the LORD came on Elijah and, tucking his cloak into his belt, he ran ahead of Ahab all the way to Jezreel.

ELIJAH FLEES TO HOREB

19 Now Ahab told Jezebel everything Elijah had done and how he had killed all the prophets with the sword. 2So Jezebel sent a messenger to Elijah to say, "May the gods deal with me, be it ever so severely, if by this time tomorrow I do not make your life like that of one of them."

3Elijah was afraid[b] and ran for his life. When he came to Beersheba in Judah, he left his servant there, 4while he himself went a day's journey into the wilderness. He came to a broom bush, sat down under it and

[a] *32* That is, probably about 24 pounds or about 11 kilograms [b] *3* Or *Elijah saw*

PRAYING SCRIPTURE

1 Kings 19

Our biggest victories are often followed by our lowest moments. This has been shown true throughout history, even among God's people. After Elijah's victory on Mount Carmel, he fled from Queen Jezebel, despairing even of his life (see verse 4). Elijah needed daily grace from God to survive. Big wins alone were not enough.

Be careful not to confuse your spiritual walk with spiritual highs. Trust God on the mountains and in the valleys.

prayed that he might die. "I have had enough, LORD," he said. "Take
my life; I am no better than my ancestors." 5Then he lay down under
the bush and fell asleep.

All at once an angel touched him and said, "Get up and eat." 6He
looked around, and there by his head was some bread baked over hot
coals, and a jar of water. He ate and drank and then lay down again.

7The angel of the LORD came back a second time and touched him
and said, "Get up and eat, for the journey is too much for you." 8So he
got up and ate and drank. Strengthened by that food, he traveled forty
days and forty nights until he reached Horeb, the mountain of God.
9There he went into a cave and spent the night.

THE LORD APPEARS TO ELIJAH

And the word of the LORD came to him: "What are you doing here, Elijah?"

10He replied, "I have been very zealous for the LORD God Almighty.
The Israelites have rejected your covenant, torn down your altars, and put your prophets to death with the sword. I am the only one left, and now they are trying to kill me too."

11The LORD said, "Go out and stand on the mountain in the presence
of the LORD, for the LORD is about to pass by."

Then a great and powerful wind tore the mountains apart and shattered the rocks before the LORD, but the LORD was not in the wind.
After the wind there was an earthquake, but the LORD was not in the
earthquake. 12After the earthquake came a fire, but the LORD was not
in the fire. And after the fire came a gentle whisper. 13When Elijah
heard it, he pulled his cloak over his face and went out and stood at the mouth of the cave.

Then a voice said to him, "What are you doing here, Elijah?"

14He replied, "I have been very zealous for the LORD God Almighty.
The Israelites have rejected your covenant, torn down your altars, and put your prophets to death with the sword. I am the only one left, and now they are trying to kill me too."

15The LORD said to him, "Go back the way you came, and go to the
Desert of Damascus. When you get there, anoint Hazael king over
Aram. 16Also, anoint Jehu son of Nimshi king over Israel, and anoint
Elisha son of Shaphat from Abel Meholah to succeed you as prophet.
17Jehu will put to death any who escape the sword of Hazael, and Eli-
sha will put to death any who escape the sword of Jehu. 18Yet I reserve
seven thousand in Israel—all whose knees have not bowed down to Baal and whose mouths have not kissed him."

THE CALL OF ELISHA

19So Elijah went from there and found Elisha son of Shaphat. He
was plowing with twelve yoke of oxen, and he himself was driving the twelfth pair. Elijah went up to him and threw his cloak around him.
20Elisha then left his oxen and ran after Elijah. "Let me kiss my father
and mother goodbye," he said, "and then I will come with you."

"Go back," Elijah replied. "What have I done to you?"

21So Elisha left him and went back. He took his yoke of oxen and slaughtered them. He burned the plowing equipment to cook the meat and gave it to the people, and they ate. Then he set out to follow Elijah and became his servant.

PRAYING SCRIPTURE

1 Kings 20

Sometimes, with all the conflicting things that happen in this world, it's hard to see how God has control. It often looks as though the bad go unpunished and the good go unrewarded, but God's plan is secure, and his power to accomplish it is unlimited.

Ask God to increase your faith as you face world events.

BEN-HADAD ATTACKS SAMARIA

20 Now Ben-Hadad king of Aram mustered his entire army. Ac-
companied by thirty-two kings with their horses and chariots,
he went up and besieged Samaria and attacked it. 2He sent messengers
into the city to Ahab king of Israel, saying, "This is what Ben-Hadad
says: 3'Your silver and gold are mine, and the best of your wives and
children are mine.'"
4The king of Israel answered, "Just as you say, my lord the king. I and
all I have are yours."
5The messengers came again and said, "This is what Ben-Hadad
says: 'I sent to demand your silver and gold, your wives and your chil-
dren. 6But about this time tomorrow I am going to send my officials
to search your palace and the houses of your officials. They will seize
everything you value and carry it away.'"
7The king of Israel summoned all the elders of the land and said to
them, "See how this man is looking for trouble! When he sent for my
wives and my children, my silver and my gold, I did not refuse him."
8The elders and the people all answered, "Don't listen to him or
agree to his demands."
9So he replied to Ben-Hadad's messengers, "Tell my lord the king,
'Your servant will do all you demanded the first time, but this demand
I cannot meet.'" They left and took the answer back to Ben-Hadad.
10Then Ben-Hadad sent another message to Ahab: "May the gods
deal with me, be it ever so severely, if enough dust remains in Samaria
to give each of my men a handful."
11The king of Israel answered, "Tell him: 'One who puts on his armor
should not boast like one who takes it off.'"
12Ben-Hadad heard this message while he and the kings were drink-
ing in their tents,[a] and he ordered his men: "Prepare to attack." So they
prepared to attack the city.

AHAB DEFEATS BEN-HADAD

13Meanwhile a prophet came to Ahab king of Israel and announced,
"This is what the LORD says: 'Do you see this vast army? I will give it
into your hand today, and then you will know that I am the LORD.'"
14"But who will do this?" asked Ahab.
The prophet replied, "This is what the LORD says: 'The junior officers
under the provincial commanders will do it.'"
"And who will start the battle?" he asked.
The prophet answered, "You will."
15So Ahab summoned the 232 junior officers under the provincial
commanders. Then he assembled the rest of the Israelites, 7,000 in all.
16They set out at noon while Ben-Hadad and the 32 kings allied with
him were in their tents getting drunk. 17The junior officers under the
provincial commanders went out first.
Now Ben-Hadad had dispatched scouts, who reported, "Men are ad-
vancing from Samaria."
18He said, "If they have come out for peace, take them alive; if they
have come out for war, take them alive."
19The junior officers under the provincial commanders marched out
of the city with the army behind them 20and each one struck down his
opponent. At that, the Arameans fled, with the Israelites in pursuit.

[a] 12 Or *in Sukkoth*; also in verse 16

But Ben-Hadad king of Aram escaped on horseback with some of his
horsemen. 21The king of Israel advanced and overpowered the horses
and chariots and inflicted heavy losses on the Arameans.
22Afterward, the prophet came to the king of Israel and said,
"Strengthen your position and see what must be done, because next
spring the king of Aram will attack you again."
23Meanwhile, the officials of the king of Aram advised him, "Their
gods are gods of the hills. That is why they were too strong for us. But if
we fight them on the plains, surely we will be stronger than they. 24Do
this: Remove all the kings from their commands and replace them
with other officers. 25You must also raise an army like the one you
lost—horse for horse and chariot for chariot—so we can fight Israel
on the plains. Then surely we will be stronger than they." He agreed
with them and acted accordingly.
26The next spring Ben-Hadad mustered the Arameans and went up
to Aphek to fight against Israel. 27When the Israelites were also mus-
tered and given provisions, they marched out to meet them. The Isra-
elites camped opposite them like two small flocks of goats, while the
Arameans covered the countryside.
28The man of God came up and told the king of Israel, "This is what
the LORD says: 'Because the Arameans think the LORD is a god of the
hills and not a god of the valleys, I will deliver this vast army into your
hands, and you will know that I am the LORD.'"
29For seven days they camped opposite each other, and on the sev-
enth day the battle was joined. The Israelites inflicted a hundred
thousand casualties on the Aramean foot soldiers in one day. 30The
rest of them escaped to the city of Aphek, where the wall collapsed on
twenty-seven thousand of them. And Ben-Hadad fled to the city and
hid in an inner room.
31His officials said to him, "Look, we have heard that the kings of Is-
rael are merciful. Let us go to the king of Israel with sackcloth around
our waists and ropes around our heads. Perhaps he will spare your life."
32Wearing sackcloth around their waists and ropes around their
heads, they went to the king of Israel and said, "Your servant
Ben-Hadad says: 'Please let me live.'"
The king answered, "Is he still alive? He is my brother."
33The men took this as a good sign and were quick to pick up his
word. "Yes, your brother Ben-Hadad!" they said.
"Go and get him," the king said. When Ben-Hadad came out, Ahab
had him come up into his chariot.
34"I will return the cities my father took from your father," Ben-Ha-
dad offered. "You may set up your own market areas in Damascus, as
my father did in Samaria."
Ahab said, "On the basis of a treaty I will set you free." So he made a
treaty with him, and let him go.

A PROPHET CONDEMNS AHAB

35By the word of the LORD one of the company of the prophets said to
his companion, "Strike me with your weapon," but he refused.
36So the prophet said, "Because you have not obeyed the LORD, as
soon as you leave me a lion will kill you." And after the man went away,
a lion found him and killed him.
37The prophet found another man and said, "Strike me, please." So the
man struck him and wounded him. 38Then the prophet went and stood

by the road waiting for the king. He disguised himself with his head-
band down over his eyes. 39As the king passed by, the prophet called out
to him, "Your servant went into the thick of the battle, and someone
came to me with a captive and said, 'Guard this man. If he is missing, it
will be your life for his life, or you must pay a talent[a] of silver.' 40While
your servant was busy here and there, the man disappeared."

"That is your sentence," the king of Israel said. "You have pro-
nounced it yourself."

41Then the prophet quickly removed the headband from his eyes,
and the king of Israel recognized him as one of the prophets. 42He said
to the king, "This is what the LORD says: 'You have set free a man I had
determined should die.[b] Therefore it is your life for his life, your peo-
ple for his people.'" 43Sullen and angry, the king of Israel went to his
palace in Samaria.

> **PRAYING SCRIPTURE**
>
> **1 Kings 21**
>
> Ahab and Jezebel's murderous scheme to steal a vineyard from Naboth showed how deep in sin the country and its leaders had sunk. Elijah pronounced judgment on Ahab who, after a life of wickedness, repented of his sin. God did not relent on his judgment but promised to judge Ahab's son's house instead.
>
> Pray for anyone you know whose heart is hard. Pray that God leads him or her to genuine repentance.

NABOTH'S VINEYARD

21 Some time later there was an incident involving a vineyard be-
longing to Naboth the Jezreelite. The vineyard was in Jezreel,
close to the palace of Ahab king of Samaria. 2Ahab said to Naboth, "Let
me have your vineyard to use for a vegetable garden, since it is close
to my palace. In exchange I will give you a better vineyard or, if you
prefer, I will pay you whatever it is worth."

3But Naboth replied, "The LORD forbid that I should give you the in-
heritance of my ancestors."

4So Ahab went home, sullen and angry because Naboth the Jezreel-
ite had said, "I will not give you the inheritance of my ancestors." He
lay on his bed sulking and refused to eat.

5His wife Jezebel came in and asked him, "Why are you so sullen?
Why won't you eat?"

6He answered her, "Because I said to Naboth the Jezreelite, 'Sell me
your vineyard; or if you prefer, I will give you another vineyard in its
place.' But he said, 'I will not give you my vineyard.'"

7Jezebel his wife said, "Is this how you act as king over Israel? Get up
and eat! Cheer up. I'll get you the vineyard of Naboth the Jezreelite."

8So she wrote letters in Ahab's name, placed his seal on them, and
sent them to the elders and nobles who lived in Naboth's city with him.
9In those letters she wrote:

> "Proclaim a day of fasting and seat Naboth in a prominent place
> among the people. 10But seat two scoundrels opposite him and
> have them bring charges that he has cursed both God and the
> king. Then take him out and stone him to death."

11So the elders and nobles who lived in Naboth's city did as Jezebel
directed in the letters she had written to them. 12They proclaimed a fast
and seated Naboth in a prominent place among the people. 13Then two
scoundrels came and sat opposite him and brought charges against
Naboth before the people, saying, "Naboth has cursed both God and
the king." So they took him outside the city and stoned him to death.
14Then they sent word to Jezebel: "Naboth has been stoned to death."

15As soon as Jezebel heard that Naboth had been stoned to death, she

[a] 39 That is, about 75 pounds or about 34 kilograms [b] 42 The Hebrew term refers to the irrevocable giving over of things or persons to the LORD, often by totally destroying them.

said to Ahab, "Get up and take possession of the vineyard of Naboth the
Jezreelite that he refused to sell you. He is no longer alive, but dead."
16 When Ahab heard that Naboth was dead, he got up and went down
to take possession of Naboth's vineyard.
17 Then the word of the LORD came to Elijah the Tishbite: 18 "Go down
to meet Ahab king of Israel, who rules in Samaria. He is now in Na-
both's vineyard, where he has gone to take possession of it. 19 Say to
him, 'This is what the LORD says: Have you not murdered a man and
seized his property?' Then say to him, 'This is what the LORD says: In
the place where dogs licked up Naboth's blood, dogs will lick up your
blood — yes, yours!' "
20 Ahab said to Elijah, "So you have found me, my enemy!"

"I have found you," he answered, "because you have sold yourself to
do evil in the eyes of the LORD. 21 He says, 'I am going to bring disaster
on you. I will wipe out your descendants and cut off from Ahab every
last male in Israel — slave or free.[a] 22 I will make your house like that of
Jeroboam son of Nebat and that of Baasha son of Ahijah, because you
have aroused my anger and have caused Israel to sin.'
23 "And also concerning Jezebel the LORD says: 'Dogs will devour Jez-
ebel by the wall of[b] Jezreel.'
24 "Dogs will eat those belonging to Ahab who die in the city, and the
birds will feed on those who die in the country."
25 (There was never anyone like Ahab, who sold himself to do evil in
the eyes of the LORD, urged on by Jezebel his wife. 26 He behaved in the
vilest manner by going after idols, like the Amorites the LORD drove
out before Israel.)
27 When Ahab heard these words, he tore his clothes, put on sackcloth
and fasted. He lay in sackcloth and went around meekly.
28 Then the word of the LORD came to Elijah the Tishbite: 29 "Have
you noticed how Ahab has humbled himself before me? Because he
has humbled himself, I will not bring this disaster in his day, but I will
bring it on his house in the days of his son."

MICAIAH PROPHESIES AGAINST AHAB

22 For three years there was no war between Aram and Israel. 2 But
in the third year Jehoshaphat king of Judah went down to see
the king of Israel. 3 The king of Israel had said to his officials, "Don't
you know that Ramoth Gilead belongs to us and yet we are doing noth-
ing to retake it from the king of Aram?"
4 So he asked Jehoshaphat, "Will you go with me to fight against Ra-
moth Gilead?"

Jehoshaphat replied to the king of Israel, "I am as you are, my peo-
ple as your people, my horses as your horses." 5 But Jehoshaphat also
said to the king of Israel, "First seek the counsel of the LORD."
6 So the king of Israel brought together the prophets — about four
hundred men — and asked them, "Shall I go to war against Ramoth
Gilead, or shall I refrain?"

"Go," they answered, "for the Lord will give it into the king's hand."
7 But Jehoshaphat asked, "Is there no longer a prophet of the LORD
here whom we can inquire of?"

[a] *21* Or *Israel — every ruler or leader* [b] *23* Most Hebrew manuscripts; a few Hebrew manuscripts, Vulgate and Syriac (see also 2 Kings 9:26) *the plot of ground at*

PRAYING SCRIPTURE

1 Kings 22

When God's people turned away from him, they turned away from prophets who spoke the truth and listened to those who told them what they wanted to hear. This is a temptation we all face. It is more comforting to be affirmed than confronted.

It is better to be corrected even if it's painful. "Wounds from a friend can be trusted" (Proverbs 27:6), so pray for friends who will tell you the truth in love.

8The king of Israel answered Jehoshaphat, "There is still one prophet through whom we can inquire of the LORD, but I hate him because he never prophesies anything good about me, but always bad. He is Micaiah son of Imlah."

"The king should not say such a thing," Jehoshaphat replied.

9So the king of Israel called one of his officials and said, "Bring Micaiah son of Imlah at once."

10Dressed in their royal robes, the king of Israel and Jehoshaphat king of Judah were sitting on their thrones at the threshing floor by the entrance of the gate of Samaria, with all the prophets prophesying before them. 11Now Zedekiah son of Kenaanah had made iron horns and he declared, "This is what the LORD says: 'With these you will gore the Arameans until they are destroyed.'"

12All the other prophets were prophesying the same thing. "Attack Ramoth Gilead and be victorious," they said, "for the LORD will give it into the king's hand."

13The messenger who had gone to summon Micaiah said to him, "Look, the other prophets without exception are predicting success for the king. Let your word agree with theirs, and speak favorably."

14But Micaiah said, "As surely as the LORD lives, I can tell him only what the LORD tells me."

15When he arrived, the king asked him, "Micaiah, shall we go to war against Ramoth Gilead, or not?"

"Attack and be victorious," he answered, "for the LORD will give it into the king's hand."

16The king said to him, "How many times must I make you swear to tell me nothing but the truth in the name of the LORD?"

17Then Micaiah answered, "I saw all Israel scattered on the hills like sheep without a shepherd, and the LORD said, 'These people have no master. Let each one go home in peace.'"

18The king of Israel said to Jehoshaphat, "Didn't I tell you that he never prophesies anything good about me, but only bad?"

19Micaiah continued, "Therefore hear the word of the LORD: I saw the LORD sitting on his throne with all the multitudes of heaven standing around him on his right and on his left. 20And the LORD said, 'Who will entice Ahab into attacking Ramoth Gilead and going to his death there?'

"One suggested this, and another that. 21Finally, a spirit came forward, stood before the LORD and said, 'I will entice him.'

22"'By what means?' the LORD asked.

"'I will go out and be a deceiving spirit in the mouths of all his prophets,' he said.

"'You will succeed in enticing him,' said the LORD. 'Go and do it.'

23"So now the LORD has put a deceiving spirit in the mouths of all these prophets of yours. The LORD has decreed disaster for you."

24Then Zedekiah son of Kenaanah went up and slapped Micaiah in the face. "Which way did the spirit from[a] the LORD go when he went from me to speak to you?" he asked.

25Micaiah replied, "You will find out on the day you go to hide in an inner room."

26The king of Israel then ordered, "Take Micaiah and send him back to Amon the ruler of the city and to Joash the king's son 27and say, 'This

[a] 24 Or *Spirit of*

is what the king says: Put this fellow in prison and give him nothing
but bread and water until I return safely.' "
[28]Micaiah declared, "If you ever return safely, the LORD has not spo-
ken through me." Then he added, "Mark my words, all you people!"

AHAB KILLED AT RAMOTH GILEAD

[29]So the king of Israel and Jehoshaphat king of Judah went up to Ra-
moth Gilead. [30]The king of Israel said to Jehoshaphat, "I will enter the
battle in disguise, but you wear your royal robes." So the king of Israel
disguised himself and went into battle.
[31]Now the king of Aram had ordered his thirty-two chariot com-
manders, "Do not fight with anyone, small or great, except the king
of Israel." [32]When the chariot commanders saw Jehoshaphat, they
thought, "Surely this is the king of Israel." So they turned to attack
him, but when Jehoshaphat cried out, [33]the chariot commanders saw
that he was not the king of Israel and stopped pursuing him.
[34]But someone drew his bow at random and hit the king of Israel
between the sections of his armor. The king told his chariot driver,
"Wheel around and get me out of the fighting. I've been wounded."
[35]All day long the battle raged, and the king was propped up in his
chariot facing the Arameans. The blood from his wound ran onto the
floor of the chariot, and that evening he died. [36]As the sun was setting,
a cry spread through the army: "Every man to his town. Every man to
his land!"
[37]So the king died and was brought to Samaria, and they buried him
there. [38]They washed the chariot at a pool in Samaria (where the pros-
titutes bathed),[a] and the dogs licked up his blood, as the word of the
LORD had declared.
[39]As for the other events of Ahab's reign, including all he did, the
palace he built and adorned with ivory, and the cities he fortified, are
they not written in the book of the annals of the kings of Israel? [40]Ahab
rested with his ancestors. And Ahaziah his son succeeded him as king.

JEHOSHAPHAT KING OF JUDAH

[41]Jehoshaphat son of Asa became king of Judah in the fourth year
of Ahab king of Israel. [42]Jehoshaphat was thirty-five years old when
he became king, and he reigned in Jerusalem twenty-five years. His
mother's name was Azubah daughter of Shilhi. [43]In everything he fol-
lowed the ways of his father Asa and did not stray from them; he did
what was right in the eyes of the LORD. The high places, however, were
not removed, and the people continued to offer sacrifices and burn
incense there.[b] [44]Jehoshaphat was also at peace with the king of Israel.
[45]As for the other events of Jehoshaphat's reign, the things he
achieved and his military exploits, are they not written in the book
of the annals of the kings of Judah? [46]He rid the land of the rest of
the male shrine prostitutes who remained there even after the reign
of his father Asa. [47]There was then no king in Edom; a provincial gov-
ernor ruled.
[48]Now Jehoshaphat built a fleet of trading ships[c] to go to Ophir for
gold, but they never set sail — they were wrecked at Ezion Geber. [49]At

[a] *38* Or *Samaria and cleaned the weapons* [b] *43* In Hebrew texts this sentence (22:43b) is numbered 22:44, and 22:44-53 is numbered 22:45-54.
[c] *48* Hebrew *of ships of Tarshish*

that time Ahaziah son of Ahab said to Jehoshaphat, "Let my men sail
with yours," but Jehoshaphat refused.
50Then Jehoshaphat rested with his ancestors and was buried with
them in the city of David his father. And Jehoram his son succeeded
him as king.

AHAZIAH KING OF ISRAEL

51Ahaziah son of Ahab became king of Israel in Samaria in the seven-
teenth year of Jehoshaphat king of Judah, and he reigned over Israel
two years. 52He did evil in the eyes of the LORD, because he followed
the ways of his father and mother and of Jeroboam son of Nebat, who
caused Israel to sin. 53He served and worshiped Baal and aroused the
anger of the LORD, the God of Israel, just as his father had done.

2 KINGS

The second half of 1 Kings took place after the kingdom divided. Both Judah and Israel faced a growing litany of monarchs who led them further down the roads of idolatry and disobedience. The Lord sent Elijah to prophesy to the rulers, calling them back from their idolatry and to faithfulness to the Lord. In 2 Kings 2, Elijah passed the prophetic mantle to his understudy Elisha. Elijah was then transported into the Lord's presence by a fiery chariot in a whirlwind.

One significant feature of 2 Kings is its evaluation of each of the kings of Judah and Israel. For the kings of Judah, the author evaluated whether he followed the Lord like David did. Then he stated whether the king removed "the high places," which is where the people would sacrifice to idols. He reported whether the kings of Israel sinned in the ways of Jeroboam, which included idolatry. The constant failure of following idols plagued both kingdoms.

The prophets of Israel continually called the people back to faithfulness to the covenant that God had made with them. He brought them out of slavery in Egypt and into this promised land. He protected them in this land and provided for them in that land. They were to live in the land according to his laws. He called them to love him, to fear him and to be set apart from the other nations of the earth. The people continually missed the mark; the prophets called them to repent.

The story of 2 Kings is the story of both houses of Israel straying further and further away from the covenant. A succession of wicked rulers in Israel—there was not a godly king among them—led to Assyria overpowering them and taking them into exile in 2 Kings 17. The author wove his assessment of what sent Israel into exile throughout the narrative, making it clear that Israel's unfaithfulness to the Lord was the culprit.

In the final chapters of 2 Kings, Judah—despite having a few periods of renewal under godly kings—experienced the same fate as Israel, though it was sadder and more dramatic. After a short-lived revival under Josiah did not dispel the Lord's anger, Babylon ransacked Judah and burned the house of the Lord. Rather than living in the land of promise with the visible symbol of God's presence, the people went into exile, ushering in one of the darkest periods in Israel's history.

The ministry of Elisha is the brightest light in the book. The succession of miracles that accompanied his prophetic ministry exceed that of any other person's ministry in the Bible except that of Jesus. Elisha ministered to ordinary people and kings. He raised the dead and made an ax-head float. In the midst of a hopeless battle, he prayed for God to intervene, and God filled the mountains with horses and chariots of fire.

Elisha's ministry reminds us that times are never too dark for prayer and that God always stands ready to answer.

PRAYING SCRIPTURE

2 Kings 1

Ahaziah's sin underscores the human tendency to look for solutions to our problems in places that God has forbidden. Seeking a sign from a false god rather than Israel's God aroused God's anger against him and brought about his own death in judgment.

Christians often turn to horoscopes, "luck" or advice from worldly sources when making decisions. Ask God for counsel. He will hear, answer and guide his people.

THE LORD'S JUDGMENT ON AHAZIAH

1 After Ahab's death, Moab rebelled against Israel. 2Now Ahaziah had
fallen through the lattice of his upper room in Samaria and injured
himself. So he sent messengers, saying to them, "Go and consult Baal-Zebub, the god of Ekron, to see if I will recover from this injury."
3But the angel of the LORD said to Elijah the Tishbite, "Go up and
meet the messengers of the king of Samaria and ask them, 'Is it because there is no God in Israel that you are going off to consult Baal-Zebub, the god of Ekron?' 4Therefore this is what the LORD says: 'You
will not leave the bed you are lying on. You will certainly die!'" So
Elijah went.
5When the messengers returned to the king, he asked them, "Why
have you come back?"
6"A man came to meet us," they replied. "And he said to us, 'Go back
to the king who sent you and tell him, "This is what the LORD says: Is
it because there is no God in Israel that you are sending messengers to
consult Baal-Zebub, the god of Ekron? Therefore you will not leave the
bed you are lying on. You will certainly die!"'"
7The king asked them, "What kind of man was it who came to meet
you and told you this?"
8They replied, "He had a garment of hair[a] and had a leather belt
around his waist."
The king said, "That was Elijah the Tishbite."
9Then he sent to Elijah a captain with his company of fifty men. The
captain went up to Elijah, who was sitting on the top of a hill, and said
to him, "Man of God, the king says, 'Come down!'"
10Elijah answered the captain, "If I am a man of God, may fire come
down from heaven and consume you and your fifty men!" Then fire
fell from heaven and consumed the captain and his men.
11At this the king sent to Elijah another captain with his fifty men.
The captain said to him, "Man of God, this is what the king says, 'Come
down at once!'"
12"If I am a man of God," Elijah replied, "may fire come down from
heaven and consume you and your fifty men!" Then the fire of God fell
from heaven and consumed him and his fifty men.
13So the king sent a third captain with his fifty men. This third captain went up and fell on his knees before Elijah. "Man of God," he
begged, "please have respect for my life and the lives of these fifty
men, your servants! 14See, fire has fallen from heaven and consumed
the first two captains and all their men. But now have respect for my
life!"
15The angel of the LORD said to Elijah, "Go down with him; do not be
afraid of him." So Elijah got up and went down with him to the king.
16He told the king, "This is what the LORD says: Is it because there
is no God in Israel for you to consult that you have sent messengers
to consult Baal-Zebub, the god of Ekron? Because you have done this,
you will never leave the bed you are lying on. You will certainly die!"
17So he died, according to the word of the LORD that Elijah had spoken.
Because Ahaziah had no son, Joram[b] succeeded him as king in the
second year of Jehoram son of Jehoshaphat king of Judah. 18As for all
the other events of Ahaziah's reign, and what he did, are they not written in the book of the annals of the kings of Israel?

[a] 8 Or *He was a hairy man* [b] 17 Hebrew *Jehoram*, a variant of *Joram*

ELIJAH TAKEN UP TO HEAVEN

2 When the LORD was about to take Elijah up to heaven in a whirl-
wind, Elijah and Elisha were on their way from Gilgal. 2Elijah said
to Elisha, "Stay here; the LORD has sent me to Bethel."
But Elisha said, "As surely as the LORD lives and as you live, I will not
leave you." So they went down to Bethel.
3The company of the prophets at Bethel came out to Elisha and
asked, "Do you know that the LORD is going to take your master from
you today?"
"Yes, I know," Elisha replied, "so be quiet."
4Then Elijah said to him, "Stay here, Elisha; the LORD has sent me
to Jericho."
And he replied, "As surely as the LORD lives and as you live, I will not
leave you." So they went to Jericho.
5The company of the prophets at Jericho went up to Elisha and asked
him, "Do you know that the LORD is going to take your master from
you today?"
"Yes, I know," he replied, "so be quiet."
6Then Elijah said to him, "Stay here; the LORD has sent me to the
Jordan."
And he replied, "As surely as the LORD lives and as you live, I will not
leave you." So the two of them walked on.
7Fifty men from the company of the prophets went and stood at a
distance, facing the place where Elijah and Elisha had stopped at the
Jordan. 8Elijah took his cloak, rolled it up and struck the water with
it. The water divided to the right and to the left, and the two of them
crossed over on dry ground.
9When they had crossed, Elijah said to Elisha, "Tell me, what can I do
for you before I am taken from you?"
"Let me inherit a double portion of your spirit," Elisha replied.
10"You have asked a difficult thing," Elijah said, "yet if you see me
when I am taken from you, it will be yours—otherwise, it will not."
11As they were walking along and talking together, suddenly a char-
iot of fire and horses of fire appeared and separated the two of them,
and Elijah went up to heaven in a whirlwind. 12Elisha saw this and cried
out, "My father! My father! The chariots and horsemen of Israel!" And
Elisha saw him no more. Then he took hold of his garment and tore
it in two.
13Elisha then picked up Elijah's cloak that had fallen from him and
went back and stood on the bank of the Jordan. 14He took the cloak
that had fallen from Elijah and struck the water with it. "Where now
is the LORD, the God of Elijah?" he asked. When he struck the water, it
divided to the right and to the left, and he crossed over.
15The company of the prophets from Jericho, who were watching,
said, "The spirit of Elijah is resting on Elisha." And they went to meet
him and bowed to the ground before him. 16"Look," they said, "we your
servants have fifty able men. Let them go and look for your master.
Perhaps the Spirit of the LORD has picked him up and set him down on
some mountain or in some valley."
"No," Elisha replied, "do not send them."
17But they persisted until he was too embarrassed to refuse. So he
said, "Send them." And they sent fifty men, who searched for three
days but did not find him. 18When they returned to Elisha, who was
staying in Jericho, he said to them, "Didn't I tell you not to go?"

PRAYING SCRIPTURE

2 Kings 2

At the end of Elijah's miraculous ministry, God called the prophet directly into his presence. In keeping with the nature of Elijah's earthly service, a chariot with horses of fire appeared; then Elijah was taken to heaven by a whirlwind (see verse 11).

Fiery chariot or not, believers will one day be in the presence of the God who loves us. In prayer, express to God how you long to be in his presence forever.

HEALING OF THE WATER

[19]The people of the city said to Elisha, "Look, our lord, this town
is well situated, as you can see, but the water is bad and the land is
unproductive."

[20]"Bring me a new bowl," he said, "and put salt in it." So they brought
it to him.

[21]Then he went out to the spring and threw the salt into it, saying,
"This is what the LORD says: 'I have healed this water. Never again will
it cause death or make the land unproductive.'" [22]And the water has
remained pure to this day, according to the word Elisha had spoken.

ELISHA IS JEERED

[23]From there Elisha went up to Bethel. As he was walking along the
road, some boys came out of the town and jeered at him. "Get out of
here, baldy!" they said. "Get out of here, baldy!" [24]He turned around,
looked at them and called down a curse on them in the name of the
LORD. Then two bears came out of the woods and mauled forty-two of
the boys. [25]And he went on to Mount Carmel and from there returned
to Samaria.

MOAB REVOLTS

3 Joram[a] son of Ahab became king of Israel in Samaria in the eigh-
teenth year of Jehoshaphat king of Judah, and he reigned twelve
years. [2]He did evil in the eyes of the LORD, but not as his father and
mother had done. He got rid of the sacred stone of Baal that his father
had made. [3]Nevertheless he clung to the sins of Jeroboam son of Nebat,
which he had caused Israel to commit; he did not turn away from them.

[4]Now Mesha king of Moab raised sheep, and he had to pay the king
of Israel a tribute of a hundred thousand lambs and the wool of a hun-
dred thousand rams. [5]But after Ahab died, the king of Moab rebelled
against the king of Israel. [6]So at that time King Joram set out from
Samaria and mobilized all Israel. [7]He also sent this message to Jehosh-
aphat king of Judah: "The king of Moab has rebelled against me. Will
you go with me to fight against Moab?"

"I will go with you," he replied. "I am as you are, my people as your
people, my horses as your horses."

[8]"By what route shall we attack?" he asked.

"Through the Desert of Edom," he answered.

[9]So the king of Israel set out with the king of Judah and the king of
Edom. After a roundabout march of seven days, the army had no more
water for themselves or for the animals with them.

[10]"What!" exclaimed the king of Israel. "Has the LORD called us three
kings together only to deliver us into the hands of Moab?"

[11]But Jehoshaphat asked, "Is there no prophet of the LORD here,
through whom we may inquire of the LORD?"

An officer of the king of Israel answered, "Elisha son of Shaphat is
here. He used to pour water on the hands of Elijah.[b]"

[12]Jehoshaphat said, "The word of the LORD is with him." So the king
of Israel and Jehoshaphat and the king of Edom went down to him.

[13]Elisha said to the king of Israel, "Why do you want to involve me?
Go to the prophets of your father and the prophets of your mother."

PRAYING SCRIPTURE

2 Kings 3

Jehoram and Jehoshaphat's plans to make war on the king of Moab were rash and not dependent on God's leading. By the time they asked for a prophet who could give guidance, the entire army and supporting animals were out of water.

Going your own way, then asking for guidance after running headlong into trouble is a sin of presumption. Commit your way to God first and depend on his leading always.

[a] *1* Hebrew *Jehoram*, a variant of *Joram*; also in verse 6 [b] *11* That is, he was Elijah's personal servant.

"No," the king of Israel answered, "because it was the LORD who
called us three kings together to deliver us into the hands of Moab."
14Elisha said, "As surely as the LORD Almighty lives, whom I serve, if
I did not have respect for the presence of Jehoshaphat king of Judah,
I would not pay any attention to you. 15But now bring me a harpist."
While the harpist was playing, the hand of the LORD came on Elisha
16and he said, "This is what the LORD says: I will fill this valley with
pools of water. 17For this is what the LORD says: You will see neither
wind nor rain, yet this valley will be filled with water, and you, your
cattle and your other animals will drink. 18This is an easy thing in the
eyes of the LORD; he will also deliver Moab into your hands. 19You will
overthrow every fortified city and every major town. You will cut down
every good tree, stop up all the springs, and ruin every good field with
stones."
20The next morning, about the time for offering the sacrifice, there
it was — water flowing from the direction of Edom! And the land was
filled with water.
21Now all the Moabites had heard that the kings had come to fight
against them; so every man, young and old, who could bear arms was
called up and stationed on the border. 22When they got up early in the
morning, the sun was shining on the water. To the Moabites across
the way, the water looked red — like blood. 23"That's blood!" they said.
"Those kings must have fought and slaughtered each other. Now to
the plunder, Moab!"
24But when the Moabites came to the camp of Israel, the Israelites
rose up and fought them until they fled. And the Israelites invaded
the land and slaughtered the Moabites. 25They destroyed the towns,
and each man threw a stone on every good field until it was covered.
They stopped up all the springs and cut down every good tree. Only Kir
Hareseth was left with its stones in place, but men armed with slings
surrounded it and attacked it.
26When the king of Moab saw that the battle had gone against him,
he took with him seven hundred swordsmen to break through to the
king of Edom, but they failed. 27Then he took his firstborn son, who
was to succeed him as king, and offered him as a sacrifice on the city
wall. The fury against Israel was great; they withdrew and returned to
their own land.

THE WIDOW'S OLIVE OIL

4 The wife of a man from the company of the prophets cried out to
Elisha, "Your servant my husband is dead, and you know that he
revered the LORD. But now his creditor is coming to take my two boys
as his slaves."
2Elisha replied to her, "How can I help you? Tell me, what do you
have in your house?"
"Your servant has nothing there at all," she said, "except a small jar
of olive oil."
3Elisha said, "Go around and ask all your neighbors for empty jars.
Don't ask for just a few. 4Then go inside and shut the door behind you
and your sons. Pour oil into all the jars, and as each is filled, put it to
one side."
5She left him and shut the door behind her and her sons. They
brought the jars to her and she kept pouring. 6When all the jars were
full, she said to her son, "Bring me another one."

PRAYING SCRIPTURE

2 Kings 4

Elijah's designated prophetic heir was Elisha, who had the faith to ask for double Elijah's spiritual power. In short order, Elisha performed miracles similar to Elijah's. He helped a widow stave off a creditor with a miraculous supply of oil (see verse 4) and raised the young son of a Shunammite family from the dead (see verses 32–35).

God confirmed Elisha's ministry by miracles. Thank God that he never leaves himself without a witness to his power.

But he replied, "There is not a jar left." Then the oil stopped flowing.
7She went and told the man of God, and he said, "Go, sell the oil and
pay your debts. You and your sons can live on what is left."

THE SHUNAMMITE'S SON RESTORED TO LIFE

8One day Elisha went to Shunem. And a well-to-do woman was there,
who urged him to stay for a meal. So whenever he came by, he stopped
there to eat. 9She said to her husband, "I know that this man who often
comes our way is a holy man of God. 10Let's make a small room on the
roof and put in it a bed and a table, a chair and a lamp for him. Then
he can stay there whenever he comes to us."

11One day when Elisha came, he went up to his room and lay down
there. 12He said to his servant Gehazi, "Call the Shunammite." So he
called her, and she stood before him. 13Elisha said to him, "Tell her,
'You have gone to all this trouble for us. Now what can be done for
you? Can we speak on your behalf to the king or the commander of
the army?'"

She replied, "I have a home among my own people."

14"What can be done for her?" Elisha asked.

Gehazi said, "She has no son, and her husband is old."

15Then Elisha said, "Call her." So he called her, and she stood in the
doorway. 16"About this time next year," Elisha said, "you will hold a
son in your arms."

"No, my lord!" she objected. "Please, man of God, don't mislead your
servant!"

17But the woman became pregnant, and the next year about that
same time she gave birth to a son, just as Elisha had told her.

18The child grew, and one day he went out to his father, who was with
the reapers. 19He said to his father, "My head! My head!"

His father told a servant, "Carry him to his mother." 20After the ser-
vant had lifted him up and carried him to his mother, the boy sat on
her lap until noon, and then he died. 21She went up and laid him on the
bed of the man of God, then shut the door and went out.

22She called her husband and said, "Please send me one of the ser-
vants and a donkey so I can go to the man of God quickly and return."

23"Why go to him today?" he asked. "It's not the New Moon or the
Sabbath."

"That's all right," she said.

24She saddled the donkey and said to her servant, "Lead on; don't
slow down for me unless I tell you." 25So she set out and came to the
man of God at Mount Carmel.

When he saw her in the distance, the man of God said to his servant
Gehazi, "Look! There's the Shunammite! 26Run to meet her and ask her,
'Are you all right? Is your husband all right? Is your child all right?'"

"Everything is all right," she said.

27When she reached the man of God at the mountain, she took hold
of his feet. Gehazi came over to push her away, but the man of God said,
"Leave her alone! She is in bitter distress, but the LORD has hidden it
from me and has not told me why."

28"Did I ask you for a son, my lord?" she said. "Didn't I tell you, 'Don't
raise my hopes'?"

29Elisha said to Gehazi, "Tuck your cloak into your belt, take my staff
in your hand and run. Don't greet anyone you meet, and if anyone
greets you, do not answer. Lay my staff on the boy's face."

[30]But the child's mother said, "As surely as the LORD lives and as you
live, I will not leave you." So he got up and followed her.
[31]Gehazi went on ahead and laid the staff on the boy's face, but there
was no sound or response. So Gehazi went back to meet Elisha and told
him, "The boy has not awakened."
[32]When Elisha reached the house, there was the boy lying dead on
his couch. [33]He went in, shut the door on the two of them and prayed
to the LORD. [34]Then he got on the bed and lay on the boy, mouth to
mouth, eyes to eyes, hands to hands. As he stretched himself out on
him, the boy's body grew warm. [35]Elisha turned away and walked back
and forth in the room and then got on the bed and stretched out on
him once more. The boy sneezed seven times and opened his eyes.
[36]Elisha summoned Gehazi and said, "Call the Shunammite." And
he did. When she came, he said, "Take your son." [37]She came in, fell at
his feet and bowed to the ground. Then she took her son and went out.

DEATH IN THE POT

[38]Elisha returned to Gilgal and there was a famine in that region.
While the company of the prophets was meeting with him, he said
to his servant, "Put on the large pot and cook some stew for these
prophets."
[39]One of them went out into the fields to gather herbs and found a
wild vine and picked as many of its gourds as his garment could hold.
When he returned, he cut them up into the pot of stew, though no one
knew what they were. [40]The stew was poured out for the men, but as
they began to eat it, they cried out, "Man of God, there is death in the
pot!" And they could not eat it.
[41]Elisha said, "Get some flour." He put it into the pot and said, "Serve
it to the people to eat." And there was nothing harmful in the pot.

FEEDING OF A HUNDRED

[42]A man came from Baal Shalishah, bringing the man of God twenty
loaves of barley bread baked from the first ripe grain, along with some
heads of new grain. "Give it to the people to eat," Elisha said.
[43]"How can I set this before a hundred men?" his servant asked.
But Elisha answered, "Give it to the people to eat. For this is what
the LORD says: 'They will eat and have some left over.'" [44]Then he set
it before them, and they ate and had some left over, according to the
word of the LORD.

NAAMAN HEALED OF LEPROSY

5 Now Naaman was commander of the army of the king of Aram.
He was a great man in the sight of his master and highly regarded,
because through him the LORD had given victory to Aram. He was a
valiant soldier, but he had leprosy.[a]
[2]Now bands of raiders from Aram had gone out and had taken cap-
tive a young girl from Israel, and she served Naaman's wife. [3]She said
to her mistress, "If only my master would see the prophet who is in
Samaria! He would cure him of his leprosy."
[4]Naaman went to his master and told him what the girl from Israel
had said. [5]"By all means, go," the king of Aram replied. "I will send a

[a] *1* The Hebrew for *leprosy* was used for various diseases affecting the skin; also in verses 3, 6, 7, 11 and 27.

PRAYING SCRIPTURE

2 Kings 5

Prejudice comes in many varieties. God revealed to Naaman, king of Syria, how his leprosy could be healed; he needed to immerse himself in the Jordan River seven times. At first he refused, preferring the "better" rivers of Damascus or that Elisha himself would heal his leprosy.

How often do we miss God's working because we are prejudiced against the message, messenger or method? Ask God for an open heart to receive his plans for you no matter the source.

letter to the king of Israel." So Naaman left, taking with him ten tal-
ents[a] of silver, six thousand shekels[b] of gold and ten sets of clothing.
6The letter that he took to the king of Israel read: "With this letter I
am sending my servant Naaman to you so that you may cure him of
his leprosy."

7As soon as the king of Israel read the letter, he tore his robes and
said, "Am I God? Can I kill and bring back to life? Why does this fellow
send someone to me to be cured of his leprosy? See how he is trying to
pick a quarrel with me!"

8When Elisha the man of God heard that the king of Israel had torn
his robes, he sent him this message: "Why have you torn your robes?
Have the man come to me and he will know that there is a prophet in
Israel." 9So Naaman went with his horses and chariots and stopped
at the door of Elisha's house. 10Elisha sent a messenger to say to him,
"Go, wash yourself seven times in the Jordan, and your flesh will be
restored and you will be cleansed."

11But Naaman went away angry and said, "I thought that he would
surely come out to me and stand and call on the name of the LORD his
God, wave his hand over the spot and cure me of my leprosy. 12Are not
Abana and Pharpar, the rivers of Damascus, better than all the waters
of Israel? Couldn't I wash in them and be cleansed?" So he turned and
went off in a rage.

13Naaman's servants went to him and said, "My father, if the prophet
had told you to do some great thing, would you not have done it? How
much more, then, when he tells you, 'Wash and be cleansed'!" 14So he
went down and dipped himself in the Jordan seven times, as the man
of God had told him, and his flesh was restored and became clean like
that of a young boy.

15Then Naaman and all his attendants went back to the man of God.
He stood before him and said, "Now I know that there is no God in all
the world except in Israel. So please accept a gift from your servant."

16The prophet answered, "As surely as the LORD lives, whom I serve,
I will not accept a thing." And even though Naaman urged him, he
refused.

17"If you will not," said Naaman, "please let me, your servant, be
given as much earth as a pair of mules can carry, for your servant will
never again make burnt offerings and sacrifices to any other god but
the LORD. 18But may the LORD forgive your servant for this one thing:
When my master enters the temple of Rimmon to bow down and he is
leaning on my arm and I have to bow there also — when I bow down
in the temple of Rimmon, may the LORD forgive your servant for this."

19"Go in peace," Elisha said.

After Naaman had traveled some distance, 20Gehazi, the servant of
Elisha the man of God, said to himself, "My master was too easy on
Naaman, this Aramean, by not accepting from him what he brought.
As surely as the LORD lives, I will run after him and get something
from him."

21So Gehazi hurried after Naaman. When Naaman saw him running
toward him, he got down from the chariot to meet him. "Is everything
all right?" he asked.

22"Everything is all right," Gehazi answered. "My master sent me to

---

[a] 5 That is, about 750 pounds or about 340 kilograms [b] 5 That is, about 150 pounds or about 69 kilograms

say, 'Two young men from the company of the prophets have just come
to me from the hill country of Ephraim. Please give them a talent[a] of
silver and two sets of clothing.'"
23"By all means, take two talents," said Naaman. He urged Gehazi
to accept them, and then tied up the two talents of silver in two bags,
with two sets of clothing. He gave them to two of his servants, and they
carried them ahead of Gehazi. 24When Gehazi came to the hill, he took
the things from the servants and put them away in the house. He sent
the men away and they left.
25When he went in and stood before his master, Elisha asked him,
"Where have you been, Gehazi?"
"Your servant didn't go anywhere," Gehazi answered.
26But Elisha said to him, "Was not my spirit with you when the
man got down from his chariot to meet you? Is this the time to take
money or to accept clothes — or olive groves and vineyards, or flocks
and herds, or male and female slaves? 27Naaman's leprosy will cling to
you and to your descendants forever." Then Gehazi went from Elisha's
presence and his skin was leprous — it had become as white as snow.

AN AXHEAD FLOATS

6 The company of the prophets said to Elisha, "Look, the place where
we meet with you is too small for us. 2Let us go to the Jordan,
where each of us can get a pole; and let us build a place there for us
to meet."
And he said, "Go."
3Then one of them said, "Won't you please come with your servants?"
"I will," Elisha replied. 4And he went with them.
They went to the Jordan and began to cut down trees. 5As one of
them was cutting down a tree, the iron axhead fell into the water. "Oh
no, my lord!" he cried out. "It was borrowed!"
6The man of God asked, "Where did it fall?" When he showed him
the place, Elisha cut a stick and threw it there, and made the iron float.
7"Lift it out," he said. Then the man reached out his hand and took it.

ELISHA TRAPS BLINDED ARAMEANS

8Now the king of Aram was at war with Israel. After conferring with
his officers, he said, "I will set up my camp in such and such a place."
9The man of God sent word to the king of Israel: "Beware of pass-
ing that place, because the Arameans are going down there." 10So the
king of Israel checked on the place indicated by the man of God. Time
and again Elisha warned the king, so that he was on his guard in such
places.
11This enraged the king of Aram. He summoned his officers and de-
manded of them, "Tell me! Which of us is on the side of the king of
Israel?"
12"None of us, my lord the king," said one of his officers, "but Elisha,
the prophet who is in Israel, tells the king of Israel the very words you
speak in your bedroom."
13"Go, find out where he is," the king ordered, "so I can send men and
capture him." The report came back: "He is in Dothan." 14Then he sent
horses and chariots and a strong force there. They went by night and
surrounded the city.

PRAYING SCRIPTURE

2 Kings 6

Outnumbered and under imminent threat by the Syrian army, the king of Israel sought advice from Elisha. His answer is a reply of faith: "Those who are with us are more than those who are with them" (verse 16). God opened the servant's eyes to see the hills covered with "horses and chariots of fire" (verse 17).

God's way is always enough to deliver his people. Asking for deliverance should be commonplace for God's children.

[a] *22* That is, about 75 pounds or about 34 kilograms

15 When the servant of the man of God got up and went out early the
next morning, an army with horses and chariots had surrounded the
city. "Oh no, my lord! What shall we do?" the servant asked.
16 "Don't be afraid," the prophet answered. "Those who are with us
are more than those who are with them."
17 And Elisha prayed, "Open his eyes, LORD, so that he may see." Then
the LORD opened the servant's eyes, and he looked and saw the hills
full of horses and chariots of fire all around Elisha.
18 As the enemy came down toward him, Elisha prayed to the LORD,
"Strike this army with blindness." So he struck them with blindness,
as Elisha had asked.
19 Elisha told them, "This is not the road and this is not the city. Fol-
low me, and I will lead you to the man you are looking for." And he led
them to Samaria.
20 After they entered the city, Elisha said, "LORD, open the eyes of
these men so they can see." Then the LORD opened their eyes and they
looked, and there they were, inside Samaria.
21 When the king of Israel saw them, he asked Elisha, "Shall I kill
them, my father? Shall I kill them?"
22 "Do not kill them," he answered. "Would you kill those you have
captured with your own sword or bow? Set food and water before them
so that they may eat and drink and then go back to their master." 23 So
he prepared a great feast for them, and after they had finished eating
and drinking, he sent them away, and they returned to their master. So
the bands from Aram stopped raiding Israel's territory.

FAMINE IN BESIEGED SAMARIA

24 Some time later, Ben-Hadad king of Aram mobilized his entire
army and marched up and laid siege to Samaria. 25 There was a great
famine in the city; the siege lasted so long that a donkey's head sold
for eighty shekels[a] of silver, and a quarter of a cab[b] of seed pods[c] for
five shekels.[d]
26 As the king of Israel was passing by on the wall, a woman cried to
him, "Help me, my lord the king!"
27 The king replied, "If the LORD does not help you, where can I get
help for you? From the threshing floor? From the winepress?" 28 Then
he asked her, "What's the matter?"

She answered, "This woman said to me, 'Give up your son so we may
eat him today, and tomorrow we'll eat my son.' 29 So we cooked my son
and ate him. The next day I said to her, 'Give up your son so we may eat
him,' but she had hidden him."
30 When the king heard the woman's words, he tore his robes. As he
went along the wall, the people looked, and they saw that, under his
robes, he had sackcloth on his body. 31 He said, "May God deal with me,
be it ever so severely, if the head of Elisha son of Shaphat remains on
his shoulders today!"
32 Now Elisha was sitting in his house, and the elders were sitting
with him. The king sent a messenger ahead, but before he arrived,
Elisha said to the elders, "Don't you see how this murderer is sending
someone to cut off my head? Look, when the messenger comes, shut
the door and hold it shut against him. Is not the sound of his master's

---

[a] *25* That is, about 2 pounds or about 920 grams [b] *25* That is, probably about 1/4 pound or about 100 grams [c] *25* Or *of doves' dung* [d] *25* That is, about 2 ounces or about 58 grams

footsteps behind him?" 33While he was still talking to them, the mes-
senger came down to him.
The king said, "This disaster is from the LORD. Why should I wait for
the LORD any longer?"
7 Elisha replied, "Hear the word of the LORD. This is what the LORD
says: About this time tomorrow, a seah[a] of the finest flour will
sell for a shekel[b] and two seahs[c] of barley for a shekel at the gate of
Samaria."
2The officer on whose arm the king was leaning said to the man of
God, "Look, even if the LORD should open the floodgates of the heav-
ens, could this happen?"
"You will see it with your own eyes," answered Elisha, "but you will
not eat any of it!"

THE SIEGE LIFTED

3Now there were four men with leprosy[d] at the entrance of the city
gate. They said to each other, "Why stay here until we die? 4If we say,
'We'll go into the city'—the famine is there, and we will die. And if we
stay here, we will die. So let's go over to the camp of the Arameans and
surrender. If they spare us, we live; if they kill us, then we die."
5At dusk they got up and went to the camp of the Arameans. When
they reached the edge of the camp, no one was there, 6for the Lord had
caused the Arameans to hear the sound of chariots and horses and a
great army, so that they said to one another, "Look, the king of Israel
has hired the Hittite and Egyptian kings to attack us!" 7So they got up
and fled in the dusk and abandoned their tents and their horses and
donkeys. They left the camp as it was and ran for their lives.
8The men who had leprosy reached the edge of the camp, entered
one of the tents and ate and drank. Then they took silver, gold and
clothes, and went off and hid them. They returned and entered an-
other tent and took some things from it and hid them also.
9Then they said to each other, "What we're doing is not right. This is
a day of good news and we are keeping it to ourselves. If we wait until
daylight, punishment will overtake us. Let's go at once and report this
to the royal palace."
10So they went and called out to the city gatekeepers and told them,
"We went into the Aramean camp and no one was there—not a sound
of anyone—only tethered horses and donkeys, and the tents left just
as they were." 11The gatekeepers shouted the news, and it was reported
within the palace.
12The king got up in the night and said to his officers, "I will tell you
what the Arameans have done to us. They know we are starving; so
they have left the camp to hide in the countryside, thinking, 'They will
surely come out, and then we will take them alive and get into the city.'"
13One of his officers answered, "Have some men take five of the
horses that are left in the city. Their plight will be like that of all the
Israelites left here—yes, they will only be like all these Israelites who
are doomed. So let us send them to find out what happened."

PRAYING SCRIPTURE

2 Kings 7

In this well-loved story, God miraculously caused the Syrians, who had implemented a stifling embargo, to abandon their military camp and supplies. The four lepers who stumbled on the scene and began plundering it realized they were selfish and in danger of judgment.

In what ways has God blessed you so that you can bless others? Ask God for wisdom to steward the resources he has put in your control.

---

[a] *1* That is, probably about 12 pounds or about 5.5 kilograms of flour; also in verses 16 and 18 [b] *1* That is, about 2/5 ounce or about 12 grams; also in verses 16 and 18 [c] *1* That is, probably about 20 pounds or about 9 kilograms of barley; also in verses 16 and 18 [d] *3* The Hebrew for *leprosy* was used for various diseases affecting the skin; also in verse 8.

14 So they selected two chariots with their horses, and the king sent them after the Aramean army. He commanded the drivers, "Go and find out what has happened." 15 They followed them as far as the Jordan, and they found the whole road strewn with the clothing and equipment the Arameans had thrown away in their headlong flight. So the messengers returned and reported to the king. 16 Then the people went out and plundered the camp of the Arameans. So a seah of the finest flour sold for a shekel, and two seahs of barley sold for a shekel, as the LORD had said.

17 Now the king had put the officer on whose arm he leaned in charge of the gate, and the people trampled him in the gateway, and he died, just as the man of God had foretold when the king came down to his house. 18 It happened as the man of God had said to the king: "About this time tomorrow, a seah of the finest flour will sell for a shekel and two seahs of barley for a shekel at the gate of Samaria."

19 The officer had said to the man of God, "Look, even if the LORD should open the floodgates of the heavens, could this happen?" The man of God had replied, "You will see it with your own eyes, but you will not eat any of it!" 20 And that is exactly what happened to him, for the people trampled him in the gateway, and he died.

PRAYING SCRIPTURE

2 Kings 8

God's providence is his non-miraculous provision for his people. The unnamed widow of this chapter experienced God's clear providence before and after the famine. With the king's direction, her land and seven years of lost proceeds were to be restored to her.

We often overlook God's providence in praying for the miraculous. While it's great to pray for miracles, let's remember to praise God for his consistent provision for us.

THE SHUNAMMITE'S LAND RESTORED

8 Now Elisha had said to the woman whose son he had restored to life, "Go away with your family and stay for a while wherever you can, because the LORD has decreed a famine in the land that will last seven years." 2 The woman proceeded to do as the man of God said. She and her family went away and stayed in the land of the Philistines seven years.

3 At the end of the seven years she came back from the land of the Philistines and went to appeal to the king for her house and land. 4 The king was talking to Gehazi, the servant of the man of God, and had said, "Tell me about all the great things Elisha has done." 5 Just as Gehazi was telling the king how Elisha had restored the dead to life, the woman whose son Elisha had brought back to life came to appeal to the king for her house and land.

Gehazi said, "This is the woman, my lord the king, and this is her son whom Elisha restored to life." 6 The king asked the woman about it, and she told him.

Then he assigned an official to her case and said to him, "Give back everything that belonged to her, including all the income from her land from the day she left the country until now."

HAZAEL MURDERS BEN-HADAD

7 Elisha went to Damascus, and Ben-Hadad king of Aram was ill. When the king was told, "The man of God has come all the way up here," 8 he said to Hazael, "Take a gift with you and go to meet the man of God. Consult the LORD through him; ask him, 'Will I recover from this illness?'"

9 Hazael went to meet Elisha, taking with him as a gift forty camel-loads of all the finest wares of Damascus. He went in and stood before him, and said, "Your son Ben-Hadad king of Aram has sent me to ask, 'Will I recover from this illness?'"

10 Elisha answered, "Go and say to him, 'You will certainly recover.' Nevertheless,[a] the LORD has revealed to me that he will in fact die." 11 He

[a] *10* The Hebrew may also be read *Go and say, 'You will certainly not recover,' for.*

stared at him with a fixed gaze until Hazael was embarrassed. Then the
man of God began to weep.
12“Why is my lord weeping?” asked Hazael.
“Because I know the harm you will do to the Israelites,” he answered.
“You will set fire to their fortified places, kill their young men with
the sword, dash their little children to the ground, and rip open their
pregnant women.”
13Hazael said, “How could your servant, a mere dog, accomplish such
a feat?”
“The LORD has shown me that you will become king of Aram,” an-
swered Elisha.
14Then Hazael left Elisha and returned to his master. When
Ben-Hadad asked, “What did Elisha say to you?” Hazael replied, “He
told me that you would certainly recover.” 15But the next day he took a
thick cloth, soaked it in water and spread it over the king’s face, so that
he died. Then Hazael succeeded him as king.

JEHORAM KING OF JUDAH

16In the fifth year of Joram son of Ahab king of Israel, when Jehosha-
phat was king of Judah, Jehoram son of Jehoshaphat began his reign as
king of Judah. 17He was thirty-two years old when he became king, and
he reigned in Jerusalem eight years. 18He followed the ways of the kings
of Israel, as the house of Ahab had done, for he married a daughter of
Ahab. He did evil in the eyes of the LORD. 19Nevertheless, for the sake
of his servant David, the LORD was not willing to destroy Judah. He had
promised to maintain a lamp for David and his descendants forever.
20In the time of Jehoram, Edom rebelled against Judah and set up its
own king. 21So Jehoram[a] went to Zair with all his chariots. The Edom-
ites surrounded him and his chariot commanders, but he rose up and
broke through by night; his army, however, fled back home. 22To this
day Edom has been in rebellion against Judah. Libnah revolted at the
same time.
23As for the other events of Jehoram’s reign, and all he did, are they
not written in the book of the annals of the kings of Judah? 24Jehoram
rested with his ancestors and was buried with them in the City of Da-
vid. And Ahaziah his son succeeded him as king.

AHAZIAH KING OF JUDAH

25In the twelfth year of Joram son of Ahab king of Israel, Ahaziah son
of Jehoram king of Judah began to reign. 26Ahaziah was twenty-two
years old when he became king, and he reigned in Jerusalem one year.
His mother’s name was Athaliah, a granddaughter of Omri king of Is-
rael. 27He followed the ways of the house of Ahab and did evil in the
eyes of the LORD, as the house of Ahab had done, for he was related by
marriage to Ahab’s family.
28Ahaziah went with Joram son of Ahab to war against Hazael king
of Aram at Ramoth Gilead. The Arameans wounded Joram; 29so King
Joram returned to Jezreel to recover from the wounds the Arameans
had inflicted on him at Ramoth[b] in his battle with Hazael king of Aram.
Then Ahaziah son of Jehoram king of Judah went down to Jezreel to
see Joram son of Ahab, because he had been wounded.

---

[a] *21* Hebrew *Joram,* a variant of *Jehoram;* also in verses 23 and 24
[b] *29* Hebrew *Ramah,* a variant of *Ramoth*

PRAYING SCRIPTURE

2 Kings 9

Although we often struggle to accept it, God ordains the rise and fall of rulers, even the ones who do not follow him with their whole hearts. In this passage, one ruler was anointed, Jehu, while a former queen, Jezebel, was judged.

God is sovereign over all his creation, including kings, queens and presidents. If you struggle with worrying about world events, ask God for faith to trust his power.

JEHU ANOINTED KING OF ISRAEL

9 The prophet Elisha summoned a man from the company of the
prophets and said to him, "Tuck your cloak into your belt, take
this flask of olive oil with you and go to Ramoth Gilead. 2When you get
there, look for Jehu son of Jehoshaphat, the son of Nimshi. Go to him,
get him away from his companions and take him into an inner room.
3Then take the flask and pour the oil on his head and declare, 'This is
what the LORD says: I anoint you king over Israel.' Then open the door
and run; don't delay!"
4So the young prophet went to Ramoth Gilead. 5When he arrived,
he found the army officers sitting together. "I have a message for you,
commander," he said.
"For which of us?" asked Jehu.
"For you, commander," he replied.
6Jehu got up and went into the house. Then the prophet poured the
oil on Jehu's head and declared, "This is what the LORD, the God of Israel, says: 'I anoint you king over the LORD's people Israel. 7You are to
destroy the house of Ahab your master, and I will avenge the blood of
my servants the prophets and the blood of all the LORD's servants shed
by Jezebel. 8The whole house of Ahab will perish. I will cut off from
Ahab every last male in Israel — slave or free.[a] 9I will make the house
of Ahab like the house of Jeroboam son of Nebat and like the house
of Baasha son of Ahijah. 10As for Jezebel, dogs will devour her on the
plot of ground at Jezreel, and no one will bury her.'" Then he opened
the door and ran.
11When Jehu went out to his fellow officers, one of them asked him,
"Is everything all right? Why did this maniac come to you?"
"You know the man and the sort of things he says," Jehu replied.
12"That's not true!" they said. "Tell us."
Jehu said, "Here is what he told me: 'This is what the LORD says: I
anoint you king over Israel.'"
13They quickly took their cloaks and spread them under him on the
bare steps. Then they blew the trumpet and shouted, "Jehu is king!"

JEHU KILLS JORAM AND AHAZIAH

14So Jehu son of Jehoshaphat, the son of Nimshi, conspired against
Joram. (Now Joram and all Israel had been defending Ramoth Gilead
against Hazael king of Aram, 15but King Joram[b] had returned to Jezreel
to recover from the wounds the Arameans had inflicted on him in the
battle with Hazael king of Aram.) Jehu said, "If you desire to make me
king, don't let anyone slip out of the city to go and tell the news in Jezreel." 16Then he got into his chariot and rode to Jezreel, because Joram
was resting there and Ahaziah king of Judah had gone down to see him.
17When the lookout standing on the tower in Jezreel saw Jehu's
troops approaching, he called out, "I see some troops coming."
"Get a horseman," Joram ordered. "Send him to meet them and ask,
'Do you come in peace?'"
18The horseman rode off to meet Jehu and said, "This is what the
king says: 'Do you come in peace?'"
"What do you have to do with peace?" Jehu replied. "Fall in behind me."

---

[a] 8 Or *Israel — every ruler or leader* [b] 15 Hebrew *Jehoram,* a variant of *Joram*; also in verses 17 and 21-24

The lookout reported, "The messenger has reached them, but he
isn't coming back."
19So the king sent out a second horseman. When he came to them he
said, "This is what the king says: 'Do you come in peace?' "
Jehu replied, "What do you have to do with peace? Fall in be-
hind me."
20The lookout reported, "He has reached them, but he isn't coming
back either. The driving is like that of Jehu son of Nimshi—he drives
like a maniac."
21"Hitch up my chariot," Joram ordered. And when it was hitched up,
Joram king of Israel and Ahaziah king of Judah rode out, each in his
own chariot, to meet Jehu. They met him at the plot of ground that had
belonged to Naboth the Jezreelite. 22When Joram saw Jehu he asked,
"Have you come in peace, Jehu?"
"How can there be peace," Jehu replied, "as long as all the idolatry
and witchcraft of your mother Jezebel abound?"
23Joram turned about and fled, calling out to Ahaziah, "Treachery,
Ahaziah!"
24Then Jehu drew his bow and shot Joram between the shoulders.
The arrow pierced his heart and he slumped down in his chariot.
25Jehu said to Bidkar, his chariot officer, "Pick him up and throw him
on the field that belonged to Naboth the Jezreelite. Remember how
you and I were riding together in chariots behind Ahab his father when
the LORD spoke this prophecy against him: 26'Yesterday I saw the blood
of Naboth and the blood of his sons, declares the LORD, and I will surely
make you pay for it on this plot of ground, declares the LORD.'[a] Now
then, pick him up and throw him on that plot, in accordance with the
word of the LORD."
27When Ahaziah king of Judah saw what had happened, he fled up
the road to Beth Haggan.[b] Jehu chased him, shouting, "Kill him too!"
They wounded him in his chariot on the way up to Gur near Ibleam,
but he escaped to Megiddo and died there. 28His servants took him by
chariot to Jerusalem and buried him with his ancestors in his tomb in
the City of David. 29(In the eleventh year of Joram son of Ahab, Ahaziah
had become king of Judah.)

JEZEBEL KILLED

30Then Jehu went to Jezreel. When Jezebel heard about it, she put on
eye makeup, arranged her hair and looked out of a window. 31As Jehu
entered the gate, she asked, "Have you come in peace, you Zimri, you
murderer of your master?"[c]
32He looked up at the window and called out, "Who is on my side?
Who?" Two or three eunuchs looked down at him. 33"Throw her down!"
Jehu said. So they threw her down, and some of her blood spattered
the wall and the horses as they trampled her underfoot.
34Jehu went in and ate and drank. "Take care of that cursed woman,"
he said, "and bury her, for she was a king's daughter." 35But when they
went out to bury her, they found nothing except her skull, her feet
and her hands. 36They went back and told Jehu, who said, "This is the
word of the LORD that he spoke through his servant Elijah the Tish-
bite: On the plot of ground at Jezreel dogs will devour Jezebel's flesh.[d]

---

[a] *26* See 1 Kings 21:19. [b] *27* Or *fled by way of the garden house* [c] *31* Or *"Was there peace for Zimri, who murdered his master?"* [d] *36* See 1 Kings 21:23.

37Jezebel's body will be like dung on the ground in the plot at Jezreel,
so that no one will be able to say, 'This is Jezebel.'"

AHAB'S FAMILY KILLED

10 Now there were in Samaria seventy sons of the house of Ahab.
So Jehu wrote letters and sent them to Samaria: to the officials
of Jezreel,[a] to the elders and to the guardians of Ahab's children. He
said, 2"You have your master's sons with you and you have chariots
and horses, a fortified city and weapons. Now as soon as this letter
reaches you, 3choose the best and most worthy of your master's sons
and set him on his father's throne. Then fight for your master's house."
4But they were terrified and said, "If two kings could not resist him,
how can we?"
5So the palace administrator, the city governor, the elders and the
guardians sent this message to Jehu: "We are your servants and we
will do anything you say. We will not appoint anyone as king; you do
whatever you think best."
6Then Jehu wrote them a second letter, saying, "If you are on my
side and will obey me, take the heads of your master's sons and come
to me in Jezreel by this time tomorrow."
Now the royal princes, seventy of them, were with the leading men
of the city, who were rearing them. 7When the letter arrived, these men
took the princes and slaughtered all seventy of them. They put their
heads in baskets and sent them to Jehu in Jezreel. 8When the messen-
ger arrived, he told Jehu, "They have brought the heads of the princes."
Then Jehu ordered, "Put them in two piles at the entrance of the city
gate until morning."
9The next morning Jehu went out. He stood before all the people
and said, "You are innocent. It was I who conspired against my master
and killed him, but who killed all these? 10Know, then, that not a word
the LORD has spoken against the house of Ahab will fail. The LORD has
done what he announced through his servant Elijah." 11So Jehu killed
everyone in Jezreel who remained of the house of Ahab, as well as all
his chief men, his close friends and his priests, leaving him no survivor.
12Jehu then set out and went toward Samaria. At Beth Eked of the
Shepherds, 13he met some relatives of Ahaziah king of Judah and
asked, "Who are you?"
They said, "We are relatives of Ahaziah, and we have come down to
greet the families of the king and of the queen mother."
14"Take them alive!" he ordered. So they took them alive and slaugh-
tered them by the well of Beth Eked — forty-two of them. He left no
survivor.
15After he left there, he came upon Jehonadab son of Rekab, who was
on his way to meet him. Jehu greeted him and said, "Are you in accord
with me, as I am with you?"
"I am," Jehonadab answered.
"If so," said Jehu, "give me your hand." So he did, and Jehu helped
him up into the chariot. 16Jehu said, "Come with me and see my zeal
for the LORD." Then he had him ride along in his chariot.
17When Jehu came to Samaria, he killed all who were left there of
Ahab's family; he destroyed them, according to the word of the LORD
spoken to Elijah.

PRAYING SCRIPTURE

2 Kings 10

God's promised judgment fell on Ahab's sons through Jehu, who put scores of them to death. Using a ruse, Jehu then assembled the prophets of Baal and had them put to death. Though Jehu portrayed zeal for the Lord, he did not turn the Israelites fully away from worshiping idols, nor did he follow God with his whole heart.

Ask God to help you follow him with your all.

[a] *1* Hebrew; some Septuagint manuscripts and Vulgate *of the city*

SERVANTS OF BAAL KILLED

18Then Jehu brought all the people together and said to them, "Ahab
served Baal a little; Jehu will serve him much. 19Now summon all the
prophets of Baal, all his servants and all his priests. See that no one is
missing, because I am going to hold a great sacrifice for Baal. Anyone
who fails to come will no longer live." But Jehu was acting deceptively
in order to destroy the servants of Baal.
20Jehu said, "Call an assembly in honor of Baal." So they proclaimed
it. 21Then he sent word throughout Israel, and all the servants of Baal
came; not one stayed away. They crowded into the temple of Baal until
it was full from one end to the other. 22And Jehu said to the keeper of
the wardrobe, "Bring robes for all the servants of Baal." So he brought
out robes for them.
23Then Jehu and Jehonadab son of Rekab went into the temple of
Baal. Jehu said to the servants of Baal, "Look around and see that no
one who serves the LORD is here with you — only servants of Baal."
24So they went in to make sacrifices and burnt offerings. Now Jehu
had posted eighty men outside with this warning: "If one of you lets
any of the men I am placing in your hands escape, it will be your life
for his life."
25As soon as Jehu had finished making the burnt offering, he or-
dered the guards and officers: "Go in and kill them; let no one escape."
So they cut them down with the sword. The guards and officers threw
the bodies out and then entered the inner shrine of the temple of Baal.
26They brought the sacred stone out of the temple of Baal and burned
it. 27They demolished the sacred stone of Baal and tore down the tem-
ple of Baal, and people have used it for a latrine to this day.
28So Jehu destroyed Baal worship in Israel. 29However, he did not
turn away from the sins of Jeroboam son of Nebat, which he had
caused Israel to commit — the worship of the golden calves at Bethel
and Dan.
30The LORD said to Jehu, "Because you have done well in accomplish-
ing what is right in my eyes and have done to the house of Ahab all I
had in mind to do, your descendants will sit on the throne of Israel to
the fourth generation." 31Yet Jehu was not careful to keep the law of the
LORD, the God of Israel, with all his heart. He did not turn away from
the sins of Jeroboam, which he had caused Israel to commit.
32In those days the LORD began to reduce the size of Israel. Hazael
overpowered the Israelites throughout their territory 33east of the Jor-
dan in all the land of Gilead (the region of Gad, Reuben and Manasseh),
from Aroer by the Arnon Gorge through Gilead to Bashan.
34As for the other events of Jehu's reign, all he did, and all his
achievements, are they not written in the book of the annals of the
kings of Israel?
35Jehu rested with his ancestors and was buried in Samaria. And Je-
hoahaz his son succeeded him as king. 36The time that Jehu reigned
over Israel in Samaria was twenty-eight years.

ATHALIAH AND JOASH

11 When Athaliah the mother of Ahaziah saw that her son was dead,
she proceeded to destroy the whole royal family. 2But Jehosh-
eba, the daughter of King Jehoram[a] and sister of Ahaziah, took Joash

PRAYING SCRIPTURE

2 Kings 11

Faithfulness to the Lord demanded that his people destroy the idols that were turning their hearts away from him. Under the priest Jehoiada, Israel rose up and destroyed the temple of Baal, breaking the altars and images that were in it.

Without wholesale forsaking of sin, repentance has not taken place. Examine your heart for any idols that need to be broken and forsaken. God will always honor those prayers.

---

[a] 2 Hebrew *Joram,* a variant of *Jehoram*

son of Ahaziah and stole him away from among the royal princes, who
were about to be murdered. She put him and his nurse in a bedroom
to hide him from Athaliah; so he was not killed. 3He remained hidden
with his nurse at the temple of the LORD for six years while Athaliah
ruled the land.

4In the seventh year Jehoiada sent for the commanders of units of
a hundred, the Carites and the guards and had them brought to him
at the temple of the LORD. He made a covenant with them and put
them under oath at the temple of the LORD. Then he showed them
the king's son. 5He commanded them, saying, "This is what you are to
do: You who are in the three companies that are going on duty on the
Sabbath — a third of you guarding the royal palace, 6a third at the Sur
Gate, and a third at the gate behind the guard, who take turns guard-
ing the temple — 7and you who are in the other two companies that
normally go off Sabbath duty are all to guard the temple for the king.
8Station yourselves around the king, each of you with weapon in hand.
Anyone who approaches your ranks[a] is to be put to death. Stay close to
the king wherever he goes."

9The commanders of units of a hundred did just as Jehoiada the
priest ordered. Each one took his men — those who were going on
duty on the Sabbath and those who were going off duty — and came
to Jehoiada the priest. 10Then he gave the commanders the spears and
shields that had belonged to King David and that were in the temple
of the LORD. 11The guards, each with weapon in hand, stationed them-
selves around the king — near the altar and the temple, from the south
side to the north side of the temple.

12Jehoiada brought out the king's son and put the crown on him; he
presented him with a copy of the covenant and proclaimed him king.
They anointed him, and the people clapped their hands and shouted,
"Long live the king!"

13When Athaliah heard the noise made by the guards and the peo-
ple, she went to the people at the temple of the LORD. 14She looked
and there was the king, standing by the pillar, as the custom was. The
officers and the trumpeters were beside the king, and all the people of
the land were rejoicing and blowing trumpets. Then Athaliah tore her
robes and called out, "Treason! Treason!"

15Jehoiada the priest ordered the commanders of units of a hundred,
who were in charge of the troops: "Bring her out between the ranks[b]
and put to the sword anyone who follows her." For the priest had said,
"She must not be put to death in the temple of the LORD." 16So they
seized her as she reached the place where the horses enter the palace
grounds, and there she was put to death.

17Jehoiada then made a covenant between the LORD and the king and
people that they would be the LORD's people. He also made a covenant
between the king and the people. 18All the people of the land went to
the temple of Baal and tore it down. They smashed the altars and idols
to pieces and killed Mattan the priest of Baal in front of the altars.

Then Jehoiada the priest posted guards at the temple of the LORD.
19He took with him the commanders of hundreds, the Carites, the
guards and all the people of the land, and together they brought the
king down from the temple of the LORD and went into the palace, en-
tering by way of the gate of the guards. The king then took his place on

---

[a] 8 Or *approaches the precincts* [b] 15 Or *out from the precincts*

the royal throne. 20 All the people of the land rejoiced, and the city was
calm, because Athaliah had been slain with the sword at the palace.
21 Joash[a] was seven years old when he began to reign.[b]

JOASH REPAIRS THE TEMPLE

12 [c] In the seventh year of Jehu, Joash[d] became king, and he reigned
in Jerusalem forty years. His mother's name was Zibiah; she
was from Beersheba. 2 Joash did what was right in the eyes of the LORD
all the years Jehoiada the priest instructed him. 3 The high places, how-
ever, were not removed; the people continued to offer sacrifices and
burn incense there.
4 Joash said to the priests, "Collect all the money that is brought as
sacred offerings to the temple of the LORD—the money collected in
the census, the money received from personal vows and the money
brought voluntarily to the temple. 5 Let every priest receive the money
from one of the treasurers, then use it to repair whatever damage is
found in the temple."
6 But by the twenty-third year of King Joash the priests still had not
repaired the temple. 7 Therefore King Joash summoned Jehoiada the
priest and the other priests and asked them, "Why aren't you repairing
the damage done to the temple? Take no more money from your trea-
surers, but hand it over for repairing the temple." 8 The priests agreed
that they would not collect any more money from the people and that
they would not repair the temple themselves.
9 Jehoiada the priest took a chest and bored a hole in its lid. He
placed it beside the altar, on the right side as one enters the temple
of the LORD. The priests who guarded the entrance put into the chest
all the money that was brought to the temple of the LORD. 10 Whenever
they saw that there was a large amount of money in the chest, the royal
secretary and the high priest came, counted the money that had been
brought into the temple of the LORD and put it into bags. 11 When the
amount had been determined, they gave the money to the men ap-
pointed to supervise the work on the temple. With it they paid those
who worked on the temple of the LORD—the carpenters and builders,
12 the masons and stonecutters. They purchased timber and blocks of
dressed stone for the repair of the temple of the LORD, and met all the
other expenses of restoring the temple.
13 The money brought into the temple was not spent for making sil-
ver basins, wick trimmers, sprinkling bowls, trumpets or any other
articles of gold or silver for the temple of the LORD; 14 it was paid to the
workers, who used it to repair the temple. 15 They did not require an
accounting from those to whom they gave the money to pay the work-
ers, because they acted with complete honesty. 16 The money from the
guilt offerings and sin offerings[e] was not brought into the temple of
the LORD; it belonged to the priests.
17 About this time Hazael king of Aram went up and attacked Gath
and captured it. Then he turned to attack Jerusalem. 18 But Joash king
of Judah took all the sacred objects dedicated by his predecessors—Je-
hoshaphat, Jehoram and Ahaziah, the kings of Judah—and the gifts

PRAYING SCRIPTURE

2 Kings 12

Although many of the people continued in idolatry, young King Jehoash followed God his entire 40-year reign. He led repairs to the temple and ensured that the repairmen were well paid for their work.

We can't always control what others do in their walk with God, but we can control our own actions. If everyone we know turns from God, he will still strengthen us to follow him if we but ask.

[a] 21 Hebrew *Jehoash,* a variant of *Joash* [b] 21 In Hebrew texts this verse (11:21) is numbered 12:1. [c] In Hebrew texts 12:1-21 is numbered 12:2-22.
[d] 1 Hebrew *Jehoash,* a variant of *Joash;* also in verses 2, 4, 6, 7 and 18
[e] 16 Or *purification offerings*

he himself had dedicated and all the gold found in the treasuries of the
temple of the LORD and of the royal palace, and he sent them to Hazael
king of Aram, who then withdrew from Jerusalem.
19As for the other events of the reign of Joash, and all he did, are
they not written in the book of the annals of the kings of Judah? 20His
officials conspired against him and assassinated him at Beth Millo, on
the road down to Silla. 21The officials who murdered him were Joza-
bad son of Shimeath and Jehozabad son of Shomer. He died and was
buried with his ancestors in the City of David. And Amaziah his son
succeeded him as king.

JEHOAHAZ KING OF ISRAEL

13 In the twenty-third year of Joash son of Ahaziah king of Judah,
Jehoahaz son of Jehu became king of Israel in Samaria, and he
reigned seventeen years. 2He did evil in the eyes of the LORD by fol-
lowing the sins of Jeroboam son of Nebat, which he had caused Israel
to commit, and he did not turn away from them. 3So the LORD's an-
ger burned against Israel, and for a long time he kept them under the
power of Hazael king of Aram and Ben-Hadad his son.
4Then Jehoahaz sought the LORD's favor, and the LORD listened to
him, for he saw how severely the king of Aram was oppressing Israel.
5The LORD provided a deliverer for Israel, and they escaped from the
power of Aram. So the Israelites lived in their own homes as they had
before. 6But they did not turn away from the sins of the house of Jero-
boam, which he had caused Israel to commit; they continued in them.
Also, the Asherah pole[a] remained standing in Samaria.
7Nothing had been left of the army of Jehoahaz except fifty horse-
men, ten chariots and ten thousand foot soldiers, for the king of Aram
had destroyed the rest and made them like the dust at threshing time.
8As for the other events of the reign of Jehoahaz, all he did and his
achievements, are they not written in the book of the annals of the
kings of Israel? 9Jehoahaz rested with his ancestors and was buried in
Samaria. And Jehoash[b] his son succeeded him as king.

JEHOASH KING OF ISRAEL

10In the thirty-seventh year of Joash king of Judah, Jehoash son of
Jehoahaz became king of Israel in Samaria, and he reigned sixteen
years. 11He did evil in the eyes of the LORD and did not turn away from
any of the sins of Jeroboam son of Nebat, which he had caused Israel
to commit; he continued in them.
12As for the other events of the reign of Jehoash, all he did and his
achievements, including his war against Amaziah king of Judah, are
they not written in the book of the annals of the kings of Israel? 13Je-
hoash rested with his ancestors, and Jeroboam succeeded him on the
throne. Jehoash was buried in Samaria with the kings of Israel.
14Now Elisha had been suffering from the illness from which he died.
Jehoash king of Israel went down to see him and wept over him. "My
father! My father!" he cried. "The chariots and horsemen of Israel!"
15Elisha said, "Get a bow and some arrows," and he did so. 16"Take the
bow in your hands," he said to the king of Israel. When he had taken it,
Elisha put his hands on the king's hands.

PRAYING SCRIPTURE
2 Kings 13

The ministry of Elisha came to an end with his death and entombment, leading to one of the most astounding miracles in Scripture. While the men of Israel were burying another man, a raiding party hurried them into placing the man in Elisha's tomb. When the dead man touched Elisha's bones, he came back to life!

God's power is always enough. Trust God for all the power you need to live for him.

---

[a] 6 That is, a wooden symbol of the goddess Asherah; here and elsewhere in 2 Kings [b] 9 Hebrew *Joash*, a variant of *Jehoash*; also in verses 12-14 and 25

17"Open the east window," he said, and he opened it. "Shoot!" Elisha said, and he shot. "The LORD's arrow of victory, the arrow of victory over Aram!" Elisha declared. "You will completely destroy the Arameans at Aphek."

18Then he said, "Take the arrows," and the king took them. Elisha told him, "Strike the ground." He struck it three times and stopped. 19The man of God was angry with him and said, "You should have struck the ground five or six times; then you would have defeated Aram and completely destroyed it. But now you will defeat it only three times."

20Elisha died and was buried.

Now Moabite raiders used to enter the country every spring. 21Once while some Israelites were burying a man, suddenly they saw a band of raiders; so they threw the man's body into Elisha's tomb. When the body touched Elisha's bones, the man came to life and stood up on his feet.

22Hazael king of Aram oppressed Israel throughout the reign of Jehoahaz. 23But the LORD was gracious to them and had compassion and showed concern for them because of his covenant with Abraham, Isaac and Jacob. To this day he has been unwilling to destroy them or banish them from his presence.

24Hazael king of Aram died, and Ben-Hadad his son succeeded him as king. 25Then Jehoash son of Jehoahaz recaptured from Ben-Hadad son of Hazael the towns he had taken in battle from his father Jehoahaz. Three times Jehoash defeated him, and so he recovered the Israelite towns.

AMAZIAH KING OF JUDAH

14 In the second year of Jehoash[a] son of Jehoahaz king of Israel, Amaziah son of Joash king of Judah began to reign. 2He was twenty-five years old when he became king, and he reigned in Jerusalem twenty-nine years. His mother's name was Jehoaddan; she was from Jerusalem. 3He did what was right in the eyes of the LORD, but not as his father David had done. In everything he followed the example of his father Joash. 4The high places, however, were not removed; the people continued to offer sacrifices and burn incense there.

5After the kingdom was firmly in his grasp, he executed the officials who had murdered his father the king. 6Yet he did not put the children of the assassins to death, in accordance with what is written in the Book of the Law of Moses where the LORD commanded: "Parents are not to be put to death for their children, nor children put to death for their parents; each will die for their own sin."[b]

7He was the one who defeated ten thousand Edomites in the Valley of Salt and captured Sela in battle, calling it Joktheel, the name it has to this day.

8Then Amaziah sent messengers to Jehoash son of Jehoahaz, the son of Jehu, king of Israel, with the challenge: "Come, let us face each other in battle."

9But Jehoash king of Israel replied to Amaziah king of Judah: "A thistle in Lebanon sent a message to a cedar in Lebanon, 'Give your daughter to my son in marriage.' Then a wild beast in Lebanon came

PRAYING SCRIPTURE

2 Kings 14

God's compassion is roused when he sees the suffering of his people. Even though they sinned over and over again, he did not abandon his covenant with them. The Old Testament frequently reminds us of God's faithfulness to his word and pity on his people.

Do you ever worry that God no longer loves you because of sins you have committed? Rejoice! He will never stop loving you.

[a] 1 Hebrew *Joash*, a variant of *Jehoash*; also in verses 13, 23 and 27
[b] 6 Deut. 24:16

along and trampled the thistle underfoot. 10You have indeed defeated Edom and now you are arrogant. Glory in your victory, but stay at home! Why ask for trouble and cause your own downfall and that of Judah also?"

11Amaziah, however, would not listen, so Jehoash king of Israel attacked. He and Amaziah king of Judah faced each other at Beth Shemesh in Judah. 12Judah was routed by Israel, and every man fled to his home. 13Jehoash king of Israel captured Amaziah king of Judah, the son of Joash, the son of Ahaziah, at Beth Shemesh. Then Jehoash went to Jerusalem and broke down the wall of Jerusalem from the Ephraim Gate to the Corner Gate — a section about four hundred cubits long.[a] 14He took all the gold and silver and all the articles found in the temple of the LORD and in the treasuries of the royal palace. He also took hostages and returned to Samaria.

15As for the other events of the reign of Jehoash, what he did and his achievements, including his war against Amaziah king of Judah, are they not written in the book of the annals of the kings of Israel? 16Jehoash rested with his ancestors and was buried in Samaria with the kings of Israel. And Jeroboam his son succeeded him as king.

17Amaziah son of Joash king of Judah lived for fifteen years after the death of Jehoash son of Jehoahaz king of Israel. 18As for the other events of Amaziah's reign, are they not written in the book of the annals of the kings of Judah?

19They conspired against him in Jerusalem, and he fled to Lachish, but they sent men after him to Lachish and killed him there. 20He was brought back by horse and was buried in Jerusalem with his ancestors, in the City of David.

21Then all the people of Judah took Azariah,[b] who was sixteen years old, and made him king in place of his father Amaziah. 22He was the one who rebuilt Elath and restored it to Judah after Amaziah rested with his ancestors.

JEROBOAM II KING OF ISRAEL

23In the fifteenth year of Amaziah son of Joash king of Judah, Jeroboam son of Jehoash king of Israel became king in Samaria, and he reigned forty-one years. 24He did evil in the eyes of the LORD and did not turn away from any of the sins of Jeroboam son of Nebat, which he had caused Israel to commit. 25He was the one who restored the boundaries of Israel from Lebo Hamath to the Dead Sea,[c] in accordance with the word of the LORD, the God of Israel, spoken through his servant Jonah son of Amittai, the prophet from Gath Hepher.

26The LORD had seen how bitterly everyone in Israel, whether slave or free, was suffering;[d] there was no one to help them. 27And since the LORD had not said he would blot out the name of Israel from under heaven, he saved them by the hand of Jeroboam son of Jehoash.

28As for the other events of Jeroboam's reign, all he did, and his military achievements, including how he recovered for Israel both Damascus and Hamath, which had belonged to Judah, are they not written in the book of the annals of the kings of Israel? 29Jeroboam rested with his ancestors, the kings of Israel. And Zechariah his son succeeded him as king.

[a] 13 That is, about 600 feet or about 180 meters [b] 21 Also called *Uzziah*
[c] 25 Hebrew *the Sea of the Arabah* [d] 26 Or *Israel was suffering. They were without a ruler or leader, and*

AZARIAH KING OF JUDAH

15 In the twenty-seventh year of Jeroboam king of Israel, Azariah[a]
son of Amaziah king of Judah began to reign. 2He was sixteen
years old when he became king, and he reigned in Jerusalem fifty-two
years. His mother's name was Jekoliah; she was from Jerusalem. 3He
did what was right in the eyes of the LORD, just as his father Amaziah
had done. 4The high places, however, were not removed; the people
continued to offer sacrifices and burn incense there.
5The LORD afflicted the king with leprosy[b] until the day he died, and
he lived in a separate house.[c] Jotham the king's son had charge of the
palace and governed the people of the land.
6As for the other events of Azariah's reign, and all he did, are they
not written in the book of the annals of the kings of Judah? 7Azariah
rested with his ancestors and was buried near them in the City of David. And Jotham his son succeeded him as king.

ZECHARIAH KING OF ISRAEL

8In the thirty-eighth year of Azariah king of Judah, Zechariah son
of Jeroboam became king of Israel in Samaria, and he reigned six
months. 9He did evil in the eyes of the LORD, as his predecessors had
done. He did not turn away from the sins of Jeroboam son of Nebat,
which he had caused Israel to commit.
10Shallum son of Jabesh conspired against Zechariah. He attacked
him in front of the people,[d] assassinated him and succeeded him as
king. 11The other events of Zechariah's reign are written in the book of
the annals of the kings of Israel. 12So the word of the LORD spoken to
Jehu was fulfilled: "Your descendants will sit on the throne of Israel to
the fourth generation."[e]

SHALLUM KING OF ISRAEL

13Shallum son of Jabesh became king in the thirty-ninth year of
Uzziah king of Judah, and he reigned in Samaria one month. 14Then
Menahem son of Gadi went from Tirzah up to Samaria. He attacked
Shallum son of Jabesh in Samaria, assassinated him and succeeded
him as king.
15The other events of Shallum's reign, and the conspiracy he led, are
written in the book of the annals of the kings of Israel.
16At that time Menahem, starting out from Tirzah, attacked Tiphsah and everyone in the city and its vicinity, because they refused to
open their gates. He sacked Tiphsah and ripped open all the pregnant
women.

MENAHEM KING OF ISRAEL

17In the thirty-ninth year of Azariah king of Judah, Menahem son of
Gadi became king of Israel, and he reigned in Samaria ten years. 18He
did evil in the eyes of the LORD. During his entire reign he did not turn
away from the sins of Jeroboam son of Nebat, which he had caused
Israel to commit.
19Then Pul[f] king of Assyria invaded the land, and Menahem gave

PRAYING SCRIPTURE

2 Kings 15

The legacy of failed kings in Israel and Judah seems to plumb the deepest depths of sin. Though their repeated failures and idolatries provoked God to anger, God's promise should point us in hope to the one true and righteous King who will rule forever on David's throne. No human ruler can stop God's purposes.

If you are tempted to worry about human leaders, thank Jesus for his eternal reign.

[a] *1* Also called *Uzziah*; also in verses 6, 7, 8, 17, 23 and 27 [b] *5* The Hebrew for *leprosy* was used for various diseases affecting the skin. [c] *5* Or *in a house where he was relieved of responsibilities* [d] *10* Hebrew; some Septuagint manuscripts *in Ibleam* [e] *12* 2 Kings 10:30 [f] *19* Also called *Tiglath-Pileser*

him a thousand talents[a] of silver to gain his support and strengthen
his own hold on the kingdom. [20]Menahem exacted this money from
Israel. Every wealthy person had to contribute fifty shekels[b] of silver
to be given to the king of Assyria. So the king of Assyria withdrew and
stayed in the land no longer.

[21]As for the other events of Menahem's reign, and all he did, are they
not written in the book of the annals of the kings of Israel? [22]Menahem
rested with his ancestors. And Pekahiah his son succeeded him as king.

PEKAHIAH KING OF ISRAEL

[23]In the fiftieth year of Azariah king of Judah, Pekahiah son of Mena-
hem became king of Israel in Samaria, and he reigned two years. [24]Pek-
ahiah did evil in the eyes of the LORD. He did not turn away from the
sins of Jeroboam son of Nebat, which he had caused Israel to commit.
[25]One of his chief officers, Pekah son of Remaliah, conspired against
him. Taking fifty men of Gilead with him, he assassinated Pekahiah,
along with Argob and Arieh, in the citadel of the royal palace at Sa-
maria. So Pekah killed Pekahiah and succeeded him as king.

[26]The other events of Pekahiah's reign, and all he did, are written in
the book of the annals of the kings of Israel.

PEKAH KING OF ISRAEL

[27]In the fifty-second year of Azariah king of Judah, Pekah son of Rem-
aliah became king of Israel in Samaria, and he reigned twenty years.
[28]He did evil in the eyes of the LORD. He did not turn away from the
sins of Jeroboam son of Nebat, which he had caused Israel to commit.

[29]In the time of Pekah king of Israel, Tiglath-Pileser king of Assyria
came and took Ijon, Abel Beth Maakah, Janoah, Kedesh and Hazor.
He took Gilead and Galilee, including all the land of Naphtali, and de-
ported the people to Assyria. [30]Then Hoshea son of Elah conspired
against Pekah son of Remaliah. He attacked and assassinated him,
and then succeeded him as king in the twentieth year of Jotham son
of Uzziah.

[31]As for the other events of Pekah's reign, and all he did, are they not
written in the book of the annals of the kings of Israel?

JOTHAM KING OF JUDAH

[32]In the second year of Pekah son of Remaliah king of Israel, Jotham
son of Uzziah king of Judah began to reign. [33]He was twenty-five years
old when he became king, and he reigned in Jerusalem sixteen years.
His mother's name was Jerusha daughter of Zadok. [34]He did what was
right in the eyes of the LORD, just as his father Uzziah had done. [35]The
high places, however, were not removed; the people continued to offer
sacrifices and burn incense there. Jotham rebuilt the Upper Gate of the
temple of the LORD.

[36]As for the other events of Jotham's reign, and what he did, are they
not written in the book of the annals of the kings of Judah? [37](In those
days the LORD began to send Rezin king of Aram and Pekah son of
Remaliah against Judah.) [38]Jotham rested with his ancestors and was
buried with them in the City of David, the city of his father. And Ahaz
his son succeeded him as king.

---

[a] *19* That is, about 38 tons or about 34 metric tons [b] *20* That is, about 1 1/4 pounds or about 575 grams

AHAZ KING OF JUDAH

16 In the seventeenth year of Pekah son of Remaliah, Ahaz son of Jotham king of Judah began to reign. 2Ahaz was twenty years old when he became king, and he reigned in Jerusalem sixteen years. Unlike David his father, he did not do what was right in the eyes of the LORD his God. 3He followed the ways of the kings of Israel and even sacrificed his son in the fire, engaging in the detestable practices of the nations the LORD had driven out before the Israelites. 4He offered sacrifices and burned incense at the high places, on the hilltops and under every spreading tree.

5Then Rezin king of Aram and Pekah son of Remaliah king of Israel marched up to fight against Jerusalem and besieged Ahaz, but they could not overpower him. 6At that time, Rezin king of Aram recovered Elath for Aram by driving out the people of Judah. Edomites then moved into Elath and have lived there to this day.

7Ahaz sent messengers to say to Tiglath-Pileser king of Assyria, "I am your servant and vassal. Come up and save me out of the hand of the king of Aram and of the king of Israel, who are attacking me." 8And Ahaz took the silver and gold found in the temple of the LORD and in the treasuries of the royal palace and sent it as a gift to the king of Assyria. 9The king of Assyria complied by attacking Damascus and capturing it. He deported its inhabitants to Kir and put Rezin to death.

10Then King Ahaz went to Damascus to meet Tiglath-Pileser king of Assyria. He saw an altar in Damascus and sent to Uriah the priest a sketch of the altar, with detailed plans for its construction. 11So Uriah the priest built an altar in accordance with all the plans that King Ahaz had sent from Damascus and finished it before King Ahaz returned. 12When the king came back from Damascus and saw the altar, he approached it and presented offerings[a] on it. 13He offered up his burnt offering and grain offering, poured out his drink offering, and splashed the blood of his fellowship offerings against the altar. 14As for the bronze altar that stood before the LORD, he brought it from the front of the temple—from between the new altar and the temple of the LORD—and put it on the north side of the new altar.

15King Ahaz then gave these orders to Uriah the priest: "On the large new altar, offer the morning burnt offering and the evening grain offering, the king's burnt offering and his grain offering, and the burnt offering of all the people of the land, and their grain offering and their drink offering. Splash against this altar the blood of all the burnt offerings and sacrifices. But I will use the bronze altar for seeking guidance." 16And Uriah the priest did just as King Ahaz had ordered.

17King Ahaz cut off the side panels and removed the basins from the movable stands. He removed the Sea from the bronze bulls that supported it and set it on a stone base. 18He took away the Sabbath canopy[b] that had been built at the temple and removed the royal entryway outside the temple of the LORD, in deference to the king of Assyria.

19As for the other events of the reign of Ahaz, and what he did, are they not written in the book of the annals of the kings of Judah? 20Ahaz rested with his ancestors and was buried with them in the City of David. And Hezekiah his son succeeded him as king.

[a] 12 Or *and went up* [b] 18 Or *the dais of his throne* (see Septuagint)

PRAYING SCRIPTURE

2 Kings 16

The kings of Israel and Judah had one thing in common: They all died. "[He] rested with his ancestors and was buried" punctuates many of the narratives of these kings (see, for example, verse 20). No king lived forever just as no wicked ruler from recent history lives forever. Their sin-stained kingdoms come to an end.

Have you prayed for your government leaders recently? Commit to praying for them to do God's will.

PRAYING
SCRIPTURE

2 Kings 17

God routinely told his people exactly how they had sinned. Before Israel went into exile in Assyria, the Lord laid out the case against them. They had refused to listen and had turned their hearts away from him.

It's easy to look at ancient Israel and say, "They should have obeyed God." But what about today? Ask God to turn the hearts of his people today back to him.

HOSHEA LAST KING OF ISRAEL

17 In the twelfth year of Ahaz king of Judah, Hoshea son of Elah
became king of Israel in Samaria, and he reigned nine years.
2He did evil in the eyes of the LORD, but not like the kings of Israel
who preceded him.
3Shalmaneser king of Assyria came up to attack Hoshea, who had
been Shalmaneser's vassal and had paid him tribute. 4But the king of
Assyria discovered that Hoshea was a traitor, for he had sent envoys
to So[a] king of Egypt, and he no longer paid tribute to the king of As-
syria, as he had done year by year. Therefore Shalmaneser seized him
and put him in prison. 5The king of Assyria invaded the entire land,
marched against Samaria and laid siege to it for three years. 6In the
ninth year of Hoshea, the king of Assyria captured Samaria and de-
ported the Israelites to Assyria. He settled them in Halah, in Gozan on
the Habor River and in the towns of the Medes.

ISRAEL EXILED BECAUSE OF SIN

7All this took place because the Israelites had sinned against the
LORD their God, who had brought them up out of Egypt from under
the power of Pharaoh king of Egypt. They worshiped other gods 8and
followed the practices of the nations the LORD had driven out before
them, as well as the practices that the kings of Israel had introduced.
9The Israelites secretly did things against the LORD their God that were
not right. From watchtower to fortified city they built themselves high
places in all their towns. 10They set up sacred stones and Asherah poles
on every high hill and under every spreading tree. 11At every high
place they burned incense, as the nations whom the LORD had driven
out before them had done. They did wicked things that aroused the
LORD's anger. 12They worshiped idols, though the LORD had said, "You
shall not do this."[b] 13The LORD warned Israel and Judah through all his
prophets and seers: "Turn from your evil ways. Observe my commands
and decrees, in accordance with the entire Law that I commanded your
ancestors to obey and that I delivered to you through my servants the
prophets."
14But they would not listen and were as stiff-necked as their an-
cestors, who did not trust in the LORD their God. 15They rejected his
decrees and the covenant he had made with their ancestors and the
statutes he had warned them to keep. They followed worthless idols
and themselves became worthless. They imitated the nations around
them although the LORD had ordered them, "Do not do as they do."
16They forsook all the commands of the LORD their God and made for
themselves two idols cast in the shape of calves, and an Asherah pole.
They bowed down to all the starry hosts, and they worshiped Baal.
17They sacrificed their sons and daughters in the fire. They practiced
divination and sought omens and sold themselves to do evil in the
eyes of the LORD, arousing his anger.
18So the LORD was very angry with Israel and removed them from
his presence. Only the tribe of Judah was left, 19and even Judah did not
keep the commands of the LORD their God. They followed the practices
Israel had introduced. 20Therefore the LORD rejected all the people of
Israel; he afflicted them and gave them into the hands of plunderers,
until he thrust them from his presence.

---

[a] 4 *So* is probably an abbreviation for *Osorkon*. [b] 12 Exodus 20:4,5

21When he tore Israel away from the house of David, they made Jer-
oboam son of Nebat their king. Jeroboam enticed Israel away from
following the LORD and caused them to commit a great sin. 22The Is-
raelites persisted in all the sins of Jeroboam and did not turn away
from them 23until the LORD removed them from his presence, as he
had warned through all his servants the prophets. So the people of
Israel were taken from their homeland into exile in Assyria, and they
are still there.

SAMARIA RESETTLED

24The king of Assyria brought people from Babylon, Kuthah, Avva,
Hamath and Sepharvaim and settled them in the towns of Samaria to
replace the Israelites. They took over Samaria and lived in its towns.
25When they first lived there, they did not worship the LORD; so he
sent lions among them and they killed some of the people. 26It was
reported to the king of Assyria: "The people you deported and reset-
tled in the towns of Samaria do not know what the god of that country
requires. He has sent lions among them, which are killing them off,
because the people do not know what he requires."

27Then the king of Assyria gave this order: "Have one of the priests
you took captive from Samaria go back to live there and teach the
people what the god of the land requires." 28So one of the priests who
had been exiled from Samaria came to live in Bethel and taught them
how to worship the LORD.

29Nevertheless, each national group made its own gods in the sev-
eral towns where they settled, and set them up in the shrines the
people of Samaria had made at the high places. 30The people from
Babylon made Sukkoth Benoth, those from Kuthah made Nergal, and
those from Hamath made Ashima; 31the Avvites made Nibhaz and Tar-
tak, and the Sepharvites burned their children in the fire as sacrifices
to Adrammelek and Anammelek, the gods of Sepharvaim. 32They wor-
shiped the LORD, but they also appointed all sorts of their own peo-
ple to officiate for them as priests in the shrines at the high places.
33They worshiped the LORD, but they also served their own gods in
accordance with the customs of the nations from which they had been
brought.

34To this day they persist in their former practices. They neither
worship the LORD nor adhere to the decrees and regulations, the laws
and commands that the LORD gave the descendants of Jacob, whom he
named Israel. 35When the LORD made a covenant with the Israelites,
he commanded them: "Do not worship any other gods or bow down
to them, serve them or sacrifice to them. 36But the LORD, who brought
you up out of Egypt with mighty power and outstretched arm, is the
one you must worship. To him you shall bow down and to him offer
sacrifices. 37You must always be careful to keep the decrees and reg-
ulations, the laws and commands he wrote for you. Do not worship
other gods. 38Do not forget the covenant I have made with you, and
do not worship other gods. 39Rather, worship the LORD your God; it is
he who will deliver you from the hand of all your enemies."

40They would not listen, however, but persisted in their former
practices. 41Even while these people were worshiping the LORD, they
were serving their idols. To this day their children and grandchildren
continue to do as their ancestors did.

PRAYING SCRIPTURE

2 Kings 18

Finally, after long years of ungodly leadership, Hezekiah took the throne in Judah. He destroyed the places of false worship and the idols—including one that had been around since the day of Moses. The bronze serpent, once a symbol of salvation, had become an object of veneration.

How easy it is for good things to come between us and God. Ask God for a heart like that of Hezekiah, who "held fast to the LORD" (verse 6).

HEZEKIAH KING OF JUDAH

18 In the third year of Hoshea son of Elah king of Israel, Hezekiah son of Ahaz king of Judah began to reign. [2]He was twenty-five years old when he became king, and he reigned in Jerusalem twenty-nine years. His mother's name was Abijah[a] daughter of Zechariah. [3]He did what was right in the eyes of the LORD, just as his father David had done. [4]He removed the high places, smashed the sacred stones and cut down the Asherah poles. He broke into pieces the bronze snake Moses had made, for up to that time the Israelites had been burning incense to it. (It was called Nehushtan.[b])

[5]Hezekiah trusted in the LORD, the God of Israel. There was no one like him among all the kings of Judah, either before him or after him. [6]He held fast to the LORD and did not stop following him; he kept the commands the LORD had given Moses. [7]And the LORD was with him; he was successful in whatever he undertook. He rebelled against the king of Assyria and did not serve him. [8]From watchtower to fortified city, he defeated the Philistines, as far as Gaza and its territory.

[9]In King Hezekiah's fourth year, which was the seventh year of Hoshea son of Elah king of Israel, Shalmaneser king of Assyria marched against Samaria and laid siege to it. [10]At the end of three years the Assyrians took it. So Samaria was captured in Hezekiah's sixth year, which was the ninth year of Hoshea king of Israel. [11]The king of Assyria deported Israel to Assyria and settled them in Halah, in Gozan on the Habor River and in towns of the Medes. [12]This happened because they had not obeyed the LORD their God, but had violated his covenant—all that Moses the servant of the LORD commanded. They neither listened to the commands nor carried them out.

[13]In the fourteenth year of King Hezekiah's reign, Sennacherib king of Assyria attacked all the fortified cities of Judah and captured them. [14]So Hezekiah king of Judah sent this message to the king of Assyria at Lachish: "I have done wrong. Withdraw from me, and I will pay whatever you demand of me." The king of Assyria exacted from Hezekiah king of Judah three hundred talents[c] of silver and thirty talents[d] of gold. [15]So Hezekiah gave him all the silver that was found in the temple of the LORD and in the treasuries of the royal palace.

[16]At this time Hezekiah king of Judah stripped off the gold with which he had covered the doors and doorposts of the temple of the LORD, and gave it to the king of Assyria.

SENNACHERIB THREATENS JERUSALEM

[17]The king of Assyria sent his supreme commander, his chief officer and his field commander with a large army, from Lachish to King Hezekiah at Jerusalem. They came up to Jerusalem and stopped at the aqueduct of the Upper Pool, on the road to the Washerman's Field. [18]They called for the king; and Eliakim son of Hilkiah the palace administrator, Shebna the secretary, and Joah son of Asaph the recorder went out to them.

[19]The field commander said to them, "Tell Hezekiah:

> "'This is what the great king, the king of Assyria, says: On what are you basing this confidence of yours? [20]You say you have the

---

[a] *2* Hebrew *Abi*, a variant of *Abijah* [b] *4* *Nehushtan* sounds like the Hebrew for both *bronze* and *snake*. [c] *14* That is, about 11 tons or about 10 metric tons [d] *14* That is, about 1 ton or about 1 metric ton

counsel and the might for war — but you speak only empty words.
On whom are you depending, that you rebel against me? 21Look, I
know you are depending on Egypt, that splintered reed of a staff,
which pierces the hand of anyone who leans on it! Such is Phar-
aoh king of Egypt to all who depend on him. 22But if you say to
me, "We are depending on the LORD our God" — isn't he the one
whose high places and altars Hezekiah removed, saying to Judah
and Jerusalem, "You must worship before this altar in Jerusalem"?
23" 'Come now, make a bargain with my master, the king of As-
syria: I will give you two thousand horses — if you can put riders
on them! 24How can you repulse one officer of the least of my mas-
ter's officials, even though you are depending on Egypt for char-
iots and horsemen[a]? 25Furthermore, have I come to attack and
destroy this place without word from the LORD? The LORD himself
told me to march against this country and destroy it.' "

26Then Eliakim son of Hilkiah, and Shebna and Joah said to the field
commander, "Please speak to your servants in Aramaic, since we un-
derstand it. Don't speak to us in Hebrew in the hearing of the people
on the wall."
27But the commander replied, "Was it only to your master and you
that my master sent me to say these things, and not to the people sit-
ting on the wall — who, like you, will have to eat their own excrement
and drink their own urine?"
28Then the commander stood and called out in Hebrew, "Hear the
word of the great king, the king of Assyria! 29This is what the king
says: Do not let Hezekiah deceive you. He cannot deliver you from my
hand. 30Do not let Hezekiah persuade you to trust in the LORD when
he says, 'The LORD will surely deliver us; this city will not be given into
the hand of the king of Assyria.'
31"Do not listen to Hezekiah. This is what the king of Assyria says:
Make peace with me and come out to me. Then each of you will eat
fruit from your own vine and fig tree and drink water from your own
cistern, 32until I come and take you to a land like your own — a land of
grain and new wine, a land of bread and vineyards, a land of olive trees
and honey. Choose life and not death!
"Do not listen to Hezekiah, for he is misleading you when he says,
'The LORD will deliver us.' 33Has the god of any nation ever delivered
his land from the hand of the king of Assyria? 34Where are the gods of
Hamath and Arpad? Where are the gods of Sepharvaim, Hena and Iv-
vah? Have they rescued Samaria from my hand? 35Who of all the gods
of these countries has been able to save his land from me? How then
can the LORD deliver Jerusalem from my hand?"
36But the people remained silent and said nothing in reply, because
the king had commanded, "Do not answer him."
37Then Eliakim son of Hilkiah the palace administrator, Shebna the
secretary, and Joah son of Asaph the recorder went to Hezekiah, with
their clothes torn, and told him what the field commander had said.

JERUSALEM'S DELIVERANCE FORETOLD

19 When King Hezekiah heard this, he tore his clothes and put on
sackcloth and went into the temple of the LORD. 2He sent Elia-
kim the palace administrator, Shebna the secretary and the leading

PRAYING SCRIPTURE

2 Kings 19

Faced with overwhelming odds against the Assyrians, who had already overcome Israel and now threatened Judah, Hezekiah prayed. Reminding God of his character and reputation, Hezekiah asked God to save them so the world would know he alone was God over all the earth.

It is not presumptuous to remind God of his character and his promises. He delights for us to approach him with his own words.

[a] 24 Or *charioteers*

priests, all wearing sackcloth, to the prophet Isaiah son of Amoz. 3They told him, "This is what Hezekiah says: This day is a day of distress and rebuke and disgrace, as when children come to the moment of birth and there is no strength to deliver them. 4It may be that the LORD your God will hear all the words of the field commander, whom his master, the king of Assyria, has sent to ridicule the living God, and that he will rebuke him for the words the LORD your God has heard. Therefore pray for the remnant that still survives."

5When King Hezekiah's officials came to Isaiah, 6Isaiah said to them, "Tell your master, 'This is what the LORD says: Do not be afraid of what you have heard — those words with which the underlings of the king of Assyria have blasphemed me. 7Listen! When he hears a certain report, I will make him want to return to his own country, and there I will have him cut down with the sword.' "

8When the field commander heard that the king of Assyria had left Lachish, he withdrew and found the king fighting against Libnah.

9Now Sennacherib received a report that Tirhakah, the king of Cush,[a] was marching out to fight against him. So he again sent messengers to Hezekiah with this word: 10"Say to Hezekiah king of Judah: Do not let the god you depend on deceive you when he says, 'Jerusalem will not be given into the hands of the king of Assyria.' 11Surely you have heard what the kings of Assyria have done to all the countries, destroying them completely. And will you be delivered? 12Did the gods of the nations that were destroyed by my predecessors deliver them — the gods of Gozan, Harran, Rezeph and the people of Eden who were in Tel Assar? 13Where is the king of Hamath or the king of Arpad? Where are the kings of Lair, Sepharvaim, Hena and Ivvah?"

HEZEKIAH'S PRAYER

14Hezekiah received the letter from the messengers and read it. Then he went up to the temple of the LORD and spread it out before the LORD. 15And Hezekiah prayed to the LORD: "LORD, the God of Israel, enthroned between the cherubim, you alone are God over all the kingdoms of the earth. You have made heaven and earth. 16Give ear, LORD, and hear; open your eyes, LORD, and see; listen to the words Sennacherib has sent to ridicule the living God.

17"It is true, LORD, that the Assyrian kings have laid waste these nations and their lands. 18They have thrown their gods into the fire and destroyed them, for they were not gods but only wood and stone, fashioned by human hands. 19Now, LORD our God, deliver us from his hand, so that all the kingdoms of the earth may know that you alone, LORD, are God."

ISAIAH PROPHESIES SENNACHERIB'S FALL

20Then Isaiah son of Amoz sent a message to Hezekiah: "This is what the LORD, the God of Israel, says: I have heard your prayer concerning Sennacherib king of Assyria. 21This is the word that the LORD has spoken against him:

" 'Virgin Daughter Zion
despises you and mocks you.
Daughter Jerusalem
tosses her head as you flee.

[a] 9 That is, the upper Nile region

22 Who is it you have ridiculed and blasphemed?
Against whom have you raised your voice
and lifted your eyes in pride?
Against the Holy One of Israel!
23 By your messengers
you have ridiculed the Lord.
And you have said,
"With my many chariots
I have ascended the heights of the mountains,
the utmost heights of Lebanon.
I have cut down its tallest cedars,
the choicest of its junipers.
I have reached its remotest parts,
the finest of its forests.
24 I have dug wells in foreign lands
and drunk the water there.
With the soles of my feet
I have dried up all the streams of Egypt."

25 " 'Have you not heard?
Long ago I ordained it.
In days of old I planned it;
now I have brought it to pass,
that you have turned fortified cities
into piles of stone.
26 Their people, drained of power,
are dismayed and put to shame.
They are like plants in the field,
like tender green shoots,
like grass sprouting on the roof,
scorched before it grows up.

27 " 'But I know where you are
and when you come and go
and how you rage against me.
28 Because you rage against me
and because your insolence has reached my ears,
I will put my hook in your nose
and my bit in your mouth,
and I will make you return
by the way you came.'

29 "This will be the sign for you, Hezekiah:

"This year you will eat what grows by itself,
and the second year what springs from that.
But in the third year sow and reap,
plant vineyards and eat their fruit.
30 Once more a remnant of the kingdom of Judah
will take root below and bear fruit above.
31 For out of Jerusalem will come a remnant,
and out of Mount Zion a band of survivors.

"The zeal of the LORD Almighty will accomplish this.

32 "Therefore this is what the LORD says concerning the king of
Assyria:

"'He will not enter this city
or shoot an arrow here.
He will not come before it with shield
or build a siege ramp against it.
33 By the way that he came he will return;
he will not enter this city,
declares the LORD.
34 I will defend this city and save it,
for my sake and for the sake of David my servant.'"

35 That night the angel of the LORD went out and put to death a hun-
dred and eighty-five thousand in the Assyrian camp. When the people
got up the next morning — there were all the dead bodies! 36 So Sen-
nacherib king of Assyria broke camp and withdrew. He returned to
Nineveh and stayed there.
37 One day, while he was worshiping in the temple of his god Nis-
rok, his sons Adrammelek and Sharezer killed him with the sword, and
they escaped to the land of Ararat. And Esarhaddon his son succeeded
him as king.

HEZEKIAH'S ILLNESS

20 In those days Hezekiah became ill and was at the point of
death. The prophet Isaiah son of Amoz went to him and said,
"This is what the LORD says: Put your house in order, because you are
going to die; you will not recover."
2 Hezekiah turned his face to the wall and prayed to the LORD, 3 "Re-
member, LORD, how I have walked before you faithfully and with
wholehearted devotion and have done what is good in your eyes." And
Hezekiah wept bitterly.
4 Before Isaiah had left the middle court, the word of the LORD came
to him: 5 "Go back and tell Hezekiah, the ruler of my people, 'This is
what the LORD, the God of your father David, says: I have heard your
prayer and seen your tears; I will heal you. On the third day from now
you will go up to the temple of the LORD. 6 I will add fifteen years to
your life. And I will deliver you and this city from the hand of the king
of Assyria. I will defend this city for my sake and for the sake of my
servant David.'"
7 Then Isaiah said, "Prepare a poultice of figs." They did so and ap-
plied it to the boil, and he recovered.
8 Hezekiah had asked Isaiah, "What will be the sign that the LORD will
heal me and that I will go up to the temple of the LORD on the third
day from now?"
9 Isaiah answered, "This is the LORD's sign to you that the LORD will
do what he has promised: Shall the shadow go forward ten steps, or
shall it go back ten steps?"
10 "It is a simple matter for the shadow to go forward ten steps," said
Hezekiah. "Rather, have it go back ten steps."
11 Then the prophet Isaiah called on the LORD, and the LORD made
the shadow go back the ten steps it had gone down on the stairway
of Ahaz.

ENVOYS FROM BABYLON

12 At that time Marduk-Baladan son of Baladan king of Babylon sent
Hezekiah letters and a gift, because he had heard of Hezekiah's illness.

PRAYING SCRIPTURE

2 Kings 20

Hezekiah, one of Judah's godly kings, was sick unto death. God even told him so, using words that endure to this day: "Put your house in order" (verse 1). In an arresting display of bold faith, Hezekiah reminded God of his faithful life and loyalty to him. God heard Hezekiah's prayer and healed him three days later.

How boldly do you pray? God is not offended when we ask big things in his name.

[13]Hezekiah received the envoys and showed them all that was in his
storehouses — the silver, the gold, the spices and the fine olive oil — his
armory and everything found among his treasures. There was nothing
in his palace or in all his kingdom that Hezekiah did not show them.
[14]Then Isaiah the prophet went to King Hezekiah and asked, "What
did those men say, and where did they come from?"
"From a distant land," Hezekiah replied. "They came from Babylon."
[15]The prophet asked, "What did they see in your palace?"
"They saw everything in my palace," Hezekiah said. "There is nothing among my treasures that I did not show them."
[16]Then Isaiah said to Hezekiah, "Hear the word of the LORD: [17]The
time will surely come when everything in your palace, and all that
your predecessors have stored up until this day, will be carried off to
Babylon. Nothing will be left, says the LORD. [18]And some of your de-
scendants, your own flesh and blood who will be born to you, will be
taken away, and they will become eunuchs in the palace of the king
of Babylon."
[19]"The word of the LORD you have spoken is good," Hezekiah replied.
For he thought, "Will there not be peace and security in my lifetime?"
[20]As for the other events of Hezekiah's reign, all his achievements
and how he made the pool and the tunnel by which he brought water
into the city, are they not written in the book of the annals of the kings
of Judah? [21]Hezekiah rested with his ancestors. And Manasseh his son
succeeded him as king.

MANASSEH KING OF JUDAH

21 Manasseh was twelve years old when he became king, and he
reigned in Jerusalem fifty-five years. His mother's name was
Hephzibah. [2]He did evil in the eyes of the LORD, following the detest-
able practices of the nations the LORD had driven out before the Israel-
ites. [3]He rebuilt the high places his father Hezekiah had destroyed; he
also erected altars to Baal and made an Asherah pole, as Ahab king of
Israel had done. He bowed down to all the starry hosts and worshiped
them. [4]He built altars in the temple of the LORD, of which the LORD
had said, "In Jerusalem I will put my Name." [5]In the two courts of the
temple of the LORD, he built altars to all the starry hosts. [6]He sacri-
ficed his own son in the fire, practiced divination, sought omens, and
consulted mediums and spiritists. He did much evil in the eyes of the
LORD, arousing his anger.
[7]He took the carved Asherah pole he had made and put it in the tem-
ple, of which the LORD had said to David and to his son Solomon, "In
this temple and in Jerusalem, which I have chosen out of all the tribes
of Israel, I will put my Name forever. [8]I will not again make the feet of
the Israelites wander from the land I gave their ancestors, if only they
will be careful to do everything I commanded them and will keep the
whole Law that my servant Moses gave them." [9]But the people did not
listen. Manasseh led them astray, so that they did more evil than the
nations the LORD had destroyed before the Israelites.
[10]The LORD said through his servants the prophets: [11]"Manasseh king
of Judah has committed these detestable sins. He has done more evil
than the Amorites who preceded him and has led Judah into sin with
his idols. [12]Therefore this is what the LORD, the God of Israel, says: I am
going to bring such disaster on Jerusalem and Judah that the ears of
everyone who hears of it will tingle. [13]I will stretch out over Jerusalem

PRAYING SCRIPTURE

2 Kings 21

True to his word, God brought calamity on Manasseh, son of Hezekiah, after the young king reestablished idol worship in Judah as much as wicked Ahab had. The people "did not listen" to God's word, becoming more evil than the nations God had already judged (see verse 9).

Sometimes Christians become guilt-ridden when their children don't follow God. Pray for your children, but know that ultimately, they are accountable to God for obedience.

the measuring line used against Samaria and the plumb line used
against the house of Ahab. I will wipe out Jerusalem as one wipes a
dish, wiping it and turning it upside down. 14I will forsake the remnant
of my inheritance and give them into the hands of enemies. They will
be looted and plundered by all their enemies; 15they have done evil in
my eyes and have aroused my anger from the day their ancestors came
out of Egypt until this day."

16Moreover, Manasseh also shed so much innocent blood that he
filled Jerusalem from end to end — besides the sin that he had caused
Judah to commit, so that they did evil in the eyes of the LORD.

17As for the other events of Manasseh's reign, and all he did, includ-
ing the sin he committed, are they not written in the book of the an-
nals of the kings of Judah? 18Manasseh rested with his ancestors and
was buried in his palace garden, the garden of Uzza. And Amon his son
succeeded him as king.

AMON KING OF JUDAH

19Amon was twenty-two years old when he became king, and he
reigned in Jerusalem two years. His mother's name was Meshullemeth
daughter of Haruz; she was from Jotbah. 20He did evil in the eyes of the
LORD, as his father Manasseh had done. 21He followed completely the
ways of his father, worshiping the idols his father had worshiped, and
bowing down to them. 22He forsook the LORD, the God of his ancestors,
and did not walk in obedience to him.

23Amon's officials conspired against him and assassinated the king
in his palace. 24Then the people of the land killed all who had plotted
against King Amon, and they made Josiah his son king in his place.

25As for the other events of Amon's reign, and what he did, are they
not written in the book of the annals of the kings of Judah? 26He was
buried in his tomb in the garden of Uzza. And Josiah his son succeeded
him as king.

THE BOOK OF THE LAW FOUND

22 Josiah was eight years old when he became king, and he
reigned in Jerusalem thirty-one years. His mother's name was
Jedidah daughter of Adaiah; she was from Bozkath. 2He did what was
right in the eyes of the LORD and followed completely the ways of his
father David, not turning aside to the right or to the left.

3In the eighteenth year of his reign, King Josiah sent the secretary,
Shaphan son of Azaliah, the son of Meshullam, to the temple of the
LORD. He said: 4"Go up to Hilkiah the high priest and have him get
ready the money that has been brought into the temple of the LORD,
which the doorkeepers have collected from the people. 5Have them
entrust it to the men appointed to supervise the work on the tem-
ple. And have these men pay the workers who repair the temple of
the LORD — 6the carpenters, the builders and the masons. Also have
them purchase timber and dressed stone to repair the temple. 7But
they need not account for the money entrusted to them, because they
are honest in their dealings."

8Hilkiah the high priest said to Shaphan the secretary, "I have found
the Book of the Law in the temple of the LORD." He gave it to Sha-
phan, who read it. 9Then Shaphan the secretary went to the king and
reported to him: "Your officials have paid out the money that was
in the temple of the LORD and have entrusted it to the workers and

PRAYING SCRIPTURE

2 Kings 22

Spiritual renewal always begins with God's Word. After Josiah became king, the discovery and reading of the Book of the Law led to an awakening. God's commands would be reinstituted with a renewed emphasis on the covenant. When you are feeling spiritually dry, where do you turn? A sure place to meet God is in his Word. Ask him to speak to you when you read it.

supervisors at the temple." 10Then Shaphan the secretary informed the
king, "Hilkiah the priest has given me a book." And Shaphan read from
it in the presence of the king.
11When the king heard the words of the Book of the Law, he tore
his robes. 12He gave these orders to Hilkiah the priest, Ahikam son of
Shaphan, Akbor son of Micaiah, Shaphan the secretary and Asaiah the
king's attendant: 13"Go and inquire of the LORD for me and for the peo-
ple and for all Judah about what is written in this book that has been
found. Great is the LORD's anger that burns against us because those
who have gone before us have not obeyed the words of this book; they
have not acted in accordance with all that is written there concern-
ing us."
14Hilkiah the priest, Ahikam, Akbor, Shaphan and Asaiah went to
speak to the prophet Huldah, who was the wife of Shallum son of Tik-
vah, the son of Harhas, keeper of the wardrobe. She lived in Jerusalem,
in the New Quarter.
15She said to them, "This is what the LORD, the God of Israel, says: Tell
the man who sent you to me, 16'This is what the LORD says: I am going
to bring disaster on this place and its people, according to everything
written in the book the king of Judah has read. 17Because they have
forsaken me and burned incense to other gods and aroused my anger
by all the idols their hands have made,[a] my anger will burn against this
place and will not be quenched.' 18Tell the king of Judah, who sent you
to inquire of the LORD, 'This is what the LORD, the God of Israel, says
concerning the words you heard: 19Because your heart was responsive
and you humbled yourself before the LORD when you heard what I
have spoken against this place and its people — that they would be-
come a curse[b] and be laid waste — and because you tore your robes
and wept in my presence, I also have heard you, declares the LORD.
20Therefore I will gather you to your ancestors, and you will be buried
in peace. Your eyes will not see all the disaster I am going to bring on
this place.'"
So they took her answer back to the king.

JOSIAH RENEWS THE COVENANT

23 Then the king called together all the elders of Judah and Jeru-
salem. 2He went up to the temple of the LORD with the people
of Judah, the inhabitants of Jerusalem, the priests and the prophets —
all the people from the least to the greatest. He read in their hearing
all the words of the Book of the Covenant, which had been found in
the temple of the LORD. 3The king stood by the pillar and renewed the
covenant in the presence of the LORD — to follow the LORD and keep
his commands, statutes and decrees with all his heart and all his soul,
thus confirming the words of the covenant written in this book. Then
all the people pledged themselves to the covenant.
4The king ordered Hilkiah the high priest, the priests next in rank
and the doorkeepers to remove from the temple of the LORD all the
articles made for Baal and Asherah and all the starry hosts. He burned
them outside Jerusalem in the fields of the Kidron Valley and took the
ashes to Bethel. 5He did away with the idolatrous priests appointed by
the kings of Judah to burn incense on the high places of the towns of

[a] 17 Or *by everything they have done* [b] 19 That is, their names would be used in cursing (see Jer. 29:22); or, others would see that they are cursed.

PRAYING SCRIPTURE

2 Kings 23

Josiah's reforms were substantial. Resolving to live for the Lord, he knew that he had to love the Lord and follow him with his whole heart. Notably, Josiah reinstituted the Passover, the annual remembrance that had long been abandoned in Israel and Judah.

Is there anything in your spiritual life that you once did but have let fall aside? Personal renewal or revival comes when we repent and restore the things of God.

Judah and on those around Jerusalem — those who burned incense to
Baal, to the sun and moon, to the constellations and to all the starry
hosts. 6He took the Asherah pole from the temple of the LORD to the
Kidron Valley outside Jerusalem and burned it there. He ground it to
powder and scattered the dust over the graves of the common people.
7He also tore down the quarters of the male shrine prostitutes that
were in the temple of the LORD, the quarters where women did weav-
ing for Asherah.

8Josiah brought all the priests from the towns of Judah and dese-
crated the high places, from Geba to Beersheba, where the priests had
burned incense. He broke down the gateway at the entrance of the
Gate of Joshua, the city governor, which was on the left of the city gate.
9Although the priests of the high places did not serve at the altar of the
LORD in Jerusalem, they ate unleavened bread with their fellow priests.

10He desecrated Topheth, which was in the Valley of Ben Hinnom,
so no one could use it to sacrifice their son or daughter in the fire to
Molek. 11He removed from the entrance to the temple of the LORD the
horses that the kings of Judah had dedicated to the sun. They were in
the court[a] near the room of an official named Nathan-Melek. Josiah
then burned the chariots dedicated to the sun.

12He pulled down the altars the kings of Judah had erected on the
roof near the upper room of Ahaz, and the altars Manasseh had built
in the two courts of the temple of the LORD. He removed them from
there, smashed them to pieces and threw the rubble into the Kidron
Valley. 13The king also desecrated the high places that were east of Je-
rusalem on the south of the Hill of Corruption — the ones Solomon
king of Israel had built for Ashtoreth the vile goddess of the Sidoni-
ans, for Chemosh the vile god of Moab, and for Molek the detestable
god of the people of Ammon. 14Josiah smashed the sacred stones and
cut down the Asherah poles and covered the sites with human bones.

15Even the altar at Bethel, the high place made by Jeroboam son of
Nebat, who had caused Israel to sin — even that altar and high place
he demolished. He burned the high place and ground it to powder, and
burned the Asherah pole also. 16Then Josiah looked around, and when
he saw the tombs that were there on the hillside, he had the bones re-
moved from them and burned on the altar to defile it, in accordance
with the word of the LORD proclaimed by the man of God who foretold
these things.

17The king asked, "What is that tombstone I see?"

The people of the city said, "It marks the tomb of the man of God
who came from Judah and pronounced against the altar of Bethel the
very things you have done to it."

18"Leave it alone," he said. "Don't let anyone disturb his bones." So
they spared his bones and those of the prophet who had come from
Samaria.

19Just as he had done at Bethel, Josiah removed all the shrines at the
high places that the kings of Israel had built in the towns of Samaria
and that had aroused the LORD's anger. 20Josiah slaughtered all the
priests of those high places on the altars and burned human bones on
them. Then he went back to Jerusalem.

21The king gave this order to all the people: "Celebrate the Passover
to the LORD your God, as it is written in this Book of the Covenant."

[a] *11* The meaning of the Hebrew for this word is uncertain.

22Neither in the days of the judges who led Israel nor in the days of the
kings of Israel and the kings of Judah had any such Passover been ob-
served. 23But in the eighteenth year of King Josiah, this Passover was
celebrated to the LORD in Jerusalem.
24Furthermore, Josiah got rid of the mediums and spiritists, the
household gods, the idols and all the other detestable things seen in
Judah and Jerusalem. This he did to fulfill the requirements of the
law written in the book that Hilkiah the priest had discovered in the
temple of the LORD. 25Neither before nor after Josiah was there a king
like him who turned to the LORD as he did — with all his heart and
with all his soul and with all his strength, in accordance with all the
Law of Moses.
26Nevertheless, the LORD did not turn away from the heat of his
fierce anger, which burned against Judah because of all that Manasseh
had done to arouse his anger. 27So the LORD said, "I will remove Judah
also from my presence as I removed Israel, and I will reject Jerusalem,
the city I chose, and this temple, about which I said, 'My Name shall
be there.'[a]"
28As for the other events of Josiah's reign, and all he did, are they not
written in the book of the annals of the kings of Judah?
29While Josiah was king, Pharaoh Necho king of Egypt went up to
the Euphrates River to help the king of Assyria. King Josiah marched
out to meet him in battle, but Necho faced him and killed him at Me-
giddo. 30Josiah's servants brought his body in a chariot from Megiddo
to Jerusalem and buried him in his own tomb. And the people of the
land took Jehoahaz son of Josiah and anointed him and made him
king in place of his father.

JEHOAHAZ KING OF JUDAH

31Jehoahaz was twenty-three years old when he became king, and he
reigned in Jerusalem three months. His mother's name was Hamutal
daughter of Jeremiah; she was from Libnah. 32He did evil in the eyes of
the LORD, just as his predecessors had done. 33Pharaoh Necho put him
in chains at Riblah in the land of Hamath so that he might not reign
in Jerusalem, and he imposed on Judah a levy of a hundred talents[b]
of silver and a talent[c] of gold. 34Pharaoh Necho made Eliakim son of
Josiah king in place of his father Josiah and changed Eliakim's name
to Jehoiakim. But he took Jehoahaz and carried him off to Egypt, and
there he died. 35Jehoiakim paid Pharaoh Necho the silver and gold he
demanded. In order to do so, he taxed the land and exacted the silver
and gold from the people of the land according to their assessments.

JEHOIAKIM KING OF JUDAH

36Jehoiakim was twenty-five years old when he became king, and
he reigned in Jerusalem eleven years. His mother's name was Zebidah
daughter of Pedaiah; she was from Rumah. 37And he did evil in the
eyes of the LORD, just as his predecessors had done.

24 During Jehoiakim's reign, Nebuchadnezzar king of Babylon
invaded the land, and Jehoiakim became his vassal for three
years. But then he turned against Nebuchadnezzar and rebelled. 2The
LORD sent Babylonian,[d] Aramean, Moabite and Ammonite raiders

[a] 27 1 Kings 8:29 [b] 33 That is, about 3 3/4 tons or about 3.4 metric tons
[c] 33 That is, about 75 pounds or about 34 kilograms [d] 2 Or *Chaldean*

PRAYING SCRIPTURE

2 Kings 24

The Lord is patient and slow to anger, but his anger will not be held back forever. Babylon carried away more than ten thousand captives from Jerusalem alone. Even this was not enough to bring repentance, as the vassal king Zedekiah also rebelled against God.

Delayed judgment does not mean that God has forgotten about sin. Intercede for those in authority to live lives that are pleasing to God.

against him to destroy Judah, in accordance with the word of the LORD
proclaimed by his servants the prophets. 3Surely these things hap-
pened to Judah according to the LORD's command, in order to remove
them from his presence because of the sins of Manasseh and all he had
done, 4including the shedding of innocent blood. For he had filled Je-
rusalem with innocent blood, and the LORD was not willing to forgive.
5As for the other events of Jehoiakim's reign, and all he did, are they
not written in the book of the annals of the kings of Judah? 6Jehoia-
kim rested with his ancestors. And Jehoiachin his son succeeded him
as king.
7The king of Egypt did not march out from his own country again,
because the king of Babylon had taken all his territory, from the Wadi
of Egypt to the Euphrates River.

JEHOIACHIN KING OF JUDAH

8Jehoiachin was eighteen years old when he became king, and he
reigned in Jerusalem three months. His mother's name was Nehushta
daughter of Elnathan; she was from Jerusalem. 9He did evil in the eyes
of the LORD, just as his father had done.
10At that time the officers of Nebuchadnezzar king of Babylon ad-
vanced on Jerusalem and laid siege to it, 11and Nebuchadnezzar
himself came up to the city while his officers were besieging it. 12Je-
hoiachin king of Judah, his mother, his attendants, his nobles and his
officials all surrendered to him.
In the eighth year of the reign of the king of Babylon, he took Jehoi-
achin prisoner. 13As the LORD had declared, Nebuchadnezzar removed
the treasures from the temple of the LORD and from the royal palace,
and cut up the gold articles that Solomon king of Israel had made for
the temple of the LORD. 14He carried all Jerusalem into exile: all the
officers and fighting men, and all the skilled workers and artisans — a
total of ten thousand. Only the poorest people of the land were left.
15Nebuchadnezzar took Jehoiachin captive to Babylon. He also
took from Jerusalem to Babylon the king's mother, his wives, his of-
ficials and the prominent people of the land. 16The king of Babylon
also deported to Babylon the entire force of seven thousand fighting
men, strong and fit for war, and a thousand skilled workers and arti-
sans. 17He made Mattaniah, Jehoiachin's uncle, king in his place and
changed his name to Zedekiah.

ZEDEKIAH KING OF JUDAH

18Zedekiah was twenty-one years old when he became king, and he
reigned in Jerusalem eleven years. His mother's name was Hamutal
daughter of Jeremiah; she was from Libnah. 19He did evil in the eyes
of the LORD, just as Jehoiakim had done. 20It was because of the LORD's
anger that all this happened to Jerusalem and Judah, and in the end he
thrust them from his presence.

THE FALL OF JERUSALEM

Now Zedekiah rebelled against the king of Babylon.
25 So in the ninth year of Zedekiah's reign, on the tenth day of
the tenth month, Nebuchadnezzar king of Babylon marched
against Jerusalem with his whole army. He encamped outside the city
and built siege works all around it. 2The city was kept under siege until
the eleventh year of King Zedekiah.

PRAYING SCRIPTURE

2 Kings 25

After the initial deportation of the Jewish leaders to Babylon, Nebuchadnezzar returned to loot the city and take Judah. With Samaria already fallen, this was the lowest point in Israel's history. The temple was stripped of its valuables, and some of the poor were left to tend vineyards.

What is your response when everything seems hopeless? Thank God that he has promised never to forsake you, his child.

3By the ninth day of the fourth[a] month the famine in the city had
become so severe that there was no food for the people to eat. 4Then
the city wall was broken through, and the whole army fled at night
through the gate between the two walls near the king's garden, though
the Babylonians[b] were surrounding the city. They fled toward the Ar-
abah,[c] 5but the Babylonian[d] army pursued the king and overtook him
in the plains of Jericho. All his soldiers were separated from him and
scattered, 6and he was captured.

He was taken to the king of Babylon at Riblah, where sentence was
pronounced on him. 7They killed the sons of Zedekiah before his eyes.
Then they put out his eyes, bound him with bronze shackles and took
him to Babylon.

8On the seventh day of the fifth month, in the nineteenth year of
Nebuchadnezzar king of Babylon, Nebuzaradan commander of the im-
perial guard, an official of the king of Babylon, came to Jerusalem. 9He
set fire to the temple of the LORD, the royal palace and all the houses
of Jerusalem. Every important building he burned down. 10The whole
Babylonian army under the commander of the imperial guard broke
down the walls around Jerusalem. 11Nebuzaradan the commander of
the guard carried into exile the people who remained in the city, along
with the rest of the populace and those who had deserted to the king of
Babylon. 12But the commander left behind some of the poorest people
of the land to work the vineyards and fields.

13The Babylonians broke up the bronze pillars, the movable stands
and the bronze Sea that were at the temple of the LORD and they car-
ried the bronze to Babylon. 14They also took away the pots, shovels,
wick trimmers, dishes and all the bronze articles used in the temple
service. 15The commander of the imperial guard took away the censers
and sprinkling bowls — all that were made of pure gold or silver.

16The bronze from the two pillars, the Sea and the movable stands,
which Solomon had made for the temple of the LORD, was more than
could be weighed. 17Each pillar was eighteen cubits[e] high. The bronze
capital on top of one pillar was three cubits[f] high and was decorated
with a network and pomegranates of bronze all around. The other pil-
lar, with its network, was similar.

18The commander of the guard took as prisoners Seraiah the chief
priest, Zephaniah the priest next in rank and the three doorkeepers.
19Of those still in the city, he took the officer in charge of the fighting
men, and five royal advisers. He also took the secretary who was chief
officer in charge of conscripting the people of the land and sixty of the
conscripts who were found in the city. 20Nebuzaradan the commander
took them all and brought them to the king of Babylon at Riblah.
21There at Riblah, in the land of Hamath, the king had them executed.

So Judah went into captivity, away from her land.

22Nebuchadnezzar king of Babylon appointed Gedaliah son of Ahi-
kam, the son of Shaphan, to be over the people he had left behind in
Judah. 23When all the army officers and their men heard that the king
of Babylon had appointed Gedaliah as governor, they came to Gedaliah

---

[a] *3* Probable reading of the original Hebrew text (see Jer. 52:6); Masoretic Text does not have *fourth.* [b] *4* Or *Chaldeans*; also in verses 13, 25 and 26
[c] *4* Or *the Jordan Valley* [d] *5* Or *Chaldean*; also in verses 10 and 24
[e] *17* That is, about 27 feet or about 8.1 meters [f] *17* That is, about 4 1/2 feet or about 1.4 meters

at Mizpah — Ishmael son of Nethaniah, Johanan son of Kareah, Seraiah
son of Tanhumeth the Netophathite, Jaazaniah the son of the Maak-
athite, and their men. 24 Gedaliah took an oath to reassure them and
their men. "Do not be afraid of the Babylonian officials," he said. "Set-
tle down in the land and serve the king of Babylon, and it will go well
with you."

25 In the seventh month, however, Ishmael son of Nethaniah, the son
of Elishama, who was of royal blood, came with ten men and assassi-
nated Gedaliah and also the men of Judah and the Babylonians who
were with him at Mizpah. 26 At this, all the people from the least to the
greatest, together with the army officers, fled to Egypt for fear of the
Babylonians.

JEHOIACHIN RELEASED

27 In the thirty-seventh year of the exile of Jehoiachin king of Judah,
in the year Awel-Marduk became king of Babylon, he released Jehoia-
chin king of Judah from prison. He did this on the twenty-seventh day
of the twelfth month. 28 He spoke kindly to him and gave him a seat
of honor higher than those of the other kings who were with him in
Babylon. 29 So Jehoiachin put aside his prison clothes and for the rest
of his life ate regularly at the king's table. 30 Day by day the king gave
Jehoiachin a regular allowance as long as he lived.

1 CHRONICLES

Just as the four Gospels tell the story of Jesus from four different vantage points and with four different emphases, so the books of 1 and 2 Chronicles tell the story of the kings of Israel from a different angle than the author of Samuel and Kings. "The Chronicler," as he is often called, includes narratives and details that cannot be found in the books of Samuel and Kings.

There is also somewhat of a distinction in that Israel's political history is covered in 2 Samuel, as well as in 1 and 2 Kings, but Israel's religious history is the focus of the Chronicles. Originally one book, the title roughly means "The Events of the Times."

Details in the Chronicler's story have led Biblical scholars to believe he wrote after the return from exile in Babylon, so he told the story of Israel from Adam to the return. While his genealogies stretch back to the beginning, the bulk of his narrative storytelling focuses on the kings of Israel, starting with Saul and David.

The first nine chapters of 1 Chronicles contain a genealogy of the people of Israel that begins with Adam. His goal was not merely to recite names but to connect the story of Israel from the beginning up to the time in which he was writing. He wanted to remind the generation returning from exile that they were part of a story that had been in process for thousands of years. They were the descendants of those who received the promises of God, and those promises had been passed down to them as well.

The final 20 chapters of 1 Chronicles focus on the life and reign of David. The author concentrated on two major themes in the work—the king and the temple. His telling of the life of David focuses on him as the prototypical king by which all the other kings should be measured. Even though David sinned and his leadership was flawed in many ways, he was the man after God's own heart, and God promised that someone from his line would sit on the throne forever. First Chronicles closes with David's death and Solomon's anointing as king of Israel.

The book includes several of David's prayers, one of which is poignantly instructive. After God refused David the privilege of building a temple, David sat down in God's presence and offered a lengthy prayer of praise and thanksgiving. At a moment when bitterness was a legitimate temptation, David found joy in the truth that God would have a temple, even if he didn't get to build it. Rather than being hurt, David thanked God for choosing a servant to build the temple and adding that he would bless that servant.

We also see David's life of repentance in prayer form, most well-known in Psalm 51. After the census debacle, David admitted doing "a very foolish thing" (21:8). David showed that being willing to prayerfully repent is aligned with God's declaration that David was "a man after my own heart" (Acts 13:22).

PRAYING SCRIPTURE

1 Chronicles 1

This genealogy traces back to Adam where God's story of redemption starts with the Bible's opening chapters. Biblical genealogies are a means to track God's activity over time in the human family. They are also a reminder that God is intimately concerned with the human family. He is not distant and detached. He is aware. Thank God for his deep love that ultimately provided his Son as a sacrifice for everyone's sins.

HISTORICAL RECORDS FROM ADAM TO ABRAHAM

TO NOAH'S SONS

1 Adam, Seth, Enosh, 2 Kenan, Mahalalel, Jared, 3 Enoch, Methuselah,
Lamech, Noah.

4 The sons of Noah:[a]
Shem, Ham and Japheth.

THE JAPHETHITES

5 The sons[b] of Japheth:
Gomer, Magog, Madai, Javan, Tubal, Meshek and Tiras.
6 The sons of Gomer:
Ashkenaz, Riphath[c] and Togarmah.
7 The sons of Javan:
Elishah, Tarshish, the Kittites and the Rodanites.

THE HAMITES

8 The sons of Ham:
Cush, Egypt, Put and Canaan.
9 The sons of Cush:
Seba, Havilah, Sabta, Raamah and Sabteka.
The sons of Raamah:
Sheba and Dedan.
10 Cush was the father[d] of
Nimrod, who became a mighty warrior on earth.
11 Egypt was the father of
the Ludites, Anamites, Lehabites, Naphtuhites, 12 Pathrusites,
Kasluhites (from whom the Philistines came) and Caphtorites.
13 Canaan was the father of
Sidon his firstborn,[e] and of the Hittites, 14 Jebusites, Amorites,
Girgashites, 15 Hivites, Arkites, Sinites, 16 Arvadites, Zemarites
and Hamathites.

THE SEMITES

17 The sons of Shem:
Elam, Ashur, Arphaxad, Lud and Aram.
The sons of Aram:[f]
Uz, Hul, Gether and Meshek.
18 Arphaxad was the father of Shelah,
and Shelah the father of Eber.
19 Two sons were born to Eber:
One was named Peleg,[g] because in his time the earth was divided; his brother was named Joktan.
20 Joktan was the father of
Almodad, Sheleph, Hazarmaveth, Jerah, 21 Hadoram, Uzal, Dik-
lah, 22 Obal,[h] Abimael, Sheba, 23 Ophir, Havilah and Jobab. All
these were sons of Joktan.

---

[a] 4 Septuagint; Hebrew does not have this line. [b] 5 *Sons* may mean *descendants* or *successors* or *nations*; also in verses 6-9, 17 and 23. [c] 6 Many Hebrew manuscripts and Vulgate (see also Septuagint and Gen. 10:3); most Hebrew manuscripts *Diphath* [d] 10 *Father* may mean *ancestor* or *predecessor* or *founder*; also in verses 11, 13, 18 and 20. [e] 13 Or *of the Sidonians, the foremost* [f] 17 One Hebrew manuscript and some Septuagint manuscripts (see also Gen. 10:23); most Hebrew manuscripts do not have this line. [g] 19 *Peleg* means *division.* [h] 22 Some Hebrew manuscripts and Syriac (see also Gen. 10:28); most Hebrew manuscripts *Ebal*

[24] Shem, Arphaxad,[a] Shelah,
[25] Eber, Peleg, Reu,
[26] Serug, Nahor, Terah
[27] and Abram (that is, Abraham).

THE FAMILY OF ABRAHAM

[28] The sons of Abraham:
Isaac and Ishmael.

DESCENDANTS OF HAGAR

[29] These were their descendants:
Nebaioth the firstborn of Ishmael, Kedar, Adbeel, Mibsam,
[30] Mishma, Dumah, Massa, Hadad, Tema, [31] Jetur, Naphish and
Kedemah. These were the sons of Ishmael.

DESCENDANTS OF KETURAH

[32] The sons born to Keturah, Abraham's concubine:
Zimran, Jokshan, Medan, Midian, Ishbak and Shuah.
The sons of Jokshan:
Sheba and Dedan.
[33] The sons of Midian:
Ephah, Epher, Hanok, Abida and Eldaah.
All these were descendants of Keturah.

DESCENDANTS OF SARAH

[34] Abraham was the father of Isaac.
The sons of Isaac:
Esau and Israel.

ESAU'S SONS

[35] The sons of Esau:
Eliphaz, Reuel, Jeush, Jalam and Korah.
[36] The sons of Eliphaz:
Teman, Omar, Zepho,[b] Gatam and Kenaz;
by Timna: Amalek.[c]
[37] The sons of Reuel:
Nahath, Zerah, Shammah and Mizzah.

THE PEOPLE OF SEIR IN EDOM

[38] The sons of Seir:
Lotan, Shobal, Zibeon, Anah, Dishon, Ezer and Dishan
[39] The sons of Lotan:
Hori and Homam. Timna was Lotan's sister.
[40] The sons of Shobal:
Alvan,[d] Manahath, Ebal, Shepho and Onam.
The sons of Zibeon:
Aiah and Anah.
[41] The son of Anah:
Dishon.

---

[a] *24* Hebrew; some Septuagint manuscripts *Arphaxad, Cainan* (see also note at Gen. 11:10) [b] *36* Many Hebrew manuscripts, some Septuagint manuscripts and Syriac (see also Gen. 36:11); most Hebrew manuscripts *Zephi* [c] *36* Some Septuagint manuscripts (see also Gen. 36:12); Hebrew *Gatam, Kenaz, Timna and Amalek* [d] *40* Many Hebrew manuscripts and some Septuagint manuscripts (see also Gen. 36:23); most Hebrew manuscripts *Alian*

The sons of Dishon:
Hemdan,[a] Eshban, Ithran and Keran.
42 The sons of Ezer:
Bilhan, Zaavan and Akan.[b]
The sons of Dishan[c]:
Uz and Aran.

THE RULERS OF EDOM

43 These were the kings who reigned in Edom before any Israelite king reigned:
Bela son of Beor, whose city was named Dinhabah.
44 When Bela died, Jobab son of Zerah from Bozrah succeeded him as king.
45 When Jobab died, Husham from the land of the Temanites succeeded him as king.
46 When Husham died, Hadad son of Bedad, who defeated Midian in the country of Moab, succeeded him as king. His city was named Avith.
47 When Hadad died, Samlah from Masrekah succeeded him as king.
48 When Samlah died, Shaul from Rehoboth on the river[d] succeeded him as king.
49 When Shaul died, Baal-Hanan son of Akbor succeeded him as king.
50 When Baal-Hanan died, Hadad succeeded him as king. His city was named Pau,[e] and his wife's name was Mehetabel daughter of Matred, the daughter of Me-Zahab. 51 Hadad also died.

The chiefs of Edom were:
Timna, Alvah, Jetheth, 52 Oholibamah, Elah, Pinon, 53 Kenaz, Teman, Mibzar, 54 Magdiel and Iram. These were the chiefs of Edom.

ISRAEL'S SONS

2 These were the sons of Israel:
Reuben, Simeon, Levi, Judah, Issachar, Zebulun, 2 Dan, Joseph, Benjamin, Naphtali, Gad and Asher.

JUDAH

TO HEZRON'S SONS

3 The sons of Judah:
Er, Onan and Shelah. These three were born to him by a Canaanite woman, the daughter of Shua. Er, Judah's firstborn, was wicked in the LORD's sight; so the LORD put him to death.
4 Judah's daughter-in-law Tamar bore Perez and Zerah to Judah. He had five sons in all.

5 The sons of Perez:
Hezron and Hamul.
6 The sons of Zerah:
Zimri, Ethan, Heman, Kalkol and Darda[f] — five in all.

PRAYING SCRIPTURE

1 Chronicles 2

This genealogy sets the sons of Israel in their place in all of Israel's history. Highlighting the line from Judah to David isolates the family through whom Messiah would come while showing the Lord's overwhelming grace in welcoming the outcast and redeeming humans' sinful pasts.

Sometimes we are tempted to dwell on our pasts to the point we cannot trust God in the present. God can help you live for today every day.

---

[a] *41* Many Hebrew manuscripts and some Septuagint manuscripts (see also Gen. 36:26); most Hebrew manuscripts *Hamran* [b] *42* Many Hebrew and Septuagint manuscripts (see also Gen. 36:27); most Hebrew manuscripts *Zaavan, Jaakan* [c] *42* See Gen. 36:28; Hebrew *Dishon*, a variant of *Dishan* [d] *48* Possibly the Euphrates [e] *50* Many Hebrew manuscripts, some Septuagint manuscripts, Vulgate and Syriac (see also Gen. 36:39); most Hebrew manuscripts *Pai* [f] *6* Many Hebrew manuscripts, some Septuagint manuscripts and Syriac (see also 1 Kings 4:31); most Hebrew manuscripts *Dara*

7 The son of Karmi:
Achar,[a] who brought trouble on Israel by violating the ban on taking devoted things.[b]
8 The son of Ethan:
Azariah.
9 The sons born to Hezron were:
Jerahmeel, Ram and Caleb.[c]

FROM RAM SON OF HEZRON

10 Ram was the father of
Amminadab, and Amminadab the father of Nahshon, the leader
of the people of Judah. 11 Nahshon was the father of Salmon,[d]
Salmon the father of Boaz, 12 Boaz the father of Obed and Obed
the father of Jesse.
13 Jesse was the father of
Eliab his firstborn; the second son was Abinadab, the third
Shimea, 14 the fourth Nethanel, the fifth Raddai, 15 the sixth
Ozem and the seventh David. 16 Their sisters were Zeruiah and
Abigail. Zeruiah's three sons were Abishai, Joab and Asahel.
17 Abigail was the mother of Amasa, whose father was Jether the
Ishmaelite.

CALEB SON OF HEZRON

18 Caleb son of Hezron had children by his wife Azubah (and by Jer-
ioth). These were her sons: Jesher, Shobab and Ardon. 19 When
Azubah died, Caleb married Ephrath, who bore him Hur. 20 Hur
was the father of Uri, and Uri the father of Bezalel.
21 Later, Hezron, when he was sixty years old, married the daugh-
ter of Makir the father of Gilead. He made love to her, and she
bore him Segub. 22 Segub was the father of Jair, who controlled
twenty-three towns in Gilead. 23 (But Geshur and Aram captured
Havvoth Jair,[e] as well as Kenath with its surrounding settle-
ments — sixty towns.) All these were descendants of Makir the
father of Gilead.
24 After Hezron died in Caleb Ephrathah, Abijah the wife of Hezron
bore him Ashhur the father[f] of Tekoa.

JERAHMEEL SON OF HEZRON

25 The sons of Jerahmeel the firstborn of Hezron:
Ram his firstborn, Bunah, Oren, Ozem and[g] Ahijah. 26 Jerahmeel
had another wife, whose name was Atarah; she was the mother
of Onam.
27 The sons of Ram the firstborn of Jerahmeel:
Maaz, Jamin and Eker.
28 The sons of Onam:
Shammai and Jada.
The sons of Shammai:
Nadab and Abishur.
29 Abishur's wife was named Abihail, who bore him Ahban and Molid.

---

[a] 7 *Achar* means *trouble*; *Achar* is called *Achan* in Joshua. [b] 7 The Hebrew term refers to the irrevocable giving over of things or persons to the LORD, often by totally destroying them. [c] 9 Hebrew *Kelubai*, a variant of *Caleb* [d] 11 Septuagint (see also Ruth 4:21); Hebrew *Salma* [e] 23 Or *captured the settlements of Jair* [f] 24 *Father* may mean *civic leader* or *military leader*; also in verses 42, 45, 49-52 and possibly elsewhere. [g] 25 Or *Oren and Ozem, by*

30 The sons of Nadab:
Seled and Appaim. Seled died without children.
31 The son of Appaim:
Ishi, who was the father of Sheshan.
Sheshan was the father of Ahlai.
32 The sons of Jada, Shammai's brother:
Jether and Jonathan. Jether died without children.
33 The sons of Jonathan:
Peleth and Zaza.
These were the descendants of Jerahmeel.
34 Sheshan had no sons — only daughters.
He had an Egyptian servant named Jarha. 35 Sheshan gave his
daughter in marriage to his servant Jarha, and she bore him
Attai.
36 Attai was the father of Nathan,
Nathan the father of Zabad,
37 Zabad the father of Ephlal,
Ephlal the father of Obed,
38 Obed the father of Jehu,
Jehu the father of Azariah,
39 Azariah the father of Helez,
Helez the father of Eleasah,
40 Eleasah the father of Sismai,
Sismai the father of Shallum,
41 Shallum the father of Jekamiah,
and Jekamiah the father of Elishama.

THE CLANS OF CALEB

42 The sons of Caleb the brother of Jerahmeel:
Mesha his firstborn, who was the father of Ziph, and his son Ma-
reshah,[a] who was the father of Hebron.
43 The sons of Hebron:
Korah, Tappuah, Rekem and Shema. 44 Shema was the father of
Raham, and Raham the father of Jorkeam. Rekem was the fa-
ther of Shammai. 45 The son of Shammai was Maon, and Maon
was the father of Beth Zur.
46 Caleb's concubine Ephah was the mother of Haran, Moza and Ga-
zez. Haran was the father of Gazez.
47 The sons of Jahdai:
Regem, Jotham, Geshan, Pelet, Ephah and Shaaph.
48 Caleb's concubine Maakah was the mother of Sheber and Tirhanah.
49 She also gave birth to Shaaph the father of Madmannah and to
Sheva the father of Makbenah and Gibea. Caleb's daughter was
Aksah. 50 These were the descendants of Caleb.

The sons of Hur the firstborn of Ephrathah:
Shobal the father of Kiriath Jearim, 51 Salma the father of Beth-
lehem, and Hareph the father of Beth Gader.
52 The descendants of Shobal the father of Kiriath Jearim were:
Haroeh, half the Manahathites, 53 and the clans of Kiriath Jea-
rim: the Ithrites, Puthites, Shumathites and Mishraites. From
these descended the Zorathites and Eshtaolites.
54 The descendants of Salma:

---

[a] 42 The meaning of the Hebrew for this phrase is uncertain.

Bethlehem, the Netophathites, Atroth Beth Joab, half the Ma-
nahathites, the Zorites, 55 and the clans of scribes[a] who lived at
Jabez: the Tirathites, Shimeathites and Sucathites. These are the
Kenites who came from Hammath, the father of the Rekabites.[b]

THE SONS OF DAVID

3 These were the sons of David born to him in Hebron:
The firstborn was Amnon the son of Ahinoam of Jezreel;
the second, Daniel the son of Abigail of Carmel;
2 the third, Absalom the son of Maakah daughter of Talmai king
of Geshur;
the fourth, Adonijah the son of Haggith;
3 the fifth, Shephatiah the son of Abital;
and the sixth, Ithream, by his wife Eglah.
4 These six were born to David in Hebron, where he reigned seven
years and six months.
David reigned in Jerusalem thirty-three years, 5 and these were the
children born to him there:
Shammua,[c] Shobab, Nathan and Solomon. These four were by
Bathsheba[d] daughter of Ammiel. 6 There were also Ibhar, Eli-
shua,[e] Eliphelet, 7 Nogah, Nepheg, Japhia, 8 Elishama, Eliada and
Eliphelet — nine in all. 9 All these were the sons of David, besides
his sons by his concubines. And Tamar was their sister.

THE KINGS OF JUDAH

10 Solomon's son was Rehoboam,
Abijah his son,
Asa his son,
Jehoshaphat his son,
11 Jehoram[f] his son,
Ahaziah his son,
Joash his son,
12 Amaziah his son,
Azariah his son,
Jotham his son,
13 Ahaz his son,
Hezekiah his son,
Manasseh his son,
14 Amon his son,
Josiah his son.
15 The sons of Josiah:
Johanan the firstborn,
Jehoiakim the second son,
Zedekiah the third,
Shallum the fourth.
16 The successors of Jehoiakim:
Jehoiachin[g] his son,
and Zedekiah.

PRAYING SCRIPTURE

1 Chronicles 3

The names of David's descendants bring to mind stories of pain, failure and sin. In a sense, this should bring a ray of hope to those who follow Jesus: No matter how troubled our families might be, God can still work his will.

If you look back through your family's past and see little of God's glory, ask him to redeem the future, producing a legacy of faith that honors him.

[a] *55* Or *of the Sopherites* [b] *55* Or *father of Beth Rekab* [c] *5* Hebrew *Shimea,* a variant of *Shammua* [d] *5* One Hebrew manuscript and Vulgate (see also Septuagint and 2 Samuel 11:3); most Hebrew manuscripts *Bathshua*
[e] *6* Two Hebrew manuscripts (see also 2 Samuel 5:15 and 1 Chron. 14:5); most Hebrew manuscripts *Elishama* [f] *11* Hebrew *Joram,* a variant of *Jehoram*
[g] *16* Hebrew *Jeconiah,* a variant of *Jehoiachin;* also in verse 17

THE ROYAL LINE AFTER THE EXILE

17 The descendants of Jehoiachin the captive:
Shealtiel his son, 18 Malkiram, Pedaiah, Shenazzar, Jekamiah,
Hoshama and Nedabiah.

19 The sons of Pedaiah:
Zerubbabel and Shimei.

The sons of Zerubbabel:
Meshullam and Hananiah.
Shelomith was their sister.

20 There were also five others:
Hashubah, Ohel, Berekiah, Hasadiah and Jushab-Hesed.

21 The descendants of Hananiah:
Pelatiah and Jeshaiah, and the sons of Rephaiah, of Arnan, of
Obadiah and of Shekaniah.

22 The descendants of Shekaniah:
Shemaiah and his sons:
Hattush, Igal, Bariah, Neariah and Shaphat — six in all.

23 The sons of Neariah:
Elioenai, Hizkiah and Azrikam — three in all.

24 The sons of Elioenai:
Hodaviah, Eliashib, Pelaiah, Akkub, Johanan, Delaiah and
Anani — seven in all.

OTHER CLANS OF JUDAH

4 The descendants of Judah:
Perez, Hezron, Karmi, Hur and Shobal.

2 Reaiah son of Shobal was the father of Jahath, and Jahath the father
of Ahumai and Lahad. These were the clans of the Zorathites.

3 These were the sons[a] of Etam:
Jezreel, Ishma and Idbash. Their sister was named Hazzelelponi.
4 Penuel was the father of Gedor, and Ezer the father of Hushah.

These were the descendants of Hur, the firstborn of Ephrathah and
father[b] of Bethlehem.

5 Ashhur the father of Tekoa had two wives, Helah and Naarah.

6 Naarah bore him Ahuzzam, Hepher, Temeni and Haahashtari.
These were the descendants of Naarah.

7 The sons of Helah:
Zereth, Zohar, Ethnan, 8 and Koz, who was the father of Anub and
Hazzobebah and of the clans of Aharhel son of Harum.

9 Jabez was more honorable than his brothers. His mother had
named him Jabez,[c] saying, "I gave birth to him in pain." 10 Jabez cried
out to the God of Israel, "Oh, that you would bless me and enlarge my
territory! Let your hand be with me, and keep me from harm so that I
will be free from pain." And God granted his request.

11 Kelub, Shuhah's brother, was the father of Mehir, who was the father
of Eshton. 12 Eshton was the father of Beth Rapha, Paseah and Te-
hinnah the father of Ir Nahash.[d] These were the men of Rekah.

13 The sons of Kenaz:
Othniel and Seraiah.

[a] 3 Some Septuagint manuscripts (see also Vulgate); Hebrew *father*
[b] 4 *Father* may mean *civic leader* or *military leader*; also in verses 12, 14, 17, 18 and possibly elsewhere. [c] 9 *Jabez* sounds like the Hebrew for *pain*.
[d] 12 Or *of the city of Nahash*

PRAYING SCRIPTURE

1 Chronicles 4

Jabez's prayer reminds us that God hears when we call on him. When Jabez asked for God's blessing on his life, for the expansion of his land, for God's presence and protection from evil, God was pleased with his prayer and granted Jabez's requests.

Are you ever afraid to bring really audacious requests to God? Let Jabez encourage you. Approach God boldly and ask in faith with God-sized petitions!

The sons of Othniel:
Hathath and Meonothai.[a] 14Meonothai was the father of Ophrah.
Seraiah was the father of Joab,
the father of Ge Harashim.[b] It was called this because its people
were skilled workers.
15The sons of Caleb son of Jephunneh:
Iru, Elah and Naam.
The son of Elah:
Kenaz.
16The sons of Jehallelel:
Ziph, Ziphah, Tiria and Asarel.
17The sons of Ezrah:
Jether, Mered, Epher and Jalon. One of Mered's wives gave birth
to Miriam, Shammai and Ishbah the father of Eshtemoa. 18(His
wife from the tribe of Judah gave birth to Jered the father of
Gedor, Heber the father of Soko, and Jekuthiel the father of Za-
noah.) These were the children of Pharaoh's daughter Bithiah,
whom Mered had married.
19The sons of Hodiah's wife, the sister of Naham:
the father of Keilah the Garmite, and Eshtemoa the Maakathite.
20The sons of Shimon:
Amnon, Rinnah, Ben-Hanan and Tilon.
The descendants of Ishi:
Zoheth and Ben-Zoheth.
21The sons of Shelah son of Judah:
Er the father of Lekah, Laadah the father of Mareshah and the
clans of the linen workers at Beth Ashbea, 22Jokim, the men of
Kozeba, and Joash and Saraph, who ruled in Moab and Jashubi
Lehem. (These records are from ancient times.) 23They were the
potters who lived at Netaim and Gederah; they stayed there and
worked for the king.

SIMEON

24The descendants of Simeon:
Nemuel, Jamin, Jarib, Zerah and Shaul;
25Shallum was Shaul's son, Mibsam his son and Mishma his son.
26The descendants of Mishma:
Hammuel his son, Zakkur his son and Shimei his son.
27Shimei had sixteen sons and six daughters, but his brothers did
not have many children; so their entire clan did not become as nu-
merous as the people of Judah. 28They lived in Beersheba, Moladah,
Hazar Shual, 29Bilhah, Ezem, Tolad, 30Bethuel, Hormah, Ziklag, 31Beth
Markaboth, Hazar Susim, Beth Biri and Shaaraim. These were their
towns until the reign of David. 32Their surrounding villages were Etam,
Ain, Rimmon, Token and Ashan — five towns — 33and all the villages
around these towns as far as Baalath.[c] These were their settlements.
And they kept a genealogical record.

34Meshobab, Jamlech, Joshah son of Amaziah, 35Joel, Jehu son of
Joshibiah, the son of Seraiah, the son of Asiel, 36also Elioenai, Jaa-
kobah, Jeshohaiah, Asaiah, Adiel, Jesimiel, Benaiah, 37and Ziza son

---

[a] *13* Some Septuagint manuscripts and Vulgate; Hebrew does not have *and Meonothai.* [b] *14* *Ge Harashim* means *valley of skilled workers.* [c] *33* Some Septuagint manuscripts (see also Joshua 19:8); Hebrew *Baal*

of Shiphi, the son of Allon, the son of Jedaiah, the son of Shimri,
the son of Shemaiah.

38 The men listed above by name were leaders of their clans. Their
families increased greatly, 39 and they went to the outskirts of Gedor to
the east of the valley in search of pasture for their flocks. 40 They found
rich, good pasture, and the land was spacious, peaceful and quiet.
Some Hamites had lived there formerly.

41 The men whose names were listed came in the days of Hezekiah
king of Judah. They attacked the Hamites in their dwellings and also
the Meunites who were there and completely destroyed[a] them, as is
evident to this day. Then they settled in their place, because there was
pasture for their flocks. 42 And five hundred of these Simeonites, led by
Pelatiah, Neariah, Rephaiah and Uzziel, the sons of Ishi, invaded the
hill country of Seir. 43 They killed the remaining Amalekites who had
escaped, and they have lived there to this day.

PRAYING SCRIPTURE

1 Chronicles 5

Fulfilling the prophecy of his father, Reuben's family inherited his instability. He lost his birthright, and despite a few military victories, Reuben's line reveals no one of lasting impact. In a single, notable event, his sons and other warriors called on God in battle and were victorious.

God's family in every era includes those who struggle to be spiritually fruitful. God loves them and will use them when they cry out to him.

REUBEN

5 The sons of Reuben the firstborn of Israel (he was the firstborn,
but when he defiled his father's marriage bed, his rights as first-
born were given to the sons of Joseph son of Israel; so he could not
be listed in the genealogical record in accordance with his birthright,
2 and though Judah was the strongest of his brothers and a ruler came
from him, the rights of the firstborn belonged to Joseph) — 3 the sons
of Reuben the firstborn of Israel:

Hanok, Pallu, Hezron and Karmi.

4 The descendants of Joel:

Shemaiah his son, Gog his son,
Shimei his son, 5 Micah his son,
Reaiah his son, Baal his son,
6 and Beerah his son, whom Tiglath-Pileser[b] king of Assyria took
into exile. Beerah was a leader of the Reubenites.

7 Their relatives by clans, listed according to their genealogical
records:

Jeiel the chief, Zechariah, 8 and Bela son of Azaz, the son of
Shema, the son of Joel. They settled in the area from Aroer to
Nebo and Baal Meon. 9 To the east they occupied the land up to
the edge of the desert that extends to the Euphrates River, be-
cause their livestock had increased in Gilead.

10 During Saul's reign they waged war against the Hagrites, who
were defeated at their hands; they occupied the dwellings of the
Hagrites throughout the entire region east of Gilead.

GAD

11 The Gadites lived next to them in Bashan, as far as Salekah:

12 Joel was the chief, Shapham the second, then Janai and Sha-
phat, in Bashan.

13 Their relatives, by families, were:

Michael, Meshullam, Sheba, Jorai, Jakan, Zia and Eber — seven
in all.

14 These were the sons of Abihail son of Huri, the son of Jaroah, the

[a] *41* The Hebrew term refers to the irrevocable giving over of things or persons to the LORD, often by totally destroying them. [b] *6* Hebrew *Tilgath-Pilneser,* a variant of *Tiglath-Pileser;* also in verse 26

son of Gilead, the son of Michael, the son of Jeshishai, the son
of Jahdo, the son of Buz.
15 Ahi son of Abdiel, the son of Guni, was head of their family.
16 The Gadites lived in Gilead, in Bashan and its outlying villages,
and on all the pasturelands of Sharon as far as they extended.
17 All these were entered in the genealogical records during the
reigns of Jotham king of Judah and Jeroboam king of Israel.

18 The Reubenites, the Gadites and the half-tribe of Manasseh had
44,760 men ready for military service — able-bodied men who could
handle shield and sword, who could use a bow, and who were trained
for battle. 19 They waged war against the Hagrites, Jetur, Naphish and
Nodab. 20 They were helped in fighting them, and God delivered the
Hagrites and all their allies into their hands, because they cried out to
him during the battle. He answered their prayers, because they trusted
in him. 21 They seized the livestock of the Hagrites — fifty thousand
camels, two hundred fifty thousand sheep and two thousand donkeys.
They also took one hundred thousand people captive, 22 and many oth-
ers fell slain, because the battle was God's. And they occupied the land
until the exile.

THE HALF-TRIBE OF MANASSEH

23 The people of the half-tribe of Manasseh were numerous; they set-
tled in the land from Bashan to Baal Hermon, that is, to Senir (Mount
Hermon).
24 These were the heads of their families: Epher, Ishi, Eliel, Azriel, Jer-
emiah, Hodaviah and Jahdiel. They were brave warriors, famous men,
and heads of their families. 25 But they were unfaithful to the God of
their ancestors and prostituted themselves to the gods of the peoples
of the land, whom God had destroyed before them. 26 So the God of Is-
rael stirred up the spirit of Pul king of Assyria (that is, Tiglath-Pileser
king of Assyria), who took the Reubenites, the Gadites and the half-
tribe of Manasseh into exile. He took them to Halah, Habor, Hara and
the river of Gozan, where they are to this day.

LEVI

6 [a] The sons of Levi:
Gershon, Kohath and Merari.
2 The sons of Kohath:
Amram, Izhar, Hebron and Uzziel.
3 The children of Amram:
Aaron, Moses and Miriam.
The sons of Aaron:
Nadab, Abihu, Eleazar and Ithamar.
4 Eleazar was the father of Phinehas,
Phinehas the father of Abishua,
5 Abishua the father of Bukki,
Bukki the father of Uzzi,
6 Uzzi the father of Zerahiah,
Zerahiah the father of Meraioth,
7 Meraioth the father of Amariah,
Amariah the father of Ahitub,

PRAYING SCRIPTURE

1 Chronicles 6

David appointed men to be "in charge of the music" because he knew the importance of music in our lives and in our worship (see verse 31). Combine this with his own musicianship and writing of psalms himself, and we see that David clearly wanted to influence others to sing praise to God.

Sometimes earthly pressures steal the song from our hearts. When we worship the Lord in song, he will move our hearts to prayerful gratitude.

[a] In Hebrew texts 6:1-15 is numbered 5:27-41, and 6:16-81 is numbered 6:1-66.

8 Ahitub the father of Zadok,
Zadok the father of Ahimaaz,
9 Ahimaaz the father of Azariah,
Azariah the father of Johanan,
10 Johanan the father of Azariah (it was he who served as priest in
the temple Solomon built in Jerusalem),
11 Azariah the father of Amariah,
Amariah the father of Ahitub,
12 Ahitub the father of Zadok,
Zadok the father of Shallum,
13 Shallum the father of Hilkiah,
Hilkiah the father of Azariah,
14 Azariah the father of Seraiah,
and Seraiah the father of Jozadak.[a]

15 Jozadak was deported when the LORD sent Judah and Jerusalem
into exile by the hand of Nebuchadnezzar.

16 The sons of Levi:
Gershon,[b] Kohath and Merari.
17 These are the names of the sons of Gershon:
Libni and Shimei.
18 The sons of Kohath:
Amram, Izhar, Hebron and Uzziel.
19 The sons of Merari:
Mahli and Mushi.
These are the clans of the Levites listed according to their fathers:
20 Of Gershon:
Libni his son, Jahath his son,
Zimmah his son, 21 Joah his son,
Iddo his son, Zerah his son
and Jeatherai his son.
22 The descendants of Kohath:
Amminadab his son, Korah his son,
Assir his son, 23 Elkanah his son,
Ebiasaph his son, Assir his son,
24 Tahath his son, Uriel his son,
Uzziah his son and Shaul his son.
25 The descendants of Elkanah:
Amasai, Ahimoth,
26 Elkanah his son,[c] Zophai his son,
Nahath his son, 27 Eliab his son,
Jeroham his son, Elkanah his son
and Samuel his son.[d]
28 The sons of Samuel:
Joel[e] the firstborn
and Abijah the second son.
29 The descendants of Merari:

[a] *14* Hebrew *Jehozadak*, a variant of *Jozadak*; also in verse 15 [b] *16* Hebrew *Gershom*, a variant of *Gershon*; also in verses 17, 20, 43, 62 and 71 [c] *26* Some Hebrew manuscripts, Septuagint and Syriac; most Hebrew manuscripts *Ahimoth* [26] *and Elkanah. The sons of Elkanah:* [d] *27* Some Septuagint manuscripts (see also 1 Samuel 1:19,20 and 1 Chron. 6:33,34); Hebrew does not have *and Samuel his son.* [e] *28* Some Septuagint manuscripts and Syriac (see also 1 Samuel 8:2 and 1 Chron. 6:33); Hebrew does not have *Joel.*

Mahli, Libni his son,
Shimei his son, Uzzah his son,
30 Shimea his son, Haggiah his son
and Asaiah his son.

THE TEMPLE MUSICIANS

31 These are the men David put in charge of the music in the house
of the LORD after the ark came to rest there. 32 They ministered with
music before the tabernacle, the tent of meeting, until Solomon built
the temple of the LORD in Jerusalem. They performed their duties according to the regulations laid down for them.
33 Here are the men who served, together with their sons:
From the Kohathites:
Heman, the musician,
the son of Joel, the son of Samuel,
34 the son of Elkanah, the son of Jeroham,
the son of Eliel, the son of Toah,
35 the son of Zuph, the son of Elkanah,
the son of Mahath, the son of Amasai,
36 the son of Elkanah, the son of Joel,
the son of Azariah, the son of Zephaniah,
37 the son of Tahath, the son of Assir,
the son of Ebiasaph, the son of Korah,
38 the son of Izhar, the son of Kohath,
the son of Levi, the son of Israel;
39 and Heman's associate Asaph, who served at his right hand:
Asaph son of Berekiah, the son of Shimea,
40 the son of Michael, the son of Baaseiah,[a]
the son of Malkijah, 41 the son of Ethni,
the son of Zerah, the son of Adaiah,
42 the son of Ethan, the son of Zimmah,
the son of Shimei, 43 the son of Jahath,
the son of Gershon, the son of Levi;
44 and from their associates, the Merarites, at his left hand:
Ethan son of Kishi, the son of Abdi,
the son of Malluk, 45 the son of Hashabiah,
the son of Amaziah, the son of Hilkiah,
46 the son of Amzi, the son of Bani,
the son of Shemer, 47 the son of Mahli,
the son of Mushi, the son of Merari,
the son of Levi.

48 Their fellow Levites were assigned to all the other duties of the tabernacle, the house of God. 49 But Aaron and his descendants were the
ones who presented offerings on the altar of burnt offering and on the
altar of incense in connection with all that was done in the Most Holy
Place, making atonement for Israel, in accordance with all that Moses
the servant of God had commanded.

50 These were the descendants of Aaron:
Eleazar his son, Phinehas his son,
Abishua his son, 51 Bukki his son,
Uzzi his son, Zerahiah his son,

---

[a] *40* Most Hebrew manuscripts; some Hebrew manuscripts, one Septuagint manuscript and Syriac *Maaseiah*

52 Meraioth his son, Amariah his son,
Ahitub his son, 53 Zadok his son
and Ahimaaz his son.

54 These were the locations of their settlements allotted as their territory (they were assigned to the descendants of Aaron who were from the Kohathite clan, because the first lot was for them):

55 They were given Hebron in Judah with its surrounding pas-
turelands. 56 But the fields and villages around the city were given
to Caleb son of Jephunneh.

57 So the descendants of Aaron were given Hebron (a city of ref-
uge), and Libnah,[a] Jattir, Eshtemoa, 58 Hilen, Debir, 59 Ashan, Jut-
tah[b] and Beth Shemesh, together with their pasturelands. 60 And
from the tribe of Benjamin they were given Gibeon,[c] Geba, Ale-
meth and Anathoth, together with their pasturelands.

The total number of towns distributed among the Kohathite clans came to thirteen.

61 The rest of Kohath's descendants were allotted ten towns from the clans of half the tribe of Manasseh.

62 The descendants of Gershon, clan by clan, were allotted thirteen towns from the tribes of Issachar, Asher and Naphtali, and from the part of the tribe of Manasseh that is in Bashan.

63 The descendants of Merari, clan by clan, were allotted twelve towns from the tribes of Reuben, Gad and Zebulun.

64 So the Israelites gave the Levites these towns and their pasture-
lands. 65 From the tribes of Judah, Simeon and Benjamin they allotted
the previously named towns.

66 Some of the Kohathite clans were given as their territory towns from the tribe of Ephraim.

67 In the hill country of Ephraim they were given Shechem (a city
of refuge), and Gezer,[d] 68 Jokmeam, Beth Horon, 69 Aijalon and Gath
Rimmon, together with their pasturelands.

70 And from half the tribe of Manasseh the Israelites gave Aner and Bileam, together with their pasturelands, to the rest of the Kohathite clans.

71 The Gershonites received the following:
From the clan of the half-tribe of Manasseh
they received Golan in Bashan and also Ashtaroth, together with their pasturelands;
72 from the tribe of Issachar
they received Kedesh, Daberath, 73 Ramoth and Anem, together
with their pasturelands;
74 from the tribe of Asher
they received Mashal, Abdon, 75 Hukok and Rehob, together with
their pasturelands;
76 and from the tribe of Naphtali
they received Kedesh in Galilee, Hammon and Kiriathaim, together with their pasturelands.

77 The Merarites (the rest of the Levites) received the following:

---

[a] 57 See Joshua 21:13; Hebrew *given the cities of refuge: Hebron, Libnah.*
[b] 59 Syriac (see also Septuagint and Joshua 21:16); Hebrew does not have *Juttah.* [c] 60 See Joshua 21:17; Hebrew does not have *Gibeon.*
[d] 67 See Joshua 21:21; Hebrew *given the cities of refuge: Shechem, Gezer.*

From the tribe of Zebulun
they received Jokneam, Kartah,[a] Rimmono and Tabor, together
with their pasturelands;
78 from the tribe of Reuben across the Jordan east of Jericho
they received Bezer in the wilderness, Jahzah, 79 Kedemoth and
Mephaath, together with their pasturelands;
80 and from the tribe of Gad
they received Ramoth in Gilead, Mahanaim, 81 Heshbon and Ja-
zer, together with their pasturelands.

ISSACHAR

7 The sons of Issachar:
Tola, Puah, Jashub and Shimron — four in all.
2 The sons of Tola:
Uzzi, Rephaiah, Jeriel, Jahmai, Ibsam and Samuel — heads of
their families. During the reign of David, the descendants of
Tola listed as fighting men in their genealogy numbered 22,600.
3 The son of Uzzi:
Izrahiah.
The sons of Izrahiah:
Michael, Obadiah, Joel and Ishiah. All five of them were chiefs.
4 According to their family genealogy, they had 36,000 men
ready for battle, for they had many wives and children.
5 The relatives who were fighting men belonging to all the clans of
Issachar, as listed in their genealogy, were 87,000 in all.

BENJAMIN

6 Three sons of Benjamin:
Bela, Beker and Jediael.
7 The sons of Bela:
Ezbon, Uzzi, Uzziel, Jerimoth and Iri, heads of families — five in
all. Their genealogical record listed 22,034 fighting men.
8 The sons of Beker:
Zemirah, Joash, Eliezer, Elioenai, Omri, Jeremoth, Abijah, An-
athoth and Alemeth. All these were the sons of Beker. 9 Their
genealogical record listed the heads of families and 20,200
fighting men.
10 The son of Jediael:
Bilhan.
The sons of Bilhan:
Jeush, Benjamin, Ehud, Kenaanah, Zethan, Tarshish and Ahish-
ahar. 11 All these sons of Jediael were heads of families. There
were 17,200 fighting men ready to go out to war.
12 The Shuppites and Huppites were the descendants of Ir, and the
Hushites[b] the descendants of Aher.

NAPHTALI

13 The sons of Naphtali:
Jahziel, Guni, Jezer and Shillem[c] — the descendants of Bilhah.

PRAYING SCRIPTURE

1 Chronicles 7

The family of God through the Old and New Testaments contains multitudes. Beyond the New Testament record, the number of people who have followed and are following God is into the billions. The genealogical record of Israel's tribes is but a few grains of the vast seashore promised to Abraham.

Think for a moment about the countless faithful who have lived through the centuries, and thank God you are among that number.

---

[a] 77 See Septuagint and Joshua 21:34; Hebrew does not have *Jokneam, Kartah.*
[b] 12 Or *Ir. The sons of Dan: Hushim,* (see Gen. 46:23); Hebrew does not have *The sons of Dan.*
[c] 13 Some Hebrew and Septuagint manuscripts (see also Gen. 46:24 and Num. 26:49); most Hebrew manuscripts *Shallum*

MANASSEH

14 The descendants of Manasseh:
Asriel was his descendant through his Aramean concubine. She
gave birth to Makir the father of Gilead. 15 Makir took a wife from
among the Huppites and Shuppites. His sister's name was Maakah.
Another descendant was named Zelophehad, who had only daughters.

16 Makir's wife Maakah gave birth to a son and named him Peresh. His brother was named Sheresh, and his sons were Ulam and Rakem.

17 The son of Ulam:
Bedan.
These were the sons of Gilead son of Makir, the son of Manasseh.
18 His sister Hammoleketh gave birth to Ishhod, Abiezer and Mahlah.

19 The sons of Shemida were:
Ahian, Shechem, Likhi and Aniam.

EPHRAIM

20 The descendants of Ephraim:
Shuthelah, Bered his son,
Tahath his son, Eleadah his son,
Tahath his son, 21 Zabad his son
and Shuthelah his son.
Ezer and Elead were killed by the native-born men of Gath,
when they went down to seize their livestock. 22 Their father
Ephraim mourned for them many days, and his relatives came
to comfort him. 23 Then he made love to his wife again, and she
became pregnant and gave birth to a son. He named him Beriah,[a]
because there had been misfortune in his family. 24 His daughter
was Sheerah, who built Lower and Upper Beth Horon as well as
Uzzen Sheerah.
25 Rephah was his son, Resheph his son,[b]
Telah his son, Tahan his son,
26 Ladan his son, Ammihud his son,
Elishama his son, 27 Nun his son
and Joshua his son.
28 Their lands and settlements included Bethel and its surrounding
villages, Naaran to the east, Gezer and its villages to the west, and She-
chem and its villages all the way to Ayyah and its villages. 29 Along the
borders of Manasseh were Beth Shan, Taanach, Megiddo and Dor, to-
gether with their villages. The descendants of Joseph son of Israel lived
in these towns.

ASHER

30 The sons of Asher:
Imnah, Ishvah, Ishvi and Beriah. Their sister was Serah.

31 The sons of Beriah:
Heber and Malkiel, who was the father of Birzaith.

32 Heber was the father of Japhlet, Shomer and Hotham and of their sister Shua.

---

[a] *23 Beriah* sounds like the Hebrew for *misfortune.* [b] *25* Some Septuagint manuscripts; Hebrew does not have *his son.*

33 The sons of Japhlet:
Pasak, Bimhal and Ashvath.
These were Japhlet's sons.
34 The sons of Shomer:
Ahi, Rohgah,[a] Hubbah and Aram.
35 The sons of his brother Helem:
Zophah, Imna, Shelesh and Amal.
36 The sons of Zophah:
Suah, Harnepher, Shual, Beri, Imrah, 37 Bezer, Hod, Shamma,
Shilshah, Ithran[b] and Beera.
38 The sons of Jether:
Jephunneh, Pispah and Ara.
39 The sons of Ulla:
Arah, Hanniel and Rizia.
40 All these were descendants of Asher — heads of families, choice
men, brave warriors and outstanding leaders. The number of men
ready for battle, as listed in their genealogy, was 26,000.

THE GENEALOGY OF SAUL THE BENJAMITE

8 Benjamin was the father of Bela his firstborn,
Ashbel the second son, Aharah the third,
2 Nohah the fourth and Rapha the fifth.
3 The sons of Bela were:
Addar, Gera, Abihud,[c] 4 Abishua, Naaman, Ahoah, 5 Gera, Shephu-
phan and Huram.
6 These were the descendants of Ehud, who were heads of families
of those living in Geba and were deported to Manahath:
7 Naaman, Ahijah, and Gera, who deported them and who was the
father of Uzza and Ahihud.
8 Sons were born to Shaharaim in Moab after he had divorced his
wives Hushim and Baara. 9 By his wife Hodesh he had Jobab,
Zibia, Mesha, Malkam, 10 Jeuz, Sakia and Mirmah. These were
his sons, heads of families. 11 By Hushim he had Abitub and
Elpaal.
12 The sons of Elpaal:
Eber, Misham, Shemed (who built Ono and Lod with its sur-
rounding villages), 13 and Beriah and Shema, who were heads of
families of those living in Aijalon and who drove out the inhab-
itants of Gath.
14 Ahio, Shashak, Jeremoth, 15 Zebadiah, Arad, Eder, 16 Michael, Ishpah
and Joha were the sons of Beriah.
17 Zebadiah, Meshullam, Hizki, Heber, 18 Ishmerai, Izliah and Jobab
were the sons of Elpaal.
19 Jakim, Zikri, Zabdi, 20 Elienai, Zillethai, Eliel, 21 Adaiah, Beraiah and
Shimrath were the sons of Shimei.
22 Ishpan, Eber, Eliel, 23 Abdon, Zikri, Hanan, 24 Hananiah, Elam, An-
thothijah, 25 Iphdeiah and Penuel were the sons of Shashak.
26 Shamsherai, Shehariah, Athaliah, 27 Jaareshiah, Elijah and Zikri
were the sons of Jeroham.
28 All these were heads of families, chiefs as listed in their genealogy,
and they lived in Jerusalem.

PRAYING SCRIPTURE

1 Chronicles 8

Israel's first king, Saul, was from the tribe of Benjamin. Other than Jonathan, there is no one of note in Saul's line. Thus, Benjamin's record is closed with only the mention of some archers in a particularly fruitful branch.

Saul's rebellious life initiated an ungodly pattern that too many kings followed. Nevertheless, God kept his promise for a Messiah, and for him we can give thanks.

---

[a] 34 Or *of his brother Shomer: Rohgah* [b] 37 Possibly a variant of *Jether*
[c] 3 Or *Gera the father of Ehud*

29 Jeiel[a] the father[b] of Gibeon lived in Gibeon.
His wife's name was Maakah, 30 and his firstborn son was Abdon,
followed by Zur, Kish, Baal, Ner,[c] Nadab, 31 Gedor, Ahio, Zeker
32 and Mikloth, who was the father of Shimeah. They too lived
near their relatives in Jerusalem.
33 Ner was the father of Kish, Kish the father of Saul, and Saul the
father of Jonathan, Malki-Shua, Abinadab and Esh-Baal.[d]
34 The son of Jonathan:
Merib-Baal,[e] who was the father of Micah.
35 The sons of Micah:
Pithon, Melek, Tarea and Ahaz.
36 Ahaz was the father of Jehoaddah, Jehoaddah was the father
of Alemeth, Azmaveth and Zimri, and Zimri was the father of
Moza. 37 Moza was the father of Binea; Raphah was his son, Elea-
sah his son and Azel his son.
38 Azel had six sons, and these were their names:
Azrikam, Bokeru, Ishmael, Sheariah, Obadiah and Hanan. All
these were the sons of Azel.
39 The sons of his brother Eshek:
Ulam his firstborn, Jeush the second son and Eliphelet the third.
40 The sons of Ulam were brave warriors who could handle the
bow. They had many sons and grandsons — 150 in all.
All these were the descendants of Benjamin.

PRAYING SCRIPTURE

1 Chronicles 9

Although both Jerusalem and Judah had fallen, a number of priests and Levites were left behind. These were few enough in number and status that the king of Babylon did not feel threatened. Daily worship activities continued in the temple.

The exiles continued to worship as the remnant did. God's people can worship him in whatever circumstances they find themselves. Call on the Lord today. He is near.

9 All Israel was listed in the genealogies recorded in the book of the
kings of Israel and Judah. They were taken captive to Babylon be-
cause of their unfaithfulness.

THE PEOPLE IN JERUSALEM

2 Now the first to resettle on their own property in their own towns
were some Israelites, priests, Levites and temple servants.
3 Those from Judah, from Benjamin, and from Ephraim and Manas-
seh who lived in Jerusalem were:
4 Uthai son of Ammihud, the son of Omri, the son of Imri, the son of
Bani, a descendant of Perez son of Judah.
5 Of the Shelanites[f]:
Asaiah the firstborn and his sons.
6 Of the Zerahites:
Jeuel.
The people from Judah numbered 690.
7 Of the Benjamites:
Sallu son of Meshullam, the son of Hodaviah, the son of
Hassenuah;
8 Ibneiah son of Jeroham; Elah son of Uzzi, the son of Mikri; and
Meshullam son of Shephatiah, the son of Reuel, the son of Ibnijah.
9 The people from Benjamin, as listed in their genealogy, num-
bered 956. All these men were heads of their families.
10 Of the priests:
Jedaiah; Jehoiarib; Jakin;

[a] *29* Some Septuagint manuscripts (see also 9:35); Hebrew does not have *Jeiel.*
[b] *29* *Father* may mean *civic leader* or *military leader.* [c] *30* Some Septuagint manuscripts (see also 9:36); Hebrew does not have *Ner.* [d] *33* Also known as *Ish-Bosheth* [e] *34* Also known as *Mephibosheth* [f] *5* See Num. 26:20; Hebrew *Shilonites.*

11 Azariah son of Hilkiah, the son of Meshullam, the son of Zadok,
the son of Meraioth, the son of Ahitub, the official in charge of
the house of God;
12 Adaiah son of Jeroham, the son of Pashhur, the son of Malkijah;
and Maasai son of Adiel, the son of Jahzerah, the son of Meshul-
lam, the son of Meshillemith, the son of Immer.
13 The priests, who were heads of families, numbered 1,760. They
were able men, responsible for ministering in the house of God.

14 Of the Levites:
Shemaiah son of Hasshub, the son of Azrikam, the son of Hash-
abiah, a Merarite; 15 Bakbakkar, Heresh, Galal and Mattaniah son
of Mika, the son of Zikri, the son of Asaph; 16 Obadiah son of
Shemaiah, the son of Galal, the son of Jeduthun; and Berekiah
son of Asa, the son of Elkanah, who lived in the villages of the
Netophathites.

17 The gatekeepers:
Shallum, Akkub, Talmon, Ahiman and their fellow Levites, Shal-
lum their chief 18 being stationed at the King's Gate on the east,
up to the present time. These were the gatekeepers belonging
to the camp of the Levites. 19 Shallum son of Kore, the son of
Ebiasaph, the son of Korah, and his fellow gatekeepers from his
family (the Korahites) were responsible for guarding the thresh-
olds of the tent just as their ancestors had been responsible for
guarding the entrance to the dwelling of the LORD. 20 In earlier
times Phinehas son of Eleazar was the official in charge of the
gatekeepers, and the LORD was with him. 21 Zechariah son of
Meshelemiah was the gatekeeper at the entrance to the tent of
meeting.

22 Altogether, those chosen to be gatekeepers at the thresholds num-
bered 212. They were registered by genealogy in their villages. The
gatekeepers had been assigned to their positions of trust by David and
Samuel the seer. 23 They and their descendants were in charge of guard-
ing the gates of the house of the LORD — the house called the tent of
meeting. 24 The gatekeepers were on the four sides: east, west, north
and south. 25 Their fellow Levites in their villages had to come from
time to time and share their duties for seven-day periods. 26 But the
four principal gatekeepers, who were Levites, were entrusted with the
responsibility for the rooms and treasuries in the house of God. 27 They
would spend the night stationed around the house of God, because
they had to guard it; and they had charge of the key for opening it
each morning.

28 Some of them were in charge of the articles used in the temple
service; they counted them when they were brought in and when they
were taken out. 29 Others were assigned to take care of the furnish-
ings and all the other articles of the sanctuary, as well as the special
flour and wine, and the olive oil, incense and spices. 30 But some of the
priests took care of mixing the spices. 31 A Levite named Mattithiah, the
firstborn son of Shallum the Korahite, was entrusted with the respon-
sibility for baking the offering bread. 32 Some of the Kohathites, their
fellow Levites, were in charge of preparing for every Sabbath the bread
set out on the table.

33 Those who were musicians, heads of Levite families, stayed in the
rooms of the temple and were exempt from other duties because they
were responsible for the work day and night.

34 All these were heads of Levite families, chiefs as listed in their ge-
nealogy, and they lived in Jerusalem.

THE GENEALOGY OF SAUL

35 Jeiel the father[a] of Gibeon lived in Gibeon.
His wife's name was Maakah, 36 and his firstborn son was Abdon,
followed by Zur, Kish, Baal, Ner, Nadab, 37 Gedor, Ahio, Zechariah
and Mikloth. 38 Mikloth was the father of Shimeam. They too
lived near their relatives in Jerusalem.
39 Ner was the father of Kish, Kish the father of Saul, and Saul the
father of Jonathan, Malki-Shua, Abinadab and Esh-Baal.[b]
40 The son of Jonathan:
Merib-Baal,[c] who was the father of Micah.
41 The sons of Micah:
Pithon, Melek, Tahrea and Ahaz.[d]
42 Ahaz was the father of Jadah, Jadah[e] was the father of Alemeth,
Azmaveth and Zimri, and Zimri was the father of Moza. 43 Moza
was the father of Binea; Rephaiah was his son, Eleasah his son
and Azel his son.
44 Azel had six sons, and these were their names:
Azrikam, Bokeru, Ishmael, Sheariah, Obadiah and Hanan. These
were the sons of Azel.

SAUL TAKES HIS LIFE

10 Now the Philistines fought against Israel; the Israelites fled be-
fore them, and many fell dead on Mount Gilboa. 2 The Philis-
tines were in hot pursuit of Saul and his sons, and they killed his sons
Jonathan, Abinadab and Malki-Shua. 3 The fighting grew fierce around
Saul, and when the archers overtook him, they wounded him.
4 Saul said to his armor-bearer, "Draw your sword and run me
through, or these uncircumcised fellows will come and abuse me."
But his armor-bearer was terrified and would not do it; so Saul took
his own sword and fell on it. 5 When the armor-bearer saw that Saul
was dead, he too fell on his sword and died. 6 So Saul and his three sons
died, and all his house died together.
7 When all the Israelites in the valley saw that the army had fled and
that Saul and his sons had died, they abandoned their towns and fled.
And the Philistines came and occupied them.
8 The next day, when the Philistines came to strip the dead, they
found Saul and his sons fallen on Mount Gilboa. 9 They stripped him
and took his head and his armor, and sent messengers throughout
the land of the Philistines to proclaim the news among their idols
and their people. 10 They put his armor in the temple of their gods and
hung up his head in the temple of Dagon.
11 When all the inhabitants of Jabesh Gilead heard what the Philis-
tines had done to Saul, 12 all their valiant men went and took the bodies
of Saul and his sons and brought them to Jabesh. Then they buried
their bones under the great tree in Jabesh, and they fasted seven days.

PRAYING SCRIPTURE

1 Chronicles 10

Saul's tragic judgment is summed up as unfaithfulness by failing to keep God's word and consulting a medium. Saul was a man with every human advantage, but he did not love God with all of his heart and did not give himself to obedience.

Think about gifted people you know who ignore God. Pray that they come to repentance and faith in Jesus so they do not meet a tragic end as Saul did.

[a] 35 *Father* may mean *civic leader* or *military leader.* [b] 39 Also known as *Ish-Bosheth* [c] 40 Also known as *Mephibosheth* [d] 41 Vulgate and Syriac (see also Septuagint and 8:35); Hebrew does not have *and Ahaz.* [e] 42 Some Hebrew manuscripts and Septuagint (see also 8:36); most Hebrew manuscripts *Jarah, Jarah*

13Saul died because he was unfaithful to the LORD; he did not keep
the word of the LORD and even consulted a medium for guidance, 14and
did not inquire of the LORD. So the LORD put him to death and turned
the kingdom over to David son of Jesse.

DAVID BECOMES KING OVER ISRAEL

11 All Israel came together to David at Hebron and said, "We are your
own flesh and blood. 2In the past, even while Saul was king, you
were the one who led Israel on their military campaigns. And the LORD
your God said to you, 'You will shepherd my people Israel, and you will
become their ruler.'"

3When all the elders of Israel had come to King David at Hebron,
he made a covenant with them at Hebron before the LORD, and they
anointed David king over Israel, as the LORD had promised through
Samuel.

DAVID CONQUERS JERUSALEM

4David and all the Israelites marched to Jerusalem (that is, Jebus).
The Jebusites who lived there 5said to David, "You will not get in here."
Nevertheless, David captured the fortress of Zion—which is the City
of David.

6David had said, "Whoever leads the attack on the Jebusites will be-
come commander in chief." Joab son of Zeruiah went up first, and so
he received the command.

7David then took up residence in the fortress, and so it was called
the City of David. 8He built up the city around it, from the terraces[a]
to the surrounding wall, while Joab restored the rest of the city. 9And
David became more and more powerful, because the LORD Almighty
was with him.

DAVID'S MIGHTY WARRIORS

10These were the chiefs of David's mighty warriors—they, together
with all Israel, gave his kingship strong support to extend it over the
whole land, as the LORD had promised— 11this is the list of David's
mighty warriors:

Jashobeam,[b] a Hakmonite, was chief of the officers[c]; he raised his
spear against three hundred men, whom he killed in one encounter.

12Next to him was Eleazar son of Dodai the Ahohite, one of the three
mighty warriors. 13He was with David at Pas Dammim when the Philis-
tines gathered there for battle. At a place where there was a field full of
barley, the troops fled from the Philistines. 14But they took their stand
in the middle of the field. They defended it and struck the Philistines
down, and the LORD brought about a great victory.

15Three of the thirty chiefs came down to David to the rock at the
cave of Adullam, while a band of Philistines was encamped in the Val-
ley of Rephaim. 16At that time David was in the stronghold, and the
Philistine garrison was at Bethlehem. 17David longed for water and
said, "Oh, that someone would get me a drink of water from the well
near the gate of Bethlehem!" 18So the Three broke through the Philis-
tine lines, drew water from the well near the gate of Bethlehem and
carried it back to David. But he refused to drink it; instead, he poured

PRAYING SCRIPTURE

1 Chronicles 11

Although David is most often remembered as a great warrior, other than fighting Goliath, he was never alone. He had scores of mighty men, many who did heroic deeds.

David's mighty men are a good reminder that all people, even kings, need help. Following God is not a solo effort; it is a team effort. Ask God to give you a team and to make you part of someone else's.

---

[a] 8 Or *the Millo* [b] 11 Possibly a variant of *Jashob-Baal* [c] 11 Or *Thirty*; some Septuagint manuscripts *Three* (see also 2 Samuel 23:8)

it out to the LORD. 19"God forbid that I should do this!" he said. "Should
I drink the blood of these men who went at the risk of their lives?" Be-
cause they risked their lives to bring it back, David would not drink it.
Such were the exploits of the three mighty warriors.
20Abishai the brother of Joab was chief of the Three. He raised his
spear against three hundred men, whom he killed, and so he became as
famous as the Three. 21He was doubly honored above the Three and be-
came their commander, even though he was not included among them.
22Benaiah son of Jehoiada, a valiant fighter from Kabzeel, performed
great exploits. He struck down Moab's two mightiest warriors. He also
went down into a pit on a snowy day and killed a lion. 23And he struck
down an Egyptian who was five cubits[a] tall. Although the Egyptian had
a spear like a weaver's rod in his hand, Benaiah went against him with
a club. He snatched the spear from the Egyptian's hand and killed him
with his own spear. 24Such were the exploits of Benaiah son of Jehoi-
ada; he too was as famous as the three mighty warriors. 25He was held
in greater honor than any of the Thirty, but he was not included among
the Three. And David put him in charge of his bodyguard.

26 The mighty warriors were:
Asahel the brother of Joab,
Elhanan son of Dodo from Bethlehem,
27 Shammoth the Harorite,
Helez the Pelonite,
28 Ira son of Ikkesh from Tekoa,
Abiezer from Anathoth,
29 Sibbekai the Hushathite,
Ilai the Ahohite,
30 Maharai the Netophathite,
Heled son of Baanah the Netophathite,
31 Ithai son of Ribai from Gibeah in Benjamin,
Benaiah the Pirathonite,
32 Hurai from the ravines of Gaash,
Abiel the Arbathite,
33 Azmaveth the Baharumite,
Eliahba the Shaalbonite,
34 the sons of Hashem the Gizonite,
Jonathan son of Shagee the Hararite,
35 Ahiam son of Sakar the Hararite,
Eliphal son of Ur,
36 Hepher the Mekerathite,
Ahijah the Pelonite,
37 Hezro the Carmelite,
Naarai son of Ezbai,
38 Joel the brother of Nathan,
Mibhar son of Hagri,
39 Zelek the Ammonite,
Naharai the Berothite, the armor-bearer of Joab son of Zeruiah,
40 Ira the Ithrite,
Gareb the Ithrite,
41 Uriah the Hittite,
Zabad son of Ahlai,

[a] *23* That is, about 7 feet 6 inches or about 2.3 meters

42 Adina son of Shiza the Reubenite, who was chief of the Reuben-
ites, and the thirty with him,
43 Hanan son of Maakah,
Joshaphat the Mithnite,
44 Uzzia the Ashterathite,
Shama and Jeiel the sons of Hotham the Aroerite,
45 Jediael son of Shimri,
his brother Joha the Tizite,
46 Eliel the Mahavite,
Jeribai and Joshaviah the sons of Elnaam,
Ithmah the Moabite,
47 Eliel, Obed and Jaasiel the Mezobaite.

WARRIORS JOIN DAVID

12 These were the men who came to David at Ziklag, while he
was banished from the presence of Saul son of Kish (they were
among the warriors who helped him in battle; 2 they were armed with
bows and were able to shoot arrows or to sling stones right-handed or
left-handed; they were relatives of Saul from the tribe of Benjamin):

3 Ahiezer their chief and Joash the sons of Shemaah the Gibeath-
ite; Jeziel and Pelet the sons of Azmaveth; Berakah, Jehu the An-
athothite, 4 and Ishmaiah the Gibeonite, a mighty warrior among
the Thirty, who was a leader of the Thirty; Jeremiah, Jahaziel,
Johanan, Jozabad the Gederathite,[a] 5 Eluzai, Jerimoth, Bealiah,
Shemariah and Shephatiah the Haruphite; 6 Elkanah, Ishiah, Az-
arel, Joezer and Jashobeam the Korahites; 7 and Joelah and Zeba-
diah the sons of Jeroham from Gedor.

8 Some Gadites defected to David at his stronghold in the wilderness.
They were brave warriors, ready for battle and able to handle the shield
and spear. Their faces were the faces of lions, and they were as swift as
gazelles in the mountains.
9 Ezer was the chief,
Obadiah the second in command, Eliab the third,
10 Mishmannah the fourth, Jeremiah the fifth,
11 Attai the sixth, Eliel the seventh,
12 Johanan the eighth, Elzabad the ninth,
13 Jeremiah the tenth and Makbannai the eleventh.
14 These Gadites were army commanders; the least was a match for a
hundred, and the greatest for a thousand. 15 It was they who crossed the
Jordan in the first month when it was overflowing all its banks, and they
put to flight everyone living in the valleys, to the east and to the west.
16 Other Benjamites and some men from Judah also came to David
in his stronghold. 17 David went out to meet them and said to them, "If
you have come to me in peace to help me, I am ready for you to join me.
But if you have come to betray me to my enemies when my hands are
free from violence, may the God of our ancestors see it and judge you."
18 Then the Spirit came on Amasai, chief of the Thirty, and he said:

"We are yours, David!
We are with you, son of Jesse!

[a] 4 In Hebrew texts the second half of this verse (*Jeremiah . . . Gederathite*) is numbered 12:5, and 12:5-40 is numbered 12:6-41.

PRAYING SCRIPTURE

1 Chronicles 12

The record of David's army at Hebron is nothing less than astounding. All manner of experts in battle weaponry, those who could maintain ranks, the stouthearted and the well-armed served with the king. They were joined by sons of Issachar who understood the times.

God's kingdom is made from all kinds of people, reflecting his multihued grace. Express thanks for those who have different skills, gifts and talents from yours.

Success, success to you,
and success to those who help you,
for your God will help you."

So David received them and made them leaders of his raiding bands.
19 Some of the tribe of Manasseh defected to David when he went
with the Philistines to fight against Saul. (He and his men did not help
the Philistines because, after consultation, their rulers sent him away.
They said, "It will cost us our heads if he deserts to his master Saul.")
20 When David went to Ziklag, these were the men of Manasseh who
defected to him: Adnah, Jozabad, Jediael, Michael, Jozabad, Elihu and
Zillethai, leaders of units of a thousand in Manasseh. 21 They helped
David against raiding bands, for all of them were brave warriors, and
they were commanders in his army. 22 Day after day men came to help
David, until he had a great army, like the army of God.[a]

OTHERS JOIN DAVID AT HEBRON

23 These are the numbers of the men armed for battle who came to
David at Hebron to turn Saul's kingdom over to him, as the LORD had
said:

24 from Judah, carrying shield and spear — 6,800 armed for battle;
25 from Simeon, warriors ready for battle — 7,100;
26 from Levi — 4,600, 27 including Jehoiada, leader of the family of Aaron, with 3,700 men, 28 and Zadok, a brave young warrior, with 22 officers from his family;
29 from Benjamin, Saul's tribe — 3,000, most of whom had remained loyal to Saul's house until then;
30 from Ephraim, brave warriors, famous in their own clans — 20,800;
31 from half the tribe of Manasseh, designated by name to come and make David king — 18,000;
32 from Issachar, men who understood the times and knew what Israel should do — 200 chiefs, with all their relatives under their command;
33 from Zebulun, experienced soldiers prepared for battle with every type of weapon, to help David with undivided loyalty — 50,000;
34 from Naphtali — 1,000 officers, together with 37,000 men carrying shields and spears;
35 from Dan, ready for battle — 28,600;
36 from Asher, experienced soldiers prepared for battle — 40,000;
37 and from east of the Jordan, from Reuben, Gad and the half-tribe of Manasseh, armed with every type of weapon — 120,000.

38 All these were fighting men who volunteered to serve in the ranks.
They came to Hebron fully determined to make David king over all Is-
rael. All the rest of the Israelites were also of one mind to make David
king. 39 The men spent three days there with David, eating and drink-
ing, for their families had supplied provisions for them. 40 Also, their
neighbors from as far away as Issachar, Zebulun and Naphtali came
bringing food on donkeys, camels, mules and oxen. There were plen-
tiful supplies of flour, fig cakes, raisin cakes, wine, olive oil, cattle and
sheep, for there was joy in Israel.

---

[a] 22 Or *a great and mighty army*

BRINGING BACK THE ARK

13 David conferred with each of his officers, the commanders of
thousands and commanders of hundreds. 2He then said to the
whole assembly of Israel, "If it seems good to you and if it is the will
of the LORD our God, let us send word far and wide to the rest of our
people throughout the territories of Israel, and also to the priests and
Levites who are with them in their towns and pasturelands, to come
and join us. 3Let us bring the ark of our God back to us, for we did not
inquire of[a] it[b] during the reign of Saul." 4The whole assembly agreed
to do this, because it seemed right to all the people.

5So David assembled all Israel, from the Shihor River in Egypt to
Lebo Hamath, to bring the ark of God from Kiriath Jearim. 6David and
all Israel went to Baalah of Judah (Kiriath Jearim) to bring up from
there the ark of God the LORD, who is enthroned between the cheru-
bim — the ark that is called by the Name.

7They moved the ark of God from Abinadab's house on a new cart,
with Uzzah and Ahio guiding it. 8David and all the Israelites were cel-
ebrating with all their might before God, with songs and with harps,
lyres, timbrels, cymbals and trumpets.

9When they came to the threshing floor of Kidon, Uzzah reached out
his hand to steady the ark, because the oxen stumbled. 10The LORD's
anger burned against Uzzah, and he struck him down because he had
put his hand on the ark. So he died there before God.

11Then David was angry because the LORD's wrath had broken out
against Uzzah, and to this day that place is called Perez Uzzah.[c]

12David was afraid of God that day and asked, "How can I ever bring
the ark of God to me?" 13He did not take the ark to be with him in the
City of David. Instead, he took it to the house of Obed-Edom the Gittite.
14The ark of God remained with the family of Obed-Edom in his house
for three months, and the LORD blessed his household and everything
he had.

PRAYING SCRIPTURE

1 Chronicles 13

Uzza's death while trying to transport the ark of the covenant to Jerusalem caused David to erupt in anger. David, too, had ignored the proper way to move the ark. He then feared he'd never be able to place the ark in the temple.

Just because things don't work out the way we wish doesn't mean God is left without a plan. Our best decision is to wait on him; his ways are always right.

DAVID'S HOUSE AND FAMILY

14 Now Hiram king of Tyre sent messengers to David, along with
cedar logs, stonemasons and carpenters to build a palace for
him. 2And David knew that the LORD had established him as king over
Israel and that his kingdom had been highly exalted for the sake of
his people Israel.

3In Jerusalem David took more wives and became the father of more
sons and daughters. 4These are the names of the children born to him
there: Shammua, Shobab, Nathan, Solomon, 5Ibhar, Elishua, Elpelet,
6Nogah, Nepheg, Japhia, 7Elishama, Beeliada[d] and Eliphelet.

DAVID DEFEATS THE PHILISTINES

8When the Philistines heard that David had been anointed king over
all Israel, they went up in full force to search for him, but David heard
about it and went out to meet them. 9Now the Philistines had come
and raided the Valley of Rephaim; 10so David inquired of God: "Shall I
go and attack the Philistines? Will you deliver them into my hands?"

The LORD answered him, "Go, I will deliver them into your hands."

11So David and his men went up to Baal Perazim, and there he

PRAYING SCRIPTURE

1 Chronicles 14

David's plan to overcome the Philistines needed a miracle. The sound of marching in the treetops indicated that God would fight for them. The victory increased David's fame, and the Lord saw to it that the nations feared David.

It is better to wait for God's promotion than to self-promote. Pride informs the latter, while humility brings the former. Ask God for a humble spirit.

[a] 3 Or *we neglected* [b] 3 Or *him* [c] 11 *Perez Uzzah* means *outbreak against Uzzah.* [d] 7 A variant of *Eliada*

PRAYING SCRIPTURE

1 Chronicles 15

After years in storage, the ark of the covenant—the physical symbol of God's presence and place of his mercy seat—was returned to Jerusalem. The procession was a celebration of God's goodness and blessing accompanied by shouting and musical instruments (see verse 28). Still one person, Saul's daughter, despised David's joy.

Guarding our hearts means we don't despise another's joy. We can and should rejoice when others experience the goodness of God.

defeated them. He said, "As waters break out, God has broken out
against my enemies by my hand." So that place was called Baal Pera-
zim.[a] [12]The Philistines had abandoned their gods there, and David gave
orders to burn them in the fire.
[13]Once more the Philistines raided the valley; [14]so David inquired
of God again, and God answered him, "Do not go directly after them,
but circle around them and attack them in front of the poplar trees.
[15]As soon as you hear the sound of marching in the tops of the poplar
trees, move out to battle, because that will mean God has gone out in
front of you to strike the Philistine army." [16]So David did as God com-
manded him, and they struck down the Philistine army, all the way
from Gibeon to Gezer.
[17]So David's fame spread throughout every land, and the LORD made
all the nations fear him.

THE ARK BROUGHT TO JERUSALEM

15 After David had constructed buildings for himself in the City of
David, he prepared a place for the ark of God and pitched a tent
for it. [2]Then David said, "No one but the Levites may carry the ark of
God, because the LORD chose them to carry the ark of the LORD and to
minister before him forever."
[3]David assembled all Israel in Jerusalem to bring up the ark of the
LORD to the place he had prepared for it. [4]He called together the de-
scendants of Aaron and the Levites:

[5]From the descendants of Kohath,
Uriel the leader and 120 relatives;
[6]from the descendants of Merari,
Asaiah the leader and 220 relatives;
[7]from the descendants of Gershon,[b]
Joel the leader and 130 relatives;
[8]from the descendants of Elizaphan,
Shemaiah the leader and 200 relatives;
[9]from the descendants of Hebron,
Eliel the leader and 80 relatives;
[10]from the descendants of Uzziel,
Amminadab the leader and 112 relatives.

[11]Then David summoned Zadok and Abiathar the priests, and Uriel,
Asaiah, Joel, Shemaiah, Eliel and Amminadab the Levites. [12]He said to
them, "You are the heads of the Levitical families; you and your fellow
Levites are to consecrate yourselves and bring up the ark of the LORD,
the God of Israel, to the place I have prepared for it. [13]It was because
you, the Levites, did not bring it up the first time that the LORD our
God broke out in anger against us. We did not inquire of him about
how to do it in the prescribed way." [14]So the priests and Levites conse-
crated themselves in order to bring up the ark of the LORD, the God of
Israel. [15]And the Levites carried the ark of God with the poles on their
shoulders, as Moses had commanded in accordance with the word of
the LORD.
[16]David told the leaders of the Levites to appoint their fellow Levites
as musicians to make a joyful sound with musical instruments: lyres,
harps and cymbals.

---

[a] 11 *Baal Perazim* means *the lord who breaks out.* [b] 7 Hebrew *Gershom,* a variant of *Gershon*

17 So the Levites appointed Heman son of Joel; from his relatives,
Asaph son of Berekiah; and from their relatives the Merarites, Ethan
son of Kushaiah; 18 and with them their relatives next in rank: Zech-
ariah,[a] Jaaziel, Shemiramoth, Jehiel, Unni, Eliab, Benaiah, Maase-
iah, Mattithiah, Eliphelehu, Mikneiah, Obed-Edom and Jeiel,[b] the
gatekeepers.

19 The musicians Heman, Asaph and Ethan were to sound the bronze
cymbals; 20 Zechariah, Jaaziel,[c] Shemiramoth, Jehiel, Unni, Eliab, Maa-
seiah and Benaiah were to play the lyres according to *alamoth*,[d] 21 and
Mattithiah, Eliphelehu, Mikneiah, Obed-Edom, Jeiel and Azaziah were
to play the harps, directing according to *sheminith*.[d] 22 Kenaniah the
head Levite was in charge of the singing; that was his responsibility
because he was skillful at it.

23 Berekiah and Elkanah were to be doorkeepers for the ark. 24 Sheba-
niah, Joshaphat, Nethanel, Amasai, Zechariah, Benaiah and Eliezer the
priests were to blow trumpets before the ark of God. Obed-Edom and
Jehiah were also to be doorkeepers for the ark.

25 So David and the elders of Israel and the commanders of units of
a thousand went to bring up the ark of the covenant of the LORD from
the house of Obed-Edom, with rejoicing. 26 Because God had helped the
Levites who were carrying the ark of the covenant of the LORD, seven
bulls and seven rams were sacrificed. 27 Now David was clothed in a
robe of fine linen, as were all the Levites who were carrying the ark,
and as were the musicians, and Kenaniah, who was in charge of the
singing of the choirs. David also wore a linen ephod. 28 So all Israel
brought up the ark of the covenant of the LORD with shouts, with the
sounding of rams' horns and trumpets, and of cymbals, and the play-
ing of lyres and harps.

29 As the ark of the covenant of the LORD was entering the City of
David, Michal daughter of Saul watched from a window. And when
she saw King David dancing and celebrating, she despised him in her
heart.

MINISTERING BEFORE THE ARK

16 They brought the ark of God and set it inside the tent that David
had pitched for it, and they presented burnt offerings and fel-
lowship offerings before God. 2 After David had finished sacrificing the
burnt offerings and fellowship offerings, he blessed the people in the
name of the LORD. 3 Then he gave a loaf of bread, a cake of dates and a
cake of raisins to each Israelite man and woman.

4 He appointed some of the Levites to minister before the ark of the
LORD, to extol,[e] thank, and praise the LORD, the God of Israel: 5 Asaph
was the chief, and next to him in rank were Zechariah, then Jaaziel,[f]
Shemiramoth, Jehiel, Mattithiah, Eliab, Benaiah, Obed-Edom and Jeiel.
They were to play the lyres and harps, Asaph was to sound the cymbals,
6 and Benaiah and Jahaziel the priests were to blow the trumpets reg-
ularly before the ark of the covenant of God.

PRAYING SCRIPTURE

1 Chronicles 16

With the ark placed in the tabernacle David had erected, the Levites commenced their ministry (see verse 4). David, ever the poet and songwriter, provided a lengthy song of thanksgiving. It recounts the faithfulness of God to his people and mentions God's goodness, power, salvation and covenant.

We need not write a song to have a song. Include the lyrics of your favorite hymn or spiritual song the next time you offer prayer.

---

[a] *18* Three Hebrew manuscripts and most Septuagint manuscripts (see also verse 20 and 16:5); most Hebrew manuscripts *Zechariah son and* or *Zechariah, Ben and* [b] *18* Hebrew; Septuagint (see also verse 21) *Jeiel and Azaziah*
[c] *20* See verse 18; Hebrew *Aziel*, a variant of *Jaaziel*. [d] *20,21* Probably a musical term [e] *4* Or *petition*; or *invoke* [f] *5* See 15:18,20; Hebrew *Jeiel*, possibly another name for *Jaaziel*.

7 That day David first appointed Asaph and his associates to give
praise to the LORD in this manner:

8 Give praise to the LORD, proclaim his name;
make known among the nations what he has done.
9 Sing to him, sing praise to him;
tell of all his wonderful acts.
10 Glory in his holy name;
let the hearts of those who seek the LORD rejoice.
11 Look to the LORD and his strength;
seek his face always.
12 Remember the wonders he has done,
his miracles, and the judgments he pronounced,
13 you his servants, the descendants of Israel,
his chosen ones, the children of Jacob.
14 He is the LORD our God;
his judgments are in all the earth.

15 He remembers[a] his covenant forever,
the promise he made, for a thousand generations,
16 the covenant he made with Abraham,
the oath he swore to Isaac.
17 He confirmed it to Jacob as a decree,
to Israel as an everlasting covenant:
18 "To you I will give the land of Canaan
as the portion you will inherit."

19 When they were but few in number,
few indeed, and strangers in it,
20 they[b] wandered from nation to nation,
from one kingdom to another.
21 He allowed no one to oppress them;
for their sake he rebuked kings:
22 "Do not touch my anointed ones;
do my prophets no harm."

23 Sing to the LORD, all the earth;
proclaim his salvation day after day.
24 Declare his glory among the nations,
his marvelous deeds among all peoples.

25 For great is the LORD and most worthy of praise;
he is to be feared above all gods.
26 For all the gods of the nations are idols,
but the LORD made the heavens.
27 Splendor and majesty are before him;
strength and joy are in his dwelling place.
28 Ascribe to the LORD, all you families of nations,
ascribe to the LORD glory and strength.
29 Ascribe to the LORD the glory due his name;
bring an offering and come before him.

---

[a] *15* Some Septuagint manuscripts (see also Psalm 105:8); Hebrew *Remember*
[b] *18-20* One Hebrew manuscript, Septuagint and Vulgate (see also Psalm 105:12); most Hebrew manuscripts *inherit, / [19]though you are but few in number, / few indeed, and strangers in it." / [20]They*

Worship the LORD in the splendor of his[a] holiness.
30 Tremble before him, all the earth!
The world is firmly established; it cannot be moved.

31 Let the heavens rejoice, let the earth be glad;
let them say among the nations, "The LORD reigns!"
32 Let the sea resound, and all that is in it;
let the fields be jubilant, and everything in them!
33 Let the trees of the forest sing,
let them sing for joy before the LORD,
for he comes to judge the earth.

34 Give thanks to the LORD, for he is good;
his love endures forever.
35 Cry out, "Save us, God our Savior;
gather us and deliver us from the nations,
that we may give thanks to your holy name,
and glory in your praise."
36 Praise be to the LORD, the God of Israel,
from everlasting to everlasting.

Then all the people said "Amen" and "Praise the LORD."

37 David left Asaph and his associates before the ark of the covenant
of the LORD to minister there regularly, according to each day's re-
quirements. 38 He also left Obed-Edom and his sixty-eight associates
to minister with them. Obed-Edom son of Jeduthun, and also Hosah,
were gatekeepers.
39 David left Zadok the priest and his fellow priests before the taber-
nacle of the LORD at the high place in Gibeon 40 to present burnt offer-
ings to the LORD on the altar of burnt offering regularly, morning and
evening, in accordance with everything written in the Law of the LORD,
which he had given Israel. 41 With them were Heman and Jeduthun
and the rest of those chosen and designated by name to give thanks to
the LORD, "for his love endures forever." 42 Heman and Jeduthun were
responsible for the sounding of the trumpets and cymbals and for the
playing of the other instruments for sacred song. The sons of Jeduthun
were stationed at the gate.
43 Then all the people left, each for their own home, and David re-
turned home to bless his family.

GOD'S PROMISE TO DAVID

17 After David was settled in his palace, he said to Nathan the
prophet, "Here I am, living in a house of cedar, while the ark of
the covenant of the LORD is under a tent."
2 Nathan replied to David, "Whatever you have in mind, do it, for God
is with you."
3 But that night the word of God came to Nathan, saying:
4 "Go and tell my servant David, 'This is what the LORD says: You
are not the one to build me a house to dwell in. 5 I have not dwelt
in a house from the day I brought Israel up out of Egypt to this day.
I have moved from one tent site to another, from one dwelling
place to another. 6 Wherever I have moved with all the Israelites,

PRAYING SCRIPTURE

1 Chronicles 17

After learning that God would not allow him to build a temple, David sat down and prayed. In this prayer David humbled himself to accept God's will. He acknowledged God's wisdom and power. David was satisfied that God's will would be done even if his wasn't.

Rejoicing for God's will in the face of personal disappointment is hard, but God can place within you a joyous heart of praise.

[a] 29 Or *LORD with the splendor of*

did I ever say to any of their leaders[a] whom I commanded to shepherd my people, “Why have you not built me a house of cedar?”’

7 “Now then, tell my servant David, ‘This is what the LORD Almighty says: I took you from the pasture, from tending the flock, and appointed you ruler over my people Israel. 8 I have been with you wherever you have gone, and I have cut off all your enemies from before you. Now I will make your name like the names of the greatest men on earth. 9 And I will provide a place for my people Israel and will plant them so that they can have a home of their own and no longer be disturbed. Wicked people will not oppress them anymore, as they did at the beginning 10 and have done ever since the time I appointed leaders over my people Israel. I will also subdue all your enemies.

“‘I declare to you that the LORD will build a house for you: 11 When your days are over and you go to be with your ancestors, I will raise up your offspring to succeed you, one of your own sons, and I will establish his kingdom. 12 He is the one who will build a house for me, and I will establish his throne forever. 13 I will be his father, and he will be my son. I will never take my love away from him, as I took it away from your predecessor. 14 I will set him over my house and my kingdom forever; his throne will be established forever.’”

15 Nathan reported to David all the words of this entire revelation.

DAVID’S PRAYER

16 Then King David went in and sat before the LORD, and he said:

“Who am I, LORD God, and what is my family, that you have brought me this far? 17 And as if this were not enough in your sight, my God, you have spoken about the future of the house of your servant. You, LORD God, have looked on me as though I were the most exalted of men.

18 “What more can David say to you for honoring your servant? For you know your servant, 19 LORD. For the sake of your servant and according to your will, you have done this great thing and made known all these great promises.

20 “There is no one like you, LORD, and there is no God but you, as we have heard with our own ears. 21 And who is like your people Israel — the one nation on earth whose God went out to redeem a people for himself, and to make a name for yourself, and to perform great and awesome wonders by driving out nations from before your people, whom you redeemed from Egypt? 22 You made your people Israel your very own forever, and you, LORD, have become their God.

23 “And now, LORD, let the promise you have made concerning your servant and his house be established forever. Do as you promised, 24 so that it will be established and that your name will be great forever. Then people will say, ‘The LORD Almighty, the God over Israel, is Israel’s God!’ And the house of your servant David will be established before you.

25 “You, my God, have revealed to your servant that you will build a house for him. So your servant has found courage to pray to you. 26 You, LORD, are God! You have promised these good things

[a] 6 Traditionally *judges*; also in verse 10

to your servant. 27Now you have been pleased to bless the house of
your servant, that it may continue forever in your sight; for you,
LORD, have blessed it, and it will be blessed forever."

DAVID'S VICTORIES

18 In the course of time, David defeated the Philistines and sub-
dued them, and he took Gath and its surrounding villages from
the control of the Philistines.
2David also defeated the Moabites, and they became subject to him
and brought him tribute.
3Moreover, David defeated Hadadezer king of Zobah, in the vicinity
of Hamath, when he went to set up his monument at[a] the Euphra-
tes River. 4David captured a thousand of his chariots, seven thousand
charioteers and twenty thousand foot soldiers. He hamstrung all but a
hundred of the chariot horses.
5When the Arameans of Damascus came to help Hadadezer king of
Zobah, David struck down twenty-two thousand of them. 6He put gar-
risons in the Aramean kingdom of Damascus, and the Arameans be-
came subject to him and brought him tribute. The LORD gave David
victory wherever he went.
7David took the gold shields carried by the officers of Hadadezer and
brought them to Jerusalem. 8From Tebah[b] and Kun, towns that belonged
to Hadadezer, David took a great quantity of bronze, which Solomon
used to make the bronze Sea, the pillars and various bronze articles.
9When Tou king of Hamath heard that David had defeated the entire
army of Hadadezer king of Zobah, 10he sent his son Hadoram to King
David to greet him and congratulate him on his victory in battle over
Hadadezer, who had been at war with Tou. Hadoram brought all kinds
of articles of gold, of silver and of bronze.
11King David dedicated these articles to the LORD, as he had done
with the silver and gold he had taken from all these nations: Edom and
Moab, the Ammonites and the Philistines, and Amalek.
12Abishai son of Zeruiah struck down eighteen thousand Edomites in
the Valley of Salt. 13He put garrisons in Edom, and all the Edomites be-
came subject to David. The LORD gave David victory wherever he went.

DAVID'S OFFICIALS

14David reigned over all Israel, doing what was just and right for all
his people. 15Joab son of Zeruiah was over the army; Jehoshaphat son
of Ahilud was recorder; 16Zadok son of Ahitub and Ahimelek[c] son of
Abiathar were priests; Shavsha was secretary; 17Benaiah son of Jehoi-
ada was over the Kerethites and Pelethites; and David's sons were chief
officials at the king's side.

DAVID DEFEATS THE AMMONITES

19 In the course of time, Nahash king of the Ammonites died, and
his son succeeded him as king. 2David thought, "I will show
kindness to Hanun son of Nahash, because his father showed kindness
to me." So David sent a delegation to express his sympathy to Hanun
concerning his father.

[a] 3 Or *to restore his control over* [b] 8 Hebrew *Tibhath*, a variant of *Tebah*
[c] 16 Some Hebrew manuscripts, Vulgate and Syriac (see also 2 Samuel 8:17); most Hebrew manuscripts *Abimelek*

PRAYING SCRIPTURE

1 Chronicles 18

While David's military exploits expanded Israel's borders, his captures brought gold, silver and bronze articles into his wealth. The Bible says, "King David dedicated these articles to the LORD" (verse 11). This had become the king's practice when capturing riches during battle.

Have you ever dedicated your possessions to God, including the things you value most? It's a great way to be reminded that all you have really belongs to him.

PRAYING SCRIPTURE

1 Chronicles 19

One prayer that seems hardest to pray is "Your will be done." When faced with a daunting foe, Joab encouraged his brother, "Be strong." Then he said, "The LORD will do what is good in his sight" (verse 13). They had no guarantee of victory; this was a prayer of faith.

Praying in faith does not always mean we know God's will. Sometimes it prepares us to accept God's will, whatever it is.

When David's envoys came to Hanun in the land of the Ammonites
to express sympathy to him, 3the Ammonite commanders said to Ha-
nun, "Do you think David is honoring your father by sending envoys
to you to express sympathy? Haven't his envoys come to you only to
explore and spy out the country and overthrow it?" 4So Hanun seized
David's envoys, shaved them, cut off their garments at the buttocks,
and sent them away.

5When someone came and told David about the men, he sent mes-
sengers to meet them, for they were greatly humiliated. The king said,
"Stay at Jericho till your beards have grown, and then come back."

6When the Ammonites realized that they had become obnoxious to
David, Hanun and the Ammonites sent a thousand talents[a] of silver
to hire chariots and charioteers from Aram Naharaim,[b] Aram Maakah
and Zobah. 7They hired thirty-two thousand chariots and charioteers,
as well as the king of Maakah with his troops, who came and camped
near Medeba, while the Ammonites were mustered from their towns
and moved out for battle.

8On hearing this, David sent Joab out with the entire army of fight-
ing men. 9The Ammonites came out and drew up in battle formation
at the entrance to their city, while the kings who had come were by
themselves in the open country.

10Joab saw that there were battle lines in front of him and behind
him; so he selected some of the best troops in Israel and deployed
them against the Arameans. 11He put the rest of the men under the
command of Abishai his brother, and they were deployed against the
Ammonites. 12Joab said, "If the Arameans are too strong for me, then
you are to rescue me; but if the Ammonites are too strong for you, then
I will rescue you. 13Be strong, and let us fight bravely for our people
and the cities of our God. The LORD will do what is good in his sight."

14Then Joab and the troops with him advanced to fight the Arame-
ans, and they fled before him. 15When the Ammonites realized that the
Arameans were fleeing, they too fled before his brother Abishai and
went inside the city. So Joab went back to Jerusalem.

16After the Arameans saw that they had been routed by Israel, they
sent messengers and had Arameans brought from beyond the Euphra-
tes River, with Shophak the commander of Hadadezer's army leading
them.

17When David was told of this, he gathered all Israel and crossed the
Jordan; he advanced against them and formed his battle lines oppo-
site them. David formed his lines to meet the Arameans in battle, and
they fought against him. 18But they fled before Israel, and David killed
seven thousand of their charioteers and forty thousand of their foot
soldiers. He also killed Shophak the commander of their army.

19When the vassals of Hadadezer saw that they had been routed by
Israel, they made peace with David and became subject to him.

So the Arameans were not willing to help the Ammonites anymore.

THE CAPTURE OF RABBAH

20 In the spring, at the time when kings go off to war, Joab led
out the armed forces. He laid waste the land of the Ammonites
and went to Rabbah and besieged it, but David remained in Jerusalem.

PRAYING SCRIPTURE

1 Chronicles 20

Absent from one battle in this chapter is King David. Verse 1 says it was the time that kings went to battle, yet David stayed home in Jerusalem while Joab defeated Rabbah. This is the preamble to David's sin with Bathsheba. David involved himself only when made aware of the significant spoils.

It is never good to presume upon God's goodness. Pray that God will keep your heart and mind on him.

[a] 6 That is, about 38 tons or about 34 metric tons [b] 6 That is, Northwest Mesopotamia

Joab attacked Rabbah and left it in ruins. 2David took the crown from
the head of their king[a] — its weight was found to be a talent[b] of gold,
and it was set with precious stones — and it was placed on David's head.
He took a great quantity of plunder from the city 3and brought out the
people who were there, consigning them to labor with saws and with
iron picks and axes. David did this to all the Ammonite towns. Then
David and his entire army returned to Jerusalem.

WAR WITH THE PHILISTINES

4In the course of time, war broke out with the Philistines, at Gezer. At
that time Sibbekai the Hushathite killed Sippai, one of the descendants
of the Rephaites, and the Philistines were subjugated.
5In another battle with the Philistines, Elhanan son of Jair killed
Lahmi the brother of Goliath the Gittite, who had a spear with a shaft
like a weaver's rod.
6In still another battle, which took place at Gath, there was a
huge man with six fingers on each hand and six toes on each
foot — twenty-four in all. He also was descended from Rapha. 7When
he taunted Israel, Jonathan son of Shimea, David's brother, killed him.
8These were descendants of Rapha in Gath, and they fell at the hands
of David and his men.

DAVID COUNTS THE FIGHTING MEN

21 Satan rose up against Israel and incited David to take a census of
Israel. 2So David said to Joab and the commanders of the troops,
"Go and count the Israelites from Beersheba to Dan. Then report back
to me so that I may know how many there are."
3But Joab replied, "May the LORD multiply his troops a hundred
times over. My lord the king, are they not all my lord's subjects? Why
does my lord want to do this? Why should he bring guilt on Israel?"
4The king's word, however, overruled Joab; so Joab left and went
throughout Israel and then came back to Jerusalem. 5Joab reported
the number of the fighting men to David: In all Israel there were one
million one hundred thousand men who could handle a sword, includ-
ing four hundred and seventy thousand in Judah.
6But Joab did not include Levi and Benjamin in the numbering, be-
cause the king's command was repulsive to him. 7This command was
also evil in the sight of God; so he punished Israel.
8Then David said to God, "I have sinned greatly by doing this. Now,
I beg you, take away the guilt of your servant. I have done a very fool-
ish thing."
9The LORD said to Gad, David's seer, 10"Go and tell David, 'This is what
the LORD says: I am giving you three options. Choose one of them for
me to carry out against you.'"
11So Gad went to David and said to him, "This is what the LORD says:
'Take your choice: 12three years of famine, three months of being swept
away[c] before your enemies, with their swords overtaking you, or three
days of the sword of the LORD — days of plague in the land, with the
angel of the LORD ravaging every part of Israel.' Now then, decide how
I should answer the one who sent me."

[a] 2 Or *of Milkom,* that is, Molek [b] 2 That is, about 75 pounds or about 34 kilograms [c] 12 Hebrew; Septuagint and Vulgate (see also 2 Samuel 24:13) *of fleeing*

PRAYING SCRIPTURE

1 Chronicles 21

David's sin of counting Israelites prompted a visit from an angel who carried out God's judgment on the people. Even though David repented of his sin, tens of thousands of Israelites died because of his actions. David feared the angel was coming for him even after he sacrificed a peace offering.

Even when sin is committed in private, public consequences are very real. Ask God to keep you from sin so neither you nor others will be hurt by it.

13 David said to Gad, "I am in deep distress. Let me fall into the hands
of the LORD, for his mercy is very great; but do not let me fall into hu-
man hands."
14 So the LORD sent a plague on Israel, and seventy thousand men of
Israel fell dead. 15 And God sent an angel to destroy Jerusalem. But as
the angel was doing so, the LORD saw it and relented concerning the
disaster and said to the angel who was destroying the people, "Enough!
Withdraw your hand." The angel of the LORD was then standing at the
threshing floor of Araunah[a] the Jebusite.
16 David looked up and saw the angel of the LORD standing be-
tween heaven and earth, with a drawn sword in his hand extended
over Jerusalem. Then David and the elders, clothed in sackcloth, fell
facedown.
17 David said to God, "Was it not I who ordered the fighting men to
be counted? I, the shepherd,[b] have sinned and done wrong. These are
but sheep. What have they done? LORD my God, let your hand fall on
me and my family, but do not let this plague remain on your people."

DAVID BUILDS AN ALTAR

18 Then the angel of the LORD ordered Gad to tell David to go up and
build an altar to the LORD on the threshing floor of Araunah the Jebu-
site. 19 So David went up in obedience to the word that Gad had spoken
in the name of the LORD.
20 While Araunah was threshing wheat, he turned and saw the an-
gel; his four sons who were with him hid themselves. 21 Then David
approached, and when Araunah looked and saw him, he left the
threshing floor and bowed down before David with his face to the
ground.
22 David said to him, "Let me have the site of your threshing floor so
I can build an altar to the LORD, that the plague on the people may be
stopped. Sell it to me at the full price."
23 Araunah said to David, "Take it! Let my lord the king do whatever
pleases him. Look, I will give the oxen for the burnt offerings, the
threshing sledges for the wood, and the wheat for the grain offering.
I will give all this."
24 But King David replied to Araunah, "No, I insist on paying the full
price. I will not take for the LORD what is yours, or sacrifice a burnt of-
fering that costs me nothing."
25 So David paid Araunah six hundred shekels[c] of gold for the site.
26 David built an altar to the LORD there and sacrificed burnt offer-
ings and fellowship offerings. He called on the LORD, and the LORD
answered him with fire from heaven on the altar of burnt offering.
27 Then the LORD spoke to the angel, and he put his sword back into
its sheath. 28 At that time, when David saw that the LORD had answered
him on the threshing floor of Araunah the Jebusite, he offered sacri-
fices there. 29 The tabernacle of the LORD, which Moses had made in
the wilderness, and the altar of burnt offering were at that time on
the high place at Gibeon. 30 But David could not go before it to inquire
of God, because he was afraid of the sword of the angel of the LORD.

---

[a] *15* Hebrew *Ornan,* a variant of *Araunah;* also in verses 18-28 [b] *17* Probable reading of the original Hebrew text (see 2 Samuel 24:17 and note); Masoretic Text does not have *the shepherd.* [c] *25* That is, about 15 pounds or about 6.9 kilograms

22 Then David said, "The house of the LORD God is to be here, and
also the altar of burnt offering for Israel."

PREPARATIONS FOR THE TEMPLE

2So David gave orders to assemble the foreigners residing in Israel,
and from among them he appointed stonecutters to prepare dressed
stone for building the house of God. 3He provided a large amount of
iron to make nails for the doors of the gateways and for the fittings,
and more bronze than could be weighed. 4He also provided more cedar
logs than could be counted, for the Sidonians and Tyrians had brought
large numbers of them to David.

5David said, "My son Solomon is young and inexperienced, and the
house to be built for the LORD should be of great magnificence and
fame and splendor in the sight of all the nations. Therefore I will make
preparations for it." So David made extensive preparations before his
death.

6Then he called for his son Solomon and charged him to build a
house for the LORD, the God of Israel. 7David said to Solomon: "My
son, I had it in my heart to build a house for the Name of the LORD
my God. 8But this word of the LORD came to me: 'You have shed much
blood and have fought many wars. You are not to build a house for my
Name, because you have shed much blood on the earth in my sight.
9But you will have a son who will be a man of peace and rest, and I
will give him rest from all his enemies on every side. His name will
be Solomon,[a] and I will grant Israel peace and quiet during his reign.
10He is the one who will build a house for my Name. He will be my son,
and I will be his father. And I will establish the throne of his kingdom
over Israel forever.'

11"Now, my son, the LORD be with you, and may you have success
and build the house of the LORD your God, as he said you would. 12May
the LORD give you discretion and understanding when he puts you in
command over Israel, so that you may keep the law of the LORD your
God. 13Then you will have success if you are careful to observe the de-
crees and laws that the LORD gave Moses for Israel. Be strong and cou-
rageous. Do not be afraid or discouraged.

14"I have taken great pains to provide for the temple of the LORD a
hundred thousand talents[b] of gold, a million talents[c] of silver, quanti-
ties of bronze and iron too great to be weighed, and wood and stone.
And you may add to them. 15You have many workers: stonecutters,
masons and carpenters, as well as those skilled in every kind of work
16in gold and silver, bronze and iron — craftsmen beyond number. Now
begin the work, and the LORD be with you."

17Then David ordered all the leaders of Israel to help his son Solo-
mon. 18He said to them, "Is not the LORD your God with you? And has
he not granted you rest on every side? For he has given the inhabitants
of the land into my hands, and the land is subject to the LORD and to his
people. 19Now devote your heart and soul to seeking the LORD your God.
Begin to build the sanctuary of the LORD God, so that you may bring
the ark of the covenant of the LORD and the sacred articles belonging
to God into the temple that will be built for the Name of the LORD."

[a] 9 *Solomon* sounds like and may be derived from the Hebrew for *peace.*
[b] *14* That is, about 3,750 tons or about 3,400 metric tons [c] *14* That is, about 37,500 tons or about 34,000 metric tons

PRAYING SCRIPTURE

1 Chronicles 22

Few things roused King David's heart like the prospect of building the temple. But because David had killed so many people, God forbade him. The honor would go to Solomon. God allowed David to secure all the building materials so it would be "of great magnificence and fame and splendor" (verse 5).

David's desire was right, but God said no. Tell God you trust his no even when you want to hear his yes.

PRAYING SCRIPTURE

1 Chronicles 22

In preparing Solomon to build the temple, David gave him an inventory of the building materials, including more gold, silver, bronze and iron than he could use. That David had a heart for a permanent place of worship is beyond dispute.

David was a generous man. While the average person cannot give millions of dollars, we all can ask God to give us generous hearts in giving.

THE LEVITES

23 When David was old and full of years, he made his son Solomon
king over Israel.
2 He also gathered together all the leaders of Israel, as well as the
priests and Levites. 3 The Levites thirty years old or more were counted,
and the total number of men was thirty-eight thousand. 4 David said,
"Of these, twenty-four thousand are to be in charge of the work of the
temple of the LORD and six thousand are to be officials and judges. 5 Four
thousand are to be gatekeepers and four thousand are to praise the
LORD with the musical instruments I have provided for that purpose."
6 David separated the Levites into divisions corresponding to the
sons of Levi: Gershon, Kohath and Merari.

GERSHONITES

7 Belonging to the Gershonites:
Ladan and Shimei.
8 The sons of Ladan:
Jehiel the first, Zetham and Joel — three in all.
9 The sons of Shimei:
Shelomoth, Haziel and Haran — three in all.
These were the heads of the families of Ladan.
10 And the sons of Shimei:
Jahath, Ziza,[a] Jeush and Beriah.
These were the sons of Shimei — four in all.
11 Jahath was the first and Ziza the second, but Jeush and Beriah
did not have many sons; so they were counted as one family
with one assignment.

KOHATHITES

12 The sons of Kohath:
Amram, Izhar, Hebron and Uzziel — four in all.
13 The sons of Amram:
Aaron and Moses.
Aaron was set apart, he and his descendants forever, to conse-
crate the most holy things, to offer sacrifices before the LORD,
to minister before him and to pronounce blessings in his name
forever. 14 The sons of Moses the man of God were counted as
part of the tribe of Levi.
15 The sons of Moses:
Gershom and Eliezer.
16 The descendants of Gershom:
Shubael was the first.
17 The descendants of Eliezer:
Rehabiah was the first.
Eliezer had no other sons, but the sons of Rehabiah were very
numerous.
18 The sons of Izhar:
Shelomith was the first.
19 The sons of Hebron:
Jeriah the first, Amariah the second, Jahaziel the third and Jek-
ameam the fourth.

[a] *10* One Hebrew manuscript, Septuagint and Vulgate (see also verse 11); most Hebrew manuscripts *Zina*

PRAYING SCRIPTURE

1 Chronicles 23

In keeping with his focus on Israel's religious history, the writer lists the Levites' assignments: workers in temple ministry and as officers and judges, gatekeepers and musicians. Worship with structured leadership was critical for Israel's survival.

The New Testament reminds us that God is a God of order. This is to be seen in the churches. Ask God to help you be a part of order in your church as a witness to him.

20 The sons of Uzziel:
Micah the first and Ishiah the second.

MERARITES

21 The sons of Merari:
Mahli and Mushi.
The sons of Mahli:
Eleazar and Kish.
22 Eleazar died without having sons: he had only daughters. Their
cousins, the sons of Kish, married them.
23 The sons of Mushi:
Mahli, Eder and Jerimoth — three in all.

24 These were the descendants of Levi by their families — the heads
of families as they were registered under their names and counted in-
dividually, that is, the workers twenty years old or more who served in
the temple of the LORD. 25 For David had said, "Since the LORD, the God
of Israel, has granted rest to his people and has come to dwell in Jerusa-
lem forever, 26 the Levites no longer need to carry the tabernacle or any
of the articles used in its service." 27 According to the last instructions of
David, the Levites were counted from those twenty years old or more.

28 The duty of the Levites was to help Aaron's descendants in the ser-
vice of the temple of the LORD: to be in charge of the courtyards, the
side rooms, the purification of all sacred things and the performance
of other duties at the house of God. 29 They were in charge of the bread
set out on the table, the special flour for the grain offerings, the thin
loaves made without yeast, the baking and the mixing, and all mea-
surements of quantity and size. 30 They were also to stand every morn-
ing to thank and praise the LORD. They were to do the same in the
evening 31 and whenever burnt offerings were presented to the LORD
on the Sabbaths, at the New Moon feasts and at the appointed festivals.
They were to serve before the LORD regularly in the proper number
and in the way prescribed for them.

32 And so the Levites carried out their responsibilities for the tent of
meeting, for the Holy Place and, under their relatives the descendants
of Aaron, for the service of the temple of the LORD.

THE DIVISIONS OF PRIESTS

24 These were the divisions of the descendants of Aaron:
The sons of Aaron were Nadab, Abihu, Eleazar and Ithamar.
2 But Nadab and Abihu died before their father did, and they had no
sons; so Eleazar and Ithamar served as the priests. 3 With the help of
Zadok a descendant of Eleazar and Ahimelek a descendant of Ithamar,
David separated them into divisions for their appointed order of min-
istering. 4 A larger number of leaders were found among Eleazar's de-
scendants than among Ithamar's, and they were divided accordingly:
sixteen heads of families from Eleazar's descendants and eight heads
of families from Ithamar's descendants. 5 They divided them impar-
tially by casting lots, for there were officials of the sanctuary and offi-
cials of God among the descendants of both Eleazar and Ithamar.

6 The scribe Shemaiah son of Nethanel, a Levite, recorded their
names in the presence of the king and of the officials: Zadok the priest,
Ahimelek son of Abiathar and the heads of families of the priests and
of the Levites — one family being taken from Eleazar and then one
from Ithamar.

PRAYING SCRIPTURE

1 Chronicles 24

The priests of Israel were responsible for carrying out ministry in the temple. To meet the needs of the people, they were put on a schedule for service. There were many priests, all of whom stood before God on behalf of the people.

Ministry to God's people is a difficult, grueling task. In some churches, this ministry falls to a single pastor. Pray fervently for God to sustain yours.

7 The first lot fell to Jehoiarib,
the second to Jedaiah,
8 the third to Harim,
the fourth to Seorim,
9 the fifth to Malkijah,
the sixth to Mijamin,
10 the seventh to Hakkoz,
the eighth to Abijah,
11 the ninth to Jeshua,
the tenth to Shekaniah,
12 the eleventh to Eliashib,
the twelfth to Jakim,
13 the thirteenth to Huppah,
the fourteenth to Jeshebeab,
14 the fifteenth to Bilgah,
the sixteenth to Immer,
15 the seventeenth to Hezir,
the eighteenth to Happizzez,
16 the nineteenth to Pethahiah,
the twentieth to Jehezkel,
17 the twenty-first to Jakin,
the twenty-second to Gamul,
18 the twenty-third to Delaiah
and the twenty-fourth to Maaziah.

19 This was their appointed order of ministering when they entered
the temple of the LORD, according to the regulations prescribed for
them by their ancestor Aaron, as the LORD, the God of Israel, had com-
manded him.

THE REST OF THE LEVITES

20 As for the rest of the descendants of Levi:
from the sons of Amram: Shubael;
from the sons of Shubael: Jehdeiah.
21 As for Rehabiah, from his sons:
Ishiah was the first.
22 From the Izharites: Shelomoth;
from the sons of Shelomoth: Jahath.
23 The sons of Hebron: Jeriah the first,[a] Amariah the second, Jahaziel
the third and Jekameam the fourth.
24 The son of Uzziel: Micah;
from the sons of Micah: Shamir.
25 The brother of Micah: Ishiah;
from the sons of Ishiah: Zechariah.
26 The sons of Merari: Mahli and Mushi.
The son of Jaaziah: Beno.
27 The sons of Merari:
from Jaaziah: Beno, Shoham, Zakkur and Ibri.
28 From Mahli: Eleazar, who had no sons.
29 From Kish: the son of Kish:
Jerahmeel.
30 And the sons of Mushi: Mahli, Eder and Jerimoth.

[a] *23* Two Hebrew manuscripts and some Septuagint manuscripts (see also 23:19); most Hebrew manuscripts *The sons of Jeriah:*

These were the Levites, according to their families. 31They also cast lots, just as their relatives the descendants of Aaron did, in the presence of King David and of Zadok, Ahimelek, and the heads of families of the priests and of the Levites. The families of the oldest brother were treated the same as those of the youngest.

THE MUSICIANS

25 David, together with the commanders of the army, set apart some of the sons of Asaph, Heman and Jeduthun for the ministry of prophesying, accompanied by harps, lyres and cymbals. Here is the list of the men who performed this service:

2From the sons of Asaph:

Zakkur, Joseph, Nethaniah and Asarelah. The sons of Asaph were under the supervision of Asaph, who prophesied under the king's supervision.

3As for Jeduthun, from his sons:

Gedaliah, Zeri, Jeshaiah, Shimei,[a] Hashabiah and Mattithiah, six in all, under the supervision of their father Jeduthun, who prophesied, using the harp in thanking and praising the LORD.

4As for Heman, from his sons:

Bukkiah, Mattaniah, Uzziel, Shubael and Jerimoth; Hananiah, Hanani, Eliathah, Giddalti and Romamti-Ezer; Joshbekashah, Mallothi, Hothir and Mahazioth. 5(All these were sons of Heman the king's seer. They were given him through the promises of God to exalt him. God gave Heman fourteen sons and three daughters.)

6All these men were under the supervision of their father for the music of the temple of the LORD, with cymbals, lyres and harps, for the ministry at the house of God.

Asaph, Jeduthun and Heman were under the supervision of the king. 7Along with their relatives—all of them trained and skilled in music for the LORD—they numbered 288. 8Young and old alike, teacher as well as student, cast lots for their duties.

9The first lot, which was for Asaph, fell to Joseph,
his sons and relatives[b] 12[c]
the second to Gedaliah,
him and his relatives and sons 12
10the third to Zakkur,
his sons and relatives 12
11the fourth to Izri,[d]
his sons and relatives 12
12the fifth to Nethaniah,
his sons and relatives 12
13the sixth to Bukkiah,
his sons and relatives 12
14the seventh to Jesarelah,[e]
his sons and relatives 12
15the eighth to Jeshaiah,
his sons and relatives 12

PRAYING SCRIPTURE

1 Chronicles 25

Israel's music training program was detailed and specific. These skilled players were said to "prophesy" with their musical instruments (see verse 1). That is an uncommon idea; in our day musicians are thought to play.

God invented music and provided that it be part of worship. He said music is a means of prophecy, thanksgiving and praise. Pray for those who prophesy musically where you worship.

[a] *3* One Hebrew manuscript and some Septuagint manuscripts (see also verse 17); most Hebrew manuscripts do not have *Shimei.* [b] *9* See Septuagint; Hebrew does not have *his sons and relatives.* [c] *9* See the total in verse 7; Hebrew does not have *twelve.* [d] *11* A variant of *Zeri* [e] *14* A variant of *Asarelah*

[16] the ninth to Mattaniah,
his sons and relatives 12
[17] the tenth to Shimei,
his sons and relatives 12
[18] the eleventh to Azarel,[a]
his sons and relatives 12
[19] the twelfth to Hashabiah,
his sons and relatives 12
[20] the thirteenth to Shubael,
his sons and relatives 12
[21] the fourteenth to Mattithiah,
his sons and relatives 12
[22] the fifteenth to Jerimoth,
his sons and relatives 12
[23] the sixteenth to Hananiah,
his sons and relatives 12
[24] the seventeenth to Joshbekashah,
his sons and relatives 12
[25] the eighteenth to Hanani,
his sons and relatives 12
[26] the nineteenth to Mallothi,
his sons and relatives 12
[27] the twentieth to Eliathah,
his sons and relatives 12
[28] the twenty-first to Hothir,
his sons and relatives 12
[29] the twenty-second to Giddalti,
his sons and relatives 12
[30] the twenty-third to Mahazioth,
his sons and relatives 12
[31] the twenty-fourth to Romamti-Ezer,
his sons and relatives 12.

THE GATEKEEPERS

26 The divisions of the gatekeepers:

From the Korahites: Meshelemiah son of Kore, one of the sons of Asaph.
[2] Meshelemiah had sons:
Zechariah the firstborn,
Jediael the second,
Zebadiah the third,
Jathniel the fourth,
[3] Elam the fifth,
Jehohanan the sixth
and Eliehoenai the seventh.
[4] Obed-Edom also had sons:
Shemaiah the firstborn,
Jehozabad the second,
Joah the third,
Sakar the fourth,
Nethanel the fifth,

PRAYING SCRIPTURE

1 Chronicles 26

Preference and potential politics were removed from the equation when the men cast lots for gatekeeping responsibilities. God's providence was often determined this way. They were submitting the assignment to him rather than making the decision themselves.

Sometimes God reveals his will to us in mundane ways. Not every answered prayer involves fire from heaven. Ask God to help you follow him in simple faith, accepting the "lot" that often guides us.

[a] 18 A variant of *Uzziel*

5 Ammiel the sixth,
Issachar the seventh
and Peullethai the eighth.
(For God had blessed Obed-Edom.)

6 Obed-Edom's son Shemaiah also had sons, who were leaders in
their father's family because they were very capable men. 7 The
sons of Shemaiah: Othni, Rephael, Obed and Elzabad; his rela-
tives Elihu and Semakiah were also able men. 8 All these were
descendants of Obed-Edom; they and their sons and their rela-
tives were capable men with the strength to do the work—de-
scendants of Obed-Edom, 62 in all.
9 Meshelemiah had sons and relatives, who were able men—18 in
all.
10 Hosah the Merarite had sons: Shimri the first (although he was
not the firstborn, his father had appointed him the first), 11 Hil-
kiah the second, Tabaliah the third and Zechariah the fourth.
The sons and relatives of Hosah were 13 in all.

12 These divisions of the gatekeepers, through their leaders, had du-
ties for ministering in the temple of the LORD, just as their relatives
had. 13 Lots were cast for each gate, according to their families, young
and old alike.
14 The lot for the East Gate fell to Shelemiah.[a] Then lots were cast
for his son Zechariah, a wise counselor, and the lot for the North Gate
fell to him. 15 The lot for the South Gate fell to Obed-Edom, and the lot
for the storehouse fell to his sons. 16 The lots for the West Gate and the
Shalleketh Gate on the upper road fell to Shuppim and Hosah.

Guard was alongside of guard: 17 There were six Levites a day on the
east, four a day on the north, four a day on the south and two at a time
at the storehouse. 18 As for the court[b] to the west, there were four at the
road and two at the court[b] itself.
19 These were the divisions of the gatekeepers who were descendants
of Korah and Merari.

THE TREASURERS AND OTHER OFFICIALS

20 Their fellow Levites were[c] in charge of the treasuries of the house
of God and the treasuries for the dedicated things.
21 The descendants of Ladan, who were Gershonites through Ladan
and who were heads of families belonging to Ladan the Gershonite,
were Jehieli, 22 the sons of Jehieli, Zetham and his brother Joel. They
were in charge of the treasuries of the temple of the LORD.
23 From the Amramites, the Izharites, the Hebronites and the
Uzzielites:

24 Shubael, a descendant of Gershom son of Moses, was the official in
charge of the treasuries. 25 His relatives through Eliezer: Reha-
biah his son, Jeshaiah his son, Joram his son, Zikri his son and
Shelomith his son. 26 Shelomith and his relatives were in charge
of all the treasuries for the things dedicated by King David, by
the heads of families who were the commanders of thousands
and commanders of hundreds, and by the other army com-
manders. 27 Some of the plunder taken in battle they dedicated

[a] 14 A variant of *Meshelemiah* [b] 18 The meaning of the Hebrew for this word is uncertain. [c] 20 Septuagint; Hebrew *As for the Levites, Ahijah was*

for the repair of the temple of the LORD. 28 And everything ded-
icated by Samuel the seer and by Saul son of Kish, Abner son of
Ner and Joab son of Zeruiah, and all the other dedicated things
were in the care of Shelomith and his relatives.
29 From the Izharites: Kenaniah and his sons were assigned duties
away from the temple, as officials and judges over Israel.
30 From the Hebronites: Hashabiah and his relatives — seventeen
hundred able men — were responsible in Israel west of the Jor-
dan for all the work of the LORD and for the king's service. 31 As
for the Hebronites, Jeriah was their chief according to the ge-
nealogical records of their families. In the fortieth year of Da-
vid's reign a search was made in the records, and capable men
among the Hebronites were found at Jazer in Gilead. 32 Jeriah
had twenty-seven hundred relatives, who were able men and
heads of families, and King David put them in charge of the
Reubenites, the Gadites and the half-tribe of Manasseh for every
matter pertaining to God and for the affairs of the king.

ARMY DIVISIONS

27 This is the list of the Israelites — heads of families, command-
ers of thousands and commanders of hundreds, and their of-
ficers, who served the king in all that concerned the army divisions
that were on duty month by month throughout the year. Each division
consisted of 24,000 men.

2 In charge of the first division, for the first month, was Jashobeam
son of Zabdiel. There were 24,000 men in his division. 3 He was a
descendant of Perez and chief of all the army officers for the first
month.
4 In charge of the division for the second month was Dodai the Aho-
hite; Mikloth was the leader of his division. There were 24,000
men in his division.
5 The third army commander, for the third month, was Benaiah son
of Jehoiada the priest. He was chief and there were 24,000 men
in his division. 6 This was the Benaiah who was a mighty warrior
among the Thirty and was over the Thirty. His son Ammizabad
was in charge of his division.
7 The fourth, for the fourth month, was Asahel the brother of Joab;
his son Zebadiah was his successor. There were 24,000 men in his
division.
8 The fifth, for the fifth month, was the commander Shamhuth the
Izrahite. There were 24,000 men in his division.
9 The sixth, for the sixth month, was Ira the son of Ikkesh the Tekoite.
There were 24,000 men in his division.
10 The seventh, for the seventh month, was Helez the Pelonite, an
Ephraimite. There were 24,000 men in his division.
11 The eighth, for the eighth month, was Sibbekai the Hushathite, a
Zerahite. There were 24,000 men in his division.
12 The ninth, for the ninth month, was Abiezer the Anathothite, a Ben-
jamite. There were 24,000 men in his division.
13 The tenth, for the tenth month, was Maharai the Netophathite, a
Zerahite. There were 24,000 men in his division.
14 The eleventh, for the eleventh month, was Benaiah the Pirathonite,
an Ephraimite. There were 24,000 men in his division.

PRAYING SCRIPTURE

1 Chronicles 27

Tucked away in this chapter of names and numbers of military officials, tribal leaders and other state officials is a reminder that the Lord had "promised to make Israel as numerous as the stars in the sky" (verse 23). The arm of the Lord alone had rescued Israel from Egypt, and he alone would continue to lead their campaigns.

Pray that rulers everywhere will campaign to honor the Lord God Almighty, allowing the Lord of hosts to lead them. With God at the helm, One is a majority.

15 The twelfth, for the twelfth month, was Heldai the Netophathite, from the family of Othniel. There were 24,000 men in his division.

LEADERS OF THE TRIBES

16 The leaders of the tribes of Israel:

over the Reubenites: Eliezer son of Zikri;
over the Simeonites: Shephatiah son of Maakah;
17 over Levi: Hashabiah son of Kemuel;
over Aaron: Zadok;
18 over Judah: Elihu, a brother of David;
over Issachar: Omri son of Michael;
19 over Zebulun: Ishmaiah son of Obadiah;
over Naphtali: Jerimoth son of Azriel;
20 over the Ephraimites: Hoshea son of Azaziah;
over half the tribe of Manasseh: Joel son of Pedaiah;
21 over the half-tribe of Manasseh in Gilead: Iddo son of Zechariah;
over Benjamin: Jaasiel son of Abner;
22 over Dan: Azarel son of Jeroham.
These were the leaders of the tribes of Israel.

23 David did not take the number of the men twenty years old or less,
because the LORD had promised to make Israel as numerous as the
stars in the sky. 24 Joab son of Zeruiah began to count the men but did
not finish. God's wrath came on Israel on account of this numbering,
and the number was not entered in the book[a] of the annals of King
David.

THE KING'S OVERSEERS

25 Azmaveth son of Adiel was in charge of the royal storehouses.
Jonathan son of Uzziah was in charge of the storehouses in the outlying districts, in the towns, the villages and the watchtowers.
26 Ezri son of Kelub was in charge of the workers who farmed the land.
27 Shimei the Ramathite was in charge of the vineyards.
Zabdi the Shiphmite was in charge of the produce of the vineyards for the wine vats.
28 Baal-Hanan the Gederite was in charge of the olive and sycamore-fig trees in the western foothills.
Joash was in charge of the supplies of olive oil.
29 Shitrai the Sharonite was in charge of the herds grazing in Sharon.
Shaphat son of Adlai was in charge of the herds in the valleys.
30 Obil the Ishmaelite was in charge of the camels.
Jehdeiah the Meronothite was in charge of the donkeys.
31 Jaziz the Hagrite was in charge of the flocks.
All these were the officials in charge of King David's property.

32 Jonathan, David's uncle, was a counselor, a man of insight and a scribe. Jehiel son of Hakmoni took care of the king's sons.
33 Ahithophel was the king's counselor.
Hushai the Arkite was the king's confidant. 34 Ahithophel was suc-
ceeded by Jehoiada son of Benaiah and by Abiathar.
Joab was the commander of the royal army.

---

[a] 24 Septuagint; Hebrew *number*

PRAYING SCRIPTURE

1 Chronicles 28

From David's many sons, God chose Solomon to build the temple. Further, God confirmed the promise he'd made to David—that his kingdom would last forever—would continue through Solomon (see verse 7). This house of the Lord was built from the finest materials and stocked with gold and silver service pieces.

The seriousness of worship was reflected in the temple's construction. As the temple of the Holy Spirit, we should take worship just as seriously.

DAVID'S PLANS FOR THE TEMPLE

28 David summoned all the officials of Israel to assemble at Jerusalem: the officers over the tribes, the commanders of the divisions in the service of the king, the commanders of thousands and commanders of hundreds, and the officials in charge of all the property and livestock belonging to the king and his sons, together with the palace officials, the warriors and all the brave fighting men.

2King David rose to his feet and said: "Listen to me, my fellow Israelites, my people. I had it in my heart to build a house as a place of rest for the ark of the covenant of the LORD, for the footstool of our God, and I made plans to build it. 3But God said to me, 'You are not to build a house for my Name, because you are a warrior and have shed blood.'

4"Yet the LORD, the God of Israel, chose me from my whole family to be king over Israel forever. He chose Judah as leader, and from the tribe of Judah he chose my family, and from my father's sons he was pleased to make me king over all Israel. 5Of all my sons — and the LORD has given me many — he has chosen my son Solomon to sit on the throne of the kingdom of the LORD over Israel. 6He said to me: 'Solomon your son is the one who will build my house and my courts, for I have chosen him to be my son, and I will be his father. 7I will establish his kingdom forever if he is unswerving in carrying out my commands and laws, as is being done at this time.'

8"So now I charge you in the sight of all Israel and of the assembly of the LORD, and in the hearing of our God: Be careful to follow all the commands of the LORD your God, that you may possess this good land and pass it on as an inheritance to your descendants forever.

9"And you, my son Solomon, acknowledge the God of your father, and serve him with wholehearted devotion and with a willing mind, for the LORD searches every heart and understands every desire and every thought. If you seek him, he will be found by you; but if you forsake him, he will reject you forever. 10Consider now, for the LORD has chosen you to build a house as the sanctuary. Be strong and do the work."

11Then David gave his son Solomon the plans for the portico of the temple, its buildings, its storerooms, its upper parts, its inner rooms and the place of atonement. 12He gave him the plans of all that the Spirit had put in his mind for the courts of the temple of the LORD and all the surrounding rooms, for the treasuries of the temple of God and for the treasuries for the dedicated things. 13He gave him instructions for the divisions of the priests and Levites, and for all the work of serving in the temple of the LORD, as well as for all the articles to be used in its service. 14He designated the weight of gold for all the gold articles to be used in various kinds of service, and the weight of silver for all the silver articles to be used in various kinds of service: 15the weight of gold for the gold lampstands and their lamps, with the weight for each lampstand and its lamps; and the weight of silver for each silver lampstand and its lamps, according to the use of each lampstand; 16the weight of gold for each table for consecrated bread; the weight of silver for the silver tables; 17the weight of pure gold for the forks, sprinkling bowls and pitchers; the weight of gold for each gold dish; the weight of silver for each silver dish; 18and the weight of the refined gold for the altar of incense. He also gave him the plan for the chariot, that is, the cherubim of gold that spread their wings and overshadow the ark of the covenant of the LORD.

19"All this," David said, "I have in writing as a result of the LORD's hand on me, and he enabled me to understand all the details of the plan."

20David also said to Solomon his son, "Be strong and courageous, and do the work. Do not be afraid or discouraged, for the LORD God, my God, is with you. He will not fail you or forsake you until all the work for the service of the temple of the LORD is finished. 21The divisions of the priests and Levites are ready for all the work on the temple of God, and every willing person skilled in any craft will help you in all the work. The officials and all the people will obey your every command."

GIFTS FOR BUILDING THE TEMPLE

29 Then King David said to the whole assembly: "My son Solomon, the one whom God has chosen, is young and inexperienced. The task is great, because this palatial structure is not for man but for the LORD God. 2With all my resources I have provided for the temple of my God—gold for the gold work, silver for the silver, bronze for the bronze, iron for the iron and wood for the wood, as well as onyx for the settings, turquoise,[a] stones of various colors, and all kinds of fine stone and marble—all of these in large quantities. 3Besides, in my devotion to the temple of my God I now give my personal treasures of gold and silver for the temple of my God, over and above everything I have provided for this holy temple: 4three thousand talents[b] of gold (gold of Ophir) and seven thousand talents[c] of refined silver, for the overlaying of the walls of the buildings, 5for the gold work and the silver work, and for all the work to be done by the craftsmen. Now, who is willing to consecrate themselves to the LORD today?"

6Then the leaders of families, the officers of the tribes of Israel, the commanders of thousands and commanders of hundreds, and the officials in charge of the king's work gave willingly. 7They gave toward the work on the temple of God five thousand talents[d] and ten thousand darics[e] of gold, ten thousand talents[f] of silver, eighteen thousand talents[g] of bronze and a hundred thousand talents[h] of iron. 8Anyone who had precious stones gave them to the treasury of the temple of the LORD in the custody of Jehiel the Gershonite. 9The people rejoiced at the willing response of their leaders, for they had given freely and wholeheartedly to the LORD. David the king also rejoiced greatly.

DAVID'S PRAYER

10David praised the LORD in the presence of the whole assembly, saying,

"Praise be to you, LORD,
the God of our father Israel,
from everlasting to everlasting.
11Yours, LORD, is the greatness and the power
and the glory and the majesty and the splendor,
for everything in heaven and earth is yours.

[a] 2 The meaning of the Hebrew for this word is uncertain. [b] 4 That is, about 110 tons or about 100 metric tons [c] 4 That is, about 260 tons or about 235 metric tons [d] 7 That is, about 190 tons or about 170 metric tons [e] 7 That is, about 185 pounds or about 84 kilograms [f] 7 That is, about 380 tons or about 340 metric tons [g] 7 That is, about 675 tons or about 610 metric tons [h] 7 That is, about 3,800 tons or about 3,400 metric tons

PRAYING SCRIPTURE

1 Chronicles 29

David took up an offering to speed the building of the temple. The giving was so generous that the construction was paid for and the treasury filled with precious stones (see verse 8). David was so joyful he burst into praise, extolling God's power, glory, victory and majesty (see verse 11).

When God answers a prayer or provides the desire of our heart, the right response is to praise him for who he is and for what he has done.

Yours, LORD, is the kingdom;
  you are exalted as head over all.
12 Wealth and honor come from you;
  you are the ruler of all things.
In your hands are strength and power
  to exalt and give strength to all.
13 Now, our God, we give you thanks,
  and praise your glorious name.

14 “But who am I, and who are my people, that we should be able to give as generously as this? Everything comes from you, and we have given you only what comes from your hand. 15 We are foreigners and strangers in your sight, as were all our ancestors. Our days on earth are like a shadow, without hope. 16 LORD our God, all this abundance that we have provided for building you a temple for your Holy Name comes from your hand, and all of it belongs to you. 17 I know, my God, that you test the heart and are pleased with integrity. All these things I have given willingly and with honest intent. And now I have seen with joy how willingly your people who are here have given to you. 18 LORD, the God of our fathers Abraham, Isaac and Israel, keep these desires and thoughts in the hearts of your people forever, and keep their hearts loyal to you. 19 And give my son Solomon the wholehearted devotion to keep your commands, statutes and decrees and to do everything to build the palatial structure for which I have provided.”

20 Then David said to the whole assembly, “Praise the LORD your God.” So they all praised the LORD, the God of their fathers; they bowed down, prostrating themselves before the LORD and the king.

SOLOMON ACKNOWLEDGED AS KING

21 The next day they made sacrifices to the LORD and presented burnt offerings to him: a thousand bulls, a thousand rams and a thousand male lambs, together with their drink offerings, and other sacrifices in abundance for all Israel. 22 They ate and drank with great joy in the presence of the LORD that day.

Then they acknowledged Solomon son of David as king a second time, anointing him before the LORD to be ruler and Zadok to be priest. 23 So Solomon sat on the throne of the LORD as king in place of his father David. He prospered and all Israel obeyed him. 24 All the officers and warriors, as well as all of King David’s sons, pledged their submission to King Solomon.

25 The LORD highly exalted Solomon in the sight of all Israel and bestowed on him royal splendor such as no king over Israel ever had before.

THE DEATH OF DAVID

26 David son of Jesse was king over all Israel. 27 He ruled over Israel forty years — seven in Hebron and thirty-three in Jerusalem. 28 He died at a good old age, having enjoyed long life, wealth and honor. His son Solomon succeeded him as king.

29 As for the events of King David’s reign, from beginning to end, they are written in the records of Samuel the seer, the records of Nathan the prophet and the records of Gad the seer, 30 together with the details of his reign and power, and the circumstances that surrounded him and Israel and the kingdoms of all the other lands.

2 CHRONICLES

The book of 2 Chronicles opens with the transition from David's reign to Solomon's. The new king's reign covers the book's first nine chapters. Rather than narrating all the events of his life and rule, the author focused particularly on the building and dedication of the first temple. The Babylonians had destroyed the temple before the exile, so the emphasis on the temple served to encourage the rebuilding of the temple after their return.

The temple occupies a central place in the Chronicler's thinking. The temple served as the visible symbol of the Lord's presence among his people. It was the center of Israelite life and worship. This focus caused the writer to mostly ignore the northern kingdom of Israel because of the ongoing false worship there. In the temple's Most Holy Place, once a year, the high priest made atonement for the people. The Chronicler believed that spiritual life in the land would be impoverished until the temple was standing again. This makes sense for a nation whose existence and blessings were contingent on keeping God's laws.

Chapters 10–36 narrate the split of the kingdom—shortly after the death of Solomon—and the downward spiral that led to exile. The tribes of Judah and Benjamin in the south were collectively called "Judah." The remaining tribes in the north were called "Israel." The kings of the northern kingdom were called the kings of "Israel," but sometimes "Israel" was used to describe the entire nation. Either way, it made clear that the kings in the north were cut off from the line of David and the promises made to him.

Many readers focus on the decline of Israel throughout the final chapters of 2 Chronicles, and rightly so. They often do this as a comparison to the degradation of their own nation of residence. However, we must not ignore the final verses of the book. In it the Chronicler showed how the exile fulfilled Jeremiah's prophecy, giving rest to the land. He also quoted from Cyrus's proclamation, which allowed Israel to return to the land. When he said, "Any of his people among you may go up" (36:23), Cyrus echoed the language of the exodus. Just as God had rescued his people from slavery, he would redeem and restore them from exile.

One of the highlights of the book is Solomon's prayer of dedication for the temple. In it he acknowledged God's greatness and majesty. He recalled God's promises to David and asked God to watch over the temple day and night and to bless it. Solomon reminded the people of their responsibility to follow God, to live rightly with their neighbors and to confess whenever they sinned. He also asked God to be faithful to forgive his people. At the end of Solomon's prayer, he dedicated and celebrated the return of the ark of the covenant. God responded by consuming the sacrificial offering with fire from heaven.

Although Solomon eventually strayed from God, the early blessings on and successes of his kingship cannot be separated from the way he regularly sought God in prayer.

PRAYING SCRIPTURE

2 Chronicles 1

When we ask the Lord for wisdom, he grants it in abundance. Incredibly, after Solomon pleased God with his request for wisdom, God blessed the king nearly beyond comprehension. So much silver and gold were brought into Jerusalem that the precious metals were as common as rocks.

Though the world denies it, wisdom is more valuable than silver and gold. Praying for wisdom in everything should be the norm for God's children.

SOLOMON ASKS FOR WISDOM

1 Solomon son of David established himself firmly over his kingdom,
for the LORD his God was with him and made him exceedingly great.
2 Then Solomon spoke to all Israel — to the commanders of thousands
and commanders of hundreds, to the judges and to all the leaders in
Israel, the heads of families — 3 and Solomon and the whole assembly
went to the high place at Gibeon, for God's tent of meeting was there,
which Moses the LORD's servant had made in the wilderness. 4 Now David
had brought up the ark of God from Kiriath Jearim to the place he had
prepared for it, because he had pitched a tent for it in Jerusalem. 5 But the
bronze altar that Bezalel son of Uri, the son of Hur, had made was in Gib-
eon in front of the tabernacle of the LORD; so Solomon and the assembly
inquired of him there. 6 Solomon went up to the bronze altar before the
LORD in the tent of meeting and offered a thousand burnt offerings on it.
7 That night God appeared to Solomon and said to him, "Ask for what-
ever you want me to give you."
8 Solomon answered God, "You have shown great kindness to David
my father and have made me king in his place. 9 Now, LORD God, let
your promise to my father David be confirmed, for you have made me
king over a people who are as numerous as the dust of the earth. 10 Give
me wisdom and knowledge, that I may lead this people, for who is able
to govern this great people of yours?"
11 God said to Solomon, "Since this is your heart's desire and you have
not asked for wealth, possessions or honor, nor for the death of your
enemies, and since you have not asked for a long life but for wisdom
and knowledge to govern my people over whom I have made you king,
12 therefore wisdom and knowledge will be given you. And I will also
give you wealth, possessions and honor, such as no king who was be-
fore you ever had and none after you will have."
13 Then Solomon went to Jerusalem from the high place at Gibeon,
from before the tent of meeting. And he reigned over Israel.
14 Solomon accumulated chariots and horses; he had fourteen hun-
dred chariots and twelve thousand horses,[a] which he kept in the chariot
cities and also with him in Jerusalem. 15 The king made silver and gold
as common in Jerusalem as stones, and cedar as plentiful as sycamore-
fig trees in the foothills. 16 Solomon's horses were imported from Egypt
and from Kue[b] — the royal merchants purchased them from Kue at the
current price. 17 They imported a chariot from Egypt for six hundred
shekels[c] of silver, and a horse for a hundred and fifty.[d] They also ex-
ported them to all the kings of the Hittites and of the Arameans.

PRAYING SCRIPTURE

2 Chronicles 2

What is the most meaningful compliment you've ever received? Maybe it was for a sporting achievement or a goal you reached, or from someone whose life you impacted. King Hiram's words to Solomon are hard to top: "Because the LORD loves his people, he has made you their king" (verse 11).

About whom would you say, "[He or she] is in my life because God loves me so much"? Praise God in prayer for them.

PREPARATIONS FOR BUILDING THE TEMPLE

2[e] Solomon gave orders to build a temple for the Name of the LORD
and a royal palace for himself. 2 He conscripted 70,000 men as
carriers and 80,000 as stonecutters in the hills and 3,600 as foremen
over them.
3 Solomon sent this message to Hiram[f] king of Tyre:

"Send me cedar logs as you did for my father David when you
sent him cedar to build a palace to live in. 4 Now I am about to

[a] 14 Or *charioteers* [b] 16 Probably Cilicia [c] 17 That is, about 15 pounds or about 6.9 kilograms [d] 17 That is, about 3 3/4 pounds or about 1.7 kilograms
[e] In Hebrew texts 2:1 is numbered 1:18, and 2:2-18 is numbered 2:1-17.
[f] 3 Hebrew *Huram*, a variant of *Hiram*; also in verses 11 and 12

build a temple for the Name of the LORD my God and to dedicate it
to him for burning fragrant incense before him, for setting out the
consecrated bread regularly, and for making burnt offerings every
morning and evening and on the Sabbaths, at the New Moons and
at the appointed festivals of the LORD our God. This is a lasting
ordinance for Israel.

5"The temple I am going to build will be great, because our God
is greater than all other gods. 6But who is able to build a temple for
him, since the heavens, even the highest heavens, cannot contain
him? Who then am I to build a temple for him, except as a place to
burn sacrifices before him?

7"Send me, therefore, a man skilled to work in gold and silver,
bronze and iron, and in purple, crimson and blue yarn, and expe-
rienced in the art of engraving, to work in Judah and Jerusalem
with my skilled workers, whom my father David provided.

8"Send me also cedar, juniper and algum[a] logs from Lebanon,
for I know that your servants are skilled in cutting timber there.
My servants will work with yours 9to provide me with plenty of
lumber, because the temple I build must be large and magnifi-
cent. 10I will give your servants, the woodsmen who cut the tim-
ber, twenty thousand cors[b] of ground wheat, twenty thousand
cors[c] of barley, twenty thousand baths[d] of wine and twenty thou-
sand baths of olive oil."

11Hiram king of Tyre replied by letter to Solomon:

"Because the LORD loves his people, he has made you their king."

12And Hiram added:

"Praise be to the LORD, the God of Israel, who made heaven and
earth! He has given King David a wise son, endowed with intelli-
gence and discernment, who will build a temple for the LORD and
a palace for himself.

13"I am sending you Huram-Abi, a man of great skill, 14whose
mother was from Dan and whose father was from Tyre. He is
trained to work in gold and silver, bronze and iron, stone and
wood, and with purple and blue and crimson yarn and fine linen.
He is experienced in all kinds of engraving and can execute any
design given to him. He will work with your skilled workers and
with those of my lord, David your father.

15"Now let my lord send his servants the wheat and barley and
the olive oil and wine he promised, 16and we will cut all the logs
from Lebanon that you need and will float them as rafts by sea
down to Joppa. You can then take them up to Jerusalem."

17Solomon took a census of all the foreigners residing in Israel, af-
ter the census his father David had taken; and they were found to be
153,600. 18He assigned 70,000 of them to be carriers and 80,000 to be
stonecutters in the hills, with 3,600 foremen over them to keep the
people working.

---

[a] *8* Probably a variant of *almug* [b] *10* That is, probably about 3,600 tons or about 3,200 metric tons of wheat [c] *10* That is, probably about 3,000 tons or about 2,700 metric tons of barley [d] *10* That is, about 120,000 gallons or about 440,000 liters

SOLOMON BUILDS THE TEMPLE

3 Then Solomon began to build the temple of the LORD in Jerusalem on Mount Moriah, where the LORD had appeared to his father David. It was on the threshing floor of Araunah[a] the Jebusite, the place provided by David. 2He began building on the second day of the second month in the fourth year of his reign.

3The foundation Solomon laid for building the temple of God was sixty cubits long and twenty cubits wide[b] (using the cubit of the old standard). 4The portico at the front of the temple was twenty cubits[c] long across the width of the building and twenty[d] cubits high.

He overlaid the inside with pure gold. 5He paneled the main hall with juniper and covered it with fine gold and decorated it with palm tree and chain designs. 6He adorned the temple with precious stones. And the gold he used was gold of Parvaim. 7He overlaid the ceiling beams, doorframes, walls and doors of the temple with gold, and he carved cherubim on the walls.

8He built the Most Holy Place, its length corresponding to the width of the temple — twenty cubits long and twenty cubits wide. He overlaid the inside with six hundred talents[e] of fine gold. 9The gold nails weighed fifty shekels.[f] He also overlaid the upper parts with gold.

10For the Most Holy Place he made a pair of sculptured cherubim and overlaid them with gold. 11The total wingspan of the cherubim was twenty cubits. One wing of the first cherub was five cubits[g] long and touched the temple wall, while its other wing, also five cubits long, touched the wing of the other cherub. 12Similarly one wing of the second cherub was five cubits long and touched the other temple wall, and its other wing, also five cubits long, touched the wing of the first cherub. 13The wings of these cherubim extended twenty cubits. They stood on their feet, facing the main hall.[h]

14He made the curtain of blue, purple and crimson yarn and fine linen, with cherubim worked into it.

15For the front of the temple he made two pillars, which together were thirty-five cubits[i] long, each with a capital five cubits high. 16He made interwoven chains[j] and put them on top of the pillars. He also made a hundred pomegranates and attached them to the chains. 17He erected the pillars in the front of the temple, one to the south and one to the north. The one to the south he named Jakin[k] and the one to the north Boaz.[l]

THE TEMPLE'S FURNISHINGS

4 He made a bronze altar twenty cubits long, twenty cubits wide and ten cubits high.[m] 2He made the Sea of cast metal, circular in shape, measuring ten cubits from rim to rim and five cubits[n] high. It took a

PRAYING SCRIPTURE

2 Chronicles 3

Among the layout and dimensions of the temple was the description of the Most Holy Place. Cherubim in this most sacred chamber were a reminder that the presence of God dwelled there.

The book of Hebrews tells us that all these things are just a pattern of a higher, heavenly reality (8:5). Thank God that his glory is now shown in his people.

PRAYING SCRIPTURE

2 Chronicles 4

Along with the tables, lampstands, bowls, ladles and censers in the temple were beasts of burden. In the temple court, twelve cast oxen held on their backs a great basin of water. Amid all the obvious symbols of worship and ritual was a reminder of God's other workers: animals.

Sacrifices are no more, but we can still honor the animals God has provided for work and companionship, and thank him for making them part of his creation.

---

[a] *1* Hebrew *Ornan,* a variant of *Araunah* [b] *3* That is, about 90 feet long and 30 feet wide or about 27 meters long and 9 meters wide [c] *4* That is, about 30 feet or about 9 meters; also in verses 8, 11 and 13 [d] *4* Some Septuagint and Syriac manuscripts; Hebrew *and a hundred and twenty* [e] *8* That is, about 23 tons or about 21 metric tons [f] *9* That is, about 1 1/4 pounds or about 575 grams [g] *11* That is, about 7 1/2 feet or about 2.3 meters; also in verse 15 [h] *13* Or *facing inward* [i] *15* That is, about 53 feet or about 16 meters [j] *16* Or possibly *made chains in the inner sanctuary;* the meaning of the Hebrew for this phrase is uncertain. [k] *17* *Jakin* probably means *he establishes.* [l] *17* *Boaz* probably means *in him is strength.* [m] *1* That is, about 30 feet long and wide and 15 feet high or about 9 meters long and wide and 4.5 meters high [n] *2* That is, about 7 1/2 feet or about 2.3 meters

line of thirty cubits[a] to measure around it. 3Below the rim, figures of
bulls encircled it — ten to a cubit.[b] The bulls were cast in two rows in
one piece with the Sea.
4The Sea stood on twelve bulls, three facing north, three facing west,
three facing south and three facing east. The Sea rested on top of them,
and their hindquarters were toward the center. 5It was a handbreadth[c]
in thickness, and its rim was like the rim of a cup, like a lily blossom.
It held three thousand baths.[d]
6He then made ten basins for washing and placed five on the south
side and five on the north. In them the things to be used for the burnt
offerings were rinsed, but the Sea was to be used by the priests for
washing.
7He made ten gold lampstands according to the specifications for
them and placed them in the temple, five on the south side and five
on the north.
8He made ten tables and placed them in the temple, five on the
south side and five on the north. He also made a hundred gold sprinkling bowls.
9He made the courtyard of the priests, and the large court and the
doors for the court, and overlaid the doors with bronze. 10He placed the
Sea on the south side, at the southeast corner.
11And Huram also made the pots and shovels and sprinkling bowls.
So Huram finished the work he had undertaken for King Solomon
in the temple of God:

12 the two pillars;
the two bowl-shaped capitals on top of the pillars;
the two sets of network decorating the two bowl-shaped capitals on top of the pillars;
13 the four hundred pomegranates for the two sets of network (two rows of pomegranates for each network, decorating the bowl-shaped capitals on top of the pillars);
14 the stands with their basins;
15 the Sea and the twelve bulls under it;
16 the pots, shovels, meat forks and all related articles.

All the objects that Huram-Abi made for King Solomon for the temple of the LORD were of polished bronze. 17The king had them cast in
clay molds in the plain of the Jordan between Sukkoth and Zarethan.[e]
18All these things that Solomon made amounted to so much that the
weight of the bronze could not be calculated.
19Solomon also made all the furnishings that were in God's temple:

the golden altar;
the tables on which was the bread of the Presence;
20 the lampstands of pure gold with their lamps, to burn in front of the inner sanctuary as prescribed;
21 the gold floral work and lamps and tongs (they were solid gold);
22 the pure gold wick trimmers, sprinkling bowls, dishes and censers; and the gold doors of the temple: the inner doors to the Most Holy Place and the doors of the main hall.

---

[a] *2* That is, about 45 feet or about 14 meters [b] *3* That is, about 18 inches or about 45 centimeters [c] *5* That is, about 3 inches or about 7.5 centimeters
[d] *5* That is, about 18,000 gallons or about 66,000 liters [e] *17* Hebrew *Zeredatha,* a variant of *Zarethan*

PRAYING SCRIPTURE

2 Chronicles 5

The ark was moved properly on the shoulders of the Levites and settled in the Most Holy Place under the wings of the cherubim. During a song of praise, the priests' ministry stopped "because of the cloud, for the glory of the LORD filled the temple of God" (verse 14).

God's work should be done God's way. When we do God's work his way, he blesses it. Pray for the humility to always do as he commands.

5 When all the work Solomon had done for the temple of the LORD was finished, he brought in the things his father David had dedicated — the silver and gold and all the furnishings — and he placed them in the treasuries of God's temple.

THE ARK BROUGHT TO THE TEMPLE

2Then Solomon summoned to Jerusalem the elders of Israel, all the heads of the tribes and the chiefs of the Israelite families, to bring up the ark of the LORD's covenant from Zion, the City of David. 3And all the Israelites came together to the king at the time of the festival in the seventh month.

4When all the elders of Israel had arrived, the Levites took up the ark, 5and they brought up the ark and the tent of meeting and all the sacred furnishings in it. The Levitical priests carried them up; 6and King Solomon and the entire assembly of Israel that had gathered about him were before the ark, sacrificing so many sheep and cattle that they could not be recorded or counted.

7The priests then brought the ark of the LORD's covenant to its place in the inner sanctuary of the temple, the Most Holy Place, and put it beneath the wings of the cherubim. 8The cherubim spread their wings over the place of the ark and covered the ark and its carrying poles. 9These poles were so long that their ends, extending from the ark, could be seen from in front of the inner sanctuary, but not from outside the Holy Place; and they are still there today. 10There was nothing in the ark except the two tablets that Moses had placed in it at Horeb, where the LORD made a covenant with the Israelites after they came out of Egypt.

11The priests then withdrew from the Holy Place. All the priests who were there had consecrated themselves, regardless of their divisions. 12All the Levites who were musicians — Asaph, Heman, Jeduthun and their sons and relatives — stood on the east side of the altar, dressed in fine linen and playing cymbals, harps and lyres. They were accompanied by 120 priests sounding trumpets. 13The trumpeters and musicians joined in unison to give praise and thanks to the LORD. Accompanied by trumpets, cymbals and other instruments, the singers raised their voices in praise to the LORD and sang:

"He is good;
his love endures forever."

Then the temple of the LORD was filled with the cloud, 14and the priests could not perform their service because of the cloud, for the glory of the LORD filled the temple of God.

PRAYING SCRIPTURE

2 Chronicles 6

Solomon recognized that it was the Lord who brought him to the dedication of the temple. In an extended prayer of dedication before all the people, he reminded them of God's blessing and preservation of them as a people. He emphasized that God answers prayer and would hear the prayers offered at his house (see verse 21).

Prayer is no longer connected to a place, but to a person: Jesus Christ. You can pray anytime and anywhere.

6 Then Solomon said, "The LORD has said that he would dwell in a dark cloud; 2I have built a magnificent temple for you, a place for you to dwell forever."

3While the whole assembly of Israel was standing there, the king turned around and blessed them. 4Then he said:

"Praise be to the LORD, the God of Israel, who with his hands has fulfilled what he promised with his mouth to my father David. For he said, 5'Since the day I brought my people out of Egypt, I have not chosen a city in any tribe of Israel to have a temple built so that my Name might be there, nor have I chosen anyone to be ruler over my people Israel. 6But now I have chosen Jerusalem for my Name to be there, and I have chosen David to rule my people Israel.'

7"My father David had it in his heart to build a temple for the
Name of the LORD, the God of Israel. 8But the LORD said to my fa-
ther David, 'You did well to have it in your heart to build a temple
for my Name. 9Nevertheless, you are not the one to build the tem-
ple, but your son, your own flesh and blood — he is the one who
will build the temple for my Name.'

10"The LORD has kept the promise he made. I have succeeded
David my father and now I sit on the throne of Israel, just as the
LORD promised, and I have built the temple for the Name of the
LORD, the God of Israel. 11There I have placed the ark, in which is
the covenant of the LORD that he made with the people of Israel."

SOLOMON'S PRAYER OF DEDICATION

12Then Solomon stood before the altar of the LORD in front of the
whole assembly of Israel and spread out his hands. 13Now he had made
a bronze platform, five cubits long, five cubits wide and three cubits
high,[a] and had placed it in the center of the outer court. He stood on
the platform and then knelt down before the whole assembly of Israel
and spread out his hands toward heaven. 14He said:

"LORD, the God of Israel, there is no God like you in heaven or
on earth — you who keep your covenant of love with your servants
who continue wholeheartedly in your way. 15You have kept your
promise to your servant David my father; with your mouth you
have promised and with your hand you have fulfilled it — as it is
today.

16"Now, LORD, the God of Israel, keep for your servant David my
father the promises you made to him when you said, 'You shall
never fail to have a successor to sit before me on the throne of Is-
rael, if only your descendants are careful in all they do to walk be-
fore me according to my law, as you have done.' 17And now, LORD,
the God of Israel, let your word that you promised your servant
David come true.

18"But will God really dwell on earth with humans? The heav-
ens, even the highest heavens, cannot contain you. How much
less this temple I have built! 19Yet, LORD my God, give attention to
your servant's prayer and his plea for mercy. Hear the cry and the
prayer that your servant is praying in your presence. 20May your
eyes be open toward this temple day and night, this place of which
you said you would put your Name there. May you hear the prayer
your servant prays toward this place. 21Hear the supplications of
your servant and of your people Israel when they pray toward this
place. Hear from heaven, your dwelling place; and when you hear,
forgive.

22"When anyone wrongs their neighbor and is required to take
an oath and they come and swear the oath before your altar in this
temple, 23then hear from heaven and act. Judge between your ser-
vants, condemning the guilty and bringing down on their heads
what they have done, and vindicating the innocent by treating
them in accordance with their innocence.

24"When your people Israel have been defeated by an enemy be-
cause they have sinned against you and when they turn back and

[a] *13* That is, about 7 1/2 feet long and wide and 4 1/2 feet high or about 2.3 meters long and wide and 1.4 meters high

give praise to your name, praying and making supplication before
you in this temple, [25]then hear from heaven and forgive the sin
of your people Israel and bring them back to the land you gave to
them and their ancestors.

[26]"When the heavens are shut up and there is no rain because
your people have sinned against you, and when they pray toward
this place and give praise to your name and turn from their sin
because you have afflicted them, [27]then hear from heaven and for-
give the sin of your servants, your people Israel. Teach them the
right way to live, and send rain on the land you gave your people
for an inheritance.

[28]"When famine or plague comes to the land, or blight or mil-
dew, locusts or grasshoppers, or when enemies besiege them in
any of their cities, whatever disaster or disease may come, [29]and
when a prayer or plea is made by anyone among your people Is-
rael — being aware of their afflictions and pains, and spreading
out their hands toward this temple — [30]then hear from heaven,
your dwelling place. Forgive, and deal with everyone according to
all they do, since you know their hearts (for you alone know the
human heart), [31]so that they will fear you and walk in obedience
to you all the time they live in the land you gave our ancestors.

[32]"As for the foreigner who does not belong to your people Is-
rael but has come from a distant land because of your great name
and your mighty hand and your outstretched arm — when they
come and pray toward this temple, [33]then hear from heaven, your
dwelling place. Do whatever the foreigner asks of you, so that all
the peoples of the earth may know your name and fear you, as do
your own people Israel, and may know that this house I have built
bears your Name.

[34]"When your people go to war against their enemies, wherever
you send them, and when they pray to you toward this city you
have chosen and the temple I have built for your Name, [35]then
hear from heaven their prayer and their plea, and uphold their
cause.

[36]"When they sin against you — for there is no one who does
not sin — and you become angry with them and give them over
to the enemy, who takes them captive to a land far away or near;
[37]and if they have a change of heart in the land where they are
held captive, and repent and plead with you in the land of their
captivity and say, 'We have sinned, we have done wrong and acted
wickedly'; [38]and if they turn back to you with all their heart and
soul in the land of their captivity where they were taken, and pray
toward the land you gave their ancestors, toward the city you have
chosen and toward the temple I have built for your Name; [39]then
from heaven, your dwelling place, hear their prayer and their
pleas, and uphold their cause. And forgive your people, who have
sinned against you.

[40]"Now, my God, may your eyes be open and your ears attentive
to the prayers offered in this place.

[41]"Now arise, LORD God, and come to your resting place,
 you and the ark of your might.
May your priests, LORD God, be clothed with salvation,
 may your faithful people rejoice in your goodness.

42 LORD God, do not reject your anointed one.
Remember the great love promised to David your servant."

THE DEDICATION OF THE TEMPLE

7 When Solomon finished praying, fire came down from heaven and
consumed the burnt offering and the sacrifices, and the glory of
the LORD filled the temple. 2 The priests could not enter the temple of
the LORD because the glory of the LORD filled it. 3 When all the Israelites
saw the fire coming down and the glory of the LORD above the temple,
they knelt on the pavement with their faces to the ground, and they
worshiped and gave thanks to the LORD, saying,

"He is good;
his love endures forever."

4 Then the king and all the people offered sacrifices before the LORD.
5 And King Solomon offered a sacrifice of twenty-two thousand head
of cattle and a hundred and twenty thousand sheep and goats. So the
king and all the people dedicated the temple of God. 6 The priests took
their positions, as did the Levites with the LORD's musical instruments,
which King David had made for praising the LORD and which were
used when he gave thanks, saying, "His love endures forever." Oppo-
site the Levites, the priests blew their trumpets, and all the Israelites
were standing.
7 Solomon consecrated the middle part of the courtyard in front of
the temple of the LORD, and there he offered burnt offerings and the
fat of the fellowship offerings, because the bronze altar he had made
could not hold the burnt offerings, the grain offerings and the fat
portions.
8 So Solomon observed the festival at that time for seven days, and
all Israel with him — a vast assembly, people from Lebo Hamath to the
Wadi of Egypt. 9 On the eighth day they held an assembly, for they had
celebrated the dedication of the altar for seven days and the festival
for seven days more. 10 On the twenty-third day of the seventh month
he sent the people to their homes, joyful and glad in heart for the good
things the LORD had done for David and Solomon and for his people
Israel.

THE LORD APPEARS TO SOLOMON

11 When Solomon had finished the temple of the LORD and the royal
palace, and had succeeded in carrying out all he had in mind to do in
the temple of the LORD and in his own palace, 12 the LORD appeared to
him at night and said:

"I have heard your prayer and have chosen this place for myself
as a temple for sacrifices.
13 "When I shut up the heavens so that there is no rain, or com-
mand locusts to devour the land or send a plague among my
people, 14 if my people, who are called by my name, will humble
themselves and pray and seek my face and turn from their wicked
ways, then I will hear from heaven, and I will forgive their sin
and will heal their land. 15 Now my eyes will be open and my ears
attentive to the prayers offered in this place. 16 I have chosen and
consecrated this temple so that my Name may be there forever.
My eyes and my heart will always be there.

PRAYING SCRIPTURE

2 Chronicles 7

Upon the dedication of the temple, the Lord appeared to Solomon, reminding him of his special relationship with Israel. On occasions when Israel was judged, they were to humble themselves, pray, seek his face and repent (see verse 14). God connected this corporate repentance to the recently dedicated temple (see verse 16).

Contrary to what some believe, God favors repentance over judgment. When in sin, go to him without delay, turn from your sin and experience his favor.

17 "As for you, if you walk before me faithfully as David your fa-
ther did, and do all I command, and observe my decrees and laws,
18 I will establish your royal throne, as I covenanted with David
your father when I said, 'You shall never fail to have a successor
to rule over Israel.'
19 "But if you[a] turn away and forsake the decrees and commands
I have given you[a] and go off to serve other gods and worship them,
20 then I will uproot Israel from my land, which I have given them,
and will reject this temple I have consecrated for my Name. I will
make it a byword and an object of ridicule among all peoples.
21 This temple will become a heap of rubble. All[b] who pass by will
be appalled and say, 'Why has the LORD done such a thing to this
land and to this temple?' 22 People will answer, 'Because they have
forsaken the LORD, the God of their ancestors, who brought them
out of Egypt, and have embraced other gods, worshiping and serv-
ing them — that is why he brought all this disaster on them.'"

SOLOMON'S OTHER ACTIVITIES

8 At the end of twenty years, during which Solomon built the temple
of the LORD and his own palace, 2 Solomon rebuilt the villages that
Hiram[c] had given him, and settled Israelites in them. 3 Solomon then
went to Hamath Zobah and captured it. 4 He also built up Tadmor in the
desert and all the store cities he had built in Hamath. 5 He rebuilt Upper
Beth Horon and Lower Beth Horon as fortified cities, with walls and with
gates and bars, 6 as well as Baalath and all his store cities, and all the cit-
ies for his chariots and for his horses[d] — whatever he desired to build in
Jerusalem, in Lebanon and throughout all the territory he ruled.
7 There were still people left from the Hittites, Amorites, Perizzites,
Hivites and Jebusites (these people were not Israelites). 8 Solomon con-
scripted the descendants of all these people remaining in the land —
whom the Israelites had not destroyed — to serve as slave labor, as it
is to this day. 9 But Solomon did not make slaves of the Israelites for
his work; they were his fighting men, commanders of his captains, and
commanders of his chariots and charioteers. 10 They were also King Sol-
omon's chief officials — two hundred and fifty officials supervising the
men.
11 Solomon brought Pharaoh's daughter up from the City of David
to the palace he had built for her, for he said, "My wife must not live
in the palace of David king of Israel, because the places the ark of the
LORD has entered are holy."
12 On the altar of the LORD that he had built in front of the portico,
Solomon sacrificed burnt offerings to the LORD, 13 according to the daily
requirement for offerings commanded by Moses for the Sabbaths, the
New Moons and the three annual festivals — the Festival of Unleav-
ened Bread, the Festival of Weeks and the Festival of Tabernacles. 14 In
keeping with the ordinance of his father David, he appointed the divi-
sions of the priests for their duties, and the Levites to lead the praise
and to assist the priests according to each day's requirement. He also
appointed the gatekeepers by divisions for the various gates, because

PRAYING SCRIPTURE

2 Chronicles 8

As was common in the ancient world, enslaved people were used to expand the cities of a kingdom. From the remaining populations of various non-Israelite tribes, Solomon conscripted forced labor for his building projects.

Even today, slavery remains one of the biggest blights on humanity, exploiting people and ignoring the image of God in them. Ask God how you can help end modern slavery while honoring those who bear his image.

[a] *19* The Hebrew is plural. [b] *21* See some Septuagint manuscripts, Old Latin, Syriac, Arabic and Targum; Hebrew *And though this temple is now so imposing, all* [c] *2* Hebrew *Huram,* a variant of *Hiram;* also in verse 18
[d] *6* Or *charioteers*

this was what David the man of God had ordered. 15They did not devi-
ate from the king's commands to the priests or to the Levites in any
matter, including that of the treasuries.
16All Solomon's work was carried out, from the day the foundation
of the temple of the LORD was laid until its completion. So the temple
of the LORD was finished.
17Then Solomon went to Ezion Geber and Elath on the coast of Edom.
18And Hiram sent him ships commanded by his own men, sailors who
knew the sea. These, with Solomon's men, sailed to Ophir and brought
back four hundred and fifty talents[a] of gold, which they delivered to
King Solomon.

THE QUEEN OF SHEBA VISITS SOLOMON

9 When the queen of Sheba heard of Solomon's fame, she came to
Jerusalem to test him with hard questions. Arriving with a very
great caravan—with camels carrying spices, large quantities of gold,
and precious stones—she came to Solomon and talked with him about
all she had on her mind. 2Solomon answered all her questions; nothing
was too hard for him to explain to her. 3When the queen of Sheba saw
the wisdom of Solomon, as well as the palace he had built, 4the food
on his table, the seating of his officials, the attending servants in their
robes, the cupbearers in their robes and the burnt offerings he made
at[b] the temple of the LORD, she was overwhelmed.
5She said to the king, "The report I heard in my own country about
your achievements and your wisdom is true. 6But I did not believe
what they said until I came and saw with my own eyes. Indeed, not
even half the greatness of your wisdom was told me; you have far
exceeded the report I heard. 7How happy your people must be! How
happy your officials, who continually stand before you and hear your
wisdom! 8Praise be to the LORD your God, who has delighted in you
and placed you on his throne as king to rule for the LORD your God.
Because of the love of your God for Israel and his desire to uphold
them forever, he has made you king over them, to maintain justice
and righteousness."
9Then she gave the king 120 talents[c] of gold, large quantities of
spices, and precious stones. There had never been such spices as those
the queen of Sheba gave to King Solomon.
10(The servants of Hiram and the servants of Solomon brought gold
from Ophir; they also brought algumwood[d] and precious stones. 11The
king used the algumwood to make steps for the temple of the LORD
and for the royal palace, and to make harps and lyres for the musi-
cians. Nothing like them had ever been seen in Judah.)
12King Solomon gave the queen of Sheba all she desired and asked
for; he gave her more than she had brought to him. Then she left and
returned with her retinue to her own country.

SOLOMON'S SPLENDOR

13The weight of the gold that Solomon received yearly was 666
talents,[e] 14not including the revenues brought in by merchants and

PRAYING SCRIPTURE

2 Chronicles 9

Solomon's wealth was so vast and his wisdom so impressive that the queen of Sheba was overwhelmed. His kingdom was filled with treasures, and he received a veritable zoo every three years.

Yet the chapter ends with the same truth that marks everyone: He died. All of Solomon's wealth could not extend his life. Wisdom is available to all, rich or poor, so ask God to give you wisdom all the days of your life.

---

[a] *18* That is, about 17 tons or about 15 metric tons [b] *4* Or *and the ascent by which he went up to* [c] *9* That is, about 4 1/2 tons or about 4 metric tons [d] *10* Probably a variant of *almugwood* [e] *13* That is, about 25 tons or about 23 metric tons

traders. Also all the kings of Arabia and the governors of the territories brought gold and silver to Solomon.

15King Solomon made two hundred large shields of hammered gold; six hundred shekels[a] of hammered gold went into each shield. 16He also made three hundred small shields of hammered gold, with three hundred shekels[b] of gold in each shield. The king put them in the Palace of the Forest of Lebanon.

17Then the king made a great throne covered with ivory and overlaid with pure gold. 18The throne had six steps, and a footstool of gold was attached to it. On both sides of the seat were armrests, with a lion standing beside each of them. 19Twelve lions stood on the six steps, one at either end of each step. Nothing like it had ever been made for any other kingdom. 20All King Solomon's goblets were gold, and all the household articles in the Palace of the Forest of Lebanon were pure gold. Nothing was made of silver, because silver was considered of little value in Solomon's day. 21The king had a fleet of trading ships[c] manned by Hiram's[d] servants. Once every three years it returned, carrying gold, silver and ivory, and apes and baboons.

22King Solomon was greater in riches and wisdom than all the other kings of the earth. 23All the kings of the earth sought audience with Solomon to hear the wisdom God had put in his heart. 24Year after year, everyone who came brought a gift—articles of silver and gold, and robes, weapons and spices, and horses and mules.

25Solomon had four thousand stalls for horses and chariots, and twelve thousand horses,[e] which he kept in the chariot cities and also with him in Jerusalem. 26He ruled over all the kings from the Euphrates River to the land of the Philistines, as far as the border of Egypt. 27The king made silver as common in Jerusalem as stones, and cedar as plentiful as sycamore-fig trees in the foothills. 28Solomon's horses were imported from Egypt and from all other countries.

SOLOMON'S DEATH

29As for the other events of Solomon's reign, from beginning to end, are they not written in the records of Nathan the prophet, in the prophecy of Ahijah the Shilonite and in the visions of Iddo the seer concerning Jeroboam son of Nebat? 30Solomon reigned in Jerusalem over all Israel forty years. 31Then he rested with his ancestors and was buried in the city of David his father. And Rehoboam his son succeeded him as king.

ISRAEL REBELS AGAINST REHOBOAM

10 Rehoboam went to Shechem, for all Israel had gone there to make him king. 2When Jeroboam son of Nebat heard this (he was in Egypt, where he had fled from King Solomon), he returned from Egypt. 3So they sent for Jeroboam, and he and all Israel went to Rehoboam and said to him: 4"Your father put a heavy yoke on us, but now lighten the harsh labor and the heavy yoke he put on us, and we will serve you."

5Rehoboam answered, "Come back to me in three days." So the people went away.

PRAYING SCRIPTURE

2 Chronicles 10

Unlike his father, Rehoboam proved to be a very foolish king. When he decided to make the people work harder and suffer more, they naturally rebelled against him. When Rehoboam sent the tax man, the people stoned him to death.

Rehoboam's first mistake was ignoring wise counsel for the advice of his friends. Wisdom is often gained by counsel, so ask God to send you good advisers to help you make good decisions.

---

[a] 15 That is, about 15 pounds or about 6.9 kilograms [b] 16 That is, about 7 1/2 pounds or about 3.5 kilograms [c] 21 Hebrew *of ships that could go to Tarshish* [d] 21 Hebrew *Huram,* a variant of *Hiram* [e] 25 Or *charioteers*

6Then King Rehoboam consulted the elders who had served his fa-
ther Solomon during his lifetime. "How would you advise me to an-
swer these people?" he asked.
7They replied, "If you will be kind to these people and please them
and give them a favorable answer, they will always be your servants."
8But Rehoboam rejected the advice the elders gave him and con-
sulted the young men who had grown up with him and were serving
him. 9He asked them, "What is your advice? How should we answer
these people who say to me, 'Lighten the yoke your father put on us'?"
10The young men who had grown up with him replied, "The people
have said to you, 'Your father put a heavy yoke on us, but make our
yoke lighter.' Now tell them, 'My little finger is thicker than my father's
waist. 11My father laid on you a heavy yoke; I will make it even heavier.
My father scourged you with whips; I will scourge you with scorpions.'"
12Three days later Jeroboam and all the people returned to Reho-
boam, as the king had said, "Come back to me in three days." 13The
king answered them harshly. Rejecting the advice of the elders, 14he
followed the advice of the young men and said, "My father made your
yoke heavy; I will make it even heavier. My father scourged you with
whips; I will scourge you with scorpions." 15So the king did not listen
to the people, for this turn of events was from God, to fulfill the word
the LORD had spoken to Jeroboam son of Nebat through Ahijah the
Shilonite.
16When all Israel saw that the king refused to listen to them, they
answered the king:

"What share do we have in David,
what part in Jesse's son?
To your tents, Israel!
Look after your own house, David!"

So all the Israelites went home. 17But as for the Israelites who were liv-
ing in the towns of Judah, Rehoboam still ruled over them.
18King Rehoboam sent out Adoniram,[a] who was in charge of forced
labor, but the Israelites stoned him to death. King Rehoboam, how-
ever, managed to get into his chariot and escape to Jerusalem. 19So
Israel has been in rebellion against the house of David to this day.
11 When Rehoboam arrived in Jerusalem, he mustered Judah and
Benjamin—a hundred and eighty thousand able young men—
to go to war against Israel and to regain the kingdom for Rehoboam.
2But this word of the LORD came to Shemaiah the man of God: 3"Say
to Rehoboam son of Solomon king of Judah and to all Israel in Ju-
dah and Benjamin, 4'This is what the LORD says: Do not go up to fight
against your fellow Israelites. Go home, every one of you, for this is my
doing.'" So they obeyed the words of the LORD and turned back from
marching against Jeroboam.

REHOBOAM FORTIFIES JUDAH

5Rehoboam lived in Jerusalem and built up towns for defense in
Judah: 6Bethlehem, Etam, Tekoa, 7Beth Zur, Soko, Adullam, 8Gath, Ma-
reshah, Ziph, 9Adoraim, Lachish, Azekah, 10Zorah, Aijalon and Hebron.
These were fortified cities in Judah and Benjamin. 11He strengthened
their defenses and put commanders in them, with supplies of food,

PRAYING SCRIPTURE

2 Chronicles 11

It is a fearful thing when God stands against someone. Rehoboam's attempt to wrest back the splintering kingdom came to an end when God told his supporting warriors to go home—and they did! Rather than repenting, Rehoboam fortified his cities to maintain control.

Repentance, not resistance, is the way back to God. Whenever you sin, don't resist the conviction that comes. That's God's grace. Instead, repent and see fellowship restored.

[a] 18 Hebrew *Hadoram*, a variant of *Adoniram*

olive oil and wine. 12He put shields and spears in all the cities, and made them very strong. So Judah and Benjamin were his.

13The priests and Levites from all their districts throughout Israel sided with him. 14The Levites even abandoned their pasturelands and property and came to Judah and Jerusalem, because Jeroboam and his sons had rejected them as priests of the LORD 15when he appointed his own priests for the high places and for the goat and calf idols he had made. 16Those from every tribe of Israel who set their hearts on seeking the LORD, the God of Israel, followed the Levites to Jerusalem to offer sacrifices to the LORD, the God of their ancestors. 17They strengthened the kingdom of Judah and supported Rehoboam son of Solomon three years, following the ways of David and Solomon during this time.

REHOBOAM'S FAMILY

18Rehoboam married Mahalath, who was the daughter of David's son Jerimoth and of Abihail, the daughter of Jesse's son Eliab. 19She bore him sons: Jeush, Shemariah and Zaham. 20Then he married Maakah daughter of Absalom, who bore him Abijah, Attai, Ziza and Shelomith. 21Rehoboam loved Maakah daughter of Absalom more than any of his other wives and concubines. In all, he had eighteen wives and sixty concubines, twenty-eight sons and sixty daughters.

22Rehoboam appointed Abijah son of Maakah as crown prince among his brothers, in order to make him king. 23He acted wisely, dispersing some of his sons throughout the districts of Judah and Benjamin, and to all the fortified cities. He gave them abundant provisions and took many wives for them.

SHISHAK ATTACKS JERUSALEM

12 After Rehoboam's position as king was established and he had become strong, he and all Israel[a] with him abandoned the law of the LORD. 2Because they had been unfaithful to the LORD, Shishak king of Egypt attacked Jerusalem in the fifth year of King Rehoboam. 3With twelve hundred chariots and sixty thousand horsemen and the innumerable troops of Libyans, Sukkites and Cushites[b] that came with him from Egypt, 4he captured the fortified cities of Judah and came as far as Jerusalem.

5Then the prophet Shemaiah came to Rehoboam and to the leaders of Judah who had assembled in Jerusalem for fear of Shishak, and he said to them, "This is what the LORD says, 'You have abandoned me; therefore, I now abandon you to Shishak.'"

6The leaders of Israel and the king humbled themselves and said, "The LORD is just."

7When the LORD saw that they humbled themselves, this word of the LORD came to Shemaiah: "Since they have humbled themselves, I will not destroy them but will soon give them deliverance. My wrath will not be poured out on Jerusalem through Shishak. 8They will, however, become subject to him, so that they may learn the difference between serving me and serving the kings of other lands."

9When Shishak king of Egypt attacked Jerusalem, he carried off the treasures of the temple of the LORD and the treasures of the royal palace. He took everything, including the gold shields Solomon had

PRAYING SCRIPTURE

2 Chronicles 12

Rehoboam's tragic reign is summarized in a single sentence: "He did evil because he had not set his heart on seeking the LORD" (verse 14). Seeking the Lord is the primary insulator against doing evil. Those who seek him with their whole hearts find him.

Rather than simply asking God to keep you from sinning, ask him to help you love and pursue him with all your heart.

[a] *1* That is, Judah, as frequently in 2 Chronicles [b] *3* That is, people from the upper Nile region

made. 10So King Rehoboam made bronze shields to replace them and
assigned these to the commanders of the guard on duty at the en-
trance to the royal palace. 11Whenever the king went to the LORD's tem-
ple, the guards went with him, bearing the shields, and afterward they
returned them to the guardroom.
12Because Rehoboam humbled himself, the LORD's anger turned
from him, and he was not totally destroyed. Indeed, there was some
good in Judah.
13King Rehoboam established himself firmly in Jerusalem and con-
tinued as king. He was forty-one years old when he became king, and
he reigned seventeen years in Jerusalem, the city the LORD had chosen
out of all the tribes of Israel in which to put his Name. His mother's
name was Naamah; she was an Ammonite. 14He did evil because he had
not set his heart on seeking the LORD.
15As for the events of Rehoboam's reign, from beginning to end, are
they not written in the records of Shemaiah the prophet and of Iddo
the seer that deal with genealogies? There was continual warfare be-
tween Rehoboam and Jeroboam. 16Rehoboam rested with his ances-
tors and was buried in the City of David. And Abijah his son succeeded
him as king.

ABIJAH KING OF JUDAH

13 In the eighteenth year of the reign of Jeroboam, Abijah became
king of Judah, 2and he reigned in Jerusalem three years. His
mother's name was Maakah,[a] a daughter[b] of Uriel of Gibeah.
There was war between Abijah and Jeroboam. 3Abijah went into bat-
tle with an army of four hundred thousand able fighting men, and
Jeroboam drew up a battle line against him with eight hundred thou-
sand able troops.
4Abijah stood on Mount Zemaraim, in the hill country of Ephraim,
and said, "Jeroboam and all Israel, listen to me! 5Don't you know that
the LORD, the God of Israel, has given the kingship of Israel to David
and his descendants forever by a covenant of salt? 6Yet Jeroboam son
of Nebat, an official of Solomon son of David, rebelled against his mas-
ter. 7Some worthless scoundrels gathered around him and opposed Re-
hoboam son of Solomon when he was young and indecisive and not
strong enough to resist them.
8"And now you plan to resist the kingdom of the LORD, which is in
the hands of David's descendants. You are indeed a vast army and have
with you the golden calves that Jeroboam made to be your gods. 9But
didn't you drive out the priests of the LORD, the sons of Aaron, and the
Levites, and make priests of your own as the peoples of other lands
do? Whoever comes to consecrate himself with a young bull and seven
rams may become a priest of what are not gods.
10"As for us, the LORD is our God, and we have not forsaken him. The
priests who serve the LORD are sons of Aaron, and the Levites assist them.
11Every morning and evening they present burnt offerings and fragrant
incense to the LORD. They set out the bread on the ceremonially clean
table and light the lamps on the gold lampstand every evening. We are
observing the requirements of the LORD our God. But you have forsaken
him. 12God is with us; he is our leader. His priests with their trumpets will

PRAYING SCRIPTURE

2 Chronicles 13

King Abijah of Judah challenged the people to remember their God, the God of Israel. Surrounded by Jeroboam's army, Abijah encouraged his people to have faith in God, and God delivered them.

We often try to fight battles that God wants to fight on our behalf. When he acts on our behalf, we are rescued and he is glorified. Commit to letting God fight your battles for you.

---

[a] 2 Most Septuagint manuscripts and Syriac (see also 11:20 and 1 Kings 15:2); Hebrew *Micaiah* [b] 2 Or *granddaughter*

sound the battle cry against you. People of Israel, do not fight against the
LORD, the God of your ancestors, for you will not succeed."
13 Now Jeroboam had sent troops around to the rear, so that while he
was in front of Judah the ambush was behind them. 14 Judah turned
and saw that they were being attacked at both front and rear. Then
they cried out to the LORD. The priests blew their trumpets 15 and the
men of Judah raised the battle cry. At the sound of their battle cry,
God routed Jeroboam and all Israel before Abijah and Judah. 16 The Is-
raelites fled before Judah, and God delivered them into their hands.
17 Abijah and his troops inflicted heavy losses on them, so that there
were five hundred thousand casualties among Israel's able men. 18 The
Israelites were subdued on that occasion, and the people of Judah were
victorious because they relied on the LORD, the God of their ancestors.
19 Abijah pursued Jeroboam and took from him the towns of Bethel,
Jeshanah and Ephron, with their surrounding villages. 20 Jeroboam did
not regain power during the time of Abijah. And the LORD struck him
down and he died.
21 But Abijah grew in strength. He married fourteen wives and had
twenty-two sons and sixteen daughters.
22 The other events of Abijah's reign, what he did and what he said,
are written in the annotations of the prophet Iddo.

14 [a] And Abijah rested with his ancestors and was buried in the City
of David. Asa his son succeeded him as king, and in his days the
country was at peace for ten years.

ASA KING OF JUDAH

2 Asa did what was good and right in the eyes of the LORD his God.
3 He removed the foreign altars and the high places, smashed the sa-
cred stones and cut down the Asherah poles.[b] 4 He commanded Judah
to seek the LORD, the God of their ancestors, and to obey his laws and
commands. 5 He removed the high places and incense altars in every
town in Judah, and the kingdom was at peace under him. 6 He built up
the fortified cities of Judah, since the land was at peace. No one was at
war with him during those years, for the LORD gave him rest.
7 "Let us build up these towns," he said to Judah, "and put walls
around them, with towers, gates and bars. The land is still ours, be-
cause we have sought the LORD our God; we sought him and he has
given us rest on every side." So they built and prospered.
8 Asa had an army of three hundred thousand men from Judah,
equipped with large shields and with spears, and two hundred and
eighty thousand from Benjamin, armed with small shields and with
bows. All these were brave fighting men.
9 Zerah the Cushite marched out against them with an army of thou-
sands upon thousands and three hundred chariots, and came as far as
Mareshah. 10 Asa went out to meet him, and they took up battle posi-
tions in the Valley of Zephathah near Mareshah.
11 Then Asa called to the LORD his God and said, "LORD, there is no
one like you to help the powerless against the mighty. Help us, LORD
our God, for we rely on you, and in your name we have come against
this vast army. LORD, you are our God; do not let mere mortals prevail
against you."

PRAYING SCRIPTURE

2 Chronicles 14

King Asa of Judah was another of the kings who loved God. He tore down the high places of idol worship, destroyed the wooden idols and oversaw years of peace. God blessed and honored Asa's obedience.

Do you ever feel as if you alone are serving God? Asa was rare among Judah's kings, but he obeyed God. God will give us faith and courage to stand for him if we ask.

[a] In Hebrew texts 14:1 is numbered 13:23, and 14:2-15 is numbered 14:1-14.
[b] 3 That is, wooden symbols of the goddess Asherah; here and elsewhere in 2 Chronicles

12The LORD struck down the Cushites before Asa and Judah. The
Cushites fled, 13and Asa and his army pursued them as far as Gerar.
Such a great number of Cushites fell that they could not recover; they
were crushed before the LORD and his forces. The men of Judah carried
off a large amount of plunder. 14They destroyed all the villages around
Gerar, for the terror of the LORD had fallen on them. They looted all
these villages, since there was much plunder there. 15They also at-
tacked the camps of the herders and carried off droves of sheep and
goats and camels. Then they returned to Jerusalem.

ASA'S REFORM

15 The Spirit of God came on Azariah son of Oded. 2He went out to
meet Asa and said to him, "Listen to me, Asa and all Judah and
Benjamin. The LORD is with you when you are with him. If you seek
him, he will be found by you, but if you forsake him, he will forsake
you. 3For a long time Israel was without the true God, without a priest
to teach and without the law. 4But in their distress they turned to the
LORD, the God of Israel, and sought him, and he was found by them. 5In
those days it was not safe to travel about, for all the inhabitants of the
lands were in great turmoil. 6One nation was being crushed by another
and one city by another, because God was troubling them with every
kind of distress. 7But as for you, be strong and do not give up, for your
work will be rewarded."

8When Asa heard these words and the prophecy of Azariah son of[a]
Oded the prophet, he took courage. He removed the detestable idols
from the whole land of Judah and Benjamin and from the towns he
had captured in the hills of Ephraim. He repaired the altar of the LORD
that was in front of the portico of the LORD's temple.

9Then he assembled all Judah and Benjamin and the people from
Ephraim, Manasseh and Simeon who had settled among them, for
large numbers had come over to him from Israel when they saw that
the LORD his God was with him.

10They assembled at Jerusalem in the third month of the fifteenth
year of Asa's reign. 11At that time they sacrificed to the LORD seven
hundred head of cattle and seven thousand sheep and goats from the
plunder they had brought back. 12They entered into a covenant to
seek the LORD, the God of their ancestors, with all their heart and soul.
13All who would not seek the LORD, the God of Israel, were to be put to
death, whether small or great, man or woman. 14They took an oath to
the LORD with loud acclamation, with shouting and with trumpets and
horns. 15All Judah rejoiced about the oath because they had sworn it
wholeheartedly. They sought God eagerly, and he was found by them.
So the LORD gave them rest on every side.

16King Asa also deposed his grandmother Maakah from her position
as queen mother, because she had made a repulsive image for the wor-
ship of Asherah. Asa cut it down, broke it up and burned it in the Kid-
ron Valley. 17Although he did not remove the high places from Israel,
Asa's heart was fully committed to the LORD all his life. 18He brought
into the temple of God the silver and gold and the articles that he and
his father had dedicated.

19There was no more war until the thirty-fifth year of Asa's reign.

[a] 8 Vulgate and Syriac (see also Septuagint and verse 1); Hebrew does not have *Azariah son of*.

PRAYING SCRIPTURE

2 Chronicles 15

King Asa was strengthened to institute reforms in Judah by God speaking through his prophet Oded. "When Asa heard these words and the prophecy . . . he took courage" (verse 8). Asa removed the idols from all over the country and restored God's altars, and the people entered a covenant to seek God with all their hearts and souls (see verse 12).

Courage should come from God's Word. It's not something we have to "work up." Seek God's Word and ask for the courage you need.

ASA'S LAST YEARS

16 In the thirty-sixth year of Asa's reign Baasha king of Israel went
up against Judah and fortified Ramah to prevent anyone from
leaving or entering the territory of Asa king of Judah.
2Asa then took the silver and gold out of the treasuries of the LORD's
temple and of his own palace and sent it to Ben-Hadad king of Aram,
who was ruling in Damascus. 3"Let there be a treaty between me and
you," he said, "as there was between my father and your father. See, I
am sending you silver and gold. Now break your treaty with Baasha
king of Israel so he will withdraw from me."
4Ben-Hadad agreed with King Asa and sent the commanders of his
forces against the towns of Israel. They conquered Ijon, Dan, Abel
Maim[a] and all the store cities of Naphtali. 5When Baasha heard this,
he stopped building Ramah and abandoned his work. 6Then King Asa
brought all the men of Judah, and they carried away from Ramah the
stones and timber Baasha had been using. With them he built up Geba
and Mizpah.
7At that time Hanani the seer came to Asa king of Judah and said to
him: "Because you relied on the king of Aram and not on the LORD your
God, the army of the king of Aram has escaped from your hand. 8Were
not the Cushites[b] and Libyans a mighty army with great numbers of
chariots and horsemen[c]? Yet when you relied on the LORD, he delivered
them into your hand. 9For the eyes of the LORD range throughout the
earth to strengthen those whose hearts are fully committed to him.
You have done a foolish thing, and from now on you will be at war."
10Asa was angry with the seer because of this; he was so enraged that
he put him in prison. At the same time Asa brutally oppressed some
of the people.
11The events of Asa's reign, from beginning to end, are written in the
book of the kings of Judah and Israel. 12In the thirty-ninth year of his
reign Asa was afflicted with a disease in his feet. Though his disease
was severe, even in his illness he did not seek help from the LORD, but
only from the physicians. 13Then in the forty-first year of his reign Asa
died and rested with his ancestors. 14They buried him in the tomb that
he had cut out for himself in the City of David. They laid him on a bier
covered with spices and various blended perfumes, and they made a
huge fire in his honor.

PRAYING SCRIPTURE

2 Chronicles 16

After years of obedience, Asa let his faith in God fail at a crucial moment. The seer Hanani's rebuke included the precious promise: "For the eyes of the LORD range throughout the earth to strengthen those whose hearts are fully committed to him" (verse 9).

This promise can be a prayer in which we commit our hearts to God and ask him to show himself strong.

JEHOSHAPHAT KING OF JUDAH

17 Jehoshaphat his son succeeded him as king and strengthened
himself against Israel. 2He stationed troops in all the fortified
cities of Judah and put garrisons in Judah and in the towns of Ephraim
that his father Asa had captured.
3The LORD was with Jehoshaphat because he followed the ways of his
father David before him. He did not consult the Baals 4but sought the
God of his father and followed his commands rather than the practices
of Israel. 5The LORD established the kingdom under his control; and all
Judah brought gifts to Jehoshaphat, so that he had great wealth and
honor. 6His heart was devoted to the ways of the LORD; furthermore, he
removed the high places and the Asherah poles from Judah.
7In the third year of his reign he sent his officials Ben-Hail, Obadiah,

PRAYING SCRIPTURE

2 Chronicles 17

The beginning narrative of Jehoshaphat highlights his obedience to God and the powerful words "the LORD established the kingdom under his control" (verse 5). The king did not establish his own kingdom. God intervened to make certain that Jehoshaphat's reign was certain.

What is one specific way you would like God to establish your life, career or ministry? As you ask him, commit to walk in his ways as you wait on him.

---

[a] 4 Also known as *Abel Beth Maakah* [b] 8 That is, people from the upper Nile region [c] 8 Or *charioteers*

Zechariah, Nethanel and Micaiah to teach in the towns of Judah. 8With
them were certain Levites — Shemaiah, Nethaniah, Zebadiah, Asahel,
Shemiramoth, Jehonathan, Adonijah, Tobijah and Tob-Adonijah — and
the priests Elishama and Jehoram. 9They taught throughout Judah,
taking with them the Book of the Law of the LORD; they went around
to all the towns of Judah and taught the people.

10The fear of the LORD fell on all the kingdoms of the lands sur-
rounding Judah, so that they did not go to war against Jehoshaphat.
11Some Philistines brought Jehoshaphat gifts and silver as tribute, and
the Arabs brought him flocks: seven thousand seven hundred rams
and seven thousand seven hundred goats.

12Jehoshaphat became more and more powerful; he built forts and
store cities in Judah 13and had large supplies in the towns of Judah. He
also kept experienced fighting men in Jerusalem. 14Their enrollment
by families was as follows:

From Judah, commanders of units of 1,000:
Adnah the commander, with 300,000 fighting men;
15next, Jehohanan the commander, with 280,000;
16next, Amasiah son of Zikri, who volunteered himself for the ser-
vice of the LORD, with 200,000.
17From Benjamin:
Eliada, a valiant soldier, with 200,000 men armed with bows
and shields;
18next, Jehozabad, with 180,000 men armed for battle.

19These were the men who served the king, besides those he stationed
in the fortified cities throughout Judah.

MICAIAH PROPHESIES AGAINST AHAB

18 Now Jehoshaphat had great wealth and honor, and he allied
himself with Ahab by marriage. 2Some years later he went down
to see Ahab in Samaria. Ahab slaughtered many sheep and cattle for
him and the people with him and urged him to attack Ramoth Gilead.
3Ahab king of Israel asked Jehoshaphat king of Judah, "Will you go
with me against Ramoth Gilead?"

Jehoshaphat replied, "I am as you are, and my people as your people;
we will join you in the war." 4But Jehoshaphat also said to the king of
Israel, "First seek the counsel of the LORD."

5So the king of Israel brought together the prophets — four hundred
men — and asked them, "Shall we go to war against Ramoth Gilead, or
shall I not?"

"Go," they answered, "for God will give it into the king's hand."

6But Jehoshaphat asked, "Is there no longer a prophet of the LORD
here whom we can inquire of?"

7The king of Israel answered Jehoshaphat, "There is still one prophet
through whom we can inquire of the LORD, but I hate him because he
never prophesies anything good about me, but always bad. He is Mi-
caiah son of Imlah."

"The king should not say such a thing," Jehoshaphat replied.

8So the king of Israel called one of his officials and said, "Bring Mi-
caiah son of Imlah at once."

9Dressed in their royal robes, the king of Israel and Jehoshaphat
king of Judah were sitting on their thrones at the threshing floor by
the entrance of the gate of Samaria, with all the prophets prophesying

PRAYING SCRIPTURE

2 Chronicles 18

God's judgment isn't always fast, but it's always sure. Long after arranging Naboth's murder, Ahab disguised himself going into a battle. A nameless archer drew his bow at random, and his arrow found a crevice in Ahab's armor, killing him. When Ahab's chariot was rinsed, dogs lapped up his blood, fulfilling the word of Elijah (1 Kings 22:38).

Don't despair when you pray for justice. Trust God's timing to be right.

before them. 10Now Zedekiah son of Kenaanah had made iron horns,
and he declared, "This is what the LORD says: 'With these you will gore
the Arameans until they are destroyed.'"
11All the other prophets were prophesying the same thing. "Attack
Ramoth Gilead and be victorious," they said, "for the LORD will give it
into the king's hand."
12The messenger who had gone to summon Micaiah said to him,
"Look, the other prophets without exception are predicting success
for the king. Let your word agree with theirs, and speak favorably."
13But Micaiah said, "As surely as the LORD lives, I can tell him only
what my God says."
14When he arrived, the king asked him, "Micaiah, shall we go to war
against Ramoth Gilead, or shall I not?"
"Attack and be victorious," he answered, "for they will be given into
your hand."
15The king said to him, "How many times must I make you swear to
tell me nothing but the truth in the name of the LORD?"
16Then Micaiah answered, "I saw all Israel scattered on the hills like
sheep without a shepherd, and the LORD said, 'These people have no
master. Let each one go home in peace.'"
17The king of Israel said to Jehoshaphat, "Didn't I tell you that he
never prophesies anything good about me, but only bad?"
18Micaiah continued, "Therefore hear the word of the LORD: I saw the
LORD sitting on his throne with all the multitudes of heaven standing
on his right and on his left. 19And the LORD said, 'Who will entice Ahab
king of Israel into attacking Ramoth Gilead and going to his death
there?'
"One suggested this, and another that. 20Finally, a spirit came for-
ward, stood before the LORD and said, 'I will entice him.'
"'By what means?' the LORD asked.
21"'I will go and be a deceiving spirit in the mouths of all his proph-
ets,' he said.
"'You will succeed in enticing him,' said the LORD. 'Go and do it.'
22"So now the LORD has put a deceiving spirit in the mouths of these
prophets of yours. The LORD has decreed disaster for you."
23Then Zedekiah son of Kenaanah went up and slapped Micaiah in
the face. "Which way did the spirit from[a] the LORD go when he went
from me to speak to you?" he asked.
24Micaiah replied, "You will find out on the day you go to hide in an
inner room."
25The king of Israel then ordered, "Take Micaiah and send him back
to Amon the ruler of the city and to Joash the king's son, 26and say,
'This is what the king says: Put this fellow in prison and give him noth-
ing but bread and water until I return safely.'"
27Micaiah declared, "If you ever return safely, the LORD has not spo-
ken through me." Then he added, "Mark my words, all you people!"

AHAB KILLED AT RAMOTH GILEAD

28So the king of Israel and Jehoshaphat king of Judah went up to Ra-
moth Gilead. 29The king of Israel said to Jehoshaphat, "I will enter the
battle in disguise, but you wear your royal robes." So the king of Israel
disguised himself and went into battle.

[a] 23 Or *Spirit of*

30 Now the king of Aram had ordered his chariot commanders, "Do
not fight with anyone, small or great, except the king of Israel." 31 When
the chariot commanders saw Jehoshaphat, they thought, "This is the
king of Israel." So they turned to attack him, but Jehoshaphat cried
out, and the LORD helped him. God drew them away from him, 32 for
when the chariot commanders saw that he was not the king of Israel,
they stopped pursuing him.
33 But someone drew his bow at random and hit the king of Israel
between the breastplate and the scale armor. The king told the chariot driver, "Wheel around and get me out of the fighting. I've been
wounded." 34 All day long the battle raged, and the king of Israel
propped himself up in his chariot facing the Arameans until evening.
Then at sunset he died.

19 When Jehoshaphat king of Judah returned safely to his palace
in Jerusalem, 2 Jehu the seer, the son of Hanani, went out to
meet him and said to the king, "Should you help the wicked and love[a]
those who hate the LORD? Because of this, the wrath of the LORD is on
you. 3 There is, however, some good in you, for you have rid the land of
the Asherah poles and have set your heart on seeking God."

JEHOSHAPHAT APPOINTS JUDGES

4 Jehoshaphat lived in Jerusalem, and he went out again among the
people from Beersheba to the hill country of Ephraim and turned them
back to the LORD, the God of their ancestors. 5 He appointed judges in
the land, in each of the fortified cities of Judah. 6 He told them, "Consider carefully what you do, because you are not judging for mere mortals but for the LORD, who is with you whenever you give a verdict.
7 Now let the fear of the LORD be on you. Judge carefully, for with the
LORD our God there is no injustice or partiality or bribery."
8 In Jerusalem also, Jehoshaphat appointed some of the Levites,
priests and heads of Israelite families to administer the law of the
LORD and to settle disputes. And they lived in Jerusalem. 9 He gave
them these orders: "You must serve faithfully and wholeheartedly in
the fear of the LORD. 10 In every case that comes before you from your
people who live in the cities—whether bloodshed or other concerns
of the law, commands, decrees or regulations—you are to warn them
not to sin against the LORD; otherwise his wrath will come on you and
your people. Do this, and you will not sin.
11 "Amariah the chief priest will be over you in any matter concerning
the LORD, and Zebadiah son of Ishmael, the leader of the tribe of Judah,
will be over you in any matter concerning the king, and the Levites will
serve as officials before you. Act with courage, and may the LORD be
with those who do well."

JEHOSHAPHAT DEFEATS MOAB AND AMMON

20 After this, the Moabites and Ammonites with some of the Meunites[b] came to wage war against Jehoshaphat.
2 Some people came and told Jehoshaphat, "A vast army is coming
against you from Edom,[c] from the other side of the Dead Sea. It is already in Hazezon Tamar" (that is, En Gedi). 3 Alarmed, Jehoshaphat

[a] 2 Or *and make alliances with* [b] 1 Some Septuagint manuscripts; Hebrew *Ammonites* [c] 2 One Hebrew manuscript; most Hebrew manuscripts, Septuagint and Vulgate *Aram*

PRAYING SCRIPTURE

2 Chronicles 19

One of Jehoshaphat's reminders was that God is fair. God does not show partiality based on any earthly criteria, nor does he act unjustly or take bribes. God does not favor the rich over the poor, the well-known over the unknown or the prince over the pauper.

God is always right because he is always righteous. This is a blessing, so thank God for his righteousness in all he does.

PRAYING SCRIPTURE

2 Chronicles 20

After Jehoshaphat led God's people into spiritual renewal, Judah was threatened by multiple nations: Moab, Ammon and others aligned themselves against Jehoshaphat (see verse 1). Upon hearing the news, he was "alarmed" and "resolved to inquire of the LORD," then called a fast throughout the entire country (see verse 3).

When calamity comes, when fear sets in, seek the Lord immediately. Whatever the threat you face, call on him without delay. Don't be ruled by fear.

resolved to inquire of the LORD, and he proclaimed a fast for all Judah. 4The people of Judah came together to seek help from the LORD; indeed, they came from every town in Judah to seek him.

5Then Jehoshaphat stood up in the assembly of Judah and Jerusalem at the temple of the LORD in the front of the new courtyard 6and said:

> "LORD, the God of our ancestors, are you not the God who is in heaven? You rule over all the kingdoms of the nations. Power and might are in your hand, and no one can withstand you. 7Our God, did you not drive out the inhabitants of this land before your people Israel and give it forever to the descendants of Abraham your friend? 8They have lived in it and have built in it a sanctuary for your Name, saying, 9'If calamity comes upon us, whether the sword of judgment, or plague or famine, we will stand in your presence before this temple that bears your Name and will cry out to you in our distress, and you will hear us and save us.'
>
> 10"But now here are men from Ammon, Moab and Mount Seir, whose territory you would not allow Israel to invade when they came from Egypt; so they turned away from them and did not destroy them. 11See how they are repaying us by coming to drive us out of the possession you gave us as an inheritance. 12Our God, will you not judge them? For we have no power to face this vast army that is attacking us. We do not know what to do, but our eyes are on you."

13All the men of Judah, with their wives and children and little ones, stood there before the LORD.

14Then the Spirit of the LORD came on Jahaziel son of Zechariah, the son of Benaiah, the son of Jeiel, the son of Mattaniah, a Levite and descendant of Asaph, as he stood in the assembly.

15He said: "Listen, King Jehoshaphat and all who live in Judah and Jerusalem! This is what the LORD says to you: 'Do not be afraid or discouraged because of this vast army. For the battle is not yours, but God's. 16Tomorrow march down against them. They will be climbing up by the Pass of Ziz, and you will find them at the end of the gorge in the Desert of Jeruel. 17You will not have to fight this battle. Take up your positions; stand firm and see the deliverance the LORD will give you, Judah and Jerusalem. Do not be afraid; do not be discouraged. Go out to face them tomorrow, and the LORD will be with you.'"

18Jehoshaphat bowed down with his face to the ground, and all the people of Judah and Jerusalem fell down in worship before the LORD. 19Then some Levites from the Kohathites and Korahites stood up and praised the LORD, the God of Israel, with a very loud voice.

20Early in the morning they left for the Desert of Tekoa. As they set out, Jehoshaphat stood and said, "Listen to me, Judah and people of Jerusalem! Have faith in the LORD your God and you will be upheld; have faith in his prophets and you will be successful." 21After consulting the people, Jehoshaphat appointed men to sing to the LORD and to praise him for the splendor of his[a] holiness as they went out at the head of the army, saying:

> "Give thanks to the LORD,
>   for his love endures forever."

---

[a] 21 Or *him with the splendor of*

22 As they began to sing and praise, the LORD set ambushes against the men of Ammon and Moab and Mount Seir who were invading Judah, and they were defeated. 23 The Ammonites and Moabites rose up against the men from Mount Seir to destroy and annihilate them. After they finished slaughtering the men from Seir, they helped to destroy one another.

24 When the men of Judah came to the place that overlooks the desert and looked toward the vast army, they saw only dead bodies lying on the ground; no one had escaped. 25 So Jehoshaphat and his men went to carry off their plunder, and they found among them a great amount of equipment and clothing[a] and also articles of value — more than they could take away. There was so much plunder that it took three days to collect it. 26 On the fourth day they assembled in the Valley of Berakah, where they praised the LORD. This is why it is called the Valley of Berakah[b] to this day.

27 Then, led by Jehoshaphat, all the men of Judah and Jerusalem returned joyfully to Jerusalem, for the LORD had given them cause to rejoice over their enemies. 28 They entered Jerusalem and went to the temple of the LORD with harps and lyres and trumpets.

29 The fear of God came on all the surrounding kingdoms when they heard how the LORD had fought against the enemies of Israel. 30 And the kingdom of Jehoshaphat was at peace, for his God had given him rest on every side.

THE END OF JEHOSHAPHAT'S REIGN

31 So Jehoshaphat reigned over Judah. He was thirty-five years old when he became king of Judah, and he reigned in Jerusalem twenty-five years. His mother's name was Azubah daughter of Shilhi. 32 He followed the ways of his father Asa and did not stray from them; he did what was right in the eyes of the LORD. 33 The high places, however, were not removed, and the people still had not set their hearts on the God of their ancestors.

34 The other events of Jehoshaphat's reign, from beginning to end, are written in the annals of Jehu son of Hanani, which are recorded in the book of the kings of Israel.

35 Later, Jehoshaphat king of Judah made an alliance with Ahaziah king of Israel, whose ways were wicked. 36 He agreed with him to construct a fleet of trading ships.[c] After these were built at Ezion Geber, 37 Eliezer son of Dodavahu of Mareshah prophesied against Jehoshaphat, saying, "Because you have made an alliance with Ahaziah, the LORD will destroy what you have made." The ships were wrecked and were not able to set sail to trade.[d]

21 Then Jehoshaphat rested with his ancestors and was buried with them in the City of David. And Jehoram his son succeeded him as king. 2 Jehoram's brothers, the sons of Jehoshaphat, were Azariah, Jehiel, Zechariah, Azariahu, Michael and Shephatiah. All these were sons of Jehoshaphat king of Israel.[e] 3 Their father had given them many gifts of silver and gold and articles of value, as well as fortified cities in Judah, but he had given the kingdom to Jehoram because he was his firstborn son.

PRAYING SCRIPTURE

2 Chronicles 21

Jehoram exemplified all that is wrong in worldly politics. He did not follow God, he led people astray, he strengthened his own base of power (rather than letting God do it) and even murdered all potential successors to the throne—including his brothers.

Hunger for worldly power usually ends in calamity. When you have an opportunity to lead, ask God for the humility to lead as Jesus would.

[a] *25* Some Hebrew manuscripts and Vulgate; most Hebrew manuscripts *corpses* [b] *26* *Berakah* means *praise.* [c] *36* Hebrew *of ships that could go to Tarshish* [d] *37* Hebrew *sail for Tarshish* [e] *2* That is, Judah, as frequently in 2 Chronicles

JEHORAM KING OF JUDAH

4 When Jehoram established himself firmly over his father's king-
dom, he put all his brothers to the sword along with some of the of-
ficials of Israel. 5 Jehoram was thirty-two years old when he became
king, and he reigned in Jerusalem eight years. 6 He followed the ways
of the kings of Israel, as the house of Ahab had done, for he married a
daughter of Ahab. He did evil in the eyes of the LORD. 7 Nevertheless,
because of the covenant the LORD had made with David, the LORD was
not willing to destroy the house of David. He had promised to main-
tain a lamp for him and his descendants forever.

8 In the time of Jehoram, Edom rebelled against Judah and set up its
own king. 9 So Jehoram went there with his officers and all his chari-
ots. The Edomites surrounded him and his chariot commanders, but
he rose up and broke through by night. 10 To this day Edom has been in
rebellion against Judah.

Libnah revolted at the same time, because Jehoram had forsaken
the LORD, the God of his ancestors. 11 He had also built high places on
the hills of Judah and had caused the people of Jerusalem to prostitute
themselves and had led Judah astray.

12 Jehoram received a letter from Elijah the prophet, which said:

> "This is what the LORD, the God of your father David, says: 'You
> have not followed the ways of your father Jehoshaphat or of Asa
> king of Judah. 13 But you have followed the ways of the kings of
> Israel, and you have led Judah and the people of Jerusalem to
> prostitute themselves, just as the house of Ahab did. You have also
> murdered your own brothers, members of your own family, men
> who were better than you. 14 So now the LORD is about to strike your
> people, your sons, your wives and everything that is yours, with a
> heavy blow. 15 You yourself will be very ill with a lingering disease
> of the bowels, until the disease causes your bowels to come out.'"

16 The LORD aroused against Jehoram the hostility of the Philistines
and of the Arabs who lived near the Cushites. 17 They attacked Judah,
invaded it and carried off all the goods found in the king's palace, to-
gether with his sons and wives. Not a son was left to him except Aha-
ziah,[a] the youngest.

18 After all this, the LORD afflicted Jehoram with an incurable dis-
ease of the bowels. 19 In the course of time, at the end of the second
year, his bowels came out because of the disease, and he died in great
pain. His people made no funeral fire in his honor, as they had for his
predecessors.

20 Jehoram was thirty-two years old when he became king, and he
reigned in Jerusalem eight years. He passed away, to no one's regret,
and was buried in the City of David, but not in the tombs of the kings.

AHAZIAH KING OF JUDAH

22 The people of Jerusalem made Ahaziah, Jehoram's youngest
son, king in his place, since the raiders, who came with the
Arabs into the camp, had killed all the older sons. So Ahaziah son of
Jehoram king of Judah began to reign.

2 Ahaziah was twenty-two[b] years old when he became king, and he

PRAYING SCRIPTURE

2 Chronicles 22

Sometimes God's working in our lives looks like what we'd read in a thriller. During Athaliah's murder spree designed to kill all heirs to the throne, one of the king's daughters took the child Joash (a target) into a room and hid him. He was hidden "at the temple of God" for six years with the king's daughter and her husband, a priest (see verse 12).

Thank God that his power is always sufficient to accomplish his plans.

[a] 17 Hebrew *Jehoahaz*, a variant of *Ahaziah* [b] 2 Some Septuagint manuscripts and Syriac (see also 2 Kings 8:26); Hebrew *forty-two*

reigned in Jerusalem one year. His mother's name was Athaliah, a
granddaughter of Omri.
3He too followed the ways of the house of Ahab, for his mother en-
couraged him to act wickedly. 4He did evil in the eyes of the LORD, as
the house of Ahab had done, for after his father's death they became
his advisers, to his undoing. 5He also followed their counsel when he
went with Joram[a] son of Ahab king of Israel to wage war against Hazael
king of Aram at Ramoth Gilead. The Arameans wounded Joram; 6so he
returned to Jezreel to recover from the wounds they had inflicted on
him at Ramoth[b] in his battle with Hazael king of Aram.

Then Ahaziah[c] son of Jehoram king of Judah went down to Jezreel
to see Joram son of Ahab because he had been wounded.
7Through Ahaziah's visit to Joram, God brought about Ahaziah's
downfall. When Ahaziah arrived, he went out with Joram to meet Jehu
son of Nimshi, whom the LORD had anointed to destroy the house of
Ahab. 8While Jehu was executing judgment on the house of Ahab, he
found the officials of Judah and the sons of Ahaziah's relatives, who
had been attending Ahaziah, and he killed them. 9He then went in
search of Ahaziah, and his men captured him while he was hiding in
Samaria. He was brought to Jehu and put to death. They buried him,
for they said, "He was a son of Jehoshaphat, who sought the LORD with
all his heart." So there was no one in the house of Ahaziah powerful
enough to retain the kingdom.

ATHALIAH AND JOASH

10When Athaliah the mother of Ahaziah saw that her son was dead,
she proceeded to destroy the whole royal family of the house of Ju-
dah. 11But Jehosheba,[d] the daughter of King Jehoram, took Joash son
of Ahaziah and stole him away from among the royal princes who were
about to be murdered and put him and his nurse in a bedroom. Be-
cause Jehosheba,[d] the daughter of King Jehoram and wife of the priest
Jehoiada, was Ahaziah's sister, she hid the child from Athaliah so she
could not kill him. 12He remained hidden with them at the temple of
God for six years while Athaliah ruled the land.

23 In the seventh year Jehoiada showed his strength. He made a
covenant with the commanders of units of a hundred: Azariah
son of Jeroham, Ishmael son of Jehohanan, Azariah son of Obed, Maa-
seiah son of Adaiah, and Elishaphat son of Zikri. 2They went through-
out Judah and gathered the Levites and the heads of Israelite families
from all the towns. When they came to Jerusalem, 3the whole assembly
made a covenant with the king at the temple of God.

Jehoiada said to them, "The king's son shall reign, as the LORD prom-
ised concerning the descendants of David. 4Now this is what you are to
do: A third of you priests and Levites who are going on duty on the Sab-
bath are to keep watch at the doors, 5a third of you at the royal palace
and a third at the Foundation Gate, and all the others are to be in the
courtyards of the temple of the LORD. 6No one is to enter the temple
of the LORD except the priests and Levites on duty; they may enter be-
cause they are consecrated, but all the others are to observe the LORD's

[a] 5 Hebrew *Jehoram*, a variant of *Joram*; also in verses 6 and 7 [b] 6 Hebrew *Ramah*, a variant of *Ramoth* [c] 6 Some Hebrew manuscripts, Septuagint, Vulgate and Syriac (see also 2 Kings 8:29); most Hebrew manuscripts *Azariah*
[d] 11 Hebrew *Jehoshabeath*, a variant of *Jehosheba*

PRAYING SCRIPTURE

2 Chronicles 23

In Joash's seventh year, the priest who had hidden him, Jehoiada, built an alliance across Judah that would secure the throne for Joash, who was of David's house. When Joash was revealed, Athaliah, author of the earlier plot to kill the heirs, revealed herself and was put to death.

A life of deceit, power-grabbing and killing is not the life of Jesus. Pray always to live according to kingdom values.

command not to enter.[a] 7The Levites are to station themselves around the king, each with weapon in hand. Anyone who enters the temple is to be put to death. Stay close to the king wherever he goes."

8The Levites and all the men of Judah did just as Jehoiada the priest ordered. Each one took his men—those who were going on duty on the Sabbath and those who were going off duty—for Jehoiada the priest had not released any of the divisions. 9Then he gave the commanders of units of a hundred the spears and the large and small shields that had belonged to King David and that were in the temple of God. 10He stationed all the men, each with his weapon in his hand, around the king—near the altar and the temple, from the south side to the north side of the temple.

11Jehoiada and his sons brought out the king's son and put the crown on him; they presented him with a copy of the covenant and proclaimed him king. They anointed him and shouted, "Long live the king!"

12When Athaliah heard the noise of the people running and cheering the king, she went to them at the temple of the LORD. 13She looked, and there was the king, standing by his pillar at the entrance. The officers and the trumpeters were beside the king, and all the people of the land were rejoicing and blowing trumpets, and musicians with their instruments were leading the praises. Then Athaliah tore her robes and shouted, "Treason! Treason!"

14Jehoiada the priest sent out the commanders of units of a hundred, who were in charge of the troops, and said to them: "Bring her out between the ranks[b] and put to the sword anyone who follows her." For the priest had said, "Do not put her to death at the temple of the LORD." 15So they seized her as she reached the entrance of the Horse Gate on the palace grounds, and there they put her to death.

16Jehoiada then made a covenant that he, the people and the king[c] would be the LORD's people. 17All the people went to the temple of Baal and tore it down. They smashed the altars and idols and killed Mattan the priest of Baal in front of the altars.

18Then Jehoiada placed the oversight of the temple of the LORD in the hands of the Levitical priests, to whom David had made assignments in the temple, to present the burnt offerings of the LORD as written in the Law of Moses, with rejoicing and singing, as David had ordered. 19He also stationed gatekeepers at the gates of the LORD's temple so that no one who was in any way unclean might enter.

20He took with him the commanders of hundreds, the nobles, the rulers of the people and all the people of the land and brought the king down from the temple of the LORD. They went into the palace through the Upper Gate and seated the king on the royal throne. 21All the people of the land rejoiced, and the city was calm, because Athaliah had been slain with the sword.

JOASH REPAIRS THE TEMPLE

24 Joash was seven years old when he became king, and he reigned in Jerusalem forty years. His mother's name was Zibiah; she was from Beersheba. 2Joash did what was right in the eyes of

PRAYING SCRIPTURE

2 Chronicles 24

Judah experienced spiritual reforms under Joash: The temple was repaired, instruments of service were replaced and the sacrifices reinstituted. Sadly, Joash's spiritual commitment lasted only as long as Jehoiada was alive. When the priest died, Joash fell hard into apostasy.

Is there anyone in your life who significantly helps you continue to follow Jesus? Ask God to help you focus on him rather than on anyone human.

[a] 6 Or *are to stand guard where the LORD has assigned them* [b] 14 Or *out from the precincts* [c] 16 Or *covenant between the LORD and the people and the king that they* (see 2 Kings 11:17)

the LORD all the years of Jehoiada the priest. 3Jehoiada chose two wives
for him, and he had sons and daughters.
4Some time later Joash decided to restore the temple of the LORD.
5He called together the priests and Levites and said to them, "Go to the
towns of Judah and collect the money due annually from all Israel, to
repair the temple of your God. Do it now." But the Levites did not act
at once.
6Therefore the king summoned Jehoiada the chief priest and said
to him, "Why haven't you required the Levites to bring in from Judah
and Jerusalem the tax imposed by Moses the servant of the LORD and
by the assembly of Israel for the tent of the covenant law?"
7Now the sons of that wicked woman Athaliah had broken into the
temple of God and had used even its sacred objects for the Baals.
8At the king's command, a chest was made and placed outside, at
the gate of the temple of the LORD. 9A proclamation was then issued
in Judah and Jerusalem that they should bring to the LORD the tax
that Moses the servant of God had required of Israel in the wilder-
ness. 10All the officials and all the people brought their contributions
gladly, dropping them into the chest until it was full. 11Whenever the
chest was brought in by the Levites to the king's officials and they saw
that there was a large amount of money, the royal secretary and the
officer of the chief priest would come and empty the chest and carry it
back to its place. They did this regularly and collected a great amount
of money. 12The king and Jehoiada gave it to those who carried out
the work required for the temple of the LORD. They hired masons and
carpenters to restore the LORD's temple, and also workers in iron and
bronze to repair the temple.
13The men in charge of the work were diligent, and the repairs pro-
gressed under them. They rebuilt the temple of God according to
its original design and reinforced it. 14When they had finished, they
brought the rest of the money to the king and Jehoiada, and with it
were made articles for the LORD's temple: articles for the service and
for the burnt offerings, and also dishes and other objects of gold and
silver. As long as Jehoiada lived, burnt offerings were presented con-
tinually in the temple of the LORD.
15Now Jehoiada was old and full of years, and he died at the age of a
hundred and thirty. 16He was buried with the kings in the City of Da-
vid, because of the good he had done in Israel for God and his temple.

THE WICKEDNESS OF JOASH

17After the death of Jehoiada, the officials of Judah came and paid
homage to the king, and he listened to them. 18They abandoned the
temple of the LORD, the God of their ancestors, and worshiped Asherah
poles and idols. Because of their guilt, God's anger came on Judah and
Jerusalem. 19Although the LORD sent prophets to the people to bring
them back to him, and though they testified against them, they would
not listen.
20Then the Spirit of God came on Zechariah son of Jehoiada the
priest. He stood before the people and said, "This is what God says:
'Why do you disobey the LORD's commands? You will not prosper. Be-
cause you have forsaken the LORD, he has forsaken you.'"
21But they plotted against him, and by order of the king they stoned
him to death in the courtyard of the LORD's temple. 22King Joash did

not remember the kindness Zechariah's father Jehoiada had shown
him but killed his son, who said as he lay dying, "May the LORD see this
and call you to account."
23At the turn of the year,[a] the army of Aram marched against Joash;
it invaded Judah and Jerusalem and killed all the leaders of the peo-
ple. They sent all the plunder to their king in Damascus. 24Although
the Aramean army had come with only a few men, the LORD delivered
into their hands a much larger army. Because Judah had forsaken the
LORD, the God of their ancestors, judgment was executed on Joash.
25When the Arameans withdrew, they left Joash severely wounded. His
officials conspired against him for murdering the son of Jehoiada the
priest, and they killed him in his bed. So he died and was buried in the
City of David, but not in the tombs of the kings.
26Those who conspired against him were Zabad,[b] son of Shimeath an
Ammonite woman, and Jehozabad, son of Shimrith[c] a Moabite woman.
27The account of his sons, the many prophecies about him, and the
record of the restoration of the temple of God are written in the an-
notations on the book of the kings. And Amaziah his son succeeded
him as king.

AMAZIAH KING OF JUDAH

25 Amaziah was twenty-five years old when he became king, and
he reigned in Jerusalem twenty-nine years. His mother's name
was Jehoaddan; she was from Jerusalem. 2He did what was right in
the eyes of the LORD, but not wholeheartedly. 3After the kingdom was
firmly in his control, he executed the officials who had murdered his
father the king. 4Yet he did not put their children to death, but acted
in accordance with what is written in the Law, in the Book of Moses,
where the LORD commanded: "Parents shall not be put to death for
their children, nor children be put to death for their parents; each will
die for their own sin."[d]
5Amaziah called the people of Judah together and assigned them ac-
cording to their families to commanders of thousands and command-
ers of hundreds for all Judah and Benjamin. He then mustered those
twenty years old or more and found that there were three hundred
thousand men fit for military service, able to handle the spear and
shield. 6He also hired a hundred thousand fighting men from Israel
for a hundred talents[e] of silver.
7But a man of God came to him and said, "Your Majesty, these troops
from Israel must not march with you, for the LORD is not with Israel—
not with any of the people of Ephraim. 8Even if you go and fight cou-
rageously in battle, God will overthrow you before the enemy, for God
has the power to help or to overthrow."
9Amaziah asked the man of God, "But what about the hundred tal-
ents I paid for these Israelite troops?"
The man of God replied, "The LORD can give you much more than
that."
10So Amaziah dismissed the troops who had come to him from
Ephraim and sent them home. They were furious with Judah and left
for home in a great rage.

PRAYING SCRIPTURE

2 Chronicles 25

An unnamed prophet was sent by God to rebuke King Amaziah. The prophet reminded him that by seeking help from false gods, he was denying help for his people!

Most temptations to trust other gods today have little to do with carved stone or wood. But we are tempted to trust in jobs, assets, reputation and other gods. Repentance from misplaced trust is a constant need for God's people.

[a] 23 Probably in the spring [b] 26 A variant of *Jozabad* [c] 26 A variant of *Shomer* [d] 4 Deut. 24:16 [e] 6 That is, about 3 3/4 tons or about 3.4 metric tons; also in verse 9

11Amaziah then marshaled his strength and led his army to the Val-
ley of Salt, where he killed ten thousand men of Seir. 12The army of
Judah also captured ten thousand men alive, took them to the top of a
cliff and threw them down so that all were dashed to pieces.
13Meanwhile the troops that Amaziah had sent back and had not al-
lowed to take part in the war raided towns belonging to Judah from
Samaria to Beth Horon. They killed three thousand people and carried
off great quantities of plunder.
14When Amaziah returned from slaughtering the Edomites, he
brought back the gods of the people of Seir. He set them up as his own
gods, bowed down to them and burned sacrifices to them. 15The anger
of the LORD burned against Amaziah, and he sent a prophet to him,
who said, "Why do you consult this people's gods, which could not save
their own people from your hand?"
16While he was still speaking, the king said to him, "Have we ap-
pointed you an adviser to the king? Stop! Why be struck down?"
So the prophet stopped but said, "I know that God has determined
to destroy you, because you have done this and have not listened to
my counsel."
17After Amaziah king of Judah consulted his advisers, he sent this
challenge to Jehoash[a] son of Jehoahaz, the son of Jehu, king of Israel:
"Come, let us face each other in battle."
18But Jehoash king of Israel replied to Amaziah king of Judah: "A
thistle in Lebanon sent a message to a cedar in Lebanon, 'Give your
daughter to my son in marriage.' Then a wild beast in Lebanon came
along and trampled the thistle underfoot. 19You say to yourself that
you have defeated Edom, and now you are arrogant and proud. But
stay at home! Why ask for trouble and cause your own downfall and
that of Judah also?"
20Amaziah, however, would not listen, for God so worked that he
might deliver them into the hands of Jehoash, because they sought
the gods of Edom. 21So Jehoash king of Israel attacked. He and Ama-
ziah king of Judah faced each other at Beth Shemesh in Judah. 22Judah
was routed by Israel, and every man fled to his home. 23Jehoash king
of Israel captured Amaziah king of Judah, the son of Joash, the son of
Ahaziah,[b] at Beth Shemesh. Then Jehoash brought him to Jerusalem
and broke down the wall of Jerusalem from the Ephraim Gate to the
Corner Gate — a section about four hundred cubits[c] long. 24He took all
the gold and silver and all the articles found in the temple of God that
had been in the care of Obed-Edom, together with the palace treasures
and the hostages, and returned to Samaria.
25Amaziah son of Joash king of Judah lived for fifteen years after
the death of Jehoash son of Jehoahaz king of Israel. 26As for the other
events of Amaziah's reign, from beginning to end, are they not writ-
ten in the book of the kings of Judah and Israel? 27From the time that
Amaziah turned away from following the LORD, they conspired against
him in Jerusalem and he fled to Lachish, but they sent men after him
to Lachish and killed him there. 28He was brought back by horse and
was buried with his ancestors in the City of Judah.[d]

[a] *17* Hebrew *Joash*, a variant of *Jehoash*; also in verses 18, 21, 23 and 25
[b] *23* Hebrew *Jehoahaz*, a variant of *Ahaziah* [c] *23* That is, about 600 feet or about 180 meters [d] *28* Most Hebrew manuscripts; some Hebrew manuscripts, Septuagint, Vulgate and Syriac (see also 2 Kings 14:20) *David*

PRAYING SCRIPTURE

2 Chronicles 26

Uzziah is an example of one whose success went to his head. He began his rule at age 16, and initially he followed God. Eventually, after achieving military victories and demonstrating ingenuity with military devices, he became arrogant and, like Saul, assumed the ministry of the priests. God was not pleased.

Pride grows when we take credit for God's blessings. Ask for the humility to acknowledge God's work.

UZZIAH KING OF JUDAH

26 Then all the people of Judah took Uzziah,[a] who was sixteen
years old, and made him king in place of his father Amaziah.
2He was the one who rebuilt Elath and restored it to Judah after Ama-
ziah rested with his ancestors.
3Uzziah was sixteen years old when he became king, and he reigned
in Jerusalem fifty-two years. His mother's name was Jekoliah; she was
from Jerusalem. 4He did what was right in the eyes of the LORD, just as
his father Amaziah had done. 5He sought God during the days of Zech-
ariah, who instructed him in the fear[b] of God. As long as he sought the
LORD, God gave him success.
6He went to war against the Philistines and broke down the walls of
Gath, Jabneh and Ashdod. He then rebuilt towns near Ashdod and else-
where among the Philistines. 7God helped him against the Philistines
and against the Arabs who lived in Gur Baal and against the Meunites.
8The Ammonites brought tribute to Uzziah, and his fame spread as far
as the border of Egypt, because he had become very powerful.
9Uzziah built towers in Jerusalem at the Corner Gate, at the Valley
Gate and at the angle of the wall, and he fortified them. 10He also built
towers in the wilderness and dug many cisterns, because he had much
livestock in the foothills and in the plain. He had people working his
fields and vineyards in the hills and in the fertile lands, for he loved
the soil.
11Uzziah had a well-trained army, ready to go out by divisions accord-
ing to their numbers as mustered by Jeiel the secretary and Maaseiah
the officer under the direction of Hananiah, one of the royal officials.
12The total number of family leaders over the fighting men was 2,600.
13Under their command was an army of 307,500 men trained for war, a
powerful force to support the king against his enemies. 14Uzziah pro-
vided shields, spears, helmets, coats of armor, bows and slingstones
for the entire army. 15In Jerusalem he made devices invented for use
on the towers and on the corner defenses so that soldiers could shoot
arrows and hurl large stones from the walls. His fame spread far and
wide, for he was greatly helped until he became powerful.
16But after Uzziah became powerful, his pride led to his downfall.
He was unfaithful to the LORD his God, and entered the temple of the
LORD to burn incense on the altar of incense. 17Azariah the priest with
eighty other courageous priests of the LORD followed him in. 18They
confronted King Uzziah and said, "It is not right for you, Uzziah, to
burn incense to the LORD. That is for the priests, the descendants of
Aaron, who have been consecrated to burn incense. Leave the sanctu-
ary, for you have been unfaithful; and you will not be honored by the
LORD God."
19Uzziah, who had a censer in his hand ready to burn incense, be-
came angry. While he was raging at the priests in their presence before
the incense altar in the LORD's temple, leprosy[c] broke out on his fore-
head. 20When Azariah the chief priest and all the other priests looked
at him, they saw that he had leprosy on his forehead, so they hurried
him out. Indeed, he himself was eager to leave, because the LORD had
afflicted him.

---

[a] *1* Also called *Azariah* [b] *5* Many Hebrew manuscripts, Septuagint and Syriac; other Hebrew manuscripts *vision* [c] *19* The Hebrew for *leprosy* was used for various diseases affecting the skin; also in verses 20, 21 and 23.

21King Uzziah had leprosy until the day he died. He lived in a sep-
arate house[a]—leprous, and banned from the temple of the LORD. Jo-
tham his son had charge of the palace and governed the people of the
land.
22The other events of Uzziah's reign, from beginning to end, are re-
corded by the prophet Isaiah son of Amoz. 23Uzziah rested with his
ancestors and was buried near them in a cemetery that belonged to
the kings, for people said, "He had leprosy." And Jotham his son suc-
ceeded him as king.

JOTHAM KING OF JUDAH

27 Jotham was twenty-five years old when he became king, and
he reigned in Jerusalem sixteen years. His mother's name was
Jerusha daughter of Zadok. 2He did what was right in the eyes of the
LORD, just as his father Uzziah had done, but unlike him he did not
enter the temple of the LORD. The people, however, continued their
corrupt practices. 3Jotham rebuilt the Upper Gate of the temple of the
LORD and did extensive work on the wall at the hill of Ophel. 4He built
towns in the hill country of Judah and forts and towers in the wooded
areas.
5Jotham waged war against the king of the Ammonites and con-
quered them. That year the Ammonites paid him a hundred talents[b]
of silver, ten thousand cors[c] of wheat and ten thousand cors[d] of barley.
The Ammonites brought him the same amount also in the second and
third years.
6Jotham grew powerful because he walked steadfastly before the
LORD his God.
7The other events in Jotham's reign, including all his wars and the
other things he did, are written in the book of the kings of Israel and
Judah. 8He was twenty-five years old when he became king, and he
reigned in Jerusalem sixteen years. 9Jotham rested with his ancestors
and was buried in the City of David. And Ahaz his son succeeded him
as king.

PRAYING SCRIPTURE

2 Chronicles 27

One of the shortest kingly sketches is that of Jotham, yet he became mighty, "because he walked steadfastly before the LORD his God" (verse 6). What a magnificent word picture of committing one's plans to God. Jotham died at the young age of 41 but made the most of the years he had.

A person's life does not have to have huge impact to have lasting impact. Ask God to help you bear fruit that outlasts your life.

AHAZ KING OF JUDAH

28 Ahaz was twenty years old when he became king, and he
reigned in Jerusalem sixteen years. Unlike David his father,
he did not do what was right in the eyes of the LORD. 2He followed
the ways of the kings of Israel and also made idols for worshiping the
Baals. 3He burned sacrifices in the Valley of Ben Hinnom and sacri-
ficed his children in the fire, engaging in the detestable practices of
the nations the LORD had driven out before the Israelites. 4He offered
sacrifices and burned incense at the high places, on the hilltops and
under every spreading tree.
5Therefore the LORD his God delivered him into the hands of the
king of Aram. The Arameans defeated him and took many of his peo-
ple as prisoners and brought them to Damascus.
He was also given into the hands of the king of Israel, who inflicted
heavy casualties on him. 6In one day Pekah son of Remaliah killed a

PRAYING SCRIPTURE

2 Chronicles 28

It is difficult to fully grasp the wickedness of King Ahaz. He made and followed false gods and set up places of false worship "at the high places, on the hilltops and under every spreading tree" (verse 4). After losing one battle, he sacrificed to the gods of the country that defeated him!

To give ourselves over to sin leads only to deep ruin. Ask God to help you overcome the degradation of sin.

---

[a] 21 Or *in a house where he was relieved of responsibilities* [b] 5 That is, about 3 3/4 tons or about 3.4 metric tons [c] 5 That is, probably about 1,800 tons or about 1,600 metric tons of wheat [d] 5 That is, probably about 1,500 tons or about 1,350 metric tons of barley

hundred and twenty thousand soldiers in Judah — because Judah had forsaken the LORD, the God of their ancestors. [7]Zikri, an Ephraimite warrior, killed Maaseiah the king's son, Azrikam the officer in charge of the palace, and Elkanah, second to the king. [8]The men of Israel took captive from their fellow Israelites who were from Judah two hundred thousand wives, sons and daughters. They also took a great deal of plunder, which they carried back to Samaria.

[9]But a prophet of the LORD named Oded was there, and he went out to meet the army when it returned to Samaria. He said to them, "Because the LORD, the God of your ancestors, was angry with Judah, he gave them into your hand. But you have slaughtered them in a rage that reaches to heaven. [10]And now you intend to make the men and women of Judah and Jerusalem your slaves. But aren't you also guilty of sins against the LORD your God? [11]Now listen to me! Send back your fellow Israelites you have taken as prisoners, for the LORD's fierce anger rests on you."

[12]Then some of the leaders in Ephraim — Azariah son of Jehohanan, Berekiah son of Meshillemoth, Jehizkiah son of Shallum, and Amasa son of Hadlai — confronted those who were arriving from the war. [13]"You must not bring those prisoners here," they said, "or we will be guilty before the LORD. Do you intend to add to our sin and guilt? For our guilt is already great, and his fierce anger rests on Israel."

[14]So the soldiers gave up the prisoners and plunder in the presence of the officials and all the assembly. [15]The men designated by name took the prisoners, and from the plunder they clothed all who were naked. They provided them with clothes and sandals, food and drink, and healing balm. All those who were weak they put on donkeys. So they took them back to their fellow Israelites at Jericho, the City of Palms, and returned to Samaria.

[16]At that time King Ahaz sent to the kings[a] of Assyria for help. [17]The Edomites had again come and attacked Judah and carried away prisoners, [18]while the Philistines had raided towns in the foothills and in the Negev of Judah. They captured and occupied Beth Shemesh, Aijalon and Gederoth, as well as Soko, Timnah and Gimzo, with their surrounding villages. [19]The LORD had humbled Judah because of Ahaz king of Israel,[b] for he had promoted wickedness in Judah and had been most unfaithful to the LORD. [20]Tiglath-Pileser[c] king of Assyria came to him, but he gave him trouble instead of help. [21]Ahaz took some of the things from the temple of the LORD and from the royal palace and from the officials and presented them to the king of Assyria, but that did not help him.

[22]In his time of trouble King Ahaz became even more unfaithful to the LORD. [23]He offered sacrifices to the gods of Damascus, who had defeated him; for he thought, "Since the gods of the kings of Aram have helped them, I will sacrifice to them so they will help me." But they were his downfall and the downfall of all Israel.

[24]Ahaz gathered together the furnishings from the temple of God and cut them in pieces. He shut the doors of the LORD's temple and set up altars at every street corner in Jerusalem. [25]In every town in Judah he built high places to burn sacrifices to other gods and aroused the anger of the LORD, the God of his ancestors.

[26]The other events of his reign and all his ways, from beginning to

[a] *16* Most Hebrew manuscripts; one Hebrew manuscript, Septuagint and Vulgate (see also 2 Kings 16:7) *king* [b] *19* That is, Judah, as frequently in 2 Chronicles [c] *20* Hebrew *Tilgath-Pilneser,* a variant of *Tiglath-Pileser*

end, are written in the book of the kings of Judah and Israel. 27Ahaz
rested with his ancestors and was buried in the city of Jerusalem, but
he was not placed in the tombs of the kings of Israel. And Hezekiah his
son succeeded him as king.

HEZEKIAH PURIFIES THE TEMPLE

29 Hezekiah was twenty-five years old when he became king, and
he reigned in Jerusalem twenty-nine years. His mother's name
was Abijah daughter of Zechariah. 2He did what was right in the eyes
of the LORD, just as his father David had done.
3In the first month of the first year of his reign, he opened the doors
of the temple of the LORD and repaired them. 4He brought in the priests
and the Levites, assembled them in the square on the east side 5and
said: "Listen to me, Levites! Consecrate yourselves now and consecrate
the temple of the LORD, the God of your ancestors. Remove all defile-
ment from the sanctuary. 6Our parents were unfaithful; they did evil in
the eyes of the LORD our God and forsook him. They turned their faces
away from the LORD's dwelling place and turned their backs on him.
7They also shut the doors of the portico and put out the lamps. They
did not burn incense or present any burnt offerings at the sanctuary to
the God of Israel. 8Therefore, the anger of the LORD has fallen on Judah
and Jerusalem; he has made them an object of dread and horror and
scorn, as you can see with your own eyes. 9This is why our fathers have
fallen by the sword and why our sons and daughters and our wives are
in captivity. 10Now I intend to make a covenant with the LORD, the God
of Israel, so that his fierce anger will turn away from us. 11My sons, do
not be negligent now, for the LORD has chosen you to stand before him
and serve him, to minister before him and to burn incense."

12Then these Levites set to work:
from the Kohathites,
Mahath son of Amasai and Joel son of Azariah;
from the Merarites,
Kish son of Abdi and Azariah son of Jehallelel;
from the Gershonites,
Joah son of Zimmah and Eden son of Joah;
13from the descendants of Elizaphan,
Shimri and Jeiel;
from the descendants of Asaph,
Zechariah and Mattaniah;
14from the descendants of Heman,
Jehiel and Shimei;
from the descendants of Jeduthun,
Shemaiah and Uzziel.

15When they had assembled their fellow Levites and consecrated
themselves, they went in to purify the temple of the LORD, as the king
had ordered, following the word of the LORD. 16The priests went into
the sanctuary of the LORD to purify it. They brought out to the court-
yard of the LORD's temple everything unclean that they found in the
temple of the LORD. The Levites took it and carried it out to the Kid-
ron Valley. 17They began the consecration on the first day of the first
month, and by the eighth day of the month they reached the portico of
the LORD. For eight more days they consecrated the temple of the LORD
itself, finishing on the sixteenth day of the first month.
18Then they went in to King Hezekiah and reported: "We have

PRAYING SCRIPTURE

2 Chronicles 29

Part of Hezekiah's reforms included restoration of the temple ministry. Judah had been so far from God that the Holy Place was filled with trash, the lamps extinguished and the temple doors locked. He called the priests and Levites back to their ministry in the house of God.

Renewal starts with an honest inventory of our spiritual condition. Confess any spiritual rubbish in your heart and ask God to cleanse you.

purified the entire temple of the LORD, the altar of burnt offering with all its utensils, and the table for setting out the consecrated bread, with all its articles. [19]We have prepared and consecrated all the articles that King Ahaz removed in his unfaithfulness while he was king. They are now in front of the LORD's altar."

[20]Early the next morning King Hezekiah gathered the city officials together and went up to the temple of the LORD. [21]They brought seven bulls, seven rams, seven male lambs and seven male goats as a sin offering[a] for the kingdom, for the sanctuary and for Judah. The king commanded the priests, the descendants of Aaron, to offer these on the altar of the LORD. [22]So they slaughtered the bulls, and the priests took the blood and splashed it against the altar; next they slaughtered the rams and splashed their blood against the altar; then they slaughtered the lambs and splashed their blood against the altar. [23]The goats for the sin offering were brought before the king and the assembly, and they laid their hands on them. [24]The priests then slaughtered the goats and presented their blood on the altar for a sin offering to atone for all Israel, because the king had ordered the burnt offering and the sin offering for all Israel.

[25]He stationed the Levites in the temple of the LORD with cymbals, harps and lyres in the way prescribed by David and Gad the king's seer and Nathan the prophet; this was commanded by the LORD through his prophets. [26]So the Levites stood ready with David's instruments, and the priests with their trumpets.

[27]Hezekiah gave the order to sacrifice the burnt offering on the altar. As the offering began, singing to the LORD began also, accompanied by trumpets and the instruments of David king of Israel. [28]The whole assembly bowed in worship, while the musicians played and the trumpets sounded. All this continued until the sacrifice of the burnt offering was completed.

[29]When the offerings were finished, the king and everyone present with him knelt down and worshiped. [30]King Hezekiah and his officials ordered the Levites to praise the LORD with the words of David and of Asaph the seer. So they sang praises with gladness and bowed down and worshiped.

[31]Then Hezekiah said, "You have now dedicated yourselves to the LORD. Come and bring sacrifices and thank offerings to the temple of the LORD." So the assembly brought sacrifices and thank offerings, and all whose hearts were willing brought burnt offerings.

[32]The number of burnt offerings the assembly brought was seventy bulls, a hundred rams and two hundred male lambs — all of them for burnt offerings to the LORD. [33]The animals consecrated as sacrifices amounted to six hundred bulls and three thousand sheep and goats. [34]The priests, however, were too few to skin all the burnt offerings; so their relatives the Levites helped them until the task was finished and until other priests had been consecrated, for the Levites had been more conscientious in consecrating themselves than the priests had been. [35]There were burnt offerings in abundance, together with the fat of the fellowship offerings and the drink offerings that accompanied the burnt offerings.

So the service of the temple of the LORD was reestablished. [36]Hezekiah and all the people rejoiced at what God had brought about for his people, because it was done so quickly.

---

[a] *21* Or *purification offering*; also in verses 23 and 24

HEZEKIAH CELEBRATES THE PASSOVER

30 Hezekiah sent word to all Israel and Judah and also wrote
letters to Ephraim and Manasseh, inviting them to come to
the temple of the LORD in Jerusalem and celebrate the Passover to the
LORD, the God of Israel. 2The king and his officials and the whole as-
sembly in Jerusalem decided to celebrate the Passover in the second
month. 3They had not been able to celebrate it at the regular time be-
cause not enough priests had consecrated themselves and the people
had not assembled in Jerusalem. 4The plan seemed right both to the
king and to the whole assembly. 5They decided to send a proclama-
tion throughout Israel, from Beersheba to Dan, calling the people to
come to Jerusalem and celebrate the Passover to the LORD, the God of
Israel. It had not been celebrated in large numbers according to what
was written.

6At the king's command, couriers went throughout Israel and Judah
with letters from the king and from his officials, which read:

> "People of Israel, return to the LORD, the God of Abraham, Isaac
> and Israel, that he may return to you who are left, who have es-
> caped from the hand of the kings of Assyria. 7Do not be like your
> parents and your fellow Israelites, who were unfaithful to the
> LORD, the God of their ancestors, so that he made them an object
> of horror, as you see. 8Do not be stiff-necked, as your ancestors
> were; submit to the LORD. Come to his sanctuary, which he has
> consecrated forever. Serve the LORD your God, so that his fierce
> anger will turn away from you. 9If you return to the LORD, then
> your fellow Israelites and your children will be shown compassion
> by their captors and will return to this land, for the LORD your God
> is gracious and compassionate. He will not turn his face from you
> if you return to him."

10The couriers went from town to town in Ephraim and Manasseh, as
far as Zebulun, but people scorned and ridiculed them. 11Nevertheless,
some from Asher, Manasseh and Zebulun humbled themselves and
went to Jerusalem. 12Also in Judah the hand of God was on the people
to give them unity of mind to carry out what the king and his officials
had ordered, following the word of the LORD.

13A very large crowd of people assembled in Jerusalem to celebrate
the Festival of Unleavened Bread in the second month. 14They removed
the altars in Jerusalem and cleared away the incense altars and threw
them into the Kidron Valley.

15They slaughtered the Passover lamb on the fourteenth day of the
second month. The priests and the Levites were ashamed and conse-
crated themselves and brought burnt offerings to the temple of the
LORD. 16Then they took up their regular positions as prescribed in
the Law of Moses the man of God. The priests splashed against the altar
the blood handed to them by the Levites. 17Since many in the crowd had
not consecrated themselves, the Levites had to kill the Passover lambs
for all those who were not ceremonially clean and could not consecrate
their lambs[a] to the LORD. 18Although most of the many people who
came from Ephraim, Manasseh, Issachar and Zebulun had not purified
themselves, yet they ate the Passover, contrary to what was written. But
Hezekiah prayed for them, saying, "May the LORD, who is good, pardon

PRAYING SCRIPTURE

2 Chronicles 30

It is sometimes forgotten that Israel and Judah did not keep the Passover annually as God had commanded. When Hezekiah became king, Judah had too few sanctified priests to observe it. When the time finally arrived, sacrifice and repentance were followed by great joy.

Ask God if there is anything in your life that is breaking fellowship. If so, repent so you can experience the joy of forgiveness.

---

[a] 17 Or *consecrate themselves*

everyone 19who sets their heart on seeking God — the LORD, the God
of their ancestors — even if they are not clean according to the rules of
the sanctuary." 20And the LORD heard Hezekiah and healed the people.
21The Israelites who were present in Jerusalem celebrated the Fes-
tival of Unleavened Bread for seven days with great rejoicing, while
the Levites and priests praised the LORD every day with resounding
instruments dedicated to the LORD.[a]
22Hezekiah spoke encouragingly to all the Levites, who showed good
understanding of the service of the LORD. For the seven days they ate
their assigned portion and offered fellowship offerings and praised[b]
the LORD, the God of their ancestors.
23The whole assembly then agreed to celebrate the festival seven
more days; so for another seven days they celebrated joyfully. 24Hez-
ekiah king of Judah provided a thousand bulls and seven thousand
sheep and goats for the assembly, and the officials provided them with
a thousand bulls and ten thousand sheep and goats. A great number
of priests consecrated themselves. 25The entire assembly of Judah re-
joiced, along with the priests and Levites and all who had assembled
from Israel, including the foreigners who had come from Israel and
also those who resided in Judah. 26There was great joy in Jerusalem,
for since the days of Solomon son of David king of Israel there had
been nothing like this in Jerusalem. 27The priests and the Levites
stood to bless the people, and God heard them, for their prayer reached
heaven, his holy dwelling place.

31 When all this had ended, the Israelites who were there went
out to the towns of Judah, smashed the sacred stones and cut
down the Asherah poles. They destroyed the high places and the altars
throughout Judah and Benjamin and in Ephraim and Manasseh. After
they had destroyed all of them, the Israelites returned to their own
towns and to their own property.

CONTRIBUTIONS FOR WORSHIP

2Hezekiah assigned the priests and Levites to divisions — each of
them according to their duties as priests or Levites — to offer burnt of-
ferings and fellowship offerings, to minister, to give thanks and to sing
praises at the gates of the LORD's dwelling. 3The king contributed from
his own possessions for the morning and evening burnt offerings and
for the burnt offerings on the Sabbaths, at the New Moons and at the
appointed festivals as written in the Law of the LORD. 4He ordered the
people living in Jerusalem to give the portion due the priests and Le-
vites so they could devote themselves to the Law of the LORD. 5As soon
as the order went out, the Israelites generously gave the firstfruits of
their grain, new wine, olive oil and honey and all that the fields pro-
duced. They brought a great amount, a tithe of everything. 6The peo-
ple of Israel and Judah who lived in the towns of Judah also brought a
tithe of their herds and flocks and a tithe of the holy things dedicated
to the LORD their God, and they piled them in heaps. 7They began do-
ing this in the third month and finished in the seventh month. 8When
Hezekiah and his officials came and saw the heaps, they praised the
LORD and blessed his people Israel.
9Hezekiah asked the priests and Levites about the heaps; 10and Az-
ariah the chief priest, from the family of Zadok, answered, "Since the

PRAYING SCRIPTURE

2 Chronicles 31

After reinstituting the Passover, King Hezekiah led the people to give offerings. From his own possessions, he gave enough to sustain the morning and evening offerings. The people followed suit, bringing all manner of fruit, grain, oxen and sheep, their tithe to the Lord.

Obedience to God means having a generous heart. Ask God to open your eyes to opportunities to bless others and support his kingdom with your possessions.

[a] 21 *Or priests sang to the LORD every day, accompanied by the LORD's instruments of praise* [b] 22 *Or and confessed their sins to*

people began to bring their contributions to the temple of the LORD,
we have had enough to eat and plenty to spare, because the LORD has
blessed his people, and this great amount is left over."
[11]Hezekiah gave orders to prepare storerooms in the temple of the
LORD, and this was done. [12]Then they faithfully brought in the con-
tributions, tithes and dedicated gifts. Konaniah, a Levite, was the
overseer in charge of these things, and his brother Shimei was next
in rank. [13]Jehiel, Azaziah, Nahath, Asahel, Jerimoth, Jozabad, Eliel, Is-
makiah, Mahath and Benaiah were assistants of Konaniah and Shimei
his brother. All these served by appointment of King Hezekiah and
Azariah the official in charge of the temple of God.
[14]Kore son of Imnah the Levite, keeper of the East Gate, was in charge
of the freewill offerings given to God, distributing the contributions
made to the LORD and also the consecrated gifts. [15]Eden, Miniamin,
Jeshua, Shemaiah, Amariah and Shekaniah assisted him faithfully in
the towns of the priests, distributing to their fellow priests according
to their divisions, old and young alike.
[16]In addition, they distributed to the males three years old or more
whose names were in the genealogical records — all who would enter
the temple of the LORD to perform the daily duties of their various
tasks, according to their responsibilities and their divisions. [17]And they
distributed to the priests enrolled by their families in the genealogical
records and likewise to the Levites twenty years old or more, accord-
ing to their responsibilities and their divisions. [18]They included all the
little ones, the wives, and the sons and daughters of the whole com-
munity listed in these genealogical records. For they were faithful in
consecrating themselves.
[19]As for the priests, the descendants of Aaron, who lived on the farm-
lands around their towns or in any other towns, men were designated
by name to distribute portions to every male among them and to all
who were recorded in the genealogies of the Levites.
[20]This is what Hezekiah did throughout Judah, doing what was good
and right and faithful before the LORD his God. [21]In everything that he
undertook in the service of God's temple and in obedience to the law
and the commands, he sought his God and worked wholeheartedly.
And so he prospered.

SENNACHERIB THREATENS JERUSALEM

32 After all that Hezekiah had so faithfully done, Sennacherib king
of Assyria came and invaded Judah. He laid siege to the fortified
cities, thinking to conquer them for himself. [2]When Hezekiah saw that
Sennacherib had come and that he intended to wage war against Jeru-
salem, [3]he consulted with his officials and military staff about blocking
off the water from the springs outside the city, and they helped him.
[4]They gathered a large group of people who blocked all the springs and
the stream that flowed through the land. "Why should the kings[a] of As-
syria come and find plenty of water?" they said. [5]Then he worked hard
repairing all the broken sections of the wall and building towers on it.
He built another wall outside that one and reinforced the terraces[b] of
the City of David. He also made large numbers of weapons and shields.
[6]He appointed military officers over the people and assembled them
before him in the square at the city gate and encouraged them with

PRAYING SCRIPTURE

2 Chronicles 32

The Assyrian king Sennacherib's attack on Judah tested the military strategy of Hezekiah and his men. After repairing the broken wall and raising another, Hezekiah encouraged the people: "With him is only the arm of flesh; but with us is the LORD our God" (verse 8).

We sometimes forget that God is stronger than anything or anyone. Thank God today that his power can overcome any "arm of flesh" that you face.

[a] 4 Hebrew; Septuagint and Syriac *king* [b] 5 Or *the Millo*

these words: 7“Be strong and courageous. Do not be afraid or discouraged because of the king of Assyria and the vast army with him, for there is a greater power with us than with him. 8With him is only the arm of flesh, but with us is the LORD our God to help us and to fight our battles.” And the people gained confidence from what Hezekiah the king of Judah said.

9Later, when Sennacherib king of Assyria and all his forces were laying siege to Lachish, he sent his officers to Jerusalem with this message for Hezekiah king of Judah and for all the people of Judah who were there:

> 10“This is what Sennacherib king of Assyria says: On what are you basing your confidence, that you remain in Jerusalem under siege? 11When Hezekiah says, ‘The LORD our God will save us from the hand of the king of Assyria,’ he is misleading you, to let you die of hunger and thirst. 12Did not Hezekiah himself remove this god’s high places and altars, saying to Judah and Jerusalem, ‘You must worship before one altar and burn sacrifices on it’?
>
> 13“Do you not know what I and my predecessors have done to all the peoples of the other lands? Were the gods of those nations ever able to deliver their land from my hand? 14Who of all the gods of these nations that my predecessors destroyed has been able to save his people from me? How then can your god deliver you from my hand? 15Now do not let Hezekiah deceive you and mislead you like this. Do not believe him, for no god of any nation or kingdom has been able to deliver his people from my hand or the hand of my predecessors. How much less will your god deliver you from my hand!”

16Sennacherib’s officers spoke further against the LORD God and against his servant Hezekiah. 17The king also wrote letters ridiculing the LORD, the God of Israel, and saying this against him: “Just as the gods of the peoples of the other lands did not rescue their people from my hand, so the god of Hezekiah will not rescue his people from my hand.” 18Then they called out in Hebrew to the people of Jerusalem who were on the wall, to terrify them and make them afraid in order to capture the city. 19They spoke about the God of Jerusalem as they did about the gods of the other peoples of the world — the work of human hands.

20King Hezekiah and the prophet Isaiah son of Amoz cried out in prayer to heaven about this. 21And the LORD sent an angel, who annihilated all the fighting men and the commanders and officers in the camp of the Assyrian king. So he withdrew to his own land in disgrace. And when he went into the temple of his god, some of his sons, his own flesh and blood, cut him down with the sword.

22So the LORD saved Hezekiah and the people of Jerusalem from the hand of Sennacherib king of Assyria and from the hand of all others. He took care of them[a] on every side. 23Many brought offerings to Jerusalem for the LORD and valuable gifts for Hezekiah king of Judah. From then on he was highly regarded by all the nations.

HEZEKIAH’S PRIDE, SUCCESS AND DEATH

24In those days Hezekiah became ill and was at the point of death. He prayed to the LORD, who answered him and gave him a miraculous

---

[a] 22 Hebrew; Septuagint and Vulgate *He gave them rest*

sign. 25But Hezekiah's heart was proud and he did not respond to the
kindness shown him; therefore the LORD's wrath was on him and on
Judah and Jerusalem. 26Then Hezekiah repented of the pride of his
heart, as did the people of Jerusalem; therefore the LORD's wrath did
not come on them during the days of Hezekiah.

27Hezekiah had very great wealth and honor, and he made treasuries
for his silver and gold and for his precious stones, spices, shields and
all kinds of valuables. 28He also made buildings to store the harvest of
grain, new wine and olive oil; and he made stalls for various kinds of
cattle, and pens for the flocks. 29He built villages and acquired great
numbers of flocks and herds, for God had given him very great riches.

30It was Hezekiah who blocked the upper outlet of the Gihon spring
and channeled the water down to the west side of the City of David. He
succeeded in everything he undertook. 31But when envoys were sent
by the rulers of Babylon to ask him about the miraculous sign that had
occurred in the land, God left him to test him and to know everything
that was in his heart.

32The other events of Hezekiah's reign and his acts of devotion are
written in the vision of the prophet Isaiah son of Amoz in the book of
the kings of Judah and Israel. 33Hezekiah rested with his ancestors and
was buried on the hill where the tombs of David's descendants are. All
Judah and the people of Jerusalem honored him when he died. And
Manasseh his son succeeded him as king.

MANASSEH KING OF JUDAH

33 Manasseh was twelve years old when he became king, and he
reigned in Jerusalem fifty-five years. 2He did evil in the eyes
of the LORD, following the detestable practices of the nations the LORD
had driven out before the Israelites. 3He rebuilt the high places his fa-
ther Hezekiah had demolished; he also erected altars to the Baals and
made Asherah poles. He bowed down to all the starry hosts and wor-
shiped them. 4He built altars in the temple of the LORD, of which the
LORD had said, "My Name will remain in Jerusalem forever." 5In both
courts of the temple of the LORD, he built altars to all the starry hosts.
6He sacrificed his children in the fire in the Valley of Ben Hinnom,
practiced divination and witchcraft, sought omens, and consulted me-
diums and spiritists. He did much evil in the eyes of the LORD, arousing
his anger.

7He took the image he had made and put it in God's temple, of which
God had said to David and to his son Solomon, "In this temple and in
Jerusalem, which I have chosen out of all the tribes of Israel, I will put
my Name forever. 8I will not again make the feet of the Israelites leave
the land I assigned to your ancestors, if only they will be careful to do
everything I commanded them concerning all the laws, decrees and
regulations given through Moses." 9But Manasseh led Judah and the
people of Jerusalem astray, so that they did more evil than the nations
the LORD had destroyed before the Israelites.

10The LORD spoke to Manasseh and his people, but they paid no at-
tention. 11So the LORD brought against them the army commanders
of the king of Assyria, who took Manasseh prisoner, put a hook in his
nose, bound him with bronze shackles and took him to Babylon. 12In
his distress he sought the favor of the LORD his God and humbled him-
self greatly before the God of his ancestors. 13And when he prayed to
him, the LORD was moved by his entreaty and listened to his plea; so

PRAYING SCRIPTURE

2 Chronicles 33

How deep and wide is the grace of God? Manasseh was one of the wickedest kings in Judah's history. He practiced witchcraft and idolatry, and he urged his people to follow the false gods of the nations. As punishment, God delivered Manasseh into Babylonian captivity.

In despair, he humbled himself, and God forgave him. There is no sin God will not forgive, so humbly call on him for his abundant grace.

he brought him back to Jerusalem and to his kingdom. Then Manas-
seh knew that the LORD is God.
14 Afterward he rebuilt the outer wall of the City of David, west of the
Gihon spring in the valley, as far as the entrance of the Fish Gate and
encircling the hill of Ophel; he also made it much higher. He stationed
military commanders in all the fortified cities in Judah.
15 He got rid of the foreign gods and removed the image from the
temple of the LORD, as well as all the altars he had built on the temple
hill and in Jerusalem; and he threw them out of the city. 16 Then he
restored the altar of the LORD and sacrificed fellowship offerings and
thank offerings on it, and told Judah to serve the LORD, the God of Is-
rael. 17 The people, however, continued to sacrifice at the high places,
but only to the LORD their God.
18 The other events of Manasseh's reign, including his prayer to his
God and the words the seers spoke to him in the name of the LORD,
the God of Israel, are written in the annals of the kings of Israel.[a] 19 His
prayer and how God was moved by his entreaty, as well as all his sins
and unfaithfulness, and the sites where he built high places and set
up Asherah poles and idols before he humbled himself — all these are
written in the records of the seers.[b] 20 Manasseh rested with his an-
cestors and was buried in his palace. And Amon his son succeeded
him as king.

AMON KING OF JUDAH

21 Amon was twenty-two years old when he became king, and he
reigned in Jerusalem two years. 22 He did evil in the eyes of the LORD,
as his father Manasseh had done. Amon worshiped and offered sacri-
fices to all the idols Manasseh had made. 23 But unlike his father Ma-
nasseh, he did not humble himself before the LORD; Amon increased
his guilt.
24 Amon's officials conspired against him and assassinated him in
his palace. 25 Then the people of the land killed all who had plotted
against King Amon, and they made Josiah his son king in his place.

JOSIAH'S REFORMS

34 Josiah was eight years old when he became king, and he
reigned in Jerusalem thirty-one years. 2 He did what was right
in the eyes of the LORD and followed the ways of his father David, not
turning aside to the right or to the left.
3 In the eighth year of his reign, while he was still young, he began to
seek the God of his father David. In his twelfth year he began to purge
Judah and Jerusalem of high places, Asherah poles and idols. 4 Under
his direction the altars of the Baals were torn down; he cut to pieces
the incense altars that were above them, and smashed the Asherah
poles and the idols. These he broke to pieces and scattered over the
graves of those who had sacrificed to them. 5 He burned the bones
of the priests on their altars, and so he purged Judah and Jerusalem.
6 In the towns of Manasseh, Ephraim and Simeon, as far as Naphtali,
and in the ruins around them, 7 he tore down the altars and the Ashe-
rah poles and crushed the idols to powder and cut to pieces all the
incense altars throughout Israel. Then he went back to Jerusalem.

PRAYING SCRIPTURE

2 Chronicles 34

Josiah's leadership brought national renewal to Judah. He recovered the Book of the Covenant, listened to the warnings of the prophet Huldah and destroyed the abominable things worshiped by the people. As a result, the people followed God as long as Josiah lived.

How can you influence others to live for Jesus? Ask God for wisdom to lead others to follow him, and be encouraged that he will use you.

---

[a] *18* That is, Judah, as frequently in 2 Chronicles [b] *19* One Hebrew manuscript and Septuagint; most Hebrew manuscripts *of Hozai*

8 In the eighteenth year of Josiah's reign, to purify the land and the temple, he sent Shaphan son of Azaliah and Maaseiah the ruler of the city, with Joah son of Joahaz, the recorder, to repair the temple of the LORD his God.

9 They went to Hilkiah the high priest and gave him the money that had been brought into the temple of God, which the Levites who were the gatekeepers had collected from the people of Manasseh, Ephraim and the entire remnant of Israel and from all the people of Judah and Benjamin and the inhabitants of Jerusalem. 10 Then they entrusted it to the men appointed to supervise the work on the LORD's temple. These men paid the workers who repaired and restored the temple. 11 They also gave money to the carpenters and builders to purchase dressed stone, and timber for joists and beams for the buildings that the kings of Judah had allowed to fall into ruin.

12 The workers labored faithfully. Over them to direct them were Jahath and Obadiah, Levites descended from Merari, and Zechariah and Meshullam, descended from Kohath. The Levites — all who were skilled in playing musical instruments — 13 had charge of the laborers and supervised all the workers from job to job. Some of the Levites were secretaries, scribes and gatekeepers.

THE BOOK OF THE LAW FOUND

14 While they were bringing out the money that had been taken into the temple of the LORD, Hilkiah the priest found the Book of the Law of the LORD that had been given through Moses. 15 Hilkiah said to Shaphan the secretary, "I have found the Book of the Law in the temple of the LORD." He gave it to Shaphan.

16 Then Shaphan took the book to the king and reported to him: "Your officials are doing everything that has been committed to them. 17 They have paid out the money that was in the temple of the LORD and have entrusted it to the supervisors and workers." 18 Then Shaphan the secretary informed the king, "Hilkiah the priest has given me a book." And Shaphan read from it in the presence of the king.

19 When the king heard the words of the Law, he tore his robes. 20 He gave these orders to Hilkiah, Ahikam son of Shaphan, Abdon son of Micah,[a] Shaphan the secretary and Asaiah the king's attendant: 21 "Go and inquire of the LORD for me and for the remnant in Israel and Judah about what is written in this book that has been found. Great is the LORD's anger that is poured out on us because those who have gone before us have not kept the word of the LORD; they have not acted in accordance with all that is written in this book."

22 Hilkiah and those the king had sent with him[b] went to speak to the prophet Huldah, who was the wife of Shallum son of Tokhath,[c] the son of Hasrah,[d] keeper of the wardrobe. She lived in Jerusalem, in the New Quarter.

23 She said to them, "This is what the LORD, the God of Israel, says: Tell the man who sent you to me, 24 'This is what the LORD says: I am going to bring disaster on this place and its people — all the curses written in the book that has been read in the presence of the king of Judah. 25 Because they have forsaken me and burned incense to other

---

[a] *20* Also called *Akbor son of Micaiah* [b] *22* One Hebrew manuscript, Vulgate and Syriac; most Hebrew manuscripts do not have *had sent with him.* [c] *22* Also called *Tikvah* [d] *22* Also called *Harhas*

gods and aroused my anger by all that their hands have made,[a] my
anger will be poured out on this place and will not be quenched.' 26Tell
the king of Judah, who sent you to inquire of the LORD, 'This is what
the LORD, the God of Israel, says concerning the words you heard: 27Be-
cause your heart was responsive and you humbled yourself before
God when you heard what he spoke against this place and its people,
and because you humbled yourself before me and tore your robes and
wept in my presence, I have heard you, declares the LORD. 28Now I will
gather you to your ancestors, and you will be buried in peace. Your
eyes will not see all the disaster I am going to bring on this place and
on those who live here.'"

So they took her answer back to the king.

29Then the king called together all the elders of Judah and Jerusa-
lem. 30He went up to the temple of the LORD with the people of Ju-
dah, the inhabitants of Jerusalem, the priests and the Levites — all the
people from the least to the greatest. He read in their hearing all the
words of the Book of the Covenant, which had been found in the tem-
ple of the LORD. 31The king stood by his pillar and renewed the cov-
enant in the presence of the LORD — to follow the LORD and keep his
commands, statutes and decrees with all his heart and all his soul, and
to obey the words of the covenant written in this book.

32Then he had everyone in Jerusalem and Benjamin pledge them-
selves to it; the people of Jerusalem did this in accordance with the
covenant of God, the God of their ancestors.

33Josiah removed all the detestable idols from all the territory be-
longing to the Israelites, and he had all who were present in Israel
serve the LORD their God. As long as he lived, they did not fail to follow
the LORD, the God of their ancestors.

PRAYING SCRIPTURE

2 Chronicles 35

After reestablishing the Passover, Josiah died in a battle with the Egyptians. His body was returned to Jerusalem, and he was entombed with the kings who had gone before him. The people loved him so much that all Jerusalem and Judah mourned. Lamenting Josiah became a custom in the land.

Ask God to raise up people who will have great impact for his kingdom, and ask him to make you one of them.

JOSIAH CELEBRATES THE PASSOVER

35 Josiah celebrated the Passover to the LORD in Jerusalem, and
the Passover lamb was slaughtered on the fourteenth day of
the first month. 2He appointed the priests to their duties and encour-
aged them in the service of the LORD's temple. 3He said to the Levites,
who instructed all Israel and who had been consecrated to the LORD:
"Put the sacred ark in the temple that Solomon son of David king of
Israel built. It is not to be carried about on your shoulders. Now serve
the LORD your God and his people Israel. 4Prepare yourselves by fam-
ilies in your divisions, according to the instructions written by David
king of Israel and by his son Solomon.

5"Stand in the holy place with a group of Levites for each subdivision
of the families of your fellow Israelites, the lay people. 6Slaughter the
Passover lambs, consecrate yourselves and prepare the lambs for your
fellow Israelites, doing what the LORD commanded through Moses."

7Josiah provided for all the lay people who were there a total of
thirty thousand lambs and goats for the Passover offerings, and also
three thousand cattle — all from the king's own possessions.

8His officials also contributed voluntarily to the people and the
priests and Levites. Hilkiah, Zechariah and Jehiel, the officials in
charge of God's temple, gave the priests twenty-six hundred Passover
offerings and three hundred cattle. 9Also Konaniah along with Shema-
iah and Nethanel, his brothers, and Hashabiah, Jeiel and Jozabad, the

[a] 25 Or *by everything they have done*

leaders of the Levites, provided five thousand Passover offerings and five hundred head of cattle for the Levites.

10The service was arranged and the priests stood in their places with the Levites in their divisions as the king had ordered. 11The Passover lambs were slaughtered, and the priests splashed against the altar the blood handed to them, while the Levites skinned the animals. 12They set aside the burnt offerings to give them to the subdivisions of the families of the people to offer to the LORD, as it is written in the Book of Moses. They did the same with the cattle. 13They roasted the Passover animals over the fire as prescribed, and boiled the holy offerings in pots, caldrons and pans and served them quickly to all the people. 14After this, they made preparations for themselves and for the priests, because the priests, the descendants of Aaron, were sacrificing the burnt offerings and the fat portions until nightfall. So the Levites made preparations for themselves and for the Aaronic priests.

15The musicians, the descendants of Asaph, were in the places prescribed by David, Asaph, Heman and Jeduthun the king's seer. The gatekeepers at each gate did not need to leave their posts, because their fellow Levites made the preparations for them.

16So at that time the entire service of the LORD was carried out for the celebration of the Passover and the offering of burnt offerings on the altar of the LORD, as King Josiah had ordered. 17The Israelites who were present celebrated the Passover at that time and observed the Festival of Unleavened Bread for seven days. 18The Passover had not been observed like this in Israel since the days of the prophet Samuel; and none of the kings of Israel had ever celebrated such a Passover as did Josiah, with the priests, the Levites and all Judah and Israel who were there with the people of Jerusalem. 19This Passover was celebrated in the eighteenth year of Josiah's reign.

THE DEATH OF JOSIAH

20After all this, when Josiah had set the temple in order, Necho king of Egypt went up to fight at Carchemish on the Euphrates, and Josiah marched out to meet him in battle. 21But Necho sent messengers to him, saying, "What quarrel is there, king of Judah, between you and me? It is not you I am attacking at this time, but the house with which I am at war. God has told me to hurry; so stop opposing God, who is with me, or he will destroy you."

22Josiah, however, would not turn away from him, but disguised himself to engage him in battle. He would not listen to what Necho had said at God's command but went to fight him on the plain of Megiddo.

23Archers shot King Josiah, and he told his officers, "Take me away; I am badly wounded." 24So they took him out of his chariot, put him in his other chariot and brought him to Jerusalem, where he died. He was buried in the tombs of his ancestors, and all Judah and Jerusalem mourned for him.

25Jeremiah composed laments for Josiah, and to this day all the male and female singers commemorate Josiah in the laments. These became a tradition in Israel and are written in the Laments.

26The other events of Josiah's reign and his acts of devotion in accordance with what is written in the Law of the LORD — 27all the events, from beginning to end, are written in the book of the kings of Israel

PRAYING SCRIPTURE

2 Chronicles 36

Many subsequent rebellions against God caused the dam to break, and God's judgment rushed over the land. The Babylonians overran Jerusalem, killing young and old, sacking the temple treasures, burning the building and breaking down the wall. The destruction was complete. Many of the citizens were carried away to Babylon.

Do you realize that Jesus has already faced judgment for all who trust him? Pause and thank God for forgiveness through Jesus.

36 and Judah. 1And the people of the land took Jehoahaz son of
Josiah and made him king in Jerusalem in place of his father.

JEHOAHAZ KING OF JUDAH

2Jehoahaz[a] was twenty-three years old when he became king, and he
reigned in Jerusalem three months. 3The king of Egypt dethroned him
in Jerusalem and imposed on Judah a levy of a hundred talents[b] of sil-
ver and a talent[c] of gold. 4The king of Egypt made Eliakim, a brother
of Jehoahaz, king over Judah and Jerusalem and changed Eliakim's
name to Jehoiakim. But Necho took Eliakim's brother Jehoahaz and
carried him off to Egypt.

JEHOIAKIM KING OF JUDAH

5Jehoiakim was twenty-five years old when he became king, and he
reigned in Jerusalem eleven years. He did evil in the eyes of the LORD
his God. 6Nebuchadnezzar king of Babylon attacked him and bound
him with bronze shackles to take him to Babylon. 7Nebuchadnezzar
also took to Babylon articles from the temple of the LORD and put them
in his temple[d] there.
8The other events of Jehoiakim's reign, the detestable things he did
and all that was found against him, are written in the book of the kings
of Israel and Judah. And Jehoiachin his son succeeded him as king.

JEHOIACHIN KING OF JUDAH

9Jehoiachin was eighteen[e] years old when he became king, and he
reigned in Jerusalem three months and ten days. He did evil in the
eyes of the LORD. 10In the spring, King Nebuchadnezzar sent for him
and brought him to Babylon, together with articles of value from the
temple of the LORD, and he made Jehoiachin's uncle,[f] Zedekiah, king
over Judah and Jerusalem.

ZEDEKIAH KING OF JUDAH

11Zedekiah was twenty-one years old when he became king, and he
reigned in Jerusalem eleven years. 12He did evil in the eyes of the LORD
his God and did not humble himself before Jeremiah the prophet, who
spoke the word of the LORD. 13He also rebelled against King Nebuchad-
nezzar, who had made him take an oath in God's name. He became
stiff-necked and hardened his heart and would not turn to the LORD,
the God of Israel. 14Furthermore, all the leaders of the priests and the
people became more and more unfaithful, following all the detestable
practices of the nations and defiling the temple of the LORD, which he
had consecrated in Jerusalem.

THE FALL OF JERUSALEM

15The LORD, the God of their ancestors, sent word to them through
his messengers again and again, because he had pity on his people and
on his dwelling place. 16But they mocked God's messengers, despised

[a] 2 Hebrew *Joahaz,* a variant of *Jehoahaz;* also in verse 4 [b] 3 That is, about 3 3/4 tons or about 3.4 metric tons [c] 3 That is, about 75 pounds or about 34 kilograms [d] 7 Or *palace* [e] 9 One Hebrew manuscript, some Septuagint manuscripts and Syriac (see also 2 Kings 24:8); most Hebrew manuscripts *eight* [f] 10 Hebrew *brother,* that is, relative (see 2 Kings 24:17) [g] 17 Or *Chaldeans*

his words and scoffed at his prophets until the wrath of the LORD was
aroused against his people and there was no remedy. 17He brought up
against them the king of the Babylonians,[g] who killed their young
men with the sword in the sanctuary, and did not spare young men
or young women, the elderly or the infirm. God gave them all into
the hands of Nebuchadnezzar. 18He carried to Babylon all the articles
from the temple of God, both large and small, and the treasures of the
LORD's temple and the treasures of the king and his officials. 19They
set fire to God's temple and broke down the wall of Jerusalem; they
burned all the palaces and destroyed everything of value there.

20He carried into exile to Babylon the remnant, who escaped from
the sword, and they became servants to him and his successors un-
til the kingdom of Persia came to power. 21The land enjoyed its sab-
bath rests; all the time of its desolation it rested, until the seventy
years were completed in fulfillment of the word of the LORD spoken
by Jeremiah.

22In the first year of Cyrus king of Persia, in order to fulfill the word
of the LORD spoken by Jeremiah, the LORD moved the heart of Cyrus
king of Persia to make a proclamation throughout his realm and also
to put it in writing:

23"This is what Cyrus king of Persia says:

"'The LORD, the God of heaven, has given me all the kingdoms
of the earth and he has appointed me to build a temple for him at
Jerusalem in Judah. Any of his people among you may go up, and
may the LORD their God be with them.'"

EZRA

Ezra focuses on the rebuilding of Jerusalem and particularly the temple after the exile. Cyrus allowed the people to return and rebuild their temple, but the work started slowly and faced many obstacles. The first six chapters tell the story of the rebuilding of the temple. The people faced open opposition in their attempts to rebuild the temple, which made them weary in the work. Zerubbabel had to exhort the scared and weary workers to finish the task.

Ezra has much to teach us about worship and prayer. In Ezra 3, when the people had laid the foundation of the temple, they gave thanks to God, saying, "He is good; his love toward Israel endures forever" (verse 11). Even though the generation who had seen the first temple mourned, the new generation knew that the temple was a sign of God's grace to them. They had been through exile, and even though the temple did not have its former glory, they praised God for what he had done. We often see this struggle in transitions today, with one generation weeping while the other rejoices. Both groups benefit from committing their new reality to God in prayer.

The last four chapters introduce the reader to Ezra and the work he did among the people. The Israelites did not just need a rebuilt temple; they needed their spiritual lives to be rebuilt as well. Ezra set his heart to know the Lord's Word and to teach it to God's people in Israel. In chapter 10, Ezra purged the Israelites of marriages to foreign wives who worshiped foreign gods. He wanted the Israelites to be pure in their pursuit of the Lord, and these marriages had a long history of turning Israel away from the Lord.

Many Christians tend to limit our prayers to our material needs and the material needs of those around us. We should pray for these, of course. Jesus modeled praying for our daily bread, Paul said we should pray about whatever makes us anxious, and James said we should seek God's will in our business endeavors. But as Ezra illustrates, we cannot neglect to pray for our spiritual lives and the spiritual health and maturity of those around us.

During one of Ezra's prayers—all through which he wept—a group of Israelites gathered to him. Scripture records that they "wept bitterly" (10:1). Ezra's prayer included confession and the people who came to him in repentance. The prayers of God's people often affect others immediately. Answers are not always in the distant future. Likely, Ezra's passion in his praying was audible, and as people heard him pouring out his heart to God, they were convicted of their own sin and brought to repentance.

Ezra was also careful to combine fasting with prayer. He proclaimed a fast for the people so they would learn to seek a safe journey on their return to Jerusalem. God answered their prayers when combined with fasting.

Ezra reminds us that no amount of political turmoil should displace prayer. God hears and answers the prayers of his people no matter the political climate.

CYRUS HELPS THE EXILES TO RETURN

1 In the first year of Cyrus king of Persia, in order to fulfill the word
of the LORD spoken by Jeremiah, the LORD moved the heart of Cyrus
king of Persia to make a proclamation throughout his realm and also
to put it in writing:

2"This is what Cyrus king of Persia says:
"'The LORD, the God of heaven, has given me all the kingdoms
of the earth and he has appointed me to build a temple for him
at Jerusalem in Judah. 3Any of his people among you may go up
to Jerusalem in Judah and build the temple of the LORD, the God
of Israel, the God who is in Jerusalem, and may their God be with
them. 4And in any locality where survivors may now be living,
the people are to provide them with silver and gold, with goods
and livestock, and with freewill offerings for the temple of God in
Jerusalem.'"

5Then the family heads of Judah and Benjamin, and the priests and
Levites — everyone whose heart God had moved — prepared to go up
and build the house of the LORD in Jerusalem. 6All their neighbors as-
sisted them with articles of silver and gold, with goods and livestock,
and with valuable gifts, in addition to all the freewill offerings.
7Moreover, King Cyrus brought out the articles belonging to the
temple of the LORD, which Nebuchadnezzar had carried away from Je-
rusalem and had placed in the temple of his god.[a] 8Cyrus king of Persia
had them brought by Mithredath the treasurer, who counted them out
to Sheshbazzar the prince of Judah.
9This was the inventory:

	gold dishes	30
	silver dishes	1,000
	silver pans[b]	29
10	gold bowls	30
	matching silver bowls	410
	other articles	1,000

11In all, there were 5,400 articles of gold and of silver. Sheshbazzar
brought all these along with the exiles when they came up from Bab-
ylon to Jerusalem.

THE LIST OF THE EXILES WHO RETURNED

2 Now these are the people of the province who came up from the
captivity of the exiles, whom Nebuchadnezzar king of Babylon
had taken captive to Babylon (they returned to Jerusalem and Judah,
each to their own town, 2in company with Zerubbabel, Joshua, Nehe-
miah, Seraiah, Reelaiah, Mordecai, Bilshan, Mispar, Bigvai, Rehum and
Baanah):

The list of the men of the people of Israel:

3	the descendants of Parosh	2,172
4	of Shephatiah	372
5	of Arah	775
6	of Pahath-Moab (through the line of Jeshua and Joab)	2,812
7	of Elam	1,254

[a] 7 Or *gods* [b] 9 The meaning of the Hebrew for this word is uncertain.

PRAYING SCRIPTURE

Ezra 1

It was a glorious day for those exiled in Babylon when King Cyrus, moved by God's Spirit, released a great number of them to return to Jerusalem so they might rebuild the temple. Additionally, he returned the articles taken from the temple so that they might be restored to use.

God can use those with political power to accomplish his ends. We should pray regularly for government leaders.

PRAYING SCRIPTURE

Ezra 2

After years of captivity in Babylon, tens of thousands of exiles traveled home to Jerusalem and all of Judah, everyone to his or her city. When the people returned, they could not restart worship until the priests built a new altar (3:2).

Aren't you glad you can readily and immediately worship God? Thank God for the blessing of going boldly to his throne.

8 of Zattu	945
9 of Zakkai	760
10 of Bani	642
11 of Bebai	623
12 of Azgad	1,222
13 of Adonikam	666
14 of Bigvai	2,056
15 of Adin	454
16 of Ater (through Hezekiah)	98
17 of Bezai	323
18 of Jorah	112
19 of Hashum	223
20 of Gibbar	95
21 the men of Bethlehem	123
22 of Netophah	56
23 of Anathoth	128
24 of Azmaveth	42
25 of Kiriath Jearim,[a] Kephirah and Beeroth	743
26 of Ramah and Geba	621
27 of Mikmash	122
28 of Bethel and Ai	223
29 of Nebo	52
30 of Magbish	156
31 of the other Elam	1,254
32 of Harim	320
33 of Lod, Hadid and Ono	725
34 of Jericho	345
35 of Senaah	3,630

36 The priests:

the descendants of Jedaiah (through the family of Jeshua)	973
37 of Immer	1,052
38 of Pashhur	1,247
39 of Harim	1,017

40 The Levites:

the descendants of Jeshua and Kadmiel (of the line of Hodaviah)	74

41 The musicians:

the descendants of Asaph	128

42 The gatekeepers of the temple:

the descendants of Shallum, Ater, Talmon, Akkub, Hatita and Shobai	139

43 The temple servants:

the descendants of
Ziha, Hasupha, Tabbaoth,

---

[a] *25* See Septuagint (see also Neh. 7:29); Hebrew *Kiriath Arim.*

[44] Keros, Siaha, Padon,
[45] Lebanah, Hagabah, Akkub,
[46] Hagab, Shalmai, Hanan,
[47] Giddel, Gahar, Reaiah,
[48] Rezin, Nekoda, Gazzam,
[49] Uzza, Paseah, Besai,
[50] Asnah, Meunim, Nephusim,
[51] Bakbuk, Hakupha, Harhur,
[52] Bazluth, Mehida, Harsha,
[53] Barkos, Sisera, Temah,
[54] Neziah and Hatipha

[55] The descendants of the servants of Solomon:

the descendants of
Sotai, Hassophereth, Peruda,
[56] Jaala, Darkon, Giddel,
[57] Shephatiah, Hattil,
Pokereth-Hazzebaim and Ami

[58] The temple servants and the descendants of the
servants of Solomon 392

[59] The following came up from the towns of Tel Melah, Tel Harsha, Kerub, Addon and Immer, but they could not show that their families were descended from Israel:

[60] The descendants of
Delaiah, Tobiah and Nekoda 652

[61] And from among the priests:

The descendants of
Hobaiah, Hakkoz and Barzillai (a man who had married a daughter of Barzillai the Gileadite and was called by that name).

[62] These searched for their family records, but they could not find them and so were excluded from the priesthood as unclean. [63] The governor ordered them not to eat any of the most sacred food until there was a priest ministering with the Urim and Thummim.

[64] The whole company numbered 42,360, [65] besides their 7,337 male and female slaves; and they also had 200 male and female singers. [66] They had 736 horses, 245 mules, [67] 435 camels and 6,720 donkeys.

[68] When they arrived at the house of the LORD in Jerusalem, some of the heads of the families gave freewill offerings toward the rebuilding of the house of God on its site. [69] According to their ability they gave to the treasury for this work 61,000 darics[a] of gold, 5,000 minas[b] of silver and 100 priestly garments.

[70] The priests, the Levites, the musicians, the gatekeepers and the temple servants settled in their own towns, along with some of the other people, and the rest of the Israelites settled in their towns.

[a] 69 That is, about 1,100 pounds or about 500 kilograms [b] 69 That is, about 3 tons or about 2.8 metric tons

PRAYING SCRIPTURE

Ezra 3

An interesting Biblical contrast is found in this chapter. When the people returned, restoration of the temple began with the laying of the foundation. Many of the older people who had seen the first temple wept. Others who had not seen it shouted joyously.

When God moves, people can interpret what they see in different ways. Comparing what God does at different times can be a problem. Ask God to keep your heart open to what he is doing.

REBUILDING THE ALTAR

3 When the seventh month came and the Israelites had settled in
their towns, the people assembled together as one in Jerusalem.
2Then Joshua son of Jozadak and his fellow priests and Zerubbabel
son of Shealtiel and his associates began to build the altar of the God
of Israel to sacrifice burnt offerings on it, in accordance with what is
written in the Law of Moses the man of God. 3Despite their fear of the
peoples around them, they built the altar on its foundation and sacri-
ficed burnt offerings on it to the LORD, both the morning and evening
sacrifices. 4Then in accordance with what is written, they celebrated
the Festival of Tabernacles with the required number of burnt offer-
ings prescribed for each day. 5After that, they presented the regular
burnt offerings, the New Moon sacrifices and the sacrifices for all the
appointed sacred festivals of the LORD, as well as those brought as free-
will offerings to the LORD. 6On the first day of the seventh month they
began to offer burnt offerings to the LORD, though the foundation of
the LORD's temple had not yet been laid.

REBUILDING THE TEMPLE

7Then they gave money to the masons and carpenters, and gave food
and drink and olive oil to the people of Sidon and Tyre, so that they
would bring cedar logs by sea from Lebanon to Joppa, as authorized
by Cyrus king of Persia.

8In the second month of the second year after their arrival at the
house of God in Jerusalem, Zerubbabel son of Shealtiel, Joshua son of
Jozadak and the rest of the people (the priests and the Levites and all
who had returned from the captivity to Jerusalem) began the work.
They appointed Levites twenty years old and older to supervise the
building of the house of the LORD. 9Joshua and his sons and brothers
and Kadmiel and his sons (descendants of Hodaviah[a]) and the sons of
Henadad and their sons and brothers — all Levites — joined together
in supervising those working on the house of God.

10When the builders laid the foundation of the temple of the LORD,
the priests in their vestments and with trumpets, and the Levites (the
sons of Asaph) with cymbals, took their places to praise the LORD, as
prescribed by David king of Israel. 11With praise and thanksgiving they
sang to the LORD:

"He is good;
his love toward Israel endures forever."

And all the people gave a great shout of praise to the LORD, because
the foundation of the house of the LORD was laid. 12But many of the
older priests and Levites and family heads, who had seen the former
temple, wept aloud when they saw the foundation of this temple be-
ing laid, while many others shouted for joy. 13No one could distinguish
the sound of the shouts of joy from the sound of weeping, because the
people made so much noise. And the sound was heard far away.

PRAYING SCRIPTURE

Ezra 4

Attempting something for God is likely to be met with resistance; it has always been this way. Here a conflict between Israelites and Samaritans halted the temple's construction for many years.

There is no guarantee of smooth sailing when serving God. Satan has any number of tactics and tools to hinder God's people. But God will empower those who call on him in faith.

OPPOSITION TO THE REBUILDING

4 When the enemies of Judah and Benjamin heard that the exiles
were building a temple for the LORD, the God of Israel, 2they came
to Zerubbabel and to the heads of the families and said, "Let us help you

[a] 9 Hebrew *Yehudah,* a variant of *Hodaviah*

build because, like you, we seek your God and have been sacrificing to
him since the time of Esarhaddon king of Assyria, who brought us here."
3But Zerubbabel, Joshua and the rest of the heads of the families of
Israel answered, "You have no part with us in building a temple to our
God. We alone will build it for the LORD, the God of Israel, as King Cy-
rus, the king of Persia, commanded us."
4Then the peoples around them set out to discourage the people of
Judah and make them afraid to go on building.[a] 5They bribed officials
to work against them and frustrate their plans during the entire reign
of Cyrus king of Persia and down to the reign of Darius king of Persia.

LATER OPPOSITION UNDER XERXES AND ARTAXERXES

6At the beginning of the reign of Xerxes,[b] they lodged an accusation
against the people of Judah and Jerusalem.
7And in the days of Artaxerxes king of Persia, Bishlam, Mithredath,
Tabeel and the rest of his associates wrote a letter to Artaxerxes. The
letter was written in Aramaic script and in the Aramaic language.[c,d]
8Rehum the commanding officer and Shimshai the secretary wrote a
letter against Jerusalem to Artaxerxes the king as follows:

9Rehum the commanding officer and Shimshai the secretary, to-
gether with the rest of their associates — the judges, officials and
administrators over the people from Persia, Uruk and Babylon,
the Elamites of Susa, 10and the other people whom the great and
honorable Ashurbanipal deported and settled in the city of Sa-
maria and elsewhere in Trans-Euphrates.

11(This is a copy of the letter they sent him.)

To King Artaxerxes,
From your servants in Trans-Euphrates:

12The king should know that the people who came up to us
from you have gone to Jerusalem and are rebuilding that rebel-
lious and wicked city. They are restoring the walls and repairing
the foundations.
13Furthermore, the king should know that if this city is built and
its walls are restored, no more taxes, tribute or duty will be paid,
and eventually the royal revenues will suffer.[e] 14Now since we are
under obligation to the palace and it is not proper for us to see the
king dishonored, we are sending this message to inform the king,
15so that a search may be made in the archives of your predeces-
sors. In these records you will find that this city is a rebellious city,
troublesome to kings and provinces, a place with a long history of
sedition. That is why this city was destroyed. 16We inform the king
that if this city is built and its walls are restored, you will be left
with nothing in Trans-Euphrates.

17The king sent this reply:

To Rehum the commanding officer, Shimshai the secretary and
the rest of their associates living in Samaria and elsewhere in
Trans-Euphrates:

---

[a] 4 Or *and troubled them as they built* [b] 6 Hebrew *Ahasuerus* [c] 7 Or *written in Aramaic and translated* [d] 7 The text of 4:8 – 6:18 is in Aramaic.
[e] 13 The meaning of the Aramaic for this clause is uncertain.

Greetings.

18 The letter you sent us has been read and translated in my presence. 19 I issued an order and a search was made, and it was found that this city has a long history of revolt against kings and has been a place of rebellion and sedition. 20 Jerusalem has had powerful kings ruling over the whole of Trans-Euphrates, and taxes, tribute and duty were paid to them. 21 Now issue an order to these men to stop work, so that this city will not be rebuilt until I so order. 22 Be careful not to neglect this matter. Why let this threat grow, to the detriment of the royal interests?

23 As soon as the copy of the letter of King Artaxerxes was read to Rehum and Shimshai the secretary and their associates, they went immediately to the Jews in Jerusalem and compelled them by force to stop.

24 Thus the work on the house of God in Jerusalem came to a standstill until the second year of the reign of Darius king of Persia.

TATTENAI'S LETTER TO DARIUS

5 Now Haggai the prophet and Zechariah the prophet, a descendant of Iddo, prophesied to the Jews in Judah and Jerusalem in the name of the God of Israel, who was over them. 2 Then Zerubbabel son of Shealtiel and Joshua son of Jozadak set to work to rebuild the house of God in Jerusalem. And the prophets of God were with them, supporting them.

3 At that time Tattenai, governor of Trans-Euphrates, and Shethar-Bozenai and their associates went to them and asked, "Who authorized you to rebuild this temple and to finish it?" 4 They[a] also asked, "What are the names of those who are constructing this building?" 5 But the eye of their God was watching over the elders of the Jews, and they were not stopped until a report could go to Darius and his written reply be received.

6 This is a copy of the letter that Tattenai, governor of Trans-Euphrates, and Shethar-Bozenai and their associates, the officials of Trans-Euphrates, sent to King Darius. 7 The report they sent him read as follows:

To King Darius:

Cordial greetings.

8 The king should know that we went to the district of Judah, to the temple of the great God. The people are building it with large stones and placing the timbers in the walls. The work is being carried on with diligence and is making rapid progress under their direction.

9 We questioned the elders and asked them, "Who authorized you to rebuild this temple and to finish it?" 10 We also asked them their names, so that we could write down the names of their leaders for your information.

11 This is the answer they gave us:

"We are the servants of the God of heaven and earth, and we are rebuilding the temple that was built many years ago, one that a great king of Israel built and finished. 12 But because our ancestors

PRAYING SCRIPTURE

Ezra 5

When the temple construction resumed, it was because a group of men led by Zerubbabel and some prophets had "the eye of their God" on them (verse 5). When threatened, they refused to stop working even in the face of reports to the Persian king Darius.

When faced with challenges to following Jesus, we should be resolute, asking God for strength to endure. His grace is sufficient if we but ask.

[a] 4 See Septuagint; Aramaic *We*.

angered the God of heaven, he gave them into the hands of Neb-
uchadnezzar the Chaldean, king of Babylon, who destroyed this
temple and deported the people to Babylon.
13 “However, in the first year of Cyrus king of Babylon, King
Cyrus issued a decree to rebuild this house of God. 14 He even re-
moved from the temple[a] of Babylon the gold and silver articles
of the house of God, which Nebuchadnezzar had taken from the
temple in Jerusalem and brought to the temple[a] in Babylon. Then
King Cyrus gave them to a man named Sheshbazzar, whom he had
appointed governor, 15 and he told him, ‘Take these articles and
go and deposit them in the temple in Jerusalem. And rebuild the
house of God on its site.’
16 “So this Sheshbazzar came and laid the foundations of the
house of God in Jerusalem. From that day to the present it has
been under construction but is not yet finished.”

17 Now if it pleases the king, let a search be made in the royal ar-
chives of Babylon to see if King Cyrus did in fact issue a decree to
rebuild this house of God in Jerusalem. Then let the king send us
his decision in this matter.

THE DECREE OF DARIUS

6 King Darius then issued an order, and they searched in the ar-
chives stored in the treasury at Babylon. 2 A scroll was found in the
citadel of Ecbatana in the province of Media, and this was written on it:

Memorandum:

3 In the first year of King Cyrus, the king issued a decree con-
cerning the temple of God in Jerusalem:

Let the temple be rebuilt as a place to present sacrifices, and let
its foundations be laid. It is to be sixty cubits[b] high and sixty cu-
bits wide, 4 with three courses of large stones and one of timbers.
The costs are to be paid by the royal treasury. 5 Also, the gold and
silver articles of the house of God, which Nebuchadnezzar took
from the temple in Jerusalem and brought to Babylon, are to be
returned to their places in the temple in Jerusalem; they are to be
deposited in the house of God.

6 Now then, Tattenai, governor of Trans-Euphrates, and Shethar-
Bozenai and you other officials of that province, stay away from
there. 7 Do not interfere with the work on this temple of God. Let
the governor of the Jews and the Jewish elders rebuild this house
of God on its site.
8 Moreover, I hereby decree what you are to do for these elders
of the Jews in the construction of this house of God:
Their expenses are to be fully paid out of the royal treasury, from
the revenues of Trans-Euphrates, so that the work will not stop.
9 Whatever is needed—young bulls, rams, male lambs for burnt of-
ferings to the God of heaven, and wheat, salt, wine and olive oil, as
requested by the priests in Jerusalem—must be given them daily
without fail, 10 so that they may offer sacrifices pleasing to the God
of heaven and pray for the well-being of the king and his sons.

PRAYING SCRIPTURE

Ezra 6

The condition of the Israelites’ spiritual life can often be understood by their Passover observances. If they were following idols, the Passover was forgotten, sometimes for decades. When they came back to God, the Passover was often restored with great joy and celebration.

What are some of the spiritual routines in your life that turn your heart to God? Set times and places that allow you consistent communion with him.

[a] 14 Or *palace* [b] 3 That is, about 90 feet or about 27 meters

11Furthermore, I decree that if anyone defies this edict, a beam
is to be pulled from their house and they are to be impaled on it.
And for this crime their house is to be made a pile of rubble. 12May
God, who has caused his Name to dwell there, overthrow any king
or people who lifts a hand to change this decree or to destroy this
temple in Jerusalem.

I Darius have decreed it. Let it be carried out with diligence.

COMPLETION AND DEDICATION OF THE TEMPLE

13Then, because of the decree King Darius had sent, Tattenai, gover-
nor of Trans-Euphrates, and Shethar-Bozenai and their associates car-
ried it out with diligence. 14So the elders of the Jews continued to build
and prosper under the preaching of Haggai the prophet and Zechariah,
a descendant of Iddo. They finished building the temple according to
the command of the God of Israel and the decrees of Cyrus, Darius and
Artaxerxes, kings of Persia. 15The temple was completed on the third
day of the month Adar, in the sixth year of the reign of King Darius.

16Then the people of Israel — the priests, the Levites and the rest of
the exiles — celebrated the dedication of the house of God with joy.
17For the dedication of this house of God they offered a hundred bulls,
two hundred rams, four hundred male lambs and, as a sin offering[a]
for all Israel, twelve male goats, one for each of the tribes of Israel.
18And they installed the priests in their divisions and the Levites in
their groups for the service of God at Jerusalem, according to what is
written in the Book of Moses.

THE PASSOVER

19On the fourteenth day of the first month, the exiles celebrated the
Passover. 20The priests and Levites had purified themselves and were
all ceremonially clean. The Levites slaughtered the Passover lamb for
all the exiles, for their relatives the priests and for themselves. 21So the
Israelites who had returned from the exile ate it, together with all who
had separated themselves from the unclean practices of their Gentile
neighbors in order to seek the LORD, the God of Israel. 22For seven days
they celebrated with joy the Festival of Unleavened Bread, because the
LORD had filled them with joy by changing the attitude of the king of
Assyria so that he assisted them in the work on the house of God, the
God of Israel.

EZRA COMES TO JERUSALEM

7 After these things, during the reign of Artaxerxes king of Persia,
Ezra son of Seraiah, the son of Azariah, the son of Hilkiah, 2the son
of Shallum, the son of Zadok, the son of Ahitub, 3the son of Amariah,
the son of Azariah, the son of Meraioth, 4the son of Zerahiah, the son
of Uzzi, the son of Bukki, 5the son of Abishua, the son of Phinehas, the
son of Eleazar, the son of Aaron the chief priest — 6this Ezra came up
from Babylon. He was a teacher well versed in the Law of Moses, which
the LORD, the God of Israel, had given. The king had granted him ev-
erything he asked, for the hand of the LORD his God was on him. 7Some
of the Israelites, including priests, Levites, musicians, gatekeepers and
temple servants, also came up to Jerusalem in the seventh year of King
Artaxerxes.

[a] 17 Or *purification offering*

PRAYING SCRIPTURE

Ezra 7

Ezra the priest, for whom the book is named, returned to Jerusalem bearing a letter of blessing from King Artaxerxes. Ezra had already "devoted himself to the study and observance of the Law of the LORD, and to teaching" it to the Israelites (verse 10).

What a tremendous pattern for all God's people to follow today! Pray for God's guidance to seek his Word, obey it and teach it to others.

8Ezra arrived in Jerusalem in the fifth month of the seventh year of
the king. 9He had begun his journey from Babylon on the first day of
the first month, and he arrived in Jerusalem on the first day of the fifth
month, for the gracious hand of his God was on him. 10For Ezra had de-
voted himself to the study and observance of the Law of the LORD, and
to teaching its decrees and laws in Israel.

KING ARTAXERXES' LETTER TO EZRA

11This is a copy of the letter King Artaxerxes had given to Ezra the
priest, a teacher of the Law, a man learned in matters concerning the
commands and decrees of the LORD for Israel:

12Artaxerxes, king of kings,

To Ezra the priest, teacher of the Law of the God of heaven:

Greetings.

13Now I decree that any of the Israelites in my kingdom, includ-
ing priests and Levites, who volunteer to go to Jerusalem with
you, may go. 14You are sent by the king and his seven advisers to
inquire about Judah and Jerusalem with regard to the Law of your
God, which is in your hand. 15Moreover, you are to take with you
the silver and gold that the king and his advisers have freely given
to the God of Israel, whose dwelling is in Jerusalem, 16together
with all the silver and gold you may obtain from the province of
Babylon, as well as the freewill offerings of the people and priests
for the temple of their God in Jerusalem. 17With this money be
sure to buy bulls, rams and male lambs, together with their grain
offerings and drink offerings, and sacrifice them on the altar of
the temple of your God in Jerusalem.

18You and your fellow Israelites may then do whatever seems
best with the rest of the silver and gold, in accordance with the
will of your God. 19Deliver to the God of Jerusalem all the articles
entrusted to you for worship in the temple of your God. 20And
anything else needed for the temple of your God that you are re-
sponsible to supply, you may provide from the royal treasury.

21Now I, King Artaxerxes, decree that all the treasurers of Trans-
Euphrates are to provide with diligence whatever Ezra the priest,
the teacher of the Law of the God of heaven, may ask of you — 22up
to a hundred talents[a] of silver, a hundred cors[b] of wheat, a hun-
dred baths[c] of wine, a hundred baths[c] of olive oil, and salt without
limit. 23Whatever the God of heaven has prescribed, let it be done
with diligence for the temple of the God of heaven. Why should his
wrath fall on the realm of the king and of his sons? 24You are also
to know that you have no authority to impose taxes, tribute or
duty on any of the priests, Levites, musicians, gatekeepers, temple
servants or other workers at this house of God.

25And you, Ezra, in accordance with the wisdom of your God,
which you possess, appoint magistrates and judges to administer
justice to all the people of Trans-Euphrates — all who know the
laws of your God. And you are to teach any who do not know them.

---

[a] *22* That is, about 3 3/4 tons or about 3.4 metric tons [b] *22* That is, probably about 18 tons or about 16 metric tons [c] *22* That is, about 600 gallons or about 2,200 liters

26 Whoever does not obey the law of your God and the law of the
king must surely be punished by death, banishment, confiscation
of property, or imprisonment.[a]

27 Praise be to the LORD, the God of our ancestors, who has put it into
the king's heart to bring honor to the house of the LORD in Jerusalem
in this way 28 and who has extended his good favor to me before the
king and his advisers and all the king's powerful officials. Because the
hand of the LORD my God was on me, I took courage and gathered lead-
ers from Israel to go up with me.

PRAYING SCRIPTURE

Ezra 8

After the people returned, Ezra proclaimed a time of fasting and prayer. He asked that they would have God's protection for themselves and their children as they traveled with all their possessions.

It is common for God's people to ask his will for themselves and for family members—but for possessions? Perhaps we would do well to seek God's will for the things he has given to our care.

LIST OF THE FAMILY HEADS RETURNING WITH EZRA

8 These are the family heads and those registered with them
who came up with me from Babylon during the reign of King
Artaxerxes:

2 of the descendants of Phinehas, Gershom;
of the descendants of Ithamar, Daniel;
of the descendants of David, Hattush 3 of the descendants of
Shekaniah;

of the descendants of Parosh, Zechariah, and with him were registered 150 men;
4 of the descendants of Pahath-Moab, Eliehoenai son of Zerahiah, and with him 200 men;
5 of the descendants of Zattu,[b] Shekaniah son of Jahaziel, and with him 300 men;
6 of the descendants of Adin, Ebed son of Jonathan, and with him 50 men;
7 of the descendants of Elam, Jeshaiah son of Athaliah, and with him 70 men;
8 of the descendants of Shephatiah, Zebadiah son of Michael, and with him 80 men;
9 of the descendants of Joab, Obadiah son of Jehiel, and with him 218 men;
10 of the descendants of Bani,[c] Shelomith son of Josiphiah, and with him 160 men;
11 of the descendants of Bebai, Zechariah son of Bebai, and with him 28 men;
12 of the descendants of Azgad, Johanan son of Hakkatan, and with him 110 men;
13 of the descendants of Adonikam, the last ones, whose names were Eliphelet, Jeuel and Shemaiah, and with them 60 men;
14 of the descendants of Bigvai, Uthai and Zakkur, and with them 70 men.

THE RETURN TO JERUSALEM

15 I assembled them at the canal that flows toward Ahava, and we
camped there three days. When I checked among the people and
the priests, I found no Levites there. 16 So I summoned Eliezer, Ariel,
Shemaiah, Elnathan, Jarib, Elnathan, Nathan, Zechariah and Meshul-
lam, who were leaders, and Joiarib and Elnathan, who were men of

[a] *26* The text of 7:12-26 is in Aramaic. [b] *5* Some Septuagint manuscripts (also 1 Esdras 8:32); Hebrew does not have *Zattu.* [c] *10* Some Septuagint manuscripts (also 1 Esdras 8:36); Hebrew does not have *Bani.*

learning, 17and I ordered them to go to Iddo, the leader in Kasiphia. I told them what to say to Iddo and his fellow Levites, the temple servants in Kasiphia, so that they might bring attendants to us for the house of our God. 18Because the gracious hand of our God was on us, they brought us Sherebiah, a capable man, from the descendants of Mahli son of Levi, the son of Israel, and Sherebiah's sons and brothers, 18 in all; 19and Hashabiah, together with Jeshaiah from the descendants of Merari, and his brothers and nephews, 20 in all. 20They also brought 220 of the temple servants — a body that David and the officials had established to assist the Levites. All were registered by name.

21There, by the Ahava Canal, I proclaimed a fast, so that we might humble ourselves before our God and ask him for a safe journey for us and our children, with all our possessions. 22I was ashamed to ask the king for soldiers and horsemen to protect us from enemies on the road, because we had told the king, "The gracious hand of our God is on everyone who looks to him, but his great anger is against all who forsake him." 23So we fasted and petitioned our God about this, and he answered our prayer.

24Then I set apart twelve of the leading priests, namely, Sherebiah, Hashabiah and ten of their brothers, 25and I weighed out to them the offering of silver and gold and the articles that the king, his advisers, his officials and all Israel present there had donated for the house of our God. 26I weighed out to them 650 talents[a] of silver, silver articles weighing 100 talents,[b] 100 talents[b] of gold, 2720 bowls of gold valued at 1,000 darics,[c] and two fine articles of polished bronze, as precious as gold.

28I said to them, "You as well as these articles are consecrated to the LORD. The silver and gold are a freewill offering to the LORD, the God of your ancestors. 29Guard them carefully until you weigh them out in the chambers of the house of the LORD in Jerusalem before the leading priests and the Levites and the family heads of Israel." 30Then the priests and Levites received the silver and gold and sacred articles that had been weighed out to be taken to the house of our God in Jerusalem.

31On the twelfth day of the first month we set out from the Ahava Canal to go to Jerusalem. The hand of our God was on us, and he protected us from enemies and bandits along the way. 32So we arrived in Jerusalem, where we rested three days.

33On the fourth day, in the house of our God, we weighed out the silver and gold and the sacred articles into the hands of Meremoth son of Uriah, the priest. Eleazar son of Phinehas was with him, and so were the Levites Jozabad son of Jeshua and Noadiah son of Binnui. 34Everything was accounted for by number and weight, and the entire weight was recorded at that time.

35Then the exiles who had returned from captivity sacrificed burnt offerings to the God of Israel: twelve bulls for all Israel, ninety-six rams, seventy-seven male lambs and, as a sin offering,[d] twelve male goats. All this was a burnt offering to the LORD. 36They also delivered the king's orders to the royal satraps and to the governors of Trans-Euphrates, who then gave assistance to the people and to the house of God.

---

[a] *26* That is, about 24 tons or about 22 metric tons [b] *26* That is, about 3 3/4 tons or about 3.4 metric tons [c] *27* That is, about 19 pounds or about 8.4 kilograms [d] *35* Or *purification offering*

PRAYING SCRIPTURE

Ezra 9

When Ezra found out that the people—including the religious leaders—had intermarried with unbelievers, he tore out part of his hair and beard, sitting "appalled until the evening sacrifice" (see verse 4). He warned the people of Israel that God would not tolerate the evil deeds they'd done.

Marriage is often an overlooked part of obedience to God. Pray for believers that they choose marriage or singleness as a way to glorify God.

EZRA'S PRAYER ABOUT INTERMARRIAGE

9 After these things had been done, the leaders came to me and
said, "The people of Israel, including the priests and the Levites,
have not kept themselves separate from the neighboring peoples with
their detestable practices, like those of the Canaanites, Hittites, Periz-
zites, Jebusites, Ammonites, Moabites, Egyptians and Amorites. 2They
have taken some of their daughters as wives for themselves and their
sons, and have mingled the holy race with the peoples around them.
And the leaders and officials have led the way in this unfaithfulness."
3When I heard this, I tore my tunic and cloak, pulled hair from my
head and beard and sat down appalled. 4Then everyone who trem-
bled at the words of the God of Israel gathered around me because
of this unfaithfulness of the exiles. And I sat there appalled until the
evening sacrifice.
5Then, at the evening sacrifice, I rose from my self-abasement, with
my tunic and cloak torn, and fell on my knees with my hands spread
out to the LORD my God 6and prayed:

> "I am too ashamed and disgraced, my God, to lift up my face
> to you, because our sins are higher than our heads and our guilt
> has reached to the heavens. 7From the days of our ancestors un-
> til now, our guilt has been great. Because of our sins, we and our
> kings and our priests have been subjected to the sword and cap-
> tivity, to pillage and humiliation at the hand of foreign kings, as
> it is today.
> 8"But now, for a brief moment, the LORD our God has been gra-
> cious in leaving us a remnant and giving us a firm place[a] in his
> sanctuary, and so our God gives light to our eyes and a little relief
> in our bondage. 9Though we are slaves, our God has not forsaken
> us in our bondage. He has shown us kindness in the sight of the
> kings of Persia: He has granted us new life to rebuild the house
> of our God and repair its ruins, and he has given us a wall of pro-
> tection in Judah and Jerusalem.
> 10"But now, our God, what can we say after this? For we have
> forsaken the commands 11you gave through your servants the
> prophets when you said: 'The land you are entering to possess is
> a land polluted by the corruption of its peoples. By their detest-
> able practices they have filled it with their impurity from one end
> to the other. 12Therefore, do not give your daughters in marriage
> to their sons or take their daughters for your sons. Do not seek
> a treaty of friendship with them at any time, that you may be
> strong and eat the good things of the land and leave it to your
> children as an everlasting inheritance.'
> 13"What has happened to us is a result of our evil deeds and
> our great guilt, and yet, our God, you have punished us less than
> our sins deserved and have given us a remnant like this. 14Shall
> we then break your commands again and intermarry with the
> peoples who commit such detestable practices? Would you not
> be angry enough with us to destroy us, leaving us no remnant or
> survivor? 15LORD, the God of Israel, you are righteous! We are left
> this day as a remnant. Here we are before you in our guilt, though
> because of it not one of us can stand in your presence."

---

[a] 8 Or *a foothold*

THE PEOPLE'S CONFESSION OF SIN

10 While Ezra was praying and confessing, weeping and throwing
himself down before the house of God, a large crowd of Isra-
elites — men, women and children — gathered around him. They too
wept bitterly. 2Then Shekaniah son of Jehiel, one of the descendants
of Elam, said to Ezra, "We have been unfaithful to our God by marrying
foreign women from the peoples around us. But in spite of this, there
is still hope for Israel. 3Now let us make a covenant before our God to
send away all these women and their children, in accordance with the
counsel of my lord and of those who fear the commands of our God. Let
it be done according to the Law. 4Rise up; this matter is in your hands.
We will support you, so take courage and do it."

5So Ezra rose up and put the leading priests and Levites and all Israel
under oath to do what had been suggested. And they took the oath.
6Then Ezra withdrew from before the house of God and went to the
room of Jehohanan son of Eliashib. While he was there, he ate no food
and drank no water, because he continued to mourn over the unfaith-
fulness of the exiles.

7A proclamation was then issued throughout Judah and Jerusalem
for all the exiles to assemble in Jerusalem. 8Anyone who failed to ap-
pear within three days would forfeit all his property, in accordance
with the decision of the officials and elders, and would himself be ex-
pelled from the assembly of the exiles.

9Within the three days, all the men of Judah and Benjamin had gath-
ered in Jerusalem. And on the twentieth day of the ninth month, all
the people were sitting in the square before the house of God, greatly
distressed by the occasion and because of the rain. 10Then Ezra the
priest stood up and said to them, "You have been unfaithful; you have
married foreign women, adding to Israel's guilt. 11Now honor[a] the
LORD, the God of your ancestors, and do his will. Separate yourselves
from the peoples around you and from your foreign wives."

12The whole assembly responded with a loud voice: "You are right!
We must do as you say. 13But there are many people here and it is the
rainy season; so we cannot stand outside. Besides, this matter cannot
be taken care of in a day or two, because we have sinned greatly in this
thing. 14Let our officials act for the whole assembly. Then let everyone
in our towns who has married a foreign woman come at a set time,
along with the elders and judges of each town, until the fierce anger
of our God in this matter is turned away from us." 15Only Jonathan son
of Asahel and Jahzeiah son of Tikvah, supported by Meshullam and
Shabbethai the Levite, opposed this.

16So the exiles did as was proposed. Ezra the priest selected men
who were family heads, one from each family division, and all of
them designated by name. On the first day of the tenth month they
sat down to investigate the cases, 17and by the first day of the first
month they finished dealing with all the men who had married for-
eign women.

THOSE GUILTY OF INTERMARRIAGE

18Among the descendants of the priests, the following had married
foreign women:

PRAYING SCRIPTURE

Ezra 10

The solution to intermarrying with the pagans was to divorce them, to put them away. To do so was evidence of the Israelites' repentance and intent to pursue God's law again.

Repentance often requires more than prayer; there should be evidence of repentance. Behavioral change must reflect heart change.

---

[a] 11 Or *Now make confession to*

From the descendants of Joshua son of Jozadak, and his brothers: Maaseiah, Eliezer, Jarib and Gedaliah. 19(They all gave their hands in pledge to put away their wives, and for their guilt they each presented a ram from the flock as a guilt offering.)
20 From the descendants of Immer:
Hanani and Zebadiah.
21 From the descendants of Harim:
Maaseiah, Elijah, Shemaiah, Jehiel and Uzziah.
22 From the descendants of Pashhur:
Elioenai, Maaseiah, Ishmael, Nethanel, Jozabad and Elasah.

23 Among the Levites:

Jozabad, Shimei, Kelaiah (that is, Kelita), Pethahiah, Judah and Eliezer.
24 From the musicians:
Eliashib.
From the gatekeepers:
Shallum, Telem and Uri.

25 And among the other Israelites:

From the descendants of Parosh:
Ramiah, Izziah, Malkijah, Mijamin, Eleazar, Malkijah and Benaiah.
26 From the descendants of Elam:
Mattaniah, Zechariah, Jehiel, Abdi, Jeremoth and Elijah.
27 From the descendants of Zattu:
Elioenai, Eliashib, Mattaniah, Jeremoth, Zabad and Aziza.
28 From the descendants of Bebai:
Jehohanan, Hananiah, Zabbai and Athlai.
29 From the descendants of Bani:
Meshullam, Malluk, Adaiah, Jashub, Sheal and Jeremoth.
30 From the descendants of Pahath-Moab:
Adna, Kelal, Benaiah, Maaseiah, Mattaniah, Bezalel, Binnui and Manasseh.
31 From the descendants of Harim:
Eliezer, Ishijah, Malkijah, Shemaiah, Shimeon, 32Benjamin, Malluk and Shemariah.
33 From the descendants of Hashum:
Mattenai, Mattattah, Zabad, Eliphelet, Jeremai, Manasseh and Shimei.
34 From the descendants of Bani:
Maadai, Amram, Uel, 35Benaiah, Bedeiah, Keluhi, 36Vaniah, Meremoth, Eliashib, 37Mattaniah, Mattenai and Jaasu.
38 From the descendants of Binnui:[a]
Shimei, 39Shelemiah, Nathan, Adaiah, 40Maknadebai, Shashai, Sharai, 41Azarel, Shelemiah, Shemariah, 42Shallum, Amariah and Joseph.
43 From the descendants of Nebo:
Jeiel, Mattithiah, Zabad, Zebina, Jaddai, Joel and Benaiah.

44All these had married foreign women, and some of them had children by these wives.[b]

[a] *37,38* See Septuagint (also 1 Esdras 9:34); Hebrew *Jaasu* [38]*and Bani and Binnui,* [b] 44 Or *and they sent them away with their children*

NEHEMIAH

Originally, Ezra and Nehemiah were one book. Where Ezra focuses on the rebuilding of the temple, Nehemiah tells the story of the rebuilding of the wall around Jerusalem. Far from writing a story centered on a construction project, Nehemiah sought a revived spiritual life among his people. The book's first seven chapters narrate the building of the wall, while the remaining chapters focus on the spiritual lives of the people.

Many Christians would be surprised to learn how much we discover about prayer in a book about building a wall. However, when you consider the immense difficulty of the work Nehemiah was undertaking and the fierce opposition that surrounded him, consistent prayer was his only recourse.

Nehemiah's prayers took two different forms—he prayed long prayers and quick, short prayers. The first long prayer occurred at the beginning of the book. Nehemiah heard of the terrible state of Jerusalem, with its wall broken down and its gates burned. He confessed his sins and those of his people.

Nehemiah did not merely pray, however. He wept and mourned for many days while fasting and praying. These were no trite words. Nehemiah was heartbroken. He approached God in that condition and remained there. Then he prayed that God would give him success. The readers do not know the identity of the man to whom Nehemiah sought blessing until the narrator informs them that Nehemiah was the king's cupbearer.

Nehemiah's long prayer in the first chapter led to the shorter prayer in the second chapter. He appeared downcast in the presence of the king, which was a serious offense. The king asked him why his face looked sad, and he informed the king about the terrible state of his people in Jerusalem. He asked Nehemiah what he would request. Rather than blurting out the first thing that came to mind, Nehemiah "prayed to the God of heaven" (2:4). The book of Nehemiah does not inform readers about the content of the prayer, but it is safe to assume that it was a prayer for him to speak wisely and for the Lord to protect his life.

Nehemiah prayed other quick, pithy petitions in the narrative. One took place when the Israelites faced stiff opposition while they built the wall. He prayed for God to take vengeance on their mockers. At other times, he prayed for God to remember him according to the work he had done for God's people.

Prayer, in fact, permeates Nehemiah. One unique aspect of prayer in the book is seen in the first-person prayers that were included in the narrative. At the end of chapter 5, Nehemiah recounted a series of events, then moved directly into prayer: "Remember me with favor, my God, for all that I have done for these people" (verse 19). We read a similar approach in 6:14, "Remember Tobiah and Sanballat, my God, because of what they have done."

Nehemiah reminds us that prayer should be as much of our daily life as breathing or working on our to do list.

PRAYING SCRIPTURE

Nehemiah 1

Nehemiah opens with a commitment to prayer and a record of prayer. Brokenhearted over the condition of Jerusalem, Nehemiah confessed his own sins and those of Israel's fathers, begging God to grant him favor with the king.

How often do you take on a project without praying? Nehemiah gives us a pattern for how to bring our concerns and requests to God in humility and faith.

NEHEMIAH'S PRAYER

1 The words of Nehemiah son of Hakaliah:

In the month of Kislev in the twentieth year, while I was in the cita-
del of Susa, [2]Hanani, one of my brothers, came from Judah with some
other men, and I questioned them about the Jewish remnant that had
survived the exile, and also about Jerusalem.
[3]They said to me, "Those who survived the exile and are back in the
province are in great trouble and disgrace. The wall of Jerusalem is
broken down, and its gates have been burned with fire."
[4]When I heard these things, I sat down and wept. For some days
I mourned and fasted and prayed before the God of heaven. [5]Then I
said:

"LORD, the God of heaven, the great and awesome God, who
keeps his covenant of love with those who love him and keep his
commandments, [6]let your ear be attentive and your eyes open to
hear the prayer your servant is praying before you day and night
for your servants, the people of Israel. I confess the sins we Isra-
elites, including myself and my father's family, have committed
against you. [7]We have acted very wickedly toward you. We have
not obeyed the commands, decrees and laws you gave your ser-
vant Moses.
[8]"Remember the instruction you gave your servant Moses, say-
ing, 'If you are unfaithful, I will scatter you among the nations,
[9]but if you return to me and obey my commands, then even if
your exiled people are at the farthest horizon, I will gather them
from there and bring them to the place I have chosen as a dwell-
ing for my Name.'
[10]"They are your servants and your people, whom you re-
deemed by your great strength and your mighty hand. [11]Lord, let
your ear be attentive to the prayer of this your servant and to the
prayer of your servants who delight in revering your name. Give
your servant success today by granting him favor in the presence
of this man."

I was cupbearer to the king.

PRAYING SCRIPTURE

Nehemiah 2

Have you ever been put on the spot? That's what happened when King Artaxerxes asked Nehemiah about his sadness. Nehemiah had already asked God to intervene, and now the king, noticing Nehemiah's countenance, put his Israelite servant in a tight spot. So, before answering, Nehemiah prayed again.

Anytime is a good time to pray. Ask God to help you remember to pray on every occasion.

ARTAXERXES SENDS NEHEMIAH TO JERUSALEM

2 In the month of Nisan in the twentieth year of King Artaxerxes,
when wine was brought for him, I took the wine and gave it to
the king. I had not been sad in his presence before, [2]so the king asked
me, "Why does your face look so sad when you are not ill? This can be
nothing but sadness of heart."
I was very much afraid, [3]but I said to the king, "May the king live for-
ever! Why should my face not look sad when the city where my ances-
tors are buried lies in ruins, and its gates have been destroyed by fire?"
[4]The king said to me, "What is it you want?"
Then I prayed to the God of heaven, [5]and I answered the king, "If it
pleases the king and if your servant has found favor in his sight, let
him send me to the city in Judah where my ancestors are buried so
that I can rebuild it."
[6]Then the king, with the queen sitting beside him, asked me, "How
long will your journey take, and when will you get back?" It pleased the
king to send me; so I set a time.

7I also said to him, "If it pleases the king, may I have letters to
the governors of Trans-Euphrates, so that they will provide me
safe-conduct until I arrive in Judah? 8And may I have a letter to Asaph,
keeper of the royal park, so he will give me timber to make beams for
the gates of the citadel by the temple and for the city wall and for the
residence I will occupy?" And because the gracious hand of my God
was on me, the king granted my requests. 9So I went to the governors
of Trans-Euphrates and gave them the king's letters. The king had also
sent army officers and cavalry with me.
10When Sanballat the Horonite and Tobiah the Ammonite official
heard about this, they were very much disturbed that someone had
come to promote the welfare of the Israelites.

NEHEMIAH INSPECTS JERUSALEM'S WALLS

11I went to Jerusalem, and after staying there three days 12I set out
during the night with a few others. I had not told anyone what my God
had put in my heart to do for Jerusalem. There were no mounts with
me except the one I was riding on.
13By night I went out through the Valley Gate toward the Jackal[a] Well
and the Dung Gate, examining the walls of Jerusalem, which had been
broken down, and its gates, which had been destroyed by fire. 14Then
I moved on toward the Fountain Gate and the King's Pool, but there
was not enough room for my mount to get through; 15so I went up
the valley by night, examining the wall. Finally, I turned back and re-
entered through the Valley Gate. 16The officials did not know where I
had gone or what I was doing, because as yet I had said nothing to the
Jews or the priests or nobles or officials or any others who would be
doing the work.
17Then I said to them, "You see the trouble we are in: Jerusalem lies
in ruins, and its gates have been burned with fire. Come, let us rebuild
the wall of Jerusalem, and we will no longer be in disgrace." 18I also
told them about the gracious hand of my God on me and what the
king had said to me.
They replied, "Let us start rebuilding." So they began this good work.
19But when Sanballat the Horonite, Tobiah the Ammonite official
and Geshem the Arab heard about it, they mocked and ridiculed us.
"What is this you are doing?" they asked. "Are you rebelling against
the king?"
20I answered them by saying, "The God of heaven will give us suc-
cess. We his servants will start rebuilding, but as for you, you have no
share in Jerusalem or any claim or historic right to it."

BUILDERS OF THE WALL

3 Eliashib the high priest and his fellow priests went to work and
rebuilt the Sheep Gate. They dedicated it and set its doors in place,
building as far as the Tower of the Hundred, which they dedicated, and
as far as the Tower of Hananel. 2The men of Jericho built the adjoining
section, and Zakkur son of Imri built next to them.

3The Fish Gate was rebuilt by the sons of Hassenaah. They laid its
beams and put its doors and bolts and bars in place. 4Meremoth son
of Uriah, the son of Hakkoz, repaired the next section. Next to him

[a] 13 Or *Serpent* or *Fig*

PRAYING SCRIPTURE

Nehemiah 3

Rebuilding Jerusalem's walls was an extensive project that required the coordination of many teams of people. The gates, doors, beams and wall sections were carefully and skillfully repaired. Nehemiah's record stands as a reminder that God uses real people in real places to do his work.

Do you ever feel as though God cannot use you in your career? Ask him to use your skills and talents to advance his kingdom.

Meshullam son of Berekiah, the son of Meshezabel, made repairs, and next to him Zadok son of Baana also made repairs. 5 The next section was repaired by the men of Tekoa, but their nobles would not put their shoulders to the work under their supervisors.[a]

6 The Jeshanah[b] Gate was repaired by Joiada son of Paseah and Meshullam son of Besodeiah. They laid its beams and put its doors with their bolts and bars in place. 7 Next to them, repairs were made by men from Gibeon and Mizpah — Melatiah of Gibeon and Jadon of Meronoth — places under the authority of the governor of Trans-Euphrates. 8 Uzziel son of Harhaiah, one of the goldsmiths, repaired the next section; and Hananiah, one of the perfume-makers, made repairs next to that. They restored Jerusalem as far as the Broad Wall. 9 Rephaiah son of Hur, ruler of a half-district of Jerusalem, repaired the next section. 10 Adjoining this, Jedaiah son of Harumaph made repairs opposite his house, and Hattush son of Hashabneiah made repairs next to him. 11 Malkijah son of Harim and Hasshub son of Pahath-Moab repaired another section and the Tower of the Ovens. 12 Shallum son of Hallohesh, ruler of a half-district of Jerusalem, repaired the next section with the help of his daughters.

13 The Valley Gate was repaired by Hanun and the residents of Zanoah. They rebuilt it and put its doors with their bolts and bars in place. They also repaired a thousand cubits[c] of the wall as far as the Dung Gate.

14 The Dung Gate was repaired by Malkijah son of Rekab, ruler of the district of Beth Hakkerem. He rebuilt it and put its doors with their bolts and bars in place.

15 The Fountain Gate was repaired by Shallun son of Kol-Hozeh, ruler of the district of Mizpah. He rebuilt it, roofing it over and putting its doors and bolts and bars in place. He also repaired the wall of the Pool of Siloam,[d] by the King's Garden, as far as the steps going down from the City of David. 16 Beyond him, Nehemiah son of Azbuk, ruler of a half-district of Beth Zur, made repairs up to a point opposite the tombs[e] of David, as far as the artificial pool and the House of the Heroes.

17 Next to him, the repairs were made by the Levites under Rehum son of Bani. Beside him, Hashabiah, ruler of half the district of Keilah, carried out repairs for his district. 18 Next to him, the repairs were made by their fellow Levites under Binnui[f] son of Henadad, ruler of the other half-district of Keilah. 19 Next to him, Ezer son of Jeshua, ruler of Mizpah, repaired another section, from a point facing the ascent to the armory as far as the angle of the wall. 20 Next to him, Baruch son of Zabbai zealously repaired another section, from the angle to the entrance of the house of Eliashib the high priest. 21 Next to him, Meremoth son of Uriah, the son of Hakkoz, repaired another section, from the entrance of Eliashib's house to the end of it.

22 The repairs next to him were made by the priests from the surrounding region. 23 Beyond them, Benjamin and Hasshub made repairs in front of their house; and next to them, Azariah son of Maaseiah, the

---

[a] *5* Or *their Lord* or *the governor* [b] *6* Or *Old* [c] *13* That is, about 1,500 feet or about 450 meters [d] *15* Hebrew *Shelah,* a variant of *Shiloah,* that is, Siloam [e] *16* Hebrew; Septuagint, some Vulgate manuscripts and Syriac *tomb* [f] *18* Two Hebrew manuscripts and Syriac (see also Septuagint and verse 24); most Hebrew manuscripts *Bavvai*

son of Ananiah, made repairs beside his house. 24Next to him, Binnui son of Henadad repaired another section, from Azariah's house to the angle and the corner, 25and Palal son of Uzai worked opposite the angle and the tower projecting from the upper palace near the court of the guard. Next to him, Pedaiah son of Parosh 26and the temple servants living on the hill of Ophel made repairs up to a point opposite the Water Gate toward the east and the projecting tower. 27Next to them, the men of Tekoa repaired another section, from the great projecting tower to the wall of Ophel.

28Above the Horse Gate, the priests made repairs, each in front of his own house. 29Next to them, Zadok son of Immer made repairs opposite his house. Next to him, Shemaiah son of Shekaniah, the guard at the East Gate, made repairs. 30Next to him, Hananiah son of Shelemiah, and Hanun, the sixth son of Zalaph, repaired another section. Next to them, Meshullam son of Berekiah made repairs opposite his living quarters. 31Next to him, Malkijah, one of the goldsmiths, made repairs as far as the house of the temple servants and the merchants, opposite the Inspection Gate, and as far as the room above the corner; 32and between the room above the corner and the Sheep Gate the goldsmiths and merchants made repairs.

OPPOSITION TO THE REBUILDING

4 [a] When Sanballat heard that we were rebuilding the wall, he became angry and was greatly incensed. He ridiculed the Jews, 2and in the presence of his associates and the army of Samaria, he said, "What are those feeble Jews doing? Will they restore their wall? Will they offer sacrifices? Will they finish in a day? Can they bring the stones back to life from those heaps of rubble — burned as they are?"

3Tobiah the Ammonite, who was at his side, said, "What they are building — even a fox climbing up on it would break down their wall of stones!"

4Hear us, our God, for we are despised. Turn their insults back on their own heads. Give them over as plunder in a land of captivity. 5Do not cover up their guilt or blot out their sins from your sight, for they have thrown insults in the face of[b] the builders.

6So we rebuilt the wall till all of it reached half its height, for the people worked with all their heart.

7But when Sanballat, Tobiah, the Arabs, the Ammonites and the people of Ashdod heard that the repairs to Jerusalem's walls had gone ahead and that the gaps were being closed, they were very angry. 8They all plotted together to come and fight against Jerusalem and stir up trouble against it. 9But we prayed to our God and posted a guard day and night to meet this threat.

10Meanwhile, the people in Judah said, "The strength of the laborers is giving out, and there is so much rubble that we cannot rebuild the wall."

11Also our enemies said, "Before they know it or see us, we will be right there among them and will kill them and put an end to the work."

12Then the Jews who lived near them came and told us ten times over, "Wherever you turn, they will attack us."

PRAYING SCRIPTURE

Nehemiah 4

God's work will frequently see opposition. Satan does what he can to hinder God's people from doing his will. Again, in this case, Nehemiah broke into prayer, and the people, with their faith in God, continued to work.

What is your normal response when you face opposition? Prayer? Fear? Worry? Remember that you can call on God when any opposition arises.

---

[a] In Hebrew texts 4:1-6 is numbered 3:33-38, and 4:7-23 is numbered 4:1-17.
[b] 5 Or *have aroused your anger before*

13Therefore I stationed some of the people behind the lowest points
of the wall at the exposed places, posting them by families, with their
swords, spears and bows. 14After I looked things over, I stood up and
said to the nobles, the officials and the rest of the people, "Don't be
afraid of them. Remember the Lord, who is great and awesome, and
fight for your families, your sons and your daughters, your wives and
your homes."
15When our enemies heard that we were aware of their plot and that
God had frustrated it, we all returned to the wall, each to our own work.
16From that day on, half of my men did the work, while the other half
were equipped with spears, shields, bows and armor. The officers posted
themselves behind all the people of Judah 17who were building the wall.
Those who carried materials did their work with one hand and held a
weapon in the other, 18and each of the builders wore his sword at his side
as he worked. But the man who sounded the trumpet stayed with me.
19Then I said to the nobles, the officials and the rest of the people,
"The work is extensive and spread out, and we are widely separated
from each other along the wall. 20Wherever you hear the sound of the
trumpet, join us there. Our God will fight for us!"
21So we continued the work with half the men holding spears, from
the first light of dawn till the stars came out. 22At that time I also said
to the people, "Have every man and his helper stay inside Jerusalem at
night, so they can serve us as guards by night and as workers by day."
23Neither I nor my brothers nor my men nor the guards with me took
off our clothes; each had his weapon, even when he went for water.[a]

NEHEMIAH HELPS THE POOR

5 Now the men and their wives raised a great outcry against their
fellow Jews. 2Some were saying, "We and our sons and daughters
are numerous; in order for us to eat and stay alive, we must get grain."
3Others were saying, "We are mortgaging our fields, our vineyards
and our homes to get grain during the famine."
4Still others were saying, "We have had to borrow money to pay the
king's tax on our fields and vineyards. 5Although we are of the same
flesh and blood as our fellow Jews and though our children are as good
as theirs, yet we have to subject our sons and daughters to slavery.
Some of our daughters have already been enslaved, but we are power-
less, because our fields and our vineyards belong to others."
6When I heard their outcry and these charges, I was very angry. 7I
pondered them in my mind and then accused the nobles and officials.
I told them, "You are charging your own people interest!" So I called
together a large meeting to deal with them 8and said: "As far as pos-
sible, we have bought back our fellow Jews who were sold to the Gen-
tiles. Now you are selling your own people, only for them to be sold
back to us!" They kept quiet, because they could find nothing to say.
9So I continued, "What you are doing is not right. Shouldn't you walk
in the fear of our God to avoid the reproach of our Gentile enemies?
10I and my brothers and my men are also lending the people money
and grain. But let us stop charging interest! 11Give back to them imme-
diately their fields, vineyards, olive groves and houses, and also the
interest you are charging them — one percent of the money, grain, new
wine and olive oil."

PRAYING SCRIPTURE

Nehemiah 5

As the exiles returned, some of them complained that their kinsmen were oppressing them. Many had to sell property to pay taxes to the king. Some of their sons and daughters were forced into slavery to cover debts. This abuse infuriated Nehemiah, who called the oppressors to cease their usury.

When your brothers and sisters in Christ suffer, how do you respond? Ask God to help you show mercy.

[a] *23* The meaning of the Hebrew for this clause is uncertain.

12“We will give it back,” they said. “And we will not demand anything
more from them. We will do as you say.”

Then I summoned the priests and made the nobles and officials take
an oath to do what they had promised. 13I also shook out the folds of
my robe and said, “In this way may God shake out of their house and
possessions anyone who does not keep this promise. So may such a
person be shaken out and emptied!”

At this the whole assembly said, “Amen,” and praised the LORD. And
the people did as they had promised.

14Moreover, from the twentieth year of King Artaxerxes, when I was
appointed to be their governor in the land of Judah, until his thirty-
second year — twelve years — neither I nor my brothers ate the food
allotted to the governor. 15But the earlier governors — those preceding
me — placed a heavy burden on the people and took forty shekels[a] of
silver from them in addition to food and wine. Their assistants also
lorded it over the people. But out of reverence for God I did not act
like that. 16Instead, I devoted myself to the work on this wall. All my
men were assembled there for the work; we[b] did not acquire any land.

17Furthermore, a hundred and fifty Jews and officials ate at my table,
as well as those who came to us from the surrounding nations. 18Each
day one ox, six choice sheep and some poultry were prepared for me,
and every ten days an abundant supply of wine of all kinds. In spite of
all this, I never demanded the food allotted to the governor, because
the demands were heavy on these people.

19Remember me with favor, my God, for all I have done for these
people.

FURTHER OPPOSITION TO THE REBUILDING

6 When word came to Sanballat, Tobiah, Geshem the Arab and the
rest of our enemies that I had rebuilt the wall and not a gap was
left in it — though up to that time I had not set the doors in the gates —
2Sanballat and Geshem sent me this message: “Come, let us meet to-
gether in one of the villages[c] on the plain of Ono.”

But they were scheming to harm me; 3so I sent messengers to them
with this reply: “I am carrying on a great project and cannot go down.
Why should the work stop while I leave it and go down to you?” 4Four
times they sent me the same message, and each time I gave them the
same answer.

5Then, the fifth time, Sanballat sent his aide to me with the same
message, and in his hand was an unsealed letter 6in which was written:

> “It is reported among the nations — and Geshem[d] says it is
> true — that you and the Jews are plotting to revolt, and therefore
> you are building the wall. Moreover, according to these reports
> you are about to become their king 7and have even appointed
> prophets to make this proclamation about you in Jerusalem:
> ‘There is a king in Judah!’ Now this report will get back to the
> king; so come, let us meet together.”

8I sent him this reply: “Nothing like what you are saying is happen-
ing; you are just making it up out of your head.”

PRAYING SCRIPTURE

Nehemiah 6

Despite the challenges and threats from enemies, the people of God completed the rebuilding project in only 52 days. When it was near completion, Nehemiah found his life was in danger, but he refused to flee or go into hiding. Why should he? He had asked God to strengthen him.

God always waits to hear and answer our cries for help. When tempted to flee your opposition, ask God for the strength to stand.

---

[a] *15* That is, about 1 pound or about 460 grams [b] *16* Most Hebrew manuscripts; some Hebrew manuscripts, Septuagint, Vulgate and Syriac *I*
[c] *2* Or *in Kephirim* [d] *6* Hebrew *Gashmu,* a variant of *Geshem*

9They were all trying to frighten us, thinking, "Their hands will get
too weak for the work, and it will not be completed."

But I prayed, "Now strengthen my hands."

10One day I went to the house of Shemaiah son of Delaiah, the son
of Mehetabel, who was shut in at his home. He said, "Let us meet in
the house of God, inside the temple, and let us close the temple doors,
because men are coming to kill you — by night they are coming to kill
you."

11But I said, "Should a man like me run away? Or should someone
like me go into the temple to save his life? I will not go!" 12I realized
that God had not sent him, but that he had prophesied against me
because Tobiah and Sanballat had hired him. 13He had been hired to
intimidate me so that I would commit a sin by doing this, and then
they would give me a bad name to discredit me.

14Remember Tobiah and Sanballat, my God, because of what they
have done; remember also the prophet Noadiah and how she and the
rest of the prophets have been trying to intimidate me. 15So the wall
was completed on the twenty-fifth of Elul, in fifty-two days.

OPPOSITION TO THE COMPLETED WALL

16When all our enemies heard about this, all the surrounding na-
tions were afraid and lost their self-confidence, because they realized
that this work had been done with the help of our God.

17Also, in those days the nobles of Judah were sending many letters
to Tobiah, and replies from Tobiah kept coming to them. 18For many
in Judah were under oath to him, since he was son-in-law to Sheka-
niah son of Arah, and his son Jehohanan had married the daughter of
Meshullam son of Berekiah. 19Moreover, they kept reporting to me his
good deeds and then telling him what I said. And Tobiah sent letters
to intimidate me.

7 After the wall had been rebuilt and I had set the doors in place,
the gatekeepers, the musicians and the Levites were appointed.
2I put in charge of Jerusalem my brother Hanani, along with Hana-
niah the commander of the citadel, because he was a man of integ-
rity and feared God more than most people do. 3I said to them, "The
gates of Jerusalem are not to be opened until the sun is hot. While the
gatekeepers are still on duty, have them shut the doors and bar them.
Also appoint residents of Jerusalem as guards, some at their posts and
some near their own houses."

THE LIST OF THE EXILES WHO RETURNED

4Now the city was large and spacious, but there were few people in
it, and the houses had not yet been rebuilt. 5So my God put it into my
heart to assemble the nobles, the officials and the common people for
registration by families. I found the genealogical record of those who
had been the first to return. This is what I found written there:

> 6These are the people of the province who came up from the
> captivity of the exiles whom Nebuchadnezzar king of Babylon had
> taken captive (they returned to Jerusalem and Judah, each to his
> own town, 7in company with Zerubbabel, Joshua, Nehemiah, Az-
> ariah, Raamiah, Nahamani, Mordecai, Bilshan, Mispereth, Bigvai,
> Nehum and Baanah):

PRAYING SCRIPTURE

Nehemiah 7

Has God ever put it in your heart to do something? Have you ever sensed an assignment from him you could not escape? This chapter is in the Bible because God put into Nehemiah's heart to register the people of Israel so the genealogy could be perpetuated.

Don't neglect to follow what God puts on your heart, even if it seems insignificant. We don't always know what small act will impact eternity.

The list of the men of Israel:

8 the descendants of Parosh	2,172
9 of Shephatiah	372
10 of Arah	652
11 of Pahath-Moab (through the line of Jeshua and Joab)	2,818
12 of Elam	1,254
13 of Zattu	845
14 of Zakkai	760
15 of Binnui	648
16 of Bebai	628
17 of Azgad	2,322
18 of Adonikam	667
19 of Bigvai	2,067
20 of Adin	655
21 of Ater (through Hezekiah)	98
22 of Hashum	328
23 of Bezai	324
24 of Hariph	112
25 of Gibeon	95
26 the men of Bethlehem and Netophah	188
27 of Anathoth	128
28 of Beth Azmaveth	42
29 of Kiriath Jearim, Kephirah and Beeroth	743
30 of Ramah and Geba	621
31 of Mikmash	122
32 of Bethel and Ai	123
33 of the other Nebo	52
34 of the other Elam	1,254
35 of Harim	320
36 of Jericho	345
37 of Lod, Hadid and Ono	721
38 of Senaah	3,930

39 The priests:

the descendants of Jedaiah (through the family of Jeshua)	973
40 of Immer	1,052
41 of Pashhur	1,247
42 of Harim	1,017

43 The Levites:

the descendants of Jeshua (through Kadmiel through the line of Hodaviah)	74

44 The musicians:

the descendants of Asaph	148

45 The gatekeepers:

the descendants of Shallum, Ater, Talmon, Akkub, Hatita and Shobai	138

46 The temple servants:

the descendants of
Ziha, Hasupha, Tabbaoth,

47 Keros, Sia, Padon,
48 Lebana, Hagaba, Shalmai,
49 Hanan, Giddel, Gahar,
50 Reaiah, Rezin, Nekoda,
51 Gazzam, Uzza, Paseah,
52 Besai, Meunim, Nephusim,
53 Bakbuk, Hakupha, Harhur,
54 Bazluth, Mehida, Harsha,
55 Barkos, Sisera, Temah,
56 Neziah and Hatipha

57 The descendants of the servants of Solomon:

the descendants of
Sotai, Sophereth, Perida,
58 Jaala, Darkon, Giddel,
59 Shephatiah, Hattil,
Pokereth-Hazzebaim and Amon

60 The temple servants and the descendants of the servants of Solomon 392

61 The following came up from the towns of Tel Melah, Tel Harsha, Kerub, Addon and Immer, but they could not show that their families were descended from Israel:

62 the descendants of
Delaiah, Tobiah and Nekoda 642

63 And from among the priests:

the descendants of
Hobaiah, Hakkoz and Barzillai (a man who had married a daughter of Barzillai the Gileadite and was called by that name).

64 These searched for their family records, but they could not find them and so were excluded from the priesthood as unclean.
65 The governor, therefore, ordered them not to eat any of the most sacred food until there should be a priest ministering with the Urim and Thummim.

66 The whole company numbered 42,360, 67 besides their 7,337 male and female slaves; and they also had 245 male and female singers. 68 There were 736 horses, 245 mules,[a] 69 435 camels and 6,720 donkeys.

70 Some of the heads of the families contributed to the work. The governor gave to the treasury 1,000 darics[b] of gold, 50 bowls and 530 garments for priests. 71 Some of the heads of the families gave to the treasury for the work 20,000 darics[c] of gold and 2,200 minas[d] of silver. 72 The total given by the rest of the people was 20,000 darics of gold, 2,000 minas[e] of silver and 67 garments for priests.

---

[a] *68* Some Hebrew manuscripts (see also Ezra 2:66); most Hebrew manuscripts do not have this verse. [b] *70* That is, about 19 pounds or about 8.4 kilograms
[c] *71* That is, about 375 pounds or about 170 kilograms; also in verse 72
[d] *71* That is, about 1 1/3 tons or about 1.2 metric tons [e] *72* That is, about 1 1/4 tons or about 1.1 metric tons

73 The priests, the Levites, the gatekeepers, the musicians and
the temple servants, along with certain of the people and the rest
of the Israelites, settled in their own towns.

EZRA READS THE LAW

When the seventh month came and the Israelites had settled in their
8 towns, 1 all the people came together as one in the square before the
Water Gate. They told Ezra the teacher of the Law to bring out the
Book of the Law of Moses, which the LORD had commanded for Israel.
2 So on the first day of the seventh month Ezra the priest brought the
Law before the assembly, which was made up of men and women and
all who were able to understand. 3 He read it aloud from daybreak till
noon as he faced the square before the Water Gate in the presence of
the men, women and others who could understand. And all the people
listened attentively to the Book of the Law.
4 Ezra the teacher of the Law stood on a high wooden platform built
for the occasion. Beside him on his right stood Mattithiah, Shema,
Anaiah, Uriah, Hilkiah and Maaseiah; and on his left were Pedaiah,
Mishael, Malkijah, Hashum, Hashbaddanah, Zechariah and Meshullam.
5 Ezra opened the book. All the people could see him because he was
standing above them; and as he opened it, the people all stood up.
6 Ezra praised the LORD, the great God; and all the people lifted their
hands and responded, "Amen! Amen!" Then they bowed down and
worshiped the LORD with their faces to the ground.
7 The Levites — Jeshua, Bani, Sherebiah, Jamin, Akkub, Shabbethai,
Hodiah, Maaseiah, Kelita, Azariah, Jozabad, Hanan and Pelaiah — in-
structed the people in the Law while the people were standing there.
8 They read from the Book of the Law of God, making it clear[a] and giv-
ing the meaning so that the people understood what was being read.
9 Then Nehemiah the governor, Ezra the priest and teacher of the
Law, and the Levites who were instructing the people said to them all,
"This day is holy to the LORD your God. Do not mourn or weep." For all
the people had been weeping as they listened to the words of the Law.
10 Nehemiah said, "Go and enjoy choice food and sweet drinks, and
send some to those who have nothing prepared. This day is holy to our
Lord. Do not grieve, for the joy of the LORD is your strength."
11 The Levites calmed all the people, saying, "Be still, for this is a holy
day. Do not grieve."
12 Then all the people went away to eat and drink, to send portions of
food and to celebrate with great joy, because they now understood the
words that had been made known to them.
13 On the second day of the month, the heads of all the families, along
with the priests and the Levites, gathered around Ezra the teacher to
give attention to the words of the Law. 14 They found written in the Law,
which the LORD had commanded through Moses, that the Israelites
were to live in temporary shelters during the festival of the seventh
month 15 and that they should proclaim this word and spread it through-
out their towns and in Jerusalem: "Go out into the hill country and
bring back branches from olive and wild olive trees, and from myrtles,
palms and shade trees, to make temporary shelters" — as it is written.[b]
16 So the people went out and brought back branches and built them-
selves temporary shelters on their own roofs, in their courtyards, in

[a] 8 Or *God, translating it* [b] 15 See Lev. 23:37-40.

PRAYING SCRIPTURE

Nehemiah 8

After more than forty-two thousand exiles had returned to the land, they gathered so Ezra could read God's law to them. Constant disobedience led them to be exiled. Now they stood listening attentively from morning until midday as Ezra read it distinctly, helping them understand it (see verses 3,8).

Keeping God's Word is key to our walk with him. As you read it, pray those passages as a way of committing to obeying them.

the courts of the house of God and in the square by the Water Gate and the one by the Gate of Ephraim. 17The whole company that had returned from exile built temporary shelters and lived in them. From the days of Joshua son of Nun until that day, the Israelites had not celebrated it like this. And their joy was very great.

18Day after day, from the first day to the last, Ezra read from the Book of the Law of God. They celebrated the festival for seven days, and on the eighth day, in accordance with the regulation, there was an assembly.

THE ISRAELITES CONFESS THEIR SINS

9 On the twenty-fourth day of the same month, the Israelites gathered together, fasting and wearing sackcloth and putting dust on their heads. 2Those of Israelite descent had separated themselves from all foreigners. They stood in their places and confessed their sins and the sins of their ancestors. 3They stood where they were and read from the Book of the Law of the LORD their God for a quarter of the day, and spent another quarter in confession and in worshiping the LORD their God. 4Standing on the stairs of the Levites were Jeshua, Bani, Kadmiel, Shebaniah, Bunni, Sherebiah, Bani and Kenani. They cried out with loud voices to the LORD their God. 5And the Levites — Jeshua, Kadmiel, Bani, Hashabneiah, Sherebiah, Hodiah, Shebaniah and Pethahiah — said: "Stand up and praise the LORD your God, who is from everlasting to everlasting.[a]"

"Blessed be your glorious name, and may it be exalted above all blessing and praise. 6You alone are the LORD. You made the heavens, even the highest heavens, and all their starry host, the earth and all that is on it, the seas and all that is in them. You give life to everything, and the multitudes of heaven worship you.

7"You are the LORD God, who chose Abram and brought him out of Ur of the Chaldeans and named him Abraham. 8You found his heart faithful to you, and you made a covenant with him to give to his descendants the land of the Canaanites, Hittites, Amorites, Perizzites, Jebusites and Girgashites. You have kept your promise because you are righteous.

9"You saw the suffering of our ancestors in Egypt; you heard their cry at the Red Sea.[b] 10You sent signs and wonders against Pharaoh, against all his officials and all the people of his land, for you knew how arrogantly the Egyptians treated them. You made a name for yourself, which remains to this day. 11You divided the sea before them, so that they passed through it on dry ground, but you hurled their pursuers into the depths, like a stone into mighty waters. 12By day you led them with a pillar of cloud, and by night with a pillar of fire to give them light on the way they were to take.

13"You came down on Mount Sinai; you spoke to them from heaven. You gave them regulations and laws that are just and right, and decrees and commands that are good. 14You made known to them your holy Sabbath and gave them commands, decrees and laws through your servant Moses. 15In their hunger you gave them bread from heaven and in their thirst you brought them water from the rock; you told them to go in and take possession of the land you had sworn with uplifted hand to give them.

[a] 5 Or *God for ever and ever* [b] 9 Or *the Sea of Reeds*

PRAYING SCRIPTURE

Nehemiah 9

With a great spirit of humility and repentance, those who were of Israelite lineage listened to the law for a quarter day, then confessed their sins and worshiped for a quarter day (see verses 2–3). Central to their worship was proclaiming "You alone are the LORD" (verse 6).

Worship should follow repentance so that our focus is on God's greatness rather than on our sin.

16"But they, our ancestors, became arrogant and stiff-necked, and they did not obey your commands. 17They refused to listen and failed to remember the miracles you performed among them. They became stiff-necked and in their rebellion appointed a leader in order to return to their slavery. But you are a forgiving God, gracious and compassionate, slow to anger and abounding in love. Therefore you did not desert them, 18even when they cast for themselves an image of a calf and said, 'This is your god, who brought you up out of Egypt,' or when they committed awful blasphemies.

19"Because of your great compassion you did not abandon them in the wilderness. By day the pillar of cloud did not fail to guide them on their path, nor the pillar of fire by night to shine on the way they were to take. 20You gave your good Spirit to instruct them. You did not withhold your manna from their mouths, and you gave them water for their thirst. 21For forty years you sustained them in the wilderness; they lacked nothing, their clothes did not wear out nor did their feet become swollen.

22"You gave them kingdoms and nations, allotting to them even the remotest frontiers. They took over the country of Sihon[a] king of Heshbon and the country of Og king of Bashan. 23You made their children as numerous as the stars in the sky, and you brought them into the land that you told their parents to enter and possess. 24Their children went in and took possession of the land. You subdued before them the Canaanites, who lived in the land; you gave the Canaanites into their hands, along with their kings and the peoples of the land, to deal with them as they pleased. 25They captured fortified cities and fertile land; they took possession of houses filled with all kinds of good things, wells already dug, vineyards, olive groves and fruit trees in abundance. They ate to the full and were well-nourished; they reveled in your great goodness.

26"But they were disobedient and rebelled against you; they turned their backs on your law. They killed your prophets, who had warned them in order to turn them back to you; they committed awful blasphemies. 27So you delivered them into the hands of their enemies, who oppressed them. But when they were oppressed they cried out to you. From heaven you heard them, and in your great compassion you gave them deliverers, who rescued them from the hand of their enemies.

28"But as soon as they were at rest, they again did what was evil in your sight. Then you abandoned them to the hand of their enemies so that they ruled over them. And when they cried out to you again, you heard from heaven, and in your compassion you delivered them time after time.

29"You warned them in order to turn them back to your law, but they became arrogant and disobeyed your commands. They sinned against your ordinances, of which you said, 'The person who obeys them will live by them.' Stubbornly they turned their backs on you, became stiff-necked and refused to listen. 30For many years you were patient with them. By your Spirit you warned them through your prophets. Yet they paid no attention,

---

[a] 22 One Hebrew manuscript and Septuagint; most Hebrew manuscripts *Sihon, that is, the country of the*

so you gave them into the hands of the neighboring peoples. 31But
in your great mercy you did not put an end to them or abandon
them, for you are a gracious and merciful God.
32"Now therefore, our God, the great God, mighty and awesome,
who keeps his covenant of love, do not let all this hardship seem
trifling in your eyes — the hardship that has come on us, on our
kings and leaders, on our priests and prophets, on our ancestors
and all your people, from the days of the kings of Assyria until
today. 33In all that has happened to us, you have remained righ-
teous; you have acted faithfully, while we acted wickedly. 34Our
kings, our leaders, our priests and our ancestors did not follow
your law; they did not pay attention to your commands or the
statutes you warned them to keep. 35Even while they were in their
kingdom, enjoying your great goodness to them in the spacious
and fertile land you gave them, they did not serve you or turn
from their evil ways.
36"But see, we are slaves today, slaves in the land you gave our
ancestors so they could eat its fruit and the other good things it
produces. 37Because of our sins, its abundant harvest goes to the
kings you have placed over us. They rule over our bodies and our
cattle as they please. We are in great distress.

THE AGREEMENT OF THE PEOPLE

38"In view of all this, we are making a binding agreement, putting
it in writing, and our leaders, our Levites and our priests are affixing
their seals to it."[a]

10 [b] Those who sealed it were:

Nehemiah the governor, the son of Hakaliah.

Zedekiah, 2Seraiah, Azariah, Jeremiah,
3Pashhur, Amariah, Malkijah,
4Hattush, Shebaniah, Malluk,
5Harim, Meremoth, Obadiah,
6Daniel, Ginnethon, Baruch,
7Meshullam, Abijah, Mijamin,
8Maaziah, Bilgai and Shemaiah.
These were the priests.

9The Levites:

Jeshua son of Azaniah, Binnui of the sons of Henadad, Kadmiel,
10and their associates: Shebaniah,
Hodiah, Kelita, Pelaiah, Hanan,
11Mika, Rehob, Hashabiah,
12Zakkur, Sherebiah, Shebaniah,
13Hodiah, Bani and Beninu.

14The leaders of the people:

Parosh, Pahath-Moab, Elam, Zattu, Bani,
15Bunni, Azgad, Bebai,
16Adonijah, Bigvai, Adin,
17Ater, Hezekiah, Azzur,

PRAYING SCRIPTURE

Nehemiah 10

After the people resettled in the land, Nehemiah and the other leaders signed the covenant Israel had long before forsaken. It was a recommitment ceremony during which the people promised to follow the Law of Moses, repenting of the sins that had condemned them to captivity.

Remembering and recommitting are powerful tools in one's spiritual journey. Recommit to God in prayer if your heart has strayed from him.

---

[a] *38* In Hebrew texts this verse (9:38) is numbered 10:1. [b] In Hebrew texts 10:1-39 is numbered 10:2-40.

18 Hodiah, Hashum, Bezai,
19 Hariph, Anathoth, Nebai,
20 Magpiash, Meshullam, Hezir,
21 Meshezabel, Zadok, Jaddua,
22 Pelatiah, Hanan, Anaiah,
23 Hoshea, Hananiah, Hasshub,
24 Hallohesh, Pilha, Shobek,
25 Rehum, Hashabnah, Maaseiah,
26 Ahiah, Hanan, Anan,
27 Malluk, Harim and Baanah.

28 "The rest of the people — priests, Levites, gatekeepers, musi-
cians, temple servants and all who separated themselves from the
neighboring peoples for the sake of the Law of God, together with
their wives and all their sons and daughters who are able to un-
derstand — 29 all these now join their fellow Israelites the nobles,
and bind themselves with a curse and an oath to follow the Law of
God given through Moses the servant of God and to obey carefully
all the commands, regulations and decrees of the LORD our Lord.

30 "We promise not to give our daughters in marriage to the peo-
ples around us or take their daughters for our sons.

31 "When the neighboring peoples bring merchandise or grain
to sell on the Sabbath, we will not buy from them on the Sabbath
or on any holy day. Every seventh year we will forgo working the
land and will cancel all debts.

32 "We assume the responsibility for carrying out the commands
to give a third of a shekel[a] each year for the service of the house of
our God: 33 for the bread set out on the table; for the regular grain
offerings and burnt offerings; for the offerings on the Sabbaths,
at the New Moon feasts and at the appointed festivals; for the holy
offerings; for sin offerings[b] to make atonement for Israel; and for
all the duties of the house of our God.

34 "We — the priests, the Levites and the people — have cast lots
to determine when each of our families is to bring to the house of
our God at set times each year a contribution of wood to burn on
the altar of the LORD our God, as it is written in the Law.

35 "We also assume responsibility for bringing to the house of
the LORD each year the firstfruits of our crops and of every fruit
tree.

36 "As it is also written in the Law, we will bring the firstborn of
our sons and of our cattle, of our herds and of our flocks to the
house of our God, to the priests ministering there.

37 "Moreover, we will bring to the storerooms of the house of
our God, to the priests, the first of our ground meal, of our grain
offerings, of the fruit of all our trees and of our new wine and
olive oil. And we will bring a tithe of our crops to the Levites, for
it is the Levites who collect the tithes in all the towns where we
work. 38 A priest descended from Aaron is to accompany the Le-
vites when they receive the tithes, and the Levites are to bring a
tenth of the tithes up to the house of our God, to the storerooms
of the treasury. 39 The people of Israel, including the Levites, are
to bring their contributions of grain, new wine and olive oil to the

[a] *32* That is, about 1/8 ounce or about 4 grams [b] *33* Or *purification offerings*

storerooms, where the articles for the sanctuary and for the min-
istering priests, the gatekeepers and the musicians are also kept.
"We will not neglect the house of our God."

THE NEW RESIDENTS OF JERUSALEM

11 Now the leaders of the people settled in Jerusalem. The rest of
the people cast lots to bring one out of every ten of them to live
in Jerusalem, the holy city, while the remaining nine were to stay in
their own towns. 2The people commended all who volunteered to live
in Jerusalem.
3These are the provincial leaders who settled in Jerusalem (now
some Israelites, priests, Levites, temple servants and descendants of
Solomon's servants lived in the towns of Judah, each on their own
property in the various towns, 4while other people from both Judah
and Benjamin lived in Jerusalem):

From the descendants of Judah:

Athaiah son of Uzziah, the son of Zechariah, the son of Amariah,
the son of Shephatiah, the son of Mahalalel, a descendant of Perez;
5and Maaseiah son of Baruch, the son of Kol-Hozeh, the son of Ha-
zaiah, the son of Adaiah, the son of Joiarib, the son of Zechariah,
a descendant of Shelah. 6The descendants of Perez who lived in
Jerusalem totaled 468 men of standing.

7From the descendants of Benjamin:

Sallu son of Meshullam, the son of Joed, the son of Pedaiah, the
son of Kolaiah, the son of Maaseiah, the son of Ithiel, the son of
Jeshaiah, 8and his followers, Gabbai and Sallai — 928 men. 9Joel
son of Zikri was their chief officer, and Judah son of Hassenuah
was over the New Quarter of the city.

10From the priests:

Jedaiah; the son of Joiarib; Jakin; 11Seraiah son of Hilkiah, the son
of Meshullam, the son of Zadok, the son of Meraioth, the son of
Ahitub, the official in charge of the house of God, 12and their asso-
ciates, who carried on work for the temple — 822 men; Adaiah son
of Jeroham, the son of Pelaliah, the son of Amzi, the son of Zecha-
riah, the son of Pashhur, the son of Malkijah, 13and his associates,
who were heads of families — 242 men; Amashsai son of Azarel,
the son of Ahzai, the son of Meshillemoth, the son of Immer, 14and
his[a] associates, who were men of standing — 128. Their chief offi-
cer was Zabdiel son of Haggedolim.

15From the Levites:

Shemaiah son of Hasshub, the son of Azrikam, the son of Hasha-
biah, the son of Bunni; 16Shabbethai and Jozabad, two of the heads
of the Levites, who had charge of the outside work of the house of
God; 17Mattaniah son of Mika, the son of Zabdi, the son of Asaph,
the director who led in thanksgiving and prayer; Bakbukiah, sec-
ond among his associates; and Abda son of Shammua, the son of
Galal, the son of Jeduthun. 18The Levites in the holy city totaled
284.

PRAYING SCRIPTURE

Nehemiah 11

Repopulating Jerusalem was accomplished by the casting of lots. Besides the leaders, 10 percent of the rest of the population would relocate there and live. The people commended all those who willingly moved to the capital city (see verse 2).

How do you respond when others are clearly following God? Ask God to let you be a channel of blessing to those who sacrifice for him.

[a] *14* Most Septuagint manuscripts; Hebrew *their*

19 The gatekeepers:

Akkub, Talmon and their associates, who kept watch at the
gates — 172 men.

20 The rest of the Israelites, with the priests and Levites, were in all
the towns of Judah, each on their ancestral property.
21 The temple servants lived on the hill of Ophel, and Ziha and Gishpa
were in charge of them.
22 The chief officer of the Levites in Jerusalem was Uzzi son of Bani,
the son of Hashabiah, the son of Mattaniah, the son of Mika. Uzzi was
one of Asaph's descendants, who were the musicians responsible for
the service of the house of God. 23 The musicians were under the king's
orders, which regulated their daily activity.
24 Pethahiah son of Meshezabel, one of the descendants of Zerah son
of Judah, was the king's agent in all affairs relating to the people.
25 As for the villages with their fields, some of the people of Judah
lived in Kiriath Arba and its surrounding settlements, in Dibon and its
settlements, in Jekabzeel and its villages, 26 in Jeshua, in Moladah, in
Beth Pelet, 27 in Hazar Shual, in Beersheba and its settlements, 28 in Zik-
lag, in Mekonah and its settlements, 29 in En Rimmon, in Zorah, in Jar-
muth, 30 Zanoah, Adullam and their villages, in Lachish and its fields,
and in Azekah and its settlements. So they were living all the way from
Beersheba to the Valley of Hinnom.
31 The descendants of the Benjamites from Geba lived in Mikmash,
Aija, Bethel and its settlements, 32 in Anathoth, Nob and Ananiah, 33 in
Hazor, Ramah and Gittaim, 34 in Hadid, Zeboim and Neballat, 35 in Lod
and Ono, and in Ge Harashim.
36 Some of the divisions of the Levites of Judah settled in Benjamin.

PRIESTS AND LEVITES

12 These were the priests and Levites who returned with Zerubba-
bel son of Shealtiel and with Joshua:

Seraiah, Jeremiah, Ezra,
2 Amariah, Malluk, Hattush,
3 Shekaniah, Rehum, Meremoth,
4 Iddo, Ginnethon,[a] Abijah,
5 Mijamin,[b] Moadiah, Bilgah,
6 Shemaiah, Joiarib, Jedaiah,
7 Sallu, Amok, Hilkiah and Jedaiah.

These were the leaders of the priests and their associates in the days
of Joshua.
8 The Levites were Jeshua, Binnui, Kadmiel, Sherebiah, Judah, and
also Mattaniah, who, together with his associates, was in charge of the
songs of thanksgiving. 9 Bakbukiah and Unni, their associates, stood
opposite them in the services.
10 Joshua was the father of Joiakim, Joiakim the father of Eliashib,
Eliashib the father of Joiada, 11 Joiada the father of Jonathan, and Jon-
athan the father of Jaddua.
12 In the days of Joiakim, these were the heads of the priestly families:

of Seraiah's family, Meraiah;
of Jeremiah's, Hananiah;

PRAYING SCRIPTURE

Nehemiah 12

The dedication of Jerusalem's wall brought singers and musicians from all over the country. Two choirs sang thanksgiving praises in the temple. The joy from the sacrifices and worship was heard far away from the city. It was truly a national day of praise to God.

Responding to God's blessings with thanksgiving and praise is the right thing to do. List ways God has blessed you recently, and then spend time in thankful prayer.

---

[a] 4 Many Hebrew manuscripts and Vulgate (see also verse 16); most Hebrew manuscripts *Ginnethoi* [b] 5 A variant of *Miniamin*

13 of Ezra's, Meshullam;
of Amariah's, Jehohanan;
14 of Malluk's, Jonathan;
of Shekaniah's,[a] Joseph;
15 of Harim's, Adna;
of Meremoth's,[b] Helkai;
16 of Iddo's, Zechariah;
of Ginnethon's, Meshullam;
17 of Abijah's, Zikri;
of Miniamin's and of Moadiah's, Piltai;
18 of Bilgah's, Shammua;
of Shemaiah's, Jehonathan;
19 of Joiarib's, Mattenai;
of Jedaiah's, Uzzi;
20 of Sallu's, Kallai;
of Amok's, Eber;
21 of Hilkiah's, Hashabiah;
of Jedaiah's, Nethanel.

22 The family heads of the Levites in the days of Eliashib, Joiada, Jo-
hanan and Jaddua, as well as those of the priests, were recorded in the
reign of Darius the Persian. 23 The family heads among the descendants
of Levi up to the time of Johanan son of Eliashib were recorded in the
book of the annals. 24 And the leaders of the Levites were Hashabiah,
Sherebiah, Jeshua son of Kadmiel, and their associates, who stood op-
posite them to give praise and thanksgiving, one section responding
to the other, as prescribed by David the man of God.

25 Mattaniah, Bakbukiah, Obadiah, Meshullam, Talmon and Akkub
were gatekeepers who guarded the storerooms at the gates. 26 They
served in the days of Joiakim son of Joshua, the son of Jozadak, and in
the days of Nehemiah the governor and of Ezra the priest, the teacher
of the Law.

DEDICATION OF THE WALL OF JERUSALEM

27 At the dedication of the wall of Jerusalem, the Levites were sought
out from where they lived and were brought to Jerusalem to celebrate
joyfully the dedication with songs of thanksgiving and with the mu-
sic of cymbals, harps and lyres. 28 The musicians also were brought to-
gether from the region around Jerusalem — from the villages of the
Netophathites, 29 from Beth Gilgal, and from the area of Geba and Az-
maveth, for the musicians had built villages for themselves around
Jerusalem. 30 When the priests and Levites had purified themselves
ceremonially, they purified the people, the gates and the wall.

31 I had the leaders of Judah go up on top of[c] the wall. I also assigned
two large choirs to give thanks. One was to proceed on top of[d] the wall
to the right, toward the Dung Gate. 32 Hoshaiah and half the leaders of
Judah followed them, 33 along with Azariah, Ezra, Meshullam, 34 Judah,
Benjamin, Shemaiah, Jeremiah, 35 as well as some priests with trum-
pets, and also Zechariah son of Jonathan, the son of Shemaiah, the
son of Mattaniah, the son of Micaiah, the son of Zakkur, the son of

---

[a] *14* Very many Hebrew manuscripts, some Septuagint manuscripts and Syriac (see also verse 3); most Hebrew manuscripts *Shebaniah's* [b] *15* Some Septuagint manuscripts (see also verse 3); Hebrew *Meraioth's* [c] *31* Or *go alongside* [d] *31* Or *proceed alongside*

Asaph, 36 and his associates — Shemaiah, Azarel, Milalai, Gilalai, Maai, Nethanel, Judah and Hanani — with musical instruments prescribed by David the man of God. Ezra the teacher of the Law led the procession. 37 At the Fountain Gate they continued directly up the steps of the City of David on the ascent to the wall and passed above the site of David's palace to the Water Gate on the east.

38 The second choir proceeded in the opposite direction. I followed them on top of[a] the wall, together with half the people — past the Tower of the Ovens to the Broad Wall, 39 over the Gate of Ephraim, the Jeshanah[b] Gate, the Fish Gate, the Tower of Hananel and the Tower of the Hundred, as far as the Sheep Gate. At the Gate of the Guard they stopped.

40 The two choirs that gave thanks then took their places in the house of God; so did I, together with half the officials, 41 as well as the priests — Eliakim, Maaseiah, Miniamin, Micaiah, Elioenai, Zechariah and Hananiah with their trumpets — 42 and also Maaseiah, Shemaiah, Eleazar, Uzzi, Jehohanan, Malkijah, Elam and Ezer. The choirs sang under the direction of Jezrahiah. 43 And on that day they offered great sacrifices, rejoicing because God had given them great joy. The women and children also rejoiced. The sound of rejoicing in Jerusalem could be heard far away.

44 At that time men were appointed to be in charge of the storerooms for the contributions, firstfruits and tithes. From the fields around the towns they were to bring into the storerooms the portions required by the Law for the priests and the Levites, for Judah was pleased with the ministering priests and Levites. 45 They performed the service of their God and the service of purification, as did also the musicians and gatekeepers, according to the commands of David and his son Solomon. 46 For long ago, in the days of David and Asaph, there had been directors for the musicians and for the songs of praise and thanksgiving to God. 47 So in the days of Zerubbabel and of Nehemiah, all Israel contributed the daily portions for the musicians and the gatekeepers. They also set aside the portion for the other Levites, and the Levites set aside the portion for the descendants of Aaron.

NEHEMIAH'S FINAL REFORMS

13 On that day the Book of Moses was read aloud in the hearing of the people and there it was found written that no Ammonite or Moabite should ever be admitted into the assembly of God, 2 because they had not met the Israelites with food and water but had hired Balaam to call a curse down on them. (Our God, however, turned the curse into a blessing.) 3 When the people heard this law, they excluded from Israel all who were of foreign descent.

4 Before this, Eliashib the priest had been put in charge of the storerooms of the house of our God. He was closely associated with Tobiah, 5 and he had provided him with a large room formerly used to store the grain offerings and incense and temple articles, and also the tithes of grain, new wine and olive oil prescribed for the Levites, musicians and gatekeepers, as well as the contributions for the priests.

6 But while all this was going on, I was not in Jerusalem, for in the thirty-second year of Artaxerxes king of Babylon I had returned to the king. Some time later I asked his permission 7 and came back to

PRAYING SCRIPTURE

Nehemiah 13

Rebuilding the wall took only a little over seven weeks, but rebuilding the lives of God's people would prove a more arduous task for Nehemiah. Returning from an out-of-country visit, he found one of the priests had befriended an enemy, misusing gifts meant for the Levites.

Anyone can turn away from God. Ask God to guard your heart that you might not slip into disobedience.

[a] 38 Or *them alongside* [b] 39 Or *Old*

Jerusalem. Here I learned about the evil thing Eliashib had done in providing Tobiah a room in the courts of the house of God. [8]I was greatly displeased and threw all Tobiah's household goods out of the room. [9]I gave orders to purify the rooms, and then I put back into them the equipment of the house of God, with the grain offerings and the incense.

[10]I also learned that the portions assigned to the Levites had not been given to them, and that all the Levites and musicians responsible for the service had gone back to their own fields. [11]So I rebuked the officials and asked them, "Why is the house of God neglected?" Then I called them together and stationed them at their posts.

[12]All Judah brought the tithes of grain, new wine and olive oil into the storerooms. [13]I put Shelemiah the priest, Zadok the scribe, and a Levite named Pedaiah in charge of the storerooms and made Hanan son of Zakkur, the son of Mattaniah, their assistant, because they were considered trustworthy. They were made responsible for distributing the supplies to their fellow Levites.

[14]Remember me for this, my God, and do not blot out what I have so faithfully done for the house of my God and its services.

[15]In those days I saw people in Judah treading winepresses on the Sabbath and bringing in grain and loading it on donkeys, together with wine, grapes, figs and all other kinds of loads. And they were bringing all this into Jerusalem on the Sabbath. Therefore I warned them against selling food on that day. [16]People from Tyre who lived in Jerusalem were bringing in fish and all kinds of merchandise and selling them in Jerusalem on the Sabbath to the people of Judah. [17]I rebuked the nobles of Judah and said to them, "What is this wicked thing you are doing — desecrating the Sabbath day? [18]Didn't your ancestors do the same things, so that our God brought all this calamity on us and on this city? Now you are stirring up more wrath against Israel by desecrating the Sabbath."

[19]When evening shadows fell on the gates of Jerusalem before the Sabbath, I ordered the doors to be shut and not opened until the Sabbath was over. I stationed some of my own men at the gates so that no load could be brought in on the Sabbath day. [20]Once or twice the merchants and sellers of all kinds of goods spent the night outside Jerusalem. [21]But I warned them and said, "Why do you spend the night by the wall? If you do this again, I will arrest you." From that time on they no longer came on the Sabbath. [22]Then I commanded the Levites to purify themselves and go and guard the gates in order to keep the Sabbath day holy.

Remember me for this also, my God, and show mercy to me according to your great love.

[23]Moreover, in those days I saw men of Judah who had married women from Ashdod, Ammon and Moab. [24]Half of their children spoke the language of Ashdod or the language of one of the other peoples, and did not know how to speak the language of Judah. [25]I rebuked them and called curses down on them. I beat some of the men and pulled out their hair. I made them take an oath in God's name and said: "You are not to give your daughters in marriage to their sons, nor are you to take their daughters in marriage for your sons or for yourselves. [26]Was it not because of marriages like these that Solomon king

of Israel sinned? Among the many nations there was no king like him.
He was loved by his God, and God made him king over all Israel, but
even he was led into sin by foreign women. 27Must we hear now that
you too are doing all this terrible wickedness and are being unfaithful
to our God by marrying foreign women?"

28One of the sons of Joiada son of Eliashib the high priest was son-in-
law to Sanballat the Horonite. And I drove him away from me.

29Remember them, my God, because they defiled the priestly office
and the covenant of the priesthood and of the Levites.

30So I purified the priests and the Levites of everything foreign, and
assigned them duties, each to his own task. 31I also made provision
for contributions of wood at designated times, and for the firstfruits.

Remember me with favor, my God.

ESTHER

Esther is the Bible's only book that does not explicitly mention the name of God. Not only is there no reference to God, but neither are there any prayers in Esther. However, this does not mean that God is completely absent from Esther's narrative. From Esther's improbable rise to the remarkable way the Israelite people are saved, it is impossible not to see God's fingerprints on this narrative.

Esther tells the story of King Xerxes who ruled over the expansive Medo-Persian Empire, divided into 127 provinces. One of the king's servants, Haman, was incensed when a Jewish resident, Mordecai, did not pay expected homage to him. This perceived slight set Haman on a murderous path of revenge.

Upon hearing that Mordecai was a Jew, Haman sought to put him to death. Haman's plan fell apart when the king was reminded that Mordecai had saved his life by uncovering a plot against him. Rather than hanging Mordecai, the king honored him in an elaborate ceremony planned by Haman—who wrongly thought the celebration was for himself. Through Esther's intercession, the Israelites were saved from Haman's planned genocide, and Haman was ultimately hanged on the gallows he had designed for Mordecai.

Esther reminds us of an important point: Even when we do not sense the direct intervention of God, he is always in the background of our lives working all things for good. Mordecai was brought to the king's attention not at the time he reported the plot, but when the king had it read to him while he was suffering from insomnia, again demonstrating God's providence.

It was Esther's relationship to the king that gave her the access needed to intervene for the Jews. Mordecai implored Esther to help—risking her own life—saying if she did not go to the king, then deliverance would come "from another place" (4:14). Mordecai recognized the hand of the unseen God and knew that he would act to save them—if not through Esther, then through someone or something else. It was here that Mordecai uttered a phrase that has stood through the centuries, "for such a time as this" (4:14). The book of Esther might not contain prayer, but Mordecai's encouragement has been repeated in prayer worldwide for centuries.

Mordecai's faith that God would save his people rested in the well-attested truth that God keeps his promises. He had delivered the people from slavery in Egypt and brought them into the land of promise. He gave them rest in the land, rest that was interrupted only by the people's unfaithfulness.

QUEEN VASHTI DEPOSED

1 This is what happened during the time of Xerxes,[a] the Xerxes who
ruled over 127 provinces stretching from India to Cush[b]: 2At that
time King Xerxes reigned from his royal throne in the citadel of Susa,
3and in the third year of his reign he gave a banquet for all his nobles
and officials. The military leaders of Persia and Media, the princes, and
the nobles of the provinces were present.
4For a full 180 days he displayed the vast wealth of his kingdom and
the splendor and glory of his majesty. 5When these days were over,
the king gave a banquet, lasting seven days, in the enclosed garden
of the king's palace, for all the people from the least to the greatest
who were in the citadel of Susa. 6The garden had hangings of white
and blue linen, fastened with cords of white linen and purple material
to silver rings on marble pillars. There were couches of gold and silver
on a mosaic pavement of porphyry, marble, mother-of-pearl and other
costly stones. 7Wine was served in goblets of gold, each one different
from the other, and the royal wine was abundant, in keeping with the
king's liberality. 8By the king's command each guest was allowed to
drink with no restrictions, for the king instructed all the wine stewards
to serve each man what he wished.
9Queen Vashti also gave a banquet for the women in the royal palace
of King Xerxes.
10On the seventh day, when King Xerxes was in high spirits from
wine, he commanded the seven eunuchs who served him — Mehuman,
Biztha, Harbona, Bigtha, Abagtha, Zethar and Karkas — 11to bring be-
fore him Queen Vashti, wearing her royal crown, in order to display
her beauty to the people and nobles, for she was lovely to look at. 12But
when the attendants delivered the king's command, Queen Vashti re-
fused to come. Then the king became furious and burned with anger.
13Since it was customary for the king to consult experts in matters of
law and justice, he spoke with the wise men who understood the times
14and were closest to the king — Karshena, Shethar, Admatha, Tarshish,
Meres, Marsena and Memukan, the seven nobles of Persia and Media
who had special access to the king and were highest in the kingdom.
15"According to law, what must be done to Queen Vashti?" he asked.
"She has not obeyed the command of King Xerxes that the eunuchs
have taken to her."
16Then Memukan replied in the presence of the king and the no-
bles, "Queen Vashti has done wrong, not only against the king but also
against all the nobles and the peoples of all the provinces of King Xer-
xes. 17For the queen's conduct will become known to all the women,
and so they will despise their husbands and say, 'King Xerxes com-
manded Queen Vashti to be brought before him, but she would not
come.' 18This very day the Persian and Median women of the nobil-
ity who have heard about the queen's conduct will respond to all the
king's nobles in the same way. There will be no end of disrespect and
discord.
19"Therefore, if it pleases the king, let him issue a royal decree and
let it be written in the laws of Persia and Media, which cannot be re-
pealed, that Vashti is never again to enter the presence of King Xerxes.
Also let the king give her royal position to someone else who is better

PRAYING SCRIPTURE

Esther 1

Sometimes God is so subtle and his providence so unseen that things that are connected don't appear to be connected. When Queen Vashti refused the king's request to appear before his friends at a royal banquet, no one could have foreseen God's plan to use her successor, Esther, to save the Jews.

Do you find it hard to maintain faith when you can't see God at work? Ask him to use Esther's story to build your faith in him.

---

[a] *1* Hebrew *Ahasuerus*; here and throughout Esther [b] *1* That is, the upper Nile region

than she. 20 Then when the king's edict is proclaimed throughout all his vast realm, all the women will respect their husbands, from the least to the greatest."

21 The king and his nobles were pleased with this advice, so the king did as Memukan proposed. 22 He sent dispatches to all parts of the kingdom, to each province in its own script and to each people in their own language, proclaiming that every man should be ruler over his own household, using his native tongue.

ESTHER MADE QUEEN

2 Later when King Xerxes' fury had subsided, he remembered Vashti and what she had done and what he had decreed about her. 2 Then the king's personal attendants proposed, "Let a search be made for beautiful young virgins for the king. 3 Let the king appoint commissioners in every province of his realm to bring all these beautiful young women into the harem at the citadel of Susa. Let them be placed under the care of Hegai, the king's eunuch, who is in charge of the women; and let beauty treatments be given to them. 4 Then let the young woman who pleases the king be queen instead of Vashti." This advice appealed to the king, and he followed it.

5 Now there was in the citadel of Susa a Jew of the tribe of Benjamin, named Mordecai son of Jair, the son of Shimei, the son of Kish, 6 who had been carried into exile from Jerusalem by Nebuchadnezzar king of Babylon, among those taken captive with Jehoiachin[a] king of Judah. 7 Mordecai had a cousin named Hadassah, whom he had brought up because she had neither father nor mother. This young woman, who was also known as Esther, had a lovely figure and was beautiful. Mordecai had taken her as his own daughter when her father and mother died.

8 When the king's order and edict had been proclaimed, many young women were brought to the citadel of Susa and put under the care of Hegai. Esther also was taken to the king's palace and entrusted to Hegai, who had charge of the harem. 9 She pleased him and won his favor. Immediately he provided her with her beauty treatments and special food. He assigned to her seven female attendants selected from the king's palace and moved her and her attendants into the best place in the harem.

10 Esther had not revealed her nationality and family background, because Mordecai had forbidden her to do so. 11 Every day he walked back and forth near the courtyard of the harem to find out how Esther was and what was happening to her.

12 Before a young woman's turn came to go in to King Xerxes, she had to complete twelve months of beauty treatments prescribed for the women, six months with oil of myrrh and six with perfumes and cosmetics. 13 And this is how she would go to the king: Anything she wanted was given her to take with her from the harem to the king's palace. 14 In the evening she would go there and in the morning return to another part of the harem to the care of Shaashgaz, the king's eunuch who was in charge of the concubines. She would not return to the king unless he was pleased with her and summoned her by name.

15 When the turn came for Esther (the young woman Mordecai had adopted, the daughter of his uncle Abihail) to go to the king, she asked for nothing other than what Hegai, the king's eunuch who was in

PRAYING SCRIPTURE

Esther 2

After a kingdom-wide search for a new queen, King Xerxes loved a young Jewish woman, Esther, more than all the other young women. Esther's cousin Mordecai counseled her in this new, providential role and reported to her an assassination plot against the king. It was foiled and recorded in the official history.

Sometimes in our spiritual journey, God seems silent or uninvolved. Trust that he knows and sees even when you cannot.

[a] 6 Hebrew *Jeconiah,* a variant of *Jehoiachin*

charge of the harem, suggested. And Esther won the favor of everyone
who saw her. [16]She was taken to King Xerxes in the royal residence in
the tenth month, the month of Tebeth, in the seventh year of his reign.
[17]Now the king was attracted to Esther more than to any of the other
women, and she won his favor and approval more than any of the
other virgins. So he set a royal crown on her head and made her queen
instead of Vashti. [18]And the king gave a great banquet, Esther's ban-
quet, for all his nobles and officials. He proclaimed a holiday through-
out the provinces and distributed gifts with royal liberality.

MORDECAI UNCOVERS A CONSPIRACY

[19]When the virgins were assembled a second time, Mordecai was sit-
ting at the king's gate. [20]But Esther had kept secret her family back-
ground and nationality just as Mordecai had told her to do, for she
continued to follow Mordecai's instructions as she had done when he
was bringing her up.
[21]During the time Mordecai was sitting at the king's gate, Bigthana[a]
and Teresh, two of the king's officers who guarded the doorway, be-
came angry and conspired to assassinate King Xerxes. [22]But Mordecai
found out about the plot and told Queen Esther, who in turn reported
it to the king, giving credit to Mordecai. [23]And when the report was
investigated and found to be true, the two officials were impaled on
poles. All this was recorded in the book of the annals in the presence
of the king.

HAMAN'S PLOT TO DESTROY THE JEWS

3 After these events, King Xerxes honored Haman son of Hamme-
datha, the Agagite, elevating him and giving him a seat of honor
higher than that of all the other nobles. [2]All the royal officials at the
king's gate knelt down and paid honor to Haman, for the king had
commanded this concerning him. But Mordecai would not kneel down
or pay him honor.
[3]Then the royal officials at the king's gate asked Mordecai, "Why do
you disobey the king's command?" [4]Day after day they spoke to him
but he refused to comply. Therefore they told Haman about it to see
whether Mordecai's behavior would be tolerated, for he had told them
he was a Jew.
[5]When Haman saw that Mordecai would not kneel down or pay him
honor, he was enraged. [6]Yet having learned who Mordecai's people
were, he scorned the idea of killing only Mordecai. Instead Haman
looked for a way to destroy all Mordecai's people, the Jews, through-
out the whole kingdom of Xerxes.
[7]In the twelfth year of King Xerxes, in the first month, the month
of Nisan, the *pur* (that is, the lot) was cast in the presence of Haman
to select a day and month. And the lot fell on[b] the twelfth month, the
month of Adar.
[8]Then Haman said to King Xerxes, "There is a certain people dis-
persed among the peoples in all the provinces of your kingdom who
keep themselves separate. Their customs are different from those of
all other people, and they do not obey the king's laws; it is not in the
king's best interest to tolerate them. [9]If it pleases the king, let a decree

PRAYING SCRIPTURE

Esther 3

One of the king's officials was a man named Haman. When Mordecai refused to join the staff in bowing before Haman—as any devout Jew would refuse to do—Haman became furious. He hatched a plot not only to kill Mordecai but to destroy every Jew in the kingdom.

Sometimes God allows evil schemes to advance before intervening. You can be confident when asking God to stop the schemes of the wicked.

---

[a] 21 Hebrew *Bigthan,* a variant of *Bigthana* [b] 7 Septuagint; Hebrew does not have *And the lot fell on.*

be issued to destroy them, and I will give ten thousand talents[a] of sil-
ver to the king's administrators for the royal treasury."
10So the king took his signet ring from his finger and gave it to Ha-
man son of Hammedatha, the Agagite, the enemy of the Jews. 11"Keep
the money," the king said to Haman, "and do with the people as you
please."
12Then on the thirteenth day of the first month the royal secretaries
were summoned. They wrote out in the script of each province and in
the language of each people all Haman's orders to the king's satraps,
the governors of the various provinces and the nobles of the various
peoples. These were written in the name of King Xerxes himself and
sealed with his own ring. 13Dispatches were sent by couriers to all the
king's provinces with the order to destroy, kill and annihilate all the
Jews — young and old, women and children — on a single day, the thir-
teenth day of the twelfth month, the month of Adar, and to plunder
their goods. 14A copy of the text of the edict was to be issued as law in
every province and made known to the people of every nationality so
they would be ready for that day.
15The couriers went out, spurred on by the king's command, and the
edict was issued in the citadel of Susa. The king and Haman sat down
to drink, but the city of Susa was bewildered.

MORDECAI PERSUADES ESTHER TO HELP

4 When Mordecai learned of all that had been done, he tore his
clothes, put on sackcloth and ashes, and went out into the city,
wailing loudly and bitterly. 2But he went only as far as the king's gate,
because no one clothed in sackcloth was allowed to enter it. 3In every
province to which the edict and order of the king came, there was great
mourning among the Jews, with fasting, weeping and wailing. Many
lay in sackcloth and ashes.
4When Esther's eunuchs and female attendants came and told her
about Mordecai, she was in great distress. She sent clothes for him to
put on instead of his sackcloth, but he would not accept them. 5Then
Esther summoned Hathak, one of the king's eunuchs assigned to at-
tend her, and ordered him to find out what was troubling Mordecai
and why.
6So Hathak went out to Mordecai in the open square of the city in
front of the king's gate. 7Mordecai told him everything that had hap-
pened to him, including the exact amount of money Haman had
promised to pay into the royal treasury for the destruction of the Jews.
8He also gave him a copy of the text of the edict for their annihilation,
which had been published in Susa, to show to Esther and explain it to
her, and he told him to instruct her to go into the king's presence to
beg for mercy and plead with him for her people.
9Hathak went back and reported to Esther what Mordecai had said.
10Then she instructed him to say to Mordecai, 11"All the king's officials
and the people of the royal provinces know that for any man or woman
who approaches the king in the inner court without being summoned
the king has but one law: that they be put to death unless the king ex-
tends the gold scepter to them and spares their lives. But thirty days
have passed since I was called to go to the king."
12When Esther's words were reported to Mordecai, 13he sent back this

PRAYING SCRIPTURE

Esther 4

This passage is pivotal to the history of the Jewish people. Queen Esther was given the opportunity to rescue her people before a vengeful plot to exterminate them came to fruition. Her plan to intervene could have led to her own death, but she said, "If I perish, I perish!" (verse 16).

Esther didn't have a death wish, but she counted the cost. Pray for God's help in counting the cost whenever you are faced with a life-changing decision.

[a] 9 That is, about 375 tons or about 340 metric tons

answer: "Do not think that because you are in the king's house you
alone of all the Jews will escape. 14For if you remain silent at this time,
relief and deliverance for the Jews will arise from another place, but
you and your father's family will perish. And who knows but that you
have come to your royal position for such a time as this?"
15Then Esther sent this reply to Mordecai: 16"Go, gather together all
the Jews who are in Susa, and fast for me. Do not eat or drink for three
days, night or day. I and my attendants will fast as you do. When this
is done, I will go to the king, even though it is against the law. And if
I perish, I perish."
17So Mordecai went away and carried out all of Esther's instructions.

ESTHER'S REQUEST TO THE KING

5 On the third day Esther put on her royal robes and stood in the in-
ner court of the palace, in front of the king's hall. The king was sit-
ting on his royal throne in the hall, facing the entrance. 2When he saw
Queen Esther standing in the court, he was pleased with her and held
out to her the gold scepter that was in his hand. So Esther approached
and touched the tip of the scepter.
3Then the king asked, "What is it, Queen Esther? What is your re-
quest? Even up to half the kingdom, it will be given you."
4"If it pleases the king," replied Esther, "let the king, together with
Haman, come today to a banquet I have prepared for him."
5"Bring Haman at once," the king said, "so that we may do what Es-
ther asks."
So the king and Haman went to the banquet Esther had prepared.
6As they were drinking wine, the king again asked Esther, "Now what
is your petition? It will be given you. And what is your request? Even
up to half the kingdom, it will be granted."
7Esther replied, "My petition and my request is this: 8If the king re-
gards me with favor and if it pleases the king to grant my petition and
fulfill my request, let the king and Haman come tomorrow to the ban-
quet I will prepare for them. Then I will answer the king's question."

HAMAN'S RAGE AGAINST MORDECAI

9Haman went out that day happy and in high spirits. But when he
saw Mordecai at the king's gate and observed that he neither rose nor
showed fear in his presence, he was filled with rage against Mordecai.
10Nevertheless, Haman restrained himself and went home.
Calling together his friends and Zeresh, his wife, 11Haman boasted to
them about his vast wealth, his many sons, and all the ways the king
had honored him and how he had elevated him above the other nobles
and officials. 12"And that's not all," Haman added. "I'm the only person
Queen Esther invited to accompany the king to the banquet she gave.
And she has invited me along with the king tomorrow. 13But all this
gives me no satisfaction as long as I see that Jew Mordecai sitting at
the king's gate."
14His wife Zeresh and all his friends said to him, "Have a pole set up,
reaching to a height of fifty cubits,[a] and ask the king in the morning
to have Mordecai impaled on it. Then go with the king to the banquet
and enjoy yourself." This suggestion delighted Haman, and he had the
pole set up.

[a] *14* That is, about 75 feet or about 23 meters

PRAYING SCRIPTURE
Esther 5

Esther's faith in this moment can hardly be overstated. She knew exactly what she needed to say and proceeded confidently with her plan to expose Haman and his wicked plot. Haman, having no idea of impending judgment, ordered a 75-foot gallows built on which to hang Mordecai.

Put yourself in Mordecai's place, knowing that God and Satan were working around him simultaneously. Thank God that he *always* has the power to overcome.

MORDECAI HONORED

6 That night the king could not sleep; so he ordered the book of the chronicles, the record of his reign, to be brought in and read to him. 2It was found recorded there that Mordecai had exposed Bigthana and Teresh, two of the king's officers who guarded the doorway, who had conspired to assassinate King Xerxes.

3"What honor and recognition has Mordecai received for this?" the king asked.

"Nothing has been done for him," his attendants answered.

4The king said, "Who is in the court?" Now Haman had just entered the outer court of the palace to speak to the king about impaling Mordecai on the pole he had set up for him.

5His attendants answered, "Haman is standing in the court."

"Bring him in," the king ordered.

6When Haman entered, the king asked him, "What should be done for the man the king delights to honor?"

Now Haman thought to himself, "Who is there that the king would rather honor than me?" 7So he answered the king, "For the man the king delights to honor, 8have them bring a royal robe the king has worn and a horse the king has ridden, one with a royal crest placed on its head. 9Then let the robe and horse be entrusted to one of the king's most noble princes. Let them robe the man the king delights to honor, and lead him on the horse through the city streets, proclaiming before him, 'This is what is done for the man the king delights to honor!'"

10"Go at once," the king commanded Haman. "Get the robe and the horse and do just as you have suggested for Mordecai the Jew, who sits at the king's gate. Do not neglect anything you have recommended."

11So Haman got the robe and the horse. He robed Mordecai, and led him on horseback through the city streets, proclaiming before him, "This is what is done for the man the king delights to honor!"

12Afterward Mordecai returned to the king's gate. But Haman rushed home, with his head covered in grief, 13and told Zeresh his wife and all his friends everything that had happened to him.

His advisers and his wife Zeresh said to him, "Since Mordecai, before whom your downfall has started, is of Jewish origin, you cannot stand against him — you will surely come to ruin!" 14While they were still talking with him, the king's eunuchs arrived and hurried Haman away to the banquet Esther had prepared.

HAMAN IMPALED

7 So the king and Haman went to Queen Esther's banquet, 2and as they were drinking wine on the second day, the king again asked, "Queen Esther, what is your petition? It will be given you. What is your request? Even up to half the kingdom, it will be granted."

3Then Queen Esther answered, "If I have found favor with you, Your Majesty, and if it pleases you, grant me my life — this is my petition. And spare my people — this is my request. 4For I and my people have been sold to be destroyed, killed and annihilated. If we had merely been sold as male and female slaves, I would have kept quiet, because no such distress would justify disturbing the king.[a]"

5King Xerxes asked Queen Esther, "Who is he? Where is he — the man who has dared to do such a thing?"

PRAYING SCRIPTURE

Esther 6

Has God ever spoken to you when you couldn't sleep? God didn't exactly speak to the king when he had insomnia, but he moved. When the king ordered that the official history be read to him, he heard of how Mordecai had saved his life.

God continued working to save the Jews, preserving the Messiah's line. Thank God for his power and wisdom.

PRAYING SCRIPTURE

Esther 7

After Haman misinterpreted the king's desire to bless an honorable man—Mordecai—and his scheme was spoiled, Esther identified Haman as the author of the plot to kill the Jews. The king angrily sentenced Haman to die on the gallows he'd constructed for Mordecai.

God is able to make evil plans against you come to nothing. Ask him to protect you from the work of the evil one.

---

[a] 4 Or *quiet, but the compensation our adversary offers cannot be compared with the loss the king would suffer*

[6]Esther said, "An adversary and enemy! This vile Haman!"

Then Haman was terrified before the king and queen. [7]The king got up in a rage, left his wine and went out into the palace garden. But Haman, realizing that the king had already decided his fate, stayed behind to beg Queen Esther for his life.

[8]Just as the king returned from the palace garden to the banquet hall, Haman was falling on the couch where Esther was reclining.

The king exclaimed, "Will he even molest the queen while she is with me in the house?"

As soon as the word left the king's mouth, they covered Haman's face. [9]Then Harbona, one of the eunuchs attending the king, said, "A pole reaching to a height of fifty cubits[a] stands by Haman's house. He had it set up for Mordecai, who spoke up to help the king."

The king said, "Impale him on it!" [10]So they impaled Haman on the pole he had set up for Mordecai. Then the king's fury subsided.

THE KING'S EDICT IN BEHALF OF THE JEWS

8 That same day King Xerxes gave Queen Esther the estate of Haman, the enemy of the Jews. And Mordecai came into the presence of the king, for Esther had told how he was related to her. [2]The king took off his signet ring, which he had reclaimed from Haman, and presented it to Mordecai. And Esther appointed him over Haman's estate.

[3]Esther again pleaded with the king, falling at his feet and weeping. She begged him to put an end to the evil plan of Haman the Agagite, which he had devised against the Jews. [4]Then the king extended the gold scepter to Esther and she arose and stood before him.

[5]"If it pleases the king," she said, "and if he regards me with favor and thinks it the right thing to do, and if he is pleased with me, let an order be written overruling the dispatches that Haman son of Hammedatha, the Agagite, devised and wrote to destroy the Jews in all the king's provinces. [6]For how can I bear to see disaster fall on my people? How can I bear to see the destruction of my family?"

[7]King Xerxes replied to Queen Esther and to Mordecai the Jew, "Because Haman attacked the Jews, I have given his estate to Esther, and they have impaled him on the pole he set up. [8]Now write another decree in the king's name in behalf of the Jews as seems best to you, and seal it with the king's signet ring — for no document written in the king's name and sealed with his ring can be revoked."

[9]At once the royal secretaries were summoned — on the twenty-third day of the third month, the month of Sivan. They wrote out all Mordecai's orders to the Jews, and to the satraps, governors and nobles of the 127 provinces stretching from India to Cush.[b] These orders were written in the script of each province and the language of each people and also to the Jews in their own script and language. [10]Mordecai wrote in the name of King Xerxes, sealed the dispatches with the king's signet ring, and sent them by mounted couriers, who rode fast horses especially bred for the king.

[11]The king's edict granted the Jews in every city the right to assemble and protect themselves; to destroy, kill and annihilate the armed men of any nationality or province who might attack them and their women and children,[c] and to plunder the property of their enemies. [12]The day

PRAYING SCRIPTURE

Esther 8

The king still did not realize he had—through Haman's plotting—authorized his forces to completely destroy the Jews. Esther again interceded, asking Xerxes to give the Jews the right to defend themselves if violence broke out.

Esther might not have known it, but God used her beyond the immediate salvation of her people. Thank God for saving the Jews in Persia and thus the Messiah's line.

---

[a] 9 That is, about 75 feet or about 23 meters [b] 9 That is, the upper Nile region [c] 11 Or *province, together with their women and children, who might attack them;*

appointed for the Jews to do this in all the provinces of King Xerxes was the thirteenth day of the twelfth month, the month of Adar. 13A copy of the text of the edict was to be issued as law in every province and made known to the people of every nationality so that the Jews would be ready on that day to avenge themselves on their enemies.

14The couriers, riding the royal horses, went out, spurred on by the king's command, and the edict was issued in the citadel of Susa.

THE TRIUMPH OF THE JEWS

15When Mordecai left the king's presence, he was wearing royal garments of blue and white, a large crown of gold and a purple robe of fine linen. And the city of Susa held a joyous celebration. 16For the Jews it was a time of happiness and joy, gladness and honor. 17In every province and in every city to which the edict of the king came, there was joy and gladness among the Jews, with feasting and celebrating. And many people of other nationalities became Jews because fear of the Jews had seized them.

9 On the thirteenth day of the twelfth month, the month of Adar, the edict commanded by the king was to be carried out. On this day the enemies of the Jews had hoped to overpower them, but now the tables were turned and the Jews got the upper hand over those who hated them. 2The Jews assembled in their cities in all the provinces of King Xerxes to attack those determined to destroy them. No one could stand against them, because the people of all the other nationalities were afraid of them. 3And all the nobles of the provinces, the satraps, the governors and the king's administrators helped the Jews, because fear of Mordecai had seized them. 4Mordecai was prominent in the palace; his reputation spread throughout the provinces, and he became more and more powerful.

5The Jews struck down all their enemies with the sword, killing and destroying them, and they did what they pleased to those who hated them. 6In the citadel of Susa, the Jews killed and destroyed five hundred men. 7They also killed Parshandatha, Dalphon, Aspatha, 8Poratha, Adalia, Aridatha, 9Parmashta, Arisai, Aridai and Vaizatha, 10the ten sons of Haman son of Hammedatha, the enemy of the Jews. But they did not lay their hands on the plunder.

11The number of those killed in the citadel of Susa was reported to the king that same day. 12The king said to Queen Esther, "The Jews have killed and destroyed five hundred men and the ten sons of Haman in the citadel of Susa. What have they done in the rest of the king's provinces? Now what is your petition? It will be given you. What is your request? It will also be granted."

13"If it pleases the king," Esther answered, "give the Jews in Susa permission to carry out this day's edict tomorrow also, and let Haman's ten sons be impaled on poles."

14So the king commanded that this be done. An edict was issued in Susa, and they impaled the ten sons of Haman. 15The Jews in Susa came together on the fourteenth day of the month of Adar, and they put to death in Susa three hundred men, but they did not lay their hands on the plunder.

16Meanwhile, the remainder of the Jews who were in the king's provinces also assembled to protect themselves and get relief from their enemies. They killed seventy-five thousand of them but did not lay their hands on the plunder. 17This happened on the thirteenth day of

PRAYING SCRIPTURE

Esther 9

When the king's previous order went into effect, the Jews defended themselves with great success. They overpowered all their attackers but did not plunder the survivors. Haman's sons were all put to death while God's faithfulness was celebrated in a new annual festival, Purim.

Celebrating what God does in our lives keeps us from becoming ungrateful. What is something you can celebrate and thank God for today?

the month of Adar, and on the fourteenth they rested and made it a
day of feasting and joy.
18The Jews in Susa, however, had assembled on the thirteenth and
fourteenth, and then on the fifteenth they rested and made it a day of
feasting and joy.
19That is why rural Jews — those living in villages — observe the
fourteenth of the month of Adar as a day of joy and feasting, a day for
giving presents to each other.

PURIM ESTABLISHED

20Mordecai recorded these events, and he sent letters to all the Jews
throughout the provinces of King Xerxes, near and far, 21to have them cel-
ebrate annually the fourteenth and fifteenth days of the month of Adar
22as the time when the Jews got relief from their enemies, and as the
month when their sorrow was turned into joy and their mourning into a
day of celebration. He wrote them to observe the days as days of feasting
and joy and giving presents of food to one another and gifts to the poor.
23So the Jews agreed to continue the celebration they had begun, do-
ing what Mordecai had written to them. 24For Haman son of Hamme-
datha, the Agagite, the enemy of all the Jews, had plotted against the
Jews to destroy them and had cast the *pur* (that is, the lot) for their ruin
and destruction. 25But when the plot came to the king's attention,[a] he
issued written orders that the evil scheme Haman had devised against
the Jews should come back onto his own head, and that he and his sons
should be impaled on poles. 26(Therefore these days were called Purim,
from the word *pur*.) Because of everything written in this letter and
because of what they had seen and what had happened to them, 27the
Jews took it on themselves to establish the custom that they and their
descendants and all who join them should without fail observe these
two days every year, in the way prescribed and at the time appointed.
28These days should be remembered and observed in every generation
by every family, and in every province and in every city. And these days
of Purim should never fail to be celebrated by the Jews — nor should
the memory of these days die out among their descendants.
29So Queen Esther, daughter of Abihail, along with Mordecai the Jew,
wrote with full authority to confirm this second letter concerning Pu-
rim. 30And Mordecai sent letters to all the Jews in the 127 provinces of
Xerxes' kingdom — words of goodwill and assurance — 31to establish
these days of Purim at their designated times, as Mordecai the Jew and
Queen Esther had decreed for them, and as they had established for
themselves and their descendants in regard to their times of fasting
and lamentation. 32Esther's decree confirmed these regulations about
Purim, and it was written down in the records.

THE GREATNESS OF MORDECAI

10 King Xerxes imposed tribute throughout the empire, to its dis-
tant shores. 2And all his acts of power and might, together with
a full account of the greatness of Mordecai, whom the king had pro-
moted, are they not written in the book of the annals of the kings of
Media and Persia? 3Mordecai the Jew was second in rank to King Xer-
xes, preeminent among the Jews, and held in high esteem by his many
fellow Jews, because he worked for the good of his people and spoke
up for the welfare of all the Jews.

[a] 25 Or *when Esther came before the king*

PRAYING SCRIPTURE

Esther 10

Mordecai's wisdom, Esther's bravery and the king's kindness resulted in Mordecai's elevation to the number two position in the kingdom. The book ends by reminding readers that Mordecai continued seeking good things for his people, advocating for their well-being.

Whose good can you seek? For whom can you advocate justice? Ask God to give you influence with the leaders who can make a difference.

JOB

The book of Job is perhaps the earliest book in the Bible and begins its wisdom literature. Job also contains the Bible's most sustained engagement with the issue of evil and suffering. The first chapter introduces Job as a righteous man whose life had been blessed with children and material property. What Job did not know was that at a meeting in heaven—of which he was the subject—the Lord pointed him out to Satan, bragging on Job's faithfulness. In two successive meetings, Satan accused Job before God, insisting that the man of God would curse God to his face if God removed his protection. The Lord indeed allowed Satan to smite Job, but he also set parameters for what the adversary could and could not do. Under an aggressive satanic assault, Job stood in his faith as his children died, his riches were plundered and his skin was covered in boils.

The book focuses on prayer in life's most heart-wrenching moments. Job's lament over the day of his birth in chapter 3 is not a mere rhetorical flourish. He had just lost everything but his life and his wife. In his anguish, Job no longer believed his life was worth much. His wife counseled him to curse God and die. Instead, Job fell to the ground and worshiped.

The bulk of Job consists of three cycles of discussion about righteousness, evil and suffering between Job and his friends. Job's friends insisted that only those who have been unrighteous suffer, while Job continually maintained his innocence. In one memorable defense (see 23:8–10), Job expressed firm confidence that even if he felt utterly abandoned and was unable to see God on any side, God still saw him. In another, Job proclaimed his absolute faith in the Redeemer (see 19:25).

The cycles of disputations with his friends led Job to challenge God to judge who among them was right. God was quick to take up the challenge. In one of God's lengthy Old Testament monologues (chs. 38–41), he rebuked Job for his arrogance. He had created the world and everything in it without Job's help; therefore Job had no standing to question him.

In a sometimes overlooked conclusion to the story, God, who strongly rebuked Job to his face, announced his vindication. To Eliphaz God said, "You have not spoken the truth about me, as my servant Job has" (42:7). In the end, the Lord restored and multiplied Job's fortunes.

We live in a fallen world where the rain falls on both the righteous and the unrighteous. Followers of Jesus die in car accidents, lose their jobs and receive cancer diagnoses. All these rightly lead us to lamentation, crying out to God for an alleviation of our suffering. This is a godly, right and understandable response to the pain we experience. Regardless of what we suffer, we can say with the confidence of Job, "The LORD gave and the LORD has taken away; may the name of the LORD be praised" (1:21).

PROLOGUE

1 In the land of Uz there lived a man whose name was Job. This man
was blameless and upright; he feared God and shunned evil. 2He
had seven sons and three daughters, 3and he owned seven thousand
sheep, three thousand camels, five hundred yoke of oxen and five hun-
dred donkeys, and had a large number of servants. He was the greatest
man among all the people of the East.
4His sons used to hold feasts in their homes on their birthdays, and
they would invite their three sisters to eat and drink with them. 5When
a period of feasting had run its course, Job would make arrangements
for them to be purified. Early in the morning he would sacrifice a
burnt offering for each of them, thinking, "Perhaps my children have
sinned and cursed God in their hearts." This was Job's regular custom.
6One day the angels[a] came to present themselves before the LORD,
and Satan[b] also came with them. 7The LORD said to Satan, "Where have
you come from?"

Satan answered the LORD, "From roaming throughout the earth, go-
ing back and forth on it."
8Then the LORD said to Satan, "Have you considered my servant Job?
There is no one on earth like him; he is blameless and upright, a man
who fears God and shuns evil."
9"Does Job fear God for nothing?" Satan replied. 10"Have you not put
a hedge around him and his household and everything he has? You
have blessed the work of his hands, so that his flocks and herds are
spread throughout the land. 11But now stretch out your hand and strike
everything he has, and he will surely curse you to your face."
12The LORD said to Satan, "Very well, then, everything he has is in
your power, but on the man himself do not lay a finger."

Then Satan went out from the presence of the LORD.
13One day when Job's sons and daughters were feasting and drinking
wine at the oldest brother's house, 14a messenger came to Job and said,
"The oxen were plowing and the donkeys were grazing nearby, 15and
the Sabeans attacked and made off with them. They put the servants to
the sword, and I am the only one who has escaped to tell you!"
16While he was still speaking, another messenger came and said,
"The fire of God fell from the heavens and burned up the sheep and
the servants, and I am the only one who has escaped to tell you!"
17While he was still speaking, another messenger came and said,
"The Chaldeans formed three raiding parties and swept down on your
camels and made off with them. They put the servants to the sword,
and I am the only one who has escaped to tell you!"
18While he was still speaking, yet another messenger came and said,
"Your sons and daughters were feasting and drinking wine at the old-
est brother's house, 19when suddenly a mighty wind swept in from the
desert and struck the four corners of the house. It collapsed on them
and they are dead, and I am the only one who has escaped to tell you!"
20At this, Job got up and tore his robe and shaved his head. Then he
fell to the ground in worship 21and said:

"Naked I came from my mother's womb,
and naked I will depart.[c]

---

[a] 6 Hebrew *the sons of God* [b] 6 Hebrew *satan* means *adversary.* [c] 21 Or *will return there*

PRAYING SCRIPTURE

Job 1

In a scene best described as a cosmic wager, Satan bet God that he could make the blameless and upright Job turn away (see verses 1,11). Satan was convinced that Job's obedience stemmed solely from the material blessings God had given Job. This was not unreasonable—many people's obedience is tied to how blessed they feel.

What could you lose and still love God? If he is not above everything, confess your need to love him more.

The LORD gave and the LORD has taken away;
may the name of the LORD be praised."

22 In all this, Job did not sin by charging God with wrongdoing.

PRAYING SCRIPTURE

Job 2

The history of God's people is filled with those who endured physical suffering yet remained faithful to him. Satan seemed convinced that Job would forsake God if he suffered bodily harm. God allowed a deep but ultimately successful test of Job's faith.

"If God loves me, why do I suffer?" is a long-standing question. But we can praise God that his love never fails even when pain and suffering come.

2 On another day the angels[a] came to present themselves before the
LORD, and Satan also came with them to present himself before
him. 2 And the LORD said to Satan, "Where have you come from?"
Satan answered the LORD, "From roaming throughout the earth, going back and forth on it."
3 Then the LORD said to Satan, "Have you considered my servant Job?
There is no one on earth like him; he is blameless and upright, a man
who fears God and shuns evil. And he still maintains his integrity,
though you incited me against him to ruin him without any reason."
4 "Skin for skin!" Satan replied. "A man will give all he has for his own
life. 5 But now stretch out your hand and strike his flesh and bones, and
he will surely curse you to your face."
6 The LORD said to Satan, "Very well, then, he is in your hands; but
you must spare his life."
7 So Satan went out from the presence of the LORD and afflicted
Job with painful sores from the soles of his feet to the crown of his
head. 8 Then Job took a piece of broken pottery and scraped himself
with it as he sat among the ashes.
9 His wife said to him, "Are you still maintaining your integrity?
Curse God and die!"
10 He replied, "You are talking like a foolish[b] woman. Shall we accept
good from God, and not trouble?"
In all this, Job did not sin in what he said.

11 When Job's three friends, Eliphaz the Temanite, Bildad the Shuhite
and Zophar the Naamathite, heard about all the troubles that had come
upon him, they set out from their homes and met together by agreement to go and sympathize with him and comfort him. 12 When they
saw him from a distance, they could hardly recognize him; they began to
weep aloud, and they tore their robes and sprinkled dust on their heads.
13 Then they sat on the ground with him for seven days and seven nights.
No one said a word to him, because they saw how great his suffering was.

PRAYING SCRIPTURE

Job 3

When suffering comes, we often don't know how to respond. Job experienced incredible loss and physical illness, and finally his emotional dam burst in a torrent of questions and complaints. He was hopeless and distraught and let his friends know exactly how he felt.

God is not offended by the frustrations we experience when life falls apart. He can handle our complaints and concerns, so go to him in confidence.

JOB SPEAKS

3 After this, Job opened his mouth and cursed the day of his birth.
2 He said:

3 "May the day of my birth perish,
and the night that said, 'A boy is conceived!'
4 That day — may it turn to darkness;
may God above not care about it;
may no light shine on it.
5 May gloom and utter darkness claim it once more;
may a cloud settle over it;
may blackness overwhelm it.
6 That night — may thick darkness seize it;
may it not be included among the days of the year
nor be entered in any of the months.

---

[a] 1 Hebrew *the sons of God* [b] 10 The Hebrew word rendered *foolish* denotes moral deficiency.

7 May that night be barren;
  may no shout of joy be heard in it.
8 May those who curse days[a] curse that day,
  those who are ready to rouse Leviathan.
9 May its morning stars become dark;
  may it wait for daylight in vain
  and not see the first rays of dawn,
10 for it did not shut the doors of the womb on me
  to hide trouble from my eyes.

11 "Why did I not perish at birth,
  and die as I came from the womb?
12 Why were there knees to receive me
  and breasts that I might be nursed?
13 For now I would be lying down in peace;
  I would be asleep and at rest
14 with kings and rulers of the earth,
  who built for themselves places now lying in ruins,
15 with princes who had gold,
  who filled their houses with silver.
16 Or why was I not hidden away in the ground like a
    stillborn child,
  like an infant who never saw the light of day?
17 There the wicked cease from turmoil,
  and there the weary are at rest.
18 Captives also enjoy their ease;
  they no longer hear the slave driver's shout.
19 The small and the great are there,
  and the slaves are freed from their owners.

20 "Why is light given to those in misery,
  and life to the bitter of soul,
21 to those who long for death that does not come,
  who search for it more than for hidden treasure,
22 who are filled with gladness
  and rejoice when they reach the grave?
23 Why is life given to a man
  whose way is hidden,
  whom God has hedged in?
24 For sighing has become my daily food;
  my groans pour out like water.
25 What I feared has come upon me;
  what I dreaded has happened to me.
26 I have no peace, no quietness;
  I have no rest, but only turmoil."

ELIPHAZ

4 Then Eliphaz the Temanite replied:

2 "If someone ventures a word with you, will you be impatient?
  But who can keep from speaking?
3 Think how you have instructed many,
  how you have strengthened feeble hands.

[a] 8 Or *curse the sea*

PRAYING SCRIPTURE

Job 4

Job's three friends Eliphaz, Bildad and Zophar tried to convince Job that he must have sinned to receive judgment. Eliphaz, who spoke first, challenged Job's assertion that he didn't deserve his suffering, citing his experience of seeing others judged for sin (see verse 8).

During times of suffering, people will sometimes make false assumptions about you. Ask God to help you love those who judge you wrongly.

4 Your words have supported those who stumbled;
you have strengthened faltering knees.
5 But now trouble comes to you, and you are discouraged;
it strikes you, and you are dismayed.
6 Should not your piety be your confidence
and your blameless ways your hope?

7 "Consider now: Who, being innocent, has ever perished?
Where were the upright ever destroyed?
8 As I have observed, those who plow evil
and those who sow trouble reap it.
9 At the breath of God they perish;
at the blast of his anger they are no more.
10 The lions may roar and growl,
yet the teeth of the great lions are broken.
11 The lion perishes for lack of prey,
and the cubs of the lioness are scattered.

12 "A word was secretly brought to me,
my ears caught a whisper of it.
13 Amid disquieting dreams in the night,
when deep sleep falls on people,
14 fear and trembling seized me
and made all my bones shake.
15 A spirit glided past my face,
and the hair on my body stood on end.
16 It stopped,
but I could not tell what it was.
A form stood before my eyes,
and I heard a hushed voice:
17 'Can a mortal be more righteous than God?
Can even a strong man be more pure than his Maker?
18 If God places no trust in his servants,
if he charges his angels with error,
19 how much more those who live in houses of clay,
whose foundations are in the dust,
who are crushed more readily than a moth!
20 Between dawn and dusk they are broken to pieces;
unnoticed, they perish forever.
21 Are not the cords of their tent pulled up,
so that they die without wisdom?'

5 "Call if you will, but who will answer you?
To which of the holy ones will you turn?
2 Resentment kills a fool,
and envy slays the simple.
3 I myself have seen a fool taking root,
but suddenly his house was cursed.
4 His children are far from safety,
crushed in court without a defender.
5 The hungry consume his harvest,
taking it even from among thorns,
and the thirsty pant after his wealth.
6 For hardship does not spring from the soil,
nor does trouble sprout from the ground.

PRAYING SCRIPTURE

Job 5

As Eliphaz continued explaining why he thought Job probably deserved his plight, he presented one piece of counsel that was beneficial: Appeal to God and present your case to him. Job's friend rightly concluded that God does infinitely great and marvelous things.

God does not fear our concerns. When you are distraught and things seem unfair, take your case directly to your Father in heaven.

7 Yet man is born to trouble
as surely as sparks fly upward.

8 "But if I were you, I would appeal to God;
I would lay my cause before him.
9 He performs wonders that cannot be fathomed,
miracles that cannot be counted.
10 He provides rain for the earth;
he sends water on the countryside.
11 The lowly he sets on high,
and those who mourn are lifted to safety.
12 He thwarts the plans of the crafty,
so that their hands achieve no success.
13 He catches the wise in their craftiness,
and the schemes of the wily are swept away.
14 Darkness comes upon them in the daytime;
at noon they grope as in the night.
15 He saves the needy from the sword in their mouth;
he saves them from the clutches of the powerful.
16 So the poor have hope,
and injustice shuts its mouth.

17 "Blessed is the one whom God corrects;
so do not despise the discipline of the Almighty.[a]
18 For he wounds, but he also binds up;
he injures, but his hands also heal.
19 From six calamities he will rescue you;
in seven no harm will touch you.
20 In famine he will deliver you from death,
and in battle from the stroke of the sword.
21 You will be protected from the lash of the tongue,
and need not fear when destruction comes.
22 You will laugh at destruction and famine,
and need not fear the wild animals.
23 For you will have a covenant with the stones of the field,
and the wild animals will be at peace with you.
24 You will know that your tent is secure;
you will take stock of your property and find nothing missing.
25 You will know that your children will be many,
and your descendants like the grass of the earth.
26 You will come to the grave in full vigor,
like sheaves gathered in season.

27 "We have examined this, and it is true.
So hear it and apply it to yourself."

JOB 6

Then Job replied:

2 "If only my anguish could be weighed
and all my misery be placed on the scales!
3 It would surely outweigh the sand of the seas —
no wonder my words have been impetuous.

[a] 17 Hebrew *Shaddai*; here and throughout Job

PRAYING SCRIPTURE

Job 6

Job's reply provides a tremendously helpful admonition. In verse 14 he said that a person in a state of despair should receive kindness from his friends, even if the person abandons God.

Think how relationships would be strengthened if everyone agreed to bear each other's burdens with kindness. Ask God to give you those friends and make you such a friend.

4 The arrows of the Almighty are in me,
my spirit drinks in their poison;
God's terrors are marshaled against me.
5 Does a wild donkey bray when it has grass,
or an ox bellow when it has fodder?
6 Is tasteless food eaten without salt,
or is there flavor in the sap of the mallow[a]?
7 I refuse to touch it;
such food makes me ill.

8 "Oh, that I might have my request,
that God would grant what I hope for,
9 that God would be willing to crush me,
to let loose his hand and cut off my life!
10 Then I would still have this consolation —
my joy in unrelenting pain —
that I had not denied the words of the Holy One.

11 "What strength do I have, that I should still hope?
What prospects, that I should be patient?
12 Do I have the strength of stone?
Is my flesh bronze?
13 Do I have any power to help myself,
now that success has been driven from me?

14 "Anyone who withholds kindness from a friend
forsakes the fear of the Almighty.
15 But my brothers are as undependable as intermittent streams,
as the streams that overflow
16 when darkened by thawing ice
and swollen with melting snow,
17 but that stop flowing in the dry season,
and in the heat vanish from their channels.
18 Caravans turn aside from their routes;
they go off into the wasteland and perish.
19 The caravans of Tema look for water,
the traveling merchants of Sheba look in hope.
20 They are distressed, because they had been confident;
they arrive there, only to be disappointed.
21 Now you too have proved to be of no help;
you see something dreadful and are afraid.
22 Have I ever said, 'Give something on my behalf,
pay a ransom for me from your wealth,
23 deliver me from the hand of the enemy,
rescue me from the clutches of the ruthless'?

24 "Teach me, and I will be quiet;
show me where I have been wrong.
25 How painful are honest words!
But what do your arguments prove?
26 Do you mean to correct what I say,
and treat my desperate words as wind?
27 You would even cast lots for the fatherless
and barter away your friend.

---

[a] 6 The meaning of the Hebrew for this phrase is uncertain.

28 "But now be so kind as to look at me.
Would I lie to your face?
29 Relent, do not be unjust;
reconsider, for my integrity is at stake.[a]
30 Is there any wickedness on my lips?
Can my mouth not discern malice?

7 "Do not mortals have hard service on earth?
Are not their days like those of hired laborers?
2 Like a slave longing for the evening shadows,
or a hired laborer waiting to be paid,
3 so I have been allotted months of futility,
and nights of misery have been assigned to me.
4 When I lie down I think, 'How long before I get up?'
The night drags on, and I toss and turn until dawn.
5 My body is clothed with worms and scabs,
my skin is broken and festering.

6 "My days are swifter than a weaver's shuttle,
and they come to an end without hope.
7 Remember, O God, that my life is but a breath;
my eyes will never see happiness again.
8 The eye that now sees me will see me no longer;
you will look for me, but I will be no more.
9 As a cloud vanishes and is gone,
so one who goes down to the grave does not return.
10 He will never come to his house again;
his place will know him no more.

11 "Therefore I will not keep silent;
I will speak out in the anguish of my spirit,
I will complain in the bitterness of my soul.
12 Am I the sea, or the monster of the deep,
that you put me under guard?
13 When I think my bed will comfort me
and my couch will ease my complaint,
14 even then you frighten me with dreams
and terrify me with visions,
15 so that I prefer strangling and death,
rather than this body of mine.
16 I despise my life; I would not live forever.
Let me alone; my days have no meaning.

17 "What is mankind that you make so much of them,
that you give them so much attention,
18 that you examine them every morning
and test them every moment?
19 Will you never look away from me,
or let me alone even for an instant?
20 If I have sinned, what have I done to you,
you who see everything we do?
Why have you made me your target?
Have I become a burden to you?[b]

PRAYING SCRIPTURE

Job 7

One thing we learn from Job is the freedom to express our raw feelings to God. Job said that he would not restrain his mouth, that he would speak out his spirit's anguish and complain of his soul's bitterness.

Job's trials should encourage us to express to God the specifics of our hurts. Does he not know about them anyway? Begin developing the habit of being completely open to God in prayer.

---

[a] 29 Or *my righteousness still stands* [b] 20 A few manuscripts of the Masoretic Text, an ancient Hebrew scribal tradition and Septuagint; most manuscripts of the Masoretic Text *I have become a burden to myself.*

21 Why do you not pardon my offenses
and forgive my sins?
For I will soon lie down in the dust;
you will search for me, but I will be no more."

BILDAD

8 Then Bildad the Shuhite replied:

2 "How long will you say such things?
Your words are a blustering wind.
3 Does God pervert justice?
Does the Almighty pervert what is right?
4 When your children sinned against him,
he gave them over to the penalty of their sin.
5 But if you will seek God earnestly
and plead with the Almighty,
6 if you are pure and upright,
even now he will rouse himself on your behalf
and restore you to your prosperous state.
7 Your beginnings will seem humble,
so prosperous will your future be.

8 "Ask the former generation
and find out what their ancestors learned,
9 for we were born only yesterday and know nothing,
and our days on earth are but a shadow.
10 Will they not instruct you and tell you?
Will they not bring forth words from their understanding?
11 Can papyrus grow tall where there is no marsh?
Can reeds thrive without water?
12 While still growing and uncut,
they wither more quickly than grass.
13 Such is the destiny of all who forget God;
so perishes the hope of the godless.
14 What they trust in is fragile[a];
what they rely on is a spider's web.
15 They lean on the web, but it gives way;
they cling to it, but it does not hold.
16 They are like a well-watered plant in the sunshine,
spreading its shoots over the garden;
17 it entwines its roots around a pile of rocks
and looks for a place among the stones.
18 But when it is torn from its spot,
that place disowns it and says, 'I never saw you.'
19 Surely its life withers away,
and[b] from the soil other plants grow.

20 "Surely God does not reject one who is blameless
or strengthen the hands of evildoers.
21 He will yet fill your mouth with laughter
and your lips with shouts of joy.
22 Your enemies will be clothed in shame,
and the tents of the wicked will be no more."

PRAYING SCRIPTURE

Job 8

Job's friend Bildad continues the attacks on Job's character and behavior, saying that Job's children got what they deserved (see verse 4). He went on essentially to accuse Job of forgetting God (see verse 13) and questioned his integrity (see verse 20).

There will always be those who think anything bad happening is a sign of God's judgment or someone's specific sin, but God isn't arbitrary. Trust him completely, even in trials.

---

[a] 14 The meaning of the Hebrew for this word is uncertain. [b] 19 Or *Surely all the joy it has / is that*

JOB

9 Then Job replied:

2 "Indeed, I know that this is true.
But how can mere mortals prove their innocence before God?
3 Though they wished to dispute with him,
they could not answer him one time out of a thousand.
4 His wisdom is profound, his power is vast.
Who has resisted him and come out unscathed?
5 He moves mountains without their knowing it
and overturns them in his anger.
6 He shakes the earth from its place
and makes its pillars tremble.
7 He speaks to the sun and it does not shine;
he seals off the light of the stars.
8 He alone stretches out the heavens
and treads on the waves of the sea.
9 He is the Maker of the Bear[a] and Orion,
the Pleiades and the constellations of the south.
10 He performs wonders that cannot be fathomed,
miracles that cannot be counted.
11 When he passes me, I cannot see him;
when he goes by, I cannot perceive him.
12 If he snatches away, who can stop him?
Who can say to him, 'What are you doing?'
13 God does not restrain his anger;
even the cohorts of Rahab cowered at his feet.

14 "How then can I dispute with him?
How can I find words to argue with him?
15 Though I were innocent, I could not answer him;
I could only plead with my Judge for mercy.
16 Even if I summoned him and he responded,
I do not believe he would give me a hearing.
17 He would crush me with a storm
and multiply my wounds for no reason.
18 He would not let me catch my breath
but would overwhelm me with misery.
19 If it is a matter of strength, he is mighty!
And if it is a matter of justice, who can challenge him[b]?
20 Even if I were innocent, my mouth would condemn me;
if I were blameless, it would pronounce me guilty.

21 "Although I am blameless,
I have no concern for myself;
I despise my own life.
22 It is all the same; that is why I say,
'He destroys both the blameless and the wicked.'
23 When a scourge brings sudden death,
he mocks the despair of the innocent.
24 When a land falls into the hands of the wicked,
he blindfolds its judges.
If it is not he, then who is it?

PRAYING SCRIPTURE

Job 9

In despair, Job began to doubt whether God heard his cries. He did not doubt God's character. He said, "[God's] wisdom is profound, his power is vast" (verse 4), but he felt his prayers were not getting through. God's greatness, Job feared, caused a gap; he lamented that there was no one to mediate on his behalf (see verse 33).

What Job did not know, we now know: Jesus Christ is our mediator who bridges the gap.

---

[a] 9 Or *of Leo* [b] 19 See Septuagint; Hebrew *me.*

25 "My days are swifter than a runner;
they fly away without a glimpse of joy.
26 They skim past like boats of papyrus,
like eagles swooping down on their prey.
27 If I say, 'I will forget my complaint,
I will change my expression, and smile,'
28 I still dread all my sufferings,
for I know you will not hold me innocent.
29 Since I am already found guilty,
why should I struggle in vain?
30 Even if I washed myself with soap
and my hands with cleansing powder,
31 you would plunge me into a slime pit
so that even my clothes would detest me.

32 "He is not a mere mortal like me that I might answer him,
that we might confront each other in court.
33 If only there were someone to mediate between us,
someone to bring us together,
34 someone to remove God's rod from me,
so that his terror would frighten me no more.
35 Then I would speak up without fear of him,
but as it now stands with me, I cannot.

PRAYING SCRIPTURE

Job 10

Job continued addressing God directly, asking if he sees us differently from the way humans see each other. Job implied that God should know he hadn't sinned and didn't deserve what had happened to him. His frustration reaches the point that he questions why he was even born.

Suffering is part and parcel of human existence. Ask God to help you trust him even when your way is as dark as death itself.

10

"I loathe my very life;
therefore I will give free rein to my complaint
and speak out in the bitterness of my soul.
2 I say to God: Do not declare me guilty,
but tell me what charges you have against me.
3 Does it please you to oppress me,
to spurn the work of your hands,
while you smile on the plans of the wicked?
4 Do you have eyes of flesh?
Do you see as a mortal sees?
5 Are your days like those of a mortal
or your years like those of a strong man,
6 that you must search out my faults
and probe after my sin—
7 though you know that I am not guilty
and that no one can rescue me from your hand?

8 "Your hands shaped me and made me.
Will you now turn and destroy me?
9 Remember that you molded me like clay.
Will you now turn me to dust again?
10 Did you not pour me out like milk
and curdle me like cheese,
11 clothe me with skin and flesh
and knit me together with bones and sinews?
12 You gave me life and showed me kindness,
and in your providence watched over my spirit.

13 "But this is what you concealed in your heart,
and I know that this was in your mind:
14 If I sinned, you would be watching me
and would not let my offense go unpunished.

15 If I am guilty — woe to me!
Even if I am innocent, I cannot lift my head,
for I am full of shame
and drowned in[a] my affliction.
16 If I hold my head high, you stalk me like a lion
and again display your awesome power against me.
17 You bring new witnesses against me
and increase your anger toward me;
your forces come against me wave upon wave.

18 "Why then did you bring me out of the womb?
I wish I had died before any eye saw me.
19 If only I had never come into being,
or had been carried straight from the womb to the grave!
20 Are not my few days almost over?
Turn away from me so I can have a moment's joy
21 before I go to the place of no return,
to the land of gloom and utter darkness,
22 to the land of deepest night,
of utter darkness and disorder,
where even the light is like darkness."

ZOPHAR

11 Then Zophar the Naamathite replied:

2 "Are all these words to go unanswered?
Is this talker to be vindicated?
3 Will your idle talk reduce others to silence?
Will no one rebuke you when you mock?
4 You say to God, 'My beliefs are flawless
and I am pure in your sight.'
5 Oh, how I wish that God would speak,
that he would open his lips against you
6 and disclose to you the secrets of wisdom,
for true wisdom has two sides.
Know this: God has even forgotten some of your sin.

7 "Can you fathom the mysteries of God?
Can you probe the limits of the Almighty?
8 They are higher than the heavens above — what can you do?
They are deeper than the depths below — what can
you know?
9 Their measure is longer than the earth
and wider than the sea.

10 "If he comes along and confines you in prison
and convenes a court, who can oppose him?
11 Surely he recognizes deceivers;
and when he sees evil, does he not take note?
12 But the witless can no more become wise
than a wild donkey's colt can be born human.[b]

13 "Yet if you devote your heart to him
and stretch out your hands to him,

PRAYING SCRIPTURE

Job 11

Have you ever tried to explain yourself only to have someone rebuke you before you could finish? Job's friend Zophar did that, accusing Job of talking too much, saying nothing and being a mocker. This is hardly the way a friend should treat one in pain.

Think for a moment about how you listen to people who are hurting. Ask God to help you lend a sympathetic ear to struggling people.

[a] 15 Or *and aware of* [b] 12 Or *wild donkey can be born tame*

14 if you put away the sin that is in your hand
and allow no evil to dwell in your tent,
15 then, free of fault, you will lift up your face;
you will stand firm and without fear.
16 You will surely forget your trouble,
recalling it only as waters gone by.
17 Life will be brighter than noonday,
and darkness will become like morning.
18 You will be secure, because there is hope;
you will look about you and take your rest in safety.
19 You will lie down, with no one to make you afraid,
and many will court your favor.
20 But the eyes of the wicked will fail,
and escape will elude them;
their hope will become a dying gasp."

JOB

12

Then Job replied:

2 "Doubtless you are the only people who matter,
and wisdom will die with you!
3 But I have a mind as well as you;
I am not inferior to you.
Who does not know all these things?

4 "I have become a laughingstock to my friends,
though I called on God and he answered —
a mere laughingstock, though righteous and blameless!
5 Those who are at ease have contempt for misfortune
as the fate of those whose feet are slipping.
6 The tents of marauders are undisturbed,
and those who provoke God are secure —
those God has in his hand.[a]

7 "But ask the animals, and they will teach you,
or the birds in the sky, and they will tell you;
8 or speak to the earth, and it will teach you,
or let the fish in the sea inform you.
9 Which of all these does not know
that the hand of the LORD has done this?
10 In his hand is the life of every creature
and the breath of all mankind.
11 Does not the ear test words
as the tongue tastes food?
12 Is not wisdom found among the aged?
Does not long life bring understanding?

13 "To God belong wisdom and power;
counsel and understanding are his.
14 What he tears down cannot be rebuilt;
those he imprisons cannot be released.
15 If he holds back the waters, there is drought;
if he lets them loose, they devastate the land.

PRAYING SCRIPTURE

Job 12

Job's defense contained a rousing defense of God himself. Asserting that even animals could teach his friends something about God, Job reminded them that God has wisdom, power, counsel and understanding. Just because they did not understand did not mean God did not understand.

No matter the lousy counsel you might get during a trial, never forget: God is aware. Rest in the assurance that he knows.

[a] 6 Or *those whose god is in their own hand*

16 To him belong strength and insight;
both deceived and deceiver are his.
17 He leads rulers away stripped
and makes fools of judges.
18 He takes off the shackles put on by kings
and ties a loincloth[a] around their waist.
19 He leads priests away stripped
and overthrows officials long established.
20 He silences the lips of trusted advisers
and takes away the discernment of elders.
21 He pours contempt on nobles
and disarms the mighty.
22 He reveals the deep things of darkness
and brings utter darkness into the light.
23 He makes nations great, and destroys them;
he enlarges nations, and disperses them.
24 He deprives the leaders of the earth of their reason;
he makes them wander in a trackless waste.
25 They grope in darkness with no light;
he makes them stagger like drunkards.

13 "My eyes have seen all this,
my ears have heard and understood it.
2 What you know, I also know;
I am not inferior to you.
3 But I desire to speak to the Almighty
and to argue my case with God.
4 You, however, smear me with lies;
you are worthless physicians, all of you!
5 If only you would be altogether silent!
For you, that would be wisdom.
6 Hear now my argument;
listen to the pleas of my lips.
7 Will you speak wickedly on God's behalf?
Will you speak deceitfully for him?
8 Will you show him partiality?
Will you argue the case for God?
9 Would it turn out well if he examined you?
Could you deceive him as you might deceive a mortal?
10 He would surely call you to account
if you secretly showed partiality.
11 Would not his splendor terrify you?
Would not the dread of him fall on you?
12 Your maxims are proverbs of ashes;
your defenses are defenses of clay.

13 "Keep silent and let me speak;
then let come to me what may.
14 Why do I put myself in jeopardy
and take my life in my hands?
15 Though he slay me, yet will I hope in him;
I will surely[b] defend my ways to his face.

PRAYING SCRIPTURE

Job 13

In a withering rebuke, Job accused his friends of assuming to speak for God but being deceitful in doing so. Then Job uttered one of the great declarations of faith in Scripture: "Though he slay me, yet will I hope in him" (verse 15).

Are you able to trust God with even your life? Stop for a moment and commit your entire life to him.

[a] 18 Or *shackles of kings / and ties a belt*

[b] 15 Or *He will surely slay me; I have no hope — / yet I will*

16 Indeed, this will turn out for my deliverance,
for no godless person would dare come before him!
17 Listen carefully to what I say;
let my words ring in your ears.
18 Now that I have prepared my case,
I know I will be vindicated.
19 Can anyone bring charges against me?
If so, I will be silent and die.

20 "Only grant me these two things, God,
and then I will not hide from you:
21 Withdraw your hand far from me,
and stop frightening me with your terrors.
22 Then summon me and I will answer,
or let me speak, and you reply to me.
23 How many wrongs and sins have I committed?
Show me my offense and my sin.
24 Why do you hide your face
and consider me your enemy?
25 Will you torment a windblown leaf?
Will you chase after dry chaff?
26 For you write down bitter things against me
and make me reap the sins of my youth.
27 You fasten my feet in shackles;
you keep close watch on all my paths
by putting marks on the soles of my feet.

28 "So man wastes away like something rotten,
like a garment eaten by moths.

14 "Mortals, born of woman,
are of few days and full of trouble.
2 They spring up like flowers and wither away;
like fleeting shadows, they do not endure.
3 Do you fix your eye on them?
Will you bring them[a] before you for judgment?
4 Who can bring what is pure from the impure?
No one!
5 A person's days are determined;
you have decreed the number of his months
and have set limits he cannot exceed.
6 So look away from him and let him alone,
till he has put in his time like a hired laborer.

7 "At least there is hope for a tree:
If it is cut down, it will sprout again,
and its new shoots will not fail.
8 Its roots may grow old in the ground
and its stump die in the soil,
9 yet at the scent of water it will bud
and put forth shoots like a plant.
10 But a man dies and is laid low;
he breathes his last and is no more.
11 As the water of a lake dries up

PRAYING SCRIPTURE

Job 14

Having transitioned to a prayer, Job confessed both his despair and his total dependence on God. He gloried in God's forgiveness, saying "My offenses will be sealed up in a bag," while admitting God's ultimate control over the end of humanity (verse 17).

Walking with God can bring conflicting feelings, including feelings that help push us to seek refuge in God. Ask God to help you seek and find him in times of trial.

[a] 3 Septuagint, Vulgate and Syriac; Hebrew *me*

or a riverbed becomes parched and dry,
12 so he lies down and does not rise;
till the heavens are no more, people will not awake
or be roused from their sleep.

13 "If only you would hide me in the grave
and conceal me till your anger has passed!
If only you would set me a time
and then remember me!
14 If someone dies, will they live again?
All the days of my hard service
I will wait for my renewal[a] to come.
15 You will call and I will answer you;
you will long for the creature your hands have made.
16 Surely then you will count my steps
but not keep track of my sin.
17 My offenses will be sealed up in a bag;
you will cover over my sin.

18 "But as a mountain erodes and crumbles
and as a rock is moved from its place,
19 as water wears away stones
and torrents wash away the soil,
so you destroy a person's hope.
20 You overpower them once for all, and they are gone;
you change their countenance and send them away.
21 If their children are honored, they do not know it;
if their offspring are brought low, they do not see it.
22 They feel but the pain of their own bodies
and mourn only for themselves."

ELIPHAZ

15 Then Eliphaz the Temanite replied:

2 "Would a wise person answer with empty notions
or fill their belly with the hot east wind?
3 Would they argue with useless words,
with speeches that have no value?
4 But you even undermine piety
and hinder devotion to God.
5 Your sin prompts your mouth;
you adopt the tongue of the crafty.
6 Your own mouth condemns you, not mine;
your own lips testify against you.

7 "Are you the first man ever born?
Were you brought forth before the hills?
8 Do you listen in on God's council?
Do you have a monopoly on wisdom?
9 What do you know that we do not know?
What insights do you have that we do not have?
10 The gray-haired and the aged are on our side,
men even older than your father.

[a] 14 Or *release*

PRAYING SCRIPTURE

Job 15

Eliphaz picked up the accusation against Job, claiming Job had turned his "rage against God" (verse 13). He accused Job of being a know-it-all who refused to listen to the wisdom of the older people around him.

Eliphaz's judgment of Job was based on his own experience rather than God's counsel. When friends offer advice, ask God to help you sift it through his Word.

11 Are God's consolations not enough for you,
words spoken gently to you?
12 Why has your heart carried you away,
and why do your eyes flash,
13 so that you vent your rage against God
and pour out such words from your mouth?

14 "What are mortals, that they could be pure,
or those born of woman, that they could be righteous?
15 If God places no trust in his holy ones,
if even the heavens are not pure in his eyes,
16 how much less mortals, who are vile and corrupt,
who drink up evil like water!

17 "Listen to me and I will explain to you;
let me tell you what I have seen,
18 what the wise have declared,
hiding nothing received from their ancestors
19 (to whom alone the land was given
when no foreigners moved among them):
20 All his days the wicked man suffers torment,
the ruthless man through all the years stored up for him.
21 Terrifying sounds fill his ears;
when all seems well, marauders attack him.
22 He despairs of escaping the realm of darkness;
he is marked for the sword.
23 He wanders about for food like a vulture;
he knows the day of darkness is at hand.
24 Distress and anguish fill him with terror;
troubles overwhelm him, like a king poised to attack,
25 because he shakes his fist at God
and vaunts himself against the Almighty,
26 defiantly charging against him
with a thick, strong shield.

27 "Though his face is covered with fat
and his waist bulges with flesh,
28 he will inhabit ruined towns
and houses where no one lives,
houses crumbling to rubble.
29 He will no longer be rich and his wealth will not endure,
nor will his possessions spread over the land.
30 He will not escape the darkness;
a flame will wither his shoots,
and the breath of God's mouth will carry him away.
31 Let him not deceive himself by trusting what is worthless,
for he will get nothing in return.
32 Before his time he will wither,
and his branches will not flourish.
33 He will be like a vine stripped of its unripe grapes,
like an olive tree shedding its blossoms.
34 For the company of the godless will be barren,
and fire will consume the tents of those who love bribes.
35 They conceive trouble and give birth to evil;
their womb fashions deceit."

JOB

16 Then Job replied:

2 "I have heard many things like these;
you are miserable comforters, all of you!
3 Will your long-winded speeches never end?
What ails you that you keep on arguing?
4 I also could speak like you,
if you were in my place;
I could make fine speeches against you
and shake my head at you.
5 But my mouth would encourage you;
comfort from my lips would bring you relief.

6 "Yet if I speak, my pain is not relieved;
and if I refrain, it does not go away.
7 Surely, God, you have worn me out;
you have devastated my entire household.
8 You have shriveled me up — and it has become a witness;
my gauntness rises up and testifies against me.
9 God assails me and tears me in his anger
and gnashes his teeth at me;
my opponent fastens on me his piercing eyes.
10 People open their mouths to jeer at me;
they strike my cheek in scorn
and unite together against me.
11 God has turned me over to the ungodly
and thrown me into the clutches of the wicked.
12 All was well with me, but he shattered me;
he seized me by the neck and crushed me.
He has made me his target;
13 his archers surround me.
Without pity, he pierces my kidneys
and spills my gall on the ground.
14 Again and again he bursts upon me;
he rushes at me like a warrior.

15 "I have sewed sackcloth over my skin
and buried my brow in the dust.
16 My face is red with weeping,
dark shadows ring my eyes;
17 yet my hands have been free of violence
and my prayer is pure.

18 "Earth, do not cover my blood;
may my cry never be laid to rest!
19 Even now my witness is in heaven;
my advocate is on high.
20 My intercessor is my friend[a]
as my eyes pour out tears to God;
21 on behalf of a man he pleads with God
as one pleads for a friend.

22 "Only a few years will pass
before I take the path of no return.

[a] 20 Or *My friends treat me with scorn*

PRAYING SCRIPTURE

Job 16

It's important to realize when people around us are not helping us get closer to God. After listening to several accusations, Job told his friends directly that they were little more than wind.

Sometimes it is hard to reject "help" when it's offered, but some counsel is simply not wise. Rest in God's love when people accuse and misjudge you.

PRAYING SCRIPTURE

Job 17

Have you ever been in a trial so difficult you did not know if you could make it another day? That's where Job was as he told God that his spirit was broken and the grave was ready to take him in.

It is Satan who wants us to despair and lose hope. Remember today that God himself is your hope and salvation, so call on him for strength to persevere.

17 1 My spirit is broken,
my days are cut short,
the grave awaits me.
2 Surely mockers surround me;
my eyes must dwell on their hostility.

3 "Give me, O God, the pledge you demand.
Who else will put up security for me?
4 You have closed their minds to understanding;
therefore you will not let them triumph.
5 If anyone denounces their friends for reward,
the eyes of their children will fail.

6 "God has made me a byword to everyone,
a man in whose face people spit.
7 My eyes have grown dim with grief;
my whole frame is but a shadow.
8 The upright are appalled at this;
the innocent are aroused against the ungodly.
9 Nevertheless, the righteous will hold to their ways,
and those with clean hands will grow stronger.

10 "But come on, all of you, try again!
I will not find a wise man among you.
11 My days have passed, my plans are shattered.
Yet the desires of my heart
12 turn night into day;
in the face of the darkness light is near.
13 If the only home I hope for is the grave,
if I spread out my bed in the realm of darkness,
14 if I say to corruption, 'You are my father,'
and to the worm, 'My mother' or 'My sister,'
15 where then is my hope —
who can see any hope for me?
16 Will it go down to the gates of death?
Will we descend together into the dust?"

PRAYING SCRIPTURE

Job 18

Bildad returned to the now familiar theme that bad things happen to bad people, not righteous people. In graphic detail he explained why Job must be guilty of some kind of wickedness, "the place of one who does not know God" (verse 21).

One thing we can learn from Job's friends is that bad assumptions don't help people who are suffering. Ask God for grace when engaging with friends in pain.

BILDAD

18 Then Bildad the Shuhite replied:

2 "When will you end these speeches?
Be sensible, and then we can talk.
3 Why are we regarded as cattle
and considered stupid in your sight?
4 You who tear yourself to pieces in your anger,
is the earth to be abandoned for your sake?
Or must the rocks be moved from their place?

5 "The lamp of a wicked man is snuffed out;
the flame of his fire stops burning.
6 The light in his tent becomes dark;
the lamp beside him goes out.
7 The vigor of his step is weakened;
his own schemes throw him down.
8 His feet thrust him into a net;
he wanders into its mesh.

9 A trap seizes him by the heel;
a snare holds him fast.
10 A noose is hidden for him on the ground;
a trap lies in his path.
11 Terrors startle him on every side
and dog his every step.
12 Calamity is hungry for him;
disaster is ready for him when he falls.
13 It eats away parts of his skin;
death's firstborn devours his limbs.
14 He is torn from the security of his tent
and marched off to the king of terrors.
15 Fire resides[a] in his tent;
burning sulfur is scattered over his dwelling.
16 His roots dry up below
and his branches wither above.
17 The memory of him perishes from the earth;
he has no name in the land.
18 He is driven from light into the realm of darkness
and is banished from the world.
19 He has no offspring or descendants among his people,
no survivor where once he lived.
20 People of the west are appalled at his fate;
those of the east are seized with horror.
21 Surely such is the dwelling of an evil man;
such is the place of one who does not know God."

JOB 19

Then Job replied:

2 "How long will you torment me
and crush me with words?
3 Ten times now you have reproached me;
shamelessly you attack me.
4 If it is true that I have gone astray,
my error remains my concern alone.
5 If indeed you would exalt yourselves above me
and use my humiliation against me,
6 then know that God has wronged me
and drawn his net around me.

7 "Though I cry, 'Violence!' I get no response;
though I call for help, there is no justice.
8 He has blocked my way so I cannot pass;
he has shrouded my paths in darkness.
9 He has stripped me of my honor
and removed the crown from my head.
10 He tears me down on every side till I am gone;
he uproots my hope like a tree.
11 His anger burns against me;
he counts me among his enemies.
12 His troops advance in force;

[a] 15 Or *Nothing he had remains*

PRAYING SCRIPTURE

Job 19

One of the most memorable declarations of faith in the Scriptures is when Job expresses certainty in a redeemer who lives (see verse 25). Not only does his redeemer live, but Job had faith that he would be resurrected in a body to stand in God's presence.

The hope of God's people is the resurrection of the body. Tell God you have faith in his resurrection power, and rejoice in that hope.

they build a siege ramp against me
and encamp around my tent.

13 "He has alienated my family from me;
my acquaintances are completely estranged from me.
14 My relatives have gone away;
my closest friends have forgotten me.
15 My guests and my female servants count me a foreigner;
they look on me as on a stranger.
16 I summon my servant, but he does not answer,
though I beg him with my own mouth.
17 My breath is offensive to my wife;
I am loathsome to my own family.
18 Even the little boys scorn me;
when I appear, they ridicule me.
19 All my intimate friends detest me;
those I love have turned against me.
20 I am nothing but skin and bones;
I have escaped only by the skin of my teeth.[a]

21 "Have pity on me, my friends, have pity,
for the hand of God has struck me.
22 Why do you pursue me as God does?
Will you never get enough of my flesh?

23 "Oh, that my words were recorded,
that they were written on a scroll,
24 that they were inscribed with an iron tool on[b] lead,
or engraved in rock forever!
25 I know that my redeemer[c] lives,
and that in the end he will stand on the earth.[d]
26 And after my skin has been destroyed,
yet[e] in[f] my flesh I will see God;
27 I myself will see him
with my own eyes — I, and not another.
How my heart yearns within me!

28 "If you say, 'How we will hound him,
since the root of the trouble lies in him,[g]'
29 you should fear the sword yourselves;
for wrath will bring punishment by the sword,
and then you will know that there is judgment.[h]"

PRAYING SCRIPTURE

Job 20

Zophar's speech about the end of the wicked contains warnings worthy of meditation: The wicked do experience only short triumphs, they do reap what they sow, their works will come to naught. He also specified that the wicked oppress the poor and leave them destitute.

God hates to see the poor mistreated. Ask God to make you aware of the needy around you so you can minister to them in his love.

ZOPHAR

20

Then Zophar the Naamathite replied:

2 "My troubled thoughts prompt me to answer
because I am greatly disturbed.
3 I hear a rebuke that dishonors me,
and my understanding inspires me to reply.

---

[a] 20 Or *only by my gums* [b] 24 Or *and* [c] 25 Or *vindicator* [d] 25 Or *on my grave* [e] 26 Or *And after I awake, / though this body has been destroyed, / then* [f] 26 Or *destroyed, / apart from* [g] 28 Many Hebrew manuscripts, Septuagint and Vulgate; most Hebrew manuscripts *me* [h] 29 Or *sword, / that you may come to know the Almighty*

4 "Surely you know how it has been from of old,
ever since mankind[a] was placed on the earth,
5 that the mirth of the wicked is brief,
the joy of the godless lasts but a moment.
6 Though the pride of the godless person reaches to the heavens
and his head touches the clouds,
7 he will perish forever, like his own dung;
those who have seen him will say, 'Where is he?'
8 Like a dream he flies away, no more to be found,
banished like a vision of the night.
9 The eye that saw him will not see him again;
his place will look on him no more.
10 His children must make amends to the poor;
his own hands must give back his wealth.
11 The youthful vigor that fills his bones
will lie with him in the dust.

12 "Though evil is sweet in his mouth
and he hides it under his tongue,
13 though he cannot bear to let it go
and lets it linger in his mouth,
14 yet his food will turn sour in his stomach;
it will become the venom of serpents within him.
15 He will spit out the riches he swallowed;
God will make his stomach vomit them up.
16 He will suck the poison of serpents;
the fangs of an adder will kill him.
17 He will not enjoy the streams,
the rivers flowing with honey and cream.
18 What he toiled for he must give back uneaten;
he will not enjoy the profit from his trading.
19 For he has oppressed the poor and left them destitute;
he has seized houses he did not build.

20 "Surely he will have no respite from his craving;
he cannot save himself by his treasure.
21 Nothing is left for him to devour;
his prosperity will not endure.
22 In the midst of his plenty, distress will overtake him;
the full force of misery will come upon him.
23 When he has filled his belly,
God will vent his burning anger against him
and rain down his blows on him.
24 Though he flees from an iron weapon,
a bronze-tipped arrow pierces him.
25 He pulls it out of his back,
the gleaming point out of his liver.
Terrors will come over him;
26 total darkness lies in wait for his treasures.
A fire unfanned will consume him
and devour what is left in his tent.
27 The heavens will expose his guilt;
the earth will rise up against him.

---

[a] 4 Or *Adam*

28 A flood will carry off his house,
rushing waters[a] on the day of God's wrath.
29 Such is the fate God allots the wicked,
the heritage appointed for them by God."

PRAYING SCRIPTURE

Job 21

After a number of discourses, Job directly challenged the theology of his friends. If suffering is always the result of God's judging wickedness, he asked, why do the wicked live long, become powerful, have large flocks and love to party?

Job rightly concluded that human beings cannot comprehend why some people live well while others die in bitterness of soul. Praise God for his wisdom that always blesses and curses rightly.

JOB 21

21 Then Job replied:

2 "Listen carefully to my words;
let this be the consolation you give me.
3 Bear with me while I speak,
and after I have spoken, mock on.

4 "Is my complaint directed to a human being?
Why should I not be impatient?
5 Look at me and be appalled;
clap your hand over your mouth.
6 When I think about this, I am terrified;
trembling seizes my body.
7 Why do the wicked live on,
growing old and increasing in power?
8 They see their children established around them,
their offspring before their eyes.
9 Their homes are safe and free from fear;
the rod of God is not on them.
10 Their bulls never fail to breed;
their cows calve and do not miscarry.
11 They send forth their children as a flock;
their little ones dance about.
12 They sing to the music of timbrel and lyre;
they make merry to the sound of the pipe.
13 They spend their years in prosperity
and go down to the grave in peace.[b]
14 Yet they say to God, 'Leave us alone!
We have no desire to know your ways.
15 Who is the Almighty, that we should serve him?
What would we gain by praying to him?'
16 But their prosperity is not in their own hands,
so I stand aloof from the plans of the wicked.

17 "Yet how often is the lamp of the wicked snuffed out?
How often does calamity come upon them,
the fate God allots in his anger?
18 How often are they like straw before the wind,
like chaff swept away by a gale?
19 It is said, 'God stores up the punishment of the wicked for their children.'
Let him repay the wicked, so that they themselves will experience it!
20 Let their own eyes see their destruction;
let them drink the cup of the wrath of the Almighty.
21 For what do they care about the families they leave behind
when their allotted months come to an end?

---

[a] 28 Or *The possessions in his house will be carried off, / washed away*
[b] 13 Or *in an instant*

22 "Can anyone teach knowledge to God,
since he judges even the highest?
23 One person dies in full vigor,
completely secure and at ease,
24 well nourished in body,[a]
bones rich with marrow.
25 Another dies in bitterness of soul,
never having enjoyed anything good.
26 Side by side they lie in the dust,
and worms cover them both.

27 "I know full well what you are thinking,
the schemes by which you would wrong me.
28 You say, 'Where now is the house of the great,
the tents where the wicked lived?'
29 Have you never questioned those who travel?
Have you paid no regard to their accounts—
30 that the wicked are spared from the day of calamity,
that they are delivered from[b] the day of wrath?
31 Who denounces their conduct to their face?
Who repays them for what they have done?
32 They are carried to the grave,
and watch is kept over their tombs.
33 The soil in the valley is sweet to them;
everyone follows after them,
and a countless throng goes[c] before them.

34 "So how can you console me with your nonsense?
Nothing is left of your answers but falsehood!"

ELIPHAZ

22 Then Eliphaz the Temanite replied:

2 "Can a man be of benefit to God?
Can even a wise person benefit him?
3 What pleasure would it give the Almighty if you were righteous?
What would he gain if your ways were blameless?

4 "Is it for your piety that he rebukes you
and brings charges against you?
5 Is not your wickedness great?
Are not your sins endless?
6 You demanded security from your relatives for no reason;
you stripped people of their clothing, leaving them naked.
7 You gave no water to the weary
and you withheld food from the hungry,
8 though you were a powerful man, owning land—
an honored man, living on it.
9 And you sent widows away empty-handed
and broke the strength of the fatherless.
10 That is why snares are all around you,
why sudden peril terrifies you,

[a] 24 The meaning of the Hebrew for this word is uncertain. [b] 30 Or *wicked are reserved for the day of calamity, / that they are brought forth to* [c] 33 Or *them, / as a countless throng went*

PRAYING SCRIPTURE

Job 22

Eliphaz returned to the debate with the strongest condemnation of Job yet: "Is not your wickedness great? Are not your sins endless?" (verse 5). Job's friends seem to have lost all empathy in their determination to convince him that he has sinned.

Sometimes, like Job, you might have attackers who grow crueler and lie. Commit their judgment to God while you continue to walk with him.

11 why it is so dark you cannot see,
and why a flood of water covers you.

12 "Is not God in the heights of heaven?
And see how lofty are the highest stars!
13 Yet you say, 'What does God know?
Does he judge through such darkness?
14 Thick clouds veil him, so he does not see us
as he goes about in the vaulted heavens.'
15 Will you keep to the old path
that the wicked have trod?
16 They were carried off before their time,
their foundations washed away by a flood.
17 They said to God, 'Leave us alone!
What can the Almighty do to us?'
18 Yet it was he who filled their houses with good things,
so I stand aloof from the plans of the wicked.
19 The righteous see their ruin and rejoice;
the innocent mock them, saying,
20 'Surely our foes are destroyed,
and fire devours their wealth.'

21 "Submit to God and be at peace with him;
in this way prosperity will come to you.
22 Accept instruction from his mouth
and lay up his words in your heart.
23 If you return to the Almighty, you will be restored:
If you remove wickedness far from your tent
24 and assign your nuggets to the dust,
your gold of Ophir to the rocks in the ravines,
25 then the Almighty will be your gold,
the choicest silver for you.
26 Surely then you will find delight in the Almighty
and will lift up your face to God.
27 You will pray to him, and he will hear you,
and you will fulfill your vows.
28 What you decide on will be done,
and light will shine on your ways.
29 When people are brought low and you say, 'Lift them up!'
then he will save the downcast.
30 He will deliver even one who is not innocent,
who will be delivered through the cleanness of your hands."

JOB 23

23 Then Job replied:

2 "Even today my complaint is bitter;
his hand[a] is heavy in spite of[b] my groaning.
3 If only I knew where to find him;
if only I could go to his dwelling!
4 I would state my case before him
and fill my mouth with arguments.
5 I would find out what he would answer me,

[a] 2 Septuagint and Syriac; Hebrew / *the hand on me* [b] 2 Or *heavy on me in*

PRAYING SCRIPTURE

Job 23

Have you ever felt abandoned by God, as if he suddenly disappeared and you were alone? Job expressed this feeling in beautiful language (see verses 8–10), saying that no matter where he looked—north, south, east or west—he couldn't see God. But Job said with confidence that God knew his way.

Even when you don't know where God is, he knows where you are. Thank him for his constant watchfulness.

and consider what he would say to me.
6 Would he vigorously oppose me?
No, he would not press charges against me.
7 There the upright can establish their innocence before him,
and there I would be delivered forever from my judge.

8 "But if I go to the east, he is not there;
if I go to the west, I do not find him.
9 When he is at work in the north, I do not see him;
when he turns to the south, I catch no glimpse of him.
10 But he knows the way that I take;
when he has tested me, I will come forth as gold.
11 My feet have closely followed his steps;
I have kept to his way without turning aside.
12 I have not departed from the commands of his lips;
I have treasured the words of his mouth more than my daily bread.

13 "But he stands alone, and who can oppose him?
He does whatever he pleases.
14 He carries out his decree against me,
and many such plans he still has in store.
15 That is why I am terrified before him;
when I think of all this, I fear him.
16 God has made my heart faint;
the Almighty has terrified me.
17 Yet I am not silenced by the darkness,
by the thick darkness that covers my face.

24 "Why does the Almighty not set times for judgment?
Why must those who know him look in vain for such days?
2 There are those who move boundary stones;
they pasture flocks they have stolen.
3 They drive away the orphan's donkey
and take the widow's ox in pledge.
4 They thrust the needy from the path
and force all the poor of the land into hiding.
5 Like wild donkeys in the desert,
the poor go about their labor of foraging food;
the wasteland provides food for their children.
6 They gather fodder in the fields
and glean in the vineyards of the wicked.
7 Lacking clothes, they spend the night naked;
they have nothing to cover themselves in the cold.
8 They are drenched by mountain rains
and hug the rocks for lack of shelter.
9 The fatherless child is snatched from the breast;
the infant of the poor is seized for a debt.
10 Lacking clothes, they go about naked;
they carry the sheaves, but still go hungry.
11 They crush olives among the terraces[a];
they tread the winepresses, yet suffer thirst.

[a] 11 The meaning of the Hebrew for this word is uncertain.

PRAYING SCRIPTURE

Job 24

Job argued that the presence of evil in this world does not mean that God is not paying attention. His friends were wrong because they didn't understand: God's judgment is not always immediate, but it always comes in the end.

Questioning the timing of God's judgment can cause us to lose faith. His timing is perfect, but our understanding is not. Ask God to strengthen your faith in his ways.

12 The groans of the dying rise from the city,
and the souls of the wounded cry out for help.
But God charges no one with wrongdoing.

13 "There are those who rebel against the light,
who do not know its ways
or stay in its paths.
14 When daylight is gone, the murderer rises up,
kills the poor and needy,
and in the night steals forth like a thief.
15 The eye of the adulterer watches for dusk;
he thinks, 'No eye will see me,'
and he keeps his face concealed.
16 In the dark, thieves break into houses,
but by day they shut themselves in;
they want nothing to do with the light.
17 For all of them, midnight is their morning;
they make friends with the terrors of darkness.

18 "Yet they are foam on the surface of the water;
their portion of the land is cursed,
so that no one goes to the vineyards.
19 As heat and drought snatch away the melted snow,
so the grave snatches away those who have sinned.
20 The womb forgets them,
the worm feasts on them;
the wicked are no longer remembered
but are broken like a tree.
21 They prey on the barren and childless woman,
and to the widow they show no kindness.
22 But God drags away the mighty by his power;
though they become established, they have no assurance
of life.
23 He may let them rest in a feeling of security,
but his eyes are on their ways.
24 For a little while they are exalted, and then they are gone;
they are brought low and gathered up like all others;
they are cut off like heads of grain.

25 "If this is not so, who can prove me false
and reduce my words to nothing?"

BILDAD

25 Then Bildad the Shuhite replied:

2 "Dominion and awe belong to God;
he establishes order in the heights of heaven.
3 Can his forces be numbered?
On whom does his light not rise?
4 How then can a mortal be righteous before God?
How can one born of woman be pure?
5 If even the moon is not bright
and the stars are not pure in his eyes,
6 how much less a mortal, who is but a maggot —
a human being, who is only a worm!"

PRAYING SCRIPTURE

Job 25

Job's friend Bildad asked the question of eternity: "How then can a mortal be righteous before God?" (verse 4). Unless we are able to answer that question rightly, we will enter eternity without the assurance that we are properly related to God. But thanks be to God that he has answered this question in Jesus!

Pause and thank God that Jesus' righteousness becomes the righteousness of all who believe in him.

JOB

26

Then Job replied:

2 "How you have helped the powerless!
How you have saved the arm that is feeble!
3 What advice you have offered to one without wisdom!
And what great insight you have displayed!
4 Who has helped you utter these words?
And whose spirit spoke from your mouth?

5 "The dead are in deep anguish,
those beneath the waters and all that live in them.
6 The realm of the dead is naked before God;
Destruction[a] lies uncovered.
7 He spreads out the northern skies over empty space;
he suspends the earth over nothing.
8 He wraps up the waters in his clouds,
yet the clouds do not burst under their weight.
9 He covers the face of the full moon,
spreading his clouds over it.
10 He marks out the horizon on the face of the waters
for a boundary between light and darkness.
11 The pillars of the heavens quake,
aghast at his rebuke.
12 By his power he churned up the sea;
by his wisdom he cut Rahab to pieces.
13 By his breath the skies became fair;
his hand pierced the gliding serpent.
14 And these are but the outer fringe of his works;
how faint the whisper we hear of him!
Who then can understand the thunder of his power?"

JOB'S FINAL WORD TO HIS FRIENDS

27

And Job continued his discourse:

2 "As surely as God lives, who has denied me justice,
the Almighty, who has made my life bitter,
3 as long as I have life within me,
the breath of God in my nostrils,
4 my lips will not say anything wicked,
and my tongue will not utter lies.
5 I will never admit you are in the right;
till I die, I will not deny my integrity.
6 I will maintain my innocence and never let go of it;
my conscience will not reproach me as long as I live.

7 "May my enemy be like the wicked,
my adversary like the unjust!
8 For what hope have the godless when they are cut off,
when God takes away their life?
9 Does God listen to their cry
when distress comes upon them?
10 Will they find delight in the Almighty?
Will they call on God at all times?

[a] 6 Hebrew *Abaddon*

PRAYING SCRIPTURE

Job 26

Job's next challenge pointed out his friends' limitations and God's omnipotence. His friends could not bring anything to life or help the powerless. God, on the other hand, is the Creator by whom the entire universe is held in place. Indeed, what we see "are but the outer fringe of his works" (verse 14).

Consider God's ability. Never hesitate to call on him. His power is limitless, and he will aid his children.

PRAYING SCRIPTURE

Job 27

Sometimes all we have to fall back on is our own integrity. When falsely accused, we know the truth. We know when we've walked forthrightly with God, when we've trusted God with our whole heart and pursued him with all our strength.

God's children do not have to receive the arrows of the wicked one. Take the enemy's complaints to God and leave them there. Trust God's loving care at all times.

11 "I will teach you about the power of God;
the ways of the Almighty I will not conceal.
12 You have all seen this yourselves.
Why then this meaningless talk?

13 "Here is the fate God allots to the wicked,
the heritage a ruthless man receives from the Almighty:
14 However many his children, their fate is the sword;
his offspring will never have enough to eat.
15 The plague will bury those who survive him,
and their widows will not weep for them.
16 Though he heaps up silver like dust
and clothes like piles of clay,
17 what he lays up the righteous will wear,
and the innocent will divide his silver.
18 The house he builds is like a moth's cocoon,
like a hut made by a watchman.
19 He lies down wealthy, but will do so no more;
when he opens his eyes, all is gone.
20 Terrors overtake him like a flood;
a tempest snatches him away in the night.
21 The east wind carries him off, and he is gone;
it sweeps him out of his place.
22 It hurls itself against him without mercy
as he flees headlong from its power.
23 It claps its hands in derision
and hisses him out of his place."

INTERLUDE: WHERE WISDOM IS FOUND

28 There is a mine for silver
and a place where gold is refined.
2 Iron is taken from the earth,
and copper is smelted from ore.
3 Mortals put an end to the darkness;
they search out the farthest recesses
for ore in the blackest darkness.
4 Far from human dwellings they cut a shaft,
in places untouched by human feet;
far from other people they dangle and sway.
5 The earth, from which food comes,
is transformed below as by fire;
6 lapis lazuli comes from its rocks,
and its dust contains nuggets of gold.
7 No bird of prey knows that hidden path,
no falcon's eye has seen it.
8 Proud beasts do not set foot on it,
and no lion prowls there.
9 People assault the flinty rock with their hands
and lay bare the roots of the mountains.
10 They tunnel through the rock;
their eyes see all its treasures.
11 They search[a] the sources of the rivers
and bring hidden things to light.

PRAYING SCRIPTURE

Job 28

Job's lengthy discourse on wisdom contains the poetry of jewels and precious metals. If humans found earth's valuables, would that bring wisdom? To find wisdom we should seek God. "The fear of the Lord—that is wisdom" (verse 28). Where are some of the places you have sought wisdom? True wisdom comes from God, its source. Fear him and you will find wisdom.

[a] 11 Septuagint, Aquila and Vulgate; Hebrew *They dam up*

12 But where can wisdom be found?
Where does understanding dwell?
13 No mortal comprehends its worth;
it cannot be found in the land of the living.
14 The deep says, "It is not in me";
the sea says, "It is not with me."
15 It cannot be bought with the finest gold,
nor can its price be weighed out in silver.
16 It cannot be bought with the gold of Ophir,
with precious onyx or lapis lazuli.
17 Neither gold nor crystal can compare with it,
nor can it be had for jewels of gold.
18 Coral and jasper are not worthy of mention;
the price of wisdom is beyond rubies.
19 The topaz of Cush cannot compare with it;
it cannot be bought with pure gold.

20 Where then does wisdom come from?
Where does understanding dwell?
21 It is hidden from the eyes of every living thing,
concealed even from the birds in the sky.
22 Destruction[a] and Death say,
"Only a rumor of it has reached our ears."
23 God understands the way to it
and he alone knows where it dwells,
24 for he views the ends of the earth
and sees everything under the heavens.
25 When he established the force of the wind
and measured out the waters,
26 when he made a decree for the rain
and a path for the thunderstorm,
27 then he looked at wisdom and appraised it;
he confirmed it and tested it.
28 And he said to the human race,
"The fear of the Lord — that is wisdom,
and to shun evil is understanding."

JOB'S FINAL DEFENSE

29 Job continued his discourse:

2 "How I long for the months gone by,
for the days when God watched over me,
3 when his lamp shone on my head
and by his light I walked through darkness!
4 Oh, for the days when I was in my prime,
when God's intimate friendship blessed my house,
5 when the Almighty was still with me
and my children were around me,
6 when my path was drenched with cream
and the rock poured out for me streams of olive oil.

7 "When I went to the gate of the city
and took my seat in the public square,

[a] 22 Hebrew *Abaddon*

PRAYING SCRIPTURE

Job 29

Have you ever thought about life and wondered what happened? As Job thought about the earlier, better days of his life, he believed all those blessings were the result of God's watching over him. He was not yet aware that even in his calamity, God watched over him still.

It's dangerous to form thoughts about God by comparing life's events. Thank God for being loving at all times.

8 the young men saw me and stepped aside
and the old men rose to their feet;
9 the chief men refrained from speaking
and covered their mouths with their hands;
10 the voices of the nobles were hushed,
and their tongues stuck to the roof of their mouths.
11 Whoever heard me spoke well of me,
and those who saw me commended me,
12 because I rescued the poor who cried for help,
and the fatherless who had none to assist them.
13 The one who was dying blessed me;
I made the widow's heart sing.
14 I put on righteousness as my clothing;
justice was my robe and my turban.
15 I was eyes to the blind
and feet to the lame.
16 I was a father to the needy;
I took up the case of the stranger.
17 I broke the fangs of the wicked
and snatched the victims from their teeth.

18 "I thought, 'I will die in my own house,
my days as numerous as the grains of sand.
19 My roots will reach to the water,
and the dew will lie all night on my branches.
20 My glory will not fade;
the bow will be ever new in my hand.'

21 "People listened to me expectantly,
waiting in silence for my counsel.
22 After I had spoken, they spoke no more;
my words fell gently on their ears.
23 They waited for me as for showers
and drank in my words as the spring rain.
24 When I smiled at them, they scarcely believed it;
the light of my face was precious to them.[a]
25 I chose the way for them and sat as their chief;
I dwelt as a king among his troops;
I was like one who comforts mourners.

30 "But now they mock me,
men younger than I,
whose fathers I would have disdained
to put with my sheep dogs.
2 Of what use was the strength of their hands to me,
since their vigor had gone from them?
3 Haggard from want and hunger,
they roamed[b] the parched land
in desolate wastelands at night.
4 In the brush they gathered salt herbs,
and their food[c] was the root of the broom bush.
5 They were banished from human society,
shouted at as if they were thieves.

PRAYING SCRIPTURE

Job 30

Job's defense turned into a lament. He cried out against God's silence in the face of the men's taunts. Having lost almost everything and everyone he loved, and now suffering with a physical illness, he described himself as churning in his suffering, his skin peeling, having a fever and crying out for help. Job was in the midst of a traumatic life event, and he was emotionally spent.

We often tell our friends exactly how we feel but somehow think God will be offended. If you are broken and hurting, tell God exactly how you feel, as Job did.

[a] 24 The meaning of the Hebrew for this clause is uncertain. [b] 3 Or *gnawed* [c] 4 Or *fuel*

6 They were forced to live in the dry stream beds,
among the rocks and in holes in the ground.
7 They brayed among the bushes
and huddled in the undergrowth.
8 A base and nameless brood,
they were driven out of the land.

9 "And now those young men mock me in song;
I have become a byword among them.
10 They detest me and keep their distance;
they do not hesitate to spit in my face.
11 Now that God has unstrung my bow and afflicted me,
they throw off restraint in my presence.
12 On my right the tribe[a] attacks;
they lay snares for my feet,
they build their siege ramps against me.
13 They break up my road;
they succeed in destroying me.
'No one can help him,' they say.
14 They advance as through a gaping breach;
amid the ruins they come rolling in.
15 Terrors overwhelm me;
my dignity is driven away as by the wind,
my safety vanishes like a cloud.

16 "And now my life ebbs away;
days of suffering grip me.
17 Night pierces my bones;
my gnawing pains never rest.
18 In his great power God becomes like clothing to me[b];
he binds me like the neck of my garment.
19 He throws me into the mud,
and I am reduced to dust and ashes.

20 "I cry out to you, God, but you do not answer;
I stand up, but you merely look at me.
21 You turn on me ruthlessly;
with the might of your hand you attack me.
22 You snatch me up and drive me before the wind;
you toss me about in the storm.
23 I know you will bring me down to death,
to the place appointed for all the living.

24 "Surely no one lays a hand on a broken man
when he cries for help in his distress.
25 Have I not wept for those in trouble?
Has not my soul grieved for the poor?
26 Yet when I hoped for good, evil came;
when I looked for light, then came darkness.
27 The churning inside me never stops;
days of suffering confront me.
28 I go about blackened, but not by the sun;
I stand up in the assembly and cry for help.

---

[a] *12* The meaning of the Hebrew for this word is uncertain. [b] *18* Hebrew; Septuagint *power he grasps my clothing*

29 I have become a brother of jackals,
a companion of owls.
30 My skin grows black and peels;
my body burns with fever.
31 My lyre is tuned to mourning,
and my pipe to the sound of wailing.

PRAYING SCRIPTURE

Job 31

Job responded to his friends in this chapter and defended his integrity against their assaults. He testified to his moral purity and the purity of his motives in the way that he treated people. His words sound strange to us, but they are his response to accusations against his character.

As you pray, ask God to examine your heart and reveal any hidden sins, and then ask him to cleanse you from them.

31 "I made a covenant with my eyes
not to look lustfully at a young woman.
2 For what is our lot from God above,
our heritage from the Almighty on high?
3 Is it not ruin for the wicked,
disaster for those who do wrong?
4 Does he not see my ways
and count my every step?

5 "If I have walked with falsehood
or my foot has hurried after deceit —
6 let God weigh me in honest scales
and he will know that I am blameless —
7 if my steps have turned from the path,
if my heart has been led by my eyes,
or if my hands have been defiled,
8 then may others eat what I have sown,
and may my crops be uprooted.

9 "If my heart has been enticed by a woman,
or if I have lurked at my neighbor's door,
10 then may my wife grind another man's grain,
and may other men sleep with her.
11 For that would have been wicked,
a sin to be judged.
12 It is a fire that burns to Destruction[a];
it would have uprooted my harvest.

13 "If I have denied justice to any of my servants,
whether male or female,
when they had a grievance against me,
14 what will I do when God confronts me?
What will I answer when called to account?
15 Did not he who made me in the womb make them?
Did not the same one form us both within our mothers?

16 "If I have denied the desires of the poor
or let the eyes of the widow grow weary,
17 if I have kept my bread to myself,
not sharing it with the fatherless —
18 but from my youth I reared them as a father would,
and from my birth I guided the widow —
19 if I have seen anyone perishing for lack of clothing,
or the needy without garments,
20 and their hearts did not bless me
for warming them with the fleece from my sheep,
21 if I have raised my hand against the fatherless,
knowing that I had influence in court,

[a] 12 Hebrew *Abaddon*

22 then let my arm fall from the shoulder,
let it be broken off at the joint.
23 For I dreaded destruction from God,
and for fear of his splendor I could not do such things.

24 "If I have put my trust in gold
or said to pure gold, 'You are my security,'
25 if I have rejoiced over my great wealth,
the fortune my hands had gained,
26 if I have regarded the sun in its radiance
or the moon moving in splendor,
27 so that my heart was secretly enticed
and my hand offered them a kiss of homage,
28 then these also would be sins to be judged,
for I would have been unfaithful to God on high.

29 "If I have rejoiced at my enemy's misfortune
or gloated over the trouble that came to him —
30 I have not allowed my mouth to sin
by invoking a curse against their life —
31 if those of my household have never said,
'Who has not been filled with Job's meat?' —
32 but no stranger had to spend the night in the street,
for my door was always open to the traveler —
33 if I have concealed my sin as people do,[a]
by hiding my guilt in my heart
34 because I so feared the crowd
and so dreaded the contempt of the clans
that I kept silent and would not go outside —

35 ("Oh, that I had someone to hear me!
I sign now my defense — let the Almighty answer me;
let my accuser put his indictment in writing.
36 Surely I would wear it on my shoulder,
I would put it on like a crown.
37 I would give him an account of my every step;
I would present it to him as to a ruler.) —

38 "if my land cries out against me
and all its furrows are wet with tears,
39 if I have devoured its yield without payment
or broken the spirit of its tenants,
40 then let briers come up instead of wheat
and stinkweed instead of barley."

The words of Job are ended.

ELIHU

32 So these three men stopped answering Job, because he was
righteous in his own eyes. 2 But Elihu son of Barakel the Bu-
zite, of the family of Ram, became very angry with Job for justifying
himself rather than God. 3 He was also angry with the three friends,
because they had found no way to refute Job, and yet had condemned
him.[b] 4 Now Elihu had waited before speaking to Job because they were

[a] *33* Or *as Adam did* [b] *3* Masoretic Text; an ancient Hebrew scribal tradition *Job, and so had condemned God*

PRAYING SCRIPTURE

Job 32

A fourth man, a friend of Job's friends, entered the conversation disagreeing with both sides. He chastened his friends that "they had found no way to refute Job, and yet had condemned him" while suggesting that Job justified himself rather than God (see verses 2–3).

When mediating an argument, don't assume the right answer is always between the disagreeing parties. Ask God to show you his way, wherever it is.

older than he. 5But when he saw that the three men had nothing more
to say, his anger was aroused.

6So Elihu son of Barakel the Buzite said:

"I am young in years,
and you are old;
that is why I was fearful,
not daring to tell you what I know.
7 I thought, 'Age should speak;
advanced years should teach wisdom.'
8 But it is the spirit[a] in a person,
the breath of the Almighty, that gives them understanding.
9 It is not only the old[b] who are wise,
not only the aged who understand what is right.

10 "Therefore I say: Listen to me;
I too will tell you what I know.
11 I waited while you spoke,
I listened to your reasoning;
while you were searching for words,
12 I gave you my full attention.
But not one of you has proved Job wrong;
none of you has answered his arguments.
13 Do not say, 'We have found wisdom;
let God, not a man, refute him.'
14 But Job has not marshaled his words against me,
and I will not answer him with your arguments.

15 "They are dismayed and have no more to say;
words have failed them.
16 Must I wait, now that they are silent,
now that they stand there with no reply?
17 I too will have my say;
I too will tell what I know.
18 For I am full of words,
and the spirit within me compels me;
19 inside I am like bottled-up wine,
like new wineskins ready to burst.
20 I must speak and find relief;
I must open my lips and reply.
21 I will show no partiality,
nor will I flatter anyone;
22 for if I were skilled in flattery,
my Maker would soon take me away.

33 "But now, Job, listen to my words;
pay attention to everything I say.
2 I am about to open my mouth;
my words are on the tip of my tongue.
3 My words come from an upright heart;
my lips sincerely speak what I know.
4 The Spirit of God has made me;
the breath of the Almighty gives me life.
5 Answer me then, if you can;
stand up and argue your case before me.

[a] 8 Or *Spirit*; also in verse 18 [b] 9 Or *many*; or *great*

PRAYING SCRIPTURE

Job 33

Elihu asserted that Job's real problem was not his argument with his friends, but his complaint that God does not respond to man's words. He believed Job was indeed guilty, and he asserted quite arrogantly that if Job would be quiet and listen, then he (Elihu) would teach him wisdom.

Try not to be the friend who thinks he or she knows everything. Everyone who is struggling should be approached humbly because God might be teaching us!

6 I am the same as you in God's sight;
I too am a piece of clay.
7 No fear of me should alarm you,
nor should my hand be heavy on you.

8 "But you have said in my hearing —
I heard the very words —
9 'I am pure, I have done no wrong;
I am clean and free from sin.
10 Yet God has found fault with me;
he considers me his enemy.
11 He fastens my feet in shackles;
he keeps close watch on all my paths.'

12 "But I tell you, in this you are not right,
for God is greater than any mortal.
13 Why do you complain to him
that he responds to no one's words[a]?
14 For God does speak — now one way, now another —
though no one perceives it.
15 In a dream, in a vision of the night,
when deep sleep falls on people
as they slumber in their beds,
16 he may speak in their ears
and terrify them with warnings,
17 to turn them from wrongdoing
and keep them from pride,
18 to preserve them from the pit,
their lives from perishing by the sword.[b]

19 "Or someone may be chastened on a bed of pain
with constant distress in their bones,
20 so that their body finds food repulsive
and their soul loathes the choicest meal.
21 Their flesh wastes away to nothing,
and their bones, once hidden, now stick out.
22 They draw near to the pit,
and their life to the messengers of death.[c]
23 Yet if there is an angel at their side,
a messenger, one out of a thousand,
sent to tell them how to be upright,
24 and he is gracious to that person and says to God,
'Spare them from going down to the pit;
I have found a ransom for them —
25 let their flesh be renewed like a child's;
let them be restored as in the days of their youth' —
26 then that person can pray to God and find favor with him,
they will see God's face and shout for joy;
he will restore them to full well-being.
27 And they will go to others and say,
'I have sinned, I have perverted what is right,
but I did not get what I deserved.

[a] 13 *Or that he does not answer for any of his actions* [b] 18 Or *from crossing the river* [c] 22 Or *to the place of the dead*

28 God has delivered me from going down to the pit,
and I shall live to enjoy the light of life.'

29 "God does all these things to a person —
twice, even three times —
30 to turn them back from the pit,
that the light of life may shine on them.

31 "Pay attention, Job, and listen to me;
be silent, and I will speak.
32 If you have anything to say, answer me;
speak up, for I want to vindicate you.
33 But if not, then listen to me;
be silent, and I will teach you wisdom."

PRAYING SCRIPTURE

Job 34

The thrust of Elihu's argument was that God will never pervert justice (which is correct), but that Job's suffering had to be punishment for sin (which was incorrect). Elihu believed people get what they deserve. He left no room for mercy.

People who know God don't get what they deserve. Thank God for his mercy that covers your sins and his grace that blesses you in abundance.

34

Then Elihu said:

2 "Hear my words, you wise men;
listen to me, you men of learning.
3 For the ear tests words
as the tongue tastes food.
4 Let us discern for ourselves what is right;
let us learn together what is good.

5 "Job says, 'I am innocent,
but God denies me justice.
6 Although I am right,
I am considered a liar;
although I am guiltless,
his arrow inflicts an incurable wound.'
7 Is there anyone like Job,
who drinks scorn like water?
8 He keeps company with evildoers;
he associates with the wicked.
9 For he says, 'There is no profit
in trying to please God.'

10 "So listen to me, you men of understanding.
Far be it from God to do evil,
from the Almighty to do wrong.
11 He repays everyone for what they have done;
he brings on them what their conduct deserves.
12 It is unthinkable that God would do wrong,
that the Almighty would pervert justice.
13 Who appointed him over the earth?
Who put him in charge of the whole world?
14 If it were his intention
and he withdrew his spirit[a] and breath,
15 all humanity would perish together
and mankind would return to the dust.

16 "If you have understanding, hear this;
listen to what I say.
17 Can someone who hates justice govern?

[a] 14 Or *Spirit*

Will you condemn the just and mighty One?
18 Is he not the One who says to kings, 'You are worthless,'
and to nobles, 'You are wicked,'
19 who shows no partiality to princes
and does not favor the rich over the poor,
for they are all the work of his hands?
20 They die in an instant, in the middle of the night;
the people are shaken and they pass away;
the mighty are removed without human hand.

21 "His eyes are on the ways of mortals;
he sees their every step.
22 There is no deep shadow, no utter darkness,
where evildoers can hide.
23 God has no need to examine people further,
that they should come before him for judgment.
24 Without inquiry he shatters the mighty
and sets up others in their place.
25 Because he takes note of their deeds,
he overthrows them in the night and they are crushed.
26 He punishes them for their wickedness
where everyone can see them,
27 because they turned from following him
and had no regard for any of his ways.
28 They caused the cry of the poor to come before him,
so that he heard the cry of the needy.
29 But if he remains silent, who can condemn him?
If he hides his face, who can see him?
Yet he is over individual and nation alike,
30 to keep the godless from ruling,
from laying snares for the people.

31 "Suppose someone says to God,
'I am guilty but will offend no more.
32 Teach me what I cannot see;
if I have done wrong, I will not do so again.'
33 Should God then reward you on your terms,
when you refuse to repent?
You must decide, not I;
so tell me what you know.

34 "Men of understanding declare,
wise men who hear me say to me,
35 'Job speaks without knowledge;
his words lack insight.'
36 Oh, that Job might be tested to the utmost
for answering like a wicked man!
37 To his sin he adds rebellion;
scornfully he claps his hands among us
and multiplies his words against God."

35

Then Elihu said:

2 "Do you think this is just?
You say, 'I am in the right, not God.'

PRAYING SCRIPTURE

Job 35

Although Elihu accused Job wrongly, he included an accurate statement about God's self-sufficiency: There is nothing we can give God, nor does he need our righteousness (see verse 7). God is wholly complete and all-knowing in everything he does.

God needs nothing, and because of that, he is and has anything we need. As you pray, ask God to handle the biggest needs in your life.

[3]Yet you ask him, 'What profit is it to me,[a]
and what do I gain by not sinning?'

[4]"I would like to reply to you
and to your friends with you.
[5]Look up at the heavens and see;
gaze at the clouds so high above you.
[6]If you sin, how does that affect him?
If your sins are many, what does that do to him?
[7]If you are righteous, what do you give to him,
or what does he receive from your hand?
[8]Your wickedness only affects humans like yourself,
and your righteousness only other people.

[9]"People cry out under a load of oppression;
they plead for relief from the arm of the powerful.
[10]But no one says, 'Where is God my Maker,
who gives songs in the night,
[11]who teaches us more than he teaches[b] the beasts of
the earth
and makes us wiser than[c] the birds in the sky?'
[12]He does not answer when people cry out
because of the arrogance of the wicked.
[13]Indeed, God does not listen to their empty plea;
the Almighty pays no attention to it.
[14]How much less, then, will he listen
when you say that you do not see him,
that your case is before him
and you must wait for him,
[15]and further, that his anger never punishes
and he does not take the least notice of wickedness.[d]
[16]So Job opens his mouth with empty talk;
without knowledge he multiplies words."

PRAYING SCRIPTURE

Job 36

When was the last time you extolled God with every superlative you could bring to mind? This chapter reminds us that our hearts are lifted toward God when we describe his attributes and majesty. His days cannot be numbered. He controls the weather. He is more powerful than storms.

Write a prayer of praise using the most extravagant ways to describe God you can think of.

36

Elihu continued:

[2]"Bear with me a little longer and I will show you
that there is more to be said in God's behalf.
[3]I get my knowledge from afar;
I will ascribe justice to my Maker.
[4]Be assured that my words are not false;
one who has perfect knowledge is with you.

[5]"God is mighty, but despises no one;
he is mighty, and firm in his purpose.
[6]He does not keep the wicked alive
but gives the afflicted their rights.
[7]He does not take his eyes off the righteous;
he enthrones them with kings
and exalts them forever.
[8]But if people are bound in chains,
held fast by cords of affliction,

[a] *3* Or *you* [b] *10,11* Or *night, / [11]who teaches us by* [c] *11* Or *us wise by*
[d] *15* Symmachus, Theodotion and Vulgate; the meaning of the Hebrew for this word is uncertain.

[9]he tells them what they have done —
that they have sinned arrogantly.
[10]He makes them listen to correction
and commands them to repent of their evil.
[11]If they obey and serve him,
they will spend the rest of their days in prosperity
and their years in contentment.
[12]But if they do not listen,
they will perish by the sword[a]
and die without knowledge.

[13]"The godless in heart harbor resentment;
even when he fetters them, they do not cry for help.
[14]They die in their youth,
among male prostitutes of the shrines.
[15]But those who suffer he delivers in their suffering;
he speaks to them in their affliction.

[16]"He is wooing you from the jaws of distress
to a spacious place free from restriction,
to the comfort of your table laden with choice food.
[17]But now you are laden with the judgment due the wicked;
judgment and justice have taken hold of you.
[18]Be careful that no one entices you by riches;
do not let a large bribe turn you aside.
[19]Would your wealth or even all your mighty efforts
sustain you so you would not be in distress?
[20]Do not long for the night,
to drag people away from their homes.[b]
[21]Beware of turning to evil,
which you seem to prefer to affliction.

[22]"God is exalted in his power.
Who is a teacher like him?
[23]Who has prescribed his ways for him,
or said to him, 'You have done wrong'?
[24]Remember to extol his work,
which people have praised in song.
[25]All humanity has seen it;
mortals gaze on it from afar.
[26]How great is God — beyond our understanding!
The number of his years is past finding out.

[27]"He draws up the drops of water,
which distill as rain to the streams[c];
[28]the clouds pour down their moisture
and abundant showers fall on mankind.
[29]Who can understand how he spreads out the clouds,
how he thunders from his pavilion?
[30]See how he scatters his lightning about him,
bathing the depths of the sea.
[31]This is the way he governs[d] the nations
and provides food in abundance.

---

[a] *12* Or *will cross the river* [b] *20* The meaning of the Hebrew for verses 18-20 is uncertain. [c] *27* Or *distill from the mist as rain* [d] *31* Or *nourishes*

32 He fills his hands with lightning
and commands it to strike its mark.
33 His thunder announces the coming storm;
even the cattle make known its approach.[a]

37

"At this my heart pounds
and leaps from its place.
2 Listen! Listen to the roar of his voice,
to the rumbling that comes from his mouth.
3 He unleashes his lightning beneath the whole heaven
and sends it to the ends of the earth.
4 After that comes the sound of his roar;
he thunders with his majestic voice.
When his voice resounds,
he holds nothing back.
5 God's voice thunders in marvelous ways;
he does great things beyond our understanding.
6 He says to the snow, 'Fall on the earth,'
and to the rain shower, 'Be a mighty downpour.'
7 So that everyone he has made may know his work,
he stops all people from their labor.[b]
8 The animals take cover;
they remain in their dens.
9 The tempest comes out from its chamber,
the cold from the driving winds.
10 The breath of God produces ice,
and the broad waters become frozen.
11 He loads the clouds with moisture;
he scatters his lightning through them.
12 At his direction they swirl around
over the face of the whole earth
to do whatever he commands them.
13 He brings the clouds to punish people,
or to water his earth and show his love.

14 "Listen to this, Job;
stop and consider God's wonders.
15 Do you know how God controls the clouds
and makes his lightning flash?
16 Do you know how the clouds hang poised,
those wonders of him who has perfect knowledge?
17 You who swelter in your clothes
when the land lies hushed under the south wind,
18 can you join him in spreading out the skies,
hard as a mirror of cast bronze?

19 "Tell us what we should say to him;
we cannot draw up our case because of our darkness.
20 Should he be told that I want to speak?
Would anyone ask to be swallowed up?
21 Now no one can look at the sun,
bright as it is in the skies
after the wind has swept them clean.

PRAYING SCRIPTURE

Job 37

Elihu closed his speech by continuing to question Job's character, based primarily on Job's lack of knowledge. If Job was not God, if he hadn't created everything and didn't control it, how could he possibly know for sure he had not offended God in some way?

While we cannot know the full mind of God, his children have assurance that he is always for us. For that we can give thanks.

[a] 33 Or *announces his coming — / the One zealous against evil*

[b] 7 Or *work, / he fills all people with fear by his power*

22 Out of the north he comes in golden splendor;
God comes in awesome majesty.
23 The Almighty is beyond our reach and exalted in power;
in his justice and great righteousness, he does not oppress.
24 Therefore, people revere him,
for does he not have regard for all the wise in heart?[a]"

THE LORD SPEAKS

38 Then the LORD spoke to Job out of the storm. He said:

2 "Who is this that obscures my plans
with words without knowledge?
3 Brace yourself like a man;
I will question you,
and you shall answer me.

4 "Where were you when I laid the earth's foundation?
Tell me, if you understand.
5 Who marked off its dimensions? Surely you know!
Who stretched a measuring line across it?
6 On what were its footings set,
or who laid its cornerstone—
7 while the morning stars sang together
and all the angels[b] shouted for joy?

8 "Who shut up the sea behind doors
when it burst forth from the womb,
9 when I made the clouds its garment
and wrapped it in thick darkness,
10 when I fixed limits for it
and set its doors and bars in place,
11 when I said, 'This far you may come and no farther;
here is where your proud waves halt'?

12 "Have you ever given orders to the morning,
or shown the dawn its place,
13 that it might take the earth by the edges
and shake the wicked out of it?
14 The earth takes shape like clay under a seal;
its features stand out like those of a garment.
15 The wicked are denied their light,
and their upraised arm is broken.

16 "Have you journeyed to the springs of the sea
or walked in the recesses of the deep?
17 Have the gates of death been shown to you?
Have you seen the gates of the deepest darkness?
18 Have you comprehended the vast expanses of the earth?
Tell me, if you know all this.

19 "What is the way to the abode of light?
And where does darkness reside?
20 Can you take them to their places?
Do you know the paths to their dwellings?

[a] 24 Or *for he does not have regard for any who think they are wise.*
[b] 7 Hebrew *the sons of God*

PRAYING SCRIPTURE

Job 38

At long last, God entered the conversation with a powerful self-defense. Spanning the breadth of creation, God asked Job whether he as a mere man created light, the waters, the stars and constellations, animals or understanding itself. To these questions Job had to answer no—and so must we.

God does not mind questions, but God's wisdom and power cannot be questioned. Reread this chapter and thank God for all he has done.

21 Surely you know, for you were already born!
You have lived so many years!

22 "Have you entered the storehouses of the snow
or seen the storehouses of the hail,
23 which I reserve for times of trouble,
for days of war and battle?
24 What is the way to the place where the lightning is dispersed,
or the place where the east winds are scattered over the earth?
25 Who cuts a channel for the torrents of rain,
and a path for the thunderstorm,
26 to water a land where no one lives,
an uninhabited desert,
27 to satisfy a desolate wasteland
and make it sprout with grass?
28 Does the rain have a father?
Who fathers the drops of dew?
29 From whose womb comes the ice?
Who gives birth to the frost from the heavens
30 when the waters become hard as stone,
when the surface of the deep is frozen?

31 "Can you bind the chains[a] of the Pleiades?
Can you loosen Orion's belt?
32 Can you bring forth the constellations in their seasons[b]
or lead out the Bear[c] with its cubs?
33 Do you know the laws of the heavens?
Can you set up God's[d] dominion over the earth?

34 "Can you raise your voice to the clouds
and cover yourself with a flood of water?
35 Do you send the lightning bolts on their way?
Do they report to you, 'Here we are'?
36 Who gives the ibis wisdom[e]
or gives the rooster understanding?[f]
37 Who has the wisdom to count the clouds?
Who can tip over the water jars of the heavens
38 when the dust becomes hard
and the clods of earth stick together?

39 "Do you hunt the prey for the lioness
and satisfy the hunger of the lions
40 when they crouch in their dens
or lie in wait in a thicket?
41 Who provides food for the raven
when its young cry out to God
and wander about for lack of food?

39

"Do you know when the mountain goats give birth?
Do you watch when the doe bears her fawn?
2 Do you count the months till they bear?
Do you know the time they give birth?

[a] *31* Septuagint; Hebrew *beauty* [b] *32* Or *the morning star in its season* [c] *32* Or *out Leo* [d] *33* Or *their* [e] *36* That is, wisdom about the flooding of the Nile [f] *36* That is, understanding of when to crow; the meaning of the Hebrew for this verse is uncertain.

PRAYING SCRIPTURE

Job 39

Continuing an elaboration on the animal kingdom, God reminded Job that he alone controls the wild and domesticated animals, those that walk and those that fly, those that go to war and those that live beyond man's reach.

There is none like God. No matter how deep, dark or long your trial is, you can never escape his presence. Turn to him in faith and seek his daily presence.

3 They crouch down and bring forth their young;
their labor pains are ended.
4 Their young thrive and grow strong in the wilds;
they leave and do not return.

5 "Who let the wild donkey go free?
Who untied its ropes?
6 I gave it the wasteland as its home,
the salt flats as its habitat.
7 It laughs at the commotion in the town;
it does not hear a driver's shout.
8 It ranges the hills for its pasture
and searches for any green thing.

9 "Will the wild ox consent to serve you?
Will it stay by your manger at night?
10 Can you hold it to the furrow with a harness?
Will it till the valleys behind you?
11 Will you rely on it for its great strength?
Will you leave your heavy work to it?
12 Can you trust it to haul in your grain
and bring it to your threshing floor?

13 "The wings of the ostrich flap joyfully,
though they cannot compare
with the wings and feathers of the stork.
14 She lays her eggs on the ground
and lets them warm in the sand,
15 unmindful that a foot may crush them,
that some wild animal may trample them.
16 She treats her young harshly, as if they were not hers;
she cares not that her labor was in vain,
17 for God did not endow her with wisdom
or give her a share of good sense.
18 Yet when she spreads her feathers to run,
she laughs at horse and rider.

19 "Do you give the horse its strength
or clothe its neck with a flowing mane?
20 Do you make it leap like a locust,
striking terror with its proud snorting?
21 It paws fiercely, rejoicing in its strength,
and charges into the fray.
22 It laughs at fear, afraid of nothing;
it does not shy away from the sword.
23 The quiver rattles against its side,
along with the flashing spear and lance.
24 In frenzied excitement it eats up the ground;
it cannot stand still when the trumpet sounds.
25 At the blast of the trumpet it snorts, 'Aha!'
It catches the scent of battle from afar,
the shout of commanders and the battle cry.

26 "Does the hawk take flight by your wisdom
and spread its wings toward the south?
27 Does the eagle soar at your command
and build its nest on high?

28 It dwells on a cliff and stays there at night;
a rocky crag is its stronghold.
29 From there it looks for food;
its eyes detect it from afar.
30 Its young ones feast on blood,
and where the slain are, there it is."

PRAYING SCRIPTURE

Job 40

Job blamed God at times for his plight and complained that God didn't respond. When God finally spoke, it was a direct challenge to his servant. Did Job think he was wiser than God?

How much of our frustration is due to thinking we know better than God? Pray for humility to submit to his will.

40

The LORD said to Job:

2 "Will the one who contends with the Almighty correct him?
Let him who accuses God answer him!"

3 Then Job answered the LORD:

4 "I am unworthy — how can I reply to you?
I put my hand over my mouth.
5 I spoke once, but I have no answer —
twice, but I will say no more."

6 Then the LORD spoke to Job out of the storm:

7 "Brace yourself like a man;
I will question you,
and you shall answer me.

8 "Would you discredit my justice?
Would you condemn me to justify yourself?
9 Do you have an arm like God's,
and can your voice thunder like his?
10 Then adorn yourself with glory and splendor,
and clothe yourself in honor and majesty.
11 Unleash the fury of your wrath,
look at all who are proud and bring them low,
12 look at all who are proud and humble them,
crush the wicked where they stand.
13 Bury them all in the dust together;
shroud their faces in the grave.
14 Then I myself will admit to you
that your own right hand can save you.

15 "Look at Behemoth,
which I made along with you
and which feeds on grass like an ox.
16 What strength it has in its loins,
what power in the muscles of its belly!
17 Its tail sways like a cedar;
the sinews of its thighs are close-knit.
18 Its bones are tubes of bronze,
its limbs like rods of iron.
19 It ranks first among the works of God,
yet its Maker can approach it with his sword.
20 The hills bring it their produce,
and all the wild animals play nearby.
21 Under the lotus plants it lies,
hidden among the reeds in the marsh.
22 The lotuses conceal it in their shadow;
the poplars by the stream surround it.

23 A raging river does not alarm it;
it is secure, though the Jordan should surge against its mouth.
24 Can anyone capture it by the eyes,
or trap it and pierce its nose?

41 [a] "Can you pull in Leviathan with a fishhook
or tie down its tongue with a rope?
2 Can you put a cord through its nose
or pierce its jaw with a hook?
3 Will it keep begging you for mercy?
Will it speak to you with gentle words?
4 Will it make an agreement with you
for you to take it as your slave for life?
5 Can you make a pet of it like a bird
or put it on a leash for the young women in your house?
6 Will traders barter for it?
Will they divide it up among the merchants?
7 Can you fill its hide with harpoons
or its head with fishing spears?
8 If you lay a hand on it,
you will remember the struggle and never do it again!
9 Any hope of subduing it is false;
the mere sight of it is overpowering.
10 No one is fierce enough to rouse it.
Who then is able to stand against me?
11 Who has a claim against me that I must pay?
Everything under heaven belongs to me.

12 "I will not fail to speak of Leviathan's limbs,
its strength and its graceful form.
13 Who can strip off its outer coat?
Who can penetrate its double coat of armor[b]?
14 Who dares open the doors of its mouth,
ringed about with fearsome teeth?
15 Its back has[c] rows of shields
tightly sealed together;
16 each is so close to the next
that no air can pass between.
17 They are joined fast to one another;
they cling together and cannot be parted.
18 Its snorting throws out flashes of light;
its eyes are like the rays of dawn.
19 Flames stream from its mouth;
sparks of fire shoot out.
20 Smoke pours from its nostrils
as from a boiling pot over burning reeds.
21 Its breath sets coals ablaze,
and flames dart from its mouth.
22 Strength resides in its neck;
dismay goes before it.
23 The folds of its flesh are tightly joined;
they are firm and immovable.

[a] In Hebrew texts 41:1-8 is numbered 40:25-32, and 41:9-34 is numbered 41:1-26.
[b] *13* Septuagint; Hebrew *double bridle* [c] *15* Or *Its pride is its*

PRAYING SCRIPTURE

Job 41

In what some believe to be descriptions of dinosaurs, God reminded Job that he made the most powerful of creatures, those unfazed by human attacks, and that Job would need God's aid to be delivered from them.

Throughout his answers to Job, God reminded his suffering son that nothing was too hard for him and that Job's doubt was ill-founded. Express thanksgiving and praise that no trial of yours overwhelms God.

[24]Its chest is hard as rock,
hard as a lower millstone.
[25]When it rises up, the mighty are terrified;
they retreat before its thrashing.
[26]The sword that reaches it has no effect,
nor does the spear or the dart or the javelin.
[27]Iron it treats like straw
and bronze like rotten wood.
[28]Arrows do not make it flee;
slingstones are like chaff to it.
[29]A club seems to it but a piece of straw;
it laughs at the rattling of the lance.
[30]Its undersides are jagged potsherds,
leaving a trail in the mud like a threshing sledge.
[31]It makes the depths churn like a boiling caldron
and stirs up the sea like a pot of ointment.
[32]It leaves a glistening wake behind it;
one would think the deep had white hair.
[33]Nothing on earth is its equal —
a creature without fear.
[34]It looks down on all that are haughty;
it is king over all that are proud."

JOB 42

42 Then Job replied to the LORD:

[2]"I know that you can do all things;
no purpose of yours can be thwarted.
[3]You asked, 'Who is this that obscures my plans without knowledge?'
Surely I spoke of things I did not understand,
things too wonderful for me to know.

[4]"You said, 'Listen now, and I will speak;
I will question you,
and you shall answer me.'
[5]My ears had heard of you
but now my eyes have seen you.
[6]Therefore I despise myself
and repent in dust and ashes."

EPILOGUE

[7]After the LORD had said these things to Job, he said to Eliphaz the
Temanite, "I am angry with you and your two friends, because you
have not spoken the truth about me, as my servant Job has. [8]So now
take seven bulls and seven rams and go to my servant Job and sacrifice
a burnt offering for yourselves. My servant Job will pray for you, and
I will accept his prayer and not deal with you according to your folly.
You have not spoken the truth about me, as my servant Job has." [9]So
Eliphaz the Temanite, Bildad the Shuhite and Zophar the Naamathite
did what the LORD told them; and the LORD accepted Job's prayer.

[10]After Job had prayed for his friends, the LORD restored his fortunes
and gave him twice as much as he had before. [11]All his brothers and
sisters and everyone who had known him before came and ate with

PRAYING SCRIPTURE

Job 42

When God finished speaking, Job repented for presuming on knowledge he didn't have. But in a heartening finale, God exonerated Job while shaming his friends. God clarified that Job's friends, not Job, were the ones who had misjudged him and spoken in error.

Job reminds us that God is in control even when we are hurting and confused. Thank God that his love and power are sufficient for us.

him in his house. They comforted and consoled him over all the trou-
ble the LORD had brought on him, and each one gave him a piece of
silver[a] and a gold ring.
12The LORD blessed the latter part of Job's life more than the former
part. He had fourteen thousand sheep, six thousand camels, a thou-
sand yoke of oxen and a thousand donkeys. 13And he also had seven
sons and three daughters. 14The first daughter he named Jemimah, the
second Keziah and the third Keren-Happuch. 15Nowhere in all the land
were there found women as beautiful as Job's daughters, and their fa-
ther granted them an inheritance along with their brothers.
16After this, Job lived a hundred and forty years; he saw his children
and their children to the fourth generation. 17And so Job died, an old
man and full of years.

[a] *11* Hebrew *him a kesitah*; a kesitah was a unit of money of unknown weight and value.

PSALMS

The Psalter, which contains the most chapters of any Biblical book, consists of prayers and songs that express the full range of human emotion. Organized into five books, the Psalms were authored by a myriad of different men, covering the span from creation through Israel's history until after the exile. The breadth of subjects addressed includes war, peace, worship, prophecies of the Messiah, praise and lament. Some contain the name of the author, and others do not. A number of David's psalms begin with superscriptions that explain the historical setting in which he composed the psalm. Many give instructions to the director of music since the psalms served as Israel's hymnbook.

Many of the psalms express difficult human emotions. One group has been classified as lament psalms. In these compositions, the psalmist complained to God about the difficulty of life or wondered whether God would rescue him. The writer conveyed that he was angry, scared, tired, abandoned and alone. Yet, in these particular psalms, the psalmist also turns to God, demonstrating confidence that he would deliver him because of God's character and faithfulness to his promises.

One section of Psalms, 120–134, is unique in that the inscription of each psalm includes "A song of ascents." These were the songs sung as worshipers ascended the road to Jerusalem in preparation for Passover.

The psalms that most Bible readers are familiar with are psalms that give praise to God. These songs not only praise God personally but often contain exhortations for other people to join the writer in giving glory to God. They often focus on attributes of God such as his power, his glory and his love for his people. They also celebrate God's acts of salvation for his people. In many cases, these use the exodus as a paradigm for how God liberates his people and looks forward to the ultimate vindication of God's people on the day of judgment.

It's clear that the Psalms, even if they are songs, are also prayers, for they address God directly. "Answer me when I call to you" (4:1). "LORD, our Lord, how majestic is your name in all the earth!" (8:1). "I love you, LORD, my strength" (18:1). "Listen to my prayer, O God, do not ignore my plea" (55:1). The longest book in the Bible contains the most prayers of any other book.

One rhythm that could help anyone learn how to pray would be to pray the Psalms. This is especially helpful for anyone who is struggling with how to pray. When praying a psalm, pray it as your own prayer to God; let the writer's words become your words. A line may arrest your attention and lead you to further prayers in your own words, or you may simply continue with the words of the psalmist. When Christians pray the Psalms, they learn both a vocabulary for prayer as well as types of petitions they can bring to God based on what they are experiencing in life.

BOOK I
PSALMS 1 – 41

PSALM 1

1 Blessed is the one
who does not walk in step with the wicked
or stand in the way that sinners take
or sit in the company of mockers,
2 but whose delight is in the law of the LORD,
and who meditates on his law day and night.
3 That person is like a tree planted by streams of water,
which yields its fruit in season
and whose leaf does not wither—
whatever they do prospers.

4 Not so the wicked!
They are like chaff
that the wind blows away.
5 Therefore the wicked will not stand in the judgment,
nor sinners in the assembly of the righteous.

6 For the LORD watches over the way of the righteous,
but the way of the wicked leads to destruction.

PRAYING SCRIPTURE

Psalm 1

The contrast between the fruitfulness of the righteous and the emptiness of the unrighteous could not be clearer. The righteous are planted near a river, constantly bearing fruit. The unrighteous are like a husk—no life, no fruit and easily blown away by the wind. They are excluded from fellowship with the people of God.

Ask God to plant you beside the river of his grace so you will thrive.

PSALM 2

1 Why do the nations conspire[a]
and the peoples plot in vain?
2 The kings of the earth rise up
and the rulers band together
against the LORD and against his anointed, saying,
3 "Let us break their chains
and throw off their shackles."

4 The One enthroned in heaven laughs;
the Lord scoffs at them.
5 He rebukes them in his anger
and terrifies them in his wrath, saying,
6 "I have installed my king
on Zion, my holy mountain."

7 I will proclaim the LORD's decree:

He said to me, "You are my son;
today I have become your father.
8 Ask me,
and I will make the nations your inheritance,
the ends of the earth your possession.
9 You will break them with a rod of iron[b];
you will dash them to pieces like pottery."

10 Therefore, you kings, be wise;
be warned, you rulers of the earth.
11 Serve the LORD with fear
and celebrate his rule with trembling.

PRAYING SCRIPTURE

Psalm 2

In every generation it appears the world is out of control, that God's plans will surely come to nothing. The psalmist reminds us that, even though the nations of the world plot against the Lord God, he will break them to pieces like a clay pot (see verse 9). No one can challenge God's sovereign reign.

When things look out of control on the world scene, pray this psalm for assurance.

---

[a] *1* Hebrew; Septuagint *rage* [b] *9* Or *will rule them with an iron scepter* (see Septuagint and Syriac)

12 Kiss his son, or he will be angry
and your way will lead to your destruction,
for his wrath can flare up in a moment.
Blessed are all who take refuge in him.

PRAYING SCRIPTURE

Psalm 3

Picture King David, hiding and afraid, as his son sought to kill him. Even in this life-threatening situation, David took time to pray, acknowledging something as simple as being able to sleep and wake again. He stated that victory over his enemy belonged to God.

Are you tempted to skip prayer during trying times? Lack of prayer leaves us unprepared for the battle. Remember to pray as a primary part of your warfare.

PSALM 3[a]

A psalm of David. When he fled from his son Absalom.

1 LORD, how many are my foes!
How many rise up against me!
2 Many are saying of me,
"God will not deliver him."[b]

3 But you, LORD, are a shield around me,
my glory, the One who lifts my head high.
4 I call out to the LORD,
and he answers me from his holy mountain.

5 I lie down and sleep;
I wake again, because the LORD sustains me.
6 I will not fear though tens of thousands
assail me on every side.

7 Arise, LORD!
Deliver me, my God!
Strike all my enemies on the jaw;
break the teeth of the wicked.

8 From the LORD comes deliverance.
May your blessing be on your people.

PRAYING SCRIPTURE

Psalm 4

Have you ever noticed that sound sleep disappears when you are worried and anxious? David's prayer acknowledged that God had given him mercy and relief, and that real gladness—often sought in drink—came from God alone.

Thank God for the safety of body and mind he brings. Anxiety is often the result of taking God's responsibility upon ourselves. Rejoice that your life is enveloped in his loving care.

PSALM 4[c]

For the director of music. With stringed instruments. A psalm of David.

1 Answer me when I call to you,
my righteous God.
Give me relief from my distress;
have mercy on me and hear my prayer.

2 How long will you people turn my glory into shame?
How long will you love delusions and seek false gods[d]?[e]
3 Know that the LORD has set apart his faithful servant for himself;
the LORD hears when I call to him.

4 Tremble and[f] do not sin;
when you are on your beds,
search your hearts and be silent.
5 Offer the sacrifices of the righteous
and trust in the LORD.

6 Many, LORD, are asking, "Who will bring us prosperity?"
Let the light of your face shine on us.
7 Fill my heart with joy
when their grain and new wine abound.

---

[a] In Hebrew texts 3:1-8 is numbered 3:2-9. [b] 2 The Hebrew has *Selah* (a word of uncertain meaning) here and at the end of verses 4 and 8. [c] In Hebrew texts 4:1-8 is numbered 4:2-9. [d] 2 Or *seek lies* [e] 2 The Hebrew has *Selah* (a word of uncertain meaning) here and at the end of verse 4. [f] 4 Or *In your anger* (see Septuagint)

8 In peace I will lie down and sleep,
for you alone, LORD,
make me dwell in safety.

PSALM 5[a]

For the director of music. For pipes. A psalm of David.

1 Listen to my words, LORD,
consider my lament.
2 Hear my cry for help,
my King and my God,
for to you I pray.

3 In the morning, LORD, you hear my voice;
in the morning I lay my requests before you
and wait expectantly.
4 For you are not a God who is pleased with wickedness;
with you, evil people are not welcome.
5 The arrogant cannot stand
in your presence.
You hate all who do wrong;
6 you destroy those who tell lies.
The bloodthirsty and deceitful
you, LORD, detest.
7 But I, by your great love,
can come into your house;
in reverence I bow down
toward your holy temple.

8 Lead me, LORD, in your righteousness
because of my enemies—
make your way straight before me.
9 Not a word from their mouth can be trusted;
their heart is filled with malice.
Their throat is an open grave;
with their tongues they tell lies.
10 Declare them guilty, O God!
Let their intrigues be their downfall.
Banish them for their many sins,
for they have rebelled against you.
11 But let all who take refuge in you be glad;
let them ever sing for joy.
Spread your protection over them,
that those who love your name may rejoice in you.

12 Surely, LORD, you bless the righteous;
you surround them with your favor as with a shield.

PSALM 6[b]

For the director of music. With stringed instruments. According to sheminith.[c] *A psalm of David.*

1 LORD, do not rebuke me in your anger
or discipline me in your wrath.

PRAYING SCRIPTURE

Psalm 5

The psalmist was discouraged by the evil of the people around him, but he drew strength from the fact that God does not take pleasure in wickedness and will ultimately judge evil. Further, he encouraged people who trust God to rejoice because God protects them (see verse 11).

Don't get so focused on evildoers that you forget God has overcome all evil. Like the psalmist, trust God and rejoice that he blesses the righteous.

PRAYING SCRIPTURE

Psalm 6

Sometimes in our human weakness we feel as though God gets frustrated with us. King David knew what it was like to walk through anger, rejection and pain. He suffered and let God know about it.

One thing David continued to do in his suffering was pray. He wept before God and sought God consistently. We never have to hesitate to bring our requests to him, believing he will hear us.

[a] In Hebrew texts 5:1-12 is numbered 5:2-13. [b] In Hebrew texts 6:1-10 is numbered 6:2-11. [c] Title: Probably a musical term

2 Have mercy on me, LORD, for I am faint;
heal me, LORD, for my bones are in agony.
3 My soul is in deep anguish.
How long, LORD, how long?

4 Turn, LORD, and deliver me;
save me because of your unfailing love.
5 Among the dead no one proclaims your name.
Who praises you from the grave?

6 I am worn out from my groaning.

All night long I flood my bed with weeping
and drench my couch with tears.
7 My eyes grow weak with sorrow;
they fail because of all my foes.

8 Away from me, all you who do evil,
for the LORD has heard my weeping.
9 The LORD has heard my cry for mercy;
the LORD accepts my prayer.
10 All my enemies will be overwhelmed with shame and anguish;
they will turn back and suddenly be put to shame.

PSALM 7[a]

A shiggaion[b] of David, which he sang to the LORD concerning Cush, a Benjamite.

1 LORD my God, I take refuge in you;
save and deliver me from all who pursue me,
2 or they will tear me apart like a lion
and rip me to pieces with no one to rescue me.

3 LORD my God, if I have done this
and there is guilt on my hands—
4 if I have repaid my ally with evil
or without cause have robbed my foe—
5 then let my enemy pursue and overtake me;
let him trample my life to the ground
and make me sleep in the dust.[c]

6 Arise, LORD, in your anger;
rise up against the rage of my enemies.
Awake, my God; decree justice.
7 Let the assembled peoples gather around you,
while you sit enthroned over them on high.
8 Let the LORD judge the peoples.
Vindicate me, LORD, according to my righteousness,
according to my integrity, O Most High.
9 Bring to an end the violence of the wicked
and make the righteous secure—
you, the righteous God
who probes minds and hearts.

10 My shield[d] is God Most High,
who saves the upright in heart.

PRAYING SCRIPTURE

Psalm 7

Sometimes God's people are tempted to think that wicked people go forever unpunished. They seem to "get away with it" more times than not. But the psalmist knew better. He realized judgment would come as it would for one who dug a pit for a foe only to fall in it themselves.

The psalmist didn't glory in the way of the wicked; he rejoiced because he trusted God's righteousness. Join the writer in giving praise to God.

---

[a] In Hebrew texts 7:1-17 is numbered 7:2-18. [b] Title: Probably a literary or musical term [c] *5* The Hebrew has *Selah* (a word of uncertain meaning) here. [d] *10* Or *sovereign*

11 God is a righteous judge,
a God who displays his wrath every day.
12 If he does not relent,
he[a] will sharpen his sword;
he will bend and string his bow.
13 He has prepared his deadly weapons;
he makes ready his flaming arrows.

14 Whoever is pregnant with evil
conceives trouble and gives birth to disillusionment.
15 Whoever digs a hole and scoops it out
falls into the pit they have made.
16 The trouble they cause recoils on them;
their violence comes down on their own heads.

17 I will give thanks to the LORD because of his righteousness;
I will sing the praises of the name of the LORD Most High.

PSALM 8[b]

For the director of music. According to gittith.[c] A psalm of David.

1 LORD, our Lord,
how majestic is your name in all the earth!

You have set your glory
in the heavens.
2 Through the praise of children and infants
you have established a stronghold against your enemies,
to silence the foe and the avenger.
3 When I consider your heavens,
the work of your fingers,
the moon and the stars,
which you have set in place,
4 what is mankind that you are mindful of them,
human beings that you care for them?[d]

5 You have made them[e] a little lower than the angels[f]
and crowned them[e] with glory and honor.
6 You made them rulers over the works of your hands;
you put everything under their[g] feet:
7 all flocks and herds,
and the animals of the wild,
8 the birds in the sky,
and the fish in the sea,
all that swim the paths of the seas.

9 LORD, our Lord,
how majestic is your name in all the earth!

PRAYING SCRIPTURE

Psalm 8

This short psalm is one of the most beautiful in the entire book, containing some of the most memorable lines in the Bible. The psalmist could not help but praise God when he thought about the great God who stoops to think about humanity.

If you are tempted to thoughts of worthlessness, know that God has crowned you with glory and honor. Rejoice in his love and praise his excellent name!

[a] 12 Or *If anyone does not repent, / God* [b] In Hebrew texts 8:1-9 is numbered 8:2-10. [c] Title: Probably a musical term [d] 4 Or *what is a human being that you are mindful of him, / a son of man that you care for him?* [e] 5 Or *him* [f] 5 Or *than God* [g] 6 Or *made him ruler . . . ; / . . . his*

PRAYING SCRIPTURE

Psalm 9

The center of this psalm says that the Lord is a "refuge for the oppressed" and "a stronghold in times of trouble" (verse 9). These are precious words of hope for those suffering from the worst this world has to offer: God is a safe place for the refugee.

To whom do you run when you are in trouble? Many seek comfort in the world, but God is a refuge for those who call on him.

PSALM 9[a,b]

For the director of music. To the tune of "The Death of the Son." A psalm of David.

1 I will give thanks to you, LORD, with all my heart;
I will tell of all your wonderful deeds.
2 I will be glad and rejoice in you;
I will sing the praises of your name, O Most High.

3 My enemies turn back;
they stumble and perish before you.
4 For you have upheld my right and my cause,
sitting enthroned as the righteous judge.
5 You have rebuked the nations and destroyed the wicked;
you have blotted out their name for ever and ever.
6 Endless ruin has overtaken my enemies,
you have uprooted their cities;
even the memory of them has perished.

7 The LORD reigns forever;
he has established his throne for judgment.
8 He rules the world in righteousness
and judges the peoples with equity.
9 The LORD is a refuge for the oppressed,
a stronghold in times of trouble.
10 Those who know your name trust in you,
for you, LORD, have never forsaken those who seek you.

11 Sing the praises of the LORD, enthroned in Zion;
proclaim among the nations what he has done.
12 For he who avenges blood remembers;
he does not ignore the cries of the afflicted.

13 LORD, see how my enemies persecute me!
Have mercy and lift me up from the gates of death,
14 that I may declare your praises
in the gates of Daughter Zion,
and there rejoice in your salvation.

15 The nations have fallen into the pit they have dug;
their feet are caught in the net they have hidden.
16 The LORD is known by his acts of justice;
the wicked are ensnared by the work of their hands.[c]
17 The wicked go down to the realm of the dead,
all the nations that forget God.
18 But God will never forget the needy;
the hope of the afflicted will never perish.

19 Arise, LORD, do not let mortals triumph;
let the nations be judged in your presence.
20 Strike them with terror, LORD;
let the nations know they are only mortal.

---

[a] Psalms 9 and 10 may originally have been a single acrostic poem in which alternating lines began with the successive letters of the Hebrew alphabet. In the Septuagint they constitute one psalm. [b] In Hebrew texts 9:1-20 is numbered 9:2-21. [c] *16* The Hebrew has *Higgaion* and *Selah* (words of uncertain meaning) here; *Selah* occurs also at the end of verse 20.

PSALM 10[a]

1 Why, LORD, do you stand far off?
Why do you hide yourself in times of trouble?

2 In his arrogance the wicked man hunts down the weak,
who are caught in the schemes he devises.
3 He boasts about the cravings of his heart;
he blesses the greedy and reviles the LORD.
4 In his pride the wicked man does not seek him;
in all his thoughts there is no room for God.
5 His ways are always prosperous;
your laws are rejected by[b] him;
he sneers at all his enemies.
6 He says to himself, "Nothing will ever shake me."
He swears, "No one will ever do me harm."

7 His mouth is full of lies and threats;
trouble and evil are under his tongue.
8 He lies in wait near the villages;
from ambush he murders the innocent.
His eyes watch in secret for his victims;
9 like a lion in cover he lies in wait.
He lies in wait to catch the helpless;
he catches the helpless and drags them off in his net.
10 His victims are crushed, they collapse;
they fall under his strength.
11 He says to himself, "God will never notice;
he covers his face and never sees."

12 Arise, LORD! Lift up your hand, O God.
Do not forget the helpless.
13 Why does the wicked man revile God?
Why does he say to himself,
"He won't call me to account"?
14 But you, God, see the trouble of the afflicted;
you consider their grief and take it in hand.
The victims commit themselves to you;
you are the helper of the fatherless.
15 Break the arm of the wicked man;
call the evildoer to account for his wickedness
that would not otherwise be found out.

16 The LORD is King for ever and ever;
the nations will perish from his land.
17 You, LORD, hear the desire of the afflicted;
you encourage them, and you listen to their cry,
18 defending the fatherless and the oppressed,
so that mere earthly mortals
will never again strike terror.

PRAYING SCRIPTURE

Psalm 10

The psalmist asked why the Lord was far off and hiding when the wicked ran amok. Descriptively, the wicked are portrayed as boasting, reviling God, lying in wait for their victims and attempting to hide from God. What is the end of the wicked? They will face the King's justice.

When tempted to question God's judgment, remember that his justice is always sure and that one day oppression will come to an end.

---

[a] Psalms 9 and 10 may originally have been a single acrostic poem in which alternating lines began with the successive letters of the Hebrew alphabet. In the Septuagint they constitute one psalm. [b] 5 See Septuagint; Hebrew */ they are haughty, and your laws are far from*

PSALM 11

For the director of music. Of David.

1 In the LORD I take refuge.
How then can you say to me:
"Flee like a bird to your mountain.
2 For look, the wicked bend their bows;
they set their arrows against the strings
to shoot from the shadows
at the upright in heart.
3 When the foundations are being destroyed,
what can the righteous do?"

4 The LORD is in his holy temple;
the LORD is on his heavenly throne.
He observes everyone on earth;
his eyes examine them.
5 The LORD examines the righteous,
but the wicked, those who love violence,
he hates with a passion.
6 On the wicked he will rain
fiery coals and burning sulfur;
a scorching wind will be their lot.

7 For the LORD is righteous,
he loves justice;
the upright will see his face.

PRAYING SCRIPTURE

Psalm 11

"In the LORD I take refuge" (verse 1). What a simple yet deep declaration. How often do we find ourselves wavering in doubt, battered by the circumstances of life? Yet we can always put our trust in the Lord because his throne is in heaven.

If you are in a period of struggle or trial, if you feel like running away, stop and tell God that you trust him in all things.

PSALM 12[a]

For the director of music. According to sheminith.[b] *A psalm of David.*

1 Help, LORD, for no one is faithful anymore;
those who are loyal have vanished from the human race.
2 Everyone lies to their neighbor;
they flatter with their lips
but harbor deception in their hearts.

3 May the LORD silence all flattering lips
and every boastful tongue—
4 those who say,
"By our tongues we will prevail;
our own lips will defend us—who is lord over us?"

5 "Because the poor are plundered and the needy groan,
I will now arise," says the LORD.
"I will protect them from those who malign them."
6 And the words of the LORD are flawless,
like silver purified in a crucible,
like gold[c] refined seven times.

7 You, LORD, will keep the needy safe
and will protect us forever from the wicked,
8 who freely strut about
when what is vile is honored by the human race.

PRAYING SCRIPTURE

Psalm 12

The assurance given in this psalm is that God's words never fail. More than silver purified in a furnace, God's words are purer still, contrasted against the flattering, lying tongues of the wicked. God's Word can be trusted through all generations.

When you come to God's Word, you can believe it with absolute confidence. Pray God's words in full certainty that he hears you and will answer.

[a] In Hebrew texts 12:1-8 is numbered 12:2-9. [b] Title: Probably a musical term
[c] 6 Probable reading of the original Hebrew text; Masoretic Text *earth*

PSALM 13[a]

For the director of music. A psalm of David.

1 How long, LORD? Will you forget me forever?
How long will you hide your face from me?
2 How long must I wrestle with my thoughts
and day after day have sorrow in my heart?
How long will my enemy triumph over me?

3 Look on me and answer, LORD my God.
Give light to my eyes, or I will sleep in death,
4 and my enemy will say, "I have overcome him,"
and my foes will rejoice when I fall.

5 But I trust in your unfailing love;
my heart rejoices in your salvation.
6 I will sing the LORD's praise,
for he has been good to me.

PSALM 14

For the director of music. Of David.

1 The fool[b] says in his heart,
"There is no God."
They are corrupt, their deeds are vile;
there is no one who does good.

2 The LORD looks down from heaven
on all mankind
to see if there are any who understand,
any who seek God.
3 All have turned away, all have become corrupt;
there is no one who does good,
not even one.

4 Do all these evildoers know nothing?

They devour my people as though eating bread;
they never call on the LORD.
5 But there they are, overwhelmed with dread,
for God is present in the company of the righteous.
6 You evildoers frustrate the plans of the poor,
but the LORD is their refuge.

7 Oh, that salvation for Israel would come out of Zion!
When the LORD restores his people,
let Jacob rejoice and Israel be glad!

PSALM 15

A psalm of David.

1 LORD, who may dwell in your sacred tent?
Who may live on your holy mountain?

2 The one whose walk is blameless,
who does what is righteous,
who speaks the truth from their heart;

[a] In Hebrew texts 13:1-6 is numbered 13:2-6. [b] *1* The Hebrew words rendered *fool* in Psalms denote one who is morally deficient.

PRAYING SCRIPTURE

Psalm 13

Our hearts often know the pain of David's plea, "How long, LORD?" (verse 1). It often seems that sorrow and hurt will last forever. God seems hidden from us while our antagonists threaten us. Yet the psalmist encourages us to seek God: "Look on me and answer, LORD my God" (verse 3).

The writer had hope because he trusted in God's mercy. Rejoice in God's mercy and in his salvation that saves you from your enemies.

PRAYING SCRIPTURE

Psalm 14

Sometimes the Bible teaches us about wise living by showing us the folly of the wicked.

Ask God to make you part of the "company of the righteous" (verse 5).

PRAYING SCRIPTURE

Psalm 15

The person who may dwell with God is upright and truthful. Such a person honors those who fear God, does not do evil and does not take bribes. These character traits demonstrate one's righteousness.

Ask God to help you live righteously so that he is glorified by your life, that you may dwell on his holy mountain.

3 whose tongue utters no slander,
   who does no wrong to a neighbor,
   and casts no slur on others;
4 who despises a vile person
   but honors those who fear the LORD;
who keeps an oath even when it hurts,
   and does not change their mind;
5 who lends money to the poor without interest;
   who does not accept a bribe against the innocent.

Whoever does these things
   will never be shaken.

PRAYING SCRIPTURE

Psalm 16

The last verse of this psalm describes the life that we can find in God alone. It exists in God's presence where he fills us with joy (see verse 11). He is the path of life.

Where have you been seeking joy? If you've sought joy outside God's presence, confess your sin and turn your heart to him.

PSALM 16

A miktam[a] of David.

1 Keep me safe, my God,
   for in you I take refuge.

2 I say to the LORD, "You are my Lord;
   apart from you I have no good thing."
3 I say of the holy people who are in the land,
   "They are the noble ones in whom is all my delight."
4 Those who run after other gods will suffer more and more.
   I will not pour out libations of blood to such gods
   or take up their names on my lips.

5 LORD, you alone are my portion and my cup;
   you make my lot secure.
6 The boundary lines have fallen for me in pleasant places;
   surely I have a delightful inheritance.
7 I will praise the LORD, who counsels me;
   even at night my heart instructs me.
8 I keep my eyes always on the LORD.
   With him at my right hand, I will not be shaken.

9 Therefore my heart is glad and my tongue rejoices;
   my body also will rest secure,
10 because you will not abandon me to the realm of the dead,
   nor will you let your faithful[b] one see decay.
11 You make known to me the path of life;
   you will fill me with joy in your presence,
   with eternal pleasures at your right hand.

PRAYING SCRIPTURE

Psalm 17

What satisfies you? What makes you content? For many people, satisfaction comes with position, power or prestige. For David, however, it was when he awakened "with seeing [God's] likeness" (verse 15). Seeing God's face would satisfy his soul completely.

Ask God to help you seek satisfaction in nothing less than God himself, no substitutes. Nothing can satisfy the way he can.

PSALM 17

A prayer of David.

1 Hear me, LORD, my plea is just;
   listen to my cry.
Hear my prayer —
   it does not rise from deceitful lips.
2 Let my vindication come from you;
   may your eyes see what is right.

3 Though you probe my heart,
   though you examine me at night and test me,

[a] Title: Probably a literary or musical term [b] *10* Or *holy*

you will find that I have planned no evil;
 my mouth has not transgressed.
4 Though people tried to bribe me,
 I have kept myself from the ways of the violent
 through what your lips have commanded.
5 My steps have held to your paths;
 my feet have not stumbled.

6 I call on you, my God, for you will answer me;
 turn your ear to me and hear my prayer.
7 Show me the wonders of your great love,
 you who save by your right hand
 those who take refuge in you from their foes.
8 Keep me as the apple of your eye;
 hide me in the shadow of your wings
9 from the wicked who are out to destroy me,
 from my mortal enemies who surround me.

10 They close up their callous hearts,
 and their mouths speak with arrogance.
11 They have tracked me down, they now surround me,
 with eyes alert, to throw me to the ground.
12 They are like a lion hungry for prey,
 like a fierce lion crouching in cover.

13 Rise up, LORD, confront them, bring them down;
 with your sword rescue me from the wicked.
14 By your hand save me from such people, LORD,
 from those of this world whose reward is in this life.
May what you have stored up for the wicked fill their bellies;
 may their children gorge themselves on it,
 and may there be leftovers for their little ones.

15 As for me, I will be vindicated and will see your face;
 when I awake, I will be satisfied with seeing your likeness.

PSALM 18[a]

For the director of music. Of David the servant of the LORD. He sang to the LORD the words of this song when the LORD delivered him from the hand of all his enemies and from the hand of Saul. He said:

1 I love you, LORD, my strength.

2 The LORD is my rock, my fortress and my deliverer;
 my God is my rock, in whom I take refuge,
 my shield[b] and the horn[c] of my salvation, my stronghold.

3 I called to the LORD, who is worthy of praise,
 and I have been saved from my enemies.
4 The cords of death entangled me;
 the torrents of destruction overwhelmed me.
5 The cords of the grave coiled around me;
 the snares of death confronted me.

6 In my distress I called to the LORD;
 I cried to my God for help.

PRAYING SCRIPTURE

Psalm 18

This psalm opens with a beautiful refrain of praise to God, a declaration of love. God is the psalmist's rock, his fortress, his deliverer. What then did the psalmist do? He called on the Lord for salvation.

Our faith is built when we call attention to God's power and majesty. Praise flows when we consider his attributes. Think about who God is and what he has done and praise him.

---

[a] In Hebrew texts 18:1-50 is numbered 18:2-51. [b] 2 Or *sovereign* [c] 2 *Horn* here symbolizes strength.

From his temple he heard my voice;
my cry came before him, into his ears.
7 The earth trembled and quaked,
and the foundations of the mountains shook;
they trembled because he was angry.
8 Smoke rose from his nostrils;
consuming fire came from his mouth,
burning coals blazed out of it.
9 He parted the heavens and came down;
dark clouds were under his feet.
10 He mounted the cherubim and flew;
he soared on the wings of the wind.
11 He made darkness his covering, his canopy around him—
the dark rain clouds of the sky.
12 Out of the brightness of his presence clouds advanced,
with hailstones and bolts of lightning.
13 The LORD thundered from heaven;
the voice of the Most High resounded.[a]
14 He shot his arrows and scattered the enemy,
with great bolts of lightning he routed them.
15 The valleys of the sea were exposed
and the foundations of the earth laid bare
at your rebuke, LORD,
at the blast of breath from your nostrils.

16 He reached down from on high and took hold of me;
he drew me out of deep waters.
17 He rescued me from my powerful enemy,
from my foes, who were too strong for me.
18 They confronted me in the day of my disaster,
but the LORD was my support.
19 He brought me out into a spacious place;
he rescued me because he delighted in me.

20 The LORD has dealt with me according to my righteousness;
according to the cleanness of my hands he has rewarded me.
21 For I have kept the ways of the LORD;
I am not guilty of turning from my God.
22 All his laws are before me;
I have not turned away from his decrees.
23 I have been blameless before him
and have kept myself from sin.
24 The LORD has rewarded me according to my righteousness,
according to the cleanness of my hands in his sight.

25 To the faithful you show yourself faithful,
to the blameless you show yourself blameless,
26 to the pure you show yourself pure,
but to the devious you show yourself shrewd.
27 You save the humble
but bring low those whose eyes are haughty.
28 You, LORD, keep my lamp burning;
my God turns my darkness into light.

---

[a] *13* Some Hebrew manuscripts and Septuagint (see also 2 Samuel 22:14); most Hebrew manuscripts *resounded, / amid hailstones and bolts of lightning*

29 With your help I can advance against a troop[a];
with my God I can scale a wall.

30 As for God, his way is perfect:
The LORD's word is flawless;
he shields all who take refuge in him.
31 For who is God besides the LORD?
And who is the Rock except our God?
32 It is God who arms me with strength
and keeps my way secure.
33 He makes my feet like the feet of a deer;
he causes me to stand on the heights.
34 He trains my hands for battle;
my arms can bend a bow of bronze.
35 You make your saving help my shield,
and your right hand sustains me;
your help has made me great.
36 You provide a broad path for my feet,
so that my ankles do not give way.

37 I pursued my enemies and overtook them;
I did not turn back till they were destroyed.
38 I crushed them so that they could not rise;
they fell beneath my feet.
39 You armed me with strength for battle;
you humbled my adversaries before me.
40 You made my enemies turn their backs in flight,
and I destroyed my foes.
41 They cried for help, but there was no one to save them—
to the LORD, but he did not answer.
42 I beat them as fine as windblown dust;
I trampled them[b] like mud in the streets.
43 You have delivered me from the attacks of the people;
you have made me the head of nations.
People I did not know now serve me,
44 foreigners cower before me;
as soon as they hear of me, they obey me.
45 They all lose heart;
they come trembling from their strongholds.

46 The LORD lives! Praise be to my Rock!
Exalted be God my Savior!
47 He is the God who avenges me,
who subdues nations under me,
48 who saves me from my enemies.
You exalted me above my foes;
from a violent man you rescued me.
49 Therefore I will praise you, LORD, among the nations;
I will sing the praises of your name.

50 He gives his king great victories;
he shows unfailing love to his anointed,
to David and to his descendants forever.

[a] 29 Or *can run through a barricade* [b] 42 Many Hebrew manuscripts, Septuagint, Syriac and Targum (see also 2 Samuel 22:43); Masoretic Text *I poured them out*

PRAYING SCRIPTURE

Psalm 19

Where God's Word is not available, God yet speaks. The creation—stars, sun, moon, quasars, supernovas, black holes—testify of his power. They don't have to say an audible word for them to reveal that God is, that he is powerful, that he is wise and that he is purposeful.

Go outside and consider creation. Look up at a clear, starry sky. Thank God for its constant testimony of his existence.

PSALM 19[a]

For the director of music. A psalm of David.

1 The heavens declare the glory of God;
the skies proclaim the work of his hands.
2 Day after day they pour forth speech;
night after night they reveal knowledge.
3 They have no speech, they use no words;
no sound is heard from them.
4 Yet their voice[b] goes out into all the earth,
their words to the ends of the world.
In the heavens God has pitched a tent for the sun.
5 It is like a bridegroom coming out of his chamber,
like a champion rejoicing to run his course.
6 It rises at one end of the heavens
and makes its circuit to the other;
nothing is deprived of its warmth.

7 The law of the LORD is perfect,
refreshing the soul.
The statutes of the LORD are trustworthy,
making wise the simple.
8 The precepts of the LORD are right,
giving joy to the heart.
The commands of the LORD are radiant,
giving light to the eyes.
9 The fear of the LORD is pure,
enduring forever.
The decrees of the LORD are firm,
and all of them are righteous.

10 They are more precious than gold,
than much pure gold;
they are sweeter than honey,
than honey from the honeycomb.
11 By them your servant is warned;
in keeping them there is great reward.
12 But who can discern their own errors?
Forgive my hidden faults.
13 Keep your servant also from willful sins;
may they not rule over me.
Then I will be blameless,
innocent of great transgression.

14 May these words of my mouth and this meditation of my heart
be pleasing in your sight,
LORD, my Rock and my Redeemer.

PRAYING SCRIPTURE

Psalm 20

We face the temptation to trust in the schemes of humankind to save us from our problems. The psalmist noted both horses and chariots—military might—as places people put their trust. But, he said, "We trust in the name of the LORD our God" (verse 7).

Who do you trust? Is your faith in might or in the Almighty? Confess to God that you are willing to trust him in times of trouble.

PSALM 20[c]

For the director of music. A psalm of David.

1 May the LORD answer you when you are in distress;
may the name of the God of Jacob protect you.

[a] In Hebrew texts 19:1-14 is numbered 19:2-15. [b] 4 Septuagint, Jerome and Syriac; Hebrew *measuring line* [c] In Hebrew texts 20:1-9 is numbered 20:2-10.

2 May he send you help from the sanctuary
and grant you support from Zion.
3 May he remember all your sacrifices
and accept your burnt offerings.[a]
4 May he give you the desire of your heart
and make all your plans succeed.
5 May we shout for joy over your victory
and lift up our banners in the name of our God.

May the LORD grant all your requests.

6 Now this I know:
The LORD gives victory to his anointed.
He answers him from his heavenly sanctuary
with the victorious power of his right hand.
7 Some trust in chariots and some in horses,
but we trust in the name of the LORD our God.
8 They are brought to their knees and fall,
but we rise up and stand firm.
9 LORD, give victory to the king!
Answer us when we call!

PSALM 21[b]

For the director of music. A psalm of David.

1 The king rejoices in your strength, LORD.
How great is his joy in the victories you give!

2 You have granted him his heart's desire
and have not withheld the request of his lips.[a]
3 You came to greet him with rich blessings
and placed a crown of pure gold on his head.
4 He asked you for life, and you gave it to him —
length of days, for ever and ever.
5 Through the victories you gave, his glory is great;
you have bestowed on him splendor and majesty.
6 Surely you have granted him unending blessings
and made him glad with the joy of your presence.
7 For the king trusts in the LORD;
through the unfailing love of the Most High
he will not be shaken.

8 Your hand will lay hold on all your enemies;
your right hand will seize your foes.
9 When you appear for battle,
you will burn them up as in a blazing furnace.
The LORD will swallow them up in his wrath,
and his fire will consume them.
10 You will destroy their descendants from the earth,
their posterity from mankind.
11 Though they plot evil against you
and devise wicked schemes, they cannot succeed.
12 You will make them turn their backs
when you aim at them with drawn bow.

PRAYING SCRIPTURE

Psalm 21

David personalized his relationship with God in a way that is instructive for us. Writing in third person, he noted how God answered his prayers, blessed him, made him glad in his presence, showed him mercy and defeated his enemies.

Don't pray generically; personalize God's blessings, thanking him for how he has blessed you. Then exclaim with David, "Be exalted in your strength, LORD" (verse 13).

---

[a] 3,2 The Hebrew has *Selah* (a word of uncertain meaning) here. [b] In Hebrew texts 21:1-13 is numbered 21:2-14.

13 Be exalted in your strength, LORD;
we will sing and praise your might.

PRAYING SCRIPTURE

Psalm 22

David's psalm of suffering is part personal and part prophecy of the Messiah's public suffering. The description of crucifixion (see verses 14–18), a punishment not invented when David wrote, provides details about Jesus' suffering that wouldn't be known for hundreds of years. God was preparing his people for how he would save them and the world.

Marvel at the wisdom of God in prophecy. Praise him for showing David what was to come.

PSALM 22[a]

For the director of music. To the tune of "The Doe of the Morning." A psalm of David.

1 My God, my God, why have you forsaken me?
Why are you so far from saving me,
so far from my cries of anguish?
2 My God, I cry out by day, but you do not answer,
by night, but I find no rest.[b]

3 Yet you are enthroned as the Holy One;
you are the one Israel praises.[c]
4 In you our ancestors put their trust;
they trusted and you delivered them.
5 To you they cried out and were saved;
in you they trusted and were not put to shame.

6 But I am a worm and not a man,
scorned by everyone, despised by the people.
7 All who see me mock me;
they hurl insults, shaking their heads.
8 "He trusts in the LORD," they say,
"let the LORD rescue him.
Let him deliver him,
since he delights in him."

9 Yet you brought me out of the womb;
you made me trust in you, even at my mother's breast.
10 From birth I was cast on you;
from my mother's womb you have been my God.

11 Do not be far from me,
for trouble is near
and there is no one to help.

12 Many bulls surround me;
strong bulls of Bashan encircle me.
13 Roaring lions that tear their prey
open their mouths wide against me.
14 I am poured out like water,
and all my bones are out of joint.
My heart has turned to wax;
it has melted within me.
15 My mouth[d] is dried up like a potsherd,
and my tongue sticks to the roof of my mouth;
you lay me in the dust of death.

16 Dogs surround me,
a pack of villains encircles me;
they pierce[e] my hands and my feet.

[a] In Hebrew texts 22:1-31 is numbered 22:2-32. [b] 2 Or *night, and am not silent* [c] 3 Or *Yet you are holy, / enthroned on the praises of Israel*
[d] 15 Probable reading of the original Hebrew text; Masoretic Text *strength*
[e] 16 Dead Sea Scrolls and some manuscripts of the Masoretic Text, Septuagint and Syriac; most manuscripts of the Masoretic Text *me, / like a lion*

17 All my bones are on display;
people stare and gloat over me.
18 They divide my clothes among them
and cast lots for my garment.

19 But you, LORD, do not be far from me.
You are my strength; come quickly to help me.
20 Deliver me from the sword,
my precious life from the power of the dogs.
21 Rescue me from the mouth of the lions;
save me from the horns of the wild oxen.

22 I will declare your name to my people;
in the assembly I will praise you.
23 You who fear the LORD, praise him!
All you descendants of Jacob, honor him!
Revere him, all you descendants of Israel!
24 For he has not despised or scorned
the suffering of the afflicted one;
he has not hidden his face from him
but has listened to his cry for help.

25 From you comes the theme of my praise in the great assembly;
before those who fear you[a] I will fulfill my vows.
26 The poor will eat and be satisfied;
those who seek the LORD will praise him—
may your hearts live forever!

27 All the ends of the earth
will remember and turn to the LORD,
and all the families of the nations
will bow down before him,
28 for dominion belongs to the LORD
and he rules over the nations.

29 All the rich of the earth will feast and worship;
all who go down to the dust will kneel before him—
those who cannot keep themselves alive.
30 Posterity will serve him;
future generations will be told about the Lord.
31 They will proclaim his righteousness,
declaring to a people yet unborn:
He has done it!

PSALM 23

A psalm of David.

1 The LORD is my shepherd, I lack nothing.
2 He makes me lie down in green pastures,
he leads me beside quiet waters,
3 he refreshes my soul.
He guides me along the right paths
for his name's sake.
4 Even though I walk
through the darkest valley,[b]

[a] 25 Hebrew *him* [b] 4 Or *the valley of the shadow of death*

PRAYING SCRIPTURE

Psalm 23

One of the more famous passages in Scripture, this psalm has soothed many an anxious heart and worried mind. The Good Shepherd's presence, protection and provision are constant assurances that he truly loves and cares for us. He is not detached and disinterested; he is near and attentive.

Pray verse 1 personally: "The LORD is my shepherd, I lack *nothing*," and believe the promise is true.

I will fear no evil,
for you are with me;
your rod and your staff,
they comfort me.

5 You prepare a table before me
in the presence of my enemies.
You anoint my head with oil;
my cup overflows.
6 Surely your goodness and love will follow me
all the days of my life,
and I will dwell in the house of the LORD
forever.

PSALM 24

Of David. A psalm.

1 The earth is the LORD's, and everything in it,
the world, and all who live in it;
2 for he founded it on the seas
and established it on the waters.

3 Who may ascend the mountain of the LORD?
Who may stand in his holy place?
4 The one who has clean hands and a pure heart,
who does not trust in an idol
or swear by a false god.[a]

5 They will receive blessing from the LORD
and vindication from God their Savior.
6 Such is the generation of those who seek him,
who seek your face, God of Jacob.[b,c]

7 Lift up your heads, you gates;
be lifted up, you ancient doors,
that the King of glory may come in.
8 Who is this King of glory?
The LORD strong and mighty,
the LORD mighty in battle.
9 Lift up your heads, you gates;
lift them up, you ancient doors,
that the King of glory may come in.
10 Who is he, this King of glory?
The LORD Almighty —
he is the King of glory.

PSALM 25[d]

Of David.

1 In you, LORD my God,
I put my trust.

PRAYING SCRIPTURE

Psalm 24

Far from being a vague or provincial god of mythology, the God of Israel is over everything: "The earth is the LORD's, and everything in it" (verse 1). Grasping this truth is key to understanding God as Creator and Sustainer of all that exists. He is the King of glory!

Pray aloud verses 7–10, and rejoice that God hears those who seek him with "clean hands and a pure heart" (verse 4).

PRAYING SCRIPTURE

Psalm 25

We need psalms like this one because we are so often weighed down with guilt and shame. A single sin can cascade into months or years of a guilty conscience even if we've confessed it to God and long forsaken it. Self-condemnation is real, spiritually deadly and a trap.

Thank God for his tender mercies, his loving-kindness, and that because of Jesus, he does not hold our sins against us.

---

[a] 4 Or *swear falsely* [b] 6 Two Hebrew manuscripts and Syriac (see also Septuagint); most Hebrew manuscripts *face, Jacob* [c] 6 The Hebrew has *Selah* (a word of uncertain meaning) here and at the end of verse 10. [d] This psalm is an acrostic poem, the verses of which begin with the successive letters of the Hebrew alphabet.

2 I trust in you;
do not let me be put to shame,
nor let my enemies triumph over me.
3 No one who hopes in you
will ever be put to shame,
but shame will come on those
who are treacherous without cause.

4 Show me your ways, LORD,
teach me your paths.
5 Guide me in your truth and teach me,
for you are God my Savior,
and my hope is in you all day long.
6 Remember, LORD, your great mercy and love,
for they are from of old.
7 Do not remember the sins of my youth
and my rebellious ways;
according to your love remember me,
for you, LORD, are good.

8 Good and upright is the LORD;
therefore he instructs sinners in his ways.
9 He guides the humble in what is right
and teaches them his way.
10 All the ways of the LORD are loving and faithful
toward those who keep the demands of his covenant.
11 For the sake of your name, LORD,
forgive my iniquity, though it is great.

12 Who, then, are those who fear the LORD?
He will instruct them in the ways they should choose.[a]
13 They will spend their days in prosperity,
and their descendants will inherit the land.
14 The LORD confides in those who fear him;
he makes his covenant known to them.
15 My eyes are ever on the LORD,
for only he will release my feet from the snare.

16 Turn to me and be gracious to me,
for I am lonely and afflicted.
17 Relieve the troubles of my heart
and free me from my anguish.
18 Look on my affliction and my distress
and take away all my sins.
19 See how numerous are my enemies
and how fiercely they hate me!

20 Guard my life and rescue me;
do not let me be put to shame,
for I take refuge in you.
21 May integrity and uprightness protect me,
because my hope, LORD,[b] is in you.

22 Deliver Israel, O God,
from all their troubles!

---

[a] 12 Or *ways he chooses* [b] 21 Septuagint; Hebrew does not have *LORD*.

PRAYING SCRIPTURE

Psalm 26

Much like Job before him, David proclaimed his integrity and invited God to examine him and prove his faithfulness. Whether David was facing the accusations of enemies or cleansing himself before going to worship, he was clearly looking for God's affirmation.

In several psalms the authors asked God to examine them so they could continue to walk in integrity. Ask God to reveal to you anything not pleasing to him.

PSALM 26

Of David.

1 Vindicate me, LORD,
for I have led a blameless life;
I have trusted in the LORD
and have not faltered.
2 Test me, LORD, and try me,
examine my heart and my mind;
3 for I have always been mindful of your unfailing love
and have lived in reliance on your faithfulness.

4 I do not sit with the deceitful,
nor do I associate with hypocrites.
5 I abhor the assembly of evildoers
and refuse to sit with the wicked.
6 I wash my hands in innocence,
and go about your altar, LORD,
7 proclaiming aloud your praise
and telling of all your wonderful deeds.

8 LORD, I love the house where you live,
the place where your glory dwells.
9 Do not take away my soul along with sinners,
my life with those who are bloodthirsty,
10 in whose hands are wicked schemes,
whose right hands are full of bribes.
11 I lead a blameless life;
deliver me and be merciful to me.

12 My feet stand on level ground;
in the great congregation I will praise the LORD.

PRAYING SCRIPTURE

Psalm 27

What an incredible psalm of assurance. The Lord is our light and our salvation. We have no reason to fear the wicked, an enemy or even an army. Our confidence is not in our circumstances but in the God who rules over circumstances, the God who is our strength.

David's final encouragement should fuel our prayers: Wait on the Lord. Have courage. He will strengthen your heart.

PSALM 27

Of David.

1 The LORD is my light and my salvation—
whom shall I fear?
The LORD is the stronghold of my life—
of whom shall I be afraid?

2 When the wicked advance against me
to devour[a] me,
it is my enemies and my foes
who will stumble and fall.
3 Though an army besiege me,
my heart will not fear;
though war break out against me,
even then I will be confident.

4 One thing I ask from the LORD,
this only do I seek:
that I may dwell in the house of the LORD
all the days of my life,
to gaze on the beauty of the LORD
and to seek him in his temple.

[a] 2 Or *slander*

5 For in the day of trouble
he will keep me safe in his dwelling;
he will hide me in the shelter of his sacred tent
and set me high upon a rock.

6 Then my head will be exalted
above the enemies who surround me;
at his sacred tent I will sacrifice with shouts of joy;
I will sing and make music to the LORD.

7 Hear my voice when I call, LORD;
be merciful to me and answer me.
8 My heart says of you, "Seek his face!"
Your face, LORD, I will seek.
9 Do not hide your face from me,
do not turn your servant away in anger;
you have been my helper.
Do not reject me or forsake me,
God my Savior.
10 Though my father and mother forsake me,
the LORD will receive me.
11 Teach me your way, LORD;
lead me in a straight path
because of my oppressors.
12 Do not turn me over to the desire of my foes,
for false witnesses rise up against me,
spouting malicious accusations.

13 I remain confident of this:
I will see the goodness of the LORD
in the land of the living.
14 Wait for the LORD;
be strong and take heart
and wait for the LORD.

PSALM 28

Of David.

1 To you, LORD, I call;
you are my Rock,
do not turn a deaf ear to me.
For if you remain silent,
I will be like those who go down to the pit.
2 Hear my cry for mercy
as I call to you for help,
as I lift up my hands
toward your Most Holy Place.

3 Do not drag me away with the wicked,
with those who do evil,
who speak cordially with their neighbors
but harbor malice in their hearts.
4 Repay them for their deeds
and for their evil work;
repay them for what their hands have done
and bring back on them what they deserve.

PRAYING SCRIPTURE

Psalm 28

Many Christians grow weary and weak while serving the Lord. David shows where we should turn: "To you, LORD, I call; you are my Rock" (verse 1). God is our rock. God is our fortress. He is the stability of our lives, so trust in him and find help.

With David we can lift holy hands in worship to the God who saves and sustains. Praise him in song, and let your heart rejoice.

5 Because they have no regard for the deeds of the LORD
and what his hands have done,
he will tear them down
and never build them up again.

6 Praise be to the LORD,
for he has heard my cry for mercy.
7 The LORD is my strength and my shield;
my heart trusts in him, and he helps me.
My heart leaps for joy,
and with my song I praise him.

8 The LORD is the strength of his people,
a fortress of salvation for his anointed one.
9 Save your people and bless your inheritance;
be their shepherd and carry them forever.

PSALM 29

A psalm of David.

1 Ascribe to the LORD, you heavenly beings,
ascribe to the LORD glory and strength.
2 Ascribe to the LORD the glory due his name;
worship the LORD in the splendor of his[a] holiness.

3 The voice of the LORD is over the waters;
the God of glory thunders,
the LORD thunders over the mighty waters.
4 The voice of the LORD is powerful;
the voice of the LORD is majestic.
5 The voice of the LORD breaks the cedars;
the LORD breaks in pieces the cedars of Lebanon.
6 He makes Lebanon leap like a calf,
Sirion[b] like a young wild ox.
7 The voice of the LORD strikes
with flashes of lightning.
8 The voice of the LORD shakes the desert;
the LORD shakes the Desert of Kadesh.
9 The voice of the LORD twists the oaks[c]
and strips the forests bare.
And in his temple all cry, "Glory!"

10 The LORD sits enthroned over the flood;
the LORD is enthroned as King forever.
11 The LORD gives strength to his people;
the LORD blesses his people with peace.

PSALM 30[d]

A psalm. A song. For the dedication of the temple.[e] Of David.

1 I will exalt you, LORD,
for you lifted me out of the depths
and did not let my enemies gloat over me.

[a] 2 Or *LORD with the splendor of* [b] 6 That is, Mount Hermon [c] 9 Or *LORD makes the deer give birth* [d] In Hebrew texts 30:1-12 is numbered 30:2-13.
[e] Title: Or *palace*

PRAYING SCRIPTURE

Psalm 29

We are prone to forget the greatness and the majesty of God. In this psalm, David extolled God's power over things considered mighty on earth. No weather, oceans, mighty trees or expanses of wilderness can compare with God's might. For this reason, God can and will give strength to his people.

Do you need strength today? Ask the One who is the source of all might.

PRAYING SCRIPTURE

Psalm 30

What is your response when God answers a prayer? Do you quickly move on to the next thing? David's response that God turned his mourning to dancing—and that his sackcloth was removed in favor of gladness—is among the most poetic in Scripture.

It is always important to acknowledge when God answers prayer, both privately to him and publicly to others. How can you bear witness to answered prayer today?

2 LORD my God, I called to you for help,
  and you healed me.
3 You, LORD, brought me up from the realm of the dead;
  you spared me from going down to the pit.

4 Sing the praises of the LORD, you his faithful people;
  praise his holy name.
5 For his anger lasts only a moment,
  but his favor lasts a lifetime;
weeping may stay for the night,
  but rejoicing comes in the morning.

6 When I felt secure, I said,
  "I will never be shaken."
7 LORD, when you favored me,
  you made my royal mountain[a] stand firm;
but when you hid your face,
  I was dismayed.

8 To you, LORD, I called;
  to the Lord I cried for mercy:
9 "What is gained if I am silenced,
  if I go down to the pit?
Will the dust praise you?
  Will it proclaim your faithfulness?
10 Hear, LORD, and be merciful to me;
  LORD, be my help."

11 You turned my wailing into dancing;
  you removed my sackcloth and clothed me with joy,
12 that my heart may sing your praises and not be silent.
  LORD my God, I will praise you forever.

PSALM 31[b]

For the director of music. A psalm of David.

1 In you, LORD, I have taken refuge;
  let me never be put to shame;
  deliver me in your righteousness.
2 Turn your ear to me,
  come quickly to my rescue;
be my rock of refuge,
  a strong fortress to save me.
3 Since you are my rock and my fortress,
  for the sake of your name lead and guide me.
4 Keep me free from the trap that is set for me,
  for you are my refuge.
5 Into your hands I commit my spirit;
  deliver me, LORD, my faithful God.

6 I hate those who cling to worthless idols;
  as for me, I trust in the LORD.
7 I will be glad and rejoice in your love,
  for you saw my affliction
  and knew the anguish of my soul.

PRAYING SCRIPTURE

Psalm 31

Whether in a time of unnamed illness or adversity, David did not forget the God who sustained him. He asked God to remember his faithfulness and acknowledged the "wonders of [God's] love" to him (verse 21).

No matter how dark a valley or the cause for it, God will sustain us. Thank God that he will hide you—in his presence—from your foes.

---

[a] 7 That is, Mount Zion [b] In Hebrew texts 31:1-24 is numbered 31:2-25.

8 You have not given me into the hands of the enemy
but have set my feet in a spacious place.

9 Be merciful to me, LORD, for I am in distress;
my eyes grow weak with sorrow,
my soul and body with grief.
10 My life is consumed by anguish
and my years by groaning;
my strength fails because of my affliction,[a]
and my bones grow weak.
11 Because of all my enemies,
I am the utter contempt of my neighbors
and an object of dread to my closest friends—
those who see me on the street flee from me.
12 I am forgotten as though I were dead;
I have become like broken pottery.
13 For I hear many whispering,
"Terror on every side!"
They conspire against me
and plot to take my life.

14 But I trust in you, LORD;
I say, "You are my God."
15 My times are in your hands;
deliver me from the hands of my enemies,
from those who pursue me.
16 Let your face shine on your servant;
save me in your unfailing love.
17 Let me not be put to shame, LORD,
for I have cried out to you;
but let the wicked be put to shame
and be silent in the realm of the dead.
18 Let their lying lips be silenced,
for with pride and contempt
they speak arrogantly against the righteous.

19 How abundant are the good things
that you have stored up for those who fear you,
that you bestow in the sight of all,
on those who take refuge in you.
20 In the shelter of your presence you hide them
from all human intrigues;
you keep them safe in your dwelling
from accusing tongues.

21 Praise be to the LORD,
for he showed me the wonders of his love
when I was in a city under siege.
22 In my alarm I said,
"I am cut off from your sight!"
Yet you heard my cry for mercy
when I called to you for help.

23 Love the LORD, all his faithful people!
The LORD preserves those who are true to him,

[a] 10 Or *guilt*

but the proud he pays back in full.
24 Be strong and take heart,
all you who hope in the LORD.

PSALM 32

Of David. A maskil.[a]

1 Blessed is the one
whose transgressions are forgiven,
whose sins are covered.
2 Blessed is the one
whose sin the LORD does not count against them
and in whose spirit is no deceit.

3 When I kept silent,
my bones wasted away
through my groaning all day long.
4 For day and night
your hand was heavy on me;
my strength was sapped
as in the heat of summer.[b]

5 Then I acknowledged my sin to you
and did not cover up my iniquity.
I said, "I will confess
my transgressions to the LORD."
And you forgave
the guilt of my sin.

6 Therefore let all the faithful pray to you
while you may be found;
surely the rising of the mighty waters
will not reach them.
7 You are my hiding place;
you will protect me from trouble
and surround me with songs of deliverance.

8 I will instruct you and teach you in the way you should go;
I will counsel you with my loving eye on you.
9 Do not be like the horse or the mule,
which have no understanding
but must be controlled by bit and bridle
or they will not come to you.
10 Many are the woes of the wicked,
but the LORD's unfailing love
surrounds the one who trusts in him.

11 Rejoice in the LORD and be glad, you righteous;
sing, all you who are upright in heart!

PSALM 33

1 Sing joyfully to the LORD, you righteous;
it is fitting for the upright to praise him.
2 Praise the LORD with the harp;
make music to him on the ten-stringed lyre.

[a] Title: Probably a literary or musical term [b] 4 The Hebrew has *Selah* (a word of uncertain meaning) here and at the end of verses 5 and 7.

PRAYING SCRIPTURE

Psalm 32

The hope of the children of God is forgiveness. Knowing that God has removed our sin, covered it and does not hold it against us should bring us great rejoicing! David wrote that the person whose sin is covered is "blessed" (verse 1).

The Psalms are filled with praise because of God's mercy toward us. As you think about God's mercy and forgiveness, let your heart be filled with praise too.

PRAYING SCRIPTURE

Psalm 33

God is paying attention. Sometimes, because things often seem out of control, we can feel as though God has let things go, that the world is spinning out on its own. But that isn't the case. This psalm assures us that God sees and God knows.

Be assured that God's eyes are on those who fear him. Thank him for seeing you, and ask him to help you love him more.

3 Sing to him a new song;
play skillfully, and shout for joy.

4 For the word of the LORD is right and true;
he is faithful in all he does.
5 The LORD loves righteousness and justice;
the earth is full of his unfailing love.

6 By the word of the LORD the heavens were made,
their starry host by the breath of his mouth.
7 He gathers the waters of the sea into jars[a];
he puts the deep into storehouses.
8 Let all the earth fear the LORD;
let all the people of the world revere him.
9 For he spoke, and it came to be;
he commanded, and it stood firm.

10 The LORD foils the plans of the nations;
he thwarts the purposes of the peoples.
11 But the plans of the LORD stand firm forever,
the purposes of his heart through all generations.

12 Blessed is the nation whose God is the LORD,
the people he chose for his inheritance.
13 From heaven the LORD looks down
and sees all mankind;
14 from his dwelling place he watches
all who live on earth—
15 he who forms the hearts of all,
who considers everything they do.

16 No king is saved by the size of his army;
no warrior escapes by his great strength.
17 A horse is a vain hope for deliverance;
despite all its great strength it cannot save.
18 But the eyes of the LORD are on those who fear him,
on those whose hope is in his unfailing love,
19 to deliver them from death
and keep them alive in famine.

20 We wait in hope for the LORD;
he is our help and our shield.
21 In him our hearts rejoice,
for we trust in his holy name.
22 May your unfailing love be with us, LORD,
even as we put our hope in you.

PSALM 34[b,c]

Of David. When he pretended to be insane before Abimelek, who drove him away, and he left.

1 I will extol the LORD at all times;
his praise will always be on my lips.
2 I will glory in the LORD;
let the afflicted hear and rejoice.

PRAYING SCRIPTURE

Psalm 34

"I sought the LORD, and he answered me" (verse 4). "Taste and see that the LORD is good" (verse 8). "The righteous cry out, and the LORD hears them" (verse 17). This psalm is filled with examples of the personal nature of our relationship with God himself. He is not distant; he is close and attentive.

Don't hesitate to pursue the God who loves you and is near you. Call on him anytime.

---

[a] 7 Or *sea as into a heap* [b] This psalm is an acrostic poem, the verses of which begin with the successive letters of the Hebrew alphabet. [c] In Hebrew texts 34:1-22 is numbered 34:2-23.

3 Glorify the LORD with me;
let us exalt his name together.

4 I sought the LORD, and he answered me;
he delivered me from all my fears.
5 Those who look to him are radiant;
their faces are never covered with shame.
6 This poor man called, and the LORD heard him;
he saved him out of all his troubles.
7 The angel of the LORD encamps around those who fear him,
and he delivers them.

8 Taste and see that the LORD is good;
blessed is the one who takes refuge in him.
9 Fear the LORD, you his holy people,
for those who fear him lack nothing.
10 The lions may grow weak and hungry,
but those who seek the LORD lack no good thing.
11 Come, my children, listen to me;
I will teach you the fear of the LORD.
12 Whoever of you loves life
and desires to see many good days,
13 keep your tongue from evil
and your lips from telling lies.
14 Turn from evil and do good;
seek peace and pursue it.

15 The eyes of the LORD are on the righteous,
and his ears are attentive to their cry;
16 but the face of the LORD is against those who do evil,
to blot out their name from the earth.

17 The righteous cry out, and the LORD hears them;
he delivers them from all their troubles.
18 The LORD is close to the brokenhearted
and saves those who are crushed in spirit.

19 The righteous person may have many troubles,
but the LORD delivers him from them all;
20 he protects all his bones,
not one of them will be broken.

21 Evil will slay the wicked;
the foes of the righteous will be condemned.
22 The LORD will rescue his servants;
no one who takes refuge in him will be condemned.

PSALM 35

Of David.

1 Contend, LORD, with those who contend with me;
fight against those who fight against me.
2 Take up shield and armor;
arise and come to my aid.
3 Brandish spear and javelin[a]
against those who pursue me.

PRAYING SCRIPTURE

Psalm 35

The psalmist called on God to help in his time of need. Acknowledging that God has indeed seen his need, he implored God not to be silent but to vindicate him and defend his cause.

We are often afraid to talk to God in a straightforward manner, as if we would hurt his feelings. But he can handle it. Never fear to pray directly from your deepest being.

[a] 3 Or *and block the way*

Say to me,
"I am your salvation."

4 May those who seek my life
be disgraced and put to shame;
may those who plot my ruin
be turned back in dismay.
5 May they be like chaff before the wind,
with the angel of the LORD driving them away;
6 may their path be dark and slippery,
with the angel of the LORD pursuing them.

7 Since they hid their net for me without cause
and without cause dug a pit for me,
8 may ruin overtake them by surprise —
may the net they hid entangle them,
may they fall into the pit, to their ruin.
9 Then my soul will rejoice in the LORD
and delight in his salvation.
10 My whole being will exclaim,
"Who is like you, LORD?
You rescue the poor from those too strong for them,
the poor and needy from those who rob them."

11 Ruthless witnesses come forward;
they question me on things I know nothing about.
12 They repay me evil for good
and leave me like one bereaved.
13 Yet when they were ill, I put on sackcloth
and humbled myself with fasting.
When my prayers returned to me unanswered,
14 I went about mourning
as though for my friend or brother.
I bowed my head in grief
as though weeping for my mother.
15 But when I stumbled, they gathered in glee;
assailants gathered against me without my knowledge.
They slandered me without ceasing.
16 Like the ungodly they maliciously mocked;[a]
they gnashed their teeth at me.

17 How long, Lord, will you look on?
Rescue me from their ravages,
my precious life from these lions.
18 I will give you thanks in the great assembly;
among the throngs I will praise you.
19 Do not let those gloat over me
who are my enemies without cause;
do not let those who hate me without reason
maliciously wink the eye.
20 They do not speak peaceably,
but devise false accusations
against those who live quietly in the land.
21 They sneer at me and say, "Aha! Aha!
With our own eyes we have seen it."

[a] *16* Septuagint; Hebrew may mean *Like an ungodly circle of mockers,*

22 LORD, you have seen this; do not be silent.
Do not be far from me, Lord.
23 Awake, and rise to my defense!
Contend for me, my God and Lord.
24 Vindicate me in your righteousness, LORD my God;
do not let them gloat over me.
25 Do not let them think, "Aha, just what we wanted!"
or say, "We have swallowed him up."

26 May all who gloat over my distress
be put to shame and confusion;
may all who exalt themselves over me
be clothed with shame and disgrace.
27 May those who delight in my vindication
shout for joy and gladness;
may they always say, "The LORD be exalted,
who delights in the well-being of his servant."

28 My tongue will proclaim your righteousness,
your praises all day long.

PSALM 36[a]

For the director of music. Of David the servant of the LORD.

1 I have a message from God in my heart
concerning the sinfulness of the wicked:[b]
There is no fear of God
before their eyes.

2 In their own eyes they flatter themselves
too much to detect or hate their sin.
3 The words of their mouths are wicked and deceitful;
they fail to act wisely or do good.
4 Even on their beds they plot evil;
they commit themselves to a sinful course
and do not reject what is wrong.

5 Your love, LORD, reaches to the heavens,
your faithfulness to the skies.
6 Your righteousness is like the highest mountains,
your justice like the great deep.
You, LORD, preserve both people and animals.
7 How priceless is your unfailing love, O God!
People take refuge in the shadow of your wings.
8 They feast on the abundance of your house;
you give them drink from your river of delights.
9 For with you is the fountain of life;
in your light we see light.

10 Continue your love to those who know you,
your righteousness to the upright in heart.
11 May the foot of the proud not come against me,
nor the hand of the wicked drive me away.
12 See how the evildoers lie fallen —
thrown down, not able to rise!

PRAYING SCRIPTURE

Psalm 36

Recognizing how much God loves his children can be shocking. The psalmist wrote that God's unfailing love caused people to trust in him and they could feast on the abundance of the temple, his house.

Note that the psalmist asked God to "continue" his love (verse 10). This is not a lack of faith, but a reiteration of his trust in God, something we should do as well.

---

[a] In Hebrew texts 36:1-12 is numbered 36:2-13. [b] 1 Or *A message from God: The transgression of the wicked / resides in their hearts.*

PRAYING SCRIPTURE

Psalm 37

Early in this psalm, David named two amazing promises of God: Take delight in him and he will provide your heart's desires; commit your way to God and trust in him, and "he will make your righteous reward shine like the dawn" (verse 6). God honors our faith and obedience by keeping his word. God cannot lie.

Is your full delight in God? To renew your delight, spend some time naming those things about God that bring you joy.

PSALM 37[a]

Of David.

1 Do not fret because of those who are evil
  or be envious of those who do wrong;
2 for like the grass they will soon wither,
  like green plants they will soon die away.

3 Trust in the LORD and do good;
  dwell in the land and enjoy safe pasture.
4 Take delight in the LORD,
  and he will give you the desires of your heart.

5 Commit your way to the LORD;
  trust in him and he will do this:
6 He will make your righteous reward shine like the dawn,
  your vindication like the noonday sun.

7 Be still before the LORD
  and wait patiently for him;
do not fret when people succeed in their ways,
  when they carry out their wicked schemes.

8 Refrain from anger and turn from wrath;
  do not fret — it leads only to evil.
9 For those who are evil will be destroyed,
  but those who hope in the LORD will inherit the land.

10 A little while, and the wicked will be no more;
  though you look for them, they will not be found.
11 But the meek will inherit the land
  and enjoy peace and prosperity.

12 The wicked plot against the righteous
  and gnash their teeth at them;
13 but the Lord laughs at the wicked,
  for he knows their day is coming.

14 The wicked draw the sword
  and bend the bow
to bring down the poor and needy,
  to slay those whose ways are upright.
15 But their swords will pierce their own hearts,
  and their bows will be broken.

16 Better the little that the righteous have
  than the wealth of many wicked;
17 for the power of the wicked will be broken,
  but the LORD upholds the righteous.

18 The blameless spend their days under the LORD's care,
  and their inheritance will endure forever.
19 In times of disaster they will not wither;
  in days of famine they will enjoy plenty.

20 But the wicked will perish:

[a] This psalm is an acrostic poem, the stanzas of which begin with the successive letters of the Hebrew alphabet.

Though the LORD's enemies are like the flowers
of the field,
they will be consumed, they will go up in smoke.

21 The wicked borrow and do not repay,
but the righteous give generously;
22 those the LORD blesses will inherit the land,
but those he curses will be destroyed.

23 The LORD makes firm the steps
of the one who delights in him;
24 though he may stumble, he will not fall,
for the LORD upholds him with his hand.

25 I was young and now I am old,
yet I have never seen the righteous forsaken
or their children begging bread.
26 They are always generous and lend freely;
their children will be a blessing.[a]

27 Turn from evil and do good;
then you will dwell in the land forever.
28 For the LORD loves the just
and will not forsake his faithful ones.

Wrongdoers will be completely destroyed[b];
the offspring of the wicked will perish.
29 The righteous will inherit the land
and dwell in it forever.

30 The mouths of the righteous utter wisdom,
and their tongues speak what is just.
31 The law of their God is in their hearts;
their feet do not slip.

32 The wicked lie in wait for the righteous,
intent on putting them to death;
33 but the LORD will not leave them in the power of the wicked
or let them be condemned when brought to trial.

34 Hope in the LORD
and keep his way.
He will exalt you to inherit the land;
when the wicked are destroyed, you will see it.

35 I have seen a wicked and ruthless man
flourishing like a luxuriant native tree,
36 but he soon passed away and was no more;
though I looked for him, he could not be found.

37 Consider the blameless, observe the upright;
a future awaits those who seek peace.[c]
38 But all sinners will be destroyed;
there will be no future[d] for the wicked.

[a] 26 Or *freely; / the names of their children will be used in blessings* (see Gen. 48:20); or *freely; / others will see that their children are blessed* [b] 28 See Septuagint; Hebrew *They will be protected forever* [c] 37 Or *upright; / those who seek peace will have posterity* [d] 38 Or *posterity*

39 The salvation of the righteous comes from the LORD;
he is their stronghold in time of trouble.
40 The LORD helps them and delivers them;
he delivers them from the wicked and saves them,
because they take refuge in him.

PRAYING SCRIPTURE

Psalm 38

Have you ever felt that when something was going wrong in your life, it was God chastening or correcting you? David knew that feeling. Whatever the cause of the discipline, he admitted that he was suffering because he'd angered God. In the middle of the trial, he yet expressed hope in God.

Scripture teaches us that God corrects his children. Don't grow weary of his discipline; it's an indication of his love for you (see Proverbs 3:12). Instead, take your hurts to God in prayer.

PSALM 38[a]

A psalm of David. A petition.

1 LORD, do not rebuke me in your anger
or discipline me in your wrath.
2 Your arrows have pierced me,
and your hand has come down on me.
3 Because of your wrath there is no health in my body;
there is no soundness in my bones because of my sin.
4 My guilt has overwhelmed me
like a burden too heavy to bear.

5 My wounds fester and are loathsome
because of my sinful folly.
6 I am bowed down and brought very low;
all day long I go about mourning.
7 My back is filled with searing pain;
there is no health in my body.
8 I am feeble and utterly crushed;
I groan in anguish of heart.

9 All my longings lie open before you, Lord;
my sighing is not hidden from you.
10 My heart pounds, my strength fails me;
even the light has gone from my eyes.
11 My friends and companions avoid me because of
my wounds;
my neighbors stay far away.
12 Those who want to kill me set their traps,
those who would harm me talk of my ruin;
all day long they scheme and lie.

13 I am like the deaf, who cannot hear,
like the mute, who cannot speak;
14 I have become like one who does not hear,
whose mouth can offer no reply.
15 LORD, I wait for you;
you will answer, Lord my God.
16 For I said, "Do not let them gloat
or exalt themselves over me when my feet slip."

17 For I am about to fall,
and my pain is ever with me.
18 I confess my iniquity;
I am troubled by my sin.
19 Many have become my enemies without cause[b];
those who hate me without reason are numerous.

---

[a] In Hebrew texts 38:1-22 is numbered 38:2-23. [b] *19* One Dead Sea Scrolls manuscript; Masoretic Text *my vigorous enemies*

20 Those who repay my good with evil
lodge accusations against me,
though I seek only to do what is good.

21 LORD, do not forsake me;
do not be far from me, my God.
22 Come quickly to help me,
my Lord and my Savior.

PSALM 39[a]

For the director of music. For Jeduthun. A psalm of David.

1 I said, "I will watch my ways
and keep my tongue from sin;
I will put a muzzle on my mouth
while in the presence of the wicked."
2 So I remained utterly silent,
not even saying anything good.
But my anguish increased;
3 my heart grew hot within me.
While I meditated, the fire burned;
then I spoke with my tongue:

4 "Show me, LORD, my life's end
and the number of my days;
let me know how fleeting my life is.
5 You have made my days a mere handbreadth;
the span of my years is as nothing before you.
Everyone is but a breath,
even those who seem secure.[b]

6 "Surely everyone goes around like a mere phantom;
in vain they rush about, heaping up wealth
without knowing whose it will finally be.

7 "But now, Lord, what do I look for?
My hope is in you.
8 Save me from all my transgressions;
do not make me the scorn of fools.
9 I was silent; I would not open my mouth,
for you are the one who has done this.
10 Remove your scourge from me;
I am overcome by the blow of your hand.
11 When you rebuke and discipline anyone for their sin,
you consume their wealth like a moth—
surely everyone is but a breath.

12 "Hear my prayer, LORD,
listen to my cry for help;
do not be deaf to my weeping.
I dwell with you as a foreigner,
a stranger, as all my ancestors were.
13 Look away from me, that I may enjoy life again
before I depart and am no more."

[a] In Hebrew texts 39:1-13 is numbered 39:2-14. [b] 5 The Hebrew has *Selah* (a word of uncertain meaning) here and at the end of verse 11.

PRAYING SCRIPTURE

Psalm 39

Have you ever spoken without considering your words and immediately wished you could take them back? Every person who has ever lived knows that experience. This psalm addresses the need to watch our speech. Sinning with the tongue is still sin.

What is your biggest challenge in speech? Ask God to help you learn when and how to hold your peace so that you do not sin with your tongue.

PRAYING SCRIPTURE

Psalm 40

It is a great delight to see God answer prayer. We often find the key: "I waited patiently for the LORD" (verse 1). It is hard to wait, hard to let God work in his own time without being anxious.

If you have a tendency to get impatient, ask God to increase your faith so you can leave the time frame in his hands.

PSALM 40[a]

For the director of music. Of David. A psalm.

1 I waited patiently for the LORD;
he turned to me and heard my cry.
2 He lifted me out of the slimy pit,
out of the mud and mire;
he set my feet on a rock
and gave me a firm place to stand.
3 He put a new song in my mouth,
a hymn of praise to our God.
Many will see and fear the LORD
and put their trust in him.

4 Blessed is the one
who trusts in the LORD,
who does not look to the proud,
to those who turn aside to false gods.[b]
5 Many, LORD my God,
are the wonders you have done,
the things you planned for us.
None can compare with you;
were I to speak and tell of your deeds,
they would be too many to declare.

6 Sacrifice and offering you did not desire—
but my ears you have opened[c]—
burnt offerings and sin offerings[d] you did not require.
7 Then I said, "Here I am, I have come—
it is written about me in the scroll.[e]
8 I desire to do your will, my God;
your law is within my heart."

9 I proclaim your saving acts in the great assembly;
I do not seal my lips, LORD,
as you know.
10 I do not hide your righteousness in my heart;
I speak of your faithfulness and your saving help.
I do not conceal your love and your faithfulness
from the great assembly.

11 Do not withhold your mercy from me, LORD;
may your love and faithfulness always protect me.
12 For troubles without number surround me;
my sins have overtaken me, and I cannot see.
They are more than the hairs of my head,
and my heart fails within me.
13 Be pleased to save me, LORD;
come quickly, LORD, to help me.

14 May all who want to take my life
be put to shame and confusion;
may all who desire my ruin
be turned back in disgrace.

[a] In Hebrew texts 40:1-17 is numbered 40:2-18. [b] 4 Or *to lies* [c] 6 Hebrew; some Septuagint manuscripts *but a body you have prepared for me* [d] 6 Or *purification offerings* [e] 7 Or *come / with the scroll written for me*

15 May those who say to me, "Aha! Aha!"
be appalled at their own shame.
16 But may all who seek you
rejoice and be glad in you;
may those who long for your saving help always say,
"The LORD is great!"

17 But as for me, I am poor and needy;
may the Lord think of me.
You are my help and my deliverer;
you are my God, do not delay.

PSALM 41[a]

For the director of music. A psalm of David.

1 Blessed are those who have regard for the weak;
the LORD delivers them in times of trouble.
2 The LORD protects and preserves them—
they are counted among the blessed in the land—
he does not give them over to the desire of their foes.
3 The LORD sustains them on their sickbed
and restores them from their bed of illness.

4 I said, "Have mercy on me, LORD;
heal me, for I have sinned against you."
5 My enemies say of me in malice,
"When will he die and his name perish?"
6 When one of them comes to see me,
he speaks falsely, while his heart gathers slander;
then he goes out and spreads it around.

7 All my enemies whisper together against me;
they imagine the worst for me, saying,
8 "A vile disease has afflicted him;
he will never get up from the place where he lies."
9 Even my close friend,
someone I trusted,
one who shared my bread,
has turned[b] against me.

10 But may you have mercy on me, LORD;
raise me up, that I may repay them.
11 I know that you are pleased with me,
for my enemy does not triumph over me.
12 Because of my integrity you uphold me
and set me in your presence forever.

13 Praise be to the LORD, the God of Israel,
from everlasting to everlasting.
Amen and Amen.

PRAYING SCRIPTURE

Psalm 41

This psalm echoes other Old Testament admonitions to care for the poor. David said God would deliver those who remember the less fortunate. Those who help will be preserved, kept alive and blessed. God's regard for the poor is to be expressed through his children.

If you are not among the poor of this world, God will bless your concern for them. Blessing the poor invites God's blessings in return.

[a] In Hebrew texts 41:1-13 is numbered 41:2-14. [b] 9 Hebrew *has lifted up his heel*

BOOK II

PSALMS 42 – 72

PRAYING SCRIPTURE

Psalm 42

How desperately do you pursue God? In whom do you place your deepest trust? When you are depressed, where do you place your hope? When you are mocked, where do you turn? For the psalmist, the answer was always the same: God alone.

Don't allow the cares of this world to take your attention from the only sure and lasting source of hope. Ask God to fill your deepest need.

PSALM 42[a,b]

For the director of music. A maskil[c] *of the Sons of Korah.*

1 As the deer pants for streams of water,
so my soul pants for you, my God.
2 My soul thirsts for God, for the living God.
When can I go and meet with God?
3 My tears have been my food
day and night,
while people say to me all day long,
"Where is your God?"
4 These things I remember
as I pour out my soul:
how I used to go to the house of God
under the protection of the Mighty One[d]
with shouts of joy and praise
among the festive throng.

5 Why, my soul, are you downcast?
Why so disturbed within me?
Put your hope in God,
for I will yet praise him,
my Savior and my God.

6 My soul is downcast within me;
therefore I will remember you
from the land of the Jordan,
the heights of Hermon — from Mount Mizar.
7 Deep calls to deep
in the roar of your waterfalls;
all your waves and breakers
have swept over me.

8 By day the LORD directs his love,
at night his song is with me —
a prayer to the God of my life.

9 I say to God my Rock,
"Why have you forgotten me?
Why must I go about mourning,
oppressed by the enemy?"
10 My bones suffer mortal agony
as my foes taunt me,
saying to me all day long,
"Where is your God?"

11 Why, my soul, are you downcast?
Why so disturbed within me?

---

[a] In many Hebrew manuscripts Psalms 42 and 43 constitute one psalm.
[b] In Hebrew texts 42:1-11 is numbered 42:2-12. [c] Title: Probably a literary or musical term [d] 4 See Septuagint and Syriac; the meaning of the Hebrew for this line is uncertain.

Put your hope in God,
for I will yet praise him,
my Savior and my God.

PSALM 43[a]

1 Vindicate me, my God,
and plead my cause
against an unfaithful nation.
Rescue me from those who are
deceitful and wicked.
2 You are God my stronghold.
Why have you rejected me?
Why must I go about mourning,
oppressed by the enemy?
3 Send me your light and your faithful care,
let them lead me;
let them bring me to your holy mountain,
to the place where you dwell.
4 Then I will go to the altar of God,
to God, my joy and my delight.
I will praise you with the lyre,
O God, my God.

5 Why, my soul, are you downcast?
Why so disturbed within me?
Put your hope in God,
for I will yet praise him,
my Savior and my God.

PSALM 44[b]

For the director of music. Of the Sons of Korah. A maskil.[c]

1 We have heard it with our ears, O God;
our ancestors have told us
what you did in their days,
in days long ago.
2 With your hand you drove out the nations
and planted our ancestors;
you crushed the peoples
and made our ancestors flourish.
3 It was not by their sword that they won the land,
nor did their arm bring them victory;
it was your right hand, your arm,
and the light of your face, for you loved them.

4 You are my King and my God,
who decrees[d] victories for Jacob.
5 Through you we push back our enemies;
through your name we trample our foes.
6 I put no trust in my bow,
my sword does not bring me victory;

PRAYING SCRIPTURE

Psalm 43

Even in pain, the psalmist prayed that God would send his light and his truth. The writer was not interested in shallow religious experiences or vain longings: He wanted God to lead him to his very presence, the place of delight and joy.

Are you stopping short of God's presence? Are you distracted from seeking his light and truth? Ask God to open your eyes and heart so all your seeking ends in his presence.

PRAYING SCRIPTURE

Psalm 44

In this sequence of psalms, the writers were baring their souls to God. They pleaded for vindication, rescue, help and redemption. God expects his children to call on him for help. Wandering around aimlessly, failing to call on God to help, is not what the Psalms instruct.

No matter how desperate your days or dark your nights, you can ask God to be with you, to help you, to strengthen you.

[a] In many Hebrew manuscripts Psalms 42 and 43 constitute one psalm.
[b] In Hebrew texts 44:1-26 is numbered 44:2-27. [c] Title: Probably a literary or musical term [d] 4 Septuagint, Aquila and Syriac; Hebrew *King, O God; / command*

7 but you give us victory over our enemies,
you put our adversaries to shame.
8 In God we make our boast all day long,
and we will praise your name forever.[a]

9 But now you have rejected and humbled us;
you no longer go out with our armies.
10 You made us retreat before the enemy,
and our adversaries have plundered us.
11 You gave us up to be devoured like sheep
and have scattered us among the nations.
12 You sold your people for a pittance,
gaining nothing from their sale.

13 You have made us a reproach to our neighbors,
the scorn and derision of those around us.
14 You have made us a byword among the nations;
the peoples shake their heads at us.
15 I live in disgrace all day long,
and my face is covered with shame
16 at the taunts of those who reproach and revile me,
because of the enemy, who is bent on revenge.

17 All this came upon us,
though we had not forgotten you;
we had not been false to your covenant.
18 Our hearts had not turned back;
our feet had not strayed from your path.
19 But you crushed us and made us a haunt for jackals;
you covered us over with deep darkness.

20 If we had forgotten the name of our God
or spread out our hands to a foreign god,
21 would not God have discovered it,
since he knows the secrets of the heart?
22 Yet for your sake we face death all day long;
we are considered as sheep to be slaughtered.

23 Awake, Lord! Why do you sleep?
Rouse yourself! Do not reject us forever.
24 Why do you hide your face
and forget our misery and oppression?

25 We are brought down to the dust;
our bodies cling to the ground.
26 Rise up and help us;
rescue us because of your unfailing love.

PSALM 45[b]

For the director of music. To the tune of "Lilies." Of the Sons of Korah. A maskil.[c] *A wedding song.*

1 My heart is stirred by a noble theme
as I recite my verses for the king;
my tongue is the pen of a skillful writer.

[a] *8* The Hebrew has *Selah* (a word of uncertain meaning) here. [b] In Hebrew texts 45:1-17 is numbered 45:2-18. [c] Title: Probably a literary or musical term

PRAYING SCRIPTURE

Psalm 45

The psalmist intended to "perpetuate [God's] memory through all generations" (verse 17). Many Christians in the past prayed for the salvation of future generations. We should do the same, striving to introduce our hope in God to those coming behind.

Even those who don't personally have descendants can pray for future generations. Make it a priority to pray for those who will be part of God's kingdom in the future.

2 You are the most excellent of men
and your lips have been anointed with grace,
since God has blessed you forever.

3 Gird your sword on your side, you mighty one;
clothe yourself with splendor and majesty.
4 In your majesty ride forth victoriously
in the cause of truth, humility and justice;
let your right hand achieve awesome deeds.
5 Let your sharp arrows pierce the hearts of the king's enemies;
let the nations fall beneath your feet.
6 Your throne, O God,[a] will last for ever and ever;
a scepter of justice will be the scepter of your kingdom.
7 You love righteousness and hate wickedness;
therefore God, your God, has set you above your companions
by anointing you with the oil of joy.
8 All your robes are fragrant with myrrh and aloes and cassia;
from palaces adorned with ivory
the music of the strings makes you glad.
9 Daughters of kings are among your honored women;
at your right hand is the royal bride in gold of Ophir.

10 Listen, daughter, and pay careful attention:
Forget your people and your father's house.
11 Let the king be enthralled by your beauty;
honor him, for he is your lord.
12 The city of Tyre will come with a gift,[b]
people of wealth will seek your favor.
13 All glorious is the princess within her chamber;
her gown is interwoven with gold.
14 In embroidered garments she is led to the king;
her virgin companions follow her —
those brought to be with her.
15 Led in with joy and gladness,
they enter the palace of the king.

16 Your sons will take the place of your fathers;
you will make them princes throughout the land.

17 I will perpetuate your memory through all generations;
therefore the nations will praise you for ever and ever.

PSALM 46[c]

For the director of music. Of the Sons of Korah. According to alamoth.[d] *A song.*

1 God is our refuge and strength,
an ever-present help in trouble.
2 Therefore we will not fear, though the earth give way
and the mountains fall into the heart of the sea,
3 though its waters roar and foam
and the mountains quake with their surging.[e]

[a] 6 Here the king is addressed as God's representative. [b] 12 Or *A Tyrian robe is among the gifts* [c] In Hebrew texts 46:1-11 is numbered 46:2-12. [d] Title: Probably a musical term [e] 3 The Hebrew has *Selah* (a word of uncertain meaning) here and at the end of verses 7 and 11.

PRAYING SCRIPTURE

Psalm 46

Are you on the run from guilt? God is your refuge. Are you weary from the constant battle against sin? God is your strength. Do you feel helpless, overcome by a circumstance you didn't ask for? God is your help right now.

When you pray in times of trouble, remind God of his promise to help, and then rest in the fact that "the LORD Almighty is with us" (verse 7).

4 There is a river whose streams make glad the city of God,
the holy place where the Most High dwells.
5 God is within her, she will not fall;
God will help her at break of day.
6 Nations are in uproar, kingdoms fall;
he lifts his voice, the earth melts.

7 The LORD Almighty is with us;
the God of Jacob is our fortress.

8 Come and see what the LORD has done,
the desolations he has brought on the earth.
9 He makes wars cease
to the ends of the earth.
He breaks the bow and shatters the spear;
he burns the shields[a] with fire.
10 He says, "Be still, and know that I am God;
I will be exalted among the nations,
I will be exalted in the earth."

11 The LORD Almighty is with us;
the God of Jacob is our fortress.

PSALM 47[b]

For the director of music. Of the Sons of Korah. A psalm.

1 Clap your hands, all you nations;
shout to God with cries of joy.

2 For the LORD Most High is awesome,
the great King over all the earth.
3 He subdued nations under us,
peoples under our feet.
4 He chose our inheritance for us,
the pride of Jacob, whom he loved.[c]

5 God has ascended amid shouts of joy,
the LORD amid the sounding of trumpets.
6 Sing praises to God, sing praises;
sing praises to our King, sing praises.
7 For God is the King of all the earth;
sing to him a psalm of praise.

8 God reigns over the nations;
God is seated on his holy throne.
9 The nobles of the nations assemble
as the people of the God of Abraham,
for the kings[d] of the earth belong to God;
he is greatly exalted.

PSALM 48[e]

A song. A psalm of the Sons of Korah.

1 Great is the LORD, and most worthy of praise,
in the city of our God, his holy mountain.

---

[a] 9 Or *chariots* [b] In Hebrew texts 47:1-9 is numbered 47:2-10. [c] 4 The Hebrew has *Selah* (a word of uncertain meaning) here. [d] 9 Or *shields* [e] In Hebrew texts 48:1-14 is numbered 48:2-15.

PRAYING SCRIPTURE

Psalm 47

This is one of many psalms where the author exhorts us to sing praises to God. This exhortation to praise is based on God's character, his power and his reign. Though emotion is involved in praise, the foundation is God himself.

Do you contemplate the person of Christ when you sing, when you praise? Seek God for who he is and for what he has done in providing salvation for all who believe.

PRAYING SCRIPTURE

Psalm 48

As the psalmist looked around Jerusalem, he saw how God had elevated the city, calling it "the joy of the whole earth" (verse 2). Yet Mount Zion was not the pinnacle; God was. God was and is above any earthly city or throne.

What was the psalmist's response? Praise. Thank God that no earthly power can rival him, and take refuge in the comfort of his preeminence.

2 Beautiful in its loftiness,
the joy of the whole earth,
like the heights of Zaphon[a] is Mount Zion,
the city of the Great King.
3 God is in her citadels;
he has shown himself to be her fortress.

4 When the kings joined forces,
when they advanced together,
5 they saw her and were astounded;
they fled in terror.
6 Trembling seized them there,
pain like that of a woman in labor.
7 You destroyed them like ships of Tarshish
shattered by an east wind.

8 As we have heard,
so we have seen
in the city of the LORD Almighty,
in the city of our God:
God makes her secure
forever.[b]

9 Within your temple, O God,
we meditate on your unfailing love.
10 Like your name, O God,
your praise reaches to the ends of the earth;
your right hand is filled with righteousness.
11 Mount Zion rejoices,
the villages of Judah are glad
because of your judgments.

12 Walk about Zion, go around her,
count her towers,
13 consider well her ramparts,
view her citadels,
that you may tell of them
to the next generation.

14 For this God is our God for ever and ever;
he will be our guide even to the end.

PSALM 49[c]

For the director of music. Of the Sons of Korah. A psalm.

1 Hear this, all you peoples;
listen, all who live in this world,
2 both low and high,
rich and poor alike:
3 My mouth will speak words of wisdom;
the meditation of my heart will give you understanding.
4 I will turn my ear to a proverb;
with the harp I will expound my riddle:

PRAYING SCRIPTURE

Psalm 49

Are you ever amazed by wealth? By the lifestyles of the superrich whose accumulation of the things of earth is beyond comprehension? The psalmist warned that no amount of money can purchase someone's salvation. It is a cost no human being can pay.

Thankfully, God has provided for salvation in his Son, Jesus Christ. If you are not sure of your relationship with God, ask him now to save you.

---

[a] 2 *Zaphon* was the most sacred mountain of the Canaanites. [b] 8 The Hebrew has *Selah* (a word of uncertain meaning) here. [c] In Hebrew texts 49:1-20 is numbered 49:2-21.

5 Why should I fear when evil days come,
when wicked deceivers surround me—
6 those who trust in their wealth
and boast of their great riches?
7 No one can redeem the life of another
or give to God a ransom for them—
8 the ransom for a life is costly,
no payment is ever enough—
9 so that they should live on forever
and not see decay.
10 For all can see that the wise die,
that the foolish and the senseless also perish,
leaving their wealth to others.
11 Their tombs will remain their houses[a] forever,
their dwellings for endless generations,
though they had[b] named lands after themselves.

12 People, despite their wealth, do not endure;
they are like the beasts that perish.

13 This is the fate of those who trust in themselves,
and of their followers, who approve their sayings.[c]
14 They are like sheep and are destined to die;
death will be their shepherd
(but the upright will prevail over them in the morning).
Their forms will decay in the grave,
far from their princely mansions.
15 But God will redeem me from the realm of the dead;
he will surely take me to himself.
16 Do not be overawed when others grow rich,
when the splendor of their houses increases;
17 for they will take nothing with them when they die,
their splendor will not descend with them.
18 Though while they live they count themselves blessed—
and people praise you when you prosper—
19 they will join those who have gone before them,
who will never again see the light of life.

20 People who have wealth but lack understanding
are like the beasts that perish.

PSALM 50

A psalm of Asaph.

1 The Mighty One, God, the LORD,
speaks and summons the earth
from the rising of the sun to where it sets.
2 From Zion, perfect in beauty,
God shines forth.
3 Our God comes
and will not be silent;
a fire devours before him,
and around him a tempest rages.

[a] 11 Septuagint and Syriac; Hebrew *In their thoughts their houses will remain* [b] 11 Or *generations, / for they have* [c] 13 The Hebrew has *Selah* (a word of uncertain meaning) here and at the end of verse 15.

PRAYING SCRIPTURE

Psalm 50

Why, when times get tough, are we often tempted to think that God has forgotten about us? Despite his ongoing and consistent provision, we doubt. Yet he owns every animal of the forest and field, "the cattle on a thousand hills" (verse 10) and even the birds of the air.

Are you struggling in some area of provision? Tell God what you need; trust his provision. He suffers no lack and will meet your needs.

4 He summons the heavens above,
and the earth, that he may judge his people:
5 "Gather to me this consecrated people,
who made a covenant with me by sacrifice."
6 And the heavens proclaim his righteousness,
for he is a God of justice.[a,b]

7 "Listen, my people, and I will speak;
I will testify against you, Israel:
I am God, your God.
8 I bring no charges against you concerning your sacrifices
or concerning your burnt offerings, which are ever before me.
9 I have no need of a bull from your stall
or of goats from your pens,
10 for every animal of the forest is mine,
and the cattle on a thousand hills.
11 I know every bird in the mountains,
and the insects in the fields are mine.
12 If I were hungry I would not tell you,
for the world is mine, and all that is in it.
13 Do I eat the flesh of bulls
or drink the blood of goats?

14 "Sacrifice thank offerings to God,
fulfill your vows to the Most High,
15 and call on me in the day of trouble;
I will deliver you, and you will honor me."

16 But to the wicked person, God says:

"What right have you to recite my laws
or take my covenant on your lips?
17 You hate my instruction
and cast my words behind you.
18 When you see a thief, you join with him;
you throw in your lot with adulterers.
19 You use your mouth for evil
and harness your tongue to deceit.
20 You sit and testify against your brother
and slander your own mother's son.
21 When you did these things and I kept silent,
you thought I was exactly[c] like you.
But I now arraign you
and set my accusations before you.

22 "Consider this, you who forget God,
or I will tear you to pieces, with no one to rescue you:
23 Those who sacrifice thank offerings honor me,
and to the blameless[d] I will show my salvation."

---

[a] *6* With a different word division of the Hebrew; Masoretic Text *for God himself is judge* [b] *6* The Hebrew has *Selah* (a word of uncertain meaning) here. [c] *21* Or *thought the 'I AM' was* [d] *23* Probable reading of the original Hebrew text; the meaning of the Masoretic Text for this phrase is uncertain.

PRAYING SCRIPTURE

Psalm 51

Nothing is more important to our walk with God than confession, agreeing with God when we sin that we have sinned. No making of excuses, no blaming others. "I know my transgressions, and my sin is always before me" (verse 3). Confession stops blaming and takes responsibility.

All sin is against God first. Confess your sin to him, and then reconcile with anyone you have wounded by your sin as quickly as possible.

PSALM 51[a]

For the director of music. A psalm of David. When the prophet Nathan came to him after David had committed adultery with Bathsheba.

1 Have mercy on me, O God,
according to your unfailing love;
according to your great compassion
blot out my transgressions.
2 Wash away all my iniquity
and cleanse me from my sin.

3 For I know my transgressions,
and my sin is always before me.
4 Against you, you only, have I sinned
and done what is evil in your sight;
so you are right in your verdict
and justified when you judge.
5 Surely I was sinful at birth,
sinful from the time my mother conceived me.
6 Yet you desired faithfulness even in the womb;
you taught me wisdom in that secret place.

7 Cleanse me with hyssop, and I will be clean;
wash me, and I will be whiter than snow.
8 Let me hear joy and gladness;
let the bones you have crushed rejoice.
9 Hide your face from my sins
and blot out all my iniquity.

10 Create in me a pure heart, O God,
and renew a steadfast spirit within me.
11 Do not cast me from your presence
or take your Holy Spirit from me.
12 Restore to me the joy of your salvation
and grant me a willing spirit, to sustain me.

13 Then I will teach transgressors your ways,
so that sinners will turn back to you.
14 Deliver me from the guilt of bloodshed, O God,
you who are God my Savior,
and my tongue will sing of your righteousness.
15 Open my lips, Lord,
and my mouth will declare your praise.
16 You do not delight in sacrifice, or I would bring it;
you do not take pleasure in burnt offerings.
17 My sacrifice, O God, is[b] a broken spirit;
a broken and contrite heart
you, God, will not despise.

18 May it please you to prosper Zion,
to build up the walls of Jerusalem.
19 Then you will delight in the sacrifices of the righteous,
in burnt offerings offered whole;
then bulls will be offered on your altar.

---

[a] In Hebrew texts 51:1-19 is numbered 51:3-21. [b] 17 Or *The sacrifices of God are*

PSALM 52[a]

For the director of music. A maskil[b] of David. When Doeg the Edomite had gone to Saul and told him: "David has gone to the house of Ahimelek."

1 Why do you boast of evil, you mighty hero?
Why do you boast all day long,
you who are a disgrace in the eyes of God?
2 You who practice deceit,
your tongue plots destruction;
it is like a sharpened razor.
3 You love evil rather than good,
falsehood rather than speaking the truth.[c]
4 You love every harmful word,
you deceitful tongue!

5 Surely God will bring you down to everlasting ruin:
He will snatch you up and pluck you from your tent;
he will uproot you from the land of the living.
6 The righteous will see and fear;
they will laugh at you, saying,
7 "Here now is the man
who did not make God his stronghold
but trusted in his great wealth
and grew strong by destroying others!"

8 But I am like an olive tree
flourishing in the house of God;
I trust in God's unfailing love
for ever and ever.
9 For what you have done I will always praise you
in the presence of your faithful people.
And I will hope in your name,
for your name is good.

PSALM 53[d]

For the director of music. According to mahalath.[e] *A maskil*[b] *of David.*

1 The fool says in his heart,
"There is no God."
They are corrupt, and their ways are vile;
there is no one who does good.

2 God looks down from heaven
on all mankind
to see if there are any who understand,
any who seek God.
3 Everyone has turned away, all have become corrupt;
there is no one who does good,
not even one.

4 Do all these evildoers know nothing?

They devour my people as though eating bread;
they never call on God.

---

[a] In Hebrew texts 52:1-9 is numbered 52:3-11. [b] Title: Probably a literary or musical term [c] 3 The Hebrew has *Selah* (a word of uncertain meaning) here and at the end of verse 5. [d] In Hebrew texts 53:1-6 is numbered 53:2-7. [e] Title: Probably a musical term

PRAYING SCRIPTURE

Psalm 52

When David was hiding from King Saul, he took the time to compose poetry. In this psalm, David contrasted the boasting of the mighty who love evil with his own trust in God's mercy. David was unafraid to acknowledge that he pursued God in a way Saul did not.

Prayerfully remind God that you trust his mercy and praise him even in the toughest times.

PRAYING SCRIPTURE

Psalm 53

The universal and pervasive presence of evil can make us feel overwhelmed. God sees and knows that people are not good in themselves and that those who are filled with iniquity attack those who fear God.

Ask God for the faith and hope to trust him and to wait for him. God ultimately will scatter evil, so we can trust that he can overcome it for us.

5 But there they are, overwhelmed with dread,
where there was nothing to dread.
God scattered the bones of those who attacked you;
you put them to shame, for God despised them.

6 Oh, that salvation for Israel would come out of Zion!
When God restores his people,
let Jacob rejoice and Israel be glad!

PRAYING SCRIPTURE

Psalm 54

There is power in remembering what God has done in our past. David often relied on God's previous acts of deliverance to strengthen him in present trials. God never changes. We can trust him now and in the future based on his past work in our lives.

When facing a trial, ask God to give you victory as he has before. Let your faith increase in his unchanging character.

PSALM 54[a]

For the director of music. With stringed instruments. A maskil[b] of David. When the Ziphites had gone to Saul and said, "Is not David hiding among us?"

1 Save me, O God, by your name;
vindicate me by your might.
2 Hear my prayer, O God;
listen to the words of my mouth.

3 Arrogant foes are attacking me;
ruthless people are trying to kill me—
people without regard for God.[c]

4 Surely God is my help;
the Lord is the one who sustains me.

5 Let evil recoil on those who slander me;
in your faithfulness destroy them.

6 I will sacrifice a freewill offering to you;
I will praise your name, LORD, for it is good.
7 You have delivered me from all my troubles,
and my eyes have looked in triumph on my foes.

PRAYING SCRIPTURE

Psalm 55

There is no pain like being abandoned or betrayed by someone you love. David knew the anguish of being betrayed by one he trusted. So does Jesus. What was David's solution? "Cast your cares on the LORD, and he will sustain you" (verse 22).

How does one cast their cares on the Lord? Verbalize to him in prayer that you are shifting your cares to him, and trust him to take them.

PSALM 55[d]

For the director of music. With stringed instruments. A maskil[b] of David.

1 Listen to my prayer, O God,
do not ignore my plea;
2 hear me and answer me.
My thoughts trouble me and I am distraught
3 because of what my enemy is saying,
because of the threats of the wicked;
for they bring down suffering on me
and assail me in their anger.

4 My heart is in anguish within me;
the terrors of death have fallen on me.
5 Fear and trembling have beset me;
horror has overwhelmed me.
6 I said, "Oh, that I had the wings of a dove!
I would fly away and be at rest.
7 I would flee far away
and stay in the desert;[e]

---

[a] In Hebrew texts 54:1-7 is numbered 54:3-9. [b] Title: Probably a literary or musical term [c] 3 The Hebrew has *Selah* (a word of uncertain meaning) here. [d] In Hebrew texts 55:1-23 is numbered 55:2-24. [e] 7 The Hebrew has *Selah* (a word of uncertain meaning) here and in the middle of verse 19.

8 I would hurry to my place of shelter,
far from the tempest and storm."

9 Lord, confuse the wicked, confound their words,
for I see violence and strife in the city.
10 Day and night they prowl about on its walls;
malice and abuse are within it.
11 Destructive forces are at work in the city;
threats and lies never leave its streets.

12 If an enemy were insulting me,
I could endure it;
if a foe were rising against me,
I could hide.
13 But it is you, a man like myself,
my companion, my close friend,
14 with whom I once enjoyed sweet fellowship
at the house of God,
as we walked about
among the worshipers.

15 Let death take my enemies by surprise;
let them go down alive to the realm of the dead,
for evil finds lodging among them.

16 As for me, I call to God,
and the LORD saves me.
17 Evening, morning and noon
I cry out in distress,
and he hears my voice.
18 He rescues me unharmed
from the battle waged against me,
even though many oppose me.
19 God, who is enthroned from of old,
who does not change—
he will hear them and humble them,
because they have no fear of God.

20 My companion attacks his friends;
he violates his covenant.
21 His talk is smooth as butter,
yet war is in his heart;
his words are more soothing than oil,
yet they are drawn swords.

22 Cast your cares on the LORD
and he will sustain you;
he will never let
the righteous be shaken.
23 But you, God, will bring down the wicked
into the pit of decay;
the bloodthirsty and deceitful
will not live out half their days.

But as for me, I trust in you.

PRAYING SCRIPTURE

Psalm 56

David begins this prayer with a raw request: "Be merciful to me, O God." David recognized that he spent all his energy simply trying to survive his enemies. In times of crisis, we may find it difficult to form well-thought-out prayers.

Sometimes we need to pray simply: "Be merciful to me" (verse 1). "I put my trust in you" (verse 3). "In God I trust and am not afraid" (verse 4). If you are in a place of emotional or spiritual exhaustion, pray simply.

PSALM 56[a]

For the director of music. To the tune of "A Dove on Distant Oaks." Of David. A miktam.[b] When the Philistines had seized him in Gath.

1 Be merciful to me, my God,
for my enemies are in hot pursuit;
all day long they press their attack.
2 My adversaries pursue me all day long;
in their pride many are attacking me.

3 When I am afraid, I put my trust in you.
4 In God, whose word I praise —
in God I trust and am not afraid.
What can mere mortals do to me?

5 All day long they twist my words;
all their schemes are for my ruin.
6 They conspire, they lurk,
they watch my steps,
hoping to take my life.
7 Because of their wickedness do not[c] let them escape;
in your anger, God, bring the nations down.

8 Record my misery;
list my tears on your scroll[d] —
are they not in your record?
9 Then my enemies will turn back
when I call for help.
By this I will know that God is for me.

10 In God, whose word I praise,
in the LORD, whose word I praise —
11 in God I trust and am not afraid.
What can man do to me?

12 I am under vows to you, my God;
I will present my thank offerings to you.
13 For you have delivered me from death
and my feet from stumbling,
that I may walk before God
in the light of life.

PRAYING SCRIPTURE

Psalm 57

David could have easily grown despondent and bitter while he was hiding from King Saul. Instead, he said, "I cry out to God Most High," the One who was able to do everything David needed (verse 2). No matter how precarious David's situation, he saw that God had prepared his steps.

Have faith! Cry out to God Most High who is able to deliver you in every situation.

PSALM 57[e]

For the director of music. To the tune of "Do Not Destroy." Of David. A miktam.[b] *When he had fled from Saul into the cave.*

1 Have mercy on me, my God, have mercy on me,
for in you I take refuge.
I will take refuge in the shadow of your wings
until the disaster has passed.

2 I cry out to God Most High,
to God, who vindicates me.
3 He sends from heaven and saves me,

---

[a] In Hebrew texts 56:1-13 is numbered 56:2-14. [b] Title: Probably a literary or musical term [c] 7 Probable reading of the original Hebrew text; Masoretic Text does not have *do not.* [d] 8 Or *misery; / put my tears in your wineskin* [e] In Hebrew texts 57:1-11 is numbered 57:2-12.

rebuking those who hotly pursue me —[a]
God sends forth his love and his faithfulness.

4 I am in the midst of lions;
I am forced to dwell among ravenous beasts —
men whose teeth are spears and arrows,
whose tongues are sharp swords.

5 Be exalted, O God, above the heavens;
let your glory be over all the earth.

6 They spread a net for my feet —
I was bowed down in distress.
They dug a pit in my path —
but they have fallen into it themselves.

7 My heart, O God, is steadfast,
my heart is steadfast;
I will sing and make music.
8 Awake, my soul!
Awake, harp and lyre!
I will awaken the dawn.

9 I will praise you, Lord, among the nations;
I will sing of you among the peoples.
10 For great is your love, reaching to the heavens;
your faithfulness reaches to the skies.

11 Be exalted, O God, above the heavens;
let your glory be over all the earth.

PSALM 58[b]

For the director of music. To the tune of "Do Not Destroy." Of David. A miktam.[c]

1 Do you rulers indeed speak justly?
Do you judge people with equity?
2 No, in your heart you devise injustice,
and your hands mete out violence on the earth.

3 Even from birth the wicked go astray;
from the womb they are wayward, spreading lies.
4 Their venom is like the venom of a snake,
like that of a cobra that has stopped its ears,
5 that will not heed the tune of the charmer,
however skillful the enchanter may be.

6 Break the teeth in their mouths, O God;
LORD, tear out the fangs of those lions!
7 Let them vanish like water that flows away;
when they draw the bow, let their arrows fall short.
8 May they be like a slug that melts away as it moves along,
like a stillborn child that never sees the sun.

9 Before your pots can feel the heat of the thorns —
whether they be green or dry — the wicked will be swept away.[d]

---

[a] 3 The Hebrew has *Selah* (a word of uncertain meaning) here and at the end of verse 6. [b] In Hebrew texts 58:1-11 is numbered 58:2-12. [c] Title: Probably a literary or musical term [d] 9 The meaning of the Hebrew for this verse is uncertain.

PRAYING SCRIPTURE

Psalm 58

We tend to question God's justice when we are suffering while those who commit injustice seem to prosper. In this imprecatory psalm, David begged God to judge the wicked because they were liars, venomous and unwilling to hear. He expressed his desire for their judgment in blunt terms.

This psalm is an example of pouring out one's soul unfiltered before God. You can ask for another's judgment, but leave justice to the Judge.

10 The righteous will be glad when they are avenged,
when they dip their feet in the blood of the wicked.
11 Then people will say,
"Surely the righteous still are rewarded;
surely there is a God who judges the earth."

PRAYING SCRIPTURE

Psalm 59

David returned to his theme of judgment for the wicked and his deliverance from them in God's power. David's writing reminds us—as it reminded him—that God is stronger than any enemy we will ever face and greater than any obstacle we struggle to overcome.

Join David in singing of God's power and mercy. As you give thanks for God's power, let your heart rejoice in song.

PSALM 59[a]

For the director of music. To the tune of "Do Not Destroy." Of David. A miktam.[b] *When Saul had sent men to watch David's house in order to kill him.*

1 Deliver me from my enemies, O God;
be my fortress against those who are attacking me.
2 Deliver me from evildoers
and save me from those who are after my blood.

3 See how they lie in wait for me!
Fierce men conspire against me
for no offense or sin of mine, LORD.
4 I have done no wrong, yet they are ready to attack me.
Arise to help me; look on my plight!
5 You, LORD God Almighty,
you who are the God of Israel,
rouse yourself to punish all the nations;
show no mercy to wicked traitors.[c]

6 They return at evening,
snarling like dogs,
and prowl about the city.
7 See what they spew from their mouths—
the words from their lips are sharp as swords,
and they think, "Who can hear us?"
8 But you laugh at them, LORD;
you scoff at all those nations.

9 You are my strength, I watch for you;
you, God, are my fortress,
10 my God on whom I can rely.

God will go before me
and will let me gloat over those who slander me.
11 But do not kill them, Lord our shield,[d]
or my people will forget.
In your might uproot them
and bring them down.
12 For the sins of their mouths,
for the words of their lips,
let them be caught in their pride.
For the curses and lies they utter,
13 consume them in your wrath,
consume them till they are no more.
Then it will be known to the ends of the earth
that God rules over Jacob.

---

[a] In Hebrew texts 59:1-17 is numbered 59:2-18. [b] Title: Probably a literary or musical term [c] 5 The Hebrew has *Selah* (a word of uncertain meaning) here and at the end of verse 13. [d] 11 Or *sovereign*

14 They return at evening,
snarling like dogs,
and prowl about the city.
15 They wander about for food
and howl if not satisfied.
16 But I will sing of your strength,
in the morning I will sing of your love;
for you are my fortress,
my refuge in times of trouble.

17 You are my strength, I sing praise to you;
you, God, are my fortress,
my God on whom I can rely.

PSALM 60[a]

For the director of music. To the tune of "The Lily of the Covenant." A miktam[b] of David. For teaching. When he fought Aram Naharaim[c] and Aram Zobah,[d] and when Joab returned and struck down twelve thousand Edomites in the Valley of Salt.

1 You have rejected us, God, and burst upon us;
you have been angry — now restore us!
2 You have shaken the land and torn it open;
mend its fractures, for it is quaking.
3 You have shown your people desperate times;
you have given us wine that makes us stagger.
4 But for those who fear you, you have raised a banner
to be unfurled against the bow.[e]

5 Save us and help us with your right hand,
that those you love may be delivered.
6 God has spoken from his sanctuary:
"In triumph I will parcel out Shechem
and measure off the Valley of Sukkoth.
7 Gilead is mine, and Manasseh is mine;
Ephraim is my helmet,
Judah is my scepter.
8 Moab is my washbasin,
on Edom I toss my sandal;
over Philistia I shout in triumph."

9 Who will bring me to the fortified city?
Who will lead me to Edom?
10 Is it not you, God, you who have now rejected us
and no longer go out with our armies?
11 Give us aid against the enemy,
for human help is worthless.
12 With God we will gain the victory,
and he will trample down our enemies.

PRAYING SCRIPTURE

Psalm 60

When you feel like the psalmist—as if God has rejected you or that he is disciplining you—remember the psalmist's hope: God will lead you to victory. God's correction lasts only until we repent and return to obedience.

Is there some sin in your life of which you have not repented? Take some time to tell God that you are turning away from sin and desire to obey him.

---

[a] In Hebrew texts 60:1-12 is numbered 60:3-14. [b] Title: Probably a literary or musical term [c] Title: That is, Arameans of Northwest Mesopotamia [d] Title: That is, Arameans of central Syria [e] 4 The Hebrew has *Selah* (a word of uncertain meaning) here.

PRAYING SCRIPTURE

Psalm 61

We often think of David only as the boy who killed Goliath or as Israel's king, but he often wrote of his weakness and weariness. Here he spoke of being overwhelmed. Can you identify? Do what David did: Confess that God is greater than your fatigue, that he is a refuge for you.

Tell God that you trust him because he is a rock that is higher than you are.

PRAYING SCRIPTURE

Psalm 62

In this psalm, David expressed two great truths—God loves us and is powerful enough to rescue us. Contemplating this, he twice said that his soul would find rest in God. Sometimes silence is necessary to understand what God is doing. Trust him even when you don't understand, and then pour out your heart to him (see verse 8).

Thank God today for being your salvation, your glory, your refuge and your rock of strength.

PSALM 61[a]

For the director of music. With stringed instruments. Of David.

1 Hear my cry, O God;
listen to my prayer.

2 From the ends of the earth I call to you,
I call as my heart grows faint;
lead me to the rock that is higher than I.
3 For you have been my refuge,
a strong tower against the foe.

4 I long to dwell in your tent forever
and take refuge in the shelter of your wings.[b]
5 For you, God, have heard my vows;
you have given me the heritage of those who fear your name.

6 Increase the days of the king's life,
his years for many generations.
7 May he be enthroned in God's presence forever;
appoint your love and faithfulness to protect him.

8 Then I will ever sing in praise of your name
and fulfill my vows day after day.

PSALM 62[c]

For the director of music. For Jeduthun. A psalm of David.

1 Truly my soul finds rest in God;
my salvation comes from him.
2 Truly he is my rock and my salvation;
he is my fortress, I will never be shaken.

3 How long will you assault me?
Would all of you throw me down—
this leaning wall, this tottering fence?
4 Surely they intend to topple me
from my lofty place;
they take delight in lies.
With their mouths they bless,
but in their hearts they curse.[d]

5 Yes, my soul, find rest in God;
my hope comes from him.
6 Truly he is my rock and my salvation;
he is my fortress, I will not be shaken.
7 My salvation and my honor depend on God[e];
he is my mighty rock, my refuge.
8 Trust in him at all times, you people;
pour out your hearts to him,
for God is our refuge.

9 Surely the lowborn are but a breath,
the highborn are but a lie.

---

[a] In Hebrew texts 61:1-8 is numbered 61:2-9. [b] 4 The Hebrew has *Selah* (a word of uncertain meaning) here. [c] In Hebrew texts 62:1-12 is numbered 62:2-13. [d] 4 The Hebrew has *Selah* (a word of uncertain meaning) here and at the end of verse 8. [e] 7 Or / *God Most High is my salvation and my honor*

If weighed on a balance, they are nothing;
together they are only a breath.
10 Do not trust in extortion
or put vain hope in stolen goods;
though your riches increase,
do not set your heart on them.

11 One thing God has spoken,
two things I have heard:
"Power belongs to you, God,
12 and with you, Lord, is unfailing love";
and, "You reward everyone
according to what they have done."

PSALM 63[a]

A psalm of David. When he was in the Desert of Judah.

1 You, God, are my God,
earnestly I seek you;
I thirst for you,
my whole being longs for you,
in a dry and parched land
where there is no water.

2 I have seen you in the sanctuary
and beheld your power and your glory.
3 Because your love is better than life,
my lips will glorify you.
4 I will praise you as long as I live,
and in your name I will lift up my hands.
5 I will be fully satisfied as with the richest of foods;
with singing lips my mouth will praise you.

6 On my bed I remember you;
I think of you through the watches of the night.
7 Because you are my help,
I sing in the shadow of your wings.
8 I cling to you;
your right hand upholds me.

9 Those who want to kill me will be destroyed;
they will go down to the depths of the earth.
10 They will be given over to the sword
and become food for jackals.

11 But the king will rejoice in God;
all who swear by God will glory in him,
while the mouths of liars will be silenced.

PSALM 64[b]

For the director of music. A psalm of David.

1 Hear me, my God, as I voice my complaint;
protect my life from the threat of the enemy.

[a] In Hebrew texts 63:1-11 is numbered 63:2-12. [b] In Hebrew texts 64:1-10 is numbered 64:2-11.

PRAYING SCRIPTURE

Psalm 63

Several insights in this psalm show how David sought God: with hunger and thirst of soul, late at night, passionately. He followed God closely and felt as if he was in the "shadow of [God's] wings," a metaphor for God's loving care (verse 7).

How do you seek God? Is he first on your mind in the morning and last thing at night? Ask him to grow your passion for him.

PRAYING SCRIPTURE

Psalm 64

The final verse of this psalm is a source of great hope and encouragement. Rejoicing in the Lord is a balm for the soul. Living uprightly brings us to glory in God. Our lives are bolstered by his divine presence and power.

Are you struggling to trust God? Make him the source of your gladness, and know the peace of his presence.

2 Hide me from the conspiracy of the wicked,
 from the plots of evildoers.
3 They sharpen their tongues like swords
 and aim cruel words like deadly arrows.
4 They shoot from ambush at the innocent;
 they shoot suddenly, without fear.

5 They encourage each other in evil plans,
 they talk about hiding their snares;
 they say, "Who will see it[a]?"
6 They plot injustice and say,
 "We have devised a perfect plan!"
 Surely the human mind and heart are cunning.

7 But God will shoot them with his arrows;
 they will suddenly be struck down.
8 He will turn their own tongues against them
 and bring them to ruin;
 all who see them will shake their heads in scorn.
9 All people will fear;
 they will proclaim the works of God
 and ponder what he has done.

10 The righteous will rejoice in the LORD
 and take refuge in him;
 all the upright in heart will glory in him!

PSALM 65[b]

For the director of music. A psalm of David. A song.

1 Praise awaits[c] you, our God, in Zion;
 to you our vows will be fulfilled.
2 You who answer prayer,
 to you all people will come.
3 When we were overwhelmed by sins,
 you forgave[d] our transgressions.
4 Blessed are those you choose
 and bring near to live in your courts!
We are filled with the good things of your house,
 of your holy temple.

5 You answer us with awesome and righteous deeds,
 God our Savior,
the hope of all the ends of the earth
 and of the farthest seas,
6 who formed the mountains by your power,
 having armed yourself with strength,
7 who stilled the roaring of the seas,
 the roaring of their waves,
 and the turmoil of the nations.
8 The whole earth is filled with awe at your wonders;
 where morning dawns, where evening fades,
 you call forth songs of joy.

PRAYING SCRIPTURE

Psalm 65

It is a blessing for us to know the true and living God, the One who rules over skies and seas, over the whole earth. Each year is crowned with his bounty, and his methods of delivery "overflow with abundance" (verse 11). He is the true God who provides salvation.

Spend some time thanking God for the blessings you remember. We can never thank the Lord too much for all he does for us.

[a] *5* Or *us* [b] In Hebrew texts 65:1-13 is numbered 65:2-14. [c] *1* Or *befits;* the meaning of the Hebrew for this word is uncertain. [d] *3* Or *made atonement for*

9 You care for the land and water it;
  you enrich it abundantly.
The streams of God are filled with water
  to provide the people with grain,
  for so you have ordained it.[a]
10 You drench its furrows and level its ridges;
  you soften it with showers and bless its crops.
11 You crown the year with your bounty,
  and your carts overflow with abundance.
12 The grasslands of the wilderness overflow;
  the hills are clothed with gladness.
13 The meadows are covered with flocks
  and the valleys are mantled with grain;
  they shout for joy and sing.

PSALM 66

For the director of music. A song. A psalm.

1 Shout for joy to God, all the earth!
2 Sing the glory of his name;
  make his praise glorious.
3 Say to God, "How awesome are your deeds!
  So great is your power
  that your enemies cringe before you.
4 All the earth bows down to you;
  they sing praise to you,
  they sing the praises of your name."[b]

5 Come and see what God has done,
  his awesome deeds for mankind!
6 He turned the sea into dry land,
  they passed through the waters on foot—
  come, let us rejoice in him.
7 He rules forever by his power,
  his eyes watch the nations—
  let not the rebellious rise up against him.

8 Praise our God, all peoples,
  let the sound of his praise be heard;
9 he has preserved our lives
  and kept our feet from slipping.
10 For you, God, tested us;
  you refined us like silver.
11 You brought us into prison
  and laid burdens on our backs.
12 You let people ride over our heads;
  we went through fire and water,
  but you brought us to a place of abundance.

13 I will come to your temple with burnt offerings
  and fulfill my vows to you—
14 vows my lips promised and my mouth spoke
  when I was in trouble.

[a] 9 Or *for that is how you prepare the land* [b] 4 The Hebrew has *Selah* (a word of uncertain meaning) here and at the end of verses 7 and 15.

PRAYING SCRIPTURE

Psalm 66

In a psalm filled with encouragement to praise, verse 18 is a stark warning for our spiritual lives: If we are content with sin, it stops our prayers from being heard. Have you ever wondered why some prayers go unanswered? Though there are other possibilities, we should not overlook sin.

Many patterns of prayer teach confession of sins before petitioning God. Open the lines of communication, and then offer your requests.

[15] I will sacrifice fat animals to you
and an offering of rams;
I will offer bulls and goats.

[16] Come and hear, all you who fear God;
let me tell you what he has done for me.
[17] I cried out to him with my mouth;
his praise was on my tongue.
[18] If I had cherished sin in my heart,
the Lord would not have listened;
[19] but God has surely listened
and has heard my prayer.
[20] Praise be to God,
who has not rejected my prayer
or withheld his love from me!

PSALM 67[a]

For the director of music. With stringed instruments. A psalm. A song.

[1] May God be gracious to us and bless us
and make his face shine on us —[b]
[2] so that your ways may be known on earth,
your salvation among all nations.

[3] May the peoples praise you, God;
may all the peoples praise you.
[4] May the nations be glad and sing for joy,
for you rule the peoples with equity
and guide the nations of the earth.
[5] May the peoples praise you, God;
may all the peoples praise you.

[6] The land yields its harvest;
God, our God, blesses us.
[7] May God bless us still,
so that all the ends of the earth will fear him.

PSALM 68[c]

For the director of music. Of David. A psalm. A song.

[1] May God arise, may his enemies be scattered;
may his foes flee before him.
[2] May you blow them away like smoke —
as wax melts before the fire,
may the wicked perish before God.
[3] But may the righteous be glad
and rejoice before God;
may they be happy and joyful.

[4] Sing to God, sing in praise of his name,
extol him who rides on the clouds[d];
rejoice before him — his name is the LORD.

[a] In Hebrew texts 67:1-7 is numbered 67:2-8. [b] *1* The Hebrew has *Selah* (a word of uncertain meaning) here and at the end of verse 4. [c] In Hebrew texts 68:1-35 is numbered 68:2-36. [d] *4* Or *name, / prepare the way for him who rides through the deserts*

PRAYING SCRIPTURE

Psalm 67

"May God be gracious to us and bless us and make his face to shine on us" is often remembered, while the goal—that God's way might be known for salvation in all the nations—is not (see verses 1–2).

God is concerned with the gospel's going to the nations. If you don't have a burden for global peoples who have never heard the gospel, ask God to help you love them the way he does.

PRAYING SCRIPTURE

Psalm 68

In this psalm of praise, David built refrain upon refrain celebrating the character, nature and works of God. God is both the One who scatters his enemies and a father to the fatherless. He is both a defender of widows and the captain of thousands of chariots. He is all-in-all.

This psalm should encourage you because God is everything you need. In faith ask him to supply your every need.

5 A father to the fatherless, a defender of widows,
is God in his holy dwelling.
6 God sets the lonely in families,[a]
he leads out the prisoners with singing;
but the rebellious live in a sun-scorched land.

7 When you, God, went out before your people,
when you marched through the wilderness,[b]
8 the earth shook, the heavens poured down rain,
before God, the One of Sinai,
before God, the God of Israel.
9 You gave abundant showers, O God;
you refreshed your weary inheritance.
10 Your people settled in it,
and from your bounty, God, you provided for the poor.

11 The Lord announces the word,
and the women who proclaim it are a mighty throng:
12 "Kings and armies flee in haste;
the women at home divide the plunder.
13 Even while you sleep among the sheep pens,[c]
the wings of my dove are sheathed with silver,
its feathers with shining gold."
14 When the Almighty[d] scattered the kings in the land,
it was like snow fallen on Mount Zalmon.

15 Mount Bashan, majestic mountain,
Mount Bashan, rugged mountain,
16 why gaze in envy, you rugged mountain,
at the mountain where God chooses to reign,
where the LORD himself will dwell forever?
17 The chariots of God are tens of thousands
and thousands of thousands;
the Lord has come from Sinai into his sanctuary.[e]
18 When you ascended on high,
you took many captives;
you received gifts from people,
even from[f] the rebellious—
that you,[g] LORD God, might dwell there.

19 Praise be to the Lord, to God our Savior,
who daily bears our burdens.
20 Our God is a God who saves;
from the Sovereign LORD comes escape from death.
21 Surely God will crush the heads of his enemies,
the hairy crowns of those who go on in their sins.
22 The Lord says, "I will bring them from Bashan;
I will bring them from the depths of the sea,
23 that your feet may wade in the blood of your foes,
while the tongues of your dogs have their share."

---

[a] 6 Or *the desolate in a homeland* [b] 7 The Hebrew has *Selah* (a word of uncertain meaning) here and at the end of verses 19 and 32. [c] 13 Or *the campfires;* or *the saddlebags* [d] 14 Hebrew *Shaddai* [e] 17 Probable reading of the original Hebrew text; Masoretic Text *Lord is among them at Sinai in holiness* [f] 18 Or *gifts for people, / even* [g] 18 Or *they*

24 Your procession, God, has come into view,
the procession of my God and King into the sanctuary.
25 In front are the singers, after them the musicians;
with them are the young women playing the timbrels.
26 Praise God in the great congregation;
praise the LORD in the assembly of Israel.
27 There is the little tribe of Benjamin, leading them,
there the great throng of Judah's princes,
and there the princes of Zebulun and of Naphtali.

28 Summon your power, God[a];
show us your strength, our God, as you have done before.
29 Because of your temple at Jerusalem
kings will bring you gifts.
30 Rebuke the beast among the reeds,
the herd of bulls among the calves of the nations.
Humbled, may the beast bring bars of silver.
Scatter the nations who delight in war.
31 Envoys will come from Egypt;
Cush[b] will submit herself to God.

32 Sing to God, you kingdoms of the earth,
sing praise to the Lord,
33 to him who rides across the highest heavens, the ancient heavens,
who thunders with mighty voice.
34 Proclaim the power of God,
whose majesty is over Israel,
whose power is in the heavens.
35 You, God, are awesome in your sanctuary;
the God of Israel gives power and strength to his people.

Praise be to God!

PRAYING SCRIPTURE

Psalm 69

The whole Bible testifies to God lifting up the poor. God desires to show his strength when his children are in need, even when they are conflicted. David confessed his foolishness and shame while being zealous for God's house in repentance.

God draws close to the humble. When you've sinned, come back to God in humility; he will meet you there and lift you up.

PSALM 69[c]

For the director of music. To the tune of "Lilies." Of David.

1 Save me, O God,
for the waters have come up to my neck.
2 I sink in the miry depths,
where there is no foothold.
I have come into the deep waters;
the floods engulf me.
3 I am worn out calling for help;
my throat is parched.
My eyes fail,
looking for my God.
4 Those who hate me without reason
outnumber the hairs of my head;
many are my enemies without cause,
those who seek to destroy me.
I am forced to restore
what I did not steal.

---

[a] *28* Many Hebrew manuscripts, Septuagint and Syriac; most Hebrew manuscripts *Your God has summoned power for you* [b] *31* That is, the upper Nile region [c] In Hebrew texts 69:1-36 is numbered 69:2-37.

5 You, God, know my folly;
my guilt is not hidden from you.

6 Lord, the LORD Almighty,
may those who hope in you
not be disgraced because of me;
God of Israel,
may those who seek you
not be put to shame because of me.
7 For I endure scorn for your sake,
and shame covers my face.
8 I am a foreigner to my own family,
a stranger to my own mother's children;
9 for zeal for your house consumes me,
and the insults of those who insult you fall on me.
10 When I weep and fast,
I must endure scorn;
11 when I put on sackcloth,
people make sport of me.
12 Those who sit at the gate mock me,
and I am the song of the drunkards.

13 But I pray to you, LORD,
in the time of your favor;
in your great love, O God,
answer me with your sure salvation.
14 Rescue me from the mire,
do not let me sink;
deliver me from those who hate me,
from the deep waters.
15 Do not let the floodwaters engulf me
or the depths swallow me up
or the pit close its mouth over me.

16 Answer me, LORD, out of the goodness of your love;
in your great mercy turn to me.
17 Do not hide your face from your servant;
answer me quickly, for I am in trouble.
18 Come near and rescue me;
deliver me because of my foes.

19 You know how I am scorned, disgraced and shamed;
all my enemies are before you.
20 Scorn has broken my heart
and has left me helpless;
I looked for sympathy, but there was none,
for comforters, but I found none.
21 They put gall in my food
and gave me vinegar for my thirst.

22 May the table set before them become a snare;
may it become retribution and[a] a trap.
23 May their eyes be darkened so they cannot see,
and their backs be bent forever.

---

[a] 22 Or *snare / and their fellowship become*

24 Pour out your wrath on them;
   let your fierce anger overtake them.
25 May their place be deserted;
   let there be no one to dwell in their tents.
26 For they persecute those you wound
   and talk about the pain of those you hurt.
27 Charge them with crime upon crime;
   do not let them share in your salvation.
28 May they be blotted out of the book of life
   and not be listed with the righteous.

29 But as for me, afflicted and in pain —
   may your salvation, God, protect me.

30 I will praise God's name in song
   and glorify him with thanksgiving.
31 This will please the LORD more than an ox,
   more than a bull with its horns and hooves.
32 The poor will see and be glad —
   you who seek God, may your hearts live!
33 The LORD hears the needy
   and does not despise his captive people.

34 Let heaven and earth praise him,
   the seas and all that move in them,
35 for God will save Zion
   and rebuild the cities of Judah.
Then people will settle there and possess it;
36 the children of his servants will inherit it,
   and those who love his name will dwell there.

PSALM 70[a]

For the director of music. Of David. A petition.

1 Hasten, O God, to save me;
   come quickly, LORD, to help me.

2 May those who want to take my life
   be put to shame and confusion;
may all who desire my ruin
   be turned back in disgrace.
3 May those who say to me, "Aha! Aha!"
   turn back because of their shame.
4 But may all who seek you
   rejoice and be glad in you;
may those who long for your saving help always say,
   "The LORD is great!"

5 But as for me, I am poor and needy;
   come quickly to me, O God.
You are my help and my deliverer;
   LORD, do not delay.

PSALM 71

1 In you, LORD, I have taken refuge;
   let me never be put to shame.

[a] In Hebrew texts 70:1-5 is numbered 70:2-6.

PRAYING SCRIPTURE

Psalm 70

Sometimes the sum of our spiritual strength is simply a short, direct prayer to God. Such prayers are not weaker than the lengthy ones we might offer in a personal devotional time. God hears and responds to these prayer flares just as certainly.

Develop the habit of calling out to God in the moment. Don't save up your requests when you can call on him anytime and anywhere.

PRAYING SCRIPTURE

Psalm 71

The Psalms note a variety of instruments that were used in the worship of God, indicating that each culture can authentically offer praise. Two of these "instruments" exist in every culture: tongues and lips. Singing is the most revelatory type of praise; it allows descriptions of God's character and work.

Have you ever sung a prayer? When you next sing a worship song, direct it to God as a prayer.

2 In your righteousness, rescue me and deliver me;
turn your ear to me and save me.
3 Be my rock of refuge,
to which I can always go;
give the command to save me,
for you are my rock and my fortress.
4 Deliver me, my God, from the hand of the wicked,
from the grasp of those who are evil and cruel.

5 For you have been my hope, Sovereign LORD,
my confidence since my youth.
6 From birth I have relied on you;
you brought me forth from my mother's womb.
I will ever praise you.
7 I have become a sign to many;
you are my strong refuge.
8 My mouth is filled with your praise,
declaring your splendor all day long.

9 Do not cast me away when I am old;
do not forsake me when my strength is gone.
10 For my enemies speak against me;
those who wait to kill me conspire together.
11 They say, "God has forsaken him;
pursue him and seize him,
for no one will rescue him."
12 Do not be far from me, my God;
come quickly, God, to help me.
13 May my accusers perish in shame;
may those who want to harm me
be covered with scorn and disgrace.

14 As for me, I will always have hope;
I will praise you more and more.
15 My mouth will tell of your righteous deeds,
of your saving acts all day long —
though I know not how to relate them all.
16 I will come and proclaim your mighty acts, Sovereign LORD;
I will proclaim your righteous deeds, yours alone.
17 Since my youth, God, you have taught me,
and to this day I declare your marvelous deeds.
18 Even when I am old and gray,
do not forsake me, my God,
till I declare your power to the next generation,
your mighty acts to all who are to come.

19 Your righteousness, God, reaches to the heavens,
you who have done great things.
Who is like you, God?
20 Though you have made me see troubles,
many and bitter,
you will restore my life again;
from the depths of the earth
you will again bring me up.
21 You will increase my honor
and comfort me once more.

22 I will praise you with the harp
for your faithfulness, my God;
I will sing praise to you with the lyre,
Holy One of Israel.
23 My lips will shout for joy
when I sing praise to you —
I whom you have delivered.
24 My tongue will tell of your righteous acts
all day long,
for those who wanted to harm me
have been put to shame and confusion.

PRAYING SCRIPTURE

Psalm 72

This psalm foreshadows the Messiah's reign. The descriptions of power, wisdom and endurance far exceed those of any earthly king. "All nations . . . will call him blessed" is the assurance all followers of Jesus have: Jesus is the Messiah for all (verse 17).

If you don't regularly pray for those who haven't heard the gospel, why not make it a practice? Whether they're across town or across the world, ask God to send gospel ambassadors to them.

PSALM 72

Of Solomon.

1 Endow the king with your justice, O God,
the royal son with your righteousness.
2 May he judge your people in righteousness,
your afflicted ones with justice.

3 May the mountains bring prosperity to the people,
the hills the fruit of righteousness.
4 May he defend the afflicted among the people
and save the children of the needy;
may he crush the oppressor.
5 May he endure[a] as long as the sun,
as long as the moon, through all generations.
6 May he be like rain falling on a mown field,
like showers watering the earth.
7 In his days may the righteous flourish
and prosperity abound till the moon is no more.

8 May he rule from sea to sea
and from the River[b] to the ends of the earth.
9 May the desert tribes bow before him
and his enemies lick the dust.
10 May the kings of Tarshish and of distant shores
bring tribute to him.
May the kings of Sheba and Seba
present him gifts.
11 May all kings bow down to him
and all nations serve him.

12 For he will deliver the needy who cry out,
the afflicted who have no one to help.
13 He will take pity on the weak and the needy
and save the needy from death.
14 He will rescue them from oppression and violence,
for precious is their blood in his sight.

15 Long may he live!
May gold from Sheba be given him.
May people ever pray for him
and bless him all day long.

---

[a] *5* Septuagint; Hebrew *You will be feared* [b] *8* That is, the Euphrates

16 May grain abound throughout the land;
  on the tops of the hills may it sway.
May the crops flourish like Lebanon
  and thrive[a] like the grass of the field.
17 May his name endure forever;
  may it continue as long as the sun.

Then all nations will be blessed through him,[b]
  and they will call him blessed.

18 Praise be to the LORD God, the God of Israel,
  who alone does marvelous deeds.
19 Praise be to his glorious name forever;
  may the whole earth be filled with his glory.
    Amen and Amen.

20 This concludes the prayers of David son of Jesse.

BOOK III

PSALMS 73 – 89

PSALM 73

A psalm of Asaph.

1 Surely God is good to Israel,
  to those who are pure in heart.

2 But as for me, my feet had almost slipped;
  I had nearly lost my foothold.
3 For I envied the arrogant
  when I saw the prosperity of the wicked.

4 They have no struggles;
  their bodies are healthy and strong.[c]
5 They are free from common human burdens;
  they are not plagued by human ills.
6 Therefore pride is their necklace;
  they clothe themselves with violence.
7 From their callous hearts comes iniquity[d];
  their evil imaginations have no limits.
8 They scoff, and speak with malice;
  with arrogance they threaten oppression.
9 Their mouths lay claim to heaven,
  and their tongues take possession of the earth.
10 Therefore their people turn to them
  and drink up waters in abundance.[e]
11 They say, "How would God know?
  Does the Most High know anything?"

[a] 16 Probable reading of the original Hebrew text; Masoretic Text *Lebanon, / from the city* [b] 17 Or *will use his name in blessings* (see Gen. 48:20)
[c] 4 With a different word division of the Hebrew; Masoretic Text *struggles at their death; / their bodies are healthy* [d] 7 Syriac (see also Septuagint); Hebrew *Their eyes bulge with fat* [e] 10 The meaning of the Hebrew for this verse is uncertain.

PRAYING SCRIPTURE

Psalm 73

This psalm has provided comfort for countless believers struggling to understand why evil people seem to prosper. The writer, Asaph, confessed that he himself nearly slipped because he concentrated on why the evil prospered.

Asaph's heart was comforted when he realized God does indeed judge the wicked. Ask God to help you focus on him and not be distracted by the state of the wicked.

[12] This is what the wicked are like —
always free of care, they go on amassing wealth.

[13] Surely in vain I have kept my heart pure
and have washed my hands in innocence.
[14] All day long I have been afflicted,
and every morning brings new punishments.

[15] If I had spoken out like that,
I would have betrayed your children.
[16] When I tried to understand all this,
it troubled me deeply
[17] till I entered the sanctuary of God;
then I understood their final destiny.

[18] Surely you place them on slippery ground;
you cast them down to ruin.
[19] How suddenly are they destroyed,
completely swept away by terrors!
[20] They are like a dream when one awakes;
when you arise, Lord,
you will despise them as fantasies.

[21] When my heart was grieved
and my spirit embittered,
[22] I was senseless and ignorant;
I was a brute beast before you.

[23] Yet I am always with you;
you hold me by my right hand.
[24] You guide me with your counsel,
and afterward you will take me into glory.
[25] Whom have I in heaven but you?
And earth has nothing I desire besides you.
[26] My flesh and my heart may fail,
but God is the strength of my heart
and my portion forever.

[27] Those who are far from you will perish;
you destroy all who are unfaithful to you.
[28] But as for me, it is good to be near God.
I have made the Sovereign LORD my refuge;
I will tell of all your deeds.

PSALM 74

A maskil[a] of Asaph.

[1] O God, why have you rejected us forever?
Why does your anger smolder against the sheep of your pasture?
[2] Remember the nation you purchased long ago,
the people of your inheritance, whom you redeemed —
Mount Zion, where you dwelt.
[3] Turn your steps toward these everlasting ruins,
all this destruction the enemy has brought on the sanctuary.

[4] Your foes roared in the place where you met with us;
they set up their standards as signs.

PRAYING SCRIPTURE

Psalm 74

Asaph wrote what many of God's people have voiced in times of despair: "Where is God?" But Asaph was not concerned only about himself. He longed to see God stop evil people from blaspheming his name.

With hope he looked to God's works of old and implored God to act in the same way again. When your way is dark, why not bring God's previous, glorious works before him in prayer?

[a] Title: Probably a literary or musical term

5 They behaved like men wielding axes
to cut through a thicket of trees.
6 They smashed all the carved paneling
with their axes and hatchets.
7 They burned your sanctuary to the ground;
they defiled the dwelling place of your Name.
8 They said in their hearts, "We will crush them completely!"
They burned every place where God was worshiped in the land.

9 We are given no signs from God;
no prophets are left,
and none of us knows how long this will be.
10 How long will the enemy mock you, God?
Will the foe revile your name forever?
11 Why do you hold back your hand, your right hand?
Take it from the folds of your garment and destroy them!

12 But God is my King from long ago;
he brings salvation on the earth.

13 It was you who split open the sea by your power;
you broke the heads of the monster in the waters.
14 It was you who crushed the heads of Leviathan
and gave it as food to the creatures of the desert.
15 It was you who opened up springs and streams;
you dried up the ever-flowing rivers.
16 The day is yours, and yours also the night;
you established the sun and moon.
17 It was you who set all the boundaries of the earth;
you made both summer and winter.

18 Remember how the enemy has mocked you, LORD,
how foolish people have reviled your name.
19 Do not hand over the life of your dove to wild beasts;
do not forget the lives of your afflicted people forever.
20 Have regard for your covenant,
because haunts of violence fill the dark places of the land.
21 Do not let the oppressed retreat in disgrace;
may the poor and needy praise your name.
22 Rise up, O God, and defend your cause;
remember how fools mock you all day long.
23 Do not ignore the clamor of your adversaries,
the uproar of your enemies, which rises continually.

PSALM 75[a]

For the director of music. To the tune of "Do Not Destroy." A psalm of Asaph. A song.

1 We praise you, God,
we praise you, for your Name is near;
people tell of your wonderful deeds.

2 You say, "I choose the appointed time;
it is I who judge with equity.
3 When the earth and all its people quake,
it is I who hold its pillars firm.[b]

[a] In Hebrew texts 75:1-10 is numbered 75:2-11. [b] 3 The Hebrew has *Selah* (a word of uncertain meaning) here.

PRAYING SCRIPTURE

Psalm 75

A phrase in verse 9 is helpful in setting our focus: "But I will declare this forever." The psalmist did not say precisely what he would declare, but given that he moved into a posture of praise from recounting God's greatness, we can infer that God was the subject of his declaration.

When you are troubled, declare who God is, what he has done and what you are asking him to do for you.

4 To the arrogant I say, 'Boast no more,'
and to the wicked, 'Do not lift up your horns.[a]
5 Do not lift your horns against heaven;
do not speak so defiantly.' "

6 No one from the east or the west
or from the desert can exalt themselves.
7 It is God who judges:
He brings one down, he exalts another.
8 In the hand of the LORD is a cup
full of foaming wine mixed with spices;
he pours it out, and all the wicked of the earth
drink it down to its very dregs.

9 As for me, I will declare this forever;
I will sing praise to the God of Jacob,
10 who says, "I will cut off the horns of all the wicked,
but the horns of the righteous will be lifted up."

PRAYING SCRIPTURE

Psalm 76

This psalm of praise reminds us that hope can arise when we remember that God will ultimately judge evil. The wicked will not have the final victory, even though they rebel against God and oppress their fellow humans.

To overcome hopelessness in a world gone wrong, focus on God's power and wisdom. Even human wrath will glorify him. Ask God to make you a witness to his justice.

PSALM 76[b]

For the director of music. With stringed instruments. A psalm of Asaph. A song.

1 God is renowned in Judah;
in Israel his name is great.
2 His tent is in Salem,
his dwelling place in Zion.
3 There he broke the flashing arrows,
the shields and the swords, the weapons of war.[c]

4 You are radiant with light,
more majestic than mountains rich with game.
5 The valiant lie plundered,
they sleep their last sleep;
not one of the warriors
can lift his hands.
6 At your rebuke, God of Jacob,
both horse and chariot lie still.

7 It is you alone who are to be feared.
Who can stand before you when you are angry?
8 From heaven you pronounced judgment,
and the land feared and was quiet—
9 when you, God, rose up to judge,
to save all the afflicted of the land.
10 Surely your wrath against mankind brings you praise,
and the survivors of your wrath are restrained.[d]

11 Make vows to the LORD your God and fulfill them;
let all the neighboring lands
bring gifts to the One to be feared.
12 He breaks the spirit of rulers;
he is feared by the kings of the earth.

---

[a] 4 *Horns* here symbolize strength; also in verses 5 and 10. [b] In Hebrew texts 76:1-12 is numbered 76:2-13. [c] 3 The Hebrew has *Selah* (a word of uncertain meaning) here and at the end of verse 9. [d] 10 Or *Surely the wrath of mankind brings you praise, / and with the remainder of wrath you arm yourself*

PSALM 77[a]

For the director of music. For Jeduthun. Of Asaph. A psalm.

1 I cried out to God for help;
I cried out to God to hear me.
2 When I was in distress, I sought the Lord;
at night I stretched out untiring hands,
and I would not be comforted.

3 I remembered you, God, and I groaned;
I meditated, and my spirit grew faint.[b]
4 You kept my eyes from closing;
I was too troubled to speak.
5 I thought about the former days,
the years of long ago;
6 I remembered my songs in the night.
My heart meditated and my spirit asked:

7 "Will the Lord reject forever?
Will he never show his favor again?
8 Has his unfailing love vanished forever?
Has his promise failed for all time?
9 Has God forgotten to be merciful?
Has he in anger withheld his compassion?"

10 Then I thought, "To this I will appeal:
the years when the Most High stretched out his right hand.
11 I will remember the deeds of the LORD;
yes, I will remember your miracles of long ago.
12 I will consider all your works
and meditate on all your mighty deeds."

13 Your ways, God, are holy.
What god is as great as our God?
14 You are the God who performs miracles;
you display your power among the peoples.
15 With your mighty arm you redeemed your people,
the descendants of Jacob and Joseph.

16 The waters saw you, God,
the waters saw you and writhed;
the very depths were convulsed.
17 The clouds poured down water,
the heavens resounded with thunder;
your arrows flashed back and forth.
18 Your thunder was heard in the whirlwind,
your lightning lit up the world;
the earth trembled and quaked.
19 Your path led through the sea,
your way through the mighty waters,
though your footprints were not seen.

20 You led your people like a flock
by the hand of Moses and Aaron.

PRAYING SCRIPTURE

Psalm 77

What a deep time of suffering the psalmist endured. In a day of trouble, he reached out, but no help was found. His soul could not be comforted. He was troubled, complaining and overwhelmed in spirit. He was so fatigued he could not stay awake or speak. Have you ever felt this low?

Why not imitate the author? Meditate on God's works, and tell others all he has done for you.

[a] In Hebrew texts 77:1-20 is numbered 77:2-21. [b] 3 The Hebrew has *Selah* (a word of uncertain meaning) here and at the end of verses 9 and 15.

PRAYING SCRIPTURE

Psalm 78

Recounting Israel's history from Jacob through the years in Egypt and the wilderness wandering, the psalmist reminded readers of God's long record of patience with his people. Despite their many rebellions, God always forgave and loved the people he'd chosen for his own.

All of God's people sin, and many experience backsliding. While you are praying, thank God for his patience when you stray.

PRAYING SCRIPTURE

Psalm 78

A question asked in doubt becomes a rhetorical question answered "yes": "Can God really spread a table in the wilderness?" (verse 19). The children of Israel did not have faith that God could provide for their needs; they saw starvation in their future. We should see provision.

God can and does provide for his children. Whether manna, quail or salad, God gives as a Father to his children. Always let him know of your needs.

PSALM 78

A maskil[a] *of Asaph.*

1 My people, hear my teaching;
listen to the words of my mouth.
2 I will open my mouth with a parable;
I will utter hidden things, things from of old—
3 things we have heard and known,
things our ancestors have told us.
4 We will not hide them from their descendants;
we will tell the next generation
the praiseworthy deeds of the LORD,
his power, and the wonders he has done.
5 He decreed statutes for Jacob
and established the law in Israel,
which he commanded our ancestors
to teach their children,
6 so the next generation would know them,
even the children yet to be born,
and they in turn would tell their children.
7 Then they would put their trust in God
and would not forget his deeds
but would keep his commands.
8 They would not be like their ancestors—
a stubborn and rebellious generation,
whose hearts were not loyal to God,
whose spirits were not faithful to him.

9 The men of Ephraim, though armed with bows,
turned back on the day of battle;
10 they did not keep God's covenant
and refused to live by his law.
11 They forgot what he had done,
the wonders he had shown them.
12 He did miracles in the sight of their ancestors
in the land of Egypt, in the region of Zoan.
13 He divided the sea and led them through;
he made the water stand up like a wall.
14 He guided them with the cloud by day
and with light from the fire all night.
15 He split the rocks in the wilderness
and gave them water as abundant as the seas;
16 he brought streams out of a rocky crag
and made water flow down like rivers.

17 But they continued to sin against him,
rebelling in the wilderness against the Most High.
18 They willfully put God to the test
by demanding the food they craved.
19 They spoke against God;
they said, "Can God really
spread a table in the wilderness?
20 True, he struck the rock,

[a] Title: Probably a literary or musical term

and water gushed out,
streams flowed abundantly,
but can he also give us bread?
Can he supply meat for his people?"
21 When the LORD heard them, he was furious;
his fire broke out against Jacob,
and his wrath rose against Israel,
22 for they did not believe in God
or trust in his deliverance.
23 Yet he gave a command to the skies above
and opened the doors of the heavens;
24 he rained down manna for the people to eat,
he gave them the grain of heaven.
25 Human beings ate the bread of angels;
he sent them all the food they could eat.
26 He let loose the east wind from the heavens
and by his power made the south wind blow.
27 He rained meat down on them like dust,
birds like sand on the seashore.
28 He made them come down inside their camp,
all around their tents.
29 They ate till they were gorged—
he had given them what they craved.
30 But before they turned from what they craved,
even while the food was still in their mouths,
31 God's anger rose against them;
he put to death the sturdiest among them,
cutting down the young men of Israel.

32 In spite of all this, they kept on sinning;
in spite of his wonders, they did not believe.
33 So he ended their days in futility
and their years in terror.
34 Whenever God slew them, they would seek him;
they eagerly turned to him again.
35 They remembered that God was their Rock,
that God Most High was their Redeemer.
36 But then they would flatter him with their mouths,
lying to him with their tongues;
37 their hearts were not loyal to him,
they were not faithful to his covenant.
38 Yet he was merciful;
he forgave their iniquities
and did not destroy them.
Time after time he restrained his anger
and did not stir up his full wrath.
39 He remembered that they were but flesh,
a passing breeze that does not return.

40 How often they rebelled against him in the wilderness
and grieved him in the wasteland!
41 Again and again they put God to the test;
they vexed the Holy One of Israel.
42 They did not remember his power—
the day he redeemed them from the oppressor,

43 the day he displayed his signs in Egypt,
his wonders in the region of Zoan.
44 He turned their river into blood;
they could not drink from their streams.
45 He sent swarms of flies that devoured them,
and frogs that devastated them.
46 He gave their crops to the grasshopper,
their produce to the locust.
47 He destroyed their vines with hail
and their sycamore-figs with sleet.
48 He gave over their cattle to the hail,
their livestock to bolts of lightning.
49 He unleashed against them his hot anger,
his wrath, indignation and hostility—
a band of destroying angels.
50 He prepared a path for his anger;
he did not spare them from death
but gave them over to the plague.
51 He struck down all the firstborn of Egypt,
the firstfruits of manhood in the tents of Ham.
52 But he brought his people out like a flock;
he led them like sheep through the wilderness.
53 He guided them safely, so they were unafraid;
but the sea engulfed their enemies.
54 And so he brought them to the border of his holy land,
to the hill country his right hand had taken.
55 He drove out nations before them
and allotted their lands to them as an inheritance;
he settled the tribes of Israel in their homes.

56 But they put God to the test
and rebelled against the Most High;
they did not keep his statutes.
57 Like their ancestors they were disloyal and faithless,
as unreliable as a faulty bow.
58 They angered him with their high places;
they aroused his jealousy with their idols.
59 When God heard them, he was furious;
he rejected Israel completely.
60 He abandoned the tabernacle of Shiloh,
the tent he had set up among humans.
61 He sent the ark of his might into captivity,
his splendor into the hands of the enemy.
62 He gave his people over to the sword;
he was furious with his inheritance.
63 Fire consumed their young men,
and their young women had no wedding songs;
64 their priests were put to the sword,
and their widows could not weep.

65 Then the Lord awoke as from sleep,
as a warrior wakes from the stupor of wine.
66 He beat back his enemies;
he put them to everlasting shame.
67 Then he rejected the tents of Joseph,
he did not choose the tribe of Ephraim;

68 but he chose the tribe of Judah,
  Mount Zion, which he loved.
69 He built his sanctuary like the heights,
  like the earth that he established forever.
70 He chose David his servant
  and took him from the sheep pens;
71 from tending the sheep he brought him
  to be the shepherd of his people Jacob,
  of Israel his inheritance.
72 And David shepherded them with integrity of heart;
  with skillful hands he led them.

PSALM 79

A psalm of Asaph.

1 O God, the nations have invaded your inheritance;
  they have defiled your holy temple,
  they have reduced Jerusalem to rubble.
2 They have left the dead bodies of your servants
  as food for the birds of the sky,
  the flesh of your own people for the animals of the wild.
3 They have poured out blood like water
  all around Jerusalem,
  and there is no one to bury the dead.
4 We are objects of contempt to our neighbors,
  of scorn and derision to those around us.

5 How long, LORD? Will you be angry forever?
  How long will your jealousy burn like fire?
6 Pour out your wrath on the nations
  that do not acknowledge you,
on the kingdoms
  that do not call on your name;
7 for they have devoured Jacob
  and devastated his homeland.

8 Do not hold against us the sins of past generations;
  may your mercy come quickly to meet us,
  for we are in desperate need.
9 Help us, God our Savior,
  for the glory of your name;
deliver us and forgive our sins
  for your name's sake.
10 Why should the nations say,
  "Where is their God?"

Before our eyes, make known among the nations
  that you avenge the outpoured blood of your servants.
11 May the groans of the prisoners come before you;
  with your strong arm preserve those condemned to die.
12 Pay back into the laps of our neighbors seven times
  the contempt they have hurled at you, Lord.
13 Then we your people, the sheep of your pasture,
  will praise you forever;
from generation to generation
  we will proclaim your praise.

PRAYING SCRIPTURE

Psalm 79

After mourning the Israelites' fallen condition—a situation caused by their own rebellion and disobedience—and begging for God's mercy, this psalm ends with a hopeful declaration that God's people are the sheep of his pasture and the ones who will never cease to praise him.

The hope we have in Christ is that God will not abandon us. Ask God today for this hope to fill your life.

PRAYING SCRIPTURE

Psalm 80

During a time when God appeared silent, three times the writer asked God to restore his people, to "make your face shine on us, that we may be saved" (verses 3,7,19). If God would look approvingly upon them, salvation would follow.

Although we can be confident that God does not get distracted, sometimes we can feel as if he is. With the psalmist, ask God to cause his face to shine on you.

PSALM 80[a]

For the director of music. To the tune of "The Lilies of the Covenant." Of Asaph. A psalm.

1 Hear us, Shepherd of Israel,
you who lead Joseph like a flock.
You who sit enthroned between the cherubim,
shine forth 2 before Ephraim, Benjamin and Manasseh.
Awaken your might;
come and save us.

3 Restore us, O God;
make your face shine on us,
that we may be saved.

4 How long, LORD God Almighty,
will your anger smolder
against the prayers of your people?
5 You have fed them with the bread of tears;
you have made them drink tears by the bowlful.
6 You have made us an object of derision[b] to our neighbors,
and our enemies mock us.

7 Restore us, God Almighty;
make your face shine on us,
that we may be saved.

8 You transplanted a vine from Egypt;
you drove out the nations and planted it.
9 You cleared the ground for it,
and it took root and filled the land.
10 The mountains were covered with its shade,
the mighty cedars with its branches.
11 Its branches reached as far as the Sea,[c]
its shoots as far as the River.[d]

12 Why have you broken down its walls
so that all who pass by pick its grapes?
13 Boars from the forest ravage it,
and insects from the fields feed on it.
14 Return to us, God Almighty!
Look down from heaven and see!
Watch over this vine,
15 the root your right hand has planted,
the son[e] you have raised up for yourself.

16 Your vine is cut down, it is burned with fire;
at your rebuke your people perish.
17 Let your hand rest on the man at your right hand,
the son of man you have raised up for yourself.
18 Then we will not turn away from you;
revive us, and we will call on your name.

19 Restore us, LORD God Almighty;
make your face shine on us,
that we may be saved.

---

[a] In Hebrew texts 80:1-19 is numbered 80:2-20. [b] *6* Probable reading of the original Hebrew text; Masoretic Text *contention* [c] *11* Probably the Mediterranean [d] *11* That is, the Euphrates [e] *15* Or *branch*

PSALM 81[a]

For the director of music. According to gittith.[b] *Of Asaph.*

1 Sing for joy to God our strength;
shout aloud to the God of Jacob!
2 Begin the music, strike the timbrel,
play the melodious harp and lyre.

3 Sound the ram's horn at the New Moon,
and when the moon is full, on the day of our festival;
4 this is a decree for Israel,
an ordinance of the God of Jacob.
5 When God went out against Egypt,
he established it as a statute for Joseph.

I heard an unknown voice say:

6 "I removed the burden from their shoulders;
their hands were set free from the basket.
7 In your distress you called and I rescued you,
I answered you out of a thundercloud;
I tested you at the waters of Meribah.[c]
8 Hear me, my people, and I will warn you—
if you would only listen to me, Israel!
9 You shall have no foreign god among you;
you shall not worship any god other than me.
10 I am the LORD your God,
who brought you up out of Egypt.
Open wide your mouth and I will fill it.

11 "But my people would not listen to me;
Israel would not submit to me.
12 So I gave them over to their stubborn hearts
to follow their own devices.

13 "If my people would only listen to me,
if Israel would only follow my ways,
14 how quickly I would subdue their enemies
and turn my hand against their foes!
15 Those who hate the LORD would cringe before him,
and their punishment would last forever.
16 But you would be fed with the finest of wheat;
with honey from the rock I would satisfy you."

PSALM 82

A psalm of Asaph.

1 God presides in the great assembly;
he renders judgment among the "gods":

2 "How long will you[d] defend the unjust
and show partiality to the wicked?[c]
3 Defend the weak and the fatherless;
uphold the cause of the poor and the oppressed.

PRAYING SCRIPTURE

Psalm 81

Asaph reminds us of two significant things about prayer: We can never ask bigger than God can answer (see verse 10), and we sometimes miss the blessings of God simply because we have forgotten God is a mighty deliver. God's people are often guilty of regarding Him too lightly.

What is the biggest thing you need from God right now? Ask him. Open to him your boldest inquiry and wait with expectation.

PRAYING SCRIPTURE

Psalm 82

Apart from God's grace, the world knows only unrighteousness and injustice. Asaph implored the people to uphold God's righteous standard: Defend the righteous, be impartial to the wicked, defend the poor and orphans and free the needy from wicked oppressors.

Make prayer for justice in this world part of your regular routine. Ask God to demonstrate his righteousness. Pray for those in need and speak on their behalf.

[a] In Hebrew texts 81:1-16 is numbered 81:2-17. [b] Title: Probably a musical term [c] *7,2* The Hebrew has *Selah* (a word of uncertain meaning) here.
[d] *2* The Hebrew is plural.

4 Rescue the weak and the needy;
deliver them from the hand of the wicked.

5 "The 'gods' know nothing, they understand nothing.
They walk about in darkness;
all the foundations of the earth are shaken.

6 "I said, 'You are "gods";
you are all sons of the Most High.'
7 But you will die like mere mortals;
you will fall like every other ruler."

8 Rise up, O God, judge the earth,
for all the nations are your inheritance.

PRAYING SCRIPTURE

Psalm 83

God is glorified when the plans of the wicked fail, so why do we so rarely pray against the wicked and their plots? Here the writer pleaded with God to interfere with his enemies, those who united against him.

Whether you use a prayer list, journal or other method of tracking requests, add specific plans of the evil one and ask God to bring them to nothing.

PSALM 83[a]

A song. A psalm of Asaph.

1 O God, do not remain silent;
do not turn a deaf ear,
do not stand aloof, O God.
2 See how your enemies growl,
how your foes rear their heads.
3 With cunning they conspire against your people;
they plot against those you cherish.
4 "Come," they say, "let us destroy them as a nation,
so that Israel's name is remembered no more."

5 With one mind they plot together;
they form an alliance against you —
6 the tents of Edom and the Ishmaelites,
of Moab and the Hagrites,
7 Byblos, Ammon and Amalek,
Philistia, with the people of Tyre.
8 Even Assyria has joined them
to reinforce Lot's descendants.[b]

9 Do to them as you did to Midian,
as you did to Sisera and Jabin at the river Kishon,
10 who perished at Endor
and became like dung on the ground.
11 Make their nobles like Oreb and Zeeb,
all their princes like Zebah and Zalmunna,
12 who said, "Let us take possession
of the pasturelands of God."

13 Make them like tumbleweed, my God,
like chaff before the wind.
14 As fire consumes the forest
or a flame sets the mountains ablaze,
15 so pursue them with your tempest
and terrify them with your storm.
16 Cover their faces with shame, LORD,
so that they will seek your name.

17 May they ever be ashamed and dismayed;
may they perish in disgrace.

[a] In Hebrew texts 83:1-18 is numbered 83:2-19. [b] *8* The Hebrew has *Selah* (a word of uncertain meaning) here.

[18] Let them know that you, whose name is the LORD —
that you alone are the Most High over all the earth.

PSALM 84[a]

For the director of music. According to gittith.[b] Of the Sons of Korah. A psalm.

[1] How lovely is your dwelling place,
LORD Almighty!
[2] My soul yearns, even faints,
for the courts of the LORD;
my heart and my flesh cry out
for the living God.
[3] Even the sparrow has found a home,
and the swallow a nest for herself,
where she may have her young —
a place near your altar,
LORD Almighty, my King and my God.
[4] Blessed are those who dwell in your house;
they are ever praising you.[c]

[5] Blessed are those whose strength is in you,
whose hearts are set on pilgrimage.
[6] As they pass through the Valley of Baka,
they make it a place of springs;
the autumn rains also cover it with pools.[d]
[7] They go from strength to strength,
till each appears before God in Zion.

[8] Hear my prayer, LORD God Almighty;
listen to me, God of Jacob.
[9] Look on our shield,[e] O God;
look with favor on your anointed one.

[10] Better is one day in your courts
than a thousand elsewhere;
I would rather be a doorkeeper in the house of my God
than dwell in the tents of the wicked.
[11] For the LORD God is a sun and shield;
the LORD bestows favor and honor;
no good thing does he withhold
from those whose walk is blameless.

[12] LORD Almighty,
blessed is the one who trusts in you.

PSALM 85[f]

For the director of music. Of the Sons of Korah. A psalm.

[1] You, LORD, showed favor to your land;
you restored the fortunes of Jacob.
[2] You forgave the iniquity of your people
and covered all their sins.[g]

[a] In Hebrew texts 84:1-12 is numbered 84:2-13. [b] Title: Probably a musical term [c] 4 The Hebrew has *Selah* (a word of uncertain meaning) here and at the end of verse 8. [d] 6 Or *blessings* [e] 9 Or *sovereign* [f] In Hebrew texts 85:1-13 is numbered 85:2-14. [g] 2 The Hebrew has *Selah* (a word of uncertain meaning) here.

PRAYING SCRIPTURE

Psalm 84

In this psalm, the sons of Korah expressed a quality worth emulating—delight in God's presence. "My soul yearns, even faints, for the courts of the LORD; my heart and my flesh cry out for the living God" (verse 2). One day in God's temple was better to these men than a thousand somewhere else. What passion!

Do you long for God more than anything? Ask God for a heart that burns with love for him.

PRAYING SCRIPTURE

Psalm 85

God is good, and he does good things for his people. This psalm, penned after the exiles returned, notes God's faithfulness while imploring the people to be obedient so God's anger would relent. The psalmist hoped they saw love and faithfulness, righteousness and peace.

God's blessings, attributes and work in us are reasons for constant praise. Praise God for rescuing you from sin's grasp and giving you new life.

3 You set aside all your wrath
and turned from your fierce anger.

4 Restore us again, God our Savior,
and put away your displeasure toward us.
5 Will you be angry with us forever?
Will you prolong your anger through all generations?
6 Will you not revive us again,
that your people may rejoice in you?
7 Show us your unfailing love, LORD,
and grant us your salvation.

8 I will listen to what God the LORD says;
he promises peace to his people, his faithful servants—
but let them not turn to folly.
9 Surely his salvation is near those who fear him,
that his glory may dwell in our land.

10 Love and faithfulness meet together;
righteousness and peace kiss each other.
11 Faithfulness springs forth from the earth,
and righteousness looks down from heaven.
12 The LORD will indeed give what is good,
and our land will yield its harvest.
13 Righteousness goes before him
and prepares the way for his steps.

PSALM 86

A prayer of David.

1 Hear me, LORD, and answer me,
for I am poor and needy.
2 Guard my life, for I am faithful to you;
save your servant who trusts in you.
You are my God; 3 have mercy on me, Lord,
for I call to you all day long.
4 Bring joy to your servant, Lord,
for I put my trust in you.

5 You, Lord, are forgiving and good,
abounding in love to all who call to you.
6 Hear my prayer, LORD;
listen to my cry for mercy.
7 When I am in distress, I call to you,
because you answer me.

8 Among the gods there is none like you, Lord;
no deeds can compare with yours.
9 All the nations you have made
will come and worship before you, Lord;
they will bring glory to your name.
10 For you are great and do marvelous deeds;
you alone are God.

11 Teach me your way, LORD,
that I may rely on your faithfulness;
give me an undivided heart,
that I may fear your name.

PRAYING SCRIPTURE

Psalm 86

The middle of this psalm contains an exaltation and a prophecy. First, among all this world's gods, there is not one like the true God. Second, there will come a time when the nations will worship him because he alone is God.

The temptation to worship false gods is a dead end. Remember that God alone is God. Pray that people in all nations will turn to him for salvation.

12 I will praise you, Lord my God, with all my heart;
I will glorify your name forever.
13 For great is your love toward me;
you have delivered me from the depths,
from the realm of the dead.

14 Arrogant foes are attacking me, O God;
ruthless people are trying to kill me —
they have no regard for you.
15 But you, Lord, are a compassionate and gracious God,
slow to anger, abounding in love and faithfulness.
16 Turn to me and have mercy on me;
show your strength in behalf of your servant;
save me, because I serve you
just as my mother did.
17 Give me a sign of your goodness,
that my enemies may see it and be put to shame,
for you, LORD, have helped me and comforted me.

PSALM 87

Of the Sons of Korah. A psalm. A song.

1 He has founded his city on the holy mountain.
2 The LORD loves the gates of Zion
more than all the other dwellings of Jacob.

3 Glorious things are said of you,
city of God:[a]
4 "I will record Rahab[b] and Babylon
among those who acknowledge me —
Philistia too, and Tyre, along with Cush[c] —
and will say, 'This one was born in Zion.' "[d]
5 Indeed, of Zion it will be said,
"This one and that one were born in her,
and the Most High himself will establish her."
6 The LORD will write in the register of the peoples:
"This one was born in Zion."

7 As they make music they will sing,
"All my fountains are in you."

PSALM 88[e]

A song. A psalm of the Sons of Korah. For the director of music. According to mahalath leannoth.[f] *A* maskil[g] *of Heman the Ezrahite.*

1 LORD, you are the God who saves me;
day and night I cry out to you.
2 May my prayer come before you;
turn your ear to my cry.

3 I am overwhelmed with troubles
and my life draws near to death.

[a] 3 The Hebrew has *Selah* (a word of uncertain meaning) here and at the end of verse 6. [b] 4 A poetic name for Egypt [c] 4 That is, the upper Nile region [d] 4 Or *"I will record concerning those who acknowledge me: / 'This one was born in Zion.' / Hear this, Rahab and Babylon, / and you too, Philistia, Tyre and Cush."* [e] In Hebrew texts 88:1-18 is numbered 88:2-19. [f] Title: Possibly a tune, "The Suffering of Affliction" [g] Title: Probably a literary or musical term

PRAYING SCRIPTURE

Psalm 87

This psalm contrasts the righteous and unrighteous, using cities as a motif. Contrasted with Babylon, Tyre and others, the children of the Most High were born in Zion, the "city of God" (verse 3). Those born in Zion were registered as the people of God.

This psalm parallels the Lamb's book of life in the New Testament. If you know Jesus Christ, thank him that your name is written there!

PRAYING SCRIPTURE

Psalm 88

Many know the pain of walking through a dark night of the soul and the despondency that often accompanies it. This psalm speaks to everyone in that spiritual place. Bitterness of soul, unanswered prayer and God's silence have brought affliction and terrors. No matter how dark the night or how distant God feels, never stop praying. If you are in a valley, look up and call his name.

4 I am counted among those who go down to the pit;
  I am like one without strength.
5 I am set apart with the dead,
  like the slain who lie in the grave,
whom you remember no more,
  who are cut off from your care.

6 You have put me in the lowest pit,
  in the darkest depths.
7 Your wrath lies heavily on me;
  you have overwhelmed me with all your waves.[a]
8 You have taken from me my closest friends
  and have made me repulsive to them.
I am confined and cannot escape;
9   my eyes are dim with grief.

I call to you, LORD, every day;
  I spread out my hands to you.
10 Do you show your wonders to the dead?
  Do their spirits rise up and praise you?
11 Is your love declared in the grave,
  your faithfulness in Destruction[b]?
12 Are your wonders known in the place of darkness,
  or your righteous deeds in the land of oblivion?

13 But I cry to you for help, LORD;
  in the morning my prayer comes before you.
14 Why, LORD, do you reject me
  and hide your face from me?

15 From my youth I have suffered and been close to death;
  I have borne your terrors and am in despair.
16 Your wrath has swept over me;
  your terrors have destroyed me.
17 All day long they surround me like a flood;
  they have completely engulfed me.
18 You have taken from me friend and neighbor—
  darkness is my closest friend.

PSALM 89[c]

A maskil[d] of Ethan the Ezrahite.

1 I will sing of the LORD's great love forever;
  with my mouth I will make your faithfulness known
  through all generations.
2 I will declare that your love stands firm forever,
  that you have established your faithfulness in
    heaven itself.
3 You said, "I have made a covenant with my chosen one,
  I have sworn to David my servant,
4 'I will establish your line forever
  and make your throne firm through all generations.'"[e]

PRAYING SCRIPTURE

Psalm 89

The psalmist, Ethan the Ezrahite, recounted the work of God related to his covenant with David. God's majesty is shown as the reason he can keep the covenant, building David's throne through all generations. This refers to the Messiah's ultimate arrival through David's line and eternal reign.

When circumstances look bleak, never forget God's power and plan. Call on him to fulfill his promises to his people, and trust him to do it.

---

[a] 7 The Hebrew has *Selah* (a word of uncertain meaning) here and at the end of verse 10. [b] 11 Hebrew *Abaddon* [c] In Hebrew texts 89:1-52 is numbered 89:2-53. [d] Title: Probably a literary or musical term [e] 4 The Hebrew has *Selah* (a word of uncertain meaning) here and at the end of verses 37, 45 and 48.

5 The heavens praise your wonders, LORD,
your faithfulness too, in the assembly of the holy ones.
6 For who in the skies above can compare with the LORD?
Who is like the LORD among the heavenly beings?
7 In the council of the holy ones God is greatly feared;
he is more awesome than all who surround him.
8 Who is like you, LORD God Almighty?
You, LORD, are mighty, and your faithfulness surrounds you.

9 You rule over the surging sea;
when its waves mount up, you still them.
10 You crushed Rahab like one of the slain;
with your strong arm you scattered your enemies.
11 The heavens are yours, and yours also the earth;
you founded the world and all that is in it.
12 You created the north and the south;
Tabor and Hermon sing for joy at your name.
13 Your arm is endowed with power;
your hand is strong, your right hand exalted.

14 Righteousness and justice are the foundation of your throne;
love and faithfulness go before you.
15 Blessed are those who have learned to acclaim you,
who walk in the light of your presence, LORD.
16 They rejoice in your name all day long;
they celebrate your righteousness.
17 For you are their glory and strength,
and by your favor you exalt our horn.[a]
18 Indeed, our shield[b] belongs to the LORD,
our king to the Holy One of Israel.

19 Once you spoke in a vision,
to your faithful people you said:
"I have bestowed strength on a warrior;
I have raised up a young man from among the people.
20 I have found David my servant;
with my sacred oil I have anointed him.
21 My hand will sustain him;
surely my arm will strengthen him.
22 The enemy will not get the better of him;
the wicked will not oppress him.
23 I will crush his foes before him
and strike down his adversaries.
24 My faithful love will be with him,
and through my name his horn[c] will be exalted.
25 I will set his hand over the sea,
his right hand over the rivers.
26 He will call out to me, 'You are my Father,
my God, the Rock my Savior.'
27 And I will appoint him to be my firstborn,
the most exalted of the kings of the earth.
28 I will maintain my love to him forever,
and my covenant with him will never fail.

---

[a] 17 *Horn* here symbolizes strong one. [b] 18 Or *sovereign* [c] 24 *Horn* here symbolizes strength.

29 I will establish his line forever,
his throne as long as the heavens endure.

30 "If his sons forsake my law
and do not follow my statutes,
31 if they violate my decrees
and fail to keep my commands,
32 I will punish their sin with the rod,
their iniquity with flogging;
33 but I will not take my love from him,
nor will I ever betray my faithfulness.
34 I will not violate my covenant
or alter what my lips have uttered.
35 Once for all, I have sworn by my holiness —
and I will not lie to David —
36 that his line will continue forever
and his throne endure before me like the sun;
37 it will be established forever like the moon,
the faithful witness in the sky."

38 But you have rejected, you have spurned,
you have been very angry with your anointed one.
39 You have renounced the covenant with your servant
and have defiled his crown in the dust.
40 You have broken through all his walls
and reduced his strongholds to ruins.
41 All who pass by have plundered him;
he has become the scorn of his neighbors.
42 You have exalted the right hand of his foes;
you have made all his enemies rejoice.
43 Indeed, you have turned back the edge of his sword
and have not supported him in battle.
44 You have put an end to his splendor
and cast his throne to the ground.
45 You have cut short the days of his youth;
you have covered him with a mantle of shame.

46 How long, LORD? Will you hide yourself forever?
How long will your wrath burn like fire?
47 Remember how fleeting is my life.
For what futility you have created all humanity!
48 Who can live and not see death,
or who can escape the power of the grave?
49 Lord, where is your former great love,
which in your faithfulness you swore to David?
50 Remember, Lord, how your servant has[a] been mocked,
how I bear in my heart the taunts of all the nations,
51 the taunts with which your enemies, LORD, have mocked,
with which they have mocked every step of your
anointed one.

52 Praise be to the LORD forever!
Amen and Amen.

[a] 50 Or *your servants have*

BOOK IV

PSALMS 90 – 106

PSALM 90

A prayer of Moses the man of God.

1 Lord, you have been our dwelling place
throughout all generations.
2 Before the mountains were born
or you brought forth the whole world,
from everlasting to everlasting you are God.

3 You turn people back to dust,
saying, "Return to dust, you mortals."
4 A thousand years in your sight
are like a day that has just gone by,
or like a watch in the night.
5 Yet you sweep people away in the sleep of death—
they are like the new grass of the morning:
6 In the morning it springs up new,
but by evening it is dry and withered.

7 We are consumed by your anger
and terrified by your indignation.
8 You have set our iniquities before you,
our secret sins in the light of your presence.
9 All our days pass away under your wrath;
we finish our years with a moan.
10 Our days may come to seventy years,
or eighty, if our strength endures;
yet the best of them are but trouble and sorrow,
for they quickly pass, and we fly away.
11 If only we knew the power of your anger!
Your wrath is as great as the fear that is your due.
12 Teach us to number our days,
that we may gain a heart of wisdom.

13 Relent, LORD! How long will it be?
Have compassion on your servants.
14 Satisfy us in the morning with your unfailing love,
that we may sing for joy and be glad all our days.
15 Make us glad for as many days as you have afflicted us,
for as many years as we have seen trouble.
16 May your deeds be shown to your servants,
your splendor to their children.

17 May the favor[a] of the Lord our God rest on us;
establish the work of our hands for us—
yes, establish the work of our hands.

PSALM 91

1 Whoever dwells in the shelter of the Most High
will rest in the shadow of the Almighty.[b]

[a] 17 Or *beauty* [b] 1 Hebrew *Shaddai*

PRAYING SCRIPTURE

Psalm 90

The psalmist asked the Lord to "teach us to number our days," the point being getting wisdom (see verse 12). Similar to the New Testament concept of redeeming the time, we should use our days wisely.

If you live an average lifespan, how many years do you have left? Ask God to help you pay attention to the time you have left so you can use it wisely.

PRAYING SCRIPTURE

Psalm 91

Verse 1 of this psalm is one of the most beautiful, encouraging and hopeful verses in the entire Bible. To dwell close to God is to know his protection. The psalm is filled with imagery to describe God's care and protection over us.

Since the psalm ends with God's promise to answer us, be with us and deliver us, it is a great psalm to pray when you are anxious or weary.

2 I will say of the LORD, "He is my refuge and my fortress,
my God, in whom I trust."

3 Surely he will save you
from the fowler's snare
and from the deadly pestilence.
4 He will cover you with his feathers,
and under his wings you will find refuge;
his faithfulness will be your shield and rampart.
5 You will not fear the terror of night,
nor the arrow that flies by day,
6 nor the pestilence that stalks in the darkness,
nor the plague that destroys at midday.
7 A thousand may fall at your side,
ten thousand at your right hand,
but it will not come near you.
8 You will only observe with your eyes
and see the punishment of the wicked.

9 If you say, "The LORD is my refuge,"
and you make the Most High your dwelling,
10 no harm will overtake you,
no disaster will come near your tent.
11 For he will command his angels concerning you
to guard you in all your ways;
12 they will lift you up in their hands,
so that you will not strike your foot against a stone.
13 You will tread on the lion and the cobra;
you will trample the great lion and the serpent.

14 "Because he[a] loves me," says the LORD, "I will rescue him;
I will protect him, for he acknowledges my name.
15 He will call on me, and I will answer him;
I will be with him in trouble,
I will deliver him and honor him.
16 With long life I will satisfy him
and show him my salvation."

PSALM 92[b]

A psalm. A song. For the Sabbath day.

1 It is good to praise the LORD
and make music to your name, O Most High,
2 proclaiming your love in the morning
and your faithfulness at night,
3 to the music of the ten-stringed lyre
and the melody of the harp.

4 For you make me glad by your deeds, LORD;
I sing for joy at what your hands have done.
5 How great are your works, LORD,
how profound your thoughts!
6 Senseless people do not know,
fools do not understand,

PRAYING SCRIPTURE

Psalm 92

"It is good to praise the LORD" (verse 1). Those simple words should serve as a compass heading for how we pray and live. How much would our spiritual, mental and emotional conditions be improved if we regularly gave God thanks?

Organize your prayer time to include periods of giving thanks, and give praise throughout each day. A quick "Thank you, Lord" keeps us pointed toward the giver of all good things.

[a] 14 That is, probably the king [b] In Hebrew texts 92:1-15 is numbered 92:2-16.

7 that though the wicked spring up like grass
and all evildoers flourish,
they will be destroyed forever.

8 But you, LORD, are forever exalted.

9 For surely your enemies, LORD,
surely your enemies will perish;
all evildoers will be scattered.
10 You have exalted my horn[a] like that of a wild ox;
fine oils have been poured on me.
11 My eyes have seen the defeat of my adversaries;
my ears have heard the rout of my wicked foes.

12 The righteous will flourish like a palm tree,
they will grow like a cedar of Lebanon;
13 planted in the house of the LORD,
they will flourish in the courts of our God.
14 They will still bear fruit in old age,
they will stay fresh and green,
15 proclaiming, "The LORD is upright;
he is my Rock, and there is no wickedness in him."

PSALM 93

1 The LORD reigns, he is robed in majesty;
the LORD is robed in majesty and armed with strength;
indeed, the world is established, firm and secure.
2 Your throne was established long ago;
you are from all eternity.

3 The seas have lifted up, LORD,
the seas have lifted up their voice;
the seas have lifted up their pounding waves.
4 Mightier than the thunder of the great waters,
mightier than the breakers of the sea —
the LORD on high is mighty.

5 Your statutes, LORD, stand firm;
holiness adorns your house
for endless days.

PSALM 94

1 The LORD is a God who avenges.
O God who avenges, shine forth.
2 Rise up, Judge of the earth;
pay back to the proud what they deserve.
3 How long, LORD, will the wicked,
how long will the wicked be jubilant?

4 They pour out arrogant words;
all the evildoers are full of boasting.
5 They crush your people, LORD;
they oppress your inheritance.
6 They slay the widow and the foreigner;
they murder the fatherless.

[a] *10 Horn* here symbolizes strength.

PRAYING SCRIPTURE

Psalm 93

Remember how the psalmists often faced troubles: They declared God's majesty. It is unwise to compare our situation to what we can accomplish. It is wise to compare our situation to what God can accomplish. Are troubles coming in like a flood? God reigns. He is clothed in strength. His throne is from everlasting.

As you pray about your circumstances, recall that God is greater than them all.

PRAYING SCRIPTURE

Psalm 94

God does not abandon his people, even when dangers multiply all around us. Why should we fear? God is a refuge for us. He is the One who renders punishment to evildoers. He breaks in pieces the might of the wicked.

The psalmist knew the power of God's law to rest our souls. Include Scripture in your prayers so you can know God's comfort in the face of wickedness.

7 They say, "The LORD does not see;
the God of Jacob takes no notice."

8 Take notice, you senseless ones among the people;
you fools, when will you become wise?
9 Does he who fashioned the ear not hear?
Does he who formed the eye not see?
10 Does he who disciplines nations not punish?
Does he who teaches mankind lack knowledge?
11 The LORD knows all human plans;
he knows that they are futile.

12 Blessed is the one you discipline, LORD,
the one you teach from your law;
13 you grant them relief from days of trouble,
till a pit is dug for the wicked.
14 For the LORD will not reject his people;
he will never forsake his inheritance.
15 Judgment will again be founded on righteousness,
and all the upright in heart will follow it.

16 Who will rise up for me against the wicked?
Who will take a stand for me against evildoers?
17 Unless the LORD had given me help,
I would soon have dwelt in the silence of death.
18 When I said, "My foot is slipping,"
your unfailing love, LORD, supported me.
19 When anxiety was great within me,
your consolation brought me joy.

20 Can a corrupt throne be allied with you —
a throne that brings on misery by its decrees?
21 The wicked band together against the righteous
and condemn the innocent to death.
22 But the LORD has become my fortress,
and my God the rock in whom I take refuge.
23 He will repay them for their sins
and destroy them for their wickedness;
the LORD our God will destroy them.

PSALM 95

1 Come, let us sing for joy to the LORD;
let us shout aloud to the Rock of our salvation.
2 Let us come before him with thanksgiving
and extol him with music and song.

3 For the LORD is the great God,
the great King above all gods.
4 In his hand are the depths of the earth,
and the mountain peaks belong to him.
5 The sea is his, for he made it,
and his hands formed the dry land.

6 Come, let us bow down in worship,
let us kneel before the LORD our Maker;
7 for he is our God
and we are the people of his pasture,
the flock under his care.

PRAYING SCRIPTURE

Psalm 95

The goodness and kindness of God should inspire singing, shouting and thanksgiving. God is the great King; he is above all gods. The earth and all that is in it are his. We are his people. We should bow down! We should worship!

If considering the majesty of God does not lead you to worship, ask him to renew your mind so that you can know him as he is.

Today, if only you would hear his voice,
8 "Do not harden your hearts as you did at Meribah,[a]
as you did that day at Massah[b] in the wilderness,
9 where your ancestors tested me;
they tried me, though they had seen what I did.
10 For forty years I was angry with that generation;
I said, 'They are a people whose hearts go astray,
and they have not known my ways.'
11 So I declared on oath in my anger,
'They shall never enter my rest.'"

PSALM 96

1 Sing to the LORD a new song;
sing to the LORD, all the earth.
2 Sing to the LORD, praise his name;
proclaim his salvation day after day.
3 Declare his glory among the nations,
his marvelous deeds among all peoples.

4 For great is the LORD and most worthy of praise;
he is to be feared above all gods.
5 For all the gods of the nations are idols,
but the LORD made the heavens.
6 Splendor and majesty are before him;
strength and glory are in his sanctuary.

7 Ascribe to the LORD, all you families of nations,
ascribe to the LORD glory and strength.
8 Ascribe to the LORD the glory due his name;
bring an offering and come into his courts.
9 Worship the LORD in the splendor of his[c] holiness;
tremble before him, all the earth.
10 Say among the nations, "The LORD reigns."
The world is firmly established, it cannot be moved;
he will judge the peoples with equity.

11 Let the heavens rejoice, let the earth be glad;
let the sea resound, and all that is in it.
12 Let the fields be jubilant, and everything in them;
let all the trees of the forest sing for joy.
13 Let all creation rejoice before the LORD, for he comes,
he comes to judge the earth.
He will judge the world in righteousness
and the peoples in his faithfulness.

PSALM 97

1 The LORD reigns, let the earth be glad;
let the distant shores rejoice.
2 Clouds and thick darkness surround him;
righteousness and justice are the foundation of his throne.
3 Fire goes before him
and consumes his foes on every side.

PRAYING SCRIPTURE

Psalm 96

In this beautiful psalm extolling God's majesty and power, the writer calls us to "worship the LORD in the splendor of his holiness!" (verse 9). This reminds us that although God loves us as we are, he expects us to pursue holiness as the way to come into his presence.

When we remember God's greatness and his grace, the right response is holiness reflecting God's character. We are then fully prepared to pray.

PRAYING SCRIPTURE

Psalm 97

Near the end of a psalm exalting God's power and character, verse 10 brings a strong admonition: "Let those who love the LORD hate evil." It's easy to say we hate evil in culture or society. It's much harder to hate the evil in us.

Do you have some sin you don't hate? Ask God to help you hate your own sin as much as you hate outside sin.

[a] 8 *Meribah* means *quarreling.* [b] 8 *Massah* means *testing.* [c] 9 Or LORD *with the splendor of*

4 His lightning lights up the world;
the earth sees and trembles.
5 The mountains melt like wax before the LORD,
before the Lord of all the earth.
6 The heavens proclaim his righteousness,
and all peoples see his glory.

7 All who worship images are put to shame,
those who boast in idols —
worship him, all you gods!

8 Zion hears and rejoices
and the villages of Judah are glad
because of your judgments, LORD.
9 For you, LORD, are the Most High over all the earth;
you are exalted far above all gods.
10 Let those who love the LORD hate evil,
for he guards the lives of his faithful ones
and delivers them from the hand of the wicked.
11 Light shines[a] on the righteous
and joy on the upright in heart.
12 Rejoice in the LORD, you who are righteous,
and praise his holy name.

PSALM 98

A psalm.

1 Sing to the LORD a new song,
for he has done marvelous things;
his right hand and his holy arm
have worked salvation for him.
2 The LORD has made his salvation known
and revealed his righteousness to the nations.
3 He has remembered his love
and his faithfulness to Israel;
all the ends of the earth have seen
the salvation of our God.

4 Shout for joy to the LORD, all the earth,
burst into jubilant song with music;
5 make music to the LORD with the harp,
with the harp and the sound of singing,
6 with trumpets and the blast of the ram's horn —
shout for joy before the LORD, the King.

7 Let the sea resound, and everything in it,
the world, and all who live in it.
8 Let the rivers clap their hands,
let the mountains sing together for joy;
9 let them sing before the LORD,
for he comes to judge the earth.
He will judge the world in righteousness
and the peoples with equity.

PRAYING SCRIPTURE

Psalm 98

Do you ever ponder that creation praises God? The Bible continues such imagery as seas roaring, mountains being joyful, rivers and trees clapping, the heavens declaring his glory. Creation always praises God as it was designed to do.

How is the praise part of your prayer life? Don't be outdone by rocks and trees! God's people are the recipients of enormous blessings, so praise him whenever you pray.

[a] *11* One Hebrew manuscript and ancient versions (see also 112:4); most Hebrew manuscripts *Light is sown*

PSALM 99

1 The LORD reigns,
let the nations tremble;
he sits enthroned between the cherubim,
let the earth shake.
2 Great is the LORD in Zion;
he is exalted over all the nations.
3 Let them praise your great and awesome name —
he is holy.

4 The King is mighty, he loves justice —
you have established equity;
in Jacob you have done
what is just and right.
5 Exalt the LORD our God
and worship at his footstool;
he is holy.

6 Moses and Aaron were among his priests,
Samuel was among those who called on his name;
they called on the LORD
and he answered them.
7 He spoke to them from the pillar of cloud;
they kept his statutes and the decrees he gave them.

8 LORD our God,
you answered them;
you were to Israel a forgiving God,
though you punished their misdeeds.[a]
9 Exalt the LORD our God
and worship at his holy mountain,
for the LORD our God is holy.

PSALM 100

A psalm. For giving grateful praise.

1 Shout for joy to the LORD, all the earth.
2 Worship the LORD with gladness;
come before him with joyful songs.
3 Know that the LORD is God.
It is he who made us, and we are his[b];
we are his people, the sheep of his pasture.

4 Enter his gates with thanksgiving
and his courts with praise;
give thanks to him and praise his name.
5 For the LORD is good and his love endures forever;
his faithfulness continues through all generations.

PRAYING SCRIPTURE

Psalm 99

God is the One who rules the world in perfect justice. More than that, we are reminded here that God loves justice, that he has established fairness. Following this, the writer said twice that we should exalt the Lord our God and worship at his feet and at his mountain—images of his strength and our weakness (see verses 5,9). Worship implies that we should love justice too.

Ask God how you can show your love for justice daily.

PRAYING SCRIPTURE

Psalm 100

This well-known psalm provides a wonderful description of the life of praise, and it builds from truths about God himself. Praise is not an act God's children raise up from sheer emotion. It's an acclamation about God based on how he has revealed himself.

Use this psalm as a pattern for praising and thanking God as you consider his creative power, goodness, mercy, truth and care for you.

---

[a] *8 Or God, / an avenger of the wrongs done to them* [b] *3 Or and not we ourselves*

PRAYING SCRIPTURE

Psalm 101

Christians should walk in integrity—blamelessness—in contrast to the deceitfulness of the world around us. In this psalm, David wrote of his own desire and commitment to stay separate from evil men, going so far as a pledge to destroy the wicked of the land (see verse 8).

Can you say that you behave blamelessly? If not, ask God to lead you to walk in the way that pleases him.

PSALM 101

Of David. A psalm.

1 I will sing of your love and justice;
to you, LORD, I will sing praise.
2 I will be careful to lead a blameless life —
when will you come to me?

I will conduct the affairs of my house
with a blameless heart.
3 I will not look with approval
on anything that is vile.

I hate what faithless people do;
I will have no part in it.
4 The perverse of heart shall be far from me;
I will have nothing to do with what is evil.

5 Whoever slanders their neighbor in secret,
I will put to silence;
whoever has haughty eyes and a proud heart,
I will not tolerate.

6 My eyes will be on the faithful in the land,
that they may dwell with me;
the one whose walk is blameless
will minister to me.

7 No one who practices deceit
will dwell in my house;
no one who speaks falsely
will stand in my presence.

8 Every morning I will put to silence
all the wicked in the land;
I will cut off every evildoer
from the city of the LORD.

PRAYING SCRIPTURE

Psalm 102

The Biblical authors treated evil as a phenomenon that would meet its end. Neither evil as a general influence nor people who practice it will last forever. God will have the final word; his mercy will flow; the nations will recognize his reign.

Are you tempted to despair over the condition of this world? Take heart! God will win, so when burdened, cast your cares on him.

PSALM 102[a]

A prayer of an afflicted person who has grown weak and pours out a lament before the LORD.

1 Hear my prayer, LORD;
let my cry for help come to you.
2 Do not hide your face from me
when I am in distress.
Turn your ear to me;
when I call, answer me quickly.

3 For my days vanish like smoke;
my bones burn like glowing embers.
4 My heart is blighted and withered like grass;
I forget to eat my food.
5 In my distress I groan aloud
and am reduced to skin and bones.
6 I am like a desert owl,
like an owl among the ruins.

[a] In Hebrew texts 102:1-28 is numbered 102:2-29.

7 I lie awake; I have become
like a bird alone on a roof.
8 All day long my enemies taunt me;
those who rail against me use my name as a curse.
9 For I eat ashes as my food
and mingle my drink with tears
10 because of your great wrath,
for you have taken me up and thrown me aside.
11 My days are like the evening shadow;
I wither away like grass.

12 But you, LORD, sit enthroned forever;
your renown endures through all generations.
13 You will arise and have compassion on Zion,
for it is time to show favor to her;
the appointed time has come.
14 For her stones are dear to your servants;
her very dust moves them to pity.
15 The nations will fear the name of the LORD,
all the kings of the earth will revere your glory.
16 For the LORD will rebuild Zion
and appear in his glory.
17 He will respond to the prayer of the destitute;
he will not despise their plea.

18 Let this be written for a future generation,
that a people not yet created may praise the LORD:
19 "The LORD looked down from his sanctuary on high,
from heaven he viewed the earth,
20 to hear the groans of the prisoners
and release those condemned to death."
21 So the name of the LORD will be declared in Zion
and his praise in Jerusalem
22 when the peoples and the kingdoms
assemble to worship the LORD.

23 In the course of my life[a] he broke my strength;
he cut short my days.
24 So I said:
"Do not take me away, my God, in the midst of my days;
your years go on through all generations.
25 In the beginning you laid the foundations of the earth,
and the heavens are the work of your hands.
26 They will perish, but you remain;
they will all wear out like a garment.
Like clothing you will change them
and they will be discarded.
27 But you remain the same,
and your years will never end.
28 The children of your servants will live in your presence;
their descendants will be established before you."

[a] 23 Or *By his power*

PRAYING SCRIPTURE

Psalm 103

In this psalm, David began exalting God's attributes and mighty acts. Then he took a personal turn: "As a father has compassion on his children, so the LORD has compassion on those who fear him" (verse 13). God is a loving Father who takes pity on us.

Do you struggle with the concept of God as Father? If so, talk to him about it. Ask him to have pity on you as loving fathers do.

PSALM 103

Of David.

1 Praise the LORD, my soul;
all my inmost being, praise his holy name.
2 Praise the LORD, my soul,
and forget not all his benefits —
3 who forgives all your sins
and heals all your diseases,
4 who redeems your life from the pit
and crowns you with love and compassion,
5 who satisfies your desires with good things
so that your youth is renewed like the eagle's.

6 The LORD works righteousness
and justice for all the oppressed.

7 He made known his ways to Moses,
his deeds to the people of Israel:
8 The LORD is compassionate and gracious,
slow to anger, abounding in love.
9 He will not always accuse,
nor will he harbor his anger forever;
10 he does not treat us as our sins deserve
or repay us according to our iniquities.
11 For as high as the heavens are above the earth,
so great is his love for those who fear him;
12 as far as the east is from the west,
so far has he removed our transgressions from us.

13 As a father has compassion on his children,
so the LORD has compassion on those who fear him;
14 for he knows how we are formed,
he remembers that we are dust.
15 The life of mortals is like grass,
they flourish like a flower of the field;
16 the wind blows over it and it is gone,
and its place remembers it no more.
17 But from everlasting to everlasting
the LORD's love is with those who fear him,
and his righteousness with their children's
children —
18 with those who keep his covenant
and remember to obey his precepts.

19 The LORD has established his throne in heaven,
and his kingdom rules over all.

20 Praise the LORD, you his angels,
you mighty ones who do his bidding,
who obey his word.
21 Praise the LORD, all his heavenly hosts,
you his servants who do his will.
22 Praise the LORD, all his works
everywhere in his dominion.

Praise the LORD, my soul.

PSALM 104

1 Praise the LORD, my soul.

LORD my God, you are very great;
you are clothed with splendor and majesty.

2 The LORD wraps himself in light as with a garment;
he stretches out the heavens like a tent
3 and lays the beams of his upper chambers on their waters.
He makes the clouds his chariot
and rides on the wings of the wind.
4 He makes winds his messengers,[a]
flames of fire his servants.

5 He set the earth on its foundations;
it can never be moved.
6 You covered it with the watery depths as with a garment;
the waters stood above the mountains.
7 But at your rebuke the waters fled,
at the sound of your thunder they took to flight;
8 they flowed over the mountains,
they went down into the valleys,
to the place you assigned for them.
9 You set a boundary they cannot cross;
never again will they cover the earth.

10 He makes springs pour water into the ravines;
it flows between the mountains.
11 They give water to all the beasts of the field;
the wild donkeys quench their thirst.
12 The birds of the sky nest by the waters;
they sing among the branches.
13 He waters the mountains from his upper chambers;
the land is satisfied by the fruit of his work.
14 He makes grass grow for the cattle,
and plants for people to cultivate—
bringing forth food from the earth:
15 wine that gladdens human hearts,
oil to make their faces shine,
and bread that sustains their hearts.
16 The trees of the LORD are well watered,
the cedars of Lebanon that he planted.
17 There the birds make their nests;
the stork has its home in the junipers.
18 The high mountains belong to the wild goats;
the crags are a refuge for the hyrax.

19 He made the moon to mark the seasons,
and the sun knows when to go down.
20 You bring darkness, it becomes night,
and all the beasts of the forest prowl.
21 The lions roar for their prey
and seek their food from God.
22 The sun rises, and they steal away;
they return and lie down in their dens.

[a] 4 Or *angels*

PRAYING SCRIPTURE

Psalm 104

When the psalmist considered God's wonderful works, he asked that his "meditation be pleasing" to God so he could "rejoice in the LORD" (verse 34).

How often do you think deeply—meditate—on who God is and what he has done in your life? Do you ever just sit with it? When you start to pray, sit quietly and think deeply about God as he has revealed himself to you.

23 Then people go out to their work,
to their labor until evening.

24 How many are your works, LORD!
In wisdom you made them all;
the earth is full of your creatures.
25 There is the sea, vast and spacious,
teeming with creatures beyond number—
living things both large and small.
26 There the ships go to and fro,
and Leviathan, which you formed to frolic there.

27 All creatures look to you
to give them their food at the proper time.
28 When you give it to them,
they gather it up;
when you open your hand,
they are satisfied with good things.
29 When you hide your face,
they are terrified;
when you take away their breath,
they die and return to the dust.
30 When you send your Spirit,
they are created,
and you renew the face of the ground.

31 May the glory of the LORD endure forever;
may the LORD rejoice in his works—
32 he who looks at the earth, and it trembles,
who touches the mountains, and they smoke.

33 I will sing to the LORD all my life;
I will sing praise to my God as long as I live.
34 May my meditation be pleasing to him,
as I rejoice in the LORD.
35 But may sinners vanish from the earth
and the wicked be no more.

Praise the LORD, my soul.

Praise the LORD.[a]

PSALM 105

1 Give praise to the LORD, proclaim his name;
make known among the nations what he has done.
2 Sing to him, sing praise to him;
tell of all his wonderful acts.
3 Glory in his holy name;
let the hearts of those who seek the LORD rejoice.
4 Look to the LORD and his strength;
seek his face always.

5 Remember the wonders he has done,
his miracles, and the judgments he pronounced,
6 you his servants, the descendants of Abraham,
his chosen ones, the children of Jacob.

[a] *35* Hebrew *Hallelu Yah*; in the Septuagint this line stands at the beginning of Psalm 105.

PRAYING SCRIPTURE

Psalm 105

Rehearsing the history of Israel from God's covenant with Abraham through Moses and the exodus, the psalmist used these events to demonstrate that God is a God of power and wonder who remembers his covenants.

That God remembers his covenants should move us to praise him! We are part of a new covenant in Jesus' blood. God will never break it; that is a reason for prayer and praise.

7 He is the LORD our God;
his judgments are in all the earth.

8 He remembers his covenant forever,
the promise he made, for a thousand generations,
9 the covenant he made with Abraham,
the oath he swore to Isaac.
10 He confirmed it to Jacob as a decree,
to Israel as an everlasting covenant:
11 "To you I will give the land of Canaan
as the portion you will inherit."

12 When they were but few in number,
few indeed, and strangers in it,
13 they wandered from nation to nation,
from one kingdom to another.
14 He allowed no one to oppress them;
for their sake he rebuked kings:
15 "Do not touch my anointed ones;
do my prophets no harm."

16 He called down famine on the land
and destroyed all their supplies of food;
17 and he sent a man before them—
Joseph, sold as a slave.
18 They bruised his feet with shackles,
his neck was put in irons,
19 till what he foretold came to pass,
till the word of the LORD proved him true.
20 The king sent and released him,
the ruler of peoples set him free.
21 He made him master of his household,
ruler over all he possessed,
22 to instruct his princes as he pleased
and teach his elders wisdom.

23 Then Israel entered Egypt;
Jacob resided as a foreigner in the land of Ham.
24 The LORD made his people very fruitful;
he made them too numerous for their foes,
25 whose hearts he turned to hate his people,
to conspire against his servants.
26 He sent Moses his servant,
and Aaron, whom he had chosen.
27 They performed his signs among them,
his wonders in the land of Ham.
28 He sent darkness and made the land dark—
for had they not rebelled against his words?
29 He turned their waters into blood,
causing their fish to die.
30 Their land teemed with frogs,
which went up into the bedrooms of their rulers.
31 He spoke, and there came swarms of flies,
and gnats throughout their country.
32 He turned their rain into hail,
with lightning throughout their land;

33 he struck down their vines and fig trees
  and shattered the trees of their country.
34 He spoke, and the locusts came,
  grasshoppers without number;
35 they ate up every green thing in their land,
  ate up the produce of their soil.
36 Then he struck down all the firstborn in their land,
  the firstfruits of all their manhood.
37 He brought out Israel, laden with silver and gold,
  and from among their tribes no one faltered.
38 Egypt was glad when they left,
  because dread of Israel had fallen on them.

39 He spread out a cloud as a covering,
  and a fire to give light at night.
40 They asked, and he brought them quail;
  he fed them well with the bread of heaven.
41 He opened the rock, and water gushed out;
  it flowed like a river in the desert.

42 For he remembered his holy promise
  given to his servant Abraham.
43 He brought out his people with rejoicing,
  his chosen ones with shouts of joy;
44 he gave them the lands of the nations,
  and they fell heir to what others had toiled for—
45 that they might keep his precepts
  and observe his laws.

Praise the LORD.[a]

PSALM 106

1 Praise the LORD.[b]

Give thanks to the LORD, for he is good;
  his love endures forever.

2 Who can proclaim the mighty acts of the LORD
  or fully declare his praise?
3 Blessed are those who act justly,
  who always do what is right.

4 Remember me, LORD, when you show favor to your people,
  come to my aid when you save them,
5 that I may enjoy the prosperity of your chosen ones,
  that I may share in the joy of your nation
  and join your inheritance in giving praise.

6 We have sinned, even as our ancestors did;
  we have done wrong and acted wickedly.
7 When our ancestors were in Egypt,
  they gave no thought to your miracles;
they did not remember your many kindnesses,
  and they rebelled by the sea, the Red Sea.[c]

PRAYING SCRIPTURE

Psalm 106

The faithfulness of God to his promises is even more amazing when we consider how faithless his people have been historically. Israel constantly rebelled. This psalm reads like a national rap sheet, recording sin after sin. But God always showed mercy even if judgment came first.

Children of God today can rejoice that God has removed our sin from us; because of Jesus no sins remain.

---

[a] 45 Hebrew *Hallelu Yah* [b] 1 Hebrew *Hallelu Yah*; also in verse 48 [c] 7 Or *the Sea of Reeds*; also in verses 9 and 22

8 Yet he saved them for his name's sake,
to make his mighty power known.
9 He rebuked the Red Sea, and it dried up;
he led them through the depths as through a desert.
10 He saved them from the hand of the foe;
from the hand of the enemy he redeemed them.
11 The waters covered their adversaries;
not one of them survived.
12 Then they believed his promises
and sang his praise.

13 But they soon forgot what he had done
and did not wait for his plan to unfold.
14 In the desert they gave in to their craving;
in the wilderness they put God to the test.
15 So he gave them what they asked for,
but sent a wasting disease among them.

16 In the camp they grew envious of Moses
and of Aaron, who was consecrated to the LORD.
17 The earth opened up and swallowed Dathan;
it buried the company of Abiram.
18 Fire blazed among their followers;
a flame consumed the wicked.
19 At Horeb they made a calf
and worshiped an idol cast from metal.
20 They exchanged their glorious God
for an image of a bull, which eats grass.
21 They forgot the God who saved them,
who had done great things in Egypt,
22 miracles in the land of Ham
and awesome deeds by the Red Sea.
23 So he said he would destroy them —
had not Moses, his chosen one,
stood in the breach before him
to keep his wrath from destroying them.

24 Then they despised the pleasant land;
they did not believe his promise.
25 They grumbled in their tents
and did not obey the LORD.
26 So he swore to them with uplifted hand
that he would make them fall in the wilderness,
27 make their descendants fall among the nations
and scatter them throughout the lands.

28 They yoked themselves to the Baal of Peor
and ate sacrifices offered to lifeless gods;
29 they aroused the LORD's anger by their wicked deeds,
and a plague broke out among them.
30 But Phinehas stood up and intervened,
and the plague was checked.
31 This was credited to him as righteousness
for endless generations to come.
32 By the waters of Meribah they angered the LORD,
and trouble came to Moses because of them;

33 for they rebelled against the Spirit of God,
and rash words came from Moses' lips.[a]

34 They did not destroy the peoples
as the LORD had commanded them,
35 but they mingled with the nations
and adopted their customs.
36 They worshiped their idols,
which became a snare to them.
37 They sacrificed their sons
and their daughters to false gods.
38 They shed innocent blood,
the blood of their sons and daughters,
whom they sacrificed to the idols of Canaan,
and the land was desecrated by their blood.
39 They defiled themselves by what they did;
by their deeds they prostituted themselves.

40 Therefore the LORD was angry with his people
and abhorred his inheritance.
41 He gave them into the hands of the nations,
and their foes ruled over them.
42 Their enemies oppressed them
and subjected them to their power.
43 Many times he delivered them,
but they were bent on rebellion
and they wasted away in their sin.
44 Yet he took note of their distress
when he heard their cry;
45 for their sake he remembered his covenant
and out of his great love he relented.
46 He caused all who held them captive
to show them mercy.

47 Save us, LORD our God,
and gather us from the nations,
that we may give thanks to your holy name
and glory in your praise.

48 Praise be to the LORD, the God of Israel,
from everlasting to everlasting.

Let all the people say, "Amen!"

Praise the LORD.

BOOK V
PSALMS 107–150

PSALM 107

1 Give thanks to the LORD, for he is good;
his love endures forever.

PRAYING SCRIPTURE

Psalm 107

Four times the psalmist pleaded for people to "give thanks to the LORD for his unfailing love and his wonderful deeds for mankind," each time for a different reason (verses 8,15,21,31). We should always praise God because he is good and he does good.

Withholding thanksgiving to God results from pride and self-sufficiency. Confession of these sins prepares us to respond to him as we should.

[a] 33 Or *against his spirit, / and rash words came from his lips*

2 Let the redeemed of the LORD tell their story—
those he redeemed from the hand of the foe,
3 those he gathered from the lands,
from east and west, from north and south.[a]

4 Some wandered in desert wastelands,
finding no way to a city where they could settle.
5 They were hungry and thirsty,
and their lives ebbed away.
6 Then they cried out to the LORD in their trouble,
and he delivered them from their distress.
7 He led them by a straight way
to a city where they could settle.
8 Let them give thanks to the LORD for his unfailing love
and his wonderful deeds for mankind,
9 for he satisfies the thirsty
and fills the hungry with good things.

10 Some sat in darkness, in utter darkness,
prisoners suffering in iron chains,
11 because they rebelled against God's commands
and despised the plans of the Most High.
12 So he subjected them to bitter labor;
they stumbled, and there was no one to help.
13 Then they cried to the LORD in their trouble,
and he saved them from their distress.
14 He brought them out of darkness, the utter darkness,
and broke away their chains.
15 Let them give thanks to the LORD for his unfailing love
and his wonderful deeds for mankind,
16 for he breaks down gates of bronze
and cuts through bars of iron.

17 Some became fools through their rebellious ways
and suffered affliction because of their iniquities.
18 They loathed all food
and drew near the gates of death.
19 Then they cried to the LORD in their trouble,
and he saved them from their distress.
20 He sent out his word and healed them;
he rescued them from the grave.
21 Let them give thanks to the LORD for his unfailing love
and his wonderful deeds for mankind.
22 Let them sacrifice thank offerings
and tell of his works with songs of joy.

23 Some went out on the sea in ships;
they were merchants on the mighty waters.
24 They saw the works of the LORD,
his wonderful deeds in the deep.
25 For he spoke and stirred up a tempest
that lifted high the waves.
26 They mounted up to the heavens and went down to the depths;
in their peril their courage melted away.

[a] 3 Hebrew *north and the sea*

27 They reeled and staggered like drunkards;
 they were at their wits' end.
28 Then they cried out to the LORD in their trouble,
 and he brought them out of their distress.
29 He stilled the storm to a whisper;
 the waves of the sea[a] were hushed.
30 They were glad when it grew calm,
 and he guided them to their desired haven.
31 Let them give thanks to the LORD for his unfailing love
 and his wonderful deeds for mankind.
32 Let them exalt him in the assembly of the people
 and praise him in the council of the elders.

33 He turned rivers into a desert,
 flowing springs into thirsty ground,
34 and fruitful land into a salt waste,
 because of the wickedness of those who lived there.
35 He turned the desert into pools of water
 and the parched ground into flowing springs;
36 there he brought the hungry to live,
 and they founded a city where they could settle.
37 They sowed fields and planted vineyards
 that yielded a fruitful harvest;
38 he blessed them, and their numbers greatly increased,
 and he did not let their herds diminish.

39 Then their numbers decreased, and they were humbled
 by oppression, calamity and sorrow;
40 he who pours contempt on nobles
 made them wander in a trackless waste.
41 But he lifted the needy out of their affliction
 and increased their families like flocks.
42 The upright see and rejoice,
 but all the wicked shut their mouths.

43 Let the one who is wise heed these things
 and ponder the loving deeds of the LORD.

PSALM 108[b]

A song. A psalm of David.

1 My heart, O God, is steadfast;
 I will sing and make music with all my soul.
2 Awake, harp and lyre!
 I will awaken the dawn.
3 I will praise you, LORD, among the nations;
 I will sing of you among the peoples.
4 For great is your love, higher than the heavens;
 your faithfulness reaches to the skies.
5 Be exalted, O God, above the heavens;
 let your glory be over all the earth.

6 Save us and help us with your right hand,
 that those you love may be delivered.

PRAYING SCRIPTURE

Psalm 108

A good pattern for the healthy spiritual life—one that has been emulated through centuries—is in verse 2: "Awake, harp and lyre! I will awaken the dawn." David met with God early in the morning, using his musical instruments to accompany his singing.

What song is on your lips in the morning? For many it is a dirge. Ask God to help you wake with songs of praise to him.

---

[a] 29 Dead Sea Scrolls; Masoretic Text / *their waves* [b] In Hebrew texts 108:1-13 is numbered 108:2-14.

7 God has spoken from his sanctuary:
“In triumph I will parcel out Shechem
and measure off the Valley of Sukkoth.
8 Gilead is mine, Manasseh is mine;
Ephraim is my helmet,
Judah is my scepter.
9 Moab is my washbasin,
on Edom I toss my sandal;
over Philistia I shout in triumph.”

10 Who will bring me to the fortified city?
Who will lead me to Edom?
11 Is it not you, God, you who have rejected us
and no longer go out with our armies?
12 Give us aid against the enemy,
for human help is worthless.
13 With God we will gain the victory,
and he will trample down our enemies.

PSALM 109

For the director of music. Of David. A psalm.

1 My God, whom I praise,
do not remain silent,
2 for people who are wicked and deceitful
have opened their mouths against me;
they have spoken against me with lying tongues.
3 With words of hatred they surround me;
they attack me without cause.
4 In return for my friendship they accuse me,
but I am a man of prayer.
5 They repay me evil for good,
and hatred for my friendship.

6 Appoint someone evil to oppose my enemy;
let an accuser stand at his right hand.
7 When he is tried, let him be found guilty,
and may his prayers condemn him.
8 May his days be few;
may another take his place of leadership.
9 May his children be fatherless
and his wife a widow.
10 May his children be wandering beggars;
may they be driven[a] from their ruined homes.
11 May a creditor seize all he has;
may strangers plunder the fruits of his labor.
12 May no one extend kindness to him
or take pity on his fatherless children.
13 May his descendants be cut off,
their names blotted out from the next generation.
14 May the iniquity of his fathers be remembered before the LORD;
may the sin of his mother never be blotted out.
15 May their sins always remain before the LORD,
that he may blot out their name from the earth.

PRAYING SCRIPTURE

Psalm 109

Scripture teaches that God watches how we treat the poor and needy. In the Old and New Testaments, attention is given to the condition of the less fortunate and how God's people should respond to them.

Ask God to open your eyes to the marginalized in your path. Ask how you can be one who shows mercy.

[a] *10* Septuagint; Hebrew *sought*

16 For he never thought of doing a kindness,
but hounded to death the poor
and the needy and the brokenhearted.
17 He loved to pronounce a curse —
may it come back on him.
He found no pleasure in blessing —
may it be far from him.
18 He wore cursing as his garment;
it entered into his body like water,
into his bones like oil.
19 May it be like a cloak wrapped about him,
like a belt tied forever around him.
20 May this be the LORD's payment to my accusers,
to those who speak evil of me.

21 But you, Sovereign LORD,
help me for your name's sake;
out of the goodness of your love, deliver me.
22 For I am poor and needy,
and my heart is wounded within me.
23 I fade away like an evening shadow;
I am shaken off like a locust.
24 My knees give way from fasting;
my body is thin and gaunt.
25 I am an object of scorn to my accusers;
when they see me, they shake their heads.

26 Help me, LORD my God;
save me according to your unfailing love.
27 Let them know that it is your hand,
that you, LORD, have done it.
28 While they curse, may you bless;
may those who attack me be put to shame,
but may your servant rejoice.
29 May my accusers be clothed with disgrace
and wrapped in shame as in a cloak.

30 With my mouth I will greatly extol the LORD;
in the great throng of worshipers I will praise him.
31 For he stands at the right hand of the needy,
to save their lives from those who would condemn them.

PSALM 110

Of David. A psalm.

1 The LORD says to my lord:[a]

"Sit at my right hand
until I make your enemies
a footstool for your feet."

2 The LORD will extend your mighty scepter from Zion, saying,
"Rule in the midst of your enemies!"
3 Your troops will be willing
on your day of battle.

PRAYING SCRIPTURE

Psalm 110

Psalm 110 is called a Messianic psalm because it is understood prophetically since David mentioned the Lord of his Lord, referring to the Father and the Son. Jesus, "my lord," represents his people as both their Priest and their King (see verse 1).

Thank the Father for his ways that are beyond finding out. Thank the Son for his obedience in dying on the cross. Thank the Holy Spirit for his daily guidance.

[a] *1* Or *Lord*

Arrayed in holy splendor,
your young men will come to you
like dew from the morning's womb.[a]

4 The LORD has sworn
and will not change his mind:
"You are a priest forever,
in the order of Melchizedek."

5 The Lord is at your right hand[b];
he will crush kings on the day of his wrath.
6 He will judge the nations, heaping up the dead
and crushing the rulers of the whole earth.
7 He will drink from a brook along the way,[c]
and so he will lift his head high.

PSALM 111[d]

1 Praise the LORD.[e]

I will extol the LORD with all my heart
in the council of the upright and in the assembly.

2 Great are the works of the LORD;
they are pondered by all who delight in them.
3 Glorious and majestic are his deeds,
and his righteousness endures forever.
4 He has caused his wonders to be remembered;
the LORD is gracious and compassionate.
5 He provides food for those who fear him;
he remembers his covenant forever.

6 He has shown his people the power of his works,
giving them the lands of other nations.
7 The works of his hands are faithful and just;
all his precepts are trustworthy.
8 They are established for ever and ever,
enacted in faithfulness and uprightness.
9 He provided redemption for his people;
he ordained his covenant forever—
holy and awesome is his name.

10 The fear of the LORD is the beginning of wisdom;
all who follow his precepts have good understanding.
To him belongs eternal praise.

PSALM 112[d]

1 Praise the LORD.[e]

Blessed are those who fear the LORD,
who find great delight in his commands.

2 Their children will be mighty in the land;
the generation of the upright will be blessed.

---

[a] *3* The meaning of the Hebrew for this sentence is uncertain. [b] *5* Or *My lord is at your right hand, LORD* [c] *7* The meaning of the Hebrew for this clause is uncertain. [d] This psalm is an acrostic poem, the lines of which begin with the successive letters of the Hebrew alphabet. [e] *1* Hebrew *Hallelu Yah*

PRAYING SCRIPTURE

Psalm 111

This psalm reminds us that we never have to choose between God's justice and his truth. God's truth informs his justice, and his justice displays the truth. His precepts (laws) stand forever. Holy and awesome is his name, indeed!

God's character and works never conflict. His perfect unity leads us to fear him and know the beginning of wisdom. This should cause us to praise God with our whole hearts.

PRAYING SCRIPTURE

Psalm 112

God promises numerous blessings for those who delight in him: blessed children, wealth and enduring righteousness. The writer also described good behavior: compassionate, righteous, generous and having integrity and a heart that trusts in God. Would you describe yourself with the qualities of good behavior? If not, ask the Holy Spirit to develop these qualities in you. He will do so, and your delight in God will increase.

3 Wealth and riches are in their houses,
and their righteousness endures forever.
4 Even in darkness light dawns for the upright,
for those who are gracious and compassionate and righteous.
5 Good will come to those who are generous and lend freely,
who conduct their affairs with justice.

6 Surely the righteous will never be shaken;
they will be remembered forever.
7 They will have no fear of bad news;
their hearts are steadfast, trusting in the LORD.
8 Their hearts are secure, they will have no fear;
in the end they will look in triumph on their foes.
9 They have freely scattered their gifts to the poor,
their righteousness endures forever;
their horn[a] will be lifted high in honor.

10 The wicked will see and be vexed,
they will gnash their teeth and waste away;
the longings of the wicked will come to nothing.

PSALM 113

1 Praise the LORD.[b]

Praise the LORD, you his servants;
praise the name of the LORD.
2 Let the name of the LORD be praised,
both now and forevermore.
3 From the rising of the sun to the place where it sets,
the name of the LORD is to be praised.

4 The LORD is exalted over all the nations,
his glory above the heavens.
5 Who is like the LORD our God,
the One who sits enthroned on high,
6 who stoops down to look
on the heavens and the earth?

7 He raises the poor from the dust
and lifts the needy from the ash heap;
8 he seats them with princes,
with the princes of his people.
9 He settles the childless woman in her home
as a happy mother of children.

Praise the LORD.

PSALM 114

1 When Israel came out of Egypt,
Jacob from a people of foreign tongue,
2 Judah became God's sanctuary,
Israel his dominion.

3 The sea looked and fled,
the Jordan turned back;

PRAYING SCRIPTURE
Psalm 113

When should we praise the Lord? "From the rising of the sun to the place where it sets" (verse 3). All day every day is a good time to praise our God. The psalmist asked who is like God, then declared that God "stoops down" to pay attention to his entire creation (verse 6).

Aren't you glad that God takes an interest in you? Thank him for his love for all of us.

PRAYING SCRIPTURE
Psalm 114

If we saw the true magnitude of God's power, we would shake in his presence. In fact, the psalmist pictured the sea, mountains and rams fleeing in fear of God's might. The earth should tremble, he wrote.

Are you afraid of God? His children can both fear (respect) him and approach him boldly in prayer because of what Jesus has done, so always pray with confidence.

[a] 9 *Horn* here symbolizes dignity. [b] 1 Hebrew *Hallelu Yah*; also in verse 9

4 the mountains leaped like rams,
the hills like lambs.

5 Why was it, sea, that you fled?
Why, Jordan, did you turn back?
6 Why, mountains, did you leap like rams,
you hills, like lambs?

7 Tremble, earth, at the presence of the Lord,
at the presence of the God of Jacob,
8 who turned the rock into a pool,
the hard rock into springs of water.

PSALM 115

1 Not to us, LORD, not to us
but to your name be the glory,
because of your love and faithfulness.

2 Why do the nations say,
"Where is their God?"
3 Our God is in heaven;
he does whatever pleases him.
4 But their idols are silver and gold,
made by human hands.
5 They have mouths, but cannot speak,
eyes, but cannot see.
6 They have ears, but cannot hear,
noses, but cannot smell.
7 They have hands, but cannot feel,
feet, but cannot walk,
nor can they utter a sound with their throats.
8 Those who make them will be like them,
and so will all who trust in them.

9 All you Israelites, trust in the LORD—
he is their help and shield.
10 House of Aaron, trust in the LORD—
he is their help and shield.
11 You who fear him, trust in the LORD—
he is their help and shield.

12 The LORD remembers us and will bless us:
He will bless his people Israel,
he will bless the house of Aaron,
13 he will bless those who fear the LORD—
small and great alike.

14 May the LORD cause you to flourish,
both you and your children.
15 May you be blessed by the LORD,
the Maker of heaven and earth.

16 The highest heavens belong to the LORD,
but the earth he has given to mankind.
17 It is not the dead who praise the LORD,
those who go down to the place of silence;

PRAYING SCRIPTURE

Psalm 115

Humans build idols and serve those idols, even though idols can do nothing for them. Idols are as dead as the wood and stone from which they are hewn. Only the God of creation is in heaven with the power to do whatever he pleases.

We know that idols are anything that we choose to worship. Ask God to reveal any idol in your life.

18 it is we who extol the LORD,
both now and forevermore.

Praise the LORD.[a]

PRAYING SCRIPTURE

Psalm 116

The psalmist proclaimed his love for God, but he didn't stop there. He then listed reasons for his love: God delivered him from trouble, saved him in a low period, dealt bountifully with him, delivered him from death and loosed his bonds.

Why do you love God? The next time you pray, take the time to tell God why you love him, no matter how long it takes.

PSALM 116

1 I love the LORD, for he heard my voice;
he heard my cry for mercy.
2 Because he turned his ear to me,
I will call on him as long as I live.

3 The cords of death entangled me,
the anguish of the grave came over me;
I was overcome by distress and sorrow.
4 Then I called on the name of the LORD:
"LORD, save me!"

5 The LORD is gracious and righteous;
our God is full of compassion.
6 The LORD protects the unwary;
when I was brought low, he saved me.

7 Return to your rest, my soul,
for the LORD has been good to you.

8 For you, LORD, have delivered me from death,
my eyes from tears,
my feet from stumbling,
9 that I may walk before the LORD
in the land of the living.

10 I trusted in the LORD when I said,
"I am greatly afflicted";
11 in my alarm I said,
"Everyone is a liar."

12 What shall I return to the LORD
for all his goodness to me?

13 I will lift up the cup of salvation
and call on the name of the LORD.
14 I will fulfill my vows to the LORD
in the presence of all his people.

15 Precious in the sight of the LORD
is the death of his faithful servants.
16 Truly I am your servant, LORD;
I serve you just as my mother did;
you have freed me from my chains.

17 I will sacrifice a thank offering to you
and call on the name of the LORD.
18 I will fulfill my vows to the LORD
in the presence of all his people,
19 in the courts of the house of the LORD —
in your midst, Jerusalem.

Praise the LORD.[a]

[a] *18,19* Hebrew *Hallelu Yah*

PSALM 117

1 Praise the LORD, all you nations;
extol him, all you peoples.
2 For great is his love toward us,
and the faithfulness of the LORD endures forever.

Praise the LORD.[a]

PSALM 118

1 Give thanks to the LORD, for he is good;
his love endures forever.

2 Let Israel say:
"His love endures forever."
3 Let the house of Aaron say:
"His love endures forever."
4 Let those who fear the LORD say:
"His love endures forever."

5 When hard pressed, I cried to the LORD;
he brought me into a spacious place.
6 The LORD is with me; I will not be afraid.
What can mere mortals do to me?
7 The LORD is with me; he is my helper.
I look in triumph on my enemies.

8 It is better to take refuge in the LORD
than to trust in humans.
9 It is better to take refuge in the LORD
than to trust in princes.
10 All the nations surrounded me,
but in the name of the LORD I cut them down.
11 They surrounded me on every side,
but in the name of the LORD I cut them down.
12 They swarmed around me like bees,
but they were consumed as quickly as burning thorns;
in the name of the LORD I cut them down.
13 I was pushed back and about to fall,
but the LORD helped me.
14 The LORD is my strength and my defense[b];
he has become my salvation.

15 Shouts of joy and victory
resound in the tents of the righteous:
"The LORD's right hand has done mighty things!
16 The LORD's right hand is lifted high;
the LORD's right hand has done mighty things!"
17 I will not die but live,
and will proclaim what the LORD has done.
18 The LORD has chastened me severely,
but he has not given me over to death.
19 Open for me the gates of the righteous;
I will enter and give thanks to the LORD.
20 This is the gate of the LORD
through which the righteous may enter.

PRAYING SCRIPTURE

Psalm 117

In this, both the shortest psalm and the shortest chapter in the Bible, the writer declared that God's merciful kindness is so great that all the Gentiles should praise God and all peoples should extol him.

Think about God's kindness filled with so much mercy. Imagine the depth and breadth of it! Praise God for his mercy and for the kindness that he has poured out abundantly on you.

PRAYING SCRIPTURE

Psalm 118

We are often tempted to trust in human ingenuity rather than God's providence. The Messianic portion of this psalm demonstrates that his ways are not ours: God chose the very One rejected by human beings to be "the cornerstone" (verse 22).

Notice how often the Psalms end with praise after talking about God's attributes. Is your response the same? When praying, practice acknowledging God's character, and then move directly to praise.

[a] 2 Hebrew *Hallelu Yah* [b] 14 Or *song*

21 I will give you thanks, for you answered me;
you have become my salvation.

22 The stone the builders rejected
has become the cornerstone;
23 the LORD has done this,
and it is marvelous in our eyes.
24 The LORD has done it this very day;
let us rejoice today and be glad.

25 LORD, save us!
LORD, grant us success!

26 Blessed is he who comes in the name of the LORD.
From the house of the LORD we bless you.[a]
27 The LORD is God,
and he has made his light shine on us.
With boughs in hand, join in the festal procession
up[b] to the horns of the altar.

28 You are my God, and I will praise you;
you are my God, and I will exalt you.

29 Give thanks to the LORD, for he is good;
his love endures forever.

PRAYING SCRIPTURE

Psalm 119

This longest chapter in all the Bible is an ode to the majesty of God's Word. Using words like "law," "precepts," "decrees," "statutes" and "commands" (verses 1,4,8,14,21), the writer drives home again and again that we will not experience God's blessings unless we are walking according to his Word.

It isn't possible to walk in God's Word if we are not in God's Word. Ask the Lord to give you a deep desire to study it.

PSALM 119[c]

א ALEPH

1 Blessed are those whose ways are blameless,
who walk according to the law of the LORD.
2 Blessed are those who keep his statutes
and seek him with all their heart—
3 they do no wrong
but follow his ways.
4 You have laid down precepts
that are to be fully obeyed.
5 Oh, that my ways were steadfast
in obeying your decrees!
6 Then I would not be put to shame
when I consider all your commands.
7 I will praise you with an upright heart
as I learn your righteous laws.
8 I will obey your decrees;
do not utterly forsake me.

ב BETH

9 How can a young person stay on the path of purity?
By living according to your word.
10 I seek you with all my heart;
do not let me stray from your commands.
11 I have hidden your word in my heart
that I might not sin against you.

---

[a] *26* The Hebrew is plural. [b] *27* Or *Bind the festal sacrifice with ropes / and take it* [c] This psalm is an acrostic poem, the stanzas of which begin with successive letters of the Hebrew alphabet; moreover, the verses of each stanza begin with the same letter of the Hebrew alphabet.

12 Praise be to you, LORD;
teach me your decrees.
13 With my lips I recount
all the laws that come from your mouth.
14 I rejoice in following your statutes
as one rejoices in great riches.
15 I meditate on your precepts
and consider your ways.
16 I delight in your decrees;
I will not neglect your word.

ג GIMEL

17 Be good to your servant while I live,
that I may obey your word.
18 Open my eyes that I may see
wonderful things in your law.
19 I am a stranger on earth;
do not hide your commands from me.
20 My soul is consumed with longing
for your laws at all times.
21 You rebuke the arrogant, who are accursed,
those who stray from your commands.
22 Remove from me their scorn and contempt,
for I keep your statutes.
23 Though rulers sit together and slander me,
your servant will meditate on your decrees.
24 Your statutes are my delight;
they are my counselors.

ד DALETH

25 I am laid low in the dust;
preserve my life according to your word.
26 I gave an account of my ways and you answered me;
teach me your decrees.
27 Cause me to understand the way of your precepts,
that I may meditate on your wonderful deeds.
28 My soul is weary with sorrow;
strengthen me according to your word.
29 Keep me from deceitful ways;
be gracious to me and teach me your law.
30 I have chosen the way of faithfulness;
I have set my heart on your laws.
31 I hold fast to your statutes, LORD;
do not let me be put to shame.
32 I run in the path of your commands,
for you have broadened my understanding.

ה HE

33 Teach me, LORD, the way of your decrees,
that I may follow it to the end.[a]
34 Give me understanding, so that I may keep your law
and obey it with all my heart.

[a] 33 Or *follow it for its reward*

PRAYING SCRIPTURE

Psalm 119

In this Psalm, we are reminded numerous times about the importance of God's Word, none more memorable than verse 11: "I have hidden your word in my heart that I might not sin against you."

Young believers are told to focus on memorizing Scripture, a practice that often falls away as we get older. Ask God for a renewed emphasis on hiding his Word in your heart.

35 Direct me in the path of your commands,
for there I find delight.
36 Turn my heart toward your statutes
and not toward selfish gain.
37 Turn my eyes away from worthless things;
preserve my life according to your word.[a]
38 Fulfill your promise to your servant,
so that you may be feared.
39 Take away the disgrace I dread,
for your laws are good.
40 How I long for your precepts!
In your righteousness preserve my life.

ו WAW

41 May your unfailing love come to me, LORD,
your salvation, according to your promise;
42 then I can answer anyone who taunts me,
for I trust in your word.
43 Never take your word of truth from my mouth,
for I have put my hope in your laws.
44 I will always obey your law,
for ever and ever.
45 I will walk about in freedom,
for I have sought out your precepts.
46 I will speak of your statutes before kings
and will not be put to shame,
47 for I delight in your commands
because I love them.
48 I reach out for your commands, which I love,
that I may meditate on your decrees.

ז ZAYIN

49 Remember your word to your servant,
for you have given me hope.
50 My comfort in my suffering is this:
Your promise preserves my life.
51 The arrogant mock me unmercifully,
but I do not turn from your law.
52 I remember, LORD, your ancient laws,
and I find comfort in them.
53 Indignation grips me because of the wicked,
who have forsaken your law.
54 Your decrees are the theme of my song
wherever I lodge.
55 In the night, LORD, I remember your name,
that I may keep your law.
56 This has been my practice:
I obey your precepts.

ח HETH

57 You are my portion, LORD;
I have promised to obey your words.

[a] *37* Two manuscripts of the Masoretic Text and Dead Sea Scrolls; most manuscripts of the Masoretic Text *life in your way*

58 I have sought your face with all my heart;
be gracious to me according to your promise.
59 I have considered my ways
and have turned my steps to your statutes.
60 I will hasten and not delay
to obey your commands.
61 Though the wicked bind me with ropes,
I will not forget your law.
62 At midnight I rise to give you thanks
for your righteous laws.
63 I am a friend to all who fear you,
to all who follow your precepts.
64 The earth is filled with your love, LORD;
teach me your decrees.

ט TETH

65 Do good to your servant
according to your word, LORD.
66 Teach me knowledge and good judgment,
for I trust your commands.
67 Before I was afflicted I went astray,
but now I obey your word.
68 You are good, and what you do is good;
teach me your decrees.
69 Though the arrogant have smeared me with lies,
I keep your precepts with all my heart.
70 Their hearts are callous and unfeeling,
but I delight in your law
71 It was good for me to be afflicted
so that I might learn your decrees.
72 The law from your mouth is more precious to me
than thousands of pieces of silver and gold.

י YODH

73 Your hands made me and formed me;
give me understanding to learn your commands.
74 May those who fear you rejoice when they see me,
for I have put my hope in your word.
75 I know, LORD, that your laws are righteous,
and that in faithfulness you have afflicted me.
76 May your unfailing love be my comfort,
according to your promise to your servant.
77 Let your compassion come to me that I may live,
for your law is my delight.
78 May the arrogant be put to shame for wronging me without cause;
but I will meditate on your precepts.
79 May those who fear you turn to me,
those who understand your statutes.
80 May I wholeheartedly follow your decrees,
that I may not be put to shame.

כ KAPH

81 My soul faints with longing for your salvation,
but I have put my hope in your word.

82 My eyes fail, looking for your promise;
I say, "When will you comfort me?"
83 Though I am like a wineskin in the smoke,
I do not forget your decrees.
84 How long must your servant wait?
When will you punish my persecutors?
85 The arrogant dig pits to trap me,
contrary to your law.
86 All your commands are trustworthy;
help me, for I am being persecuted without cause.
87 They almost wiped me from the earth,
but I have not forsaken your precepts.
88 In your unfailing love preserve my life,
that I may obey the statutes of your mouth.

ל LAMEDH

89 Your word, LORD, is eternal;
it stands firm in the heavens.
90 Your faithfulness continues through all generations;
you established the earth, and it endures.
91 Your laws endure to this day,
for all things serve you.
92 If your law had not been my delight,
I would have perished in my affliction.
93 I will never forget your precepts,
for by them you have preserved my life.
94 Save me, for I am yours;
I have sought out your precepts.
95 The wicked are waiting to destroy me,
but I will ponder your statutes.
96 To all perfection I see a limit,
but your commands are boundless.

מ MEM

97 Oh, how I love your law!
I meditate on it all day long.
98 Your commands are always with me
and make me wiser than my enemies.
99 I have more insight than all my teachers,
for I meditate on your statutes.
100 I have more understanding than the elders,
for I obey your precepts.
101 I have kept my feet from every evil path
so that I might obey your word.
102 I have not departed from your laws,
for you yourself have taught me.
103 How sweet are your words to my taste,
sweeter than honey to my mouth!
104 I gain understanding from your precepts;
therefore I hate every wrong path.

נ NUN

105 Your word is a lamp for my feet,
a light on my path.

PRAYING SCRIPTURE

Psalm 119

It's important to remember that God's Word is not arbitrary. It did not come on a whim, nor did it arise from human devising. "Your word, LORD, is eternal; it stands firm in the heavens" (verse 89). God's laws, commands, exhortations and promises are first settled with him, then given to us.

Thank God for revealing himself to us through his Word.

106 I have taken an oath and confirmed it,
that I will follow your righteous laws.
107 I have suffered much;
preserve my life, LORD, according to your word.
108 Accept, LORD, the willing praise of my mouth,
and teach me your laws.
109 Though I constantly take my life in my hands,
I will not forget your law.
110 The wicked have set a snare for me,
but I have not strayed from your precepts.
111 Your statutes are my heritage forever;
they are the joy of my heart.
112 My heart is set on keeping your decrees
to the very end.[a]

ס SAMEKH

113 I hate double-minded people,
but I love your law.
114 You are my refuge and my shield;
I have put my hope in your word.
115 Away from me, you evildoers,
that I may keep the commands of my God!
116 Sustain me, my God, according to your promise, and
I will live;
do not let my hopes be dashed.
117 Uphold me, and I will be delivered;
I will always have regard for your decrees.
118 You reject all who stray from your decrees,
for their delusions come to nothing.
119 All the wicked of the earth you discard like dross;
therefore I love your statutes.
120 My flesh trembles in fear of you;
I stand in awe of your laws.

ע AYIN

121 I have done what is righteous and just;
do not leave me to my oppressors.
122 Ensure your servant's well-being;
do not let the arrogant oppress me.
123 My eyes fail, looking for your salvation,
looking for your righteous promise.
124 Deal with your servant according to your love
and teach me your decrees.
125 I am your servant; give me discernment
that I may understand your statutes.
126 It is time for you to act, LORD;
your law is being broken.
127 Because I love your commands
more than gold, more than pure gold,
128 and because I consider all your precepts right,
I hate every wrong path.

---

[a] 112 Or *decrees / for their enduring reward*

פ PE

129 Your statutes are wonderful;
therefore I obey them.
130 The unfolding of your words gives light;
it gives understanding to the simple.
131 I open my mouth and pant,
longing for your commands.
132 Turn to me and have mercy on me,
as you always do to those who love your name.
133 Direct my footsteps according to your word;
let no sin rule over me.
134 Redeem me from human oppression,
that I may obey your precepts.
135 Make your face shine on your servant
and teach me your decrees.
136 Streams of tears flow from my eyes,
for your law is not obeyed.

צ TSADHE

137 You are righteous, LORD,
and your laws are right.
138 The statutes you have laid down are righteous;
they are fully trustworthy.
139 My zeal wears me out,
for my enemies ignore your words.
140 Your promises have been thoroughly tested,
and your servant loves them.
141 Though I am lowly and despised,
I do not forget your precepts.
142 Your righteousness is everlasting
and your law is true.
143 Trouble and distress have come upon me,
but your commands give me delight.
144 Your statutes are always righteous;
give me understanding that I may live.

ק QOPH

145 I call with all my heart; answer me, LORD,
and I will obey your decrees.
146 I call out to you; save me
and I will keep your statutes.
147 I rise before dawn and cry for help;
I have put my hope in your word.
148 My eyes stay open through the watches of the night,
that I may meditate on your promises.
149 Hear my voice in accordance with your love;
preserve my life, LORD, according to your laws.
150 Those who devise wicked schemes are near,
but they are far from your law.
151 Yet you are near, LORD,
and all your commands are true.
152 Long ago I learned from your statutes
that you established them to last forever.

ר RESH

153 Look on my suffering and deliver me,
for I have not forgotten your law.
154 Defend my cause and redeem me;
preserve my life according to your promise.
155 Salvation is far from the wicked,
for they do not seek out your decrees.
156 Your compassion, LORD, is great;
preserve my life according to your laws.
157 Many are the foes who persecute me,
but I have not turned from your statutes.
158 I look on the faithless with loathing,
for they do not obey your word.
159 See how I love your precepts;
preserve my life, LORD, in accordance with your love.
160 All your words are true;
all your righteous laws are eternal.

ש SIN AND SHIN

161 Rulers persecute me without cause,
but my heart trembles at your word.
162 I rejoice in your promise
like one who finds great spoil.
163 I hate and detest falsehood
but I love your law.
164 Seven times a day I praise you
for your righteous laws.
165 Great peace have those who love your law,
and nothing can make them stumble.
166 I wait for your salvation, LORD,
and I follow your commands.
167 I obey your statutes,
for I love them greatly.
168 I obey your precepts and your statutes,
for all my ways are known to you.

ת TAW

169 May my cry come before you, LORD;
give me understanding according to your word.
170 May my supplication come before you;
deliver me according to your promise.
171 May my lips overflow with praise,
for you teach me your decrees.
172 May my tongue sing of your word,
for all your commands are righteous.
173 May your hand be ready to help me,
for I have chosen your precepts.
174 I long for your salvation, LORD,
and your law gives me delight.
175 Let me live that I may praise you,
and may your laws sustain me.
176 I have strayed like a lost sheep.
Seek your servant,
for I have not forgotten your commands.

PRAYING SCRIPTURE

Psalm 120

When you are in distress, what do you do? Do you complain to your spouse or a friend? Do you text someone and ask for help? Do you become worried? Here the psalmist teaches us a crucial practice: Cry out to God.

God is never too busy for his children, and he is always interested in our plight, so call to him immediately whenever you are anxious.

PRAYING SCRIPTURE

Psalm 121

This second of the songs of ascents (so named because they were sung by the people traveling up to Jerusalem) promises that God will help those who seek him. Though we often grow tired and weary, the Lord who watches over us never sleeps. He watches our coming and going.

Do you ever consider God's constant watch over your daily routine? Thank God for his attention and protection over you in life's normal activities.

PRAYING SCRIPTURE

Psalm 122

The first verse of this psalm has welcomed generations of God's people to worship. For Israel, to love the house of the Lord—the temple—was to love the Lord of the temple. Those ascending pilgrims were joyful to see it as they entered Jerusalem.

How do you respond when you gather with God's people? We truly should rejoice and be glad, because God dwells in his people's praises.

PSALM 120

A song of ascents.

1 I call on the LORD in my distress,
and he answers me.
2 Save me, LORD,
from lying lips
and from deceitful tongues.

3 What will he do to you,
and what more besides,
you deceitful tongue?
4 He will punish you with a warrior's sharp arrows,
with burning coals of the broom bush.

5 Woe to me that I dwell in Meshek,
that I live among the tents of Kedar!
6 Too long have I lived
among those who hate peace.
7 I am for peace;
but when I speak, they are for war.

PSALM 121

A song of ascents.

1 I lift up my eyes to the mountains —
where does my help come from?
2 My help comes from the LORD,
the Maker of heaven and earth.

3 He will not let your foot slip —
he who watches over you will not slumber;
4 indeed, he who watches over Israel
will neither slumber nor sleep.

5 The LORD watches over you —
the LORD is your shade at your right hand;
6 the sun will not harm you by day,
nor the moon by night.

7 The LORD will keep you from all harm —
he will watch over your life;
8 the LORD will watch over your coming and going
both now and forevermore.

PSALM 122

A song of ascents. Of David.

1 I rejoiced with those who said to me,
"Let us go to the house of the LORD."
2 Our feet are standing
in your gates, Jerusalem.

3 Jerusalem is built like a city
that is closely compacted together.
4 That is where the tribes go up —
the tribes of the LORD —
to praise the name of the LORD
according to the statute given to Israel.

5 There stand the thrones for judgment,
the thrones of the house of David.

6 Pray for the peace of Jerusalem:
"May those who love you be secure.
7 May there be peace within your walls
and security within your citadels."
8 For the sake of my family and friends,
I will say, "Peace be within you."
9 For the sake of the house of the LORD our God,
I will seek your prosperity.

PSALM 123

A song of ascents.

1 I lift up my eyes to you,
to you who sit enthroned in heaven.
2 As the eyes of slaves look to the hand of their master,
as the eyes of a female slave look to the hand of
her mistress,
so our eyes look to the LORD our God,
till he shows us his mercy.

3 Have mercy on us, LORD, have mercy on us,
for we have endured no end of contempt.
4 We have endured no end
of ridicule from the arrogant,
of contempt from the proud.

PSALM 124

A song of ascents. Of David.

1 If the LORD had not been on our side —
let Israel say —
2 if the LORD had not been on our side
when people attacked us,
3 they would have swallowed us alive
when their anger flared against us;
4 the flood would have engulfed us,
the torrent would have swept over us,
5 the raging waters
would have swept us away.

6 Praise be to the LORD,
who has not let us be torn by their teeth.
7 We have escaped like a bird
from the fowler's snare;
the snare has been broken,
and we have escaped.
8 Our help is in the name of the LORD,
the Maker of heaven and earth.

PSALM 125

A song of ascents.

1 Those who trust in the LORD are like Mount Zion,
which cannot be shaken but endures forever.

PRAYING SCRIPTURE

Psalm 123

How does it make you feel when wealthy or esteemed people mistreat others? If you ever feel contempt toward them, you are not alone; so did the writer of this psalm. But that is not the end. "Have mercy on us, LORD," he prayed (verse 3).

Sometimes our responses to earthly evils are not godly. But God can make them godly when we ask him to help us.

PRAYING SCRIPTURE

Psalm 124

Every time we escape from trouble, it is because our help comes from the Lord; there are no exceptions to this wonderful truth. "If the LORD had not been on our side," we would have been swept away, destroyed (verse 1).

We can bless the Lord because it is in his name that we find help. Whenever you are in any kind of trouble, call on God first, and he will aid you.

PRAYING SCRIPTURE

Psalm 125

The Lord is always with us and does good things for us because we trust him. How trustworthy is God? Those who trust him cannot be moved; they are like the fortress, Mount Zion, which Israel's pilgrims sought as they ascended to Jerusalem.

The psalmist asked God to do good to people who do good—a blessing for obedience. We can join that prayer.

2 As the mountains surround Jerusalem,
so the LORD surrounds his people
both now and forevermore.

3 The scepter of the wicked will not remain
over the land allotted to the righteous,
for then the righteous might use
their hands to do evil.

4 LORD, do good to those who are good,
to those who are upright in heart.
5 But those who turn to crooked ways
the LORD will banish with the evildoers.

Peace be on Israel.

PSALM 126

A song of ascents.

1 When the LORD restored the fortunes of[a] Zion,
we were like those who dreamed.[b]
2 Our mouths were filled with laughter,
our tongues with songs of joy.
Then it was said among the nations,
"The LORD has done great things for them."
3 The LORD has done great things for us,
and we are filled with joy.

4 Restore our fortunes,[c] LORD,
like streams in the Negev.
5 Those who sow with tears
will reap with songs of joy.
6 Those who go out weeping,
carrying seed to sow,
will return with songs of joy,
carrying sheaves with them.

PRAYING SCRIPTURE

Psalm 126

The end of this psalm is a common prayer for those who share the gospel of Jesus: Honor our brokenhearted weeping, and let us know the joy of a great harvest of souls.

When was the last time you told someone what Christ has done for you and invited that person to know him? Ask God for such an opportunity today.

PSALM 127

A song of ascents. Of Solomon.

1 Unless the LORD builds the house,
the builders labor in vain.
Unless the LORD watches over the city,
the guards stand watch in vain.
2 In vain you rise early
and stay up late,
toiling for food to eat—
for he grants sleep to[d] those he loves.

3 Children are a heritage from the LORD,
offspring a reward from him.
4 Like arrows in the hands of a warrior
are children born in one's youth.
5 Blessed is the man
whose quiver is full of them.

PRAYING SCRIPTURE

Psalm 127

This beautiful psalm recalls the twin blessings of a life of trusting God and children. The writer called children "a heritage from the LORD," that is, an inheritance (verse 3). He also warned us that our attempts to do things without God are vain, as are our long days of labor.

Do you ever feel as though every pressure is on you? Tell God specifically that you trust him to "build the house."

[a] 1 Or *LORD brought back the captives to* [b] 1 Or *those restored to health* [c] 4 Or *Bring back our captives* [d] 2 Or *eat— / for while they sleep he provides for*

They will not be put to shame
  when they contend with their opponents in court.

PSALM 128

A song of ascents.

1 Blessed are all who fear the LORD,
  who walk in obedience to him.
2 You will eat the fruit of your labor;
  blessings and prosperity will be yours.
3 Your wife will be like a fruitful vine
  within your house;
your children will be like olive shoots
  around your table.
4 Yes, this will be the blessing
  for the man who fears the LORD.

5 May the LORD bless you from Zion;
  may you see the prosperity of Jerusalem
  all the days of your life.
6 May you live to see your children's children—
  peace be on Israel.

PSALM 129

A song of ascents.

1 "They have greatly oppressed me from my youth,"
  let Israel say;
2 "they have greatly oppressed me from my youth,
  but they have not gained the victory over me.
3 Plowmen have plowed my back
  and made their furrows long.
4 But the LORD is righteous;
  he has cut me free from the cords of the wicked."

5 May all who hate Zion
  be turned back in shame.
6 May they be like grass on the roof,
  which withers before it can grow;
7 a reaper cannot fill his hands with it,
  nor one who gathers fill his arms.
8 May those who pass by not say to them,
  "The blessing of the LORD be on you;
  we bless you in the name of the LORD."

PSALM 130

A song of ascents.

1 Out of the depths I cry to you, LORD;
2   Lord, hear my voice.
Let your ears be attentive
  to my cry for mercy.

3 If you, LORD, kept a record of sins,
  Lord, who could stand?
4 But with you there is forgiveness,
  so that we can, with reverence, serve you.

PRAYING SCRIPTURE

Psalm 128

The Lord blesses his people, not merely spiritually, but also materially. He blesses the labor of our hands, he is the source of true happiness and he strengthens families. He blesses those who fear him.

How do you currently need God to bless you? Is there a void you've been trying to fill? Ask God to bless everything in your life for his glory.

PRAYING SCRIPTURE

Psalm 129

In this, the tenth song of ascents, the writer called on God to punish his enemies who had persecuted him severely. He likened his suffering to having someone plow long furrows down his back. He asked God to shame and repel those who hated Israel.

Even though the wicked had prevailed thus far, the writer continued to have faith. Regardless of how strong your enemies are, trust God to take care of you.

PRAYING SCRIPTURE

Psalm 130

Many believe that God is tracking our good and bad acts with some kind of recordkeeping system. The psalmist was aware, though, that if God did that, no one would be saved. Instead, He offers forgiveness to us.

Have you experienced God's forgiveness in Jesus? If not, ask him now to forgive your sins.

5 I wait for the LORD, my whole being waits,
and in his word I put my hope.
6 I wait for the Lord
more than watchmen wait for the morning,
more than watchmen wait for the morning.

7 Israel, put your hope in the LORD,
for with the LORD is unfailing love
and with him is full redemption.
8 He himself will redeem Israel
from all their sins.

PRAYING SCRIPTURE

Psalm 131

In an image to which we can all relate, the psalmist compares his contentment in the Lord to a child in his mother's lap. He has a "calmed and quieted" soul (verse 2). He experienced this in part because he refused to concern himself with things that are God's responsibility.

How often are you calm and quiet? If you find yourself trying to play God, cast your cares and concerns on him in prayer.

PSALM 131

A song of ascents. Of David.

1 My heart is not proud, LORD,
my eyes are not haughty;
I do not concern myself with great matters
or things too wonderful for me.
2 But I have calmed and quieted myself,
I am like a weaned child with its mother;
like a weaned child I am content.

3 Israel, put your hope in the LORD
both now and forevermore.

PRAYING SCRIPTURE

Psalm 132

The author of this psalm knew there was no hope apart from God keeping his promises. He recounted God's remembering David, swearing his covenant with David, and choosing Zion for the dwelling place of his house, the temple.

Do not be afraid to remind God of his promises for he delights to keep them. Then you can shout with joy with all the saints who know his sure word.

PSALM 132

A song of ascents.

1 LORD, remember David
and all his self-denial.

2 He swore an oath to the LORD,
he made a vow to the Mighty One of Jacob:
3 "I will not enter my house
or go to my bed,
4 I will allow no sleep to my eyes
or slumber to my eyelids,
5 till I find a place for the LORD,
a dwelling for the Mighty One of Jacob."

6 We heard it in Ephrathah,
we came upon it in the fields of Jaar:[a]
7 "Let us go to his dwelling place,
let us worship at his footstool, saying,
8 'Arise, LORD, and come to your resting place,
you and the ark of your might.
9 May your priests be clothed with your righteousness;
may your faithful people sing for joy.' "

10 For the sake of your servant David,
do not reject your anointed one.

11 The LORD swore an oath to David,
a sure oath he will not revoke:

[a] 6 Or *heard of it in Ephrathah, / we found it in the fields of Jearim.* (See 1 Chron. 13:5,6) (And no quotation marks around verses 7-9)

"One of your own descendants
I will place on your throne.
12 If your sons keep my covenant
and the statutes I teach them,
then their sons will sit
on your throne for ever and ever."

13 For the LORD has chosen Zion,
he has desired it for his dwelling, saying,
14 "This is my resting place for ever and ever;
here I will sit enthroned, for I have desired it.
15 I will bless her with abundant provisions;
her poor I will satisfy with food.
16 I will clothe her priests with salvation,
and her faithful people will ever sing for joy.

17 "Here I will make a horn[a] grow for David
and set up a lamp for my anointed one.
18 I will clothe his enemies with shame,
but his head will be adorned with a radiant crown."

PSALM 133

A song of ascents. Of David.

1 How good and pleasant it is
when God's people live together in unity!

2 It is like precious oil poured on the head,
running down on the beard,
running down on Aaron's beard,
down on the collar of his robe.
3 It is as if the dew of Hermon
were falling on Mount Zion.
For there the LORD bestows his blessing,
even life forevermore.

PSALM 134

A song of ascents.

1 Praise the LORD, all you servants of the LORD
who minister by night in the house of the LORD.
2 Lift up your hands in the sanctuary
and praise the LORD.

3 May the LORD bless you from Zion,
he who is the Maker of heaven and earth.

PSALM 135

1 Praise the LORD.[b]

Praise the name of the LORD;
praise him, you servants of the LORD,
2 you who minister in the house of the LORD,
in the courts of the house of our God.

[a] 17 *Horn* here symbolizes strong one, that is, king. [b] 1 Hebrew *Hallelu Yah*; also in verses 3 and 21

PRAYING SCRIPTURE

Psalm 133

One of the greatest blessings Christians can enjoy is unity in the family of God. The psalmist likened it to the holy anointing oil that flowed off Aaron's head, down his beard and onto his priestly robes. Unity is good, unity is pleasant and unity should be pursued.

Are you living in unity with the Christians around you? Ask God to help you seek harmony with others and to be one who brings peace.

PRAYING SCRIPTURE

Psalm 134

Imagine the people arriving in Jerusalem and the majestic temple of God first coming into view. Some, arriving in the evening, would bless those priests and other servants who were ministering in God's house, encouraging them to lift their hands in praise.

It's important that we encourage others in prayer because people are hurting in all kinds of ways. Pray with someone and encourage him or her to praise God.

PRAYING SCRIPTURE

Psalm 135

The Psalms consistently invite us to see the power of God and to respond in praise. Over and over we are commanded to praise and bless God. The reason is always related to God's character and his work in the world.

Praise is amplified in community, so pray with others when you can, and join together in praising the Lord.

3 Praise the LORD, for the LORD is good;
sing praise to his name, for that is pleasant.
4 For the LORD has chosen Jacob to be his own,
Israel to be his treasured possession.

5 I know that the LORD is great,
that our Lord is greater than all gods.
6 The LORD does whatever pleases him,
in the heavens and on the earth,
in the seas and all their depths.
7 He makes clouds rise from the ends of the earth;
he sends lightning with the rain
and brings out the wind from his storehouses.

8 He struck down the firstborn of Egypt,
the firstborn of people and animals.
9 He sent his signs and wonders into your midst, Egypt,
against Pharaoh and all his servants.
10 He struck down many nations
and killed mighty kings —
11 Sihon king of the Amorites,
Og king of Bashan,
and all the kings of Canaan —
12 and he gave their land as an inheritance,
an inheritance to his people Israel.

13 Your name, LORD, endures forever,
your renown, LORD, through all generations.
14 For the LORD will vindicate his people
and have compassion on his servants.

15 The idols of the nations are silver and gold,
made by human hands.
16 They have mouths, but cannot speak,
eyes, but cannot see.
17 They have ears, but cannot hear,
nor is there breath in their mouths.
18 Those who make them will be like them,
and so will all who trust in them.

19 All you Israelites, praise the LORD;
house of Aaron, praise the LORD;
20 house of Levi, praise the LORD;
you who fear him, praise the LORD.
21 Praise be to the LORD from Zion,
to him who dwells in Jerusalem.

Praise the LORD.

PSALM 136

1 Give thanks to the LORD, for he is good.
His love endures forever.

2 Give thanks to the God of gods.
His love endures forever.

3 Give thanks to the Lord of lords:
His love endures forever.

PRAYING SCRIPTURE

Psalm 136

The refrain running through this psalm, "His love endures forever," can give us direction (verse 1). It follows reminders of God's miracles, especially related to the exodus and Israel's wilderness wandering. Everything God did was a call to praise his mercy.

How would it change your prayers to include "Your love endures forever" after thanking God for all the blessings he gives? Include it the next time you pray.

4 to him who alone does great wonders,
His love endures forever.
5 who by his understanding made the heavens,
His love endures forever.
6 who spread out the earth upon the waters,
His love endures forever.
7 who made the great lights —
His love endures forever.
8 the sun to govern the day,
His love endures forever.
9 the moon and stars to govern the night;
His love endures forever.

10 to him who struck down the firstborn of Egypt
His love endures forever.
11 and brought Israel out from among them
His love endures forever.
12 with a mighty hand and outstretched arm;
His love endures forever.

13 to him who divided the Red Sea[a] asunder
His love endures forever.
14 and brought Israel through the midst of it,
His love endures forever.
15 but swept Pharaoh and his army into the Red Sea;
His love endures forever.

16 to him who led his people through the wilderness;
His love endures forever.

17 to him who struck down great kings,
His love endures forever.
18 and killed mighty kings —
His love endures forever.
19 Sihon king of the Amorites
His love endures forever.
20 and Og king of Bashan —
His love endures forever.
21 and gave their land as an inheritance,
His love endures forever.
22 an inheritance to his servant Israel.
His love endures forever.

23 He remembered us in our low estate
His love endures forever.
24 and freed us from our enemies.
His love endures forever.
25 He gives food to every creature.
His love endures forever.

26 Give thanks to the God of heaven.
His love endures forever.

[a] *13* Or *the Sea of Reeds*; also in verse 15

PRAYING SCRIPTURE

Psalm 137

This psalm looks back on the pain God's people felt during their exile in Babylon. It can also describe our condition when we are in sin: How can we sing God's songs if we are living our lives in ways that displease him? How can joy fill a rebellious spirit?

In our sin we should return to God. If you find yourself spiritually in a "foreign land," ask him to restore you.

PSALM 137

1 By the rivers of Babylon we sat and wept
  when we remembered Zion.
2 There on the poplars
  we hung our harps,
3 for there our captors asked us for songs,
  our tormentors demanded songs of joy;
  they said, "Sing us one of the songs of Zion!"

4 How can we sing the songs of the LORD
  while in a foreign land?
5 If I forget you, Jerusalem,
  may my right hand forget its skill.
6 May my tongue cling to the roof of my mouth
  if I do not remember you,
if I do not consider Jerusalem
  my highest joy.

7 Remember, LORD, what the Edomites did
  on the day Jerusalem fell.
"Tear it down," they cried,
  "tear it down to its foundations!"
8 Daughter Babylon, doomed to destruction,
  happy is the one who repays you
  according to what you have done to us.
9 Happy is the one who seizes your infants
  and dashes them against the rocks.

PRAYING SCRIPTURE

Psalm 138

Are you committed to spending time with God's words? For many Christians, Bible reading has become optional. But God has magnified his promises above even his name! How can we value God's words too little when God values them so much?

If you've allowed things to distract you from God's words, ask him to revive your love for them. Pray for open eyes when you read them.

PSALM 138

Of David.

1 I will praise you, LORD, with all my heart;
  before the "gods" I will sing your praise.
2 I will bow down toward your holy temple
  and will praise your name
  for your unfailing love and your faithfulness,
for you have so exalted your solemn decree
  that it surpasses your fame.
3 When I called, you answered me;
  you greatly emboldened me.

4 May all the kings of the earth praise you, LORD,
  when they hear what you have decreed.
5 May they sing of the ways of the LORD,
  for the glory of the LORD is great.

6 Though the LORD is exalted, he looks kindly on the lowly;
  though lofty, he sees them from afar.
7 Though I walk in the midst of trouble,
  you preserve my life.
You stretch out your hand against the anger of my foes;
  with your right hand you save me.
8 The LORD will vindicate me;
  your love, LORD, endures forever —
  do not abandon the works of your hands.

PSALM 139

For the director of music. Of David. A psalm.

1 You have searched me, LORD,
and you know me.
2 You know when I sit and when I rise;
you perceive my thoughts from afar.
3 You discern my going out and my lying down;
you are familiar with all my ways.
4 Before a word is on my tongue
you, LORD, know it completely.
5 You hem me in behind and before,
and you lay your hand upon me.
6 Such knowledge is too wonderful for me,
too lofty for me to attain.

7 Where can I go from your Spirit?
Where can I flee from your presence?
8 If I go up to the heavens, you are there;
if I make my bed in the depths, you are there.
9 If I rise on the wings of the dawn,
if I settle on the far side of the sea,
10 even there your hand will guide me,
your right hand will hold me fast.
11 If I say, "Surely the darkness will hide me
and the light become night around me,"
12 even the darkness will not be dark to you;
the night will shine like the day,
for darkness is as light to you.

13 For you created my inmost being;
you knit me together in my mother's womb.
14 I praise you because I am fearfully and wonderfully made;
your works are wonderful,
I know that full well.
15 My frame was not hidden from you
when I was made in the secret place,
when I was woven together in the depths of the earth.
16 Your eyes saw my unformed body;
all the days ordained for me were written in your book
before one of them came to be.
17 How precious to me are your thoughts,[a] God!
How vast is the sum of them!
18 Were I to count them,
they would outnumber the grains of sand—
when I awake, I am still with you.

19 If only you, God, would slay the wicked!
Away from me, you who are bloodthirsty!
20 They speak of you with evil intent;
your adversaries misuse your name.
21 Do I not hate those who hate you, LORD,
and abhor those who are in rebellion against you?
22 I have nothing but hatred for them;

[a] 17 Or *How amazing are your thoughts concerning me*

PRAYING SCRIPTURE

Psalm 139

God is always ever-present, a reality that should give full confidence to his children. Whether we fly to heaven or make our bed in the depths, we cannot escape his presence. The highest mountain, deepest sea, darkness, light—he is there in them all. To the innermost part of our person, he knows us (see verse 1).

Everyone knows the feeling of being alone, but God's children can take heart. He is always near, so ask him to help you sense his presence today.

I count them my enemies.
23 Search me, God, and know my heart;
test me and know my anxious thoughts.
24 See if there is any offensive way in me,
and lead me in the way everlasting.

PRAYING SCRIPTURE

Psalm 140

One of the ways God preserves his people is by preventing wicked people from accomplishing evil. God preserved Israel until the coming of the Messiah. God will preserve the church until the second coming of the Messiah. All the upright will indeed dwell in his presence.

Thank God for his protection from evil, for he will preserve his people today and forever.

PSALM 140[a]

For the director of music. A psalm of David.

1 Rescue me, LORD, from evildoers;
protect me from the violent,
2 who devise evil plans in their hearts
and stir up war every day.
3 They make their tongues as sharp as a serpent's;
the poison of vipers is on their lips.[b]

4 Keep me safe, LORD, from the hands of the wicked;
protect me from the violent,
who devise ways to trip my feet.
5 The arrogant have hidden a snare for me;
they have spread out the cords of their net
and have set traps for me along my path.

6 I say to the LORD, "You are my God."
Hear, LORD, my cry for mercy.
7 Sovereign LORD, my strong deliverer,
you shield my head in the day of battle.
8 Do not grant the wicked their desires, LORD;
do not let their plans succeed.

9 Those who surround me proudly rear their heads;
may the mischief of their lips engulf them.
10 May burning coals fall on them;
may they be thrown into the fire,
into miry pits, never to rise.
11 May slanderers not be established in the land;
may disaster hunt down the violent.

12 I know that the LORD secures justice for the poor
and upholds the cause of the needy.
13 Surely the righteous will praise your name,
and the upright will live in your presence.

PRAYING SCRIPTURE

Psalm 141

Do you have any friends whom you rely on to tell you difficult truths? David longed for the righteous to "strike" and "rebuke" him because he knew the end result was his own righteousness (verse 5).

Who can confront you about sin or ask about the condition of your soul? Thank God for those faithful friends.

PSALM 141

A psalm of David.

1 I call to you, LORD, come quickly to me;
hear me when I call to you.
2 May my prayer be set before you like incense;
may the lifting up of my hands be like the evening sacrifice.

3 Set a guard over my mouth, LORD;
keep watch over the door of my lips.
4 Do not let my heart be drawn to what is evil
so that I take part in wicked deeds

---

[a] In Hebrew texts 140:1-13 is numbered 140:2-14. [b] *3* The Hebrew has *Selah* (a word of uncertain meaning) here and at the end of verses 5 and 8.

along with those who are evildoers;
do not let me eat their delicacies.

5 Let a righteous man strike me — that is a kindness;
let him rebuke me — that is oil on my head.
My head will not refuse it,
for my prayer will still be against the deeds of evildoers.

6 Their rulers will be thrown down from the cliffs,
and the wicked will learn that my words were well spoken.
7 They will say, "As one plows and breaks up the earth,
so our bones have been scattered at the mouth of the grave."

8 But my eyes are fixed on you, Sovereign LORD;
in you I take refuge — do not give me over to death.
9 Keep me safe from the traps set by evildoers,
from the snares they have laid for me.
10 Let the wicked fall into their own nets,
while I pass by in safety.

PSALM 142[a]

A maskil[b] of David. When he was in the cave. A prayer.

1 I cry aloud to the LORD;
I lift up my voice to the LORD for mercy.
2 I pour out before him my complaint;
before him I tell my trouble.

3 When my spirit grows faint within me,
it is you who watch over my way.
In the path where I walk
people have hidden a snare for me.
4 Look and see, there is no one at my right hand;
no one is concerned for me.
I have no refuge;
no one cares for my life.

5 I cry to you, LORD;
I say, "You are my refuge,
my portion in the land of the living."

6 Listen to my cry,
for I am in desperate need;
rescue me from those who pursue me,
for they are too strong for me.
7 Set me free from my prison,
that I may praise your name.
Then the righteous will gather about me
because of your goodness to me.

PSALM 143

A psalm of David.

1 LORD, hear my prayer,
listen to my cry for mercy;

[a] In Hebrew texts 142:1-7 is numbered 142:2-8. [b] Title: Probably a literary or musical term

PRAYING SCRIPTURE

Psalm 142

When David believed no one was looking out for him, he cried out to the Lord. He viewed the Lord as his "portion in the land of the living" (verse 5). The Lord was as sure to him as an inheritance of land in Israel. The Lord is real.

Is the Lord real to you? Spend some time reflecting on your relationship with the God of the universe.

PRAYING SCRIPTURE

Psalm 143

In this psalm of David's, a plea for help was a crucial reminder of humanity's need for a Savior: "No one living is righteous before you" (verse 2). If we can be righteous on our own, why plead for God's mercies or be concerned with his judgment? We need righteousness, and ours is insufficient.

Have you called on Jesus for salvation? If not, stop now and ask him to save you.

in your faithfulness and righteousness
come to my relief.
2 Do not bring your servant into judgment,
for no one living is righteous before you.
3 The enemy pursues me,
he crushes me to the ground;
he makes me dwell in the darkness
like those long dead.
4 So my spirit grows faint within me;
my heart within me is dismayed.
5 I remember the days of long ago;
I meditate on all your works
and consider what your hands have done.
6 I spread out my hands to you;
I thirst for you like a parched land.[a]

7 Answer me quickly, LORD;
my spirit fails.
Do not hide your face from me
or I will be like those who go down to the pit.
8 Let the morning bring me word of your unfailing love,
for I have put my trust in you.
Show me the way I should go,
for to you I entrust my life.
9 Rescue me from my enemies, LORD,
for I hide myself in you.
10 Teach me to do your will,
for you are my God;
may your good Spirit
lead me on level ground.

11 For your name's sake, LORD, preserve my life;
in your righteousness, bring me out of trouble.
12 In your unfailing love, silence my enemies;
destroy all my foes,
for I am your servant.

PRAYING SCRIPTURE

Psalm 144

When we consider the grandeur and the holiness of God, we are astounded that he loves and provides for humanity. His majesty should do more than astound; it should make us happy. "Blessed is the people whose God is the LORD" (verse 15).

When you consider God's majesty, how do you feel? God loves his children. Express your love for him when you pray.

PSALM 144

Of David.

1 Praise be to the LORD my Rock,
who trains my hands for war,
my fingers for battle.
2 He is my loving God and my fortress,
my stronghold and my deliverer,
my shield, in whom I take refuge,
who subdues peoples[b] under me.

3 LORD, what are human beings that you care for them,
mere mortals that you think of them?
4 They are like a breath;
their days are like a fleeting shadow.

[a] 6 The Hebrew has *Selah* (a word of uncertain meaning) here. [b] 2 Many manuscripts of the Masoretic Text, Dead Sea Scrolls, Aquila, Jerome and Syriac; most manuscripts of the Masoretic Text *subdues my people*

5 Part your heavens, LORD, and come down;
touch the mountains, so that they smoke.
6 Send forth lightning and scatter the enemy;
shoot your arrows and rout them.
7 Reach down your hand from on high;
deliver me and rescue me
from the mighty waters,
from the hands of foreigners
8 whose mouths are full of lies,
whose right hands are deceitful.

9 I will sing a new song to you, my God;
on the ten-stringed lyre I will make music to you,
10 to the One who gives victory to kings,
who delivers his servant David.

From the deadly sword 11 deliver me;
rescue me from the hands of foreigners
whose mouths are full of lies,
whose right hands are deceitful.

12 Then our sons in their youth
will be like well-nurtured plants,
and our daughters will be like pillars
carved to adorn a palace.
13 Our barns will be filled
with every kind of provision.
Our sheep will increase by thousands,
by tens of thousands in our fields;
14 our oxen will draw heavy loads.[a]
There will be no breaching of walls,
no going into captivity,
no cry of distress in our streets.
15 Blessed is the people of whom this is true;
blessed is the people whose God is the LORD.

PSALM 145[b]

A psalm of praise. Of David.

1 I will exalt you, my God the King;
I will praise your name for ever and ever.
2 Every day I will praise you
and extol your name for ever and ever.

3 Great is the LORD and most worthy of praise;
his greatness no one can fathom.
4 One generation commends your works to another;
they tell of your mighty acts.
5 They speak of the glorious splendor of your majesty—
and I will meditate on your wonderful works.[c]

[a] 14 Or *our chieftains will be firmly established* [b] This psalm is an acrostic poem, the verses of which (including verse 13b) begin with the successive letters of the Hebrew alphabet. [c] 5 Dead Sea Scrolls and Syriac (see also Septuagint); Masoretic Text *On the glorious splendor of your majesty / and on your wonderful works I will meditate*

PRAYING SCRIPTURE

Psalm 145

A series of personal promises bring God's character into focus: He upholds all who fall and raises those who are bowed down and provides for those who look to him. We should never forget God's care for his children.

"The LORD is near to all who call on him," so call on him (verse 18). He hears you when you pray.

6 They tell of the power of your awesome works—
and I will proclaim your great deeds.
7 They celebrate your abundant goodness
and joyfully sing of your righteousness.

8 The LORD is gracious and compassionate,
slow to anger and rich in love.

9 The LORD is good to all;
he has compassion on all he has made.
10 All your works praise you, LORD;
your faithful people extol you.
11 They tell of the glory of your kingdom
and speak of your might,
12 so that all people may know of your mighty acts
and the glorious splendor of your kingdom.
13 Your kingdom is an everlasting kingdom,
and your dominion endures through all generations.

The LORD is trustworthy in all he promises
and faithful in all he does.[a]
14 The LORD upholds all who fall
and lifts up all who are bowed down.
15 The eyes of all look to you,
and you give them their food at the proper time.
16 You open your hand
and satisfy the desires of every living thing.

17 The LORD is righteous in all his ways
and faithful in all he does.
18 The LORD is near to all who call on him,
to all who call on him in truth.
19 He fulfills the desires of those who fear him;
he hears their cry and saves them.
20 The LORD watches over all who love him,
but all the wicked he will destroy.

21 My mouth will speak in praise of the LORD.
Let every creature praise his holy name
for ever and ever.

PSALM 146

1 Praise the LORD.[b]

Praise the LORD, my soul.

2 I will praise the LORD all my life;
I will sing praise to my God as long as I live.
3 Do not put your trust in princes,
in human beings, who cannot save.
4 When their spirit departs, they return to the ground;
on that very day their plans come to nothing.
5 Blessed are those whose help is the God of Jacob,
whose hope is in the LORD their God.

PRAYING SCRIPTURE

Psalm 146

The psalmist warned against putting trust in princes or in any human. Why? Because humans do not have eternal wisdom or power. Ultimately, they all die, so put your trust in God alone.

Where is your trust for daily living? If it's not in the One with eternal wisdom, ask him for faith.

[a] 13 One manuscript of the Masoretic Text, Dead Sea Scrolls and Syriac (see also Septuagint); most manuscripts of the Masoretic Text do not have the last two lines of verse 13. [b] 1 Hebrew *Hallelu Yah*; also in verse 10

6 He is the Maker of heaven and earth,
the sea, and everything in them —
he remains faithful forever.
7 He upholds the cause of the oppressed
and gives food to the hungry.
The LORD sets prisoners free,
8 the LORD gives sight to the blind,
the LORD lifts up those who are bowed down,
the LORD loves the righteous.
9 The LORD watches over the foreigner
and sustains the fatherless and the widow,
but he frustrates the ways of the wicked.

10 The LORD reigns forever,
your God, O Zion, for all generations.

Praise the LORD.

PSALM 147

1 Praise the LORD.[a]

How good it is to sing praises to our God,
how pleasant and fitting to praise him!

2 The LORD builds up Jerusalem;
he gathers the exiles of Israel.
3 He heals the brokenhearted
and binds up their wounds.
4 He determines the number of the stars
and calls them each by name.
5 Great is our Lord and mighty in power;
his understanding has no limit.
6 The LORD sustains the humble
but casts the wicked to the ground.

7 Sing to the LORD with grateful praise;
make music to our God on the harp.

8 He covers the sky with clouds;
he supplies the earth with rain
and makes grass grow on the hills.
9 He provides food for the cattle
and for the young ravens when they call.

10 His pleasure is not in the strength of the horse,
nor his delight in the legs of the warrior;
11 the LORD delights in those who fear him,
who put their hope in his unfailing love.

12 Extol the LORD, Jerusalem;
praise your God, Zion.

13 He strengthens the bars of your gates
and blesses your people within you.
14 He grants peace to your borders
and satisfies you with the finest of wheat.

[a] 1 Hebrew *Hallelu Yah*; also in verse 20

PRAYING SCRIPTURE

Psalm 147

The psalmist contrasted the limitless power of God—he named and counted the stars—with his gentleness—he "sustains the humble" (verse 6). No wonder we are commanded to sing to the Lord "with grateful praise" (verse 7).

Have you ever experienced God's sustaining hand? "His understanding has no limit" (verse 5). Never hesitate to humble yourself before him, for he understands where you are and what you need, and he will lift you up.

15 He sends his command to the earth;
his word runs swiftly.
16 He spreads the snow like wool
and scatters the frost like ashes.
17 He hurls down his hail like pebbles.
Who can withstand his icy blast?
18 He sends his word and melts them;
he stirs up his breezes, and the waters flow.

19 He has revealed his word to Jacob,
his laws and decrees to Israel.
20 He has done this for no other nation;
they do not know his laws.[a]

Praise the LORD.

PRAYING SCRIPTURE

Psalm 148

This psalm calls upon all creation to sing of the greatness of God. The planets, our atmosphere, the creatures of the sea, land animals, weather patterns, land, hills, mountains, birds and creeping things—God made them all, rules them all and deserves their praise.

The righteous thing for humans to do is join creation in praise. Start your prayer today by praising God.

PSALM 148

1 Praise the LORD.[b]

Praise the LORD from the heavens;
praise him in the heights above.
2 Praise him, all his angels;
praise him, all his heavenly hosts.
3 Praise him, sun and moon;
praise him, all you shining stars.
4 Praise him, you highest heavens
and you waters above the skies.

5 Let them praise the name of the LORD,
for at his command they were created,
6 and he established them for ever and ever—
he issued a decree that will never pass away.

7 Praise the LORD from the earth,
you great sea creatures and all ocean depths,
8 lightning and hail, snow and clouds,
stormy winds that do his bidding,
9 you mountains and all hills,
fruit trees and all cedars,
10 wild animals and all cattle,
small creatures and flying birds,
11 kings of the earth and all nations,
you princes and all rulers on earth,
12 young men and women,
old men and children.

13 Let them praise the name of the LORD,
for his name alone is exalted;
his splendor is above the earth and the heavens.
14 And he has raised up for his people a horn,[c]
the praise of all his faithful servants,
of Israel, the people close to his heart.

Praise the LORD.

[a] *20* Masoretic Text; Dead Sea Scrolls and Septuagint *nation; / he has not made his laws known to them* [b] *1* Hebrew *Hallelu Yah*; also in verse 14
[c] *14* *Horn* here symbolizes strength.

PSALM 149

1 Praise the LORD.[a]

Sing to the LORD a new song,
his praise in the assembly of his faithful people.

2 Let Israel rejoice in their Maker;
let the people of Zion be glad in their King.
3 Let them praise his name with dancing
and make music to him with timbrel and harp.
4 For the LORD takes delight in his people;
he crowns the humble with victory.
5 Let his faithful people rejoice in this honor
and sing for joy on their beds.

6 May the praise of God be in their mouths
and a double-edged sword in their hands,
7 to inflict vengeance on the nations
and punishment on the peoples,
8 to bind their kings with fetters,
their nobles with shackles of iron,
9 to carry out the sentence written against them—
this is the glory of all his faithful people.

Praise the LORD.

PSALM 150

1 Praise the LORD.[b]

Praise God in his sanctuary;
praise him in his mighty heavens.
2 Praise him for his acts of power;
praise him for his surpassing greatness.
3 Praise him with the sounding of the trumpet,
praise him with the harp and lyre,
4 praise him with timbrel and dancing,
praise him with the strings and pipe,
5 praise him with the clash of cymbals,
praise him with resounding cymbals.

6 Let everything that has breath praise the LORD.

Praise the LORD.

PRAYING SCRIPTURE

Psalm 149

The Psalms make clear that our fullest praise includes the body: voices, hands raised, dancing, playing musical instruments and singing loudly. Praise is not merely mental acknowledgment of facts but includes the will, emotions and body.

How can you express praise to God during your prayer time? By singing? Raising your hands? Kneeling? Lying prostrate? We should praise God bodily, not simply verbally.

PRAYING SCRIPTURE

Psalm 150

The final psalm summarizes the entire book by inviting every living thing to praise the Lord. This is a fitting end to a hymnbook that teaches all creation the proper way to praise the God of all creation.

If you are a musician, play something in praise. If you aren't, play a recorded song of praise and join in with singing to the Lord. Let your praise be a prayer to God.

[a] 1 Hebrew *Hallelu Yah*; also in verse 9 [b] 1 Hebrew *Hallelu Yah*; also in verse 6

PROVERBS

The book of Proverbs is a collection of sayings, or proverbs, that give counsel about life with a goal of imparting *wisdom*, a word mentioned throughout. Wisdom can be defined as "skillfully applying knowledge to life," touching all the practical aspects of living that we encounter. The sayings herein teach the reader about God, family, neighbors and government.

Sections of Proverbs read like a letter from a father to a son. Solomon, the principal author, hoped his son would live as a wise and discerning leader; these proverbs were recorded to teach him how to be that leader. The first nine chapters of Proverbs constitute Solomon's call for his son to hear wisdom; wisdom is personified in many verses. He laid out before his son two paths—the path of wisdom and the path of folly. The path of wisdom leads to life and joy, but the path of folly leads to death and misery. If Solomon's son did not set his heart to live wisely, he would not listen to the wise advice that follows.

The second large section of Proverbs consists of the short, pithy statements that we associate with Proverbs. Using memorable sayings, Solomon taught his son about a wide range of issues that would help him live a wise and full life. These proverbs touch on wisdom for marriage and family. He instructed his son on how to live with integrity in work and business dealings. These proverbs also dispense wisdom for self-control concerning money, anger and our words.

The instructions we find in Proverbs remind us of an important truth—all of life is spiritual. There is no area of life, no matter how mundane, that is not connected to our spiritual lives. Because of this, we need wisdom in every area of life. Christians need to know how to treat their neighbors and how to be good employees. Every follower of Jesus stands in need of wisdom about how to treat other people and how to exercise self-control.

Proverbs does not teach us how to pray by teaching a pattern of prayer. It teaches us to pray by showing us how we should live; it gives us patterns of living we should then pray to live out. While reading Proverbs, who would not pray for wisdom? Who would not pray for their children to avoid evil? Who would not pray for their husband or wife?

There is a long Biblical tradition of praying for wisdom. We see this when Solomon was anointed king. Solomon asked God for a discerning heart to lead God's people. In James, which has been called "the Proverbs of the New Testament," the apostle instructed Christians who lack wisdom to pray and ask for it. He promised that when Christians ask for wisdom, God will give it "generously to all without finding fault" (James 1:5).

God always answers and honors the prayer for wisdom. Proverbs provides scores of examples of business interactions, family challenges and personal temptations to pray over—and the assurance that God will provide the wisdom needed to make decisions that please him.

PURPOSE AND THEME

1 The proverbs of Solomon son of David, king of Israel:

2 for gaining wisdom and instruction;
for understanding words of insight;
3 for receiving instruction in prudent behavior,
doing what is right and just and fair;
4 for giving prudence to those who are simple,[a]
knowledge and discretion to the young —
5 let the wise listen and add to their learning,
and let the discerning get guidance —
6 for understanding proverbs and parables,
the sayings and riddles of the wise.[b]

7 The fear of the LORD is the beginning of knowledge,
but fools[c] despise wisdom and instruction.

PROLOGUE: EXHORTATIONS TO EMBRACE WISDOM

WARNING AGAINST THE INVITATION OF SINFUL MEN

8 Listen, my son, to your father's instruction
and do not forsake your mother's teaching.
9 They are a garland to grace your head
and a chain to adorn your neck.

10 My son, if sinful men entice you,
do not give in to them.
11 If they say, "Come along with us;
let's lie in wait for innocent blood,
let's ambush some harmless soul;
12 let's swallow them alive, like the grave,
and whole, like those who go down to the pit;
13 we will get all sorts of valuable things
and fill our houses with plunder;
14 cast lots with us;
we will all share the loot" —
15 my son, do not go along with them,
do not set foot on their paths;
16 for their feet rush into evil,
they are swift to shed blood.
17 How useless to spread a net
where every bird can see it!
18 These men lie in wait for their own blood;
they ambush only themselves!
19 Such are the paths of all who go after ill-gotten gain;
it takes away the life of those who get it.

WISDOM'S REBUKE

20 Out in the open wisdom calls aloud,
she raises her voice in the public square;

---

[a] 4 The Hebrew word rendered *simple* in Proverbs denotes a person who is gullible, without moral direction and inclined to evil. [b] 6 Or *understanding a proverb, namely, a parable, / and the sayings of the wise, their riddles*
[c] 7 The Hebrew words rendered *fool* in Proverbs, and often elsewhere in the Old Testament, denote a person who is morally deficient.

PRAYING SCRIPTURE

Proverbs 1

Many seek wisdom only in books or from life experience, but Solomon says, "The fear of the LORD is the beginning of knowledge" (verse 7). Everything we seek to learn should be grounded in reverent respect for the Lord. Fools, on the other hand, despise both wisdom and instruction.

Ask God for a reverential fear of him. When you pray for wisdom, bow in awe of the One who has it all.

21 on top of the wall[a] she cries out,
at the city gate she makes her speech:

22 "How long will you who are simple love your simple ways?
How long will mockers delight in mockery
and fools hate knowledge?
23 Repent at my rebuke!
Then I will pour out my thoughts to you,
I will make known to you my teachings.
24 But since you refuse to listen when I call
and no one pays attention when I stretch out my hand,
25 since you disregard all my advice
and do not accept my rebuke,
26 I in turn will laugh when disaster strikes you;
I will mock when calamity overtakes you —
27 when calamity overtakes you like a storm,
when disaster sweeps over you like a whirlwind,
when distress and trouble overwhelm you.

28 "Then they will call to me but I will not answer;
they will look for me but will not find me,
29 since they hated knowledge
and did not choose to fear the LORD.
30 Since they would not accept my advice
and spurned my rebuke,
31 they will eat the fruit of their ways
and be filled with the fruit of their schemes.
32 For the waywardness of the simple will kill them,
and the complacency of fools will destroy them;
33 but whoever listens to me will live in safety
and be at ease, without fear of harm."

MORAL BENEFITS OF WISDOM

2 My son, if you accept my words
and store up my commands within you,
2 turning your ear to wisdom
and applying your heart to understanding —
3 indeed, if you call out for insight
and cry aloud for understanding,
4 and if you look for it as for silver
and search for it as for hidden treasure,
5 then you will understand the fear of the LORD
and find the knowledge of God.
6 For the LORD gives wisdom;
from his mouth come knowledge and understanding.
7 He holds success in store for the upright,
he is a shield to those whose walk is blameless,
8 for he guards the course of the just
and protects the way of his faithful ones.

9 Then you will understand what is right and just
and fair — every good path.

PRAYING SCRIPTURE

Proverbs 2

When we set our hearts to pursue wisdom, the Lord gives it generously. He says the first steps are the key: "stor[ing] up my commands" (verse 1), "turning your ear to wisdom and applying your heart to understanding" (verse 2). We have to want wisdom for God to give it.

You can evaluate your desire for wisdom by your desire for God's Word. Ask God to speak through it to you.

[a] *21* Septuagint; Hebrew / *at noisy street corners*

10 For wisdom will enter your heart,
and knowledge will be pleasant to your soul.
11 Discretion will protect you,
and understanding will guard you.

12 Wisdom will save you from the ways of wicked men,
from men whose words are perverse,
13 who have left the straight paths
to walk in dark ways,
14 who delight in doing wrong
and rejoice in the perverseness of evil,
15 whose paths are crooked
and who are devious in their ways.

16 Wisdom will save you also from the adulterous woman,
from the wayward woman with her seductive words,
17 who has left the partner of her youth
and ignored the covenant she made before God.[a]
18 Surely her house leads down to death
and her paths to the spirits of the dead.
19 None who go to her return
or attain the paths of life.

20 Thus you will walk in the ways of the good
and keep to the paths of the righteous.
21 For the upright will live in the land,
and the blameless will remain in it;
22 but the wicked will be cut off from the land,
and the unfaithful will be torn from it.

WISDOM BESTOWS WELL-BEING

3 My son, do not forget my teaching,
but keep my commands in your heart,
2 for they will prolong your life many years
and bring you peace and prosperity.

3 Let love and faithfulness never leave you;
bind them around your neck,
write them on the tablet of your heart.
4 Then you will win favor and a good name
in the sight of God and man.

5 Trust in the Lord with all your heart
and lean not on your own understanding;
6 in all your ways submit to him,
and he will make your paths straight.[b]

7 Do not be wise in your own eyes;
fear the Lord and shun evil.
8 This will bring health to your body
and nourishment to your bones.

9 Honor the Lord with your wealth,
with the firstfruits of all your crops;

PRAYING SCRIPTURE

Proverbs 3

It is counterintuitive to see generosity as a means to blessing, but that's what God promises (see verses 9–10). He also reminds us not to withhold good things from people who deserve it if the blessing is in our power to bestow it (see verse 27).

We live generously when we keep God's commands. Ask God to make your life a blessing to others both in word and in deed.

[a] 17 Or *covenant of her God* [b] 6 Or *will direct your paths*

10 then your barns will be filled to overflowing,
and your vats will brim over with new wine.

11 My son, do not despise the LORD's discipline,
and do not resent his rebuke,
12 because the LORD disciplines those he loves,
as a father the son he delights in.[a]

13 Blessed are those who find wisdom,
those who gain understanding,
14 for she is more profitable than silver
and yields better returns than gold.
15 She is more precious than rubies;
nothing you desire can compare with her.
16 Long life is in her right hand;
in her left hand are riches and honor.
17 Her ways are pleasant ways,
and all her paths are peace.
18 She is a tree of life to those who take hold of her;
those who hold her fast will be blessed.

19 By wisdom the LORD laid the earth's foundations,
by understanding he set the heavens in place;
20 by his knowledge the watery depths were divided,
and the clouds let drop the dew.

21 My son, do not let wisdom and understanding out of your sight,
preserve sound judgment and discretion;
22 they will be life for you,
an ornament to grace your neck.
23 Then you will go on your way in safety,
and your foot will not stumble.
24 When you lie down, you will not be afraid;
when you lie down, your sleep will be sweet.
25 Have no fear of sudden disaster
or of the ruin that overtakes the wicked,
26 for the LORD will be at your side
and will keep your foot from being snared.

27 Do not withhold good from those to whom it is due,
when it is in your power to act.
28 Do not say to your neighbor,
"Come back tomorrow and I'll give it to you"—
when you already have it with you.
29 Do not plot harm against your neighbor,
who lives trustfully near you.
30 Do not accuse anyone for no reason—
when they have done you no harm.

31 Do not envy the violent
or choose any of their ways.

32 For the LORD detests the perverse
but takes the upright into his confidence.
33 The LORD's curse is on the house of the wicked,
but he blesses the home of the righteous.

[a] 12 Hebrew; Septuagint *loves, / and he chastens everyone he accepts as his child*

34 He mocks proud mockers
but shows favor to the humble and oppressed.
35 The wise inherit honor,
but fools get only shame.

GET WISDOM AT ANY COST

4 Listen, my sons, to a father's instruction;
pay attention and gain understanding.
2 I give you sound learning,
so do not forsake my teaching.
3 For I too was a son to my father,
still tender, and cherished by my mother.
4 Then he taught me, and he said to me,
"Take hold of my words with all your heart;
keep my commands, and you will live.
5 Get wisdom, get understanding;
do not forget my words or turn away from them.
6 Do not forsake wisdom, and she will protect you;
love her, and she will watch over you.
7 The beginning of wisdom is this: Get[a] wisdom.
Though it cost all you have,[b] get understanding.
8 Cherish her, and she will exalt you;
embrace her, and she will honor you.
9 She will give you a garland to grace your head
and present you with a glorious crown."

10 Listen, my son, accept what I say,
and the years of your life will be many.
11 I instruct you in the way of wisdom
and lead you along straight paths.
12 When you walk, your steps will not be hampered;
when you run, you will not stumble.
13 Hold on to instruction, do not let it go;
guard it well, for it is your life.
14 Do not set foot on the path of the wicked
or walk in the way of evildoers.
15 Avoid it, do not travel on it;
turn from it and go on your way.
16 For they cannot rest until they do evil;
they are robbed of sleep till they make someone stumble.
17 They eat the bread of wickedness
and drink the wine of violence.

18 The path of the righteous is like the morning sun,
shining ever brighter till the full light of day.
19 But the way of the wicked is like deep darkness;
they do not know what makes them stumble.

20 My son, pay attention to what I say;
turn your ear to my words.
21 Do not let them out of your sight,
keep them within your heart;
22 for they are life to those who find them
and health to one's whole body.

PRAYING SCRIPTURE

Proverbs 4

Your heart—the deep, innermost part of your being—is the seat of your thinking, character and will. It drives what you love and what you do. We cannot have a heart that is far from God and hope to accomplish his purposes. The book of Proverbs helps us keep our hearts aligned with God's will.

Ask God to guide your heart and commit to love him wholeheartedly.

[a] 7 Or *Wisdom is supreme; therefore get* [b] 7 Or *wisdom. / Whatever else you get*

23 Above all else, guard your heart,
for everything you do flows from it.
24 Keep your mouth free of perversity;
keep corrupt talk far from your lips.
25 Let your eyes look straight ahead;
fix your gaze directly before you.
26 Give careful thought to the[a] paths for your feet
and be steadfast in all your ways.
27 Do not turn to the right or the left;
keep your foot from evil.

WARNING AGAINST ADULTERY

5 My son, pay attention to my wisdom,
turn your ear to my words of insight,
2 that you may maintain discretion
and your lips may preserve knowledge.
3 For the lips of the adulterous woman drip honey,
and her speech is smoother than oil;
4 but in the end she is bitter as gall,
sharp as a double-edged sword.
5 Her feet go down to death;
her steps lead straight to the grave.
6 She gives no thought to the way of life;
her paths wander aimlessly, but she does not know it.

7 Now then, my sons, listen to me;
do not turn aside from what I say.
8 Keep to a path far from her,
do not go near the door of her house,
9 lest you lose your honor to others
and your dignity[b] to one who is cruel,
10 lest strangers feast on your wealth
and your toil enrich the house of another.
11 At the end of your life you will groan,
when your flesh and body are spent.
12 You will say, "How I hated discipline!
How my heart spurned correction!
13 I would not obey my teachers
or turn my ear to my instructors.
14 And I was soon in serious trouble
in the assembly of God's people."

15 Drink water from your own cistern,
running water from your own well.
16 Should your springs overflow in the streets,
your streams of water in the public squares?
17 Let them be yours alone,
never to be shared with strangers.
18 May your fountain be blessed,
and may you rejoice in the wife of your youth.
19 A loving doe, a graceful deer —
may her breasts satisfy you always,
may you ever be intoxicated with her love.

PRAYING SCRIPTURE

Proverbs 5

King Solomon, with his numerous wives and concubines, would have known something about immorality. Here Solomon, in picturesque language, cautioned his son to be vigilant about the health of his marriage, saying, "Drink water from your own cistern" and "be intoxicated with" his wife's love (verses 15,19).

Marital health is a challenge for husbands and wives. If you are married, ask God to keep your mind pure and your marriage focused on him.

[a] 26 Or *Make level* [b] 9 Or *years*

20 Why, my son, be intoxicated with another man's wife?
Why embrace the bosom of a wayward woman?

21 For your ways are in full view of the LORD,
and he examines all your paths.
22 The evil deeds of the wicked ensnare them;
the cords of their sins hold them fast.
23 For lack of discipline they will die,
led astray by their own great folly.

WARNINGS AGAINST FOLLY

6 My son, if you have put up security for your neighbor,
if you have shaken hands in pledge for a stranger,
2 you have been trapped by what you said,
ensnared by the words of your mouth.
3 So do this, my son, to free yourself,
since you have fallen into your neighbor's hands:
Go — to the point of exhaustion — [a]
and give your neighbor no rest!
4 Allow no sleep to your eyes,
no slumber to your eyelids.
5 Free yourself, like a gazelle from the hand of the hunter,
like a bird from the snare of the fowler.

6 Go to the ant, you sluggard;
consider its ways and be wise!
7 It has no commander,
no overseer or ruler,
8 yet it stores its provisions in summer
and gathers its food at harvest.

9 How long will you lie there, you sluggard?
When will you get up from your sleep?
10 A little sleep, a little slumber,
a little folding of the hands to rest —
11 and poverty will come on you like a thief
and scarcity like an armed man.

12 A troublemaker and a villain,
who goes about with a corrupt mouth,
13 who winks maliciously with his eye,
signals with his feet
and motions with his fingers,
14 who plots evil with deceit in his heart —
he always stirs up conflict.
15 Therefore disaster will overtake him in an instant;
he will suddenly be destroyed — without remedy.

16 There are six things the LORD hates,
seven that are detestable to him:
17 haughty eyes,
a lying tongue,
hands that shed innocent blood,
18 a heart that devises wicked schemes,
feet that are quick to rush into evil,

[a] 3 Or *Go and humble yourself,*

PRAYING SCRIPTURE

Proverbs 6

Proverbs teaches wisdom seekers about the virtue of hard work and the vice of laziness. The lazy person, the "sluggard," is guilty of sleeping the day away with "a little sleep, a little slumber" (verses 6,10). The result of laziness is poverty.

Laziness is always seen as sin in Scripture because it is neglecting the purposes of God. Ask God to give you a mind to work. Consider the ant and be wise.

19 a false witness who pours out lies
and a person who stirs up conflict in the community.

WARNING AGAINST ADULTERY

20 My son, keep your father's command
and do not forsake your mother's teaching.
21 Bind them always on your heart;
fasten them around your neck.
22 When you walk, they will guide you;
when you sleep, they will watch over you;
when you awake, they will speak to you.
23 For this command is a lamp,
this teaching is a light,
and correction and instruction
are the way to life,
24 keeping you from your neighbor's wife,
from the smooth talk of a wayward woman.

25 Do not lust in your heart after her beauty
or let her captivate you with her eyes.

26 For a prostitute can be had for a loaf of bread,
but another man's wife preys on your very life.
27 Can a man scoop fire into his lap
without his clothes being burned?
28 Can a man walk on hot coals
without his feet being scorched?
29 So is he who sleeps with another man's wife;
no one who touches her will go unpunished.

30 People do not despise a thief if he steals
to satisfy his hunger when he is starving.
31 Yet if he is caught, he must pay sevenfold,
though it costs him all the wealth of his house.
32 But a man who commits adultery has no sense;
whoever does so destroys himself.
33 Blows and disgrace are his lot,
and his shame will never be wiped away.

34 For jealousy arouses a husband's fury,
and he will show no mercy when he takes revenge.
35 He will not accept any compensation;
he will refuse a bribe, however great it is.

PRAYING SCRIPTURE

Proverbs 7

Temptations to sexual sin fill this chapter. Solomon warned his son and his other children against the deception of a seductress. How does one stay pure? Keep God's Word, thinking of God's law as "the apple of your eye" (verse 2) and writing his commands on your heart.

God's Word is key to overcoming any temptation. Ask God to help you write his commands on your heart.

WARNING AGAINST THE ADULTEROUS WOMAN

7 My son, keep my words
and store up my commands within you.
2 Keep my commands and you will live;
guard my teachings as the apple of your eye.
3 Bind them on your fingers;
write them on the tablet of your heart.
4 Say to wisdom, "You are my sister,"
and to insight, "You are my relative."
5 They will keep you from the adulterous woman,
from the wayward woman with her seductive words.

6 At the window of my house
I looked down through the lattice.
7 I saw among the simple,
I noticed among the young men,
a youth who had no sense.
8 He was going down the street near her corner,
walking along in the direction of her house
9 at twilight, as the day was fading,
as the dark of night set in.

10 Then out came a woman to meet him,
dressed like a prostitute and with crafty intent.
11 (She is unruly and defiant,
her feet never stay at home;
12 now in the street, now in the squares,
at every corner she lurks.)
13 She took hold of him and kissed him
and with a brazen face she said:

14 "Today I fulfilled my vows,
and I have food from my fellowship offering at home.
15 So I came out to meet you;
I looked for you and have found you!
16 I have covered my bed
with colored linens from Egypt.
17 I have perfumed my bed
with myrrh, aloes and cinnamon.
18 Come, let's drink deeply of love till morning;
let's enjoy ourselves with love!
19 My husband is not at home;
he has gone on a long journey.
20 He took his purse filled with money
and will not be home till full moon."

21 With persuasive words she led him astray;
she seduced him with her smooth talk.
22 All at once he followed her
like an ox going to the slaughter,
like a deer[a] stepping into a noose[b]
23 till an arrow pierces his liver,
like a bird darting into a snare,
little knowing it will cost him his life.

24 Now then, my sons, listen to me;
pay attention to what I say.
25 Do not let your heart turn to her ways
or stray into her paths.
26 Many are the victims she has brought down;
her slain are a mighty throng.
27 Her house is a highway to the grave,
leading down to the chambers of death.

---

[a] 22 Syriac (see also Septuagint); Hebrew *fool* [b] 22 The meaning of the Hebrew for this line is uncertain.

PRAYING SCRIPTURE

Proverbs 8

Wisdom is personified in this chapter, pictured as a woman on a hill calling out, as one at the city gates trying to get the attention of the men doing business there and as one who has been with God "at the very beginning, when the world came to be" (verse 23).

Genuine wisdom is found in Jesus Christ. Little wonder the writer says, "Those who find me find life" (verse 35). Ask God to lead you in the way of wisdom.

WISDOM'S CALL

8 Does not wisdom call out?
Does not understanding raise her voice?
2 At the highest point along the way,
where the paths meet, she takes her stand;
3 beside the gate leading into the city,
at the entrance, she cries aloud:
4 "To you, O people, I call out;
I raise my voice to all mankind.
5 You who are simple, gain prudence;
you who are foolish, set your hearts on it.[a]
6 Listen, for I have trustworthy things to say;
I open my lips to speak what is right.
7 My mouth speaks what is true,
for my lips detest wickedness.
8 All the words of my mouth are just;
none of them is crooked or perverse.
9 To the discerning all of them are right;
they are upright to those who have found knowledge.
10 Choose my instruction instead of silver,
knowledge rather than choice gold,
11 for wisdom is more precious than rubies,
and nothing you desire can compare with her.

12 "I, wisdom, dwell together with prudence;
I possess knowledge and discretion.
13 To fear the LORD is to hate evil;
I hate pride and arrogance,
evil behavior and perverse speech.
14 Counsel and sound judgment are mine;
I have insight, I have power.
15 By me kings reign
and rulers issue decrees that are just;
16 by me princes govern,
and nobles — all who rule on earth.[b]
17 I love those who love me,
and those who seek me find me.
18 With me are riches and honor,
enduring wealth and prosperity.
19 My fruit is better than fine gold;
what I yield surpasses choice silver.
20 I walk in the way of righteousness,
along the paths of justice,
21 bestowing a rich inheritance on those who love me
and making their treasuries full.

22 "The LORD brought me forth as the first of his works,[c,d]
before his deeds of old;
23 I was formed long ages ago,
at the very beginning, when the world came to be.

---

[a] 5 Septuagint; Hebrew *foolish, instruct your minds* [b] 16 Some Hebrew manuscripts and Septuagint; other Hebrew manuscripts *all righteous rulers* [c] 22 Or *way*; or *dominion* [d] 22 Or *The LORD possessed me at the beginning of his work*; or *The LORD brought me forth at the beginning of his work*

24 When there were no watery depths, I was given birth,
when there were no springs overflowing with water;
25 before the mountains were settled in place,
before the hills, I was given birth,
26 before he made the world or its fields
or any of the dust of the earth.
27 I was there when he set the heavens in place,
when he marked out the horizon on the face of the deep,
28 when he established the clouds above
and fixed securely the fountains of the deep,
29 when he gave the sea its boundary
so the waters would not overstep his command,
and when he marked out the foundations of the earth.
30 Then I was constantly[a] at his side.
I was filled with delight day after day,
rejoicing always in his presence,
31 rejoicing in his whole world
and delighting in mankind.

32 "Now then, my children, listen to me;
blessed are those who keep my ways.
33 Listen to my instruction and be wise;
do not disregard it.
34 Blessed are those who listen to me,
watching daily at my doors,
waiting at my doorway.
35 For those who find me find life
and receive favor from the LORD.
36 But those who fail to find me harm themselves;
all who hate me love death."

INVITATIONS OF WISDOM AND FOLLY

9 Wisdom has built her house;
she has set up[b] its seven pillars.
2 She has prepared her meat and mixed her wine;
she has also set her table.
3 She has sent out her servants, and she calls
from the highest point of the city,
4 "Let all who are simple come to my house!"
To those who have no sense she says,
5 "Come, eat my food
and drink the wine I have mixed.
6 Leave your simple ways and you will live;
walk in the way of insight."

7 Whoever corrects a mocker invites insults;
whoever rebukes the wicked incurs abuse.
8 Do not rebuke mockers or they will hate you;
rebuke the wise and they will love you.
9 Instruct the wise and they will be wiser still;
teach the righteous and they will add to their learning.

PRAYING SCRIPTURE

Proverbs 9

King Solomon showed a choice everyone has: We can follow the path of wisdom, which leads to life, or the path of folly leading to death. Wisdom begins with the fear of the Lord. The foolish pass by wisdom to continue on a path to destruction.

Do you regularly pursue wisdom and seek to live by it? God rejoices to give wisdom, so ask when you need it.

[a] *30* Or *was the artisan*; or *was a little child* [b] *1* Septuagint, Syriac and Targum; Hebrew *has hewn out*

10 The fear of the LORD is the beginning of wisdom,
and knowledge of the Holy One is understanding.
11 For through wisdom[a] your days will be many,
and years will be added to your life.
12 If you are wise, your wisdom will reward you;
if you are a mocker, you alone will suffer.

13 Folly is an unruly woman;
she is simple and knows nothing.
14 She sits at the door of her house,
on a seat at the highest point of the city,
15 calling out to those who pass by,
who go straight on their way,
16 "Let all who are simple come to my house!"
To those who have no sense she says,
17 "Stolen water is sweet;
food eaten in secret is delicious!"
18 But little do they know that the dead are there,
that her guests are deep in the realm of the dead.

PROVERBS OF SOLOMON

10 The proverbs of Solomon:

A wise son brings joy to his father,
but a foolish son brings grief to his mother.

2 Ill-gotten treasures have no lasting value,
but righteousness delivers from death.

3 The LORD does not let the righteous go hungry,
but he thwarts the craving of the wicked.

4 Lazy hands make for poverty,
but diligent hands bring wealth.

5 He who gathers crops in summer is a prudent son,
but he who sleeps during harvest is a disgraceful son.

6 Blessings crown the head of the righteous,
but violence overwhelms the mouth of the wicked.[b]

7 The name of the righteous is used in blessings,[c]
but the name of the wicked will rot.

8 The wise in heart accept commands,
but a chattering fool comes to ruin.

9 Whoever walks in integrity walks securely,
but whoever takes crooked paths will be found out.

10 Whoever winks maliciously causes grief,
and a chattering fool comes to ruin.

11 The mouth of the righteous is a fountain of life,
but the mouth of the wicked conceals violence.

PRAYING SCRIPTURE

Proverbs 10

Contrasting the righteous and the wicked, this chapter warns that the treasures of the wicked "have no lasting value" while "righteousness delivers from death" (verse 2). The righteous are blessed while the wicked are violent; and wealth comes as a blessing from God with no added sorrow.

God's way is always the best way. Ask him to help you walk in his ways so you can experience his blessings.

---

[a] *11* Septuagint, Syriac and Targum; Hebrew *me* [b] *6* Or *righteous, / but the mouth of the wicked conceals violence* [c] *7* See Gen. 48:20.

12 Hatred stirs up conflict,
but love covers over all wrongs.

13 Wisdom is found on the lips of the discerning,
but a rod is for the back of one who has no sense.

14 The wise store up knowledge,
but the mouth of a fool invites ruin.

15 The wealth of the rich is their fortified city,
but poverty is the ruin of the poor.

16 The wages of the righteous is life,
but the earnings of the wicked are sin and death.

17 Whoever heeds discipline shows the way to life,
but whoever ignores correction leads others astray.

18 Whoever conceals hatred with lying lips
and spreads slander is a fool.

19 Sin is not ended by multiplying words,
but the prudent hold their tongues.

20 The tongue of the righteous is choice silver,
but the heart of the wicked is of little value.

21 The lips of the righteous nourish many,
but fools die for lack of sense.

22 The blessing of the LORD brings wealth,
without painful toil for it.

23 A fool finds pleasure in wicked schemes,
but a person of understanding delights in wisdom.

24 What the wicked dread will overtake them;
what the righteous desire will be granted.

25 When the storm has swept by, the wicked are gone,
but the righteous stand firm forever.

26 As vinegar to the teeth and smoke to the eyes,
so are sluggards to those who send them.

27 The fear of the LORD adds length to life,
but the years of the wicked are cut short.

28 The prospect of the righteous is joy,
but the hopes of the wicked come to nothing.

29 The way of the LORD is a refuge for the blameless,
but it is the ruin of those who do evil.

30 The righteous will never be uprooted,
but the wicked will not remain in the land.

31 From the mouth of the righteous comes the fruit of wisdom,
but a perverse tongue will be silenced.

32 The lips of the righteous know what finds favor,
but the mouth of the wicked only what is perverse.

PRAYING SCRIPTURE

Proverbs 11

Genuine wisdom always demonstrates itself in our treating other people with dignity. We should walk with integrity, keep people's secrets and be merciful and generous to others. "The fruit of the righteous is a tree of life" from which many people are blessed (verse 30).

Every person bears the image of God even though marred by sin. Ask God to help you treat every person with dignity and respect.

11 The LORD detests dishonest scales,
but accurate weights find favor with him.

2 When pride comes, then comes disgrace,
but with humility comes wisdom.

3 The integrity of the upright guides them,
but the unfaithful are destroyed by their duplicity.

4 Wealth is worthless in the day of wrath,
but righteousness delivers from death.

5 The righteousness of the blameless makes their paths straight,
but the wicked are brought down by their own wickedness.

6 The righteousness of the upright delivers them,
but the unfaithful are trapped by evil desires.

7 Hopes placed in mortals die with them;
all the promise of[a] their power comes to nothing.

8 The righteous person is rescued from trouble,
and it falls on the wicked instead.

9 With their mouths the godless destroy their neighbors,
but through knowledge the righteous escape.

10 When the righteous prosper, the city rejoices;
when the wicked perish, there are shouts of joy.

11 Through the blessing of the upright a city is exalted,
but by the mouth of the wicked it is destroyed.

12 Whoever derides their neighbor has no sense,
but the one who has understanding holds their tongue.

13 A gossip betrays a confidence,
but a trustworthy person keeps a secret.

14 For lack of guidance a nation falls,
but victory is won through many advisers.

15 Whoever puts up security for a stranger will surely suffer,
but whoever refuses to shake hands in pledge is safe.

16 A kindhearted woman gains honor,
but ruthless men gain only wealth.

17 Those who are kind benefit themselves,
but the cruel bring ruin on themselves.

18 A wicked person earns deceptive wages,
but the one who sows righteousness reaps a sure reward.

19 Truly the righteous attain life,
but whoever pursues evil finds death.

20 The LORD detests those whose hearts are perverse,
but he delights in those whose ways are blameless.

21 Be sure of this: The wicked will not go unpunished,
but those who are righteous will go free.

---

[a] 7 Two Hebrew manuscripts; most Hebrew manuscripts, Vulgate, Syriac and Targum *When the wicked die, their hope perishes; / all they expected from*

22 Like a gold ring in a pig's snout
is a beautiful woman who shows no discretion.

23 The desire of the righteous ends only in good,
but the hope of the wicked only in wrath.

24 One person gives freely, yet gains even more;
another withholds unduly, but comes to poverty.

25 A generous person will prosper;
whoever refreshes others will be refreshed.

26 People curse the one who hoards grain,
but they pray God's blessing on the one who is willing to sell.

27 Whoever seeks good finds favor,
but evil comes to one who searches for it.

28 Those who trust in their riches will fall,
but the righteous will thrive like a green leaf.

29 Whoever brings ruin on their family will inherit only wind,
and the fool will be servant to the wise.

30 The fruit of the righteous is a tree of life,
and the one who is wise saves lives.

31 If the righteous receive their due on earth,
how much more the ungodly and the sinner!

12 Whoever loves discipline loves knowledge,
but whoever hates correction is stupid.

2 Good people obtain favor from the LORD,
but he condemns those who devise wicked schemes.

3 No one can be established through wickedness,
but the righteous cannot be uprooted.

4 A wife of noble character is her husband's crown,
but a disgraceful wife is like decay in his bones.

5 The plans of the righteous are just,
but the advice of the wicked is deceitful.

6 The words of the wicked lie in wait for blood,
but the speech of the upright rescues them.

7 The wicked are overthrown and are no more,
but the house of the righteous stands firm.

8 A person is praised according to their prudence,
and one with a warped mind is despised.

9 Better to be a nobody and yet have a servant
than pretend to be somebody and have no food.

10 The righteous care for the needs of their animals,
but the kindest acts of the wicked are cruel.

11 Those who work their land will have abundant food,
but those who chase fantasies have no sense.

12 The wicked desire the stronghold of evildoers,
but the root of the righteous endures.

PRAYING SCRIPTURE

Proverbs 12

Near the end of this chapter filled with contrasts between wickedness and righteousness is this dire warning: "The LORD detests lying lips" (verse 22). In God's economy, there is no such thing as a little white lie. What brings God delight? Those who deal truthfully.

Commit to being a person of truth, a person who brings God delight. Ask God to help you guard your words with truth.

13 Evildoers are trapped by their sinful talk,
and so the innocent escape trouble.

14 From the fruit of their lips people are filled with good things,
and the work of their hands brings them reward.

15 The way of fools seems right to them,
but the wise listen to advice.

16 Fools show their annoyance at once,
but the prudent overlook an insult.

17 An honest witness tells the truth,
but a false witness tells lies.

18 The words of the reckless pierce like swords,
but the tongue of the wise brings healing.

19 Truthful lips endure forever,
but a lying tongue lasts only a moment.

20 Deceit is in the hearts of those who plot evil,
but those who promote peace have joy.

21 No harm overtakes the righteous,
but the wicked have their fill of trouble.

22 The LORD detests lying lips,
but he delights in people who are trustworthy.

23 The prudent keep their knowledge to themselves,
but a fool's heart blurts out folly.

24 Diligent hands will rule,
but laziness ends in forced labor.

25 Anxiety weighs down the heart,
but a kind word cheers it up.

26 The righteous choose their friends carefully,
but the way of the wicked leads them astray.

27 The lazy do not roast[a] any game,
but the diligent feed on the riches of the hunt.

28 In the way of righteousness there is life;
along that path is immortality.

13 A wise son heeds his father's instruction,
but a mocker does not respond to rebukes.

2 From the fruit of their lips people enjoy good things,
but the unfaithful have an appetite for violence.

3 Those who guard their lips preserve their lives,
but those who speak rashly will come to ruin.

4 A sluggard's appetite is never filled,
but the desires of the diligent are fully satisfied.

5 The righteous hate what is false,
but the wicked make themselves a stench
and bring shame on themselves.

PRAYING SCRIPTURE

Proverbs 13

Do you ever think about how your close friends influence you? What is the character of the people closest to you, the ones who know you best? Verse 20 contains both a promise, "Walk with the wise and become wise," and a warning, "A companion of fools suffers harm."

The people we let close to us are important to our spiritual formation. Ask God for wisdom in choosing close friends.

---

[a] *27* The meaning of the Hebrew for this word is uncertain.

6 Righteousness guards the person of integrity,
but wickedness overthrows the sinner.

7 One person pretends to be rich, yet has nothing;
another pretends to be poor, yet has great wealth.

8 A person's riches may ransom their life,
but the poor cannot respond to threatening rebukes.

9 The light of the righteous shines brightly,
but the lamp of the wicked is snuffed out.

10 Where there is strife, there is pride,
but wisdom is found in those who take advice.

11 Dishonest money dwindles away,
but whoever gathers money little by little makes it grow.

12 Hope deferred makes the heart sick,
but a longing fulfilled is a tree of life.

13 Whoever scorns instruction will pay for it,
but whoever respects a command is rewarded.

14 The teaching of the wise is a fountain of life,
turning a person from the snares of death.

15 Good judgment wins favor,
but the way of the unfaithful leads to their destruction.[a]

16 All who are prudent act with[b] knowledge,
but fools expose their folly.

17 A wicked messenger falls into trouble,
but a trustworthy envoy brings healing.

18 Whoever disregards discipline comes to poverty and shame,
but whoever heeds correction is honored.

19 A longing fulfilled is sweet to the soul,
but fools detest turning from evil.

20 Walk with the wise and become wise,
for a companion of fools suffers harm.

21 Trouble pursues the sinner,
but the righteous are rewarded with good things.

22 A good person leaves an inheritance for their children's children,
but a sinner's wealth is stored up for the righteous.

23 An unplowed field produces food for the poor,
but injustice sweeps it away.

24 Whoever spares the rod hates their children,
but the one who loves their children is careful to
discipline them.

25 The righteous eat to their hearts' content,
but the stomach of the wicked goes hungry.

---

[a] *15* Septuagint and Syriac; the meaning of the Hebrew for this phrase is uncertain. [b] *16* Or *prudent protect themselves through*

PRAYING SCRIPTURE

Proverbs 14

Solomon, one of the richest men who ever lived, king of Israel, who had all that his heart could desire, reminds us that mistreating the poor is the same as mistreating God. Having mercy on the needy is evidence that we honor God.

Poor people often feel invisible, but God sees. He sees who shows mercy. Ask God to open your eyes and heart to needy people you meet this week.

14 The wise woman builds her house,
but with her own hands the foolish one tears hers down.

2 Whoever fears the LORD walks uprightly,
but those who despise him are devious in their ways.

3 A fool's mouth lashes out with pride,
but the lips of the wise protect them.

4 Where there are no oxen, the manger is empty,
but from the strength of an ox come abundant harvests.

5 An honest witness does not deceive,
but a false witness pours out lies.

6 The mocker seeks wisdom and finds none,
but knowledge comes easily to the discerning.

7 Stay away from a fool,
for you will not find knowledge on their lips.

8 The wisdom of the prudent is to give thought to their ways,
but the folly of fools is deception.

9 Fools mock at making amends for sin,
but goodwill is found among the upright.

10 Each heart knows its own bitterness,
and no one else can share its joy.

11 The house of the wicked will be destroyed,
but the tent of the upright will flourish.

12 There is a way that appears to be right,
but in the end it leads to death.

13 Even in laughter the heart may ache,
and rejoicing may end in grief.

14 The faithless will be fully repaid for their ways,
and the good rewarded for theirs.

15 The simple believe anything,
but the prudent give thought to their steps.

16 The wise fear the LORD and shun evil,
but a fool is hotheaded and yet feels secure.

17 A quick-tempered person does foolish things,
and the one who devises evil schemes is hated.

18 The simple inherit folly,
but the prudent are crowned with knowledge.

19 Evildoers will bow down in the presence of the good,
and the wicked at the gates of the righteous.

20 The poor are shunned even by their neighbors,
but the rich have many friends.

21 It is a sin to despise one's neighbor,
but blessed is the one who is kind to the needy.

22 Do not those who plot evil go astray?
But those who plan what is good find[a] love and faithfulness.

23 All hard work brings a profit,
but mere talk leads only to poverty.

24 The wealth of the wise is their crown,
but the folly of fools yields folly.

25 A truthful witness saves lives,
but a false witness is deceitful.

26 Whoever fears the LORD has a secure fortress,
and for their children it will be a refuge.

27 The fear of the LORD is a fountain of life,
turning a person from the snares of death.

28 A large population is a king's glory,
but without subjects a prince is ruined.

29 Whoever is patient has great understanding,
but one who is quick-tempered displays folly.

30 A heart at peace gives life to the body,
but envy rots the bones.

31 Whoever oppresses the poor shows contempt for their Maker,
but whoever is kind to the needy honors God.

32 When calamity comes, the wicked are brought down,
but even in death the righteous seek refuge in God.

33 Wisdom reposes in the heart of the discerning
and even among fools she lets herself be known.[b]

34 Righteousness exalts a nation,
but sin condemns any people.

35 A king delights in a wise servant,
but a shameful servant arouses his fury.

15 A gentle answer turns away wrath,
but a harsh word stirs up anger.

2 The tongue of the wise adorns knowledge,
but the mouth of the fool gushes folly.

3 The eyes of the LORD are everywhere,
keeping watch on the wicked and the good.

4 The soothing tongue is a tree of life,
but a perverse tongue crushes the spirit.

5 A fool spurns a parent's discipline,
but whoever heeds correction shows prudence.

6 The house of the righteous contains great treasure,
but the income of the wicked brings ruin.

[a] 22 Or *show* [b] 33 Hebrew; Septuagint and Syriac *discerning / but in the heart of fools she is not known*

PRAYING SCRIPTURE

Proverbs 15

Proverbs contains many warnings about being a scoffer, one who derides or mocks the truth. Scoffers are unwilling to learn or to receive correction. Scoffers think they know everything and thus mock anyone who tries to help.

Guard your heart against scoffing. Ask God for a heart that seeks wisdom instead of mocking it.

7 The lips of the wise spread knowledge,
but the hearts of fools are not upright.

8 The LORD detests the sacrifice of the wicked,
but the prayer of the upright pleases him.

9 The LORD detests the way of the wicked,
but he loves those who pursue righteousness.

10 Stern discipline awaits anyone who leaves the path;
the one who hates correction will die.

11 Death and Destruction[a] lie open before the LORD—
how much more do human hearts!

12 Mockers resent correction,
so they avoid the wise.

13 A happy heart makes the face cheerful,
but heartache crushes the spirit.

14 The discerning heart seeks knowledge,
but the mouth of a fool feeds on folly.

15 All the days of the oppressed are wretched,
but the cheerful heart has a continual feast.

16 Better a little with the fear of the LORD
than great wealth with turmoil.

17 Better a small serving of vegetables with love
than a fattened calf with hatred.

18 A hot-tempered person stirs up conflict,
but the one who is patient calms a quarrel.

19 The way of the sluggard is blocked with thorns,
but the path of the upright is a highway.

20 A wise son brings joy to his father,
but a foolish man despises his mother.

21 Folly brings joy to one who has no sense,
but whoever has understanding keeps a straight course.

22 Plans fail for lack of counsel,
but with many advisers they succeed.

23 A person finds joy in giving an apt reply—
and how good is a timely word!

24 The path of life leads upward for the prudent
to keep them from going down to the realm of the dead.

25 The LORD tears down the house of the proud,
but he sets the widow's boundary stones in place.

26 The LORD detests the thoughts of the wicked,
but gracious words are pure in his sight.

27 The greedy bring ruin to their households,
but the one who hates bribes will live.

[a] *11* Hebrew *Abaddon*

28 The heart of the righteous weighs its answers,
but the mouth of the wicked gushes evil.

29 The LORD is far from the wicked,
but he hears the prayer of the righteous.

30 Light in a messenger's eyes brings joy to the heart,
and good news gives health to the bones.

31 Whoever heeds life-giving correction
will be at home among the wise.

32 Those who disregard discipline despise themselves,
but the one who heeds correction gains understanding.

33 Wisdom's instruction is to fear the LORD,
and humility comes before honor.

16 To humans belong the plans of the heart,
but from the LORD comes the proper answer of the tongue.

2 All a person's ways seem pure to them,
but motives are weighed by the LORD.

3 Commit to the LORD whatever you do,
and he will establish your plans.

4 The LORD works out everything to its proper end—
even the wicked for a day of disaster.

5 The LORD detests all the proud of heart.
Be sure of this: They will not go unpunished.

6 Through love and faithfulness sin is atoned for;
through the fear of the LORD evil is avoided.

7 When the LORD takes pleasure in anyone's way,
he causes their enemies to make peace with them.

8 Better a little with righteousness
than much gain with injustice.

9 In their hearts humans plan their course,
but the LORD establishes their steps.

10 The lips of a king speak as an oracle,
and his mouth does not betray justice.

11 Honest scales and balances belong to the LORD;
all the weights in the bag are of his making.

12 Kings detest wrongdoing,
for a throne is established through righteousness.

13 Kings take pleasure in honest lips;
they value the one who speaks what is right.

14 A king's wrath is a messenger of death,
but the wise will appease it.

15 When a king's face brightens, it means life;
his favor is like a rain cloud in spring.

16 How much better to get wisdom than gold,
to get insight rather than silver!

PRAYING SCRIPTURE

Proverbs 16

This chapter contains a warning for everyone: "There is a way that appears to be right, but in the end it leads to death" (verse 25). It seems right that a person can do enough good to enter heaven. But that's the way of death; no one is good enough.

Where is your hope? If it's in good works, realize that is a death sentence. Ask God for forgiveness, even for sinful good works.

17 The highway of the upright avoids evil;
those who guard their ways preserve their lives.

18 Pride goes before destruction,
a haughty spirit before a fall.

19 Better to be lowly in spirit along with the oppressed
than to share plunder with the proud.

20 Whoever gives heed to instruction prospers,[a]
and blessed is the one who trusts in the LORD.

21 The wise in heart are called discerning,
and gracious words promote instruction.[b]

22 Prudence is a fountain of life to the prudent,
but folly brings punishment to fools.

23 The hearts of the wise make their mouths prudent,
and their lips promote instruction.[c]

24 Gracious words are a honeycomb,
sweet to the soul and healing to the bones.

25 There is a way that appears to be right,
but in the end it leads to death.

26 The appetite of laborers works for them;
their hunger drives them on.

27 A scoundrel plots evil,
and on their lips it is like a scorching fire.

28 A perverse person stirs up conflict,
and a gossip separates close friends.

29 A violent person entices their neighbor
and leads them down a path that is not good.

30 Whoever winks with their eye is plotting perversity;
whoever purses their lips is bent on evil.

31 Gray hair is a crown of splendor;
it is attained in the way of righteousness.

32 Better a patient person than a warrior,
one with self-control than one who takes a city.

33 The lot is cast into the lap,
but its every decision is from the LORD.

17 Better a dry crust with peace and quiet
than a house full of feasting, with strife.

2 A prudent servant will rule over a disgraceful son
and will share the inheritance as one of the family.

3 The crucible for silver and the furnace for gold,
but the LORD tests the heart.

4 A wicked person listens to deceitful lips;
a liar pays attention to a destructive tongue.

PRAYING SCRIPTURE

Proverbs 17

Which is worse: giving a pass to the guilty or condemning the innocent? "The LORD detests them both" (verse 15). God is watching how laws and mores can be used to the benefit of the haves and to the detriment of the have-nots. God is not pleased when justice is perverted in either direction.

Ask God to help you pursue justice so people around you can know his character.

[a] 20 Or *whoever speaks prudently finds what is good* [b] 21 Or *words make a person persuasive* [c] 23 Or *prudent / and make their lips persuasive*

5 Whoever mocks the poor shows contempt for their Maker;
whoever gloats over disaster will not go unpunished.

6 Children's children are a crown to the aged,
and parents are the pride of their children.

7 Eloquent lips are unsuited to a godless fool—
how much worse lying lips to a ruler!

8 A bribe is seen as a charm by the one who gives it;
they think success will come at every turn.

9 Whoever would foster love covers over an offense,
but whoever repeats the matter separates close friends.

10 A rebuke impresses a discerning person
more than a hundred lashes a fool.

11 Evildoers foster rebellion against God;
the messenger of death will be sent against them.

12 Better to meet a bear robbed of her cubs
than a fool bent on folly.

13 Evil will never leave the house
of one who pays back evil for good.

14 Starting a quarrel is like breaching a dam;
so drop the matter before a dispute breaks out.

15 Acquitting the guilty and condemning the innocent—
the LORD detests them both.

16 Why should fools have money in hand to buy wisdom,
when they are not able to understand it?

17 A friend loves at all times,
and a brother is born for a time of adversity.

18 One who has no sense shakes hands in pledge
and puts up security for a neighbor.

19 Whoever loves a quarrel loves sin;
whoever builds a high gate invites destruction.

20 One whose heart is corrupt does not prosper;
one whose tongue is perverse falls into trouble.

21 To have a fool for a child brings grief;
there is no joy for the parent of a godless fool.

22 A cheerful heart is good medicine,
but a crushed spirit dries up the bones.

23 The wicked accept bribes in secret
to pervert the course of justice.

24 A discerning person keeps wisdom in view,
but a fool's eyes wander to the ends of the earth.

25 A foolish son brings grief to his father
and bitterness to the mother who bore him.

26 If imposing a fine on the innocent is not good,
surely to flog honest officials is not right.

PRAYING SCRIPTURE

Proverbs 18

If we speak without giving consideration to our words, we can hurt the people around us and show our own foolishness. A fool's words cause contention, call for destruction and are a snare to his or her own life. Speech is a primary revealer of foolishness.

Have you asked yourself how others are affected by your words? Ask God to make your words a source of blessing.

27 The one who has knowledge uses words with restraint,
and whoever has understanding is even-tempered.

28 Even fools are thought wise if they keep silent,
and discerning if they hold their tongues.

18

An unfriendly person pursues selfish ends
and against all sound judgment starts quarrels.

2 Fools find no pleasure in understanding
but delight in airing their own opinions.

3 When wickedness comes, so does contempt,
and with shame comes reproach.

4 The words of the mouth are deep waters,
but the fountain of wisdom is a rushing stream.

5 It is not good to be partial to the wicked
and so deprive the innocent of justice.

6 The lips of fools bring them strife,
and their mouths invite a beating.

7 The mouths of fools are their undoing,
and their lips are a snare to their very lives.

8 The words of a gossip are like choice morsels;
they go down to the inmost parts.

9 One who is slack in his work
is brother to one who destroys.

10 The name of the LORD is a fortified tower;
the righteous run to it and are safe.

11 The wealth of the rich is their fortified city;
they imagine it a wall too high to scale.

12 Before a downfall the heart is haughty,
but humility comes before honor.

13 To answer before listening —
that is folly and shame.

14 The human spirit can endure in sickness,
but a crushed spirit who can bear?

15 The heart of the discerning acquires knowledge,
for the ears of the wise seek it out.

16 A gift opens the way
and ushers the giver into the presence of the great.

17 In a lawsuit the first to speak seems right,
until someone comes forward and cross-examines.

18 Casting the lot settles disputes
and keeps strong opponents apart.

19 A brother wronged is more unyielding than a fortified city;
disputes are like the barred gates of a citadel.

20 From the fruit of their mouth a person's stomach is filled;
with the harvest of their lips they are satisfied.

21 The tongue has the power of life and death,
and those who love it will eat its fruit.

22 He who finds a wife finds what is good
and receives favor from the LORD.

23 The poor plead for mercy,
but the rich answer harshly.

24 One who has unreliable friends soon comes to ruin,
but there is a friend who sticks closer than a brother.

19

Better the poor whose walk is blameless
than a fool whose lips are perverse.

2 Desire without knowledge is not good —
how much more will hasty feet miss the way!

3 A person's own folly leads to their ruin,
yet their heart rages against the LORD.

4 Wealth attracts many friends,
but even the closest friend of the poor person deserts them.

5 A false witness will not go unpunished,
and whoever pours out lies will not go free.

6 Many curry favor with a ruler,
and everyone is the friend of one who gives gifts.

7 The poor are shunned by all their relatives —
how much more do their friends avoid them!
Though the poor pursue them with pleading,
they are nowhere to be found.[a]

8 The one who gets wisdom loves life;
the one who cherishes understanding will soon prosper.

9 A false witness will not go unpunished,
and whoever pours out lies will perish.

10 It is not fitting for a fool to live in luxury —
how much worse for a slave to rule over princes!

11 A person's wisdom yields patience;
it is to one's glory to overlook an offense.

12 A king's rage is like the roar of a lion,
but his favor is like dew on the grass.

13 A foolish child is a father's ruin,
and a quarrelsome wife is like
the constant dripping of a leaky roof.

14 Houses and wealth are inherited from parents,
but a prudent wife is from the LORD.

15 Laziness brings on deep sleep,
and the shiftless go hungry.

16 Whoever keeps commandments keeps their life,
but whoever shows contempt for their ways will die.

[a] 7 The meaning of the Hebrew for this sentence is uncertain.

PRAYING SCRIPTURE

Proverbs 19

We are assured that though many plans might be in our hearts, it is the Lord's purpose that will ultimately prevail. That should give us confidence to move forward in faith.

Are you struggling with direction in life? Ask God to make his way clear, for it is the way that will stand.

17 Whoever is kind to the poor lends to the LORD,
and he will reward them for what they have done.

18 Discipline your children, for in that there is hope;
do not be a willing party to their death.

19 A hot-tempered person must pay the penalty;
rescue them, and you will have to do it again.

20 Listen to advice and accept discipline,
and at the end you will be counted among the wise.

21 Many are the plans in a person's heart,
but it is the LORD's purpose that prevails.

22 What a person desires is unfailing love[a];
better to be poor than a liar.

23 The fear of the LORD leads to life;
then one rests content, untouched by trouble.

24 A sluggard buries his hand in the dish;
he will not even bring it back to his mouth!

25 Flog a mocker, and the simple will learn prudence;
rebuke the discerning, and they will gain knowledge.

26 Whoever robs their father and drives out their mother
is a child who brings shame and disgrace.

27 Stop listening to instruction, my son,
and you will stray from the words of knowledge.

28 A corrupt witness mocks at justice,
and the mouth of the wicked gulps down evil.

29 Penalties are prepared for mockers,
and beatings for the backs of fools.

20

Wine is a mocker and beer a brawler;
whoever is led astray by them is not wise.

2 A king's wrath strikes terror like the roar of a lion;
those who anger him forfeit their lives.

3 It is to one's honor to avoid strife,
but every fool is quick to quarrel.

4 Sluggards do not plow in season;
so at harvest time they look but find nothing.

5 The purposes of a person's heart are deep waters,
but one who has insight draws them out.

6 Many claim to have unfailing love,
but a faithful person who can find?

7 The righteous lead blameless lives;
blessed are their children after them.

8 When a king sits on his throne to judge,
he winnows out all evil with his eyes.

[a] 22 Or *Greed is a person's shame*

PRAYING SCRIPTURE

Proverbs 20

Often in business, people will do whatever it takes to close a deal or climb the ladder, even if it means ignoring God's commands. But God wants us to be honest. Shady dealings in business are an abomination to the Lord.

Do you find it hard to be honest? Ask God to help you choose integrity whenever you have the chance to lie or cheat to get ahead.

9 Who can say, "I have kept my heart pure;
I am clean and without sin"?

10 Differing weights and differing measures —
the LORD detests them both.

11 Even small children are known by their actions,
so is their conduct really pure and upright?

12 Ears that hear and eyes that see —
the LORD has made them both.

13 Do not love sleep or you will grow poor;
stay awake and you will have food to spare.

14 "It's no good, it's no good!" says the buyer —
then goes off and boasts about the purchase.

15 Gold there is, and rubies in abundance,
but lips that speak knowledge are a rare jewel.

16 Take the garment of one who puts up security for a stranger;
hold it in pledge if it is done for an outsider.

17 Food gained by fraud tastes sweet,
but one ends up with a mouth full of gravel.

18 Plans are established by seeking advice;
so if you wage war, obtain guidance.

19 A gossip betrays a confidence;
so avoid anyone who talks too much.

20 If someone curses their father or mother,
their lamp will be snuffed out in pitch darkness.

21 An inheritance claimed too soon
will not be blessed at the end.

22 Do not say, "I'll pay you back for this wrong!"
Wait for the LORD, and he will avenge you.

23 The LORD detests differing weights,
and dishonest scales do not please him.

24 A person's steps are directed by the LORD.
How then can anyone understand their own way?

25 It is a trap to dedicate something rashly
and only later to consider one's vows.

26 A wise king winnows out the wicked;
he drives the threshing wheel over them.

27 The human spirit is[a] the lamp of the LORD
that sheds light on one's inmost being.

28 Love and faithfulness keep a king safe;
through love his throne is made secure.

29 The glory of young men is their strength,
gray hair the splendor of the old.

---

[a] 27 Or *A person's words are*

30 Blows and wounds scrub away evil,
and beatings purge the inmost being.

PRAYING SCRIPTURE

Proverbs 21

Those who walk on God's path find "life, prosperity and honor" (verse 21). This is an echo of the promise that "goodness and love shall follow" God's people for all eternity (Psalm 23:6). Though life here is hard, God promises a reward.

Are you following righteousness and love? Ask God to orient your life around that pursuit.

21 In the LORD's hand the king's heart is a stream of water
that he channels toward all who please him.

2 A person may think their own ways are right,
but the LORD weighs the heart.

3 To do what is right and just
is more acceptable to the LORD than sacrifice.

4 Haughty eyes and a proud heart —
the unplowed field of the wicked — produce sin.

5 The plans of the diligent lead to profit
as surely as haste leads to poverty.

6 A fortune made by a lying tongue
is a fleeting vapor and a deadly snare.[a]

7 The violence of the wicked will drag them away,
for they refuse to do what is right.

8 The way of the guilty is devious,
but the conduct of the innocent is upright.

9 Better to live on a corner of the roof
than share a house with a quarrelsome wife.

10 The wicked crave evil;
their neighbors get no mercy from them.

11 When a mocker is punished, the simple gain wisdom;
by paying attention to the wise they get knowledge.

12 The Righteous One[b] takes note of the house of the wicked
and brings the wicked to ruin.

13 Whoever shuts their ears to the cry of the poor
will also cry out and not be answered.

14 A gift given in secret soothes anger,
and a bribe concealed in the cloak pacifies great wrath.

15 When justice is done, it brings joy to the righteous
but terror to evildoers.

16 Whoever strays from the path of prudence
comes to rest in the company of the dead.

17 Whoever loves pleasure will become poor;
whoever loves wine and olive oil will never be rich.

18 The wicked become a ransom for the righteous,
and the unfaithful for the upright.

19 Better to live in a desert
than with a quarrelsome and nagging wife.

20 The wise store up choice food and olive oil,
but fools gulp theirs down.

---

[a] 6 Some Hebrew manuscripts, Septuagint and Vulgate; most Hebrew manuscripts *vapor for those who seek death* [b] 12 Or *The righteous person*

21 Whoever pursues righteousness and love
finds life, prosperity[a] and honor.

22 One who is wise can go up against the city of the mighty
and pull down the stronghold in which they trust.

23 Those who guard their mouths and their tongues
keep themselves from calamity.

24 The proud and arrogant person — "Mocker" is his name —
behaves with insolent fury.

25 The craving of a sluggard will be the death of him,
because his hands refuse to work.
26 All day long he craves for more,
but the righteous give without sparing.

27 The sacrifice of the wicked is detestable —
how much more so when brought with evil intent!

28 A false witness will perish,
but a careful listener will testify successfully.

29 The wicked put up a bold front,
but the upright give thought to their ways.

30 There is no wisdom, no insight, no plan
that can succeed against the LORD.

31 The horse is made ready for the day of battle,
but victory rests with the LORD.

22 A good name is more desirable than great riches;
to be esteemed is better than silver or gold.

2 Rich and poor have this in common:
The LORD is the Maker of them all.

3 The prudent see danger and take refuge,
but the simple keep going and pay the penalty.

4 Humility is the fear of the LORD;
its wages are riches and honor and life.

5 In the paths of the wicked are snares and pitfalls,
but those who would preserve their life stay far from them.

6 Start children off on the way they should go,
and even when they are old they will not turn from it.

7 The rich rule over the poor,
and the borrower is slave to the lender.

8 Whoever sows injustice reaps calamity,
and the rod they wield in fury will be broken.

9 The generous will themselves be blessed,
for they share their food with the poor.

10 Drive out the mocker, and out goes strife;
quarrels and insults are ended.

PRAYING SCRIPTURE

Proverbs 22

We learn early that one's reputation is directly connected to a person's name. Solomon recognized this and wrote that a good name is more desirable than great riches. Such a statement conveys even more meaning when we remember Solomon's immense wealth.

What do you want people to think when they hear your name? Pray that your name will remind people of your love for God and that your reputation will reflect his character.

[a] 21 Or *righteousness*

[11] One who loves a pure heart and who speaks with grace
will have the king for a friend.

[12] The eyes of the LORD keep watch over knowledge,
but he frustrates the words of the unfaithful.

[13] The sluggard says, "There's a lion outside!
I'll be killed in the public square!"

[14] The mouth of an adulterous woman is a deep pit;
a man who is under the LORD's wrath falls into it.

[15] Folly is bound up in the heart of a child,
but the rod of discipline will drive it far away.

[16] One who oppresses the poor to increase his wealth
and one who gives gifts to the rich — both come to poverty.

THIRTY SAYINGS OF THE WISE

SAYING 1

[17] Pay attention and turn your ear to the sayings of the wise;
apply your heart to what I teach,
[18] for it is pleasing when you keep them in your heart
and have all of them ready on your lips.
[19] So that your trust may be in the LORD,
I teach you today, even you.
[20] Have I not written thirty sayings for you,
sayings of counsel and knowledge,
[21] teaching you to be honest and to speak the truth,
so that you bring back truthful reports
to those you serve?

SAYING 2

[22] Do not exploit the poor because they are poor
and do not crush the needy in court,
[23] for the LORD will take up their case
and will exact life for life.

SAYING 3

[24] Do not make friends with a hot-tempered person,
do not associate with one easily angered,
[25] or you may learn their ways
and get yourself ensnared.

SAYING 4

[26] Do not be one who shakes hands in pledge
or puts up security for debts;
[27] if you lack the means to pay,
your very bed will be snatched from under you.

SAYING 5

[28] Do not move an ancient boundary stone
set up by your ancestors.

SAYING 6

[29] Do you see someone skilled in their work?
They will serve before kings;
they will not serve before officials of low rank.

SAYING 7

23 When you sit to dine with a ruler,
note well what[a] is before you,
2 and put a knife to your throat
if you are given to gluttony.
3 Do not crave his delicacies,
for that food is deceptive.

SAYING 8

4 Do not wear yourself out to get rich;
do not trust your own cleverness.
5 Cast but a glance at riches, and they are gone,
for they will surely sprout wings
and fly off to the sky like an eagle.

SAYING 9

6 Do not eat the food of a begrudging host,
do not crave his delicacies;
7 for he is the kind of person
who is always thinking about the cost.[b]
"Eat and drink," he says to you,
but his heart is not with you.
8 You will vomit up the little you have eaten
and will have wasted your compliments.

SAYING 10

9 Do not speak to fools,
for they will scorn your prudent words.

SAYING 11

10 Do not move an ancient boundary stone
or encroach on the fields of the fatherless,
11 for their Defender is strong;
he will take up their case against you.

SAYING 12

12 Apply your heart to instruction
and your ears to words of knowledge.

SAYING 13

13 Do not withhold discipline from a child;
if you punish them with the rod, they will not die.
14 Punish them with the rod
and save them from death.

SAYING 14

15 My son, if your heart is wise,
then my heart will be glad indeed;
16 my inmost being will rejoice
when your lips speak what is right.

SAYING 15

17 Do not let your heart envy sinners,
but always be zealous for the fear of the LORD.
18 There is surely a future hope for you,
and your hope will not be cut off.

---

[a] 1 Or *who* [b] 7 Or *for as he thinks within himself, / so he is*; or *for as he puts on a feast, / so he is*

PRAYING SCRIPTURE

Proverbs 23

More than half of this chapter can be classified as parental guidance for instructing kids: Be wise, don't envy sinners, be zealous to fear the Lord, listen to your parents, seek the truth and beware of alcoholic drink.

It is best to teach kids the path of righteousness when they are young. Pray for guidance to imprint God's ways on their hearts.

SAYING 16

19 Listen, my son, and be wise,
and set your heart on the right path:
20 Do not join those who drink too much wine
or gorge themselves on meat,
21 for drunkards and gluttons become poor,
and drowsiness clothes them in rags.

SAYING 17

22 Listen to your father, who gave you life,
and do not despise your mother when she is old.
23 Buy the truth and do not sell it —
wisdom, instruction and insight as well.
24 The father of a righteous child has great joy;
a man who fathers a wise son rejoices in him.
25 May your father and mother rejoice;
may she who gave you birth be joyful!

SAYING 18

26 My son, give me your heart
and let your eyes delight in my ways,
27 for an adulterous woman is a deep pit,
and a wayward wife is a narrow well.
28 Like a bandit she lies in wait
and multiplies the unfaithful among men.

SAYING 19

29 Who has woe? Who has sorrow?
Who has strife? Who has complaints?
Who has needless bruises? Who has bloodshot eyes?
30 Those who linger over wine,
who go to sample bowls of mixed wine.
31 Do not gaze at wine when it is red,
when it sparkles in the cup,
when it goes down smoothly!
32 In the end it bites like a snake
and poisons like a viper.
33 Your eyes will see strange sights,
and your mind will imagine confusing things.
34 You will be like one sleeping on the high seas,
lying on top of the rigging.
35 "They hit me," you will say, "but I'm not hurt!
They beat me, but I don't feel it!
When will I wake up
so I can find another drink?"

SAYING 20

24 Do not envy the wicked,
do not desire their company;
2 for their hearts plot violence,
and their lips talk about making trouble.

SAYING 21

3 By wisdom a house is built,
and through understanding it is established;
4 through knowledge its rooms are filled
with rare and beautiful treasures.

PRAYING SCRIPTURE

Proverbs 24

A principle with physical and spiritual application is in verses 11–12. When we see someone "staggering toward slaughter," we have a responsibility to intervene. Slaughter could refer to physical danger from unwise living or spiritual danger from unbelief.

Do you know people who are staggering? Ask God for wisdom to know the best way to deliver them from slaughter.

SAYING 22

5 The wise prevail through great power,
and those who have knowledge muster their strength.
6 Surely you need guidance to wage war,
and victory is won through many advisers.

SAYING 23

7 Wisdom is too high for fools;
in the assembly at the gate they must not open their mouths.

SAYING 24

8 Whoever plots evil
will be known as a schemer.
9 The schemes of folly are sin,
and people detest a mocker.

SAYING 25

10 If you falter in a time of trouble,
how small is your strength!
11 Rescue those being led away to death;
hold back those staggering toward slaughter.
12 If you say, "But we knew nothing about this,"
does not he who weighs the heart perceive it?
Does not he who guards your life know it?
Will he not repay everyone according to what they have done?

SAYING 26

13 Eat honey, my son, for it is good;
honey from the comb is sweet to your taste.
14 Know also that wisdom is like honey for you:
If you find it, there is a future hope for you,
and your hope will not be cut off.

SAYING 27

15 Do not lurk like a thief near the house of the righteous,
do not plunder their dwelling place;
16 for though the righteous fall seven times, they rise again,
but the wicked stumble when calamity strikes.

SAYING 28

17 Do not gloat when your enemy falls;
when they stumble, do not let your heart rejoice,
18 or the LORD will see and disapprove
and turn his wrath away from them.

SAYING 29

19 Do not fret because of evildoers
or be envious of the wicked,
20 for the evildoer has no future hope,
and the lamp of the wicked will be snuffed out.

SAYING 30

21 Fear the LORD and the king, my son,
and do not join with rebellious officials,
22 for those two will send sudden destruction on them,
and who knows what calamities they can bring?

FURTHER SAYINGS OF THE WISE

23 These also are sayings of the wise:

To show partiality in judging is not good:
24 Whoever says to the guilty, "You are innocent,"
will be cursed by peoples and denounced by nations.
25 But it will go well with those who convict the guilty,
and rich blessing will come on them.

26 An honest answer
is like a kiss on the lips.

27 Put your outdoor work in order
and get your fields ready;
after that, build your house.

28 Do not testify against your neighbor without cause —
would you use your lips to mislead?
29 Do not say, "I'll do to them as they have done to me;
I'll pay them back for what they did."

30 I went past the field of a sluggard,
past the vineyard of someone who has no sense;
31 thorns had come up everywhere,
the ground was covered with weeds,
and the stone wall was in ruins.
32 I applied my heart to what I observed
and learned a lesson from what I saw:
33 A little sleep, a little slumber,
a little folding of the hands to rest —
34 and poverty will come on you like a thief
and scarcity like an armed man.

MORE PROVERBS OF SOLOMON

25 These are more proverbs of Solomon, compiled by the men of Hezekiah king of Judah:

2 It is the glory of God to conceal a matter;
to search out a matter is the glory of kings.
3 As the heavens are high and the earth is deep,
so the hearts of kings are unsearchable.

4 Remove the dross from the silver,
and a silversmith can produce a vessel;
5 remove wicked officials from the king's presence,
and his throne will be established through righteousness.

6 Do not exalt yourself in the king's presence,
and do not claim a place among his great men;
7 it is better for him to say to you, "Come up here,"
than for him to humiliate you before his nobles.

What you have seen with your eyes
8 do not bring[a] hastily to court,
for what will you do in the end
if your neighbor puts you to shame?

PRAYING SCRIPTURE

Proverbs 25

In a passage that foreshadows the Sermon on the Mount, Solomon said the way to treat our enemies is to meet their physical needs: food when they are hungry and water when they are thirsty. When we repay evil with good, they are shamed.

Being kind to an enemy is very hard. Sometimes it feels impossible, but God rewards it. Ask him for his love to help you respond as Jesus did.

[a] 7,8 Or *nobles / on whom you had set your eyes. /* [8]*Do not go*

9 If you take your neighbor to court,
do not betray another's confidence,
10 or the one who hears it may shame you
and the charge against you will stand.

11 Like apples[a] of gold in settings of silver
is a ruling rightly given.
12 Like an earring of gold or an ornament of fine gold
is the rebuke of a wise judge to a listening ear.

13 Like a snow-cooled drink at harvest time
is a trustworthy messenger to the one who sends him;
he refreshes the spirit of his master.
14 Like clouds and wind without rain
is one who boasts of gifts never given.

15 Through patience a ruler can be persuaded,
and a gentle tongue can break a bone.

16 If you find honey, eat just enough —
too much of it, and you will vomit.
17 Seldom set foot in your neighbor's house —
too much of you, and they will hate you.

18 Like a club or a sword or a sharp arrow
is one who gives false testimony against a neighbor.
19 Like a broken tooth or a lame foot
is reliance on the unfaithful in a time of trouble.
20 Like one who takes away a garment on a cold day,
or like vinegar poured on a wound,
is one who sings songs to a heavy heart.

21 If your enemy is hungry, give him food to eat;
if he is thirsty, give him water to drink.
22 In doing this, you will heap burning coals on his head,
and the LORD will reward you.

23 Like a north wind that brings unexpected rain
is a sly tongue — which provokes a horrified look.

24 Better to live on a corner of the roof
than share a house with a quarrelsome wife.

25 Like cold water to a weary soul
is good news from a distant land.
26 Like a muddied spring or a polluted well
are the righteous who give way to the wicked.

27 It is not good to eat too much honey,
nor is it honorable to search out matters that are too deep.

28 Like a city whose walls are broken through
is a person who lacks self-control.

26 Like snow in summer or rain in harvest,
honor is not fitting for a fool.
2 Like a fluttering sparrow or a darting swallow,
an undeserved curse does not come to rest.

[a] *11* Or possibly *apricots*

PRAYING SCRIPTURE

Proverbs 26

Do you correct foolish people or stay silent? This chapter teaches that our response depends on the context. Sometimes it is better to answer and sometimes it isn't. Don't let the fool think himself wise, but don't be like a fool in answering.

Ask God for wisdom whenever you encounter a fool.

3 A whip for the horse, a bridle for the donkey,
and a rod for the backs of fools!
4 Do not answer a fool according to his folly,
or you yourself will be just like him.
5 Answer a fool according to his folly,
or he will be wise in his own eyes.
6 Sending a message by the hands of a fool
is like cutting off one's feet or drinking poison.
7 Like the useless legs of one who is lame
is a proverb in the mouth of a fool.
8 Like tying a stone in a sling
is the giving of honor to a fool.
9 Like a thornbush in a drunkard's hand
is a proverb in the mouth of a fool.
10 Like an archer who wounds at random
is one who hires a fool or any passer-by.
11 As a dog returns to its vomit,
so fools repeat their folly.
12 Do you see a person wise in their own eyes?
There is more hope for a fool than for them.

13 A sluggard says, "There's a lion in the road,
a fierce lion roaming the streets!"
14 As a door turns on its hinges,
so a sluggard turns on his bed.
15 A sluggard buries his hand in the dish;
he is too lazy to bring it back to his mouth.
16 A sluggard is wiser in his own eyes
than seven people who answer discreetly.

17 Like one who grabs a stray dog by the ears
is someone who rushes into a quarrel not their own.

18 Like a maniac shooting
flaming arrows of death
19 is one who deceives their neighbor
and says, "I was only joking!"

20 Without wood a fire goes out;
without a gossip a quarrel dies down.
21 As charcoal to embers and as wood to fire,
so is a quarrelsome person for kindling strife.
22 The words of a gossip are like choice morsels;
they go down to the inmost parts.

23 Like a coating of silver dross on earthenware
are fervent[a] lips with an evil heart.
24 Enemies disguise themselves with their lips,
but in their hearts they harbor deceit.
25 Though their speech is charming, do not believe them,
for seven abominations fill their hearts.
26 Their malice may be concealed by deception,
but their wickedness will be exposed in the assembly.
27 Whoever digs a pit will fall into it;
if someone rolls a stone, it will roll back on them.

[a] 23 Hebrew; Septuagint *smooth*

28 A lying tongue hates those it hurts,
and a flattering mouth works ruin.

27

Do not boast about tomorrow,
for you do not know what a day may bring.

2 Let someone else praise you, and not your own mouth;
an outsider, and not your own lips.

3 Stone is heavy and sand a burden,
but a fool's provocation is heavier than both.

4 Anger is cruel and fury overwhelming,
but who can stand before jealousy?

5 Better is open rebuke
than hidden love.

6 Wounds from a friend can be trusted,
but an enemy multiplies kisses.

7 One who is full loathes honey from the comb,
but to the hungry even what is bitter tastes sweet.

8 Like a bird that flees its nest
is anyone who flees from home.

9 Perfume and incense bring joy to the heart,
and the pleasantness of a friend
springs from their heartfelt advice.

10 Do not forsake your friend or a friend of your family,
and do not go to your relative's house when disaster strikes you—
better a neighbor nearby than a relative far away.

11 Be wise, my son, and bring joy to my heart;
then I can answer anyone who treats me with contempt.

12 The prudent see danger and take refuge,
but the simple keep going and pay the penalty.

13 Take the garment of one who puts up security for a stranger;
hold it in pledge if it is done for an outsider.

14 If anyone loudly blesses their neighbor early in the morning,
it will be taken as a curse.

15 A quarrelsome wife is like the dripping
of a leaky roof in a rainstorm;
16 restraining her is like restraining the wind
or grasping oil with the hand.

17 As iron sharpens iron,
so one person sharpens another.

18 The one who guards a fig tree will eat its fruit,
and whoever protects their master will be honored.

19 As water reflects the face,
so one's life reflects the heart.[a]

PRAYING SCRIPTURE

Proverbs 27

To manage possessions, "give careful attention" to the condition of your flocks and herds (verse 23), that is, pay attention to your finances and other possessions, tending them well. Do not be obsessed with them.

Do you struggle between managing possessions and focusing on heavenly things? Ask God how to be wise in both endeavors.

[a] 19 *Or so others reflect your heart back to you*

20 Death and Destruction[a] are never satisfied,
and neither are human eyes.

21 The crucible for silver and the furnace for gold,
but people are tested by their praise.

22 Though you grind a fool in a mortar,
grinding them like grain with a pestle,
you will not remove their folly from them.

23 Be sure you know the condition of your flocks,
give careful attention to your herds;
24 for riches do not endure forever,
and a crown is not secure for all generations.
25 When the hay is removed and new growth appears
and the grass from the hills is gathered in,
26 the lambs will provide you with clothing,
and the goats with the price of a field.
27 You will have plenty of goats' milk to feed your family
and to nourish your female servants.

28 The wicked flee though no one pursues,
but the righteous are as bold as a lion.

2 When a country is rebellious, it has many rulers,
but a ruler with discernment and knowledge
maintains order.

3 A ruler[b] who oppresses the poor
is like a driving rain that leaves no crops.
4 Those who forsake instruction praise the wicked,
but those who heed it resist them.

5 Evildoers do not understand what is right,
but those who seek the LORD understand it fully.

6 Better the poor whose walk is blameless
than the rich whose ways are perverse.

7 A discerning son heeds instruction,
but a companion of gluttons disgraces his father.

8 Whoever increases wealth by taking interest or profit from the
poor
amasses it for another, who will be kind to the poor.

9 If anyone turns a deaf ear to my instruction,
even their prayers are detestable.

10 Whoever leads the upright along an evil path
will fall into their own trap,
but the blameless will receive a good inheritance.

11 The rich are wise in their own eyes;
one who is poor and discerning sees how deluded they are.

12 When the righteous triumph, there is great elation;
but when the wicked rise to power, people go into hiding.

PRAYING SCRIPTURE

Proverbs 28

This chapter returns to the ongoing theme of the poor. Solomon included both a warning—needy people should not oppress other needy people—and an encouragement for poor people to live with integrity because that is better than being rich and perverse.

Whether rich, poor or in between, we can all embrace God's righteousness as the standard for living. Pray for a greater desire for integrity than for wealth.

[a] 20 Hebrew *Abaddon* [b] 3 Or *A poor person*

13 Whoever conceals their sins does not prosper,
but the one who confesses and renounces them finds mercy.

14 Blessed is the one who always trembles before God,
but whoever hardens their heart falls into trouble.

15 Like a roaring lion or a charging bear
is a wicked ruler over a helpless people.

16 A tyrannical ruler practices extortion,
but one who hates ill-gotten gain will enjoy a long reign.

17 Anyone tormented by the guilt of murder
will seek refuge in the grave;
let no one hold them back.

18 The one whose walk is blameless is kept safe,
but the one whose ways are perverse will fall into the pit.[a]

19 Those who work their land will have abundant food,
but those who chase fantasies will have their fill of poverty.

20 A faithful person will be richly blessed,
but one eager to get rich will not go unpunished.

21 To show partiality is not good—
yet a person will do wrong for a piece of bread.

22 The stingy are eager to get rich
and are unaware that poverty awaits them.

23 Whoever rebukes a person will in the end gain favor
rather than one who has a flattering tongue.

24 Whoever robs their father or mother
and says, "It's not wrong,"
is partner to one who destroys.

25 The greedy stir up conflict,
but those who trust in the LORD will prosper.

26 Those who trust in themselves are fools,
but those who walk in wisdom are kept safe.

27 Those who give to the poor will lack nothing,
but those who close their eyes to them receive many curses.

28 When the wicked rise to power, people go into hiding;
but when the wicked perish, the righteous thrive.

29 Whoever remains stiff-necked after many rebukes
will suddenly be destroyed—without remedy.

2 When the righteous thrive, the people rejoice;
when the wicked rule, the people groan.

3 A man who loves wisdom brings joy to his father,
but a companion of prostitutes squanders his wealth.

4 By justice a king gives a country stability,
but those who are greedy for[b] bribes tear it down.

[a] 18 Syriac (see Septuagint); Hebrew *into one* [b] 4 Or *who give*

PRAYING SCRIPTURE

Proverbs 29

A recurring theme in Proverbs is self-control, especially in our speech. We are warned against using flattery (see verse 5), against venting our feelings (see verse 11) and against speaking angrily (see verse 22). How we speak reveals what is inside of us and witnesses, either positively or negatively, to the Lord in us.

Do you find yourself frequently apologizing for things you say? Ask God to slow your speech so it always honors him.

5 Those who flatter their neighbors
are spreading nets for their feet.

6 Evildoers are snared by their own sin,
but the righteous shout for joy and are glad.

7 The righteous care about justice for the poor,
but the wicked have no such concern.

8 Mockers stir up a city,
but the wise turn away anger.

9 If a wise person goes to court with a fool,
the fool rages and scoffs, and there is no peace.

10 The bloodthirsty hate a person of integrity
and seek to kill the upright.

11 Fools give full vent to their rage,
but the wise bring calm in the end.

12 If a ruler listens to lies,
all his officials become wicked.

13 The poor and the oppressor have this in common:
The LORD gives sight to the eyes of both.

14 If a king judges the poor with fairness,
his throne will be established forever.

15 A rod and a reprimand impart wisdom,
but a child left undisciplined disgraces its mother.

16 When the wicked thrive, so does sin,
but the righteous will see their downfall.

17 Discipline your children, and they will give you peace;
they will bring you the delights you desire.

18 Where there is no revelation, people cast off restraint;
but blessed is the one who heeds wisdom's instruction.

19 Servants cannot be corrected by mere words;
though they understand, they will not respond.

20 Do you see someone who speaks in haste?
There is more hope for a fool than for them.

21 A servant pampered from youth
will turn out to be insolent.

22 An angry person stirs up conflict,
and a hot-tempered person commits many sins.

23 Pride brings a person low,
but the lowly in spirit gain honor.

24 The accomplices of thieves are their own enemies;
they are put under oath and dare not testify.

25 Fear of man will prove to be a snare,
but whoever trusts in the LORD is kept safe.

26 Many seek an audience with a ruler,
but it is from the LORD that one gets justice.

27 The righteous detest the dishonest;
the wicked detest the upright.

SAYINGS OF AGUR

30 The sayings of Agur son of Jakeh — an inspired utterance.

This man's utterance to Ithiel:

"I am weary, God,
but I can prevail.[a]
2 Surely I am only a brute, not a man;
I do not have human understanding.
3 I have not learned wisdom,
nor have I attained to the knowledge of the Holy One.
4 Who has gone up to heaven and come down?
Whose hands have gathered up the wind?
Who has wrapped up the waters in a cloak?
Who has established all the ends of the earth?
What is his name, and what is the name of his son?
Surely you know!

5 "Every word of God is flawless;
he is a shield to those who take refuge in him.
6 Do not add to his words,
or he will rebuke you and prove you a liar.

7 "Two things I ask of you, LORD;
do not refuse me before I die:
8 Keep falsehood and lies far from me;
give me neither poverty nor riches,
but give me only my daily bread.
9 Otherwise, I may have too much and disown you
and say, 'Who is the LORD?'
Or I may become poor and steal,
and so dishonor the name of my God.

10 "Do not slander a servant to their master,
or they will curse you, and you will pay for it.

11 "There are those who curse their fathers
and do not bless their mothers;
12 those who are pure in their own eyes
and yet are not cleansed of their filth;
13 those whose eyes are ever so haughty,
whose glances are so disdainful;
14 those whose teeth are swords
and whose jaws are set with knives
to devour the poor from the earth
and the needy from among mankind.

15 "The leech has two daughters.
'Give! Give!' they cry.
"There are three things that are never satisfied,
four that never say, 'Enough!':

[a] *1* With a different word division of the Hebrew; Masoretic Text *utterance to Ithiel, / to Ithiel and Ukal:*

PRAYING SCRIPTURE

Proverbs 30

Agur's reflections in this chapter exalt God, showing his all-surpassing wisdom. No one equals God's power to govern creation. His words are complete. His ways are beyond human understanding. Agur's requests were only two: He wanted to maintain his integrity and see his daily needs met.

Are you as content as Agur? When you pray for things, are they mostly needs or mostly extra blessings?

16 the grave, the barren womb,
land, which is never satisfied with water,
and fire, which never says, 'Enough!'

17 "The eye that mocks a father,
that scorns an aged mother,
will be pecked out by the ravens of the valley,
will be eaten by the vultures.

18 "There are three things that are too amazing for me,
four that I do not understand:
19 the way of an eagle in the sky,
the way of a snake on a rock,
the way of a ship on the high seas,
and the way of a man with a young woman.

20 "This is the way of an adulterous woman:
She eats and wipes her mouth
and says, 'I've done nothing wrong.'

21 "Under three things the earth trembles,
under four it cannot bear up:
22 a servant who becomes king,
a godless fool who gets plenty to eat,
23 a contemptible woman who gets married,
and a servant who displaces her mistress.

24 "Four things on earth are small,
yet they are extremely wise:
25 Ants are creatures of little strength,
yet they store up their food in the summer;
26 hyraxes are creatures of little power,
yet they make their home in the crags;
27 locusts have no king,
yet they advance together in ranks;
28 a lizard can be caught with the hand,
yet it is found in kings' palaces.

29 "There are three things that are stately in their stride,
four that move with stately bearing:
30 a lion, mighty among beasts,
who retreats before nothing;
31 a strutting rooster, a he-goat,
and a king secure against revolt.[a]

32 "If you play the fool and exalt yourself,
or if you plan evil,
clap your hand over your mouth!
33 For as churning cream produces butter,
and as twisting the nose produces blood,
so stirring up anger produces strife."

SAYINGS OF KING LEMUEL

31 The sayings of King Lemuel — an inspired utterance his mother taught him.

2 Listen, my son! Listen, son of my womb!

[a] 31 The meaning of the Hebrew for this phrase is uncertain.

PRAYING SCRIPTURE

Proverbs 31

Whether King Lemuel's mother had a specific woman in mind for her holistic description of "a wife of noble character" is unknown (verse 10). We need to remember that the list is something to which women can aspire but not necessarily fulfill. It's a guide, not a checklist.

Have you ever struggled with the description of the virtuous woman? Ask God for wisdom, and commit your growth in virtue to his providence and care.

Listen, my son, the answer to my prayers!
3 Do not spend your strength[a] on women,
your vigor on those who ruin kings.

4 It is not for kings, Lemuel—
it is not for kings to drink wine,
not for rulers to crave beer,
5 lest they drink and forget what has been decreed,
and deprive all the oppressed of their rights.
6 Let beer be for those who are perishing,
wine for those who are in anguish!
7 Let them drink and forget their poverty
and remember their misery no more.

8 Speak up for those who cannot speak for themselves,
for the rights of all who are destitute.
9 Speak up and judge fairly;
defend the rights of the poor and needy.

EPILOGUE: THE WIFE OF NOBLE CHARACTER

10 [b]A wife of noble character who can find?
She is worth far more than rubies.
11 Her husband has full confidence in her
and lacks nothing of value.
12 She brings him good, not harm,
all the days of her life.
13 She selects wool and flax
and works with eager hands.
14 She is like the merchant ships,
bringing her food from afar.
15 She gets up while it is still night;
she provides food for her family
and portions for her female servants.
16 She considers a field and buys it;
out of her earnings she plants a vineyard.
17 She sets about her work vigorously;
her arms are strong for her tasks.
18 She sees that her trading is profitable,
and her lamp does not go out at night.
19 In her hand she holds the distaff
and grasps the spindle with her fingers.
20 She opens her arms to the poor
and extends her hands to the needy.
21 When it snows, she has no fear for her household;
for all of them are clothed in scarlet.
22 She makes coverings for her bed;
she is clothed in fine linen and purple.
23 Her husband is respected at the city gate,
where he takes his seat among the elders of the land.
24 She makes linen garments and sells them,
and supplies the merchants with sashes.

[a] 3 Or *wealth* [b] 10 Verses 10-31 are an acrostic poem, the verses of which begin with the successive letters of the Hebrew alphabet.

25 She is clothed with strength and dignity;
she can laugh at the days to come.
26 She speaks with wisdom,
and faithful instruction is on her tongue.
27 She watches over the affairs of her household
and does not eat the bread of idleness.
28 Her children arise and call her blessed;
her husband also, and he praises her:
29 "Many women do noble things,
but you surpass them all."
30 Charm is deceptive, and beauty is fleeting;
but a woman who fears the LORD is to be praised.
31 Honor her for all that her hands have done,
and let her works bring her praise at the city gate.

ECCLESIASTES

Solomon wrote Proverbs when he was middle-aged and Song of Songs in his younger days. Ecclesiastes—which is traditionally thought to be authored by Solomon—offered his reflections near the end of his life. He looked back over the endeavors to which he had devoted his life, only to declare that they were all meaningless. It's possible the tenor of the book, vainglory and its emptiness, is how Solomon experienced life after he had turned to idols and was no longer serving the God of Israel. The key word *meaningless*, then, could reflect an attempt to secure lasting happiness apart from God.

Solomon called himself "the Teacher" throughout, perhaps as a way to establish spiritual authority rather than relying on political authority as king.

Even though Ecclesiastes contains some of the Bible's most well-known quotations and reflections on life that have resonated with untold people throughout the centuries, some people have wondered why it is in the Bible at all. It is not a book of hope, not a book that stirs the heart to praise, nor a book that elevates the work of God in the world. The Teacher's meditation on death in 3:20–21, for instance, equates the death of humans with the death of animals.

To give one example of Solomon's reflections on the meaningless nature of certain aspects of life, consider his thoughts about riches. He understood the subject well considering the preponderance of riches he had accumulated. His verdict? "Whoever loves money never has enough" (5:10). He warned that for those who have an abundance of riches, sleep will be fleeting because of worries about the security of their possessions. Further, he reasoned that he came naked from his mother's womb and would take nothing with him into the afterlife. Solomon was the original "you can't take it with you" realist.

Solomon's reflections on life led him to an exhortation for all young people who listen: "Remember your Creator in the days of your youth" (12:1). In a thread of arresting images, he pleaded with his listeners to seek the Lord before it was too late. Before they knew what had happened, the days of their youth would be gone, and they would be older and full of regret. He concluded "the matter" with a straightforward charge: "Fear God and keep his commandments, for this is the duty of all mankind" (12:13). And don't forget judgment is coming.

The brevity of life, as well as the inherent futility of many of our pursuits, should drive us to fervent and constant prayer. Rather than being overcome with emptiness, however, we should focus on the eternal. We can truly enjoy life when we remember there is "a season for every activity under the heavens" (3:1), and that all seasons are under God's control.

Remembering the brevity of life gives us a seriousness and urgency about life that drives us to pray. When we remember that we are living a short life "under the sun," we focus on what actually matters in life. When we do this, we will recognize the limitations of our own efforts and be driven to prayer.

PRAYING SCRIPTURE

Ecclesiastes 1

The Teacher loved learning but concluded that his human wisdom led only to futility: "Utterly meaningless! Everything is meaningless" (verse 2). His lifelong search ended this way because somewhere he lost God's perspective and sought knowledge for its own sake.

If you ever feel that life is empty, that there is no purpose in existence, implore God to bring his perspective to you, and be filled with his love.

EVERYTHING IS MEANINGLESS

1 The words of the Teacher,[a] son of David, king in Jerusalem:

2 "Meaningless! Meaningless!"
says the Teacher.
"Utterly meaningless!
Everything is meaningless."

3 What do people gain from all their labors
at which they toil under the sun?
4 Generations come and generations go,
but the earth remains forever.
5 The sun rises and the sun sets,
and hurries back to where it rises.
6 The wind blows to the south
and turns to the north;
round and round it goes,
ever returning on its course.
7 All streams flow into the sea,
yet the sea is never full.
To the place the streams come from,
there they return again.
8 All things are wearisome,
more than one can say.
The eye never has enough of seeing,
nor the ear its fill of hearing.
9 What has been will be again,
what has been done will be done again;
there is nothing new under the sun.
10 Is there anything of which one can say,
"Look! This is something new"?
It was here already, long ago;
it was here before our time.
11 No one remembers the former generations,
and even those yet to come
will not be remembered
by those who follow them.

WISDOM IS MEANINGLESS

12 I, the Teacher, was king over Israel in Jerusalem. 13 I applied my
mind to study and to explore by wisdom all that is done under the
heavens. What a heavy burden God has laid on mankind! 14 I have seen
all the things that are done under the sun; all of them are meaningless,
a chasing after the wind.

15 What is crooked cannot be straightened;
what is lacking cannot be counted.

16 I said to myself, "Look, I have increased in wisdom more than
anyone who has ruled over Jerusalem before me; I have experienced
much of wisdom and knowledge." 17 Then I applied myself to the un-
derstanding of wisdom, and also of madness and folly, but I learned
that this, too, is a chasing after the wind.

[a] 1 Or *the leader of the assembly*; also in verses 2 and 12

18 For with much wisdom comes much sorrow;
the more knowledge, the more grief.

PLEASURES ARE MEANINGLESS

2 I said to myself, "Come now, I will test you with pleasure to find out
what is good." But that also proved to be meaningless. 2 "Laugh-
ter," I said, "is madness. And what does pleasure accomplish?" 3 I tried
cheering myself with wine, and embracing folly — my mind still guid-
ing me with wisdom. I wanted to see what was good for people to do
under the heavens during the few days of their lives.

4 I undertook great projects: I built houses for myself and planted
vineyards. 5 I made gardens and parks and planted all kinds of fruit
trees in them. 6 I made reservoirs to water groves of flourishing trees.
7 I bought male and female slaves and had other slaves who were born
in my house. I also owned more herds and flocks than anyone in Jeru-
salem before me. 8 I amassed silver and gold for myself, and the trea-
sure of kings and provinces. I acquired male and female singers, and
a harem[a] as well — the delights of a man's heart. 9 I became greater by
far than anyone in Jerusalem before me. In all this my wisdom stayed
with me.

10 I denied myself nothing my eyes desired;
I refused my heart no pleasure.
My heart took delight in all my labor,
and this was the reward for all my toil.
11 Yet when I surveyed all that my hands had done
and what I had toiled to achieve,
everything was meaningless, a chasing after the wind;
nothing was gained under the sun.

WISDOM AND FOLLY ARE MEANINGLESS

12 Then I turned my thoughts to consider wisdom,
and also madness and folly.
What more can the king's successor do
than what has already been done?
13 I saw that wisdom is better than folly,
just as light is better than darkness.
14 The wise have eyes in their heads,
while the fool walks in the darkness;
but I came to realize
that the same fate overtakes them both.

15 Then I said to myself,

"The fate of the fool will overtake me also.
What then do I gain by being wise?"
I said to myself,
"This too is meaningless."
16 For the wise, like the fool, will not be long remembered;
the days have already come when both have been
forgotten.
Like the fool, the wise too must die!

[a] 8 The meaning of the Hebrew for this phrase is uncertain.

PRAYING SCRIPTURE

Ecclesiastes 2

Many people live as if pleasure will somehow, finally satisfy them, but it only leaves them wanting. The Teacher even found laughter to be madness and mirth to be futile. Like "chasing after the wind" (verse 11).

The temptation is to settle for lesser pleasures than God's best. Pray that your pursuit of God will keep pleasure in its proper place.

TOIL IS MEANINGLESS

17So I hated life, because the work that is done under the sun was
grievous to me. All of it is meaningless, a chasing after the wind. 18I
hated all the things I had toiled for under the sun, because I must leave
them to the one who comes after me. 19And who knows whether that
person will be wise or foolish? Yet they will have control over all the
fruit of my toil into which I have poured my effort and skill under the
sun. This too is meaningless. 20So my heart began to despair over all
my toilsome labor under the sun. 21For a person may labor with wis-
dom, knowledge and skill, and then they must leave all they own to
another who has not toiled for it. This too is meaningless and a great
misfortune. 22What do people get for all the toil and anxious striving
with which they labor under the sun? 23All their days their work is grief
and pain; even at night their minds do not rest. This too is meaningless.
24A person can do nothing better than to eat and drink and find sat-
isfaction in their own toil. This too, I see, is from the hand of God, 25for
without him, who can eat or find enjoyment? 26To the person who pleases
him, God gives wisdom, knowledge and happiness, but to the sinner he
gives the task of gathering and storing up wealth to hand it over to the
one who pleases God. This too is meaningless, a chasing after the wind.

A TIME FOR EVERYTHING

3 There is a time for everything,
and a season for every activity under the heavens:

2 a time to be born and a time to die,
a time to plant and a time to uproot,
3 a time to kill and a time to heal,
a time to tear down and a time to build,
4 a time to weep and a time to laugh,
a time to mourn and a time to dance,
5 a time to scatter stones and a time to gather them,
a time to embrace and a time to refrain from embracing,
6 a time to search and a time to give up,
a time to keep and a time to throw away,
7 a time to tear and a time to mend,
a time to be silent and a time to speak,
8 a time to love and a time to hate,
a time for war and a time for peace.

9What do workers gain from their toil? 10I have seen the burden God
has laid on the human race. 11He has made everything beautiful in
its time. He has also set eternity in the human heart; yet[a] no one can
fathom what God has done from beginning to end. 12I know that there
is nothing better for people than to be happy and to do good while they
live. 13That each of them may eat and drink, and find satisfaction in all
their toil — this is the gift of God. 14I know that everything God does
will endure forever; nothing can be added to it and nothing taken from
it. God does it so that people will fear him.

15 Whatever is has already been,
and what will be has been before;
and God will call the past to account.[b]

[a] 11 *Or also placed ignorance in the human heart, so that* [b] 15 Or *God calls back the past*

PRAYING SCRIPTURE

Ecclesiastes 3

In one of the most beautiful passages ever written, the Teacher reminds us that life is comprised of seasons. Much of our frustration in life comes from not recognizing the cycles, often feeling trapped in the difficult times of weeping, mourning and death.

We do well to remember a single word from verse 1: "season." Ask God to help you remember that seasons change, but God remains the same.

16 And I saw something else under the sun:

In the place of judgment — wickedness was there,
  in the place of justice — wickedness was there.

17 I said to myself,

"God will bring into judgment
  both the righteous and the wicked,
for there will be a time for every activity,
  a time to judge every deed."

18 I also said to myself, "As for humans, God tests them so that they
may see that they are like the animals. 19 Surely the fate of human be-
ings is like that of the animals; the same fate awaits them both: As
one dies, so dies the other. All have the same breath[a]; humans have
no advantage over animals. Everything is meaningless. 20 All go to the
same place; all come from dust, and to dust all return. 21 Who knows
if the human spirit rises upward and if the spirit of the animal goes
down into the earth?"
22 So I saw that there is nothing better for a person than to enjoy their
work, because that is their lot. For who can bring them to see what will
happen after them?

OPPRESSION, TOIL, FRIENDLESSNESS

4 Again I looked and saw all the oppression that was taking place
under the sun:

I saw the tears of the oppressed —
  and they have no comforter;
power was on the side of their oppressors —
  and they have no comforter.
2 And I declared that the dead,
  who had already died,
are happier than the living,
  who are still alive.
3 But better than both
  is the one who has never been born,
who has not seen the evil
  that is done under the sun.

4 And I saw that all toil and all achievement spring from one person's
envy of another. This too is meaningless, a chasing after the wind.

5 Fools fold their hands
  and ruin themselves.
6 Better one handful with tranquillity
  than two handfuls with toil
  and chasing after the wind.

7 Again I saw something meaningless under the sun:

8 There was a man all alone;
  he had neither son nor brother.
There was no end to his toil,
  yet his eyes were not content with his wealth.

[a] 19 Or *spirit*

PRAYING SCRIPTURE

Ecclesiastes 4

Seeing the injustice that surrounds us can be overwhelming, but the Teacher ensured we don't look away. He saw "the tears of the oppressed" and invited us to consider: "They have no comforter" (verse 1). Their oppressors had power over them.

How often are we guilty of looking away when challenged by injustice? Ask God to make you attentive and responsive to injustices.

"For whom am I toiling," he asked,
"and why am I depriving myself of enjoyment?"
This too is meaningless —
a miserable business!

9 Two are better than one,
because they have a good return for their labor:
10 If either of them falls down,
one can help the other up.
But pity anyone who falls
and has no one to help them up.
11 Also, if two lie down together, they will keep warm.
But how can one keep warm alone?
12 Though one may be overpowered,
two can defend themselves.
A cord of three strands is not quickly broken.

ADVANCEMENT IS MEANINGLESS

13 Better a poor but wise youth than an old but foolish king who no
longer knows how to heed a warning. 14 The youth may have come from
prison to the kingship, or he may have been born in poverty within his
kingdom. 15 I saw that all who lived and walked under the sun followed
the youth, the king's successor. 16 There was no end to all the people
who were before them. But those who came later were not pleased
with the successor. This too is meaningless, a chasing after the wind.

FULFILL YOUR VOW TO GOD

5[a] Guard your steps when you go to the house of God. Go near to
listen rather than to offer the sacrifice of fools, who do not know
that they do wrong.

2 Do not be quick with your mouth,
do not be hasty in your heart
to utter anything before God.
God is in heaven
and you are on earth,
so let your words be few.
3 A dream comes when there are many cares,
and many words mark the speech of a fool.

4 When you make a vow to God, do not delay to fulfill it. He has no
pleasure in fools; fulfill your vow. 5 It is better not to make a vow than
to make one and not fulfill it. 6 Do not let your mouth lead you into sin.
And do not protest to the temple messenger, "My vow was a mistake."
Why should God be angry at what you say and destroy the work of your
hands? 7 Much dreaming and many words are meaningless. Therefore
fear God.

RICHES ARE MEANINGLESS

8 If you see the poor oppressed in a district, and justice and rights
denied, do not be surprised at such things; for one official is eyed by a
higher one, and over them both are others higher still. 9 The increase
from the land is taken by all; the king himself profits from the fields.

PRAYING SCRIPTURE

Ecclesiastes 5

Contentment is one of God's good gifts. The Teacher commended those who worked hard, affirming that it is good and right for people to enjoy the fruits of their labor (see verse 18). But, he warned, those who love money will not be satisfied even if they accumulate more.

Is your life marked by contentment? Ask God to help you enjoy the fruit of your labor, rejoicing in his provision.

[a] In Hebrew texts 5:1 is numbered 4:17, and 5:2-20 is numbered 5:1-19.

10 Whoever loves money never has enough;
whoever loves wealth is never satisfied with their income.
This too is meaningless.

11 As goods increase,
so do those who consume them.
And what benefit are they to the owners
except to feast their eyes on them?

12 The sleep of a laborer is sweet,
whether they eat little or much,
but as for the rich, their abundance
permits them no sleep.

13 I have seen a grievous evil under the sun:

wealth hoarded to the harm of its owners,
14 or wealth lost through some misfortune,
so that when they have children
there is nothing left for them to inherit.
15 Everyone comes naked from their mother's womb,
and as everyone comes, so they depart.
They take nothing from their toil
that they can carry in their hands.

16 This too is a grievous evil:

As everyone comes, so they depart,
and what do they gain,
since they toil for the wind?
17 All their days they eat in darkness,
with great frustration, affliction and anger.

18 This is what I have observed to be good: that it is appropriate for a
person to eat, to drink and to find satisfaction in their toilsome labor
under the sun during the few days of life God has given them — for this
is their lot. 19 Moreover, when God gives someone wealth and posses-
sions, and the ability to enjoy them, to accept their lot and be happy
in their toil — this is a gift of God. 20 They seldom reflect on the days
of their life, because God keeps them occupied with gladness of heart.

6 I have seen another evil under the sun, and it weighs heavily on
mankind: 2 God gives some people wealth, possessions and honor,
so that they lack nothing their hearts desire, but God does not grant
them the ability to enjoy them, and strangers enjoy them instead. This
is meaningless, a grievous evil.
3 A man may have a hundred children and live many years; yet no mat-
ter how long he lives, if he cannot enjoy his prosperity and does not
receive proper burial, I say that a stillborn child is better off than he.
4 It comes without meaning, it departs in darkness, and in darkness its
name is shrouded. 5 Though it never saw the sun or knew anything, it has
more rest than does that man — 6 even if he lives a thousand years twice
over but fails to enjoy his prosperity. Do not all go to the same place?

7 Everyone's toil is for their mouth,
yet their appetite is never satisfied.
8 What advantage have the wise over fools?
What do the poor gain
by knowing how to conduct themselves before others?

PRAYING SCRIPTURE

Ecclesiastes 6

The Teacher's feelings of futility were displayed as he wrestled with the meaning of life. He realized life was passing but had no confidence in what came next (see verse 12). The wealthy person might lose everything or live a long life, but death comes; possessions are left behind.

Do you ever feel that life is futile? God's Word assures us of our purpose, so take all your feelings of emptiness to him.

9 Better what the eye sees
than the roving of the appetite.
This too is meaningless,
a chasing after the wind.

10 Whatever exists has already been named,
and what humanity is has been known;
no one can contend
with someone who is stronger.
11 The more the words,
the less the meaning,
and how does that profit anyone?

12 For who knows what is good for a person in life, during the few and
meaningless days they pass through like a shadow? Who can tell them
what will happen under the sun after they are gone?

WISDOM

7 A good name is better than fine perfume,
and the day of death better than the day of birth.
2 It is better to go to a house of mourning
than to go to a house of feasting,
for death is the destiny of everyone;
the living should take this to heart.
3 Frustration is better than laughter,
because a sad face is good for the heart.
4 The heart of the wise is in the house of mourning,
but the heart of fools is in the house of pleasure.
5 It is better to heed the rebuke of a wise person
than to listen to the song of fools.
6 Like the crackling of thorns under the pot,
so is the laughter of fools.
This too is meaningless.
7 Extortion turns a wise person into a fool,
and a bribe corrupts the heart.

8 The end of a matter is better than its beginning,
and patience is better than pride.
9 Do not be quickly provoked in your spirit,
for anger resides in the lap of fools.
10 Do not say, "Why were the old days better than these?"
For it is not wise to ask such questions.

11 Wisdom, like an inheritance, is a good thing
and benefits those who see the sun.
12 Wisdom is a shelter
as money is a shelter,
but the advantage of knowledge is this:
Wisdom preserves those who have it.

13 Consider what God has done:

Who can straighten
what he has made crooked?
14 When times are good, be happy;
but when times are bad, consider this:

PRAYING SCRIPTURE

Ecclesiastes 7

Gaining wisdom comes at a cost. The heart of the fool is glad, but that of the wise holds mourning. The Teacher also warned that the wise face unique temptations like bribery, which "corrupts the heart" (verse 7). True wisdom needs practical application, not merely a mental library.

Are you facing a challenge for which you need wisdom? Ask God for it, knowing it might not be an easy road.

God has made the one
as well as the other.
Therefore, no one can discover
anything about their future.

15 In this meaningless life of mine I have seen both of these:

the righteous perishing in their righteousness,
and the wicked living long in their wickedness.
16 Do not be overrighteous,
neither be overwise —
why destroy yourself?
17 Do not be overwicked,
and do not be a fool —
why die before your time?
18 It is good to grasp the one
and not let go of the other.
Whoever fears God will avoid all extremes.[a]

19 Wisdom makes one wise person more powerful
than ten rulers in a city.

20 Indeed, there is no one on earth who is righteous,
no one who does what is right and never sins.

21 Do not pay attention to every word people say,
or you may hear your servant cursing you —
22 for you know in your heart
that many times you yourself have cursed others.

23 All this I tested by wisdom and I said,

"I am determined to be wise" —
but this was beyond me.
24 Whatever exists is far off and most profound —
who can discover it?
25 So I turned my mind to understand,
to investigate and to search out wisdom and the scheme of things
and to understand the stupidity of wickedness
and the madness of folly.
26 I find more bitter than death
the woman who is a snare,
whose heart is a trap
and whose hands are chains.
The man who pleases God will escape her,
but the sinner she will ensnare.

27 "Look," says the Teacher,[b] "this is what I have discovered:

"Adding one thing to another to discover the scheme of things —
28 while I was still searching
but not finding —
I found one upright man among a thousand,
but not one upright woman among them all.

---

[a] 18 Or *will follow them both* [b] 27 Or *the leader of the assembly*

29 This only have I found:
God created mankind upright,
but they have gone in search of many schemes."

PRAYING SCRIPTURE

Ecclesiastes 8

In this chapter, the Teacher contemplated one of the most persistent mysteries of life: Why do bad things happen to good people and vice versa? But his solution—eat, drink and be glad—was as empty as the problem vexing him.

Does it bother you when the cosmic scales seem out of balance? Nothing God does is in vain, so commit to fully trust him.

8 Who is like the wise?
Who knows the explanation of things?
A person's wisdom brightens their face
and changes its hard appearance.

OBEY THE KING

2 Obey the king's command, I say, because you took an oath before
God. 3 Do not be in a hurry to leave the king's presence. Do not stand up
for a bad cause, for he will do whatever he pleases. 4 Since a king's word
is supreme, who can say to him, "What are you doing?"

5 Whoever obeys his command will come to no harm,
and the wise heart will know the proper time and procedure.
6 For there is a proper time and procedure for every matter,
though a person may be weighed down by misery.

7 Since no one knows the future,
who can tell someone else what is to come?
8 As no one has power over the wind to contain it,
so[a] no one has power over the time of their death.
As no one is discharged in time of war,
so wickedness will not release those who practice it.

9 All this I saw, as I applied my mind to everything done under the
sun. There is a time when a man lords it over others to his own[b] hurt.
10 Then too, I saw the wicked buried—those who used to come and go
from the holy place and receive praise[c] in the city where they did this.
This too is meaningless.
11 When the sentence for a crime is not quickly carried out, people's
hearts are filled with schemes to do wrong. 12 Although a wicked per-
son who commits a hundred crimes may live a long time, I know that
it will go better with those who fear God, who are reverent before him.
13 Yet because the wicked do not fear God, it will not go well with them,
and their days will not lengthen like a shadow.
14 There is something else meaningless that occurs on earth: the righ-
teous who get what the wicked deserve, and the wicked who get what
the righteous deserve. This too, I say, is meaningless. 15 So I commend
the enjoyment of life, because there is nothing better for a person un-
der the sun than to eat and drink and be glad. Then joy will accompany
them in their toil all the days of the life God has given them under the
sun.
16 When I applied my mind to know wisdom and to observe the labor
that is done on earth—people getting no sleep day or night— 17 then
I saw all that God has done. No one can comprehend what goes on
under the sun. Despite all their efforts to search it out, no one can
discover its meaning. Even if the wise claim they know, they cannot
really comprehend it.

[a] 8 Or *over the human spirit to retain it, / and so* [b] 9 Or *to their*
[c] 10 Some Hebrew manuscripts and Septuagint (Aquila); most Hebrew manuscripts *and are forgotten*

A COMMON DESTINY FOR ALL

9 So I reflected on all this and concluded that the righteous and
the wise and what they do are in God's hands, but no one knows
whether love or hate awaits them. 2All share a common destiny — the
righteous and the wicked, the good and the bad,[a] the clean and the
unclean, those who offer sacrifices and those who do not.

As it is with the good,
  so with the sinful;
as it is with those who take oaths,
  so with those who are afraid to take them.

3This is the evil in everything that happens under the sun: The same
destiny overtakes all. The hearts of people, moreover, are full of evil
and there is madness in their hearts while they live, and afterward
they join the dead. 4Anyone who is among the living has hope[b] — even
a live dog is better off than a dead lion!

5For the living know that they will die,
  but the dead know nothing;
they have no further reward,
  and even their name is forgotten.
6Their love, their hate
  and their jealousy have long since vanished;
never again will they have a part
  in anything that happens under the sun.

7Go, eat your food with gladness, and drink your wine with a joyful
heart, for God has already approved what you do. 8Always be clothed in
white, and always anoint your head with oil. 9Enjoy life with your wife,
whom you love, all the days of this meaningless life that God has given
you under the sun — all your meaningless days. For this is your lot in life
and in your toilsome labor under the sun. 10Whatever your hand finds to
do, do it with all your might, for in the realm of the dead, where you are
going, there is neither working nor planning nor knowledge nor wisdom.

11I have seen something else under the sun:

The race is not to the swift
  or the battle to the strong,
nor does food come to the wise
  or wealth to the brilliant
  or favor to the learned;
but time and chance happen to them all.

12Moreover, no one knows when their hour will come:

As fish are caught in a cruel net,
  or birds are taken in a snare,
so people are trapped by evil times
  that fall unexpectedly upon them.

WISDOM BETTER THAN FOLLY

13I also saw under the sun this example of wisdom that greatly im-
pressed me: 14There was once a small city with only a few people in

[a] 2 Septuagint (Aquila), Vulgate and Syriac; Hebrew does not have *and the bad.* [b] 4 Or *What then is to be chosen? With all who live, there is hope*

PRAYING SCRIPTURE

Ecclesiastes 9

Here the Teacher reverted to one of his favorite themes: human mortality. The righteous and the wicked, the clean and unclean, the good and the sinner, the ones who sacrifice and those who don't all die. Everyone "join[s] the dead" (verse 3). The Teacher was hopeless because he'd forgotten the Lord.

The Teacher might have been hopeless, but we can call on Jesus in whom is our hope.

it. And a powerful king came against it, surrounded it and built huge
siege works against it. [15]Now there lived in that city a man poor but
wise, and he saved the city by his wisdom. But nobody remembered
that poor man. [16]So I said, "Wisdom is better than strength." But the
poor man's wisdom is despised, and his words are no longer heeded.

17 The quiet words of the wise are more to be heeded
than the shouts of a ruler of fools.
18 Wisdom is better than weapons of war,
but one sinner destroys much good.

10 As dead flies give perfume a bad smell,
so a little folly outweighs wisdom and honor.
2 The heart of the wise inclines to the right,
but the heart of the fool to the left.
3 Even as fools walk along the road,
they lack sense
and show everyone how stupid they are.
4 If a ruler's anger rises against you,
do not leave your post;
calmness can lay great offenses to rest.

5 There is an evil I have seen under the sun,
the sort of error that arises from a ruler:
6 Fools are put in many high positions,
while the rich occupy the low ones.
7 I have seen slaves on horseback,
while princes go on foot like slaves.
8 Whoever digs a pit may fall into it;
whoever breaks through a wall may be bitten by a snake.
9 Whoever quarries stones may be injured by them;
whoever splits logs may be endangered by them.

10 If the ax is dull
and its edge unsharpened,
more strength is needed,
but skill will bring success.

11 If a snake bites before it is charmed,
the charmer receives no fee.

12 Words from the mouth of the wise are gracious,
but fools are consumed by their own lips.
13 At the beginning their words are folly;
at the end they are wicked madness —
14 and fools multiply words.

No one knows what is coming —
who can tell someone else what will happen after them?

15 The toil of fools wearies them;
they do not know the way to town.

16 Woe to the land whose king was a servant[a]
and whose princes feast in the morning.
17 Blessed is the land whose king is of noble birth

PRAYING SCRIPTURE

Ecclesiastes 10

In this chapter, the Teacher used a series of contrasts to distinguish wisdom and folly, with multiple warnings about the latter. Even a little folly lowers the respect for a wise man the way dead flies in perfume ruin its smell (see verse 1). Fools talk more than they should but make little sense for all they say.

One can hardly scratch the surface of Scripture without seeing the need to pray for wisdom.

[a] 16 Or *king is a child*

and whose princes eat at a proper time —
for strength and not for drunkenness.

18 Through laziness, the rafters sag;
because of idle hands, the house leaks.

19 A feast is made for laughter,
wine makes life merry,
and money is the answer for everything.

20 Do not revile the king even in your thoughts,
or curse the rich in your bedroom,
because a bird in the sky may carry your words,
and a bird on the wing may report what you say.

INVEST IN MANY VENTURES

11 Ship your grain across the sea;
after many days you may receive a return.
2 Invest in seven ventures, yes, in eight;
you do not know what disaster may come upon the land.

3 If clouds are full of water,
they pour rain on the earth.
Whether a tree falls to the south or to the north,
in the place where it falls, there it will lie.
4 Whoever watches the wind will not plant;
whoever looks at the clouds will not reap.

5 As you do not know the path of the wind,
or how the body is formed[a] in a mother's womb,
so you cannot understand the work of God,
the Maker of all things.

6 Sow your seed in the morning,
and at evening let your hands not be idle,
for you do not know which will succeed,
whether this or that,
or whether both will do equally well.

REMEMBER YOUR CREATOR WHILE YOUNG

7 Light is sweet,
and it pleases the eyes to see the sun.
8 However many years anyone may live,
let them enjoy them all.
But let them remember the days of darkness,
for there will be many.
Everything to come is meaningless.

9 You who are young, be happy while you are young,
and let your heart give you joy in the days of your youth.
Follow the ways of your heart
and whatever your eyes see,
but know that for all these things
God will bring you into judgment.
10 So then, banish anxiety from your heart

[a] 5 Or *know how life* (or *the spirit*) / *enters the body being formed*

PRAYING SCRIPTURE

Ecclesiastes 11

The Teacher echoed some of Job's themes, reminding us that we don't know everything. Whether clouds, rain, the wind, or the secrets of how a child develops in the womb, "You cannot understand the work of God, the Maker of all things" (verse 5).

God's ways are as far beyond ours as the expanse of the universe, but we can learn from them. Ask God for the wisdom to discern his hand at work.

and cast off the troubles of your body,
for youth and vigor are meaningless.

PRAYING SCRIPTURE

Ecclesiastes 12

In this well-known and well-loved chapter, the Teacher encouraged people to seek God while they were young, before adulthood and age brought unending challenges. Sadly, he then reverted to his familiar refrain, "Meaningless! Meaningless!" (verse 8).

Hopelessness is like poison, killing one's spiritual vitality. Call on God in faith. Trust him. Hope in him to give your life meaning. That is the essence of wisdom.

12 Remember your Creator
in the days of your youth,
before the days of trouble come
and the years approach when you will say,
"I find no pleasure in them" —
2 before the sun and the light
and the moon and the stars grow dark,
and the clouds return after the rain;
3 when the keepers of the house tremble,
and the strong men stoop,
when the grinders cease because they are few,
and those looking through the windows grow dim;
4 when the doors to the street are closed
and the sound of grinding fades;
when people rise up at the sound of birds,
but all their songs grow faint;
5 when people are afraid of heights
and of dangers in the streets;
when the almond tree blossoms
and the grasshopper drags itself along
and desire no longer is stirred.
Then people go to their eternal home
and mourners go about the streets.

6 Remember him — before the silver cord is severed,
and the golden bowl is broken;
before the pitcher is shattered at the spring,
and the wheel broken at the well,
7 and the dust returns to the ground it came from,
and the spirit returns to God who gave it.

8 "Meaningless! Meaningless!" says the Teacher.[a]
"Everything is meaningless!"

THE CONCLUSION OF THE MATTER

9 Not only was the Teacher wise, but he also imparted knowledge to
the people. He pondered and searched out and set in order many prov-
erbs. 10 The Teacher searched to find just the right words, and what he
wrote was upright and true.

11 The words of the wise are like goads, their collected sayings like
firmly embedded nails — given by one shepherd.[b] 12 Be warned, my
son, of anything in addition to them.

Of making many books there is no end, and much study wearies the body.

13 Now all has been heard;
here is the conclusion of the matter:
Fear God and keep his commandments,
for this is the duty of all mankind.
14 For God will bring every deed into judgment,
including every hidden thing,
whether it is good or evil.

---

[a] 8 Or *the leader of the assembly*; also in verses 9 and 10 [b] 11 Or *Shepherd*

SONG OF SONGS

The events in Song of Songs take place in the days of Solomon's youth. As the first line implies, it is meant to be the love song that exceeds every other love song ever written. It pictures the wooing and courting of the two main characters in the book—Solomon and his soon-to-be bride, a shepherdess.

The songs begin before the wedding. The bride sings of her love and expectations for her future husband. She looks forward to becoming his wife and wonders that he should love her. He sings of his love and sexual desire for her. He loves her and finds her to be lovely.

As the book moves from songs during the engagement to songs about the marriage bed, the sexual ethic becomes clear. The bride has reserved herself for her future husband. While Solomon would eventually, sadly, adopt cultural views on polygamous marriage and pagan views by marrying politically advantageous, foreign wives, his song paints the beautiful picture of the pure love a husband and wife should have for each other.

Traditionally, Song of Songs has been interpreted both as actual history and as an allegory, often at the same time. It is the literal story of a woman betrothed to Solomon. The two are deeply in love, as shown through the series of songs and romantic comments to each other, and they long for the physical relationship marriage hallows. Many Christians throughout the centuries have also read Song of Songs as an allegory of the relationship between Christ and his church. While there are good reasons for choosing the literal over the allegorical reading, it is good and spiritually healthy for us to see our human relationships pointing to the deep relationship we enjoy with the Lord Jesus. If a husband and wife rejoice in each other, how much more does Christ rejoice over his people, and how much more should we celebrate the love of Christ for us?

It is fitting that there is an entire book of the Bible devoted to celebrating marriage. Christian marriages point to the relationship between Christ and his church. Loving and healthy marriages are a source of great joy to the husband and wife, as well as to the people who surround them. Strong marriages lead to healthier churches and a stabler society. Christians should pray for their own marriages and for the health and joy of the marriages of those around them.

Song of Songs should drive us to prayer on behalf of our own marriage or the marriages of people we know. Prayer is the air that keeps relationships breathing. It is in prayer that husbands and wives dedicate themselves to each other and to God over and over. Prayer keeps hearts in love with spouses and love pure between dating or engaged couples. There is no era in which marriage relationships are easy; prayer is needed as much now as in the ancient days of Solomon and the woman who was the object of his delight.

PRAYING SCRIPTURE

Song of Songs 1

Solomon's song celebrates the beauty of marital love. Exchanged compliments and expressions of love fill this chapter. The lover and her beloved display the passion of a woman and man thoroughly enamored with each other.

If you are married or hope to be one day, ask God to let you give and receive the love shown here.

1 Solomon's Song of Songs.

SHE[a]

[2] Let him kiss me with the kisses of his mouth —
for your love is more delightful than wine.
[3] Pleasing is the fragrance of your perfumes;
your name is like perfume poured out.
No wonder the young women love you!
[4] Take me away with you — let us hurry!
Let the king bring me into his chambers.

FRIENDS

We rejoice and delight in you[b];
we will praise your love more than wine.

SHE

How right they are to adore you!

[5] Dark am I, yet lovely,
daughters of Jerusalem,
dark like the tents of Kedar,
like the tent curtains of Solomon.[c]
[6] Do not stare at me because I am dark,
because I am darkened by the sun.
My mother's sons were angry with me
and made me take care of the vineyards;
my own vineyard I had to neglect.
[7] Tell me, you whom I love,
where you graze your flock
and where you rest your sheep at midday.
Why should I be like a veiled woman
beside the flocks of your friends?

FRIENDS

[8] If you do not know, most beautiful of women,
follow the tracks of the sheep
and graze your young goats
by the tents of the shepherds.

HE

[9] I liken you, my darling, to a mare
among Pharaoh's chariot horses.
[10] Your cheeks are beautiful with earrings,
your neck with strings of jewels.
[11] We will make you earrings of gold,
studded with silver.

SHE

[12] While the king was at his table,
my perfume spread its fragrance.
[13] My beloved is to me a sachet of myrrh
resting between my breasts.

---

[a] The main male and female speakers (identified primarily on the basis of the gender of the relevant Hebrew forms) are indicated by the captions *He* and *She* respectively. The words of others are marked *Friends.* In some instances the divisions and their captions are debatable. [b] 4 The Hebrew is masculine singular. [c] 5 Or *Salma*

14 My beloved is to me a cluster of henna blossoms
from the vineyards of En Gedi.

HE

15 How beautiful you are, my darling!
Oh, how beautiful!
Your eyes are doves.

SHE

16 How handsome you are, my beloved!
Oh, how charming!
And our bed is verdant.

HE

17 The beams of our house are cedars;
our rafters are firs.

SHE[a]

2 I am a rose[b] of Sharon,
a lily of the valleys.

HE

2 Like a lily among thorns
is my darling among the young women.

SHE

3 Like an apple[c] tree among the trees of the forest
is my beloved among the young men.
I delight to sit in his shade,
and his fruit is sweet to my taste.
4 Let him lead me to the banquet hall,
and let his banner over me be love.
5 Strengthen me with raisins,
refresh me with apples,
for I am faint with love.
6 His left arm is under my head,
and his right arm embraces me.
7 Daughters of Jerusalem, I charge you
by the gazelles and by the does of the field:
Do not arouse or awaken love
until it so desires.

8 Listen! My beloved!
Look! Here he comes,
leaping across the mountains,
bounding over the hills.
9 My beloved is like a gazelle or a young stag.
Look! There he stands behind our wall,
gazing through the windows,
peering through the lattice.
10 My beloved spoke and said to me,
"Arise, my darling,
my beautiful one, come with me.
11 See! The winter is past;
the rains are over and gone.

[a] Or *He* [b] *1* Probably a member of the crocus family [c] *3* Or possibly *apricot*; here and elsewhere in Song of Songs

PRAYING SCRIPTURE

Song of Songs 2

Invoking examples from the created world, these songs mention mountains and hills, rain and flowers, gazelles and foxes—which are said to spoil the vineyards. The latter is an allusion to the things we might be tempted to overlook—habits, attitudes, sins—that end up causing damage.

Search your life for those "little foxes that ruin the vineyards," and ask God to "catch" them for your protection (verse 15).

12 Flowers appear on the earth;
the season of singing has come,
the cooing of doves
is heard in our land.
13 The fig tree forms its early fruit;
the blossoming vines spread their fragrance.
Arise, come, my darling;
my beautiful one, come with me."

HE

14 My dove in the clefts of the rock,
in the hiding places on the mountainside,
show me your face,
let me hear your voice;
for your voice is sweet,
and your face is lovely.
15 Catch for us the foxes,
the little foxes
that ruin the vineyards,
our vineyards that are in bloom.

SHE

16 My beloved is mine and I am his;
he browses among the lilies.
17 Until the day breaks
and the shadows flee,
turn, my beloved,
and be like a gazelle
or like a young stag
on the rugged hills.[a]

3 All night long on my bed
I looked for the one my heart loves;
I looked for him but did not find him.
2 I will get up now and go about the city,
through its streets and squares;
I will search for the one my heart loves.
So I looked for him but did not find him.
3 The watchmen found me
as they made their rounds in the city.
"Have you seen the one my heart loves?"
4 Scarcely had I passed them
when I found the one my heart loves.
I held him and would not let him go
till I had brought him to my mother's house,
to the room of the one who conceived me.
5 Daughters of Jerusalem, I charge you
by the gazelles and by the does of the field:
Do not arouse or awaken love
until it so desires.

6 Who is this coming up from the wilderness
like a column of smoke,
perfumed with myrrh and incense
made from all the spices of the merchant?

[a] 17 Or *the hills of Bether*

PRAYING SCRIPTURE

Song of Songs 3

In a night of fitful sleep, the lover arose to look for her beloved, identified as King Solomon. This passage is understood to describe their wedding day as King Solomon came forth in splendor accompanied by five dozen valiant men brandishing swords. This is not a chapel ceremony with suspendered groomsmen.

Whether you are married or not, think about how it feels to look for love. Ask God to help you love him with that sort of longing.

7 Look! It is Solomon's carriage,
escorted by sixty warriors,
the noblest of Israel,
8 all of them wearing the sword,
all experienced in battle,
each with his sword at his side,
prepared for the terrors of the night.
9 King Solomon made for himself the carriage;
he made it of wood from Lebanon.
10 Its posts he made of silver,
its base of gold.
Its seat was upholstered with purple,
its interior inlaid with love.
Daughters of Jerusalem, 11 come out,
and look, you daughters of Zion.
Look[a] on King Solomon wearing a crown,
the crown with which his mother crowned him
on the day of his wedding,
the day his heart rejoiced.

HE

4 How beautiful you are, my darling!
Oh, how beautiful!
Your eyes behind your veil are doves.
Your hair is like a flock of goats
descending from the hills of Gilead.
2 Your teeth are like a flock of sheep just shorn,
coming up from the washing.
Each has its twin;
not one of them is alone.
3 Your lips are like a scarlet ribbon;
your mouth is lovely.
Your temples behind your veil
are like the halves of a pomegranate.
4 Your neck is like the tower of David,
built with courses of stone[b];
on it hang a thousand shields,
all of them shields of warriors.
5 Your breasts are like two fawns,
like twin fawns of a gazelle
that browse among the lilies.
6 Until the day breaks
and the shadows flee,
I will go to the mountain of myrrh
and to the hill of incense.
7 You are altogether beautiful, my darling;
there is no flaw in you.

8 Come with me from Lebanon, my bride,
come with me from Lebanon.
Descend from the crest of Amana,
from the top of Senir, the summit of Hermon,

[a] 10,11 Or *interior lovingly inlaid / by the daughters of Jerusalem. / 11Come out, you daughters of Zion, / and look* [b] 4 The meaning of the Hebrew for this phrase is uncertain.

PRAYING SCRIPTURE

Song of Songs 4

This chapter shows Solomon following his own advice from Proverbs and delighting in the wife of his youth. His romantic comparisons to sheep, pomegranates and lilies sound odd to modern ears but were fitting in their agrarian time.

Strange sounding to us or not, this chapter reminds us of the importance that romance continues in marriage. If you are married, pray for new and creative ways to express your love.

from the lions' dens
and the mountain haunts of leopards.
9 You have stolen my heart, my sister, my bride;
you have stolen my heart
with one glance of your eyes,
with one jewel of your necklace.
10 How delightful is your love, my sister, my bride!
How much more pleasing is your love than wine,
and the fragrance of your perfume
more than any spice!
11 Your lips drop sweetness as the honeycomb, my bride;
milk and honey are under your tongue.
The fragrance of your garments
is like the fragrance of Lebanon.
12 You are a garden locked up, my sister, my bride;
you are a spring enclosed, a sealed fountain.
13 Your plants are an orchard of pomegranates
with choice fruits,
with henna and nard,
14 nard and saffron,
calamus and cinnamon,
with every kind of incense tree,
with myrrh and aloes
and all the finest spices.
15 You are[a] a garden fountain,
a well of flowing water
streaming down from Lebanon.

SHE

16 Awake, north wind,
and come, south wind!
Blow on my garden,
that its fragrance may spread everywhere.
Let my beloved come into his garden
and taste its choice fruits.

HE

5 I have come into my garden, my sister, my bride;
I have gathered my myrrh with my spice.
I have eaten my honeycomb and my honey;
I have drunk my wine and my milk.

FRIENDS

Eat, friends, and drink;
drink your fill of love.

SHE

2 I slept but my heart was awake.
Listen! My beloved is knocking:
"Open to me, my sister, my darling,
my dove, my flawless one.
My head is drenched with dew,
my hair with the dampness of the night."

PRAYING SCRIPTURE
Song of Songs 5

Many Christians through history have interpreted Solomon's Song as an allegory about the relationship between Christ and the church. The lover's superlative description of her beloved as "outstanding among ten thousand" (verse 10) lends itself to such a thought.

Jesus exceeds Solomon by ten thousand times ten thousand. Pray that God will elevate your thinking about Jesus as the bridegroom for the church. He is the most excellent of all.

[a] 15 Or *I am* (spoken by *She*)

3 I have taken off my robe —
must I put it on again?
I have washed my feet —
must I soil them again?
4 My beloved thrust his hand through the latch-opening;
my heart began to pound for him.
5 I arose to open for my beloved,
and my hands dripped with myrrh,
my fingers with flowing myrrh,
on the handles of the bolt.
6 I opened for my beloved,
but my beloved had left; he was gone.
My heart sank at his departure.[a]
I looked for him but did not find him.
I called him but he did not answer.
7 The watchmen found me
as they made their rounds in the city.
They beat me, they bruised me;
they took away my cloak,
those watchmen of the walls!
8 Daughters of Jerusalem, I charge you —
if you find my beloved,
what will you tell him?
Tell him I am faint with love.

FRIENDS

9 How is your beloved better than others,
most beautiful of women?
How is your beloved better than others,
that you so charge us?

SHE

10 My beloved is radiant and ruddy,
outstanding among ten thousand.
11 His head is purest gold;
his hair is wavy
and black as a raven.
12 His eyes are like doves
by the water streams,
washed in milk,
mounted like jewels.
13 His cheeks are like beds of spice
yielding perfume.
His lips are like lilies
dripping with myrrh.
14 His arms are rods of gold
set with topaz.
His body is like polished ivory
decorated with lapis lazuli.
15 His legs are pillars of marble
set on bases of pure gold.
His appearance is like Lebanon,
choice as its cedars.

[a] 6 Or *heart had gone out to him when he spoke*

16 His mouth is sweetness itself;
he is altogether lovely.
This is my beloved, this is my friend,
daughters of Jerusalem.

PRAYING SCRIPTURE

Song of Songs 6

One tender section of the song celebrates the simple act of going to a garden to gather lilies. Solomon's feeding of a flock, a daily routine, was lauded and brought the Shulamite to exclaim, "I am my beloved's and my beloved is mine" (verse 3).

Do you celebrate the simple things in a relationship, such as sharing dessert or watching your spouse enjoy a hobby? Seek love that celebrates such things.

FRIENDS

6 Where has your beloved gone,
most beautiful of women?
Which way did your beloved turn,
that we may look for him with you?

SHE

2 My beloved has gone down to his garden,
to the beds of spices,
to browse in the gardens
and to gather lilies.
3 I am my beloved's and my beloved is mine;
he browses among the lilies.

HE

4 You are as beautiful as Tirzah, my darling,
as lovely as Jerusalem,
as majestic as troops with banners.
5 Turn your eyes from me;
they overwhelm me.
Your hair is like a flock of goats
descending from Gilead.
6 Your teeth are like a flock of sheep
coming up from the washing.
Each has its twin,
not one of them is missing.
7 Your temples behind your veil
are like the halves of a pomegranate.
8 Sixty queens there may be,
and eighty concubines,
and virgins beyond number;
9 but my dove, my perfect one, is unique,
the only daughter of her mother,
the favorite of the one who bore her.
The young women saw her and called her blessed;
the queens and concubines praised her.

FRIENDS

10 Who is this that appears like the dawn,
fair as the moon, bright as the sun,
majestic as the stars in procession?

HE

11 I went down to the grove of nut trees
to look at the new growth in the valley,
to see if the vines had budded
or the pomegranates were in bloom.
12 Before I realized it,
my desire set me among the royal chariots of my people.[a]

[a] 12 Or *among the chariots of Amminadab*; or *among the chariots of the people of the prince*

FRIENDS

13 Come back, come back, O Shulammite;
come back, come back, that we may gaze on you!

HE

Why would you gaze on the Shulammite
as on the dance of Mahanaim?[a]

7 [b] How beautiful your sandaled feet,
O prince's daughter!
Your graceful legs are like jewels,
the work of an artist's hands.
2 Your navel is a rounded goblet
that never lacks blended wine.
Your waist is a mound of wheat
encircled by lilies.
3 Your breasts are like two fawns,
like twin fawns of a gazelle.
4 Your neck is like an ivory tower.
Your eyes are the pools of Heshbon
by the gate of Bath Rabbim.
Your nose is like the tower of Lebanon
looking toward Damascus.
5 Your head crowns you like Mount Carmel.
Your hair is like royal tapestry;
the king is held captive by its tresses.
6 How beautiful you are and how pleasing,
my love, with your delights!
7 Your stature is like that of the palm,
and your breasts like clusters of fruit.
8 I said, "I will climb the palm tree;
I will take hold of its fruit."
May your breasts be like clusters of grapes on the vine,
the fragrance of your breath like apples,
9 and your mouth like the best wine.

SHE

May the wine go straight to my beloved,
flowing gently over lips and teeth.[c]
10 I belong to my beloved,
and his desire is for me.
11 Come, my beloved, let us go to the countryside,
let us spend the night in the villages.[d]
12 Let us go early to the vineyards
to see if the vines have budded,
if their blossoms have opened,
and if the pomegranates are in bloom —
there I will give you my love.
13 The mandrakes send out their fragrance,
and at our door is every delicacy,
both new and old,
that I have stored up for you, my beloved.

PRAYING SCRIPTURE

Song of Songs 7

In a particularly descriptive chapter, Solomon and his bride each express their strong desire for the other's body. God created the human body so that one sex generally appeals visually to the other. This is not the sum of a marriage, but it is an important component.

Those who are married should give close attention to their physical relationship. Pray that God will always bring you closer together through it.

[a] *13* In Hebrew texts this verse (6:13) is numbered 7:1. [b] In Hebrew texts 7:1-13 is numbered 7:2-14. [c] *9* Septuagint, Aquila, Vulgate and Syriac; Hebrew *lips of sleepers* [d] *11* Or *the henna bushes*

PRAYING SCRIPTURE

Song of Songs 8

The book ends with multiple voices coming together, including those of the lover's friends and her beloved. Healthy marriages are a source of great joy to all who encounter them, and those who claim Christ should be most joyful of all.

Whether you are married or not, ask God for your present (or potential) marriage to be a living example of Jesus and the church, bearing witness to the eternal glory of his saving power.

8 If only you were to me like a brother,
who was nursed at my mother's breasts!
Then, if I found you outside,
I would kiss you,
and no one would despise me.
2 I would lead you
and bring you to my mother's house —
she who has taught me.
I would give you spiced wine to drink,
the nectar of my pomegranates.
3 His left arm is under my head
and his right arm embraces me.
4 Daughters of Jerusalem, I charge you:
Do not arouse or awaken love
until it so desires.

FRIENDS

5 Who is this coming up from the wilderness
leaning on her beloved?

SHE

Under the apple tree I roused you;
there your mother conceived you,
there she who was in labor gave you birth.
6 Place me like a seal over your heart,
like a seal on your arm;
for love is as strong as death,
its jealousy[a] unyielding as the grave.
It burns like blazing fire,
like a mighty flame.[b]
7 Many waters cannot quench love;
rivers cannot sweep it away.
If one were to give
all the wealth of one's house for love,
it[c] would be utterly scorned.

FRIENDS

8 We have a little sister,
and her breasts are not yet grown.
What shall we do for our sister
on the day she is spoken for?
9 If she is a wall,
we will build towers of silver on her.
If she is a door,
we will enclose her with panels of cedar.

SHE

10 I am a wall,
and my breasts are like towers.
Thus I have become in his eyes
like one bringing contentment.
11 Solomon had a vineyard in Baal Hamon;
he let out his vineyard to tenants.

[a] 6 Or *ardor* [b] 6 Or *fire, / like the very flame of the LORD* [c] 7 Or *he*

Each was to bring for its fruit
a thousand shekels[a] of silver.
12 But my own vineyard is mine to give;
the thousand shekels are for you, Solomon,
and two hundred[b] are for those who tend its fruit.

HE

13 You who dwell in the gardens
with friends in attendance,
let me hear your voice!

SHE

14 Come away, my beloved,
and be like a gazelle
or like a young stag
on the spice-laden mountains.

[a] *11* That is, about 25 pounds or about 12 kilograms; also in verse 12
[b] *12* That is, about 5 pounds or about 2.3 kilograms

ISAIAH

Isaiah's prophecy begins the prophetic books and is the first of the Major Prophets. He served as a prophet during the reigns of King Uzziah, Jotham, Ahaz and Hezekiah. The book's concerns pair with the narratives of these kings in both 1 and 2 Kings and 1 and 2 Chronicles. Isaiah warned his people of the judgment that was coming upon them and then offered comfort when the harm was realized. Some of the most familiar Biblical prophecies are in Isaiah.

The first 39 chapters chronicle warnings to Israel and conclude with the deportation of Israel to Assyria. Then, beginning with chapter 40, the tone of the book completely changes. Isaiah offered comfort to the people of God, showing that God was going to restore his people and bring them back into the land. He was also going to send his "servant" to his people. The servant would execute justice and make all things right, but first he would bear his people's sins and take their guilt upon himself. These chapters (especially 52:13—53:12) include some of the most detailed prophecies of the Messiah in the Old Testament. We read that he would be physically abused, despised and rejected, oppressed and afflicted, then put to death. He suffered these things not for himself but for his people.

Another well-known portion of Isaiah is the narrative of his own call to service in chapter 6. Isaiah saw the Lord sitting in the temple. He was particularly entranced by God's holiness, which Isaiah emphasized three times. Six-winged angelic beings called seraphim alternately stood and flew around the throne, proclaiming the holiness of God. Seeing the magnificence of God caused Isaiah to see his sinfulness and led him to confess his own sins and those of his people. His prayer of confession was not the end of the story, however, for one of the seraphim touched a live coal to his lips and absolved him of his sin.

One of the major emphases in the book is justice. Early in the record, as God was pronouncing impending judgment, he commanded the people, "Learn to do right; seek justice. Defend the oppressed. Take up the cause of the fatherless; plead the case of the widow" (1:17). Each was a longstanding principle for God's people to live justly in their community. God further promised that Zion would be delivered with justice and that there would be condemnation for plundering the poor, for oppression and for denying justice to the innocent. These themes teach us proper subjects for our own prayer life.

The call of Isaiah draws our attention to the glory and sovereignty of God as well as to his kindness and grace. God is high above us and possesses incredible power, yet he is also near to his people. We need both truths about God when we pray. Because God is kind and gracious, we know that he will listen when we call out to him. His power and his sovereignty assure us that he is able to answer.

1 The vision concerning Judah and Jerusalem that Isaiah son of Amoz saw during the reigns of Uzziah, Jotham, Ahaz and Hezekiah, kings of Judah.

A REBELLIOUS NATION

2 Hear me, you heavens! Listen, earth!
For the LORD has spoken:
"I reared children and brought them up,
but they have rebelled against me.
3 The ox knows its master,
the donkey its owner's manger,
but Israel does not know,
my people do not understand."

4 Woe to the sinful nation,
a people whose guilt is great,
a brood of evildoers,
children given to corruption!
They have forsaken the LORD;
they have spurned the Holy One of Israel
and turned their backs on him.

5 Why should you be beaten anymore?
Why do you persist in rebellion?
Your whole head is injured,
your whole heart afflicted.
6 From the sole of your foot to the top of your head
there is no soundness—
only wounds and welts
and open sores,
not cleansed or bandaged
or soothed with olive oil.

7 Your country is desolate,
your cities burned with fire;
your fields are being stripped by foreigners
right before you,
laid waste as when overthrown by strangers.
8 Daughter Zion is left
like a shelter in a vineyard,
like a hut in a cucumber field,
like a city under siege.
9 Unless the LORD Almighty
had left us some survivors,
we would have become like Sodom,
we would have been like Gomorrah.

10 Hear the word of the LORD,
you rulers of Sodom;
listen to the instruction of our God,
you people of Gomorrah!
11 "The multitude of your sacrifices—
what are they to me?" says the LORD.
"I have more than enough of burnt offerings,
of rams and the fat of fattened animals;
I have no pleasure
in the blood of bulls and lambs and goats.

PRAYING SCRIPTURE

Isaiah 1

In the opening chapter, Isaiah condemned heartless worship as being offensive to the Lord. God's people had sinned in many ways. The prophet summed it up: They had "turned their backs on him" (verse 4). They hadn't just turned their backs; they'd forsaken God completely.

Pause for a few minutes of personal reflection. Are you currently facing God or not? Ask God to orient your life toward him.

12 When you come to appear before me,
who has asked this of you,
this trampling of my courts?
13 Stop bringing meaningless offerings!
Your incense is detestable to me.
New Moons, Sabbaths and convocations —
I cannot bear your worthless assemblies.
14 Your New Moon feasts and your appointed festivals
I hate with all my being.
They have become a burden to me;
I am weary of bearing them.
15 When you spread out your hands in prayer,
I hide my eyes from you;
even when you offer many prayers,
I am not listening.

Your hands are full of blood!

16 Wash and make yourselves clean.
Take your evil deeds out of my sight;
stop doing wrong.
17 Learn to do right; seek justice.
Defend the oppressed.[a]
Take up the cause of the fatherless;
plead the case of the widow.

18 "Come now, let us settle the matter,"
says the LORD.
"Though your sins are like scarlet,
they shall be as white as snow;
though they are red as crimson,
they shall be like wool.
19 If you are willing and obedient,
you will eat the good things of the land;
20 but if you resist and rebel,
you will be devoured by the sword."
For the mouth of the LORD has spoken.

21 See how the faithful city
has become a prostitute!
She once was full of justice;
righteousness used to dwell in her —
but now murderers!
22 Your silver has become dross,
your choice wine is diluted with water.
23 Your rulers are rebels,
partners with thieves;
they all love bribes
and chase after gifts.
They do not defend the cause of the fatherless;
the widow's case does not come before them.

24 Therefore the Lord, the LORD Almighty,
the Mighty One of Israel, declares:

---

[a] 17 Or *justice. / Correct the oppressor*

"Ah! I will vent my wrath on my foes
and avenge myself on my enemies.
25 I will turn my hand against you;[a]
I will thoroughly purge away your dross
and remove all your impurities.
26 I will restore your leaders as in days of old,
your rulers as at the beginning.
Afterward you will be called
the City of Righteousness,
the Faithful City."

27 Zion will be delivered with justice,
her penitent ones with righteousness.
28 But rebels and sinners will both be broken,
and those who forsake the LORD will perish.

29 "You will be ashamed because of the sacred oaks
in which you have delighted;
you will be disgraced because of the gardens
that you have chosen.
30 You will be like an oak with fading leaves,
like a garden without water.
31 The mighty man will become tinder
and his work a spark;
both will burn together,
with no one to quench the fire."

THE MOUNTAIN OF THE LORD

2 This is what Isaiah son of Amoz saw concerning Judah and Jerusalem:

2 In the last days

the mountain of the LORD's temple will be established
as the highest of the mountains;
it will be exalted above the hills,
and all nations will stream to it.

3 Many peoples will come and say,

"Come, let us go up to the mountain of the LORD,
to the temple of the God of Jacob.
He will teach us his ways,
so that we may walk in his paths."
The law will go out from Zion,
the word of the LORD from Jerusalem.
4 He will judge between the nations
and will settle disputes for many peoples.
They will beat their swords into plowshares
and their spears into pruning hooks.
Nation will not take up sword against nation,
nor will they train for war anymore.

5 Come, descendants of Jacob,
let us walk in the light of the LORD.

[a] *25* That is, against Jerusalem

PRAYING SCRIPTURE

Isaiah 2

Isaiah quickly pivoted to a future day when the nations will flock to God's house to worship him and learn his ways. The day will come when humankind's pride will be "brought low and . . . humbled"; only God "will be exalted in that day" (verse 17).

There is nothing wrong with praying for Jesus' coming. In fact, we are encouraged to look for it! Spend some time expressing longing to see Jesus.

THE DAY OF THE LORD

6 You, LORD, have abandoned your people,
the descendants of Jacob.
They are full of superstitions from the East;
they practice divination like the Philistines
and embrace pagan customs.
7 Their land is full of silver and gold;
there is no end to their treasures.
Their land is full of horses;
there is no end to their chariots.
8 Their land is full of idols;
they bow down to the work of their hands,
to what their fingers have made.
9 So people will be brought low
and everyone humbled —
do not forgive them.[a]

10 Go into the rocks, hide in the ground
from the fearful presence of the LORD
and the splendor of his majesty!
11 The eyes of the arrogant will be humbled
and human pride brought low;
the LORD alone will be exalted in that day.

12 The LORD Almighty has a day in store
for all the proud and lofty,
for all that is exalted
(and they will be humbled),
13 for all the cedars of Lebanon, tall and lofty,
and all the oaks of Bashan,
14 for all the towering mountains
and all the high hills,
15 for every lofty tower
and every fortified wall,
16 for every trading ship[b]
and every stately vessel.
17 The arrogance of man will be brought low
and human pride humbled;
the LORD alone will be exalted in that day,
18 and the idols will totally disappear.

19 People will flee to caves in the rocks
and to holes in the ground
from the fearful presence of the LORD
and the splendor of his majesty,
when he rises to shake the earth.
20 In that day people will throw away
to the moles and bats
their idols of silver and idols of gold,
which they made to worship.
21 They will flee to caverns in the rocks
and to the overhanging crags
from the fearful presence of the LORD

[a] 9 Or *not raise them up* [b] 16 Hebrew *every ship of Tarshish*

and the splendor of his majesty,
when he rises to shake the earth.

22 Stop trusting in mere humans,
who have but a breath in their nostrils.
Why hold them in esteem?

JUDGMENT ON JERUSALEM AND JUDAH

3 See now, the Lord,
the LORD Almighty,
is about to take from Jerusalem and Judah
both supply and support:
all supplies of food and all supplies of water,
2 the hero and the warrior,
the judge and the prophet,
the diviner and the elder,
3 the captain of fifty and the man of rank,
the counselor, skilled craftsman and clever enchanter.

4 "I will make mere youths their officials;
children will rule over them."
5 People will oppress each other —
man against man, neighbor against neighbor.
The young will rise up against the old,
the nobody against the honored.

6 A man will seize one of his brothers
in his father's house, and say,
"You have a cloak, you be our leader;
take charge of this heap of ruins!"
7 But in that day he will cry out,
"I have no remedy.
I have no food or clothing in my house;
do not make me the leader of the people."

8 Jerusalem staggers,
Judah is falling;
their words and deeds are against the LORD,
defying his glorious presence.
9 The look on their faces testifies against them;
they parade their sin like Sodom;
they do not hide it.
Woe to them!
They have brought disaster upon themselves.

10 Tell the righteous it will be well with them,
for they will enjoy the fruit of their deeds.
11 Woe to the wicked!
Disaster is upon them!
They will be paid back
for what their hands have done.

12 Youths oppress my people,
women rule over them.
My people, your guides lead you astray;
they turn you from the path.

PRAYING SCRIPTURE

Isaiah 3

One of the Lord's judgments was on the elders and princes. In a withering indictment, he condemned them for ruining the vineyard, plundering, crushing God's people and "grinding the face of the poor" (verse 15). It was a judgment from which there was no escape.

Not knowing how to help the poor is one thing, but it is sinful to oppress them. Pray God will give you his heart for the poor.

13 The LORD takes his place in court;
he rises to judge the people.
14 The LORD enters into judgment
against the elders and leaders of his people:
"It is you who have ruined my vineyard;
the plunder from the poor is in your houses.
15 What do you mean by crushing my people
and grinding the faces of the poor?"
declares the Lord, the LORD Almighty.

16 The LORD says,
"The women of Zion are haughty,
walking along with outstretched necks,
flirting with their eyes,
strutting along with swaying hips,
with ornaments jingling on their ankles.
17 Therefore the Lord will bring sores on the heads of the women of Zion;
the LORD will make their scalps bald."

18 In that day the Lord will snatch away their finery: the bangles and
headbands and crescent necklaces, 19 the earrings and bracelets and
veils, 20 the headdresses and anklets and sashes, the perfume bottles
and charms, 21 the signet rings and nose rings, 22 the fine robes and the
capes and cloaks, the purses 23 and mirrors, and the linen garments
and tiaras and shawls.

24 Instead of fragrance there will be a stench;
instead of a sash, a rope;
instead of well-dressed hair, baldness;
instead of fine clothing, sackcloth;
instead of beauty, branding.
25 Your men will fall by the sword,
your warriors in battle.
26 The gates of Zion will lament and mourn;
destitute, she will sit on the ground.

4 1 In that day seven women
will take hold of one man
and say, "We will eat our own food
and provide our own clothes;
only let us be called by your name.
Take away our disgrace!"

PRAYING SCRIPTURE

Isaiah 4

Despite the coming judgment, God promised future salvation for his people. Recalling the Messiah's name, the Branch, Isaiah told of a day when the Messiah will rule, his people will be washed and cleansed and God's glory will cover Mount Zion.

Even on our worst days, we are not beyond the reach of grace. When you feel furthest from God, call on him.

THE BRANCH OF THE LORD

2 In that day the Branch of the LORD will be beautiful and glorious, and
the fruit of the land will be the pride and glory of the survivors in Israel.
3 Those who are left in Zion, who remain in Jerusalem, will be called holy,
all who are recorded among the living in Jerusalem. 4 The Lord will wash
away the filth of the women of Zion; he will cleanse the bloodstains from
Jerusalem by a spirit[a] of judgment and a spirit[a] of fire. 5 Then the LORD
will create over all of Mount Zion and over those who assemble there a
cloud of smoke by day and a glow of flaming fire by night; over every-
thing the glory[b] will be a canopy. 6 It will be a shelter and shade from the
heat of the day, and a refuge and hiding place from the storm and rain.

[a] 4 Or *the Spirit* [b] 5 Or *over all the glory there*

THE SONG OF THE VINEYARD

5 I will sing for the one I love
a song about his vineyard:
My loved one had a vineyard
on a fertile hillside.
2 He dug it up and cleared it of stones
and planted it with the choicest vines.
He built a watchtower in it
and cut out a winepress as well.
Then he looked for a crop of good grapes,
but it yielded only bad fruit.

3 "Now you dwellers in Jerusalem and people of Judah,
judge between me and my vineyard.
4 What more could have been done for my vineyard
than I have done for it?
When I looked for good grapes,
why did it yield only bad?
5 Now I will tell you
what I am going to do to my vineyard:
I will take away its hedge,
and it will be destroyed;
I will break down its wall,
and it will be trampled.
6 I will make it a wasteland,
neither pruned nor cultivated,
and briers and thorns will grow there.
I will command the clouds
not to rain on it."

7 The vineyard of the LORD Almighty
is the nation of Israel,
and the people of Judah
are the vines he delighted in.
And he looked for justice, but saw bloodshed;
for righteousness, but heard cries of distress.

WOES AND JUDGMENTS

8 Woe to you who add house to house
and join field to field
till no space is left
and you live alone in the land.

9 The LORD Almighty has declared in my hearing:

"Surely the great houses will become desolate,
the fine mansions left without occupants.
10 A ten-acre vineyard will produce only a bath[a] of wine;
a homer[b] of seed will yield only an ephah[c] of grain."

11 Woe to those who rise early in the morning
to run after their drinks,
who stay up late at night
till they are inflamed with wine.

PRAYING SCRIPTURE

Isaiah 5

In this chapter, God revealed one reason for his judgment on Jerusalem: his disappointment with his people. He planted a vineyard to cultivate "good grapes," but instead it brought forth "only bad fruit" (verse 2). Rather than sweetness, bitterness was his harvest.

God has a purpose for all of us and empowers us to fulfill it. If you are producing wild rather than good grapes, confess it and ask God to restore you.

[a] *10* That is, about 6 gallons or about 22 liters [b] *10* That is, probably about 360 pounds or about 160 kilograms [c] *10* That is, probably about 36 pounds or about 16 kilograms

12 They have harps and lyres at their banquets,
pipes and timbrels and wine,
but they have no regard for the deeds of the LORD,
no respect for the work of his hands.
13 Therefore my people will go into exile
for lack of understanding;
those of high rank will die of hunger
and the common people will be parched with thirst.
14 Therefore Death expands its jaws,
opening wide its mouth;
into it will descend their nobles and masses
with all their brawlers and revelers.
15 So people will be brought low
and everyone humbled,
the eyes of the arrogant humbled.
16 But the LORD Almighty will be exalted by his justice,
and the holy God will be proved holy by his righteous acts.
17 Then sheep will graze as in their own pasture;
lambs will feed[a] among the ruins of the rich.

18 Woe to those who draw sin along with cords of deceit,
and wickedness as with cart ropes,
19 to those who say, "Let God hurry;
let him hasten his work
so we may see it.
The plan of the Holy One of Israel—
let it approach, let it come into view,
so we may know it."

20 Woe to those who call evil good
and good evil,
who put darkness for light
and light for darkness,
who put bitter for sweet
and sweet for bitter.

21 Woe to those who are wise in their own eyes
and clever in their own sight.

22 Woe to those who are heroes at drinking wine
and champions at mixing drinks,
23 who acquit the guilty for a bribe,
but deny justice to the innocent.
24 Therefore, as tongues of fire lick up straw
and as dry grass sinks down in the flames,
so their roots will decay
and their flowers blow away like dust;
for they have rejected the law of the LORD Almighty
and spurned the word of the Holy One of Israel.
25 Therefore the LORD's anger burns against his people;
his hand is raised and he strikes them down.
The mountains shake,
and the dead bodies are like refuse in the streets.

Yet for all this, his anger is not turned away,
his hand is still upraised.

[a] 17 Septuagint; Hebrew / *strangers will eat*

26 He lifts up a banner for the distant nations,
he whistles for those at the ends of the earth.
Here they come,
swiftly and speedily!
27 Not one of them grows tired or stumbles,
not one slumbers or sleeps;
not a belt is loosened at the waist,
not a sandal strap is broken.
28 Their arrows are sharp,
all their bows are strung;
their horses' hooves seem like flint,
their chariot wheels like a whirlwind.
29 Their roar is like that of the lion,
they roar like young lions;
they growl as they seize their prey
and carry it off with no one to rescue.
30 In that day they will roar over it
like the roaring of the sea.
And if one looks at the land,
there is only darkness and distress;
even the sun will be darkened by clouds.

ISAIAH'S COMMISSION

6 In the year that King Uzziah died, I saw the Lord, high and exalted,
seated on a throne; and the train of his robe filled the temple.
2 Above him were seraphim, each with six wings: With two wings they
covered their faces, with two they covered their feet, and with two they
were flying. 3 And they were calling to one another:

"Holy, holy, holy is the LORD Almighty;
the whole earth is full of his glory."

4 At the sound of their voices the doorposts and thresholds shook and
the temple was filled with smoke.

5 "Woe to me!" I cried. "I am ruined! For I am a man of unclean lips,
and I live among a people of unclean lips, and my eyes have seen the
King, the LORD Almighty."

6 Then one of the seraphim flew to me with a live coal in his hand,
which he had taken with tongs from the altar. 7 With it he touched my
mouth and said, "See, this has touched your lips; your guilt is taken
away and your sin atoned for."

8 Then I heard the voice of the Lord saying, "Whom shall I send? And
who will go for us?"

And I said, "Here am I. Send me!"
9 He said, "Go and tell this people:
"'Be ever hearing, but never understanding;
be ever seeing, but never perceiving.'
10 Make the heart of this people calloused;
make their ears dull
and close their eyes.[a]
Otherwise they might see with their eyes,

PRAYING SCRIPTURE

Isaiah 6

Aside from Moses' call at the burning bush, Isaiah's call is the most glorious for the sheer weight of what he experienced. He was a personal eyewitness to the throne room of the Lord of hosts, which is filled with seraphim who endlessly proclaim the holiness of God.

This Lord who called Isaiah is the same Lord who calls children from every corner of the earth. Praise God for his majesty that humbles even the angelic beings.

[a] 9,10 Hebrew; Septuagint *'You will be ever hearing, but never understanding; / you will be ever seeing, but never perceiving.' / [10]This people's heart has become calloused; / they hardly hear with their ears, / and they have closed their eyes*

hear with their ears,
understand with their hearts,
and turn and be healed."

11 Then I said, "For how long, Lord?"
And he answered:

"Until the cities lie ruined
and without inhabitant,
until the houses are left deserted
and the fields ruined and ravaged,
12 until the LORD has sent everyone far away
and the land is utterly forsaken.
13 And though a tenth remains in the land,
it will again be laid waste.
But as the terebinth and oak
leave stumps when they are cut down,
so the holy seed will be the stump in the land."

THE SIGN OF IMMANUEL

7 When Ahaz son of Jotham, the son of Uzziah, was king of Judah,
King Rezin of Aram and Pekah son of Remaliah king of Israel
marched up to fight against Jerusalem, but they could not overpower it.
2 Now the house of David was told, "Aram has allied itself with[a]
Ephraim"; so the hearts of Ahaz and his people were shaken, as the
trees of the forest are shaken by the wind.
3 Then the LORD said to Isaiah, "Go out, you and your son
Shear-Jashub,[b] to meet Ahaz at the end of the aqueduct of the Upper
Pool, on the road to the Launderer's Field. 4 Say to him, 'Be careful,
keep calm and don't be afraid. Do not lose heart because of these two
smoldering stubs of firewood — because of the fierce anger of Rezin
and Aram and of the son of Remaliah. 5 Aram, Ephraim and Remaliah's
son have plotted your ruin, saying, 6 "Let us invade Judah; let us tear it
apart and divide it among ourselves, and make the son of Tabeel king
over it." 7 Yet this is what the Sovereign LORD says:

" 'It will not take place,
it will not happen,
8 for the head of Aram is Damascus,
and the head of Damascus is only Rezin.
Within sixty-five years
Ephraim will be too shattered to be a people.
9 The head of Ephraim is Samaria,
and the head of Samaria is only Remaliah's son.
If you do not stand firm in your faith,
you will not stand at all.' "

10 Again the LORD spoke to Ahaz, 11 "Ask the LORD your God for a sign,
whether in the deepest depths or in the highest heights."
12 But Ahaz said, "I will not ask; I will not put the LORD to the test."
13 Then Isaiah said, "Hear now, you house of David! Is it not enough
to try the patience of humans? Will you try the patience of my God
also? 14 Therefore the Lord himself will give you[c] a sign: The virgin[d]

PRAYING SCRIPTURE

Isaiah 7

Hundreds of years before the coming of Jesus, God gave the sign of his coming: "The virgin will conceive and give birth to a son" (verse 14). His very name, Immanuel, revealed his person: God with us. The hope of the world rests on God fulfilling this prophecy in his Son.

People are as shocked today as they were then that God would become human. Thank him for stooping to become like us to save us.

---

[a] 2 Or *has set up camp in* [b] 3 *Shear-Jashub* means *a remnant will return.*
[c] 14 The Hebrew is plural. [d] 14 Or *young woman*

will conceive and give birth to a son, and[a] will call him Immanuel.[b]
15 He will be eating curds and honey when he knows enough to reject
the wrong and choose the right, 16 for before the boy knows enough to
reject the wrong and choose the right, the land of the two kings you
dread will be laid waste. 17 The LORD will bring on you and on your peo-
ple and on the house of your father a time unlike any since Ephraim
broke away from Judah — he will bring the king of Assyria."

ASSYRIA, THE LORD'S INSTRUMENT

18 In that day the LORD will whistle for flies from the Nile delta in
Egypt and for bees from the land of Assyria. 19 They will all come and
settle in the steep ravines and in the crevices in the rocks, on all the
thornbushes and at all the water holes. 20 In that day the Lord will use
a razor hired from beyond the Euphrates River — the king of Assyria —
to shave your head and private parts, and to cut off your beard also.
21 In that day, a person will keep alive a young cow and two goats. 22 And
because of the abundance of the milk they give, there will be curds to
eat. All who remain in the land will eat curds and honey. 23 In that day,
in every place where there were a thousand vines worth a thousand
silver shekels,[c] there will be only briers and thorns. 24 Hunters will go
there with bow and arrow, for the land will be covered with briers and
thorns. 25 As for all the hills once cultivated by the hoe, you will no lon-
ger go there for fear of the briers and thorns; they will become places
where cattle are turned loose and where sheep run.

ISAIAH AND HIS CHILDREN AS SIGNS

8 The LORD said to me, "Take a large scroll and write on it with an
ordinary pen: Maher-Shalal-Hash-Baz."[d] 2 So I called in Uriah the
priest and Zechariah son of Jeberekiah as reliable witnesses for me.
3 Then I made love to the prophetess, and she conceived and gave birth
to a son. And the LORD said to me, "Name him Maher-Shalal-Hash-Baz.
4 For before the boy knows how to say 'My father' or 'My mother,' the
wealth of Damascus and the plunder of Samaria will be carried off by
the king of Assyria."

5 The LORD spoke to me again:

6 "Because this people has rejected
the gently flowing waters of Shiloah
and rejoices over Rezin
and the son of Remaliah,
7 therefore the Lord is about to bring against them
the mighty floodwaters of the Euphrates —
the king of Assyria with all his pomp.
It will overflow all its channels,
run over all its banks
8 and sweep on into Judah, swirling over it,
passing through it and reaching up to the neck.
Its outspread wings will cover the breadth of your land,
Immanuel[b]!"

[a] *14* Masoretic Text; Dead Sea Scrolls *son, and he* or *son, and they*
[b] *14,8* *Immanuel* means *God with us.*
[c] *23* That is, about 25 pounds or about 12 kilograms
[d] *1* *Maher-Shalal-Hash-Baz* means *quick to the plunder, swift to the spoil*; also in verse 3.

PRAYING SCRIPTURE

Isaiah 8

A unique warning from the Lord challenges us to be people of truth: Don't fall for conspiracy talk (see verse 12). Focusing on fantastic tales and never-ending mysteries damages our witness as people who are of the way, the truth and the life. The fearmongering of conspiracy promoters should be rejected.

Do you set your mind on fantasy or reality? To pursue God is to pursue truth. Ask him to guide you to truth.

9 Raise the war cry,[a] you nations, and be shattered!
Listen, all you distant lands.
Prepare for battle, and be shattered!
Prepare for battle, and be shattered!
10 Devise your strategy, but it will be thwarted;
propose your plan, but it will not stand,
for God is with us.[b]

11 This is what the LORD says to me with his strong hand upon me, warning me not to follow the way of this people:

12 "Do not call conspiracy
everything this people calls a conspiracy;
do not fear what they fear,
and do not dread it.
13 The LORD Almighty is the one you are to regard as holy,
he is the one you are to fear,
he is the one you are to dread.
14 He will be a holy place;
for both Israel and Judah he will be
a stone that causes people to stumble
and a rock that makes them fall.
And for the people of Jerusalem he will be
a trap and a snare.
15 Many of them will stumble;
they will fall and be broken,
they will be snared and captured."

16 Bind up this testimony of warning
and seal up God's instruction among my disciples.
17 I will wait for the LORD,
who is hiding his face from the descendants of Jacob.
I will put my trust in him.

18 Here am I, and the children the LORD has given me. We are signs and symbols in Israel from the LORD Almighty, who dwells on Mount Zion.

THE DARKNESS TURNS TO LIGHT

19 When someone tells you to consult mediums and spiritists, who whisper and mutter, should not a people inquire of their God? Why consult the dead on behalf of the living? 20 Consult God's instruction and the testimony of warning. If anyone does not speak according to this word, they have no light of dawn. 21 Distressed and hungry, they will roam through the land; when they are famished, they will become enraged and, looking upward, will curse their king and their God. 22 Then they will look toward the earth and see only distress and darkness and fearful gloom, and they will be thrust into utter darkness.

9[c] Nevertheless, there will be no more gloom for those who were in distress. In the past he humbled the land of Zebulun and the land of Naphtali, but in the future he will honor Galilee of the nations, by the Way of the Sea, beyond the Jordan—

PRAYING SCRIPTURE

Isaiah 9

This chapter anticipates the joy that God's people will experience when Christ comes to make all things new. The prophesied child to be born and son to be given has quickened the hearts of God's people through the centuries. Jesus is the One who will sit on David's throne forever!

Let your heart rejoice in the wisdom and might of God. Praise him for Jesus, our Prince of Peace.

---

[a] 9 Or *Do your worst* [b] 10 Hebrew *Immanuel* [c] In Hebrew texts 9:1 is numbered 8:23, and 9:2-21 is numbered 9:1-20.

2 The people walking in darkness
have seen a great light;
on those living in the land of deep darkness
a light has dawned.
3 You have enlarged the nation
and increased their joy;
they rejoice before you
as people rejoice at the harvest,
as warriors rejoice
when dividing the plunder.
4 For as in the day of Midian's defeat,
you have shattered
the yoke that burdens them,
the bar across their shoulders,
the rod of their oppressor.
5 Every warrior's boot used in battle
and every garment rolled in blood
will be destined for burning,
will be fuel for the fire.
6 For to us a child is born,
to us a son is given,
and the government will be on his shoulders.
And he will be called
Wonderful Counselor, Mighty God,
Everlasting Father, Prince of Peace.
7 Of the greatness of his government and peace
there will be no end.
He will reign on David's throne
and over his kingdom,
establishing and upholding it
with justice and righteousness
from that time on and forever.
The zeal of the LORD Almighty
will accomplish this.

THE LORD'S ANGER AGAINST ISRAEL

8 The Lord has sent a message against Jacob;
it will fall on Israel.
9 All the people will know it —
Ephraim and the inhabitants of Samaria —
who say with pride
and arrogance of heart,
10 "The bricks have fallen down,
but we will rebuild with dressed stone;
the fig trees have been felled,
but we will replace them with cedars."
11 But the LORD has strengthened Rezin's foes against them
and has spurred their enemies on.
12 Arameans from the east and Philistines from the west
have devoured Israel with open mouth.

Yet for all this, his anger is not turned away,
his hand is still upraised.

13 But the people have not returned to him who struck them,
nor have they sought the LORD Almighty.

14 So the LORD will cut off from Israel both head and tail,
both palm branch and reed in a single day;
15 the elders and dignitaries are the head,
the prophets who teach lies are the tail.
16 Those who guide this people mislead them,
and those who are guided are led astray.
17 Therefore the Lord will take no pleasure in the young men,
nor will he pity the fatherless and widows,
for everyone is ungodly and wicked,
every mouth speaks folly.

Yet for all this, his anger is not turned away,
his hand is still upraised.

18 Surely wickedness burns like a fire;
it consumes briers and thorns,
it sets the forest thickets ablaze,
so that it rolls upward in a column of smoke.
19 By the wrath of the LORD Almighty
the land will be scorched
and the people will be fuel for the fire;
they will not spare one another.
20 On the right they will devour,
but still be hungry;
on the left they will eat,
but not be satisfied.
Each will feed on the flesh of their own offspring[a]:
21 Manasseh will feed on Ephraim, and Ephraim on Manasseh;
together they will turn against Judah.

Yet for all this, his anger is not turned away,
his hand is still upraised.

PRAYING SCRIPTURE

Isaiah 10

Even when God's enemies seem victorious, their time will come to an end. The Bible is filled with judgments on the people of Israel and Judah, their enemies and various surrounding nations. God not only judges those who sin against his people; he judges whoever sins against him.

We can be thankful that Jesus has borne judgment for us while we acknowledge consequences for sin. Ask God for both wisdom and power to walk righteously.

10 Woe to those who make unjust laws,
to those who issue oppressive decrees,
2 to deprive the poor of their rights
and withhold justice from the oppressed of my people,
making widows their prey
and robbing the fatherless.
3 What will you do on the day of reckoning,
when disaster comes from afar?
To whom will you run for help?
Where will you leave your riches?
4 Nothing will remain but to cringe among the captives
or fall among the slain.

Yet for all this, his anger is not turned away,
his hand is still upraised.

GOD'S JUDGMENT ON ASSYRIA

5 "Woe to the Assyrian, the rod of my anger,
in whose hand is the club of my wrath!
6 I send him against a godless nation,
I dispatch him against a people who anger me,

[a] 20 Or *arm*

to seize loot and snatch plunder,
and to trample them down like mud in the streets.
7 But this is not what he intends,
this is not what he has in mind;
his purpose is to destroy,
to put an end to many nations.
8 'Are not my commanders all kings?' he says.
9 'Has not Kalno fared like Carchemish?
Is not Hamath like Arpad,
and Samaria like Damascus?
10 As my hand seized the kingdoms of the idols,
kingdoms whose images excelled those of Jerusalem and Samaria —
11 shall I not deal with Jerusalem and her images
as I dealt with Samaria and her idols?'"

12 When the Lord has finished all his work against Mount Zion and
Jerusalem, he will say, "I will punish the king of Assyria for the willful
pride of his heart and the haughty look in his eyes. 13 For he says:

"'By the strength of my hand I have done this,
and by my wisdom, because I have understanding.
I removed the boundaries of nations,
I plundered their treasures;
like a mighty one I subdued[a] their kings.
14 As one reaches into a nest,
so my hand reached for the wealth of the nations;
as people gather abandoned eggs,
so I gathered all the countries;
not one flapped a wing,
or opened its mouth to chirp.'"

15 Does the ax raise itself above the person who swings it,
or the saw boast against the one who uses it?
As if a rod were to wield the person who lifts it up,
or a club brandish the one who is not wood!
16 Therefore, the Lord, the LORD Almighty,
will send a wasting disease upon his sturdy warriors;
under his pomp a fire will be kindled
like a blazing flame.
17 The Light of Israel will become a fire,
their Holy One a flame;
in a single day it will burn and consume
his thorns and his briers.
18 The splendor of his forests and fertile fields
it will completely destroy,
as when a sick person wastes away.
19 And the remaining trees of his forests will be so few
that a child could write them down.

THE REMNANT OF ISRAEL

20 In that day the remnant of Israel,
the survivors of Jacob,

[a] 13 Or *treasures; / I subdued the mighty,*

will no longer rely on him
who struck them down
but will truly rely on the LORD,
the Holy One of Israel.
21 A remnant will return,[a] a remnant of Jacob
will return to the Mighty God.
22 Though your people be like the sand by the sea, Israel,
only a remnant will return.
Destruction has been decreed,
overwhelming and righteous.
23 The Lord, the LORD Almighty, will carry out
the destruction decreed upon the whole land.

24 Therefore this is what the Lord, the LORD Almighty, says:

"My people who live in Zion,
do not be afraid of the Assyrians,
who beat you with a rod
and lift up a club against you, as Egypt did.
25 Very soon my anger against you will end
and my wrath will be directed to their destruction."

26 The LORD Almighty will lash them with a whip,
as when he struck down Midian at the rock of Oreb;
and he will raise his staff over the waters,
as he did in Egypt.
27 In that day their burden will be lifted from your shoulders,
their yoke from your neck;
the yoke will be broken
because you have grown so fat.[b]

28 They enter Aiath;
they pass through Migron;
they store supplies at Mikmash.
29 They go over the pass, and say,
"We will camp overnight at Geba."
Ramah trembles;
Gibeah of Saul flees.
30 Cry out, Daughter Gallim!
Listen, Laishah!
Poor Anathoth!
31 Madmenah is in flight;
the people of Gebim take cover.
32 This day they will halt at Nob;
they will shake their fist
at the mount of Daughter Zion,
at the hill of Jerusalem.

33 See, the Lord, the LORD Almighty,
will lop off the boughs with great power.
The lofty trees will be felled,
the tall ones will be brought low.
34 He will cut down the forest thickets with an ax;
Lebanon will fall before the Mighty One.

---

[a] *21* Hebrew *shear-jashub* (see 7:3 and note); also in verse 22 [b] *27* Hebrew; Septuagint *broken / from your shoulders*

THE BRANCH FROM JESSE

11 A shoot will come up from the stump of Jesse;
from his roots a Branch will bear fruit.
2 The Spirit of the LORD will rest on him—
the Spirit of wisdom and of understanding,
the Spirit of counsel and of might,
the Spirit of the knowledge and fear of the LORD—
3 and he will delight in the fear of the LORD.

He will not judge by what he sees with his eyes,
or decide by what he hears with his ears;
4 but with righteousness he will judge the needy,
with justice he will give decisions for the poor of the earth.
He will strike the earth with the rod of his mouth;
with the breath of his lips he will slay the wicked.
5 Righteousness will be his belt
and faithfulness the sash around his waist.

6 The wolf will live with the lamb,
the leopard will lie down with the goat,
the calf and the lion and the yearling[a] together;
and a little child will lead them.
7 The cow will feed with the bear,
their young will lie down together,
and the lion will eat straw like the ox.
8 The infant will play near the cobra's den,
and the young child will put its hand into the viper's nest.
9 They will neither harm nor destroy
on all my holy mountain,
for the earth will be filled with the knowledge of the LORD
as the waters cover the sea.

10 In that day the Root of Jesse will stand as a banner for the peoples;
the nations will rally to him, and his resting place will be glorious. 11 In
that day the Lord will reach out his hand a second time to reclaim the
surviving remnant of his people from Assyria, from Lower Egypt, from
Upper Egypt, from Cush,[b] from Elam, from Babylonia,[c] from Hamath
and from the islands of the Mediterranean.

12 He will raise a banner for the nations
and gather the exiles of Israel;
he will assemble the scattered people of Judah
from the four quarters of the earth.
13 Ephraim's jealousy will vanish,
and Judah's enemies[d] will be destroyed;
Ephraim will not be jealous of Judah,
nor Judah hostile toward Ephraim.
14 They will swoop down on the slopes of Philistia to the west;
together they will plunder the people to the east.
They will subdue Edom and Moab,
and the Ammonites will be subject to them.
15 The LORD will dry up
the gulf of the Egyptian sea;

[a] 6 Hebrew; Septuagint *lion will feed* [b] 11 That is, the upper Nile region
[c] 11 Hebrew *Shinar* [d] 13 Or *hostility*

PRAYING SCRIPTURE

Isaiah 11

Because of Jesus Christ—the "shoot . . . from the stump of Jesse," the Branch from his roots—one day there will be no more violence or war (see verse 1). Animals that now devour will befriend their prey; venomous snakes will no longer bite children. All of creation will be at peace.

Don't you just long for that day? Tell God all the different reasons you long for his just reign to come to earth.

with a scorching wind he will sweep his hand
over the Euphrates River.
He will break it up into seven streams
so that anyone can cross over in sandals.
16 There will be a highway for the remnant of his people
that is left from Assyria,
as there was for Israel
when they came up from Egypt.

SONGS OF PRAISE

12 In that day you will say:

"I will praise you, LORD.
Although you were angry with me,
your anger has turned away
and you have comforted me.
2 Surely God is my salvation;
I will trust and not be afraid.
The LORD, the LORD himself, is my strength and my defense[a];
he has become my salvation."
3 With joy you will draw water
from the wells of salvation.

4 In that day you will say:

"Give praise to the LORD, proclaim his name;
make known among the nations what he has done,
and proclaim that his name is exalted.
5 Sing to the LORD, for he has done glorious things;
let this be known to all the world.
6 Shout aloud and sing for joy, people of Zion,
for great is the Holy One of Israel among you."

PRAYING SCRIPTURE

Isaiah 12

Our private praise should always spill over into public witness. We must tell others what God has done for us; we must "make known among the nations what he has done" (verse 4). Without our witness, people who do not know God might not recognize his common grace in their lives.

We are to praise the Lord and call on his name. Simply, we are to pray. We cannot rightly praise God without prayer.

A PROPHECY AGAINST BABYLON

13 A prophecy against Babylon that Isaiah son of Amoz saw:

2 Raise a banner on a bare hilltop,
shout to them;
beckon to them
to enter the gates of the nobles.
3 I have commanded those I prepared for battle;
I have summoned my warriors to carry out my wrath—
those who rejoice in my triumph.

4 Listen, a noise on the mountains,
like that of a great multitude!
Listen, an uproar among the kingdoms,
like nations massing together!
The LORD Almighty is mustering
an army for war.
5 They come from faraway lands,
from the ends of the heavens—
the LORD and the weapons of his wrath—
to destroy the whole country.

PRAYING SCRIPTURE

Isaiah 13

The "day of the LORD" referenced in this chapter is not a onetime event (see verse 6). It's the name given for any day of judgment, this time upon Babylon, a wicked city. God promises judgment so severe that everyone who does not flee will die.

Sin exacts an awful price. Ask God to keep you from sin, and thank him that his final judgment will destroy sin forever.

[a] 2 Or *song*

6 Wail, for the day of the LORD is near;
it will come like destruction from the Almighty.[a]
7 Because of this, all hands will go limp,
every heart will melt with fear.
8 Terror will seize them,
pain and anguish will grip them;
they will writhe like a woman in labor.
They will look aghast at each other,
their faces aflame.

9 See, the day of the LORD is coming
—a cruel day, with wrath and fierce anger—
to make the land desolate
and destroy the sinners within it.
10 The stars of heaven and their constellations
will not show their light.
The rising sun will be darkened
and the moon will not give its light.
11 I will punish the world for its evil,
the wicked for their sins.
I will put an end to the arrogance of the haughty
and will humble the pride of the ruthless.
12 I will make people scarcer than pure gold,
more rare than the gold of Ophir.
13 Therefore I will make the heavens tremble;
and the earth will shake from its place
at the wrath of the LORD Almighty,
in the day of his burning anger.

14 Like a hunted gazelle,
like sheep without a shepherd,
they will all return to their own people,
they will flee to their native land.
15 Whoever is captured will be thrust through;
all who are caught will fall by the sword.
16 Their infants will be dashed to pieces before their eyes;
their houses will be looted and their wives violated.

17 See, I will stir up against them the Medes,
who do not care for silver
and have no delight in gold.
18 Their bows will strike down the young men;
they will have no mercy on infants,
nor will they look with compassion on children.
19 Babylon, the jewel of kingdoms,
the pride and glory of the Babylonians,[b]
will be overthrown by God
like Sodom and Gomorrah.
20 She will never be inhabited
or lived in through all generations;
there no nomads will pitch their tents,
there no shepherds will rest their flocks.
21 But desert creatures will lie there,
jackals will fill her houses;

[a] 6 Hebrew *Shaddai* [b] 19 Or *Chaldeans*

there the owls will dwell,
and there the wild goats will leap about.
22 Hyenas will inhabit her strongholds,
jackals her luxurious palaces.
Her time is at hand,
and her days will not be prolonged.

PRAYING SCRIPTURE

Isaiah 14

Pride has long been called the sin of the devil because of a passage in this chapter. Verses 13–15 recount the fall of Lucifer, who tried to exalt himself to be like God. The result was judgment, being cast "to the depths of the pit" (verse 15).

Pride can be disguised as confidence or boldness. Do an honest self-assessment. If God convicts you of pride, repent and seek humility instead.

14

The LORD will have compassion on Jacob;
once again he will choose Israel
and will settle them in their own land.
Foreigners will join them
and unite with the descendants of Jacob.
2 Nations will take them
and bring them to their own place.
And Israel will take possession of the nations
and make them male and female servants in the LORD's land.
They will make captives of their captors
and rule over their oppressors.

3 On the day the LORD gives you relief from your suffering and tur-
moil and from the harsh labor forced on you, 4 you will take up this
taunt against the king of Babylon:

How the oppressor has come to an end!
How his fury[a] has ended!
5 The LORD has broken the rod of the wicked,
the scepter of the rulers,
6 which in anger struck down peoples
with unceasing blows,
and in fury subdued nations
with relentless aggression.
7 All the lands are at rest and at peace;
they break into singing.
8 Even the junipers and the cedars of Lebanon
gloat over you and say,
"Now that you have been laid low,
no one comes to cut us down."
9 The realm of the dead below is all astir
to meet you at your coming;
it rouses the spirits of the departed to greet you —
all those who were leaders in the world;
it makes them rise from their thrones —
all those who were kings over the nations.
10 They will all respond,
they will say to you,
"You also have become weak, as we are;
you have become like us."
11 All your pomp has been brought down to the grave,
along with the noise of your harps;
maggots are spread out beneath you
and worms cover you.

[a] 4 Dead Sea Scrolls, Septuagint and Syriac; the meaning of the word in the Masoretic Text is uncertain.

12 How you have fallen from heaven,
morning star, son of the dawn!
You have been cast down to the earth,
you who once laid low the nations!
13 You said in your heart,
"I will ascend to the heavens;
I will raise my throne
above the stars of God;
I will sit enthroned on the mount of assembly,
on the utmost heights of Mount Zaphon.[a]
14 I will ascend above the tops of the clouds;
I will make myself like the Most High."
15 But you are brought down to the realm of the dead,
to the depths of the pit.

16 Those who see you stare at you,
they ponder your fate:
"Is this the man who shook the earth
and made kingdoms tremble,
17 the man who made the world a wilderness,
who overthrew its cities
and would not let his captives go home?"

18 All the kings of the nations lie in state,
each in his own tomb.
19 But you are cast out of your tomb
like a rejected branch;
you are covered with the slain,
with those pierced by the sword,
those who descend to the stones of the pit.
Like a corpse trampled underfoot,
20 you will not join them in burial,
for you have destroyed your land
and killed your people.

Let the offspring of the wicked
never be mentioned again.
21 Prepare a place to slaughter his children
for the sins of their ancestors;
they are not to rise to inherit the land
and cover the earth with their cities.

22 "I will rise up against them,"
declares the LORD Almighty.
"I will wipe out Babylon's name and survivors,
her offspring and descendants,"
declares the LORD.
23 "I will turn her into a place for owls
and into swampland;
I will sweep her with the broom of destruction,"
declares the LORD Almighty.

24 The LORD Almighty has sworn,

---

[a] *13* Or *of the north*; Zaphon was the most sacred mountain of the Canaanites.

“Surely, as I have planned, so it will be,
and as I have purposed, so it will happen.
25 I will crush the Assyrian in my land;
on my mountains I will trample him down.
His yoke will be taken from my people,
and his burden removed from their shoulders.”

26 This is the plan determined for the whole world;
this is the hand stretched out over all nations.
27 For the LORD Almighty has purposed, and who can thwart him?
His hand is stretched out, and who can turn it back?

A PROPHECY AGAINST THE PHILISTINES

28 This prophecy came in the year King Ahaz died:

29 Do not rejoice, all you Philistines,
that the rod that struck you is broken;
from the root of that snake will spring up a viper,
its fruit will be a darting, venomous serpent.
30 The poorest of the poor will find pasture,
and the needy will lie down in safety.
But your root I will destroy by famine;
it will slay your survivors.

31 Wail, you gate! Howl, you city!
Melt away, all you Philistines!
A cloud of smoke comes from the north,
and there is not a straggler in its ranks.
32 What answer shall be given
to the envoys of that nation?
“The LORD has established Zion,
and in her his afflicted people will find refuge.”

A PROPHECY AGAINST MOAB

15 A prophecy against Moab:

Ar in Moab is ruined,
destroyed in a night!
Kir in Moab is ruined,
destroyed in a night!
2 Dibon goes up to its temple,
to its high places to weep;
Moab wails over Nebo and Medeba.
Every head is shaved
and every beard cut off.
3 In the streets they wear sackcloth;
on the roofs and in the public squares
they all wail,
prostrate with weeping.
4 Heshbon and Elealeh cry out,
their voices are heard all the way to Jahaz.
Therefore the armed men of Moab cry out,
and their hearts are faint.

5 My heart cries out over Moab;
her fugitives flee as far as Zoar,

PRAYING SCRIPTURE

Isaiah 15

Isaiah mourned over the destruction of Moab, even though the nation was an enemy of Israel. He was sympathetic to the suffering of the people who had clothed themselves in sackcloth, weeping bitterly. The prophet reminds us we should not rejoice when calamity befalls people, even if they are suffering righteous judgment.

Ask God to help you live with mercy for the suffering, even if they are reaping their own harvest.

as far as Eglath Shelishiyah.
They go up the hill to Luhith,
weeping as they go;
on the road to Horonaim
they lament their destruction.
6 The waters of Nimrim are dried up
and the grass is withered;
the vegetation is gone
and nothing green is left.
7 So the wealth they have acquired and stored up
they carry away over the Ravine of the Poplars.
8 Their outcry echoes along the border of Moab;
their wailing reaches as far as Eglaim,
their lamentation as far as Beer Elim.
9 The waters of Dimon[a] are full of blood,
but I will bring still more upon Dimon[a] —
a lion upon the fugitives of Moab
and upon those who remain in the land.

16 Send lambs as tribute
to the ruler of the land,
from Sela, across the desert,
to the mount of Daughter Zion.
2 Like fluttering birds
pushed from the nest,
so are the women of Moab
at the fords of the Arnon.
3 "Make up your mind," Moab says.
"Render a decision.
Make your shadow like night —
at high noon.
Hide the fugitives,
do not betray the refugees.
4 Let the Moabite fugitives stay with you;
be their shelter from the destroyer."

The oppressor will come to an end,
and destruction will cease;
the aggressor will vanish from the land.
5 In love a throne will be established;
in faithfulness a man will sit on it —
one from the house[b] of David —
one who in judging seeks justice
and speeds the cause of righteousness.

6 We have heard of Moab's pride —
how great is her arrogance! —
of her conceit, her pride and her insolence;
but her boasts are empty.
7 Therefore the Moabites wail,
they wail together for Moab.

PRAYING SCRIPTURE

Isaiah 16

Isaiah testified that Moab, judged because of its lies, haughtiness and pride, would be nearly obliterated and "her survivors [would] be very few and feeble" (verse 14). God's judgment would be thorough, for Moab's sin was so great that even the nation's prayer would prove futile (see verse 12).

Nothing is more destructive to our spiritual life than pride. Ask God to cleanse you from every prideful thought and act.

---

[a] 9 *Dimon,* a wordplay on *Dibon* (see verse 2), sounds like the Hebrew for *blood.* [b] 5 Hebrew *tent*

Lament and grieve
for the raisin cakes of Kir Hareseth.
8 The fields of Heshbon wither,
the vines of Sibmah also.
The rulers of the nations
have trampled down the choicest vines,
which once reached Jazer
and spread toward the desert.
Their shoots spread out
and went as far as the sea.[a]
9 So I weep, as Jazer weeps,
for the vines of Sibmah.
Heshbon and Elealeh,
I drench you with tears!
The shouts of joy over your ripened fruit
and over your harvests have been stilled.
10 Joy and gladness are taken away from the orchards;
no one sings or shouts in the vineyards;
no one treads out wine at the presses,
for I have put an end to the shouting.
11 My heart laments for Moab like a harp,
my inmost being for Kir Hareseth.
12 When Moab appears at her high place,
she only wears herself out;
when she goes to her shrine to pray,
it is to no avail.

13 This is the word the LORD has already spoken concerning Moab.
14 But now the LORD says: "Within three years, as a servant bound by
contract would count them, Moab's splendor and all her many people
will be despised, and her survivors will be very few and feeble."

A PROPHECY AGAINST DAMASCUS

17 A prophecy against Damascus:

"See, Damascus will no longer be a city
but will become a heap of ruins.
2 The cities of Aroer will be deserted
and left to flocks, which will lie down,
with no one to make them afraid.
3 The fortified city will disappear from Ephraim,
and royal power from Damascus;
the remnant of Aram will be
like the glory of the Israelites,"
declares the LORD Almighty.

4 "In that day the glory of Jacob will fade;
the fat of his body will waste away.
5 It will be as when reapers harvest the standing grain,
gathering the grain in their arms —
as when someone gleans heads of grain
in the Valley of Rephaim.
6 Yet some gleanings will remain,
as when an olive tree is beaten,

PRAYING SCRIPTURE

Isaiah 17

The oracle against Damascus warns against the danger of forgetting the goodness and loving-kindness of God. Eventually everyone will "look to their Maker" and have respect for Israel's Holy One (verse 7). Repentance and revival always bring us to a clearer, closer relationship with God.

Do you feel as though you need to be spiritually revived? Spend time in a prayer of confession, and then ask God to revive your spirit in him.

---

[a] 8 Probably the Dead Sea

leaving two or three olives on the topmost branches,
four or five on the fruitful boughs,"
declares the LORD, the God of Israel.

7 In that day people will look to their Maker
and turn their eyes to the Holy One of Israel.
8 They will not look to the altars,
the work of their hands,
and they will have no regard for the Asherah poles[a]
and the incense altars their fingers have made.

9 In that day their strong cities, which they left because of the Israel-
ites, will be like places abandoned to thickets and undergrowth. And
all will be desolation.

10 You have forgotten God your Savior;
you have not remembered the Rock, your fortress.
Therefore, though you set out the finest plants
and plant imported vines,
11 though on the day you set them out, you make them grow,
and on the morning when you plant them, you bring them to bud,
yet the harvest will be as nothing
in the day of disease and incurable pain.

12 Woe to the many nations that rage—
they rage like the raging sea!
Woe to the peoples who roar—
they roar like the roaring of great waters!
13 Although the peoples roar like the roar of surging waters,
when he rebukes them they flee far away,
driven before the wind like chaff on the hills,
like tumbleweed before a gale.
14 In the evening, sudden terror!
Before the morning, they are gone!
This is the portion of those who loot us,
the lot of those who plunder us.

A PROPHECY AGAINST CUSH

18 Woe to the land of whirring wings[b]
along the rivers of Cush,[c]
2 which sends envoys by sea
in papyrus boats over the water.

Go, swift messengers,
to a people tall and smooth-skinned,
to a people feared far and wide,
an aggressive nation of strange speech,
whose land is divided by rivers.

3 All you people of the world,
you who live on the earth,
when a banner is raised on the mountains,
you will see it,

PRAYING SCRIPTURE

Isaiah 18

Messengers from Ethiopia foreshadow the inhabitants of earth who will one day come to Zion for salvation. Isaiah echoed other prophets who saw that God's salvation would spread to all nations. God will be glorified with some from every nation, tribe and tongue around his throne for eternity.

Do you have a burden for the nations to know Christ? Find a list of peoples who haven't heard the gospel and pray for them.

[a] 8 That is, wooden symbols of the goddess Asherah [b] 1 Or *of locusts*
[c] 1 That is, the upper Nile region

and when a trumpet sounds,
you will hear it.
4 This is what the LORD says to me:
"I will remain quiet and will look on from my dwelling place,
like shimmering heat in the sunshine,
like a cloud of dew in the heat of harvest."
5 For, before the harvest, when the blossom is gone
and the flower becomes a ripening grape,
he will cut off the shoots with pruning knives,
and cut down and take away the spreading branches.
6 They will all be left to the mountain birds of prey
and to the wild animals;
the birds will feed on them all summer,
the wild animals all winter.

7 At that time gifts will be brought to the LORD Almighty

from a people tall and smooth-skinned,
from a people feared far and wide,
an aggressive nation of strange speech,
whose land is divided by rivers—

the gifts will be brought to Mount Zion, the place of the Name of the LORD Almighty.

A PROPHECY AGAINST EGYPT

19 A prophecy against Egypt:

See, the LORD rides on a swift cloud
and is coming to Egypt.
The idols of Egypt tremble before him,
and the hearts of the Egyptians melt with fear.

2 "I will stir up Egyptian against Egyptian—
brother will fight against brother,
neighbor against neighbor,
city against city,
kingdom against kingdom.
3 The Egyptians will lose heart,
and I will bring their plans to nothing;
they will consult the idols and the spirits of the dead,
the mediums and the spiritists.
4 I will hand the Egyptians over
to the power of a cruel master,
and a fierce king will rule over them,"
declares the Lord, the LORD Almighty.

5 The waters of the river will dry up,
and the riverbed will be parched and dry.
6 The canals will stink;
the streams of Egypt will dwindle and dry up.
The reeds and rushes will wither,
7 also the plants along the Nile,
at the mouth of the river.
Every sown field along the Nile
will become parched, will blow away and be no more.
8 The fishermen will groan and lament,

PRAYING SCRIPTURE

Isaiah 19

In a continuing list of nations that would come under God's judgment, Egypt came next. Yet another nation would learn that God is superior to its idols. He will cause them to "tremble before him," and their hearts will melt because of his power (verse 1).

God shows his love and grace when he destroys the idols of our hearts. Implore God to examine your heart, cause the idols to totter and show himself greater.

all who cast hooks into the Nile;
those who throw nets on the water
will pine away.
9 Those who work with combed flax will despair,
the weavers of fine linen will lose hope.
10 The workers in cloth will be dejected,
and all the wage earners will be sick at heart.

11 The officials of Zoan are nothing but fools;
the wise counselors of Pharaoh give senseless advice.
How can you say to Pharaoh,
"I am one of the wise men,
a disciple of the ancient kings"?
12 Where are your wise men now?
Let them show you and make known
what the LORD Almighty
has planned against Egypt.
13 The officials of Zoan have become fools,
the leaders of Memphis are deceived;
the cornerstones of her peoples
have led Egypt astray.
14 The LORD has poured into them
a spirit of dizziness;
they make Egypt stagger in all that she does,
as a drunkard staggers around in his vomit.
15 There is nothing Egypt can do —
head or tail, palm branch or reed.

16 In that day the Egyptians will become weaklings. They will shud-
der with fear at the uplifted hand that the LORD Almighty raises against
them. 17 And the land of Judah will bring terror to the Egyptians; every-
one to whom Judah is mentioned will be terrified, because of what the
LORD Almighty is planning against them.

18 In that day five cities in Egypt will speak the language of Canaan
and swear allegiance to the LORD Almighty. One of them will be called
the City of the Sun.[a]

19 In that day there will be an altar to the LORD in the heart of Egypt,
and a monument to the LORD at its border. 20 It will be a sign and wit-
ness to the LORD Almighty in the land of Egypt. When they cry out to
the LORD because of their oppressors, he will send them a savior and
defender, and he will rescue them. 21 So the LORD will make himself
known to the Egyptians, and in that day they will acknowledge the
LORD. They will worship with sacrifices and grain offerings; they will
make vows to the LORD and keep them. 22 The LORD will strike Egypt
with a plague; he will strike them and heal them. They will turn to the
LORD, and he will respond to their pleas and heal them.

23 In that day there will be a highway from Egypt to Assyria. The As-
syrians will go to Egypt and the Egyptians to Assyria. The Egyptians
and Assyrians will worship together. 24 In that day Israel will be the
third, along with Egypt and Assyria, a blessing[b] on the earth. 25 The

---

[a] 18 Some manuscripts of the Masoretic Text, Dead Sea Scrolls, Symmachus and Vulgate; most manuscripts of the Masoretic Text *City of Destruction*
[b] 24 Or *Assyria, whose names will be used in blessings* (see Gen. 48:20); or *Assyria, who will be seen by others as blessed*

Lord Almighty will bless them, saying, "Blessed be Egypt my people,
Assyria my handiwork, and Israel my inheritance."

A PROPHECY AGAINST EGYPT AND CUSH

20 In the year that the supreme commander, sent by Sargon king
of Assyria, came to Ashdod and attacked and captured it—
2at that time the Lord spoke through Isaiah son of Amoz. He said to
him, "Take off the sackcloth from your body and the sandals from your
feet." And he did so, going around stripped and barefoot.
3Then the Lord said, "Just as my servant Isaiah has gone stripped
and barefoot for three years, as a sign and portent against Egypt and
Cush,[a] 4so the king of Assyria will lead away stripped and barefoot the
Egyptian captives and Cushite exiles, young and old, with buttocks
bared—to Egypt's shame. 5Those who trusted in Cush and boasted in
Egypt will be dismayed and put to shame. 6In that day the people who
live on this coast will say, 'See what has happened to those we relied
on, those we fled to for help and deliverance from the king of Assyria!
How then can we escape?'"

A PROPHECY AGAINST BABYLON

21 A prophecy against the Desert by the Sea:

Like whirlwinds sweeping through the southland,
an invader comes from the desert,
from a land of terror.

2 A dire vision has been shown to me:
The traitor betrays, the looter takes loot.
Elam, attack! Media, lay siege!
I will bring to an end all the groaning she caused.

3 At this my body is racked with pain,
pangs seize me, like those of a woman in labor;
I am staggered by what I hear,
I am bewildered by what I see.
4 My heart falters,
fear makes me tremble;
the twilight I longed for
has become a horror to me.

5 They set the tables,
they spread the rugs,
they eat, they drink!
Get up, you officers,
oil the shields!

6This is what the Lord says to me:

"Go, post a lookout
and have him report what he sees.
7 When he sees chariots
with teams of horses,
riders on donkeys
or riders on camels,

PRAYING SCRIPTURE

Isaiah 20

In one of the more unusual passages in all Scripture, God commanded Isaiah to be a living parable for God's judgment against Egypt and Ethiopia. The king of the Assyrians would shame the two countries, taking them captive and showing their nakedness.

Though God's judgment is sure, his desire is to show mercy. Ask him to show grace to those who are in danger of his judgment.

PRAYING SCRIPTURE

Isaiah 21

Think about the mental and emotional anguish a prophet must have endured by constantly telling people that judgment was coming and people were going to die. Isaiah's visions put him in great distress as he agonized over the fate of Israel and the nations (see verses 3–4).

Sometimes we wrongly think of our spiritual leaders as above all the mess and pain of life. They need prayer. Commit to praying for those who shepherd your spiritual life.

---

[a] *3* That is, the upper Nile region; also in verse 5

let him be alert,
fully alert."

8 And the lookout[a] shouted,

"Day after day, my lord, I stand on the watchtower;
every night I stay at my post.
9 Look, here comes a man in a chariot
with a team of horses.
And he gives back the answer:
'Babylon has fallen, has fallen!
All the images of its gods
lie shattered on the ground!' "
10 My people who are crushed on the threshing floor,
I tell you what I have heard
from the LORD Almighty,
from the God of Israel.

A PROPHECY AGAINST EDOM

11 A prophecy against Dumah[b]:

Someone calls to me from Seir,
"Watchman, what is left of the night?
Watchman, what is left of the night?"
12 The watchman replies,
"Morning is coming, but also the night.
If you would ask, then ask;
and come back yet again."

A PROPHECY AGAINST ARABIA

13 A prophecy against Arabia:

You caravans of Dedanites,
who camp in the thickets of Arabia,
14 bring water for the thirsty;
you who live in Tema,
bring food for the fugitives.
15 They flee from the sword,
from the drawn sword,
from the bent bow
and from the heat of battle.

16 This is what the Lord says to me: "Within one year, as a servant
bound by contract would count it, all the splendor of Kedar will come
to an end. 17 The survivors of the archers, the warriors of Kedar, will be
few." The LORD, the God of Israel, has spoken.

A PROPHECY ABOUT JERUSALEM

22 A prophecy against the Valley of Vision:

What troubles you now,
that you have all gone up on the roofs,
2 you town so full of commotion,
you city of tumult and revelry?

[a] 8 Dead Sea Scrolls and Syriac; Masoretic Text *A lion* [b] 11 *Dumah*, a wordplay on *Edom*, means *silence* or *stillness*.

PRAYING SCRIPTURE

Isaiah 22

It's heartrending enough that God's judgment falls on so many who are outside the faith. Too many times his people suffer the consequences of their sin. All sin calls for mourning, but especially sin among God's people who should be walking in the light.

Does your sin or that of another grieve you most? God's people should always seek to walk in the light and pray to be empowered by the Holy Spirit to do so.

Your slain were not killed by the sword,
  nor did they die in battle.
3 All your leaders have fled together;
  they have been captured without using the bow.
All you who were caught were taken prisoner together,
  having fled while the enemy was still far away.
4 Therefore I said, "Turn away from me;
  let me weep bitterly.
Do not try to console me
  over the destruction of my people."

5 The Lord, the LORD Almighty, has a day
  of tumult and trampling and terror
  in the Valley of Vision,
a day of battering down walls
  and of crying out to the mountains.
6 Elam takes up the quiver,
  with her charioteers and horses;
  Kir uncovers the shield.
7 Your choicest valleys are full of chariots,
  and horsemen are posted at the city gates.

8 The Lord stripped away the defenses of Judah,
  and you looked in that day
  to the weapons in the Palace of the Forest.
9 You saw that the walls of the City of David
  were broken through in many places;
you stored up water
  in the Lower Pool.
10 You counted the buildings in Jerusalem
  and tore down houses to strengthen the wall.
11 You built a reservoir between the two walls
  for the water of the Old Pool,
but you did not look to the One who made it,
  or have regard for the One who planned it long ago.

12 The Lord, the LORD Almighty,
  called you on that day
to weep and to wail,
  to tear out your hair and put on sackcloth.
13 But see, there is joy and revelry,
  slaughtering of cattle and killing of sheep,
  eating of meat and drinking of wine!
"Let us eat and drink," you say,
  "for tomorrow we die!"

14 The LORD Almighty has revealed this in my hearing: "Till your dying
day this sin will not be atoned for," says the Lord, the LORD Almighty.

15 This is what the Lord, the LORD Almighty, says:

"Go, say to this steward,
  to Shebna the palace administrator:
16 What are you doing here and who gave you permission
  to cut out a grave for yourself here,
hewing your grave on the height
  and chiseling your resting place in the rock?

17 "Beware, the LORD is about to take firm hold of you
and hurl you away, you mighty man.
18 He will roll you up tightly like a ball
and throw you into a large country.
There you will die
and there the chariots you were so proud of
will become a disgrace to your master's house.
19 I will depose you from your office,
and you will be ousted from your position.

20 "In that day I will summon my servant, Eliakim son of Hilkiah. 21 I
will clothe him with your robe and fasten your sash around him and
hand your authority over to him. He will be a father to those who live
in Jerusalem and to the people of Judah. 22 I will place on his shoulder
the key to the house of David; what he opens no one can shut, and
what he shuts no one can open. 23 I will drive him like a peg into a firm
place; he will become a seat[a] of honor for the house of his father. 24 All
the glory of his family will hang on him: its offspring and offshoots—
all its lesser vessels, from the bowls to all the jars.

25 "In that day," declares the LORD Almighty, "the peg driven into the firm place will give way; it will be sheared off and will fall, and the load hanging on it will be cut down." The LORD has spoken.

A PROPHECY AGAINST TYRE

23 A prophecy against Tyre:

Wail, you ships of Tarshish!
For Tyre is destroyed
and left without house or harbor.
From the land of Cyprus
word has come to them.
2 Be silent, you people of the island
and you merchants of Sidon,
whom the seafarers have enriched.
3 On the great waters
came the grain of the Shihor;
the harvest of the Nile[b] was the revenue of Tyre,
and she became the marketplace of the nations.

4 Be ashamed, Sidon, and you fortress of the sea,
for the sea has spoken:
"I have neither been in labor nor given birth;
I have neither reared sons nor brought up daughters."
5 When word comes to Egypt,
they will be in anguish at the report from Tyre.

6 Cross over to Tarshish;
wail, you people of the island.
7 Is this your city of revelry,
the old, old city,
whose feet have taken her
to settle in far-off lands?

PRAYING SCRIPTURE

Isaiah 23

The Lord judged Tyre for two reasons: because of its pride and so that he might display his power over the "renowned on the earth" and "humble" them (verse 9). God's judgment is never arbitrary. He doesn't punish for punishment's sake but to reveal his righteousness.

Every country will face judgment in the future. Pray that God will strengthen you as a witness to his saving power for everyone.

---

[a] *23* Or *throne* [b] *2,3* Masoretic Text; Dead Sea Scrolls *Sidon, / who cross over the sea; / your envoys* [3]*are on the great waters. / The grain of the Shihor, / the harvest of the Nile,*

8 Who planned this against Tyre,
the bestower of crowns,
whose merchants are princes,
whose traders are renowned in the earth?
9 The LORD Almighty planned it,
to bring down her pride in all her splendor
and to humble all who are renowned on the earth.

10 Till[a] your land as they do along the Nile,
Daughter Tarshish,
for you no longer have a harbor.
11 The LORD has stretched out his hand over the sea
and made its kingdoms tremble.
He has given an order concerning Phoenicia
that her fortresses be destroyed.
12 He said, "No more of your reveling,
Virgin Daughter Sidon, now crushed!
"Up, cross over to Cyprus;
even there you will find no rest."
13 Look at the land of the Babylonians,[b]
this people that is now of no account!
The Assyrians have made it
a place for desert creatures;
they raised up their siege towers,
they stripped its fortresses bare
and turned it into a ruin.

14 Wail, you ships of Tarshish;
your fortress is destroyed!

15 At that time Tyre will be forgotten for seventy years, the span of a
king's life. But at the end of these seventy years, it will happen to Tyre
as in the song of the prostitute:

16 "Take up a harp, walk through the city,
you forgotten prostitute;
play the harp well, sing many a song,
so that you will be remembered."

17 At the end of seventy years, the LORD will deal with Tyre. She will
return to her lucrative prostitution and will ply her trade with all the
kingdoms on the face of the earth. 18 Yet her profit and her earnings
will be set apart for the LORD; they will not be stored up or hoarded.
Her profits will go to those who live before the LORD, for abundant food
and fine clothes.

THE LORD'S DEVASTATION OF THE EARTH

24 See, the LORD is going to lay waste the earth
and devastate it;
he will ruin its face
and scatter its inhabitants —
2 it will be the same
for priest as for people,

PRAYING SCRIPTURE

Isaiah 24

Isaiah made it clear: Nations will not be alone in receiving God's judgment; individuals will too. Priests, slaves, masters, maids, buyers, sellers, borrowers, lenders, debtors and creditors alike will be judged. The folly of human rebellion becomes evident when we see God in his glory.

Scripture makes clear that God is concerned about every facet of life, so commit all of your life to his control again today.

[a] *10* Dead Sea Scrolls and some Septuagint manuscripts; Masoretic Text *Go through* [b] *13* Or *Chaldeans*

for the master as for his servant,
for the mistress as for her servant,
for seller as for buyer,
for borrower as for lender,
for debtor as for creditor.
3 The earth will be completely laid waste
and totally plundered.
The LORD has spoken this word.

4 The earth dries up and withers,
the world languishes and withers,
the heavens languish with the earth.
5 The earth is defiled by its people;
they have disobeyed the laws,
violated the statutes
and broken the everlasting covenant.
6 Therefore a curse consumes the earth;
its people must bear their guilt.
Therefore earth's inhabitants are burned up,
and very few are left.
7 The new wine dries up and the vine withers;
all the merrymakers groan.
8 The joyful timbrels are stilled,
the noise of the revelers has stopped,
the joyful harp is silent.
9 No longer do they drink wine with a song;
the beer is bitter to its drinkers.
10 The ruined city lies desolate;
the entrance to every house is barred.
11 In the streets they cry out for wine;
all joy turns to gloom,
all joyful sounds are banished from the earth.
12 The city is left in ruins,
its gate is battered to pieces.
13 So will it be on the earth
and among the nations,
as when an olive tree is beaten,
or as when gleanings are left after the grape harvest.

14 They raise their voices, they shout for joy;
from the west they acclaim the LORD's majesty.
15 Therefore in the east give glory to the LORD;
exalt the name of the LORD, the God of Israel,
in the islands of the sea.
16 From the ends of the earth we hear singing:
"Glory to the Righteous One."

But I said, "I waste away, I waste away!
Woe to me!
The treacherous betray!
With treachery the treacherous betray!"
17 Terror and pit and snare await you,
people of the earth.
18 Whoever flees at the sound of terror
will fall into a pit;

whoever climbs out of the pit
will be caught in a snare.

The floodgates of the heavens are opened,
the foundations of the earth shake.
19 The earth is broken up,
the earth is split asunder,
the earth is violently shaken.
20 The earth reels like a drunkard,
it sways like a hut in the wind;
so heavy upon it is the guilt of its rebellion
that it falls — never to rise again.

21 In that day the LORD will punish
the powers in the heavens above
and the kings on the earth below.
22 They will be herded together
like prisoners bound in a dungeon;
they will be shut up in prison
and be punished[a] after many days.
23 The moon will be dismayed,
the sun ashamed;
for the LORD Almighty will reign
on Mount Zion and in Jerusalem,
and before its elders — with great glory.

PRAISE TO THE LORD

25 LORD, you are my God;
I will exalt you and praise your name,
for in perfect faithfulness
you have done wonderful things,
things planned long ago.
2 You have made the city a heap of rubble,
the fortified town a ruin,
the foreigners' stronghold a city no more;
it will never be rebuilt.
3 Therefore strong peoples will honor you;
cities of ruthless nations will revere you.
4 You have been a refuge for the poor,
a refuge for the needy in their distress,
a shelter from the storm
and a shade from the heat.
For the breath of the ruthless
is like a storm driving against a wall
5 and like the heat of the desert.
You silence the uproar of foreigners;
as heat is reduced by the shadow of a cloud,
so the song of the ruthless is stilled.

6 On this mountain the LORD Almighty will prepare
a feast of rich food for all peoples,
a banquet of aged wine —
the best of meats and the finest of wines.

PRAYING SCRIPTURE

Isaiah 25

The Lord's glory is a terror to sinners but a refuge to those who humble themselves before him. If we don't think God as Judge is a reason for praise, then we miss a great emphasis of the prophets. It's due to his power that he will one day "swallow up death forever" and "wipe away the tears from all faces" (verse 8).

Spend time praising God for his perfect judgment.

[a] 22 Or *released*

7 On this mountain he will destroy
the shroud that enfolds all peoples,
the sheet that covers all nations;
8 he will swallow up death forever.
The Sovereign LORD will wipe away the tears
from all faces;
he will remove his people's disgrace
from all the earth.
The LORD has spoken.

9 In that day they will say,

"Surely this is our God;
we trusted in him, and he saved us.
This is the LORD, we trusted in him;
let us rejoice and be glad in his salvation."

10 The hand of the LORD will rest on this mountain;
but Moab will be trampled in their land
as straw is trampled down in the manure.
11 They will stretch out their hands in it,
as swimmers stretch out their hands to swim.
God will bring down their pride
despite the cleverness[a] of their hands.
12 He will bring down your high fortified walls
and lay them low;
he will bring them down to the ground,
to the very dust.

A SONG OF PRAISE

26 In that day this song will be sung in the land of Judah:

We have a strong city;
God makes salvation
its walls and ramparts.
2 Open the gates
that the righteous nation may enter,
the nation that keeps faith.
3 You will keep in perfect peace
those whose minds are steadfast,
because they trust in you.
4 Trust in the LORD forever,
for the LORD, the LORD himself, is the Rock eternal.
5 He humbles those who dwell on high,
he lays the lofty city low;
he levels it to the ground
and casts it down to the dust.
6 Feet trample it down—
the feet of the oppressed,
the footsteps of the poor.

7 The path of the righteous is level;
you, the Upright One, make the way of the righteous smooth.
8 Yes, LORD, walking in the way of your laws,[b]
we wait for you;

PRAYING SCRIPTURE

Isaiah 26

A chapter of great hope for future Judah reminds us that the Lord gives us peace when our hearts rest in him. "LORD, you establish peace for us," Isaiah said (verse 12). God's people are always invited into his protection regardless of what's going on in the world.

When the world is coming apart all around you, rest in him. Ask God to cover you with his peace, and he will.

[a] *11* The meaning of the Hebrew for this word is uncertain. [b] *8* Or *judgments*

your name and renown
  are the desire of our hearts.
9 My soul yearns for you in the night;
  in the morning my spirit longs for you.
When your judgments come upon the earth,
  the people of the world learn righteousness.
10 But when grace is shown to the wicked,
  they do not learn righteousness;
even in a land of uprightness they go on doing evil
  and do not regard the majesty of the LORD.
11 LORD, your hand is lifted high,
  but they do not see it.
Let them see your zeal for your people and be put to shame;
  let the fire reserved for your enemies consume them.

12 LORD, you establish peace for us;
  all that we have accomplished you have done for us.
13 LORD our God, other lords besides you have ruled over us,
  but your name alone do we honor.
14 They are now dead, they live no more;
  their spirits do not rise.
You punished them and brought them to ruin;
  you wiped out all memory of them.
15 You have enlarged the nation, LORD;
  you have enlarged the nation.
You have gained glory for yourself;
  you have extended all the borders of the land.

16 LORD, they came to you in their distress;
  when you disciplined them,
  they could barely whisper a prayer.[a]
17 As a pregnant woman about to give birth
  writhes and cries out in her pain,
  so were we in your presence, LORD.
18 We were with child, we writhed in labor,
  but we gave birth to wind.
We have not brought salvation to the earth,
  and the people of the world have not come to life.

19 But your dead will live, LORD;
  their bodies will rise—
let those who dwell in the dust
  wake up and shout for joy—
your dew is like the dew of the morning;
  the earth will give birth to her dead.

20 Go, my people, enter your rooms
  and shut the doors behind you;
hide yourselves for a little while
  until his wrath has passed by.
21 See, the LORD is coming out of his dwelling
  to punish the people of the earth for their sins.
The earth will disclose the blood shed on it;
  the earth will conceal its slain no longer.

[a] *16* The meaning of the Hebrew for this clause is uncertain.

DELIVERANCE OF ISRAEL

27 In that day,

the LORD will punish with his sword—
his fierce, great and powerful sword—
Leviathan the gliding serpent,
Leviathan the coiling serpent;
he will slay the monster of the sea.

2 In that day—

"Sing about a fruitful vineyard:
3 I, the LORD, watch over it;
I water it continually.
I guard it day and night
so that no one may harm it.
4 I am not angry.
If only there were briers and thorns confronting me!
I would march against them in battle;
I would set them all on fire.
5 Or else let them come to me for refuge;
let them make peace with me,
yes, let them make peace with me."

6 In days to come Jacob will take root,
Israel will bud and blossom
and fill all the world with fruit.

7 Has the LORD struck her
as he struck down those who struck her?
Has she been killed
as those were killed who killed her?
8 By warfare[a] and exile you contend with her—
with his fierce blast he drives her out,
as on a day the east wind blows.
9 By this, then, will Jacob's guilt be atoned for,
and this will be the full fruit of the removal of his sin:
When he makes all the altar stones
to be like limestone crushed to pieces,
no Asherah poles[b] or incense altars
will be left standing.
10 The fortified city stands desolate,
an abandoned settlement, forsaken like the wilderness;
there the calves graze,
there they lie down;
they strip its branches bare.
11 When its twigs are dry, they are broken off
and women come and make fires with them.
For this is a people without understanding;
so their Maker has no compassion on them,
and their Creator shows them no favor.

12 In that day the LORD will thresh from the flowing Euphrates to the
Wadi of Egypt, and you, Israel, will be gathered up one by one. 13 And

[a] 8 See Septuagint; the meaning of the Hebrew for this word is uncertain.
[b] 9 That is, wooden symbols of the goddess Asherah

PRAYING SCRIPTURE

Isaiah 27

In a pattern common to the prophets, Isaiah alternated between narratives of judgment and curses to promises of blessing and restoration. That often feels like the pattern of life, doesn't it? We descend from mountaintop to valley, then rise from trial to triumph. God never promised his way would be easy, but he will hear our prayers for strength to walk the narrow way.

in that day a great trumpet will sound. Those who were perishing in
Assyria and those who were exiled in Egypt will come and worship the
LORD on the holy mountain in Jerusalem.

WOE TO THE LEADERS OF EPHRAIM AND JUDAH

28 Woe to that wreath, the pride of Ephraim's drunkards,
to the fading flower, his glorious beauty,
set on the head of a fertile valley—
to that city, the pride of those laid low by wine!
2 See, the Lord has one who is powerful and strong.
Like a hailstorm and a destructive wind,
like a driving rain and a flooding downpour,
he will throw it forcefully to the ground.
3 That wreath, the pride of Ephraim's drunkards,
will be trampled underfoot.
4 That fading flower, his glorious beauty,
set on the head of a fertile valley,
will be like figs ripe before harvest—
as soon as people see them and take them in hand,
they swallow them.

5 In that day the LORD Almighty
will be a glorious crown,
a beautiful wreath
for the remnant of his people.
6 He will be a spirit of justice
to the one who sits in judgment,
a source of strength
to those who turn back the battle at the gate.

7 And these also stagger from wine
and reel from beer:
Priests and prophets stagger from beer
and are befuddled with wine;
they reel from beer,
they stagger when seeing visions,
they stumble when rendering decisions.
8 All the tables are covered with vomit
and there is not a spot without filth.

9 "Who is it he is trying to teach?
To whom is he explaining his message?
To children weaned from their milk,
to those just taken from the breast?
10 For it is:
Do this, do that,
a rule for this, a rule for that[a];
a little here, a little there."

11 Very well then, with foreign lips and strange tongues
God will speak to this people,
12 to whom he said,
"This is the resting place, let the weary rest";

[a] *10* Hebrew / *sav lasav sav lasav / kav lakav kav lakav* (probably meaningless sounds mimicking the prophet's words); also in verse 13

PRAYING SCRIPTURE

Isaiah 28

One of Isaiah's most well-known Messianic prophecies is in verse 16, regarding the "precious cornerstone for a sure foundation." God's assurance is that whoever believes in this stone, the Messiah, will not act hastily but will hold to faith in God's promise.

Do you live daily with Jesus as the cornerstone, the sure foundation of your life? If not, ask God to help you build every decision on him.

and, "This is the place of repose" —
but they would not listen.
13 So then, the word of the LORD to them will become:
Do this, do that,
a rule for this, a rule for that;
a little here, a little there —
so that as they go they will fall backward;
they will be injured and snared and captured.

14 Therefore hear the word of the LORD, you scoffers
who rule this people in Jerusalem.
15 You boast, "We have entered into a covenant with death,
with the realm of the dead we have made an agreement.
When an overwhelming scourge sweeps by,
it cannot touch us,
for we have made a lie our refuge
and falsehood[a] our hiding place."

16 So this is what the Sovereign LORD says:

"See, I lay a stone in Zion, a tested stone,
a precious cornerstone for a sure foundation;
the one who relies on it
will never be stricken with panic.
17 I will make justice the measuring line
and righteousness the plumb line;
hail will sweep away your refuge, the lie,
and water will overflow your hiding place.
18 Your covenant with death will be annulled;
your agreement with the realm of the dead will not stand.
When the overwhelming scourge sweeps by,
you will be beaten down by it.
19 As often as it comes it will carry you away;
morning after morning, by day and by night,
it will sweep through."

The understanding of this message
will bring sheer terror.
20 The bed is too short to stretch out on,
the blanket too narrow to wrap around you.
21 The LORD will rise up as he did at Mount Perazim,
he will rouse himself as in the Valley of Gibeon —
to do his work, his strange work,
and perform his task, his alien task.
22 Now stop your mocking,
or your chains will become heavier;
the Lord, the LORD Almighty, has told me
of the destruction decreed against the whole land.

23 Listen and hear my voice;
pay attention and hear what I say.
24 When a farmer plows for planting, does he plow continually?
Does he keep on breaking up and working the soil?
25 When he has leveled the surface,
does he not sow caraway and scatter cumin?

[a] 15 Or *false gods*

Does he not plant wheat in its place,[a]
barley in its plot,[a]
and spelt in its field?
26 His God instructs him
and teaches him the right way.

27 Caraway is not threshed with a sledge,
nor is the wheel of a cart rolled over cumin;
caraway is beaten out with a rod,
and cumin with a stick.
28 Grain must be ground to make bread;
so one does not go on threshing it forever.
The wheels of a threshing cart may be rolled over it,
but one does not use horses to grind grain.
29 All this also comes from the LORD Almighty,
whose plan is wonderful,
whose wisdom is magnificent.

WOE TO DAVID'S CITY

29 Woe to you, Ariel, Ariel,
the city where David settled!
Add year to year
and let your cycle of festivals go on.
2 Yet I will besiege Ariel;
she will mourn and lament,
she will be to me like an altar hearth.[b]
3 I will encamp against you on all sides;
I will encircle you with towers
and set up my siege works against you.
4 Brought low, you will speak from the ground;
your speech will mumble out of the dust.
Your voice will come ghostlike from the earth;
out of the dust your speech will whisper.

5 But your many enemies will become like fine dust,
the ruthless hordes like blown chaff.
Suddenly, in an instant,
6 the LORD Almighty will come
with thunder and earthquake and great noise,
with windstorm and tempest and flames of a devouring fire.
7 Then the hordes of all the nations that fight against Ariel,
that attack her and her fortress and besiege her,
will be as it is with a dream,
with a vision in the night—
8 as when a hungry person dreams of eating,
but awakens hungry still;
as when a thirsty person dreams of drinking,
but awakens faint and thirsty still.
So will it be with the hordes of all the nations
that fight against Mount Zion.

9 Be stunned and amazed,
blind yourselves and be sightless;

PRAYING SCRIPTURE

Isaiah 29

Jesus' New Testament condemnation of the religious leaders was taken from verse 13: "These people come near to me with their mouth and honor me with their lips, but their hearts are far from me." The danger of this hypocrisy is that one can still appear committed with a distant heart. What people think of us feeds our pride, keeping us from repenting.

Are your inner and outer lives aligned? If not, repent and ask God for integrity.

[a] *25* The meaning of the Hebrew for this word is uncertain. [b] *2* The Hebrew for *altar hearth* sounds like the Hebrew for *Ariel.*

be drunk, but not from wine,
stagger, but not from beer.
10 The LORD has brought over you a deep sleep:
He has sealed your eyes (the prophets);
he has covered your heads (the seers).

11 For you this whole vision is nothing but words sealed in a scroll.
And if you give the scroll to someone who can read, and say, "Read
this, please," they will answer, "I can't; it is sealed." 12 Or if you give the
scroll to someone who cannot read, and say, "Read this, please," they
will answer, "I don't know how to read."

13 The Lord says:

"These people come near to me with their mouth
and honor me with their lips,
but their hearts are far from me.
Their worship of me
is based on merely human rules they have been taught.[a]
14 Therefore once more I will astound these people
with wonder upon wonder;
the wisdom of the wise will perish,
the intelligence of the intelligent will vanish."
15 Woe to those who go to great depths
to hide their plans from the LORD,
who do their work in darkness and think,
"Who sees us? Who will know?"
16 You turn things upside down,
as if the potter were thought to be like the clay!
Shall what is formed say to the one who formed it,
"You did not make me"?
Can the pot say to the potter,
"You know nothing"?

17 In a very short time, will not Lebanon be turned into a fertile field
and the fertile field seem like a forest?
18 In that day the deaf will hear the words of the scroll,
and out of gloom and darkness
the eyes of the blind will see.
19 Once more the humble will rejoice in the LORD;
the needy will rejoice in the Holy One of Israel.
20 The ruthless will vanish,
the mockers will disappear,
and all who have an eye for evil will be cut down—
21 those who with a word make someone out to be guilty,
who ensnare the defender in court
and with false testimony deprive the innocent of justice.

22 Therefore this is what the LORD, who redeemed Abraham, says to
the descendants of Jacob:

"No longer will Jacob be ashamed;
no longer will their faces grow pale.
23 When they see among them their children,
the work of my hands,

---

[a] 13 Hebrew; Septuagint *They worship me in vain; / their teachings are merely human rules*

they will keep my name holy;
they will acknowledge the holiness of the Holy One of Jacob,
and will stand in awe of the God of Israel.
24 Those who are wayward in spirit will gain understanding;
those who complain will accept instruction."

PRAYING SCRIPTURE

Isaiah 30

The Lord called his people "obstinate children" for carrying out plans that were not his (verse 1). Since it didn't come from God's Spirit, their alliance added sin to their already existing sin. The protection they gained would be turned to shame.

Pray for the repentance that leads to salvation and the quietness and trust in the Lord that brings strength. Always seek counsel from God's Word, and ask his Spirit for wisdom for righteous living.

WOE TO THE OBSTINATE NATION

30 "Woe to the obstinate children,"
declares the LORD,
"to those who carry out plans that are not mine,
forming an alliance, but not by my Spirit,
heaping sin upon sin;
2 who go down to Egypt
without consulting me;
who look for help to Pharaoh's protection,
to Egypt's shade for refuge.
3 But Pharaoh's protection will be to your shame,
Egypt's shade will bring you disgrace.
4 Though they have officials in Zoan
and their envoys have arrived in Hanes,
5 everyone will be put to shame
because of a people useless to them,
who bring neither help nor advantage,
but only shame and disgrace."

6 A prophecy concerning the animals of the Negev:

Through a land of hardship and distress,
of lions and lionesses,
of adders and darting snakes,
the envoys carry their riches on donkeys' backs,
their treasures on the humps of camels,
to that unprofitable nation,
7 to Egypt, whose help is utterly useless.
Therefore I call her
Rahab the Do-Nothing.

8 Go now, write it on a tablet for them,
inscribe it on a scroll,
that for the days to come
it may be an everlasting witness.
9 For these are rebellious people, deceitful children,
children unwilling to listen to the LORD's instruction.
10 They say to the seers,
"See no more visions!"
and to the prophets,
"Give us no more visions of what is right!
Tell us pleasant things,
prophesy illusions.
11 Leave this way,
get off this path,
and stop confronting us
with the Holy One of Israel!"

12 Therefore this is what the Holy One of Israel says:

"Because you have rejected this message,
relied on oppression
and depended on deceit,
13 this sin will become for you
like a high wall, cracked and bulging,
that collapses suddenly, in an instant.
14 It will break in pieces like pottery,
shattered so mercilessly
that among its pieces not a fragment will be found
for taking coals from a hearth
or scooping water out of a cistern."

15 This is what the Sovereign LORD, the Holy One of Israel, says:

"In repentance and rest is your salvation,
in quietness and trust is your strength,
but you would have none of it.
16 You said, 'No, we will flee on horses.'
Therefore you will flee!
You said, 'We will ride off on swift horses.'
Therefore your pursuers will be swift!
17 A thousand will flee
at the threat of one;
at the threat of five
you will all flee away,
till you are left
like a flagstaff on a mountaintop,
like a banner on a hill."

18 Yet the LORD longs to be gracious to you;
therefore he will rise up to show you compassion.
For the LORD is a God of justice.
Blessed are all who wait for him!

19 People of Zion, who live in Jerusalem, you will weep no more.
How gracious he will be when you cry for help! As soon as he hears,
he will answer you. 20 Although the Lord gives you the bread of ad-
versity and the water of affliction, your teachers will be hidden no
more; with your own eyes you will see them. 21 Whether you turn
to the right or to the left, your ears will hear a voice behind you,
saying, "This is the way; walk in it." 22 Then you will desecrate your
idols overlaid with silver and your images covered with gold; you
will throw them away like a menstrual cloth and say to them, "Away
with you!"

23 He will also send you rain for the seed you sow in the ground,
and the food that comes from the land will be rich and plentiful. In
that day your cattle will graze in broad meadows. 24 The oxen and
donkeys that work the soil will eat fodder and mash, spread out with
fork and shovel. 25 In the day of great slaughter, when the towers fall,
streams of water will flow on every high mountain and every lofty
hill. 26 The moon will shine like the sun, and the sunlight will be
seven times brighter, like the light of seven full days, when the LORD
binds up the bruises of his people and heals the wounds he inflicted.

27 See, the Name of the LORD comes from afar,
with burning anger and dense clouds of smoke;

his lips are full of wrath,
and his tongue is a consuming fire.
28 His breath is like a rushing torrent,
rising up to the neck.
He shakes the nations in the sieve of destruction;
he places in the jaws of the peoples
a bit that leads them astray.
29 And you will sing
as on the night you celebrate a holy festival;
your hearts will rejoice
as when people playing pipes go up
to the mountain of the LORD,
to the Rock of Israel.
30 The LORD will cause people to hear his majestic voice
and will make them see his arm coming down
with raging anger and consuming fire,
with cloudburst, thunderstorm and hail.
31 The voice of the LORD will shatter Assyria;
with his rod he will strike them down.
32 Every stroke the LORD lays on them
with his punishing club
will be to the music of timbrels and harps,
as he fights them in battle with the blows of his arm.
33 Topheth has long been prepared;
it has been made ready for the king.
Its fire pit has been made deep and wide,
with an abundance of fire and wood;
the breath of the LORD,
like a stream of burning sulfur,
sets it ablaze.

WOE TO THOSE WHO RELY ON EGYPT

31 Woe to those who go down to Egypt for help,
who rely on horses,
who trust in the multitude of their chariots
and in the great strength of their horsemen,
but do not look to the Holy One of Israel,
or seek help from the LORD.
2 Yet he too is wise and can bring disaster;
he does not take back his words.
He will rise up against that wicked nation,
against those who help evildoers.
3 But the Egyptians are mere mortals and not God;
their horses are flesh and not spirit.
When the LORD stretches out his hand,
those who help will stumble,
those who are helped will fall;
all will perish together.

4 This is what the LORD says to me:

"As a lion growls,
a great lion over its prey —
and though a whole band of shepherds
is called together against it,

PRAYING SCRIPTURE

Isaiah 31

A common temptation for God's people is placing our faith in what we can see. Israel was tempted to rely on earthly help, like neighboring Egypt with its military power, rather than calling on the Holy One who has all power and wisdom.

Faith is seeing all of reality as God sees; it's seeing his working though the invisible. Pray for the faith to trust God's unseen hand rather than human might.

it is not frightened by their shouts
or disturbed by their clamor —
so the LORD Almighty will come down
to do battle on Mount Zion and on its heights.
5 Like birds hovering overhead,
the LORD Almighty will shield Jerusalem;
he will shield it and deliver it,
he will 'pass over' it and will rescue it."

6 Return, you Israelites, to the One you have so greatly revolted
against. 7 For in that day every one of you will reject the idols of silver
and gold your sinful hands have made.

8 "Assyria will fall by no human sword;
a sword, not of mortals, will devour them.
They will flee before the sword
and their young men will be put to forced labor.
9 Their stronghold will fall because of terror;
at the sight of the battle standard their commanders will panic,"
declares the LORD,
whose fire is in Zion,
whose furnace is in Jerusalem.

THE KINGDOM OF RIGHTEOUSNESS

32 See, a king will reign in righteousness
and rulers will rule with justice.
2 Each one will be like a shelter from the wind
and a refuge from the storm,
like streams of water in the desert
and the shadow of a great rock in a thirsty land.

3 Then the eyes of those who see will no longer be closed,
and the ears of those who hear will listen.
4 The fearful heart will know and understand,
and the stammering tongue will be fluent and clear.
5 No longer will the fool be called noble
nor the scoundrel be highly respected.
6 For fools speak folly,
their hearts are bent on evil:
They practice ungodliness
and spread error concerning the LORD;
the hungry they leave empty
and from the thirsty they withhold water.
7 Scoundrels use wicked methods,
they make up evil schemes
to destroy the poor with lies,
even when the plea of the needy is just.
8 But the noble make noble plans,
and by noble deeds they stand.

THE WOMEN OF JERUSALEM

9 You women who are so complacent,
rise up and listen to me;
you daughters who feel secure,
hear what I have to say!

PRAYING SCRIPTURE

Isaiah 32

The hope of God's future righteous reign should stoke a fire in us for living with it in view. Looking around can lead to distraction and despair. Looking forward can lead to hope and passion for God's kingdom where "a king will reign in righteousness" (verse 1).

Focusing on God's kingdom brings hope as we recognize that God hasn't lost. Ask him to help you live in the victory he's already won.

10 In little more than a year
you who feel secure will tremble;
the grape harvest will fail,
and the harvest of fruit will not come.
11 Tremble, you complacent women;
shudder, you daughters who feel secure!
Strip off your fine clothes
and wrap yourselves in rags.
12 Beat your breasts for the pleasant fields,
for the fruitful vines
13 and for the land of my people,
a land overgrown with thorns and briers—
yes, mourn for all houses of merriment
and for this city of revelry.
14 The fortress will be abandoned,
the noisy city deserted;
citadel and watchtower will become a wasteland forever,
the delight of donkeys, a pasture for flocks,
15 till the Spirit is poured on us from on high,
and the desert becomes a fertile field,
and the fertile field seems like a forest.
16 The LORD's justice will dwell in the desert,
his righteousness live in the fertile field.
17 The fruit of that righteousness will be peace;
its effect will be quietness and confidence forever.
18 My people will live in peaceful dwelling places,
in secure homes,
in undisturbed places of rest.
19 Though hail flattens the forest
and the city is leveled completely,
20 how blessed you will be,
sowing your seed by every stream,
and letting your cattle and donkeys range free.

DISTRESS AND HELP

33 Woe to you, destroyer,
you who have not been destroyed!
Woe to you, betrayer,
you who have not been betrayed!
When you stop destroying,
you will be destroyed;
when you stop betraying,
you will be betrayed.

2 LORD, be gracious to us;
we long for you.
Be our strength every morning,
our salvation in time of distress.
3 At the uproar of your army, the peoples flee;
when you rise up, the nations scatter.
4 Your plunder, O nations, is harvested as by young locusts;
like a swarm of locusts people pounce on it.

5 The LORD is exalted, for he dwells on high;
he will fill Zion with his justice and righteousness.

PRAYING SCRIPTURE
Isaiah 33

Even when God's people had been unfaithful to him, Isaiah remained convinced that God was for them. God promised they would "see the king in his beauty" as well as the land of Zion that was still far off to them (verse 17).

This is the essence of our sojourn. God remains faithful even when we are unfaithful, and at times, when we seek him in prayer, we glimpse his kingdom afar off.

6 He will be the sure foundation for your times,
a rich store of salvation and wisdom and knowledge;
the fear of the LORD is the key to this treasure.[a]

7 Look, their brave men cry aloud in the streets;
the envoys of peace weep bitterly.
8 The highways are deserted,
no travelers are on the roads.
The treaty is broken,
its witnesses[b] are despised,
no one is respected.
9 The land dries up and wastes away,
Lebanon is ashamed and withers;
Sharon is like the Arabah,
and Bashan and Carmel drop their leaves.

10 "Now will I arise," says the LORD.
"Now will I be exalted;
now will I be lifted up.
11 You conceive chaff,
you give birth to straw;
your breath is a fire that consumes you.
12 The peoples will be burned to ashes;
like cut thornbushes they will be set ablaze."

13 You who are far away, hear what I have done;
you who are near, acknowledge my power!
14 The sinners in Zion are terrified;
trembling grips the godless:
"Who of us can dwell with the consuming fire?
Who of us can dwell with everlasting burning?"
15 Those who walk righteously
and speak what is right,
who reject gain from extortion
and keep their hands from accepting bribes,
who stop their ears against plots of murder
and shut their eyes against contemplating evil—
16 they are the ones who will dwell on the heights,
whose refuge will be the mountain fortress.
Their bread will be supplied,
and water will not fail them.

17 Your eyes will see the king in his beauty
and view a land that stretches afar.
18 In your thoughts you will ponder the former terror:
"Where is that chief officer?
Where is the one who took the revenue?
Where is the officer in charge of the towers?"
19 You will see those arrogant people no more,
people whose speech is obscure,
whose language is strange and incomprehensible.

20 Look on Zion, the city of our festivals;
your eyes will see Jerusalem,
a peaceful abode, a tent that will not be moved;

[a] 6 Or *is a treasure from him* [b] 8 Dead Sea Scrolls; Masoretic Text / *the cities*

its stakes will never be pulled up,
nor any of its ropes broken.
21 There the LORD will be our Mighty One.
It will be like a place of broad rivers and streams.
No galley with oars will ride them,
no mighty ship will sail them.
22 For the LORD is our judge,
the LORD is our lawgiver,
the LORD is our king;
it is he who will save us.

23 Your rigging hangs loose:
The mast is not held secure,
the sail is not spread.
Then an abundance of spoils will be divided
and even the lame will carry off plunder.
24 No one living in Zion will say, "I am ill";
and the sins of those who dwell there will be forgiven.

JUDGMENT AGAINST THE NATIONS

34 Come near, you nations, and listen;
pay attention, you peoples!
Let the earth hear, and all that is in it,
the world, and all that comes out of it!
2 The LORD is angry with all nations;
his wrath is on all their armies.
He will totally destroy[a] them,
he will give them over to slaughter.
3 Their slain will be thrown out,
their dead bodies will stink;
the mountains will be soaked with their blood.
4 All the stars in the sky will be dissolved
and the heavens rolled up like a scroll;
all the starry host will fall
like withered leaves from the vine,
like shriveled figs from the fig tree.

5 My sword has drunk its fill in the heavens;
see, it descends in judgment on Edom,
the people I have totally destroyed.
6 The sword of the LORD is bathed in blood,
it is covered with fat—
the blood of lambs and goats,
fat from the kidneys of rams.
For the LORD has a sacrifice in Bozrah
and a great slaughter in the land of Edom.
7 And the wild oxen will fall with them,
the bull calves and the great bulls.
Their land will be drenched with blood,
and the dust will be soaked with fat.

8 For the LORD has a day of vengeance,
a year of retribution, to uphold Zion's cause.

PRAYING SCRIPTURE

Isaiah 34

When the Lord's anger is aroused, the nations should give him their attention. Using graphic language, Isaiah described dead bodies and their stench, blood, vengeance and burning sulfur. The sword of the Lord would be severe. And where did God point the Israelites for assurance? The "scroll of the LORD" (verse 16).

God's Word is where we should always go to be reassured of God's plan. Every time you open it, ask God's Spirit for wisdom.

[a] 2 The Hebrew term refers to the irrevocable giving over of things or persons to the LORD, often by totally destroying them; also in verse 5.

9 Edom's streams will be turned into pitch,
her dust into burning sulfur;
her land will become blazing pitch!
10 It will not be quenched night or day;
its smoke will rise forever.
From generation to generation it will lie desolate;
no one will ever pass through it again.
11 The desert owl[a] and screech owl[a] will possess it;
the great owl[a] and the raven will nest there.
God will stretch out over Edom
the measuring line of chaos
and the plumb line of desolation.
12 Her nobles will have nothing there to be called a kingdom,
all her princes will vanish away.
13 Thorns will overrun her citadels,
nettles and brambles her strongholds.
She will become a haunt for jackals,
a home for owls.
14 Desert creatures will meet with hyenas,
and wild goats will bleat to each other;
there the night creatures will also lie down
and find for themselves places of rest.
15 The owl will nest there and lay eggs,
she will hatch them, and care for her young
under the shadow of her wings;
there also the falcons will gather,
each with its mate.

16 Look in the scroll of the LORD and read:

None of these will be missing,
not one will lack her mate.
For it is his mouth that has given the order,
and his Spirit will gather them together.
17 He allots their portions;
his hand distributes them by measure.
They will possess it forever
and dwell there from generation to generation.

JOY OF THE REDEEMED

35 The desert and the parched land will be glad;
the wilderness will rejoice and blossom.
Like the crocus, 2 it will burst into bloom;
it will rejoice greatly and shout for joy.
The glory of Lebanon will be given to it,
the splendor of Carmel and Sharon;
they will see the glory of the LORD,
the splendor of our God.

3 Strengthen the feeble hands,
steady the knees that give way;
4 say to those with fearful hearts,
"Be strong, do not fear;

[a] 11 The precise identification of these birds is uncertain.

PRAYING SCRIPTURE

Isaiah 35

God's glorious future for his children is pictured in this: The desert will bloom (see verse 1); the blind, deaf and lame will be healed (see verses 5–6); the Way of Holiness will be established (see verse 8); no danger creatures will be there (see verse 9); and his people will return to Zion with singing and joy (see verse 10).

Bookmark this chapter for whenever you go through a hard time. Pray this chapter as an expression of hope to the Lord.

your God will come,
he will come with vengeance;
with divine retribution
he will come to save you."

5 Then will the eyes of the blind be opened
and the ears of the deaf unstopped.
6 Then will the lame leap like a deer,
and the mute tongue shout for joy.
Water will gush forth in the wilderness
and streams in the desert.
7 The burning sand will become a pool,
the thirsty ground bubbling springs.
In the haunts where jackals once lay,
grass and reeds and papyrus will grow.

8 And a highway will be there;
it will be called the Way of Holiness;
it will be for those who walk on that Way.
The unclean will not journey on it;
wicked fools will not go about on it.
9 No lion will be there,
nor any ravenous beast;
they will not be found there.
But only the redeemed will walk there,
10 and those the LORD has rescued will return.
They will enter Zion with singing;
everlasting joy will crown their heads.
Gladness and joy will overtake them,
and sorrow and sighing will flee away.

SENNACHERIB THREATENS JERUSALEM

36 In the fourteenth year of King Hezekiah's reign, Sennacherib
king of Assyria attacked all the fortified cities of Judah and
captured them. 2 Then the king of Assyria sent his field commander
with a large army from Lachish to King Hezekiah at Jerusalem. When
the commander stopped at the aqueduct of the Upper Pool, on the
road to the Launderer's Field, 3 Eliakim son of Hilkiah the palace ad-
ministrator, Shebna the secretary, and Joah son of Asaph the recorder
went out to him.
4 The field commander said to them, "Tell Hezekiah:

" 'This is what the great king, the king of Assyria, says: On what
are you basing this confidence of yours? 5 You say you have counsel
and might for war — but you speak only empty words. On whom
are you depending, that you rebel against me? 6 Look, I know you
are depending on Egypt, that splintered reed of a staff, which
pierces the hand of anyone who leans on it! Such is Pharaoh king
of Egypt to all who depend on him. 7 But if you say to me, "We are
depending on the LORD our God" — isn't he the one whose high
places and altars Hezekiah removed, saying to Judah and Jerusa-
lem, "You must worship before this altar"?
8 " 'Come now, make a bargain with my master, the king of As-
syria: I will give you two thousand horses — if you can put riders
on them! 9 How then can you repulse one officer of the least of
my master's officials, even though you are depending on Egypt

PRAYING SCRIPTURE

Isaiah 36

During King Hezekiah's reign, Sennacherib, king of the Assyrians, mounted an assault on Judah, overtaking all its fortified cities. The attack obviously had political intent, but for Hezekiah it was a test: Would he trust God to deliver them?

Whenever external forces press down on us, our faith often fails if we listen to bad counsel. Resist the temptation to trust in human beings, and pray instead for God's strength.

for chariots and horsemen[a]? 10 Furthermore, have I come to attack
and destroy this land without the LORD? The LORD himself told me
to march against this country and destroy it.'"

11 Then Eliakim, Shebna and Joah said to the field commander,
"Please speak to your servants in Aramaic, since we understand it.
Don't speak to us in Hebrew in the hearing of the people on the wall."
12 But the commander replied, "Was it only to your master and you
that my master sent me to say these things, and not to the people sit-
ting on the wall — who, like you, will have to eat their own excrement
and drink their own urine?"
13 Then the commander stood and called out in Hebrew, "Hear the
words of the great king, the king of Assyria! 14 This is what the king
says: Do not let Hezekiah deceive you. He cannot deliver you! 15 Do not
let Hezekiah persuade you to trust in the LORD when he says, 'The LORD
will surely deliver us; this city will not be given into the hand of the
king of Assyria.'
16 "Do not listen to Hezekiah. This is what the king of Assyria says:
Make peace with me and come out to me. Then each of you will eat
fruit from your own vine and fig tree and drink water from your own
cistern, 17 until I come and take you to a land like your own — a land of
grain and new wine, a land of bread and vineyards.
18 "Do not let Hezekiah mislead you when he says, 'The LORD will de-
liver us.' Have the gods of any nations ever delivered their lands from
the hand of the king of Assyria? 19 Where are the gods of Hamath and
Arpad? Where are the gods of Sepharvaim? Have they rescued Samaria
from my hand? 20 Who of all the gods of these countries have been able
to save their lands from me? How then can the LORD deliver Jerusalem
from my hand?"
21 But the people remained silent and said nothing in reply, because
the king had commanded, "Do not answer him."
22 Then Eliakim son of Hilkiah the palace administrator, Shebna the
secretary and Joah son of Asaph the recorder went to Hezekiah, with
their clothes torn, and told him what the field commander had said.

JERUSALEM'S DELIVERANCE FORETOLD

37 When King Hezekiah heard this, he tore his clothes and put on
sackcloth and went into the temple of the LORD. 2 He sent Eli-
akim the palace administrator, Shebna the secretary, and the leading
priests, all wearing sackcloth, to the prophet Isaiah son of Amoz. 3 They
told him, "This is what Hezekiah says: This day is a day of distress and
rebuke and disgrace, as when children come to the moment of birth
and there is no strength to deliver them. 4 It may be that the LORD your
God will hear the words of the field commander, whom his master, the
king of Assyria, has sent to ridicule the living God, and that he will re-
buke him for the words the LORD your God has heard. Therefore pray
for the remnant that still survives."
5 When King Hezekiah's officials came to Isaiah, 6 Isaiah said to them,
"Tell your master, 'This is what the LORD says: Do not be afraid of what
you have heard — those words with which the underlings of the king
of Assyria have blasphemed me. 7 Listen! When he hears a certain re-
port, I will make him want to return to his own country, and there I
will have him cut down with the sword.'"

[a] 9 Or *charioteers*

PRAYING SCRIPTURE

Isaiah 37

After trusting in chariots and horses had failed, the people finally turned in prayer to the Lord and witnessed a supernatural victory. The angel of the Lord went forth, killing 185,000 of the encamped Assyrian warriors in a single night (see verse 36).

We often fail to remember that God can act outside the breadth of our imagination. When things are bleakest, call on him to intervene for you.

8When the field commander heard that the king of Assyria had left
Lachish, he withdrew and found the king fighting against Libnah.
9Now Sennacherib received a report that Tirhakah, the king of Cush,[a]
was marching out to fight against him. When he heard it, he sent mes-
sengers to Hezekiah with this word: 10"Say to Hezekiah king of Judah:
Do not let the god you depend on deceive you when he says, 'Jerusalem
will not be given into the hands of the king of Assyria.' 11Surely you
have heard what the kings of Assyria have done to all the countries,
destroying them completely. And will you be delivered? 12Did the gods
of the nations that were destroyed by my predecessors deliver them —
the gods of Gozan, Harran, Rezeph and the people of Eden who were in
Tel Assar? 13Where is the king of Hamath or the king of Arpad? Where
are the kings of Lair, Sepharvaim, Hena and Ivvah?"

HEZEKIAH'S PRAYER

14Hezekiah received the letter from the messengers and read it. Then
he went up to the temple of the LORD and spread it out before the
LORD. 15And Hezekiah prayed to the LORD: 16"LORD Almighty, the God of
Israel, enthroned between the cherubim, you alone are God over all the
kingdoms of the earth. You have made heaven and earth. 17Give ear,
LORD, and hear; open your eyes, LORD, and see; listen to all the words
Sennacherib has sent to ridicule the living God.

18"It is true, LORD, that the Assyrian kings have laid waste all these
peoples and their lands. 19They have thrown their gods into the fire
and destroyed them, for they were not gods but only wood and stone,
fashioned by human hands. 20Now, LORD our God, deliver us from his
hand, so that all the kingdoms of the earth may know that you, LORD,
are the only God.[b]"

SENNACHERIB'S FALL

21Then Isaiah son of Amoz sent a message to Hezekiah: "This is what
the LORD, the God of Israel, says: Because you have prayed to me con-
cerning Sennacherib king of Assyria, 22this is the word the LORD has
spoken against him:

"Virgin Daughter Zion
  despises and mocks you.
Daughter Jerusalem
  tosses her head as you flee.
23Who is it you have ridiculed and blasphemed?
  Against whom have you raised your voice
and lifted your eyes in pride?
  Against the Holy One of Israel!
24By your messengers
  you have ridiculed the Lord.
And you have said,
  'With my many chariots
I have ascended the heights of the mountains,
  the utmost heights of Lebanon.
I have cut down its tallest cedars,
  the choicest of its junipers.

[a] 9 That is, the upper Nile region [b] 20 Dead Sea Scrolls (see also 2 Kings 19:19); Masoretic Text *you alone are the LORD*

I have reached its remotest heights,
the finest of its forests.
25 I have dug wells in foreign lands[a]
and drunk the water there.
With the soles of my feet
I have dried up all the streams of Egypt.'

26 "Have you not heard?
Long ago I ordained it.
In days of old I planned it;
now I have brought it to pass,
that you have turned fortified cities
into piles of stone.
27 Their people, drained of power,
are dismayed and put to shame.
They are like plants in the field,
like tender green shoots,
like grass sprouting on the roof,
scorched[b] before it grows up.

28 "But I know where you are
and when you come and go
and how you rage against me.
29 Because you rage against me
and because your insolence has reached my ears,
I will put my hook in your nose
and my bit in your mouth,
and I will make you return
by the way you came.

30 "This will be the sign for you, Hezekiah:

"This year you will eat what grows by itself,
and the second year what springs from that.
But in the third year sow and reap,
plant vineyards and eat their fruit.
31 Once more a remnant of the kingdom of Judah
will take root below and bear fruit above.
32 For out of Jerusalem will come a remnant,
and out of Mount Zion a band of survivors.
The zeal of the LORD Almighty
will accomplish this.

33 "Therefore this is what the LORD says concerning the king of Assyria:

"He will not enter this city
or shoot an arrow here.
He will not come before it with shield
or build a siege ramp against it.
34 By the way that he came he will return;
he will not enter this city,"
declares the LORD.

---

[a] *25* Dead Sea Scrolls (see also 2 Kings 19:24); Masoretic Text does not have *in foreign lands.* [b] *27* Some manuscripts of the Masoretic Text, Dead Sea Scrolls and some Septuagint manuscripts (see also 2 Kings 19:26); most manuscripts of the Masoretic Text *roof / and terraced fields*

35 "I will defend this city and save it,
for my sake and for the sake of David my servant!"

36 Then the angel of the LORD went out and put to death a hundred
and eighty-five thousand in the Assyrian camp. When the people got
up the next morning — there were all the dead bodies! 37 So Sennach-
erib king of Assyria broke camp and withdrew. He returned to Nineveh
and stayed there.
38 One day, while he was worshiping in the temple of his god Nis-
rok, his sons Adrammelek and Sharezer killed him with the sword, and
they escaped to the land of Ararat. And Esarhaddon his son succeeded
him as king.

HEZEKIAH'S ILLNESS

38 In those days Hezekiah became ill and was at the point of
death. The prophet Isaiah son of Amoz went to him and said,
"This is what the LORD says: Put your house in order, because you are
going to die; you will not recover."
2 Hezekiah turned his face to the wall and prayed to the LORD, 3 "Re-
member, LORD, how I have walked before you faithfully and with
wholehearted devotion and have done what is good in your eyes." And
Hezekiah wept bitterly.
4 Then the word of the LORD came to Isaiah: 5 "Go and tell Hezekiah,
'This is what the LORD, the God of your father David, says: I have heard
your prayer and seen your tears; I will add fifteen years to your life.
6 And I will deliver you and this city from the hand of the king of As-
syria. I will defend this city.
7 " 'This is the LORD's sign to you that the LORD will do what he has
promised: 8 I will make the shadow cast by the sun go back the ten
steps it has gone down on the stairway of Ahaz.' " So the sunlight went
back the ten steps it had gone down.

9 A writing of Hezekiah king of Judah after his illness and recovery:

10 I said, "In the prime of my life
must I go through the gates of death
and be robbed of the rest of my years?"
11 I said, "I will not again see the LORD himself
in the land of the living;
no longer will I look on my fellow man,
or be with those who now dwell in this world.
12 Like a shepherd's tent my house
has been pulled down and taken from me.
Like a weaver I have rolled up my life,
and he has cut me off from the loom;
day and night you made an end of me.
13 I waited patiently till dawn,
but like a lion he broke all my bones;
day and night you made an end of me.
14 I cried like a swift or thrush,
I moaned like a mourning dove.
My eyes grew weak as I looked to the heavens.
I am being threatened; Lord, come to my aid!"
15 But what can I say?
He has spoken to me, and he himself has done this.

PRAYING SCRIPTURE

Isaiah 38

Have you ever wrestled with God in prayer to get an answer, exerting physical energy like Jacob or emotional energy like Hezekiah? When God's prophet warned him of impending death, Hezekiah went to his room, faced a wall and prayed with bitter weeping. God gave the king his desire, promising him 15 more years.

If God heard only your prayers accompanied by wrestling or tears, how many would be answered?

I will walk humbly all my years
  because of this anguish of my soul.
16 Lord, by such things people live;
  and my spirit finds life in them too.
You restored me to health
  and let me live.
17 Surely it was for my benefit
  that I suffered such anguish.
In your love you kept me
  from the pit of destruction;
you have put all my sins
  behind your back.
18 For the grave cannot praise you,
  death cannot sing your praise;
those who go down to the pit
  cannot hope for your faithfulness.
19 The living, the living — they praise you,
  as I am doing today;
parents tell their children
  about your faithfulness.

20 The LORD will save me,
  and we will sing with stringed instruments
all the days of our lives
  in the temple of the LORD.

21 Isaiah had said, "Prepare a poultice of figs and apply it to the boil,
and he will recover."
22 Hezekiah had asked, "What will be the sign that I will go up to the
temple of the LORD?"

ENVOYS FROM BABYLON

39 At that time Marduk-Baladan son of Baladan king of Babylon
sent Hezekiah letters and a gift, because he had heard of his
illness and recovery. 2 Hezekiah received the envoys gladly and showed
them what was in his storehouses — the silver, the gold, the spices,
the fine olive oil — his entire armory and everything found among his
treasures. There was nothing in his palace or in all his kingdom that
Hezekiah did not show them.
3 Then Isaiah the prophet went to King Hezekiah and asked, "What
did those men say, and where did they come from?"
"From a distant land," Hezekiah replied. "They came to me from
Babylon."
4 The prophet asked, "What did they see in your palace?"
"They saw everything in my palace," Hezekiah said. "There is noth-
ing among my treasures that I did not show them."
5 Then Isaiah said to Hezekiah, "Hear the word of the LORD Almighty:
6 The time will surely come when everything in your palace, and all
that your predecessors have stored up until this day, will be carried
off to Babylon. Nothing will be left, says the LORD. 7 And some of your
descendants, your own flesh and blood who will be born to you, will
be taken away, and they will become eunuchs in the palace of the king
of Babylon."
8 "The word of the LORD you have spoken is good," Hezekiah replied.
For he thought, "There will be peace and security in my lifetime."

PRAYING SCRIPTURE

Isaiah 39

It did not take long for Hezekiah's miraculous answer to prayer to give way to pride. Desirous to make himself look strong before a political envoy by showing off his riches, he crossed a line. In response, Isaiah prophesied that some of Hezekiah's sons would become servants in Babylonia.

It is common for Satan to bring stumbling after a great victory. Ask God to keep you free from pride, always giving him full credit for victories.

PRAYING SCRIPTURE

Isaiah 40

This chapter is packed with familiar passages of God's greatness—from the coming of the Messiah (see verses 1–5) to the blessings of his kingdom (see verses 6–11), to his power over the nations (see verses 12–17), to God's incomparability (see verses 18–23), to his omnipotence (see verses 28–31). It is little wonder those who wait on the Lord will be empowered!

When you are struggling, open your Bible to this chapter. Pray this list of exaltations of God and rejoice in his majesty.

COMFORT FOR GOD'S PEOPLE

40 Comfort, comfort my people,
says your God.
2 Speak tenderly to Jerusalem,
and proclaim to her
that her hard service has been completed,
that her sin has been paid for,
that she has received from the LORD's hand
double for all her sins.

3 A voice of one calling:
"In the wilderness prepare
the way for the LORD[a];
make straight in the desert
a highway for our God.[b]
4 Every valley shall be raised up,
every mountain and hill made low;
the rough ground shall become level,
the rugged places a plain.
5 And the glory of the LORD will be revealed,
and all people will see it together.
For the mouth of the LORD has spoken."

6 A voice says, "Cry out."
And I said, "What shall I cry?"

"All people are like grass,
and all their faithfulness is like the flowers of the field.
7 The grass withers and the flowers fall,
because the breath of the LORD blows on them.
Surely the people are grass.
8 The grass withers and the flowers fall,
but the word of our God endures forever."

9 You who bring good news to Zion,
go up on a high mountain.
You who bring good news to Jerusalem,[c]
lift up your voice with a shout,
lift it up, do not be afraid;
say to the towns of Judah,
"Here is your God!"
10 See, the Sovereign LORD comes with power,
and he rules with a mighty arm.
See, his reward is with him,
and his recompense accompanies him.
11 He tends his flock like a shepherd:
He gathers the lambs in his arms
and carries them close to his heart;
he gently leads those that have young.

12 Who has measured the waters in the hollow of his hand,
or with the breadth of his hand marked off the heavens?

[a] 3 Or *A voice of one calling in the wilderness: / "Prepare the way for the LORD*
[b] 3 Hebrew; Septuagint *make straight the paths of our God* [c] 9 Or *Zion, bringer of good news, / go up on a high mountain. / Jerusalem, bringer of good news*

Who has held the dust of the earth in a basket,
  or weighed the mountains on the scales
  and the hills in a balance?
13 Who can fathom the Spirit[a] of the LORD,
  or instruct the LORD as his counselor?
14 Whom did the LORD consult to enlighten him,
  and who taught him the right way?
Who was it that taught him knowledge,
  or showed him the path of understanding?

15 Surely the nations are like a drop in a bucket;
  they are regarded as dust on the scales;
  he weighs the islands as though they were fine dust.
16 Lebanon is not sufficient for altar fires,
  nor its animals enough for burnt offerings.
17 Before him all the nations are as nothing;
  they are regarded by him as worthless
  and less than nothing.

18 With whom, then, will you compare God?
  To what image will you liken him?
19 As for an idol, a metalworker casts it,
  and a goldsmith overlays it with gold
  and fashions silver chains for it.
20 A person too poor to present such an offering
  selects wood that will not rot;
they look for a skilled worker
  to set up an idol that will not topple.

21 Do you not know?
  Have you not heard?
Has it not been told you from the beginning?
  Have you not understood since the earth was founded?
22 He sits enthroned above the circle of the earth,
  and its people are like grasshoppers.
He stretches out the heavens like a canopy,
  and spreads them out like a tent to live in.
23 He brings princes to naught
  and reduces the rulers of this world to nothing.
24 No sooner are they planted,
  no sooner are they sown,
  no sooner do they take root in the ground,
than he blows on them and they wither,
  and a whirlwind sweeps them away like chaff.

25 "To whom will you compare me?
  Or who is my equal?" says the Holy One.
26 Lift up your eyes and look to the heavens:
  Who created all these?
He who brings out the starry host one by one
  and calls forth each of them by name.
Because of his great power and mighty strength,
  not one of them is missing.

---

[a] 13 Or *mind*

27 Why do you complain, Jacob?
Why do you say, Israel,
"My way is hidden from the LORD;
my cause is disregarded by my God"?
28 Do you not know?
Have you not heard?
The LORD is the everlasting God,
the Creator of the ends of the earth.
He will not grow tired or weary,
and his understanding no one can fathom.
29 He gives strength to the weary
and increases the power of the weak.
30 Even youths grow tired and weary,
and young men stumble and fall;
31 but those who hope in the LORD
will renew their strength.
They will soar on wings like eagles;
they will run and not grow weary,
they will walk and not be faint.

THE HELPER OF ISRAEL

41 "Be silent before me, you islands!
Let the nations renew their strength!
Let them come forward and speak;
let us meet together at the place of judgment.

2 "Who has stirred up one from the east,
calling him in righteousness to his service[a]?
He hands nations over to him
and subdues kings before him.
He turns them to dust with his sword,
to windblown chaff with his bow.
3 He pursues them and moves on unscathed,
by a path his feet have not traveled before.
4 Who has done this and carried it through,
calling forth the generations from the beginning?
I, the LORD—with the first of them
and with the last—I am he."

5 The islands have seen it and fear;
the ends of the earth tremble.
They approach and come forward;
6 they help each other
and say to their companions, "Be strong!"
7 The metalworker encourages the goldsmith,
and the one who smooths with the hammer
spurs on the one who strikes the anvil.
One says of the welding, "It is good."
The other nails down the idol so it will not topple.

8 "But you, Israel, my servant,
Jacob, whom I have chosen,
you descendants of Abraham my friend,

PRAYING SCRIPTURE

Isaiah 41

Verse 10 is one of the most comforting, faith-building promises in all of Scripture. Are you fearful? Don't be, because God is with you. Don't be dismayed; he is your God. He will strengthen, help and uphold you with his mighty, righteous hand.

God loves and cares for all his children. Call on him. Lean into him. Prayer is our way to the Father's care.

[a] 2 Or *east, / whom victory meets at every step*

9 I took you from the ends of the earth,
from its farthest corners I called you.
I said, 'You are my servant';
I have chosen you and have not rejected you.
10 So do not fear, for I am with you;
do not be dismayed, for I am your God.
I will strengthen you and help you;
I will uphold you with my righteous right hand.

11 "All who rage against you
will surely be ashamed and disgraced;
those who oppose you
will be as nothing and perish.
12 Though you search for your enemies,
you will not find them.
Those who wage war against you
will be as nothing at all.
13 For I am the LORD your God
who takes hold of your right hand
and says to you, Do not fear;
I will help you.
14 Do not be afraid, you worm Jacob,
little Israel, do not fear,
for I myself will help you," declares the LORD,
your Redeemer, the Holy One of Israel.
15 "See, I will make you into a threshing sledge,
new and sharp, with many teeth.
You will thresh the mountains and crush them,
and reduce the hills to chaff.
16 You will winnow them, the wind will pick them up,
and a gale will blow them away.
But you will rejoice in the LORD
and glory in the Holy One of Israel.

17 "The poor and needy search for water,
but there is none;
their tongues are parched with thirst.
But I the LORD will answer them;
I, the God of Israel, will not forsake them.
18 I will make rivers flow on barren heights,
and springs within the valleys.
I will turn the desert into pools of water,
and the parched ground into springs.
19 I will put in the desert
the cedar and the acacia, the myrtle and the olive.
I will set junipers in the wasteland,
the fir and the cypress together,
20 so that people may see and know,
may consider and understand,
that the hand of the LORD has done this,
that the Holy One of Israel has created it.

21 "Present your case," says the LORD.
"Set forth your arguments," says Jacob's King.
22 "Tell us, you idols,
what is going to happen.

Tell us what the former things were,
so that we may consider them
and know their final outcome.
Or declare to us the things to come,
23 tell us what the future holds,
so we may know that you are gods.
Do something, whether good or bad,
so that we will be dismayed and filled with fear.
24 But you are less than nothing
and your works are utterly worthless;
whoever chooses you is detestable.

25 "I have stirred up one from the north, and he comes—
one from the rising sun who calls on my name.
He treads on rulers as if they were mortar,
as if he were a potter treading the clay.
26 Who told of this from the beginning, so we could know,
or beforehand, so we could say, 'He was right'?
No one told of this,
no one foretold it,
no one heard any words from you.
27 I was the first to tell Zion, 'Look, here they are!'
I gave to Jerusalem a messenger of good news.
28 I look but there is no one—
no one among the gods to give counsel,
no one to give answer when I ask them.
29 See, they are all false!
Their deeds amount to nothing;
their images are but wind and confusion.

THE SERVANT OF THE LORD

42 "Here is my servant, whom I uphold,
my chosen one in whom I delight;
I will put my Spirit on him,
and he will bring justice to the nations.
2 He will not shout or cry out,
or raise his voice in the streets.
3 A bruised reed he will not break,
and a smoldering wick he will not snuff out.
In faithfulness he will bring forth justice;
4 he will not falter or be discouraged
till he establishes justice on earth.
In his teaching the islands will put their hope."

5 This is what God the LORD says—
the Creator of the heavens, who stretches them out,
who spreads out the earth with all that springs from it,
who gives breath to its people,
and life to those who walk on it:
6 "I, the LORD, have called you in righteousness;
I will take hold of your hand.
I will keep you and will make you
to be a covenant for the people
and a light for the Gentiles,
7 to open eyes that are blind,

PRAYING SCRIPTURE

Isaiah 42

The promise of the Messiah resounds through the first part of this chapter. He will bring justice, and he will not fail (verses 1,4). Further revealed is how the Lord is gentle with his people: "A bruised reed he will not break" (verse 3).

Do you ever feel as if going to God with your concerns wearies him? Do not fear. He loves to hear from his children and has patience with us.

to free captives from prison
and to release from the dungeon those who sit in darkness.

8 "I am the LORD; that is my name!
I will not yield my glory to another
or my praise to idols.
9 See, the former things have taken place,
and new things I declare;
before they spring into being
I announce them to you."

SONG OF PRAISE TO THE LORD

10 Sing to the LORD a new song,
his praise from the ends of the earth,
you who go down to the sea, and all that is in it,
you islands, and all who live in them.
11 Let the wilderness and its towns raise their voices;
let the settlements where Kedar lives rejoice.
Let the people of Sela sing for joy;
let them shout from the mountaintops.
12 Let them give glory to the LORD
and proclaim his praise in the islands.
13 The LORD will march out like a champion,
like a warrior he will stir up his zeal;
with a shout he will raise the battle cry
and will triumph over his enemies.

14 "For a long time I have kept silent,
I have been quiet and held myself back.
But now, like a woman in childbirth,
I cry out, I gasp and pant.
15 I will lay waste the mountains and hills
and dry up all their vegetation;
I will turn rivers into islands
and dry up the pools.
16 I will lead the blind by ways they have not known,
along unfamiliar paths I will guide them;
I will turn the darkness into light before them
and make the rough places smooth.
These are the things I will do;
I will not forsake them.
17 But those who trust in idols,
who say to images, 'You are our gods,'
will be turned back in utter shame.

ISRAEL BLIND AND DEAF

18 "Hear, you deaf;
look, you blind, and see!
19 Who is blind but my servant,
and deaf like the messenger I send?
Who is blind like the one in covenant with me,
blind like the servant of the LORD?
20 You have seen many things, but you pay no attention;
your ears are open, but you do not listen."
21 It pleased the LORD

for the sake of his righteousness
to make his law great and glorious.
22 But this is a people plundered and looted,
all of them trapped in pits
or hidden away in prisons.
They have become plunder,
with no one to rescue them;
they have been made loot,
with no one to say, "Send them back."

23 Which of you will listen to this
or pay close attention in time to come?
24 Who handed Jacob over to become loot,
and Israel to the plunderers?
Was it not the LORD,
against whom we have sinned?
For they would not follow his ways;
they did not obey his law.
25 So he poured out on them his burning anger,
the violence of war.
It enveloped them in flames, yet they did not understand;
it consumed them, but they did not take it to heart.

ISRAEL'S ONLY SAVIOR

43 But now, this is what the LORD says—
he who created you, Jacob,
he who formed you, Israel:
"Do not fear, for I have redeemed you;
I have summoned you by name; you are mine.
2 When you pass through the waters,
I will be with you;
and when you pass through the rivers,
they will not sweep over you.
When you walk through the fire,
you will not be burned;
the flames will not set you ablaze.
3 For I am the LORD your God,
the Holy One of Israel, your Savior;
I give Egypt for your ransom,
Cush[a] and Seba in your stead.
4 Since you are precious and honored in my sight,
and because I love you,
I will give people in exchange for you,
nations in exchange for your life.
5 Do not be afraid, for I am with you;
I will bring your children from the east
and gather you from the west.
6 I will say to the north, 'Give them up!'
and to the south, 'Do not hold them back.'
Bring my sons from afar
and my daughters from the ends of the earth—
7 everyone who is called by my name,

PRAYING SCRIPTURE

Isaiah 43

Isaiah relayed many words of hope to the Israelites before God bared his heart about their unfaithfulness. Despite all he did to show his love and care, he had to chastise them, saying, "You have not called on me, Jacob, you have not wearied yourselves for me, Israel" (verse 22).

We belong to the Lord because he redeemed us and created us for his glory. Pray that you might always remember his love for you.

[a] *3* That is, the upper Nile region

whom I created for my glory,
whom I formed and made."

8 Lead out those who have eyes but are blind,
who have ears but are deaf.
9 All the nations gather together
and the peoples assemble.
Which of their gods foretold this
and proclaimed to us the former things?
Let them bring in their witnesses to prove they were right,
so that others may hear and say, "It is true."
10 "You are my witnesses," declares the LORD,
"and my servant whom I have chosen,
so that you may know and believe me
and understand that I am he.
Before me no god was formed,
nor will there be one after me.
11 I, even I, am the LORD,
and apart from me there is no savior.
12 I have revealed and saved and proclaimed—
I, and not some foreign god among you.
You are my witnesses," declares the LORD, "that I am God.
13 Yes, and from ancient days I am he.
No one can deliver out of my hand.
When I act, who can reverse it?"

GOD'S MERCY AND ISRAEL'S UNFAITHFULNESS

14 This is what the LORD says—
your Redeemer, the Holy One of Israel:
"For your sake I will send to Babylon
and bring down as fugitives all the Babylonians,[a]
in the ships in which they took pride.
15 I am the LORD, your Holy One,
Israel's Creator, your King."

16 This is what the LORD says—
he who made a way through the sea,
a path through the mighty waters,
17 who drew out the chariots and horses,
the army and reinforcements together,
and they lay there, never to rise again,
extinguished, snuffed out like a wick:
18 "Forget the former things;
do not dwell on the past.
19 See, I am doing a new thing!
Now it springs up; do you not perceive it?
I am making a way in the wilderness
and streams in the wasteland.
20 The wild animals honor me,
the jackals and the owls,
because I provide water in the wilderness
and streams in the wasteland,
to give drink to my people, my chosen,

[a] 14 Or *Chaldeans*

21 the people I formed for myself
    that they may proclaim my praise.

22 "Yet you have not called on me, Jacob,
    you have not wearied yourselves for[a] me, Israel.
23 You have not brought me sheep for burnt offerings,
    nor honored me with your sacrifices.
I have not burdened you with grain offerings
    nor wearied you with demands for incense.
24 You have not bought any fragrant calamus for me,
    or lavished on me the fat of your sacrifices.
But you have burdened me with your sins
    and wearied me with your offenses.

25 "I, even I, am he who blots out
    your transgressions, for my own sake,
    and remembers your sins no more.
26 Review the past for me,
    let us argue the matter together;
    state the case for your innocence.
27 Your first father sinned;
    those I sent to teach you rebelled against me.
28 So I disgraced the dignitaries of your temple;
    I consigned Jacob to destruction[b]
    and Israel to scorn.

ISRAEL THE CHOSEN

44 "But now listen, Jacob, my servant,
    Israel, whom I have chosen.
2 This is what the LORD says—
    he who made you, who formed you in the womb,
    and who will help you:
Do not be afraid, Jacob, my servant,
    Jeshurun,[c] whom I have chosen.
3 For I will pour water on the thirsty land,
    and streams on the dry ground;
I will pour out my Spirit on your offspring,
    and my blessing on your descendants.
4 They will spring up like grass in a meadow,
    like poplar trees by flowing streams.
5 Some will say, 'I belong to the LORD';
    others will call themselves by the name of Jacob;
still others will write on their hand, 'The LORD's,'
    and will take the name Israel.

THE LORD, NOT IDOLS

6 "This is what the LORD says—
    Israel's King and Redeemer, the LORD Almighty:
I am the first and I am the last;
    apart from me there is no God.

PRAYING SCRIPTURE

Isaiah 44

Between a reminder of God's blessings and the promise of restoration, God castigated those who would trust in idols. Idols are useless. Those who made them did not understand; God had plastered their eyes shut and closed their hearts (see verse 18). What leads to idolatry? "A deluded heart" (verse 20).

Idolatry's deceptiveness is subtle. We must always be on the lookout. Ask God to protect your heart that you might keep yourself from idols.

[a] 22 Or *Jacob; / surely you have grown weary of* [b] 28 The Hebrew term refers to the irrevocable giving over of things or persons to the LORD, often by totally destroying them. [c] 2 *Jeshurun* means *the upright one*, that is, Israel.

7 Who then is like me? Let him proclaim it.
Let him declare and lay out before me
what has happened since I established my ancient people,
and what is yet to come —
yes, let them foretell what will come.
8 Do not tremble, do not be afraid.
Did I not proclaim this and foretell it long ago?
You are my witnesses. Is there any God besides me?
No, there is no other Rock; I know not one."

9 All who make idols are nothing,
and the things they treasure are worthless.
Those who would speak up for them are blind;
they are ignorant, to their own shame.
10 Who shapes a god and casts an idol,
which can profit nothing?
11 People who do that will be put to shame;
such craftsmen are only human beings.
Let them all come together and take their stand;
they will be brought down to terror and shame.

12 The blacksmith takes a tool
and works with it in the coals;
he shapes an idol with hammers,
he forges it with the might of his arm.
He gets hungry and loses his strength;
he drinks no water and grows faint.
13 The carpenter measures with a line
and makes an outline with a marker;
he roughs it out with chisels
and marks it with compasses.
He shapes it in human form,
human form in all its glory,
that it may dwell in a shrine.
14 He cut down cedars,
or perhaps took a cypress or oak.
He let it grow among the trees of the forest,
or planted a pine, and the rain made it grow.
15 It is used as fuel for burning;
some of it he takes and warms himself,
he kindles a fire and bakes bread.
But he also fashions a god and worships it;
he makes an idol and bows down to it.
16 Half of the wood he burns in the fire;
over it he prepares his meal,
he roasts his meat and eats his fill.
He also warms himself and says,
"Ah! I am warm; I see the fire."
17 From the rest he makes a god, his idol;
he bows down to it and worships.
He prays to it and says,
"Save me! You are my god!"
18 They know nothing, they understand nothing;
their eyes are plastered over so they cannot see,
and their minds closed so they cannot understand.

19 No one stops to think,
no one has the knowledge or understanding to say,
"Half of it I used for fuel;
I even baked bread over its coals,
I roasted meat and I ate.
Shall I make a detestable thing from what is left?
Shall I bow down to a block of wood?"
20 Such a person feeds on ashes; a deluded heart misleads him;
he cannot save himself, or say,
"Is not this thing in my right hand a lie?"

21 "Remember these things, Jacob,
for you, Israel, are my servant.
I have made you, you are my servant;
Israel, I will not forget you.
22 I have swept away your offenses like a cloud,
your sins like the morning mist.
Return to me,
for I have redeemed you."

23 Sing for joy, you heavens, for the LORD has done this;
shout aloud, you earth beneath.
Burst into song, you mountains,
you forests and all your trees,
for the LORD has redeemed Jacob,
he displays his glory in Israel.

JERUSALEM TO BE INHABITED

24 "This is what the LORD says—
your Redeemer, who formed you in the womb:

I am the LORD,
the Maker of all things,
who stretches out the heavens,
who spreads out the earth by myself,
25 who foils the signs of false prophets
and makes fools of diviners,
who overthrows the learning of the wise
and turns it into nonsense,
26 who carries out the words of his servants
and fulfills the predictions of his messengers,

who says of Jerusalem, 'It shall be inhabited,'
of the towns of Judah, 'They shall be rebuilt,'
and of their ruins, 'I will restore them,'
27 who says to the watery deep, 'Be dry,
and I will dry up your streams,'
28 who says of Cyrus, 'He is my shepherd
and will accomplish all that I please;
he will say of Jerusalem, "Let it be rebuilt,"
and of the temple, "Let its foundations be laid."'

45 "This is what the LORD says to his anointed,
to Cyrus, whose right hand I take hold of
to subdue nations before him
and to strip kings of their armor,

PRAYING SCRIPTURE

Isaiah 45

It is traditionally believed that King Cyrus was a pagan leader whom the Lord used to accomplish his plans. He didn't need to explain, but he did, showing that he can use anyone he pleases whenever he pleases for whatever end he pleases.

When tempted to wonder if things are out of control, thank God that his plans are perfect, power unrivaled and wisdom unsurpassed.

to open doors before him
so that gates will not be shut:
2 I will go before you
and will level the mountains[a];
I will break down gates of bronze
and cut through bars of iron.
3 I will give you hidden treasures,
riches stored in secret places,
so that you may know that I am the LORD,
the God of Israel, who summons you by name.
4 For the sake of Jacob my servant,
of Israel my chosen,
I summon you by name
and bestow on you a title of honor,
though you do not acknowledge me.
5 I am the LORD, and there is no other;
apart from me there is no God.
I will strengthen you,
though you have not acknowledged me,
6 so that from the rising of the sun
to the place of its setting
people may know there is none besides me.
I am the LORD, and there is no other.
7 I form the light and create darkness,
I bring prosperity and create disaster;
I, the LORD, do all these things.

8 "You heavens above, rain down my righteousness;
let the clouds shower it down.
Let the earth open wide,
let salvation spring up,
let righteousness flourish with it;
I, the LORD, have created it.

9 "Woe to those who quarrel with their Maker,
those who are nothing but potsherds
among the potsherds on the ground.
Does the clay say to the potter,
'What are you making?'
Does your work say,
'The potter has no hands'?
10 Woe to the one who says to a father,
'What have you begotten?'
or to a mother,
'What have you brought to birth?'

11 "This is what the LORD says —
the Holy One of Israel, and its Maker:
Concerning things to come,
do you question me about my children,
or give me orders about the work of my hands?
12 It is I who made the earth
and created mankind on it.

---

[a] 2 Dead Sea Scrolls and Septuagint; the meaning of the word in the Masoretic Text is uncertain.

My own hands stretched out the heavens;
I marshaled their starry hosts.
13 I will raise up Cyrus[a] in my righteousness:
I will make all his ways straight.
He will rebuild my city
and set my exiles free,
but not for a price or reward,
says the LORD Almighty."

14 This is what the LORD says:

"The products of Egypt and the merchandise of Cush,[b]
and those tall Sabeans —
they will come over to you
and will be yours;
they will trudge behind you,
coming over to you in chains.
They will bow down before you
and plead with you, saying,
'Surely God is with you, and there is no other;
there is no other god.'"

15 Truly you are a God who has been hiding himself,
the God and Savior of Israel.
16 All the makers of idols will be put to shame and disgraced;
they will go off into disgrace together.
17 But Israel will be saved by the LORD
with an everlasting salvation;
you will never be put to shame or disgraced,
to ages everlasting.

18 For this is what the LORD says —
he who created the heavens,
he is God;
he who fashioned and made the earth,
he founded it;
he did not create it to be empty,
but formed it to be inhabited —
he says:
"I am the LORD,
and there is no other.
19 I have not spoken in secret,
from somewhere in a land of darkness;
I have not said to Jacob's descendants,
'Seek me in vain.'
I, the LORD, speak the truth;
I declare what is right.

20 "Gather together and come;
assemble, you fugitives from the nations.
Ignorant are those who carry about idols of wood,
who pray to gods that cannot save.
21 Declare what is to be, present it —
let them take counsel together.

---

[a] 13 Hebrew *him* [b] 14 That is, the upper Nile region

Who foretold this long ago,
who declared it from the distant past?
Was it not I, the LORD?
And there is no God apart from me,
a righteous God and a Savior;
there is none but me.

22 "Turn to me and be saved,
all you ends of the earth;
for I am God, and there is no other.
23 By myself I have sworn,
my mouth has uttered in all integrity
a word that will not be revoked:
Before me every knee will bow;
by me every tongue will swear.
24 They will say of me, 'In the LORD alone
are deliverance and strength.'"
All who have raged against him
will come to him and be put to shame.
25 But all the descendants of Israel
will find deliverance in the LORD
and will make their boast in him.

GODS OF BABYLON

46 Bel bows down, Nebo stoops low;
their idols are borne by beasts of burden.[a]
The images that are carried about are burdensome,
a burden for the weary.
2 They stoop and bow down together;
unable to rescue the burden,
they themselves go off into captivity.

3 "Listen to me, you descendants of Jacob,
all the remnant of the people of Israel,
you whom I have upheld since your birth,
and have carried since you were born.
4 Even to your old age and gray hairs
I am he, I am he who will sustain you.
I have made you and I will carry you;
I will sustain you and I will rescue you.

5 "With whom will you compare me or count me equal?
To whom will you liken me that we may be compared?
6 Some pour out gold from their bags
and weigh out silver on the scales;
they hire a goldsmith to make it into a god,
and they bow down and worship it.
7 They lift it to their shoulders and carry it;
they set it up in its place, and there it stands.
From that spot it cannot move.
Even though someone cries out to it, it cannot answer;
it cannot save them from their troubles.

8 "Remember this, keep it in mind,
take it to heart, you rebels.

PRAYING SCRIPTURE

Isaiah 46

God truly desires for people to repent and be reconciled to him. Here he implored the people to listen and abandon their stubborn ways while he brought his righteousness near them. His "salvation will not be delayed" (verse 13). Never think that God wants to keep you at arm's length. He wants us to repent because his ways are best! Thank him that he persistently draws us to himself.

[a] 1 Or *are but beasts and cattle*

9 Remember the former things, those of long ago;
  I am God, and there is no other;
  I am God, and there is none like me.
10 I make known the end from the beginning,
  from ancient times, what is still to come.
I say, 'My purpose will stand,
  and I will do all that I please.'
11 From the east I summon a bird of prey;
  from a far-off land, a man to fulfill my purpose.
What I have said, that I will bring about;
  what I have planned, that I will do.
12 Listen to me, you stubborn-hearted,
  you who are now far from my righteousness.
13 I am bringing my righteousness near,
  it is not far away;
  and my salvation will not be delayed.
I will grant salvation to Zion,
  my splendor to Israel.

THE FALL OF BABYLON

47 "Go down, sit in the dust,
  Virgin Daughter Babylon;
sit on the ground without a throne,
  queen city of the Babylonians.[a]
No more will you be called
  tender or delicate.
2 Take millstones and grind flour;
  take off your veil.
Lift up your skirts, bare your legs,
  and wade through the streams.
3 Your nakedness will be exposed
  and your shame uncovered.
I will take vengeance;
  I will spare no one."

4 Our Redeemer — the LORD Almighty is his name —
  is the Holy One of Israel.

5 "Sit in silence, go into darkness,
  queen city of the Babylonians;
no more will you be called
  queen of kingdoms.
6 I was angry with my people
  and desecrated my inheritance;
I gave them into your hand,
  and you showed them no mercy.
Even on the aged
  you laid a very heavy yoke.
7 You said, 'I am forever —
  the eternal queen!'
But you did not consider these things
  or reflect on what might happen.

8 "Now then, listen, you lover of pleasure,
  lounging in your security

PRAYING SCRIPTURE

Isaiah 47

God's judgment on Babylon was due in part to secret sin. They said, "No one sees me." In addition, they embraced Lucifer's pride, saying, "There is none besides me" (verse 10). The power of secret sins is the guilt we expect will come if exposed. We feel condemned if we don't repent and condemned at the prospect of it. Confess any secret sin to God, and then walk in freedom.

[a] 1 Or *Chaldeans;* also in verse 5

and saying to yourself,
'I am, and there is none besides me.
I will never be a widow
or suffer the loss of children.'
9 Both of these will overtake you
in a moment, on a single day:
loss of children and widowhood.
They will come upon you in full measure,
in spite of your many sorceries
and all your potent spells.
10 You have trusted in your wickedness
and have said, 'No one sees me.'
Your wisdom and knowledge mislead you
when you say to yourself,
'I am, and there is none besides me.'
11 Disaster will come upon you,
and you will not know how to conjure it away.
A calamity will fall upon you
that you cannot ward off with a ransom;
a catastrophe you cannot foresee
will suddenly come upon you.

12 "Keep on, then, with your magic spells
and with your many sorceries,
which you have labored at since childhood.
Perhaps you will succeed,
perhaps you will cause terror.
13 All the counsel you have received has only worn you out!
Let your astrologers come forward,
those stargazers who make predictions month by month,
let them save you from what is coming upon you.
14 Surely they are like stubble;
the fire will burn them up.
They cannot even save themselves
from the power of the flame.
These are not coals for warmth;
this is not a fire to sit by.
15 That is all they are to you —
these you have dealt with
and labored with since childhood.
All of them go on in their error;
there is not one that can save you.

STUBBORN ISRAEL

48 "Listen to this, you descendants of Jacob,
you who are called by the name of Israel
and come from the line of Judah,
you who take oaths in the name of the LORD
and invoke the God of Israel —
but not in truth or righteousness —
2 you who call yourselves citizens of the holy city
and claim to rely on the God of Israel —
the LORD Almighty is his name:
3 I foretold the former things long ago,
my mouth announced them and I made them known;

PRAYING SCRIPTURE

Isaiah 48

The Lord frequently reminded Israel that he was not a far-off, disinterested deity but their Lord and their God. Intimately connected to this reality is that God refines his people, burning off dross and bringing them to a state of greater purity.

God's testing is never for the sake of seeing us hurt, but to purify us for his service. Ask God to show you the dross in your life.

then suddenly I acted, and they came to pass.
4 For I knew how stubborn you were;
your neck muscles were iron,
your forehead was bronze.
5 Therefore I told you these things long ago;
before they happened I announced them to you
so that you could not say,
'My images brought them about;
my wooden image and metal god ordained them.'
6 You have heard these things; look at them all.
Will you not admit them?

"From now on I will tell you of new things,
of hidden things unknown to you.
7 They are created now, and not long ago;
you have not heard of them before today.
So you cannot say,
'Yes, I knew of them.'
8 You have neither heard nor understood;
from of old your ears have not been open.
Well do I know how treacherous you are;
you were called a rebel from birth.
9 For my own name's sake I delay my wrath;
for the sake of my praise I hold it back from you,
so as not to destroy you completely.
10 See, I have refined you, though not as silver;
I have tested you in the furnace of affliction.
11 For my own sake, for my own sake, I do this.
How can I let myself be defamed?
I will not yield my glory to another.

ISRAEL FREED

12 "Listen to me, Jacob,
Israel, whom I have called:
I am he;
I am the first and I am the last.
13 My own hand laid the foundations of the earth,
and my right hand spread out the heavens;
when I summon them,
they all stand up together.

14 "Come together, all of you, and listen:
Which of the idols has foretold these things?
The LORD's chosen ally
will carry out his purpose against Babylon;
his arm will be against the Babylonians.[a]
15 I, even I, have spoken;
yes, I have called him.
I will bring him,
and he will succeed in his mission.

16 "Come near me and listen to this:

"From the first announcement I have not spoken in secret;
at the time it happens, I am there."

[a] 14 Or *Chaldeans*; also in verse 20

And now the Sovereign LORD has sent me,
endowed with his Spirit.

17 This is what the LORD says —
your Redeemer, the Holy One of Israel:
"I am the LORD your God,
who teaches you what is best for you,
who directs you in the way you should go.
18 If only you had paid attention to my commands,
your peace would have been like a river,
your well-being like the waves of the sea.
19 Your descendants would have been like the sand,
your children like its numberless grains;
their name would never be blotted out
nor destroyed from before me."

20 Leave Babylon,
flee from the Babylonians!
Announce this with shouts of joy
and proclaim it.
Send it out to the ends of the earth;
say, "The LORD has redeemed his servant Jacob."
21 They did not thirst when he led them through the deserts;
he made water flow for them from the rock;
he split the rock
and water gushed out.

22 "There is no peace," says the LORD, "for the wicked."

THE SERVANT OF THE LORD

49 Listen to me, you islands;
hear this, you distant nations:
Before I was born the LORD called me;
from my mother's womb he has spoken my name.
2 He made my mouth like a sharpened sword,
in the shadow of his hand he hid me;
he made me into a polished arrow
and concealed me in his quiver.
3 He said to me, "You are my servant,
Israel, in whom I will display my splendor."
4 But I said, "I have labored in vain;
I have spent my strength for nothing at all.
Yet what is due me is in the LORD's hand,
and my reward is with my God."

5 And now the LORD says —
he who formed me in the womb to be his servant
to bring Jacob back to him
and gather Israel to himself,
for I am[a] honored in the eyes of the LORD
and my God has been my strength —
6 he says:
"It is too small a thing for you to be my servant
to restore the tribes of Jacob
and bring back those of Israel I have kept.

PRAYING SCRIPTURE

Isaiah 49

Promised from the Old Testament was this truth: The Messiah, God's servant, would not only be the Savior for Israel, but he would also be the Savior for the Gentiles. His salvation would not be regional but "to the ends of the earth" (verse 6).

Those who are not Jewish can be reconciled to God because Jesus came for Gentiles too. Thank God today that he loves all the world.

[a] 5 Or *him, / but Israel would not be gathered; / yet I will be*

I will also make you a light for the Gentiles,
that my salvation may reach to the ends of the earth."

7 This is what the LORD says—
the Redeemer and Holy One of Israel—
to him who was despised and abhorred by the nation,
to the servant of rulers:
"Kings will see you and stand up,
princes will see and bow down,
because of the LORD, who is faithful,
the Holy One of Israel, who has chosen you."

RESTORATION OF ISRAEL

8 This is what the LORD says:

"In the time of my favor I will answer you,
and in the day of salvation I will help you;
I will keep you and will make you
to be a covenant for the people,
to restore the land
and to reassign its desolate inheritances,
9 to say to the captives, 'Come out,'
and to those in darkness, 'Be free!'

"They will feed beside the roads
and find pasture on every barren hill.
10 They will neither hunger nor thirst,
nor will the desert heat or the sun beat down on them.
He who has compassion on them will guide them
and lead them beside springs of water.
11 I will turn all my mountains into roads,
and my highways will be raised up.
12 See, they will come from afar—
some from the north, some from the west,
some from the region of Aswan.[a]"

13 Shout for joy, you heavens;
rejoice, you earth;
burst into song, you mountains!
For the LORD comforts his people
and will have compassion on his afflicted ones.

14 But Zion said, "The LORD has forsaken me,
the Lord has forgotten me."

15 "Can a mother forget the baby at her breast
and have no compassion on the child she has borne?
Though she may forget,
I will not forget you!
16 See, I have engraved you on the palms of my hands;
your walls are ever before me.
17 Your children hasten back,
and those who laid you waste depart from you.
18 Lift up your eyes and look around;
all your children gather and come to you.

---

[a] *12* Dead Sea Scrolls; Masoretic Text *Sinim*

As surely as I live," declares the LORD,
"you will wear them all as ornaments;
you will put them on, like a bride.

19 "Though you were ruined and made desolate
and your land laid waste,
now you will be too small for your people,
and those who devoured you will be far away.
20 The children born during your bereavement
will yet say in your hearing,
'This place is too small for us;
give us more space to live in.'
21 Then you will say in your heart,
'Who bore me these?
I was bereaved and barren;
I was exiled and rejected.
Who brought these up?
I was left all alone,
but these — where have they come from?'"

22 This is what the Sovereign LORD says:

"See, I will beckon to the nations,
I will lift up my banner to the peoples;
they will bring your sons in their arms
and carry your daughters on their hips.
23 Kings will be your foster fathers,
and their queens your nursing mothers.
They will bow down before you with their faces to the ground;
they will lick the dust at your feet.
Then you will know that I am the LORD;
those who hope in me will not be disappointed."

24 Can plunder be taken from warriors,
or captives be rescued from the fierce[a]?

25 But this is what the LORD says:

"Yes, captives will be taken from warriors,
and plunder retrieved from the fierce;
I will contend with those who contend with you,
and your children I will save.
26 I will make your oppressors eat their own flesh;
they will be drunk on their own blood, as with wine.
Then all mankind will know
that I, the LORD, am your Savior,
your Redeemer, the Mighty One of Jacob."

ISRAEL'S SIN AND THE SERVANT'S OBEDIENCE

50 This is what the LORD says:

"Where is your mother's certificate of divorce
with which I sent her away?
Or to which of my creditors
did I sell you?

[a] *24* Dead Sea Scrolls, Vulgate and Syriac (see also Septuagint and verse 25); Masoretic Text *righteous*

PRAYING SCRIPTURE

Isaiah 50

The Lord speaks to start this chapter, using a series of questions and statements designed to show he is stronger than any human. Is his hand shortened that he cannot save? No. Does he lack power to redeem? No. God uses hyperbole at times because simple comparisons won't do.

We never have reason to doubt God's might. Spend some time in prayer listing God's attributes, and praise him for his greatness.

Because of your sins you were sold;
because of your transgressions your mother was sent away.
2 When I came, why was there no one?
When I called, why was there no one to answer?
Was my arm too short to deliver you?
Do I lack the strength to rescue you?
By a mere rebuke I dry up the sea,
I turn rivers into a desert;
their fish rot for lack of water
and die of thirst.
3 I clothe the heavens with darkness
and make sackcloth its covering."

4 The Sovereign LORD has given me a well-instructed tongue,
to know the word that sustains the weary.
He wakens me morning by morning,
wakens my ear to listen like one being instructed.
5 The Sovereign LORD has opened my ears;
I have not been rebellious,
I have not turned away.
6 I offered my back to those who beat me,
my cheeks to those who pulled out my beard;
I did not hide my face
from mocking and spitting.
7 Because the Sovereign LORD helps me,
I will not be disgraced.
Therefore have I set my face like flint,
and I know I will not be put to shame.
8 He who vindicates me is near.
Who then will bring charges against me?
Let us face each other!
Who is my accuser?
Let him confront me!
9 It is the Sovereign LORD who helps me.
Who will condemn me?
They will all wear out like a garment;
the moths will eat them up.

10 Who among you fears the LORD
and obeys the word of his servant?
Let the one who walks in the dark,
who has no light,
trust in the name of the LORD
and rely on their God.
11 But now, all you who light fires
and provide yourselves with flaming torches,
go, walk in the light of your fires
and of the torches you have set ablaze.
This is what you shall receive from my hand:
You will lie down in torment.

EVERLASTING SALVATION FOR ZION

51 "Listen to me, you who pursue righteousness
and who seek the LORD:
Look to the rock from which you were cut

PRAYING SCRIPTURE

Isaiah 51

"Listen to me" (verse 4); "Lift up your eyes to the heavens" (verse 6); "Awake, awake," the Lord commanded (verse 9). He used these imperatives to invite his people into close relationship with him. And he reminded his people that it is precisely because of his power that his comfort is real (see verses 12–16).

No other comfort in the world compares to the Lord's. If you are anxious or worried, ask him to comfort you.

and to the quarry from which you were hewn;
2 look to Abraham, your father,
and to Sarah, who gave you birth.
When I called him he was only one man,
and I blessed him and made him many.
3 The LORD will surely comfort Zion
and will look with compassion on all her ruins;
he will make her deserts like Eden,
her wastelands like the garden of the LORD.
Joy and gladness will be found in her,
thanksgiving and the sound of singing.

4 "Listen to me, my people;
hear me, my nation:
Instruction will go out from me;
my justice will become a light to the nations.
5 My righteousness draws near speedily,
my salvation is on the way,
and my arm will bring justice to the nations.
The islands will look to me
and wait in hope for my arm.
6 Lift up your eyes to the heavens,
look at the earth beneath;
the heavens will vanish like smoke,
the earth will wear out like a garment
and its inhabitants die like flies.
But my salvation will last forever,
my righteousness will never fail.

7 "Hear me, you who know what is right,
you people who have taken my instruction to heart:
Do not fear the reproach of mere mortals
or be terrified by their insults.
8 For the moth will eat them up like a garment;
the worm will devour them like wool.
But my righteousness will last forever,
my salvation through all generations."

9 Awake, awake, arm of the LORD,
clothe yourself with strength!
Awake, as in days gone by,
as in generations of old.
Was it not you who cut Rahab to pieces,
who pierced that monster through?
10 Was it not you who dried up the sea,
the waters of the great deep,
who made a road in the depths of the sea
so that the redeemed might cross over?
11 Those the LORD has rescued will return.
They will enter Zion with singing;
everlasting joy will crown their heads.
Gladness and joy will overtake them,
and sorrow and sighing will flee away.

12 "I, even I, am he who comforts you.
Who are you that you fear mere mortals,

human beings who are but grass,
13 that you forget the LORD your Maker,
who stretches out the heavens
and who lays the foundations of the earth,
that you live in constant terror every day
because of the wrath of the oppressor,
who is bent on destruction?
For where is the wrath of the oppressor?
14 The cowering prisoners will soon be set free;
they will not die in their dungeon,
nor will they lack bread.
15 For I am the LORD your God,
who stirs up the sea so that its waves roar —
the LORD Almighty is his name.
16 I have put my words in your mouth
and covered you with the shadow of my hand —
I who set the heavens in place,
who laid the foundations of the earth,
and who say to Zion, 'You are my people.' "

THE CUP OF THE LORD'S WRATH

17 Awake, awake!
Rise up, Jerusalem,
you who have drunk from the hand of the LORD
the cup of his wrath,
you who have drained to its dregs
the goblet that makes people stagger.
18 Among all the children she bore
there was none to guide her;
among all the children she reared
there was none to take her by the hand.
19 These double calamities have come upon you —
who can comfort you? —
ruin and destruction, famine and sword —
who can[a] console you?
20 Your children have fainted;
they lie at every street corner,
like antelope caught in a net.
They are filled with the wrath of the LORD,
with the rebuke of your God.

21 Therefore hear this, you afflicted one,
made drunk, but not with wine.
22 This is what your Sovereign LORD says,
your God, who defends his people:
"See, I have taken out of your hand
the cup that made you stagger;
from that cup, the goblet of my wrath,
you will never drink again.
23 I will put it into the hands of your tormentors,
who said to you,
'Fall prostrate that we may walk on you.'

[a] 19 Dead Sea Scrolls, Septuagint, Vulgate and Syriac; Masoretic Text / *how can I*

And you made your back like the ground,
like a street to be walked on."

52 Awake, awake, Zion,
clothe yourself with strength!
Put on your garments of splendor,
Jerusalem, the holy city.
The uncircumcised and defiled
will not enter you again.
2 Shake off your dust;
rise up, sit enthroned, Jerusalem.
Free yourself from the chains on your neck,
Daughter Zion, now a captive.

3 For this is what the LORD says:

"You were sold for nothing,
and without money you will be redeemed."

4 For this is what the Sovereign LORD says:

"At first my people went down to Egypt to live;
lately, Assyria has oppressed them.

5 "And now what do I have here?" declares the LORD.

"For my people have been taken away for nothing,
and those who rule them mock,[a]"
declares the LORD.
"And all day long
my name is constantly blasphemed.
6 Therefore my people will know my name;
therefore in that day they will know
that it is I who foretold it.
Yes, it is I."

7 How beautiful on the mountains
are the feet of those who bring good news,
who proclaim peace,
who bring good tidings,
who proclaim salvation,
who say to Zion,
"Your God reigns!"
8 Listen! Your watchmen lift up their voices;
together they shout for joy.
When the LORD returns to Zion,
they will see it with their own eyes.
9 Burst into songs of joy together,
you ruins of Jerusalem,
for the LORD has comforted his people,
he has redeemed Jerusalem.
10 The LORD will lay bare his holy arm
in the sight of all the nations,
and all the ends of the earth will see
the salvation of our God.

PRAYING SCRIPTURE

Isaiah 52

The salvation the Lord brings should thrill the hearts of his people and be good news in their ears. Everything about the Good News is good. The feet that bring good news, the voice that proclaims peace and the one who says, "Your God reigns," are all part of God's salvation (verse 7).

Have you taken the Good News to anyone lately? Ask God for beautiful feet that take the gospel to the lost.

[a] 5 Dead Sea Scrolls and Vulgate; Masoretic Text *wail*

11 Depart, depart, go out from there!
Touch no unclean thing!
Come out from it and be pure,
you who carry the articles of the LORD's house.
12 But you will not leave in haste
or go in flight;
for the LORD will go before you,
the God of Israel will be your rear guard.

THE SUFFERING AND GLORY OF THE SERVANT

13 See, my servant will act wisely[a];
he will be raised and lifted up and highly exalted.
14 Just as there were many who were appalled at him[b]—
his appearance was so disfigured beyond that of any human being
and his form marred beyond human likeness—
15 so he will sprinkle many nations,[c]
and kings will shut their mouths because of him.
For what they were not told, they will see,
and what they have not heard, they will understand.

53 Who has believed our message
and to whom has the arm of the LORD been revealed?
2 He grew up before him like a tender shoot,
and like a root out of dry ground.
He had no beauty or majesty to attract us to him,
nothing in his appearance that we should desire him.
3 He was despised and rejected by mankind,
a man of suffering, and familiar with pain.
Like one from whom people hide their faces
he was despised, and we held him in low esteem.

4 Surely he took up our pain
and bore our suffering,
yet we considered him punished by God,
stricken by him, and afflicted.
5 But he was pierced for our transgressions,
he was crushed for our iniquities;
the punishment that brought us peace was on him,
and by his wounds we are healed.
6 We all, like sheep, have gone astray,
each of us has turned to our own way;
and the LORD has laid on him
the iniquity of us all.

7 He was oppressed and afflicted,
yet he did not open his mouth;
he was led like a lamb to the slaughter,
and as a sheep before its shearers is silent,
so he did not open his mouth.
8 By oppression[d] and judgment he was taken away.
Yet who of his generation protested?

PRAYING SCRIPTURE

Isaiah 53

The ancient idea of the Messiah was that of a warrior-king who could lead Israel in battle. The concept of a suffering Messiah, one who would die as a sacrifice, was not something most people were ready to accept. God, through Isaiah, made it clear that the Messiah's suffering was God's plan.

Jesus suffered so that we could be reconciled to God. Praise him for his love so strong that he suffered for us.

[a] 13 Or *will prosper* [b] 14 Hebrew *you* [c] 15 Or *so will many nations be amazed at him* (see also Septuagint) [d] 8 Or *From arrest*

For he was cut off from the land of the living;
for the transgression of my people he was punished.[a]
9 He was assigned a grave with the wicked,
and with the rich in his death,
though he had done no violence,
nor was any deceit in his mouth.

10 Yet it was the LORD's will to crush him and cause him to suffer,
and though the LORD makes[b] his life an offering for sin,
he will see his offspring and prolong his days,
and the will of the LORD will prosper in his hand.
11 After he has suffered,
he will see the light of life[c] and be satisfied[d];
by his knowledge[e] my righteous servant will justify many,
and he will bear their iniquities.
12 Therefore I will give him a portion among the great,[f]
and he will divide the spoils with the strong,[g]
because he poured out his life unto death,
and was numbered with the transgressors.
For he bore the sin of many,
and made intercession for the transgressors.

THE FUTURE GLORY OF ZION

54 "Sing, barren woman,
you who never bore a child;
burst into song, shout for joy,
you who were never in labor;
because more are the children of the desolate woman
than of her who has a husband,"
says the LORD.

2 "Enlarge the place of your tent,
stretch your tent curtains wide,
do not hold back;
lengthen your cords,
strengthen your stakes.
3 For you will spread out to the right and to the left;
your descendants will dispossess nations
and settle in their desolate cities.

4 "Do not be afraid; you will not be put to shame.
Do not fear disgrace; you will not be humiliated.
You will forget the shame of your youth
and remember no more the reproach of your widowhood.
5 For your Maker is your husband —
the LORD Almighty is his name —
the Holy One of Israel is your Redeemer;
he is called the God of all the earth.
6 The LORD will call you back
as if you were a wife deserted and distressed in spirit —

[a] 8 Or *generation considered / that he was cut off from the land of the living, / that he was punished for the transgression of my people?* [b] 10 Hebrew *though you make* [c] 11 Dead Sea Scrolls (see also Septuagint); Masoretic Text does not have *the light of life.* [d] 11 Or (with Masoretic Text) *"He will see the fruit of his suffering / and will be satisfied* [e] 11 Or *by knowledge of him* [f] 12 Or *many* [g] 12 Or *numerous*

PRAYING SCRIPTURE

Isaiah 54

The Lord often describes his relationship with his people in the language of a marriage covenant. "For your Maker is your husband— the LORD Almighty is his name" (verse 5). Since God uses this imagery metaphorically about himself, it is instructive to those who are married.

Our view of marriage should reflect that of God himself. Whether you are married or not, ask God to help you honor it as he does.

a wife who married young,
only to be rejected," says your God.
7 "For a brief moment I abandoned you,
but with deep compassion I will bring you back.
8 In a surge of anger
I hid my face from you for a moment,
but with everlasting kindness
I will have compassion on you,"
says the LORD your Redeemer.

9 "To me this is like the days of Noah,
when I swore that the waters of Noah would never again cover
the earth.
So now I have sworn not to be angry with you,
never to rebuke you again.
10 Though the mountains be shaken
and the hills be removed,
yet my unfailing love for you will not be shaken
nor my covenant of peace be removed,"
says the LORD, who has compassion on you.

11 "Afflicted city, lashed by storms and not comforted,
I will rebuild you with stones of turquoise,[a]
your foundations with lapis lazuli.
12 I will make your battlements of rubies,
your gates of sparkling jewels,
and all your walls of precious stones.
13 All your children will be taught by the LORD,
and great will be their peace.
14 In righteousness you will be established:
Tyranny will be far from you;
you will have nothing to fear.
Terror will be far removed;
it will not come near you.
15 If anyone does attack you, it will not be my doing;
whoever attacks you will surrender to you.

16 "See, it is I who created the blacksmith
who fans the coals into flame
and forges a weapon fit for its work.
And it is I who have created the destroyer to wreak havoc;
17 no weapon forged against you will prevail,
and you will refute every tongue that accuses you.
This is the heritage of the servants of the LORD,
and this is their vindication from me,"
declares the LORD.

INVITATION TO THE THIRSTY

55 "Come, all you who are thirsty,
come to the waters;
and you who have no money,
come, buy and eat!
Come, buy wine and milk
without money and without cost.

PRAYING SCRIPTURE

Isaiah 55

The sheer beauty of the opening verses of this chapter should raise us to the heights of thankfulness and wonder. Whenever we are tired and weary, when we have nothing to give, we can go to the Lord, and he will gladly meet our needs. Come without money and eat; enjoy the best God offers; listen to his words and live.

God lavishes his unending grace upon us. Praise and thank him for it.

[a] 11 The meaning of the Hebrew for this word is uncertain.

2 Why spend money on what is not bread,
and your labor on what does not satisfy?
Listen, listen to me, and eat what is good,
and you will delight in the richest of fare.
3 Give ear and come to me;
listen, that you may live.
I will make an everlasting covenant with you,
my faithful love promised to David.
4 See, I have made him a witness to the peoples,
a ruler and commander of the peoples.
5 Surely you will summon nations you know not,
and nations you do not know will come running to you,
because of the LORD your God,
the Holy One of Israel,
for he has endowed you with splendor."

6 Seek the LORD while he may be found;
call on him while he is near.
7 Let the wicked forsake their ways
and the unrighteous their thoughts.
Let them turn to the LORD, and he will have mercy on them,
and to our God, for he will freely pardon.

8 "For my thoughts are not your thoughts,
neither are your ways my ways,"
declares the LORD.
9 "As the heavens are higher than the earth,
so are my ways higher than your ways
and my thoughts than your thoughts.
10 As the rain and the snow
come down from heaven,
and do not return to it
without watering the earth
and making it bud and flourish,
so that it yields seed for the sower and bread for the eater,
11 so is my word that goes out from my mouth:
It will not return to me empty,
but will accomplish what I desire
and achieve the purpose for which I sent it.
12 You will go out in joy
and be led forth in peace;
the mountains and hills
will burst into song before you,
and all the trees of the field
will clap their hands.
13 Instead of the thornbush will grow the juniper,
and instead of briers the myrtle will grow.
This will be for the LORD's renown,
for an everlasting sign,
that will endure forever."

SALVATION FOR OTHERS

56 This is what the LORD says:

"Maintain justice
and do what is right,

PRAYING SCRIPTURE

Isaiah 56

Throughout the prophets' books, the Lord reserved harsh judgment for Israel and Judah's rulers who led the people astray. Priests and false prophets alike receive his judgment for fleecing the flock, mistreating the oppressed and using their offices to enrich themselves (see verses 9–12). With such, God is not pleased.

Every era has its false prophets, bad leaders and hypocritical shepherds. Ask God for wisdom to discern and avoid them.

for my salvation is close at hand
  and my righteousness will soon be revealed.
2 Blessed is the one who does this —
  the person who holds it fast,
who keeps the Sabbath without desecrating it,
  and keeps their hands from doing any evil."

3 Let no foreigner who is bound to the LORD say,
  "The LORD will surely exclude me from his people."
And let no eunuch complain,
  "I am only a dry tree."

4 For this is what the LORD says:

"To the eunuchs who keep my Sabbaths,
  who choose what pleases me
  and hold fast to my covenant —
5 to them I will give within my temple and its walls
  a memorial and a name
  better than sons and daughters;
I will give them an everlasting name
  that will endure forever.
6 And foreigners who bind themselves to the LORD
  to minister to him,
to love the name of the LORD,
  and to be his servants,
all who keep the Sabbath without desecrating it
  and who hold fast to my covenant —
7 these I will bring to my holy mountain
  and give them joy in my house of prayer.
Their burnt offerings and sacrifices
  will be accepted on my altar;
for my house will be called
  a house of prayer for all nations."
8 The Sovereign LORD declares —
  he who gathers the exiles of Israel:
"I will gather still others to them
  besides those already gathered."

GOD'S ACCUSATION AGAINST THE WICKED

9 Come, all you beasts of the field,
  come and devour, all you beasts of the forest!
10 Israel's watchmen are blind,
  they all lack knowledge;
they are all mute dogs,
  they cannot bark;
they lie around and dream,
  they love to sleep.
11 They are dogs with mighty appetites;
  they never have enough.
They are shepherds who lack understanding;
  they all turn to their own way,
  they seek their own gain.
12 "Come," each one cries, "let me get wine!
  Let us drink our fill of beer!

And tomorrow will be like today,
 or even far better."

57 The righteous perish,
 and no one takes it to heart;
the devout are taken away,
 and no one understands
that the righteous are taken away
 to be spared from evil.
2 Those who walk uprightly
 enter into peace;
 they find rest as they lie in death.

3 "But you — come here, you children of a sorceress,
 you offspring of adulterers and prostitutes!
4 Who are you mocking?
 At whom do you sneer
 and stick out your tongue?
Are you not a brood of rebels,
 the offspring of liars?
5 You burn with lust among the oaks
 and under every spreading tree;
you sacrifice your children in the ravines
 and under the overhanging crags.
6 The idols among the smooth stones of the ravines are your portion;
 indeed, they are your lot.
Yes, to them you have poured out drink offerings
 and offered grain offerings.
 In view of all this, should I relent?
7 You have made your bed on a high and lofty hill;
 there you went up to offer your sacrifices.
8 Behind your doors and your doorposts
 you have put your pagan symbols.
Forsaking me, you uncovered your bed,
 you climbed into it and opened it wide;
you made a pact with those whose beds you love,
 and you looked with lust on their naked bodies.
9 You went to Molek[a] with olive oil
 and increased your perfumes.
You sent your ambassadors[b] far away;
 you descended to the very realm of the dead!
10 You wearied yourself by such going about,
 but you would not say, 'It is hopeless.'
You found renewal of your strength,
 and so you did not faint.

11 "Whom have you so dreaded and feared
 that you have not been true to me,
and have neither remembered me
 nor taken this to heart?
Is it not because I have long been silent
 that you do not fear me?

[a] 9 Or *to the king* [b] 9 Or *idols*

PRAYING SCRIPTURE

Isaiah 57

Nothing so grieves the heart of God as when his people ignore bad things happening to the righteous. Isaiah said, "No one takes it to heart" (verse 1). In our connected world, it is easy for all Christians to be aware of when our brothers and sisters are being persecuted in another country.

Train yourself to heed news stories about persecution. Pray for the suffering as you read about them.

12 I will expose your righteousness and your works,
and they will not benefit you.
13 When you cry out for help,
let your collection of idols save you!
The wind will carry all of them off,
a mere breath will blow them away.
But whoever takes refuge in me
will inherit the land
and possess my holy mountain."

COMFORT FOR THE CONTRITE

14 And it will be said:

"Build up, build up, prepare the road!
Remove the obstacles out of the way of my people."
15 For this is what the high and exalted One says —
he who lives forever, whose name is holy:
"I live in a high and holy place,
but also with the one who is contrite and lowly in spirit,
to revive the spirit of the lowly
and to revive the heart of the contrite.
16 I will not accuse them forever,
nor will I always be angry,
for then they would faint away because of me —
the very people I have created.
17 I was enraged by their sinful greed;
I punished them, and hid my face in anger,
yet they kept on in their willful ways.
18 I have seen their ways, but I will heal them;
I will guide them and restore comfort to Israel's mourners,
19 creating praise on their lips.
Peace, peace, to those far and near,"
says the LORD. "And I will heal them."
20 But the wicked are like the tossing sea,
which cannot rest,
whose waves cast up mire and mud.
21 "There is no peace," says my God, "for the wicked."

TRUE FASTING

58 "Shout it aloud, do not hold back.
Raise your voice like a trumpet.
Declare to my people their rebellion
and to the descendants of Jacob their sins.
2 For day after day they seek me out;
they seem eager to know my ways,
as if they were a nation that does what is right
and has not forsaken the commands of its God.
They ask me for just decisions
and seem eager for God to come near them.
3 'Why have we fasted,' they say,
'and you have not seen it?
Why have we humbled ourselves,
and you have not noticed?'

"Yet on the day of your fasting, you do as you please
and exploit all your workers.

PRAYING SCRIPTURE

Isaiah 58

Fasting, the denial of physical food for a period of time to engage in intense pursuit of God, is a long-standing practice. The Lord warns, though, fasting that is not sincere is worthless (see verses 3–4).

Do you include fasting as part of your spiritual growth? When performed from the heart and with care, fasting and prayer loose bonds, release burdens, break yokes and lead to life.

4 Your fasting ends in quarreling and strife,
and in striking each other with wicked fists.
You cannot fast as you do today
and expect your voice to be heard on high.
5 Is this the kind of fast I have chosen,
only a day for people to humble themselves?
Is it only for bowing one's head like a reed
and for lying in sackcloth and ashes?
Is that what you call a fast,
a day acceptable to the LORD?

6 "Is not this the kind of fasting I have chosen:
to loose the chains of injustice
and untie the cords of the yoke,
to set the oppressed free
and break every yoke?
7 Is it not to share your food with the hungry
and to provide the poor wanderer with shelter—
when you see the naked, to clothe them,
and not to turn away from your own flesh and blood?
8 Then your light will break forth like the dawn,
and your healing will quickly appear;
then your righteousness[a] will go before you,
and the glory of the LORD will be your rear guard.
9 Then you will call, and the LORD will answer;
you will cry for help, and he will say: Here am I.

"If you do away with the yoke of oppression,
with the pointing finger and malicious talk,
10 and if you spend yourselves in behalf of the hungry
and satisfy the needs of the oppressed,
then your light will rise in the darkness,
and your night will become like the noonday.
11 The LORD will guide you always;
he will satisfy your needs in a sun-scorched land
and will strengthen your frame.
You will be like a well-watered garden,
like a spring whose waters never fail.
12 Your people will rebuild the ancient ruins
and will raise up the age-old foundations;
you will be called Repairer of Broken Walls,
Restorer of Streets with Dwellings.

13 "If you keep your feet from breaking the Sabbath
and from doing as you please on my holy day,
if you call the Sabbath a delight
and the LORD's holy day honorable,
and if you honor it by not going your own way
and not doing as you please or speaking idle words,
14 then you will find your joy in the LORD,
and I will cause you to ride in triumph on the heights of the land
and to feast on the inheritance of your father Jacob."
For the mouth of the LORD has spoken.

---

[a] 8 Or *your righteous One*

PRAYING SCRIPTURE

Isaiah 59

The number of times the Lord warns of judgment due to injustice is staggering. "No one pleads a case with integrity" (verse 4). "There is no justice in their paths" (verse 8). "So justice is far from us" (verse 9). "Justice is driven back" (verse 14). The Lord is angered when justice is abandoned.

Because justice was forsaken, God purposed to send his Redeemer to Zion (see verse 20). Until final judgment comes, injustice remains. Ask the Lord how you can call for justice.

SIN, CONFESSION AND REDEMPTION

59 Surely the arm of the LORD is not too short to save,
nor his ear too dull to hear.
2 But your iniquities have separated
you from your God;
your sins have hidden his face from you,
so that he will not hear.
3 For your hands are stained with blood,
your fingers with guilt.
Your lips have spoken falsely,
and your tongue mutters wicked things.
4 No one calls for justice;
no one pleads a case with integrity.
They rely on empty arguments, they utter lies;
they conceive trouble and give birth to evil.
5 They hatch the eggs of vipers
and spin a spider's web.
Whoever eats their eggs will die,
and when one is broken, an adder is hatched.
6 Their cobwebs are useless for clothing;
they cannot cover themselves with what they make.
Their deeds are evil deeds,
and acts of violence are in their hands.
7 Their feet rush into sin;
they are swift to shed innocent blood.
They pursue evil schemes;
acts of violence mark their ways.
8 The way of peace they do not know;
there is no justice in their paths.
They have turned them into crooked roads;
no one who walks along them will know peace.

9 So justice is far from us,
and righteousness does not reach us.
We look for light, but all is darkness;
for brightness, but we walk in deep shadows.
10 Like the blind we grope along the wall,
feeling our way like people without eyes.
At midday we stumble as if it were twilight;
among the strong, we are like the dead.
11 We all growl like bears;
we moan mournfully like doves.
We look for justice, but find none;
for deliverance, but it is far away.

12 For our offenses are many in your sight,
and our sins testify against us.
Our offenses are ever with us,
and we acknowledge our iniquities:
13 rebellion and treachery against the LORD,
turning our backs on our God,
inciting revolt and oppression,
uttering lies our hearts have conceived.
14 So justice is driven back,
and righteousness stands at a distance;

truth has stumbled in the streets,
  honesty cannot enter.
15 Truth is nowhere to be found,
  and whoever shuns evil becomes a prey.

The LORD looked and was displeased
  that there was no justice.
16 He saw that there was no one,
  he was appalled that there was no one to intervene;
so his own arm achieved salvation for him,
  and his own righteousness sustained him.
17 He put on righteousness as his breastplate,
  and the helmet of salvation on his head;
he put on the garments of vengeance
  and wrapped himself in zeal as in a cloak.
18 According to what they have done,
  so will he repay
wrath to his enemies
  and retribution to his foes;
  he will repay the islands their due.
19 From the west, people will fear the name of the LORD,
  and from the rising of the sun, they will revere his glory.
For he will come like a pent-up flood
  that the breath of the LORD drives along.[a]

20 "The Redeemer will come to Zion,
  to those in Jacob who repent of their sins,"
declares the LORD.

21 "As for me, this is my covenant with them," says the LORD. "My
Spirit, who is on you, will not depart from you, and my words that I
have put in your mouth will always be on your lips, on the lips of your
children and on the lips of their descendants — from this time on and
forever," says the LORD.

THE GLORY OF ZION

60 "Arise, shine, for your light has come,
  and the glory of the LORD rises upon you.
2 See, darkness covers the earth
  and thick darkness is over the peoples,
but the LORD rises upon you
  and his glory appears over you.
3 Nations will come to your light,
  and kings to the brightness of your dawn.

4 "Lift up your eyes and look about you:
  All assemble and come to you;
your sons come from afar,
  and your daughters are carried on the hip.
5 Then you will look and be radiant,
  your heart will throb and swell with joy;
the wealth on the seas will be brought to you,
  to you the riches of the nations will come.

PRAYING SCRIPTURE

Isaiah 60

God's people are a light to the nations so the latter might see God. God sets up a light for the purpose of illumination. What is our light? "The LORD will be your everlasting light" (verse 20). When we live as God intends, his glory is on display through us.

Jesus addressed this, saying, "Let your light shine before others" (Matthew 5:16). Pray that God will help you reveal his full light.

[a] 19 Or *When enemies come in like a flood, / the Spirit of the LORD will put them to flight*

6 Herds of camels will cover your land,
young camels of Midian and Ephah.
And all from Sheba will come,
bearing gold and incense
and proclaiming the praise of the LORD.
7 All Kedar's flocks will be gathered to you,
the rams of Nebaioth will serve you;
they will be accepted as offerings on my altar,
and I will adorn my glorious temple.

8 "Who are these that fly along like clouds,
like doves to their nests?
9 Surely the islands look to me;
in the lead are the ships of Tarshish,[a]
bringing your children from afar,
with their silver and gold,
to the honor of the LORD your God,
the Holy One of Israel,
for he has endowed you with splendor.

10 "Foreigners will rebuild your walls,
and their kings will serve you.
Though in anger I struck you,
in favor I will show you compassion.
11 Your gates will always stand open,
they will never be shut, day or night,
so that people may bring you the wealth of the nations —
their kings led in triumphal procession.
12 For the nation or kingdom that will not serve you will perish;
it will be utterly ruined.

13 "The glory of Lebanon will come to you,
the juniper, the fir and the cypress together,
to adorn my sanctuary;
and I will glorify the place for my feet.
14 The children of your oppressors will come bowing before you;
all who despise you will bow down at your feet
and will call you the City of the LORD,
Zion of the Holy One of Israel.

15 "Although you have been forsaken and hated,
with no one traveling through,
I will make you the everlasting pride
and the joy of all generations.
16 You will drink the milk of nations
and be nursed at royal breasts.
Then you will know that I, the LORD, am your Savior,
your Redeemer, the Mighty One of Jacob.
17 Instead of bronze I will bring you gold,
and silver in place of iron.
Instead of wood I will bring you bronze,
and iron in place of stones.
I will make peace your governor
and well-being your ruler.

---

[a] 9 Or *the trading ships*

18 No longer will violence be heard in your land,
nor ruin or destruction within your borders,
but you will call your walls Salvation
and your gates Praise.
19 The sun will no more be your light by day,
nor will the brightness of the moon shine on you,
for the LORD will be your everlasting light,
and your God will be your glory.
20 Your sun will never set again,
and your moon will wane no more;
the LORD will be your everlasting light,
and your days of sorrow will end.
21 Then all your people will be righteous
and they will possess the land forever.
They are the shoot I have planted,
the work of my hands,
for the display of my splendor.
22 The least of you will become a thousand,
the smallest a mighty nation.
I am the LORD;
in its time I will do this swiftly."

THE YEAR OF THE LORD'S FAVOR

61 The Spirit of the Sovereign LORD is on me,
because the LORD has anointed me
to proclaim good news to the poor.
He has sent me to bind up the brokenhearted,
to proclaim freedom for the captives
and release from darkness for the prisoners,[a]
2 to proclaim the year of the LORD's favor
and the day of vengeance of our God,
to comfort all who mourn,
3 and provide for those who grieve in Zion—
to bestow on them a crown of beauty
instead of ashes,
the oil of joy
instead of mourning,
and a garment of praise
instead of a spirit of despair.
They will be called oaks of righteousness,
a planting of the LORD
for the display of his splendor.

4 They will rebuild the ancient ruins
and restore the places long devastated;
they will renew the ruined cities
that have been devastated for generations.
5 Strangers will shepherd your flocks;
foreigners will work your fields and vineyards.
6 And you will be called priests of the LORD,
you will be named ministers of our God.
You will feed on the wealth of nations,
and in their riches you will boast.

PRAYING SCRIPTURE

Isaiah 61

Jesus' first public sermon was taken from this chapter and set the stage for his entire ministry. After reading the first few verses, He explained to his hearers that he was the fulfillment of these words. Among the promises is "the oil of joy instead of mourning" (verse 3).

Are you in mourning about a job loss, bad health or a broken relationship? Ask Jesus to be your oil of joy.

[a] 1 Hebrew; Septuagint *the blind*

7 Instead of your shame
you will receive a double portion,
and instead of disgrace
you will rejoice in your inheritance.
And so you will inherit a double portion in your land,
and everlasting joy will be yours.

8 "For I, the LORD, love justice;
I hate robbery and wrongdoing.
In my faithfulness I will reward my people
and make an everlasting covenant with them.
9 Their descendants will be known among the nations
and their offspring among the peoples.
All who see them will acknowledge
that they are a people the LORD has blessed."

10 I delight greatly in the LORD;
my soul rejoices in my God.
For he has clothed me with garments of salvation
and arrayed me in a robe of his righteousness,
as a bridegroom adorns his head like a priest,
and as a bride adorns herself with her jewels.
11 For as the soil makes the sprout come up
and a garden causes seeds to grow,
so the Sovereign LORD will make righteousness
and praise spring up before all nations.

ZION'S NEW NAME

62 For Zion's sake I will not keep silent,
for Jerusalem's sake I will not remain quiet,
till her vindication shines out like the dawn,
her salvation like a blazing torch.
2 The nations will see your vindication,
and all kings your glory;
you will be called by a new name
that the mouth of the LORD will bestow.
3 You will be a crown of splendor in the LORD's hand,
a royal diadem in the hand of your God.
4 No longer will they call you Deserted,
or name your land Desolate.
But you will be called Hephzibah,[a]
and your land Beulah[b];
for the LORD will take delight in you,
and your land will be married.
5 As a young man marries a young woman,
so will your Builder marry you;
as a bridegroom rejoices over his bride,
so will your God rejoice over you.
6 I have posted watchmen on your walls, Jerusalem;
they will never be silent day or night.
You who call on the LORD,
give yourselves no rest,

PRAYING SCRIPTURE

Isaiah 62

In this joyful chapter of Israel's future glory, God promised that his kingdom would show his righteousness to the Gentiles. There will be no more judgment. Israel will be a "crown of splendor" and "a royal diadem" in the hand of God (verse 3). Never again will Israel be called "Deserted" or "Desolate" (verse 4).

God's promises are sure. We can bank on them. When you read promises in God's Word, pray them as your own.

[a] 4 *Hephzibah* means *my delight is in her.* [b] 4 *Beulah* means *married.*

7 and give him no rest till he establishes Jerusalem
and makes her the praise of the earth.

8 The LORD has sworn by his right hand
and by his mighty arm:
"Never again will I give your grain
as food for your enemies,
and never again will foreigners drink the new wine
for which you have toiled;
9 but those who harvest it will eat it
and praise the LORD,
and those who gather the grapes will drink it
in the courts of my sanctuary."

10 Pass through, pass through the gates!
Prepare the way for the people.
Build up, build up the highway!
Remove the stones.
Raise a banner for the nations.

11 The LORD has made proclamation
to the ends of the earth:
"Say to Daughter Zion,
'See, your Savior comes!
See, his reward is with him,
and his recompense accompanies him.'"
12 They will be called the Holy People,
the Redeemed of the LORD;
and you will be called Sought After,
the City No Longer Deserted.

GOD'S DAY OF VENGEANCE AND REDEMPTION

63 Who is this coming from Edom,
from Bozrah, with his garments stained crimson?
Who is this, robed in splendor,
striding forward in the greatness of his strength?

"It is I, proclaiming victory,
mighty to save."

2 Why are your garments red,
like those of one treading the winepress?
3 "I have trodden the winepress alone;
from the nations no one was with me.
I trampled them in my anger
and trod them down in my wrath;
their blood spattered my garments,
and I stained all my clothing.
4 It was for me the day of vengeance;
the year for me to redeem had come.
5 I looked, but there was no one to help,
I was appalled that no one gave support;
so my own arm achieved salvation for me,
and my own wrath sustained me.
6 I trampled the nations in my anger;
in my wrath I made them drunk
and poured their blood on the ground."

PRAYING SCRIPTURE

Isaiah 63

When we pray, we interact with God as our Father, a relationship emphasized in this chapter (see verse 16). Some struggle with the concept of God as Father because of strained relationships with their earthly fathers. But God as Father is a good thing, even if our understanding is limited.

A father who loves unconditionally, shows grace and mercy and never abandons his children is a Father we can bring every concern to in prayer.

PRAISE AND PRAYER

7 I will tell of the kindnesses of the LORD,
the deeds for which he is to be praised,
according to all the LORD has done for us —
yes, the many good things
he has done for Israel,
according to his compassion and many kindnesses.
8 He said, "Surely they are my people,
children who will be true to me";
and so he became their Savior.
9 In all their distress he too was distressed,
and the angel of his presence saved them.[a]
In his love and mercy he redeemed them;
he lifted them up and carried them
all the days of old.
10 Yet they rebelled
and grieved his Holy Spirit.
So he turned and became their enemy
and he himself fought against them.

11 Then his people recalled[b] the days of old,
the days of Moses and his people —
where is he who brought them through the sea,
with the shepherd of his flock?
Where is he who set
his Holy Spirit among them,
12 who sent his glorious arm of power
to be at Moses' right hand,
who divided the waters before them,
to gain for himself everlasting renown,
13 who led them through the depths?
Like a horse in open country,
they did not stumble;
14 like cattle that go down to the plain,
they were given rest by the Spirit of the LORD.
This is how you guided your people
to make for yourself a glorious name.

15 Look down from heaven and see,
from your lofty throne, holy and glorious.
Where are your zeal and your might?
Your tenderness and compassion are withheld from us.
16 But you are our Father,
though Abraham does not know us
or Israel acknowledge us;
you, LORD, are our Father,
our Redeemer from of old is your name.
17 Why, LORD, do you make us wander from your ways
and harden our hearts so we do not revere you?
Return for the sake of your servants,
the tribes that are your inheritance.
18 For a little while your people possessed your holy place,
but now our enemies have trampled down your sanctuary.

---

[a] 9 Or *Savior* [9]*in their distress. / It was no envoy or angel / but his own presence that saved them* [b] 11 Or *But may he recall*

19 We are yours from of old;
but you have not ruled over them,
they have not been called[a] by your name.

64 [b] Oh, that you would rend the heavens and come down,
that the mountains would tremble before you!
2 As when fire sets twigs ablaze
and causes water to boil,
come down to make your name known to your enemies
and cause the nations to quake before you!
3 For when you did awesome things that we did not expect,
you came down, and the mountains trembled before you.
4 Since ancient times no one has heard,
no ear has perceived,
no eye has seen any God besides you,
who acts on behalf of those who wait for him.
5 You come to the help of those who gladly do right,
who remember your ways.
But when we continued to sin against them,
you were angry.
How then can we be saved?
6 All of us have become like one who is unclean,
and all our righteous acts are like filthy rags;
we all shrivel up like a leaf,
and like the wind our sins sweep us away.
7 No one calls on your name
or strives to lay hold of you;
for you have hidden your face from us
and have given us over to[c] our sins.

8 Yet you, LORD, are our Father.
We are the clay, you are the potter;
we are all the work of your hand.
9 Do not be angry beyond measure, LORD;
do not remember our sins forever.
Oh, look on us, we pray,
for we are all your people.
10 Your sacred cities have become a wasteland;
even Zion is a wasteland, Jerusalem a desolation.
11 Our holy and glorious temple, where our ancestors
praised you,
has been burned with fire,
and all that we treasured lies in ruins.
12 After all this, LORD, will you hold yourself back?
Will you keep silent and punish us beyond measure?

JUDGMENT AND SALVATION

65 "I revealed myself to those who did not ask for me;
I was found by those who did not seek me.
To a nation that did not call on my name,
I said, 'Here am I, here am I.'

PRAYING SCRIPTURE

Isaiah 64

One of the most important lessons we can learn is that God is in control of our lives; we aren't. He is the potter, and we are the clay. We all are the work of the Master Potter's hands. Though we are scarred and flawed, he is fashioning his children into something beautiful.

Sometimes it takes faith to believe that God is making us into a masterwork. Prayerfully submit to the Master Potter's shaping work.

PRAYING SCRIPTURE

Isaiah 65

"New heavens and a new earth" (verse 17). Just the words should stir the heart of every child of God. Weeping will be no more in the new Jerusalem. Life as the Lord intended it shall fill the earth. Every vain thing will be removed; all will be flourishing.

Don't you long for that day? We all should. Tell God you want the day to come when all will be righteousness and peace.

[a] 19 Or *We are like those you have never ruled, / like those never called* [b] In Hebrew texts 64:1 is numbered 63:19b, and 64:2-12 is numbered 64:1-11.
[c] 7 Septuagint, Syriac and Targum; Hebrew *have made us melt because of*

2 All day long I have held out my hands
to an obstinate people,
who walk in ways not good,
pursuing their own imaginations—
3 a people who continually provoke me
to my very face,
offering sacrifices in gardens
and burning incense on altars of brick;
4 who sit among the graves
and spend their nights keeping secret vigil;
who eat the flesh of pigs,
and whose pots hold broth of impure meat;
5 who say, 'Keep away; don't come near me,
for I am too sacred for you!'
Such people are smoke in my nostrils,
a fire that keeps burning all day.

6 "See, it stands written before me:
I will not keep silent but will pay back in full;
I will pay it back into their laps—
7 both your sins and the sins of your ancestors,"
says the LORD.
"Because they burned sacrifices on the mountains
and defied me on the hills,
I will measure into their laps
the full payment for their former deeds."

8 This is what the LORD says:

"As when juice is still found in a cluster of grapes
and people say, 'Don't destroy it,
there is still a blessing in it,'
so will I do in behalf of my servants;
I will not destroy them all.
9 I will bring forth descendants from Jacob,
and from Judah those who will possess my mountains;
my chosen people will inherit them,
and there will my servants live.
10 Sharon will become a pasture for flocks,
and the Valley of Achor a resting place for herds,
for my people who seek me.

11 "But as for you who forsake the LORD
and forget my holy mountain,
who spread a table for Fortune
and fill bowls of mixed wine for Destiny,
12 I will destine you for the sword,
and all of you will fall in the slaughter;
for I called but you did not answer,
I spoke but you did not listen.
You did evil in my sight
and chose what displeases me."

13 Therefore this is what the Sovereign LORD says:

"My servants will eat,
but you will go hungry;

my servants will drink,
but you will go thirsty;
my servants will rejoice,
but you will be put to shame.
14 My servants will sing
out of the joy of their hearts,
but you will cry out
from anguish of heart
and wail in brokenness of spirit.
15 You will leave your name
for my chosen ones to use in their curses;
the Sovereign LORD will put you to death,
but to his servants he will give another name.
16 Whoever invokes a blessing in the land
will do so by the one true God;
whoever takes an oath in the land
will swear by the one true God.
For the past troubles will be forgotten
and hidden from my eyes.

NEW HEAVENS AND A NEW EARTH

17 "See, I will create
new heavens and a new earth.
The former things will not be remembered,
nor will they come to mind.
18 But be glad and rejoice forever
in what I will create,
for I will create Jerusalem to be a delight
and its people a joy.
19 I will rejoice over Jerusalem
and take delight in my people;
the sound of weeping and of crying
will be heard in it no more.

20 "Never again will there be in it
an infant who lives but a few days,
or an old man who does not live out his years;
the one who dies at a hundred
will be thought a mere child;
the one who fails to reach[a] a hundred
will be considered accursed.
21 They will build houses and dwell in them;
they will plant vineyards and eat their fruit.
22 No longer will they build houses and others live in them,
or plant and others eat.
For as the days of a tree,
so will be the days of my people;
my chosen ones will long enjoy
the work of their hands.
23 They will not labor in vain,
nor will they bear children doomed to misfortune;
for they will be a people blessed by the LORD,
they and their descendants with them.

---

[a] 20 Or *the sinner who reaches*

24 Before they call I will answer;
while they are still speaking I will hear.
25 The wolf and the lamb will feed together,
and the lion will eat straw like the ox,
and dust will be the serpent's food.
They will neither harm nor destroy
on all my holy mountain,"
says the LORD.

JUDGMENT AND HOPE

66 This is what the LORD says:

"Heaven is my throne,
and the earth is my footstool.
Where is the house you will build for me?
Where will my resting place be?
2 Has not my hand made all these things,
and so they came into being?"
declares the LORD.

"These are the ones I look on with favor:
those who are humble and contrite in spirit,
and who tremble at my word.
3 But whoever sacrifices a bull
is like one who kills a person,
and whoever offers a lamb
is like one who breaks a dog's neck;
whoever makes a grain offering
is like one who presents pig's blood,
and whoever burns memorial incense
is like one who worships an idol.
They have chosen their own ways,
and they delight in their abominations;
4 so I also will choose harsh treatment for them
and will bring on them what they dread.
For when I called, no one answered,
when I spoke, no one listened.
They did evil in my sight
and chose what displeases me."

5 Hear the word of the LORD,
you who tremble at his word:
"Your own people who hate you,
and exclude you because of my name, have said,
'Let the LORD be glorified,
that we may see your joy!'
Yet they will be put to shame.
6 Hear that uproar from the city,
hear that noise from the temple!
It is the sound of the LORD
repaying his enemies all they deserve.

7 "Before she goes into labor,
she gives birth;
before the pains come upon her,
she delivers a son.

PRAYING SCRIPTURE

Isaiah 66

Isaiah continued the theme of the new heavens and new earth, closing his book by reminding us that God will establish them so that "all mankind will come and bow down before [him]" (verse 23). Eternity will not be endless nothingness. We will worship in person the One we worship now by faith.

Don't wait for eternity to worship the Lord. He's at work in your life. Worship him for it! Declare his worth every time you pray.

8 Who has ever heard of such things?
Who has ever seen things like this?
Can a country be born in a day
or a nation be brought forth in a moment?
Yet no sooner is Zion in labor
than she gives birth to her children.
9 Do I bring to the moment of birth
and not give delivery?" says the LORD.
"Do I close up the womb
when I bring to delivery?" says your God.
10 "Rejoice with Jerusalem and be glad for her,
all you who love her;
rejoice greatly with her,
all you who mourn over her.
11 For you will nurse and be satisfied
at her comforting breasts;
you will drink deeply
and delight in her overflowing abundance."

12 For this is what the LORD says:

"I will extend peace to her like a river,
and the wealth of nations like a flooding stream;
you will nurse and be carried on her arm
and dandled on her knees.
13 As a mother comforts her child,
so will I comfort you;
and you will be comforted over Jerusalem."

14 When you see this, your heart will rejoice
and you will flourish like grass;
the hand of the LORD will be made known to his servants,
but his fury will be shown to his foes.
15 See, the LORD is coming with fire,
and his chariots are like a whirlwind;
he will bring down his anger with fury,
and his rebuke with flames of fire.
16 For with fire and with his sword
the LORD will execute judgment on all people,
and many will be those slain by the LORD.

17 "Those who consecrate and purify themselves to go into the gardens, following one who is among those who eat the flesh of pigs, rats and other unclean things — they will meet their end together with the one they follow," declares the LORD.

18 "And I, because of what they have planned and done, am about to come[a] and gather the people of all nations and languages, and they will come and see my glory.

19 "I will set a sign among them, and I will send some of those who survive to the nations — to Tarshish, to the Libyans[b] and Lydians (famous as archers), to Tubal and Greece, and to the distant islands that have not heard of my fame or seen my glory. They will proclaim my glory among the nations.
20 And they will bring all your people, from

---

[a] *18* The meaning of the Hebrew for this clause is uncertain. [b] *19* Some Septuagint manuscripts *Put* (Libyans); Hebrew *Pul*

all the nations, to my holy mountain in Jerusalem as an offering to
the LORD — on horses, in chariots and wagons, and on mules and cam-
els," says the LORD. "They will bring them, as the Israelites bring their
grain offerings, to the temple of the LORD in ceremonially clean ves-
sels. 21And I will select some of them also to be priests and Levites,"
says the LORD.

22"As the new heavens and the new earth that I make will endure
before me," declares the LORD, "so will your name and descendants
endure. 23From one New Moon to another and from one Sabbath to
another, all mankind will come and bow down before me," says the
LORD. 24"And they will go out and look on the dead bodies of those
who rebelled against me; the worms that eat them will not die, the
fire that burns them will not be quenched, and they will be loathsome
to all mankind."

JEREMIAH

Jeremiah has rightfully been nicknamed "the weeping prophet," as most of his prophecy centers on the fall of Jerusalem to Babylonian invaders. He received his prophetic call before the reign of King Josiah, and he did see some reform in his lifetime. But mostly he witnessed the slow and steady descent of Judah into apostasy and sin.

Jeremiah spent a great deal of his prophecy warning Israel of the judgment to come, calling them to repentance. In this section of the book, Jeremiah spoke as if repentance was a real possibility for Israel. Then the tone of the book changed when judgment became certain. During this period, Jeremiah preached the righteousness of God in sending his people into exile. However, judgment was not the final word—the prophet showed that the exile would eventually lead to the restoration of God's people.

During exile, God directed his people to seek the peace of the city where they had been carried away, and to pray for it (see 29:7). Several verses later, God promised to hear them when they prayed to him. God clearly wanted his people to pray for peace where they were, rather than growing despondent in their circumstances. If the city prospered, they would prosper along with it. Later, when a group of Jewish exiles hoped to flee into Egypt, Jeremiah prayed for God's guidance. Much to the group's displeasure, they were told to stay (see 42:10–12; 43:2).

Chapter 31 is one of the most well-known and theologically important passages in the book. It promises a "new covenant" that God would make with his people. This new covenant would not be like the old covenant, which the people broke. Instead, God would be the God of his people, putting his Spirit in them. Further, he would no longer remember the sins they had committed. No one would have to tell another to "know the LORD" (verse 34), because they would all know him and be known by him.

The new covenant promise helps Christians understand the privilege of prayer. God is our God; he is the Father who listens. He knows us, loves us and makes himself known to us. We no longer need a human mediator to approach God; we have the eternal Son of God. We need not wave our arms to get his attention; we can boldly approach his throne. When we struggle in prayer, the Holy Spirit helps us. He gives us the words to say, and he can also intercede for us when we don't have the words.

Jeremiah also models for Christians how to pray in a culture that does not know God. It is fully appropriate for God's people to mourn over the depravity, sin and unfaithfulness in their culture. It is a tragedy when people run from God and spend their lives in sin. An ungodly culture often resents both the message and the messenger, so we should pray for boldness. When Christians face pressure in secular spaces, we need God's help to stand strong in the faith.

PRAYING SCRIPTURE

Jeremiah 1

Have you ever thought about how the Lord knew every one of our days before we had consciously experienced even one of them? God has a purpose for each of us from our mother's womb. God told Jeremiah, "I appointed you a prophet to the nations" (verse 5).

Do you know your purpose? God has a unique plan for each person. If you aren't sure of your purpose, ask him to show you, and then follow in that path.

PRAYING SCRIPTURE

Jeremiah 2

Human beings tend to abandon God for worldliness—a temptation that affects even his people. The children of Israel had succumbed once again to idolatry and injustice, abandoning God and embracing false teaching—all this even though God had previously corrected them (see verse 30).

Search your heart for any remnant of idolatry, injustice or worldliness. Confess to God when you are tempted to abandon his ways. Seek his forgiveness and receive it by faith.

1 The words of Jeremiah son of Hilkiah, one of the priests at Anathoth
in the territory of Benjamin. 2The word of the LORD came to him in
the thirteenth year of the reign of Josiah son of Amon king of Judah,
3and through the reign of Jehoiakim son of Josiah king of Judah, down
to the fifth month of the eleventh year of Zedekiah son of Josiah king
of Judah, when the people of Jerusalem went into exile.

THE CALL OF JEREMIAH

4The word of the LORD came to me, saying,

5"Before I formed you in the womb I knew[a] you,
before you were born I set you apart;
I appointed you as a prophet to the nations."

6"Alas, Sovereign LORD," I said, "I do not know how to speak; I am
too young."
7But the LORD said to me, "Do not say, 'I am too young.' You must go
to everyone I send you to and say whatever I command you. 8Do not be
afraid of them, for I am with you and will rescue you," declares the LORD.
9Then the LORD reached out his hand and touched my mouth and
said to me, "I have put my words in your mouth. 10See, today I appoint
you over nations and kingdoms to uproot and tear down, to destroy
and overthrow, to build and to plant."
11The word of the LORD came to me: "What do you see, Jeremiah?"
"I see the branch of an almond tree," I replied.
12The LORD said to me, "You have seen correctly, for I am watching[b]
to see that my word is fulfilled."
13The word of the LORD came to me again: "What do you see?"
"I see a pot that is boiling," I answered. "It is tilting toward us from
the north."
14The LORD said to me, "From the north disaster will be poured out
on all who live in the land. 15I am about to summon all the peoples of
the northern kingdoms," declares the LORD.

"Their kings will come and set up their thrones
in the entrance of the gates of Jerusalem;
they will come against all her surrounding walls
and against all the towns of Judah.
16I will pronounce my judgments on my people
because of their wickedness in forsaking me,
in burning incense to other gods
and in worshiping what their hands have made.

17"Get yourself ready! Stand up and say to them whatever I command
you. Do not be terrified by them, or I will terrify you before them. 18Today
I have made you a fortified city, an iron pillar and a bronze wall to stand
against the whole land—against the kings of Judah, its officials, its priests
and the people of the land. 19They will fight against you but will not over-
come you, for I am with you and will rescue you," declares the LORD.

ISRAEL FORSAKES GOD

2 The word of the LORD came to me: 2"Go and proclaim in the hear-
ing of Jerusalem:

"This is what the LORD says:

[a] 5 Or *chose* [b] 12 The Hebrew for *watching* sounds like the Hebrew for *almond tree.*

"'I remember the devotion of your youth,
how as a bride you loved me
and followed me through the wilderness,
through a land not sown.
3 Israel was holy to the LORD,
the firstfruits of his harvest;
all who devoured her were held guilty,
and disaster overtook them,'"
declares the LORD.

4 Hear the word of the LORD, you descendants
of Jacob,
all you clans of Israel.

5 This is what the LORD says:

"What fault did your ancestors find in me,
that they strayed so far from me?
They followed worthless idols
and became worthless themselves.
6 They did not ask, 'Where is the LORD,
who brought us up out of Egypt
and led us through the barren wilderness,
through a land of deserts and ravines,
a land of drought and utter darkness,
a land where no one travels and no one lives?'
7 I brought you into a fertile land
to eat its fruit and rich produce.
But you came and defiled my land
and made my inheritance detestable.
8 The priests did not ask,
'Where is the LORD?'
Those who deal with the law did not know me;
the leaders rebelled against me.
The prophets prophesied by Baal,
following worthless idols.

9 "Therefore I bring charges against you again,"
declares the LORD.
"And I will bring charges against your
children's children.
10 Cross over to the coasts of Cyprus and look,
send to Kedar[a] and observe closely;
see if there has ever been anything like this:
11 Has a nation ever changed its gods?
(Yet they are not gods at all.)
But my people have exchanged their glorious God
for worthless idols.
12 Be appalled at this, you heavens,
and shudder with great horror,"
declares the LORD.
13 "My people have committed two sins:
They have forsaken me,
the spring of living water,

[a] *10* In the Syro-Arabian desert

and have dug their own cisterns,
broken cisterns that cannot hold water.
14 Is Israel a servant, a slave by birth?
Why then has he become plunder?
15 Lions have roared;
they have growled at him.
They have laid waste his land;
his towns are burned and deserted.
16 Also, the men of Memphis and Tahpanhes
have cracked your skull.
17 Have you not brought this on yourselves
by forsaking the LORD your God
when he led you in the way?
18 Now why go to Egypt
to drink water from the Nile[a]?
And why go to Assyria
to drink water from the Euphrates?
19 Your wickedness will punish you;
your backsliding will rebuke you.
Consider then and realize
how evil and bitter it is for you
when you forsake the LORD your God
and have no awe of me,"
declares the Lord, the LORD Almighty.

20 "Long ago you broke off your yoke
and tore off your bonds;
you said, 'I will not serve you!'
Indeed, on every high hill
and under every spreading tree
you lay down as a prostitute.
21 I had planted you like a choice vine
of sound and reliable stock.
How then did you turn against me
into a corrupt, wild vine?
22 Although you wash yourself with soap
and use an abundance of cleansing powder,
the stain of your guilt is still before me,"
declares the Sovereign LORD.
23 "How can you say, 'I am not defiled;
I have not run after the Baals'?
See how you behaved in the valley;
consider what you have done.
You are a swift she-camel
running here and there,
24 a wild donkey accustomed to the desert,
sniffing the wind in her craving—
in her heat who can restrain her?
Any males that pursue her need not tire themselves;
at mating time they will find her.
25 Do not run until your feet are bare
and your throat is dry.

---

[a] 18 Hebrew *Shihor*; that is, a branch of the Nile

But you said, 'It's no use!
I love foreign gods,
and I must go after them.'

26 "As a thief is disgraced when he is caught,
so the people of Israel are disgraced —
they, their kings and their officials,
their priests and their prophets.
27 They say to wood, 'You are my father,'
and to stone, 'You gave me birth.'
They have turned their backs to me
and not their faces;
yet when they are in trouble, they say,
'Come and save us!'
28 Where then are the gods you made for yourselves?
Let them come if they can save you
when you are in trouble!
For you, Judah, have as many gods
as you have towns.

29 "Why do you bring charges against me?
You have all rebelled against me,"
declares the LORD.

30 "In vain I punished your people;
they did not respond to correction.
Your sword has devoured your prophets
like a ravenous lion.

31 "You of this generation, consider the word of the LORD:

"Have I been a desert to Israel
or a land of great darkness?
Why do my people say, 'We are free to roam;
we will come to you no more'?
32 Does a young woman forget her jewelry,
a bride her wedding ornaments?
Yet my people have forgotten me,
days without number.
33 How skilled you are at pursuing love!
Even the worst of women can learn from your ways.
34 On your clothes is found
the lifeblood of the innocent poor,
though you did not catch them breaking in.
Yet in spite of all this
35 you say, 'I am innocent;
he is not angry with me.'
But I will pass judgment on you
because you say, 'I have not sinned.'
36 Why do you go about so much,
changing your ways?
You will be disappointed by Egypt
as you were by Assyria.
37 You will also leave that place
with your hands on your head,
for the LORD has rejected those you trust;
you will not be helped by them.

PRAYING SCRIPTURE

Jeremiah 3

During the reign of King Josiah, God called Jeremiah to prophesy to Israel. Even though the Lord was angry with his people, He remained merciful and beckoned them to return from their backsliding. If they would return, he promised them "shepherds after [his] own heart" (verse 15).

God is patient when we stray. Thank him for the mercy that always invites us back and the love he lavishes on his children.

3 "If a man divorces his wife
and she leaves him and marries another man,
should he return to her again?
Would not the land be completely defiled?
But you have lived as a prostitute with many lovers —
would you now return to me?"
declares the LORD.
2 "Look up to the barren heights and see.
Is there any place where you have not been ravished?
By the roadside you sat waiting for lovers,
sat like a nomad in the desert.
You have defiled the land
with your prostitution and wickedness.
3 Therefore the showers have been withheld,
and no spring rains have fallen.
Yet you have the brazen look of a prostitute;
you refuse to blush with shame.
4 Have you not just called to me:
'My Father, my friend from my youth,
5 will you always be angry?
Will your wrath continue forever?'
This is how you talk,
but you do all the evil you can."

UNFAITHFUL ISRAEL

6 During the reign of King Josiah, the LORD said to me, "Have you
seen what faithless Israel has done? She has gone up on every high hill
and under every spreading tree and has committed adultery there. 7 I
thought that after she had done all this she would return to me but she
did not, and her unfaithful sister Judah saw it. 8 I gave faithless Israel
her certificate of divorce and sent her away because of all her adulter-
ies. Yet I saw that her unfaithful sister Judah had no fear; she also went
out and committed adultery. 9 Because Israel's immorality mattered so
little to her, she defiled the land and committed adultery with stone
and wood. 10 In spite of all this, her unfaithful sister Judah did not re-
turn to me with all her heart, but only in pretense," declares the LORD.
11 The LORD said to me, "Faithless Israel is more righteous than un-
faithful Judah. 12 Go, proclaim this message toward the north:

"'Return, faithless Israel,' declares the LORD,
'I will frown on you no longer,
for I am faithful,' declares the LORD,
'I will not be angry forever.
13 Only acknowledge your guilt —
you have rebelled against the LORD your God,
you have scattered your favors to foreign gods
under every spreading tree,
and have not obeyed me,'"
declares the LORD.

14 "Return, faithless people," declares the LORD, "for I am your hus-
band. I will choose you — one from a town and two from a clan — and
bring you to Zion. 15 Then I will give you shepherds after my own heart,
who will lead you with knowledge and understanding. 16 In those days,
when your numbers have increased greatly in the land," declares the

LORD, "people will no longer say, 'The ark of the covenant of the LORD.'
It will never enter their minds or be remembered; it will not be missed,
nor will another one be made. 17At that time they will call Jerusalem
The Throne of the LORD, and all nations will gather in Jerusalem to
honor the name of the LORD. No longer will they follow the stubborn-
ness of their evil hearts. 18In those days the people of Judah will join
the people of Israel, and together they will come from a northern land
to the land I gave your ancestors as an inheritance.

19"I myself said,

"'How gladly would I treat you like my children
and give you a pleasant land,
the most beautiful inheritance of any nation.'
I thought you would call me 'Father'
and not turn away from following me.
20 But like a woman unfaithful to her husband,
so you, Israel, have been unfaithful to me,"
declares the LORD.

21 A cry is heard on the barren heights,
the weeping and pleading of the people of Israel,
because they have perverted their ways
and have forgotten the LORD their God.

22 "Return, faithless people;
I will cure you of backsliding."

"Yes, we will come to you,
for you are the LORD our God.
23 Surely the idolatrous commotion on the hills
and mountains is a deception;
surely in the LORD our God
is the salvation of Israel.
24 From our youth shameful gods have consumed
the fruits of our ancestors' labor—
their flocks and herds,
their sons and daughters.
25 Let us lie down in our shame,
and let our disgrace cover us.
We have sinned against the LORD our God,
both we and our ancestors;
from our youth till this day
we have not obeyed the LORD our God."

4 "If you, Israel, will return,
then return to me,"
declares the LORD.
"If you put your detestable idols out of my sight
and no longer go astray,
2 and if in a truthful, just and righteous way
you swear, 'As surely as the LORD lives,'
then the nations will invoke blessings by him
and in him they will boast."

3This is what the LORD says to the people of Judah and to Jerusalem:

"Break up your unplowed ground
and do not sow among thorns.

PRAYING SCRIPTURE

Jeremiah 4

Repentance is our way of returning to the Lord. The Israelites had rebelled, yet God beckoned them back. Still, they could not return unrepentant. *If* they put away their abominations and committed themselves to the Lord, they would be blessed.

God will not be mocked; obedience precedes blessing. When we sin, our return must be accompanied by repentance. Come clean before God and seek his mercy. Commit to following him obediently.

4 Circumcise yourselves to the LORD,
circumcise your hearts,
you people of Judah and inhabitants of Jerusalem,
or my wrath will flare up and burn like fire
because of the evil you have done —
burn with no one to quench it.

DISASTER FROM THE NORTH

5 "Announce in Judah and proclaim in Jerusalem and say:
'Sound the trumpet throughout the land!'
Cry aloud and say:
'Gather together!
Let us flee to the fortified cities!'
6 Raise the signal to go to Zion!
Flee for safety without delay!
For I am bringing disaster from the north,
even terrible destruction."

7 A lion has come out of his lair;
a destroyer of nations has set out.
He has left his place
to lay waste your land.
Your towns will lie in ruins
without inhabitant.
8 So put on sackcloth,
lament and wail,
for the fierce anger of the LORD
has not turned away from us.

9 "In that day," declares the LORD,
"the king and the officials will lose heart,
the priests will be horrified,
and the prophets will be appalled."

10 Then I said, "Alas, Sovereign LORD! How completely you have de-
ceived this people and Jerusalem by saying, 'You will have peace,'
when the sword is at our throats!"
11 At that time this people and Jerusalem will be told, "A scorching
wind from the barren heights in the desert blows toward my people,
but not to winnow or cleanse; 12 a wind too strong for that comes from
me. Now I pronounce my judgments against them."

13 Look! He advances like the clouds,
his chariots come like a whirlwind,
his horses are swifter than eagles.
Woe to us! We are ruined!
14 Jerusalem, wash the evil from your heart and be saved.
How long will you harbor wicked thoughts?
15 A voice is announcing from Dan,
proclaiming disaster from the hills of Ephraim.
16 "Tell this to the nations,
proclaim concerning Jerusalem:
'A besieging army is coming from a distant land,
raising a war cry against the cities of Judah.
17 They surround her like men guarding a field,
because she has rebelled against me,'"
declares the LORD.

18 "Your own conduct and actions
have brought this on you.
This is your punishment.
How bitter it is!
How it pierces to the heart!"

19 Oh, my anguish, my anguish!
I writhe in pain.
Oh, the agony of my heart!
My heart pounds within me,
I cannot keep silent.
For I have heard the sound of the trumpet;
I have heard the battle cry.
20 Disaster follows disaster;
the whole land lies in ruins.
In an instant my tents are destroyed,
my shelter in a moment.
21 How long must I see the battle standard
and hear the sound of the trumpet?

22 "My people are fools;
they do not know me.
They are senseless children;
they have no understanding.
They are skilled in doing evil;
they know not how to do good."

23 I looked at the earth,
and it was formless and empty;
and at the heavens,
and their light was gone.
24 I looked at the mountains,
and they were quaking;
all the hills were swaying.
25 I looked, and there were no people;
every bird in the sky had flown away.
26 I looked, and the fruitful land was a desert;
all its towns lay in ruins
before the LORD, before his fierce anger.

27 This is what the LORD says:

"The whole land will be ruined,
though I will not destroy it completely.
28 Therefore the earth will mourn
and the heavens above grow dark,
because I have spoken and will not relent,
I have decided and will not turn back."

29 At the sound of horsemen and archers
every town takes to flight.
Some go into the thickets;
some climb up among the rocks.
All the towns are deserted;
no one lives in them.

30 What are you doing, you devastated one?
Why dress yourself in scarlet

and put on jewels of gold?
Why highlight your eyes with makeup?
You adorn yourself in vain.
Your lovers despise you;
they want to kill you.

31 I hear a cry as of a woman in labor,
a groan as of one bearing her first child —
the cry of Daughter Zion gasping for breath,
stretching out her hands and saying,
"Alas! I am fainting;
my life is given over to murderers."

NOT ONE IS UPRIGHT

5 "Go up and down the streets of Jerusalem,
look around and consider,
search through her squares.
If you can find but one person
who deals honestly and seeks the truth,
I will forgive this city.
2 Although they say, 'As surely as the LORD lives,'
still they are swearing falsely."

3 LORD, do not your eyes look for truth?
You struck them, but they felt no pain;
you crushed them, but they refused correction.
They made their faces harder than stone
and refused to repent.
4 I thought, "These are only the poor;
they are foolish,
for they do not know the way of the LORD,
the requirements of their God.
5 So I will go to the leaders
and speak to them;
surely they know the way of the LORD,
the requirements of their God."
But with one accord they too had broken off the yoke
and torn off the bonds.
6 Therefore a lion from the forest will attack them,
a wolf from the desert will ravage them,
a leopard will lie in wait near their towns
to tear to pieces any who venture out,
for their rebellion is great
and their backslidings many.
7 "Why should I forgive you?
Your children have forsaken me
and sworn by gods that are not gods.
I supplied all their needs,
yet they committed adultery
and thronged to the houses of prostitutes.
8 They are well-fed, lusty stallions,
each neighing for another man's wife.
9 Should I not punish them for this?"
declares the LORD.

PRAYING SCRIPTURE

Jeremiah 5

The chapter recounts many of the reasons the Lord brought judgment on the people of Israel. He had often warned about false teachers leading them astray. Here, after criticizing false prophets and priests who rule by their own authority, the Lord warned, "My people love it this way" (verse 31).

"But what will you do in the end?" Don't succumb to deceitful words. Ask God to give you ears to hear his Word.

"Should I not avenge myself
  on such a nation as this?

10 "Go through her vineyards and ravage them,
  but do not destroy them completely.
Strip off her branches,
  for these people do not belong to the LORD.
11 The people of Israel and the people of Judah
  have been utterly unfaithful to me,"
declares the LORD.

12 They have lied about the LORD;
  they said, "He will do nothing!
No harm will come to us;
  we will never see sword or famine.
13 The prophets are but wind
  and the word is not in them;
  so let what they say be done to them."

14 Therefore this is what the LORD God Almighty says:

"Because the people have spoken these words,
  I will make my words in your mouth a fire
  and these people the wood it consumes.
15 People of Israel," declares the LORD,
  "I am bringing a distant nation against you—
an ancient and enduring nation,
  a people whose language you do not know,
  whose speech you do not understand.
16 Their quivers are like an open grave;
  all of them are mighty warriors.
17 They will devour your harvests and food,
  devour your sons and daughters;
they will devour your flocks and herds,
  devour your vines and fig trees.
With the sword they will destroy
  the fortified cities in which you trust.

18 "Yet even in those days," declares the LORD, "I will not destroy you
completely. 19 And when the people ask, 'Why has the LORD our God
done all this to us?' you will tell them, 'As you have forsaken me and
served foreign gods in your own land, so now you will serve foreigners
in a land not your own.'

20 "Announce this to the descendants of Jacob
  and proclaim it in Judah:
21 Hear this, you foolish and senseless people,
  who have eyes but do not see,
  who have ears but do not hear:
22 Should you not fear me?" declares the LORD.
  "Should you not tremble in my presence?
I made the sand a boundary for the sea,
  an everlasting barrier it cannot cross.
The waves may roll, but they cannot prevail;
  they may roar, but they cannot cross it.
23 But these people have stubborn and rebellious hearts;
  they have turned aside and gone away.

24 They do not say to themselves,
'Let us fear the LORD our God,
who gives autumn and spring rains in season,
who assures us of the regular weeks of harvest.'
25 Your wrongdoings have kept these away;
your sins have deprived you of good.

26 "Among my people are the wicked
who lie in wait like men who snare birds
and like those who set traps to catch people.
27 Like cages full of birds,
their houses are full of deceit;
they have become rich and powerful
28 and have grown fat and sleek.
Their evil deeds have no limit;
they do not seek justice.
They do not promote the case of the fatherless;
they do not defend the just cause of the poor.
29 Should I not punish them for this?"
declares the LORD.
"Should I not avenge myself
on such a nation as this?

30 "A horrible and shocking thing
has happened in the land:
31 The prophets prophesy lies,
the priests rule by their own authority,
and my people love it this way.
But what will you do in the end?

JERUSALEM UNDER SIEGE

6 "Flee for safety, people of Benjamin!
Flee from Jerusalem!
Sound the trumpet in Tekoa!
Raise the signal over Beth Hakkerem!
For disaster looms out of the north,
even terrible destruction.
2 I will destroy Daughter Zion,
so beautiful and delicate.
3 Shepherds with their flocks will come against her;
they will pitch their tents around her,
each tending his own portion."

4 "Prepare for battle against her!
Arise, let us attack at noon!
But, alas, the daylight is fading,
and the shadows of evening grow long.
5 So arise, let us attack at night
and destroy her fortresses!"

6 This is what the LORD Almighty says:

"Cut down the trees
and build siege ramps against Jerusalem.
This city must be punished;
it is filled with oppression.

PRAYING SCRIPTURE

Jeremiah 6

The Lord said that it is good for our souls when we walk in "the ancient paths" (verse 16). Some wrongly think this refers to old ways of doing things from bygone eras of their church experience. Those ways might bring comfort, but they do not bring rest.

Seek "the ancient paths," such as the Word of God, which is a light to your path. Seek his ways; then you will find rest for your soul.

7 As a well pours out its water,
so she pours out her wickedness.
Violence and destruction resound in her;
her sickness and wounds are ever before me.
8 Take warning, Jerusalem,
or I will turn away from you
and make your land desolate
so no one can live in it."

9 This is what the LORD Almighty says:

"Let them glean the remnant of Israel
as thoroughly as a vine;
pass your hand over the branches again,
like one gathering grapes."

10 To whom can I speak and give warning?
Who will listen to me?
Their ears are closed[a]
so they cannot hear.
The word of the LORD is offensive to them;
they find no pleasure in it.
11 But I am full of the wrath of the LORD,
and I cannot hold it in.

"Pour it out on the children in the street
and on the young men gathered together;
both husband and wife will be caught in it,
and the old, those weighed down with years.
12 Their houses will be turned over to others,
together with their fields and their wives,
when I stretch out my hand
against those who live in the land,"
declares the LORD.

13 "From the least to the greatest,
all are greedy for gain;
prophets and priests alike,
all practice deceit.
14 They dress the wound of my people
as though it were not serious.
'Peace, peace,' they say,
when there is no peace.
15 Are they ashamed of their detestable conduct?
No, they have no shame at all;
they do not even know how to blush.
So they will fall among the fallen;
they will be brought down when I punish them,"
says the LORD.

16 This is what the LORD says:

"Stand at the crossroads and look;
ask for the ancient paths,
ask where the good way is, and walk in it,
and you will find rest for your souls.

[a] 10 Hebrew *uncircumcised*

But you said, 'We will not walk in it.'
17 I appointed watchmen over you and said,
'Listen to the sound of the trumpet!'
But you said, 'We will not listen.'
18 Therefore hear, you nations;
you who are witnesses,
observe what will happen to them.
19 Hear, you earth:
I am bringing disaster on this people,
the fruit of their schemes,
because they have not listened to my words
and have rejected my law.
20 What do I care about incense from Sheba
or sweet calamus from a distant land?
Your burnt offerings are not acceptable;
your sacrifices do not please me."

21 Therefore this is what the LORD says:

"I will put obstacles before this people.
Parents and children alike will stumble over them;
neighbors and friends will perish."

22 This is what the LORD says:

"Look, an army is coming
from the land of the north;
a great nation is being stirred up
from the ends of the earth.
23 They are armed with bow and spear;
they are cruel and show no mercy.
They sound like the roaring sea
as they ride on their horses;
they come like men in battle formation
to attack you, Daughter Zion."

24 We have heard reports about them,
and our hands hang limp.
Anguish has gripped us,
pain like that of a woman in labor.
25 Do not go out to the fields
or walk on the roads,
for the enemy has a sword,
and there is terror on every side.
26 Put on sackcloth, my people,
and roll in ashes;
mourn with bitter wailing
as for an only son,
for suddenly the destroyer
will come upon us.

27 "I have made you a tester of metals
and my people the ore,
that you may observe
and test their ways.
28 They are all hardened rebels,
going about to slander.

They are bronze and iron;
  they all act corruptly.
29 The bellows blow fiercely
  to burn away the lead with fire,
but the refining goes on in vain;
  the wicked are not purged out.
30 They are called rejected silver,
  because the LORD has rejected them."

FALSE RELIGION WORTHLESS

7 This is the word that came to Jeremiah from the LORD: 2"Stand
at the gate of the LORD's house and there proclaim this message:
"'Hear the word of the LORD, all you people of Judah who come
through these gates to worship the LORD. 3This is what the LORD Al-
mighty, the God of Israel, says: Reform your ways and your actions, and
I will let you live in this place. 4Do not trust in deceptive words and say,
"This is the temple of the LORD, the temple of the LORD, the temple of
the LORD!" 5If you really change your ways and your actions and deal
with each other justly, 6if you do not oppress the foreigner, the father-
less or the widow and do not shed innocent blood in this place, and if
you do not follow other gods to your own harm, 7then I will let you live
in this place, in the land I gave your ancestors for ever and ever. 8But
look, you are trusting in deceptive words that are worthless.
9"'Will you steal and murder, commit adultery and perjury,[a] burn
incense to Baal and follow other gods you have not known, 10and then
come and stand before me in this house, which bears my Name, and
say, "We are safe"—safe to do all these detestable things? 11Has this
house, which bears my Name, become a den of robbers to you? But I
have been watching! declares the LORD.
12"'Go now to the place in Shiloh where I first made a dwelling for
my Name, and see what I did to it because of the wickedness of my
people Israel. 13While you were doing all these things, declares the
LORD, I spoke to you again and again, but you did not listen; I called
you, but you did not answer. 14Therefore, what I did to Shiloh I will now
do to the house that bears my Name, the temple you trust in, the place
I gave to you and your ancestors. 15I will thrust you from my presence,
just as I did all your fellow Israelites, the people of Ephraim.'
16"So do not pray for this people nor offer any plea or petition for
them; do not plead with me, for I will not listen to you. 17Do you not
see what they are doing in the towns of Judah and in the streets of
Jerusalem? 18The children gather wood, the fathers light the fire, and
the women knead the dough and make cakes to offer to the Queen of
Heaven. They pour out drink offerings to other gods to arouse my an-
ger. 19But am I the one they are provoking? declares the LORD. Are they
not rather harming themselves, to their own shame?
20"'Therefore this is what the Sovereign LORD says: My anger and
my wrath will be poured out on this place—on man and beast, on the
trees of the field and on the crops of your land—and it will burn and
not be quenched.
21"'This is what the LORD Almighty, the God of Israel, says: Go ahead,
add your burnt offerings to your other sacrifices and eat the meat your-
selves! 22For when I brought your ancestors out of Egypt and spoke to

[a] 9 Or *and swear by false gods*

PRAYING SCRIPTURE

Jeremiah 7

Israel's history is littered with their pursuit of false gods. On more than one occasion, the people chose to worship gods with human sacrifices: the burning of their own children. Through Jeremiah, God made very clear that this was not his design (see verse 31).

We should not be deceived that idolatry is only about wood or stone images. Anything we prioritize over God's place in our lives can be an idol. Check your heart to see if you have idols that you need to turn away from.

them, I did not just give them commands about burnt offerings and sacrifices, 23 but I gave them this command: Obey me, and I will be your God and you will be my people. Walk in obedience to all I command you, that it may go well with you. 24 But they did not listen or pay attention; instead, they followed the stubborn inclinations of their evil hearts. They went backward and not forward. 25 From the time your ancestors left Egypt until now, day after day, again and again I sent you my servants the prophets. 26 But they did not listen to me or pay attention. They were stiff-necked and did more evil than their ancestors.'

27 "When you tell them all this, they will not listen to you; when you call to them, they will not answer. 28 Therefore say to them, 'This is the nation that has not obeyed the LORD its God or responded to correction. Truth has perished; it has vanished from their lips.

29 " 'Cut off your hair and throw it away; take up a lament on the barren heights, for the LORD has rejected and abandoned this generation that is under his wrath.

THE VALLEY OF SLAUGHTER

30 " 'The people of Judah have done evil in my eyes, declares the LORD. They have set up their detestable idols in the house that bears my Name and have defiled it. 31 They have built the high places of Topheth in the Valley of Ben Hinnom to burn their sons and daughters in the fire — something I did not command, nor did it enter my mind. 32 So beware, the days are coming, declares the LORD, when people will no longer call it Topheth or the Valley of Ben Hinnom, but the Valley of Slaughter, for they will bury the dead in Topheth until there is no more room. 33 Then the carcasses of this people will become food for the birds and the wild animals, and there will be no one to frighten them away. 34 I will bring an end to the sounds of joy and gladness and to the voices of bride and bridegroom in the towns of Judah and the streets of Jerusalem, for the land will become desolate.

8 " 'At that time, declares the LORD, the bones of the kings and officials of Judah, the bones of the priests and prophets, and the bones of the people of Jerusalem will be removed from their graves. 2 They will be exposed to the sun and the moon and all the stars of the heavens, which they have loved and served and which they have followed and consulted and worshiped. They will not be gathered up or buried, but will be like dung lying on the ground. 3 Wherever I banish them, all the survivors of this evil nation will prefer death to life, declares the LORD Almighty.'

SIN AND PUNISHMENT

4 "Say to them, 'This is what the LORD says:

" 'When people fall down, do they not get up?
  When someone turns away, do they not return?
5 Why then have these people turned away?
  Why does Jerusalem always turn away?
They cling to deceit;
  they refuse to return.
6 I have listened attentively,
  but they do not say what is right.
None of them repent of their wickedness,
  saying, "What have I done?"

PRAYING SCRIPTURE

Jeremiah 8

God mourns over our disobedience and sin, longing for us to come back to him. God's anger was so severe that Jeremiah was driven to mourning. When he asked, "Is there no balm in Gilead? Is there no physician there?" (verse 22), his hopelessness was laid bare.

Do you ever feel hopeless? Call on the Lord who is the Great Physician and a balm for your weary soul. Rejoice in his healing and hope.

Each pursues their own course
like a horse charging into battle.
7 Even the stork in the sky
knows her appointed seasons,
and the dove, the swift and the thrush
observe the time of their migration.
But my people do not know
the requirements of the LORD.

8 "'How can you say, "We are wise,
for we have the law of the LORD,"
when actually the lying pen of the scribes
has handled it falsely?
9 The wise will be put to shame;
they will be dismayed and trapped.
Since they have rejected the word of the LORD,
what kind of wisdom do they have?
10 Therefore I will give their wives to other men
and their fields to new owners.
From the least to the greatest,
all are greedy for gain;
prophets and priests alike,
all practice deceit.
11 They dress the wound of my people
as though it were not serious.
"Peace, peace," they say,
when there is no peace.
12 Are they ashamed of their detestable conduct?
No, they have no shame at all;
they do not even know how to blush.
So they will fall among the fallen;
they will be brought down when they are punished,
says the LORD.

13 "'I will take away their harvest,
declares the LORD.
There will be no grapes on the vine.
There will be no figs on the tree,
and their leaves will wither.
What I have given them
will be taken from them.[a]'"

14 Why are we sitting here?
Gather together!
Let us flee to the fortified cities
and perish there!
For the LORD our God has doomed us to perish
and given us poisoned water to drink,
because we have sinned against him.
15 We hoped for peace
but no good has come,
for a time of healing
but there is only terror.

---

[a] 13 The meaning of the Hebrew for this sentence is uncertain.

16 The snorting of the enemy's horses
is heard from Dan;
at the neighing of their stallions
the whole land trembles.
They have come to devour
the land and everything in it,
the city and all who live there.

17 "See, I will send venomous snakes among you,
vipers that cannot be charmed,
and they will bite you,"
declares the LORD.

18 You who are my Comforter[a] in sorrow,
my heart is faint within me.
19 Listen to the cry of my people
from a land far away:
"Is the LORD not in Zion?
Is her King no longer there?"

"Why have they aroused my anger with their images,
with their worthless foreign idols?"

20 "The harvest is past,
the summer has ended,
and we are not saved."

21 Since my people are crushed, I am crushed;
I mourn, and horror grips me.
22 Is there no balm in Gilead?
Is there no physician there?
Why then is there no healing
for the wound of my people?

9 [b] 1 Oh, that my head were a spring of water
and my eyes a fountain of tears!
I would weep day and night
for the slain of my people.
2 Oh, that I had in the desert
a lodging place for travelers,
so that I might leave my people
and go away from them;
for they are all adulterers,
a crowd of unfaithful people.

3 "They make ready their tongue
like a bow, to shoot lies;
it is not by truth
that they triumph[c] in the land.
They go from one sin to another;
they do not acknowledge me,"
declares the LORD.

4 "Beware of your friends;
do not trust anyone in your clan.

PRAYING SCRIPTURE

Jeremiah 9

Here we see the reason for Jeremiah's nickname: the weeping prophet. The burden for his people finally broke his emotional dam, and he prayed that he could "weep day and night" for his dead countrymen and those who "go from one sin to another" (verses 1,3).

The sin and folly that surround us should break our hearts and move us to prayer. Pray for the people around you who need to repent and believe.

---

[a] *18* The meaning of the Hebrew for this word is uncertain. [b] In Hebrew texts 9:1 is numbered 8:23, and 9:2-26 is numbered 9:1-25. [c] *3* Or *lies; / they are not valiant for truth*

For every one of them is a deceiver,[a]
and every friend a slanderer.
5 Friend deceives friend,
and no one speaks the truth.
They have taught their tongues to lie;
they weary themselves with sinning.
6 You[b] live in the midst of deception;
in their deceit they refuse to acknowledge me,"
declares the LORD.

7 Therefore this is what the LORD Almighty says:

"See, I will refine and test them,
for what else can I do
because of the sin of my people?
8 Their tongue is a deadly arrow;
it speaks deceitfully.
With their mouths they all speak cordially to their neighbors,
but in their hearts they set traps for them.
9 Should I not punish them for this?"
declares the LORD.
"Should I not avenge myself
on such a nation as this?"

10 I will weep and wail for the mountains
and take up a lament concerning the wilderness grasslands.
They are desolate and untraveled,
and the lowing of cattle is not heard.
The birds have all fled
and the animals are gone.

11 "I will make Jerusalem a heap of ruins,
a haunt of jackals;
and I will lay waste the towns of Judah
so no one can live there."

12 Who is wise enough to understand this? Who has been instructed
by the LORD and can explain it? Why has the land been ruined and laid
waste like a desert that no one can cross?
13 The LORD said, "It is because they have forsaken my law, which I
set before them; they have not obeyed me or followed my law. 14 In-
stead, they have followed the stubbornness of their hearts; they have
followed the Baals, as their ancestors taught them." 15 Therefore this is
what the LORD Almighty, the God of Israel, says: "See, I will make this
people eat bitter food and drink poisoned water. 16 I will scatter them
among nations that neither they nor their ancestors have known, and
I will pursue them with the sword until I have made an end of them."

17 This is what the LORD Almighty says:

"Consider now! Call for the wailing women to come;
send for the most skillful of them.
18 Let them come quickly
and wail over us
till our eyes overflow with tears
and water streams from our eyelids.

---

[a] 4 Or *a deceiving Jacob* [b] 6 That is, Jeremiah (the Hebrew is singular)

19 The sound of wailing is heard from Zion:
'How ruined we are!
How great is our shame!
We must leave our land
because our houses are in ruins.'"

20 Now, you women, hear the word of the LORD;
open your ears to the words of his mouth.
Teach your daughters how to wail;
teach one another a lament.
21 Death has climbed in through our windows
and has entered our fortresses;
it has removed the children from the streets
and the young men from the public squares.

22 Say, "This is what the LORD declares:

" 'Dead bodies will lie
like dung on the open field,
like cut grain behind the reaper,
with no one to gather them.' "

23 This is what the LORD says:

"Let not the wise boast of their wisdom
or the strong boast of their strength
or the rich boast of their riches,
24 but let the one who boasts boast about this:
that they have the understanding to know me,
that I am the LORD, who exercises kindness,
justice and righteousness on earth,
for in these I delight,"
declares the LORD.

25 "The days are coming," declares the LORD, "when I will punish all
who are circumcised only in the flesh — 26 Egypt, Judah, Edom, Am-
mon, Moab and all who live in the wilderness in distant places.[a] For all
these nations are really uncircumcised, and even the whole house of
Israel is uncircumcised in heart."

PRAYING SCRIPTURE

Jeremiah 10

After much preaching to a rebellious people, it seems some took revenge on the prophet by stealing his goods and destroying his living quarters (see verse 20). Jeremiah reminded God that the people's shepherds were "senseless," not having concern for their sheep on their hearts (verse 21).

Expect persecution when you stand on God's Word. But rather than taking revenge, take your persecutors to God in prayer, asking for the light of the gospel to break in on them.

GOD AND IDOLS

10 Hear what the LORD says to you, people of Israel. 2 This is what
the LORD says:

"Do not learn the ways of the nations
or be terrified by signs in the heavens,
though the nations are terrified by them.
3 For the practices of the peoples are worthless;
they cut a tree out of the forest,
and a craftsman shapes it with his chisel.
4 They adorn it with silver and gold;
they fasten it with hammer and nails
so it will not totter.
5 Like a scarecrow in a cucumber field,
their idols cannot speak;

[a] 26 Or *wilderness and who clip the hair by their foreheads*

they must be carried
because they cannot walk.
Do not fear them;
they can do no harm
nor can they do any good."

6 No one is like you, LORD;
you are great,
and your name is mighty in power.
7 Who should not fear you,
King of the nations?
This is your due.
Among all the wise leaders of the nations
and in all their kingdoms,
there is no one like you.

8 They are all senseless and foolish;
they are taught by worthless wooden idols.
9 Hammered silver is brought from Tarshish
and gold from Uphaz.
What the craftsman and goldsmith have made
is then dressed in blue and purple —
all made by skilled workers.
10 But the LORD is the true God;
he is the living God, the eternal King.
When he is angry, the earth trembles;
the nations cannot endure his wrath.

11 "Tell them this: 'These gods, who did not make the heavens and
the earth, will perish from the earth and from under the heavens.'"[a]

12 But God made the earth by his power;
he founded the world by his wisdom
and stretched out the heavens by his understanding.
13 When he thunders, the waters in the heavens roar;
he makes clouds rise from the ends of the earth.
He sends lightning with the rain
and brings out the wind from his storehouses.

14 Everyone is senseless and without knowledge;
every goldsmith is shamed by his idols.
The images he makes are a fraud;
they have no breath in them.
15 They are worthless, the objects of mockery;
when their judgment comes, they will perish.
16 He who is the Portion of Jacob is not like these,
for he is the Maker of all things,
including Israel, the people of his inheritance —
the LORD Almighty is his name.

COMING DESTRUCTION

17 Gather up your belongings to leave the land,
you who live under siege.
18 For this is what the LORD says:

[a] 11 The text of this verse is in Aramaic.

"At this time I will hurl out
those who live in this land;
I will bring distress on them
so that they may be captured."

19 Woe to me because of my injury!
My wound is incurable!
Yet I said to myself,
"This is my sickness, and I must endure it."
20 My tent is destroyed;
all its ropes are snapped.
My children are gone from me and are no more;
no one is left now to pitch my tent
or to set up my shelter.
21 The shepherds are senseless
and do not inquire of the LORD;
so they do not prosper
and all their flock is scattered.
22 Listen! The report is coming —
a great commotion from the land of the north!
It will make the towns of Judah desolate,
a haunt of jackals.

JEREMIAH'S PRAYER

23 LORD, I know that people's lives are not their own;
it is not for them to direct their steps.
24 Discipline me, LORD, but only in due measure —
not in your anger,
or you will reduce me to nothing.
25 Pour out your wrath on the nations
that do not acknowledge you,
on the peoples who do not call on your name.
For they have devoured Jacob;
they have devoured him completely
and destroyed his homeland.

THE COVENANT IS BROKEN

11 This is the word that came to Jeremiah from the LORD: 2"Listen
to the terms of this covenant and tell them to the people of Ju-
dah and to those who live in Jerusalem. 3Tell them that this is what
the LORD, the God of Israel, says: 'Cursed is the one who does not obey
the terms of this covenant — 4the terms I commanded your ancestors
when I brought them out of Egypt, out of the iron-smelting furnace.' I
said, 'Obey me and do everything I command you, and you will be my
people, and I will be your God. 5Then I will fulfill the oath I swore to
your ancestors, to give them a land flowing with milk and honey' —
the land you possess today."

I answered, "Amen, LORD."

6The LORD said to me, "Proclaim all these words in the towns of Ju-
dah and in the streets of Jerusalem: 'Listen to the terms of this cov-
enant and follow them. 7From the time I brought your ancestors up
from Egypt until today, I warned them again and again, saying, "Obey
me." 8But they did not listen or pay attention; instead, they followed
the stubbornness of their evil hearts. So I brought on them all the

PRAYING SCRIPTURE

Jeremiah 11

Ignoring the voice of the Lord has disastrous consequences. God's ways are good, holy, helpful and right. When we walk in them, we find life. When we disobey, we reap the evil we sow. In Jeremiah's words, those who did not obey the words of God's covenant were "cursed" (verse 3).

Those who do not believe in Jesus Christ are still under a curse. Pray for their obedience to faith in him.

curses of the covenant I had commanded them to follow but that they did not keep.' "

9Then the LORD said to me, "There is a conspiracy among the peo-
ple of Judah and those who live in Jerusalem. 10They have returned
to the sins of their ancestors, who refused to listen to my words. They
have followed other gods to serve them. Both Israel and Judah have
broken the covenant I made with their ancestors. 11Therefore this is
what the LORD says: 'I will bring on them a disaster they cannot escape.
Although they cry out to me, I will not listen to them. 12The towns of
Judah and the people of Jerusalem will go and cry out to the gods to
whom they burn incense, but they will not help them at all when di-
saster strikes. 13You, Judah, have as many gods as you have towns; and
the altars you have set up to burn incense to that shameful god Baal
are as many as the streets of Jerusalem.'

14"Do not pray for this people or offer any plea or petition for them,
because I will not listen when they call to me in the time of their
distress.

15 "What is my beloved doing in my temple
as she, with many others, works out her evil schemes?
Can consecrated meat avert your punishment?
When you engage in your wickedness,
then you rejoice.[a]"

16 The LORD called you a thriving olive tree
with fruit beautiful in form.
But with the roar of a mighty storm
he will set it on fire,
and its branches will be broken.

17The LORD Almighty, who planted you, has decreed disaster for you, because the people of both Israel and Judah have done evil and aroused my anger by burning incense to Baal.

PLOT AGAINST JEREMIAH

18Because the LORD revealed their plot to me, I knew it, for at that
time he showed me what they were doing. 19I had been like a gen-
tle lamb led to the slaughter; I did not realize that they had plotted
against me, saying,

"Let us destroy the tree and its fruit;
let us cut him off from the land of the living,
that his name be remembered no more."
20 But you, LORD Almighty, who judge righteously
and test the heart and mind,
let me see your vengeance on them,
for to you I have committed my cause.

21Therefore this is what the LORD says about the people of Anathoth
who are threatening to kill you, saying, "Do not prophesy in the name
of the LORD or you will die by our hands"— 22therefore this is what the
LORD Almighty says: "I will punish them. Their young men will die by
the sword, their sons and daughters by famine. 23Not even a remnant
will be left to them, because I will bring disaster on the people of Ana-
thoth in the year of their punishment."

[a] 15 Or *Could consecrated meat avert your punishment? / Then you would rejoice*

PRAYING SCRIPTURE

Jeremiah 12

Do you get weary during trials? After a little suffering, are you ready to throw in the towel? After listening to Jeremiah complain, God didn't promise ease: If you get tired of running with men, he asked, how will you keep up with horses (see verse 5)?

The Lord wasn't chiding Jeremiah as much as he was preparing him. Ask God to make you ready for whatever comes.

JEREMIAH'S COMPLAINT

12 You are always righteous, LORD,
when I bring a case before you.
Yet I would speak with you about your justice:
Why does the way of the wicked prosper?
Why do all the faithless live at ease?
2 You have planted them, and they have taken root;
they grow and bear fruit.
You are always on their lips
but far from their hearts.
3 Yet you know me, LORD;
you see me and test my thoughts about you.
Drag them off like sheep to be butchered!
Set them apart for the day of slaughter!
4 How long will the land lie parched
and the grass in every field be withered?
Because those who live in it are wicked,
the animals and birds have perished.
Moreover, the people are saying,
"He will not see what happens to us."

GOD'S ANSWER

5 "If you have raced with men on foot
and they have worn you out,
how can you compete with horses?
If you stumble[a] in safe country,
how will you manage in the thickets by[b] the Jordan?
6 Your relatives, members of your own family —
even they have betrayed you;
they have raised a loud cry against you.
Do not trust them,
though they speak well of you.

7 "I will forsake my house,
abandon my inheritance;
I will give the one I love
into the hands of her enemies.
8 My inheritance has become to me
like a lion in the forest.
She roars at me;
therefore I hate her.
9 Has not my inheritance become to me
like a speckled bird of prey
that other birds of prey surround and attack?
Go and gather all the wild beasts;
bring them to devour.
10 Many shepherds will ruin my vineyard
and trample down my field;
they will turn my pleasant field
into a desolate wasteland.
11 It will be made a wasteland,
parched and desolate before me;

---

[a] 5 Or *you feel secure only* [b] 5 Or *the flooding of*

the whole land will be laid waste
because there is no one who cares.
12 Over all the barren heights in the desert
destroyers will swarm,
for the sword of the LORD will devour
from one end of the land to the other;
no one will be safe.
13 They will sow wheat but reap thorns;
they will wear themselves out but gain nothing.
They will bear the shame of their harvest
because of the LORD's fierce anger."

14 This is what the LORD says: "As for all my wicked neighbors who
seize the inheritance I gave my people Israel, I will uproot them from
their lands and I will uproot the people of Judah from among them.
15 But after I uproot them, I will again have compassion and will bring
each of them back to their own inheritance and their own country.
16 And if they learn well the ways of my people and swear by my name,
saying, 'As surely as the LORD lives' — even as they once taught my peo-
ple to swear by Baal — then they will be established among my people.
17 But if any nation does not listen, I will completely uproot and destroy
it," declares the LORD.

A LINEN BELT

13 This is what the LORD said to me: "Go and buy a linen belt and
put it around your waist, but do not let it touch water." 2 So I
bought a belt, as the LORD directed, and put it around my waist.
3 Then the word of the LORD came to me a second time: 4 "Take the
belt you bought and are wearing around your waist, and go now to Pe-
rath[a] and hide it there in a crevice in the rocks." 5 So I went and hid it
at Perath, as the LORD told me.
6 Many days later the LORD said to me, "Go now to Perath and get the
belt I told you to hide there." 7 So I went to Perath and dug up the belt
and took it from the place where I had hidden it, but now it was ruined
and completely useless.
8 Then the word of the LORD came to me: 9 "This is what the LORD
says: 'In the same way I will ruin the pride of Judah and the great
pride of Jerusalem. 10 These wicked people, who refuse to listen to my
words, who follow the stubbornness of their hearts and go after other
gods to serve and worship them, will be like this belt — completely
useless! 11 For as a belt is bound around the waist, so I bound all the
people of Israel and all the people of Judah to me,' declares the LORD,
'to be my people for my renown and praise and honor. But they have
not listened.'

WINESKINS

12 "Say to them: 'This is what the LORD, the God of Israel, says: Every
wineskin should be filled with wine.' And if they say to you, 'Don't we
know that every wineskin should be filled with wine?' 13 then tell them,
'This is what the LORD says: I am going to fill with drunkenness all who
live in this land, including the kings who sit on David's throne, the
priests, the prophets and all those living in Jerusalem. 14 I will smash

PRAYING SCRIPTURE

Jeremiah 13

A pattern in the prophets' books is the Lord's using physical meta phors to accompany prophecies. The linen sash Jeremiah obtained represented Israel, its ruin, the coming fall of Judah and Jerusalem. The Lord desired for his people to be bound to him like the sash to its wearer (verse 11).

The Lord longs for his people's love. He brings judgment to bring repentance to show mercy. Remember to tell the Lord that you love him when you pray.

[a] 4 Or possibly *to the Euphrates*; similarly in verses 5-7

them one against the other, parents and children alike, declares the LORD. I will allow no pity or mercy or compassion to keep me from destroying them.'"

THREAT OF CAPTIVITY

15 Hear and pay attention,
do not be arrogant,
for the LORD has spoken.
16 Give glory to the LORD your God
before he brings the darkness,
before your feet stumble
on the darkening hills.
You hope for light,
but he will turn it to utter darkness
and change it to deep gloom.
17 If you do not listen,
I will weep in secret
because of your pride;
my eyes will weep bitterly,
overflowing with tears,
because the LORD's flock will be taken captive.

18 Say to the king and to the queen mother,
"Come down from your thrones,
for your glorious crowns
will fall from your heads."
19 The cities in the Negev will be shut up,
and there will be no one to open them.
All Judah will be carried into exile,
carried completely away.
20 Look up and see
those who are coming from the north.
Where is the flock that was entrusted to you,
the sheep of which you boasted?
21 What will you say when the LORD sets over you
those you cultivated as your special allies?
Will not pain grip you
like that of a woman in labor?
22 And if you ask yourself,
"Why has this happened to me?"—
it is because of your many sins
that your skirts have been torn off
and your body mistreated.
23 Can an Ethiopian[a] change his skin
or a leopard its spots?
Neither can you do good
who are accustomed to doing evil.
24 "I will scatter you like chaff
driven by the desert wind.
25 This is your lot,
the portion I have decreed for you,"
declares the LORD,

[a] 23 Hebrew *Cushite* (probably a person from the upper Nile region)

"because you have forgotten me
and trusted in false gods.
26 I will pull up your skirts over your face
that your shame may be seen —
27 your adulteries and lustful neighings,
your shameless prostitution!
I have seen your detestable acts
on the hills and in the fields.
Woe to you, Jerusalem!
How long will you be unclean?"

DROUGHT, FAMINE, SWORD

14 This is the word of the LORD that came to Jeremiah concerning
the drought:

2 "Judah mourns,
her cities languish;
they wail for the land,
and a cry goes up from Jerusalem.
3 The nobles send their servants for water;
they go to the cisterns
but find no water.
They return with their jars unfilled;
dismayed and despairing,
they cover their heads.
4 The ground is cracked
because there is no rain in the land;
the farmers are dismayed
and cover their heads.
5 Even the doe in the field
deserts her newborn fawn
because there is no grass.
6 Wild donkeys stand on the barren heights
and pant like jackals;
their eyes fail
for lack of food."

7 Although our sins testify against us,
do something, LORD, for the sake of your name.
For we have often rebelled;
we have sinned against you.
8 You who are the hope of Israel,
its Savior in times of distress,
why are you like a stranger in the land,
like a traveler who stays only a night?
9 Why are you like a man taken by surprise,
like a warrior powerless to save?
You are among us, LORD,
and we bear your name;
do not forsake us!

10 This is what the LORD says about this people:

"They greatly love to wander;
they do not restrain their feet.
So the LORD does not accept them;

PRAYING SCRIPTURE

Jeremiah 14

How angry was the Lord, even beyond drought, famine and plague? He directed Jeremiah not even to pray for the people or for their good (verse 11). The Lord further promised not to hear their prayers or accept their offerings. But the people cried for mercy, reminding him of his covenant with them.

Do you ever feel as though God doesn't hear you? Remind him that he has promised to hear you, and then tell him your burdens.

he will now remember their wickedness
and punish them for their sins."

11Then the LORD said to me, "Do not pray for the well-being of this
people. 12Although they fast, I will not listen to their cry; though they
offer burnt offerings and grain offerings, I will not accept them. Instead, I will destroy them with the sword, famine and plague."

13But I said, "Alas, Sovereign LORD! The prophets keep telling them,
'You will not see the sword or suffer famine. Indeed, I will give you lasting peace in this place.'"

14Then the LORD said to me, "The prophets are prophesying lies in
my name. I have not sent them or appointed them or spoken to them. They are prophesying to you false visions, divinations, idolatries[a] and
the delusions of their own minds. 15Therefore this is what the LORD
says about the prophets who are prophesying in my name: I did not send them, yet they are saying, 'No sword or famine will touch this
land.' Those same prophets will perish by sword and famine. 16And the
people they are prophesying to will be thrown out into the streets of Jerusalem because of the famine and sword. There will be no one to bury them, their wives, their sons and their daughters. I will pour out on them the calamity they deserve.

17"Speak this word to them:

"'Let my eyes overflow with tears
night and day without ceasing;
for the Virgin Daughter, my people,
has suffered a grievous wound,
a crushing blow.
18 If I go into the country,
I see those slain by the sword;
if I go into the city,
I see the ravages of famine.
Both prophet and priest
have gone to a land they know not.'"

19 Have you rejected Judah completely?
Do you despise Zion?
Why have you afflicted us
so that we cannot be healed?
We hoped for peace
but no good has come,
for a time of healing
but there is only terror.
20 We acknowledge our wickedness, LORD,
and the guilt of our ancestors;
we have indeed sinned against you.
21 For the sake of your name do not despise us;
do not dishonor your glorious throne.
Remember your covenant with us
and do not break it.
22 Do any of the worthless idols of the nations bring rain?
Do the skies themselves send down showers?
No, it is you, LORD our God.

[a] 14 Or *visions, worthless divinations*

Therefore our hope is in you,
for you are the one who does all this.

15 Then the LORD said to me: "Even if Moses and Samuel were
to stand before me, my heart would not go out to this people.
Send them away from my presence! Let them go! 2And if they ask you,
'Where shall we go?' tell them, 'This is what the LORD says:

"'Those destined for death, to death;
those for the sword, to the sword;
those for starvation, to starvation;
those for captivity, to captivity.'

3"I will send four kinds of destroyers against them," declares the
LORD, "the sword to kill and the dogs to drag away and the birds and
the wild animals to devour and destroy. 4I will make them abhorrent
to all the kingdoms of the earth because of what Manasseh son of Hez-
ekiah king of Judah did in Jerusalem.

5"Who will have pity on you, Jerusalem?
Who will mourn for you?
Who will stop to ask how you are?
6You have rejected me," declares the LORD.
"You keep on backsliding.
So I will reach out and destroy you;
I am tired of holding back.
7I will winnow them with a winnowing fork
at the city gates of the land.
I will bring bereavement and destruction on my people,
for they have not changed their ways.
8I will make their widows more numerous
than the sand of the sea.
At midday I will bring a destroyer
against the mothers of their young men;
suddenly I will bring down on them
anguish and terror.
9The mother of seven will grow faint
and breathe her last.
Her sun will set while it is still day;
she will be disgraced and humiliated.
I will put the survivors to the sword
before their enemies,"
declares the LORD.

10Alas, my mother, that you gave me birth,
a man with whom the whole land strives and contends!
I have neither lent nor borrowed,
yet everyone curses me.

11The LORD said,

"Surely I will deliver you for a good purpose;
surely I will make your enemies plead with you
in times of disaster and times of distress.

12"Can a man break iron —
iron from the north — or bronze?

PRAYING SCRIPTURE

Jeremiah 15

As the Lord continued to pronounce judgment, Jeremiah fell into despair. Bearing God's burden for an unrepentant nation wore heavily on him, but the Lord "delivered [Jeremiah] for a good purpose" (verse 11).

Despair is a dangerous place of emotion. It consumes the spirit and makes us rue the day we were born. Call on God and ask him for renewal in your mind and spirit.

13 "Your wealth and your treasures
I will give as plunder, without charge,
because of all your sins
throughout your country.
14 I will enslave you to your enemies
in[a] a land you do not know,
for my anger will kindle a fire
that will burn against you."

15 LORD, you understand;
remember me and care for me.
Avenge me on my persecutors.
You are long-suffering — do not take me away;
think of how I suffer reproach for your sake.
16 When your words came, I ate them;
they were my joy and my heart's delight,
for I bear your name,
LORD God Almighty.
17 I never sat in the company of revelers,
never made merry with them;
I sat alone because your hand was on me
and you had filled me with indignation.
18 Why is my pain unending
and my wound grievous and incurable?
You are to me like a deceptive brook,
like a spring that fails.

19 Therefore this is what the LORD says:

"If you repent, I will restore you
that you may serve me;
if you utter worthy, not worthless, words,
you will be my spokesman.
Let this people turn to you,
but you must not turn to them.
20 I will make you a wall to this people,
a fortified wall of bronze;
they will fight against you
but will not overcome you,
for I am with you
to rescue and save you,"

declares the LORD.

21 "I will save you from the hands of the wicked
and deliver you from the grasp of the cruel."

DAY OF DISASTER

16 Then the word of the LORD came to me: 2"You must not marry
and have sons or daughters in this place." 3For this is what the
LORD says about the sons and daughters born in this land and about the
women who are their mothers and the men who are their fathers: 4"They
will die of deadly diseases. They will not be mourned or buried but will be
like dung lying on the ground. They will perish by sword and famine, and
their dead bodies will become food for the birds and the wild animals."

PRAYING SCRIPTURE

Jeremiah 16

Too often sons and daughters walk in the sins of their fathers and mothers. The Lord pronounced judgment on all of them (see verse 4), while warning Jeremiah himself not to marry because of the judgment he was about to bring on the people.

Yet even as God announced judgment, he promised restoration. Bring all your requests to him in faith that he will hear and answer.

[a] 14 Some Hebrew manuscripts, Septuagint and Syriac (see also 17:4); most Hebrew manuscripts *I will cause your enemies to bring you / into*

5For this is what the LORD says: "Do not enter a house where there is
a funeral meal; do not go to mourn or show sympathy, because I have
withdrawn my blessing, my love and my pity from this people," de-
clares the LORD. 6"Both high and low will die in this land. They will not
be buried or mourned, and no one will cut themselves or shave their
head for the dead. 7No one will offer food to comfort those who mourn
for the dead — not even for a father or a mother — nor will anyone give
them a drink to console them.

8"And do not enter a house where there is feasting and sit down to eat
and drink. 9For this is what the LORD Almighty, the God of Israel, says:
Before your eyes and in your days I will bring an end to the sounds of
joy and gladness and to the voices of bride and bridegroom in this place.

10"When you tell these people all this and they ask you, 'Why has the
LORD decreed such a great disaster against us? What wrong have we
done? What sin have we committed against the LORD our God?' 11then
say to them, 'It is because your ancestors forsook me,' declares the LORD,
'and followed other gods and served and worshiped them. They forsook
me and did not keep my law. 12But you have behaved more wickedly
than your ancestors. See how all of you are following the stubbornness
of your evil hearts instead of obeying me. 13So I will throw you out of this
land into a land neither you nor your ancestors have known, and there
you will serve other gods day and night, for I will show you no favor.'

14"However, the days are coming," declares the LORD, "when it will no
longer be said, 'As surely as the LORD lives, who brought the Israelites
up out of Egypt,' 15but it will be said, 'As surely as the LORD lives, who
brought the Israelites up out of the land of the north and out of all the
countries where he had banished them.' For I will restore them to the
land I gave their ancestors.

16"But now I will send for many fishermen," declares the LORD, "and
they will catch them. After that I will send for many hunters, and they
will hunt them down on every mountain and hill and from the crev-
ices of the rocks. 17My eyes are on all their ways; they are not hidden
from me, nor is their sin concealed from my eyes. 18I will repay them
double for their wickedness and their sin, because they have defiled
my land with the lifeless forms of their vile images and have filled my
inheritance with their detestable idols."

19 LORD, my strength and my fortress,
my refuge in time of distress,
to you the nations will come
from the ends of the earth and say,
"Our ancestors possessed nothing but false gods,
worthless idols that did them no good.
20 Do people make their own gods?
Yes, but they are not gods!"

21 "Therefore I will teach them —
this time I will teach them
my power and might.
Then they will know
that my name is the LORD.

17 "Judah's sin is engraved with an iron tool,
inscribed with a flint point,
on the tablets of their hearts
and on the horns of their altars.

PRAYING SCRIPTURE

Jeremiah 17

The person who has an abiding walk with the Lord will not be shaken in the day of trouble. One who trusts in human beings, who "draws strength from mere flesh," will shrivel like a desert shrub. But those who trust in the Lord will be like a tree planted by a stream (see verses 5–8).

What is the source of your strength? Commit to trusting God, and seek him the way a tree seeks water.

2 Even their children remember
their altars and Asherah poles[a]
beside the spreading trees
and on the high hills.
3 My mountain in the land
and your[b] wealth and all your treasures
I will give away as plunder,
together with your high places,
because of sin throughout your country.
4 Through your own fault you will lose
the inheritance I gave you.
I will enslave you to your enemies
in a land you do not know,
for you have kindled my anger,
and it will burn forever."

5 This is what the LORD says:

"Cursed is the one who trusts in man,
who draws strength from mere flesh
and whose heart turns away from the LORD.
6 That person will be like a bush in the wastelands;
they will not see prosperity when it comes.
They will dwell in the parched places of the desert,
in a salt land where no one lives.

7 "But blessed is the one who trusts in the LORD,
whose confidence is in him.
8 They will be like a tree planted by the water
that sends out its roots by the stream.
It does not fear when heat comes;
its leaves are always green.
It has no worries in a year of drought
and never fails to bear fruit."

9 The heart is deceitful above all things
and beyond cure.
Who can understand it?

10 "I the LORD search the heart
and examine the mind,
to reward each person according to their conduct,
according to what their deeds deserve."

11 Like a partridge that hatches eggs it did not lay
are those who gain riches by unjust means.
When their lives are half gone, their riches will desert them,
and in the end they will prove to be fools.

12 A glorious throne, exalted from the beginning,
is the place of our sanctuary.
13 LORD, you are the hope of Israel;
all who forsake you will be put to shame.
Those who turn away from you will be written in the dust

---

[a] *2* That is, wooden symbols of the goddess Asherah [b] *2,3* Or *hills / [3]and the mountains of the land. / Your*

because they have forsaken the LORD,
the spring of living water.

14 Heal me, LORD, and I will be healed;
save me and I will be saved,
for you are the one I praise.
15 They keep saying to me,
"Where is the word of the LORD?
Let it now be fulfilled!"
16 I have not run away from being your shepherd;
you know I have not desired the day of despair.
What passes my lips is open before you.
17 Do not be a terror to me;
you are my refuge in the day of disaster.
18 Let my persecutors be put to shame,
but keep me from shame;
let them be terrified,
but keep me from terror.
Bring on them the day of disaster;
destroy them with double destruction.

KEEPING THE SABBATH DAY HOLY

19This is what the LORD said to me: "Go and stand at the Gate of the
People,[a] through which the kings of Judah go in and out; stand also
at all the other gates of Jerusalem. 20Say to them, 'Hear the word of
the LORD, you kings of Judah and all people of Judah and everyone
living in Jerusalem who come through these gates. 21This is what the
LORD says: Be careful not to carry a load on the Sabbath day or bring
it through the gates of Jerusalem. 22Do not bring a load out of your
houses or do any work on the Sabbath, but keep the Sabbath day holy,
as I commanded your ancestors. 23Yet they did not listen or pay atten-
tion; they were stiff-necked and would not listen or respond to disci-
pline. 24But if you are careful to obey me, declares the LORD, and bring
no load through the gates of this city on the Sabbath, but keep the
Sabbath day holy by not doing any work on it, 25then kings who sit
on David's throne will come through the gates of this city with their
officials. They and their officials will come riding in chariots and on
horses, accompanied by the men of Judah and those living in Jerusa-
lem, and this city will be inhabited forever. 26People will come from
the towns of Judah and the villages around Jerusalem, from the terri-
tory of Benjamin and the western foothills, from the hill country and
the Negev, bringing burnt offerings and sacrifices, grain offerings and
incense, and bringing thank offerings to the house of the LORD. 27But if
you do not obey me to keep the Sabbath day holy by not carrying any
load as you come through the gates of Jerusalem on the Sabbath day,
then I will kindle an unquenchable fire in the gates of Jerusalem that
will consume her fortresses.'"

AT THE POTTER'S HOUSE

18 This is the word that came to Jeremiah from the LORD: 2"Go
down to the potter's house, and there I will give you my mes-
sage." 3So I went down to the potter's house, and I saw him working

[a] 19 Or *Army*

PRAYING SCRIPTURE

Jeremiah 18

God is the great potter who forms and shapes the lives of his people. Jeremiah pictured God, the Creator, in a potter's house forming a pot on the potter's wheel. When the pot became marred, the potter decided to reshape the clay into another pot.

This parable served as a warning to Israel: God can uproot, tear down, or destroy a nation. It is unwise to assume that God will overlook sin, so confess any sin you have to him.

at the wheel. 4But the pot he was shaping from the clay was marred
in his hands; so the potter formed it into another pot, shaping it as
seemed best to him.

5Then the word of the LORD came to me. 6He said, "Can I not do
with you, Israel, as this potter does?" declares the LORD. "Like clay in
the hand of the potter, so are you in my hand, Israel. 7If at any time I
announce that a nation or kingdom is to be uprooted, torn down and
destroyed, 8and if that nation I warned repents of its evil, then I will
relent and not inflict on it the disaster I had planned. 9And if at an-
other time I announce that a nation or kingdom is to be built up and
planted, 10and if it does evil in my sight and does not obey me, then I
will reconsider the good I had intended to do for it.

11"Now therefore say to the people of Judah and those living in Jeru-
salem, 'This is what the LORD says: Look! I am preparing a disaster for
you and devising a plan against you. So turn from your evil ways, each
one of you, and reform your ways and your actions.' 12But they will re-
ply, 'It's no use. We will continue with our own plans; we will all follow
the stubbornness of our evil hearts.'"

13Therefore this is what the LORD says:

"Inquire among the nations:
  Who has ever heard anything like this?
A most horrible thing has been done
  by Virgin Israel.
14 Does the snow of Lebanon
  ever vanish from its rocky slopes?
Do its cool waters from distant sources
  ever stop flowing?[a]
15 Yet my people have forgotten me;
  they burn incense to worthless idols,
which made them stumble in their ways,
  in the ancient paths.
They made them walk in byways,
  on roads not built up.
16 Their land will be an object of horror
  and of lasting scorn;
all who pass by will be appalled
  and will shake their heads.
17 Like a wind from the east,
  I will scatter them before their enemies;
I will show them my back and not my face
  in the day of their disaster."

18They said, "Come, let's make plans against Jeremiah; for the teach-
ing of the law by the priest will not cease, nor will counsel from the
wise, nor the word from the prophets. So come, let's attack him with
our tongues and pay no attention to anything he says."

19 Listen to me, LORD;
  hear what my accusers are saying!
20 Should good be repaid with evil?
  Yet they have dug a pit for me.
Remember that I stood before you

[a] *14* The meaning of the Hebrew for this sentence is uncertain.

and spoke in their behalf
to turn your wrath away from them.
21 So give their children over to famine;
hand them over to the power of the sword.
Let their wives be made childless and widows;
let their men be put to death,
their young men slain by the sword in battle.
22 Let a cry be heard from their houses
when you suddenly bring invaders against them,
for they have dug a pit to capture me
and have hidden snares for my feet.
23 But you, LORD, know
all their plots to kill me.
Do not forgive their crimes
or blot out their sins from your sight.
Let them be overthrown before you;
deal with them in the time of your anger.

19 This is what the LORD says: "Go and buy a clay jar from a potter.
Take along some of the elders of the people and of the priests
2 and go out to the Valley of Ben Hinnom, near the entrance of the Pot-
sherd Gate. There proclaim the words I tell you, 3 and say, 'Hear the
word of the LORD, you kings of Judah and people of Jerusalem. This is
what the LORD Almighty, the God of Israel, says: Listen! I am going to
bring a disaster on this place that will make the ears of everyone who
hears of it tingle. 4 For they have forsaken me and made this a place
of foreign gods; they have burned incense in it to gods that neither
they nor their ancestors nor the kings of Judah ever knew, and they
have filled this place with the blood of the innocent. 5 They have built
the high places of Baal to burn their children in the fire as offerings to
Baal — something I did not command or mention, nor did it enter my
mind. 6 So beware, the days are coming, declares the LORD, when peo-
ple will no longer call this place Topheth or the Valley of Ben Hinnom,
but the Valley of Slaughter.

7 " 'In this place I will ruin[a] the plans of Judah and Jerusalem. I will
make them fall by the sword before their enemies, at the hands of
those who want to kill them, and I will give their carcasses as food to
the birds and the wild animals. 8 I will devastate this city and make it
an object of horror and scorn; all who pass by will be appalled and will
scoff because of all its wounds. 9 I will make them eat the flesh of their
sons and daughters, and they will eat one another's flesh because their
enemies will press the siege so hard against them to destroy them.'

10 "Then break the jar while those who go with you are watching,
11 and say to them, 'This is what the LORD Almighty says: I will smash
this nation and this city just as this potter's jar is smashed and cannot
be repaired. They will bury the dead in Topheth until there is no more
room. 12 This is what I will do to this place and to those who live here,
declares the LORD. I will make this city like Topheth. 13 The houses in Je-
rusalem and those of the kings of Judah will be defiled like this place,
Topheth — all the houses where they burned incense on the roofs to all
the starry hosts and poured out drink offerings to other gods.' "

14 Jeremiah then returned from Topheth, where the LORD had sent

[a] 7 The Hebrew for *ruin* sounds like the Hebrew for *jar* (see verses 1 and 10).

PRAYING SCRIPTURE

Jeremiah 19

Unlike a previous metaphor in which a pot marred on the potter's wheel was reshaped into a new one, the Lord told Jeremiah to break a clay jar in the sight of some of the elders. The warning in this case: "I will smash this nation and this city just as this potter's jar is smashed and cannot be repaired" (verse 11).

Sometimes sin is so costly that the damage it causes cannot be repaired. Pray that sin does not ruin you.

him to prophesy, and stood in the court of the LORD's temple and
said to all the people, 15"This is what the LORD Almighty, the God of
Israel, says: 'Listen! I am going to bring on this city and all the villages
around it every disaster I pronounced against them, because they were
stiff-necked and would not listen to my words.'"

JEREMIAH AND PASHHUR

20 When the priest Pashhur son of Immer, the official in charge
of the temple of the LORD, heard Jeremiah prophesying these
things, 2he had Jeremiah the prophet beaten and put in the stocks
at the Upper Gate of Benjamin at the LORD's temple. 3The next day,
when Pashhur released him from the stocks, Jeremiah said to him,
"The LORD's name for you is not Pashhur, but Terror on Every Side.
4For this is what the LORD says: 'I will make you a terror to yourself
and to all your friends; with your own eyes you will see them fall by
the sword of their enemies. I will give all Judah into the hands of the
king of Babylon, who will carry them away to Babylon or put them to
the sword. 5I will deliver all the wealth of this city into the hands of
their enemies — all its products, all its valuables and all the treasures
of the kings of Judah. They will take it away as plunder and carry it off
to Babylon. 6And you, Pashhur, and all who live in your house will go
into exile to Babylon. There you will die and be buried, you and all your
friends to whom you have prophesied lies.'"

JEREMIAH'S COMPLAINT

7 You deceived[a] me, LORD, and I was deceived[a];
 you overpowered me and prevailed.
I am ridiculed all day long;
 everyone mocks me.
8 Whenever I speak, I cry out
 proclaiming violence and destruction.
So the word of the LORD has brought me
 insult and reproach all day long.
9 But if I say, "I will not mention his word
 or speak anymore in his name,"
his word is in my heart like a fire,
 a fire shut up in my bones.
I am weary of holding it in;
 indeed, I cannot.
10 I hear many whispering,
 "Terror on every side!
 Denounce him! Let's denounce him!"
All my friends
 are waiting for me to slip, saying,
"Perhaps he will be deceived;
 then we will prevail over him
 and take our revenge on him."
11 But the LORD is with me like a mighty warrior;
 so my persecutors will stumble and not prevail.
They will fail and be thoroughly disgraced;
 their dishonor will never be forgotten.
12 LORD Almighty, you who examine the righteous

[a] 7 Or *persuaded*

PRAYING SCRIPTURE

Jeremiah 20

It is noteworthy how Jeremiah wrestled with God in prayer, how straightforward he was. He accused the Lord of deceiving him (see verse 7). He complained about being mocked and ridiculed by the people (see verse 7). Then Jeremiah threatened not to speak any more of the Lord.

We often are afraid to pray with our whole heart. We guard our emotions and words as if God can't see them. Learn to pray openly and authentically.

and probe the heart and mind,
let me see your vengeance on them,
for to you I have committed my cause.

13 Sing to the LORD!
Give praise to the LORD!
He rescues the life of the needy
from the hands of the wicked.

14 Cursed be the day I was born!
May the day my mother bore me not be blessed!
15 Cursed be the man who brought my father the news,
who made him very glad, saying,
"A child is born to you — a son!"
16 May that man be like the towns
the LORD overthrew without pity.
May he hear wailing in the morning,
a battle cry at noon.
17 For he did not kill me in the womb,
with my mother as my grave,
her womb enlarged forever.
18 Why did I ever come out of the womb
to see trouble and sorrow
and to end my days in shame?

GOD REJECTS ZEDEKIAH'S REQUEST

21 The word came to Jeremiah from the LORD when King Zedekiah
sent to him Pashhur son of Malkijah and the priest Zephaniah son
of Maaseiah. They said: 2 "Inquire now of the LORD for us because Nebu-
chadnezzar[a] king of Babylon is attacking us. Perhaps the LORD will per-
form wonders for us as in times past so that he will withdraw from us."
3 But Jeremiah answered them, "Tell Zedekiah, 4 'This is what the
LORD, the God of Israel, says: I am about to turn against you the weap-
ons of war that are in your hands, which you are using to fight the king
of Babylon and the Babylonians[b] who are outside the wall besieging
you. And I will gather them inside this city. 5 I myself will fight against
you with an outstretched hand and a mighty arm in furious anger and
in great wrath. 6 I will strike down those who live in this city — both
man and beast — and they will die of a terrible plague. 7 After that, de-
clares the LORD, I will give Zedekiah king of Judah, his officials and the
people in this city who survive the plague, sword and famine, into the
hands of Nebuchadnezzar king of Babylon and to their enemies who
want to kill them. He will put them to the sword; he will show them no
mercy or pity or compassion.'
8 "Furthermore, tell the people, 'This is what the LORD says: See, I am
setting before you the way of life and the way of death. 9 Whoever stays
in this city will die by the sword, famine or plague. But whoever goes
out and surrenders to the Babylonians who are besieging you will live;
they will escape with their lives. 10 I have determined to do this city
harm and not good, declares the LORD. It will be given into the hands
of the king of Babylon, and he will destroy it with fire.'
11 "Moreover, say to the royal house of Judah, 'Hear the word of the
LORD. 12 This is what the LORD says to you, house of David:

PRAYING SCRIPTURE

Jeremiah 21

Sometimes we have to leave what we know in order to be obedient to the Lord. Jeremiah prophesied that anyone who remained in the city would be destroyed by the Babylonians who were set to besiege the city. Those who surrendered would live.

God provided his people a way of escape, even though it might humiliate them. Remember the cost of obedience, and ask God for faith to obey.

[a] 2 Hebrew *Nebuchadrezzar,* of which *Nebuchadnezzar* is a variant; here and often in Jeremiah and Ezekiel [b] 4 Or *Chaldeans;* also in verse 9

"'Administer justice every morning;
rescue from the hand of the oppressor
the one who has been robbed,
or my wrath will break out and burn like fire
because of the evil you have done —
burn with no one to quench it.
13 I am against you, Jerusalem,
you who live above this valley
on the rocky plateau, declares the LORD —
you who say, "Who can come against us?
Who can enter our refuge?"
14 I will punish you as your deeds deserve,
declares the LORD.
I will kindle a fire in your forests
that will consume everything around you.'"

JUDGMENT AGAINST WICKED KINGS

22 This is what the LORD says: "Go down to the palace of the king
of Judah and proclaim this message there: 2'Hear the word of
the LORD to you, king of Judah, you who sit on David's throne — you,
your officials and your people who come through these gates. 3This is
what the LORD says: Do what is just and right. Rescue from the hand of
the oppressor the one who has been robbed. Do no wrong or violence
to the foreigner, the fatherless or the widow, and do not shed innocent
blood in this place. 4For if you are careful to carry out these commands,
then kings who sit on David's throne will come through the gates of
this palace, riding in chariots and on horses, accompanied by their of-
ficials and their people. 5But if you do not obey these commands, de-
clares the LORD, I swear by myself that this palace will become a ruin.'"
6For this is what the LORD says about the palace of the king of Judah:

"Though you are like Gilead to me,
like the summit of Lebanon,
I will surely make you like a wasteland,
like towns not inhabited.
7 I will send destroyers against you,
each man with his weapons,
and they will cut up your fine cedar beams
and throw them into the fire.

8"People from many nations will pass by this city and will ask one
another, 'Why has the LORD done such a thing to this great city?' 9And
the answer will be: 'Because they have forsaken the covenant of the
LORD their God and have worshiped and served other gods.'"

10 Do not weep for the dead king or mourn his loss;
rather, weep bitterly for him who is exiled,
because he will never return
nor see his native land again.

11For this is what the LORD says about Shallum[a] son of Josiah, who suc-
ceeded his father as king of Judah but has gone from this place: "He
will never return. 12He will die in the place where they have led him
captive; he will not see this land again."

PRAYING SCRIPTURE

Jeremiah 22

One of the repeated commands to the kings of Israel and Judah was that they should judge righteously. No favoritism was to be shown to the rich and powerful. The most vulnerable—foreigners, orphans, widows—were to be protected. Thereby God's justice would be displayed.

The way we treat the people made in God's image is a reflection of our attitude toward him. Ask God to love the vulnerable through you.

---

[a] 11 Also called *Jehoahaz*

13 "Woe to him who builds his palace by unrighteousness,
his upper rooms by injustice,
making his own people work for nothing,
not paying them for their labor.
14 He says, 'I will build myself a great palace
with spacious upper rooms.'
So he makes large windows in it,
panels it with cedar
and decorates it in red.

15 "Does it make you a king
to have more and more cedar?
Did not your father have food and drink?
He did what was right and just,
so all went well with him.
16 He defended the cause of the poor and needy,
and so all went well.
Is that not what it means to know me?"
declares the LORD.
17 "But your eyes and your heart
are set only on dishonest gain,
on shedding innocent blood
and on oppression and extortion."

18 Therefore this is what the LORD says about Jehoiakim son of Josiah
king of Judah:

"They will not mourn for him:
'Alas, my brother! Alas, my sister!'
They will not mourn for him:
'Alas, my master! Alas, his splendor!'
19 He will have the burial of a donkey —
dragged away and thrown
outside the gates of Jerusalem."

20 "Go up to Lebanon and cry out,
let your voice be heard in Bashan,
cry out from Abarim,
for all your allies are crushed.
21 I warned you when you felt secure,
but you said, 'I will not listen!'
This has been your way from your youth;
you have not obeyed me.
22 The wind will drive all your shepherds away,
and your allies will go into exile.
Then you will be ashamed and disgraced
because of all your wickedness.
23 You who live in 'Lebanon,'[a]
who are nestled in cedar buildings,
how you will groan when pangs come upon you,
pain like that of a woman in labor!

24 "As surely as I live," declares the LORD, "even if you, Jehoiachin[b]
son of Jehoiakim king of Judah, were a signet ring on my right hand,

---

[a] *23* That is, the palace in Jerusalem (see 1 Kings 7:2) [b] *24* Hebrew *Koniah*, a variant of *Jehoiachin*; also in verse 28

I would still pull you off. 25I will deliver you into the hands of those
who want to kill you, those you fear — Nebuchadnezzar king of Bab-
ylon and the Babylonians.[a] 26I will hurl you and the mother who gave
you birth into another country, where neither of you was born, and
there you both will die. 27You will never come back to the land you
long to return to."

28 Is this man Jehoiachin a despised, broken pot,
  an object no one wants?
Why will he and his children be hurled out,
  cast into a land they do not know?
29 O land, land, land,
  hear the word of the LORD!
30 This is what the LORD says:
"Record this man as if childless,
  a man who will not prosper in his lifetime,
for none of his offspring will prosper,
  none will sit on the throne of David
  or rule anymore in Judah."

PRAYING SCRIPTURE

Jeremiah 23

Even as his people walked in disobedience, the Lord revealed their salvation and deliverance. Despite shepherds who had scattered the flock, God promised "a righteous Branch, a King who will reign wisely and do what is just and right in the land" (verse 5). The promise? The Messiah would come and make things right again.

God's promises never expire. Because he is faithful to his Word, we can trust him to answer us when we call on him.

THE RIGHTEOUS BRANCH

23 "Woe to the shepherds who are destroying and scattering the
sheep of my pasture!" declares the LORD. 2Therefore this is
what the LORD, the God of Israel, says to the shepherds who tend my
people: "Because you have scattered my flock and driven them away
and have not bestowed care on them, I will bestow punishment on you
for the evil you have done," declares the LORD. 3"I myself will gather
the remnant of my flock out of all the countries where I have driven
them and will bring them back to their pasture, where they will be
fruitful and increase in number. 4I will place shepherds over them who
will tend them, and they will no longer be afraid or terrified, nor will
any be missing," declares the LORD.

5 "The days are coming," declares the LORD,
  "when I will raise up for David[b] a righteous Branch,
a King who will reign wisely
  and do what is just and right in the land.
6 In his days Judah will be saved
  and Israel will live in safety.
This is the name by which he will be called:
  The LORD Our Righteous Savior.

7"So then, the days are coming," declares the LORD, "when people will
no longer say, 'As surely as the LORD lives, who brought the Israelites
up out of Egypt,' 8but they will say, 'As surely as the LORD lives, who
brought the descendants of Israel up out of the land of the north and
out of all the countries where he had banished them.' Then they will
live in their own land."

LYING PROPHETS

9Concerning the prophets:
My heart is broken within me;
  all my bones tremble.

[a] 25 Or *Chaldeans* [b] 5 Or *up from David's line*

I am like a drunken man,
like a strong man overcome by wine,
because of the LORD
and his holy words.
10 The land is full of adulterers;
because of the curse[a] the land lies parched
and the pastures in the wilderness are withered.
The prophets follow an evil course
and use their power unjustly.

11 "Both prophet and priest are godless;
even in my temple I find their wickedness,"
declares the LORD.
12 "Therefore their path will become slippery;
they will be banished to darkness
and there they will fall.
I will bring disaster on them
in the year they are punished,"
declares the LORD.

13 "Among the prophets of Samaria
I saw this repulsive thing:
They prophesied by Baal
and led my people Israel astray.
14 And among the prophets of Jerusalem
I have seen something horrible:
They commit adultery and live a lie.
They strengthen the hands of evildoers,
so that not one of them turns from their wickedness.
They are all like Sodom to me;
the people of Jerusalem are like Gomorrah."

15 Therefore this is what the LORD Almighty says concerning the prophets:

"I will make them eat bitter food
and drink poisoned water,
because from the prophets of Jerusalem
ungodliness has spread throughout the land."

16 This is what the LORD Almighty says:

"Do not listen to what the prophets are prophesying to you;
they fill you with false hopes.
They speak visions from their own minds,
not from the mouth of the LORD.
17 They keep saying to those who despise me,
'The LORD says: You will have peace.'
And to all who follow the stubbornness of their hearts
they say, 'No harm will come to you.'
18 But which of them has stood in the council of the LORD
to see or to hear his word?
Who has listened and heard his word?
19 See, the storm of the LORD
will burst out in wrath,

---

[a] 10 Or *because of these things*

a whirlwind swirling down
  on the heads of the wicked.
20 The anger of the LORD will not turn back
  until he fully accomplishes
  the purposes of his heart.
In days to come
  you will understand it clearly.
21 I did not send these prophets,
  yet they have run with their message;
I did not speak to them,
  yet they have prophesied.
22 But if they had stood in my council,
  they would have proclaimed my words to my people
and would have turned them from their evil ways
  and from their evil deeds.

23 "Am I only a God nearby,"
declares the LORD,
  "and not a God far away?
24 Who can hide in secret places
  so that I cannot see them?"
declares the LORD.
  "Do not I fill heaven and earth?"
declares the LORD.

25 "I have heard what the prophets say who prophesy lies in my name.
They say, 'I had a dream! I had a dream!' 26 How long will this continue
in the hearts of these lying prophets, who prophesy the delusions of
their own minds? 27 They think the dreams they tell one another will
make my people forget my name, just as their ancestors forgot my
name through Baal worship. 28 Let the prophet who has a dream re-
count the dream, but let the one who has my word speak it faithfully.
For what has straw to do with grain?" declares the LORD. 29 "Is not my
word like fire," declares the LORD, "and like a hammer that breaks a
rock in pieces?

30 "Therefore," declares the LORD, "I am against the prophets who
steal from one another words supposedly from me. 31 Yes," declares the
LORD, "I am against the prophets who wag their own tongues and yet
declare, 'The LORD declares.' 32 Indeed, I am against those who proph-
esy false dreams," declares the LORD. "They tell them and lead my peo-
ple astray with their reckless lies, yet I did not send or appoint them.
They do not benefit these people in the least," declares the LORD.

FALSE PROPHECY

33 "When these people, or a prophet or a priest, ask you, 'What is the
message from the LORD?' say to them, 'What message? I will forsake
you, declares the LORD.' 34 If a prophet or a priest or anyone else claims,
'This is a message from the LORD,' I will punish them and their house-
hold. 35 This is what each of you keeps saying to your friends and other
Israelites: 'What is the LORD's answer?' or 'What has the LORD spoken?'
36 But you must not mention 'a message from the LORD' again, because
each one's word becomes their own message. So you distort the words
of the living God, the LORD Almighty, our God. 37 This is what you keep
saying to a prophet: 'What is the LORD's answer to you?' or 'What has
the LORD spoken?' 38 Although you claim, 'This is a message from the

LORD,' this is what the LORD says: You used the words, 'This is a mes-
sage from the LORD,' even though I told you that you must not claim,
'This is a message from the LORD.' 39Therefore, I will surely forget you
and cast you out of my presence along with the city I gave to you and
your ancestors. 40I will bring on you everlasting disgrace — everlasting
shame that will not be forgotten."

TWO BASKETS OF FIGS

24 After Jehoiachin[a] son of Jehoiakim king of Judah and the of-
ficials, the skilled workers and the artisans of Judah were car-
ried into exile from Jerusalem to Babylon by Nebuchadnezzar king
of Babylon, the LORD showed me two baskets of figs placed in front
of the temple of the LORD. 2One basket had very good figs, like those
that ripen early; the other basket had very bad figs, so bad they could
not be eaten.
3Then the LORD asked me, "What do you see, Jeremiah?"
"Figs," I answered. "The good ones are very good, but the bad ones
are so bad they cannot be eaten."
4Then the word of the LORD came to me: 5"This is what the LORD,
the God of Israel, says: 'Like these good figs, I regard as good the ex-
iles from Judah, whom I sent away from this place to the land of the
Babylonians.[b] 6My eyes will watch over them for their good, and I will
bring them back to this land. I will build them up and not tear them
down; I will plant them and not uproot them. 7I will give them a heart
to know me, that I am the LORD. They will be my people, and I will be
their God, for they will return to me with all their heart.
8" 'But like the bad figs, which are so bad they cannot be eaten,' says
the LORD, 'so will I deal with Zedekiah king of Judah, his officials and
the survivors from Jerusalem, whether they remain in this land or live
in Egypt. 9I will make them abhorrent and an offense to all the king-
doms of the earth, a reproach and a byword, a curse[c] and an object of
ridicule, wherever I banish them. 10I will send the sword, famine and
plague against them until they are destroyed from the land I gave to
them and their ancestors.' "

PRAYING SCRIPTURE

Jeremiah 24

The two baskets of figs represent the condition of God's people. The bad figs represent those who God made abhorrent and an offense to others. The good figs were those God would bless, those he would watch over "for their good" (verse 6), those to whom he would give "a heart to know me, that I am the LORD" (verse 7).

God wants his people to know him, so pray that God will give you a heart to seek him.

SEVENTY YEARS OF CAPTIVITY

25 The word came to Jeremiah concerning all the people of Judah
in the fourth year of Jehoiakim son of Josiah king of Judah,
which was the first year of Nebuchadnezzar king of Babylon. 2So Jere-
miah the prophet said to all the people of Judah and to all those living
in Jerusalem: 3For twenty-three years — from the thirteenth year of
Josiah son of Amon king of Judah until this very day — the word of the
LORD has come to me and I have spoken to you again and again, but
you have not listened.
4And though the LORD has sent all his servants the prophets to you
again and again, you have not listened or paid any attention. 5They
said, "Turn now, each of you, from your evil ways and your evil prac-
tices, and you can stay in the land the LORD gave to you and your ances-
tors for ever and ever. 6Do not follow other gods to serve and worship
them; do not arouse my anger with what your hands have made. Then
I will not harm you."

PRAYING SCRIPTURE

Jeremiah 25

The people's disobedience could not outdo God's willingness to bring them back to himself. Their exile would be limited to 70 years of captivity. God's rescue of Israel would come through the defeat of the very ones who took them captive.

When people we love walk in disobedience, let us cry out to God on their behalf, that they may come to repentance rather than live out of fellowship for years.

---

[a] 1 Hebrew *Jeconiah,* a variant of *Jehoiachin* [b] 5 Or *Chaldeans* [c] 9 That is, their names will be used in cursing (see 29:22); or, others will see that they are cursed.

7“But you did not listen to me,” declares the LORD, “and you have
aroused my anger with what your hands have made, and you have
brought harm to yourselves.”
8Therefore the LORD Almighty says this: “Because you have not lis-
tened to my words, 9I will summon all the peoples of the north and
my servant Nebuchadnezzar king of Babylon,” declares the LORD, “and
I will bring them against this land and its inhabitants and against all
the surrounding nations. I will completely destroy[a] them and make
them an object of horror and scorn, and an everlasting ruin. 10I will
banish from them the sounds of joy and gladness, the voices of bride
and bridegroom, the sound of millstones and the light of the lamp.
11This whole country will become a desolate wasteland, and these na-
tions will serve the king of Babylon seventy years.
12“But when the seventy years are fulfilled, I will punish the king of
Babylon and his nation, the land of the Babylonians,[b] for their guilt,”
declares the LORD, “and will make it desolate forever. 13I will bring on
that land all the things I have spoken against it, all that are written in
this book and prophesied by Jeremiah against all the nations. 14They
themselves will be enslaved by many nations and great kings; I will
repay them according to their deeds and the work of their hands.”

THE CUP OF GOD’S WRATH

15This is what the LORD, the God of Israel, said to me: “Take from
my hand this cup filled with the wine of my wrath and make all the
nations to whom I send you drink it. 16When they drink it, they will
stagger and go mad because of the sword I will send among them.”
17So I took the cup from the LORD’s hand and made all the nations
to whom he sent me drink it: 18Jerusalem and the towns of Judah, its
kings and officials, to make them a ruin and an object of horror and
scorn, a curse[c] — as they are today; 19Pharaoh king of Egypt, his at-
tendants, his officials and all his people, 20and all the foreign people
there; all the kings of Uz; all the kings of the Philistines (those of Ash-
kelon, Gaza, Ekron, and the people left at Ashdod); 21Edom, Moab and
Ammon; 22all the kings of Tyre and Sidon; the kings of the coastlands
across the sea; 23Dedan, Tema, Buz and all who are in distant places[d];
24all the kings of Arabia and all the kings of the foreign people who
live in the wilderness; 25all the kings of Zimri, Elam and Media; 26and
all the kings of the north, near and far, one after the other — all the
kingdoms on the face of the earth. And after all of them, the king of
Sheshak[e] will drink it too.
27“Then tell them, ‘This is what the LORD Almighty, the God of Israel,
says: Drink, get drunk and vomit, and fall to rise no more because of
the sword I will send among you.’ 28But if they refuse to take the cup
from your hand and drink, tell them, ‘This is what the LORD Almighty
says: You must drink it! 29See, I am beginning to bring disaster on the
city that bears my Name, and will you indeed go unpunished? You will
not go unpunished, for I am calling down a sword on all who live on
the earth, declares the LORD Almighty.’
30“Now prophesy all these words against them and say to them:

---

[a] 9 The Hebrew term refers to the irrevocable giving over of things or persons to the LORD, often by totally destroying them. [b] 12 Or *Chaldeans*
[c] 18 That is, their names to be used in cursing (see 29:22); or, to be seen by others as cursed [d] 23 Or *who clip the hair by their foreheads*
[e] 26 *Sheshak* is a cryptogram for Babylon.

"'The LORD will roar from on high;
he will thunder from his holy dwelling
and roar mightily against his land.
He will shout like those who tread the grapes,
shout against all who live on the earth.
31 The tumult will resound to the ends of the earth,
for the LORD will bring charges against the nations;
he will bring judgment on all mankind
and put the wicked to the sword,'"
declares the LORD.

32 This is what the LORD Almighty says:

"Look! Disaster is spreading
from nation to nation;
a mighty storm is rising
from the ends of the earth."

33 At that time those slain by the LORD will be everywhere — from one
end of the earth to the other. They will not be mourned or gathered up
or buried, but will be like dung lying on the ground.

34 Weep and wail, you shepherds;
roll in the dust, you leaders of the flock.
For your time to be slaughtered has come;
you will fall like the best of the rams.[a]
35 The shepherds will have nowhere to flee,
the leaders of the flock no place to escape.
36 Hear the cry of the shepherds,
the wailing of the leaders of the flock,
for the LORD is destroying their pasture.
37 The peaceful meadows will be laid waste
because of the fierce anger of the LORD.
38 Like a lion he will leave his lair,
and their land will become desolate
because of the sword[b] of the oppressor
and because of the LORD's fierce anger.

JEREMIAH THREATENED WITH DEATH

26 Early in the reign of Jehoiakim son of Josiah king of Judah,
this word came from the LORD: 2"This is what the LORD says:
Stand in the courtyard of the LORD's house and speak to all the people
of the towns of Judah who come to worship in the house of the LORD.
Tell them everything I command you; do not omit a word. 3Perhaps
they will listen and each will turn from their evil ways. Then I will re-
lent and not inflict on them the disaster I was planning because of the
evil they have done. 4Say to them, 'This is what the LORD says: If you do
not listen to me and follow my law, which I have set before you, 5and
if you do not listen to the words of my servants the prophets, whom I
have sent to you again and again (though you have not listened), 6then
I will make this house like Shiloh and this city a curse[c] among all the
nations of the earth.'"

PRAYING SCRIPTURE

Jeremiah 26

One short sentence in this chapter illuminates the immense responsibility God's prophets held. Before another prophecy, God warned Jeremiah: "Do not omit a word" (verse 2). What a tremendous burden the prophets bore. The weight of being God's instrument is heavy.

When giving God's word to others, it is important to give them the entire truth of his law and his love. Pray on those occasions that you speak all of God's words.

---

[a] 34 Septuagint; Hebrew *fall and be shattered like fine pottery* [b] 38 Some Hebrew manuscripts and Septuagint (see also 46:16 and 50:16); most Hebrew manuscripts *anger* [c] 6 That is, its name will be used in cursing (see 29:22); or, others will see that it is cursed.

7The priests, the prophets and all the people heard Jeremiah speak
these words in the house of the LORD. 8But as soon as Jeremiah fin-
ished telling all the people everything the LORD had commanded him
to say, the priests, the prophets and all the people seized him and
said, "You must die! 9Why do you prophesy in the LORD's name that
this house will be like Shiloh and this city will be desolate and de-
serted?" And all the people crowded around Jeremiah in the house
of the LORD.

10When the officials of Judah heard about these things, they went
up from the royal palace to the house of the LORD and took their
places at the entrance of the New Gate of the LORD's house. 11Then the
priests and the prophets said to the officials and all the people, "This
man should be sentenced to death because he has prophesied against
this city. You have heard it with your own ears!"

12Then Jeremiah said to all the officials and all the people: "The
LORD sent me to prophesy against this house and this city all the
things you have heard. 13Now reform your ways and your actions and
obey the LORD your God. Then the LORD will relent and not bring the
disaster he has pronounced against you. 14As for me, I am in your
hands; do with me whatever you think is good and right. 15Be assured,
however, that if you put me to death, you will bring the guilt of inno-
cent blood on yourselves and on this city and on those who live in it,
for in truth the LORD has sent me to you to speak all these words in
your hearing."

16Then the officials and all the people said to the priests and the
prophets, "This man should not be sentenced to death! He has spoken
to us in the name of the LORD our God."

17Some of the elders of the land stepped forward and said to the
entire assembly of people, 18"Micah of Moresheth prophesied in the
days of Hezekiah king of Judah. He told all the people of Judah, 'This
is what the LORD Almighty says:

"'Zion will be plowed like a field,
Jerusalem will become a heap of rubble,
the temple hill a mound overgrown with thickets.'[a]

19"Did Hezekiah king of Judah or anyone else in Judah put him to
death? Did not Hezekiah fear the LORD and seek his favor? And did not
the LORD relent, so that he did not bring the disaster he pronounced
against them? We are about to bring a terrible disaster on ourselves!"

20(Now Uriah son of Shemaiah from Kiriath Jearim was another
man who prophesied in the name of the LORD; he prophesied the
same things against this city and this land as Jeremiah did. 21When
King Jehoiakim and all his officers and officials heard his words, the
king was determined to put him to death. But Uriah heard of it and
fled in fear to Egypt. 22King Jehoiakim, however, sent Elnathan son
of Akbor to Egypt, along with some other men. 23They brought Uriah
out of Egypt and took him to King Jehoiakim, who had him struck
down with a sword and his body thrown into the burial place of the
common people.)

24Furthermore, Ahikam son of Shaphan supported Jeremiah, and so
he was not handed over to the people to be put to death.

---

[a] *18* Micah 3:12

JUDAH TO SERVE NEBUCHADNEZZAR

27 Early in the reign of Zedekiah[a] son of Josiah king of Judah,
this word came to Jeremiah from the LORD: 2 This is what the
LORD said to me: "Make a yoke out of straps and crossbars and put it
on your neck. 3 Then send word to the kings of Edom, Moab, Ammon,
Tyre and Sidon through the envoys who have come to Jerusalem to
Zedekiah king of Judah. 4 Give them a message for their masters and
say, 'This is what the LORD Almighty, the God of Israel, says: "Tell this
to your masters: 5 With my great power and outstretched arm I made
the earth and its people and the animals that are on it, and I give it to
anyone I please. 6 Now I will give all your countries into the hands of
my servant Nebuchadnezzar king of Babylon; I will make even the wild
animals subject to him. 7 All nations will serve him and his son and his
grandson until the time for his land comes; then many nations and
great kings will subjugate him.

8 " ' "If, however, any nation or kingdom will not serve Nebuchadnez-
zar king of Babylon or bow its neck under his yoke, I will punish that
nation with the sword, famine and plague, declares the LORD, until I
destroy it by his hand. 9 So do not listen to your prophets, your divin-
ers, your interpreters of dreams, your mediums or your sorcerers who
tell you, 'You will not serve the king of Babylon.' 10 They prophesy lies
to you that will only serve to remove you far from your lands; I will
banish you and you will perish. 11 But if any nation will bow its neck un-
der the yoke of the king of Babylon and serve him, I will let that nation
remain in its own land to till it and to live there, declares the LORD." ' "

12 I gave the same message to Zedekiah king of Judah. I said, "Bow
your neck under the yoke of the king of Babylon; serve him and his
people, and you will live. 13 Why will you and your people die by the
sword, famine and plague with which the LORD has threatened any
nation that will not serve the king of Babylon? 14 Do not listen to the
words of the prophets who say to you, 'You will not serve the king of
Babylon,' for they are prophesying lies to you. 15 'I have not sent them,'
declares the LORD. 'They are prophesying lies in my name. Therefore,
I will banish you and you will perish, both you and the prophets who
prophesy to you.' "

16 Then I said to the priests and all these people, "This is what the
LORD says: Do not listen to the prophets who say, 'Very soon now the
articles from the LORD's house will be brought back from Babylon.'
They are prophesying lies to you. 17 Do not listen to them. Serve the
king of Babylon, and you will live. Why should this city become a ruin?
18 If they are prophets and have the word of the LORD, let them plead
with the LORD Almighty that the articles remaining in the house of the
LORD and in the palace of the king of Judah and in Jerusalem not be
taken to Babylon. 19 For this is what the LORD Almighty says about the
pillars, the bronze Sea, the movable stands and the other articles that
are left in this city, 20 which Nebuchadnezzar king of Babylon did not
take away when he carried Jehoiachin[b] son of Jehoiakim king of Ju-
dah into exile from Jerusalem to Babylon, along with all the nobles of
Judah and Jerusalem — 21 yes, this is what the LORD Almighty, the God
of Israel, says about the things that are left in the house of the LORD

PRAYING SCRIPTURE

Jeremiah 27

God's people need to heed his words of warning; otherwise we could find ourselves overcome. God never simplistically warned his people; he always pled with them to return to him. He reasoned with them as here, "Why should this city become a ruin?" (verse 17).

The Lord deals with his people through relationship. He isn't an ogre; he's our Father. Thank him for the kindness and love he shows to us.

---

[a] *1* A few Hebrew manuscripts and Syriac (see also 27:3,12 and 28:1); most Hebrew manuscripts *Jehoiakim* (Most Septuagint manuscripts do not have this verse.) [b] *20* Hebrew *Jeconiah*, a variant of *Jehoiachin*

and in the palace of the king of Judah and in Jerusalem: 22'They will
be taken to Babylon and there they will remain until the day I come
for them,' declares the LORD. 'Then I will bring them back and restore
them to this place.'"

THE FALSE PROPHET HANANIAH

28 In the fifth month of that same year, the fourth year, early in
the reign of Zedekiah king of Judah, the prophet Hananiah son
of Azzur, who was from Gibeon, said to me in the house of the LORD in
the presence of the priests and all the people: 2"This is what the LORD
Almighty, the God of Israel, says: 'I will break the yoke of the king of
Babylon. 3Within two years I will bring back to this place all the articles
of the LORD's house that Nebuchadnezzar king of Babylon removed
from here and took to Babylon. 4I will also bring back to this place
Jehoiachin[a] son of Jehoiakim king of Judah and all the other exiles
from Judah who went to Babylon,' declares the LORD, 'for I will break
the yoke of the king of Babylon.'"
5Then the prophet Jeremiah replied to the prophet Hananiah before
the priests and all the people who were standing in the house of the
LORD. 6He said, "Amen! May the LORD do so! May the LORD fulfill the
words you have prophesied by bringing the articles of the LORD's house
and all the exiles back to this place from Babylon. 7Nevertheless, listen
to what I have to say in your hearing and in the hearing of all the peo-
ple: 8From early times the prophets who preceded you and me have
prophesied war, disaster and plague against many countries and great
kingdoms. 9But the prophet who prophesies peace will be recognized
as one truly sent by the LORD only if his prediction comes true."
10Then the prophet Hananiah took the yoke off the neck of the
prophet Jeremiah and broke it, 11and he said before all the people,
"This is what the LORD says: 'In the same way I will break the yoke of
Nebuchadnezzar king of Babylon off the neck of all the nations within
two years.'" At this, the prophet Jeremiah went on his way.
12After the prophet Hananiah had broken the yoke off the neck of the
prophet Jeremiah, the word of the LORD came to Jeremiah: 13"Go and
tell Hananiah, 'This is what the LORD says: You have broken a wooden
yoke, but in its place you will get a yoke of iron. 14This is what the
LORD Almighty, the God of Israel, says: I will put an iron yoke on the
necks of all these nations to make them serve Nebuchadnezzar king
of Babylon, and they will serve him. I will even give him control over
the wild animals.'"
15Then the prophet Jeremiah said to Hananiah the prophet, "Listen,
Hananiah! The LORD has not sent you, yet you have persuaded this na-
tion to trust in lies. 16Therefore this is what the LORD says: 'I am about
to remove you from the face of the earth. This very year you are going
to die, because you have preached rebellion against the LORD.'"
17In the seventh month of that same year, Hananiah the prophet
died.

A LETTER TO THE EXILES

29 This is the text of the letter that the prophet Jeremiah sent
from Jerusalem to the surviving elders among the exiles and
to the priests, the prophets and all the other people Nebuchadnezzar

PRAYING SCRIPTURE
Jeremiah 28

The Lord was serious about the truth of the words his prophets spoke. When Hananiah attempted to steal Jeremiah's prophetic office and lessen the severity of his prophecies, God intervened with a promise of harsher judgment.

Claiming to speak for God is bold, so prophets had better be accurate. God does not excuse those who lie in his name. Ask for the wisdom to understand and speak what is true.

PRAYING SCRIPTURE
Jeremiah 29

In a verse that can be easily misunderstood, God instructed his people to seek the peace and prosperity of the cities they inhabited while they were in exile (see verse 7). They were to build families, but they should not feel at home because they would eventually be returned to their land (see verses 6,10).

Truly this world is a home away from home for the Christian. We can build blessed lives and families here while praying for the world to come.

[a] 4 Hebrew *Jeconiah,* a variant of *Jehoiachin*

had carried into exile from Jerusalem to Babylon. 2(This was after King
Jehoiachin[a] and the queen mother, the court officials and the leaders
of Judah and Jerusalem, the skilled workers and the artisans had gone
into exile from Jerusalem.) 3He entrusted the letter to Elasah son of
Shaphan and to Gemariah son of Hilkiah, whom Zedekiah king of Ju-
dah sent to King Nebuchadnezzar in Babylon. It said:

4This is what the LORD Almighty, the God of Israel, says to all
those I carried into exile from Jerusalem to Babylon: 5"Build
houses and settle down; plant gardens and eat what they produce.
6Marry and have sons and daughters; find wives for your sons and
give your daughters in marriage, so that they too may have sons
and daughters. Increase in number there; do not decrease. 7Also,
seek the peace and prosperity of the city to which I have carried
you into exile. Pray to the LORD for it, because if it prospers, you
too will prosper." 8Yes, this is what the LORD Almighty, the God
of Israel, says: "Do not let the prophets and diviners among you
deceive you. Do not listen to the dreams you encourage them to
have. 9They are prophesying lies to you in my name. I have not
sent them," declares the LORD.

10This is what the LORD says: "When seventy years are com-
pleted for Babylon, I will come to you and fulfill my good promise
to bring you back to this place. 11For I know the plans I have for
you," declares the LORD, "plans to prosper you and not to harm
you, plans to give you hope and a future. 12Then you will call on
me and come and pray to me, and I will listen to you. 13You will
seek me and find me when you seek me with all your heart. 14I will
be found by you," declares the LORD, "and will bring you back from
captivity.[b] I will gather you from all the nations and places where
I have banished you," declares the LORD, "and will bring you back
to the place from which I carried you into exile."

15You may say, "The LORD has raised up prophets for us in Bab-
ylon," 16but this is what the LORD says about the king who sits on
David's throne and all the people who remain in this city, your
fellow citizens who did not go with you into exile— 17yes, this is
what the LORD Almighty says: "I will send the sword, famine and
plague against them and I will make them like figs that are so bad
they cannot be eaten. 18I will pursue them with the sword, famine
and plague and will make them abhorrent to all the kingdoms of
the earth, a curse[c] and an object of horror, of scorn and reproach,
among all the nations where I drive them. 19For they have not lis-
tened to my words," declares the LORD, "words that I sent to them
again and again by my servants the prophets. And you exiles have
not listened either," declares the LORD.

20Therefore, hear the word of the LORD, all you exiles whom
I have sent away from Jerusalem to Babylon. 21This is what the
LORD Almighty, the God of Israel, says about Ahab son of Kolaiah
and Zedekiah son of Maaseiah, who are prophesying lies to you
in my name: "I will deliver them into the hands of Nebuchadnez-
zar king of Babylon, and he will put them to death before your
very eyes. 22Because of them, all the exiles from Judah who are

---

[a] 2 Hebrew *Jeconiah*, a variant of *Jehoiachin* [b] 14 Or *will restore your fortunes* [c] 18 That is, their names will be used in cursing (see verse 22); or, others will see that they are cursed.

in Babylon will use this curse: 'May the LORD treat you like Zede-
kiah and Ahab, whom the king of Babylon burned in the fire.' [23]For
they have done outrageous things in Israel; they have committed
adultery with their neighbors' wives, and in my name they have
uttered lies — which I did not authorize. I know it and am a wit-
ness to it," declares the LORD.

MESSAGE TO SHEMAIAH

[24]Tell Shemaiah the Nehelamite, [25]"This is what the LORD Almighty,
the God of Israel, says: You sent letters in your own name to all the
people in Jerusalem, to the priest Zephaniah son of Maaseiah, and to
all the other priests. You said to Zephaniah, [26]'The LORD has appointed
you priest in place of Jehoiada to be in charge of the house of the LORD;
you should put any maniac who acts like a prophet into the stocks and
neck-irons. [27]So why have you not reprimanded Jeremiah from Ana-
thoth, who poses as a prophet among you? [28]He has sent this message
to us in Babylon: It will be a long time. Therefore build houses and
settle down; plant gardens and eat what they produce.'"

[29]Zephaniah the priest, however, read the letter to Jeremiah the
prophet. [30]Then the word of the LORD came to Jeremiah: [31]"Send this
message to all the exiles: 'This is what the LORD says about Shema-
iah the Nehelamite: Because Shemaiah has prophesied to you, even
though I did not send him, and has persuaded you to trust in lies, [32]this
is what the LORD says: I will surely punish Shemaiah the Nehelamite
and his descendants. He will have no one left among this people, nor
will he see the good things I will do for my people, declares the LORD,
because he has preached rebellion against me.'"

RESTORATION OF ISRAEL

30 This is the word that came to Jeremiah from the LORD: [2]"This
is what the LORD, the God of Israel, says: 'Write in a book all the
words I have spoken to you. [3]The days are coming,' declares the LORD,
'when I will bring my people Israel and Judah back from captivity[a] and
restore them to the land I gave their ancestors to possess,' says the LORD."

[4]These are the words the LORD spoke concerning Israel and Judah:
[5]"This is what the LORD says:

"'Cries of fear are heard —
  terror, not peace.
[6]Ask and see:
  Can a man bear children?
Then why do I see every strong man
  with his hands on his stomach like a woman in labor,
  every face turned deathly pale?
[7]How awful that day will be!
  No other will be like it.
It will be a time of trouble for Jacob,
  but he will be saved out of it.

[8]"'In that day,' declares the LORD Almighty,
  'I will break the yoke off their necks
and will tear off their bonds;
  no longer will foreigners enslave them.

PRAYING SCRIPTURE

Jeremiah 30

The Lord again remembered his promise to restore Israel and Judah while using graphic language of labor, seed-sowing, wounding and hunting to describe their suffering and judgment. He warned that the judgment he brought would not end until he fully accomplished the purposes of his heart (see verse 24).

For judgment or for blessing, God does what he intends. Ask for the grace and power to live the kind of life he blesses.

---

[a] 3 Or *will restore the fortunes of my people Israel and Judah*

9 Instead, they will serve the LORD their God
and David their king,
whom I will raise up for them.

10 " 'So do not be afraid, Jacob my servant;
do not be dismayed, Israel,'
declares the LORD.

'I will surely save you out of a distant place,
your descendants from the land of their exile.
Jacob will again have peace and security,
and no one will make him afraid.
11 I am with you and will save you,'
declares the LORD.
'Though I completely destroy all the nations
among which I scatter you,
I will not completely destroy you.
I will discipline you but only in due measure;
I will not let you go entirely unpunished.'

12 "This is what the LORD says:

" 'Your wound is incurable,
your injury beyond healing.
13 There is no one to plead your cause,
no remedy for your sore,
no healing for you.
14 All your allies have forgotten you;
they care nothing for you.
I have struck you as an enemy would
and punished you as would the cruel,
because your guilt is so great
and your sins so many.
15 Why do you cry out over your wound,
your pain that has no cure?
Because of your great guilt and many sins
I have done these things to you.

16 " 'But all who devour you will be devoured;
all your enemies will go into exile.
Those who plunder you will be plundered;
all who make spoil of you I will despoil.
17 But I will restore you to health
and heal your wounds,'
declares the LORD,

'because you are called an outcast,
Zion for whom no one cares.'

18 "This is what the LORD says:

" 'I will restore the fortunes of Jacob's tents
and have compassion on his dwellings;
the city will be rebuilt on her ruins,
and the palace will stand in its proper place.
19 From them will come songs of thanksgiving
and the sound of rejoicing.
I will add to their numbers,
and they will not be decreased;

I will bring them honor,
and they will not be disdained.
20 Their children will be as in days of old,
and their community will be established before me;
I will punish all who oppress them.
21 Their leader will be one of their own;
their ruler will arise from among them.
I will bring him near and he will come close to me —
for who is he who will devote himself
to be close to me?'

declares the LORD.

22 " 'So you will be my people,
and I will be your God.' "

23 See, the storm of the LORD
will burst out in wrath,
a driving wind swirling down
on the heads of the wicked.
24 The fierce anger of the LORD will not turn back
until he fully accomplishes
the purposes of his heart.
In days to come
you will understand this.

31

"At that time," declares the LORD, "I will be the God of all the
families of Israel, and they will be my people."
2 This is what the LORD says:

"The people who survive the sword
will find favor in the wilderness;
I will come to give rest to Israel."

3 The LORD appeared to us in the past,[a] saying:

"I have loved you with an everlasting love;
I have drawn you with unfailing kindness.
4 I will build you up again,
and you, Virgin Israel, will be rebuilt.
Again you will take up your timbrels
and go out to dance with the joyful.
5 Again you will plant vineyards
on the hills of Samaria;
the farmers will plant them
and enjoy their fruit.
6 There will be a day when watchmen cry out
on the hills of Ephraim,
'Come, let us go up to Zion,
to the LORD our God.' "

7 This is what the LORD says:

"Sing with joy for Jacob;
shout for the foremost of the nations.
Make your praises heard, and say,
'LORD, save your people,
the remnant of Israel.'

PRAYING SCRIPTURE

Jeremiah 31

Before the institution of a new covenant, God prepared his people for its coming and even described it: God's law would be in their minds and on their hearts (see verse 33). The covenant would be based on relationship, specifically that God's children would know him personally (see verse 34).

This is such a glorious truth! If you are in Christ, you pray to One who knows you; you are not a stranger to him.

[a] 3 Or *LORD has appeared to us from afar*

8 See, I will bring them from the land of the north
and gather them from the ends of the earth.
Among them will be the blind and the lame,
expectant mothers and women in labor;
a great throng will return.
9 They will come with weeping;
they will pray as I bring them back.
I will lead them beside streams of water
on a level path where they will not stumble,
because I am Israel's father,
and Ephraim is my firstborn son.

10 "Hear the word of the LORD, you nations;
proclaim it in distant coastlands:
'He who scattered Israel will gather them
and will watch over his flock like a shepherd.'
11 For the LORD will deliver Jacob
and redeem them from the hand of those stronger than they.
12 They will come and shout for joy on the heights of Zion;
they will rejoice in the bounty of the LORD —
the grain, the new wine and the olive oil,
the young of the flocks and herds.
They will be like a well-watered garden,
and they will sorrow no more.
13 Then young women will dance and be glad,
young men and old as well.
I will turn their mourning into gladness;
I will give them comfort and joy instead of sorrow.
14 I will satisfy the priests with abundance,
and my people will be filled with my bounty,"
declares the LORD.

15 This is what the LORD says:

"A voice is heard in Ramah,
mourning and great weeping,
Rachel weeping for her children
and refusing to be comforted,
because they are no more."

16 This is what the LORD says:
"Restrain your voice from weeping
and your eyes from tears,
for your work will be rewarded,"
declares the LORD.
"They will return from the land of the enemy.
17 So there is hope for your descendants,"
declares the LORD.
"Your children will return to their own land.

18 "I have surely heard Ephraim's moaning:
'You disciplined me like an unruly calf,
and I have been disciplined.
Restore me, and I will return,
because you are the LORD my God.
19 After I strayed,
I repented;

after I came to understand,
I beat my breast.
I was ashamed and humiliated
because I bore the disgrace of my youth.'
20 Is not Ephraim my dear son,
the child in whom I delight?
Though I often speak against him,
I still remember him.
Therefore my heart yearns for him;
I have great compassion for him,"
declares the LORD.

21 "Set up road signs;
put up guideposts.
Take note of the highway,
the road that you take.
Return, Virgin Israel,
return to your towns.
22 How long will you wander,
unfaithful Daughter Israel?
The LORD will create a new thing on earth—
the woman will return to[a] the man."

23 This is what the LORD Almighty, the God of Israel, says: "When I
bring them back from captivity,[b] the people in the land of Judah and
in its towns will once again use these words: 'The LORD bless you, you
prosperous city, you sacred mountain.' 24 People will live together in Ju-
dah and all its towns—farmers and those who move about with their
flocks. 25 I will refresh the weary and satisfy the faint."
26 At this I awoke and looked around. My sleep had been pleasant
to me.
27 "The days are coming," declares the LORD, "when I will plant the
kingdoms of Israel and Judah with the offspring of people and of an-
imals. 28 Just as I watched over them to uproot and tear down, and
to overthrow, destroy and bring disaster, so I will watch over them to
build and to plant," declares the LORD. 29 "In those days people will no
longer say,

'The parents have eaten sour grapes,
and the children's teeth are set on edge.'

30 Instead, everyone will die for their own sin; whoever eats sour
grapes—their own teeth will be set on edge.

31 "The days are coming," declares the LORD,
"when I will make a new covenant
with the people of Israel
and with the people of Judah.
32 It will not be like the covenant
I made with their ancestors
when I took them by the hand
to lead them out of Egypt,
because they broke my covenant,
though I was a husband to[c] them,[d]"
declares the LORD.

[a] 22 Or *will protect* [b] 23 Or *I restore their fortunes* [c] 32 Hebrew; Septuagint and Syriac / *and I turned away from* [d] 32 Or *was their master*

33 "This is the covenant I will make with the people of Israel
after that time," declares the LORD.
"I will put my law in their minds
and write it on their hearts.
I will be their God,
and they will be my people.
34 No longer will they teach their neighbor,
or say to one another, 'Know the LORD,'
because they will all know me,
from the least of them to the greatest,"
declares the LORD.

"For I will forgive their wickedness
and will remember their sins no more."

35 This is what the LORD says,

he who appoints the sun
to shine by day,
who decrees the moon and stars
to shine by night,
who stirs up the sea
so that its waves roar—
the LORD Almighty is his name:
36 "Only if these decrees vanish from my sight,"
declares the LORD,
"will Israel ever cease
being a nation before me."

37 This is what the LORD says:

"Only if the heavens above can be measured
and the foundations of the earth below be searched out
will I reject all the descendants of Israel
because of all they have done,"
declares the LORD.

38 "The days are coming," declares the LORD, "when this city will be
rebuilt for me from the Tower of Hananel to the Corner Gate. 39 The
measuring line will stretch from there straight to the hill of Gareb and
then turn to Goah. 40 The whole valley where dead bodies and ashes are
thrown, and all the terraces out to the Kidron Valley on the east as far
as the corner of the Horse Gate, will be holy to the LORD. The city will
never again be uprooted or demolished."

JEREMIAH BUYS A FIELD

32 This is the word that came to Jeremiah from the LORD in the
tenth year of Zedekiah king of Judah, which was the eigh-
teenth year of Nebuchadnezzar. 2 The army of the king of Babylon was
then besieging Jerusalem, and Jeremiah the prophet was confined in
the courtyard of the guard in the royal palace of Judah.
3 Now Zedekiah king of Judah had imprisoned him there, saying,
"Why do you prophesy as you do? You say, 'This is what the LORD says:
I am about to give this city into the hands of the king of Babylon, and
he will capture it. 4 Zedekiah king of Judah will not escape the Babylo-
nians[a] but will certainly be given into the hands of the king of Babylon,

PRAYING SCRIPTURE

Jeremiah 32

While Jeremiah was imprisoned in exile and Nebuchadnezzar attacked Jerusalem, the Lord told his prophet to purchase a plot of land in his homeland from his uncle. The purchase was a physical promise from God: This was not a wasted investment—he would return his people to their home.

Aren't the promises of God life-giving, sustaining and encouraging? Lean on them today and whenever you feel hopeless. He will not forget you.

[a] 4 Or *Chaldeans*; also in verses 5, 24, 25, 28, 29 and 43

and will speak with him face to face and see him with his own eyes.
[5]He will take Zedekiah to Babylon, where he will remain until I deal
with him, declares the LORD. If you fight against the Babylonians, you
will not succeed.'"

[6]Jeremiah said, "The word of the LORD came to me: [7]Hanamel son
of Shallum your uncle is going to come to you and say, 'Buy my field at
Anathoth, because as nearest relative it is your right and duty to buy it.'

[8]"Then, just as the LORD had said, my cousin Hanamel came to me in
the courtyard of the guard and said, 'Buy my field at Anathoth in the
territory of Benjamin. Since it is your right to redeem it and possess
it, buy it for yourself.'

"I knew that this was the word of the LORD; [9]so I bought the field
at Anathoth from my cousin Hanamel and weighed out for him sev-
enteen shekels[a] of silver. [10]I signed and sealed the deed, had it wit-
nessed, and weighed out the silver on the scales. [11]I took the deed of
purchase — the sealed copy containing the terms and conditions, as
well as the unsealed copy — [12]and I gave this deed to Baruch son of Ne-
riah, the son of Mahseiah, in the presence of my cousin Hanamel and
of the witnesses who had signed the deed and of all the Jews sitting in
the courtyard of the guard.

[13]"In their presence I gave Baruch these instructions: [14]'This is what
the LORD Almighty, the God of Israel, says: Take these documents, both
the sealed and unsealed copies of the deed of purchase, and put them
in a clay jar so they will last a long time. [15]For this is what the LORD Al-
mighty, the God of Israel, says: Houses, fields and vineyards will again
be bought in this land.'

[16]"After I had given the deed of purchase to Baruch son of Neriah, I
prayed to the LORD:

[17]"Ah, Sovereign LORD, you have made the heavens and the earth
by your great power and outstretched arm. Nothing is too hard for
you. [18]You show love to thousands but bring the punishment for
the parents' sins into the laps of their children after them. Great
and mighty God, whose name is the LORD Almighty, [19]great are
your purposes and mighty are your deeds. Your eyes are open to
the ways of all mankind; you reward each person according to
their conduct and as their deeds deserve. [20]You performed signs
and wonders in Egypt and have continued them to this day, in
Israel and among all mankind, and have gained the renown that
is still yours. [21]You brought your people Israel out of Egypt with
signs and wonders, by a mighty hand and an outstretched arm
and with great terror. [22]You gave them this land you had sworn to
give their ancestors, a land flowing with milk and honey. [23]They
came in and took possession of it, but they did not obey you or
follow your law; they did not do what you commanded them to
do. So you brought all this disaster on them.

[24]"See how the siege ramps are built up to take the city. Because
of the sword, famine and plague, the city will be given into the
hands of the Babylonians who are attacking it. What you said has
happened, as you now see. [25]And though the city will be given into
the hands of the Babylonians, you, Sovereign LORD, say to me, 'Buy
the field with silver and have the transaction witnessed.'"

[a] 9 That is, about 7 ounces or about 200 grams

26Then the word of the LORD came to Jeremiah: 27"I am the LORD,
the God of all mankind. Is anything too hard for me? 28Therefore this
is what the LORD says: I am about to give this city into the hands of the
Babylonians and to Nebuchadnezzar king of Babylon, who will capture
it. 29The Babylonians who are attacking this city will come in and set it
on fire; they will burn it down, along with the houses where the peo-
ple aroused my anger by burning incense on the roofs to Baal and by
pouring out drink offerings to other gods.

30"The people of Israel and Judah have done nothing but evil in my
sight from their youth; indeed, the people of Israel have done nothing
but arouse my anger with what their hands have made, declares the
LORD. 31From the day it was built until now, this city has so aroused my
anger and wrath that I must remove it from my sight. 32The people of
Israel and Judah have provoked me by all the evil they have done—
they, their kings and officials, their priests and prophets, the people
of Judah and those living in Jerusalem. 33They turned their backs to
me and not their faces; though I taught them again and again, they
would not listen or respond to discipline. 34They set up their vile im-
ages in the house that bears my Name and defiled it. 35They built high
places for Baal in the Valley of Ben Hinnom to sacrifice their sons and
daughters to Molek, though I never commanded—nor did it enter my
mind—that they should do such a detestable thing and so make Ju-
dah sin.

36"You are saying about this city, 'By the sword, famine and plague
it will be given into the hands of the king of Babylon'; but this is what
the LORD, the God of Israel, says: 37I will surely gather them from all
the lands where I banish them in my furious anger and great wrath;
I will bring them back to this place and let them live in safety. 38They
will be my people, and I will be their God. 39I will give them singleness
of heart and action, so that they will always fear me and that all will
then go well for them and for their children after them. 40I will make
an everlasting covenant with them: I will never stop doing good to
them, and I will inspire them to fear me, so that they will never turn
away from me. 41I will rejoice in doing them good and will assuredly
plant them in this land with all my heart and soul.

42"This is what the LORD says: As I have brought all this great calam-
ity on this people, so I will give them all the prosperity I have promised
them. 43Once more fields will be bought in this land of which you say,
'It is a desolate waste, without people or animals, for it has been given
into the hands of the Babylonians.' 44Fields will be bought for silver,
and deeds will be signed, sealed and witnessed in the territory of Ben-
jamin, in the villages around Jerusalem, in the towns of Judah and in
the towns of the hill country, of the western foothills and of the Negev,
because I will restore their fortunes,[a] declares the LORD."

PROMISE OF RESTORATION

33 While Jeremiah was still confined in the courtyard of the
guard, the word of the LORD came to him a second time: 2"This
is what the LORD says, he who made the earth, the LORD who formed
it and established it—the LORD is his name: 3'Call to me and I will an-
swer you and tell you great and unsearchable things you do not know.'
4For this is what the LORD, the God of Israel, says about the houses in

[a] 44 Or *will bring them back from captivity*

PRAYING SCRIPTURE

Jeremiah 33

God's promise to Jeremiah is the hope of every person praying to God: "Call to me and I will answer you and tell you great and unsearchable things you do not know" (verse 3).

How big are your prayer requests? What "great and unsearchable things" are you asking the Lord to do? Take him your biggest requests; don't hold back even a little. And when he answers, glorify his name.

this city and the royal palaces of Judah that have been torn down to be
used against the siege ramps and the sword 5in the fight with the Bab-
ylonians[a]: 'They will be filled with the dead bodies of the people I will
slay in my anger and wrath. I will hide my face from this city because
of all its wickedness.

6" 'Nevertheless, I will bring health and healing to it; I will heal my
people and will let them enjoy abundant peace and security. 7I will
bring Judah and Israel back from captivity[b] and will rebuild them as
they were before. 8I will cleanse them from all the sin they have com-
mitted against me and will forgive all their sins of rebellion against
me. 9Then this city will bring me renown, joy, praise and honor before
all nations on earth that hear of all the good things I do for it; and they
will be in awe and will tremble at the abundant prosperity and peace
I provide for it.'

10"This is what the LORD says: 'You say about this place, "It is a deso-
late waste, without people or animals." Yet in the towns of Judah and
the streets of Jerusalem that are deserted, inhabited by neither peo-
ple nor animals, there will be heard once more 11the sounds of joy and
gladness, the voices of bride and bridegroom, and the voices of those
who bring thank offerings to the house of the LORD, saying,

"Give thanks to the LORD Almighty,
for the LORD is good;
his love endures forever."

For I will restore the fortunes of the land as they were before,' says
the LORD.

12"This is what the LORD Almighty says: 'In this place, desolate
and without people or animals — in all its towns there will again be
pastures for shepherds to rest their flocks. 13In the towns of the hill
country, of the western foothills and of the Negev, in the territory of
Benjamin, in the villages around Jerusalem and in the towns of Judah,
flocks will again pass under the hand of the one who counts them,'
says the LORD.

14" 'The days are coming,' declares the LORD, 'when I will fulfill the
good promise I made to the people of Israel and Judah.

15" 'In those days and at that time
I will make a righteous Branch sprout from David's line;
he will do what is just and right in the land.
16In those days Judah will be saved
and Jerusalem will live in safety.
This is the name by which it[c] will be called:
The LORD Our Righteous Savior.'

17For this is what the LORD says: 'David will never fail to have a man
to sit on the throne of Israel, 18nor will the Levitical priests ever fail to
have a man to stand before me continually to offer burnt offerings, to
burn grain offerings and to present sacrifices.' "

19The word of the LORD came to Jeremiah: 20"This is what the LORD
says: 'If you can break my covenant with the day and my covenant with
the night, so that day and night no longer come at their appointed
time, 21then my covenant with David my servant — and my covenant

[a] 5 Or *Chaldeans* [b] 7 Or *will restore the fortunes of Judah and Israel*
[c] 16 Or *he*

with the Levites who are priests ministering before me — can be bro-
ken and David will no longer have a descendant to reign on his throne.
22 I will make the descendants of David my servant and the Levites who
minister before me as countless as the stars in the sky and as measure-
less as the sand on the seashore.' "

23 The word of the LORD came to Jeremiah: 24 "Have you not noticed
that these people are saying, 'The LORD has rejected the two kingdoms[a]
he chose'? So they despise my people and no longer regard them as a
nation. 25 This is what the LORD says: 'If I have not made my covenant
with day and night and established the laws of heaven and earth,
26 then I will reject the descendants of Jacob and David my servant and
will not choose one of his sons to rule over the descendants of Abra-
ham, Isaac and Jacob. For I will restore their fortunes[b] and have com-
passion on them.' "

WARNING TO ZEDEKIAH

34 While Nebuchadnezzar king of Babylon and all his army and
all the kingdoms and peoples in the empire he ruled were
fighting against Jerusalem and all its surrounding towns, this word
came to Jeremiah from the LORD: 2 "This is what the LORD, the God of
Israel, says: Go to Zedekiah king of Judah and tell him, 'This is what
the LORD says: I am about to give this city into the hands of the king of
Babylon, and he will burn it down. 3 You will not escape from his grasp
but will surely be captured and given into his hands. You will see the
king of Babylon with your own eyes, and he will speak with you face to
face. And you will go to Babylon.

4 " ' 'Yet hear the LORD's promise to you, Zedekiah king of Judah. This
is what the LORD says concerning you: You will not die by the sword;
5 you will die peacefully. As people made a funeral fire in honor of your
predecessors, the kings who ruled before you, so they will make a fire
in your honor and lament, "Alas, master!" I myself make this promise,
declares the LORD.' "

6 Then Jeremiah the prophet told all this to Zedekiah king of Judah,
in Jerusalem, 7 while the army of the king of Babylon was fighting
against Jerusalem and the other cities of Judah that were still holding
out — Lachish and Azekah. These were the only fortified cities left in
Judah.

FREEDOM FOR SLAVES

8 The word came to Jeremiah from the LORD after King Zedekiah had
made a covenant with all the people in Jerusalem to proclaim freedom
for the slaves. 9 Everyone was to free their Hebrew slaves, both male and
female; no one was to hold a fellow Hebrew in bondage. 10 So all the offi-
cials and people who entered into this covenant agreed that they would
free their male and female slaves and no longer hold them in bond-
age. They agreed, and set them free. 11 But afterward they changed their
minds and took back the slaves they had freed and enslaved them again.

12 Then the word of the LORD came to Jeremiah: 13 "This is what the
LORD, the God of Israel, says: I made a covenant with your ancestors
when I brought them out of Egypt, out of the land of slavery. I said,
14 'Every seventh year each of you must free any fellow Hebrews who
have sold themselves to you. After they have served you six years, you

PRAYING SCRIPTURE

Jeremiah 34

God cares about those who are on the lowest rungs of society. He demands that they be treated justly and fairly. When his people disobeyed him, again enslaving people they had previously freed, God promised to send the sword, plague and famine (see verse 17). His desire is for each person to live in liberty with others.

God wants freedom for all. Pray for those today in our world who are enslaved physically and spiritually.

[a] 24 Or *families* [b] 26 Or *will bring them back from captivity*

must let them go free.’[a] Your ancestors, however, did not listen to me
or pay attention to me. 15Recently you repented and did what is right
in my sight: Each of you proclaimed freedom to your own people. You
even made a covenant before me in the house that bears my Name.
16But now you have turned around and profaned my name; each of
you has taken back the male and female slaves you had set free to go
where they wished. You have forced them to become your slaves again.
17“Therefore this is what the LORD says: You have not obeyed me; you
have not proclaimed freedom to your own people. So I now proclaim
‘freedom’ for you, declares the LORD — ‘freedom’ to fall by the sword,
plague and famine. I will make you abhorrent to all the kingdoms of
the earth. 18Those who have violated my covenant and have not ful-
filled the terms of the covenant they made before me, I will treat like
the calf they cut in two and then walked between its pieces. 19The lead-
ers of Judah and Jerusalem, the court officials, the priests and all the
people of the land who walked between the pieces of the calf, 20I will
deliver into the hands of their enemies who want to kill them. Their
dead bodies will become food for the birds and the wild animals.
21“I will deliver Zedekiah king of Judah and his officials into the
hands of their enemies who want to kill them, to the army of the king
of Babylon, which has withdrawn from you. 22I am going to give the
order, declares the LORD, and I will bring them back to this city. They
will fight against it, take it and burn it down. And I will lay waste the
towns of Judah so no one can live there.”

THE REKABITES

35 This is the word that came to Jeremiah from the LORD during
the reign of Jehoiakim son of Josiah king of Judah: 2“Go to the
Rekabite family and invite them to come to one of the side rooms of
the house of the LORD and give them wine to drink.”
3So I went to get Jaazaniah son of Jeremiah, the son of Habazziniah,
and his brothers and all his sons — the whole family of the Rekabites.
4I brought them into the house of the LORD, into the room of the sons
of Hanan son of Igdaliah the man of God. It was next to the room of
the officials, which was over that of Maaseiah son of Shallum the door-
keeper. 5Then I set bowls full of wine and some cups before the Rekab-
ites and said to them, “Drink some wine.”
6But they replied, “We do not drink wine, because our forefather Je-
honadab[b] son of Rekab gave us this command: ‘Neither you nor your
descendants must ever drink wine. 7Also you must never build houses,
sow seed or plant vineyards; you must never have any of these things,
but must always live in tents. Then you will live a long time in the
land where you are nomads.’ 8We have obeyed everything our forefa-
ther Jehonadab son of Rekab commanded us. Neither we nor our wives
nor our sons and daughters have ever drunk wine 9or built houses to
live in or had vineyards, fields or crops. 10We have lived in tents and
have fully obeyed everything our forefather Jehonadab commanded
us. 11But when Nebuchadnezzar king of Babylon invaded this land, we
said, ‘Come, we must go to Jerusalem to escape the Babylonian[c] and
Aramean armies.’ So we have remained in Jerusalem.”
12Then the word of the LORD came to Jeremiah, saying: 13“This is

PRAYING SCRIPTURE

Jeremiah 35

Despite the obvious and ongoing rebellion of his people, the Lord always preserved a remnant who followed and obeyed him. In this case, the house of the Rekabites obeyed their father’s direction to serve the Lord, so God promised to honor them forever (see verse 19).

God never leaves himself without a witness, no matter how bleak things seem. Seek his way no matter what everyone else around you might do.

[a] *14* Deut. 15:12 [b] *6* Hebrew *Jonadab,* a variant of *Jehonadab*; here and often in this chapter [c] *11* Or *Chaldean*

what the LORD Almighty, the God of Israel, says: Go and tell the people
of Judah and those living in Jerusalem, 'Will you not learn a lesson and
obey my words?' declares the LORD. 14'Jehonadab son of Rekab ordered
his descendants not to drink wine and this command has been kept. To
this day they do not drink wine, because they obey their forefather's
command. But I have spoken to you again and again, yet you have not
obeyed me. 15Again and again I sent all my servants the prophets to
you. They said, "Each of you must turn from your wicked ways and
reform your actions; do not follow other gods to serve them. Then you
will live in the land I have given to you and your ancestors." But you
have not paid attention or listened to me. 16The descendants of Jehon-
adab son of Rekab have carried out the command their forefather gave
them, but these people have not obeyed me.'

17"Therefore this is what the LORD God Almighty, the God of Israel,
says: 'Listen! I am going to bring on Judah and on everyone living in
Jerusalem every disaster I pronounced against them. I spoke to them,
but they did not listen; I called to them, but they did not answer.'"

18Then Jeremiah said to the family of the Rekabites, "This is what
the LORD Almighty, the God of Israel, says: 'You have obeyed the com-
mand of your forefather Jehonadab and have followed all his instruc-
tions and have done everything he ordered.' 19Therefore this is what
the LORD Almighty, the God of Israel, says: 'Jehonadab son of Rekab
will never fail to have a descendant to serve me.'"

JEHOIAKIM BURNS JEREMIAH'S SCROLL

36 In the fourth year of Jehoiakim son of Josiah king of Judah,
this word came to Jeremiah from the LORD: 2"Take a scroll and
write on it all the words I have spoken to you concerning Israel, Judah
and all the other nations from the time I began speaking to you in the
reign of Josiah till now. 3Perhaps when the people of Judah hear about
every disaster I plan to inflict on them, they will each turn from their
wicked ways; then I will forgive their wickedness and their sin."

4So Jeremiah called Baruch son of Neriah, and while Jeremiah dic-
tated all the words the LORD had spoken to him, Baruch wrote them
on the scroll. 5Then Jeremiah told Baruch, "I am restricted; I am not al-
lowed to go to the LORD's temple. 6So you go to the house of the LORD on
a day of fasting and read to the people from the scroll the words of the
LORD that you wrote as I dictated. Read them to all the people of Judah
who come in from their towns. 7Perhaps they will bring their petition
before the LORD and will each turn from their wicked ways, for the an-
ger and wrath pronounced against this people by the LORD are great."

8Baruch son of Neriah did everything Jeremiah the prophet told him
to do; at the LORD's temple he read the words of the LORD from the
scroll. 9In the ninth month of the fifth year of Jehoiakim son of Josiah
king of Judah, a time of fasting before the LORD was proclaimed for
all the people in Jerusalem and those who had come from the towns
of Judah. 10From the room of Gemariah son of Shaphan the secretary,
which was in the upper courtyard at the entrance of the New Gate of
the temple, Baruch read to all the people at the LORD's temple the
words of Jeremiah from the scroll.

11When Micaiah son of Gemariah, the son of Shaphan, heard all the
words of the LORD from the scroll, 12he went down to the secretary's
room in the royal palace, where all the officials were sitting: Elish-
ama the secretary, Delaiah son of Shemaiah, Elnathan son of Akbor,

PRAYING SCRIPTURE

Jeremiah 36

A literal event in this chapter is an all-too-real metaphor of how some people treat God's Word: They destroy it. After Baruch recorded God's words as spoken through Jeremiah, the scribe took the scroll to King Jehoiakim. As the king's servant read, the king took a knife to the scroll and cast all the pieces into a fire.

Pray that you will never be among those who destroy God's Word through disobedience or ignorance.

Gemariah son of Shaphan, Zedekiah son of Hananiah, and all the other officials. 13After Micaiah told them everything he had heard Baruch read to the people from the scroll, 14all the officials sent Jehudi son of Nethaniah, the son of Shelemiah, the son of Cushi, to say to Baruch, "Bring the scroll from which you have read to the people and come." So Baruch son of Neriah went to them with the scroll in his hand. 15They said to him, "Sit down, please, and read it to us."

So Baruch read it to them. 16When they heard all these words, they looked at each other in fear and said to Baruch, "We must report all these words to the king." 17Then they asked Baruch, "Tell us, how did you come to write all this? Did Jeremiah dictate it?"

18"Yes," Baruch replied, "he dictated all these words to me, and I wrote them in ink on the scroll."

19Then the officials said to Baruch, "You and Jeremiah, go and hide. Don't let anyone know where you are."

20After they put the scroll in the room of Elishama the secretary, they went to the king in the courtyard and reported everything to him. 21The king sent Jehudi to get the scroll, and Jehudi brought it from the room of Elishama the secretary and read it to the king and all the officials standing beside him. 22It was the ninth month and the king was sitting in the winter apartment, with a fire burning in the firepot in front of him. 23Whenever Jehudi had read three or four columns of the scroll, the king cut them off with a scribe's knife and threw them into the firepot, until the entire scroll was burned in the fire. 24The king and all his attendants who heard all these words showed no fear, nor did they tear their clothes. 25Even though Elnathan, Delaiah and Gemariah urged the king not to burn the scroll, he would not listen to them. 26Instead, the king commanded Jerahmeel, a son of the king, Seraiah son of Azriel and Shelemiah son of Abdeel to arrest Baruch the scribe and Jeremiah the prophet. But the LORD had hidden them.

27After the king burned the scroll containing the words that Baruch had written at Jeremiah's dictation, the word of the LORD came to Jeremiah: 28"Take another scroll and write on it all the words that were on the first scroll, which Jehoiakim king of Judah burned up. 29Also tell Jehoiakim king of Judah, 'This is what the LORD says: You burned that scroll and said, "Why did you write on it that the king of Babylon would certainly come and destroy this land and wipe from it both man and beast?" 30Therefore this is what the LORD says about Jehoiakim king of Judah: He will have no one to sit on the throne of David; his body will be thrown out and exposed to the heat by day and the frost by night. 31I will punish him and his children and his attendants for their wickedness; I will bring on them and those living in Jerusalem and the people of Judah every disaster I pronounced against them, because they have not listened.'"

32So Jeremiah took another scroll and gave it to the scribe Baruch son of Neriah, and as Jeremiah dictated, Baruch wrote on it all the words of the scroll that Jehoiakim king of Judah had burned in the fire. And many similar words were added to them.

JEREMIAH IN PRISON

37 Zedekiah son of Josiah was made king of Judah by Nebuchadnezzar king of Babylon; he reigned in place of Jehoiachin[a] son of Jehoiakim. 2Neither he nor his attendants nor the people of the land

PRAYING SCRIPTURE
Jeremiah 37

Suffering persecution for the faith has been a hallmark of God's people for centuries. Jeremiah found himself in prison after being falsely accused (see verse 13), then speaking truthfully to the king—who did not like the prophet's message (see verse 21).

When the wicked are in power (in government, business, family), God's people must always be aware that persecution is a possibility. Pray for the faith to stand firm if you are punished for following Jesus.

[a] 1 Hebrew *Koniah*, a variant of *Jehoiachin*

paid any attention to the words the LORD had spoken through Jere-
miah the prophet.
3King Zedekiah, however, sent Jehukal son of Shelemiah with the
priest Zephaniah son of Maaseiah to Jeremiah the prophet with this
message: "Please pray to the LORD our God for us."
4Now Jeremiah was free to come and go among the people, for he
had not yet been put in prison. 5Pharaoh's army had marched out of
Egypt, and when the Babylonians[a] who were besieging Jerusalem
heard the report about them, they withdrew from Jerusalem.
6Then the word of the LORD came to Jeremiah the prophet: 7"This is
what the LORD, the God of Israel, says: Tell the king of Judah, who sent
you to inquire of me, 'Pharaoh's army, which has marched out to sup-
port you, will go back to its own land, to Egypt. 8Then the Babylonians
will return and attack this city; they will capture it and burn it down.'
9"This is what the LORD says: Do not deceive yourselves, thinking,
'The Babylonians will surely leave us.' They will not! 10Even if you were
to defeat the entire Babylonian[b] army that is attacking you and only
wounded men were left in their tents, they would come out and burn
this city down."
11After the Babylonian army had withdrawn from Jerusalem because
of Pharaoh's army, 12Jeremiah started to leave the city to go to the ter-
ritory of Benjamin to get his share of the property among the people
there. 13But when he reached the Benjamin Gate, the captain of the
guard, whose name was Irijah son of Shelemiah, the son of Hananiah,
arrested him and said, "You are deserting to the Babylonians!"
14"That's not true!" Jeremiah said. "I am not deserting to the Bab-
ylonians." But Irijah would not listen to him; instead, he arrested
Jeremiah and brought him to the officials. 15They were angry with Jer-
emiah and had him beaten and imprisoned in the house of Jonathan
the secretary, which they had made into a prison.
16Jeremiah was put into a vaulted cell in a dungeon, where he re-
mained a long time. 17Then King Zedekiah sent for him and had him
brought to the palace, where he asked him privately, "Is there any word
from the LORD?"
"Yes," Jeremiah replied, "you will be delivered into the hands of the
king of Babylon."
18Then Jeremiah said to King Zedekiah, "What crime have I commit-
ted against you or your attendants or this people, that you have put me
in prison? 19Where are your prophets who prophesied to you, 'The king
of Babylon will not attack you or this land'? 20But now, my lord the
king, please listen. Let me bring my petition before you: Do not send
me back to the house of Jonathan the secretary, or I will die there."
21King Zedekiah then gave orders for Jeremiah to be placed in the
courtyard of the guard and given a loaf of bread from the street of the
bakers each day until all the bread in the city was gone. So Jeremiah
remained in the courtyard of the guard.

JEREMIAH THROWN INTO A CISTERN

38 Shephatiah son of Mattan, Gedaliah son of Pashhur, Jehukal[c]
son of Shelemiah, and Pashhur son of Malkijah heard what Jer-
emiah was telling all the people when he said, 2"This is what the LORD
says: 'Whoever stays in this city will die by the sword, famine or plague,

PRAYING SCRIPTURE

Jeremiah 38

Jeremiah had warned of the danger facing the people of Judah if they did not repent; now their destruction was imminent. Jeremiah's warning only angered the king, who responded by having the prophet thrown into a cistern. The king wanted "prophecies" that would encourage his army, words of comfort rather than judgment.

People often want to hear what confirms their feelings. Ask God to make you one who lovingly speaks truth.

[a] 5 Or *Chaldeans*; also in verses 8, 9, 13 and 14 [b] 10 Or *Chaldean*; also in verse 11 [c] 1 Hebrew *Jukal*, a variant of *Jehukal*

but whoever goes over to the Babylonians[a] will live. They will escape
with their lives; they will live.' 3And this is what the LORD says: 'This
city will certainly be given into the hands of the army of the king of
Babylon, who will capture it.' "

4Then the officials said to the king, "This man should be put to
death. He is discouraging the soldiers who are left in this city, as well
as all the people, by the things he is saying to them. This man is not
seeking the good of these people but their ruin."

5"He is in your hands," King Zedekiah answered. "The king can do
nothing to oppose you."

6So they took Jeremiah and put him into the cistern of Malkijah,
the king's son, which was in the courtyard of the guard. They lowered
Jeremiah by ropes into the cistern; it had no water in it, only mud, and
Jeremiah sank down into the mud.

7But Ebed-Melek, a Cushite,[b] an official[c] in the royal palace, heard
that they had put Jeremiah into the cistern. While the king was sitting
in the Benjamin Gate, 8Ebed-Melek went out of the palace and said to
him, 9"My lord the king, these men have acted wickedly in all they
have done to Jeremiah the prophet. They have thrown him into a cis-
tern, where he will starve to death when there is no longer any bread
in the city."

10Then the king commanded Ebed-Melek the Cushite, "Take thirty
men from here with you and lift Jeremiah the prophet out of the cis-
tern before he dies."

11So Ebed-Melek took the men with him and went to a room under
the treasury in the palace. He took some old rags and worn-out clothes
from there and let them down with ropes to Jeremiah in the cistern.
12Ebed-Melek the Cushite said to Jeremiah, "Put these old rags and
worn-out clothes under your arms to pad the ropes." Jeremiah did so,
13and they pulled him up with the ropes and lifted him out of the cis-
tern. And Jeremiah remained in the courtyard of the guard.

ZEDEKIAH QUESTIONS JEREMIAH AGAIN

14Then King Zedekiah sent for Jeremiah the prophet and had him
brought to the third entrance to the temple of the LORD. "I am going
to ask you something," the king said to Jeremiah. "Do not hide any-
thing from me."

15Jeremiah said to Zedekiah, "If I give you an answer, will you not
kill me? Even if I did give you counsel, you would not listen to me."

16But King Zedekiah swore this oath secretly to Jeremiah: "As surely
as the LORD lives, who has given us breath, I will neither kill you nor
hand you over to those who want to kill you."

17Then Jeremiah said to Zedekiah, "This is what the LORD God Al-
mighty, the God of Israel, says: 'If you surrender to the officers of
the king of Babylon, your life will be spared and this city will not be
burned down; you and your family will live. 18But if you will not sur-
render to the officers of the king of Babylon, this city will be given into
the hands of the Babylonians and they will burn it down; you yourself
will not escape from them.' "

19King Zedekiah said to Jeremiah, "I am afraid of the Jews who have
gone over to the Babylonians, for the Babylonians may hand me over
to them and they will mistreat me."

---

[a] *2* Or *Chaldeans*; also in verses 18, 19 and 23 [b] *7* Probably from the upper Nile region [c] *7* Or *a eunuch*

[20]"They will not hand you over," Jeremiah replied. "Obey the LORD
by doing what I tell you. Then it will go well with you, and your life
will be spared. [21]But if you refuse to surrender, this is what the LORD
has revealed to me: [22]All the women left in the palace of the king of
Judah will be brought out to the officials of the king of Babylon. Those
women will say to you:

"'They misled you and overcame you—
those trusted friends of yours.
Your feet are sunk in the mud;
your friends have deserted you.'

[23]"All your wives and children will be brought out to the Babyloni-
ans. You yourself will not escape from their hands but will be captured
by the king of Babylon; and this city will[a] be burned down."
[24]Then Zedekiah said to Jeremiah, "Do not let anyone know about
this conversation, or you may die. [25]If the officials hear that I talked
with you, and they come to you and say, 'Tell us what you said to the
king and what the king said to you; do not hide it from us or we will
kill you,' [26]then tell them, 'I was pleading with the king not to send me
back to Jonathan's house to die there.'"
[27]All the officials did come to Jeremiah and question him, and he
told them everything the king had ordered him to say. So they said
no more to him, for no one had heard his conversation with the king.
[28]And Jeremiah remained in the courtyard of the guard until the day
Jerusalem was captured.

THE FALL OF JERUSALEM

39 This is how Jerusalem was taken: [1]In the ninth year of Zede-
kiah king of Judah, in the tenth month, Nebuchadnezzar king
of Babylon marched against Jerusalem with his whole army and laid
siege to it. [2]And on the ninth day of the fourth month of Zedekiah's
eleventh year, the city wall was broken through. [3]Then all the officials
of the king of Babylon came and took seats in the Middle Gate: Nergal-
Sharezer of Samgar, Nebo-Sarsekim a chief officer, Nergal-Sharezer a
high official and all the other officials of the king of Babylon. [4]When
Zedekiah king of Judah and all the soldiers saw them, they fled; they
left the city at night by way of the king's garden, through the gate be-
tween the two walls, and headed toward the Arabah.[b]
[5]But the Babylonian[c] army pursued them and overtook Zedekiah
in the plains of Jericho. They captured him and took him to Nebu-
chadnezzar king of Babylon at Riblah in the land of Hamath, where
he pronounced sentence on him. [6]There at Riblah the king of Babylon
slaughtered the sons of Zedekiah before his eyes and also killed all the
nobles of Judah. [7]Then he put out Zedekiah's eyes and bound him with
bronze shackles to take him to Babylon.
[8]The Babylonians[d] set fire to the royal palace and the houses of the
people and broke down the walls of Jerusalem. [9]Nebuzaradan com-
mander of the imperial guard carried into exile to Babylon the people
who remained in the city, along with those who had gone over to him,
and the rest of the people. [10]But Nebuzaradan the commander of the
guard left behind in the land of Judah some of the poor people, who
owned nothing; and at that time he gave them vineyards and fields.

PRAYING SCRIPTURE

Jeremiah 39

God's judgment on Judah was horrific. After a siege of around a year and a half, Jerusalem fell to the Babylonians. King Zedekiah's sons were killed in front of him before he was forcibly blinded by his enemy. In God's provision, Nebuchadnezzar treated Jeremiah better than his own king had.

Despite the fall, God promised to "rescue . . . on that day" (verse 17). Always look to God's faithfulness even when your world is falling apart.

---

[a] 23 Or *and you will cause this city to* [b] 4 Or *the Jordan Valley* [c] 5 Or *Chaldean* [d] 8 Or *Chaldeans*

11Now Nebuchadnezzar king of Babylon had given these orders about Jeremiah through Nebuzaradan commander of the imperial guard: 12"Take him and look after him; don't harm him but do for him whatever he asks." 13So Nebuzaradan the commander of the guard, Nebushazban a chief officer, Nergal-Sharezer a high official and all the other officers of the king of Babylon 14sent and had Jeremiah taken out of the courtyard of the guard. They turned him over to Gedaliah son of Ahikam, the son of Shaphan, to take him back to his home. So he remained among his own people.

15While Jeremiah had been confined in the courtyard of the guard, the word of the LORD came to him: 16"Go and tell Ebed-Melek the Cushite, 'This is what the LORD Almighty, the God of Israel, says: I am about to fulfill my words against this city — words concerning disaster, not prosperity. At that time they will be fulfilled before your eyes. 17But I will rescue you on that day, declares the LORD; you will not be given into the hands of those you fear. 18I will save you; you will not fall by the sword but will escape with your life, because you trust in me, declares the LORD.'"

JEREMIAH FREED

40 The word came to Jeremiah from the LORD after Nebuzaradan commander of the imperial guard had released him at Ramah. He had found Jeremiah bound in chains among all the captives from Jerusalem and Judah who were being carried into exile to Babylon. 2When the commander of the guard found Jeremiah, he said to him, "The LORD your God decreed this disaster for this place. 3And now the LORD has brought it about; he has done just as he said he would. All this happened because you people sinned against the LORD and did not obey him. 4But today I am freeing you from the chains on your wrists. Come with me to Babylon, if you like, and I will look after you; but if you do not want to, then don't come. Look, the whole country lies before you; go wherever you please." 5However, before Jeremiah turned to go,[a] Nebuzaradan added, "Go back to Gedaliah son of Ahikam, the son of Shaphan, whom the king of Babylon has appointed over the towns of Judah, and live with him among the people, or go anywhere else you please."

Then the commander gave him provisions and a present and let him go. 6So Jeremiah went to Gedaliah son of Ahikam at Mizpah and stayed with him among the people who were left behind in the land.

PRAYING SCRIPTURE

Jeremiah 40

As was common, not all the population of Judah was taken into captivity. Many were left behind, among them men, women, children and the poor—those who would be no threat to the occupying leaders. The Lord left Jeremiah in Judah to preach hope to those who remained in the city.

God provides for his people, even when they are low. Ask him for a heart to minister to those in need.

GEDALIAH ASSASSINATED

7When all the army officers and their men who were still in the open country heard that the king of Babylon had appointed Gedaliah son of Ahikam as governor over the land and had put him in charge of the men, women and children who were the poorest in the land and who had not been carried into exile to Babylon, 8they came to Gedaliah at Mizpah — Ishmael son of Nethaniah, Johanan and Jonathan the sons of Kareah, Seraiah son of Tanhumeth, the sons of Ephai the Netophathite, and Jaazaniah[b] the son of the Maakathite, and their men. 9Gedaliah son of Ahikam, the son of Shaphan, took an oath to reassure them and their men. "Do not be afraid to serve the Babylonians,[c]" he said.

[a] 5 Or *Jeremiah answered* [b] 8 Hebrew *Jezaniah,* a variant of *Jaazaniah*
[c] 9 Or *Chaldeans;* also in verse 10

"Settle down in the land and serve the king of Babylon, and it will go
well with you. [10]I myself will stay at Mizpah to represent you before the
Babylonians who come to us, but you are to harvest the wine, summer
fruit and olive oil, and put them in your storage jars, and live in the
towns you have taken over."
[11]When all the Jews in Moab, Ammon, Edom and all the other coun-
tries heard that the king of Babylon had left a remnant in Judah and
had appointed Gedaliah son of Ahikam, the son of Shaphan, as gover-
nor over them, [12]they all came back to the land of Judah, to Gedaliah
at Mizpah, from all the countries where they had been scattered. And
they harvested an abundance of wine and summer fruit.
[13]Johanan son of Kareah and all the army officers still in the open
country came to Gedaliah at Mizpah [14]and said to him, "Don't you know
that Baalis king of the Ammonites has sent Ishmael son of Nethaniah
to take your life?" But Gedaliah son of Ahikam did not believe them.
[15]Then Johanan son of Kareah said privately to Gedaliah in Mizpah,
"Let me go and kill Ishmael son of Nethaniah, and no one will know it.
Why should he take your life and cause all the Jews who are gathered
around you to be scattered and the remnant of Judah to perish?"
[16]But Gedaliah son of Ahikam said to Johanan son of Kareah, "Don't
do such a thing! What you are saying about Ishmael is not true."

41 In the seventh month Ishmael son of Nethaniah, the son of
Elishama, who was of royal blood and had been one of the king's
officers, came with ten men to Gedaliah son of Ahikam at Mizpah.
While they were eating together there, [2]Ishmael son of Nethaniah and
the ten men who were with him got up and struck down Gedaliah son
of Ahikam, the son of Shaphan, with the sword, killing the one whom
the king of Babylon had appointed as governor over the land. [3]Ishmael
also killed all the men of Judah who were with Gedaliah at Mizpah, as
well as the Babylonian[a] soldiers who were there.
[4]The day after Gedaliah's assassination, before anyone knew about it,
[5]eighty men who had shaved off their beards, torn their clothes and cut
themselves came from Shechem, Shiloh and Samaria, bringing grain
offerings and incense with them to the house of the LORD. [6]Ishmael
son of Nethaniah went out from Mizpah to meet them, weeping as he
went. When he met them, he said, "Come to Gedaliah son of Ahikam."
[7]When they went into the city, Ishmael son of Nethaniah and the men
who were with him slaughtered them and threw them into a cistern.
[8]But ten of them said to Ishmael, "Don't kill us! We have wheat and
barley, olive oil and honey, hidden in a field." So he let them alone and
did not kill them with the others. [9]Now the cistern where he threw all
the bodies of the men he had killed along with Gedaliah was the one
King Asa had made as part of his defense against Baasha king of Israel.
Ishmael son of Nethaniah filled it with the dead.
[10]Ishmael made captives of all the rest of the people who were in
Mizpah — the king's daughters along with all the others who were left
there, over whom Nebuzaradan commander of the imperial guard had
appointed Gedaliah son of Ahikam. Ishmael son of Nethaniah took
them captive and set out to cross over to the Ammonites.
[11]When Johanan son of Kareah and all the army officers who were
with him heard about all the crimes Ishmael son of Nethaniah had
committed, [12]they took all their men and went to fight Ishmael son

[a] 3 Or *Chaldean*

PRAYING SCRIPTURE

Jeremiah 41

Ishmael's insurrection ended with a number of people murdered, including the governor Nebuchadnezzar had installed over the region. He then took a number of the people prisoner and led them to the land of the Ammonites, where they were kept until being rescued.

Violence is usually not a solution because the ways of humankind do not accomplish the will of God. Commit to follow God's will when you are in hard places.

of Nethaniah. They caught up with him near the great pool in Gibeon.
13When all the people Ishmael had with him saw Johanan son of Ka-
reah and the army officers who were with him, they were glad. 14All the
people Ishmael had taken captive at Mizpah turned and went over to
Johanan son of Kareah. 15But Ishmael son of Nethaniah and eight of
his men escaped from Johanan and fled to the Ammonites.

FLIGHT TO EGYPT

16Then Johanan son of Kareah and all the army officers who were
with him led away all the people of Mizpah who had survived, whom
Johanan had recovered from Ishmael son of Nethaniah after Ishmael
had assassinated Gedaliah son of Ahikam — the soldiers, women, chil-
dren and court officials he had recovered from Gibeon. 17And they went
on, stopping at Geruth Kimham near Bethlehem on their way to Egypt
18to escape the Babylonians.[a] They were afraid of them because Ish-
mael son of Nethaniah had killed Gedaliah son of Ahikam, whom the
king of Babylon had appointed as governor over the land.

42 Then all the army officers, including Johanan son of Kareah
and Jezaniah[b] son of Hoshaiah, and all the people from the
least to the greatest approached 2Jeremiah the prophet and said to
him, "Please hear our petition and pray to the LORD your God for this
entire remnant. For as you now see, though we were once many, now
only a few are left. 3Pray that the LORD your God will tell us where we
should go and what we should do."

4"I have heard you," replied Jeremiah the prophet. "I will certainly
pray to the LORD your God as you have requested; I will tell you every-
thing the LORD says and will keep nothing back from you."

5Then they said to Jeremiah, "May the LORD be a true and faithful
witness against us if we do not act in accordance with everything the
LORD your God sends you to tell us. 6Whether it is favorable or unfavor-
able, we will obey the LORD our God, to whom we are sending you, so
that it will go well with us, for we will obey the LORD our God."

7Ten days later the word of the LORD came to Jeremiah. 8So he called
together Johanan son of Kareah and all the army officers who were
with him and all the people from the least to the greatest. 9He said to
them, "This is what the LORD, the God of Israel, to whom you sent me
to present your petition, says: 10'If you stay in this land, I will build you
up and not tear you down; I will plant you and not uproot you, for I
have relented concerning the disaster I have inflicted on you. 11Do not
be afraid of the king of Babylon, whom you now fear. Do not be afraid
of him, declares the LORD, for I am with you and will save you and de-
liver you from his hands. 12I will show you compassion so that he will
have compassion on you and restore you to your land.'

13"However, if you say, 'We will not stay in this land,' and so disobey
the LORD your God, 14and if you say, 'No, we will go and live in Egypt,
where we will not see war or hear the trumpet or be hungry for bread,'
15then hear the word of the LORD, you remnant of Judah. This is what
the LORD Almighty, the God of Israel, says: 'If you are determined to
go to Egypt and you do go to settle there, 16then the sword you fear
will overtake you there, and the famine you dread will follow you into
Egypt, and there you will die. 17Indeed, all who are determined to go
to Egypt to settle there will die by the sword, famine and plague; not

PRAYING SCRIPTURE

Jeremiah 42

The people of Judah were restless and tired of occupation, so they hatched a scheme to flee to Egypt. They asked Jeremiah to discern God's will, saying, "Whether it is favorable or unfavorable, we will obey" (verse 6). Ten days later, God spoke to his prophet.

Praying "Your will be done" is always the correct path. God's answers need not please us to be the best for us, so seek his will.

---

[a] 18 Or *Chaldeans* [b] 1 Hebrew; Septuagint (see also 43:2) *Azariah*

one of them will survive or escape the disaster I will bring on them.'
18 This is what the LORD Almighty, the God of Israel, says: 'As my anger
and wrath have been poured out on those who lived in Jerusalem, so
will my wrath be poured out on you when you go to Egypt. You will be
a curse[a] and an object of horror, a curse[a] and an object of reproach; you
will never see this place again.'
19 "Remnant of Judah, the LORD has told you, 'Do not go to Egypt.' Be
sure of this: I warn you today 20 that you made a fatal mistake when
you sent me to the LORD your God and said, 'Pray to the LORD our God
for us; tell us everything he says and we will do it.' 21 I have told you to-
day, but you still have not obeyed the LORD your God in all he sent me
to tell you. 22 So now, be sure of this: You will die by the sword, famine
and plague in the place where you want to go to settle."

43 When Jeremiah had finished telling the people all the words
of the LORD their God—everything the LORD had sent him to
tell them— 2 Azariah son of Hoshaiah and Johanan son of Kareah and
all the arrogant men said to Jeremiah, "You are lying! The LORD our
God has not sent you to say, 'You must not go to Egypt to settle there.'
3 But Baruch son of Neriah is inciting you against us to hand us over to
the Babylonians,[b] so they may kill us or carry us into exile to Babylon."
4 So Johanan son of Kareah and all the army officers and all the peo-
ple disobeyed the LORD's command to stay in the land of Judah. 5 In-
stead, Johanan son of Kareah and all the army officers led away all the
remnant of Judah who had come back to live in the land of Judah from
all the nations where they had been scattered. 6 They also led away
all those whom Nebuzaradan commander of the imperial guard had
left with Gedaliah son of Ahikam, the son of Shaphan—the men, the
women, the children and the king's daughters. And they took Jeremiah
the prophet and Baruch son of Neriah along with them. 7 So they en-
tered Egypt in disobedience to the LORD and went as far as Tahpanhes.
8 In Tahpanhes the word of the LORD came to Jeremiah: 9 "While the
Jews are watching, take some large stones with you and bury them
in clay in the brick pavement at the entrance to Pharaoh's palace in
Tahpanhes. 10 Then say to them, 'This is what the LORD Almighty, the
God of Israel, says: I will send for my servant Nebuchadnezzar king of
Babylon, and I will set his throne over these stones I have buried here;
he will spread his royal canopy above them. 11 He will come and attack
Egypt, bringing death to those destined for death, captivity to those
destined for captivity, and the sword to those destined for the sword.
12 He will set fire to the temples of the gods of Egypt; he will burn their
temples and take their gods captive. As a shepherd picks his garment
clean of lice, so he will pick Egypt clean and depart. 13 There in the tem-
ple of the sun[c] in Egypt he will demolish the sacred pillars and will
burn down the temples of the gods of Egypt.'"

DISASTER BECAUSE OF IDOLATRY

44 This word came to Jeremiah concerning all the Jews living
in Lower Egypt—in Migdol, Tahpanhes and Memphis—and
in Upper Egypt: 2 "This is what the LORD Almighty, the God of Israel,
says: You saw the great disaster I brought on Jerusalem and on all the
towns of Judah. Today they lie deserted and in ruins 3 because of the

[a] 18 That is, your name will be used in cursing (see 29:22); or, others will see that you are cursed. [b] 3 Or *Chaldeans* [c] 13 Or *in Heliopolis*

PRAYING SCRIPTURE

Jeremiah 43

Sadly, after committing to obeying God's will no matter what it would be, "the arrogant men" refused to accept God's decree. Instead, they accused Jeremiah of speaking falsely (verse 2).

Pride is always at the root when we don't accept God's will or when we assume in advance that his ways automatically align with our own. Part of prayer is submitting to God. Prayer should change us to agree with him.

PRAYING SCRIPTURE

Jeremiah 44

Jerusalem was overrun. Judah was desolate (see verse 6). Because of the people's prolonged disobedience, God spoke to Jeremiah again. He reminded them that they were bringing disaster on themselves (see verse 7). Their sin and judgment are their own doing.

How often are the bad things that happen to us a result of our own choices? Ask God to show you where you have damaged yourself with sin. Repent and turn from it.

evil they have done. They aroused my anger by burning incense to and worshiping other gods that neither they nor you nor your ancestors ever knew. 4Again and again I sent my servants the prophets, who said, 'Do not do this detestable thing that I hate!' 5But they did not listen or pay attention; they did not turn from their wickedness or stop burning incense to other gods. 6Therefore, my fierce anger was poured out; it raged against the towns of Judah and the streets of Jerusalem and made them the desolate ruins they are today.

7"Now this is what the LORD God Almighty, the God of Israel, says: Why bring such great disaster on yourselves by cutting off from Judah the men and women, the children and infants, and so leave yourselves without a remnant? 8Why arouse my anger with what your hands have made, burning incense to other gods in Egypt, where you have come to live? You will destroy yourselves and make yourselves a curse[a] and an object of reproach among all the nations on earth. 9Have you forgotten the wickedness committed by your ancestors and by the kings and queens of Judah and the wickedness committed by you and your wives in the land of Judah and the streets of Jerusalem? 10To this day they have not humbled themselves or shown reverence, nor have they followed my law and the decrees I set before you and your ancestors.

11"Therefore this is what the LORD Almighty, the God of Israel, says: I am determined to bring disaster on you and to destroy all Judah. 12I will take away the remnant of Judah who were determined to go to Egypt to settle there. They will all perish in Egypt; they will fall by the sword or die from famine. From the least to the greatest, they will die by sword or famine. They will become a curse and an object of horror, a curse and an object of reproach. 13I will punish those who live in Egypt with the sword, famine and plague, as I punished Jerusalem. 14None of the remnant of Judah who have gone to live in Egypt will escape or survive to return to the land of Judah, to which they long to return and live; none will return except a few fugitives."

15Then all the men who knew that their wives were burning incense to other gods, along with all the women who were present — a large assembly — and all the people living in Lower and Upper Egypt, said to Jeremiah, 16"We will not listen to the message you have spoken to us in the name of the LORD! 17We will certainly do everything we said we would: We will burn incense to the Queen of Heaven and will pour out drink offerings to her just as we and our ancestors, our kings and our officials did in the towns of Judah and in the streets of Jerusalem. At that time we had plenty of food and were well off and suffered no harm. 18But ever since we stopped burning incense to the Queen of Heaven and pouring out drink offerings to her, we have had nothing and have been perishing by sword and famine."

19The women added, "When we burned incense to the Queen of Heaven and poured out drink offerings to her, did not our husbands know that we were making cakes impressed with her image and pouring out drink offerings to her?"

20Then Jeremiah said to all the people, both men and women, who were answering him, 21"Did not the LORD remember and call to mind the incense burned in the towns of Judah and the streets of Jerusalem by you and your ancestors, your kings and your officials and the people

[a] *8* That is, your name will be used in cursing (see 29:22); or, others will see that you are cursed; also in verse 12; similarly in verse 22.

of the land? 22When the LORD could no longer endure your wicked ac-
tions and the detestable things you did, your land became a curse and
a desolate waste without inhabitants, as it is today. 23Because you have
burned incense and have sinned against the LORD and have not obeyed
him or followed his law or his decrees or his stipulations, this disaster
has come upon you, as you now see."

24Then Jeremiah said to all the people, including the women, "Hear
the word of the LORD, all you people of Judah in Egypt. 25This is what
the LORD Almighty, the God of Israel, says: You and your wives have
done what you said you would do when you promised, 'We will cer-
tainly carry out the vows we made to burn incense and pour out drink
offerings to the Queen of Heaven.'

"Go ahead then, do what you promised! Keep your vows! 26But hear
the word of the LORD, all you Jews living in Egypt: 'I swear by my great
name,' says the LORD, 'that no one from Judah living anywhere in Egypt
will ever again invoke my name or swear, "As surely as the Sovereign
LORD lives." 27For I am watching over them for harm, not for good; the
Jews in Egypt will perish by sword and famine until they are all de-
stroyed. 28Those who escape the sword and return to the land of Judah
from Egypt will be very few. Then the whole remnant of Judah who
came to live in Egypt will know whose word will stand—mine or theirs.

29" 'This will be the sign to you that I will punish you in this place,'
declares the LORD, 'so that you will know that my threats of harm
against you will surely stand.' 30This is what the LORD says: 'I am going
to deliver Pharaoh Hophra king of Egypt into the hands of his enemies
who want to kill him, just as I gave Zedekiah king of Judah into the
hands of Nebuchadnezzar king of Babylon, the enemy who wanted to
kill him.' "

A MESSAGE TO BARUCH

45 When Baruch son of Neriah wrote on a scroll the words Jer-
emiah the prophet dictated in the fourth year of Jehoiakim
son of Josiah king of Judah, Jeremiah said this to Baruch: 2"This is
what the LORD, the God of Israel, says to you, Baruch: 3You said, 'Woe
to me! The LORD has added sorrow to my pain; I am worn out with
groaning and find no rest.' 4But the LORD has told me to say to you,
'This is what the LORD says: I will overthrow what I have built and up-
root what I have planted, throughout the earth. 5Should you then seek
great things for yourself? Do not seek them. For I will bring disaster on
all people, declares the LORD, but wherever you go I will let you escape
with your life.' "

A MESSAGE ABOUT EGYPT

46 This is the word of the LORD that came to Jeremiah the prophet
concerning the nations:

2Concerning Egypt:

This is the message against the army of Pharaoh Necho king of
Egypt, which was defeated at Carchemish on the Euphrates River by
Nebuchadnezzar king of Babylon in the fourth year of Jehoiakim son
of Josiah king of Judah:

3"Prepare your shields, both large and small,
and march out for battle!

PRAYING SCRIPTURE

Jeremiah 45

In Jeremiah's rebuke to Baruch, we are reminded of this: The Lord does whatever he pleases. "I will overthrow what I have built and uproot what I have planted" (verse 4). God can destroy every pretension to greatness—in nations and people alike—in a moment.

Humility is the way to life. Ask God for a humble heart that obeys him. Repent of pride; it only brings judgment.

PRAYING SCRIPTURE

Jeremiah 46

It isn't always possible to know with certainty how God is moving in the world. As nations rise against nations and kingdoms against kingdoms, even in our darkest moments, we should never fear or be dismayed for the Lord is with us.

Does fear come upon you when the news turns bad? Always turn to the Lord, taking your fears to him and resting in his power and wisdom.

4 Harness the horses,
  mount the steeds!
Take your positions
  with helmets on!
Polish your spears,
  put on your armor!
5 What do I see?
  They are terrified,
they are retreating,
  their warriors are defeated.
They flee in haste
  without looking back,
  and there is terror on every side,"
    declares the LORD.
6 "The swift cannot flee
  nor the strong escape.
In the north by the River Euphrates
  they stumble and fall.

7 "Who is this that rises like the Nile,
  like rivers of surging waters?
8 Egypt rises like the Nile,
  like rivers of surging waters.
She says, 'I will rise and cover the earth;
  I will destroy cities and their people.'
9 Charge, you horses!
  Drive furiously, you charioteers!
March on, you warriors — men of Cush[a] and Put who carry shields,
  men of Lydia who draw the bow.
10 But that day belongs to the Lord, the LORD Almighty —
  a day of vengeance, for vengeance on his foes.
The sword will devour till it is satisfied,
  till it has quenched its thirst with blood.
For the Lord, the LORD Almighty, will offer sacrifice
  in the land of the north by the River Euphrates.

11 "Go up to Gilead and get balm,
  Virgin Daughter Egypt.
But you try many medicines in vain;
  there is no healing for you.
12 The nations will hear of your shame;
  your cries will fill the earth.
One warrior will stumble over another;
  both will fall down together."

13 This is the message the LORD spoke to Jeremiah the prophet about
the coming of Nebuchadnezzar king of Babylon to attack Egypt:

14 "Announce this in Egypt, and proclaim it in Migdol;
  proclaim it also in Memphis and Tahpanhes:
'Take your positions and get ready,
  for the sword devours those around you.'
15 Why will your warriors be laid low?
  They cannot stand, for the LORD will push them down.

---

[a] 9 That is, the upper Nile region

16 They will stumble repeatedly;
they will fall over each other.
They will say, 'Get up, let us go back
to our own people and our native lands,
away from the sword of the oppressor.'
17 There they will exclaim,
'Pharaoh king of Egypt is only a loud noise;
he has missed his opportunity.'

18 "As surely as I live," declares the King,
whose name is the LORD Almighty,
"one will come who is like Tabor among the mountains,
like Carmel by the sea.
19 Pack your belongings for exile,
you who live in Egypt,
for Memphis will be laid waste
and lie in ruins without inhabitant.

20 "Egypt is a beautiful heifer,
but a gadfly is coming
against her from the north.
21 The mercenaries in her ranks
are like fattened calves.
They too will turn and flee together,
they will not stand their ground,
for the day of disaster is coming upon them,
the time for them to be punished.
22 Egypt will hiss like a fleeing serpent
as the enemy advances in force;
they will come against her with axes,
like men who cut down trees.
23 They will chop down her forest,"
declares the LORD,
"dense though it be.
They are more numerous than locusts,
they cannot be counted.
24 Daughter Egypt will be put to shame,
given into the hands of the people of the north."

25 The LORD Almighty, the God of Israel, says: "I am about to bring
punishment on Amon god of Thebes, on Pharaoh, on Egypt and her
gods and her kings, and on those who rely on Pharaoh. 26 I will give
them into the hands of those who want to kill them — Nebuchadnezzar
king of Babylon and his officers. Later, however, Egypt will be inhab
ited as in times past," declares the LORD.

27 "Do not be afraid, Jacob my servant;
do not be dismayed, Israel.
I will surely save you out of a distant place,
your descendants from the land of their exile.
Jacob will again have peace and security,
and no one will make him afraid.
28 Do not be afraid, Jacob my servant,
for I am with you," declares the LORD.
"Though I completely destroy all the nations

among which I scatter you,
I will not completely destroy you.
I will discipline you but only in due measure;
I will not let you go entirely unpunished."

A MESSAGE ABOUT THE PHILISTINES

PRAYING SCRIPTURE

Jeremiah 47

Following a prophecy of devastation on the Philistines, Jeremiah lamented God's continuing judgment on the lands: "Alas, sword of the LORD, how long till you rest?" (verse 6). Jeremiah was weary, but he understood things were not yet set right.

God's judgments are never wrong, but it can be wearying to see God's wrath fall on people. When we express in prayer that we trust God in his wisdom, peace will follow.

47 This is the word of the LORD that came to Jeremiah the prophet concerning the Philistines before Pharaoh attacked Gaza:

2 This is what the LORD says:

"See how the waters are rising in the north;
they will become an overflowing torrent.
They will overflow the land and everything in it,
the towns and those who live in them.
The people will cry out;
all who dwell in the land will wail
3 at the sound of the hooves of galloping steeds,
at the noise of enemy chariots
and the rumble of their wheels.
Parents will not turn to help their children;
their hands will hang limp.
4 For the day has come
to destroy all the Philistines
and to remove all survivors
who could help Tyre and Sidon.
The LORD is about to destroy the Philistines,
the remnant from the coasts of Caphtor.[a]
5 Gaza will shave her head in mourning;
Ashkelon will be silenced.
You remnant on the plain,
how long will you cut yourselves?

6 " 'Alas, sword of the LORD,
how long till you rest?
Return to your sheath;
cease and be still.'
7 But how can it rest
when the LORD has commanded it,
when he has ordered it
to attack Ashkelon and the coast?"

PRAYING SCRIPTURE

Jeremiah 48

The judgment on the Moabites is one of the most extended and explicit in Jeremiah. Their many cities and places would not be immune. God even called out their false god, Chemosh, and said it would be brought low, reminding us there is no place over which God is not Lord.

God sets up kings, takes down nations and will eventually destroy all false gods, including idols of the heart. Remain prayerful and trust in God's sovereignty.

A MESSAGE ABOUT MOAB

48 Concerning Moab:

This is what the LORD Almighty, the God of Israel, says:

"Woe to Nebo, for it will be ruined.
Kiriathaim will be disgraced and captured;
the stronghold[b] will be disgraced and shattered.
2 Moab will be praised no more;
in Heshbon[c] people will plot her downfall:
'Come, let us put an end to that nation.'

[a] 4 That is, Crete [b] 1 Or *captured; / Misgab* [c] 2 The Hebrew for *Heshbon* sounds like the Hebrew for *plot*.

You, the people of Madmen,[a] will also be silenced;
the sword will pursue you.
3 Cries of anguish arise from Horonaim,
cries of great havoc and destruction.
4 Moab will be broken;
her little ones will cry out.[b]
5 They go up the hill to Luhith,
weeping bitterly as they go;
on the road down to Horonaim
anguished cries over the destruction are heard.
6 Flee! Run for your lives;
become like a bush[c] in the desert.
7 Since you trust in your deeds and riches,
you too will be taken captive,
and Chemosh will go into exile,
together with his priests and officials.
8 The destroyer will come against every town,
and not a town will escape.
The valley will be ruined
and the plateau destroyed,
because the LORD has spoken.
9 Put salt on Moab,
for she will be laid waste[d];
her towns will become desolate,
with no one to live in them.

10 "A curse on anyone who is lax in doing the LORD's work!
A curse on anyone who keeps their sword from bloodshed!

11 "Moab has been at rest from youth,
like wine left on its dregs,
not poured from one jar to another—
she has not gone into exile.
So she tastes as she did,
and her aroma is unchanged.
12 But days are coming,"
declares the LORD,
"when I will send men who pour from pitchers,
and they will pour her out;
they will empty her pitchers
and smash her jars.
13 Then Moab will be ashamed of Chemosh,
as Israel was ashamed
when they trusted in Bethel.

14 "How can you say, 'We are warriors,
men valiant in battle'?
15 Moab will be destroyed and her towns invaded;
her finest young men will go down in the slaughter,"
declares the King, whose name is the LORD Almighty.
16 "The fall of Moab is at hand;
her calamity will come quickly.

[a] 2 The name of the Moabite town Madmen sounds like the Hebrew for *be silenced.* [b] 4 Hebrew; Septuagint / *proclaim it to Zoar* [c] 6 Or *like Aroer*
[d] 9 Or *Give wings to Moab, / for she will fly away*

17 Mourn for her, all who live around her,
all who know her fame;
say, 'How broken is the mighty scepter,
how broken the glorious staff!'

18 "Come down from your glory
and sit on the parched ground,
you inhabitants of Daughter Dibon,
for the one who destroys Moab
will come up against you
and ruin your fortified cities.
19 Stand by the road and watch,
you who live in Aroer.
Ask the man fleeing and the woman escaping,
ask them, 'What has happened?'
20 Moab is disgraced, for she is shattered.
Wail and cry out!
Announce by the Arnon
that Moab is destroyed.
21 Judgment has come to the plateau —
to Holon, Jahzah and Mephaath,
22 to Dibon, Nebo and Beth Diblathaim,
23 to Kiriathaim, Beth Gamul and Beth Meon,
24 to Kerioth and Bozrah —
to all the towns of Moab, far and near.
25 Moab's horn[a] is cut off;
her arm is broken,"
declares the LORD.

26 "Make her drunk,
for she has defied the LORD.
Let Moab wallow in her vomit;
let her be an object of ridicule.
27 Was not Israel the object of your ridicule?
Was she caught among thieves,
that you shake your head in scorn
whenever you speak of her?
28 Abandon your towns and dwell among the rocks,
you who live in Moab.
Be like a dove that makes its nest
at the mouth of a cave.

29 "We have heard of Moab's pride —
how great is her arrogance! —
of her insolence, her pride, her conceit
and the haughtiness of her heart.
30 I know her insolence but it is futile,"
declares the LORD,

"and her boasts accomplish nothing.
31 Therefore I wail over Moab,
for all Moab I cry out,
I moan for the people of Kir Hareseth.
32 I weep for you, as Jazer weeps,
you vines of Sibmah.

[a] 25 *Horn* here symbolizes strength.

Your branches spread as far as the sea[a];
  they reached as far as[b] Jazer.
The destroyer has fallen
  on your ripened fruit and grapes.
33 Joy and gladness are gone
  from the orchards and fields of Moab.
I have stopped the flow of wine from the presses;
  no one treads them with shouts of joy.
Although there are shouts,
  they are not shouts of joy.

34 "The sound of their cry rises
  from Heshbon to Elealeh and Jahaz,
from Zoar as far as Horonaim and Eglath Shelishiyah,
  for even the waters of Nimrim are dried up.
35 In Moab I will put an end
  to those who make offerings on the high places
  and burn incense to their gods,"
declares the LORD.

36 "So my heart laments for Moab like the music of a pipe;
  it laments like a pipe for the people of Kir Hareseth.
  The wealth they acquired is gone.
37 Every head is shaved
  and every beard cut off;
every hand is slashed
  and every waist is covered with sackcloth.
38 On all the roofs in Moab
  and in the public squares
there is nothing but mourning,
  for I have broken Moab
  like a jar that no one wants,"
declares the LORD.

39 "How shattered she is! How they wail!
  How Moab turns her back in shame!
Moab has become an object of ridicule,
  an object of horror to all those around her."

40 This is what the LORD says:

"Look! An eagle is swooping down,
  spreading its wings over Moab.
41 Kerioth[c] will be captured
  and the strongholds taken.
In that day the hearts of Moab's warriors
  will be like the heart of a woman in labor.
42 Moab will be destroyed as a nation
  because she defied the LORD.
43 Terror and pit and snare await you,
  you people of Moab,"
declares the LORD.

44 "Whoever flees from the terror
  will fall into a pit,

---

[a] 32 Probably the Dead Sea [b] 32 Two Hebrew manuscripts and Septuagint; most Hebrew manuscripts *as far as the Sea of* [c] 41 Or *The cities*

whoever climbs out of the pit
will be caught in a snare;
for I will bring on Moab
the year of her punishment,"
declares the LORD.

45 "In the shadow of Heshbon
the fugitives stand helpless,
for a fire has gone out from Heshbon,
a blaze from the midst of Sihon;
it burns the foreheads of Moab,
the skulls of the noisy boasters.
46 Woe to you, Moab!
The people of Chemosh are destroyed;
your sons are taken into exile
and your daughters into captivity.

47 "Yet I will restore the fortunes of Moab
in days to come,"
declares the LORD.

Here ends the judgment on Moab.

A MESSAGE ABOUT AMMON

49 Concerning the Ammonites:

This is what the LORD says:

"Has Israel no sons?
Has Israel no heir?
Why then has Molek[a] taken possession of Gad?
Why do his people live in its towns?
2 But the days are coming,"
declares the LORD,
"when I will sound the battle cry
against Rabbah of the Ammonites;
it will become a mound of ruins,
and its surrounding villages will be set on fire.
Then Israel will drive out
those who drove her out,"
says the LORD.

3 "Wail, Heshbon, for Ai is destroyed!
Cry out, you inhabitants of Rabbah!
Put on sackcloth and mourn;
rush here and there inside the walls,
for Molek will go into exile,
together with his priests and officials.
4 Why do you boast of your valleys,
boast of your valleys so fruitful?
Unfaithful Daughter Ammon,
you trust in your riches and say,
'Who will attack me?'
5 I will bring terror on you

PRAYING SCRIPTURE

Jeremiah 49

Even when there is great darkness, we should look for the glimmer of God's grace. The gospel is a light that cannot be ultimately suppressed; it shines wherever there is one who bears witness to it. The evil of the nations did not overcome God's ability to work.

Rejoice because the light of the world cannot be extinguished. Ask God to let his grace shine through you in every circumstance of your life.

[a] 1 Or *their king*; also in verse 3

from all those around you,"
declares the Lord, the LORD Almighty.
"Every one of you will be driven away,
and no one will gather the fugitives.

6 "Yet afterward, I will restore the fortunes of the Ammonites,"
declares the LORD.

A MESSAGE ABOUT EDOM

7 Concerning Edom:

This is what the LORD Almighty says:

"Is there no longer wisdom in Teman?
Has counsel perished from the prudent?
Has their wisdom decayed?
8 Turn and flee, hide in deep caves,
you who live in Dedan,
for I will bring disaster on Esau
at the time when I punish him.
9 If grape pickers came to you,
would they not leave a few grapes?
If thieves came during the night,
would they not steal only as much as they wanted?
10 But I will strip Esau bare;
I will uncover his hiding places,
so that he cannot conceal himself.
His armed men are destroyed,
also his allies and neighbors,
so there is no one to say,
11 'Leave your fatherless children; I will keep them alive.
Your widows too can depend on me.'"

12 This is what the LORD says: "If those who do not deserve to drink
the cup must drink it, why should you go unpunished? You will not go
unpunished, but must drink it. 13 I swear by myself," declares the LORD,
"that Bozrah will become a ruin and a curse,[a] an object of horror and
reproach; and all its towns will be in ruins forever."

14 I have heard a message from the LORD;
an envoy was sent to the nations to say,
"Assemble yourselves to attack it!
Rise up for battle!"

15 "Now I will make you small among the nations,
despised by mankind.
16 The terror you inspire
and the pride of your heart have deceived you,
you who live in the clefts of the rocks,
who occupy the heights of the hill.
Though you build your nest as high as the eagle's,
from there I will bring you down,"
declares the LORD.

---

[a] *13* That is, its name will be used in cursing (see 29:22); or, others will see that it is cursed.

17 "Edom will become an object of horror;
all who pass by will be appalled and will scoff
because of all its wounds.
18 As Sodom and Gomorrah were overthrown,
along with their neighboring towns,"
says the LORD,
"so no one will live there;
no people will dwell in it.

19 "Like a lion coming up from Jordan's thickets
to a rich pastureland,
I will chase Edom from its land in an instant.
Who is the chosen one I will appoint for this?
Who is like me and who can challenge me?
And what shepherd can stand against me?"

20 Therefore, hear what the LORD has planned against Edom,
what he has purposed against those who live in Teman:
The young of the flock will be dragged away;
their pasture will be appalled at their fate.
21 At the sound of their fall the earth will tremble;
their cry will resound to the Red Sea.[a]
22 Look! An eagle will soar and swoop down,
spreading its wings over Bozrah.
In that day the hearts of Edom's warriors
will be like the heart of a woman in labor.

A MESSAGE ABOUT DAMASCUS

23 Concerning Damascus:

"Hamath and Arpad are dismayed,
for they have heard bad news.
They are disheartened,
troubled like[b] the restless sea.
24 Damascus has become feeble,
she has turned to flee
and panic has gripped her;
anguish and pain have seized her,
pain like that of a woman in labor.
25 Why has the city of renown not been abandoned,
the town in which I delight?
26 Surely, her young men will fall in the streets;
all her soldiers will be silenced in that day,"
declares the LORD Almighty.
27 "I will set fire to the walls of Damascus;
it will consume the fortresses of Ben-Hadad."

A MESSAGE ABOUT KEDAR AND HAZOR

28 Concerning Kedar and the kingdoms of Hazor, which Nebuchad-
nezzar king of Babylon attacked:

This is what the LORD says:

"Arise, and attack Kedar
and destroy the people of the East.

---

[a] 21 Or *the Sea of Reeds* [b] 23 Hebrew *on* or *by*

29 Their tents and their flocks will be taken;
their shelters will be carried off
with all their goods and camels.
People will shout to them,
'Terror on every side!'

30 "Flee quickly away!
Stay in deep caves, you who live in Hazor,"
declares the LORD.

"Nebuchadnezzar king of Babylon has plotted against you;
he has devised a plan against you.

31 "Arise and attack a nation at ease,
which lives in confidence,"
declares the LORD,

"a nation that has neither gates nor bars;
its people live far from danger.
32 Their camels will become plunder,
and their large herds will be spoils of war.
I will scatter to the winds those who are in distant places[a]
and will bring disaster on them from every side,"
declares the LORD.

33 "Hazor will become a haunt of jackals,
a desolate place forever.
No one will live there;
no people will dwell in it."

A MESSAGE ABOUT ELAM

34 This is the word of the LORD that came to Jeremiah the prophet
concerning Elam, early in the reign of Zedekiah king of Judah:

35 This is what the LORD Almighty says:

"See, I will break the bow of Elam,
the mainstay of their might.
36 I will bring against Elam the four winds
from the four quarters of heaven;
I will scatter them to the four winds,
and there will not be a nation
where Elam's exiles do not go.
37 I will shatter Elam before their foes,
before those who want to kill them;
I will bring disaster on them,
even my fierce anger,"
declares the LORD.

"I will pursue them with the sword
until I have made an end of them.
38 I will set my throne in Elam
and destroy her king and officials,"
declares the LORD.

39 "Yet I will restore the fortunes of Elam
in days to come,"
declares the LORD.

---

[a] 32 Or *who clip the hair by their foreheads*

PRAYING SCRIPTURE

Jeremiah 50

In the midst of judgment, God staked his ability to redeem Israel on a single thing: himself. While recounting the suffering of Israel and Judah, he assured them that "their Redeemer is strong; the LORD Almighty is his name" (verse 34). The Lord never needs assistance from others.

Think about this: God never needs your help. He is strong; he is omnipotent; he is good. Rejoice, rest and rely on these awesome truths.

A MESSAGE ABOUT BABYLON

50 This is the word the LORD spoke through Jeremiah the prophet concerning Babylon and the land of the Babylonians[a]:

2 "Announce and proclaim among the nations,
lift up a banner and proclaim it;
keep nothing back, but say,
'Babylon will be captured;
Bel will be put to shame,
Marduk filled with terror.
Her images will be put to shame
and her idols filled with terror.'
3 A nation from the north will attack her
and lay waste her land.
No one will live in it;
both people and animals will flee away.

4 "In those days, at that time,"
declares the LORD,
"the people of Israel and the people of Judah together
will go in tears to seek the LORD their God.
5 They will ask the way to Zion
and turn their faces toward it.
They will come and bind themselves to the LORD
in an everlasting covenant
that will not be forgotten.

6 "My people have been lost sheep;
their shepherds have led them astray
and caused them to roam on the mountains.
They wandered over mountain and hill
and forgot their own resting place.
7 Whoever found them devoured them;
their enemies said, 'We are not guilty,
for they sinned against the LORD, their verdant pasture,
the LORD, the hope of their ancestors.'

8 "Flee out of Babylon;
leave the land of the Babylonians,
and be like the goats that lead the flock.
9 For I will stir up and bring against Babylon
an alliance of great nations from the land of the north.
They will take up their positions against her,
and from the north she will be captured.
Their arrows will be like skilled warriors
who do not return empty-handed.
10 So Babylonia[b] will be plundered;
all who plunder her will have their fill,"
declares the LORD.

11 "Because you rejoice and are glad,
you who pillage my inheritance,
because you frolic like a heifer threshing grain
and neigh like stallions,

---

[a] *1* Or *Chaldeans*; also in verses 8, 25, 35 and 45 [b] *10* Or *Chaldea*

12 your mother will be greatly ashamed;
she who gave you birth will be disgraced.
She will be the least of the nations—
a wilderness, a dry land, a desert.
13 Because of the LORD's anger she will not be inhabited
but will be completely desolate.
All who pass Babylon will be appalled;
they will scoff because of all her wounds.

14 "Take up your positions around Babylon,
all you who draw the bow.
Shoot at her! Spare no arrows,
for she has sinned against the LORD.
15 Shout against her on every side!
She surrenders, her towers fall,
her walls are torn down.
Since this is the vengeance of the LORD,
take vengeance on her;
do to her as she has done to others.
16 Cut off from Babylon the sower,
and the reaper with his sickle at harvest.
Because of the sword of the oppressor
let everyone return to their own people,
let everyone flee to their own land.

17 "Israel is a scattered flock
that lions have chased away.
The first to devour them
was the king of Assyria;
the last to crush their bones
was Nebuchadnezzar king of Babylon."

18 Therefore this is what the LORD Almighty, the God of Israel, says:

"I will punish the king of Babylon and his land
as I punished the king of Assyria.
19 But I will bring Israel back to their own pasture,
and they will graze on Carmel and Bashan;
their appetite will be satisfied
on the hills of Ephraim and Gilead.
20 In those days, at that time,"
declares the LORD,
"search will be made for Israel's guilt,
but there will be none,
and for the sins of Judah,
but none will be found,
for I will forgive the remnant I spare.

21 "Attack the land of Merathaim
and those who live in Pekod.
Pursue, kill and completely destroy[a] them,"
declares the LORD.
"Do everything I have commanded you.

[a] *21* The Hebrew term refers to the irrevocable giving over of things or persons to the LORD, often by totally destroying them; also in verse 26.

22 The noise of battle is in the land,
the noise of great destruction!
23 How broken and shattered
is the hammer of the whole earth!
How desolate is Babylon
among the nations!
24 I set a trap for you, Babylon,
and you were caught before you knew it;
you were found and captured
because you opposed the LORD.
25 The LORD has opened his arsenal
and brought out the weapons of his wrath,
for the Sovereign LORD Almighty has work to do
in the land of the Babylonians.
26 Come against her from afar.
Break open her granaries;
pile her up like heaps of grain.
Completely destroy her
and leave her no remnant.
27 Kill all her young bulls;
let them go down to the slaughter!
Woe to them! For their day has come,
the time for them to be punished.
28 Listen to the fugitives and refugees from Babylon
declaring in Zion
how the LORD our God has taken vengeance,
vengeance for his temple.

29 "Summon archers against Babylon,
all those who draw the bow.
Encamp all around her;
let no one escape.
Repay her for her deeds;
do to her as she has done.
For she has defied the LORD,
the Holy One of Israel.
30 Therefore, her young men will fall in the streets;
all her soldiers will be silenced in that day,"
declares the LORD.
31 "See, I am against you, you arrogant one,"
declares the Lord, the LORD Almighty,
"for your day has come,
the time for you to be punished.
32 The arrogant one will stumble and fall
and no one will help her up;
I will kindle a fire in her towns
that will consume all who are around her."

33 This is what the LORD Almighty says:

"The people of Israel are oppressed,
and the people of Judah as well.
All their captors hold them fast,
refusing to let them go.
34 Yet their Redeemer is strong;
the LORD Almighty is his name.

He will vigorously defend their cause
so that he may bring rest to their land,
but unrest to those who live in Babylon.

35 "A sword against the Babylonians!"
declares the LORD —
"against those who live in Babylon
and against her officials and wise men!
36 A sword against her false prophets!
They will become fools.
A sword against her warriors!
They will be filled with terror.
37 A sword against her horses and chariots
and all the foreigners in her ranks!
They will become weaklings.
A sword against her treasures!
They will be plundered.
38 A drought on[a] her waters!
They will dry up.
For it is a land of idols,
idols that will go mad with terror.

39 "So desert creatures and hyenas will live there,
and there the owl will dwell.
It will never again be inhabited
or lived in from generation to generation.
40 As I overthrew Sodom and Gomorrah
along with their neighboring towns,"
declares the LORD,
"so no one will live there;
no people will dwell in it.

41 "Look! An army is coming from the north;
a great nation and many kings
are being stirred up from the ends of the earth.
42 They are armed with bows and spears;
they are cruel and without mercy.
They sound like the roaring sea
as they ride on their horses;
they come like men in battle formation
to attack you, Daughter Babylon.
43 The king of Babylon has heard reports about them,
and his hands hang limp.
Anguish has gripped him,
pain like that of a woman in labor.
44 Like a lion coming up from Jordan's thickets
to a rich pastureland,
I will chase Babylon from its land in an instant.
Who is the chosen one I will appoint for this?
Who is like me and who can challenge me?
And what shepherd can stand against me?"

45 Therefore, hear what the LORD has planned against Babylon,
what he has purposed against the land of the Babylonians:

[a] 38 Or *A sword against*

The young of the flock will be dragged away;
their pasture will be appalled at their fate.
46 At the sound of Babylon's capture the earth will tremble;
its cry will resound among the nations.

PRAYING SCRIPTURE

Jeremiah 51

In one of the most devastating prophecies of judgment in all of Scripture, God described the total obliteration he would bring upon Babylon. So intent was he that after Jeremiah wrote down the prophecy, he instructed Seraiah to tie a rock to the scroll and sink it in the Euphrates River, representing the sinking of Babylon.

God's judgment on sin was borne by Jesus. Ask him for freedom from the fear of judgment.

51

This is what the LORD says:

"See, I will stir up the spirit of a destroyer
against Babylon and the people of Leb Kamai.[a]
2 I will send foreigners to Babylon
to winnow her and to devastate her land;
they will oppose her on every side
in the day of her disaster.
3 Let not the archer string his bow,
nor let him put on his armor.
Do not spare her young men;
completely destroy[b] her army.
4 They will fall down slain in Babylon,[c]
fatally wounded in her streets.
5 For Israel and Judah have not been forsaken
by their God, the LORD Almighty,
though their land[d] is full of guilt
before the Holy One of Israel.

6 "Flee from Babylon!
Run for your lives!
Do not be destroyed because of her sins.
It is time for the LORD's vengeance;
he will repay her what she deserves.
7 Babylon was a gold cup in the LORD's hand;
she made the whole earth drunk.
The nations drank her wine;
therefore they have now gone mad.
8 Babylon will suddenly fall and be broken.
Wail over her!
Get balm for her pain;
perhaps she can be healed.

9 " 'We would have healed Babylon,
but she cannot be healed;
let us leave her and each go to our own land,
for her judgment reaches to the skies,
it rises as high as the heavens.'

10 " 'The LORD has vindicated us;
come, let us tell in Zion
what the LORD our God has done.'

11 "Sharpen the arrows,
take up the shields!
The LORD has stirred up the kings of the Medes,
because his purpose is to destroy Babylon.

[a] 1 *Leb Kamai* is a cryptogram for Chaldea, that is, Babylonia. [b] 3 The Hebrew term refers to the irrevocable giving over of things or persons to the LORD, often by totally destroying them. [c] 4 Or *Chaldea* [d] 5 Or *Almighty, / and the land of the Babylonians*

The LORD will take vengeance,
  vengeance for his temple.
12 Lift up a banner against the walls of Babylon!
  Reinforce the guard,
station the watchmen,
  prepare an ambush!
The LORD will carry out his purpose,
  his decree against the people of Babylon.
13 You who live by many waters
  and are rich in treasures,
your end has come,
  the time for you to be destroyed.
14 The LORD Almighty has sworn by himself:
  I will surely fill you with troops, as with a swarm of locusts,
  and they will shout in triumph over you.

15 "He made the earth by his power;
  he founded the world by his wisdom
  and stretched out the heavens by his understanding.
16 When he thunders, the waters in the heavens roar;
  he makes clouds rise from the ends of the earth.
He sends lightning with the rain
  and brings out the wind from his storehouses.

17 "Everyone is senseless and without knowledge;
  every goldsmith is shamed by his idols.
The images he makes are a fraud;
  they have no breath in them.
18 They are worthless, the objects of mockery;
  when their judgment comes, they will perish.
19 He who is the Portion of Jacob is not like these,
  for he is the Maker of all things,
including the people of his inheritance—
  the LORD Almighty is his name.

20 "You are my war club,
  my weapon for battle—
with you I shatter nations,
  with you I destroy kingdoms,
21 with you I shatter horse and rider,
  with you I shatter chariot and driver,
22 with you I shatter man and woman,
  with you I shatter old man and youth,
  with you I shatter young man and young woman,
23 with you I shatter shepherd and flock,
  with you I shatter farmer and oxen,
  with you I shatter governors and officials.

24 "Before your eyes I will repay Babylon and all who live in Babylonia[a] for all the wrong they have done in Zion," declares the LORD.

25 "I am against you, you destroying mountain,
  you who destroy the whole earth,"
    declares the LORD.

---

[a] 24 Or *Chaldea*; also in verse 35

"I will stretch out my hand against you,
  roll you off the cliffs,
  and make you a burned-out mountain.
26 No rock will be taken from you for a cornerstone,
  nor any stone for a foundation,
  for you will be desolate forever,"
  declares the LORD.

27 "Lift up a banner in the land!
  Blow the trumpet among the nations!
Prepare the nations for battle against her;
  summon against her these kingdoms:
  Ararat, Minni and Ashkenaz.
Appoint a commander against her;
  send up horses like a swarm of locusts.
28 Prepare the nations for battle against her —
  the kings of the Medes,
their governors and all their officials,
  and all the countries they rule.
29 The land trembles and writhes,
  for the LORD's purposes against Babylon stand —
to lay waste the land of Babylon
  so that no one will live there.
30 Babylon's warriors have stopped fighting;
  they remain in their strongholds.
Their strength is exhausted;
  they have become weaklings.
Her dwellings are set on fire;
  the bars of her gates are broken.
31 One courier follows another
  and messenger follows messenger
to announce to the king of Babylon
  that his entire city is captured,
32 the river crossings seized,
  the marshes set on fire,
  and the soldiers terrified."

33 This is what the LORD Almighty, the God of Israel, says:

"Daughter Babylon is like a threshing floor
  at the time it is trampled;
  the time to harvest her will soon come."

34 "Nebuchadnezzar king of Babylon has devoured us,
  he has thrown us into confusion,
  he has made us an empty jar.
Like a serpent he has swallowed us
  and filled his stomach with our delicacies,
  and then has spewed us out.
35 May the violence done to our flesh[a] be on Babylon,"
  say the inhabitants of Zion.
"May our blood be on those who live in Babylonia,"
  says Jerusalem.

---

[a] 35 Or *done to us and to our children*

36 Therefore this is what the LORD says:

"See, I will defend your cause
and avenge you;
I will dry up her sea
and make her springs dry.
37 Babylon will be a heap of ruins,
a haunt of jackals,
an object of horror and scorn,
a place where no one lives.
38 Her people all roar like young lions,
they growl like lion cubs.
39 But while they are aroused,
I will set out a feast for them
and make them drunk,
so that they shout with laughter —
then sleep forever and not awake,"
declares the LORD.

40 "I will bring them down
like lambs to the slaughter,
like rams and goats.

41 "How Sheshak[a] will be captured,
the boast of the whole earth seized!
How desolate Babylon will be
among the nations!
42 The sea will rise over Babylon;
its roaring waves will cover her.
43 Her towns will be desolate,
a dry and desert land,
a land where no one lives,
through which no one travels.
44 I will punish Bel in Babylon
and make him spew out what he has swallowed.
The nations will no longer stream to him.
And the wall of Babylon will fall.

45 "Come out of her, my people!
Run for your lives!
Run from the fierce anger of the LORD.
46 Do not lose heart or be afraid
when rumors are heard in the land;
one rumor comes this year, another the next,
rumors of violence in the land
and of ruler against ruler.
47 For the time will surely come
when I will punish the idols of Babylon;
her whole land will be disgraced
and her slain will all lie fallen within her.
48 Then heaven and earth and all that is in them
will shout for joy over Babylon,
for out of the north
destroyers will attack her,"
declares the LORD.

[a] 41 *Sheshak* is a cryptogram for Babylon.

49 "Babylon must fall because of Israel's slain,
just as the slain in all the earth
have fallen because of Babylon.
50 You who have escaped the sword,
leave and do not linger!
Remember the LORD in a distant land,
and call to mind Jerusalem."

51 "We are disgraced,
for we have been insulted
and shame covers our faces,
because foreigners have entered
the holy places of the LORD's house."

52 "But days are coming," declares the LORD,
"when I will punish her idols,
and throughout her land
the wounded will groan.
53 Even if Babylon ascends to the heavens
and fortifies her lofty stronghold,
I will send destroyers against her,"
declares the LORD.

54 "The sound of a cry comes from Babylon,
the sound of great destruction
from the land of the Babylonians.[a]
55 The LORD will destroy Babylon;
he will silence her noisy din.
Waves of enemies will rage like great waters;
the roar of their voices will resound.
56 A destroyer will come against Babylon;
her warriors will be captured,
and their bows will be broken.
For the LORD is a God of retribution;
he will repay in full.
57 I will make her officials and wise men drunk,
her governors, officers and warriors as well;
they will sleep forever and not awake,"
declares the King, whose name is the LORD Almighty.

58 This is what the LORD Almighty says:

"Babylon's thick wall will be leveled
and her high gates set on fire;
the peoples exhaust themselves for nothing,
the nations' labor is only fuel for the flames."

59 This is the message Jeremiah the prophet gave to the staff officer
Seraiah son of Neriah, the son of Mahseiah, when he went to Babylon
with Zedekiah king of Judah in the fourth year of his reign. 60 Jere-
miah had written on a scroll about all the disasters that would come
upon Babylon — all that had been recorded concerning Babylon.
61 He said to Seraiah, "When you get to Babylon, see that you read all
these words aloud. 62 Then say, 'LORD, you have said you will destroy
this place, so that neither people nor animals will live in it; it will be

[a] 54 Or *Chaldeans*

desolate forever.' 63When you finish reading this scroll, tie a stone to
it and throw it into the Euphrates. 64Then say, 'So will Babylon sink to
rise no more because of the disaster I will bring on her. And her peo-
ple will fall.'"

The words of Jeremiah end here.

THE FALL OF JERUSALEM

52 Zedekiah was twenty-one years old when he became king, and
he reigned in Jerusalem eleven years. His mother's name was
Hamutal daughter of Jeremiah; she was from Libnah. 2He did evil in
the eyes of the LORD, just as Jehoiakim had done. 3It was because of the
LORD's anger that all this happened to Jerusalem and Judah, and in the
end he thrust them from his presence.

Now Zedekiah rebelled against the king of Babylon.

4So in the ninth year of Zedekiah's reign, on the tenth day of the
tenth month, Nebuchadnezzar king of Babylon marched against Jeru-
salem with his whole army. They encamped outside the city and built
siege works all around it. 5The city was kept under siege until the elev-
enth year of King Zedekiah.

6By the ninth day of the fourth month the famine in the city had be-
come so severe that there was no food for the people to eat. 7Then the
city wall was broken through, and the whole army fled. They left the
city at night through the gate between the two walls near the king's
garden, though the Babylonians[a] were surrounding the city. They fled
toward the Arabah,[b] 8but the Babylonian[c] army pursued King Zedekiah
and overtook him in the plains of Jericho. All his soldiers were sepa-
rated from him and scattered, 9and he was captured.

He was taken to the king of Babylon at Riblah in the land of Hamath,
where he pronounced sentence on him. 10There at Riblah the king of
Babylon killed the sons of Zedekiah before his eyes; he also killed all
the officials of Judah. 11Then he put out Zedekiah's eyes, bound him
with bronze shackles and took him to Babylon, where he put him in
prison till the day of his death.

12On the tenth day of the fifth month, in the nineteenth year of Neb-
uchadnezzar king of Babylon, Nebuzaradan commander of the impe-
rial guard, who served the king of Babylon, came to Jerusalem. 13He
set fire to the temple of the LORD, the royal palace and all the houses
of Jerusalem. Every important building he burned down. 14The whole
Babylonian army, under the commander of the imperial guard, broke
down all the walls around Jerusalem. 15Nebuzaradan the commander
of the guard carried into exile some of the poorest people and those
who remained in the city, along with the rest of the craftsmen[d] and
those who had deserted to the king of Babylon. 16But Nebuzaradan
left behind the rest of the poorest people of the land to work the vine-
yards and fields.

17The Babylonians broke up the bronze pillars, the movable stands
and the bronze Sea that were at the temple of the LORD and they car-
ried all the bronze to Babylon. 18They also took away the pots, shov-
els, wick trimmers, sprinkling bowls, dishes and all the bronze articles
used in the temple service. 19The commander of the imperial guard

PRAYING SCRIPTURE

Jeremiah 52

Judgment on Jerusalem finally came after much warning. Its fall was Israel's darkest hour. Jerusalem, the city of God, was overrun by marauders. But the Lord had shown hope for the future. All along, while God warned of inevitable judgment, he reminded his people of his love and deliverance.

God's love is without end. It is even more boundless than the oceans of the world. Meditate on and thank God for his never-failing love.

[a] 7 Or *Chaldeans*; also in verse 17 [b] 7 Or *the Jordan Valley* [c] 8 Or *Chaldean*; also in verse 14 [d] 15 Or *the populace*

took away the basins, censers, sprinkling bowls, pots, lampstands,
dishes and bowls used for drink offerings — all that were made of pure
gold or silver.
20 The bronze from the two pillars, the Sea and the twelve bronze
bulls under it, and the movable stands, which King Solomon had made
for the temple of the LORD, was more than could be weighed. 21 Each
pillar was eighteen cubits high and twelve cubits in circumference[a];
each was four fingers thick, and hollow. 22 The bronze capital on top of
one pillar was five cubits[b] high and was decorated with a network and
pomegranates of bronze all around. The other pillar, with its pome-
granates, was similar. 23 There were ninety-six pomegranates on the
sides; the total number of pomegranates above the surrounding net-
work was a hundred.
24 The commander of the guard took as prisoners Seraiah the chief
priest, Zephaniah the priest next in rank and the three doorkeepers.
25 Of those still in the city, he took the officer in charge of the fight-
ing men, and seven royal advisers. He also took the secretary who was
chief officer in charge of conscripting the people of the land, sixty of
whom were found in the city. 26 Nebuzaradan the commander took
them all and brought them to the king of Babylon at Riblah. 27 There at
Riblah, in the land of Hamath, the king had them executed.
So Judah went into captivity, away from her land. 28 This is the num-
ber of the people Nebuchadnezzar carried into exile:

in the seventh year, 3,023 Jews;
29 in Nebuchadnezzar's eighteenth year,
832 people from Jerusalem;
30 in his twenty-third year,
745 Jews taken into exile by Nebuzaradan the commander of the imperial guard.
There were 4,600 people in all.

JEHOIACHIN RELEASED

31 In the thirty-seventh year of the exile of Jehoiachin king of Judah,
in the year Awel-Marduk became king of Babylon, on the twenty-fifth
day of the twelfth month, he released Jehoiachin king of Judah and
freed him from prison. 32 He spoke kindly to him and gave him a seat
of honor higher than those of the other kings who were with him in
Babylon. 33 So Jehoiachin put aside his prison clothes and for the rest
of his life ate regularly at the king's table. 34 Day by day the king of
Babylon gave Jehoiachin a regular allowance as long as he lived, till
the day of his death.

[a] *21* That is, about 27 feet high and 18 feet in circumference or about 8.1 meters high and 5.4 meters in circumference [b] *22* That is, about 7 1/2 feet or about 2.3 meters

LAMENTATIONS

Lamentations' authorship has traditionally been attributed to Jeremiah the prophet. This squares with Jeremiah's propensity for lament in the book bearing his name as well as a lament attributed to him during the reign of King Josiah (see 2 Chronicles 35:25). While the book of Jeremiah focuses on Judah before their deportation to Babylon, Lamentations is situated in the aftermath of their humiliating defeat. Most of the survivors who remained were deported to Babylon. The Babylonians destroyed Solomon's temple and left much of the city in rubble.

Each chapter of Lamentations is a separate poem. The structure works poetically through the letters of the Hebrew alphabet as if Jeremiah was mourning his way through it. The book has been called "the funeral of a city" for it grieves what the people lost in the destruction of Jerusalem. It ponders the meaning of God's judgment on his people, expressing repentance and remorse for their sin. Some of the poetry contains expressions of hope in God's future work among the people of Israel.

Like many of the Psalms, Lamentations captures how God's people express their sorrows and grief. "The hearts of the people cry out to the Lord" (2:18), "Arise, cry out in the night" (2:19), "Do not close your ears to my cry for relief" (3:56). The deep hurt of the writer and the wounds of God's people are on full display.

Lamentations reminds us that although God does not always provide a ready answer, neither does he disparage our desires for an explanation nor our cries for help. In chapter 3, Jeremiah despaired that God wasn't hearing the prayers he offered: "Even when I call out or cry for help, he shuts out my prayer" (verse 8); "You have covered yourself with a cloud so that no prayer can get through" (verse 44). Yet Jeremiah retained faith that "the LORD is good to those whose hope is in him" (verse 25).

The New Testament teaches the same. In Philippians 4, Paul said that Christians should make their requests known to God instead of being anxious. Peter implored Christians to cast their anxieties on God, "because he cares for you" (1 Peter 5:7). From the totality of Scripture, we can easily see that God invites his people to lament, mourn and cry in his presence. When we do, he hears, answers and gives us peace.

Lamentations also teaches God's people how to mourn with hope. Just as the author lamented the fall of Jerusalem yet spoke of God's new morning mercies, so Christians, weary at the effects of sin in our lives and in the world, should look for evidence of God's grace at work around us.

One of the great hymns of the faith, "Great Is Thy Faithfulness," finds its inspiration in these verses: "Because of the LORD's great love we are not consumed, for his compassions never fail. They are new every morning; great is your faithfulness" (3:22–23). When we pray during times of trouble, crying out to God and expressing our hurt and pain, we pray in hope knowing that God is making all things new.

PRAYING SCRIPTURE

Lamentations 1

It is appropriate for us to mourn the devastating effects of sin on the culture in which we live. Jeremiah showed us how, personifying Jerusalem's sorrow: "she weeps," "tears are on her cheeks," "the roads to Zion mourn" (verses 2,4). The rightness of judgment did not remove the sorrow it brought Jeremiah.

Lament is an appropriate response to sin's devastation, so take the time for it and pray for the objects of your sorrow.

1[a] How deserted lies the city,
once so full of people!
How like a widow is she,
who once was great among the nations!
She who was queen among the provinces
has now become a slave.

2 Bitterly she weeps at night,
tears are on her cheeks.
Among all her lovers
there is no one to comfort her.
All her friends have betrayed her;
they have become her enemies.

3 After affliction and harsh labor,
Judah has gone into exile.
She dwells among the nations;
she finds no resting place.
All who pursue her have overtaken her
in the midst of her distress.

4 The roads to Zion mourn,
for no one comes to her appointed festivals.
All her gateways are desolate,
her priests groan,
her young women grieve,
and she is in bitter anguish.

5 Her foes have become her masters;
her enemies are at ease.
The LORD has brought her grief
because of her many sins.
Her children have gone into exile,
captive before the foe.

6 All the splendor has departed
from Daughter Zion.
Her princes are like deer
that find no pasture;
in weakness they have fled
before the pursuer.

7 In the days of her affliction and wandering
Jerusalem remembers all the treasures
that were hers in days of old.
When her people fell into enemy hands,
there was no one to help her.
Her enemies looked at her
and laughed at her destruction.

8 Jerusalem has sinned greatly
and so has become unclean.
All who honored her despise her,
for they have all seen her naked;

[a] This chapter is an acrostic poem, the verses of which begin with the successive letters of the Hebrew alphabet.

she herself groans
  and turns away.

9 Her filthiness clung to her skirts;
  she did not consider her future.
Her fall was astounding;
  there was none to comfort her.
"Look, LORD, on my affliction,
  for the enemy has triumphed."

10 The enemy laid hands
  on all her treasures;
she saw pagan nations
  enter her sanctuary—
those you had forbidden
  to enter your assembly.

11 All her people groan
  as they search for bread;
they barter their treasures for food
  to keep themselves alive.
"Look, LORD, and consider,
  for I am despised."

12 "Is it nothing to you, all you who pass by?
  Look around and see.
Is any suffering like my suffering
  that was inflicted on me,
that the LORD brought on me
  in the day of his fierce anger?

13 "From on high he sent fire,
  sent it down into my bones.
He spread a net for my feet
  and turned me back.
He made me desolate,
  faint all the day long.

14 "My sins have been bound into a yoke[a];
  by his hands they were woven together.
They have been hung on my neck,
  and the Lord has sapped my strength.
He has given me into the hands
  of those I cannot withstand.

15 "The Lord has rejected
  all the warriors in my midst;
he has summoned an army against me
  to[b] crush my young men.
In his winepress the Lord has trampled
  Virgin Daughter Judah.

16 "This is why I weep
  and my eyes overflow with tears.

[a] 14 Most Hebrew manuscripts; many Hebrew manuscripts and Septuagint *He kept watch over my sins* [b] 15 Or *has set a time for me / when he will*

No one is near to comfort me,
 no one to restore my spirit.
My children are destitute
 because the enemy has prevailed."

17 Zion stretches out her hands,
 but there is no one to comfort her.
The LORD has decreed for Jacob
 that his neighbors become his foes;
Jerusalem has become
 an unclean thing among them.

18 "The LORD is righteous,
 yet I rebelled against his command.
Listen, all you peoples;
 look on my suffering.
My young men and young women
 have gone into exile.

19 "I called to my allies
 but they betrayed me.
My priests and my elders
 perished in the city
while they searched for food
 to keep themselves alive.

20 "See, LORD, how distressed I am!
 I am in torment within,
and in my heart I am disturbed,
 for I have been most rebellious.
Outside, the sword bereaves;
 inside, there is only death.

21 "People have heard my groaning,
 but there is no one to comfort me.
All my enemies have heard of my distress;
 they rejoice at what you have done.
May you bring the day you have announced
 so they may become like me.

22 "Let all their wickedness come before you;
 deal with them
as you have dealt with me
 because of all my sins.
My groans are many
 and my heart is faint."

2[a] How the Lord has covered Daughter Zion
 with the cloud of his anger[b]!
He has hurled down the splendor of Israel
 from heaven to earth;
he has not remembered his footstool
 in the day of his anger.

PRAYING SCRIPTURE

Lamentations 2

The Lord's warnings about sin's consequences are not idle. His holiness does not allow his judgment to rest forever. But the proper response is lament. Zion's elders sat "on the ground . . . [and] sprinkled dust on their heads and put on sackcloth" (verse 10).

We can't act as if sin is unimportant; that's the attitude of the world. We should pray to take sin just as seriously as God does.

[a] This chapter is an acrostic poem, the verses of which begin with the successive letters of the Hebrew alphabet. [b] 1 Or *How the Lord in his anger / has treated Daughter Zion with contempt*

2 Without pity the Lord has swallowed up
all the dwellings of Jacob;
in his wrath he has torn down
the strongholds of Daughter Judah.
He has brought her kingdom and its princes
down to the ground in dishonor.

3 In fierce anger he has cut off
every horn[a,b] of Israel.
He has withdrawn his right hand
at the approach of the enemy.
He has burned in Jacob like a flaming fire
that consumes everything around it.

4 Like an enemy he has strung his bow;
his right hand is ready.
Like a foe he has slain
all who were pleasing to the eye;
he has poured out his wrath like fire
on the tent of Daughter Zion.

5 The Lord is like an enemy;
he has swallowed up Israel.
He has swallowed up all her palaces
and destroyed her strongholds.
He has multiplied mourning and lamentation
for Daughter Judah.

6 He has laid waste his dwelling like a garden;
he has destroyed his place of meeting.
The LORD has made Zion forget
her appointed festivals and her Sabbaths;
in his fierce anger he has spurned
both king and priest.

7 The Lord has rejected his altar
and abandoned his sanctuary.
He has given the walls of her palaces
into the hands of the enemy;
they have raised a shout in the house of the LORD
as on the day of an appointed festival.

8 The LORD determined to tear down
the wall around Daughter Zion.
He stretched out a measuring line
and did not withhold his hand from destroying.
He made ramparts and walls lament;
together they wasted away.

9 Her gates have sunk into the ground;
their bars he has broken and destroyed.
Her king and her princes are exiled among the nations,
the law is no more,
and her prophets no longer find
visions from the LORD.

---

[a] 3 Or *off / all the strength*; or *every king* [b] 3 *Horn* here symbolizes strength.

10 The elders of Daughter Zion
sit on the ground in silence;
they have sprinkled dust on their heads
and put on sackcloth.
The young women of Jerusalem
have bowed their heads to the ground.

11 My eyes fail from weeping,
I am in torment within;
my heart is poured out on the ground
because my people are destroyed,
because children and infants faint
in the streets of the city.

12 They say to their mothers,
"Where is bread and wine?"
as they faint like the wounded
in the streets of the city,
as their lives ebb away
in their mothers' arms.

13 What can I say for you?
With what can I compare you,
Daughter Jerusalem?
To what can I liken you,
that I may comfort you,
Virgin Daughter Zion?
Your wound is as deep as the sea.
Who can heal you?

14 The visions of your prophets
were false and worthless;
they did not expose your sin
to ward off your captivity.
The prophecies they gave you
were false and misleading.

15 All who pass your way
clap their hands at you;
they scoff and shake their heads
at Daughter Jerusalem:
"Is this the city that was called
the perfection of beauty,
the joy of the whole earth?"

16 All your enemies open their mouths
wide against you;
they scoff and gnash their teeth
and say, "We have swallowed her up.
This is the day we have waited for;
we have lived to see it."

17 The LORD has done what he planned;
he has fulfilled his word,
which he decreed long ago.
He has overthrown you without pity,

he has let the enemy gloat over you,
  he has exalted the horn[a] of your foes.

18 The hearts of the people
  cry out to the Lord.
You walls of Daughter Zion,
  let your tears flow like a river
  day and night;
give yourself no relief,
  your eyes no rest.

19 Arise, cry out in the night,
  as the watches of the night begin;
pour out your heart like water
  in the presence of the Lord.
Lift up your hands to him
  for the lives of your children,
who faint from hunger
  at every street corner.

20 "Look, LORD, and consider:
  Whom have you ever treated like this?
Should women eat their offspring,
  the children they have cared for?
Should priest and prophet be killed
  in the sanctuary of the Lord?

21 "Young and old lie together
  in the dust of the streets;
my young men and young women
  have fallen by the sword.
You have slain them in the day of your anger;
  you have slaughtered them without pity.

22 "As you summon to a feast day,
  so you summoned against me terrors on every side.
In the day of the LORD's anger
  no one escaped or survived;
those I cared for and reared
  my enemy has destroyed."

3[b] I am the man who has seen affliction
  by the rod of the LORD's wrath.
2 He has driven me away and made me walk
  in darkness rather than light;
3 indeed, he has turned his hand against me
  again and again, all day long.

4 He has made my skin and my flesh grow old
  and has broken my bones.
5 He has besieged me and surrounded me
  with bitterness and hardship.

[a] 17 *Horn* here symbolizes strength. [b] This chapter is an acrostic poem; the verses of each stanza begin with the successive letters of the Hebrew alphabet, and the verses within each stanza begin with the same letter.

PRAYING SCRIPTURE

Lamentations 3

Jeremiah didn't merely lament God's judgment on the nation; he mourned his own experience. "He has made my skin and my flesh grow old and has broken my bones . . . He has broken my teeth with gravel" (verses 4,16). How did Jeremiah survive his personal trauma? He received God's mercies and compassion every day.

No matter how bad your circumstances, God's mercies and compassion are new each day. Commit yourself to him in hope of his goodness.

6 He has made me dwell in darkness
like those long dead.

7 He has walled me in so I cannot escape;
he has weighed me down with chains.
8 Even when I call out or cry for help,
he shuts out my prayer.
9 He has barred my way with blocks of stone;
he has made my paths crooked.

10 Like a bear lying in wait,
like a lion in hiding,
11 he dragged me from the path and mangled me
and left me without help.
12 He drew his bow
and made me the target for his arrows.

13 He pierced my heart
with arrows from his quiver.
14 I became the laughingstock of all my people;
they mock me in song all day long.
15 He has filled me with bitter herbs
and given me gall to drink.

16 He has broken my teeth with gravel;
he has trampled me in the dust.
17 I have been deprived of peace;
I have forgotten what prosperity is.
18 So I say, "My splendor is gone
and all that I had hoped from the LORD."

19 I remember my affliction and my wandering,
the bitterness and the gall.
20 I well remember them,
and my soul is downcast within me.
21 Yet this I call to mind
and therefore I have hope:

22 Because of the LORD's great love we are not consumed,
for his compassions never fail.
23 They are new every morning;
great is your faithfulness.
24 I say to myself, "The LORD is my portion;
therefore I will wait for him."

25 The LORD is good to those whose hope is in him,
to the one who seeks him;
26 it is good to wait quietly
for the salvation of the LORD.
27 It is good for a man to bear the yoke
while he is young.

28 Let him sit alone in silence,
for the LORD has laid it on him.
29 Let him bury his face in the dust —
there may yet be hope.
30 Let him offer his cheek to one who would strike him,
and let him be filled with disgrace.

31 For no one is cast off
by the Lord forever.
32 Though he brings grief, he will show compassion,
so great is his unfailing love.
33 For he does not willingly bring affliction
or grief to anyone.

34 To crush underfoot
all prisoners in the land,
35 to deny people their rights
before the Most High,
36 to deprive them of justice —
would not the Lord see such things?

37 Who can speak and have it happen
if the Lord has not decreed it?
38 Is it not from the mouth of the Most High
that both calamities and good things come?
39 Why should the living complain
when punished for their sins?

40 Let us examine our ways and test them,
and let us return to the LORD.
41 Let us lift up our hearts and our hands
to God in heaven, and say:
42 "We have sinned and rebelled
and you have not forgiven.

43 "You have covered yourself with anger and pursued us;
you have slain without pity.
44 You have covered yourself with a cloud
so that no prayer can get through.
45 You have made us scum and refuse
among the nations.

46 "All our enemies have opened their mouths
wide against us.
47 We have suffered terror and pitfalls,
ruin and destruction."
48 Streams of tears flow from my eyes
because my people are destroyed.

49 My eyes will flow unceasingly,
without relief,
50 until the LORD looks down
from heaven and sees.
51 What I see brings grief to my soul
because of all the women of my city.

52 Those who were my enemies without cause
hunted me like a bird.
53 They tried to end my life in a pit
and threw stones at me;
54 the waters closed over my head,
and I thought I was about to perish.

55 I called on your name, LORD,
from the depths of the pit.

56 You heard my plea: "Do not close your ears
to my cry for relief."
57 You came near when I called you,
and you said, "Do not fear."

58 You, Lord, took up my case;
you redeemed my life.
59 LORD, you have seen the wrong done to me.
Uphold my cause!
60 You have seen the depth of their vengeance,
all their plots against me.

61 LORD, you have heard their insults,
all their plots against me—
62 what my enemies whisper and mutter
against me all day long.
63 Look at them! Sitting or standing,
they mock me in their songs.

64 Pay them back what they deserve, LORD,
for what their hands have done.
65 Put a veil over their hearts,
and may your curse be on them!
66 Pursue them in anger and destroy them
from under the heavens of the LORD.

PRAYING SCRIPTURE

Lamentations 4

This chapter holds an important insight about how people think. All the kings and nations around Israel did not believe an enemy could take down Jerusalem. They thought the city was invincible. Israel's collapse, however, wasn't due to economic troubles—it was due to sin, rebellion against God.

To understand what God is doing in the world requires seeing as he sees. Ask him for wisdom to understand his ways.

4

[a] How the gold has lost its luster,
the fine gold become dull!
The sacred gems are scattered
at every street corner.

2 How the precious children of Zion,
once worth their weight in gold,
are now considered as pots of clay,
the work of a potter's hands!

3 Even jackals offer their breasts
to nurse their young,
but my people have become heartless
like ostriches in the desert.

4 Because of thirst the infant's tongue
sticks to the roof of its mouth;
the children beg for bread,
but no one gives it to them.

5 Those who once ate delicacies
are destitute in the streets.
Those brought up in royal purple
now lie on ash heaps.

6 The punishment of my people
is greater than that of Sodom,
which was overthrown in a moment
without a hand turned to help her.

---

[a] This chapter is an acrostic poem, the verses of which begin with the successive letters of the Hebrew alphabet.

7 Their princes were brighter than snow
and whiter than milk,
their bodies more ruddy than rubies,
their appearance like lapis lazuli.

8 But now they are blacker than soot;
they are not recognized in the streets.
Their skin has shriveled on their bones;
it has become as dry as a stick.

9 Those killed by the sword are better off
than those who die of famine;
racked with hunger, they waste away
for lack of food from the field.

10 With their own hands compassionate women
have cooked their own children,
who became their food
when my people were destroyed.

11 The LORD has given full vent to his wrath;
he has poured out his fierce anger.
He kindled a fire in Zion
that consumed her foundations.

12 The kings of the earth did not believe,
nor did any of the peoples of the world,
that enemies and foes could enter
the gates of Jerusalem.

13 But it happened because of the sins of her prophets
and the iniquities of her priests,
who shed within her
the blood of the righteous.

14 Now they grope through the streets
as if they were blind.
They are so defiled with blood
that no one dares to touch their garments.

15 "Go away! You are unclean!" people cry to them.
"Away! Away! Don't touch us!"
When they flee and wander about,
people among the nations say,
"They can stay here no longer."

16 The LORD himself has scattered them;
he no longer watches over them.
The priests are shown no honor,
the elders no favor.

17 Moreover, our eyes failed,
looking in vain for help;
from our towers we watched
for a nation that could not save us.

18 People stalked us at every step,
so we could not walk in our streets.
Our end was near, our days were numbered,
for our end had come.

19 Our pursuers were swifter
than eagles in the sky;
they chased us over the mountains
and lay in wait for us in the desert.

20 The LORD's anointed, our very life breath,
was caught in their traps.
We thought that under his shadow
we would live among the nations.

21 Rejoice and be glad, Daughter Edom,
you who live in the land of Uz.
But to you also the cup will be passed;
you will be drunk and stripped naked.

22 Your punishment will end, Daughter Zion;
he will not prolong your exile.
But he will punish your sin, Daughter Edom,
and expose your wickedness.

PRAYING SCRIPTURE

Lamentations 5

The Lord reigns over the earth forever and is able to deliver us when we call on him—but we must call on him. Jeremiah acknowledged God's power, expressed his own sorrow and asked for Israel to be renewed (verses 19–21). Expressing lament is necessary, but we also need to ask for deliverance.

Is there anything in your life you need to ask God to renew? Include it in your next prayer time.

5

Remember, LORD, what has happened to us;
look, and see our disgrace.
2 Our inheritance has been turned over to strangers,
our homes to foreigners.
3 We have become fatherless,
our mothers are widows.
4 We must buy the water we drink;
our wood can be had only at a price.
5 Those who pursue us are at our heels;
we are weary and find no rest.
6 We submitted to Egypt and Assyria
to get enough bread.
7 Our ancestors sinned and are no more,
and we bear their punishment.
8 Slaves rule over us,
and there is no one to free us from their hands.
9 We get our bread at the risk of our lives
because of the sword in the desert.
10 Our skin is hot as an oven,
feverish from hunger.
11 Women have been violated in Zion,
and virgins in the towns of Judah.
12 Princes have been hung up by their hands;
elders are shown no respect.
13 Young men toil at the millstones;
boys stagger under loads of wood.
14 The elders are gone from the city gate;
the young men have stopped their music.
15 Joy is gone from our hearts;
our dancing has turned to mourning.
16 The crown has fallen from our head.
Woe to us, for we have sinned!
17 Because of this our hearts are faint,
because of these things our eyes grow dim
18 for Mount Zion, which lies desolate,
with jackals prowling over it.

19 You, LORD, reign forever;
your throne endures from generation to generation.
20 Why do you always forget us?
Why do you forsake us so long?
21 Restore us to yourself, LORD, that we may return;
renew our days as of old
22 unless you have utterly rejected us
and are angry with us beyond measure.

EZEKIEL

The book of Ezekiel is set after the initial exile of Judah in Babylon before the final destruction of Jerusalem. Ezekiel received his call to prophetic service in Babylon through a vision that for centuries has puzzled many. We need not grasp every detail of the vision to grasp the main point—God is not limited to working only in Judah. He is the God of the entire world, and his glory inhabits all the world that he has created.

The first half of Ezekiel warns God's people about the judgment that is going to come upon them. Chapters 25–32 begin God's words of deliverance. First he promised deliverance for Israel by bringing judgment upon their enemies. Then, in chapters 33–48, Ezekiel pictured the salvation that God would bring to his people in the new covenant. The book ends with the vision of a restored temple.

One of the most well-known passages in Ezekiel is in chapter 36, the description of the new covenant. God promised that he would take the heart of stone from his people and give them a heart of flesh. He also promised to put a new Spirit in his people. This new covenant promise reminds us that as we pray, we also are approaching God as his people. He has given us his Spirit. We pray in the power of the Holy Spirit and pray for the same Holy Spirit to guide and strengthen us to follow him.

Prayer is infrequently referenced explicitly in Ezekiel. It is usually paired with Ezekiel's common expression of abject humility before the Lord: falling on his face. During God's judgment on the wicked of Jerusalem, Ezekiel found himself alone. Crying out to God, he fell on his face, asking whether God would kill the remnant of the faithful in his fury toward the city (see 9:8). Soon after, when one of the princes was killed, Ezekiel, voicing the same concern, said, "Then, I fell facedown and cried in a loud voice, 'Alas, Sovereign LORD! Will you completely destroy the remnant of Israel?'" (11:13). Prayer should be our natural response in our most dire circumstances.

The most frequent refrain throughout Ezekiel is "then you will know that I am the LORD." God works in the world so that he might receive the glory he deserves. In Ezekiel God disciplined his people, saved his people and brought judgment upon the enemies of his people all for his glory. As believers we should pray that God would receive the glory due his name. We do this first by praying that God would be glorified in our own lives. We ask the Lord to work through us so that our lives point to him. Also, believers should pray that God's name receives glory through the gospel going to the nations so we have extra incentive to rejoice when those from every nation, tribe, tongue and language are before the throne of God.

EZEKIEL'S INAUGURAL VISION

1 In my thirtieth year, in the fourth month on the fifth day, while I was among the exiles by the Kebar River, the heavens were opened and I saw visions of God.

2On the fifth of the month—it was the fifth year of the exile of King Jehoiachin— 3the word of the LORD came to Ezekiel the priest, the son of Buzi, by the Kebar River in the land of the Babylonians.[a] There the hand of the LORD was on him.

4I looked, and I saw a windstorm coming out of the north—an immense cloud with flashing lightning and surrounded by brilliant light. The center of the fire looked like glowing metal, 5and in the fire was what looked like four living creatures. In appearance their form was human, 6but each of them had four faces and four wings. 7Their legs were straight; their feet were like those of a calf and gleamed like burnished bronze. 8Under their wings on their four sides they had human hands. All four of them had faces and wings, 9and the wings of one touched the wings of another. Each one went straight ahead; they did not turn as they moved.

10Their faces looked like this: Each of the four had the face of a human being, and on the right side each had the face of a lion, and on the left the face of an ox; each also had the face of an eagle. 11Such were their faces. They each had two wings spreading out upward, each wing touching that of the creature on either side; and each had two other wings covering its body. 12Each one went straight ahead. Wherever the spirit would go, they would go, without turning as they went. 13The appearance of the living creatures was like burning coals of fire or like torches. Fire moved back and forth among the creatures; it was bright, and lightning flashed out of it. 14The creatures sped back and forth like flashes of lightning.

15As I looked at the living creatures, I saw a wheel on the ground beside each creature with its four faces. 16This was the appearance and structure of the wheels: They sparkled like topaz, and all four looked alike. Each appeared to be made like a wheel intersecting a wheel. 17As they moved, they would go in any one of the four directions the creatures faced; the wheels did not change direction as the creatures went. 18Their rims were high and awesome, and all four rims were full of eyes all around.

19When the living creatures moved, the wheels beside them moved; and when the living creatures rose from the ground, the wheels also rose. 20Wherever the spirit would go, they would go, and the wheels would rise along with them, because the spirit of the living creatures was in the wheels. 21When the creatures moved, they also moved; when the creatures stood still, they also stood still; and when the creatures rose from the ground, the wheels rose along with them, because the spirit of the living creatures was in the wheels.

22Spread out above the heads of the living creatures was what looked something like a vault, sparkling like crystal, and awesome. 23Under the vault their wings were stretched out one toward the other, and each had two wings covering its body. 24When the creatures moved, I heard the sound of their wings, like the roar of rushing waters, like the voice of the Almighty,[b] like the tumult of an army. When they stood still, they lowered their wings.

[a] 3 Or *Chaldeans* [b] 24 Hebrew *Shaddai*

PRAYING SCRIPTURE

Ezekiel 1

The book of Ezekiel is filled with imagery, and its meaning isn't always readily apparent. The descriptions here of beings with human faces, wings, straight legs with calves' feet and the like don't lend themselves to easy interpretation. Yet Ezekiel knew God was speaking to him. Even though his prophet was in exile, God remained in control.

Unlike Ezekiel, today we are blessed with God's full Word. We can pray in complete confidence in his truth.

25Then there came a voice from above the vault over their heads as they stood with lowered wings. 26Above the vault over their heads was what looked like a throne of lapis lazuli, and high above on the throne was a figure like that of a man. 27I saw that from what appeared to be his waist up he looked like glowing metal, as if full of fire, and that from there down he looked like fire; and brilliant light surrounded him. 28Like the appearance of a rainbow in the clouds on a rainy day, so was the radiance around him.

This was the appearance of the likeness of the glory of the LORD. When I saw it, I fell facedown, and I heard the voice of one speaking.

EZEKIEL'S CALL TO BE A PROPHET

2 He said to me, "Son of man,[a] stand up on your feet and I will speak to you." 2As he spoke, the Spirit came into me and raised me to my feet, and I heard him speaking to me.

3He said: "Son of man, I am sending you to the Israelites, to a rebellious nation that has rebelled against me; they and their ancestors have been in revolt against me to this very day. 4The people to whom I am sending you are obstinate and stubborn. Say to them, 'This is what the Sovereign LORD says.' 5And whether they listen or fail to listen—for they are a rebellious people—they will know that a prophet has been among them. 6And you, son of man, do not be afraid of them or their words. Do not be afraid, though briers and thorns are all around you and you live among scorpions. Do not be afraid of what they say or be terrified by them, though they are a rebellious people. 7You must speak my words to them, whether they listen or fail to listen, for they are rebellious. 8But you, son of man, listen to what I say to you. Do not rebel like that rebellious people; open your mouth and eat what I give you."

9Then I looked, and I saw a hand stretched out to me. In it was a scroll, 10which he unrolled before me. On both sides of it were written words of lament and mourning and woe.

3 And he said to me, "Son of man, eat what is before you, eat this scroll; then go and speak to the people of Israel." 2So I opened my mouth, and he gave me the scroll to eat.

3Then he said to me, "Son of man, eat this scroll I am giving you and fill your stomach with it." So I ate it, and it tasted as sweet as honey in my mouth.

4He then said to me: "Son of man, go now to the people of Israel and speak my words to them. 5You are not being sent to a people of obscure speech and strange language, but to the people of Israel— 6not to many peoples of obscure speech and strange language, whose words you cannot understand. Surely if I had sent you to them, they would have listened to you. 7But the people of Israel are not willing to listen to you because they are not willing to listen to me, for all the Israelites are hardened and obstinate. 8But I will make you as unyielding and hardened as they are. 9I will make your forehead like the hardest stone, harder than flint. Do not be afraid of them or terrified by them, though they are a rebellious people."

10And he said to me, "Son of man, listen carefully and take to heart all the words I speak to you. 11Go now to your people in exile and speak

PRAYING SCRIPTURE
Ezekiel 2

The Lord does not call us to any task without providing the power to accomplish it, even if it does not look successful to us. The Lord prepared Ezekiel for how his audience—rebellious, impudent, stubborn and transgressors—would respond. Yet God said, "Do not be afraid of them" (verse 6).

We sometimes fear people who are aggressively disobedient to God. But don't fear! Ask God for the confidence to trust him.

PRAYING SCRIPTURE
Ezekiel 3

Many Christians envision themselves as the "watchman on the wall," warning everyone around them about the dangers in their present time. The fact is, Christians have a watchman, the Holy Spirit, who is actively applying the Word of God to our hearts and minds so we might avoid the wickedness about which Ezekiel warned.

Ask the Holy Spirit to warn you away from the evils facing you today.

[a] *1* The Hebrew phrase *ben adam* means *human being.* The phrase *son of man* is retained as a form of address here and throughout Ezekiel because of its possible association with "Son of Man" in the New Testament.

to them. Say to them, 'This is what the Sovereign LORD says,' whether
they listen or fail to listen."
12Then the Spirit lifted me up, and I heard behind me a loud rum-
bling sound as the glory of the LORD rose from the place where it was
standing.[a] 13It was the sound of the wings of the living creatures brush-
ing against each other and the sound of the wheels beside them, a loud
rumbling sound. 14The Spirit then lifted me up and took me away, and
I went in bitterness and in the anger of my spirit, with the strong hand
of the LORD on me. 15I came to the exiles who lived at Tel Aviv near the
Kebar River. And there, where they were living, I sat among them for
seven days — deeply distressed.

EZEKIEL'S TASK AS WATCHMAN

16At the end of seven days the word of the LORD came to me: 17"Son
of man, I have made you a watchman for the people of Israel; so hear
the word I speak and give them warning from me. 18When I say to
a wicked person, 'You will surely die,' and you do not warn them or
speak out to dissuade them from their evil ways in order to save their
life, that wicked person will die for[b] their sin, and I will hold you ac-
countable for their blood. 19But if you do warn the wicked person and
they do not turn from their wickedness or from their evil ways, they
will die for their sin; but you will have saved yourself.
20"Again, when a righteous person turns from their righteousness
and does evil, and I put a stumbling block before them, they will die.
Since you did not warn them, they will die for their sin. The righteous
things that person did will not be remembered, and I will hold you
accountable for their blood. 21But if you do warn the righteous person
not to sin and they do not sin, they will surely live because they took
warning, and you will have saved yourself."
22The hand of the LORD was on me there, and he said to me, "Get up
and go out to the plain, and there I will speak to you." 23So I got up and
went out to the plain. And the glory of the LORD was standing there,
like the glory I had seen by the Kebar River, and I fell facedown.
24Then the Spirit came into me and raised me to my feet. He spoke
to me and said: "Go, shut yourself inside your house. 25And you, son of
man, they will tie with ropes; you will be bound so that you cannot go
out among the people. 26I will make your tongue stick to the roof of
your mouth so that you will be silent and unable to rebuke them, for
they are a rebellious people. 27But when I speak to you, I will open your
mouth and you shall say to them, 'This is what the Sovereign LORD
says.' Whoever will listen let them listen, and whoever will refuse let
them refuse; for they are a rebellious people.

SIEGE OF JERUSALEM SYMBOLIZED

4 "Now, son of man, take a block of clay, put it in front of you and
draw the city of Jerusalem on it. 2Then lay siege to it: Erect siege
works against it, build a ramp up to it, set up camps against it and put
battering rams around it. 3Then take an iron pan, place it as an iron wall
between you and the city and turn your face toward it. It will be under
siege, and you shall besiege it. This will be a sign to the people of Israel.

PRAYING SCRIPTURE

Ezekiel 4

God did not allow Ezekiel merely to prophesy verbally to the people. Ezekiel became a physical manifestation of the judgment God would bring. Ezekiel built "siege works" against Jerusalem (verse 2). Then he had to lay on his left and then right side to portray the long years they had spent in sin (see verses 3–8).

In ministering to others, God might require uncomfortable things of us. Humble yourself to the full obedience God requires of his messengers.

---

[a] 12 Probable reading of the original Hebrew text; Masoretic Text *sound — may the glory of the LORD be praised from his place* [b] 18 Or *in*; also in verses 19 and 20

4“Then lie on your left side and put the sin of the people of Israel upon yourself.[a] You are to bear their sin for the number of days you lie on your side. 5I have assigned you the same number of days as the years of their sin. So for 390 days you will bear the sin of the people of Israel.

6“After you have finished this, lie down again, this time on your right side, and bear the sin of the people of Judah. I have assigned you 40 days, a day for each year. 7Turn your face toward the siege of Jerusalem and with bared arm prophesy against her. 8I will tie you up with ropes so that you cannot turn from one side to the other until you have finished the days of your siege.

9“Take wheat and barley, beans and lentils, millet and spelt; put them in a storage jar and use them to make bread for yourself. You are to eat it during the 390 days you lie on your side. 10Weigh out twenty shekels[b] of food to eat each day and eat it at set times. 11Also measure out a sixth of a hin[c] of water and drink it at set times. 12Eat the food as you would a loaf of barley bread; bake it in the sight of the people, using human excrement for fuel.” 13The LORD said, “In this way the people of Israel will eat defiled food among the nations where I will drive them.”

14Then I said, “Not so, Sovereign LORD! I have never defiled myself. From my youth until now I have never eaten anything found dead or torn by wild animals. No impure meat has ever entered my mouth.”

15“Very well,” he said, “I will let you bake your bread over cow dung instead of human excrement.”

16He then said to me: “Son of man, I am about to cut off the food supply in Jerusalem. The people will eat rationed food in anxiety and drink rationed water in despair, 17for food and water will be scarce. They will be appalled at the sight of each other and will waste away because of[d] their sin.

GOD’S RAZOR OF JUDGMENT

5 “Now, son of man, take a sharp sword and use it as a barber’s razor to shave your head and your beard. Then take a set of scales and divide up the hair. 2When the days of your siege come to an end, burn a third of the hair inside the city. Take a third and strike it with the sword all around the city. And scatter a third to the wind. For I will pursue them with drawn sword. 3But take a few hairs and tuck them away in the folds of your garment. 4Again, take a few of these and throw them into the fire and burn them up. A fire will spread from there to all Israel.

5“This is what the Sovereign LORD says: This is Jerusalem, which I have set in the center of the nations, with countries all around her. 6Yet in her wickedness she has rebelled against my laws and decrees more than the nations and countries around her. She has rejected my laws and has not followed my decrees.

7“Therefore this is what the Sovereign LORD says: You have been more unruly than the nations around you and have not followed my decrees or kept my laws. You have not even[e] conformed to the standards of the nations around you.

PRAYING SCRIPTURE

Ezekiel 5

Israel’s place in the middle of the nations did not allow it to yield to their influence. God placed Israel as a light to the nations, but it regularly extinguished the light by embracing the sin of the surrounding peoples. Israel’s knowledge of the light made its judgment that much harsher.

Shining God’s light—his Word, will and ways—is his command. Pray for the boldness to let your light shine.

[a] 4 Or *upon your side* [b] 10 That is, about 8 ounces or about 230 grams [c] 11 That is, about 2/3 quart or about 0.6 liter [d] 17 Or *away in* [e] 7 Most Hebrew manuscripts; some Hebrew manuscripts and Syriac *You have*

8“Therefore this is what the Sovereign LORD says: I myself am against
you, Jerusalem, and I will inflict punishment on you in the sight of the
nations. 9Because of all your detestable idols, I will do to you what I
have never done before and will never do again. 10Therefore in your
midst parents will eat their children, and children will eat their parents.
I will inflict punishment on you and will scatter all your survivors to
the winds. 11Therefore as surely as I live, declares the Sovereign LORD,
because you have defiled my sanctuary with all your vile images and
detestable practices, I myself will shave you; I will not look on you with
pity or spare you. 12A third of your people will die of the plague or perish
by famine inside you; a third will fall by the sword outside your walls;
and a third I will scatter to the winds and pursue with drawn sword.

13“Then my anger will cease and my wrath against them will subside,
and I will be avenged. And when I have spent my wrath on them, they
will know that I the LORD have spoken in my zeal.

14“I will make you a ruin and a reproach among the nations around
you, in the sight of all who pass by. 15You will be a reproach and a taunt,
a warning and an object of horror to the nations around you when I
inflict punishment on you in anger and in wrath and with stinging
rebuke. I the LORD have spoken. 16When I shoot at you with my deadly
and destructive arrows of famine, I will shoot to destroy you. I will
bring more and more famine upon you and cut off your supply of food.
17I will send famine and wild beasts against you, and they will leave
you childless. Plague and bloodshed will sweep through you, and I will
bring the sword against you. I the LORD have spoken.”

DOOM FOR THE MOUNTAINS OF ISRAEL

6 The word of the LORD came to me: 2“Son of man, set your face
against the mountains of Israel; prophesy against them 3and say:
‘You mountains of Israel, hear the word of the Sovereign LORD. This
is what the Sovereign LORD says to the mountains and hills, to the ra-
vines and valleys: I am about to bring a sword against you, and I will
destroy your high places. 4Your altars will be demolished and your in-
cense altars will be smashed; and I will slay your people in front of
your idols. 5I will lay the dead bodies of the Israelites in front of their
idols, and I will scatter your bones around your altars. 6Wherever you
live, the towns will be laid waste and the high places demolished, so
that your altars will be laid waste and devastated, your idols smashed
and ruined, your incense altars broken down, and what you have made
wiped out. 7Your people will fall slain among you, and you will know
that I am the LORD.

8“ ‘But I will spare some, for some of you will escape the sword when
you are scattered among the lands and nations. 9Then in the nations
where they have been carried captive, those who escape will remember
me—how I have been grieved by their adulterous hearts, which have
turned away from me, and by their eyes, which have lusted after their
idols. They will loathe themselves for the evil they have done and for
all their detestable practices. 10And they will know that I am the LORD;
I did not threaten in vain to bring this calamity on them.

11“ ‘This is what the Sovereign LORD says: Strike your hands together
and stamp your feet and cry out “Alas!” because of all the wicked and
detestable practices of the people of Israel, for they will fall by the
sword, famine and plague. 12One who is far away will die of the plague,
and one who is near will fall by the sword, and anyone who survives

PRAYING SCRIPTURE

Ezekiel 6

The “high places” the prophets regularly condemned were the places where altars and temples to false gods were often constructed (see verse 3). Whether on high hills or mountaintops, under spreading trees or thick oaks or anywhere else, God condemned the entire incense-burning, idolatrous enterprise (see verses 13–14).

The Lord’s warnings to his people against idolatry are warnings against present deception and future judgment. Ask God to protect your heart and mind from idols.

and is spared will die of famine. So will I pour out my wrath on them.
13And they will know that I am the LORD, when their people lie slain among their idols around their altars, on every high hill and on all the mountaintops, under every spreading tree and every leafy oak — places where they offered fragrant incense to all their idols.
14And I will stretch out my hand against them and make the land a desolate waste from the desert to Diblah[a] — wherever they live. Then they will know that I am the LORD.' "

PRAYING SCRIPTURE

Ezekiel 7

It is difficult to read the repeated descriptions of the many nations' sins without seeing the same sins in almost every culture in every age. Humanity is beset continually by all manner of sinning against God. We routinely break his laws and express no humility or sorrow over our sin nor repentance to set things right.

No sin is new or unique. Pray for the repentance of the nations that God might be glorified.

THE END HAS COME

7 The word of the LORD came to me: 2"Son of man, this is what the Sovereign LORD says to the land of Israel:

" 'The end! The end has come
upon the four corners of the land!
3The end is now upon you,
and I will unleash my anger against you.
I will judge you according to your conduct
and repay you for all your detestable practices.
4I will not look on you with pity;
I will not spare you.
I will surely repay you for your conduct
and for the detestable practices among you.
" 'Then you will know that I am the LORD.'

5"This is what the Sovereign LORD says:

" 'Disaster! Unheard-of[b] disaster!
See, it comes!
6The end has come!
The end has come!
It has roused itself against you.
See, it comes!
7Doom has come upon you,
upon you who dwell in the land.
The time has come! The day is near!
There is panic, not joy, on the mountains.
8I am about to pour out my wrath on you
and spend my anger against you.
I will judge you according to your conduct
and repay you for all your detestable practices.
9I will not look on you with pity;
I will not spare you.
I will repay you for your conduct
and for the detestable practices among you.
" 'Then you will know that it is I the LORD who strikes you.

10" 'See, the day!
See, it comes!
Doom has burst forth,
the rod has budded,
arrogance has blossomed!

[a] 14 Most Hebrew manuscripts; a few Hebrew manuscripts *Riblah* [b] 5 Most Hebrew manuscripts; some Hebrew manuscripts and Syriac *Disaster after*

11 Violence has arisen,[a]
a rod to punish the wicked.
None of the people will be left,
none of that crowd —
none of their wealth,
nothing of value.
12 The time has come!
The day has arrived!
Let not the buyer rejoice
nor the seller grieve,
for my wrath is on the whole crowd.
13 The seller will not recover
the property that was sold —
as long as both buyer and seller live.
For the vision concerning the whole crowd
will not be reversed.
Because of their sins, not one of them
will preserve their life.

14 " 'They have blown the trumpet,
they have made all things ready,
but no one will go into battle,
for my wrath is on the whole crowd.
15 Outside is the sword;
inside are plague and famine.
Those in the country
will die by the sword;
those in the city
will be devoured by famine and plague.
16 The fugitives who escape
will flee to the mountains.
Like doves of the valleys,
they will all moan,
each for their own sins.
17 Every hand will go limp;
every leg will be wet with urine.
18 They will put on sackcloth
and be clothed with terror.
Every face will be covered with shame,
and every head will be shaved.

19 " 'They will throw their silver into the streets,
and their gold will be treated as a thing unclean.
Their silver and gold
will not be able to deliver them
in the day of the LORD's wrath.
It will not satisfy their hunger
or fill their stomachs,
for it has caused them to stumble into sin.
20 They took pride in their beautiful jewelry
and used it to make their detestable idols.
They made it into vile images;
therefore I will make it a thing unclean for them.

[a] 11 Or *The violent one has become*

21 I will give their wealth as plunder to foreigners
and as loot to the wicked of the earth,
who will defile it.
22 I will turn my face away from the people,
and robbers will desecrate the place I treasure.
They will enter it
and will defile it.

23 " 'Prepare chains!
For the land is full of bloodshed,
and the city is full of violence.
24 I will bring the most wicked of nations
to take possession of their houses.
I will put an end to the pride of the mighty,
and their sanctuaries will be desecrated.
25 When terror comes,
they will seek peace in vain.
26 Calamity upon calamity will come,
and rumor upon rumor.
They will go searching for a vision from the prophet,
priestly instruction in the law will cease,
the counsel of the elders will come to an end.
27 The king will mourn,
the prince will be clothed with despair,
and the hands of the people of the land will tremble.
I will deal with them according to their conduct,
and by their own standards I will judge them.

" 'Then they will know that I am the LORD.' "

PRAYING SCRIPTURE

Ezekiel 8

Idolatry bled over into people's homes where idols were being displayed in shrines (see verse 12). By moving inside to worship, the people thought they were hiding their idolatry from Yahweh—but he saw. Even worse, the prophet was shown women who were weeping for a false god, Tammuz (see verse 14).

The depths to which our hearts can sink into idolatry should scare us. Keep your eyes on the Lord God of heaven, and worship him alone.

IDOLATRY IN THE TEMPLE

8 In the sixth year, in the sixth month on the fifth day, while I was
sitting in my house and the elders of Judah were sitting before
me, the hand of the Sovereign LORD came on me there. 2 I looked, and
I saw a figure like that of a man.[a] From what appeared to be his waist
down he was like fire, and from there up his appearance was as bright
as glowing metal. 3 He stretched out what looked like a hand and took
me by the hair of my head. The Spirit lifted me up between earth and
heaven and in visions of God he took me to Jerusalem, to the entrance
of the north gate of the inner court, where the idol that provokes to
jealousy stood. 4 And there before me was the glory of the God of Israel,
as in the vision I had seen in the plain.
5 Then he said to me, "Son of man, look toward the north." So I
looked, and in the entrance north of the gate of the altar I saw this
idol of jealousy.
6 And he said to me, "Son of man, do you see what they are doing—
the utterly detestable things the Israelites are doing here, things that
will drive me far from my sanctuary? But you will see things that are
even more detestable."
7 Then he brought me to the entrance to the court. I looked, and I saw
a hole in the wall. 8 He said to me, "Son of man, now dig into the wall."
So I dug into the wall and saw a doorway there.
9 And he said to me, "Go in and see the wicked and detestable things

[a] 2 Or *saw a fiery figure*

they are doing here." 10So I went in and looked, and I saw portrayed all over the walls all kinds of crawling things and unclean animals and all the idols of Israel. 11In front of them stood seventy elders of Israel, and Jaazaniah son of Shaphan was standing among them. Each had a censer in his hand, and a fragrant cloud of incense was rising.

12He said to me, "Son of man, have you seen what the elders of Israel are doing in the darkness, each at the shrine of his own idol? They say, 'The LORD does not see us; the LORD has forsaken the land.'" 13Again, he said, "You will see them doing things that are even more detestable."

14Then he brought me to the entrance of the north gate of the house of the LORD, and I saw women sitting there, mourning the god Tammuz. 15He said to me, "Do you see this, son of man? You will see things that are even more detestable than this."

16He then brought me into the inner court of the house of the LORD, and there at the entrance to the temple, between the portico and the altar, were about twenty-five men. With their backs toward the temple of the LORD and their faces toward the east, they were bowing down to the sun in the east.

17He said to me, "Have you seen this, son of man? Is it a trivial matter for the people of Judah to do the detestable things they are doing here? Must they also fill the land with violence and continually arouse my anger? Look at them putting the branch to their nose! 18Therefore I will deal with them in anger; I will not look on them with pity or spare them. Although they shout in my ears, I will not listen to them."

JUDGMENT ON THE IDOLATERS

9 Then I heard him call out in a loud voice, "Bring near those who are appointed to execute judgment on the city, each with a weapon in his hand." 2And I saw six men coming from the direction of the upper gate, which faces north, each with a deadly weapon in his hand. With them was a man clothed in linen who had a writing kit at his side. They came in and stood beside the bronze altar.

3Now the glory of the God of Israel went up from above the cherubim, where it had been, and moved to the threshold of the temple. Then the LORD called to the man clothed in linen who had the writing kit at his side 4and said to him, "Go throughout the city of Jerusalem and put a mark on the foreheads of those who grieve and lament over all the detestable things that are done in it."

5As I listened, he said to the others, "Follow him through the city and kill, without showing pity or compassion. 6Slaughter the old men, the young men and women, the mothers and children, but do not touch anyone who has the mark. Begin at my sanctuary." So they began with the old men who were in front of the temple.

7Then he said to them, "Defile the temple and fill the courts with the slain. Go!" So they went out and began killing throughout the city. 8While they were killing and I was left alone, I fell facedown, crying out, "Alas, Sovereign LORD! Are you going to destroy the entire remnant of Israel in this outpouring of your wrath on Jerusalem?"

9He answered me, "The sin of the people of Israel and Judah is exceedingly great; the land is full of bloodshed and the city is full of injustice. They say, 'The LORD has forsaken the land; the LORD does not see.' 10So I will not look on them with pity or spare them, but I will bring down on their own heads what they have done."

PRAYING SCRIPTURE

Ezekiel 9

We should always remember that we live under the watchful eye of our heavenly Father. In this gruesome passage, everyone in the city was killed, young and old, unless they were already grieved over the detestable things done in the city. Ezekiel was grieved to the point of asking whether God intended to destroy everyone!

Don't hesitate to express your emotions to God. Talk to him honestly for he already knows what you think.

PRAYING SCRIPTURE

Ezekiel 10

This chapter contains one of the most chilling passages in Scripture. The judgment of God reached its apex when his glory—that which had accompanied the temple's dedication—was taken away from the temple into heaven. As a result of his people's sin, God left his house barren.

Sin separates from God. It always has and always will. Ask God daily, hourly if needed, to help you avoid sin.

11 Then the man in linen with the writing kit at his side brought back
word, saying, "I have done as you commanded."

GOD'S GLORY DEPARTS FROM THE TEMPLE

10 I looked, and I saw the likeness of a throne of lapis lazuli above
the vault that was over the heads of the cherubim. 2 The LORD
said to the man clothed in linen, "Go in among the wheels beneath the
cherubim. Fill your hands with burning coals from among the cheru-
bim and scatter them over the city." And as I watched, he went in.
3 Now the cherubim were standing on the south side of the temple
when the man went in, and a cloud filled the inner court. 4 Then the
glory of the LORD rose from above the cherubim and moved to the
threshold of the temple. The cloud filled the temple, and the court was
full of the radiance of the glory of the LORD. 5 The sound of the wings
of the cherubim could be heard as far away as the outer court, like the
voice of God Almighty[a] when he speaks.
6 When the LORD commanded the man in linen, "Take fire from
among the wheels, from among the cherubim," the man went in and
stood beside a wheel. 7 Then one of the cherubim reached out his hand
to the fire that was among them. He took up some of it and put it into
the hands of the man in linen, who took it and went out. 8 (Under the
wings of the cherubim could be seen what looked like human hands.)
9 I looked, and I saw beside the cherubim four wheels, one beside
each of the cherubim; the wheels sparkled like topaz. 10 As for their
appearance, the four of them looked alike; each was like a wheel inter-
secting a wheel. 11 As they moved, they would go in any one of the four
directions the cherubim faced; the wheels did not turn about[b] as the
cherubim went. The cherubim went in whatever direction the head
faced, without turning as they went. 12 Their entire bodies, including
their backs, their hands and their wings, were completely full of eyes,
as were their four wheels. 13 I heard the wheels being called "the whirl-
ing wheels." 14 Each of the cherubim had four faces: One face was that
of a cherub, the second the face of a human being, the third the face of
a lion, and the fourth the face of an eagle.
15 Then the cherubim rose upward. These were the living creatures I
had seen by the Kebar River. 16 When the cherubim moved, the wheels
beside them moved; and when the cherubim spread their wings to
rise from the ground, the wheels did not leave their side. 17 When the
cherubim stood still, they also stood still; and when the cherubim rose,
they rose with them, because the spirit of the living creatures was in
them.
18 Then the glory of the LORD departed from over the threshold of
the temple and stopped above the cherubim. 19 While I watched, the
cherubim spread their wings and rose from the ground, and as they
went, the wheels went with them. They stopped at the entrance of the
east gate of the LORD's house, and the glory of the God of Israel was
above them.
20 These were the living creatures I had seen beneath the God of Is-
rael by the Kebar River, and I realized that they were cherubim. 21 Each
had four faces and four wings, and under their wings was what looked
like human hands. 22 Their faces had the same appearance as those I
had seen by the Kebar River. Each one went straight ahead.

[a] 5 Hebrew *El-Shaddai* [b] 11 Or *aside*

GOD'S SURE JUDGMENT ON JERUSALEM

11 Then the Spirit lifted me up and brought me to the gate of the
house of the LORD that faces east. There at the entrance of the
gate were twenty-five men, and I saw among them Jaazaniah son of
Azzur and Pelatiah son of Benaiah, leaders of the people. 2The LORD
said to me, "Son of man, these are the men who are plotting evil and
giving wicked advice in this city. 3They say, 'Haven't our houses been
recently rebuilt? This city is a pot, and we are the meat in it.' 4Therefore
prophesy against them; prophesy, son of man."
5Then the Spirit of the LORD came on me, and he told me to say:
"This is what the LORD says: That is what you are saying, you leaders in
Israel, but I know what is going through your mind. 6You have killed
many people in this city and filled its streets with the dead.
7"Therefore this is what the Sovereign LORD says: The bodies you
have thrown there are the meat and this city is the pot, but I will drive
you out of it. 8You fear the sword, and the sword is what I will bring
against you, declares the Sovereign LORD. 9I will drive you out of the
city and deliver you into the hands of foreigners and inflict punish-
ment on you. 10You will fall by the sword, and I will execute judgment
on you at the borders of Israel. Then you will know that I am the LORD.
11This city will not be a pot for you, nor will you be the meat in it; I will
execute judgment on you at the borders of Israel. 12And you will know
that I am the LORD, for you have not followed my decrees or kept my
laws but have conformed to the standards of the nations around you."
13Now as I was prophesying, Pelatiah son of Benaiah died. Then I fell
facedown and cried out in a loud voice, "Alas, Sovereign LORD! Will you
completely destroy the remnant of Israel?"

THE PROMISE OF ISRAEL'S RETURN

14The word of the LORD came to me: 15"Son of man, the people of Jeru-
salem have said of your fellow exiles and all the other Israelites, 'They
are far away from the LORD; this land was given to us as our possession.'
16"Therefore say: 'This is what the Sovereign LORD says: Although I
sent them far away among the nations and scattered them among the
countries, yet for a little while I have been a sanctuary for them in the
countries where they have gone.'
17"Therefore say: 'This is what the Sovereign LORD says: I will gather
you from the nations and bring you back from the countries where you
have been scattered, and I will give you back the land of Israel again.'
18"They will return to it and remove all its vile images and detest-
able idols. 19I will give them an undivided heart and put a new spirit
in them; I will remove from them their heart of stone and give them
a heart of flesh. 20Then they will follow my decrees and be careful to
keep my laws. They will be my people, and I will be their God. 21But as
for those whose hearts are devoted to their vile images and detestable
idols, I will bring down on their own heads what they have done, de-
clares the Sovereign LORD."
22Then the cherubim, with the wheels beside them, spread their
wings, and the glory of the God of Israel was above them. 23The glory
of the LORD went up from within the city and stopped above the moun-
tain east of it. 24The Spirit lifted me up and brought me to the exiles in
Babylonia[a] in the vision given by the Spirit of God.

PRAYING SCRIPTURE

Ezekiel 11

Virtually everyone at some time in life depends on the counsel of others. We grow by listening to counselors and often pass that knowledge along to others. Israel's counselors had grown so wicked that God blamed them for those killed who filled the streets (see verses 2–6).

We need to make sure our counselors are good. Are they in the Word? Led by the Spirit? Do they pray? Ask God to give you counselors who know him.

[a] 24 Or *Chaldea*

Then the vision I had seen went up from me, 25and I told the exiles everything the LORD had shown me.

THE EXILE SYMBOLIZED

12 The word of the LORD came to me: 2"Son of man, you are living among a rebellious people. They have eyes to see but do not see and ears to hear but do not hear, for they are a rebellious people.

3"Therefore, son of man, pack your belongings for exile and in the daytime, as they watch, set out and go from where you are to another place. Perhaps they will understand, though they are a rebellious people. 4During the daytime, while they watch, bring out your belongings packed for exile. Then in the evening, while they are watching, go out like those who go into exile. 5While they watch, dig through the wall and take your belongings out through it. 6Put them on your shoulder as they are watching and carry them out at dusk. Cover your face so that you cannot see the land, for I have made you a sign to the Israelites."

7So I did as I was commanded. During the day I brought out my things packed for exile. Then in the evening I dug through the wall with my hands. I took my belongings out at dusk, carrying them on my shoulders while they watched.

8In the morning the word of the LORD came to me: 9"Son of man, did not the Israelites, that rebellious people, ask you, 'What are you doing?'

10"Say to them, 'This is what the Sovereign LORD says: This prophecy concerns the prince in Jerusalem and all the Israelites who are there.' 11Say to them, 'I am a sign to you.'

"As I have done, so it will be done to them. They will go into exile as captives.

12"The prince among them will put his things on his shoulder at dusk and leave, and a hole will be dug in the wall for him to go through. He will cover his face so that he cannot see the land. 13I will spread my net for him, and he will be caught in my snare; I will bring him to Babylonia, the land of the Chaldeans, but he will not see it, and there he will die. 14I will scatter to the winds all those around him — his staff and all his troops — and I will pursue them with drawn sword.

15"They will know that I am the LORD, when I disperse them among the nations and scatter them through the countries. 16But I will spare a few of them from the sword, famine and plague, so that in the nations where they go they may acknowledge all their detestable practices. Then they will know that I am the LORD."

17The word of the LORD came to me: 18"Son of man, tremble as you eat your food, and shudder in fear as you drink your water. 19Say to the people of the land: 'This is what the Sovereign LORD says about those living in Jerusalem and in the land of Israel: They will eat their food in anxiety and drink their water in despair, for their land will be stripped of everything in it because of the violence of all who live there. 20The inhabited towns will be laid waste and the land will be desolate. Then you will know that I am the LORD.'"

THERE WILL BE NO DELAY

21The word of the LORD came to me: 22"Son of man, what is this proverb you have in the land of Israel: 'The days go by and every vision comes to nothing'? 23Say to them, 'This is what the Sovereign LORD says: I am going to put an end to this proverb, and they will no longer quote

PRAYING SCRIPTURE

Ezekiel 12

Like Jeremiah, Ezekiel was commanded by God to perform actions that served as visual aids to God's pronouncements. By digging through the wall, then carrying his belongings through it, he portrayed their coming exile when they would be removed from the land.

God's judgment on sin was certain, but he went to extraordinary lengths to warn his people how to escape it. Never doubt God's desire for us to be holy.

it in Israel.' Say to them, 'The days are near when every vision will be
fulfilled. 24For there will be no more false visions or flattering divina-
tions among the people of Israel. 25But I the LORD will speak what I will,
and it shall be fulfilled without delay. For in your days, you rebellious
people, I will fulfill whatever I say, declares the Sovereign LORD.'"
26The word of the LORD came to me: 27"Son of man, the Israelites are
saying, 'The vision he sees is for many years from now, and he proph-
esies about the distant future.'
28"Therefore say to them, 'This is what the Sovereign LORD says:
None of my words will be delayed any longer; whatever I say will be
fulfilled, declares the Sovereign LORD.'"

FALSE PROPHETS CONDEMNED

13 The word of the LORD came to me: 2"Son of man, prophesy
against the prophets of Israel who are now prophesying. Say to
those who prophesy out of their own imagination: 'Hear the word of
the LORD! 3This is what the Sovereign LORD says: Woe to the foolish[a]
prophets who follow their own spirit and have seen nothing! 4Your
prophets, Israel, are like jackals among ruins. 5You have not gone up to
the breaches in the wall to repair it for the people of Israel so that it will
stand firm in the battle on the day of the LORD. 6Their visions are false
and their divinations a lie. Even though the LORD has not sent them,
they say, "The LORD declares," and expect him to fulfill their words.
7Have you not seen false visions and uttered lying divinations when
you say, "The LORD declares," though I have not spoken?
8"'Therefore this is what the Sovereign LORD says: Because of your
false words and lying visions, I am against you, declares the Sovereign
LORD. 9My hand will be against the prophets who see false visions and
utter lying divinations. They will not belong to the council of my peo-
ple or be listed in the records of Israel, nor will they enter the land of
Israel. Then you will know that I am the Sovereign LORD.
10"'Because they lead my people astray, saying, "Peace," when there
is no peace, and because, when a flimsy wall is built, they cover it with
whitewash, 11therefore tell those who cover it with whitewash that it
is going to fall. Rain will come in torrents, and I will send hailstones
hurtling down, and violent winds will burst forth. 12When the wall col-
lapses, will people not ask you, "Where is the whitewash you covered
it with?"
13"'Therefore this is what the Sovereign LORD says: In my wrath I will
unleash a violent wind, and in my anger hailstones and torrents of rain
will fall with destructive fury. 14I will tear down the wall you have cov-
ered with whitewash and will level it to the ground so that its founda-
tion will be laid bare. When it[b] falls, you will be destroyed in it; and you
will know that I am the LORD. 15So I will pour out my wrath against the
wall and against those who covered it with whitewash. I will say to you,
"The wall is gone and so are those who whitewashed it, 16those proph-
ets of Israel who prophesied to Jerusalem and saw visions of peace for
her when there was no peace, declares the Sovereign LORD."'
17"Now, son of man, set your face against the daughters of your peo-
ple who prophesy out of their own imagination. Prophesy against
them 18and say, 'This is what the Sovereign LORD says: Woe to the
women who sew magic charms on all their wrists and make veils of

PRAYING SCRIPTURE

Ezekiel 13

When Israel multiplied false prophets and divinations, it discouraged and disheartened those who trusted in the Lord. The foolishness of her prophets was a curse, not a blessing. God called them "foolish prophets who follow their own spirit and have seen nothing!" (verse 3).

Following our own spirit is always a temptation; it feels normal. Pray for the guidance of the Holy Spirit rather than that of your own spirit, and know God's truth.

[a] 3 Or *wicked* [b] 14 Or *the city*

various lengths for their heads in order to ensnare people. Will you
ensnare the lives of my people but preserve your own? 19You have pro-
faned me among my people for a few handfuls of barley and scraps of
bread. By lying to my people, who listen to lies, you have killed those
who should not have died and have spared those who should not live.
20" 'Therefore this is what the Sovereign LORD says: I am against your
magic charms with which you ensnare people like birds and I will tear
them from your arms; I will set free the people that you ensnare like
birds. 21I will tear off your veils and save my people from your hands,
and they will no longer fall prey to your power. Then you will know
that I am the LORD. 22Because you disheartened the righteous with
your lies, when I had brought them no grief, and because you encour-
aged the wicked not to turn from their evil ways and so save their lives,
23therefore you will no longer see false visions or practice divination.
I will save my people from your hands. And then you will know that I
am the LORD.' "

IDOLATERS CONDEMNED

14 Some of the elders of Israel came to me and sat down in front
of me. 2Then the word of the LORD came to me: 3"Son of man,
these men have set up idols in their hearts and put wicked stumbling
blocks before their faces. Should I let them inquire of me at all? 4There-
fore speak to them and tell them, 'This is what the Sovereign LORD
says: When any of the Israelites set up idols in their hearts and put a
wicked stumbling block before their faces and then go to a prophet, I
the LORD will answer them myself in keeping with their great idolatry.
5I will do this to recapture the hearts of the people of Israel, who have
all deserted me for their idols.'
6"Therefore say to the people of Israel, 'This is what the Sovereign
LORD says: Repent! Turn from your idols and renounce all your detest-
able practices!
7" 'When any of the Israelites or any foreigner residing in Israel sep-
arate themselves from me and set up idols in their hearts and put a
wicked stumbling block before their faces and then go to a prophet to
inquire of me, I the LORD will answer them myself. 8I will set my face
against them and make them an example and a byword. I will remove
them from my people. Then you will know that I am the LORD.
9" 'And if the prophet is enticed to utter a prophecy, I the LORD have
enticed that prophet, and I will stretch out my hand against him and
destroy him from among my people Israel. 10They will bear their
guilt — the prophet will be as guilty as the one who consults him.
11Then the people of Israel will no longer stray from me, nor will they
defile themselves anymore with all their sins. They will be my people,
and I will be their God, declares the Sovereign LORD.' "

JERUSALEM'S JUDGMENT INESCAPABLE

12The word of the LORD came to me: 13"Son of man, if a country sins
against me by being unfaithful and I stretch out my hand against it to
cut off its food supply and send famine upon it and kill its people and
their animals, 14even if these three men — Noah, Daniel[a] and Job —
were in it, they could save only themselves by their righteousness, de-
clares the Sovereign LORD.

[a] *14* Or *Danel*, a man of renown in ancient literature; also in verse 20

PRAYING SCRIPTURE

Ezekiel 14

As we read passages having to do with God's judgment, his wrath poured out on nations, it can be easy to conclude (wrongly) that God is anxious to judge. But he reminds Ezekiel it is "being unfaithful" in a land that brings judgment (see verse 13). God's desire is mercy.

Think about the patience God shows time and time again. If you are harboring idols in your heart (see verse 3), repent and turn back to the Lord.

15“Or if I send wild beasts through that country and they leave it
childless and it becomes desolate so that no one can pass through it
because of the beasts, 16as surely as I live, declares the Sovereign LORD,
even if these three men were in it, they could not save their own sons or
daughters. They alone would be saved, but the land would be desolate.
17“Or if I bring a sword against that country and say, ‘Let the sword
pass throughout the land,’ and I kill its people and their animals, 18as
surely as I live, declares the Sovereign LORD, even if these three men
were in it, they could not save their own sons or daughters. They alone
would be saved.
19“Or if I send a plague into that land and pour out my wrath on it
through bloodshed, killing its people and their animals, 20as surely as
I live, declares the Sovereign LORD, even if Noah, Daniel and Job were
in it, they could save neither son nor daughter. They would save only
themselves by their righteousness.
21“For this is what the Sovereign LORD says: How much worse will
it be when I send against Jerusalem my four dreadful judgments —
sword and famine and wild beasts and plague — to kill its men and
their animals! 22Yet there will be some survivors — sons and daughters
who will be brought out of it. They will come to you, and when you see
their conduct and their actions, you will be consoled regarding the di-
saster I have brought on Jerusalem — every disaster I have brought on
it. 23You will be consoled when you see their conduct and their actions,
for you will know that I have done nothing in it without cause, declares
the Sovereign LORD.”

JERUSALEM AS A USELESS VINE

15 The word of the LORD came to me: 2“Son of man, how is the
wood of a vine different from that of a branch from any of
the trees in the forest? 3Is wood ever taken from it to make anything
useful? Do they make pegs from it to hang things on? 4And after it is
thrown on the fire as fuel and the fire burns both ends and chars the
middle, is it then useful for anything? 5If it was not useful for anything
when it was whole, how much less can it be made into something use-
ful when the fire has burned it and it is charred?
6“Therefore this is what the Sovereign LORD says: As I have given the
wood of the vine among the trees of the forest as fuel for the fire, so
will I treat the people living in Jerusalem. 7I will set my face against
them. Although they have come out of the fire, the fire will yet con-
sume them. And when I set my face against them, you will know that
I am the LORD. 8I will make the land desolate because they have been
unfaithful, declares the Sovereign LORD.”

JERUSALEM AS AN ADULTEROUS WIFE

16 The word of the LORD came to me: 2“Son of man, confront Jeru-
salem with her detestable practices 3and say, ‘This is what the
Sovereign LORD says to Jerusalem: Your ancestry and birth were in the
land of the Canaanites; your father was an Amorite and your mother a
Hittite. 4On the day you were born your cord was not cut, nor were you
washed with water to make you clean, nor were you rubbed with salt or
wrapped in cloths. 5No one looked on you with pity or had compassion
enough to do any of these things for you. Rather, you were thrown out
into the open field, for on the day you were born you were despised.
6“ ‘Then I passed by and saw you kicking about in your blood, and as

PRAYING SCRIPTURE

Ezekiel 15

It is erroneous to think of judgment as geographically distant from us or well into the future, a cosmic end to this world. But judgment was usually temporal; it happened to the ones who were warned about it. The Lord compared his people to a woody grapevine from which nothing could be built; it was good only for burning.

Sin’s consequences can be immediate, so pray for the wisdom to live righteously.

PRAYING SCRIPTURE

Ezekiel 16

The Lord’s love for his people is deep and all-encompassing. Jerusalem is compared to a child born but neglected—unwashed, unwrapped, uncared for, cast aside. But God said, “I spread the corner of my garment over you and covered your naked body . . . bathed you with water . . . and put ointments on you” (verses 8–9). God loved Jerusalem despite who she was, not because of it.

Rejoice in the magnificent love of God revealed in Jesus Christ and poured out on the world.

you lay there in your blood I said to you, "Live!"[a] 7I made you grow like a plant of the field. You grew and developed and entered puberty. Your breasts had formed and your hair had grown, yet you were stark naked.

8"'Later I passed by, and when I looked at you and saw that you were old enough for love, I spread the corner of my garment over you and covered your naked body. I gave you my solemn oath and entered into a covenant with you, declares the Sovereign LORD, and you became mine.

9"'I bathed you with water and washed the blood from you and put ointments on you. 10I clothed you with an embroidered dress and put sandals of fine leather on you. I dressed you in fine linen and covered you with costly garments. 11I adorned you with jewelry: I put bracelets on your arms and a necklace around your neck, 12and I put a ring on your nose, earrings on your ears and a beautiful crown on your head. 13So you were adorned with gold and silver; your clothes were of fine linen and costly fabric and embroidered cloth. Your food was honey, olive oil and the finest flour. You became very beautiful and rose to be a queen. 14And your fame spread among the nations on account of your beauty, because the splendor I had given you made your beauty perfect, declares the Sovereign LORD.

15"'But you trusted in your beauty and used your fame to become a prostitute. You lavished your favors on anyone who passed by and your beauty became his. 16You took some of your garments to make gaudy high places, where you carried on your prostitution. You went to him, and he possessed your beauty.[b] 17You also took the fine jewelry I gave you, the jewelry made of my gold and silver, and you made for yourself male idols and engaged in prostitution with them. 18And you took your embroidered clothes to put on them, and you offered my oil and incense before them. 19Also the food I provided for you—the flour, olive oil and honey I gave you to eat—you offered as fragrant incense before them. That is what happened, declares the Sovereign LORD.

20"'And you took your sons and daughters whom you bore to me and sacrificed them as food to the idols. Was your prostitution not enough? 21You slaughtered my children and sacrificed them to the idols. 22In all your detestable practices and your prostitution you did not remember the days of your youth, when you were naked and bare, kicking about in your blood.

23"'Woe! Woe to you, declares the Sovereign LORD. In addition to all your other wickedness, 24you built a mound for yourself and made a lofty shrine in every public square. 25At every street corner you built your lofty shrines and degraded your beauty, spreading your legs with increasing promiscuity to anyone who passed by. 26You engaged in prostitution with the Egyptians, your neighbors with large genitals, and aroused my anger with your increasing promiscuity. 27So I stretched out my hand against you and reduced your territory; I gave you over to the greed of your enemies, the daughters of the Philistines, who were shocked by your lewd conduct. 28You engaged in prostitution with the Assyrians too, because you were insatiable; and even after that, you still were not satisfied. 29Then you increased your promiscuity to include Babylonia,[c] a land of merchants, but even with this you were not satisfied.

---

[a] 6 A few Hebrew manuscripts, Septuagint and Syriac; most Hebrew manuscripts repeat *and as you lay there in your blood I said to you, "Live!"*
[b] 16 The meaning of the Hebrew for this sentence is uncertain. [c] 29 Or *Chaldea*

30" 'I am filled with fury against you,[a] declares the Sovereign LORD,
when you do all these things, acting like a brazen prostitute! 31When
you built your mounds at every street corner and made your lofty
shrines in every public square, you were unlike a prostitute, because
you scorned payment.
32" 'You adulterous wife! You prefer strangers to your own husband!
33All prostitutes receive gifts, but you give gifts to all your lovers, brib-
ing them to come to you from everywhere for your illicit favors. 34So
in your prostitution you are the opposite of others; no one runs after
you for your favors. You are the very opposite, for you give payment
and none is given to you.
35" 'Therefore, you prostitute, hear the word of the LORD! 36This is
what the Sovereign LORD says: Because you poured out your lust and
exposed your naked body in your promiscuity with your lovers, and
because of all your detestable idols, and because you gave them your
children's blood, 37therefore I am going to gather all your lovers, with
whom you found pleasure, those you loved as well as those you hated. I
will gather them against you from all around and will strip you in front
of them, and they will see you stark naked. 38I will sentence you to the
punishment of women who commit adultery and who shed blood; I
will bring on you the blood vengeance of my wrath and jealous anger.
39Then I will deliver you into the hands of your lovers, and they will
tear down your mounds and destroy your lofty shrines. They will strip
you of your clothes and take your fine jewelry and leave you stark na-
ked. 40They will bring a mob against you, who will stone you and hack
you to pieces with their swords. 41They will burn down your houses
and inflict punishment on you in the sight of many women. I will put
a stop to your prostitution, and you will no longer pay your lovers.
42Then my wrath against you will subside and my jealous anger will
turn away from you; I will be calm and no longer angry.
43" 'Because you did not remember the days of your youth but en-
raged me with all these things, I will surely bring down on your head
what you have done, declares the Sovereign LORD. Did you not add
lewdness to all your other detestable practices?
44" 'Everyone who quotes proverbs will quote this proverb about
you: "Like mother, like daughter." 45You are a true daughter of your
mother, who despised her husband and her children; and you are a
true sister of your sisters, who despised their husbands and their chil-
dren. Your mother was a Hittite and your father an Amorite. 46Your
older sister was Samaria, who lived to the north of you with her daugh-
ters; and your younger sister, who lived to the south of you with her
daughters, was Sodom. 47You not only followed their ways and copied
their detestable practices, but in all your ways you soon became more
depraved than they. 48As surely as I live, declares the Sovereign LORD,
your sister Sodom and her daughters never did what you and your
daughters have done.
49" 'Now this was the sin of your sister Sodom: She and her daughters
were arrogant, overfed and unconcerned; they did not help the poor
and needy. 50They were haughty and did detestable things before me.
Therefore I did away with them as you have seen. 51Samaria did not
commit half the sins you did. You have done more detestable things
than they, and have made your sisters seem righteous by all these things

[a] 30 Or *How feverish is your heart,*

you have done. [52]Bear your disgrace, for you have furnished some justification for your sisters. Because your sins were more vile than theirs, they appear more righteous than you. So then, be ashamed and bear your disgrace, for you have made your sisters appear righteous.

[53]" 'However, I will restore the fortunes of Sodom and her daughters and of Samaria and her daughters, and your fortunes along with them, [54]so that you may bear your disgrace and be ashamed of all you have done in giving them comfort. [55]And your sisters, Sodom with her daughters and Samaria with her daughters, will return to what they were before; and you and your daughters will return to what you were before. [56]You would not even mention your sister Sodom in the day of your pride, [57]before your wickedness was uncovered. Even so, you are now scorned by the daughters of Edom[a] and all her neighbors and the daughters of the Philistines — all those around you who despise you. [58]You will bear the consequences of your lewdness and your detestable practices, declares the LORD.

[59]" 'This is what the Sovereign LORD says: I will deal with you as you deserve, because you have despised my oath by breaking the covenant. [60]Yet I will remember the covenant I made with you in the days of your youth, and I will establish an everlasting covenant with you. [61]Then you will remember your ways and be ashamed when you receive your sisters, both those who are older than you and those who are younger. I will give them to you as daughters, but not on the basis of my covenant with you. [62]So I will establish my covenant with you, and you will know that I am the LORD. [63]Then, when I make atonement for you for all you have done, you will remember and be ashamed and never again open your mouth because of your humiliation, declares the Sovereign LORD.' "

TWO EAGLES AND A VINE

17 The word of the LORD came to me: [2]"Son of man, set forth an allegory and tell it to the Israelites as a parable. [3]Say to them, 'This is what the Sovereign LORD says: A great eagle with powerful wings, long feathers and full plumage of varied colors came to Lebanon. Taking hold of the top of a cedar, [4]he broke off its topmost shoot and carried it away to a land of merchants, where he planted it in a city of traders.

[5]" 'He took one of the seedlings of the land and put it in fertile soil. He planted it like a willow by abundant water, [6]and it sprouted and became a low, spreading vine. Its branches turned toward him, but its roots remained under it. So it became a vine and produced branches and put out leafy boughs.

[7]" 'But there was another great eagle with powerful wings and full plumage. The vine now sent out its roots toward him from the plot where it was planted and stretched out its branches to him for water. [8]It had been planted in good soil by abundant water so that it would produce branches, bear fruit and become a splendid vine.'

[9]"Say to them, 'This is what the Sovereign LORD says: Will it thrive? Will it not be uprooted and stripped of its fruit so that it withers? All its new growth will wither. It will not take a strong arm or many people to pull it up by the roots. [10]It has been planted, but will it thrive? Will it not wither completely when the east wind strikes it — wither away in the plot where it grew?' "

PRAYING SCRIPTURE

Ezekiel 17

Ending another pronouncement of judgment, the Lord returned to his theme of future promised blessing. Israel will be revived. All God has cut down will be replanted. His people will provide shade, shelter and sustenance. The dry tree will turn green, and the low tree will be made tall.

God's gracious blessing restores what has been destroyed, even what he destroys. Thank God for his love that can overcome the most devastating effects of sin.

[a] *57* Many Hebrew manuscripts and Syriac; most Hebrew manuscripts, Septuagint and Vulgate *Aram*

11Then the word of the LORD came to me: 12"Say to this rebellious
people, 'Do you not know what these things mean?' Say to them: 'The
king of Babylon went to Jerusalem and carried off her king and her no-
bles, bringing them back with him to Babylon. 13Then he took a mem-
ber of the royal family and made a treaty with him, putting him under
oath. He also carried away the leading men of the land, 14so that the
kingdom would be brought low, unable to rise again, surviving only by
keeping his treaty. 15But the king rebelled against him by sending his
envoys to Egypt to get horses and a large army. Will he succeed? Will he
who does such things escape? Will he break the treaty and yet escape?

16" 'As surely as I live, declares the Sovereign LORD, he shall die in
Babylon, in the land of the king who put him on the throne, whose
oath he despised and whose treaty he broke. 17Pharaoh with his mighty
army and great horde will be of no help to him in war, when ramps
are built and siege works erected to destroy many lives. 18He despised
the oath by breaking the covenant. Because he had given his hand in
pledge and yet did all these things, he shall not escape.

19" 'Therefore this is what the Sovereign LORD says: As surely as I live,
I will repay him for despising my oath and breaking my covenant. 20I
will spread my net for him, and he will be caught in my snare. I will
bring him to Babylon and execute judgment on him there because he
was unfaithful to me. 21All his choice troops will fall by the sword, and
the survivors will be scattered to the winds. Then you will know that I
the LORD have spoken.

22" 'This is what the Sovereign LORD says: I myself will take a shoot
from the very top of a cedar and plant it; I will break off a tender sprig
from its topmost shoots and plant it on a high and lofty mountain.
23On the mountain heights of Israel I will plant it; it will produce
branches and bear fruit and become a splendid cedar. Birds of every
kind will nest in it; they will find shelter in the shade of its branches.
24All the trees of the forest will know that I the LORD bring down the
tall tree and make the low tree grow tall. I dry up the green tree and
make the dry tree flourish.

" 'I the LORD have spoken, and I will do it.' "

THE ONE WHO SINS WILL DIE

18 The word of the LORD came to me: 2"What do you people mean
by quoting this proverb about the land of Israel:

" 'The parents eat sour grapes,
  and the children's teeth are set on edge'?

3"As surely as I live, declares the Sovereign LORD, you will no longer
quote this proverb in Israel. 4For everyone belongs to me, the parent
as well as the child—both alike belong to me. The one who sins is the
one who will die.

5"Suppose there is a righteous man
  who does what is just and right.
6He does not eat at the mountain shrines
  or look to the idols of Israel.
He does not defile his neighbor's wife
  or have sexual relations with a woman during her period.
7He does not oppress anyone,
  but returns what he took in pledge for a loan.

PRAYING SCRIPTURE

Ezekiel 18

In this chapter, the Lord confirmed an important truth: Every person is responsible for his or her own sin; we cannot blame our sin on another person. Our sin nature is inherited from Adam, but sin does not pass on to generations. "The child will not share the guilt of the parent" (verse 20).

Have you blamed others for sins you've committed? Take your sins to the Father, admit your own guilt, and receive his abundant forgiveness.

He does not commit robbery
but gives his food to the hungry
and provides clothing for the naked.
8 He does not lend to them at interest
or take a profit from them.
He withholds his hand from doing wrong
and judges fairly between two parties.
9 He follows my decrees
and faithfully keeps my laws.
That man is righteous;
he will surely live,
declares the Sovereign LORD.

10 "Suppose he has a violent son, who sheds blood or does any of
these other things[a] 11 (though the father has done none of them):

"He eats at the mountain shrines.
He defiles his neighbor's wife.
12 He oppresses the poor and needy.
He commits robbery.
He does not return what he took in pledge.
He looks to the idols.
He does detestable things.
13 He lends at interest and takes a profit.

Will such a man live? He will not! Because he has done all these detestable things, he is to be put to death; his blood will be on his own head.
14 "But suppose this son has a son who sees all the sins his father
commits, and though he sees them, he does not do such things:

15 "He does not eat at the mountain shrines
or look to the idols of Israel.
He does not defile his neighbor's wife.
16 He does not oppress anyone
or require a pledge for a loan.
He does not commit robbery
but gives his food to the hungry
and provides clothing for the naked.
17 He withholds his hand from mistreating the poor
and takes no interest or profit from them.
He keeps my laws and follows my decrees.

He will not die for his father's sin; he will surely live. 18 But his father
will die for his own sin, because he practiced extortion, robbed his
brother and did what was wrong among his people.
19 "Yet you ask, 'Why does the son not share the guilt of his father?'
Since the son has done what is just and right and has been careful to
keep all my decrees, he will surely live. 20 The one who sins is the one
who will die. The child will not share the guilt of the parent, nor will the parent share the guilt of the child. The righteousness of the righteous will be credited to them, and the wickedness of the wicked will be charged against them.
21 "But if a wicked person turns away from all the sins they have committed and keeps all my decrees and does what is just and right, that
person will surely live; they will not die. 22 None of the offenses they

[a] 10 Or *things to a brother*

have committed will be remembered against them. Because of the
righteous things they have done, they will live. 23Do I take any plea-
sure in the death of the wicked? declares the Sovereign LORD. Rather,
am I not pleased when they turn from their ways and live?
24"But if a righteous person turns from their righteousness and com-
mits sin and does the same detestable things the wicked person does,
will they live? None of the righteous things that person has done will
be remembered. Because of the unfaithfulness they are guilty of and
because of the sins they have committed, they will die.
25"Yet you say, 'The way of the Lord is not just.' Hear, you Israelites:
Is my way unjust? Is it not your ways that are unjust? 26If a righteous
person turns from their righteousness and commits sin, they will die
for it; because of the sin they have committed they will die. 27But if a
wicked person turns away from the wickedness they have committed
and does what is just and right, they will save their life. 28Because they
consider all the offenses they have committed and turn away from
them, that person will surely live; they will not die. 29Yet the Israelites
say, 'The way of the Lord is not just.' Are my ways unjust, people of Is-
rael? Is it not your ways that are unjust?
30"Therefore, you Israelites, I will judge each of you according to
your own ways, declares the Sovereign LORD. Repent! Turn away from
all your offenses; then sin will not be your downfall. 31Rid yourselves
of all the offenses you have committed, and get a new heart and a new
spirit. Why will you die, people of Israel? 32For I take no pleasure in the
death of anyone, declares the Sovereign LORD. Repent and live!

A LAMENT OVER ISRAEL'S PRINCES

19 "Take up a lament concerning the princes of Israel 2and say:

"'What a lioness was your mother
among the lions!
She lay down among them
and reared her cubs.
3She brought up one of her cubs,
and he became a strong lion.
He learned to tear the prey
and he became a man-eater.
4The nations heard about him,
and he was trapped in their pit.
They led him with hooks
to the land of Egypt.
5"'When she saw her hope unfulfilled,
her expectation gone,
she took another of her cubs
and made him a strong lion.
6He prowled among the lions,
for he was now a strong lion.
He learned to tear the prey
and he became a man-eater.
7He broke down[a] their strongholds
and devastated their towns.

PRAYING SCRIPTURE

Ezekiel 19

The most insidious pride is revealed when someone says, "It can't happen to me" or "I would never do that." Most people can become trapped in sin, and many do become trapped. Israel's princes found this out the hard way: in the courts of Babylon.

Don't be among those who get as close to sin as they can, thinking they are safe. Let God's mercy be a barrier from sinning against him.

[a] 7 Targum (see Septuagint); Hebrew *He knew*

The land and all who were in it
  were terrified by his roaring.
8 Then the nations came against him,
  those from regions round about.
They spread their net for him,
  and he was trapped in their pit.
9 With hooks they pulled him into a cage
  and brought him to the king of Babylon.
They put him in prison,
  so his roar was heard no longer
  on the mountains of Israel.

10 " 'Your mother was like a vine in your vineyard[a]
  planted by the water;
it was fruitful and full of branches
  because of abundant water.
11 Its branches were strong,
  fit for a ruler's scepter.
It towered high
  above the thick foliage,
conspicuous for its height
  and for its many branches.
12 But it was uprooted in fury
  and thrown to the ground.
The east wind made it shrivel,
  it was stripped of its fruit;
its strong branches withered
  and fire consumed them.
13 Now it is planted in the desert,
  in a dry and thirsty land.
14 Fire spread from one of its main[b] branches
  and consumed its fruit.
No strong branch is left on it
  fit for a ruler's scepter.'

"This is a lament and is to be used as a lament."

REBELLIOUS ISRAEL PURGED

20 In the seventh year, in the fifth month on the tenth day, some
of the elders of Israel came to inquire of the LORD, and they
sat down in front of me.
2Then the word of the LORD came to me: 3"Son of man, speak to the
elders of Israel and say to them, 'This is what the Sovereign LORD says:
Have you come to inquire of me? As surely as I live, I will not let you
inquire of me, declares the Sovereign LORD.'
4"Will you judge them? Will you judge them, son of man? Then con-
front them with the detestable practices of their ancestors 5and say to
them: 'This is what the Sovereign LORD says: On the day I chose Israel, I
swore with uplifted hand to the descendants of Jacob and revealed my-
self to them in Egypt. With uplifted hand I said to them, "I am the LORD
your God." 6On that day I swore to them that I would bring them out of
Egypt into a land I had searched out for them, a land flowing with milk

PRAYING SCRIPTURE
Ezekiel 20

The elders of the land engaged Ezekiel to determine the Lord's will. The prophet did not hold back the Lord's words: "I would pour out my wrath on them and spend my anger against them" (verse 8). After multiple prophecies of judgment, an exasperated Ezekiel complained, "They are saying of me, 'Isn't he just telling parables?'" (verse 49).

To people in rebellion, God's correction doesn't always seem serious. Pray people you know take him seriously.

[a] 10 Two Hebrew manuscripts; most Hebrew manuscripts *your blood*
[b] 14 Or *from under its*

and honey, the most beautiful of all lands. 7And I said to them, "Each
of you, get rid of the vile images you have set your eyes on, and do
not defile yourselves with the idols of Egypt. I am the LORD your God."
8"'But they rebelled against me and would not listen to me; they
did not get rid of the vile images they had set their eyes on, nor did
they forsake the idols of Egypt. So I said I would pour out my wrath on
them and spend my anger against them in Egypt. 9But for the sake of
my name, I brought them out of Egypt. I did it to keep my name from
being profaned in the eyes of the nations among whom they lived and
in whose sight I had revealed myself to the Israelites. 10Therefore I
led them out of Egypt and brought them into the wilderness. 11I gave
them my decrees and made known to them my laws, by which the
person who obeys them will live. 12Also I gave them my Sabbaths as a
sign between us, so they would know that I the LORD made them holy.
13"'Yet the people of Israel rebelled against me in the wilderness.
They did not follow my decrees but rejected my laws — by which the
person who obeys them will live — and they utterly desecrated my
Sabbaths. So I said I would pour out my wrath on them and destroy
them in the wilderness. 14But for the sake of my name I did what would
keep it from being profaned in the eyes of the nations in whose sight
I had brought them out. 15Also with uplifted hand I swore to them in
the wilderness that I would not bring them into the land I had given
them — a land flowing with milk and honey, the most beautiful of all
lands — 16because they rejected my laws and did not follow my decrees
and desecrated my Sabbaths. For their hearts were devoted to their
idols. 17Yet I looked on them with pity and did not destroy them or put
an end to them in the wilderness. 18I said to their children in the wil-
derness, "Do not follow the statutes of your parents or keep their laws
or defile yourselves with their idols. 19I am the LORD your God; follow
my decrees and be careful to keep my laws. 20Keep my Sabbaths holy,
that they may be a sign between us. Then you will know that I am the
LORD your God."
21"'But the children rebelled against me: They did not follow my
decrees, they were not careful to keep my laws, of which I said, "The
person who obeys them will live by them," and they desecrated my
Sabbaths. So I said I would pour out my wrath on them and spend
my anger against them in the wilderness. 22But I withheld my hand,
and for the sake of my name I did what would keep it from being pro-
faned in the eyes of the nations in whose sight I had brought them
out. 23Also with uplifted hand I swore to them in the wilderness that
I would disperse them among the nations and scatter them through
the countries, 24because they had not obeyed my laws but had rejected
my decrees and desecrated my Sabbaths, and their eyes lusted after
their parents' idols. 25So I gave them other statutes that were not good
and laws through which they could not live; 26I defiled them through
their gifts — the sacrifice of every firstborn — that I might fill them
with horror so they would know that I am the LORD.'
27"Therefore, son of man, speak to the people of Israel and say to
them, 'This is what the Sovereign LORD says: In this also your ancestors
blasphemed me by being unfaithful to me: 28When I brought them
into the land I had sworn to give them and they saw any high hill or
any leafy tree, there they offered their sacrifices, made offerings that
aroused my anger, presented their fragrant incense and poured out

their drink offerings. [29]Then I said to them: What is this high place you go to?'" (It is called Bamah[a] to this day.)

REBELLIOUS ISRAEL RENEWED

[30]"Therefore say to the Israelites: 'This is what the Sovereign LORD says: Will you defile yourselves the way your ancestors did and lust after their vile images? [31]When you offer your gifts — the sacrifice of your children in the fire — you continue to defile yourselves with all your idols to this day. Am I to let you inquire of me, you Israelites? As surely as I live, declares the Sovereign LORD, I will not let you inquire of me.

[32]" 'You say, "We want to be like the nations, like the peoples of the world, who serve wood and stone." But what you have in mind will never happen. [33]As surely as I live, declares the Sovereign LORD, I will reign over you with a mighty hand and an outstretched arm and with outpoured wrath. [34]I will bring you from the nations and gather you from the countries where you have been scattered — with a mighty hand and an outstretched arm and with outpoured wrath. [35]I will bring you into the wilderness of the nations and there, face to face, I will execute judgment upon you. [36]As I judged your ancestors in the wilderness of the land of Egypt, so I will judge you, declares the Sovereign LORD. [37]I will take note of you as you pass under my rod, and I will bring you into the bond of the covenant. [38]I will purge you of those who revolt and rebel against me. Although I will bring them out of the land where they are living, yet they will not enter the land of Israel. Then you will know that I am the LORD.

[39]" 'As for you, people of Israel, this is what the Sovereign LORD says: Go and serve your idols, every one of you! But afterward you will surely listen to me and no longer profane my holy name with your gifts and idols. [40]For on my holy mountain, the high mountain of Israel, declares the Sovereign LORD, there in the land all the people of Israel will serve me, and there I will accept them. There I will require your offerings and your choice gifts,[b] along with all your holy sacrifices. [41]I will accept you as fragrant incense when I bring you out from the nations and gather you from the countries where you have been scattered, and I will be proved holy through you in the sight of the nations. [42]Then you will know that I am the LORD, when I bring you into the land of Israel, the land I had sworn with uplifted hand to give to your ancestors. [43]There you will remember your conduct and all the actions by which you have defiled yourselves, and you will loathe yourselves for all the evil you have done. [44]You will know that I am the LORD, when I deal with you for my name's sake and not according to your evil ways and your corrupt practices, you people of Israel, declares the Sovereign LORD.' "

PROPHECY AGAINST THE SOUTH

[45]The word of the LORD came to me: [46]"Son of man, set your face toward the south; preach against the south and prophesy against the forest of the southland. [47]Say to the southern forest: 'Hear the word of the LORD. This is what the Sovereign LORD says: I am about to set fire to you, and it will consume all your trees, both green and dry. The blazing flame will not be quenched, and every face from south to north will be scorched by it. [48]Everyone will see that I the LORD have kindled it; it will not be quenched.' "

---

[a] 29 *Bamah* means *high place.* [b] 40 Or *and the gifts of your firstfruits*

[49]Then I said, "Sovereign LORD, they are saying of me, 'Isn't he just
telling parables?' "[a]

BABYLON AS GOD'S SWORD OF JUDGMENT

21 [b] The word of the LORD came to me: [2]"Son of man, set your face
against Jerusalem and preach against the sanctuary. Prophesy
against the land of Israel [3]and say to her: 'This is what the LORD says: I
am against you. I will draw my sword from its sheath and cut off from
you both the righteous and the wicked. [4]Because I am going to cut off
the righteous and the wicked, my sword will be unsheathed against
everyone from south to north. [5]Then all people will know that I the
LORD have drawn my sword from its sheath; it will not return again.'
[6]"Therefore groan, son of man! Groan before them with broken
heart and bitter grief. [7]And when they ask you, 'Why are you groaning?'
you shall say, 'Because of the news that is coming. Every heart will melt
with fear and every hand go limp; every spirit will become faint and
every leg will be wet with urine.' It is coming! It will surely take place,
declares the Sovereign LORD."
[8]The word of the LORD came to me: [9]"Son of man, prophesy and say,
'This is what the Lord says:

" 'A sword, a sword,
sharpened and polished—
[10]sharpened for the slaughter,
polished to flash like lightning!

" 'Shall we rejoice in the scepter of my royal son? The sword despises
every such stick.

[11]" 'The sword is appointed to be polished,
to be grasped with the hand;
it is sharpened and polished,
made ready for the hand of the slayer.
[12]Cry out and wail, son of man,
for it is against my people;
it is against all the princes of Israel.
They are thrown to the sword
along with my people.
Therefore beat your breast.

[13]" 'Testing will surely come. And what if even the scepter, which the
sword despises, does not continue? declares the Sovereign LORD.'

[14]"So then, son of man, prophesy
and strike your hands together.
Let the sword strike twice,
even three times.
It is a sword for slaughter—
a sword for great slaughter,
closing in on them from every side.
[15]So that hearts may melt with fear
and the fallen be many,
I have stationed the sword for slaughter[c]
at all their gates.

PRAYING SCRIPTURE

Ezekiel 21

Many people read of the "sword of the Lord" and think of God's Word. But in passages of judgment, "sword" is often used to describe a nation. It's used here of Babylon, set against both the Israelites and the Ammonites. God's judgment is both swift and sure against evil.

God can be trusted to wield his sword justly. Pray for those it is wielded against to come to repentance.

---

[a] 49 In Hebrew texts 20:45-49 is numbered 21:1-5. [b] In Hebrew texts 21:1-32 is numbered 21:6-37. [c] 15 Septuagint; the meaning of the Hebrew for this word is uncertain.

Look! It is forged to strike like lightning,
 it is grasped for slaughter.
16 Slash to the right, you sword,
 then to the left,
 wherever your blade is turned.
17 I too will strike my hands together,
 and my wrath will subside.
I the LORD have spoken."

18The word of the LORD came to me: 19"Son of man, mark out two
roads for the sword of the king of Babylon to take, both starting from
the same country. Make a signpost where the road branches off to the
city. 20Mark out one road for the sword to come against Rabbah of the
Ammonites and another against Judah and fortified Jerusalem. 21For
the king of Babylon will stop at the fork in the road, at the junction of
the two roads, to seek an omen: He will cast lots with arrows, he will
consult his idols, he will examine the liver. 22Into his right hand will
come the lot for Jerusalem, where he is to set up battering rams, to
give the command to slaughter, to sound the battle cry, to set battering
rams against the gates, to build a ramp and to erect siege works. 23It
will seem like a false omen to those who have sworn allegiance to him,
but he will remind them of their guilt and take them captive.

24"Therefore this is what the Sovereign LORD says: 'Because you peo-
ple have brought to mind your guilt by your open rebellion, revealing
your sins in all that you do — because you have done this, you will be
taken captive.

25" 'You profane and wicked prince of Israel, whose day has come,
whose time of punishment has reached its climax, 26this is what the
Sovereign LORD says: Take off the turban, remove the crown. It will not
be as it was: The lowly will be exalted and the exalted will be brought
low. 27A ruin! A ruin! I will make it a ruin! The crown will not be re-
stored until he to whom it rightfully belongs shall come; to him I will
give it.'

28"And you, son of man, prophesy and say, 'This is what the Sover-
eign LORD says about the Ammonites and their insults:

" 'A sword, a sword,
 drawn for the slaughter,
polished to consume
 and to flash like lightning!
29 Despite false visions concerning you
 and lying divinations about you,
it will be laid on the necks
 of the wicked who are to be slain,
whose day has come,
 whose time of punishment has reached its climax.

30 " 'Let the sword return to its sheath.
 In the place where you were created,
in the land of your ancestry,
 I will judge you.
31 I will pour out my wrath on you
 and breathe out my fiery anger against you;
I will deliver you into the hands of brutal men,
 men skilled in destruction.

32You will be fuel for the fire,
your blood will be shed in your land,
you will be remembered no more;
for I the LORD have spoken.'"

JUDGMENT ON JERUSALEM'S SINS

22 The word of the LORD came to me:
2"Son of man, will you judge her? Will you judge this city of blood-
shed? Then confront her with all her detestable practices 3and say:
'This is what the Sovereign LORD says: You city that brings on herself
doom by shedding blood in her midst and defiles herself by making
idols, 4you have become guilty because of the blood you have shed and
have become defiled by the idols you have made. You have brought
your days to a close, and the end of your years has come. Therefore I
will make you an object of scorn to the nations and a laughingstock to
all the countries. 5Those who are near and those who are far away will
mock you, you infamous city, full of turmoil.
6"'See how each of the princes of Israel who are in you uses his power
to shed blood. 7In you they have treated father and mother with con-
tempt; in you they have oppressed the foreigner and mistreated the
fatherless and the widow. 8You have despised my holy things and des-
ecrated my Sabbaths. 9In you are slanderers who are bent on shedding
blood; in you are those who eat at the mountain shrines and commit
lewd acts. 10In you are those who dishonor their father's bed; in you
are those who violate women during their period, when they are cere-
monially unclean. 11In you one man commits a detestable offense with
his neighbor's wife, another shamefully defiles his daughter-in-law,
and another violates his sister, his own father's daughter. 12In you are
people who accept bribes to shed blood; you take interest and make a
profit from the poor. You extort unjust gain from your neighbors. And
you have forgotten me, declares the Sovereign LORD.
13"'I will surely strike my hands together at the unjust gain you have
made and at the blood you have shed in your midst. 14Will your cour-
age endure or your hands be strong in the day I deal with you? I the
LORD have spoken, and I will do it. 15I will disperse you among the
nations and scatter you through the countries; and I will put an end
to your uncleanness. 16When you have been defiled[a] in the eyes of the
nations, you will know that I am the LORD.'"
17Then the word of the LORD came to me: 18"Son of man, the people
of Israel have become dross to me; all of them are the copper, tin, iron
and lead left inside a furnace. They are but the dross of silver. 19There-
fore this is what the Sovereign LORD says: 'Because you have all be-
come dross, I will gather you into Jerusalem. 20As silver, copper, iron,
lead and tin are gathered into a furnace to be melted with a fiery blast,
so will I gather you in my anger and my wrath and put you inside the
city and melt you. 21I will gather you and I will blow on you with my
fiery wrath, and you will be melted inside her. 22As silver is melted in a
furnace, so you will be melted inside her, and you will know that I the
LORD have poured out my wrath on you.'"
23Again the word of the LORD came to me: 24"Son of man, say to the
land, 'You are a land that has not been cleansed or rained on in the

PRAYING SCRIPTURE
Ezekiel 22

The leaders of God's people have a particular responsibility to demonstrate obedience and faithfulness to the Lord. When they fail, God's people are scattered like sheep without a shepherd. The land was so bereft of spiritual leadership that when the Lord looked for a man to stand in the gap, he found none (see verse 30).

God is always looking for those who will live for him. Pray to be that person.

[a] 16 Or *When I have allotted you your inheritance*

day of wrath.' 25There is a conspiracy of her princes[a] within her like a roaring lion tearing its prey; they devour people, take treasures and precious things and make many widows within her. 26Her priests do violence to my law and profane my holy things; they do not distinguish between the holy and the common; they teach that there is no difference between the unclean and the clean; and they shut their eyes to the keeping of my Sabbaths, so that I am profaned among them. 27Her officials within her are like wolves tearing their prey; they shed blood and kill people to make unjust gain. 28Her prophets whitewash these deeds for them by false visions and lying divinations. They say, 'This is what the Sovereign LORD says'—when the LORD has not spoken. 29The people of the land practice extortion and commit robbery; they oppress the poor and needy and mistreat the foreigner, denying them justice.

30"I looked for someone among them who would build up the wall and stand before me in the gap on behalf of the land so I would not have to destroy it, but I found no one. 31So I will pour out my wrath on them and consume them with my fiery anger, bringing down on their own heads all they have done, declares the Sovereign LORD."

TWO ADULTEROUS SISTERS

23 The word of the LORD came to me: 2"Son of man, there were two women, daughters of the same mother. 3They became prostitutes in Egypt, engaging in prostitution from their youth. In that land their breasts were fondled and their virgin bosoms caressed. 4The older was named Oholah, and her sister was Oholibah. They were mine and gave birth to sons and daughters. Oholah is Samaria, and Oholibah is Jerusalem.

5"Oholah engaged in prostitution while she was still mine; and she lusted after her lovers, the Assyrians—warriors 6clothed in blue, governors and commanders, all of them handsome young men, and mounted horsemen. 7She gave herself as a prostitute to all the elite of the Assyrians and defiled herself with all the idols of everyone she lusted after. 8She did not give up the prostitution she began in Egypt, when during her youth men slept with her, caressed her virgin bosom and poured out their lust on her.

9"Therefore I delivered her into the hands of her lovers, the Assyrians, for whom she lusted. 10They stripped her naked, took away her sons and daughters and killed her with the sword. She became a byword among women, and punishment was inflicted on her.

11"Her sister Oholibah saw this, yet in her lust and prostitution she was more depraved than her sister. 12She too lusted after the Assyrians—governors and commanders, warriors in full dress, mounted horsemen, all handsome young men. 13I saw that she too defiled herself; both of them went the same way.

14"But she carried her prostitution still further. She saw men portrayed on a wall, figures of Chaldeans[b] portrayed in red, 15with belts around their waists and flowing turbans on their heads; all of them looked like Babylonian chariot officers, natives of Chaldea.[c] 16As soon as she saw them, she lusted after them and sent messengers to them in Chaldea. 17Then the Babylonians came to her, to the bed of love, and in their lust they defiled her. After she had been defiled by them, she

PRAYING SCRIPTURE
Ezekiel 23

Israel's relationship with the Lord was so intimate he used marriage metaphors to illustrate it. Specifically, he often used unfaithfulness to portray Israel's chasing after other gods; in graphic language of prostitution and loose morals, he spoke about nations with whom "she was a prostitute" (verse 19).

Our relationship with Jesus is that of bride to groom. How faithful are you to Jesus the groom? Search your heart and, if needed, return to your first love.

[a] *25* Septuagint; Hebrew *prophets* [b] *14* Or *Babylonians* [c] *15* Or *Babylonia;* also in verse 16

turned away from them in disgust. 18When she carried on her prosti-
tution openly and exposed her naked body, I turned away from her
in disgust, just as I had turned away from her sister. 19Yet she became
more and more promiscuous as she recalled the days of her youth,
when she was a prostitute in Egypt. 20There she lusted after her lovers,
whose genitals were like those of donkeys and whose emission was like
that of horses. 21So you longed for the lewdness of your youth, when
in Egypt your bosom was caressed and your young breasts fondled.[a]
22"Therefore, Oholibah, this is what the Sovereign LORD says: I will
stir up your lovers against you, those you turned away from in disgust,
and I will bring them against you from every side— 23the Babyloni-
ans and all the Chaldeans, the men of Pekod and Shoa and Koa, and all
the Assyrians with them, handsome young men, all of them governors
and commanders, chariot officers and men of high rank, all mounted
on horses. 24They will come against you with weapons,[b] chariots and
wagons and with a throng of people; they will take up positions against
you on every side with large and small shields and with helmets. I will
turn you over to them for punishment, and they will punish you ac-
cording to their standards. 25I will direct my jealous anger against you,
and they will deal with you in fury. They will cut off your noses and
your ears, and those of you who are left will fall by the sword. They will
take away your sons and daughters, and those of you who are left will
be consumed by fire. 26They will also strip you of your clothes and take
your fine jewelry. 27So I will put a stop to the lewdness and prostitution
you began in Egypt. You will not look on these things with longing or
remember Egypt anymore.
28"For this is what the Sovereign LORD says: I am about to deliver
you into the hands of those you hate, to those you turned away from in
disgust. 29They will deal with you in hatred and take away everything
you have worked for. They will leave you stark naked, and the shame
of your prostitution will be exposed. Your lewdness and promiscuity
30have brought this on you, because you lusted after the nations and
defiled yourself with their idols. 31You have gone the way of your sister;
so I will put her cup into your hand.
32"This is what the Sovereign LORD says:

"You will drink your sister's cup,
  a cup large and deep;
it will bring scorn and derision,
  for it holds so much.
33You will be filled with drunkenness and sorrow,
  the cup of ruin and desolation,
  the cup of your sister Samaria.
34You will drink it and drain it dry
  and chew on its pieces—
  and you will tear your breasts.

I have spoken, declares the Sovereign LORD.

35"Therefore this is what the Sovereign LORD says: Since you have
forgotten me and turned your back on me, you must bear the conse-
quences of your lewdness and prostitution."

[a] *21* Syriac (see also verse 3); Hebrew *caressed because of your young breasts*
[b] *24* The meaning of the Hebrew for this word is uncertain.

36The LORD said to me: "Son of man, will you judge Oholah and Oholi-
bah? Then confront them with their detestable practices, 37for they have
committed adultery and blood is on their hands. They committed adul-
tery with their idols; they even sacrificed their children, whom they
bore to me, as food for them. 38They have also done this to me: At that
same time they defiled my sanctuary and desecrated my Sabbaths. 39On
the very day they sacrificed their children to their idols, they entered
my sanctuary and desecrated it. That is what they did in my house.

40"They even sent messengers for men who came from far away, and
when they arrived you bathed yourself for them, applied eye makeup
and put on your jewelry. 41You sat on an elegant couch, with a table
spread before it on which you had placed the incense and olive oil that
belonged to me.

42"The noise of a carefree crowd was around her; drunkards were
brought from the desert along with men from the rabble, and they
put bracelets on the wrists of the woman and her sister and beautiful
crowns on their heads. 43Then I said about the one worn out by adul-
tery, 'Now let them use her as a prostitute, for that is all she is.' 44And
they slept with her. As men sleep with a prostitute, so they slept with
those lewd women, Oholah and Oholibah. 45But righteous judges will
sentence them to the punishment of women who commit adultery and
shed blood, because they are adulterous and blood is on their hands.

46"This is what the Sovereign LORD says: Bring a mob against them
and give them over to terror and plunder. 47The mob will stone them
and cut them down with their swords; they will kill their sons and
daughters and burn down their houses.

48"So I will put an end to lewdness in the land, that all women may
take warning and not imitate you. 49You will suffer the penalty for
your lewdness and bear the consequences of your sins of idolatry. Then
you will know that I am the Sovereign LORD."

JERUSALEM AS A COOKING POT

24 In the ninth year, in the tenth month on the tenth day, the
word of the LORD came to me: 2"Son of man, record this date,
this very date, because the king of Babylon has laid siege to Jerusalem
this very day. 3Tell this rebellious people a parable and say to them:
'This is what the Sovereign LORD says:

"'Put on the cooking pot; put it on
 and pour water into it.
4Put into it the pieces of meat,
 all the choice pieces — the leg and the shoulder.
Fill it with the best of these bones;
5 take the pick of the flock.
Pile wood beneath it for the bones;
 bring it to a boil
 and cook the bones in it.

6"'For this is what the Sovereign LORD says:

"'Woe to the city of bloodshed,
 to the pot now encrusted,
 whose deposit will not go away!
Take the meat out piece by piece
 in whatever order it comes.

PRAYING SCRIPTURE

Ezekiel 24

One of the hardest lessons God ever put upon his people is this: Ezekiel's wife died, and God commanded him not to mourn. "Ezekiel will be a sign to you" (verse 24). The prophet was the visible symbol that Israel would know that he is the Lord.

Following the Lord is not always easy; we are called to suffer for him. Pray now for the faith to follow him no matter how deep the valley.

7 " 'For the blood she shed is in her midst:
She poured it on the bare rock;
she did not pour it on the ground,
where the dust would cover it.
8 To stir up wrath and take revenge
I put her blood on the bare rock,
so that it would not be covered.

9 " 'Therefore this is what the Sovereign LORD says:

" 'Woe to the city of bloodshed!
I, too, will pile the wood high.
10 So heap on the wood
and kindle the fire.
Cook the meat well,
mixing in the spices;
and let the bones be charred.
11 Then set the empty pot on the coals
till it becomes hot and its copper glows,
so that its impurities may be melted
and its deposit burned away.
12 It has frustrated all efforts;
its heavy deposit has not been removed,
not even by fire.

13 " 'Now your impurity is lewdness. Because I tried to cleanse you but you would not be cleansed from your impurity, you will not be clean again until my wrath against you has subsided.

14 " 'I the LORD have spoken. The time has come for me to act. I will not hold back; I will not have pity, nor will I relent. You will be judged according to your conduct and your actions, declares the Sovereign LORD.' "

EZEKIEL'S WIFE DIES

15 The word of the LORD came to me: 16 "Son of man, with one blow I
am about to take away from you the delight of your eyes. Yet do not
lament or weep or shed any tears. 17 Groan quietly; do not mourn for
the dead. Keep your turban fastened and your sandals on your feet;
do not cover your mustache and beard or eat the customary food of
mourners."
18 So I spoke to the people in the morning, and in the evening my
wife died. The next morning I did as I had been commanded.
19 Then the people asked me, "Won't you tell us what these things
have to do with us? Why are you acting like this?"
20 So I said to them, "The word of the LORD came to me. 21 Say to the
people of Israel, 'This is what the Sovereign LORD says: I am about to
desecrate my sanctuary — the stronghold in which you take pride, the
delight of your eyes, the object of your affection. The sons and daugh-
ters you left behind will fall by the sword. 22 And you will do as I have
done. You will not cover your mustache and beard or eat the customary
food of mourners. 23 You will keep your turbans on your heads and your
sandals on your feet. You will not mourn or weep but will waste away
because of[a] your sins and groan among yourselves. 24 Ezekiel will be a

[a] 23 Or *away in*

sign to you; you will do just as he has done. When this happens, you
will know that I am the Sovereign LORD.’
25“And you, son of man, on the day I take away their stronghold,
their joy and glory, the delight of their eyes, their heart’s desire, and
their sons and daughters as well — 26on that day a fugitive will come
to tell you the news. 27At that time your mouth will be opened; you
will speak with him and will no longer be silent. So you will be a sign
to them, and they will know that I am the LORD.”

PRAYING SCRIPTURE

Ezekiel 25

God, through Ezekiel, proclaimed coming judgment for four nations: Ammon, Moab, Edom and Philistia. These judgments were not random or pointless. For each one he gives the reason: so the peoples of these countries would know that the Lord is God.

Praise the God who is powerful enough to bring judgment but loving enough to get people’s attention over sin. That God’s wisdom is beyond comprehension should humble us to rejoicing.

A PROPHECY AGAINST AMMON

25 The word of the LORD came to me: 2“Son of man, set your face
against the Ammonites and prophesy against them. 3Say to
them, ‘Hear the word of the Sovereign LORD. This is what the Sover-
eign LORD says: Because you said “Aha!” over my sanctuary when it
was desecrated and over the land of Israel when it was laid waste and
over the people of Judah when they went into exile, 4therefore I am
going to give you to the people of the East as a possession. They will
set up their camps and pitch their tents among you; they will eat your
fruit and drink your milk. 5I will turn Rabbah into a pasture for camels
and Ammon into a resting place for sheep. Then you will know that I
am the LORD. 6For this is what the Sovereign LORD says: Because you
have clapped your hands and stamped your feet, rejoicing with all the
malice of your heart against the land of Israel, 7therefore I will stretch
out my hand against you and give you as plunder to the nations. I will
wipe you out from among the nations and exterminate you from the
countries. I will destroy you, and you will know that I am the LORD.’”

A PROPHECY AGAINST MOAB

8“This is what the Sovereign LORD says: ‘Because Moab and Seir said,
“Look, Judah has become like all the other nations,” 9therefore I will
expose the flank of Moab, beginning at its frontier towns — Beth Jesh-
imoth, Baal Meon and Kiriathaim — the glory of that land. 10I will give
Moab along with the Ammonites to the people of the East as a pos-
session, so that the Ammonites will not be remembered among the
nations; 11and I will inflict punishment on Moab. Then they will know
that I am the LORD.’”

A PROPHECY AGAINST EDOM

12“This is what the Sovereign LORD says: ‘Because Edom took revenge
on Judah and became very guilty by doing so, 13therefore this is what
the Sovereign LORD says: I will stretch out my hand against Edom and
kill both man and beast. I will lay it waste, and from Teman to Dedan
they will fall by the sword. 14I will take vengeance on Edom by the hand
of my people Israel, and they will deal with Edom in accordance with
my anger and my wrath; they will know my vengeance, declares the
Sovereign LORD.’”

A PROPHECY AGAINST PHILISTIA

15“This is what the Sovereign LORD says: ‘Because the Philistines
acted in vengeance and took revenge with malice in their hearts, and
with ancient hostility sought to destroy Judah, 16therefore this is what
the Sovereign LORD says: I am about to stretch out my hand against
the Philistines, and I will wipe out the Kerethites and destroy those
remaining along the coast. 17I will carry out great vengeance on them

and punish them in my wrath. Then they will know that I am the LORD,
when I take vengeance on them.’ ”

A PROPHECY AGAINST TYRE

26 In the eleventh month of the twelfth[a] year, on the first day of
the month, the word of the LORD came to me: 2“Son of man,
because Tyre has said of Jerusalem, ‘Aha! The gate to the nations is bro-
ken, and its doors have swung open to me; now that she lies in ruins
I will prosper,’ 3therefore this is what the Sovereign LORD says: I am
against you, Tyre, and I will bring many nations against you, like the
sea casting up its waves. 4They will destroy the walls of Tyre and pull
down her towers; I will scrape away her rubble and make her a bare
rock. 5Out in the sea she will become a place to spread fishnets, for I
have spoken, declares the Sovereign LORD. She will become plunder for
the nations, 6and her settlements on the mainland will be ravaged by
the sword. Then they will know that I am the LORD.
7“For this is what the Sovereign LORD says: From the north I am going
to bring against Tyre Nebuchadnezzar[b] king of Babylon, king of kings,
with horses and chariots, with horsemen and a great army. 8He will rav-
age your settlements on the mainland with the sword; he will set up siege
works against you, build a ramp up to your walls and raise his shields
against you. 9He will direct the blows of his battering rams against your
walls and demolish your towers with his weapons. 10His horses will be
so many that they will cover you with dust. Your walls will tremble at
the noise of the warhorses, wagons and chariots when he enters your
gates as men enter a city whose walls have been broken through. 11The
hooves of his horses will trample all your streets; he will kill your people
with the sword, and your strong pillars will fall to the ground. 12They will
plunder your wealth and loot your merchandise; they will break down
your walls and demolish your fine houses and throw your stones, timber
and rubble into the sea. 13I will put an end to your noisy songs, and the
music of your harps will be heard no more. 14I will make you a bare rock,
and you will become a place to spread fishnets. You will never be rebuilt,
for I the LORD have spoken, declares the Sovereign LORD.
15“This is what the Sovereign LORD says to Tyre: Will not the coast-
lands tremble at the sound of your fall, when the wounded groan and
the slaughter takes place in you? 16Then all the princes of the coast
will step down from their thrones and lay aside their robes and take
off their embroidered garments. Clothed with terror, they will sit on
the ground, trembling every moment, appalled at you. 17Then they will
take up a lament concerning you and say to you:

“ ‘How you are destroyed, city of renown,
  peopled by men of the sea!
You were a power on the seas,
  you and your citizens;
you put your terror
  on all who lived there.
18 Now the coastlands tremble
  on the day of your fall;
the islands in the sea
  are terrified at your collapse.’

[a] 1 Probable reading of the original Hebrew text; Masoretic Text does not have *month of the twelfth*. [b] 7 Hebrew *Nebuchadrezzar*, of which *Nebuchadnezzar* is a variant; here and often in Ezekiel and Jeremiah

PRAYING SCRIPTURE

Ezekiel 26

Judgment reveals how transient the nature of possessions really is. The people of Tyre would have their riches and merchandise plundered by their enemies. Their houses would be destroyed; the materials used to build them would be scattered.

Sin and rebellion rot nations to the core. God’s judgment strikes to the heart of everything that usurps his rightful place. Pray that you don’t idolize earthly possessions.

[19]"This is what the Sovereign LORD says: When I make you a deso-
late city, like cities no longer inhabited, and when I bring the ocean
depths over you and its vast waters cover you, [20]then I will bring you
down with those who go down to the pit, to the people of long ago. I
will make you dwell in the earth below, as in ancient ruins, with those
who go down to the pit, and you will not return or take your place[a] in
the land of the living. [21]I will bring you to a horrible end and you will
be no more. You will be sought, but you will never again be found, de-
clares the Sovereign LORD."

PRAYING SCRIPTURE

Ezekiel 27

Gathering riches for ourselves accomplishes nothing if we do not know and love God. Many of the nations that experienced God's judgment were fabulously wealthy. Tyre, who benefited from coastal trade with numerous cities, was "perfect in beauty" (verse 3).

Earthly possessions might impress those around us, but they are little more than fuel for God's fire. Pray for the right outlook on the things God has entrusted to your care.

A LAMENT OVER TYRE

27 The word of the LORD came to me: [2]"Son of man, take up a
lament concerning Tyre. [3]Say to Tyre, situated at the gateway
to the sea, merchant of peoples on many coasts, 'This is what the Sov-
ereign LORD says:

"'You say, Tyre,
"I am perfect in beauty."
[4]Your domain was on the high seas;
your builders brought your beauty to perfection.
[5]They made all your timbers
of juniper from Senir[b];
they took a cedar from Lebanon
to make a mast for you.
[6]Of oaks from Bashan
they made your oars;
of cypress wood[c] from the coasts of Cyprus
they made your deck, adorned with ivory.
[7]Fine embroidered linen from Egypt was your sail
and served as your banner;
your awnings were of blue and purple
from the coasts of Elishah.
[8]Men of Sidon and Arvad were your oarsmen;
your skilled men, Tyre, were aboard as your sailors.
[9]Veteran craftsmen of Byblos were on board
as shipwrights to caulk your seams.
All the ships of the sea and their sailors
came alongside to trade for your wares.
[10]"'Men of Persia, Lydia and Put
served as soldiers in your army.
They hung their shields and helmets on your walls,
bringing you splendor.
[11]Men of Arvad and Helek
guarded your walls on every side;
men of Gammad
were in your towers.
They hung their shields around your walls;
they brought your beauty to perfection.

[12]"'Tarshish did business with you because of your great wealth of
goods; they exchanged silver, iron, tin and lead for your merchandise.

---

[a] 20 Septuagint; Hebrew *return, and I will give glory* [b] 5 That is, Mount Hermon [c] 6 Targum; the Masoretic Text has a different division of the consonants.

13“ ‘Greece, Tubal and Meshek did business with you; they traded hu-
man beings and articles of bronze for your wares.
14“ ‘Men of Beth Togarmah exchanged chariot horses, cavalry horses
and mules for your merchandise.
15“ ‘The men of Rhodes[a] traded with you, and many coastlands were
your customers; they paid you with ivory tusks and ebony.
16“ ‘Aram[b] did business with you because of your many products;
they exchanged turquoise, purple fabric, embroidered work, fine
linen, coral and rubies for your merchandise.
17“ ‘Judah and Israel traded with you; they exchanged wheat from
Minnith and confections,[c] honey, olive oil and balm for your wares.
18“ ‘Damascus did business with you because of your many prod-
ucts and great wealth of goods. They offered wine from Helbon, wool
from Zahar 19and casks of wine from Izal in exchange for your wares:
wrought iron, cassia and calamus.
20“ ‘Dedan traded in saddle blankets with you.
21“ ‘Arabia and all the princes of Kedar were your customers; they did
business with you in lambs, rams and goats.
22“ ‘The merchants of Sheba and Raamah traded with you; for your
merchandise they exchanged the finest of all kinds of spices and pre-
cious stones, and gold.
23“ ‘Harran, Kanneh and Eden and merchants of Sheba, Ashur and
Kilmad traded with you. 24In your marketplace they traded with you
beautiful garments, blue fabric, embroidered work and multicolored
rugs with cords twisted and tightly knotted.

25“ ‘The ships of Tarshish serve
as carriers for your wares.
You are filled with heavy cargo
as you sail the sea.
26Your oarsmen take you
out to the high seas.
But the east wind will break you to pieces
far out at sea.
27Your wealth, merchandise and wares,
your mariners, sailors and shipwrights,
your merchants and all your soldiers,
and everyone else on board
will sink into the heart of the sea
on the day of your shipwreck.
28The shorelands will quake
when your sailors cry out.
29All who handle the oars
will abandon their ships;
the mariners and all the sailors
will stand on the shore.
30They will raise their voice
and cry bitterly over you;
they will sprinkle dust on their heads
and roll in ashes.
31They will shave their heads because of you
and will put on sackcloth.

[a] *15* Septuagint; Hebrew *Dedan* [b] *16* Most Hebrew manuscripts; some Hebrew manuscripts and Syriac *Edom* [c] *17* The meaning of the Hebrew for this word is uncertain.

They will weep over you with anguish of soul
and with bitter mourning.
32 As they wail and mourn over you,
they will take up a lament concerning you:
"Who was ever silenced like Tyre,
surrounded by the sea?"
33 When your merchandise went out on the seas,
you satisfied many nations;
with your great wealth and your wares
you enriched the kings of the earth.
34 Now you are shattered by the sea
in the depths of the waters;
your wares and all your company
have gone down with you.
35 All who live in the coastlands
are appalled at you;
their kings shudder with horror
and their faces are distorted with fear.
36 The merchants among the nations scoff at you;
you have come to a horrible end
and will be no more.' "

A PROPHECY AGAINST THE KING OF TYRE

PRAYING SCRIPTURE

Ezekiel 28

The middle of this chapter contains a reference to the king of Tyre that is also commonly understood as a depiction of Satan (see verses 12–17). Proud because of beauty, the one who had been exalted and anointed was cast down to shame.

Pride is rightly called the sin of the devil. Pride pits us against God, claiming for ourselves the position of lordship that belongs to him alone. Ask God for deliverance from pride's destruction.

28 The word of the LORD came to me: 2"Son of man, say to the ruler of Tyre, 'This is what the Sovereign LORD says:

" 'In the pride of your heart
you say, "I am a god;
I sit on the throne of a god
in the heart of the seas."
But you are a mere mortal and not a god,
though you think you are as wise as a god.
3 Are you wiser than Daniel[a]?
Is no secret hidden from you?
4 By your wisdom and understanding
you have gained wealth for yourself
and amassed gold and silver
in your treasuries.
5 By your great skill in trading
you have increased your wealth,
and because of your wealth
your heart has grown proud.

6 " 'Therefore this is what the Sovereign LORD says:

" 'Because you think you are wise,
as wise as a god,
7 I am going to bring foreigners against you,
the most ruthless of nations;
they will draw their swords against your beauty and wisdom
and pierce your shining splendor.
8 They will bring you down to the pit,
and you will die a violent death
in the heart of the seas.

[a] 3 Or *Danel*, a man of renown in ancient literature

9 Will you then say, "I am a god,"
in the presence of those who kill you?
You will be but a mortal, not a god,
in the hands of those who slay you.
10 You will die the death of the uncircumcised
at the hands of foreigners.

I have spoken, declares the Sovereign LORD.'"

11 The word of the LORD came to me: 12 "Son of man, take up a lament
concerning the king of Tyre and say to him: 'This is what the Sovereign
LORD says:

"'You were the seal of perfection,
full of wisdom and perfect in beauty.
13 You were in Eden,
the garden of God;
every precious stone adorned you:
carnelian, chrysolite and emerald,
topaz, onyx and jasper,
lapis lazuli, turquoise and beryl.[a]
Your settings and mountings[b] were made of gold;
on the day you were created they were prepared.
14 You were anointed as a guardian cherub,
for so I ordained you.
You were on the holy mount of God;
you walked among the fiery stones.
15 You were blameless in your ways
from the day you were created
till wickedness was found in you.
16 Through your widespread trade
you were filled with violence,
and you sinned.
So I drove you in disgrace from the mount of God,
and I expelled you, guardian cherub,
from among the fiery stones.
17 Your heart became proud
on account of your beauty,
and you corrupted your wisdom
because of your splendor.
So I threw you to the earth;
I made a spectacle of you before kings.
18 By your many sins and dishonest trade
you have desecrated your sanctuaries.
So I made a fire come out from you,
and it consumed you,
and I reduced you to ashes on the ground
in the sight of all who were watching.
19 All the nations who knew you
are appalled at you;
you have come to a horrible end
and will be no more.'"

---

[a] 13 The precise identification of some of these precious stones is uncertain.
[b] 13 The meaning of the Hebrew for this phrase is uncertain.

A PROPHECY AGAINST SIDON

20The word of the LORD came to me: 21"Son of man, set your face
against Sidon; prophesy against her 22and say: 'This is what the Sov-
ereign LORD says:

"'I am against you, Sidon,
and among you I will display my glory.
You will know that I am the LORD,
when I inflict punishment on you
and within you am proved to be holy.
23 I will send a plague upon you
and make blood flow in your streets.
The slain will fall within you,
with the sword against you on every side.
Then you will know that I am the LORD.

24"'No longer will the people of Israel have malicious neighbors who
are painful briers and sharp thorns. Then they will know that I am the
Sovereign LORD.

25"'This is what the Sovereign LORD says: When I gather the people
of Israel from the nations where they have been scattered, I will be
proved holy through them in the sight of the nations. Then they will
live in their own land, which I gave to my servant Jacob. 26They will
live there in safety and will build houses and plant vineyards; they
will live in safety when I inflict punishment on all their neighbors who
maligned them. Then they will know that I am the LORD their God.'"

A PROPHECY AGAINST EGYPT

JUDGMENT ON PHARAOH

29 In the tenth year, in the tenth month on the twelfth day, the
word of the LORD came to me: 2"Son of man, set your face
against Pharaoh king of Egypt and prophesy against him and against
all Egypt. 3Speak to him and say: 'This is what the Sovereign LORD says:

"'I am against you, Pharaoh king of Egypt,
you great monster lying among your streams.
You say, "The Nile belongs to me;
I made it for myself."
4 But I will put hooks in your jaws
and make the fish of your streams stick to your scales.
I will pull you out from among your streams,
with all the fish sticking to your scales.
5 I will leave you in the desert,
you and all the fish of your streams.
You will fall on the open field
and not be gathered or picked up.
I will give you as food
to the beasts of the earth and the birds of the sky.
6Then all who live in Egypt will know that I am the LORD.

"'You have been a staff of reed for the people of Israel. 7When they
grasped you with their hands, you splintered and you tore open their
shoulders; when they leaned on you, you broke and their backs were
wrenched.[a]

[a] 7 Syriac (see also Septuagint and Vulgate); Hebrew *and you caused their backs to stand*

PRAYING SCRIPTURE

Ezekiel 29

A common Old Testament pattern is that God used one nation to judge another, then later used a third nation to judge the first. This is not a result of uncertainty; it is a result of sin being punished. God judges on his own timeline and purposes.

The good news for God's people today is that we will never face judgment. Thank God his judgment has already been reconciled at the cross.

8“ ‘Therefore this is what the Sovereign LORD says: I will bring a
sword against you and kill both man and beast. 9Egypt will become a
desolate wasteland. Then they will know that I am the LORD.

“ ‘Because you said, “The Nile is mine; I made it,” 10therefore I am
against you and against your streams, and I will make the land of
Egypt a ruin and a desolate waste from Migdol to Aswan, as far as the
border of Cush.[a] 11The foot of neither man nor beast will pass through
it; no one will live there for forty years. 12I will make the land of Egypt
desolate among devastated lands, and her cities will lie desolate forty
years among ruined cities. And I will disperse the Egyptians among
the nations and scatter them through the countries.

13“ ‘Yet this is what the Sovereign LORD says: At the end of forty years
I will gather the Egyptians from the nations where they were scattered.
14I will bring them back from captivity and return them to Upper
Egypt, the land of their ancestry. There they will be a lowly kingdom.
15It will be the lowliest of kingdoms and will never again exalt itself
above the other nations. I will make it so weak that it will never again
rule over the nations. 16Egypt will no longer be a source of confidence
for the people of Israel but will be a reminder of their sin in turning
to her for help. Then they will know that I am the Sovereign LORD.’ ”

NEBUCHADNEZZAR'S REWARD

17In the twenty-seventh year, in the first month on the first day, the
word of the LORD came to me: 18“Son of man, Nebuchadnezzar king of
Babylon drove his army in a hard campaign against Tyre; every head
was rubbed bare and every shoulder made raw. Yet he and his army got
no reward from the campaign he led against Tyre. 19Therefore this is
what the Sovereign LORD says: I am going to give Egypt to Nebuchad-
nezzar king of Babylon, and he will carry off its wealth. He will loot
and plunder the land as pay for his army. 20I have given him Egypt as
a reward for his efforts because he and his army did it for me, declares
the Sovereign LORD.

21“On that day I will make a horn[b] grow for the Israelites, and I will
open your mouth among them. Then they will know that I am the LORD.”

A LAMENT OVER EGYPT

30 The word of the LORD came to me: 2“Son of man, prophesy and
say: ‘This is what the Sovereign LORD says:

“ ‘Wail and say,
“Alas for that day!”
3For the day is near,
the day of the LORD is near —
a day of clouds,
a time of doom for the nations.
4A sword will come against Egypt,
and anguish will come upon Cush.[c]
When the slain fall in Egypt,
her wealth will be carried away
and her foundations torn down.

5Cush and Libya, Lydia and all Arabia, Kub and the people of the cov-
enant land will fall by the sword along with Egypt.

[a] 10 That is, the upper Nile region [b] 21 *Horn* here symbolizes strength.
[c] 4 That is, the upper Nile region; also in verses 5 and 9

PRAYING SCRIPTURE

Ezekiel 30

God exercises his power and sovereignty over the rise and fall of nations. Neither the rise of nations nor their decline catches him by surprise; nor do their sin and repentance. He knows the nations, their names, their boundaries and their duration before they are even formed.

Thank God that he knows all and that nothing catches him off guard. You can trust him to know all about you too.

6" 'This is what the LORD says:

" 'The allies of Egypt will fall
and her proud strength will fail.
From Migdol to Aswan
they will fall by the sword within her,
declares the Sovereign LORD.
7" 'They will be desolate
among desolate lands,
and their cities will lie
among ruined cities.
8 Then they will know that I am the LORD,
when I set fire to Egypt
and all her helpers are crushed.

9" 'On that day messengers will go out from me in ships to frighten
Cush out of her complacency. Anguish will take hold of them on the
day of Egypt's doom, for it is sure to come.

10" 'This is what the Sovereign LORD says:

" 'I will put an end to the hordes of Egypt
by the hand of Nebuchadnezzar king of Babylon.
11 He and his army — the most ruthless of nations —
will be brought in to destroy the land.
They will draw their swords against Egypt
and fill the land with the slain.
12 I will dry up the waters of the Nile
and sell the land to an evil nation;
by the hand of foreigners
I will lay waste the land and everything in it.

I the LORD have spoken.

13" 'This is what the Sovereign LORD says:

" 'I will destroy the idols
and put an end to the images in Memphis.
No longer will there be a prince in Egypt,
and I will spread fear throughout the land.
14 I will lay waste Upper Egypt,
set fire to Zoan
and inflict punishment on Thebes.
15 I will pour out my wrath on Pelusium,
the stronghold of Egypt,
and wipe out the hordes of Thebes.
16 I will set fire to Egypt;
Pelusium will writhe in agony.
Thebes will be taken by storm;
Memphis will be in constant distress.
17 The young men of Heliopolis and Bubastis
will fall by the sword,
and the cities themselves will go into captivity.
18 Dark will be the day at Tahpanhes
when I break the yoke of Egypt;
there her proud strength will come to an end.
She will be covered with clouds,
and her villages will go into captivity.

19 So I will inflict punishment on Egypt,
and they will know that I am the LORD.' "

PHARAOH'S ARMS ARE BROKEN

20 In the eleventh year, in the first month on the seventh day, the
word of the LORD came to me: 21 "Son of man, I have broken the arm of
Pharaoh king of Egypt. It has not been bound up to be healed or put in
a splint so that it may become strong enough to hold a sword. 22 There-
fore this is what the Sovereign LORD says: I am against Pharaoh king
of Egypt. I will break both his arms, the good arm as well as the broken
one, and make the sword fall from his hand. 23 I will disperse the Egyp-
tians among the nations and scatter them through the countries. 24 I
will strengthen the arms of the king of Babylon and put my sword in
his hand, but I will break the arms of Pharaoh, and he will groan before
him like a mortally wounded man. 25 I will strengthen the arms of the
king of Babylon, but the arms of Pharaoh will fall limp. Then they will
know that I am the LORD, when I put my sword into the hand of the
king of Babylon and he brandishes it against Egypt. 26 I will disperse
the Egyptians among the nations and scatter them through the coun-
tries. Then they will know that I am the LORD."

PHARAOH AS A FELLED CEDAR OF LEBANON

31 In the eleventh year, in the third month on the first day, the
word of the LORD came to me: 2 "Son of man, say to Pharaoh king
of Egypt and to his hordes:

" 'Who can be compared with you in majesty?
3 Consider Assyria, once a cedar in Lebanon,
with beautiful branches overshadowing the forest;
it towered on high,
its top above the thick foliage.
4 The waters nourished it,
deep springs made it grow tall;
their streams flowed
all around its base
and sent their channels
to all the trees of the field.
5 So it towered higher
than all the trees of the field;
its boughs increased
and its branches grew long,
spreading because of abundant waters.
6 All the birds of the sky
nested in its boughs,
all the animals of the wild
gave birth under its branches;
all the great nations
lived in its shade.
7 It was majestic in beauty,
with its spreading boughs,
for its roots went down
to abundant waters.
8 The cedars in the garden of God
could not rival it,
nor could the junipers
equal its boughs,

PRAYING SCRIPTURE

Ezekiel 31

In an unusual reference, the Lord compares Egypt's judgment to his judgment on the Garden of Eden. Having pictured Egypt as a great tree, he reminded them they couldn't compare to the trees of Eden. He promised to cut Egypt down "to the earth below" (verse 18).

Think of all that was lost when Adam and Eve sinned, and long for the time when Eden's promise is restored to God's people.

nor could the plane trees
compare with its branches—
no tree in the garden of God
could match its beauty.
9I made it beautiful
with abundant branches,
the envy of all the trees of Eden
in the garden of God.

10" 'Therefore this is what the Sovereign LORD says: Because the great
cedar towered over the thick foliage, and because it was proud of its
height, 11I gave it into the hands of the ruler of the nations, for him to
deal with according to its wickedness. I cast it aside, 12and the most
ruthless of foreign nations cut it down and left it. Its boughs fell on
the mountains and in all the valleys; its branches lay broken in all the
ravines of the land. All the nations of the earth came out from under
its shade and left it. 13All the birds settled on the fallen tree, and all the
wild animals lived among its branches. 14Therefore no other trees by
the waters are ever to tower proudly on high, lifting their tops above
the thick foliage. No other trees so well-watered are ever to reach such
a height; they are all destined for death, for the earth below, among
mortals who go down to the realm of the dead.

15" 'This is what the Sovereign LORD says: On the day it was brought
down to the realm of the dead I covered the deep springs with mourn-
ing for it; I held back its streams, and its abundant waters were re-
strained. Because of it I clothed Lebanon with gloom, and all the trees
of the field withered away. 16I made the nations tremble at the sound
of its fall when I brought it down to the realm of the dead to be with
those who go down to the pit. Then all the trees of Eden, the choicest
and best of Lebanon, the well-watered trees, were consoled in the earth
below. 17They too, like the great cedar, had gone down to the realm of
the dead, to those killed by the sword, along with the armed men who
lived in its shade among the nations.

18" 'Which of the trees of Eden can be compared with you in splendor
and majesty? Yet you, too, will be brought down with the trees of Eden
to the earth below; you will lie among the uncircumcised, with those
killed by the sword.

" 'This is Pharaoh and all his hordes, declares the Sovereign LORD.' "

PRAYING SCRIPTURE

Ezekiel 32

Instructing a prophet to take up a lamentation was God's way of revealing who was to be judged. Even in the face of judgment of sin and iniquity, there was room for lament. God has no pleasure in the death of the wicked (Ezekiel 18:23). Lament over their deaths is right for God's people.

How do you respond when wicked people die? We should learn to rejoice when sin is stopped but lament when sinners die.

A LAMENT OVER PHARAOH

32 In the twelfth year, in the twelfth month on the first day, the
word of the LORD came to me: 2"Son of man, take up a lament
concerning Pharaoh king of Egypt and say to him:

" 'You are like a lion among the nations;
you are like a monster in the seas
thrashing about in your streams,
churning the water with your feet
and muddying the streams.

3" 'This is what the Sovereign LORD says:

" 'With a great throng of people
I will cast my net over you,
and they will haul you up in my net.
4I will throw you on the land
and hurl you on the open field.

I will let all the birds of the sky settle on you
  and all the animals of the wild gorge themselves on you.
5 I will spread your flesh on the mountains
  and fill the valleys with your remains.
6 I will drench the land with your flowing blood
  all the way to the mountains,
  and the ravines will be filled with your flesh.
7 When I snuff you out, I will cover the heavens
  and darken their stars;
I will cover the sun with a cloud,
  and the moon will not give its light.
8 All the shining lights in the heavens
  I will darken over you;
  I will bring darkness over your land,
    declares the Sovereign LORD.
9 I will trouble the hearts of many peoples
  when I bring about your destruction among the nations,
  among[a] lands you have not known.
10 I will cause many peoples to be appalled at you,
  and their kings will shudder with horror because of you
  when I brandish my sword before them.
On the day of your downfall
  each of them will tremble
  every moment for his life.

11 " 'For this is what the Sovereign LORD says:

" 'The sword of the king of Babylon
  will come against you.
12 I will cause your hordes to fall
  by the swords of mighty men—
  the most ruthless of all nations.
They will shatter the pride of Egypt,
  and all her hordes will be overthrown.
13 I will destroy all her cattle
  from beside abundant waters
no longer to be stirred by the foot of man
  or muddied by the hooves of cattle.
14 Then I will let her waters settle
  and make her streams flow like oil,
    declares the Sovereign LORD.
15 When I make Egypt desolate
  and strip the land of everything in it,
when I strike down all who live there,
  then they will know that I am the LORD.'

16 "This is the lament they will chant for her. The daughters of the
nations will chant it; for Egypt and all her hordes they will chant it,
declares the Sovereign LORD."

EGYPT'S DESCENT INTO THE REALM OF THE DEAD

17 In the twelfth year, on the fifteenth day of the month, the word
of the LORD came to me: 18 "Son of man, wail for the hordes of Egypt
and consign to the earth below both her and the daughters of mighty

---

[a] 9 Hebrew; Septuagint *bring you into captivity among the nations, / to*

nations, along with those who go down to the pit. 19Say to them, 'Are you more favored than others? Go down and be laid among the uncircumcised.' 20They will fall among those killed by the sword. The sword is drawn; let her be dragged off with all her hordes. 21From within the realm of the dead the mighty leaders will say of Egypt and her allies, 'They have come down and they lie with the uncircumcised, with those killed by the sword.'

22"Assyria is there with her whole army; she is surrounded by the graves of all her slain, all who have fallen by the sword. 23Their graves are in the depths of the pit and her army lies around her grave. All who had spread terror in the land of the living are slain, fallen by the sword.

24"Elam is there, with all her hordes around her grave. All of them are slain, fallen by the sword. All who had spread terror in the land of the living went down uncircumcised to the earth below. They bear their shame with those who go down to the pit. 25A bed is made for her among the slain, with all her hordes around her grave. All of them are uncircumcised, killed by the sword. Because their terror had spread in the land of the living, they bear their shame with those who go down to the pit; they are laid among the slain.

26"Meshek and Tubal are there, with all their hordes around their graves. All of them are uncircumcised, killed by the sword because they spread their terror in the land of the living. 27But they do not lie with the fallen warriors of old,[a] who went down to the realm of the dead with their weapons of war — their swords placed under their heads and their shields[b] resting on their bones — though these warriors also had terrorized the land of the living.

28"You too, Pharaoh, will be broken and will lie among the uncircumcised, with those killed by the sword.

29"Edom is there, her kings and all her princes; despite their power, they are laid with those killed by the sword. They lie with the uncircumcised, with those who go down to the pit.

30"All the princes of the north and all the Sidonians are there; they went down with the slain in disgrace despite the terror caused by their power. They lie uncircumcised with those killed by the sword and bear their shame with those who go down to the pit.

31"Pharaoh — he and all his army — will see them and he will be consoled for all his hordes that were killed by the sword, declares the Sovereign LORD. 32Although I had him spread terror in the land of the living, Pharaoh and all his hordes will be laid among the uncircumcised, with those killed by the sword, declares the Sovereign LORD."

RENEWAL OF EZEKIEL'S CALL AS WATCHMAN

33 The word of the LORD came to me: 2"Son of man, speak to your people and say to them: 'When I bring the sword against a land, and the people of the land choose one of their men and make him their watchman, 3and he sees the sword coming against the land and blows the trumpet to warn the people, 4then if anyone hears the trumpet but does not heed the warning and the sword comes and takes their life, their blood will be on their own head. 5Since they heard the sound of the trumpet but did not heed the warning, their blood will be on their own head. If they had heeded the warning, they

PRAYING SCRIPTURE

Ezekiel 33

Central to God's judgment is the hope of repentance. His purpose is to lead the wicked to turn from their ways so that "they will not die" (verse 15). Referencing God's complete forgiveness, Ezekiel said, "None of the sins that person has committed will be remembered against them" (verse 16).

What a glorious promise for all who turn from sin! God doesn't simply forgive; he totally removes the offense. Thank him for such thorough cleansing.

[a] 27 Septuagint; Hebrew *warriors who were uncircumcised* [b] 27 Probable reading of the original Hebrew text; Masoretic Text *punishment*

would have saved themselves. [6]But if the watchman sees the sword
coming and does not blow the trumpet to warn the people and the
sword comes and takes someone's life, that person's life will be taken
because of their sin, but I will hold the watchman accountable for their
blood.'

[7]"Son of man, I have made you a watchman for the people of Israel;
so hear the word I speak and give them warning from me. [8]When I say
to the wicked, 'You wicked person, you will surely die,' and you do not
speak out to dissuade them from their ways, that wicked person will
die for[a] their sin, and I will hold you accountable for their blood. [9]But
if you do warn the wicked person to turn from their ways and they do
not do so, they will die for their sin, though you yourself will be saved.

[10]"Son of man, say to the Israelites, 'This is what you are saying: "Our
offenses and sins weigh us down, and we are wasting away because
of[b] them. How then can we live?"' [11]Say to them, 'As surely as I live,
declares the Sovereign LORD, I take no pleasure in the death of the
wicked, but rather that they turn from their ways and live. Turn! Turn
from your evil ways! Why will you die, people of Israel?'

[12]"Therefore, son of man, say to your people, 'If someone who is
righteous disobeys, that person's former righteousness will count for
nothing. And if someone who is wicked repents, that person's former
wickedness will not bring condemnation. The righteous person who
sins will not be allowed to live even though they were formerly righ-
teous.' [13]If I tell a righteous person that they will surely live, but then
they trust in their righteousness and do evil, none of the righteous
things that person has done will be remembered; they will die for the
evil they have done. [14]And if I say to a wicked person, 'You will surely
die,' but they then turn away from their sin and do what is just and
right — [15]if they give back what they took in pledge for a loan, return
what they have stolen, follow the decrees that give life, and do no
evil — that person will surely live; they will not die. [16]None of the sins
that person has committed will be remembered against them. They
have done what is just and right; they will surely live.

[17]"Yet your people say, 'The way of the Lord is not just.' But it is their
way that is not just. [18]If a righteous person turns from their righteous-
ness and does evil, they will die for it. [19]And if a wicked person turns
away from their wickedness and does what is just and right, they will
live by doing so. [20]Yet you Israelites say, 'The way of the Lord is not
just.' But I will judge each of you according to your own ways."

JERUSALEM'S FALL EXPLAINED

[21]In the twelfth year of our exile, in the tenth month on the fifth day,
a man who had escaped from Jerusalem came to me and said, "The city
has fallen!" [22]Now the evening before the man arrived, the hand of the
LORD was on me, and he opened my mouth before the man came to me
in the morning. So my mouth was opened and I was no longer silent.

[23]Then the word of the LORD came to me: [24]"Son of man, the people
living in those ruins in the land of Israel are saying, 'Abraham was only
one man, yet he possessed the land. But we are many; surely the land
has been given to us as our possession.' [25]Therefore say to them, 'This
is what the Sovereign LORD says: Since you eat meat with the blood still
in it and look to your idols and shed blood, should you then possess

[a] *8* Or *in*; also in verse 9 [b] *10* Or *away in*

the land? 26You rely on your sword, you do detestable things, and each
of you defiles his neighbor's wife. Should you then possess the land?'
27"Say this to them: 'This is what the Sovereign LORD says: As surely
as I live, those who are left in the ruins will fall by the sword, those
out in the country I will give to the wild animals to be devoured, and
those in strongholds and caves will die of a plague. 28I will make the
land a desolate waste, and her proud strength will come to an end,
and the mountains of Israel will become desolate so that no one will
cross them. 29Then they will know that I am the LORD, when I have
made the land a desolate waste because of all the detestable things
they have done.'
30"As for you, son of man, your people are talking together about
you by the walls and at the doors of the houses, saying to each other,
'Come and hear the message that has come from the LORD.' 31My people
come to you, as they usually do, and sit before you to hear your words,
but they do not put them into practice. Their mouths speak of love,
but their hearts are greedy for unjust gain. 32Indeed, to them you are
nothing more than one who sings love songs with a beautiful voice
and plays an instrument well, for they hear your words but do not put
them into practice.
33"When all this comes true—and it surely will—then they will
know that a prophet has been among them."

THE LORD WILL BE ISRAEL'S SHEPHERD

34 The word of the LORD came to me: 2"Son of man, prophesy
against the shepherds of Israel; prophesy and say to them:
'This is what the Sovereign LORD says: Woe to you shepherds of Is-
rael who only take care of yourselves! Should not shepherds take care
of the flock? 3You eat the curds, clothe yourselves with the wool and
slaughter the choice animals, but you do not take care of the flock.
4You have not strengthened the weak or healed the sick or bound up
the injured. You have not brought back the strays or searched for the
lost. You have ruled them harshly and brutally. 5So they were scattered
because there was no shepherd, and when they were scattered they
became food for all the wild animals. 6My sheep wandered over all the
mountains and on every high hill. They were scattered over the whole
earth, and no one searched or looked for them.
7"'Therefore, you shepherds, hear the word of the LORD: 8As surely as
I live, declares the Sovereign LORD, because my flock lacks a shepherd
and so has been plundered and has become food for all the wild ani-
mals, and because my shepherds did not search for my flock but cared
for themselves rather than for my flock, 9therefore, you shepherds,
hear the word of the LORD: 10This is what the Sovereign LORD says: I am
against the shepherds and will hold them accountable for my flock. I
will remove them from tending the flock so that the shepherds can no
longer feed themselves. I will rescue my flock from their mouths, and
it will no longer be food for them.
11"'For this is what the Sovereign LORD says: I myself will search for
my sheep and look after them. 12As a shepherd looks after his scat-
tered flock when he is with them, so will I look after my sheep. I will
rescue them from all the places where they were scattered on a day
of clouds and darkness. 13I will bring them out from the nations and
gather them from the countries, and I will bring them into their own
land. I will pasture them on the mountains of Israel, in the ravines and

PRAYING SCRIPTURE

Ezekiel 34

Every shepherd of God's people bears the burden of caring for the flock rather than only looking out for himself or herself. The prophets directed some of the harshest words toward the shepherds—priests and other spiritual leaders—who enriched or otherwise elevated themselves at the expense of their sheep.

If you're a shepherd, examine your priorities. Are your sheep first? If not, ask God to reorient your heart to a heart like his.

in all the settlements in the land. [14]I will tend them in a good pasture, and the mountain heights of Israel will be their grazing land. There they will lie down in good grazing land, and there they will feed in a rich pasture on the mountains of Israel. [15]I myself will tend my sheep and have them lie down, declares the Sovereign LORD. [16]I will search for the lost and bring back the strays. I will bind up the injured and strengthen the weak, but the sleek and the strong I will destroy. I will shepherd the flock with justice.

[17]" 'As for you, my flock, this is what the Sovereign LORD says: I will judge between one sheep and another, and between rams and goats. [18]Is it not enough for you to feed on the good pasture? Must you also trample the rest of your pasture with your feet? Is it not enough for you to drink clear water? Must you also muddy the rest with your feet? [19]Must my flock feed on what you have trampled and drink what you have muddied with your feet?

[20]" 'Therefore this is what the Sovereign LORD says to them: See, I myself will judge between the fat sheep and the lean sheep. [21]Because you shove with flank and shoulder, butting all the weak sheep with your horns until you have driven them away, [22]I will save my flock, and they will no longer be plundered. I will judge between one sheep and another. [23]I will place over them one shepherd, my servant David, and he will tend them; he will tend them and be their shepherd. [24]I the LORD will be their God, and my servant David will be prince among them. I the LORD have spoken.

[25]" 'I will make a covenant of peace with them and rid the land of savage beasts so that they may live in the wilderness and sleep in the forests in safety. [26]I will make them and the places surrounding my hill a blessing.[a] I will send down showers in season; there will be showers of blessing. [27]The trees will yield their fruit and the ground will yield its crops; the people will be secure in their land. They will know that I am the LORD, when I break the bars of their yoke and rescue them from the hands of those who enslaved them. [28]They will no longer be plundered by the nations, nor will wild animals devour them. They will live in safety, and no one will make them afraid. [29]I will provide for them a land renowned for its crops, and they will no longer be victims of famine in the land or bear the scorn of the nations. [30]Then they will know that I, the LORD their God, am with them and that they, the Israelites, are my people, declares the Sovereign LORD. [31]You are my sheep, the sheep of my pasture, and I am your God, declares the Sovereign LORD.' "

A PROPHECY AGAINST EDOM

35 The word of the LORD came to me: [2]"Son of man, set your face against Mount Seir; prophesy against it [3]and say: 'This is what the Sovereign LORD says: I am against you, Mount Seir, and I will stretch out my hand against you and make you a desolate waste. [4]I will turn your towns into ruins and you will be desolate. Then you will know that I am the LORD.

[5]" 'Because you harbored an ancient hostility and delivered the Israelites over to the sword at the time of their calamity, the time their punishment reached its climax, [6]therefore as surely as I live, declares

[a] 26 Or *I will cause them and the places surrounding my hill to be named in blessings* (see Gen. 48:20); or *I will cause them and the places surrounding my hill to be seen as blessed*

PRAYING SCRIPTURE

Ezekiel 35

The prophets repeatedly made it clear that they were speaking for God. Their words of judgment didn't arise from within themselves. They also made clear that the nations were judged for their own sins: "I will treat you in accordance with the anger and jealousy you showed" (verse 11).

God's judgment saw its ultimate fulfillment when Jesus bore the sins of all for all time. Thank God for his work at the cross.

the Sovereign LORD, I will give you over to bloodshed and it will pursue
you. Since you did not hate bloodshed, bloodshed will pursue you. 7I
will make Mount Seir a desolate waste and cut off from it all who come
and go. 8I will fill your mountains with the slain; those killed by the
sword will fall on your hills and in your valleys and in all your ravines.
9I will make you desolate forever; your towns will not be inhabited.
Then you will know that I am the LORD.

10" 'Because you have said, "These two nations and countries will be
ours and we will take possession of them," even though I the LORD
was there, 11therefore as surely as I live, declares the Sovereign LORD,
I will treat you in accordance with the anger and jealousy you showed
in your hatred of them and I will make myself known among them
when I judge you. 12Then you will know that I the LORD have heard all
the contemptible things you have said against the mountains of Israel.
You said, "They have been laid waste and have been given over to us to
devour." 13You boasted against me and spoke against me without re-
straint, and I heard it. 14This is what the Sovereign LORD says: While the
whole earth rejoices, I will make you desolate. 15Because you rejoiced
when the inheritance of Israel became desolate, that is how I will treat
you. You will be desolate, Mount Seir, you and all of Edom. Then they
will know that I am the LORD.' "

HOPE FOR THE MOUNTAINS OF ISRAEL

36 "Son of man, prophesy to the mountains of Israel and say,
'Mountains of Israel, hear the word of the LORD. 2This is what
the Sovereign LORD says: The enemy said of you, "Aha! The ancient
heights have become our possession." ' 3Therefore prophesy and say,
'This is what the Sovereign LORD says: Because they ravaged and
crushed you from every side so that you became the possession of the
rest of the nations and the object of people's malicious talk and slan-
der, 4therefore, mountains of Israel, hear the word of the Sovereign
LORD: This is what the Sovereign LORD says to the mountains and hills,
to the ravines and valleys, to the desolate ruins and the deserted towns
that have been plundered and ridiculed by the rest of the nations
around you— 5this is what the Sovereign LORD says: In my burning
zeal I have spoken against the rest of the nations, and against all Edom,
for with glee and with malice in their hearts they made my land their
own possession so that they might plunder its pastureland.' 6Therefore
prophesy concerning the land of Israel and say to the mountains and
hills, to the ravines and valleys: 'This is what the Sovereign LORD says:
I speak in my jealous wrath because you have suffered the scorn of the
nations. 7Therefore this is what the Sovereign LORD says: I swear with
uplifted hand that the nations around you will also suffer scorn.

8" 'But you, mountains of Israel, will produce branches and fruit for
my people Israel, for they will soon come home. 9I am concerned for
you and will look on you with favor; you will be plowed and sown,
10and I will cause many people to live on you—yes, all of Israel. The
towns will be inhabited and the ruins rebuilt. 11I will increase the num-
ber of people and animals living on you, and they will be fruitful and
become numerous. I will settle people on you as in the past and will
make you prosper more than before. Then you will know that I am the
LORD. 12I will cause people, my people Israel, to live on you. They will
possess you, and you will be their inheritance; you will never again
deprive them of their children.

PRAYING SCRIPTURE

Ezekiel 36

The promise of the new covenant, the hope of new life, is God's replacing our old stony hearts with hearts of flesh. Moreover, God promised, "I will put my Spirit in you and move you to follow my decrees and be careful to keep my laws" (verse 27). The advantages we have in the new covenant are almost too good to believe.

The presence of the Holy Spirit in us should be a source of ongoing thanksgiving.

13"'This is what the Sovereign LORD says: Because some say to you,
"You devour people and deprive your nation of its children," 14there-
fore you will no longer devour people or make your nation childless,
declares the Sovereign LORD. 15No longer will I make you hear the
taunts of the nations, and no longer will you suffer the scorn of the
peoples or cause your nation to fall, declares the Sovereign LORD.'"

ISRAEL'S RESTORATION ASSURED

16Again the word of the LORD came to me: 17"Son of man, when the
people of Israel were living in their own land, they defiled it by their
conduct and their actions. Their conduct was like a woman's monthly
uncleanness in my sight. 18So I poured out my wrath on them because
they had shed blood in the land and because they had defiled it with
their idols. 19I dispersed them among the nations, and they were scat-
tered through the countries; I judged them according to their conduct
and their actions. 20And wherever they went among the nations they
profaned my holy name, for it was said of them, 'These are the LORD's
people, and yet they had to leave his land.' 21I had concern for my holy
name, which the people of Israel profaned among the nations where
they had gone.

22"Therefore say to the Israelites, 'This is what the Sovereign LORD
says: It is not for your sake, people of Israel, that I am going to do these
things, but for the sake of my holy name, which you have profaned
among the nations where you have gone. 23I will show the holiness
of my great name, which has been profaned among the nations, the
name you have profaned among them. Then the nations will know
that I am the LORD, declares the Sovereign LORD, when I am proved
holy through you before their eyes.

24"'For I will take you out of the nations; I will gather you from all
the countries and bring you back into your own land. 25I will sprinkle
clean water on you, and you will be clean; I will cleanse you from all
your impurities and from all your idols. 26I will give you a new heart
and put a new spirit in you; I will remove from you your heart of stone
and give you a heart of flesh. 27And I will put my Spirit in you and
move you to follow my decrees and be careful to keep my laws. 28Then
you will live in the land I gave your ancestors; you will be my people,
and I will be your God. 29I will save you from all your uncleanness. I
will call for the grain and make it plentiful and will not bring famine
upon you. 30I will increase the fruit of the trees and the crops of the
field, so that you will no longer suffer disgrace among the nations be-
cause of famine. 31Then you will remember your evil ways and wicked
deeds, and you will loathe yourselves for your sins and detestable prac-
tices. 32I want you to know that I am not doing this for your sake, de-
clares the Sovereign LORD. Be ashamed and disgraced for your conduct,
people of Israel!

33"'This is what the Sovereign LORD says: On the day I cleanse you
from all your sins, I will resettle your towns, and the ruins will be re-
built. 34The desolate land will be cultivated instead of lying desolate in
the sight of all who pass through it. 35They will say, "This land that was
laid waste has become like the garden of Eden; the cities that were ly-
ing in ruins, desolate and destroyed, are now fortified and inhabited."
36Then the nations around you that remain will know that I the LORD
have rebuilt what was destroyed and have replanted what was deso-
late. I the LORD have spoken, and I will do it.'

37“This is what the Sovereign LORD says: Once again I will yield to
Israel’s plea and do this for them: I will make their people as numerous
as sheep, 38as numerous as the flocks for offerings at Jerusalem during
her appointed festivals. So will the ruined cities be filled with flocks of
people. Then they will know that I am the LORD.”

THE VALLEY OF DRY BONES

37 The hand of the LORD was on me, and he brought me out by
the Spirit of the LORD and set me in the middle of a valley; it
was full of bones. 2He led me back and forth among them, and I saw a
great many bones on the floor of the valley, bones that were very dry.
3He asked me, “Son of man, can these bones live?”
I said, “Sovereign LORD, you alone know.”
4Then he said to me, “Prophesy to these bones and say to them, ‘Dry
bones, hear the word of the LORD! 5This is what the Sovereign LORD
says to these bones: I will make breath[a] enter you, and you will come
to life. 6I will attach tendons to you and make flesh come upon you and
cover you with skin; I will put breath in you, and you will come to life.
Then you will know that I am the LORD.’ ”
7So I prophesied as I was commanded. And as I was prophesying,
there was a noise, a rattling sound, and the bones came together, bone
to bone. 8I looked, and tendons and flesh appeared on them and skin
covered them, but there was no breath in them.
9Then he said to me, “Prophesy to the breath; prophesy, son of man,
and say to it, ‘This is what the Sovereign LORD says: Come, breath, from
the four winds and breathe into these slain, that they may live.’ ” 10So
I prophesied as he commanded me, and breath entered them; they
came to life and stood up on their feet—a vast army.
11Then he said to me: “Son of man, these bones are the people of Is-
rael. They say, ‘Our bones are dried up and our hope is gone; we are cut
off.’ 12Therefore prophesy and say to them: ‘This is what the Sovereign
LORD says: My people, I am going to open your graves and bring you
up from them; I will bring you back to the land of Israel. 13Then you,
my people, will know that I am the LORD, when I open your graves and
bring you up from them. 14I will put my Spirit in you and you will live,
and I will settle you in your own land. Then you will know that I the
LORD have spoken, and I have done it, declares the LORD.’ ”

ONE NATION UNDER ONE KING

15The word of the LORD came to me: 16“Son of man, take a stick of
wood and write on it, ‘Belonging to Judah and the Israelites associated
with him.’ Then take another stick of wood, and write on it, ‘Belonging
to Joseph (that is, to Ephraim) and all the Israelites associated with
him.’ 17Join them together into one stick so that they will become one
in your hand.
18“When your people ask you, ‘Won’t you tell us what you mean by
this?’ 19say to them, ‘This is what the Sovereign LORD says: I am going
to take the stick of Joseph—which is in Ephraim’s hand—and of the
Israelite tribes associated with him, and join it to Judah’s stick. I will
make them into a single stick of wood, and they will become one in my
hand.’ 20Hold before their eyes the sticks you have written on 21and say
to them, ‘This is what the Sovereign LORD says: I will take the Israelites

PRAYING SCRIPTURE

Ezekiel 37

Few Biblical stories are as vivid as Ezekiel’s valley of dry bones. Prophesying in an open graveyard, God reassembled these fallen people piecemeal by bone, sinew and skin. When breath entered them, they came to life! God did this as a sign; he would indeed restore Israel.

God is able to raise the physical dead and the spiritual dead. If you do not know God, ask him to raise you to spiritual life.

[a] 5 The Hebrew for this word can also mean *wind* or *spirit* (see verses 6-14).

out of the nations where they have gone. I will gather them from all around and bring them back into their own land. 22I will make them one nation in the land, on the mountains of Israel. There will be one king over all of them and they will never again be two nations or be divided into two kingdoms. 23They will no longer defile themselves with their idols and vile images or with any of their offenses, for I will save them from all their sinful backsliding,[a] and I will cleanse them. They will be my people, and I will be their God.

24" 'My servant David will be king over them, and they will all have one shepherd. They will follow my laws and be careful to keep my decrees. 25They will live in the land I gave to my servant Jacob, the land where your ancestors lived. They and their children and their children's children will live there forever, and David my servant will be their prince forever. 26I will make a covenant of peace with them; it will be an everlasting covenant. I will establish them and increase their numbers, and I will put my sanctuary among them forever. 27My dwelling place will be with them; I will be their God, and they will be my people. 28Then the nations will know that I the LORD make Israel holy, when my sanctuary is among them forever.' "

THE LORD'S GREAT VICTORY OVER THE NATIONS

38 The word of the LORD came to me: 2"Son of man, set your face against Gog, of the land of Magog, the chief prince of[b] Meshek and Tubal; prophesy against him 3and say: 'This is what the Sovereign LORD says: I am against you, Gog, chief prince of[c] Meshek and Tubal. 4I will turn you around, put hooks in your jaws and bring you out with your whole army—your horses, your horsemen fully armed, and a great horde with large and small shields, all of them brandishing their swords. 5Persia, Cush[d] and Put will be with them, all with shields and helmets, 6also Gomer with all its troops, and Beth Togarmah from the far north with all its troops—the many nations with you.

7" 'Get ready; be prepared, you and all the hordes gathered about you, and take command of them. 8After many days you will be called to arms. In future years you will invade a land that has recovered from war, whose people were gathered from many nations to the mountains of Israel, which had long been desolate. They had been brought out from the nations, and now all of them live in safety. 9You and all your troops and the many nations with you will go up, advancing like a storm; you will be like a cloud covering the land.

10" 'This is what the Sovereign LORD says: On that day thoughts will come into your mind and you will devise an evil scheme. 11You will say, "I will invade a land of unwalled villages; I will attack a peaceful and unsuspecting people—all of them living without walls and without gates and bars. 12I will plunder and loot and turn my hand against the resettled ruins and the people gathered from the nations, rich in livestock and goods, living at the center of the land.[e]" 13Sheba and Dedan and the merchants of Tarshish and all her villages[f] will say to you, "Have you come to plunder? Have you gathered your hordes to loot, to carry off silver and gold, to take away livestock and goods and to seize much plunder?" '

PRAYING SCRIPTURE

Ezekiel 38

The centuries have proven fertile ground for endless speculation as to the identities and actions of Gog, Magog, Rosh, Meshech, Tubal and Gomer, and whether these prophecies apply to the generations through time. Even so, God said "I will show my greatness and my holiness, and I will make myself known in the sight of many nations" (verse 23).

Thank God for his glory so great that eventually every nation will bow to him.

---

[a] *23* Many Hebrew manuscripts (see also Septuagint); most Hebrew manuscripts *all their dwelling places where they sinned* [b] *2* Or *the prince of Rosh,* [c] *3* Or *Gog, prince of Rosh,* [d] *5* That is, the upper Nile region [e] *12* The Hebrew for this phrase means *the navel of the earth.* [f] *13* Or *her strong lions*

14“Therefore, son of man, prophesy and say to Gog: ‘This is what the
Sovereign LORD says: In that day, when my people Israel are living in
safety, will you not take notice of it? 15You will come from your place
in the far north, you and many nations with you, all of them riding on
horses, a great horde, a mighty army. 16You will advance against my
people Israel like a cloud that covers the land. In days to come, Gog, I
will bring you against my land, so that the nations may know me when
I am proved holy through you before their eyes.
17“ ‘This is what the Sovereign LORD says: You are the one I spoke
of in former days by my servants the prophets of Israel. At that time
they prophesied for years that I would bring you against them. 18This
is what will happen in that day: When Gog attacks the land of Israel, my
hot anger will be aroused, declares the Sovereign LORD. 19In my zeal
and fiery wrath I declare that at that time there shall be a great earth-
quake in the land of Israel. 20The fish in the sea, the birds in the sky,
the beasts of the field, every creature that moves along the ground,
and all the people on the face of the earth will tremble at my presence.
The mountains will be overturned, the cliffs will crumble and every
wall will fall to the ground. 21I will summon a sword against Gog on all
my mountains, declares the Sovereign LORD. Every man’s sword will be
against his brother. 22I will execute judgment on him with plague and
bloodshed; I will pour down torrents of rain, hailstones and burning
sulfur on him and on his troops and on the many nations with him.
23And so I will show my greatness and my holiness, and I will make
myself known in the sight of many nations. Then they will know that
I am the LORD.’

39 “Son of man, prophesy against Gog and say: ‘This is what the
Sovereign LORD says: I am against you, Gog, chief prince of[a]
Meshek and Tubal. 2I will turn you around and drag you along. I will
bring you from the far north and send you against the mountains of
Israel. 3Then I will strike your bow from your left hand and make your
arrows drop from your right hand. 4On the mountains of Israel you will
fall, you and all your troops and the nations with you. I will give you as
food to all kinds of carrion birds and to the wild animals. 5You will fall
in the open field, for I have spoken, declares the Sovereign LORD. 6I will
send fire on Magog and on those who live in safety in the coastlands,
and they will know that I am the LORD.
7“ ‘I will make known my holy name among my people Israel. I will
no longer let my holy name be profaned, and the nations will know that
I the LORD am the Holy One in Israel. 8It is coming! It will surely take
place, declares the Sovereign LORD. This is the day I have spoken of.
9“ ‘Then those who live in the towns of Israel will go out and use the
weapons for fuel and burn them up — the small and large shields, the
bows and arrows, the war clubs and spears. For seven years they will
use them for fuel. 10They will not need to gather wood from the fields
or cut it from the forests, because they will use the weapons for fuel.
And they will plunder those who plundered them and loot those who
looted them, declares the Sovereign LORD.
11“ ‘On that day I will give Gog a burial place in Israel, in the valley
of those who travel east of the Sea. It will block the way of travelers,
because Gog and all his hordes will be buried there. So it will be called
the Valley of Hamon Gog.[b]

PRAYING SCRIPTURE
Ezekiel 39

In the midst of the Lord’s warning to Gog, he said, “I will no longer let my holy name be profaned” (verse 7). The name of the Lord should always be counted as holy because it represents the holy, righteous, all-powerful God of Israel.

How long has it been since you worshiped the name of the Lord? Spend some time today honoring his holy name.

[a] 1 Or *Gog, prince of Rosh,* [b] 11 *Hamon Gog* means *hordes of Gog.*

12"'For seven months the Israelites will be burying them in order to cleanse the land. 13All the people of the land will bury them, and the day I display my glory will be a memorable day for them, declares the Sovereign LORD. 14People will be continually employed in cleansing the land. They will spread out across the land and, along with others, they will bury any bodies that are lying on the ground.

"'After the seven months they will carry out a more detailed search. 15As they go through the land, anyone who sees a human bone will leave a marker beside it until the gravediggers bury it in the Valley of Hamon Gog, 16near a town called Hamonah.[a] And so they will cleanse the land.'

17"Son of man, this is what the Sovereign LORD says: Call out to every kind of bird and all the wild animals: 'Assemble and come together from all around to the sacrifice I am preparing for you, the great sacrifice on the mountains of Israel. There you will eat flesh and drink blood. 18You will eat the flesh of mighty men and drink the blood of the princes of the earth as if they were rams and lambs, goats and bulls — all of them fattened animals from Bashan. 19At the sacrifice I am preparing for you, you will eat fat till you are glutted and drink blood till you are drunk. 20At my table you will eat your fill of horses and riders, mighty men and soldiers of every kind,' declares the Sovereign LORD.

21"I will display my glory among the nations, and all the nations will see the punishment I inflict and the hand I lay on them. 22From that day forward the people of Israel will know that I am the LORD their God. 23And the nations will know that the people of Israel went into exile for their sin, because they were unfaithful to me. So I hid my face from them and handed them over to their enemies, and they all fell by the sword. 24I dealt with them according to their uncleanness and their offenses, and I hid my face from them.

25"Therefore this is what the Sovereign LORD says: I will now restore the fortunes of Jacob[b] and will have compassion on all the people of Israel, and I will be zealous for my holy name. 26They will forget their shame and all the unfaithfulness they showed toward me when they lived in safety in their land with no one to make them afraid. 27When I have brought them back from the nations and have gathered them from the countries of their enemies, I will be proved holy through them in the sight of many nations. 28Then they will know that I am the LORD their God, for though I sent them into exile among the nations, I will gather them to their own land, not leaving any behind. 29I will no longer hide my face from them, for I will pour out my Spirit on the people of Israel, declares the Sovereign LORD."

THE TEMPLE AREA RESTORED

40 In the twenty-fifth year of our exile, at the beginning of the year, on the tenth of the month, in the fourteenth year after the fall of the city — on that very day the hand of the LORD was on me and he took me there. 2In visions of God he took me to the land of Israel and set me on a very high mountain, on whose south side were some buildings that looked like a city. 3He took me there, and I saw a man whose appearance was like bronze; he was standing in the gateway with a linen cord and a measuring rod in his hand. 4The man said

[a] 16 *Hamonah* means *horde.* [b] 25 *Or now bring Jacob back from captivity*

PRAYING SCRIPTURE

Ezekiel 40

Ezekiel received a vision in which he saw life in Israel as it should be under God's rule, an extensive and detailed vision of the temple. The passage seems to prefigure a similar narrative in Revelation where God told John to go and measure the temple in Jerusalem.

Worship will be central to the eternal kingdom, so start practicing now by including worship in every prayer you offer to God.

to me, "Son of man, look carefully and listen closely and pay attention to everything I am going to show you, for that is why you have been brought here. Tell the people of Israel everything you see."

THE EAST GATE TO THE OUTER COURT

5 I saw a wall completely surrounding the temple area. The length of the measuring rod in the man's hand was six long cubits,[a] each of which was a cubit and a handbreadth. He measured the wall; it was one measuring rod thick and one rod high.

6 Then he went to the east gate. He climbed its steps and measured the threshold of the gate; it was one rod deep. 7 The alcoves for the guards were one rod long and one rod wide, and the projecting walls between the alcoves were five cubits[b] thick. And the threshold of the gate next to the portico facing the temple was one rod deep.

8 Then he measured the portico of the gateway; 9 it[c] was eight cubits[d] deep and its jambs were two cubits[e] thick. The portico of the gateway faced the temple.

10 Inside the east gate were three alcoves on each side; the three had the same measurements, and the faces of the projecting walls on each side had the same measurements. 11 Then he measured the width of the entrance of the gateway; it was ten cubits and its length was thirteen cubits.[f] 12 In front of each alcove was a wall one cubit high, and the alcoves were six cubits square. 13 Then he measured the gateway from the top of the rear wall of one alcove to the top of the opposite one; the distance was twenty-five cubits[g] from one parapet opening to the opposite one. 14 He measured along the faces of the projecting walls all around the inside of the gateway — sixty cubits.[h] The measurement was up to the portico[i] facing the courtyard.[j] 15 The distance from the entrance of the gateway to the far end of its portico was fifty cubits.[k] 16 The alcoves and the projecting walls inside the gateway were surmounted by narrow parapet openings all around, as was the portico; the openings all around faced inward. The faces of the projecting walls were decorated with palm trees.

THE OUTER COURT

17 Then he brought me into the outer court. There I saw some rooms and a pavement that had been constructed all around the court; there were thirty rooms along the pavement. 18 It abutted the sides of the gateways and was as wide as they were long; this was the lower pavement. 19 Then he measured the distance from the inside of the lower gateway to the outside of the inner court; it was a hundred cubits[l] on the east side as well as on the north.

---

[a] *5* That is, about 11 feet or about 3.2 meters; also in verse 12. The long cubit of about 21 inches or about 53 centimeters is the basic unit of measurement of length throughout chapters 40 – 48. [b] *7* That is, about 8 3/4 feet or about 2.7 meters; also in verse 48 [c] *8,9* Many Hebrew manuscripts, Septuagint, Vulgate and Syriac; most Hebrew manuscripts *gateway facing the temple; it was one rod deep. 9Then he measured the portico of the gateway; it* [d] *9* That is, about 14 feet or about 4.2 meters [e] *9* That is, about 3 1/2 feet or about 1 meter [f] *11* That is, about 18 feet wide and 23 feet long or about 5.3 meters wide and 6.9 meters long [g] *13* That is, about 44 feet or about 13 meters; also in verses 21, 25, 29, 30, 33 and 36 [h] *14* That is, about 105 feet or about 32 meters [i] *14* Septuagint; Hebrew *projecting wall* [j] *14* The meaning of the Hebrew for this verse is uncertain. [k] *15* That is, about 88 feet or about 27 meters; also in verses 21, 25, 29, 33 and 36 [l] *19* That is, about 175 feet or about 53 meters; also in verses 23, 27 and 47

THE NORTH GATE

20Then he measured the length and width of the north gate, leading
into the outer court. 21Its alcoves — three on each side — its project-
ing walls and its portico had the same measurements as those of the
first gateway. It was fifty cubits long and twenty-five cubits wide. 22Its
openings, its portico and its palm tree decorations had the same mea-
surements as those of the gate facing east. Seven steps led up to it, with
its portico opposite them. 23There was a gate to the inner court facing
the north gate, just as there was on the east. He measured from one
gate to the opposite one; it was a hundred cubits.

THE SOUTH GATE

24Then he led me to the south side and I saw the south gate. He mea-
sured its jambs and its portico, and they had the same measurements
as the others. 25The gateway and its portico had narrow openings all
around, like the openings of the others. It was fifty cubits long and
twenty-five cubits wide. 26Seven steps led up to it, with its portico op-
posite them; it had palm tree decorations on the faces of the projecting
walls on each side. 27The inner court also had a gate facing south, and
he measured from this gate to the outer gate on the south side; it was
a hundred cubits.

THE GATES TO THE INNER COURT

28Then he brought me into the inner court through the south gate,
and he measured the south gate; it had the same measurements as the
others. 29Its alcoves, its projecting walls and its portico had the same
measurements as the others. The gateway and its portico had openings
all around. It was fifty cubits long and twenty-five cubits wide. 30(The
porticoes of the gateways around the inner court were twenty-five cu-
bits wide and five cubits deep.) 31Its portico faced the outer court; palm
trees decorated its jambs, and eight steps led up to it.

32Then he brought me to the inner court on the east side, and he
measured the gateway; it had the same measurements as the others.
33Its alcoves, its projecting walls and its portico had the same mea-
surements as the others. The gateway and its portico had openings
all around. It was fifty cubits long and twenty-five cubits wide. 34Its
portico faced the outer court; palm trees decorated the jambs on either
side, and eight steps led up to it.

35Then he brought me to the north gate and measured it. It had the
same measurements as the others, 36as did its alcoves, its projecting
walls and its portico, and it had openings all around. It was fifty cu-
bits long and twenty five cubits wide. 37Its portico[a] faced the outer
court; palm trees decorated the jambs on either side, and eight steps
led up to it.

THE ROOMS FOR PREPARING SACRIFICES

38A room with a doorway was by the portico in each of the inner
gateways, where the burnt offerings were washed. 39In the portico of
the gateway were two tables on each side, on which the burnt offer-
ings, sin offerings[b] and guilt offerings were slaughtered. 40By the out-
side wall of the portico of the gateway, near the steps at the entrance of
the north gateway were two tables, and on the other side of the steps
were two tables. 41So there were four tables on one side of the gateway

[a] *37* Septuagint (see also verses 31 and 34); Hebrew *jambs* [b] *39* Or *purification offerings*

and four on the other — eight tables in all — on which the sacrifices were slaughtered. 42 There were also four tables of dressed stone for the burnt offerings, each a cubit and a half long, a cubit and a half wide and a cubit high.[a] On them were placed the utensils for slaughtering the burnt offerings and the other sacrifices. 43 And double-pronged hooks, each a handbreadth[b] long, were attached to the wall all around. The tables were for the flesh of the offerings.

THE ROOMS FOR THE PRIESTS

44 Outside the inner gate, within the inner court, were two rooms, one[c] at the side of the north gate and facing south, and another at the side of the south[d] gate and facing north. 45 He said to me, "The room facing south is for the priests who guard the temple, 46 and the room facing north is for the priests who guard the altar. These are the sons of Zadok, who are the only Levites who may draw near to the LORD to minister before him."

47 Then he measured the court: It was square — a hundred cubits long and a hundred cubits wide. And the altar was in front of the temple.

THE NEW TEMPLE

48 He brought me to the portico of the temple and measured the jambs of the portico; they were five cubits wide on either side. The width of the entrance was fourteen cubits[e] and its projecting walls were[f] three cubits[g] wide on either side. 49 The portico was twenty cubits[h] wide, and twelve[i] cubits[j] from front to back. It was reached by a flight of stairs,[k] and there were pillars on each side of the jambs.

41 Then the man brought me to the main hall and measured the jambs; the width of the jambs was six cubits[l] on each side.[m] 2 The entrance was ten cubits[n] wide, and the projecting walls on each side of it were five cubits[o] wide. He also measured the main hall; it was forty cubits long and twenty cubits wide.[p]

3 Then he went into the inner sanctuary and measured the jambs of the entrance; each was two cubits[q] wide. The entrance was six cubits wide, and the projecting walls on each side of it were seven cubits[r] wide. 4 And he measured the length of the inner sanctuary; it was twenty cubits, and its width was twenty cubits across the end of the main hall. He said to me, "This is the Most Holy Place."

5 Then he measured the wall of the temple; it was six cubits thick, and each side room around the temple was four cubits[s] wide. 6 The side rooms were on three levels, one above another, thirty on each level.

PRAYING SCRIPTURE

Ezekiel 41

The detailed measurements of the temple would encourage the exiled Israelites; they could see by faith that God had not forgotten them. Their place of worship awaited. On this side of Calvary, because of Christ, every Christian—not only the high priest—has access to the Most Holy Place.

God's presence is the Most Holy Place. God invites his children there. Spend time today talking to your Father in his presence.

[a] 42 That is, about 2 2/3 feet long and wide and 21 inches high or about 80 centimeters long and wide and 53 centimeters high [b] 43 That is, about 3 1/2 inches or about 9 centimeters [c] 44 Septuagint; Hebrew *were rooms for singers, which were* [d] 44 Septuagint; Hebrew *east* [e] 48 That is, about 25 feet or about 7.4 meters [f] 48 Septuagint; Hebrew *entrance was* [g] 48 That is, about 5 1/4 feet or about 1.6 meters [h] 49 That is, about 35 feet or about 11 meters [i] 49 Septuagint; Hebrew *eleven* [j] 49 That is, about 21 feet or about 6.4 meters [k] 49 Hebrew; Septuagint *Ten steps led up to it* [l] 1 That is, about 11 feet or about 3.2 meters; also in verses 3, 5 and 8 [m] 1 One Hebrew manuscript and Septuagint; most Hebrew manuscripts *side, the width of the tent* [n] 2 That is, about 18 feet or about 5.3 meters [o] 2 That is, about 8 3/4 feet or about 2.7 meters; also in verses 9, 11 and 12 [p] 2 That is, about 70 feet long and 35 feet wide or about 21 meters long and 11 meters wide [q] 3 That is, about 3 1/2 feet or about 1.1 meters; also in verse 22 [r] 3 That is, about 12 feet or about 3.7 meters [s] 5 That is, about 7 feet or about 2.1 meters

There were ledges all around the wall of the temple to serve as sup-
ports for the side rooms, so that the supports were not inserted into
the wall of the temple. 7The side rooms all around the temple were
wider at each successive level. The structure surrounding the tem-
ple was built in ascending stages, so that the rooms widened as one
went upward. A stairway went up from the lowest floor to the top floor
through the middle floor.

8I saw that the temple had a raised base all around it, forming the
foundation of the side rooms. It was the length of the rod, six long cu-
bits. 9The outer wall of the side rooms was five cubits thick. The open
area between the side rooms of the temple 10and the priests' rooms
was twenty cubits wide all around the temple. 11There were entrances
to the side rooms from the open area, one on the north and another
on the south; and the base adjoining the open area was five cubits
wide all around.

12The building facing the temple courtyard on the west side was
seventy cubits[a] wide. The wall of the building was five cubits thick all
around, and its length was ninety cubits.[b]

13Then he measured the temple; it was a hundred cubits[c] long, and
the temple courtyard and the building with its walls were also a hun-
dred cubits long. 14The width of the temple courtyard on the east, in-
cluding the front of the temple, was a hundred cubits.

15Then he measured the length of the building facing the courtyard
at the rear of the temple, including its galleries on each side; it was a
hundred cubits.

The main hall, the inner sanctuary and the portico facing the court,
16as well as the thresholds and the narrow windows and galleries
around the three of them — everything beyond and including the
threshold was covered with wood. The floor, the wall up to the win-
dows, and the windows were covered. 17In the space above the outside
of the entrance to the inner sanctuary and on the walls at regular inter-
vals all around the inner and outer sanctuary 18were carved cherubim
and palm trees. Palm trees alternated with cherubim. Each cherub had
two faces: 19the face of a human being toward the palm tree on one
side and the face of a lion toward the palm tree on the other. They
were carved all around the whole temple. 20From the floor to the area
above the entrance, cherubim and palm trees were carved on the wall
of the main hall.

21The main hall had a rectangular doorframe, and the one at the
front of the Most Holy Place was similar. 22There was a wooden altar
three cubits[d] high and two cubits square[e]; its corners, its base[f] and its
sides were of wood. The man said to me, "This is the table that is before
the LORD." 23Both the main hall and the Most Holy Place had double
doors. 24Each door had two leaves — two hinged leaves for each door.
25And on the doors of the main hall were carved cherubim and palm
trees like those carved on the walls, and there was a wooden overhang
on the front of the portico. 26On the sidewalls of the portico were nar-
row windows with palm trees carved on each side. The side rooms of
the temple also had overhangs.

---

[a] *12* That is, about 123 feet or about 37 meters [b] *12* That is, about 158 feet or about 48 meters [c] *13* That is, about 175 feet or about 53 meters; also in verses 14 and 15 [d] *22* That is, about 5 1/4 feet or about 1.5 meters [e] *22* Septuagint; Hebrew *long* [f] *22* Septuagint; Hebrew *length*

PRAYING SCRIPTURE

Ezekiel 42

Ezekiel's measuring assignment reminds us both that the temple was central to Old Testament worship and that the temple and its ministries foreshadowed the ministry of Jesus. Jesus, our great high priest, is our mediator, the One who intercedes for us to the Father.

Intercession, praying for others, is to be a major part of the Christian life. Be intentional about praying for other people's needs.

THE ROOMS FOR THE PRIESTS

42 Then the man led me northward into the outer court and brought me to the rooms opposite the temple courtyard and opposite the outer wall on the north side. 2The building whose door faced north was a hundred cubits long and fifty cubits wide.[a] 3Both in the section twenty cubits[b] from the inner court and in the section opposite the pavement of the outer court, gallery faced gallery at the three levels. 4In front of the rooms was an inner passageway ten cubits wide and a hundred cubits[c] long.[d] Their doors were on the north. 5Now the upper rooms were narrower, for the galleries took more space from them than from the rooms on the lower and middle floors of the building. 6The rooms on the top floor had no pillars, as the courts had; so they were smaller in floor space than those on the lower and middle floors. 7There was an outer wall parallel to the rooms and the outer court; it extended in front of the rooms for fifty cubits. 8While the row of rooms on the side next to the outer court was fifty cubits long, the row on the side nearest the sanctuary was a hundred cubits long. 9The lower rooms had an entrance on the east side as one enters them from the outer court.

10On the south side[e] along the length of the wall of the outer court, adjoining the temple courtyard and opposite the outer wall, were rooms 11with a passageway in front of them. These were like the rooms on the north; they had the same length and width, with similar exits and dimensions. Similar to the doorways on the north 12were the doorways of the rooms on the south. There was a doorway at the beginning of the passageway that was parallel to the corresponding wall extending eastward, by which one enters the rooms.

13Then he said to me, "The north and south rooms facing the temple courtyard are the priests' rooms, where the priests who approach the LORD will eat the most holy offerings. There they will put the most holy offerings — the grain offerings, the sin offerings[f] and the guilt offerings — for the place is holy. 14Once the priests enter the holy precincts, they are not to go into the outer court until they leave behind the garments in which they minister, for these are holy. They are to put on other clothes before they go near the places that are for the people."

15When he had finished measuring what was inside the temple area, he led me out by the east gate and measured the area all around: 16He measured the east side with the measuring rod; it was five hundred cubits.[g,h] 17He measured the north side; it was five hundred cubits[i] by the measuring rod. 18He measured the south side; it was five hundred cubits by the measuring rod. 19Then he turned to the west side and measured; it was five hundred cubits by the measuring rod. 20So he measured the area on all four sides. It had a wall around it, five hundred cubits long and five hundred cubits wide, to separate the holy from the common.

---

[a] *2* That is, about 175 feet long and 88 feet wide or about 53 meters long and 27 meters wide [b] *3* That is, about 35 feet or about 11 meters [c] *4* Septuagint and Syriac; Hebrew *and one cubit* [d] *4* That is, about 18 feet wide and 175 feet long or about 5.3 meters wide and 53 meters long [e] *10* Septuagint; Hebrew *Eastward* [f] *13* Or *purification offerings* [g] *16* See Septuagint of verse 17; Hebrew *rods;* also in verses 18 and 19. [h] *16* Five hundred cubits equal about 875 feet or about 265 meters; also in verses 17, 18 and 19. [i] *17* Septuagint; Hebrew *rods*

GOD'S GLORY RETURNS TO THE TEMPLE

43 Then the man brought me to the gate facing east, 2and I saw the glory of the God of Israel coming from the east. His voice was like the roar of rushing waters, and the land was radiant with his glory. 3The vision I saw was like the vision I had seen when he[a] came to destroy the city and like the visions I had seen by the Kebar River, and I fell facedown. 4The glory of the LORD entered the temple through the gate facing east. 5Then the Spirit lifted me up and brought me into the inner court, and the glory of the LORD filled the temple.

6While the man was standing beside me, I heard someone speaking to me from inside the temple. 7He said: "Son of man, this is the place of my throne and the place for the soles of my feet. This is where I will live among the Israelites forever. The people of Israel will never again defile my holy name — neither they nor their kings — by their prostitution and the funeral offerings[b] for their kings at their death.[c] 8When they placed their threshold next to my threshold and their doorposts beside my doorposts, with only a wall between me and them, they defiled my holy name by their detestable practices. So I destroyed them in my anger. 9Now let them put away from me their prostitution and the funeral offerings for their kings, and I will live among them forever.

10"Son of man, describe the temple to the people of Israel, that they may be ashamed of their sins. Let them consider its perfection, 11and if they are ashamed of all they have done, make known to them the design of the temple — its arrangement, its exits and entrances — its whole design and all its regulations[d] and laws. Write these down before them so that they may be faithful to its design and follow all its regulations.

12"This is the law of the temple: All the surrounding area on top of the mountain will be most holy. Such is the law of the temple.

THE GREAT ALTAR RESTORED

13"These are the measurements of the altar in long cubits,[e] that cubit being a cubit and a handbreadth: Its gutter is a cubit deep and a cubit wide, with a rim of one span[f] around the edge. And this is the height of the altar: 14From the gutter on the ground up to the lower ledge that goes around the altar it is two cubits high, and the ledge is a cubit wide.[g] From this lower ledge to the upper ledge that goes around the altar it is four cubits high, and that ledge is also a cubit wide.[h] 15Above that, the altar hearth is four cubits high, and four horns project upward from the hearth. 16The altar hearth is square, twelve cubits[i] long and twelve cubits wide. 17The upper ledge also is square, fourteen cubits[j] long and fourteen cubits wide. All around the altar is a gutter of one cubit with a rim of half a cubit.[f] The steps of the altar face east."

18Then he said to me, "Son of man, this is what the Sovereign LORD says: These will be the regulations for sacrificing burnt offerings and

PRAYING SCRIPTURE

Ezekiel 43

Three mentions of "the glory" of the Lord (verses 2,4–5) remind us that the display of his power and majesty are meant to provoke awe in his people. When we remember God's glory, we are reminded of our own sinfulness and need for him, and our weakness is contrasted with his might.

God's people are to demonstrate his glory. We bear witness to his power. Ask God to let his glory be on display in your life.

---

[a] *3* Some Hebrew manuscripts and Vulgate; most Hebrew manuscripts *I*
[b] *7* Or *the memorial monuments*; also in verse 9 [c] *7* Or *their high places*
[d] *11* Some Hebrew manuscripts and Septuagint; most Hebrew manuscripts *regulations and its whole design* [e] *13* That is, about 21 inches or about 53 centimeters; also in verses 14 and 17. The long cubit is the basic unit for linear measurement throughout Ezekiel 40–48. [f] *13,17* That is, about 11 inches or about 27 centimeters [g] *14* That is, about 3 1/2 feet high and 1 3/4 feet wide or about 105 centimeters high and 53 centimeters wide [h] *14* That is, about 7 feet high and 1 3/4 feet wide or about 2.1 meters high and 53 centimeters wide [i] *16* That is, about 21 feet or about 6.4 meters [j] *17* That is, about 25 feet or about 7.4 meters

splashing blood against the altar when it is built: 19You are to give a young bull as a sin offering[a] to the Levitical priests of the family of Zadok, who come near to minister before me, declares the Sovereign LORD. 20You are to take some of its blood and put it on the four horns of the altar and on the four corners of the upper ledge and all around the rim, and so purify the altar and make atonement for it. 21You are to take the bull for the sin offering and burn it in the designated part of the temple area outside the sanctuary.

22"On the second day you are to offer a male goat without defect for a sin offering, and the altar is to be purified as it was purified with the bull. 23When you have finished purifying it, you are to offer a young bull and a ram from the flock, both without defect. 24You are to offer them before the LORD, and the priests are to sprinkle salt on them and sacrifice them as a burnt offering to the LORD.

25"For seven days you are to provide a male goat daily for a sin offering; you are also to provide a young bull and a ram from the flock, both without defect. 26For seven days they are to make atonement for the altar and cleanse it; thus they will dedicate it. 27At the end of these days, from the eighth day on, the priests are to present your burnt offerings and fellowship offerings on the altar. Then I will accept you, declares the Sovereign LORD."

THE PRIESTHOOD RESTORED

44 Then the man brought me back to the outer gate of the sanctuary, the one facing east, and it was shut. 2The LORD said to me, "This gate is to remain shut. It must not be opened; no one may enter through it. It is to remain shut because the LORD, the God of Israel, has entered through it. 3The prince himself is the only one who may sit inside the gateway to eat in the presence of the LORD. He is to enter by way of the portico of the gateway and go out the same way."

4Then the man brought me by way of the north gate to the front of the temple. I looked and saw the glory of the LORD filling the temple of the LORD, and I fell facedown.

5The LORD said to me, "Son of man, look carefully, listen closely and give attention to everything I tell you concerning all the regulations and instructions regarding the temple of the LORD. Give attention to the entrance to the temple and all the exits of the sanctuary. 6Say to rebellious Israel, 'This is what the Sovereign LORD says: Enough of your detestable practices, people of Israel! 7In addition to all your other detestable practices, you brought foreigners uncircumcised in heart and flesh into my sanctuary, desecrating my temple while you offered me food, fat and blood, and you broke my covenant. 8Instead of carrying out your duty in regard to my holy things, you put others in charge of my sanctuary. 9This is what the Sovereign LORD says: No foreigner uncircumcised in heart and flesh is to enter my sanctuary, not even the foreigners who live among the Israelites.

10" 'The Levites who went far from me when Israel went astray and who wandered from me after their idols must bear the consequences of their sin. 11They may serve in my sanctuary, having charge of the gates of the temple and serving in it; they may slaughter the burnt offerings and sacrifices for the people and stand before the people and serve them. 12But because they served them in the presence of their idols and made the people of Israel fall into sin, therefore I have sworn

PRAYING SCRIPTURE

Ezekiel 44

In the reconstructed temple, one gate was closed off because God used it. Still, "the prince himself is the only one who may sit inside the gateway" and eat in God's presence (verse 3). When we believe our sin keeps us from entering God's presence in prayer, we should look to Christ who is worthy.

The prince obviously represents Jesus, the Mediator between God and humanity. Entrust your prayers to his intercession for you.

---

[a] 19 Or *purification offering;* also in verses 21, 22 and 25

with uplifted hand that they must bear the consequences of their sin, declares the Sovereign LORD. 13 They are not to come near to serve me as priests or come near any of my holy things or my most holy offerings; they must bear the shame of their detestable practices. 14 And I will appoint them to guard the temple for all the work that is to be done in it.

15 “‘But the Levitical priests, who are descendants of Zadok and who guarded my sanctuary when the Israelites went astray from me, are to come near to minister before me; they are to stand before me to offer sacrifices of fat and blood, declares the Sovereign LORD. 16 They alone are to enter my sanctuary; they alone are to come near my table to minister before me and serve me as guards.

17 “‘When they enter the gates of the inner court, they are to wear linen clothes; they must not wear any woolen garment while ministering at the gates of the inner court or inside the temple. 18 They are to wear linen turbans on their heads and linen undergarments around their waists. They must not wear anything that makes them perspire. 19 When they go out into the outer court where the people are, they are to take off the clothes they have been ministering in and are to leave them in the sacred rooms, and put on other clothes, so that the people are not consecrated through contact with their garments.

20 “‘They must not shave their heads or let their hair grow long, but they are to keep the hair of their heads trimmed. 21 No priest is to drink wine when he enters the inner court. 22 They must not marry widows or divorced women; they may marry only virgins of Israelite descent or widows of priests. 23 They are to teach my people the difference between the holy and the common and show them how to distinguish between the unclean and the clean.

24 “‘In any dispute, the priests are to serve as judges and decide it according to my ordinances. They are to keep my laws and my decrees for all my appointed festivals, and they are to keep my Sabbaths holy.

25 “‘A priest must not defile himself by going near a dead person; however, if the dead person was his father or mother, son or daughter, brother or unmarried sister, then he may defile himself. 26 After he is cleansed, he must wait seven days. 27 On the day he goes into the inner court of the sanctuary to minister in the sanctuary, he is to offer a sin offering[a] for himself, declares the Sovereign LORD.

28 “‘I am to be the only inheritance the priests have. You are to give them no possession in Israel; I will be their possession. 29 They will eat the grain offerings, the sin offerings and the guilt offerings; and everything in Israel devoted[b] to the LORD will belong to them. 30 The best of all the firstfruits and of all your special gifts will belong to the priests. You are to give them the first portion of your ground meal so that a blessing may rest on your household. 31 The priests must not eat anything, whether bird or animal, found dead or torn by wild animals.

ISRAEL FULLY RESTORED

45 “‘When you allot the land as an inheritance, you are to present to the LORD a portion of the land as a sacred district, 25,000 cubits[c] long and 20,000[d] cubits[e] wide; the entire area will be holy. 2 Of

[a] *27* Or *purification offering*; also in verse 29 [b] *29* The Hebrew term refers to the irrevocable giving over of things or persons to the LORD. [c] *1* That is, about 8 miles or about 13 kilometers; also in verses 3, 5 and 6 [d] *1* Septuagint (see also verses 3 and 5 and 48:9); Hebrew *10,000* [e] *1* That is, about 6 1/2 miles or about 11 kilometers

PRAYING SCRIPTURE

Ezekiel 45

God’s anger toward injustice poured out in a rebuke against Israel’s leaders: “Give up your violence and oppression and do what is just and right. Stop dispossessing my people” (verse 9). How we treat people is a window into how we understand God’s holiness, and our response to injustice around us reflects our passion for God’s justice.

Pray that God’s will be done for the mistreated and dispossessed and those who suffer violence of all kinds.

this, a section 500 cubits[a] square is to be for the sanctuary, with 50
cubits[b] around it for open land. 3In the sacred district, measure off a
section 25,000 cubits long and 10,000 cubits[c] wide. In it will be the
sanctuary, the Most Holy Place. 4It will be the sacred portion of the
land for the priests, who minister in the sanctuary and who draw near
to minister before the LORD. It will be a place for their houses as well as
a holy place for the sanctuary. 5An area 25,000 cubits long and 10,000
cubits wide will belong to the Levites, who serve in the temple, as their
possession for towns to live in.[d]

6" 'You are to give the city as its property an area 5,000 cubits[e] wide
and 25,000 cubits long, adjoining the sacred portion; it will belong to
all Israel.

7" 'The prince will have the land bordering each side of the area
formed by the sacred district and the property of the city. It will extend
westward from the west side and eastward from the east side, running
lengthwise from the western to the eastern border parallel to one of
the tribal portions. 8This land will be his possession in Israel. And my
princes will no longer oppress my people but will allow the people of
Israel to possess the land according to their tribes.

9" 'This is what the Sovereign LORD says: You have gone far enough,
princes of Israel! Give up your violence and oppression and do what
is just and right. Stop dispossessing my people, declares the Sover-
eign LORD. 10You are to use accurate scales, an accurate ephah[f] and an
accurate bath.[g] 11The ephah and the bath are to be the same size, the
bath containing a tenth of a homer and the ephah a tenth of a homer;
the homer is to be the standard measure for both. 12The shekel[h] is to
consist of twenty gerahs. Twenty shekels plus twenty-five shekels plus
fifteen shekels equal one mina.[i]

13" 'This is the special gift you are to offer: a sixth of an ephah[j] from
each homer of wheat and a sixth of an ephah[k] from each homer of
barley. 14The prescribed portion of olive oil, measured by the bath, is a
tenth of a bath[l] from each cor (which consists of ten baths or one ho-
mer, for ten baths are equivalent to a homer). 15Also one sheep is to be
taken from every flock of two hundred from the well-watered pastures
of Israel. These will be used for the grain offerings, burnt offerings
and fellowship offerings to make atonement for the people, declares
the Sovereign LORD. 16All the people of the land will be required to
give this special offering to the prince in Israel. 17It will be the duty of
the prince to provide the burnt offerings, grain offerings and drink
offerings at the festivals, the New Moons and the Sabbaths — at all the
appointed festivals of Israel. He will provide the sin offerings,[m] grain
offerings, burnt offerings and fellowship offerings to make atonement
for the Israelites.

---

[a] *2* That is, about 875 feet or about 265 meters [b] *2* That is, about 88 feet or about 27 meters [c] *3* That is, about 3 1/3 miles or about 5.3 kilometers; also in verse 5 [d] *5* Septuagint; Hebrew *temple; they will have as their possession 20 rooms* [e] *6* That is, about 1 2/3 miles or about 2.7 kilometers [f] *10* An ephah was a dry measure having the capacity of about 3/5 bushel or about 22 liters. [g] *10* A bath was a liquid measure equaling about 6 gallons or about 22 liters. [h] *12* A shekel weighed about 2/5 ounce or about 12 grams. [i] *12* That is, 60 shekels; the common mina was 50 shekels. Sixty shekels were about 1 1/2 pounds or about 690 grams. [j] *13* That is, probably about 6 pounds or about 2.7 kilograms [k] *13* That is, probably about 5 pounds or about 2.3 kilograms [l] *14* That is, about 2 1/2 quarts or about 2.2 liters [m] *17* Or *purification offerings*; also in verses 19, 22, 23 and 25

18“‘This is what the Sovereign LORD says: In the first month on the
first day you are to take a young bull without defect and purify the sanc-
tuary. 19The priest is to take some of the blood of the sin offering and put
it on the doorposts of the temple, on the four corners of the upper ledge
of the altar and on the gateposts of the inner court. 20You are to do the
same on the seventh day of the month for anyone who sins unintention-
ally or through ignorance; so you are to make atonement for the temple.
21“‘In the first month on the fourteenth day you are to observe the
Passover, a festival lasting seven days, during which you shall eat bread
made without yeast. 22On that day the prince is to provide a bull as a sin
offering for himself and for all the people of the land. 23Every day during
the seven days of the festival he is to provide seven bulls and seven rams
without defect as a burnt offering to the LORD, and a male goat for a sin
offering. 24He is to provide as a grain offering an ephah for each bull
and an ephah for each ram, along with a hin[a] of olive oil for each ephah.
25“‘During the seven days of the festival, which begins in the seventh
month on the fifteenth day, he is to make the same provision for sin
offerings, burnt offerings, grain offerings and oil.

46 “‘This is what the Sovereign LORD says: The gate of the inner
court facing east is to be shut on the six working days, but on
the Sabbath day and on the day of the New Moon it is to be opened.
2The prince is to enter from the outside through the portico of the
gateway and stand by the gatepost. The priests are to sacrifice his
burnt offering and his fellowship offerings. He is to bow down in wor-
ship at the threshold of the gateway and then go out, but the gate will
not be shut until evening. 3On the Sabbaths and New Moons the people
of the land are to worship in the presence of the LORD at the entrance
of that gateway. 4The burnt offering the prince brings to the LORD on
the Sabbath day is to be six male lambs and a ram, all without defect.
5The grain offering given with the ram is to be an ephah,[b] and the grain
offering with the lambs is to be as much as he pleases, along with a hin[c]
of olive oil for each ephah. 6On the day of the New Moon he is to offer a
young bull, six lambs and a ram, all without defect. 7He is to provide as
a grain offering one ephah with the bull, one ephah with the ram, and
with the lambs as much as he wants to give, along with a hin of oil for
each ephah. 8When the prince enters, he is to go in through the portico
of the gateway, and he is to come out the same way.
9“‘When the people of the land come before the LORD at the ap-
pointed festivals, whoever enters by the north gate to worship is to
go out the south gate; and whoever enters by the south gate is to go
out the north gate. No one is to return through the gate by which they
entered, but each is to go out the opposite gate. 10The prince is to be
among them, going in when they go in and going out when they go
out. 11At the feasts and the appointed festivals, the grain offering is to
be an ephah with a bull, an ephah with a ram, and with the lambs as
much as he pleases, along with a hin of oil for each ephah.
12“‘When the prince provides a freewill offering to the LORD—
whether a burnt offering or fellowship offerings—the gate facing east
is to be opened for him. He shall offer his burnt offering or his fellow-
ship offerings as he does on the Sabbath day. Then he shall go out, and
after he has gone out, the gate will be shut.

PRAYING SCRIPTURE

Ezekiel 46

No one enters the presence of the Lord without offering a sacrifice. Through the Old Testament this was a first-order teaching. Priests offered sacrifices every day for the sins of the people. The priests also had sacrifices offered for themselves. No one is perfect; no one is exempt.

Jesus fulfilled this system perfectly. Every sacrifice of every animal pointed to him. Praise God that it is finished!

---

[a] *24* That is, about 1 gallon or about 3.8 liters [b] *5* That is, probably about 35 pounds or about 16 kilograms; also in verses 7 and 11 [c] *5* That is, about 1 gallon or about 3.8 liters; also in verses 7 and 11

13“ ‘Every day you are to provide a year-old lamb without defect for a
burnt offering to the LORD; morning by morning you shall provide it.
14You are also to provide with it morning by morning a grain offering,
consisting of a sixth of an ephah[a] with a third of a hin[b] of oil to moisten
the flour. The presenting of this grain offering to the LORD is a lasting
ordinance. 15So the lamb and the grain offering and the oil shall be pro-
vided morning by morning for a regular burnt offering.
16“ ‘This is what the Sovereign LORD says: If the prince makes a gift
from his inheritance to one of his sons, it will also belong to his descen-
dants; it is to be their property by inheritance. 17If, however, he makes
a gift from his inheritance to one of his servants, the servant may keep
it until the year of freedom; then it will revert to the prince. His inher-
itance belongs to his sons only; it is theirs. 18The prince must not take
any of the inheritance of the people, driving them off their property.
He is to give his sons their inheritance out of his own property, so that
not one of my people will be separated from their property.’ ”
19Then the man brought me through the entrance at the side of the
gate to the sacred rooms facing north, which belonged to the priests,
and showed me a place at the western end. 20He said to me, “This is
the place where the priests are to cook the guilt offering and the sin
offering[c] and bake the grain offering, to avoid bringing them into the
outer court and consecrating the people.”
21He then brought me to the outer court and led me around to its
four corners, and I saw in each corner another court. 22In the four cor-
ners of the outer court were enclosed[d] courts, forty cubits long and
thirty cubits wide;[e] each of the courts in the four corners was the same
size. 23Around the inside of each of the four courts was a ledge of stone,
with places for fire built all around under the ledge. 24He said to me,
“These are the kitchens where those who minister at the temple are to
cook the sacrifices of the people.”

THE RIVER FROM THE TEMPLE

47 The man brought me back to the entrance to the temple, and
I saw water coming out from under the threshold of the tem-
ple toward the east (for the temple faced east). The water was coming
down from under the south side of the temple, south of the altar. 2He
then brought me out through the north gate and led me around the
outside to the outer gate facing east, and the water was trickling from
the south side.
3As the man went eastward with a measuring line in his hand, he
measured off a thousand cubits[f] and then led me through water that
was ankle-deep. 4He measured off another thousand cubits and led me
through water that was knee-deep. He measured off another thousand
and led me through water that was up to the waist. 5He measured off
another thousand, but now it was a river that I could not cross, because
the water had risen and was deep enough to swim in — a river that no
one could cross. 6He asked me, “Son of man, do you see this?”
Then he led me back to the bank of the river. 7When I arrived there,
I saw a great number of trees on each side of the river. 8He said to me,

PRAYING SCRIPTURE

Ezekiel 47

In the new creation, the world will not know decay, famine, disease or sin. Every wrong thing will be made right; every wicked thing will be gone; only righteousness will remain. The trees of verse 12 represent the fruitfulness and blessing of God's kingdom.

God's promised restoration of Israel, the means of ensuring the Messiah's coming, is at the heart of the salvation story. Ponder the wisdom of God in bringing salvation.

[a] *14* That is, probably about 6 pounds or about 2.7 kilograms [b] *14* That is, about 1 1/2 quarts or about 1.3 liters [c] *20* Or *purification offering* [d] *22* The meaning of the Hebrew for this word is uncertain. [e] *22* That is, about 70 feet long and 53 feet wide or about 21 meters long and 16 meters wide [f] *3* That is, about 1,700 feet or about 530 meters

"This water flows toward the eastern region and goes down into the
Arabah,[a] where it enters the Dead Sea. When it empties into the sea,
the salty water there becomes fresh. 9Swarms of living creatures will
live wherever the river flows. There will be large numbers of fish, be-
cause this water flows there and makes the salt water fresh; so where
the river flows everything will live. 10Fishermen will stand along the
shore; from En Gedi to En Eglaim there will be places for spreading
nets. The fish will be of many kinds — like the fish of the Mediterra-
nean Sea. 11But the swamps and marshes will not become fresh; they
will be left for salt. 12Fruit trees of all kinds will grow on both banks
of the river. Their leaves will not wither, nor will their fruit fail. Every
month they will bear fruit, because the water from the sanctuary flows
to them. Their fruit will serve for food and their leaves for healing."

THE BOUNDARIES OF THE LAND

13This is what the Sovereign LORD says: "These are the boundaries of
the land that you will divide among the twelve tribes of Israel as their
inheritance, with two portions for Joseph. 14You are to divide it equally
among them. Because I swore with uplifted hand to give it to your an-
cestors, this land will become your inheritance.

15"This is to be the boundary of the land:

"On the north side it will run from the Mediterranean Sea by the
Hethlon road past Lebo Hamath to Zedad, 16Berothah[b] and Sib-
raim (which lies on the border between Damascus and Hamath),
as far as Hazer Hattikon, which is on the border of Hauran. 17The
boundary will extend from the sea to Hazar Enan,[c] along the
northern border of Damascus, with the border of Hamath to the
north. This will be the northern boundary.

18"On the east side the boundary will run between Hauran and Damas-
cus, along the Jordan between Gilead and the land of Israel, to the
Dead Sea and as far as Tamar.[d] This will be the eastern boundary.

19"On the south side it will run from Tamar as far as the waters of Mer-
ibah Kadesh, then along the Wadi of Egypt to the Mediterranean
Sea. This will be the southern boundary.

20"On the west side, the Mediterranean Sea will be the boundary to a
point opposite Lebo Hamath. This will be the western boundary.

21"You are to distribute this land among yourselves according to the
tribes of Israel. 22You are to allot it as an inheritance for yourselves and
for the foreigners residing among you and who have children. You are
to consider them as native-born Israelites; along with you they are to
be allotted an inheritance among the tribes of Israel. 23In whatever
tribe a foreigner resides, there you are to give them their inheritance,"
declares the Sovereign LORD.

THE DIVISION OF THE LAND

48 "These are the tribes, listed by name: At the northern frontier,
Dan will have one portion; it will follow the Hethlon road to
Lebo Hamath; Hazar Enan and the northern border of Damascus next
to Hamath will be part of its border from the east side to the west side.

[a] 8 Or *the Jordan Valley* [b] 15,16 See Septuagint and 48:1; Hebrew *road to go into Zedad, 16Hamath, Berothah.* [c] 17 Hebrew *Enon*, a variant of *Enan*
[d] 18 See Syriac; Hebrew *Israel. You will measure to the Dead Sea.*

PRAYING SCRIPTURE

Ezekiel 48

Ezekiel closed his prophecy with instructions that echo Israel's taking of the promised land centuries before. The land assignments, borders and layout details would have reminded them of the Torah. The prominence of the city prefigured the heavenly city down to its name: "The LORD Is There" (verse 35).

A city is coming that will descend from God in heaven. Until then, pray that God's will is done on earth as it is in heaven.

2"Asher will have one portion; it will border the territory of Dan from
east to west.
3"Naphtali will have one portion; it will border the territory of Asher
from east to west.
4"Manasseh will have one portion; it will border the territory of
Naphtali from east to west.
5"Ephraim will have one portion; it will border the territory of Ma-
nasseh from east to west.
6"Reuben will have one portion; it will border the territory of
Ephraim from east to west.
7"Judah will have one portion; it will border the territory of Reuben
from east to west.
8"Bordering the territory of Judah from east to west will be the por-
tion you are to present as a special gift. It will be 25,000 cubits[a] wide,
and its length from east to west will equal one of the tribal portions;
the sanctuary will be in the center of it.
9"The special portion you are to offer to the LORD will be 25,000 cu-
bits long and 10,000 cubits[b] wide. 10This will be the sacred portion
for the priests. It will be 25,000 cubits long on the north side, 10,000
cubits wide on the west side, 10,000 cubits wide on the east side and
25,000 cubits long on the south side. In the center of it will be the
sanctuary of the LORD. 11This will be for the consecrated priests, the
Zadokites, who were faithful in serving me and did not go astray as
the Levites did when the Israelites went astray. 12It will be a special
gift to them from the sacred portion of the land, a most holy portion,
bordering the territory of the Levites.
13"Alongside the territory of the priests, the Levites will have an al-
lotment 25,000 cubits long and 10,000 cubits wide. Its total length will
be 25,000 cubits and its width 10,000 cubits. 14They must not sell or
exchange any of it. This is the best of the land and must not pass into
other hands, because it is holy to the LORD.
15"The remaining area, 5,000 cubits[c] wide and 25,000 cubits long,
will be for the common use of the city, for houses and for pastureland.
The city will be in the center of it 16and will have these measurements:
the north side 4,500 cubits,[d] the south side 4,500 cubits, the east side
4,500 cubits, and the west side 4,500 cubits. 17The pastureland for the
city will be 250 cubits[e] on the north, 250 cubits on the south, 250 cu-
bits on the east, and 250 cubits on the west. 18What remains of the
area, bordering on the sacred portion and running the length of it, will
be 10,000 cubits on the east side and 10,000 cubits on the west side.
Its produce will supply food for the workers of the city. 19The workers
from the city who farm it will come from all the tribes of Israel. 20The
entire portion will be a square, 25,000 cubits on each side. As a special
gift you will set aside the sacred portion, along with the property of
the city.
21"What remains on both sides of the area formed by the sacred
portion and the property of the city will belong to the prince. It will
extend eastward from the 25,000 cubits of the sacred portion to the

[a] *8* That is, about 8 miles or about 13 kilometers; also in verses 9, 10, 13, 15, 20 and 21 [b] *9* That is, about 3 1/3 miles or about 5.3 kilometers; also in verses 10, 13 and 18 [c] *15* That is, about 1 2/3 miles or about 2.7 kilometers
[d] *16* That is, about 1 1/2 miles or about 2.4 kilometers; also in verses 30, 32, 33 and 34 [e] *17* That is, about 440 feet or about 135 meters

eastern border, and westward from the 25,000 cubits to the western border. Both these areas running the length of the tribal portions will belong to the prince, and the sacred portion with the temple sanctuary will be in the center of them.
22So the property of the Levites and the property of the city will lie in the center of the area that belongs to the prince. The area belonging to the prince will lie between the border of Judah and the border of Benjamin.

23"As for the rest of the tribes: Benjamin will have one portion; it will extend from the east side to the west side.

24"Simeon will have one portion; it will border the territory of Benjamin from east to west.

25"Issachar will have one portion; it will border the territory of Simeon from east to west.

26"Zebulun will have one portion; it will border the territory of Issachar from east to west.

27"Gad will have one portion; it will border the territory of Zebulun from east to west.

28"The southern boundary of Gad will run south from Tamar to the waters of Meribah Kadesh, then along the Wadi of Egypt to the Mediterranean Sea.

29"This is the land you are to allot as an inheritance to the tribes of Israel, and these will be their portions," declares the Sovereign LORD.

THE GATES OF THE NEW CITY

30"These will be the exits of the city: Beginning on the north side, which is 4,500 cubits long,
31the gates of the city will be named after the tribes of Israel. The three gates on the north side will be the gate of Reuben, the gate of Judah and the gate of Levi.

32"On the east side, which is 4,500 cubits long, will be three gates: the gate of Joseph, the gate of Benjamin and the gate of Dan.

33"On the south side, which measures 4,500 cubits, will be three gates: the gate of Simeon, the gate of Issachar and the gate of Zebulun.

34"On the west side, which is 4,500 cubits long, will be three gates: the gate of Gad, the gate of Asher and the gate of Naphtali.

35"The distance all around will be 18,000 cubits.[a]

"And the name of the city from that time on will be:

THE LORD IS THERE."

---

[a] *35* That is, about 6 miles or about 9.5 kilometers

DANIEL

If there was ever a book written that teaches the power and necessity of prayer, it is the book of Daniel. It tells two distinct stories of four young Jewish men living in exile in Babylon, in a narrative that includes multiple subplots involving dreams, interpretations, idolatry, thwarted capital punishment, angelic warriors and lycanthropy—a man acting like a wild animal.

The first half of the book is told in the third person and largely narrates events from the lives of these four men and King Nebuchadnezzar. The second half explains visions the Lord had given Daniel and frequently uses the first person. God's sovereignty over all nations, including pagan empires, is a theme of the book.

The narrative of Shadrach, Meshach and Abednego shows God's providential care over his faithful servants as they live in a culture that is indifferent to God and unaware of his ways. When Shadrach, Meshach and Abednego refused to bow before a giant idol King Nebuchadnezzar erected, the Lord intervened miraculously to protect them. While inside a superheated furnace used for melting metal—a death sentence to be sure—a fourth man appeared with them. The king recognized the man as a divine being. Many believe this to be a preincarnate appearance of the Lord Jesus Christ, showing that he does not abandon those who sacrifice for him.

Another example of living counterculturally is when Daniel continued to pray three times a day even though the new king, Darius, caught in a scheme hatched by wicked advisers, had forbidden it. As punishment Daniel was tossed in a den of lions, where he was fully expected to meet his demise. But the Lord shut the lions' mouths, and Daniel was not harmed.

These two incidents in Daniel's narrative help Christians understand how to pray in an ungodly culture. We pray for the Lord to help us remain faithful to him, even when the world around us misunderstands our obedience or persecutes us for faithfulness. As Nebuchadnezzar's heart was convicted by the reality of who God is, we pray that those around us who oppose the gospel would come to see who God is through our witness.

The need to persist in prayer is seen in chapter 10, in which an angel informed Daniel that the answer to his prayer had been delayed due to spiritual warfare in the heavens. While this vignette might seem unimaginable, it should drive us never to stop praying until our petitions are answered.

Daniel's narrative also demonstrates God's absolute providence over the rising and falling of the world's nations and its leaders. This encourages us to pray diligently for our governmental leaders. Their lives are in God's hands, so we ask the Lord to move upon them. We pray for him to convict them when they are wrong and for them to have the wisdom they need to lead. Most importantly, we pray that they have the humility to know that their power comes from God and not from themselves.

DANIEL'S TRAINING IN BABYLON

1 In the third year of the reign of Jehoiakim king of Judah, Nebuchadnezzar king of Babylon came to Jerusalem and besieged it. 2And the Lord delivered Jehoiakim king of Judah into his hand, along with some of the articles from the temple of God. These he carried off to the temple of his god in Babylonia[a] and put in the treasure house of his god.

3Then the king ordered Ashpenaz, chief of his court officials, to bring into the king's service some of the Israelites from the royal family and the nobility — 4young men without any physical defect, handsome, showing aptitude for every kind of learning, well informed, quick to understand, and qualified to serve in the king's palace. He was to teach them the language and literature of the Babylonians.[b] 5The king assigned them a daily amount of food and wine from the king's table. They were to be trained for three years, and after that they were to enter the king's service.

6Among those who were chosen were some from Judah: Daniel, Hananiah, Mishael and Azariah. 7The chief official gave them new names: to Daniel, the name Belteshazzar; to Hananiah, Shadrach; to Mishael, Meshach; and to Azariah, Abednego.

8But Daniel resolved not to defile himself with the royal food and wine, and he asked the chief official for permission not to defile himself this way. 9Now God had caused the official to show favor and compassion to Daniel, 10but the official told Daniel, "I am afraid of my lord the king, who has assigned your[c] food and drink. Why should he see you looking worse than the other young men your age? The king would then have my head because of you."

11Daniel then said to the guard whom the chief official had appointed over Daniel, Hananiah, Mishael and Azariah, 12"Please test your servants for ten days: Give us nothing but vegetables to eat and water to drink. 13Then compare our appearance with that of the young men who eat the royal food, and treat your servants in accordance with what you see." 14So he agreed to this and tested them for ten days.

15At the end of the ten days they looked healthier and better nourished than any of the young men who ate the royal food. 16So the guard took away their choice food and the wine they were to drink and gave them vegetables instead.

17To these four young men God gave knowledge and understanding of all kinds of literature and learning. And Daniel could understand visions and dreams of all kinds.

18At the end of the time set by the king to bring them into his service, the chief official presented them to Nebuchadnezzar. 19The king talked with them, and he found none equal to Daniel, Hananiah, Mishael and Azariah; so they entered the king's service. 20In every matter of wisdom and understanding about which the king questioned them, he found them ten times better than all the magicians and enchanters in his whole kingdom.

21And Daniel remained there until the first year of King Cyrus.

NEBUCHADNEZZAR'S DREAM

2 In the second year of his reign, Nebuchadnezzar had dreams; his mind was troubled and he could not sleep. 2So the king summoned the magicians, enchanters, sorcerers and astrologers[d] to tell

[a] 2 Hebrew *Shinar* [b] 4 Or *Chaldeans* [c] 10 The Hebrew for *your* and *you* in this verse is plural. [d] 2 Or *Chaldeans*; also in verses 4, 5 and 10

PRAYING SCRIPTURE

Daniel 1

While in exile, several young Jewish men were chosen for special training for the king. Among them was Daniel. When asked to violate their conscience by eating certain foods, they faithfully obeyed the Lord with their refusal and their wisdom.

Sometimes we can do the right thing but in a way that reflects poorly on the Lord. Pray for the wisdom to choose right and to act graciously.

PRAYING SCRIPTURE

Daniel 2

Daniel earned his reputation as an accurate interpreter of dreams in service to Nebuchadnezzar. Disturbed by a dream he could not interpret, the king demanded that his wise men not only interpret his dream but also tell him what the dream was in the first place without first revealing any of its details!

While the wise men faltered, Daniel prevailed after praying for God's help. God is willing and able to give us wisdom, so ask him whenever it's needed (see James 1:5).

him what he had dreamed. When they came in and stood before the
king, 3he said to them, "I have had a dream that troubles me and I want
to know what it means.[a]"

4Then the astrologers answered the king,[b] "May the king live for-
ever! Tell your servants the dream, and we will interpret it."

5The king replied to the astrologers, "This is what I have firmly de-
cided: If you do not tell me what my dream was and interpret it, I will
have you cut into pieces and your houses turned into piles of rubble.
6But if you tell me the dream and explain it, you will receive from me
gifts and rewards and great honor. So tell me the dream and interpret
it for me."

7Once more they replied, "Let the king tell his servants the dream,
and we will interpret it."

8Then the king answered, "I am certain that you are trying to gain
time, because you realize that this is what I have firmly decided: 9If
you do not tell me the dream, there is only one penalty for you. You
have conspired to tell me misleading and wicked things, hoping the
situation will change. So then, tell me the dream, and I will know that
you can interpret it for me."

10The astrologers answered the king, "There is no one on earth who
can do what the king asks! No king, however great and mighty, has
ever asked such a thing of any magician or enchanter or astrologer.
11What the king asks is too difficult. No one can reveal it to the king
except the gods, and they do not live among humans."

12This made the king so angry and furious that he ordered the exe-
cution of all the wise men of Babylon. 13So the decree was issued to put
the wise men to death, and men were sent to look for Daniel and his
friends to put them to death.

14When Arioch, the commander of the king's guard, had gone out
to put to death the wise men of Babylon, Daniel spoke to him with
wisdom and tact. 15He asked the king's officer, "Why did the king issue
such a harsh decree?" Arioch then explained the matter to Daniel. 16At
this, Daniel went in to the king and asked for time, so that he might
interpret the dream for him.

17Then Daniel returned to his house and explained the matter to his
friends Hananiah, Mishael and Azariah. 18He urged them to plead for
mercy from the God of heaven concerning this mystery, so that he and
his friends might not be executed with the rest of the wise men of Bab-
ylon. 19During the night the mystery was revealed to Daniel in a vision.
Then Daniel praised the God of heaven 20and said:

"Praise be to the name of God for ever and ever;
    wisdom and power are his.
21 He changes times and seasons;
    he deposes kings and raises up others.
He gives wisdom to the wise
    and knowledge to the discerning.
22 He reveals deep and hidden things;
    he knows what lies in darkness,
    and light dwells with him.
23 I thank and praise you, God of my ancestors:
    You have given me wisdom and power,

---

[a] 3 Or *was* [b] 4 At this point the Hebrew text has *in Aramaic,* indicating
that the text from here through the end of chapter 7 is in Aramaic.

you have made known to me what we asked of you,
you have made known to us the dream of the king."

DANIEL INTERPRETS THE DREAM

24Then Daniel went to Arioch, whom the king had appointed to
execute the wise men of Babylon, and said to him, "Do not execute
the wise men of Babylon. Take me to the king, and I will interpret his
dream for him."

25Arioch took Daniel to the king at once and said, "I have found
a man among the exiles from Judah who can tell the king what his
dream means."

26The king asked Daniel (also called Belteshazzar), "Are you able to
tell me what I saw in my dream and interpret it?"

27Daniel replied, "No wise man, enchanter, magician or diviner can
explain to the king the mystery he has asked about, 28but there is a
God in heaven who reveals mysteries. He has shown King Nebuchadnezzar what will happen in days to come. Your dream and the visions
that passed through your mind as you were lying in bed are these:

29"As Your Majesty was lying there, your mind turned to things to
come, and the revealer of mysteries showed you what is going to happen. 30As for me, this mystery has been revealed to me, not because I
have greater wisdom than anyone else alive, but so that Your Majesty
may know the interpretation and that you may understand what went
through your mind.

31"Your Majesty looked, and there before you stood a large statue—
an enormous, dazzling statue, awesome in appearance. 32The head of
the statue was made of pure gold, its chest and arms of silver, its belly
and thighs of bronze, 33its legs of iron, its feet partly of iron and partly
of baked clay. 34While you were watching, a rock was cut out, but not
by human hands. It struck the statue on its feet of iron and clay and
smashed them. 35Then the iron, the clay, the bronze, the silver and the
gold were all broken to pieces and became like chaff on a threshing
floor in the summer. The wind swept them away without leaving a
trace. But the rock that struck the statue became a huge mountain and
filled the whole earth.

36"This was the dream, and now we will interpret it to the king.
37Your Majesty, you are the king of kings. The God of heaven has given
you dominion and power and might and glory; 38in your hands he has
placed all mankind and the beasts of the field and the birds in the sky.
Wherever they live, he has made you ruler over them all. You are that
head of gold.

39"After you, another kingdom will arise, inferior to yours. Next, a
third kingdom, one of bronze, will rule over the whole earth. 40Finally,
there will be a fourth kingdom, strong as iron—for iron breaks and
smashes everything—and as iron breaks things to pieces, so it will
crush and break all the others. 41Just as you saw that the feet and toes
were partly of baked clay and partly of iron, so this will be a divided
kingdom; yet it will have some of the strength of iron in it, even as you
saw iron mixed with clay. 42As the toes were partly iron and partly clay,
so this kingdom will be partly strong and partly brittle. 43And just as
you saw the iron mixed with baked clay, so the people will be a mixture and will not remain united, any more than iron mixes with clay.

44"In the time of those kings, the God of heaven will set up a kingdom that will never be destroyed, nor will it be left to another people.

It will crush all those kingdoms and bring them to an end, but it will
itself endure forever. 45This is the meaning of the vision of the rock cut
out of a mountain, but not by human hands — a rock that broke the
iron, the bronze, the clay, the silver and the gold to pieces.
"The great God has shown the king what will take place in the future.
The dream is true and its interpretation is trustworthy."
46Then King Nebuchadnezzar fell prostrate before Daniel and paid
him honor and ordered that an offering and incense be presented to
him. 47The king said to Daniel, "Surely your God is the God of gods and
the Lord of kings and a revealer of mysteries, for you were able to re-
veal this mystery."
48Then the king placed Daniel in a high position and lavished many
gifts on him. He made him ruler over the entire province of Babylon
and placed him in charge of all its wise men. 49Moreover, at Daniel's
request the king appointed Shadrach, Meshach and Abednego admin-
istrators over the province of Babylon, while Daniel himself remained
at the royal court.

PRAYING SCRIPTURE

Daniel 3

From the time of Shadrach, Meshach and Abednego, God's people have marveled at the power of God to save his people according to his will. His rescue was so thorough that not even the smell of smoke clung to them when they exited the flames.

There is never a bad time to pray for God to rescue you. You cannot drain his power with your circumstance, so never be slow to ask.

THE IMAGE OF GOLD AND THE BLAZING FURNACE

3 King Nebuchadnezzar made an image of gold, sixty cubits high
and six cubits wide,[a] and set it up on the plain of Dura in the prov-
ince of Babylon. 2He then summoned the satraps, prefects, governors,
advisers, treasurers, judges, magistrates and all the other provincial of-
ficials to come to the dedication of the image he had set up. 3So the sa-
traps, prefects, governors, advisers, treasurers, judges, magistrates and
all the other provincial officials assembled for the dedication of the
image that King Nebuchadnezzar had set up, and they stood before it.
4Then the herald loudly proclaimed, "Nations and peoples of every
language, this is what you are commanded to do: 5As soon as you hear
the sound of the horn, flute, zither, lyre, harp, pipe and all kinds of
music, you must fall down and worship the image of gold that King
Nebuchadnezzar has set up. 6Whoever does not fall down and worship
will immediately be thrown into a blazing furnace."
7Therefore, as soon as they heard the sound of the horn, flute, zither,
lyre, harp and all kinds of music, all the nations and peoples of every
language fell down and worshiped the image of gold that King Nebu-
chadnezzar had set up.
8At this time some astrologers[b] came forward and denounced the
Jews. 9They said to King Nebuchadnezzar, "May the king live forever!
10Your Majesty has issued a decree that everyone who hears the sound
of the horn, flute, zither, lyre, harp, pipe and all kinds of music must
fall down and worship the image of gold, 11and that whoever does not
fall down and worship will be thrown into a blazing furnace. 12But
there are some Jews whom you have set over the affairs of the prov-
ince of Babylon — Shadrach, Meshach and Abednego — who pay no at-
tention to you, Your Majesty. They neither serve your gods nor worship
the image of gold you have set up."
13Furious with rage, Nebuchadnezzar summoned Shadrach, Meshach
and Abednego. So these men were brought before the king, 14and Neb-
uchadnezzar said to them, "Is it true, Shadrach, Meshach and Abed-
nego, that you do not serve my gods or worship the image of gold I
have set up? 15Now when you hear the sound of the horn, flute, zither,

[a] *1* That is, about 90 feet high and 9 feet wide or about 27 meters high and 2.7 meters wide [b] *8* Or *Chaldeans*

lyre, harp, pipe and all kinds of music, if you are ready to fall down and
worship the image I made, very good. But if you do not worship it, you
will be thrown immediately into a blazing furnace. Then what god will
be able to rescue you from my hand?"
16Shadrach, Meshach and Abednego replied to him, "King Nebuchad-
nezzar, we do not need to defend ourselves before you in this matter.
17If we are thrown into the blazing furnace, the God we serve is able to
deliver us from it, and he will deliver us[a] from Your Majesty's hand.
18But even if he does not, we want you to know, Your Majesty, that we
will not serve your gods or worship the image of gold you have set up."
19Then Nebuchadnezzar was furious with Shadrach, Meshach and
Abednego, and his attitude toward them changed. He ordered the fur-
nace heated seven times hotter than usual 20and commanded some
of the strongest soldiers in his army to tie up Shadrach, Meshach and
Abednego and throw them into the blazing furnace. 21So these men,
wearing their robes, trousers, turbans and other clothes, were bound
and thrown into the blazing furnace. 22The king's command was so
urgent and the furnace so hot that the flames of the fire killed the sol-
diers who took up Shadrach, Meshach and Abednego, 23and these three
men, firmly tied, fell into the blazing furnace.
24Then King Nebuchadnezzar leaped to his feet in amazement and
asked his advisers, "Weren't there three men that we tied up and threw
into the fire?"
They replied, "Certainly, Your Majesty."
25He said, "Look! I see four men walking around in the fire, unbound
and unharmed, and the fourth looks like a son of the gods."
26Nebuchadnezzar then approached the opening of the blazing fur-
nace and shouted, "Shadrach, Meshach and Abednego, servants of the
Most High God, come out! Come here!"
So Shadrach, Meshach and Abednego came out of the fire, 27and the
satraps, prefects, governors and royal advisers crowded around them.
They saw that the fire had not harmed their bodies, nor was a hair of
their heads singed; their robes were not scorched, and there was no
smell of fire on them.
28Then Nebuchadnezzar said, "Praise be to the God of Shadrach, Me-
shach and Abednego, who has sent his angel and rescued his servants!
They trusted in him and defied the king's command and were willing
to give up their lives rather than serve or worship any god except their
own God. 29Therefore I decree that the people of any nation or lan-
guage who say anything against the God of Shadrach, Meshach and
Abednego be cut into pieces and their houses be turned into piles of
rubble, for no other god can save in this way."
30Then the king promoted Shadrach, Meshach and Abednego in the
province of Babylon.

NEBUCHADNEZZAR'S DREAM OF A TREE

4 [b] King Nebuchadnezzar,

To the nations and peoples of every language, who live in all the earth:

May you prosper greatly!

[a] 17 Or *If the God we serve is able to deliver us, then he will deliver us from the blazing furnace and* [b] In Aramaic texts 4:1-3 is numbered 3:31-33, and 4:4-37 is numbered 4:1-34.

PRAYING SCRIPTURE

Daniel 4

Nowhere in Scripture is the truth that when we exalt ourselves, the Lord will surely humble us, more clearly displayed than in the story of Nebuchadnezzar's becoming like a beast of the field. Rather than humbling himself after learning from his dreams, the king grew proud of his kingdom, glorifying himself instead of God.

Taking credit for God's acts is dangerous. Examine your heart for any arrogance, and repent when you pray.

2It is my pleasure to tell you about the miraculous signs and
wonders that the Most High God has performed for me.

3How great are his signs,
how mighty his wonders!
His kingdom is an eternal kingdom;
his dominion endures from generation to generation.

4I, Nebuchadnezzar, was at home in my palace, contented and
prosperous. 5I had a dream that made me afraid. As I was lying in
bed, the images and visions that passed through my mind terrified
me. 6So I commanded that all the wise men of Babylon be brought
before me to interpret the dream for me. 7When the magicians,
enchanters, astrologers[a] and diviners came, I told them the dream,
but they could not interpret it for me. 8Finally, Daniel came into
my presence and I told him the dream. (He is called Belteshazzar,
after the name of my god, and the spirit of the holy gods is in him.)
9I said, "Belteshazzar, chief of the magicians, I know that the
spirit of the holy gods is in you, and no mystery is too difficult for
you. Here is my dream; interpret it for me. 10These are the visions
I saw while lying in bed: I looked, and there before me stood a tree
in the middle of the land. Its height was enormous. 11The tree grew
large and strong and its top touched the sky; it was visible to the
ends of the earth. 12Its leaves were beautiful, its fruit abundant,
and on it was food for all. Under it the wild animals found shelter,
and the birds lived in its branches; from it every creature was fed.
13"In the visions I saw while lying in bed, I looked, and there be-
fore me was a holy one, a messenger,[b] coming down from heaven.
14He called in a loud voice: 'Cut down the tree and trim off its
branches; strip off its leaves and scatter its fruit. Let the animals
flee from under it and the birds from its branches. 15But let the
stump and its roots, bound with iron and bronze, remain in the
ground, in the grass of the field.

"'Let him be drenched with the dew of heaven, and let him live
with the animals among the plants of the earth. 16Let his mind be
changed from that of a man and let him be given the mind of an
animal, till seven times[c] pass by for him.
17"'The decision is announced by messengers, the holy ones de-
clare the verdict, so that the living may know that the Most High
is sovereign over all kingdoms on earth and gives them to anyone
he wishes and sets over them the lowliest of people.'

18"This is the dream that I, King Nebuchadnezzar, had. Now, Bel-
teshazzar, tell me what it means, for none of the wise men in my
kingdom can interpret it for me. But you can, because the spirit of
the holy gods is in you."

DANIEL INTERPRETS THE DREAM

19Then Daniel (also called Belteshazzar) was greatly perplexed
for a time, and his thoughts terrified him. So the king said, "Belte-
shazzar, do not let the dream or its meaning alarm you."
Belteshazzar answered, "My lord, if only the dream applied to
your enemies and its meaning to your adversaries! 20The tree you

[a] 7 Or *Chaldeans* [b] 13 Or *watchman*; also in verses 17 and 23 [c] 16 Or *years*; also in verses 23, 25 and 32

saw, which grew large and strong, with its top touching the sky,
visible to the whole earth, 21with beautiful leaves and abundant
fruit, providing food for all, giving shelter to the wild animals,
and having nesting places in its branches for the birds — 22Your
Majesty, you are that tree! You have become great and strong; your
greatness has grown until it reaches the sky, and your dominion
extends to distant parts of the earth.

23"Your Majesty saw a holy one, a messenger, coming down
from heaven and saying, 'Cut down the tree and destroy it, but
leave the stump, bound with iron and bronze, in the grass of the
field, while its roots remain in the ground. Let him be drenched
with the dew of heaven; let him live with the wild animals, until
seven times pass by for him.'

24"This is the interpretation, Your Majesty, and this is the decree
the Most High has issued against my lord the king: 25You will be
driven away from people and will live with the wild animals; you
will eat grass like the ox and be drenched with the dew of heaven.
Seven times will pass by for you until you acknowledge that the
Most High is sovereign over all kingdoms on earth and gives them
to anyone he wishes. 26The command to leave the stump of the
tree with its roots means that your kingdom will be restored to
you when you acknowledge that Heaven rules. 27Therefore, Your
Majesty, be pleased to accept my advice: Renounce your sins by
doing what is right, and your wickedness by being kind to the oppressed. It may be that then your prosperity will continue."

THE DREAM IS FULFILLED

28All this happened to King Nebuchadnezzar. 29Twelve months
later, as the king was walking on the roof of the royal palace of
Babylon, 30he said, "Is not this the great Babylon I have built as
the royal residence, by my mighty power and for the glory of my
majesty?"

31Even as the words were on his lips, a voice came from heaven,
"This is what is decreed for you, King Nebuchadnezzar: Your royal
authority has been taken from you. 32You will be driven away
from people and will live with the wild animals; you will eat grass
like the ox. Seven times will pass by for you until you acknowledge
that the Most High is sovereign over all kingdoms on earth and
gives them to anyone he wishes."

33Immediately what had been said about Nebuchadnezzar was
fulfilled. He was driven away from people and ate grass like the ox.
His body was drenched with the dew of heaven until his hair grew
like the feathers of an eagle and his nails like the claws of a bird.

34At the end of that time, I, Nebuchadnezzar, raised my eyes toward heaven, and my sanity was restored. Then I praised the Most
High; I honored and glorified him who lives forever.

His dominion is an eternal dominion;
    his kingdom endures from generation to generation.
35 All the peoples of the earth
    are regarded as nothing.
He does as he pleases
    with the powers of heaven
    and the peoples of the earth.

No one can hold back his hand
  or say to him: "What have you done?"

36At the same time that my sanity was restored, my honor and
splendor were returned to me for the glory of my kingdom. My ad-
visers and nobles sought me out, and I was restored to my throne
and became even greater than before. 37Now I, Nebuchadnezzar,
praise and exalt and glorify the King of heaven, because every-
thing he does is right and all his ways are just. And those who walk
in pride he is able to humble.

THE WRITING ON THE WALL

5 King Belshazzar gave a great banquet for a thousand of his nobles
and drank wine with them. 2While Belshazzar was drinking his
wine, he gave orders to bring in the gold and silver goblets that Neb-
uchadnezzar his father[a] had taken from the temple in Jerusalem, so
that the king and his nobles, his wives and his concubines might drink
from them. 3So they brought in the gold goblets that had been taken
from the temple of God in Jerusalem, and the king and his nobles,
his wives and his concubines drank from them. 4As they drank the
wine, they praised the gods of gold and silver, of bronze, iron, wood
and stone.

5Suddenly the fingers of a human hand appeared and wrote on the
plaster of the wall, near the lampstand in the royal palace. The king
watched the hand as it wrote. 6His face turned pale and he was so
frightened that his legs became weak and his knees were knocking.

7The king summoned the enchanters, astrologers[b] and diviners.
Then he said to these wise men of Babylon, "Whoever reads this writ-
ing and tells me what it means will be clothed in purple and have a
gold chain placed around his neck, and he will be made the third high-
est ruler in the kingdom."

8Then all the king's wise men came in, but they could not read the
writing or tell the king what it meant. 9So King Belshazzar became
even more terrified and his face grew more pale. His nobles were
baffled.

10The queen,[c] hearing the voices of the king and his nobles, came
into the banquet hall. "May the king live forever!" she said. "Don't be
alarmed! Don't look so pale! 11There is a man in your kingdom who
has the spirit of the holy gods in him. In the time of your father he
was found to have insight and intelligence and wisdom like that of
the gods. Your father, King Nebuchadnezzar, appointed him chief of
the magicians, enchanters, astrologers and diviners. 12He did this be-
cause Daniel, whom the king called Belteshazzar, was found to have a
keen mind and knowledge and understanding, and also the ability to
interpret dreams, explain riddles and solve difficult problems. Call for
Daniel, and he will tell you what the writing means."

13So Daniel was brought before the king, and the king said to him,
"Are you Daniel, one of the exiles my father the king brought from
Judah? 14I have heard that the spirit of the gods is in you and that you
have insight, intelligence and outstanding wisdom. 15The wise men
and enchanters were brought before me to read this writing and tell
me what it means, but they could not explain it. 16Now I have heard

PRAYING SCRIPTURE

Daniel 5

Even the greatest earthly rulers will return to the dust one day, as is portrayed in the narrative of the "handwriting on the wall." King Belshazzar, before a feast of a thousand lords and his wives and concubines, was called to account for his iniquity. Daniel interpreted the words to mean that Belshazzar's kingdom was ending—and it did that night.

Pray for government leaders to follow the Lord so they can avoid judgment.

---

[a] *2* Or *ancestor*; or *predecessor*; also in verses 11, 13 and 18 [b] *7* Or *Chaldeans*; also in verse 11 [c] *10* Or *queen mother*

that you are able to give interpretations and to solve difficult prob-
lems. If you can read this writing and tell me what it means, you will be
clothed in purple and have a gold chain placed around your neck, and
you will be made the third highest ruler in the kingdom."
17 Then Daniel answered the king, "You may keep your gifts for your-
self and give your rewards to someone else. Nevertheless, I will read
the writing for the king and tell him what it means.
18 "Your Majesty, the Most High God gave your father Nebuchadnez-
zar sovereignty and greatness and glory and splendor. 19 Because of the
high position he gave him, all the nations and peoples of every language
dreaded and feared him. Those the king wanted to put to death, he put
to death; those he wanted to spare, he spared; those he wanted to pro-
mote, he promoted; and those he wanted to humble, he humbled. 20 But
when his heart became arrogant and hardened with pride, he was de-
posed from his royal throne and stripped of his glory. 21 He was driven
away from people and given the mind of an animal; he lived with the
wild donkeys and ate grass like the ox; and his body was drenched with
the dew of heaven, until he acknowledged that the Most High God is sov-
ereign over all kingdoms on earth and sets over them anyone he wishes.
22 "But you, Belshazzar, his son,[a] have not humbled yourself, though
you knew all this. 23 Instead, you have set yourself up against the Lord
of heaven. You had the goblets from his temple brought to you, and
you and your nobles, your wives and your concubines drank wine
from them. You praised the gods of silver and gold, of bronze, iron,
wood and stone, which cannot see or hear or understand. But you did
not honor the God who holds in his hand your life and all your ways.
24 Therefore he sent the hand that wrote the inscription.
25 "This is the inscription that was written:

MENE, MENE, TEKEL, PARSIN

26 "Here is what these words mean:

Mene[b]: God has numbered the days of your reign and brought it to an end.

27 *Tekel*[c]: You have been weighed on the scales and found wanting.

28 *Peres*[d]: Your kingdom is divided and given to the Medes and Persians."

29 Then at Belshazzar's command, Daniel was clothed in purple, a
gold chain was placed around his neck, and he was proclaimed the
third highest ruler in the kingdom.
30 That very night Belshazzar, king of the Babylonians,[e] was slain,
31 and Darius the Mede took over the kingdom, at the age of sixty-two.[f]

DANIEL IN THE DEN OF LIONS

6 [g] It pleased Darius to appoint 120 satraps to rule throughout the
kingdom, 2 with three administrators over them, one of whom
was Daniel. The satraps were made accountable to them so that the
king might not suffer loss. 3 Now Daniel so distinguished himself

PRAYING SCRIPTURE

Daniel 6

Nowhere in Scripture is God's care for his people clearer than when he shut the mouths of a den of lions so that his prophet Daniel could have a restful night. The deceived king who ordered Daniel's death was both surprised and glad that God brought salvation to Daniel.

God allows testing to demonstrate His power and care to those around us. Pray for endurance, knowing those around you may be watching.

---

[a] 22 Or *descendant*; or *successor* [b] 26 *Mene* can mean *numbered* or *mina* (a unit of money). [c] 27 *Tekel* can mean *weighed* or *shekel.* [d] 28 *Peres* (the singular of *Parsin*) can mean *divided* or *Persia* or *a half mina* or *a half shekel.* [e] 30 Or *Chaldeans* [f] 31 In Aramaic texts this verse (5:31) is numbered 6:1. [g] In Aramaic texts 6:1-28 is numbered 6:2-29.

among the administrators and the satraps by his exceptional qualities
that the king planned to set him over the whole kingdom. 4At this,
the administrators and the satraps tried to find grounds for charges
against Daniel in his conduct of government affairs, but they were un-
able to do so. They could find no corruption in him, because he was
trustworthy and neither corrupt nor negligent. 5Finally these men
said, "We will never find any basis for charges against this man Daniel
unless it has something to do with the law of his God."

6So these administrators and satraps went as a group to the king and
said: "May King Darius live forever! 7The royal administrators, prefects,
satraps, advisers and governors have all agreed that the king should
issue an edict and enforce the decree that anyone who prays to any god
or human being during the next thirty days, except to you, Your Maj-
esty, shall be thrown into the lions' den. 8Now, Your Majesty, issue the
decree and put it in writing so that it cannot be altered — in accordance
with the law of the Medes and Persians, which cannot be repealed." 9So
King Darius put the decree in writing.

10Now when Daniel learned that the decree had been published, he
went home to his upstairs room where the windows opened toward
Jerusalem. Three times a day he got down on his knees and prayed,
giving thanks to his God, just as he had done before. 11Then these men
went as a group and found Daniel praying and asking God for help. 12So
they went to the king and spoke to him about his royal decree: "Did
you not publish a decree that during the next thirty days anyone who
prays to any god or human being except to you, Your Majesty, would
be thrown into the lions' den?"

The king answered, "The decree stands — in accordance with the law
of the Medes and Persians, which cannot be repealed."

13Then they said to the king, "Daniel, who is one of the exiles from
Judah, pays no attention to you, Your Majesty, or to the decree you
put in writing. He still prays three times a day." 14When the king heard
this, he was greatly distressed; he was determined to rescue Daniel and
made every effort until sundown to save him.

15Then the men went as a group to King Darius and said to him, "Re-
member, Your Majesty, that according to the law of the Medes and Per-
sians no decree or edict that the king issues can be changed."

16So the king gave the order, and they brought Daniel and threw him
into the lions' den. The king said to Daniel, "May your God, whom you
serve continually, rescue you!"

17A stone was brought and placed over the mouth of the den, and the
king sealed it with his own signet ring and with the rings of his no-
bles, so that Daniel's situation might not be changed. 18Then the king
returned to his palace and spent the night without eating and without
any entertainment being brought to him. And he could not sleep.

19At the first light of dawn, the king got up and hurried to the lions'
den. 20When he came near the den, he called to Daniel in an anguished
voice, "Daniel, servant of the living God, has your God, whom you serve
continually, been able to rescue you from the lions?"

21Daniel answered, "May the king live forever! 22My God sent his
angel, and he shut the mouths of the lions. They have not hurt me,
because I was found innocent in his sight. Nor have I ever done any
wrong before you, Your Majesty."

23The king was overjoyed and gave orders to lift Daniel out of the
den. And when Daniel was lifted from the den, no wound was found
on him, because he had trusted in his God.

24 At the king's command, the men who had falsely accused Daniel
were brought in and thrown into the lions' den, along with their wives
and children. And before they reached the floor of the den, the lions
overpowered them and crushed all their bones.
25 Then King Darius wrote to all the nations and peoples of every
language in all the earth:

"May you prosper greatly!

26 "I issue a decree that in every part of my kingdom people
must fear and reverence the God of Daniel.

"For he is the living God
and he endures forever;
his kingdom will not be destroyed,
his dominion will never end.
27 He rescues and he saves;
he performs signs and wonders
in the heavens and on the earth.
He has rescued Daniel
from the power of the lions."

28 So Daniel prospered during the reign of Darius and the reign of
Cyrus[a] the Persian.

DANIEL'S DREAM OF FOUR BEASTS

7 In the first year of Belshazzar king of Babylon, Daniel had a dream,
and visions passed through his mind as he was lying in bed. He
wrote down the substance of his dream.
2 Daniel said: "In my vision at night I looked, and there before me
were the four winds of heaven churning up the great sea. 3 Four great
beasts, each different from the others, came up out of the sea.
4 "The first was like a lion, and it had the wings of an eagle. I watched
until its wings were torn off and it was lifted from the ground so that
it stood on two feet like a human being, and the mind of a human was
given to it.
5 "And there before me was a second beast, which looked like a bear.
It was raised up on one of its sides, and it had three ribs in its mouth
between its teeth. It was told, 'Get up and eat your fill of flesh!'
6 "After that, I looked, and there before me was another beast, one
that looked like a leopard. And on its back it had four wings like those
of a bird. This beast had four heads, and it was given authority to rule.
7 "After that, in my vision at night I looked, and there before me was
a fourth beast — terrifying and frightening and very powerful. It had
large iron teeth; it crushed and devoured its victims and trampled un-
derfoot whatever was left. It was different from all the former beasts,
and it had ten horns.
8 "While I was thinking about the horns, there before me was another
horn, a little one, which came up among them; and three of the first
horns were uprooted before it. This horn had eyes like the eyes of a
human being and a mouth that spoke boastfully.
9 "As I looked,

"thrones were set in place,
and the Ancient of Days took his seat.

PRAYING SCRIPTURE

Daniel 7

Daniel's vision of the four great beasts (see verses 3–8) resolves into the appearance of "the Ancient of Days" upon his throne (verse 9). As the scene unfolded, "one like a son of man" approached the Ancient of Days, and to him "was given authority, glory and sovereign power" (verses 13–14).

God's plan has always been for some from all nations and peoples to worship him. God be praised for prophecy and prophecy fulfilled.

[a] 28 Or *Darius, that is, the reign of Cyrus*

His clothing was as white as snow;
 the hair of his head was white like wool.
His throne was flaming with fire,
 and its wheels were all ablaze.
10 A river of fire was flowing,
 coming out from before him.
Thousands upon thousands attended him;
 ten thousand times ten thousand stood before him.
The court was seated,
 and the books were opened.

11 “Then I continued to watch because of the boastful words the horn was speaking. I kept looking until the beast was slain and its body destroyed and thrown into the blazing fire. 12 (The other beasts had been stripped of their authority, but were allowed to live for a period of time.)

13 “In my vision at night I looked, and there before me was one like a son of man,[a] coming with the clouds of heaven. He approached the Ancient of Days and was led into his presence. 14 He was given authority, glory and sovereign power; all nations and peoples of every language worshiped him. His dominion is an everlasting dominion that will not pass away, and his kingdom is one that will never be destroyed.

THE INTERPRETATION OF THE DREAM

15 “I, Daniel, was troubled in spirit, and the visions that passed through my mind disturbed me. 16 I approached one of those standing there and asked him the meaning of all this.

“So he told me and gave me the interpretation of these things: 17 ‘The four great beasts are four kings that will rise from the earth. 18 But the holy people of the Most High will receive the kingdom and will possess it forever — yes, for ever and ever.’

19 “Then I wanted to know the meaning of the fourth beast, which was different from all the others and most terrifying, with its iron teeth and bronze claws — the beast that crushed and devoured its victims and trampled underfoot whatever was left. 20 I also wanted to know about the ten horns on its head and about the other horn that came up, before which three of them fell — the horn that looked more imposing than the others and that had eyes and a mouth that spoke boastfully. 21 As I watched, this horn was waging war against the holy people and defeating them, 22 until the Ancient of Days came and pronounced judgment in favor of the holy people of the Most High, and the time came when they possessed the kingdom.

23 “He gave me this explanation: ‘The fourth beast is a fourth kingdom that will appear on earth. It will be different from all the other kingdoms and will devour the whole earth, trampling it down and crushing it. 24 The ten horns are ten kings who will come from this kingdom. After them another king will arise, different from the earlier ones; he will subdue three kings. 25 He will speak against the Most High and oppress his holy people and try to change the set times and the laws. The holy people will be delivered into his hands for a time, times and half a time.[b]

[a] *13* The Aramaic phrase *bar enash* means *human being.* The phrase *son of man* is retained here because of its use in the New Testament as a title of Jesus, probably based largely on this verse. [b] *25* Or *for a year, two years and half a year*

26“‘But the court will sit, and his power will be taken away and
completely destroyed forever. 27Then the sovereignty, power and
greatness of all the kingdoms under heaven will be handed over to
the holy people of the Most High. His kingdom will be an everlasting
kingdom, and all rulers will worship and obey him.’
28“This is the end of the matter. I, Daniel, was deeply troubled
by my thoughts, and my face turned pale, but I kept the matter to
myself.”

DANIEL’S VISION OF A RAM AND A GOAT

8 In the third year of King Belshazzar’s reign, I, Daniel, had a vision,
after the one that had already appeared to me. 2In my vision I saw
myself in the citadel of Susa in the province of Elam; in the vision I
was beside the Ulai Canal. 3I looked up, and there before me was a
ram with two horns, standing beside the canal, and the horns were
long. One of the horns was longer than the other but grew up later. 4I
watched the ram as it charged toward the west and the north and the
south. No animal could stand against it, and none could rescue from
its power. It did as it pleased and became great.
5As I was thinking about this, suddenly a goat with a prominent
horn between its eyes came from the west, crossing the whole earth
without touching the ground. 6It came toward the two-horned ram I
had seen standing beside the canal and charged at it in great rage. 7I
saw it attack the ram furiously, striking the ram and shattering its two
horns. The ram was powerless to stand against it; the goat knocked it
to the ground and trampled on it, and none could rescue the ram from
its power. 8The goat became very great, but at the height of its power
the large horn was broken off, and in its place four prominent horns
grew up toward the four winds of heaven.
9Out of one of them came another horn, which started small but
grew in power to the south and to the east and toward the Beautiful
Land. 10It grew until it reached the host of the heavens, and it threw
some of the starry host down to the earth and trampled on them. 11It
set itself up to be as great as the commander of the army of the LORD;
it took away the daily sacrifice from the LORD, and his sanctuary was
thrown down. 12Because of rebellion, the LORD’s people[a] and the daily
sacrifice were given over to it. It prospered in everything it did, and
truth was thrown to the ground.
13Then I heard a holy one speaking, and another holy one said to
him, “How long will it take for the vision to be fulfilled — the vision
concerning the daily sacrifice, the rebellion that causes desolation,
the surrender of the sanctuary and the trampling underfoot of the
LORD’s people?”
14He said to me, “It will take 2,300 evenings and mornings; then the
sanctuary will be reconsecrated.”

THE INTERPRETATION OF THE VISION

15While I, Daniel, was watching the vision and trying to understand
it, there before me stood one who looked like a man. 16And I heard a
man’s voice from the Ulai calling, “Gabriel, tell this man the meaning
of the vision.”
17As he came near the place where I was standing, I was terrified and

[a] 12 Or *rebellion, the armies*

PRAYING SCRIPTURE

Daniel 8

In an ironic turn of events, the one who interpreted visions needed his own vision interpreted. God sent the angel Gabriel to reveal the rise and fall of kingdoms, including the rise of an extremely cunning and deceitful king. The impact of the vision caused Daniel to lie “exhausted for several days” (verse 27).

Many today have lost the ability to be shocked at wickedness; Daniel had not. Shocked or not, we should plead with God to overthrow the wicked.

fell prostrate. "Son of man,"[a] he said to me, "understand that the vision
concerns the time of the end."
18 While he was speaking to me, I was in a deep sleep, with my face to
the ground. Then he touched me and raised me to my feet.
19 He said: "I am going to tell you what will happen later in the time
of wrath, because the vision concerns the appointed time of the end.[b]
20 The two-horned ram that you saw represents the kings of Media and
Persia. 21 The shaggy goat is the king of Greece, and the large horn be-
tween its eyes is the first king. 22 The four horns that replaced the one
that was broken off represent four kingdoms that will emerge from his
nation but will not have the same power.
23 "In the latter part of their reign, when rebels have become com-
pletely wicked, a fierce-looking king, a master of intrigue, will arise.
24 He will become very strong, but not by his own power. He will cause
astounding devastation and will succeed in whatever he does. He will
destroy those who are mighty, the holy people. 25 He will cause deceit to
prosper, and he will consider himself superior. When they feel secure,
he will destroy many and take his stand against the Prince of princes.
Yet he will be destroyed, but not by human power.
26 "The vision of the evenings and mornings that has been given you
is true, but seal up the vision, for it concerns the distant future."
27 I, Daniel, was worn out. I lay exhausted for several days. Then I got
up and went about the king's business. I was appalled by the vision; it
was beyond understanding.

DANIEL'S PRAYER

9 In the first year of Darius son of Xerxes[c] (a Mede by descent), who
was made ruler over the Babylonian[d] kingdom — 2 in the first year
of his reign, I, Daniel, understood from the Scriptures, according to the
word of the LORD given to Jeremiah the prophet, that the desolation of
Jerusalem would last seventy years. 3 So I turned to the Lord God and
pleaded with him in prayer and petition, in fasting, and in sackcloth
and ashes.
4 I prayed to the LORD my God and confessed:

> "Lord, the great and awesome God, who keeps his covenant of
> love with those who love him and keep his commandments, 5 we
> have sinned and done wrong. We have been wicked and have re-
> belled; we have turned away from your commands and laws. 6 We
> have not listened to your servants the prophets, who spoke in your
> name to our kings, our princes and our ancestors, and to all the
> people of the land.
> 7 "Lord, you are righteous, but this day we are covered with
> shame — the people of Judah and the inhabitants of Jerusalem
> and all Israel, both near and far, in all the countries where you
> have scattered us because of our unfaithfulness to you. 8 We and
> our kings, our princes and our ancestors are covered with shame,
> LORD, because we have sinned against you. 9 The Lord our God is
> merciful and forgiving, even though we have rebelled against
> him; 10 we have not obeyed the LORD our God or kept the laws he

PRAYING SCRIPTURE
Daniel 9

Daniel's prophecy of the 70 weeks is surrounded by more speculation than almost any other passage in Scripture. Regardless of the correct interpretation, the most important thing we learn from it is that all of time is in God's control. Nothing escapes his power.

The eyes of God's people should ever be on his Word. That's where our assurance is. Ask God to help you hold steadfastly to his promises.

[a] *17* The Hebrew phrase *ben adam* means *human being.* The phrase *son of man* is retained as a form of address here because of its possible association with "Son of Man" in the New Testament. [b] *19* Or *because the end will be at the appointed time* [c] *1* Hebrew *Ahasuerus* [d] *1* Or *Chaldean*

gave us through his servants the prophets. 11All Israel has trans-
gressed your law and turned away, refusing to obey you.
"Therefore the curses and sworn judgments written in the Law
of Moses, the servant of God, have been poured out on us, because
we have sinned against you. 12You have fulfilled the words spoken
against us and against our rulers by bringing on us great disaster.
Under the whole heaven nothing has ever been done like what has
been done to Jerusalem. 13Just as it is written in the Law of Moses,
all this disaster has come on us, yet we have not sought the favor
of the LORD our God by turning from our sins and giving attention
to your truth. 14The LORD did not hesitate to bring the disaster on
us, for the LORD our God is righteous in everything he does; yet we
have not obeyed him.
15"Now, Lord our God, who brought your people out of Egypt
with a mighty hand and who made for yourself a name that en-
dures to this day, we have sinned, we have done wrong. 16Lord, in
keeping with all your righteous acts, turn away your anger and
your wrath from Jerusalem, your city, your holy hill. Our sins and
the iniquities of our ancestors have made Jerusalem and your
people an object of scorn to all those around us.
17"Now, our God, hear the prayers and petitions of your servant.
For your sake, Lord, look with favor on your desolate sanctuary.
18Give ear, our God, and hear; open your eyes and see the desola-
tion of the city that bears your Name. We do not make requests of
you because we are righteous, but because of your great mercy.
19Lord, listen! Lord, forgive! Lord, hear and act! For your sake, my
God, do not delay, because your city and your people bear your
Name."

THE SEVENTY "SEVENS"

20While I was speaking and praying, confessing my sin and the sin
of my people Israel and making my request to the LORD my God for his
holy hill — 21while I was still in prayer, Gabriel, the man I had seen in
the earlier vision, came to me in swift flight about the time of the eve-
ning sacrifice. 22He instructed me and said to me, "Daniel, I have now
come to give you insight and understanding. 23As soon as you began to
pray, a word went out, which I have come to tell you, for you are highly
esteemed. Therefore, consider the word and understand the vision:
24"Seventy 'sevens'[a] are decreed for your people and your holy city
to finish[b] transgression, to put an end to sin, to atone for wickedness,
to bring in everlasting righteousness, to seal up vision and prophecy
and to anoint the Most Holy Place.[c]
25"Know and understand this: From the time the word goes out to re-
store and rebuild Jerusalem until the Anointed One,[d] the ruler, comes,
there will be seven 'sevens,' and sixty-two 'sevens.' It will be rebuilt
with streets and a trench, but in times of trouble. 26After the sixty-two
'sevens,' the Anointed One will be put to death and will have nothing.[e]
The people of the ruler who will come will destroy the city and the
sanctuary. The end will come like a flood: War will continue until the
end, and desolations have been decreed. 27He will confirm a covenant

[a] 24 Or *'weeks'*; also in verses 25 and 26 [b] 24 Or *restrain* [c] 24 Or *the most holy One* [d] 25 Or *an anointed one*; also in verse 26 [e] 26 Or *death and will have no one*; or *death, but not for himself*

with many for one 'seven.'[a] In the middle of the 'seven'[a] he will put
an end to sacrifice and offering. And at the temple[b] he will set up an
abomination that causes desolation, until the end that is decreed is
poured out on him.[c]"[d]

DANIEL'S VISION OF A MAN

10 In the third year of Cyrus king of Persia, a revelation was given
to Daniel (who was called Belteshazzar). Its message was true
and it concerned a great war.[e] The understanding of the message came
to him in a vision.

2 At that time I, Daniel, mourned for three weeks. 3 I ate no choice
food; no meat or wine touched my lips; and I used no lotions at all un-
til the three weeks were over.

4 On the twenty-fourth day of the first month, as I was standing on
the bank of the great river, the Tigris, 5 I looked up and there before me
was a man dressed in linen, with a belt of fine gold from Uphaz around
his waist. 6 His body was like topaz, his face like lightning, his eyes like
flaming torches, his arms and legs like the gleam of burnished bronze,
and his voice like the sound of a multitude.

7 I, Daniel, was the only one who saw the vision; those who were with
me did not see it, but such terror overwhelmed them that they fled
and hid themselves. 8 So I was left alone, gazing at this great vision; I
had no strength left, my face turned deathly pale and I was helpless.
9 Then I heard him speaking, and as I listened to him, I fell into a deep
sleep, my face to the ground.

10 A hand touched me and set me trembling on my hands and knees.
11 He said, "Daniel, you who are highly esteemed, consider carefully the
words I am about to speak to you, and stand up, for I have now been
sent to you." And when he said this to me, I stood up trembling.

12 Then he continued, "Do not be afraid, Daniel. Since the first day
that you set your mind to gain understanding and to humble your-
self before your God, your words were heard, and I have come in re-
sponse to them. 13 But the prince of the Persian kingdom resisted me
twenty-one days. Then Michael, one of the chief princes, came to help
me, because I was detained there with the king of Persia. 14 Now I have
come to explain to you what will happen to your people in the future,
for the vision concerns a time yet to come."

15 While he was saying this to me, I bowed with my face toward
the ground and was speechless. 16 Then one who looked like a man[f]
touched my lips, and I opened my mouth and began to speak. I said
to the one standing before me, "I am overcome with anguish because
of the vision, my lord, and I feel very weak. 17 How can I, your servant,
talk with you, my lord? My strength is gone and I can hardly breathe."

18 Again the one who looked like a man touched me and gave me
strength. 19 "Do not be afraid, you who are highly esteemed," he said.
"Peace! Be strong now; be strong."

When he spoke to me, I was strengthened and said, "Speak, my lord,
since you have given me strength."

[a] 27 Or *'week'* [b] 27 Septuagint and Theodotion; Hebrew *wing* [c] 27 Or *it*
[d] 27 Or *And one who causes desolation will come upon the wing of the abominable temple, until the end that is decreed is poured out on the desolated city* [e] 1 Or *true and burdensome* [f] 16 Most manuscripts of the Masoretic Text; one manuscript of the Masoretic Text, Dead Sea Scrolls and Septuagint *Then something that looked like a human hand*

PRAYING SCRIPTURE

Daniel 10

Have you ever prayed for something for a long time, until you began wondering if God had heard you? Daniel prayed and fasted for three weeks after the prophecy of the 70 weeks. When the answer finally arrived via an angel, Daniel found it had been delayed due to spiritual warfare in heavenly places.

We neglect the reality of spiritual warfare to our peril. Be diligent in prayer like Daniel until the answer comes.

20 So he said, "Do you know why I have come to you? Soon I will re-
turn to fight against the prince of Persia, and when I go, the prince of
Greece will come; 21 but first I will tell you what is written in the Book of
Truth. (No one supports me against them except Michael, your prince.
11 1 And in the first year of Darius the Mede, I took my stand to sup-
port and protect him.)

THE KINGS OF THE SOUTH AND THE NORTH

2 "Now then, I tell you the truth: Three more kings will arise in Per-
sia, and then a fourth, who will be far richer than all the others. When
he has gained power by his wealth, he will stir up everyone against the
kingdom of Greece. 3 Then a mighty king will arise, who will rule with
great power and do as he pleases. 4 After he has arisen, his empire will
be broken up and parceled out toward the four winds of heaven. It will
not go to his descendants, nor will it have the power he exercised, be-
cause his empire will be uprooted and given to others.

5 "The king of the South will become strong, but one of his com-
manders will become even stronger than he and will rule his own
kingdom with great power. 6 After some years, they will become allies.
The daughter of the king of the South will go to the king of the North
to make an alliance, but she will not retain her power, and he and his
power[a] will not last. In those days she will be betrayed, together with
her royal escort and her father[b] and the one who supported her.

7 "One from her family line will arise to take her place. He will attack
the forces of the king of the North and enter his fortress; he will fight
against them and be victorious. 8 He will also seize their gods, their
metal images and their valuable articles of silver and gold and carry
them off to Egypt. For some years he will leave the king of the North
alone. 9 Then the king of the North will invade the realm of the king of
the South but will retreat to his own country. 10 His sons will prepare for
war and assemble a great army, which will sweep on like an irresistible
flood and carry the battle as far as his fortress.

11 "Then the king of the South will march out in a rage and fight
against the king of the North, who will raise a large army, but it will
be defeated. 12 When the army is carried off, the king of the South will
be filled with pride and will slaughter many thousands, yet he will not
remain triumphant. 13 For the king of the North will muster another
army, larger than the first; and after several years, he will advance with
a huge army fully equipped.

14 "In those times many will rise against the king of the South. Those
who are violent among your own people will rebel in fulfillment of the
vision, but without success. 15 Then the king of the North will come and
build up siege ramps and will capture a fortified city. The forces of the
South will be powerless to resist; even their best troops will not have
the strength to stand. 16 The invader will do as he pleases; no one will
be able to stand against him. He will establish himself in the Beautiful
Land and will have the power to destroy it. 17 He will determine to come
with the might of his entire kingdom and will make an alliance with
the king of the South. And he will give him a daughter in marriage
in order to overthrow the kingdom, but his plans[c] will not succeed or
help him. 18 Then he will turn his attention to the coastlands and will
take many of them, but a commander will put an end to his insolence

[a] 6 Or *offspring* [b] 6 Or *child* (see Vulgate and Syriac) [c] 17 Or *but she*

PRAYING SCRIPTURE

Daniel 11

Darius the Mede was but one of many kings who came and went under the sovereignty of God. Nothing that happens in the future will catch God off guard or render him immobilized. No king will ever be beyond the authority of the King of the universe.

One reason we pray for those in authority is that they will give an account to God. List your governmental leaders and pray regularly for them.

and will turn his insolence back on him. 19 After this, he will turn back toward the fortresses of his own country but will stumble and fall, to be seen no more.

20 "His successor will send out a tax collector to maintain the royal splendor. In a few years, however, he will be destroyed, yet not in anger or in battle.

21 "He will be succeeded by a contemptible person who has not been given the honor of royalty. He will invade the kingdom when its people feel secure, and he will seize it through intrigue. 22 Then an overwhelming army will be swept away before him; both it and a prince of the covenant will be destroyed. 23 After coming to an agreement with him, he will act deceitfully, and with only a few people he will rise to power. 24 When the richest provinces feel secure, he will invade them and will achieve what neither his fathers nor his forefathers did. He will distribute plunder, loot and wealth among his followers. He will plot the overthrow of fortresses — but only for a time.

25 "With a large army he will stir up his strength and courage against the king of the South. The king of the South will wage war with a large and very powerful army, but he will not be able to stand because of the plots devised against him. 26 Those who eat from the king's provisions will try to destroy him; his army will be swept away, and many will fall in battle. 27 The two kings, with their hearts bent on evil, will sit at the same table and lie to each other, but to no avail, because an end will still come at the appointed time. 28 The king of the North will return to his own country with great wealth, but his heart will be set against the holy covenant. He will take action against it and then return to his own country.

29 "At the appointed time he will invade the South again, but this time the outcome will be different from what it was before. 30 Ships of the western coastlands will oppose him, and he will lose heart. Then he will turn back and vent his fury against the holy covenant. He will return and show favor to those who forsake the holy covenant.

31 "His armed forces will rise up to desecrate the temple fortress and will abolish the daily sacrifice. Then they will set up the abomination that causes desolation. 32 With flattery he will corrupt those who have violated the covenant, but the people who know their God will firmly resist him.

33 "Those who are wise will instruct many, though for a time they will fall by the sword or be burned or captured or plundered. 34 When they fall, they will receive a little help, and many who are not sincere will join them. 35 Some of the wise will stumble, so that they may be refined, purified and made spotless until the time of the end, for it will still come at the appointed time.

THE KING WHO EXALTS HIMSELF

36 "The king will do as he pleases. He will exalt and magnify himself above every god and will say unheard-of things against the God of gods. He will be successful until the time of wrath is completed, for what has been determined must take place. 37 He will show no regard for the gods of his ancestors or for the one desired by women, nor will he regard any god, but will exalt himself above them all. 38 Instead of them, he will honor a god of fortresses; a god unknown to his ancestors he will honor with gold and silver, with precious stones and costly gifts. 39 He will attack the mightiest fortresses with the help of a foreign

god and will greatly honor those who acknowledge him. He will make
them rulers over many people and will distribute the land at a price.[a]
40“At the time of the end the king of the South will engage him
in battle, and the king of the North will storm out against him with
chariots and cavalry and a great fleet of ships. He will invade many
countries and sweep through them like a flood. 41He will also invade
the Beautiful Land. Many countries will fall, but Edom, Moab and the
leaders of Ammon will be delivered from his hand. 42He will extend
his power over many countries; Egypt will not escape. 43He will gain
control of the treasures of gold and silver and all the riches of Egypt,
with the Libyans and Cushites[b] in submission. 44But reports from the
east and the north will alarm him, and he will set out in a great rage
to destroy and annihilate many. 45He will pitch his royal tents between
the seas at[c] the beautiful holy mountain. Yet he will come to his end,
and no one will help him.

THE END TIMES

12 “At that time Michael, the great prince who protects your people,
will arise. There will be a time of distress such as has not hap-
pened from the beginning of nations until then. But at that time your
people — everyone whose name is found written in the book — will be
delivered. 2Multitudes who sleep in the dust of the earth will awake:
some to everlasting life, others to shame and everlasting contempt.
3Those who are wise[d] will shine like the brightness of the heavens, and
those who lead many to righteousness, like the stars for ever and ever.
4But you, Daniel, roll up and seal the words of the scroll until the time
of the end. Many will go here and there to increase knowledge.”

5Then I, Daniel, looked, and there before me stood two others, one
on this bank of the river and one on the opposite bank. 6One of them
said to the man clothed in linen, who was above the waters of the river,
“How long will it be before these astonishing things are fulfilled?”
7The man clothed in linen, who was above the waters of the river,
lifted his right hand and his left hand toward heaven, and I heard him
swear by him who lives forever, saying, “It will be for a time, times and
half a time.[e] When the power of the holy people has been finally bro-
ken, all these things will be completed.”
8I heard, but I did not understand. So I asked, “My lord, what will the
outcome of all this be?”
9He replied, “Go your way, Daniel, because the words are rolled up
and sealed until the time of the end. 10Many will be purified, made
spotless and refined, but the wicked will continue to be wicked. None
of the wicked will understand, but those who are wise will understand.
11“From the time that the daily sacrifice is abolished and the abom-
ination that causes desolation is set up, there will be 1,290 days.
12Blessed is the one who waits for and reaches the end of the 1,335 days.
13“As for you, go your way till the end. You will rest, and then at the
end of the days you will rise to receive your allotted inheritance.”

PRAYING SCRIPTURE

Daniel 12

Daniel’s prophecy closes with a word of hope and warning: Some people will be raised to everlasting life while others will be raised to “shame and everlasting contempt” (verse 2). God’s plans and purposes will not be thwarted. He will bring many to himself in righteousness, and “those who lead many to righteousness” will shine forever (verse 3).

Pray that God will bless you with opportunities to turn many to righteousness and to his glory.

---

[a] 39 Or *land for a reward* [b] 43 That is, people from the upper Nile region
[c] 45 Or *the sea and* [d] 3 Or *who impart wisdom* [e] 7 Or *a year, two years and half a year*

HOSEA

Most of the prophets begin with a list of the kings who reigned when they carried out their ministry. A quick reference to 1 and 2 Kings and the other prophets helps readers understand the world in which the prophet ministered. Hosea proclaimed God's word during the reign of Uzziah, Jotham, Ahaz and Hezekiah in Judah and Jeroboam, son of Joash, in Israel. Hosea was a contemporary of the better-known prophet Isaiah.

Hosea prophesied in the years before Israel went into Assyrian exile. His message warned of the judgment to come but also pointed to the grace that comes from covenant faithfulness to the Lord. The Lord called Hosea not only to preach his message to the people but also to embody the message he was preaching by enduring suffering and difficulty in his own life.

In the book, the relationship between God and his people is portrayed as a marriage. Israel broke their vows and ran toward other gods who were unable to deliver them. This image first reminds us of the intimate relationship that exists between the Lord and his people, how desperately he loves us. He is our beloved who gave his Son as a sacrifice for our sins to bring us to himself. When we pray, we do not pray to a distant, uncaring god, but rather to a God who truly loves us and stays faithful to us until the end.

The Lord called Hosea to marry a prostitute named Gomer. The names they gave their children—Jezreel, Lo-Ruhamah and Lo-Ammi—picture the judgment of God upon his people for their sins against him. He called to mind their bloodshed in the Valley of Jezreel and rejected them for their continued rebellion and idolatry. Then Gomer—whom God had commanded Hosea to marry—committed adultery. Hosea was forced not only to take her back but to purchase her, as she had apparently become a slave to her new lover. Hosea and Gomer were a living parable, reminding Israel of how time and time again the Lord showed them mercy in spite of their repeated unfaithfulness.

Although the book of Hosea is often reduced to the summary of Hosea and Gomer's relationship, the largest portion of the book consists of prophetic charges, pronounced judgments, calls to repentance and reminders of God's love of his people and his anger toward sin. Both Israel and Judah stood condemned by their rebellion. In the final chapter, God's restoration is promised: "I will heal their waywardness and love them freely, for my anger has turned away from them" (14:4).

There is little mention of prayer, indicative of the spiritual condition of the nation. The people did not call on God in repentance or for deliverance. The nation was spiritually dead. The people did not pursue God, but still God pursued his people.

Hosea's theme, despite rebellion and judgment, is ultimately one of hope: God will never stop loving his people.

1 The word of the LORD that came to Hosea son of Beeri during the
reigns of Uzziah, Jotham, Ahaz and Hezekiah, kings of Judah, and
during the reign of Jeroboam son of Jehoash[a] king of Israel:

HOSEA'S WIFE AND CHILDREN

2When the LORD began to speak through Hosea, the LORD said to
him, "Go, marry a promiscuous woman and have children with her,
for like an adulterous wife this land is guilty of unfaithfulness to the
LORD." 3So he married Gomer daughter of Diblaim, and she conceived
and bore him a son.
4Then the LORD said to Hosea, "Call him Jezreel, because I will soon
punish the house of Jehu for the massacre at Jezreel, and I will put an
end to the kingdom of Israel. 5In that day I will break Israel's bow in
the Valley of Jezreel."
6Gomer conceived again and gave birth to a daughter. Then the LORD
said to Hosea, "Call her Lo-Ruhamah (which means "not loved"), for I will
no longer show love to Israel, that I should at all forgive them. 7Yet I will
show love to Judah; and I will save them — not by bow, sword or battle,
or by horses and horsemen, but I, the LORD their God, will save them."
8After she had weaned Lo-Ruhamah, Gomer had another son. 9Then
the LORD said, "Call him Lo-Ammi (which means "not my people"), for
you are not my people, and I am not your God.[b]
10"Yet the Israelites will be like the sand on the seashore, which can-
not be measured or counted. In the place where it was said to them,
'You are not my people,' they will be called 'children of the living God.'
11The people of Judah and the people of Israel will come together; they
will appoint one leader and will come up out of the land, for great will
be the day of Jezreel.[c]

2 [d] "Say of your brothers, 'My people,' and of your sisters, 'My loved
one.'

ISRAEL PUNISHED AND RESTORED

2 "Rebuke your mother, rebuke her,
  for she is not my wife,
  and I am not her husband.
Let her remove the adulterous look from her face
  and the unfaithfulness from between her breasts.
3 Otherwise I will strip her naked
  and make her as bare as on the day she was born;
I will make her like a desert,
  turn her into a parched land,
  and slay her with thirst.
4 I will not show my love to her children,
  because they are the children of adultery.
5 Their mother has been unfaithful
  and has conceived them in disgrace.
She said, 'I will go after my lovers,
  who give me my food and my water,
  my wool and my linen, my olive oil and my drink.'
6 Therefore I will block her path with thornbushes;
  I will wall her in so that she cannot find her way.

[a] *1* Hebrew *Joash,* a variant of *Jehoash* [b] *9* Or *your I AM* [c] *11* In Hebrew texts 1:10,11 is numbered 2:1,2. [d] In Hebrew texts 2:1-23 is numbered 2:3-25.

PRAYING SCRIPTURE

Hosea 1

In another turn where the Lord used a prophet as a physical sermon, not merely verbal prophecy, Hosea was instructed to marry a woman who would be unfaithful to him. The Lord used Hosea's troubled marriage to show his relationship with Israel. Even their children taught Israel a lesson.

As with the Lord and Israel, we are the bride of Christ. Confess your deepest love to him when you pray.

PRAYING SCRIPTURE

Hosea 2

God's wrath toward Israel culminated in a strong charge: "She is not my wife, and I am not her husband" (verse 2). Israel's unfaithfulness was her undoing. Still, despite her wandering, the Lord committed to pursuing her: "I am now going to allure her . . . and speak tenderly to her" (verse 14).

The Lord's wrath and his mercy are not contradictory. Without the latter, Israel never would have withstood the former. Thank God every day for his mercy to you.

7 She will chase after her lovers but not catch them;
she will look for them but not find them.
Then she will say,
'I will go back to my husband as at first,
for then I was better off than now.'
8 She has not acknowledged that I was the one
who gave her the grain, the new wine and oil,
who lavished on her the silver and gold—
which they used for Baal.

9 "Therefore I will take away my grain when it ripens,
and my new wine when it is ready.
I will take back my wool and my linen,
intended to cover her naked body.
10 So now I will expose her lewdness
before the eyes of her lovers;
no one will take her out of my hands.
11 I will stop all her celebrations:
her yearly festivals, her New Moons,
her Sabbath days—all her appointed festivals.
12 I will ruin her vines and her fig trees,
which she said were her pay from her lovers;
I will make them a thicket,
and wild animals will devour them.
13 I will punish her for the days
she burned incense to the Baals;
she decked herself with rings and jewelry,
and went after her lovers,
but me she forgot,"
declares the LORD.

14 "Therefore I am now going to allure her;
I will lead her into the wilderness
and speak tenderly to her.
15 There I will give her back her vineyards,
and will make the Valley of Achor[a] a door of hope.
There she will respond[b] as in the days of her youth,
as in the day she came up out of Egypt.

16 "In that day," declares the LORD,
"you will call me 'my husband';
you will no longer call me 'my master.[c]'
17 I will remove the names of the Baals from her lips;
no longer will their names be invoked.
18 In that day I will make a covenant for them
with the beasts of the field, the birds in the sky
and the creatures that move along the ground.
Bow and sword and battle
I will abolish from the land,
so that all may lie down in safety.
19 I will betroth you to me forever;
I will betroth you in[d] righteousness and justice,
in[d] love and compassion.

[a] 15 *Achor* means *trouble.* [b] 15 Or *sing* [c] 16 Hebrew *baal* [d] 19 Or *with*

20 I will betroth you in[a] faithfulness,
and you will acknowledge the LORD.

21 "In that day I will respond,"
declares the LORD—
"I will respond to the skies,
and they will respond to the earth;
22 and the earth will respond to the grain,
the new wine and the olive oil,
and they will respond to Jezreel.[b]
23 I will plant her for myself in the land;
I will show my love to the one I called 'Not my loved one.[c]'
I will say to those called 'Not my people,[d]' 'You are my people';
and they will say, 'You are my God.' "

HOSEA'S RECONCILIATION WITH HIS WIFE

3 The LORD said to me, "Go, show your love to your wife again,
though she is loved by another man and is an adulteress. Love her
as the LORD loves the Israelites, though they turn to other gods and
love the sacred raisin cakes."
2 So I bought her for fifteen shekels[e] of silver and about a homer and
a lethek[f] of barley. 3 Then I told her, "You are to live with me many days;
you must not be a prostitute or be intimate with any man, and I will
behave the same way toward you."
4 For the Israelites will live many days without king or prince, with-
out sacrifice or sacred stones, without ephod or household gods. 5 Af-
terward the Israelites will return and seek the LORD their God and
David their king. They will come trembling to the LORD and to his
blessings in the last days.

THE CHARGE AGAINST ISRAEL

4 Hear the word of the LORD, you Israelites,
because the LORD has a charge to bring
against you who live in the land:
"There is no faithfulness, no love,
no acknowledgment of God in the land.
2 There is only cursing,[g] lying and murder,
stealing and adultery;
they break all bounds,
and bloodshed follows bloodshed.
3 Because of this the land dries up,
and all who live in it waste away;
the beasts of the field, the birds in the sky
and the fish in the sea are swept away.

4 "But let no one bring a charge,
let no one accuse another,
for your people are like those
who bring charges against a priest.
5 You stumble day and night,
and the prophets stumble with you.

[a] 20 Or *with* [b] 22 *Jezreel* means *God plants.* [c] 23 Hebrew *Lo-Ruhamah* (see 1:6) [d] 23 Hebrew *Lo-Ammi* (see 1:9) [e] 2 That is, about 6 ounces or about 170 grams [f] 2 A homer and a lethek possibly weighed about 430 pounds or about 195 kilograms. [g] 2 That is, to pronounce a curse on

PRAYING SCRIPTURE

Hosea 3

Hosea's love for wayward Gomer pictures God's love for Israel, with this major difference: God commanded Hosea, "Go, show your love to. . . an adulteress" (verse 1). God did not need to be instructed to love Israel. God's love is self-generated. He can do no other, for he is love.

We are never more like God than when we love. Pray that his loving nature will flow through you to everyone around you.

PRAYING SCRIPTURE

Hosea 4

Because we often compare God's love to our love, we find it hard to believe he could love Israel—or us—after we repeatedly sin against him. But as we learn from Hosea, God never waivers in his redemptive love toward his people.

God loves because God is love; he can't not love. Thank God for his love for us that cannot be overcome by sin and never ends.

So I will destroy your mother —
6 my people are destroyed from lack of knowledge.

"Because you have rejected knowledge,
I also reject you as my priests;
because you have ignored the law of your God,
I also will ignore your children.
7 The more priests there were,
the more they sinned against me;
they exchanged their glorious God[a] for something disgraceful.
8 They feed on the sins of my people
and relish their wickedness.
9 And it will be: Like people, like priests.
I will punish both of them for their ways
and repay them for their deeds.

10 "They will eat but not have enough;
they will engage in prostitution but not flourish,
because they have deserted the LORD
to give themselves 11 to prostitution;
old wine and new wine
take away their understanding.
12 My people consult a wooden idol,
and a diviner's rod speaks to them.
A spirit of prostitution leads them astray;
they are unfaithful to their God.
13 They sacrifice on the mountaintops
and burn offerings on the hills,
under oak, poplar and terebinth,
where the shade is pleasant.
Therefore your daughters turn to prostitution
and your daughters-in-law to adultery.

14 "I will not punish your daughters
when they turn to prostitution,
nor your daughters-in-law
when they commit adultery,
because the men themselves consort with harlots
and sacrifice with shrine prostitutes —
a people without understanding will come to ruin!

15 "Though you, Israel, commit adultery,
do not let Judah become guilty.

"Do not go to Gilgal;
do not go up to Beth Aven.[b]
And do not swear, 'As surely as the LORD lives!'
16 The Israelites are stubborn,
like a stubborn heifer.
How then can the LORD pasture them
like lambs in a meadow?
17 Ephraim is joined to idols;
leave him alone!

---

[a] 7 Syriac (see also an ancient Hebrew scribal tradition); Masoretic Text *me; / I will exchange their glory* [b] 15 *Beth Aven* means *house of wickedness* (a derogatory name for Bethel, which means *house of God*).

18 Even when their drinks are gone,
they continue their prostitution;
their rulers dearly love shameful ways.
19 A whirlwind will sweep them away,
and their sacrifices will bring them shame.

JUDGMENT AGAINST ISRAEL

5 "Hear this, you priests!
Pay attention, you Israelites!
Listen, royal house!
This judgment is against you:
You have been a snare at Mizpah,
a net spread out on Tabor.
2 The rebels are knee-deep in slaughter.
I will discipline all of them.
3 I know all about Ephraim;
Israel is not hidden from me.
Ephraim, you have now turned to prostitution;
Israel is corrupt.

4 "Their deeds do not permit them
to return to their God.
A spirit of prostitution is in their heart;
they do not acknowledge the LORD.
5 Israel's arrogance testifies against them;
the Israelites, even Ephraim, stumble in their sin;
Judah also stumbles with them.
6 When they go with their flocks and herds
to seek the LORD,
they will not find him;
he has withdrawn himself from them.
7 They are unfaithful to the LORD;
they give birth to illegitimate children.
When they celebrate their New Moon feasts,
he will devour[a] their fields.

8 "Sound the trumpet in Gibeah,
the horn in Ramah.
Raise the battle cry in Beth Aven[b];
lead on, Benjamin.
9 Ephraim will be laid waste
on the day of reckoning.
Among the tribes of Israel
I proclaim what is certain.
10 Judah's leaders are like those
who move boundary stones.
I will pour out my wrath on them
like a flood of water.
11 Ephraim is oppressed,
trampled in judgment,
intent on pursuing idols.[c]

[a] 7 Or *Now their New Moon feasts / will devour them and* [b] 8 *Beth Aven* means *house of wickedness* (a derogatory name for Bethel, which means *house of God*). [c] 11 The meaning of the Hebrew for this word is uncertain.

PRAYING SCRIPTURE

Hosea 5

Turning away from the Lord when searching for solutions to problems is a common temptation. Pride—thinking we know better than God how to live—is the reason. God rebuked Israel from the top down for their sin: the priests, the king and the entire ruling house (see verse 1).

Satan always has ready an alternative to God's best. He did it in the Garden of Eden; he does it today. Commit your way to the Lord.

12 I am like a moth to Ephraim,
like rot to the people of Judah.

13 "When Ephraim saw his sickness,
and Judah his sores,
then Ephraim turned to Assyria,
and sent to the great king for help.
But he is not able to cure you,
not able to heal your sores.
14 For I will be like a lion to Ephraim,
like a great lion to Judah.
I will tear them to pieces and go away;
I will carry them off, with no one to rescue them.
15 Then I will return to my lair
until they have borne their guilt
and seek my face —
in their misery
they will earnestly seek me."

ISRAEL UNREPENTANT

6 "Come, let us return to the LORD.
He has torn us to pieces
but he will heal us;
he has injured us
but he will bind up our wounds.
2 After two days he will revive us;
on the third day he will restore us,
that we may live in his presence.
3 Let us acknowledge the LORD;
let us press on to acknowledge him.
As surely as the sun rises,
he will appear;
he will come to us like the winter rains,
like the spring rains that water the earth."

4 "What can I do with you, Ephraim?
What can I do with you, Judah?
Your love is like the morning mist,
like the early dew that disappears.
5 Therefore I cut you in pieces with my prophets,
I killed you with the words of my mouth —
then my judgments go forth like the sun.[a]
6 For I desire mercy, not sacrifice,
and acknowledgment of God rather than burnt offerings.
7 As at Adam,[b] they have broken the covenant;
they were unfaithful to me there.
8 Gilead is a city of evildoers,
stained with footprints of blood.
9 As marauders lie in ambush for a victim,
so do bands of priests;
they murder on the road to Shechem,
carrying out their wicked schemes.

PRAYING SCRIPTURE
Hosea 6

"Come, let us return to the LORD" are sweet words (verse 1). Let God's people—tired of running away, of being apart from him, of facing judgment—return. Repentance is one of God's good gifts to his people. It is the road of returning to him.

No matter how far you have strayed, bring your repentance to the Lord and live full in the light of restored fellowship.

[a] 5 The meaning of the Hebrew for this line is uncertain. [b] 7 Or *Like Adam;* or *Like human beings*

10 I have seen a horrible thing in Israel:
There Ephraim is given to prostitution,
Israel is defiled.

11 "Also for you, Judah,
a harvest is appointed.

"Whenever I would restore the fortunes of my people,

7 1 whenever I would heal Israel,
the sins of Ephraim are exposed
and the crimes of Samaria revealed.
They practice deceit,
thieves break into houses,
bandits rob in the streets;
2 but they do not realize
that I remember all their evil deeds.
Their sins engulf them;
they are always before me.

3 "They delight the king with their wickedness,
the princes with their lies.
4 They are all adulterers,
burning like an oven
whose fire the baker need not stir
from the kneading of the dough till it rises.
5 On the day of the festival of our king
the princes become inflamed with wine,
and he joins hands with the mockers.
6 Their hearts are like an oven;
they approach him with intrigue.
Their passion smolders all night;
in the morning it blazes like a flaming fire.
7 All of them are hot as an oven;
they devour their rulers.
All their kings fall,
and none of them calls on me.

8 "Ephraim mixes with the nations;
Ephraim is a flat loaf not turned over.
9 Foreigners sap his strength,
but he does not realize it.
His hair is sprinkled with gray,
but he does not notice.
10 Israel's arrogance testifies against him,
but despite all this
he does not return to the LORD his God
or search for him.

11 "Ephraim is like a dove,
easily deceived and senseless —
now calling to Egypt,
now turning to Assyria.
12 When they go, I will throw my net over them;
I will pull them down like the birds in the sky.
When I hear them flocking together,
I will catch them.

PRAYING SCRIPTURE

Hosea 7

Because of the grace God has shown us, there should be a clear difference between our character and the character of the unbelieving world. The description of Ephraim was not different than that of the nations like Egypt and Assyria that God had judged or would judge. Israel was not bearing witness to the Lord their God.

Can people tell you belong to Jesus? Pray for your life to be a testimony of God's salvation.

13 Woe to them,
because they have strayed from me!
Destruction to them,
because they have rebelled against me!
I long to redeem them
but they speak about me falsely.
14 They do not cry out to me from their hearts
but wail on their beds.
They slash themselves,[a] appealing to their gods
for grain and new wine,
but they turn away from me.
15 I trained them and strengthened their arms,
but they plot evil against me.
16 They do not turn to the Most High;
they are like a faulty bow.
Their leaders will fall by the sword
because of their insolent words.
For this they will be ridiculed
in the land of Egypt.

ISRAEL TO REAP THE WHIRLWIND

8 "Put the trumpet to your lips!
An eagle is over the house of the LORD
because the people have broken my covenant
and rebelled against my law.
2 Israel cries out to me,
'Our God, we acknowledge you!'
3 But Israel has rejected what is good;
an enemy will pursue him.
4 They set up kings without my consent;
they choose princes without my approval.
With their silver and gold
they make idols for themselves
to their own destruction.
5 Samaria, throw out your calf-idol!
My anger burns against them.
How long will they be incapable of purity?
6 They are from Israel!
This calf — a metalworker has made it;
it is not God.
It will be broken in pieces,
that calf of Samaria.

7 "They sow the wind
and reap the whirlwind.
The stalk has no head;
it will produce no flour.
Were it to yield grain,
foreigners would swallow it up.
8 Israel is swallowed up;
now she is among the nations
like something no one wants.

[a] 14 Some Hebrew manuscripts and Septuagint; most Hebrew manuscripts *They gather together*

PRAYING SCRIPTURE
Hosea 8

Many passages in the Bible implore God's people not to "forget" him. The people of Israel showed they had forgotten God even though they claimed him; they rejected things that were good (see verse 3). They would reap more judgment than the evil they had sown. For the wind they would reap the whirlwind.

Many people want to sow their wild oats, then hope the crops fail. Ask God for boldness to warn those around you living in sin.

9 For they have gone up to Assyria
like a wild donkey wandering alone.
Ephraim has sold herself to lovers.
10 Although they have sold themselves among the nations,
I will now gather them together.
They will begin to waste away
under the oppression of the mighty king.

11 "Though Ephraim built many altars for sin offerings,
these have become altars for sinning.
12 I wrote for them the many things of my law,
but they regarded them as something foreign.
13 Though they offer sacrifices as gifts to me,
and though they eat the meat,
the LORD is not pleased with them.
Now he will remember their wickedness
and punish their sins:
They will return to Egypt.
14 Israel has forgotten their Maker
and built palaces;
Judah has fortified many towns.
But I will send fire on their cities
that will consume their fortresses."

PUNISHMENT FOR ISRAEL

9 Do not rejoice, Israel;
do not be jubilant like the other nations.
For you have been unfaithful to your God;
you love the wages of a prostitute
at every threshing floor.
2 Threshing floors and winepresses will not feed the people;
the new wine will fail them.
3 They will not remain in the LORD's land;
Ephraim will return to Egypt
and eat unclean food in Assyria.
4 They will not pour out wine offerings to the LORD,
nor will their sacrifices please him.
Such sacrifices will be to them like the bread of mourners;
all who eat them will be unclean.
This food will be for themselves;
it will not come into the temple of the LORD.

5 What will you do on the day of your appointed festivals,
on the feast days of the LORD?
6 Even if they escape from destruction,
Egypt will gather them,
and Memphis will bury them.
Their treasures of silver will be taken over by briers,
and thorns will overrun their tents.
7 The days of punishment are coming,
the days of reckoning are at hand.
Let Israel know this.
Because your sins are so many
and your hostility so great,
the prophet is considered a fool,
the inspired person a maniac.

PRAYING SCRIPTURE

Hosea 9

In an arresting rebuke, Hosea told the Israelites not to rejoice. This was no time for parties, feasting or festivals. They had "been unfaithful to [their] God" (verse 1). Any joy Israel showed would have been for the pleasure of sin, and God would have grieved. Better to be silent than to rejoice over the wrong things.

Ask God to help you recognize what pleases him, and rejoice over his righteousness.

8 The prophet, along with my God,
is the watchman over Ephraim,[a]
yet snares await him on all his paths,
and hostility in the house of his God.
9 They have sunk deep into corruption,
as in the days of Gibeah.
God will remember their wickedness
and punish them for their sins.

10 "When I found Israel,
it was like finding grapes in the desert;
when I saw your ancestors,
it was like seeing the early fruit on the fig tree.
But when they came to Baal Peor,
they consecrated themselves to that shameful idol
and became as vile as the thing they loved.
11 Ephraim's glory will fly away like a bird —
no birth, no pregnancy, no conception.
12 Even if they rear children,
I will bereave them of every one.
Woe to them
when I turn away from them!
13 I have seen Ephraim, like Tyre,
planted in a pleasant place.
But Ephraim will bring out
their children to the slayer."

14 Give them, LORD —
what will you give them?
Give them wombs that miscarry
and breasts that are dry.

15 "Because of all their wickedness in Gilgal,
I hated them there.
Because of their sinful deeds,
I will drive them out of my house.
I will no longer love them;
all their leaders are rebellious.
16 Ephraim is blighted,
their root is withered,
they yield no fruit.
Even if they bear children,
I will slay their cherished offspring."

17 My God will reject them
because they have not obeyed him;
they will be wanderers among the nations.

10 Israel was a spreading vine;
he brought forth fruit for himself.
As his fruit increased,
he built more altars;
as his land prospered,
he adorned his sacred stones.

[a] 8 Or *The prophet is the watchman over Ephraim, / the people of my God*

PRAYING SCRIPTURE

Hosea 10

Hosea presented Israel with what could very well be called an invitation hymn: "Sow righteousness for yourselves, reap the fruit of unfailing love, and break up your unplowed ground; for it is time to seek the LORD" (verse 12). The Lord always calls to his people. His offer of fellowship is always open. His mercy is always near.

Are you sowing in righteousness so you can reap in mercy? Pray for a harvest that glorifies God.

2 Their heart is deceitful,
and now they must bear their guilt.
The LORD will demolish their altars
and destroy their sacred stones.

3 Then they will say, "We have no king
because we did not revere the LORD.
But even if we had a king,
what could he do for us?"
4 They make many promises,
take false oaths
and make agreements;
therefore lawsuits spring up
like poisonous weeds in a plowed field.
5 The people who live in Samaria fear
for the calf-idol of Beth Aven.[a]
Its people will mourn over it,
and so will its idolatrous priests,
those who had rejoiced over its splendor,
because it is taken from them into exile.
6 It will be carried to Assyria
as tribute for the great king.
Ephraim will be disgraced;
Israel will be ashamed of its foreign alliances.
7 Samaria's king will be destroyed,
swept away like a twig on the surface of the waters.
8 The high places of wickedness[b] will be destroyed —
it is the sin of Israel.
Thorns and thistles will grow up
and cover their altars.
Then they will say to the mountains, "Cover us!"
and to the hills, "Fall on us!"

9 "Since the days of Gibeah, you have sinned, Israel,
and there you have remained.[c]
Will not war again overtake
the evildoers in Gibeah?
10 When I please, I will punish them;
nations will be gathered against them
to put them in bonds for their double sin.
11 Ephraim is a trained heifer
that loves to thresh;
so I will put a yoke
on her fair neck.
I will drive Ephraim,
Judah must plow,
and Jacob must break up the ground.
12 Sow righteousness for yourselves,
reap the fruit of unfailing love,
and break up your unplowed ground;
for it is time to seek the LORD,
until he comes

---

[a] *5* *Beth Aven* means *house of wickedness* (a derogatory name for Bethel, which means *house of God*). [b] *8* Hebrew *aven*, a reference to Beth Aven (a derogatory name for Bethel); see verse 5. [c] *9* Or *there a stand was taken*

and showers his righteousness on you.
13 But you have planted wickedness,
you have reaped evil,
you have eaten the fruit of deception.
Because you have depended on your own strength
and on your many warriors,
14 the roar of battle will rise against your people,
so that all your fortresses will be devastated —
as Shalman devastated Beth Arbel on the day of battle,
when mothers were dashed to the ground with their children.
15 So will it happen to you, Bethel,
because your wickedness is great.
When that day dawns,
the king of Israel will be completely destroyed.

GOD'S LOVE FOR ISRAEL

11 "When Israel was a child, I loved him,
and out of Egypt I called my son.
2 But the more they were called,
the more they went away from me.[a]
They sacrificed to the Baals
and they burned incense to images.
3 It was I who taught Ephraim to walk,
taking them by the arms;
but they did not realize
it was I who healed them.
4 I led them with cords of human kindness,
with ties of love.
To them I was like one who lifts
a little child to the cheek,
and I bent down to feed them.

5 "Will they not return to Egypt
and will not Assyria rule over them
because they refuse to repent?
6 A sword will flash in their cities;
it will devour their false prophets
and put an end to their plans.
7 My people are determined to turn from me.
Even though they call me God Most High,
I will by no means exalt them.

8 "How can I give you up, Ephraim?
How can I hand you over, Israel?
How can I treat you like Admah?
How can I make you like Zeboyim?
My heart is changed within me;
all my compassion is aroused.
9 I will not carry out my fierce anger,
nor will I devastate Ephraim again.
For I am God, and not a man —
the Holy One among you.
I will not come against their cities.

PRAYING SCRIPTURE

Hosea 11

Verse 1 reveals the prophecy invoked by Matthew in reference to Joseph, Mary and Jesus fleeing Herod: "Out of Egypt I called my son." Hosea likely was not aware of its significance beyond God's expression of love for Israel in those days, but he was faithful to speak God's words nonetheless.

God's Word foretold the first coming of Christ and foretells Christ's second coming. Pray for a longing for his return.

---

[a] 2 Septuagint; Hebrew *them*

10 They will follow the LORD;
he will roar like a lion.
When he roars,
his children will come trembling from the west.
11 They will come from Egypt,
trembling like sparrows,
from Assyria, fluttering like doves.
I will settle them in their homes,"
declares the LORD.

ISRAEL'S SIN

12 Ephraim has surrounded me with lies,
Israel with deceit.
And Judah is unruly against God,
even against the faithful Holy One.[a]

12[b] 1 Ephraim feeds on the wind;
he pursues the east wind all day
and multiplies lies and violence.
He makes a treaty with Assyria
and sends olive oil to Egypt.
2 The LORD has a charge to bring against Judah;
he will punish Jacob[c] according to his ways
and repay him according to his deeds.
3 In the womb he grasped his brother's heel;
as a man he struggled with God.
4 He struggled with the angel and overcame him;
he wept and begged for his favor.
He found him at Bethel
and talked with him there —
5 the LORD God Almighty,
the LORD is his name!
6 But you must return to your God;
maintain love and justice,
and wait for your God always.

7 The merchant uses dishonest scales
and loves to defraud.
8 Ephraim boasts,
"I am very rich; I have become wealthy.
With all my wealth they will not find in me
any iniquity or sin."

9 "I have been the LORD your God
ever since you came out of Egypt;
I will make you live in tents again,
as in the days of your appointed festivals.
10 I spoke to the prophets,
gave them many visions
and told parables through them."

11 Is Gilead wicked?
Its people are worthless!

PRAYING SCRIPTURE

Hosea 12

God commands his people to treat all people with the justice and equity they deserve as God's image bearers. When the people of Judah returned, they were to "maintain love and justice" in society and "wait for [their] God always" (verse 6), a reference to obedience.

We cannot please God unless we are showing love and justice wherever we live. It's one of the ways God shows his mercy to those who don't know him.

---

[a] *12* In Hebrew texts this verse (11:12) is numbered 12:1. [b] In Hebrew texts 12:1-14 is numbered 12:2-15. [c] *2* *Jacob* means *he grasps the heel*, a Hebrew idiom for *he takes advantage of* or *he deceives*.

Do they sacrifice bulls in Gilgal?
Their altars will be like piles of stones
on a plowed field.
12 Jacob fled to the country of Aram[a];
Israel served to get a wife,
and to pay for her he tended sheep.
13 The LORD used a prophet to bring Israel up from Egypt,
by a prophet he cared for him.
14 But Ephraim has aroused his bitter anger;
his Lord will leave on him the guilt of his bloodshed
and will repay him for his contempt.

THE LORD'S ANGER AGAINST ISRAEL

13 When Ephraim spoke, people trembled;
he was exalted in Israel.
But he became guilty of Baal worship and died.
2 Now they sin more and more;
they make idols for themselves from their silver,
cleverly fashioned images,
all of them the work of craftsmen.
It is said of these people,
"They offer human sacrifices!
They kiss[b] calf-idols!"
3 Therefore they will be like the morning mist,
like the early dew that disappears,
like chaff swirling from a threshing floor,
like smoke escaping through a window.

4 "But I have been the LORD your God
ever since you came out of Egypt.
You shall acknowledge no God but me,
no Savior except me.
5 I cared for you in the wilderness,
in the land of burning heat.
6 When I fed them, they were satisfied;
when they were satisfied, they became proud;
then they forgot me.
7 So I will be like a lion to them,
like a leopard I will lurk by the path.
8 Like a bear robbed of her cubs,
I will attack them and rip them open;
like a lion I will devour them —
a wild animal will tear them apart.

9 "You are destroyed, Israel,
because you are against me, against your helper.
10 Where is your king, that he may save you?
Where are your rulers in all your towns,
of whom you said,
'Give me a king and princes'?
11 So in my anger I gave you a king,
and in my wrath I took him away.
12 The guilt of Ephraim is stored up,
his sins are kept on record.

PRAYING SCRIPTURE

Hosea 13

While pronouncing judgment on the Israelites, God reminded them that he alone was their God, that he delivered them from Egypt and that he was their only Savior. He reminded them that he didn't even forget them in their wilderness wanderings. Still, despite his provision, they forgot him (see verse 6).

How often do we forget God by not praising him, not thanking him, not loving him wholeheartedly? Remember God's deliverance when you are praying this week.

---

[a] *12* That is, Northwest Mesopotamia [b] *2* Or *"Men who sacrifice / kiss*

13 Pains as of a woman in childbirth come to him,
but he is a child without wisdom;
when the time arrives,
he doesn't have the sense to come out of the womb.

14 "I will deliver this people from the power of the grave;
I will redeem them from death.
Where, O death, are your plagues?
Where, O grave, is your destruction?

"I will have no compassion,
15 even though he thrives among his brothers.
An east wind from the LORD will come,
blowing in from the desert;
his spring will fail
and his well dry up.
His storehouse will be plundered
of all its treasures.
16 The people of Samaria must bear their guilt,
because they have rebelled against their God.
They will fall by the sword;
their little ones will be dashed to the ground,
their pregnant women ripped open."[a]

REPENTANCE TO BRING BLESSING

14 [b] Return, Israel, to the LORD your God.
Your sins have been your downfall!
2 Take words with you
and return to the LORD.
Say to him:
"Forgive all our sins
and receive us graciously,
that we may offer the fruit of our lips.[c]
3 Assyria cannot save us;
we will not mount warhorses.
We will never again say 'Our gods'
to what our own hands have made,
for in you the fatherless find compassion."

4 "I will heal their waywardness
and love them freely,
for my anger has turned away from them.
5 I will be like the dew to Israel;
he will blossom like a lily.
Like a cedar of Lebanon
he will send down his roots;
6 his young shoots will grow.
His splendor will be like an olive tree,
his fragrance like a cedar of Lebanon.
7 People will dwell again in his shade;
they will flourish like the grain,
they will blossom like the vine —
Israel's fame will be like the wine of Lebanon.

PRAYING SCRIPTURE

Hosea 14

Hosea's prompting for the Israelites is filled with the language of hope. If they returned to the Lord, admitted their stumbling, asked for iniquity to be removed, admitted that the nations around them were powerless and forsook idols, they would find that "the fatherless find compassion" (verse 3).

God responded that he would heal the Israelites' waywardness and love them freely. Praise God for his relentless, passionate love for all of his children.

[a] *16* In Hebrew texts this verse (13:16) is numbered 14:1. [b] In Hebrew texts 14:1-9 is numbered 14:2-10. [c] *2* Or *offer our lips as sacrifices of bulls*

8 Ephraim, what more have I[a] to do with idols?
  I will answer him and care for him.
I am like a flourishing juniper;
  your fruitfulness comes from me."

9 Who is wise? Let them realize these things.
  Who is discerning? Let them understand.
The ways of the LORD are right;
  the righteous walk in them,
  but the rebellious stumble in them.

[a] 8 Or Hebrew; Septuagint *What more has Ephraim*

JOEL

Unlike many of the other prophets, Joel doesn't list in his introduction any of the kings who reigned during his ministry. However, this doesn't leave readers completely in the dark as to the times in which he prophesied. From the warnings he issued in chapter 3, many scholars conclude that his ministry took place during the reign of Joash (835–796 BC). This was a dark time in the life of God's people, and to make matters worse, they had experienced a plague of locusts that destroyed a full year's worth of crops. As Joel's prophecies made clear, the coming judgment would make the locusts seem like nothing in comparison.

Joel's message was a response to the difficult time facing Israel, using it as a call to repentance. The people should see the terrible state of their land as a wake-up call regarding their broken fellowship with God. Indeed, the destruction of the temple and the plague of locusts were symbolic of the broken relationship between God and his people. They had sinned against him, bringing these terrible consequences upon themselves. Their only hope was mourning over their sin—the kind of mourning that leads to repentance. The prophet recorded: "'Even now,' declares the LORD, 'return to me with all your heart, with fasting and weeping and mourning. Rend your heart and not your garments. Return to the LORD your God, for he is gracious and compassionate, slow to anger and abounding in love, and he relents from sending calamity'" (2:12–13). Joel reminded the people that God, being gracious and merciful, would rather forgive than judge.

Joel's prophecy points to a time when the Spirit of God would be poured out on everyone rather than primarily working through the prophets. His words echoed the promises of Jeremiah and Ezekiel, looking forward to a day when God would make a new covenant with his people. God would be their God, they would be his people, and he would fill them with his Spirit and remember their sins no more. When the apostle Peter preached on the day of Pentecost in Acts 2, he quoted Joel 2:28–32. Peter told his listeners that Joel's prophecy was being fulfilled then and there.

Prayer was an integral part of the national repentance God commanded. Blowing trumpets, consecrating a time of fasting, calling a sacred assembly, gathering the elders and the people to sanctify them and weeping preceded their asking the Lord to spare them from being overtaken by their enemies (see 2:15–17). It behooves us to humble ourselves in the same way when we approach God in prayer.

Christians live in an era when the Holy Spirit indwells each follower of Jesus and is active in our lives. As we pray, we pray in the power of the Holy Spirit and with the aid of the Holy Spirit. Christians ought to pray for a renewed sense of the Spirit's work in our lives and for a growing understanding of how the Spirit helps us when we pray.

PRAYING SCRIPTURE

Joel 1

The description of judgment in this chapter is so detailed and thorough that it left little doubt as to its severity: swarming locusts, great locusts, young locusts, each wave adding to the damage of the ones before. By the end, God was saying, there would be nothing left.

When you are disturbed over judgment, follow Joel's example (see verse 19), "To you, LORD, I call."

1 The word of the LORD that came to Joel son of Pethuel.

AN INVASION OF LOCUSTS

2 Hear this, you elders;
listen, all who live in the land.
Has anything like this ever happened in your days
or in the days of your ancestors?
3 Tell it to your children,
and let your children tell it to their children,
and their children to the next generation.
4 What the locust swarm has left
the great locusts have eaten;
what the great locusts have left
the young locusts have eaten;
what the young locusts have left
other locusts[a] have eaten.

5 Wake up, you drunkards, and weep!
Wail, all you drinkers of wine;
wail because of the new wine,
for it has been snatched from your lips.
6 A nation has invaded my land,
a mighty army without number;
it has the teeth of a lion,
the fangs of a lioness.
7 It has laid waste my vines
and ruined my fig trees.
It has stripped off their bark
and thrown it away,
leaving their branches white.

8 Mourn like a virgin in sackcloth
grieving for the betrothed of her youth.
9 Grain offerings and drink offerings
are cut off from the house of the LORD.
The priests are in mourning,
those who minister before the LORD.
10 The fields are ruined,
the ground is dried up;
the grain is destroyed,
the new wine is dried up,
the olive oil fails.

11 Despair, you farmers,
wail, you vine growers;
grieve for the wheat and the barley,
because the harvest of the field is destroyed.
12 The vine is dried up
and the fig tree is withered;
the pomegranate, the palm and the apple[b] tree —
all the trees of the field — are dried up.
Surely the people's joy
is withered away.

---

[a] 4 The precise meaning of the four Hebrew words used here for locusts is uncertain. [b] 12 Or possibly *apricot*

A CALL TO LAMENTATION

13 Put on sackcloth, you priests, and mourn;
wail, you who minister before the altar.
Come, spend the night in sackcloth,
you who minister before my God;
for the grain offerings and drink offerings
are withheld from the house of your God.
14 Declare a holy fast;
call a sacred assembly.
Summon the elders
and all who live in the land
to the house of the LORD your God,
and cry out to the LORD.

15 Alas for that day!
For the day of the LORD is near;
it will come like destruction from the Almighty.[a]

16 Has not the food been cut off
before our very eyes —
joy and gladness
from the house of our God?
17 The seeds are shriveled
beneath the clods.[b]
The storehouses are in ruins,
the granaries have been broken down,
for the grain has dried up.
18 How the cattle moan!
The herds mill about
because they have no pasture;
even the flocks of sheep are suffering.

19 To you, LORD, I call,
for fire has devoured the pastures in the wilderness
and flames have burned up all the trees of the field.
20 Even the wild animals pant for you;
the streams of water have dried up
and fire has devoured the pastures in the wilderness.

AN ARMY OF LOCUSTS

2 Blow the trumpet in Zion;
sound the alarm on my holy hill.

Let all who live in the land tremble,
for the day of the LORD is coming.
It is close at hand —
2 a day of darkness and gloom,
a day of clouds and blackness.
Like dawn spreading across the mountains
a large and mighty army comes,
such as never was in ancient times
nor ever will be in ages to come.

[a] 15 Hebrew *Shaddai* [b] 17 The meaning of the Hebrew for this word is uncertain.

PRAYING SCRIPTURE

Joel 2

The call to repentance always involves the heart. The Lord admonished his people to turn with their whole hearts, to fast, weep and mourn. And rather than the common sign of repentance—the tearing of clothes—the Lord told them to rend their hearts instead (see verses 12–13). He was not interested in a show.

Repentance is not a performance. When you go to God, make sure your heart bears the weight.

3 Before them fire devours,
behind them a flame blazes.
Before them the land is like the garden of Eden,
behind them, a desert waste —
nothing escapes them.
4 They have the appearance of horses;
they gallop along like cavalry.
5 With a noise like that of chariots
they leap over the mountaintops,
like a crackling fire consuming stubble,
like a mighty army drawn up for battle.

6 At the sight of them, nations are in anguish;
every face turns pale.
7 They charge like warriors;
they scale walls like soldiers.
They all march in line,
not swerving from their course.
8 They do not jostle each other;
each marches straight ahead.
They plunge through defenses
without breaking ranks.
9 They rush upon the city;
they run along the wall.
They climb into the houses;
like thieves they enter through the windows.

10 Before them the earth shakes,
the heavens tremble,
the sun and moon are darkened,
and the stars no longer shine.
11 The LORD thunders
at the head of his army;
his forces are beyond number,
and mighty is the army that obeys his command.
The day of the LORD is great;
it is dreadful.
Who can endure it?

REND YOUR HEART

12 "Even now," declares the LORD,
"return to me with all your heart,
with fasting and weeping and mourning."

13 Rend your heart
and not your garments.
Return to the LORD your God,
for he is gracious and compassionate,
slow to anger and abounding in love,
and he relents from sending calamity.
14 Who knows? He may turn and relent
and leave behind a blessing —
grain offerings and drink offerings
for the LORD your God.
15 Blow the trumpet in Zion,

declare a holy fast,
call a sacred assembly.
16 Gather the people,
consecrate the assembly;
bring together the elders,
gather the children,
those nursing at the breast.
Let the bridegroom leave his room
and the bride her chamber.
17 Let the priests, who minister before the LORD,
weep between the portico and the altar.
Let them say, "Spare your people, LORD.
Do not make your inheritance an object of scorn,
a byword among the nations.
Why should they say among the peoples,
'Where is their God?' "

THE LORD'S ANSWER

18 Then the LORD was jealous for his land
and took pity on his people.

19 The LORD replied[a] to them:

"I am sending you grain, new wine and olive oil,
enough to satisfy you fully;
never again will I make you
an object of scorn to the nations.

20 "I will drive the northern horde far from you,
pushing it into a parched and barren land;
its eastern ranks will drown in the Dead Sea
and its western ranks in the Mediterranean Sea.
And its stench will go up;
its smell will rise."

Surely he has done great things!
21 Do not be afraid, land of Judah;
be glad and rejoice.
Surely the LORD has done great things!
22 Do not be afraid, you wild animals,
for the pastures in the wilderness are becoming green.
The trees are bearing their fruit;
the fig tree and the vine yield their riches.
23 Be glad, people of Zion,
rejoice in the LORD your God,
for he has given you the autumn rains
because he is faithful.
He sends you abundant showers,
both autumn and spring rains, as before.
24 The threshing floors will be filled with grain;
the vats will overflow with new wine and oil.

25 "I will repay you for the years the locusts have eaten —
the great locust and the young locust,

[a] 18,19 Or *LORD will be jealous . . . / and take pity . . . / 19The LORD will reply*

the other locusts and the locust swarm[a] —
my great army that I sent among you.
26 You will have plenty to eat, until you are full,
and you will praise the name of the LORD your God,
who has worked wonders for you;
never again will my people be shamed.
27 Then you will know that I am in Israel,
that I am the LORD your God,
and that there is no other;
never again will my people be shamed.

THE DAY OF THE LORD

28 "And afterward,
I will pour out my Spirit on all people.
Your sons and daughters will prophesy,
your old men will dream dreams,
your young men will see visions.
29 Even on my servants, both men and women,
I will pour out my Spirit in those days.
30 I will show wonders in the heavens
and on the earth,
blood and fire and billows of smoke.
31 The sun will be turned to darkness
and the moon to blood
before the coming of the great and dreadful day of the LORD.
32 And everyone who calls
on the name of the LORD will be saved;
for on Mount Zion and in Jerusalem
there will be deliverance,
as the LORD has said,
even among the survivors
whom the LORD calls.[b]

THE NATIONS JUDGED

3[c] "In those days and at that time,
when I restore the fortunes of Judah and Jerusalem,
2 I will gather all nations
and bring them down to the Valley of Jehoshaphat.[d]
There I will put them on trial
for what they did to my inheritance, my people Israel,
because they scattered my people among the nations
and divided up my land.
3 They cast lots for my people
and traded boys for prostitutes;
they sold girls for wine to drink.

4 "Now what have you against me, Tyre and Sidon and all you regions
of Philistia? Are you repaying me for something I have done? If you
are paying me back, I will swiftly and speedily return on your own
heads what you have done. 5 For you took my silver and my gold and

PRAYING SCRIPTURE

Joel 3

When the prophets spoke of God's restoring his people, it always involved abundance. The mountains will "drip new wine, and the hills will flow with milk; all the ravines of Judah will run with water" (verse 18). A fountain shall flow from God's house and water the land.

Restoration of creation is the final act of the redemption drama. Trust God to complete all that he has started in Christ, praying to that end.

[a] *25* The precise meaning of the four Hebrew words used here for locusts is uncertain. [b] *32* In Hebrew texts 2:28-32 is numbered 3:1-5. [c] In Hebrew texts 3:1-21 is numbered 4:1-21. [d] *2* *Jehoshaphat* means *the LORD judges*; also in verse 12.

carried off my finest treasures to your temples.[a] 6You sold the people
of Judah and Jerusalem to the Greeks, that you might send them far
from their homeland.

7"See, I am going to rouse them out of the places to which you sold
them, and I will return on your own heads what you have done. 8I will
sell your sons and daughters to the people of Judah, and they will sell
them to the Sabeans, a nation far away." The LORD has spoken.

9 Proclaim this among the nations:
Prepare for war!
Rouse the warriors!
Let all the fighting men draw near and attack.
10 Beat your plowshares into swords
and your pruning hooks into spears.
Let the weakling say,
"I am strong!"
11 Come quickly, all you nations from every side,
and assemble there.

Bring down your warriors, LORD!

12 "Let the nations be roused;
let them advance into the Valley of Jehoshaphat,
for there I will sit
to judge all the nations on every side.
13 Swing the sickle,
for the harvest is ripe.
Come, trample the grapes,
for the winepress is full
and the vats overflow—
so great is their wickedness!"

14 Multitudes, multitudes
in the valley of decision!
For the day of the LORD is near
in the valley of decision.
15 The sun and moon will be darkened,
and the stars no longer shine.
16 The LORD will roar from Zion
and thunder from Jerusalem;
the earth and the heavens will tremble.
But the LORD will be a refuge for his people,
a stronghold for the people of Israel.

BLESSINGS FOR GOD'S PEOPLE

17 "Then you will know that I, the LORD your God,
dwell in Zion, my holy hill.
Jerusalem will be holy;
never again will foreigners invade her.

18 "In that day the mountains will drip new wine,
and the hills will flow with milk;
all the ravines of Judah will run with water.
A fountain will flow out of the LORD's house
and will water the valley of acacias.[b]

---

[a] 5 Or *palaces* [b] 18 Or *Valley of Shittim*

19 But Egypt will be desolate,
Edom a desert waste,
because of violence done to the people of Judah,
in whose land they shed innocent blood.
20 Judah will be inhabited forever
and Jerusalem through all generations.
21 Shall I leave their innocent blood unavenged?
No, I will not."

The LORD dwells in Zion!

AMOS

The titular prophet of this book was not a priest or other kind of religious leader. While prophesying in Bethel, the local priest, Amaziah, complained about his message. Amos admitted that he had never been a prophet, nor had his father; rather, he "was a shepherd, and [he] also took care of sycamore-fig trees" when God chose him specifically for prophetic ministry (7:14–15). This minor prophet contains a verse that is likely among the most heard in the English-speaking world, due to its inclusion in a speech by Martin Luther King Jr. in 1963: "But let justice roll on like a river, righteousness like a never-failing stream!" (5:24).

Amos carried out his ministry during the reign of King Uzziah in Judah and Jeroboam, the son of Joash, in Israel. This places Amos's ministry in the same general time period as Isaiah and Hosea. He specified that he had prophesied two years before "the earthquake." Current scholarship does not have a date for the earthquake, but the people in Amos's day would have been well-acquainted with the seismic activity he was describing. This reference shows how the Bible's narrative is rooted in actual historical events.

In addition to the usual concerns that we see from the Old Testament prophets, Amos emphasized the need for people to treat each other justly. Amos covered a wide range of injustices taking place in Israel. He shared the Lord's displeasure with the poor being mistreated in the courts. Amos, reiterating a concern of Solomon's in Proverbs, condemned those who used dishonest scales and measurements in their place of business to cheat their customers (see 8:5). He also pronounced "woe" upon the rich who are complacent and secure while mistreating and taking advantage of the poor. Israel's lack of obedience to God's demand for justice led to warnings of deep and brutal judgment from God.

Amos reminds us that our relationships with other people should be a major focus of our prayer lives. We spend a significant portion of each day interacting with other people, so therefore we should spend time praying that we will treat people in a way that accords with God's commands and character.

Amos helps Christians understand how to pray for a just society. Christians often pray for revival, and rightly so, yet we do not often pray about how revival should affect the places in which we live. A godly society would treat the poor and vulnerable with dignity and respect rather than contempt. In a just society, the poor receive the same treatment in the courts as the rich. Business owners give their customers a fair deal, and leaders look out for the people entrusted to their care rather than themselves. When we pray "your kingdom come," we should pray specifically for these types of outcomes.

The book ends with a promise of restoration. Descriptive language of a repaired tabernacle, a revived spiritual life, bountiful harvests, rebuilt cities and renewed residence await the people when their days of punishment are accomplished.

PRAYING SCRIPTURE

Amos 1

Amos was unique in his lack of any noticeable prophetic pedigree. The book opens with Amos, "one of the shepherds of Tekoa" (verse 1), and mentions later that he was "neither a prophet nor the son of a prophet" (7:14). Sin lurked beneath the surface of Israel's economic well-being, and God called Amos to speak to God's people.

Scripture teaches us that God delights in using the simple to confound the wise. Make yourself available to him and watch him use you.

1 The words of Amos, one of the shepherds of Tekoa — the vision
he saw concerning Israel two years before the earthquake, when
Uzziah was king of Judah and Jeroboam son of Jehoash[a] was king of
Israel.

2 He said:

"The LORD roars from Zion
and thunders from Jerusalem;
the pastures of the shepherds dry up,
and the top of Carmel withers."

JUDGMENT ON ISRAEL'S NEIGHBORS

3 This is what the LORD says:

"For three sins of Damascus,
even for four, I will not relent.
Because she threshed Gilead
with sledges having iron teeth,
4 I will send fire on the house of Hazael
that will consume the fortresses of Ben-Hadad.
5 I will break down the gate of Damascus;
I will destroy the king who is in[b] the Valley of Aven[c]
and the one who holds the scepter in Beth Eden.
The people of Aram will go into exile to Kir,"
says the LORD.

6 This is what the LORD says:

"For three sins of Gaza,
even for four, I will not relent.
Because she took captive whole communities
and sold them to Edom,
7 I will send fire on the walls of Gaza
that will consume her fortresses.
8 I will destroy the king[d] of Ashdod
and the one who holds the scepter in Ashkelon.
I will turn my hand against Ekron,
till the last of the Philistines are dead,"
says the Sovereign LORD.

9 This is what the LORD says:

"For three sins of Tyre,
even for four, I will not relent.
Because she sold whole communities of captives to Edom,
disregarding a treaty of brotherhood,
10 I will send fire on the walls of Tyre
that will consume her fortresses."

11 This is what the LORD says:

"For three sins of Edom,
even for four, I will not relent.
Because he pursued his brother with a sword
and slaughtered the women of the land,

---

[a] 1 Hebrew *Joash*, a variant of *Jehoash* [b] 5 Or *the inhabitants of* [c] 5 *Aven* means *wickedness.* [d] 8 Or *inhabitants*

because his anger raged continually
 and his fury flamed unchecked,
12 I will send fire on Teman
 that will consume the fortresses of Bozrah."

13 This is what the LORD says:

"For three sins of Ammon,
 even for four, I will not relent.
Because he ripped open the pregnant women of Gilead
 in order to extend his borders,
14 I will set fire to the walls of Rabbah
 that will consume her fortresses
amid war cries on the day of battle,
 amid violent winds on a stormy day.
15 Her king[a] will go into exile,
 he and his officials together,"
 says the LORD.

2 This is what the LORD says:

"For three sins of Moab,
 even for four, I will not relent.
Because he burned to ashes
 the bones of Edom's king,
2 I will send fire on Moab
 that will consume the fortresses of Kerioth.[b]
Moab will go down in great tumult
 amid war cries and the blast of the trumpet.
3 I will destroy her ruler
 and kill all her officials with him,"
 says the LORD.

4 This is what the LORD says:

"For three sins of Judah,
 even for four, I will not relent.
Because they have rejected the law of the LORD
 and have not kept his decrees,
because they have been led astray by false gods,[c]
 the gods[d] their ancestors followed,
5 I will send fire on Judah
 that will consume the fortresses of Jerusalem."

JUDGMENT ON ISRAEL

6 This is what the LORD says:

"For three sins of Israel,
 even for four, I will not relent.
They sell the innocent for silver,
 and the needy for a pair of sandals.
7 They trample on the heads of the poor
 as on the dust of the ground
 and deny justice to the oppressed.
Father and son use the same girl

PRAYING SCRIPTURE

Amos 2

The Lord's anger against Moab, Judah and Israel was palpable. A long list of sins—breaking commandments, exploitation of the righteous and the poor, sexual sins that defiled God's name, alcohol abuse and disregard for the prophets—had brought God's judgment.

When sin is rampant in society, people suffer greatly. Pray for the strength to stand against the sins that dominate our times and context, and bear witness to Christ.

---

[a] 15 Or / *Molek* [b] 2 Or *of her cities* [c] 4 Or *by lies* [d] 4 Or *lies*

and so profane my holy name.
8 They lie down beside every altar
on garments taken in pledge.
In the house of their god
they drink wine taken as fines.

9 "Yet I destroyed the Amorites before them,
though they were tall as the cedars
and strong as the oaks.
I destroyed their fruit above
and their roots below.
10 I brought you up out of Egypt
and led you forty years in the wilderness
to give you the land of the Amorites.

11 "I also raised up prophets from among your children
and Nazirites from among your youths.
Is this not true, people of Israel?"

declares the LORD.

12 "But you made the Nazirites drink wine
and commanded the prophets not to prophesy.

13 "Now then, I will crush you
as a cart crushes when loaded with grain.
14 The swift will not escape,
the strong will not muster their strength,
and the warrior will not save his life.
15 The archer will not stand his ground,
the fleet-footed soldier will not get away,
and the horseman will not save his life.
16 Even the bravest warriors
will flee naked on that day,"

declares the LORD.

WITNESSES SUMMONED AGAINST ISRAEL

3 Hear this word, people of Israel, the word the LORD has spoken
against you — against the whole family I brought up out of Egypt:

2 "You only have I chosen
of all the families of the earth;
therefore I will punish you
for all your sins."

3 Do two walk together
unless they have agreed to do so?
4 Does a lion roar in the thicket
when it has no prey?
Does it growl in its den
when it has caught nothing?
5 Does a bird swoop down to a trap on the ground
when no bait is there?
Does a trap spring up from the ground
if it has not caught anything?
6 When a trumpet sounds in a city,
do not the people tremble?
When disaster comes to a city,
has not the LORD caused it?

PRAYING SCRIPTURE

Amos 3

"Do two walk together unless they have agreed to do so?" is often asked about people (verse 3). But here it refers to God and his children. The question then is: Can we walk with God unless we agree with him? God doesn't need to agree with us, but we need to agree with him.

How close are you to God? Are you in agreement with him constantly? If not, ask him for a heart that stays close to him.

7 Surely the Sovereign LORD does nothing
without revealing his plan
to his servants the prophets.

8 The lion has roared—
who will not fear?
The Sovereign LORD has spoken—
who can but prophesy?

9 Proclaim to the fortresses of Ashdod
and to the fortresses of Egypt:
"Assemble yourselves on the mountains of Samaria;
see the great unrest within her
and the oppression among her people."

10 "They do not know how to do right," declares the LORD,
"who store up in their fortresses
what they have plundered and looted."

11 Therefore this is what the Sovereign LORD says:

"An enemy will overrun your land,
pull down your strongholds
and plunder your fortresses."

12 This is what the LORD says:

"As a shepherd rescues from the lion's mouth
only two leg bones or a piece of an ear,
so will the Israelites living in Samaria be rescued,
with only the head of a bed
and a piece of fabric[a] from a couch.[b]"

13 "Hear this and testify against the descendants of Jacob," declares
the Lord, the LORD God Almighty.

14 "On the day I punish Israel for her sins,
I will destroy the altars of Bethel;
the horns of the altar will be cut off
and fall to the ground.
15 I will tear down the winter house
along with the summer house;
the houses adorned with ivory will be destroyed
and the mansions will be demolished,"
declares the LORD.

ISRAEL HAS NOT RETURNED TO GOD

4 Hear this word, you cows of Bashan on Mount Samaria,
you women who oppress the poor and crush the needy
and say to your husbands, "Bring us some drinks!"
2 The Sovereign LORD has sworn by his holiness:
"The time will surely come
when you will be taken away with hooks,
the last of you with fishhooks.[c]

PRAYING SCRIPTURE

Amos 4

Not only were the various kings, princes and priests evil—the women in Israel were evil too. They oppressed the poor, crushed the needy and generally lacked compassion (see verse 1). In addition to Israel's sin that brought God's wrath, they refused the correction he sent (see verse 6). In fact, they doubled down on their sin.

When we hear a sermon, read a book or have a conversation that confronts our sin, that's God working to bring us to repentance.

[a] 12 The meaning of the Hebrew for this phrase is uncertain. [b] 12 Or *Israelites be rescued, / those who sit in Samaria / on the edge of their beds / and in Damascus on their couches.* [c] 2 Or *away in baskets, / the last of you in fish baskets*

3 You will each go straight out
through breaches in the wall,
and you will be cast out toward Harmon,[a]"
declares the LORD.

4 "Go to Bethel and sin;
go to Gilgal and sin yet more.
Bring your sacrifices every morning,
your tithes every three years.[b]
5 Burn leavened bread as a thank offering
and brag about your freewill offerings —
boast about them, you Israelites,
for this is what you love to do,"
declares the Sovereign LORD.

6 "I gave you empty stomachs in every city
and lack of bread in every town,
yet you have not returned to me,"
declares the LORD.

7 "I also withheld rain from you
when the harvest was still three months away.
I sent rain on one town,
but withheld it from another.
One field had rain;
another had none and dried up.
8 People staggered from town to town for water
but did not get enough to drink,
yet you have not returned to me,"
declares the LORD.

9 "Many times I struck your gardens and vineyards,
destroying them with blight and mildew.
Locusts devoured your fig and olive trees,
yet you have not returned to me,"
declares the LORD.

10 "I sent plagues among you
as I did to Egypt.
I killed your young men with the sword,
along with your captured horses.
I filled your nostrils with the stench of your camps,
yet you have not returned to me,"
declares the LORD.

11 "I overthrew some of you
as I overthrew Sodom and Gomorrah.
You were like a burning stick snatched from the fire,
yet you have not returned to me,"
declares the LORD.

12 "Therefore this is what I will do to you, Israel,
and because I will do this to you, Israel,
prepare to meet your God."

---

[a] 3 Masoretic Text; with a different word division of the Hebrew (see Septuagint) *out, you mountain of oppression* [b] 4 Or *days*

13 He who forms the mountains,
who creates the wind,
and who reveals his thoughts to mankind,
who turns dawn to darkness,
and treads on the heights of the earth—
the LORD God Almighty is his name.

A LAMENT AND CALL TO REPENTANCE

5 Hear this word, Israel, this lament I take up concerning you:

2 "Fallen is Virgin Israel,
never to rise again,
deserted in her own land,
with no one to lift her up."

3 This is what the Sovereign LORD says to Israel:

"Your city that marches out a thousand strong
will have only a hundred left;
your town that marches out a hundred strong
will have only ten left."

4 This is what the LORD says to Israel:

"Seek me and live;
5 do not seek Bethel,
do not go to Gilgal,
do not journey to Beersheba.
For Gilgal will surely go into exile,
and Bethel will be reduced to nothing.[a]"
6 Seek the LORD and live,
or he will sweep through the tribes of Joseph like a fire;
it will devour them,
and Bethel will have no one to quench it.

7 There are those who turn justice into bitterness
and cast righteousness to the ground.

8 He who made the Pleiades and Orion,
who turns midnight into dawn
and darkens day into night,
who calls for the waters of the sea
and pours them out over the face of the land—
the LORD is his name.
9 With a blinding flash he destroys the stronghold
and brings the fortified city to ruin.

10 There are those who hate the one who upholds justice in court
and detest the one who tells the truth.

11 You levy a straw tax on the poor
and impose a tax on their grain.
Therefore, though you have built stone mansions,
you will not live in them;

PRAYING SCRIPTURE

Amos 5

One of the verses recognized outside of churches is a call for God's judgment to fall: "But let justice roll on like a river, righteousness like a never-failing stream!" (verse 24). Sometimes the only response we have to the wickedness around us is to pray for God's judgment to fall.

When you look around your culture, what invites God's judgment? Pray for justice to run down so God's righteousness can be demonstrated.

---

[a] 5 Hebrew *aven*, a reference to Beth Aven (a derogatory name for Bethel); see Hosea 4:15.

though you have planted lush vineyards,
you will not drink their wine.
12 For I know how many are your offenses
and how great your sins.

There are those who oppress the innocent and take bribes
and deprive the poor of justice in the courts.
13 Therefore the prudent keep quiet in such times,
for the times are evil.

14 Seek good, not evil,
that you may live.
Then the LORD God Almighty will be with you,
just as you say he is.
15 Hate evil, love good;
maintain justice in the courts.
Perhaps the LORD God Almighty will have mercy
on the remnant of Joseph.

16 Therefore this is what the Lord, the LORD God Almighty, says:

"There will be wailing in all the streets
and cries of anguish in every public square.
The farmers will be summoned to weep
and the mourners to wail.
17 There will be wailing in all the vineyards,
for I will pass through your midst,"
says the LORD.

THE DAY OF THE LORD

18 Woe to you who long
for the day of the LORD!
Why do you long for the day of the LORD?
That day will be darkness, not light.
19 It will be as though a man fled from a lion
only to meet a bear,
as though he entered his house
and rested his hand on the wall
only to have a snake bite him.
20 Will not the day of the LORD be darkness, not light —
pitch-dark, without a ray of brightness?

21 "I hate, I despise your religious festivals;
your assemblies are a stench to me.
22 Even though you bring me burnt offerings and grain offerings,
I will not accept them.
Though you bring choice fellowship offerings,
I will have no regard for them.
23 Away with the noise of your songs!
I will not listen to the music of your harps.
24 But let justice roll on like a river,
righteousness like a never-failing stream!

25 "Did you bring me sacrifices and offerings
forty years in the wilderness, people of Israel?
26 You have lifted up the shrine of your king,
the pedestal of your idols,

the star of your god[a] —
which you made for yourselves.
27 Therefore I will send you into exile beyond Damascus,"
says the LORD, whose name is God Almighty.

WOE TO THE COMPLACENT

6 Woe to you who are complacent in Zion,
and to you who feel secure on Mount Samaria,
you notable men of the foremost nation,
to whom the people of Israel come!
2 Go to Kalneh and look at it;
go from there to great Hamath,
and then go down to Gath in Philistia.
Are they better off than your two kingdoms?
Is their land larger than yours?
3 You put off the day of disaster
and bring near a reign of terror.
4 You lie on beds adorned with ivory
and lounge on your couches.
You dine on choice lambs
and fattened calves.
5 You strum away on your harps like David
and improvise on musical instruments.
6 You drink wine by the bowlful
and use the finest lotions,
but you do not grieve over the ruin of Joseph.
7 Therefore you will be among the first to go into exile;
your feasting and lounging will end.

THE LORD ABHORS THE PRIDE OF ISRAEL

8 The Sovereign LORD has sworn by himself — the LORD God Al-
mighty declares:

"I abhor the pride of Jacob
and detest his fortresses;
I will deliver up the city
and everything in it."

9 If ten people are left in one house, they too will die. 10 And if the
relative who comes to carry the bodies out of the house to burn them[b]
asks anyone who might be hiding there, "Is anyone else with you?" and
he says, "No," then he will go on to say, "Hush! We must not mention
the name of the LORD."

11 For the LORD has given the command,
and he will smash the great house into pieces
and the small house into bits.

12 Do horses run on the rocky crags?
Does one plow the sea[c] with oxen?
But you have turned justice into poison

PRAYING SCRIPTURE

Amos 6

God's people should be careful that lives of comfort do not lead them to be apathetic about following him. When people with authority neglect God's standard of justice and righteousness, he will bring about judgment. He said, "I abhor the pride of Jacob and detest his fortresses," and judgment came (verse 8).

God expects his people to act like his people. Pray that you obey him in all things for his good pleasure.

---

[a] 26 Or *lifted up Sakkuth your king / and Kaiwan your idols, / your star-gods*; Septuagint *lifted up the shrine of Molek / and the star of your god Rephan, / their idols* [b] 10 Or *to make a funeral fire in honor of the dead* [c] 12 With a different word division of the Hebrew; Masoretic Text *plow there*

and the fruit of righteousness into bitterness —
13 you who rejoice in the conquest of Lo Debar[a]
and say, "Did we not take Karnaim[b] by our own strength?"

14 For the LORD God Almighty declares,
"I will stir up a nation against you, Israel,
that will oppress you all the way
from Lebo Hamath to the valley of the Arabah."

LOCUSTS, FIRE AND A PLUMB LINE

7 This is what the Sovereign LORD showed me: He was preparing
swarms of locusts after the king's share had been harvested and
just as the late crops were coming up. 2 When they had stripped the
land clean, I cried out, "Sovereign LORD, forgive! How can Jacob sur-
vive? He is so small!"
3 So the LORD relented.
"This will not happen," the LORD said.
4 This is what the Sovereign LORD showed me: The Sovereign LORD
was calling for judgment by fire; it dried up the great deep and de-
voured the land. 5 Then I cried out, "Sovereign LORD, I beg you, stop!
How can Jacob survive? He is so small!"
6 So the LORD relented.
"This will not happen either," the Sovereign LORD said.

7 This is what he showed me: The Lord was standing by a wall that
had been built true to plumb,[c] with a plumb line[d] in his hand. 8 And
the LORD asked me, "What do you see, Amos?"
"A plumb line," I replied.
Then the Lord said, "Look, I am setting a plumb line among my peo-
ple Israel; I will spare them no longer.

9 "The high places of Isaac will be destroyed
and the sanctuaries of Israel will be ruined;
with my sword I will rise against the house of Jeroboam."

AMOS AND AMAZIAH

10 Then Amaziah the priest of Bethel sent a message to Jeroboam
king of Israel: "Amos is raising a conspiracy against you in the very
heart of Israel. The land cannot bear all his words. 11 For this is what
Amos is saying:

"'Jeroboam will die by the sword,
and Israel will surely go into exile,
away from their native land.'"

12 Then Amaziah said to Amos, "Get out, you seer! Go back to the land
of Judah. Earn your bread there and do your prophesying there. 13 Don't
prophesy anymore at Bethel, because this is the king's sanctuary and
the temple of the kingdom."
14 Amos answered Amaziah, "I was neither a prophet nor the son of
a prophet, but I was a shepherd, and I also took care of sycamore-fig
trees. 15 But the LORD took me from tending the flock and said to me,

PRAYING SCRIPTURE

Amos 7

In addition to military intervention and conquest, the Lord will judge sinful nations by natural disasters like fires, floods and plague. Sometimes he uses threats. In this passage, God threatened a swarm of devouring locusts and a destructive fire but relented when Amos interceded.

Amos's intercession instructs us about prayer. God doesn't reject us when we ask him to do something different. Pray with the assurance that he really does listen.

---

[a] 13 *Lo Debar* means *nothing.* [b] 13 *Karnaim* means *horns*; *horn* here symbolizes strength. [c] 7 The meaning of the Hebrew for this phrase is uncertain. [d] 7 The meaning of the Hebrew for this phrase is uncertain; also in verse 8.

'Go, prophesy to my people Israel.' 16 Now then, hear the word of the
LORD. You say,

"'Do not prophesy against Israel,
and stop preaching against the descendants of Isaac.'

17 "Therefore this is what the LORD says:

"'Your wife will become a prostitute in the city,
and your sons and daughters will fall by the sword.
Your land will be measured and divided up,
and you yourself will die in a pagan[a] country.
And Israel will surely go into exile,
away from their native land.'"

A BASKET OF RIPE FRUIT

8 This is what the Sovereign LORD showed me: a basket of ripe fruit.
2 "What do you see, Amos?" he asked.
"A basket of ripe fruit," I answered.
Then the LORD said to me, "The time is ripe for my people Israel; I
will spare them no longer.
3 "In that day," declares the Sovereign LORD, "the songs in the temple
will turn to wailing.[b] Many, many bodies — flung everywhere! Silence!"

4 Hear this, you who trample the needy
and do away with the poor of the land,

5 saying,

"When will the New Moon be over
that we may sell grain,
and the Sabbath be ended
that we may market wheat?" —
skimping on the measure,
boosting the price
and cheating with dishonest scales,
6 buying the poor with silver
and the needy for a pair of sandals,
selling even the sweepings with the wheat.

7 The LORD has sworn by himself, the Pride of Jacob: "I will never
forget anything they have done.

8 "Will not the land tremble for this,
and all who live in it mourn?
The whole land will rise like the Nile;
it will be stirred up and then sink
like the river of Egypt.

9 "In that day," declares the Sovereign LORD,

"I will make the sun go down at noon
and darken the earth in broad daylight.
10 I will turn your religious festivals into mourning
and all your singing into weeping.
I will make all of you wear sackcloth
and shave your heads.

PRAYING SCRIPTURE

Amos 8

One of the greatest gifts God has given us is his words. Israel's wickedness was so complete that God promised a famine, "not a famine of food or a thirst for water, but a famine of hearing the words of the LORD" (verse 11). Even when they longed for it, they wouldn't find it. Thank God you have access to his written Word, and pray for those who do not.

---

[a] 17 Hebrew *an unclean* [b] 3 Or *"the temple singers will wail*

I will make that time like mourning for an only son
and the end of it like a bitter day.

11 "The days are coming," declares the Sovereign LORD,
"when I will send a famine through the land—
not a famine of food or a thirst for water,
but a famine of hearing the words of the LORD.
12 People will stagger from sea to sea
and wander from north to east,
searching for the word of the LORD,
but they will not find it.

13 "In that day

"the lovely young women and strong young men
will faint because of thirst.
14 Those who swear by the sin of Samaria—
who say, 'As surely as your god lives, Dan,'
or, 'As surely as the god[a] of Beersheba lives'—
they will fall, never to rise again."

ISRAEL TO BE DESTROYED

9 I saw the Lord standing by the altar, and he said:

"Strike the tops of the pillars
so that the thresholds shake.
Bring them down on the heads of all the people;
those who are left I will kill with the sword.
Not one will get away,
none will escape.
2 Though they dig down to the depths below,
from there my hand will take them.
Though they climb up to the heavens above,
from there I will bring them down.
3 Though they hide themselves on the top of Carmel,
there I will hunt them down and seize them.
Though they hide from my eyes at the bottom of the sea,
there I will command the serpent to bite them.
4 Though they are driven into exile by their enemies,
there I will command the sword to slay them.

"I will keep my eye on them
for harm and not for good."

5 The Lord, the LORD Almighty—
he touches the earth and it melts,
and all who live in it mourn;
the whole land rises like the Nile,
then sinks like the river of Egypt;
6 he builds his lofty palace[b] in the heavens
and sets its foundation[c] on the earth;
he calls for the waters of the sea
and pours them out over the face of the land—
the LORD is his name.

PRAYING SCRIPTURE

Amos 9

Even in the darkest of days, the Lord upholds and sustains his people through promises of future blessing. After his warning of impending judgment for those who failed to repent, God promised to bless those who did, allowing them to enjoy harvests bountiful beyond all expectation.

God is a God of blessing. He longs to give his people good things. It is good and right to ask God for good things and to live accordingly.

[a] 14 Hebrew *the way* [b] 6 The meaning of the Hebrew for this phrase is uncertain. [c] 6 The meaning of the Hebrew for this word is uncertain.

7 "Are not you Israelites
the same to me as the Cushites[a]?"
declares the LORD.

"Did I not bring Israel up from Egypt,
the Philistines from Caphtor[b]
and the Arameans from Kir?

8 "Surely the eyes of the Sovereign LORD
are on the sinful kingdom.
I will destroy it
from the face of the earth.
Yet I will not totally destroy
the descendants of Jacob,"
declares the LORD.

9 "For I will give the command,
and I will shake the people of Israel
among all the nations
as grain is shaken in a sieve,
and not a pebble will reach the ground.
10 All the sinners among my people
will die by the sword,
all those who say,
'Disaster will not overtake or meet us.'

ISRAEL'S RESTORATION

11 "In that day

"I will restore David's fallen shelter —
I will repair its broken walls
and restore its ruins —
and will rebuild it as it used to be,
12 so that they may possess the remnant of Edom
and all the nations that bear my name,[c]"
declares the LORD, who will do these things.

13 "The days are coming," declares the LORD,

"when the reaper will be overtaken by the plowman
and the planter by the one treading grapes.
New wine will drip from the mountains
and flow from all the hills,
14 and I will bring my people Israel back from exile.[d]

"They will rebuild the ruined cities and live in them.
They will plant vineyards and drink their wine;
they will make gardens and eat their fruit.
15 I will plant Israel in their own land,
never again to be uprooted
from the land I have given them,"

says the LORD your God.

---

[a] 7 That is, people from the upper Nile region [b] 7 That is, Crete
[c] 12 Hebrew; Septuagint *so that the remnant of people / and all the nations that bear my name may seek me* [d] 14 Or *will restore the fortunes of my people Israel*

OBADIAH

Obadiah's one chapter consists of an oracle against Edom, a vision of God returning the deeds of Israel's enemies on their own heads, and a restoration of God's people. It's unfortunate that so few Christians are familiar with the contents of the Old Testament's shortest book for it addresses both judgment and deliverance.

Biblical scholars are uncertain of the specific date and occasion for Obadiah's oracle. He is not mentioned in any other books of the Bible, though Edom (the descendants of Esau) frequently harassed Israel (the descendants of his brother, Jacob). However, the book of 1 Esdras in the Apocrypha blames the Edomites for destroying Jerusalem at the behest of the Babylonians. This provides context for the reader to understand why Obadiah has a vision of the Edomites' destruction and why he sees their deeds coming back to haunt them.

Both God's judgment and Israel's deliverance are assured, and both are accomplished. "The day of the LORD is near for all nations . . . They will drink and drink and be as if they had never been" (verses 15–16). Yet, "on Mount Zion will be deliverance; it will be holy, and Jacob will possess his inheritance" (verse 17). God's promise to deliver Jacob (Israel) and destroy the house of Esau to stubble with no survivors is true to this day. There is no nation of Edom; the descendants of Esau are gone to history.

Living on this side of the cross, Christians often struggle to understand how we should apply passages calling for or celebrating the downfall of ancient enemies. First, we should recognize that Christians are right to cry out to God for freedom from their oppressors. When those who reject God and hate his people use persecution as a tool, the only possible remedy is for us to call out to God in prayer. As we pray for deliverance and justice, all Christians do well to remember our brothers and sisters around the world who are also suffering for the gospel.

Even as we pray for justice and deliverance for ourselves and others, we must do so with a posture of forgiveness. We pray for the salvation of our persecutors. We pray for God to forgive them and change them. We pray that if given the opportunity, we would forgive them of their sins against us and live at peace with them, just as we live at peace with God. Failure to pray for our enemies inevitably leads to pride or hatred.

Jesus taught this. The work he did in forgiving us and reconciling us to himself demands it. We once were far from God, sinning against him and rebelling against his goodness. He sent Jesus to die in our place. By his own grace, he brought us back to himself and saved us, not by our good works but by faith alone. He forgave all our sins and became our friend. Jesus experienced judgment so all who believe in him can know deliverance.

OBADIAH'S VISION

1 The vision of Obadiah.

This is what the Sovereign LORD says about Edom—

We have heard a message from the LORD:
An envoy was sent to the nations to say,
"Rise, let us go against her for battle"—

2 "See, I will make you small among the nations;
you will be utterly despised.
3 The pride of your heart has deceived you,
you who live in the clefts of the rocks[a]
and make your home on the heights,
you who say to yourself,
'Who can bring me down to the ground?'
4 Though you soar like the eagle
and make your nest among the stars,
from there I will bring you down,"
declares the LORD.

5 "If thieves came to you,
if robbers in the night—
oh, what a disaster awaits you!—
would they not steal only as much as they wanted?
If grape pickers came to you,
would they not leave a few grapes?
6 But how Esau will be ransacked,
his hidden treasures pillaged!
7 All your allies will force you to the border;
your friends will deceive and overpower you;
those who eat your bread will set a trap for you,[b]
but you will not detect it.

8 "In that day," declares the LORD,
"will I not destroy the wise men of Edom,
those of understanding in the mountains of Esau?
9 Your warriors, Teman, will be terrified,
and everyone in Esau's mountains
will be cut down in the slaughter.
10 Because of the violence against your brother Jacob,
you will be covered with shame;
you will be destroyed forever.
11 On the day you stood aloof
while strangers carried off his wealth
and foreigners entered his gates
and cast lots for Jerusalem,
you were like one of them.
12 You should not gloat over your brother
in the day of his misfortune,
nor rejoice over the people of Judah
in the day of their destruction,
nor boast so much
in the day of their trouble.

[a] 3 Or *of Sela* [b] 7 The meaning of the Hebrew for this clause is uncertain.

PRAYING SCRIPTURE

Obadiah

Obadiah provided a short but strong emphasis on the day of the Lord. Judgment would fall, but Israel, God's chosen one, would endure and again possess the land. In language prophetic of a still-coming day, the prophet concluded, "And the kingdom will be the LORD's" (verse 21).

How glorious it is to contemplate the return of Christ, who will reign forever from David's throne. Pray for the day when the kingdom is visibly his.

13 You should not march through the gates of my people
in the day of their disaster,
nor gloat over them in their calamity
in the day of their disaster,
nor seize their wealth
in the day of their disaster.
14 You should not wait at the crossroads
to cut down their fugitives,
nor hand over their survivors
in the day of their trouble.

15 "The day of the LORD is near
for all nations.
As you have done, it will be done to you;
your deeds will return upon your own head.
16 Just as you drank on my holy hill,
so all the nations will drink continually;
they will drink and drink
and be as if they had never been.
17 But on Mount Zion will be deliverance;
it will be holy,
and Jacob will possess his inheritance.
18 Jacob will be a fire
and Joseph a flame;
Esau will be stubble,
and they will set him on fire and destroy him.
There will be no survivors
from Esau."

The LORD has spoken.

19 People from the Negev will occupy
the mountains of Esau,
and people from the foothills will possess
the land of the Philistines.
They will occupy the fields of Ephraim and Samaria,
and Benjamin will possess Gilead.
20 This company of Israelite exiles who are in Canaan
will possess the land as far as Zarephath;
the exiles from Jerusalem who are in Sepharad
will possess the towns of the Negev.
21 Deliverers will go up on[a] Mount Zion
to govern the mountains of Esau.
And the kingdom will be the LORD's.

[a] *21* Or *from*

JONAH

The story of Jonah stands as one of the best-known narratives in all of Scripture. However, many are only familiar with the first half. The Lord called the prophet Jonah to go to Nineveh and proclaim that the Lord would destroy it in three days. However, Jonah refused to go and, instead, tried to escape from God's presence, securing passage on a ship that was going in the opposite direction. While Jonah was still on the ship, the Lord sent a great storm, a judgment on Jonah. The sailors offloaded the cargo, but the storm was only calmed when they—at Jonah's suggestion—threw him overboard.

That sounds extreme! But the Lord had already prepared a huge fish to swallow Jonah. While many interpret the fish as God's judgment on the prophet, Jonah saw it as the Lord's salvation. While in the fish's stomach, Jonah prayed earnestly. In fact, the entirety of the second chapter consists of Jonah's prayer. Jonah admitted his disobedience and need, then thanked the Lord for his mercy. In faith he thanked God for saving him *before* the fish spit him out onto dry land (see 2:9–10). In a tragic irony, however, Jonah wanted to deny the salvation he enjoyed to others God intended to save.

When the Lord called him a second time to go to Nineveh, Jonah obeyed. For three days, he proclaimed the Lord's judgment from one end of the city to the other. The people responded with wholehearted repentance; even the king humbled himself and repented in sackcloth and dust. It was a genuine revival. God turned away his wrath, and the people's lives were spared.

The final chapter shows that this revival angered Jonah, who deep down wanted the people destroyed. It may have been that he feared they would attack Israel at some future point, or perhaps Jonah was simply prejudiced against the Ninevites. Orchestrating a series of events, including a hot sun, a shady plant, a scorching wind and a hungry worm, God revealed Jonah's hateful spirit. When Jonah complained bitterly about his discomfort, God reminded him that Nineveh and its people—and even its livestock—were more valuable than Jonah's personal comfort.

The main character in Jonah is not the prophet nor the fish, but God, who shows compassion to thousands and delights in the salvation of wayward people. In the beginning, God saved Jonah from his rebellion through the storm and from death through the fish. Then he used Jonah's preaching to save the city of Nineveh from his own wrath.

When we pray, our thoughts are often consumed with what we need from God. In one sense, this is completely understandable and right. Christians should pray about everything that brings us anxiety. At the same time, our prayers should also focus on the needs of others. Christians have a special responsibility to pray for the salvation of those who are far from God, asking God to show them the same compassion that he has shown to us.

PRAYING SCRIPTURE

Jonah 1

What happens when God's prophet doesn't want to prophesy? Amid so many books where nations were judged for disobedience sits Jonah, in which a prophet was judged for disobedience. It seems Jonah was less concerned about Nineveh's repentance than God was. Imagine an evangelist who does not want converts!

Does your heart burn for the lost to know Christ? If not, ask God to renew your prayers for those without him.

PRAYING SCRIPTURE

Jonah 2

In Jonah's life, judgment and deliverance met at the same time and in an unusual way. Tossed into the sea by frightened sailors and reconciled to his death, Jonah was doubtless shocked to find that what he reckoned a punishment was instead his transportation.

As the old saying goes, God does move in mysterious ways. Pray for eyes that are open to the mysterious things God might do for you.

JONAH FLEES FROM THE LORD

1 The word of the LORD came to Jonah son of Amittai: [2]"Go to the
great city of Nineveh and preach against it, because its wickedness
has come up before me."
[3]But Jonah ran away from the LORD and headed for Tarshish. He
went down to Joppa, where he found a ship bound for that port. After
paying the fare, he went aboard and sailed for Tarshish to flee from
the LORD.
[4]Then the LORD sent a great wind on the sea, and such a violent
storm arose that the ship threatened to break up. [5]All the sailors were
afraid and each cried out to his own god. And they threw the cargo into
the sea to lighten the ship.
But Jonah had gone below deck, where he lay down and fell into a
deep sleep. [6]The captain went to him and said, "How can you sleep?
Get up and call on your god! Maybe he will take notice of us so that we
will not perish."
[7]Then the sailors said to each other, "Come, let us cast lots to find out
who is responsible for this calamity." They cast lots and the lot fell on
Jonah. [8]So they asked him, "Tell us, who is responsible for making all
this trouble for us? What kind of work do you do? Where do you come
from? What is your country? From what people are you?"
[9]He answered, "I am a Hebrew and I worship the LORD, the God of
heaven, who made the sea and the dry land."
[10]This terrified them and they asked, "What have you done?" (They
knew he was running away from the LORD, because he had already
told them so.)
[11]The sea was getting rougher and rougher. So they asked him, "What
should we do to you to make the sea calm down for us?"
[12]"Pick me up and throw me into the sea," he replied, "and it will
become calm. I know that it is my fault that this great storm has come
upon you."
[13]Instead, the men did their best to row back to land. But they could
not, for the sea grew even wilder than before. [14]Then they cried out to
the LORD, "Please, LORD, do not let us die for taking this man's life. Do
not hold us accountable for killing an innocent man, for you, LORD,
have done as you pleased." [15]Then they took Jonah and threw him
overboard, and the raging sea grew calm. [16]At this the men greatly
feared the LORD, and they offered a sacrifice to the LORD and made
vows to him.

JONAH'S PRAYER

[17]Now the LORD provided a huge fish to swallow Jonah, and Jonah
2[a] was in the belly of the fish three days and three nights. [1]From in-
side the fish Jonah prayed to the LORD his God. [2]He said:

"In my distress I called to the LORD,
and he answered me.
From deep in the realm of the dead I called for help,
and you listened to my cry.
[3]You hurled me into the depths,
into the very heart of the seas,
and the currents swirled about me;

---

[a] In Hebrew texts 2:1 is numbered 1:17, and 2:1-10 is numbered 2:2-11.

all your waves and breakers
    swept over me.
4 I said, 'I have been banished
    from your sight;
yet I will look again
    toward your holy temple.'
5 The engulfing waters threatened me,[a]
    the deep surrounded me;
    seaweed was wrapped around my head.
6 To the roots of the mountains I sank down;
    the earth beneath barred me in forever.
But you, LORD my God,
    brought my life up from the pit.

7 "When my life was ebbing away,
    I remembered you, LORD,
and my prayer rose to you,
    to your holy temple.

8 "Those who cling to worthless idols
    turn away from God's love for them.
9 But I, with shouts of grateful praise,
    will sacrifice to you.
What I have vowed I will make good.
    I will say, 'Salvation comes from the LORD.'"

10 And the LORD commanded the fish, and it vomited Jonah onto dry
land.

JONAH GOES TO NINEVEH

3 Then the word of the LORD came to Jonah a second time: 2 "Go
to the great city of Nineveh and proclaim to it the message I
give you."

3 Jonah obeyed the word of the LORD and went to Nineveh. Now Nin-
eveh was a very large city; it took three days to go through it. 4 Jonah
began by going a day's journey into the city, proclaiming, "Forty more
days and Nineveh will be overthrown." 5 The Ninevites believed God.
A fast was proclaimed, and all of them, from the greatest to the least,
put on sackcloth.

6 When Jonah's warning reached the king of Nineveh, he rose from
his throne, took off his royal robes, covered himself with sackcloth and
sat down in the dust. 7 This is the proclamation he issued in Nineveh:

"By the decree of the king and his nobles:

Do not let people or animals, herds or flocks, taste anything; do
not let them eat or drink. 8 But let people and animals be covered
with sackcloth. Let everyone call urgently on God. Let them give
up their evil ways and their violence. 9 Who knows? God may yet
relent and with compassion turn from his fierce anger so that we
will not perish."

10 When God saw what they did and how they turned from their evil
ways, he relented and did not bring on them the destruction he had
threatened.

PRAYING SCRIPTURE

Jonah 3

When Nineveh heard the word of the Lord that Jonah proclaimed, the people—from the king down to the least—all turned to God in repentance. The king proclaimed a fast and a display of humility from all the people to acknowledge their sin before God.

Until Jesus returns, every generation will live in a time when spiritual awakening is needed. Ask God to bring it to your community and country.

---

[a] 5 Or *waters were at my throat*

JONAH'S ANGER AT THE LORD'S COMPASSION

4 But to Jonah this seemed very wrong, and he became angry. 2He prayed to the LORD, "Isn't this what I said, LORD, when I was still at home? That is what I tried to forestall by fleeing to Tarshish. I knew that you are a gracious and compassionate God, slow to anger and abounding in love, a God who relents from sending calamity. 3Now, LORD, take away my life, for it is better for me to die than to live."

4But the LORD replied, "Is it right for you to be angry?"

5Jonah had gone out and sat down at a place east of the city. There he made himself a shelter, sat in its shade and waited to see what would happen to the city. 6Then the LORD God provided a leafy plant[a] and made it grow up over Jonah to give shade for his head to ease his discomfort, and Jonah was very happy about the plant. 7But at dawn the next day God provided a worm, which chewed the plant so that it withered. 8When the sun rose, God provided a scorching east wind, and the sun blazed on Jonah's head so that he grew faint. He wanted to die, and said, "It would be better for me to die than to live."

9But God said to Jonah, "Is it right for you to be angry about the plant?"

"It is," he said. "And I'm so angry I wish I were dead."

10But the LORD said, "You have been concerned about this plant, though you did not tend it or make it grow. It sprang up overnight and died overnight. 11And should I not have concern for the great city of Nineveh, in which there are more than a hundred and twenty thousand people who cannot tell their right hand from their left — and also many animals?"

PRAYING SCRIPTURE

Jonah 4

It would have been easy for Jonah to be triumphalist about the great revival of Nineveh, but there was a problem: Jonah wanted God to rain down fire and judgment on them! He was frustrated because he knew God would show mercy.

Hoping for judgment on people because we don't like them is not Biblical justice. We need the mind of God, who purposes to show mercy when people repent.

[a] 6 The precise identification of this plant is uncertain; also in verses 7, 9 and 10.

MICAH

The opening sentence of Micah places him as a contemporary of Isaiah, Hosea and Amos. Micah proclaimed his message in the period before Assyria overran the northern kingdom in 722 BC and carried them off into exile. He lived in a period of apostasy, idolatry and injustice.

Micah's prophecy consists of three series of oracles about the state of Israel and the future glory that was to follow. In the first series, Micah spoke of God gathering a remnant that would remain faithful to him. Then he prophesied of a future day when the remnant would lie in a restored Jerusalem. Finally, Micah denounced the sin of Israel and looked forward to a time when God's forgiveness would cleanse the people.

Injustice and oppression were clearly on the prophet's mind in conveying God's anger. He pronounced woe on those who planned and plotted evil (see 2:1), on those who coveted and seized fields, thereby oppressing people (see 2:2), and on the rulers who exploited God's people (see 3:2–3). Further, Micah condemned other prophets who led the people astray and preached hypocritically of peace while going to war (see 3:5).

Micah expressed the depth of his own soul's pain, "What misery is mine!" He viewed his ministry as a failure: "I am like one who gathers summer fruit at the gleaning of the vineyard; there is no cluster of grapes to eat, none of the early figs that I crave" (7:1). Micah was not receiving accolades or awards for his prophetic ministry, but he stood firm.

One of the most notable Messianic prophecies that is recounted every Christmas is in 5:2, in which it is written that the birth of the Messiah is to be in Bethlehem. Though an insignificant town, the One to come from there would be "ruler over Israel, whose origins are from of old, from ancient times." A further part of the prophecy proclaimed that "his greatness will reach to the ends of the earth. And he will be our peace" (5:4–5). This, of course, is Jesus Christ, the Prince of Peace.

The book ends with one of the most encouraging promises in all of God's Word. God is revealed as the One who pardons sin, does not stay angry and delights to show mercy (see 7:18). He is compassionate and will "hurl all our iniquities into the depths of the sea" (7:19). This promise has brought many saints through long valleys of discouragement.

Christians can live faithfully in difficult times because of the sureness of our future hope. We know that our hope is in heaven, so we are willing to accept marginalized status in this present world. Christ is making all things new now and will one day return to ultimately make all things new. We look forward to this blessed hope in all our prayers, asking God to help us live in light of it.

PRAYING SCRIPTURE

Micah 1

One thing that becomes ever clearer in reading the books of the prophets is God's patience to warn the nations about their sin. Prophet after prophet raised the alarm that God's wrath would be unleashed against their sins. "The LORD is coming from his dwelling place," Micah warned (verse 3).

Part of God's judgment was shaming the nations (see verses 8–10). Those who shamelessly sin will be brought to shame. God will see to it.

1 The word of the LORD that came to Micah of Moresheth during the reigns of Jotham, Ahaz and Hezekiah, kings of Judah — the vision he saw concerning Samaria and Jerusalem.

2 Hear, you peoples, all of you,
listen, earth and all who live in it,
that the Sovereign LORD may bear witness against you,
the Lord from his holy temple.

JUDGMENT AGAINST SAMARIA AND JERUSALEM

3 Look! The LORD is coming from his dwelling place;
he comes down and treads on the heights of the earth.
4 The mountains melt beneath him
and the valleys split apart,
like wax before the fire,
like water rushing down a slope.
5 All this is because of Jacob's transgression,
because of the sins of the people of Israel.
What is Jacob's transgression?
Is it not Samaria?
What is Judah's high place?
Is it not Jerusalem?

6 "Therefore I will make Samaria a heap of rubble,
a place for planting vineyards.
I will pour her stones into the valley
and lay bare her foundations.
7 All her idols will be broken to pieces;
all her temple gifts will be burned with fire;
I will destroy all her images.
Since she gathered her gifts from the wages of prostitutes,
as the wages of prostitutes they will again be used."

WEEPING AND MOURNING

8 Because of this I will weep and wail;
I will go about barefoot and naked.
I will howl like a jackal
and moan like an owl.
9 For Samaria's plague is incurable;
it has spread to Judah.
It has reached the very gate of my people,
even to Jerusalem itself.
10 Tell it not in Gath[a];
weep not at all.
In Beth Ophrah[b]
roll in the dust.
11 Pass by naked and in shame,
you who live in Shaphir.[c]
Those who live in Zaanan[d]
will not come out.
Beth Ezel is in mourning;
it no longer protects you.

---

[a] 10 *Gath* sounds like the Hebrew for *tell*. [b] 10 *Beth Ophrah* means *house of dust*. [c] 11 *Shaphir* means *pleasant*. [d] 11 *Zaanan* sounds like the Hebrew for *come out*.

12 Those who live in Maroth[a] writhe in pain,
waiting for relief,
because disaster has come from the LORD,
even to the gate of Jerusalem.
13 You who live in Lachish,
harness fast horses to the chariot.
You are where the sin of Daughter Zion began,
for the transgressions of Israel were found in you.
14 Therefore you will give parting gifts
to Moresheth Gath.
The town of Akzib[b] will prove deceptive
to the kings of Israel.
15 I will bring a conqueror against you
who live in Mareshah.[c]
The nobles of Israel
will flee to Adullam.
16 Shave your head in mourning
for the children in whom you delight;
make yourself as bald as the vulture,
for they will go from you into exile.

HUMAN PLANS AND GOD'S PLANS

2 Woe to those who plan iniquity,
to those who plot evil on their beds!
At morning's light they carry it out
because it is in their power to do it.
2 They covet fields and seize them,
and houses, and take them.
They defraud people of their homes,
they rob them of their inheritance.

3 Therefore, the LORD says:

"I am planning disaster against this people,
from which you cannot save yourselves.
You will no longer walk proudly,
for it will be a time of calamity.
4 In that day people will ridicule you;
they will taunt you with this mournful song:
'We are utterly ruined;
my people's possession is divided up.
He takes it from me!
He assigns our fields to traitors.'"

5 Therefore you will have no one in the assembly of the LORD
to divide the land by lot.

FALSE PROPHETS

6 "Do not prophesy," their prophets say.
"Do not prophesy about these things;
disgrace will not overtake us."
7 You descendants of Jacob, should it be said,

PRAYING SCRIPTURE

Micah 2

A metaphor many scriptural writers use is of the Lord as a shepherd. Micah returned to it as God said that he will gather the remnant of Israel and bring them all together like a flock in pasture. God's people need him at all times.

Have you recently confessed to the Lord your absolute need for him? Thank him for his provision and confess that you need him constantly.

---

[a] 12 *Maroth* sounds like the Hebrew for *bitter.* [b] 14 *Akzib* means *deception.*
[c] 15 *Mareshah* sounds like the Hebrew for *conqueror.*

"Does the LORD become[a] impatient?
Does he do such things?"

"Do not my words do good
to the one whose ways are upright?
8 Lately my people have risen up
like an enemy.
You strip off the rich robe
from those who pass by without a care,
like men returning from battle.
9 You drive the women of my people
from their pleasant homes.
You take away my blessing
from their children forever.
10 Get up, go away!
For this is not your resting place,
because it is defiled,
it is ruined, beyond all remedy.
11 If a liar and deceiver comes and says,
'I will prophesy for you plenty of wine and beer,'
that would be just the prophet for this people!

DELIVERANCE PROMISED

12 "I will surely gather all of you, Jacob;
I will surely bring together the remnant of Israel.
I will bring them together like sheep in a pen,
like a flock in its pasture;
the place will throng with people.
13 The One who breaks open the way will go up before them;
they will break through the gate and go out.
Their King will pass through before them,
the LORD at their head."

LEADERS AND PROPHETS REBUKED

3 Then I said,

"Listen, you leaders of Jacob,
you rulers of Israel.
Should you not embrace justice,
2 you who hate good and love evil;
who tear the skin from my people
and the flesh from their bones;
3 who eat my people's flesh,
strip off their skin
and break their bones in pieces;
who chop them up like meat for the pan,
like flesh for the pot?"

4 Then they will cry out to the LORD,
but he will not answer them.
At that time he will hide his face from them
because of the evil they have done.

5 This is what the LORD says:

[a] 7 Or *Is the Spirit of the LORD*

PRAYING SCRIPTURE
Micah 3

A consistent theme in the prophets' books is God's call for his people to act justly. God described the unjust as those who "hate good and love evil; who tear the skin from my people and the flesh from their bones" (verse 2), then continued the description in even more graphic language.

We should expect the world to be unjust, but God's people are to seek justice. Ask God for courage to stand for the suffering.

"As for the prophets
who lead my people astray,
they proclaim 'peace'
if they have something to eat,
but prepare to wage war against anyone
who refuses to feed them.
6 Therefore night will come over you, without visions,
and darkness, without divination.
The sun will set for the prophets,
and the day will go dark for them.
7 The seers will be ashamed
and the diviners disgraced.
They will all cover their faces
because there is no answer from God."
8 But as for me, I am filled with power,
with the Spirit of the LORD,
and with justice and might,
to declare to Jacob his transgression,
to Israel his sin.

9 Hear this, you leaders of Jacob,
you rulers of Israel,
who despise justice
and distort all that is right;
10 who build Zion with bloodshed,
and Jerusalem with wickedness.
11 Her leaders judge for a bribe,
her priests teach for a price,
and her prophets tell fortunes for money.
Yet they look for the LORD's support and say,
"Is not the LORD among us?
No disaster will come upon us."
12 Therefore because of you,
Zion will be plowed like a field,
Jerusalem will become a heap of rubble,
the temple hill a mound overgrown with thickets.

THE MOUNTAIN OF THE LORD

4 In the last days

the mountain of the LORD's temple will be established
as the highest of the mountains;
it will be exalted above the hills,
and peoples will stream to it.

2 Many nations will come and say,

"Come, let us go up to the mountain of the LORD,
to the temple of the God of Jacob.
He will teach us his ways,
so that we may walk in his paths."
The law will go out from Zion,
the word of the LORD from Jerusalem.
3 He will judge between many peoples
and will settle disputes for strong nations far and wide.

PRAYING SCRIPTURE

Micah 4

To show his love for outsiders, the Lord promised "in that day" to gather the lame, outcast and grief-stricken (see verse 6). He will build his remnant from those thought unworthy by earthly standards.

The whole of Scripture teaches us that God loves the lost, those far from him, sheep gone astray, prodigal children—every outcast. Thank God that he found and loves you regardless of social standing or economic status.

They will beat their swords into plowshares
and their spears into pruning hooks.
Nation will not take up sword against nation,
nor will they train for war anymore.
4 Everyone will sit under their own vine
and under their own fig tree,
and no one will make them afraid,
for the LORD Almighty has spoken.
5 All the nations may walk
in the name of their gods,
but we will walk in the name of the LORD
our God for ever and ever.

THE LORD'S PLAN

6 "In that day," declares the LORD,

"I will gather the lame;
I will assemble the exiles
and those I have brought to grief.
7 I will make the lame my remnant,
those driven away a strong nation.
The LORD will rule over them in Mount Zion
from that day and forever.
8 As for you, watchtower of the flock,
stronghold[a] of Daughter Zion,
the former dominion will be restored to you;
kingship will come to Daughter Jerusalem."

9 Why do you now cry aloud —
have you no king[b]?
Has your ruler[c] perished,
that pain seizes you like that of a woman in labor?
10 Writhe in agony, Daughter Zion,
like a woman in labor,
for now you must leave the city
to camp in the open field.
You will go to Babylon;
there you will be rescued.
There the LORD will redeem you
out of the hand of your enemies.

11 But now many nations
are gathered against you.
They say, "Let her be defiled,
let our eyes gloat over Zion!"
12 But they do not know
the thoughts of the LORD;
they do not understand his plan,
that he has gathered them like sheaves to the threshing floor.
13 "Rise and thresh, Daughter Zion,
for I will give you horns of iron;
I will give you hooves of bronze,
and you will break to pieces many nations."

---

[a] 8 Or *hill* [b] 9 Or *King* [c] 9 Or *Ruler*

You will devote their ill-gotten gains to the LORD,
their wealth to the Lord of all the earth.

A PROMISED RULER FROM BETHLEHEM

5 [a] Marshal your troops now, city of troops,
for a siege is laid against us.
They will strike Israel's ruler
on the cheek with a rod.

2 "But you, Bethlehem Ephrathah,
though you are small among the clans[b] of Judah,
out of you will come for me
one who will be ruler over Israel,
whose origins are from of old,
from ancient times."

3 Therefore Israel will be abandoned
until the time when she who is in labor bears a son,
and the rest of his brothers return
to join the Israelites.

4 He will stand and shepherd his flock
in the strength of the LORD,
in the majesty of the name of the LORD his God.
And they will live securely, for then his greatness
will reach to the ends of the earth.

5 And he will be our peace
when the Assyrians invade our land
and march through our fortresses.
We will raise against them seven shepherds,
even eight commanders,
6 who will rule[c] the land of Assyria with the sword,
the land of Nimrod with drawn sword.[d]
He will deliver us from the Assyrians
when they invade our land
and march across our borders.
7 The remnant of Jacob will be
in the midst of many peoples
like dew from the LORD,
like showers on the grass,
which do not wait for anyone
or depend on man.
8 The remnant of Jacob will be among the nations,
in the midst of many peoples,
like a lion among the beasts of the forest,
like a young lion among flocks of sheep,
which mauls and mangles as it goes,
and no one can rescue.
9 Your hand will be lifted up in triumph over your enemies,
and all your foes will be destroyed.

10 "In that day," declares the LORD,

PRAYING SCRIPTURE

Micah 5

God named the birthplace of the "one who will be ruler over Israel, whose origins are from of old, from ancient times" as Bethlehem, a little town in Judah (verse 2). Jesus' New Testament birth narrative identifies this as a prophecy of the birthplace of the Lord and Messiah of Israel.

God was gracious to his people, giving them many prophecies of the promised Messiah. Thank God for his promises that never fail.

[a] In Hebrew texts 5:1 is numbered 4:14, and 5:2-15 is numbered 5:1-14. [b] 2 Or *rulers* [c] 6 Or *crush* [d] 6 Or *Nimrod in its gates*

"I will destroy your horses from among you
and demolish your chariots.
11 I will destroy the cities of your land
and tear down all your strongholds.
12 I will destroy your witchcraft
and you will no longer cast spells.
13 I will destroy your idols
and your sacred stones from among you;
you will no longer bow down
to the work of your hands.
14 I will uproot from among you your Asherah poles[a]
when I demolish your cities.
15 I will take vengeance in anger and wrath
on the nations that have not obeyed me."

THE LORD'S CASE AGAINST ISRAEL

6 Listen to what the LORD says:

"Stand up, plead my case before the mountains;
let the hills hear what you have to say.

2 "Hear, you mountains, the LORD's accusation;
listen, you everlasting foundations of the earth.
For the LORD has a case against his people;
he is lodging a charge against Israel.

3 "My people, what have I done to you?
How have I burdened you? Answer me.
4 I brought you up out of Egypt
and redeemed you from the land of slavery.
I sent Moses to lead you,
also Aaron and Miriam.
5 My people, remember
what Balak king of Moab plotted
and what Balaam son of Beor answered.
Remember your journey from Shittim to Gilgal,
that you may know the righteous acts of the LORD."

6 With what shall I come before the LORD
and bow down before the exalted God?
Shall I come before him with burnt offerings,
with calves a year old?
7 Will the LORD be pleased with thousands of rams,
with ten thousand rivers of olive oil?
Shall I offer my firstborn for my transgression,
the fruit of my body for the sin of my soul?
8 He has shown you, O mortal, what is good.
And what does the LORD require of you?
To act justly and to love mercy
and to walk humbly[b] with your God.

ISRAEL'S GUILT AND PUNISHMENT

9 Listen! The LORD is calling to the city—
and to fear your name is wisdom—

PRAYING SCRIPTURE

Micah 6

The emotion God showed in expressing love for his people might catch some people off guard: "My people, what have I done to you? How have I burdened you? Answer me" (verse 3). The Lord's speech was direct and personal. This is far from the distant, overbearing tyrant many envision when they think of God.

God loves, God is love and God loves you. Humbly thank and praise him for it.

[a] 14 That is, wooden symbols of the goddess Asherah [b] 8 Or *prudently*

"Heed the rod and the One who appointed it.[a]
10 Am I still to forget your ill-gotten treasures, you wicked house,
and the short ephah,[b] which is accursed?
11 Shall I acquit someone with dishonest scales,
with a bag of false weights?
12 Your rich people are violent;
your inhabitants are liars
and their tongues speak deceitfully.
13 Therefore, I have begun to destroy you,
to ruin[c] you because of your sins.
14 You will eat but not be satisfied;
your stomach will still be empty.[d]
You will store up but save nothing,
because what you save[e] I will give to the sword.
15 You will plant but not harvest;
you will press olives but not use the oil,
you will crush grapes but not drink the wine.
16 You have observed the statutes of Omri
and all the practices of Ahab's house;
you have followed their traditions.
Therefore I will give you over to ruin
and your people to derision;
you will bear the scorn of the nations.[f]"

ISRAEL'S MISERY

7 What misery is mine!
I am like one who gathers summer fruit
at the gleaning of the vineyard;
there is no cluster of grapes to eat,
none of the early figs that I crave.
2 The faithful have been swept from the land;
not one upright person remains.
Everyone lies in wait to shed blood;
they hunt each other with nets.
3 Both hands are skilled in doing evil;
the ruler demands gifts,
the judge accepts bribes,
the powerful dictate what they desire —
they all conspire together.
4 The best of them is like a brier,
the most upright worse than a thorn hedge.
The day God visits you has come,
the day your watchmen sound the alarm.
Now is the time of your confusion.
5 Do not trust a neighbor;
put no confidence in a friend.
Even with the woman who lies in your embrace
guard the words of your lips.

PRAYING SCRIPTURE

Micah 7

There are no more blessed verses than those that end Micah: "Who is a God like you, who pardons sin and forgives the transgression of the remnant of his inheritance? . . . You will again have compassion on us . . . and hurl all our iniquities into the depths of the sea" (verses 18–19). The hope of God's forgiveness sets the book aglow.

If you are a child of God worried that God is holding your sin against you, take heart! Rejoice in his full forgiveness.

---

[a] *9* The meaning of the Hebrew for this line is uncertain. [b] *10* An ephah was a dry measure. [c] *13* Or *Therefore, I will make you ill and destroy you; / I will ruin* [d] *14* The meaning of the Hebrew for this word is uncertain. [e] *14* Or *You will press toward birth but not give birth, / and what you bring to birth* [f] *16* Septuagint; Hebrew *scorn due my people*

6 For a son dishonors his father,
a daughter rises up against her mother,
a daughter-in-law against her mother-in-law—
a man's enemies are the members of his own household.

7 But as for me, I watch in hope for the LORD,
I wait for God my Savior;
my God will hear me.

ISRAEL WILL RISE

8 Do not gloat over me, my enemy!
Though I have fallen, I will rise.
Though I sit in darkness,
the LORD will be my light.
9 Because I have sinned against him,
I will bear the LORD's wrath,
until he pleads my case
and upholds my cause.
He will bring me out into the light;
I will see his righteousness.
10 Then my enemy will see it
and will be covered with shame,
she who said to me,
"Where is the LORD your God?"
My eyes will see her downfall;
even now she will be trampled underfoot
like mire in the streets.

11 The day for building your walls will come,
the day for extending your boundaries.
12 In that day people will come to you
from Assyria and the cities of Egypt,
even from Egypt to the Euphrates
and from sea to sea
and from mountain to mountain.
13 The earth will become desolate because of its inhabitants,
as the result of their deeds.

PRAYER AND PRAISE

14 Shepherd your people with your staff,
the flock of your inheritance,
which lives by itself in a forest,
in fertile pasturelands.[a]
Let them feed in Bashan and Gilead
as in days long ago.

15 "As in the days when you came out of Egypt,
I will show them my wonders."

16 Nations will see and be ashamed,
deprived of all their power.
They will put their hands over their mouths
and their ears will become deaf.
17 They will lick dust like a snake,

[a] 14 Or *in the middle of Carmel*

like creatures that crawl on the ground.
They will come trembling out of their dens;
they will turn in fear to the LORD our God
and will be afraid of you.
18 Who is a God like you,
who pardons sin and forgives the transgression
of the remnant of his inheritance?
You do not stay angry forever
but delight to show mercy.
19 You will again have compassion on us;
you will tread our sins underfoot
and hurl all our iniquities into the depths of the sea.
20 You will be faithful to Jacob,
and show love to Abraham,
as you pledged on oath to our ancestors
in days long ago.

NAHUM

Nahum shared little of his personal story in the book that bears his name. No other Biblical books mention his name. The first verse identifies his home as "Elkosh," but so far, its location has not been established. While the details behind the author of the book remain a mystery, Nahum conveyed a simple and straightforward message.

Like so many throughout history, the revival of Nineveh under Jonah's preaching did not last. One hundred years later, God's judgment was near. Nahum devoted significant attention to the fall of Nineveh, which took place in 612 BC. As Nahum referenced the collapse of Thebes in 663 BC, it seems likely he delivered his prophecy between these two events.

The first chapter of Nahum presents God in the beauty of his complex character. First, Nahum stressed God's wondrous holiness and his wrath against sin. He described God as jealous. This should not be understood as typical human desire, as if God could want what someone else has. Instead, God's jealousy is the desire of a husband for his wife. Just as the husband does not want his wife to take another lover or to commit herself to another man, so the Lord is jealous for his people to love and follow him rather than giving themselves over to idols or false religion.

Nahum echoed Moses (see Exodus 34:6–7), reminding his hearers that the Lord is "slow to anger." Then he made the case that the Lord had been patient for a long time and would not hold his anger back forever. That God "will not leave the guilty unpunished" (1:3) remains true, though faith in Jesus changed the calculus. Those who believe in him are forgiven and considered righteous.

Indeed, the gospel is foreshadowed in Nahum: "Look, there on the mountains, the feet of one who brings good news, who proclaims peace!" (1:15). Paul connected this prophecy (and that of Isaiah 52:7) to the preaching of the gospel. He asked in Romans 10:15, "And how can anyone preach unless they are sent?" before quoting the Old Testament prophecies. Those who bring the gospel bring peace between God and humankind. It is good news!

As with many of the Minor Prophets, there is no direct teaching on prayer in Nahum. The pronouncement of judgment was so certain in Nahum, even right at hand, that the time for repentance was past. The Lord is good, and he is a refuge when trouble comes (see 1:7). However, when the Lord has set himself against a people, the results could be horrific: He would show them as naked and ashamed before other nations and kingdoms (see 3:5); he would pelt them with filth and treat them with contempt; and he would turn them into a spectacle that no one wanted to see (see 3:6–7). Our hope in God is that we will not face judgment because of Jesus.

We pray for friends, neighbors and family members, for all who are separated from God remain under judgment. Because God will not acquit the wicked, it is important to pray that they come to Christ. Remembering the brevity of our time here on earth and the reality of God's wrath ought to drive us to our knees to plead for the souls of those we love.

1 A prophecy concerning Nineveh. The book of the vision of Nahum the Elkoshite.

THE LORD'S ANGER AGAINST NINEVEH

2 The LORD is a jealous and avenging God;
the LORD takes vengeance and is filled with wrath.
The LORD takes vengeance on his foes
and vents his wrath against his enemies.
3 The LORD is slow to anger but great in power;
the LORD will not leave the guilty unpunished.
His way is in the whirlwind and the storm,
and clouds are the dust of his feet.
4 He rebukes the sea and dries it up;
he makes all the rivers run dry.
Bashan and Carmel wither
and the blossoms of Lebanon fade.
5 The mountains quake before him
and the hills melt away.
The earth trembles at his presence,
the world and all who live in it.
6 Who can withstand his indignation?
Who can endure his fierce anger?
His wrath is poured out like fire;
the rocks are shattered before him.

7 The LORD is good,
a refuge in times of trouble.
He cares for those who trust in him,
8 but with an overwhelming flood
he will make an end of Nineveh;
he will pursue his foes into the realm of darkness.

9 Whatever they plot against the LORD
he will bring[a] to an end;
trouble will not come a second time.
10 They will be entangled among thorns
and drunk from their wine;
they will be consumed like dry stubble.[b]
11 From you, Nineveh, has one come forth
who plots evil against the LORD
and devises wicked plans.

12 This is what the LORD says:

"Although they have allies and are numerous,
they will be destroyed and pass away.
Although I have afflicted you, Judah,
I will afflict you no more.
13 Now I will break their yoke from your neck
and tear your shackles away."

14 The LORD has given a command concerning you, Nineveh:
"You will have no descendants to bear your name.

[a] 9 Or *What do you foes plot against the LORD? / He will bring it* [b] 10 The meaning of the Hebrew for this verse is uncertain.

PRAYING SCRIPTURE

Nahum 1

Nahum wasted no time and jumped right into the character of God as an avenger and as One who is good. Many mistakenly think God is one or the other, but Scripture teaches that he is both. God's character is perfect and complete. He never becomes unbalanced at any time.

Think for a while about how good it is that God is perfect in his characteristics. Be thankful that he is never out of control.

I will destroy the images and idols
that are in the temple of your gods.
I will prepare your grave,
for you are vile."

15 Look, there on the mountains,
the feet of one who brings good news,
who proclaims peace!
Celebrate your festivals, Judah,
and fulfill your vows.
No more will the wicked invade you;
they will be completely destroyed.[a]

NINEVEH TO FALL

2 [b] An attacker advances against you, Nineveh.
Guard the fortress,
watch the road,
brace yourselves,
marshal all your strength!

2 The LORD will restore the splendor of Jacob
like the splendor of Israel,
though destroyers have laid them waste
and have ruined their vines.

3 The shields of the soldiers are red;
the warriors are clad in scarlet.
The metal on the chariots flashes
on the day they are made ready;
the spears of juniper are brandished.[c]
4 The chariots storm through the streets,
rushing back and forth through the squares.
They look like flaming torches;
they dart about like lightning.

5 Nineveh summons her picked troops,
yet they stumble on their way.
They dash to the city wall;
the protective shield is put in place.
6 The river gates are thrown open
and the palace collapses.
7 It is decreed[d] that Nineveh
be exiled and carried away.
Her female slaves moan like doves
and beat on their breasts.
8 Nineveh is like a pool
whose water is draining away.
"Stop! Stop!" they cry,
but no one turns back.
9 Plunder the silver!
Plunder the gold!
The supply is endless,
the wealth from all its treasures!

PRAYING SCRIPTURE
Nahum 2

To restore the splendor of Jacob like the splendor of Israel, Nineveh would come under judgment (see verse 2). God set his face against the Ninevites, and they fled. Perhaps this is the judgment that was averted when revival came to Nineveh under Jonah's earlier preaching.

Sustained obedience is important to God. Obedience then rebellion always arouses God's anger. Pray for the wisdom and humility to seek God each day.

[a] *15* In Hebrew texts this verse (1:15) is numbered 2:1. [b] In Hebrew texts 2:1-13 is numbered 2:2-14. [c] *3* Hebrew; Septuagint and Syriac *ready; / the horsemen rush to and fro.* [d] *7* The meaning of the Hebrew for this word is uncertain.

10 She is pillaged, plundered, stripped!
Hearts melt, knees give way,
bodies tremble, every face grows pale.

11 Where now is the lions' den,
the place where they fed their young,
where the lion and lioness went,
and the cubs, with nothing to fear?
12 The lion killed enough for his cubs
and strangled the prey for his mate,
filling his lairs with the kill
and his dens with the prey.

13 "I am against you,"
declares the LORD Almighty.
"I will burn up your chariots in smoke,
and the sword will devour your young lions.
I will leave you no prey on the earth.
The voices of your messengers
will no longer be heard."

WOE TO NINEVEH

3 Woe to the city of blood,
full of lies,
full of plunder,
never without victims!
2 The crack of whips,
the clatter of wheels,
galloping horses
and jolting chariots!
3 Charging cavalry,
flashing swords
and glittering spears!
Many casualties,
piles of dead,
bodies without number,
people stumbling over the corpses —
4 all because of the wanton lust of a prostitute,
alluring, the mistress of sorceries,
who enslaved nations by her prostitution
and peoples by her witchcraft.

5 "I am against you," declares the LORD Almighty.
"I will lift your skirts over your face.
I will show the nations your nakedness
and the kingdoms your shame.
6 I will pelt you with filth,
I will treat you with contempt
and make you a spectacle.
7 All who see you will flee from you and say,
'Nineveh is in ruins — who will mourn for her?'
Where can I find anyone to comfort you?"

8 Are you better than Thebes,
situated on the Nile,
with water around her?

PRAYING SCRIPTURE

Nahum 3

Again, Scripture shows the futility of trusting in the strength of human beings rather than in the Lord. Nineveh's destruction was horrific: "many casualties, piles of dead, bodies without number, people stumbling over the corpses" (verse 3). So many were killed that people tripped over the bodies in the street.

Even the possibility of judgment of countries and peoples should drive us to intercede that God would pour his abundant mercy out on them.

The river was her defense,
the waters her wall.
9 Cush[a] and Egypt were her boundless strength;
Put and Libya were among her allies.
10 Yet she was taken captive
and went into exile.
Her infants were dashed to pieces
at every street corner.
Lots were cast for her nobles,
and all her great men were put in chains.
11 You too will become drunk;
you will go into hiding
and seek refuge from the enemy.

12 All your fortresses are like fig trees
with their first ripe fruit;
when they are shaken,
the figs fall into the mouth of the eater.
13 Look at your troops —
they are all weaklings.
The gates of your land
are wide open to your enemies;
fire has consumed the bars of your gates.

14 Draw water for the siege,
strengthen your defenses!
Work the clay,
tread the mortar,
repair the brickwork!
15 There the fire will consume you;
the sword will cut you down —
they will devour you like a swarm of locusts.
Multiply like grasshoppers,
multiply like locusts!
16 You have increased the number of your merchants
till they are more numerous than the stars in the sky,
but like locusts they strip the land
and then fly away.
17 Your guards are like locusts,
your officials like swarms of locusts
that settle in the walls on a cold day —
but when the sun appears they fly away,
and no one knows where.

18 King of Assyria, your shepherds[b] slumber;
your nobles lie down to rest.
Your people are scattered on the mountains
with no one to gather them.
19 Nothing can heal you;
your wound is fatal.
All who hear the news about you
clap their hands at your fall,
for who has not felt
your endless cruelty?

---

[a] *9* That is, the upper Nile region [b] *18* That is, rulers

HABAKKUK

Habakkuk gave little personal detail in his prophecy; his biography is nonexistent. He did not provide his father's name, a story of his calling or a list of the kings who reigned while he prophesied. The only possible hint to the timing of his ministry is the reference in Habakkuk 1:6 to God raising up the Babylonians, who destroyed Jerusalem and sent Judah into exile in 587 BC. Habakkuk delivered his message prior to this date.

Chapters 1 and 2 contain a remarkable address from the prophet to the Lord. Ordinarily, people question God because they wonder how a loving God could allow suffering. Habakkuk's issue is different: He wanted to know why a just and holy God would allow people to continue sinning. He appealed to God's righteous character and asked how long he would wait to act.

When Christians plead with God in prayer, it is wise to do so based on what he teaches about himself in his Word. We pray for God to save people based on his love and compassion, not because they are "good neighbors" who deserve to be saved. And, because God is just and righteous, we can pray for just and righteous outcomes for godly people who are suffering.

Habakkuk also serves as a reminder that we are allowed to question God in prayer. If we are to pray about whatever makes us anxious (see Philippians 4:6–7), we can pray about aspects of God's will for us that we don't understand. This is what Habakkuk did in 3:2: "I have heard of your fame; I stand in awe of your deeds, LORD." There is nothing inherently spiritual about sterile prayers that don't exhibit open, honest communication with the Lord. Pleading with God for answers or expressing our feelings is a benefit of being his child.

A foundational verse for Christian living, quoted three times in the New Testament, is in 2:4: "the righteous person will live by his faithfulness," contrasted with the sinful soul of the proud (see Romans 1:17; Galatians 3:11; Hebrews 10:38). The just not only are saved by faith, but they are to live by faith. Salvation is not a "believe once and be done" relationship. The way we come to God, by faith, is the way we live with him day by day.

Chapter 3 closes with a hymn of praise to God, expressing trust in him. Habakkuk knows that because of God's righteous character and eternal purpose, he should be praised even when the tree does not bud, the vines do not bear fruit, the fields produce no food and there are no cattle in the stalls (see 3:17–18). Because God is simultaneously all-powerful and all-loving, we can express trust in him even when our world seems to be falling apart.

Habakkuk's parting thought informs our prayers and strengthens our faith when we are walking in difficult times. God is our strength. He has the power to make our feet sure like the feet of a deer so we can tread on the heights. Ask God for the faith to walk with him through any valley or over any mountain where he leads.

PRAYING SCRIPTURE

Habakkuk 1

Habakkuk reminds us of a harsh reality: The wicked are often in charge, and when they are "justice is perverted" (verse 4). He complained that God was waiting too long to bring justice to the violent plundering he witnessed.

"How long" (verse 2) is the prayer of lament seen over and over in Scripture. It should be the prayer of those today who want God to stop the injustices and violence that pervade our world.

1 The prophecy that Habakkuk the prophet received.

HABAKKUK'S COMPLAINT

2 How long, LORD, must I call for help,
but you do not listen?
Or cry out to you, "Violence!"
but you do not save?
3 Why do you make me look at injustice?
Why do you tolerate wrongdoing?
Destruction and violence are before me;
there is strife, and conflict abounds.
4 Therefore the law is paralyzed,
and justice never prevails.
The wicked hem in the righteous,
so that justice is perverted.

THE LORD'S ANSWER

5 "Look at the nations and watch—
and be utterly amazed.
For I am going to do something in your days
that you would not believe,
even if you were told.
6 I am raising up the Babylonians,[a]
that ruthless and impetuous people,
who sweep across the whole earth
to seize dwellings not their own.
7 They are a feared and dreaded people;
they are a law to themselves
and promote their own honor.
8 Their horses are swifter than leopards,
fiercer than wolves at dusk.
Their cavalry gallops headlong;
their horsemen come from afar.
They fly like an eagle swooping to devour;
9 they all come intent on violence.
Their hordes[b] advance like a desert wind
and gather prisoners like sand.
10 They mock kings
and scoff at rulers.
They laugh at all fortified cities;
by building earthen ramps they capture them.
11 Then they sweep past like the wind and go on—
guilty people, whose own strength is their god."

HABAKKUK'S SECOND COMPLAINT

12 LORD, are you not from everlasting?
My God, my Holy One, you[c] will never die.
You, LORD, have appointed them to execute judgment;
you, my Rock, have ordained them to punish.
13 Your eyes are too pure to look on evil;
you cannot tolerate wrongdoing.

---

[a] 6 Or *Chaldeans* [b] 9 The meaning of the Hebrew for this word is uncertain. [c] 12 An ancient Hebrew scribal tradition; Masoretic Text *we*

Why then do you tolerate the treacherous?
  Why are you silent while the wicked
  swallow up those more righteous than themselves?
14 You have made people like the fish in the sea,
  like the sea creatures that have no ruler.
15 The wicked foe pulls all of them up with hooks,
  he catches them in his net,
he gathers them up in his dragnet;
  and so he rejoices and is glad.
16 Therefore he sacrifices to his net
  and burns incense to his dragnet,
for by his net he lives in luxury
  and enjoys the choicest food.
17 Is he to keep on emptying his net,
  destroying nations without mercy?

2 I will stand at my watch
  and station myself on the ramparts;
I will look to see what he will say to me,
  and what answer I am to give to this complaint.[a]

THE LORD'S ANSWER

2 Then the LORD replied:

"Write down the revelation
  and make it plain on tablets
  so that a herald[b] may run with it.
3 For the revelation awaits an appointed time;
  it speaks of the end
  and will not prove false.
Though it linger, wait for it;
  it[c] will certainly come
  and will not delay.

4 "See, the enemy is puffed up;
  his desires are not upright—
  but the righteous person will live by his faithfulness[d]—
5 indeed, wine betrays him;
  he is arrogant and never at rest.
Because he is as greedy as the grave
  and like death is never satisfied,
he gathers to himself all the nations
  and takes captive all the peoples.

6 "Will not all of them taunt him with ridicule and scorn, saying,

" 'Woe to him who piles up stolen goods
  and makes himself wealthy by extortion!
  How long must this go on?'
7 Will not your creditors suddenly arise?
  Will they not wake up and make you tremble?
  Then you will become their prey.
8 Because you have plundered many nations,
  the peoples who are left will plunder you.

[a] 1 Or *and what to answer when I am rebuked* [b] 2 Or *so that whoever reads it* [c] 3 Or *Though he linger, wait for him; / he* [d] 4 Or *faith*

PRAYING SCRIPTURE

Habakkuk 2

After a devastating series of woes pronounced on the wicked and a summary of the futility of idol worship, Habakkuk rendered a beautiful reminder of hope and assurance: "The LORD is in his holy temple; let all the earth be silence before him" (verse 20).

What a faith-building verse. When you are anxious, begin prayer with the acknowledgment that God is where he's supposed to be and in total control of his creation.

For you have shed human blood;
you have destroyed lands and cities and everyone in them.

9 "Woe to him who builds his house by unjust gain,
setting his nest on high
to escape the clutches of ruin!
10 You have plotted the ruin of many peoples,
shaming your own house and forfeiting your life.
11 The stones of the wall will cry out,
and the beams of the woodwork will echo it.

12 "Woe to him who builds a city with bloodshed
and establishes a town by injustice!
13 Has not the LORD Almighty determined
that the people's labor is only fuel for the fire,
that the nations exhaust themselves for nothing?
14 For the earth will be filled with the knowledge of the glory of the LORD
as the waters cover the sea.

15 "Woe to him who gives drink to his neighbors,
pouring it from the wineskin till they are drunk,
so that he can gaze on their naked bodies!
16 You will be filled with shame instead of glory.
Now it is your turn! Drink and let your nakedness be exposed[a]!
The cup from the LORD's right hand is coming around to you,
and disgrace will cover your glory.
17 The violence you have done to Lebanon will overwhelm you,
and your destruction of animals will terrify you.
For you have shed human blood;
you have destroyed lands and cities and everyone in them.

18 "Of what value is an idol carved by a craftsman?
Or an image that teaches lies?
For the one who makes it trusts in his own creation;
he makes idols that cannot speak.
19 Woe to him who says to wood, 'Come to life!'
Or to lifeless stone, 'Wake up!'
Can it give guidance?
It is covered with gold and silver;
there is no breath in it."

20 The LORD is in his holy temple;
let all the earth be silent before him.

HABAKKUK'S PRAYER

3 A prayer of Habakkuk the prophet. On *shigionoth.*[b]

2 LORD, I have heard of your fame;
I stand in awe of your deeds, LORD.
Repeat them in our day,
in our time make them known;
in wrath remember mercy.

[a] *16* Masoretic Text; Dead Sea Scrolls, Aquila, Vulgate and Syriac (see also Septuagint) *and stagger* [b] *1* Probably a literary or musical term

PRAYING SCRIPTURE

Habakkuk 3

The brief hymn of assurance that ends Habakkuk (see verses 17–19) is among the most encouraging in Scripture. Even if nothing returns to normal, no fruit comes from the vines and the stalls are empty, we can rejoice in God. He is our strength, giving us surefootedness to walk even in the high places.

Do you take time in trials, as Habakkuk did, to express your hope in God? Your faith will be strengthened if you do.

3 God came from Teman,
the Holy One from Mount Paran.[a]
His glory covered the heavens
and his praise filled the earth.
4 His splendor was like the sunrise;
rays flashed from his hand,
where his power was hidden.
5 Plague went before him;
pestilence followed his steps.
6 He stood, and shook the earth;
he looked, and made the nations tremble.
The ancient mountains crumbled
and the age-old hills collapsed —
but he marches on forever.
7 I saw the tents of Cushan in distress,
the dwellings of Midian in anguish.

8 Were you angry with the rivers, LORD?
Was your wrath against the streams?
Did you rage against the sea
when you rode your horses
and your chariots to victory?
9 You uncovered your bow,
you called for many arrows.
You split the earth with rivers;
10 the mountains saw you and writhed.
Torrents of water swept by;
the deep roared
and lifted its waves on high.

11 Sun and moon stood still in the heavens
at the glint of your flying arrows,
at the lightning of your flashing spear.
12 In wrath you strode through the earth
and in anger you threshed the nations.
13 You came out to deliver your people,
to save your anointed one.
You crushed the leader of the land of wickedness,
you stripped him from head to foot.
14 With his own spear you pierced his head
when his warriors stormed out to scatter us,
gloating as though about to devour
the wretched who were in hiding.
15 You trampled the sea with your horses,
churning the great waters.

16 I heard and my heart pounded,
my lips quivered at the sound;
decay crept into my bones,
and my legs trembled.
Yet I will wait patiently for the day of calamity
to come on the nation invading us.

---

[a] *3* The Hebrew has *Selah* (a word of uncertain meaning) here and at the middle of verse 9 and at the end of verse 13.

17 Though the fig tree does not bud
and there are no grapes on the vines,
though the olive crop fails
and the fields produce no food,
though there are no sheep in the pen
and no cattle in the stalls,
18 yet I will rejoice in the LORD,
I will be joyful in God my Savior.

19 The Sovereign LORD is my strength;
he makes my feet like the feet of a deer,
he enables me to tread on the heights.

For the director of music. On my stringed instruments.

ZEPHANIAH

Zephaniah prophesied during the reign of King Josiah in Judah. Josiah reformed life in Judah after reading the scroll containing the book of Deuteronomy. He abolished idolatrous practices and reinstated worship according to God's Word. It was celebrated as a time of revival in the midst of the darkening days of the kings, as Josiah was one of the few kings who led the people to follow God.

Zephaniah centered his prophecy on God's judgment. In 1:2 he related God's words, "I will sweep away everything from the face of the earth," including animals, fish, birds and humans. Then he expounded on the coming "day of the LORD" followed by a time of hope for Israel's remnant who will experience God's faithfulness (see 1:14—3:8; 3:9–20).

Zephaniah possessed a double-sided vision of the day of the Lord. First, he saw it as a day of judgment in which those who had opposed God and his people would receive what they were justly due. Gaza, Ashkelon, Ashdod, Ekron and others would be uprooted and destroyed (see 2:4–5). At the same time, he saw it as a day of salvation for God's people, not just because they would be welcomed into God's presence, but because they would be delivered from the harassment and persecution of the nations and be given recompense. Some from Judah would even live in their enemies' abandoned homes (see 2:7).

It was not only surrounding nations, however, that were in sin. God pronounced judgment on Jerusalem for being oppressive, rebellious and defiled. Her officials, prophets and priests were all ungodly and wicked. Yet, while the surrounding nations would be destroyed, Jerusalem would ultimately be saved.

Persecution of God's people is not limited to Old Testament Israel and Judah. Since the birth of the church at Pentecost, God's people have been subject to persecution. Jesus promised persecution would come (see John 15:20). Paul's journeys in Acts and list of the persecuted in Hebrews 11 shows that faith is not always an easy walk with God. When we face persecution or harassment, we can pray several different ways. First, we can pray for God to awaken our harassers to repent and turn to him. Also, we can pray that God will help us to bless those who persecute us and not to curse them (see Luke 6:28). Finally, even though God's people can expect to suffer persecution, we can pray both for the strength to endure and for deliverance to come. God hears both pleas.

Similar to ancient Israel, we also look forward to another day of the Lord: The return of the Lord Jesus Christ to gather his own to himself. It is a day of salvation for us; we will be like him and see him as he is. We will experience the final release from pain and suffering, delivered not only from the penalty of sin but from its very presence. We should also pray for the Lord to hasten this day, knowing that when Jesus returns, all things will be made new.

PRAYING SCRIPTURE

Zephaniah 1

In Zephaniah's prophecy against Josiah, it is clear that the Lord's patience is spent. A time of judgment is coming in which he will utterly consume everything from the face of the earth and completely destroy idolatrous Judah (see verse 3). It would be called a "day of the LORD."

There is yet coming a day of the Lord during which all wickedness will be destroyed forever. Pray for those you know to repent and seek Jesus today.

1 The word of the LORD that came to Zephaniah son of Cushi, the son of Gedaliah, the son of Amariah, the son of Hezekiah, during the reign of Josiah son of Amon king of Judah:

JUDGMENT ON THE WHOLE EARTH IN THE DAY OF THE LORD

2 "I will sweep away everything
from the face of the earth,"
declares the LORD.

3 "I will sweep away both man and beast;
I will sweep away the birds in the sky
and the fish in the sea —
and the idols that cause the wicked to stumble."[a]
"When I destroy all mankind
on the face of the earth,"
declares the LORD,
4 "I will stretch out my hand against Judah
and against all who live in Jerusalem.
I will destroy every remnant of Baal worship in this place,
the very names of the idolatrous priests —
5 those who bow down on the roofs
to worship the starry host,
those who bow down and swear by the LORD
and who also swear by Molek,[b]
6 those who turn back from following the LORD
and neither seek the LORD nor inquire of him."

7 Be silent before the Sovereign LORD,
for the day of the LORD is near.
The LORD has prepared a sacrifice;
he has consecrated those he has invited.

8 "On the day of the LORD's sacrifice
I will punish the officials
and the king's sons
and all those clad
in foreign clothes.
9 On that day I will punish
all who avoid stepping on the threshold,[c]
who fill the temple of their gods
with violence and deceit.

10 "On that day,"
declares the LORD,
"a cry will go up from the Fish Gate,
wailing from the New Quarter,
and a loud crash from the hills.
11 Wail, you who live in the market district[d];
all your merchants will be wiped out,
all who trade with[e] silver will be destroyed.
12 At that time I will search Jerusalem with lamps
and punish those who are complacent,
who are like wine left on its dregs,

[a] 3 The meaning of the Hebrew for this line is uncertain. [b] 5 Hebrew *Malkam* [c] 9 See 1 Samuel 5:5. [d] 11 Or *the Mortar* [e] 11 Or *in*

who think, 'The LORD will do nothing,
either good or bad.'
13 Their wealth will be plundered,
their houses demolished.
Though they build houses,
they will not live in them;
though they plant vineyards,
they will not drink the wine."

14 The great day of the LORD is near—
near and coming quickly.
The cry on the day of the LORD is bitter;
the Mighty Warrior shouts his battle cry.
15 That day will be a day of wrath—
a day of distress and anguish,
a day of trouble and ruin,
a day of darkness and gloom,
a day of clouds and blackness—
16 a day of trumpet and battle cry
against the fortified cities
and against the corner towers.

17 "I will bring such distress on all people
that they will grope about like those who are blind,
because they have sinned against the LORD.
Their blood will be poured out like dust
and their entrails like dung.
18 Neither their silver nor their gold
will be able to save them
on the day of the LORD's wrath."

In the fire of his jealousy
the whole earth will be consumed,
for he will make a sudden end
of all who live on the earth.

JUDAH AND JERUSALEM JUDGED ALONG WITH THE NATIONS

JUDAH SUMMONED TO REPENT

2 Gather together, gather yourselves together,
you shameful nation,
2 before the decree takes effect
and that day passes like windblown chaff,
before the LORD's fierce anger
comes upon you,
before the day of the LORD's wrath
comes upon you.
3 Seek the LORD, all you humble of the land,
you who do what he commands.
Seek righteousness, seek humility;
perhaps you will be sheltered
on the day of the LORD's anger.

PHILISTIA

4 Gaza will be abandoned
and Ashkelon left in ruins.

PRAYING SCRIPTURE

Zephaniah 2

Again, prior to judging the nations, God provided an opportunity for repentance. He implored those who sought righteousness to gather "before the decree takes effect and that day passes like windblown chaff . . . Seek the LORD, all you humble of the land" (verses 2–3). Even those who were otherwise humble needed to be aware of the severity of God's anger.

The Lord is always a hiding place for those who fear him. Seek him at all times.

At midday Ashdod will be emptied
and Ekron uprooted.
5 Woe to you who live by the sea,
you Kerethite people;
the word of the LORD is against you,
Canaan, land of the Philistines.
He says, "I will destroy you,
and none will be left."
6 The land by the sea will become pastures
having wells for shepherds
and pens for flocks.
7 That land will belong
to the remnant of the people of Judah;
there they will find pasture.
In the evening they will lie down
in the houses of Ashkelon.
The LORD their God will care for them;
he will restore their fortunes.[a]

MOAB AND AMMON

8 "I have heard the insults of Moab
and the taunts of the Ammonites,
who insulted my people
and made threats against their land.
9 Therefore, as surely as I live,"
declares the LORD Almighty,
the God of Israel,
"surely Moab will become like Sodom,
the Ammonites like Gomorrah —
a place of weeds and salt pits,
a wasteland forever.
The remnant of my people will plunder them;
the survivors of my nation will inherit their land."
10 This is what they will get in return for their pride,
for insulting and mocking
the people of the LORD Almighty.
11 The LORD will be awesome to them
when he destroys all the gods of the earth.
Distant nations will bow down to him,
all of them in their own lands.

CUSH

12 "You Cushites,[b] too,
will be slain by my sword."

ASSYRIA

13 He will stretch out his hand against the north
and destroy Assyria,
leaving Nineveh utterly desolate
and dry as the desert.
14 Flocks and herds will lie down there,
creatures of every kind.

---

[a] 7 Or *will bring back their captives*
[b] 12 That is, people from the upper Nile region

The desert owl and the screech owl
  will roost on her columns.
Their hooting will echo through the windows,
  rubble will fill the doorways,
  the beams of cedar will be exposed.
15 This is the city of revelry
  that lived in safety.
She said to herself,
  "I am the one! And there is none besides me."
What a ruin she has become,
  a lair for wild beasts!
All who pass by her scoff
  and shake their fists.

JERUSALEM

3 Woe to the city of oppressors,
  rebellious and defiled!
2 She obeys no one,
  she accepts no correction.
She does not trust in the LORD,
  she does not draw near to her God.
3 Her officials within her
  are roaring lions;
her rulers are evening wolves,
  who leave nothing for the morning.
4 Her prophets are unprincipled;
  they are treacherous people.
Her priests profane the sanctuary
  and do violence to the law.
5 The LORD within her is righteous;
  he does no wrong.
Morning by morning he dispenses his justice,
  and every new day he does not fail,
  yet the unrighteous know no shame.

JERUSALEM REMAINS UNREPENTANT

6 "I have destroyed nations;
  their strongholds are demolished.
I have left their streets deserted,
  with no one passing through.
Their cities are laid waste;
  they are deserted and empty.
7 Of Jerusalem I thought,
  'Surely you will fear me
  and accept correction!'
Then her place of refuge[a] would not be destroyed,
  nor all my punishments come upon[b] her.
But they were still eager
  to act corruptly in all they did.
8 Therefore wait for me,"
  declares the LORD,
  "for the day I will stand up to testify.[c]

PRAYING SCRIPTURE

Zephaniah 3

As horrific and sure as God's judgment sounds, he reminds his people that there is an end purpose: their restoration. The people will once again worship their Lord. They will again bring offerings. They will again be meek, humble and filled with faith. This remnant will trust God.

Every living child of God is part of a remnant God is reserving for himself. Let your worship be a testimony of his mercy and grace.

---

[a] 7 Or *her sanctuary* [b] 7 Or *all those I appointed over* [c] 8 Septuagint and Syriac; Hebrew *will rise up to plunder*

I have decided to assemble the nations,
to gather the kingdoms
and to pour out my wrath on them —
all my fierce anger.
The whole world will be consumed
by the fire of my jealous anger.

RESTORATION OF ISRAEL'S REMNANT

9 "Then I will purify the lips of the peoples,
that all of them may call on the name of the LORD
and serve him shoulder to shoulder.
10 From beyond the rivers of Cush[a]
my worshipers, my scattered people,
will bring me offerings.
11 On that day you, Jerusalem, will not be put to shame
for all the wrongs you have done to me,
because I will remove from you
your arrogant boasters.
Never again will you be haughty
on my holy hill.
12 But I will leave within you
the meek and humble.
The remnant of Israel
will trust in the name of the LORD.
13 They will do no wrong;
they will tell no lies.
A deceitful tongue
will not be found in their mouths.
They will eat and lie down
and no one will make them afraid."

14 Sing, Daughter Zion;
shout aloud, Israel!
Be glad and rejoice with all your heart,
Daughter Jerusalem!
15 The LORD has taken away your punishment,
he has turned back your enemy.
The LORD, the King of Israel, is with you;
never again will you fear any harm.
16 On that day
they will say to Jerusalem,
"Do not fear, Zion;
do not let your hands hang limp.
17 The LORD your God is with you,
the Mighty Warrior who saves.
He will take great delight in you;
in his love he will no longer rebuke you,
but will rejoice over you with singing."

18 "I will remove from you
all who mourn over the loss of your appointed festivals,
which is a burden and reproach for you.
19 At that time I will deal
with all who oppressed you.

---

[a] *10* That is, the upper Nile region

I will rescue the lame;
  I will gather the exiles.
I will give them praise and honor
  in every land where they have suffered shame.
20 At that time I will gather you;
  at that time I will bring you home.
I will give you honor and praise
  among all the peoples of the earth
when I restore your fortunes[a]
  before your very eyes,"

says the LORD.

[a] 20 Or *I bring back your captives*

HAGGAI

Haggai identified the setting for his prophecy as the second year of King Darius's reign. By consulting other passages of Scripture, we can identify the contemporary events leading to Haggai's preaching. Babylon ransacked Jerusalem and sent Judah to exile in 586 BC. Exiles returned 50 years later to begin rebuilding the temple, but their work ceased when they ran into opposition (see Ezra 1–3). Notable is Haggai's use of specific dates (see 1:1,15; 2:1,10,20), reminding us of how the Bible's events are located in real-world history.

When Haggai's ministry began, the people were working on their houses and neglecting work on the temple, the house of God. His first message was directed to Zerubbabel, the governor of Judah, and Joshua, the chief priest. After challenging them on the lack of work on God's house—the delay was 16 years—he linked their present distress in the land to their neglect in rebuilding. The Lord told his people to consider the results of their ways: "You have planted much, but harvested little. You eat, but never have enough. You drink, but never have your fill" (1:6). The woes continued still.

As the people resumed their work on the temple, Haggai focused his message on reassuring them that the Lord would be with them, that he would strengthen them in their work. He promised that the Lord would restore their fortunes and the land's productivity. Although the rebuilt temple did not have the glory of the former temple (see 2:3), God assured them that his Spirit remained with them just as when they escaped from Egypt.

God's future judgment would feature a shaking of all nations. Then what is desired by all nations would come, and God's house would once again be filled with glory (see 2:6–7). That which is "desired by all nations" has been interpreted as Jesus the Messiah, who would fill the eternal temple—his people—with a glory greater than any structural temple.

These promises of hope did not alleviate the reality of the people's sin. God likened their attempts at holiness with a priest doing ministry. God explained that if the priest carried consecrated meat in the fold of his garment and accidentally touched some other food, the latter food would not be consecrated. They could not be "holiness adjacent."

While we are not saved by our good works, we recognize that blessings are associated with obedience to God. Our lives tend to be marked more by joy and blessing when we love God with our whole heart and walk with a clear conscience before him. Even though we live in community, we must pursue holiness personally.

Although God pronounced judgment and called for repentance through the prophet Haggai, no corporate repentance is recorded. There is no record of prayer, sackcloth, ashes or fasting, even though God forgives those who call on him. Scripture is clear that the only response to sin is repentance. We do well to confess any sin among us, knowing the one who is desired by all nations sits enthroned as Lord over every tribe, people and language in the world.

A CALL TO BUILD THE HOUSE OF THE LORD

1 In the second year of King Darius, on the first day of the sixth month, the word of the LORD came through the prophet Haggai to Zerubbabel son of Shealtiel, governor of Judah, and to Joshua son of Jozadak,[a] the high priest:

2This is what the LORD Almighty says: "These people say, 'The time has not yet come to rebuild the LORD's house.'"

3Then the word of the LORD came through the prophet Haggai: 4"Is it a time for you yourselves to be living in your paneled houses, while this house remains a ruin?"

5Now this is what the LORD Almighty says: "Give careful thought to your ways. 6You have planted much, but harvested little. You eat, but never have enough. You drink, but never have your fill. You put on clothes, but are not warm. You earn wages, only to put them in a purse with holes in it."

7This is what the LORD Almighty says: "Give careful thought to your ways. 8Go up into the mountains and bring down timber and build my house, so that I may take pleasure in it and be honored," says the LORD. 9"You expected much, but see, it turned out to be little. What you brought home, I blew away. Why?" declares the LORD Almighty. "Because of my house, which remains a ruin, while each of you is busy with your own house. 10Therefore, because of you the heavens have withheld their dew and the earth its crops. 11I called for a drought on the fields and the mountains, on the grain, the new wine, the olive oil and everything else the ground produces, on people and livestock, and on all the labor of your hands."

12Then Zerubbabel son of Shealtiel, Joshua son of Jozadak, the high priest, and the whole remnant of the people obeyed the voice of the LORD their God and the message of the prophet Haggai, because the LORD their God had sent him. And the people feared the LORD.

13Then Haggai, the LORD's messenger, gave this message of the LORD to the people: "I am with you," declares the LORD. 14So the LORD stirred up the spirit of Zerubbabel son of Shealtiel, governor of Judah, and the spirit of Joshua son of Jozadak, the high priest, and the spirit of the whole remnant of the people. They came and began to work on the house of the LORD Almighty, their God, 15on the twenty-fourth day of the sixth month.

THE PROMISED GLORY OF THE NEW HOUSE

2 In the second year of King Darius, 1on the twenty-first day of the seventh month, the word of the LORD came through the prophet Haggai: 2"Speak to Zerubbabel son of Shealtiel, governor of Judah, to Joshua son of Jozadak,[b] the high priest, and to the remnant of the people. Ask them, 3'Who of you is left who saw this house in its former glory? How does it look to you now? Does it not seem to you like nothing? 4But now be strong, Zerubbabel,' declares the LORD. 'Be strong, Joshua son of Jozadak, the high priest. Be strong, all you people of the land,' declares the LORD, 'and work. For I am with you,' declares the LORD Almighty. 5'This is what I covenanted with you when you came out of Egypt. And my Spirit remains among you. Do not fear.'

PRAYING SCRIPTURE

Haggai 1

Sometimes we are so busy tending our own comforts that we forget to give our attention to the Lord's work. God's people had given heed to their well-being, but the temple had been neglected, reflecting a lack of worshipful hearts. So the Lord called them to account.

Worship cannot be neglected in favor of material accumulation. If this part of your life has been reversed, confess it to God, and then spend time worshiping him.

PRAYING SCRIPTURE

Haggai 2

God's people were convicted to restore God's house, and so they began the work. Haggai continued to prophesy and included a magnificent promise of the Messiah's coming (see verse 7). God promised to fill the temple with glory, even greater than that of the former temple.

Sometimes God's latter blessing surpasses his earlier blessings. Always call to God in faith that greater things are yet to come.

[a] 1 Hebrew *Jehozadak*, a variant of *Jozadak*; also in verses 12 and 14
[b] 2 Hebrew *Jehozadak*, a variant of *Jozadak*; also in verse 4

6"This is what the LORD Almighty says: 'In a little while I will once more shake the heavens and the earth, the sea and the dry land. 7I will shake all nations, and what is desired by all nations will come, and I will fill this house with glory,' says the LORD Almighty. 8'The silver is mine and the gold is mine,' declares the LORD Almighty. 9'The glory of this present house will be greater than the glory of the former house,' says the LORD Almighty. 'And in this place I will grant peace,' declares the LORD Almighty."

BLESSINGS FOR A DEFILED PEOPLE

10On the twenty-fourth day of the ninth month, in the second year of Darius, the word of the LORD came to the prophet Haggai: 11"This is what the LORD Almighty says: 'Ask the priests what the law says: 12If someone carries consecrated meat in the fold of their garment, and that fold touches some bread or stew, some wine, olive oil or other food, does it become consecrated?'"

The priests answered, "No."

13Then Haggai said, "If a person defiled by contact with a dead body touches one of these things, does it become defiled?"

"Yes," the priests replied, "it becomes defiled."

14Then Haggai said, "'So it is with this people and this nation in my sight,' declares the LORD. 'Whatever they do and whatever they offer there is defiled.

15"'Now give careful thought to this from this day on[a] — consider how things were before one stone was laid on another in the LORD's temple. 16When anyone came to a heap of twenty measures, there were only ten. When anyone went to a wine vat to draw fifty measures, there were only twenty. 17I struck all the work of your hands with blight, mildew and hail, yet you did not return to me,' declares the LORD. 18'From this day on, from this twenty-fourth day of the ninth month, give careful thought to the day when the foundation of the LORD's temple was laid. Give careful thought: 19Is there yet any seed left in the barn? Until now, the vine and the fig tree, the pomegranate and the olive tree have not borne fruit.

"'From this day on I will bless you.'"

ZERUBBABEL THE LORD'S SIGNET RING

20The word of the LORD came to Haggai a second time on the twenty-fourth day of the month: 21"Tell Zerubbabel governor of Judah that I am going to shake the heavens and the earth. 22I will overturn royal thrones and shatter the power of the foreign kingdoms. I will overthrow chariots and their drivers; horses and their riders will fall, each by the sword of his brother.

23"'On that day,' declares the LORD Almighty, 'I will take you, my servant Zerubbabel son of Shealtiel,' declares the LORD, 'and I will make you like my signet ring, for I have chosen you,' declares the LORD Almighty."

---

[a] 15 Or *to the days past*

ZECHARIAH

Along with Haggai, Zechariah's prophecy is situated during the second year of the reign of King Darius. Some Israelites had begun trickling back into Jerusalem after a half century in exile. They began work on the rebuilding of the temple, but opposition caused them to stop. They accepted this status quo and went to work on their homes rather than the house of God.

Zechariah used visionary and symbolic imagery to convey his message. From a macro level, Zechariah can be divided into two major sections: chapters 1–8 and chapters 9–14.

The first six chapters of the prophecy contain eight visions, showing that God is "jealous" for the loyalty of his people. God's jealous desire for his people's hearts to belong to him alone is rooted in his rule over all creation and his special presence among his people through the temple. The remaining eight chapters of the book focus on God as the Shepherd and protector of Israel who will dwell and reign in Jerusalem through the coming Messiah.

In chapter 7, the Lord, speaking through the prophet, reminded the people as he had years before, that obedience is better than sacrifice. He castigated them for not heeding the words of the prophets he'd already sent and questioned their motives for the fasting and mourning they had done: "When you fasted . . . was it really for me?" (7:5–7). God is not impressed by religious acts devoid of holy devotion.

Zechariah centered his prophecy on the idea of God's kingdom. Throughout the book, God's jealousy for Jerusalem is related to the city's role as the seat of his kingdom. He emphasized the need to build the temple because it would be where the Lord would establish his dwelling place among his people. Zechariah foretold of a coming "Branch" who would build the temple of the Lord, but he would also bear the glory of God, sitting and ruling from God's throne as both a king and a priest (see 6:12–13). This prophesied Branch can only be the Messiah, Jesus Christ.

Similarly, when Jesus taught his disciples to pray "Your kingdom come," he was reminding his followers to pray for the expansion of God's kingdom here on earth. If God's kingdom is initiated, as many have defined it—within the rule and reign of God in the hearts of his people—then many of our prayers for the kingdom to come will focus on prayers for more people to come to know Jesus. His kingdom grows one life at a time.

Zechariah closed with an opportunity for repentance and blessing for the nations that came against Jerusalem. They shall annually come to the feast. Pray for that day of the Lord, that the glory of the Lord may be revealed to all.

PRAYING SCRIPTURE

Zechariah 1

The Lord spoke through yet another prophet to assure his people of his love for them. He said, "I am very jealous for Jerusalem and Zion" (verse 14). We miss the measure of God's love when we don't consider the words he uses to describe its intensity.

Express to God your gratitude for how deeply and passionately he loves you. Rejoice in our Lord who is eager to express his love.

A CALL TO RETURN TO THE LORD

1 In the eighth month of the second year of Darius, the word of the
LORD came to the prophet Zechariah son of Berekiah, the son of
Iddo:
2 "The LORD was very angry with your ancestors. 3 Therefore tell the
people: This is what the LORD Almighty says: 'Return to me,' declares
the LORD Almighty, 'and I will return to you,' says the LORD Almighty.
4 Do not be like your ancestors, to whom the earlier prophets pro-
claimed: This is what the LORD Almighty says: 'Turn from your evil
ways and your evil practices.' But they would not listen or pay atten-
tion to me, declares the LORD. 5 Where are your ancestors now? And
the prophets, do they live forever? 6 But did not my words and my de-
crees, which I commanded my servants the prophets, overtake your
ancestors?
"Then they repented and said, 'The LORD Almighty has done to us
what our ways and practices deserve, just as he determined to do.'"

THE MAN AMONG THE MYRTLE TREES

7 On the twenty-fourth day of the eleventh month, the month of She-
bat, in the second year of Darius, the word of the LORD came to the
prophet Zechariah son of Berekiah, the son of Iddo.
8 During the night I had a vision, and there before me was a man
mounted on a red horse. He was standing among the myrtle trees in a
ravine. Behind him were red, brown and white horses.
9 I asked, "What are these, my lord?"
The angel who was talking with me answered, "I will show you what
they are."
10 Then the man standing among the myrtle trees explained, "They
are the ones the LORD has sent to go throughout the earth."
11 And they reported to the angel of the LORD who was standing
among the myrtle trees, "We have gone throughout the earth and
found the whole world at rest and in peace."
12 Then the angel of the LORD said, "LORD Almighty, how long will you
withhold mercy from Jerusalem and from the towns of Judah, which
you have been angry with these seventy years?" 13 So the LORD spoke
kind and comforting words to the angel who talked with me.
14 Then the angel who was speaking to me said, "Proclaim this word:
This is what the LORD Almighty says: 'I am very jealous for Jerusalem
and Zion, 15 and I am very angry with the nations that feel secure. I was
only a little angry, but they went too far with the punishment.'
16 "Therefore this is what the LORD says: 'I will return to Jerusalem
with mercy, and there my house will be rebuilt. And the measuring
line will be stretched out over Jerusalem,' declares the LORD Almighty.
17 "Proclaim further: This is what the LORD Almighty says: 'My towns
will again overflow with prosperity, and the LORD will again comfort
Zion and choose Jerusalem.'"

FOUR HORNS AND FOUR CRAFTSMEN

18 Then I looked up, and there before me were four horns. 19 I asked
the angel who was speaking to me, "What are these?"
He answered me, "These are the horns that scattered Judah, Israel
and Jerusalem."
20 Then the LORD showed me four craftsmen. 21 I asked, "What are
these coming to do?"

He answered, "These are the horns that scattered Judah so that no
one could raise their head, but the craftsmen have come to terrify
them and throw down these horns of the nations who lifted up their
horns against the land of Judah to scatter its people."[a]

A MAN WITH A MEASURING LINE

2[b] Then I looked up, and there before me was a man with a measur-
ing line in his hand. 2 I asked, "Where are you going?"
He answered me, "To measure Jerusalem, to find out how wide and
how long it is."
3 While the angel who was speaking to me was leaving, another angel
came to meet him 4 and said to him: "Run, tell that young man, 'Jerusa-
lem will be a city without walls because of the great number of people
and animals in it. 5 And I myself will be a wall of fire around it,' declares
the LORD, 'and I will be its glory within.'
6 "Come! Come! Flee from the land of the north," declares the LORD,
"for I have scattered you to the four winds of heaven," declares the
LORD.
7 "Come, Zion! Escape, you who live in Daughter Babylon!" 8 For this
is what the LORD Almighty says: "After the Glorious One has sent me
against the nations that have plundered you — for whoever touches
you touches the apple of his eye — 9 I will surely raise my hand against
them so that their slaves will plunder them.[c] Then you will know that
the LORD Almighty has sent me.
10 "Shout and be glad, Daughter Zion. For I am coming, and I will live
among you," declares the LORD. 11 "Many nations will be joined with
the LORD in that day and will become my people. I will live among you
and you will know that the LORD Almighty has sent me to you. 12 The
LORD will inherit Judah as his portion in the holy land and will again
choose Jerusalem. 13 Be still before the LORD, all mankind, because he
has roused himself from his holy dwelling."

CLEAN GARMENTS FOR THE HIGH PRIEST

3 Then he showed me Joshua the high priest standing before the
angel of the LORD, and Satan[d] standing at his right side to accuse
him. 2 The LORD said to Satan, "The LORD rebuke you, Satan! The LORD,
who has chosen Jerusalem, rebuke you! Is not this man a burning stick
snatched from the fire?"
3 Now Joshua was dressed in filthy clothes as he stood before the an-
gel. 4 The angel said to those who were standing before him, "Take off
his filthy clothes."
Then he said to Joshua, "See, I have taken away your sin, and I will
put fine garments on you."
5 Then I said, "Put a clean turban on his head." So they put a clean tur-
ban on his head and clothed him, while the angel of the LORD stood by.
6 The angel of the LORD gave this charge to Joshua: 7 "This is what the
LORD Almighty says: 'If you will walk in obedience to me and keep my
requirements, then you will govern my house and have charge of my
courts, and I will give you a place among these standing here.
8 " 'Listen, High Priest Joshua, you and your associates seated before

PRAYING SCRIPTURE

Zechariah 2

One of the repeated promises of the Old Testament, which Israel didn't always understand, was the heart of God for the peoples of all nations. God's purpose in calling Israel was to save not only Israel, but to save the people of other nations who would turn to God as a result of Israel's light.

The church now has the responsibility to take the gospel to all people. Ask God to use you in this task.

PRAYING SCRIPTURE

Zechariah 3

God's people have no reason to fear his return. He promised a time of redemption and restoration. His servant, "the Branch," a reference to Jesus the Messiah, would come to make things new (see verse 8). Further, the Lord promised a day of prosperity and peace for his people.

The future glory of the restored creation, the new heaven and the new earth, is the hope of God's people. Pray with confidence for that time.

---

[a] *21* In Hebrew texts 1:18-21 is numbered 2:1-4. [b] In Hebrew texts 2:1-13 is numbered 2:5-17. [c] *8,9* Or *says after . . . eye:* [9] "*I . . . plunder them.*"
[d] *1* Hebrew *satan* means *adversary.*

you, who are men symbolic of things to come: I am going to bring my
servant, the Branch. 9See, the stone I have set in front of Joshua! There
are seven eyes[a] on that one stone, and I will engrave an inscription on
it,' says the LORD Almighty, 'and I will remove the sin of this land in a
single day.
10" 'In that day each of you will invite your neighbor to sit under your
vine and fig tree,' declares the LORD Almighty."

THE GOLD LAMPSTAND AND THE TWO OLIVE TREES

4 Then the angel who talked with me returned and woke me up, like
someone awakened from sleep. 2He asked me, "What do you see?"
I answered, "I see a solid gold lampstand with a bowl at the top and
seven lamps on it, with seven channels to the lamps. 3Also there are
two olive trees by it, one on the right of the bowl and the other on its
left."
4I asked the angel who talked with me, "What are these, my lord?"
5He answered, "Do you not know what these are?"
"No, my lord," I replied.
6So he said to me, "This is the word of the LORD to Zerubbabel: 'Not
by might nor by power, but by my Spirit,' says the LORD Almighty.
7"What are you, mighty mountain? Before Zerubbabel you will be-
come level ground. Then he will bring out the capstone to shouts of
'God bless it! God bless it!' "
8Then the word of the LORD came to me: 9"The hands of Zerubbabel
have laid the foundation of this temple; his hands will also complete
it. Then you will know that the LORD Almighty has sent me to you.
10"Who dares despise the day of small things, since the seven eyes
of the LORD that range throughout the earth will rejoice when they see
the chosen capstone[b] in the hand of Zerubbabel?"
11Then I asked the angel, "What are these two olive trees on the right
and the left of the lampstand?"
12Again I asked him, "What are these two olive branches beside the
two gold pipes that pour out golden oil?"
13He replied, "Do you not know what these are?"
"No, my lord," I said.
14So he said, "These are the two who are anointed to[c] serve the Lord
of all the earth."

THE FLYING SCROLL

5 I looked again, and there before me was a flying scroll.
2He asked me, "What do you see?"
I answered, "I see a flying scroll, twenty cubits long and ten cubits
wide.[d]"
3And he said to me, "This is the curse that is going out over the
whole land; for according to what it says on one side, every thief will
be banished, and according to what it says on the other, everyone who
swears falsely will be banished. 4The LORD Almighty declares, 'I will
send it out, and it will enter the house of the thief and the house of
anyone who swears falsely by my name. It will remain in that house
and destroy it completely, both its timbers and its stones.' "

---

[a] 9 Or *facets* [b] 10 Or *the plumb line* [c] 14 Or *two who bring oil and*
[d] 2 That is, about 30 feet long and 15 feet wide or about 9 meters long and 4.5 meters wide

PRAYING SCRIPTURE

Zechariah 4

The power of God for his people always comes the same way, "Not by might nor by power, but by [God's] Spirit" (verse 6). God is not interested in his people's using worldly power to gain authority or position, because God's Spirit is sufficient for our every need.

Examine your heart for any lust for secular might or power. Forsake it and trust the Spirit of God to be your strength.

PRAYING SCRIPTURE

Zechariah 5

A series of visions helped Zechariah understand the breadth of coming judgment. A flying scroll announced a curse that would span the face of the whole land (see verse 3) followed by a basket with a lead cover and a woman in the basket. An angel speaking with Zechariah provided a succinct interpretation: "This is wickedness" (verse 8).

The ways God announces judgment vary. Pray for wisdom to hear his voice and recognize his works.

THE WOMAN IN A BASKET

5Then the angel who was speaking to me came forward and said to
me, "Look up and see what is appearing."
6I asked, "What is it?"
He replied, "It is a basket." And he added, "This is the iniquity[a] of the
people throughout the land."
7Then the cover of lead was raised, and there in the basket sat a
woman! 8He said, "This is wickedness," and he pushed her back into
the basket and pushed its lead cover down on it.
9Then I looked up — and there before me were two women, with
the wind in their wings! They had wings like those of a stork, and they
lifted up the basket between heaven and earth.
10"Where are they taking the basket?" I asked the angel who was
speaking to me.
11He replied, "To the country of Babylonia[b] to build a house for it.
When the house is ready, the basket will be set there in its place."

FOUR CHARIOTS

6 I looked up again, and there before me were four chariots coming
out from between two mountains — mountains of bronze. 2The
first chariot had red horses, the second black, 3the third white, and
the fourth dappled — all of them powerful. 4I asked the angel who was
speaking to me, "What are these, my lord?"
5The angel answered me, "These are the four spirits[c] of heaven, go-
ing out from standing in the presence of the Lord of the whole world.
6The one with the black horses is going toward the north country, the
one with the white horses toward the west,[d] and the one with the dap-
pled horses toward the south."
7When the powerful horses went out, they were straining to go
throughout the earth. And he said, "Go throughout the earth!" So they
went throughout the earth.
8Then he called to me, "Look, those going toward the north country
have given my Spirit[e] rest in the land of the north."

A CROWN FOR JOSHUA

9The word of the LORD came to me: 10"Take silver and gold from the
exiles Heldai, Tobijah and Jedaiah, who have arrived from Babylon. Go
the same day to the house of Josiah son of Zephaniah. 11Take the silver
and gold and make a crown, and set it on the head of the high priest,
Joshua son of Jozadak.[f] 12Tell him this is what the LORD Almighty says:
'Here is the man whose name is the Branch, and he will branch out
from his place and build the temple of the LORD. 13It is he who will
build the temple of the LORD, and he will be clothed with majesty and
will sit and rule on his throne. And he[g] will be a priest on his throne.
And there will be harmony between the two.' 14The crown will be given
to Heldai,[h] Tobijah, Jedaiah and Hen[i] son of Zephaniah as a memorial
in the temple of the LORD. 15Those who are far away will come and
help to build the temple of the LORD, and you will know that the LORD
Almighty has sent me to you. This will happen if you diligently obey
the LORD your God."

PRAYING SCRIPTURE

Zechariah 6

Joshua, the son of the high priest, was a type of Jesus Christ. Types were often used to teach truths related to future persons or ministries. The prophecies of this chapter are elsewhere used of the Messiah, and a king is represented by the crown, which served as a memorial in the Lord's temple (see verse 14).

As you pray through verses 12–13, praise God for Jesus' Messiahship and his glory.

[a] 6 Or *appearance* [b] 11 Hebrew *Shinar* [c] 5 Or *winds* [d] 6 Or *horses after them* [e] 8 Or *spirit* [f] 11 Hebrew *Jehozadak*, a variant of *Jozadak* [g] 13 Or *there* [h] 14 Syriac; Hebrew *Helem* [i] 14 Or *and the gracious one, the*

JUSTICE AND MERCY, NOT FASTING

7 In the fourth year of King Darius, the word of the LORD came to
Zechariah on the fourth day of the ninth month, the month of
Kislev. 2The people of Bethel had sent Sharezer and Regem-Melek, to-
gether with their men, to entreat the LORD 3by asking the priests of the
house of the LORD Almighty and the prophets, "Should I mourn and
fast in the fifth month, as I have done for so many years?"
4Then the word of the LORD Almighty came to me: 5"Ask all the peo-
ple of the land and the priests, 'When you fasted and mourned in the
fifth and seventh months for the past seventy years, was it really for
me that you fasted? 6And when you were eating and drinking, were
you not just feasting for yourselves? 7Are these not the words the LORD
proclaimed through the earlier prophets when Jerusalem and its sur-
rounding towns were at rest and prosperous, and the Negev and the
western foothills were settled?'"
8And the word of the LORD came again to Zechariah: 9"This is what
the LORD Almighty said: 'Administer true justice; show mercy and com-
passion to one another. 10Do not oppress the widow or the fatherless,
the foreigner or the poor. Do not plot evil against each other.'
11"But they refused to pay attention; stubbornly they turned their
backs and covered their ears. 12They made their hearts as hard as flint
and would not listen to the law or to the words that the LORD Almighty
had sent by his Spirit through the earlier prophets. So the LORD Al-
mighty was very angry.
13" 'When I called, they did not listen; so when they called, I would
not listen,' says the LORD Almighty. 14'I scattered them with a whirl-
wind among all the nations, where they were strangers. The land they
left behind them was so desolate that no one traveled through it. This
is how they made the pleasant land desolate.'"

PRAYING SCRIPTURE

Zechariah 7

This chapter provides the core doctrine of justice: Do not oppress the vulnerable (widows, orphans, immigrants, the poor), and do not plot wickedness against your brother, which likely includes countrymen (see verses 8–10). Rather than exploitation, God demands compassion, mercy and true justice.

At its foundation, practicing justice means treating people fairly according to God's righteous standard. Pray for the compassion to treat people justly and for the courage to stand against injustice.

THE LORD PROMISES TO BLESS JERUSALEM

8 The word of the LORD Almighty came to me.
2This is what the LORD Almighty says: "I am very jealous for Zion;
I am burning with jealousy for her."
3This is what the LORD says: "I will return to Zion and dwell in Jeru-
salem. Then Jerusalem will be called the Faithful City, and the moun-
tain of the LORD Almighty will be called the Holy Mountain."
4This is what the LORD Almighty says: "Once again men and women
of ripe old age will sit in the streets of Jerusalem, each of them with
cane in hand because of their age. 5The city streets will be filled with
boys and girls playing there."
6This is what the LORD Almighty says: "It may seem marvelous to the
remnant of this people at that time, but will it seem marvelous to me?"
declares the LORD Almighty.
7This is what the LORD Almighty says: "I will save my people from
the countries of the east and the west. 8I will bring them back to live in
Jerusalem; they will be my people, and I will be faithful and righteous
to them as their God."
9This is what the LORD Almighty says: "Now hear these words, 'Let
your hands be strong so that the temple may be built.' This is also
what the prophets said who were present when the foundation was
laid for the house of the LORD Almighty. 10Before that time there were
no wages for people or hire for animals. No one could go about their
business safely because of their enemies, since I had turned everyone

PRAYING SCRIPTURE

Zechariah 8

In a promise about future Jerusalem, the Lord reminded his people that he punished their ancestors' disobedience. But in days to come he would "do good again to Jerusalem and Judah." Giving them instructions on how to live, he said, "Do not be afraid" (verse 15).

Serving God should never bring fear to his people. It should bring confidence in his goodness. Ask the Lord to help you live well in him.

against their neighbor. 11But now I will not deal with the remnant of
this people as I did in the past," declares the LORD Almighty.
12"The seed will grow well, the vine will yield its fruit, the ground
will produce its crops, and the heavens will drop their dew. I will give
all these things as an inheritance to the remnant of this people. 13Just
as you, Judah and Israel, have been a curse[a] among the nations, so I
will save you, and you will be a blessing.[b] Do not be afraid, but let your
hands be strong."
14This is what the LORD Almighty says: "Just as I had determined to
bring disaster on you and showed no pity when your ancestors angered
me," says the LORD Almighty, 15"so now I have determined to do good
again to Jerusalem and Judah. Do not be afraid. 16These are the things
you are to do: Speak the truth to each other, and render true and sound
judgment in your courts; 17do not plot evil against each other, and do
not love to swear falsely. I hate all this," declares the LORD.
18The word of the LORD Almighty came to me.
19This is what the LORD Almighty says: "The fasts of the fourth, fifth,
seventh and tenth months will become joyful and glad occasions and
happy festivals for Judah. Therefore love truth and peace."
20This is what the LORD Almighty says: "Many peoples and the in-
habitants of many cities will yet come, 21and the inhabitants of one city
will go to another and say, 'Let us go at once to entreat the LORD and
seek the LORD Almighty. I myself am going.' 22And many peoples and
powerful nations will come to Jerusalem to seek the LORD Almighty
and to entreat him."
23This is what the LORD Almighty says: "In those days ten people
from all languages and nations will take firm hold of one Jew by the
hem of his robe and say, 'Let us go with you, because we have heard
that God is with you.'"

JUDGMENT ON ISRAEL'S ENEMIES

9 A prophecy:

The word of the LORD is against the land of Hadrak
 and will come to rest on Damascus —
for the eyes of all people and all the tribes of Israel
 are on the LORD —[c]
2 and on Hamath too, which borders on it,
 and on Tyre and Sidon, though they are very skillful.
3 Tyre has built herself a stronghold;
 she has heaped up silver like dust,
 and gold like the dirt of the streets.
4 But the Lord will take away her possessions
 and destroy her power on the sea,
 and she will be consumed by fire.
5 Ashkelon will see it and fear;
 Gaza will writhe in agony,
 and Ekron too, for her hope will wither.
Gaza will lose her king
 and Ashkelon will be deserted.

PRAYING SCRIPTURE

Zechariah 9

The writers of the New Testament Gospels recognized something a lot of people missed: The Messiah would come to Israel humbly, without fanfare or acclaim. Zechariah prophesied that their King would come "righteous and victorious, lowly and riding on a donkey" (verse 9). This prophecy was fulfilled in Jesus Christ.

Does your life reflect the humility of Jesus? Ask God to remove every root of pride or self-sufficiency. Ask for the humble disposition of the Messiah.

---

[a] *13* That is, your name has been used in cursing (see Jer. 29:22); or, you have been regarded as under a curse. [b] *13* Or *and your name will be used in blessings* (see Gen. 48:20); or *and you will be seen as blessed* [c] *1* Or *Damascus. / For the eye of the LORD is on all people, / as well as on the tribes of Israel,*

6 A mongrel people will occupy Ashdod,
and I will put an end to the pride of the Philistines.
7 I will take the blood from their mouths,
the forbidden food from between their teeth.
Those who are left will belong to our God
and become a clan in Judah,
and Ekron will be like the Jebusites.
8 But I will encamp at my temple
to guard it against marauding forces.
Never again will an oppressor overrun my people,
for now I am keeping watch.

THE COMING OF ZION'S KING

9 Rejoice greatly, Daughter Zion!
Shout, Daughter Jerusalem!
See, your king comes to you,
righteous and victorious,
lowly and riding on a donkey,
on a colt, the foal of a donkey.
10 I will take away the chariots from Ephraim
and the warhorses from Jerusalem,
and the battle bow will be broken.
He will proclaim peace to the nations.
His rule will extend from sea to sea
and from the River[a] to the ends of the earth.
11 As for you, because of the blood of my covenant with you,
I will free your prisoners from the waterless pit.
12 Return to your fortress, you prisoners of hope;
even now I announce that I will restore twice as much to you.
13 I will bend Judah as I bend my bow
and fill it with Ephraim.
I will rouse your sons, Zion,
against your sons, Greece,
and make you like a warrior's sword.

THE LORD WILL APPEAR

14 Then the LORD will appear over them;
his arrow will flash like lightning.
The Sovereign LORD will sound the trumpet;
he will march in the storms of the south,
15 and the LORD Almighty will shield them.
They will destroy
and overcome with slingstones.
They will drink and roar as with wine;
they will be full like a bowl
used for sprinkling[b] the corners of the altar.
16 The LORD their God will save his people on that day
as a shepherd saves his flock.
They will sparkle in his land
like jewels in a crown.
17 How attractive and beautiful they will be!
Grain will make the young men thrive,
and new wine the young women.

---

[a] *10* That is, the Euphrates [b] *15* Or *bowl, / like*

THE LORD WILL CARE FOR JUDAH

10 Ask the LORD for rain in the springtime;
it is the LORD who sends the thunderstorms.
He gives showers of rain to all people,
and plants of the field to everyone.
2 The idols speak deceitfully,
diviners see visions that lie;
they tell dreams that are false,
they give comfort in vain.
Therefore the people wander like sheep
oppressed for lack of a shepherd.

3 "My anger burns against the shepherds,
and I will punish the leaders;
for the LORD Almighty will care
for his flock, the people of Judah,
and make them like a proud horse in battle.
4 From Judah will come the cornerstone,
from him the tent peg,
from him the battle bow,
from him every ruler.
5 Together they[a] will be like warriors in battle
trampling their enemy into the mud of the streets.
They will fight because the LORD is with them,
and they will put the enemy horsemen to shame.

6 "I will strengthen Judah
and save the tribes of Joseph.
I will restore them
because I have compassion on them.
They will be as though
I had not rejected them,
for I am the LORD their God
and I will answer them.
7 The Ephraimites will become like warriors,
and their hearts will be glad as with wine.
Their children will see it and be joyful;
their hearts will rejoice in the LORD.
8 I will signal for them
and gather them in.
Surely I will redeem them;
they will be as numerous as before.
9 Though I scatter them among the peoples,
yet in distant lands they will remember me.
They and their children will survive,
and they will return.
10 I will bring them back from Egypt
and gather them from Assyria.
I will bring them to Gilead and Lebanon,
and there will not be room enough for them.
11 They will pass through the sea of trouble;
the surging sea will be subdued
and all the depths of the Nile will dry up.

[a] 4,5 Or *ruler, all of them together.* / [5]*They*

PRAYING SCRIPTURE

Zechariah 10

The Lord loves his people and answers when we call on him. Even as the Lord condemned idols and unfaithful shepherds, he promised his people mercy. He promised strength and "and in his name they will live securely" (verse 12).

Does your life reflect the name of the Lord? When people think of you, are their thoughts turned to Jesus' presence? Pray that you will live in his name.

Assyria's pride will be brought down
  and Egypt's scepter will pass away.
12 I will strengthen them in the LORD
  and in his name they will live securely,"
    declares the LORD.

11 Open your doors, Lebanon,
  so that fire may devour your cedars!
2 Wail, you juniper, for the cedar has fallen;
  the stately trees are ruined!
Wail, oaks of Bashan;
  the dense forest has been cut down!
3 Listen to the wail of the shepherds;
  their rich pastures are destroyed!
Listen to the roar of the lions;
  the lush thicket of the Jordan is ruined!

TWO SHEPHERDS

4 This is what the LORD my God says: "Shepherd the flock marked
for slaughter. 5 Their buyers slaughter them and go unpunished. Those
who sell them say, 'Praise the LORD, I am rich!' Their own shepherds
do not spare them. 6 For I will no longer have pity on the people of the
land," declares the LORD. "I will give everyone into the hands of their
neighbors and their king. They will devastate the land, and I will not
rescue anyone from their hands."

7 So I shepherded the flock marked for slaughter, particularly the op-
pressed of the flock. Then I took two staffs and called one Favor and
the other Union, and I shepherded the flock. 8 In one month I got rid
of the three shepherds.

The flock detested me, and I grew weary of them 9 and said, "I will
not be your shepherd. Let the dying die, and the perishing perish. Let
those who are left eat one another's flesh."

10 Then I took my staff called Favor and broke it, revoking the cov-
enant I had made with all the nations. 11 It was revoked on that day,
and so the oppressed of the flock who were watching me knew it was
the word of the LORD.

12 I told them, "If you think it best, give me my pay; but if not, keep
it." So they paid me thirty pieces of silver.

13 And the LORD said to me, "Throw it to the potter"—the handsome
price at which they valued me! So I took the thirty pieces of silver and
threw them to the potter at the house of the LORD.

14 Then I broke my second staff called Union, breaking the family
bond between Judah and Israel.

15 Then the LORD said to me, "Take again the equipment of a foolish
shepherd. 16 For I am going to raise up a shepherd over the land who
will not care for the lost, or seek the young, or heal the injured, or feed
the healthy, but will eat the meat of the choice sheep, tearing off their
hooves.

17 "Woe to the worthless shepherd,
  who deserts the flock!
May the sword strike his arm and his right eye!
  May his arm be completely withered,
  his right eye totally blinded!"

PRAYING SCRIPTURE

Zechariah 11

In a heartbreaking prophecy, God not only condemned Israel's evil spiritual shepherds as he had before as part of a devastating judgment, but he promised to send a shepherd who would not care for them. They would reap the wicked harvest they had sown with the poor and weak bearing the brunt.

Sin's corrosive effects cannot be stopped except through repentance and obedience. Don't let some sin of yours bring harm to those you love.

JERUSALEM'S ENEMIES TO BE DESTROYED

12 A prophecy: The word of the LORD concerning Israel.

The LORD, who stretches out the heavens, who lays the foundation of the earth, and who forms the human spirit within a person, declares: 2"I am going to make Jerusalem a cup that sends all the surrounding peoples reeling. Judah will be besieged as well as Jerusalem. 3On that day, when all the nations of the earth are gathered against her, I will make Jerusalem an immovable rock for all the nations. All who try to move it will injure themselves. 4On that day I will strike every horse with panic and its rider with madness," declares the LORD. "I will keep a watchful eye over Judah, but I will blind all the horses of the nations. 5Then the clans of Judah will say in their hearts, 'The people of Jerusalem are strong, because the LORD Almighty is their God.'

6"On that day I will make the clans of Judah like a firepot in a woodpile, like a flaming torch among sheaves. They will consume all the surrounding peoples right and left, but Jerusalem will remain intact in her place.

7"The LORD will save the dwellings of Judah first, so that the honor of the house of David and of Jerusalem's inhabitants may not be greater than that of Judah. 8On that day the LORD will shield those who live in Jerusalem, so that the feeblest among them will be like David, and the house of David will be like God, like the angel of the LORD going before them. 9On that day I will set out to destroy all the nations that attack Jerusalem.

MOURNING FOR THE ONE THEY PIERCED

10"And I will pour out on the house of David and the inhabitants of Jerusalem a spirit[a] of grace and supplication. They will look on[b] me, the one they have pierced, and they will mourn for him as one mourns for an only child, and grieve bitterly for him as one grieves for a firstborn son. 11On that day the weeping in Jerusalem will be as great as the weeping of Hadad Rimmon in the plain of Megiddo. 12The land will mourn, each clan by itself, with their wives by themselves: the clan of the house of David and their wives, the clan of the house of Nathan and their wives, 13the clan of the house of Levi and their wives, the clan of Shimei and their wives, 14and all the rest of the clans and their wives.

CLEANSING FROM SIN

13 "On that day a fountain will be opened to the house of David and the inhabitants of Jerusalem, to cleanse them from sin and impurity.

2"On that day, I will banish the names of the idols from the land, and they will be remembered no more," declares the LORD Almighty. "I will remove both the prophets and the spirit of impurity from the land. 3And if anyone still prophesies, their father and mother, to whom they were born, will say to them, 'You must die, because you have told lies in the LORD's name.' Then their own parents will stab the one who prophesies.

4"On that day every prophet will be ashamed of their prophetic vision. They will not put on a prophet's garment of hair in order to deceive. 5Each will say, 'I am not a prophet. I am a farmer; the land has

[a] 10 Or *the Spirit* [b] 10 Or *to*

PRAYING SCRIPTURE

Zechariah 12

Zechariah prophesied of a future day when his people would experience a Spirit of grace and supplication. God would empower them to pray! In that day, they would recognize Jesus who was pierced. And they would grieve.

Our obedience often comes late, but late is better than not at all. Ask God for a spirit of prayer, and bring all of your concerns to him.

PRAYING SCRIPTURE

Zechariah 13

In this chapter, we find another prophecy pointing to the Messiah. "Strike the shepherd, and the sheep will be scattered" (verse 7) is applied to the scattering of the fearful disciples between Jesus' arrest and his resurrection. When the sheep were regathered, they would all say, "The LORD is our God" (verse 9).

God's purposes always aim to turn people to him. Pray for any sheep you know who are wandering from the Shepherd.

been my livelihood since my youth.[a] 6 If someone asks, 'What are these
wounds on your body[b]?' they will answer, 'The wounds I was given at
the house of my friends.'

THE SHEPHERD STRUCK, THE SHEEP SCATTERED

7 "Awake, sword, against my shepherd,
  against the man who is close to me!"
  declares the LORD Almighty.
"Strike the shepherd,
  and the sheep will be scattered,
  and I will turn my hand against the little ones.
8 In the whole land," declares the LORD,
  "two-thirds will be struck down and perish;
  yet one-third will be left in it.
9 This third I will put into the fire;
  I will refine them like silver
  and test them like gold.
They will call on my name
  and I will answer them;
I will say, 'They are my people,'
  and they will say, 'The LORD is our God.'"

THE LORD COMES AND REIGNS

14 A day of the LORD is coming, Jerusalem, when your possessions
will be plundered and divided up within your very walls.
2 I will gather all the nations to Jerusalem to fight against it; the city
will be captured, the houses ransacked, and the women raped. Half of
the city will go into exile, but the rest of the people will not be taken
from the city. 3 Then the LORD will go out and fight against those na-
tions, as he fights on a day of battle. 4 On that day his feet will stand on
the Mount of Olives, east of Jerusalem, and the Mount of Olives will
be split in two from east to west, forming a great valley, with half of
the mountain moving north and half moving south. 5 You will flee by
my mountain valley, for it will extend to Azel. You will flee as you fled
from the earthquake[c] in the days of Uzziah king of Judah. Then the
LORD my God will come, and all the holy ones with him.
6 On that day there will be neither sunlight nor cold, frosty darkness.
7 It will be a unique day — a day known only to the LORD — with no
distinction between day and night. When evening comes, there will
be light.
8 On that day living water will flow out from Jerusalem, half of it
east to the Dead Sea and half of it west to the Mediterranean Sea, in
summer and in winter.
9 The LORD will be king over the whole earth. On that day there will
be one LORD, and his name the only name.
10 The whole land, from Geba to Rimmon, south of Jerusalem, will
become like the Arabah. But Jerusalem will be raised up high from
the Benjamin Gate to the site of the First Gate, to the Corner Gate, and
from the Tower of Hananel to the royal winepresses, and will remain
in its place. 11 It will be inhabited; never again will it be destroyed. Je-
rusalem will be secure.

PRAYING SCRIPTURE

Zechariah 14

In another "day of the LORD" prophecy, Zechariah foretold the ultimate day of the Lord after which judgment would no longer be needed. At that time, "the LORD will be king over the whole earth." No more divided allegiance. The Lord would be worshiped, and his name would be the only name (see verse 9).

The final day of the Lord is coming. Ask for wisdom to live according to the Lord's present reign, a witness to his coming reign.

---

[a] 5 *Or farmer; a man sold me in my youth* [b] 6 *Or wounds between your hands* [c] 5 Or [5] *My mountain valley will be blocked and will extend to Azel. It will be blocked as it was blocked because of the earthquake*

12This is the plague with which the LORD will strike all the nations
that fought against Jerusalem: Their flesh will rot while they are still
standing on their feet, their eyes will rot in their sockets, and their
tongues will rot in their mouths. 13On that day people will be stricken
by the LORD with great panic. They will seize each other by the hand
and attack one another. 14Judah too will fight at Jerusalem. The wealth
of all the surrounding nations will be collected — great quantities of
gold and silver and clothing. 15A similar plague will strike the horses
and mules, the camels and donkeys, and all the animals in those
camps.

16Then the survivors from all the nations that have attacked Jerusa-
lem will go up year after year to worship the King, the LORD Almighty,
and to celebrate the Festival of Tabernacles. 17If any of the peoples of
the earth do not go up to Jerusalem to worship the King, the LORD Al-
mighty, they will have no rain. 18If the Egyptian people do not go up
and take part, they will have no rain. The LORD[a] will bring on them
the plague he inflicts on the nations that do not go up to celebrate the
Festival of Tabernacles. 19This will be the punishment of Egypt and
the punishment of all the nations that do not go up to celebrate the
Festival of Tabernacles.

20On that day HOLY TO THE LORD will be inscribed on the bells of the
horses, and the cooking pots in the LORD's house will be like the sacred
bowls in front of the altar. 21Every pot in Jerusalem and Judah will be
holy to the LORD Almighty, and all who come to sacrifice will take some
of the pots and cook in them. And on that day there will no longer be
a Canaanite[b] in the house of the LORD Almighty.

---

[a] 18 Or *part, then the LORD* [b] 21 Or *merchant*

MALACHI

The final book of the Old Testament identifies its author but doesn't explicitly tell the setting for his prophecy. This doesn't mean that we are without clues to his times, though. In several verses, Malachi mentions the temple as if it were still standing, doubtless referencing the second temple that was built after the return from exile. Malachi shares some of the same concerns and themes as the books of Ezra and Nehemiah.

Unlike the concerns about the temple expressed in Haggai and Zechariah, no immediate crises occasioned Malachi's prophecy. The people were barely back from exile, and already they were dealing with priestly corruption, abominations and presuming on God's grace. Malachi, the prophet called by God to address it, was concerned about these sins that could destroy Israel from within. Malachi showed how the people were either going through the mere formality of religion or failing to carry out the basic aspects of their faith. They claimed God was their Father, but they failed to honor him in the ways they should.

It was God who called them to account. Seven times in the book, the people question whether God was being truthful with them, challenging his charges against them. "How have you loved us?" (1:2); "How have we shown contempt for your name?" (1:6); "Why?" was God concerned about their lack of marital commitment (2:14); "How have we wearied him?" (2:17); "How are we to return?" (3:7); "How are we robbing you?" (3:8); "What have we said against you?" (3:13). Only God's relentless grace kept him from destroying them.

Malachi's emphasis on hypocrisy reminds us of the foolishness of neglecting prayer and devotion in our own lives. If we call ourselves followers of Jesus who love God the Father, then we cannot neglect prayer. When we neglect prayer—the glorious opportunity to commune with the Creator of the universe who loves us and redeemed us—we invite sin to take over. Soon we will be marked by hypocritical play-acting about our faith.

Our sin can cause us to neglect our prayer lives. We feel guilty for our sins, and this causes us to avoid God's presence. Then we are overwhelmed with shame because we have not prayed. This drives us further away from the Lord, which leads to more sin and even less prayer than before. However, if we will come into his presence and confess our sins and receive his forgiveness, true fellowship will be restored.

Like so many of the prophets before him, Malachi turned to a future day of the Lord. Judgment is coming, he said, but "the sun of righteousness will arise with healing in its rays" (4:2). The book ends with a final promise that God will send a prophet, a type of Elijah, to turn the hearts of parents to their children and the hearts of the children to their parents so they can avoid God's curse on the earth.

1 A prophecy: The word of the LORD to Israel through Malachi.[a]

ISRAEL DOUBTS GOD'S LOVE

2"I have loved you," says the LORD.
"But you ask, 'How have you loved us?'
"Was not Esau Jacob's brother?" declares the LORD. "Yet I have loved
Jacob, 3but Esau I have hated, and I have turned his hill country into a
wasteland and left his inheritance to the desert jackals."
4Edom may say, "Though we have been crushed, we will rebuild the
ruins."
But this is what the LORD Almighty says: "They may build, but I will
demolish. They will be called the Wicked Land, a people always under
the wrath of the LORD. 5You will see it with your own eyes and say,
'Great is the LORD — even beyond the borders of Israel!'

BREAKING COVENANT THROUGH BLEMISHED SACRIFICES

6"A son honors his father, and a slave his master. If I am a father,
where is the honor due me? If I am a master, where is the respect due
me?" says the LORD Almighty.
"It is you priests who show contempt for my name.
"But you ask, 'How have we shown contempt for your name?'
7"By offering defiled food on my altar.
"But you ask, 'How have we defiled you?'
"By saying that the LORD's table is contemptible. 8When you offer
blind animals for sacrifice, is that not wrong? When you sacrifice lame
or diseased animals, is that not wrong? Try offering them to your gov-
ernor! Would he be pleased with you? Would he accept you?" says the
LORD Almighty.
9"Now plead with God to be gracious to us. With such offerings from
your hands, will he accept you?" — says the LORD Almighty.
10"Oh, that one of you would shut the temple doors, so that you
would not light useless fires on my altar! I am not pleased with you,"
says the LORD Almighty, "and I will accept no offering from your hands.
11My name will be great among the nations, from where the sun rises
to where it sets. In every place incense and pure offerings will be
brought to me, because my name will be great among the nations,"
says the LORD Almighty.
12"But you profane it by saying, 'The Lord's table is defiled,' and, 'Its
food is contemptible.' 13And you say, 'What a burden!' and you sniff at
it contemptuously," says the LORD Almighty.
"When you bring injured, lame or diseased animals and offer them
as sacrifices, should I accept them from your hands?" says the LORD.
14"Cursed is the cheat who has an acceptable male in his flock and vows
to give it, but then sacrifices a blemished animal to the Lord. For I am
a great king," says the LORD Almighty, "and my name is to be feared
among the nations.

ADDITIONAL WARNING TO THE PRIESTS

2 "And now, you priests, this warning is for you. 2If you do not lis-
ten, and if you do not resolve to honor my name," says the LORD
Almighty, "I will send a curse on you, and I will curse your blessings.

[a] 1 *Malachi* means *my messenger.*

PRAYING SCRIPTURE

Malachi 1

Despite the doubts and disobedience of his people, God promised that his name would be great not merely in Israel but among the Gentiles. "In every place," God said, incense would be offered to his name and pure offerings unlike the tainted offerings of Israel (verse 11).

The name of the Lord *will be* magnified among the nations. Pray to be an instrument of his glory in the spread of the gospel.

PRAYING SCRIPTURE

Malachi 2

The rebukes in Malachi took place after God returned the people to the land. It was less than a generation before they were deep in sin again, standing at the brink of judgment. Their priests were corrupt, their women were mistreated and divorce was a problem.

God takes marriage seriously and wants his people to do the same. Pray for God's people to honor him and reflect Jesus in marriage.

Yes, I have already cursed them, because you have not resolved to
honor me.

3"Because of you I will rebuke your descendants[a]; I will smear on
your faces the dung from your festival sacrifices, and you will be car-
ried off with it. 4And you will know that I have sent you this warning
so that my covenant with Levi may continue," says the LORD Almighty.
5"My covenant was with him, a covenant of life and peace, and I gave
them to him; this called for reverence and he revered me and stood in
awe of my name. 6True instruction was in his mouth and nothing false
was found on his lips. He walked with me in peace and uprightness,
and turned many from sin.

7"For the lips of a priest ought to preserve knowledge, because he is
the messenger of the LORD Almighty and people seek instruction from
his mouth. 8But you have turned from the way and by your teaching
have caused many to stumble; you have violated the covenant with
Levi," says the LORD Almighty. 9"So I have caused you to be despised
and humiliated before all the people, because you have not followed
my ways but have shown partiality in matters of the law."

BREAKING COVENANT THROUGH DIVORCE

10Do we not all have one Father[b]? Did not one God create us? Why
do we profane the covenant of our ancestors by being unfaithful to
one another?

11Judah has been unfaithful. A detestable thing has been commit-
ted in Israel and in Jerusalem: Judah has desecrated the sanctuary the
LORD loves by marrying women who worship a foreign god. 12As for
the man who does this, whoever he may be, may the LORD remove
him from the tents of Jacob[c]—even though he brings an offering to
the LORD Almighty.

13Another thing you do: You flood the LORD's altar with tears. You
weep and wail because he no longer looks with favor on your offerings
or accepts them with pleasure from your hands. 14You ask, "Why?" It
is because the LORD is the witness between you and the wife of your
youth. You have been unfaithful to her, though she is your partner, the
wife of your marriage covenant.

15Has not the one God made you? You belong to him in body and
spirit. And what does the one God seek? Godly offspring.[d] So be on your
guard, and do not be unfaithful to the wife of your youth.

16"The man who hates and divorces his wife," says the LORD, the God
of Israel, "does violence to the one he should protect,"[e] says the LORD
Almighty.

So be on your guard, and do not be unfaithful.

BREAKING COVENANT THROUGH INJUSTICE

17You have wearied the LORD with your words.

"How have we wearied him?" you ask.

By saying, "All who do evil are good in the eyes of the LORD, and he
is pleased with them" or "Where is the God of justice?"

---

[a] 3 Or *will blight your grain* [b] 10 Or *father* [c] 12 Or [12]*May the LORD remove from the tents of Jacob anyone who gives testimony in behalf of the man who does this* [d] 15 The meaning of the Hebrew for the first part of this verse is uncertain. [e] 16 Or *"I hate divorce," says the LORD, the God of Israel, "because the man who divorces his wife covers his garment with violence,"*

3 "I will send my messenger, who will prepare the way before me.
Then suddenly the Lord you are seeking will come to his temple;
the messenger of the covenant, whom you desire, will come," says the
LORD Almighty.
2But who can endure the day of his coming? Who can stand when
he appears? For he will be like a refiner's fire or a launderer's soap.
3He will sit as a refiner and purifier of silver; he will purify the Levites
and refine them like gold and silver. Then the LORD will have men
who will bring offerings in righteousness, 4and the offerings of Judah
and Jerusalem will be acceptable to the LORD, as in days gone by, as in
former years.
5"So I will come to put you on trial. I will be quick to testify against
sorcerers, adulterers and perjurers, against those who defraud laborers of their wages, who oppress the widows and the fatherless, and
deprive the foreigners among you of justice, but do not fear me," says
the LORD Almighty.

BREAKING COVENANT BY WITHHOLDING TITHES

6"I the LORD do not change. So you, the descendants of Jacob, are
not destroyed. 7Ever since the time of your ancestors you have turned
away from my decrees and have not kept them. Return to me, and I
will return to you," says the LORD Almighty.

"But you ask, 'How are we to return?'

8"Will a mere mortal rob God? Yet you rob me.

"But you ask, 'How are we robbing you?'

"In tithes and offerings. 9You are under a curse — your whole nation — because you are robbing me. 10Bring the whole tithe into the
storehouse, that there may be food in my house. Test me in this," says
the LORD Almighty, "and see if I will not throw open the floodgates
of heaven and pour out so much blessing that there will not be room
enough to store it. 11I will prevent pests from devouring your crops,
and the vines in your fields will not drop their fruit before it is ripe,"
says the LORD Almighty. 12"Then all the nations will call you blessed,
for yours will be a delightful land," says the LORD Almighty.

ISRAEL SPEAKS ARROGANTLY AGAINST GOD

13"You have spoken arrogantly against me," says the LORD.

"Yet you ask, 'What have we said against you?'

14"You have said, 'It is futile to serve God. What do we gain by carrying out his requirements and going about like mourners before the
LORD Almighty? 15But now we call the arrogant blessed. Certainly evildoers prosper, and even when they put God to the test, they get away
with it.'"

THE FAITHFUL REMNANT

16Then those who feared the LORD talked with each other, and the
LORD listened and heard. A scroll of remembrance was written in his
presence concerning those who feared the LORD and honored his
name.
17"On the day when I act," says the LORD Almighty, "they will be my
treasured possession. I will spare them, just as a father has compassion and spares his son who serves him. 18And you will again see the
distinction between the righteous and the wicked, between those who
serve God and those who do not.

PRAYING SCRIPTURE
Malachi 3

"I the LORD do not change," he said to the sons of Jacob (verse 6). This is the greatest hope we have. We never have to wonder whether God will be the same today or tomorrow as he was in the days of Israel.

The Lord is always the same, always faithful. Praise him and trust him when you take requests to him.

PRAYING SCRIPTURE

Malachi 4

The day of the Lord Malachi spoke of is unique in two ways: A "sun of righteousness" would arise to heal his people (see verse 2). This is commonly understood to be Jesus. And Elijah the prophet would precede him as a messenger to God's people. This is reckoned to be John the Baptist.

The coming of Jesus brought judgment on sin. If you do not know Jesus, call on him for forgiveness of your sins.

JUDGMENT AND COVENANT RENEWAL

4 [a] "Surely the day is coming; it will burn like a furnace. All the arro-
gant and every evildoer will be stubble, and the day that is com-
ing will set them on fire," says the LORD Almighty. "Not a root or a
branch will be left to them. 2But for you who revere my name, the sun
of righteousness will rise with healing in its rays. And you will go out
and frolic like well-fed calves. 3Then you will trample on the wicked;
they will be ashes under the soles of your feet on the day when I act,"
says the LORD Almighty.
4"Remember the law of my servant Moses, the decrees and laws I
gave him at Horeb for all Israel.
5"See, I will send the prophet Elijah to you before that great and
dreadful day of the LORD comes. 6He will turn the hearts of the parents
to their children, and the hearts of the children to their parents; or else
I will come and strike the land with total destruction."

[a] In Hebrew texts 4:1-6 is numbered 3:19-24.

NEW TESTAMENT

MATTHEW

The Gospel of Matthew stands as the first of the four historical and theological accounts of Jesus' life. The four Gospels, which lead off the New Testament, contain what we need to know about the life of Jesus so that we can know who he is and understand what he came to do so that we might trust him, love him, follow him and obey him. The Gospels do not tell us everything about Jesus' life because, as John said, "the whole world would not have room for the books" if they did (John 21:25). However, they do tell us everything we need to know about Jesus.

Matthew's purpose in writing was to show Jesus as the Son of David, the Messiah. The Jewish people awaited the One who would come from David's line to reign on the throne forever, as God had promised through the prophets. Matthew makes extensive use of the Hebrew Scriptures via quotations and allusions—more than any of the other Gospels—to show that Jesus fulfilled their prophetic words and was, in fact, the One for whom the Jews had been waiting.

Matthew contains one of the most straightforward teachings on prayer in the Bible. In the middle of the Sermon on the Mount (see 6:5–15), the longest block of Jesus' teaching in the Gospels, Jesus taught his disciples how to pray. We can certainly pray the words of the Lord's Prayer; some people say it when entering into prayer. However, in the Lord's Prayer, we see a pattern for prayer: We praise God, ask for forgiveness, request that God give us our daily provision and seek growth as followers of Jesus.

A few verses later in the same sermon, Jesus taught his disciples to persist in prayer: "Ask and it will be given to you; seek and you will find; knock and the door will be opened to you" (7:7). God is willing and eager to hear, answer and give good gifts to his children.

Jesus further taught his followers the difference between godliness and hypocrisy, contrasting how, and even where, people prayed. He told them that when they prayed, they should not pray like the hypocrites to be seen by people. Their public, showy prayer detracted from God's glory and focused glory instead on themselves. Jesus warned when our prayers are combined with fasting, we should take care not to advertise it with long, tired faces (see 6:16–18).

Prayer should not consist of mindlessly saying the same things over and over in hopes that we will win God over by magical incantation. Prayer engages the heart and mind, connecting us to God for real conversation and requests that spring from our lives and the lives of those around us. Merely chanting before God is no different than saying nothing; that's why Jesus called it "babbling" (6:7).

Of the seven sayings of Jesus from the cross recorded in the four Gospels, Matthew includes the prayer: "Why have you forsaken me?" (27:46). Only in this statement do we hear the agony of the loss of fellowship with God that humanity's sin created and which Christ bore. Matthew's record of that moment was a reminder to his readers of Jesus' dynamic as both the Messiah and the Son of God.

PRAYING SCRIPTURE

Matthew 1

God with us. Can you imagine a more glorious answer to a centuries-old prophecy than God's stepping out of heaven, descending to earth, not as a god of mythology, but as a human babe? He was born to normal people, among livestock, with poor shepherds as an audience. Immanuel.

Stop and reflect on this glorious truth. Thank God that he is not distant but close to those he came to save.

THE GENEALOGY OF JESUS THE MESSIAH

1 This is the genealogy[a] of Jesus the Messiah[b] the son of David, the son of Abraham:

2 Abraham was the father of Isaac,
Isaac the father of Jacob,
Jacob the father of Judah and his brothers,
3 Judah the father of Perez and Zerah, whose mother was Tamar,
Perez the father of Hezron,
Hezron the father of Ram,
4 Ram the father of Amminadab,
Amminadab the father of Nahshon,
Nahshon the father of Salmon,
5 Salmon the father of Boaz, whose mother was Rahab,
Boaz the father of Obed, whose mother was Ruth,
Obed the father of Jesse,
6 and Jesse the father of King David.

David was the father of Solomon, whose mother had been Uriah's wife,
7 Solomon the father of Rehoboam,
Rehoboam the father of Abijah,
Abijah the father of Asa,
8 Asa the father of Jehoshaphat,
Jehoshaphat the father of Jehoram,
Jehoram the father of Uzziah,
9 Uzziah the father of Jotham,
Jotham the father of Ahaz,
Ahaz the father of Hezekiah,
10 Hezekiah the father of Manasseh,
Manasseh the father of Amon,
Amon the father of Josiah,
11 and Josiah the father of Jeconiah[c] and his brothers at the time of the exile to Babylon.

12 After the exile to Babylon:
Jeconiah was the father of Shealtiel,
Shealtiel the father of Zerubbabel,
13 Zerubbabel the father of Abihud,
Abihud the father of Eliakim,
Eliakim the father of Azor,
14 Azor the father of Zadok,
Zadok the father of Akim,
Akim the father of Elihud,
15 Elihud the father of Eleazar,
Eleazar the father of Matthan,
Matthan the father of Jacob,
16 and Jacob the father of Joseph, the husband of Mary, and Mary was the mother of Jesus who is called the Messiah.

17 Thus there were fourteen generations in all from Abraham to David, fourteen from David to the exile to Babylon, and fourteen from the exile to the Messiah.

---

[a] *1* Or *is an account of the origin* [b] *1* Or *Jesus Christ. Messiah* (Hebrew) and *Christ* (Greek) both mean *Anointed One*; also in verse 18. [c] *11* That is, Jehoiachin; also in verse 12

JOSEPH ACCEPTS JESUS AS HIS SON

18This is how the birth of Jesus the Messiah came about[a]: His mother Mary was pledged to be married to Joseph, but before they came together, she was found to be pregnant through the Holy Spirit. 19Because Joseph her husband was faithful to the law, and yet[b] did not want to expose her to public disgrace, he had in mind to divorce her quietly.

20But after he had considered this, an angel of the Lord appeared to him in a dream and said, "Joseph son of David, do not be afraid to take Mary home as your wife, because what is conceived in her is from the Holy Spirit. 21She will give birth to a son, and you are to give him the name Jesus,[c] because he will save his people from their sins."

22All this took place to fulfill what the Lord had said through the prophet: 23"The virgin will conceive and give birth to a son, and they will call him Immanuel"[d] (which means "God with us").

24When Joseph woke up, he did what the angel of the Lord had commanded him and took Mary home as his wife. 25But he did not consummate their marriage until she gave birth to a son. And he gave him the name Jesus.

THE MAGI VISIT THE MESSIAH

2 After Jesus was born in Bethlehem in Judea, during the time of King Herod, Magi[e] from the east came to Jerusalem 2and asked, "Where is the one who has been born king of the Jews? We saw his star when it rose and have come to worship him."

3When King Herod heard this he was disturbed, and all Jerusalem with him. 4When he had called together all the people's chief priests and teachers of the law, he asked them where the Messiah was to be born. 5"In Bethlehem in Judea," they replied, "for this is what the prophet has written:

6" 'But you, Bethlehem, in the land of Judah,
 are by no means least among the rulers of Judah;
for out of you will come a ruler
 who will shepherd my people Israel.'[f]"

7Then Herod called the Magi secretly and found out from them the exact time the star had appeared. 8He sent them to Bethlehem and said, "Go and search carefully for the child. As soon as you find him, report to me, so that I too may go and worship him."

9After they had heard the king, they went on their way, and the star they had seen when it rose went ahead of them until it stopped over the place where the child was. 10When they saw the star, they were overjoyed. 11On coming to the house, they saw the child with his mother Mary, and they bowed down and worshiped him. Then they opened their treasures and presented him with gifts of gold, frankincense and myrrh. 12And having been warned in a dream not to go back to Herod, they returned to their country by another route.

THE ESCAPE TO EGYPT

13When they had gone, an angel of the Lord appeared to Joseph in a dream. "Get up," he said, "take the child and his mother and escape to

PRAYING SCRIPTURE

Matthew 2

The story of the wise men looking for Jesus is the story of everyone who encountered a witness to Jesus and sought him. The wise men did not start off on their own; God illumined their interest and guided their way. They found Jesus because God first shone a starlight.

How did you first hear of Jesus? Someone somewhere probably shined the light of Jesus. Praise God for their faithful witness.

---

[a] 18 Or *The origin of Jesus the Messiah was like this* [b] 19 Or *was a righteous man and* [c] 21 *Jesus* is the Greek form of *Joshua*, which means *the LORD saves.* [d] 23 Isaiah 7:14 [e] 1 Traditionally *wise men* [f] 6 Micah 5:2,4

Egypt. Stay there until I tell you, for Herod is going to search for the
child to kill him."
14So he got up, took the child and his mother during the night and
left for Egypt, 15where he stayed until the death of Herod. And so was
fulfilled what the Lord had said through the prophet: "Out of Egypt I
called my son."[a]
16When Herod realized that he had been outwitted by the Magi, he
was furious, and he gave orders to kill all the boys in Bethlehem and
its vicinity who were two years old and under, in accordance with the
time he had learned from the Magi. 17Then what was said through the
prophet Jeremiah was fulfilled:

18 "A voice is heard in Ramah,
  weeping and great mourning,
Rachel weeping for her children
  and refusing to be comforted,
  because they are no more."[b]

THE RETURN TO NAZARETH

19After Herod died, an angel of the Lord appeared in a dream to Jo-
seph in Egypt 20and said, "Get up, take the child and his mother and
go to the land of Israel, for those who were trying to take the child's
life are dead."
21So he got up, took the child and his mother and went to the land
of Israel. 22But when he heard that Archelaus was reigning in Judea
in place of his father Herod, he was afraid to go there. Having been
warned in a dream, he withdrew to the district of Galilee, 23and he
went and lived in a town called Nazareth. So was fulfilled what was said
through the prophets, that he would be called a Nazarene.

JOHN THE BAPTIST PREPARES THE WAY

3 In those days John the Baptist came, preaching in the wilderness
of Judea 2and saying, "Repent, for the kingdom of heaven has
come near." 3This is he who was spoken of through the prophet Isaiah:

"A voice of one calling in the wilderness,
'Prepare the way for the Lord,
  make straight paths for him.'"[c]

4John's clothes were made of camel's hair, and he had a leather belt
around his waist. His food was locusts and wild honey. 5People went
out to him from Jerusalem and all Judea and the whole region of the
Jordan. 6Confessing their sins, they were baptized by him in the Jor-
dan River.
7But when he saw many of the Pharisees and Sadducees coming to
where he was baptizing, he said to them: "You brood of vipers! Who
warned you to flee from the coming wrath? 8Produce fruit in keeping
with repentance. 9And do not think you can say to yourselves, 'We have
Abraham as our father.' I tell you that out of these stones God can raise
up children for Abraham. 10The ax is already at the root of the trees,
and every tree that does not produce good fruit will be cut down and
thrown into the fire.
11"I baptize you with[d] water for repentance. But after me comes one

PRAYING SCRIPTURE

Matthew 3

Matthew references Isaiah's prophecy, the promise of John the Baptist, who would prepare the way of Jesus (see verse 3). The story of Jesus includes many players, but none more important than John. He is the one who introduced Jesus to his people as the Lamb of God.

Have you thanked God lately for Jesus, the Lamb who gave himself for you? We can never thank him enough for the forgiveness he has given.

[a] *15* Hosea 11:1 [b] *18* Jer. 31:15 [c] *3* Isaiah 40:3 [d] *11* Or *in*

who is more powerful than I, whose sandals I am not worthy to carry.
He will baptize you with[a] the Holy Spirit and fire. 12 His winnowing fork
is in his hand, and he will clear his threshing floor, gathering his wheat
into the barn and burning up the chaff with unquenchable fire."

THE BAPTISM OF JESUS

13 Then Jesus came from Galilee to the Jordan to be baptized by John.
14 But John tried to deter him, saying, "I need to be baptized by you,
and do you come to me?"

15 Jesus replied, "Let it be so now; it is proper for us to do this to fulfill
all righteousness." Then John consented.

16 As soon as Jesus was baptized, he went up out of the water. At that
moment heaven was opened, and he saw the Spirit of God descending
like a dove and alighting on him. 17 And a voice from heaven said, "This
is my Son, whom I love; with him I am well pleased."

JESUS IS TESTED IN THE WILDERNESS

4 Then Jesus was led by the Spirit into the wilderness to be tempted[b]
by the devil. 2 After fasting forty days and forty nights, he was hun-
gry. 3 The tempter came to him and said, "If you are the Son of God, tell
these stones to become bread."

4 Jesus answered, "It is written: 'Man shall not live on bread alone,
but on every word that comes from the mouth of God.'[c]"

5 Then the devil took him to the holy city and had him stand on
the highest point of the temple. 6 "If you are the Son of God," he said,
"throw yourself down. For it is written:

"'He will command his angels concerning you,
and they will lift you up in their hands,
so that you will not strike your foot against a stone.'[d]"

7 Jesus answered him, "It is also written: 'Do not put the Lord your
God to the test.'[e]"

8 Again, the devil took him to a very high mountain and showed him
all the kingdoms of the world and their splendor. 9 "All this I will give
you," he said, "if you will bow down and worship me."

10 Jesus said to him, "Away from me, Satan! For it is written: 'Worship
the Lord your God, and serve him only.'[f]"

11 Then the devil left him, and angels came and attended him.

JESUS BEGINS TO PREACH

12 When Jesus heard that John had been put in prison, he withdrew
to Galilee. 13 Leaving Nazareth, he went and lived in Capernaum, which
was by the lake in the area of Zebulun and Naphtali — 14 to fulfill what
was said through the prophet Isaiah:

15 "Land of Zebulun and land of Naphtali,
the Way of the Sea, beyond the Jordan,
Galilee of the Gentiles —
16 the people living in darkness
have seen a great light;
on those living in the land of the shadow of death
a light has dawned."[g]

PRAYING SCRIPTURE

Matthew 4

Jesus' temptations remind us that he truly lived like one of us. Jesus wasn't immune to temptation. He endured temptation. His pattern of using Scripture to combat Satan is for all of us. We cannot withstand temptation apart from the "it is written" God has provided for us.

Do you have an area of temptation where you often fail? Memorize and pray Scripture about it to be strengthened to overcome.

---

[a] *11* Or *in* [b] *1* The Greek for *tempted* can also mean *tested.* [c] *4* Deut. 8:3
[d] *6* Psalm 91:11,12 [e] *7* Deut. 6:16 [f] *10* Deut. 6:13 [g] *16* Isaiah 9:1,2

17 From that time on Jesus began to preach, "Repent, for the kingdom
of heaven has come near."

JESUS CALLS HIS FIRST DISCIPLES

18 As Jesus was walking beside the Sea of Galilee, he saw two broth-
ers, Simon called Peter and his brother Andrew. They were casting a
net into the lake, for they were fishermen. 19 "Come, follow me," Jesus
said, "and I will send you out to fish for people." 20 At once they left
their nets and followed him.
21 Going on from there, he saw two other brothers, James son of Zeb-
edee and his brother John. They were in a boat with their father Zeb-
edee, preparing their nets. Jesus called them, 22 and immediately they
left the boat and their father and followed him.

JESUS HEALS THE SICK

23 Jesus went throughout Galilee, teaching in their synagogues, pro-
claiming the good news of the kingdom, and healing every disease and
sickness among the people. 24 News about him spread all over Syria,
and people brought to him all who were ill with various diseases, those
suffering severe pain, the demon-possessed, those having seizures,
and the paralyzed; and he healed them. 25 Large crowds from Galilee,
the Decapolis,[a] Jerusalem, Judea and the region across the Jordan fol-
lowed him.

INTRODUCTION TO THE SERMON ON THE MOUNT

5 Now when Jesus saw the crowds, he went up on a mountainside
and sat down. His disciples came to him, 2 and he began to teach
them.

PRAYING SCRIPTURE

Matthew 5

The Beatitudes are far from the detailed regulations of Moses' Law given to Israel. In them Jesus has given an ethic for all people everywhere who desire to be a part of his rule and reign. These are the blessings that belong to all who strive to live like Jesus.

Read and pray through this oft-quoted passage, asking God to make each beatitude a reality in your life.

THE BEATITUDES

He said:

3 "Blessed are the poor in spirit,
for theirs is the kingdom of heaven.
4 Blessed are those who mourn,
for they will be comforted.
5 Blessed are the meek,
for they will inherit the earth.
6 Blessed are those who hunger and thirst for righteousness,
for they will be filled.
7 Blessed are the merciful,
for they will be shown mercy.
8 Blessed are the pure in heart,
for they will see God.
9 Blessed are the peacemakers,
for they will be called children of God.
10 Blessed are those who are persecuted because of righteousness,
for theirs is the kingdom of heaven.

11 "Blessed are you when people insult you, persecute you and falsely
say all kinds of evil against you because of me. 12 Rejoice and be glad,
because great is your reward in heaven, for in the same way they per-
secuted the prophets who were before you.

[a] *25* That is, the Ten Cities

SALT AND LIGHT

13 “You are the salt of the earth. But if the salt loses its saltiness, how
can it be made salty again? It is no longer good for anything, except to
be thrown out and trampled underfoot.
14 “You are the light of the world. A town built on a hill cannot be hid-
den. 15 Neither do people light a lamp and put it under a bowl. Instead
they put it on its stand, and it gives light to everyone in the house. 16 In
the same way, let your light shine before others, that they may see your
good deeds and glorify your Father in heaven.

THE FULFILLMENT OF THE LAW

17 “Do not think that I have come to abolish the Law or the Proph-
ets; I have not come to abolish them but to fulfill them. 18 For truly I
tell you, until heaven and earth disappear, not the smallest letter, not
the least stroke of a pen, will by any means disappear from the Law
until everything is accomplished. 19 Therefore anyone who sets aside
one of the least of these commands and teaches others accordingly
will be called least in the kingdom of heaven, but whoever practices
and teaches these commands will be called great in the kingdom of
heaven. 20 For I tell you that unless your righteousness surpasses that
of the Pharisees and the teachers of the law, you will certainly not enter
the kingdom of heaven.

MURDER

21 “You have heard that it was said to the people long ago, ‘You shall
not murder,[a] and anyone who murders will be subject to judgment.’
22 But I tell you that anyone who is angry with a brother or sister[b,c] will
be subject to judgment. Again, anyone who says to a brother or sister,
‘Raca,’[d] is answerable to the court. And anyone who says, ‘You fool!’ will
be in danger of the fire of hell.
23 “Therefore, if you are offering your gift at the altar and there re-
member that your brother or sister has something against you, 24 leave
your gift there in front of the altar. First go and be reconciled to them;
then come and offer your gift.
25 “Settle matters quickly with your adversary who is taking you to
court. Do it while you are still together on the way, or your adversary
may hand you over to the judge, and the judge may hand you over to
the officer, and you may be thrown into prison. 26 Truly I tell you, you
will not get out until you have paid the last penny.

ADULTERY

27 “You have heard that it was said, ‘You shall not commit adultery.’[e]
28 But I tell you that anyone who looks at a woman lustfully has already
committed adultery with her in his heart. 29 If your right eye causes you
to stumble, gouge it out and throw it away. It is better for you to lose
one part of your body than for your whole body to be thrown into hell.
30 And if your right hand causes you to stumble, cut it off and throw
it away. It is better for you to lose one part of your body than for your
whole body to go into hell.

---

[a] *21* Exodus 20:13 [b] *22* The Greek word for *brother or sister* (*adelphos*) refers here to a fellow disciple, whether man or woman; also in verse 23.
[c] *22* Some manuscripts *brother or sister without cause* [d] *22* An Aramaic term of contempt [e] *27* Exodus 20:14

DIVORCE

31"It has been said, 'Anyone who divorces his wife must give her a certificate of divorce.'[a] 32But I tell you that anyone who divorces his wife, except for sexual immorality, makes her the victim of adultery, and anyone who marries a divorced woman commits adultery.

OATHS

33"Again, you have heard that it was said to the people long ago, 'Do not break your oath, but fulfill to the Lord the vows you have made.' 34But I tell you, do not swear an oath at all: either by heaven, for it is God's throne; 35or by the earth, for it is his footstool; or by Jerusalem, for it is the city of the Great King. 36And do not swear by your head, for you cannot make even one hair white or black. 37All you need to say is simply 'Yes' or 'No'; anything beyond this comes from the evil one.[b]

EYE FOR EYE

38"You have heard that it was said, 'Eye for eye, and tooth for tooth.'[c] 39But I tell you, do not resist an evil person. If anyone slaps you on the right cheek, turn to them the other cheek also. 40And if anyone wants to sue you and take your shirt, hand over your coat as well. 41If anyone forces you to go one mile, go with them two miles. 42Give to the one who asks you, and do not turn away from the one who wants to borrow from you.

LOVE FOR ENEMIES

43"You have heard that it was said, 'Love your neighbor[d] and hate your enemy.' 44But I tell you, love your enemies and pray for those who persecute you, 45that you may be children of your Father in heaven. He causes his sun to rise on the evil and the good, and sends rain on the righteous and the unrighteous. 46If you love those who love you, what reward will you get? Are not even the tax collectors doing that? 47And if you greet only your own people, what are you doing more than others? Do not even pagans do that? 48Be perfect, therefore, as your heavenly Father is perfect.

GIVING TO THE NEEDY

6 "Be careful not to practice your righteousness in front of others to be seen by them. If you do, you will have no reward from your Father in heaven.

2"So when you give to the needy, do not announce it with trumpets, as the hypocrites do in the synagogues and on the streets, to be honored by others. Truly I tell you, they have received their reward in full. 3But when you give to the needy, do not let your left hand know what your right hand is doing, 4so that your giving may be in secret. Then your Father, who sees what is done in secret, will reward you.

PRAYER

5"And when you pray, do not be like the hypocrites, for they love to pray standing in the synagogues and on the street corners to be seen by others. Truly I tell you, they have received their reward in full. 6But when you pray, go into your room, close the door and pray to your

PRAYING SCRIPTURE

Matthew 6

In a world that drives us to worry, with its dangers, disease and death, Jesus tells us not to worry. Even more, he teaches us that worry is a waste. It changes nothing about our lives, leaving the world unchanged and us worse off. Instead, he says, learn from creation that God takes care of everything.

Are you consumed with worry? Remember: God is in control. Ask him for daily assurance.

---

[a] *31* Deut. 24:1 [b] *37* Or *from evil* [c] *38* Exodus 21:24; Lev. 24:20; Deut. 19:21
[d] *43* Lev. 19:18

Father, who is unseen. Then your Father, who sees what is done in se-
cret, will reward you. 7And when you pray, do not keep on babbling
like pagans, for they think they will be heard because of their many
words. 8Do not be like them, for your Father knows what you need
before you ask him.
9"This, then, is how you should pray:

"'Our Father in heaven,
hallowed be your name,
10 your kingdom come,
your will be done,
on earth as it is in heaven.
11 Give us today our daily bread.
12 And forgive us our debts,
as we also have forgiven our debtors.
13 And lead us not into temptation,[a]
but deliver us from the evil one.[b]'

14For if you forgive other people when they sin against you, your heav-
enly Father will also forgive you. 15But if you do not forgive others their
sins, your Father will not forgive your sins.

FASTING

16"When you fast, do not look somber as the hypocrites do, for they
disfigure their faces to show others they are fasting. Truly I tell you,
they have received their reward in full. 17But when you fast, put oil on
your head and wash your face, 18so that it will not be obvious to others
that you are fasting, but only to your Father, who is unseen; and your
Father, who sees what is done in secret, will reward you.

TREASURES IN HEAVEN

19"Do not store up for yourselves treasures on earth, where moths
and vermin destroy, and where thieves break in and steal. 20But store
up for yourselves treasures in heaven, where moths and vermin do not
destroy, and where thieves do not break in and steal. 21For where your
treasure is, there your heart will be also.
22"The eye is the lamp of the body. If your eyes are healthy,[c] your
whole body will be full of light. 23But if your eyes are unhealthy,[d] your
whole body will be full of darkness. If then the light within you is dark-
ness, how great is that darkness!
24"No one can serve two masters. Either you will hate the one and
love the other, or you will be devoted to the one and despise the other.
You cannot serve both God and money.

DO NOT WORRY

25"Therefore I tell you, do not worry about your life, what you will
eat or drink; or about your body, what you will wear. Is not life more
than food, and the body more than clothes? 26Look at the birds of the
air; they do not sow or reap or store away in barns, and yet your heav-
enly Father feeds them. Are you not much more valuable than they?
27Can any one of you by worrying add a single hour to your life[e]?

---

[a] 13 The Greek for *temptation* can also mean *testing.* [b] 13 Or *from evil*; some late manuscripts *one, / for yours is the kingdom and the power and the glory forever. Amen.* [c] 22 The Greek for *healthy* here implies *generous.* [d] 23 The Greek for *unhealthy* here implies *stingy.* [e] 27 Or *single cubit to your height*

28“And why do you worry about clothes? See how the flowers of the field grow. They do not labor or spin. 29Yet I tell you that not even Solomon in all his splendor was dressed like one of these. 30If that is how God clothes the grass of the field, which is here today and tomorrow is thrown into the fire, will he not much more clothe you—you of little faith? 31So do not worry, saying, ‘What shall we eat?’ or ‘What shall we drink?’ or ‘What shall we wear?’ 32For the pagans run after all these things, and your heavenly Father knows that you need them. 33But seek first his kingdom and his righteousness, and all these things will be given to you as well. 34Therefore do not worry about tomorrow, for tomorrow will worry about itself. Each day has enough trouble of its own.

JUDGING OTHERS

7 “Do not judge, or you too will be judged. 2For in the same way you judge others, you will be judged, and with the measure you use, it will be measured to you.

3“Why do you look at the speck of sawdust in your brother’s eye and pay no attention to the plank in your own eye? 4How can you say to your brother, ‘Let me take the speck out of your eye,’ when all the time there is a plank in your own eye? 5You hypocrite, first take the plank out of your own eye, and then you will see clearly to remove the speck from your brother’s eye.

6“Do not give dogs what is sacred; do not throw your pearls to pigs. If you do, they may trample them under their feet, and turn and tear you to pieces.

PRAYING SCRIPTURE

Matthew 7

Prayer is not always a one-and-done proposition. To build our faith, the Lord often challenges our persistence. If he doesn’t answer right away, we are to keep asking, keep seeking, keep knocking. As he builds our faith, our lives become like a house built on a rock that life’s storms cannot destroy.

Be persistent in prayer. Whatever burdens you, whatever you want to see the Lord do, ask, seek and knock until he answers.

ASK, SEEK, KNOCK

7“Ask and it will be given to you; seek and you will find; knock and the door will be opened to you. 8For everyone who asks receives; the one who seeks finds; and to the one who knocks, the door will be opened.

9“Which of you, if your son asks for bread, will give him a stone? 10Or if he asks for a fish, will give him a snake? 11If you, then, though you are evil, know how to give good gifts to your children, how much more will your Father in heaven give good gifts to those who ask him! 12So in everything, do to others what you would have them do to you, for this sums up the Law and the Prophets.

THE NARROW AND WIDE GATES

13“Enter through the narrow gate. For wide is the gate and broad is the road that leads to destruction, and many enter through it. 14But small is the gate and narrow the road that leads to life, and only a few find it.

TRUE AND FALSE PROPHETS

15“Watch out for false prophets. They come to you in sheep’s clothing, but inwardly they are ferocious wolves. 16By their fruit you will recognize them. Do people pick grapes from thornbushes, or figs from thistles? 17Likewise, every good tree bears good fruit, but a bad tree bears bad fruit. 18A good tree cannot bear bad fruit, and a bad tree cannot bear good fruit. 19Every tree that does not bear good fruit is cut down and thrown into the fire. 20Thus, by their fruit you will recognize them.

TRUE AND FALSE DISCIPLES

21“Not everyone who says to me, ‘Lord, Lord,’ will enter the kingdom of heaven, but only the one who does the will of my Father who is in heaven. 22Many will say to me on that day, ‘Lord, Lord, did we not prophesy in your name and in your name drive out demons and in your name perform many miracles?’ 23Then I will tell them plainly, ‘I never knew you. Away from me, you evildoers!’

THE WISE AND FOOLISH BUILDERS

24“Therefore everyone who hears these words of mine and puts them into practice is like a wise man who built his house on the rock. 25The rain came down, the streams rose, and the winds blew and beat against that house; yet it did not fall, because it had its foundation on the rock. 26But everyone who hears these words of mine and does not put them into practice is like a foolish man who built his house on sand. 27The rain came down, the streams rose, and the winds blew and beat against that house, and it fell with a great crash.”

28When Jesus had finished saying these things, the crowds were amazed at his teaching, 29because he taught as one who had authority, and not as their teachers of the law.

JESUS HEALS A MAN WITH LEPROSY

8 When Jesus came down from the mountainside, large crowds followed him. 2A man with leprosy[a] came and knelt before him and said, “Lord, if you are willing, you can make me clean.”

3Jesus reached out his hand and touched the man. “I am willing,” he said. “Be clean!” Immediately he was cleansed of his leprosy. 4Then Jesus said to him, “See that you don’t tell anyone. But go, show yourself to the priest and offer the gift Moses commanded, as a testimony to them.”

THE FAITH OF THE CENTURION

5When Jesus had entered Capernaum, a centurion came to him, asking for help. 6“Lord,” he said, “my servant lies at home paralyzed, suffering terribly.”

7Jesus said to him, “Shall I come and heal him?”

8The centurion replied, “Lord, I do not deserve to have you come under my roof. But just say the word, and my servant will be healed. 9For I myself am a man under authority, with soldiers under me. I tell this one, ‘Go,’ and he goes; and that one, ‘Come,’ and he comes. I say to my servant, ‘Do this,’ and he does it.”

10When Jesus heard this, he was amazed and said to those following him, “Truly I tell you, I have not found anyone in Israel with such great faith. 11I say to you that many will come from the east and the west, and will take their places at the feast with Abraham, Isaac and Jacob in the kingdom of heaven. 12But the subjects of the kingdom will be thrown outside, into the darkness, where there will be weeping and gnashing of teeth.”

13Then Jesus said to the centurion, “Go! Let it be done just as you believed it would.” And his servant was healed at that moment.

---

[a] *2* The Greek word traditionally translated *leprosy* was used for various diseases affecting the skin.

PRAYING SCRIPTURE

Matthew 8

This packed chapter emphasizes Jesus’ healing power and his authority over nature, but central to his gospel message is one of his strongest discipleship challenges: “Follow me, and leave the dead to bury their own dead” (verse 22). The call to discipleship is a call to die to all of our worldly desires.

Do you find it difficult to deny yourself? Ask God to help you make the sacrifices discipleship requires.

JESUS HEALS MANY

14When Jesus came into Peter's house, he saw Peter's mother-in-law
lying in bed with a fever. 15He touched her hand and the fever left her,
and she got up and began to wait on him.
16When evening came, many who were demon-possessed were
brought to him, and he drove out the spirits with a word and healed all
the sick. 17This was to fulfill what was spoken through the prophet Isaiah:

"He took up our infirmities
and bore our diseases."[a]

THE COST OF FOLLOWING JESUS

18When Jesus saw the crowd around him, he gave orders to cross to
the other side of the lake. 19Then a teacher of the law came to him and
said, "Teacher, I will follow you wherever you go."
20Jesus replied, "Foxes have dens and birds have nests, but the Son
of Man has no place to lay his head."
21Another disciple said to him, "Lord, first let me go and bury my
father."
22But Jesus told him, "Follow me, and let the dead bury their own
dead."

JESUS CALMS THE STORM

23Then he got into the boat and his disciples followed him. 24Sud-
denly a furious storm came up on the lake, so that the waves swept
over the boat. But Jesus was sleeping. 25The disciples went and woke
him, saying, "Lord, save us! We're going to drown!"
26He replied, "You of little faith, why are you so afraid?" Then he got
up and rebuked the winds and the waves, and it was completely calm.
27The men were amazed and asked, "What kind of man is this? Even
the winds and the waves obey him!"

JESUS RESTORES TWO DEMON-POSSESSED MEN

28When he arrived at the other side in the region of the Gadarenes,[b]
two demon-possessed men coming from the tombs met him. They
were so violent that no one could pass that way. 29"What do you want
with us, Son of God?" they shouted. "Have you come here to torture us
before the appointed time?"
30Some distance from them a large herd of pigs was feeding. 31The de-
mons begged Jesus, "If you drive us out, send us into the herd of pigs."
32He said to them, "Go!" So they came out and went into the pigs, and
the whole herd rushed down the steep bank into the lake and died in
the water. 33Those tending the pigs ran off, went into the town and re-
ported all this, including what had happened to the demon-possessed
men. 34Then the whole town went out to meet Jesus. And when they
saw him, they pleaded with him to leave their region.

JESUS FORGIVES AND HEALS A PARALYZED MAN

9 Jesus stepped into a boat, crossed over and came to his own town.
2Some men brought to him a paralyzed man, lying on a mat. When
Jesus saw their faith, he said to the man, "Take heart, son; your sins
are forgiven."

PRAYING SCRIPTURE

Matthew 9

The paralyzed man brought to Jesus by his friends put Jesus front and center before the religious leaders. Jesus didn't shy away from his mission: He not only healed the man, he first forgave his sins. To the leaders it was blasphemy, but for Jesus it was why he came.

Jesus came both to heal and forgive, and he still provides both of these needs today. So come to him in faith on behalf of yourself or someone else in need.

---

[a] *17* Isaiah 53:4 (see Septuagint) [b] *28* Some manuscripts *Gergesenes*; other manuscripts *Gerasenes*

3 At this, some of the teachers of the law said to themselves, "This
fellow is blaspheming!"
4 Knowing their thoughts, Jesus said, "Why do you entertain evil
thoughts in your hearts? 5 Which is easier: to say, 'Your sins are for-
given,' or to say, 'Get up and walk'? 6 But I want you to know that the
Son of Man has authority on earth to forgive sins." So he said to the
paralyzed man, "Get up, take your mat and go home." 7 Then the man
got up and went home. 8 When the crowd saw this, they were filled
with awe; and they praised God, who had given such authority to man.

THE CALLING OF MATTHEW

9 As Jesus went on from there, he saw a man named Matthew sitting
at the tax collector's booth. "Follow me," he told him, and Matthew got
up and followed him.
10 While Jesus was having dinner at Matthew's house, many tax col-
lectors and sinners came and ate with him and his disciples. 11 When
the Pharisees saw this, they asked his disciples, "Why does your teacher
eat with tax collectors and sinners?"
12 On hearing this, Jesus said, "It is not the healthy who need a doc-
tor, but the sick. 13 But go and learn what this means: 'I desire mercy,
not sacrifice.'[a] For I have not come to call the righteous, but sinners."

JESUS QUESTIONED ABOUT FASTING

14 Then John's disciples came and asked him, "How is it that we and
the Pharisees fast often, but your disciples do not fast?"
15 Jesus answered, "How can the guests of the bridegroom mourn
while he is with them? The time will come when the bridegroom will
be taken from them; then they will fast.
16 "No one sews a patch of unshrunk cloth on an old garment, for the
patch will pull away from the garment, making the tear worse. 17 Nei-
ther do people pour new wine into old wineskins. If they do, the skins
will burst; the wine will run out and the wineskins will be ruined. No,
they pour new wine into new wineskins, and both are preserved."

JESUS RAISES A DEAD GIRL AND HEALS A SICK WOMAN

18 While he was saying this, a synagogue leader came and knelt be-
fore him and said, "My daughter has just died. But come and put your
hand on her, and she will live." 19 Jesus got up and went with him, and
so did his disciples.
20 Just then a woman who had been subject to bleeding for twelve
years came up behind him and touched the edge of his cloak. 21 She
said to herself, "If I only touch his cloak, I will be healed."
22 Jesus turned and saw her. "Take heart, daughter," he said, "your
faith has healed you." And the woman was healed at that moment.
23 When Jesus entered the synagogue leader's house and saw the
noisy crowd and people playing pipes, 24 he said, "Go away. The girl is
not dead but asleep." But they laughed at him. 25 After the crowd had
been put outside, he went in and took the girl by the hand, and she got
up. 26 News of this spread through all that region.

JESUS HEALS THE BLIND AND THE MUTE

27 As Jesus went on from there, two blind men followed him, calling
out, "Have mercy on us, Son of David!"

[a] *13* Hosea 6:6

28When he had gone indoors, the blind men came to him, and he
asked them, "Do you believe that I am able to do this?"
"Yes, Lord," they replied.
29Then he touched their eyes and said, "According to your faith let
it be done to you"; 30and their sight was restored. Jesus warned them
sternly, "See that no one knows about this." 31But they went out and
spread the news about him all over that region.
32While they were going out, a man who was demon-possessed and
could not talk was brought to Jesus. 33And when the demon was driven
out, the man who had been mute spoke. The crowd was amazed and
said, "Nothing like this has ever been seen in Israel."
34But the Pharisees said, "It is by the prince of demons that he drives
out demons."

THE WORKERS ARE FEW

35Jesus went through all the towns and villages, teaching in their
synagogues, proclaiming the good news of the kingdom and healing
every disease and sickness. 36When he saw the crowds, he had com-
passion on them, because they were harassed and helpless, like sheep
without a shepherd. 37Then he said to his disciples, "The harvest is
plentiful but the workers are few. 38Ask the Lord of the harvest, there-
fore, to send out workers into his harvest field."

JESUS SENDS OUT THE TWELVE

10 Jesus called his twelve disciples to him and gave them author-
ity to drive out impure spirits and to heal every disease and
sickness.
2These are the names of the twelve apostles: first, Simon (who is
called Peter) and his brother Andrew; James son of Zebedee, and his
brother John; 3Philip and Bartholomew; Thomas and Matthew the tax
collector; James son of Alphaeus, and Thaddaeus; 4Simon the Zealot
and Judas Iscariot, who betrayed him.
5These twelve Jesus sent out with the following instructions: "Do
not go among the Gentiles or enter any town of the Samaritans. 6Go
rather to the lost sheep of Israel. 7As you go, proclaim this message:
'The kingdom of heaven has come near.' 8Heal the sick, raise the dead,
cleanse those who have leprosy,[a] drive out demons. Freely you have
received; freely give.
9"Do not get any gold or silver or copper to take with you in your
belts — 10no bag for the journey or extra shirt or sandals or a staff,
for the worker is worth his keep. 11Whatever town or village you enter,
search there for some worthy person and stay at their house until you
leave. 12As you enter the home, give it your greeting. 13If the home is
deserving, let your peace rest on it; if it is not, let your peace return to
you. 14If anyone will not welcome you or listen to your words, leave
that home or town and shake the dust off your feet. 15Truly I tell you,
it will be more bearable for Sodom and Gomorrah on the day of judg-
ment than for that town.
16"I am sending you out like sheep among wolves. Therefore be as
shrewd as snakes and as innocent as doves. 17Be on your guard; you will
be handed over to the local councils and be flogged in the synagogues.

PRAYING SCRIPTURE

Matthew 10

One of the assurances we have in following Christ is that we will face trials. Jesus warned the Twelve of possible mistreatment while on their preaching mission (see verses 16–26). Jesus said he himself is a cause of division (see verses 34–37). The Christian life is not a life of ease if we are authentically following Christ.

Thank God for opportunities to suffer for Christ and for the strength to endure the trials that come your way.

[a] *8* The Greek word traditionally translated *leprosy* was used for various diseases affecting the skin.

18On my account you will be brought before governors and kings as witnesses to them and to the Gentiles. 19But when they arrest you, do not worry about what to say or how to say it. At that time you will be given what to say, 20for it will not be you speaking, but the Spirit of your Father speaking through you.

21"Brother will betray brother to death, and a father his child; children will rebel against their parents and have them put to death. 22You will be hated by everyone because of me, but the one who stands firm to the end will be saved. 23When you are persecuted in one place, flee to another. Truly I tell you, you will not finish going through the towns of Israel before the Son of Man comes.

24"The student is not above the teacher, nor a servant above his master. 25It is enough for students to be like their teachers, and servants like their masters. If the head of the house has been called Beelzebul, how much more the members of his household!

26"So do not be afraid of them, for there is nothing concealed that will not be disclosed, or hidden that will not be made known. 27What I tell you in the dark, speak in the daylight; what is whispered in your ear, proclaim from the roofs. 28Do not be afraid of those who kill the body but cannot kill the soul. Rather, be afraid of the One who can destroy both soul and body in hell. 29Are not two sparrows sold for a penny? Yet not one of them will fall to the ground outside your Father's care.[a] 30And even the very hairs of your head are all numbered. 31So don't be afraid; you are worth more than many sparrows.

32"Whoever acknowledges me before others, I will also acknowledge before my Father in heaven. 33But whoever disowns me before others, I will disown before my Father in heaven.

34"Do not suppose that I have come to bring peace to the earth. I did not come to bring peace, but a sword. 35For I have come to turn

"'a man against his father,
  a daughter against her mother,
a daughter-in-law against her mother-in-law—
36 a man's enemies will be the members of his own household.'[b]

37"Anyone who loves their father or mother more than me is not worthy of me; anyone who loves their son or daughter more than me is not worthy of me. 38Whoever does not take up their cross and follow me is not worthy of me. 39Whoever finds their life will lose it, and whoever loses their life for my sake will find it.

40"Anyone who welcomes you welcomes me, and anyone who welcomes me welcomes the one who sent me. 41Whoever welcomes a prophet as a prophet will receive a prophet's reward, and whoever welcomes a righteous person as a righteous person will receive a righteous person's reward. 42And if anyone gives even a cup of cold water to one of these little ones who is my disciple, truly I tell you, that person will certainly not lose their reward."

JESUS AND JOHN THE BAPTIST

11 After Jesus had finished instructing his twelve disciples, he went on from there to teach and preach in the towns of Galilee.[c]

2When John, who was in prison, heard about the deeds of the Messiah, he sent his disciples 3to ask him, "Are you the one who is to come, or should we expect someone else?"

[a] *29* Or *will;* or *knowledge* [b] *36* Micah 7:6 [c] *1* Greek *in their towns*

PRAYING SCRIPTURE

Matthew 11

The most well-known prophet of Jesus' day, the one whose birth prophecy was intertwined with Jesus' own, had been thrown into prison. After hearing about Jesus' ministry, John was curious as to whether Jesus was the Messiah. Jesus used his ministry as proof.

When people around you have questions about Jesus, answer the way he did: with the gospel. Ask God for wisdom to point every seeking person to Jesus.

4Jesus replied, "Go back and report to John what you hear and see: 5The
blind receive sight, the lame walk, those who have leprosy[a] are cleansed,
the deaf hear, the dead are raised, and the good news is proclaimed to
the poor. 6Blessed is anyone who does not stumble on account of me."

7As John's disciples were leaving, Jesus began to speak to the crowd
about John: "What did you go out into the wilderness to see? A reed
swayed by the wind? 8If not, what did you go out to see? A man dressed
in fine clothes? No, those who wear fine clothes are in kings' palaces.
9Then what did you go out to see? A prophet? Yes, I tell you, and more
than a prophet. 10This is the one about whom it is written:

" 'I will send my messenger ahead of you,
   who will prepare your way before you.'[b]

11Truly I tell you, among those born of women there has not risen any-
one greater than John the Baptist; yet whoever is least in the kingdom
of heaven is greater than he. 12From the days of John the Baptist until
now, the kingdom of heaven has been subjected to violence,[c] and vi-
olent people have been raiding it. 13For all the Prophets and the Law
prophesied until John. 14And if you are willing to accept it, he is the
Elijah who was to come. 15Whoever has ears, let them hear.

16"To what can I compare this generation? They are like children sit-
ting in the marketplaces and calling out to others:

17" 'We played the pipe for you,
   and you did not dance;
we sang a dirge,
   and you did not mourn.'

18For John came neither eating nor drinking, and they say, 'He has a de-
mon.' 19The Son of Man came eating and drinking, and they say, 'Here
is a glutton and a drunkard, a friend of tax collectors and sinners.' But
wisdom is proved right by her deeds."

WOE ON UNREPENTANT TOWNS

20Then Jesus began to denounce the towns in which most of his
miracles had been performed, because they did not repent. 21"Woe
to you, Chorazin! Woe to you, Bethsaida! For if the miracles that were
performed in you had been performed in Tyre and Sidon, they would
have repented long ago in sackcloth and ashes. 22But I tell you, it will
be more bearable for Tyre and Sidon on the day of judgment than for
you. 23And you, Capernaum, will you be lifted to the heavens? No, you
will go down to Hades.[d] For if the miracles that were performed in you
had been performed in Sodom, it would have remained to this day.
24But I tell you that it will be more bearable for Sodom on the day of
judgment than for you."

THE FATHER REVEALED IN THE SON

25At that time Jesus said, "I praise you, Father, Lord of heaven
and earth, because you have hidden these things from the wise and
learned, and revealed them to little children. 26Yes, Father, for this is
what you were pleased to do.

27"All things have been committed to me by my Father. No one

---

[a] *5* The Greek word traditionally translated *leprosy* was used for various diseases affecting the skin. [b] *10* Mal. 3:1 [c] *12* Or *been forcefully advancing* [d] *23* That is, the realm of the dead

knows the Son except the Father, and no one knows the Father except
the Son and those to whom the Son chooses to reveal him.
28“Come to me, all you who are weary and burdened, and I will give
you rest. 29Take my yoke upon you and learn from me, for I am gentle
and humble in heart, and you will find rest for your souls. 30For my
yoke is easy and my burden is light.”

JESUS IS LORD OF THE SABBATH

12 At that time Jesus went through the grainfields on the Sabbath.
His disciples were hungry and began to pick some heads of grain
and eat them. 2When the Pharisees saw this, they said to him, “Look!
Your disciples are doing what is unlawful on the Sabbath.”
3He answered, “Haven’t you read what David did when he and his
companions were hungry? 4He entered the house of God, and he and
his companions ate the consecrated bread — which was not lawful for
them to do, but only for the priests. 5Or haven’t you read in the Law
that the priests on Sabbath duty in the temple desecrate the Sabbath
and yet are innocent? 6I tell you that something greater than the tem-
ple is here. 7If you had known what these words mean, ‘I desire mercy,
not sacrifice,’[a] you would not have condemned the innocent. 8For the
Son of Man is Lord of the Sabbath.”
9Going on from that place, he went into their synagogue, 10and a man
with a shriveled hand was there. Looking for a reason to bring charges
against Jesus, they asked him, “Is it lawful to heal on the Sabbath?”
11He said to them, “If any of you has a sheep and it falls into a pit on
the Sabbath, will you not take hold of it and lift it out? 12How much
more valuable is a person than a sheep! Therefore it is lawful to do
good on the Sabbath.”
13Then he said to the man, “Stretch out your hand.” So he stretched it
out and it was completely restored, just as sound as the other. 14But the
Pharisees went out and plotted how they might kill Jesus.

GOD’S CHOSEN SERVANT

15Aware of this, Jesus withdrew from that place. A large crowd fol-
lowed him, and he healed all who were ill. 16He warned them not to
tell others about him. 17This was to fulfill what was spoken through
the prophet Isaiah:

18 “Here is my servant whom I have chosen,
  the one I love, in whom I delight;
I will put my Spirit on him,
  and he will proclaim justice to the nations.
19 He will not quarrel or cry out;
  no one will hear his voice in the streets.
20 A bruised reed he will not break,
  and a smoldering wick he will not snuff out,
till he has brought justice through to victory.
21 In his name the nations will put their hope.”[b]

JESUS AND BEELZEBUL

22Then they brought him a demon-possessed man who was blind and
mute, and Jesus healed him, so that he could both talk and see. 23All
the people were astonished and said, “Could this be the Son of David?”

[a] 7 Hosea 6:6 [b] 21 Isaiah 42:1-4

PRAYING SCRIPTURE

Matthew 12

Jesus’ public ministry consistently aroused the ire of religious leaders—never more than when he violated their ideas of the law’s requirements. Here Jesus healed a man on the Sabbath. This miracle angered the leaders so much that they began plotting to kill him.

As Jesus warned, his life and work cause division. Pray for the strength to follow Christ even when it causes tension in your relationships.

24 But when the Pharisees heard this, they said, "It is only by Beelzebul, the prince of demons, that this fellow drives out demons."

25 Jesus knew their thoughts and said to them, "Every kingdom divided against itself will be ruined, and every city or household divided against itself will not stand. 26 If Satan drives out Satan, he is divided against himself. How then can his kingdom stand? 27 And if I drive out demons by Beelzebul, by whom do your people drive them out? So then, they will be your judges. 28 But if it is by the Spirit of God that I drive out demons, then the kingdom of God has come upon you.

29 "Or again, how can anyone enter a strong man's house and carry off his possessions unless he first ties up the strong man? Then he can plunder his house.

30 "Whoever is not with me is against me, and whoever does not gather with me scatters. 31 And so I tell you, every kind of sin and slander can be forgiven, but blasphemy against the Spirit will not be forgiven. 32 Anyone who speaks a word against the Son of Man will be forgiven, but anyone who speaks against the Holy Spirit will not be forgiven, either in this age or in the age to come.

33 "Make a tree good and its fruit will be good, or make a tree bad and its fruit will be bad, for a tree is recognized by its fruit. 34 You brood of vipers, how can you who are evil say anything good? For the mouth speaks what the heart is full of. 35 A good man brings good things out of the good stored up in him, and an evil man brings evil things out of the evil stored up in him. 36 But I tell you that everyone will have to give account on the day of judgment for every empty word they have spoken. 37 For by your words you will be acquitted, and by your words you will be condemned."

THE SIGN OF JONAH

38 Then some of the Pharisees and teachers of the law said to him, "Teacher, we want to see a sign from you."

39 He answered, "A wicked and adulterous generation asks for a sign! But none will be given it except the sign of the prophet Jonah. 40 For as Jonah was three days and three nights in the belly of a huge fish, so the Son of Man will be three days and three nights in the heart of the earth. 41 The men of Nineveh will stand up at the judgment with this generation and condemn it; for they repented at the preaching of Jonah, and now something greater than Jonah is here. 42 The Queen of the South will rise at the judgment with this generation and condemn it; for she came from the ends of the earth to listen to Solomon's wisdom, and now something greater than Solomon is here.

43 "When an impure spirit comes out of a person, it goes through arid places seeking rest and does not find it. 44 Then it says, 'I will return to the house I left.' When it arrives, it finds the house unoccupied, swept clean and put in order. 45 Then it goes and takes with it seven other spirits more wicked than itself, and they go in and live there. And the final condition of that person is worse than the first. That is how it will be with this wicked generation."

JESUS' MOTHER AND BROTHERS

46 While Jesus was still talking to the crowd, his mother and brothers stood outside, wanting to speak to him. 47 Someone told him, "Your mother and brothers are standing outside, wanting to speak to you."

48 He replied to him, "Who is my mother, and who are my brothers?"

49Pointing to his disciples, he said, "Here are my mother and my broth-
ers. 50For whoever does the will of my Father in heaven is my brother
and sister and mother."

THE PARABLE OF THE SOWER

13 That same day Jesus went out of the house and sat by the lake.
2Such large crowds gathered around him that he got into a boat
and sat in it, while all the people stood on the shore. 3Then he told
them many things in parables, saying: "A farmer went out to sow his
seed. 4As he was scattering the seed, some fell along the path, and the
birds came and ate it up. 5Some fell on rocky places, where it did not
have much soil. It sprang up quickly, because the soil was shallow. 6But
when the sun came up, the plants were scorched, and they withered
because they had no root. 7Other seed fell among thorns, which grew
up and choked the plants. 8Still other seed fell on good soil, where it
produced a crop—a hundred, sixty or thirty times what was sown.
9Whoever has ears, let them hear."

10The disciples came to him and asked, "Why do you speak to the
people in parables?"

11He replied, "Because the knowledge of the secrets of the kingdom
of heaven has been given to you, but not to them. 12Whoever has will
be given more, and they will have an abundance. Whoever does not
have, even what they have will be taken from them. 13This is why I
speak to them in parables:

"Though seeing, they do not see;
  though hearing, they do not hear or understand.

14In them is fulfilled the prophecy of Isaiah:

"'You will be ever hearing but never understanding;
  you will be ever seeing but never perceiving.
15 For this people's heart has become calloused;
  they hardly hear with their ears,
  and they have closed their eyes.
Otherwise they might see with their eyes,
  hear with their ears,
  understand with their hearts
and turn, and I would heal them.'[a]

16But blessed are your eyes because they see, and your ears because
they hear. 17For truly I tell you, many prophets and righteous people
longed to see what you see but did not see it, and to hear what you hear
but did not hear it.

18"Listen then to what the parable of the sower means: 19When
anyone hears the message about the kingdom and does not under-
stand it, the evil one comes and snatches away what was sown in their
heart. This is the seed sown along the path. 20The seed falling on rocky
ground refers to someone who hears the word and at once receives
it with joy. 21But since they have no root, they last only a short time.
When trouble or persecution comes because of the word, they quickly
fall away. 22The seed falling among the thorns refers to someone who
hears the word, but the worries of this life and the deceitfulness of
wealth choke the word, making it unfruitful. 23But the seed falling on

PRAYING SCRIPTURE

Matthew 13

The parable of the sower doesn't merely teach us about soils and seeds; it reminds us that our evangelistic efforts will not always bear fruit. For the child of God, obedience to share the gospel is what matters; the results are always up to the Lord of the harvest.

If you are not sharing the gospel because you are disappointed with results, pray for obedience and leave the harvest to Jesus.

---

[a] *15* Isaiah 6:9,10 (see Septuagint)

good soil refers to someone who hears the word and understands it.
This is the one who produces a crop, yielding a hundred, sixty or thirty
times what was sown."

THE PARABLE OF THE WEEDS

24Jesus told them another parable: "The kingdom of heaven is like a
man who sowed good seed in his field. 25But while everyone was sleep-
ing, his enemy came and sowed weeds among the wheat, and went
away. 26When the wheat sprouted and formed heads, then the weeds
also appeared.

27"The owner's servants came to him and said, 'Sir, didn't you sow
good seed in your field? Where then did the weeds come from?'

28" 'An enemy did this,' he replied.

"The servants asked him, 'Do you want us to go and pull them up?'

29" 'No,' he answered, 'because while you are pulling the weeds, you
may uproot the wheat with them. 30Let both grow together until the
harvest. At that time I will tell the harvesters: First collect the weeds
and tie them in bundles to be burned; then gather the wheat and bring
it into my barn.' "

THE PARABLES OF THE MUSTARD SEED AND THE YEAST

31He told them another parable: "The kingdom of heaven is like a
mustard seed, which a man took and planted in his field. 32Though it
is the smallest of all seeds, yet when it grows, it is the largest of gar-
den plants and becomes a tree, so that the birds come and perch in its
branches."

33He told them still another parable: "The kingdom of heaven is like
yeast that a woman took and mixed into about sixty pounds[a] of flour
until it worked all through the dough."

34Jesus spoke all these things to the crowd in parables; he did not say
anything to them without using a parable. 35So was fulfilled what was
spoken through the prophet:

"I will open my mouth in parables,
I will utter things hidden since the creation of the world."[b]

THE PARABLE OF THE WEEDS EXPLAINED

36Then he left the crowd and went into the house. His disciples came
to him and said, "Explain to us the parable of the weeds in the field."

37He answered, "The one who sowed the good seed is the Son of Man.
38The field is the world, and the good seed stands for the people of the
kingdom. The weeds are the people of the evil one, 39and the enemy
who sows them is the devil. The harvest is the end of the age, and the
harvesters are angels.

40"As the weeds are pulled up and burned in the fire, so it will be
at the end of the age. 41The Son of Man will send out his angels, and
they will weed out of his kingdom everything that causes sin and all
who do evil. 42They will throw them into the blazing furnace, where
there will be weeping and gnashing of teeth. 43Then the righteous will
shine like the sun in the kingdom of their Father. Whoever has ears,
let them hear.

---

[a] *33* Or about 27 kilograms [b] *35* Psalm 78:2

THE PARABLES OF THE HIDDEN TREASURE AND THE PEARL

44"The kingdom of heaven is like treasure hidden in a field. When a
man found it, he hid it again, and then in his joy went and sold all he
had and bought that field.

45"Again, the kingdom of heaven is like a merchant looking for fine
pearls. 46When he found one of great value, he went away and sold ev-
erything he had and bought it.

THE PARABLE OF THE NET

47"Once again, the kingdom of heaven is like a net that was let down
into the lake and caught all kinds of fish. 48When it was full, the fish-
ermen pulled it up on the shore. Then they sat down and collected the
good fish in baskets, but threw the bad away. 49This is how it will be at
the end of the age. The angels will come and separate the wicked from
the righteous 50and throw them into the blazing furnace, where there
will be weeping and gnashing of teeth.

51"Have you understood all these things?" Jesus asked.

"Yes," they replied.

52He said to them, "Therefore every teacher of the law who has be-
come a disciple in the kingdom of heaven is like the owner of a house
who brings out of his storeroom new treasures as well as old."

A PROPHET WITHOUT HONOR

53When Jesus had finished these parables, he moved on from there.
54Coming to his hometown, he began teaching the people in their syn-
agogue, and they were amazed. "Where did this man get this wisdom
and these miraculous powers?" they asked. 55"Isn't this the carpenter's
son? Isn't his mother's name Mary, and aren't his brothers James, Jo-
seph, Simon and Judas? 56Aren't all his sisters with us? Where then did
this man get all these things?" 57And they took offense at him.

But Jesus said to them, "A prophet is not without honor except in his own town and in his own home."

58And he did not do many miracles there because of their lack of
faith.

JOHN THE BAPTIST BEHEADED

14 At that time Herod the tetrarch heard the reports about Jesus,
2and he said to his attendants, "This is John the Baptist; he has
risen from the dead! That is why miraculous powers are at work in him."

3Now Herod had arrested John and bound him and put him in prison
because of Herodias, his brother Philip's wife, 4for John had been say-
ing to him: "It is not lawful for you to have her." 5Herod wanted to kill
John, but he was afraid of the people, because they considered John
a prophet.

6On Herod's birthday the daughter of Herodias danced for the guests
and pleased Herod so much 7that he promised with an oath to give her
whatever she asked. 8Prompted by her mother, she said, "Give me here
on a platter the head of John the Baptist." 9The king was distressed,
but because of his oaths and his dinner guests, he ordered that her
request be granted 10and had John beheaded in the prison. 11His head
was brought in on a platter and given to the girl, who carried it to her
mother. 12John's disciples came and took his body and buried it. Then
they went and told Jesus.

PRAYING SCRIPTURE

Matthew 14

One of the most memorable events in Jesus' ministry is his walking on water. The disciples—fearing for their lives in a storm—were so shocked to see Jesus coming to them walking on top of the sea that they thought he was a ghost. After calming the storm and getting into the boat, Jesus chided them for their lack of faith.

Do you need God's intervention? Pray in faith, and he will answer you.

JESUS FEEDS THE FIVE THOUSAND

13When Jesus heard what had happened, he withdrew by boat privately to a solitary place. Hearing of this, the crowds followed him on foot from the towns. 14When Jesus landed and saw a large crowd, he had compassion on them and healed their sick.

15As evening approached, the disciples came to him and said, "This is a remote place, and it's already getting late. Send the crowds away, so they can go to the villages and buy themselves some food."

16Jesus replied, "They do not need to go away. You give them something to eat."

17"We have here only five loaves of bread and two fish," they answered.

18"Bring them here to me," he said. 19And he directed the people to sit down on the grass. Taking the five loaves and the two fish and looking up to heaven, he gave thanks and broke the loaves. Then he gave them to the disciples, and the disciples gave them to the people. 20They all ate and were satisfied, and the disciples picked up twelve basketfuls of broken pieces that were left over. 21The number of those who ate was about five thousand men, besides women and children.

JESUS WALKS ON THE WATER

22Immediately Jesus made the disciples get into the boat and go on ahead of him to the other side, while he dismissed the crowd. 23After he had dismissed them, he went up on a mountainside by himself to pray. Later that night, he was there alone, 24and the boat was already a considerable distance from land, buffeted by the waves because the wind was against it.

25Shortly before dawn Jesus went out to them, walking on the lake. 26When the disciples saw him walking on the lake, they were terrified. "It's a ghost," they said, and cried out in fear.

27But Jesus immediately said to them: "Take courage! It is I. Don't be afraid."

28"Lord, if it's you," Peter replied, "tell me to come to you on the water."

29"Come," he said.

Then Peter got down out of the boat, walked on the water and came toward Jesus. 30But when he saw the wind, he was afraid and, beginning to sink, cried out, "Lord, save me!"

31Immediately Jesus reached out his hand and caught him. "You of little faith," he said, "why did you doubt?"

32And when they climbed into the boat, the wind died down. 33Then those who were in the boat worshiped him, saying, "Truly you are the Son of God."

34When they had crossed over, they landed at Gennesaret. 35And when the men of that place recognized Jesus, they sent word to all the surrounding country. People brought all their sick to him 36and begged him to let the sick just touch the edge of his cloak, and all who touched it were healed.

PRAYING SCRIPTURE

Matthew 15

We can easily forget the sheer volume of ministry Jesus accomplished over three years. The Gospels mention a good number, but then verses like 29–31 remind us that Jesus healed multitudes of people whose individual stories are not recorded.

God's ministry in your life may never be publicized, but you can praise him just the same. List the ways God has worked in your life recently. Praise him for each one.

THAT WHICH DEFILES

15 Then some Pharisees and teachers of the law came to Jesus from Jerusalem and asked, 2"Why do your disciples break the tradition of the elders? They don't wash their hands before they eat!"

3Jesus replied, "And why do you break the command of God for the

sake of your tradition? 4 For God said, 'Honor your father and mother'[a]
and 'Anyone who curses their father or mother is to be put to death.'[b]
5 But you say that if anyone declares that what might have been used to
help their father or mother is 'devoted to God,' 6 they are not to 'honor
their father or mother' with it. Thus you nullify the word of God for
the sake of your tradition. 7 You hypocrites! Isaiah was right when he
prophesied about you:

8 " 'These people honor me with their lips,
but their hearts are far from me.
9 They worship me in vain;
their teachings are merely human rules.'[c]"

10 Jesus called the crowd to him and said, "Listen and understand.
11 What goes into someone's mouth does not defile them, but what
comes out of their mouth, that is what defiles them."

12 Then the disciples came to him and asked, "Do you know that the
Pharisees were offended when they heard this?"

13 He replied, "Every plant that my heavenly Father has not planted
will be pulled up by the roots. 14 Leave them; they are blind guides.[d] If
the blind lead the blind, both will fall into a pit."

15 Peter said, "Explain the parable to us."

16 "Are you still so dull?" Jesus asked them. 17 "Don't you see that
whatever enters the mouth goes into the stomach and then out of
the body? 18 But the things that come out of a person's mouth come
from the heart, and these defile them. 19 For out of the heart come
evil thoughts — murder, adultery, sexual immorality, theft, false tes-
timony, slander. 20 These are what defile a person; but eating with un-
washed hands does not defile them."

THE FAITH OF A CANAANITE WOMAN

21 Leaving that place, Jesus withdrew to the region of Tyre and Si-
don. 22 A Canaanite woman from that vicinity came to him, crying
out, "Lord, Son of David, have mercy on me! My daughter is demon-
possessed and suffering terribly."

23 Jesus did not answer a word. So his disciples came to him and
urged him, "Send her away, for she keeps crying out after us."

24 He answered, "I was sent only to the lost sheep of Israel."

25 The woman came and knelt before him. "Lord, help me!" she said.

26 He replied, "It is not right to take the children's bread and toss it
to the dogs."

27 "Yes it is, Lord," she said. "Even the dogs eat the crumbs that fall
from their master's table."

28 Then Jesus said to her, "Woman, you have great faith! Your request
is granted." And her daughter was healed at that moment.

JESUS FEEDS THE FOUR THOUSAND

29 Jesus left there and went along the Sea of Galilee. Then he went up
on a mountainside and sat down. 30 Great crowds came to him, bring-
ing the lame, the blind, the crippled, the mute and many others, and
laid them at his feet; and he healed them. 31 The people were amazed
when they saw the mute speaking, the crippled made well, the lame
walking and the blind seeing. And they praised the God of Israel.

---

[a] 4 Exodus 20:12; Deut. 5:16 [b] 4 Exodus 21:17; Lev. 20:9 [c] 9 Isaiah 29:13
[d] 14 Some manuscripts *blind guides of the blind*

32 Jesus called his disciples to him and said, "I have compassion for
these people; they have already been with me three days and have
nothing to eat. I do not want to send them away hungry, or they may
collapse on the way."
33 His disciples answered, "Where could we get enough bread in this
remote place to feed such a crowd?"
34 "How many loaves do you have?" Jesus asked.
"Seven," they replied, "and a few small fish."
35 He told the crowd to sit down on the ground. 36 Then he took the
seven loaves and the fish, and when he had given thanks, he broke
them and gave them to the disciples, and they in turn to the people.
37 They all ate and were satisfied. Afterward the disciples picked up
seven basketfuls of broken pieces that were left over. 38 The number of
those who ate was four thousand men, besides women and children.
39 After Jesus had sent the crowd away, he got into the boat and went
to the vicinity of Magadan.

THE DEMAND FOR A SIGN

16 The Pharisees and Sadducees came to Jesus and tested him by
asking him to show them a sign from heaven.
2 He replied, "When evening comes, you say, 'It will be fair weather,
for the sky is red,' 3 and in the morning, 'Today it will be stormy, for the
sky is red and overcast.' You know how to interpret the appearance of
the sky, but you cannot interpret the signs of the times.[a] 4 A wicked and
adulterous generation looks for a sign, but none will be given it except
the sign of Jonah." Jesus then left them and went away.

THE YEAST OF THE PHARISEES AND SADDUCEES

5 When they went across the lake, the disciples forgot to take bread.
6 "Be careful," Jesus said to them. "Be on your guard against the yeast
of the Pharisees and Sadducees."
7 They discussed this among themselves and said, "It is because we
didn't bring any bread."
8 Aware of their discussion, Jesus asked, "You of little faith, why are
you talking among yourselves about having no bread? 9 Do you still
not understand? Don't you remember the five loaves for the five thou-
sand, and how many basketfuls you gathered? 10 Or the seven loaves for
the four thousand, and how many basketfuls you gathered? 11 How is
it you don't understand that I was not talking to you about bread? But
be on your guard against the yeast of the Pharisees and Sadducees."
12 Then they understood that he was not telling them to guard against
the yeast used in bread, but against the teaching of the Pharisees and
Sadducees.

PETER DECLARES THAT JESUS IS THE MESSIAH

13 When Jesus came to the region of Caesarea Philippi, he asked his
disciples, "Who do people say the Son of Man is?"
14 They replied, "Some say John the Baptist; others say Elijah; and
still others, Jeremiah or one of the prophets."
15 "But what about you?" he asked. "Who do you say I am?"
16 Simon Peter answered, "You are the Messiah, the Son of the living
God."

PRAYING SCRIPTURE

Matthew 16

Many people desire an idea of Jesus without understanding the deep commitment his cross requires. The cross, having become a piece of jewelry detached of meaning, should represent that we have died to our own passions, desires and lusts.

Are you dying daily on the cross you bear? Ask God to orient your daily life as one who is dead to sin but alive to him in Jesus Christ.

[a] 2,3 Some early manuscripts do not have *When evening comes . . . of the times.*

17 Jesus replied, “Blessed are you, Simon son of Jonah, for this was
not revealed to you by flesh and blood, but by my Father in heaven.
18 And I tell you that you are Peter,[a] and on this rock I will build my
church, and the gates of Hades[b] will not overcome it. 19 I will give you
the keys of the kingdom of heaven; whatever you bind on earth will
be[c] bound in heaven, and whatever you loose on earth will be[c] loosed
in heaven.” 20 Then he ordered his disciples not to tell anyone that he
was the Messiah.

JESUS PREDICTS HIS DEATH

21 From that time on Jesus began to explain to his disciples that he
must go to Jerusalem and suffer many things at the hands of the el-
ders, the chief priests and the teachers of the law, and that he must be
killed and on the third day be raised to life.
22 Peter took him aside and began to rebuke him. “Never, Lord!” he
said. “This shall never happen to you!”
23 Jesus turned and said to Peter, “Get behind me, Satan! You are a
stumbling block to me; you do not have in mind the concerns of God,
but merely human concerns.”
24 Then Jesus said to his disciples, “Whoever wants to be my disciple
must deny themselves and take up their cross and follow me. 25 For
whoever wants to save their life[d] will lose it, but whoever loses their
life for me will find it. 26 What good will it be for someone to gain the
whole world, yet forfeit their soul? Or what can anyone give in ex-
change for their soul? 27 For the Son of Man is going to come in his
Father’s glory with his angels, and then he will reward each person
according to what they have done.
28 “Truly I tell you, some who are standing here will not taste death
before they see the Son of Man coming in his kingdom.”

THE TRANSFIGURATION

17 After six days Jesus took with him Peter, James and John the
brother of James, and led them up a high mountain by them-
selves. 2 There he was transfigured before them. His face shone like
the sun, and his clothes became as white as the light. 3 Just then there
appeared before them Moses and Elijah, talking with Jesus.
4 Peter said to Jesus, “Lord, it is good for us to be here. If you wish,
I will put up three shelters — one for you, one for Moses and one for
Elijah.”
5 While he was still speaking, a bright cloud covered them, and a
voice from the cloud said, “This is my Son, whom I love; with him I am
well pleased. Listen to him!”
6 When the disciples heard this, they fell facedown to the ground,
terrified. 7 But Jesus came and touched them. “Get up,” he said. “Don’t
be afraid.” 8 When they looked up, they saw no one except Jesus.
9 As they were coming down the mountain, Jesus instructed them,
“Don’t tell anyone what you have seen, until the Son of Man has been
raised from the dead.”
10 The disciples asked him, “Why then do the teachers of the law say
that Elijah must come first?”

PRAYING SCRIPTURE

Matthew 17

In this chapter, Jesus revealed to Peter, James and John the reality of who he was. On a mountain, Jesus was “transfigured” before them (verse 2). For a few moments, Jesus displayed at least some of the glory he had known with the Father before his incarnation. Take some time to think about Jesus in his glory, and think about seeing that glory for eternity. Praise God for the glory that you will share with him.

---

[a] *18* The Greek word for *Peter* means *rock*. [b] *18* That is, the realm of the dead [c] *19* Or *will have been* [d] *25* The Greek word means either *life* or *soul*; also in verse 26.

11Jesus replied, "To be sure, Elijah comes and will restore all things.
12But I tell you, Elijah has already come, and they did not recognize
him, but have done to him everything they wished. In the same way
the Son of Man is going to suffer at their hands." 13Then the disciples
understood that he was talking to them about John the Baptist.

JESUS HEALS A DEMON-POSSESSED BOY

14When they came to the crowd, a man approached Jesus and knelt
before him. 15"Lord, have mercy on my son," he said. "He has seizures
and is suffering greatly. He often falls into the fire or into the water. 16I
brought him to your disciples, but they could not heal him."

17"You unbelieving and perverse generation," Jesus replied, "how
long shall I stay with you? How long shall I put up with you? Bring the
boy here to me." 18Jesus rebuked the demon, and it came out of the
boy, and he was healed at that moment.

19Then the disciples came to Jesus in private and asked, "Why
couldn't we drive it out?"

20He replied, "Because you have so little faith. Truly I tell you, if you
have faith as small as a mustard seed, you can say to this mountain,
'Move from here to there,' and it will move. Nothing will be impossible
for you." [21][a]

JESUS PREDICTS HIS DEATH A SECOND TIME

22When they came together in Galilee, he said to them, "The Son of
Man is going to be delivered into the hands of men. 23They will kill
him, and on the third day he will be raised to life." And the disciples
were filled with grief.

THE TEMPLE TAX

24After Jesus and his disciples arrived in Capernaum, the collectors
of the two-drachma temple tax came to Peter and asked, "Doesn't your
teacher pay the temple tax?"

25"Yes, he does," he replied.

When Peter came into the house, Jesus was the first to speak. "What
do you think, Simon?" he asked. "From whom do the kings of the earth
collect duty and taxes — from their own children or from others?"

26"From others," Peter answered.

"Then the children are exempt," Jesus said to him. 27"But so that we
may not cause offense, go to the lake and throw out your line. Take the
first fish you catch; open its mouth and you will find a four-drachma
coin. Take it and give it to them for my tax and yours."

THE GREATEST IN THE KINGDOM OF HEAVEN

18 At that time the disciples came to Jesus and asked, "Who, then,
is the greatest in the kingdom of heaven?"

2He called a little child to him, and placed the child among them.
3And he said: "Truly I tell you, unless you change and become like lit-
tle children, you will never enter the kingdom of heaven. 4Therefore,
whoever takes the lowly position of this child is the greatest in the
kingdom of heaven. 5And whoever welcomes one such child in my
name welcomes me.

PRAYING SCRIPTURE

Matthew 18

In this powerful chapter, Jesus subverts the worldly idea of greatness, teaches the extent to which the Father will go to save a sheep and reminds us that forgiveness is the way of his kingdom. In fact, everything about the kingdom of God is the reverse of what earthly kingdoms emphasize.

Have you prioritized worldly ambitions over kingdom ethics? If so, repent and ask God to reset your priorities to align with his.

[a] *21* Some manuscripts include here words similar to Mark 9:29.

CAUSING TO STUMBLE

6“If anyone causes one of these little ones — those who believe in
me — to stumble, it would be better for them to have a large millstone
hung around their neck and to be drowned in the depths of the sea.
7Woe to the world because of the things that cause people to stumble!
Such things must come, but woe to the person through whom they
come! 8If your hand or your foot causes you to stumble, cut it off and
throw it away. It is better for you to enter life maimed or crippled than
to have two hands or two feet and be thrown into eternal fire. 9And if
your eye causes you to stumble, gouge it out and throw it away. It is
better for you to enter life with one eye than to have two eyes and be
thrown into the fire of hell.

THE PARABLE OF THE WANDERING SHEEP

10“See that you do not despise one of these little ones. For I tell you that
their angels in heaven always see the face of my Father in heaven. [11][a]

12“What do you think? If a man owns a hundred sheep, and one of
them wanders away, will he not leave the ninety-nine on the hills and
go to look for the one that wandered off? 13And if he finds it, truly I tell
you, he is happier about that one sheep than about the ninety-nine
that did not wander off. 14In the same way your Father in heaven is not
willing that any of these little ones should perish.

DEALING WITH SIN IN THE CHURCH

15“If your brother or sister[b] sins,[c] go and point out their fault, just
between the two of you. If they listen to you, you have won them over.
16But if they will not listen, take one or two others along, so that ‘every
matter may be established by the testimony of two or three witnesses.’[d]
17If they still refuse to listen, tell it to the church; and if they refuse to
listen even to the church, treat them as you would a pagan or a tax
collector.

18“Truly I tell you, whatever you bind on earth will be[e] bound in
heaven, and whatever you loose on earth will be[e] loosed in heaven.

19“Again, truly I tell you that if two of you on earth agree about any-
thing they ask for, it will be done for them by my Father in heaven.
20For where two or three gather in my name, there am I with them.”

THE PARABLE OF THE UNMERCIFUL SERVANT

21Then Peter came to Jesus and asked, “Lord, how many times shall I
forgive my brother or sister who sins against me? Up to seven times?”

22Jesus answered, “I tell you, not seven times, but seventy-seven
times.[f]

23“Therefore, the kingdom of heaven is like a king who wanted to
settle accounts with his servants. 24As he began the settlement, a man
who owed him ten thousand bags of gold[g] was brought to him. 25Since
he was not able to pay, the master ordered that he and his wife and his
children and all that he had be sold to repay the debt.

---

[a] *11* Some manuscripts include here the words of Luke 19:10. [b] *15* The Greek word for *brother or sister* (*adelphos*) refers here to a fellow disciple, whether man or woman; also in verses 21 and 35. [c] *15* Some manuscripts *sins against you* [d] *16* Deut. 19:15 [e] *18* Or *will have been* [f] *22* Or *seventy times seven* [g] *24* Greek *ten thousand talents*; a talent was worth about 20 years of a day laborer’s wages.

26“At this the servant fell on his knees before him. ‘Be patient with
me,’ he begged, ‘and I will pay back everything.’ 27The servant’s master
took pity on him, canceled the debt and let him go.
28“But when that servant went out, he found one of his fellow ser-
vants who owed him a hundred silver coins.[a] He grabbed him and be-
gan to choke him. ‘Pay back what you owe me!’ he demanded.
29“His fellow servant fell to his knees and begged him, ‘Be patient
with me, and I will pay it back.’
30“But he refused. Instead, he went off and had the man thrown into
prison until he could pay the debt. 31When the other servants saw what
had happened, they were outraged and went and told their master ev-
erything that had happened.
32“Then the master called the servant in. ‘You wicked servant,’ he
said, ‘I canceled all that debt of yours because you begged me to.
33Shouldn’t you have had mercy on your fellow servant just as I had
on you?’ 34In anger his master handed him over to the jailers to be tor-
tured, until he should pay back all he owed.
35“This is how my heavenly Father will treat each of you unless you
forgive your brother or sister from your heart.”

DIVORCE

19 When Jesus had finished saying these things, he left Galilee and
went into the region of Judea to the other side of the Jordan.
2Large crowds followed him, and he healed them there.
3Some Pharisees came to him to test him. They asked, “Is it lawful
for a man to divorce his wife for any and every reason?”
4“Haven’t you read,” he replied, “that at the beginning the Creator
‘made them male and female,’[b] 5and said, ‘For this reason a man will
leave his father and mother and be united to his wife, and the two will
become one flesh’[c]? 6So they are no longer two, but one flesh. There-
fore what God has joined together, let no one separate.”
7“Why then,” they asked, “did Moses command that a man give his
wife a certificate of divorce and send her away?”
8Jesus replied, “Moses permitted you to divorce your wives because
your hearts were hard. But it was not this way from the beginning. 9I
tell you that anyone who divorces his wife, except for sexual immoral-
ity, and marries another woman commits adultery.”
10The disciples said to him, “If this is the situation between a hus-
band and wife, it is better not to marry.”
11Jesus replied, “Not everyone can accept this word, but only those
to whom it has been given. 12For there are eunuchs who were born that
way, and there are eunuchs who have been made eunuchs by others—
and there are those who choose to live like eunuchs for the sake of
the kingdom of heaven. The one who can accept this should accept it.”

PRAYING SCRIPTURE

Matthew 19

Engaged by a wealthy, young community leader, Jesus fielded the question, “What good thing must I do to get eternal life?” (verse 16). In response, Jesus gave one of the most challenging teachings of his entire ministry, one the young man was unwilling to accept.

Is there anything you are unwilling to give up for Jesus? If so, acknowledge it is an obstacle to following him and repent of it.

THE LITTLE CHILDREN AND JESUS

13Then people brought little children to Jesus for him to place his
hands on them and pray for them. But the disciples rebuked them.
14Jesus said, “Let the little children come to me, and do not hinder
them, for the kingdom of heaven belongs to such as these.” 15When he
had placed his hands on them, he went on from there.

[a] 28 Greek *a hundred denarii*; a denarius was the usual daily wage of a day laborer (see 20:2). [b] 4 Gen. 1:27 [c] 5 Gen. 2:24

THE RICH AND THE KINGDOM OF GOD

16 Just then a man came up to Jesus and asked, "Teacher, what good
thing must I do to get eternal life?"
17 "Why do you ask me about what is good?" Jesus replied.
"There is only One who is good. If you want to enter life, keep the
commandments."
18 "Which ones?" he inquired.
Jesus replied, " 'You shall not murder, you shall not commit adultery,
you shall not steal, you shall not give false testimony, 19 honor your fa-
ther and mother,'[a] and 'love your neighbor as yourself.'[b]"
20 "All these I have kept," the young man said. "What do I still lack?"
21 Jesus answered, "If you want to be perfect, go, sell your possessions
and give to the poor, and you will have treasure in heaven. Then come,
follow me."
22 When the young man heard this, he went away sad, because he
had great wealth.
23 Then Jesus said to his disciples, "Truly I tell you, it is hard for
someone who is rich to enter the kingdom of heaven. 24 Again I tell
you, it is easier for a camel to go through the eye of a needle than for
someone who is rich to enter the kingdom of God."
25 When the disciples heard this, they were greatly astonished and
asked, "Who then can be saved?"
26 Jesus looked at them and said, "With man this is impossible, but
with God all things are possible."
27 Peter answered him, "We have left everything to follow you! What
then will there be for us?"
28 Jesus said to them, "Truly I tell you, at the renewal of all things,
when the Son of Man sits on his glorious throne, you who have fol-
lowed me will also sit on twelve thrones, judging the twelve tribes of
Israel. 29 And everyone who has left houses or brothers or sisters or
father or mother or wife[c] or children or fields for my sake will receive
a hundred times as much and will inherit eternal life. 30 But many who
are first will be last, and many who are last will be first.

THE PARABLE OF THE WORKERS IN THE VINEYARD

20 "For the kingdom of heaven is like a landowner who went
out early in the morning to hire workers for his vineyard. 2 He
agreed to pay them a denarius[d] for the day and sent them into his
vineyard.
3 "About nine in the morning he went out and saw others standing in
the marketplace doing nothing. 4 He told them, 'You also go and work
in my vineyard, and I will pay you whatever is right.' 5 So they went.
"He went out again about noon and about three in the afternoon
and did the same thing. 6 About five in the afternoon he went out and
found still others standing around. He asked them, 'Why have you
been standing here all day long doing nothing?'
7 " 'Because no one has hired us,' they answered.
"He said to them, 'You also go and work in my vineyard.'
8 "When evening came, the owner of the vineyard said to his fore-
man, 'Call the workers and pay them their wages, beginning with the
last ones hired and going on to the first.'

PRAYING SCRIPTURE

Matthew 20

The parable of the workers in the field is generally understood not as a story about wages but as a metaphor of salvation. Those who come to the kingdom late do not receive a lesser reward than those who are in the kingdom for a long time. And all who do come find that serving, not ruling, is the way of the kingdom (see verse 26).

Ask God to cultivate a servant's heart in you.

[a] *19* Exodus 20:12-16; Deut. 5:16-20 [b] *19* Lev. 19:18 [c] *29* Some manuscripts do not have *or wife.* [d] *2* A denarius was the usual daily wage of a day laborer.

9“The workers who were hired about five in the afternoon came and
each received a denarius. 10So when those came who were hired first,
they expected to receive more. But each one of them also received a
denarius. 11When they received it, they began to grumble against the
landowner. 12‘These who were hired last worked only one hour,’ they
said, ‘and you have made them equal to us who have borne the burden
of the work and the heat of the day.’

13“But he answered one of them, ‘I am not being unfair to you,
friend. Didn’t you agree to work for a denarius? 14Take your pay and
go. I want to give the one who was hired last the same as I gave you.
15Don’t I have the right to do what I want with my own money? Or are
you envious because I am generous?’

16“So the last will be first, and the first will be last.”

JESUS PREDICTS HIS DEATH A THIRD TIME

17Now Jesus was going up to Jerusalem. On the way, he took the
Twelve aside and said to them, 18“We are going up to Jerusalem, and
the Son of Man will be delivered over to the chief priests and the teach-
ers of the law. They will condemn him to death 19and will hand him
over to the Gentiles to be mocked and flogged and crucified. On the
third day he will be raised to life!”

A MOTHER’S REQUEST

20Then the mother of Zebedee’s sons came to Jesus with her sons
and, kneeling down, asked a favor of him.

21“What is it you want?” he asked.

She said, “Grant that one of these two sons of mine may sit at your
right and the other at your left in your kingdom.”

22“You don’t know what you are asking,” Jesus said to them. “Can
you drink the cup I am going to drink?”

“We can,” they answered.

23Jesus said to them, “You will indeed drink from my cup, but to sit
at my right or left is not for me to grant. These places belong to those
for whom they have been prepared by my Father.”

24When the ten heard about this, they were indignant with the two
brothers. 25Jesus called them together and said, “You know that the
rulers of the Gentiles lord it over them, and their high officials exer-
cise authority over them. 26Not so with you. Instead, whoever wants to
become great among you must be your servant, 27and whoever wants
to be first must be your slave— 28just as the Son of Man did not come
to be served, but to serve, and to give his life as a ransom for many.”

TWO BLIND MEN RECEIVE SIGHT

29As Jesus and his disciples were leaving Jericho, a large crowd fol-
lowed him. 30Two blind men were sitting by the roadside, and when
they heard that Jesus was going by, they shouted, “Lord, Son of David,
have mercy on us!”

31The crowd rebuked them and told them to be quiet, but they
shouted all the louder, “Lord, Son of David, have mercy on us!”

32Jesus stopped and called them. “What do you want me to do for
you?” he asked.

33“Lord,” they answered, “we want our sight.”

34Jesus had compassion on them and touched their eyes. Immedi-
ately they received their sight and followed him.

JESUS COMES TO JERUSALEM AS KING

21 As they approached Jerusalem and came to Bethphage on the
Mount of Olives, Jesus sent two disciples, 2saying to them, "Go to
the village ahead of you, and at once you will find a donkey tied there,
with her colt by her. Untie them and bring them to me. 3If anyone says
anything to you, say that the Lord needs them, and he will send them
right away."
4This took place to fulfill what was spoken through the prophet:

5"Say to Daughter Zion,
'See, your king comes to you,
gentle and riding on a donkey,
and on a colt, the foal of a donkey.'"[a]

6The disciples went and did as Jesus had instructed them. 7They
brought the donkey and the colt and placed their cloaks on them for
Jesus to sit on. 8A very large crowd spread their cloaks on the road,
while others cut branches from the trees and spread them on the
road. 9The crowds that went ahead of him and those that followed
shouted,

"Hosanna[b] to the Son of David!"

"Blessed is he who comes in the name of the Lord!"[c]

"Hosanna[b] in the highest heaven!"

10When Jesus entered Jerusalem, the whole city was stirred and
asked, "Who is this?"
11The crowds answered, "This is Jesus, the prophet from Nazareth
in Galilee."

JESUS AT THE TEMPLE

12Jesus entered the temple courts and drove out all who were buying
and selling there. He overturned the tables of the money changers and
the benches of those selling doves. 13"It is written," he said to them,
"'My house will be called a house of prayer,'[d] but you are making it 'a
den of robbers.'[e]"
14The blind and the lame came to him at the temple, and he healed
them. 15But when the chief priests and the teachers of the law saw
the wonderful things he did and the children shouting in the temple
courts, "Hosanna to the Son of David," they were indignant.
16"Do you hear what these children are saying?" they asked him.
"Yes," replied Jesus, "have you never read,
"'From the lips of children and infants
you, Lord, have called forth your praise'[f]?"

17And he left them and went out of the city to Bethany, where he
spent the night.

JESUS CURSES A FIG TREE

18Early in the morning, as Jesus was on his way back to the city, he
was hungry. 19Seeing a fig tree by the road, he went up to it but found

PRAYING SCRIPTURE

Matthew 21

Arriving in Jerusalem for the Passover, Jesus, like all devout Jews, made his way to the temple. But Jesus did not like what he found. The money changers and those who sold doves for sacrifice had turned the temple into "a den of robbers" (verse 13). Righteously angry, Jesus drove them out.

How often do we defile our worship with things of this world? Pray to be righteously angry at any sin in your heart.

[a] *5* Zech. 9:9 [b] *9* A Hebrew expression meaning "Save!" which became an exclamation of praise; also in verse 15 [c] *9* Psalm 118:25,26 [d] *13* Isaiah 56:7 [e] *13* Jer. 7:11 [f] *16* Psalm 8:2 (see Septuagint)

nothing on it except leaves. Then he said to it, "May you never bear
fruit again!" Immediately the tree withered.
20 When the disciples saw this, they were amazed. "How did the fig
tree wither so quickly?" they asked.
21 Jesus replied, "Truly I tell you, if you have faith and do not doubt,
not only can you do what was done to the fig tree, but also you can say
to this mountain, 'Go, throw yourself into the sea,' and it will be done.
22 If you believe, you will receive whatever you ask for in prayer."

THE AUTHORITY OF JESUS QUESTIONED

23 Jesus entered the temple courts, and, while he was teaching, the chief
priests and the elders of the people came to him. "By what authority are
you doing these things?" they asked. "And who gave you this authority?"
24 Jesus replied, "I will also ask you one question. If you answer
me, I will tell you by what authority I am doing these things. 25 John's
baptism — where did it come from? Was it from heaven, or of human
origin?"
They discussed it among themselves and said, "If we say, 'From
heaven,' he will ask, 'Then why didn't you believe him?' 26 But if we say,
'Of human origin' — we are afraid of the people, for they all hold that
John was a prophet."
27 So they answered Jesus, "We don't know."
Then he said, "Neither will I tell you by what authority I am doing
these things.

THE PARABLE OF THE TWO SONS

28 "What do you think? There was a man who had two sons. He went
to the first and said, 'Son, go and work today in the vineyard.'
29 " 'I will not,' he answered, but later he changed his mind and went.
30 "Then the father went to the other son and said the same thing. He
answered, 'I will, sir,' but he did not go.
31 "Which of the two did what his father wanted?"
"The first," they answered.
Jesus said to them, "Truly I tell you, the tax collectors and the pros-
titutes are entering the kingdom of God ahead of you. 32 For John came
to you to show you the way of righteousness, and you did not believe
him, but the tax collectors and the prostitutes did. And even after you
saw this, you did not repent and believe him.

THE PARABLE OF THE TENANTS

33 "Listen to another parable: There was a landowner who planted
a vineyard. He put a wall around it, dug a winepress in it and built a
watchtower. Then he rented the vineyard to some farmers and moved
to another place. 34 When the harvest time approached, he sent his ser-
vants to the tenants to collect his fruit.
35 "The tenants seized his servants; they beat one, killed another, and
stoned a third. 36 Then he sent other servants to them, more than the
first time, and the tenants treated them the same way. 37 Last of all, he
sent his son to them. 'They will respect my son,' he said.
38 "But when the tenants saw the son, they said to each other, 'This is
the heir. Come, let's kill him and take his inheritance.' 39 So they took
him and threw him out of the vineyard and killed him.
40 "Therefore, when the owner of the vineyard comes, what will he
do to those tenants?"

41“He will bring those wretches to a wretched end,” they replied,
“and he will rent the vineyard to other tenants, who will give him his
share of the crop at harvest time.”
42Jesus said to them, “Have you never read in the Scriptures:

“ ‘The stone the builders rejected
has become the cornerstone;
the Lord has done this,
and it is marvelous in our eyes’[a]?

43“Therefore I tell you that the kingdom of God will be taken away
from you and given to a people who will produce its fruit. 44Anyone
who falls on this stone will be broken to pieces; anyone on whom it
falls will be crushed.”[b]
45When the chief priests and the Pharisees heard Jesus’ parables,
they knew he was talking about them. 46They looked for a way to ar-
rest him, but they were afraid of the crowd because the people held
that he was a prophet.

THE PARABLE OF THE WEDDING BANQUET

22 Jesus spoke to them again in parables, saying: 2“The kingdom
of heaven is like a king who prepared a wedding banquet for
his son. 3He sent his servants to those who had been invited to the ban-
quet to tell them to come, but they refused to come.
4“Then he sent some more servants and said, ‘Tell those who have
been invited that I have prepared my dinner: My oxen and fattened
cattle have been butchered, and everything is ready. Come to the wed-
ding banquet.’
5“But they paid no attention and went off — one to his field, another
to his business. 6The rest seized his servants, mistreated them and
killed them. 7The king was enraged. He sent his army and destroyed
those murderers and burned their city.
8“Then he said to his servants, ‘The wedding banquet is ready, but
those I invited did not deserve to come. 9So go to the street corners
and invite to the banquet anyone you find.’ 10So the servants went out
into the streets and gathered all the people they could find, the bad as
well as the good, and the wedding hall was filled with guests.
11“But when the king came in to see the guests, he noticed a man
there who was not wearing wedding clothes. 12He asked, ‘How did you
get in here without wedding clothes, friend?’ The man was speechless.
13“Then the king told the attendants, ‘Tie him hand and foot, and
throw him outside, into the darkness, where there will be weeping and
gnashing of teeth.’
14“For many are invited, but few are chosen.”

PAYING THE IMPERIAL TAX TO CAESAR

15Then the Pharisees went out and laid plans to trap him in his words.
16They sent their disciples to him along with the Herodians. “Teacher,”
they said, “we know that you are a man of integrity and that you teach
the way of God in accordance with the truth. You aren’t swayed by oth-
ers, because you pay no attention to who they are. 17Tell us then, what
is your opinion? Is it right to pay the imperial tax[c] to Caesar or not?”

PRAYING SCRIPTURE

Matthew 22

After a series of challenges from various religious groups, including the Pharisees and Sadducees, Jesus closed with his own challenge: If King David called the Messiah “Lord,” how could the Messiah be David’s descendant, “his son”? (verse 45). They were unable to answer.

Who do you think Jesus is? Do you believe he is the Son of God who died for you? If you haven’t, place your faith in him to be saved.

[a] 42 Psalm 118:22,23 [b] 44 Some manuscripts do not have verse 44.
[c] 17 A special tax levied on subject peoples, not on Roman citizens

18 But Jesus, knowing their evil intent, said, "You hypocrites, why are
you trying to trap me? 19 Show me the coin used for paying the tax."
They brought him a denarius, 20 and he asked them, "Whose image is
this? And whose inscription?"
21 "Caesar's," they replied.

Then he said to them, "So give back to Caesar what is Caesar's, and
to God what is God's."

22 When they heard this, they were amazed. So they left him and
went away.

MARRIAGE AT THE RESURRECTION

23 That same day the Sadducees, who say there is no resurrection,
came to him with a question. 24 "Teacher," they said, "Moses told us
that if a man dies without having children, his brother must marry the
widow and raise up offspring for him. 25 Now there were seven brothers
among us. The first one married and died, and since he had no chil-
dren, he left his wife to his brother. 26 The same thing happened to the
second and third brother, right on down to the seventh. 27 Finally, the
woman died. 28 Now then, at the resurrection, whose wife will she be of
the seven, since all of them were married to her?"

29 Jesus replied, "You are in error because you do not know the Scrip-
tures or the power of God. 30 At the resurrection people will neither
marry nor be given in marriage; they will be like the angels in heaven.
31 But about the resurrection of the dead—have you not read what God
said to you, 32 'I am the God of Abraham, the God of Isaac, and the God
of Jacob'[a]? He is not the God of the dead but of the living."

33 When the crowds heard this, they were astonished at his teaching.

THE GREATEST COMMANDMENT

34 Hearing that Jesus had silenced the Sadducees, the Pharisees got
together. 35 One of them, an expert in the law, tested him with this
question: 36 "Teacher, which is the greatest commandment in the Law?"

37 Jesus replied: "'Love the Lord your God with all your heart and
with all your soul and with all your mind.'[b] 38 This is the first and
greatest commandment. 39 And the second is like it: 'Love your neigh-
bor as yourself.'[c] 40 All the Law and the Prophets hang on these two
commandments."

WHOSE SON IS THE MESSIAH?

41 While the Pharisees were gathered together, Jesus asked them,
42 "What do you think about the Messiah? Whose son is he?"

"The son of David," they replied.

43 He said to them, "How is it then that David, speaking by the Spirit,
calls him 'Lord'? For he says,

44 "'The Lord said to my Lord:
"Sit at my right hand
until I put your enemies
under your feet."'[d]

45 If then David calls him 'Lord,' how can he be his son?" 46 No one could
say a word in reply, and from that day on no one dared to ask him any
more questions.

[a] 32 Exodus 3:6 [b] 37 Deut. 6:5 [c] 39 Lev. 19:18 [d] 44 Psalm 110:1

A WARNING AGAINST HYPOCRISY

23 Then Jesus said to the crowds and to his disciples: 2“The teach-
ers of the law and the Pharisees sit in Moses’ seat. 3So you must
be careful to do everything they tell you. But do not do what they do,
for they do not practice what they preach. 4They tie up heavy, cumber-
some loads and put them on other people’s shoulders, but they them-
selves are not willing to lift a finger to move them.
5“Everything they do is done for people to see: They make their phy-
lacteries[a] wide and the tassels on their garments long; 6they love the
place of honor at banquets and the most important seats in the syna-
gogues; 7they love to be greeted with respect in the marketplaces and
to be called ‘Rabbi’ by others.
8“But you are not to be called ‘Rabbi,’ for you have one Teacher, and
you are all brothers. 9And do not call anyone on earth ‘father,’ for you
have one Father, and he is in heaven. 10Nor are you to be called instruc-
tors, for you have one Instructor, the Messiah. 11The greatest among
you will be your servant. 12For those who exalt themselves will be
humbled, and those who humble themselves will be exalted.

SEVEN WOES ON THE TEACHERS OF THE LAW AND THE PHARISEES

13“Woe to you, teachers of the law and Pharisees, you hypocrites! You
shut the door of the kingdom of heaven in people’s faces. You your-
selves do not enter, nor will you let those enter who are trying to. [14][b]
15“Woe to you, teachers of the law and Pharisees, you hypocrites! You
travel over land and sea to win a single convert, and when you have
succeeded, you make them twice as much a child of hell as you are.
16“Woe to you, blind guides! You say, ‘If anyone swears by the temple,
it means nothing; but anyone who swears by the gold of the temple is
bound by that oath.’ 17You blind fools! Which is greater: the gold, or the
temple that makes the gold sacred? 18You also say, ‘If anyone swears
by the altar, it means nothing; but anyone who swears by the gift on
the altar is bound by that oath.’ 19You blind men! Which is greater: the
gift, or the altar that makes the gift sacred? 20Therefore, anyone who
swears by the altar swears by it and by everything on it. 21And anyone
who swears by the temple swears by it and by the one who dwells in
it. 22And anyone who swears by heaven swears by God’s throne and by
the one who sits on it.
23“Woe to you, teachers of the law and Pharisees, you hypocrites!
You give a tenth of your spices—mint, dill and cumin. But you have
neglected the more important matters of the law—justice, mercy and
faithfulness. You should have practiced the latter, without neglecting
the former. 24You blind guides! You strain out a gnat but swallow a
camel.
25“Woe to you, teachers of the law and Pharisees, you hypocrites! You
clean the outside of the cup and dish, but inside they are full of greed
and self-indulgence. 26Blind Pharisee! First clean the inside of the cup
and dish, and then the outside also will be clean.
27“Woe to you, teachers of the law and Pharisees, you hypocrites! You
are like whitewashed tombs, which look beautiful on the outside but

PRAYING SCRIPTURE

Matthew 23

This chapter contains more of Jesus’ condemnations than any other in the Gospels. In repeated woes, he pointed to the hypocrisy of the scribes and Pharisees, warning them of eternal condemnation in hell. All their religious works did not move them any closer to salvation.

Is your faith in Jesus alone for salvation? If not, stop now, repent of your sins and place your faith in him alone to be saved.

[a] *5* That is, boxes containing Scripture verses, worn on forehead and arm
[b] *14* Some manuscripts include here words similar to Mark 12:40 and Luke 20:47.

on the inside are full of the bones of the dead and everything unclean. 28In the same way, on the outside you appear to people as righteous but on the inside you are full of hypocrisy and wickedness.

29"Woe to you, teachers of the law and Pharisees, you hypocrites! You build tombs for the prophets and decorate the graves of the righteous. 30And you say, 'If we had lived in the days of our ancestors, we would not have taken part with them in shedding the blood of the prophets.' 31So you testify against yourselves that you are the descendants of those who murdered the prophets. 32Go ahead, then, and complete what your ancestors started!

33"You snakes! You brood of vipers! How will you escape being condemned to hell? 34Therefore I am sending you prophets and sages and teachers. Some of them you will kill and crucify; others you will flog in your synagogues and pursue from town to town. 35And so upon you will come all the righteous blood that has been shed on earth, from the blood of righteous Abel to the blood of Zechariah son of Berekiah, whom you murdered between the temple and the altar. 36Truly I tell you, all this will come on this generation.

37"Jerusalem, Jerusalem, you who kill the prophets and stone those sent to you, how often I have longed to gather your children together, as a hen gathers her chicks under her wings, and you were not willing. 38Look, your house is left to you desolate. 39For I tell you, you will not see me again until you say, 'Blessed is he who comes in the name of the Lord.'[a]"

THE DESTRUCTION OF THE TEMPLE AND SIGNS OF THE END TIMES

24 Jesus left the temple and was walking away when his disciples came up to him to call his attention to its buildings. 2"Do you see all these things?" he asked. "Truly I tell you, not one stone here will be left on another; every one will be thrown down."

3As Jesus was sitting on the Mount of Olives, the disciples came to him privately. "Tell us," they said, "when will this happen, and what will be the sign of your coming and of the end of the age?"

4Jesus answered: "Watch out that no one deceives you. 5For many will come in my name, claiming, 'I am the Messiah,' and will deceive many. 6You will hear of wars and rumors of wars, but see to it that you are not alarmed. Such things must happen, but the end is still to come. 7Nation will rise against nation, and kingdom against kingdom. There will be famines and earthquakes in various places. 8All these are the beginning of birth pains.

9"Then you will be handed over to be persecuted and put to death, and you will be hated by all nations because of me. 10At that time many will turn away from the faith and will betray and hate each other, 11and many false prophets will appear and deceive many people. 12Because of the increase of wickedness, the love of most will grow cold, 13but the one who stands firm to the end will be saved. 14And this gospel of the kingdom will be preached in the whole world as a testimony to all nations, and then the end will come.

15"So when you see standing in the holy place 'the abomination that causes desolation,'[b] spoken of through the prophet Daniel—let the reader understand— 16then let those who are in Judea flee to the

PRAYING SCRIPTURE

Matthew 24

As it has been since the days of Jesus, the disciples wanted a sign of the end. Jesus told them a number of signs have to be accomplished, including the spread of the gospel to all nations, "then the end will come" (verse 14). Today, in faith, we await the same return as those early disciples.

We should live with Christ's return in mind and pray to be watchful and ready for him.

[a] *39* Psalm 118:26 [b] *15* Daniel 9:27; 11:31; 12:11

mountains. 17Let no one on the housetop go down to take anything
out of the house. 18Let no one in the field go back to get their cloak.
19How dreadful it will be in those days for pregnant women and nurs-
ing mothers! 20Pray that your flight will not take place in winter or on
the Sabbath. 21For then there will be great distress, unequaled from
the beginning of the world until now — and never to be equaled again.

22"If those days had not been cut short, no one would survive, but
for the sake of the elect those days will be shortened. 23At that time
if anyone says to you, 'Look, here is the Messiah!' or, 'There he is!' do
not believe it. 24For false messiahs and false prophets will appear and
perform great signs and wonders to deceive, if possible, even the elect.
25See, I have told you ahead of time.

26"So if anyone tells you, 'There he is, out in the wilderness,' do not
go out; or, 'Here he is, in the inner rooms,' do not believe it. 27For as
lightning that comes from the east is visible even in the west, so will
be the coming of the Son of Man. 28Wherever there is a carcass, there
the vultures will gather.

29"Immediately after the distress of those days

"'the sun will be darkened,
    and the moon will not give its light;
the stars will fall from the sky,
    and the heavenly bodies will be shaken.'[a]

30"Then will appear the sign of the Son of Man in heaven. And then
all the peoples of the earth[b] will mourn when they see the Son of Man
coming on the clouds of heaven, with power and great glory.[c] 31And he
will send his angels with a loud trumpet call, and they will gather his
elect from the four winds, from one end of the heavens to the other.

32"Now learn this lesson from the fig tree: As soon as its twigs get
tender and its leaves come out, you know that summer is near. 33Even
so, when you see all these things, you know that it[d] is near, right at the
door. 34Truly I tell you, this generation will certainly not pass away un-
til all these things have happened. 35Heaven and earth will pass away,
but my words will never pass away.

THE DAY AND HOUR UNKNOWN

36"But about that day or hour no one knows, not even the angels
in heaven, nor the Son,[e] but only the Father. 37As it was in the days of
Noah, so it will be at the coming of the Son of Man. 38For in the days
before the flood, people were eating and drinking, marrying and giving
in marriage, up to the day Noah entered the ark; 39and they knew noth-
ing about what would happen until the flood came and took them all
away. That is how it will be at the coming of the Son of Man. 40Two men
will be in the field; one will be taken and the other left. 41Two women
will be grinding with a hand mill; one will be taken and the other left.

42"Therefore keep watch, because you do not know on what day your
Lord will come. 43But understand this: If the owner of the house had
known at what time of night the thief was coming, he would have kept
watch and would not have let his house be broken into. 44So you also
must be ready, because the Son of Man will come at an hour when you
do not expect him.

---

[a] *29* Isaiah 13:10; 34:4 [b] *30* Or *the tribes of the land* [c] *30* See Daniel 7:13-14. [d] *33* Or *he* [e] *36* Some manuscripts do not have *nor the Son.*

[45]"Who then is the faithful and wise servant, whom the master has put in charge of the servants in his household to give them their food at the proper time? [46]It will be good for that servant whose master finds him doing so when he returns. [47]Truly I tell you, he will put him in charge of all his possessions. [48]But suppose that servant is wicked and says to himself, 'My master is staying away a long time,' [49]and he then begins to beat his fellow servants and to eat and drink with drunkards. [50]The master of that servant will come on a day when he does not expect him and at an hour he is not aware of. [51]He will cut him to pieces and assign him a place with the hypocrites, where there will be weeping and gnashing of teeth.

PRAYING SCRIPTURE

Matthew 25

This series of three parables shows us that God makes eternal judgments based on our temporal lives. There will be some at the judgment he does not know. Some will be cast into outer darkness. All are expected to treat the downtrodden as if they were Jesus himself.

How does your daily life reflect what you say you believe about eternity? Ask God to help you make decisions with an eternal outlook.

THE PARABLE OF THE TEN VIRGINS

25 "At that time the kingdom of heaven will be like ten virgins who took their lamps and went out to meet the bridegroom. [2]Five of them were foolish and five were wise. [3]The foolish ones took their lamps but did not take any oil with them. [4]The wise ones, however, took oil in jars along with their lamps. [5]The bridegroom was a long time in coming, and they all became drowsy and fell asleep.

[6]"At midnight the cry rang out: 'Here's the bridegroom! Come out to meet him!'

[7]"Then all the virgins woke up and trimmed their lamps. [8]The foolish ones said to the wise, 'Give us some of your oil; our lamps are going out.'

[9]" 'No,' they replied, 'there may not be enough for both us and you. Instead, go to those who sell oil and buy some for yourselves.'

[10]"But while they were on their way to buy the oil, the bridegroom arrived. The virgins who were ready went in with him to the wedding banquet. And the door was shut.

[11]"Later the others also came. 'Lord, Lord,' they said, 'open the door for us!'

[12]"But he replied, 'Truly I tell you, I don't know you.'

[13]"Therefore keep watch, because you do not know the day or the hour.

THE PARABLE OF THE BAGS OF GOLD

[14]"Again, it will be like a man going on a journey, who called his servants and entrusted his wealth to them. [15]To one he gave five bags of gold, to another two bags, and to another one bag,[a] each according to his ability. Then he went on his journey. [16]The man who had received five bags of gold went at once and put his money to work and gained five bags more. [17]So also, the one with two bags of gold gained two more. [18]But the man who had received one bag went off, dug a hole in the ground and hid his master's money.

[19]"After a long time the master of those servants returned and settled accounts with them. [20]The man who had received five bags of gold brought the other five. 'Master,' he said, 'you entrusted me with five bags of gold. See, I have gained five more.'

[21]"His master replied, 'Well done, good and faithful servant! You have been faithful with a few things; I will put you in charge of many things. Come and share your master's happiness!'

---

[a] *15* Greek *five talents . . . two talents . . . one talent*; also throughout this parable; a talent was worth about 20 years of a day laborer's wage.

22“The man with two bags of gold also came. ‘Master,’ he said, ‘you
entrusted me with two bags of gold; see, I have gained two more.’
23“His master replied, ‘Well done, good and faithful servant! You
have been faithful with a few things; I will put you in charge of many
things. Come and share your master’s happiness!’
24“Then the man who had received one bag of gold came. ‘Master,’
he said, ‘I knew that you are a hard man, harvesting where you have
not sown and gathering where you have not scattered seed. 25So I was
afraid and went out and hid your gold in the ground. See, here is what
belongs to you.’
26“His master replied, ‘You wicked, lazy servant! So you knew that I
harvest where I have not sown and gather where I have not scattered
seed? 27Well then, you should have put my money on deposit with the
bankers, so that when I returned I would have received it back with
interest.
28“ ‘So take the bag of gold from him and give it to the one who has
ten bags. 29For whoever has will be given more, and they will have an
abundance. Whoever does not have, even what they have will be taken
from them. 30And throw that worthless servant outside, into the dark-
ness, where there will be weeping and gnashing of teeth.’

THE SHEEP AND THE GOATS

31“When the Son of Man comes in his glory, and all the angels with
him, he will sit on his glorious throne. 32All the nations will be gath-
ered before him, and he will separate the people one from another as
a shepherd separates the sheep from the goats. 33He will put the sheep
on his right and the goats on his left.
34“Then the King will say to those on his right, ‘Come, you who are
blessed by my Father; take your inheritance, the kingdom prepared
for you since the creation of the world. 35For I was hungry and you
gave me something to eat, I was thirsty and you gave me something
to drink, I was a stranger and you invited me in, 36I needed clothes and
you clothed me, I was sick and you looked after me, I was in prison and
you came to visit me.’
37“Then the righteous will answer him, ‘Lord, when did we see you
hungry and feed you, or thirsty and give you something to drink?
38When did we see you a stranger and invite you in, or needing clothes
and clothe you? 39When did we see you sick or in prison and go to visit
you?’
40“The King will reply, ‘Truly I tell you, whatever you did for one of
the least of these brothers and sisters of mine, you did for me.’
41“Then he will say to those on his left, ‘Depart from me, you who are
cursed, into the eternal fire prepared for the devil and his angels. 42For
I was hungry and you gave me nothing to eat, I was thirsty and you
gave me nothing to drink, 43I was a stranger and you did not invite me
in, I needed clothes and you did not clothe me, I was sick and in prison
and you did not look after me.’
44“They also will answer, ‘Lord, when did we see you hungry or
thirsty or a stranger or needing clothes or sick or in prison, and did
not help you?’
45“He will reply, ‘Truly I tell you, whatever you did not do for one of
the least of these, you did not do for me.’
46“Then they will go away to eternal punishment, but the righteous
to eternal life.”

PRAYING SCRIPTURE

Matthew 25

Contrary to the belief that all but the truly wicked will make it to heaven, Jesus taught that the entirety of humanity—all the nations—will be divided among those who believe and those who do not. The works that identify the goats are not genocide and mass murder, but lack of compassion toward the suffering. “Lesser sins” condemn like greater ones.

Sheep or goat: What does the fruit of your life reveal?

THE PLOT AGAINST JESUS

26 When Jesus had finished saying all these things, he said to his disciples, 2“As you know, the Passover is two days away — and the Son of Man will be handed over to be crucified.”

3Then the chief priests and the elders of the people assembled in the palace of the high priest, whose name was Caiaphas, 4and they schemed to arrest Jesus secretly and kill him. 5“But not during the festival,” they said, “or there may be a riot among the people.”

JESUS ANOINTED AT BETHANY

6While Jesus was in Bethany in the home of Simon the Leper, 7a woman came to him with an alabaster jar of very expensive perfume, which she poured on his head as he was reclining at the table.

8When the disciples saw this, they were indignant. “Why this waste?” they asked. 9“This perfume could have been sold at a high price and the money given to the poor.”

10Aware of this, Jesus said to them, “Why are you bothering this woman? She has done a beautiful thing to me. 11The poor you will always have with you,[a] but you will not always have me. 12When she poured this perfume on my body, she did it to prepare me for burial. 13Truly I tell you, wherever this gospel is preached throughout the world, what she has done will also be told, in memory of her.”

JUDAS AGREES TO BETRAY JESUS

14Then one of the Twelve — the one called Judas Iscariot — went to the chief priests 15and asked, “What are you willing to give me if I deliver him over to you?” So they counted out for him thirty pieces of silver. 16From then on Judas watched for an opportunity to hand him over.

THE LAST SUPPER

17On the first day of the Festival of Unleavened Bread, the disciples came to Jesus and asked, “Where do you want us to make preparations for you to eat the Passover?”

18He replied, “Go into the city to a certain man and tell him, ‘The Teacher says: My appointed time is near. I am going to celebrate the Passover with my disciples at your house.’ ” 19So the disciples did as Jesus had directed them and prepared the Passover.

20When evening came, Jesus was reclining at the table with the Twelve. 21And while they were eating, he said, “Truly I tell you, one of you will betray me.”

22They were very sad and began to say to him one after the other, “Surely you don’t mean me, Lord?”

23Jesus replied, “The one who has dipped his hand into the bowl with me will betray me. 24The Son of Man will go just as it is written about him. But woe to that man who betrays the Son of Man! It would be better for him if he had not been born.”

25Then Judas, the one who would betray him, said, “Surely you don’t mean me, Rabbi?”

Jesus answered, “You have said so.”

26While they were eating, Jesus took bread, and when he had given thanks, he broke it and gave it to his disciples, saying, “Take and eat; this is my body.”

[a] *11* See Deut. 15:11.

PRAYING SCRIPTURE

Matthew 26

In his final Passover with his disciples, Jesus shared the meal with one who would betray him, one who would deny him and many who would abandon him. Peter, the one most likely to brag, had assured Jesus that he would stay with the Messiah to the end. But he ended up publicly denying Jesus three times.

Ask the Lord for the strength to remain faithful whatever may come.

27Then he took a cup, and when he had given thanks, he gave it to
them, saying, "Drink from it, all of you. 28This is my blood of the[a] cov-
enant, which is poured out for many for the forgiveness of sins. 29I tell
you, I will not drink from this fruit of the vine from now on until that
day when I drink it new with you in my Father's kingdom."
30When they had sung a hymn, they went out to the Mount of Olives.

JESUS PREDICTS PETER'S DENIAL

31Then Jesus told them, "This very night you will all fall away on ac-
count of me, for it is written:

> "'I will strike the shepherd,
> and the sheep of the flock will be scattered.'[b]

32But after I have risen, I will go ahead of you into Galilee."
33Peter replied, "Even if all fall away on account of you, I never will."
34"Truly I tell you," Jesus answered, "this very night, before the
rooster crows, you will disown me three times."
35But Peter declared, "Even if I have to die with you, I will never dis-
own you." And all the other disciples said the same.

GETHSEMANE

36Then Jesus went with his disciples to a place called Gethsemane, and
he said to them, "Sit here while I go over there and pray." 37He took Peter
and the two sons of Zebedee along with him, and he began to be sor-
rowful and troubled. 38Then he said to them, "My soul is overwhelmed
with sorrow to the point of death. Stay here and keep watch with me."
39Going a little farther, he fell with his face to the ground and prayed,
"My Father, if it is possible, may this cup be taken from me. Yet not as
I will, but as you will."
40Then he returned to his disciples and found them sleeping.
"Couldn't you men keep watch with me for one hour?" he asked Peter.
41"Watch and pray so that you will not fall into temptation. The spirit
is willing, but the flesh is weak."
42He went away a second time and prayed, "My Father, if it is not
possible for this cup to be taken away unless I drink it, may your will
be done."
43When he came back, he again found them sleeping, because their
eyes were heavy. 44So he left them and went away once more and
prayed the third time, saying the same thing.
45Then he returned to the disciples and said to them, "Are you still
sleeping and resting? Look, the hour has come, and the Son of Man is
delivered into the hands of sinners. 46Rise! Let us go! Here comes my
betrayer!"

JESUS ARRESTED

47While he was still speaking, Judas, one of the Twelve, arrived. With
him was a large crowd armed with swords and clubs, sent from the
chief priests and the elders of the people. 48Now the betrayer had ar-
ranged a signal with them: "The one I kiss is the man; arrest him." 49Go-
ing at once to Jesus, Judas said, "Greetings, Rabbi!" and kissed him.
50Jesus replied, "Do what you came for, friend."[c]

---

[a] *28* Some manuscripts *the new* [b] *31* Zech. 13:7 [c] *50* Or *"Why have you come, friend?"*

Then the men stepped forward, seized Jesus and arrested him.
51With that, one of Jesus' companions reached for his sword, drew it
out and struck the servant of the high priest, cutting off his ear.
52"Put your sword back in its place," Jesus said to him, "for all who
draw the sword will die by the sword. 53Do you think I cannot call on
my Father, and he will at once put at my disposal more than twelve le-
gions of angels? 54But how then would the Scriptures be fulfilled that
say it must happen in this way?"

55In that hour Jesus said to the crowd, "Am I leading a rebellion, that
you have come out with swords and clubs to capture me? Every day I
sat in the temple courts teaching, and you did not arrest me. 56But this
has all taken place that the writings of the prophets might be fulfilled."
Then all the disciples deserted him and fled.

JESUS BEFORE THE SANHEDRIN

57Those who had arrested Jesus took him to Caiaphas the high priest,
where the teachers of the law and the elders had assembled. 58But Pe-
ter followed him at a distance, right up to the courtyard of the high
priest. He entered and sat down with the guards to see the outcome.

59The chief priests and the whole Sanhedrin were looking for false
evidence against Jesus so that they could put him to death. 60But they
did not find any, though many false witnesses came forward.

Finally two came forward 61and declared, "This fellow said, 'I am
able to destroy the temple of God and rebuild it in three days.'"

62Then the high priest stood up and said to Jesus, "Are you not going
to answer? What is this testimony that these men are bringing against
you?" 63But Jesus remained silent.

The high priest said to him, "I charge you under oath by the living
God: Tell us if you are the Messiah, the Son of God."

64"You have said so," Jesus replied. "But I say to all of you: From now
on you will see the Son of Man sitting at the right hand of the Mighty
One and coming on the clouds of heaven."[a]

65Then the high priest tore his clothes and said, "He has spoken
blasphemy! Why do we need any more witnesses? Look, now you have
heard the blasphemy. 66What do you think?"

"He is worthy of death," they answered.

67Then they spit in his face and struck him with their fists. Others
slapped him 68and said, "Prophesy to us, Messiah. Who hit you?"

PETER DISOWNS JESUS

69Now Peter was sitting out in the courtyard, and a servant girl came
to him. "You also were with Jesus of Galilee," she said.

70But he denied it before them all. "I don't know what you're talking
about," he said.

71Then he went out to the gateway, where another servant girl
saw him and said to the people there, "This fellow was with Jesus of
Nazareth."

72He denied it again, with an oath: "I don't know the man!"

73After a little while, those standing there went up to Peter and said,
"Surely you are one of them; your accent gives you away."

74Then he began to call down curses, and he swore to them, "I don't
know the man!"

---

[a] *64* See Psalm 110:1; Daniel 7:13.

Immediately a rooster crowed. 75Then Peter remembered the word
Jesus had spoken: "Before the rooster crows, you will disown me three
times." And he went outside and wept bitterly.

JUDAS HANGS HIMSELF

27 Early in the morning, all the chief priests and the elders of the
people made their plans how to have Jesus executed. 2So they
bound him, led him away and handed him over to Pilate the governor.
3When Judas, who had betrayed him, saw that Jesus was condemned,
he was seized with remorse and returned the thirty pieces of silver to
the chief priests and the elders. 4"I have sinned," he said, "for I have
betrayed innocent blood."
"What is that to us?" they replied. "That's your responsibility."
5So Judas threw the money into the temple and left. Then he went
away and hanged himself.
6The chief priests picked up the coins and said, "It is against the law
to put this into the treasury, since it is blood money." 7So they decided
to use the money to buy the potter's field as a burial place for foreign-
ers. 8That is why it has been called the Field of Blood to this day. 9Then
what was spoken by Jeremiah the prophet was fulfilled: "They took the
thirty pieces of silver, the price set on him by the people of Israel, 10and
they used them to buy the potter's field, as the Lord commanded me."[a]

JESUS BEFORE PILATE

11Meanwhile Jesus stood before the governor, and the governor
asked him, "Are you the king of the Jews?"
"You have said so," Jesus replied.
12When he was accused by the chief priests and the elders, he gave
no answer. 13Then Pilate asked him, "Don't you hear the testimony they
are bringing against you?" 14But Jesus made no reply, not even to a sin-
gle charge — to the great amazement of the governor.
15Now it was the governor's custom at the festival to release a pris-
oner chosen by the crowd. 16At that time they had a well-known
prisoner whose name was Jesus[b] Barabbas. 17So when the crowd had
gathered, Pilate asked them, "Which one do you want me to release
to you: Jesus Barabbas, or Jesus who is called the Messiah?" 18For he
knew it was out of self-interest that they had handed Jesus over to him.
19While Pilate was sitting on the judge's seat, his wife sent him this
message: "Don't have anything to do with that innocent man, for I
have suffered a great deal today in a dream because of him."
20But the chief priests and the elders persuaded the crowd to ask for
Barabbas and to have Jesus executed.
21"Which of the two do you want me to release to you?" asked the
governor.
"Barabbas," they answered.
22"What shall I do, then, with Jesus who is called the Messiah?" Pi-
late asked.
They all answered, "Crucify him!"
23"Why? What crime has he committed?" asked Pilate.
But they shouted all the louder, "Crucify him!"
24When Pilate saw that he was getting nowhere, but that instead

[a] *10* See Zech. 11:12,13; Jer. 19:1-13; 32:6-9. [b] *16* Many manuscripts do not have *Jesus*; also in verse 17.

PRAYING SCRIPTURE

Matthew 27

The Lamb of God, the innocent, spotless One, the One in whom there was no guile, was crucified like a common criminal, a political rebel. Jesus was not crucified because of his sin (he had none) but because of ours.

Have you trusted in Jesus Christ alone to remove your sins? If not, pray now. He will hear, answer and forgive.

an uproar was starting, he took water and washed his hands in front
of the crowd. "I am innocent of this man's blood," he said. "It is your
responsibility!"
25 All the people answered, "His blood is on us and on our children!"
26 Then he released Barabbas to them. But he had Jesus flogged, and
handed him over to be crucified.

THE SOLDIERS MOCK JESUS

27 Then the governor's soldiers took Jesus into the Praetorium and
gathered the whole company of soldiers around him. 28 They stripped
him and put a scarlet robe on him, 29 and then twisted together a crown
of thorns and set it on his head. They put a staff in his right hand. Then
they knelt in front of him and mocked him. "Hail, king of the Jews!"
they said. 30 They spit on him, and took the staff and struck him on
the head again and again. 31 After they had mocked him, they took off
the robe and put his own clothes on him. Then they led him away to
crucify him.

THE CRUCIFIXION OF JESUS

32 As they were going out, they met a man from Cyrene, named Si-
mon, and they forced him to carry the cross. 33 They came to a place
called Golgotha (which means "the place of the skull"). 34 There they
offered Jesus wine to drink, mixed with gall; but after tasting it, he
refused to drink it. 35 When they had crucified him, they divided up his
clothes by casting lots. 36 And sitting down, they kept watch over him
there. 37 Above his head they placed the written charge against him:
THIS IS JESUS, THE KING OF THE JEWS.
38 Two rebels were crucified with him, one on his right and one on his
left. 39 Those who passed by hurled insults at him, shaking their heads
40 and saying, "You who are going to destroy the temple and build it
in three days, save yourself! Come down from the cross, if you are the
Son of God!" 41 In the same way the chief priests, the teachers of the
law and the elders mocked him. 42 "He saved others," they said, "but
he can't save himself! He's the king of Israel! Let him come down now
from the cross, and we will believe in him. 43 He trusts in God. Let God
rescue him now if he wants him, for he said, 'I am the Son of God.'"
44 In the same way the rebels who were crucified with him also heaped
insults on him.

THE DEATH OF JESUS

45 From noon until three in the afternoon darkness came over all the
land. 46 About three in the afternoon Jesus cried out in a loud voice,
"Eli, Eli,[a] *lema sabachthani?"* (which means "My God, my God, why have
you forsaken me?").[b]
47 When some of those standing there heard this, they said, "He's call-
ing Elijah."
48 Immediately one of them ran and got a sponge. He filled it with
wine vinegar, put it on a staff, and offered it to Jesus to drink. 49 The
rest said, "Now leave him alone. Let's see if Elijah comes to save him."
50 And when Jesus had cried out again in a loud voice, he gave up
his spirit.
51 At that moment the curtain of the temple was torn in two from

---

[a] 46 Some manuscripts *Eloi, Eloi* [b] 46 Psalm 22:1

top to bottom. The earth shook, the rocks split 52and the tombs broke
open. The bodies of many holy people who had died were raised to life.
53They came out of the tombs after Jesus' resurrection and[a] went into
the holy city and appeared to many people.
54When the centurion and those with him who were guarding Jesus
saw the earthquake and all that had happened, they were terrified, and
exclaimed, "Surely he was the Son of God!"
55Many women were there, watching from a distance. They had fol-
lowed Jesus from Galilee to care for his needs. 56Among them were
Mary Magdalene, Mary the mother of James and Joseph,[b] and the
mother of Zebedee's sons.

THE BURIAL OF JESUS

57As evening approached, there came a rich man from Arimathea,
named Joseph, who had himself become a disciple of Jesus. 58Going to
Pilate, he asked for Jesus' body, and Pilate ordered that it be given to
him. 59Joseph took the body, wrapped it in a clean linen cloth, 60and
placed it in his own new tomb that he had cut out of the rock. He rolled
a big stone in front of the entrance to the tomb and went away. 61Mary
Magdalene and the other Mary were sitting there opposite the tomb.

THE GUARD AT THE TOMB

62The next day, the one after Preparation Day, the chief priests and
the Pharisees went to Pilate. 63"Sir," they said, "we remember that
while he was still alive that deceiver said, 'After three days I will rise
again.' 64So give the order for the tomb to be made secure until the
third day. Otherwise, his disciples may come and steal the body and tell
the people that he has been raised from the dead. This last deception
will be worse than the first."
65"Take a guard," Pilate answered. "Go, make the tomb as secure as
you know how." 66So they went and made the tomb secure by putting
a seal on the stone and posting the guard.

JESUS HAS RISEN

28 After the Sabbath, at dawn on the first day of the week, Mary
Magdalene and the other Mary went to look at the tomb.
2There was a violent earthquake, for an angel of the Lord came down
from heaven and, going to the tomb, rolled back the stone and sat on
it. 3His appearance was like lightning, and his clothes were white as
snow. 4The guards were so afraid of him that they shook and became
like dead men.
5The angel said to the women, "Do not be afraid, for I know that you
are looking for Jesus, who was crucified. 6He is not here; he has risen,
just as he said. Come and see the place where he lay. 7Then go quickly
and tell his disciples: 'He has risen from the dead and is going ahead of
you into Galilee. There you will see him.' Now I have told you."
8So the women hurried away from the tomb, afraid yet filled with
joy, and ran to tell his disciples. 9Suddenly Jesus met them. "Greet-
ings," he said. They came to him, clasped his feet and worshiped him.
10Then Jesus said to them, "Do not be afraid. Go and tell my brothers
to go to Galilee; there they will see me."

[a] 53 Or *tombs, and after Jesus' resurrection they* [b] 56 Greek *Joses*, a variant of *Joseph*

PRAYING SCRIPTURE

Matthew 28

The greatest news in history is this: Jesus did not stay dead. As the angel told the women seeking Jesus' body, "He is not here; he has risen, just as he said." Jesus' resurrection from the dead is also our guarantee of life with him.

Eternal life is his life given to us. If you do not have this life, ask God to give it to you, and receive it in faith.

THE GUARDS' REPORT

11 While the women were on their way, some of the guards went into
the city and reported to the chief priests everything that had hap-
pened. 12 When the chief priests had met with the elders and devised
a plan, they gave the soldiers a large sum of money, 13 telling them,
"You are to say, 'His disciples came during the night and stole him
away while we were asleep.' 14 If this report gets to the governor, we
will satisfy him and keep you out of trouble." 15 So the soldiers took the
money and did as they were instructed. And this story has been widely
circulated among the Jews to this very day.

THE GREAT COMMISSION

16 Then the eleven disciples went to Galilee, to the mountain where
Jesus had told them to go. 17 When they saw him, they worshiped him;
but some doubted. 18 Then Jesus came to them and said, "All authority
in heaven and on earth has been given to me. 19 Therefore go and make
disciples of all nations, baptizing them in the name of the Father and
of the Son and of the Holy Spirit, 20 and teaching them to obey every-
thing I have commanded you. And surely I am with you always, to the
very end of the age."

PRAYING SCRIPTURE

Matthew 28

The church's central mission is stated in this chapter. The spread of the gospel of Jesus comes from going, baptizing, teaching, obeying and living in the presence of Jesus through the Holy Spirit. Jesus charges his disciples by virtue of his own authority, given to him by the Father with whom he is one.

Look for ways to be intentional this week to spread the gospel with those around you.

MARK

The Gospel of Mark moves quickly through the life of Jesus. Mark focuses on Jesus' deeds and does not contain many long blocks of his teaching. Mark uses the word "immediately" more than 30 times as his Gospel follows Jesus from place to place. Mark does not contain a narrative of Jesus' birth and does not tell the story of Jesus' ascension into heaven. Still, some scholars believe both Matthew and Luke patterned their Gospel narratives on Mark's. Some scholars further believe Mark's Gospel is the witness of the apostle Peter—that it bears his account of the life and ministry of Jesus.

Two significant teachings of Jesus that Mark includes are in 1:15, "The time has come . . . The kingdom of God has come near. Repent and believe the good news!" and in 10:45, seen as the theme of his Gospel: "For even the Son of Man did not come to be served, but to serve, and to give his life as a ransom for many." Taken together, Jesus portrayed a kingdom entered through repentance and faith, then exemplified through serving.

For all its focus on action, however, Mark also records Jesus going out to a desolate place to pray alone (see 1:35). Mark says it was "very early in the morning, while it was still dark." Jesus didn't merely roll over for a quick "quiet time" before facing the day. He spent meaningful time in prayer with the Father. The day before, he had healed many people. His time in prayer was interrupted by his disciples who were imploring him to come help others. Soon he was on his way to other nearby villages to heal more people and preach God's Word to them.

Jesus not only prayed himself; he instructed his disciples to pray. He told them that whatever they prayed for, if they believed, God would provide it (see 11:24). In a prophesied time of persecution, Jesus told them to pray that their escape would not take place in the winter (see 13:18). When he was agonizing in the garden prayer before his arrest and crucifixion, he told his sleepy disciples, "Watch and pray so that you will not fall into temptation" (14:38). If we pay attention to Jesus, we learn that all of life is subject to prayer.

In his ministry, Jesus could have been healing people or preaching during the time he spent in prayer, but his dedication to spending time with the Father before embarking on his next ministry assignment demonstrates the importance of prayer. If the perfect Son of God, who never sinned and never knew failure, set aside time out of a busy schedule to pray, how much more should we? We cannot claim that we lack time to pray; we have all the time we need if we prioritize it as Jesus did. In fact, if our lives are so busy that we think we don't have time to pray, it is likely a good sign of how badly we need to pray.

PRAYING SCRIPTURE

Mark 1

Mark's Gospel is unique in that Mark jumped almost directly into Jesus' public ministry, including his earliest preaching, which revealed God's kingdom at hand and implored people to repent and believe in the gospel. Jesus' message aligned with his ministry from the outset.

Our emphasis should mirror Jesus' emphasis. Ask God to help you keep his kingdom and the Good News of Jesus as the emphasis of your life.

JOHN THE BAPTIST PREPARES THE WAY

1 The beginning of the good news about Jesus the Messiah,[a] the Son of God,[b] 2as it is written in Isaiah the prophet:

"I will send my messenger ahead of you,
  who will prepare your way"[c] —
3"a voice of one calling in the wilderness,
'Prepare the way for the Lord,
  make straight paths for him.'"[d]

4And so John the Baptist appeared in the wilderness, preaching a baptism of repentance for the forgiveness of sins. 5The whole Judean countryside and all the people of Jerusalem went out to him. Confessing their sins, they were baptized by him in the Jordan River. 6John wore clothing made of camel's hair, with a leather belt around his waist, and he ate locusts and wild honey. 7And this was his message: "After me comes the one more powerful than I, the straps of whose sandals I am not worthy to stoop down and untie. 8I baptize you with[e] water, but he will baptize you with[e] the Holy Spirit."

THE BAPTISM AND TESTING OF JESUS

9At that time Jesus came from Nazareth in Galilee and was baptized by John in the Jordan. 10Just as Jesus was coming up out of the water, he saw heaven being torn open and the Spirit descending on him like a dove. 11And a voice came from heaven: "You are my Son, whom I love; with you I am well pleased."

12At once the Spirit sent him out into the wilderness, 13and he was in the wilderness forty days, being tempted[f] by Satan. He was with the wild animals, and angels attended him.

JESUS ANNOUNCES THE GOOD NEWS

14After John was put in prison, Jesus went into Galilee, proclaiming the good news of God. 15"The time has come," he said. "The kingdom of God has come near. Repent and believe the good news!"

JESUS CALLS HIS FIRST DISCIPLES

16As Jesus walked beside the Sea of Galilee, he saw Simon and his brother Andrew casting a net into the lake, for they were fishermen. 17"Come, follow me," Jesus said, "and I will send you out to fish for people." 18At once they left their nets and followed him.

19When he had gone a little farther, he saw James son of Zebedee and his brother John in a boat, preparing their nets. 20Without delay he called them, and they left their father Zebedee in the boat with the hired men and followed him.

JESUS DRIVES OUT AN IMPURE SPIRIT

21They went to Capernaum, and when the Sabbath came, Jesus went into the synagogue and began to teach. 22The people were amazed at his teaching, because he taught them as one who had authority, not as the teachers of the law. 23Just then a man in their synagogue who was possessed by an impure spirit cried out, 24"What do you want with

---

[a] *1* Or *Jesus Christ. Messiah* (Hebrew) and *Christ* (Greek) both mean *Anointed One.* [b] *1* Some manuscripts do not have *the Son of God.* [c] *2* Mal. 3:1 [d] *3* Isaiah 40:3 [e] *8* Or *in* [f] *13* The Greek for *tempted* can also mean *tested.*

us, Jesus of Nazareth? Have you come to destroy us? I know who you
are — the Holy One of God!"
25"Be quiet!" said Jesus sternly. "Come out of him!" 26The impure
spirit shook the man violently and came out of him with a shriek.
27The people were all so amazed that they asked each other, "What
is this? A new teaching — and with authority! He even gives orders to
impure spirits and they obey him." 28News about him spread quickly
over the whole region of Galilee.

JESUS HEALS MANY

29As soon as they left the synagogue, they went with James and John
to the home of Simon and Andrew. 30Simon's mother-in-law was in bed
with a fever, and they immediately told Jesus about her. 31So he went
to her, took her hand and helped her up. The fever left her and she be-
gan to wait on them.
32That evening after sunset the people brought to Jesus all the sick
and demon-possessed. 33The whole town gathered at the door, 34and
Jesus healed many who had various diseases. He also drove out many
demons, but he would not let the demons speak because they knew
who he was.

JESUS PRAYS IN A SOLITARY PLACE

35Very early in the morning, while it was still dark, Jesus got up, left
the house and went off to a solitary place, where he prayed. 36Simon
and his companions went to look for him, 37and when they found him,
they exclaimed: "Everyone is looking for you!"
38Jesus replied, "Let us go somewhere else — to the nearby vil-
lages — so I can preach there also. That is why I have come." 39So he
traveled throughout Galilee, preaching in their synagogues and driv-
ing out demons.

JESUS HEALS A MAN WITH LEPROSY

40A man with leprosy[a] came to him and begged him on his knees, "If
you are willing, you can make me clean."
41Jesus was indignant.[b] He reached out his hand and touched the
man. "I am willing," he said. "Be clean!" 42Immediately the leprosy left
him and he was cleansed.
43Jesus sent him away at once with a strong warning: 44"See that you
don't tell this to anyone. But go, show yourself to the priest and offer
the sacrifices that Moses commanded for your cleansing, as a testi-
mony to them." 45Instead he went out and began to talk freely, spread-
ing the news. As a result, Jesus could no longer enter a town openly
but stayed outside in lonely places. Yet the people still came to him
from everywhere.

JESUS FORGIVES AND HEALS A PARALYZED MAN

2 A few days later, when Jesus again entered Capernaum, the peo-
ple heard that he had come home. 2They gathered in such large
numbers that there was no room left, not even outside the door, and
he preached the word to them. 3Some men came, bringing to him a

[a] *40* The Greek word traditionally translated *leprosy* was used for various diseases affecting the skin. [b] *41* Many manuscripts *Jesus was filled with compassion*

PRAYING SCRIPTURE

Mark 2

Jesus' ministry was a continuous challenge to the religious leaders as part of the ongoing unveiling of himself as the Messiah. Jesus connected the healing of the paralytic with the forgiveness of the man's sins. Since only God can forgive sin, the conclusion is inescapable: Jesus is the Son of God, the Father of Israel (see verse 10).

Have you believed in Jesus, the Savior of the world? He will forgive your sins as he forgave the sins of the paralyzed man.

paralyzed man, carried by four of them. 4Since they could not get him
to Jesus because of the crowd, they made an opening in the roof above
Jesus by digging through it and then lowered the mat the man was
lying on. 5When Jesus saw their faith, he said to the paralyzed man,
"Son, your sins are forgiven."

6Now some teachers of the law were sitting there, thinking to them-
selves, 7"Why does this fellow talk like that? He's blaspheming! Who
can forgive sins but God alone?"

8Immediately Jesus knew in his spirit that this was what they were
thinking in their hearts, and he said to them, "Why are you thinking
these things? 9Which is easier: to say to this paralyzed man, 'Your sins
are forgiven,' or to say, 'Get up, take your mat and walk'? 10But I want
you to know that the Son of Man has authority on earth to forgive
sins." So he said to the man, 11"I tell you, get up, take your mat and go
home." 12He got up, took his mat and walked out in full view of them
all. This amazed everyone and they praised God, saying, "We have
never seen anything like this!"

JESUS CALLS LEVI AND EATS WITH SINNERS

13Once again Jesus went out beside the lake. A large crowd came to
him, and he began to teach them. 14As he walked along, he saw Levi
son of Alphaeus sitting at the tax collector's booth. "Follow me," Jesus
told him, and Levi got up and followed him.

15While Jesus was having dinner at Levi's house, many tax collec-
tors and sinners were eating with him and his disciples, for there were
many who followed him. 16When the teachers of the law who were
Pharisees saw him eating with the sinners and tax collectors, they
asked his disciples: "Why does he eat with tax collectors and sinners?"

17On hearing this, Jesus said to them, "It is not the healthy who
need a doctor, but the sick. I have not come to call the righteous, but
sinners."

JESUS QUESTIONED ABOUT FASTING

18Now John's disciples and the Pharisees were fasting. Some people
came and asked Jesus, "How is it that John's disciples and the disciples
of the Pharisees are fasting, but yours are not?"

19Jesus answered, "How can the guests of the bridegroom fast while
he is with them? They cannot, so long as they have him with them.
20But the time will come when the bridegroom will be taken from
them, and on that day they will fast.

21"No one sews a patch of unshrunk cloth on an old garment. Other-
wise, the new piece will pull away from the old, making the tear worse.
22And no one pours new wine into old wineskins. Otherwise, the wine
will burst the skins, and both the wine and the wineskins will be ru-
ined. No, they pour new wine into new wineskins."

JESUS IS LORD OF THE SABBATH

23One Sabbath Jesus was going through the grainfields, and as his
disciples walked along, they began to pick some heads of grain. 24The
Pharisees said to him, "Look, why are they doing what is unlawful on
the Sabbath?"

25He answered, "Have you never read what David did when he and
his companions were hungry and in need? 26In the days of Abiathar
the high priest, he entered the house of God and ate the consecrated

bread, which is lawful only for priests to eat. And he also gave some to
his companions."
27Then he said to them, "The Sabbath was made for man, not man
for the Sabbath. 28So the Son of Man is Lord even of the Sabbath."

JESUS HEALS ON THE SABBATH

3 Another time Jesus went into the synagogue, and a man with a
shriveled hand was there. 2Some of them were looking for a rea-
son to accuse Jesus, so they watched him closely to see if he would heal
him on the Sabbath. 3Jesus said to the man with the shriveled hand,
"Stand up in front of everyone."
4Then Jesus asked them, "Which is lawful on the Sabbath: to do good
or to do evil, to save life or to kill?" But they remained silent.
5He looked around at them in anger and, deeply distressed at their
stubborn hearts, said to the man, "Stretch out your hand." He stretched
it out, and his hand was completely restored. 6Then the Pharisees went
out and began to plot with the Herodians how they might kill Jesus.

CROWDS FOLLOW JESUS

7Jesus withdrew with his disciples to the lake, and a large crowd
from Galilee followed. 8When they heard about all he was doing, many
people came to him from Judea, Jerusalem, Idumea, and the regions
across the Jordan and around Tyre and Sidon. 9Because of the crowd he
told his disciples to have a small boat ready for him, to keep the people
from crowding him. 10For he had healed many, so that those with dis-
eases were pushing forward to touch him. 11Whenever the impure spir-
its saw him, they fell down before him and cried out, "You are the Son
of God." 12But he gave them strict orders not to tell others about him.

JESUS APPOINTS THE TWELVE

13Jesus went up on a mountainside and called to him those he
wanted, and they came to him. 14He appointed twelve[a] that they might
be with him and that he might send them out to preach 15and to have
authority to drive out demons. 16These are the twelve he appointed:
Simon (to whom he gave the name Peter), 17James son of Zebedee and
his brother John (to them he gave the name Boanerges, which means
"sons of thunder"), 18Andrew, Philip, Bartholomew, Matthew, Thomas,
James son of Alphaeus, Thaddaeus, Simon the Zealot 19and Judas Is-
cariot, who betrayed him.

JESUS ACCUSED BY HIS FAMILY AND BY TEACHERS OF THE LAW

20Then Jesus entered a house, and again a crowd gathered, so that
he and his disciples were not even able to eat. 21When his family[b] heard
about this, they went to take charge of him, for they said, "He is out
of his mind."
22And the teachers of the law who came down from Jerusalem said,
"He is possessed by Beelzebul! By the prince of demons he is driving
out demons."
23So Jesus called them over to him and began to speak to them in
parables: "How can Satan drive out Satan? 24If a kingdom is divided

[a] 14 Some manuscripts *twelve — designating them apostles —* [b] 21 Or *his associates*

PRAYING SCRIPTURE

Mark 3

As God's Son, Jesus could have chosen to go it alone and still have worked miracles, preached the gospel and had a successful ministry. Instead, he chose to pour his time and message into 12 men, 11 of whom would continue spreading the gospel message after he returned to the Father.

Are you involved in a discipleship relationship? If not, ask God to bless you with the opportunity to disciple others.

against itself, that kingdom cannot stand. 25If a house is divided against itself, that house cannot stand. 26And if Satan opposes himself and is divided, he cannot stand; his end has come. 27In fact, no one can enter a strong man's house without first tying him up. Then he can plunder the strong man's house. 28Truly I tell you, people can be forgiven all their sins and every slander they utter, 29but whoever blasphemes against the Holy Spirit will never be forgiven; they are guilty of an eternal sin."

30He said this because they were saying, "He has an impure spirit."

31Then Jesus' mother and brothers arrived. Standing outside, they sent someone in to call him. 32A crowd was sitting around him, and they told him, "Your mother and brothers are outside looking for you."

33"Who are my mother and my brothers?" he asked.

34Then he looked at those seated in a circle around him and said, "Here are my mother and my brothers! 35Whoever does God's will is my brother and sister and mother."

THE PARABLE OF THE SOWER

4 Again Jesus began to teach by the lake. The crowd that gathered around him was so large that he got into a boat and sat in it out on the lake, while all the people were along the shore at the water's edge. 2He taught them many things by parables, and in his teaching said: 3"Listen! A farmer went out to sow his seed. 4As he was scattering the seed, some fell along the path, and the birds came and ate it up. 5Some fell on rocky places, where it did not have much soil. It sprang up quickly, because the soil was shallow. 6But when the sun came up, the plants were scorched, and they withered because they had no root. 7Other seed fell among thorns, which grew up and choked the plants, so that they did not bear grain. 8Still other seed fell on good soil. It came up, grew and produced a crop, some multiplying thirty, some sixty, some a hundred times."

9Then Jesus said, "Whoever has ears to hear, let them hear."

10When he was alone, the Twelve and the others around him asked him about the parables. 11He told them, "The secret of the kingdom of God has been given to you. But to those on the outside everything is said in parables 12so that,

"'they may be ever seeing but never perceiving,
and ever hearing but never understanding;
otherwise they might turn and be forgiven!'[a]"

13Then Jesus said to them, "Don't you understand this parable? How then will you understand any parable? 14The farmer sows the word. 15Some people are like seed along the path, where the word is sown. As soon as they hear it, Satan comes and takes away the word that was sown in them. 16Others, like seed sown on rocky places, hear the word and at once receive it with joy. 17But since they have no root, they last only a short time. When trouble or persecution comes because of the word, they quickly fall away. 18Still others, like seed sown among thorns, hear the word; 19but the worries of this life, the deceitfulness of wealth and the desires for other things come in and choke the word, making it unfruitful. 20Others, like seed sown on good soil, hear the word, accept it, and produce a crop—some thirty, some sixty, some a hundred times what was sown."

PRAYING SCRIPTURE

Mark 4

Among a series of parables, Jesus emphasized the light of the kingdom that exposes and reveals. The kingdom is also like a mustard seed—it begins very small—but it grows large enough that birds perch in its shade. God's kingdom looked small, but it would grow as Jesus' light shone in the darkness.

There is nothing that will not be revealed in the light of the kingdom. Pray for that light to guide you.

[a] *12* Isaiah 6:9,10

A LAMP ON A STAND

21He said to them, "Do you bring in a lamp to put it under a bowl or
a bed? Instead, don't you put it on its stand? 22For whatever is hidden
is meant to be disclosed, and whatever is concealed is meant to be
brought out into the open. 23If anyone has ears to hear, let them hear."
24"Consider carefully what you hear," he continued. "With the mea-
sure you use, it will be measured to you — and even more. 25Whoever
has will be given more; whoever does not have, even what they have
will be taken from them."

THE PARABLE OF THE GROWING SEED

26He also said, "This is what the kingdom of God is like. A man scat-
ters seed on the ground. 27Night and day, whether he sleeps or gets up,
the seed sprouts and grows, though he does not know how. 28All by
itself the soil produces grain — first the stalk, then the head, then the
full kernel in the head. 29As soon as the grain is ripe, he puts the sickle
to it, because the harvest has come."

THE PARABLE OF THE MUSTARD SEED

30Again he said, "What shall we say the kingdom of God is like, or
what parable shall we use to describe it? 31It is like a mustard seed,
which is the smallest of all seeds on earth. 32Yet when planted, it grows
and becomes the largest of all garden plants, with such big branches
that the birds can perch in its shade."
33With many similar parables Jesus spoke the word to them, as much
as they could understand. 34He did not say anything to them without
using a parable. But when he was alone with his own disciples, he ex-
plained everything.

JESUS CALMS THE STORM

35That day when evening came, he said to his disciples, "Let us go
over to the other side." 36Leaving the crowd behind, they took him
along, just as he was, in the boat. There were also other boats with
him. 37A furious squall came up, and the waves broke over the boat,
so that it was nearly swamped. 38Jesus was in the stern, sleeping on a
cushion. The disciples woke him and said to him, "Teacher, don't you
care if we drown?"
39He got up, rebuked the wind and said to the waves, "Quiet! Be still!"
Then the wind died down and it was completely calm.
40He said to his disciples, "Why are you so afraid? Do you still have
no faith?"
41They were terrified and asked each other, "Who is this? Even the
wind and the waves obey him!"

JESUS RESTORES A DEMON-POSSESSED MAN

5 They went across the lake to the region of the Gerasenes.[a] 2When
Jesus got out of the boat, a man with an impure spirit came from the
tombs to meet him. 3This man lived in the tombs, and no one could bind
him anymore, not even with a chain. 4For he had often been chained
hand and foot, but he tore the chains apart and broke the irons on his
feet. No one was strong enough to subdue him. 5Night and day among
the tombs and in the hills he would cry out and cut himself with stones.

PRAYING SCRIPTURE

Mark 5

The spirit world was important to the times in which Jesus lived, and Jesus affirmed the reality of both angels and demons during his ministry. In a provocative encounter on the shore of the Sea of Galilee, Jesus cast a multitude ("Legion") of demons out of a tormented man into a herd of pigs (see verses 9–13).

Does the spirit world make you fearful? Trust Jesus' power; call on him when you are afraid.

[a] *1* Some manuscripts *Gadarenes*; other manuscripts *Gergesenes*

6When he saw Jesus from a distance, he ran and fell on his knees in front of him. 7He shouted at the top of his voice, "What do you want with me, Jesus, Son of the Most High God? In God's name don't torture me!" 8For Jesus had said to him, "Come out of this man, you impure spirit!"

9Then Jesus asked him, "What is your name?"

"My name is Legion," he replied, "for we are many." 10And he begged Jesus again and again not to send them out of the area.

11A large herd of pigs was feeding on the nearby hillside. 12The demons begged Jesus, "Send us among the pigs; allow us to go into them." 13He gave them permission, and the impure spirits came out and went into the pigs. The herd, about two thousand in number, rushed down the steep bank into the lake and were drowned.

14Those tending the pigs ran off and reported this in the town and countryside, and the people went out to see what had happened. 15When they came to Jesus, they saw the man who had been possessed by the legion of demons, sitting there, dressed and in his right mind; and they were afraid. 16Those who had seen it told the people what had happened to the demon-possessed man—and told about the pigs as well. 17Then the people began to plead with Jesus to leave their region.

18As Jesus was getting into the boat, the man who had been demon-possessed begged to go with him. 19Jesus did not let him, but said, "Go home to your own people and tell them how much the Lord has done for you, and how he has had mercy on you." 20So the man went away and began to tell in the Decapolis[a] how much Jesus had done for him. And all the people were amazed.

JESUS RAISES A DEAD GIRL AND HEALS A SICK WOMAN

21When Jesus had again crossed over by boat to the other side of the lake, a large crowd gathered around him while he was by the lake. 22Then one of the synagogue leaders, named Jairus, came, and when he saw Jesus, he fell at his feet. 23He pleaded earnestly with him, "My little daughter is dying. Please come and put your hands on her so that she will be healed and live." 24So Jesus went with him.

A large crowd followed and pressed around him. 25And a woman was there who had been subject to bleeding for twelve years. 26She had suffered a great deal under the care of many doctors and had spent all she had, yet instead of getting better she grew worse. 27When she heard about Jesus, she came up behind him in the crowd and touched his cloak, 28because she thought, "If I just touch his clothes, I will be healed." 29Immediately her bleeding stopped and she felt in her body that she was freed from her suffering.

30At once Jesus realized that power had gone out from him. He turned around in the crowd and asked, "Who touched my clothes?"

31"You see the people crowding against you," his disciples answered, "and yet you can ask, 'Who touched me?' "

32But Jesus kept looking around to see who had done it. 33Then the woman, knowing what had happened to her, came and fell at his feet and, trembling with fear, told him the whole truth. 34He said to her, "Daughter, your faith has healed you. Go in peace and be freed from your suffering."

35While Jesus was still speaking, some people came from the house

[a] *20* That is, the Ten Cities

of Jairus, the synagogue leader. "Your daughter is dead," they said.
"Why bother the teacher anymore?"
36Overhearing[a] what they said, Jesus told him, "Don't be afraid; just
believe."
37He did not let anyone follow him except Peter, James and John the
brother of James. 38When they came to the home of the synagogue
leader, Jesus saw a commotion, with people crying and wailing loudly.
39He went in and said to them, "Why all this commotion and wailing?
The child is not dead but asleep." 40But they laughed at him.
After he put them all out, he took the child's father and mother and
the disciples who were with him, and went in where the child was. 41He
took her by the hand and said to her, *"Talitha koum!"* (which means
"Little girl, I say to you, get up!"). 42Immediately the girl stood up and
began to walk around (she was twelve years old). At this they were
completely astonished. 43He gave strict orders not to let anyone know
about this, and told them to give her something to eat.

A PROPHET WITHOUT HONOR

6 Jesus left there and went to his hometown, accompanied by his
disciples. 2When the Sabbath came, he began to teach in the syn-
agogue, and many who heard him were amazed.
"Where did this man get these things?" they asked. "What's this wis-
dom that has been given him? What are these remarkable miracles he
is performing? 3Isn't this the carpenter? Isn't this Mary's son and the
brother of James, Joseph,[b] Judas and Simon? Aren't his sisters here
with us?" And they took offense at him.
4Jesus said to them, "A prophet is not without honor except in his
own town, among his relatives and in his own home." 5He could not do
any miracles there, except lay his hands on a few sick people and heal
them. 6He was amazed at their lack of faith.

JESUS SENDS OUT THE TWELVE

Then Jesus went around teaching from village to village. 7Calling the
Twelve to him, he began to send them out two by two and gave them
authority over impure spirits.
8These were his instructions: "Take nothing for the journey except a
staff—no bread, no bag, no money in your belts. 9Wear sandals but not
an extra shirt. 10Whenever you enter a house, stay there until you leave
that town. 11And if any place will not welcome you or listen to you, leave
that place and shake the dust off your feet as a testimony against them."
12They went out and preached that people should repent. 13They
drove out many demons and anointed many sick people with oil and
healed them.

JOHN THE BAPTIST BEHEADED

14King Herod heard about this, for Jesus' name had become well
known. Some were saying,[c] "John the Baptist has been raised from the
dead, and that is why miraculous powers are at work in him."
15Others said, "He is Elijah."
And still others claimed, "He is a prophet, like one of the prophets
of long ago."

PRAYING SCRIPTURE

Mark 6

One of Jesus' most dramatic miracles is when he walked across the Sea of Galilee to his disciples who were in a boat struggling against a storm. Though they feared the storm and Jesus himself, thinking him a ghost, he encouraged them not to fear.

"Do not be afraid" is a life lesson God's people need to remember. God is always near; cry out to him when the storms come.

---

[a] 36 Or *Ignoring* [b] 3 Greek *Joses,* a variant of *Joseph* [c] 14 Some early manuscripts *He was saying*

16But when Herod heard this, he said, "John, whom I beheaded, has
been raised from the dead!"
17For Herod himself had given orders to have John arrested, and he
had him bound and put in prison. He did this because of Herodias, his
brother Philip's wife, whom he had married. 18For John had been say-
ing to Herod, "It is not lawful for you to have your brother's wife." 19So
Herodias nursed a grudge against John and wanted to kill him. But
she was not able to, 20because Herod feared John and protected him,
knowing him to be a righteous and holy man. When Herod heard John,
he was greatly puzzled[a]; yet he liked to listen to him.
21Finally the opportune time came. On his birthday Herod gave a
banquet for his high officials and military commanders and the lead-
ing men of Galilee. 22When the daughter of[b] Herodias came in and
danced, she pleased Herod and his dinner guests.

The king said to the girl, "Ask me for anything you want, and I'll give
it to you." 23And he promised her with an oath, "Whatever you ask I will
give you, up to half my kingdom."
24She went out and said to her mother, "What shall I ask for?"

"The head of John the Baptist," she answered.
25At once the girl hurried in to the king with the request: "I want you
to give me right now the head of John the Baptist on a platter."
26The king was greatly distressed, but because of his oaths and his
dinner guests, he did not want to refuse her. 27So he immediately sent
an executioner with orders to bring John's head. The man went, be-
headed John in the prison, 28and brought back his head on a platter.
He presented it to the girl, and she gave it to her mother. 29On hearing
of this, John's disciples came and took his body and laid it in a tomb.

JESUS FEEDS THE FIVE THOUSAND

30The apostles gathered around Jesus and reported to him all they
had done and taught. 31Then, because so many people were coming
and going that they did not even have a chance to eat, he said to them,
"Come with me by yourselves to a quiet place and get some rest."
32So they went away by themselves in a boat to a solitary place. 33But
many who saw them leaving recognized them and ran on foot from all
the towns and got there ahead of them. 34When Jesus landed and saw a
large crowd, he had compassion on them, because they were like sheep
without a shepherd. So he began teaching them many things.
35By this time it was late in the day, so his disciples came to him.
"This is a remote place," they said, "and it's already very late. 36Send
the people away so that they can go to the surrounding countryside
and villages and buy themselves something to eat."
37But he answered, "You give them something to eat."

They said to him, "That would take more than half a year's wages[c]!
Are we to go and spend that much on bread and give it to them to eat?"
38"How many loaves do you have?" he asked. "Go and see."

When they found out, they said, "Five — and two fish."
39Then Jesus directed them to have all the people sit down in
groups on the green grass. 40So they sat down in groups of hundreds
and fifties. 41Taking the five loaves and the two fish and looking up to
heaven, he gave thanks and broke the loaves. Then he gave them to

---

[a] 20 Some early manuscripts *he did many things* [b] 22 Some early manuscripts *When his daughter* [c] 37 Greek *take two hundred denarii*

his disciples to distribute to the people. He also divided the two fish
among them all. 42They all ate and were satisfied, 43and the disciples
picked up twelve basketfuls of broken pieces of bread and fish. 44The
number of the men who had eaten was five thousand.

JESUS WALKS ON THE WATER

45Immediately Jesus made his disciples get into the boat and go on
ahead of him to Bethsaida, while he dismissed the crowd. 46After leav-
ing them, he went up on a mountainside to pray.

47Later that night, the boat was in the middle of the lake, and he was
alone on land. 48He saw the disciples straining at the oars, because
the wind was against them. Shortly before dawn he went out to them,
walking on the lake. He was about to pass by them, 49but when they
saw him walking on the lake, they thought he was a ghost. They cried
out, 50because they all saw him and were terrified.

Immediately he spoke to them and said, "Take courage! It is I. Don't
be afraid." 51Then he climbed into the boat with them, and the wind
died down. They were completely amazed, 52for they had not under-
stood about the loaves; their hearts were hardened.

53When they had crossed over, they landed at Gennesaret and an-
chored there. 54As soon as they got out of the boat, people recognized
Jesus. 55They ran throughout that whole region and carried the sick on
mats to wherever they heard he was. 56And wherever he went — into
villages, towns or countryside — they placed the sick in the market-
places. They begged him to let them touch even the edge of his cloak,
and all who touched it were healed.

THAT WHICH DEFILES

7 The Pharisees and some of the teachers of the law who had come
from Jerusalem gathered around Jesus 2and saw some of his disci-
ples eating food with hands that were defiled, that is, unwashed. 3(The
Pharisees and all the Jews do not eat unless they give their hands a
ceremonial washing, holding to the tradition of the elders. 4When they
come from the marketplace they do not eat unless they wash. And they
observe many other traditions, such as the washing of cups, pitchers
and kettles.[a])

5So the Pharisees and teachers of the law asked Jesus, "Why don't
your disciples live according to the tradition of the elders instead of
eating their food with defiled hands?"

6He replied, "Isaiah was right when he prophesied about you hypo-
crites; as it is written:

"'These people honor me with their lips,
but their hearts are far from me.
7They worship me in vain;
their teachings are merely human rules.'[b]

8You have let go of the commands of God and are holding on to human
traditions."

9And he continued, "You have a fine way of setting aside the com-
mands of God in order to observe[c] your own traditions! 10For Moses
said, 'Honor your father and mother,'[d] and, 'Anyone who curses their

[a] 4 Some early manuscripts *pitchers, kettles and dining couches* [b] 6,7 Isaiah 29:13 [c] 9 Some manuscripts *set up* [d] 10 Exodus 20:12; Deut. 5:16

PRAYING SCRIPTURE

Mark 7

Blaming others for our sin is easy—too easy. Jesus' instruction to the Pharisees and scribes was intended to focus on the true cause of human wickedness. It is not the result of dirty hands or unwashed pots and pans. It is the result of the sinfulness of each heart. We are defiled from the inside, not the outside.

Pray for the blood of Jesus to constantly cleanse you from all unrighteousness.

father or mother is to be put to death.'[a] 11But you say that if anyone declares that what might have been used to help their father or mother is Corban (that is, devoted to God)— 12then you no longer let them do anything for their father or mother. 13Thus you nullify the word of God by your tradition that you have handed down. And you do many things like that."

14Again Jesus called the crowd to him and said, "Listen to me, everyone, and understand this. 15Nothing outside a person can defile them by going into them. Rather, it is what comes out of a person that defiles them." [16][b]

17After he had left the crowd and entered the house, his disciples asked him about this parable. 18"Are you so dull?" he asked. "Don't you see that nothing that enters a person from the outside can defile them? 19For it doesn't go into their heart but into their stomach, and then out of the body." (In saying this, Jesus declared all foods clean.)

20He went on: "What comes out of a person is what defiles them. 21For it is from within, out of a person's heart, that evil thoughts come—sexual immorality, theft, murder, 22adultery, greed, malice, deceit, lewdness, envy, slander, arrogance and folly. 23All these evils come from inside and defile a person."

JESUS HONORS A SYROPHOENICIAN WOMAN'S FAITH

24Jesus left that place and went to the vicinity of Tyre.[c] He entered a house and did not want anyone to know it; yet he could not keep his presence secret. 25In fact, as soon as she heard about him, a woman whose little daughter was possessed by an impure spirit came and fell at his feet. 26The woman was a Greek, born in Syrian Phoenicia. She begged Jesus to drive the demon out of her daughter.

27"First let the children eat all they want," he told her, "for it is not right to take the children's bread and toss it to the dogs."

28"Lord," she replied, "even the dogs under the table eat the children's crumbs."

29Then he told her, "For such a reply, you may go; the demon has left your daughter."

30She went home and found her child lying on the bed, and the demon gone.

JESUS HEALS A DEAF AND MUTE MAN

31Then Jesus left the vicinity of Tyre and went through Sidon, down to the Sea of Galilee and into the region of the Decapolis.[d] 32There some people brought to him a man who was deaf and could hardly talk, and they begged Jesus to place his hand on him.

33After he took him aside, away from the crowd, Jesus put his fingers into the man's ears. Then he spit and touched the man's tongue. 34He looked up to heaven and with a deep sigh said to him, *"Ephphatha!"* (which means "Be opened!"). 35At this, the man's ears were opened, his tongue was loosened and he began to speak plainly.

36Jesus commanded them not to tell anyone. But the more he did so, the more they kept talking about it. 37People were overwhelmed with amazement. "He has done everything well," they said. "He even makes the deaf hear and the mute speak."

[a] *10* Exodus 21:17; Lev. 20:9 [b] *16* Some manuscripts include here the words of 4:23. [c] *24* Many early manuscripts *Tyre and Sidon* [d] *31* That is, the Ten Cities

JESUS FEEDS THE FOUR THOUSAND

8 During those days another large crowd gathered. Since they had
nothing to eat, Jesus called his disciples to him and said, 2"I have
compassion for these people; they have already been with me three
days and have nothing to eat. 3If I send them home hungry, they will
collapse on the way, because some of them have come a long distance."
4His disciples answered, "But where in this remote place can anyone
get enough bread to feed them?"
5"How many loaves do you have?" Jesus asked.
"Seven," they replied.
6He told the crowd to sit down on the ground. When he had taken
the seven loaves and given thanks, he broke them and gave them to
his disciples to distribute to the people, and they did so. 7They had a
few small fish as well; he gave thanks for them also and told the disci-
ples to distribute them. 8The people ate and were satisfied. Afterward
the disciples picked up seven basketfuls of broken pieces that were
left over. 9About four thousand were present. After he had sent them
away, 10he got into the boat with his disciples and went to the region
of Dalmanutha.
11The Pharisees came and began to question Jesus. To test him, they
asked him for a sign from heaven. 12He sighed deeply and said, "Why
does this generation ask for a sign? Truly I tell you, no sign will be
given to it." 13Then he left them, got back into the boat and crossed to
the other side.

THE YEAST OF THE PHARISEES AND HEROD

14The disciples had forgotten to bring bread, except for one loaf they
had with them in the boat. 15"Be careful," Jesus warned them. "Watch
out for the yeast of the Pharisees and that of Herod."
16They discussed this with one another and said, "It is because we
have no bread."
17Aware of their discussion, Jesus asked them: "Why are you talking
about having no bread? Do you still not see or understand? Are your
hearts hardened? 18Do you have eyes but fail to see, and ears but fail
to hear? And don't you remember? 19When I broke the five loaves for
the five thousand, how many basketfuls of pieces did you pick up?"
"Twelve," they replied.
20"And when I broke the seven loaves for the four thousand, how
many basketfuls of pieces did you pick up?"
They answered, "Seven."
21He said to them, "Do you still not understand?"

JESUS HEALS A BLIND MAN AT BETHSAIDA

22They came to Bethsaida, and some people brought a blind
man and begged Jesus to touch him. 23He took the blind man by the
hand and led him outside the village. When he had spit on the man's
eyes and put his hands on him, Jesus asked, "Do you see anything?"
24He looked up and said, "I see people; they look like trees walking
around."
25Once more Jesus put his hands on the man's eyes. Then his eyes
were opened, his sight was restored, and he saw everything clearly.
26Jesus sent him home, saying, "Don't even go into[a] the village."

[a] 26 Some manuscripts *go and tell anyone in*

PRAYING SCRIPTURE

Mark 8

The healing of this blind man is the only miracle Jesus did in stages. Perhaps this is a reminder to us that the Lord does not always act immediately. Even miracles are not bound to a single moment in time. Things can go from fuzzy to clear as he continues to work.

God does not leave his work half finished. Ask for patience as the Lord works his will for you.

PETER DECLARES THAT JESUS IS THE MESSIAH

27 Jesus and his disciples went on to the villages around Caesarea Philippi. On the way he asked them, "Who do people say I am?"

28 They replied, "Some say John the Baptist; others say Elijah; and still others, one of the prophets."

29 "But what about you?" he asked. "Who do you say I am?"

Peter answered, "You are the Messiah."

30 Jesus warned them not to tell anyone about him.

JESUS PREDICTS HIS DEATH

31 He then began to teach them that the Son of Man must suffer many things and be rejected by the elders, the chief priests and the teachers of the law, and that he must be killed and after three days rise again. 32 He spoke plainly about this, and Peter took him aside and began to rebuke him.

33 But when Jesus turned and looked at his disciples, he rebuked Peter. "Get behind me, Satan!" he said. "You do not have in mind the concerns of God, but merely human concerns."

THE WAY OF THE CROSS

34 Then he called the crowd to him along with his disciples and said: "Whoever wants to be my disciple must deny themselves and take up their cross and follow me. 35 For whoever wants to save their life[a] will lose it, but whoever loses their life for me and for the gospel will save it. 36 What good is it for someone to gain the whole world, yet forfeit their soul? 37 Or what can anyone give in exchange for their soul? 38 If anyone is ashamed of me and my words in this adulterous and sinful generation, the Son of Man will be ashamed of them when he comes in his Father's glory with the holy angels."

9 And he said to them, "Truly I tell you, some who are standing here will not taste death before they see that the kingdom of God has come with power."

THE TRANSFIGURATION

2 After six days Jesus took Peter, James and John with him and led them up a high mountain, where they were all alone. There he was transfigured before them. 3 His clothes became dazzling white, whiter than anyone in the world could bleach them. 4 And there appeared before them Elijah and Moses, who were talking with Jesus.

5 Peter said to Jesus, "Rabbi, it is good for us to be here. Let us put up three shelters — one for you, one for Moses and one for Elijah." 6 (He did not know what to say, they were so frightened.)

7 Then a cloud appeared and covered them, and a voice came from the cloud: "This is my Son, whom I love. Listen to him!"

8 Suddenly, when they looked around, they no longer saw anyone with them except Jesus.

9 As they were coming down the mountain, Jesus gave them orders not to tell anyone what they had seen until the Son of Man had risen from the dead. 10 They kept the matter to themselves, discussing what "rising from the dead" meant.

11 And they asked him, "Why do the teachers of the law say that Elijah must come first?"

PRAYING SCRIPTURE

Mark 9

Twice in the story of the deliverance of the demon-possessed boy, Jesus challenged his listeners' faith. He called them "unbelieving" (verse 19), then told the boy's uncertain father, "Everything is possible for one who believes" (verse 23). Faith is the way of the kingdom. It is the assurance that God can make the invisible visible.

How strong is your faith? Are you prepared for God to do the impossible because of it?

[a] *35* The Greek word means either *life* or *soul*; also in verses 36 and 37.

12Jesus replied, "To be sure, Elijah does come first, and restores all
things. Why then is it written that the Son of Man must suffer much
and be rejected? 13But I tell you, Elijah has come, and they have done to
him everything they wished, just as it is written about him."

JESUS HEALS A BOY POSSESSED BY AN IMPURE SPIRIT

14When they came to the other disciples, they saw a large crowd
around them and the teachers of the law arguing with them. 15As soon
as all the people saw Jesus, they were overwhelmed with wonder and
ran to greet him.

16"What are you arguing with them about?" he asked.

17A man in the crowd answered, "Teacher, I brought you my son,
who is possessed by a spirit that has robbed him of speech. 18When-
ever it seizes him, it throws him to the ground. He foams at the mouth,
gnashes his teeth and becomes rigid. I asked your disciples to drive out
the spirit, but they could not."

19"You unbelieving generation," Jesus replied, "how long shall I stay
with you? How long shall I put up with you? Bring the boy to me."

20So they brought him. When the spirit saw Jesus, it immediately
threw the boy into a convulsion. He fell to the ground and rolled
around, foaming at the mouth.

21Jesus asked the boy's father, "How long has he been like this?"

"From childhood," he answered. 22"It has often thrown him into fire
or water to kill him. But if you can do anything, take pity on us and
help us."

23" 'If you can'?" said Jesus. "Everything is possible for one who
believes."

24Immediately the boy's father exclaimed, "I do believe; help me
overcome my unbelief!"

25When Jesus saw that a crowd was running to the scene, he rebuked
the impure spirit. "You deaf and mute spirit," he said, "I command you,
come out of him and never enter him again."

26The spirit shrieked, convulsed him violently and came out. The
boy looked so much like a corpse that many said, "He's dead." 27But
Jesus took him by the hand and lifted him to his feet, and he stood up.

28After Jesus had gone indoors, his disciples asked him privately,
"Why couldn't we drive it out?"

29He replied, "This kind can come out only by prayer.[a]"

JESUS PREDICTS HIS DEATH A SECOND TIME

30They left that place and passed through Galilee. Jesus did not want
anyone to know where they were, 31because he was teaching his dis-
ciples. He said to them, "The Son of Man is going to be delivered into
the hands of men. They will kill him, and after three days he will rise."
32But they did not understand what he meant and were afraid to ask
him about it.

33They came to Capernaum. When he was in the house, he asked
them, "What were you arguing about on the road?" 34But they kept
quiet because on the way they had argued about who was the greatest.

35Sitting down, Jesus called the Twelve and said, "Anyone who wants
to be first must be the very last, and the servant of all."

36He took a little child whom he placed among them. Taking the

---

[a] *29* Some manuscripts *prayer and fasting*

child in his arms, he said to them, 37“Whoever welcomes one of these
little children in my name welcomes me; and whoever welcomes me
does not welcome me but the one who sent me.”

WHOEVER IS NOT AGAINST US IS FOR US

38“Teacher,” said John, “we saw someone driving out demons in your
name and we told him to stop, because he was not one of us.”

39“Do not stop him,” Jesus said. “For no one who does a miracle in
my name can in the next moment say anything bad about me, 40for
whoever is not against us is for us. 41Truly I tell you, anyone who gives
you a cup of water in my name because you belong to the Messiah will
certainly not lose their reward.

CAUSING TO STUMBLE

42“If anyone causes one of these little ones — those who believe in
me — to stumble, it would be better for them if a large millstone were
hung around their neck and they were thrown into the sea. 43If your
hand causes you to stumble, cut it off. It is better for you to enter life
maimed than with two hands to go into hell, where the fire never goes
out. [44][a] 45And if your foot causes you to stumble, cut it off. It is better
for you to enter life crippled than to have two feet and be thrown into
hell. [46][a] 47And if your eye causes you to stumble, pluck it out. It is bet-
ter for you to enter the kingdom of God with one eye than to have two
eyes and be thrown into hell, 48where

> “ ‘the worms that eat them do not die,
> and the fire is not quenched.’[b]

49Everyone will be salted with fire.

50“Salt is good, but if it loses its saltiness, how can you make it salty
again? Have salt among yourselves, and be at peace with each other.”

DIVORCE

10 Jesus then left that place and went into the region of Judea and
across the Jordan. Again crowds of people came to him, and as
was his custom, he taught them.

2Some Pharisees came and tested him by asking, “Is it lawful for a
man to divorce his wife?”

3“What did Moses command you?” he replied.

4They said, “Moses permitted a man to write a certificate of divorce
and send her away.”

5“It was because your hearts were hard that Moses wrote you this
law,” Jesus replied. 6“But at the beginning of creation God ‘made
them male and female.’[c] 7‘For this reason a man will leave his father
and mother and be united to his wife,[d] 8and the two will become one
flesh.’[e] So they are no longer two, but one flesh. 9Therefore what God
has joined together, let no one separate.”

10When they were in the house again, the disciples asked Jesus about
this. 11He answered, “Anyone who divorces his wife and marries an-
other woman commits adultery against her. 12And if she divorces her
husband and marries another man, she commits adultery.”

PRAYING SCRIPTURE

Mark 10

Trust in earthly deeds and earthly goods is a hindrance to the way of God’s kingdom. This wealthy young leader believed his life of law-keeping was sufficient for eternal life, but Jesus revealed the man’s ongoing flaw: His trust was in things, and he was not willing to part with them.

No possession is worth eternity. Things pass; Jesus does not. Are you willing to abandon everything to receive the life Jesus offers?

---

[a] 44,46 Some manuscripts include here the words of verse 48. [b] 48 Isaiah 66:24 [c] 6 Gen. 1:27 [d] 7 Some early manuscripts do not have *and be united to his wife.* [e] 8 Gen. 2:24

THE LITTLE CHILDREN AND JESUS

13 People were bringing little children to Jesus for him to place his
hands on them, but the disciples rebuked them. 14 When Jesus saw this,
he was indignant. He said to them, "Let the little children come to me,
and do not hinder them, for the kingdom of God belongs to such as
these. 15 Truly I tell you, anyone who will not receive the kingdom of
God like a little child will never enter it." 16 And he took the children in
his arms, placed his hands on them and blessed them.

THE RICH AND THE KINGDOM OF GOD

17 As Jesus started on his way, a man ran up to him and fell on his
knees before him. "Good teacher," he asked, "what must I do to inherit
eternal life?"

18 "Why do you call me good?" Jesus answered. "No one is good—
except God alone. 19 You know the commandments: 'You shall not
murder, you shall not commit adultery, you shall not steal, you shall
not give false testimony, you shall not defraud, honor your father and
mother.'[a]"

20 "Teacher," he declared, "all these I have kept since I was a boy."

21 Jesus looked at him and loved him. "One thing you lack," he said.
"Go, sell everything you have and give to the poor, and you will have
treasure in heaven. Then come, follow me."

22 At this the man's face fell. He went away sad, because he had great
wealth.

23 Jesus looked around and said to his disciples, "How hard it is for
the rich to enter the kingdom of God!"

24 The disciples were amazed at his words. But Jesus said again, "Chil-
dren, how hard it is[b] to enter the kingdom of God! 25 It is easier for a
camel to go through the eye of a needle than for someone who is rich
to enter the kingdom of God."

26 The disciples were even more amazed, and said to each other,
"Who then can be saved?"

27 Jesus looked at them and said, "With man this is impossible, but
not with God; all things are possible with God."

28 Then Peter spoke up, "We have left everything to follow you!"

29 "Truly I tell you," Jesus replied, "no one who has left home or
brothers or sisters or mother or father or children or fields for me and
the gospel 30 will fail to receive a hundred times as much in this pres-
ent age: homes, brothers, sisters, mothers, children and fields—along
with persecutions—and in the age to come eternal life. 31 But many
who are first will be last, and the last first."

JESUS PREDICTS HIS DEATH A THIRD TIME

32 They were on their way up to Jerusalem, with Jesus leading the
way, and the disciples were astonished, while those who followed were
afraid. Again he took the Twelve aside and told them what was going
to happen to him. 33 "We are going up to Jerusalem," he said, "and the
Son of Man will be delivered over to the chief priests and the teachers
of the law. They will condemn him to death and will hand him over to
the Gentiles, 34 who will mock him and spit on him, flog him and kill
him. Three days later he will rise."

---

[a] 19 Exodus 20:12-16; Deut. 5:16-20 [b] 24 Some manuscripts *is for those who trust in riches*

THE REQUEST OF JAMES AND JOHN

35 Then James and John, the sons of Zebedee, came to him. "Teacher,"
they said, "we want you to do for us whatever we ask."
36 "What do you want me to do for you?" he asked.
37 They replied, "Let one of us sit at your right and the other at your
left in your glory."
38 "You don't know what you are asking," Jesus said. "Can you drink
the cup I drink or be baptized with the baptism I am baptized with?"
39 "We can," they answered.
Jesus said to them, "You will drink the cup I drink and be baptized
with the baptism I am baptized with, 40 but to sit at my right or left is
not for me to grant. These places belong to those for whom they have
been prepared."
41 When the ten heard about this, they became indignant with James
and John. 42 Jesus called them together and said, "You know that those
who are regarded as rulers of the Gentiles lord it over them, and their
high officials exercise authority over them. 43 Not so with you. Instead,
whoever wants to become great among you must be your servant,
44 and whoever wants to be first must be slave of all. 45 For even the Son
of Man did not come to be served, but to serve, and to give his life as
a ransom for many."

BLIND BARTIMAEUS RECEIVES HIS SIGHT

46 Then they came to Jericho. As Jesus and his disciples, together with
a large crowd, were leaving the city, a blind man, Bartimaeus (which
means "son of Timaeus"), was sitting by the roadside begging. 47 When
he heard that it was Jesus of Nazareth, he began to shout, "Jesus, Son
of David, have mercy on me!"
48 Many rebuked him and told him to be quiet, but he shouted all the
more, "Son of David, have mercy on me!"
49 Jesus stopped and said, "Call him."
So they called to the blind man, "Cheer up! On your feet! He's calling you." 50 Throwing his cloak aside, he jumped to his feet and came
to Jesus.
51 "What do you want me to do for you?" Jesus asked him.
The blind man said, "Rabbi, I want to see."
52 "Go," said Jesus, "your faith has healed you." Immediately he received his sight and followed Jesus along the road.

PRAYING SCRIPTURE

Mark 11

Often in Jesus' ministry he implored people not to reveal his identity, but this time it was different. Approaching Jerusalem shortly before the time of his betrayal, a crowd of his disciples, spreading clothes and branches on the road, publicly announced the arrival of the Messiah.

When was the last time you praised Jesus publicly, drawing attention to his greatness? Seek opportunities to elevate his name before others.

JESUS COMES TO JERUSALEM AS KING

11 As they approached Jerusalem and came to Bethphage and Bethany at the Mount of Olives, Jesus sent two of his disciples, 2 saying
to them, "Go to the village ahead of you, and just as you enter it, you
will find a colt tied there, which no one has ever ridden. Untie it and
bring it here. 3 If anyone asks you, 'Why are you doing this?' say, 'The
Lord needs it and will send it back here shortly.'"
4 They went and found a colt outside in the street, tied at a doorway.
As they untied it, 5 some people standing there asked, "What are you
doing, untying that colt?" 6 They answered as Jesus had told them to,
and the people let them go. 7 When they brought the colt to Jesus and
threw their cloaks over it, he sat on it. 8 Many people spread their cloaks
on the road, while others spread branches they had cut in the fields.
9 Those who went ahead and those who followed shouted,

"Hosanna![a]"

"Blessed is he who comes in the name of the Lord!"[b]

10 "Blessed is the coming kingdom of our father David!"

"Hosanna in the highest heaven!"

11 Jesus entered Jerusalem and went into the temple courts. He
looked around at everything, but since it was already late, he went out
to Bethany with the Twelve.

JESUS CURSES A FIG TREE AND CLEARS THE TEMPLE COURTS

12 The next day as they were leaving Bethany, Jesus was hungry.
13 Seeing in the distance a fig tree in leaf, he went to find out if it had
any fruit. When he reached it, he found nothing but leaves, because it
was not the season for figs. 14 Then he said to the tree, "May no one ever
eat fruit from you again." And his disciples heard him say it.

15 On reaching Jerusalem, Jesus entered the temple courts and began
driving out those who were buying and selling there. He overturned
the tables of the money changers and the benches of those selling
doves, 16 and would not allow anyone to carry merchandise through
the temple courts. 17 And as he taught them, he said, "Is it not written:
'My house will be called a house of prayer for all nations'[c]? But you
have made it 'a den of robbers.'[d]"

18 The chief priests and the teachers of the law heard this and began
looking for a way to kill him, for they feared him, because the whole
crowd was amazed at his teaching.

19 When evening came, Jesus and his disciples[e] went out of the city.

20 In the morning, as they went along, they saw the fig tree withered
from the roots. 21 Peter remembered and said to Jesus, "Rabbi, look!
The fig tree you cursed has withered!"

22 "Have faith in God," Jesus answered. 23 "Truly[f] I tell you, if anyone
says to this mountain, 'Go, throw yourself into the sea,' and does not
doubt in their heart but believes that what they say will happen, it will
be done for them. 24 Therefore I tell you, whatever you ask for in prayer,
believe that you have received it, and it will be yours. 25 And when you
stand praying, if you hold anything against anyone, forgive them, so
that your Father in heaven may forgive you your sins." [26][g]

THE AUTHORITY OF JESUS QUESTIONED

27 They arrived again in Jerusalem, and while Jesus was walking in
the temple courts, the chief priests, the teachers of the law and the el-
ders came to him. 28 "By what authority are you doing these things?"
they asked. "And who gave you authority to do this?"

29 Jesus replied, "I will ask you one question. Answer me, and I will
tell you by what authority I am doing these things. 30 John's baptism—
was it from heaven, or of human origin? Tell me!"

31 They discussed it among themselves and said, "If we say, 'From
heaven,' he will ask, 'Then why didn't you believe him?' 32 But if we say,

---

[a] 9 A Hebrew expression meaning "Save!" which became an exclamation of praise; also in verse 10 [b] 9 Psalm 118:25,26 [c] 17 Isaiah 56:7 [d] 17 Jer. 7:11 [e] 19 Some early manuscripts *came, Jesus* [f] 22,23 Some early manuscripts *"If you have faith in God," Jesus answered, [23]"truly* [g] 26 Some manuscripts include here words similar to Matt. 6:15.

'Of human origin' . . ." (They feared the people, for everyone held that
John really was a prophet.)
33So they answered Jesus, "We don't know."
Jesus said, "Neither will I tell you by what authority I am doing these
things."

THE PARABLE OF THE TENANTS

12 Jesus then began to speak to them in parables: "A man planted
a vineyard. He put a wall around it, dug a pit for the winepress
and built a watchtower. Then he rented the vineyard to some farmers
and moved to another place. 2At harvest time he sent a servant to the
tenants to collect from them some of the fruit of the vineyard. 3But
they seized him, beat him and sent him away empty-handed. 4Then
he sent another servant to them; they struck this man on the head and
treated him shamefully. 5He sent still another, and that one they killed.
He sent many others; some of them they beat, others they killed.
6"He had one left to send, a son, whom he loved. He sent him last of
all, saying, 'They will respect my son.'
7"But the tenants said to one another, 'This is the heir. Come, let's
kill him, and the inheritance will be ours.' 8So they took him and killed
him, and threw him out of the vineyard.
9"What then will the owner of the vineyard do? He will come and kill
those tenants and give the vineyard to others. 10Haven't you read this
passage of Scripture:

"'The stone the builders rejected
has become the cornerstone;
11 the Lord has done this,
and it is marvelous in our eyes'[a]?"

12Then the chief priests, the teachers of the law and the elders looked
for a way to arrest him because they knew he had spoken the parable
against them. But they were afraid of the crowd; so they left him and
went away.

PRAYING SCRIPTURE

Mark 12

While teaching in Jerusalem, Jesus was confronted by the religious leaders. When asked about the "most important [commandment]" (verse 28), Jesus responded that we should love God with all our heart, soul, mind and strength, and our neighbor as we love ourselves (see verses 29–31). These were his top two priorities.

How much do you love God? Your neighbors? Is either love waning? Ask God to help you keep your priorities of love in order.

PAYING THE IMPERIAL TAX TO CAESAR

13Later they sent some of the Pharisees and Herodians to Jesus to
catch him in his words. 14They came to him and said, "Teacher, we
know that you are a man of integrity. You aren't swayed by others, be-
cause you pay no attention to who they are; but you teach the way of
God in accordance with the truth. Is it right to pay the imperial tax[b] to
Caesar or not? 15Should we pay or shouldn't we?"
But Jesus knew their hypocrisy. "Why are you trying to trap me?" he
asked. "Bring me a denarius and let me look at it." 16They brought the
coin, and he asked them, "Whose image is this? And whose inscription?"
"Caesar's," they replied.
17Then Jesus said to them, "Give back to Caesar what is Caesar's and
to God what is God's."
And they were amazed at him.

MARRIAGE AT THE RESURRECTION

18Then the Sadducees, who say there is no resurrection, came to him
with a question. 19"Teacher," they said, "Moses wrote for us that if a

[a] *11* Psalm 118:22,23 [b] *14* A special tax levied on subject peoples, not on Roman citizens

man's brother dies and leaves a wife but no children, the man must
marry the widow and raise up offspring for his brother. 20Now there
were seven brothers. The first one married and died without leaving
any children. 21The second one married the widow, but he also died,
leaving no child. It was the same with the third. 22In fact, none of the
seven left any children. Last of all, the woman died too. 23At the resur-
rection[a] whose wife will she be, since the seven were married to her?"
24Jesus replied, "Are you not in error because you do not know the
Scriptures or the power of God? 25When the dead rise, they will neither
marry nor be given in marriage; they will be like the angels in heaven.
26Now about the dead rising — have you not read in the Book of Moses,
in the account of the burning bush, how God said to him, 'I am the God
of Abraham, the God of Isaac, and the God of Jacob'[b]? 27He is not the
God of the dead, but of the living. You are badly mistaken!"

THE GREATEST COMMANDMENT

28One of the teachers of the law came and heard them debating. No-
ticing that Jesus had given them a good answer, he asked him, "Of all
the commandments, which is the most important?"
29"The most important one," answered Jesus, "is this: 'Hear, O Israel:
The Lord our God, the Lord is one.[c] 30Love the Lord your God with all
your heart and with all your soul and with all your mind and with all
your strength.'[d] 31The second is this: 'Love your neighbor as yourself.'[e]
There is no commandment greater than these."
32"Well said, teacher," the man replied. "You are right in saying that
God is one and there is no other but him. 33To love him with all your
heart, with all your understanding and with all your strength, and to
love your neighbor as yourself is more important than all burnt offer-
ings and sacrifices."
34When Jesus saw that he had answered wisely, he said to him, "You
are not far from the kingdom of God." And from then on no one dared
ask him any more questions.

WHOSE SON IS THE MESSIAH?

35While Jesus was teaching in the temple courts, he asked, "Why do
the teachers of the law say that the Messiah is the son of David? 36David
himself, speaking by the Holy Spirit, declared:

"'The Lord said to my Lord:
  "Sit at my right hand
until I put your enemies
  under your feet."'[f]

37David himself calls him 'Lord.' How then can he be his son?"
The large crowd listened to him with delight.

WARNING AGAINST THE TEACHERS OF THE LAW

38As he taught, Jesus said, "Watch out for the teachers of the law.
They like to walk around in flowing robes and be greeted with respect
in the marketplaces, 39and have the most important seats in the syn-
agogues and the places of honor at banquets. 40They devour widows'

---

[a] *23* Some manuscripts *resurrection, when people rise from the dead,*
[b] *26* Exodus 3:6 [c] *29* Or *The Lord our God is one Lord* [d] *30* Deut. 6:4,5
[e] *31* Lev. 19:18 [f] *36* Psalm 110:1

houses and for a show make lengthy prayers. These men will be punished most severely."

THE WIDOW'S OFFERING

41 Jesus sat down opposite the place where the offerings were put and watched the crowd putting their money into the temple treasury. Many rich people threw in large amounts. 42 But a poor widow came and put in two very small copper coins, worth only a few cents.

43 Calling his disciples to him, Jesus said, "Truly I tell you, this poor widow has put more into the treasury than all the others. 44 They all gave out of their wealth; but she, out of her poverty, put in everything—all she had to live on."

THE DESTRUCTION OF THE TEMPLE AND SIGNS OF THE END TIMES

13 As Jesus was leaving the temple, one of his disciples said to him, "Look, Teacher! What massive stones! What magnificent buildings!"

2 "Do you see all these great buildings?" replied Jesus. "Not one stone here will be left on another; every one will be thrown down."

3 As Jesus was sitting on the Mount of Olives opposite the temple, Peter, James, John and Andrew asked him privately, 4 "Tell us, when will these things happen? And what will be the sign that they are all about to be fulfilled?"

5 Jesus said to them: "Watch out that no one deceives you. 6 Many will come in my name, claiming, 'I am he,' and will deceive many. 7 When you hear of wars and rumors of wars, do not be alarmed. Such things must happen, but the end is still to come. 8 Nation will rise against nation, and kingdom against kingdom. There will be earthquakes in various places, and famines. These are the beginning of birth pains.

9 "You must be on your guard. You will be handed over to the local councils and flogged in the synagogues. On account of me you will stand before governors and kings as witnesses to them. 10 And the gospel must first be preached to all nations. 11 Whenever you are arrested and brought to trial, do not worry beforehand about what to say. Just say whatever is given you at the time, for it is not you speaking, but the Holy Spirit.

12 "Brother will betray brother to death, and a father his child. Children will rebel against their parents and have them put to death. 13 Everyone will hate you because of me, but the one who stands firm to the end will be saved.

14 "When you see 'the abomination that causes desolation'[a] standing where it[b] does not belong—let the reader understand—then let those who are in Judea flee to the mountains. 15 Let no one on the housetop go down or enter the house to take anything out. 16 Let no one in the field go back to get their cloak. 17 How dreadful it will be in those days for pregnant women and nursing mothers! 18 Pray that this will not take place in winter, 19 because those will be days of distress unequaled from the beginning, when God created the world, until now—and never to be equaled again.

20 "If the Lord had not cut short those days, no one would survive. But for the sake of the elect, whom he has chosen, he has shortened

PRAYING SCRIPTURE

Mark 13

In one of the most studied chapters in the Bible, Jesus gave a discourse on the last days, including prophecies concerning the temple's destruction, a time of great tribulation and his coming in the clouds. Summing it up, he made clear the knowledge of these things belongs to the Father only.

When the upheaval of this world begins to bother you, turn to the Father whom Jesus also trusted completely.

---

[a] *14* Daniel 9:27; 11:31; 12:11 [b] *14* Or *he*

them. 21At that time if anyone says to you, 'Look, here is the Messiah!'
or, 'Look, there he is!' do not believe it. 22For false messiahs and false
prophets will appear and perform signs and wonders to deceive, if pos-
sible, even the elect. 23So be on your guard; I have told you everything
ahead of time.
24"But in those days, following that distress,

"'the sun will be darkened,
and the moon will not give its light;
25the stars will fall from the sky,
and the heavenly bodies will be shaken.'[a]

26"At that time people will see the Son of Man coming in clouds with
great power and glory. 27And he will send his angels and gather his
elect from the four winds, from the ends of the earth to the ends of
the heavens.
28"Now learn this lesson from the fig tree: As soon as its twigs get
tender and its leaves come out, you know that summer is near. 29Even
so, when you see these things happening, you know that it[b] is near,
right at the door. 30Truly I tell you, this generation will certainly not
pass away until all these things have happened. 31Heaven and earth
will pass away, but my words will never pass away.

THE DAY AND HOUR UNKNOWN

32"But about that day or hour no one knows, not even the angels in
heaven, nor the Son, but only the Father. 33Be on guard! Be alert[c]! You
do not know when that time will come. 34It's like a man going away:
He leaves his house and puts his servants in charge, each with their
assigned task, and tells the one at the door to keep watch.
35"Therefore keep watch because you do not know when the owner
of the house will come back — whether in the evening, or at midnight,
or when the rooster crows, or at dawn. 36If he comes suddenly, do
not let him find you sleeping. 37What I say to you, I say to everyone:
'Watch!'"

JESUS ANOINTED AT BETHANY

14 Now the Passover and the Festival of Unleavened Bread were
only two days away, and the chief priests and the teachers of
the law were scheming to arrest Jesus secretly and kill him. 2"But not
during the festival," they said, "or the people may riot."
3While he was in Bethany, reclining at the table in the home of Si-
mon the Leper, a woman came with an alabaster jar of very expensive
perfume, made of pure nard. She broke the jar and poured the per-
fume on his head.
4Some of those present were saying indignantly to one another,
"Why this waste of perfume? 5It could have been sold for more than
a year's wages[d] and the money given to the poor." And they rebuked
her harshly.
6"Leave her alone," said Jesus. "Why are you bothering her? She has
done a beautiful thing to me. 7The poor you will always have with you,[e]
and you can help them any time you want. But you will not always
have me. 8She did what she could. She poured perfume on my body

PRAYING SCRIPTURE

Mark 14

The final Passover Jesus shared with his disciples is the one we remember as the Last Supper. Knowing he was about to be arrested and crucified, Jesus still took the time to eat with and teach the Twelve—including Judas who was prepared to betray him.

Jesus never faltered in his commitment to the men he'd called. Thank God that his love for you never fails; Jesus is the proof.

---

[a] 25 Isaiah 13:10; 34:4 [b] 29 Or *he* [c] 33 Some manuscripts *alert and pray*
[d] 5 Greek *than three hundred denarii* [e] 7 See Deut. 15:11.

beforehand to prepare for my burial. [9]Truly I tell you, wherever the
gospel is preached throughout the world, what she has done will also
be told, in memory of her."
[10]Then Judas Iscariot, one of the Twelve, went to the chief priests to
betray Jesus to them. [11]They were delighted to hear this and promised
to give him money. So he watched for an opportunity to hand him
over.

THE LAST SUPPER

[12]On the first day of the Festival of Unleavened Bread, when it was
customary to sacrifice the Passover lamb, Jesus' disciples asked him,
"Where do you want us to go and make preparations for you to eat the
Passover?"
[13]So he sent two of his disciples, telling them, "Go into the city, and
a man carrying a jar of water will meet you. Follow him. [14]Say to the
owner of the house he enters, 'The Teacher asks: Where is my guest
room, where I may eat the Passover with my disciples?' [15]He will show
you a large room upstairs, furnished and ready. Make preparations for
us there."
[16]The disciples left, went into the city and found things just as Jesus
had told them. So they prepared the Passover.
[17]When evening came, Jesus arrived with the Twelve. [18]While they
were reclining at the table eating, he said, "Truly I tell you, one of you
will betray me — one who is eating with me."
[19]They were saddened, and one by one they said to him, "Surely you
don't mean me?"
[20]"It is one of the Twelve," he replied, "one who dips bread into the
bowl with me. [21]The Son of Man will go just as it is written about him.
But woe to that man who betrays the Son of Man! It would be better for
him if he had not been born."
[22]While they were eating, Jesus took bread, and when he had given
thanks, he broke it and gave it to his disciples, saying, "Take it; this is
my body."
[23]Then he took a cup, and when he had given thanks, he gave it to
them, and they all drank from it.
[24]"This is my blood of the[a] covenant, which is poured out for many,"
he said to them. [25]"Truly I tell you, I will not drink again from the fruit
of the vine until that day when I drink it new in the kingdom of God."
[26]When they had sung a hymn, they went out to the Mount of Olives.

JESUS PREDICTS PETER'S DENIAL

[27]"You will all fall away," Jesus told them, "for it is written:

"'I will strike the shepherd,
and the sheep will be scattered.'[b]

[28]But after I have risen, I will go ahead of you into Galilee."
[29]Peter declared, "Even if all fall away, I will not."
[30]"Truly I tell you," Jesus answered, "today — yes, tonight — before
the rooster crows twice[c] you yourself will disown me three times."
[31]But Peter insisted emphatically, "Even if I have to die with you, I
will never disown you." And all the others said the same.

---

[a] *24* Some manuscripts *the new* [b] *27* Zech. 13:7 [c] *30* Some early manuscripts do not have *twice.*

GETHSEMANE

32They went to a place called Gethsemane, and Jesus said to his disci-
ples, "Sit here while I pray." 33He took Peter, James and John along with
him, and he began to be deeply distressed and troubled. 34"My soul is
overwhelmed with sorrow to the point of death," he said to them. "Stay
here and keep watch."

35Going a little farther, he fell to the ground and prayed that if pos-
sible the hour might pass from him. 36"*Abba*,[a] Father," he said, "every-
thing is possible for you. Take this cup from me. Yet not what I will,
but what you will."

37Then he returned to his disciples and found them sleeping. "Si-
mon," he said to Peter, "are you asleep? Couldn't you keep watch for
one hour? 38Watch and pray so that you will not fall into temptation.
The spirit is willing, but the flesh is weak."

39Once more he went away and prayed the same thing. 40When he
came back, he again found them sleeping, because their eyes were
heavy. They did not know what to say to him.

41Returning the third time, he said to them, "Are you still sleeping
and resting? Enough! The hour has come. Look, the Son of Man is de-
livered into the hands of sinners. 42Rise! Let us go! Here comes my
betrayer!"

JESUS ARRESTED

43Just as he was speaking, Judas, one of the Twelve, appeared. With
him was a crowd armed with swords and clubs, sent from the chief
priests, the teachers of the law, and the elders.

44Now the betrayer had arranged a signal with them: "The one I kiss
is the man; arrest him and lead him away under guard." 45Going at
once to Jesus, Judas said, "Rabbi!" and kissed him. 46The men seized
Jesus and arrested him. 47Then one of those standing near drew his
sword and struck the servant of the high priest, cutting off his ear.

48"Am I leading a rebellion," said Jesus, "that you have come out with
swords and clubs to capture me? 49Every day I was with you, teaching
in the temple courts, and you did not arrest me. But the Scriptures
must be fulfilled." 50Then everyone deserted him and fled.

51A young man, wearing nothing but a linen garment, was follow-
ing Jesus. When they seized him, 52he fled naked, leaving his garment
behind.

JESUS BEFORE THE SANHEDRIN

53They took Jesus to the high priest, and all the chief priests, the el-
ders and the teachers of the law came together. 54Peter followed him
at a distance, right into the courtyard of the high priest. There he sat
with the guards and warmed himself at the fire.

55The chief priests and the whole Sanhedrin were looking for evi-
dence against Jesus so that they could put him to death, but they did
not find any. 56Many testified falsely against him, but their statements
did not agree.

57Then some stood up and gave this false testimony against him:
58"We heard him say, 'I will destroy this temple made with human
hands and in three days will build another, not made with hands.'"
59Yet even then their testimony did not agree.

---

[a] *36* Aramaic for *father*

60Then the high priest stood up before them and asked Jesus, "Are
you not going to answer? What is this testimony that these men are
bringing against you?" 61But Jesus remained silent and gave no answer.
Again the high priest asked him, "Are you the Messiah, the Son of
the Blessed One?"
62"I am," said Jesus. "And you will see the Son of Man sitting at the
right hand of the Mighty One and coming on the clouds of heaven."
63The high priest tore his clothes. "Why do we need any more wit-
nesses?" he asked. 64"You have heard the blasphemy. What do you
think?"
They all condemned him as worthy of death. 65Then some began to
spit at him; they blindfolded him, struck him with their fists, and said,
"Prophesy!" And the guards took him and beat him.

PETER DISOWNS JESUS

66While Peter was below in the courtyard, one of the servant girls of
the high priest came by. 67When she saw Peter warming himself, she
looked closely at him.
"You also were with that Nazarene, Jesus," she said.
68But he denied it. "I don't know or understand what you're talking
about," he said, and went out into the entryway.[a]
69When the servant girl saw him there, she said again to those stand-
ing around, "This fellow is one of them." 70Again he denied it.
After a little while, those standing near said to Peter, "Surely you are
one of them, for you are a Galilean."
71He began to call down curses, and he swore to them, "I don't know
this man you're talking about."
72Immediately the rooster crowed the second time.[b] Then Peter
remembered the word Jesus had spoken to him: "Before the rooster
crows twice[c] you will disown me three times." And he broke down and
wept.

JESUS BEFORE PILATE

15 Very early in the morning, the chief priests, with the elders, the
teachers of the law and the whole Sanhedrin, made their plans.
So they bound Jesus, led him away and handed him over to Pilate.
2"Are you the king of the Jews?" asked Pilate.
"You have said so," Jesus replied.
3The chief priests accused him of many things. 4So again Pilate asked
him, "Aren't you going to answer? See how many things they are ac-
cusing you of."
5But Jesus still made no reply, and Pilate was amazed.
6Now it was the custom at the festival to release a prisoner whom the
people requested. 7A man called Barabbas was in prison with the in-
surrectionists who had committed murder in the uprising. 8The crowd
came up and asked Pilate to do for them what he usually did.
9"Do you want me to release to you the king of the Jews?" asked
Pilate, 10knowing it was out of self-interest that the chief priests had
handed Jesus over to him. 11But the chief priests stirred up the crowd
to have Pilate release Barabbas instead.

PRAYING SCRIPTURE

Mark 15

Nowhere is the substitutionary nature of Jesus' death for sinners any clearer than in the choice Pilate offered the crowd: Who should be set free—the innocent, perfect Lamb of God or Barabbas, a murderous seditionist? The crowd, stoked by the religious leaders, chose Barabbas.

Have you thought lately about the fact Jesus died in your place? Thank God for sending the perfect Lamb to take judgment for you personally.

[a] 68 Some early manuscripts *entryway and the rooster crowed* [b] 72 Some early manuscripts do not have *the second time.* [c] 72 Some early manuscripts do not have *twice.*

[12]“What shall I do, then, with the one you call the king of the Jews?”
Pilate asked them.
[13]“Crucify him!” they shouted.
[14]“Why? What crime has he committed?” asked Pilate.
But they shouted all the louder, “Crucify him!”
[15]Wanting to satisfy the crowd, Pilate released Barabbas to them. He
had Jesus flogged, and handed him over to be crucified.

THE SOLDIERS MOCK JESUS

[16]The soldiers led Jesus away into the palace (that is, the Praetorium)
and called together the whole company of soldiers. [17]They put a purple
robe on him, then twisted together a crown of thorns and set it on him.
[18]And they began to call out to him, “Hail, king of the Jews!” [19]Again
and again they struck him on the head with a staff and spit on him.
Falling on their knees, they paid homage to him. [20]And when they had
mocked him, they took off the purple robe and put his own clothes on
him. Then they led him out to crucify him.

THE CRUCIFIXION OF JESUS

[21]A certain man from Cyrene, Simon, the father of Alexander and
Rufus, was passing by on his way in from the country, and they forced
him to carry the cross. [22]They brought Jesus to the place called Golgo-
tha (which means “the place of the skull”). [23]Then they offered him
wine mixed with myrrh, but he did not take it. [24]And they crucified
him. Dividing up his clothes, they cast lots to see what each would get.
[25]It was nine in the morning when they crucified him. [26]The written
notice of the charge against him read: THE KING OF THE JEWS.
[27]They crucified two rebels with him, one on his right and one on his
left. [28][a] [29]Those who passed by hurled insults at him, shaking their
heads and saying, “So! You who are going to destroy the temple and
build it in three days, [30]come down from the cross and save yourself!”
[31]In the same way the chief priests and the teachers of the law mocked
him among themselves. “He saved others,” they said, “but he can’t save
himself! [32]Let this Messiah, this king of Israel, come down now from
the cross, that we may see and believe.” Those crucified with him also
heaped insults on him.

THE DEATH OF JESUS

[33]At noon, darkness came over the whole land until three in the af-
ternoon. [34]And at three in the afternoon Jesus cried out in a loud voice,
“Eloi, Eloi, lema sabachthani?” (which means “My God, my God, why
have you forsaken me?”).[b]
[35]When some of those standing near heard this, they said, “Listen,
he’s calling Elijah.”
[36]Someone ran, filled a sponge with wine vinegar, put it on a staff,
and offered it to Jesus to drink. “Now leave him alone. Let’s see if Elijah
comes to take him down,” he said.
[37]With a loud cry, Jesus breathed his last.
[38]The curtain of the temple was torn in two from top to bottom.
[39]And when the centurion, who stood there in front of Jesus, saw how
he died,[c] he said, “Surely this man was the Son of God!”

[a] *28* Some manuscripts include here words similar to Luke 22:37.
[b] *34* Psalm 22:1 [c] *39* Some manuscripts *saw that he died with such a cry*

40Some women were watching from a distance. Among them were Mary Magdalene, Mary the mother of James the younger and of Joseph,[a] and Salome. 41In Galilee these women had followed him and cared for his needs. Many other women who had come up with him to Jerusalem were also there.

THE BURIAL OF JESUS

42It was Preparation Day (that is, the day before the Sabbath). So as evening approached, 43Joseph of Arimathea, a prominent member of the Council, who was himself waiting for the kingdom of God, went boldly to Pilate and asked for Jesus' body. 44Pilate was surprised to hear that he was already dead. Summoning the centurion, he asked him if Jesus had already died. 45When he learned from the centurion that it was so, he gave the body to Joseph. 46So Joseph bought some linen cloth, took down the body, wrapped it in the linen, and placed it in a tomb cut out of rock. Then he rolled a stone against the entrance of the tomb. 47Mary Magdalene and Mary the mother of Joseph saw where he was laid.

JESUS HAS RISEN

16 When the Sabbath was over, Mary Magdalene, Mary the mother of James, and Salome bought spices so that they might go to anoint Jesus' body. 2Very early on the first day of the week, just after sunrise, they were on their way to the tomb 3and they asked each other, "Who will roll the stone away from the entrance of the tomb?"

4But when they looked up, they saw that the stone, which was very large, had been rolled away. 5As they entered the tomb, they saw a young man dressed in a white robe sitting on the right side, and they were alarmed.

6"Don't be alarmed," he said. "You are looking for Jesus the Nazarene, who was crucified. He has risen! He is not here. See the place where they laid him. 7But go, tell his disciples and Peter, 'He is going ahead of you into Galilee. There you will see him, just as he told you.'"

8Trembling and bewildered, the women went out and fled from the tomb. They said nothing to anyone, because they were afraid.[b]

[The earliest manuscripts and some other ancient witnesses do not have verses 9 – 20.]

9When Jesus rose early on the first day of the week, he appeared first to Mary Magdalene, out of whom he had driven seven demons. 10She went and told those who had been with him and who were mourning and weeping. 11When they heard that Jesus was alive and that she had seen him, they did not believe it.

12Afterward Jesus appeared in a different form to two of them while they were walking in the country. 13These returned and reported it to the rest; but they did not believe them either.

PRAYING SCRIPTURE

Mark 16

Mark's version of the Great Commission, while it includes the assurance of miraculous provisions, is primarily about one imperative: "Go into all the world and preach the gospel to all creation" (verse 15). This charge has not changed since Jesus returned to heaven. Every generation of Christians inherits the same command.

Are you focused on fulfilling the Great Commission? Pray for opportunities to teach the gospel, and trust Jesus' authority as you proclaim it each day.

---

[a] 40 Greek *Joses*, a variant of *Joseph*; also in verse 47 [b] 8 Some manuscripts have the following ending between verses 8 and 9, and one manuscript has it after verse 8 (omitting verses 9-20): *Then they quickly reported all these instructions to those around Peter. After this, Jesus himself also sent out through them from east to west the sacred and imperishable proclamation of eternal salvation. Amen.*

14 *Later Jesus appeared to the Eleven as they were eating; he rebuked them*
for their lack of faith and their stubborn refusal to believe those who had seen
him after he had risen.
15 *He said to them, "Go into all the world and preach the gospel to all crea-*
tion. 16 *Whoever believes and is baptized will be saved, but whoever does not*
believe will be condemned. 17 *And these signs will accompany those who be-*
lieve: In my name they will drive out demons; they will speak in new tongues;
18 *they will pick up snakes with their hands; and when they drink deadly poison,*
it will not hurt them at all; they will place their hands on sick people, and they
will get well."
19 *After the Lord Jesus had spoken to them, he was taken up into heaven and*
he sat at the right hand of God. 20 *Then the disciples went out and preached ev-*
erywhere, and the Lord worked with them and confirmed his word by the signs
that accompanied it.

LUKE

It is traditionally accepted that Luke wrote his Gospel and Acts as a two-part work intended to narrate the details of Jesus' life and to reaffirm the things eyewitnesses of Jesus taught while he was in the world. Luke addressed the work to Theophilus, but it is uncertain whether this was a historical person or simply a figurative term representing all those who love God, which is what the word *theophilus* means.

Outside of the Lord's Prayer in chapter 11, Luke relates Jesus' teaching about prayer through his parables. Through the parable of the Pharisee and the tax collector and the parable of the persistent widow, Jesus depicted the heart attitudes his followers should bring to the practice of prayer.

The latter, also known as the parable of the persistent widow, is found in Luke 18:1–8. In this parable, a widow continually pleaded for justice before a judge who neither feared God nor cared what people thought. In other words, the judge did not pay attention to God's law nor to the cries of those in his court. Though he denied her justice, she continued to return, pleading with him until he realized that he had to issue justice on her behalf or else she might attack him. Jesus taught that if the unjust judge gave justice in response to continual pleading, how much more would God avenge his people who cry out to him continually?

The parable of the Pharisee and the tax collector (see 18:9–14) was directed to "some who were confident of their own righteousness and looked down on everyone else." The Pharisee prayed proudly in the temple, boasting of his goodness. He contrasted himself favorably with the tax collector who stood at a distance. It is telling that Jesus indicated that the Pharisee's prayers did not justify him before God. The tax collector, by contrast, did not look at anyone or look up. Rather, he hung his head and prayed that God would have mercy on him because of his sin. Jesus' conclusion was that the tax collector, rather than the Pharisee, went home having been made right with God.

Luke wrote that Jesus' praying was so strenuous and that he was under such duress, and perhaps anxiety, that an angel came to strengthen him. Being in even more anguish (see 22:44), Jesus prayed earnestly, so much so that sweat like blood dropped from his body to the ground. When Jesus had finished praying, the place of his agony was literally marked by his blood.

The emphasis on prayer in this Gospel reminds us that though we are sinners and have no reason to expect that God should hear us, he does. When we come before him humbly yet boldly, even in extreme anguish, we are reminded that he is just, not unjust, and that we "should always pray and not give up" (18:1).

INTRODUCTION

1 Many have undertaken to draw up an account of the things that have been fulfilled[a] among us, 2just as they were handed down to us by those who from the first were eyewitnesses and servants of the word. 3With this in mind, since I myself have carefully investigated everything from the beginning, I too decided to write an orderly account for you, most excellent Theophilus, 4so that you may know the certainty of the things you have been taught.

THE BIRTH OF JOHN THE BAPTIST FORETOLD

5In the time of Herod king of Judea there was a priest named Zechariah, who belonged to the priestly division of Abijah; his wife Elizabeth was also a descendant of Aaron. 6Both of them were righteous in the sight of God, observing all the Lord's commands and decrees blamelessly. 7But they were childless because Elizabeth was not able to conceive, and they were both very old.

8Once when Zechariah's division was on duty and he was serving as priest before God, 9he was chosen by lot, according to the custom of the priesthood, to go into the temple of the Lord and burn incense. 10And when the time for the burning of incense came, all the assembled worshipers were praying outside.

11Then an angel of the Lord appeared to him, standing at the right side of the altar of incense. 12When Zechariah saw him, he was startled and was gripped with fear. 13But the angel said to him: "Do not be afraid, Zechariah; your prayer has been heard. Your wife Elizabeth will bear you a son, and you are to call him John. 14He will be a joy and delight to you, and many will rejoice because of his birth, 15for he will be great in the sight of the Lord. He is never to take wine or other fermented drink, and he will be filled with the Holy Spirit even before he is born. 16He will bring back many of the people of Israel to the Lord their God. 17And he will go on before the Lord, in the spirit and power of Elijah, to turn the hearts of the parents to their children and the disobedient to the wisdom of the righteous — to make ready a people prepared for the Lord."

18Zechariah asked the angel, "How can I be sure of this? I am an old man and my wife is well along in years."

19The angel said to him, "I am Gabriel. I stand in the presence of God, and I have been sent to speak to you and to tell you this good news. 20And now you will be silent and not able to speak until the day this happens, because you did not believe my words, which will come true at their appointed time."

21Meanwhile, the people were waiting for Zechariah and wondering why he stayed so long in the temple. 22When he came out, he could not speak to them. They realized he had seen a vision in the temple, for he kept making signs to them but remained unable to speak.

23When his time of service was completed, he returned home. 24After this his wife Elizabeth became pregnant and for five months remained in seclusion. 25"The Lord has done this for me," she said. "In these days he has shown his favor and taken away my disgrace among the people."

PRAYING SCRIPTURE

Luke 1

The *Magnificat* is among the most beautiful and theologically rich songs in all Scripture. Having received the promise that she would bear the Messiah, Mary recalled God's work in Israel, acknowledged the Lord's ability to keep his promises and exhibited humble faith in his strength.

Do you respond with joy when God calls you to a surprising task? Learn from Mary. Praise God when he does great things through you.

[a] *1* Or *been surely believed*

THE BIRTH OF JESUS FORETOLD

26In the sixth month of Elizabeth's pregnancy, God sent the angel Ga-
briel to Nazareth, a town in Galilee, 27to a virgin pledged to be married
to a man named Joseph, a descendant of David. The virgin's name was
Mary. 28The angel went to her and said, "Greetings, you who are highly
favored! The Lord is with you."

29Mary was greatly troubled at his words and wondered what kind of
greeting this might be. 30But the angel said to her, "Do not be afraid,
Mary; you have found favor with God. 31You will conceive and give
birth to a son, and you are to call him Jesus. 32He will be great and
will be called the Son of the Most High. The Lord God will give him the
throne of his father David, 33and he will reign over Jacob's descendants
forever; his kingdom will never end."

34"How will this be," Mary asked the angel, "since I am a virgin?"

35The angel answered, "The Holy Spirit will come on you, and the
power of the Most High will overshadow you. So the holy one to be
born will be called[a] the Son of God. 36Even Elizabeth your relative is go-
ing to have a child in her old age, and she who was said to be unable to
conceive is in her sixth month. 37For no word from God will ever fail."

38"I am the Lord's servant," Mary answered. "May your word to me
be fulfilled." Then the angel left her.

MARY VISITS ELIZABETH

39At that time Mary got ready and hurried to a town in the hill coun-
try of Judea, 40where she entered Zechariah's home and greeted Eliz-
abeth. 41When Elizabeth heard Mary's greeting, the baby leaped in
her womb, and Elizabeth was filled with the Holy Spirit. 42In a loud
voice she exclaimed: "Blessed are you among women, and blessed is
the child you will bear! 43But why am I so favored, that the mother of
my Lord should come to me? 44As soon as the sound of your greeting
reached my ears, the baby in my womb leaped for joy. 45Blessed is she
who has believed that the Lord would fulfill his promises to her!"

MARY'S SONG

46And Mary said:

"My soul glorifies the Lord
47 and my spirit rejoices in God my Savior,
48 for he has been mindful
of the humble state of his servant.
From now on all generations will call me blessed,
49 for the Mighty One has done great things for me—
holy is his name.
50 His mercy extends to those who fear him,
from generation to generation.
51 He has performed mighty deeds with his arm;
he has scattered those who are proud in their inmost thoughts.
52 He has brought down rulers from their thrones
but has lifted up the humble.
53 He has filled the hungry with good things
but has sent the rich away empty.
54 He has helped his servant Israel,
remembering to be merciful

---

[a] *35* Or *So the child to be born will be called holy,*

55 to Abraham and his descendants forever,
just as he promised our ancestors."

56 Mary stayed with Elizabeth for about three months and then re-
turned home.

THE BIRTH OF JOHN THE BAPTIST

57 When it was time for Elizabeth to have her baby, she gave birth to a
son. 58 Her neighbors and relatives heard that the Lord had shown her
great mercy, and they shared her joy.
59 On the eighth day they came to circumcise the child, and they were
going to name him after his father Zechariah, 60 but his mother spoke
up and said, "No! He is to be called John."
61 They said to her, "There is no one among your relatives who has
that name."
62 Then they made signs to his father, to find out what he would like
to name the child. 63 He asked for a writing tablet, and to everyone's
astonishment he wrote, "His name is John." 64 Immediately his mouth
was opened and his tongue set free, and he began to speak, praising
God. 65 All the neighbors were filled with awe, and throughout the hill
country of Judea people were talking about all these things. 66 Every-
one who heard this wondered about it, asking, "What then is this child
going to be?" For the Lord's hand was with him.

ZECHARIAH'S SONG

67 His father Zechariah was filled with the Holy Spirit and prophesied:

68 "Praise be to the Lord, the God of Israel,
because he has come to his people and redeemed them.
69 He has raised up a horn[a] of salvation for us
in the house of his servant David
70 (as he said through his holy prophets of long ago),
71 salvation from our enemies
and from the hand of all who hate us—
72 to show mercy to our ancestors
and to remember his holy covenant,
73 the oath he swore to our father Abraham:
74 to rescue us from the hand of our enemies,
and to enable us to serve him without fear
75 in holiness and righteousness before him all our days.

76 And you, my child, will be called a prophet of the Most High;
for you will go on before the Lord to prepare the way for him,
77 to give his people the knowledge of salvation
through the forgiveness of their sins,
78 because of the tender mercy of our God,
by which the rising sun will come to us from heaven
79 to shine on those living in darkness
and in the shadow of death,
to guide our feet into the path of peace."

80 And the child grew and became strong in spirit[b]; and he lived in
the wilderness until he appeared publicly to Israel.

---

[a] *69* *Horn* here symbolizes a strong king. [b] *80* Or *in the Spirit*

PRAYING SCRIPTURE

Luke 2

Never was there a birth like that of Jesus Christ. A night like any other night outside Bethlehem, a nondescript Middle Eastern town in a nondescript Roman province, became a night like no other night in history. Angels announced to a group of lowly shepherds that "a Savior has been born to you; he is the Messiah, the Lord" (verse 11).

Thank God for bringing a Messiah not only for the powerful, but for all people.

THE BIRTH OF JESUS

2 In those days Caesar Augustus issued a decree that a census should be taken of the entire Roman world. 2(This was the first census that took place while[a] Quirinius was governor of Syria.) 3And everyone went to their own town to register.

4So Joseph also went up from the town of Nazareth in Galilee to Judea, to Bethlehem the town of David, because he belonged to the house and line of David. 5He went there to register with Mary, who was pledged to be married to him and was expecting a child. 6While they were there, the time came for the baby to be born, 7and she gave birth to her firstborn, a son. She wrapped him in cloths and placed him in a manger, because there was no guest room available for them.

8And there were shepherds living out in the fields nearby, keeping watch over their flocks at night. 9An angel of the Lord appeared to them, and the glory of the Lord shone around them, and they were terrified. 10But the angel said to them, "Do not be afraid. I bring you good news that will cause great joy for all the people. 11Today in the town of David a Savior has been born to you; he is the Messiah, the Lord. 12This will be a sign to you: You will find a baby wrapped in cloths and lying in a manger."

13Suddenly a great company of the heavenly host appeared with the angel, praising God and saying,

14"Glory to God in the highest heaven,
and on earth peace to those on whom his favor rests."

15When the angels had left them and gone into heaven, the shepherds said to one another, "Let's go to Bethlehem and see this thing that has happened, which the Lord has told us about."

16So they hurried off and found Mary and Joseph, and the baby, who was lying in the manger. 17When they had seen him, they spread the word concerning what had been told them about this child, 18and all who heard it were amazed at what the shepherds said to them. 19But Mary treasured up all these things and pondered them in her heart. 20The shepherds returned, glorifying and praising God for all the things they had heard and seen, which were just as they had been told.

21On the eighth day, when it was time to circumcise the child, he was named Jesus, the name the angel had given him before he was conceived.

JESUS PRESENTED IN THE TEMPLE

22When the time came for the purification rites required by the Law of Moses, Joseph and Mary took him to Jerusalem to present him to the Lord 23(as it is written in the Law of the Lord, "Every firstborn male is to be consecrated to the Lord"[b]), 24and to offer a sacrifice in keeping with what is said in the Law of the Lord: "a pair of doves or two young pigeons."[c]

25Now there was a man in Jerusalem called Simeon, who was righteous and devout. He was waiting for the consolation of Israel, and the Holy Spirit was on him. 26It had been revealed to him by the Holy Spirit that he would not die before he had seen the Lord's Messiah. 27Moved by the Spirit, he went into the temple courts. When the parents brought in the child Jesus to do for him what the custom of the Law required, 28Simeon took him in his arms and praised God, saying:

---

[a] 2 Or *This census took place before* [b] *23* Exodus 13:2,12 [c] *24* Lev. 12:8

29 "Sovereign Lord, as you have promised,
you may now dismiss[a] your servant in peace.
30 For my eyes have seen your salvation,
31 which you have prepared in the sight of all nations:
32 a light for revelation to the Gentiles,
and the glory of your people Israel."

33 The child's father and mother marveled at what was said about
him. 34 Then Simeon blessed them and said to Mary, his mother: "This
child is destined to cause the falling and rising of many in Israel, and
to be a sign that will be spoken against, 35 so that the thoughts of many
hearts will be revealed. And a sword will pierce your own soul too."
36 There was also a prophet, Anna, the daughter of Penuel, of the tribe
of Asher. She was very old; she had lived with her husband seven years
after her marriage, 37 and then was a widow until she was eighty-four.[b]
She never left the temple but worshiped night and day, fasting and
praying. 38 Coming up to them at that very moment, she gave thanks
to God and spoke about the child to all who were looking forward to
the redemption of Jerusalem.
39 When Joseph and Mary had done everything required by the Law
of the Lord, they returned to Galilee to their own town of Nazareth.
40 And the child grew and became strong; he was filled with wisdom,
and the grace of God was on him.

THE BOY JESUS AT THE TEMPLE

41 Every year Jesus' parents went to Jerusalem for the Festival of the
Passover. 42 When he was twelve years old, they went up to the festi-
val, according to the custom. 43 After the festival was over, while his
parents were returning home, the boy Jesus stayed behind in Jerusa-
lem, but they were unaware of it. 44 Thinking he was in their company,
they traveled on for a day. Then they began looking for him among
their relatives and friends. 45 When they did not find him, they went
back to Jerusalem to look for him. 46 After three days they found him
in the temple courts, sitting among the teachers, listening to them
and asking them questions. 47 Everyone who heard him was amazed at
his understanding and his answers. 48 When his parents saw him, they
were astonished. His mother said to him, "Son, why have you treated
us like this? Your father and I have been anxiously searching for you."
49 "Why were you searching for me?" he asked. "Didn't you know I
had to be in my Father's house?"[c] 50 But they did not understand what
he was saying to them.
51 Then he went down to Nazareth with them and was obedient to
them. But his mother treasured all these things in her heart. 52 And
Jesus grew in wisdom and stature, and in favor with God and man.

JOHN THE BAPTIST PREPARES THE WAY

3 In the fifteenth year of the reign of Tiberius Caesar — when Pon-
tius Pilate was governor of Judea, Herod tetrarch of Galilee, his
brother Philip tetrarch of Iturea and Traconitis, and Lysanias tetrarch
of Abilene — 2 during the high-priesthood of Annas and Caiaphas, the
word of God came to John son of Zechariah in the wilderness. 3 He
went into all the country around the Jordan, preaching a baptism of

PRAYING SCRIPTURE

Luke 3

The ministry of John the Baptist set the stage for the ministry of Jesus. Preaching a gospel of repentance, John was used by God to get the attention of tax collectors, Roman soldiers and other common people. He also raised the ire of the religious leaders, leading eventually to his imprisonment.

Kingdom ministry is costly. Think about what following Jesus has cost you. If nothing, ask God to lead you into deeper waters.

[a] 29 Or *promised, / now dismiss* [b] 37 Or *then had been a widow for eighty-four years.* [c] 49 Or *be about my Father's business*

repentance for the forgiveness of sins. 4As it is written in the book of the words of Isaiah the prophet:

"A voice of one calling in the wilderness,
'Prepare the way for the Lord,
make straight paths for him.
5Every valley shall be filled in,
every mountain and hill made low.
The crooked roads shall become straight,
the rough ways smooth.
6And all people will see God's salvation.'"[a]

7John said to the crowds coming out to be baptized by him, "You brood of vipers! Who warned you to flee from the coming wrath? 8Produce fruit in keeping with repentance. And do not begin to say to yourselves, 'We have Abraham as our father.' For I tell you that out of these stones God can raise up children for Abraham. 9The ax is already at the root of the trees, and every tree that does not produce good fruit will be cut down and thrown into the fire."

10"What should we do then?" the crowd asked.

11John answered, "Anyone who has two shirts should share with the one who has none, and anyone who has food should do the same."

12Even tax collectors came to be baptized. "Teacher," they asked, "what should we do?"

13"Don't collect any more than you are required to," he told them.

14Then some soldiers asked him, "And what should we do?"

He replied, "Don't extort money and don't accuse people falsely—be content with your pay."

15The people were waiting expectantly and were all wondering in their hearts if John might possibly be the Messiah. 16John answered them all, "I baptize you with[b] water. But one who is more powerful than I will come, the straps of whose sandals I am not worthy to untie. He will baptize you with[b] the Holy Spirit and fire. 17His winnowing fork is in his hand to clear his threshing floor and to gather the wheat into his barn, but he will burn up the chaff with unquenchable fire." 18And with many other words John exhorted the people and proclaimed the good news to them.

19But when John rebuked Herod the tetrarch because of his marriage to Herodias, his brother's wife, and all the other evil things he had done, 20Herod added this to them all: He locked John up in prison.

THE BAPTISM AND GENEALOGY OF JESUS

21When all the people were being baptized, Jesus was baptized too. And as he was praying, heaven was opened 22and the Holy Spirit descended on him in bodily form like a dove. And a voice came from heaven: "You are my Son, whom I love; with you I am well pleased."

23Now Jesus himself was about thirty years old when he began his ministry. He was the son, so it was thought, of Joseph,

the son of Heli, 24the son of Matthat,
the son of Levi, the son of Melki,
the son of Jannai, the son of Joseph,
25the son of Mattathias, the son of Amos,
the son of Nahum, the son of Esli,

[a] 6 Isaiah 40:3-5 [b] 16 Or *in*

the son of Naggai, 26 the son of Maath,
the son of Mattathias, the son of Semein,
the son of Josek, the son of Joda,
27 the son of Joanan, the son of Rhesa,
the son of Zerubbabel, the son of Shealtiel,
the son of Neri, 28 the son of Melki,
the son of Addi, the son of Cosam,
the son of Elmadam, the son of Er,
29 the son of Joshua, the son of Eliezer,
the son of Jorim, the son of Matthat,
the son of Levi, 30 the son of Simeon,
the son of Judah, the son of Joseph,
the son of Jonam, the son of Eliakim,
31 the son of Melea, the son of Menna,
the son of Mattatha, the son of Nathan,
the son of David, 32 the son of Jesse,
the son of Obed, the son of Boaz,
the son of Salmon,[a] the son of Nahshon,
33 the son of Amminadab, the son of Ram,[b]
the son of Hezron, the son of Perez,
the son of Judah, 34 the son of Jacob,
the son of Isaac, the son of Abraham,
the son of Terah, the son of Nahor,
35 the son of Serug, the son of Reu,
the son of Peleg, the son of Eber,
the son of Shelah, 36 the son of Cainan,
the son of Arphaxad, the son of Shem,
the son of Noah, the son of Lamech,
37 the son of Methuselah, the son of Enoch,
the son of Jared, the son of Mahalalel,
the son of Kenan, 38 the son of Enosh,
the son of Seth, the son of Adam,
the son of God.

JESUS IS TESTED IN THE WILDERNESS

4 Jesus, full of the Holy Spirit, left the Jordan and was led by the
Spirit into the wilderness, 2 where for forty days he was tempted[c]
by the devil. He ate nothing during those days, and at the end of them
he was hungry.
3 The devil said to him, "If you are the Son of God, tell this stone to
become bread."
4 Jesus answered, "It is written: 'Man shall not live on bread alone.'[d]"
5 The devil led him up to a high place and showed him in an instant
all the kingdoms of the world. 6 And he said to him, "I will give you all
their authority and splendor; it has been given to me, and I can give it
to anyone I want to. 7 If you worship me, it will all be yours."
8 Jesus answered, "It is written: 'Worship the Lord your God and serve
him only.'[e]"
9 The devil led him to Jerusalem and had him stand on the highest
point of the temple. "If you are the Son of God," he said, "throw your-
self down from here. 10 For it is written:

---

[a] *32* Some early manuscripts *Sala* [b] *33* Some manuscripts *Amminadab, the son of Admin, the son of Arni*; other manuscripts vary widely. [c] *2* The Greek for *tempted* can also mean *tested.* [d] *4* Deut. 8:3 [e] *8* Deut. 6:13

PRAYING SCRIPTURE

Luke 4

Despite the miraculous announcement of his birth, Jesus' entrance into the world by a virgin girl and the public announcement of his ministry at his baptism, Jesus was not welcome in his hometown synagogue. The people rejected his warning of judgment on Israel and the promise of a kingdom that included all people.

Do not be among those who restrict the kingdom. Jesus' invitation is open to all. Pray for everyone around you to enter through him.

"'He will command his angels concerning you
to guard you carefully;
11 they will lift you up in their hands,
so that you will not strike your foot against a stone.'[a]"

12 Jesus answered, "It is said: 'Do not put the Lord your God to the
test.'[b]"

13 When the devil had finished all this tempting, he left him until an
opportune time.

JESUS REJECTED AT NAZARETH

14 Jesus returned to Galilee in the power of the Spirit, and news about
him spread through the whole countryside. 15 He was teaching in their
synagogues, and everyone praised him.

16 He went to Nazareth, where he had been brought up, and on the
Sabbath day he went into the synagogue, as was his custom. He stood
up to read, 17 and the scroll of the prophet Isaiah was handed to him.
Unrolling it, he found the place where it is written:

18 "The Spirit of the Lord is on me,
because he has anointed me
to proclaim good news to the poor.
He has sent me to proclaim freedom for the prisoners
and recovery of sight for the blind,
to set the oppressed free,
19 to proclaim the year of the Lord's favor."[c]

20 Then he rolled up the scroll, gave it back to the attendant and sat
down. The eyes of everyone in the synagogue were fastened on him.
21 He began by saying to them, "Today this scripture is fulfilled in your
hearing."

22 All spoke well of him and were amazed at the gracious words that
came from his lips. "Isn't this Joseph's son?" they asked.

23 Jesus said to them, "Surely you will quote this proverb to me: 'Phy-
sician, heal yourself!' And you will tell me, 'Do here in your hometown
what we have heard that you did in Capernaum.'"

24 "Truly I tell you," he continued, "no prophet is accepted in his
hometown. 25 I assure you that there were many widows in Israel in
Elijah's time, when the sky was shut for three and a half years and
there was a severe famine throughout the land. 26 Yet Elijah was not
sent to any of them, but to a widow in Zarephath in the region of Sidon.
27 And there were many in Israel with leprosy[d] in the time of Elisha the
prophet, yet not one of them was cleansed—only Naaman the Syrian."

28 All the people in the synagogue were furious when they heard this.
29 They got up, drove him out of the town, and took him to the brow of
the hill on which the town was built, in order to throw him off the cliff.
30 But he walked right through the crowd and went on his way.

JESUS DRIVES OUT AN IMPURE SPIRIT

31 Then he went down to Capernaum, a town in Galilee, and on the
Sabbath he taught the people. 32 They were amazed at his teaching, be-
cause his words had authority.

---

[a] *11* Psalm 91:11,12 [b] *12* Deut. 6:16 [c] *19* Isaiah 61:1,2 (see Septuagint); Isaiah 58:6 [d] *27* The Greek word traditionally translated *leprosy* was used for various diseases affecting the skin.

33 In the synagogue there was a man possessed by a demon, an im-
pure spirit. He cried out at the top of his voice, 34 "Go away! What do you
want with us, Jesus of Nazareth? Have you come to destroy us? I know
who you are — the Holy One of God!"
35 "Be quiet!" Jesus said sternly. "Come out of him!" Then the demon
threw the man down before them all and came out without injuring
him.
36 All the people were amazed and said to each other, "What words
these are! With authority and power he gives orders to impure spirits
and they come out!" 37 And the news about him spread throughout the
surrounding area.

JESUS HEALS MANY

38 Jesus left the synagogue and went to the home of Simon. Now Si-
mon's mother-in-law was suffering from a high fever, and they asked
Jesus to help her. 39 So he bent over her and rebuked the fever, and it
left her. She got up at once and began to wait on them.
40 At sunset, the people brought to Jesus all who had various kinds
of sickness, and laying his hands on each one, he healed them. 41 More-
over, demons came out of many people, shouting, "You are the Son
of God!" But he rebuked them and would not allow them to speak,
because they knew he was the Messiah.
42 At daybreak, Jesus went out to a solitary place. The people were
looking for him and when they came to where he was, they tried to
keep him from leaving them. 43 But he said, "I must proclaim the good
news of the kingdom of God to the other towns also, because that is
why I was sent." 44 And he kept on preaching in the synagogues of
Judea.

JESUS CALLS HIS FIRST DISCIPLES

5 One day as Jesus was standing by the Lake of Gennesaret,[a] the peo-
ple were crowding around him and listening to the word of God.
2 He saw at the water's edge two boats, left there by the fishermen, who
were washing their nets. 3 He got into one of the boats, the one belong-
ing to Simon, and asked him to put out a little from shore. Then he sat
down and taught the people from the boat.
4 When he had finished speaking, he said to Simon, "Put out into
deep water, and let down the nets for a catch."
5 Simon answered, "Master, we've worked hard all night and haven't
caught anything. But because you say so, I will let down the nets."
6 When they had done so, they caught such a large number of fish
that their nets began to break. 7 So they signaled their partners in the
other boat to come and help them, and they came and filled both boats
so full that they began to sink.
8 When Simon Peter saw this, he fell at Jesus' knees and said, "Go
away from me, Lord; I am a sinful man!" 9 For he and all his compan-
ions were astonished at the catch of fish they had taken, 10 and so were
James and John, the sons of Zebedee, Simon's partners.
Then Jesus said to Simon, "Don't be afraid; from now on you will fish
for people." 11 So they pulled their boats up on shore, left everything
and followed him.

[a] 1 That is, the Sea of Galilee

PRAYING SCRIPTURE

Luke 5

Jesus' calling of his first disciples was miraculous and prophetic. The miracle was a great catch of fish after a night of empty toil. The prophetic part was that they would leave their nets and catch men for the kingdom. Jesus chose men whom other rabbis would have considered unqualified.

Do you ever feel unworthy or useless in God's kingdom? Rejoice! Jesus intentionally uses the unexpected of this world. Thank him for it!

JESUS HEALS A MAN WITH LEPROSY

12 While Jesus was in one of the towns, a man came along who was cov-
ered with leprosy.[a] When he saw Jesus, he fell with his face to the ground
and begged him, "Lord, if you are willing, you can make me clean."
13 Jesus reached out his hand and touched the man. "I am willing," he
said. "Be clean!" And immediately the leprosy left him.
14 Then Jesus ordered him, "Don't tell anyone, but go, show yourself
to the priest and offer the sacrifices that Moses commanded for your
cleansing, as a testimony to them."
15 Yet the news about him spread all the more, so that crowds of peo-
ple came to hear him and to be healed of their sicknesses. 16 But Jesus
often withdrew to lonely places and prayed.

JESUS FORGIVES AND HEALS A PARALYZED MAN

17 One day Jesus was teaching, and Pharisees and teachers of the law
were sitting there. They had come from every village of Galilee and
from Judea and Jerusalem. And the power of the Lord was with Jesus
to heal the sick. 18 Some men came carrying a paralyzed man on a mat
and tried to take him into the house to lay him before Jesus. 19 When
they could not find a way to do this because of the crowd, they went
up on the roof and lowered him on his mat through the tiles into the
middle of the crowd, right in front of Jesus.
20 When Jesus saw their faith, he said, "Friend, your sins are forgiven."
21 The Pharisees and the teachers of the law began thinking to them-
selves, "Who is this fellow who speaks blasphemy? Who can forgive
sins but God alone?"
22 Jesus knew what they were thinking and asked, "Why are you
thinking these things in your hearts? 23 Which is easier: to say, 'Your
sins are forgiven,' or to say, 'Get up and walk'? 24 But I want you to know
that the Son of Man has authority on earth to forgive sins." So he said
to the paralyzed man, "I tell you, get up, take your mat and go home."
25 Immediately he stood up in front of them, took what he had been
lying on and went home praising God. 26 Everyone was amazed and
gave praise to God. They were filled with awe and said, "We have seen
remarkable things today."

JESUS CALLS LEVI AND EATS WITH SINNERS

27 After this, Jesus went out and saw a tax collector by the name of
Levi sitting at his tax booth. "Follow me," Jesus said to him, 28 and Levi
got up, left everything and followed him.
29 Then Levi held a great banquet for Jesus at his house, and a large
crowd of tax collectors and others were eating with them. 30 But the
Pharisees and the teachers of the law who belonged to their sect com-
plained to his disciples, "Why do you eat and drink with tax collectors
and sinners?"
31 Jesus answered them, "It is not the healthy who need a doctor, but the
sick. 32 I have not come to call the righteous, but sinners to repentance."

JESUS QUESTIONED ABOUT FASTING

33 They said to him, "John's disciples often fast and pray, and so do
the disciples of the Pharisees, but yours go on eating and drinking."

---

[a] *12* The Greek word traditionally translated *leprosy* was used for various diseases affecting the skin.

34 Jesus answered, "Can you make the friends of the bridegroom fast
while he is with them? 35 But the time will come when the bridegroom
will be taken from them; in those days they will fast."
36 He told them this parable: "No one tears a piece out of a new gar-
ment to patch an old one. Otherwise, they will have torn the new gar-
ment, and the patch from the new will not match the old. 37 And no
one pours new wine into old wineskins. Otherwise, the new wine will
burst the skins; the wine will run out and the wineskins will be ruined.
38 No, new wine must be poured into new wineskins. 39 And no one af-
ter drinking old wine wants the new, for they say, 'The old is better.'"

JESUS IS LORD OF THE SABBATH

6 One Sabbath Jesus was going through the grainfields, and his dis-
ciples began to pick some heads of grain, rub them in their hands
and eat the kernels. 2 Some of the Pharisees asked, "Why are you doing
what is unlawful on the Sabbath?"
3 Jesus answered them, "Have you never read what David did when
he and his companions were hungry? 4 He entered the house of God,
and taking the consecrated bread, he ate what is lawful only for priests
to eat. And he also gave some to his companions." 5 Then Jesus said to
them, "The Son of Man is Lord of the Sabbath."
6 On another Sabbath he went into the synagogue and was teaching,
and a man was there whose right hand was shriveled. 7 The Pharisees
and the teachers of the law were looking for a reason to accuse Jesus,
so they watched him closely to see if he would heal on the Sabbath.
8 But Jesus knew what they were thinking and said to the man with
the shriveled hand, "Get up and stand in front of everyone." So he got
up and stood there.
9 Then Jesus said to them, "I ask you, which is lawful on the Sabbath:
to do good or to do evil, to save life or to destroy it?"
10 He looked around at them all, and then said to the man, "Stretch
out your hand." He did so, and his hand was completely restored. 11 But
the Pharisees and the teachers of the law were furious and began to
discuss with one another what they might do to Jesus.

THE TWELVE APOSTLES

12 One of those days Jesus went out to a mountainside to pray, and
spent the night praying to God. 13 When morning came, he called his
disciples to him and chose twelve of them, whom he also designated
apostles: 14 Simon (whom he named Peter), his brother Andrew, James,
John, Philip, Bartholomew, 15 Matthew, Thomas, James son of Alphaeus,
Simon who was called the Zealot, 16 Judas son of James, and Judas Is-
cariot, who became a traitor.

BLESSINGS AND WOES

17 He went down with them and stood on a level place. A large crowd of
his disciples was there and a great number of people from all over Judea,
from Jerusalem, and from the coastal region around Tyre and Sidon,
18 who had come to hear him and to be healed of their diseases. Those
troubled by impure spirits were cured, 19 and the people all tried to touch
him, because power was coming from him and healing them all.
20 Looking at his disciples, he said:

"Blessed are you who are poor,
for yours is the kingdom of God.

PRAYING SCRIPTURE

Luke 6

Perhaps the hardest command Jesus ever gave was to love our enemies. We are to pray for those who mistreat us, bless those who curse us and do good to those who hate us (see verses 27–28). He goes even further, removing any doubt that the way of the kingdom is opposite the way of the world. Retaliation has no place in the kingdom.

Pray that you might love everyone, especially those who hate and mistreat you.

21 Blessed are you who hunger now,
for you will be satisfied.
Blessed are you who weep now,
for you will laugh.
22 Blessed are you when people hate you,
when they exclude you and insult you
and reject your name as evil,
because of the Son of Man.

23“Rejoice in that day and leap for joy, because great is your reward
in heaven. For that is how their ancestors treated the prophets.

24“But woe to you who are rich,
for you have already received your comfort.
25 Woe to you who are well fed now,
for you will go hungry.
Woe to you who laugh now,
for you will mourn and weep.
26 Woe to you when everyone speaks well of you,
for that is how their ancestors treated the false prophets.

LOVE FOR ENEMIES

27“But to you who are listening I say: Love your enemies, do good to
those who hate you, 28bless those who curse you, pray for those who
mistreat you. 29If someone slaps you on one cheek, turn to them the
other also. If someone takes your coat, do not withhold your shirt from
them. 30Give to everyone who asks you, and if anyone takes what be-
longs to you, do not demand it back. 31Do to others as you would have
them do to you.

32“If you love those who love you, what credit is that to you? Even
sinners love those who love them. 33And if you do good to those who
are good to you, what credit is that to you? Even sinners do that. 34And
if you lend to those from whom you expect repayment, what credit
is that to you? Even sinners lend to sinners, expecting to be repaid in
full. 35But love your enemies, do good to them, and lend to them with-
out expecting to get anything back. Then your reward will be great,
and you will be children of the Most High, because he is kind to the
ungrateful and wicked. 36Be merciful, just as your Father is merciful.

JUDGING OTHERS

37“Do not judge, and you will not be judged. Do not condemn, and
you will not be condemned. Forgive, and you will be forgiven. 38Give,
and it will be given to you. A good measure, pressed down, shaken
together and running over, will be poured into your lap. For with the
measure you use, it will be measured to you.”

39He also told them this parable: “Can the blind lead the blind? Will
they not both fall into a pit? 40The student is not above the teacher, but
everyone who is fully trained will be like their teacher.

41“Why do you look at the speck of sawdust in your brother’s eye and
pay no attention to the plank in your own eye? 42How can you say to
your brother, ‘Brother, let me take the speck out of your eye,’ when you
yourself fail to see the plank in your own eye? You hypocrite, first take
the plank out of your eye, and then you will see clearly to remove the
speck from your brother’s eye.

A TREE AND ITS FRUIT

43"No good tree bears bad fruit, nor does a bad tree bear good fruit.
44Each tree is recognized by its own fruit. People do not pick figs from
thornbushes, or grapes from briers. 45A good man brings good things
out of the good stored up in his heart, and an evil man brings evil
things out of the evil stored up in his heart. For the mouth speaks what
the heart is full of.

THE WISE AND FOOLISH BUILDERS

46"Why do you call me, 'Lord, Lord,' and do not do what I say? 47As
for everyone who comes to me and hears my words and puts them
into practice, I will show you what they are like. 48They are like a man
building a house, who dug down deep and laid the foundation on rock.
When a flood came, the torrent struck that house but could not shake
it, because it was well built. 49But the one who hears my words and
does not put them into practice is like a man who built a house on
the ground without a foundation. The moment the torrent struck that
house, it collapsed and its destruction was complete."

THE FAITH OF THE CENTURION

7 When Jesus had finished saying all this to the people who were
listening, he entered Capernaum. 2There a centurion's servant,
whom his master valued highly, was sick and about to die. 3The cen-
turion heard of Jesus and sent some elders of the Jews to him, asking
him to come and heal his servant. 4When they came to Jesus, they
pleaded earnestly with him, "This man deserves to have you do this,
5because he loves our nation and has built our synagogue." 6So Jesus
went with them.

He was not far from the house when the centurion sent friends to say
to him: "Lord, don't trouble yourself, for I do not deserve to have you
come under my roof. 7That is why I did not even consider myself wor-
thy to come to you. But say the word, and my servant will be healed.
8For I myself am a man under authority, with soldiers under me. I tell
this one, 'Go,' and he goes; and that one, 'Come,' and he comes. I say to
my servant, 'Do this,' and he does it."

9When Jesus heard this, he was amazed at him, and turning to the
crowd following him, he said, "I tell you, I have not found such great
faith even in Israel." 10Then the men who had been sent returned to
the house and found the servant well.

PRAYING SCRIPTURE

Luke 7

Unique in the story of the centurion's sick servant is this military leader's recognition of Jesus as one with the authority to command by his word. He knew there was no need for Jesus to make a trip to his house when Jesus could heal verbally. Jesus marveled at such faith.

Do you have the kind of faith that provides insight into God's ways? Ask God to increase your faith.

JESUS RAISES A WIDOW'S SON

11Soon afterward, Jesus went to a town called Nain, and his disci-
ples and a large crowd went along with him. 12As he approached the
town gate, a dead person was being carried out — the only son of his
mother, and she was a widow. And a large crowd from the town was
with her. 13When the Lord saw her, his heart went out to her and he
said, "Don't cry."

14Then he went up and touched the bier they were carrying him on,
and the bearers stood still. He said, "Young man, I say to you, get up!"
15The dead man sat up and began to talk, and Jesus gave him back to
his mother.

16They were all filled with awe and praised God. "A great prophet has
appeared among us," they said. "God has come to help his people." 17This
news about Jesus spread throughout Judea and the surrounding country.

JESUS AND JOHN THE BAPTIST

18John's disciples told him about all these things. Calling two of them, 19he sent them to the Lord to ask, "Are you the one who is to come, or should we expect someone else?"

20When the men came to Jesus, they said, "John the Baptist sent us to you to ask, 'Are you the one who is to come, or should we expect someone else?'"

21At that very time Jesus cured many who had diseases, sicknesses and evil spirits, and gave sight to many who were blind. 22So he replied to the messengers, "Go back and report to John what you have seen and heard: The blind receive sight, the lame walk, those who have leprosy[a] are cleansed, the deaf hear, the dead are raised, and the good news is proclaimed to the poor. 23Blessed is anyone who does not stumble on account of me."

24After John's messengers left, Jesus began to speak to the crowd about John: "What did you go out into the wilderness to see? A reed swayed by the wind? 25If not, what did you go out to see? A man dressed in fine clothes? No, those who wear expensive clothes and indulge in luxury are in palaces. 26But what did you go out to see? A prophet? Yes, I tell you, and more than a prophet. 27This is the one about whom it is written:

"'I will send my messenger ahead of you,
who will prepare your way before you.'[b]

28I tell you, among those born of women there is no one greater than John; yet the one who is least in the kingdom of God is greater than he."

29(All the people, even the tax collectors, when they heard Jesus' words, acknowledged that God's way was right, because they had been baptized by John. 30But the Pharisees and the experts in the law rejected God's purpose for themselves, because they had not been baptized by John.)

31Jesus went on to say, "To what, then, can I compare the people of this generation? What are they like? 32They are like children sitting in the marketplace and calling out to each other:

"'We played the pipe for you,
and you did not dance;
we sang a dirge,
and you did not cry.'

33For John the Baptist came neither eating bread nor drinking wine, and you say, 'He has a demon.' 34The Son of Man came eating and drinking, and you say, 'Here is a glutton and a drunkard, a friend of tax collectors and sinners.' 35But wisdom is proved right by all her children."

JESUS ANOINTED BY A SINFUL WOMAN

36When one of the Pharisees invited Jesus to have dinner with him, he went to the Pharisee's house and reclined at the table. 37A woman in that town who lived a sinful life learned that Jesus was eating at the Pharisee's house, so she came there with an alabaster jar of perfume.

[a] *22* The Greek word traditionally translated *leprosy* was used for various diseases affecting the skin. [b] *27* Mal. 3:1

38 As she stood behind him at his feet weeping, she began to wet his
feet with her tears. Then she wiped them with her hair, kissed them
and poured perfume on them.
39 When the Pharisee who had invited him saw this, he said to him-
self, "If this man were a prophet, he would know who is touching him
and what kind of woman she is — that she is a sinner."
40 Jesus answered him, "Simon, I have something to tell you."
"Tell me, teacher," he said.
41 "Two people owed money to a certain moneylender. One owed him
five hundred denarii,[a] and the other fifty.
42 Neither of them had the
money to pay him back, so he forgave the debts of both. Now which of
them will love him more?"
43 Simon replied, "I suppose the one who had the bigger debt
forgiven."
"You have judged correctly," Jesus said.
44 Then he turned toward the woman and said to Simon, "Do you see
this woman? I came into your house. You did not give me any water
for my feet, but she wet my feet with her tears and wiped them with
her hair.
45 You did not give me a kiss, but this woman, from the time I
entered, has not stopped kissing my feet.
46 You did not put oil on my
head, but she has poured perfume on my feet.
47 Therefore, I tell you,
her many sins have been forgiven — as her great love has shown. But
whoever has been forgiven little loves little."
48 Then Jesus said to her, "Your sins are forgiven."
49 The other guests began to say among themselves, "Who is this who
even forgives sins?"
50 Jesus said to the woman, "Your faith has saved you; go in peace."

THE PARABLE OF THE SOWER

8 After this, Jesus traveled about from one town and village to an-
other, proclaiming the good news of the kingdom of God. The
Twelve were with him,
2 and also some women who had been cured of
evil spirits and diseases: Mary (called Magdalene) from whom seven
demons had come out;
3 Joanna the wife of Chuza, the manager of Her-
od's household; Susanna; and many others. These women were help-
ing to support them out of their own means.
4 While a large crowd was gathering and people were coming to Jesus
from town after town, he told this parable:
5 "A farmer went out to sow
his seed. As he was scattering the seed, some fell along the path; it was
trampled on, and the birds ate it up.
6 Some fell on rocky ground, and
when it came up, the plants withered because they had no moisture.
7 Other seed fell among thorns, which grew up with it and choked the
plants.
8 Still other seed fell on good soil. It came up and yielded a crop,
a hundred times more than was sown."
When he said this, he called out, "Whoever has ears to hear, let them
hear."
9 His disciples asked him what this parable meant.
10 He said, "The
knowledge of the secrets of the kingdom of God has been given to you,
but to others I speak in parables, so that,

"'though seeing, they may not see;
though hearing, they may not understand.'[b]

PRAYING SCRIPTURE

Luke 8

The earthly ministry of Jesus was strongly supported by women. As he ministered with the Twelve, some formerly demon-possessed women, the wife of King Herod's steward and others "were helping to support them out of their own means," that is, their possessions (verses 2–3).

Women were not prominent in Jesus' day. Women today can be confident: God will use you. Ask God how you can best serve him.

---

[a] *41* A denarius was the usual daily wage of a day laborer (see Matt. 20:2).
[b] *10* Isaiah 6:9

11"This is the meaning of the parable: The seed is the word of God. 12Those along the path are the ones who hear, and then the devil comes and takes away the word from their hearts, so that they may not believe and be saved. 13Those on the rocky ground are the ones who receive the word with joy when they hear it, but they have no root. They believe for a while, but in the time of testing they fall away. 14The seed that fell among thorns stands for those who hear, but as they go on their way they are choked by life's worries, riches and pleasures, and they do not mature. 15But the seed on good soil stands for those with a noble and good heart, who hear the word, retain it, and by persevering produce a crop.

A LAMP ON A STAND

16"No one lights a lamp and hides it in a clay jar or puts it under a bed. Instead, they put it on a stand, so that those who come in can see the light. 17For there is nothing hidden that will not be disclosed, and nothing concealed that will not be known or brought out into the open. 18Therefore consider carefully how you listen. Whoever has will be given more; whoever does not have, even what they think they have will be taken from them."

JESUS' MOTHER AND BROTHERS

19Now Jesus' mother and brothers came to see him, but they were not able to get near him because of the crowd. 20Someone told him, "Your mother and brothers are standing outside, wanting to see you."

21He replied, "My mother and brothers are those who hear God's word and put it into practice."

JESUS CALMS THE STORM

22One day Jesus said to his disciples, "Let us go over to the other side of the lake." So they got into a boat and set out. 23As they sailed, he fell asleep. A squall came down on the lake, so that the boat was being swamped, and they were in great danger.

24The disciples went and woke him, saying, "Master, Master, we're going to drown!"

He got up and rebuked the wind and the raging waters; the storm subsided, and all was calm. 25"Where is your faith?" he asked his disciples.

In fear and amazement they asked one another, "Who is this? He commands even the winds and the water, and they obey him."

JESUS RESTORES A DEMON-POSSESSED MAN

26They sailed to the region of the Gerasenes,[a] which is across the lake from Galilee. 27When Jesus stepped ashore, he was met by a demon-possessed man from the town. For a long time this man had not worn clothes or lived in a house, but had lived in the tombs. 28When he saw Jesus, he cried out and fell at his feet, shouting at the top of his voice, "What do you want with me, Jesus, Son of the Most High God? I beg you, don't torture me!" 29For Jesus had commanded the impure spirit to come out of the man. Many times it had seized him, and though he was chained hand and foot and kept under guard, he had broken his chains and had been driven by the demon into solitary places.

---

[a] *26* Some manuscripts *Gadarenes*; other manuscripts *Gergesenes*; also in verse 37

30Jesus asked him, "What is your name?"
"Legion," he replied, because many demons had gone into him.
31And they begged Jesus repeatedly not to order them to go into the
Abyss.
32A large herd of pigs was feeding there on the hillside. The demons
begged Jesus to let them go into the pigs, and he gave them permission.
33When the demons came out of the man, they went into the pigs, and
the herd rushed down the steep bank into the lake and was drowned.
34When those tending the pigs saw what had happened, they ran
off and reported this in the town and countryside, 35and the people
went out to see what had happened. When they came to Jesus, they
found the man from whom the demons had gone out, sitting at Jesus'
feet, dressed and in his right mind; and they were afraid. 36Those who
had seen it told the people how the demon-possessed man had been
cured. 37Then all the people of the region of the Gerasenes asked Jesus
to leave them, because they were overcome with fear. So he got into
the boat and left.
38The man from whom the demons had gone out begged to go with
him, but Jesus sent him away, saying, 39"Return home and tell how
much God has done for you." So the man went away and told all over
town how much Jesus had done for him.

JESUS RAISES A DEAD GIRL AND HEALS A SICK WOMAN

40Now when Jesus returned, a crowd welcomed him, for they were
all expecting him. 41Then a man named Jairus, a synagogue leader,
came and fell at Jesus' feet, pleading with him to come to his house
42because his only daughter, a girl of about twelve, was dying.
As Jesus was on his way, the crowds almost crushed him. 43And a
woman was there who had been subject to bleeding for twelve years,[a]
but no one could heal her. 44She came up behind him and touched the
edge of his cloak, and immediately her bleeding stopped.
45"Who touched me?" Jesus asked.
When they all denied it, Peter said, "Master, the people are crowding
and pressing against you."
46But Jesus said, "Someone touched me; I know that power has gone
out from me."
47Then the woman, seeing that she could not go unnoticed, came
trembling and fell at his feet. In the presence of all the people, she
told why she had touched him and how she had been instantly healed.
48Then he said to her, "Daughter, your faith has healed you. Go in
peace."
49While Jesus was still speaking, someone came from the house of
Jairus, the synagogue leader. "Your daughter is dead," he said. "Don't
bother the teacher anymore."
50Hearing this, Jesus said to Jairus, "Don't be afraid; just believe, and
she will be healed."
51When he arrived at the house of Jairus, he did not let anyone go
in with him except Peter, John and James, and the child's father and
mother. 52Meanwhile, all the people were wailing and mourning for
her. "Stop wailing," Jesus said. "She is not dead but asleep."
53They laughed at him, knowing that she was dead. 54But he took her
by the hand and said, "My child, get up!" 55Her spirit returned, and at

[a] *43* Many manuscripts *years, and she had spent all she had on doctors*

once she stood up. Then Jesus told them to give her something to eat.
56 Her parents were astonished, but he ordered them not to tell anyone
what had happened.

JESUS SENDS OUT THE TWELVE

9 When Jesus had called the Twelve together, he gave them power
and authority to drive out all demons and to cure diseases, 2 and he
sent them out to proclaim the kingdom of God and to heal the sick. 3 He
told them: "Take nothing for the journey—no staff, no bag, no bread,
no money, no extra shirt. 4 Whatever house you enter, stay there until
you leave that town. 5 If people do not welcome you, leave their town
and shake the dust off your feet as a testimony against them." 6 So they
set out and went from village to village, proclaiming the good news
and healing people everywhere.
7 Now Herod the tetrarch heard about all that was going on. And he
was perplexed because some were saying that John had been raised
from the dead, 8 others that Elijah had appeared, and still others that
one of the prophets of long ago had come back to life. 9 But Herod said,
"I beheaded John. Who, then, is this I hear such things about?" And he
tried to see him.

JESUS FEEDS THE FIVE THOUSAND

10 When the apostles returned, they reported to Jesus what they had
done. Then he took them with him and they withdrew by themselves
to a town called Bethsaida, 11 but the crowds learned about it and fol-
lowed him. He welcomed them and spoke to them about the kingdom
of God, and healed those who needed healing.
12 Late in the afternoon the Twelve came to him and said, "Send the
crowd away so they can go to the surrounding villages and countryside
and find food and lodging, because we are in a remote place here."
13 He replied, "You give them something to eat."
They answered, "We have only five loaves of bread and two fish—
unless we go and buy food for all this crowd." 14 (About five thousand
men were there.)
But he said to his disciples, "Have them sit down in groups of about
fifty each." 15 The disciples did so, and everyone sat down. 16 Taking the
five loaves and the two fish and looking up to heaven, he gave thanks
and broke them. Then he gave them to the disciples to distribute to
the people. 17 They all ate and were satisfied, and the disciples picked
up twelve basketfuls of broken pieces that were left over.

PETER DECLARES THAT JESUS IS THE MESSIAH

18 Once when Jesus was praying in private and his disciples were with
him, he asked them, "Who do the crowds say I am?"
19 They replied, "Some say John the Baptist; others say Elijah; and
still others, that one of the prophets of long ago has come back to life."
20 "But what about you?" he asked. "Who do you say I am?"
Peter answered, "God's Messiah."

JESUS PREDICTS HIS DEATH

21 Jesus strictly warned them not to tell this to anyone. 22 And he said,
"The Son of Man must suffer many things and be rejected by the el-
ders, the chief priests and the teachers of the law, and he must be killed
and on the third day be raised to life."

PRAYING SCRIPTURE

Luke 9

Nothing is too hard for God. Faced with a hungry crowd and barely enough food to feed a child, Jesus took five loaves and two fish and miraculously multiplied them many times over, feeding more than five thousand people. There were more leftovers than food that had been available at the start.

The Lord is able to take what little we have and multiply it. Pray not according to your resources but according to his power.

[23]Then he said to them all: "Whoever wants to be my disciple must
deny themselves and take up their cross daily and follow me. [24]For
whoever wants to save their life will lose it, but whoever loses their
life for me will save it. [25]What good is it for someone to gain the whole
world, and yet lose or forfeit their very self? [26]Whoever is ashamed of
me and my words, the Son of Man will be ashamed of them when he
comes in his glory and in the glory of the Father and of the holy angels.
[27]"Truly I tell you, some who are standing here will not taste death
before they see the kingdom of God."

THE TRANSFIGURATION

[28]About eight days after Jesus said this, he took Peter, John and
James with him and went up onto a mountain to pray. [29]As he was
praying, the appearance of his face changed, and his clothes became as
bright as a flash of lightning. [30]Two men, Moses and Elijah, appeared
in glorious splendor, talking with Jesus. [31]They spoke about his depar-
ture,[a] which he was about to bring to fulfillment at Jerusalem. [32]Pe-
ter and his companions were very sleepy, but when they became fully
awake, they saw his glory and the two men standing with him. [33]As the
men were leaving Jesus, Peter said to him, "Master, it is good for us to
be here. Let us put up three shelters — one for you, one for Moses and
one for Elijah." (He did not know what he was saying.)
[34]While he was speaking, a cloud appeared and covered them, and
they were afraid as they entered the cloud. [35]A voice came from the
cloud, saying, "This is my Son, whom I have chosen; listen to him."
[36]When the voice had spoken, they found that Jesus was alone. The
disciples kept this to themselves and did not tell anyone at that time
what they had seen.

JESUS HEALS A DEMON-POSSESSED BOY

[37]The next day, when they came down from the mountain, a large
crowd met him. [38]A man in the crowd called out, "Teacher, I beg you to
look at my son, for he is my only child. [39]A spirit seizes him and he sud-
denly screams; it throws him into convulsions so that he foams at the
mouth. It scarcely ever leaves him and is destroying him. [40]I begged
your disciples to drive it out, but they could not."
[41]"You unbelieving and perverse generation," Jesus replied, "how
long shall I stay with you and put up with you? Bring your son here."
[42]Even while the boy was coming, the demon threw him to the
ground in a convulsion. But Jesus rebuked the impure spirit, healed
the boy and gave him back to his father. [43]And they were all amazed at
the greatness of God.

JESUS PREDICTS HIS DEATH A SECOND TIME

While everyone was marveling at all that Jesus did, he said to his
disciples, [44]"Listen carefully to what I am about to tell you: The Son of
Man is going to be delivered into the hands of men." [45]But they did not
understand what this meant. It was hidden from them, so that they did
not grasp it, and they were afraid to ask him about it.
[46]An argument started among the disciples as to which of them
would be the greatest. [47]Jesus, knowing their thoughts, took a little
child and had him stand beside him. [48]Then he said to them, "Whoever

[a] 31 Greek *exodos*

welcomes this little child in my name welcomes me; and whoever welcomes me welcomes the one who sent me. For it is the one who is least among you all who is the greatest.”

49“Master,” said John, “we saw someone driving out demons in your name and we tried to stop him, because he is not one of us.”

50“Do not stop him,” Jesus said, “for whoever is not against you is for you.”

SAMARITAN OPPOSITION

51As the time approached for him to be taken up to heaven, Jesus resolutely set out for Jerusalem. 52And he sent messengers on ahead, who went into a Samaritan village to get things ready for him; 53but the people there did not welcome him, because he was heading for Jerusalem. 54When the disciples James and John saw this, they asked, “Lord, do you want us to call fire down from heaven to destroy them[a]?” 55But Jesus turned and rebuked them. 56Then he and his disciples went to another village.

THE COST OF FOLLOWING JESUS

57As they were walking along the road, a man said to him, “I will follow you wherever you go.”

58Jesus replied, “Foxes have dens and birds have nests, but the Son of Man has no place to lay his head.”

59He said to another man, “Follow me.”

But he replied, “Lord, first let me go and bury my father.”

60Jesus said to him, “Let the dead bury their own dead, but you go and proclaim the kingdom of God.”

61Still another said, “I will follow you, Lord; but first let me go back and say goodbye to my family.”

62Jesus replied, “No one who puts a hand to the plow and looks back is fit for service in the kingdom of God.”

JESUS SENDS OUT THE SEVENTY-TWO

10 After this the Lord appointed seventy-two[b] others and sent them two by two ahead of him to every town and place where he was about to go. 2He told them, “The harvest is plentiful, but the workers are few. Ask the Lord of the harvest, therefore, to send out workers into his harvest field. 3Go! I am sending you out like lambs among wolves. 4Do not take a purse or bag or sandals; and do not greet anyone on the road.

5“When you enter a house, first say, ‘Peace to this house.’ 6If someone who promotes peace is there, your peace will rest on them; if not, it will return to you. 7Stay there, eating and drinking whatever they give you, for the worker deserves his wages. Do not move around from house to house.

8“When you enter a town and are welcomed, eat what is offered to you. 9Heal the sick who are there and tell them, ‘The kingdom of God has come near to you.’ 10But when you enter a town and are not welcomed, go into its streets and say, 11‘Even the dust of your town we wipe from our feet as a warning to you. Yet be sure of this: The kingdom of God has come near.’ 12I tell you, it will be more bearable on that day for Sodom than for that town.

PRAYING SCRIPTURE

Luke 10

The parable of the Good Samaritan answers the question “Who is my neighbor?” for all time. The Samaritan man, being part of a class of despised people, was an unlikely hero of the story. The conclusion we find is that hurting people need neighbors, and neighbors are those who help. Being a neighbor is not about where we live; it is about helping.

Ask God to give you the heart of a good neighbor.

[a] 54 Some manuscripts *them, just as Elijah did* [b] 1 Some manuscripts *seventy*; also in verse 17

13"Woe to you, Chorazin! Woe to you, Bethsaida! For if the miracles
that were performed in you had been performed in Tyre and Sidon,
they would have repented long ago, sitting in sackcloth and ashes.
14But it will be more bearable for Tyre and Sidon at the judgment than
for you. 15And you, Capernaum, will you be lifted to the heavens? No,
you will go down to Hades.[a]
16"Whoever listens to you listens to me; whoever rejects you rejects
me; but whoever rejects me rejects him who sent me."
17The seventy-two returned with joy and said, "Lord, even the de-
mons submit to us in your name."
18He replied, "I saw Satan fall like lightning from heaven. 19I have
given you authority to trample on snakes and scorpions and to over-
come all the power of the enemy; nothing will harm you. 20However,
do not rejoice that the spirits submit to you, but rejoice that your
names are written in heaven."
21At that time Jesus, full of joy through the Holy Spirit, said, "I praise
you, Father, Lord of heaven and earth, because you have hidden these
things from the wise and learned, and revealed them to little children.
Yes, Father, for this is what you were pleased to do.
22"All things have been committed to me by my Father. No one
knows who the Son is except the Father, and no one knows who the
Father is except the Son and those to whom the Son chooses to reveal
him."
23Then he turned to his disciples and said privately, "Blessed are the
eyes that see what you see. 24For I tell you that many prophets and
kings wanted to see what you see but did not see it, and to hear what
you hear but did not hear it."

THE PARABLE OF THE GOOD SAMARITAN

25On one occasion an expert in the law stood up to test Jesus.
"Teacher," he asked, "what must I do to inherit eternal life?"
26"What is written in the Law?" he replied. "How do you read it?"
27He answered, " 'Love the Lord your God with all your heart and with
all your soul and with all your strength and with all your mind'[b]; and,
'Love your neighbor as yourself.'[c]"
28"You have answered correctly," Jesus replied. "Do this and you will
live."
29But he wanted to justify himself, so he asked Jesus, "And who is
my neighbor?"
30In reply Jesus said: "A man was going down from Jerusalem to
Jericho, when he was attacked by robbers. They stripped him of his
clothes, beat him and went away, leaving him half dead. 31A priest hap-
pened to be going down the same road, and when he saw the man, he
passed by on the other side. 32So too, a Levite, when he came to the
place and saw him, passed by on the other side. 33But a Samaritan, as
he traveled, came where the man was; and when he saw him, he took
pity on him. 34He went to him and bandaged his wounds, pouring on
oil and wine. Then he put the man on his own donkey, brought him to
an inn and took care of him. 35The next day he took out two denarii[d]
and gave them to the innkeeper. 'Look after him,' he said, 'and when
I return, I will reimburse you for any extra expense you may have.'

---

[a] *15* That is, the realm of the dead [b] *27* Deut. 6:5 [c] *27* Lev. 19:18
[d] *35* A denarius was the usual daily wage of a day laborer (see Matt. 20:2).

36“Which of these three do you think was a neighbor to the man who
fell into the hands of robbers?”
37The expert in the law replied, “The one who had mercy on him.”
Jesus told him, “Go and do likewise.”

AT THE HOME OF MARTHA AND MARY

38As Jesus and his disciples were on their way, he came to a village
where a woman named Martha opened her home to him. 39She had a
sister called Mary, who sat at the Lord’s feet listening to what he said.
40But Martha was distracted by all the preparations that had to be
made. She came to him and asked, “Lord, don’t you care that my sister
has left me to do the work by myself? Tell her to help me!”
41“Martha, Martha,” the Lord answered, “you are worried and up-
set about many things, 42but few things are needed — or indeed only
one.[a] Mary has chosen what is better, and it will not be taken away
from her.”

JESUS’ TEACHING ON PRAYER

11 One day Jesus was praying in a certain place. When he finished,
one of his disciples said to him, “Lord, teach us to pray, just as
John taught his disciples.”
2He said to them, “When you pray, say:

“ ‘Father,[b]
hallowed be your name,
your kingdom come.[c]
3Give us each day our daily bread.
4Forgive us our sins,
for we also forgive everyone who sins against us.[d]
And lead us not into temptation.[e]’ ”

5Then Jesus said to them, “Suppose you have a friend, and you go
to him at midnight and say, ‘Friend, lend me three loaves of bread;
6a friend of mine on a journey has come to me, and I have no food
to offer him.’ 7And suppose the one inside answers, ‘Don’t bother me.
The door is already locked, and my children and I are in bed. I can’t
get up and give you anything.’ 8I tell you, even though he will not
get up and give you the bread because of friendship, yet because of
your shameless audacity[f] he will surely get up and give you as much
as you need.
9“So I say to you: Ask and it will be given to you; seek and you will
find; knock and the door will be opened to you. 10For everyone who
asks receives; the one who seeks finds; and to the one who knocks, the
door will be opened.
11“Which of you fathers, if your son asks for[g] a fish, will give him a
snake instead? 12Or if he asks for an egg, will give him a scorpion? 13If
you then, though you are evil, know how to give good gifts to your chil-
dren, how much more will your Father in heaven give the Holy Spirit
to those who ask him!”

PRAYING SCRIPTURE

Luke 11

In this passage are two significant teachings on prayer. Both the story of the friend’s arrival at midnight and the admonition to ask, seek and knock encourage us to be bold and persistent when we pray.

When you ask God to answer prayer, do you bombard him, or are your prayers more like one and done? Doing the latter is not wrong, but God invites us to ask him again and again.

---

[a] 42 Some manuscripts *but only one thing is needed* [b] 2 Some manuscripts *Our Father in heaven* [c] 2 Some manuscripts *come. May your will be done on earth as it is in heaven.* [d] 4 Greek *everyone who is indebted to us* [e] 4 Some manuscripts *temptation, but deliver us from the evil one* [f] 8 Or *yet to preserve his good name* [g] 11 Some manuscripts *for bread, will give him a stone? Or if he asks for*

JESUS AND BEELZEBUL

14Jesus was driving out a demon that was mute. When the demon
left, the man who had been mute spoke, and the crowd was amazed.
15But some of them said, "By Beelzebul, the prince of demons, he is
driving out demons." 16Others tested him by asking for a sign from
heaven.
17Jesus knew their thoughts and said to them: "Any kingdom divided
against itself will be ruined, and a house divided against itself will fall.
18If Satan is divided against himself, how can his kingdom stand? I say
this because you claim that I drive out demons by Beelzebul. 19Now if I
drive out demons by Beelzebul, by whom do your followers drive them
out? So then, they will be your judges. 20But if I drive out demons by
the finger of God, then the kingdom of God has come upon you.
21"When a strong man, fully armed, guards his own house, his pos-
sessions are safe. 22But when someone stronger attacks and overpow-
ers him, he takes away the armor in which the man trusted and divides
up his plunder.
23"Whoever is not with me is against me, and whoever does not
gather with me scatters.
24"When an impure spirit comes out of a person, it goes through arid
places seeking rest and does not find it. Then it says, 'I will return to
the house I left.' 25When it arrives, it finds the house swept clean and
put in order. 26Then it goes and takes seven other spirits more wicked
than itself, and they go in and live there. And the final condition of
that person is worse than the first."
27As Jesus was saying these things, a woman in the crowd called out,
"Blessed is the mother who gave you birth and nursed you."
28He replied, "Blessed rather are those who hear the word of God
and obey it."

THE SIGN OF JONAH

29As the crowds increased, Jesus said, "This is a wicked generation.
It asks for a sign, but none will be given it except the sign of Jonah.
30For as Jonah was a sign to the Ninevites, so also will the Son of Man
be to this generation. 31The Queen of the South will rise at the judg-
ment with the people of this generation and condemn them, for she
came from the ends of the earth to listen to Solomon's wisdom; and
now something greater than Solomon is here. 32The men of Nineveh
will stand up at the judgment with this generation and condemn it, for
they repented at the preaching of Jonah; and now something greater
than Jonah is here.

THE LAMP OF THE BODY

33"No one lights a lamp and puts it in a place where it will be hidden,
or under a bowl. Instead they put it on its stand, so that those who
come in may see the light. 34Your eye is the lamp of your body. When
your eyes are healthy,[a] your whole body also is full of light. But when
they are unhealthy,[b] your body also is full of darkness. 35See to it, then,
that the light within you is not darkness. 36Therefore, if your whole
body is full of light, and no part of it dark, it will be just as full of light
as when a lamp shines its light on you."

[a] 34 The Greek for *healthy* here implies *generous*. [b] 34 The Greek for *unhealthy* here implies *stingy*.

WOES ON THE PHARISEES AND THE EXPERTS IN THE LAW

37 When Jesus had finished speaking, a Pharisee invited him to eat
with him; so he went in and reclined at the table. 38 But the Pharisee
was surprised when he noticed that Jesus did not first wash before
the meal.

39 Then the Lord said to him, "Now then, you Pharisees clean the
outside of the cup and dish, but inside you are full of greed and wick-
edness. 40 You foolish people! Did not the one who made the outside
make the inside also? 41 But now as for what is inside you — be gener-
ous to the poor, and everything will be clean for you.

42 "Woe to you Pharisees, because you give God a tenth of your mint,
rue and all other kinds of garden herbs, but you neglect justice and
the love of God. You should have practiced the latter without leaving
the former undone.

43 "Woe to you Pharisees, because you love the most important seats
in the synagogues and respectful greetings in the marketplaces.

44 "Woe to you, because you are like unmarked graves, which people
walk over without knowing it."

45 One of the experts in the law answered him, "Teacher, when you
say these things, you insult us also."

46 Jesus replied, "And you experts in the law, woe to you, because you
load people down with burdens they can hardly carry, and you your-
selves will not lift one finger to help them.

47 "Woe to you, because you build tombs for the prophets, and it was
your ancestors who killed them. 48 So you testify that you approve of
what your ancestors did; they killed the prophets, and you build their
tombs. 49 Because of this, God in his wisdom said, 'I will send them
prophets and apostles, some of whom they will kill and others they
will persecute.' 50 Therefore this generation will be held responsible for
the blood of all the prophets that has been shed since the beginning of
the world, 51 from the blood of Abel to the blood of Zechariah, who was
killed between the altar and the sanctuary. Yes, I tell you, this genera-
tion will be held responsible for it all.

52 "Woe to you experts in the law, because you have taken away the
key to knowledge. You yourselves have not entered, and you have hin-
dered those who were entering."

53 When Jesus went outside, the Pharisees and the teachers of the
law began to oppose him fiercely and to besiege him with questions,
54 waiting to catch him in something he might say.

WARNINGS AND ENCOURAGEMENTS

12 Meanwhile, when a crowd of many thousands had gathered, so
that they were trampling on one another, Jesus began to speak
first to his disciples, saying: "Be[a] on your guard against the yeast of the
Pharisees, which is hypocrisy. 2 There is nothing concealed that will not
be disclosed, or hidden that will not be made known. 3 What you have
said in the dark will be heard in the daylight, and what you have whis-
pered in the ear in the inner rooms will be proclaimed from the roofs.
4 "I tell you, my friends, do not be afraid of those who kill the body
and after that can do no more. 5 But I will show you whom you should
fear: Fear him who, after your body has been killed, has authority to

PRAYING SCRIPTURE

Luke 12

In Jesus' parable, one difference between faithful and unfaithful servants is that the former prepare themselves to serve the master until he returns, while the latter takes advantage of the master's absence, abusing the other servants and debasing himself with wine. Faithfulness reveals itself by concern over the master's will, but worldly concerns lead to wickedness.

Are you faithfully awaiting Christ's return? If not, confess where you have become an unfaithful servant.

[a] 1 Or *speak to his disciples, saying: "First of all, be*

throw you into hell. Yes, I tell you, fear him. 6Are not five sparrows
sold for two pennies? Yet not one of them is forgotten by God. 7Indeed,
the very hairs of your head are all numbered. Don't be afraid; you are
worth more than many sparrows.
8"I tell you, whoever publicly acknowledges me before others, the
Son of Man will also acknowledge before the angels of God. 9But who-
ever disowns me before others will be disowned before the angels of
God. 10And everyone who speaks a word against the Son of Man will
be forgiven, but anyone who blasphemes against the Holy Spirit will
not be forgiven.
11"When you are brought before synagogues, rulers and authorities,
do not worry about how you will defend yourselves or what you will
say, 12for the Holy Spirit will teach you at that time what you should
say."

THE PARABLE OF THE RICH FOOL

13Someone in the crowd said to him, "Teacher, tell my brother to di-
vide the inheritance with me."
14Jesus replied, "Man, who appointed me a judge or an arbiter be-
tween you?" 15Then he said to them, "Watch out! Be on your guard
against all kinds of greed; life does not consist in an abundance of
possessions."
16And he told them this parable: "The ground of a certain rich man
yielded an abundant harvest. 17He thought to himself, 'What shall I do?
I have no place to store my crops.'
18"Then he said, 'This is what I'll do. I will tear down my barns and
build bigger ones, and there I will store my surplus grain. 19And I'll say
to myself, "You have plenty of grain laid up for many years. Take life
easy; eat, drink and be merry." '
20"But God said to him, 'You fool! This very night your life will be
demanded from you. Then who will get what you have prepared for
yourself?'
21"This is how it will be with whoever stores up things for themselves
but is not rich toward God."

DO NOT WORRY

22Then Jesus said to his disciples: "Therefore I tell you, do not worry
about your life, what you will eat; or about your body, what you will
wear. 23For life is more than food, and the body more than clothes.
24Consider the ravens: They do not sow or reap, they have no store-
room or barn; yet God feeds them. And how much more valuable you
are than birds! 25Who of you by worrying can add a single hour to your
life[a]? 26Since you cannot do this very little thing, why do you worry
about the rest?
27"Consider how the wild flowers grow. They do not labor or spin.
Yet I tell you, not even Solomon in all his splendor was dressed like
one of these. 28If that is how God clothes the grass of the field, which
is here today, and tomorrow is thrown into the fire, how much more
will he clothe you — you of little faith! 29And do not set your heart on
what you will eat or drink; do not worry about it. 30For the pagan world
runs after all such things, and your Father knows that you need them.
31But seek his kingdom, and these things will be given to you as well.

---

[a] 25 Or *single cubit to your height*

32“Do not be afraid, little flock, for your Father has been pleased to
give you the kingdom. 33Sell your possessions and give to the poor.
Provide purses for yourselves that will not wear out, a treasure in
heaven that will never fail, where no thief comes near and no moth
destroys. 34For where your treasure is, there your heart will be also.

WATCHFULNESS

35“Be dressed ready for service and keep your lamps burning, 36like
servants waiting for their master to return from a wedding banquet,
so that when he comes and knocks they can immediately open the
door for him. 37It will be good for those servants whose master finds
them watching when he comes. Truly I tell you, he will dress himself
to serve, will have them recline at the table and will come and wait on
them. 38It will be good for those servants whose master finds them
ready, even if he comes in the middle of the night or toward daybreak.
39But understand this: If the owner of the house had known at what
hour the thief was coming, he would not have let his house be broken
into. 40You also must be ready, because the Son of Man will come at an
hour when you do not expect him.”

**41Peter asked, “Lord, are you telling this parable to us, or to
everyone?”**

42The Lord answered, “Who then is the faithful and wise manager,
whom the master puts in charge of his servants to give them their food
allowance at the proper time? 43It will be good for that servant whom
the master finds doing so when he returns. 44Truly I tell you, he will
put him in charge of all his possessions. 45But suppose the servant says
to himself, ‘My master is taking a long time in coming,’ and he then
begins to beat the other servants, both men and women, and to eat
and drink and get drunk. 46The master of that servant will come on a
day when he does not expect him and at an hour he is not aware of.
He will cut him to pieces and assign him a place with the unbelievers.

47“The servant who knows the master’s will and does not get ready
or does not do what the master wants will be beaten with many blows.
48But the one who does not know and does things deserving punish-
ment will be beaten with few blows. From everyone who has been
given much, much will be demanded; and from the one who has been
entrusted with much, much more will be asked.

NOT PEACE BUT DIVISION

49“I have come to bring fire on the earth, and how I wish it were
already kindled! 50But I have a baptism to undergo, and what con-
straint I am under until it is completed! 51Do you think I came to bring
peace on earth? No, I tell you, but division. 52From now on there will
be five in one family divided against each other, three against two and
two against three. 53They will be divided, father against son and son
against father, mother against daughter and daughter against mother,
mother-in-law against daughter-in-law and daughter-in-law against
mother-in-law.”

INTERPRETING THE TIMES

54He said to the crowd: “When you see a cloud rising in the west, im-
mediately you say, ‘It’s going to rain,’ and it does. 55And when the south
wind blows, you say, ‘It’s going to be hot,’ and it is. 56Hypocrites! You

know how to interpret the appearance of the earth and the sky. How is
it that you don't know how to interpret this present time?
57"Why don't you judge for yourselves what is right? 58As you are go-
ing with your adversary to the magistrate, try hard to be reconciled on
the way, or your adversary may drag you off to the judge, and the judge
turn you over to the officer, and the officer throw you into prison. 59I
tell you, you will not get out until you have paid the last penny."

REPENT OR PERISH

13 Now there were some present at that time who told Jesus about
the Galileans whose blood Pilate had mixed with their sacrifices.
2Jesus answered, "Do you think that these Galileans were worse sin-
ners than all the other Galileans because they suffered this way? 3I tell
you, no! But unless you repent, you too will all perish. 4Or those eigh-
teen who died when the tower in Siloam fell on them—do you think
they were more guilty than all the others living in Jerusalem? 5I tell
you, no! But unless you repent, you too will all perish."
6Then he told this parable: "A man had a fig tree growing in his vine-
yard, and he went to look for fruit on it but did not find any. 7So he said
to the man who took care of the vineyard, 'For three years now I've
been coming to look for fruit on this fig tree and haven't found any.
Cut it down! Why should it use up the soil?'
8" 'Sir,' the man replied, 'leave it alone for one more year, and I'll dig
around it and fertilize it. 9If it bears fruit next year, fine! If not, then
cut it down.' "

JESUS HEALS A CRIPPLED WOMAN ON THE SABBATH

10On a Sabbath Jesus was teaching in one of the synagogues, 11and a
woman was there who had been crippled by a spirit for eighteen years.
She was bent over and could not straighten up at all. 12When Jesus saw
her, he called her forward and said to her, "Woman, you are set free
from your infirmity." 13Then he put his hands on her, and immediately
she straightened up and praised God.
14Indignant because Jesus had healed on the Sabbath, the synagogue
leader said to the people, "There are six days for work. So come and be
healed on those days, not on the Sabbath."
15The Lord answered him, "You hypocrites! Doesn't each of you on
the Sabbath untie your ox or donkey from the stall and lead it out to
give it water? 16Then should not this woman, a daughter of Abraham,
whom Satan has kept bound for eighteen long years, be set free on the
Sabbath day from what bound her?"
17When he said this, all his opponents were humiliated, but the peo-
ple were delighted with all the wonderful things he was doing.

THE PARABLES OF THE MUSTARD SEED AND THE YEAST

18Then Jesus asked, "What is the kingdom of God like? What shall
I compare it to? 19It is like a mustard seed, which a man took and
planted in his garden. It grew and became a tree, and the birds perched
in its branches."
20Again he asked, "What shall I compare the kingdom of God to? 21It
is like yeast that a woman took and mixed into about sixty pounds[a] of
flour until it worked all through the dough."

[a] *21* Or about 27 kilograms

PRAYING SCRIPTURE

Luke 13

While traveling to Jerusalem, Jesus taught in various cities and villages. He warned that some would not enter his kingdom and that to do so one must choose "the narrow door" (verse 24). Jesus was always clear that the majority would not enter his kingdom.

If you have never prayed to be on the narrow way, confirm your route with God today.

THE NARROW DOOR

22Then Jesus went through the towns and villages, teaching as he made his way to Jerusalem. 23Someone asked him, "Lord, are only a few people going to be saved?"

He said to them, 24"Make every effort to enter through the narrow door, because many, I tell you, will try to enter and will not be able to. 25Once the owner of the house gets up and closes the door, you will stand outside knocking and pleading, 'Sir, open the door for us.'

"But he will answer, 'I don't know you or where you come from.'

26"Then you will say, 'We ate and drank with you, and you taught in our streets.'

27"But he will reply, 'I don't know you or where you come from. Away from me, all you evildoers!'

28"There will be weeping there, and gnashing of teeth, when you see Abraham, Isaac and Jacob and all the prophets in the kingdom of God, but you yourselves thrown out. 29People will come from east and west and north and south, and will take their places at the feast in the kingdom of God. 30Indeed there are those who are last who will be first, and first who will be last."

JESUS' SORROW FOR JERUSALEM

31At that time some Pharisees came to Jesus and said to him, "Leave this place and go somewhere else. Herod wants to kill you."

32He replied, "Go tell that fox, 'I will keep on driving out demons and healing people today and tomorrow, and on the third day I will reach my goal.' 33In any case, I must press on today and tomorrow and the next day — for surely no prophet can die outside Jerusalem!

34"Jerusalem, Jerusalem, you who kill the prophets and stone those sent to you, how often I have longed to gather your children together, as a hen gathers her chicks under her wings, and you were not willing. 35Look, your house is left to you desolate. I tell you, you will not see me again until you say, 'Blessed is he who comes in the name of the Lord.'[a]"

JESUS AT A PHARISEE'S HOUSE

14 One Sabbath, when Jesus went to eat in the house of a prominent Pharisee, he was being carefully watched. 2There in front of him was a man suffering from abnormal swelling of his body. 3Jesus asked the Pharisees and experts in the law, "Is it lawful to heal on the Sabbath or not?" 4But they remained silent. So taking hold of the man, he healed him and sent him on his way.

5Then he asked them, "If one of you has a child[b] or an ox that falls into a well on the Sabbath day, will you not immediately pull it out?" 6And they had nothing to say.

7When he noticed how the guests picked the places of honor at the table, he told them this parable: 8"When someone invites you to a wedding feast, do not take the place of honor, for a person more distinguished than you may have been invited. 9If so, the host who invited both of you will come and say to you, 'Give this person your seat.' Then, humiliated, you will have to take the least important place. 10But when you are invited, take the lowest place, so that when your host comes, he will say to you, 'Friend, move up to a better place.' Then you will

PRAYING SCRIPTURE

Luke 14

Jesus' humanity was often revealed in eating and drinking. Here he used two images of meals to portray the reality of his kingdom. Both involved participation by those who otherwise would be counted unworthy to attend: the poor, the lame and the blind.

Often when we think about this passage, we forget that we are the needy ones invited to the banquet! Praise God for his all-sufficient grace.

---

[a] *35* Psalm 118:26 [b] *5* Some manuscripts *donkey*

be honored in the presence of all the other guests. 11For all those who
exalt themselves will be humbled, and those who humble themselves
will be exalted."

12Then Jesus said to his host, "When you give a luncheon or dinner,
do not invite your friends, your brothers or sisters, your relatives, or
your rich neighbors; if you do, they may invite you back and so you will
be repaid. 13But when you give a banquet, invite the poor, the crippled,
the lame, the blind, 14and you will be blessed. Although they cannot re-
pay you, you will be repaid at the resurrection of the righteous."

THE PARABLE OF THE GREAT BANQUET

15When one of those at the table with him heard this, he said to
Jesus, "Blessed is the one who will eat at the feast in the kingdom of
God."

16Jesus replied: "A certain man was preparing a great banquet and
invited many guests. 17At the time of the banquet he sent his servant
to tell those who had been invited, 'Come, for everything is now ready.'

18"But they all alike began to make excuses. The first said, 'I have just
bought a field, and I must go and see it. Please excuse me.'

19"Another said, 'I have just bought five yoke of oxen, and I'm on my
way to try them out. Please excuse me.'

20"Still another said, 'I just got married, so I can't come.'

21"The servant came back and reported this to his master. Then the
owner of the house became angry and ordered his servant, 'Go out
quickly into the streets and alleys of the town and bring in the poor,
the crippled, the blind and the lame.'

22"'Sir,' the servant said, 'what you ordered has been done, but there
is still room.'

23"Then the master told his servant, 'Go out to the roads and coun-
try lanes and compel them to come in, so that my house will be full.
24I tell you, not one of those who were invited will get a taste of my
banquet.'"

THE COST OF BEING A DISCIPLE

25Large crowds were traveling with Jesus, and turning to them he
said: 26"If anyone comes to me and does not hate father and mother,
wife and children, brothers and sisters — yes, even their own life —
such a person cannot be my disciple. 27And whoever does not carry
their cross and follow me cannot be my disciple.

28"Suppose one of you wants to build a tower. Won't you first sit
down and estimate the cost to see if you have enough money to com-
plete it? 29For if you lay the foundation and are not able to finish it,
everyone who sees it will ridicule you, 30saying, 'This person began to
build and wasn't able to finish.'

31"Or suppose a king is about to go to war against another king. Won't
he first sit down and consider whether he is able with ten thousand
men to oppose the one coming against him with twenty thousand?
32If he is not able, he will send a delegation while the other is still a
long way off and will ask for terms of peace. 33In the same way, those
of you who do not give up everything you have cannot be my disciples.

34"Salt is good, but if it loses its saltiness, how can it be made salty
again? 35It is fit neither for the soil nor for the manure pile; it is thrown
out.

"Whoever has ears to hear, let them hear."

PRAYING SCRIPTURE

Luke 15

This chapter is one of things lost and found. A sheep is lost and found. A coin is lost and found. A son is lost and found. Jesus is in the finding business, but seen in each vignette is that he is also in the searching business: The wilderness, the house, and the road were searched.

Where did Jesus find you? If you are still lost, call on him in faith.

THE PARABLE OF THE LOST SHEEP

15 Now the tax collectors and sinners were all gathering around to
hear Jesus. 2But the Pharisees and the teachers of the law mut-
tered, "This man welcomes sinners and eats with them."
3Then Jesus told them this parable: 4"Suppose one of you has a hun-
dred sheep and loses one of them. Doesn't he leave the ninety-nine
in the open country and go after the lost sheep until he finds it? 5And
when he finds it, he joyfully puts it on his shoulders 6and goes home.
Then he calls his friends and neighbors together and says, 'Rejoice
with me; I have found my lost sheep.' 7I tell you that in the same way
there will be more rejoicing in heaven over one sinner who repents
than over ninety-nine righteous persons who do not need to repent.

THE PARABLE OF THE LOST COIN

8"Or suppose a woman has ten silver coins[a] and loses one. Doesn't
she light a lamp, sweep the house and search carefully until she finds
it? 9And when she finds it, she calls her friends and neighbors together
and says, 'Rejoice with me; I have found my lost coin.' 10In the same
way, I tell you, there is rejoicing in the presence of the angels of God
over one sinner who repents."

THE PARABLE OF THE LOST SON

11Jesus continued: "There was a man who had two sons. 12The youn-
ger one said to his father, 'Father, give me my share of the estate.' So
he divided his property between them.
13"Not long after that, the younger son got together all he had, set
off for a distant country and there squandered his wealth in wild liv-
ing. 14After he had spent everything, there was a severe famine in that
whole country, and he began to be in need. 15So he went and hired
himself out to a citizen of that country, who sent him to his fields to
feed pigs. 16He longed to fill his stomach with the pods that the pigs
were eating, but no one gave him anything.
17"When he came to his senses, he said, 'How many of my father's
hired servants have food to spare, and here I am starving to death!
18I will set out and go back to my father and say to him: Father, I have
sinned against heaven and against you. 19I am no longer worthy to be
called your son; make me like one of your hired servants.' 20So he got
up and went to his father.
"But while he was still a long way off, his father saw him and was
filled with compassion for him; he ran to his son, threw his arms
around him and kissed him.
21"The son said to him, 'Father, I have sinned against heaven and
against you. I am no longer worthy to be called your son.'
22"But the father said to his servants, 'Quick! Bring the best robe and
put it on him. Put a ring on his finger and sandals on his feet. 23Bring
the fattened calf and kill it. Let's have a feast and celebrate. 24For this
son of mine was dead and is alive again; he was lost and is found.' So
they began to celebrate.
25"Meanwhile, the older son was in the field. When he came near
the house, he heard music and dancing. 26So he called one of the ser-
vants and asked him what was going on. 27'Your brother has come,' he

---

[a] 8 Greek *ten drachmas*, each worth about a day's wages

replied, ‘and your father has killed the fattened calf because he has
him back safe and sound.’
28“The older brother became angry and refused to go in. So his father
went out and pleaded with him. 29But he answered his father, ‘Look!
All these years I’ve been slaving for you and never disobeyed your or-
ders. Yet you never gave me even a young goat so I could celebrate
with my friends. 30But when this son of yours who has squandered
your property with prostitutes comes home, you kill the fattened calf
for him!’
31“ ‘My son,’ the father said, ‘you are always with me, and everything
I have is yours. 32But we had to celebrate and be glad, because this
brother of yours was dead and is alive again; he was lost and is found.’ ”

THE PARABLE OF THE SHREWD MANAGER

16 Jesus told his disciples: “There was a rich man whose manager
was accused of wasting his possessions. 2So he called him in
and asked him, ‘What is this I hear about you? Give an account of your
management, because you cannot be manager any longer.’
3“The manager said to himself, ‘What shall I do now? My master is
taking away my job. I’m not strong enough to dig, and I’m ashamed to
beg — 4I know what I’ll do so that, when I lose my job here, people will
welcome me into their houses.’
5“So he called in each one of his master’s debtors. He asked the first,
‘How much do you owe my master?’
6“ ‘Nine hundred gallons[a] of olive oil,’ he replied.
“The manager told him, ‘Take your bill, sit down quickly, and make
it four hundred and fifty.’
7“Then he asked the second, ‘And how much do you owe?’
“ ‘A thousand bushels[b] of wheat,’ he replied.
“He told him, ‘Take your bill and make it eight hundred.’
8“The master commended the dishonest manager because he had
acted shrewdly. For the people of this world are more shrewd in deal-
ing with their own kind than are the people of the light. 9I tell you, use
worldly wealth to gain friends for yourselves, so that when it is gone,
you will be welcomed into eternal dwellings.
10“Whoever can be trusted with very little can also be trusted with
much, and whoever is dishonest with very little will also be dishonest
with much. 11So if you have not been trustworthy in handling worldly
wealth, who will trust you with true riches? 12And if you have not been
trustworthy with someone else’s property, who will give you property
of your own?
13“No one can serve two masters. Either you will hate the one and
love the other, or you will be devoted to the one and despise the other.
You cannot serve both God and money.”
14The Pharisees, who loved money, heard all this and were sneering
at Jesus. 15He said to them, “You are the ones who justify yourselves
in the eyes of others, but God knows your hearts. What people value
highly is detestable in God’s sight.

ADDITIONAL TEACHINGS

16“The Law and the Prophets were proclaimed until John. Since that
time, the good news of the kingdom of God is being preached, and

PRAYING SCRIPTURE

Luke 16

This is the most graphic, explicit narrative about hell in Scripture. In it we read of flames, torment and separation. This is a human story of judgment and reward. Significant to Jesus’ warning is that the rich man did not want others to join his torments.

God’s people must warn others about the horrors of hell and prayerfully share the gospel with them.

[a] 6 Or about 3,000 liters [b] 7 Or about 30 tons

everyone is forcing their way into it. 17 It is easier for heaven and earth
to disappear than for the least stroke of a pen to drop out of the Law.
18 "Anyone who divorces his wife and marries another woman com-
mits adultery, and the man who marries a divorced woman commits
adultery.

THE RICH MAN AND LAZARUS

19 "There was a rich man who was dressed in purple and fine linen
and lived in luxury every day. 20 At his gate was laid a beggar named
Lazarus, covered with sores 21 and longing to eat what fell from the rich
man's table. Even the dogs came and licked his sores.
22 "The time came when the beggar died and the angels carried him
to Abraham's side. The rich man also died and was buried. 23 In Hades,
where he was in torment, he looked up and saw Abraham far away,
with Lazarus by his side. 24 So he called to him, 'Father Abraham, have
pity on me and send Lazarus to dip the tip of his finger in water and
cool my tongue, because I am in agony in this fire.'
25 "But Abraham replied, 'Son, remember that in your lifetime you
received your good things, while Lazarus received bad things, but now
he is comforted here and you are in agony. 26 And besides all this, be-
tween us and you a great chasm has been set in place, so that those
who want to go from here to you cannot, nor can anyone cross over
from there to us.'
27 "He answered, 'Then I beg you, father, send Lazarus to my family,
28 for I have five brothers. Let him warn them, so that they will not also
come to this place of torment.'
29 "Abraham replied, 'They have Moses and the Prophets; let them
listen to them.'
30 " 'No, father Abraham,' he said, 'but if someone from the dead goes
to them, they will repent.'
31 "He said to him, 'If they do not listen to Moses and the Prophets,
they will not be convinced even if someone rises from the dead.' "

SIN, FAITH, DUTY

17 Jesus said to his disciples: "Things that cause people to stum-
ble are bound to come, but woe to anyone through whom they
come. 2 It would be better for them to be thrown into the sea with a
millstone tied around their neck than to cause one of these little ones
to stumble. 3 So watch yourselves.
"If your brother or sister[a] sins against you, rebuke them; and if they
repent, forgive them. 4 Even if they sin against you seven times in a
day and seven times come back to you saying 'I repent,' you must for-
give them."
5 The apostles said to the Lord, "Increase our faith!"
6 He replied, "If you have faith as small as a mustard seed, you can
say to this mulberry tree, 'Be uprooted and planted in the sea,' and it
will obey you.
7 "Suppose one of you has a servant plowing or looking after the
sheep. Will he say to the servant when he comes in from the field,
'Come along now and sit down to eat'? 8 Won't he rather say, 'Prepare
my supper, get yourself ready and wait on me while I eat and drink;

[a] 3 The Greek word for *brother or sister* (*adelphos*) refers here to a fellow disciple, whether man or woman.

PRAYING SCRIPTURE

Luke 17

Few things were as horrible in ancient Israel as leprosy. Those who were not healed of this condition were forced to live as exiles in their own homeland, separated from the healthy population. Ten such men beseeched Jesus for healing and were granted it at his word. Nine of them never returned, but the tenth—a Samaritan—returned to thank Jesus.

Recognize the source of blessing. Ask God to make you grateful.

after that you may eat and drink'? [9]Will he thank the servant because
he did what he was told to do? [10]So you also, when you have done ev-
erything you were told to do, should say, 'We are unworthy servants;
we have only done our duty.'"

JESUS HEALS TEN MEN WITH LEPROSY

[11]Now on his way to Jerusalem, Jesus traveled along the border be-
tween Samaria and Galilee. [12]As he was going into a village, ten men
who had leprosy[a] met him. They stood at a distance [13]and called out in
a loud voice, "Jesus, Master, have pity on us!"

[14]When he saw them, he said, "Go, show yourselves to the priests."
And as they went, they were cleansed.

[15]One of them, when he saw he was healed, came back, praising God
in a loud voice. [16]He threw himself at Jesus' feet and thanked him—
and he was a Samaritan.

[17]Jesus asked, "Were not all ten cleansed? Where are the other nine?
[18]Has no one returned to give praise to God except this foreigner?"
[19]Then he said to him, "Rise and go; your faith has made you well."

THE COMING OF THE KINGDOM OF GOD

[20]Once, on being asked by the Pharisees when the kingdom of God
would come, Jesus replied, "The coming of the kingdom of God is not
something that can be observed, [21]nor will people say, 'Here it is,' or
'There it is,' because the kingdom of God is in your midst."[b]

[22]Then he said to his disciples, "The time is coming when you will
long to see one of the days of the Son of Man, but you will not see it.
[23]People will tell you, 'There he is!' or 'Here he is!' Do not go running off
after them. [24]For the Son of Man in his day[c] will be like the lightning,
which flashes and lights up the sky from one end to the other. [25]But
first he must suffer many things and be rejected by this generation.

[26]"Just as it was in the days of Noah, so also will it be in the days of
the Son of Man. [27]People were eating, drinking, marrying and being
given in marriage up to the day Noah entered the ark. Then the flood
came and destroyed them all.

[28]"It was the same in the days of Lot. People were eating and drink-
ing, buying and selling, planting and building. [29]But the day Lot
left Sodom, fire and sulfur rained down from heaven and destroyed
them all.

[30]"It will be just like this on the day the Son of Man is revealed.
[31]On that day no one who is on the housetop, with possessions inside,
should go down to get them. Likewise, no one in the field should go
back for anything. [32]Remember Lot's wife! [33]Whoever tries to keep
their life will lose it, and whoever loses their life will preserve it. [34]I
tell you, on that night two people will be in one bed; one will be taken
and the other left. [35]Two women will be grinding grain together; one
will be taken and the other left." [36][d]

[37]"Where, Lord?" they asked.

He replied, "Where there is a dead body, there the vultures will gather."

---

[a] *12* The Greek word traditionally translated *leprosy* was used for various diseases affecting the skin. [b] *21* Or *is within you* [c] *24* Some manuscripts do not have *in his day.* [d] *36* Some manuscripts include here words similar to Matt. 24:40.

PRAYING SCRIPTURE

Luke 18

Do you keep praying until God provides an answer? This widow was determined to get the legal justice she deserved concerning someone who had wronged her. The judge, who really did not care about her, did not want to spend all his time dealing with her, so he granted her the relief she wanted.

In Jesus' teaching, this is how we should pray. Are you persistent in prayer?

THE PARABLE OF THE PERSISTENT WIDOW

18 Then Jesus told his disciples a parable to show them that they
should always pray and not give up. 2He said: "In a certain
town there was a judge who neither feared God nor cared what people
thought. 3And there was a widow in that town who kept coming to him
with the plea, 'Grant me justice against my adversary.'
4"For some time he refused. But finally he said to himself, 'Even
though I don't fear God or care what people think, 5yet because this
widow keeps bothering me, I will see that she gets justice, so that she
won't eventually come and attack me!'"
6And the Lord said, "Listen to what the unjust judge says. 7And will
not God bring about justice for his chosen ones, who cry out to him day
and night? Will he keep putting them off? 8I tell you, he will see that
they get justice, and quickly. However, when the Son of Man comes,
will he find faith on the earth?"

THE PARABLE OF THE PHARISEE AND THE TAX COLLECTOR

9To some who were confident of their own righteousness and looked
down on everyone else, Jesus told this parable: 10"Two men went up to
the temple to pray, one a Pharisee and the other a tax collector. 11The
Pharisee stood by himself and prayed: 'God, I thank you that I am not
like other people — robbers, evildoers, adulterers — or even like this
tax collector. 12I fast twice a week and give a tenth of all I get.'
13"But the tax collector stood at a distance. He would not even look
up to heaven, but beat his breast and said, 'God, have mercy on me, a
sinner.'
14"I tell you that this man, rather than the other, went home justified
before God. For all those who exalt themselves will be humbled, and
those who humble themselves will be exalted."

THE LITTLE CHILDREN AND JESUS

15People were also bringing babies to Jesus for him to place his
hands on them. When the disciples saw this, they rebuked them. 16But
Jesus called the children to him and said, "Let the little children come
to me, and do not hinder them, for the kingdom of God belongs to such
as these. 17Truly I tell you, anyone who will not receive the kingdom of
God like a little child will never enter it."

THE RICH AND THE KINGDOM OF GOD

18A certain ruler asked him, "Good teacher, what must I do to inherit
eternal life?"
19"Why do you call me good?" Jesus answered. "No one is good — ex-
cept God alone. 20You know the commandments: 'You shall not com-
mit adultery, you shall not murder, you shall not steal, you shall not
give false testimony, honor your father and mother.'[a]"
21"All these I have kept since I was a boy," he said.
22When Jesus heard this, he said to him, "You still lack one thing. Sell
everything you have and give to the poor, and you will have treasure
in heaven. Then come, follow me."
23When he heard this, he became very sad, because he was very
wealthy. 24Jesus looked at him and said, "How hard it is for the rich
to enter the kingdom of God! 25Indeed, it is easier for a camel to go

[a] *20* Exodus 20:12-16; Deut. 5:16-20

through the eye of a needle than for someone who is rich to enter the
kingdom of God."
26Those who heard this asked, "Who then can be saved?"
27Jesus replied, "What is impossible with man is possible with God."
28Peter said to him, "We have left all we had to follow you!"
29"Truly I tell you," Jesus said to them, "no one who has left home
or wife or brothers or sisters or parents or children for the sake of the
kingdom of God 30will fail to receive many times as much in this age,
and in the age to come eternal life."

JESUS PREDICTS HIS DEATH A THIRD TIME

31Jesus took the Twelve aside and told them, "We are going up to
Jerusalem, and everything that is written by the prophets about the
Son of Man will be fulfilled. 32He will be delivered over to the Gentiles.
They will mock him, insult him and spit on him; 33they will flog him
and kill him. On the third day he will rise again."
34The disciples did not understand any of this. Its meaning was hid-
den from them, and they did not know what he was talking about.

A BLIND BEGGAR RECEIVES HIS SIGHT

35As Jesus approached Jericho, a blind man was sitting by the road-
side begging. 36When he heard the crowd going by, he asked what was
happening. 37They told him, "Jesus of Nazareth is passing by."
38He called out, "Jesus, Son of David, have mercy on me!"
39Those who led the way rebuked him and told him to be quiet, but
he shouted all the more, "Son of David, have mercy on me!"
40Jesus stopped and ordered the man to be brought to him. When he
came near, Jesus asked him, 41"What do you want me to do for you?"
"Lord, I want to see," he replied.
42Jesus said to him, "Receive your sight; your faith has healed you."
43Immediately he received his sight and followed Jesus, praising God.
When all the people saw it, they also praised God.

ZACCHAEUS THE TAX COLLECTOR

19 Jesus entered Jericho and was passing through. 2A man was
there by the name of Zacchaeus; he was a chief tax collector and
was wealthy. 3He wanted to see who Jesus was, but because he was
short he could not see over the crowd. 4So he ran ahead and climbed a
sycamore-fig tree to see him, since Jesus was coming that way.
5When Jesus reached the spot, he looked up and said to him, "Zac-
chaeus, come down immediately. I must stay at your house today." 6So
he came down at once and welcomed him gladly.
7All the people saw this and began to mutter, "He has gone to be the
guest of a sinner."
8But Zacchaeus stood up and said to the Lord, "Look, Lord! Here and
now I give half of my possessions to the poor, and if I have cheated
anybody out of anything, I will pay back four times the amount."
9Jesus said to him, "Today salvation has come to this house, because
this man, too, is a son of Abraham. 10For the Son of Man came to seek
and to save the lost."

THE PARABLE OF THE TEN MINAS

11While they were listening to this, he went on to tell them a parable,
because he was near Jerusalem and the people thought that the king-
dom of God was going to appear at once. 12He said: "A man of noble

PRAYING SCRIPTURE

Luke 19

Many Christians will remember singing a kid's song about Zacchaeus, a tax collector in Jericho who desired to see Jesus. Because the song focused more on Zacchaeus's short stature, we often missed the primary point: He repented after meeting Jesus (see verse 8).

Repentance as part of the gospel message is missed still in our day. If you are living with a "hope so" faith, turn from your sins and ask God to save you.

birth went to a distant country to have himself appointed king and then to return. 13So he called ten of his servants and gave them ten minas.[a] 'Put this money to work,' he said, 'until I come back.'

14"But his subjects hated him and sent a delegation after him to say, 'We don't want this man to be our king.'

15"He was made king, however, and returned home. Then he sent for the servants to whom he had given the money, in order to find out what they had gained with it.

16"The first one came and said, 'Sir, your mina has earned ten more.'

17" 'Well done, my good servant!' his master replied. 'Because you have been trustworthy in a very small matter, take charge of ten cities.'

18"The second came and said, 'Sir, your mina has earned five more.'

19"His master answered, 'You take charge of five cities.'

20"Then another servant came and said, 'Sir, here is your mina; I have kept it laid away in a piece of cloth. 21I was afraid of you, because you are a hard man. You take out what you did not put in and reap what you did not sow.'

22"His master replied, 'I will judge you by your own words, you wicked servant! You knew, did you, that I am a hard man, taking out what I did not put in, and reaping what I did not sow? 23Why then didn't you put my money on deposit, so that when I came back, I could have collected it with interest?'

24"Then he said to those standing by, 'Take his mina away from him and give it to the one who has ten minas.'

25" 'Sir,' they said, 'he already has ten!'

26"He replied, 'I tell you that to everyone who has, more will be given, but as for the one who has nothing, even what they have will be taken away. 27But those enemies of mine who did not want me to be king over them — bring them here and kill them in front of me.' "

JESUS COMES TO JERUSALEM AS KING

28After Jesus had said this, he went on ahead, going up to Jerusalem. 29As he approached Bethphage and Bethany at the hill called the Mount of Olives, he sent two of his disciples, saying to them, 30"Go to the village ahead of you, and as you enter it, you will find a colt tied there, which no one has ever ridden. Untie it and bring it here. 31If anyone asks you, 'Why are you untying it?' say, 'The Lord needs it.' "

32Those who were sent ahead went and found it just as he had told them. 33As they were untying the colt, its owners asked them, "Why are you untying the colt?"

34They replied, "The Lord needs it."

35They brought it to Jesus, threw their cloaks on the colt and put Jesus on it. 36As he went along, people spread their cloaks on the road.

37When he came near the place where the road goes down the Mount of Olives, the whole crowd of disciples began joyfully to praise God in loud voices for all the miracles they had seen:

38"Blessed is the king who comes in the name of the Lord!"[b]

"Peace in heaven and glory in the highest!"

39Some of the Pharisees in the crowd said to Jesus, "Teacher, rebuke your disciples!"

40"I tell you," he replied, "if they keep quiet, the stones will cry out."

---

[a] *13* A mina was about three months' wages. [b] *38* Psalm 118:26

41 As he approached Jerusalem and saw the city, he wept over it 42 and said, "If you, even you, had only known on this day what would bring you peace — but now it is hidden from your eyes. 43 The days will come upon you when your enemies will build an embankment against you and encircle you and hem you in on every side. 44 They will dash you to the ground, you and the children within your walls. They will not leave one stone on another, because you did not recognize the time of God's coming to you."

JESUS AT THE TEMPLE

45 When Jesus entered the temple courts, he began to drive out those who were selling. 46 "It is written," he said to them, "'My house will be a house of prayer'[a]; but you have made it 'a den of robbers.'[b]"

47 Every day he was teaching at the temple. But the chief priests, the teachers of the law and the leaders among the people were trying to kill him. 48 Yet they could not find any way to do it, because all the people hung on his words.

THE AUTHORITY OF JESUS QUESTIONED

20 One day as Jesus was teaching the people in the temple courts and proclaiming the good news, the chief priests and the teachers of the law, together with the elders, came up to him. 2 "Tell us by what authority you are doing these things," they said. "Who gave you this authority?"

3 He replied, "I will also ask you a question. Tell me: 4 John's baptism — was it from heaven, or of human origin?"

5 They discussed it among themselves and said, "If we say, 'From heaven,' he will ask, 'Why didn't you believe him?' 6 But if we say, 'Of human origin,' all the people will stone us, because they are persuaded that John was a prophet."

7 So they answered, "We don't know where it was from."

8 Jesus said, "Neither will I tell you by what authority I am doing these things."

THE PARABLE OF THE TENANTS

9 He went on to tell the people this parable: "A man planted a vineyard, rented it to some farmers and went away for a long time. 10 At harvest time he sent a servant to the tenants so they would give him some of the fruit of the vineyard. But the tenants beat him and sent him away empty-handed. 11 He sent another servant, but that one also they beat and treated shamefully and sent away empty-handed. 12 He sent still a third, and they wounded him and threw him out.

13 "Then the owner of the vineyard said, 'What shall I do? I will send my son, whom I love; perhaps they will respect him.'

14 "But when the tenants saw him, they talked the matter over. 'This is the heir,' they said. 'Let's kill him, and the inheritance will be ours.' 15 So they threw him out of the vineyard and killed him.

"What then will the owner of the vineyard do to them? 16 He will come and kill those tenants and give the vineyard to others."

When the people heard this, they said, "God forbid!"

17 Jesus looked directly at them and asked, "Then what is the meaning of that which is written:

PRAYING SCRIPTURE

Luke 20

People in the twenty-first century aren't the only ones who have had to deal with taxes. Taxation was the basis of a political situation turned theological question for Jesus: Should the Jews pay taxes to the Romans? Jesus' wisdom exceeded their expectations: Give to Caesar what belongs to Caesar and to God what belongs to God.

Ask God to give you a clear understanding of the requirements of earthly and heavenly citizenship.

[a] 46 Isaiah 56:7 [b] 46 Jer. 7:11

"'The stone the builders rejected
has become the cornerstone'[a]?

18Everyone who falls on that stone will be broken to pieces; anyone on
whom it falls will be crushed."

19The teachers of the law and the chief priests looked for a way to ar-
rest him immediately, because they knew he had spoken this parable
against them. But they were afraid of the people.

PAYING TAXES TO CAESAR

20Keeping a close watch on him, they sent spies, who pretended to
be sincere. They hoped to catch Jesus in something he said, so that
they might hand him over to the power and authority of the governor.
21So the spies questioned him: "Teacher, we know that you speak and
teach what is right, and that you do not show partiality but teach the
way of God in accordance with the truth. 22Is it right for us to pay taxes
to Caesar or not?"

23He saw through their duplicity and said to them, 24"Show me a de-
narius. Whose image and inscription are on it?"

"Caesar's," they replied.

25He said to them, "Then give back to Caesar what is Caesar's, and to
God what is God's."

26They were unable to trap him in what he had said there in public.
And astonished by his answer, they became silent.

THE RESURRECTION AND MARRIAGE

27Some of the Sadducees, who say there is no resurrection, came to
Jesus with a question. 28"Teacher," they said, "Moses wrote for us that
if a man's brother dies and leaves a wife but no children, the man must
marry the widow and raise up offspring for his brother. 29Now there
were seven brothers. The first one married a woman and died child-
less. 30The second 31and then the third married her, and in the same
way the seven died, leaving no children. 32Finally, the woman died too.
33Now then, at the resurrection whose wife will she be, since the seven
were married to her?"

34Jesus replied, "The people of this age marry and are given in mar-
riage. 35But those who are considered worthy of taking part in the age
to come and in the resurrection from the dead will neither marry nor
be given in marriage, 36and they can no longer die; for they are like the
angels. They are God's children, since they are children of the resurrec-
tion. 37But in the account of the burning bush, even Moses showed that
the dead rise, for he calls the Lord 'the God of Abraham, and the God of
Isaac, and the God of Jacob.'[b] 38He is not the God of the dead, but of the
living, for to him all are alive."

39Some of the teachers of the law responded, "Well said, teacher!"
40And no one dared to ask him any more questions.

WHOSE SON IS THE MESSIAH?

41Then Jesus said to them, "Why is it said that the Messiah is the son
of David? 42David himself declares in the Book of Psalms:

"'The Lord said to my Lord:
"Sit at my right hand

---

[a] 17 Psalm 118:22 [b] 37 Exodus 3:6

43until I make your enemies
a footstool for your feet."'[a]
44David calls him 'Lord.' How then can he be his son?"

WARNING AGAINST THE TEACHERS OF THE LAW

45While all the people were listening, Jesus said to his disciples,
46"Beware of the teachers of the law. They like to walk around in flow-
ing robes and love to be greeted with respect in the marketplaces and
have the most important seats in the synagogues and the places of
honor at banquets. 47They devour widows' houses and for a show make
lengthy prayers. These men will be punished most severely."

THE WIDOW'S OFFERING

21 As Jesus looked up, he saw the rich putting their gifts into the
temple treasury. 2He also saw a poor widow put in two very
small copper coins. 3"Truly I tell you," he said, "this poor widow has
put in more than all the others. 4All these people gave their gifts out
of their wealth; but she out of her poverty put in all she had to live on."

THE DESTRUCTION OF THE TEMPLE AND SIGNS OF THE END TIMES

5Some of his disciples were remarking about how the temple was
adorned with beautiful stones and with gifts dedicated to God. But
Jesus said, 6"As for what you see here, the time will come when not one
stone will be left on another; every one of them will be thrown down."
7"Teacher," they asked, "when will these things happen? And what
will be the sign that they are about to take place?"
8He replied: "Watch out that you are not deceived. For many will
come in my name, claiming, 'I am he,' and, 'The time is near.' Do not
follow them. 9When you hear of wars and uprisings, do not be fright-
ened. These things must happen first, but the end will not come right
away."
10Then he said to them: "Nation will rise against nation, and king-
dom against kingdom. 11There will be great earthquakes, famines and
pestilences in various places, and fearful events and great signs from
heaven.
12"But before all this, they will seize you and persecute you. They will
hand you over to synagogues and put you in prison, and you will be
brought before kings and governors, and all on account of my name.
13And so you will bear testimony to me. 14But make up your mind not
to worry beforehand how you will defend yourselves. 15For I will give
you words and wisdom that none of your adversaries will be able to re-
sist or contradict. 16You will be betrayed even by parents, brothers and
sisters, relatives and friends, and they will put some of you to death.
17Everyone will hate you because of me. 18But not a hair of your head
will perish. 19Stand firm, and you will win life.
20"When you see Jerusalem being surrounded by armies, you will
know that its desolation is near. 21Then let those who are in Judea flee
to the mountains, let those in the city get out, and let those in the coun-
try not enter the city. 22For this is the time of punishment in fulfillment
of all that has been written. 23How dreadful it will be in those days for

[a] 43 Psalm 110:1

PRAYING SCRIPTURE

Luke 21

Ever since the widow dropped her two coins into the temple treasury, we have been reminded that Jesus is watching how we give. How we give is not merely an expression of our financial standing; it's an expression of our hearts. How much do we hold on to possessions?

In Jesus' estimation, the widow gave more than all the wealthy contributors. Regardless of how much you have, ask God to grow in you a generous heart.

pregnant women and nursing mothers! There will be great distress in the land and wrath against this people. 24They will fall by the sword and will be taken as prisoners to all the nations. Jerusalem will be trampled on by the Gentiles until the times of the Gentiles are fulfilled.

25"There will be signs in the sun, moon and stars. On the earth, nations will be in anguish and perplexity at the roaring and tossing of the sea. 26People will faint from terror, apprehensive of what is coming on the world, for the heavenly bodies will be shaken. 27At that time they will see the Son of Man coming in a cloud with power and great glory. 28When these things begin to take place, stand up and lift up your heads, because your redemption is drawing near."

29He told them this parable: "Look at the fig tree and all the trees. 30When they sprout leaves, you can see for yourselves and know that summer is near. 31Even so, when you see these things happening, you know that the kingdom of God is near.

32"Truly I tell you, this generation will certainly not pass away until all these things have happened. 33Heaven and earth will pass away, but my words will never pass away.

34"Be careful, or your hearts will be weighed down with carousing, drunkenness and the anxieties of life, and that day will close on you suddenly like a trap. 35For it will come on all those who live on the face of the whole earth. 36Be always on the watch, and pray that you may be able to escape all that is about to happen, and that you may be able to stand before the Son of Man."

37Each day Jesus was teaching at the temple, and each evening he went out to spend the night on the hill called the Mount of Olives, 38and all the people came early in the morning to hear him at the temple.

JUDAS AGREES TO BETRAY JESUS

22 Now the Festival of Unleavened Bread, called the Passover, was approaching, 2and the chief priests and the teachers of the law were looking for some way to get rid of Jesus, for they were afraid of the people. 3Then Satan entered Judas, called Iscariot, one of the Twelve. 4And Judas went to the chief priests and the officers of the temple guard and discussed with them how he might betray Jesus. 5They were delighted and agreed to give him money. 6He consented, and watched for an opportunity to hand Jesus over to them when no crowd was present.

THE LAST SUPPER

7Then came the day of Unleavened Bread on which the Passover lamb had to be sacrificed. 8Jesus sent Peter and John, saying, "Go and make preparations for us to eat the Passover."

9"Where do you want us to prepare for it?" they asked.

10He replied, "As you enter the city, a man carrying a jar of water will meet you. Follow him to the house that he enters, 11and say to the owner of the house, 'The Teacher asks: Where is the guest room, where I may eat the Passover with my disciples?' 12He will show you a large room upstairs, all furnished. Make preparations there."

13They left and found things just as Jesus had told them. So they prepared the Passover.

14When the hour came, Jesus and his apostles reclined at the table. 15And he said to them, "I have eagerly desired to eat this Passover with

PRAYING SCRIPTURE

Luke 22

After the religious leaders who had paid for Jesus' betrayal questioned and accused him, they asked him point-blank whether he was the Messiah. Jesus initially refused to answer because he knew they would not believe him. Eventually he told them directly.

Jesus' identity is not a secret, and he calls on people to believe on him. Pray for those around you to recognize Jesus as the Savior.

you before I suffer. 16For I tell you, I will not eat it again until it finds fulfillment in the kingdom of God."

17After taking the cup, he gave thanks and said, "Take this and divide it among you. 18For I tell you I will not drink again from the fruit of the vine until the kingdom of God comes."

19And he took bread, gave thanks and broke it, and gave it to them, saying, "This is my body given for you; do this in remembrance of me."

20In the same way, after the supper he took the cup, saying, "This cup is the new covenant in my blood, which is poured out for you.[a] 21But the hand of him who is going to betray me is with mine on the table. 22The Son of Man will go as it has been decreed. But woe to that man who betrays him!" 23They began to question among themselves which of them it might be who would do this.

24A dispute also arose among them as to which of them was considered to be greatest. 25Jesus said to them, "The kings of the Gentiles lord it over them; and those who exercise authority over them call themselves Benefactors. 26But you are not to be like that. Instead, the greatest among you should be like the youngest, and the one who rules like the one who serves. 27For who is greater, the one who is at the table or the one who serves? Is it not the one who is at the table? But I am among you as one who serves. 28You are those who have stood by me in my trials. 29And I confer on you a kingdom, just as my Father conferred one on me, 30so that you may eat and drink at my table in my kingdom and sit on thrones, judging the twelve tribes of Israel.

31"Simon, Simon, Satan has asked to sift all of you as wheat. 32But I have prayed for you, Simon, that your faith may not fail. And when you have turned back, strengthen your brothers."

33But he replied, "Lord, I am ready to go with you to prison and to death."

34Jesus answered, "I tell you, Peter, before the rooster crows today, you will deny three times that you know me."

35Then Jesus asked them, "When I sent you without purse, bag or sandals, did you lack anything?"

"Nothing," they answered.

36He said to them, "But now if you have a purse, take it, and also a bag; and if you don't have a sword, sell your cloak and buy one. 37It is written: 'And he was numbered with the transgressors'[b]; and I tell you that this must be fulfilled in me. Yes, what is written about me is reaching its fulfillment."

38The disciples said, "See, Lord, here are two swords."

"That's enough!" he replied.

JESUS PRAYS ON THE MOUNT OF OLIVES

39Jesus went out as usual to the Mount of Olives, and his disciples followed him. 40On reaching the place, he said to them, "Pray that you will not fall into temptation." 41He withdrew about a stone's throw beyond them, knelt down and prayed, 42"Father, if you are willing, take this cup from me; yet not my will, but yours be done." 43An angel from heaven appeared to him and strengthened him. 44And being in anguish, he prayed more earnestly, and his sweat was like drops of blood falling to the ground.[c]

---

[a] *19,20* Some manuscripts do not have *given for you . . . poured out for you.*
[b] *37* Isaiah 53:12 [c] *43,44* Many early manuscripts do not have verses 43 and 44.

45 When he rose from prayer and went back to the disciples, he found them asleep, exhausted from sorrow. 46 "Why are you sleeping?" he asked them. "Get up and pray so that you will not fall into temptation."

JESUS ARRESTED

47 While he was still speaking a crowd came up, and the man who was called Judas, one of the Twelve, was leading them. He approached Jesus to kiss him, 48 but Jesus asked him, "Judas, are you betraying the Son of Man with a kiss?"

49 When Jesus' followers saw what was going to happen, they said, "Lord, should we strike with our swords?" 50 And one of them struck the servant of the high priest, cutting off his right ear.

51 But Jesus answered, "No more of this!" And he touched the man's ear and healed him.

52 Then Jesus said to the chief priests, the officers of the temple guard, and the elders, who had come for him, "Am I leading a rebellion, that you have come with swords and clubs? 53 Every day I was with you in the temple courts, and you did not lay a hand on me. But this is your hour — when darkness reigns."

PETER DISOWNS JESUS

54 Then seizing him, they led him away and took him into the house of the high priest. Peter followed at a distance. 55 And when some there had kindled a fire in the middle of the courtyard and had sat down together, Peter sat down with them. 56 A servant girl saw him seated there in the firelight. She looked closely at him and said, "This man was with him."

57 But he denied it. "Woman, I don't know him," he said.

58 A little later someone else saw him and said, "You also are one of them."

"Man, I am not!" Peter replied.

59 About an hour later another asserted, "Certainly this fellow was with him, for he is a Galilean."

60 Peter replied, "Man, I don't know what you're talking about!" Just as he was speaking, the rooster crowed. 61 The Lord turned and looked straight at Peter. Then Peter remembered the word the Lord had spoken to him: "Before the rooster crows today, you will disown me three times." 62 And he went outside and wept bitterly.

THE GUARDS MOCK JESUS

63 The men who were guarding Jesus began mocking and beating him. 64 They blindfolded him and demanded, "Prophesy! Who hit you?" 65 And they said many other insulting things to him.

JESUS BEFORE PILATE AND HEROD

66 At daybreak the council of the elders of the people, both the chief priests and the teachers of the law, met together, and Jesus was led before them. 67 "If you are the Messiah," they said, "tell us."

Jesus answered, "If I tell you, you will not believe me, 68 and if I asked you, you would not answer. 69 But from now on, the Son of Man will be seated at the right hand of the mighty God."

70 They all asked, "Are you then the Son of God?"

He replied, "You say that I am."

71Then they said, "Why do we need any more testimony? We have
heard it from his own lips."

23 Then the whole assembly rose and led him off to Pilate. 2And
they began to accuse him, saying, "We have found this man
subverting our nation. He opposes payment of taxes to Caesar and
claims to be Messiah, a king."
3So Pilate asked Jesus, "Are you the king of the Jews?"
"You have said so," Jesus replied.
4Then Pilate announced to the chief priests and the crowd, "I find no
basis for a charge against this man."
5But they insisted, "He stirs up the people all over Judea by his teach-
ing. He started in Galilee and has come all the way here."
6On hearing this, Pilate asked if the man was a Galilean. 7When
he learned that Jesus was under Herod's jurisdiction, he sent him to
Herod, who was also in Jerusalem at that time.
8When Herod saw Jesus, he was greatly pleased, because for a long
time he had been wanting to see him. From what he had heard about
him, he hoped to see him perform a sign of some sort. 9He plied him
with many questions, but Jesus gave him no answer. 10The chief priests
and the teachers of the law were standing there, vehemently accusing
him. 11Then Herod and his soldiers ridiculed and mocked him. Dress-
ing him in an elegant robe, they sent him back to Pilate. 12That day
Herod and Pilate became friends — before this they had been enemies.
13Pilate called together the chief priests, the rulers and the people,
14and said to them, "You brought me this man as one who was inciting
the people to rebellion. I have examined him in your presence and
have found no basis for your charges against him. 15Neither has Herod,
for he sent him back to us; as you can see, he has done nothing to de-
serve death. 16Therefore, I will punish him and then release him." [17][a]
18But the whole crowd shouted, "Away with this man! Release Barab-
bas to us!" 19(Barabbas had been thrown into prison for an insurrection
in the city, and for murder.)
20Wanting to release Jesus, Pilate appealed to them again. 21But they
kept shouting, "Crucify him! Crucify him!"
22For the third time he spoke to them: "Why? What crime has this
man committed? I have found in him no grounds for the death pen-
alty. Therefore I will have him punished and then release him."
23But with loud shouts they insistently demanded that he be cru-
cified, and their shouts prevailed. 24So Pilate decided to grant their
demand. 25He released the man who had been thrown into prison for
insurrection and murder, the one they asked for, and surrendered
Jesus to their will.

THE CRUCIFIXION OF JESUS

26As the soldiers led him away, they seized Simon from Cyrene, who
was on his way in from the country, and put the cross on him and made
him carry it behind Jesus. 27A large number of people followed him, in-
cluding women who mourned and wailed for him. 28Jesus turned and
said to them, "Daughters of Jerusalem, do not weep for me; weep for
yourselves and for your children. 29For the time will come when you
will say, 'Blessed are the childless women, the wombs that never bore
and the breasts that never nursed!' 30Then

[a] 17 Some manuscripts include here words similar to Matt. 27:15 and Mark 15:6.

PRAYING SCRIPTURE

Luke 23

The "trial" of Jesus was a kangaroo court to convict the perfect One who had never sinned, much less committed a crime worthy of death. Yet it was, in God's sovereignty, how the Lamb would be slain for the sins of the world.

Think about what Jesus suffered in sacrificing himself so people can be reconciled to God. Thank him for his great love and total obedience to the Father.

> "'they will say to the mountains, "Fall on us!"
> and to the hills, "Cover us!"'[a]

31For if people do these things when the tree is green, what will happen when it is dry?"

32Two other men, both criminals, were also led out with him to be executed. 33When they came to the place called the Skull, they crucified him there, along with the criminals — one on his right, the other on his left. 34Jesus said, "Father, forgive them, for they do not know what they are doing."[b] And they divided up his clothes by casting lots.

35The people stood watching, and the rulers even sneered at him. They said, "He saved others; let him save himself if he is God's Messiah, the Chosen One."

36The soldiers also came up and mocked him. They offered him wine vinegar 37and said, "If you are the king of the Jews, save yourself."

38There was a written notice above him, which read: THIS IS THE KING OF THE JEWS.

39One of the criminals who hung there hurled insults at him: "Aren't you the Messiah? Save yourself and us!"

40But the other criminal rebuked him. "Don't you fear God," he said, "since you are under the same sentence? 41We are punished justly, for we are getting what our deeds deserve. But this man has done nothing wrong."

42Then he said, "Jesus, remember me when you come into your kingdom.[c]"

43Jesus answered him, "Truly I tell you, today you will be with me in paradise."

THE DEATH OF JESUS

44It was now about noon, and darkness came over the whole land until three in the afternoon, 45for the sun stopped shining. And the curtain of the temple was torn in two. 46Jesus called out with a loud voice, "Father, into your hands I commit my spirit."[d] When he had said this, he breathed his last.

47The centurion, seeing what had happened, praised God and said, "Surely this was a righteous man." 48When all the people who had gathered to witness this sight saw what took place, they beat their breasts and went away. 49But all those who knew him, including the women who had followed him from Galilee, stood at a distance, watching these things.

THE BURIAL OF JESUS

50Now there was a man named Joseph, a member of the Council, a good and upright man, 51who had not consented to their decision and action. He came from the Judean town of Arimathea, and he himself was waiting for the kingdom of God. 52Going to Pilate, he asked for Jesus' body. 53Then he took it down, wrapped it in linen cloth and placed it in a tomb cut in the rock, one in which no one had yet been laid. 54It was Preparation Day, and the Sabbath was about to begin.

55The women who had come with Jesus from Galilee followed Joseph and saw the tomb and how his body was laid in it. 56Then they went home and prepared spices and perfumes. But they rested on the Sabbath in obedience to the commandment.

---

[a] *30* Hosea 10:8 [b] *34* Some early manuscripts do not have this sentence.
[c] *42* Some manuscripts *come with your kingly power* [d] *46* Psalm 31:5

JESUS HAS RISEN

24 On the first day of the week, very early in the morning, the
women took the spices they had prepared and went to the
tomb. 2They found the stone rolled away from the tomb, 3but when
they entered, they did not find the body of the Lord Jesus. 4While they
were wondering about this, suddenly two men in clothes that gleamed
like lightning stood beside them. 5In their fright the women bowed
down with their faces to the ground, but the men said to them, "Why
do you look for the living among the dead? 6He is not here; he has
risen! Remember how he told you, while he was still with you in Gali-
lee: 7'The Son of Man must be delivered over to the hands of sinners,
be crucified and on the third day be raised again.' " 8Then they remem-
bered his words.

9When they came back from the tomb, they told all these things
to the Eleven and to all the others. 10It was Mary Magdalene, Joanna,
Mary the mother of James, and the others with them who told this to
the apostles. 11But they did not believe the women, because their words
seemed to them like nonsense. 12Peter, however, got up and ran to the
tomb. Bending over, he saw the strips of linen lying by themselves, and
he went away, wondering to himself what had happened.

ON THE ROAD TO EMMAUS

13Now that same day two of them were going to a village called Em-
maus, about seven miles[a] from Jerusalem. 14They were talking with
each other about everything that had happened. 15As they talked and
discussed these things with each other, Jesus himself came up and
walked along with them; 16but they were kept from recognizing him.

17He asked them, "What are you discussing together as you walk
along?"

They stood still, their faces downcast. 18One of them, named Cleo-
pas, asked him, "Are you the only one visiting Jerusalem who does not
know the things that have happened there in these days?"

19"What things?" he asked.

"About Jesus of Nazareth," they replied. "He was a prophet, powerful
in word and deed before God and all the people. 20The chief priests and
our rulers handed him over to be sentenced to death, and they cruci-
fied him; 21but we had hoped that he was the one who was going to
redeem Israel. And what is more, it is the third day since all this took
place. 22In addition, some of our women amazed us. They went to the
tomb early this morning 23but didn't find his body. They came and told
us that they had seen a vision of angels, who said he was alive. 24Then
some of our companions went to the tomb and found it just as the
women had said, but they did not see Jesus."

25He said to them, "How foolish you are, and how slow to believe all
that the prophets have spoken! 26Did not the Messiah have to suffer
these things and then enter his glory?" 27And beginning with Moses
and all the Prophets, he explained to them what was said in all the
Scriptures concerning himself.

28As they approached the village to which they were going, Jesus
continued on as if he were going farther. 29But they urged him
strongly, "Stay with us, for it is nearly evening; the day is almost over."
So he went in to stay with them.

---

[a] *13* Or about 11 kilometers

PRAYING SCRIPTURE

Luke 24

After revealing himself to two disciples walking to the town of Emmaus and then to the eleven disciples on the shore of Galilee, Jesus reminded them that he was the fulfillment of the Law and the Prophets.

Jesus did not leave his disciples in the dark. He confirmed who he was again and again. Jesus told us who he is. Pray in faith based on who he is.

30When he was at the table with them, he took bread, gave thanks,
broke it and began to give it to them. 31Then their eyes were opened
and they recognized him, and he disappeared from their sight. 32They
asked each other, "Were not our hearts burning within us while he
talked with us on the road and opened the Scriptures to us?"

33They got up and returned at once to Jerusalem. There they found
the Eleven and those with them, assembled together 34and saying, "It
is true! The Lord has risen and has appeared to Simon." 35Then the two
told what had happened on the way, and how Jesus was recognized by
them when he broke the bread.

JESUS APPEARS TO THE DISCIPLES

36While they were still talking about this, Jesus himself stood among
them and said to them, "Peace be with you."

37They were startled and frightened, thinking they saw a ghost. 38He
said to them, "Why are you troubled, and why do doubts rise in your
minds? 39Look at my hands and my feet. It is I myself! Touch me and
see; a ghost does not have flesh and bones, as you see I have."

40When he had said this, he showed them his hands and feet. 41And
while they still did not believe it because of joy and amazement, he
asked them, "Do you have anything here to eat?" 42They gave him a
piece of broiled fish, 43and he took it and ate it in their presence.

44He said to them, "This is what I told you while I was still with you:
Everything must be fulfilled that is written about me in the Law of
Moses, the Prophets and the Psalms."

45Then he opened their minds so they could understand the Scrip-
tures. 46He told them, "This is what is written: The Messiah will suffer
and rise from the dead on the third day, 47and repentance for the for-
giveness of sins will be preached in his name to all nations, beginning
at Jerusalem. 48You are witnesses of these things. 49I am going to send
you what my Father has promised; but stay in the city until you have
been clothed with power from on high."

THE ASCENSION OF JESUS

50When he had led them out to the vicinity of Bethany, he lifted
up his hands and blessed them. 51While he was blessing them, he left
them and was taken up into heaven. 52Then they worshiped him and
returned to Jerusalem with great joy. 53And they stayed continually at
the temple, praising God.

JOHN

The Gospel of John is unique among the four Gospels, not because it tells a different story than the others, but because he organized his content by theme more than chronology. John's aim was to show Jesus as the Son of God so people would "believe that Jesus is the Messiah, the Son of God, and that by believing you may have life in his name" (20:30–31).

John used a particular literary device to accomplish his purpose, focusing on seven miracles and seven "I AM" declarations of Jesus. The latter directly connect Jesus to the God who revealed himself as "I AM WHO I AM" to Moses in Exodus 3. The seven miracles, sometimes called "the seven signs," which are changing water into wine (see 2:1–11); healing an official's son (see 4:46–54); healing the paralyzed man by the pool of Bethesda (see 5:1–15); feeding the five thousand (see 6:1–14); walking on water (see 6:15–21); healing a man born blind (see 9:1–12); and raising Lazarus from the dead (see 11:1–44), reveal the power and the authority of Jesus.

The seven I AMs of Jesus are: "I am the bread of life" (6:35); "I am the light of the world" (8:12); "I am the gate" (10:9); "I am the good shepherd" (10:11); "I am the resurrection and the life" (11:25); "I am the way and the truth and the life" (14:6); and "I am the true vine" (15:1). Jesus made no secret of his claim to be one with the Father.

John's Gospel features the longest prayer of Jesus recorded in Scripture, the "high priestly prayer," in chapter 17. In it Jesus prayed for his followers because they were about to face difficulty during the three days between his death and resurrection. He prayed that the Father would keep them through that hour of trial so that they might have unity together as the Son has unity with the Father.

But Jesus did not only pray for the disciples' unity then. He also prayed to protect the unity of everyone who would come to believe in him through their message. That includes you and me. Jesus' prayer shows his enduring love for all his disciples and his concern for the continuing bond of brotherhood through their faith

Jesus also recounted his relationship with the Father. He referenced the glory he shared with his Father before the foundation of the world, praying it would soon be restored to him. Through the entire prayer, he showed his love for his Father and prayed that he would be glorified as he had glorified his Father.

Our prayers can be marked with the same intimacy with the Father that Jesus expressed. When we trust in Christ, we are adopted into God's family. Other believers are our brothers and sisters. God is our Father, and we are his children. Jesus' emphasis on God as our Father opens wide a door merely cracked in the Old Testament.

We also pray for the advancement of the mission of God through the church since Jesus has sent us in the same way the Father sent him (see 20:21). God created the world that he might glorify himself. As more people come to know Jesus, he receives the glory he is due. Therefore, we ought to pray that the church would bring glory to the Father by living in unity and working to spread the gospel at home and abroad.

PRAYING SCRIPTURE

John 1

The introduction of Jesus as "the Word" includes a range of theological truths. He is eternal. He has been with God always. He is God. He manifests the glory of God. He is filled with grace and truth. In short, John used the word *logos* to present Jesus as God's ultimate communication to the world: The Word became flesh.

Praise God for communicating himself to us in Jesus Christ, the eternal Word made human.

THE WORD BECAME FLESH

1 In the beginning was the Word, and the Word was with God, and the
Word was God. 2He was with God in the beginning. 3Through him
all things were made; without him nothing was made that has been
made. 4In him was life, and that life was the light of all mankind. 5The
light shines in the darkness, and the darkness has not overcome[a] it.

6There was a man sent from God whose name was John. 7He came
as a witness to testify concerning that light, so that through him all
might believe. 8He himself was not the light; he came only as a wit-
ness to the light.

9The true light that gives light to everyone was coming into the
world. 10He was in the world, and though the world was made through
him, the world did not recognize him. 11He came to that which was his
own, but his own did not receive him. 12Yet to all who did receive him,
to those who believed in his name, he gave the right to become chil-
dren of God— 13children born not of natural descent, nor of human
decision or a husband's will, but born of God.

14The Word became flesh and made his dwelling among us. We have
seen his glory, the glory of the one and only Son, who came from the
Father, full of grace and truth.

15(John testified concerning him. He cried out, saying, "This is the
one I spoke about when I said, 'He who comes after me has surpassed
me because he was before me.'") 16Out of his fullness we have all re-
ceived grace in place of grace already given. 17For the law was given
through Moses; grace and truth came through Jesus Christ. 18No one
has ever seen God, but the one and only Son, who is himself God and[b]
is in closest relationship with the Father, has made him known.

JOHN THE BAPTIST DENIES BEING THE MESSIAH

19Now this was John's testimony when the Jewish leaders[c] in Jerusa-
lem sent priests and Levites to ask him who he was. 20He did not fail to
confess, but confessed freely, "I am not the Messiah."

21They asked him, "Then who are you? Are you Elijah?"

He said, "I am not."

"Are you the Prophet?"

He answered, "No."

22Finally they said, "Who are you? Give us an answer to take back to
those who sent us. What do you say about yourself?"

23John replied in the words of Isaiah the prophet, "I am the voice of
one calling in the wilderness, 'Make straight the way for the Lord.'"[d]

24Now the Pharisees who had been sent 25questioned him, "Why
then do you baptize if you are not the Messiah, nor Elijah, nor the
Prophet?"

26"I baptize with[e] water," John replied, "but among you stands one
you do not know. 27He is the one who comes after me, the straps of
whose sandals I am not worthy to untie."

28This all happened at Bethany on the other side of the Jordan,
where John was baptizing.

---

[a] *5* Or *understood* [b] *18* Some manuscripts *but the only Son, who* [c] *19* The Greek term traditionally translated *the Jews* (*hoi Ioudaioi*) refers here and elsewhere in John's Gospel to those Jewish leaders who opposed Jesus; also in 5:10,15,16; 7:1,11,13; 9:22; 18:14,28,36; 19:7,12,31,38; 20:19. [d] *23* Isaiah 40:3 [e] *26* Or *in*; also in verses 31 and 33 (twice)

JOHN TESTIFIES ABOUT JESUS

29 The next day John saw Jesus coming toward him and said, "Look,
the Lamb of God, who takes away the sin of the world! 30 This is the one
I meant when I said, 'A man who comes after me has surpassed me be-
cause he was before me.' 31 I myself did not know him, but the reason
I came baptizing with water was that he might be revealed to Israel."

32 Then John gave this testimony: "I saw the Spirit come down from
heaven as a dove and remain on him. 33 And I myself did not know him,
but the one who sent me to baptize with water told me, 'The man on
whom you see the Spirit come down and remain is the one who will
baptize with the Holy Spirit.' 34 I have seen and I testify that this is God's
Chosen One."[a]

JOHN'S DISCIPLES FOLLOW JESUS

35 The next day John was there again with two of his disciples.
36 When he saw Jesus passing by, he said, "Look, the Lamb of God!"

37 When the two disciples heard him say this, they followed Jesus.
38 Turning around, Jesus saw them following and asked, "What do you
want?"

They said, "Rabbi" (which means "Teacher"), "where are you staying?"

39 "Come," he replied, "and you will see."

So they went and saw where he was staying, and they spent that day
with him. It was about four in the afternoon.

40 Andrew, Simon Peter's brother, was one of the two who heard what
John had said and who had followed Jesus. 41 The first thing Andrew
did was to find his brother Simon and tell him, "We have found the
Messiah" (that is, the Christ). 42 And he brought him to Jesus.

Jesus looked at him and said, "You are Simon son of John. You will
be called Cephas" (which, when translated, is Peter[b]).

JESUS CALLS PHILIP AND NATHANAEL

43 The next day Jesus decided to leave for Galilee. Finding Philip, he
said to him, "Follow me."

44 Philip, like Andrew and Peter, was from the town of Bethsaida.
45 Philip found Nathanael and told him, "We have found the one Moses
wrote about in the Law, and about whom the prophets also wrote—
Jesus of Nazareth, the son of Joseph."

46 "Nazareth! Can anything good come from there?" Nathanael asked.

"Come and see," said Philip.

47 When Jesus saw Nathanael approaching, he said of him, "Here
truly is an Israelite in whom there is no deceit."

48 "How do you know me?" Nathanael asked.

Jesus answered, "I saw you while you were still under the fig tree
before Philip called you."

49 Then Nathanael declared, "Rabbi, you are the Son of God; you are
the king of Israel."

50 Jesus said, "You believe[c] because I told you I saw you under the fig
tree. You will see greater things than that." 51 He then added, "Very truly
I tell you,[d] you[d] will see 'heaven open, and the angels of God ascending
and descending on'[e] the Son of Man."

[a] *34* See Isaiah 42:1; many manuscripts *is the Son of God.* [b] *42* *Cephas* (Aramaic) and *Peter* (Greek) both mean *rock.* [c] *50* Or *Do you believe . . . ?*
[d] *51* The Greek is plural. [e] *51* Gen. 28:12

PRAYING SCRIPTURE

John 2

Jesus' very first miracle involved blessing a wedding party by saving the host from the embarrassment of running out of wine. At his mother's behest, Jesus changed ordinary water into wine so extraordinary that the master of the feast declared it better than the previous wine that was served.

Jesus always does better than we expect. He is not offended when we ask for his blessings, so ask with big faith!

JESUS CHANGES WATER INTO WINE

2 On the third day a wedding took place at Cana in Galilee. Jesus'
mother was there, 2and Jesus and his disciples had also been in-
vited to the wedding. 3When the wine was gone, Jesus' mother said to
him, "They have no more wine."
4"Woman,[a] why do you involve me?" Jesus replied. "My hour has
not yet come."
5His mother said to the servants, "Do whatever he tells you."
6Nearby stood six stone water jars, the kind used by the Jews for cer-
emonial washing, each holding from twenty to thirty gallons.[b]
7Jesus said to the servants, "Fill the jars with water"; so they filled
them to the brim.
8Then he told them, "Now draw some out and take it to the master
of the banquet."
They did so, 9and the master of the banquet tasted the water that
had been turned into wine. He did not realize where it had come from,
though the servants who had drawn the water knew. Then he called
the bridegroom aside 10and said, "Everyone brings out the choice wine
first and then the cheaper wine after the guests have had too much to
drink; but you have saved the best till now."
11What Jesus did here in Cana of Galilee was the first of the signs
through which he revealed his glory; and his disciples believed in him.
12After this he went down to Capernaum with his mother and broth-
ers and his disciples. There they stayed for a few days.

JESUS CLEARS THE TEMPLE COURTS

13When it was almost time for the Jewish Passover, Jesus went up to
Jerusalem. 14In the temple courts he found people selling cattle, sheep
and doves, and others sitting at tables exchanging money. 15So he made
a whip out of cords, and drove all from the temple courts, both sheep
and cattle; he scattered the coins of the money changers and over-
turned their tables. 16To those who sold doves he said, "Get these out
of here! Stop turning my Father's house into a market!" 17His disciples
remembered that it is written: "Zeal for your house will consume me."[c]
18The Jews then responded to him, "What sign can you show us to
prove your authority to do all this?"
19Jesus answered them, "Destroy this temple, and I will raise it again
in three days."
20They replied, "It has taken forty-six years to build this temple, and
you are going to raise it in three days?" 21But the temple he had spo-
ken of was his body. 22After he was raised from the dead, his disciples
recalled what he had said. Then they believed the scripture and the
words that Jesus had spoken.
23Now while he was in Jerusalem at the Passover Festival, many people
saw the signs he was performing and believed in his name.[d] 24But Jesus
would not entrust himself to them, for he knew all people. 25He did not
need any testimony about mankind, for he knew what was in each person.

JESUS TEACHES NICODEMUS

3 Now there was a Pharisee, a man named Nicodemus who was a
member of the Jewish ruling council. 2He came to Jesus at night
and said, "Rabbi, we know that you are a teacher who has come from

PRAYING SCRIPTURE

John 3

What does it mean to be born again? Many people are interested in the answer to that question, just as the religious leader Nicodemus was. Jesus made plain that he did not mean a second physical birth, but a spiritual birth. It's not merely a second birth, but a second kind of birth. Human birth is good; heavenly birth is better.

Whoever believes in Jesus will receive everlasting life, so ask him for the new birth he promises.

---

[a] 4 The Greek for *Woman* does not denote any disrespect. [b] 6 Or from about 75 to about 115 liters [c] 17 Psalm 69:9 [d] 23 Or *in him*

God. For no one could perform the signs you are doing if God were
not with him."
3Jesus replied, "Very truly I tell you, no one can see the kingdom of
God unless they are born again.[a]"
4"How can someone be born when they are old?" Nicodemus asked.
"Surely they cannot enter a second time into their mother's womb to
be born!"
5Jesus answered, "Very truly I tell you, no one can enter the kingdom
of God unless they are born of water and the Spirit. 6Flesh gives birth to
flesh, but the Spirit[b] gives birth to spirit. 7You should not be surprised
at my saying, 'You[c] must be born again.' 8The wind blows wherever it
pleases. You hear its sound, but you cannot tell where it comes from or
where it is going. So it is with everyone born of the Spirit."[d]
9"How can this be?" Nicodemus asked.
10"You are Israel's teacher," said Jesus, "and do you not understand
these things? 11Very truly I tell you, we speak of what we know, and
we testify to what we have seen, but still you people do not accept our
testimony. 12I have spoken to you of earthly things and you do not be-
lieve; how then will you believe if I speak of heavenly things? 13No one
has ever gone into heaven except the one who came from heaven—
the Son of Man.[e] 14Just as Moses lifted up the snake in the wilderness,
so the Son of Man must be lifted up,[f] 15that everyone who believes may
have eternal life in him."[g]
16For God so loved the world that he gave his one and only Son, that
whoever believes in him shall not perish but have eternal life. 17For
God did not send his Son into the world to condemn the world, but
to save the world through him. 18Whoever believes in him is not con-
demned, but whoever does not believe stands condemned already
because they have not believed in the name of God's one and only
Son. 19This is the verdict: Light has come into the world, but people
loved darkness instead of light because their deeds were evil. 20Every-
one who does evil hates the light, and will not come into the light for
fear that their deeds will be exposed. 21But whoever lives by the truth
comes into the light, so that it may be seen plainly that what they have
done has been done in the sight of God.

JOHN TESTIFIES AGAIN ABOUT JESUS

22After this, Jesus and his disciples went out into the Judean coun-
tryside, where he spent some time with them, and baptized. 23Now
John also was baptizing at Aenon near Salim, because there was plenty
of water, and people were coming and being baptized. 24(This was be-
fore John was put in prison.) 25An argument developed between some
of John's disciples and a certain Jew over the matter of ceremonial
washing. 26They came to John and said to him, "Rabbi, that man who
was with you on the other side of the Jordan—the one you testified
about—look, he is baptizing, and everyone is going to him."
27To this John replied, "A person can receive only what is given them
from heaven. 28You yourselves can testify that I said, 'I am not the Mes-
siah but am sent ahead of him.' 29The bride belongs to the bridegroom.

[a] 3 The Greek for *again* also means *from above*; also in verse 7. [b] 6 Or *but spirit* [c] 7 The Greek is plural. [d] 8 The Greek for *Spirit* is the same as that for *wind*. [e] 13 Some manuscripts *Man, who is in heaven* [f] 14 The Greek for *lifted up* also means *exalted*. [g] 15 Some interpreters end the quotation with verse 21.

The friend who attends the bridegroom waits and listens for him, and is full of joy when he hears the bridegroom's voice. That joy is mine, and it is now complete. 30 He must become greater; I must become less."[a]

31 The one who comes from above is above all; the one who is from the earth belongs to the earth, and speaks as one from the earth. The one who comes from heaven is above all. 32 He testifies to what he has seen and heard, but no one accepts his testimony. 33 Whoever has accepted it has certified that God is truthful. 34 For the one whom God has sent speaks the words of God, for God[b] gives the Spirit without limit. 35 The Father loves the Son and has placed everything in his hands. 36 Whoever believes in the Son has eternal life, but whoever rejects the Son will not see life, for God's wrath remains on them.

PRAYING SCRIPTURE

John 4

To help his disciples grasp the desperate need for people who would share the gospel, Jesus used the image of harvest. The grain is ready; now is the time. "Open your eyes" (verse 35) means "pay attention." Jesus encouraged both sowing and reaping because both bring rejoicing.

The harvest is no less urgent today than in the days of Jesus. Ask the Father to make you a faithful harvester.

JESUS TALKS WITH A SAMARITAN WOMAN

4 Now Jesus learned that the Pharisees had heard that he was gaining and baptizing more disciples than John — 2 although in fact it was not Jesus who baptized, but his disciples. 3 So he left Judea and went back once more to Galilee.

4 Now he had to go through Samaria. 5 So he came to a town in Samaria called Sychar, near the plot of ground Jacob had given to his son Joseph. 6 Jacob's well was there, and Jesus, tired as he was from the journey, sat down by the well. It was about noon.

7 When a Samaritan woman came to draw water, Jesus said to her, "Will you give me a drink?" 8 (His disciples had gone into the town to buy food.)

9 The Samaritan woman said to him, "You are a Jew and I am a Samaritan woman. How can you ask me for a drink?" (For Jews do not associate with Samaritans.[c])

10 Jesus answered her, "If you knew the gift of God and who it is that asks you for a drink, you would have asked him and he would have given you living water."

11 "Sir," the woman said, "you have nothing to draw with and the well is deep. Where can you get this living water? 12 Are you greater than our father Jacob, who gave us the well and drank from it himself, as did also his sons and his livestock?"

13 Jesus answered, "Everyone who drinks this water will be thirsty again, 14 but whoever drinks the water I give them will never thirst. Indeed, the water I give them will become in them a spring of water welling up to eternal life."

15 The woman said to him, "Sir, give me this water so that I won't get thirsty and have to keep coming here to draw water."

16 He told her, "Go, call your husband and come back."

17 "I have no husband," she replied.

Jesus said to her, "You are right when you say you have no husband. 18 The fact is, you have had five husbands, and the man you now have is not your husband. What you have just said is quite true."

19 "Sir," the woman said, "I can see that you are a prophet. 20 Our ancestors worshiped on this mountain, but you Jews claim that the place where we must worship is in Jerusalem."

21 "Woman," Jesus replied, "believe me, a time is coming when you will worship the Father neither on this mountain nor in Jerusalem.

---

[a] *30* Some interpreters end the quotation with verse 36. [b] *34* Greek *he*
[c] *9* Or *do not use dishes Samaritans have used*

22You Samaritans worship what you do not know; we worship what we
do know, for salvation is from the Jews. 23Yet a time is coming and has
now come when the true worshipers will worship the Father in the Spirit
and in truth, for they are the kind of worshipers the Father seeks. 24God
is spirit, and his worshipers must worship in the Spirit and in truth."

25The woman said, "I know that Messiah" (called Christ) "is coming.
When he comes, he will explain everything to us."

26Then Jesus declared, "I, the one speaking to you — I am he."

THE DISCIPLES REJOIN JESUS

27Just then his disciples returned and were surprised to find him
talking with a woman. But no one asked, "What do you want?" or "Why
are you talking with her?"

28Then, leaving her water jar, the woman went back to the town and
said to the people, 29"Come, see a man who told me everything I ever
did. Could this be the Messiah?" 30They came out of the town and made
their way toward him.

31Meanwhile his disciples urged him, "Rabbi, eat something."

32But he said to them, "I have food to eat that you know nothing
about."

33Then his disciples said to each other, "Could someone have brought
him food?"

34"My food," said Jesus, "is to do the will of him who sent me and to
finish his work. 35Don't you have a saying, 'It's still four months until
harvest'? I tell you, open your eyes and look at the fields! They are ripe
for harvest. 36Even now the one who reaps draws a wage and harvests
a crop for eternal life, so that the sower and the reaper may be glad to-
gether. 37Thus the saying 'One sows and another reaps' is true. 38I sent
you to reap what you have not worked for. Others have done the hard
work, and you have reaped the benefits of their labor."

MANY SAMARITANS BELIEVE

39Many of the Samaritans from that town believed in him because of
the woman's testimony, "He told me everything I ever did." 40So when
the Samaritans came to him, they urged him to stay with them, and
he stayed two days. 41And because of his words many more became
believers.

42They said to the woman, "We no longer believe just because of
what you said; now we have heard for ourselves, and we know that
this man really is the Savior of the world."

JESUS HEALS AN OFFICIAL'S SON

43After the two days he left for Galilee. 44(Now Jesus himself had
pointed out that a prophet has no honor in his own country.) 45When
he arrived in Galilee, the Galileans welcomed him. They had seen all
that he had done in Jerusalem at the Passover Festival, for they also
had been there.

46Once more he visited Cana in Galilee, where he had turned the wa-
ter into wine. And there was a certain royal official whose son lay sick
at Capernaum. 47When this man heard that Jesus had arrived in Galilee
from Judea, he went to him and begged him to come and heal his son,
who was close to death.

48"Unless you people see signs and wonders," Jesus told him, "you
will never believe."

49The royal official said, "Sir, come down before my child dies."
50"Go," Jesus replied, "your son will live."
The man took Jesus at his word and departed. 51While he was still on
the way, his servants met him with the news that his boy was living.
52When he inquired as to the time when his son got better, they said to
him, "Yesterday, at one in the afternoon, the fever left him."
53Then the father realized that this was the exact time at which Jesus
had said to him, "Your son will live." So he and his whole household
believed.
54This was the second sign Jesus performed after coming from Judea to Galilee.

PRAYING SCRIPTURE

John 5

The healing of the man by the pool contains an important truth for prayer: Ask for what you want. When Jesus asked the man if he wanted to be healed, the man explained *why* he'd not yet been healed. The man did not directly answer Jesus' question.

The Word contains many promises from God. God offers to meet our needs, so when God offers, answer with a resounding yes!

THE HEALING AT THE POOL

5 Some time later, Jesus went up to Jerusalem for one of the Jewish
festivals. 2Now there is in Jerusalem near the Sheep Gate a pool,
which in Aramaic is called Bethesda[a] and which is surrounded by five
covered colonnades. 3Here a great number of disabled people used to
lie — the blind, the lame, the paralyzed. [4][b] 5One who was there had
been an invalid for thirty-eight years. 6When Jesus saw him lying
there and learned that he had been in this condition for a long time,
he asked him, "Do you want to get well?"
7"Sir," the invalid replied, "I have no one to help me into the pool
when the water is stirred. While I am trying to get in, someone else
goes down ahead of me."
8Then Jesus said to him, "Get up! Pick up your mat and walk." 9At
once the man was cured; he picked up his mat and walked.
The day on which this took place was a Sabbath, 10and so the Jewish
leaders said to the man who had been healed, "It is the Sabbath; the
law forbids you to carry your mat."
11But he replied, "The man who made me well said to me, 'Pick up
your mat and walk.' "
12So they asked him, "Who is this fellow who told you to pick it up
and walk?"
13The man who was healed had no idea who it was, for Jesus had
slipped away into the crowd that was there.
14Later Jesus found him at the temple and said to him, "See, you are
well again. Stop sinning or something worse may happen to you." 15The
man went away and told the Jewish leaders that it was Jesus who had
made him well.

THE AUTHORITY OF THE SON

16So, because Jesus was doing these things on the Sabbath, the Jew-
ish leaders began to persecute him. 17In his defense Jesus said to them,
"My Father is always at his work to this very day, and I too am work-
ing." 18For this reason they tried all the more to kill him; not only was
he breaking the Sabbath, but he was even calling God his own Father,
making himself equal with God.
19Jesus gave them this answer: "Very truly I tell you, the Son can
do nothing by himself; he can do only what he sees his Father doing,

---

[a] 2 Some manuscripts *Bethzatha*; other manuscripts *Bethsaida* [b] 3,4 Some manuscripts include here, wholly or in part, *paralyzed — and they waited for the moving of the waters. 4From time to time an angel of the Lord would come down and stir up the waters. The first one into the pool after each such disturbance would be cured of whatever disease they had.*

because whatever the Father does the Son also does. 20For the Father loves the Son and shows him all he does. Yes, and he will show him even greater works than these, so that you will be amazed. 21For just as the Father raises the dead and gives them life, even so the Son gives life to whom he is pleased to give it. 22Moreover, the Father judges no one, but has entrusted all judgment to the Son, 23that all may honor the Son just as they honor the Father. Whoever does not honor the Son does not honor the Father, who sent him.

24"Very truly I tell you, whoever hears my word and believes him who sent me has eternal life and will not be judged but has crossed over from death to life. 25Very truly I tell you, a time is coming and has now come when the dead will hear the voice of the Son of God and those who hear will live. 26For as the Father has life in himself, so he has granted the Son also to have life in himself. 27And he has given him authority to judge because he is the Son of Man.

28"Do not be amazed at this, for a time is coming when all who are in their graves will hear his voice 29and come out — those who have done what is good will rise to live, and those who have done what is evil will rise to be condemned. 30By myself I can do nothing; I judge only as I hear, and my judgment is just, for I seek not to please myself but him who sent me.

TESTIMONIES ABOUT JESUS

31"If I testify about myself, my testimony is not true. 32There is another who testifies in my favor, and I know that his testimony about me is true.

33"You have sent to John and he has testified to the truth. 34Not that I accept human testimony; but I mention it that you may be saved. 35John was a lamp that burned and gave light, and you chose for a time to enjoy his light.

36"I have testimony weightier than that of John. For the works that the Father has given me to finish — the very works that I am doing — testify that the Father has sent me. 37And the Father who sent me has himself testified concerning me. You have never heard his voice nor seen his form, 38nor does his word dwell in you, for you do not believe the one he sent. 39You study[a] the Scriptures diligently because you think that in them you have eternal life. These are the very Scriptures that testify about me, 40yet you refuse to come to me to have life.

41"I do not accept glory from human beings, 42but I know you. I know that you do not have the love of God in your hearts. 43I have come in my Father's name, and you do not accept me; but if someone else comes in his own name, you will accept him. 44How can you believe since you accept glory from one another but do not seek the glory that comes from the only God[b]?

45"But do not think I will accuse you before the Father. Your accuser is Moses, on whom your hopes are set. 46If you believed Moses, you would believe me, for he wrote about me. 47But since you do not believe what he wrote, how are you going to believe what I say?"

JESUS FEEDS THE FIVE THOUSAND

6 Some time after this, Jesus crossed to the far shore of the Sea of Galilee (that is, the Sea of Tiberias), 2and a great crowd of people followed him because they saw the signs he had performed by healing

PRAYING SCRIPTURE

John 6

"I am the bread of life," Jesus said (verse 35). The discourse in the middle of this chapter brings vividly to life a central metaphor Jesus used of himself—one that we still use today. Jesus is the bread from heaven. Bread as the symbol of his broken body is memorialized during the Lord's Supper.

Have you thought lately about Jesus' broken, crucified physical body? Praise him for his suffering on your behalf that secured your salvation.

---

[a] 39 Or [39]*Study* [b] 44 Some early manuscripts *the Only One*

the sick. 3Then Jesus went up on a mountainside and sat down with his
disciples. 4The Jewish Passover Festival was near.
5When Jesus looked up and saw a great crowd coming toward him,
he said to Philip, "Where shall we buy bread for these people to eat?"
6He asked this only to test him, for he already had in mind what he
was going to do.
7Philip answered him, "It would take more than half a year's wages[a]
to buy enough bread for each one to have a bite!"
8Another of his disciples, Andrew, Simon Peter's brother, spoke up,
9"Here is a boy with five small barley loaves and two small fish, but
how far will they go among so many?"
10Jesus said, "Have the people sit down." There was plenty of grass
in that place, and they sat down (about five thousand men were there).
11Jesus then took the loaves, gave thanks, and distributed to those who
were seated as much as they wanted. He did the same with the fish.
12When they had all had enough to eat, he said to his disciples,
"Gather the pieces that are left over. Let nothing be wasted." 13So they
gathered them and filled twelve baskets with the pieces of the five
barley loaves left over by those who had eaten.
14After the people saw the sign Jesus performed, they began to say,
"Surely this is the Prophet who is to come into the world." 15Jesus,
knowing that they intended to come and make him king by force,
withdrew again to a mountain by himself.

JESUS WALKS ON THE WATER

16When evening came, his disciples went down to the lake, 17where
they got into a boat and set off across the lake for Capernaum. By now
it was dark, and Jesus had not yet joined them. 18A strong wind was
blowing and the waters grew rough. 19When they had rowed about
three or four miles,[b] they saw Jesus approaching the boat, walking on
the water; and they were frightened. 20But he said to them, "It is I;
don't be afraid." 21Then they were willing to take him into the boat,
and immediately the boat reached the shore where they were heading.
22The next day the crowd that had stayed on the opposite shore of
the lake realized that only one boat had been there, and that Jesus had
not entered it with his disciples, but that they had gone away alone.
23Then some boats from Tiberias landed near the place where the peo-
ple had eaten the bread after the Lord had given thanks. 24Once the
crowd realized that neither Jesus nor his disciples were there, they got
into the boats and went to Capernaum in search of Jesus.

JESUS THE BREAD OF LIFE

25When they found him on the other side of the lake, they asked
him, "Rabbi, when did you get here?"
26Jesus answered, "Very truly I tell you, you are looking for me, not
because you saw the signs I performed but because you ate the loaves
and had your fill. 27Do not work for food that spoils, but for food that
endures to eternal life, which the Son of Man will give you. For on him
God the Father has placed his seal of approval."
28Then they asked him, "What must we do to do the works God
requires?"
29Jesus answered, "The work of God is this: to believe in the one he
has sent."

---

[a] 7 Greek *take two hundred denarii* [b] 19 Or about 5 or 6 kilometers

30So they asked him, "What sign then will you give that we may see it
and believe you? What will you do? 31Our ancestors ate the manna in the
wilderness; as it is written: 'He gave them bread from heaven to eat.'[a]"
32Jesus said to them, "Very truly I tell you, it is not Moses who has
given you the bread from heaven, but it is my Father who gives you the
true bread from heaven. 33For the bread of God is the bread that comes
down from heaven and gives life to the world."
34"Sir," they said, "always give us this bread."
35Then Jesus declared, "I am the bread of life. Whoever comes to me
will never go hungry, and whoever believes in me will never be thirsty.
36But as I told you, you have seen me and still you do not believe. 37All
those the Father gives me will come to me, and whoever comes to me
I will never drive away. 38For I have come down from heaven not to do
my will but to do the will of him who sent me. 39And this is the will of
him who sent me, that I shall lose none of all those he has given me,
but raise them up at the last day. 40For my Father's will is that everyone
who looks to the Son and believes in him shall have eternal life, and I
will raise them up at the last day."
41At this the Jews there began to grumble about him because he said,
"I am the bread that came down from heaven." 42They said, "Is this not
Jesus, the son of Joseph, whose father and mother we know? How can
he now say, 'I came down from heaven'?"
43"Stop grumbling among yourselves," Jesus answered. 44"No one
can come to me unless the Father who sent me draws them, and I will
raise them up at the last day. 45It is written in the Prophets: 'They will
all be taught by God.'[b] Everyone who has heard the Father and learned
from him comes to me. 46No one has seen the Father except the one
who is from God; only he has seen the Father. 47Very truly I tell you,
the one who believes has eternal life. 48I am the bread of life. 49Your
ancestors ate the manna in the wilderness, yet they died. 50But here is
the bread that comes down from heaven, which anyone may eat and
not die. 51I am the living bread that came down from heaven. Whoever
eats this bread will live forever. This bread is my flesh, which I will give
for the life of the world."
52Then the Jews began to argue sharply among themselves, "How
can this man give us his flesh to eat?"
53Jesus said to them, "Very truly I tell you, unless you eat the flesh
of the Son of Man and drink his blood, you have no life in you. 54Who-
ever eats my flesh and drinks my blood has eternal life, and I will raise
them up at the last day. 55For my flesh is real food and my blood is real
drink. 56Whoever eats my flesh and drinks my blood remains in me,
and I in them. 57Just as the living Father sent me and I live because of
the Father, so the one who feeds on me will live because of me. 58This
is the bread that came down from heaven. Your ancestors ate manna
and died, but whoever feeds on this bread will live forever." 59He said
this while teaching in the synagogue in Capernaum.

MANY DISCIPLES DESERT JESUS

60On hearing it, many of his disciples said, "This is a hard teaching.
Who can accept it?"
61Aware that his disciples were grumbling about this, Jesus said to
them, "Does this offend you? 62Then what if you see the Son of Man as-
cend to where he was before! 63The Spirit gives life; the flesh counts for

[a] *31* Exodus 16:4; Neh. 9:15; Psalm 78:24,25 [b] *45* Isaiah 54:13

nothing. The words I have spoken to you — they are full of the Spirit[a]
and life. 64Yet there are some of you who do not believe." For Jesus had
known from the beginning which of them did not believe and who
would betray him. 65He went on to say, "This is why I told you that no
one can come to me unless the Father has enabled them."
66From this time many of his disciples turned back and no longer
followed him.
67"You do not want to leave too, do you?" Jesus asked the Twelve.
68Simon Peter answered him, "Lord, to whom shall we go? You have
the words of eternal life. 69We have come to believe and to know that
you are the Holy One of God."
70Then Jesus replied, "Have I not chosen you, the Twelve? Yet one
of you is a devil!" 71(He meant Judas, the son of Simon Iscariot, who,
though one of the Twelve, was later to betray him.)

JESUS GOES TO THE FESTIVAL OF TABERNACLES

7 After this, Jesus went around in Galilee. He did not want[b] to go about
in Judea because the Jewish leaders there were looking for a way to
kill him. 2But when the Jewish Festival of Tabernacles was near, 3Jesus'
brothers said to him, "Leave Galilee and go to Judea, so that your dis-
ciples there may see the works you do. 4No one who wants to become
a public figure acts in secret. Since you are doing these things, show
yourself to the world." 5For even his own brothers did not believe in him.
6Therefore Jesus told them, "My time is not yet here; for you any
time will do. 7The world cannot hate you, but it hates me because I
testify that its works are evil. 8You go to the festival. I am not[c] going
up to this festival, because my time has not yet fully come." 9After he
had said this, he stayed in Galilee.
10However, after his brothers had left for the festival, he went also,
not publicly, but in secret. 11Now at the festival the Jewish leaders were
watching for Jesus and asking, "Where is he?"
12Among the crowds there was widespread whispering about him.
Some said, "He is a good man."
Others replied, "No, he deceives the people." 13But no one would say
anything publicly about him for fear of the leaders.

PRAYING SCRIPTURE

John 7

The religious leaders of Jesus' day were primarily responsible for his death. They delivered him to the Romans to be arrested, but why? Clearly they feared his growing influence (see verses 46–47) and tried to sway people from believing in him (see verse 52).

Jesus' death did not catch the Father by surprise. Thank God for his all-surpassing wisdom that provided salvation through Jesus.

JESUS TEACHES AT THE FESTIVAL

14Not until halfway through the festival did Jesus go up to the tem-
ple courts and begin to teach. 15The Jews there were amazed and asked,
"How did this man get such learning without having been taught?"
16Jesus answered, "My teaching is not my own. It comes from the
one who sent me. 17Anyone who chooses to do the will of God will find
out whether my teaching comes from God or whether I speak on my
own. 18Whoever speaks on their own does so to gain personal glory, but
he who seeks the glory of the one who sent him is a man of truth; there
is nothing false about him. 19Has not Moses given you the law? Yet not
one of you keeps the law. Why are you trying to kill me?"
20"You are demon-possessed," the crowd answered. "Who is trying
to kill you?"
21Jesus said to them, "I did one miracle, and you are all amazed.
22Yet, because Moses gave you circumcision (though actually it did not
come from Moses, but from the patriarchs), you circumcise a boy on

[a] *63* Or *are Spirit;* or *are spirit* [b] *1* Some manuscripts *not have authority*
[c] *8* Some manuscripts *not yet*

the Sabbath. 23Now if a boy can be circumcised on the Sabbath so that
the law of Moses may not be broken, why are you angry with me for
healing a man's whole body on the Sabbath? 24Stop judging by mere
appearances, but instead judge correctly."

DIVISION OVER WHO JESUS IS

25At that point some of the people of Jerusalem began to ask, "Isn't
this the man they are trying to kill? 26Here he is, speaking publicly,
and they are not saying a word to him. Have the authorities really con-
cluded that he is the Messiah? 27But we know where this man is from;
when the Messiah comes, no one will know where he is from."

28Then Jesus, still teaching in the temple courts, cried out, "Yes, you
know me, and you know where I am from. I am not here on my own
authority, but he who sent me is true. You do not know him, 29but I
know him because I am from him and he sent me."

30At this they tried to seize him, but no one laid a hand on him, be-
cause his hour had not yet come. 31Still, many in the crowd believed in
him. They said, "When the Messiah comes, will he perform more signs
than this man?"

32The Pharisees heard the crowd whispering such things about him.
Then the chief priests and the Pharisees sent temple guards to arrest
him.

33Jesus said, "I am with you for only a short time, and then I am
going to the one who sent me. 34You will look for me, but you will not
find me; and where I am, you cannot come."

35The Jews said to one another, "Where does this man intend to go
that we cannot find him? Will he go where our people live scattered
among the Greeks, and teach the Greeks? 36What did he mean when
he said, 'You will look for me, but you will not find me,' and 'Where I
am, you cannot come'?"

37On the last and greatest day of the festival, Jesus stood and said in
a loud voice, "Let anyone who is thirsty come to me and drink. 38Who-
ever believes in me, as Scripture has said, rivers of living water will
flow from within them."[a] 39By this he meant the Spirit, whom those
who believed in him were later to receive. Up to that time the Spirit
had not been given, since Jesus had not yet been glorified.

40On hearing his words, some of the people said, "Surely this man
is the Prophet."

41Others said, "He is the Messiah."

Still others asked, "How can the Messiah come from Galilee? 42Does
not Scripture say that the Messiah will come from David's descendants
and from Bethlehem, the town where David lived?" 43Thus the people
were divided because of Jesus. 44Some wanted to seize him, but no one
laid a hand on him.

UNBELIEF OF THE JEWISH LEADERS

45Finally the temple guards went back to the chief priests and the
Pharisees, who asked them, "Why didn't you bring him in?"

46"No one ever spoke the way this man does," the guards replied.

47"You mean he has deceived you also?" the Pharisees retorted.
48"Have any of the rulers or of the Pharisees believed in him? 49No! But
this mob that knows nothing of the law — there is a curse on them."

---

[a] 37,38 Or *me. And let anyone drink* 38*who believes in me." As Scripture has said, "Out of him (or them) will flow rivers of living water."*

50 Nicodemus, who had gone to Jesus earlier and who was one of
their own number, asked, 51 "Does our law condemn a man without
first hearing him to find out what he has been doing?"
52 They replied, "Are you from Galilee, too? Look into it, and you will
find that a prophet does not come out of Galilee."

[The earliest manuscripts and many other ancient witnesses do not have John 7:53—8:11. A few manuscripts include these verses, wholly or in part, after John 7:36, John 21:25, Luke 21:38 or Luke 24:53.]

8 *53 Then they all went home, 1 but Jesus went to the Mount of Olives.*
2 At dawn he appeared again in the temple courts, where all the people gath-
ered around him, and he sat down to teach them. 3 The teachers of the law and
the Pharisees brought in a woman caught in adultery. They made her stand be-
fore the group 4 and said to Jesus, "Teacher, this woman was caught in the act of
adultery. 5 In the Law Moses commanded us to stone such women. Now what do
you say?" 6 They were using this question as a trap, in order to have a basis for
accusing him.
But Jesus bent down and started to write on the ground with his finger. 7 When
they kept on questioning him, he straightened up and said to them, "Let any one
of you who is without sin be the first to throw a stone at her." 8 Again he stooped
down and wrote on the ground.
9 At this, those who heard began to go away one at a time, the older ones first,
until only Jesus was left, with the woman still standing there. 10 Jesus straight-
ened up and asked her, "Woman, where are they? Has no one condemned you?"
11 "No one, sir," she said.
"Then neither do I condemn you," Jesus declared. "Go now and leave your life of sin."

PRAYING SCRIPTURE

John 8

In one of the most beautiful and moving stories in all of Scripture, a woman caught in adultery was taken to Jesus for judgment (see verses 1–11). The scribes and Pharisees tested Jesus based on the law's requirement that adulterers be stoned. Jesus showed her mercy while challenging her accusers to prove themselves sinless. They could not.

Ask God to help you show the same kind of love and mercy for sinners that Jesus exemplified.

DISPUTE OVER JESUS' TESTIMONY

12 When Jesus spoke again to the people, he said, "I am the light of
the world. Whoever follows me will never walk in darkness, but will
have the light of life."
13 The Pharisees challenged him, "Here you are, appearing as your
own witness; your testimony is not valid."
14 Jesus answered, "Even if I testify on my own behalf, my testimony
is valid, for I know where I came from and where I am going. But you
have no idea where I come from or where I am going. 15 You judge by
human standards; I pass judgment on no one. 16 But if I do judge, my
decisions are true, because I am not alone. I stand with the Father, who
sent me. 17 In your own Law it is written that the testimony of two wit-
nesses is true. 18 I am one who testifies for myself; my other witness is
the Father, who sent me."
19 Then they asked him, "Where is your father?"
"You do not know me or my Father," Jesus replied. "If you knew me,
you would know my Father also." 20 He spoke these words while teach-
ing in the temple courts near the place where the offerings were put.
Yet no one seized him, because his hour had not yet come.

DISPUTE OVER WHO JESUS IS

21 Once more Jesus said to them, "I am going away, and you will look
for me, and you will die in your sin. Where I go, you cannot come."
22 This made the Jews ask, "Will he kill himself? Is that why he says,
'Where I go, you cannot come'?"

23But he continued, "You are from below; I am from above. You are of
this world; I am not of this world. 24I told you that you would die in your
sins; if you do not believe that I am he, you will indeed die in your sins."
25"Who are you?" they asked.
"Just what I have been telling you from the beginning," Jesus re-
plied. 26"I have much to say in judgment of you. But he who sent me is
trustworthy, and what I have heard from him I tell the world."
27They did not understand that he was telling them about his Father.
28So Jesus said, "When you have lifted up[a] the Son of Man, then you
will know that I am he and that I do nothing on my own but speak just
what the Father has taught me. 29The one who sent me is with me; he
has not left me alone, for I always do what pleases him." 30Even as he
spoke, many believed in him.

DISPUTE OVER WHOSE CHILDREN JESUS' OPPONENTS ARE

31To the Jews who had believed him, Jesus said, "If you hold to my
teaching, you are really my disciples. 32Then you will know the truth,
and the truth will set you free."
33They answered him, "We are Abraham's descendants and have
never been slaves of anyone. How can you say that we shall be set free?"
34Jesus replied, "Very truly I tell you, everyone who sins is a slave to
sin. 35Now a slave has no permanent place in the family, but a son be-
longs to it forever. 36So if the Son sets you free, you will be free indeed.
37I know that you are Abraham's descendants. Yet you are looking for
a way to kill me, because you have no room for my word. 38I am telling
you what I have seen in the Father's presence, and you are doing what
you have heard from your father.[b]"
39"Abraham is our father," they answered.
"If you were Abraham's children," said Jesus, "then you would[c] do
what Abraham did. 40As it is, you are looking for a way to kill me, a
man who has told you the truth that I heard from God. Abraham did
not do such things. 41You are doing the works of your own father."
"We are not illegitimate children," they protested. "The only Father
we have is God himself."
42Jesus said to them, "If God were your Father, you would love me,
for I have come here from God. I have not come on my own; God sent
me. 43Why is my language not clear to you? Because you are unable to
hear what I say. 44You belong to your father, the devil, and you want to
carry out your father's desires. He was a murderer from the beginning,
not holding to the truth, for there is no truth in him. When he lies, he
speaks his native language, for he is a liar and the father of lies. 45Yet
because I tell the truth, you do not believe me! 46Can any of you prove
me guilty of sin? If I am telling the truth, why don't you believe me?
47Whoever belongs to God hears what God says. The reason you do not
hear is that you do not belong to God."

JESUS' CLAIMS ABOUT HIMSELF

48The Jews answered him, "Aren't we right in saying that you are a
Samaritan and demon-possessed?"

---

[a] 28 The Greek for *lifted up* also means *exalted.* [b] 38 Or *presence. Therefore do what you have heard from the Father.* [c] 39 Some early manuscripts *"If you are Abraham's children," said Jesus, "then*

49"I am not possessed by a demon," said Jesus, "but I honor my Fa-
ther and you dishonor me. 50I am not seeking glory for myself; but
there is one who seeks it, and he is the judge. 51Very truly I tell you,
whoever obeys my word will never see death."

52At this they exclaimed, "Now we know that you are demon-possessed!
Abraham died and so did the prophets, yet you say that whoever obeys
your word will never taste death. 53Are you greater than our father Abra-
ham? He died, and so did the prophets. Who do you think you are?"

54Jesus replied, "If I glorify myself, my glory means nothing. My Fa-
ther, whom you claim as your God, is the one who glorifies me. 55Though
you do not know him, I know him. If I said I did not, I would be a liar
like you, but I do know him and obey his word. 56Your father Abraham
rejoiced at the thought of seeing my day; he saw it and was glad."

57"You are not yet fifty years old," they said to him, "and you have
seen Abraham!"

58"Very truly I tell you," Jesus answered, "before Abraham was born,
I am!" 59At this, they picked up stones to stone him, but Jesus hid him-
self, slipping away from the temple grounds.

JESUS HEALS A MAN BORN BLIND

9 As he went along, he saw a man blind from birth. 2His disciples
asked him, "Rabbi, who sinned, this man or his parents, that he
was born blind?"

3"Neither this man nor his parents sinned," said Jesus, "but this hap-
pened so that the works of God might be displayed in him. 4As long as
it is day, we must do the works of him who sent me. Night is coming,
when no one can work. 5While I am in the world, I am the light of the
world."

6After saying this, he spit on the ground, made some mud with
the saliva, and put it on the man's eyes. 7"Go," he told him, "wash in
the Pool of Siloam" (this word means "Sent"). So the man went and
washed, and came home seeing.

8His neighbors and those who had formerly seen him begging asked,
"Isn't this the same man who used to sit and beg?" 9Some claimed that
he was.

Others said, "No, he only looks like him."

But he himself insisted, "I am the man."

10"How then were your eyes opened?" they asked.

11He replied, "The man they call Jesus made some mud and put it on
my eyes. He told me to go to Siloam and wash. So I went and washed,
and then I could see."

12"Where is this man?" they asked him.

"I don't know," he said.

THE PHARISEES INVESTIGATE THE HEALING

13They brought to the Pharisees the man who had been blind. 14Now
the day on which Jesus had made the mud and opened the man's eyes
was a Sabbath. 15Therefore the Pharisees also asked him how he had
received his sight. "He put mud on my eyes," the man replied, "and I
washed, and now I see."

16Some of the Pharisees said, "This man is not from God, for he does
not keep the Sabbath."

But others asked, "How can a sinner perform such signs?" So they
were divided.

PRAYING SCRIPTURE

John 9

The relationship of sin and suffering is not a new quandary. People have long believed that bad things always stem directly from bad actions, that cosmic repayment is always a straight line. Jesus said this was not so. In answer to this question, Jesus said sometimes sickness happens so God can be glorified in the healing.

Never hesitate to pray for someone to be healed. God will glorify himself by healing in Jesus' name.

17 Then they turned again to the blind man, "What have you to say
about him? It was your eyes he opened."
The man replied, "He is a prophet."
18 They still did not believe that he had been blind and had received
his sight until they sent for the man's parents. 19 "Is this your son?"
they asked. "Is this the one you say was born blind? How is it that now
he can see?"
20 "We know he is our son," the parents answered, "and we know he
was born blind. 21 But how he can see now, or who opened his eyes,
we don't know. Ask him. He is of age; he will speak for himself." 22 His
parents said this because they were afraid of the Jewish leaders, who
already had decided that anyone who acknowledged that Jesus was the
Messiah would be put out of the synagogue. 23 That was why his parents
said, "He is of age; ask him."
24 A second time they summoned the man who had been blind. "Give
glory to God by telling the truth," they said. "We know this man is a
sinner."
25 He replied, "Whether he is a sinner or not, I don't know. One thing
I do know. I was blind but now I see!"
26 Then they asked him, "What did he do to you? How did he open
your eyes?"
27 He answered, "I have told you already and you did not listen. Why
do you want to hear it again? Do you want to become his disciples too?"
28 Then they hurled insults at him and said, "You are this fellow's
disciple! We are disciples of Moses! 29 We know that God spoke to Mo-
ses, but as for this fellow, we don't even know where he comes from."
30 The man answered, "Now that is remarkable! You don't know
where he comes from, yet he opened my eyes. 31 We know that God
does not listen to sinners. He listens to the godly person who does his
will. 32 Nobody has ever heard of opening the eyes of a man born blind.
33 If this man were not from God, he could do nothing."
34 To this they replied, "You were steeped in sin at birth; how dare
you lecture us!" And they threw him out.

SPIRITUAL BLINDNESS

35 Jesus heard that they had thrown him out, and when he found
him, he said, "Do you believe in the Son of Man?"
36 "Who is he, sir?" the man asked. "Tell me so that I may believe in
him."
37 Jesus said, "You have now seen him; in fact, he is the one speaking
with you."
38 Then the man said, "Lord, I believe," and he worshiped him.
39 Jesus said,[a] "For judgment I have come into this world, so that the
blind will see and those who see will become blind."
40 Some Pharisees who were with him heard him say this and asked,
"What? Are we blind too?"
41 Jesus said, "If you were blind, you would not be guilty of sin; but
now that you claim you can see, your guilt remains.

THE GOOD SHEPHERD AND HIS SHEEP

10 "Very truly I tell you Pharisees, anyone who does not enter the
sheep pen by the gate, but climbs in by some other way, is a
thief and a robber. 2 The one who enters by the gate is the shepherd

[a] *38,39* Some early manuscripts do not have *Then the man said . . . 39 Jesus said.*

PRAYING SCRIPTURE

John 10

Sheep always know the voice of their shepherd. Those who hear Jesus know Jesus. His sheep will listen for his voice over the din of noise that surrounds us daily. We do well to seek out times and places where we can better hear his voice so we can follow him more readily.

As you read the Word of God, pray to hear the Good Shepherd's voice, and then follow him.

of the sheep. 3 The gatekeeper opens the gate for him, and the sheep listen to his voice. He calls his own sheep by name and leads them out. 4 When he has brought out all his own, he goes on ahead of them, and his sheep follow him because they know his voice. 5 But they will never follow a stranger; in fact, they will run away from him because they do not recognize a stranger's voice." 6 Jesus used this figure of speech, but the Pharisees did not understand what he was telling them.

7 Therefore Jesus said again, "Very truly I tell you, I am the gate for the sheep. 8 All who have come before me are thieves and robbers, but the sheep have not listened to them. 9 I am the gate; whoever enters through me will be saved.[a] They will come in and go out, and find pasture. 10 The thief comes only to steal and kill and destroy; I have come that they may have life, and have it to the full.

11 "I am the good shepherd. The good shepherd lays down his life for the sheep. 12 The hired hand is not the shepherd and does not own the sheep. So when he sees the wolf coming, he abandons the sheep and runs away. Then the wolf attacks the flock and scatters it. 13 The man runs away because he is a hired hand and cares nothing for the sheep.

14 "I am the good shepherd; I know my sheep and my sheep know me— 15 just as the Father knows me and I know the Father—and I lay down my life for the sheep. 16 I have other sheep that are not of this sheep pen. I must bring them also. They too will listen to my voice, and there shall be one flock and one shepherd. 17 The reason my Father loves me is that I lay down my life—only to take it up again. 18 No one takes it from me, but I lay it down of my own accord. I have authority to lay it down and authority to take it up again. This command I received from my Father."

19 The Jews who heard these words were again divided. 20 Many of them said, "He is demon-possessed and raving mad. Why listen to him?"

21 But others said, "These are not the sayings of a man possessed by a demon. Can a demon open the eyes of the blind?"

FURTHER CONFLICT OVER JESUS' CLAIMS

22 Then came the Festival of Dedication[b] at Jerusalem. It was winter, 23 and Jesus was in the temple courts walking in Solomon's Colonnade. 24 The Jews who were there gathered around him, saying, "How long will you keep us in suspense? If you are the Messiah, tell us plainly."

25 Jesus answered, "I did tell you, but you do not believe. The works I do in my Father's name testify about me, 26 but you do not believe because you are not my sheep. 27 My sheep listen to my voice; I know them, and they follow me. 28 I give them eternal life, and they shall never perish; no one will snatch them out of my hand. 29 My Father, who has given them to me, is greater than all[c]; no one can snatch them out of my Father's hand. 30 I and the Father are one."

31 Again his Jewish opponents picked up stones to stone him, 32 but Jesus said to them, "I have shown you many good works from the Father. For which of these do you stone me?"

33 "We are not stoning you for any good work," they replied, "but for blasphemy, because you, a mere man, claim to be God."

34 Jesus answered them, "Is it not written in your Law, 'I have said you are "gods"'[d]? 35 If he called them 'gods,' to whom the word of God

---

[a] 9 Or *kept safe* [b] 22 That is, Hanukkah [c] 29 Many early manuscripts *What my Father has given me is greater than all* [d] 34 Psalm 82:6

came — and Scripture cannot be set aside — 36what about the one whom the Father set apart as his very own and sent into the world? Why then do you accuse me of blasphemy because I said, 'I am God's Son'? 37Do not believe me unless I do the works of my Father. 38But if I do them, even though you do not believe me, believe the works, that you may know and understand that the Father is in me, and I in the Father." 39Again they tried to seize him, but he escaped their grasp.

40Then Jesus went back across the Jordan to the place where John had been baptizing in the early days. There he stayed, 41and many people came to him. They said, "Though John never performed a sign, all that John said about this man was true." 42And in that place many believed in Jesus.

THE DEATH OF LAZARUS

11 Now a man named Lazarus was sick. He was from Bethany, the village of Mary and her sister Martha. 2(This Mary, whose brother Lazarus now lay sick, was the same one who poured perfume on the Lord and wiped his feet with her hair.) 3So the sisters sent word to Jesus, "Lord, the one you love is sick."

4When he heard this, Jesus said, "This sickness will not end in death. No, it is for God's glory so that God's Son may be glorified through it." 5Now Jesus loved Martha and her sister and Lazarus. 6So when he heard that Lazarus was sick, he stayed where he was two more days, 7and then he said to his disciples, "Let us go back to Judea."

8"But Rabbi," they said, "a short while ago the Jews there tried to stone you, and yet you are going back?"

9Jesus answered, "Are there not twelve hours of daylight? Anyone who walks in the daytime will not stumble, for they see by this world's light. 10It is when a person walks at night that they stumble, for they have no light."

11After he had said this, he went on to tell them, "Our friend Lazarus has fallen asleep; but I am going there to wake him up."

12His disciples replied, "Lord, if he sleeps, he will get better." 13Jesus had been speaking of his death, but his disciples thought he meant natural sleep.

14So then he told them plainly, "Lazarus is dead, 15and for your sake I am glad I was not there, so that you may believe. But let us go to him."

16Then Thomas (also known as Didymus[a]) said to the rest of the disciples, "Let us also go, that we may die with him."

JESUS COMFORTS THE SISTERS OF LAZARUS

17On his arrival, Jesus found that Lazarus had already been in the tomb for four days. 18Now Bethany was less than two miles[b] from Jerusalem, 19and many Jews had come to Martha and Mary to comfort them in the loss of their brother. 20When Martha heard that Jesus was coming, she went out to meet him, but Mary stayed at home.

21"Lord," Martha said to Jesus, "if you had been here, my brother would not have died. 22But I know that even now God will give you whatever you ask."

23Jesus said to her, "Your brother will rise again."

24Martha answered, "I know he will rise again in the resurrection at the last day."

---

[a] *16 Thomas* (Aramaic) and *Didymus* (Greek) both mean *twin.* [b] *18* Or about 3 kilometers

PRAYING SCRIPTURE

John 11

The close relationship between Jesus and Lazarus' family reveals one of Jesus' most human moments: weeping over the death of a friend. He was God in flesh with the full range of our emotions. Jesus showed us how to be sad with those who are sad. He also told us that in him there is always hope.

Jesus is the resurrection and the life (see verses 25–26). Trust him for life; pray for people you know to know his life.

25 Jesus said to her, "I am the resurrection and the life. The one who believes in me will live, even though they die; 26 and whoever lives by believing in me will never die. Do you believe this?"

27 "Yes, Lord," she replied, "I believe that you are the Messiah, the Son of God, who is to come into the world."

28 After she had said this, she went back and called her sister Mary aside. "The Teacher is here," she said, "and is asking for you." 29 When Mary heard this, she got up quickly and went to him. 30 Now Jesus had not yet entered the village, but was still at the place where Martha had met him. 31 When the Jews who had been with Mary in the house, comforting her, noticed how quickly she got up and went out, they followed her, supposing she was going to the tomb to mourn there.

32 When Mary reached the place where Jesus was and saw him, she fell at his feet and said, "Lord, if you had been here, my brother would not have died."

33 When Jesus saw her weeping, and the Jews who had come along with her also weeping, he was deeply moved in spirit and troubled. 34 "Where have you laid him?" he asked.

"Come and see, Lord," they replied.

35 Jesus wept.

36 Then the Jews said, "See how he loved him!"

37 But some of them said, "Could not he who opened the eyes of the blind man have kept this man from dying?"

JESUS RAISES LAZARUS FROM THE DEAD

38 Jesus, once more deeply moved, came to the tomb. It was a cave with a stone laid across the entrance. 39 "Take away the stone," he said.

"But, Lord," said Martha, the sister of the dead man, "by this time there is a bad odor, for he has been there four days."

40 Then Jesus said, "Did I not tell you that if you believe, you will see the glory of God?"

41 So they took away the stone. Then Jesus looked up and said, "Father, I thank you that you have heard me. 42 I knew that you always hear me, but I said this for the benefit of the people standing here, that they may believe that you sent me."

43 When he had said this, Jesus called in a loud voice, "Lazarus, come out!" 44 The dead man came out, his hands and feet wrapped with strips of linen, and a cloth around his face.

Jesus said to them, "Take off the grave clothes and let him go."

THE PLOT TO KILL JESUS

45 Therefore many of the Jews who had come to visit Mary, and had seen what Jesus did, believed in him. 46 But some of them went to the Pharisees and told them what Jesus had done. 47 Then the chief priests and the Pharisees called a meeting of the Sanhedrin.

"What are we accomplishing?" they asked. "Here is this man performing many signs. 48 If we let him go on like this, everyone will believe in him, and then the Romans will come and take away both our temple and our nation."

49 Then one of them, named Caiaphas, who was high priest that year, spoke up, "You know nothing at all! 50 You do not realize that it is better for you that one man die for the people than that the whole nation perish."

51 He did not say this on his own, but as high priest that year he

prophesied that Jesus would die for the Jewish nation, 52and not only
for that nation but also for the scattered children of God, to bring them
together and make them one. 53So from that day on they plotted to
take his life.

54Therefore Jesus no longer moved about publicly among the people
of Judea. Instead he withdrew to a region near the wilderness, to a vil-
lage called Ephraim, where he stayed with his disciples.

55When it was almost time for the Jewish Passover, many went up
from the country to Jerusalem for their ceremonial cleansing before
the Passover. 56They kept looking for Jesus, and as they stood in the
temple courts they asked one another, "What do you think? Isn't he
coming to the festival at all?" 57But the chief priests and the Pharisees
had given orders that anyone who found out where Jesus was should
report it so that they might arrest him.

JESUS ANOINTED AT BETHANY

12 Six days before the Passover, Jesus came to Bethany, where Laz-
arus lived, whom Jesus had raised from the dead. 2Here a dinner
was given in Jesus' honor. Martha served, while Lazarus was among
those reclining at the table with him. 3Then Mary took about a pint[a]
of pure nard, an expensive perfume; she poured it on Jesus' feet and
wiped his feet with her hair. And the house was filled with the fra-
grance of the perfume.

4But one of his disciples, Judas Iscariot, who was later to betray
him, objected, 5"Why wasn't this perfume sold and the money given
to the poor? It was worth a year's wages.[b]" 6He did not say this because
he cared about the poor but because he was a thief; as keeper of the
money bag, he used to help himself to what was put into it.

7"Leave her alone," Jesus replied. "It was intended that she should
save this perfume for the day of my burial. 8You will always have the
poor among you,[c] but you will not always have me."

9Meanwhile a large crowd of Jews found out that Jesus was there
and came, not only because of him but also to see Lazarus, whom he
had raised from the dead. 10So the chief priests made plans to kill Laz-
arus as well, 11for on account of him many of the Jews were going over
to Jesus and believing in him.

PRAYING SCRIPTURE

John 12

What does it mean to walk in the light? Jesus is the One who came from the Father, who spoke with the authority of the Father (see verse 49) and was the light who came into the world. Accepting the teaching of Jesus as having divine authority and living by his teaching is to walk in the light.

Jesus has overcome the darkness. Walk by his words to walk in the light.

JESUS COMES TO JERUSALEM AS KING

12The next day the great crowd that had come for the festival heard
that Jesus was on his way to Jerusalem. 13They took palm branches and
went out to meet him, shouting,

"Hosanna![d]"

"Blessed is he who comes in the name of the Lord!"[e]

"Blessed is the king of Israel!"

14Jesus found a young donkey and sat on it, as it is written:

15"Do not be afraid, Daughter Zion;
see, your king is coming,
seated on a donkey's colt."[f]

---

[a] *3* Or about 0.5 liter [b] *5* Greek *three hundred denarii* [c] *8* See Deut. 15:11.
[d] *13* A Hebrew expression meaning "Save!" which became an exclamation of praise [e] *13* Psalm 118:25,26 [f] *15* Zech. 9:9

16At first his disciples did not understand all this. Only after Jesus
was glorified did they realize that these things had been written about
him and that these things had been done to him.

17Now the crowd that was with him when he called Lazarus from
the tomb and raised him from the dead continued to spread the word.
18Many people, because they had heard that he had performed this
sign, went out to meet him. 19So the Pharisees said to one another,
"See, this is getting us nowhere. Look how the whole world has gone
after him!"

JESUS PREDICTS HIS DEATH

20Now there were some Greeks among those who went up to worship
at the festival. 21They came to Philip, who was from Bethsaida in Gali-
lee, with a request. "Sir," they said, "we would like to see Jesus." 22Philip
went to tell Andrew; Andrew and Philip in turn told Jesus.

23Jesus replied, "The hour has come for the Son of Man to be glori-
fied. 24Very truly I tell you, unless a kernel of wheat falls to the ground
and dies, it remains only a single seed. But if it dies, it produces many
seeds. 25Anyone who loves their life will lose it, while anyone who
hates their life in this world will keep it for eternal life. 26Whoever
serves me must follow me; and where I am, my servant also will be.
My Father will honor the one who serves me.

27"Now my soul is troubled, and what shall I say? 'Father, save me
from this hour'? No, it was for this very reason I came to this hour.
28Father, glorify your name!"

Then a voice came from heaven, "I have glorified it, and will glorify
it again." 29The crowd that was there and heard it said it had thun-
dered; others said an angel had spoken to him.

30Jesus said, "This voice was for your benefit, not mine. 31Now is the
time for judgment on this world; now the prince of this world will be
driven out. 32And I, when I am lifted up[a] from the earth, will draw all
people to myself." 33He said this to show the kind of death he was go-
ing to die.

34The crowd spoke up, "We have heard from the Law that the Mes-
siah will remain forever, so how can you say, 'The Son of Man must be
lifted up'? Who is this 'Son of Man'?"

35Then Jesus told them, "You are going to have the light just a little
while longer. Walk while you have the light, before darkness overtakes
you. Whoever walks in the dark does not know where they are going.
36Believe in the light while you have the light, so that you may become
children of light." When he had finished speaking, Jesus left and hid
himself from them.

BELIEF AND UNBELIEF AMONG THE JEWS

37Even after Jesus had performed so many signs in their presence,
they still would not believe in him. 38This was to fulfill the word of
Isaiah the prophet:

> "Lord, who has believed our message
> and to whom has the arm of the Lord been revealed?"[b]

39For this reason they could not believe, because, as Isaiah says
elsewhere:

[a] *32* The Greek for *lifted up* also means *exalted*. [b] *38* Isaiah 53:1

40 "He has blinded their eyes
and hardened their hearts,
so they can neither see with their eyes,
nor understand with their hearts,
nor turn — and I would heal them."[a]

41 Isaiah said this because he saw Jesus' glory and spoke about him.
42 Yet at the same time many even among the leaders believed in
him. But because of the Pharisees they would not openly acknowledge
their faith for fear they would be put out of the synagogue; 43 for they
loved human praise more than praise from God.
44 Then Jesus cried out, "Whoever believes in me does not believe
in me only, but in the one who sent me. 45 The one who looks at me is
seeing the one who sent me. 46 I have come into the world as a light, so
that no one who believes in me should stay in darkness.
47 "If anyone hears my words but does not keep them, I do not judge
that person. For I did not come to judge the world, but to save the
world. 48 There is a judge for the one who rejects me and does not ac-
cept my words; the very words I have spoken will condemn them at
the last day. 49 For I did not speak on my own, but the Father who sent
me commanded me to say all that I have spoken. 50 I know that his
command leads to eternal life. So whatever I say is just what the Father
has told me to say."

JESUS WASHES HIS DISCIPLES' FEET

13 It was just before the Passover Festival. Jesus knew that the hour
had come for him to leave this world and go to the Father. Hav-
ing loved his own who were in the world, he loved them to the end.
2 The evening meal was in progress, and the devil had already
prompted Judas, the son of Simon Iscariot, to betray Jesus. 3 Jesus knew
that the Father had put all things under his power, and that he had
come from God and was returning to God; 4 so he got up from the meal,
took off his outer clothing, and wrapped a towel around his waist. 5 After
that, he poured water into a basin and began to wash his disciples' feet,
drying them with the towel that was wrapped around him.
6 He came to Simon Peter, who said to him, "Lord, are you going to
wash my feet?"
7 Jesus replied, "You do not realize now what I am doing, but later
you will understand."
8 "No," said Peter, "you shall never wash my feet."
Jesus answered, "Unless I wash you, you have no part with me."
9 "Then, Lord," Simon Peter replied, "not just my feet but my hands
and my head as well!"
10 Jesus answered, "Those who have had a bath need only to wash
their feet; their whole body is clean. And you are clean, though not ev-
ery one of you." 11 For he knew who was going to betray him, and that
was why he said not every one was clean.
12 When he had finished washing their feet, he put on his clothes and
returned to his place. "Do you understand what I have done for you?"
he asked them. 13 "You call me 'Teacher' and 'Lord,' and rightly so, for
that is what I am. 14 Now that I, your Lord and Teacher, have washed
your feet, you also should wash one another's feet. 15 I have set you an
example that you should do as I have done for you. 16 Very truly I tell

PRAYING SCRIPTURE

John 13

At the solemn moment of the Last Supper, which would become a new memorial for his followers, Jesus gave a new commandment: His disciples were to love one another as he has loved them. Love was to be the distinguishing characteristic of Jesus' people throughout the ages.

Do you love other believers the way Jesus loves you? It can be a challenge, so ask Jesus to help you love others the way he has shown us.

[a] *40* Isaiah 6:10

you, no servant is greater than his master, nor is a messenger greater
than the one who sent him. 17Now that you know these things, you will
be blessed if you do them.

JESUS PREDICTS HIS BETRAYAL

18"I am not referring to all of you; I know those I have chosen. But
this is to fulfill this passage of Scripture: 'He who shared my bread has
turned[a] against me.'[b]
19"I am telling you now before it happens, so that when it does hap-
pen you will believe that I am who I am. 20Very truly I tell you, whoever
accepts anyone I send accepts me; and whoever accepts me accepts the
one who sent me."
21After he had said this, Jesus was troubled in spirit and testified,
"Very truly I tell you, one of you is going to betray me."
22His disciples stared at one another, at a loss to know which of them
he meant. 23One of them, the disciple whom Jesus loved, was reclining
next to him. 24Simon Peter motioned to this disciple and said, "Ask
him which one he means."
25Leaning back against Jesus, he asked him, "Lord, who is it?"
26Jesus answered, "It is the one to whom I will give this piece of
bread when I have dipped it in the dish." Then, dipping the piece of
bread, he gave it to Judas, the son of Simon Iscariot. 27As soon as Judas
took the bread, Satan entered into him.

So Jesus told him, "What you are about to do, do quickly." 28But no
one at the meal understood why Jesus said this to him. 29Since Judas
had charge of the money, some thought Jesus was telling him to buy
what was needed for the festival, or to give something to the poor.
30As soon as Judas had taken the bread, he went out. And it was night.

JESUS PREDICTS PETER'S DENIAL

31When he was gone, Jesus said, "Now the Son of Man is glorified and
God is glorified in him. 32If God is glorified in him,[c] God will glorify the
Son in himself, and will glorify him at once.
33"My children, I will be with you only a little longer. You will look
for me, and just as I told the Jews, so I tell you now: Where I am going,
you cannot come.
34"A new command I give you: Love one another. As I have loved you,
so you must love one another. 35By this everyone will know that you
are my disciples, if you love one another."
36Simon Peter asked him, "Lord, where are you going?"
Jesus replied, "Where I am going, you cannot follow now, but you
will follow later."
37Peter asked, "Lord, why can't I follow you now? I will lay down my
life for you."
38Then Jesus answered, "Will you really lay down your life for me?
Very truly I tell you, before the rooster crows, you will disown me three
times!

JESUS COMFORTS HIS DISCIPLES

14 "Do not let your hearts be troubled. You believe in God[d]; believe
also in me. 2My Father's house has many rooms; if that were not
so, would I have told you that I am going there to prepare a place for

PRAYING SCRIPTURE

John 14

As Jesus continued teaching during the Last Supper, he assured the Twelve of his peace. He promised a heavenly home that he was about to prepare for them, confirming that he is the only way to it. Sensing their anxiety, he also promised a kind of peace that only he could provide.

When you are anxious, call on Jesus. Do not simply ask for peace; ask him for his peace.

[a] 18 Greek *has lifted up his heel* [b] 18 Psalm 41:9 [c] 32 Many early manuscripts do not have *If God is glorified in him.* [d] 1 Or *Believe in God*

you? [3]And if I go and prepare a place for you, I will come back and take
you to be with me that you also may be where I am. [4]You know the way
to the place where I am going."

JESUS THE WAY TO THE FATHER

[5]Thomas said to him, "Lord, we don't know where you are going, so
how can we know the way?"
[6]Jesus answered, "I am the way and the truth and the life. No one
comes to the Father except through me. [7]If you really know me, you
will know[a] my Father as well. From now on, you do know him and
have seen him."
[8]Philip said, "Lord, show us the Father and that will be enough
for us."
[9]Jesus answered: "Don't you know me, Philip, even after I have been
among you such a long time? Anyone who has seen me has seen the
Father. How can you say, 'Show us the Father'? [10]Don't you believe that
I am in the Father, and that the Father is in me? The words I say to you
I do not speak on my own authority. Rather, it is the Father, living in
me, who is doing his work. [11]Believe me when I say that I am in the Fa-
ther and the Father is in me; or at least believe on the evidence of the
works themselves. [12]Very truly I tell you, whoever believes in me will
do the works I have been doing, and they will do even greater things
than these, because I am going to the Father. [13]And I will do whatever
you ask in my name, so that the Father may be glorified in the Son.
[14]You may ask me for anything in my name, and I will do it.

JESUS PROMISES THE HOLY SPIRIT

[15]"If you love me, keep my commands. [16]And I will ask the Father,
and he will give you another advocate to help you and be with you for-
ever — [17]the Spirit of truth. The world cannot accept him, because it
neither sees him nor knows him. But you know him, for he lives with
you and will be[b] in you. [18]I will not leave you as orphans; I will come
to you. [19]Before long, the world will not see me anymore, but you will
see me. Because I live, you also will live. [20]On that day you will realize
that I am in my Father, and you are in me, and I am in you. [21]Whoever
has my commands and keeps them is the one who loves me. The one
who loves me will be loved by my Father, and I too will love them and
show myself to them."
[22]Then Judas (not Judas Iscariot) said, "But, Lord, why do you intend
to show yourself to us and not to the world?"
[23]Jesus replied, "Anyone who loves me will obey my teaching. My
Father will love them, and we will come to them and make our home
with them. [24]Anyone who does not love me will not obey my teaching.
These words you hear are not my own; they belong to the Father who
sent me.
[25]"All this I have spoken while still with you. [26]But the Advocate, the
Holy Spirit, whom the Father will send in my name, will teach you all
things and will remind you of everything I have said to you. [27]Peace I
leave with you; my peace I give you. I do not give to you as the world
gives. Do not let your hearts be troubled and do not be afraid.
[28]"You heard me say, 'I am going away and I am coming back to you.'

---

[a] 7 Some manuscripts *If you really knew me, you would know* [b] 17 Some
early manuscripts *and is*

If you loved me, you would be glad that I am going to the Father, for the Father is greater than I. 29I have told you now before it happens, so that when it does happen you will believe. 30I will not say much more to you, for the prince of this world is coming. He has no hold over me, 31but he comes so that the world may learn that I love the Father and do exactly what my Father has commanded me.

"Come now; let us leave.

THE VINE AND THE BRANCHES

15 "I am the true vine, and my Father is the gardener. 2He cuts off every branch in me that bears no fruit, while every branch that does bear fruit he prunes[a] so that it will be even more fruitful. 3You are already clean because of the word I have spoken to you. 4Remain in me, as I also remain in you. No branch can bear fruit by itself; it must remain in the vine. Neither can you bear fruit unless you remain in me.

5"I am the vine; you are the branches. If you remain in me and I in you, you will bear much fruit; apart from me you can do nothing. 6If you do not remain in me, you are like a branch that is thrown away and withers; such branches are picked up, thrown into the fire and burned. 7If you remain in me and my words remain in you, ask whatever you wish, and it will be done for you. 8This is to my Father's glory, that you bear much fruit, showing yourselves to be my disciples.

9"As the Father has loved me, so have I loved you. Now remain in my love. 10If you keep my commands, you will remain in my love, just as I have kept my Father's commands and remain in his love. 11I have told you this so that my joy may be in you and that your joy may be complete. 12My command is this: Love each other as I have loved you. 13Greater love has no one than this: to lay down one's life for one's friends. 14You are my friends if you do what I command. 15I no longer call you servants, because a servant does not know his master's business. Instead, I have called you friends, for everything that I learned from my Father I have made known to you. 16You did not choose me, but I chose you and appointed you so that you might go and bear fruit — fruit that will last — and so that whatever you ask in my name the Father will give you. 17This is my command: Love each other.

THE WORLD HATES THE DISCIPLES

18"If the world hates you, keep in mind that it hated me first. 19If you belonged to the world, it would love you as its own. As it is, you do not belong to the world, but I have chosen you out of the world. That is why the world hates you. 20Remember what I told you: 'A servant is not greater than his master.'[b] If they persecuted me, they will persecute you also. If they obeyed my teaching, they will obey yours also. 21They will treat you this way because of my name, for they do not know the one who sent me. 22If I had not come and spoken to them, they would not be guilty of sin; but now they have no excuse for their sin. 23Whoever hates me hates my Father as well. 24If I had not done among them the works no one else did, they would not be guilty of sin. As it is, they have seen, and yet they have hated both me and my Father. 25But this is to fulfill what is written in their Law: 'They hated me without reason.'[c]

PRAYING SCRIPTURE

John 15

Wherever we invest our time and energy, there we abide. For the Christian, we are either abiding in this world or abiding in Christ. We cannot claim to abide in Christ if all our love and effort prioritizes things that do not count for eternity.

In what or whom are you abiding? To bear spiritual fruit that lasts, pray to abide in Christ.

[a] *2* The Greek for *he prunes* also means *he cleans.* [b] *20* John 13:16
[c] *25* Psalms 35:19; 69:4

THE WORK OF THE HOLY SPIRIT

26“When the Advocate comes, whom I will send to you from the Fa-
ther — the Spirit of truth who goes out from the Father — he will testify
about me. 27And you also must testify, for you have been with me from
the beginning.

16 “All this I have told you so that you will not fall away. 2They
will put you out of the synagogue; in fact, the time is coming
when anyone who kills you will think they are offering a service to
God. 3They will do such things because they have not known the Father
or me. 4I have told you this, so that when their time comes you will
remember that I warned you about them. I did not tell you this from
the beginning because I was with you, 5but now I am going to him who
sent me. None of you asks me, ‘Where are you going?’ 6Rather, you
are filled with grief because I have said these things. 7But very truly
I tell you, it is for your good that I am going away. Unless I go away,
the Advocate will not come to you; but if I go, I will send him to you.
8When he comes, he will prove the world to be in the wrong about sin
and righteousness and judgment: 9about sin, because people do not
believe in me; 10about righteousness, because I am going to the Father,
where you can see me no longer; 11and about judgment, because the
prince of this world now stands condemned.

12“I have much more to say to you, more than you can now bear.
13But when he, the Spirit of truth, comes, he will guide you into all the
truth. He will not speak on his own; he will speak only what he hears,
and he will tell you what is yet to come. 14He will glorify me because it
is from me that he will receive what he will make known to you. 15All
that belongs to the Father is mine. That is why I said the Spirit will re-
ceive from me what he will make known to you.”

THE DISCIPLES’ GRIEF WILL TURN TO JOY

16Jesus went on to say, “In a little while you will see me no more, and
then after a little while you will see me.”

17At this, some of his disciples said to one another, “What does he
mean by saying, ‘In a little while you will see me no more, and then
after a little while you will see me,’ and ‘Because I am going to the Fa-
ther’?” 18They kept asking, “What does he mean by ‘a little while’? We
don’t understand what he is saying.”

19Jesus saw that they wanted to ask him about this, so he said to
them, “Are you asking one another what I meant when I said, ‘In a little
while you will see me no more, and then after a little while you will see
me’? 20Very truly I tell you, you will weep and mourn while the world
rejoices. You will grieve, but your grief will turn to joy. 21A woman giv-
ing birth to a child has pain because her time has come; but when her
baby is born she forgets the anguish because of her joy that a child is
born into the world. 22So with you: Now is your time of grief, but I will
see you again and you will rejoice, and no one will take away your joy.
23In that day you will no longer ask me anything. Very truly I tell you,
my Father will give you whatever you ask in my name. 24Until now you
have not asked for anything in my name. Ask and you will receive, and
your joy will be complete.

25“Though I have been speaking figuratively, a time is coming when
I will no longer use this kind of language but will tell you plainly about
my Father. 26In that day you will ask in my name. I am not saying that
I will ask the Father on your behalf. 27No, the Father himself loves you

PRAYING SCRIPTURE

John 16

If Jesus’ followers meditate on this truth, it will bring great joy: He has overcome the world (see verse 33). We need not overcome the world. Instead, we walk in the victory he has already won. That is why we can have peace even in tribulation. Jesus has won, and we win in him.

Are you trusting daily in Christ’s victory? Confess that he has overcome, and walk in that truth.

because you have loved me and have believed that I came from God. [28]I came from the Father and entered the world; now I am leaving the world and going back to the Father."

[29]Then Jesus' disciples said, "Now you are speaking clearly and without figures of speech. [30]Now we can see that you know all things and that you do not even need to have anyone ask you questions. This makes us believe that you came from God."

[31]"Do you now believe?" Jesus replied. [32]"A time is coming and in fact has come when you will be scattered, each to your own home. You will leave me all alone. Yet I am not alone, for my Father is with me.

[33]"I have told you these things, so that in me you may have peace. In this world you will have trouble. But take heart! I have overcome the world."

PRAYING SCRIPTURE

John 17

This prayer of Jesus the hour before his arrest gives insight to what was on his mind as he approached the cross. After praying briefly for himself, he prayed extensively for his disciples and for all who would believe in him because of their testimony. Jesus prayed for all his followers for all time that night.

How are your prayers divided between your concerns and others' needs? Let Jesus' prayer guide you.

JESUS PRAYS TO BE GLORIFIED

17 After Jesus said this, he looked toward heaven and prayed:

"Father, the hour has come. Glorify your Son, that your Son may glorify you. [2]For you granted him authority over all people that he might give eternal life to all those you have given him. [3]Now this is eternal life: that they know you, the only true God, and Jesus Christ, whom you have sent. [4]I have brought you glory on earth by finishing the work you gave me to do. [5]And now, Father, glorify me in your presence with the glory I had with you before the world began.

JESUS PRAYS FOR HIS DISCIPLES

[6]"I have revealed you[a] to those whom you gave me out of the world. They were yours; you gave them to me and they have obeyed your word. [7]Now they know that everything you have given me comes from you. [8]For I gave them the words you gave me and they accepted them. They knew with certainty that I came from you, and they believed that you sent me. [9]I pray for them. I am not praying for the world, but for those you have given me, for they are yours. [10]All I have is yours, and all you have is mine. And glory has come to me through them. [11]I will remain in the world no longer, but they are still in the world, and I am coming to you. Holy Father, protect them by the power of[b] your name, the name you gave me, so that they may be one as we are one. [12]While I was with them, I protected them and kept them safe by[c] that name you gave me. None has been lost except the one doomed to destruction so that Scripture would be fulfilled.

[13]"I am coming to you now, but I say these things while I am still in the world, so that they may have the full measure of my joy within them. [14]I have given them your word and the world has hated them, for they are not of the world any more than I am of the world. [15]My prayer is not that you take them out of the world but that you protect them from the evil one. [16]They are not of the world, even as I am not of it. [17]Sanctify them by[d] the truth; your word is truth. [18]As you sent me into the world, I have sent them into the world. [19]For them I sanctify myself, that they too may be truly sanctified.

[a] 6 Greek *your name* [b] 11 Or *Father, keep them faithful to* [c] 12 Or *kept them faithful to* [d] 17 Or *them to live in accordance with*

JESUS PRAYS FOR ALL BELIEVERS

20“My prayer is not for them alone. I pray also for those who will
believe in me through their message, 21that all of them may be
one, Father, just as you are in me and I am in you. May they also
be in us so that the world may believe that you have sent me. 22I
have given them the glory that you gave me, that they may be one
as we are one — 23I in them and you in me — so that they may be
brought to complete unity. Then the world will know that you sent
me and have loved them even as you have loved me.
24“Father, I want those you have given me to be with me where I
am, and to see my glory, the glory you have given me because you
loved me before the creation of the world.
25“Righteous Father, though the world does not know you, I
know you, and they know that you have sent me. 26I have made
you[a] known to them, and will continue to make you known in or-
der that the love you have for me may be in them and that I myself
may be in them.”

JESUS ARRESTED

18 When he had finished praying, Jesus left with his disciples and
crossed the Kidron Valley. On the other side there was a garden,
and he and his disciples went into it.
2Now Judas, who betrayed him, knew the place, because Jesus had
often met there with his disciples. 3So Judas came to the garden, guid-
ing a detachment of soldiers and some officials from the chief priests
and the Pharisees. They were carrying torches, lanterns and weapons.
4Jesus, knowing all that was going to happen to him, went out and
asked them, “Who is it you want?”
5“Jesus of Nazareth,” they replied.
“I am he,” Jesus said. (And Judas the traitor was standing there with
them.) 6When Jesus said, “I am he,” they drew back and fell to the
ground.
7Again he asked them, “Who is it you want?”
“Jesus of Nazareth,” they said.
8Jesus answered, “I told you that I am he. If you are looking for me,
then let these men go.” 9This happened so that the words he had spo-
ken would be fulfilled: “I have not lost one of those you gave me.”[b]
10Then Simon Peter, who had a sword, drew it and struck the high
priest’s servant, cutting off his right ear. (The servant’s name was
Malchus.)
11Jesus commanded Peter, “Put your sword away! Shall I not drink
the cup the Father has given me?”
12Then the detachment of soldiers with its commander and the Jew-
ish officials arrested Jesus. They bound him 13and brought him first
to Annas, who was the father-in-law of Caiaphas, the high priest that
year. 14Caiaphas was the one who had advised the Jewish leaders that
it would be good if one man died for the people.

PETER’S FIRST DENIAL

15Simon Peter and another disciple were following Jesus. Because
this disciple was known to the high priest, he went with Jesus into the
high priest’s courtyard, 16but Peter had to wait outside at the door. The

PRAYING SCRIPTURE

John 18

The narrative of Jesus’ betrayal, arrest and trial reveals the depths to which the leaders went to remove their perceived enemy. Yet Jesus showed nothing but honesty about his mission: “I have spoken openly . . . I always taught in synagogues or at the temple” (verse 20). They had already heard everything he had taught.

Some people look for any excuse not to believe. Pray for unbelievers you know to heed Jesus’ words in faith.

[a] 26 Greek *your name* [b] 9 John 6:39

other disciple, who was known to the high priest, came back, spoke to
the servant girl on duty there and brought Peter in.

17“You aren’t one of this man’s disciples too, are you?” she asked
Peter.

He replied, “I am not.”

18It was cold, and the servants and officials stood around a fire they
had made to keep warm. Peter also was standing with them, warming
himself.

THE HIGH PRIEST QUESTIONS JESUS

19Meanwhile, the high priest questioned Jesus about his disciples
and his teaching.

20“I have spoken openly to the world,” Jesus replied. “I always taught
in synagogues or at the temple, where all the Jews come together. I
said nothing in secret. 21Why question me? Ask those who heard me.
Surely they know what I said.”

22When Jesus said this, one of the officials nearby slapped him in
the face. “Is this the way you answer the high priest?” he demanded.

23“If I said something wrong,” Jesus replied, “testify as to what is
wrong. But if I spoke the truth, why did you strike me?” 24Then Annas
sent him bound to Caiaphas the high priest.

PETER’S SECOND AND THIRD DENIALS

25Meanwhile, Simon Peter was still standing there warming himself.
So they asked him, “You aren’t one of his disciples too, are you?”

He denied it, saying, “I am not.”

26One of the high priest’s servants, a relative of the man whose ear
Peter had cut off, challenged him, “Didn’t I see you with him in the
garden?” 27Again Peter denied it, and at that moment a rooster began
to crow.

JESUS BEFORE PILATE

28Then the Jewish leaders took Jesus from Caiaphas to the palace
of the Roman governor. By now it was early morning, and to avoid
ceremonial uncleanness they did not enter the palace, because they
wanted to be able to eat the Passover. 29So Pilate came out to them and
asked, “What charges are you bringing against this man?”

30“If he were not a criminal,” they replied, “we would not have
handed him over to you.”

31Pilate said, “Take him yourselves and judge him by your own law.”

“But we have no right to execute anyone,” they objected. 32This took
place to fulfill what Jesus had said about the kind of death he was go-
ing to die.

33Pilate then went back inside the palace, summoned Jesus and
asked him, “Are you the king of the Jews?”

34“Is that your own idea,” Jesus asked, “or did others talk to you
about me?”

35“Am I a Jew?” Pilate replied. “Your own people and chief priests
handed you over to me. What is it you have done?”

36Jesus said, “My kingdom is not of this world. If it were, my servants
would fight to prevent my arrest by the Jewish leaders. But now my
kingdom is from another place.”

37“You are a king, then!” said Pilate.

Jesus answered, “You say that I am a king. In fact, the reason I was there was a garden, and in the garden a new tomb, in which no one had ever been laid. 42Because it was the Jewish day of Preparation and since the tomb was nearby, they laid Jesus there.

THE EMPTY TOMB

20 Early on the first day of the week, while it was still dark, Mary Magdalene went to the tomb and saw that the stone had been removed from the entrance. 2So she came running to Simon Peter and the other disciple, the one Jesus loved, and said, "They have taken the Lord out of the tomb, and we don't know where they have put him!"

3So Peter and the other disciple started for the tomb. 4Both were running, but the other disciple outran Peter and reached the tomb first. 5He bent over and looked in at the strips of linen lying there but did not go in. 6Then Simon Peter came along behind him and went straight into the tomb. He saw the strips of linen lying there, 7as well as the cloth that had been wrapped around Jesus' head. The cloth was still lying in its place, separate from the linen. 8Finally the other disciple, who had reached the tomb first, also went inside. He saw and believed. 9(They still did not understand from Scripture that Jesus had to rise from the dead.) 10Then the disciples went back to where they were staying.

JESUS APPEARS TO MARY MAGDALENE

11Now Mary stood outside the tomb crying. As she wept, she bent over to look into the tomb 12and saw two angels in white, seated where Jesus' body had been, one at the head and the other at the foot.

13They asked her, "Woman, why are you crying?"

"They have taken my Lord away," she said, "and I don't know where they have put him." 14At this, she turned around and saw Jesus standing there, but she did not realize that it was Jesus.

15He asked her, "Woman, why are you crying? Who is it you are looking for?"

Thinking he was the gardener, she said, "Sir, if you have carried him away, tell me where you have put him, and I will get him."

16Jesus said to her, "Mary."

She turned toward him and cried out in Aramaic, "Rabboni!" (which means "Teacher").

17Jesus said, "Do not hold on to me, for I have not yet ascended to the Father. Go instead to my brothers and tell them, 'I am ascending to my Father and your Father, to my God and your God.'"

18Mary Magdalene went to the disciples with the news: "I have seen the Lord!" And she told them that he had said these things to her.

JESUS APPEARS TO HIS DISCIPLES

19On the evening of that first day of the week, when the disciples were together, with the doors locked for fear of the Jewish leaders, Jesus came and stood among them and said, "Peace be with you!" 20After he said this, he showed them his hands and side. The disciples were overjoyed when they saw the Lord.

21Again Jesus said, "Peace be with you! As the Father has sent me, I am sending you." 22And with that he breathed on them and said, "Receive the Holy Spirit. 23If you forgive anyone's sins, their sins are forgiven; if you do not forgive them, they are not forgiven."

PRAYING SCRIPTURE

John 20

Christian faith hinges on the empty tomb. Did Jesus really rise from the dead? Did he defeat sin, death, hell and the grave? If all these things are true, our lives can be changed forever.

The blessing of faith is here: "Blessed are those who have not seen and yet have believed" (verse 29). Trust God to do the invisible; ask him for faith when yours wavers.

JESUS APPEARS TO THOMAS

24Now Thomas (also known as Didymus[a]), one of the Twelve, was not
with the disciples when Jesus came. 25So the other disciples told him,
"We have seen the Lord!"

But he said to them, "Unless I see the nail marks in his hands and put my finger where the nails were, and put my hand into his side, I will not believe."

26A week later his disciples were in the house again, and Thomas
was with them. Though the doors were locked, Jesus came and stood
among them and said, "Peace be with you!" 27Then he said to Thomas,
"Put your finger here; see my hands. Reach out your hand and put it into my side. Stop doubting and believe."

28Thomas said to him, "My Lord and my God!"

29Then Jesus told him, "Because you have seen me, you have believed; blessed are those who have not seen and yet have believed."

THE PURPOSE OF JOHN'S GOSPEL

30Jesus performed many other signs in the presence of his disciples,
which are not recorded in this book. 31But these are written that you
may believe[b] that Jesus is the Messiah, the Son of God, and that by believing you may have life in his name.

JESUS AND THE MIRACULOUS CATCH OF FISH

21 Afterward Jesus appeared again to his disciples, by the Sea
of Galilee.[c] It happened this way: 2Simon Peter, Thomas (also
known as Didymus[a]), Nathanael from Cana in Galilee, the sons of Zebedee, and two other disciples were together. 3"I'm going out to fish,"
Simon Peter told them, and they said, "We'll go with you." So they went out and got into the boat, but that night they caught nothing.

4Early in the morning, Jesus stood on the shore, but the disciples did not realize that it was Jesus.

5He called out to them, "Friends, haven't you any fish?"

"No," they answered.

6He said, "Throw your net on the right side of the boat and you will find some." When they did, they were unable to haul the net in because of the large number of fish.

7Then the disciple whom Jesus loved said to Peter, "It is the Lord!"
As soon as Simon Peter heard him say, "It is the Lord," he wrapped his outer garment around him (for he had taken it off) and jumped into
the water. 8The other disciples followed in the boat, towing the net
full of fish, for they were not far from shore, about a hundred yards.[d]
9When they landed, they saw a fire of burning coals there with fish on it, and some bread.

10Jesus said to them, "Bring some of the fish you have just caught."
11So Simon Peter climbed back into the boat and dragged the net
ashore. It was full of large fish, 153, but even with so many the net was
not torn. 12Jesus said to them, "Come and have breakfast." None of the
disciples dared ask him, "Who are you?" They knew it was the Lord.
13Jesus came, took the bread and gave it to them, and did the same
with the fish. 14This was now the third time Jesus appeared to his disciples after he was raised from the dead.

PRAYING SCRIPTURE
John 21

It seems appropriate that Peter, having denied Jesus three times, was given the opportunity by Jesus to affirm him three times. Before the other disciples, three times Jesus asked Peter to confess his love for the Savior. Peter did. Jesus thus openly restored the one who denied him only days before.

Jesus forgives and restores. If you are living in shame from denying Christ, express your love, and then feed his sheep.

[a] 24,2 *Thomas* (Aramaic) and *Didymus* (Greek) both mean *twin.* [b] 31 Or *may continue to believe* [c] 1 Greek *Tiberias* [d] 8 Or about 90 meters

JESUS REINSTATES PETER

15 When they had finished eating, Jesus said to Simon Peter, "Simon
son of John, do you love me more than these?"
"Yes, Lord," he said, "you know that I love you."
Jesus said, "Feed my lambs."
16 Again Jesus said, "Simon son of John, do you love me?"
He answered, "Yes, Lord, you know that I love you."
Jesus said, "Take care of my sheep."
17 The third time he said to him, "Simon son of John, do you love me?"
Peter was hurt because Jesus asked him the third time, "Do you love
me?" He said, "Lord, you know all things; you know that I love you."
Jesus said, "Feed my sheep. 18 Very truly I tell you, when you were
younger you dressed yourself and went where you wanted; but when
you are old you will stretch out your hands, and someone else will
dress you and lead you where you do not want to go." 19 Jesus said this
to indicate the kind of death by which Peter would glorify God. Then
he said to him, "Follow me!"

20 Peter turned and saw that the disciple whom Jesus loved was fol-
lowing them. (This was the one who had leaned back against Jesus at
the supper and had said, "Lord, who is going to betray you?") 21 When
Peter saw him, he asked, "Lord, what about him?"
22 Jesus answered, "If I want him to remain alive until I return,
what is that to you? You must follow me." 23 Because of this, the rumor
spread among the believers that this disciple would not die. But Jesus
did not say that he would not die; he only said, "If I want him to re-
main alive until I return, what is that to you?"
24 This is the disciple who testifies to these things and who wrote
them down. We know that his testimony is true.
25 Jesus did many other things as well. If every one of them were
written down, I suppose that even the whole world would not have
room for the books that would be written.

ACTS

The book of Acts is addressed to Theophilus like its companion piece, the Gospel of Luke. Acts details the release of the Holy Spirit into humankind, and the expansive growth of the church headed by Jesus Christ.

Jesus had appeared to the apostles for a period of 40 days between his resurrection and ascension, and he taught them what they needed to know about the mission they were to fulfill until he returned. He told the disciples that they would be his witnesses in "Jerusalem, and in all Judea and Samaria, and to the ends of the earth" (1:8).

When the Holy Spirit descended upon them, they experienced the power from on high, and the church exploded into existence. Almost immediately we read of the conversion of three thousand people after a powerful sermon given by Peter.

The power of God seen in the explosive expansion of the early church was ushered in through the prayers of the apostles and early believers. Prayer was an integral part of the daily lives of those in the early church. Daily believers met, eating together, studying together, fellowshiping and praying. Indeed, there simply would not have been the early church we have come to know without the prayers of God's people.

Prayer plays a pivotal role in the church's mission. These early followers of Jesus prayed to fill the office left vacant by the betrayal and death of Judas. They were in a room praying when God sent the Holy Spirit. They prayed for boldness to spread God's Word. The apostles prayed over the men they set apart to serve tables. Leaders fasted and prayed before sending out Paul and Barnabas on the first missionary journey. Paul and Silas, imprisoned at Philippi, were praying and singing hymns at midnight when an earthquake broke their chains, freeing them to share the gospel with their jailer. Apostles prayed for people to be healed, and Paul prayed with the Ephesian elders as he told them he might never see them again.

Prayer was not tied to just one aspect of the church's life together. Rather, it propelled every area—mission, leadership, healing and personal witness. This set a model for Jesus' followers today. The church cannot carry out its mission without prayer. The church prays for wisdom in selecting its leaders and then prays for those leaders. Christians pray for boldness to spread God's Word in their daily lives and ask God to protect them as they do so. They pray for other Christians who are suffering with sickness and ask God to heal them. The church prays for people who will go to remote corners of the globe to share the gospel and then prays over those who are called out to go.

JESUS TAKEN UP INTO HEAVEN

1 In my former book, Theophilus, I wrote about all that Jesus began
to do and to teach 2until the day he was taken up to heaven, after
giving instructions through the Holy Spirit to the apostles he had cho-
sen. 3After his suffering, he presented himself to them and gave many
convincing proofs that he was alive. He appeared to them over a period
of forty days and spoke about the kingdom of God. 4On one occasion,
while he was eating with them, he gave them this command: "Do not
leave Jerusalem, but wait for the gift my Father promised, which you
have heard me speak about. 5For John baptized with[a] water, but in a
few days you will be baptized with[a] the Holy Spirit."
6Then they gathered around him and asked him, "Lord, are you at
this time going to restore the kingdom to Israel?"
7He said to them: "It is not for you to know the times or dates the Fa-
ther has set by his own authority. 8But you will receive power when the
Holy Spirit comes on you; and you will be my witnesses in Jerusalem,
and in all Judea and Samaria, and to the ends of the earth."
9After he said this, he was taken up before their very eyes, and a
cloud hid him from their sight.
10They were looking intently up into the sky as he was going, when
suddenly two men dressed in white stood beside them. 11"Men of Gali-
lee," they said, "why do you stand here looking into the sky? This same
Jesus, who has been taken from you into heaven, will come back in the
same way you have seen him go into heaven."

MATTHIAS CHOSEN TO REPLACE JUDAS

12Then the apostles returned to Jerusalem from the hill called the
Mount of Olives, a Sabbath day's walk[b] from the city. 13When they ar-
rived, they went upstairs to the room where they were staying. Those
present were Peter, John, James and Andrew; Philip and Thomas, Bar-
tholomew and Matthew; James son of Alphaeus and Simon the Zealot,
and Judas son of James. 14They all joined together constantly in prayer,
along with the women and Mary the mother of Jesus, and with his
brothers.
15In those days Peter stood up among the believers (a group num-
bering about a hundred and twenty) 16and said, "Brothers and sisters,[c]
the Scripture had to be fulfilled in which the Holy Spirit spoke long ago
through David concerning Judas, who served as guide for those who
arrested Jesus. 17He was one of our number and shared in our ministry."
18(With the payment he received for his wickedness, Judas bought a
field; there he fell headlong, his body burst open and all his intestines
spilled out. 19Everyone in Jerusalem heard about this, so they called
that field in their language Akeldama, that is, Field of Blood.)
20"For," said Peter, "it is written in the Book of Psalms:

"'May his place be deserted;
let there be no one to dwell in it,'[d]

and,

"'May another take his place of leadership.'[e]

PRAYING SCRIPTURE

Acts 1

The return of Jesus to heaven—the ascension—is sometimes overlooked because it is between Christ's charge in Acts 1:8 and the coming of the Holy Spirit at Pentecost. But, it is his ascension that both opened the door to the Spirit's coming and Jesus' taking his seat at the Father's right hand.

Have you reflected on Christ's position in heaven on your behalf? Take your requests to him confidently; he intercedes for you!

---

[a] *5* Or *in* [b] *12* That is, about 5/8 mile or about 1 kilometer [c] *16* The Greek word for *brothers and sisters* (*adelphoi*) refers here to believers, both men and women, as part of God's family; also in 6:3; 11:29; 12:17; 16:40; 18:18,27; 21:7,17; 28:14,15. [d] *20* Psalm 69:25 [e] *20* Psalm 109:8

21 Therefore it is necessary to choose one of the men who have been
with us the whole time the Lord Jesus was living among us, 22 be-
ginning from John's baptism to the time when Jesus was taken
up from us. For one of these must become a witness with us of his
resurrection."
23 So they nominated two men: Joseph called Barsabbas (also known
as Justus) and Matthias. 24 Then they prayed, "Lord, you know every-
one's heart. Show us which of these two you have chosen 25 to take
over this apostolic ministry, which Judas left to go where he belongs."
26 Then they cast lots, and the lot fell to Matthias; so he was added to
the eleven apostles.

THE HOLY SPIRIT COMES AT PENTECOST

2 When the day of Pentecost came, they were all together in one
place. 2 Suddenly a sound like the blowing of a violent wind came
from heaven and filled the whole house where they were sitting. 3 They
saw what seemed to be tongues of fire that separated and came to rest
on each of them. 4 All of them were filled with the Holy Spirit and be-
gan to speak in other tongues[a] as the Spirit enabled them.
5 Now there were staying in Jerusalem God-fearing Jews from every
nation under heaven. 6 When they heard this sound, a crowd came to-
gether in bewilderment, because each one heard their own language
being spoken. 7 Utterly amazed, they asked: "Aren't all these who are
speaking Galileans? 8 Then how is it that each of us hears them in our
native language? 9 Parthians, Medes and Elamites; residents of Meso-
potamia, Judea and Cappadocia, Pontus and Asia,[b] 10 Phrygia and Pam-
phylia, Egypt and the parts of Libya near Cyrene; visitors from Rome
11 (both Jews and converts to Judaism); Cretans and Arabs — we hear
them declaring the wonders of God in our own tongues!" 12 Amazed
and perplexed, they asked one another, "What does this mean?"
13 Some, however, made fun of them and said, "They have had too
much wine."

PRAYING SCRIPTURE

Acts 2

On the day of Pentecost, the Holy Spirit arrived like a "blowing of a violent wind," bringing "tongues of fire" to the disciples (verses 2,3). And what was on their tongues? The wonders of God in many languages! (see verse 11).

Ask God to use your tongue to speak his wonders among those you encounter and to rekindle your fire for the glory of his great name.

PETER ADDRESSES THE CROWD

14 Then Peter stood up with the Eleven, raised his voice and ad-
dressed the crowd: "Fellow Jews and all of you who live in Jerusalem,
let me explain this to you; listen carefully to what I say. 15 These people
are not drunk, as you suppose. It's only nine in the morning! 16 No, this
is what was spoken by the prophet Joel:

17 " 'In the last days, God says,
I will pour out my Spirit on all people.
Your sons and daughters will prophesy,
your young men will see visions,
your old men will dream dreams.
18 Even on my servants, both men and women,
I will pour out my Spirit in those days,
and they will prophesy.
19 I will show wonders in the heavens above
and signs on the earth below,
blood and fire and billows of smoke.

[a] 4 Or *languages*; also in verse 11 [b] 9 That is, the Roman province by that name

20 The sun will be turned to darkness
and the moon to blood
before the coming of the great and glorious day of the Lord.
21 And everyone who calls
on the name of the Lord will be saved.'[a]

22 "Fellow Israelites, listen to this: Jesus of Nazareth was a man ac-
credited by God to you by miracles, wonders and signs, which God
did among you through him, as you yourselves know. 23 This man was
handed over to you by God's deliberate plan and foreknowledge; and
you, with the help of wicked men,[b] put him to death by nailing him to
the cross. 24 But God raised him from the dead, freeing him from the
agony of death, because it was impossible for death to keep its hold on
him. 25 David said about him:

"'I saw the Lord always before me.
Because he is at my right hand,
I will not be shaken.
26 Therefore my heart is glad and my tongue rejoices;
my body also will rest in hope,
27 because you will not abandon me to the realm of the dead,
you will not let your holy one see decay.
28 You have made known to me the paths of life;
you will fill me with joy in your presence.'[c]

29 "Fellow Israelites, I can tell you confidently that the patriarch Da-
vid died and was buried, and his tomb is here to this day. 30 But he was
a prophet and knew that God had promised him on oath that he would
place one of his descendants on his throne. 31 Seeing what was to come,
he spoke of the resurrection of the Messiah, that he was not abandoned
to the realm of the dead, nor did his body see decay. 32 God has raised
this Jesus to life, and we are all witnesses of it. 33 Exalted to the right
hand of God, he has received from the Father the promised Holy Spirit
and has poured out what you now see and hear. 34 For David did not
ascend to heaven, and yet he said,

"'The Lord said to my Lord:
"Sit at my right hand
35 until I make your enemies
a footstool for your feet."'[d]

36 "Therefore let all Israel be assured of this: God has made this Jesus,
whom you crucified, both Lord and Messiah."
37 When the people heard this, they were cut to the heart and said to
Peter and the other apostles, "Brothers, what shall we do?"
38 Peter replied, "Repent and be baptized, every one of you, in the
name of Jesus Christ for the forgiveness of your sins. And you will re-
ceive the gift of the Holy Spirit. 39 The promise is for you and your chil-
dren and for all who are far off — for all whom the Lord our God will
call."
40 With many other words he warned them; and he pleaded with
them, "Save yourselves from this corrupt generation." 41 Those who
accepted his message were baptized, and about three thousand were
added to their number that day.

---

[a] *21* Joel 2:28-32 [b] *23* Or *of those not having the law* (that is, Gentiles)
[c] *28* Psalm 16:8-11 (see Septuagint) [d] *35* Psalm 110:1

PRAYING SCRIPTURE

Acts 2

God's indwelling presence brought the life of Jesus to the believers, clothing them with power from on high (Luke 24:49). The Spirit would lead and guide believers to bring God's kingdom to the ends of the earth.

Is your daily life marked by the direction of God's Spirit? Ask him for sensitivity to his leading so his will may be done through your life.

PRAYING SCRIPTURE

Acts 3

From the earliest days of the church, the apostles' preaching emphasized the deity of Jesus. In a sermon near Solomon's Colonnade, Peter identified Jesus as the Prophet who was prophesied by Moses (see verse 22). Peter also echoed Jesus' message of repentance (see verse 19).

We should always keep Jesus at the forefront of our message. He is the Son of God who saves all who believe in him. Pray that those you know will believe in him.

THE FELLOWSHIP OF THE BELIEVERS

42They devoted themselves to the apostles' teaching and to fellowship, to the breaking of bread and to prayer. 43Everyone was filled with awe at the many wonders and signs performed by the apostles. 44All the believers were together and had everything in common. 45They sold property and possessions to give to anyone who had need. 46Every day they continued to meet together in the temple courts. They broke bread in their homes and ate together with glad and sincere hearts, 47praising God and enjoying the favor of all the people. And the Lord added to their number daily those who were being saved.

PETER HEALS A LAME BEGGAR

3 One day Peter and John were going up to the temple at the time of prayer — at three in the afternoon. 2Now a man who was lame from birth was being carried to the temple gate called Beautiful, where he was put every day to beg from those going into the temple courts. 3When he saw Peter and John about to enter, he asked them for money. 4Peter looked straight at him, as did John. Then Peter said, "Look at us!" 5So the man gave them his attention, expecting to get something from them.

6Then Peter said, "Silver or gold I do not have, but what I do have I give you. In the name of Jesus Christ of Nazareth, walk." 7Taking him by the right hand, he helped him up, and instantly the man's feet and ankles became strong. 8He jumped to his feet and began to walk. Then he went with them into the temple courts, walking and jumping, and praising God. 9When all the people saw him walking and praising God, 10they recognized him as the same man who used to sit begging at the temple gate called Beautiful, and they were filled with wonder and amazement at what had happened to him.

PETER SPEAKS TO THE ONLOOKERS

11While the man held on to Peter and John, all the people were astonished and came running to them in the place called Solomon's Colonnade. 12When Peter saw this, he said to them: "Fellow Israelites, why does this surprise you? Why do you stare at us as if by our own power or godliness we had made this man walk? 13The God of Abraham, Isaac and Jacob, the God of our fathers, has glorified his servant Jesus. You handed him over to be killed, and you disowned him before Pilate, though he had decided to let him go. 14You disowned the Holy and Righteous One and asked that a murderer be released to you. 15You killed the author of life, but God raised him from the dead. We are witnesses of this. 16By faith in the name of Jesus, this man whom you see and know was made strong. It is Jesus' name and the faith that comes through him that has completely healed him, as you can all see.

17"Now, fellow Israelites, I know that you acted in ignorance, as did your leaders. 18But this is how God fulfilled what he had foretold through all the prophets, saying that his Messiah would suffer. 19Repent, then, and turn to God, so that your sins may be wiped out, that times of refreshing may come from the Lord, 20and that he may send the Messiah, who has been appointed for you — even Jesus. 21Heaven must receive him until the time comes for God to restore everything, as he promised long ago through his holy prophets. 22For Moses said, 'The Lord your God will raise up for you a prophet like me from among your

own people; you must listen to everything he tells you. 23Anyone who
does not listen to him will be completely cut off from their people.'[a]
24"Indeed, beginning with Samuel, all the prophets who have spoken
have foretold these days. 25And you are heirs of the prophets and of the
covenant God made with your fathers. He said to Abraham, 'Through
your offspring all peoples on earth will be blessed.'[b] 26When God raised
up his servant, he sent him first to you to bless you by turning each of
you from your wicked ways."

PETER AND JOHN BEFORE THE SANHEDRIN

4 The priests and the captain of the temple guard and the Sadducees
came up to Peter and John while they were speaking to the peo-
ple. 2They were greatly disturbed because the apostles were teaching
the people, proclaiming in Jesus the resurrection of the dead. 3They
seized Peter and John and, because it was evening, they put them in
jail until the next day. 4But many who heard the message believed; so
the number of men who believed grew to about five thousand.
5The next day the rulers, the elders and the teachers of the law met
in Jerusalem. 6Annas the high priest was there, and so were Caiaphas,
John, Alexander and others of the high priest's family. 7They had Peter
and John brought before them and began to question them: "By what
power or what name did you do this?"
8Then Peter, filled with the Holy Spirit, said to them: "Rulers and
elders of the people! 9If we are being called to account today for an act
of kindness shown to a man who was lame and are being asked how he
was healed, 10then know this, you and all the people of Israel: It is by the
name of Jesus Christ of Nazareth, whom you crucified but whom God
raised from the dead, that this man stands before you healed. 11Jesus is

"'the stone you builders rejected,
which has become the cornerstone.'[c]

12Salvation is found in no one else, for there is no other name under
heaven given to mankind by which we must be saved."
13When they saw the courage of Peter and John and realized that
they were unschooled, ordinary men, they were astonished and they
took note that these men had been with Jesus. 14But since they could
see the man who had been healed standing there with them, there
was nothing they could say. 15So they ordered them to withdraw from
the Sanhedrin and then conferred together. 16"What are we going to
do with these men?" they asked. "Everyone living in Jerusalem knows
they have performed a notable sign, and we cannot deny it. 17But to
stop this thing from spreading any further among the people, we must
warn them to speak no longer to anyone in this name."
18Then they called them in again and commanded them not to
speak or teach at all in the name of Jesus. 19But Peter and John re-
plied, "Which is right in God's eyes: to listen to you, or to him? You be
the judges! 20As for us, we cannot help speaking about what we have
seen and heard."
21After further threats they let them go. They could not decide how
to punish them, because all the people were praising God for what had
happened. 22For the man who was miraculously healed was over forty
years old.

[a] 23 Deut. 18:15,18,19 [b] 25 Gen. 22:18; 26:4 [c] 11 Psalm 118:22

PRAYING SCRIPTURE

Acts 4

"All the believers were one in heart and mind" (verse 32). These early believers were so united in the Lord that they were willing to share everything they had, refusing any longer to claim ownership over it. Truly, they were living in light of another kingdom.

Few things are more important to God's people than unity, and we should constantly be praying for it.

THE BELIEVERS PRAY

23On their release, Peter and John went back to their own people
and reported all that the chief priests and the elders had said to them.
24When they heard this, they raised their voices together in prayer to
God. “Sovereign Lord,” they said, “you made the heavens and the earth
and the sea, and everything in them. 25You spoke by the Holy Spirit
through the mouth of your servant, our father David:

“ ‘Why do the nations rage
and the peoples plot in vain?
26 The kings of the earth rise up
and the rulers band together
against the Lord
and against his anointed one.[a]’[b]

27Indeed Herod and Pontius Pilate met together with the Gentiles
and the people of Israel in this city to conspire against your holy ser-
vant Jesus, whom you anointed. 28They did what your power and will
had decided beforehand should happen. 29Now, Lord, consider their
threats and enable your servants to speak your word with great bold-
ness. 30Stretch out your hand to heal and perform signs and wonders
through the name of your holy servant Jesus.”

31After they prayed, the place where they were meeting was shaken.
And they were all filled with the Holy Spirit and spoke the word of
God boldly.

THE BELIEVERS SHARE THEIR POSSESSIONS

32All the believers were one in heart and mind. No one claimed that
any of their possessions was their own, but they shared everything
they had. 33With great power the apostles continued to testify to the
resurrection of the Lord Jesus. And God’s grace was so powerfully at
work in them all 34that there were no needy persons among them. For
from time to time those who owned land or houses sold them, brought
the money from the sales 35and put it at the apostles’ feet, and it was
distributed to anyone who had need.

36Joseph, a Levite from Cyprus, whom the apostles called Barnabas
(which means “son of encouragement”), 37sold a field he owned and
brought the money and put it at the apostles’ feet.

ANANIAS AND SAPPHIRA

5 Now a man named Ananias, together with his wife Sapphira, also
sold a piece of property. 2With his wife’s full knowledge he kept
back part of the money for himself, but brought the rest and put it at
the apostles’ feet.

3Then Peter said, “Ananias, how is it that Satan has so filled your
heart that you have lied to the Holy Spirit and have kept for yourself
some of the money you received for the land? 4Didn’t it belong to you
before it was sold? And after it was sold, wasn’t the money at your dis-
posal? What made you think of doing such a thing? You have not lied
just to human beings but to God.”

5When Ananias heard this, he fell down and died. And great fear
seized all who heard what had happened. 6Then some young men came
forward, wrapped up his body, and carried him out and buried him.

PRAYING SCRIPTURE

Acts 5

Riding the wave of property selling to support God’s church, one couple decided to lie about their gift. Ananias and Sapphira both were struck dead at Peter’s feet for lying to the Holy Spirit. All giving was voluntary, and there was no reason for them to lie—except pride.

When we lie to the body of Christ we lie to the Holy Spirit of God. Pray to always be truthful.

[a] *26* That is, Messiah or Christ [b] *26* Psalm 2:1,2

7About three hours later his wife came in, not knowing what had happened. 8Peter asked her, "Tell me, is this the price you and Ananias got for the land?"

"Yes," she said, "that is the price."

9Peter said to her, "How could you conspire to test the Spirit of the Lord? Listen! The feet of the men who buried your husband are at the door, and they will carry you out also."

10At that moment she fell down at his feet and died. Then the young men came in and, finding her dead, carried her out and buried her beside her husband. 11Great fear seized the whole church and all who heard about these events.

THE APOSTLES HEAL MANY

12The apostles performed many signs and wonders among the people. And all the believers used to meet together in Solomon's Colonnade. 13No one else dared join them, even though they were highly regarded by the people. 14Nevertheless, more and more men and women believed in the Lord and were added to their number. 15As a result, people brought the sick into the streets and laid them on beds and mats so that at least Peter's shadow might fall on some of them as he passed by. 16Crowds gathered also from the towns around Jerusalem, bringing their sick and those tormented by impure spirits, and all of them were healed.

THE APOSTLES PERSECUTED

17Then the high priest and all his associates, who were members of the party of the Sadducees, were filled with jealousy. 18They arrested the apostles and put them in the public jail. 19But during the night an angel of the Lord opened the doors of the jail and brought them out. 20"Go, stand in the temple courts," he said, "and tell the people all about this new life."

21At daybreak they entered the temple courts, as they had been told, and began to teach the people.

When the high priest and his associates arrived, they called together the Sanhedrin — the full assembly of the elders of Israel — and sent to the jail for the apostles. 22But on arriving at the jail, the officers did not find them there. So they went back and reported, 23"We found the jail securely locked, with the guards standing at the doors; but when we opened them, we found no one inside." 24On hearing this report, the captain of the temple guard and the chief priests were at a loss, wondering what this might lead to.

25Then someone came and said, "Look! The men you put in jail are standing in the temple courts teaching the people." 26At that, the captain went with his officers and brought the apostles. They did not use force, because they feared that the people would stone them.

27The apostles were brought in and made to appear before the Sanhedrin to be questioned by the high priest. 28"We gave you strict orders not to teach in this name," he said. "Yet you have filled Jerusalem with your teaching and are determined to make us guilty of this man's blood."

29Peter and the other apostles replied: "We must obey God rather than human beings! 30The God of our ancestors raised Jesus from the dead — whom you killed by hanging him on a cross. 31God exalted him to his own right hand as Prince and Savior that he might bring Israel

to repentance and forgive their sins. 32We are witnesses of these things,
and so is the Holy Spirit, whom God has given to those who obey him."
33When they heard this, they were furious and wanted to put them
to death. 34But a Pharisee named Gamaliel, a teacher of the law, who
was honored by all the people, stood up in the Sanhedrin and ordered
that the men be put outside for a little while. 35Then he addressed the
Sanhedrin: "Men of Israel, consider carefully what you intend to do to
these men. 36Some time ago Theudas appeared, claiming to be some-
body, and about four hundred men rallied to him. He was killed, all
his followers were dispersed, and it all came to nothing. 37After him,
Judas the Galilean appeared in the days of the census and led a band of
people in revolt. He too was killed, and all his followers were scattered.
38Therefore, in the present case I advise you: Leave these men alone!
Let them go! For if their purpose or activity is of human origin, it will
fail. 39But if it is from God, you will not be able to stop these men; you
will only find yourselves fighting against God."
40His speech persuaded them. They called the apostles in and had
them flogged. Then they ordered them not to speak in the name of
Jesus, and let them go.
41The apostles left the Sanhedrin, rejoicing because they had been
counted worthy of suffering disgrace for the Name. 42Day after day, in
the temple courts and from house to house, they never stopped teach-
ing and proclaiming the good news that Jesus is the Messiah.

THE CHOOSING OF THE SEVEN

6 In those days when the number of disciples was increasing, the
Hellenistic Jews[a] among them complained against the Hebraic
Jews because their widows were being overlooked in the daily distri-
bution of food. 2So the Twelve gathered all the disciples together and
said, "It would not be right for us to neglect the ministry of the word
of God in order to wait on tables. 3Brothers and sisters, choose seven
men from among you who are known to be full of the Spirit and wis-
dom. We will turn this responsibility over to them 4and will give our
attention to prayer and the ministry of the word."
5This proposal pleased the whole group. They chose Stephen, a man
full of faith and of the Holy Spirit; also Philip, Procorus, Nicanor, Ti-
mon, Parmenas, and Nicolas from Antioch, a convert to Judaism.
6They presented these men to the apostles, who prayed and laid their
hands on them.
7So the word of God spread. The number of disciples in Jerusalem
increased rapidly, and a large number of priests became obedient to
the faith.

STEPHEN SEIZED

8Now Stephen, a man full of God's grace and power, performed great
wonders and signs among the people. 9Opposition arose, however,
from members of the Synagogue of the Freedmen (as it was called) —
Jews of Cyrene and Alexandria as well as the provinces of Cilicia and
Asia — who began to argue with Stephen. 10But they could not stand
up against the wisdom the Spirit gave him as he spoke.
11Then they secretly persuaded some men to say, "We have heard
Stephen speak blasphemous words against Moses and against God."

PRAYING SCRIPTURE

Acts 6

The early ministry of the church was threatened with derailment by discrimination (Hellenist widows were not receiving the food distribution), so the apostles created a leadership position that would eventually be adopted as a church standard: deacons. These servants shared practical ministry burdens so that ministry of the Word continued as the apostles' primary aim.

Pray that your pastor and deacons serve well together so the needs of the flock are met.

[a] *1* That is, Jews who had adopted the Greek language and culture

12So they stirred up the people and the elders and the teachers of
the law. They seized Stephen and brought him before the Sanhedrin.
13They produced false witnesses, who testified, "This fellow never stops
speaking against this holy place and against the law. 14For we have
heard him say that this Jesus of Nazareth will destroy this place and
change the customs Moses handed down to us."
15All who were sitting in the Sanhedrin looked intently at Stephen,
and they saw that his face was like the face of an angel.

STEPHEN'S SPEECH TO THE SANHEDRIN

7 Then the high priest asked Stephen, "Are these charges true?"
2To this he replied: "Brothers and fathers, listen to me! The God of
glory appeared to our father Abraham while he was still in Mesopota-
mia, before he lived in Harran. 3'Leave your country and your people,'
God said, 'and go to the land I will show you.'[a]
4"So he left the land of the Chaldeans and settled in Harran. After the
death of his father, God sent him to this land where you are now liv-
ing. 5He gave him no inheritance here, not even enough ground to set
his foot on. But God promised him that he and his descendants after
him would possess the land, even though at that time Abraham had
no child. 6God spoke to him in this way: 'For four hundred years your
descendants will be strangers in a country not their own, and they will
be enslaved and mistreated. 7But I will punish the nation they serve as
slaves,' God said, 'and afterward they will come out of that country and
worship me in this place.'[b] 8Then he gave Abraham the covenant of cir-
cumcision. And Abraham became the father of Isaac and circumcised
him eight days after his birth. Later Isaac became the father of Jacob,
and Jacob became the father of the twelve patriarchs.
9"Because the patriarchs were jealous of Joseph, they sold him as a
slave into Egypt. But God was with him 10and rescued him from all his
troubles. He gave Joseph wisdom and enabled him to gain the good-
will of Pharaoh king of Egypt. So Pharaoh made him ruler over Egypt
and all his palace.
11"Then a famine struck all Egypt and Canaan, bringing great suf-
fering, and our ancestors could not find food. 12When Jacob heard
that there was grain in Egypt, he sent our forefathers on their first
visit. 13On their second visit, Joseph told his brothers who he was, and
Pharaoh learned about Joseph's family. 14After this, Joseph sent for
his father Jacob and his whole family, seventy-five in all. 15Then Jacob
went down to Egypt, where he and our ancestors died. 16Their bodies
were brought back to Shechem and placed in the tomb that Abraham
had bought from the sons of Hamor at Shechem for a certain sum of
money.
17"As the time drew near for God to fulfill his promise to Abraham,
the number of our people in Egypt had greatly increased. 18Then 'a new
king, to whom Joseph meant nothing, came to power in Egypt.'[c] 19He
dealt treacherously with our people and oppressed our ancestors by
forcing them to throw out their newborn babies so that they would die.
20"At that time Moses was born, and he was no ordinary child.[d] For
three months he was cared for by his family. 21When he was placed
outside, Pharaoh's daughter took him and brought him up as her own

PRAYING SCRIPTURE

Acts 7

Stephen was an early servant in the church. When facing a false accusation from religious opponents, he relied on Scripture as his defense, preaching a sermon that covered the working of God through Israel's history and concluding that his listeners were guilty of resisting the Holy Spirit (see verse 51).

Resisting the work of the Spirit is dangerous because he was sent by Jesus to continue his ministry. Ask God for obedience to the Spirit's leading.

---

[a] *3* Gen. 12:1 [b] *7* Gen. 15:13,14 [c] *18* Exodus 1:8 [d] *20* Or *was fair in the sight of God*

son. 22Moses was educated in all the wisdom of the Egyptians and was
powerful in speech and action.

23"When Moses was forty years old, he decided to visit his own
people, the Israelites. 24He saw one of them being mistreated by an
Egyptian, so he went to his defense and avenged him by killing the
Egyptian. 25Moses thought that his own people would realize that God
was using him to rescue them, but they did not. 26The next day Moses
came upon two Israelites who were fighting. He tried to reconcile them
by saying, 'Men, you are brothers; why do you want to hurt each other?'

27"But the man who was mistreating the other pushed Moses aside
and said, 'Who made you ruler and judge over us? 28Are you thinking of
killing me as you killed the Egyptian yesterday?'[a] 29When Moses heard
this, he fled to Midian, where he settled as a foreigner and had two sons.

30"After forty years had passed, an angel appeared to Moses in the
flames of a burning bush in the desert near Mount Sinai. 31When he saw
this, he was amazed at the sight. As he went over to get a closer look, he
heard the Lord say: 32'I am the God of your fathers, the God of Abraham,
Isaac and Jacob.'[b] Moses trembled with fear and did not dare to look.

33"Then the Lord said to him, 'Take off your sandals, for the place
where you are standing is holy ground. 34I have indeed seen the op-
pression of my people in Egypt. I have heard their groaning and have
come down to set them free. Now come, I will send you back to Egypt.'[c]

35"This is the same Moses they had rejected with the words, 'Who
made you ruler and judge?' He was sent to be their ruler and deliverer
by God himself, through the angel who appeared to him in the bush.
36He led them out of Egypt and performed wonders and signs in Egypt,
at the Red Sea and for forty years in the wilderness.

37"This is the Moses who told the Israelites, 'God will raise up for you
a prophet like me from your own people.'[d] 38He was in the assembly
in the wilderness, with the angel who spoke to him on Mount Sinai,
and with our ancestors; and he received living words to pass on to us.

39"But our ancestors refused to obey him. Instead, they rejected him
and in their hearts turned back to Egypt. 40They told Aaron, 'Make us
gods who will go before us. As for this fellow Moses who led us out of
Egypt — we don't know what has happened to him!'[e] 41That was the
time they made an idol in the form of a calf. They brought sacrifices
to it and reveled in what their own hands had made. 42But God turned
away from them and gave them over to the worship of the sun, moon
and stars. This agrees with what is written in the book of the prophets:

" 'Did you bring me sacrifices and offerings
forty years in the wilderness, people of Israel?
43You have taken up the tabernacle of Molek
and the star of your god Rephan,
the idols you made to worship.
Therefore I will send you into exile'[f] beyond Babylon.

44"Our ancestors had the tabernacle of the covenant law with them
in the wilderness. It had been made as God directed Moses, according
to the pattern he had seen. 45After receiving the tabernacle, our ances-
tors under Joshua brought it with them when they took the land from
the nations God drove out before them. It remained in the land until

---

[a] 28 Exodus 2:14 [b] 32 Exodus 3:6 [c] 34 Exodus 3:5,7,8,10 [d] 37 Deut. 18:15
[e] 40 Exodus 32:1 [f] 43 Amos 5:25-27 (see Septuagint)

the time of David, 46who enjoyed God's favor and asked that he might
provide a dwelling place for the God of Jacob.[a] 47But it was Solomon
who built a house for him.
48"However, the Most High does not live in houses made by human
hands. As the prophet says:

49" 'Heaven is my throne,
and the earth is my footstool.
What kind of house will you build for me?
says the Lord.
Or where will my resting place be?
50 Has not my hand made all these things?'[b]

51"You stiff-necked people! Your hearts and ears are still uncircum-
cised. You are just like your ancestors: You always resist the Holy Spirit!
52Was there ever a prophet your ancestors did not persecute? They even
killed those who predicted the coming of the Righteous One. And now
you have betrayed and murdered him — 53you who have received the
law that was given through angels but have not obeyed it."

THE STONING OF STEPHEN

54When the members of the Sanhedrin heard this, they were furious
and gnashed their teeth at him. 55But Stephen, full of the Holy Spirit,
looked up to heaven and saw the glory of God, and Jesus standing at
the right hand of God. 56"Look," he said, "I see heaven open and the
Son of Man standing at the right hand of God."
57At this they covered their ears and, yelling at the top of their voices,
they all rushed at him, 58dragged him out of the city and began to
stone him. Meanwhile, the witnesses laid their coats at the feet of a
young man named Saul.
59While they were stoning him, Stephen prayed, "Lord Jesus, receive
my spirit." 60Then he fell on his knees and cried out, "Lord, do not hold
this sin against them." When he had said this, he fell asleep.
8 And Saul approved of their killing him.

THE CHURCH PERSECUTED AND SCATTERED

On that day a great persecution broke out against the church in
Jerusalem, and all except the apostles were scattered throughout Ju-
dea and Samaria. 2Godly men buried Stephen and mourned deeply
for him. 3But Saul began to destroy the church. Going from house to
house, he dragged off both men and women and put them in prison.

PHILIP IN SAMARIA

4Those who had been scattered preached the word wherever they
went. 5Philip went down to a city in Samaria and proclaimed the Mes-
siah there. 6When the crowds heard Philip and saw the signs he per-
formed, they all paid close attention to what he said. 7For with shrieks,
impure spirits came out of many, and many who were paralyzed or
lame were healed. 8So there was great joy in that city.

SIMON THE SORCERER

9Now for some time a man named Simon had practiced sorcery in
the city and amazed all the people of Samaria. He boasted that he was

PRAYING SCRIPTURE

Acts 8

In the midst of God's continuing work, Philip, one of the early church servants, was called by an angel to another place. A government official from Ethiopia was returning home from Jerusalem. He was a spiritual seeker but lacked a full understanding about Jesus. Philip explained the Scriptures to the man, who believed in Jesus and was immediately baptized.

Ask God to use you like he did Philip to touch others with the gospel.

[a] 46 Some early manuscripts *the house of Jacob* [b] 50 Isaiah 66:1,2

someone great, [10]and all the people, both high and low, gave him their
attention and exclaimed, "This man is rightly called the Great Power
of God." [11]They followed him because he had amazed them for a long
time with his sorcery. [12]But when they believed Philip as he proclaimed
the good news of the kingdom of God and the name of Jesus Christ,
they were baptized, both men and women. [13]Simon himself believed
and was baptized. And he followed Philip everywhere, astonished by
the great signs and miracles he saw.

[14]When the apostles in Jerusalem heard that Samaria had accepted
the word of God, they sent Peter and John to Samaria. [15]When they ar-
rived, they prayed for the new believers there that they might receive
the Holy Spirit, [16]because the Holy Spirit had not yet come on any of
them; they had simply been baptized in the name of the Lord Jesus.
[17]Then Peter and John placed their hands on them, and they received
the Holy Spirit.

[18]When Simon saw that the Spirit was given at the laying on of the
apostles' hands, he offered them money [19]and said, "Give me also this
ability so that everyone on whom I lay my hands may receive the Holy
Spirit."

[20]Peter answered: "May your money perish with you, because you
thought you could buy the gift of God with money! [21]You have no part
or share in this ministry, because your heart is not right before God.
[22]Repent of this wickedness and pray to the Lord in the hope that he
may forgive you for having such a thought in your heart. [23]For I see
that you are full of bitterness and captive to sin."

[24]Then Simon answered, "Pray to the Lord for me so that nothing
you have said may happen to me."

[25]After they had further proclaimed the word of the Lord and testi-
fied about Jesus, Peter and John returned to Jerusalem, preaching the
gospel in many Samaritan villages.

PHILIP AND THE ETHIOPIAN

[26]Now an angel of the Lord said to Philip, "Go south to the road —
the desert road — that goes down from Jerusalem to Gaza." [27]So he
started out, and on his way he met an Ethiopian[a] eunuch, an impor-
tant official in charge of all the treasury of the Kandake (which means
"queen of the Ethiopians"). This man had gone to Jerusalem to wor-
ship, [28]and on his way home was sitting in his chariot reading the Book
of Isaiah the prophet. [29]The Spirit told Philip, "Go to that chariot and
stay near it."

[30]Then Philip ran up to the chariot and heard the man reading Isaiah
the prophet. "Do you understand what you are reading?" Philip asked.

[31]"How can I," he said, "unless someone explains it to me?" So he
invited Philip to come up and sit with him.

[32]This is the passage of Scripture the eunuch was reading:

"He was led like a sheep to the slaughter,
    and as a lamb before its shearer is silent,
    so he did not open his mouth.
[33]In his humiliation he was deprived of justice.
    Who can speak of his descendants?
    For his life was taken from the earth."[b]

---

[a] *27* That is, from the southern Nile region [b] *33* Isaiah 53:7,8 (see Septuagint)

[34]The eunuch asked Philip, "Tell me, please, who is the prophet talking about, himself or someone else?" [35]Then Philip began with that very passage of Scripture and told him the good news about Jesus.

[36]As they traveled along the road, they came to some water and the eunuch said, "Look, here is water. What can stand in the way of my being baptized?" [37][a] [38]And he gave orders to stop the chariot. Then both Philip and the eunuch went down into the water and Philip baptized him. [39]When they came up out of the water, the Spirit of the Lord suddenly took Philip away, and the eunuch did not see him again, but went on his way rejoicing. [40]Philip, however, appeared at Azotus and traveled about, preaching the gospel in all the towns until he reached Caesarea.

SAUL'S CONVERSION

9 Meanwhile, Saul was still breathing out murderous threats against the Lord's disciples. He went to the high priest [2]and asked him for letters to the synagogues in Damascus, so that if he found any there who belonged to the Way, whether men or women, he might take them as prisoners to Jerusalem. [3]As he neared Damascus on his journey, suddenly a light from heaven flashed around him. [4]He fell to the ground and heard a voice say to him, "Saul, Saul, why do you persecute me?"

[5]"Who are you, Lord?" Saul asked.

"I am Jesus, whom you are persecuting," he replied. [6]"Now get up and go into the city, and you will be told what you must do."

[7]The men traveling with Saul stood there speechless; they heard the sound but did not see anyone. [8]Saul got up from the ground, but when he opened his eyes he could see nothing. So they led him by the hand into Damascus. [9]For three days he was blind, and did not eat or drink anything.

[10]In Damascus there was a disciple named Ananias. The Lord called to him in a vision, "Ananias!"

"Yes, Lord," he answered.

[11]The Lord told him, "Go to the house of Judas on Straight Street and ask for a man from Tarsus named Saul, for he is praying. [12]In a vision he has seen a man named Ananias come and place his hands on him to restore his sight."

[13]"Lord," Ananias answered, "I have heard many reports about this man and all the harm he has done to your holy people in Jerusalem. [14]And he has come here with authority from the chief priests to arrest all who call on your name."

[15]But the Lord said to Ananias, "Go! This man is my chosen instrument to proclaim my name to the Gentiles and their kings and to the people of Israel. [16]I will show him how much he must suffer for my name."

[17]Then Ananias went to the house and entered it. Placing his hands on Saul, he said, "Brother Saul, the Lord — Jesus, who appeared to you on the road as you were coming here — has sent me so that you may see again and be filled with the Holy Spirit." [18]Immediately, something like scales fell from Saul's eyes, and he could see again. He got up and was baptized, [19]and after taking some food, he regained his strength.

PRAYING SCRIPTURE

Acts 9

The conversion of Saul was so dramatic it spawned its own language for an eye-opening, life-changing event: a "Damascus road experience." To get Saul's attention, Jesus stopped him in his tracks, blinded him and confronted him (see verse 3–5). By persecuting Christians, Saul was persecuting Jesus.

"'Who are you, Lord?' Saul asked" (verse 5). Have you asked this question too? Believe on Jesus and surrender to him, just like Saul did, and your life also will be changed.

[a] 37 Some manuscripts include here *Philip said, "If you believe with all your heart, you may." The eunuch answered, "I believe that Jesus Christ is the Son of God."*

SAUL IN DAMASCUS AND JERUSALEM

Saul spent several days with the disciples in Damascus. 20At once
he began to preach in the synagogues that Jesus is the Son of God.
21All those who heard him were astonished and asked, "Isn't he the
man who raised havoc in Jerusalem among those who call on this
name? And hasn't he come here to take them as prisoners to the chief
priests?" 22Yet Saul grew more and more powerful and baffled the Jews
living in Damascus by proving that Jesus is the Messiah.

23After many days had gone by, there was a conspiracy among the
Jews to kill him, 24but Saul learned of their plan. Day and night they
kept close watch on the city gates in order to kill him. 25But his follow-
ers took him by night and lowered him in a basket through an opening
in the wall.

26When he came to Jerusalem, he tried to join the disciples, but they
were all afraid of him, not believing that he really was a disciple. 27But
Barnabas took him and brought him to the apostles. He told them how
Saul on his journey had seen the Lord and that the Lord had spoken to
him, and how in Damascus he had preached fearlessly in the name of
Jesus. 28So Saul stayed with them and moved about freely in Jerusa-
lem, speaking boldly in the name of the Lord. 29He talked and debated
with the Hellenistic Jews,[a] but they tried to kill him. 30When the be-
lievers learned of this, they took him down to Caesarea and sent him
off to Tarsus.

31Then the church throughout Judea, Galilee and Samaria enjoyed a
time of peace and was strengthened. Living in the fear of the Lord and
encouraged by the Holy Spirit, it increased in numbers.

AENEAS AND DORCAS

32As Peter traveled about the country, he went to visit the Lord's peo-
ple who lived in Lydda. 33There he found a man named Aeneas, who
was paralyzed and had been bedridden for eight years. 34"Aeneas," Pe-
ter said to him, "Jesus Christ heals you. Get up and roll up your mat."
Immediately Aeneas got up. 35All those who lived in Lydda and Sharon
saw him and turned to the Lord.

36In Joppa there was a disciple named Tabitha (in Greek her name is
Dorcas); she was always doing good and helping the poor. 37About that
time she became sick and died, and her body was washed and placed
in an upstairs room. 38Lydda was near Joppa; so when the disciples
heard that Peter was in Lydda, they sent two men to him and urged
him, "Please come at once!"

39Peter went with them, and when he arrived he was taken upstairs
to the room. All the widows stood around him, crying and showing
him the robes and other clothing that Dorcas had made while she was
still with them.

40Peter sent them all out of the room; then he got down on his
knees and prayed. Turning toward the dead woman, he said, "Tabi-
tha, get up." She opened her eyes, and seeing Peter she sat up. 41He
took her by the hand and helped her to her feet. Then he called for
the believers, especially the widows, and presented her to them alive.
42This became known all over Joppa, and many people believed in
the Lord. 43Peter stayed in Joppa for some time with a tanner named
Simon.

---

[a] *29* That is, Jews who had adopted the Greek language and culture

CORNELIUS CALLS FOR PETER

10 At Caesarea there was a man named Cornelius, a centurion in
what was known as the Italian Regiment. 2He and all his family
were devout and God-fearing; he gave generously to those in need and
prayed to God regularly. 3One day at about three in the afternoon he
had a vision. He distinctly saw an angel of God, who came to him and
said, "Cornelius!"
4Cornelius stared at him in fear. "What is it, Lord?" he asked.
The angel answered, "Your prayers and gifts to the poor have come
up as a memorial offering before God. 5Now send men to Joppa to
bring back a man named Simon who is called Peter. 6He is staying with
Simon the tanner, whose house is by the sea."
7When the angel who spoke to him had gone, Cornelius called two
of his servants and a devout soldier who was one of his attendants.
8He told them everything that had happened and sent them to Joppa.

PETER'S VISION

9About noon the following day as they were on their journey and
approaching the city, Peter went up on the roof to pray. 10He became
hungry and wanted something to eat, and while the meal was being
prepared, he fell into a trance. 11He saw heaven opened and something
like a large sheet being let down to earth by its four corners. 12It con-
tained all kinds of four-footed animals, as well as reptiles and birds.
13Then a voice told him, "Get up, Peter. Kill and eat."
14"Surely not, Lord!" Peter replied. "I have never eaten anything im-
pure or unclean."
15The voice spoke to him a second time, "Do not call anything im-
pure that God has made clean."
16This happened three times, and immediately the sheet was taken
back to heaven.
17While Peter was wondering about the meaning of the vision,
the men sent by Cornelius found out where Simon's house was and
stopped at the gate. 18They called out, asking if Simon who was known
as Peter was staying there.
19While Peter was still thinking about the vision, the Spirit said to
him, "Simon, three[a] men are looking for you. 20So get up and go down-
stairs. Do not hesitate to go with them, for I have sent them."
21Peter went down and said to the men, "I'm the one you're looking
for. Why have you come?"
22The men replied, "We have come from Cornelius the centurion. He
is a righteous and God-fearing man, who is respected by all the Jewish
people. A holy angel told him to ask you to come to his house so that
he could hear what you have to say." 23Then Peter invited the men into
the house to be his guests.

PETER AT CORNELIUS'S HOUSE

The next day Peter started out with them, and some of the believers
from Joppa went along. 24The following day he arrived in Caesarea.
Cornelius was expecting them and had called together his relatives
and close friends. 25As Peter entered the house, Cornelius met him and
fell at his feet in reverence. 26But Peter made him get up. "Stand up,"
he said, "I am only a man myself."

PRAYING SCRIPTURE

Acts 10

A question confronting the early Jewish believers was whether Gentiles would also be part of God's family. Did Jesus come for them too? God clarified to Peter that the gospel is also for the Gentiles. The Lord then sent Peter to see Cornelius, a Roman soldier who wanted to know the Lord.

Praise God that the Good News is good news for everyone! We can pray for everyone to hear it.

---

[a] 19 One early manuscript *two*; other manuscripts do not have the number.

27While talking with him, Peter went inside and found a large gather-
ing of people. 28He said to them: "You are well aware that it is against our
law for a Jew to associate with or visit a Gentile. But God has shown me
that I should not call anyone impure or unclean. 29So when I was sent for,
I came without raising any objection. May I ask why you sent for me?"
30Cornelius answered: "Three days ago I was in my house praying at
this hour, at three in the afternoon. Suddenly a man in shining clothes
stood before me 31and said, 'Cornelius, God has heard your prayer and
remembered your gifts to the poor. 32Send to Joppa for Simon who is
called Peter. He is a guest in the home of Simon the tanner, who lives
by the sea.' 33So I sent for you immediately, and it was good of you to
come. Now we are all here in the presence of God to listen to every-
thing the Lord has commanded you to tell us."
34Then Peter began to speak: "I now realize how true it is that God
does not show favoritism 35but accepts from every nation the one who
fears him and does what is right. 36You know the message God sent to
the people of Israel, announcing the good news of peace through Jesus
Christ, who is Lord of all. 37You know what has happened throughout
the province of Judea, beginning in Galilee after the baptism that John
preached — 38how God anointed Jesus of Nazareth with the Holy Spirit
and power, and how he went around doing good and healing all who
were under the power of the devil, because God was with him.
39"We are witnesses of everything he did in the country of the Jews
and in Jerusalem. They killed him by hanging him on a cross, 40but
God raised him from the dead on the third day and caused him to be
seen. 41He was not seen by all the people, but by witnesses whom God
had already chosen — by us who ate and drank with him after he rose
from the dead. 42He commanded us to preach to the people and to
testify that he is the one whom God appointed as judge of the living
and the dead. 43All the prophets testify about him that everyone who
believes in him receives forgiveness of sins through his name."
44While Peter was still speaking these words, the Holy Spirit came
on all who heard the message. 45The circumcised believers who had
come with Peter were astonished that the gift of the Holy Spirit had
been poured out even on Gentiles. 46For they heard them speaking in
tongues[a] and praising God.
Then Peter said, 47"Surely no one can stand in the way of their be-
ing baptized with water. They have received the Holy Spirit just as
we have." 48So he ordered that they be baptized in the name of Jesus
Christ. Then they asked Peter to stay with them for a few days.

PETER EXPLAINS HIS ACTIONS

11 The apostles and the believers throughout Judea heard that the
Gentiles also had received the word of God. 2So when Peter went
up to Jerusalem, the circumcised believers criticized him 3and said,
"You went into the house of uncircumcised men and ate with them."
4Starting from the beginning, Peter told them the whole story: 5"I
was in the city of Joppa praying, and in a trance I saw a vision. I saw
something like a large sheet being let down from heaven by its four
corners, and it came down to where I was. 6I looked into it and saw
four-footed animals of the earth, wild beasts, reptiles and birds. 7Then
I heard a voice telling me, 'Get up, Peter. Kill and eat.'

[a] 46 Or *other languages*

PRAYING SCRIPTURE

Acts 11

What happened in this chapter reinforces the promise in Isaiah 42:6, that Jesus would be a light for the Gentiles. Here God revealed to Peter that non-Jews are included in the kingdom of God. For Peter, a devout Jew, this was a life-shifting change of perception. Peter then taught that God had given to Gentiles "repentance that leads to life" (verse 18).

The inclusion of both Jews and Gentiles in the kingdom is truly good news, so thank God for his inclusive grace.

8“I replied, ‘Surely not, Lord! Nothing impure or unclean has ever
entered my mouth.’
9“The voice spoke from heaven a second time, ‘Do not call anything
impure that God has made clean.’ 10This happened three times, and
then it was all pulled up to heaven again.
11“Right then three men who had been sent to me from Caesarea
stopped at the house where I was staying. 12The Spirit told me to have
no hesitation about going with them. These six brothers also went
with me, and we entered the man’s house. 13He told us how he had
seen an angel appear in his house and say, ‘Send to Joppa for Simon
who is called Peter. 14He will bring you a message through which you
and all your household will be saved.’
15“As I began to speak, the Holy Spirit came on them as he had come
on us at the beginning. 16Then I remembered what the Lord had said:
‘John baptized with[a] water, but you will be baptized with[a] the Holy
Spirit.’ 17So if God gave them the same gift he gave us who believed in
the Lord Jesus Christ, who was I to think that I could stand in God’s
way?”
18When they heard this, they had no further objections and praised
God, saying, “So then, even to Gentiles God has granted repentance
that leads to life.”

THE CHURCH IN ANTIOCH

19Now those who had been scattered by the persecution that broke
out when Stephen was killed traveled as far as Phoenicia, Cyprus and
Antioch, spreading the word only among Jews. 20Some of them, how-
ever, men from Cyprus and Cyrene, went to Antioch and began to
speak to Greeks also, telling them the good news about the Lord Jesus.
21The Lord’s hand was with them, and a great number of people be-
lieved and turned to the Lord.
22News of this reached the church in Jerusalem, and they sent Barna-
bas to Antioch. 23When he arrived and saw what the grace of God had
done, he was glad and encouraged them all to remain true to the Lord
with all their hearts. 24He was a good man, full of the Holy Spirit and
faith, and a great number of people were brought to the Lord.
25Then Barnabas went to Tarsus to look for Saul, 26and when he
found him, he brought him to Antioch. So for a whole year Barnabas
and Saul met with the church and taught great numbers of people. The
disciples were called Christians first at Antioch.
27During this time some prophets came down from Jerusalem to An-
tioch. 28One of them, named Agabus, stood up and through the Spirit
predicted that a severe famine would spread over the entire Roman
world. (This happened during the reign of Claudius.) 29The disciples,
as each one was able, decided to provide help for the brothers and sis-
ters living in Judea. 30This they did, sending their gift to the elders by
Barnabas and Saul.

PETER’S MIRACULOUS ESCAPE FROM PRISON

12 It was about this time that King Herod arrested some who be-
longed to the church, intending to persecute them. 2He had
James, the brother of John, put to death with the sword. 3When he
saw that this met with approval among the Jews, he proceeded to seize

[a] 16 Or *in*

PRAYING SCRIPTURE

Acts 12

Here is one of the most encouraging examples of prayer in the Bible. While Peter was in prison for preaching the gospel, the church prayed constantly for him. God sent an angel to release Peter, but upon the apostle’s arrival at the home of local believers, they did not believe it was him!

Sometimes God answers our prayers despite weak faith. Take your requests to God even when you are not sure of the outcome.

Peter also. This happened during the Festival of Unleavened Bread.
4After arresting him, he put him in prison, handing him over to be
guarded by four squads of four soldiers each. Herod intended to bring
him out for public trial after the Passover.

5So Peter was kept in prison, but the church was earnestly praying
to God for him.

6The night before Herod was to bring him to trial, Peter was sleeping
between two soldiers, bound with two chains, and sentries stood guard
at the entrance. 7Suddenly an angel of the Lord appeared and a light
shone in the cell. He struck Peter on the side and woke him up. "Quick,
get up!" he said, and the chains fell off Peter's wrists.

8Then the angel said to him, "Put on your clothes and sandals." And
Peter did so. "Wrap your cloak around you and follow me," the angel
told him. 9Peter followed him out of the prison, but he had no idea that
what the angel was doing was really happening; he thought he was
seeing a vision. 10They passed the first and second guards and came
to the iron gate leading to the city. It opened for them by itself, and
they went through it. When they had walked the length of one street,
suddenly the angel left him.

11Then Peter came to himself and said, "Now I know without a doubt
that the Lord has sent his angel and rescued me from Herod's clutches
and from everything the Jewish people were hoping would happen."

12When this had dawned on him, he went to the house of Mary the
mother of John, also called Mark, where many people had gathered
and were praying. 13Peter knocked at the outer entrance, and a servant
named Rhoda came to answer the door. 14When she recognized Peter's
voice, she was so overjoyed she ran back without opening it and ex-
claimed, "Peter is at the door!"

15"You're out of your mind," they told her. When she kept insisting
that it was so, they said, "It must be his angel."

16But Peter kept on knocking, and when they opened the door and
saw him, they were astonished. 17Peter motioned with his hand for
them to be quiet and described how the Lord had brought him out of
prison. "Tell James and the other brothers and sisters about this," he
said, and then he left for another place.

18In the morning, there was no small commotion among the soldiers
as to what had become of Peter. 19After Herod had a thorough search
made for him and did not find him, he cross-examined the guards and
ordered that they be executed.

HEROD'S DEATH

Then Herod went from Judea to Caesarea and stayed there. 20He
had been quarreling with the people of Tyre and Sidon; they now
joined together and sought an audience with him. After securing the
support of Blastus, a trusted personal servant of the king, they asked
for peace, because they depended on the king's country for their food
supply.

21On the appointed day Herod, wearing his royal robes, sat on his
throne and delivered a public address to the people. 22They shouted,
"This is the voice of a god, not of a man." 23Immediately, because Herod
did not give praise to God, an angel of the Lord struck him down, and
he was eaten by worms and died.

24But the word of God continued to spread and flourish.

BARNABAS AND SAUL SENT OFF

25When Barnabas and Saul had finished their mission, they returned from[a] Jerusalem, taking with them John, also called Mark.

13 1Now in the church at Antioch there were prophets and teachers: Barnabas, Simeon called Niger, Lucius of Cyrene, Manaen (who had been brought up with Herod the tetrarch) and Saul. 2While they were worshiping the Lord and fasting, the Holy Spirit said, "Set apart for me Barnabas and Saul for the work to which I have called them." 3So after they had fasted and prayed, they placed their hands on them and sent them off.

ON CYPRUS

4The two of them, sent on their way by the Holy Spirit, went down to Seleucia and sailed from there to Cyprus. 5When they arrived at Salamis, they proclaimed the word of God in the Jewish synagogues. John was with them as their helper.

6They traveled through the whole island until they came to Paphos. There they met a Jewish sorcerer and false prophet named Bar-Jesus, 7who was an attendant of the proconsul, Sergius Paulus. The proconsul, an intelligent man, sent for Barnabas and Saul because he wanted to hear the word of God. 8But Elymas the sorcerer (for that is what his name means) opposed them and tried to turn the proconsul from the faith. 9Then Saul, who was also called Paul, filled with the Holy Spirit, looked straight at Elymas and said, 10"You are a child of the devil and an enemy of everything that is right! You are full of all kinds of deceit and trickery. Will you never stop perverting the right ways of the Lord? 11Now the hand of the Lord is against you. You are going to be blind for a time, not even able to see the light of the sun."

Immediately mist and darkness came over him, and he groped about, seeking someone to lead him by the hand. 12When the proconsul saw what had happened, he believed, for he was amazed at the teaching about the Lord.

IN PISIDIAN ANTIOCH

13From Paphos, Paul and his companions sailed to Perga in Pamphylia, where John left them to return to Jerusalem. 14From Perga they went on to Pisidian Antioch. On the Sabbath they entered the synagogue and sat down. 15After the reading from the Law and the Prophets, the leaders of the synagogue sent word to them, saying, "Brothers, if you have a word of exhortation for the people, please speak."

16Standing up, Paul motioned with his hand and said: "Fellow Israelites and you Gentiles who worship God, listen to me! 17The God of the people of Israel chose our ancestors; he made the people prosper during their stay in Egypt; with mighty power he led them out of that country; 18for about forty years he endured their conduct[b] in the wilderness; 19and he overthrew seven nations in Canaan, giving their land to his people as their inheritance. 20All this took about 450 years.

"After this, God gave them judges until the time of Samuel the prophet. 21Then the people asked for a king, and he gave them Saul son of Kish, of the tribe of Benjamin, who ruled forty years. 22After removing Saul, he made David their king. God testified concerning him: 'I have found David son of Jesse, a man after my own heart; he will do everything I want him to do.'

[a] *25* Some manuscripts *to* [b] *18* Some manuscripts *he cared for them*

PRAYING SCRIPTURE

Acts 13

Saul and Barnabas were the first missionaries sent out by a church. Though they were commissioned to their work by the church at Antioch, Scripture says they were "sent on their way by the Holy Spirit" (verse 4). It is the Holy Spirit who empowers the church to fulfill the mission of God in this world.

Is the Holy Spirit inviting you to join him in the spread of the kingdom in some specific way? Seek his guidance and be obedient to it.

23“From this man’s descendants God has brought to Israel the Savior Jesus, as he promised. 24Before the coming of Jesus, John preached repentance and baptism to all the people of Israel. 25As John was completing his work, he said: ‘Who do you suppose I am? I am not the one you are looking for. But there is one coming after me whose sandals I am not worthy to untie.’

26“Fellow children of Abraham and you God-fearing Gentiles, it is to us that this message of salvation has been sent. 27The people of Jerusalem and their rulers did not recognize Jesus, yet in condemning him they fulfilled the words of the prophets that are read every Sabbath. 28Though they found no proper ground for a death sentence, they asked Pilate to have him executed. 29When they had carried out all that was written about him, they took him down from the cross and laid him in a tomb. 30But God raised him from the dead, 31and for many days he was seen by those who had traveled with him from Galilee to Jerusalem. They are now his witnesses to our people.

32“We tell you the good news: What God promised our ancestors 33he has fulfilled for us, their children, by raising up Jesus. As it is written in the second Psalm:

> “ ‘You are my son;
> today I have become your father.’[a]

34God raised him from the dead so that he will never be subject to decay. As God has said,

> “ ‘I will give you the holy and sure blessings promised to David.’[b]

35So it is also stated elsewhere:

> “ ‘You will not let your holy one see decay.’[c]

36“Now when David had served God’s purpose in his own generation, he fell asleep; he was buried with his ancestors and his body decayed. 37But the one whom God raised from the dead did not see decay.

38“Therefore, my friends, I want you to know that through Jesus the forgiveness of sins is proclaimed to you. 39Through him everyone who believes is set free from every sin, a justification you were not able to obtain under the law of Moses. 40Take care that what the prophets have said does not happen to you:

> 41“ ‘Look, you scoffers,
> wonder and perish,
> for I am going to do something in your days
> that you would never believe,
> even if someone told you.’[d]”

42As Paul and Barnabas were leaving the synagogue, the people invited them to speak further about these things on the next Sabbath. 43When the congregation was dismissed, many of the Jews and devout converts to Judaism followed Paul and Barnabas, who talked with them and urged them to continue in the grace of God.

44On the next Sabbath almost the whole city gathered to hear the word of the Lord. 45When the Jews saw the crowds, they were filled with jealousy. They began to contradict what Paul was saying and heaped abuse on him.

---

[a] *33* Psalm 2:7 [b] *34* Isaiah 55:3 [c] *35* Psalm 16:10 (see Septuagint)
[d] *41* Hab. 1:5

[46]Then Paul and Barnabas answered them boldly: "We had to speak
the word of God to you first. Since you reject it and do not consider
yourselves worthy of eternal life, we now turn to the Gentiles. [47]For this
is what the Lord has commanded us:

"'I have made you[a] a light for the Gentiles,
that you[a] may bring salvation to the ends of the earth.'[b]"

[48]When the Gentiles heard this, they were glad and honored the
word of the Lord; and all who were appointed for eternal life believed.
[49]The word of the Lord spread through the whole region. [50]But the
Jewish leaders incited the God-fearing women of high standing and
the leading men of the city. They stirred up persecution against Paul
and Barnabas, and expelled them from their region. [51]So they shook
the dust off their feet as a warning to them and went to Iconium. [52]And
the disciples were filled with joy and with the Holy Spirit.

IN ICONIUM

14 At Iconium Paul and Barnabas went as usual into the Jewish
synagogue. There they spoke so effectively that a great num-
ber of Jews and Greeks believed. [2]But the Jews who refused to be-
lieve stirred up the other Gentiles and poisoned their minds against
the brothers. [3]So Paul and Barnabas spent considerable time there,
speaking boldly for the Lord, who confirmed the message of his grace
by enabling them to perform signs and wonders. [4]The people of the
city were divided; some sided with the Jews, others with the apostles.
[5]There was a plot afoot among both Gentiles and Jews, together with
their leaders, to mistreat them and stone them. [6]But they found out
about it and fled to the Lycaonian cities of Lystra and Derbe and to
the surrounding country, [7]where they continued to preach the gospel.

IN LYSTRA AND DERBE

[8]In Lystra there sat a man who was lame. He had been that way from
birth and had never walked. [9]He listened to Paul as he was speaking.
Paul looked directly at him, saw that he had faith to be healed [10]and
called out, "Stand up on your feet!" At that, the man jumped up and
began to walk.

[11]When the crowd saw what Paul had done, they shouted in the Lyc-
aonian language, "The gods have come down to us in human form!"
[12]Barnabas they called Zeus, and Paul they called Hermes because he
was the chief speaker. [13]The priest of Zeus, whose temple was just out-
side the city, brought bulls and wreaths to the city gates because he
and the crowd wanted to offer sacrifices to them.

[14]But when the apostles Barnabas and Paul heard of this, they tore
their clothes and rushed out into the crowd, shouting: [15]"Friends, why
are you doing this? We too are only human, like you. We are bringing
you good news, telling you to turn from these worthless things to the
living God, who made the heavens and the earth and the sea and ev-
erything in them. [16]In the past, he let all nations go their own way. [17]Yet
he has not left himself without testimony: He has shown kindness by
giving you rain from heaven and crops in their seasons; he provides
you with plenty of food and fills your hearts with joy." [18]Even with these
words, they had difficulty keeping the crowd from sacrificing to them.

PRAYING SCRIPTURE

Acts 14

Life in the early church was not only about miracles and numerical growth. There was suffering and persecution too. In this chapter, Paul and Barnabas were hailed as Greek gods by some (see verses 12–13), while Paul was nearly stoned to death by a different group immediately following.

Resolve to follow God whether people are encouraging you or persecuting you. Pray for the power to walk with him at all times.

[a] 47 The Greek is singular. [b] 47 Isaiah 49:6

19Then some Jews came from Antioch and Iconium and won the
crowd over. They stoned Paul and dragged him outside the city, think-
ing he was dead. 20But after the disciples had gathered around him,
he got up and went back into the city. The next day he and Barnabas
left for Derbe.

THE RETURN TO ANTIOCH IN SYRIA

21They preached the gospel in that city and won a large num-
ber of disciples. Then they returned to Lystra, Iconium and Antioch,
22strengthening the disciples and encouraging them to remain true to
the faith. "We must go through many hardships to enter the kingdom
of God," they said. 23Paul and Barnabas appointed elders[a] for them
in each church and, with prayer and fasting, committed them to the
Lord, in whom they had put their trust. 24After going through Pisidia,
they came into Pamphylia, 25and when they had preached the word in
Perga, they went down to Attalia.

26From Attalia they sailed back to Antioch, where they had been com-
mitted to the grace of God for the work they had now completed. 27On
arriving there, they gathered the church together and reported all that
God had done through them and how he had opened a door of faith
to the Gentiles. 28And they stayed there a long time with the disciples.

THE COUNCIL AT JERUSALEM

15 Certain people came down from Judea to Antioch and were
teaching the believers: "Unless you are circumcised, according
to the custom taught by Moses, you cannot be saved." 2This brought
Paul and Barnabas into sharp dispute and debate with them. So Paul
and Barnabas were appointed, along with some other believers, to go
up to Jerusalem to see the apostles and elders about this question.
3The church sent them on their way, and as they traveled through
Phoenicia and Samaria, they told how the Gentiles had been converted.
This news made all the believers very glad. 4When they came to Jerusa-
lem, they were welcomed by the church and the apostles and elders, to
whom they reported everything God had done through them.

5Then some of the believers who belonged to the party of the Phar-
isees stood up and said, "The Gentiles must be circumcised and re-
quired to keep the law of Moses."

6The apostles and elders met to consider this question. 7After much
discussion, Peter got up and addressed them: "Brothers, you know that
some time ago God made a choice among you that the Gentiles might
hear from my lips the message of the gospel and believe. 8God, who
knows the heart, showed that he accepted them by giving the Holy
Spirit to them, just as he did to us. 9He did not discriminate between
us and them, for he purified their hearts by faith. 10Now then, why do
you try to test God by putting on the necks of Gentiles a yoke that nei-
ther we nor our ancestors have been able to bear? 11No! We believe it is
through the grace of our Lord Jesus that we are saved, just as they are."

12The whole assembly became silent as they listened to Barnabas
and Paul telling about the signs and wonders God had done among the
Gentiles through them. 13When they finished, James spoke up. "Broth-
ers," he said, "listen to me. 14Simon[b] has described to us how God first

PRAYING SCRIPTURE

Acts 15

The first church council was convened over the matter of circumcision, addressing the question of whether Gentiles needed to keep the Mosaic Law to be fully converted. Some Pharisees said yes (see verse 5). The answer to that question, which would affect the church forever, was no. The council issued a short letter with a few restrictions.

The Holy Spirit led the church away from law-keeping toward freedom. Prayerfully thank God for freedom in Christ.

[a] *23* Or *Barnabas ordained elders*; or *Barnabas had elders elected* [b] *14* Greek *Simeon*, a variant of *Simon*; that is, Peter

intervened to choose a people for his name from the Gentiles. 15The
words of the prophets are in agreement with this, as it is written:

16"'After this I will return
and rebuild David's fallen tent.
Its ruins I will rebuild,
and I will restore it,
17that the rest of mankind may seek the Lord,
even all the Gentiles who bear my name,
says the Lord, who does these things'[a]—
18 things known from long ago.[b]

19"It is my judgment, therefore, that we should not make it difficult
for the Gentiles who are turning to God. 20Instead we should write to
them, telling them to abstain from food polluted by idols, from sex-
ual immorality, from the meat of strangled animals and from blood.
21For the law of Moses has been preached in every city from the earliest
times and is read in the synagogues on every Sabbath."

THE COUNCIL'S LETTER TO GENTILE BELIEVERS

22Then the apostles and elders, with the whole church, decided to
choose some of their own men and send them to Antioch with Paul
and Barnabas. They chose Judas (called Barsabbas) and Silas, men who
were leaders among the believers. 23With them they sent the follow-
ing letter:

The apostles and elders, your brothers,

To the Gentile believers in Antioch, Syria and Cilicia:

Greetings.

24We have heard that some went out from us without our au-
thorization and disturbed you, troubling your minds by what they
said. 25So we all agreed to choose some men and send them to
you with our dear friends Barnabas and Paul— 26men who have
risked their lives for the name of our Lord Jesus Christ. 27There-
fore we are sending Judas and Silas to confirm by word of mouth
what we are writing. 28It seemed good to the Holy Spirit and to us
not to burden you with anything beyond the following require-
ments: 29You are to abstain from food sacrificed to idols, from
blood, from the meat of strangled animals and from sexual im-
morality. You will do well to avoid these things.

Farewell.

30So the men were sent off and went down to Antioch, where they
gathered the church together and delivered the letter. 31The people read
it and were glad for its encouraging message. 32Judas and Silas, who
themselves were prophets, said much to encourage and strengthen the
believers. 33After spending some time there, they were sent off by the
believers with the blessing of peace to return to those who had sent
them. [34][c] 35But Paul and Barnabas remained in Antioch, where they
and many others taught and preached the word of the Lord.

[a] 17 Amos 9:11,12 (see Septuagint) [b] 17,18 Some manuscripts *things'— / 18the Lord's work is known to him from long ago* [c] 34 Some manuscripts include here *But Silas decided to remain there.*

DISAGREEMENT BETWEEN PAUL AND BARNABAS

[36]Some time later Paul said to Barnabas, "Let us go back and visit the believers in all the towns where we preached the word of the Lord and see how they are doing." [37]Barnabas wanted to take John, also called Mark, with them, [38]but Paul did not think it wise to take him, because he had deserted them in Pamphylia and had not continued with them in the work. [39]They had such a sharp disagreement that they parted company. Barnabas took Mark and sailed for Cyprus, [40]but Paul chose Silas and left, commended by the believers to the grace of the Lord. [41]He went through Syria and Cilicia, strengthening the churches.

TIMOTHY JOINS PAUL AND SILAS

16 Paul came to Derbe and then to Lystra, where a disciple named Timothy lived, whose mother was Jewish and a believer but whose father was a Greek. [2]The believers at Lystra and Iconium spoke well of him. [3]Paul wanted to take him along on the journey, so he circumcised him because of the Jews who lived in that area, for they all knew that his father was a Greek. [4]As they traveled from town to town, they delivered the decisions reached by the apostles and elders in Jerusalem for the people to obey. [5]So the churches were strengthened in the faith and grew daily in numbers.

PRAYING SCRIPTURE

Acts 16

Sometimes the Lord uses ordinary means to guide, and sometimes he uses drastic ones. Intending to preach the gospel in Asia, Paul was rebuffed by the Spirit. The Spirit gave Paul a vision: a man in Macedonia calling for help. Recognizing it as a message from the Lord, Paul's team went there to preach the gospel.

Pay attention to both the ordinary and drastic means God uses, and pray for obedience.

PAUL'S VISION OF THE MAN OF MACEDONIA

[6]Paul and his companions traveled throughout the region of Phrygia and Galatia, having been kept by the Holy Spirit from preaching the word in the province of Asia. [7]When they came to the border of Mysia, they tried to enter Bithynia, but the Spirit of Jesus would not allow them to. [8]So they passed by Mysia and went down to Troas. [9]During the night Paul had a vision of a man of Macedonia standing and begging him, "Come over to Macedonia and help us." [10]After Paul had seen the vision, we got ready at once to leave for Macedonia, concluding that God had called us to preach the gospel to them.

LYDIA'S CONVERSION IN PHILIPPI

[11]From Troas we put out to sea and sailed straight for Samothrace, and the next day we went on to Neapolis. [12]From there we traveled to Philippi, a Roman colony and the leading city of that district[a] of Macedonia. And we stayed there several days.

[13]On the Sabbath we went outside the city gate to the river, where we expected to find a place of prayer. We sat down and began to speak to the women who had gathered there. [14]One of those listening was a woman from the city of Thyatira named Lydia, a dealer in purple cloth. She was a worshiper of God. The Lord opened her heart to respond to Paul's message. [15]When she and the members of her household were baptized, she invited us to her home. "If you consider me a believer in the Lord," she said, "come and stay at my house." And she persuaded us.

PAUL AND SILAS IN PRISON

[16]Once when we were going to the place of prayer, we were met by a female slave who had a spirit by which she predicted the future. She earned a great deal of money for her owners by fortune-telling. [17]She

[a] *12* The text and meaning of the Greek for *the leading city of that district* are uncertain.

followed Paul and the rest of us, shouting, "These men are servants of
the Most High God, who are telling you the way to be saved." [18]She kept
this up for many days. Finally Paul became so annoyed that he turned
around and said to the spirit, "In the name of Jesus Christ I command
you to come out of her!" At that moment the spirit left her.

[19]When her owners realized that their hope of making money was
gone, they seized Paul and Silas and dragged them into the market-
place to face the authorities. [20]They brought them before the magis-
trates and said, "These men are Jews, and are throwing our city into
an uproar [21]by advocating customs unlawful for us Romans to accept
or practice."

[22]The crowd joined in the attack against Paul and Silas, and the mag-
istrates ordered them to be stripped and beaten with rods. [23]After they
had been severely flogged, they were thrown into prison, and the jailer
was commanded to guard them carefully. [24]When he received these or-
ders, he put them in the inner cell and fastened their feet in the stocks.

[25]About midnight Paul and Silas were praying and singing hymns
to God, and the other prisoners were listening to them. [26]Suddenly
there was such a violent earthquake that the foundations of the prison
were shaken. At once all the prison doors flew open, and everyone's
chains came loose. [27]The jailer woke up, and when he saw the prison
doors open, he drew his sword and was about to kill himself because
he thought the prisoners had escaped. [28]But Paul shouted, "Don't harm
yourself! We are all here!"

[29]The jailer called for lights, rushed in and fell trembling before Paul
and Silas. [30]He then brought them out and asked, "Sirs, what must I
do to be saved?"

[31]They replied, "Believe in the Lord Jesus, and you will be saved —
you and your household." [32]Then they spoke the word of the Lord to
him and to all the others in his house. [33]At that hour of the night the
jailer took them and washed their wounds; then immediately he and
all his household were baptized. [34]The jailer brought them into his
house and set a meal before them; he was filled with joy because he
had come to believe in God — he and his whole household.

[35]When it was daylight, the magistrates sent their officers to the
jailer with the order: "Release those men." [36]The jailer told Paul, "The
magistrates have ordered that you and Silas be released. Now you can
leave. Go in peace."

[37]But Paul said to the officers: "They beat us publicly without a trial,
even though we are Roman citizens, and threw us into prison. And now
do they want to get rid of us quietly? No! Let them come themselves
and escort us out."

[38]The officers reported this to the magistrates, and when they heard
that Paul and Silas were Roman citizens, they were alarmed. [39]They
came to appease them and escorted them from the prison, requesting
them to leave the city. [40]After Paul and Silas came out of the prison,
they went to Lydia's house, where they met with the brothers and sis-
ters and encouraged them. Then they left.

IN THESSALONICA

17 When Paul and his companions had passed through Amphipo-
lis and Apollonia, they came to Thessalonica, where there was a
Jewish synagogue. [2]As was his custom, Paul went into the synagogue,
and on three Sabbath days he reasoned with them from the Scriptures,

PRAYING SCRIPTURE

Acts 17

Paul's ministry at Athens is instructive in how we can engage culture with the gospel message. To witness to the Jews, Paul taught the Scriptures in the synagogue for three Sabbaths. To witness to the pagan philosophers, Paul explained that their Unknown God was the Lord God who can be known through Jesus.

Ask God to give you wisdom in bringing the gospel to people of different beliefs.

3explaining and proving that the Messiah had to suffer and rise from
the dead. "This Jesus I am proclaiming to you is the Messiah," he said.
4Some of the Jews were persuaded and joined Paul and Silas, as did a
large number of God-fearing Greeks and quite a few prominent women.
5But other Jews were jealous; so they rounded up some bad char-
acters from the marketplace, formed a mob and started a riot in the
city. They rushed to Jason's house in search of Paul and Silas in order
to bring them out to the crowd.[a] 6But when they did not find them,
they dragged Jason and some other believers before the city officials,
shouting: "These men who have caused trouble all over the world have
now come here, 7and Jason has welcomed them into his house. They
are all defying Caesar's decrees, saying that there is another king, one
called Jesus." 8When they heard this, the crowd and the city officials
were thrown into turmoil. 9Then they made Jason and the others post
bond and let them go.

IN BEREA

10As soon as it was night, the believers sent Paul and Silas away to
Berea. On arriving there, they went to the Jewish synagogue. 11Now
the Berean Jews were of more noble character than those in Thessa-
lonica, for they received the message with great eagerness and exam-
ined the Scriptures every day to see if what Paul said was true. 12As
a result, many of them believed, as did also a number of prominent
Greek women and many Greek men.
13But when the Jews in Thessalonica learned that Paul was preaching
the word of God at Berea, some of them went there too, agitating the
crowds and stirring them up. 14The believers immediately sent Paul to
the coast, but Silas and Timothy stayed at Berea. 15Those who escorted
Paul brought him to Athens and then left with instructions for Silas
and Timothy to join him as soon as possible.

IN ATHENS

16While Paul was waiting for them in Athens, he was greatly dis-
tressed to see that the city was full of idols. 17So he reasoned in the
synagogue with both Jews and God-fearing Greeks, as well as in the
marketplace day by day with those who happened to be there. 18A
group of Epicurean and Stoic philosophers began to debate with
him. Some of them asked, "What is this babbler trying to say?" Oth-
ers remarked, "He seems to be advocating foreign gods." They said
this because Paul was preaching the good news about Jesus and the
resurrection. 19Then they took him and brought him to a meeting of
the Areopagus, where they said to him, "May we know what this new
teaching is that you are presenting? 20You are bringing some strange
ideas to our ears, and we would like to know what they mean." 21(All
the Athenians and the foreigners who lived there spent their time do-
ing nothing but talking about and listening to the latest ideas.)
22Paul then stood up in the meeting of the Areopagus and said: "Peo-
ple of Athens! I see that in every way you are very religious. 23For as I
walked around and looked carefully at your objects of worship, I even
found an altar with this inscription: TO AN UNKNOWN GOD. So you are
ignorant of the very thing you worship — and this is what I am going
to proclaim to you.

[a] 5 Or *the assembly of the people*

24"The God who made the world and everything in it is the Lord of
heaven and earth and does not live in temples built by human hands.
25And he is not served by human hands, as if he needed anything.
Rather, he himself gives everyone life and breath and everything else.
26From one man he made all the nations, that they should inhabit the
whole earth; and he marked out their appointed times in history and
the boundaries of their lands. 27God did this so that they would seek
him and perhaps reach out for him and find him, though he is not
far from any one of us. 28'For in him we live and move and have our
being.'[a] As some of your own poets have said, 'We are his offspring.'[b]

29"Therefore since we are God's offspring, we should not think that
the divine being is like gold or silver or stone — an image made by
human design and skill. 30In the past God overlooked such ignorance,
but now he commands all people everywhere to repent. 31For he has
set a day when he will judge the world with justice by the man he has
appointed. He has given proof of this to everyone by raising him from
the dead."

32When they heard about the resurrection of the dead, some of them
sneered, but others said, "We want to hear you again on this subject."
33At that, Paul left the Council. 34Some of the people became followers
of Paul and believed. Among them was Dionysius, a member of the
Areopagus, also a woman named Damaris, and a number of others.

IN CORINTH

18 After this, Paul left Athens and went to Corinth. 2There he met
a Jew named Aquila, a native of Pontus, who had recently come
from Italy with his wife Priscilla, because Claudius had ordered all Jews
to leave Rome. Paul went to see them, 3and because he was a tent-
maker as they were, he stayed and worked with them. 4Every Sabbath
he reasoned in the synagogue, trying to persuade Jews and Greeks.

5When Silas and Timothy came from Macedonia, Paul devoted him-
self exclusively to preaching, testifying to the Jews that Jesus was the
Messiah. 6But when they opposed Paul and became abusive, he shook
out his clothes in protest and said to them, "Your blood be on your
own heads! I am innocent of it. From now on I will go to the Gentiles."

7Then Paul left the synagogue and went next door to the house of
Titius Justus, a worshiper of God. 8Crispus, the synagogue leader, and
his entire household believed in the Lord; and many of the Corinthians
who heard Paul believed and were baptized.

9One night the Lord spoke to Paul in a vision: "Do not be afraid;
keep on speaking, do not be silent. 10For I am with you, and no one
is going to attack and harm you, because I have many people in this
city." 11So Paul stayed in Corinth for a year and a half, teaching them
the word of God.

12While Gallio was proconsul of Achaia, the Jews of Corinth made
a united attack on Paul and brought him to the place of judgment.
13"This man," they charged, "is persuading the people to worship God
in ways contrary to the law."

14Just as Paul was about to speak, Gallio said to them, "If you Jews
were making a complaint about some misdemeanor or serious crime,
it would be reasonable for me to listen to you. 15But since it involves

[a] *28* From the Cretan philosopher Epimenides [b] *28* From the Cilician Stoic philosopher Aratus

PRAYING SCRIPTURE

Acts 18

Here we learn of the ministry of Apollos. We can be encouraged that God uses those whose theology is not fully formed. This eloquent speaker spoke with "great fervor" (verse 25), but he had not learned much beyond John's baptizing ministry. Two believers spent time with Apollos, teaching him more details.

God can use you even with limited theology. Why not ask him to send someone to teach you more?

questions about words and names and your own law — settle the mat-
ter yourselves. I will not be a judge of such things." 16So he drove them
off. 17Then the crowd there turned on Sosthenes the synagogue leader
and beat him in front of the proconsul; and Gallio showed no concern
whatever.

PRISCILLA, AQUILA AND APOLLOS

18Paul stayed on in Corinth for some time. Then he left the brothers
and sisters and sailed for Syria, accompanied by Priscilla and Aquila. Be-
fore he sailed, he had his hair cut off at Cenchreae because of a vow he
had taken. 19They arrived at Ephesus, where Paul left Priscilla and Aq-
uila. He himself went into the synagogue and reasoned with the Jews.
20When they asked him to spend more time with them, he declined.
21But as he left, he promised, "I will come back if it is God's will." Then
he set sail from Ephesus. 22When he landed at Caesarea, he went up
to Jerusalem and greeted the church and then went down to Antioch.

23After spending some time in Antioch, Paul set out from there and
traveled from place to place throughout the region of Galatia and
Phrygia, strengthening all the disciples.

24Meanwhile a Jew named Apollos, a native of Alexandria, came to
Ephesus. He was a learned man, with a thorough knowledge of the
Scriptures. 25He had been instructed in the way of the Lord, and he
spoke with great fervor[a] and taught about Jesus accurately, though he
knew only the baptism of John. 26He began to speak boldly in the syn-
agogue. When Priscilla and Aquila heard him, they invited him to their
home and explained to him the way of God more adequately.

27When Apollos wanted to go to Achaia, the brothers and sisters en-
couraged him and wrote to the disciples there to welcome him. When
he arrived, he was a great help to those who by grace had believed.
28For he vigorously refuted his Jewish opponents in public debate,
proving from the Scriptures that Jesus was the Messiah.

PAUL IN EPHESUS

19 While Apollos was at Corinth, Paul took the road through the
interior and arrived at Ephesus. There he found some disciples
2and asked them, "Did you receive the Holy Spirit when[b] you believed?"

They answered, "No, we have not even heard that there is a Holy
Spirit."

3So Paul asked, "Then what baptism did you receive?"

"John's baptism," they replied.

4Paul said, "John's baptism was a baptism of repentance. He told the
people to believe in the one coming after him, that is, in Jesus." 5On
hearing this, they were baptized in the name of the Lord Jesus. 6When
Paul placed his hands on them, the Holy Spirit came on them, and they
spoke in tongues[c] and prophesied. 7There were about twelve men in all.

8Paul entered the synagogue and spoke boldly there for three
months, arguing persuasively about the kingdom of God. 9But some
of them became obstinate; they refused to believe and publicly ma-
ligned the Way. So Paul left them. He took the disciples with him and
had discussions daily in the lecture hall of Tyrannus. 10This went on
for two years, so that all the Jews and Greeks who lived in the province
of Asia heard the word of the Lord.

PRAYING SCRIPTURE

Acts 19

The unusual replication of Pentecost that took place in Ephesus, where believers knew of John the Baptist but not of Jesus, was accompanied both by the arrival of the Holy Spirit and speaking in tongues. The Lord confirmed that the Gentiles were in the same family of Jesus as were the Jews.

There is only one family of God. Pray for people you know who are not in God's family to believe in Jesus.

[a] 25 Or *with fervor in the Spirit* [b] 2 Or *after* [c] 6 Or *other languages*

11God did extraordinary miracles through Paul, 12so that even handkerchiefs and aprons that had touched him were taken to the sick, and their illnesses were cured and the evil spirits left them.

13Some Jews who went around driving out evil spirits tried to invoke the name of the Lord Jesus over those who were demon-possessed. They would say, "In the name of the Jesus whom Paul preaches, I command you to come out." 14Seven sons of Sceva, a Jewish chief priest, were doing this. 15One day the evil spirit answered them, "Jesus I know, and Paul I know about, but who are you?" 16Then the man who had the evil spirit jumped on them and overpowered them all. He gave them such a beating that they ran out of the house naked and bleeding.

17When this became known to the Jews and Greeks living in Ephesus, they were all seized with fear, and the name of the Lord Jesus was held in high honor. 18Many of those who believed now came and openly confessed what they had done. 19A number who had practiced sorcery brought their scrolls together and burned them publicly. When they calculated the value of the scrolls, the total came to fifty thousand drachmas.[a] 20In this way the word of the Lord spread widely and grew in power.

21After all this had happened, Paul decided[b] to go to Jerusalem, passing through Macedonia and Achaia. "After I have been there," he said, "I must visit Rome also." 22He sent two of his helpers, Timothy and Erastus, to Macedonia, while he stayed in the province of Asia a little longer.

THE RIOT IN EPHESUS

23About that time there arose a great disturbance about the Way. 24A silversmith named Demetrius, who made silver shrines of Artemis, brought in a lot of business for the craftsmen there. 25He called them together, along with the workers in related trades, and said: "You know, my friends, that we receive a good income from this business. 26And you see and hear how this fellow Paul has convinced and led astray large numbers of people here in Ephesus and in practically the whole province of Asia. He says that gods made by human hands are no gods at all. 27There is danger not only that our trade will lose its good name, but also that the temple of the great goddess Artemis will be discredited; and the goddess herself, who is worshiped throughout the province of Asia and the world, will be robbed of her divine majesty."

28When they heard this, they were furious and began shouting: "Great is Artemis of the Ephesians!" 29Soon the whole city was in an uproar. The people seized Gaius and Aristarchus, Paul's traveling companions from Macedonia, and all of them rushed into the theater together. 30Paul wanted to appear before the crowd, but the disciples would not let him. 31Even some of the officials of the province, friends of Paul, sent him a message begging him not to venture into the theater.

32The assembly was in confusion: Some were shouting one thing, some another. Most of the people did not even know why they were there. 33The Jews in the crowd pushed Alexander to the front, and they shouted instructions to him. He motioned for silence in order to make a defense before the people. 34But when they realized he was a Jew, they all shouted in unison for about two hours: "Great is Artemis of the Ephesians!"

---

[a] 19 A drachma was a silver coin worth about a day's wages. [b] 21 Or *decided in the Spirit*

[35]The city clerk quieted the crowd and said: "Fellow Ephesians,
doesn't all the world know that the city of Ephesus is the guardian
of the temple of the great Artemis and of her image, which fell from
heaven? [36]Therefore, since these facts are undeniable, you ought to
calm down and not do anything rash. [37]You have brought these men
here, though they have neither robbed temples nor blasphemed our
goddess. [38]If, then, Demetrius and his fellow craftsmen have a griev-
ance against anybody, the courts are open and there are proconsuls.
They can press charges. [39]If there is anything further you want to bring
up, it must be settled in a legal assembly. [40]As it is, we are in danger
of being charged with rioting because of what happened today. In that
case we would not be able to account for this commotion, since there
is no reason for it." [41]After he had said this, he dismissed the assembly.

THROUGH MACEDONIA AND GREECE

20 When the uproar had ended, Paul sent for the disciples and,
after encouraging them, said goodbye and set out for Macedo-
nia. [2]He traveled through that area, speaking many words of encour-
agement to the people, and finally arrived in Greece, [3]where he stayed
three months. Because some Jews had plotted against him just as he
was about to sail for Syria, he decided to go back through Macedo-
nia. [4]He was accompanied by Sopater son of Pyrrhus from Berea, Aris-
tarchus and Secundus from Thessalonica, Gaius from Derbe, Timothy
also, and Tychicus and Trophimus from the province of Asia. [5]These
men went on ahead and waited for us at Troas. [6]But we sailed from Phi-
lippi after the Festival of Unleavened Bread, and five days later joined
the others at Troas, where we stayed seven days.

PRAYING SCRIPTURE

Acts 20

Paul's multifaceted ministry through Greece, Troas and Miletus gives us insight into how he spent his life for the gospel. In his well-known charge to the Ephesian elders (see verses 17–38), he included these words from Jesus: "It is more blessed to give than to receive" (verse 35). Paul's life exemplified giving until his final breath.

Ask God for a heart to give, and you too will be blessed.

EUTYCHUS RAISED FROM THE DEAD AT TROAS

[7]On the first day of the week we came together to break bread. Paul
spoke to the people and, because he intended to leave the next day,
kept on talking until midnight. [8]There were many lamps in the up-
stairs room where we were meeting. [9]Seated in a window was a young
man named Eutychus, who was sinking into a deep sleep as Paul talked
on and on. When he was sound asleep, he fell to the ground from the
third story and was picked up dead. [10]Paul went down, threw himself
on the young man and put his arms around him. "Don't be alarmed,"
he said. "He's alive!" [11]Then he went upstairs again and broke bread
and ate. After talking until daylight, he left. [12]The people took the
young man home alive and were greatly comforted.

PAUL'S FAREWELL TO THE EPHESIAN ELDERS

[13]We went on ahead to the ship and sailed for Assos, where we were
going to take Paul aboard. He had made this arrangement because
he was going there on foot. [14]When he met us at Assos, we took him
aboard and went on to Mitylene. [15]The next day we set sail from there
and arrived off Chios. The day after that we crossed over to Samos, and
on the following day arrived at Miletus. [16]Paul had decided to sail past
Ephesus to avoid spending time in the province of Asia, for he was in a
hurry to reach Jerusalem, if possible, by the day of Pentecost.

[17]From Miletus, Paul sent to Ephesus for the elders of the church.
[18]When they arrived, he said to them: "You know how I lived the whole
time I was with you, from the first day I came into the province of Asia.
[19]I served the Lord with great humility and with tears and in the midst

of severe testing by the plots of my Jewish opponents. 20 You know
that I have not hesitated to preach anything that would be helpful to
you but have taught you publicly and from house to house. 21 I have
declared to both Jews and Greeks that they must turn to God in repen-
tance and have faith in our Lord Jesus.

22 "And now, compelled by the Spirit, I am going to Jerusalem, not
knowing what will happen to me there. 23 I only know that in every
city the Holy Spirit warns me that prison and hardships are facing me.
24 However, I consider my life worth nothing to me; my only aim is to
finish the race and complete the task the Lord Jesus has given me—
the task of testifying to the good news of God's grace.

25 "Now I know that none of you among whom I have gone about
preaching the kingdom will ever see me again. 26 Therefore, I declare
to you today that I am innocent of the blood of any of you. 27 For I have
not hesitated to proclaim to you the whole will of God. 28 Keep watch
over yourselves and all the flock of which the Holy Spirit has made you
overseers. Be shepherds of the church of God,[a] which he bought with
his own blood.[b] 29 I know that after I leave, savage wolves will come in
among you and will not spare the flock. 30 Even from your own number
men will arise and distort the truth in order to draw away disciples af-
ter them. 31 So be on your guard! Remember that for three years I never
stopped warning each of you night and day with tears.

32 "Now I commit you to God and to the word of his grace, which
can build you up and give you an inheritance among all those who
are sanctified. 33 I have not coveted anyone's silver or gold or cloth-
ing. 34 You yourselves know that these hands of mine have supplied
my own needs and the needs of my companions. 35 In everything I did,
I showed you that by this kind of hard work we must help the weak,
remembering the words the Lord Jesus himself said: 'It is more blessed
to give than to receive.' "

36 When Paul had finished speaking, he knelt down with all of them
and prayed. 37 They all wept as they embraced him and kissed him.
38 What grieved them most was his statement that they would never
see his face again. Then they accompanied him to the ship.

ON TO JERUSALEM

21 After we had torn ourselves away from them, we put out to sea
and sailed straight to Kos. The next day we went to Rhodes and
from there to Patara. 2 We found a ship crossing over to Phoenicia, went
on board and set sail. 3 After sighting Cyprus and passing to the south
of it, we sailed on to Syria. We landed at Tyre, where our ship was to
unload its cargo. 4 We sought out the disciples there and stayed with
them seven days. Through the Spirit they urged Paul not to go on to
Jerusalem. 5 When it was time to leave, we left and continued on our
way. All of them, including wives and children, accompanied us out of
the city, and there on the beach we knelt to pray. 6 After saying goodbye
to each other, we went aboard the ship, and they returned home.

7 We continued our voyage from Tyre and landed at Ptolemais, where
we greeted the brothers and sisters and stayed with them for a day.
8 Leaving the next day, we reached Caesarea and stayed at the house of
Philip the evangelist, one of the Seven. 9 He had four unmarried daugh-
ters who prophesied.

[a] *28* Many manuscripts *of the Lord* [b] *28* Or *with the blood of his own Son*

PRAYING SCRIPTURE

Acts 21

Paul's life continued on unpredictable paths as he spread the gospel across the empire. Due to opposition from religious leaders and others, he faced regular physical abuse. After being arrested in Jerusalem, some believed him to be an Egyptian who led an insurrection. But even under arrest, Paul preached the gospel (see verses 37–40).

Commit to suffer well for Jesus. Ask God for courage to spread the gospel always.

10After we had been there a number of days, a prophet named Agabus came down from Judea. 11Coming over to us, he took Paul's belt, tied his own hands and feet with it and said, "The Holy Spirit says, 'In this way the Jewish leaders in Jerusalem will bind the owner of this belt and will hand him over to the Gentiles.'"

12When we heard this, we and the people there pleaded with Paul not to go up to Jerusalem. 13Then Paul answered, "Why are you weeping and breaking my heart? I am ready not only to be bound, but also to die in Jerusalem for the name of the Lord Jesus." 14When he would not be dissuaded, we gave up and said, "The Lord's will be done."

15After this, we started on our way up to Jerusalem. 16Some of the disciples from Caesarea accompanied us and brought us to the home of Mnason, where we were to stay. He was a man from Cyprus and one of the early disciples.

PAUL'S ARRIVAL AT JERUSALEM

17When we arrived at Jerusalem, the brothers and sisters received us warmly. 18The next day Paul and the rest of us went to see James, and all the elders were present. 19Paul greeted them and reported in detail what God had done among the Gentiles through his ministry.

20When they heard this, they praised God. Then they said to Paul: "You see, brother, how many thousands of Jews have believed, and all of them are zealous for the law. 21They have been informed that you teach all the Jews who live among the Gentiles to turn away from Moses, telling them not to circumcise their children or live according to our customs. 22What shall we do? They will certainly hear that you have come, 23so do what we tell you. There are four men with us who have made a vow. 24Take these men, join in their purification rites and pay their expenses, so that they can have their heads shaved. Then everyone will know there is no truth in these reports about you, but that you yourself are living in obedience to the law. 25As for the Gentile believers, we have written to them our decision that they should abstain from food sacrificed to idols, from blood, from the meat of strangled animals and from sexual immorality."

26The next day Paul took the men and purified himself along with them. Then he went to the temple to give notice of the date when the days of purification would end and the offering would be made for each of them.

PAUL ARRESTED

27When the seven days were nearly over, some Jews from the province of Asia saw Paul at the temple. They stirred up the whole crowd and seized him, 28shouting, "Fellow Israelites, help us! This is the man who teaches everyone everywhere against our people and our law and this place. And besides, he has brought Greeks into the temple and defiled this holy place." 29(They had previously seen Trophimus the Ephesian in the city with Paul and assumed that Paul had brought him into the temple.)

30The whole city was aroused, and the people came running from all directions. Seizing Paul, they dragged him from the temple, and immediately the gates were shut. 31While they were trying to kill him, news reached the commander of the Roman troops that the whole city of Jerusalem was in an uproar. 32He at once took some officers and soldiers and ran down to the crowd. When the rioters saw the commander and his soldiers, they stopped beating Paul.

33The commander came up and arrested him and ordered him to be
bound with two chains. Then he asked who he was and what he had
done. 34Some in the crowd shouted one thing and some another, and
since the commander could not get at the truth because of the uproar,
he ordered that Paul be taken into the barracks. 35When Paul reached
the steps, the violence of the mob was so great he had to be carried by
the soldiers. 36The crowd that followed kept shouting, "Get rid of him!"

PAUL SPEAKS TO THE CROWD

37As the soldiers were about to take Paul into the barracks, he asked
the commander, "May I say something to you?"
"Do you speak Greek?" he replied. 38"Aren't you the Egyptian who
started a revolt and led four thousand terrorists out into the wilder-
ness some time ago?"
39Paul answered, "I am a Jew, from Tarsus in Cilicia, a citizen of no
ordinary city. Please let me speak to the people."
40After receiving the commander's permission, Paul stood on the
steps and motioned to the crowd. When they were all silent, he said to
22 them in Aramaic[a]: 1"Brothers and fathers, listen now to my
defense."
2When they heard him speak to them in Aramaic, they became very
quiet.
Then Paul said: 3"I am a Jew, born in Tarsus of Cilicia, but brought
up in this city. I studied under Gamaliel and was thoroughly trained in
the law of our ancestors. I was just as zealous for God as any of you are
today. 4I persecuted the followers of this Way to their death, arresting
both men and women and throwing them into prison, 5as the high
priest and all the Council can themselves testify. I even obtained letters
from them to their associates in Damascus, and went there to bring
these people as prisoners to Jerusalem to be punished.
6"About noon as I came near Damascus, suddenly a bright light from
heaven flashed around me. 7I fell to the ground and heard a voice say
to me, 'Saul! Saul! Why do you persecute me?'
8"'Who are you, Lord?' I asked.
"'I am Jesus of Nazareth, whom you are persecuting,' he replied. 9My
companions saw the light, but they did not understand the voice of
him who was speaking to me.
10"'What shall I do, Lord?' I asked.
"'Get up,' the Lord said, 'and go into Damascus. There you will be
told all that you have been assigned to do.' 11My companions led me
by the hand into Damascus, because the brilliance of the light had
blinded me.
12"A man named Ananias came to see me. He was a devout observer
of the law and highly respected by all the Jews living there. 13He stood
beside me and said, 'Brother Saul, receive your sight!' And at that very
moment I was able to see him.
14"Then he said: 'The God of our ancestors has chosen you to know
his will and to see the Righteous One and to hear words from his
mouth. 15You will be his witness to all people of what you have seen
and heard. 16And now what are you waiting for? Get up, be baptized
and wash your sins away, calling on his name.'
17"When I returned to Jerusalem and was praying at the temple, I fell

PRAYING SCRIPTURE

Acts 22

Paul was arrested in Jerusalem for preaching and teaching about Jesus. The more he spoke of the Way, the more agitated and bloodthirsty the crowd became. Finally, upon being brought into a barracks, Paul invoked his Roman citizenship, which led to his release the next day.

Standing for the gospel has cost many their freedom or their lives. Pray for faith to bear the gospel no matter the cost.

---

[a] 40 Or possibly *Hebrew*; also in 22:2

into a trance 18and saw the Lord speaking to me. 'Quick!' he said. 'Leave
Jerusalem immediately, because the people here will not accept your
testimony about me.'
19" 'Lord,' I replied, 'these people know that I went from one syna-
gogue to another to imprison and beat those who believe in you. 20And
when the blood of your martyr[a] Stephen was shed, I stood there giving
my approval and guarding the clothes of those who were killing him.'
21"Then the Lord said to me, 'Go; I will send you far away to the
Gentiles.' "

PAUL THE ROMAN CITIZEN

22The crowd listened to Paul until he said this. Then they raised their
voices and shouted, "Rid the earth of him! He's not fit to live!"
23As they were shouting and throwing off their cloaks and flinging
dust into the air, 24the commander ordered that Paul be taken into
the barracks. He directed that he be flogged and interrogated in or-
der to find out why the people were shouting at him like this. 25As
they stretched him out to flog him, Paul said to the centurion standing
there, "Is it legal for you to flog a Roman citizen who hasn't even been
found guilty?"
26When the centurion heard this, he went to the commander and
reported it. "What are you going to do?" he asked. "This man is a Ro-
man citizen."
27The commander went to Paul and asked, "Tell me, are you a Ro-
man citizen?"
"Yes, I am," he answered.
28Then the commander said, "I had to pay a lot of money for my
citizenship."
"But I was born a citizen," Paul replied.
29Those who were about to interrogate him withdrew immediately.
The commander himself was alarmed when he realized that he had
put Paul, a Roman citizen, in chains.

PAUL BEFORE THE SANHEDRIN

30The commander wanted to find out exactly why Paul was being
accused by the Jews. So the next day he released him and ordered the
chief priests and all the members of the Sanhedrin to assemble. Then
he brought Paul and had him stand before them.

23 Paul looked straight at the Sanhedrin and said, "My brothers,
I have fulfilled my duty to God in all good conscience to this
day." 2At this the high priest Ananias ordered those standing near Paul
to strike him on the mouth. 3Then Paul said to him, "God will strike
you, you whitewashed wall! You sit there to judge me according to the
law, yet you yourself violate the law by commanding that I be struck!"
4Those who were standing near Paul said, "How dare you insult God's
high priest!"
5Paul replied, "Brothers, I did not realize that he was the high priest;
for it is written: 'Do not speak evil about the ruler of your people.'[b]"
6Then Paul, knowing that some of them were Sadducees and the oth-
ers Pharisees, called out in the Sanhedrin, "My brothers, I am a Phari-
see, descended from Pharisees. I stand on trial because of the hope of
the resurrection of the dead." 7When he said this, a dispute broke out

PRAYING SCRIPTURE

Acts 23

Paul's life continued as a series of defenses before political leaders. Some of them never quite understood why he had been arrested. Paul leveraged his heritage—Jewish birth and Roman citizenship—as needed to defend himself, even as God encouraged him to "take courage" (verse 11).

How much better would our lives be if we were consistently of good cheer? Ask God to give you a joyful heart no matter your circumstances.

---

[a] 20 Or *witness* [b] 5 Exodus 22:28

between the Pharisees and the Sadducees, and the assembly was divided. 8(The Sadducees say that there is no resurrection, and that there are neither angels nor spirits, but the Pharisees believe all these things.)

9There was a great uproar, and some of the teachers of the law who were Pharisees stood up and argued vigorously. "We find nothing wrong with this man," they said. "What if a spirit or an angel has spoken to him?" 10The dispute became so violent that the commander was afraid Paul would be torn to pieces by them. He ordered the troops to go down and take him away from them by force and bring him into the barracks.

11The following night the Lord stood near Paul and said, "Take courage! As you have testified about me in Jerusalem, so you must also testify in Rome."

THE PLOT TO KILL PAUL

12The next morning some Jews formed a conspiracy and bound themselves with an oath not to eat or drink until they had killed Paul. 13More than forty men were involved in this plot. 14They went to the chief priests and the elders and said, "We have taken a solemn oath not to eat anything until we have killed Paul. 15Now then, you and the Sanhedrin petition the commander to bring him before you on the pretext of wanting more accurate information about his case. We are ready to kill him before he gets here."

16But when the son of Paul's sister heard of this plot, he went into the barracks and told Paul.

17Then Paul called one of the centurions and said, "Take this young man to the commander; he has something to tell him." 18So he took him to the commander.

The centurion said, "Paul, the prisoner, sent for me and asked me to bring this young man to you because he has something to tell you."

19The commander took the young man by the hand, drew him aside and asked, "What is it you want to tell me?"

20He said: "Some Jews have agreed to ask you to bring Paul before the Sanhedrin tomorrow on the pretext of wanting more accurate information about him. 21Don't give in to them, because more than forty of them are waiting in ambush for him. They have taken an oath not to eat or drink until they have killed him. They are ready now, waiting for your consent to their request."

22The commander dismissed the young man with this warning: "Don't tell anyone that you have reported this to me."

PAUL TRANSFERRED TO CAESAREA

23Then he called two of his centurions and ordered them, "Get ready a detachment of two hundred soldiers, seventy horsemen and two hundred spearmen[a] to go to Caesarea at nine tonight. 24Provide horses for Paul so that he may be taken safely to Governor Felix."

25He wrote a letter as follows:

26Claudius Lysias,

To His Excellency, Governor Felix:

Greetings.

---

[a] *23* The meaning of the Greek for this word is uncertain.

27This man was seized by the Jews and they were about to kill
him, but I came with my troops and rescued him, for I had learned
that he is a Roman citizen. 28I wanted to know why they were ac-
cusing him, so I brought him to their Sanhedrin. 29I found that
the accusation had to do with questions about their law, but there
was no charge against him that deserved death or imprisonment.
30When I was informed of a plot to be carried out against the man,
I sent him to you at once. I also ordered his accusers to present to
you their case against him.

31So the soldiers, carrying out their orders, took Paul with them dur-
ing the night and brought him as far as Antipatris. 32The next day they
let the cavalry go on with him, while they returned to the barracks.
33When the cavalry arrived in Caesarea, they delivered the letter to the
governor and handed Paul over to him. 34The governor read the letter
and asked what province he was from. Learning that he was from Cili-
cia, 35he said, "I will hear your case when your accusers get here." Then
he ordered that Paul be kept under guard in Herod's palace.

PAUL'S TRIAL BEFORE FELIX

24 Five days later the high priest Ananias went down to Caesarea
with some of the elders and a lawyer named Tertullus, and
they brought their charges against Paul before the governor. 2When
Paul was called in, Tertullus presented his case before Felix: "We have
enjoyed a long period of peace under you, and your foresight has
brought about reforms in this nation. 3Everywhere and in every way,
most excellent Felix, we acknowledge this with profound gratitude.
4But in order not to weary you further, I would request that you be
kind enough to hear us briefly.

5"We have found this man to be a troublemaker, stirring up riots
among the Jews all over the world. He is a ringleader of the Nazarene
sect 6and even tried to desecrate the temple; so we seized him. [7][a] 8By
examining him yourself you will be able to learn the truth about all
these charges we are bringing against him."

9The other Jews joined in the accusation, asserting that these things
were true.

10When the governor motioned for him to speak, Paul replied: "I
know that for a number of years you have been a judge over this na-
tion; so I gladly make my defense. 11You can easily verify that no more
than twelve days ago I went up to Jerusalem to worship. 12My accusers
did not find me arguing with anyone at the temple, or stirring up a
crowd in the synagogues or anywhere else in the city. 13And they can-
not prove to you the charges they are now making against me. 14How-
ever, I admit that I worship the God of our ancestors as a follower of the
Way, which they call a sect. I believe everything that is in accordance
with the Law and that is written in the Prophets, 15and I have the same
hope in God as these men themselves have, that there will be a resur-
rection of both the righteous and the wicked. 16So I strive always to
keep my conscience clear before God and man.

17"After an absence of several years, I came to Jerusalem to bring my

PRAYING SCRIPTURE

Acts 24

The narrative of Paul's persecutions continues with his defense before the governor, Felix. Paul's defense, however, consisted of his testimony of salvation in Jesus. He claimed his arrest was based on theological, not criminal, reasons (see verse 21). Felix, fearful of the implications, delayed his ruling until later.

Never underestimate the power of your testimony of faith in Christ. Ask God for opportunities to tell your faith story, and trust him to use it.

[a] 6-8 Some manuscripts include here *him, and we would have judged him in accordance with our law. 7But the commander Lysias came and took him from us with much violence, 8ordering his accusers to come before you.*

people gifts for the poor and to present offerings. 18I was ceremonially clean when they found me in the temple courts doing this. There was no crowd with me, nor was I involved in any disturbance. 19But there are some Jews from the province of Asia, who ought to be here before you and bring charges if they have anything against me. 20Or these who are here should state what crime they found in me when I stood before the Sanhedrin— 21unless it was this one thing I shouted as I stood in their presence: 'It is concerning the resurrection of the dead that I am on trial before you today.'"

22Then Felix, who was well acquainted with the Way, adjourned the proceedings. "When Lysias the commander comes," he said, "I will decide your case." 23He ordered the centurion to keep Paul under guard but to give him some freedom and permit his friends to take care of his needs.

24Several days later Felix came with his wife Drusilla, who was Jewish. He sent for Paul and listened to him as he spoke about faith in Christ Jesus. 25As Paul talked about righteousness, self-control and the judgment to come, Felix was afraid and said, "That's enough for now! You may leave. When I find it convenient, I will send for you." 26At the same time he was hoping that Paul would offer him a bribe, so he sent for him frequently and talked with him.

27When two years had passed, Felix was succeeded by Porcius Festus, but because Felix wanted to grant a favor to the Jews, he left Paul in prison.

PAUL'S TRIAL BEFORE FESTUS

25 Three days after arriving in the province, Festus went up from Caesarea to Jerusalem, 2where the chief priests and the Jewish leaders appeared before him and presented the charges against Paul. 3They requested Festus, as a favor to them, to have Paul transferred to Jerusalem, for they were preparing an ambush to kill him along the way. 4Festus answered, "Paul is being held at Caesarea, and I myself am going there soon. 5Let some of your leaders come with me, and if the man has done anything wrong, they can press charges against him there."

6After spending eight or ten days with them, Festus went down to Caesarea. The next day he convened the court and ordered that Paul be brought before him. 7When Paul came in, the Jews who had come down from Jerusalem stood around him. They brought many serious charges against him, but they could not prove them.

8Then Paul made his defense: "I have done nothing wrong against the Jewish law or against the temple or against Caesar."

9Festus, wishing to do the Jews a favor, said to Paul, "Are you willing to go up to Jerusalem and stand trial before me there on these charges?"

10Paul answered: "I am now standing before Caesar's court, where I ought to be tried. I have not done any wrong to the Jews, as you yourself know very well. 11If, however, I am guilty of doing anything deserving death, I do not refuse to die. But if the charges brought against me by these Jews are not true, no one has the right to hand me over to them. I appeal to Caesar!"

12After Festus had conferred with his council, he declared: "You have appealed to Caesar. To Caesar you will go!"

PRAYING SCRIPTURE

Acts 25

Paul's appeal to Caesar was dramatic: "I am now standing before Caesar's court, where I ought to be tried" (verse 10). His Roman judge was all too happy to oblige, "To Caesar you will go!" (verse 12).

The Bible is not against working within the legal system according to one's rights. Pray for those who are struggling against unfair legal practices. Ask God to show his strength on their behalf.

FESTUS CONSULTS KING AGRIPPA

13A few days later King Agrippa and Bernice arrived at Caesarea to
pay their respects to Festus. 14Since they were spending many days
there, Festus discussed Paul's case with the king. He said: "There is a
man here whom Felix left as a prisoner. 15When I went to Jerusalem,
the chief priests and the elders of the Jews brought charges against
him and asked that he be condemned.

16"I told them that it is not the Roman custom to hand over anyone
before they have faced their accusers and have had an opportunity to
defend themselves against the charges. 17When they came here with
me, I did not delay the case, but convened the court the next day and
ordered the man to be brought in. 18When his accusers got up to speak,
they did not charge him with any of the crimes I had expected. 19In-
stead, they had some points of dispute with him about their own reli-
gion and about a dead man named Jesus who Paul claimed was alive.
20I was at a loss how to investigate such matters; so I asked if he would
be willing to go to Jerusalem and stand trial there on these charges.
21But when Paul made his appeal to be held over for the Emperor's de-
cision, I ordered him held until I could send him to Caesar."

22Then Agrippa said to Festus, "I would like to hear this man myself."

He replied, "Tomorrow you will hear him."

PAUL BEFORE AGRIPPA

23The next day Agrippa and Bernice came with great pomp and en-
tered the audience room with the high-ranking military officers and
the prominent men of the city. At the command of Festus, Paul was
brought in. 24Festus said: "King Agrippa, and all who are present with
us, you see this man! The whole Jewish community has petitioned me
about him in Jerusalem and here in Caesarea, shouting that he ought
not to live any longer. 25I found he had done nothing deserving of
death, but because he made his appeal to the Emperor I decided to
send him to Rome. 26But I have nothing definite to write to His Majesty
about him. Therefore I have brought him before all of you, and espe-
cially before you, King Agrippa, so that as a result of this investigation
I may have something to write. 27For I think it is unreasonable to send
a prisoner on to Rome without specifying the charges against him."

26 Then Agrippa said to Paul, "You have permission to speak for
yourself."

So Paul motioned with his hand and began his defense: 2"King
Agrippa, I consider myself fortunate to stand before you today as I
make my defense against all the accusations of the Jews, 3and espe-
cially so because you are well acquainted with all the Jewish customs
and controversies. Therefore, I beg you to listen to me patiently.

4"The Jewish people all know the way I have lived ever since I was
a child, from the beginning of my life in my own country, and also in
Jerusalem. 5They have known me for a long time and can testify, if
they are willing, that I conformed to the strictest sect of our religion,
living as a Pharisee. 6And now it is because of my hope in what God
has promised our ancestors that I am on trial today. 7This is the prom-
ise our twelve tribes are hoping to see fulfilled as they earnestly serve
God day and night. King Agrippa, it is because of this hope that these
Jews are accusing me. 8Why should any of you consider it incredible
that God raises the dead?

PRAYING SCRIPTURE

Acts 26

Among Paul's defenses of his preaching was one before Herod Agrippa. Paul gave a testimony of salvation, the pattern of which has been copied ever since: his life before Christ (see verses 4–11), how he was converted (see verse 12–18) and his life since conversion (see verse 19–23).

Can you share your faith journey following the same pattern? Take a few minutes to write down your story. Then ask the Lord for opportunities to share it with others.

9"I too was convinced that I ought to do all that was possible to op-
pose the name of Jesus of Nazareth. 10And that is just what I did in Je-
rusalem. On the authority of the chief priests I put many of the Lord's
people in prison, and when they were put to death, I cast my vote
against them. 11Many a time I went from one synagogue to another
to have them punished, and I tried to force them to blaspheme. I was
so obsessed with persecuting them that I even hunted them down in
foreign cities.

12"On one of these journeys I was going to Damascus with the author-
ity and commission of the chief priests. 13About noon, King Agrippa,
as I was on the road, I saw a light from heaven, brighter than the sun,
blazing around me and my companions. 14We all fell to the ground,
and I heard a voice saying to me in Aramaic,[a] 'Saul, Saul, why do you
persecute me? It is hard for you to kick against the goads.'

15"Then I asked, 'Who are you, Lord?'

"'I am Jesus, whom you are persecuting,' the Lord replied. 16'Now
get up and stand on your feet. I have appeared to you to appoint you
as a servant and as a witness of what you have seen and will see of me.
17I will rescue you from your own people and from the Gentiles. I am
sending you to them 18to open their eyes and turn them from dark-
ness to light, and from the power of Satan to God, so that they may
receive forgiveness of sins and a place among those who are sanctified
by faith in me.'

19"So then, King Agrippa, I was not disobedient to the vision from
heaven. 20First to those in Damascus, then to those in Jerusalem and
in all Judea, and then to the Gentiles, I preached that they should re-
pent and turn to God and demonstrate their repentance by their deeds.
21That is why some Jews seized me in the temple courts and tried to
kill me. 22But God has helped me to this very day; so I stand here and
testify to small and great alike. I am saying nothing beyond what the
prophets and Moses said would happen — 23that the Messiah would
suffer and, as the first to rise from the dead, would bring the message
of light to his own people and to the Gentiles."

24At this point Festus interrupted Paul's defense. "You are out of your
mind, Paul!" he shouted. "Your great learning is driving you insane."

25"I am not insane, most excellent Festus," Paul replied. "What I am
saying is true and reasonable. 26The king is familiar with these things,
and I can speak freely to him. I am convinced that none of this has es-
caped his notice, because it was not done in a corner. 27King Agrippa,
do you believe the prophets? I know you do."

28Then Agrippa said to Paul, "Do you think that in such a short time
you can persuade me to be a Christian?"

29Paul replied, "Short time or long — I pray to God that not only you
but all who are listening to me today may become what I am, except
for these chains."

30The king rose, and with him the governor and Bernice and those
sitting with them. 31After they left the room, they began saying to
one another, "This man is not doing anything that deserves death or
imprisonment."

32Agrippa said to Festus, "This man could have been set free if he had
not appealed to Caesar."

---

[a] 14 Or *Hebrew*

PRAYING SCRIPTURE

Acts 27

The storm at sea and shipwreck are among the incredible challenges of Paul's ministry. Paul built the faith of the 276 passengers by telling them God promised that he, Paul, would appear before Caesar. To do that, he had to survive, which meant they, too, would survive.

When we talk about the "storms of life," we often speak metaphorically. But God is with us in all storms, so call on him for help.

PAUL SAILS FOR ROME

27 When it was decided that we would sail for Italy, Paul and some other prisoners were handed over to a centurion named Julius, who belonged to the Imperial Regiment. 2We boarded a ship from Adramyttium about to sail for ports along the coast of the province of Asia, and we put out to sea. Aristarchus, a Macedonian from Thessalonica, was with us.

3The next day we landed at Sidon; and Julius, in kindness to Paul, allowed him to go to his friends so they might provide for his needs. 4From there we put out to sea again and passed to the lee of Cyprus because the winds were against us. 5When we had sailed across the open sea off the coast of Cilicia and Pamphylia, we landed at Myra in Lycia. 6There the centurion found an Alexandrian ship sailing for Italy and put us on board. 7We made slow headway for many days and had difficulty arriving off Cnidus. When the wind did not allow us to hold our course, we sailed to the lee of Crete, opposite Salmone. 8We moved along the coast with difficulty and came to a place called Fair Havens, near the town of Lasea.

9Much time had been lost, and sailing had already become dangerous because by now it was after the Day of Atonement.[a] So Paul warned them, 10"Men, I can see that our voyage is going to be disastrous and bring great loss to ship and cargo, and to our own lives also." 11But the centurion, instead of listening to what Paul said, followed the advice of the pilot and of the owner of the ship. 12Since the harbor was unsuitable to winter in, the majority decided that we should sail on, hoping to reach Phoenix and winter there. This was a harbor in Crete, facing both southwest and northwest.

THE STORM

13When a gentle south wind began to blow, they saw their opportunity; so they weighed anchor and sailed along the shore of Crete. 14Before very long, a wind of hurricane force, called the Northeaster, swept down from the island. 15The ship was caught by the storm and could not head into the wind; so we gave way to it and were driven along. 16As we passed to the lee of a small island called Cauda, we were hardly able to make the lifeboat secure, 17so the men hoisted it aboard. Then they passed ropes under the ship itself to hold it together. Because they were afraid they would run aground on the sandbars of Syrtis, they lowered the sea anchor[b] and let the ship be driven along. 18We took such a violent battering from the storm that the next day they began to throw the cargo overboard. 19On the third day, they threw the ship's tackle overboard with their own hands. 20When neither sun nor stars appeared for many days and the storm continued raging, we finally gave up all hope of being saved.

21After they had gone a long time without food, Paul stood up before them and said: "Men, you should have taken my advice not to sail from Crete; then you would have spared yourselves this damage and loss. 22But now I urge you to keep up your courage, because not one of you will be lost; only the ship will be destroyed. 23Last night an angel of the God to whom I belong and whom I serve stood beside me 24and said, 'Do not be afraid, Paul. You must stand trial before Caesar; and God has graciously given you the lives of all who sail with you.' 25So keep

[a] 9 That is, Yom Kippur [b] 17 Or *the sails*

up your courage, men, for I have faith in God that it will happen just
as he told me. 26Nevertheless, we must run aground on some island."

THE SHIPWRECK

27On the fourteenth night we were still being driven across the Adria-
tic[a] Sea, when about midnight the sailors sensed they were approaching
land. 28They took soundings and found that the water was a hundred
and twenty feet[b] deep. A short time later they took soundings again
and found it was ninety feet[c] deep. 29Fearing that we would be dashed
against the rocks, they dropped four anchors from the stern and prayed
for daylight. 30In an attempt to escape from the ship, the sailors let the
lifeboat down into the sea, pretending they were going to lower some
anchors from the bow. 31Then Paul said to the centurion and the sol-
diers, "Unless these men stay with the ship, you cannot be saved." 32So
the soldiers cut the ropes that held the lifeboat and let it drift away.

33Just before dawn Paul urged them all to eat. "For the last fourteen
days," he said, "you have been in constant suspense and have gone
without food — you haven't eaten anything. 34Now I urge you to take
some food. You need it to survive. Not one of you will lose a single
hair from his head." 35After he said this, he took some bread and gave
thanks to God in front of them all. Then he broke it and began to eat.
36They were all encouraged and ate some food themselves. 37Altogether
there were 276 of us on board. 38When they had eaten as much as they
wanted, they lightened the ship by throwing the grain into the sea.

39When daylight came, they did not recognize the land, but they saw
a bay with a sandy beach, where they decided to run the ship aground
if they could. 40Cutting loose the anchors, they left them in the sea and
at the same time untied the ropes that held the rudders. Then they
hoisted the foresail to the wind and made for the beach. 41But the ship
struck a sandbar and ran aground. The bow stuck fast and would not
move, and the stern was broken to pieces by the pounding of the surf.

42The soldiers planned to kill the prisoners to prevent any of them
from swimming away and escaping. 43But the centurion wanted to
spare Paul's life and kept them from carrying out their plan. He or-
dered those who could swim to jump overboard first and get to land.
44The rest were to get there on planks or on other pieces of the ship. In
this way everyone reached land safely.

PAUL ASHORE ON MALTA

28 Once safely on shore, we found out that the island was called
Malta. 2The islanders showed us unusual kindness. They built
a fire and welcomed us all because it was raining and cold. 3Paul gath-
ered a pile of brushwood and, as he put it on the fire, a viper, driven
out by the heat, fastened itself on his hand. 4When the islanders saw
the snake hanging from his hand, they said to each other, "This man
must be a murderer; for though he escaped from the sea, the god-
dess Justice has not allowed him to live." 5But Paul shook the snake
off into the fire and suffered no ill effects. 6The people expected him
to swell up or suddenly fall dead; but after waiting a long time and
seeing nothing unusual happen to him, they changed their minds and
said he was a god.

PRAYING SCRIPTURE

Acts 28

After a long, arduous journey, Paul arrived in Rome. He was allowed to stay with the soldier who guarded him (see verse 16). The book of Acts ends with Paul in a rented house (see verse 30). Thus, the church's beginning continued, and Paul emphasized the kingdom of God and "taught about the Lord Jesus Christ" (verse 31).

The church grew by the gospel of Jesus. Pray that the Good News will compel your growth, too.

[a] *27* In ancient times the name referred to an area extending well south of Italy. [b] *28* Or about 37 meters [c] *28* Or about 27 meters

[7]There was an estate nearby that belonged to Publius, the chief offi-
cial of the island. He welcomed us to his home and showed us generous
hospitality for three days. [8]His father was sick in bed, suffering from
fever and dysentery. Paul went in to see him and, after prayer, placed
his hands on him and healed him. [9]When this had happened, the rest
of the sick on the island came and were cured. [10]They honored us in
many ways; and when we were ready to sail, they furnished us with
the supplies we needed.

PAUL'S ARRIVAL AT ROME

[11]After three months we put out to sea in a ship that had wintered
in the island — it was an Alexandrian ship with the figurehead of the
twin gods Castor and Pollux. [12]We put in at Syracuse and stayed there
three days. [13]From there we set sail and arrived at Rhegium. The next
day the south wind came up, and on the following day we reached
Puteoli. [14]There we found some brothers and sisters who invited us to
spend a week with them. And so we came to Rome. [15]The brothers and
sisters there had heard that we were coming, and they traveled as far as
the Forum of Appius and the Three Taverns to meet us. At the sight of
these people Paul thanked God and was encouraged. [16]When we got to
Rome, Paul was allowed to live by himself, with a soldier to guard him.

PAUL PREACHES AT ROME UNDER GUARD

[17]Three days later he called together the local Jewish leaders. When
they had assembled, Paul said to them: "My brothers, although I have
done nothing against our people or against the customs of our an-
cestors, I was arrested in Jerusalem and handed over to the Romans.
[18]They examined me and wanted to release me, because I was not
guilty of any crime deserving death. [19]The Jews objected, so I was com-
pelled to make an appeal to Caesar. I certainly did not intend to bring
any charge against my own people. [20]For this reason I have asked to
see you and talk with you. It is because of the hope of Israel that I am
bound with this chain."

[21]They replied, "We have not received any letters from Judea con-
cerning you, and none of our people who have come from there
has reported or said anything bad about you. [22]But we want to hear
what your views are, for we know that people everywhere are talking
against this sect."

[23]They arranged to meet Paul on a certain day, and came in even
larger numbers to the place where he was staying. He witnessed to
them from morning till evening, explaining about the kingdom of
God, and from the Law of Moses and from the Prophets he tried to
persuade them about Jesus. [24]Some were convinced by what he said,
but others would not believe. [25]They disagreed among themselves and
began to leave after Paul had made this final statement: "The Holy
Spirit spoke the truth to your ancestors when he said through Isaiah
the prophet:

[26]" 'Go to this people and say,
"You will be ever hearing but never understanding;
you will be ever seeing but never perceiving."
[27]For this people's heart has become calloused;
they hardly hear with their ears,
and they have closed their eyes.

Otherwise they might see with their eyes,
hear with their ears,
understand with their hearts
and turn, and I would heal them.'[a]

28"Therefore I want you to know that God's salvation has been sent
to the Gentiles, and they will listen!" [29][b]
30For two whole years Paul stayed there in his own rented house and
welcomed all who came to see him. 31He proclaimed the kingdom of
God and taught about the Lord Jesus Christ—with all boldness and
without hindrance!

[a] 27 Isaiah 6:9,10 (see Septuagint) [b] 29 Some manuscripts include here *After he said this, the Jews left, arguing vigorously among themselves.*

ROMANS

It would be impossible to overstate the role Paul's letter to the Romans has played in the history of the church. This letter, Paul's theological magnum opus, lays out the theology of salvation in greater depth than any of his other writings. It led to the salvation of Augustine, and in large part, sparked the Protestant Reformation. Paul did not know the church at Rome, so he intended this letter to serve as an introduction to himself and to the message he preached. After visiting those in Rome, he would then go and preach the gospel in Spain.

In almost every Pauline letter, he included a prayer for the church or individual to whom he was writing. These prayers focus on the recipients' growth in Christ and progress in the faith and provide a helpful framework for how Christians can pray for each other and for their churches. They often focus on the evidence of grace in the believer and offer specific petitions for continuing spiritual growth.

Paul's prayer for the Romans begins in the way that so many of his prayers do—with thanksgiving for his readers. Thanksgiving is a major theme throughout Paul's letters, so it is fitting that he included it here. Because of the news of their conversion and growth in Christ, he expressed his thankfulness for the believers in Rome. Christians are grateful for every new believer, every new church and every evidence of God's grace in a person's life.

In Romans 8, the apostle laid a foundational understanding of prayer after contrasting the person who walks by the flesh and the person who walks by the Spirit. This is important, he explained, because it is the Spirit who fills us and reminds us of our adoption as God's children. Our spiritual adoption leads us to cry out to God the Father in prayer. The word used for "Father" pictures a child's use of "daddy" or even "dada." It shows us the childlikeness with which we can and should approach our heavenly Father in prayer.

When we don't know how to pray, the Spirit steps in and intercedes for us, giving words to the internal groaning of our hearts. He literally prays on our behalf with sighs that are too deep for any words we could pray. The Spirit ministers in us while Jesus intercedes for us. How can we doubt that our prayers will be answered?

Romans includes Paul's standard closing of a letter: listing the names of fellow workers who send greetings, greeting many individual church members who will read or hear the letter and giving final instructions. Here he warned the Roman believers to "watch out for those who cause divisions and put obstacles in your way that are contrary to the teaching you have learned. Keep away from them" (16:17). Paul did not think that remaining connected to people who lived divisively would encourage spiritual growth. Thus, he commanded those who followed Jesus to take note of those who caused division and avoid them.

1 Paul, a servant of Christ Jesus, called to be an apostle and set
apart for the gospel of God — 2the gospel he promised beforehand
through his prophets in the Holy Scriptures 3regarding his Son, who
as to his earthly life[a] was a descendant of David, 4and who through
the Spirit of holiness was appointed the Son of God in power[b] by his
resurrection from the dead: Jesus Christ our Lord. 5Through him we
received grace and apostleship to call all the Gentiles to the obedience
that comes from[c] faith for his name's sake. 6And you also are among
those Gentiles who are called to belong to Jesus Christ.

7To all in Rome who are loved by God and called to be his holy people:

Grace and peace to you from God our Father and from the Lord Jesus
Christ.

PAUL'S LONGING TO VISIT ROME

8First, I thank my God through Jesus Christ for all of you, because
your faith is being reported all over the world. 9God, whom I serve in
my spirit in preaching the gospel of his Son, is my witness how con-
stantly I remember you 10in my prayers at all times; and I pray that
now at last by God's will the way may be opened for me to come to you.

11I long to see you so that I may impart to you some spiritual gift to
make you strong — 12that is, that you and I may be mutually encour-
aged by each other's faith. 13I do not want you to be unaware, brothers
and sisters,[d] that I planned many times to come to you (but have been
prevented from doing so until now) in order that I might have a har-
vest among you, just as I have had among the other Gentiles.

14I am obligated both to Greeks and non-Greeks, both to the wise and
the foolish. 15That is why I am so eager to preach the gospel also to you
who are in Rome.

16For I am not ashamed of the gospel, because it is the power of God
that brings salvation to everyone who believes: first to the Jew, then to
the Gentile. 17For in the gospel the righteousness of God is revealed — a
righteousness that is by faith from first to last,[e] just as it is written:
"The righteous will live by faith."[f]

GOD'S WRATH AGAINST SINFUL HUMANITY

18The wrath of God is being revealed from heaven against all the
godlessness and wickedness of people, who suppress the truth by their
wickedness, 19since what may be known about God is plain to them,
because God has made it plain to them. 20For since the creation of
the world God's invisible qualities — his eternal power and divine na-
ture — have been clearly seen, being understood from what has been
made, so that people are without excuse.

21For although they knew God, they neither glorified him as God nor
gave thanks to him, but their thinking became futile and their foolish
hearts were darkened. 22Although they claimed to be wise, they became
fools 23and exchanged the glory of the immortal God for images made
to look like a mortal human being and birds and animals and reptiles.

PRAYING SCRIPTURE

Romans 1

In this chapter, Paul taught us that the gospel is the power of God that brings salvation to both Jews and Gentiles (see verse 16). There is no one who cannot be saved by the gospel of Jesus if they but believe.

Have you believed in the gospel of Jesus Christ? Do you believe Jesus died for you, was buried and rose from the dead? If not, call on him to save you today.

[a] 3 Or *who according to the flesh* [b] 4 Or *was declared with power to be the Son of God* [c] 5 Or *that is* [d] 13 The Greek word for *brothers and sisters* (*adelphoi*) refers here to believers, both men and women, as part of God's family; also in 7:1,4; 8:12,29; 10:1; 11:25; 12:1; 15:14,30; 16:14,17. [e] 17 Or *is from faith to faith* [f] 17 Hab. 2:4

24 Therefore God gave them over in the sinful desires of their hearts
to sexual impurity for the degrading of their bodies with one another.
25 They exchanged the truth about God for a lie, and worshiped and
served created things rather than the Creator — who is forever praised.
Amen.
26 Because of this, God gave them over to shameful lusts. Even their
women exchanged natural sexual relations for unnatural ones. 27 In
the same way the men also abandoned natural relations with women
and were inflamed with lust for one another. Men committed shame-
ful acts with other men, and received in themselves the due penalty
for their error.
28 Furthermore, just as they did not think it worthwhile to retain the
knowledge of God, so God gave them over to a depraved mind, so that
they do what ought not to be done. 29 They have become filled with
every kind of wickedness, evil, greed and depravity. They are full of
envy, murder, strife, deceit and malice. They are gossips, 30 slanderers,
God-haters, insolent, arrogant and boastful; they invent ways of doing
evil; they disobey their parents; 31 they have no understanding, no fi-
delity, no love, no mercy. 32 Although they know God's righteous decree
that those who do such things deserve death, they not only continue
to do these very things but also approve of those who practice them.

GOD'S RIGHTEOUS JUDGMENT

PRAYING SCRIPTURE

Romans 2

Have you met people who do not believe they could be under God's judgment because they don't think they have done anything worthy of judgment? Here we are warned that no one—whether Jew, Gentile, or self-righteous person—will escape God's judgment.

Thanks be to God that Jesus bore the judgment of God for all who believe. Thank God for his grace that provides the salvation Christ has borne.

2 You, therefore, have no excuse, you who pass judgment on some-
one else, for at whatever point you judge another, you are con-
demning yourself, because you who pass judgment do the same things.
2 Now we know that God's judgment against those who do such things
is based on truth. 3 So when you, a mere human being, pass judgment
on them and yet do the same things, do you think you will escape God's
judgment? 4 Or do you show contempt for the riches of his kindness,
forbearance and patience, not realizing that God's kindness is intended
to lead you to repentance?
5 But because of your stubbornness and your unrepentant heart, you
are storing up wrath against yourself for the day of God's wrath, when
his righteous judgment will be revealed. 6 God "will repay each person
according to what they have done."[a] 7 To those who by persistence in
doing good seek glory, honor and immortality, he will give eternal
life. 8 But for those who are self-seeking and who reject the truth and
follow evil, there will be wrath and anger. 9 There will be trouble and
distress for every human being who does evil: first for the Jew, then
for the Gentile; 10 but glory, honor and peace for everyone who does
good: first for the Jew, then for the Gentile. 11 For God does not show
favoritism.
12 All who sin apart from the law will also perish apart from the law,
and all who sin under the law will be judged by the law. 13 For it is not
those who hear the law who are righteous in God's sight, but it is those
who obey the law who will be declared righteous. 14 (Indeed, when
Gentiles, who do not have the law, do by nature things required by
the law, they are a law for themselves, even though they do not have
the law. 15 They show that the requirements of the law are written on
their hearts, their consciences also bearing witness, and their thoughts
sometimes accusing them and at other times even defending them.)

[a] 6 Psalm 62:12; Prov. 24:12

16This will take place on the day when God judges people's secrets
through Jesus Christ, as my gospel declares.

THE JEWS AND THE LAW

17Now you, if you call yourself a Jew; if you rely on the law and boast
in God; 18if you know his will and approve of what is superior because
you are instructed by the law; 19if you are convinced that you are a guide
for the blind, a light for those who are in the dark, 20an instructor of the
foolish, a teacher of little children, because you have in the law the em-
bodiment of knowledge and truth— 21you, then, who teach others, do
you not teach yourself? You who preach against stealing, do you steal?
22You who say that people should not commit adultery, do you commit
adultery? You who abhor idols, do you rob temples? 23You who boast
in the law, do you dishonor God by breaking the law? 24As it is written:
"God's name is blasphemed among the Gentiles because of you."[a]

25Circumcision has value if you observe the law, but if you break the
law, you have become as though you had not been circumcised. 26So
then, if those who are not circumcised keep the law's requirements,
will they not be regarded as though they were circumcised? 27The one
who is not circumcised physically and yet obeys the law will condemn
you who, even though you have the[b] written code and circumcision,
are a lawbreaker.

28A person is not a Jew who is one only outwardly, nor is circumci-
sion merely outward and physical. 29No, a person is a Jew who is one
inwardly; and circumcision is circumcision of the heart, by the Spirit,
not by the written code. Such a person's praise is not from other peo-
ple, but from God.

GOD'S FAITHFULNESS

3 What advantage, then, is there in being a Jew, or what value is
there in circumcision? 2Much in every way! First of all, the Jews
have been entrusted with the very words of God.

3What if some were unfaithful? Will their unfaithfulness nullify
God's faithfulness? 4Not at all! Let God be true, and every human be-
ing a liar. As it is written:

> "So that you may be proved right when you speak
> and prevail when you judge."[c]

5But if our unrighteousness brings out God's righteousness more
clearly, what shall we say? That God is unjust in bringing his wrath on
us? (I am using a human argument.) 6Certainly not! If that were so,
how could God judge the world? 7Someone might argue, "If my false-
hood enhances God's truthfulness and so increases his glory, why am
I still condemned as a sinner?" 8Why not say—as some slanderously
claim that we say—"Let us do evil that good may result"? Their con-
demnation is just!

NO ONE IS RIGHTEOUS

9What shall we conclude then? Do we have any advantage? Not at all!
For we have already made the charge that Jews and Gentiles alike are
all under the power of sin. 10As it is written:

PRAYING SCRIPTURE

Romans 3

Before being given the Good News, people need to understand the bad news: Sin affects every human being. Paul wrote that Jews and Gentiles alike are guilty (see verse 9). Those who had access to the law were not better than those who did not. All have sinned and fall short of God's glory.

The only way to be forgiven is through Jesus Christ. If you have not done so already, ask him today to save you.

---

[a] 24 Isaiah 52:5 (see Septuagint); Ezek. 36:20,22 [b] 27 Or *who, by means of a*
[c] 4 Psalm 51:4

"There is no one righteous, not even one;
11 there is no one who understands;
there is no one who seeks God.
12 All have turned away,
they have together become worthless;
there is no one who does good,
not even one."[a]
13 "Their throats are open graves;
their tongues practice deceit."[b]
"The poison of vipers is on their lips."[c]
14 "Their mouths are full of cursing and bitterness."[d]
15 "Their feet are swift to shed blood;
16 ruin and misery mark their ways,
17 and the way of peace they do not know."[e]
18 "There is no fear of God before their eyes."[f]

19 Now we know that whatever the law says, it says to those who are
under the law, so that every mouth may be silenced and the whole
world held accountable to God. 20 Therefore no one will be declared
righteous in God's sight by the works of the law; rather, through the
law we become conscious of our sin.

RIGHTEOUSNESS THROUGH FAITH

21 But now apart from the law the righteousness of God has been made
known, to which the Law and the Prophets testify. 22 This righteousness
is given through faith in[g] Jesus Christ to all who believe. There is no
difference between Jew and Gentile, 23 for all have sinned and fall short
of the glory of God, 24 and all are justified freely by his grace through the
redemption that came by Christ Jesus. 25 God presented Christ as a sacri-
fice of atonement,[h] through the shedding of his blood — to be received
by faith. He did this to demonstrate his righteousness, because in his
forbearance he had left the sins committed beforehand unpunished —
26 he did it to demonstrate his righteousness at the present time, so as
to be just and the one who justifies those who have faith in Jesus.

27 Where, then, is boasting? It is excluded. Because of what law? The
law that requires works? No, because of the law that requires faith.
28 For we maintain that a person is justified by faith apart from the
works of the law. 29 Or is God the God of Jews only? Is he not the God
of Gentiles too? Yes, of Gentiles too, 30 since there is only one God, who
will justify the circumcised by faith and the uncircumcised through
that same faith. 31 Do we, then, nullify the law by this faith? Not at all!
Rather, we uphold the law.

PRAYING SCRIPTURE

Romans 4

Few things are more misunderstood in Scripture than the relationship of the law and faith in salvation. Paul made clear that Abraham, who lived before the law, was justified by faith, not works. Therefore, keeping the law could not be a requirement for justification.

There is nothing any person can do to gain salvation by their works. Pray that the unbelievers you know may place their faith in Jesus.

ABRAHAM JUSTIFIED BY FAITH

4 What then shall we say that Abraham, our forefather according to
the flesh, discovered in this matter? 2 If, in fact, Abraham was jus-
tified by works, he had something to boast about — but not before God.
3 What does Scripture say? "Abraham believed God, and it was credited
to him as righteousness."[i]

[a] *12* Psalms 14:1-3; 53:1-3; Eccles. 7:20 [b] *13* Psalm 5:9 [c] *13* Psalm 140:3
[d] *14* Psalm 10:7 (see Septuagint) [e] *17* Isaiah 59:7,8 [f] *18* Psalm 36:1
[g] *22* Or *through the faithfulness of* [h] *25* The Greek for *sacrifice of atonement* refers to the atonement cover on the ark of the covenant (see Lev. 16:15,16).
[i] *3* Gen. 15:6; also in verse 22

4 Now to the one who works, wages are not credited as a gift but as
an obligation. 5 However, to the one who does not work but trusts God
who justifies the ungodly, their faith is credited as righteousness. 6 Da-
vid says the same thing when he speaks of the blessedness of the one
to whom God credits righteousness apart from works:

7 "Blessed are those
whose transgressions are forgiven,
whose sins are covered.
8 Blessed is the one
whose sin the Lord will never count against them."[a]

9 Is this blessedness only for the circumcised, or also for the uncir-
cumcised? We have been saying that Abraham's faith was credited to
him as righteousness. 10 Under what circumstances was it credited? Was
it after he was circumcised, or before? It was not after, but before! 11 And
he received circumcision as a sign, a seal of the righteousness that he
had by faith while he was still uncircumcised. So then, he is the father
of all who believe but have not been circumcised, in order that righ-
teousness might be credited to them. 12 And he is then also the father
of the circumcised who not only are circumcised but who also follow
in the footsteps of the faith that our father Abraham had before he
was circumcised.

13 It was not through the law that Abraham and his offspring received
the promise that he would be heir of the world, but through the righ-
teousness that comes by faith. 14 For if those who depend on the law are
heirs, faith means nothing and the promise is worthless, 15 because the
law brings wrath. And where there is no law there is no transgression.

16 Therefore, the promise comes by faith, so that it may be by grace
and may be guaranteed to all Abraham's offspring — not only to those
who are of the law but also to those who have the faith of Abraham.
He is the father of us all. 17 As it is written: "I have made you a father of
many nations."[b] He is our father in the sight of God, in whom he be-
lieved — the God who gives life to the dead and calls into being things
that were not.

18 Against all hope, Abraham in hope believed and so became the
father of many nations, just as it had been said to him, "So shall your
offspring be."[c] 19 Without weakening in his faith, he faced the fact that
his body was as good as dead — since he was about a hundred years
old — and that Sarah's womb was also dead. 20 Yet he did not waver
through unbelief regarding the promise of God, but was strengthened
in his faith and gave glory to God, 21 being fully persuaded that God
had power to do what he had promised. 22 This is why "it was credited
to him as righteousness." 23 The words "it was credited to him" were
written not for him alone, 24 but also for us, to whom God will credit
righteousness — for us who believe in him who raised Jesus our Lord
from the dead. 25 He was delivered over to death for our sins and was
raised to life for our justification.

PEACE AND HOPE

5 Therefore, since we have been justified through faith, we[d] have
peace with God through our Lord Jesus Christ, 2 through whom we
have gained access by faith into this grace in which we now stand. And

PRAYING SCRIPTURE

Romans 5

Justification speaks to our legal standing before God. Whereas God's people were once condemned, through faith in the finished work of Christ, they are declared righteous in him. Everything that was lost because of Adam's sin was regained in Christ's obedience. We have peace and access to the grace of God (see verses 1–2).

Justification means we can live without guilt and shame. Thank God that you have been set right in Jesus.

[a] *8* Psalm 32:1,2 [b] *17* Gen. 17:5 [c] *18* Gen. 15:5 [d] *1* Many manuscripts *let us*

we[a] boast in the hope of the glory of God. 3Not only so, but we[a] also glory in our sufferings, because we know that suffering produces perseverance; 4perseverance, character; and character, hope. 5And hope does not put us to shame, because God's love has been poured out into our hearts through the Holy Spirit, who has been given to us.

6You see, at just the right time, when we were still powerless, Christ died for the ungodly. 7Very rarely will anyone die for a righteous person, though for a good person someone might possibly dare to die. 8But God demonstrates his own love for us in this: While we were still sinners, Christ died for us.

9Since we have now been justified by his blood, how much more shall we be saved from God's wrath through him! 10For if, while we were God's enemies, we were reconciled to him through the death of his Son, how much more, having been reconciled, shall we be saved through his life! 11Not only is this so, but we also boast in God through our Lord Jesus Christ, through whom we have now received reconciliation.

DEATH THROUGH ADAM, LIFE THROUGH CHRIST

12Therefore, just as sin entered the world through one man, and death through sin, and in this way death came to all people, because all sinned—

13To be sure, sin was in the world before the law was given, but sin is not charged against anyone's account where there is no law. 14Nevertheless, death reigned from the time of Adam to the time of Moses, even over those who did not sin by breaking a command, as did Adam, who is a pattern of the one to come.

15But the gift is not like the trespass. For if the many died by the trespass of the one man, how much more did God's grace and the gift that came by the grace of the one man, Jesus Christ, overflow to the many! 16Nor can the gift of God be compared with the result of one man's sin: The judgment followed one sin and brought condemnation, but the gift followed many trespasses and brought justification. 17For if, by the trespass of the one man, death reigned through that one man, how much more will those who receive God's abundant provision of grace and of the gift of righteousness reign in life through the one man, Jesus Christ!

18Consequently, just as one trespass resulted in condemnation for all people, so also one righteous act resulted in justification and life for all people. 19For just as through the disobedience of the one man the many were made sinners, so also through the obedience of the one man the many will be made righteous.

20The law was brought in so that the trespass might increase. But where sin increased, grace increased all the more, 21so that, just as sin reigned in death, so also grace might reign through righteousness to bring eternal life through Jesus Christ our Lord.

DEAD TO SIN, ALIVE IN CHRIST

6 What shall we say, then? Shall we go on sinning so that grace may increase? 2By no means! We are those who have died to sin; how can we live in it any longer? 3Or don't you know that all of us who were baptized into Christ Jesus were baptized into his death? 4We were therefore buried with him through baptism into death in order that,

PRAYING SCRIPTURE

Romans 6

Sanctification follows justification as one day follows the next. It is that continued working of the Holy Spirit in the believer whereby we sin less and obey more. The process of sanctification results in God's children looking more like Jesus and less like the world.

Are you cooperating with the Spirit in your spiritual growth? Ask him for humility, obedience and Christlikeness in your life.

[a] 2,3 Or *let us*

just as Christ was raised from the dead through the glory of the Father,
we too may live a new life.
5For if we have been united with him in a death like his, we will cer-
tainly also be united with him in a resurrection like his. 6For we know
that our old self was crucified with him so that the body ruled by sin
might be done away with,[a] that we should no longer be slaves to sin —
7because anyone who has died has been set free from sin.
8Now if we died with Christ, we believe that we will also live with
him. 9For we know that since Christ was raised from the dead, he can-
not die again; death no longer has mastery over him. 10The death he
died, he died to sin once for all; but the life he lives, he lives to God.
11In the same way, count yourselves dead to sin but alive to God in
Christ Jesus. 12Therefore do not let sin reign in your mortal body so
that you obey its evil desires. 13Do not offer any part of yourself to sin
as an instrument of wickedness, but rather offer yourselves to God as
those who have been brought from death to life; and offer every part
of yourself to him as an instrument of righteousness. 14For sin shall no
longer be your master, because you are not under the law, but under
grace.

SLAVES TO RIGHTEOUSNESS

15What then? Shall we sin because we are not under the law but under
grace? By no means! 16Don't you know that when you offer yourselves
to someone as obedient slaves, you are slaves of the one you obey —
whether you are slaves to sin, which leads to death, or to obedience,
which leads to righteousness? 17But thanks be to God that, though you
used to be slaves to sin, you have come to obey from your heart the pat-
tern of teaching that has now claimed your allegiance. 18You have been
set free from sin and have become slaves to righteousness.
19I am using an example from everyday life because of your human
limitations. Just as you used to offer yourselves as slaves to impurity
and to ever-increasing wickedness, so now offer yourselves as slaves
to righteousness leading to holiness. 20When you were slaves to sin,
you were free from the control of righteousness. 21What benefit did
you reap at that time from the things you are now ashamed of? Those
things result in death! 22But now that you have been set free from sin
and have become slaves of God, the benefit you reap leads to holiness,
and the result is eternal life. 23For the wages of sin is death, but the gift
of God is eternal life in[b] Christ Jesus our Lord.

RELEASED FROM THE LAW, BOUND TO CHRIST

7 Do you not know, brothers and sisters — for I am speaking to those
who know the law — that the law has authority over someone only
as long as that person lives? 2For example, by law a married woman is
bound to her husband as long as he is alive, but if her husband dies,
she is released from the law that binds her to him. 3So then, if she has
sexual relations with another man while her husband is still alive, she
is called an adulteress. But if her husband dies, she is released from
that law and is not an adulteress if she marries another man.
4So, my brothers and sisters, you also died to the law through the
body of Christ, that you might belong to another, to him who was
raised from the dead, in order that we might bear fruit for God. 5For

[a] 6 Or *be rendered powerless* [b] 23 Or *through*

PRAYING SCRIPTURE

Romans 7

Paul's wrestling with his fleshly nature comprises one of the most challenging passages in the Bible (see verses 7–25). In his struggle, what he hated, he did; his only hope was in the law of God. This wrestling brought him first to despair—"What a wretched man I am!"—and then to gratitude through Jesus Christ—"Thanks be to God" (verses 24–25).

When you feel you are losing the battle with sin, ask God for his power and trust him for victory.

when we were in the realm of the flesh,[a] the sinful passions aroused
by the law were at work in us, so that we bore fruit for death. 6 But now,
by dying to what once bound us, we have been released from the law
so that we serve in the new way of the Spirit, and not in the old way of
the written code.

THE LAW AND SIN

7 What shall we say, then? Is the law sinful? Certainly not! Neverthe-
less, I would not have known what sin was had it not been for the law.
For I would not have known what coveting really was if the law had
not said, "You shall not covet."[b] 8 But sin, seizing the opportunity af-
forded by the commandment, produced in me every kind of coveting.
For apart from the law, sin was dead. 9 Once I was alive apart from the
law; but when the commandment came, sin sprang to life and I died.
10 I found that the very commandment that was intended to bring life
actually brought death. 11 For sin, seizing the opportunity afforded by
the commandment, deceived me, and through the commandment put
me to death. 12 So then, the law is holy, and the commandment is holy,
righteous and good.

13 Did that which is good, then, become death to me? By no means!
Nevertheless, in order that sin might be recognized as sin, it used what
is good to bring about my death, so that through the commandment
sin might become utterly sinful.

14 We know that the law is spiritual; but I am unspiritual, sold as a
slave to sin. 15 I do not understand what I do. For what I want to do I
do not do, but what I hate I do. 16 And if I do what I do not want to do,
I agree that the law is good. 17 As it is, it is no longer I myself who do it,
but it is sin living in me. 18 For I know that good itself does not dwell
in me, that is, in my sinful nature.[c] For I have the desire to do what is
good, but I cannot carry it out. 19 For I do not do the good I want to do,
but the evil I do not want to do—this I keep on doing. 20 Now if I do
what I do not want to do, it is no longer I who do it, but it is sin living
in me that does it.

21 So I find this law at work: Although I want to do good, evil is right
there with me. 22 For in my inner being I delight in God's law; 23 but
I see another law at work in me, waging war against the law of my
mind and making me a prisoner of the law of sin at work within me.
24 What a wretched man I am! Who will rescue me from this body that
is subject to death? 25 Thanks be to God, who delivers me through Jesus
Christ our Lord!

So then, I myself in my mind am a slave to God's law, but in my sinful
nature[d] a slave to the law of sin.

LIFE THROUGH THE SPIRIT

8 Therefore, there is now no condemnation for those who are in
Christ Jesus, 2 because through Christ Jesus the law of the Spirit
who gives life has set you[e] free from the law of sin and death. 3 For what
the law was powerless to do because it was weakened by the flesh,[f]

PRAYING SCRIPTURE

Romans 8

The hope of the redeemed is glorification. Our physical bodies as well as our inner person will be fully like Jesus. All that is of earth will be burned away so only glory remains. Anything we suffer on this earth cannot compare to the glory that awaits (see verse 18).

If we suffer with Christ, we, as sons of glory, will be glorified together as heirs (see verse 17). Praise God today for the glory that will be revealed in us. May your faith in him instruct your good works.

---

[a] *5* In contexts like this, the Greek word for *flesh* (*sarx*) refers to the sinful state of human beings, often presented as a power in opposition to the Spirit. [b] *7* Exodus 20:17; Deut. 5:21 [c] *18* Or *my flesh* [d] *25* Or *in the flesh*
[e] *2* The Greek is singular; some manuscripts *me* [f] *3* In contexts like this, the Greek word for *flesh* (*sarx*) refers to the sinful state of human beings, often presented as a power in opposition to the Spirit; also in verses 4-13.

God did by sending his own Son in the likeness of sinful flesh to be a
sin offering.[a] And so he condemned sin in the flesh, 4in order that the
righteous requirement of the law might be fully met in us, who do not
live according to the flesh but according to the Spirit.
5Those who live according to the flesh have their minds set on what
the flesh desires; but those who live in accordance with the Spirit have
their minds set on what the Spirit desires. 6The mind governed by the
flesh is death, but the mind governed by the Spirit is life and peace.
7The mind governed by the flesh is hostile to God; it does not submit
to God's law, nor can it do so. 8Those who are in the realm of the flesh
cannot please God.
9You, however, are not in the realm of the flesh but are in the realm
of the Spirit, if indeed the Spirit of God lives in you. And if anyone
does not have the Spirit of Christ, they do not belong to Christ. 10But
if Christ is in you, then even though your body is subject to death be-
cause of sin, the Spirit gives life[b] because of righteousness. 11And if the
Spirit of him who raised Jesus from the dead is living in you, he who
raised Christ from the dead will also give life to your mortal bodies
because of[c] his Spirit who lives in you.
12Therefore, brothers and sisters, we have an obligation — but it is
not to the flesh, to live according to it. 13For if you live according to the
flesh, you will die; but if by the Spirit you put to death the misdeeds of
the body, you will live.
14For those who are led by the Spirit of God are the children of God.
15The Spirit you received does not make you slaves, so that you live in
fear again; rather, the Spirit you received brought about your adop-
tion to sonship.[d] And by him we cry, *"Abba,*[e] Father." 16The Spirit him-
self testifies with our spirit that we are God's children. 17Now if we are
children, then we are heirs — heirs of God and co-heirs with Christ, if
indeed we share in his sufferings in order that we may also share in
his glory.

PRESENT SUFFERING AND FUTURE GLORY

18I consider that our present sufferings are not worth comparing
with the glory that will be revealed in us. 19For the creation waits in
eager expectation for the children of God to be revealed. 20For the cre-
ation was subjected to frustration, not by its own choice, but by the
will of the one who subjected it, in hope 21that[f] the creation itself will
be liberated from its bondage to decay and brought into the freedom
and glory of the children of God.
22We know that the whole creation has been groaning as in the pains
of childbirth right up to the present time. 23Not only so, but we our-
selves, who have the firstfruits of the Spirit, groan inwardly as we wait
eagerly for our adoption to sonship, the redemption of our bodies.
24For in this hope we were saved. But hope that is seen is no hope at
all. Who hopes for what they already have? 25But if we hope for what
we do not yet have, we wait for it patiently.
26In the same way, the Spirit helps us in our weakness. We do not
know what we ought to pray for, but the Spirit himself intercedes for

---

[a] *3* Or *flesh, for sin* [b] *10* Or *you, your body is dead because of sin, yet your spirit is alive* [c] *11* Some manuscripts *bodies through* [d] *15* The Greek word for *adoption to sonship* is a term referring to the full legal standing of an adopted male heir in Roman culture; also in verse 23. [e] *15* Aramaic for *father* [f] *20,21* Or *subjected it in hope.* [21]*For*

us through wordless groans. 27And he who searches our hearts knows
the mind of the Spirit, because the Spirit intercedes for God's people
in accordance with the will of God.

28And we know that in all things God works for the good of those
who love him, who[a] have been called according to his purpose. 29For
those God foreknew he also predestined to be conformed to the image
of his Son, that he might be the firstborn among many brothers and
sisters. 30And those he predestined, he also called; those he called, he
also justified; those he justified, he also glorified.

MORE THAN CONQUERORS

31What, then, shall we say in response to these things? If God is for
us, who can be against us? 32He who did not spare his own Son, but
gave him up for us all — how will he not also, along with him, gra-
ciously give us all things? 33Who will bring any charge against those
whom God has chosen? It is God who justifies. 34Who then is the one
who condemns? No one. Christ Jesus who died — more than that, who
was raised to life — is at the right hand of God and is also interceding
for us. 35Who shall separate us from the love of Christ? Shall trouble or
hardship or persecution or famine or nakedness or danger or sword?
36As it is written:

> "For your sake we face death all day long;
> we are considered as sheep to be slaughtered."[b]

37No, in all these things we are more than conquerors through him who
loved us. 38For I am convinced that neither death nor life, neither an-
gels nor demons,[c] neither the present nor the future, nor any powers,
39neither height nor depth, nor anything else in all creation, will be
able to separate us from the love of God that is in Christ Jesus our Lord.

PAUL'S ANGUISH OVER ISRAEL

9 I speak the truth in Christ — I am not lying, my conscience con-
firms it through the Holy Spirit — 2I have great sorrow and un-
ceasing anguish in my heart. 3For I could wish that I myself were
cursed and cut off from Christ for the sake of my people, those of my
own race, 4the people of Israel. Theirs is the adoption to sonship; theirs
the divine glory, the covenants, the receiving of the law, the temple
worship and the promises. 5Theirs are the patriarchs, and from them
is traced the human ancestry of the Messiah, who is God over all, for-
ever praised![d] Amen.

GOD'S SOVEREIGN CHOICE

6It is not as though God's word had failed. For not all who are de-
scended from Israel are Israel. 7Nor because they are his descendants
are they all Abraham's children. On the contrary, "It is through Isaac
that your offspring will be reckoned."[e] 8In other words, it is not the
children by physical descent who are God's children, but it is the chil-
dren of the promise who are regarded as Abraham's offspring. 9For this

PRAYING SCRIPTURE

Romans 9

The role of Israel in God's plan reminds us that God's plans cannot ultimately be destroyed. Though God chose Israel as the place where Jesus will sit enthroned as King, through Jesus, anyone—Jew or Gentile—can come to the stumbling stone, and a rock of offense. "The one who believes in him will never be put to shame" (verse 33).

God's ways are not always our ways, but we can pray to understand, and often he will reveal them.

---

[a] 28 *Or that all things work together for good to those who love God, who;* or *that in all things God works together with those who love him to bring about what is good — with those who* [b] 36 Psalm 44:22 [c] 38 *Or nor heavenly rulers* [d] 5 Or *Messiah, who is over all. God be forever praised!* Or *Messiah. God who is over all be forever praised!* [e] 7 Gen. 21:12

was how the promise was stated: "At the appointed time I will return,
and Sarah will have a son."[a]
10Not only that, but Rebekah's children were conceived at the same
time by our father Isaac. 11Yet, before the twins were born or had done
anything good or bad — in order that God's purpose in election might
stand: 12not by works but by him who calls — she was told, "The older
will serve the younger."[b] 13Just as it is written: "Jacob I loved, but Esau
I hated."[c]
14What then shall we say? Is God unjust? Not at all! 15For he says to
Moses,

"I will have mercy on whom I have mercy,
and I will have compassion on whom I have compassion."[d]

16It does not, therefore, depend on human desire or effort, but on
God's mercy. 17For Scripture says to Pharaoh: "I raised you up for this
very purpose, that I might display my power in you and that my name
might be proclaimed in all the earth."[e] 18Therefore God has mercy on
whom he wants to have mercy, and he hardens whom he wants to
harden.
19One of you will say to me: "Then why does God still blame us? For
who is able to resist his will?" 20But who are you, a human being, to
talk back to God? "Shall what is formed say to the one who formed it,
'Why did you make me like this?' "[f] 21Does not the potter have the right
to make out of the same lump of clay some pottery for special purposes
and some for common use?
22What if God, although choosing to show his wrath and make his
power known, bore with great patience the objects of his wrath — pre-
pared for destruction? 23What if he did this to make the riches of his
glory known to the objects of his mercy, whom he prepared in advance
for glory — 24even us, whom he also called, not only from the Jews but
also from the Gentiles? 25As he says in Hosea:

"I will call them 'my people' who are not my people;
and I will call her 'my loved one' who is not my loved one,"[g]

26and,

"In the very place where it was said to them,
'You are not my people,'
there they will be called 'children of the living God.' "[h]

27Isaiah cries out concerning Israel:

"Though the number of the Israelites be like the sand by the sea,
only the remnant will be saved.
28For the Lord will carry out
his sentence on earth with speed and finality."[i]

29It is just as Isaiah said previously:

"Unless the Lord Almighty
had left us descendants,
we would have become like Sodom,
we would have been like Gomorrah."[j]

---

[a] *9* Gen. 18:10,14 [b] *12* Gen. 25:23 [c] *13* Mal. 1:2,3 [d] *15* Exodus 33:19
[e] *17* Exodus 9:16 [f] *20* Isaiah 29:16; 45:9 [g] *25* Hosea 2:23 [h] *26* Hosea 1:10
[i] *28* Isaiah 10:22,23 (see Septuagint) [j] *29* Isaiah 1:9

ISRAEL'S UNBELIEF

30What then shall we say? That the Gentiles, who did not pursue
righteousness, have obtained it, a righteousness that is by faith; 31but
the people of Israel, who pursued the law as the way of righteousness,
have not attained their goal. 32Why not? Because they pursued it not
by faith but as if it were by works. They stumbled over the stumbling
stone. 33As it is written:

"See, I lay in Zion a stone that causes people to stumble
  and a rock that makes them fall,
  and the one who believes in him will never be put to shame."[a]

PRAYING SCRIPTURE

Romans 10

The "Romans Road to Salvation" has long been used by Christians to present how a person can be saved. All have sinned (3:23). Death is the result of sin (6:23). But if you declare with your mouth that Jesus is Lord and believe in your heart that God raised him from the dead, you will be saved (10:9–10). The promise of salvation is for whoever will ask (see verse 13).

Memorize these five verses. Then pray for opportunities to share the gospel.

10 Brothers and sisters, my heart's desire and prayer to God for
the Israelites is that they may be saved. 2For I can testify about
them that they are zealous for God, but their zeal is not based on
knowledge. 3Since they did not know the righteousness of God and
sought to establish their own, they did not submit to God's righteous-
ness. 4Christ is the culmination of the law so that there may be righ-
teousness for everyone who believes.
5Moses writes this about the righteousness that is by the law: "The
person who does these things will live by them."[b] 6But the righteous-
ness that is by faith says: "Do not say in your heart, 'Who will ascend
into heaven?'"[c] (that is, to bring Christ down) 7"or 'Who will descend
into the deep?'"[d] (that is, to bring Christ up from the dead). 8But what
does it say? "The word is near you; it is in your mouth and in your
heart,"[e] that is, the message concerning faith that we proclaim: 9If you
declare with your mouth, "Jesus is Lord," and believe in your heart that
God raised him from the dead, you will be saved. 10For it is with your
heart that you believe and are justified, and it is with your mouth that
you profess your faith and are saved. 11As Scripture says, "Anyone who
believes in him will never be put to shame."[f] 12For there is no differ-
ence between Jew and Gentile — the same Lord is Lord of all and richly
blesses all who call on him, 13for, "Everyone who calls on the name of
the Lord will be saved."[g]
14How, then, can they call on the one they have not believed in? And
how can they believe in the one of whom they have not heard? And
how can they hear without someone preaching to them? 15And how
can anyone preach unless they are sent? As it is written: "How beauti-
ful are the feet of those who bring good news!"[h]
16But not all the Israelites accepted the good news. For Isaiah says,
"Lord, who has believed our message?"[i] 17Consequently, faith comes
from hearing the message, and the message is heard through the word
about Christ. 18But I ask: Did they not hear? Of course they did:

"Their voice has gone out into all the earth,
  their words to the ends of the world."[j]

19Again I ask: Did Israel not understand? First, Moses says,

"I will make you envious by those who are not a nation;
  I will make you angry by a nation that has no understanding."[k]

20And Isaiah boldly says,

---

[a] *33* Isaiah 8:14; 28:16 [b] *5* Lev. 18:5 [c] *6* Deut. 30:12 [d] *7* Deut. 30:13
[e] *8* Deut. 30:14 [f] *11* Isaiah 28:16 (see Septuagint) [g] *13* Joel 2:32
[h] *15* Isaiah 52:7 [i] *16* Isaiah 53:1 [j] *18* Psalm 19:4 [k] *19* Deut. 32:21

"I was found by those who did not seek me;
  I revealed myself to those who did not ask for me."[a]

21But concerning Israel he says,

"All day long I have held out my hands
  to a disobedient and obstinate people."[b]

THE REMNANT OF ISRAEL

11 I ask then: Did God reject his people? By no means! I am an Israel-
ite myself, a descendant of Abraham, from the tribe of Benjamin.
2God did not reject his people, whom he foreknew. Don't you know
what Scripture says in the passage about Elijah — how he appealed
to God against Israel: 3"Lord, they have killed your prophets and torn
down your altars; I am the only one left, and they are trying to kill
me"[c]? 4And what was God's answer to him? "I have reserved for myself
seven thousand who have not bowed the knee to Baal."[d] 5So too, at the
present time there is a remnant chosen by grace. 6And if by grace, then
it cannot be based on works; if it were, grace would no longer be grace.

7What then? What the people of Israel sought so earnestly they did
not obtain. The elect among them did, but the others were hardened,
8as it is written:

"God gave them a spirit of stupor,
  eyes that could not see
  and ears that could not hear,
to this very day."[e]

9And David says:

"May their table become a snare and a trap,
  a stumbling block and a retribution for them.
10May their eyes be darkened so they cannot see,
  and their backs be bent forever."[f]

INGRAFTED BRANCHES

11Again I ask: Did they stumble so as to fall beyond recovery? Not
at all! Rather, because of their transgression, salvation has come to
the Gentiles to make Israel envious. 12But if their transgression means
riches for the world, and their loss means riches for the Gentiles, how
much greater riches will their full inclusion bring!

13I am talking to you Gentiles. Inasmuch as I am the apostle to the
Gentiles, I take pride in my ministry 14in the hope that I may somehow
arouse my own people to envy and save some of them. 15For if their
rejection brought reconciliation to the world, what will their accep-
tance be but life from the dead? 16If the part of the dough offered as
firstfruits is holy, then the whole batch is holy; if the root is holy, so
are the branches.

17If some of the branches have been broken off, and you, though a
wild olive shoot, have been grafted in among the others and now share
in the nourishing sap from the olive root, 18do not consider yourself
to be superior to those other branches. If you do, consider this: You do
not support the root, but the root supports you. 19You will say then,

[a] *20* Isaiah 65:1 [b] *21* Isaiah 65:2 [c] *3* 1 Kings 19:10,14 [d] *4* 1 Kings 19:18
[e] *8* Deut. 29:4; Isaiah 29:10 [f] *10* Psalm 69:22,23

PRAYING SCRIPTURE

Romans 11

The Lord's interactions with Israel, replete throughout the Old Testament, are significantly fewer once we read past the Gospels. Jesus made clear that his church includes people from all nations. The Gentiles have been "grafted in" (verse 17) to God's promise to Israel. God is not done with the Jews and will save Israel in the end (see verse 26).

Salvation for Jew or Gentile is all of grace. Praise Jesus for saving all who come to him.

"Branches were broken off so that I could be grafted in." 20Granted. But they were broken off because of unbelief, and you stand by faith. Do not be arrogant, but tremble. 21For if God did not spare the natural branches, he will not spare you either.

22Consider therefore the kindness and sternness of God: sternness to those who fell, but kindness to you, provided that you continue in his kindness. Otherwise, you also will be cut off. 23And if they do not persist in unbelief, they will be grafted in, for God is able to graft them in again. 24After all, if you were cut out of an olive tree that is wild by nature, and contrary to nature were grafted into a cultivated olive tree, how much more readily will these, the natural branches, be grafted into their own olive tree!

ALL ISRAEL WILL BE SAVED

25I do not want you to be ignorant of this mystery, brothers and sisters, so that you may not be conceited: Israel has experienced a hardening in part until the full number of the Gentiles has come in, 26and in this way[a] all Israel will be saved. As it is written:

"The deliverer will come from Zion;
he will turn godlessness away from Jacob.
27And this is[b] my covenant with them
when I take away their sins."[c]

28As far as the gospel is concerned, they are enemies for your sake; but as far as election is concerned, they are loved on account of the patriarchs, 29for God's gifts and his call are irrevocable. 30Just as you who were at one time disobedient to God have now received mercy as a result of their disobedience, 31so they too have now become disobedient in order that they too may now[d] receive mercy as a result of God's mercy to you. 32For God has bound everyone over to disobedience so that he may have mercy on them all.

DOXOLOGY

33Oh, the depth of the riches of the wisdom and[e] knowledge of God!
How unsearchable his judgments,
and his paths beyond tracing out!
34"Who has known the mind of the Lord?
Or who has been his counselor?"[f]
35"Who has ever given to God,
that God should repay them?"[g]
36For from him and through him and for him are all things.
To him be the glory forever! Amen.

A LIVING SACRIFICE

12 Therefore, I urge you, brothers and sisters, in view of God's mercy, to offer your bodies as a living sacrifice, holy and pleasing to God—this is your true and proper worship. 2Do not conform to the pattern of this world, but be transformed by the renewing of your mind. Then you will be able to test and approve what God's will is—his good, pleasing and perfect will.

[a] 26 Or *and so* [b] 27 Or *will be* [c] 27 Isaiah 59:20,21; 27:9 (see Septuagint); Jer. 31:33,34 [d] 31 Some manuscripts do not have *now.* [e] 33 Or *riches and the wisdom and the* [f] 34 Isaiah 40:13 [g] 35 Job 41:11

PRAYING SCRIPTURE

Romans 12

The thought of offering up a sheep or goat for sacrifice is easier than the thought of presenting yourself as the sacrifice. God does not intend to kill his people, but he does intend that we live as dead to the desires of the world. Our transformation occurs as we renew our minds through the Word of God and prayer so that we may demonstrate "his good, pleasing and perfect, will" (verse 2).

The way of Jesus is to be a living sacrifice. Pray for your desires, hopes, dreams and plans to be his.

HUMBLE SERVICE IN THE BODY OF CHRIST

[3]For by the grace given me I say to every one of you: Do not think
of yourself more highly than you ought, but rather think of yourself
with sober judgment, in accordance with the faith God has distributed
to each of you. [4]For just as each of us has one body with many members,
and these members do not all have the same function, [5]so in Christ we,
though many, form one body, and each member belongs to all the oth-
ers. [6]We have different gifts, according to the grace given to each of us. If
your gift is prophesying, then prophesy in accordance with your[a] faith;
[7]if it is serving, then serve; if it is teaching, then teach; [8]if it is to encour-
age, then give encouragement; if it is giving, then give generously; if it
is to lead,[b] do it diligently; if it is to show mercy, do it cheerfully.

LOVE IN ACTION

[9]Love must be sincere. Hate what is evil; cling to what is good. [10]Be
devoted to one another in love. Honor one another above yourselves.
[11]Never be lacking in zeal, but keep your spiritual fervor, serving the
Lord. [12]Be joyful in hope, patient in affliction, faithful in prayer. [13]Share
with the Lord's people who are in need. Practice hospitality.

[14]Bless those who persecute you; bless and do not curse. [15]Rejoice
with those who rejoice; mourn with those who mourn. [16]Live in har-
mony with one another. Do not be proud, but be willing to associate
with people of low position.[c] Do not be conceited.

[17]Do not repay anyone evil for evil. Be careful to do what is right in
the eyes of everyone. [18]If it is possible, as far as it depends on you, live
at peace with everyone. [19]Do not take revenge, my dear friends, but
leave room for God's wrath, for it is written: "It is mine to avenge; I will
repay,"[d] says the Lord. [20]On the contrary:

"If your enemy is hungry, feed him;
  if he is thirsty, give him something to drink.
In doing this, you will heap burning coals on his head."[e]

[21]Do not be overcome by evil, but overcome evil with good.

SUBMISSION TO GOVERNING AUTHORITIES

13 Let everyone be subject to the governing authorities, for there
is no authority except that which God has established. The
authorities that exist have been established by God. [2]Consequently,
whoever rebels against the authority is rebelling against what God has
instituted, and those who do so will bring judgment on themselves.
[3]For rulers hold no terror for those who do right, but for those who do
wrong. Do you want to be free from fear of the one in authority? Then
do what is right and you will be commended. [4]For the one in author-
ity is God's servant for your good. But if you do wrong, be afraid, for
rulers do not bear the sword for no reason. They are God's servants,
agents of wrath to bring punishment on the wrongdoer. [5]Therefore, it
is necessary to submit to the authorities, not only because of possible
punishment but also as a matter of conscience.

[6]This is also why you pay taxes, for the authorities are God's ser-
vants, who give their full time to governing. [7]Give to everyone what
you owe them: If you owe taxes, pay taxes; if revenue, then revenue; if
respect, then respect; if honor, then honor.

PRAYING SCRIPTURE

Romans 13

Love your neighbor. Why is such a simple command often hard to live out? Here Paul wrote that the summation of the Ten Commandments is found in "Love your neighbor as yourself." Love does no harm; therefore it fulfills the law (see verses 9–10).

Think about the neighbors God has put around you. Ask him to help you love them as yourself so that you, too, fulfill the law.

[a] *6* Or *the* [b] *8* Or *to provide for others* [c] *16* Or *willing to do menial work*
[d] *19* Deut. 32:35 [e] *20* Prov. 25:21,22

LOVE FULFILLS THE LAW

8Let no debt remain outstanding, except the continuing debt to love
one another, for whoever loves others has fulfilled the law. 9The com-
mandments, "You shall not commit adultery," "You shall not murder,"
"You shall not steal," "You shall not covet,"[a] and whatever other com-
mand there may be, are summed up in this one command: "Love your
neighbor as yourself."[b] 10Love does no harm to a neighbor. Therefore
love is the fulfillment of the law.

THE DAY IS NEAR

11And do this, understanding the present time: The hour has already
come for you to wake up from your slumber, because our salvation is
nearer now than when we first believed. 12The night is nearly over;
the day is almost here. So let us put aside the deeds of darkness and
put on the armor of light. 13Let us behave decently, as in the daytime,
not in carousing and drunkenness, not in sexual immorality and de-
bauchery, not in dissension and jealousy. 14Rather, clothe yourselves
with the Lord Jesus Christ, and do not think about how to gratify the
desires of the flesh.[c]

THE WEAK AND THE STRONG

14 Accept the one whose faith is weak, without quarreling over
disputable matters. 2One person's faith allows them to eat any-
thing, but another, whose faith is weak, eats only vegetables. 3The one
who eats everything must not treat with contempt the one who does
not, and the one who does not eat everything must not judge the one
who does, for God has accepted them. 4Who are you to judge someone
else's servant? To their own master, servants stand or fall. And they will
stand, for the Lord is able to make them stand.

5One person considers one day more sacred than another; another
considers every day alike. Each of them should be fully convinced in
their own mind. 6Whoever regards one day as special does so to the
Lord. Whoever eats meat does so to the Lord, for they give thanks to
God; and whoever abstains does so to the Lord and gives thanks to
God. 7For none of us lives for ourselves alone, and none of us dies for
ourselves alone. 8If we live, we live for the Lord; and if we die, we die
for the Lord. So, whether we live or die, we belong to the Lord. 9For this
very reason, Christ died and returned to life so that he might be the
Lord of both the dead and the living.

10You, then, why do you judge your brother or sister[d]? Or why do you
treat them with contempt? For we will all stand before God's judgment
seat. 11It is written:

"'As surely as I live,' says the Lord,
'every knee will bow before me;
every tongue will acknowledge God.'"[e]

12So then, each of us will give an account of ourselves to God.

13Therefore let us stop passing judgment on one another. Instead,
make up your mind not to put any stumbling block or obstacle in the

PRAYING SCRIPTURE

Romans 14

If God's people would learn the two truths here, the church would be in better condition. There is a law of liberty. God's people are free! And there is a law of love that provides guidance to the law of liberty. Love keeps us from using liberty in a way that hurts others.

Which is more important to you, love or freedom? Ask God to let love be your primary law.

---

[a] *9* Exodus 20:13-15,17; Deut. 5:17-19,21 [b] *9* Lev. 19:18 [c] *14* In contexts like this, the Greek word for *flesh* (*sarx*) refers to the sinful state of human beings, often presented as a power in opposition to the Spirit. [d] *10* The Greek word for *brother or sister* (*adelphos*) refers here to a believer, whether man or woman, as part of God's family; also in verses 13, 15 and 21. [e] *11* Isaiah 45:23

way of a brother or sister. 14I am convinced, being fully persuaded in
the Lord Jesus, that nothing is unclean in itself. But if anyone regards
something as unclean, then for that person it is unclean. 15If your
brother or sister is distressed because of what you eat, you are no lon-
ger acting in love. Do not by your eating destroy someone for whom
Christ died. 16Therefore do not let what you know is good be spoken of
as evil. 17For the kingdom of God is not a matter of eating and drink-
ing, but of righteousness, peace and joy in the Holy Spirit, 18because
anyone who serves Christ in this way is pleasing to God and receives
human approval.

19Let us therefore make every effort to do what leads to peace and
to mutual edification. 20Do not destroy the work of God for the sake of
food. All food is clean, but it is wrong for a person to eat anything that
causes someone else to stumble. 21It is better not to eat meat or drink
wine or to do anything else that will cause your brother or sister to fall.

22So whatever you believe about these things keep between yourself
and God. Blessed is the one who does not condemn himself by what he
approves. 23But whoever has doubts is condemned if they eat, because
their eating is not from faith; and everything that does not come from
faith is sin.[a]

15 We who are strong ought to bear with the failings of the weak
and not to please ourselves. 2Each of us should please our neigh
bors for their good, to build them up. 3For even Christ did not please
himself but, as it is written: "The insults of those who insult you have
fallen on me."[b] 4For everything that was written in the past was written
to teach us, so that through the endurance taught in the Scriptures and
the encouragement they provide we might have hope.

5May the God who gives endurance and encouragement give you the
same attitude of mind toward each other that Christ Jesus had, 6so that
with one mind and one voice you may glorify the God and Father of
our Lord Jesus Christ.

7Accept one another, then, just as Christ accepted you, in order to
bring praise to God. 8For I tell you that Christ has become a servant of
the Jews[c] on behalf of God's truth, so that the promises made to the pa-
triarchs might be confirmed 9and, moreover, that the Gentiles might
glorify God for his mercy. As it is written:

"Therefore I will praise you among the Gentiles;
I will sing the praises of your name."[d]

10Again, it says,

"Rejoice, you Gentiles, with his people."[e]

11And again,

"Praise the Lord, all you Gentiles;
let all the peoples extol him."[f]

12And again, Isaiah says,

"The Root of Jesse will spring up,
one who will arise to rule over the nations;
in him the Gentiles will hope."[g]

PRAYING SCRIPTURE

Romans 15

The admonition for the strong to bear with the weak is a crucial "upside-down" of the Christian life, much like whoever wants to be greatest should serve. Worldly thinking says the strong get what they can while the weak get what they deserve. That is not the way of Jesus.

If you have been walking with Jesus for a while, pray for the wisdom and humility to edify the weak.

---

[a] 23 Some manuscripts place 16:25-27 here; others after 15:33. [b] 3 Psalm 69:9
[c] 8 Greek *circumcision* [d] 9 2 Samuel 22:50; Psalm 18:49 [e] 10 Deut. 32:43
[f] 11 Psalm 117:1 [g] 12 Isaiah 11:10 (see Septuagint)

13May the God of hope fill you with all joy and peace as you trust in him, so that you may overflow with hope by the power of the Holy Spirit.

PAUL THE MINISTER TO THE GENTILES

14I myself am convinced, my brothers and sisters, that you yourselves are full of goodness, filled with knowledge and competent to instruct one another. 15Yet I have written you quite boldly on some points to remind you of them again, because of the grace God gave me 16to be a minister of Christ Jesus to the Gentiles. He gave me the priestly duty of proclaiming the gospel of God, so that the Gentiles might become an offering acceptable to God, sanctified by the Holy Spirit.

17Therefore I glory in Christ Jesus in my service to God. 18I will not venture to speak of anything except what Christ has accomplished through me in leading the Gentiles to obey God by what I have said and done — 19by the power of signs and wonders, through the power of the Spirit of God. So from Jerusalem all the way around to Illyricum, I have fully proclaimed the gospel of Christ. 20It has always been my ambition to preach the gospel where Christ was not known, so that I would not be building on someone else's foundation. 21Rather, as it is written:

> "Those who were not told about him will see,
> and those who have not heard will understand."[a]

22This is why I have often been hindered from coming to you.

PAUL'S PLAN TO VISIT ROME

23But now that there is no more place for me to work in these regions, and since I have been longing for many years to visit you, 24I plan to do so when I go to Spain. I hope to see you while passing through and to have you assist me on my journey there, after I have enjoyed your company for a while. 25Now, however, I am on my way to Jerusalem in the service of the Lord's people there. 26For Macedonia and Achaia were pleased to make a contribution for the poor among the Lord's people in Jerusalem. 27They were pleased to do it, and indeed they owe it to them. For if the Gentiles have shared in the Jews' spiritual blessings, they owe it to the Jews to share with them their material blessings. 28So after I have completed this task and have made sure that they have received this contribution, I will go to Spain and visit you on the way. 29I know that when I come to you, I will come in the full measure of the blessing of Christ.

30I urge you, brothers and sisters, by our Lord Jesus Christ and by the love of the Spirit, to join me in my struggle by praying to God for me. 31Pray that I may be kept safe from the unbelievers in Judea and that the contribution I take to Jerusalem may be favorably received by the Lord's people there, 32so that I may come to you with joy, by God's will, and in your company be refreshed. 33The God of peace be with you all. Amen.

PERSONAL GREETINGS

16 I commend to you our sister Phoebe, a deacon[b,c] of the church in Cenchreae. 2I ask you to receive her in the Lord in a way worthy of his people and to give her any help she may need from you, for she has been the benefactor of many people, including me.

---

[a] *21* Isaiah 52:15 (see Septuagint) [b] *1* Or *servant* [c] *1* The word *deacon* refers here to a Christian designated to serve with the overseers/elders of the church in a variety of ways; similarly in Phil. 1:1 and 1 Tim. 3:8,12.

PRAYING SCRIPTURE
Romans 16

Closing his letter to the Romans shows us how far Paul's circle of influence broadened, as he mentioned almost 40 people by name. His encouragement must have had a lasting impact on them; it is apparent that they had imprinted themselves on his heart.

Think of the people God has allowed you to influence for the gospel. Ask him how you might continue to bless them in his name.

3 Greet Priscilla[a] and Aquila, my co-workers in Christ Jesus. 4 They risked their lives for me. Not only I but all the churches of the Gentiles are grateful to them.
5 Greet also the church that meets at their house.
Greet my dear friend Epenetus, who was the first convert to Christ in the province of Asia.
6 Greet Mary, who worked very hard for you.
7 Greet Andronicus and Junia, my fellow Jews who have been in prison with me. They are outstanding among[b] the apostles, and they were in Christ before I was.
8 Greet Ampliatus, my dear friend in the Lord.
9 Greet Urbanus, our co-worker in Christ, and my dear friend Stachys.
10 Greet Apelles, whose fidelity to Christ has stood the test.
Greet those who belong to the household of Aristobulus.
11 Greet Herodion, my fellow Jew.
Greet those in the household of Narcissus who are in the Lord.
12 Greet Tryphena and Tryphosa, those women who work hard in the Lord.
Greet my dear friend Persis, another woman who has worked very hard in the Lord.
13 Greet Rufus, chosen in the Lord, and his mother, who has been a mother to me, too.
14 Greet Asyncritus, Phlegon, Hermes, Patrobas, Hermas and the other brothers and sisters with them.
15 Greet Philologus, Julia, Nereus and his sister, and Olympas and all the Lord's people who are with them.
16 Greet one another with a holy kiss.
All the churches of Christ send greetings.

17 I urge you, brothers and sisters, to watch out for those who cause
divisions and put obstacles in your way that are contrary to the teach-
ing you have learned. Keep away from them. 18 For such people are not
serving our Lord Christ, but their own appetites. By smooth talk and
flattery they deceive the minds of naive people. 19 Everyone has heard
about your obedience, so I rejoice because of you; but I want you to be
wise about what is good, and innocent about what is evil.

20 The God of peace will soon crush Satan under your feet.
The grace of our Lord Jesus be with you.

21 Timothy, my co-worker, sends his greetings to you, as do Lucius,
Jason and Sosipater, my fellow Jews.

22 I, Tertius, who wrote down this letter, greet you in the Lord.

23 Gaius, whose hospitality I and the whole church here enjoy, sends
you his greetings.
Erastus, who is the city's director of public works, and our brother
Quartus send you their greetings. [24][c]

25 Now to him who is able to establish you in accordance with my gos-
pel, the message I proclaim about Jesus Christ, in keeping with the rev-
elation of the mystery hidden for long ages past, 26 but now revealed
and made known through the prophetic writings by the command
of the eternal God, so that all the Gentiles might come to the obedi-
ence that comes from[d] faith— 27 to the only wise God be glory forever
through Jesus Christ! Amen.

---

[a] 3 Greek *Prisca,* a variant of *Priscilla* [b] 7 Or *are esteemed by* [c] 24 Some manuscripts include here *May the grace of our Lord Jesus Christ be with all of you. Amen.* [d] 26 Or *that is*

1 CORINTHIANS

Paul wrote the letter we know as 1 Corinthians to a church he established through his missionary efforts. He had met Priscilla and Aquila in Corinth and worked as a tentmaker while he shared the gospel. His efforts to preach the gospel in the synagogue were met with opposition, but the Lord, appearing to him in a dream, told him to keep working and not to be afraid. Paul stayed there for 18 months.

Afterward the church in Corinth experienced many internal struggles in Paul's absence. They faced internal division, factions, immorality, quarrels about spiritual gifts, people being greedy and even getting drunk at the Lord's Supper and members questioning the resurrection of believers. The letter can be understood as a long series of correctives. The Corinthian church was not a body of hungry Christians desiring to grow spiritually. It was a body of rebellious Christians stuck in carnality.

Even though the church was beset with problems, Paul began his letter with a prayer expressing his thankfulness for them. He praised God for showing grace to them and expressed his gratitude that God had not withheld any "gift" from them. Their spiritual gifts were the cause of some of their conflicts; however, Paul encouraged them to use their gifts as members, or parts, of the same body of Christ.

Early instruction in the letter reminded the Corinthians where true power lies: in the cross of Jesus. Its message is the power of God for those who are being saved (see 1:18). This wisdom of God is viewed as foolishness by the world. But, Paul said, Christ is the wisdom of God for the called (see 1:24).

Paul also dealt with public prayer in answering questions about the church's controversy over tongues. While Christians differ in their understanding of speaking in tongues, we can all agree on Paul's emphasis that public prayers should be a blessing to the Christians who hear them. Far from an "anything goes" approach, Paul expected things to be done "in a fitting and orderly way," noting that "God is not a God of disorder but of peace," a reality that is to be manifested in all churches (14:40,33).

Paul especially emphasized that public speaking in the gathered assembly should be understandable in order to edify the church body. There is a similar application about how we pray: Public prayers should not be weighed down with such flowery language or theological jargon that the average Christian cannot understand them. Praying to be heard (and applauded) by listeners is prideful, not spiritual.

One of the ways disciples learn to pray is by hearing those with healthy prayer lives model prayer. As Christians hear how other brothers and sisters approach the Lord, what they pray for and how they incorporate Scripture into prayer, they will learn how to pray. Therefore, we should give attention to how we pray in public settings, because our prayers are to be a blessing to those who are listening.

1 Paul, called to be an apostle of Christ Jesus by the will of God, and
our brother Sosthenes,

2To the church of God in Corinth, to those sanctified in Christ Jesus
and called to be his holy people, together with all those everywhere
who call on the name of our Lord Jesus Christ — their Lord and ours:

3Grace and peace to you from God our Father and the Lord Jesus
Christ.

THANKSGIVING

4I always thank my God for you because of his grace given you in
Christ Jesus. 5For in him you have been enriched in every way — with
all kinds of speech and with all knowledge — 6God thus confirming
our testimony about Christ among you. 7Therefore you do not lack
any spiritual gift as you eagerly wait for our Lord Jesus Christ to be
revealed. 8He will also keep you firm to the end, so that you will be
blameless on the day of our Lord Jesus Christ. 9God is faithful, who has
called you into fellowship with his Son, Jesus Christ our Lord.

A CHURCH DIVIDED OVER LEADERS

10I appeal to you, brothers and sisters,[a] in the name of our Lord Jesus
Christ, that all of you agree with one another in what you say and that
there be no divisions among you, but that you be perfectly united in
mind and thought. 11My brothers and sisters, some from Chloe's house-
hold have informed me that there are quarrels among you. 12What I
mean is this: One of you says, "I follow Paul"; another, "I follow Apol-
los"; another, "I follow Cephas[b]"; still another, "I follow Christ."

13Is Christ divided? Was Paul crucified for you? Were you baptized in
the name of Paul? 14I thank God that I did not baptize any of you ex-
cept Crispus and Gaius, 15so no one can say that you were baptized in
my name. 16(Yes, I also baptized the household of Stephanas; beyond
that, I don't remember if I baptized anyone else.) 17For Christ did not
send me to baptize, but to preach the gospel — not with wisdom and
eloquence, lest the cross of Christ be emptied of its power.

CHRIST CRUCIFIED IS GOD'S POWER AND WISDOM

18For the message of the cross is foolishness to those who are per-
ishing, but to us who are being saved it is the power of God. 19For it is
written:

"I will destroy the wisdom of the wise;
the intelligence of the intelligent I will frustrate."[c]

20Where is the wise person? Where is the teacher of the law? Where
is the philosopher of this age? Has not God made foolish the wisdom
of the world? 21For since in the wisdom of God the world through its
wisdom did not know him, God was pleased through the foolishness
of what was preached to save those who believe. 22Jews demand signs
and Greeks look for wisdom, 23but we preach Christ crucified: a stum-
bling block to Jews and foolishness to Gentiles, 24but to those whom

PRAYING SCRIPTURE

1 Corinthians 1

After a brief greeting, Paul jumped directly into the first issue facing the Corinthians: They were divided into factions based on their preferred spiritual leader. Whether influenced by Paul, Apollos or Peter, they all needed to remember they were first and foremost of Christ.

Factions based on spiritual heroes have long been a problem among God's people. Ask God to protect you from hero worship, and keep your focus on Jesus alone.

---

[a] *10* The Greek word for *brothers and sisters* (*adelphoi*) refers here to believers, both men and women, as part of God's family; also in verses 11 and 26; and in 2:1; 3:1; 4:6; 6:8; 7:24,29; 10:1; 11:33; 12:1; 14:6,20,26,39; 15:1,6,50,58; 16:15,20. [b] *12* That is, Peter [c] *19* Isaiah 29:14

God has called, both Jews and Greeks, Christ the power of God and the wisdom of God. 25For the foolishness of God is wiser than human wisdom, and the weakness of God is stronger than human strength.

26Brothers and sisters, think of what you were when you were called. Not many of you were wise by human standards; not many were influential; not many were of noble birth. 27But God chose the foolish things of the world to shame the wise; God chose the weak things of the world to shame the strong. 28God chose the lowly things of this world and the despised things — and the things that are not — to nullify the things that are, 29so that no one may boast before him. 30It is because of him that you are in Christ Jesus, who has become for us wisdom from God — that is, our righteousness, holiness and redemption. 31Therefore, as it is written: "Let the one who boasts boast in the Lord."[a]

2 And so it was with me, brothers and sisters. When I came to you, I did not come with eloquence or human wisdom as I proclaimed to you the testimony about God.[b] 2For I resolved to know nothing while I was with you except Jesus Christ and him crucified. 3I came to you in weakness with great fear and trembling. 4My message and my preaching were not with wise and persuasive words, but with a demonstration of the Spirit's power, 5so that your faith might not rest on human wisdom, but on God's power.

GOD'S WISDOM REVEALED BY THE SPIRIT

6We do, however, speak a message of wisdom among the mature, but not the wisdom of this age or of the rulers of this age, who are coming to nothing. 7No, we declare God's wisdom, a mystery that has been hidden and that God destined for our glory before time began. 8None of the rulers of this age understood it, for if they had, they would not have crucified the Lord of glory. 9However, as it is written:

"What no eye has seen,
  what no ear has heard,
and what no human mind has conceived"[c] —
  the things God has prepared for those who love him —

10these are the things God has revealed to us by his Spirit.

The Spirit searches all things, even the deep things of God. 11For who knows a person's thoughts except their own spirit within them? In the same way no one knows the thoughts of God except the Spirit of God. 12What we have received is not the spirit of the world, but the Spirit who is from God, so that we may understand what God has freely given us. 13This is what we speak, not in words taught us by human wisdom but in words taught by the Spirit, explaining spiritual realities with Spirit-taught words.[d] 14The person without the Spirit does not accept the things that come from the Spirit of God but considers them foolishness, and cannot understand them because they are discerned only through the Spirit. 15The person with the Spirit makes judgments about all things, but such a person is not subject to merely human judgments, 16for,

"Who has known the mind of the Lord
  so as to instruct him?"[e]

But we have the mind of Christ.

[a] *31* Jer. 9:24 [b] *1* Some manuscripts *proclaimed to you God's mystery* [c] *9* Isaiah 64:4 [d] *13* Or *Spirit, interpreting spiritual truths to those who are spiritual* [e] *16* Isaiah 40:13

PRAYING SCRIPTURE

1 Corinthians 2

Do you have spiritual wisdom? It is the "mystery that has been hidden and that God destined for our glory before time began" that Paul said God established for our glory (verse 7). It is the wisdom neither of this age nor of this world, but from God through the Holy Spirit to his people. Unbelievers cannot obtain it; it is foolishness to them.

God's people have obtained spiritual wisdom in Christ. Pray that it will always be increasing in you.

THE CHURCH AND ITS LEADERS

3 Brothers and sisters, I could not address you as people who live
by the Spirit but as people who are still worldly — mere infants in
Christ. 2I gave you milk, not solid food, for you were not yet ready for
it. Indeed, you are still not ready. 3You are still worldly. For since there
is jealousy and quarreling among you, are you not worldly? Are you
not acting like mere humans? 4For when one says, "I follow Paul," and
another, "I follow Apollos," are you not mere human beings?
5What, after all, is Apollos? And what is Paul? Only servants, through
whom you came to believe — as the Lord has assigned to each his task.
6I planted the seed, Apollos watered it, but God has been making it
grow. 7So neither the one who plants nor the one who waters is any-
thing, but only God, who makes things grow. 8The one who plants and
the one who waters have one purpose, and they will each be rewarded
according to their own labor. 9For we are co-workers in God's service;
you are God's field, God's building.
10By the grace God has given me, I laid a foundation as a wise
builder, and someone else is building on it. But each one should build
with care. 11For no one can lay any foundation other than the one al-
ready laid, which is Jesus Christ. 12If anyone builds on this foundation
using gold, silver, costly stones, wood, hay or straw, 13their work will be
shown for what it is, because the Day will bring it to light. It will be re-
vealed with fire, and the fire will test the quality of each person's work.
14If what has been built survives, the builder will receive a reward. 15If
it is burned up, the builder will suffer loss but yet will be saved — even
though only as one escaping through the flames.
16Don't you know that you yourselves are God's temple and that
God's Spirit dwells in your midst? 17If anyone destroys God's temple,
God will destroy that person; for God's temple is sacred, and you to-
gether are that temple.
18Do not deceive yourselves. If any of you think you are wise by the
standards of this age, you should become "fools" so that you may be-
come wise. 19For the wisdom of this world is foolishness in God's sight.
As it is written: "He catches the wise in their craftiness"[a]; 20and again,
"The Lord knows that the thoughts of the wise are futile."[b] 21So then,
no more boasting about human leaders! All things are yours, 22whether
Paul or Apollos or Cephas[c] or the world or life or death or the present or
the future — all are yours, 23and you are of Christ, and Christ is of God.

THE NATURE OF TRUE APOSTLESHIP

4 This, then, is how you ought to regard us: as servants of Christ and
as those entrusted with the mysteries God has revealed. 2Now it is
required that those who have been given a trust must prove faithful.
3I care very little if I am judged by you or by any human court; indeed,
I do not even judge myself. 4My conscience is clear, but that does not
make me innocent. It is the Lord who judges me. 5Therefore judge
nothing before the appointed time; wait until the Lord comes. He will
bring to light what is hidden in darkness and will expose the motives
of the heart. At that time each will receive their praise from God.
6Now, brothers and sisters, I have applied these things to myself and
Apollos for your benefit, so that you may learn from us the meaning
of the saying, "Do not go beyond what is written." Then you will not be

[a] 19 Job 5:13 [b] 20 Psalm 94:11 [c] 22 That is, Peter

PRAYING SCRIPTURE

1 Corinthians 3

The complement to gaining spiritual wisdom is avoiding worldly wisdom that leads people to believe they are truly wise. Worldly wisdom is crafty in the things of this age, emphasizing temporal goals as the way to succeed in this life. Better to be thought a fool and have spiritual wisdom than to be caught in your own craftiness (see verse 19).

If you are living by worldly wisdom, confess it and spend time with the spiritually wise.

PRAYING SCRIPTURE

1 Corinthians 4

In giving part of his ministry biography, Paul reminded the Corinthians of his sacrifice on their behalf (see verse 11). They hungered and suffered thirst. They were poorly clothed. They had been beaten. They were homeless. Yet Paul saw them as his beloved children, having become their father "through the gospel" (verse 15).

No sacrifice is too great in our efforts to disciple others. Ask God for a spirit of sacrifice focused on others' spiritual growth.

puffed up in being a follower of one of us over against the other. [7]For
who makes you different from anyone else? What do you have that you
did not receive? And if you did receive it, why do you boast as though
you did not?
[8]Already you have all you want! Already you have become rich! You
have begun to reign — and that without us! How I wish that you really
had begun to reign so that we also might reign with you! [9]For it seems
to me that God has put us apostles on display at the end of the proces-
sion, like those condemned to die in the arena. We have been made a
spectacle to the whole universe, to angels as well as to human beings.
[10]We are fools for Christ, but you are so wise in Christ! We are weak, but
you are strong! You are honored, we are dishonored! [11]To this very hour
we go hungry and thirsty, we are in rags, we are brutally treated, we are
homeless. [12]We work hard with our own hands. When we are cursed, we
bless; when we are persecuted, we endure it; [13]when we are slandered,
we answer kindly. We have become the scum of the earth, the garbage
of the world — right up to this moment.

PAUL'S APPEAL AND WARNING

[14]I am writing this not to shame you but to warn you as my dear chil-
dren. [15]Even if you had ten thousand guardians in Christ, you do not
have many fathers, for in Christ Jesus I became your father through
the gospel. [16]Therefore I urge you to imitate me. [17]For this reason I
have sent to you Timothy, my son whom I love, who is faithful in the
Lord. He will remind you of my way of life in Christ Jesus, which agrees
with what I teach everywhere in every church.
[18]Some of you have become arrogant, as if I were not coming to you.
[19]But I will come to you very soon, if the Lord is willing, and then I
will find out not only how these arrogant people are talking, but what
power they have. [20]For the kingdom of God is not a matter of talk but
of power. [21]What do you prefer? Shall I come to you with a rod of disci-
pline, or shall I come in love and with a gentle spirit?

DEALING WITH A CASE OF INCEST

5 It is actually reported that there is sexual immorality among you,
and of a kind that even pagans do not tolerate: A man is sleeping
with his father's wife. [2]And you are proud! Shouldn't you rather have
gone into mourning and have put out of your fellowship the man who
has been doing this? [3]For my part, even though I am not physically
present, I am with you in spirit. As one who is present with you in this
way, I have already passed judgment in the name of our Lord Jesus on
the one who has been doing this. [4]So when you are assembled and I
am with you in spirit, and the power of our Lord Jesus is present, [5]hand
this man over to Satan for the destruction of the flesh,[a,b] so that his
spirit may be saved on the day of the Lord.
[6]Your boasting is not good. Don't you know that a little yeast leavens
the whole batch of dough? [7]Get rid of the old yeast, so that you may be
a new unleavened batch — as you really are. For Christ, our Passover
lamb, has been sacrificed. [8]Therefore let us keep the Festival, not with
the old bread leavened with malice and wickedness, but with the un-
leavened bread of sincerity and truth.

PRAYING SCRIPTURE

1 Corinthians 5

Incredibly, the church at Corinth allowed a man to call himself part of that body while living in an immoral relationship so obscene that not even the unbelievers in the community would commit it. Their unwillingness to call him to repentance was a blight on their witness. God's people are responsible to hold one another to holy living. If you are confronted about sin, humbly repent and seek God's forgiveness.

---

[a] 5 In contexts like this, the Greek word for *flesh* (*sarx*) refers to the sinful state of human beings, often presented as a power in opposition to the Spirit.
[b] 5 Or *of his body*

9 I wrote to you in my letter not to associate with sexually immoral people — 10 not at all meaning the people of this world who are immoral, or the greedy and swindlers, or idolaters. In that case you would have to leave this world. 11 But now I am writing to you that you must not associate with anyone who claims to be a brother or sister[a] but is sexually immoral or greedy, an idolater or slanderer, a drunkard or swindler. Do not even eat with such people.

12 What business is it of mine to judge those outside the church? Are you not to judge those inside? 13 God will judge those outside. "Expel the wicked person from among you."[b]

LAWSUITS AMONG BELIEVERS

6 If any of you has a dispute with another, do you dare to take it before the ungodly for judgment instead of before the Lord's people? 2 Or do you not know that the Lord's people will judge the world? And if you are to judge the world, are you not competent to judge trivial cases? 3 Do you not know that we will judge angels? How much more the things of this life! 4 Therefore, if you have disputes about such matters, do you ask for a ruling from those whose way of life is scorned in the church? 5 I say this to shame you. Is it possible that there is nobody among you wise enough to judge a dispute between believers? 6 But instead, one brother takes another to court — and this in front of unbelievers!

7 The very fact that you have lawsuits among you means you have been completely defeated already. Why not rather be wronged? Why not rather be cheated? 8 Instead, you yourselves cheat and do wrong, and you do this to your brothers and sisters. 9 Or do you not know that wrongdoers will not inherit the kingdom of God? Do not be deceived: Neither the sexually immoral nor idolaters nor adulterers nor men who have sex with men[c] 10 nor thieves nor the greedy nor drunkards nor slanderers nor swindlers will inherit the kingdom of God. 11 And that is what some of you were. But you were washed, you were sanctified, you were justified in the name of the Lord Jesus Christ and by the Spirit of our God.

SEXUAL IMMORALITY

12 "I have the right to do anything," you say — but not everything is beneficial. "I have the right to do anything" — but I will not be mastered by anything. 13 You say, "Food for the stomach and the stomach for food, and God will destroy them both." The body, however, is not meant for sexual immorality but for the Lord, and the Lord for the body. 14 By his power God raised the Lord from the dead, and he will raise us also. 15 Do you not know that your bodies are members of Christ himself? Shall I then take the members of Christ and unite them with a prostitute? Never! 16 Do you not know that he who unites himself with a prostitute is one with her in body? For it is said, "The two will become one flesh."[d] 17 But whoever is united with the Lord is one with him in spirit.[e]

18 Flee from sexual immorality. All other sins a person commits are outside the body, but whoever sins sexually, sins against their own body.

PRAYING SCRIPTURE

1 Corinthians 6

A significant teaching that applies across our lives is that we as God's people are not our own. Because of Jesus' death and resurrection, we belong to God. Paul called our bodies "temples of the Holy Spirit" (verse 19).

Are you engaged in any behavior that implies your body is not God's? If so, repent and acknowledge that he owns you.

---

[a] *11* The Greek word for *brother or sister* (*adelphos*) refers here to a believer, whether man or woman, as part of God's family; also in 8:11,13.
[b] *13* Deut. 13:5; 17:7; 19:19; 21:21; 22:21,24; 24:7
[c] *9* The words *men who have sex with men* translate two Greek words that refer to the passive and active participants in homosexual acts.
[d] *16* Gen. 2:24
[e] *17* Or *in the Spirit*

19 Do you not know that your bodies are temples of the Holy Spirit, who is in you, whom you have received from God? You are not your own; 20 you were bought at a price. Therefore honor God with your bodies.

CONCERNING MARRIED LIFE

PRAYING SCRIPTURE

1 Corinthians 7

Marriages that reflect Christ are important, but so are single lives that reflect Christ. Paul made clear that married people can serve Christ together and single people can serve Christ alone. He commended both, while making it clear that singleness is to be preferred at certain times.

Marriage reflects Christ and his church while singleness reflects Christ's life on earth. Ask God to make you content as you are right now.

7 Now for the matters you wrote about: "It is good for a man not to have sexual relations with a woman." 2 But since sexual immorality is occurring, each man should have sexual relations with his own wife, and each woman with her own husband. 3 The husband should fulfill his marital duty to his wife, and likewise the wife to her husband. 4 The wife does not have authority over her own body but yields it to her husband. In the same way, the husband does not have authority over his own body but yields it to his wife. 5 Do not deprive each other except perhaps by mutual consent and for a time, so that you may devote yourselves to prayer. Then come together again so that Satan will not tempt you because of your lack of self-control. 6 I say this as a concession, not as a command. 7 I wish that all of you were as I am. But each of you has your own gift from God; one has this gift, another has that.

8 Now to the unmarried[a] and the widows I say: It is good for them to stay unmarried, as I do. 9 But if they cannot control themselves, they should marry, for it is better to marry than to burn with passion.

10 To the married I give this command (not I, but the Lord): A wife must not separate from her husband. 11 But if she does, she must remain unmarried or else be reconciled to her husband. And a husband must not divorce his wife.

12 To the rest I say this (I, not the Lord): If any brother has a wife who is not a believer and she is willing to live with him, he must not divorce her. 13 And if a woman has a husband who is not a believer and he is willing to live with her, she must not divorce him. 14 For the unbelieving husband has been sanctified through his wife, and the unbelieving wife has been sanctified through her believing husband. Otherwise your children would be unclean, but as it is, they are holy.

15 But if the unbeliever leaves, let it be so. The brother or the sister is not bound in such circumstances; God has called us to live in peace. 16 How do you know, wife, whether you will save your husband? Or, how do you know, husband, whether you will save your wife?

CONCERNING CHANGE OF STATUS

17 Nevertheless, each person should live as a believer in whatever situation the Lord has assigned to them, just as God has called them. This is the rule I lay down in all the churches. 18 Was a man already circumcised when he was called? He should not become uncircumcised. Was a man uncircumcised when he was called? He should not be circumcised. 19 Circumcision is nothing and uncircumcision is nothing. Keeping God's commands is what counts. 20 Each person should remain in the situation they were in when God called them.

21 Were you a slave when you were called? Don't let it trouble you — although if you can gain your freedom, do so. 22 For the one who was a slave when called to faith in the Lord is the Lord's freed person; similarly, the one who was free when called is Christ's slave. 23 You were bought at a price; do not become slaves of human beings. 24 Brothers and sisters, each person, as responsible to God, should remain in the situation they were in when God called them.

---

[a] 8 Or *widowers*

CONCERNING THE UNMARRIED

25Now about virgins: I have no command from the Lord, but I give a judgment as one who by the Lord's mercy is trustworthy. 26Because of the present crisis, I think that it is good for a man to remain as he is. 27Are you pledged to a woman? Do not seek to be released. Are you free from such a commitment? Do not look for a wife. 28But if you do marry, you have not sinned; and if a virgin marries, she has not sinned. But those who marry will face many troubles in this life, and I want to spare you this.

29What I mean, brothers and sisters, is that the time is short. From now on those who have wives should live as if they do not; 30those who mourn, as if they did not; those who are happy, as if they were not; those who buy something, as if it were not theirs to keep; 31those who use the things of the world, as if not engrossed in them. For this world in its present form is passing away.

32I would like you to be free from concern. An unmarried man is concerned about the Lord's affairs — how he can please the Lord. 33But a married man is concerned about the affairs of this world — how he can please his wife — 34and his interests are divided. An unmarried woman or virgin is concerned about the Lord's affairs: Her aim is to be devoted to the Lord in both body and spirit. But a married woman is concerned about the affairs of this world — how she can please her husband. 35I am saying this for your own good, not to restrict you, but that you may live in a right way in undivided devotion to the Lord.

36If anyone is worried that he might not be acting honorably toward the virgin he is engaged to, and if his passions are too strong[a] and he feels he ought to marry, he should do as he wants. He is not sinning. They should get married. 37But the man who has settled the matter in his own mind, who is under no compulsion but has control over his own will, and who has made up his mind not to marry the virgin — this man also does the right thing. 38So then, he who marries the virgin does right, but he who does not marry her does better.[b]

39A woman is bound to her husband as long as he lives. But if her husband dies, she is free to marry anyone she wishes, but he must belong to the Lord. 40In my judgment, she is happier if she stays as she is — and I think that I too have the Spirit of God.

CONCERNING FOOD SACRIFICED TO IDOLS

8 Now about food sacrificed to idols: We know that "We all possess knowledge." But knowledge puffs up while love builds up. 2Those who think they know something do not yet know as they ought to know. 3But whoever loves God is known by God.[c]

4So then, about eating food sacrificed to idols: We know that "An idol is nothing at all in the world" and that "There is no God but one."

[a] 36 Or *if she is getting beyond the usual age for marriage* [b] 36-38 Or *36If anyone thinks he is not treating his daughter properly, and if she is getting along in years* (or *if her passions are too strong*), *and he feels she ought to marry, he should do as he wants. He is not sinning. He should let her get married. 37But the man who has settled the matter in his own mind, who is under no compulsion but has control over his own will, and who has made up his mind to keep the virgin unmarried — this man also does the right thing. 38So then, he who gives his virgin in marriage does right, but he who does not give her in marriage does better.* [c] 2,3 An early manuscript and another ancient witness *think they have knowledge do not yet know as they ought to know. 3But whoever loves truly knows.*

PRAYING SCRIPTURE

1 Corinthians 8

In a crucial section of this letter dealing with gray or convictional areas, Paul began with a simple principle—do not use your freedom in Christ to cause another Christian to sin. For the Christian, freedom in all things does not mean freedom for all things. Wisdom is needed.

Has a brother or sister in Christ ever been offended when you exercised your freedom in Christ? Pray for an opportunity to seek forgiveness from them.

5For even if there are so-called gods, whether in heaven or on earth (as indeed there are many "gods" and many "lords"), 6yet for us there is but one God, the Father, from whom all things came and for whom we live; and there is but one Lord, Jesus Christ, through whom all things came and through whom we live.

7But not everyone possesses this knowledge. Some people are still so accustomed to idols that when they eat sacrificial food they think of it as having been sacrificed to a god, and since their conscience is weak, it is defiled. 8But food does not bring us near to God; we are no worse if we do not eat, and no better if we do.

9Be careful, however, that the exercise of your rights does not become a stumbling block to the weak. 10For if someone with a weak conscience sees you, with all your knowledge, eating in an idol's temple, won't that person be emboldened to eat what is sacrificed to idols? 11So this weak brother or sister, for whom Christ died, is destroyed by your knowledge. 12When you sin against them in this way and wound their weak conscience, you sin against Christ. 13Therefore, if what I eat causes my brother or sister to fall into sin, I will never eat meat again, so that I will not cause them to fall.

PRAYING SCRIPTURE

1 Corinthians 9

We often find it difficult to leave our comfort zone. Seeking comfort is opposed to faith because faith requires us to trust God in the middle of uncertainty. Paul used himself and Barnabas as examples of self-denial for the sake of the gospel.

Freedom in Christ was given that we might serve others. If you struggle with the faith to step into the unknown, trust the God who knows all.

PAUL'S RIGHTS AS AN APOSTLE

9 Am I not free? Am I not an apostle? Have I not seen Jesus our Lord? Are you not the result of my work in the Lord? 2Even though I may not be an apostle to others, surely I am to you! For you are the seal of my apostleship in the Lord.

3This is my defense to those who sit in judgment on me. 4Don't we have the right to food and drink? 5Don't we have the right to take a believing wife along with us, as do the other apostles and the Lord's brothers and Cephas[a]? 6Or is it only I and Barnabas who lack the right to not work for a living?

7Who serves as a soldier at his own expense? Who plants a vineyard and does not eat its grapes? Who tends a flock and does not drink the milk? 8Do I say this merely on human authority? Doesn't the Law say the same thing? 9For it is written in the Law of Moses: "Do not muzzle an ox while it is treading out the grain."[b] Is it about oxen that God is concerned? 10Surely he says this for us, doesn't he? Yes, this was written for us, because whoever plows and threshes should be able to do so in the hope of sharing in the harvest. 11If we have sown spiritual seed among you, is it too much if we reap a material harvest from you? 12If others have this right of support from you, shouldn't we have it all the more?

But we did not use this right. On the contrary, we put up with anything rather than hinder the gospel of Christ.

13Don't you know that those who serve in the temple get their food from the temple, and that those who serve at the altar share in what is offered on the altar? 14In the same way, the Lord has commanded that those who preach the gospel should receive their living from the gospel.

15But I have not used any of these rights. And I am not writing this in the hope that you will do such things for me, for I would rather die than allow anyone to deprive me of this boast. 16For when I preach the gospel, I cannot boast, since I am compelled to preach. Woe to me if I

[a] 5 That is, Peter [b] 9 Deut. 25:4

do not preach the gospel! 17If I preach voluntarily, I have a reward; if
not voluntarily, I am simply discharging the trust committed to me.
18What then is my reward? Just this: that in preaching the gospel I
may offer it free of charge, and so not make full use of my rights as a
preacher of the gospel.

PAUL'S USE OF HIS FREEDOM

19Though I am free and belong to no one, I have made myself a slave
to everyone, to win as many as possible. 20To the Jews I became like a
Jew, to win the Jews. To those under the law I became like one under
the law (though I myself am not under the law), so as to win those un-
der the law. 21To those not having the law I became like one not having
the law (though I am not free from God's law but am under Christ's
law), so as to win those not having the law. 22To the weak I became
weak, to win the weak. I have become all things to all people so that by
all possible means I might save some. 23I do all this for the sake of the
gospel, that I may share in its blessings.

THE NEED FOR SELF-DISCIPLINE

24Do you not know that in a race all the runners run, but only one
gets the prize? Run in such a way as to get the prize. 25Everyone who
competes in the games goes into strict training. They do it to get a
crown that will not last, but we do it to get a crown that will last for-
ever. 26Therefore I do not run like someone running aimlessly; I do not
fight like a boxer beating the air. 27No, I strike a blow to my body and
make it my slave so that after I have preached to others, I myself will
not be disqualified for the prize.

WARNINGS FROM ISRAEL'S HISTORY

10 For I do not want you to be ignorant of the fact, brothers and sis-
ters, that our ancestors were all under the cloud and that they all
passed through the sea. 2They were all baptized into Moses in the cloud
and in the sea. 3They all ate the same spiritual food 4and drank the same
spiritual drink; for they drank from the spiritual rock that accompanied
them, and that rock was Christ. 5Nevertheless, God was not pleased with
most of them; their bodies were scattered in the wilderness.

6Now these things occurred as examples to keep us from setting our
hearts on evil things as they did. 7Do not be idolaters, as some of them
were; as it is written: "The people sat down to eat and drink and got
up to indulge in revelry."[a] 8We should not commit sexual immorality,
as some of them did — and in one day twenty-three thousand of them
died. 9We should not test Christ,[b] as some of them did — and were
killed by snakes. 10And do not grumble, as some of them did — and
were killed by the destroying angel.

11These things happened to them as examples and were written
down as warnings for us, on whom the culmination of the ages has
come. 12So, if you think you are standing firm, be careful that you don't
fall! 13No temptation[c] has overtaken you except what is common to
mankind. And God is faithful; he will not let you be tempted[c] beyond
what you can bear. But when you are tempted,[c] he will also provide a
way out so that you can endure it.

[a] 7 Exodus 32:6 [b] 9 Some manuscripts *test the Lord* [c] 13 The Greek for *temptation* and *tempted* can also mean *testing* and *tested.*

PRAYING SCRIPTURE

1 Corinthians 10

This chapter contains one of the most precious promises God's children can ever claim: We will never face a temptation so strong that God will not provide a way to escape from it (see verse 13). Many Christians memorize this verse to recall it during temptation.

Do you ever feel overwhelmed by temptation? Pray this verse and trust that God will not allow you to be tempted too far.

IDOL FEASTS AND THE LORD'S SUPPER

14Therefore, my dear friends, flee from idolatry. 15I speak to sensible
people; judge for yourselves what I say. 16Is not the cup of thanksgiving
for which we give thanks a participation in the blood of Christ? And
is not the bread that we break a participation in the body of Christ?
17Because there is one loaf, we, who are many, are one body, for we all
share the one loaf.

18Consider the people of Israel: Do not those who eat the sacrifices
participate in the altar? 19Do I mean then that food sacrificed to an
idol is anything, or that an idol is anything? 20No, but the sacrifices of
pagans are offered to demons, not to God, and I do not want you to be
participants with demons. 21You cannot drink the cup of the Lord and
the cup of demons too; you cannot have a part in both the Lord's table
and the table of demons. 22Are we trying to arouse the Lord's jealousy?
Are we stronger than he?

THE BELIEVER'S FREEDOM

23"I have the right to do anything," you say—but not everything is
beneficial. "I have the right to do anything"—but not everything is con-
structive. 24No one should seek their own good, but the good of others.

25Eat anything sold in the meat market without raising questions of
conscience, 26for, "The earth is the Lord's, and everything in it."[a]

27If an unbeliever invites you to a meal and you want to go, eat what-
ever is put before you without raising questions of conscience. 28But if
someone says to you, "This has been offered in sacrifice," then do not
eat it, both for the sake of the one who told you and for the sake of con-
science. 29I am referring to the other person's conscience, not yours.
For why is my freedom being judged by another's conscience? 30If I
take part in the meal with thankfulness, why am I denounced because
of something I thank God for?

31So whether you eat or drink or whatever you do, do it all for the
glory of God. 32Do not cause anyone to stumble, whether Jews, Greeks
or the church of God—33even as I try to please everyone in every
way. For I am not seeking my own good but the good of many, so that
11 they may be saved. 1Follow my example, as I follow the example
of Christ.

ON COVERING THE HEAD IN WORSHIP

2I praise you for remembering me in everything and for holding to
the traditions just as I passed them on to you. 3But I want you to realize
that the head of every man is Christ, and the head of the woman is man,[b]
and the head of Christ is God. 4Every man who prays or prophesies with
his head covered dishonors his head. 5But every woman who prays or
prophesies with her head uncovered dishonors her head—it is the same
as having her head shaved. 6For if a woman does not cover her head, she
might as well have her hair cut off; but if it is a disgrace for a woman to
have her hair cut off or her head shaved, then she should cover her head.
7A man ought not to cover his head,[c] since he is the image and glory

PRAYING SCRIPTURE

1 Corinthians 11

The Lord's Supper, also called Communion or the Eucharist, is that ongoing memorial of Jesus' death, burial and resurrection. The physical elements of bread and wine, received in the context of a church's fellowship meal, remind us of the salvation Christ has provided for us. We are encouraged to approach it in unity and with clean hearts.

When you next take the Lord's Supper, pray to be a worthy participant.

---

[a] *26* Psalm 24:1 [b] *3* Or *of the wife is her husband* [c] *4-7* Or *4Every man who prays or prophesies with long hair dishonors his head. 5But every woman who prays or prophesies with no covering of hair dishonors her head—she is just like one of the "shorn women." 6If a woman has no covering, let her be for now with short hair; but since it is a disgrace for a woman to have her hair shorn or shaved, she should grow it again. 7A man ought not to have long hair*

of God; but woman is the glory of man. 8For man did not come from woman, but woman from man; 9neither was man created for woman, but woman for man. 10It is for this reason that a woman ought to have authority over her own[a] head, because of the angels. 11Nevertheless, in the Lord woman is not independent of man, nor is man independent of woman. 12For as woman came from man, so also man is born of woman. But everything comes from God.

13Judge for yourselves: Is it proper for a woman to pray to God with her head uncovered? 14Does not the very nature of things teach you that if a man has long hair, it is a disgrace to him, 15but that if a woman has long hair, it is her glory? For long hair is given to her as a covering. 16If anyone wants to be contentious about this, we have no other practice — nor do the churches of God.

CORRECTING AN ABUSE OF THE LORD'S SUPPER

17In the following directives I have no praise for you, for your meetings do more harm than good. 18In the first place, I hear that when you come together as a church, there are divisions among you, and to some extent I believe it. 19No doubt there have to be differences among you to show which of you have God's approval. 20So then, when you come together, it is not the Lord's Supper you eat, 21for when you are eating, some of you go ahead with your own private suppers. As a result, one person remains hungry and another gets drunk. 22Don't you have homes to eat and drink in? Or do you despise the church of God by humiliating those who have nothing? What shall I say to you? Shall I praise you? Certainly not in this matter!

23For I received from the Lord what I also passed on to you: The Lord Jesus, on the night he was betrayed, took bread, 24and when he had given thanks, he broke it and said, "This is my body, which is for you; do this in remembrance of me." 25In the same way, after supper he took the cup, saying, "This cup is the new covenant in my blood; do this, whenever you drink it, in remembrance of me." 26For whenever you eat this bread and drink this cup, you proclaim the Lord's death until he comes.

27So then, whoever eats the bread or drinks the cup of the Lord in an unworthy manner will be guilty of sinning against the body and blood of the Lord. 28Everyone ought to examine themselves before they eat of the bread and drink from the cup. 29For those who eat and drink without discerning the body of Christ eat and drink judgment on themselves. 30That is why many among you are weak and sick, and a number of you have fallen asleep. 31But if we were more discerning with regard to ourselves, we would not come under such judgment. 32Nevertheless, when we are judged in this way by the Lord, we are being disciplined so that we will not be finally condemned with the world.

33So then, my brothers and sisters, when you gather to eat, you should all eat together. 34Anyone who is hungry should eat something at home, so that when you meet together it may not result in judgment.

And when I come I will give further directions.

CONCERNING SPIRITUAL GIFTS

12 Now about the gifts of the Spirit, brothers and sisters, I do not want you to be uninformed. 2You know that when you were pagans, somehow or other you were influenced and led astray to mute

PRAYING SCRIPTURE

1 Corinthians 12

The Lord does not leave his church foundering without the support it needs to accomplish its mission. The Holy Spirit gives strength to the body in the form of gifts to its members. The gifts differ but all exist for the benefit of building up the whole church, not merely the ones possessing a gift.

Do you know your giftedness? Pray to exercise what God has given you to benefit your local church.

[a] 10 Or *have a sign of authority on her*

idols. 3Therefore I want you to know that no one who is speaking by
the Spirit of God says, "Jesus be cursed," and no one can say, "Jesus is
Lord," except by the Holy Spirit.
4There are different kinds of gifts, but the same Spirit distributes
them. 5There are different kinds of service, but the same Lord. 6There
are different kinds of working, but in all of them and in everyone it
is the same God at work.
7Now to each one the manifestation of the Spirit is given for the
common good. 8To one there is given through the Spirit a message
of wisdom, to another a message of knowledge by means of the same
Spirit, 9to another faith by the same Spirit, to another gifts of healing
by that one Spirit, 10to another miraculous powers, to another proph-
ecy, to another distinguishing between spirits, to another speaking in
different kinds of tongues,[a] and to still another the interpretation of
tongues.[a] 11All these are the work of one and the same Spirit, and he
distributes them to each one, just as he determines.

UNITY AND DIVERSITY IN THE BODY

12Just as a body, though one, has many parts, but all its many parts
form one body, so it is with Christ. 13For we were all baptized by[b] one
Spirit so as to form one body — whether Jews or Gentiles, slave or
free — and we were all given the one Spirit to drink. 14Even so the
body is not made up of one part but of many.
15Now if the foot should say, "Because I am not a hand, I do not
belong to the body," it would not for that reason stop being part of
the body. 16And if the ear should say, "Because I am not an eye, I
do not belong to the body," it would not for that reason stop being
part of the body. 17If the whole body were an eye, where would the
sense of hearing be? If the whole body were an ear, where would the
sense of smell be? 18But in fact God has placed the parts in the body,
every one of them, just as he wanted them to be. 19If they were all
one part, where would the body be? 20As it is, there are many parts,
but one body.
21The eye cannot say to the hand, "I don't need you!" And the head
cannot say to the feet, "I don't need you!" 22On the contrary, those
parts of the body that seem to be weaker are indispensable, 23and the
parts that we think are less honorable we treat with special honor.
And the parts that are unpresentable are treated with special mod-
esty, 24while our presentable parts need no special treatment. But
God has put the body together, giving greater honor to the parts that
lacked it, 25so that there should be no division in the body, but that its
parts should have equal concern for each other. 26If one part suffers,
every part suffers with it; if one part is honored, every part rejoices
with it.
27Now you are the body of Christ, and each one of you is a part of it.
28And God has placed in the church first of all apostles, second proph-
ets, third teachers, then miracles, then gifts of healing, of helping, of
guidance, and of different kinds of tongues. 29Are all apostles? Are all
prophets? Are all teachers? Do all work miracles? 30Do all have gifts
of healing? Do all speak in tongues[c]? Do all interpret? 31Now eagerly
desire the greater gifts.

[a] *10* Or *languages*; also in verse 28 [b] *13* Or *with*; or *in* [c] *30* Or *other languages*

LOVE IS INDISPENSABLE

And yet I will show you the most excellent way.
13 If I speak in the tongues[a] of men or of angels, but do not have
love, I am only a resounding gong or a clanging cymbal. 2If I
have the gift of prophecy and can fathom all mysteries and all knowl-
edge, and if I have a faith that can move mountains, but do not have
love, I am nothing. 3If I give all I possess to the poor and give over my
body to hardship that I may boast,[b] but do not have love, I gain nothing.
4Love is patient, love is kind. It does not envy, it does not boast, it is
not proud. 5It does not dishonor others, it is not self-seeking, it is not
easily angered, it keeps no record of wrongs. 6Love does not delight
in evil but rejoices with the truth. 7It always protects, always trusts,
always hopes, always perseveres.
8Love never fails. But where there are prophecies, they will cease;
where there are tongues, they will be stilled; where there is knowl-
edge, it will pass away. 9For we know in part and we prophesy in part,
10but when completeness comes, what is in part disappears. 11When I
was a child, I talked like a child, I thought like a child, I reasoned like
a child. When I became a man, I put the ways of childhood behind me.
12For now we see only a reflection as in a mirror; then we shall see face
to face. Now I know in part; then I shall know fully, even as I am fully
known.
13And now these three remain: faith, hope and love. But the greatest
of these is love.

PRAYING SCRIPTURE

1 Corinthians 13

Love is the great motivating factor of the Christian life. Hope is important because we cannot live without it. Faith is important because it is the means of living in the invisible kingdom. But love is greater than either of them (see verse 13). Without love even our greatest actions for God are vain and out of tune.

Do you love like God? Ask him for a love big enough to include everyone you meet.

INTELLIGIBILITY IN WORSHIP

14 Follow the way of love and eagerly desire gifts of the Spirit, es-
pecially prophecy. 2For anyone who speaks in a tongue[c] does
not speak to people but to God. Indeed, no one understands them;
they utter mysteries by the Spirit. 3But the one who prophesies speaks
to people for their strengthening, encouraging and comfort. 4Anyone
who speaks in a tongue edifies themselves, but the one who proph-
esies edifies the church. 5I would like every one of you to speak in
tongues,[d] but I would rather have you prophesy. The one who proph-
esies is greater than the one who speaks in tongues,[d] unless someone
interprets, so that the church may be edified.
6Now, brothers and sisters, if I come to you and speak in tongues,
what good will I be to you, unless I bring you some revelation or
knowledge or prophecy or word of instruction? 7Even in the case of
lifeless things that make sounds, such as the pipe or harp, how will
anyone know what tune is being played unless there is a distinction in
the notes? 8Again, if the trumpet does not sound a clear call, who will
get ready for battle? 9So it is with you. Unless you speak intelligible
words with your tongue, how will anyone know what you are saying?
You will just be speaking into the air. 10Undoubtedly there are all sorts
of languages in the world, yet none of them is without meaning. 11If
then I do not grasp the meaning of what someone is saying, I am a
foreigner to the speaker, and the speaker is a foreigner to me. 12So it is
with you. Since you are eager for gifts of the Spirit, try to excel in those
that build up the church.

PRAYING SCRIPTURE

1 Corinthians 14

For many Christians, spiritual gifts are as mysterious as a black hole. We learn with the Corinthians that spiritual gifts do not exist to build ourselves up or draw attention to ourselves, but to build up the body of Christ. The gifts are for the church.

If you don't know your spiritual gifting, ask other believers to help you discover it. Then ask God to use it for building the body.

---

[a] *1* Or *languages* [b] *3* Some manuscripts *body to the flames* [c] *2* Or *in another language*; also in verses 4, 13, 14, 19, 26 and 27 [d] *5* Or *in other languages*; also in verses 6, 18, 22, 23 and 39

13For this reason the one who speaks in a tongue should pray that they may interpret what they say. 14For if I pray in a tongue, my spirit prays, but my mind is unfruitful. 15So what shall I do? I will pray with my spirit, but I will also pray with my understanding; I will sing with my spirit, but I will also sing with my understanding. 16Otherwise when you are praising God in the Spirit, how can someone else, who is now put in the position of an inquirer,[a] say "Amen" to your thanksgiving, since they do not know what you are saying? 17You are giving thanks well enough, but no one else is edified.

18I thank God that I speak in tongues more than all of you. 19But in the church I would rather speak five intelligible words to instruct others than ten thousand words in a tongue.

20Brothers and sisters, stop thinking like children. In regard to evil be infants, but in your thinking be adults. 21In the Law it is written:

"With other tongues
  and through the lips of foreigners
I will speak to this people,
  but even then they will not listen to me,
    says the Lord."[b]

22Tongues, then, are a sign, not for believers but for unbelievers; prophecy, however, is not for unbelievers but for believers. 23So if the whole church comes together and everyone speaks in tongues, and inquirers or unbelievers come in, will they not say that you are out of your mind? 24But if an unbeliever or an inquirer comes in while everyone is prophesying, they are convicted of sin and are brought under judgment by all, 25as the secrets of their hearts are laid bare. So they will fall down and worship God, exclaiming, "God is really among you!"

GOOD ORDER IN WORSHIP

26What then shall we say, brothers and sisters? When you come together, each of you has a hymn, or a word of instruction, a revelation, a tongue or an interpretation. Everything must be done so that the church may be built up. 27If anyone speaks in a tongue, two — or at the most three — should speak, one at a time, and someone must interpret. 28If there is no interpreter, the speaker should keep quiet in the church and speak to himself and to God.

29Two or three prophets should speak, and the others should weigh carefully what is said. 30And if a revelation comes to someone who is sitting down, the first speaker should stop. 31For you can all prophesy in turn so that everyone may be instructed and encouraged. 32The spirits of prophets are subject to the control of prophets. 33For God is not a God of disorder but of peace — as in all the congregations of the Lord's people.

34Women[c] should remain silent in the churches. They are not allowed to speak, but must be in submission, as the law says. 35If they want to inquire about something, they should ask their own husbands at home; for it is disgraceful for a woman to speak in the church.[d]

36Or did the word of God originate with you? Or are you the only people it has reached? 37If anyone thinks they are a prophet or otherwise gifted by the Spirit, let them acknowledge that what I am writing

---

[a] *16* The Greek word for *inquirer* is a technical term for someone not fully initiated into a religion; also in verses 23 and 24. [b] *21* Isaiah 28:11,12
[c] *33,34* Or *peace. As in all the congregations of the Lord's people, 34women*
[d] *34,35* In a few manuscripts these verses come after verse 40.

to you is the Lord's command. [38]But if anyone ignores this, they will themselves be ignored.[a]

[39]Therefore, my brothers and sisters, be eager to prophesy, and do not forbid speaking in tongues. [40]But everything should be done in a fitting and orderly way.

THE RESURRECTION OF CHRIST

15 Now, brothers and sisters, I want to remind you of the gospel I preached to you, which you received and on which you have taken your stand. [2]By this gospel you are saved, if you hold firmly to the word I preached to you. Otherwise, you have believed in vain.

[3]For what I received I passed on to you as of first importance[b]: that Christ died for our sins according to the Scriptures, [4]that he was buried, that he was raised on the third day according to the Scriptures, [5]and that he appeared to Cephas,[c] and then to the Twelve. [6]After that, he appeared to more than five hundred of the brothers and sisters at the same time, most of whom are still living, though some have fallen asleep. [7]Then he appeared to James, then to all the apostles, [8]and last of all he appeared to me also, as to one abnormally born.

[9]For I am the least of the apostles and do not even deserve to be called an apostle, because I persecuted the church of God. [10]But by the grace of God I am what I am, and his grace to me was not without effect. No, I worked harder than all of them — yet not I, but the grace of God that was with me. [11]Whether, then, it is I or they, this is what we preach, and this is what you believed.

THE RESURRECTION OF THE DEAD

[12]But if it is preached that Christ has been raised from the dead, how can some of you say that there is no resurrection of the dead? [13]If there is no resurrection of the dead, then not even Christ has been raised. [14]And if Christ has not been raised, our preaching is useless and so is your faith. [15]More than that, we are then found to be false witnesses about God, for we have testified about God that he raised Christ from the dead. But he did not raise him if in fact the dead are not raised. [16]For if the dead are not raised, then Christ has not been raised either. [17]And if Christ has not been raised, your faith is futile; you are still in your sins. [18]Then those also who have fallen asleep in Christ are lost. [19]If only for this life we have hope in Christ, we are of all people most to be pitied.

[20]But Christ has indeed been raised from the dead, the firstfruits of those who have fallen asleep. [21]For since death came through a man, the resurrection of the dead comes also through a man. [22]For as in Adam all die, so in Christ all will be made alive. [23]But each in turn: Christ, the firstfruits; then, when he comes, those who belong to him. [24]Then the end will come, when he hands over the kingdom to God the Father after he has destroyed all dominion, authority and power. [25]For he must reign until he has put all his enemies under his feet. [26]The last enemy to be destroyed is death. [27]For he "has put everything under his feet."[d] Now when it says that "everything" has been put under him, it is clear that this does not include God himself, who put everything under Christ. [28]When he has done this, then the Son himself will be made subject to him who put everything under him, so that God may be all in all.

PRAYING SCRIPTURE

1 Corinthians 15

The victory of the Christian is in the death, burial and resurrection of Jesus. Paul called this the gospel he preached (see verses 1–4). Though in Adam all die, in Christ all are made alive! Hallelujah!

If you need reassurance of your salvation, look to the finished work of Jesus. He is making all things new; you can rejoice in that daily.

---

[a] *38* Some manuscripts *But anyone who is ignorant of this will be ignorant*
[b] *3* Or *you at the first* [c] *5* That is, Peter [d] *27* Psalm 8:6

29Now if there is no resurrection, what will those do who are baptized for the dead? If the dead are not raised at all, why are people baptized for them? 30And as for us, why do we endanger ourselves every hour? 31I face death every day — yes, just as surely as I boast about you in Christ Jesus our Lord. 32If I fought wild beasts in Ephesus with no more than human hopes, what have I gained? If the dead are not raised,

"Let us eat and drink,
 for tomorrow we die."[a]

33Do not be misled: "Bad company corrupts good character."[b] 34Come back to your senses as you ought, and stop sinning; for there are some who are ignorant of God — I say this to your shame.

THE RESURRECTION BODY

35But someone will ask, "How are the dead raised? With what kind of body will they come?" 36How foolish! What you sow does not come to life unless it dies. 37When you sow, you do not plant the body that will be, but just a seed, perhaps of wheat or of something else. 38But God gives it a body as he has determined, and to each kind of seed he gives its own body. 39Not all flesh is the same: People have one kind of flesh, animals have another, birds another and fish another. 40There are also heavenly bodies and there are earthly bodies; but the splendor of the heavenly bodies is one kind, and the splendor of the earthly bodies is another. 41The sun has one kind of splendor, the moon another and the stars another; and star differs from star in splendor.

42So will it be with the resurrection of the dead. The body that is sown is perishable, it is raised imperishable; 43it is sown in dishonor, it is raised in glory; it is sown in weakness, it is raised in power; 44it is sown a natural body, it is raised a spiritual body.

If there is a natural body, there is also a spiritual body. 45So it is written: "The first man Adam became a living being"[c]; the last Adam, a life-giving spirit. 46The spiritual did not come first, but the natural, and after that the spiritual. 47The first man was of the dust of the earth; the second man is of heaven. 48As was the earthly man, so are those who are of the earth; and as is the heavenly man, so also are those who are of heaven. 49And just as we have borne the image of the earthly man, so shall we[d] bear the image of the heavenly man.

50I declare to you, brothers and sisters, that flesh and blood cannot inherit the kingdom of God, nor does the perishable inherit the imperishable. 51Listen, I tell you a mystery: We will not all sleep, but we will all be changed — 52in a flash, in the twinkling of an eye, at the last trumpet. For the trumpet will sound, the dead will be raised imperishable, and we will be changed. 53For the perishable must clothe itself with the imperishable, and the mortal with immortality. 54When the perishable has been clothed with the imperishable, and the mortal with immortality, then the saying that is written will come true: "Death has been swallowed up in victory."[e]

55"Where, O death, is your victory?
 Where, O death, is your sting?"[f]

[a] 32 Isaiah 22:13 [b] 33 From the Greek poet Menander [c] 45 Gen. 2:7
[d] 49 Some early manuscripts *so let us* [e] 54 Isaiah 25:8 [f] 55 Hosea 13:14

PRAYING SCRIPTURE

1 Corinthians 15

These perishable, flesh and blood bodies we inhabit cannot inherit the kingdom of God. But one day the perishable must put on the imperishable, and what is mortal must put on what is immortal. In that moment, we will stand victorious in our Christ and scoff at death, saying, "Where, O death, is your sting?" (verse 55).

Mindful of the inheritance that can never perish, spoil or fade awaiting us (1 Peter 1:4), let us pray as Paul wrote, "Let nothing move you. Always give yourselves fully to the work of the Lord, because you know that your labor in the Lord is not in vain" (verse 58).

56The sting of death is sin, and the power of sin is the law. 57But thanks
be to God! He gives us the victory through our Lord Jesus Christ.
58Therefore, my dear brothers and sisters, stand firm. Let nothing
move you. Always give yourselves fully to the work of the Lord, be-
cause you know that your labor in the Lord is not in vain.

THE COLLECTION FOR THE LORD'S PEOPLE

16 Now about the collection for the Lord's people: Do what I told
the Galatian churches to do. 2On the first day of every week,
each one of you should set aside a sum of money in keeping with your
income, saving it up, so that when I come no collections will have to
be made. 3Then, when I arrive, I will give letters of introduction to the
men you approve and send them with your gift to Jerusalem. 4If it
seems advisable for me to go also, they will accompany me.

PERSONAL REQUESTS

5After I go through Macedonia, I will come to you — for I will be go-
ing through Macedonia. 6Perhaps I will stay with you for a while, or
even spend the winter, so that you can help me on my journey, wher-
ever I go. 7For I do not want to see you now and make only a passing
visit; I hope to spend some time with you, if the Lord permits. 8But I
will stay on at Ephesus until Pentecost, 9because a great door for ef-
fective work has opened to me, and there are many who oppose me.
10When Timothy comes, see to it that he has nothing to fear while
he is with you, for he is carrying on the work of the Lord, just as I am.
11No one, then, should treat him with contempt. Send him on his way
in peace so that he may return to me. I am expecting him along with
the brothers.
12Now about our brother Apollos: I strongly urged him to go to you
with the brothers. He was quite unwilling to go now, but he will go
when he has the opportunity.
13Be on your guard; stand firm in the faith; be courageous; be strong.
14Do everything in love.
15You know that the household of Stephanas were the first converts
in Achaia, and they have devoted themselves to the service of the
Lord's people. I urge you, brothers and sisters, 16to submit to such peo-
ple and to everyone who joins in the work and labors at it. 17I was glad
when Stephanas, Fortunatus and Achaicus arrived, because they have
supplied what was lacking from you. 18For they refreshed my spirit and
yours also. Such men deserve recognition.

FINAL GREETINGS

19The churches in the province of Asia send you greetings. Aquila
and Priscilla[a] greet you warmly in the Lord, and so does the church
that meets at their house. 20All the brothers and sisters here send you
greetings. Greet one another with a holy kiss.
21I, Paul, write this greeting in my own hand.
22If anyone does not love the Lord, let that person be cursed! Come,
Lord[b]!
23The grace of the Lord Jesus be with you.
24My love to all of you in Christ Jesus. Amen.[c]

---

[a] 19 Greek *Prisca,* a variant of *Priscilla* [b] 22 The Greek for *Come, Lord* reproduces an Aramaic expression (*Marana tha*) used by early Christians.
[c] 24 Some manuscripts do not have *Amen.*

PRAYING SCRIPTURE

1 Corinthians 16

In the closing chapter of this letter, Paul commended those who faithfully served in the name of Jesus and implored the Corinthian church to do the same, saying, "Be on your guard; stand firm in the faith; be courageous; be strong" (verse 13). He further told them that love should be the basis of all they do (see verse 14).

This list of qualities—watchfulness, steadfastness, courage, strength and love—is worth asking God to build in us as we serve him.

2 CORINTHIANS

Paul's second letter to the Corinthians is one of three letters to the church in Corinth. His first letter and his third letter are presented in Scripture as 1 and 2 Corinthians. His middle letter, referenced in 2:4, Paul penned with much affliction, an anguished heart and tears.

One major change had taken place in the church in Corinth since Paul's first letter to them: A group who considered themselves apostles rose up in the church, challenging Paul's credentials as an apostle. They pointed to his sufferings as an indictment of his apostleship and seem to have used his appearance and manner of speaking against him. Paul's defense of his ministry and obvious heart for the people in Corinth provide a master class in mature Christian ministry.

In what is perhaps the most well-known passage in the letter, Paul offered immense help for Christians who were walking through suffering. He said that because he had experienced such tremendous revelations as an apostle, God gave him a "thorn in my flesh," which was also a "messenger of Satan," to keep him humble (12:7). Paul's humble endurance of suffering invites us to apply the grace found in 2 Corinthians 12 to all our suffering.

Paul did not specify what this thorn in the flesh was, but he pleaded with God three times to take the thorn away. Instead of removing his pain, though, God told Paul that his grace was sufficient. In one of the paradoxes of the Christian life, we learn that God's strength is made perfect in our weakness. We suffer so that God can be glorified as he strengthens us in our trials and his power is manifest in us and through us.

As with Paul and his thorn, God does not always answer our prayers with the results we want. Often God's answer to our prayers for deliverance is to leave us in the trial. We do not always know what he desires to accomplish in us and through us during the trial. The ultimate aim of any trial is that we would draw closer to him in our weakness, learning to depend fully on his strength.

When God does not answer our prayer immediately or exactly as we prayed, it does not necessarily indicate a deficiency in our prayers or sin in our lives. God is not being cruel, playing games or withholding what we need. Instead, in his goodness, the Father is teaching us how much we need him. Our continued prayers are an acknowledgment of that deep-seated need as well as a request for relief.

As he often did, Paul closed his letter with a prayer that his readers "will not do anything wrong" (13:7). He told them it is better for him to write to them "that when I come I may not have to be harsh" (13:10). Even in correction, Paul desired to be gentle, loving and edifying.

1 Paul, an apostle of Christ Jesus by the will of God, and Timothy our
brother,

To the church of God in Corinth, together with all his holy people
throughout Achaia:

2Grace and peace to you from God our Father and the Lord Jesus
Christ.

PRAISE TO THE GOD OF ALL COMFORT

3Praise be to the God and Father of our Lord Jesus Christ, the Father of
compassion and the God of all comfort, 4who comforts us in all our trou-
bles, so that we can comfort those in any trouble with the comfort we
ourselves receive from God. 5For just as we share abundantly in the suf-
ferings of Christ, so also our comfort abounds through Christ. 6If we are
distressed, it is for your comfort and salvation; if we are comforted, it is
for your comfort, which produces in you patient endurance of the same
sufferings we suffer. 7And our hope for you is firm, because we know
that just as you share in our sufferings, so also you share in our comfort.
8We do not want you to be uninformed, brothers and sisters,[a] about
the troubles we experienced in the province of Asia. We were under
great pressure, far beyond our ability to endure, so that we despaired
of life itself. 9Indeed, we felt we had received the sentence of death.
But this happened that we might not rely on ourselves but on God,
who raises the dead. 10He has delivered us from such a deadly peril,
and he will deliver us again. On him we have set our hope that he will
continue to deliver us, 11as you help us by your prayers. Then many will
give thanks on our behalf for the gracious favor granted us in answer
to the prayers of many.

PAUL'S CHANGE OF PLANS

12Now this is our boast: Our conscience testifies that we have con-
ducted ourselves in the world, and especially in our relations with you,
with integrity[b] and godly sincerity. We have done so, relying not on
worldly wisdom but on God's grace. 13For we do not write you anything
you cannot read or understand. And I hope that, 14as you have under-
stood us in part, you will come to understand fully that you can boast
of us just as we will boast of you in the day of the Lord Jesus.
15Because I was confident of this, I wanted to visit you first so that
you might benefit twice. 16I wanted to visit you on my way to Mace-
donia and to come back to you from Macedonia, and then to have you
send me on my way to Judea. 17Was I fickle when I intended to do this?
Or do I make my plans in a worldly manner so that in the same breath
I say both "Yes, yes" and "No, no"?
18But as surely as God is faithful, our message to you is not "Yes"
and "No." 19For the Son of God, Jesus Christ, who was preached among
you by us — by me and Silas[c] and Timothy — was not "Yes" and "No,"
but in him it has always been "Yes." 20For no matter how many prom-
ises God has made, they are "Yes" in Christ. And so through him the
"Amen" is spoken by us to the glory of God. 21Now it is God who makes
both us and you stand firm in Christ. He anointed us, 22set his seal of

PRAYING SCRIPTURE

2 Corinthians 1

Paul's second letter to the Corinthian church begins with an explanation for suffering. God comforts us when we are in pain so that we might comfort others in their pain. Our pain is not in vain when we view it as a tutor that prepares us to help others.

When you think your suffering is in vain, pray for opportunities to tell others who are suffering about the comfort God provides.

---

[a] 8 The Greek word for *brothers and sisters* (*adelphoi*) refers here to believers, both men and women, as part of God's family; also in 8:1; 13:11. [b] 12 Many manuscripts *holiness* [c] 19 Greek *Silvanus*, a variant of *Silas*

ownership on us, and put his Spirit in our hearts as a deposit, guaran-
teeing what is to come.
23 I call God as my witness — and I stake my life on it — that it was in
order to spare you that I did not return to Corinth. 24 Not that we lord
it over your faith, but we work with you for your joy, because it is by
2 faith you stand firm. 1 So I made up my mind that I would not
make another painful visit to you. 2 For if I grieve you, who is left
to make me glad but you whom I have grieved? 3 I wrote as I did, so
that when I came I would not be distressed by those who should have
made me rejoice. I had confidence in all of you, that you would all
share my joy. 4 For I wrote you out of great distress and anguish of heart
and with many tears, not to grieve you but to let you know the depth
of my love for you.

FORGIVENESS FOR THE OFFENDER

5 If anyone has caused grief, he has not so much grieved me as he
has grieved all of you to some extent — not to put it too severely. 6 The
punishment inflicted on him by the majority is sufficient. 7 Now in-
stead, you ought to forgive and comfort him, so that he will not be
overwhelmed by excessive sorrow. 8 I urge you, therefore, to reaffirm
your love for him. 9 Another reason I wrote you was to see if you would
stand the test and be obedient in everything. 10 Anyone you forgive, I
also forgive. And what I have forgiven — if there was anything to for-
give — I have forgiven in the sight of Christ for your sake, 11 in order
that Satan might not outwit us. For we are not unaware of his schemes.

MINISTERS OF THE NEW COVENANT

12 Now when I went to Troas to preach the gospel of Christ and found
that the Lord had opened a door for me, 13 I still had no peace of mind,
because I did not find my brother Titus there. So I said goodbye to
them and went on to Macedonia.
14 But thanks be to God, who always leads us as captives in Christ's tri-
umphal procession and uses us to spread the aroma of the knowledge
of him everywhere. 15 For we are to God the pleasing aroma of Christ
among those who are being saved and those who are perishing. 16 To
the one we are an aroma that brings death; to the other, an aroma that
brings life. And who is equal to such a task? 17 Unlike so many, we do not
peddle the word of God for profit. On the contrary, in Christ we speak
before God with sincerity, as those sent from God.
3 Are we beginning to commend ourselves again? Or do we need,
like some people, letters of recommendation to you or from you?
2 You yourselves are our letter, written on our hearts, known and read
by everyone. 3 You show that you are a letter from Christ, the result of
our ministry, written not with ink but with the Spirit of the living God,
not on tablets of stone but on tablets of human hearts.
4 Such confidence we have through Christ before God. 5 Not that we
are competent in ourselves to claim anything for ourselves, but our
competence comes from God. 6 He has made us competent as ministers
of a new covenant — not of the letter but of the Spirit; for the letter
kills, but the Spirit gives life.

THE GREATER GLORY OF THE NEW COVENANT

7 Now if the ministry that brought death, which was engraved in let-
ters on stone, came with glory, so that the Israelites could not look

PRAYING SCRIPTURE

2 Corinthians 2

When we share the gospel, some people will receive it as the best news they have ever heard. Others, however, will think it carries the stench of death. It is the same gospel and the same messenger. The condition of the hearer's heart is the deciding factor.

Who, then, is sufficient? In Christ, we are. Call on him for the faith you need to share the gospel with boldness.

PRAYING SCRIPTURE

2 Corinthians 3

It might be hard to comprehend how blessed we are to live in the New Testament era, but verses 7–18 paint an amazing picture. Every Christian is being changed into the image of Christ little by little. The glory we experience in Jesus far exceeds the glory of Moses (the law).

Read through verses 7–18 and list ways the Spirit's ministry is more glorious than the law (see verse 8), and praise God for these ways.

steadily at the face of Moses because of its glory, transitory though it
was, 8will not the ministry of the Spirit be even more glorious? 9If the
ministry that brought condemnation was glorious, how much more
glorious is the ministry that brings righteousness! 10For what was glo-
rious has no glory now in comparison with the surpassing glory. 11And
if what was transitory came with glory, how much greater is the glory
of that which lasts!

12Therefore, since we have such a hope, we are very bold. 13We are not
like Moses, who would put a veil over his face to prevent the Israelites
from seeing the end of what was passing away. 14But their minds were
made dull, for to this day the same veil remains when the old covenant
is read. It has not been removed, because only in Christ is it taken
away. 15Even to this day when Moses is read, a veil covers their hearts.
16But whenever anyone turns to the Lord, the veil is taken away. 17Now
the Lord is the Spirit, and where the Spirit of the Lord is, there is free-
dom. 18And we all, who with unveiled faces contemplate[a] the Lord's
glory, are being transformed into his image with ever-increasing glory,
which comes from the Lord, who is the Spirit.

PRESENT WEAKNESS AND RESURRECTION LIFE

4 Therefore, since through God's mercy we have this ministry, we do
not lose heart. 2Rather, we have renounced secret and shameful
ways; we do not use deception, nor do we distort the word of God. On
the contrary, by setting forth the truth plainly we commend ourselves
to everyone's conscience in the sight of God. 3And even if our gospel is
veiled, it is veiled to those who are perishing. 4The god of this age has
blinded the minds of unbelievers, so that they cannot see the light of
the gospel that displays the glory of Christ, who is the image of God.
5For what we preach is not ourselves, but Jesus Christ as Lord, and our-
selves as your servants for Jesus' sake. 6For God, who said, "Let light
shine out of darkness,"[b] made his light shine in our hearts to give us
the light of the knowledge of God's glory displayed in the face of Christ.

7But we have this treasure in jars of clay to show that this all-
surpassing power is from God and not from us. 8We are hard pressed on
every side, but not crushed; perplexed, but not in despair; 9persecuted,
but not abandoned; struck down, but not destroyed. 10We always carry
around in our body the death of Jesus, so that the life of Jesus may also
be revealed in our body. 11For we who are alive are always being given
over to death for Jesus' sake, so that his life may also be revealed in our
mortal body. 12So then, death is at work in us, but life is at work in you.

13It is written: "I believed; therefore I have spoken."[c] Since we have
that same spirit of[d] faith, we also believe and therefore speak, 14be-
cause we know that the one who raised the Lord Jesus from the dead
will also raise us with Jesus and present us with you to himself. 15All
this is for your benefit, so that the grace that is reaching more and
more people may cause thanksgiving to overflow to the glory of God.

16Therefore we do not lose heart. Though outwardly we are wasting
away, yet inwardly we are being renewed day by day. 17For our light and
momentary troubles are achieving for us an eternal glory that far out-
weighs them all. 18So we fix our eyes not on what is seen, but on what is
unseen, since what is seen is temporary, but what is unseen is eternal.

PRAYING SCRIPTURE

2 Corinthians 4

Scripture often encourages Christians through difficult times by reminding them of the eternal glory that awaits them. This entails walking by faith that God is working in us to his glory even when we do not see it. Let us look to "what is unseen" (verse 18).

Ask God to help get your attention off what is seen and, by faith, claim the invisible, eternal work of glory.

---

[a] 18 Or *reflect* [b] 6 Gen. 1:3 [c] 13 Psalm 116:10 (see Septuagint) [d] 13 Or *Spirit-given*

PRAYING SCRIPTURE

2 Corinthians 5

The bad news is that the sin of Adam passed on to all people, resulting in separation from God. The good news is that we can be reconciled to God through Jesus. Even more, those who are reconciled become ambassadors of reconciliation, taking the gospel of Jesus to the world (see verse 20).

Are you an effective ambassador? Pray for effectiveness and for opportunities to take the Good News to those who have not heard.

AWAITING THE NEW BODY

5 For we know that if the earthly tent we live in is destroyed, we have
a building from God, an eternal house in heaven, not built by hu-
man hands. 2Meanwhile we groan, longing to be clothed instead with
our heavenly dwelling, 3because when we are clothed, we will not be
found naked. 4For while we are in this tent, we groan and are burdened,
because we do not wish to be unclothed but to be clothed instead with
our heavenly dwelling, so that what is mortal may be swallowed up by
life. 5Now the one who has fashioned us for this very purpose is God,
who has given us the Spirit as a deposit, guaranteeing what is to come.
6Therefore we are always confident and know that as long as we are
at home in the body we are away from the Lord. 7For we live by faith,
not by sight. 8We are confident, I say, and would prefer to be away
from the body and at home with the Lord. 9So we make it our goal to
please him, whether we are at home in the body or away from it. 10For
we must all appear before the judgment seat of Christ, so that each of
us may receive what is due us for the things done while in the body,
whether good or bad.

THE MINISTRY OF RECONCILIATION

11Since, then, we know what it is to fear the Lord, we try to persuade
others. What we are is plain to God, and I hope it is also plain to your
conscience. 12We are not trying to commend ourselves to you again,
but are giving you an opportunity to take pride in us, so that you can
answer those who take pride in what is seen rather than in what is
in the heart. 13If we are "out of our mind," as some say, it is for God;
if we are in our right mind, it is for you. 14For Christ's love compels
us, because we are convinced that one died for all, and therefore all
died. 15And he died for all, that those who live should no longer live
for themselves but for him who died for them and was raised again.
16So from now on we regard no one from a worldly point of view.
Though we once regarded Christ in this way, we do so no longer.
17Therefore, if anyone is in Christ, the new creation has come:[a] The
old has gone, the new is here! 18All this is from God, who reconciled us
to himself through Christ and gave us the ministry of reconciliation:
19that God was reconciling the world to himself in Christ, not counting
people's sins against them. And he has committed to us the message of
reconciliation. 20We are therefore Christ's ambassadors, as though God
were making his appeal through us. We implore you on Christ's behalf:
Be reconciled to God. 21God made him who had no sin to be sin[b] for us,
so that in him we might become the righteousness of God.

6 As God's co-workers we urge you not to receive God's grace in vain.
2For he says,

"In the time of my favor I heard you,
and in the day of salvation I helped you."[c]

I tell you, now is the time of God's favor, now is the day of salvation.

PAUL'S HARDSHIPS

3We put no stumbling block in anyone's path, so that our minis-
try will not be discredited. 4Rather, as servants of God we commend

PRAYING SCRIPTURE

2 Corinthians 6

Paul expected that the lives of believers would stand in stark contrast to the unbelieving world around them. He explained that those who know Christ should not be in unequal relationships with unbelievers. Those who are holy (set apart for God) should guard themselves and not allow those who are of the world to persuade them to unrighteousness.

Seek sincere fellowship with children of God so that you may encourage one another to stay steadfast in the faith.

---

[a] 17 Or *Christ, that person is a new creation.* [b] 21 Or *be a sin offering*
[c] 2 Isaiah 49:8

ourselves in every way: in great endurance; in troubles, hardships
and distresses; 5in beatings, imprisonments and riots; in hard work,
sleepless nights and hunger; 6in purity, understanding, patience and
kindness; in the Holy Spirit and in sincere love; 7in truthful speech
and in the power of God; with weapons of righteousness in the right
hand and in the left; 8through glory and dishonor, bad report and good
report; genuine, yet regarded as impostors; 9known, yet regarded as
unknown; dying, and yet we live on; beaten, and yet not killed; 10sor-
rowful, yet always rejoicing; poor, yet making many rich; having noth-
ing, and yet possessing everything.
11We have spoken freely to you, Corinthians, and opened wide our
hearts to you. 12We are not withholding our affection from you, but you
are withholding yours from us. 13As a fair exchange — I speak as to my
children — open wide your hearts also.

WARNING AGAINST IDOLATRY

14Do not be yoked together with unbelievers. For what do righteous-
ness and wickedness have in common? Or what fellowship can light
have with darkness? 15What harmony is there between Christ and Be-
lial[a]? Or what does a believer have in common with an unbeliever?
16What agreement is there between the temple of God and idols? For
we are the temple of the living God. As God has said:

"I will live with them
 and walk among them,
and I will be their God,
 and they will be my people."[b]

17Therefore,

"Come out from them
 and be separate,
 says the Lord.
Touch no unclean thing,
 and I will receive you."[c]

18And,

"I will be a Father to you,
 and you will be my sons and daughters,
 says the Lord Almighty."[d]

7 Therefore, since we have these promises, dear friends, let us purify
ourselves from everything that contaminates body and spirit, per-
fecting holiness out of reverence for God.

PAUL'S JOY OVER THE CHURCH'S REPENTANCE

2Make room for us in your hearts. We have wronged no one, we have
corrupted no one, we have exploited no one. 3I do not say this to con-
demn you; I have said before that you have such a place in our hearts
that we would live or die with you. 4I have spoken to you with great
frankness; I take great pride in you. I am greatly encouraged; in all our
troubles my joy knows no bounds.
5For when we came into Macedonia, we had no rest, but we were

[a] *15* Greek *Beliar*, a variant of *Belial* [b] *16* Lev. 26:12; Jer. 32:38; Ezek. 37:27
[c] *17* Isaiah 52:11; Ezek. 20:34,41 [d] *18* 2 Samuel 7:14; 7:8

PRAYING SCRIPTURE

2 Corinthians 7

Godly sorrow leads us to genuine repentance from our sins. Much of the time we consider neither the cost nor the payment of sin, so we tend not to give it proper attention. When we properly sorrow over our sin, we will be led to genuine repentance.

Are you tempted to gloss over your sin, neglecting its seriousness? Ask God to lead you to be sorry (see verse 8) and to give you an awareness of sin so you can genuinely repent.

harassed at every turn — conflicts on the outside, fears within. 6But God, who comforts the downcast, comforted us by the coming of Titus, 7and not only by his coming but also by the comfort you had given him. He told us about your longing for me, your deep sorrow, your ardent concern for me, so that my joy was greater than ever.

8Even if I caused you sorrow by my letter, I do not regret it. Though I did regret it — I see that my letter hurt you, but only for a little while — 9yet now I am happy, not because you were made sorry, but because your sorrow led you to repentance. For you became sorrowful as God intended and so were not harmed in any way by us. 10Godly sorrow brings repentance that leads to salvation and leaves no regret, but worldly sorrow brings death. 11See what this godly sorrow has produced in you: what earnestness, what eagerness to clear yourselves, what indignation, what alarm, what longing, what concern, what readiness to see justice done. At every point you have proved yourselves to be innocent in this matter. 12So even though I wrote to you, it was neither on account of the one who did the wrong nor on account of the injured party, but rather that before God you could see for yourselves how devoted to us you are. 13By all this we are encouraged.

In addition to our own encouragement, we were especially delighted to see how happy Titus was, because his spirit has been refreshed by all of you. 14I had boasted to him about you, and you have not embarrassed me. But just as everything we said to you was true, so our boasting about you to Titus has proved to be true as well. 15And his affection for you is all the greater when he remembers that you were all obedient, receiving him with fear and trembling. 16I am glad I can have complete confidence in you.

THE COLLECTION FOR THE LORD'S PEOPLE

8 And now, brothers and sisters, we want you to know about the grace that God has given the Macedonian churches. 2In the midst of a very severe trial, their overflowing joy and their extreme poverty welled up in rich generosity. 3For I testify that they gave as much as they were able, and even beyond their ability. Entirely on their own, 4they urgently pleaded with us for the privilege of sharing in this service to the Lord's people. 5And they exceeded our expectations: They gave themselves first of all to the Lord, and then by the will of God also to us. 6So we urged Titus, just as he had earlier made a beginning, to bring also to completion this act of grace on your part. 7But since you excel in everything — in faith, in speech, in knowledge, in complete earnestness and in the love we have kindled in you[a] — see that you also excel in this grace of giving.

8I am not commanding you, but I want to test the sincerity of your love by comparing it with the earnestness of others. 9For you know the grace of our Lord Jesus Christ, that though he was rich, yet for your sake he became poor, so that you through his poverty might become rich.

10And here is my judgment about what is best for you in this matter. Last year you were the first not only to give but also to have the desire to do so. 11Now finish the work, so that your eager willingness to do it may be matched by your completion of it, according to your means. 12For if the willingness is there, the gift is acceptable according to what one has, not according to what one does not have.

PRAYING SCRIPTURE

2 Corinthians 8

Christians are motivated to give because we have joyfully received the gift of Jesus. Generosity is not something we "work up" out of emotional appeals. It is a loving response to the blessing God has given us. If our heavenly Father gave his Son, Jesus, for us, how can we not give to others?

How often do you think about being generous? Ask God to open your eyes and your heart for opportunities to demonstrate his goodness.

[a] 7 Some manuscripts *and in your love for us*

13Our desire is not that others might be relieved while you are hard
pressed, but that there might be equality. 14At the present time your
plenty will supply what they need, so that in turn their plenty will sup-
ply what you need. The goal is equality, 15as it is written: "The one who
gathered much did not have too much, and the one who gathered little
did not have too little."[a]

TITUS SENT TO RECEIVE THE COLLECTION

16Thanks be to God, who put into the heart of Titus the same con-
cern I have for you. 17For Titus not only welcomed our appeal, but he is
coming to you with much enthusiasm and on his own initiative. 18And
we are sending along with him the brother who is praised by all the
churches for his service to the gospel. 19What is more, he was chosen
by the churches to accompany us as we carry the offering, which we ad-
minister in order to honor the Lord himself and to show our eagerness
to help. 20We want to avoid any criticism of the way we administer this
liberal gift. 21For we are taking pains to do what is right, not only in the
eyes of the Lord but also in the eyes of man.

22In addition, we are sending with them our brother who has often
proved to us in many ways that he is zealous, and now even more so
because of his great confidence in you. 23As for Titus, he is my partner
and co-worker among you; as for our brothers, they are representatives
of the churches and an honor to Christ. 24Therefore show these men
the proof of your love and the reason for our pride in you, so that the
churches can see it.

9 There is no need for me to write to you about this service to the
Lord's people. 2For I know your eagerness to help, and I have been
boasting about it to the Macedonians, telling them that since last year
you in Achaia were ready to give; and your enthusiasm has stirred
most of them to action. 3But I am sending the brothers in order that
our boasting about you in this matter should not prove hollow, but
that you may be ready, as I said you would be. 4For if any Macedo-
nians come with me and find you unprepared, we — not to say any-
thing about you — would be ashamed of having been so confident. 5So
I thought it necessary to urge the brothers to visit you in advance and
finish the arrangements for the generous gift you had promised. Then
it will be ready as a generous gift, not as one grudgingly given.

GENEROSITY ENCOURAGED

6Remember this: Whoever sows sparingly will also reap sparingly,
and whoever sows generously will also reap generously. 7Each of you
should give what you have decided in your heart to give, not reluc-
tantly or under compulsion, for God loves a cheerful giver. 8And God is
able to bless you abundantly, so that in all things at all times, having
all that you need, you will abound in every good work. 9As it is written:

"They have freely scattered their gifts to the poor;
their righteousness endures forever."[b]

10Now he who supplies seed to the sower and bread for food will also
supply and increase your store of seed and will enlarge the harvest of
your righteousness. 11You will be enriched in every way so that you can
be generous on every occasion, and through us your generosity will
result in thanksgiving to God.

[a] 15 Exodus 16:18 [b] 9 Psalm 112:9

PRAYING SCRIPTURE

2 Corinthians 9

Paul continued the theme of generosity, expanding its blessings. Using a seed/fruit metaphor, he said that sowing generously will "enlarge the harvest of your righteousness" (verse 10).

While the Scriptures do not teach "give to get rich," they do clearly teach that God honors generous giving. Ask God to help you understand your income and giving as his blessing, sowing and fruit. Give intentionally, and watch him multiply what you give.

12This service that you perform is not only supplying the needs
of the Lord's people but is also overflowing in many expressions of
thanks to God. 13Because of the service by which you have proved your-
selves, others will praise God for the obedience that accompanies your
confession of the gospel of Christ, and for your generosity in sharing
with them and with everyone else. 14And in their prayers for you their
hearts will go out to you, because of the surpassing grace God has given
you. 15Thanks be to God for his indescribable gift!

PAUL'S DEFENSE OF HIS MINISTRY

10 By the humility and gentleness of Christ, I appeal to you—I,
Paul, who am "timid" when face to face with you, but "bold"
toward you when away! 2I beg you that when I come I may not have to
be as bold as I expect to be toward some people who think that we live
by the standards of this world. 3For though we live in the world, we do
not wage war as the world does. 4The weapons we fight with are not
the weapons of the world. On the contrary, they have divine power to
demolish strongholds. 5We demolish arguments and every pretension
that sets itself up against the knowledge of God, and we take captive
every thought to make it obedient to Christ. 6And we will be ready to
punish every act of disobedience, once your obedience is complete.
7You are judging by appearances.[a] If anyone is confident that they
belong to Christ, they should consider again that we belong to Christ
just as much as they do. 8So even if I boast somewhat freely about
the authority the Lord gave us for building you up rather than tearing
you down, I will not be ashamed of it. 9I do not want to seem to be
trying to frighten you with my letters. 10For some say, "His letters are
weighty and forceful, but in person he is unimpressive and his speak-
ing amounts to nothing." 11Such people should realize that what we
are in our letters when we are absent, we will be in our actions when
we are present.
12We do not dare to classify or compare ourselves with some who
commend themselves. When they measure themselves by them-
selves and compare themselves with themselves, they are not wise.
13We, however, will not boast beyond proper limits, but will confine
our boasting to the sphere of service God himself has assigned to us, a
sphere that also includes you. 14We are not going too far in our boast-
ing, as would be the case if we had not come to you, for we did get as far
as you with the gospel of Christ. 15Neither do we go beyond our limits
by boasting of work done by others. Our hope is that, as your faith con-
tinues to grow, our sphere of activity among you will greatly expand,
16so that we can preach the gospel in the regions beyond you. For we
do not want to boast about work already done in someone else's ter-
ritory. 17But, "Let the one who boasts boast in the Lord."[b] 18For it is not
the one who commends himself who is approved, but the one whom
the Lord commends.

PAUL AND THE FALSE APOSTLES

11 I hope you will put up with me in a little foolishness. Yes, please
put up with me! 2I am jealous for you with a godly jealousy. I
promised you to one husband, to Christ, so that I might present you as
a pure virgin to him. 3But I am afraid that just as Eve was deceived by

[a] 7 Or *Look at the obvious facts* [b] 17 Jer. 9:24

PRAYING SCRIPTURE

2 Corinthians 10

Winning the spiritual war is a daily moment-by-moment, thought-by-thought effort. We must cast down any philosophy that goes against what Scripture teaches us about God. Any sinful thought we have must be taken "captive" so it cannot lead us away from God (see verse 5).

Is your thought life under God's control? If so, thank him for the victory. If not, pray to bring every thought into the obedience of Jesus Christ.

PRAYING SCRIPTURE

2 Corinthians 11

Paul's catalog of sufferings was not written to draw attention to himself but to demonstrate his credentials in the gospel. No one who claimed superiority over him had as much standing in ministry or suffering for it.

This passage should draw attention to our brothers and sisters around the world suffering for their faith. Make interceding for the persecuted church part of your regular prayer time.

the serpent's cunning, your minds may somehow be led astray from your sincere and pure devotion to Christ. 4For if someone comes to you and preaches a Jesus other than the Jesus we preached, or if you receive a different spirit from the Spirit you received, or a different gospel from the one you accepted, you put up with it easily enough.

5I do not think I am in the least inferior to those "super-apostles."[a] 6I may indeed be untrained as a speaker, but I do have knowledge. We have made this perfectly clear to you in every way. 7Was it a sin for me to lower myself in order to elevate you by preaching the gospel of God to you free of charge? 8I robbed other churches by receiving support from them so as to serve you. 9And when I was with you and needed something, I was not a burden to anyone, for the brothers who came from Macedonia supplied what I needed. I have kept myself from being a burden to you in any way, and will continue to do so. 10As surely as the truth of Christ is in me, nobody in the regions of Achaia will stop this boasting of mine. 11Why? Because I do not love you? God knows I do!

12And I will keep on doing what I am doing in order to cut the ground from under those who want an opportunity to be considered equal with us in the things they boast about. 13For such people are false apostles, deceitful workers, masquerading as apostles of Christ. 14And no wonder, for Satan himself masquerades as an angel of light. 15It is not surprising, then, if his servants also masquerade as servants of righteousness. Their end will be what their actions deserve.

PAUL BOASTS ABOUT HIS SUFFERINGS

16I repeat: Let no one take me for a fool. But if you do, then tolerate me just as you would a fool, so that I may do a little boasting. 17In this self-confident boasting I am not talking as the Lord would, but as a fool. 18Since many are boasting in the way the world does, I too will boast. 19You gladly put up with fools since you are so wise! 20In fact, you even put up with anyone who enslaves you or exploits you or takes advantage of you or puts on airs or slaps you in the face. 21To my shame I admit that we were too weak for that!

Whatever anyone else dares to boast about — I am speaking as a fool — I also dare to boast about. 22Are they Hebrews? So am I. Are they Israelites? So am I. Are they Abraham's descendants? So am I. 23Are they servants of Christ? (I am out of my mind to talk like this.) I am more. I have worked much harder, been in prison more frequently, been flogged more severely, and been exposed to death again and again. 24Five times I received from the Jews the forty lashes minus one. 25Three times I was beaten with rods, once I was pelted with stones, three times I was shipwrecked, I spent a night and a day in the open sea, 26I have been constantly on the move. I have been in danger from rivers, in danger from bandits, in danger from my fellow Jews, in danger from Gentiles; in danger in the city, in danger in the country, in danger at sea; and in danger from false believers. 27I have labored and toiled and have often gone without sleep; I have known hunger and thirst and have often gone without food; I have been cold and naked. 28Besides everything else, I face daily the pressure of my concern for all the churches. 29Who is weak, and I do not feel weak? Who is led into sin, and I do not inwardly burn?

[a] 5 Or *to the most eminent apostles*

30If I must boast, I will boast of the things that show my weakness. 31The God and Father of the Lord Jesus, who is to be praised forever, knows that I am not lying. 32In Damascus the governor under King Aretas had the city of the Damascenes guarded in order to arrest me. 33But I was lowered in a basket from a window in the wall and slipped through his hands.

PAUL'S VISION AND HIS THORN

12 I must go on boasting. Although there is nothing to be gained, I will go on to visions and revelations from the Lord. 2I know a man in Christ who fourteen years ago was caught up to the third heaven. Whether it was in the body or out of the body I do not know — God knows. 3And I know that this man — whether in the body or apart from the body I do not know, but God knows — 4was caught up to paradise and heard inexpressible things, things that no one is permitted to tell. 5I will boast about a man like that, but I will not boast about myself, except about my weaknesses. 6Even if I should choose to boast, I would not be a fool, because I would be speaking the truth. But I refrain, so no one will think more of me than is warranted by what I do or say, 7or because of these surpassingly great revelations. Therefore, in order to keep me from becoming conceited, I was given a thorn in my flesh, a messenger of Satan, to torment me. 8Three times I pleaded with the Lord to take it away from me. 9But he said to me, "My grace is sufficient for you, for my power is made perfect in weakness." Therefore I will boast all the more gladly about my weaknesses, so that Christ's power may rest on me. 10That is why, for Christ's sake, I delight in weaknesses, in insults, in hardships, in persecutions, in difficulties. For when I am weak, then I am strong.

PAUL'S CONCERN FOR THE CORINTHIANS

11I have made a fool of myself, but you drove me to it. I ought to have been commended by you, for I am not in the least inferior to the "super-apostles,"[a] even though I am nothing. 12I persevered in demonstrating among you the marks of a true apostle, including signs, wonders and miracles. 13How were you inferior to the other churches, except that I was never a burden to you? Forgive me this wrong!

14Now I am ready to visit you for the third time, and I will not be a burden to you, because what I want is not your possessions but you. After all, children should not have to save up for their parents, but parents for their children. 15So I will very gladly spend for you everything I have and expend myself as well. If I love you more, will you love me less? 16Be that as it may, I have not been a burden to you. Yet, crafty fellow that I am, I caught you by trickery! 17Did I exploit you through any of the men I sent to you? 18I urged Titus to go to you and I sent our brother with him. Titus did not exploit you, did he? Did we not walk in the same footsteps by the same Spirit?

19Have you been thinking all along that we have been defending ourselves to you? We have been speaking in the sight of God as those in Christ; and everything we do, dear friends, is for your strengthening. 20For I am afraid that when I come I may not find you as I want you to be, and you may not find me as you want me to be. I fear that there may be discord, jealousy, fits of rage, selfish ambition, slander, gossip,

PRAYING SCRIPTURE

2 Corinthians 12

The apostle Paul had some kind of issue he called "a thorn in my flesh." We are not told whether it was an actual ailment or a problematic person. We are told it was a "messenger of Satan" to keep Paul from becoming proud (verse 7).

Whenever you are afflicted, ask if it is for a reason. Rejoice in it even if it is not pleasant, that God might be glorified.

---

[a] 11 Or *the most eminent apostles*

arrogance and disorder. [21]I am afraid that when I come again my God
will humble me before you, and I will be grieved over many who have
sinned earlier and have not repented of the impurity, sexual sin and
debauchery in which they have indulged.

FINAL WARNINGS

13 This will be my third visit to you. "Every matter must be estab-
lished by the testimony of two or three witnesses."[a] [2]I already
gave you a warning when I was with you the second time. I now repeat
it while absent: On my return I will not spare those who sinned ear-
lier or any of the others, [3]since you are demanding proof that Christ is
speaking through me. He is not weak in dealing with you, but is pow-
erful among you. [4]For to be sure, he was crucified in weakness, yet he
lives by God's power. Likewise, we are weak in him, yet by God's power
we will live with him in our dealing with you.
[5]Examine yourselves to see whether you are in the faith; test your-
selves. Do you not realize that Christ Jesus is in you — unless, of course,
you fail the test? [6]And I trust that you will discover that we have not
failed the test. [7]Now we pray to God that you will not do anything
wrong — not so that people will see that we have stood the test but so
that you will do what is right even though we may seem to have failed.
[8]For we cannot do anything against the truth, but only for the truth.
[9]We are glad whenever we are weak but you are strong; and our prayer
is that you may be fully restored. [10]This is why I write these things
when I am absent, that when I come I may not have to be harsh in my
use of authority — the authority the Lord gave me for building you up,
not for tearing you down.

FINAL GREETINGS

[11]Finally, brothers and sisters, rejoice! Strive for full restoration, en-
courage one another, be of one mind, live in peace. And the God of love
and peace will be with you.
[12]Greet one another with a holy kiss. [13]All God's people here send
their greetings.
[14]May the grace of the Lord Jesus Christ, and the love of God, and the
fellowship of the Holy Spirit be with you all.

PRAYING SCRIPTURE

2 Corinthians 13

Paul urged all his readers to exercise thoughtful introspection concerning their spiritual condition: "Examine yourselves to see whether you are in the faith" (verse 5). And he wrote this to believers! All believers should test themselves for union with Christ lest they be disqualified.

Our relationship with Jesus should never be taken for granted. Regularly ask God to examine your heart and motives so that your love through faith in him may be complete.

[a] 1 Deut. 19:15

GALATIANS

Paul's letter to the church in Galatia does not begin with his customary prayer of thanksgiving. Instead, Paul launched into a discourse expressing astonishment that the church had already abandoned the gospel of God's grace, substituting self-righteousness for it. Rather than advancing in the Spirit, they had returned to trying to please God by keeping the Law of Moses. Paul was as clear as possible that the gospel of Jesus—the gospel he had preached to them—is the one true gospel. They should not hear any other gospel and, in fact, should consider any messenger who brings a different gospel accursed by God.

The rest of Galatians is a defense of the gospel: People are saved by the grace of God alone through faith in Jesus Christ alone. Paul warned the Galatians against falling back on works because "if righteousness could be gained through the law, Christ died for nothing" (2:21). He called the Galatians "foolish" and "bewitched" for allowing themselves to be deceived into this lie (3:1), reminding them of the curse and foolishness of trying to keep the law (see 3:10–11). And referencing Abraham, he confirmed that Abraham was saved by faith, not by the Law of Moses that came 430 years later (see 3:17).

After explaining the purpose of the law to the Galatians, Paul began chapter 4 with a discussion of the spiritual state of every Christian. He said that the one whose faith is in Christ is "no longer a slave, but God's child" (verse 7). In an era during which slaves were not considered family, Paul's use of sonship language would have greatly affected the readers. God's redemption and adoption were wrought by Jesus, born of a virgin in the fullness of time, who gave his life for us. Therefore, every person who trusts in Jesus is a child of God. Since we are the children of God, we have become joint heirs with the Lord Jesus. He will reign forever with the Father, and we will reign with him.

The truth of adoption is important for our prayer lives because it reminds us of the access that we have to the Father through the Lord Jesus. Just as children do not need to make an appointment to ask their earthly father for a glass of water, so the Christian now needs no special permission to enter the presence of God. Our sonship gives us immediate access to God the Father. He beckons us to enter his presence and make our requests known to him. The Holy Spirit reminds us of our adoption as God's children and helps us pray when we enter his presence.

Paul closed the letter with an appeal that sets us free from works: the cross of Jesus. The cross is our only source of boasting. It is where the world is crucified to us and where we are crucified to the world, and where all that matters is being a new creation in Jesus.

1 Paul, an apostle — sent not from men nor by a man, but by Jesus
Christ and God the Father, who raised him from the dead — 2and
all the brothers and sisters[a] with me,

To the churches in Galatia:

3Grace and peace to you from God our Father and the Lord Jesus
Christ, 4who gave himself for our sins to rescue us from the present
evil age, according to the will of our God and Father, 5to whom be glory
for ever and ever. Amen.

NO OTHER GOSPEL

6I am astonished that you are so quickly deserting the one who called
you to live in the grace of Christ and are turning to a different gospel —
7which is really no gospel at all. Evidently some people are throwing
you into confusion and are trying to pervert the gospel of Christ. 8But
even if we or an angel from heaven should preach a gospel other than
the one we preached to you, let them be under God's curse! 9As we have
already said, so now I say again: If anybody is preaching to you a gospel
other than what you accepted, let them be under God's curse!

10Am I now trying to win the approval of human beings, or of God?
Or am I trying to please people? If I were still trying to please people,
I would not be a servant of Christ.

PAUL CALLED BY GOD

11I want you to know, brothers and sisters, that the gospel I preached
is not of human origin. 12I did not receive it from any man, nor was I
taught it; rather, I received it by revelation from Jesus Christ.

13For you have heard of my previous way of life in Judaism, how in-
tensely I persecuted the church of God and tried to destroy it. 14I was
advancing in Judaism beyond many of my own age among my people
and was extremely zealous for the traditions of my fathers. 15But when
God, who set me apart from my mother's womb and called me by his
grace, was pleased 16to reveal his Son in me so that I might preach him
among the Gentiles, my immediate response was not to consult any hu-
man being. 17I did not go up to Jerusalem to see those who were apos-
tles before I was, but I went into Arabia. Later I returned to Damascus.

18Then after three years, I went up to Jerusalem to get acquainted
with Cephas[b] and stayed with him fifteen days. 19I saw none of the
other apostles — only James, the Lord's brother. 20I assure you before
God that what I am writing you is no lie.

21Then I went to Syria and Cilicia. 22I was personally unknown to the
churches of Judea that are in Christ. 23They only heard the report: "The
man who formerly persecuted us is now preaching the faith he once
tried to destroy." 24And they praised God because of me.

PAUL ACCEPTED BY THE APOSTLES

2 Then after fourteen years, I went up again to Jerusalem, this time
with Barnabas. I took Titus along also. 2I went in response to a rev-
elation and, meeting privately with those esteemed as leaders, I pre-
sented to them the gospel that I preach among the Gentiles. I wanted

PRAYING SCRIPTURE

Galatians 1

For Paul, the gospel of Jesus Christ was the one absolute nonnegotiable of life and ministry. He was so convinced of the gospel that he warned against even an angel bringing another gospel other than the one he preached: the gospel of Jesus.

Do you have that much confidence in the gospel? If not, ask God to bring you the assurance you need.

PRAYING SCRIPTURE

Galatians 2

One of the deepest verses in Scripture, reminds us of a simple but profound truth: Jesus Christ lives in those who believe. "I have been crucified with Christ and I no longer live, but Christ lives in me" (verse 20). This life of Christ is lived by faith in Christ. Everything is of Jesus!

Pause and praise God for the new life he gives in Jesus.

[a] *2* The Greek word for *brothers and sisters* (*adelphoi*) refers here to believers, both men and women, as part of God's family; also in verse 11; and in 3:15; 4:12,28,31; 5:11,13; 6:1,18. [b] *18* That is, Peter

to be sure I was not running and had not been running my race in vain.
3Yet not even Titus, who was with me, was compelled to be circum-
cised, even though he was a Greek. 4This matter arose because some
false believers had infiltrated our ranks to spy on the freedom we have
in Christ Jesus and to make us slaves. 5We did not give in to them for
a moment, so that the truth of the gospel might be preserved for you.
6As for those who were held in high esteem — whatever they were
makes no difference to me; God does not show favoritism — they
added nothing to my message. 7On the contrary, they recognized that
I had been entrusted with the task of preaching the gospel to the un-
circumcised,[a] just as Peter had been to the circumcised.[b] 8For God, who
was at work in Peter as an apostle to the circumcised, was also at work
in me as an apostle to the Gentiles. 9James, Cephas[c] and John, those
esteemed as pillars, gave me and Barnabas the right hand of fellow-
ship when they recognized the grace given to me. They agreed that we
should go to the Gentiles, and they to the circumcised. 10All they asked
was that we should continue to remember the poor, the very thing I
had been eager to do all along.

PAUL OPPOSES CEPHAS

11When Cephas came to Antioch, I opposed him to his face, because he
stood condemned. 12For before certain men came from James, he used
to eat with the Gentiles. But when they arrived, he began to draw back
and separate himself from the Gentiles because he was afraid of those
who belonged to the circumcision group. 13The other Jews joined him
in his hypocrisy, so that by their hypocrisy even Barnabas was led astray.
14When I saw that they were not acting in line with the truth of the
gospel, I said to Cephas in front of them all, "You are a Jew, yet you live
like a Gentile and not like a Jew. How is it, then, that you force Gentiles
to follow Jewish customs?
15"We who are Jews by birth and not sinful Gentiles 16know that a
person is not justified by the works of the law, but by faith in Jesus
Christ. So we, too, have put our faith in Christ Jesus that we may be
justified by faith in[d] Christ and not by the works of the law, because by
the works of the law no one will be justified.
17"But if, in seeking to be justified in Christ, we Jews find ourselves
also among the sinners, doesn't that mean that Christ promotes sin?
Absolutely not! 18If I rebuild what I destroyed, then I really would be
a lawbreaker.
19"For through the law I died to the law so that I might live for God.
20I have been crucified with Christ and I no longer live, but Christ lives
in me. The life I now live in the body, I live by faith in the Son of God,
who loved me and gave himself for me. 21I do not set aside the grace of
God, for if righteousness could be gained through the law, Christ died
for nothing!"[e]

FAITH OR WORKS OF THE LAW

3 You foolish Galatians! Who has bewitched you? Before your very
eyes Jesus Christ was clearly portrayed as crucified. 2I would like to
learn just one thing from you: Did you receive the Spirit by the works

PRAYING SCRIPTURE

Galatians 3

Many early Christians remained confused about the role of the law after Christ's coming. The law could not save; it could only bring a curse (see verse 10). The blessing of Abraham, brought through Jesus Christ, was received by faith. Thus, Jew and Gentile alike could participate in the same blessing of Abraham who was justified by faith, not by the works of the law.

Thank God that all who believe in Jesus are saved.

[a] 7 That is, Gentiles [b] 7 That is, Jews; also in verses 8 and 9 [c] 9 That is, Peter; also in verses 11 and 14 [d] 16 Or *but through the faithfulness of . . . justified on the basis of the faithfulness of* [e] 21 Some interpreters end the quotation after verse 14.

of the law, or by believing what you heard? 3Are you so foolish? Af-
ter beginning by means of the Spirit, are you now trying to finish by
means of the flesh?[a] 4Have you experienced[b] so much in vain — if it
really was in vain? 5So again I ask, does God give you his Spirit and
work miracles among you by the works of the law, or by your believing
what you heard? 6So also Abraham "believed God, and it was credited
to him as righteousness."[c]

7Understand, then, that those who have faith are children of Abra-
ham. 8Scripture foresaw that God would justify the Gentiles by faith,
and announced the gospel in advance to Abraham: "All nations will be
blessed through you."[d] 9So those who rely on faith are blessed along
with Abraham, the man of faith.

10For all who rely on the works of the law are under a curse, as it is
written: "Cursed is everyone who does not continue to do everything
written in the Book of the Law."[e] 11Clearly no one who relies on the law
is justified before God, because "the righteous will live by faith."[f] 12The
law is not based on faith; on the contrary, it says, "The person who does
these things will live by them."[g] 13Christ redeemed us from the curse of
the law by becoming a curse for us, for it is written: "Cursed is everyone
who is hung on a pole."[h] 14He redeemed us in order that the blessing
given to Abraham might come to the Gentiles through Christ Jesus, so
that by faith we might receive the promise of the Spirit.

THE LAW AND THE PROMISE

15Brothers and sisters, let me take an example from everyday life.
Just as no one can set aside or add to a human covenant that has been
duly established, so it is in this case. 16The promises were spoken to
Abraham and to his seed. Scripture does not say "and to seeds," mean-
ing many people, but "and to your seed,"[i] meaning one person, who is
Christ. 17What I mean is this: The law, introduced 430 years later, does
not set aside the covenant previously established by God and thus do
away with the promise. 18For if the inheritance depends on the law,
then it no longer depends on the promise; but God in his grace gave it
to Abraham through a promise.

19Why, then, was the law given at all? It was added because of trans-
gressions until the Seed to whom the promise referred had come. The
law was given through angels and entrusted to a mediator. 20A media-
tor, however, implies more than one party; but God is one.

21Is the law, therefore, opposed to the promises of God? Absolutely
not! For if a law had been given that could impart life, then righteous-
ness would certainly have come by the law. 22But Scripture has locked up
everything under the control of sin, so that what was promised, being
given through faith in Jesus Christ, might be given to those who believe.

CHILDREN OF GOD

23Before the coming of this faith,[j] we were held in custody under the
law, locked up until the faith that was to come would be revealed. 24So
the law was our guardian until Christ came that we might be justified by
faith. 25Now that this faith has come, we are no longer under a guardian.

---

[a] *3* In contexts like this, the Greek word for *flesh* (*sarx*) refers to the sinful state of human beings, often presented as a power in opposition to the Spirit.
[b] *4* Or *suffered* [c] *6* Gen. 15:6 [d] *8* Gen. 12:3; 18:18; 22:18 [e] *10* Deut. 27:26
[f] *11* Hab. 2:4 [g] *12* Lev. 18:5 [h] *13* Deut. 21:23 [i] *16* Gen. 12:7; 13:15; 24:7
[j] *22,23* Or *through the faithfulness of Jesus . . . 23Before faith came*

26So in Christ Jesus you are all children of God through faith, 27for
all of you who were baptized into Christ have clothed yourselves with
Christ. 28There is neither Jew nor Gentile, neither slave nor free, nor
is there male and female, for you are all one in Christ Jesus. 29If you
belong to Christ, then you are Abraham's seed, and heirs according to
the promise.

PRAYING SCRIPTURE

Galatians 4

It is a great privilege to have the assurance that we are the children of God. So important is this relationship that one of the reasons the Holy Spirit was sent to us is so we can cry "*Abba*, Father" (verse 6). The Spirit of the Son teaches us to call on the Father.

Have you considered the privilege of calling God "Father" rather than only "God"? Ponder the significance such intimacy brings.

4 What I am saying is that as long as an heir is underage, he is no
different from a slave, although he owns the whole estate. 2The
heir is subject to guardians and trustees until the time set by his fa-
ther. 3So also, when we were underage, we were in slavery under the
elemental spiritual forces[a] of the world. 4But when the set time had
fully come, God sent his Son, born of a woman, born under the law, 5to
redeem those under the law, that we might receive adoption to son-
ship.[b] 6Because you are his sons, God sent the Spirit of his Son into our
hearts, the Spirit who calls out, *"Abba,*[c] Father." 7So you are no longer
a slave, but God's child; and since you are his child, God has made you
also an heir.

PAUL'S CONCERN FOR THE GALATIANS

8Formerly, when you did not know God, you were slaves to those
who by nature are not gods. 9But now that you know God — or rather
are known by God — how is it that you are turning back to those weak
and miserable forces[d]? Do you wish to be enslaved by them all over
again? 10You are observing special days and months and seasons and
years! 11I fear for you, that somehow I have wasted my efforts on you.

12I plead with you, brothers and sisters, become like me, for I be-
came like you. You did me no wrong. 13As you know, it was because of
an illness that I first preached the gospel to you, 14and even though
my illness was a trial to you, you did not treat me with contempt or
scorn. Instead, you welcomed me as if I were an angel of God, as if I
were Christ Jesus himself. 15Where, then, is your blessing of me now?
I can testify that, if you could have done so, you would have torn out
your eyes and given them to me. 16Have I now become your enemy by
telling you the truth?

17Those people are zealous to win you over, but for no good. What
they want is to alienate you from us, so that you may have zeal for
them. 18It is fine to be zealous, provided the purpose is good, and to be
so always, not just when I am with you. 19My dear children, for whom I
am again in the pains of childbirth until Christ is formed in you, 20how
I wish I could be with you now and change my tone, because I am per-
plexed about you!

HAGAR AND SARAH

21Tell me, you who want to be under the law, are you not aware of
what the law says? 22For it is written that Abraham had two sons, one
by the slave woman and the other by the free woman. 23His son by the
slave woman was born according to the flesh, but his son by the free
woman was born as the result of a divine promise.

24These things are being taken figuratively: The women represent
two covenants. One covenant is from Mount Sinai and bears children

[a] 3 Or *under the basic principles* [b] 5 The Greek word for *adoption to sonship* is a legal term referring to the full legal standing of an adopted male heir in Roman culture. [c] 6 Aramaic for *Father* [d] 9 Or *principles*

who are to be slaves: This is Hagar. 25Now Hagar stands for Mount Sinai
in Arabia and corresponds to the present city of Jerusalem, because
she is in slavery with her children. 26But the Jerusalem that is above is
free, and she is our mother. 27For it is written:

"Be glad, barren woman,
 you who never bore a child;
shout for joy and cry aloud,
 you who were never in labor;
because more are the children of the desolate woman
 than of her who has a husband."[a]

28Now you, brothers and sisters, like Isaac, are children of promise.
29At that time the son born according to the flesh persecuted the son
born by the power of the Spirit. It is the same now. 30But what does
Scripture say? "Get rid of the slave woman and her son, for the slave
woman's son will never share in the inheritance with the free woman's
son."[b] 31Therefore, brothers and sisters, we are not children of the slave
woman, but of the free woman.

FREEDOM IN CHRIST

5 It is for freedom that Christ has set us free. Stand firm, then, and
do not let yourselves be burdened again by a yoke of slavery.
2Mark my words! I, Paul, tell you that if you let yourselves be circum-
cised, Christ will be of no value to you at all. 3Again I declare to every
man who lets himself be circumcised that he is obligated to obey the
whole law. 4You who are trying to be justified by the law have been
alienated from Christ; you have fallen away from grace. 5For through
the Spirit we eagerly await by faith the righteousness for which we
hope. 6For in Christ Jesus neither circumcision nor uncircumcision has
any value. The only thing that counts is faith expressing itself through
love.
7You were running a good race. Who cut in on you to keep you from
obeying the truth? 8That kind of persuasion does not come from the
one who calls you. 9"A little yeast works through the whole batch of
dough." 10I am confident in the Lord that you will take no other view.
The one who is throwing you into confusion, whoever that may be, will
have to pay the penalty. 11Brothers and sisters, if I am still preaching
circumcision, why am I still being persecuted? In that case the offense
of the cross has been abolished. 12As for those agitators, I wish they
would go the whole way and emasculate themselves!

LIFE BY THE SPIRIT

13You, my brothers and sisters, were called to be free. But do not use
your freedom to indulge the flesh[c]; rather, serve one another humbly
in love. 14For the entire law is fulfilled in keeping this one command:
"Love your neighbor as yourself."[d] 15If you bite and devour each other,
watch out or you will be destroyed by each other.
16So I say, walk by the Spirit, and you will not gratify the desires of
the flesh. 17For the flesh desires what is contrary to the Spirit, and the

PRAYING SCRIPTURE

Galatians 5

The Christian life is known by its fruit. Although verbal testimony is important—we should talk about Jesus—authentic conversion shows itself in the way we live in addition to what we say. Fruit can be inspected by all who know you.

Does your life demonstrate love, joy, peace, forbearance, kindness, goodness, faithfulness, gentleness and self-control (see verses 22–23)? Examine yourself for this fruit. Ask the Holy Spirit to bear his fruit in you at all times.

[a] *27* Isaiah 54:1 [b] *30* Gen. 21:10 [c] *13* In contexts like this, the Greek word for *flesh* (*sarx*) refers to the sinful state of human beings, often presented as a power in opposition to the Spirit; also in verses 16, 17, 19 and 24; and in 6:8.
[d] *14* Lev. 19:18

Spirit what is contrary to the flesh. They are in conflict with each other, so that you are not to do whatever[a] you want. 18But if you are led by the Spirit, you are not under the law.

19The acts of the flesh are obvious: sexual immorality, impurity and debauchery; 20idolatry and witchcraft; hatred, discord, jealousy, fits of rage, selfish ambition, dissensions, factions 21and envy; drunkenness, orgies, and the like. I warn you, as I did before, that those who live like this will not inherit the kingdom of God.

22But the fruit of the Spirit is love, joy, peace, forbearance, kindness, goodness, faithfulness, 23gentleness and self-control. Against such things there is no law. 24Those who belong to Christ Jesus have crucified the flesh with its passions and desires. 25Since we live by the Spirit, let us keep in step with the Spirit. 26Let us not become conceited, provoking and envying each other.

DOING GOOD TO ALL

6 Brothers and sisters, if someone is caught in a sin, you who live by the Spirit should restore that person gently. But watch yourselves, or you also may be tempted. 2Carry each other's burdens, and in this way you will fulfill the law of Christ. 3If anyone thinks they are something when they are not, they deceive themselves. 4Each one should test their own actions. Then they can take pride in themselves alone, without comparing themselves to someone else, 5for each one should carry their own load. 6Nevertheless, the one who receives instruction in the word should share all good things with their instructor.

7Do not be deceived: God cannot be mocked. A man reaps what he sows. 8Whoever sows to please their flesh, from the flesh will reap destruction; whoever sows to please the Spirit, from the Spirit will reap eternal life. 9Let us not become weary in doing good, for at the proper time we will reap a harvest if we do not give up. 10Therefore, as we have opportunity, let us do good to all people, especially to those who belong to the family of believers.

NOT CIRCUMCISION BUT THE NEW CREATION

11See what large letters I use as I write to you with my own hand!

12Those who want to impress people by means of the flesh are trying to compel you to be circumcised. The only reason they do this is to avoid being persecuted for the cross of Christ. 13Not even those who are circumcised keep the law, yet they want you to be circumcised that they may boast about your circumcision in the flesh. 14May I never boast except in the cross of our Lord Jesus Christ, through which[b] the world has been crucified to me, and I to the world. 15Neither circumcision nor uncircumcision means anything; what counts is the new creation. 16Peace and mercy to all who follow this rule — to[c] the Israel of God.

17From now on, let no one cause me trouble, for I bear on my body the marks of Jesus.

18The grace of our Lord Jesus Christ be with your spirit, brothers and sisters. Amen.

PRAYING SCRIPTURE

Galatians 6

Paul ended this brief yet powerful letter with a stirring exhortation on the importance of the cross of Jesus. Paul, as the most successful of early Christian missionaries, said his only boasting was "in the cross of our Lord Jesus Christ" (verse 14). The cross was the source of Paul's death to the world.

Are you struggling with worldly temptations and appeals? Ask God to crucify your sinful desires to the cross of Christ.

[a] 17 Or *you do not do what* [b] 14 Or *whom* [c] 16 Or *rule and to*

EPHESIANS

Paul's letter to the Ephesians marries Christian doctrine and practice. Many scholars conclude that the letter is an encyclical, that it was not intended for a single church but for churches all over Asia. That explains why it does not address a specific issue like Paul's other letters but includes general spiritual encouragement and deep theological instruction.

The first three chapters of the letter expound on the beauty of Christian salvation. Verses 3–14 of chapter 1 contain one of the most lyrical hymns in all of Scripture. Paul described how God has "blessed us in the heavenly realms with every spiritual blessing in Christ" (verse 3). Paul gloried in the fact that we have been chosen, predestined, accepted and forgiven. We have an inheritance, salvation, wisdom and understanding, and we have been adopted as God's children.

Paul's prayer for the Ephesians at the end of chapter 1 centered on his desire for them to have the wisdom and enlightenment to understand the hope they have in Christ, the inheritance they share with him and the power available to them through the Holy Spirit—the same things available to us. Paul was eager for these believers to understand who they are in Christ so they might enjoy the fullness of walking with him.

Paul offered another prayer for the believers in chapter 3. Motivated by his desire for them not to be discouraged in following Christ because of his sufferings, he prayed for them to be strengthened with the power God supplies. He prayed that God's strength would lead them to grow in the faith and gain a greater understanding of the love that God had shown them in Jesus. Paul was so moved by the mystery of the gospel that he knelt in prayer to the Father.

After offering prayers, Paul guided the Ephesians in their personal prayer lives. At the conclusion of the armor of God passage in chapter 6, Paul implored them always to keep on praying for the Lord's people. Paul believed that a crucial element in following Jesus was for the body of Christ constantly to pray for each other. To this end, Paul included a petition to the Ephesians to pray for him, that he might proclaim the gospel without fear.

Intercessory prayer is an important part of the Christian life. If we love our neighbors as ourselves, we are going to be concerned that they know Jesus and follow him. We know that their salvation and continuing growth in grace depends on the work of the Holy Spirit within them. We understand the frailty of human nature and how easily they can be discouraged. Therefore, we have no choice but to pray for the salvation of our neighbors and for the Lord to be at work in the lives of our brothers and sisters. We ask him to help them put sin to death, grow in righteousness and know the joy of following Jesus.

PRAYING SCRIPTURE

Ephesians 1

A significant theological mystery is revealed here: The Father, Son and Holy Spirit work in unison to secure our salvation and heavenly hope. No members of the Trinity were coerced, confused or left out. Eternal salvation is a work of the triune God.

It is right and Biblical to pray to any member of the Godhead, so thank the Father, Son and Holy Spirit for their work in your salvation.

1 Paul, an apostle of Christ Jesus by the will of God,

To God's holy people in Ephesus,[a] the faithful in Christ Jesus:

2Grace and peace to you from God our Father and the Lord Jesus
Christ.

PRAISE FOR SPIRITUAL BLESSINGS IN CHRIST

3Praise be to the God and Father of our Lord Jesus Christ, who has
blessed us in the heavenly realms with every spiritual blessing in
Christ. 4For he chose us in him before the creation of the world to be
holy and blameless in his sight. In love 5he[b] predestined us for adop-
tion to sonship[c] through Jesus Christ, in accordance with his pleasure
and will — 6to the praise of his glorious grace, which he has freely
given us in the One he loves. 7In him we have redemption through his
blood, the forgiveness of sins, in accordance with the riches of God's
grace 8that he lavished on us. With all wisdom and understanding,
9he[d] made known to us the mystery of his will according to his good
pleasure, which he purposed in Christ, 10to be put into effect when the
times reach their fulfillment — to bring unity to all things in heaven
and on earth under Christ.

11In him we were also chosen,[e] having been predestined according
to the plan of him who works out everything in conformity with the
purpose of his will, 12in order that we, who were the first to put our
hope in Christ, might be for the praise of his glory. 13And you also were
included in Christ when you heard the message of truth, the gospel
of your salvation. When you believed, you were marked in him with a
seal, the promised Holy Spirit, 14who is a deposit guaranteeing our in-
heritance until the redemption of those who are God's possession — to
the praise of his glory.

THANKSGIVING AND PRAYER

15For this reason, ever since I heard about your faith in the Lord Jesus
and your love for all God's people, 16I have not stopped giving thanks
for you, remembering you in my prayers. 17I keep asking that the God
of our Lord Jesus Christ, the glorious Father, may give you the Spirit[f]
of wisdom and revelation, so that you may know him better. 18I pray
that the eyes of your heart may be enlightened in order that you may
know the hope to which he has called you, the riches of his glorious
inheritance in his holy people, 19and his incomparably great power for
us who believe. That power is the same as the mighty strength 20he
exerted when he raised Christ from the dead and seated him at his
right hand in the heavenly realms, 21far above all rule and authority,
power and dominion, and every name that is invoked, not only in the
present age but also in the one to come. 22And God placed all things
under his feet and appointed him to be head over everything for the
church, 23which is his body, the fullness of him who fills everything
in every way.

---

[a] *1* Some early manuscripts do not have *in Ephesus.* [b] *4,5* Or *sight in love. 5He* [c] *5* The Greek word for *adoption to sonship* is a legal term referring to the full legal standing of an adopted male heir in Roman culture. [d] *8,9* Or *us with all wisdom and understanding. 9And he* [e] *11* Or *were made heirs* [f] *17* Or *a spirit*

MADE ALIVE IN CHRIST

2 As for you, you were dead in your transgressions and sins, 2in which you used to live when you followed the ways of this world and of the ruler of the kingdom of the air, the spirit who is now at work in those who are disobedient. 3All of us also lived among them at one time, gratifying the cravings of our flesh[a] and following its desires and thoughts. Like the rest, we were by nature deserving of wrath. 4But because of his great love for us, God, who is rich in mercy, 5made us alive with Christ even when we were dead in transgressions — it is by grace you have been saved. 6And God raised us up with Christ and seated us with him in the heavenly realms in Christ Jesus, 7in order that in the coming ages he might show the incomparable riches of his grace, expressed in his kindness to us in Christ Jesus. 8For it is by grace you have been saved, through faith — and this is not from yourselves, it is the gift of God — 9not by works, so that no one can boast. 10For we are God's handiwork, created in Christ Jesus to do good works, which God prepared in advance for us to do.

PRAYING SCRIPTURE

Ephesians 2

A most joy-inducing truth is that we are not saved by works. While it runs opposite of the way people tend to think, if salvation were through good deeds, how would we ever have assurance of it? When would we tally enough credits to secure an eternity with God?

Thank God that salvation is of his grace. Praise him for loving us enough to make salvation sure in Jesus Christ.

JEW AND GENTILE RECONCILED THROUGH CHRIST

11Therefore, remember that formerly you who are Gentiles by birth and called "uncircumcised" by those who call themselves "the circumcision" (which is done in the body by human hands) — 12remember that at that time you were separate from Christ, excluded from citizenship in Israel and foreigners to the covenants of the promise, without hope and without God in the world. 13But now in Christ Jesus you who once were far away have been brought near by the blood of Christ.

14For he himself is our peace, who has made the two groups one and has destroyed the barrier, the dividing wall of hostility, 15by setting aside in his flesh the law with its commands and regulations. His purpose was to create in himself one new humanity out of the two, thus making peace, 16and in one body to reconcile both of them to God through the cross, by which he put to death their hostility. 17He came and preached peace to you who were far away and peace to those who were near. 18For through him we both have access to the Father by one Spirit.

19Consequently, you are no longer foreigners and strangers, but fellow citizens with God's people and also members of his household, 20built on the foundation of the apostles and prophets, with Christ Jesus himself as the chief cornerstone. 21In him the whole building is joined together and rises to become a holy temple in the Lord. 22And in him you too are being built together to become a dwelling in which God lives by his Spirit.

GOD'S MARVELOUS PLAN FOR THE GENTILES

3 For this reason I, Paul, the prisoner of Christ Jesus for the sake of you Gentiles —

2Surely you have heard about the administration of God's grace that was given to me for you, 3that is, the mystery made known to me by revelation, as I have already written briefly. 4In reading this, then, you will be able to understand my insight into the mystery of Christ,

PRAYING SCRIPTURE

Ephesians 3

When you are unsure of how to pray, use the prayers in the pages of Scripture. Including the depth of Paul's rejoicing can fuel your own petitions. As your prayers are bolstered by the inspired words of the holy text, prayers birthed from your heart will grow deeper.

Verse 20 is a great Scripture to read in prayer. Pray it when asking in faith for God to do something big!

[a] *3* In contexts like this, the Greek word for *flesh* (*sarx*) refers to the sinful state of human beings, often presented as a power in opposition to the Spirit.

5which was not made known to people in other generations as it has
now been revealed by the Spirit to God's holy apostles and prophets.
6This mystery is that through the gospel the Gentiles are heirs together
with Israel, members together of one body, and sharers together in the
promise in Christ Jesus.

7I became a servant of this gospel by the gift of God's grace given
me through the working of his power. 8Although I am less than the
least of all the Lord's people, this grace was given me: to preach to the
Gentiles the boundless riches of Christ, 9and to make plain to everyone
the administration of this mystery, which for ages past was kept hid-
den in God, who created all things. 10His intent was that now, through
the church, the manifold wisdom of God should be made known to
the rulers and authorities in the heavenly realms, 11according to his
eternal purpose that he accomplished in Christ Jesus our Lord. 12In
him and through faith in him we may approach God with freedom and
confidence. 13I ask you, therefore, not to be discouraged because of my
sufferings for you, which are your glory.

A PRAYER FOR THE EPHESIANS

14For this reason I kneel before the Father, 15from whom every fam-
ily[a] in heaven and on earth derives its name. 16I pray that out of his
glorious riches he may strengthen you with power through his Spirit
in your inner being, 17so that Christ may dwell in your hearts through
faith. And I pray that you, being rooted and established in love, 18may
have power, together with all the Lord's holy people, to grasp how wide
and long and high and deep is the love of Christ, 19and to know this
love that surpasses knowledge — that you may be filled to the measure
of all the fullness of God.

20Now to him who is able to do immeasurably more than all we ask
or imagine, according to his power that is at work within us, 21to him
be glory in the church and in Christ Jesus throughout all generations,
for ever and ever! Amen.

UNITY AND MATURITY IN THE BODY OF CHRIST

4 As a prisoner for the Lord, then, I urge you to live a life worthy of
the calling you have received. 2Be completely humble and gen-
tle; be patient, bearing with one another in love. 3Make every effort to
keep the unity of the Spirit through the bond of peace. 4There is one
body and one Spirit, just as you were called to one hope when you were
called; 5one Lord, one faith, one baptism; 6one God and Father of all,
who is over all and through all and in all.

7But to each one of us grace has been given as Christ apportioned it.
8This is why it[b] says:

"When he ascended on high,
he took many captives
and gave gifts to his people."[c]

9(What does "he ascended" mean except that he also descended to the
lower, earthly regions[d]? 10He who descended is the very one who as-
cended higher than all the heavens, in order to fill the whole universe.)
11So Christ himself gave the apostles, the prophets, the evangelists, the

PRAYING SCRIPTURE

Ephesians 4

We help show the unity of Christ's body through exercising our spiritual gifts to serve his church. Spiritual gifts are not given by God primarily to build up individuals. They are given to build up the entire body. The body is a whole; spiritual gifts do not only affect a finger or toe.

Thank God not only for your gifting that makes the body whole, but also for others' gifts helping you to mature spiritually.

[a] 15 The Greek for *family* (*patria*) is derived from the Greek for *father* (*pater*).
[b] 8 Or *God* [c] 8 Psalm 68:18 [d] 9 Or *the depths of the earth*

pastors and teachers, 12to equip his people for works of service, so that
the body of Christ may be built up 13until we all reach unity in the faith
and in the knowledge of the Son of God and become mature, attaining
to the whole measure of the fullness of Christ.
14Then we will no longer be infants, tossed back and forth by the
waves, and blown here and there by every wind of teaching and by the
cunning and craftiness of people in their deceitful scheming. 15Instead,
speaking the truth in love, we will grow to become in every respect the
mature body of him who is the head, that is, Christ. 16From him the
whole body, joined and held together by every supporting ligament,
grows and builds itself up in love, as each part does its work.

INSTRUCTIONS FOR CHRISTIAN LIVING

17So I tell you this, and insist on it in the Lord, that you must no longer
live as the Gentiles do, in the futility of their thinking. 18They are dark-
ened in their understanding and separated from the life of God because
of the ignorance that is in them due to the hardening of their hearts.
19Having lost all sensitivity, they have given themselves over to sensual-
ity so as to indulge in every kind of impurity, and they are full of greed.
20That, however, is not the way of life you learned 21when you heard
about Christ and were taught in him in accordance with the truth that
is in Jesus. 22You were taught, with regard to your former way of life,
to put off your old self, which is being corrupted by its deceitful de-
sires; 23to be made new in the attitude of your minds; 24and to put on
the new self, created to be like God in true righteousness and holiness.
25Therefore each of you must put off falsehood and speak truthfully
to your neighbor, for we are all members of one body. 26"In your anger
do not sin"[a]: Do not let the sun go down while you are still angry, 27and
do not give the devil a foothold. 28Anyone who has been stealing must
steal no longer, but must work, doing something useful with their own
hands, that they may have something to share with those in need.
29Do not let any unwholesome talk come out of your mouths, but
only what is helpful for building others up according to their needs,
that it may benefit those who listen. 30And do not grieve the Holy Spirit
of God, with whom you were sealed for the day of redemption. 31Get rid
of all bitterness, rage and anger, brawling and slander, along with every
form of malice. 32Be kind and compassionate to one another, forgiving
5 each other, just as in Christ God forgave you. 1Follow God's exam-
ple, therefore, as dearly loved children 2and walk in the way of
love, just as Christ loved us and gave himself up for us as a fragrant
offering and sacrifice to God.
3But among you there must not be even a hint of sexual immorality,
or of any kind of impurity, or of greed, because these are improper for
God's holy people. 4Nor should there be obscenity, foolish talk or coarse
joking, which are out of place, but rather thanksgiving. 5For of this you
can be sure: No immoral, impure or greedy person — such a person
is an idolater — has any inheritance in the kingdom of Christ and of
God.[b] 6Let no one deceive you with empty words, for because of such
things God's wrath comes on those who are disobedient. 7Therefore do
not be partners with them.
8For you were once darkness, but now you are light in the Lord. Live
as children of light 9(for the fruit of the light consists in all goodness,

[a] 26 Psalm 4:4 (see Septuagint) [b] 5 Or *kingdom of the Messiah and God*

PRAYING SCRIPTURE

Ephesians 5

Living out the Christian life is often portrayed as walking. "Walking with God" is a common way to express living by faith. Paul wrote that we are to walk in love, in light and in wisdom, meaning that each should mark our lives. Our walk takes us where love, light and wisdom are the pathway.

Walking with God is intentional, not accidental. Look for his way, and then pray to walk in it.

righteousness and truth) 10and find out what pleases the Lord. 11Have
nothing to do with the fruitless deeds of darkness, but rather expose
them. 12It is shameful even to mention what the disobedient do in
secret. 13But everything exposed by the light becomes visible — and
everything that is illuminated becomes a light. 14This is why it is said:

"Wake up, sleeper,
  rise from the dead,
  and Christ will shine on you."

15Be very careful, then, how you live — not as unwise but as wise,
16making the most of every opportunity, because the days are evil.
17Therefore do not be foolish, but understand what the Lord's will is.
18Do not get drunk on wine, which leads to debauchery. Instead, be
filled with the Spirit, 19speaking to one another with psalms, hymns,
and songs from the Spirit. Sing and make music from your heart to the
Lord, 20always giving thanks to God the Father for everything, in the
name of our Lord Jesus Christ.

INSTRUCTIONS FOR CHRISTIAN HOUSEHOLDS

21Submit to one another out of reverence for Christ.
22Wives, submit yourselves to your own husbands as you do to the
Lord. 23For the husband is the head of the wife as Christ is the head of the
church, his body, of which he is the Savior. 24Now as the church submits
to Christ, so also wives should submit to their husbands in everything.
25Husbands, love your wives, just as Christ loved the church and gave
himself up for her 26to make her holy, cleansing[a] her by the washing
with water through the word, 27and to present her to himself as a ra-
diant church, without stain or wrinkle or any other blemish, but holy
and blameless. 28In this same way, husbands ought to love their wives
as their own bodies. He who loves his wife loves himself. 29After all, no
one ever hated their own body, but they feed and care for their body,
just as Christ does the church — 30for we are members of his body.
31"For this reason a man will leave his father and mother and be united
to his wife, and the two will become one flesh."[b] 32This is a profound
mystery — but I am talking about Christ and the church. 33However,
each one of you also must love his wife as he loves himself, and the
wife must respect her husband.

6 Children, obey your parents in the Lord, for this is right. 2"Honor
your father and mother" — which is the first commandment with
a promise — 3"so that it may go well with you and that you may enjoy
long life on the earth."[c]
4Fathers,[d] do not exasperate your children; instead, bring them up
in the training and instruction of the Lord.
5Slaves, obey your earthly masters with respect and fear, and with sin-
cerity of heart, just as you would obey Christ. 6Obey them not only to
win their favor when their eye is on you, but as slaves of Christ, doing
the will of God from your heart. 7Serve wholeheartedly, as if you were
serving the Lord, not people, 8because you know that the Lord will re-
ward each one for whatever good they do, whether they are slave or free.
9And masters, treat your slaves in the same way. Do not threaten
them, since you know that he who is both their Master and yours is in
heaven, and there is no favoritism with him.

PRAYING SCRIPTURE

Ephesians 6

The only way we can be spiritually victorious is to be properly armed for the spiritual battle taking place all around us all the time. The god of this world seeks control, and his attacks require us to be prepared from head to toe. The Holy Spirit provides all the armor and weaponry we need to stand victorious. Read verses 10–20, prayerfully taking on the armor God provides.

---

[a] 26 Or *having cleansed* [b] 31 Gen. 2:24 [c] 3 Deut. 5:16 [d] 4 Or *Parents*

THE ARMOR OF GOD

10Finally, be strong in the Lord and in his mighty power. 11Put on the full armor of God, so that you can take your stand against the devil's schemes. 12For our struggle is not against flesh and blood, but against the rulers, against the authorities, against the powers of this dark world and against the spiritual forces of evil in the heavenly realms. 13Therefore put on the full armor of God, so that when the day of evil comes, you may be able to stand your ground, and after you have done everything, to stand. 14Stand firm then, with the belt of truth buckled around your waist, with the breastplate of righteousness in place, 15and with your feet fitted with the readiness that comes from the gospel of peace. 16In addition to all this, take up the shield of faith, with which you can extinguish all the flaming arrows of the evil one. 17Take the helmet of salvation and the sword of the Spirit, which is the word of God.

18And pray in the Spirit on all occasions with all kinds of prayers and requests. With this in mind, be alert and always keep on praying for all the Lord's people. 19Pray also for me, that whenever I speak, words may be given me so that I will fearlessly make known the mystery of the gospel, 20for which I am an ambassador in chains. Pray that I may declare it fearlessly, as I should.

FINAL GREETINGS

21Tychicus, the dear brother and faithful servant in the Lord, will tell you everything, so that you also may know how I am and what I am doing. 22I am sending him to you for this very purpose, that you may know how we are, and that he may encourage you.

23Peace to the brothers and sisters,[a] and love with faith from God the Father and the Lord Jesus Christ. 24Grace to all who love our Lord Jesus Christ with an undying love.[b]

---

[a] *23* The Greek word for *brothers and sisters* (*adelphoi*) refers here to believers, both men and women, as part of God's family. [b] *24* Or *Grace and immortality to all who love our Lord Jesus Christ.*

PHILIPPIANS

In Philippians, we read the apostle Paul's thank-you letter to a church he loved. Written while Paul was imprisoned, the letter radiates with hope that Christians can find joy in every situation, including the worst they could imagine. Beyond merely hoping for joy, Paul directed the Philippians to "rejoice in the Lord always" (4:4).

The letter moves quickly from Paul's standard greeting to expressions of prayer: "I thank my God every time I remember you" with reasons why: their partnership in the gospel, God's ability to complete his work in them and their sharing of God's grace with him (see 1:3–7). He then named things he was praying for them: that their love might abound, that they would increase in knowledge and discernment and that their spiritual growth would continue (see 1:9–11). Paul's prayer life overflowed into his letter.

Chapter 2 presents the teaching about Jesus' humility in being born as a man while remaining God. As a result of his obedience to crucifixion, Jesus was and is highly exalted by the Father, who has given his Son "the name that is above every name" (verse 9). Everyone will bow at that name. Every tongue will one day confess "that Jesus Christ is Lord, to the glory of God the Father" (verse 11).

Philippians also contains one of Paul's most important and encouraging teachings on personal prayer. After telling his Philippian brothers and sisters that they should always rejoice, Paul wrote that they should not let anxiousness be part of their lives. Too often Christians wonder if they are even allowed to pray about some of the seemingly small concerns they have. Philippians answers this question. If something causes you stress, anxiety or pain, you should pray about it. Rather than allowing yourself to be wracked with worry, bring your cares and pains to the Lord. Just as loving parents long to know what concerns their children, the Lord wants to take our anxieties from us and carry them. In exchange, he gives Christians a peace we cannot explain; a peace that transcends all understanding, which will guard our hearts and minds in Christ Jesus (see 4:7).

Paul also emphasized that Christians should present their requests to the Lord "with thanksgiving" (4:6). Thanksgiving is a consistent theme throughout the book of Philippians. This might seem strange because Paul wrote this letter from a prison cell. However, Paul knew what God has done for his children in Jesus. When we consider how God remains with his people in their sufferings or hears when they cry out to him, how could we not express our thankfulness to him in our prayers? We make requests, thankful that God hears us and thankful that we know he will answer from heaven.

1 Paul and Timothy, servants of Christ Jesus,

To all God's holy people in Christ Jesus at Philippi, together with the overseers and deacons[a]:

[2]Grace and peace to you from God our Father and the Lord Jesus Christ.

THANKSGIVING AND PRAYER

[3]I thank my God every time I remember you. [4]In all my prayers for all of you, I always pray with joy [5]because of your partnership in the gospel from the first day until now, [6]being confident of this, that he who began a good work in you will carry it on to completion until the day of Christ Jesus.

[7]It is right for me to feel this way about all of you, since I have you in my heart and, whether I am in chains or defending and confirming the gospel, all of you share in God's grace with me. [8]God can testify how I long for all of you with the affection of Christ Jesus.

[9]And this is my prayer: that your love may abound more and more in knowledge and depth of insight, [10]so that you may be able to discern what is best and may be pure and blameless for the day of Christ, [11]filled with the fruit of righteousness that comes through Jesus Christ — to the glory and praise of God.

PAUL'S CHAINS ADVANCE THE GOSPEL

[12]Now I want you to know, brothers and sisters,[b] that what has happened to me has actually served to advance the gospel. [13]As a result, it has become clear throughout the whole palace guard[c] and to everyone else that I am in chains for Christ. [14]And because of my chains, most of the brothers and sisters have become confident in the Lord and dare all the more to proclaim the gospel without fear.

[15]It is true that some preach Christ out of envy and rivalry, but others out of goodwill. [16]The latter do so out of love, knowing that I am put here for the defense of the gospel. [17]The former preach Christ out of selfish ambition, not sincerely, supposing that they can stir up trouble for me while I am in chains. [18]But what does it matter? The important thing is that in every way, whether from false motives or true, Christ is preached. And because of this I rejoice.

Yes, and I will continue to rejoice, [19]for I know that through your prayers and God's provision of the Spirit of Jesus Christ what has happened to me will turn out for my deliverance.[d] [20]I eagerly expect and hope that I will in no way be ashamed, but will have sufficient courage so that now as always Christ will be exalted in my body, whether by life or by death. [21]For to me, to live is Christ and to die is gain. [22]If I am to go on living in the body, this will mean fruitful labor for me. Yet what shall I choose? I do not know! [23]I am torn between the two: I desire to depart and be with Christ, which is better by far; [24]but it is more necessary for you that I remain in the body. [25]Convinced of this, I know

[a] *1* The word *deacons* refers here to Christians designated to serve with the overseers/elders of the church in a variety of ways; similarly in Romans 16:1 and 1 Tim. 3:8,12. [b] *12* The Greek word for *brothers and sisters* (*adelphoi*) refers here to believers, both men and women, as part of God's family; also in verse 14; and in 3:1,13,17; 4:1,8,21. [c] *13* Or *whole palace* [d] *19* Or *vindication*; or *salvation*

PRAYING SCRIPTURE

Philippians 1

One of God's most awesome promises is that he will not stop working in our lives until he finishes the good work he has started in us (see verse 6). The joyous thing about this good work is that it depends solely on him; he starts the work, and he will complete it.

If any part of our salvation depended on us, what terrible shape we would be in. Thank God that your salvation is his design and his doing.

that I will remain, and I will continue with all of you for your progress
and joy in the faith, 26so that through my being with you again your
boasting in Christ Jesus will abound on account of me.

LIFE WORTHY OF THE GOSPEL

27Whatever happens, conduct yourselves in a manner worthy of the
gospel of Christ. Then, whether I come and see you or only hear about
you in my absence, I will know that you stand firm in the one Spirit,[a]
striving together as one for the faith of the gospel 28without being
frightened in any way by those who oppose you. This is a sign to them
that they will be destroyed, but that you will be saved — and that by
God. 29For it has been granted to you on behalf of Christ not only to
believe in him, but also to suffer for him, 30since you are going through
the same struggle you saw I had, and now hear that I still have.

IMITATING CHRIST'S HUMILITY

2 Therefore if you have any encouragement from being united with
Christ, if any comfort from his love, if any common sharing in the
Spirit, if any tenderness and compassion, 2then make my joy complete
by being like-minded, having the same love, being one in spirit and of
one mind. 3Do nothing out of selfish ambition or vain conceit. Rather,
in humility value others above yourselves, 4not looking to your own
interests but each of you to the interests of the others.

5In your relationships with one another, have the same mindset as
Christ Jesus:

6 Who, being in very nature[b] God,
did not consider equality with God something to be used to his
own advantage;
7 rather, he made himself nothing
by taking the very nature[c] of a servant,
being made in human likeness.
8 And being found in appearance as a man,
he humbled himself
by becoming obedient to death —
even death on a cross!

9 Therefore God exalted him to the highest place
and gave him the name that is above every name,
10 that at the name of Jesus every knee should bow,
in heaven and on earth and under the earth,
11 and every tongue acknowledge that Jesus Christ is Lord,
to the glory of God the Father.

DO EVERYTHING WITHOUT GRUMBLING

12Therefore, my dear friends, as you have always obeyed — not only
in my presence, but now much more in my absence — continue to
work out your salvation with fear and trembling, 13for it is God who
works in you to will and to act in order to fulfill his good purpose.

14Do everything without grumbling or arguing, 15so that you may
become blameless and pure, "children of God without fault in a warped
and crooked generation."[d] Then you will shine among them like stars
in the sky 16as you hold firmly to the word of life. And then I will be

PRAYING SCRIPTURE

Philippians 2

Humility goes against the grain of human nature. Pride moves us to "look out for number one," even while the needs of others around us go unmet. This is unlike the way of Jesus, who humbled himself, taking on the form of a servant to bear our sins on the cross.

Can people around you say you are a servant? Ask Jesus for the same humility he embraced for us.

[a] 27 Or *in one spirit* [b] 6 Or *in the form of* [c] 7 Or *the form* [d] 15 Deut. 32:5

able to boast on the day of Christ that I did not run or labor in vain.
[17]But even if I am being poured out like a drink offering on the sacrifice
and service coming from your faith, I am glad and rejoice with all of
you. [18]So you too should be glad and rejoice with me.

TIMOTHY AND EPAPHRODITUS

[19]I hope in the Lord Jesus to send Timothy to you soon, that I also
may be cheered when I receive news about you. [20]I have no one else
like him, who will show genuine concern for your welfare. [21]For every-
one looks out for their own interests, not those of Jesus Christ. [22]But
you know that Timothy has proved himself, because as a son with his
father he has served with me in the work of the gospel. [23]I hope, there-
fore, to send him as soon as I see how things go with me. [24]And I am
confident in the Lord that I myself will come soon.

[25]But I think it is necessary to send back to you Epaphroditus, my
brother, co-worker and fellow soldier, who is also your messenger,
whom you sent to take care of my needs. [26]For he longs for all of you
and is distressed because you heard he was ill. [27]Indeed he was ill, and
almost died. But God had mercy on him, and not on him only but also
on me, to spare me sorrow upon sorrow. [28]Therefore I am all the more
eager to send him, so that when you see him again you may be glad
and I may have less anxiety. [29]So then, welcome him in the Lord with
great joy, and honor people like him, [30]because he almost died for the
work of Christ. He risked his life to make up for the help you yourselves
could not give me.

NO CONFIDENCE IN THE FLESH

3 Further, my brothers and sisters, rejoice in the Lord! It is no trouble
for me to write the same things to you again, and it is a safeguard
for you. [2]Watch out for those dogs, those evildoers, those mutilators of
the flesh. [3]For it is we who are the circumcision, we who serve God by
his Spirit, who boast in Christ Jesus, and who put no confidence in the
flesh — [4]though I myself have reasons for such confidence.

If someone else thinks they have reasons to put confidence in the
flesh, I have more: [5]circumcised on the eighth day, of the people of
Israel, of the tribe of Benjamin, a Hebrew of Hebrews; in regard to the
law, a Pharisee; [6]as for zeal, persecuting the church; as for righteous-
ness based on the law, faultless.

[7]But whatever were gains to me I now consider loss for the sake of
Christ. [8]What is more, I consider everything a loss because of the sur-
passing worth of knowing Christ Jesus my Lord, for whose sake I have
lost all things. I consider them garbage, that I may gain Christ [9]and be
found in him, not having a righteousness of my own that comes from
the law, but that which is through faith in[a] Christ — the righteousness
that comes from God on the basis of faith. [10]I want to know Christ —
yes, to know the power of his resurrection and participation in his suf-
ferings, becoming like him in his death, [11]and so, somehow, attaining
to the resurrection from the dead.

[12]Not that I have already obtained all this, or have already arrived
at my goal, but I press on to take hold of that for which Christ Jesus
took hold of me. [13]Brothers and sisters, I do not consider myself yet to
have taken hold of it. But one thing I do: Forgetting what is behind and

[a] 9 Or *through the faithfulness of*

PRAYING SCRIPTURE

Philippians 3

It is easy to get distracted in the walk of faith. The world offers so much that pursuit of the invisible kingdom often takes second or third place. Paul's solution was to forget those things which are behind so we might "press on toward the goal to win the prize for which God has called [us] heavenward in Christ Jesus" (verse 14).

Do you have the same goal as Paul? Ask God for focus to keep him first always.

straining toward what is ahead, 14I press on toward the goal to win the prize for which God has called me heavenward in Christ Jesus.

FOLLOWING PAUL'S EXAMPLE

15All of us, then, who are mature should take such a view of things. And if on some point you think differently, that too God will make clear to you. 16Only let us live up to what we have already attained.

17Join together in following my example, brothers and sisters, and just as you have us as a model, keep your eyes on those who live as we do. 18For, as I have often told you before and now tell you again even with tears, many live as enemies of the cross of Christ. 19Their destiny is destruction, their god is their stomach, and their glory is in their shame. Their mind is set on earthly things. 20But our citizenship is in heaven. And we eagerly await a Savior from there, the Lord Jesus Christ, 21who, by the power that enables him to bring everything under his control, will transform our lowly bodies so that they will be like his glorious body.

CLOSING APPEAL FOR STEADFASTNESS AND UNITY

4 Therefore, my brothers and sisters, you whom I love and long for, my joy and crown, stand firm in the Lord in this way, dear friends!

2I plead with Euodia and I plead with Syntyche to be of the same mind in the Lord. 3Yes, and I ask you, my true companion, help these women since they have contended at my side in the cause of the gospel, along with Clement and the rest of my co-workers, whose names are in the book of life.

FINAL EXHORTATIONS

4Rejoice in the Lord always. I will say it again: Rejoice! 5Let your gentleness be evident to all. The Lord is near. 6Do not be anxious about anything, but in every situation, by prayer and petition, with thanksgiving, present your requests to God. 7And the peace of God, which transcends all understanding, will guard your hearts and your minds in Christ Jesus.

8Finally, brothers and sisters, whatever is true, whatever is noble, whatever is right, whatever is pure, whatever is lovely, whatever is admirable — if anything is excellent or praiseworthy — think about such things. 9Whatever you have learned or received or heard from me, or seen in me — put it into practice. And the God of peace will be with you.

THANKS FOR THEIR GIFTS

10I rejoiced greatly in the Lord that at last you renewed your concern for me. Indeed, you were concerned, but you had no opportunity to show it. 11I am not saying this because I am in need, for I have learned to be content whatever the circumstances. 12I know what it is to be in need, and I know what it is to have plenty. I have learned the secret of being content in any and every situation, whether well fed or hungry, whether living in plenty or in want. 13I can do all this through him who gives me strength.

14Yet it was good of you to share in my troubles. 15Moreover, as you Philippians know, in the early days of your acquaintance with the gospel, when I set out from Macedonia, not one church shared with me in the matter of giving and receiving, except you only; 16for even when

PRAYING SCRIPTURE

Philippians 4

When you feel anxious, God invites you to lay your burdens on him in prayer. Paul wrote that "in every situation" you should "present your requests to God" (verse 6). It is when you take everything to God in prayer with thanksgiving that the "peace of God, which transcends all understanding" guards your heart (verse 7).

Is there anything worrying you? Take it to God in prayer; thank him for taking your burden.

I was in Thessalonica, you sent me aid more than once when I was in
need. [17]Not that I desire your gifts; what I desire is that more be cred-
ited to your account. [18]I have received full payment and have more
than enough. I am amply supplied, now that I have received from
Epaphroditus the gifts you sent. They are a fragrant offering, an ac-
ceptable sacrifice, pleasing to God. [19]And my God will meet all your
needs according to the riches of his glory in Christ Jesus.

[20]To our God and Father be glory for ever and ever. Amen.

FINAL GREETINGS

[21]Greet all God's people in Christ Jesus. The brothers and sisters who
are with me send greetings. [22]All God's people here send you greetings,
especially those who belong to Caesar's household.

[23]The grace of the Lord Jesus Christ be with your spirit. Amen.[a]

---

[a] *23* Some manuscripts do not have *Amen.*

COLOSSIANS

Paul wrote to the church at Colossae as they were struggling with an onslaught of false teaching. From reading Paul's admonitions, it appears false teachers had mixed pagan mysticism with Jewish legalism, forming a confusing hybrid that burdened these new believers. The church did not have a clear view of who Jesus is in his nature, majesty or power. They were thus enslaved rather than freed in their walk with Jesus.

Paul asked the Lord that the Colossian believers might be filled with the knowledge of his will. He did not ask this so they could simply accumulate knowledge, but that they might walk worthy of their calling. He also prayed that they would bear fruit in every good work and grow in their knowledge of God.

Since heresy assaulted the Colossians on all sides, Paul asked the Lord to give them spiritual wisdom—a request that our prayers should include. Because we live in an error-filled, broken world, we need the Lord's wisdom to follow him. The price of being deceived can be steep and long-lasting. Therefore, when we think of each other, we should pray for each other accordingly.

In the middle of Colossians, Paul contrasted the temporal and the eternal in terms of death and life, and heaven ("above") and earth. If we have died with Christ, he said, we should not live according to the world's regulations. Merely following guidelines about handling food, for instance, brings no spiritual value (see 2:20–23). "Since, then, you have been raised with Christ," he wrote, "set your hearts on things above, where Christ is, seated at the right hand of God" (3:1). Seeking Christ's life should lead us to "put to death" our earthly nature (see 3:5–10).

A beautiful passage follows (see 3:12–17), instructing us how our lives should look when contrasted with how they should not. We should put on compassion, kindness, humility, gentleness and patience. Peace should rule in the body of Christ, as we are thankful for every one of God's blessings, and with the word of Christ dwelling among us richly.

Addressing the subject of prayer again in chapter 4, Paul admonished the Colossians "to devote themselves to prayer" (verse 2). They needed always to be at the ready, like a military sentry on watch. For the Colossians, prayer was to be their first decision, not their last resort. They needed this instruction because the temptation to neglect prayer for a life of self-sufficiency is real. It affects every generation of Christians.

Most believers struggle to pray consistently; and when we do pray, wrestling with a wandering mind is normal. The most serious requests are interrupted by the most trivial thoughts. Every Christian who desires to grow must pay heed to Paul's words in this letter, committing ourselves to prayer at regular intervals and at all waking hours.

1 Paul, an apostle of Christ Jesus by the will of God, and Timothy our brother,

2To God's holy people in Colossae, the faithful brothers and sisters[a] in Christ:

Grace and peace to you from God our Father.[b]

THANKSGIVING AND PRAYER

3We always thank God, the Father of our Lord Jesus Christ, when we pray for you, 4because we have heard of your faith in Christ Jesus and of the love you have for all God's people — 5the faith and love that spring from the hope stored up for you in heaven and about which you have already heard in the true message of the gospel 6that has come to you. In the same way, the gospel is bearing fruit and growing throughout the whole world — just as it has been doing among you since the day you heard it and truly understood God's grace. 7You learned it from Epaphras, our dear fellow servant,[c] who is a faithful minister of Christ on our[d] behalf, 8and who also told us of your love in the Spirit.

9For this reason, since the day we heard about you, we have not stopped praying for you. We continually ask God to fill you with the knowledge of his will through all the wisdom and understanding that the Spirit gives,[e] 10so that you may live a life worthy of the Lord and please him in every way: bearing fruit in every good work, growing in the knowledge of God, 11being strengthened with all power according to his glorious might so that you may have great endurance and patience, 12and giving joyful thanks to the Father, who has qualified you[f] to share in the inheritance of his holy people in the kingdom of light. 13For he has rescued us from the dominion of darkness and brought us into the kingdom of the Son he loves, 14in whom we have redemption, the forgiveness of sins.

THE SUPREMACY OF THE SON OF GOD

15The Son is the image of the invisible God, the firstborn over all creation. 16For in him all things were created: things in heaven and on earth, visible and invisible, whether thrones or powers or rulers or authorities; all things have been created through him and for him. 17He is before all things, and in him all things hold together. 18And he is the head of the body, the church; he is the beginning and the firstborn from among the dead, so that in everything he might have the supremacy. 19For God was pleased to have all his fullness dwell in him, 20and through him to reconcile to himself all things, whether things on earth or things in heaven, by making peace through his blood, shed on the cross.

21Once you were alienated from God and were enemies in your minds because of[g] your evil behavior. 22But now he has reconciled you by Christ's physical body through death to present you holy in his sight, without blemish and free from accusation — 23if you continue in your faith, established and firm, and do not move from the hope held

PRAYING SCRIPTURE

Colossians 1

Central to the Christian's faith is that Jesus Christ is God, one with the Father and the Spirit, in whom is everything and for whom everything holds together (see verse 17). Jesus is greater than all prophets and teachers, and it is through him alone that people can be forgiven of their sins and made right with God (see verse 14).

Jesus is not one god among many. He is the only true God. Praise the Father, Son and Holy Spirit for salvation in Christ.

[a] 2 The Greek word for *brothers and sisters* (*adelphoi*) refers here to believers, both men and women, as part of God's family; also in 4:15. [b] 2 Some manuscripts *Father and the Lord Jesus Christ* [c] 7 Or *slave* [d] 7 Some manuscripts *your* [e] 9 Or *all spiritual wisdom and understanding* [f] 12 Some manuscripts *us* [g] 21 Or *minds, as shown by*

out in the gospel. This is the gospel that you heard and that has been
proclaimed to every creature under heaven, and of which I, Paul, have
become a servant.

PAUL'S LABOR FOR THE CHURCH

24Now I rejoice in what I am suffering for you, and I fill up in my
flesh what is still lacking in regard to Christ's afflictions, for the sake
of his body, which is the church. 25I have become its servant by the
commission God gave me to present to you the word of God in its full-
ness — 26the mystery that has been kept hidden for ages and gener-
ations, but is now disclosed to the Lord's people. 27To them God has
chosen to make known among the Gentiles the glorious riches of this
mystery, which is Christ in you, the hope of glory.
28He is the one we proclaim, admonishing and teaching everyone
with all wisdom, so that we may present everyone fully mature in
Christ. 29To this end I strenuously contend with all the energy Christ
so powerfully works in me.

2 I want you to know how hard I am contending for you and for
those at Laodicea, and for all who have not met me personally.
2My goal is that they may be encouraged in heart and united in love,
so that they may have the full riches of complete understanding, in
order that they may know the mystery of God, namely, Christ, 3in
whom are hidden all the treasures of wisdom and knowledge. 4I tell
you this so that no one may deceive you by fine-sounding arguments.
5For though I am absent from you in body, I am present with you in
spirit and delight to see how disciplined you are and how firm your
faith in Christ is.

SPIRITUAL FULLNESS IN CHRIST

6So then, just as you received Christ Jesus as Lord, continue to live
your lives in him, 7rooted and built up in him, strengthened in the
faith as you were taught, and overflowing with thankfulness.
8See to it that no one takes you captive through hollow and decep-
tive philosophy, which depends on human tradition and the elemental
spiritual forces[a] of this world rather than on Christ.
9For in Christ all the fullness of the Deity lives in bodily form, 10and
in Christ you have been brought to fullness. He is the head over every
power and authority. 11In him you were also circumcised with a cir-
cumcision not performed by human hands. Your whole self ruled by
the flesh[b] was put off when you were circumcised by[c] Christ, 12having
been buried with him in baptism, in which you were also raised with
him through your faith in the working of God, who raised him from
the dead.
13When you were dead in your sins and in the uncircumcision of your
flesh, God made you[d] alive with Christ. He forgave us all our sins, 14hav-
ing canceled the charge of our legal indebtedness, which stood against
us and condemned us; he has taken it away, nailing it to the cross.
15And having disarmed the powers and authorities, he made a public
spectacle of them, triumphing over them by the cross.[e]

PRAYING SCRIPTURE

Colossians 2

The world is filled with false philosophies that draw the believer away from Jesus. Our protection against them is to live in Jesus the same way we received Jesus (see verse 6). As we walk in him, we become rooted, built up in him and strengthened in the faith (see verse 7). Protection is not a matter of wishing; it is a matter of walking.

Ask God to help you discern ideologies that would lead you away from Christ.

---

[a] *8* Or *the basic principles*; also in verse 20 [b] *11* In contexts like this, the Greek word for *flesh* (*sarx*) refers to the sinful state of human beings, often presented as a power in opposition to the Spirit; also in verse 13. [c] *11* Or *put off in the circumcision of* [d] *13* Some manuscripts *us* [e] *15* Or *them in him*

FREEDOM FROM HUMAN RULES

16 Therefore do not let anyone judge you by what you eat or drink, or
with regard to a religious festival, a New Moon celebration or a Sabbath
day. 17 These are a shadow of the things that were to come; the reality,
however, is found in Christ. 18 Do not let anyone who delights in false
humility and the worship of angels disqualify you. Such a person also
goes into great detail about what they have seen; they are puffed up
with idle notions by their unspiritual mind. 19 They have lost connec-
tion with the head, from whom the whole body, supported and held
together by its ligaments and sinews, grows as God causes it to grow.
20 Since you died with Christ to the elemental spiritual forces of this
world, why, as though you still belonged to the world, do you submit to
its rules: 21 "Do not handle! Do not taste! Do not touch!"? 22 These rules,
which have to do with things that are all destined to perish with use,
are based on merely human commands and teachings. 23 Such regula-
tions indeed have an appearance of wisdom, with their self-imposed
worship, their false humility and their harsh treatment of the body,
but they lack any value in restraining sensual indulgence.

LIVING AS THOSE MADE ALIVE IN CHRIST

3 Since, then, you have been raised with Christ, set your hearts on
things above, where Christ is, seated at the right hand of God. 2 Set
your minds on things above, not on earthly things. 3 For you died, and
your life is now hidden with Christ in God. 4 When Christ, who is your[a]
life, appears, then you also will appear with him in glory.
5 Put to death, therefore, whatever belongs to your earthly nature:
sexual immorality, impurity, lust, evil desires and greed, which is idol-
atry. 6 Because of these, the wrath of God is coming.[b] 7 You used to walk
in these ways, in the life you once lived. 8 But now you must also rid
yourselves of all such things as these: anger, rage, malice, slander, and
filthy language from your lips. 9 Do not lie to each other, since you have
taken off your old self with its practices 10 and have put on the new
self, which is being renewed in knowledge in the image of its Creator.
11 Here there is no Gentile or Jew, circumcised or uncircumcised, bar-
barian, Scythian, slave or free, but Christ is all, and is in all.
12 Therefore, as God's chosen people, holy and dearly loved, clothe your-
selves with compassion, kindness, humility, gentleness and patience.
13 Bear with each other and forgive one another if any of you has a griev-
ance against someone. Forgive as the Lord forgave you. 14 And over all
these virtues put on love, which binds them all together in perfect unity.
15 Let the peace of Christ rule in your hearts, since as members of one
body you were called to peace. And be thankful. 16 Let the message of
Christ dwell among you richly as you teach and admonish one another
with all wisdom through psalms, hymns, and songs from the Spirit,
singing to God with gratitude in your hearts. 17 And whatever you do,
whether in word or deed, do it all in the name of the Lord Jesus, giving
thanks to God the Father through him.

INSTRUCTIONS FOR CHRISTIAN HOUSEHOLDS

18 Wives, submit yourselves to your husbands, as is fitting in the Lord.
19 Husbands, love your wives and do not be harsh with them.

[a] 4 Some manuscripts *our* [b] 6 Some early manuscripts *coming on those who are disobedient*

PRAYING SCRIPTURE

Colossians 3

What is the solution for worldliness? Seek those things that are above where Jesus is. We cannot seek the things of the world and the things of God at the same time. We will either seek one or the other. Who should seek the things that are above? Those who "have been raised with Christ" (verse 1).

If your mind is not regularly set "on things above," confess that, and then ask God to help you seek those things every day.

20Children, obey your parents in everything, for this pleases the
Lord.
21Fathers,[a] do not embitter your children, or they will become
discouraged.
22Slaves, obey your earthly masters in everything; and do it, not only
when their eye is on you and to curry their favor, but with sincerity of
heart and reverence for the Lord. 23Whatever you do, work at it with all
your heart, as working for the Lord, not for human masters, 24since you
know that you will receive an inheritance from the Lord as a reward.
It is the Lord Christ you are serving. 25Anyone who does wrong will be
repaid for their wrongs, and there is no favoritism.

4 Masters, provide your slaves with what is right and fair, because
you know that you also have a Master in heaven.

FURTHER INSTRUCTIONS

2Devote yourselves to prayer, being watchful and thankful. 3And
pray for us, too, that God may open a door for our message, so that we
may proclaim the mystery of Christ, for which I am in chains. 4Pray
that I may proclaim it clearly, as I should. 5Be wise in the way you act
toward outsiders; make the most of every opportunity. 6Let your con-
versation be always full of grace, seasoned with salt, so that you may
know how to answer everyone.

FINAL GREETINGS

7Tychicus will tell you all the news about me. He is a dear brother, a
faithful minister and fellow servant[b] in the Lord. 8I am sending him
to you for the express purpose that you may know about our[c] circum-
stances and that he may encourage your hearts. 9He is coming with
Onesimus, our faithful and dear brother, who is one of you. They will
tell you everything that is happening here.
10My fellow prisoner Aristarchus sends you his greetings, as does
Mark, the cousin of Barnabas. (You have received instructions about
him; if he comes to you, welcome him.) 11Jesus, who is called Justus,
also sends greetings. These are the only Jews[d] among my co-workers
for the kingdom of God, and they have proved a comfort to me. 12Epa-
phras, who is one of you and a servant of Christ Jesus, sends greetings.
He is always wrestling in prayer for you, that you may stand firm in
all the will of God, mature and fully assured. 13I vouch for him that
he is working hard for you and for those at Laodicea and Hierapolis.
14Our dear friend Luke, the doctor, and Demas send greetings. 15Give
my greetings to the brothers and sisters at Laodicea, and to Nympha
and the church in her house.
16After this letter has been read to you, see that it is also read in the
church of the Laodiceans and that you in turn read the letter from
Laodicea.
17Tell Archippus: "See to it that you complete the ministry you have
received in the Lord."
18I, Paul, write this greeting in my own hand. Remember my chains.
Grace be with you.

PRAYING SCRIPTURE

Colossians 4

Paul closed Colossians as he did most of his letters, with commendation for his fellow laborers. Mentioned here are Onesimus, who would soon be reconciled to Philemon, and Luke, the author of two New Testament books. God had given Paul a team, and he knew they were responsible for a great amount of ministry.

Who around you can you commend? Always be ready to elevate your co-laborers in the gospel.

[a] 21 Or *Parents* [b] 7 Or *slave*; also in verse 12 [c] 8 Some manuscripts *that he may know about your* [d] 11 Greek *only ones of the circumcision group*

1 THESSALONIANS

Paul's first letter to the church in Thessalonica is one of his earliest letters, written to a church he founded in Acts 17. No one great trouble in the church seems to have prompted the letter, though there do seem to be some issues around the resurrection, sexual morality and some members of the community not pulling their weight in ministry.

In the letter's opening, Paul mentioned that he often prayed for this church, remembering how they had labored in the faith. Paul recalled that they "welcomed the message in the midst of severe suffering" (1:6), which is no minor mention given the prevalence of persecution in the early church era. They needed to be encouraged in their suffering, and their spiritual father provided it.

Paul expressed his thankfulness for God's salvation in their lives from first to last. He celebrated their conversion to Christ through the proclamation of the gospel, as well as their continued growth in the grace of Christ. As we pray for other Christians, we give thanks for the evidence of God's grace in their lives. We praise him for their salvation and for the progress that we see them making in the faith. Sanctification comes with trust in God, the ministry of the Spirit and the surrender and learning of his children. Rejoicing in the growth of another is evidence of our own sanctification.

In the last paragraph of chapter 3, Paul prayed that God would help the Thessalonians have increasing love for each other and for the world, the same kind of love they had seen in Paul. This desire echoes Jesus' words in John 13, that everyone would know we are his disciples because we love one another. Similarly, our prayers for each other should promote growth in this central virtue of the Christian life. Christians cannot say they are growing in faith toward God if they are not likewise growing in love for others. Praying to this end—for ourselves and others—follows the hearts of both Jesus and Paul.

Paul's best-known teaching on prayer in 1 Thessalonians is found in one of the book's shortest verses. In 5:17 he admonished the Thessalonian Christians to "pray continually." The idea here is not that followers of Jesus spend all their time in their prayer closets, never going to work or engaging with the world. Instead, the force of the command is that Christians pray consistently throughout the day. We pray as we work, interact with others and go through the normal routines of our day, all the while praying for God's strength, confessing sin, thanking God for his goodness and lifting up others as they come to our minds or across our paths.

One practical way to pray continually is to develop the habit of praying in the moment with someone who asks for prayer. Rather than only saying, "I'll be praying for you," a promise that often goes unremembered, stop where you are and pray for that person then and there.

PRAYING SCRIPTURE

1 Thessalonians 1

Paul began most of his letters by thanking God for his brothers and sisters in Christ. Here he went even further, recounting their history together in the gospel. While many people have friendships and relationships, only Christians can claim fellowship in the gospel of Jesus.

When you read Paul's bragging on the Thessalonians, what comes to mind? Ask God to help you encourage your partners in the gospel.

1 Paul, Silas[a] and Timothy,

To the church of the Thessalonians in God the Father and the Lord Jesus Christ:

Grace and peace to you.

THANKSGIVING FOR THE THESSALONIANS' FAITH

2 We always thank God for all of you and continually mention you in our prayers. 3 We remember before our God and Father your work produced by faith, your labor prompted by love, and your endurance inspired by hope in our Lord Jesus Christ.

4 For we know, brothers and sisters[b] loved by God, that he has chosen you, 5 because our gospel came to you not simply with words but also with power, with the Holy Spirit and deep conviction. You know how we lived among you for your sake. 6 You became imitators of us and of the Lord, for you welcomed the message in the midst of severe suffering with the joy given by the Holy Spirit. 7 And so you became a model to all the believers in Macedonia and Achaia. 8 The Lord's message rang out from you not only in Macedonia and Achaia — your faith in God has become known everywhere. Therefore we do not need to say anything about it, 9 for they themselves report what kind of reception you gave us. They tell how you turned to God from idols to serve the living and true God, 10 and to wait for his Son from heaven, whom he raised from the dead — Jesus, who rescues us from the coming wrath.

PRAYING SCRIPTURE

1 Thessalonians 2

Few sections of Scripture describe the pains and joys of discipleship better than verses 7–12. Paul used descriptions like "nursing," "toil and hardship," "encouraging," "comforting" and "urging." No Christian can read this and take lightly the idea of real discipleship or be fooled into thinking it does not require great personal investment.

Would you describe your discipling relationships with words like those? If not, ask God to deepen your discipleship opportunities like Paul's with the Thessalonians.

PAUL'S MINISTRY IN THESSALONICA

2 You know, brothers and sisters, that our visit to you was not without results. 2 We had previously suffered and been treated outrageously in Philippi, as you know, but with the help of our God we dared to tell you his gospel in the face of strong opposition. 3 For the appeal we make does not spring from error or impure motives, nor are we trying to trick you. 4 On the contrary, we speak as those approved by God to be entrusted with the gospel. We are not trying to please people but God, who tests our hearts. 5 You know we never used flattery, nor did we put on a mask to cover up greed — God is our witness. 6 We were not looking for praise from people, not from you or anyone else, even though as apostles of Christ we could have asserted our authority. 7 Instead, we were like young children[c] among you.

Just as a nursing mother cares for her children, 8 so we cared for you. Because we loved you so much, we were delighted to share with you not only the gospel of God but our lives as well. 9 Surely you remember, brothers and sisters, our toil and hardship; we worked night and day in order not to be a burden to anyone while we preached the gospel of God to you. 10 You are witnesses, and so is God, of how holy, righteous and blameless we were among you who believed. 11 For you know that we dealt with each of you as a father deals with his own children, 12 encouraging, comforting and urging you to live lives worthy of God, who calls you into his kingdom and glory.

13 And we also thank God continually because, when you received the

[a] *1* Greek *Silvanus*, a variant of *Silas* [b] *4* The Greek word for *brothers and sisters* (*adelphoi*) refers here to believers, both men and women, as part of God's family; also in 2:1,9,14,17; 3:7; 4:1,10,13; 5:1,4,12,14,25,27. [c] *7* Some manuscripts *were gentle*

word of God, which you heard from us, you accepted it not as a human
word, but as it actually is, the word of God, which is indeed at work in
you who believe. 14For you, brothers and sisters, became imitators of
God's churches in Judea, which are in Christ Jesus: You suffered from
your own people the same things those churches suffered from the
Jews 15who killed the Lord Jesus and the prophets and also drove us
out. They displease God and are hostile to everyone 16in their effort to
keep us from speaking to the Gentiles so that they may be saved. In
this way they always heap up their sins to the limit. The wrath of God
has come upon them at last.[a]

PAUL'S LONGING TO SEE THE THESSALONIANS

17But, brothers and sisters, when we were orphaned by being sep-
arated from you for a short time (in person, not in thought), out of
our intense longing we made every effort to see you. 18For we wanted
to come to you — certainly I, Paul, did, again and again — but Satan
blocked our way. 19For what is our hope, our joy, or the crown in which
we will glory in the presence of our Lord Jesus when he comes? Is it not
you? 20Indeed, you are our glory and joy.

3 So when we could stand it no longer, we thought it best to be left
by ourselves in Athens. 2We sent Timothy, who is our brother
and co-worker in God's service in spreading the gospel of Christ, to
strengthen and encourage you in your faith, 3so that no one would be
unsettled by these trials. For you know quite well that we are destined
for them. 4In fact, when we were with you, we kept telling you that we
would be persecuted. And it turned out that way, as you well know. 5For
this reason, when I could stand it no longer, I sent to find out about
your faith. I was afraid that in some way the tempter had tempted you
and that our labors might have been in vain.

TIMOTHY'S ENCOURAGING REPORT

6But Timothy has just now come to us from you and has brought good
news about your faith and love. He has told us that you always have
pleasant memories of us and that you long to see us, just as we also
long to see you. 7Therefore, brothers and sisters, in all our distress and
persecution we were encouraged about you because of your faith. 8For
now we really live, since you are standing firm in the Lord. 9How can we
thank God enough for you in return for all the joy we have in the pres-
ence of our God because of you? 10Night and day we pray most earnestly
that we may see you again and supply what is lacking in your faith.

11Now may our God and Father himself and our Lord Jesus clear the
way for us to come to you. 12May the Lord make your love increase and
overflow for each other and for everyone else, just as ours does for you.
13May he strengthen your hearts so that you will be blameless and holy
in the presence of our God and Father when our Lord Jesus comes with
all his holy ones.

LIVING TO PLEASE GOD

4 As for other matters, brothers and sisters, we instructed you how
to live in order to please God, as in fact you are living. Now we ask
you and urge you in the Lord Jesus to do this more and more. 2For you
know what instructions we gave you by the authority of the Lord Jesus.

[a] 16 Or *them fully*

PRAYING SCRIPTURE

1 Thessalonians 3

Paul ended this chapter with a brief yet beautiful prayer for the spiritual growth of the Thessalonian believers. He asked that God the Father would make a way for him to visit them, that they would love each other increasingly and that he would strengthen their hearts to be blameless and holy in the presence of the Father at the coming of the Lord Jesus (see verses 12–13).

When you pray for others, what do you pray for them? Paul's prayer is a good pattern to follow or include with any intercession.

PRAYING SCRIPTURE

1 Thessalonians 4

For two thousand years, this passage has given hope to weary souls. If Jesus died and rose again—and he did—we can be assured of his coming again. It is the word of the Lord that Christ will return and gather to himself all who have not yet passed through death to heaven (see verse 15).

When life gets heavy and you are worn down, lift your eyes and pray for Jesus to return soon.

3It is God's will that you should be sanctified: that you should avoid sexual immorality; 4that each of you should learn to control your own body[a] in a way that is holy and honorable, 5not in passionate lust like the pagans, who do not know God; 6and that in this matter no one should wrong or take advantage of a brother or sister.[b] The Lord will punish all those who commit such sins, as we told you and warned you before. 7For God did not call us to be impure, but to live a holy life. 8Therefore, anyone who rejects this instruction does not reject a human being but God, the very God who gives you his Holy Spirit.

9Now about your love for one another we do not need to write to you, for you yourselves have been taught by God to love each other. 10And in fact, you do love all of God's family throughout Macedonia. Yet we urge you, brothers and sisters, to do so more and more, 11and to make it your ambition to lead a quiet life: You should mind your own business and work with your hands, just as we told you, 12so that your daily life may win the respect of outsiders and so that you will not be dependent on anybody.

BELIEVERS WHO HAVE DIED

13Brothers and sisters, we do not want you to be uninformed about those who sleep in death, so that you do not grieve like the rest of mankind, who have no hope. 14For we believe that Jesus died and rose again, and so we believe that God will bring with Jesus those who have fallen asleep in him. 15According to the Lord's word, we tell you that we who are still alive, who are left until the coming of the Lord, will certainly not precede those who have fallen asleep. 16For the Lord himself will come down from heaven, with a loud command, with the voice of the archangel and with the trumpet call of God, and the dead in Christ will rise first. 17After that, we who are still alive and are left will be caught up together with them in the clouds to meet the Lord in the air. And so we will be with the Lord forever. 18Therefore encourage one another with these words.

THE DAY OF THE LORD

5 Now, brothers and sisters, about times and dates we do not need to write to you, 2for you know very well that the day of the Lord will come like a thief in the night. 3While people are saying, "Peace and safety," destruction will come on them suddenly, as labor pains on a pregnant woman, and they will not escape.

4But you, brothers and sisters, are not in darkness so that this day should surprise you like a thief. 5You are all children of the light and children of the day. We do not belong to the night or to the darkness. 6So then, let us not be like others, who are asleep, but let us be awake and sober. 7For those who sleep, sleep at night, and those who get drunk, get drunk at night. 8But since we belong to the day, let us be sober, putting on faith and love as a breastplate, and the hope of salvation as a helmet. 9For God did not appoint us to suffer wrath but to receive salvation through our Lord Jesus Christ. 10He died for us so that, whether we are awake or asleep, we may live together with him. 11Therefore encourage one another and build each other up, just as in fact you are doing.

PRAYING SCRIPTURE

1 Thessalonians 5

The Lord wants his people to look for opportunities to encourage one another, and Paul did just that to close out this letter. Verses 16–22 are like bullet-point reminders of basic spiritual principles to us all. Among them is that we "pray continually" (verse 17).

Unceasing prayer does not mean staying on our knees 24 hours a day. It means always taking everything to God in prayer. Strive to make that your practice.

[a] 4 Or *learn to live with your own wife*; or *learn to acquire a wife* [b] 6 The Greek word for *brother or sister* (*adelphos*) refers here to a believer, whether man or woman, as part of God's family.

FINAL INSTRUCTIONS

12Now we ask you, brothers and sisters, to acknowledge those who
work hard among you, who care for you in the Lord and who admonish
you. 13Hold them in the highest regard in love because of their work.
Live in peace with each other. 14And we urge you, brothers and sisters,
warn those who are idle and disruptive, encourage the disheartened,
help the weak, be patient with everyone. 15Make sure that nobody pays
back wrong for wrong, but always strive to do what is good for each
other and for everyone else.

16Rejoice always, 17pray continually, 18give thanks in all circum-
stances; for this is God's will for you in Christ Jesus.

19Do not quench the Spirit. 20Do not treat prophecies with contempt
21but test them all; hold on to what is good, 22reject every kind of evil.

23May God himself, the God of peace, sanctify you through and
through. May your whole spirit, soul and body be kept blameless at
the coming of our Lord Jesus Christ. 24The one who calls you is faith-
ful, and he will do it.

25Brothers and sisters, pray for us. 26Greet all God's people with a
holy kiss. 27I charge you before the Lord to have this letter read to all
the brothers and sisters.

28The grace of our Lord Jesus Christ be with you.

2 THESSALONIANS

Paul's second letter to the Thessalonian church takes a more serious tone than the first. It appears the church was facing ongoing persecution, as Paul referenced their "perseverance and faith in all the persecutions and trials" endured for the gospel (1:4). News of their suffering was an occasion for Paul to pray. He wrote that he and his co-laborers prayed always that God would make the Thessalonians worthy of the calling he placed on them, by bringing to fruition every desire for goodness and every deed prompted by faith (see 1:11–12).

Paul also spoke of those who were troubling the Thessalonians as they tried to follow Jesus. He reminded the church that God is the ultimate Judge who will make all things right in the end. The false teachers would meet the same end as Satan, being "punished with everlasting destruction" (1:9).

The deception that had infiltrated their thinking seems to have concerned the return of Jesus (see 2:1–12). Paul encouraged them to be neither unsettled nor alarmed by reports that "the day of the Lord," commonly understood to be the second coming, had happened but they had somehow missed it. Paul then laid out a series of events that must happen first, a series that has been subject to endless speculation since Paul wrote it. After assuring them things were in God's control, he attempted to comfort them with the knowledge that God chose them for salvation; they need not worry.

Paul not only prayed for this church that he loved, but he also wanted them to be praying for him. It was not a one-way street. In particular, he coveted their prayers that his team would "be delivered from wicked and evil people" (3:2). In essence, Paul was asking for prayer that his missionary efforts would not be hindered. These efforts were twofold. First, Paul planted churches everywhere he went, getting the gospel out to those who had never heard and assembling those who believed into local house churches. Second, we see from his journeys recorded in Acts and from the content of his letters that he carried a tremendous burden for Christians to grow in their faith and was committed to helping it happen.

When Paul asked the Thessalonians to pray that God's word might "spread rapidly" and "be honored," it was not a mystery to them—that is what happened in their midst. As such, they should long to see it happen with others. Paul wanted them to pray that God's word would quickly pierce the hearts of men, women, boys and girls so that they might cry out to God and be saved.

In this, Paul provided a good example for how we can pray for our own local congregations. We can and should pray that our churches would be filled with evangelistic fervor, spreading the good news of the gospel everywhere we go. As we go, we pray that our efforts will be blessed by the Spirit so that people will respond. We should also pray that the Lord will protect our churches from heresy and divisiveness that would undercut our evangelistic mission.

1 Paul, Silas[a] and Timothy,

To the church of the Thessalonians in God our Father and the Lord
Jesus Christ:

2 Grace and peace to you from God the Father and the Lord Jesus
Christ.

THANKSGIVING AND PRAYER

3 We ought always to thank God for you, brothers and sisters,[b] and
rightly so, because your faith is growing more and more, and the love
all of you have for one another is increasing. 4 Therefore, among God's
churches we boast about your perseverance and faith in all the perse-
cutions and trials you are enduring.

5 All this is evidence that God's judgment is right, and as a result
you will be counted worthy of the kingdom of God, for which you are
suffering. 6 God is just: He will pay back trouble to those who trouble
you 7 and give relief to you who are troubled, and to us as well. This
will happen when the Lord Jesus is revealed from heaven in blazing
fire with his powerful angels. 8 He will punish those who do not know
God and do not obey the gospel of our Lord Jesus. 9 They will be pun-
ished with everlasting destruction and shut out from the presence of
the Lord and from the glory of his might 10 on the day he comes to be
glorified in his holy people and to be marveled at among all those who
have believed. This includes you, because you believed our testimony
to you.

11 With this in mind, we constantly pray for you, that our God may
make you worthy of his calling, and that by his power he may bring to
fruition your every desire for goodness and your every deed prompted
by faith. 12 We pray this so that the name of our Lord Jesus may be glo-
rified in you, and you in him, according to the grace of our God and
the Lord Jesus Christ.[c]

THE MAN OF LAWLESSNESS

2 Concerning the coming of our Lord Jesus Christ and our being
gathered to him, we ask you, brothers and sisters, 2 not to be-
come easily unsettled or alarmed by the teaching allegedly from us—
whether by a prophecy or by word of mouth or by letter—asserting
that the day of the Lord has already come. 3 Don't let anyone deceive
you in any way, for that day will not come until the rebellion occurs
and the man of lawlessness[d] is revealed, the man doomed to destruc-
tion. 4 He will oppose and will exalt himself over everything that is
called God or is worshiped, so that he sets himself up in God's temple,
proclaiming himself to be God.

5 Don't you remember that when I was with you I used to tell you
these things? 6 And now you know what is holding him back, so that
he may be revealed at the proper time. 7 For the secret power of law-
lessness is already at work; but the one who now holds it back will con-
tinue to do so till he is taken out of the way. 8 And then the lawless one
will be revealed, whom the Lord Jesus will overthrow with the breath

[a] *1* Greek *Silvanus*, a variant of *Silas* [b] *3* The Greek word for *brothers and sisters* (*adelphoi*) refers here to believers, both men and women, as part of God's family; also in 2:1,13,15; 3:1,6,13. [c] *12* Or *God and Lord, Jesus Christ*
[d] *3* Some manuscripts *sin*

PRAYING SCRIPTURE

2 Thessalonians 1

Paul began this second letter to the church at Thessalonica much the same as the first, commending them "because your faith is growing more and more" (verse 3). Everywhere he went, he bragged on them for their love for each other and for their patience and faith in suffering (see verse 4).

Imagine the kind of faith that draws an apostle's commendation twice! Ask God for the kind of faith, love and endurance that affects everyone who knows you.

PRAYING SCRIPTURE

2 Thessalonians 2

To the Thessalonian believers, who were apparently concerned that they had somehow missed Jesus' return, Paul gave this preview: First, there would be a falling away from the faith, confirmed by the rise of the "man of lawlessness . . . the man doomed to destruction" (verse 3). This is commonly understood as a reference to the Antichrist.

Things will get worse before the return of Christ. Pray for the Spirit's strength if you live until those days.

of his mouth and destroy by the splendor of his coming. 9The coming
of the lawless one will be in accordance with how Satan works. He will
use all sorts of displays of power through signs and wonders that serve
the lie, 10and all the ways that wickedness deceives those who are per-
ishing. They perish because they refused to love the truth and so be
saved. 11For this reason God sends them a powerful delusion so that
they will believe the lie 12and so that all will be condemned who have
not believed the truth but have delighted in wickedness.

STAND FIRM

13But we ought always to thank God for you, brothers and sisters
loved by the Lord, because God chose you as firstfruits[a] to be saved
through the sanctifying work of the Spirit and through belief in the
truth. 14He called you to this through our gospel, that you might share
in the glory of our Lord Jesus Christ.
15So then, brothers and sisters, stand firm and hold fast to the teach-
ings[b] we passed on to you, whether by word of mouth or by letter.
16May our Lord Jesus Christ himself and God our Father, who loved
us and by his grace gave us eternal encouragement and good hope,
17encourage your hearts and strengthen you in every good deed and
word.

REQUEST FOR PRAYER

3 As for other matters, brothers and sisters, pray for us that the mes-
sage of the Lord may spread rapidly and be honored, just as it was
with you. 2And pray that we may be delivered from wicked and evil
people, for not everyone has faith. 3But the Lord is faithful, and he will
strengthen you and protect you from the evil one. 4We have confidence
in the Lord that you are doing and will continue to do the things we
command. 5May the Lord direct your hearts into God's love and Christ's
perseverance.

WARNING AGAINST IDLENESS

6In the name of the Lord Jesus Christ, we command you, brothers
and sisters, to keep away from every believer who is idle and disruptive
and does not live according to the teaching[c] you received from us. 7For
you yourselves know how you ought to follow our example. We were
not idle when we were with you, 8nor did we eat anyone's food without
paying for it. On the contrary, we worked night and day, laboring and
toiling so that we would not be a burden to any of you. 9We did this, not
because we do not have the right to such help, but in order to offer our-
selves as a model for you to imitate. 10For even when we were with you,
we gave you this rule: "The one who is unwilling to work shall not eat."
11We hear that some among you are idle and disruptive. They are not
busy; they are busybodies. 12Such people we command and urge in the
Lord Jesus Christ to settle down and earn the food they eat. 13And as for
you, brothers and sisters, never tire of doing what is good.
14Take special note of anyone who does not obey our instruction
in this letter. Do not associate with them, in order that they may feel
ashamed. 15Yet do not regard them as an enemy, but warn them as you
would a fellow believer.

PRAYING SCRIPTURE

2 Thessalonians 3

The Lord sympathizes with our weakness and knows our tendency to grow weary in doing the right thing. Paul and his team were no exceptions. In asking the Thessalonians for prayer, Paul admitted his own need. He could not minister, and the word could not "be honored" without God's presence (see verse 1).

When tempted to self-sufficiency, it is worth remembering that not even the apostles depended on themselves. Submit yourself to the Spirit and depend on him in all things.

---

[a] 13 Some manuscripts *because from the beginning God chose you* [b] 15 Or *traditions* [c] 6 Or *tradition*

FINAL GREETINGS

16Now may the Lord of peace himself give you peace at all times and
in every way. The Lord be with all of you.
17I, Paul, write this greeting in my own hand, which is the distin-
guishing mark in all my letters. This is how I write.
18The grace of our Lord Jesus Christ be with you all.

1 TIMOTHY

First Timothy is the first of Paul's four letters, along with 2 Timothy, Titus and Philemon, written to individuals rather than churches. The first three of these letters are commonly known as the "Pastoral Letters" and deal with aspects of leading and shepherding God's people.

Timothy served as a pastor at the church in Ephesus, which Paul founded while on a missionary journey (see Acts 18). Paul knew the church well and loved Timothy as a son in the ministry, but he wrote because the church faced a host of issues. The church dealt with false teaching, unqualified leaders and members who were taking advantage of others' goodness. Paul's letter helped Timothy navigate these issues so that everything in the house of God might be done in a fitting and orderly way.

Paul told his young protégé that he wanted the church to pray for all people, but he specifically mentioned people who were in "authority," referencing kings in particular. That is, Christians everywhere should pray for their government leaders. When Paul wrote this letter, the church lived under the authority of the Roman emperor. It would be nearly three hundred years before a church-friendly emperor arose, and many in the intervening years were hostile. Paul's example shows us that Christians cannot excuse themselves from praying for leaders simply because we do not agree with their politics, their personalities or even their persecution.

A specific reason we should pray for our leaders is so that Jesus' people may live quiet lives that are pleasing to God. As we pray for our leaders, we should ask God to lead them to make wise decisions that would enable Christians to follow Jesus and carry out the mission of the church without threat of violence or government interference. Christianity need not have exclusivity for believers to advance the gospel, but doors are opened when leaders have wisdom and permit it.

In many places, Christians desire the freedom to worship; in other places Christians are concerned about losing that freedom. Paul's call to pray provides instruction. Regardless of the goodness of leaders, we should pray for them to do good. Humbly we bow our knees in prayer and ask God to bless them. When we gather as the body, we pray for God to give our leaders wisdom and courage. Then we go about our business of following Jesus, and we live in a way that honors him. We entrust our leaders and their decisions to the Lord and trust him to protect his people.

Another emphasis on prayer relates to those who would place unbiblical regulations on God's people, even telling them whether they could marry and what they could and could not eat (see 4:5). This struggle is mentioned in several New Testament books, but here Paul says all good "is consecrated by the word of God and prayer." Prayers of thanksgiving for our food are as important as the food itself.

1 Paul, an apostle of Christ Jesus by the command of God our Savior
and of Christ Jesus our hope,
2To Timothy my true son in the faith:
Grace, mercy and peace from God the Father and Christ Jesus our Lord.

TIMOTHY CHARGED TO OPPOSE FALSE TEACHERS

3As I urged you when I went into Macedonia, stay there in Ephesus
so that you may command certain people not to teach false doctrines
any longer 4or to devote themselves to myths and endless genealogies.
Such things promote controversial speculations rather than advanc-
ing God's work — which is by faith. 5The goal of this command is love,
which comes from a pure heart and a good conscience and a sincere
faith. 6Some have departed from these and have turned to meaning-
less talk. 7They want to be teachers of the law, but they do not know
what they are talking about or what they so confidently affirm.
8We know that the law is good if one uses it properly. 9We also know
that the law is made not for the righteous but for lawbreakers and reb-
els, the ungodly and sinful, the unholy and irreligious, for those who
kill their fathers or mothers, for murderers, 10for the sexually immoral,
for those practicing homosexuality, for slave traders and liars and per-
jurers — and for whatever else is contrary to the sound doctrine 11that
conforms to the gospel concerning the glory of the blessed God, which
he entrusted to me.

THE LORD'S GRACE TO PAUL

12I thank Christ Jesus our Lord, who has given me strength, that
he considered me trustworthy, appointing me to his service. 13Even
though I was once a blasphemer and a persecutor and a violent man,
I was shown mercy because I acted in ignorance and unbelief. 14The
grace of our Lord was poured out on me abundantly, along with the
faith and love that are in Christ Jesus.
15Here is a trustworthy saying that deserves full acceptance: Christ
Jesus came into the world to save sinners — of whom I am the worst.
16But for that very reason I was shown mercy so that in me, the worst of
sinners, Christ Jesus might display his immense patience as an exam-
ple for those who would believe in him and receive eternal life. 17Now
to the King eternal, immortal, invisible, the only God, be honor and
glory for ever and ever. Amen.

THE CHARGE TO TIMOTHY RENEWED

18Timothy, my son, I am giving you this command in keeping with
the prophecies once made about you, so that by recalling them you
may fight the battle well, 19holding on to faith and a good conscience,
which some have rejected and so have suffered shipwreck with regard
to the faith. 20Among them are Hymenaeus and Alexander, whom I
have handed over to Satan to be taught not to blaspheme.

INSTRUCTIONS ON WORSHIP

2 I urge, then, first of all, that petitions, prayers, intercession and
thanksgiving be made for all people — 2for kings and all those in
authority, that we may live peaceful and quiet lives in all godliness and
holiness. 3This is good, and pleases God our Savior, 4who wants all peo-
ple to be saved and to come to a knowledge of the truth. 5For there is

PRAYING SCRIPTURE

1 Timothy 1

Paul's first letter to Timothy starts with a reminder to encourage those in Ephesus to keep their doctrine, "the gospel concerning the glory of the blessed God," pure (verse 11). They had a responsibility to prevent "some" from changing from what they had been taught. Given the clarity and directness Paul used, it seems likely that "some" were already causing problems.

Attempts to change the gospel are the challenge of every generation. Ask God to help you keep the glorious gospel in your daily living.

PRAYING SCRIPTURE

1 Timothy 2

As citizens of the kingdom of heaven living as citizens of earthly nations, we should pray for our leaders and ask God to fill them with wisdom. Our temptation is to pray for the leaders we like or with whom we agree, but against those with whom we disagree.

Pray that leaders may come to be saved, because "this is good, and pleases God our Savior" (verse 3).

one God and one mediator between God and mankind, the man Christ Jesus, 6 who gave himself as a ransom for all people. This has now been witnessed to at the proper time. 7 And for this purpose I was appointed a herald and an apostle — I am telling the truth, I am not lying — and a true and faithful teacher of the Gentiles.

8 Therefore I want the men everywhere to pray, lifting up holy hands without anger or disputing. 9 I also want the women to dress modestly, with decency and propriety, adorning themselves, not with elaborate hairstyles or gold or pearls or expensive clothes, 10 but with good deeds, appropriate for women who profess to worship God.

11 A woman[a] should learn in quietness and full submission. 12 I do not permit a woman to teach or to assume authority over a man;[b] she must be quiet. 13 For Adam was formed first, then Eve. 14 And Adam was not the one deceived; it was the woman who was deceived and became a sinner. 15 But women[c] will be saved through childbearing — if they continue in faith, love and holiness with propriety.

QUALIFICATIONS FOR OVERSEERS AND DEACONS

3 Here is a trustworthy saying: Whoever aspires to be an overseer desires a noble task. 2 Now the overseer is to be above reproach, faithful to his wife, temperate, self-controlled, respectable, hospitable, able to teach, 3 not given to drunkenness, not violent but gentle, not quarrelsome, not a lover of money. 4 He must manage his own family well and see that his children obey him, and he must do so in a manner worthy of full[d] respect. 5 (If anyone does not know how to manage his own family, how can he take care of God's church?) 6 He must not be a recent convert, or he may become conceited and fall under the same judgment as the devil. 7 He must also have a good reputation with outsiders, so that he will not fall into disgrace and into the devil's trap.

8 In the same way, deacons[e] are to be worthy of respect, sincere, not indulging in much wine, and not pursuing dishonest gain. 9 They must keep hold of the deep truths of the faith with a clear conscience. 10 They must first be tested; and then if there is nothing against them, let them serve as deacons.

11 In the same way, the women[f] are to be worthy of respect, not malicious talkers but temperate and trustworthy in everything.

12 A deacon must be faithful to his wife and must manage his children and his household well. 13 Those who have served well gain an excellent standing and great assurance in their faith in Christ Jesus.

REASONS FOR PAUL'S INSTRUCTIONS

14 Although I hope to come to you soon, I am writing you these instructions so that, 15 if I am delayed, you will know how people ought to conduct themselves in God's household, which is the church of the living God, the pillar and foundation of the truth. 16 Beyond all question, the mystery from which true godliness springs is great:

He appeared in the flesh,
  was vindicated by the Spirit,[g]

PRAYING SCRIPTURE

1 Timothy 3

How we organize our churches and how leaders tend to those in their care is important because the church is "the pillar and foundation of the truth" (verse 15). While churches in different cultures may vary in some respects, the basic leadership structure should follow Biblical patterns.

How frequently do you pray for the leaders of your church? It might help to make a list of their names. Then lift them daily to God in prayer.

---

[a] *11* Or *wife*; also in verse 12 [b] *12* Or *over her husband* [c] *15* Greek *she* [d] *4* Or *him with proper* [e] *8* The word *deacons* refers here to Christians designated to serve with the overseers/elders of the church in a variety of ways; similarly in verse 12; and in Romans 16:1 and Phil. 1:1. [f] *11* Possibly deacons' wives or women who are deacons [g] *16* Or *vindicated in spirit*

was seen by angels,
 was preached among the nations,
was believed on in the world,
 was taken up in glory.

4 The Spirit clearly says that in later times some will abandon the
faith and follow deceiving spirits and things taught by demons.
[2]Such teachings come through hypocritical liars, whose consciences
have been seared as with a hot iron. [3]They forbid people to marry and
order them to abstain from certain foods, which God created to be
received with thanksgiving by those who believe and who know the
truth. [4]For everything God created is good, and nothing is to be re-
jected if it is received with thanksgiving, [5]because it is consecrated by
the word of God and prayer.

[6]If you point these things out to the brothers and sisters,[a] you will be
a good minister of Christ Jesus, nourished on the truths of the faith and
of the good teaching that you have followed. [7]Have nothing to do with
godless myths and old wives' tales; rather, train yourself to be godly.
[8]For physical training is of some value, but godliness has value for all
things, holding promise for both the present life and the life to come.
[9]This is a trustworthy saying that deserves full acceptance. [10]That is
why we labor and strive, because we have put our hope in the living
God, who is the Savior of all people, and especially of those who believe.

[11]Command and teach these things. [12]Don't let anyone look down
on you because you are young, but set an example for the believers in
speech, in conduct, in love, in faith and in purity. [13]Until I come, devote
yourself to the public reading of Scripture, to preaching and to teach-
ing. [14]Do not neglect your gift, which was given you through prophecy
when the body of elders laid their hands on you.

[15]Be diligent in these matters; give yourself wholly to them, so that
everyone may see your progress. [16]Watch your life and doctrine closely.
Persevere in them, because if you do, you will save both yourself and
your hearers.

WIDOWS, ELDERS AND SLAVES

5 Do not rebuke an older man harshly, but exhort him as if he were
your father. Treat younger men as brothers, [2]older women as
mothers, and younger women as sisters, with absolute purity.

[3]Give proper recognition to those widows who are really in need.
[4]But if a widow has children or grandchildren, these should learn first
of all to put their religion into practice by caring for their own family
and so repaying their parents and grandparents, for this is pleasing
to God. [5]The widow who is really in need and left all alone puts her
hope in God and continues night and day to pray and to ask God for
help. [6]But the widow who lives for pleasure is dead even while she
lives. [7]Give the people these instructions, so that no one may be open
to blame. [8]Anyone who does not provide for their relatives, and espe-
cially for their own household, has denied the faith and is worse than
an unbeliever.

[9]No widow may be put on the list of widows unless she is over sixty,
has been faithful to her husband, [10]and is well known for her good

[a] 6 The Greek word for *brothers and sisters* (*adelphoi*) refers here to believers, both men and women, as part of God's family.

PRAYING SCRIPTURE

1 Timothy 4

Similar to a warning Paul made about the falling away and rise of the Antichrist, Paul warned that some will "abandon the faith" in the latter days (verse 1). Being filled with rebellion and false teaching, they will forbid people to marry and order them to abstain from certain foods (see verse 3).

God's children should be on guard for false teaching. In these days, pray and remain closer to the Word than ever.

PRAYING SCRIPTURE

1 Timothy 5

Paul gave instruction on how churches should both respect and care for their vulnerable members: Older men should not be rebuked, and older women should be treated as mothers. We also read how easily young widows—unmarried Christians—could be turned aside after Satan.

Local churches are better examples of the gospel when members love and treat each other like family, so pray with that kind of heart.

deeds, such as bringing up children, showing hospitality, washing the
feet of the Lord's people, helping those in trouble and devoting herself
to all kinds of good deeds.
11As for younger widows, do not put them on such a list. For when
their sensual desires overcome their dedication to Christ, they want
to marry. 12Thus they bring judgment on themselves, because they
have broken their first pledge. 13Besides, they get into the habit of be-
ing idle and going about from house to house. And not only do they
become idlers, but also busybodies who talk nonsense, saying things
they ought not to. 14So I counsel younger widows to marry, to have chil-
dren, to manage their homes and to give the enemy no opportunity
for slander. 15Some have in fact already turned away to follow Satan.
16If any woman who is a believer has widows in her care, she should
continue to help them and not let the church be burdened with them,
so that the church can help those widows who are really in need.
17The elders who direct the affairs of the church well are worthy of
double honor, especially those whose work is preaching and teaching.
18For Scripture says, "Do not muzzle an ox while it is treading out the
grain,"[a] and "The worker deserves his wages."[b] 19Do not entertain an
accusation against an elder unless it is brought by two or three wit-
nesses. 20But those elders who are sinning you are to reprove before
everyone, so that the others may take warning. 21I charge you, in the
sight of God and Christ Jesus and the elect angels, to keep these in-
structions without partiality, and to do nothing out of favoritism.
22Do not be hasty in the laying on of hands, and do not share in the
sins of others. Keep yourself pure.
23Stop drinking only water, and use a little wine because of your
stomach and your frequent illnesses.
24The sins of some are obvious, reaching the place of judgment
ahead of them; the sins of others trail behind them. 25In the same way,
good deeds are obvious, and even those that are not obvious cannot
remain hidden forever.

6 All who are under the yoke of slavery should consider their mas-
ters worthy of full respect, so that God's name and our teaching
may not be slandered. 2Those who have believing masters should not
show them disrespect just because they are fellow believers. Instead,
they should serve them even better because their masters are dear to
them as fellow believers and are devoted to the welfare[c] of their slaves.

FALSE TEACHERS AND THE LOVE OF MONEY

These are the things you are to teach and insist on. 3If anyone
teaches otherwise and does not agree to the sound instruction of our
Lord Jesus Christ and to godly teaching, 4they are conceited and un-
derstand nothing. They have an unhealthy interest in controversies
and quarrels about words that result in envy, strife, malicious talk, evil
suspicions 5and constant friction between people of corrupt mind, who
have been robbed of the truth and who think that godliness is a means
to financial gain.
6But godliness with contentment is great gain. 7For we brought
nothing into the world, and we can take nothing out of it. 8But if we
have food and clothing, we will be content with that. 9Those who want
to get rich fall into temptation and a trap and into many foolish and

PRAYING SCRIPTURE

1 Timothy 6

Contentment is one of the most difficult lessons in the Christian life. For many the lure of materialism is a constant temptation to trust in things rather than trusting in God. Paul returned to the basics, teaching the early Christians to be content with something to eat and wear.

How much does it take to satisfy you? Ask God to help you be content in him and not to depend on other things to bring you joy.

[a] 18 Deut. 25:4 [b] 18 Luke 10:7 [c] 2 Or *and benefit from the service*

harmful desires that plunge people into ruin and destruction. 10For
the love of money is a root of all kinds of evil. Some people, eager for
money, have wandered from the faith and pierced themselves with
many griefs.

FINAL CHARGE TO TIMOTHY

11But you, man of God, flee from all this, and pursue righteousness,
godliness, faith, love, endurance and gentleness. 12Fight the good fight
of the faith. Take hold of the eternal life to which you were called when
you made your good confession in the presence of many witnesses.
13In the sight of God, who gives life to everything, and of Christ Jesus,
who while testifying before Pontius Pilate made the good confession,
I charge you 14to keep this command without spot or blame until the
appearing of our Lord Jesus Christ, 15which God will bring about in his
own time — God, the blessed and only Ruler, the King of kings and
Lord of lords, 16who alone is immortal and who lives in unapproach-
able light, whom no one has seen or can see. To him be honor and
might forever. Amen.

17Command those who are rich in this present world not to be arro-
gant nor to put their hope in wealth, which is so uncertain, but to put
their hope in God, who richly provides us with everything for our en-
joyment. 18Command them to do good, to be rich in good deeds, and to
be generous and willing to share. 19In this way they will lay up treasure
for themselves as a firm foundation for the coming age, so that they
may take hold of the life that is truly life.

20Timothy, guard what has been entrusted to your care. Turn away
from godless chatter and the opposing ideas of what is falsely called
knowledge, 21which some have professed and in so doing have de-
parted from the faith.

Grace be with you all.

2 TIMOTHY

Many believe that 2 Timothy is the last letter Paul wrote. He appears to have written this letter from prison, not house arrest, as he was chained. He asked for his cloak, which suggests that he was in a cold space. He also asked for his books and parchments, perhaps to continue studying the Scriptures and encouraging the churches (see 4:13).

Paul's letter does not mention Timothy's exact situation, but its contents lead us to believe that Timothy was facing stiff opposition in his ministry. Paul encouraged the young pastor to continue preaching the Word when it was convenient and when it was not, "in season and out of season" (4:2); to have courage in the face of difficulty, to "endure hardship" (4:5); and to correct his opponents with humility, "leading them to a knowledge of the truth" (2:25).

In his prayer for Timothy, the apostle thanked God for Timothy's sincere faith in Christ, remembering that Timothy's faith was passed down to him through the teaching of his grandmother and mother. Christians today do well to remember the formative role of the family in passing down the basics of the faith. Followers of Christ who have children need to pray not only for their children but also in anticipation for their grandchildren and great-grandchildren even before they are born. Beseeching God for one's descendants to come to faith in Jesus and live to honor him is the first step to building a godly family.

One important theme in 2 Timothy is the role of courage in the Christian life. Paul wanted Timothy to be courageous, but not in his own strength. He reminded Timothy that the Spirit is the One who brings power, love and self-discipline; fear is not of the Spirit of God.

One of the clearest descriptions of the disciple-making process is included in chapter 2: "You then, my son, be strong in the grace that is in Christ Jesus. And the things that you have heard me say in the presence of many witnesses entrust to reliable people who will also be qualified to teach others" (verses 1–2). Making disciples, the core of the Great Commission, happens generationally as the disciple's life is passed from one to the next. Though proclamation or teaching is important in the disciple's growth, truth is transmitted best life to life.

Christians face many situations where we must display the courage of our convictions in the face of mockery, adversity and opposition. Timothy was not left without instruction on this point. In these times, we would do well to remember that the strength to stand does not come from ourselves but from the Lord. We pray and ask him in advance for the courage to live for him and to make uncomfortable stands, to "[suffer], like a good soldier of Christ Jesus" (2:3). We also pray in the moment of testing, asking the Lord to give us courage in the moment, love for those who oppose us and the wisdom to know what we ought to say and do.

1 Paul, an apostle of Christ Jesus by the will of God, in keeping with
the promise of life that is in Christ Jesus,

[2]To Timothy, my dear son:

Grace, mercy and peace from God the Father and Christ Jesus our
Lord.

THANKSGIVING

[3]I thank God, whom I serve, as my ancestors did, with a clear con-
science, as night and day I constantly remember you in my prayers.
[4]Recalling your tears, I long to see you, so that I may be filled with joy.
[5]I am reminded of your sincere faith, which first lived in your grand-
mother Lois and in your mother Eunice and, I am persuaded, now lives
in you also.

APPEAL FOR LOYALTY TO PAUL AND THE GOSPEL

[6]For this reason I remind you to fan into flame the gift of God, which
is in you through the laying on of my hands. [7]For the Spirit God gave
us does not make us timid, but gives us power, love and self-discipline.
[8]So do not be ashamed of the testimony about our Lord or of me his
prisoner. Rather, join with me in suffering for the gospel, by the power
of God. [9]He has saved us and called us to a holy life — not because of
anything we have done but because of his own purpose and grace. This
grace was given us in Christ Jesus before the beginning of time, [10]but
it has now been revealed through the appearing of our Savior, Christ
Jesus, who has destroyed death and has brought life and immortality
to light through the gospel. [11]And of this gospel I was appointed a her-
ald and an apostle and a teacher. [12]That is why I am suffering as I am.
Yet this is no cause for shame, because I know whom I have believed,
and am convinced that he is able to guard what I have entrusted to
him until that day.

[13]What you heard from me, keep as the pattern of sound teaching,
with faith and love in Christ Jesus. [14]Guard the good deposit that was
entrusted to you — guard it with the help of the Holy Spirit who lives
in us.

EXAMPLES OF DISLOYALTY AND LOYALTY

[15]You know that everyone in the province of Asia has deserted me,
including Phygelus and Hermogenes.

[16]May the Lord show mercy to the household of Onesiphorus, be-
cause he often refreshed me and was not ashamed of my chains. [17]On
the contrary, when he was in Rome, he searched hard for me until he
found me. [18]May the Lord grant that he will find mercy from the Lord
on that day! You know very well in how many ways he helped me in
Ephesus.

THE APPEAL RENEWED

2 You then, my son, be strong in the grace that is in Christ Jesus.
[2]And the things you have heard me say in the presence of many
witnesses entrust to reliable people who will also be qualified to teach
others. [3]Join with me in suffering, like a good soldier of Christ Jesus.
[4]No one serving as a soldier gets entangled in civilian affairs, but
rather tries to please his commanding officer. [5]Similarly, anyone who
competes as an athlete does not receive the victor's crown except by

PRAYING SCRIPTURE

2 Timothy 1

God's people are better equipped to walk through difficulties when they are secure in the salvation God has given. God has called us "to a holy life—not because of anything we have done," meaning we can do nothing to secure salvation. It is always because of "his own purpose and grace" (verse 9).

Many believe good works should get people to heaven, but that is not God's plan. Thank God that salvation depends solely on him.

PRAYING SCRIPTURE

2 Timothy 2

Paul commanded his young protégé, Timothy, to "join with me in suffering, like a good soldier of Christ Jesus" (verse 3). The wartime metaphor includes remaining disentangled from civilian affairs (see verse 4). Our goal should be to please the One who calls us to service no matter how difficult the way might become.

Are you committed to endure hardship? Ask God for the strength of a good soldier who stays focused on that battle.

competing according to the rules. 6The hardworking farmer should be
the first to receive a share of the crops. 7Reflect on what I am saying,
for the Lord will give you insight into all this.
8Remember Jesus Christ, raised from the dead, descended from Da-
vid. This is my gospel, 9for which I am suffering even to the point of
being chained like a criminal. But God's word is not chained. 10There-
fore I endure everything for the sake of the elect, that they too may
obtain the salvation that is in Christ Jesus, with eternal glory.
11Here is a trustworthy saying:

If we died with him,
    we will also live with him;
12 if we endure,
    we will also reign with him.
If we disown him,
    he will also disown us;
13 if we are faithless,
    he remains faithful,
    for he cannot disown himself.

DEALING WITH FALSE TEACHERS

14Keep reminding God's people of these things. Warn them before
God against quarreling about words; it is of no value, and only ruins
those who listen. 15Do your best to present yourself to God as one ap-
proved, a worker who does not need to be ashamed and who correctly
handles the word of truth. 16Avoid godless chatter, because those who
indulge in it will become more and more ungodly. 17Their teaching
will spread like gangrene. Among them are Hymenaeus and Philetus,
18who have departed from the truth. They say that the resurrection has
already taken place, and they destroy the faith of some. 19Neverthe-
less, God's solid foundation stands firm, sealed with this inscription:
"The Lord knows those who are his," and, "Everyone who confesses the
name of the Lord must turn away from wickedness."
20In a large house there are articles not only of gold and silver, but
also of wood and clay; some are for special purposes and some for com-
mon use. 21Those who cleanse themselves from the latter will be in-
struments for special purposes, made holy, useful to the Master and
prepared to do any good work.
22Flee the evil desires of youth and pursue righteousness, faith, love
and peace, along with those who call on the Lord out of a pure heart.
23Don't have anything to do with foolish and stupid arguments, be-
cause you know they produce quarrels. 24And the Lord's servant must
not be quarrelsome but must be kind to everyone, able to teach, not
resentful. 25Opponents must be gently instructed, in the hope that God
will grant them repentance leading them to a knowledge of the truth,
26and that they will come to their senses and escape from the trap of
the devil, who has taken them captive to do his will.

3 But mark this: There will be terrible times in the last days. 2People
will be lovers of themselves, lovers of money, boastful, proud, abu-
sive, disobedient to their parents, ungrateful, unholy, 3without love,
unforgiving, slanderous, without self-control, brutal, not lovers of the
good, 4treacherous, rash, conceited, lovers of pleasure rather than lov-
ers of God— 5having a form of godliness but denying its power. Have
nothing to do with such people.

PRAYING SCRIPTURE

2 Timothy 3

The days that precede the return of Christ will be perilous. The world will be filled with every imaginable immorality as people race further and further from God. Some people will even claim a form of godliness, but Paul warned that they lack the power of God. We should turn away from such people, lest we be led away (see verses 5–6). Without Jesus, we would face the same doom to destruction as the world. Seek your refuge in him.

6 They are the kind who worm their way into homes and gain control
over gullible women, who are loaded down with sins and are swayed
by all kinds of evil desires, 7 always learning but never able to come to
a knowledge of the truth. 8 Just as Jannes and Jambres opposed Mo-
ses, so also these teachers oppose the truth. They are men of depraved
minds, who, as far as the faith is concerned, are rejected. 9 But they will
not get very far because, as in the case of those men, their folly will be
clear to everyone.

A FINAL CHARGE TO TIMOTHY

10 You, however, know all about my teaching, my way of life, my
purpose, faith, patience, love, endurance, 11 persecutions, sufferings—
what kinds of things happened to me in Antioch, Iconium and Lys-
tra, the persecutions I endured. Yet the Lord rescued me from all of
them. 12 In fact, everyone who wants to live a godly life in Christ Jesus
will be persecuted, 13 while evildoers and impostors will go from bad
to worse, deceiving and being deceived. 14 But as for you, continue in
what you have learned and have become convinced of, because you
know those from whom you learned it, 15 and how from infancy you
have known the Holy Scriptures, which are able to make you wise for
salvation through faith in Christ Jesus. 16 All Scripture is God-breathed
and is useful for teaching, rebuking, correcting and training in righ-
teousness, 17 so that the servant of God[a] may be thoroughly equipped
for every good work.

4 In the presence of God and of Christ Jesus, who will judge the liv-
ing and the dead, and in view of his appearing and his kingdom, I
give you this charge: 2 Preach the word; be prepared in season and out
of season; correct, rebuke and encourage—with great patience and
careful instruction. 3 For the time will come when people will not put
up with sound doctrine. Instead, to suit their own desires, they will
gather around them a great number of teachers to say what their itch-
ing ears want to hear. 4 They will turn their ears away from the truth
and turn aside to myths. 5 But you, keep your head in all situations,
endure hardship, do the work of an evangelist, discharge all the duties
of your ministry.

6 For I am already being poured out like a drink offering, and the
time for my departure is near. 7 I have fought the good fight, I have
finished the race, I have kept the faith. 8 Now there is in store for me
the crown of righteousness, which the Lord, the righteous Judge, will
award to me on that day—and not only to me, but also to all who have
longed for his appearing.

PERSONAL REMARKS

9 Do your best to come to me quickly, 10 for Demas, because he loved
this world, has deserted me and has gone to Thessalonica. Crescens has
gone to Galatia, and Titus to Dalmatia. 11 Only Luke is with me. Get Mark
and bring him with you, because he is helpful to me in my ministry.
12 I sent Tychicus to Ephesus. 13 When you come, bring the cloak that I
left with Carpus at Troas, and my scrolls, especially the parchments.

14 Alexander the metalworker did me a great deal of harm. The Lord
will repay him for what he has done. 15 You too should be on your guard
against him, because he strongly opposed our message.

PRAYING SCRIPTURE

2 Timothy 4

Paul was able to endure the sufferings he faced in prison because he knew the Lord had laid up a crown of righteousness for him. This crown is not unique for Paul. He told Timothy that everyone who loves Jesus' appearing will also gain this reward.

Do you look forward to the return of Jesus? Do you long to see him? Pray that your heart will be in tune with his return.

---

[a] 17 Or *that you, a man of God,*

16At my first defense, no one came to my support, but everyone de-
serted me. May it not be held against them. 17But the Lord stood at my
side and gave me strength, so that through me the message might be
fully proclaimed and all the Gentiles might hear it. And I was delivered
from the lion's mouth. 18The Lord will rescue me from every evil attack
and will bring me safely to his heavenly kingdom. To him be glory for
ever and ever. Amen.

FINAL GREETINGS

19Greet Priscilla[a] and Aquila and the household of Onesiphorus.
20Erastus stayed in Corinth, and I left Trophimus sick in Miletus. 21Do
your best to get here before winter. Eubulus greets you, and so do Pu-
dens, Linus, Claudia and all the brothers and sisters.[b]
22The Lord be with your spirit. Grace be with you all.

[a] 19 Greek *Prisca*, a variant of *Priscilla* [b] 21 The Greek word for *brothers and sisters* (*adelphoi*) refers here to believers, both men and women, as part of God's family.

TITUS

Paul wrote the letter of Titus to a son in the faith who was organizing the church on the island of Crete. Many of the believers there came out of pagan backgrounds. The culture had the reputation of Cretans being liars and gluttons. Even their own "prophets" said as much. Paul left Titus on Crete to teach the church about Christian living and to appoint qualified leaders for the church in each city.

Paul's letter to Titus devotes significant space to the qualifications of church leaders (see 1:5–16). These instructions provide a framework for us to pray for our leaders. Our prayers for them should focus on asking the Lord to protect their character. As scandals involving church leaders grow more common, we should pray for the Lord to convict pastors and elders of sin so that they will continue growing in holiness. Their teaching is another area our prayers can focus on. Since pastors have been charged with teaching God's Word, we should be strategic about lifting them up as they prepare to preach the Word, praying that they would deal effectively with questions from those who are skeptical about the faith. Paul called it "hold[ing] firmly to the trustworthy message as it has been taught" (1:9).

Titus also received instruction from Paul about the importance of intergenerational discipleship. Paul spoke of older men training younger men and older women teaching younger women. The older generation was to model and demonstrate how to follow Jesus and live in ways that bring him glory.

Two passages that stand out for their clarity and hope are 2:11–14 and 3:3–7. In the former, Paul reminded us to deny the ungodliness of this world because we have hope in Christ. Here hope is a noun rather than a verb. Christ is our hope; that's why our hope is sound. It is not the power of our hoping but the object of our hope that gives us assurance that Christ will return in power and glory.

This is an excellent pattern for praying about discipling relationships that grow and increase in the church. If we care about the growth and progress of the church in the world—including our own churches—then our prayers should reflect it. Let us pray for older men who pour their lives into younger men, helping them grow into mature followers of Jesus. Ask the Father to raise up spiritual mothers who will teach and train younger women to follow Jesus as they are called so "that no one will malign the word of God" (2:5).

Then Paul contrasted the church's lives before Jesus—which describes those of us who are saved as well: "foolish, disobedient, deceived and enslaved by all kinds of passions and pleasures. We lived in malice and envy, being hated and hating one another" (3:3). But, he wrote, when Jesus appeared, he brought justification. It is not by any conceivable good deed we can do, but according to his mercy that he saves us. And not only that, but he pours out his Spirit on his children. This is gloriously good news!

PRAYING SCRIPTURE

Titus 1

It is imperative that churches have leaders who have both godly character and sound doctrine. Being upright but doctrinally suspect will not work. Neither will being doctrinally straight but morally corrupted be effective. Both right beliefs and right practice are required to lead the people of God.

Pray diligently for the leaders in your church. If you are blessed with those whose beliefs and practices are right, encourage them in the Lord.

1 Paul, a servant of God and an apostle of Jesus Christ to further the faith of God's elect and their knowledge of the truth that leads to godliness— 2in the hope of eternal life, which God, who does not lie, promised before the beginning of time, 3and which now at his appointed season he has brought to light through the preaching entrusted to me by the command of God our Savior,

4To Titus, my true son in our common faith:

Grace and peace from God the Father and Christ Jesus our Savior.

APPOINTING ELDERS WHO LOVE WHAT IS GOOD

5The reason I left you in Crete was that you might put in order what was left unfinished and appoint[a] elders in every town, as I directed you. 6An elder must be blameless, faithful to his wife, a man whose children believe[b] and are not open to the charge of being wild and disobedient. 7Since an overseer manages God's household, he must be blameless—not overbearing, not quick-tempered, not given to drunkenness, not violent, not pursuing dishonest gain. 8Rather, he must be hospitable, one who loves what is good, who is self-controlled, upright, holy and disciplined. 9He must hold firmly to the trustworthy message as it has been taught, so that he can encourage others by sound doctrine and refute those who oppose it.

REBUKING THOSE WHO FAIL TO DO GOOD

10For there are many rebellious people, full of meaningless talk and deception, especially those of the circumcision group. 11They must be silenced, because they are disrupting whole households by teaching things they ought not to teach—and that for the sake of dishonest gain. 12One of Crete's own prophets has said it: "Cretans are always liars, evil brutes, lazy gluttons."[c] 13This saying is true. Therefore rebuke them sharply, so that they will be sound in the faith 14and will pay no attention to Jewish myths or to the merely human commands of those who reject the truth. 15To the pure, all things are pure, but to those who are corrupted and do not believe, nothing is pure. In fact, both their minds and consciences are corrupted. 16They claim to know God, but by their actions they deny him. They are detestable, disobedient and unfit for doing anything good.

PRAYING SCRIPTURE

Titus 2

Every generation must teach and model godly living for the generations behind them. Scripture makes it clear that Jesus redeems people from wickedness that they might be eager to do what is good. There are behaviors to be embraced and behaviors to be denied. We are not to live like the world.

Does your life reflect new life in Christ? If not, deny yourself those things that hinder you, and ask Jesus to help you live a self-controlled, upright and godly life.

DOING GOOD FOR THE SAKE OF THE GOSPEL

2 You, however, must teach what is appropriate to sound doctrine. 2Teach the older men to be temperate, worthy of respect, self-controlled, and sound in faith, in love and in endurance.

3Likewise, teach the older women to be reverent in the way they live, not to be slanderers or addicted to much wine, but to teach what is good. 4Then they can urge the younger women to love their husbands and children, 5to be self-controlled and pure, to be busy at home, to be kind, and to be subject to their husbands, so that no one will malign the word of God.

6Similarly, encourage the young men to be self-controlled. 7In everything set them an example by doing what is good. In your teaching show integrity, seriousness 8and soundness of speech that cannot be

---

[a] 5 Or *ordain* [b] 6 Or *children are trustworthy* [c] 12 From the Cretan philosopher Epimenides

condemned, so that those who oppose you may be ashamed because
they have nothing bad to say about us.
9Teach slaves to be subject to their masters in everything, to try to
please them, not to talk back to them, 10and not to steal from them,
but to show that they can be fully trusted, so that in every way they will
make the teaching about God our Savior attractive.
11For the grace of God has appeared that offers salvation to all people.
12It teaches us to say "No" to ungodliness and worldly passions, and to
live self-controlled, upright and godly lives in this present age, 13while
we wait for the blessed hope — the appearing of the glory of our great
God and Savior, Jesus Christ, 14who gave himself for us to redeem us
from all wickedness and to purify for himself a people that are his very
own, eager to do what is good.
15These, then, are the things you should teach. Encourage and re-
buke with all authority. Do not let anyone despise you.

SAVED IN ORDER TO DO GOOD

3 Remind the people to be subject to rulers and authorities, to
be obedient, to be ready to do whatever is good, 2to slander no
one, to be peaceable and considerate, and always to be gentle toward
everyone.
3At one time we too were foolish, disobedient, deceived and en-
slaved by all kinds of passions and pleasures. We lived in malice and
envy, being hated and hating one another. 4But when the kindness and
love of God our Savior appeared, 5he saved us, not because of righteous
things we had done, but because of his mercy. He saved us through the
washing of rebirth and renewal by the Holy Spirit, 6whom he poured
out on us generously through Jesus Christ our Savior, 7so that, having
been justified by his grace, we might become heirs having the hope
of eternal life. 8This is a trustworthy saying. And I want you to stress
these things, so that those who have trusted in God may be careful to
devote themselves to doing what is good. These things are excellent
and profitable for everyone.
9But avoid foolish controversies and genealogies and arguments
and quarrels about the law, because these are unprofitable and use-
less. 10Warn a divisive person once, and then warn them a second time.
After that, have nothing to do with them. 11You may be sure that such
people are warped and sinful; they are self-condemned.

FINAL REMARKS

12As soon as I send Artemas or Tychicus to you, do your best to come
to me at Nicopolis, because I have decided to winter there. 13Do every-
thing you can to help Zenas the lawyer and Apollos on their way and
see that they have everything they need. 14Our people must learn to
devote themselves to doing what is good, in order to provide for ur-
gent needs and not live unproductive lives.
15Everyone with me sends you greetings. Greet those who love us
in the faith.
Grace be with you all.

PRAYING SCRIPTURE

Titus 3

At the very end of this pastoral letter, Paul gave a brief exhortation that Christians must "devote themselves to doing what is good" and "provide for urgent needs" so the life of a believer would be fruitful rather than barren (verse 14).

Helping cases of urgent needs is not often thought of as a Biblical imperative, but it is. Those who meet urgent needs are bearing fruit. Ask God to help you be attentive and responsive to needs around you.

PHILEMON

The most personal of Paul's letters, Philemon was written to a brother who hosted a church in his house. In his prayer for Philemon (see verses 4–6), Paul praised God for Philemon's faith and the love he had for all the saints. In this, Paul expressed his thankfulness at seeing a brother grow in the basics of the Christian faith. When we read Paul's prayers for churches and individuals, this was frequently in the forefront of his mind.

Paul prayed for another aspect of Philemon's spiritual growth. He said he asked God to make Philemon's generosity in sharing his faith effective through "every good thing we share for the sake of Christ" (verse 6). Paul's joy in Philemon's life was refreshed by the latter's treatment of the saints in his life. Paul mentioned this early, setting the stage for a request he was about to make.

In addition to being the most personal letter, it is possibly the most subversive. It subtly but clearly changes the conversation on a subject that would be controversial and misunderstood for centuries to come: slavery.

While imprisoned, Paul met Onesimus, a slave who had apparently fled from Philemon, his master. Onesimus had become a follower of Jesus and, under circumstances not made clear, he had ministered to and with Paul. When Paul sent Onesimus home, he bore the letter to Philemon and the letter to the Colossians (see Colossians 4:7–9). Charged with the responsibility to update everyone, it is clear that Paul had bigger plans for Onesimus than Philemon could imagine.

The heart of this short note, called by some a "postcard," is the new relationship Paul hoped to foster between the former slave and master. Paul implored Philemon to receive Onesimus ("useful") as a brother rather than a slave and to allow the one who "has become useful both to you and to me" (verse 11) to be free to serve with Paul. In doing so, Paul challenged the social order, showing through the relationship between the two men that in Christ Jesus there is neither slave nor free.

Philemon shows that love for our brothers, generosity, hospitality and a strong faith in God produce healthy and vibrant congregations. It also helps us define "brother" and "sister" in Christ as going beyond social or class categories to bonds in the Spirit shared by all believers in all places in all times.

We should pray for our brothers and sisters and for ourselves to be loving and hospitable. The reality of the gospel is seen clearly when those who were formerly separated live as brothers and sisters regardless of class, gender, ethnicity or nationality.

1 Paul, a prisoner of Christ Jesus, and Timothy our brother,

To Philemon our dear friend and fellow worker — 2 also to Apphia
our sister and Archippus our fellow soldier — and to the church that
meets in your home:

3 Grace and peace to you[a] from God our Father and the Lord Jesus
Christ.

THANKSGIVING AND PRAYER

4 I always thank my God as I remember you in my prayers, 5 because
I hear about your love for all his holy people and your faith in the Lord
Jesus. 6 I pray that your partnership with us in the faith may be effec-
tive in deepening your understanding of every good thing we share
for the sake of Christ. 7 Your love has given me great joy and encour-
agement, because you, brother, have refreshed the hearts of the Lord's
people.

PAUL'S PLEA FOR ONESIMUS

8 Therefore, although in Christ I could be bold and order you to do
what you ought to do, 9 yet I prefer to appeal to you on the basis of love.
It is as none other than Paul — an old man and now also a prisoner of
Christ Jesus — 10 that I appeal to you for my son Onesimus,[b] who be-
came my son while I was in chains. 11 Formerly he was useless to you,
but now he has become useful both to you and to me.

12 I am sending him — who is my very heart — back to you. 13 I would
have liked to keep him with me so that he could take your place in
helping me while I am in chains for the gospel. 14 But I did not want to
do anything without your consent, so that any favor you do would not
seem forced but would be voluntary. 15 Perhaps the reason he was sepa-
rated from you for a little while was that you might have him back for-
ever — 16 no longer as a slave, but better than a slave, as a dear brother.
He is very dear to me but even dearer to you, both as a fellow man and
as a brother in the Lord.

17 So if you consider me a partner, welcome him as you would wel-
come me. 18 If he has done you any wrong or owes you anything,
charge it to me. 19 I, Paul, am writing this with my own hand. I will pay
it back — not to mention that you owe me your very self. 20 I do wish,
brother, that I may have some benefit from you in the Lord; refresh my
heart in Christ. 21 Confident of your obedience, I write to you, knowing
that you will do even more than I ask.

22 And one thing more: Prepare a guest room for me, because I hope
to be restored to you in answer to your prayers.

23 Epaphras, my fellow prisoner in Christ Jesus, sends you greetings.
24 And so do Mark, Aristarchus, Demas and Luke, my fellow workers.

25 The grace of the Lord Jesus Christ be with your spirit.

[a] 3 The Greek is plural; also in verses 22 and 25; elsewhere in this letter "you" is singular. [b] 10 *Onesimus* means *useful*.

PRAYING SCRIPTURE

Philemon

In Christ, people who previously would have been our enemies have become family. Paul challenged Philemon regarding his relationship with the slave Onesimus, calling the latter "a dear brother" to both Philemon and Paul (verse 16).

The gospel has the power to break down every human-made barrier. Ask God to reveal to you how the gospel changes all your relationships.

HEBREWS

The authorship of the book of Hebrews has puzzled Biblical scholars and teachers for centuries. It is one of the most famous anonymous books in the history of the world. The author demonstrates a deep knowledge of the Old Testament Scriptures and a sophisticated grasp of the Greek language. The letter was written to Jewish Christians, perhaps including converted priests, who had suffered persecution and were thinking of abandoning their faith in Christ and returning to their former religious life.

The author of Hebrews pleaded with these Christians not to turn away from the enlightenment they had in Christ. Throughout the book, he showed that Jesus is better: better than Moses, better than the tabernacle, better than the priests, better than the entire old covenant. These people and places were not unimportant; they were the core of Judaism. The author demonstrated over and again how these people and aspects of the Jewish faith pointed to the reality of what God would accomplish for us in the Lord Jesus. Jesus not only fulfilled the Old Testament prophecies and types; he exceeded them in every possible way.

One of the writer's purposes was to show the access Christians have to God through Christ. In chapter 12, he showed that Christians have not approached a mountain that cannot be touched, which was the Israelites' dilemma at Sinai. Instead, we have been brought into the city of God. Christians do not have to worship at a distance; through Jesus' blood we can draw near to God in worship and prayer.

The writer's emphasis on Jesus' superior priesthood has tremendous implications for our prayer lives. At the end of chapter 2, he wrote that Jesus suffered all the things that we suffer, but without sin, so that he might be for us a high priest both faithful and merciful.

Hebrews also teaches us that we should pray boldly, not hesitantly, because Jesus is sympathetic to us: "Let us then approach God's throne of grace with confidence, so that we may receive mercy and find grace to help us in our time of need" (4:16). Jesus knows all our weaknesses, loves us anyway and ministers to us through them. Since he has known temptation, he is able to come to our aid when we are tempted. Since he knows our needs, he is able to supply them when we ask.

Our boldness is rooted not in pride but in the knowledge that Jesus has opened the way for us to come before the Father. When we come before the throne, we take advantage of the blessing God himself promises us. We cannot presume upon the grace and mercy God offers to give us when we pray; it is his gift.

Closing the book is another call to prayer. The writer encouraged us through Jesus to "continually offer to God a sacrifice of praise—the fruit of lips that openly profess his name" (13:15). The primacy of giving thanks in prayer cannot be overstated. It is foundational to prayer and to spiritual growth, acknowledging our total dependence on the One who made us.

GOD'S FINAL WORD: HIS SON

1 In the past God spoke to our ancestors through the prophets at many
times and in various ways, 2but in these last days he has spoken to
us by his Son, whom he appointed heir of all things, and through whom
also he made the universe. 3The Son is the radiance of God's glory and
the exact representation of his being, sustaining all things by his pow-
erful word. After he had provided purification for sins, he sat down at
the right hand of the Majesty in heaven. 4So he became as much su-
perior to the angels as the name he has inherited is superior to theirs.

THE SON SUPERIOR TO ANGELS

5For to which of the angels did God ever say,

"You are my Son;
today I have become your Father"[a]?

Or again,

"I will be his Father,
and he will be my Son"[b]?

6And again, when God brings his firstborn into the world, he says,

"Let all God's angels worship him."[c]

7In speaking of the angels he says,

"He makes his angels spirits,
and his servants flames of fire."[d]

8But about the Son he says,

"Your throne, O God, will last for ever and ever;
a scepter of justice will be the scepter of your kingdom.
9 You have loved righteousness and hated wickedness;
therefore God, your God, has set you above your companions
by anointing you with the oil of joy."[e]

10He also says,

"In the beginning, Lord, you laid the foundations of the earth,
and the heavens are the work of your hands.
11 They will perish, but you remain;
they will all wear out like a garment.
12 You will roll them up like a robe;
like a garment they will be changed.
But you remain the same,
and your years will never end."[f]

13To which of the angels did God ever say,

"Sit at my right hand
until I make your enemies
a footstool for your feet"[g]?

14Are not all angels ministering spirits sent to serve those who will inherit salvation?

PRAYING SCRIPTURE

Hebrews 1

This magisterial book opens with an explanation that Jesus is superior to angels. Not only is he superior to them, but he is also equal with God. The author's defense regards the divinity of Christ; he is the One who sits on God's throne.

A common misconception is that Jesus is simply an angelic being, but Hebrews makes it clear that he is God. Ask God to open your eyes to the deep riches of this book.

---

[a] *5* Psalm 2:7 [b] *5* 2 Samuel 7:14; 1 Chron. 17:13 [c] *6* Deut. 32:43 (see Dead Sea Scrolls and Septuagint) [d] *7* Psalm 104:4 [e] *9* Psalm 45:6,7 [f] *12* Psalm 102:25-27 [g] *13* Psalm 110:1

PRAYING SCRIPTURE

Hebrews 2

The sufferings of Jesus prepared him to be our great high priest, the One who represents us before the Lord. The writer of Hebrews said "it was fitting that [Jesus]" be made perfect through suffering (verse 10). Why? For the purpose of bringing many to glory.

The work of Jesus in saving sinners would be beyond comprehension if Scripture did not reveal it. Praise God for his wisdom and work in bringing many to himself.

WARNING TO PAY ATTENTION

2 We must pay the most careful attention, therefore, to what we
have heard, so that we do not drift away. 2For since the message
spoken through angels was binding, and every violation and disobe-
dience received its just punishment, 3how shall we escape if we ignore
so great a salvation? This salvation, which was first announced by the
Lord, was confirmed to us by those who heard him. 4God also testified
to it by signs, wonders and various miracles, and by gifts of the Holy
Spirit distributed according to his will.

JESUS MADE FULLY HUMAN

5It is not to angels that he has subjected the world to come, about
which we are speaking. 6But there is a place where someone has
testified:

"What is mankind that you are mindful of them,
a son of man that you care for him?
7You made them a little[a] lower than the angels;
you crowned them with glory and honor
8 and put everything under their feet."[b,c]

In putting everything under them,[d] God left nothing that is not subject
to them.[d] Yet at present we do not see everything subject to them.[d]
9But we do see Jesus, who was made lower than the angels for a little
while, now crowned with glory and honor because he suffered death,
so that by the grace of God he might taste death for everyone.
10In bringing many sons and daughters to glory, it was fitting that
God, for whom and through whom everything exists, should make
the pioneer of their salvation perfect through what he suffered. 11Both
the one who makes people holy and those who are made holy are
of the same family. So Jesus is not ashamed to call them brothers and
sisters.[e] 12He says,

"I will declare your name to my brothers and sisters;
in the assembly I will sing your praises."[f]

13And again,

"I will put my trust in him."[g]

And again he says,

"Here am I, and the children God has given me."[h]

14Since the children have flesh and blood, he too shared in their hu-
manity so that by his death he might break the power of him who
holds the power of death — that is, the devil — 15and free those who
all their lives were held in slavery by their fear of death. 16For surely it
is not angels he helps, but Abraham's descendants. 17For this reason he
had to be made like them,[i] fully human in every way, in order that he
might become a merciful and faithful high priest in service to God, and

---

[a] *7* Or *them for a little while* [b] *6-8* Psalm 8:4-6 [c] *7,8* Or *7You made him a little lower than the angels;/ you crowned him with glory and honor/ 8and put everything under his feet."* [d] *8* Or *him* [e] *11* The Greek word for *brothers and sisters* (*adelphoi*) refers here to believers, both men and women, as part of God's family; also in verse 12; and in 3:1,12; 10:19; 13:22. [f] *12* Psalm 22:22 [g] *13* Isaiah 8:17 [h] *13* Isaiah 8:18 [i] *17* Or *like his brothers*

that he might make atonement for the sins of the people. 18Because he
himself suffered when he was tempted, he is able to help those who
are being tempted.

JESUS GREATER THAN MOSES

3 Therefore, holy brothers and sisters, who share in the heavenly
calling, fix your thoughts on Jesus, whom we acknowledge as our
apostle and high priest. 2He was faithful to the one who appointed him,
just as Moses was faithful in all God's house. 3Jesus has been found
worthy of greater honor than Moses, just as the builder of a house has
greater honor than the house itself. 4For every house is built by some-
one, but God is the builder of everything. 5"Moses was faithful as a
servant in all God's house,"[a] bearing witness to what would be spoken
by God in the future. 6But Christ is faithful as the Son over God's house.
And we are his house, if indeed we hold firmly to our confidence and
the hope in which we glory.

WARNING AGAINST UNBELIEF

7So, as the Holy Spirit says:

"Today, if you hear his voice,
8 do not harden your hearts
as you did in the rebellion,
during the time of testing in the wilderness,
9 where your ancestors tested and tried me,
though for forty years they saw what I did.
10 That is why I was angry with that generation;
I said, 'Their hearts are always going astray,
and they have not known my ways.'
11 So I declared on oath in my anger,
'They shall never enter my rest.'"[b]

12See to it, brothers and sisters, that none of you has a sinful, unbe-
lieving heart that turns away from the living God. 13But encourage one
another daily, as long as it is called "Today," so that none of you may
be hardened by sin's deceitfulness. 14We have come to share in Christ,
if indeed we hold our original conviction firmly to the very end. 15As
has just been said:

"Today, if you hear his voice,
do not harden your hearts
as you did in the rebellion."[c]

16Who were they who heard and rebelled? Were they not all those
Moses led out of Egypt? 17And with whom was he angry for forty years?
Was it not with those who sinned, whose bodies perished in the wil-
derness? 18And to whom did God swear that they would never enter his
rest if not to those who disobeyed? 19So we see that they were not able
to enter, because of their unbelief.

A SABBATH-REST FOR THE PEOPLE OF GOD

4 Therefore, since the promise of entering his rest still stands, let us
be careful that none of you be found to have fallen short of it. 2For
we also have had the good news proclaimed to us, just as they did; but

[a] *5* Num. 12:7 [b] *11* Psalm 95:7-11 [c] *15* Psalm 95:7,8

PRAYING SCRIPTURE

Hebrews 3

Faithfulness is a key spiritual component of the Christian life. Here we read that Moses was faithful, though he was due less glory than Jesus since "the builder of a house has more honor than the house itself" (verse 3). The Spirit is given to believers so we might be faithful, not unbelieving.

The children of Israel failed to follow God because of unbelief. Ask God daily for the faith to walk with him.

PRAYING SCRIPTURE

Hebrews 4

One of the most blessed truths about Jesus is that he is a merciful high priest who sympathizes with us in our weakness. Although he never sinned, he knows exactly what it is like to be tempted. Jesus is not wearied by our frailty; He is moved to compassion by it.

Always go to Jesus. He understands our struggles and listens to our prayers as One who has been there himself.

the message they heard was of no value to them, because they did not
share the faith of those who obeyed.[a] 3Now we who have believed enter
that rest, just as God has said,

"So I declared on oath in my anger,
'They shall never enter my rest.'"[b]

And yet his works have been finished since the creation of the world.
4For somewhere he has spoken about the seventh day in these words:
"On the seventh day God rested from all his works."[c] 5And again in the
passage above he says, "They shall never enter my rest."

6Therefore since it still remains for some to enter that rest, and since
those who formerly had the good news proclaimed to them did not go
in because of their disobedience, 7God again set a certain day, calling it
"Today." This he did when a long time later he spoke through David, as
in the passage already quoted:

"Today, if you hear his voice,
do not harden your hearts."[d]

8For if Joshua had given them rest, God would not have spoken later
about another day. 9There remains, then, a Sabbath-rest for the people
of God; 10for anyone who enters God's rest also rests from their works,[e]
just as God did from his. 11Let us, therefore, make every effort to en-
ter that rest, so that no one will perish by following their example of
disobedience.

12For the word of God is alive and active. Sharper than any double-
edged sword, it penetrates even to dividing soul and spirit, joints and
marrow; it judges the thoughts and attitudes of the heart. 13Nothing
in all creation is hidden from God's sight. Everything is uncovered and
laid bare before the eyes of him to whom we must give account.

JESUS THE GREAT HIGH PRIEST

14Therefore, since we have a great high priest who has ascended into
heaven,[f] Jesus the Son of God, let us hold firmly to the faith we profess.
15For we do not have a high priest who is unable to empathize with our
weaknesses, but we have one who has been tempted in every way, just
as we are—yet he did not sin. 16Let us then approach God's throne of
grace with confidence, so that we may receive mercy and find grace to
help us in our time of need.

5 Every high priest is selected from among the people and is ap-
pointed to represent the people in matters related to God, to offer
gifts and sacrifices for sins. 2He is able to deal gently with those who
are ignorant and are going astray, since he himself is subject to weak-
ness. 3This is why he has to offer sacrifices for his own sins, as well as
for the sins of the people. 4And no one takes this honor on himself, but
he receives it when called by God, just as Aaron was.

5In the same way, Christ did not take on himself the glory of becom-
ing a high priest. But God said to him,

"You are my Son;
today I have become your Father."[g]

PRAYING SCRIPTURE

Hebrews 5

The Law of Moses instituted a priesthood with Aaron, Moses' brother, as its head. But we also learn of another less known priesthood, that of Melchizedek. The difference between the two is that Aaron's priesthood was temporary, while Melchizedek's is eternal. Jesus is a priest like the latter. Because he ever lives to respond, there will never be a time when you can bring a request to Jesus that he will not answer.

[a] 2 Some manuscripts *because those who heard did not combine it with faith*
[b] 3 Psalm 95:11; also in verse 5 [c] 4 Gen. 2:2 [d] 7 Psalm 95:7,8 [e] 10 Or *labor* [f] 14 Greek *has gone through the heavens* [g] 5 Psalm 2:7

6And he says in another place,

"You are a priest forever,
in the order of Melchizedek."[a]

7During the days of Jesus' life on earth, he offered up prayers and
petitions with fervent cries and tears to the one who could save him
from death, and he was heard because of his reverent submission. 8Son
though he was, he learned obedience from what he suffered 9and, once
made perfect, he became the source of eternal salvation for all who
obey him 10and was designated by God to be high priest in the order
of Melchizedek.

WARNING AGAINST FALLING AWAY

11We have much to say about this, but it is hard to make it clear to
you because you no longer try to understand. 12In fact, though by this
time you ought to be teachers, you need someone to teach you the
elementary truths of God's word all over again. You need milk, not
solid food! 13Anyone who lives on milk, being still an infant, is not
acquainted with the teaching about righteousness. 14But solid food is
for the mature, who by constant use have trained themselves to dis-
tinguish good from evil.

6 Therefore let us move beyond the elementary teachings about
Christ and be taken forward to maturity, not laying again the
foundation of repentance from acts that lead to death,[b] and of faith
in God, 2instruction about cleansing rites,[c] the laying on of hands, the
resurrection of the dead, and eternal judgment. 3And God permitting,
we will do so.

4It is impossible for those who have once been enlightened, who
have tasted the heavenly gift, who have shared in the Holy Spirit, 5who
have tasted the goodness of the word of God and the powers of the
coming age 6and who have fallen[d] away, to be brought back to repen-
tance. To their loss they are crucifying the Son of God all over again
and subjecting him to public disgrace. 7Land that drinks in the rain
often falling on it and that produces a crop useful to those for whom it
is farmed receives the blessing of God. 8But land that produces thorns
and thistles is worthless and is in danger of being cursed. In the end
it will be burned.

9Even though we speak like this, dear friends, we are convinced of
better things in your case — the things that have to do with salvation.
10God is not unjust; he will not forget your work and the love you have
shown him as you have helped his people and continue to help them.
11We want each of you to show this same diligence to the very end, so
that what you hope for may be fully realized. 12We do not want you to
become lazy, but to imitate those who through faith and patience in-
herit what has been promised.

THE CERTAINTY OF GOD'S PROMISE

13When God made his promise to Abraham, since there was no one
greater for him to swear by, he swore by himself, 14saying, "I will surely
bless you and give you many descendants."[e] 15And so after waiting pa-
tiently, Abraham received what was promised.

PRAYING SCRIPTURE

Hebrews 6

The hope that we have in Jesus Christ is a strong and sure anchor of our souls. To establish this, God gave us promises based on his character: He cannot lie, and he is a refuge for us (see verse 18). From these truths we see that Jesus has entered God's presence as a forerunner for us, leaving us the Holy Spirit as our guarantee.

Even when things look utterly uncertain, you can call on Jesus, who is eternally immovable.

---

[a] 6 Psalm 110:4 [b] 1 Or *from useless rituals* [c] 2 Or *about baptisms*
[d] 6 Or *age,* 6*if they fall* [e] 14 Gen. 22:17

16People swear by someone greater than themselves, and the oath confirms what is said and puts an end to all argument. 17Because God wanted to make the unchanging nature of his purpose very clear to the heirs of what was promised, he confirmed it with an oath. 18God did this so that, by two unchangeable things in which it is impossible for God to lie, we who have fled to take hold of the hope set before us may be greatly encouraged. 19We have this hope as an anchor for the soul, firm and secure. It enters the inner sanctuary behind the curtain, 20where our forerunner, Jesus, has entered on our behalf. He has become a high priest forever, in the order of Melchizedek.

MELCHIZEDEK THE PRIEST

7 This Melchizedek was king of Salem and priest of God Most High. He met Abraham returning from the defeat of the kings and blessed him, 2and Abraham gave him a tenth of everything. First, the name Melchizedek means "king of righteousness"; then also, "king of Salem" means "king of peace." 3Without father or mother, without genealogy, without beginning of days or end of life, resembling the Son of God, he remains a priest forever.

4Just think how great he was: Even the patriarch Abraham gave him a tenth of the plunder! 5Now the law requires the descendants of Levi who become priests to collect a tenth from the people — that is, from their fellow Israelites — even though they also are descended from Abraham. 6This man, however, did not trace his descent from Levi, yet he collected a tenth from Abraham and blessed him who had the promises. 7And without doubt the lesser is blessed by the greater. 8In the one case, the tenth is collected by people who die; but in the other case, by him who is declared to be living. 9One might even say that Levi, who collects the tenth, paid the tenth through Abraham, 10because when Melchizedek met Abraham, Levi was still in the body of his ancestor.

JESUS LIKE MELCHIZEDEK

11If perfection could have been attained through the Levitical priesthood — and indeed the law given to the people established that priesthood — why was there still need for another priest to come, one in the order of Melchizedek, not in the order of Aaron? 12For when the priesthood is changed, the law must be changed also. 13He of whom these things are said belonged to a different tribe, and no one from that tribe has ever served at the altar. 14For it is clear that our Lord descended from Judah, and in regard to that tribe Moses said nothing about priests. 15And what we have said is even more clear if another priest like Melchizedek appears, 16one who has become a priest not on the basis of a regulation as to his ancestry but on the basis of the power of an indestructible life. 17For it is declared:

> "You are a priest forever,
> in the order of Melchizedek."[a]

18The former regulation is set aside because it was weak and useless 19(for the law made nothing perfect), and a better hope is introduced, by which we draw near to God.

20And it was not without an oath! Others became priests without any oath, 21but he became a priest with an oath when God said to him:

PRAYING SCRIPTURE

Hebrews 7

Meditate on this nearly unfathomable truth: Jesus' perfect sacrifice and perfect priesthood offer us perpetual access to the throne of God. Through Jesus, we can enter the presence of the God of the entire universe, the Creator and Sustainer of all there is.

If you are God's child, never hesitate to call on him. As a child approaches his or her father, so can we come to God and ask of him with confidence that he listens.

[a] 17 Psalm 110:4

"The Lord has sworn
 and will not change his mind:
 'You are a priest forever.' "[a]

22Because of this oath, Jesus has become the guarantor of a better
covenant.
23Now there have been many of those priests, since death prevented
them from continuing in office; 24but because Jesus lives forever, he
has a permanent priesthood. 25Therefore he is able to save completely[b]
those who come to God through him, because he always lives to inter-
cede for them.
26Such a high priest truly meets our need — one who is holy, blame-
less, pure, set apart from sinners, exalted above the heavens. 27Unlike
the other high priests, he does not need to offer sacrifices day after
day, first for his own sins, and then for the sins of the people. He sac-
rificed for their sins once for all when he offered himself. 28For the
law appoints as high priests men in all their weakness; but the oath,
which came after the law, appointed the Son, who has been made per-
fect forever.

THE HIGH PRIEST OF A NEW COVENANT

8 Now the main point of what we are saying is this: We do have such
a high priest, who sat down at the right hand of the throne of the
Majesty in heaven, 2and who serves in the sanctuary, the true taberna-
cle set up by the Lord, not by a mere human being.
3Every high priest is appointed to offer both gifts and sacrifices, and
so it was necessary for this one also to have something to offer. 4If he
were on earth, he would not be a priest, for there are already priests
who offer the gifts prescribed by the law. 5They serve at a sanctuary
that is a copy and shadow of what is in heaven. This is why Moses was
warned when he was about to build the tabernacle: "See to it that you
make everything according to the pattern shown you on the moun-
tain."[c] 6But in fact the ministry Jesus has received is as superior to
theirs as the covenant of which he is mediator is superior to the old
one, since the new covenant is established on better promises.
7For if there had been nothing wrong with that first covenant, no
place would have been sought for another. 8But God found fault with
the people and said[d]:

"The days are coming, declares the Lord,
 when I will make a new covenant
with the people of Israel
 and with the people of Judah.
9It will not be like the covenant
 I made with their ancestors
when I took them by the hand
 to lead them out of Egypt,
because they did not remain faithful to my covenant,
 and I turned away from them,
 declares the Lord.
10This is the covenant I will establish with the people of Israel
 after that time, declares the Lord.

---

[a] 21 Psalm 110:4 [b] 25 Or *forever* [c] 5 Exodus 25:40 [d] 8 Some
manuscripts may be translated *fault and said to the people.*

PRAYING SCRIPTURE
Hebrews 8

Under the new covenant, the Holy Spirit permanently dwells within us. This is a reality no Old Testament saint ever knew: not Moses, Jeremiah, Deborah, or Isaiah. The new covenant we live under in Jesus has surpassed the old covenant, which is here described as "obsolete and outdated" (verse 13).

Consider the benefits like eternal forgiveness and the indwelling of the Spirit that come from living under a better covenant. Thank God for blessing you with the better promises that come with it.

I will put my laws in their minds
  and write them on their hearts.
I will be their God,
  and they will be my people.
11 No longer will they teach their neighbor,
  or say to one another, 'Know the Lord,'
because they will all know me,
  from the least of them to the greatest.
12 For I will forgive their wickedness
  and will remember their sins no more."[a]

13 By calling this covenant "new," he has made the first one obsolete; and what is obsolete and outdated will soon disappear.

WORSHIP IN THE EARTHLY TABERNACLE

9 Now the first covenant had regulations for worship and also an earthly sanctuary. 2 A tabernacle was set up. In its first room were the lampstand and the table with its consecrated bread; this was called the Holy Place. 3 Behind the second curtain was a room called the Most Holy Place, 4 which had the golden altar of incense and the gold-covered ark of the covenant. This ark contained the gold jar of manna, Aaron's staff that had budded, and the stone tablets of the covenant. 5 Above the ark were the cherubim of the Glory, overshadowing the atonement cover. But we cannot discuss these things in detail now.

6 When everything had been arranged like this, the priests entered regularly into the outer room to carry on their ministry. 7 But only the high priest entered the inner room, and that only once a year, and never without blood, which he offered for himself and for the sins the people had committed in ignorance. 8 The Holy Spirit was showing by this that the way into the Most Holy Place had not yet been disclosed as long as the first tabernacle was still functioning. 9 This is an illustration for the present time, indicating that the gifts and sacrifices being offered were not able to clear the conscience of the worshiper. 10 They are only a matter of food and drink and various ceremonial washings — external regulations applying until the time of the new order.

PRAYING SCRIPTURE

Hebrews 9

Many under the old covenant probably did not realize that the offerings they continuously offered were insufficient to remove sin. The blood of bulls and goats could not sufficiently deal with sin; another sacrifice always lay ahead. Jesus Christ finally and completely put away our sins by offering himself as a sacrifice.

Remember that all your sins—past, present and future—are forgiven in Jesus. Take some time in prayer to praise his name for forgiveness.

THE BLOOD OF CHRIST

11 But when Christ came as high priest of the good things that are now already here,[b] he went through the greater and more perfect tabernacle that is not made with human hands, that is to say, is not a part of this creation. 12 He did not enter by means of the blood of goats and calves; but he entered the Most Holy Place once for all by his own blood, thus obtaining[c] eternal redemption. 13 The blood of goats and bulls and the ashes of a heifer sprinkled on those who are ceremonially unclean sanctify them so that they are outwardly clean. 14 How much more, then, will the blood of Christ, who through the eternal Spirit offered himself unblemished to God, cleanse our consciences from acts that lead to death,[d] so that we may serve the living God!

15 For this reason Christ is the mediator of a new covenant, that those who are called may receive the promised eternal inheritance — now that he has died as a ransom to set them free from the sins committed under the first covenant.

---

[a] 12 Jer. 31:31-34 [b] 11 Some early manuscripts *are to come* [c] 12 Or *blood, having obtained* [d] 14 Or *from useless rituals*

16In the case of a will,[a] it is necessary to prove the death of the one
who made it, 17because a will is in force only when somebody has died;
it never takes effect while the one who made it is living. 18This is why
even the first covenant was not put into effect without blood. 19When
Moses had proclaimed every command of the law to all the people,
he took the blood of calves, together with water, scarlet wool and
branches of hyssop, and sprinkled the scroll and all the people. 20He
said, "This is the blood of the covenant, which God has commanded
you to keep."[b] 21In the same way, he sprinkled with the blood both the
tabernacle and everything used in its ceremonies. 22In fact, the law re-
quires that nearly everything be cleansed with blood, and without the
shedding of blood there is no forgiveness.

23It was necessary, then, for the copies of the heavenly things to be
purified with these sacrifices, but the heavenly things themselves with
better sacrifices than these. 24For Christ did not enter a sanctuary made
with human hands that was only a copy of the true one; he entered
heaven itself, now to appear for us in God's presence. 25Nor did he enter
heaven to offer himself again and again, the way the high priest enters
the Most Holy Place every year with blood that is not his own. 26Other-
wise Christ would have had to suffer many times since the creation of
the world. But he has appeared once for all at the culmination of the
ages to do away with sin by the sacrifice of himself. 27Just as people
are destined to die once, and after that to face judgment, 28so Christ
was sacrificed once to take away the sins of many; and he will appear
a second time, not to bear sin, but to bring salvation to those who are
waiting for him.

CHRIST'S SACRIFICE ONCE FOR ALL

10 The law is only a shadow of the good things that are coming—
not the realities themselves. For this reason it can never, by the
same sacrifices repeated endlessly year after year, make perfect those
who draw near to worship. 2Otherwise, would they not have stopped
being offered? For the worshipers would have been cleansed once for
all, and would no longer have felt guilty for their sins. 3But those sacri-
fices are an annual reminder of sins. 4It is impossible for the blood of
bulls and goats to take away sins.

5Therefore, when Christ came into the world, he said:

"Sacrifice and offering you did not desire,
 but a body you prepared for me;
6with burnt offerings and sin offerings
 you were not pleased.
7Then I said, 'Here I am—it is written about me in the scroll—
 I have come to do your will, my God.'"[c]

8First he said, "Sacrifices and offerings, burnt offerings and sin offer-
ings you did not desire, nor were you pleased with them"—though
they were offered in accordance with the law. 9Then he said, "Here I
am, I have come to do your will." He sets aside the first to establish the
second. 10And by that will, we have been made holy through the sacri-
fice of the body of Jesus Christ once for all.

11Day after day every priest stands and performs his religious duties;

PRAYING SCRIPTURE

Hebrews 10

The Old Testament sacrifices—even with all their guidelines and frequency—could never save. Lasting redemption of sin through the blood of bulls and goats simply was not possible, nor was it God's design (see verse 4). Those sacrifices pointed to the ultimate sacrifice, the Lamb of God, Jesus.

When you are burdened with the temptation to perform for God's acceptance or approval, remember that Jesus, in his love and obedience to the Father, has paid the price on your behalf. Take time to thank him for this gift.

[a] *16* Same Greek word as *covenant*; also in verse 17 [b] *20* Exodus 24:8
[c] *7* Psalm 40:6-8 (see Septuagint)

again and again he offers the same sacrifices, which can never take
away sins. 12 But when this priest had offered for all time one sacrifice
for sins, he sat down at the right hand of God, 13 and since that time he
waits for his enemies to be made his footstool. 14 For by one sacrifice he
has made perfect forever those who are being made holy.
15 The Holy Spirit also testifies to us about this. First he says:

16 "This is the covenant I will make with them
after that time, says the Lord.
I will put my laws in their hearts,
and I will write them on their minds."[a]

17 Then he adds:

"Their sins and lawless acts
I will remember no more."[b]

18 And where these have been forgiven, sacrifice for sin is no longer
necessary.

A CALL TO PERSEVERE IN FAITH

19 Therefore, brothers and sisters, since we have confidence to enter
the Most Holy Place by the blood of Jesus, 20 by a new and living way
opened for us through the curtain, that is, his body, 21 and since we have
a great priest over the house of God, 22 let us draw near to God with a
sincere heart and with the full assurance that faith brings, having our
hearts sprinkled to cleanse us from a guilty conscience and having our
bodies washed with pure water. 23 Let us hold unswervingly to the hope
we profess, for he who promised is faithful. 24 And let us consider how
we may spur one another on toward love and good deeds, 25 not giving
up meeting together, as some are in the habit of doing, but encourag-
ing one another — and all the more as you see the Day approaching.
26 If we deliberately keep on sinning after we have received the
knowledge of the truth, no sacrifice for sins is left, 27 but only a fear-
ful expectation of judgment and of raging fire that will consume the
enemies of God. 28 Anyone who rejected the law of Moses died without
mercy on the testimony of two or three witnesses. 29 How much more
severely do you think someone deserves to be punished who has tram-
pled the Son of God underfoot, who has treated as an unholy thing the
blood of the covenant that sanctified them, and who has insulted the
Spirit of grace? 30 For we know him who said, "It is mine to avenge; I
will repay,"[c] and again, "The Lord will judge his people."[d] 31 It is a dread-
ful thing to fall into the hands of the living God.
32 Remember those earlier days after you had received the light,
when you endured in a great conflict full of suffering. 33 Sometimes
you were publicly exposed to insult and persecution; at other times
you stood side by side with those who were so treated. 34 You suffered
along with those in prison and joyfully accepted the confiscation of
your property, because you knew that you yourselves had better and
lasting possessions. 35 So do not throw away your confidence; it will be
richly rewarded.
36 You need to persevere so that when you have done the will of God,
you will receive what he has promised. 37 For,

PRAYING SCRIPTURE
Hebrews 10

Christians can be tempted to falter in their commitment to Christ, so we should stir up each other to love and good works. The primary way we do that is by regularly gathering as the body of Christ. It is in this gathering that we exhort each other as the return of Christ approaches.

When you pray with other believers, remind them to obey because Christ may return at any time.

---

[a] *16* Jer. 31:33 [b] *17* Jer. 31:34 [c] *30* Deut. 32:35 [d] *30* Deut. 32:36; Psalm 135:14

"In just a little while,
he who is coming will come
and will not delay."[a]

38 And,

"But my righteous[b] one will live by faith.
And I take no pleasure
in the one who shrinks back."[c]

39 But we do not belong to those who shrink back and are destroyed,
but to those who have faith and are saved.

FAITH IN ACTION

11 Now faith is confidence in what we hope for and assurance
about what we do not see. 2 This is what the ancients were com-
mended for.
3 By faith we understand that the universe was formed at God's com-
mand, so that what is seen was not made out of what was visible.
4 By faith Abel brought God a better offering than Cain did. By faith
he was commended as righteous, when God spoke well of his offerings.
And by faith Abel still speaks, even though he is dead.
5 By faith Enoch was taken from this life, so that he did not experi-
ence death: "He could not be found, because God had taken him away."[d]
For before he was taken, he was commended as one who pleased God.
6 And without faith it is impossible to please God, because anyone who
comes to him must believe that he exists and that he rewards those
who earnestly seek him.
7 By faith Noah, when warned about things not yet seen, in holy fear
built an ark to save his family. By his faith he condemned the world
and became heir of the righteousness that is in keeping with faith.
8 By faith Abraham, when called to go to a place he would later re-
ceive as his inheritance, obeyed and went, even though he did not
know where he was going. 9 By faith he made his home in the prom-
ised land like a stranger in a foreign country; he lived in tents, as did
Isaac and Jacob, who were heirs with him of the same promise. 10 For he
was looking forward to the city with foundations, whose architect and
builder is God. 11 And by faith even Sarah, who was past childbearing
age, was enabled to bear children because she[e] considered him faith-
ful who had made the promise. 12 And so from this one man, and he as
good as dead, came descendants as numerous as the stars in the sky
and as countless as the sand on the seashore.
13 All these people were still living by faith when they died. They did
not receive the things promised; they only saw them and welcomed
them from a distance, admitting that they were foreigners and strang-
ers on earth. 14 People who say such things show that they are looking
for a country of their own. 15 If they had been thinking of the country
they had left, they would have had opportunity to return. 16 Instead,
they were longing for a better country — a heavenly one. Therefore
God is not ashamed to be called their God, for he has prepared a city
for them.

PRAYING SCRIPTURE

Hebrews 11

Meditate on this for a minute: "Without faith it is impossible to please God" (verse 6). What a stirring challenge. God rewards those who believe him and diligently seek him. The famed Hall of Faith recounts name after name of people who lived by faith and with patient endurance in their walks with God to receive promises yet unseen.

Is your faith weak? Commit to prayer and the Word, and then watch it flourish.

---

[a] *37* Isaiah 26:20; Hab. 2:3 [b] *38* Some early manuscripts *But the righteous* [c] *38* Hab. 2:4 (see Septuagint) [d] *5* Gen. 5:24 [e] *11* Or *By faith Abraham, even though he was too old to have children — and Sarah herself was not able to conceive — was enabled to become a father because he*

17 By faith Abraham, when God tested him, offered Isaac as a sacrifice.
He who had embraced the promises was about to sacrifice his one and
only son, 18 even though God had said to him, "It is through Isaac that
your offspring will be reckoned."[a] 19 Abraham reasoned that God could
even raise the dead, and so in a manner of speaking he did receive
Isaac back from death.
20 By faith Isaac blessed Jacob and Esau in regard to their future.
21 By faith Jacob, when he was dying, blessed each of Joseph's sons,
and worshiped as he leaned on the top of his staff.
22 By faith Joseph, when his end was near, spoke about the exodus of
the Israelites from Egypt and gave instructions concerning the burial
of his bones.
23 By faith Moses' parents hid him for three months after he was
born, because they saw he was no ordinary child, and they were not
afraid of the king's edict.
24 By faith Moses, when he had grown up, refused to be known as the
son of Pharaoh's daughter. 25 He chose to be mistreated along with the
people of God rather than to enjoy the fleeting pleasures of sin. 26 He
regarded disgrace for the sake of Christ as of greater value than the
treasures of Egypt, because he was looking ahead to his reward. 27 By
faith he left Egypt, not fearing the king's anger; he persevered because
he saw him who is invisible. 28 By faith he kept the Passover and the
application of blood, so that the destroyer of the firstborn would not
touch the firstborn of Israel.
29 By faith the people passed through the Red Sea as on dry land; but
when the Egyptians tried to do so, they were drowned.
30 By faith the walls of Jericho fell, after the army had marched
around them for seven days.
31 By faith the prostitute Rahab, because she welcomed the spies, was
not killed with those who were disobedient.[b]
32 And what more shall I say? I do not have time to tell about Gid-
eon, Barak, Samson and Jephthah, about David and Samuel and the
prophets, 33 who through faith conquered kingdoms, administered
justice, and gained what was promised; who shut the mouths of li-
ons, 34 quenched the fury of the flames, and escaped the edge of the
sword; whose weakness was turned to strength; and who became pow-
erful in battle and routed foreign armies. 35 Women received back their
dead, raised to life again. There were others who were tortured, refus-
ing to be released so that they might gain an even better resurrection.
36 Some faced jeers and flogging, and even chains and imprisonment.
37 They were put to death by stoning;[c] they were sawed in two; they
were killed by the sword. They went about in sheepskins and goat-
skins, destitute, persecuted and mistreated— 38 the world was not
worthy of them. They wandered in deserts and mountains, living in
caves and in holes in the ground.
39 These were all commended for their faith, yet none of them re-
ceived what had been promised, 40 since God had planned something
better for us so that only together with us would they be made perfect.
12 Therefore, since we are surrounded by such a great cloud of wit-
nesses, let us throw off everything that hinders and the sin that
so easily entangles. And let us run with perseverance the race marked

PRAYING SCRIPTURE

Hebrews 12

Discipline is usually not enjoyable, but it is necessary. Whether it is correction due to bad behavior or an exercise regimen to keep our bodies in shape, discipline hurts. When we are corrected by God, it is also painful, but the result is "a harvest of righteousness and peace" *if* we are trained by the discipline (see verse 11).

Righteous living is the way to avoid correction. But when discipline comes, learn from it, and enjoy peace afterward.

[a] 18 Gen. 21:12 [b] 31 Or *unbelieving* [c] 37 Some early manuscripts *stoning; they were put to the test;*

out for us, 2fixing our eyes on Jesus, the pioneer and perfecter of faith.
For the joy set before him he endured the cross, scorning its shame,
and sat down at the right hand of the throne of God. 3Consider him
who endured such opposition from sinners, so that you will not grow
weary and lose heart.

GOD DISCIPLINES HIS CHILDREN

4In your struggle against sin, you have not yet resisted to the point
of shedding your blood. 5And have you completely forgotten this word
of encouragement that addresses you as a father addresses his son? It
says,

"My son, do not make light of the Lord's discipline,
  and do not lose heart when he rebukes you,
6because the Lord disciplines the one he loves,
  and he chastens everyone he accepts as his son."[a]

7Endure hardship as discipline; God is treating you as his children.
For what children are not disciplined by their father? 8If you are not
disciplined — and everyone undergoes discipline — then you are not
legitimate, not true sons and daughters at all. 9Moreover, we have all
had human fathers who disciplined us and we respected them for it.
How much more should we submit to the Father of spirits and live!
10They disciplined us for a little while as they thought best; but God
disciplines us for our good, in order that we may share in his holiness.
11No discipline seems pleasant at the time, but painful. Later on, how-
ever, it produces a harvest of righteousness and peace for those who
have been trained by it.
12Therefore, strengthen your feeble arms and weak knees. 13"Make
level paths for your feet,"[b] so that the lame may not be disabled, but
rather healed.

WARNING AND ENCOURAGEMENT

14Make every effort to live in peace with everyone and to be holy;
without holiness no one will see the Lord. 15See to it that no one falls
short of the grace of God and that no bitter root grows up to cause
trouble and defile many. 16See that no one is sexually immoral, or is
godless like Esau, who for a single meal sold his inheritance rights as
the oldest son. 17Afterward, as you know, when he wanted to inherit
this blessing, he was rejected. Even though he sought the blessing with
tears, he could not change what he had done.

THE MOUNTAIN OF FEAR AND THE MOUNTAIN OF JOY

18You have not come to a mountain that can be touched and that is
burning with fire; to darkness, gloom and storm; 19to a trumpet blast
or to such a voice speaking words that those who heard it begged that
no further word be spoken to them, 20because they could not bear
what was commanded: "If even an animal touches the mountain, it
must be stoned to death."[c] 21The sight was so terrifying that Moses said,
"I am trembling with fear."[d]
22But you have come to Mount Zion, to the city of the living God,
the heavenly Jerusalem. You have come to thousands upon thousands

[a] *5,6* Prov. 3:11,12 (see Septuagint) [b] *13* Prov. 4:26 [c] *20* Exodus 19:12,13
[d] *21* See Deut. 9:19.

of angels in joyful assembly, 23to the church of the firstborn, whose
names are written in heaven. You have come to God, the Judge of all,
to the spirits of the righteous made perfect, 24to Jesus the mediator of
a new covenant, and to the sprinkled blood that speaks a better word
than the blood of Abel.
25See to it that you do not refuse him who speaks. If they did not
escape when they refused him who warned them on earth, how much
less will we, if we turn away from him who warns us from heaven?
26At that time his voice shook the earth, but now he has promised,
"Once more I will shake not only the earth but also the heavens."[a] 27The
words "once more" indicate the removing of what can be shaken —
that is, created things — so that what cannot be shaken may remain.
28Therefore, since we are receiving a kingdom that cannot be shaken,
let us be thankful, and so worship God acceptably with reverence and
awe, 29for our "God is a consuming fire."[b]

CONCLUDING EXHORTATIONS

13 Keep on loving one another as brothers and sisters. 2Do not for-
get to show hospitality to strangers, for by so doing some peo-
ple have shown hospitality to angels without knowing it. 3Continue to
remember those in prison as if you were together with them in prison,
and those who are mistreated as if you yourselves were suffering.
4Marriage should be honored by all, and the marriage bed kept pure,
for God will judge the adulterer and all the sexually immoral. 5Keep
your lives free from the love of money and be content with what you
have, because God has said,

> "Never will I leave you;
> never will I forsake you."[c]

6So we say with confidence,

> "The Lord is my helper; I will not be afraid.
> What can mere mortals do to me?"[d]

7Remember your leaders, who spoke the word of God to you. Con-
sider the outcome of their way of life and imitate their faith. 8Jesus
Christ is the same yesterday and today and forever.
9Do not be carried away by all kinds of strange teachings. It is good
for our hearts to be strengthened by grace, not by eating ceremonial
foods, which is of no benefit to those who do so. 10We have an altar
from which those who minister at the tabernacle have no right to eat.
11The high priest carries the blood of animals into the Most Holy
Place as a sin offering, but the bodies are burned outside the camp.
12And so Jesus also suffered outside the city gate to make the people
holy through his own blood. 13Let us, then, go to him outside the camp,
bearing the disgrace he bore. 14For here we do not have an enduring
city, but we are looking for the city that is to come.
15Through Jesus, therefore, let us continually offer to God a sacrifice
of praise — the fruit of lips that openly profess his name. 16And do not
forget to do good and to share with others, for with such sacrifices God
is pleased.
17Have confidence in your leaders and submit to their authority, be-
cause they keep watch over you as those who must give an account. Do

PRAYING SCRIPTURE

Hebrews 13

The writer closes with a series of practical encouragements but soon returns to the sacrifice of Jesus for his people. His blood established an "eternal covenant," equipped us "with everything good," and means he is working in us "what is pleasing to him" (verses 20–21).

Without the death of Christ, we would still be lost. Thank God for the sacrifice of Jesus that accomplished so much for his people.

[a] 26 Haggai 2:6 [b] 29 Deut. 4:24 [c] 5 Deut. 31:6 [d] 6 Psalm 118:6,7

this so that their work will be a joy, not a burden, for that would be of
no benefit to you.
18Pray for us. We are sure that we have a clear conscience and desire
to live honorably in every way. 19I particularly urge you to pray so that
I may be restored to you soon.

BENEDICTION AND FINAL GREETINGS

20Now may the God of peace, who through the blood of the eternal
covenant brought back from the dead our Lord Jesus, that great Shep-
herd of the sheep, 21equip you with everything good for doing his will,
and may he work in us what is pleasing to him, through Jesus Christ,
to whom be glory for ever and ever. Amen.

22Brothers and sisters, I urge you to bear with my word of exhorta-
tion, for in fact I have written to you quite briefly.
23I want you to know that our brother Timothy has been released. If
he arrives soon, I will come with him to see you.
24Greet all your leaders and all the Lord's people. Those from Italy
send you their greetings.
25Grace be with you all.

JAMES

James, the half brother of Jesus, wrote to help Christians understand how to live out their faith with justice and wisdom. James wrote to a scattered church (see 1:1) that was still largely Jewish. They were followers of Jesus the Messiah who were suffering persecution. As such, James helped them navigate their trials in a Christ-honoring way. Many Christians have called James's letter "the Proverbs of the New Testament" because of its emphasis on practical living.

In the first paragraph of his letter, James connected wisdom to our prayer lives—if you need wisdom, ask from God in faith, and it will be given (see 1:5–6).

James called believers to embrace their trials with joy, knowing that the Lord uses our trials to create perseverance in us. The growth that we experience as we learn perseverance helps us to face trials, temptations and any difficulty life might throw at us. The apostle went so far as to say, "Blessed is the one who perseveres under trial" (1:12). We don't often think of temptation as an opportunity to know happiness, but we can when we endure without sinning.

Addressing the sin of partiality, James reminded these believers not to show favoritism to the wealthy over the poor. God has chosen the poor of this world to be heirs of his kingdom so they should not be despised. James further reminded the church of how they have often been oppressed and dragged to court by the rich (see 2:1–13). It seems that their favoritism toward the rich was an attempt to gain favor from them, but James did not let them off the hook. Neither did he let the rich off the hook, warning them about their materialism and profits gained in part from exploiting their workers (see 5:1–6).

One of the most significant commentaries on the nature of faith is found in this letter. James said we should "not merely listen to the word," which leads to self-deception, but we should "do what it says" (1:22). He further taught that a faith not accompanied by God-honoring good works is no faith at all (see 2:14–26). This teaching is essential to a holistic understanding of faith. Faith is not simply believing with all one's heart that something is so. Biblical faith believes in the character and promises of God and is accompanied by works that show our faith. Without works, faith is dead.

Being a book on practical spirituality, James includes teaching on prayer. Believers who are struggling with sickness should call for the elders of the church to pray for them and anoint them with oil. He said, "The prayer offered in faith will make the sick person well" (5:15). While our prayers should never merely focus on our physical needs, we should always bring our physical needs to the Lord.

Our prayers should be like that of Elijah: earnest and bold. If God answered Elijah, a human being like us, then he will answer our prayers of faith as well.

1 James, a servant of God and of the Lord Jesus Christ,
To the twelve tribes scattered among the nations:
Greetings.

TRIALS AND TEMPTATIONS

2Consider it pure joy, my brothers and sisters,[a] whenever you face
trials of many kinds, 3because you know that the testing of your faith
produces perseverance. 4Let perseverance finish its work so that you
may be mature and complete, not lacking anything. 5If any of you lacks
wisdom, you should ask God, who gives generously to all without find-
ing fault, and it will be given to you. 6But when you ask, you must be-
lieve and not doubt, because the one who doubts is like a wave of the
sea, blown and tossed by the wind. 7That person should not expect to
receive anything from the Lord. 8Such a person is double-minded and
unstable in all they do.
9Believers in humble circumstances ought to take pride in their high
position. 10But the rich should take pride in their humiliation — since
they will pass away like a wild flower. 11For the sun rises with scorch-
ing heat and withers the plant; its blossom falls and its beauty is de-
stroyed. In the same way, the rich will fade away even while they go
about their business.
12Blessed is the one who perseveres under trial because, having
stood the test, that person will receive the crown of life that the Lord
has promised to those who love him.
13When tempted, no one should say, "God is tempting me." For God
cannot be tempted by evil, nor does he tempt anyone; 14but each per-
son is tempted when they are dragged away by their own evil desire
and enticed. 15Then, after desire has conceived, it gives birth to sin; and
sin, when it is full-grown, gives birth to death.
16Don't be deceived, my dear brothers and sisters. 17Every good and
perfect gift is from above, coming down from the Father of the heav-
enly lights, who does not change like shifting shadows. 18He chose to
give us birth through the word of truth, that we might be a kind of
firstfruits of all he created.

LISTENING AND DOING

19My dear brothers and sisters, take note of this: Everyone should
be quick to listen, slow to speak and slow to become angry, 20because
human anger does not produce the righteousness that God desires.
21Therefore, get rid of all moral filth and the evil that is so prevalent
and humbly accept the word planted in you, which can save you.
22Do not merely listen to the word, and so deceive yourselves. Do
what it says. 23Anyone who listens to the word but does not do what it
says is like someone who looks at his face in a mirror 24and, after look-
ing at himself, goes away and immediately forgets what he looks like.
25But whoever looks intently into the perfect law that gives freedom,
and continues in it — not forgetting what they have heard, but doing
it — they will be blessed in what they do.

[a] *2* The Greek word for *brothers and sisters* (*adelphoi*) refers here to believers, both men and women, as part of God's family; also in verses 16 and 19; and in 2:1,5,14; 3:10,12; 4:11; 5:7,9,10,12,19.

PRAYING SCRIPTURE

James 1

In a chapter that covers a lot of ground about temptation, a reward is promised: the crown of life. But though the crown is promised for those who persevere under trial, endurance is equated with those who love God (see verse 12). The power to endure temptation does not come from our will. It comes when we love God more than sin.

Ask God to help you love him so much that temptations to sin will be completely unappealing.

26Those who consider themselves religious and yet do not keep a tight rein on their tongues deceive themselves, and their religion is worthless. 27Religion that God our Father accepts as pure and faultless is this: to look after orphans and widows in their distress and to keep oneself from being polluted by the world.

PRAYING SCRIPTURE

James 2

Because our actions do not earn us salvation does not mean there is no place for them in the Christian life. James teaches us that when we claim to have faith, if that faith is not accompanied by our actions, as we read about through the lives of people like Abraham and Rahab, for example, our faith is dead. God does not see action apart from faith; people cannot see faith apart from action.

We need to act upon our faith, but we cannot trust our actions to save us. Ask God for faith and the courage to believe him while you act.

FAVORITISM FORBIDDEN

2 My brothers and sisters, believers in our glorious Lord Jesus Christ must not show favoritism. 2Suppose a man comes into your meeting wearing a gold ring and fine clothes, and a poor man in filthy old clothes also comes in. 3If you show special attention to the man wearing fine clothes and say, "Here's a good seat for you," but say to the poor man, "You stand there" or "Sit on the floor by my feet," 4have you not discriminated among yourselves and become judges with evil thoughts?

5Listen, my dear brothers and sisters: Has not God chosen those who are poor in the eyes of the world to be rich in faith and to inherit the kingdom he promised those who love him? 6But you have dishonored the poor. Is it not the rich who are exploiting you? Are they not the ones who are dragging you into court? 7Are they not the ones who are blaspheming the noble name of him to whom you belong?

8If you really keep the royal law found in Scripture, "Love your neighbor as yourself,"[a] you are doing right. 9But if you show favoritism, you sin and are convicted by the law as lawbreakers. 10For whoever keeps the whole law and yet stumbles at just one point is guilty of breaking all of it. 11For he who said, "You shall not commit adultery,"[b] also said, "You shall not murder."[c] If you do not commit adultery but do commit murder, you have become a lawbreaker.

12Speak and act as those who are going to be judged by the law that gives freedom, 13because judgment without mercy will be shown to anyone who has not been merciful. Mercy triumphs over judgment.

FAITH AND DEEDS

14What good is it, my brothers and sisters, if someone claims to have faith but has no deeds? Can such faith save them? 15Suppose a brother or a sister is without clothes and daily food. 16If one of you says to them, "Go in peace; keep warm and well fed," but does nothing about their physical needs, what good is it? 17In the same way, faith by itself, if it is not accompanied by action, is dead.

18But someone will say, "You have faith; I have deeds."

Show me your faith without deeds, and I will show you my faith by my deeds. 19You believe that there is one God. Good! Even the demons believe that — and shudder.

20You foolish person, do you want evidence that faith without deeds is useless[d]? 21Was not our father Abraham considered righteous for what he did when he offered his son Isaac on the altar? 22You see that his faith and his actions were working together, and his faith was made complete by what he did. 23And the scripture was fulfilled that says, "Abraham believed God, and it was credited to him as righteousness,"[e] and he was called God's friend. 24You see that a person is considered righteous by what they do and not by faith alone.

---

[a] *8* Lev. 19:18 [b] *11* Exodus 20:14; Deut. 5:18 [c] *11* Exodus 20:13; Deut. 5:17
[d] *20* Some early manuscripts *dead* [e] *23* Gen. 15:6

25 In the same way, was not even Rahab the prostitute considered righteous for what she did when she gave lodging to the spies and sent them off in a different direction? 26 As the body without the spirit is dead, so faith without deeds is dead.

TAMING THE TONGUE

3 Not many of you should become teachers, my fellow believers, because you know that we who teach will be judged more strictly. 2 We all stumble in many ways. Anyone who is never at fault in what they say is perfect, able to keep their whole body in check.

3 When we put bits into the mouths of horses to make them obey us, we can turn the whole animal. 4 Or take ships as an example. Although they are so large and are driven by strong winds, they are steered by a very small rudder wherever the pilot wants to go. 5 Likewise, the tongue is a small part of the body, but it makes great boasts. Consider what a great forest is set on fire by a small spark. 6 The tongue also is a fire, a world of evil among the parts of the body. It corrupts the whole body, sets the whole course of one's life on fire, and is itself set on fire by hell.

7 All kinds of animals, birds, reptiles and sea creatures are being tamed and have been tamed by mankind, 8 but no human being can tame the tongue. It is a restless evil, full of deadly poison.

9 With the tongue we praise our Lord and Father, and with it we curse human beings, who have been made in God's likeness. 10 Out of the same mouth come praise and cursing. My brothers and sisters, this should not be. 11 Can both fresh water and salt water flow from the same spring? 12 My brothers and sisters, can a fig tree bear olives, or a grapevine bear figs? Neither can a salt spring produce fresh water.

TWO KINDS OF WISDOM

13 Who is wise and understanding among you? Let them show it by their good life, by deeds done in the humility that comes from wisdom. 14 But if you harbor bitter envy and selfish ambition in your hearts, do not boast about it or deny the truth. 15 Such "wisdom" does not come down from heaven but is earthly, unspiritual, demonic. 16 For where you have envy and selfish ambition, there you find disorder and every evil practice.

17 But the wisdom that comes from heaven is first of all pure; then peace-loving, considerate, submissive, full of mercy and good fruit, impartial and sincere. 18 Peacemakers who sow in peace reap a harvest of righteousness.

SUBMIT YOURSELVES TO GOD

4 What causes fights and quarrels among you? Don't they come from your desires that battle within you? 2 You desire but do not have, so you kill. You covet but you cannot get what you want, so you quarrel and fight. You do not have because you do not ask God. 3 When you ask, you do not receive, because you ask with wrong motives, that you may spend what you get on your pleasures.

4 You adulterous people,[a] don't you know that friendship with the world means enmity against God? Therefore, anyone who chooses to be a friend of the world becomes an enemy of God. 5 Or do you think Scripture says without reason that he jealously longs for the spirit he

PRAYING SCRIPTURE

James 3

James seems to have been familiar with church members. His brief address on the danger of an unbridled tongue, if heeded by every Christian, would stop gossip in its tracks. The out-of-control tongue is "a fire, a world of evil" (verse 6). Gossip and slander are not mere chatter to occupy one's time. They are sins that destroy.

Does your speech glorify God at all times? Pray for a tongue that honors God.

PRAYING SCRIPTURE

James 4

One of the most beautiful, hope-filled promises in God's Word is found here: When we come near to God, he responds by coming near to us. God waits for us; he desires us. God never runs from his seeking children. He comes toward us.

Do you ever feel abandoned by God? Come near to him. Pray. He will come near to you.

[a] 4 An allusion to covenant unfaithfulness; see Hosea 3:1.

has caused to dwell in us[a]? 6 But he gives us more grace. That is why
Scripture says:

> "God opposes the proud
> but shows favor to the humble."[b]

7 Submit yourselves, then, to God. Resist the devil, and he will flee
from you. 8 Come near to God and he will come near to you. Wash
your hands, you sinners, and purify your hearts, you double-minded.
9 Grieve, mourn and wail. Change your laughter to mourning and your
joy to gloom. 10 Humble yourselves before the Lord, and he will lift
you up.

11 Brothers and sisters, do not slander one another. Anyone who
speaks against a brother or sister[c] or judges them speaks against the
law and judges it. When you judge the law, you are not keeping it, but
sitting in judgment on it. 12 There is only one Lawgiver and Judge, the
one who is able to save and destroy. But you—who are you to judge
your neighbor?

BOASTING ABOUT TOMORROW

13 Now listen, you who say, "Today or tomorrow we will go to this
or that city, spend a year there, carry on business and make money."
14 Why, you do not even know what will happen tomorrow. What is your
life? You are a mist that appears for a little while and then vanishes.
15 Instead, you ought to say, "If it is the Lord's will, we will live and do
this or that." 16 As it is, you boast in your arrogant schemes. All such
boasting is evil. 17 If anyone, then, knows the good they ought to do and
doesn't do it, it is sin for them.

WARNING TO RICH OPPRESSORS

5 Now listen, you rich people, weep and wail because of the misery
that is coming on you. 2 Your wealth has rotted, and moths have
eaten your clothes. 3 Your gold and silver are corroded. Their corrosion
will testify against you and eat your flesh like fire. You have hoarded
wealth in the last days. 4 Look! The wages you failed to pay the workers
who mowed your fields are crying out against you. The cries of the har-
vesters have reached the ears of the Lord Almighty. 5 You have lived on
earth in luxury and self-indulgence. You have fattened yourselves in
the day of slaughter.[d] 6 You have condemned and murdered the inno-
cent one, who was not opposing you.

PATIENCE IN SUFFERING

7 Be patient, then, brothers and sisters, until the Lord's coming. See
how the farmer waits for the land to yield its valuable crop, patiently
waiting for the autumn and spring rains. 8 You too, be patient and
stand firm, because the Lord's coming is near. 9 Don't grumble against
one another, brothers and sisters, or you will be judged. The Judge is
standing at the door!

10 Brothers and sisters, as an example of patience in the face of suf-
fering, take the prophets who spoke in the name of the Lord. 11 As you

PRAYING SCRIPTURE

James 5

The final chapter of this letter encourages us to pray, reminding us that God works through the prayers of his people. It also reminds us to pray in faith. For it is the "prayer offered in faith" that God hears on behalf of the sick, saving and raising them up (verse 15).

Do not be tempted to draw on prayer as a last resort. Make it your first option, inviting God to be involved in all your needs.

---

[a] 5 Or *that the spirit he caused to dwell in us envies intensely;* or *that the Spirit he caused to dwell in us longs jealously* [b] 6 Prov. 3:34 [c] 11 The Greek word for *brother or sister* (*adelphos*) refers here to a believer, whether man or woman, as part of God's family. [d] 5 Or *yourselves as in a day of feasting*

know, we count as blessed those who have persevered. You have heard
of Job's perseverance and have seen what the Lord finally brought
about. The Lord is full of compassion and mercy.
12Above all, my brothers and sisters, do not swear — not by heaven
or by earth or by anything else. All you need to say is a simple "Yes" or
"No." Otherwise you will be condemned.

THE PRAYER OF FAITH

13Is anyone among you in trouble? Let them pray. Is anyone happy?
Let them sing songs of praise. 14Is anyone among you sick? Let them
call the elders of the church to pray over them and anoint them with
oil in the name of the Lord. 15And the prayer offered in faith will make
the sick person well; the Lord will raise them up. If they have sinned,
they will be forgiven. 16Therefore confess your sins to each other and
pray for each other so that you may be healed. The prayer of a righteous person is powerful and effective.
17Elijah was a human being, even as we are. He prayed earnestly that
it would not rain, and it did not rain on the land for three and a half
years. 18Again he prayed, and the heavens gave rain, and the earth produced its crops.
19My brothers and sisters, if one of you should wander from the truth
and someone should bring that person back, 20remember this: Whoever turns a sinner from the error of their way will save them from
death and cover over a multitude of sins.

1 PETER

The recipients of Peter's first letter were being persecuted because of their faith in Jesus. He identified them as exiles who had been scattered throughout "Pontus, Galatia, Cappadocia, Asia and Bithynia" (1:1). Rather than leaving them with the reality of being dispersed like exiles, Peter immediately reminded them that they were chosen according to the Father's foreknowledge. They might have been scattered, but they were not lost to God.

The bulk of Peter's admonition to these believers focused on helping them to be faithful followers of Jesus who brought glory to him, testifying to his name even in the midst of persecution. An important key to every believer's spiritual growth is in the apostle's encouragement that even in suffering they need not despair. "In all this you greatly rejoice," he wrote, "though now for a little while you may have had to suffer grief in all kinds of trials" (1:6). They could rejoice even in suffering because it would just be for a while; it would not last forever. And there was another benefit: "that the proven genuineness of your faith—of greater worth than gold that perishes . . . may result in praise, glory and honor when Jesus Christ is revealed" (1:7). Their suffering was not in vain. When Jesus returns, they will be rewarded for enduring faithfully. Their genuine faith would honor and praise Christ, bringing glory to him.

The theme of suffering resurfaces in the second half of the book as well. Peter told the church, "Do not be surprised at the fiery ordeal that has come on you to test you, as though something strange were happening to you" (4:12). And rather than complain, they should rejoice that they were suffering as Jesus did. What a difference to the way many believers today react to the slightest discomfort to living for Christ. This helps us know how to pray when we are under pressure for our faith. Before we pray for the suffering to go away, we first pray that the Lord would use us to be a witness in our trials. We pray for the courage to speak the gospel clearly and for a heart that speaks the gospel with grace. We ask the Lord to help us model kindness and compassion, even when we are on the receiving end of hatred and vitriol.

Because "the end of all things is near" (4:7), Peter commanded these saints to be serious about praying. It is significant that, in chapter 5, he told these suffering believers to cast all their anxieties on God because he cares for them. Part of prayer is casting our cares on the Lord. God does not leave his children to deal with our frustrations, fears or difficulties on our own. Instead of carrying the weight of our anxieties, the Lord bears them for us. He does this for us because he cares for us.

Since God promises to care for us, our prayers should not merely include our requests; they should also include our thanksgiving.

1 Peter, an apostle of Jesus Christ,

To God's elect, exiles scattered throughout the provinces of Pontus,
Galatia, Cappadocia, Asia and Bithynia, 2who have been chosen accord-
ing to the foreknowledge of God the Father, through the sanctifying
work of the Spirit, to be obedient to Jesus Christ and sprinkled with
his blood:

Grace and peace be yours in abundance.

PRAISE TO GOD FOR A LIVING HOPE

3Praise be to the God and Father of our Lord Jesus Christ! In his great
mercy he has given us new birth into a living hope through the resur-
rection of Jesus Christ from the dead, 4and into an inheritance that can
never perish, spoil or fade. This inheritance is kept in heaven for you,
5who through faith are shielded by God's power until the coming of the
salvation that is ready to be revealed in the last time. 6In all this you
greatly rejoice, though now for a little while you may have had to suffer
grief in all kinds of trials. 7These have come so that the proven genu-
ineness of your faith — of greater worth than gold, which perishes even
though refined by fire — may result in praise, glory and honor when
Jesus Christ is revealed. 8Though you have not seen him, you love him;
and even though you do not see him now, you believe in him and are
filled with an inexpressible and glorious joy, 9for you are receiving the
end result of your faith, the salvation of your souls.

10Concerning this salvation, the prophets, who spoke of the grace
that was to come to you, searched intently and with the greatest care,
11trying to find out the time and circumstances to which the Spirit of
Christ in them was pointing when he predicted the sufferings of the
Messiah and the glories that would follow. 12It was revealed to them
that they were not serving themselves but you, when they spoke of the
things that have now been told you by those who have preached the
gospel to you by the Holy Spirit sent from heaven. Even angels long to
look into these things.

BE HOLY

13Therefore, with minds that are alert and fully sober, set your hope
on the grace to be brought to you when Jesus Christ is revealed at his
coming. 14As obedient children, do not conform to the evil desires you
had when you lived in ignorance. 15But just as he who called you is holy,
so be holy in all you do; 16for it is written: "Be holy, because I am holy."[a]

17Since you call on a Father who judges each person's work impar-
tially, live out your time as foreigners here in reverent fear. 18For you
know that it was not with perishable things such as silver or gold that
you were redeemed from the empty way of life handed down to you
from your ancestors, 19but with the precious blood of Christ, a lamb
without blemish or defect. 20He was chosen before the creation of the
world, but was revealed in these last times for your sake. 21Through
him you believe in God, who raised him from the dead and glorified
him, and so your faith and hope are in God.

22Now that you have purified yourselves by obeying the truth so that
you have sincere love for each other, love one another deeply, from

[a] *16* Lev. 11:44,45; 19:2

PRAYING SCRIPTURE

1 Peter 1

The blessings we enjoy in Jesus are nearly incomprehensible: abundant mercy, living hope and an inheritance that can never perish, spoil or fade, kept for us in heaven. And we are shielded by the power of God (see verses 4–5).

We often thank God for physical or material blessings, but do you regularly thank God for the blessings of being saved? Give thanks for the spiritual blessings you have in Christ.

the heart.[a] 23For you have been born again, not of perishable seed, but
of imperishable, through the living and enduring word of God. 24For,

> "All people are like grass,
>   and all their glory is like the flowers of the field;
> the grass withers and the flowers fall,
> 25 but the word of the Lord endures forever."[b]

And this is the word that was preached to you.

2 Therefore, rid yourselves of all malice and all deceit, hypocrisy,
envy, and slander of every kind. 2Like newborn babies, crave pure
spiritual milk, so that by it you may grow up in your salvation, 3now
that you have tasted that the Lord is good.

THE LIVING STONE AND A CHOSEN PEOPLE

4As you come to him, the living Stone — rejected by humans but
chosen by God and precious to him — 5you also, like living stones,
are being built into a spiritual house[c] to be a holy priesthood, offer-
ing spiritual sacrifices acceptable to God through Jesus Christ. 6For in
Scripture it says:

> "See, I lay a stone in Zion,
>   a chosen and precious cornerstone,
> and the one who trusts in him
>   will never be put to shame."[d]

7Now to you who believe, this stone is precious. But to those who do
not believe,

> "The stone the builders rejected
>   has become the cornerstone,"[e]

8and,

> "A stone that causes people to stumble
>   and a rock that makes them fall."[f]

They stumble because they disobey the message — which is also what
they were destined for.

9But you are a chosen people, a royal priesthood, a holy nation, God's
special possession, that you may declare the praises of him who called
you out of darkness into his wonderful light. 10Once you were not a
people, but now you are the people of God; once you had not received
mercy, but now you have received mercy.

LIVING GODLY LIVES IN A PAGAN SOCIETY

11Dear friends, I urge you, as foreigners and exiles, to abstain from
sinful desires, which wage war against your soul. 12Live such good lives
among the pagans that, though they accuse you of doing wrong, they
may see your good deeds and glorify God on the day he visits us.

13Submit yourselves for the Lord's sake to every human authority:
whether to the emperor, as the supreme authority, 14or to governors,
who are sent by him to punish those who do wrong and to commend
those who do right. 15For it is God's will that by doing good you should

PRAYING SCRIPTURE

1 Peter 2

Just as God chose ancient Israel for a people, he has chosen the church, a global people from every nation, tribe and language: a chosen people, a royal priesthood, a holy nation, the special people of God (see verse 9). The people God blesses today are his church, which infiltrates all earthly nations with the gospel.

God's people, having obtained mercy, are chosen to glorify him. Pray moment by moment to live accordingly.

---

[a] *22* Some early manuscripts *from a pure heart* [b] *25* Isaiah 40:6-8 (see Septuagint) [c] *5* Or *into a temple of the Spirit* [d] *6* Isaiah 28:16 [e] *7* Psalm 118:22 [f] *8* Isaiah 8:14

silence the ignorant talk of foolish people. 16Live as free people, but do not use your freedom as a cover-up for evil; live as God's slaves. 17Show proper respect to everyone, love the family of believers, fear God, honor the emperor.

18Slaves, in reverent fear of God submit yourselves to your masters, not only to those who are good and considerate, but also to those who are harsh. 19For it is commendable if someone bears up under the pain of unjust suffering because they are conscious of God. 20But how is it to your credit if you receive a beating for doing wrong and endure it? But if you suffer for doing good and you endure it, this is commendable before God. 21To this you were called, because Christ suffered for you, leaving you an example, that you should follow in his steps.

22 "He committed no sin,
 and no deceit was found in his mouth."[a]

23When they hurled their insults at him, he did not retaliate; when he suffered, he made no threats. Instead, he entrusted himself to him who judges justly. 24"He himself bore our sins" in his body on the cross, so that we might die to sins and live for righteousness; "by his wounds you have been healed." 25For "you were like sheep going astray,"[b] but now you have returned to the Shepherd and Overseer of your souls.

3 Wives, in the same way submit yourselves to your own husbands so that, if any of them do not believe the word, they may be won over without words by the behavior of their wives, 2when they see the purity and reverence of your lives. 3Your beauty should not come from outward adornment, such as elaborate hairstyles and the wearing of gold jewelry or fine clothes. 4Rather, it should be that of your inner self, the unfading beauty of a gentle and quiet spirit, which is of great worth in God's sight. 5For this is the way the holy women of the past who put their hope in God used to adorn themselves. They submitted themselves to their own husbands, 6like Sarah, who obeyed Abraham and called him her lord. You are her daughters if you do what is right and do not give way to fear.

7Husbands, in the same way be considerate as you live with your wives, and treat them with respect as the weaker partner and as heirs with you of the gracious gift of life, so that nothing will hinder your prayers.

SUFFERING FOR DOING GOOD

8Finally, all of you, be like-minded, be sympathetic, love one another, be compassionate and humble. 9Do not repay evil with evil or insult with insult. On the contrary, repay evil with blessing, because to this you were called so that you may inherit a blessing. 10For,

"Whoever would love life
 and see good days
must keep their tongue from evil
 and their lips from deceitful speech.
11 They must turn from evil and do good;
 they must seek peace and pursue it.
12 For the eyes of the Lord are on the righteous
 and his ears are attentive to their prayer,
but the face of the Lord is against those who do evil."[c]

PRAYING SCRIPTURE

1 Peter 3

Peter instructed believers to be prepared to give an answer for the reason of our hope whenever we are asked. But this is prefaced by the command, "But in your hearts revere Christ as Lord" (verse 15). We best prepare to answer others when our hearts are right with God. It is easy for other things to tempt our hearts away from the Lord. Confess any idols and set God apart in your affections.

---

[a] 22 Isaiah 53:9 [b] 24,25 Isaiah 53:4,5,6 (see Septuagint) [c] 12 Psalm 34:12-16

13Who is going to harm you if you are eager to do good? 14But even if you should suffer for what is right, you are blessed. "Do not fear their threats[a]; do not be frightened."[b] 15But in your hearts revere Christ as Lord. Always be prepared to give an answer to everyone who asks you to give the reason for the hope that you have. But do this with gentleness and respect, 16keeping a clear conscience, so that those who speak maliciously against your good behavior in Christ may be ashamed of their slander. 17For it is better, if it is God's will, to suffer for doing good than for doing evil. 18For Christ also suffered once for sins, the righteous for the unrighteous, to bring you to God. He was put to death in the body but made alive in the Spirit. 19After being made alive,[c] he went and made proclamation to the imprisoned spirits — 20to those who were disobedient long ago when God waited patiently in the days of Noah while the ark was being built. In it only a few people, eight in all, were saved through water, 21and this water symbolizes baptism that now saves you also — not the removal of dirt from the body but the pledge of a clear conscience toward God.[d] It saves you by the resurrection of Jesus Christ, 22who has gone into heaven and is at God's right hand — with angels, authorities and powers in submission to him.

LIVING FOR GOD

4 Therefore, since Christ suffered in his body, arm yourselves also with the same attitude, because whoever suffers in the body is done with sin. 2As a result, they do not live the rest of their earthly lives for evil human desires, but rather for the will of God. 3For you have spent enough time in the past doing what pagans choose to do — living in debauchery, lust, drunkenness, orgies, carousing and detestable idolatry. 4They are surprised that you do not join them in their reckless, wild living, and they heap abuse on you. 5But they will have to give account to him who is ready to judge the living and the dead. 6For this is the reason the gospel was preached even to those who are now dead, so that they might be judged according to human standards in regard to the body, but live according to God in regard to the spirit.

7The end of all things is near. Therefore be alert and of sober mind so that you may pray. 8Above all, love each other deeply, because love covers over a multitude of sins. 9Offer hospitality to one another without grumbling. 10Each of you should use whatever gift you have received to serve others, as faithful stewards of God's grace in its various forms. 11If anyone speaks, they should do so as one who speaks the very words of God. If anyone serves, they should do so with the strength God provides, so that in all things God may be praised through Jesus Christ. To him be the glory and the power for ever and ever. Amen.

PRAYING SCRIPTURE

1 Peter 4

Since Jesus' return to heaven, God's people have longed for the day when he will come again. Here Peter connected this expectation to prayer: We should remain serious and attentive to prayer.

Sometimes life on earth seems utterly hopeless. However, every generation of believers lives in these end times in the power of the Spirit. Ask God to help you stay focused on him, and commit to praying daily for Christ's return.

SUFFERING FOR BEING A CHRISTIAN

12Dear friends, do not be surprised at the fiery ordeal that has come on you to test you, as though something strange were happening to you. 13But rejoice inasmuch as you participate in the sufferings of Christ, so that you may be overjoyed when his glory is revealed. 14If you are insulted because of the name of Christ, you are blessed, for the Spirit of glory and of God rests on you. 15If you suffer, it should not be as a murderer or thief or any other kind of criminal, or even as

[a] 14 Or *fear what they fear* [b] 14 Isaiah 8:12 [c] 18,19 Or *but made alive in the spirit, 19in which also* [d] 21 Or *but an appeal to God for a clear conscience*

a meddler. 16However, if you suffer as a Christian, do not be ashamed,
but praise God that you bear that name. 17For it is time for judgment
to begin with God's household; and if it begins with us, what will the
outcome be for those who do not obey the gospel of God? 18And,

"If it is hard for the righteous to be saved,
what will become of the ungodly and the sinner?"[a]

19So then, those who suffer according to God's will should commit
themselves to their faithful Creator and continue to do good.

TO THE ELDERS AND THE FLOCK

5 To the elders among you, I appeal as a fellow elder and a witness of
Christ's sufferings who also will share in the glory to be revealed:
2Be shepherds of God's flock that is under your care, watching over
them — not because you must, but because you are willing, as God
wants you to be; not pursuing dishonest gain, but eager to serve; 3not
lording it over those entrusted to you, but being examples to the flock.
4And when the Chief Shepherd appears, you will receive the crown of
glory that will never fade away.
5In the same way, you who are younger, submit yourselves to your
elders. All of you, clothe yourselves with humility toward one another,
because,

"God opposes the proud
but shows favor to the humble."[b]

6Humble yourselves, therefore, under God's mighty hand, that he may
lift you up in due time. 7Cast all your anxiety on him because he cares
for you.
8Be alert and of sober mind. Your enemy the devil prowls around
like a roaring lion looking for someone to devour. 9Resist him, stand-
ing firm in the faith, because you know that the family of believers
throughout the world is undergoing the same kind of sufferings.
10And the God of all grace, who called you to his eternal glory in
Christ, after you have suffered a little while, will himself restore you
and make you strong, firm and steadfast. 11To him be the power for
ever and ever. Amen.

FINAL GREETINGS

12With the help of Silas,[c] whom I regard as a faithful brother, I have
written to you briefly, encouraging you and testifying that this is the
true grace of God. Stand fast in it.
13She who is in Babylon, chosen together with you, sends you her
greetings, and so does my son Mark. 14Greet one another with a kiss
of love.
Peace to all of you who are in Christ.

PRAYING SCRIPTURE

1 Peter 5

Verse 7 gives us one of the greatest hopes in Scripture: God invites us as his people to cast all our anxiety on him because he cares for us. God does not desire that we, his people, live with burdens and cares too devastating to manage. He invites us to cast them on him. We do not even need to be orderly about it.

Are you anxious? Burdened? Cast your concerns on Jesus; he cares for you.

---

[a] *18* Prov. 11:31 (see Septuagint) [b] *5* Prov. 3:34 [c] *12* Greek *Silvanus*, a variant of *Silas*

2 PETER

Peter's second letter addresses a much different problem than the first. In his first letter, Peter's audience faced trouble from without in the form of pressure and persecution. The recipients of his second letter needed to be warned about the danger of false prophets who would arise and lead them astray from within. In particular, Peter was concerned about false teachers who would undermine these believers' faith in the second coming of the Lord Jesus.

To encourage the church in the turbulent times they lived in, Peter reminded them that they had a common faith in Jesus (see 1:1). He then said that God's divine power would provide them with everything they needed to live and be godly. And if that was not enough, God gave them "very great and precious promises, so that through them you may participate in the divine nature" (1:3–4). God has promised and provided everything we need in him to live how he calls us to live. He calls those who lack these virtues "nearsighted and blind" (1:9), having forgotten what the Lord did for them.

Peter also wanted his readers to be assured of the Scriptures. Using his personal experience on the Mount of Transfiguration (see 1:18) as a place one could surely say, "God has spoken," he immediately turned their attention to Scripture: It is not a private interpretation, rather, holy men were moved by the Holy Spirit. The Word of God stands counter to false prophets.

The whole of the second chapter deals with the destructiveness and destruction of false teachers. Peter called them "unreasoning animals," "springs without water," "slaves of depravity," and dogs who return to their vomit. The warning was reminiscent of the Old Testament prophets and their soundings of judgment. Our prayers should often include petitions to stay in the truth and avoid false teachings and false teachers.

To put the false teachers in perspective, Peter reminded his readers that the Lord's timetable is not ours. Instead, a day is like a thousand years and a thousand years is like a day to God. He answers prayers and fulfills plans according to his will and timing; there are no other factors in play. This truth is important to remember for the believers' prayer life. Too often, we act as if every prayer deserves an immediate answer; we expect God to answer according to our will instead of his. But the Lord simply does not work this way. He operates in his own perfect timing, and we must learn to trust him.

Peter closed his letter with a reminder about the return of Jesus. "But the day of the Lord will come like a thief," he said, before reminding them of new heavens and a new earth that will be marked by righteousness (see 3:10–13). Peter encouraged the church to look forward to this day and live blameless and in peace. The return of Christ, with the living it should inspire, should be a strong motivation for us to pray until his return.

1 Simon Peter, a servant and apostle of Jesus Christ,

To those who through the righteousness of our God and Savior Jesus Christ have received a faith as precious as ours:

2Grace and peace be yours in abundance through the knowledge of God and of Jesus our Lord.

CONFIRMING ONE'S CALLING AND ELECTION

3His divine power has given us everything we need for a godly life
through our knowledge of him who called us by his own glory and
goodness. 4Through these he has given us his very great and precious
promises, so that through them you may participate in the divine
nature, having escaped the corruption in the world caused by evil
desires.

5For this very reason, make every effort to add to your faith good-
ness; and to goodness, knowledge; 6and to knowledge, self-control;
and to self-control, perseverance; and to perseverance, godliness;
7and to godliness, mutual affection; and to mutual affection, love.
8For if you possess these qualities in increasing measure, they will
keep you from being ineffective and unproductive in your knowledge
of our Lord Jesus Christ. 9But whoever does not have them is near-
sighted and blind, forgetting that they have been cleansed from their
past sins.

10Therefore, my brothers and sisters,[a] make every effort to confirm
your calling and election. For if you do these things, you will never
stumble, 11and you will receive a rich welcome into the eternal king-
dom of our Lord and Savior Jesus Christ.

PROPHECY OF SCRIPTURE

12So I will always remind you of these things, even though you know
them and are firmly established in the truth you now have. 13I think
it is right to refresh your memory as long as I live in the tent of this
body, 14because I know that I will soon put it aside, as our Lord Jesus
Christ has made clear to me. 15And I will make every effort to see that
after my departure you will always be able to remember these things.

16For we did not follow cleverly devised stories when we told you
about the coming of our Lord Jesus Christ in power, but we were eye-
witnesses of his majesty. 17He received honor and glory from God the
Father when the voice came to him from the Majestic Glory, saying,
"This is my Son, whom I love; with him I am well pleased."[b] 18We our-
selves heard this voice that came from heaven when we were with him
on the sacred mountain.

19We also have the prophetic message as something completely re-
liable, and you will do well to pay attention to it, as to a light shining
in a dark place, until the day dawns and the morning star rises in
your hearts. 20Above all, you must understand that no prophecy of
Scripture came about by the prophet's own interpretation of things.
21For prophecy never had its origin in the human will, but prophets,
though human, spoke from God as they were carried along by the
Holy Spirit.

PRAYING SCRIPTURE

2 Peter 1

The reality of our faith is demonstrated by our continued progression into godly, Christlike character. Peter listed a synopsis of peace with the Spirit, including faith, goodness, knowledge, self-control, perseverance, godliness, mutual affection and love. Without this maturing process, we will forget our past sinful life (verses 5–9).

As a rule, do you focus more on your spiritual growth or your failures? Pray to focus on the path of growth.

[a] *10* The Greek word for *brothers and sisters* (*adelphoi*) refers here to believers, both men and women, as part of God's family. [b] *17* Matt. 17:5; Mark 9:7; Luke 9:35

PRAYING SCRIPTURE

2 Peter 2

The tenor of the entire Scriptures is that God will bring judgment on false teachers. Those who lead people astray with "destructive heresies," who "exploit you with fabricated stories," and are "full of adultery," and "experts in greed," will find their condemnation to be all too real (verses 1–3,14).

Are you careful about the teachers you listen to? Ask God for the discernment to avoid the lies of those whose destruction is assured.

FALSE TEACHERS AND THEIR DESTRUCTION

2 But there were also false prophets among the people, just as there
will be false teachers among you. They will secretly introduce
destructive heresies, even denying the sovereign Lord who bought
them—bringing swift destruction on themselves. 2Many will follow
their depraved conduct and will bring the way of truth into disrepute.
3In their greed these teachers will exploit you with fabricated stories.
Their condemnation has long been hanging over them, and their de-
struction has not been sleeping.

4For if God did not spare angels when they sinned, but sent them to
hell,[a] putting them in chains of darkness[b] to be held for judgment; 5if
he did not spare the ancient world when he brought the flood on its
ungodly people, but protected Noah, a preacher of righteousness, and
seven others; 6if he condemned the cities of Sodom and Gomorrah by
burning them to ashes, and made them an example of what is going
to happen to the ungodly; 7and if he rescued Lot, a righteous man,
who was distressed by the depraved conduct of the lawless 8(for that
righteous man, living among them day after day, was tormented in
his righteous soul by the lawless deeds he saw and heard)— 9if this
is so, then the Lord knows how to rescue the godly from trials and to
hold the unrighteous for punishment on the day of judgment. 10This
is especially true of those who follow the corrupt desire of the flesh[c]
and despise authority.

Bold and arrogant, they are not afraid to heap abuse on celestial be-
ings; 11yet even angels, although they are stronger and more powerful,
do not heap abuse on such beings when bringing judgment on them
from[d] the Lord. 12But these people blaspheme in matters they do not
understand. They are like unreasoning animals, creatures of instinct,
born only to be caught and destroyed, and like animals they too will
perish.

13They will be paid back with harm for the harm they have done.
Their idea of pleasure is to carouse in broad daylight. They are blots
and blemishes, reveling in their pleasures while they feast with you.[e]
14With eyes full of adultery, they never stop sinning; they seduce the
unstable; they are experts in greed—an accursed brood! 15They have
left the straight way and wandered off to follow the way of Balaam son
of Bezer,[f] who loved the wages of wickedness. 16But he was rebuked for
his wrongdoing by a donkey—an animal without speech—who spoke
with a human voice and restrained the prophet's madness.

17These people are springs without water and mists driven by a
storm. Blackest darkness is reserved for them. 18For they mouth empty,
boastful words and, by appealing to the lustful desires of the flesh,
they entice people who are just escaping from those who live in error.
19They promise them freedom, while they themselves are slaves of de-
pravity—for "people are slaves to whatever has mastered them." 20If
they have escaped the corruption of the world by knowing our Lord
and Savior Jesus Christ and are again entangled in it and are over-
come, they are worse off at the end than they were at the beginning.

[a] 4 Greek *Tartarus* [b] 4 Some manuscripts *in gloomy dungeons* [c] *10* In contexts like this, the Greek word for *flesh* (*sarx*) refers to the sinful state of human beings, often presented as a power in opposition to the Spirit; also in verse 18. [d] *11* Many manuscripts *beings in the presence of* [e] *13* Some manuscripts *in their love feasts* [f] *15* Greek *Bosor*

21It would have been better for them not to have known the way of
righteousness, than to have known it and then to turn their backs on
the sacred command that was passed on to them. 22Of them the prov-
erbs are true: "A dog returns to its vomit,"[a] and, "A sow that is washed
returns to her wallowing in the mud."

THE DAY OF THE LORD

3 Dear friends, this is now my second letter to you. I have written
both of them as reminders to stimulate you to wholesome think-
ing. 2I want you to recall the words spoken in the past by the holy
prophets and the command given by our Lord and Savior through your
apostles.
3Above all, you must understand that in the last days scoffers will
come, scoffing and following their own evil desires. 4They will say,
"Where is this 'coming' he promised? Ever since our ancestors died,
everything goes on as it has since the beginning of creation." 5But they
deliberately forget that long ago by God's word the heavens came into
being and the earth was formed out of water and by water. 6By these
waters also the world of that time was deluged and destroyed. 7By the
same word the present heavens and earth are reserved for fire, being
kept for the day of judgment and destruction of the ungodly.
8But do not forget this one thing, dear friends: With the Lord a day
is like a thousand years, and a thousand years are like a day. 9The Lord
is not slow in keeping his promise, as some understand slowness. In-
stead he is patient with you, not wanting anyone to perish, but every-
one to come to repentance.
10But the day of the Lord will come like a thief. The heavens will
disappear with a roar; the elements will be destroyed by fire, and the
earth and everything done in it will be laid bare.[b]
11Since everything will be destroyed in this way, what kind of people
ought you to be? You ought to live holy and godly lives 12as you look
forward to the day of God and speed its coming.[c] That day will bring
about the destruction of the heavens by fire, and the elements will
melt in the heat. 13But in keeping with his promise we are looking for-
ward to a new heaven and a new earth, where righteousness dwells.
14So then, dear friends, since you are looking forward to this, make
every effort to be found spotless, blameless and at peace with him.
15Bear in mind that our Lord's patience means salvation, just as our
dear brother Paul also wrote you with the wisdom that God gave him.
16He writes the same way in all his letters, speaking in them of these
matters. His letters contain some things that are hard to understand,
which ignorant and unstable people distort, as they do the other Scrip-
tures, to their own destruction.
17Therefore, dear friends, since you have been forewarned, be on
your guard so that you may not be carried away by the error of the
lawless and fall from your secure position. 18But grow in the grace and
knowledge of our Lord and Savior Jesus Christ. To him be glory both
now and forever! Amen.

PRAYING SCRIPTURE

2 Peter 3

In his patience, the Lord has delayed his return so more people will have time to repent and come to him. God loves the lost. His strong desire is that people place their faith in Jesus (see verse 9).

Pray for those you know who do not know Jesus, that they might avail themselves of God's patience and trust him for salvation.

[a] 22 Prov. 26:11 [b] 10 Some manuscripts *be burned up* [c] 12 Or *as you wait eagerly for the day of God to come*

1 JOHN

The apostle John did not identify the recipients of this letter, though we see his affection by calling them his "dear children" (2:1). Many Christians have believed that this letter was intended for the church at Ephesus. Apparently the community of believers to whom John was writing was dealing with a form of Gnosticism. Proponents of this heresy believed that matter (including the human body) was evil, while spirit was good. They taught that Jesus had not come in a human body, in flesh. John immediately addressed such thinking, describing Jesus as One "which we have heard, which we have seen with our eyes, which we have looked at and our hands have touched" (1:1). John had interacted with the human Jesus. The "Word of life" was not a mere apparition; he was flesh, blood and bone.

Using three beautiful metaphors, John called God light (see 1:5), love (see 4:7–8) and life (see 5:11). To know God means "we walk in the light, as he is in the light" (1:7). To know God means we "love one another, for love comes from God" (4:7). And to have the Son of God is to have life (see 5:12).

John used other images—little children, young men, old men, fathers—and the Father to demonstrate stages of spiritual growth. Each correlates to maturity. Little children are saved. Young men have overcome the evil one. Fathers know God.

An important theme of 1 John regards the Antichrist and antichrists. John seemed more concerned about the "spirit of the antichrist" who does not confess that Jesus has come in flesh (see 4:3) than he was about an individual known as *the* Antichrist. This is instructive for us. A spirit that permeates culture and denies Jesus is to be guarded against more than a single individual. Regardless of the spirit or the person, John assured God's children that they "have overcome them, because the one who is in you is greater than the one who is in the world" (4:4).

In chapter 3, John addressed a vital issue: condemnation. Condemnation from both Satan and our hearts is a lifelong challenge for many. Self-condemnation over past sins or current struggles beset the growth of many. But when our hearts condemn us, we can trust that God is greater than our hearts. He knows everything about his children yet still refuses to condemn them (see verse 20).

In the final chapter, John revealed one motivation for what he had written: that his readers who believe in Jesus might know they have eternal life. How could they know something like that? Because "whoever has the Son has life; whoever does not have the Son of God does not have life" (5:12). Jesus is life; to have him is to live.

The book closes with a strong emphasis on prayer, promising that we can have confidence in God that if we ask anything according to his will, he hears us and answers our petitions (see 5:14–15). What an incredible promise. God's children should not hesitate to call on him in faith.

THE INCARNATION OF THE WORD OF LIFE

1 That which was from the beginning, which we have heard, which
we have seen with our eyes, which we have looked at and our hands
have touched — this we proclaim concerning the Word of life. 2The life
appeared; we have seen it and testify to it, and we proclaim to you the
eternal life, which was with the Father and has appeared to us. 3We pro-
claim to you what we have seen and heard, so that you also may have
fellowship with us. And our fellowship is with the Father and with his
Son, Jesus Christ. 4We write this to make our[a] joy complete.

LIGHT AND DARKNESS, SIN AND FORGIVENESS

5This is the message we have heard from him and declare to you:
God is light; in him there is no darkness at all. 6If we claim to have fel-
lowship with him and yet walk in the darkness, we lie and do not live
out the truth. 7But if we walk in the light, as he is in the light, we have
fellowship with one another, and the blood of Jesus, his Son, purifies
us from all[b] sin.
8If we claim to be without sin, we deceive ourselves and the truth is
not in us. 9If we confess our sins, he is faithful and just and will forgive
us our sins and purify us from all unrighteousness. 10If we claim we
have not sinned, we make him out to be a liar and his word is not in us.

2 My dear children, I write this to you so that you will not sin. But
if anybody does sin, we have an advocate with the Father — Jesus
Christ, the Righteous One. 2He is the atoning sacrifice for our sins, and
not only for ours but also for the sins of the whole world.

LOVE AND HATRED FOR FELLOW BELIEVERS

3We know that we have come to know him if we keep his commands.
4Whoever says, "I know him," but does not do what he commands is a
liar, and the truth is not in that person. 5But if anyone obeys his word,
love for God[c] is truly made complete in them. This is how we know
we are in him: 6Whoever claims to live in him must live as Jesus did.
7Dear friends, I am not writing you a new command but an old one,
which you have had since the beginning. This old command is the
message you have heard. 8Yet I am writing you a new command; its
truth is seen in him and in you, because the darkness is passing and
the true light is already shining.
9Anyone who claims to be in the light but hates a brother or sister[d]
is still in the darkness. 10Anyone who loves their brother and sister[e]
lives in the light, and there is nothing in them to make them stumble.
11But anyone who hates a brother or sister is in the darkness and walks
around in the darkness. They do not know where they are going, be-
cause the darkness has blinded them.

REASONS FOR WRITING

12I am writing to you, dear children,
because your sins have been forgiven on account of his name.

---

[a] 4 Some manuscripts *your* [b] 7 Or *every* [c] 5 Or *word, God's love*
[d] 9 The Greek word for *brother or sister* (*adelphos*) refers here to a believer, whether man or woman, as part of God's family; also in verse 11; and in 3:15,17; 4:20; 5:16. [e] 10 The Greek word for *brother and sister* (*adelphos*) refers here to a believer, whether man or woman, as part of God's family; also in 3:10; 4:20,21.

PRAYING SCRIPTURE

1 John 1

John's personal experience with the Savior gave testimony to the fellowship Jesus came to bring: We can fellowship with each other because we have fellowship with God. Fellowship implies unity of purpose and direction. This fellowship is demonstrated when we walk in the light as he is in the light.

We cannot be right with God while being wrong with God's people. Seek to fellowship with all of God's people.

PRAYING SCRIPTURE

1 John 2

Scripture has much to say about love. The two great commandments are to love God and love our neighbor. In John's Gospel, he wrote about God's great love for the world. We read that it is impossible to hate a brother in Christ while walking in the light.

Do you have any brothers or sisters you struggle to love? If so, pray that the Father will help you love them as he does.

13 I am writing to you, fathers,
because you know him who is from the beginning.
I am writing to you, young men,
because you have overcome the evil one.

14 I write to you, dear children,
because you know the Father.
I write to you, fathers,
because you know him who is from the beginning.
I write to you, young men,
because you are strong,
and the word of God lives in you,
and you have overcome the evil one.

ON NOT LOVING THE WORLD

15 Do not love the world or anything in the world. If anyone loves
the world, love for the Father[a] is not in them. 16 For everything in the
world — the lust of the flesh, the lust of the eyes, and the pride of
life — comes not from the Father but from the world. 17 The world and
its desires pass away, but whoever does the will of God lives forever.

WARNINGS AGAINST DENYING THE SON

18 Dear children, this is the last hour; and as you have heard that the
antichrist is coming, even now many antichrists have come. This is
how we know it is the last hour. 19 They went out from us, but they
did not really belong to us. For if they had belonged to us, they would
have remained with us; but their going showed that none of them be-
longed to us.

20 But you have an anointing from the Holy One, and all of you know
the truth.[b] 21 I do not write to you because you do not know the truth,
but because you do know it and because no lie comes from the truth.
22 Who is the liar? It is whoever denies that Jesus is the Christ. Such a
person is the antichrist — denying the Father and the Son. 23 No one
who denies the Son has the Father; whoever acknowledges the Son
has the Father also.

24 As for you, see that what you have heard from the beginning re-
mains in you. If it does, you also will remain in the Son and in the Fa-
ther. 25 And this is what he promised us — eternal life.

26 I am writing these things to you about those who are trying to lead
you astray. 27 As for you, the anointing you received from him remains
in you, and you do not need anyone to teach you. But as his anointing
teaches you about all things and as that anointing is real, not counter-
feit — just as it has taught you, remain in him.

GOD'S CHILDREN AND SIN

28 And now, dear children, continue in him, so that when he appears
we may be confident and unashamed before him at his coming.

29 If you know that he is righteous, you know that everyone who does
what is right has been born of him.

3 See what great love the Father has lavished on us, that we should
be called children of God! And that is what we are! The reason the
world does not know us is that it did not know him. 2 Dear friends, now

PRAYING SCRIPTURE

1 John 3

John wrote that we understand love because Jesus laid down his life for us (see verse 16). The application of loving the family of God is that we meet the physical needs of others. If we do not, John asked, "How can the love of God be in that person?" (verse 17).

Love defined as emotion is easy. But love defined by action is harder. Ask God to help you truly love others—in deed not only in word.

[a] 15 Or *world, the Father's love* [b] 20 Some manuscripts *and you know all things*

we are children of God, and what we will be has not yet been made
known. But we know that when Christ appears,[a] we shall be like him,
for we shall see him as he is. 3All who have this hope in him purify
themselves, just as he is pure.
4Everyone who sins breaks the law; in fact, sin is lawlessness. 5But
you know that he appeared so that he might take away our sins. And in
him is no sin. 6No one who lives in him keeps on sinning. No one who
continues to sin has either seen him or known him.
7Dear children, do not let anyone lead you astray. The one who does
what is right is righteous, just as he is righteous. 8The one who does
what is sinful is of the devil, because the devil has been sinning from
the beginning. The reason the Son of God appeared was to destroy the
devil's work. 9No one who is born of God will continue to sin, because
God's seed remains in them; they cannot go on sinning, because they
have been born of God. 10This is how we know who the children of God
are and who the children of the devil are: Anyone who does not do
what is right is not God's child, nor is anyone who does not love their
brother and sister.

MORE ON LOVE AND HATRED

11For this is the message you heard from the beginning: We should
love one another. 12Do not be like Cain, who belonged to the evil one
and murdered his brother. And why did he murder him? Because his
own actions were evil and his brother's were righteous. 13Do not be sur-
prised, my brothers and sisters,[b] if the world hates you. 14We know that
we have passed from death to life, because we love each other. Anyone
who does not love remains in death. 15Anyone who hates a brother or
sister is a murderer, and you know that no murderer has eternal life
residing in him.
16This is how we know what love is: Jesus Christ laid down his life for
us. And we ought to lay down our lives for our brothers and sisters. 17If
anyone has material possessions and sees a brother or sister in need
but has no pity on them, how can the love of God be in that person?
18Dear children, let us not love with words or speech but with actions
and in truth.
19This is how we know that we belong to the truth and how we set
our hearts at rest in his presence: 20If our hearts condemn us, we know
that God is greater than our hearts, and he knows everything. 21Dear
friends, if our hearts do not condemn us, we have confidence before
God 22and receive from him anything we ask, because we keep his
commands and do what pleases him. 23And this is his command: to
believe in the name of his Son, Jesus Christ, and to love one another as
he commanded us. 24The one who keeps God's commands lives in him,
and he in them. And this is how we know that he lives in us: We know
it by the Spirit he gave us.

ON DENYING THE INCARNATION

4 Dear friends, do not believe every spirit, but test the spirits to see
whether they are from God, because many false prophets have
gone out into the world. 2This is how you can recognize the Spirit of

PRAYING SCRIPTURE

1 John 4

The practical nature of love continues here where we are told that "God is love," a truth we should long savor (verse 8). God's love is not a theory nor based only on emotion. God showed his love to us by sending his Son that we might have life.

Loving like God loves means loving practically. Pray for opportunities to love practically by serving people you come into contact with.

[a] 2 Or *when it is made known* [b] 13 The Greek word for *brothers and sisters* (*adelphoi*) refers here to believers, both men and women, as part of God's family; also in verse 16.

God: Every spirit that acknowledges that Jesus Christ has come in the flesh is from God, 3but every spirit that does not acknowledge Jesus is not from God. This is the spirit of the antichrist, which you have heard is coming and even now is already in the world.

4You, dear children, are from God and have overcome them, because the one who is in you is greater than the one who is in the world. 5They are from the world and therefore speak from the viewpoint of the world, and the world listens to them. 6We are from God, and whoever knows God listens to us; but whoever is not from God does not listen to us. This is how we recognize the Spirit[a] of truth and the spirit of falsehood.

GOD'S LOVE AND OURS

7Dear friends, let us love one another, for love comes from God. Everyone who loves has been born of God and knows God. 8Whoever does not love does not know God, because God is love. 9This is how God showed his love among us: He sent his one and only Son into the world that we might live through him. 10This is love: not that we loved God, but that he loved us and sent his Son as an atoning sacrifice for our sins. 11Dear friends, since God so loved us, we also ought to love one another. 12No one has ever seen God; but if we love one another, God lives in us and his love is made complete in us.

13This is how we know that we live in him and he in us: He has given us of his Spirit. 14And we have seen and testify that the Father has sent his Son to be the Savior of the world. 15If anyone acknowledges that Jesus is the Son of God, God lives in them and they in God. 16And so we know and rely on the love God has for us.

God is love. Whoever lives in love lives in God, and God in them. 17This is how love is made complete among us so that we will have confidence on the day of judgment: In this world we are like Jesus. 18There is no fear in love. But perfect love drives out fear, because fear has to do with punishment. The one who fears is not made perfect in love.

19We love because he first loved us. 20Whoever claims to love God yet hates a brother or sister is a liar. For whoever does not love their brother and sister, whom they have seen, cannot love God, whom they have not seen. 21And he has given us this command: Anyone who loves God must also love their brother and sister.

PRAYING SCRIPTURE

1 John 5

Do you ever wonder whether God loves you eternally? John told us that God's love is intertwined with Jesus, the Son. Whoever has Jesus has life. Whoever does not, does not have life. John wrote that God's people can "know that [they] have eternal life" because of Jesus (verse 13).

Whenever you doubt God's ability to keep you, remember Jesus and thank him. It is his power, not ours, that makes us children of God.

FAITH IN THE INCARNATE SON OF GOD

5 Everyone who believes that Jesus is the Christ is born of God, and everyone who loves the father loves his child as well. 2This is how we know that we love the children of God: by loving God and carrying out his commands. 3In fact, this is love for God: to keep his commands. And his commands are not burdensome, 4for everyone born of God overcomes the world. This is the victory that has overcome the world, even our faith. 5Who is it that overcomes the world? Only the one who believes that Jesus is the Son of God.

6This is the one who came by water and blood — Jesus Christ. He did not come by water only, but by water and blood. And it is the Spirit who testifies, because the Spirit is the truth. 7For there are three that testify: 8the[b] Spirit, the water and the blood; and the three are in agreement.

[a] 6 Or *spirit* [b] 7,8 Late manuscripts of the Vulgate *testify in heaven: the Father, the Word and the Holy Spirit, and these three are one. 8And there are three that testify on earth: the* (not found in any Greek manuscript before the fourteenth century)

9We accept human testimony, but God's testimony is greater because
it is the testimony of God, which he has given about his Son. 10Who-
ever believes in the Son of God accepts this testimony. Whoever does
not believe God has made him out to be a liar, because they have not
believed the testimony God has given about his Son. 11And this is the
testimony: God has given us eternal life, and this life is in his Son.
12Whoever has the Son has life; whoever does not have the Son of God
does not have life.

CONCLUDING AFFIRMATIONS

13I write these things to you who believe in the name of the Son of
God so that you may know that you have eternal life. 14This is the con-
fidence we have in approaching God: that if we ask anything according
to his will, he hears us. 15And if we know that he hears us—whatever
we ask—we know that we have what we asked of him.

16If you see any brother or sister commit a sin that does not lead
to death, you should pray and God will give them life. I refer to those
whose sin does not lead to death. There is a sin that leads to death. I
am not saying that you should pray about that. 17All wrongdoing is sin,
and there is sin that does not lead to death.

18We know that anyone born of God does not continue to sin; the
One who was born of God keeps them safe, and the evil one cannot
harm them. 19We know that we are children of God, and that the whole
world is under the control of the evil one. 20We know also that the Son
of God has come and has given us understanding, so that we may know
him who is true. And we are in him who is true by being in his Son
Jesus Christ. He is the true God and eternal life.

21Dear children, keep yourselves from idols.

2 JOHN

John's last two letters, 2 John and 3 John, are the two shortest books in the New Testament by number of words in the Greek text. Second John includes 245 words while 3 John contains only 219. These short letters—almost notes—from John echo the concerns of his first letter applied to immediate concerns in this Christian community.

John desired that these children of his would live in truth and love. He hoped they would beware of false teachers who denied that Jesus had come in the flesh, a concern also expressed in 1 John. He had "great joy" that his children were walking in truth, just as the "the Father commanded us" (verse 4). John reminded them that he wasn't writing anything new, but that which they had heard from the beginning: Love one another (see verse 5).

As with the recipients of John's first letter, this local body of believers was finding Gnosticism a challenge to their spiritual growth. While Gnosticism might seem a remote concern today, the incarnation of Jesus has tremendous implications for our prayer lives. If Jesus did not come in the flesh, then he did not really live on this earth, suffering the trials and temptations that we do. If he did not live in a physical human body, then he could not have died a physical death on the cross for our sins and his body was not raised from the dead. Thus, he did not ascend bodily into heaven and is not interceding at the right hand of God for us. Nor do we have a merciful and faithful high priest who offers grace to help in time of need. Jesus Christ, a real man with a fleshly body like ours, sits at the right hand of the Father as our mediator.

John called anyone who denies this "the deceiver and the antichrist" (verse 7), echoing language from his earlier letter. He told this "lady chosen by God" (verse 1), alternately interpreted as a woman in whose house the church met or the church itself, not to allow a deceiver into "your house" (that is, the church's meeting), lest she be sharing in their wicked work (see verses 10–11).

John further encouraged the church to remain diligent in the faith that they "may be rewarded fully" (1:8), doubtless a reference to the judgment seat of Christ. If they succumbed to the false teaching of the deceivers, they risked losing those things they had worked for.

John's love for his children became clear when, at the end of the letter, he expressed his hope to see them face-to-face so his letter would not be the sum of their communication. Meeting in person would bring them all fullness of joy.

John clearly prayed for these disciples. The loving character of his tone and his deep desire for their spiritual obedience would have been accompanied by fervent prayer for them. As God blesses us with spiritual children, we will likewise find ourselves praying for their full obedience to Christ.

1 The elder,

To the lady chosen by God and to her children, whom I love in the
truth — and not I only, but also all who know the truth — 2 because of
the truth, which lives in us and will be with us forever:

3 Grace, mercy and peace from God the Father and from Jesus Christ,
the Father's Son, will be with us in truth and love.

4 It has given me great joy to find some of your children walking in
the truth, just as the Father commanded us. 5 And now, dear lady, I am
not writing you a new command but one we have had from the begin-
ning. I ask that we love one another. 6 And this is love: that we walk in
obedience to his commands. As you have heard from the beginning,
his command is that you walk in love.

7 I say this because many deceivers, who do not acknowledge Jesus
Christ as coming in the flesh, have gone out into the world. Any such
person is the deceiver and the antichrist. 8 Watch out that you do not
lose what we[a] have worked for, but that you may be rewarded fully.
9 Anyone who runs ahead and does not continue in the teaching of
Christ does not have God; whoever continues in the teaching has both
the Father and the Son. 10 If anyone comes to you and does not bring
this teaching, do not take them into your house or welcome them.
11 Anyone who welcomes them shares in their wicked work.

12 I have much to write to you, but I do not want to use paper and ink.
Instead, I hope to visit you and talk with you face to face, so that our
joy may be complete.

13 The children of your sister, who is chosen by God, send their
greetings.

PRAYING SCRIPTURE

2 John

John's second letter emphasizes some familiar ground: The Christian life is evidenced by walking in love, so be diligent in identifying teaching that strays from the Savior's love expressed in Christ's life. The love of God requires us to reject false doctrine that denies the deity of Jesus. Anyone who teaches such is "the antichrist" (verse 7).

It is important to remember that the spirit of antichrist is more prevalent than an individual identified as the Antichrist. Pray that God protects you from the spirit of this age.

---

[a] 8 Some manuscripts *you*

3 JOHN

Third John differs from John's first two letters in that it was written to a named individual, Gaius, rather than an entire church, although it partially addresses trouble in a church. Four times John said that Gaius was "a dear friend," also translated "beloved," demonstrating John's great affection for this fellow servant and perhaps recalling how multiple times he referred to himself as "the disciple whom Jesus loved" in his Gospel (see John 13:23; 19:26; 20:2; 21:7,20).

John began the letter with a prayer for Gaius's physical health and general well-being, a theme completely appropriate for all Christian prayers. We are unified beings: body, soul and spirit. However, John's prayer for Gaius also included the desire that "all may go well with you" (verse 2), just as his soul prospered.

In verse 4, John wrote, "I have no greater joy than to hear that my children are walking in the truth." This reveals Gaius as one of John's children, one whom he had discipled to some extent. This "walking in truth" seems to be John's greatest burden. It is worth noting that John did not simply say it made him happy. There was nothing in his life that brought him greater *joy* than the spiritual fidelity of his spiritual children. All Christians should reflect this concern, praying that each of us would walk with him who is the Truth.

Halfway through the short book, John revealed his reason for writing. One member of the church, Diotrephes, was dominating the body, refusing to receive John and his brethren and removing from membership those who would have received them. John clarified that Diotrephes, even though he had some authority in the church, did not know God. His evil actions revealed an evil heart. John commended Demetrius instead.

This might seem that John was offended because of a perceived or actual slight, but the problem was much worse. The truth of the gospel in those early days following the return of Christ was entrusted to the apostles of Jesus. To reject them was to reject the Way and put the early followers of Jesus in the peril of spiritual decline and deception. It was imperative for John to correct this problem, even if from a distance, and reestablish his apostolic authority before the church, lest they be drawn from the truth.

Third John ends just like 2 John, with the apostle expressing his desire to see Gaius in addition to writing the letter. He had more to say, and his strong desire to see the one he loved could not be contained by pen and ink.

1The elder,

To my dear friend Gaius, whom I love in the truth.

2Dear friend, I pray that you may enjoy good health and that all may
go well with you, even as your soul is getting along well. 3It gave me
great joy when some believers came and testified about your faith-
fulness to the truth, telling how you continue to walk in it. 4I have
no greater joy than to hear that my children are walking in the truth.
5Dear friend, you are faithful in what you are doing for the brothers
and sisters,[a] even though they are strangers to you. 6They have told
the church about your love. Please send them on their way in a man-
ner that honors God. 7It was for the sake of the Name that they went
out, receiving no help from the pagans. 8We ought therefore to show
hospitality to such people so that we may work together for the truth.
9I wrote to the church, but Diotrephes, who loves to be first, will not
welcome us. 10So when I come, I will call attention to what he is do-
ing, spreading malicious nonsense about us. Not satisfied with that, he
even refuses to welcome other believers. He also stops those who want
to do so and puts them out of the church.
11Dear friend, do not imitate what is evil but what is good. Anyone
who does what is good is from God. Anyone who does what is evil has
not seen God. 12Demetrius is well spoken of by everyone — and even
by the truth itself. We also speak well of him, and you know that our
testimony is true.
13I have much to write you, but I do not want to do so with pen and
ink. 14I hope to see you soon, and we will talk face to face.

15Peace to you. The friends here send their greetings. Greet the
friends there by name.

PRAYING SCRIPTURE

3 John

John walked alongside Jesus for three years, learning from him daily. It seems normal, then, that John's greatest joy would be hearing reports that his spiritual children walked in truth (see verse 4). Walking in truth refers to their spiritual growth in following Jesus. The practical aspects of their lives bore witness to the gospel (see verses 5–8).

Christian discipleship is a never-ending source of joy. If you are discipling someone, pray for their continued growth, and then rejoice as it happens.

---

[a] 5 The Greek word for *brothers and sisters* (*adelphoi*) refers here to believers, both men and women, as part of God's family.

JUDE

Like James, Jude was written by a half brother of the Lord Jesus. He wrote to warn a Christian community about the imminent danger of false prophets who were among them and would lead them astray. Where 2 Peter foresaw false prophets who were to come, Jude announced that they were there already. The early believers were in constant spiritual peril from false teachers.

Jude warned his readers about the ungodly character of the false prophets. They scoffed at the truth and chased after their own ungodly passions. False prophets disturb God's people by stirring up divisions within the church. They are in love with this present world and do not possess the Holy Spirit.

Jude wanted his readers to model a different reality, where their love of the truth was demonstrated by their lives. Before he told them what their lives should look like to a watching world, Jude instructed them to build themselves up in the faith and to pray in the Holy Spirit. While Jude did not give a definition of praying in the Spirit, we can reasonably conclude from other Scripture that he was referring to prayer offered in the power of the Spirit and aided by the Spirit. Praying in the Holy Spirit isn't a mystical gift accessible by a chosen few; it is a blessing available to all God's people who will pray.

Jude features two of the most unusual passages in the Bible (see verses 6,9). Many people would agree that the "angels who did not keep their positions of authority" refer to those angels who were part of Satan's rebellion. But what do the "everlasting chains for judgment" mean? Then, in a story never mentioned in the Old Testament, we learn that Michael the archangel disputed with the devil about Moses's body after the great leader of Israel died. But the account of this mysterious narrative is not the main point. Jude wanted his readers to know that believers who contend for the faith do well to remember God's authority over all creation, upholding his ways, even if—as in the case of the archangel Michael—the devil tries to incite the sin of slander. It is enough to resist the temptation to argue.

In keeping with John and Peter, Jude warned of apostates and false teachers who "divide you, who follow mere natural instincts and do not have the Spirit" (verse 19). Rather, the church should keep themselves in the love of God. In the midst of a world following after its lusts, Jude exhorted the church, "Building yourselves up in your most holy faith and praying in the Holy spirit, keep yourselves in God's love as you wait for the mercy of our Lord Jesus Christ to bring you to eternal life" (verses 20–21).

If followers of Jesus are going to stand out from the present world around us, it is not going to happen in judgment of unbelievers who behave like unbelievers. Instead, Christians must demonstrate the fruit of the Spirit's work in us. This will only happen as we bring all our requests to God. Without the empowering of the Spirit, we do not have the ability to continue following Jesus.

In a similar vein, Jude closed his letter with a benediction addressed to "him who is able to keep you from stumbling" (verse 24). While we might grow and mature in the faith, Christians never move beyond our need for the grace, guidance and strength that only God can give.

1 Jude, a servant of Jesus Christ and a brother of James,

To those who have been called, who are loved in God the Father and
kept for[a] Jesus Christ:

2 Mercy, peace and love be yours in abundance.

THE SIN AND DOOM OF UNGODLY PEOPLE

3 Dear friends, although I was very eager to write to you about the
salvation we share, I felt compelled to write and urge you to contend
for the faith that was once for all entrusted to God's holy people. 4 For
certain individuals whose condemnation was written about[b] long ago
have secretly slipped in among you. They are ungodly people, who per-
vert the grace of our God into a license for immorality and deny Jesus
Christ our only Sovereign and Lord.
5 Though you already know all this, I want to remind you that the
Lord[c] at one time delivered his people out of Egypt, but later destroyed
those who did not believe. 6 And the angels who did not keep their posi-
tions of authority but abandoned their proper dwelling — these he has
kept in darkness, bound with everlasting chains for judgment on the
great Day. 7 In a similar way, Sodom and Gomorrah and the surrounding
towns gave themselves up to sexual immorality and perversion. They
serve as an example of those who suffer the punishment of eternal fire.
8 In the very same way, on the strength of their dreams these un-
godly people pollute their own bodies, reject authority and heap abuse
on celestial beings. 9 But even the archangel Michael, when he was dis-
puting with the devil about the body of Moses, did not himself dare
to condemn him for slander but said, "The Lord rebuke you!"[d] 10 Yet
these people slander whatever they do not understand, and the very
things they do understand by instinct — as irrational animals do — will
destroy them.
11 Woe to them! They have taken the way of Cain; they have rushed for
profit into Balaam's error; they have been destroyed in Korah's rebellion.
12 These people are blemishes at your love feasts, eating with you
without the slightest qualm — shepherds who feed only themselves.
They are clouds without rain, blown along by the wind; autumn trees,
without fruit and uprooted — twice dead. 13 They are wild waves of the
sea, foaming up their shame; wandering stars, for whom blackest dark-
ness has been reserved forever.
14 Enoch, the seventh from Adam, prophesied about them: "See, the
Lord is coming with thousands upon thousands of his holy ones 15 to
judge everyone, and to convict all of them of all the ungodly acts they
have committed in their ungodliness, and of all the defiant words un-
godly sinners have spoken against him."[e] 16 These people are grumblers
and faultfinders; they follow their own evil desires; they boast about
themselves and flatter others for their own advantage.

A CALL TO PERSEVERE

17 But, dear friends, remember what the apostles of our Lord Jesus
Christ foretold. 18 They said to you, "In the last times there will be

[a] *1* Or *by*; or *in* [b] *4* Or *individuals who were marked out for condemnation* [c] *5* Some early manuscripts *Jesus* [d] *9* Jude is alluding to the Jewish *Testament of Moses* (approximately the first century A.D.). [e] *14,15* From the Jewish *First Book of Enoch* (approximately the first century B.C.)

PRAYING SCRIPTURE

Jude

Jude's brief letter reminds us that false teachers do not arise in a vacuum. They are influenced and used by the forces of darkness, indeed by fallen angels. They are marked by lewdness, false doctrine, greed and self-centeredness.

Teachers are not of God when they violate the Word. Seek the wisdom that allows you to evaluate teachers by the Word. Reject all whose lives do not match up with it.

PRAYING SCRIPTURE

Jude

While it sometimes seems as if the volume of false teachers and false doctrines is higher than ever, Jude reminded us that apostates have always been with us, beginning with the rebellious angels through Israel's history until the very day when Jude warned the church. We avoid them by praying in the Holy Spirit.

When you pray, submit yourself to the Holy Spirit. He guides, informs and empowers us when we pray.

scoffers who will follow their own ungodly desires." 19These are the
people who divide you, who follow mere natural instincts and do not
have the Spirit.

20But you, dear friends, by building yourselves up in your most holy
faith and praying in the Holy Spirit, 21keep yourselves in God's love as
you wait for the mercy of our Lord Jesus Christ to bring you to eternal
life.

22Be merciful to those who doubt; 23save others by snatching them
from the fire; to others show mercy, mixed with fear—hating even the
clothing stained by corrupted flesh.[a]

DOXOLOGY

24To him who is able to keep you from stumbling and to present
you before his glorious presence without fault and with great joy—
25to the only God our Savior be glory, majesty, power and authority,
through Jesus Christ our Lord, before all ages, now and forevermore!
Amen.

[a] *22,23* The Greek manuscripts of these verses vary at several points.

REVELATION

The revelation ("unveiling") of Jesus Christ was a vision given to John by an angel while exiled on the island of Patmos. What he saw in the vision is sometimes called "the Apocalypse," from the Greek word behind the title. John wrote the symbolism-filled book to comfort the Christians of his day and beyond about the things that would take place concerning the end of our era and the return of Jesus. John addressed it to seven churches located in seven cities in Asia.

Despite the mysterious nature of much of the book, Revelation is largely a work of hope. Before describing the massive judgments poured out on earth's rebellious inhabitants, John, in chapters 1, 4 and 5, showed that God is in complete control. Jesus is "the Alpha and the Omega . . . who is, and who was, and who is to come, the Almighty" (1:8). The One on the throne is attended by four six-winged creatures who see everything (see 4:8). Because of his redeeming work, the Lamb is deemed worthy to take the scroll of judgment from the Father's hand (see 5:9). The throne room scene demonstrates the absolute sovereignty of God over all that is revealed in the rest of the book.

Several important themes emerge that enlighten our understanding of prayer. First, we see that prayer is integral to churches continuing to be faithful to Jesus. Chapters 2 and 3 bring messages from Jesus to churches in Ephesus, Smyrna, Pergamum, Thyatira, Sardis, Philadelphia and Laodicea. Just as today, the spiritual lives of these churches were a mixed bag. False teaching and false teachers—ever a plague in the New Testament—were a problem. Only the church at Philadelphia received no rebuke. These chapters serve to remind us that the church will not be all that Jesus has called it to be if we are negligent in the duty of prayer.

Also, Revelation reminds us that Christians ought to pray that we would be faithful to Jesus in the face of opposition and difficulty. Many of the Christians during the time of John's letter were facing persecution because of their faith. They would have understood the descriptions of martyrdom and persecution for the sake of the gospel (see 6:9–11) as what they might experience. John urged them not to fear because Jesus is "the First and the Last" (1:17).

Through the centuries, Revelation has compelled Christians to pray for their unbelieving friends, neighbors and families. Jesus will come again one day to judge the living and the dead, after which there will be no more opportunities for people to repent and trust in him for salvation. Because we do not know the time of his return, it is imperative that people believe in Jesus now. We must pray that God will open their eyes to the truth so they may be saved and we might stand together proclaiming, "Worthy is the Lamb, who was slain" (5:12).

PRAYING SCRIPTURE

Revelation 1

John began his unveiling of Jesus Christ with a testimony of how the letter came to be ("On the Lord's Day, I was in the Spirit"; verse 10) and for whom it was intended (the seven churches in Asia; verse 11). John's description of the glorified Jesus is without equal in the New Testament.

As you read verses 10–20, think about how overwhelmed John was (see verse 17). Seek to know Jesus in such a way that you are humbled by his glory.

PROLOGUE

1 The revelation from Jesus Christ, which God gave him to show his
servants what must soon take place. He made it known by sending
his angel to his servant John, 2who testifies to everything he saw—
that is, the word of God and the testimony of Jesus Christ. 3Blessed is
the one who reads aloud the words of this prophecy, and blessed are
those who hear it and take to heart what is written in it, because the
time is near.

GREETINGS AND DOXOLOGY

4John,

To the seven churches in the province of Asia:

Grace and peace to you from him who is, and who was, and who is to
come, and from the seven spirits[a] before his throne, 5and from Jesus
Christ, who is the faithful witness, the firstborn from the dead, and the
ruler of the kings of the earth.

To him who loves us and has freed us from our sins by his blood,
6and has made us to be a kingdom and priests to serve his God and
Father—to him be glory and power for ever and ever! Amen.

7"Look, he is coming with the clouds,"[b]
and "every eye will see him,
even those who pierced him";
and all peoples on earth "will mourn because of him."[c]
So shall it be! Amen.

8"I am the Alpha and the Omega," says the Lord God, "who is, and
who was, and who is to come, the Almighty."

JOHN'S VISION OF CHRIST

9I, John, your brother and companion in the suffering and kingdom
and patient endurance that are ours in Jesus, was on the island of Pat-
mos because of the word of God and the testimony of Jesus. 10On the
Lord's Day I was in the Spirit, and I heard behind me a loud voice like
a trumpet, 11which said: "Write on a scroll what you see and send it to
the seven churches: to Ephesus, Smyrna, Pergamum, Thyatira, Sardis,
Philadelphia and Laodicea."

12I turned around to see the voice that was speaking to me. And
when I turned I saw seven golden lampstands, 13and among the lamp-
stands was someone like a son of man,[d] dressed in a robe reaching
down to his feet and with a golden sash around his chest. 14The hair on
his head was white like wool, as white as snow, and his eyes were like
blazing fire. 15His feet were like bronze glowing in a furnace, and his
voice was like the sound of rushing waters. 16In his right hand he held
seven stars, and coming out of his mouth was a sharp, double-edged
sword. His face was like the sun shining in all its brilliance.

17When I saw him, I fell at his feet as though dead. Then he placed
his right hand on me and said: "Do not be afraid. I am the First and
the Last. 18I am the Living One; I was dead, and now look, I am alive for
ever and ever! And I hold the keys of death and Hades.

---

[a] *4* That is, the sevenfold Spirit [b] *7* Daniel 7:13 [c] *7* Zech. 12:10 [d] *13* See Daniel 7:13.

19"Write, therefore, what you have seen, what is now and what will
take place later. 20The mystery of the seven stars that you saw in my
right hand and of the seven golden lampstands is this: The seven stars
are the angels[a] of the seven churches, and the seven lampstands are
the seven churches.

TO THE CHURCH IN EPHESUS

2 "To the angel[b] of the church in Ephesus write:

These are the words of him who holds the seven stars in his
right hand and walks among the seven golden lampstands. 2I
know your deeds, your hard work and your perseverance. I know
that you cannot tolerate wicked people, that you have tested those
who claim to be apostles but are not, and have found them false.
3You have persevered and have endured hardships for my name,
and have not grown weary.
4Yet I hold this against you: You have forsaken the love you
had at first. 5Consider how far you have fallen! Repent and do the
things you did at first. If you do not repent, I will come to you and
remove your lampstand from its place. 6But you have this in your
favor: You hate the practices of the Nicolaitans, which I also hate.
7Whoever has ears, let them hear what the Spirit says to the
churches. To the one who is victorious, I will give the right to eat
from the tree of life, which is in the paradise of God.

TO THE CHURCH IN SMYRNA

8"To the angel of the church in Smyrna write:

These are the words of him who is the First and the Last, who
died and came to life again. 9I know your afflictions and your pov-
erty — yet you are rich! I know about the slander of those who say
they are Jews and are not, but are a synagogue of Satan. 10Do not
be afraid of what you are about to suffer. I tell you, the devil will
put some of you in prison to test you, and you will suffer persecu-
tion for ten days. Be faithful, even to the point of death, and I will
give you life as your victor's crown.
11Whoever has ears, let them hear what the Spirit says to the
churches. The one who is victorious will not be hurt at all by the
second death.

TO THE CHURCH IN PERGAMUM

12"To the angel of the church in Pergamum write:

These are the words of him who has the sharp, double-edged
sword. 13I know where you live — where Satan has his throne. Yet
you remain true to my name. You did not renounce your faith in
me, not even in the days of Antipas, my faithful witness, who was
put to death in your city — where Satan lives.
14Nevertheless, I have a few things against you: There are some
among you who hold to the teaching of Balaam, who taught Ba-
lak to entice the Israelites to sin so that they ate food sacrificed
to idols and committed sexual immorality. 15Likewise, you also
have those who hold to the teaching of the Nicolaitans. 16Repent

PRAYING SCRIPTURE

Revelation 2

The four churches named in this chapter are guilty of various sins against the Lord: forsaking their first love, blasphemy, holding to false doctrine and tolerating a wicked prophet identified as Jezebel (see verse 20). Doctrinal issues in churches are not unique to modern times but have existed since the early church.

Heresy in churches must be dealt with for God to be pleased. Ask God to make you an adherent of truth.

[a] 20 Or *messengers* [b] 1 Or *messenger*; also in verses 8, 12 and 18

therefore! Otherwise, I will soon come to you and will fight against
them with the sword of my mouth.
17 Whoever has ears, let them hear what the Spirit says to the
churches. To the one who is victorious, I will give some of the hid-
den manna. I will also give that person a white stone with a new
name written on it, known only to the one who receives it.

TO THE CHURCH IN THYATIRA

18 "To the angel of the church in Thyatira write:

These are the words of the Son of God, whose eyes are like blaz-
ing fire and whose feet are like burnished bronze. 19 I know your
deeds, your love and faith, your service and perseverance, and that
you are now doing more than you did at first.
20 Nevertheless, I have this against you: You tolerate that woman
Jezebel, who calls herself a prophet. By her teaching she misleads
my servants into sexual immorality and the eating of food sacri-
ficed to idols. 21 I have given her time to repent of her immorality,
but she is unwilling. 22 So I will cast her on a bed of suffering, and
I will make those who commit adultery with her suffer intensely,
unless they repent of her ways. 23 I will strike her children dead.
Then all the churches will know that I am he who searches hearts
and minds, and I will repay each of you according to your deeds.
24 Now I say to the rest of you in Thyatira, to you who do not
hold to her teaching and have not learned Satan's so-called deep
secrets, 'I will not impose any other burden on you, 25 except to
hold on to what you have until I come.'
26 To the one who is victorious and does my will to the end, I will
give authority over the nations — 27 that one 'will rule them with
an iron scepter and will dash them to pieces like pottery'[a] — just
as I have received authority from my Father. 28 I will also give that
one the morning star. 29 Whoever has ears, let them hear what the
Spirit says to the churches.

TO THE CHURCH IN SARDIS

3 "To the angel[b] of the church in Sardis write:

These are the words of him who holds the seven spirits[c] of God
and the seven stars. I know your deeds; you have a reputation of
being alive, but you are dead. 2 Wake up! Strengthen what remains
and is about to die, for I have found your deeds unfinished in the
sight of my God. 3 Remember, therefore, what you have received
and heard; hold it fast, and repent. But if you do not wake up, I
will come like a thief, and you will not know at what time I will
come to you.
4 Yet you have a few people in Sardis who have not soiled their
clothes. They will walk with me, dressed in white, for they are
worthy. 5 The one who is victorious will, like them, be dressed in
white. I will never blot out the name of that person from the book
of life, but will acknowledge that name before my Father and his
angels. 6 Whoever has ears, let them hear what the Spirit says to
the churches.

PRAYING SCRIPTURE

Revelation 3

Jesus identified two churches with deadly problems, Sardis and Laodicea, while commending one church, Philadelphia, for its faithfulness. The repeated phrase in chapters 2 and 3, "I know your deeds," should bring us to fear and trembling at how Jesus might evaluate our churches today.

What would you do differently today if Jesus was watching? He is watching, so ask for wisdom to live pleasing to him.

[a] *27* Psalm 2:9 [b] *1* Or *messenger*; also in verses 7 and 14 [c] *1* That is, the sevenfold Spirit

TO THE CHURCH IN PHILADELPHIA

7"To the angel of the church in Philadelphia write:

These are the words of him who is holy and true, who holds
the key of David. What he opens no one can shut, and what he
shuts no one can open. 8I know your deeds. See, I have placed be-
fore you an open door that no one can shut. I know that you have
little strength, yet you have kept my word and have not denied
my name. 9I will make those who are of the synagogue of Satan,
who claim to be Jews though they are not, but are liars — I will
make them come and fall down at your feet and acknowledge that
I have loved you. 10Since you have kept my command to endure
patiently, I will also keep you from the hour of trial that is going
to come on the whole world to test the inhabitants of the earth.

11I am coming soon. Hold on to what you have, so that no one
will take your crown. 12The one who is victorious I will make a pil-
lar in the temple of my God. Never again will they leave it. I will
write on them the name of my God and the name of the city of
my God, the new Jerusalem, which is coming down out of heaven
from my God; and I will also write on them my new name. 13Who-
ever has ears, let them hear what the Spirit says to the churches.

TO THE CHURCH IN LAODICEA

14"To the angel of the church in Laodicea write:

These are the words of the Amen, the faithful and true witness,
the ruler of God's creation. 15I know your deeds, that you are nei-
ther cold nor hot. I wish you were either one or the other! 16So,
because you are lukewarm — neither hot nor cold — I am about
to spit you out of my mouth. 17You say, 'I am rich; I have acquired
wealth and do not need a thing.' But you do not realize that you
are wretched, pitiful, poor, blind and naked. 18I counsel you to
buy from me gold refined in the fire, so you can become rich; and
white clothes to wear, so you can cover your shameful nakedness;
and salve to put on your eyes, so you can see.

19Those whom I love I rebuke and discipline. So be earnest and
repent. 20Here I am! I stand at the door and knock. If anyone hears
my voice and opens the door, I will come in and eat with that per-
son, and they with me.

21To the one who is victorious, I will give the right to sit with me
on my throne, just as I was victorious and sat down with my Father
on his throne. 22Whoever has ears, let them hear what the Spirit
says to the churches."

THE THRONE IN HEAVEN

4 After this I looked, and there before me was a door standing
open in heaven. And the voice I had first heard speaking to me
like a trumpet said, "Come up here, and I will show you what must
take place after this." 2At once I was in the Spirit, and there before
me was a throne in heaven with someone sitting on it. 3And the one
who sat there had the appearance of jasper and ruby. A rainbow that
shone like an emerald encircled the throne. 4Surrounding the throne
were twenty-four other thrones, and seated on them were twenty-four
elders. They were dressed in white and had crowns of gold on their
heads. 5From the throne came flashes of lightning, rumblings and

PRAYING SCRIPTURE

Revelation 4

The scene is the throne room of heaven. What an awe-inspiring sight beyond comprehension. God is seated on his throne and is radiant in his appearance. Verse 8 reminds us of Isaiah's experience with winged creatures and unceasing praise (Isaiah 6:2–3).

As you read this chapter, envision what John relates. This is not imagination; it is real. Tell God how much you long to be in his presence.

peals of thunder. In front of the throne, seven lamps were blazing.
These are the seven spirits[a] of God. 6Also in front of the throne there
was what looked like a sea of glass, clear as crystal.

In the center, around the throne, were four living creatures, and they
were covered with eyes, in front and in back. 7The first living creature
was like a lion, the second was like an ox, the third had a face like a
man, the fourth was like a flying eagle. 8Each of the four living crea-
tures had six wings and was covered with eyes all around, even under
its wings. Day and night they never stop saying:

"'Holy, holy, holy
is the Lord God Almighty,'[b]
who was, and is, and is to come."

9Whenever the living creatures give glory, honor and thanks to him who
sits on the throne and who lives for ever and ever, 10the twenty-four el-
ders fall down before him who sits on the throne and worship him who
lives for ever and ever. They lay their crowns before the throne and say:

11"You are worthy, our Lord and God,
to receive glory and honor and power,
for you created all things,
and by your will they were created
and have their being."

THE SCROLL AND THE LAMB

5 Then I saw in the right hand of him who sat on the throne a scroll
with writing on both sides and sealed with seven seals. 2And I saw
a mighty angel proclaiming in a loud voice, "Who is worthy to break
the seals and open the scroll?" 3But no one in heaven or on earth or
under the earth could open the scroll or even look inside it. 4I wept and
wept because no one was found who was worthy to open the scroll or
look inside. 5Then one of the elders said to me, "Do not weep! See, the
Lion of the tribe of Judah, the Root of David, has triumphed. He is able
to open the scroll and its seven seals."

6Then I saw a Lamb, looking as if it had been slain, standing at the
center of the throne, encircled by the four living creatures and the el-
ders. The Lamb had seven horns and seven eyes, which are the seven
spirits[a] of God sent out into all the earth. 7He went and took the scroll
from the right hand of him who sat on the throne. 8And when he had
taken it, the four living creatures and the twenty-four elders fell down
before the Lamb. Each one had a harp and they were holding golden
bowls full of incense, which are the prayers of God's people. 9And they
sang a new song, saying:

"You are worthy to take the scroll
and to open its seals,
because you were slain,
and with your blood you purchased for God
persons from every tribe and language and people and nation.
10You have made them to be a kingdom and priests to serve our God,
and they will reign[c] on the earth."

PRAYING SCRIPTURE

Revelation 5

All of human history is heading toward the scene in heaven depicted here. The Lamb is revealed and affirmed as the only one worthy to pronounce final judgment. The gods of this world to which people have entrusted their lives and hopes have no place and are proven frauds. Only Jesus is worthy!

Read this chapter thoroughly, praising God for everything revealed about the worthiness of his Lamb who redeems.

---

[a] *5,6* That is, the sevenfold Spirit [b] *8* Isaiah 6:3 [c] *10* Some manuscripts *they reign*

11 Then I looked and heard the voice of many angels, numbering thousands upon thousands, and ten thousand times ten thousand. They encircled the throne and the living creatures and the elders. 12 In a loud voice they were saying:

"Worthy is the Lamb, who was slain,
to receive power and wealth and wisdom and strength
and honor and glory and praise!"

13 Then I heard every creature in heaven and on earth and under the earth and on the sea, and all that is in them, saying:

"To him who sits on the throne and to the Lamb
be praise and honor and glory and power,
for ever and ever!"

14 The four living creatures said, "Amen," and the elders fell down and worshiped.

THE SEALS

6 I watched as the Lamb opened the first of the seven seals. Then I heard one of the four living creatures say in a voice like thunder, "Come!" 2 I looked, and there before me was a white horse! Its rider held a bow, and he was given a crown, and he rode out as a conqueror bent on conquest.

3 When the Lamb opened the second seal, I heard the second living creature say, "Come!" 4 Then another horse came out, a fiery red one. Its rider was given power to take peace from the earth and to make people kill each other. To him was given a large sword.

5 When the Lamb opened the third seal, I heard the third living creature say, "Come!" I looked, and there before me was a black horse! Its rider was holding a pair of scales in his hand. 6 Then I heard what sounded like a voice among the four living creatures, saying, "Two pounds[a] of wheat for a day's wages,[b] and six pounds[c] of barley for a day's wages,[b] and do not damage the oil and the wine!"

7 When the Lamb opened the fourth seal, I heard the voice of the fourth living creature say, "Come!" 8 I looked, and there before me was a pale horse! Its rider was named Death, and Hades was following close behind him. They were given power over a fourth of the earth to kill by sword, famine and plague, and by the wild beasts of the earth.

9 When he opened the fifth seal, I saw under the altar the souls of those who had been slain because of the word of God and the testimony they had maintained. 10 They called out in a loud voice, "How long, Sovereign Lord, holy and true, until you judge the inhabitants of the earth and avenge our blood?" 11 Then each of them was given a white robe, and they were told to wait a little longer, until the full number of their fellow servants, their brothers and sisters,[d] were killed just as they had been.

12 I watched as he opened the sixth seal. There was a great earthquake. The sun turned black like sackcloth made of goat hair, the whole moon turned blood red, 13 and the stars in the sky fell to earth, as figs drop from a fig tree when shaken by a strong wind. 14 The heavens

PRAYING SCRIPTURE

Revelation 6

The seals of Revelation have been the source of endless wondering through the centuries. Their opening sounds terrible because of what they unleash. We do not have to know exactly every detail of their opening to know that tragedy and judgment accompany them.

What is clear in the seal judgments is that God is doing the judging (see verse 9). If you are in Christ, you will escape judgment. That is a reason for praise!

---

[a] 6 Or about 1 kilogram [b] 6 Greek *a denarius* [c] 6 Or about 3 kilograms
[d] 11 The Greek word for *brothers and sisters* (*adelphoi*) refers here to believers, both men and women, as part of God's family; also in 12:10; 19:10.

receded like a scroll being rolled up, and every mountain and island
was removed from its place.
15 Then the kings of the earth, the princes, the generals, the rich, the
mighty, and everyone else, both slave and free, hid in caves and among
the rocks of the mountains. 16 They called to the mountains and the
rocks, "Fall on us and hide us[a] from the face of him who sits on the
throne and from the wrath of the Lamb! 17 For the great day of their[b]
wrath has come, and who can withstand it?"

144,000 SEALED

PRAYING SCRIPTURE

Revelation 7

While much emphasis has been given to the 144,000—who they are, when they might appear and everything they might do—we should remember the One who is the focus: "Salvation belongs to our God, who sits on the throne, and to the Lamb" (verse 10). The testimony of all the saints is to Jesus.

Never forget that Jesus is the focus of history. Make him the focus of your life and prayers.

7 After this I saw four angels standing at the four corners of the
earth, holding back the four winds of the earth to prevent any
wind from blowing on the land or on the sea or on any tree. 2 Then I
saw another angel coming up from the east, having the seal of the liv-
ing God. He called out in a loud voice to the four angels who had been
given power to harm the land and the sea: 3 "Do not harm the land
or the sea or the trees until we put a seal on the foreheads of the ser-
vants of our God." 4 Then I heard the number of those who were sealed:
144,000 from all the tribes of Israel.

5 From the tribe of Judah 12,000 were sealed,
from the tribe of Reuben 12,000,
from the tribe of Gad 12,000,
6 from the tribe of Asher 12,000,
from the tribe of Naphtali 12,000,
from the tribe of Manasseh 12,000,
7 from the tribe of Simeon 12,000,
from the tribe of Levi 12,000,
from the tribe of Issachar 12,000,
8 from the tribe of Zebulun 12,000,
from the tribe of Joseph 12,000,
from the tribe of Benjamin 12,000.

THE GREAT MULTITUDE IN WHITE ROBES

9 After this I looked, and there before me was a great multitude that
no one could count, from every nation, tribe, people and language,
standing before the throne and before the Lamb. They were wearing
white robes and were holding palm branches in their hands. 10 And
they cried out in a loud voice:

"Salvation belongs to our God,
who sits on the throne,
and to the Lamb."

11 All the angels were standing around the throne and around the elders
and the four living creatures. They fell down on their faces before the
throne and worshiped God, 12 saying:

"Amen!
Praise and glory
and wisdom and thanks and honor
and power and strength
be to our God for ever and ever.
Amen!"

[a] 16 See Hosea 10:8. [b] 17 Some manuscripts *his*

13Then one of the elders asked me, "These in white robes — who are
they, and where did they come from?"
14I answered, "Sir, you know."
And he said, "These are they who have come out of the great tribula-
tion; they have washed their robes and made them white in the blood
of the Lamb. 15Therefore,

"they are before the throne of God
  and serve him day and night in his temple;
and he who sits on the throne
  will shelter them with his presence.
16 'Never again will they hunger;
  never again will they thirst.
The sun will not beat down on them,'[a]
  nor any scorching heat.
17 For the Lamb at the center of the throne
  will be their shepherd;
'he will lead them to springs of living water.'[a]
  'And God will wipe away every tear from their eyes.'[b]"

THE SEVENTH SEAL AND THE GOLDEN CENSER

8 When he opened the seventh seal, there was silence in heaven for
about half an hour.
2And I saw the seven angels who stand before God, and seven trum-
pets were given to them.
3Another angel, who had a golden censer, came and stood at the al-
tar. He was given much incense to offer, with the prayers of all God's
people, on the golden altar in front of the throne. 4The smoke of the
incense, together with the prayers of God's people, went up before God
from the angel's hand. 5Then the angel took the censer, filled it with
fire from the altar, and hurled it on the earth; and there came peals of
thunder, rumblings, flashes of lightning and an earthquake.

THE TRUMPETS

6Then the seven angels who had the seven trumpets prepared to
sound them.
7The first angel sounded his trumpet, and there came hail and fire
mixed with blood, and it was hurled down on the earth. A third of the
earth was burned up, a third of the trees were burned up, and all the
green grass was burned up.
8The second angel sounded his trumpet, and something like a huge
mountain, all ablaze, was thrown into the sea. A third of the sea turned
into blood, 9a third of the living creatures in the sea died, and a third
of the ships were destroyed.
10The third angel sounded his trumpet, and a great star, blazing like a
torch, fell from the sky on a third of the rivers and on the springs of wa-
ter — 11the name of the star is Wormwood.[c] A third of the waters turned
bitter, and many people died from the waters that had become bitter.
12The fourth angel sounded his trumpet, and a third of the sun was
struck, a third of the moon, and a third of the stars, so that a third of
them turned dark. A third of the day was without light, and also a third
of the night.

PRAYING SCRIPTURE
Revelation 8

In revealing the seventh seal, an angel was seen with incense mingled with the prayers of God's people. The imagery is a clear reference to the altar in the Old Testament temple, but rather than simply sacrificial smoke, the prayers of God's people are mingled in.

Does knowing that your prayers are received In God's throne motivate you to pray more? Think about how your prayers honor God when you offer them to him.

[a] *16,17* Isaiah 49:10 [b] *17* Isaiah 25:8 [c] *11* Wormwood is a bitter substance.

13As I watched, I heard an eagle that was flying in midair call out in a loud voice: "Woe! Woe! Woe to the inhabitants of the earth, because of the trumpet blasts about to be sounded by the other three angels!"

9 The fifth angel sounded his trumpet, and I saw a star that had fallen from the sky to the earth. The star was given the key to the shaft of the Abyss. 2When he opened the Abyss, smoke rose from it like the smoke from a gigantic furnace. The sun and sky were darkened by the smoke from the Abyss. 3And out of the smoke locusts came down on the earth and were given power like that of scorpions of the earth. 4They were told not to harm the grass of the earth or any plant or tree, but only those people who did not have the seal of God on their foreheads. 5They were not allowed to kill them but only to torture them for five months. And the agony they suffered was like that of the sting of a scorpion when it strikes. 6During those days people will seek death but will not find it; they will long to die, but death will elude them.

7The locusts looked like horses prepared for battle. On their heads they wore something like crowns of gold, and their faces resembled human faces. 8Their hair was like women's hair, and their teeth were like lions' teeth. 9They had breastplates like breastplates of iron, and the sound of their wings was like the thundering of many horses and chariots rushing into battle. 10They had tails with stingers, like scorpions, and in their tails they had power to torment people for five months. 11They had as king over them the angel of the Abyss, whose name in Hebrew is Abaddon and in Greek is Apollyon (that is, Destroyer).

12The first woe is past; two other woes are yet to come.

13The sixth angel sounded his trumpet, and I heard a voice coming from the four horns of the golden altar that is before God. 14It said to the sixth angel who had the trumpet, "Release the four angels who are bound at the great river Euphrates." 15And the four angels who had been kept ready for this very hour and day and month and year were released to kill a third of mankind. 16The number of the mounted troops was twice ten thousand times ten thousand. I heard their number.

17The horses and riders I saw in my vision looked like this: Their breastplates were fiery red, dark blue, and yellow as sulfur. The heads of the horses resembled the heads of lions, and out of their mouths came fire, smoke and sulfur. 18A third of mankind was killed by the three plagues of fire, smoke and sulfur that came out of their mouths. 19The power of the horses was in their mouths and in their tails; for their tails were like snakes, having heads with which they inflict injury.

20The rest of mankind who were not killed by these plagues still did not repent of the work of their hands; they did not stop worshiping demons, and idols of gold, silver, bronze, stone and wood — idols that cannot see or hear or walk. 21Nor did they repent of their murders, their magic arts, their sexual immorality or their thefts.

THE ANGEL AND THE LITTLE SCROLL

10 Then I saw another mighty angel coming down from heaven. He was robed in a cloud, with a rainbow above his head; his face was like the sun, and his legs were like fiery pillars. 2He was holding a little scroll, which lay open in his hand. He planted his right foot on the sea and his left foot on the land, 3and he gave a loud shout like the roar of a lion. When he shouted, the voices of the seven thunders spoke. 4And when the seven thunders spoke, I was about to write; but I heard

PRAYING SCRIPTURE

Revelation 9

The narrative of judgments continues with one of the more descriptive and creatively interpreted passages in all of Scripture. Locusts that looked like horses wearing crowns on their heads, with men's faces and women's hair, with a breastplate like iron and tails like scorpions appear (see verses 7–10). But the focal point is not the creatures; it is those being judged: unrepentant people.

God saves through faith in Jesus and repentance from sin. Ask God to bring your unbelieving friends and family to faith in Christ.

PRAYING SCRIPTURE

Revelation 10

The "little scroll" brought to John by the angel is less mysterious than other parts of the Apocalypse. Eating the scroll (see verse 9) hearkens back to Ezekiel 3:1–3, where the prophet ate God's words in order that he might speak to the house of Israel. Similarly, the little book here is God's Word, given to John in order that he might also prophesy (see verse 11).

The Word of God is our means of making sense of the world. Ask him to help you consume it to grow.

a voice from heaven say, "Seal up what the seven thunders have said
and do not write it down."
5Then the angel I had seen standing on the sea and on the land raised
his right hand to heaven. 6And he swore by him who lives for ever and
ever, who created the heavens and all that is in them, the earth and all
that is in it, and the sea and all that is in it, and said, "There will be no
more delay! 7But in the days when the seventh angel is about to sound
his trumpet, the mystery of God will be accomplished, just as he an-
nounced to his servants the prophets."
8Then the voice that I had heard from heaven spoke to me once
more: "Go, take the scroll that lies open in the hand of the angel who
is standing on the sea and on the land."
9So I went to the angel and asked him to give me the little scroll. He
said to me, "Take it and eat it. It will turn your stomach sour, but 'in
your mouth it will be as sweet as honey.'[a]" 10I took the little scroll from
the angel's hand and ate it. It tasted as sweet as honey in my mouth,
but when I had eaten it, my stomach turned sour. 11Then I was told,
"You must prophesy again about many peoples, nations, languages
and kings."

THE TWO WITNESSES

11 I was given a reed like a measuring rod and was told, "Go and
measure the temple of God and the altar, with its worshipers.
2But exclude the outer court; do not measure it, because it has been
given to the Gentiles. They will trample on the holy city for 42 months.
3And I will appoint my two witnesses, and they will prophesy for 1,260
days, clothed in sackcloth." 4They are "the two olive trees" and the two
lampstands, and "they stand before the Lord of the earth."[b] 5If anyone
tries to harm them, fire comes from their mouths and devours their
enemies. This is how anyone who wants to harm them must die. 6They
have power to shut up the heavens so that it will not rain during the
time they are prophesying; and they have power to turn the waters
into blood and to strike the earth with every kind of plague as often
as they want.
7Now when they have finished their testimony, the beast that comes
up from the Abyss will attack them, and overpower and kill them.
8Their bodies will lie in the public square of the great city — which
is figuratively called Sodom and Egypt — where also their Lord was
crucified. 9For three and a half days some from every people, tribe,
language and nation will gaze on their bodies and refuse them burial.
10The inhabitants of the earth will gloat over them and will celebrate
by sending each other gifts, because these two prophets had tormented
those who live on the earth.
11But after the three and a half days the breath[c] of life from God en-
tered them, and they stood on their feet, and terror struck those who
saw them. 12Then they heard a loud voice from heaven saying to them,
"Come up here." And they went up to heaven in a cloud, while their
enemies looked on.
13At that very hour there was a severe earthquake and a tenth of the
city collapsed. Seven thousand people were killed in the earthquake,
and the survivors were terrified and gave glory to the God of heaven.
14The second woe has passed; the third woe is coming soon.

PRAYING SCRIPTURE

Revelation 11

As the period of tribulation and judgment continues, God sends two witnesses to prophesy for a period of roughly three and a half years. Their ministries are like those of Moses and Elijah, causing some to wonder if this is who they are. At the end of their prophesying, they are put to death. Then, as witnesses to the power of Christ and his resurrection, God resurrects them three and a half days later.

Thank God that his wisdom is beyond comprehension.

---

[a] 9 Ezek. 3:3 [b] 4 See Zech. 4:3,11,14. [c] 11 Or *Spirit* (see Ezek. 37:5,14)

THE SEVENTH TRUMPET

15The seventh angel sounded his trumpet, and there were loud
voices in heaven, which said:

"The kingdom of the world has become
  the kingdom of our Lord and of his Messiah,
  and he will reign for ever and ever."

16And the twenty-four elders, who were seated on their thrones before
God, fell on their faces and worshiped God, 17saying:

"We give thanks to you, Lord God Almighty,
  the One who is and who was,
because you have taken your great power
  and have begun to reign.
18The nations were angry,
  and your wrath has come.
The time has come for judging the dead,
  and for rewarding your servants the prophets
and your people who revere your name,
  both great and small —
and for destroying those who destroy the earth."

19Then God's temple in heaven was opened, and within his temple
was seen the ark of his covenant. And there came flashes of lightning,
rumblings, peals of thunder, an earthquake and a severe hailstorm.

THE WOMAN AND THE DRAGON

12 A great sign appeared in heaven: a woman clothed with the sun,
with the moon under her feet and a crown of twelve stars on
her head. 2She was pregnant and cried out in pain as she was about to
give birth. 3Then another sign appeared in heaven: an enormous red
dragon with seven heads and ten horns and seven crowns on its heads.
4Its tail swept a third of the stars out of the sky and flung them to the
earth. The dragon stood in front of the woman who was about to give
birth, so that it might devour her child the moment he was born. 5She
gave birth to a son, a male child, who "will rule all the nations with an
iron scepter."[a] And her child was snatched up to God and to his throne.
6The woman fled into the wilderness to a place prepared for her by
God, where she might be taken care of for 1,260 days.

7Then war broke out in heaven. Michael and his angels fought
against the dragon, and the dragon and his angels fought back. 8But
he was not strong enough, and they lost their place in heaven. 9The
great dragon was hurled down — that ancient serpent called the devil,
or Satan, who leads the whole world astray. He was hurled to the earth,
and his angels with him.

10Then I heard a loud voice in heaven say:

"Now have come the salvation and the power
  and the kingdom of our God,
  and the authority of his Messiah.
For the accuser of our brothers and sisters,
  who accuses them before our God day and night,
  has been hurled down.

PRAYING SCRIPTURE

Revelation 12

Like much of Revelation the woman of this chapter is the subject of speculation. Is she Mary? Israel? The church? Between two sections about her, John recounted a war in heaven during which Satan, the accuser of the brethren, is hurled to the earth (see verse 9) where he persecutes the saints of God.

When accused by Satan, plead the blood of the Lamb, share your testimony and love Jesus more than life itself.

---

[a] 5 Psalm 2:9

11 They triumphed over him
by the blood of the Lamb
and by the word of their testimony;
they did not love their lives so much
as to shrink from death.
12 Therefore rejoice, you heavens
and you who dwell in them!
But woe to the earth and the sea,
because the devil has gone down to you!
He is filled with fury,
because he knows that his time is short."

13 When the dragon saw that he had been hurled to the earth, he pur-
sued the woman who had given birth to the male child. 14 The woman
was given the two wings of a great eagle, so that she might fly to the
place prepared for her in the wilderness, where she would be taken
care of for a time, times and half a time, out of the serpent's reach.
15 Then from his mouth the serpent spewed water like a river, to over-
take the woman and sweep her away with the torrent. 16 But the earth
helped the woman by opening its mouth and swallowing the river that
the dragon had spewed out of his mouth. 17 Then the dragon was en-
raged at the woman and went off to wage war against the rest of her
offspring — those who keep God's commands and hold fast their tes-
timony about Jesus.

THE BEAST OUT OF THE SEA

13 The dragon[a] stood on the shore of the sea. And I saw a beast
coming out of the sea. It had ten horns and seven heads, with
ten crowns on its horns, and on each head a blasphemous name. 2 The
beast I saw resembled a leopard, but had feet like those of a bear and
a mouth like that of a lion. The dragon gave the beast his power and
his throne and great authority. 3 One of the heads of the beast seemed
to have had a fatal wound, but the fatal wound had been healed. The
whole world was filled with wonder and followed the beast. 4 People
worshiped the dragon because he had given authority to the beast, and
they also worshiped the beast and asked, "Who is like the beast? Who
can wage war against it?"

5 The beast was given a mouth to utter proud words and blasphe-
mies and to exercise its authority for forty-two months. 6 It opened its
mouth to blaspheme God, and to slander his name and his dwelling
place and those who live in heaven. 7 It was given power to wage war
against God's holy people and to conquer them. And it was given au-
thority over every tribe, people, language and nation. 8 All inhabitants
of the earth will worship the beast — all whose names have not been
written in the Lamb's book of life, the Lamb who was slain from the
creation of the world.[b]
9 Whoever has ears, let them hear.

10 "If anyone is to go into captivity,
into captivity they will go.
If anyone is to be killed[c] with the sword,
with the sword they will be killed."[d]

PRAYING SCRIPTURE

Revelation 13

Two beasts make their way to the stage: one from the sea, and the other from the earth. This tandem of evil is empowered by the dragon, Satan. According to John, all those on earth "whose names have not been written in the Lamb's book of life" will worship the first beast (see verse 8).

Judgment passages like this one should remind God's people to pray for unbelievers to come to faith in Christ.

---

[a] *1* Some manuscripts *And I* [b] *8* Or *written from the creation of the world in the book of life belonging to the Lamb who was slain* [c] *10* Some manuscripts *anyone kills* [d] *10* Jer. 15:2

This calls for patient endurance and faithfulness on the part of God's people.

THE BEAST OUT OF THE EARTH

11 Then I saw a second beast, coming out of the earth. It had two horns like a lamb, but it spoke like a dragon. 12 It exercised all the authority of the first beast on its behalf, and made the earth and its inhabitants worship the first beast, whose fatal wound had been healed. 13 And it performed great signs, even causing fire to come down from heaven to the earth in full view of the people. 14 Because of the signs it was given power to perform on behalf of the first beast, it deceived the inhabitants of the earth. It ordered them to set up an image in honor of the beast who was wounded by the sword and yet lived. 15 The second beast was given power to give breath to the image of the first beast, so that the image could speak and cause all who refused to worship the image to be killed. 16 It also forced all people, great and small, rich and poor, free and slave, to receive a mark on their right hands or on their foreheads, 17 so that they could not buy or sell unless they had the mark, which is the name of the beast or the number of its name.

18 This calls for wisdom. Let the person who has insight calculate the number of the beast, for it is the number of a man.[a] That number is 666.

THE LAMB AND THE 144,000

14 Then I looked, and there before me was the Lamb, standing on Mount Zion, and with him 144,000 who had his name and his Father's name written on their foreheads. 2 And I heard a sound from heaven like the roar of rushing waters and like a loud peal of thunder. The sound I heard was like that of harpists playing their harps. 3 And they sang a new song before the throne and before the four living creatures and the elders. No one could learn the song except the 144,000 who had been redeemed from the earth. 4 These are those who did not defile themselves with women, for they remained virgins. They follow the Lamb wherever he goes. They were purchased from among mankind and offered as firstfruits to God and the Lamb. 5 No lie was found in their mouths; they are blameless.

> **PRAYING SCRIPTURE**
>
> **Revelation 14**
>
> In a passage filled with graphic imagery like burning sulfur (see verse 10), angels with sickles reaping the earth (see verse 16) and blood flowing from a press for 180 miles (see verse 20), we are reminded of the saints: "the people of God who keep his commands and remain faithful to Jesus" (verse 12).
>
> God's saints have always been marked by obedience and faith; our faith and our actions go hand in hand. Ask God to help you remain steadfast in your walk with him.

THE THREE ANGELS

6 Then I saw another angel flying in midair, and he had the eternal gospel to proclaim to those who live on the earth—to every nation, tribe, language and people. 7 He said in a loud voice, "Fear God and give him glory, because the hour of his judgment has come. Worship him who made the heavens, the earth, the sea and the springs of water."

8 A second angel followed and said, "'Fallen! Fallen is Babylon the Great,'[b] which made all the nations drink the maddening wine of her adulteries."

9 A third angel followed them and said in a loud voice: "If anyone worships the beast and its image and receives its mark on their forehead or on their hand, 10 they, too, will drink the wine of God's fury, which has been poured full strength into the cup of his wrath. They will be tormented with burning sulfur in the presence of the holy angels and of the Lamb. 11 And the smoke of their torment will rise for

[a] 18 Or *is humanity's number* [b] 8 Isaiah 21:9

ever and ever. There will be no rest day or night for those who worship
the beast and its image, or for anyone who receives the mark of its
name." 12This calls for patient endurance on the part of the people of
God who keep his commands and remain faithful to Jesus.
13Then I heard a voice from heaven say, "Write this: Blessed are the
dead who die in the Lord from now on."

"Yes," says the Spirit, "they will rest from their labor, for their deeds
will follow them."

HARVESTING THE EARTH AND TRAMPLING THE WINEPRESS

14I looked, and there before me was a white cloud, and seated on the
cloud was one like a son of man[a] with a crown of gold on his head and
a sharp sickle in his hand. 15Then another angel came out of the temple
and called in a loud voice to him who was sitting on the cloud, "Take
your sickle and reap, because the time to reap has come, for the har-
vest of the earth is ripe." 16So he who was seated on the cloud swung
his sickle over the earth, and the earth was harvested.
17Another angel came out of the temple in heaven, and he too had
a sharp sickle. 18Still another angel, who had charge of the fire, came
from the altar and called in a loud voice to him who had the sharp
sickle, "Take your sharp sickle and gather the clusters of grapes from
the earth's vine, because its grapes are ripe." 19The angel swung his
sickle on the earth, gathered its grapes and threw them into the great
winepress of God's wrath. 20They were trampled in the winepress out-
side the city, and blood flowed out of the press, rising as high as the
horses' bridles for a distance of 1,600 stadia.[b]

SEVEN ANGELS WITH SEVEN PLAGUES

15 I saw in heaven another great and marvelous sign: seven an-
gels with the seven last plagues — last, because with them God's
wrath is completed. 2And I saw what looked like a sea of glass glowing
with fire and, standing beside the sea, those who had been victorious
over the beast and its image and over the number of its name. They
held harps given them by God 3and sang the song of God's servant Mo-
ses and of the Lamb:

"Great and marvelous are your deeds,
  Lord God Almighty.
Just and true are your ways,
  King of the nations.[c]
4Who will not fear you, Lord,
  and bring glory to your name?
For you alone are holy.
All nations will come
  and worship before you,
for your righteous acts have been revealed."[d]

5After this I looked, and I saw in heaven the temple — that is, the tab-
ernacle of the covenant law — and it was opened. 6Out of the temple
came the seven angels with the seven plagues. They were dressed in

PRAYING SCRIPTURE

Revelation 15

As the judgments shift to a series of seven bowls, a scene reminiscent of Exodus 40:34–35 unfolds. The heavenly temple is "filled with smoke from the glory of God and from his power" (verse 8). God's glory was so overwhelming that no one could enter the temple or stand in his presence, much like the priests in Exodus were unable to minister.

Ask God to help you live in light of his glorious presence.

---

[a] *14* See Daniel 7:13. [b] *20* That is, about 180 miles or about 300 kilometers
[c] *3* Some manuscripts *ages* [d] *3,4* Phrases in this song are drawn from
Psalm 111:2,3; Deut. 32:4; Jer. 10:7; Psalms 86:9; 98:2.

clean, shining linen and wore golden sashes around their chests. 7Then one of the four living creatures gave to the seven angels seven golden bowls filled with the wrath of God, who lives for ever and ever. 8And the temple was filled with smoke from the glory of God and from his power, and no one could enter the temple until the seven plagues of the seven angels were completed.

THE SEVEN BOWLS OF GOD'S WRATH

16 Then I heard a loud voice from the temple saying to the seven angels, "Go, pour out the seven bowls of God's wrath on the earth."

2The first angel went and poured out his bowl on the land, and ugly, festering sores broke out on the people who had the mark of the beast and worshiped its image.

3The second angel poured out his bowl on the sea, and it turned into blood like that of a dead person, and every living thing in the sea died.

4The third angel poured out his bowl on the rivers and springs of water, and they became blood. 5Then I heard the angel in charge of the waters say:

"You are just in these judgments, O Holy One,
you who are and who were;
6for they have shed the blood of your holy people and your prophets,
and you have given them blood to drink as they deserve."

7And I heard the altar respond:

"Yes, Lord God Almighty,
true and just are your judgments."

8The fourth angel poured out his bowl on the sun, and the sun was allowed to scorch people with fire. 9They were seared by the intense heat and they cursed the name of God, who had control over these plagues, but they refused to repent and glorify him.

10The fifth angel poured out his bowl on the throne of the beast, and its kingdom was plunged into darkness. People gnawed their tongues in agony 11and cursed the God of heaven because of their pains and their sores, but they refused to repent of what they had done.

12The sixth angel poured out his bowl on the great river Euphrates, and its water was dried up to prepare the way for the kings from the East. 13Then I saw three impure spirits that looked like frogs; they came out of the mouth of the dragon, out of the mouth of the beast and out of the mouth of the false prophet. 14They are demonic spirits that perform signs, and they go out to the kings of the whole world, to gather them for the battle on the great day of God Almighty.

15"Look, I come like a thief! Blessed is the one who stays awake and remains clothed, so as not to go naked and be shamefully exposed."

16Then they gathered the kings together to the place that in Hebrew is called Armageddon.

17The seventh angel poured out his bowl into the air, and out of the temple came a loud voice from the throne, saying, "It is done!" 18Then there came flashes of lightning, rumblings, peals of thunder and a severe earthquake. No earthquake like it has ever occurred since mankind has been on earth, so tremendous was the quake. 19The great city

PRAYING SCRIPTURE

Revelation 16

As God's judgments on the earth grow worse and worse and as the battle of all battles—Armageddon—draws near, Jesus speaks from heaven, saying that he will return as a thief and that those who watch and are ready will be blessed (see verse 15).

There is no part of God's plan outside his control; nothing is left to chance. Praise God for his sovereign rule over his creation.

split into three parts, and the cities of the nations collapsed. God remembered Babylon the Great and gave her the cup filled with the wine of the fury of his wrath. 20Every island fled away and the mountains could not be found. 21From the sky huge hailstones, each weighing about a hundred pounds,[a] fell on people. And they cursed God on account of the plague of hail, because the plague was so terrible.

BABYLON, THE PROSTITUTE ON THE BEAST

17 One of the seven angels who had the seven bowls came and said to me, "Come, I will show you the punishment of the great prostitute, who sits by many waters. 2With her the kings of the earth committed adultery, and the inhabitants of the earth were intoxicated with the wine of her adulteries."

3Then the angel carried me away in the Spirit into a wilderness. There I saw a woman sitting on a scarlet beast that was covered with blasphemous names and had seven heads and ten horns. 4The woman was dressed in purple and scarlet, and was glittering with gold, precious stones and pearls. She held a golden cup in her hand, filled with abominable things and the filth of her adulteries. 5The name written on her forehead was a mystery:

BABYLON THE GREAT
THE MOTHER OF PROSTITUTES
AND OF THE ABOMINATIONS OF THE EARTH.

6I saw that the woman was drunk with the blood of God's holy people, the blood of those who bore testimony to Jesus.

When I saw her, I was greatly astonished. 7Then the angel said to me: "Why are you astonished? I will explain to you the mystery of the woman and of the beast she rides, which has the seven heads and ten horns. 8The beast, which you saw, once was, now is not, and yet will come up out of the Abyss and go to its destruction. The inhabitants of the earth whose names have not been written in the book of life from the creation of the world will be astonished when they see the beast, because it once was, now is not, and yet will come.

9"This calls for a mind with wisdom. The seven heads are seven hills on which the woman sits. 10They are also seven kings. Five have fallen, one is, the other has not yet come; but when he does come, he must remain for only a little while. 11The beast who once was, and now is not, is an eighth king. He belongs to the seven and is going to his destruction.

12"The ten horns you saw are ten kings who have not yet received a kingdom, but who for one hour will receive authority as kings along with the beast. 13They have one purpose and will give their power and authority to the beast. 14They will wage war against the Lamb, but the Lamb will triumph over them because he is Lord of lords and King of kings — and with him will be his called, chosen and faithful followers."

15Then the angel said to me, "The waters you saw, where the prostitute sits, are peoples, multitudes, nations and languages. 16The beast and the ten horns you saw will hate the prostitute. They will bring her to ruin and leave her naked; they will eat her flesh and burn her with fire. 17For God has put it into their hearts to accomplish his purpose by agreeing to hand over to the beast their royal authority, until God's words are fulfilled. 18The woman you saw is the great city that rules over the kings of the earth."

[a] *21* Or about 45 kilograms

PRAYING SCRIPTURE

Revelation 17

Babylon is that city throughout Scripture that represents all that is against God. Here it is described in a litany of negative ways, including the one drunk with the blood of the saints and martyrs. It is crucial to understand that God does all this to fulfill his purpose (see verse 17).

The horrid judgments that are visited upon the planet and the wickedest people do not surprise God. Pray for those still unbelieving to meet Jesus.

PRAYING SCRIPTURE

Revelation 18

Babylon is destroyed. Babylon, that unfaithful city that committed adultery with all the kings of the earth, that tempted the merchants of the earth with her materialism and that was responsible for the blood of the prophets and God's holy people, will "never . . . be found again" (verse 21).

It is easy for Christians to get caught up in the systems and priorities of this world. Pray for God to keep your heart fixed on things above.

LAMENT OVER FALLEN BABYLON

18 After this I saw another angel coming down from heaven. He
had great authority, and the earth was illuminated by his splen-
dor. 2With a mighty voice he shouted:

"'Fallen! Fallen is Babylon the Great!'[a]
She has become a dwelling for demons
and a haunt for every impure spirit,
a haunt for every unclean bird,
a haunt for every unclean and detestable animal.
3For all the nations have drunk
the maddening wine of her adulteries.
The kings of the earth committed adultery with her,
and the merchants of the earth grew rich from her excessive luxuries."

WARNING TO ESCAPE BABYLON'S JUDGMENT

4Then I heard another voice from heaven say:

"'Come out of her, my people,'[b]
so that you will not share in her sins,
so that you will not receive any of her plagues;
5for her sins are piled up to heaven,
and God has remembered her crimes.
6Give back to her as she has given;
pay her back double for what she has done.
Pour her a double portion from her own cup.
7Give her as much torment and grief
as the glory and luxury she gave herself.
In her heart she boasts,
'I sit enthroned as queen.
I am not a widow;[c]
I will never mourn.'
8Therefore in one day her plagues will overtake her:
death, mourning and famine.
She will be consumed by fire,
for mighty is the Lord God who judges her.

THREEFOLD WOE OVER BABYLON'S FALL

9"When the kings of the earth who committed adultery with her and
shared her luxury see the smoke of her burning, they will weep and
mourn over her. 10Terrified at her torment, they will stand far off and cry:

"'Woe! Woe to you, great city,
you mighty city of Babylon!
In one hour your doom has come!'

11"The merchants of the earth will weep and mourn over her because
no one buys their cargoes anymore — 12cargoes of gold, silver, precious
stones and pearls; fine linen, purple, silk and scarlet cloth; every sort
of citron wood, and articles of every kind made of ivory, costly wood,
bronze, iron and marble; 13cargoes of cinnamon and spice, of incense,
myrrh and frankincense, of wine and olive oil, of fine flour and wheat;
cattle and sheep; horses and carriages; and human beings sold as slaves.

---

[a] 2 Isaiah 21:9 [b] 4 Jer. 51:45 [c] 7 See Isaiah 47:7,8.

14"They will say, 'The fruit you longed for is gone from you. All your
luxury and splendor have vanished, never to be recovered.' 15The mer-
chants who sold these things and gained their wealth from her will
stand far off, terrified at her torment. They will weep and mourn 16and
cry out:

"'Woe! Woe to you, great city,
dressed in fine linen, purple and scarlet,
and glittering with gold, precious stones and pearls!
17 In one hour such great wealth has been brought to ruin!'

"Every sea captain, and all who travel by ship, the sailors, and all who
earn their living from the sea, will stand far off. 18When they see the
smoke of her burning, they will exclaim, 'Was there ever a city like this
great city?' 19They will throw dust on their heads, and with weeping
and mourning cry out:

"'Woe! Woe to you, great city,
where all who had ships on the sea
became rich through her wealth!
In one hour she has been brought to ruin!'

20 "Rejoice over her, you heavens!
Rejoice, you people of God!
Rejoice, apostles and prophets!
For God has judged her
with the judgment she imposed on you."

THE FINALITY OF BABYLON'S DOOM

21Then a mighty angel picked up a boulder the size of a large mill-
stone and threw it into the sea, and said:

"With such violence
the great city of Babylon will be thrown down,
never to be found again.
22 The music of harpists and musicians, pipers and trumpeters,
will never be heard in you again.
No worker of any trade
will ever be found in you again.
The sound of a millstone
will never be heard in you again.
23 The light of a lamp
will never shine in you again.
The voice of bridegroom and bride
will never be heard in you again.
Your merchants were the world's important people.
By your magic spell all the nations were led astray.
24 In her was found the blood of prophets and of God's holy people,
of all who have been slaughtered on the earth."

THREEFOLD HALLELUJAH OVER BABYLON'S FALL

19 After this I heard what sounded like the roar of a great multi-
tude in heaven shouting:

"Hallelujah!
Salvation and glory and power belong to our God,
2 for true and just are his judgments.

PRAYING SCRIPTURE

Revelation 19

People debate the specifics of Christ's return, but one thing is abundantly clear: Jesus will return to destroy all who are allied against him. Sin was paid for at the cross and will ultimately be punished eternally. Those who remain in rebellion against God will not escape his judgment. Indeed, they cannot.

God's children need not fear Christ's return. Pray for all you know to be saved so that they can avoid judgment.

He has condemned the great prostitute
who corrupted the earth by her adulteries.
He has avenged on her the blood of his servants."
3 And again they shouted:

"Hallelujah!
The smoke from her goes up for ever and ever."

4 The twenty-four elders and the four living creatures fell down and
worshiped God, who was seated on the throne. And they cried:

"Amen, Hallelujah!"

5 Then a voice came from the throne, saying:

"Praise our God,
all you his servants,
you who fear him,
both great and small!"

6 Then I heard what sounded like a great multitude, like the roar of
rushing waters and like loud peals of thunder, shouting:

"Hallelujah!
For our Lord God Almighty reigns.
7 Let us rejoice and be glad
and give him glory!
For the wedding of the Lamb has come,
and his bride has made herself ready.
8 Fine linen, bright and clean,
was given her to wear."
(Fine linen stands for the righteous acts of God's holy people.)

9 Then the angel said to me, "Write this: Blessed are those who are
invited to the wedding supper of the Lamb!" And he added, "These are
the true words of God."
10 At this I fell at his feet to worship him. But he said to me, "Don't do
that! I am a fellow servant with you and with your brothers and sisters
who hold to the testimony of Jesus. Worship God! For it is the Spirit of
prophecy who bears testimony to Jesus."

THE HEAVENLY WARRIOR DEFEATS THE BEAST

11 I saw heaven standing open and there before me was a white
horse, whose rider is called Faithful and True. With justice he judges
and wages war. 12 His eyes are like blazing fire, and on his head are
many crowns. He has a name written on him that no one knows but
he himself. 13 He is dressed in a robe dipped in blood, and his name is
the Word of God. 14 The armies of heaven were following him, riding on
white horses and dressed in fine linen, white and clean. 15 Coming out
of his mouth is a sharp sword with which to strike down the nations.
"He will rule them with an iron scepter."[a] He treads the winepress of
the fury of the wrath of God Almighty. 16 On his robe and on his thigh
he has this name written:

KING OF KINGS AND LORD OF LORDS.

[a] *15* Psalm 2:9

17 And I saw an angel standing in the sun, who cried in a loud voice
to all the birds flying in midair, “Come, gather together for the great
supper of God, 18 so that you may eat the flesh of kings, generals, and
the mighty, of horses and their riders, and the flesh of all people, free
and slave, great and small.”
19 Then I saw the beast and the kings of the earth and their armies
gathered together to wage war against the rider on the horse and his
army. 20 But the beast was captured, and with it the false prophet who
had performed the signs on its behalf. With these signs he had deluded
those who had received the mark of the beast and worshiped its image. The two of them were thrown alive into the fiery lake of burning
sulfur. 21 The rest were killed with the sword coming out of the mouth
of the rider on the horse, and all the birds gorged themselves on their
flesh.

THE THOUSAND YEARS

20 And I saw an angel coming down out of heaven, having the
key to the Abyss and holding in his hand a great chain. 2 He
seized the dragon, that ancient serpent, who is the devil, or Satan, and
bound him for a thousand years. 3 He threw him into the Abyss, and
locked and sealed it over him, to keep him from deceiving the nations
anymore until the thousand years were ended. After that, he must be
set free for a short time.
4 I saw thrones on which were seated those who had been given authority to judge. And I saw the souls of those who had been beheaded
because of their testimony about Jesus and because of the word of
God. They[a] had not worshiped the beast or its image and had not received its mark on their foreheads or their hands. They came to life and
reigned with Christ a thousand years. 5 (The rest of the dead did not
come to life until the thousand years were ended.) This is the first resurrection. 6 Blessed and holy are those who share in the first resurrection. The second death has no power over them, but they will be priests
of God and of Christ and will reign with him for a thousand years.

THE JUDGMENT OF SATAN

7 When the thousand years are over, Satan will be released from his
prison 8 and will go out to deceive the nations in the four corners of
the earth — Gog and Magog — and to gather them for battle. In number they are like the sand on the seashore. 9 They marched across the
breadth of the earth and surrounded the camp of God’s people, the city
he loves. But fire came down from heaven and devoured them. 10 And
the devil, who deceived them, was thrown into the lake of burning sulfur, where the beast and the false prophet had been thrown. They will
be tormented day and night for ever and ever.

THE JUDGMENT OF THE DEAD

11 Then I saw a great white throne and him who was seated on it.
The earth and the heavens fled from his presence, and there was no
place for them. 12 And I saw the dead, great and small, standing before
the throne, and books were opened. Another book was opened, which
is the book of life. The dead were judged according to what they had
done as recorded in the books. 13 The sea gave up the dead that were in

[a] 4 Or *God; I also saw those who*

PRAYING SCRIPTURE

Revelation 20

The great white throne judgment is the most solemn and tragic event a human being can face. A place of neither grace nor mercy, the wicked are found guilty according to what they had done (see verse 12) and condemned to eternal judgment. God’s judgment is not arbitrary. Sinners bring judgment upon themselves by rejecting God’s grace.

This judgment of sin should stir us to pray for everyone we know who does not know Jesus as Lord.

it, and death and Hades gave up the dead that were in them, and each
person was judged according to what they had done. 14Then death and
Hades were thrown into the lake of fire. The lake of fire is the second
death. 15Anyone whose name was not found written in the book of life
was thrown into the lake of fire.

A NEW HEAVEN AND A NEW EARTH

21 Then I saw "a new heaven and a new earth,"[a] for the first heaven
and the first earth had passed away, and there was no longer
any sea. 2I saw the Holy City, the new Jerusalem, coming down out of
heaven from God, prepared as a bride beautifully dressed for her hus-
band. 3And I heard a loud voice from the throne saying, "Look! God's
dwelling place is now among the people, and he will dwell with them.
They will be his people, and God himself will be with them and be their
God. 4'He will wipe every tear from their eyes. There will be no more
death'[b] or mourning or crying or pain, for the old order of things has
passed away."
5He who was seated on the throne said, "I am making everything
new!" Then he said, "Write this down, for these words are trustworthy
and true."
6He said to me: "It is done. I am the Alpha and the Omega, the Be-
ginning and the End. To the thirsty I will give water without cost from
the spring of the water of life. 7Those who are victorious will inherit all
this, and I will be their God and they will be my children. 8But the cow-
ardly, the unbelieving, the vile, the murderers, the sexually immoral,
those who practice magic arts, the idolaters and all liars — they will be
consigned to the fiery lake of burning sulfur. This is the second death."

THE NEW JERUSALEM, THE BRIDE OF THE LAMB

9One of the seven angels who had the seven bowls full of the seven
last plagues came and said to me, "Come, I will show you the bride, the
wife of the Lamb." 10And he carried me away in the Spirit to a moun-
tain great and high, and showed me the Holy City, Jerusalem, coming
down out of heaven from God. 11It shone with the glory of God, and its
brilliance was like that of a very precious jewel, like a jasper, clear as
crystal. 12It had a great, high wall with twelve gates, and with twelve
angels at the gates. On the gates were written the names of the twelve
tribes of Israel. 13There were three gates on the east, three on the north,
three on the south and three on the west. 14The wall of the city had
twelve foundations, and on them were the names of the twelve apos-
tles of the Lamb.
15The angel who talked with me had a measuring rod of gold to
measure the city, its gates and its walls. 16The city was laid out like a
square, as long as it was wide. He measured the city with the rod and
found it to be 12,000 stadia[c] in length, and as wide and high as it is
long. 17The angel measured the wall using human measurement, and
it was 144 cubits[d] thick.[e] 18The wall was made of jasper, and the city of
pure gold, as pure as glass. 19The foundations of the city walls were
decorated with every kind of precious stone. The first foundation was
jasper, the second sapphire, the third agate, the fourth emerald, 20the

PRAYING SCRIPTURE

Revelation 21

Finally, after millennia of sin, degradation, destruction and pain, God restores everything he has redeemed. A new heaven and a new earth replace those corrupted by the fall. God's people will live eternally with him in a new creation that has not been, and cannot be, affected by sin.

Think about that day! Worship God, thanking him for our eternity with him.

[a] *1* Isaiah 65:17 [b] *4* Isaiah 25:8 [c] *16* That is, about 1,400 miles or about 2,200 kilometers [d] *17* That is, about 200 feet or about 65 meters [e] *17* Or *high*

fifth onyx, the sixth ruby, the seventh chrysolite, the eighth beryl, the
ninth topaz, the tenth turquoise, the eleventh jacinth, and the twelfth
amethyst.[a] 21 The twelve gates were twelve pearls, each gate made of a
single pearl. The great street of the city was of gold, as pure as trans-
parent glass.
22 I did not see a temple in the city, because the Lord God Almighty
and the Lamb are its temple. 23 The city does not need the sun or the
moon to shine on it, for the glory of God gives it light, and the Lamb is
its lamp. 24 The nations will walk by its light, and the kings of the earth
will bring their splendor into it. 25 On no day will its gates ever be shut,
for there will be no night there. 26 The glory and honor of the nations
will be brought into it. 27 Nothing impure will ever enter it, nor will
anyone who does what is shameful or deceitful, but only those whose
names are written in the Lamb's book of life.

EDEN RESTORED

22 Then the angel showed me the river of the water of life, as clear
as crystal, flowing from the throne of God and of the Lamb
2 down the middle of the great street of the city. On each side of the
river stood the tree of life, bearing twelve crops of fruit, yielding its
fruit every month. And the leaves of the tree are for the healing of
the nations. 3 No longer will there be any curse. The throne of God and
of the Lamb will be in the city, and his servants will serve him. 4 They
will see his face, and his name will be on their foreheads. 5 There will
be no more night. They will not need the light of a lamp or the light
of the sun, for the Lord God will give them light. And they will reign
for ever and ever.

JOHN AND THE ANGEL

6 The angel said to me, "These words are trustworthy and true. The
Lord, the God who inspires the prophets, sent his angel to show his
servants the things that must soon take place."

7 "Look, I am coming soon! Blessed is the one who keeps the words
of the prophecy written in this scroll."

8 I, John, am the one who heard and saw these things. And when I
had heard and seen them, I fell down to worship at the feet of the angel
who had been showing them to me. 9 But he said to me, "Don't do that!
I am a fellow servant with you and with your fellow prophets and with
all who keep the words of this scroll. Worship God!"
10 Then he told me, "Do not seal up the words of the prophecy of this
scroll, because the time is near. 11 Let the one who does wrong continue
to do wrong; let the vile person continue to be vile; let the one who
does right continue to do right; and let the holy person continue to
be holy."

EPILOGUE: INVITATION AND WARNING

12 "Look, I am coming soon! My reward is with me, and I will give to
each person according to what they have done. 13 I am the Alpha and
the Omega, the First and the Last, the Beginning and the End.
14 "Blessed are those who wash their robes, that they may have the
right to the tree of life and may go through the gates into the city.

PRAYING SCRIPTURE

Revelation 22

In this last chapter of the Scriptures, we return to an Eden-like setting, a city in which God again dwells with his people. Both the river of life and the tree of life are in its midst. The city is resplendent because the glory of the Lord has risen upon its inhabitants (Is. 60:1).

Let our hearts rejoice at our good King Jesus, the ruler of heaven now with earth. Join in with the countless voices of those who anticipate the day of his place among us: "Come, Lord Jesus!"

---

[a] 20 The precise identification of some of these precious stones is uncertain.

15Outside are the dogs, those who practice magic arts, the sexually im-
moral, the murderers, the idolaters and everyone who loves and prac-
tices falsehood.
16"I, Jesus, have sent my angel to give you[a] this testimony for the
churches. I am the Root and the Offspring of David, and the bright
Morning Star."

17The Spirit and the bride say, "Come!" And let the one who hears say,
"Come!" Let the one who is thirsty come; and let the one who wishes
take the free gift of the water of life.

18I warn everyone who hears the words of the prophecy of this scroll:
If anyone adds anything to them, God will add to that person the
plagues described in this scroll. 19And if anyone takes words away from
this scroll of prophecy, God will take away from that person any share
in the tree of life and in the Holy City, which are described in this scroll.
20He who testifies to these things says, "Yes, I am coming soon."
Amen. Come, Lord Jesus.
21The grace of the Lord Jesus be with God's people. Amen.

[a] *16* The Greek is plural.

TABLE OF WEIGHTS AND MEASURES

	Biblical Unit	Approximate American Equivalent	Approximate Metric Equivalent
Weights	talent (60 minas)	75 pounds	34 kilograms
	mina (50 shekels)	1 1/4 pounds	560 grams
	shekel (2 bekas)	2/5 ounce	11.5 grams
	pim (2/3 shekel)	1/4 ounce	7.8 grams
	beka (10 gerahs)	1/5 ounce	5.7 grams
	gerah	1/50 ounce	0.6 gram
	daric	1/3 ounce	8.4 grams
Length	cubit	18 inches	45 centimeters
	span	9 inches	23 centimeters
	handbreadth	3 inches	7.5 centimeters
	stadion (pl. stadia)	600 feet	183 meters
Capacity			
Dry Measure	cor [homer] (10 ephahs)	6 bushels	220 liters
	lethek (5 ephahs)	3 bushels	110 liters
	ephah (10 omers)	3/5 bushel	22 liters
	seah (1/3 ephah)	7 quarts	7.5 liters
	omer (1/10 ephah)	2 quarts	2 liters
	cab (1/18 ephah)	1 quart	1 liter
Liquid Measure	bath (1 ephah)	6 gallons	22 liters
	hin (1/6 bath)	1 gallon	3.8 liters
	log (1/72 bath)	1/3 quart	0.3 liter

The figures of the table are calculated on the basis of a shekel equaling 11.5 grams, a cubit equaling 18 inches and an ephah equaling 22 liters. The quart referred to is either a dry quart (slightly larger than a liter) or a liquid quart (slightly smaller than a liter), whichever is applicable. The ton referred to in the footnotes is the American ton of 2,000 pounds. These weights are calculated relative to the particular commodity involved. Accordingly, the same measure of capacity in the text may be converted into different weights in the footnotes.

This table is based upon the best available information, but it is not intended to be mathematically precise; like the measurement equivalents in the footnotes, it merely gives approximate amounts and distances. Weights and measures differed somewhat at various times and places in the ancient world. There is uncertainty particularly about the ephah and the bath; further discoveries may shed more light on these units of capacity.

PRAYERS OF THE BIBLE

PRAYERS OF THE OLD TESTAMENT

Abraham pleads for Sodom *Genesis 18:22–33*
Abraham's servant prays for guidance *Genesis 24:12–14*
Isaac blesses Jacob and Esau *Genesis 27*
Jacob's vow at Bethel *Genesis 28*
Jacob's prayer before encountering Esau at Peniel *Genesis 32*
Jacob blessings on his twelve sons *Genesis 48–49*
Moses' song of thanksgiving for deliverance from Egypt *Exodus 15*
Moses' plea for the Israelites regarding the golden calf *Exodus 32; Deuteronomy 9*
Moses request to see God's glory *Exodus 33*
The Aaronic blessing *Numbers 6*
Moses begs God's forgiveness for the Israelites' rebellious response to Canaan *Numbers 14*
Balaam, on God's instruction, blesses the Israelites *Numbers 22–24*
Moses' song: God and his people *Deuteronomy 32*
Moses blessing on the tribes of Israel before his death *Deuteronomy 33*
Joshua's prayer after Achan's sin and Israel's defeat at Ai *Joshua 7*
Joshua prays for time to complete his victory *Joshua 10*
Deborah's song of thanksgiving for victory *Judges 5*
Gideon's prayer for reassurance of victory *Judges 6*
Hannah's prayer for a son *1 Samuel 1*
Hannah's thanksgiving for Samuel *1 Samuel 2*
Samuel's prayer for the nation *1 Samuel 7*
David's response to God's promise of an eternal kingdom *2 Samuel 7; 1 Chronicles 17*
David's song of thanksgiving for deliverance *2 Samuel 22; Psalm 18*
Solomon's prayer for wisdom *1 Kings 3; 2 Chronicles 1*
Solomon's prayer at the dedication of the temple *1 Kings 8; 2 Chronicles 6*
Elijah petitions God at Mount Carmel among the priests of Baal *1 Kings 18*
Hezekiah's prayer at the time of Sennacherib's siege *2 Kings 19; Isaiah 37*
Thanksgiving as the ark is brought to Jerusalem *1 Chronicles 16*
David's prayer for Solomon *2 Chronicles 29*
Ezra's confession of the nation's sin *Ezra 9*
Nehemiah's prayer for the Jewish remnant and for Jerusalem *Nehemiah 1*
Ezra leads the Israelites in public confession *Nehemiah 9*
Job seeks the reason for his suffering *Job 10*
Job pleads his case *Job 13–14*
Job's confession *Job 42*

SOME PRAYERS FROM THE PSALMS

Evening prayer *Psalm 4*
Morning prayer *Psalm 5*
The Shepherd Psalm *Psalm 23*
Praise and worship *Psalms 24; 67; 92; 95–98; 100; 113; 145; 148; 150*
Guidance *Psalm 25*
Trust *Psalms 37; 62*
Deliverance *Psalms 40; 116*
Longing for God *Psalms 27; 42; 63; 84*
Forgiveness *Psalms 51; 130*

Thanksgiving *Psalms 65; 111; 136*
Help in trouble *Psalms 66; 69; 86; 88; 102; 140; 143*
God's constant love and care *Psalms 89; 103; 107; 146*
God's majesty and glory *Psalms 8; 29; 93; 104*
God's knowledge and presence *Psalm 139*
God's Word *Psalms 19; 119*
God's protection *Psalms 46; 91; 125*

PRAYERS FROM THE PROPHETS

Isaiah's prayers *Isaiah 25; 33; 63–64*
Hezekiah's prayer in his illness *Isaiah 38*
Jeremiah's prayers *Jeremiah 11; 14; 20; 32*
Laments for the fall of Jerusalem *Lamentations 1–4*
Prayer for restoration *Lamentations 5*
Nebuchadnezzar's dream; Daniel's prayer *Daniel 2*
Nebuchadnezzar praises God *Daniel 4*
Daniel's prayer at the end of the exile *Daniel 9*
Jonah's prayer *Jonah 2*
Habakkuk questions God *Habakkuk 1*
Habakkuk's prayer *Habakkuk 3*

PRAYERS OF JESUS

The Lord's Prayer *Matthew 6:9–13; Luke 11:2–4*
Praise that God reveals his nature to children *Matthew 11:25–26; Luke 10:21*
In the garden of Gethsemane *Matthew 26:36–44; Mark 14:32–39; Luke 22:46*
From the cross *Matthew 27:46; Mark 15:34; Luke 23:34,46*
At the raising of Lazarus *John 11:41–42*
Facing death *John 12:27–28*
For his followers *John 17*

PRAYERS OF THE NEW TESTAMENT

Mary's thanksgiving *Luke 1:46–55*
Zechariah's prayer *Luke 1:68–79*
Simeon's prayer *Luke 2:29–35*
Prayers of the Pharisee and the tax collector *Luke 18:10–13*
The church's prayer in the face of threats *Acts 4:24–30*
Stephen's prayer at his death *Acts 7:59–60*
Peter's thanksgiving *2 Peter 1:3–5*
John's prayer for Gaius *3 John 2*

PRAYERS OF PAUL

For the Christians at Rome *Romans 1:8–10*
For the people of Israel *Romans 10:1*
For the church at Corinth *1 Corinthians 1:4–9; 2 Corinthians 13:7–9*
Thanksgiving for God's comfort in trouble *2 Corinthians 1:3–4*
Thanksgiving for spiritual riches in Christ *Ephesians 1:8–14*
For the Ephesian Christians *Ephesians 1:16–23; 3:14–19*
For the Philippian Christians *Philippians 1:8–11*
For the church at Colossae *Colossians 1:3–14*
For the Thessalonian Christians *1 Thessalonians 1:2–3; 2:13; 3:9–13; 5:23; 2 Thessalonians 1:3; 2:13,16–17; 3:16*
For Timothy *2 Timothy 1:3–4*
For Philemon *Philemon 4–6*

CLOSING BLESSINGS

To establish you in the gospel of Jesus Christ *Romans 16:25–27*
To him who is able to do immeasurably more than we ask *Ephesians 3:20–21*
To increase and abound in love to one another *1 Thessalonians 3:11–13*
To equip you for everything good for doing his will *Hebrews 13:20–21*
For restoration and strength after suffering *1 Peter 5:10–11*
To grow in the grace and knowledge of Jesus Christ *2 Peter 3:18*
To him who is able to keep you from stumbling *Jude 24–25*

WHY READ THE BIBLE?

Why is the Bible so vital to spiritual growth? Because we are part of the big picture of God's story. Every part of the Bible must be understood in the context of one story line: God redeeming all things so all things are once again in relationship with him. The Bible is not to be read as a jumble of history and poetry lessons in morality and theology, dramatic narratives, comforting promises, guiding principles and commands. Instead, we are to connect each individual part (each proverb, song, letter, prophecy or parable) to the bigger story of God revealing himself to us and redeeming all things to himself.

The Bible

- is "active and powerful" (Hebrews 4:12–13).
- blesses those who obey it (see James 1:25).
- makes truth known (see Psalm 19:7–11).
- gives wisdom, joy, and enlightenment (see Psalm 19:7–8).
- teaches us how to combat sin (see Psalm 119:11).
- equips for every good work (see 2 Timothy 3:16–17).
- transforms lives (see Romans 12:1–2).

All this and more are true, but perhaps the most important reason the Bible is vital to spiritual growth is because it is the Word of God. It is a revelation from God and of God. Every time we come to the Bible, we can meet and know God.

God speaks through Scripture, so Scripture has God's authority. All authority comes from God (see Romans 13:1–2). We read the Bible to learn what is true and to come under the influence of God's authority. As we engage God's Word, we engage God himself.

Biblical inspiration is the process whereby "prophets, though human, spoke from God as they were carried along by the Holy Spirit" (2 Peter 1:21). When we come to the Bible, we remember that the words are filled with the very Spirit of God. The Holy Spirit is our teacher, and Scripture is what he teaches us. Wanting the work of the Holy Spirit in our lives without making Scripture central to that pursuit limits the Spirit. As we approach Scripture, we need to ask the Holy Spirit to come alongside us to illuminate what we read. Listening to God's Spirit is like having the author of a book sitting next to us, explaining what is written; then we are motivated to obey what we read.

The Bible is God's fully divine written Word communicated through real people in real-life contexts. It is one means by which we can know God and his salvation. The Bible is for every person to use so he or she can know and follow God.

Despite the sufficiency and clarity of the Bible, sometimes understanding Scripture still requires effort. Each person willing to do the work can understand the general meaning of the Bible. We still need teachers; the Bible tells us that teachers are gifts to us from God (see 1 Corinthians 12:28; Ephesians 4:11). Jesus himself came as the Teacher (see John 13:13).

As we engage the Bible through personal study and biblical teaching, we realize afresh that the Bible contains God's words. Therefore, it is vital to our daily lives as we seek to reflect him.

STEPS TO ENGAGE

You might ask, *Why employ the Scripture engagement process?* Simply reading the Bible doesn't automatically result in a person's loving God and others. Reflecting on a Bible passage after reading it is imperative for spiritual growth. Similarly, reading a math book doesn't mean you understand the math or are able to use it. You must engage and try the calculations. Therefore, Scripture engagement serves to make passages more personally meaningful to you so they can result in godly living.

Here are some steps to help you prepare to engage with God's Word.

READY YOUR HEART

Your heart is the center of your being. God will not force his presence upon you. He will call to you and wait for you to open your heart to him (see Revelation 3:20).

As you shape your attitude, much of the rest of the process will naturally follow. For example, the way you choose to approach someone influences the outcome of your meeting. Your attitude as you go for a job interview, meet potential in-laws, interact with a teacher or even talk with a friend makes a difference in your experience. The same is true for your experience with the Bible. Expect engagement; expect good things to result from your encounter with God. Ready your heart for dialogue and interaction.

PREPARE TO MEET WITH THE LORD

Here you prepare to meet someone specific—God himself. The foundational premise of Scripture engagement is that when you engage the Bible, you engage God. Spiritual reading of the Bible is a relational process; we primarily read to meet and know God.

If you had the chance to be in the physical, visible presence of Jesus, would you go? It would probably be terrifying; think of all the times in the Bible where "do not be afraid" was needed to calm the hearts of people who had a direct experience with God. But if you went, what should your attitude be? How would you prepare to meet God?

This meeting might cause your sinfulness to surface. Perhaps your reaction would be to confess your sins and ask forgiveness before your meeting. You also might come into Jesus' presence with gratitude and joy at the chance to meet with your Lord and Savior. Surely your focus would be on him alone. You would probably be quick to listen to whatever he would say, ready to pay attention to every detail and nuance. Psalm 123:1–2 gives us a good image of how we can prepare ourselves to meet with God: we look to God with the attentiveness of a servant and wait expectantly for instructions from our master, not wanting to miss a single direction or signal.

We have access to God through Jesus by the Holy Spirit—what an amazing biblical truth (see Ephesians 2:18; 3:12). The more we prepare our hearts and minds for meeting God in his Word, just as if we were coming into the physical presence of Jesus, the more life-changing and powerful our experiences with Scripture will be.

GET PRACTICAL

Please understand that you won't necessarily have an emotional experience every time you engage the Bible. The disciples didn't appear to have been overwhelmed by Jesus' presence every moment they were with him. But each time can be significant (see Isaiah 55:11). To prepare to engage with Scripture, do the following:

Pick a time. Set aside a specific amount of time in your weekly calendar to engage the Bible so that it becomes a rhythm in your life. Make it a habit just like brushing your teeth or eating three meals a day.

Pick the best time. Use your prime time of the day to engage with the Bible. Don't save it for when you're the most exhausted or distracted. Are you a morning person or a night person? Plan your time accordingly.

Pick a place. Go wherever you naturally go when you want to focus on something important. Using the same place repeatedly trains your brain to set itself to the proper mode when you go there.

Pray. Briefly ask God's Spirit to teach you, meet you and bless your time in his Word (see 1 Corinthians 2:16). Commit to obey what you discover about his will.

Start small. It is better to start with modest goals and continue the practice than to start with huge goals, get disappointed and stop.

Find a method that works for you. There is no single engagement tool that every person should use.

DEAL WITH DISTRACTIONS

Distraction is a lively topic for most of us. We have a difficult time slowing down and spending time with the Bible. Distractions seem to pop out of nowhere: external chaos, internal stress, weariness or an undisciplined mind. With diligent effort, you will grow in your ability to give attention to the Bible. Try these tips:

Get rid of things that usually distract you. Or choose a place for engagement that offers the fewest objects that distract.

Journal before you enter the Word. Take a minute to write out your troubles, disappointments, frustrations, joys. Start a conversation with God and then turn to Scripture for what to do.

Keep paper handy so you can jot down things that come to mind. Do this throughout your reading. This gets thoughts out of your head as quickly as possible so you can refocus.

Change up your routine to a new Scripture engagement practice.

Read the passage aloud if you get distracted when silently reading the Bible.

Stop feeling guilty about distraction. It's okay. It happens to all of us. Feeling guilty just adds another distraction. Ask God to redirect your thoughts to the Word.

Practice. Don't give up. Scripture engagement, like all spiritual disciplines, gets easier with time. Disciplining the mind is work, but the chance to interact with God through his Word is definitely worth the focused effort.

CHOOSE HOW MUCH TO READ

Is reading larger quantities of the Bible (perhaps whole books at a time or the Bible in a year) better because you can see the big picture? Or is it better to read one book of the Bible over and over? Or should you take in small portions of the Bible (just a few verses or a paragraph) because you can go into more depth?

The answer is yes! You'll want to take different approaches at different times. Perhaps begin with smaller portions and work up to larger ones. Experiment to find what is most effective for you.

No matter how much you read, remember the purpose of engaging Scripture: to meet, know and obey God. Over time God will use his Word to transform you into his image if you let it soak into your life. If you don't see an immediate change or the practice feels a bit dry, don't give up engaging the Bible. Let God work in your life as he wants to work. Following these steps will help you get the most from each encounter you have with God in his Word.

SCRIPTURE ENGAGEMENT VS. BIBLE STUDY

Engaging the Bible is not the same as studying the Bible; it *complements* deep study of the Scriptures. The relational reading of Scripture engagement should not detract from Bible study. Second Timothy 2:15 teaches us to correctly handle "the word of truth." The apostle Paul was a scholar (see Acts 22:3). So, we need to study *and* engage.

Inductive study of the Bible—the process of observing, interpreting and applying—is how we understand what the Bible means and how to obey it. We must know what the Bible says in order to gain an accurate understanding of God. Though Bible study is important, it is not enough. It is possible to study the Bible as a mere academic exercise, to read it in a way that does not impact life because we have no encounter with God. You have probably met people who have head knowledge of a topic without a heart or life change, a kind of empty scholasticism.

On the other hand, the goal of Scripture engagement is not to be so subjective with the Bible that we move away from the original meaning of the passage. The sole question can never be, *What does the passage mean to me?* Scripture engagement calls us to both analyze and apply the Bible, to be both students and followers. The goal is to listen with our minds and with our hearts. The ideal process is to come to the Bible, working hard to study what it means, and then to reflect, in the power of the Holy Spirit, on the meaning of the passage for our lives and communities.

Ideally reflection brings up more questions about the meaning of the text, and study brings up fodder for reflection. The two practices work synergistically to bring you closer to God.

LEARN HOW TO READ *AND* REFLECT

Few would disagree about the need to teach people how to study the Bible, learning the principles of Bible interpretation (*hermeneutics*), understanding the historical and cultural settings of the Bible and discerning the meanings of words in the original biblical languages. But aren't people naturally reflective? Once they understand what the Bible says intellectually, won't they examine and act on that understanding? No, reflection and application need to be taught too. In some ways, understanding the Bible intellectually is the easier of the two processes. The reflection process through which we are mostly likely to meet God and be changed by him is what we especially need to learn.

Why is reflecting on the Scriptures sometimes challenging? One reason is our natural tendency to avoid anything that brings change. Meeting and knowing God are always for our good but obeying him involves death to ourselves (see Matthew 16:24). Meeting with God will change our lives. Being willing to change is a critical first step in the spiritual reading of the Bible.

Scripture engagement is also difficult because reflecting on Scripture is a whole-person process. We offer our intellect and our emotions. We contemplate personal and community life changes. We yield our attitudes and our actions to God's direction. It's much easier to use a corner of our brains to skim the surface of a Bible passage, preventing it from penetrating our lives.

Scripture uses a number of words to show us ways to reflect:

- "meditate" (Joshua 1:8; Psalm 1:2);
- "reflect" (2 Timothy 2:7);
- "look into" (James 1:25);

- "dwell" (Colossians 3:16);
- "consider" (Jeremiah 2:31);
- "talk about" (Deuteronomy 6:7);
- "hold firmly" (1 Corinthians 15:2);
- eat (see Jeremiah 15:16).

These basic actions can be mixed and matched in different ways, using different practices based on our needs. But all are needed for the best results.

The basic idea of soccer seems fairly simple: kick the ball into the goal. Even children can play the game. But with practice and good coaching, kids can grow up to be brilliant World Cup–level athletes, masters of the game. Similarly, everyone can engage the Bible at some level. But with practice and coaching we can grow in the life-changing skills of Scripture engagement and experience real transformation.

Just as we need good instruction about how to study the Bible, we need good coaching in how to reflect on and apply it. The bottom line is that Scripture study and engagement are equally important practices. With *The Prayer Bible* you can put both to work!

SPIRITUAL DISCIPLINES AND SCRIPTURE ENGAGEMENT

Spiritual disciplines include service, solitude, study, celebration, worship, holiness, confession, silence, fasting, simplicity, chastity, evangelism and submission. Bible engagement is foundational to each. Spiritual disciplines are never the end goal; instead, they help us grow in relationship with God and with people. As we become like Christ, we love well and live well. Spiritual disciplines are important because they deliberately build habits that show love for God and for people.

Spiritual disciplines are joyful work. They aren't the kind of work by which you seek to earn God's favor, where you try to please an angry, demanding taskmaster. Instead, they are the work you do to please a coach you love and trust. God knows you better than you know yourself. He believes in you, pushing you wisely, developing you into the kind of person you only hoped you could be. As you see how disciplines change you, you double down with anticipation and kindness.

The question is not whether to engage the Bible, but how to engage it so God can transform your life. Spiritual disciplines must be motivated by, informed by and performed through a reflective approach to Scripture. Spiritual disciplines put you in a place to meet God and obey him. They rightly develop your heart, body and mind. They show you how to give people godly love that grows them into loving people. Disciplines let Scripture engagement become Scripture living.

ABOUT THE TAYLOR UNIVERSITY CENTER FOR SCRIPTURE ENGAGEMENT

ENGAGE SCRIPTURE, ENGAGE GOD

The Taylor University Center for Scripture Engagement (TUCSE) started in 2009 through a number of people who were hungry to help others meet and be transformed by Jesus Christ through the Bible. Those involved had all experienced deep life change through their reading of the Scriptures, and they wanted to equip others to know Christ in a similar life-changing manner. The core question was, *How do we teach people to engage the Bible in such a manner that they meet and are transformed by God?*

Two things seemed true to us. One, people within Christian communities were often told reading/listening to the Bible is important to their spiritual lives (to which we agree). Two, that people were seldom actually taught how to read the Bible—they were almost universally left alone to figure it out by themselves (which broke our hearts). Out of a desire to be a part of the solution and to help people engage Scripture so that they could engage God, the TUCSE was born.

Joining with many others around the world, the dream of the TUCSE is that Scripture engagement will become one of the most broadly applied missional concepts in the Christian world. The mission of the TUCSE is to carry out four distinct Scripture engagement programs:

- Learning—helping all ages learn how to engage Scripture for themselves.
- Training—providing ministry leaders with resources to teach others how to engage Scripture.
- Research—conducting original research to better understand how to best engage Scripture and to ground all programs in the daily lives of real people.
- Clearinghouse of Resources—to help provide access to Scripture engagement resources to a wide audience (found on Bible Gateway).

It is our deepest hope that the materials in the Abide line of resources will be used by God to help you experience for yourself the reality that engaging well with Scripture is truly life changing.

TAYLOR UNIVERSITY CENTER FOR
SCRIPTURE
ENGAGEMENT

Phil Collins, PhD

Executive Director, Taylor University
Center for Scripture Engagement
(tucse.taylor.edu)

Professor of Christian Ministries, Taylor University
(taylor.edu)

A NOTE REGARDING THE TYPE

This Bible was set in the Zondervan NIV Typeface, commissioned by Zondervan, a division of HarperCollins Christian Publishing, and designed in Aarhus, Denmark by Klaus Krogh and Magnus Gaarde of 2K/DENMARK. The design takes inspiration from the vision of the New International Version (NIV) to be a modern translation that gives the reader the most accurate Bible text possible, reflects the very best of biblical scholarship, and uses contemporary global English. The designers of the Zondervan NIV Typeface sought to reflect this rich, half-century-old tradition of accuracy, readability, and clarity while also embodying the best advancements in modern Bible typography. The result is a distinctive Bible typeface that is uncompromisingly beautiful, clear, readable at any size, and perfectly suited to the New International Version.